Integrating Voice and Data Networks

Scott Keagy

Cisco Press

Cisco Press
201 W 103rd Street
Indianapolis, IN 46290 USA

Integrating Voice and Data Networks

Scott Keagy

Copyright© 2000 Cisco Press

Published by:
Cisco Press
201 West 103rd Street
Indianapolis, IN 46290 USA

Printed in the United States of America 3 4 5 6 7 8 9 0

Library of Congress Cataloging-in-Publication Number: 99-67924

ISBN: 1-57870-196-1

Third Printing   October 2002

Warning and Disclaimer

This book is designed to provide information about Voice and Data Integration. Every effort has been made to make this book as complete and as accurate as possible, but no warranty or fitness is implied.

The information is provided on an "as is" basis. The author, Cisco Press, and Cisco Systems, Inc. shall have neither liability nor responsibility to any person or entity with respect to any loss or damages arising from the information contained in this book or from the use of the discs or programs that may accompany it.

The opinions expressed in this book belong to the author and are not necessarily those of Cisco Systems, Inc.

Trademark Acknowledgments

All terms mentioned in this book that are known to be trademarks or service marks have been appropriately capitalized. Cisco Press or Cisco Systems, Inc. cannot attest to the accuracy of this information. Use of a term in this book should not be regarded as affecting the validity of any trademark or service mark.

Feedback Information

At Cisco Press, our goal is to create in-depth technical books of the highest quality and value. Each book is crafted with care and precision, undergoing rigorous development that involves the unique expertise of members from the professional technical community.

Readers' feedback is a natural continuation of this process. If you have any comments regarding how we could improve the quality of this book, or otherwise alter it to better suit your needs, you can contact us through e-mail at feedback@ciscopress.com. Please make sure to include the book title and ISBN in your message.

We greatly appreciate your assistance.

Publisher	John Wait
Editor-in-Chief	John Kane
Cisco Representative	Anthony Wolfenden
Cisco Press Program Manager	Sonia Torres Chavez
Cisco Marketing Communications Manager	Tom Geitner
Cisco Marketing Program Manager	Edie Quiroz
Production Manager	Patrick Kanouse
Acquisitions Editor	Tracy Hughes
Production Editor	Marc Fowler
Copy Editor	Jessica McCarty
Technical Editors	Priscilla Oppenheimer
	Brian Gracely
	Steve Kalman
Book Designer	Gina Rexrode
Cover Designer	Louisa Adair
Composition	Argosy Publishing
Indexer	Tim Wright

CISCO SYSTEMS

Corporate Headquarters
Cisco Systems, Inc.
170 West Tasman Drive
San Jose, CA 95134-1706
USA
http://www.cisco.com
Tel: 408 526-4000
     800 553-NETS (6387)
Fax: 408 526-4100

European Headquarters
Cisco Systems Europe
11 Rue Camille Desmoulins
92782 Issy-les-Moulineaux
Cedex 9
France
http://www-europe.cisco.com
Tel: 33 1 58 04 60 00
Fax: 33 1 58 04 61 00

Americas Headquarters
Cisco Systems, Inc.
170 West Tasman Drive
San Jose, CA 95134-1706
USA
http://www.cisco.com
Tel: 408 526-7660
Fax: 408 527-0883

Asia Pacific Headquarters
Cisco Systems Australia,
Pty., Ltd
Level 17, 99 Walker Street
North Sydney
NSW 2059 Australia
http://www.cisco.com
Tel: +61 2 8448 7100
Fax: +61 2 9957 4350

Cisco Systems has more than 200 offices in the following countries. Addresses, phone numbers, and fax numbers are listed on the Cisco Web site at www.cisco.com/go/offices

Argentina • Australia • Austria • Belgium • Brazil • Bulgaria • Canada • Chile • China • Colombia • Costa Rica • Croatia • Czech Republic • Denmark • Dubai, UAE • Finland • France • Germany • Greece • Hong Kong • Hungary • India • Indonesia • Ireland Israel • Italy • Japan • Korea • Luxembourg • Malaysia • Mexico • The Netherlands • New Zealand • Norway • Peru • Philippines Poland • Portugal • Puerto Rico • Romania • Russia • Saudi Arabia • Scotland • Singapore • Slovakia • Slovenia • South Africa • Spain Sweden • Switzerland • Taiwan • Thailand • Turkey • Ukraine • United Kingdom • United States • Venezuela • Vietnam • Zimbabwe

About the Author

Scott Keagy (CCIE# 3985) is a cofounder of SK Networks, Inc., which specializes in voice/data network consulting. While on assignment at Cisco Systems in 1997 and 1998, he implemented the first VoFR and VoIP connectivity in its production network, for the sales offices in South and Central America. Since 1998 he has been on assignment at Pacific Bell and SBC, designing and implementing VoFR, VoATM, and VoIP solutions for their customers. He is a member of the IEEE Communications society, and he has been in the networking and computer industries for nine years. You can contact Scott at cisco-book1@sknetworks.com.

About the Technical Reviewers

Brian Gracely (CCIE #3077) is a Technical Marketing Engineer for Cisco Systems, Inc., working on VoIP, VoATM, and VoFR initiatives. His current projects involve H.323 and SIP, as well as IP telephony, unified messaging, and VoIP QoS for both enterprise and service provider customers. Previously, Brian worked with Cisco customers on LAN and ATM switching networks.

Steven Kalman is the principal office at Esquire Micro Consultants which operates in lecturing, writing, and consulting. Mr. Kalman has over thirty years experience in data processing with strengths in network design and implementation. Mr. Kalman is an instructor and author for Learning Tree International and has written and reviewed many networking related titles. Mr. Kalman holds his CCNA, CCDA, ECNE, CEN and CNI certifications.

Priscilla Oppenheimer has been developing data communications and networking systems since 1980 when she recieved her master's degree in Information Science from the University of Michigan. After many years as a software developer, she became a technical instructor and training developer and taught more than 2,000 network engineers from most of the Fortune 500 companies. Her employment at such companies as Apple Computer, Network General, and Cisco Systems gave her a change to troubleshoot real-world network design problems, and the opportunity to develop a pracitcal methodology for enterprise network design. Priscilla holds the following certifications: CNX, CCFP, CCNP, CCNP Voice Access Specialiation.

Acknowledgments

My first acknowledgment goes to the Cisco TAC groups. After working with them as an external customer for several years, I have been very impressed with their high level of technical expertise, the efficiency with which they solve problems, and their professional attitude. They are a model support organization, and I believe, a big part of Cisco's success.

There is more to writing a book than putting the words on the page. Lynette Quinn, Kathy Trace, and Tracy Hughes have helped me navigate through the editing process, and they have managed all sorts of details that I don't even want to know about.

My technical reviewers, Steve Kalman, Brian Gracely, and Priscilla Oppenheimer, have done a great job of finding my mistakes and suggesting better ways of explaining things. I have asked Brian numerous questions about Cisco technology and new developments, and he has answered them all or found people within Cisco who could answer them. Among these technical gurus within Cisco, I am grateful to Dhaval Shah, Hongchi Shih, and Stephen Liu for their contributions. Early in my writing efforts, David Oroshnic and Sachin Gupta also gave me good information.

While on assignment at Pacific Bell and SBC, I have enjoyed working for Mark Smith, an early CCIE and the Vice President of Professional Services for SBC Datacomm. I am also grateful to Larry Nelson, a former manager of a Pacific Bell Central Office, who has been a great source of telephony information and contacts.

While at Cisco, I enjoyed suffering with the local SEs in Central and South America to get their VoIP and VoFR connections working, after the PBX guy quit and left us hanging. I learned a lot about telephony during that time, including how to navigate a Portuguese voice-mail system.

Thanks go to Kamal Bakshi and Bruce McMurdo from the Enterprise Solutions Center (also known as the ESC or Escape Lab) in Building D of Cisco, San Jose. I made some of the configuration examples in this book using their routers.

A special thanks is also in order for Robert Fenerty, a former manager at Hewlett-Packard Company, who guided me early in my career. If not for his influence, I would not be in the networking industry today.

Most of all, I thank my wife Surbhi Kaul. It is difficult to be a family member of someone who maintains a day job and writes a book in the evenings and on the weekends. A few lines of praise and thanks do not make up for the last year and a half, but Surbhi, I really appreciate your encouragement, patience, and love. I'm lucky to be your husband.

Contents at a Glance

Contents

Preface

When I began writing this book nearly a year and a half ago, the technological landscape of integrated voice and data networks was very different. While adequate for most projects, the technology offerings were fragmented across different product lines, and there were numerous caveats with respect to feature support and hardware requirements. For example, the smallest Cisco router that supported T-1 voice connections and VoIP was the AS5300 Access Server. For companies that did not have the call volume or network size to justify the price point of the AS5300, the only reasonable option was the MC3810. At that time, the MC3810 did not support VoIP, so smaller companies that required digital PBX connections had to choose between VoFR and VoATM.

Scaling MC3810 hub-and-spoke networks was also very awkward. Many network topologies require a single voice T-1 between the router and PBX at remote locations. To support the voice-port densities at the central site, these designs often required stacks of MC3810 routers, tied together via back-to-back serial connections using Frame Relay switching. For larger networks, the remote MC3810 routers could be connected to a carrier-class IGX Frame Relay switch at the central site. There was a huge price and technology gap between the small-scale stacks of MC3810s to the large-scale carrier class WAN switch.

Since that time, there has been a mind-boggling frenzy of product development within Cisco. Even while focusing on voice/data integration, I have been challenged to keep abreast of new product developments and feature support. As of this writing, there are hardware solutions to fit any price point and technology scale, from small-office/home-office (SOHO) applications to large carrier-class, high-density voice gateways and controllers. The Cisco IOS software supports a variety of voice signaling options across many hardware platforms, and more features are constantly being added. Aside from these gateway advances, the Cisco AVVID program has added new dimensions to the array of products, creating new applications that are unparalleled in old-world voice networks.

Many solid voice/data networks have been built with previous generations of Cisco IOS software and equipment. It stands to reason that the current generation of Cisco offerings, which incorporate a multitude of improvements, is quite robust in terms of reliability and feature support.

The largest obstacle to the development of voice/data networks is not the maturity of the products or the technology, but the lack of experienced people who understand the technology and can take advantage of the features that Cisco routers support. It is my hope that you will learn from this book, which in turn will advance the field of voice/data networking.

Introduction

Voice and data services have traditionally developed as isolated communications systems. In order to integrate these systems, you must thoroughly understand how an integrated solution meets the goals and requirements of each system.

Objectives

This book explains the goals and requirements of traditional voice networks, and provides information to help you develop integrated voice/data networks that can meet these goals and requirements. Using illustrations and detailed examples, this book explains the strengths and weaknesses of VoFR, VoATM, and VoIP as packet voice solutions.

After reading this book, you should be able to perform the following functions:

- Analyze a traditional telephony environment and propose an enhanced packet voice solution to reduce circuit expenses and enable new applications

- Design a telephone-numbering and call-routing plan that spans traditional telephone switches and packet voice routers

- Enable quality of service (QoS) features on Cisco routers to ensure excellent voice quality

- Establish connectivity between Cisco routers and PBXs, key systems, or Central Office (CO) phone switches using a variety of traditional telephony signaling protocols

- Establish any-to-any calling connectivity across traditional and packet voice networks, using appropriate connection modes to preserve features as appropriate (for example, hook-flash, stutter dial-tone for voice mail)

- Isolate and resolve voice quality issues that may be caused by any number of factors, including audio signal levels, tandem routing, codec processing, and network QoS

Audience

This book is most relevant to data network engineers and managers who will design, implement, or maintain integrated voice/data networks. This book is also appropriate for sales engineers, systems engineers, project managers, and others in the networking industry who are involved with voice/data integration projects or wish to increase their knowledge of voice and data networking.

You are not expected to be familiar with any aspect of traditional voice networking, except perhaps as an end user of a business telephone with features such as call forward, transfer, and conference.

You will absorb more information from this book if you are familiar with basic data networking concepts such as the OSI 7 layer model, TCP/IP routing and addressing, and wide area networking (WAN) technologies such as T-1/E-1, ISDN, Frame Relay, and ATM. To facilitate discussions of VoFR, VoATM, and VoIP, this book briefly reviews WAN technologies and examines advanced IP features in detail. You are not expected to understand QoS issues prior to reading this book.

Organization

This book is organized to accommodate readers with different objectives and different technical backgrounds. The Cisco IOS configuration details are isolated in the last part of the book, so that readers who do not need hands-on configuration knowledge may learn the concepts without the burden of configuration details. For readers who need specific guidance while working in the trenches, ample space is devoted to detailed explanations of Cisco IOS configuration. In addition, the book offers practical advice that is distilled from the author's design and implementation experience in numerous production network environments.

Part I is an in-depth examination of traditional telephony standards, protocols, and methodologies as they apply to corporate enterprises, and to a limited extent, service providers.

Part II builds the conceptual foundation for real-time packet voice communication over data networks, including QoS issues and call signaling requirements. The operation of VoFR, VoATM, and VoIP (including H.323 and SIP) are described in this part of the book.

Part III considers the early phases of a voice/data integration project, including discovery, analysis, planning, and design issues.

Part IV is devoted to the implementation phase of voice/data integration projects, and delves into the specifics of Cisco IOS router configuration. Several appendixes provide useful troubleshooting information that is inadequately documented in other sources.

Approach

This book is intended to complement the documentation that is currently available from Cisco Connection Online (CCO). Given the detailed references that are already available for individual commands, this book does not exhaustively define the configuration options for each voice-related command. Rather, the most relevant commands are described from the perspective of what functions they enable or what problems they solve. The focus of this book is to build an organized conceptual framework that helps you make sense of many interrelated technologies.

I learn new topics and retain knowledge better when I understand how and why something works. I do not like to memorize command sequences or follow a ritualized process unless I know what I am doing and why I am doing it. For this reason, I have tried to emphasize the why and how wherever possible in this book.

I recognize that there are many ways to think and learn, and that some people prefer to learn the essentials without laboring through details. However, if you try to learn this material by memorizing a set sequence of tasks, then you may be stuck when you encounter a new situation or a variation of a familiar situation. I have endeavored to instill in you a deeper level of knowledge that you can use to resolve unfamiliar obstacles and more quickly grasp related subjects.

PART I

Traditional Voice Networks

This book begins with an exploration of voice networking subjects to which data network engineers have traditionally had little exposure.

Chapter 1 provides an overview of traditional voice networks. The chapter defines various calling features available to telephony users, the equipment that provides these features, and the services available from telephony service providers to connect the equipment and provide calling features between sites.

Chapter 2 delves into the protocols that connect and disconnect calls in traditional enterprise voice networks, and provides an overview of the protocols that enable advanced calling features.

Chapter 3 discusses Signaling System 7, which operates in the signaling networks used by telephony service providers around the globe. The chapter provides an overview of typical network topologies, addressing, protocols, and shows the relationship between SS7 and ISDN.

Chapter 4 examines telephone number assignments at a variety of scales, including the international numbering plan identified in ITU Recommendation E.164, and the North American Numbering Plan (NANP). The design of private numbering plans is explored, with consideration for the impacts of the numbering plan assignment on network administration and call routing. The chapter introduces the "dial peer" construct, which is how Cisco routers implement call routing and apply features to calls.

Chapter 5 explores the most significant variables that affect voice quality, several subjective and objective methods of measuring voice quality, and standard methods of predicting voice quality that result from a given network design.

Chapter 6 examines the conversion of voice signals from the analog to the digital domain. This discussion includes a variety of Digital Signal Processing (DSP) techniques to compress voice signals, including waveform, source, and hybrid codecs. The chapter concludes with a comparison of the standard ITU G.700 series audio codecs.

CHAPTER 1

The State of Voice Communications

Most telephony books either begin with a history of telecommunications, or have a chapter dedicated to the subject. There is generally a discussion of the United States telephone provider monopoly, and the subsequent government intervention that created the Regional Bell Operating Companies (RBOCs). This is generally followed by a discussion of government regulations in the telephone industry, within the United States and other countries, as well.

In this book, the preceding paragraph is about the most you will see on telecom history and regulations. This is a technology book—not a history or legal book. Leave it to the lawyers to sort out legal issues in the fast-changing telecom regulatory environment. The aim of this book is to help you understand the underlying technologies of two different worlds, and minimize the obstacles you will encounter along the path to integrating your voice and data networks.

After reading this chapter, you should have a good understanding of the voice communications services currently available in traditional telephony environments. It is important that you understand the telephony features you may be required to support across the voice/data network. It is also important that you understand how these features are provisioned—from the perspective of the telephony equipment at your sites and from the perspective of the voice circuits and services provided by circuit vendors. This chapter is organized into the following sections:

- Telephony Systems
- Trunk Circuit
- Calling Features & Services

Telephony Systems

The focus of the following sections is on the systems that implement calling features and services. The sections are segregated into the following types of telephone systems:

- Residential
- On-premise business
- Off-premise Centrex

Residential Systems

Residential systems are the simplest of the systems described here. The basic elements of the residential telephony system are illustrated in Figure 1-1.

NOTE   With the widespread adoption of Signaling System #7 (SS7) in the core public phone networks, residential customers have access to many advanced calling features. These features were not available before SS7 was widely adopted among carriers, because there was no standard way to signal the feature requests between different carrier networks. SS7 is explored in Chapter 3, "Signaling System #7."

Figure 1-1   *Basic Elements of Residential Telephony Systems*

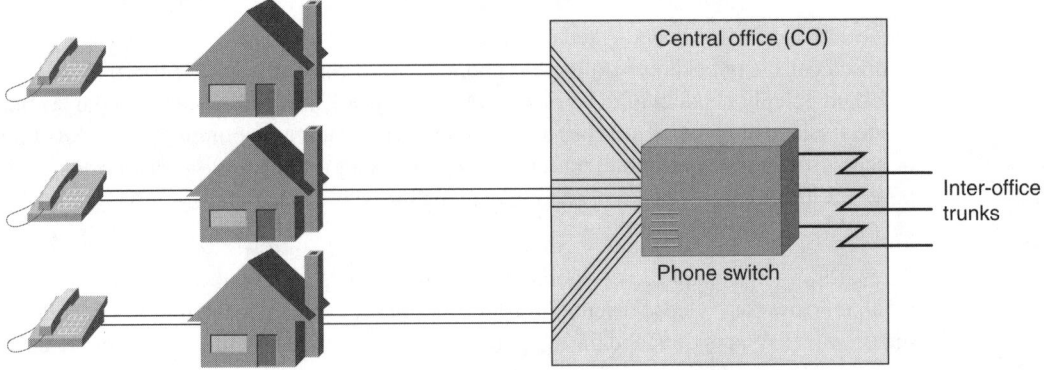

All of the telephone jacks in your house are wired in parallel (similar to the old coaxial Ethernet LANs) with a few pairs of wires. Each phone circuit requires a single wire pair. There is a continuous wired connection from the telephone jacks in your house to the central office (CO). At your house, you use a simple single-line telephone that provides plain old telephone service (POTS). Your telephone only provides a speaker, microphone, ringer, keypad, and a Dual Tone Multi-Frequency (DTMF) generator. The battery power required to power the phone is gleaned from the same wire pair, connected to the CO, that provides the audio path and call signaling. All of the network intelligence comes from the core network switch in the CO. The CO is a secured building, managed by a local exchange carrier (LEC), that terminates physical wires from thousands or tens of thousands of households. To facilitate signal transmission and reduce noise, these wires may have repeaters and/or loading coils (inductors that block high-frequency signals) placed anywhere along the path between your house and the CO.

In addition to the wire terminations, the CO has trunks to other COs and tandem switching nodes in the carrier's network. The residential wires, business wires, and the interoffice trunks (for example, voice circuits between telephone switches in the carrier's network) terminate on large voice switches made by a few vendors. If you have ever configured ISDN on a Cisco router, the **ISDN switch-type** command identifies the type of switch in the CO—examples include 5ess and dms100.

On-Premise Business Systems

Businesses and other organizations have more complex telecommunications needs than residential customers, because there are more people to consider and because there is a greater focus on personal productivity. Just as businesses can vary greatly in size and communications requirements, the systems to support these businesses vary greatly.

Figure 1-2 provides a voice network overview of a typical organization with multiple sites. The sites are typically connected via tie lines that provide a dedicated physical path for calls between the sites. These dedicated circuits are less expensive to use than paying for public switched calls between sites. At least one of these sites must have trunks to the Public Switched Telephone Network (PSTN). It is a good idea to have at least one analog POTS phone at each site directly attached to the PSTN (that is, not going through a private voice switch) to maintain communications during emergencies like long power outages or voice switch failure.

On-premise business telephony systems may be composed of the following elements:

- Business telephones
- Analog devices
- Key System Units (KSUs) and hybrids
- Private Branch Exchanges (PBXs)
- Automatic Call Distributors (ACDs)
- Interactive Voice Response (IVR) units
- Voice mail and Auto-Attendant systems

Figure 1-2   *Typical Business Voice Network with Multiple Sites*

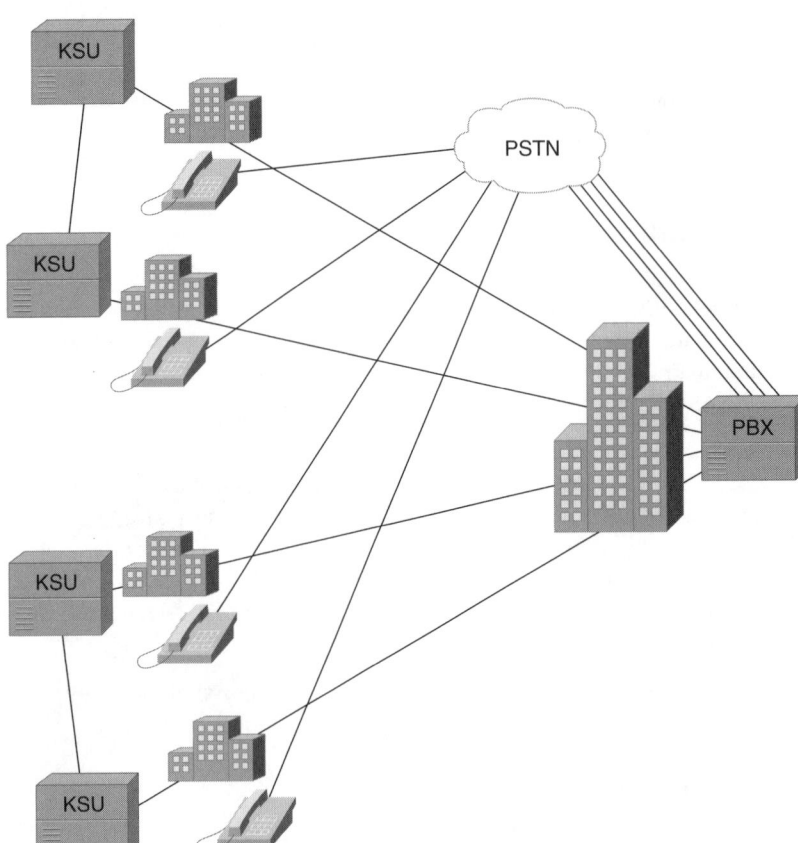

Business Telephones

A business telephone is typically designed to operate with the specific key system or PBX installed at that location. A key system or PBX manufacturer may offer a variety of telephone models for use with the particular system—from single-line telephones with no display, to multiline telephones with a large display and an attendant console. Business telephones offer more features than standard analog telephones, but the instruments are much more expensive—each telephone can cost hundreds of dollars. The telephones usually have a message-waiting indicator lamp that lights whenever the user receives a voice-mail message. Many business telephones have display screens where information such as caller ID or date/time is displayed. Most telephones accommodate multiple telephone lines, or appearances, so that you can juggle multiple conversations simultaneously. In addition to the keys from an analog keypad, a digital telephone may have a hold button, numerous function keys that provide quick access to advanced calling features, and numerous keys to select lines or outside trunks. The power for the phones comes from the wires that connect to the key system or PBX. The telephones are called digital because the audio signals are transmitted to and from the key system or PBX in digital form. The telephone has a codec to convert between the analog and digital signals.

Analog Devices

Analog devices in a business telephony environment include fax machines, modems, and standard analog phones. These devices require special ports to connect to the key system or PBX because they do not understand the proprietary digital signals from the phone switch. They are designed to plug directly into a POTS line. This is just another name for a regular residential line or a loop-start trunk in a business environment.

Key System Units and Hybrids

Key systems and *hybrids* are devices that enable businesses to share a small number of outside telephone lines among a larger number of employees. Since all employees are not constantly using their phones, businesses can reduce phone circuit expenses by using a fewer number of lines more efficiently. In a traditional key system, users can access any one of the analog telephone lines (for example, 1-MB circuits) that are connected to the system by pressing a button on their telephone. There is no routing logic within a traditional key system. Each button is strictly associated with a port to an outside line.

Key systems are typically scoped for businesses that need from ten to 100 telephones. A starter system might support up to 16 telephones and 6 outside trunks. A larger system might support up to 80 telephones.

In one standard key system implementation, all of the telephones are squared. (The origin of the term, squared, is unclear, but it is associated with the earliest electronic key systems.) When a telephone is squared, it means that every telephone is identically configured with a button for each outside line. In such a scenario, each of ten users might have the same three outside lines accessible from the same three-button locations. An LED or an LCD display indicates to other users when a given line is busy.

One of the defining characteristics of a key system is that there is no call routing or digit manipulation. When you press a button on the telephone for an outside line, you instantly seize the trunk associated with that button and hear a dial tone from the central office. Traditional key systems do not support T1 trunks—they generally use loop-start trunks. The key system may be optionally configured to let you dial 9 to seize the next available trunk instead of pressing a button for a specific outside line.

Key systems have evolved into hybrid key systems, which offer services more like PBXs, and in some cases offer a number of integrated voice applications. These systems may provide advanced calling features, support for T1, PRI, and direct inward dialing (DID) trunks, and may have self-contained voice mail, auto-attendant, ACD, and IVR systems.

These systems really have more functionality than a PBX, but the name hybrid key system is still used because the system may support fewer lines or trunks than a traditional PBX.

Private Branch Exchanges

A *private branch exchange (PBX)*, which is sometimes called a *private automatic branch exchange (PABX)*, is a true call-routing switch. Unlike a traditional key system that has buttons for specific outside lines, a PBX maintains a call-routing table. This may be a static table, or it may be a complex set of rules that define a *Least Cost Routing (LCR)* scheme. Do not confuse LCR with any concepts from dynamic data routing protocols. LCR simply refers to routing calls based on the least financial cost. The LCR scheme generally considers the destination number and the time of day to decide which trunk will provide the lowest per-minute cost for the call. The set of rules is statically defined in the PBX configuration.

From a physical perspective, a PBX is one or more shelves (or carriers according to AT&T/Lucent terminology) with a backplane that accepts cards. Types of cards that you are likely to encounter include digital station cards, analog station cards, and trunk cards. There may be a number of other card types, including CPU cards, echo cancellers, and so on. Figure 1-3 illustrates the functional components of a PBX. Most PBX systems enable cards to be hot-swapped, with only the corresponding section of the PBX configuration needing to be modified. Some PBX cards are reconfigured by setting DIP switches on the sides of the cards. Often you have to remove a card to see the DIP switches.

WARNING   Be careful to follow the procedures defined by a PBX vendor before removing cards in a PBX. You may need to unplug the card to set DIP switches, or simply to reset the card while troubleshooting problems. In some cases you must toggle a switch on the card before removing it, or you risk damaging the card and the entire phone system. In some PBXs, if you do not remove system power from a card (via a toggle switch, for example), the telephone switch can literally catch on fire when you unplug the card.

Automatic Call Distributors

An *automatic call distributor (ACD)* is just a specialized PBX. ACDs are typically associated with call centers, such as sales or support organizations. Inbound calls are distributed to call agents according to a set of rules. A call may be sent to the longest idle agent, or to the agent with the most experience with a particular product or service, for example. Agents must log on to the ACD system, so make sure that the logon process is supported as part of the voice/data integration design.

Figure 1-3 *Functional Components of a PBX*

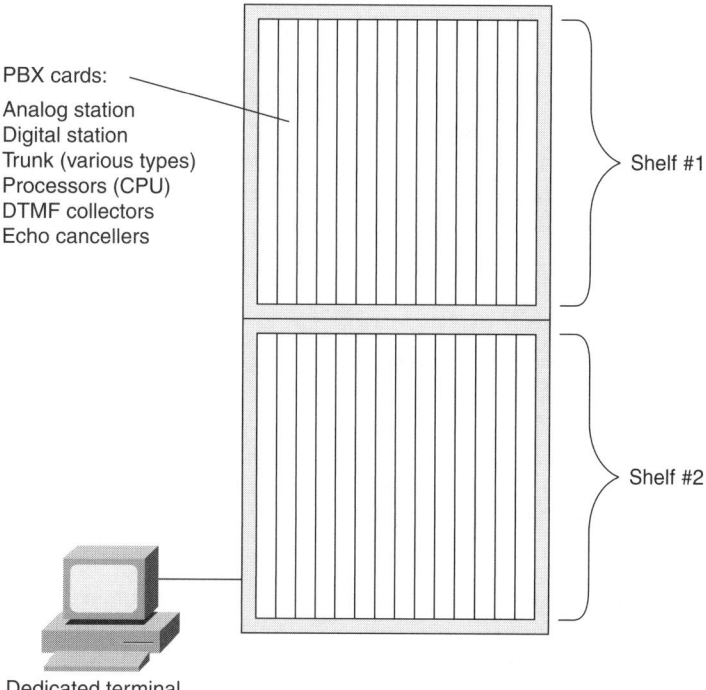

PBX cards:

Analog station
Digital station
Trunk (various types)
Processors (CPU)
DTMF collectors
Echo cancellers

Shelf #1

Shelf #2

Dedicated terminal

How does the ACD get data to make call-distributing decisions? The dialed number identification service (DNIS) value from the inbound call is a start. The automatic number identification (ANI) can often provide unique customer identification. The caller may also interact with an interactive voice response (IVR) unit that collects information, such as account numbers or product serial numbers, prior to the caller reaching a live agent. This information is used as a key to search a database, and the appropriate record may be presented to the call agent via a computer application. The term *screen pop* is commonly used to describe the information that appears on the call agent's computer screen.

One interesting feature of an ACD system is that there may be more trunks than there are call agents to service the trunks! Whenever you call a business and hear, "We are experiencing unusually high call volumes—please wait for...," you are one of the callers in queue. ACD systems offer a simple priority queuing mechanism to move favored customers to the front of the line. Conversely, customers calling to discontinue a service may be pushed to the back of the line. So be wary the next time an automated system gives you the option to discontinue a service. Good ACD systems can tell you how long to expect to be on hold, or how many callers are ahead of you. Bad ACD systems, or poorly implemented ACD systems, can provide dead air that makes you think you have been disconnected.

Interactive Voice Response

Aside from collecting information for call center agents, an Interactive Voice Response (IVR) system can also offload some traffic from the call center. Simple queries like store hours or directions can be automatically processed, so call agents have more time to manage complex calls. IVR systems, when linked with back-end databases, can provide real-time and customer-specific data that further offload call centers. Processing requests such as account balance inquiries and appointment scheduling are ideally suited to IVR systems. Call center agents are happier when they do not have to perform such repetitive tasks.

Voice Messaging and Auto-Attendant

A voice-messaging (or voice-mail) system stores spoken messages destined for users that have a voice-mail account on the system. The system is normally a standalone device that connects to a PBX, though it may be bundled into a hybrid key system. Standalone–voice-mail systems normally connect to a PBX via standard phone lines or trunks for the audio path and call signaling (such as loop start, E&M), and via an RS-232 serial connection (such as Simplified Message Desk Interface [SMDI]) for signaling about which voice mailbox to access.

When a PBX forwards a call to a voice-mail system (for example, when the destination is busy or not answering), the voice-mail system needs to know the destination mailbox. This information enables the voice-mail system to play a personalized greeting, and to record a message from the caller so that the intended recipient can retrieve it at a later time. The PBX may be programmed to provide the destination mailbox to the voice-mail system via the serial SMDI connection. If the PBX is not programmed for this functionality, then it cannot forward calls to a personalized voice mailbox for each user; it can only forward calls to the main voice-mail number, where an auto-attendant processes the call.

The voice-mail system auto-attendant provides a recorded greeting such as, "Welcome to company X; please enter a mailbox number or press 1 to spell by name." Callers can then interact with the voice-mail system by pressing keys on their phone in response to voice prompts. The auto-attendant processes digit input from the caller, recalls the personalized voice-mail greeting of the intended destination, and records a message from the caller. The auto-attendant may then accept additional input from the caller to leave a message for a different recipient.

Off-Premise Centrex Systems

Carriers and service providers offer Centrex service to their customers as an outsourced telecommunications solution. Traditional Centrex service provides the functionality of a customer's PBXs from the phone switches in a CO. Centrex service can support direct inward dial (DID), abbreviated dialing between customer sites, call transfer, forward, conference, hold, and call waiting—all of the normal PBX functions. Centrex also supports voice mail, though most phones used with Centrex service are not equipped to take advantage of the message-waiting lamp. A stutter dial tone is normally used to indicate a waiting voice-mail message.

The telephones are the only equipment located at the customer sites when Centrex service is used. Customers may use normal telephones, or they may connect a PBX to the Centrex service to enable employees to use telephones with more features (for example, number display, multiple lines, message-waiting lamp, buttons dedicated to features, and so on).

Centrex is a very compelling service for some businesses, but it does have its limitations. The month-to-month service lease is a small financial commitment compared to purchasing an expensive PBX. The service is provided by highly reliable CO telephone switches that are monitored and maintained 24 hours per day, with no dependence on electricity from the customer's location. For widely distributed campuses, Centrex may be more cost effective than installing phone switches in multiple buildings or ordering off-premise extension (OPX) circuits. Centrex is conceptually more scalable than a small phone system for rapidly growing companies, in that the CO phone switch can accommodate many Centrex lines.

On the less appealing side of Centrex, you are at the whim of a phone company whenever you add an employee who needs a phone. The carrier may have a provisioning backlog or run out of Centrex lines in a busy exchange, which leaves you few options when you have new users that need a telephone. You must have a separate copper wire pair for each phone connected to the Centrex service, and the explosion of wiring becomes impractical as an organization grows.

Trunk Circuits

To provide useful communication, the telephony equipment at your site needs to interface with the equipment at other sites and with the PSTN. This is analogous to having WAN data circuits at each site and a connection to the public Internet. The types of circuits used for voice communications bear resemblance to data circuits at the most basic level—that is framing, line coding, and channelization—but the similarities end there.

The physical facility for a voice circuit is either a DS0 that delivers a single analog voice channel, or a time division multiplexing (TDM) digital facility that delivers many voice channels. In the United States, a T1 delivers 24 voice channels with in-band signaling. Most of the world uses an E1 to provide 30 voice channels, a framing channel, and a signaling channel. A digital facility can be directly connected to a T1/E1 card in the PBX, but an external channel service unit (CSU) commonly serves as a point of demarcation between the carrier-owned circuit and the customer-owned wiring and equipment. If the PBX or key system does not have a T1/E1 card, then a Channel Bank can split the T1 into separate DS0s and provide a wire pair to each analog port in the voice switch.

In the United States, you can order the following types of voice circuits from circuit vendors:

- Dial-tone lines
- Both-way trunks
- DID trunks
- ISDN PRI trunks
- Point-to-point tie lines
- Off-premise extensions
- Foreign-exchange trunks

Dial-tone lines are circuits that provide analog connectivity to the CO via a single pair of wires. Each dial-tone line is uniquely associated with a phone number that is assigned by the circuit vendor. This type of connection is used in residential phone lines. In a business environment, this circuit may also be called a *loop-start trunk* if it is connected to a key system or PBX. These types of circuits are more commonly associated with key systems than with PBXs.

Both-way trunks, also called *combination trunks*, must be connected to a key system or PBX. Ground-start signaling is normally used to prevent inbound and outbound calls from seizing the trunk at the same time. Chapter 2, "Enterprise Telephony Signaling," examines loop-start and ground-start signaling. A common way that companies use both-way trunks is for outbound calling only. This is because another circuit provides direct inward dial, so the both-way trunk effectively becomes a direct outward dial (DOD) trunk.

A *direct inward dial (DID) trunk* enables callers to directly reach employees without being transferred by an attendant. Consider a business without DID trunks that is assigned 555-1000 as the main number, and uses three-digit extensions for its employees. If you want to reach someone in this company, you must first dial the main number, and then be transferred to the extension—say, x132. If the company ordered DID trunks and reserved the number block of 555-1xxx, then you could call the person directly by dialing 555-1132.

So why is this so special? What makes it different from residential lines where you can directly reach someone? DID trunks enable more telephone numbers to be assigned than the number of trunks. You can order 24 DID trunks (a full T1) with a block of 100 phone numbers for the employees in your office, and give each of them a unique phone number for the outside world. With normal dial-tone trunks, you only get one phone number for each trunk, and the phone number is always associated with a specific physical line. DID trunk lines accept calls for any of the dialed numbers in the DID block, and the PBX forwards the call to the appropriate extension. This enables inbound calls to use any trunk for any destination in the DID block.

One disadvantage of standard DID trunks is that they only allow inbound calling. This means that you must pay for additional trunks for outbound calling. If your voice services are provisioned on a T1 local loop, then you can use some channels for a DID trunk group, and some channels for a both-way trunk group. The both-way trunks would be used for outbound calls only.

An ISDN *Primary Rate Interface (PRI)* circuit provides a 23B+D service in the United States. This means that you get 23 bearer channels that carry voice traffic, and a data channel that carries signaling traffic. ISDN can provide sophisticated calling features and services because there is a full DS0 for signaling traffic. One of the fancier calling features supported by voice PRI circuits is two-way DID. The same trunks can provide DID and enable outbound calls. On inbound calls, automatic number identification (ANI) is available before ringing begins, because it is delivered as part of the call-setup message. ISDN PRI circuits also pass the private switch automatic location identification (PS/ALI) information required for emergency services. In general, the ISDN PRI connection is the conduit that will enable integration of advanced calling features in private voice networks and the PSTN. PBX vendors may continue to use proprietary signaling schemes with their digital telephones. The public voice network has embraced SS7 to support advanced calling features. An ISDN PRI enables these features to function through both networks.

NOTE   DID, ANI, and PS/ALI are described later in this chapter in the section entitled "Calling Features and Services."

Point-to-point circuits, or tie lines, are clear channel circuits that can be used for voice or data communication. You may be accustomed to T1 data circuits that use extended super-framing (ESF) and binary-8 zero substitution (B8ZS) line coding. It is more common in the voice world to use d4 super-framing and alternate mark inversion (AMI) line coding. Use ESF/B8ZS if your PBXs support it. Just make sure that you use the same framing and line coding that the circuit vendor is using.

Across the tie line, PBXs peer directly with each other—not with the local CO. The PBXs use E&M signaling, discussed in Chapter 2, for call setup and teardown. In a typical implementation, you dial a short-trunk access code to seize a specific tie line. When the PBX at the other end of the tie line provides dial tone, you then dial extensions at that site, or dial 9 to reach an outside line from that office. This is called *tail-end hop-off*, or *toll bypass*, and it can save you a lot of money on toll calls.

In a larger tie-line network, you might have to traverse multiple tie lines to reach the intended destination. The process for doing this is analogous to source routing—every hop of the voice network must be specified as part of the dialed number. Consider Figure 1-4. In this scenario, you are a caller at site B trying to reach someone at site C. You first dial the trunk access code (TAC) for site A. After you hear a dial tone from the PBX at site A, you dial the TAC for site C. When you hear a dial tone from the PBX at site C, you can call extensions of users at the site.

Figure 1-4   *Tie-Line Network with a TAC Numbering Plan*

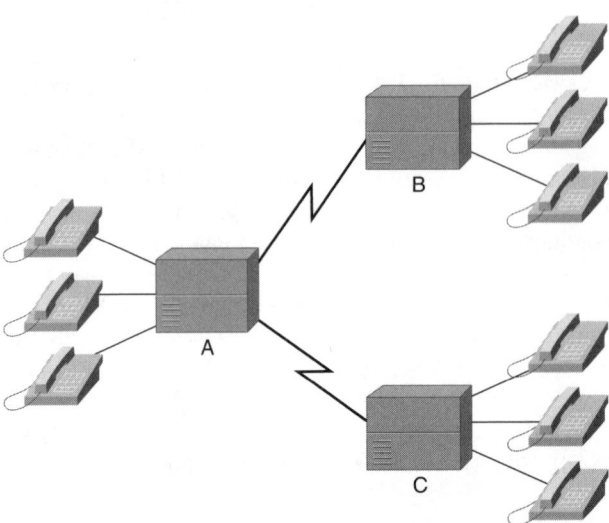

The process just described illustrates one of the key differences between a traditional key system and PBX. The key system does not have call-routing capabilities, so you must source route all of your calls through the network. As a workaround, a button on your telephone might be configured to dial a sequence of TACs interspersed with suitable pauses. Then, you would press a single button to get dial tone from office X. However, you still need to know which button to push to dial which office, so there is still a routing choice you must manually make with each call.

When you have a PBX network, you no longer need to know where your call is routed. You just need to know the extension of the user you want to reach. The PBX network is preconfigured to route the call out the appropriate trunk at each hop. You dial x231 to reach Chris in the San Jose office, but you do not know what path the call takes (unless you configured the PBX). The call could traverse a tie line, or the PBX may append 1-408-555-1 and send the full 11 digits to the PSTN.

You might have a network with both key systems and PBXs. In one scenario, the central site has a PBX that maintains call-routing information for the entire hub-and-spoke network. The remote sites have key systems, dial-tone trunks to the PSTN, and tie trunks to the central site. The telephones at the remote sites have buttons for dial tone from the PSTN, and dial tone from the tie lines. From a remote site, you can seize a tie trunk and dial an extension in any office directly. The PBX at the central site receives the digits that you dial, and routes the call to the proper destination. This is analogous to a hub-and-spoke data network where the central site has routes for the entire network, but the remote sites only have a default route to the central site.

Off-premise extensions, or *OPX lines*, are useful when you want to integrate remote users into your voice network. At the main site, you terminate the OPX line into your PBX. You assign an extension to that line as if a telephone is locally attached. The other end of the OPX line is directly connected to a telephone at an employee's residence, or a satellite office with a few users. Centrex systems are essentially OPX lines at business locations connected to a CO phone switch.

Remote telephones connected via OPX lines can place calls and receive calls as if they were directly connected to the phone switch at the main site. They do not have all of the features of digital telephones, but they can use hook-flash or key sequences, like *70, to take advantage of PBX features. A voice-mail–alert lamp will not work, but a stutter dial tone can be used to indicate voice mail.

Foreign exchange lines, or *FX lines*, give an organization a local telephone presence in areas where it may not have a local physical presence. Imagine that you have a business with offices in San Francisco but many clients in Los Angeles. You may not want your clients in Los Angeles to make long-distance calls to speak with you. In this case, you can order an FX line from your business office to the circuit vendor's CO in Los Angeles. You then have a local number for Los Angeles callers, but it rings directly to you in San Francisco. This is basically a back-hauled voice line. This application for FX lines is not commonly used now, because 800-number service provides the same function and more. With 800 service, callers have toll-free access to your business, and you have the same 800 number for many different geographic regions.

FX lines are still useful if your business makes a large number of calls to a specific remote destination. If you have a tie line to a business office in that location, you can use tail-end hop-off. If you do not have a business office in the area, then you can order an FX line and use that line for local calls to the area.

Figure 1-5 summarizes the relationship between tie lines, OPX lines, and FX lines. Remote connections between key systems or PBXs are provided with tie lines. Remote connections between a voice switch and a telephone are provided with OPX lines. Remote connections between a voice switch and a distant CO are provided with FX lines.

Figure 1-5   *Relationship Between Tie, OPX, and FX Lines*

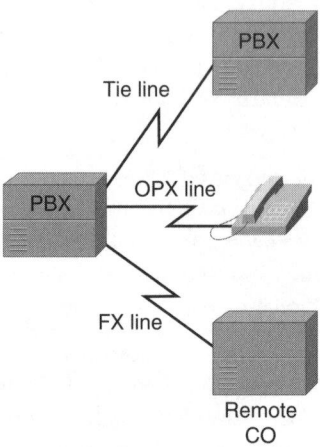

Calling Features & Services

In addition to basic call connection and disconnection, a variety of additional calling features and services are available for residential and business telephone users. The most common features and services are grouped here according to the following categories:

- Call Session Management
- User Identification
- Convenience
- Security
- Emergency Response

Call Session Management

These features help you control how new or existing call connections are handled, and how additional call connections are handled when other connections already exist. You have real-time control over where calls are terminated—whether to a different phone set, multiple phone sets, or to a voice mailbox. These features are provided by the phone switch (for example, hybrid key system or PBX) at each site.

Call hold places an active connection in an idle state without disconnecting the call. The endpoint of the call is temporarily suspended, but it is not moved. At this point, you can receive or place a call on another line, or perform some action while the other party waits.

Call hold is often implemented with music on hold, to reassure the holding party that the connection is still active.

Call park is used to transfer an active call connection to a temporary holding point, from which you may retrieve the call. An extension identifies the temporary holding point, or where the call is parked. Call park is often used in conjunction with an intercom system that notifies users of calls that are waiting. For example, a loudspeaker might announce, "Pat, you have a call parked on 101." Pat would then retrieve the call by pressing a button on the phone (for example, Intercom) and entering the extension 101. This feature is similar to call transfer, except that you manually accept the call from any telephone instead of passively receiving the call when your phone rings. This is beneficial in environments where you need to receive calls but may not be close to your own phone. Instead of trying to track your present location, the attendant can notify you over the loudspeaker.

Call transfer enables you to transfer your end of an active call connection to another user without disconnecting the remote party. Attendants (or receptionists) use this feature extensively to direct calls to various extensions. This feature saves the remote party from having to redial a different number in your organization. If you only have an extension and no direct phone number, then a party from outside of your network cannot call you without being transferred.

Call conference enables three or more people to simultaneously communicate. There are two types of audio conferencing: spontaneous and planned. The spontaneous type (that is, ad hoc conference) enables an active call connection to be converted to a conference call by the addition of other parties at any time. A PBX or hybrid key system typically supports this feature. A planned conference (or meet-me bridge) normally has a "conference bridge" phone number to which all parties must connect, and a passcode that identifies the specific conference. Planned conferences are usually provisioned on specialized equipment that accommodates more participants than spontaneous conferences. Spontaneous conferences have the advantage that participants need not be notified prior to the conference.

Call waiting notifies you of inbound calls when you are already engaged in an active call connection. This feature is useful when you do not want to miss calls. In business environments, this feature is typically implemented with multiline phones. With Centrex or residential phone service, you can be notified via an audible tone during your active conversation.

Call forwarding enables calls destined for your phone to be directed elsewhere in response to different conditions. Calls can be forwarded to your voice mailbox when your line is busy or you do not answer after a preset number of rings. This feature can function with call waiting. You can also specify a number to which all calls should be forwarded, such as another call agent, or your mobile phone. Some systems offer additional options for conditionally forwarding calls.

Do not disturb (DND) creates the appearance that your phone is busy. If you have voice mail provisioned, all calls will be forwarded to your voice mailbox. This feature is useful when you are woefully behind at work and need to get out of interrupt mode to get some work done.

Voice messaging provides the basic functions of a phone answering machine and more. Callers may have the option of marking messages as urgent or private, reaching a live person by pressing a key sequence (normally 0), or transferring to a different extension. You may be notified when you have voice messages by a lamp indicator on your desk telephone or a stutter dial tone when you pick up the phone. These notifications are called Message Waiting Indicators, or MWI. In addition, the voice-mail system may send an alert to your pager based on conditions that you define (for example, all messages, or only urgent messages). When you connect to your password-protected–voice-mail account and listen to your messages, the urgent messages are played before the normal messages. You can sometimes control how messages are played back—faster or slower, rewind, fast forward, repeat, and so on. You have the option of replying to a message or forwarding it to others, unless the message has been marked private. You may be able to send messages to people in your voice-mail network by spelling their names as opposed to entering their extension numbers. This voice-mail network may extend between all of the sites in your organization, or each site may have an independent voice-mail system.

Identification

Several technologies provide identity information about the party that originates a call and the party that receives a call. This information can be used by the calling and called party in a number of ways.

Caller ID is provided on loop-start trunks by telephone circuit vendors (Chapter 2 describes loop-start circuits in detail). This service is available to residential phone subscribers, as well. The actual telephone number at the source of the call is passed to the receiver as an analog signal between the first and second ring. This means that calls answered during the first ring may not be identified. The party that originates the call has the option of blocking the source telephone number, except when the call is destined for 800 or 900 numbers. The exceptions are intended to allow billing reconciliation.

Automatic Number Identification (ANI) is a service available on ground-start, T1, or PRI trunks (each of these circuit types is discussed in detail in Chapter 2). For calls from a residence, the ANI and caller ID may be the same, but for calls from a business, the ANI delivers the bill-to number (BTN) of the calling party to the destination. ANI does not deliver the exact phone number that placed the call unless this is the same as the BTN. Parties that originate calls to toll-free (that is, 800 numbers in North America) or premium rate services (that is, 900 or 976 numbers in North America) cannot block their ANI, because this information is required by the receiving side of the connection for billing purposes.

Dialed Number Identification Service (DNIS) is generally used when multiple 800 or 900 numbers are routed by the telephone circuit vendor to the same trunk group. An organization might advertise separate phone numbers for different types of calls, but the same call center might receive all of the calls. The DNIS value enables the call center to track which number the caller dialed, and to route the call to an appropriate call agent.

Custom ringing uses the calling party information to generate special ringing tones when the call is from a predefined party. This helps you identify who is calling you even if you do not have a display to see the phone number of the calling party. A common feature of key systems and PBXs is to provide a separate ringing tone for calls from within the private network and calls from the PSTN. This enables businesses to prioritize customer calls ahead of internal calls. In a residential context, custom ringing is also used to identify which number is called when multiple phone numbers are associated with the same line. This is a popular service to provide a separate "teenager phone number" without physically ordering two separate phone circuits.

Call return is the service commonly invoked by dialing *69 on a POTS phone in the United States. When you dial *69, the number that last attempted to call you is dialed. Even if the last call attempt to your number was not established (for example, the call is abandoned after two rings), the number is still considered the last number to call you. If that number uses caller ID blocking, then the phone network is unable to complete the call.

A variety of quite useful call logging features are now available. Intelligent phone sets or computer-based telephony terminals can track a list of recent missed calls, received calls, and placed calls. Calls can be returned to numbers from any of these lists. These logging features depend on the availability of caller ID or ANI.

Caller ID blocking allows you to maintain a degree of privacy by not revealing your number to destinations that use caller ID. This privacy cannot be maintained when you call 800 numbers, because the destinations have a right to know who is making the calls for which they pay. Similarly, you cannot maintain your privacy while dialing 900 numbers because they must know whom to bill.

NOTE   The Advanced Intelligent Network (AIN) features that are accessed by dialing *<digit><digit> in North America, such as *69 and *70, are referred to as Custom Local Access Signaling Services, or CLASS.

Convenience

Though several of the features that make use of calling- and called-party identification can be considered features of convenience, they are discussed in the preceding section because of their dependence on identification functions. The features of this section are convenience features that do not require special information from the network. Generally, these features save you from the tedium of dialing long digit sequences when alternatives exist.

The *intercom/paging* functions of a key system enable users of the system to communicate without using outside lines. The phone connection may be switched directly between the user phones or to an audio broadcast system in the building. Predefined text messages may also be sent to users with display phones. Each local user is accessed via a short extension, typically three or four digits.

Systemwide and personal speed dialing plans use short key sequences to specify calling destinations. The key system or PBX recognizes the short key sequence and substitutes the correct expanded destination number.

Redial enables you to call the last number that you dialed again, even if the connection was not completed. This is useful to retry a busy number, to resume a conversation that was accidentally disconnected, or whenever you want to speak to the same party again.

Repeat dialing is useful when the intended destination of a call is busy. A key system, PBX, or a service from the circuit vendor will attempt to place the call at predefined intervals, and ring your phone set when the destination line is no longer busy. When a telephone circuit vendor provides this service, you may have instant knowledge of when the destination line is free. With a computer-based telephone terminal, key system, or PBX, you will not know that the destination is free until the predefined interval arrives for the call-retry mechanism.

Voice activated dialing is an emerging feature that frees your hands from the keypad. A digital signal processor (DSP) recognizes a characteristic audio sample, and dials the number associated with the audio sample. The audio sample can be the name of a person to call, or it can be an open-ended system where you speak the actual numbers to be dialed. Do not confuse this feature with voice activity detection (VAD), which is a bandwidth-saving technique used in digital voice transmission.

Security

A number of telephony features are designed to reduce your exposure to threatening or harassing calls, or to prevent unauthorized use of your phone system. These features enable you to stop receiving unwanted calls, or to identify threatening and harassing callers. They can also discourage dishonest employees and phreakers (telecom hackers) from exploiting your phone system for toll fraud.

Anonymous call rejection (ACR) stops all calls to your number that originate from numbers that use caller ID blocking. The caller hears a system message indicating that such calls are not accepted, followed by instructions to remove caller ID blocking for the specific call.

Call screening prevents calls from numbers that you have identified to be threatening or harassing. The caller hears a system message indicating that the desired destination will not accept the call.

Call trace is a service that must be specially ordered from the phone company. With this feature, call detail reports are immediately sent to law enforcement officials for criminal investigation. Some organizations, like public school facilities, often have requirements for this service.

Number restrictions are often used to prevent calls from your facility to 900 numbers, international numbers, or long-distance numbers. Most key systems and PBXs have a mechanism to create multiple restriction profiles, and assign those profiles specific users. For example, your company executives may need to place international calls to arrange business meetings, but members in the sales department only need to make domestic calls.

Emergency Response

This is an important service that should not be neglected in the process of integrating your voice and data networks. Table 1-1 lists the emergency response telephone numbers for various countries.

Table 1-1   *Emergency Response Telephone Numbers in Different Countries*

Country	Ambulance	Fire	Police
Armenia	03	01	02
Australia	000	000	000
Brazil	193	193	190
Canada	911	911	911
China	120	119	110
Czech Republic	155	150	158
Denmark	112	112	112
Egypt	123	180	122
Germany	115	112	110
Hong Kong	999	999	999
Iceland	112	112	112
India	102	101	100
Israel	101	102	100
Italy	118	115	112
Japan	119	119	110
Korea	119	119	112
Malaysia	999	994	999

continues

Table 1-1 *Emergency Response Telephone Numbers in Different Countries (Continued)*

Country	Ambulance	Fire	Police
Mexico City	080	080	080
New Zealand	111	111	111
Portugal	112	112	112
Singapore	995	995	999
South Africa	112	112	112
Sweden	112	112	112
United Kingdom	999	999	999
USA	911	911	911

You can find a more comprehensive list at the following URL:

www.ambulance.ie.eu.org/Numbers/Index.htm

In North America, it is not enough that you provide call routing for 911; you must also ensure that the Public Safety Answering Point (PSAP), or equivalent agency, receives information from your site to properly dispatch emergency services.

Consider the simple case of a business operating in a small building. When someone at this business site places a call to 911, the ANI information can be used by the PSAP to uniquely identify the location from which the call is placed. But for larger organizations, the ANI information is not sufficient. Consider a campus with multiple buildings, multiple floors in each building, and multiple rooms on each floor. The ANI information could be the same for a 911 call sourced from any room in any of these buildings! How would an ambulance know where to go?

Telephone circuit vendors offer a service that enables PBXs to provide more information about the location of the call. PBXs can send a Private Switch Automatic Location Identifier (PS/ALI) message as part of the call to 911, so emergency dispatchers can identify the building, room, and location from which the emergency call was placed. In some networking environments, there are big liability issues associated with maintaining the customer records of which extension is in which location. In these environments, extra care must be exercised when designing an integrated voice/data network.

Summary

This chapter has reviewed a variety of telephone features and services, the telecom equipment that provides the features, and the types of circuits that connect the equipment between sites. Chapter 3 explores the signaling details for the trunk types presented here.

CHAPTER 2

Enterprise Telephony Signaling

This chapter explores the telephone trunk connections between customer premises equipment (CPE) and the central offices (CO) managed by a circuit vendor. In a typical business environment, the CPE is a private branch exchange (PBX) that connects users to the Public Switched Telephone Network (PSTN) via the CO. The CPE can also be a simple telephone like the one in your home, or a key system for a small office.

In some cases, the CO is not involved with the telephony signaling, other than to provide the transmission facility (for example, T-1/E-1) between customer sites. In such cases, the phone switches at each customer location peer directly with each other through the CO switches. The trunk signaling used across these tie lines or tie trunks also falls within the scope of this chapter.

This chapter is divided into the following sections:

- Signaling Functions
- Analog Trunk Signaling
- Digital Trunk Signaling
- Signaling System Release 2 (R2)

The first section explores the various functions and signaling features that must be provided by telephone trunks, while the remaining sections explore how these features are provided with various trunk facilities and protocols.

Signaling Functions

Aside from the transmission of a two-way audio path, there are a number of important signaling functions that a telephone trunk or line must provide. As used in this chapter, a *trunk* refers to a connection between telephone switches (for example, PBX, key systems, or CO), and a *line* refers to a connection between a telephone and a phone switch. The following types of signaling are explored in this section:

- On-hook/off-hook detection
- Start-dial supervision
- Digit transmission

- Number identification
- Call progress tones
- Answer and disconnect supervision

In addition to the fundamental signaling functions described here, other signaling is required to enable advanced calling features. You can find more information about advanced feature signaling in books dedicated to SS7, Advanced Intelligent Network (AIN), and ISDN.

On-Hook/Off-Hook Detection

As the name implies, on-hook/off-hook signaling requires only two states: on-hook and off-hook. The telephone is *on the hook* when the handset portion (the microphone and speaker) is resting on the base of the telephone. The telephone is *off the hook* when the handset is lifted from the telephone base to place or receive a call. Telephone trunk endpoints must be able to transmit and receive signals that indicate the on-hook and off-hook status. The method of signaling the on-hook and off-hook state differs between trunk types.

On-hook/off-hook signaling is mandatory for all trunk types except for permanent trunk connections (for example, always-on or hoot-n-holler connections). Permanent trunks are usually implemented by permanently setting the trunk interface to an off-hook state.

Start-Dial Supervision

Start-dial supervision ensures that the receiving telephone switch is ready to interpret digits (that is, the destination telephone number) that are transmitted by the sending phone switch. Without start-dial supervision, the receiving phone switch may miss the first digits of a destination address, which results in a failed call attempt. For this reason, you should use a trunk signaling type that includes start-dial supervision whenever possible. For analog trunks, E&M wink-start is the best option that is widely available. Some digital trunks that use common channel signaling (CCS) provide the functionality of start-dial supervision.

While start-dial supervision provides positive confirmation that the remote switch is ready to receive digits, it does not provide confirmation that the digits have been received properly. Confirmation of receipt for individual digits is not a feature of signaling protocols used in North America, but R2 MFC signaling, which is used in many countries (and described later in this chapter), does provide this added reliability.

Digit Transmission

Telephones and telephone switches transmit digits to represent destination addresses, and to provide input from users to automated systems such as voice mail, auto-attendant, automatic call distributors (ACD), and interactive voice response (IVR) systems.

Telephony systems commonly use two classes of digit transmission:

- Pulse dialing
- Tone dialing

Pulse Dialing

The original telephones and circuits did not have a method to transmit digits. Human operators in a central office would answer the phone as soon as you went off-hook, and they would use patch cords to physically connect your phone circuit to the destination party's phone circuit. The original pulse scheme was implemented with rotary dial phones, which were designed to work with the existing loop-start lines and to enable the originating party to automatically dial the destination party without operator intervention.

Each number is signaled in the pulse dialing scheme as a series of make/break pulses, where the make portion is the off-hook state (about 60 percent of the pulse time), and the break portion is the on-hook state (about 40 percent of the pulse time). Each digit is represented by a corresponding number of breaks in the circuit. Zero is represented as ten pulses. Figure 2-1 illustrates the line state over time when 1234 is dialed.

Figure 2-1 *Pulse Dialing Transmits a Series of On-Hook Pulses to Represent Dialed Digits*

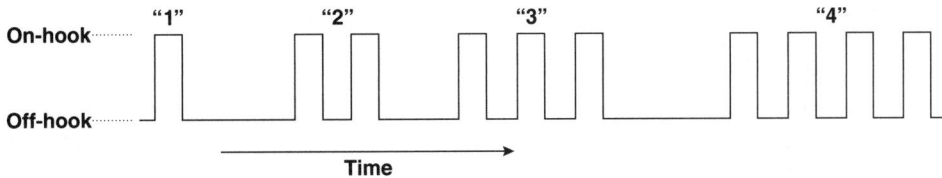

Per the EIA/TIA-470 specification, North American pulse dialing systems operate at a nominal rate of 10 pulses per second (PPS), but engineering tolerances allow operation from 8 to 11 PPS. Different standards and pulse rates apply in other countries, such as the nominal 20 PPS used in Japan.

Dialing Plans

Consider for a moment a seemingly unrelated topic: dialing plans. The assignment of area codes in the North American Numbering Plan is inexplicable from a routing perspective. Why would numerically adjacent area codes be placed on opposite sides of the United States (for example, 212 in New York, and 213 in Los Angeles)? This arrangement seems appalling to anyone that understands routing, but routing is not the only concern.

At the time that the North American Numbering Plan was developed, pulse dialing was the norm. Note that in the pulse-dialing scheme, smaller digits are transmitted faster than larger digits. For example, a 1 requires 100 ms to transmit one pulse, and a 9 requires 900 ms to transmit nine pulses (based on the ten PPS standard). In an effort to reduce the average amount of time and rotary dialing effort required by users across the continent, the major metropolitan areas of North America were assigned the area codes that resulted in the smallest amount of delay. The largest metropolitan area, New York, was assigned the area code with the shortest transmission delay that obeyed the numbering rules, which was 212. Los Angeles and Chicago were the next largest metropolitan areas, so they each received the next shortest area codes, which were 213 and 312.

With the advent of dual tone multi-frequency (DTMF) digit transmission, the motivation to arrange area codes based on digit transmission time had evaporated. The numbering plan legacy remains, however, shaped by a past which is no longer relevant.

Tone Dialing

There are a variety of standards for transmitting digits via audible tones:

- Dual tone multi-frequency (DTMF)
- Multi-frequency pulse (MF-P)
- Multi-frequency compelled (MF-C)

Multi-frequency (MF) digit transmission standards are generally a subset of broader signaling protocols based on audible MF tones. These broader signaling protocols describe digit transmission, supervisory signals, line signals, and other types of call control and information. These broader standards are mentioned where appropriate.

Dual Tone Multi-Frequency

Dual Tone Multi-Frequency (DTMF) is the most widely used method for digit transmission, both for destination number transmission and for in-band information exchange between callers and automated telephony systems (voice mail, IVR, ACD, auto-attendant, and so on).

The mapping between digits and audible frequencies is based on the physical layout of a standard telephone keypad. A separate frequency is assigned to each row and column of the keypad, such that any key corresponds with exactly two frequencies, as shown in Table 2-1.

Table 2-1   *DTMF Frequencies Assigned to a Standard Telephone Keypad*

	1209 Hz	1336 Hz	1477 Hz	1633 Hz
697 Hz	**1**	**2**	**3**	**A**
770 Hz	**4**	**5**	**6**	**B**
852 Hz	**7**	**8**	**9**	**C**
941 Hz	*****	**0**	**#**	**D**

The * key is commonly used to signal feature requests from the user to the public network. Many PBX manufacturers follow this convention for private networks as well. The # key is commonly used as a termination digit in public networks, so that call setup can begin without waiting for the digit timeout to expire.

The keys in the last column are not present on standard telephone keypads, but they are used in some applications, such as the Automatic Voice Network (AUTOVON) of the U.S. Department of Defense. In this application (see Table 2-2), the letters A through D represent call priority and preemption rules that regulate the use of congested facilities.

Table 2-2   *DTMF Extended Keys as Used in AUTOVON Defense Network*

Digit	Priority
A	Flash override
B	Flash
C	Immediate
D	Priority

Note that these priority names have been inherited by the IP precedence values 1 through 4.

Multi-Frequency Pulse

The allocation of frequencies for DTMF signaling was designed to simplify the construction of the first DTMF telephones. While the arrangement is intuitive, it is not the most efficient use of signaling frequencies. Multi-frequency (MF) allocation schemes generally use a set of six frequencies, from which two different frequencies are selected to represent each value. Though the mapping between digits and frequency is less intuitive, the common MF schemes use two less frequency components than the DTMF scheme. Table 2-3 illustrates the allocation of frequencies in the CCITT SS#5 and R1 MF protocols.

Table 2-3   *MF Allocation for CCITT SS#5 and R1 MF Digit Transmission*

	700 Hz	900 Hz	1100 Hz	1300 Hz	1500 Hz	1700 Hz
700 Hz	1	2	4	7	ST3
900 Hz		3	5	8	ST1
1100 Hz			6	9	KP (*)
1300 Hz				0	ST2
1500 HZ					ST (#)
1700 Hz					

In France and Spain, the Socotel protocol uses the same frequency allocation to represent digits, but the other aspects of the MF signaling operation are different.

So what is the relevance of pulse in multi-frequency pulse? In MF pulse signaling, the audible MF tone is played for a short duration to represent each signal. Contrast this behavior with multi-frequency compelled, where each tone is played continuously until it is acknowledged by the opposite end of the trunk.

Multi-Frequency Compelled

The most common multi-frequency compelled (MF-C) protocol for digit transmission is the CCITT R2 signaling protocol, specified in the CCITT Blue Book of 1988, Fascicle VI, Part 4 (now known as ITU-T Recommendations Q.400 through Q.490). Actually, the R2 signaling protocols are divided into the line signaling parts, which transmit supervisory signals, and the interregister signaling parts, which transmit call setup and control signals. The MF-C portion is the interregister signaling. Table 2-4 illustrates the frequency allocation for digit transmission via R2 MF interregister signals in the forward direction.

The signaling is called *multi-frequency compelled* because the MF tones are played continuously until the remote side is compelled to acknowledge them with another MF tone. This fact is important because it means that both ends of the trunk must transmit MF tones during the same call setup. You may also see information about *semi-compelled signaling*. A semi-compelled trunk uses compelled signaling in one direction and pulsed signaling in the other direction.

Table 2-4 *MF Compelled Digit Transmission as Used in CCITT R2 Signaling*

	1380 Hz	1500 Hz	1620 Hz	1740 Hz	1860 Hz	1980 Hz
1380 Hz	1	2	4	7	Code 11
1500 Hz		3	5	8	Code 12
1620 Hz			6	9	Code 13
1740 Hz				0	Code 14
1860 Hz					Code 15
1980 Hz					

Because both ends of an MF-C trunk need to transmit MF tones across the same audio path during the same conversation, there is a potential for confusion. An endpoint may receive a reflection of its own MF signals that are similar to the expected signals from the remote end. To combat the potential problem, MF-C systems (and more generally, bidirectional MF systems) often use different frequency ranges for the forward and backward directions of the call. This means that twice as many frequencies must be used, while staying within the voice-band frequencies. Note that the CCITT R2 frequencies are more closely spaced than the CCITT R1 frequencies for this very reason.

A final note on compelled signaling for digit transmission: For networks with long transmission delays (for example, satellite networks, or VoX networks), the individual acknowledgment of each digit can lead to a very high call-setup time. This situation is analogous to a TCP/IP data transfer with a window size of 1 packet. Consider for example, a network with 200+ ms delays in each direction. An 11-digit number requires a minimum of 4.4 seconds for transmission (400 ms for each digit with acknowledgment), assuming that the digits can be instantaneously detected. Accounting for the 50 to 60 ms required to detect each digit, the overall delay of compelled MF digit transmission is quite long when compared with pulsed MF digit transmission.

Number Identification

There are a variety of signaling methods to provide the telephone number of the party that places a call (the calling party), and the party that receives a call (the called party).

Calling Party Identification

Calling party identification can represent the technical origin of the call (that is, the exact telephone number of the outgoing trunk/line from the CPE), or it can represent the administrative origin of the call (that is, the party that pays the phone bills). *Caller ID*

(CID), sometimes called *Called Number Delivery (CND)*, provides the technical origin of a call, and *Automatic Number Identification (ANI)* provides the administrative origin of a call.

For residential subscribers, the CID and ANI values are generally the same. For business subscribers with multiple trunks/lines at a location, the CID and ANI are probably different. The ANI is the same for each trunk, assuming that the business phone bill is consolidated under a single bill-to number (BTN). The CID represents the actual telephone number of the originating trunk, which is different for each trunk.

Caller ID

Though multiple formatting standards exist for CID functions, this book focuses on the Custom Local Area Signaling Services (CLASS) standard for caller ID published by Bellcore. Examples of other CID standards include Calling Line Identity Presentation (CLIP) in the United Kingdom, and Analog Calling Line Identity Presentation (ACLIP) in Singapore.

Caller ID information is transmitted to the destination party between the first and second ringing tones, as indicated in Figure 2-2. Note that this format assumes the North American ringing cadence of 2 seconds on, 4 seconds off. Countries with a shorter silence interval in the ringing cadence must modify this standard to fit the time constraint.

Figure 2-2   *Overview of Caller ID Signaling*

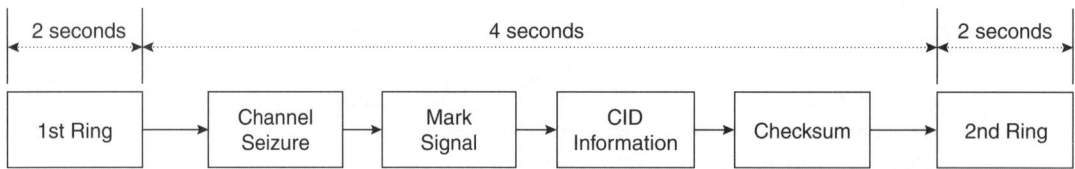

The CID information is a synchronous serial bit-stream that operates at 1200 bits per second (bps). A logical 0 is represented by a 2200-Hz tone at –13.5 decibels per milliwatt (dBm), and a logical 1 is represented by a 1200-Hz tone at –13.5 dBm. The fancy name for this type of signaling is *continuous binary frequency shift key (FSK) modulation*.

At least 500 ms after the first ring, the CO sends a channel seizure signal, which is an alternating series of 0s and 1s for 250 ms (exactly 300 bits, beginning with a 0 and ending with a 1). The channel seizure is followed by a mark signal that lasts for 150 ms. These two information elements are essentially a preamble to the actual CID information.

The actual CID information can take two formats:

- SDMF—Single Data Message Format
- MDMF—Multiple Data Message Format

Both the SDMF and the MDMF formats include the date and the time of the call. The MDMF format includes the telephone number and an ASCII string for the name of the calling party, while the SDMF format only identifies the telephone number of the calling party. The CID information is followed by a checksum.

Automatic Number Identification

Automatic Number Identification (ANI) can be provided on both analog and digital trunks from the carrier's switch to the CPE. The ANI is passed through carrier SS7 networks via the Initial Address Message (IAM) of the ISUP protocol (see next chapter), or through in-band multi-frequency (MF) tones when the network does not support SS7. The carrier's signaling network, as well as the trunk connection from the CO to the CPE, determine how the ANI is passed from the carrier to the CPE. The two basic ANI transmission methods from the CO to the CPE are:

- ISDN Q.931 SETUP message
- CAS MF tones with Feature Group D (FGD)

If the carrier has an SS7 network, and the subscriber has an ISDN connection to the carrier, then the ANI is passed in a Q.931 SETUP message. The information in the SETUP message is directly mapped from the IAM message in the SS7 network.

When the subscriber does not have an ISDN connection to the carrier, or the carrier does not have an SS7 signaling network, then the ANI can only be transmitted across trunks that are enabled for Feature Group D (FGD) signaling. With FGD, the actual ANI information is passed in-band using analog multi-frequency (MF) tones, according to the R1 MF specification (explained later in this chapter). FGD is generally provisioned on E&M wink-start trunks with a wink acknowledgment of the ANI information (explained later in this chapter).

FGD signaling was originally designed for the trunks between a Local Exchange carrier (LEC) and an Inter-Exchange Carrier (IXC), to provide telephone subscribers convenient access to long-distance service providers. Without FGD, a subscriber would have to dial a telephone number for a long-distance provider (for example, 1-800-CALL-ATT), enter a pin number to specify the billing account, and then dial the destination number. With FGD, a subscriber dials a prefix code of 10XXXXX along with the destination phone number. There are no intermediate dial tones, and no need to provide billing account information, because the signaling on the FGD trunk automatically provides this information. FGD also enables subscribers to choose a default IXC through which long-distance calls are placed when no prefix code is dialed. The use of FGD has subsequently been expanded to provide ANI from a CO to subscribers, and to provide ANI information from an E-911 Tandem Office to the Public Safety Answering Point (PSAP) for Emergency-911 calls in North America.

You can learn more about North American Emergency-911 protocols and data formats used at the following URL:

www.nena9-1-1.org/

Called Party Identification

Called party identification provides the number that the caller dialed to the destination of the call. This feature seems ridiculous at first thought: "If somebody calls you, why would you need to know the number they called? You can be fairly certain that they called your number!" This service is actually very useful for subscribers that have multiple phone numbers associated with the same trunk(s)/line(s). In a residential setting, the application can be separate phone numbers for parents and children, with a distinctive ring to indicate the desired party. In a business setting, the applications include direct inward dialing (DID) and call centers.

There are two classes of called party identification:

- Direct inward dial (DID)
- Dialed number identification service (DNIS)

The DID class is generally used to steer calls to a specific subscriber in an organization that shares phone lines. Direct inward dial can be provided on analog or digital trunks, using just about any digit transmission mechanism:

- Dial pulse (DP)
- Dual tone multi-frequency (DTMF)
- R1 multi-frequency (MF)
- R2 multi-frequency compelled (MF-C)

The DNIS class is generally used to steer calls through an automatic call distributor (ACD) system to an appropriate agent group, or to provide enhanced screen-pop information in call-center environments. DNIS is provided in an ISDN Q.931 SETUP message (based on the content of an ISUP IAM message in the SS7 network). DNIS can also be provided via MF tones.

Call Progress Tones

Voice networks signal a variety of conditions to users through audible call progress tones. Call progress tones are familiar to users within a country, but vary between countries. Table 2-5 contains a sampling of the call progress tones that are common in North America.

Table 2-5 *Call Progress Tones Used in North America*

Call Progress Signal	Frequency	Cadence
Dial Tone	350 Hz + 440 Hz	Continuous
PBX Ring-Back	440 Hz + 480 Hz	1 second on, 3 seconds off (repeated)
PSTN Ring-Back	440 Hz + 480 Hz	2 seconds on, 4 seconds off (repeated)
Busy Signal	480 Hz + 620 Hz	500 ms on, 500 ms off (repeated)
PBX Reorder	480 Hz + 620 Hz	250 ms on, 250 ms off (repeated)
PSTN Reorder	480 Hz + 620 Hz	300 ms on, 250 ms off (repeated)
Congestion	480 Hz + 620 Hz	200 ms on, 300 ms off (repeated)
Invalid Number	200 Hz, 300 Hz, 400 Hz	1 second for each frequency
Receiver Off-Hook	1,400 Hz + 2,060 Hz + 2,450 Hz + 2,600 Hz	100 ms on, 100 ms off (repeated)

When integrating networks on a global scale, it is important that the equipment in each country provides the call progress tones that are customary for the country. This ensures that users within each country have a consistent and familiar experience when using the telephone system.

Answer and Disconnect Supervision

Far-end answer supervision and disconnect supervision are features that provide positive confirmation of the beginning and end of call sessions. These features are important to service providers for billing and accounting purposes. Telephone companies are not the only service providers; other examples of service providers that benefit from answer and disconnect supervision include companies that implement departmental charge-back programs for telecom expenses, and hotels that charge guests for telephone calls.

Without answer supervision, service providers do not have a fixed point to begin billing for a connection. In such cases, the service provider may commence billing 20 or 30 seconds after the number is dialed, with the assumption that the destination would have answered by this time. In other cases, the service provider may begin billing immediately after the number is dialed. The problem with these approaches is that incomplete calls are also billed, much to the chagrin of the subscribers.

The Importance of Answer Supervision

On one trip outside the United States, I had poor luck calling back home from the hotel where I was staying. Every time I tried to place a call, I would get an automated announcement that indicated "all circuits are busy." I must have tried ten times to get through. Upon checkout from the hotel, I was surprised to discover charges of more than US$50 for phone calls to the United States, although I never had a successful connection! I have since approached answer supervision with more respect.

Analog Voice Trunks

Analog trunks are used when a telephone switch does not support digital connections, or when few voice channels are required. For example, small offices with key systems traditionally use analog trunks for tie lines and PSTN connections. Large offices with PBXs use analog tie lines to connect small remote offices. Analog trunks are also common for international tie lines because the cost of T1/E1 facilities is prohibitive for many organizations.

There are three common analog trunk types:

- Loop start
- Ground start
- E&M

Descriptions in the following sections consider the CO telephone switch and the CPE as the trunk endpoints, but other combinations are possible. For example, a PBX analog station port can act like the CO for the following connected devices:

- Plain old telephone service (POTS) telephone (for example, a residential telephone)
- Fax machine
- Modem
- Office or trunk port on a PBX or key system
- FXO port on a Cisco router

Alternatively, an FXS port on a Cisco router can act as the CO for the same set of devices. In general, the labels office and station are more appropriate than CO and CPE. Remember that FXS ports on Cisco routers provide battery and dial tone to stations, and FXO ports on Cisco routers expect battery and dial tone from the office.

Loop Start

Residential telephony systems around the world use loop-start signaling. Because trunks connect between telephone switches, and lines connect a telephone switch to a telephone, residential facilities are called loop-start lines. A circuit between a CO and a PBX may be called a trunk from the customer's perspective, or a line from the circuit vendor's perspective. In the United States, the loop-start trunk/line service may be called a 1-MB; it identifies a single measured business rate telephone circuit. The name indicates that telephone service is measured and billed based on usage, as opposed to the flat rate charged for local residential telephone service in the United States.

Idle Circuit

Analog loop-start signaling uses a single pair of wires between the phone switch in a CO and the telephone or telephone switch known as the CPE. Figure 2-3 illustrates an idle loop-start circuit with no active calls.

Figure 2-3   *Loop-Start Circuit in an Idle State*

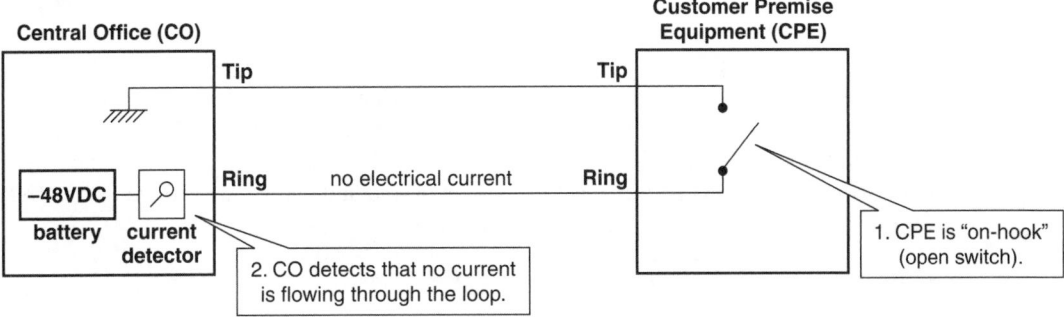

The CO provides a –48–volt (V) direct current (DC) battery, which sources electrical current through the circuit loop. Residential telephones do not require separate power sources for this reason. The CO also provides a dial tone generator and an alternating current (AC) ringing generator to signal the CPE. Electrical current flows from the battery in the CO to the CPE via the ring wire, and returns through the CPE to the CO ground via the tip wire. The CO knows when current is flowing through the loop via a current detector on the tip wire. Note that the CPE does not require an electrical ground.

Outbound Connections from the CPE

When the CPE is in the on-hook state (that is, the phone is hung up), there is an open electrical switch that prevents electricity from flowing through the circuit loop. When the

CPE initiates a call by changing to the off-hook state (that is, the phone is picked up), the electrical switch is closed, and current flows through the circuit loop. When current flows through the loop, the CO detects the CPE off-hook condition. The CO responds by transmitting a dial tone on the loop, which informs the CPE that the CO is ready to receive digits of the destination telephone number. This is a form of start-dial supervision. The off-hook detection and start-dial supervision for loop-start trunks is illustrated in Figure 2-4.

Figure 2-4   *CPE Initiates a Connection in a Loop-Start Trunk*

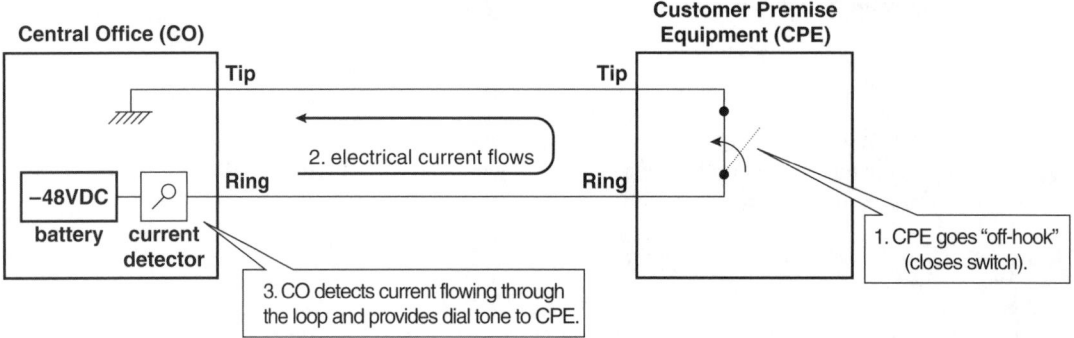

Following the digit transmission (via pulse or DTMF) and progress tones, the answer supervision signal is transmitted when the distant party answers the call. The local CO transmits the answer supervision signal as a polarity reversal on the tip and ring wires. In other words, the tip and ring connections to the ground and battery are reversed at the CO for the duration of the call, as shown in Figure 2-5.

Figure 2-5   *Answer Supervision for Loop-Start Trunks Provided as Tip and Ring Polarity Reversal*

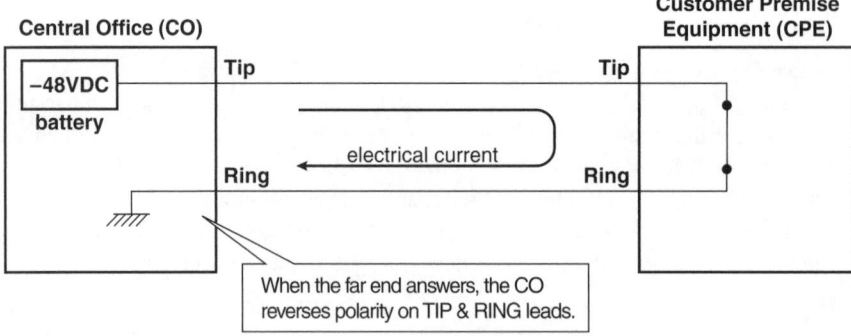

The CPE is designed to function with either signal polarity, but old equipment may not be able to transmit DTMF signals when the polarity is reversed. Because loop-start answer supervision reverses the signal polarity for the duration of the call, old equipment cannot use voice mail, auto-attendant, and IVR systems when answer supervision is present. For more information about loop-start answer supervision in the United States, read ANSI T1.401.01.

Inbound Connections from CO

The CO signals an inbound call destined for the CPE by sending an AC ringing voltage (between 90V and 140V) on the loop along with the –48VDC battery. If the CPE is a standard telephone, the AC voltage is translated to an audible ring that alerts the subscriber. If the CPE is a phone switch, the connection to the CO is automatically established after a predetermined number of rings. When the CPE changes to an off-hook state, the electrical switch is closed and current flows through the circuit loop. The CO detects that current is flowing through the loop, and the audio connection is established. Figure 2-6 illustrates this process.

Figure 2-6   *CO Initiates a Connection in a Loop-Start Trunk*

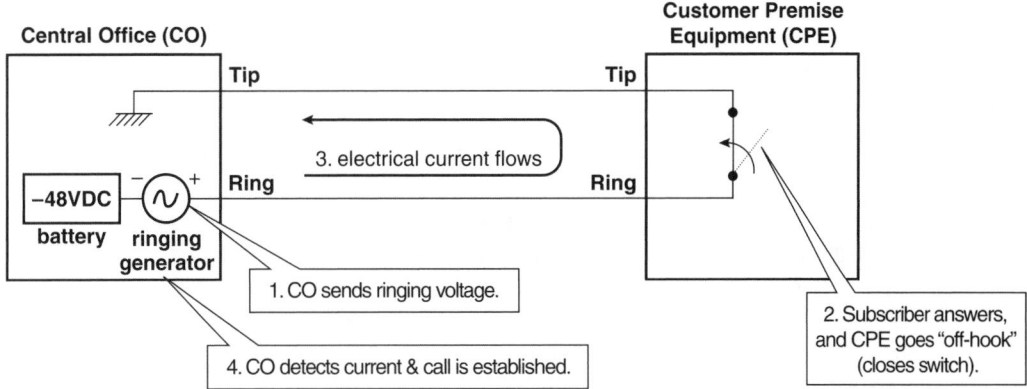

If the CPE is not a simple telephone, the CPE may provide an auto-attendant or a dial tone over the established audio path from the CO to the CPE. This signals the remote calling party to enter additional addressing information (for example, a phone extension) to complete the call to the final destination.

Disconnect Supervision

There are several methods for a CO to provide disconnect supervision to the CPE on loop-start trunks:

- Battery reversal
- Battery denial
- Supervisory tone disconnect (STD)

Battery reversal for disconnect supervision is similar to battery reversal for loop-start answer supervision. The tip and ring wires are reversed at the CO, which provides positive confirmation to the CPE that the far-end party has returned to an on-hook state. The FXO ports on Cisco routers recognize battery reversal as a form of supervisory disconnect beginning in IOS 12.0(7)XK. Note that VIC-2FXO cards must be replaced with VIC-2FXO-M1 cards (in Cisco 2600/3600 series routers) to incorporate hardware fixes, but the Cisco MC3810 supports the feature without a hardware upgrade.

Battery denial is when the local CO removes the –48VDC battery from the loop for at least 350 ms when the remote party disconnects. The battery denial must be greater than 350 ms to avoid confusion with pulse dialed digit transmission. FXO ports on Cisco routers recognize battery denial as a disconnect supervision signal.

Supervisory tone disconnect (STD) is an audible call progress tone that indicates the remote party has disconnected. A busy signal is the most commonly used STD; the actual signal varies from country to country, but is generally a tone of 600 Hz or less with a periodic on-off cadence. As of IOS 12.1(1)T, FXO ports on Cisco routers recognize STD as a form of disconnect supervision only for calls that have not yet been answered. STD will be available for active calls in a future IOS release; it may be available by the time you read this.

Ground-Start

Loop-start trunks are susceptible to a problem known as *glare*. This problem occurs when an inbound call is received from the CO at the same time that an outbound call is attempted from the CPE. The result is that the called party unknowingly answers the inbound call before a ringing tone is generated. This scenario is usually accompanied by a fair amount of confusion, because the calling party may have heard a ring-back tone and is unaware of the problem, while the called party dials digits into the calling party's ear and expects to be speaking with someone else. The called party may also be an automatic system such as a PBX that expects to place an outgoing call. In such cases, the outbound call on the PBX fails, and the calling party hears dial pulses or DTMF tones.

The competing calls need not arrive at opposite ends of the trunk at exactly the same time to cause problems. In reality, calls may arrive on both ends of the trunk and cause glare problems during a small time window. This time window is normally the duration of the silent period in the ringing cadence. In a typical PBX (and CO switch for that matter), the ringing cadence is driven by an oscillator that operates independently of when calls actually arrive. (Note that the PBX provides the ringing tone to the attached devices—the ringing tone is not passed from the remote end). A call may arrive during a silent period in the ringing cadence generated by the PBX, so the subscriber is not alerted until the beginning of an audible period in the ringing cadence. In the United States, this silent period during which inbound calls may not be announced is 4 seconds. Countries that use a short period of silence in the ringing cadence are less susceptible to glare problems.

Some PBXs support ring splash to combat the glare problem on loop-start trunks. In such cases, the PBX provides a brief ringing tone within 200 ms after the trunk is seized, following which the normal ringing cadence resumes. While the likelihood of glare is reduced, the ringing cadence sounds strange because the initial ring is not synchronized with the following rings.

Ground-start trunks, which can be provisioned from a CO, combat glare by introducing a low-delay three-way handshake. The fast handshake reduces the window of glare possibility to less than 100 ms. Both ends know sooner when a call is coming from the other side, so the glare condition can mostly be avoided. For example, a PBX may return a busy tone or use a different trunk instead of seizing the trunk in a glare condition. The following process outlines a ground-start trunk seizure by the CPE:

1 The CPE signals to the CO that it wants to seize the trunk.

2 The CO acknowledges the CPE request to seize the trunk.

3 The CPE completes the circuit loop, or seizes the trunk.

When the CO must deliver an inbound call, one less step is required:

1 The CO signals to the CPE that there is an inbound call.

2 The CPE acknowledges the request to seize the trunk by completing the circuit loop.

In both cases, the CO detects the current as soon as the loop circuit is completed by the CPE, and the call proceeds as in the case of a loop-start trunk. The following sections provide more detailed description of the ground-start signaling process.

Idle Circuit

Analog ground-start trunks use two wires between the CO and the CPE. Ground-start trunks do not function properly unless the tip and ring wires are connected with the correct polarity (that is, tip to ground, ring to –48VDC). Figure 2-7 illustrates a ground-start circuit in the idle state.

Figure 2-7 *Ground-Start Trunk in an Idle State*

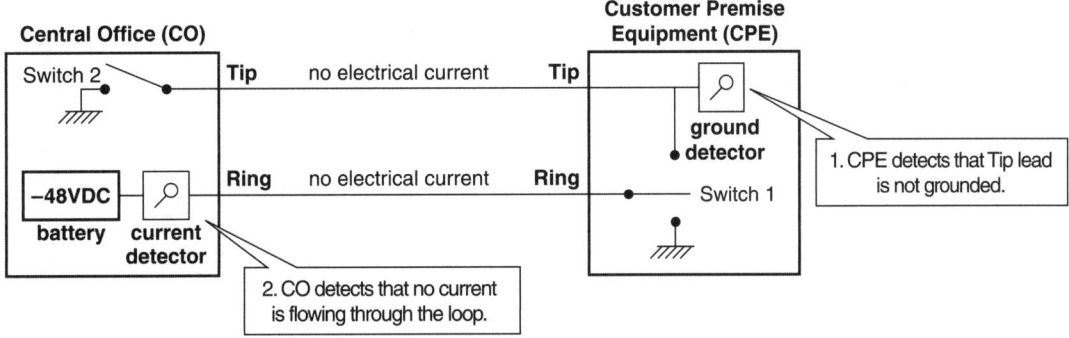

Ground-start trunks are more difficult than loop-start trunks to provision at the physical layer. Whereas loop-start trunks are unaffected by tip/ring polarity, ground-start trunks depend on proper polarity. This means that crossed wires on a punch-down block in a wiring closet will not affect a loop-start trunk, but they may be the source of failure for a ground-start trunk. Also note that for ground-start trunks, the electrical ground potential must be the same at both locations. In practice, the only way to achieve this requirement is to ensure that the electrical systems at both locations are well grounded, such as to a metal grounding rod rammed into the earth, or to a cold water pipe.

Outbound Connections from CPE

When the PBX or key system must seize the trunk for an outbound call, it moves Switch 1 to the ground position, which provides an electrical current path from the battery in the CO to the ground in the CPE. The CO detects the flowing current, and acknowledges the CPE request for trunk seizure by closing Switch 2. This provides a path for electrical current from the CPE ground detector to the CO ground. Figure 2-8 illustrates this process.

Figure 2-8 *CPE Grounds Ring Lead to Request Trunk; CO Replies by Grounding the Tip Lead*

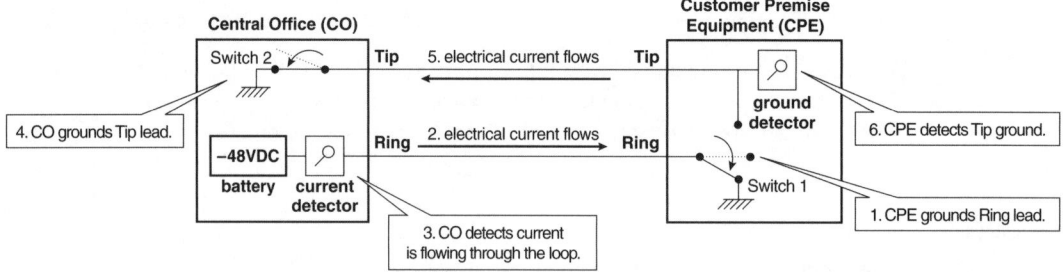

Figure 2-9 illustrates the remaining steps of the trunk seizure. When the CPE detects that the CO has grounded the tip wire, the CPE completes the circuit loop (just as in loop start), and removes the local ground signal. At this stage, the trunk is seized and it appears exactly like a loop-start trunk.

Recall that the motivation for this back-and-forth signaling is to minimize the time window during which both ends of the trunk may simultaneously seize the circuit (an undesirable condition known as *glare*).

Figure 2-9   *CPE Completes the Circuit Loop, Which Now Appears the Same as a Loop-Start Trunk*

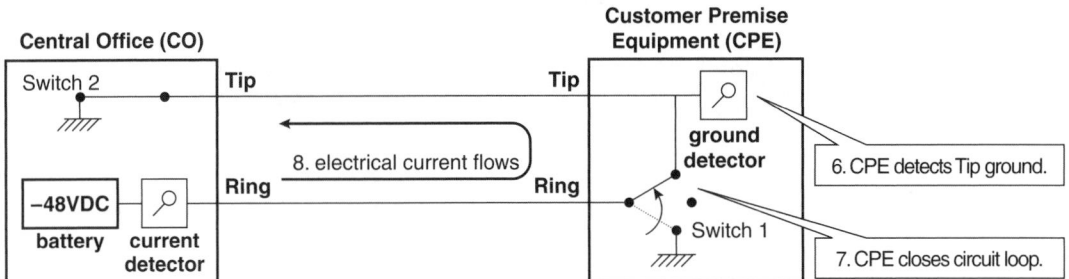

Inbound Connections from CO

Figure 2-10 illustrates the first steps that occur when a CO delivers an inbound call to the CPE. The CO closes Switch 2, which grounds the tip lead, and sends AC ringing voltage on the ring lead. The CPE senses the grounded tip wire and the AC ringing voltage on the ring wire, and completes the circuit loop in response. At this point, the call proceeds as it would on a loop-start trunk.

Figure 2-10   *CO Signals Call for CPE by Grounding the Tip and Sending an AC Ringing Signal on the Ring*

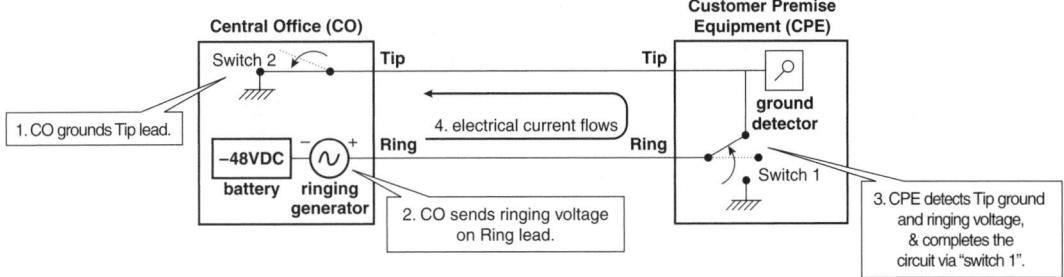

E&M

Depending on whom you ask, E&M is an acronym for Ear and Mouth, Earth and Magneto, or nothing at all. E&M circuit diagrams have wires that are labeled with E and M (as well as a few other letters), so the name is relevant in any case.

Recall that loop-start and ground-start trunks use the same wire pair for both the audio path and signaling functions. E&M trunks isolate these functions into separate wire pairs.

Depending on the E&M circuit configuration, the trunk signals and the audio path may each require one or two wire pairs, for a total of four to eight wires. Given that the trunk operation depends on correct arrangement of all the wires, E&M trunks are more challenging to implement at the physical layer than other trunk types.

The sections that follow explore several facets of analog E&M trunks, including:

- Interface wiring
- Audio path
- Circuit types
- Start-dial supervision

Interface Wiring

Table 2-6 identifies the wiring leads that are used in analog E&M trunk interfaces. If you are familiar with the wiring leads, you will have a greater understanding of the E&M circuit types that are presented in subsequent sections. Some of the terms in the table descriptions may be unfamiliar, but they will be defined in the sections that follow. You can refer back to this table as you explore the various E&M circuit types.

Table 2-6   *Electrical Leads Used for Analog E&M Trunks*

Lead	Name	Description
E	Ear or Earth	The ear of the PBX listens for signals from the CO on this wire.
		Signal state is either: (1) current is flowing; or (2) no current is flowing.
M	Mouth or Magneto	The mouth of the PBX talks to the CO on this wire.
		Signal state is either: (1) current is flowing; or (2) no current is flowing.
SG	Signal Ground	Forms a loop with the E lead through which current can flow in ground-isolation configurations.
SB	Signal Battery	Forms a loop with the M lead through which current can flow in ground-isolation configurations.
T1/R1	Tip-1/ring-1	Provides inbound audio to the PBX in four-wire E&M circuits, or both-way audio in two-wire E&M circuits.

Table 2-6   *Electrical Leads Used for Analog E&M Trunks (Continued)*

Lead	Name	Description
T/R	Tip/ring	Provides outbound audio from the PBX in four-wire E&M circuits; not used for two-wire E&M circuits.

You must connect the wiring leads to a punch-down block to interface with some vendors' equipment, while other vendors require that the individual wires be directly attached to holes in the chassis. All Cisco routers that support analog E&M interfaces use RJ-45 jacks, which are convenient when moves/adds/changes are necessary. Figure 2-11 illustrates the RJ-45 cabling pin for analog E&M interfaces connecting to Cisco routers. Note that this diagram illustrates a male RJ-45 connector on the end of a cable that connects to the Cisco router. Pin 1 is on the right side when looking straight at the cable in this manner. Looking at the female RJ-45 receptacle on a Cisco router (with the spot for the click-tab on the bottom), pin 1 appears on the left side.

Figure 2-11   *Analog E&M Cabling Pinout for Cisco Routers*

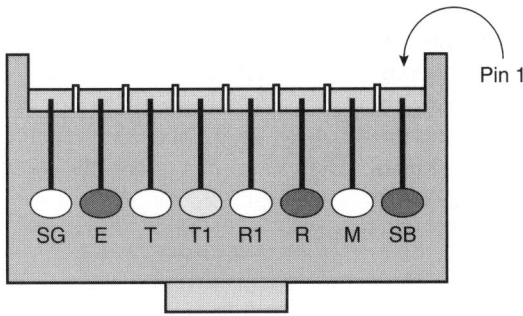

Audio Path

An analog E&M trunk can operate in either a *two-wire E&M* mode or a *four-wire E&M* mode. This distinction only refers to the number of wires used in the audio portion of the circuit. Two-wire E&M circuits accommodate both the transmit and receive directions of the audio path over a single pair of wires. Four-wire E&M circuits use one pair of wires for the transmit direction, and another pair of wires for the receive direction of the audio path. The decision to use two-wire or four-wire audio paths may be made independently of the E&M circuit type.

It is important that both ends of the trunk agree on either two-wire or four-wire operation. If the trunk configurations are mismatched, then the side configured for two-wire audio will not hear the remote party. The side configured with four-wire audio will appear to operate normally. This problem is referred to as *one-way audio*.

NOTE   In case you are wondering, both the two-wire and four-wire versions of an analog E&M trunk only support a single phone connection. You cannot use a four-wire E&M circuit to place two simultaneous calls.

Circuit Types

There are five primary E&M circuit configurations, which are distinguished by the degree of electrical ground isolation and the ability to operate in a back-to-back configuration.

Back-to-back operation of trunk interfaces is desirable for lab testing purposes, and when analog E&M connections must be established between collocated PBXs. Trunk interfaces can operate in a back-to-back design when the signaling systems are symmetrical. This means that the transmit signaling loop must send the same signals as are expected on the receive signaling loop.

Ground isolation is important when the voltage (that is, the electrical potential) of electrical ground is different at opposite ends of an E&M trunk. For example, suppose a voltmeter registers 0.1 volts (V) for the chassis ground (relative to the absolute ground) at one end of the trunk, and –0.1V for the chassis ground at the other end of the trunk. The 0.2V difference is enough to cause electrical current to flow through undesired paths in the electrical system, which may cause erratic signals on the wiring leads. Other electromagnetic devices that share the grounding system can also affect the ground voltage and cause interference.

To avoid the problems associated with different ground potentials, ground-isolated E&M trunk interfaces are designed such that the electrical systems are only connected to a ground at the same end of the trunk. This means that current cannot flow from a battery at one end of the trunk to a ground at the other end of the trunk. To pass the desired current (or the signal) across the trunk, a loop must be formed from two wires, with the battery and ground signals on one side of the trunk (as in loop-start circuits). This trick keeps current flowing between both ends of the trunk, without mixing the ground potentials. The remote side may then modulate the signal (block or enable electrical current) via a simple electrical switch that opens and closes. Note that both ends of a ground-isolated system may have a battery and ground, as long as current does not flow from a battery at one end to a ground at the other end.

TIP   E&M circuits without ground isolation require two signaling wires, and circuits with ground isolation require two pairs of signaling wires.

There are several strategies of on-hook/off-hook sequences used for E&M trunk seizure that apply to all of the E&M circuit types. Though trunk seizure is not discussed here with respect to each circuit type, the signals that represent on-hook and off-hook states are described for each E&M circuit configuration. The process of seizing an E&M trunk, in terms of on-hook/off-hook states, is described in more detail later in this chapter (see the "E&M Start-Dial Supervision" section later in this chapter.)

E&M Type I

Figure 2-12 illustrates the circuit configuration for E&M Type I trunks.

Figure 2-12 *E&M Type I Circuit*

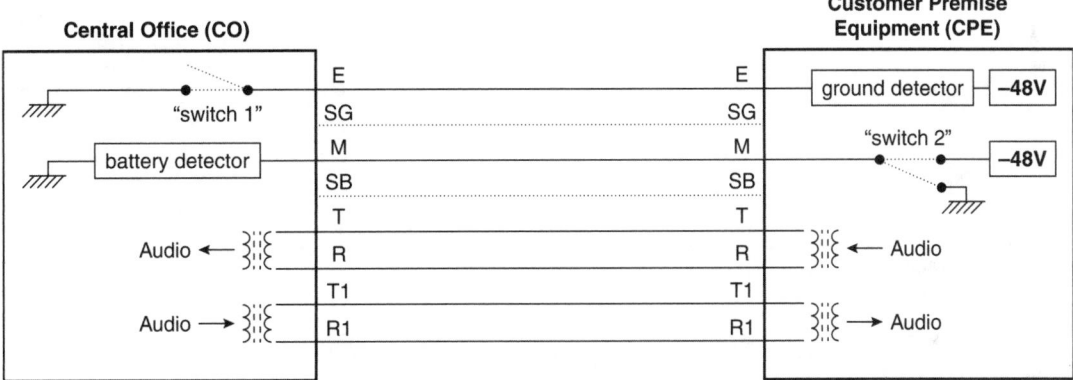

The CO signals an idle on-hook state to the PBX by leaving Switch 1 in the open position. The PBX detects this signal as the absence of current flowing across the E lead. The CO signals an off-hook state to the PBX by closing Switch 1, which causes current to flow across the E lead. The PBX interprets current on the E lead as the off-hook signal from the CO.

The PBX signals an idle on-hook state to the CO by leaving Switch 2 in the ground position, which grounds the M lead. No current flows on the M lead in this condition, because each end of the wire is connected to ground. The CO interprets the lack of current on the M lead as the on-hook signal from the PBX. The PBX signals an off-hook state to the CO by connecting the M lead to a battery, which causes current to flow across the M lead. The CO interprets the current flowing on the M lead as the off-hook signal from the PBX.

You can deduce that E&M Type I trunks do not provide ground isolation, because current flows from battery in the PBX to ground in the CO. You can also deduce that back-to-back connections of the PBX interface or CO interface are not possible for E&M Type I, because no current can flow in such configurations. In order for current to flow, there must be a battery and a ground on each circuit loop. If the E lead and M lead are crossed over between back-to-back PBXs, each wire has two batteries to source the current, but no ground to drain it. Crossed-over connections on back-to-back CO interfaces result in two grounds, but no battery to source the current.

Even though E&M Type I does not provide ground isolation and is not suitable for back-to-back configurations, it is the most commonly used E&M circuit in the United States.

E&M Type II

Figure 2-13 illustrates the circuit configuration for E&M Type II circuits.

Figure 2-13   *E&M Type II Circuit*

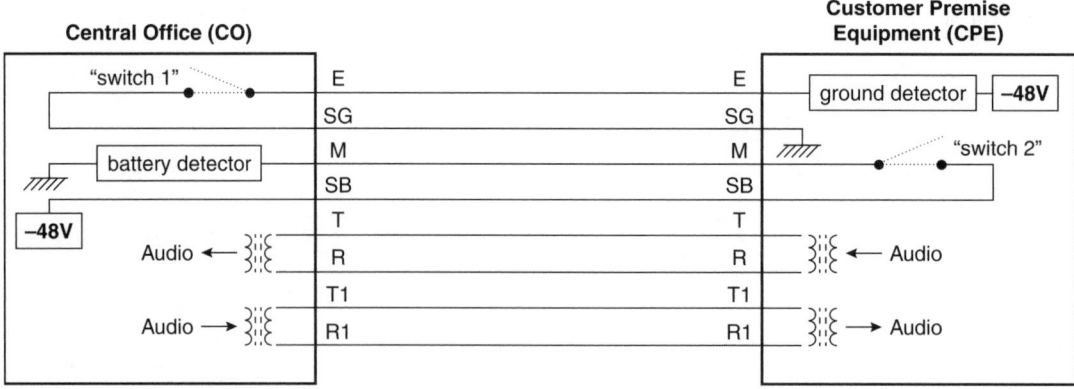

Just as in E&M Type I signaling, the CO signals an idle on-hook state to the PBX by leaving Switch 1 in the open position. The CO signals an off-hook state by closing Switch 1, which causes current to flow on the E lead (and SG lead), where it is detected by the PBX. The PBX signals the idle on-hook state to the CO by leaving Switch 2 in the open position, which causes no current to flow across the M lead. The PBX signals an off-hook state by closing Switch 2, which enables current to flow from the CO battery across the SB lead, and back over the M lead to the current detector in the CO.

E&M Type II circuits operate the same as E&M Type I circuits, with the addition of a ground-isolation feature. Instead of placing the ground for the E lead at the CO premises (which violates the principles of ground isolation because the E lead battery is in the PBX), the SG lead acts as an extension cord to carry the current back to the ground in the PBX. Instead of placing the battery for the M lead in the PBX (which violates ground isolation because the M-lead ground is in the CO), the SB lead acts as an extension cord to carry current from a battery at the CO. The extension cord concept places the battery and ground at the same ends of the trunk as the current detectors (or signal receivers), while enabling the remote ends of the trunk to control the current with simple switches (such as signal transmitters). This design prevents differences in ground potential between opposite ends of the trunk from interfering with the current detector function, while still enabling current to flow across the trunk and represent signaling states.

E&M Type III

The E&M Type III interface is primarily used between phone company switches in the upper tiers of the hierarchy. (As such, the CO and CPE labels are not applicable—think of the CO as the master and the CPE as the slave.) Because digital signaling (for example, SS7) has largely replaced analog signaling at the core of telephone networks, the E&M Type III interface is becoming obsolete.

Figure 2-14 illustrates the circuit configuration for E&M Type III circuits.

Figure 2-14   *E&M Type III Circuit*

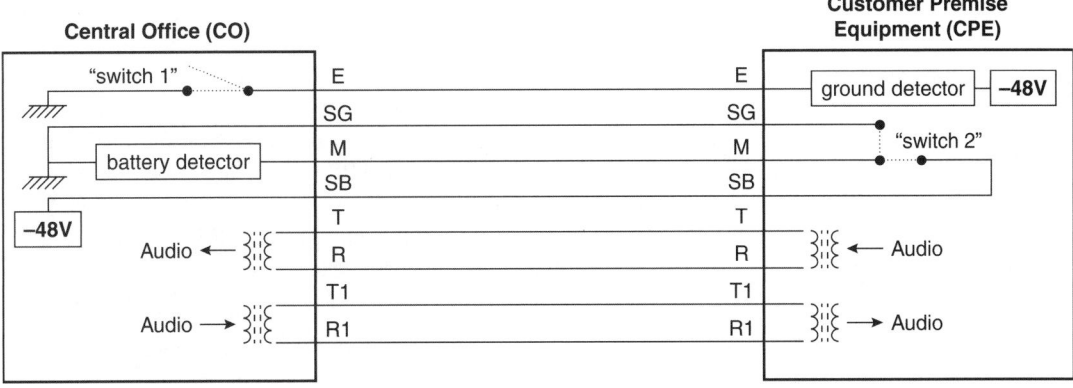

An interesting feature of this E&M circuit type is that the signals from the CPE to the CO require three wires (M/SG/SB), while the signals from the CO to the CPE only require a single wire. This asymmetry enables the CPE side to operate normally in the absence of a good ground reference.

The CO controls what signal is sent to the CPE via the E lead exactly as in the case of E&M Type I circuits (that is, via Switch 1). The CPE controls what signal is sent to the CO via the M lead by setting Switch 2 such that M is connected to SB or SG. The CPE connects M to SB to signal an off-hook state, and connects M to SG to signal an on-hook state. In either case, the ground or battery on the M lead originates from the CO side.

E&M Type IV

Figure 2-15 illustrates the circuit configuration for E&M Type IV circuits.

Figure 2-15 *E&M Type IV Circuit.*

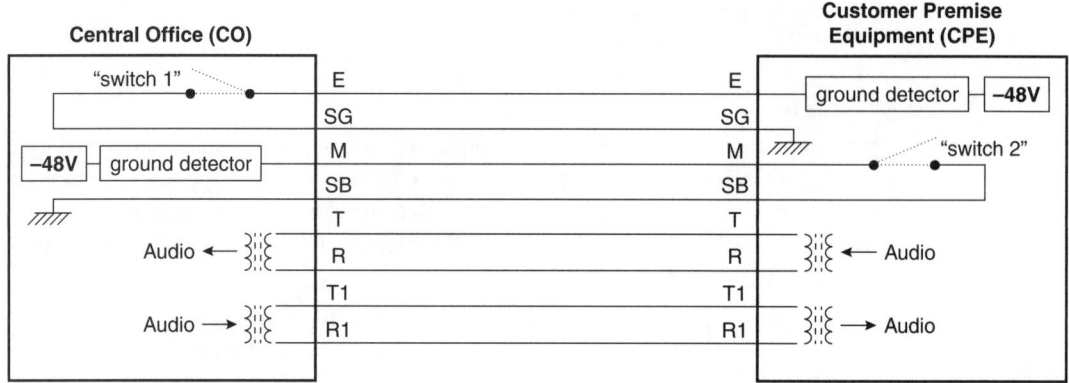

E&M Type IV circuits are nearly identical to E&M type II circuits. The circuit loop formed by the E lead and SG lead operates the same as in an E&M Type II circuit. The loop formed by the M lead and the SB lead is slightly different, because the positions of the battery and ground are swapped and the polarity of the current detector is reversed. The switches still perform the same functions as in E&M Type II (that is, open switch is on-hook, closed switch is off-hook). However, an off-hook state from the PBX yields a ground level voltage on the M lead and SB lead, as opposed to the battery level voltage in the case of E&M Type II. This means that there is never a battery level voltage on any of the PBX signaling leads, which reduces the likelihood of equipment damage from excessive current if wires are improperly connected.

While E&M Type IV circuits are safer to provision than E&M Type II, they are also more difficult to troubleshoot. If you connect a voltmeter to the pins of an E&M Type IV interface (for example, the associated wires on a punch-down block) and read ground signals on multiple pins, it is difficult to know which pins represent which signals. If the trunks interface fails to function properly, it is difficult to isolate whether the wires are crossed or if some other problem is present. Cisco routers do not support E&M Type IV circuits.

E&M Type V

E&M Type V combines the wiring simplicity of E&M Type I, with the benefits of ground isolation and back-to-back capabilities of the more complicated signaling types. Recall that ground isolation is a good feature because it prevents electrical current from leaking through the circuit at undesired times. (This concept will be explained better shortly.) E&M

Type V does not provide ground isolation, but it does address the problem of leaking current. Figure 2-16 illustrates the circuit configuration for E&M Type V circuits.

Figure 2-16 *E&M Type V Circuit*

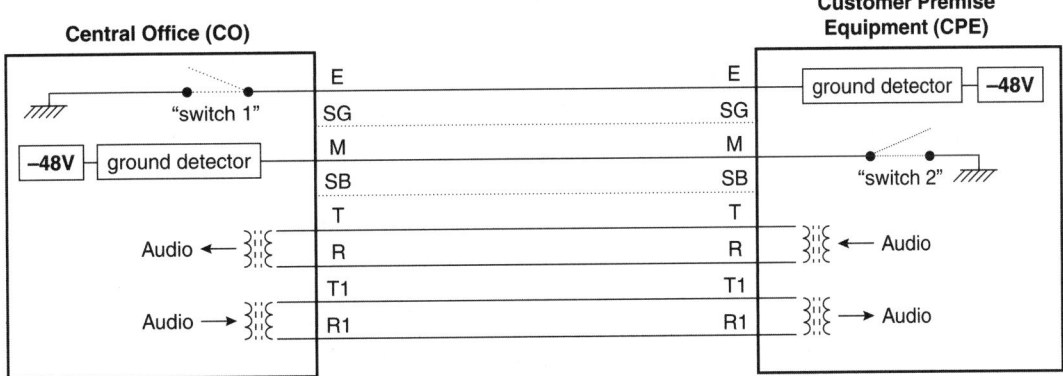

Switches 1 and 2 are open when the PBX and CO are sending an idle on-hook state. Switch 1 closes when the CO signals an off-hook to the PBX, and switch 2 closes when the PBX signals an off-hook to the CO.

To understand how E&M Type V combats the leaking current, it is important to understand how current leaks in the E&M Type I circuit (refer to Figure 2-12). In E&M Type I circuits, the PBX grounds the M lead in an on-hook state. If the ground voltages on either end of the M wire are not exactly equal, then some current crosses the wire, which may cause the current detector in the CO to think that the PBX is going off-hook. The larger the disparity between the ground voltages, the larger the leaking current. A solution to this problem, which is employed in E&M Type V circuits, is to leave the M-lead signal as open instead of ground during the on-hook condition. This prevents current from flowing across the wire, even if the grounds are at different voltage potentials.

To allow back-to-back operation of either the PBX or the CO interface, E&M Type V circuits provide battery on one lead and ground on the other lead for each end of the trunk. Recall that E&M Type I circuits cannot operate back-to-back because the PBX side of the trunk provides a battery on both leads. Such a back-to-back configuration would result in a wire with a battery on either end, which would not allow current to flow.

Circuit Type Summary

Table 2-7 summarizes the characteristics of the five analog E&M circuit types.

Table 2-7 *Characteristics of Analog E&M Circuit Configurations*

	Type I	Type II	Type III	Type IV	Type V
Typical Use	North America (most PBXs)	Centrex, some Nortel PBXs	Older CO switches	Compatible with Type II, but safer	Common outside of United States
Signaling Leads	E,M	E,M,SB,SG	E,M,SB,SG	E,M,SB,SG	E,M
Ground Isolation?	No	Yes	Yes	Yes	No
Back-to-Back Configurations?	No	Yes	No	Yes	Yes

Note that other variants of E&M circuits do exist, such as the SSDC5 signaling used by British Telecom. SSDC5 is very similar to E&M Type V, with impedance added in series between the electrical switches and ground. Cisco routers do not support SSDC5 signaling.

A voltmeter can help verify the proper wiring and operation of an analog E&M trunk. With the black probe of the voltmeter connected to the SG lead on the PBX trunk interface, touch the red probe to each of the other leads on the PBX trunk interface. Table 2-8 summarizes what you should expect to measure for analog E&M trunks that are operating correctly.

Table 2-8 *Requirements to Generate On-Hook/Off-Hook Signaling States in Analog E&M Circuits*

	Type I	Type II	Type III	Type IV	Type V
E/SG (on-hook)	Open	Open	Open	Open	Open
E/SG (off-hook)	Ground	Ground	Ground	Ground	Ground
M/SB (on-hook)	Ground	Open	Ground	Open	Open
M/SB (off-hook)	Battery	Battery	Battery	Ground	Ground

Note that the ground signal may not measure exactly 0V, and the battery signal may not measure exactly –48V. Also, the voltage on the E lead and SG lead may not be the same, but they should both be close to the same state (that is, ground, battery, or open). The same rule applies for the M lead and the SB lead. Such are the vagaries of the real world.

Start-Dial Supervision

The preceding section addressed how different types of E&M circuits represent on-hook and off-hook states. This section explores the following methods for a PBX or CO to seize an E&M trunk and begin transmitting digits, each of which involve on-hook and off-hook signaling:

- Immediate start
- Delay start
- Wink start
- Tone start

Immediate Start

E&M *immediate start* is the simplest form of start-dial supervision, and is almost the same as no supervision. The originating side of the trunk sends the off-hook signal, and after 150 ms, begins transmitting the digits of the destination address (in other words, the called number). The idea is that the 150-ms pause is enough for the receiver to be ready, but there is no method for the receiving side to indicate that it is actually ready to receive digits. After the pause, the originating side of the trunk just transmits the digits whether or not the receiving side is ready.

Delay Start

An example of a situation in which the receiver may not be ready within 150 ms is a PBX that oversubscribes DTMF digit collectors across multiple trunks. For example, a PBX may have four digit collectors for a T-1 circuit that can accept 24 calls. If all of the DTMF collectors are in use by other trunks, and a call arrives on an otherwise available trunk, the PBX must indicate to the CO that it is not ready to receive the digits until a DTMF collector becomes available. Delay-start signaling is one way to accomplish this goal.

In *delay-start signaling*, the originating side of the E&M trunk goes off-hook, and checks the state of the receiving side after 75 to 300 ms. If the receiver is off-hook during this check, then the originating side waits until the receiver changes to an on-hook state. In systems without delay-dial integrity, the originating side transmits the digits after a predefined amount of time even if the receiver is not ready (similar to immediate start). Systems with delay-dial integrity operate similarly to wink-start systems. That is, the originating side of the trunk waits for the remote side to transition from off-hook to on-hook before it transmits the digits.

Wink Start

Wink-start signaling is the most common method of start-dial supervision. It should be your first choice when provisioning an E&M interface (analog or digital). Figure 2-17 illustrates the process of trunk seizure and preparation for digit transmission.

Figure 2-17   *Wink-Start Signaling Provides Confirmation that Receiver Is Ready to Receive Digits*

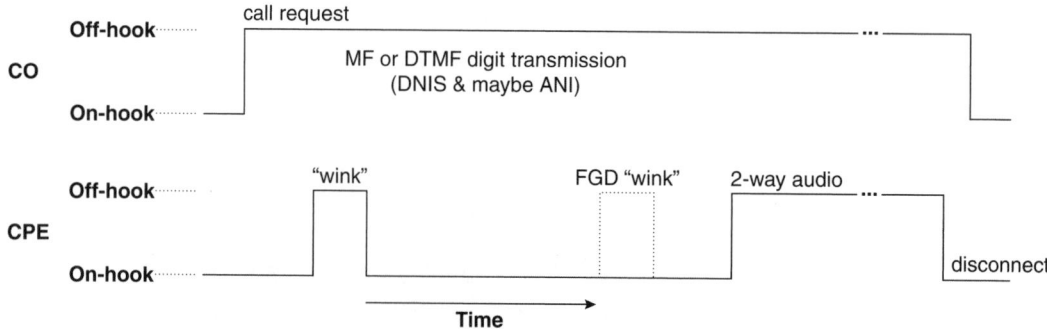

1   The originating side of the E&M trunk sends the off-hook signal, and waits for an acknowledgment from the receiver.

2   The receiver detects the off-hook signal, and replies with a wink (an off-hook pulse that lasts from 140 to 290 ms, followed by a return to an on-hook state).

3   The originating side detects the wink acknowledgment from the receiver, pauses for at least 210 ms, and then transmits the digits.

4   If Feature Group D (FGD) is enabled for the trunk, the receiving side acknowledges the digits with another wink. This type of signaling is called E&M wink start with wink acknowledgment. Feature Group B (FGB) does not use the wink acknowledgment.

5   The receiver changes to an off-hook state when the called party answers the connection and the audio path is built.

Tone Start

E&M *tone-start signaling* is sometimes used between PBXs in private networks. It is similar to loop-start and ground-start signaling, in that the receiver responds to a trunk seizure request with a dial tone. The originating side can automatically transmit the digits when it detects the dial tone. If the digit buffer in the originating side of the trunk is empty, then the calling party hears the dial tone and dials additional digits to complete the call.

Digital Trunk Types

When there is sufficient call volume to justify the cost of hardware and recurring circuit charges, digital trunks are the facilities of choice. T-1 and E-1 circuits are the standard digital facilities that interface with PBXs and hybrid key systems.

This book assumes that you are familiar with T-1 and E-1 circuit technology as it is used for data-only transmission (that is, WAN connections between routers). For T-1 circuits, this includes alternate mark inversion (AMI) line coding with D4 super-framing (SF), as well as bipolar 8-zero substitution (B8ZS) line coding with extended super-framing (ESF). For E-1 circuits, this includes AMI or high-density bipolar 3 (HDB3) line coding, and timeslot 0 framing with or without CRC-4 multiframes.

This book does not assume that you are familiar with the telephony signaling features available for T-1 and E-1 circuits. The remainder of this chapter explores the types of telephony signaling that are used in conjunction with T-1 and E-1 circuits, divided into two broad classes:

- Channel-associated signaling (CAS)
- Common-channel signaling (CCS)

TIP

You should be aware that CAS and CCS are both acronyms for other voice-related concepts, so be careful when adjusting PBX parameters with these labels. For example, NEC telephone switches have a configuration parameter called Trunk Class that may be assigned as CAS. The CAS option actually refers to centralized attendant service. *Centi-call seconds (CCS)* is often used to describe the amount of busy-hour traffic on a PBX.

Channel-Associated Signaling

In channel-associated signaling (CAS), there is a deterministic relationship between the call-control signals and the TDM audio channels that they control. The basic frame structures of both T-1 and E-1 facilities include specific bit positions that represent the signaling information for specific audio channels. For T-1 facilities, the signaling bits are colocated on the same timeslot as the audio path that they control. For E-1 facilities, the signaling bits are arranged in timeslot 16 with a multiframe structure, such that specific bits in specific frames of the multiframe represent the signals for a given TDM channel. A simple algorithm can interpret the signaling state of each TDM audio channel by reading specific bit positions in a T-1/E-1 multiframe. The specific bit positions are constant for each T-1 super-frame or E-1 multiframe structure.

The following sections explore how call-control-signaling bits are embedded in T-1/E-1 frames, and how the values of these bits map to call-control signaling states:

- T-1: Robbed Bit Signaling
- E-1: Timeslot-16 Multiframes
- ABCD Signaling Schemes

T-1: Robbed-Bit Signaling

T-1 *robbed-bit signaling (RBS)*, which is common in North America, is so named because some of the bits from the audio payload in each TDM timeslot are robbed and reused for signaling information. Every six frames (0.75 ms), the bits that represent the signaling state for each timeslot overwrite the encoded audio information in the least significant bit of their respective timeslots.

Because only the least significant bit of some frames is overwritten, and because the PSTN standard pulse code modulation (PCM) encoding is resilient to bit errors, RBS has no noticeable effect on voice quality. However, RBS has a significant impact on timeslots that are used for data (as opposed to voice) transmission. If RBS cannot be disabled for a channel, then the effective bandwidth of the channel is reduced from 64 to 56 kbps. This is why some ISDN data calls in the United States must be configured to only use 56 kbps for each B-channel.

Figure 2-18 illustrates how audio bits are robbed and reused for signaling in conjunction with D4 super-framing on T-1 facilities.

Note that D4 super-frames allow only 2 signaling bits for each audio channel, because every six frames yield 1 signaling bit. These bits are called the A and B bits, and the CAS scheme for D4 super-frames is called AB signaling. Extended super-frames, which are composed of twice as many frames as standard D4 super-frames, allow 4 signaling bits for each audio channel. Figure 2-19 illustrates the ABCD bit arrangement in an extended super-frame.

The extended super-frame CAS scheme where all 4 bits are used for signaling is called ABCD signaling. If only the first 2 bits are required, then the last 2 bits are set to follow the first 2 bits in a scheme known as ABAB signaling. If only a single bit is required for signaling, then the last 3 bits are set to follow the first in a scheme known as AAAA signaling.

Figure 2-18 *Robbed-Bit Signaling Used with D4 Super-Frames (SF) on T-1 Circuits*

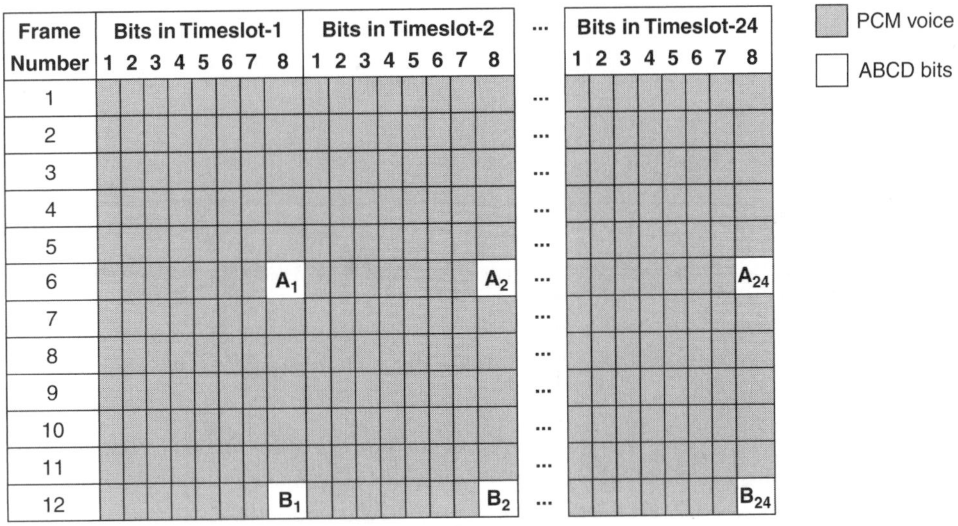

E-1: Timeslot-16 Multiframes

Channel-associated signaling seems somewhat counter-intuitive for E-1 circuits, because all of the signaling information is contained in timeslot 16. Although the signals are all in a single timeslot (which would seem to indicate a common-channel signaling scheme), the bit positions in that timeslot have a fixed meaning that is an inherent part of the frame structure. In other words, all signaling states are defined at the frame level, and are continuously encoded whether or not there are active calls or signaling requirements. Contrast this with CCS methods, in which a specific timeslot is used as a serial bit-stream for event-driven messages that require a higher layer protocol to interpret.

Figure 2-20 illustrates a single E-1 frame, in which timeslot zero (TS-0) provides the facility framing functions, timeslot 16 (TS-16) provides the CAS functions, and the remaining timeslots contain pulse code modulated (PCM) voice signals.

Figure 2-19   *Robbed-Bit Signaling Used with Extended Super-Frames (ESF) on T-1 Circuits*

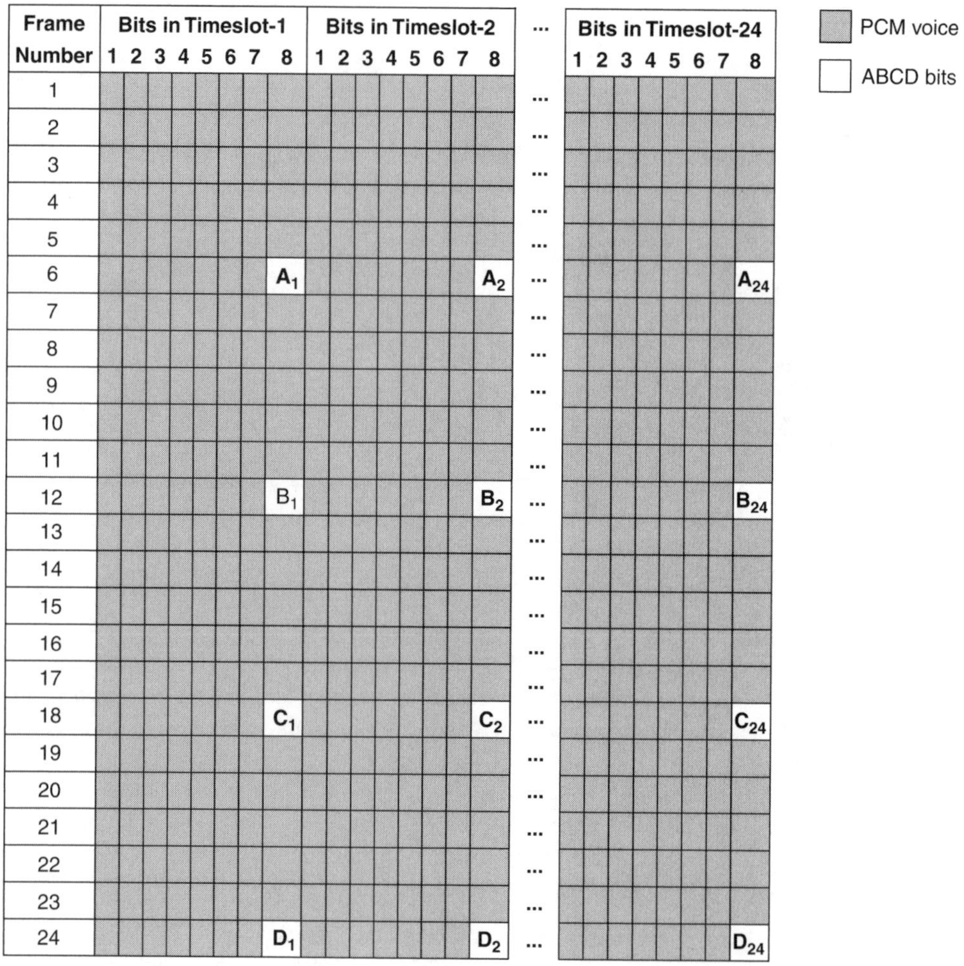

Frame Number	Bits in Timeslot-1 1 2 3 4 5 6 7 8	Bits in Timeslot-2 1 2 3 4 5 6 7 8	...	Bits in Timeslot-24 1 2 3 4 5 6 7 8
1			...	
2			...	
3			...	
4			...	
5			...	
6	A_1	A_2	...	A_{24}
7			...	
8			...	
9			...	
10			...	
11			...	
12	B_1	B_2	...	B_{24}
13			...	
14			...	
15			...	
16			...	
17			...	
18	C_1	C_2	...	C_{24}
19			...	
20			...	
21			...	
22			...	
23			...	
24	D_1	D_2	...	D_{24}

■ PCM voice
□ ABCD bits

Figure 2-20   *Allocation of E-1 Timeslots for Framing, Data, and Signaling*

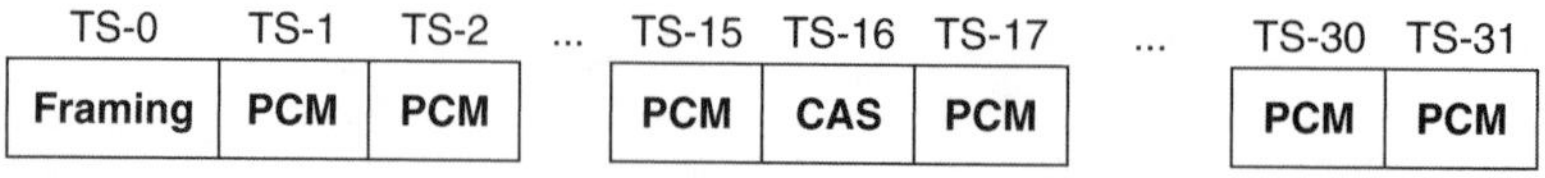

TS-0	TS-1	TS-2	...	TS-15	TS-16	TS-17	...	TS-30	TS-31
Framing	PCM	PCM		PCM	CAS	PCM		PCM	PCM

There are two types of multiframe structures for E-1 circuits. The first structure, which should be familiar to you if you have worked with E-1 data circuits, is based on the CRC-4 bits in TS-0. This structure serves the same function as a super-frame or extended super-frame over T-1 facilities: to maintain the clocking integrity of the synchronous circuit and provide facilities for link layer testing (for example, loop-back signals, alarms, and so on). The second multiframe structure is based on TS-16, and is independent of the multiframes in TS-0. That is, the first frame of a TS-16 multiframe is not required to be the first frame of the TS-0 multiframe. In practice, many vendors do align these multiframe structures for simplicity. Figure 2-21 illustrates how the CAS bits are arranged in timeslot 16 of the TS-16 multiframe.

Figure 2-21   *Allocation of ABCD Bits Within a Timeslot-16 Multiframe*

Frame Number	Bits in Timeslot-16							
	1	2	3	4	5	6	7	8
0	0	0	0	0	X	Y	X	X
1	A_1	B_1	C_1	D_1	A_{17}	B_{17}	C_{17}	D_{17}
2	A_2	B_2	C_2	D_2	A_{18}	B_{18}	C_{18}	D_{18}
3	A_3	B_3	C_3	D_3	A_{19}	B_{19}	C_{19}	D_{19}
4	A_4	B_4	C_4	D_4	A_{20}	B_{20}	C_{20}	D_{20}
5	A_5	B_5	C_5	D_5	A_{21}	B_{21}	C_{21}	D_{21}
6	A_6	B_6	C_6	D_6	A_{22}	B_{22}	C_{22}	D_{22}
7	A_7	B_7	C_7	D_7	A_{23}	B_{23}	C_{23}	D_{23}
8	A_8	B_8	C_8	D_8	A_{24}	B_{24}	C_{24}	D_{24}
9	A_9	B_9	C_9	D_9	A_{25}	B_{25}	C_{25}	D_{25}
10	A_{10}	B_{10}	C_{10}	D_{10}	A_{26}	B_{26}	C_{26}	D_{26}
11	A_{11}	B_{11}	C_{11}	D_{11}	A_{27}	B_{27}	C_{27}	D_{27}
12	A_{12}	B_{12}	C_{12}	D_{12}	A_{28}	B_{28}	C_{28}	D_{28}
13	A_{13}	B_{13}	C_{13}	D_{13}	A_{29}	B_{29}	C_{29}	D_{29}
14	A_{14}	B_{14}	C_{14}	D_{14}	A_{30}	B_{30}	C_{30}	D_{30}
15	A_{15}	B_{15}	C_{15}	D_{15}	A_{31}	B_{31}	C_{31}	D_{31}

The first frame of the TS-16 multiframe provides synchronization for the multiframe and limited facility signaling. The Y bit indicates the presence or absence of a yellow alarm (which is a remote-side red alarm), and the X bits are unused and reserved for future or country-specific use. The second frame of the TS-16 multiframe begins the CAS bit encoding. The first 4 bits encode the ABCD bits for TS-1, and the last 4 bits encode the ABCD bits for TS-17. In the next frame, the ABCD bits for TS-2 and TS-18 are encoded. TS-16 of each successive frame encodes the ABCD bits for the remaining timeslots. In Figure 2-21, the subscripts of the ABCD bits indicate which timeslots they govern.

ABCD Signaling States

Many CAS variations use only the A and B bits to emulate the common analog signaling types:

- Loop start
- Ground start
- E&M immediate start
- E&M delay dial
- E&M wink start

Digital Loop Start

Digital loop-start signaling requires the A and B signaling bits. The CPE controls the A bit, which represents the state of the circuit loop (A=0 open, A=1 closed). The CO controls the B bit, which represents the state of the ringing tone (B=0 ringing, B=1 no ringing). Both the CO and the CPE echo the bit values they receive for the bits that they do not control, so the AB bit values are the same in each direction. Refer back to Figures 2-6 through 2-9 for a review of analog loop-start signaling.

The CPE initiates a loop-start trunk seizure by closing the circuit loop. The bit transitions for this process are illustrated in Table 2-9.

Table 2-9   *Digital Loop-Start Seizure Initiated by the CPE*

	CO			CPE	
Description	**A**	**B**	**Direction**	**A**	**B**
Idle	0	1		0	1
CPE closes loop			←	1	1
Active call	1	1		1	1

The CO initiates a loop-start trunk seizure by sending a ringing tone on the tip lead. When the subscriber lifts the handset (or the phone switch automatically answers the incoming call), the loop is closed and the audio path is active. Table 2-10 illustrates the signaling bit transitions.

Table 2-10   *Digital Loop-Start Seizure Initiated by the CO*

	CO			CPE	
Description	**A**	**B**	**Direction**	**A**	**B**
Idle	0	1		0	1
CO sends ringing	0	0	→		

Table 2-10 *Digital Loop-Start Seizure Initiated by the CO (Continued)*

	CO			CPE	
Description	**A**	**B**	**Direction**	**A**	**B**
CPE closes loop			←	1	0
CO stops sending the ringing	1	1	→		
Active call	1	1		1	1

Digital Ground Start

Digital ground-start signaling also requires the A and B signaling bits. In digital loop-start signaling, the CO and CPE each control one of the two signaling bits, which have the same meaning in both directions of transmission. Digital ground start differs because the bits have different meanings and are set independently in each direction. The CO and CPE each have full control of both signaling bits that they transmit. Refer to Figures 2-7 through 2-12 to review the operation of analog ground-start signaling.

From the CO side, the A bit indicates the state of the tip lead (A=0 grounded, A=1 open), and the B bit indicates the presence or absence of ringing tone (B=0 ringing, B=1 no ringing).

From the CPE side, both the A bit and B bit relate to the operation of switch 1 in Figures 2-7 through 2-10. Because switch 1 can connect the ring lead to one of three positions (open, grounded, or loop closed with tip), 2 bits (A and B) are required to represent its state. The A bit indicates whether the circuit loop is open or closed (A=0 open, A=1 closed), and the B bit indicates whether or not the ring wire is grounded (B=0 grounded, B=1 not grounded). Note that the ring wire should never be grounded by the CPE when the loop is closed; hence {A=1, B=0} is an invalid state from the CPE.

The following is a summary of the ground-start trunk seizure by the CPE:

- In the idle state, the CO leaves the tip open and provides no ringing tone, while the CPE leaves switch 1 in the open position (loop open, ring lead not grounded).

- To initiate trunk seizure, the CPE connects the ring lead to ground, which alerts the CO.

- The CO grounds the tip lead as an acknowledgment and indication to proceed.

- The CPE closes the circuit loop, which activates the audio path.

Table 2-11 illustrates the AB bit transitions of this process.

Table 2-11 *Ground-Start Seizure Initiated by the CPE*

	CO			CPE	
Description	**A**	**B**	**Direction**	**A**	**B**
Idle	1	1		0	1
CPE grounds ring			←	0	0
CO grounds tip	0	1	→		
CPE closes loop			←	1	1
Active call	0	1		1	1

The following is a summary of the ground-start trunk seizure by the CO:

- In the idle state, the CO leaves the tip open and provides no ringing tone, while the CPE leaves switch 1 in the open position (loop open, ring lead not grounded).

- To initiate trunk seizure, the CO grounds the tip and sends a ringing tone to the CPE.

- The CPE replies to the tip ground and ringing tone by closing the loop on the ring lead. Note that the CPE never grounds the ring lead on inbound calls.

- The call is activated when the CPE closes the loop.

Table 2-12 illustrates the AB bit transitions of this process.

Table 2-12 *Ground-Start Seizure Initiated by the CO*

	CO			CPE	
Description	**A**	**B**	**Direction**	**A**	**B**
Idle	1	1		0	1
CO grounds tip, sends ringing	0	0	→		
CPE closes loop			←	1	1
CO stops sending the ringing	0	1	→		
Active call	0	1		1	1

Digital E&M Immediate Start

Digital E&M signaling only requires 1 signaling bit in each direction to represent two signaling states: A=0 is on-hook, and A=1 is off-hook. The B bit, which is not required, is generally set to follow the A bit, even for systems that otherwise follow ITU-T Recommendations (for example, setting C=0 and D=1). The physical complexity of analog E&M circuits disappears in digital E&M signaling, because the analog circuit wiring variations and voltage levels are abstracted into the value of a single signaling bit. Several variations of digital E&M signaling allow for different methods of start-dial supervision.

Table 2-13 illustrates the bit transitions when the CPE initiates seizure of a digital E&M immediate-start trunk.

Table 2-13   *Digital E&M Immediate-Start Seizure Initiated by the CPE*

Description	CO		Direction	CPE	
	A	**B**	**Direction**	**A**	**B**
Idle	0	0		0	0
CPE goes off-hook, sends digits			←	1	1
CO receives digits, party answers	1	1	→		
Active call	1	1		1	1

The process is very similar when the CO initiates trunk seizure as in Table 2-14.

Table 2-14   *Digital E&M Immediate-Start Seizure Initiated by the CO*

Description	CO		Direction	CPE	
	A	**B**	**Direction**	**A**	**B**
Idle	0	0		0	0
CO goes off-hook, sends digits	1	1	→		
CPE receives digits, party answers			←	1	1
Active call	1	1		1	1

Digital E&M Delay Start

Table 2-15 illustrates the bit transitions of a digital E&M delay-start trunk (with integrity) when the CPE initiates trunk seizure.

Table 2-15   *Digital E&M Delay-Start (with Integrity) Seizure Initiated by the CPE*

Description	CO		Direction	CPE	
	A	**B**	**Direction**	**A**	**B**
Idle	0	0		0	0
CPE goes off-hook			←	1	1
CO begins delay-start acknowledgment	0	0	→		
CO sends delay signal	1	1	→		
CO ready for digits	0	0	→		

continues

Table 2-15 *Digital E&M Delay-Start (with Integrity) Seizure Initiated by the CPE (Continued)*

	CO			CPE	
Description	**A**	**B**	**Direction**	**A**	**B**
(CPE sends digits)					
CO receives digits, party answers	1	1	→		
Active call	1	1		1	1

The CPE sends an off-hook signal to the CO to indicate that it is ready to place a call. The CO responds with an off-hook signal to acknowledge the request. The CPE is not allowed to transmit digits until the CO has a digit collector ready to receive the digits. The CO indicates readiness to receive digits with a return to an on-hook state. When the CO receives the digits and the remote party answers, the CO signals the off-hook state, and the call is active.

The mirror image of this process occurs when the CO initiates trunk seizure on a digital E&M delay-start trunk (with integrity). Table 2-16 illustrates the bit transitions.

Table 2-16 *Digital E&M Delay-Start (with Integrity) Seizure Initiated by the CO*

	CO			CPE	
Description	**A**	**B**	**Direction**	**A**	**B**
Idle	0	0		0	0
CO goes off-hook	1	1	→		
CPE begins "delay-start" acknowledgment			←	0	0
CPE sends delay signal			←	1	1
CPE ready for digits			←	0	0
(CO sends digits)					
CPE receives digits, party answers			←	1	1
Active call	1	1		1	1

Digital E&M Wink Start

Table 2-17 illustrates the bit transitions of a digital E&M immediate-start trunk when the CPE initiates trunk seizure.

Table 2-17 *E&M Wink-Start Seizure Initiation by the CPE*

Description	CO		Direction	CPE	
	A	B		A	B
Idle	0	0		0	0
CPE goes off-hook			←	1	1
CO begins wink acknowledgment	0	0	→		
Actual wink	1	1	→		
Wink completed	0	0	→		
(CPE sends digits)					
CO begins second wink (FGD only)	0	0	→		
Actual wink	1	1	→		
Wink completed	0	0	→		
CO receives digits, party answers	1	1	→		
Active call	1	1		1	1

The CPE sends an off-hook signal to the CO to indicate that it is ready to place a call. The CO acknowledges the trunk-seizure request with a wink. After the CPE transmits the digits, the CO may provide another wink acknowledgment that the digits were properly received. The second wink is associated with Feature Group D (FGD) signaling, which is commonly used on trunks between an LEC and an IXC in North America. When the remote party answers, the CO signals an off-hook state, and the call is active.

As illustrated in Table 2-18, the mirror image of this process occurs when the CO initiates trunk seizure.

Table 2-18 *E&M Wink-Start Seizure Initiation by the CO*

Description	CO		Direction	CPE	
	A	B		A	B
Idle	0	0		0	0
CO goes off-hook	1	1	→		
CPE begins wink acknowledgment			←	0	0
Actual wink				1	1
Wink completed			←	0	0
(CO sends digits)					

continues

Table 2-18   *E&M Wink-Start Seizure Initiation by the CO (Continued)*

Description	CO A	CO B	Direction	CPE A	CPE B
CPE begins second wink (FGD only)			←	0	0
Actual wink			←	1	1
Wink completed			←	0	0
CPE receives digits, party answers			←	1	1
Active call	1	1		1	1

National Variants

The A and the B bits generally follow one of the CAS schemes described in the preceding sections, but the C and D bits are set according to the type of digital facility and national or international standards. For T-1 voice interfaces that follow EIA/TIA-464B, the C and D bits normally follow the state of the A and B bits. For E-1 interfaces, an ITU-T specification indicates that the ABCD bits should be set to A101 if only 1 signaling bit is required, or AB01 if 2 signaling bits are required. E-1 CAS circuits generally follow this specification when 2 signaling bits are required, but may differ when only 1 signaling bit is required, by setting B=A instead of B=1. Some countries follow national standards for E-1 signaling, instead of the ITU-T standard. The Mercury Exchange Limited CAS (MELCAS) from the United Kingdom follows the ITU-T specifications for unused signaling bits, but the actively used signaling bits are inverted from the normal CAS values. It should be clear that local practices vary greatly, which presents a significant challenge when integrating voice/data networks on a global scale. You are well advised to verify the standard signaling practices for each country in which you operate.

Channel Banks in Voice Applications

For phone switches that do not support digital interfaces, a *channel service unit (CSU)*, commonly called a *channel bank*, demultiplexes a digital CAS circuit into discreet analog outputs. For example, a CSU may terminate four analog E&M trunks from a PBX, and convert the signals into the first four channels of a T-1 CAS circuit. In this scenario, the CSU acts as the CO side of the analog E&M trunks to the PBX, and as the PBX side of the T-1 CAS circuit to the CO. The CSU is responsible for converting the analog audio information into a digital bit-stream, and converting the signals from the analog E&M signaling leads into the appropriate ABCD signal bits of the digital circuit.

Common Channel Signaling

In *common channel signaling (CCS)*, a dedicated timeslot of a T-1/E-1 circuit transports an arbitrary serial bit-stream between the trunk endpoints. This timeslot is often called the *data channel* (or *D-channel* in the case of ISDN). CCS trunk endpoints use the channel to transmit telephony signaling and control information, via a message-oriented protocol with HDLC-like encapsulation. By using a message-oriented protocol, CCS schemes offer an almost unlimited array of possibilities for telephony signaling and control. Examples of features that CCS provides include message-waiting indicator lamps on properly equipped telephones, calling- and called-party identification, and even call-routing information exchanged between PBXs.

Messages are only transmitted across the CCS data channel when there is information to send, such as a state transition on a trunk interface (for example, on-hook to off-hook), or an acknowledgment of previous information. Contrast this behavior with CAS, which provides a constant stream of information about each audio channel via the signaling bits that are built into the frame structure.

There are three categories of CCS protocols that you will encounter in the world of telephony:

- Vendor proprietary
- ISDN
- Private Signaling System #1 (PSS1 or Q.SIG)

Vendor Proprietary

Many PBX vendors have developed proprietary messaging protocols for use across a CCS data channel. Because of the proprietary nature of these protocols, switches from different vendors are not interoperable. As a result, the same vendor generally provides phone switches for both ends of the trunk. Whereas CAS trunks may be terminated at the CO for access to the PSTN, CCS trunks are generally tie-lines that the carrier provides as a clear channel circuit between customer locations.

Examples of proprietary CCS protocols include Nortel's Meridian Customer Defined Network (MCDN), Siemens' Corporate Network N & NQ (CorNet-N & CorNet-NQ), and NEC's Events-Based Common Channel Interface Signaling (E-CCIS).

ISDN

The *Integrated Services Digital Network (ISDN)* specifications are the most prevalent standards for enabling advanced telephony signaling across network boundaries. ISDN interfaces are required for subscribers to take advantage of the capabilities in the Advanced Intelligent Network (AIN) of North America, and similar SS7 networks around the globe.

(In some areas, internetworking between SS7 and MF protocols in the service provider's backbone enable non-ISDN interfaces to have limited interaction with SS7 network features.)

ISDN is a user-network interface (UNI) specification that enables CPE to exchange signals and information with the SS7 networks of service providers, while maintaining the security and integrity of the SS7 networks. ISDN uses a message-oriented protocol, specified in ITU-T Recommendations Q.921 and Q.931, across a data or D channel. The framework supports many data types in the bearer or B channels, such as 3.1 kHz audio, speech, video, unrestricted data, and so on. This book is primarily concerned with the voice applications of ISDN (that is, bearer types speech and 3.1 kHz audio), though ISDN data applications are relevant for VoIP implementations.

The following ISDN concepts are explored in this section:

- Interfaces and topologies
- ISDN Link Layer (Q.921)
- ISDN network layer (Q.931)

Interfaces and Topologies

The most common ISDN interfaces are the basic rate interface (BRI) and the primary rate interface (PRI). The BRI is a 2B+D service, which means that two bearer channels are bundled with a data channel. The PRI service is 23B+D for a T-1 facility, and 30B+D for an E-1 facility. The 24th channel of a T-1 facility or the 17th channel of an E-1 facility (for example, timeslot 16) is allocated for the D-channel. For large-scale or high-density applications, multiple T-1/E-1 facilities may be controlled by a single D-channel (with back-up D-channel configurations possible). This arrangement, known as *non-facility associated signaling (NFAS)*, increases the number of B-channels available for traffic throughput, because some facilities do not require a D-channel. NFAS employs economies of scale in a manner similar to SS7 signaling links.

ISDN interfaces are not symmetrical; that is, the user side and the network side have different operations. In traditional data networks, a router always acts as the user side of the interface, while the CO switch acts as the network side of the interface. Similarly in traditional voice networks, a PBX acts as the user side while the CO switch acts as the network side. Figure 2-22 illustrates these points.

Figure 2-22   *Router and PBX Act as User Side of ISDN Interface in Traditional Applications*

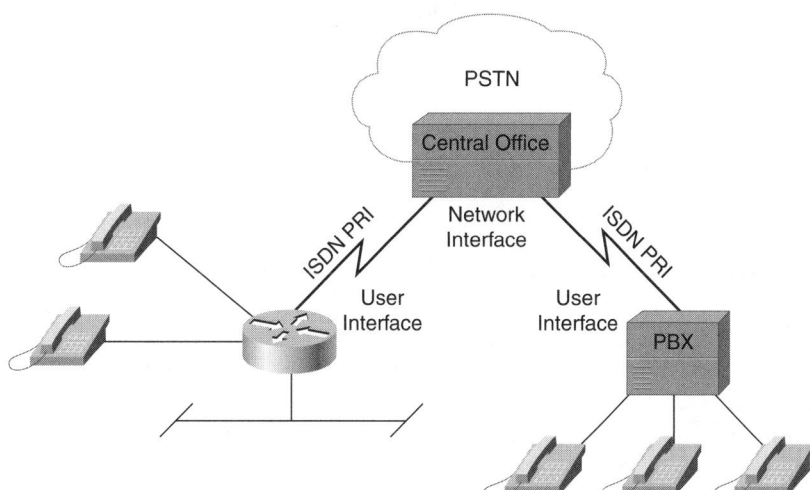

For ISDN connections between a router and a PBX, it is common for the router to act as the network side of the interface. (See Figure 2-23.) This topology enables the PBX to operate as if it is connected to the PSTN via a CO.

Figure 2-23   *Router Acts as the CO Side of an ISDN Connection to a PBX*

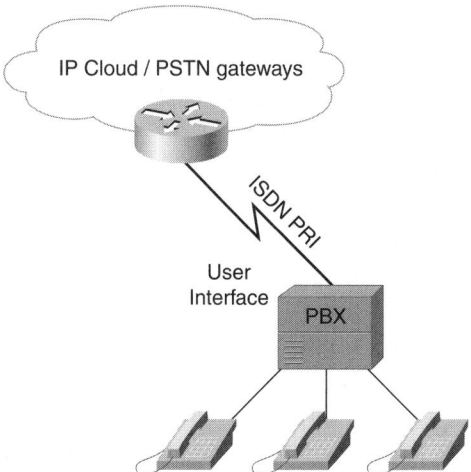

The network side of the ISDN interface is called the local exchange (LE), and the user side of the ISDN connection is called the terminal endpoint (TE). This explanation is a simplification of the ISDN reference points, where the TE is actually behind the S reference point, as illustrated in Figure 2-24. A PBX connected to an ISDN circuit sits between the S and T reference points, providing connections to TE1 devices (such as ISDN phones) and TE2 devices (such as POTS phones).

Figure 2-24 *ISDN Reference Points and Functional Devices*

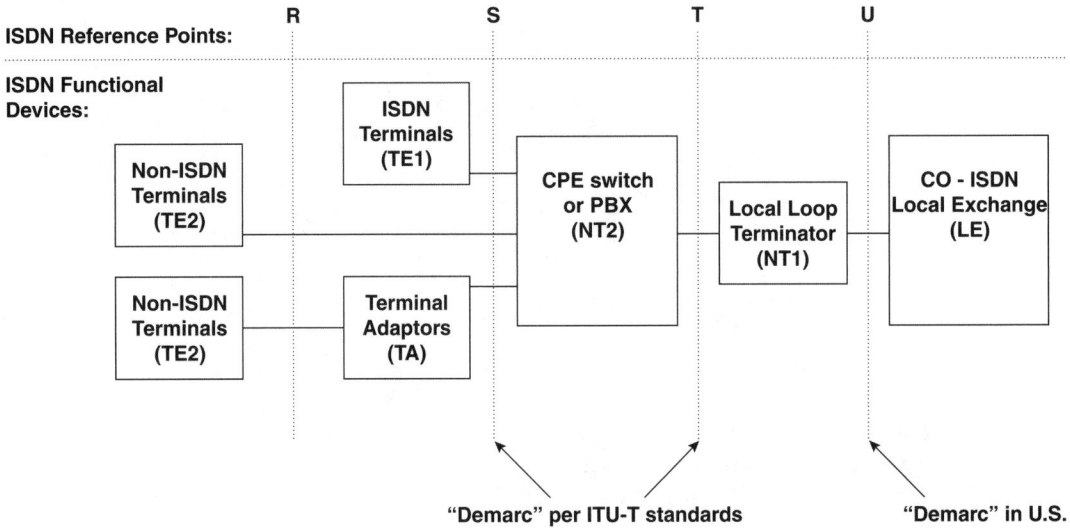

ISDN Link Layer (Q.921)

ITU-T Recommendation Q.921 specifies the Link Access Procedures on the D-channel (LAPD) as the Layer 2 protocol for the ISDN D-channel. LAPD provides the normal Layer 2 functions, such as framing, sequencing, addressing, acknowledgment, error control, and flow control. From an implementation and troubleshooting perspective, your concerns will most likely be limited to the addressing functions. ISDN Layer 2 requires two forms of addressing:

- Terminal endpoint identifier (TEI)
- Service access point identifier (SAPI)

Each terminal on an ISDN interface requires a unique terminal endpoint identifier (TEI). The TEI may be manually assigned (TEI= 0 to 63), or assigned by the network (TEI= 64 to 126) to each terminal device on the user side of the ISDN interface. Though not required, multiple TEIs may be assigned to the same device to differentiate similar services running on the same endpoint (for example, two instances of an X.25 packet over D-channel service from an endpoint).

Messages that flow across the D-channel may be user data, call control signaling, layer 2 administrative functions, and so on. The service access point identifier (SAPI) identifies the type of information (or service) that is encoded in the message. SAPI numbers are well defined for each service, though only a few are commonly used. Table 2-19 lists some of these.

Table 2-19   *Common ISDN Services Identified in Layer 2 Addressing*

SAPI	Associated Layer 3 Service
0	Q.931 call control messages (circuit switched)
1	Q.931 call control messages (packet mode)
16	X.25 packet over D-channel (Always on ISDN)
63	Layer 2 management

For ISDN connections between a router and a PBX, the SAPI field of the Q.931 call control messages is set to zero.

When an ISDN link is activated, the following process occurs:

- A terminal endpoint (TE) requests a TEI from the local exchange (LE).
- The local exchange assigns a TEI to the terminal endpoint.
- The terminal endpoint initializes a logical link for each active service with a Set Asynchronous Balanced Mode Extended (SABME) frame.
- For each logical link that is initialized by the terminal endpoint, the local exchange replies with an Unnumbered Acknowledgment (UA) frame.

Figure 2-25 illustrates an example of this process.

Figure 2-25 *ISDN Layer 2 Is Initialized when the Link Is Activated*

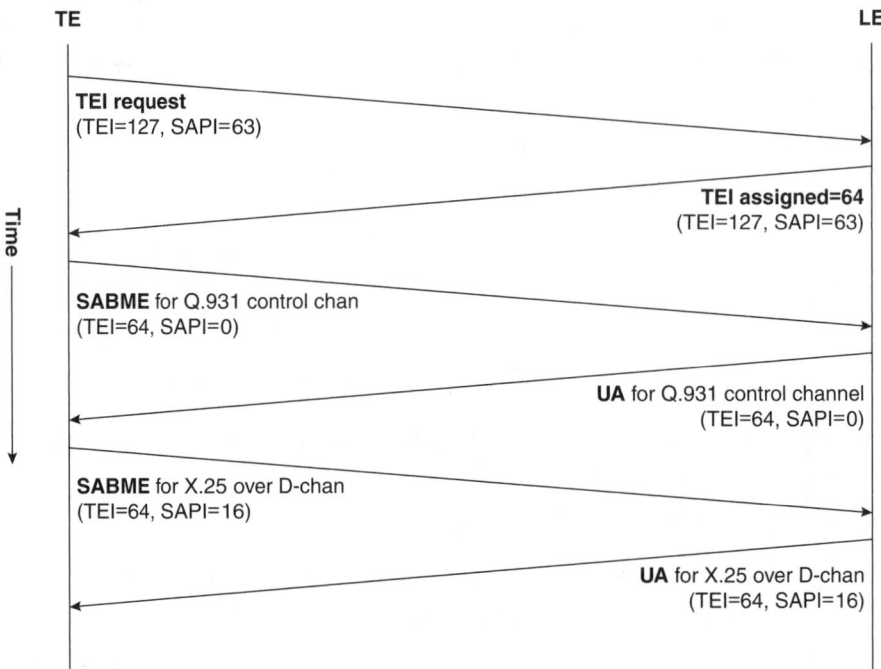

ISDN Network Layer (Q.931)

ITU-T Recommendation Q.931 specifies the network layer for the messages that cross the D-channel of an ISDN interface. The variety of call control and signaling functions are encoded as different message types with relevant information fields.

The following process, illustrated in Figure 2-26, describes an ISDN call setup and teardown for an outbound call from a TE to the LE:

- The TE detects that the calling party goes off-hook, which causes the TE to transmit a SETUP message to the LE. The SETUP message contains the calling party's identification, the bearer type, and a desired B channel to use.

- The LE replies with a SETUP ACKNOWLEDGE message, indicating that more information is required to process the call.

- The TE provides a dial tone to the calling party and collects the called party's address.

- The TE uses either the en bloc or the overlap method to transmit the destination phone number to the LE. If the en bloc method is used, all of the digits are sent in a single INFORMATION message. If the overlap method is used, separate INFORMATION messages encode each of the digits.

- The LE processes the call and responds to the TE with a CALL PROCEEDING message.

- When the LE receives confirmation that the destination side received the number, the LE sends an ALERTING message to the TE.

- When the remote party answers the call, the LE sends a CONNECT message to the TE. At this point, the bearer channel is activated and the parties have an active audio path for communication.

- When the calling party hangs up, the TE sends a DISCONNECT message to the LE and disengages the B-channel.

- The LE acknowledges with a RELEASE message, and processes the call termination through the network (to notify the remote party).

- The TE acknowledges the RELEASE message with a RELEASE COMPLETE message, and the local interface is free to initiate another call.

The process is similar for an inbound call from the LE to the TE:

- The LE transmits a SETUP message to the TE, which includes mostly the same information as the SETUP from the TE to the LE at the originating end of the connection.

- The TE replies with a CALL PROCEEDING message, while the PBX determines how to complete the call.

- The TE sends an ALERTING message to the LE, which is a translated version of the ring-back tone from the PBX. The LE forwards the notification back through the network.

- When the called party answers the phone, the TE sends a CONNECT message to the LE.

- The LE replies with a CONNECT ACKNOWLEDGE message and establishes the B-channel. At this point, the audio path is activated.

- When the LE receives an indication through the network that the remote party has disconnected, the LE sends a DISCONNECT message to the TE.

- The TE acknowledges the DISCONNECT message with a RELEASE message.

- The LE deactivates the B-channel, and sends a RELEASE COMPLETE message to the TE. The B-channel can now be reused for another call.

Most Q.931 messages at the ISDN interface correspond with ISUP messages in an SS7 network. Figure 3-20 in the next chapter illustrates the interaction between ISUP and Q.931 messages.

Figure 2-26   *Q.931 Messages for a Call Setup and Teardown*

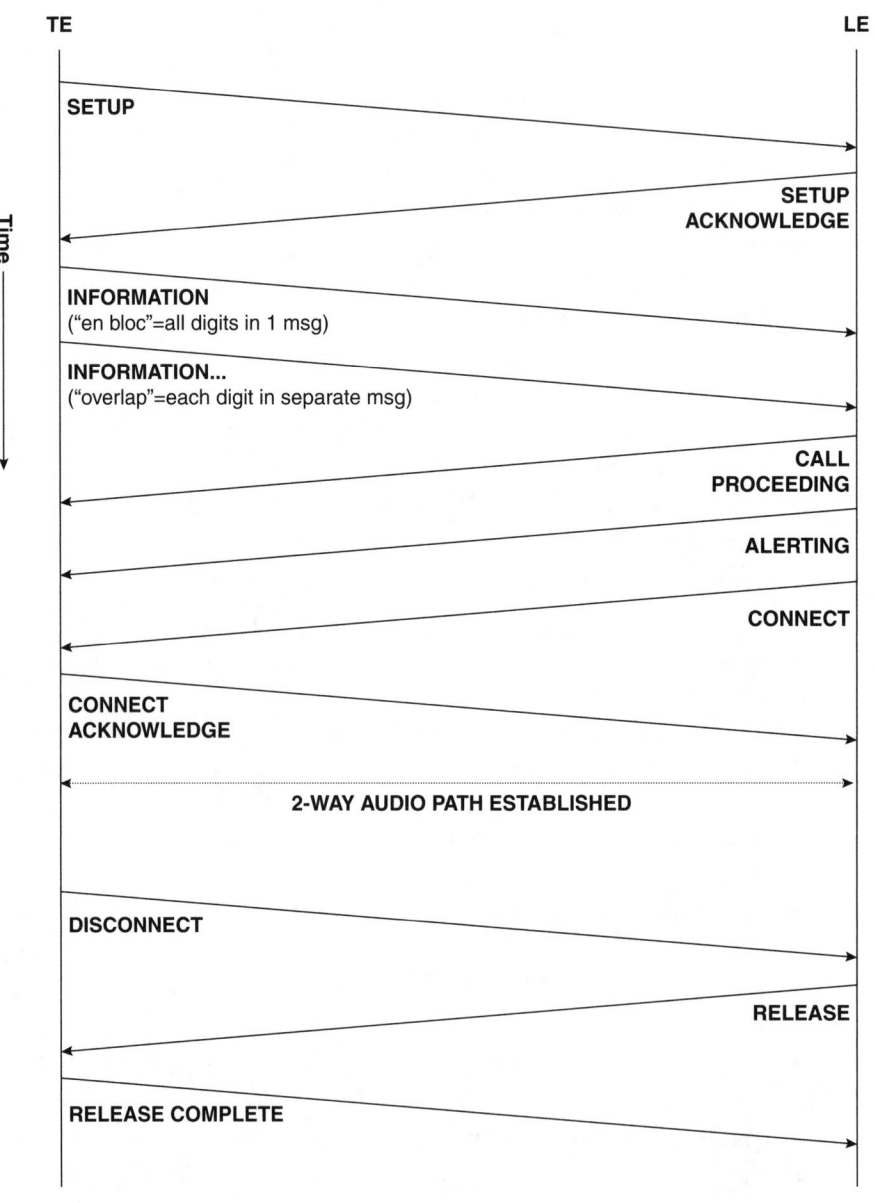

Q.SIG—Private Signaling System #1

Q.SIG, which is formally known as Private Signaling System #1 (PSS1), is a set of extensions to the ISDN protocols specified by the ITU-T. The PSS1 message types are modeled after the ITU-T Q series signaling recommendations, hence the name Q.SIG. The goal of PSS1 is to enable advanced calling features between private telephone networks that use different phone switch vendors.

Traditionally, advanced calling features have been available within a private network, as long as all of the phone switches communicate via a proprietary CCS protocol (or CAS MF tones in some cases). Communication across trunks with different vendors' hardware at each endpoint has been traditionally limited to the minimal functions that can be provided via analog trunks (that is, call setup and teardown).

A collection of vendors formed the ISDN PBX Network Specification (IPNS) Forum to ensure that all phone switches that implement Q.SIG are interoperable for the set of supported Q.SIG features. Telephone switches may support all or a subset of the Q.SIG features. The features are defined in a collection of standards that are published by the European Computer Manufacturers Association (ECMA). Table 2-20 highlights a sampling of the Q.SIG feature specifications.

Table 2-20 *A Sampling of ECMA Standards for Q.SIG Feature Implementation*

Standard	Description
ECMA-142/143	Basic call services
ECMA-148	Calling and connected line presentation and restriction (number only)
ECMA-163/164	Calling and connected name presentation and restriction
ECMA-165	Generic functional procedures (signaling framework for other calling features)
ECMA-173/174	Call forwarding for busy/no reply and call deflection
ECMA-175/176	Path replacement (optimizing the call path when transferring a call)
ECMA-177/178	Call transfer
ECMA-193/194	Do not disturb/override
ECMA-202/203	Call intrusion
ECMA-211/212	Advice of charges
ECMA-241/242	Message-waiting indication (voice-mail light on telephone)

As of this writing, Cisco routers support ECMA-142/143 and ECMA-165. Note that the primary focus of Q.SIG is to provide advanced feature support across vendors in traditional telephony environments. These standards are not applicable for packet telephony environments, but they offer clear benefits in mixed packet and traditional voice networks. Q.SIG features can greatly improve the set of features and functionality that are supported across an integrated voice and data network. As an example, consider a call that is transferred between different locations of a business. In a good PBX network, the audio path may be pruned during the transfer to eliminate unnecessary switch hops. (See Figure 2-27.)

Figure 2-27   *Audio Path Optimized on Call Transfer Using Vendor-Proprietary PBX Technology*

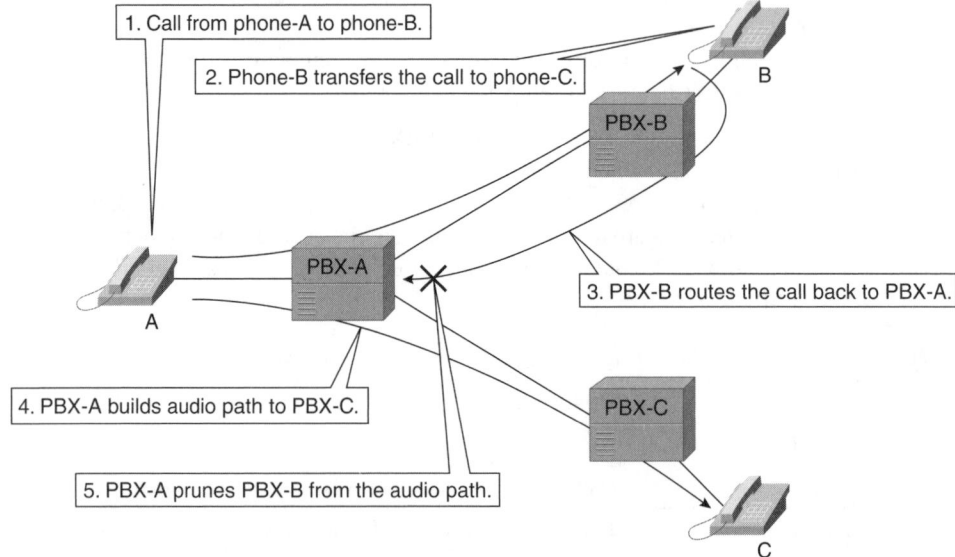

In a voice/data network, the same scenario often results in an audio path that follows each office from which the call was transferred. (See Figure 2-28.) The resulting audio quality is quite poor because of codec processing and signal loss insertion at numerous router/PBX interfaces, as well as cumulative delay, jitter, and packet loss. These topics are explored in greater detail throughout this book.

If routers and phone switches in your network support ECMA-176, you can enjoy the best of both worlds in a transitional VoX network. This may be an important step if you do not immediately migrate to a pure IP telephony environment, which supports all of the traditional calling features in addition to many exciting new applications.

You can read more about the ECMA standards and download them from the following URL:

www.ecma.ch/

You can read more about the QSIG forum at:

www.qsig.ie/

Figure 2-28   *Audio Path Not Optimized During Call Transfer in a VoX Network*

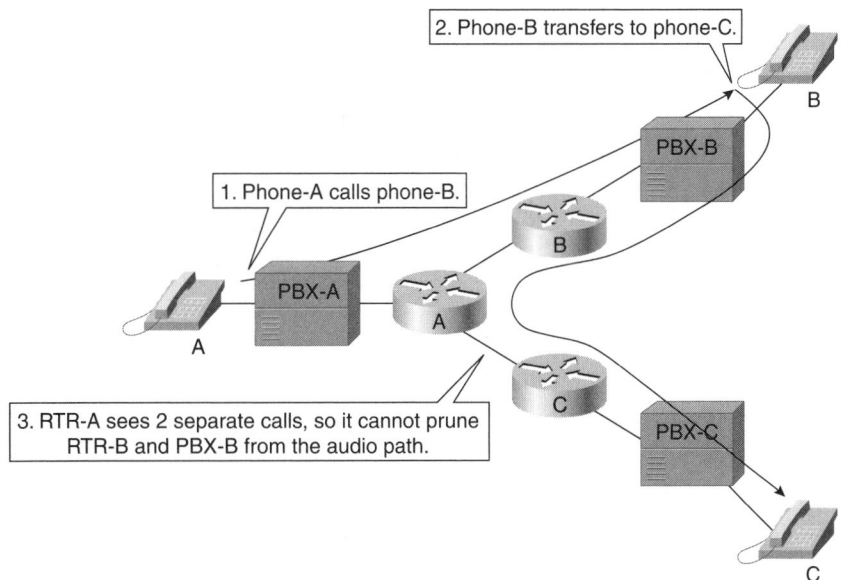

Signaling System Release 2 Signaling

Signaling System Release 2, known more simply as *R2*, was last updated in the CCITT 1988 Blue Book. In the new nomenclature, you can find the R2 specifications in ITU-T Recommendations Q.400 through Q.490.

The R2 signaling system is composed of two complementary signaling types:

- Line signaling
- Interregister signaling

Line Signaling

R2 line signaling performs supervisory functions, such as trunk seizure, release, and clearing. There is an analog version of R2 line signaling that uses low-level continuous tones (that is, frequency division multiplexing, or FDM), but this book addresses only the digital version, which is a form of E1 CAS.

The R2 digital line signals are represented as the A and B signaling bits in timeslot 16 of an E-1 multiframe (per ITU-T Recommendation G.732). The line signals have different meanings in the forward and backward directions of the call. The forward direction is generally from the CO to the CPE, but in a bidirectional implementation, the forward direction may be from the originating switch toward the destination switch. The A and B bits are sometimes referred to as A_f and B_f in the forward direction, and A_b and B_b in the backward direction.

Table 2-21 shows the R2 line signaling bit transitions in the forward and backward directions for a call setup, teardown, and blocking.

Table 2-21   *Call Setup and Teardown with R2 Digital Line Signaling*

	Forward			Backward	
Description	**A**	**B**	**Direction**	**A**	**B**
Idle	1	0		1	0
Seizure	0	0	→		
Seizure Acknowledgment			←	1	1
(Inter-Register MF signaling for address information, and so on)					
Answering			←	0	1
(Active call)	0	0		0	1
If called party disconnects:					
Clear backward			←	1	1
Forward switch releases circuit	1	0	→		
Backward switch releases circuit			←	1	0
(Both switches are idle)	1	0		1	0
If calling party disconnects:					
Clear forward	1	0	→		
Backward switch releases circuit			←	1	0
(Both switches are idle)	1	0		1	0
Blocking			←	1	1
(Forward calls are now blocked)					
Unblocking			←	1	0
(Forward calls are allowed again)					

Interregister Signaling

R2 interregister signaling, also called *R2 MF signaling*, performs all of the signaling functions that are not part of seizing, releasing, or blocking a trunk. These functions include address transmission for the called and calling parties, identification of calling-party group (for example, subscriber, operator, maintenance equipment,), circuit information regarding satellites or echo suppressors, and any information that is specified within a country's national standards.

This section explores the following aspects of R2 MF interregister signaling:

- Naming conventions
- Signal generation
- Signal interpretation
- Signal acknowledgment modes

The section ends with an example of R2 MF signaling for a Direct Dialing In (DDI) application.

Naming Conventions

For applications such as Direct Dialing In (DDI), the CO is labeled the outgoing register, and the CPE is labeled the incoming register. For two-way trunks, the outgoing register may be whichever side originates the call, and the receiving side becomes the incoming register. Forward signals originate from the outgoing register, and backward signals originate from the incoming register. Figure 2-29 illustrates these conventions.

Figure 2-29 *Naming Conventions for Registers and Signaling Directions*

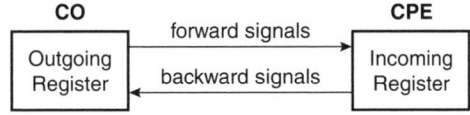

Signal Generation

R2 MF signals are composed of two frequencies from a group of six frequencies. The six frequencies in the forward direction are different than the six frequencies in the backward direction, so that reflected signals cannot be mistaken as signals from the opposite end of the trunk.

Table 2-22 illustrates the MF signals used in the forward direction.

Table 2-22 *R2 MF Signals in the Forward Direction*

	1380 Hz	1500 Hz	1620 Hz	1740 Hz	1860 Hz	1980 Hz
1380 Hz		Code-1	Code-2	Code-4	Code-7	Code-11
1500 Hz			Code-3	Code-5	Code-8	Code-12
1620 Hz				Code-6	Code-9	Code-13
1740 Hz					Code-10	Code-14
1860 Hz						Code-15
1980 Hz						

Table 2-23 illustrates the MF signals used in the backward direction.

Table 2-23 *R2 MF Signals in the Backward Direction*

	1140 Hz	1020 Hz	900 Hz	780 Hz	660 Hz	540 Hz
1140 Hz		Code-1	Code-2	Code-4	Code-7	Code-11
1020 Hz			Code-3	Code-5	Code-8	Code-12
900 Hz				Code-6	Code-9	Code-13
780 Hz					Code-10	Code-14
660 Hz						Code-15
540 Hz						

Signal Interpretation

Signals in both the forward and backward directions can be interpreted in two different contexts. Forward signals are classified as either Group I or Group II signals, and backward signals are classified as either Group A or Group B signals. Figure 2-30 illustrates the different signal groups.

In the forward direction, Group I signals provide addressing information, and information about the circuit such as the presence of a satellite hop in a previous link, or the requirement for an echo suppressor. Group II signals identify the priority level and category of the calling party, such as subscriber, operator, or maintenance equipment. Many Group II signals are available for country-specific use.

Figure 2-30 *R2 Interregister Signals Are Classified into Four Groups*

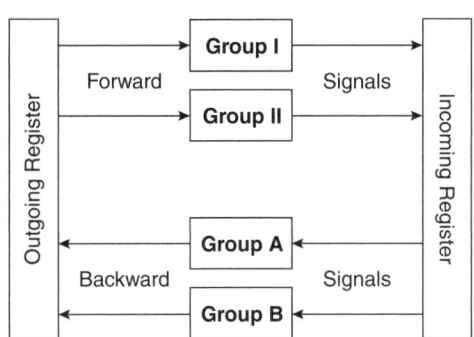

In the backward direction, Group A signals confirm the receipt of Group I signals, or request retransmission of any of the three previous digits. Group A signals can also request Group II signals from the outgoing register, such as a desired spoken language for the operator, or additional information about the calling party or circuit. Group B signals acknowledge Group II signals, and provide call progress tones or charge information. Many Group B signals are available for country-specific use.

The Group I forward signals are defined in Table 2-24.

Table 2-24 *Definition of R2 MF Group I Forward Interregister Signals*

MF Code	Primary Definition	Other Definitions
1	Digit 1	Request French Language
2	Digit 2	Request English Language
3	Digit 3	Request German Language
4	Digit 4	Request Russian Language
5	Digit 5	Request Spanish Language
6	Digit 6	Request Language (spare)
7	Digit 7	Request Language (spare)
8	Digit 8	Request Language (spare)
9	Digit 9	Discriminating digit (spare)
10	Digit 0	Discriminating digit
11	Access to incoming operator	Country code; outgoing echo-suppressor required

continues

Table 2-24   *Definition of R2 MF Group I Forward Interregister Signals (Continued)*

MF Code	Primary Definition	Other Definitions
12	Access to delay operator	Country code; no echo suppressor required; request rejected
13	Test call indicator	Access to test equipment; no satellite link in use
14	Incoming echo-suppressor required	Satellite link in use; outgoing echo-suppressor inserted
15	End of address	

The Group II forward signals are defined in Table 2-25.

Table 2-25   *Definition of R2 MF Group II Forward Interregister Signals*

MF Code	Primary Definition
1	National: Calling party is a subscriber with priority
2	National: Calling party is a subscriber without priority
3	National: Calling party is maintenance equipment
4	Spare (country-specific)
5	National: Calling party is an operator
6	National: Call will be used for data transmission (for example, data modems)
7	International: Calling party does not support forward-transfer (subscriber, operator, or maintenance equipment)
8	International: Call will be used for data transmission (for example, data modems)
9	International: Calling party is a subscriber with priority
10	International: Calling party supports forward-transfer (used by operators for international assistance)
11	Spare (country-specific)
12	Spare (country-specific)
13	Spare (country-specific)
14	Spare (country-specific)
15	Spare (country-specific)

The Group A backward signals are defined in Table 2-26.

Table 2-26   *Definition of R2 MF Group A Backward Interregister Signals*

MF Code	Primary Definition
1	Requests next digit (n+1)
2	Requests previous digit (n–1) (not to be used over satellite links)
3	Address complete; changing to Group B signals (cannot switch back to Group A signals after this)
4	Experienced congestion in national network
5	Requests calling party's group information (for example, subscriber, operator, maintenance equipment)
6	Call will be charged on answer, no Group B signals to follow
7	Requests previous digit (n–2) (not to be used over satellite links)
8	Requests previous digit (n–3) (not to be used over satellite links)
9	Spare (country-specific)
10	Spare (country-specific)
11	Requests a country code on international calls (not to be used over satellite links)
12	Requests a desired language or discrimination digit
13	Requests information about the circuit (such as, Are there satellite links? Are echo-suppressors needed?)
14	Acknowledges a language or discrimination digit; indicates that echo-suppressor is available if needed
15	Congestion in an international exchange or at its output

The Group B backward signals are defined in Table 2-27.

Table 2-27   *Definition of R2 MF Group B Backward Interregister Signals*

MF Code	Primary Definition
1	Spare (country-specific)
2	Requests a special tone to be sent to calling party (called party cannot be reached for long-term)
3	Called-party line is busy

continues

Table 2-27 *Definition of R2 MF Group B Backward Interregister Signals (Continued)*

MF Code	Primary Definition
4	Congestion encountered
5	Unallocated (invalid) number
6	Indicates that call will be charged, and called-party's line is available
7	Indicates that call will not be charged, and called-party's line is available
8	Called-party line is out of order
9	Spare (country-specific)
10	Spare (country-specific)
11	Spare (country-specific)
12	Spare (country-specific)
13	Spare (country-specific)
14	Spare (country-specific)
15	Spare (country-specific)

Signal Acknowledgment Modes

Inter-register signals are transmitted more reliably if they are acknowledged, but an excessive amount of time may be required if the circuit uses satellite links or crosses a voice/data network with low bit-rate codecs.

MF Compelled

The ITU-T international specifications for R2 signaling indicate that all interregister signals operate in the compelled mode. Each MF tone is played continuously until the opposite end of the trunk acknowledges the signal. In other words, the remote end is compelled to acknowledge a signal to make it stop. Figure 2-31 illustrates this point.

Figure 2-31   *MF-Compelled Signaling—Tones Played Continuously Until Acknowledged*

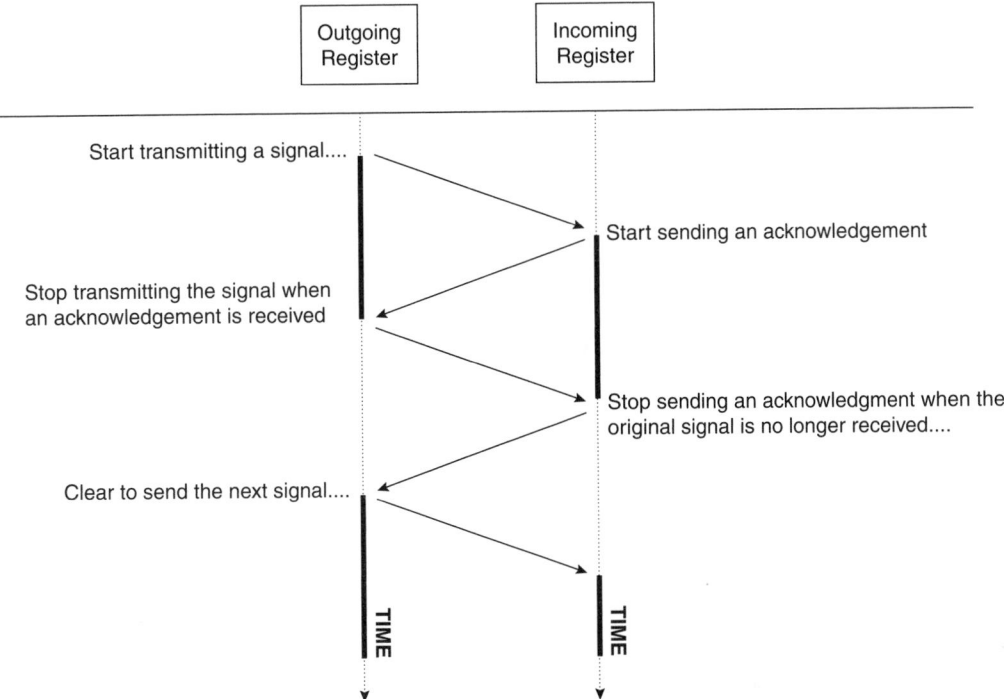

The acknowledgment signal may provide information in addition to the acknowledgment function. Figure 2-32 illustrates this point with a Direct Dialing In (DDI) application, which is similar to the DID service in North America.

The called-party number 1234 is transmitted as a series of Group I signals. The incoming register sends a Group A signal to confirm receipt of all digits and a conversion to Group B signals. The outgoing register replies with a Group II message that provides additional information about the calling party, which is acknowledged with a Group B signal that provides call progress and billing information.

Figure 2-32   *R2 MF Example Application—Direct Dialing In*

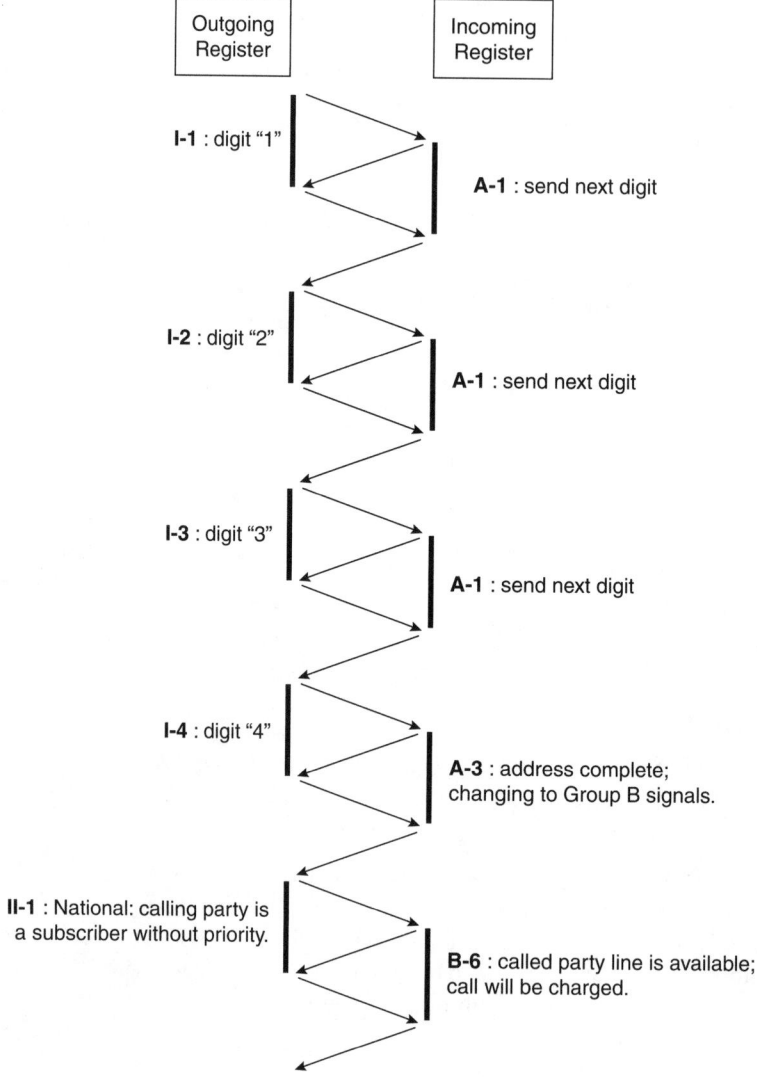

MF Pulsed (Non-compelled)

In some countries and some applications (for example, satellite links, voice/data networks, or high-latency circuits in general), R2 MF interregister signals are transmitted for a specified duration, in a similar manner as standard DTMF tones. Group I signals do not require a Group A acknowledgment, which saves considerable time during the call setup for high-latency circuits. This also means that the services associated with Group A are not available when non-compelled MF signaling is used.

MF Semi-compelled

Some countries use a modified form of MF-compelled signaling, where the MF signals from the CO to the CPE are compelled, but the responses from the CPE to the CO are pulsed. This technique reduces the call setup time without eliminating the features that are accessed via Group A signaling.

Summary

This chapter has covered many topics in a fair amount of depth, so it is important to take a rest and review the subjects:

- Signaling functions
- Analog trunk signaling
- Digital trunk signaling
- Signaling System Release 2 (R2)

The section on signaling functions addressed the types of information that must be conveyed through various types of call signaling, such as line supervision, digit transmission, number identification, and call-progress tones. The analog trunk signaling section explored loop start, ground start, and E&M variations. The section on digital trunk signaling explored CAS implementations of the analog signaling types, as well as several CCS methods such as vendor-proprietary implementations, ISDN, and Q.SIG. Finally, E1 R2 signaling was examined from the perspectives of line signaling and interregister signaling. If you encounter R1 MF signaling in your work and you need more information, the most complete (though not necessarily most readable) sources are the ITU-T Q-series specifications. You can also search Cisco Connection Online, as information about various signaling schemes and country variants is constantly being added.

CHAPTER 3

Signaling System #7

Signaling System #7, or SS7, is a suite of protocols used by telephony service providers to support out-of-band call signaling and advanced calling features. It is the international standard for circuit-switched signaling between telephony service providers, although the framework allows for variations from country to country. SS7 networks do not transport customer data (except in the case of Q.931 messages generated by customer premises equipment, or CPE). Rather, they transport call setup and teardown messages, database queries, trunk status, instructions for remote phone switches, and so on. An SS7 network is sometimes referred to as an Intelligent Network (IN), or an Advanced Intelligent Network (AIN), because the signaling message structure enables many more functions than simple call setup and teardown.

Because SS7 traffic originates and terminates within service-provider networks, the vast majority of enterprises need not be concerned with the inner workings of SS7. Internet service providers that develop VoIP offerings do require SS7 for large-scale interconnection to traditional telephony service providers (LECs, CLECs, IXCs, and PTTs). Large enterprises that require many ISDN Primary Rate Interface (PRI) circuits at a point of presence (POP) may benefit from SS7 connections to a traditional telephony service provider. In general, a large amount of voice (including fax or modem) traffic is required to economically justify a pair of SS7 links.

This chapter provides an overview of SS7, and is organized into the following sections:

- Signaling network entities
- Network topologies
- Addressing
- Protocols
- Subscriber interface to SS7 networks

Signaling Network Entities

The entities that connect to an SS7 network are classified as follows:

- Service Switching Points (SSPs)
- Signal Transfer Points (STPs)
- Service Control Points (SCPs)

Service Switching Points

Customers of a service provider usually connect to the service provider network near the *Service Switching Points (SSPs)*. The SSP can be a computer attached to a Class-5 voice switch in an end office, or it can be built into the voice switch itself, such as the Nortel DMS-100, or the Lucent 5ess. The SSP function is often implemented as a separate computer attached to the voice switch, so that the SS7 functionality can be upgraded separately from the voice-switching hardware and software.

SSPs serve as the originating and terminating points of call signaling in SS7 networks. Call signaling from customer networks (that is, PBX signaling) must be translated at the SSP for transmission across the SS7 network. The SSP also initiates queries to service provider databases, initiates actions in remote SSPs, and performs actions in response to requests from SSPs and other signaling entities.

Signal Transfer Points

Signal Transfer Points (STPs) provide many functions in an SS7 network. They route traffic between signaling entities, translate between different SS7 protocol variants, and provide traffic and usage measurements for network monitoring and billing functions. If an SSP does not know the SS7 address to which it must send traffic—a database, for example—the STP can use the dialed digits to resolve the SS7 address for the SSP. In the United States, the STP functionality is usually provided by a computer attached to a Class-4 switch in a tandem office. There is at least one tandem office in every local access and transport area (LATA) in the United States of America.

There are three types of STPs:

- National
- International
- Gateway

National STPs use the national variant of SS7 protocols within a country (such as the ANSI or Bellcore versions of SS7 within the United States). *International STPs* use the international SS7 protocols specified in the ITU-T Q.700 series recommendations. In addition to providing routing and translation between national and international standards,

Gateway STPs provide the interface between different provider networks. *Gateway STPs can also measure SS7 signaling traffic and track circuit usage by monitoring call connect/ disconnect messages.* This information can be used to provide centralized billing.

Service Control Points

Service Control Points (SCPs) connect applications and databases to the SS7 network. This connection enables a wide range of services that are not otherwise possible, such as intelligent phone number translation. For example, a business can have different locations served by a single 800 number that is easy for its customers to remember. In this scenario, local phone switches all over the country route the dialed digits to an 800 database, which also receives the ANI of the calling party. The database then redirects the call to the actual destination, based on geography (the nearest call center), time of day (a call center in a different time zone if after local business hours), or other considerations such as call-center congestion.

SCPs are typically implemented on a UNIX platform, and packaged in pairs for redundancy. There is usually a Service Creation Environment (SCE) associated with the SCP, so that telecom providers can quickly develop new services to differentiate themselves in the marketplace. The SCE is a programming environment that includes a programming language and prebuilt functions to perform common tasks such as digit manipulation or database queries. Vendors offer integrated SCP packages that have the SCE, database, and management functions preconfigured. The SCP may also have X.25 or IP connections to external databases or servers that are not part of the SS7 network. In this way, the SCP is a gateway between SS7 and other networks. Examples of services that the SCP provides include:

* Location registration for mobile telephones
* Line information database (for maintaining profiles of each subscriber)
* Calling-card authentication
* Billing instructions (for example, collect calling, or third-party billing)
* Number translation for Local Number Portability

Network Topologies

The primary design goal for an SS7 network is high availability. Equipment and links are provisioned in mated pairs to provide redundancy at all points of the network. Link pairs are designed to share the traffic load and operate at 40 percent capacity or less, so that if one of the paired links fails, the other link can accommodate the combined load without experiencing congestion. Traffic routing is based on link sets, which are groups of links between the same two nodes. Traffic is shared equally among all of the links in a link set.

The links carry signaling traffic, similar to a D-channel in a PRI circuit, or the signaling channel of a CCS voice trunk. The main difference here is that SS7 protocols are used, and the physical path of the signaling channel is not necessarily parallel to the actual audio path. The relationship between the signaling path and the audio path falls into three categories:

- Associated signaling
- Quasi-associated signaling
- Nonassociated signaling

As Figure 3-1 illustrates, the voice trunks and signaling trunks share the same physical path in *associated signaling*. A more complicated model enables the audio path to be directly connected between two nodes, while the signaling path traverses an intermediate node. This scenario, called *quasi-associated signaling*, is common when two end offices in the same LATA have dedicated trunks between them. For calls between the offices, the audio path flows across the direct fiber connection, but the call setup and signaling is routed through a tandem office to provide billing and accounting. *Nonassociated signaling* is the norm when end offices are directly connected, but remote databases provide calling services. In this scenario, call signals traverse multiple STPs, while the audio path is connected directly or through a fewer number of hops. To ensure short call-setup times and minimize signaling delay, the number of STP hops should be minimized. As SS7 networks migrate from time division multiplexing (TDM) to asynchronous transfer mode (ATM) facilities, associated signaling via emulated circuits will become the norm.

Signaling links operate at much lower rates than voice trunks, because setting up and tearing down calls is not a bandwidth-intensive process. Most countries and international links use 64-kbps DS-0 facilities (which supports about 80 ISDN User Part (ISUP) messages per second), while the United States uses 56-kbps DS-0A or T1 (1536 kbps) facilities. The amount of signaling traffic is increasing as more features are added to SS7 networks. The ATM Broadband ISDN Inter-Carrier Interface (ATM B-ICI) specifications provide the migration path to higher bandwidth ATM circuit facilities for SS7 signaling.

Figure 3-2 depicts a high-level topology diagram for an SS7 network, illustrating the signaling network entities and the types of links between them.

Figure 3-1 *Relationships Between the Signaling Path and Audio Path*

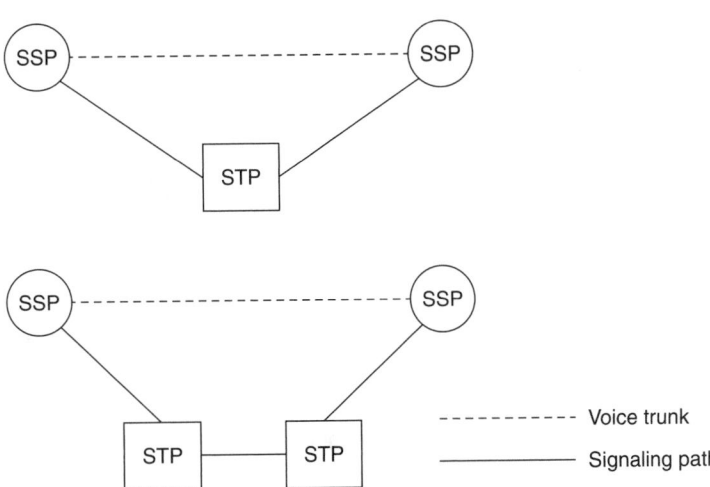

Note that the different types of signaling links all function in exactly the same manner. Different labels are assigned to the links to identify their logical location and purpose, and to indicate which entities are attached to the links:

- *A links*, or access links, connect the SSP or SCP to the nearest STP. In other words, the phone switches and databases connect to local SS7 routers via A links.

- *B links*, or bridge links, connect pairs of STPs at the same level of hierarchy. For example, a pair of SS7 routers in a toll office may connect to a pair of SS7 routers in another toll office, via a full mesh of B links.

Figure 3-2 *Topology of an SS7 Network*

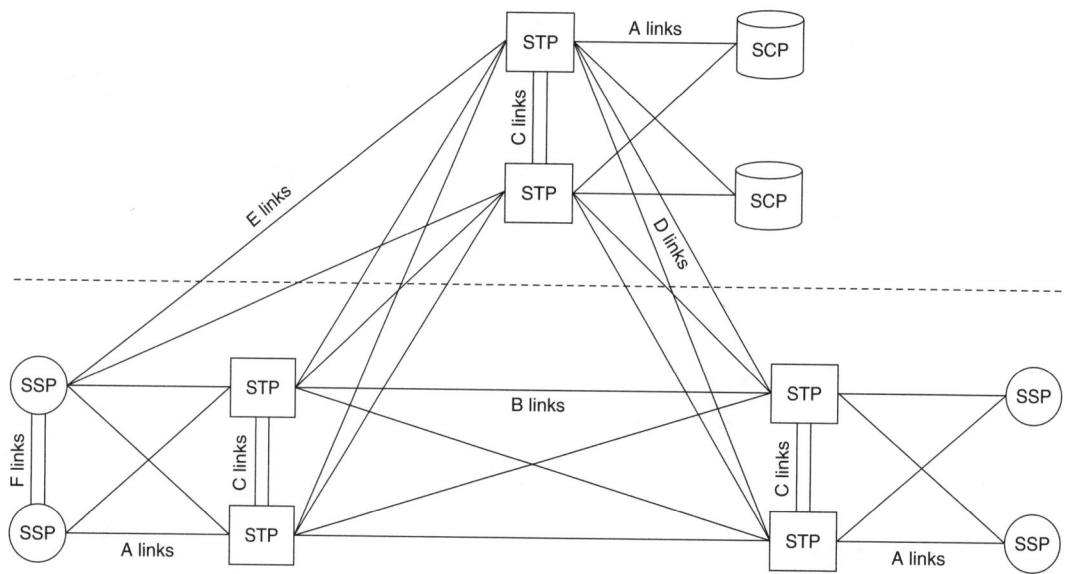

- *C links*, or cross links, provide connectivity with a pair of STPs. These links provide backup connectivity in case of congestion or failures of the B links or D links. C links are not used for call-related traffic under normal circumstances.

- *D links*, also called diagonal links, connect pairs of STPs at different levels of hierarchy in the network. If an SS7 network has a flat topology, then there are no D links in the network.

- *E links*, or extended links, connect phone switches to remote STPs. These links are used as a backup if the local SS7 routers are too congested.

- *F links*, or fully associated links, provide direct signaling connectivity between SSPs. If there is a lot of traffic between two end offices, then the signaling traffic may be passed on the same facilities as the voice traffic.

Addressing

Just like in TCP/IP or any network protocol suite, SS7 networks need addresses to identify entities on the network and the services available within each entity. SS7 uses the following address types:

- Telephone numbers
- Point codes

- Subsystem numbers
- Signaling link codes
- Circuit identification codes

Telephone Numbers

Telephone numbers identify subscribers, but they do not identify entities within the provider SS7 network. Telephone numbers are not SS7 addresses, even though SS7 uses them in many functions. Think of telephone numbers as labels that must be converted to SS7 addresses. The call-routing table in an SSP is organized according to the dialed digits of the telephone number, but at some point an STP must translate the dialed digits to a destination point code (and perhaps a subsystem number). This simplifies call routing for the SSPs, and concentrates the network intelligence into fewer well-managed devices (STPs). This also facilitates security in the service provider SS7 network, because the STP can be used as a firewall to: (1) hide the actual point code and subsystem number addresses from other networks; and (2) regulate who has access to certain point codes and subsystem addresses.

The dialed digits of the telephone number (the destination) are often referred to as Global Title digits, and Global Title Translation is the process of determining the destination point code and subsystem number from the dialed digits.

Point Codes

Point codes provide unique identities for SSPs, STPs, and SCPs in an SS7 network. Point codes in SS7 networks are the functional equivalent of IP addresses in TCP/IP networks. The format for the point code is not uniform in all SS7 networks. The ITU-T international version of the point code structure is a 14-bit address, as illustrated in Figure 3-3. The zone identifies the country or group of countries, the area identifies a specific network within the zone, and the remaining bits identify individual signaling points within the network.

Figure 3-3   *Point-Code Structure for ITU-T International SS7*

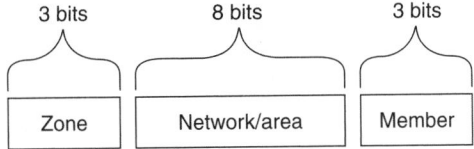

The point-code address space is not very large at this level, because it is only used among international signaling gateways. Unlike IPv4 address allocation in the global Internet, which partitions a single address space, the global SS7 network uses a different address space at the national and international levels. Gateway STPs translate between the international point-code structure and a national point-code structure. As a result, SS7 networks can use a smaller address space and operate independently within a given level of the global hierarchy.

Each country can define the organization of the national version of the point-code structure. Many countries follow the ITU-T structure and use a 14-bit point code. This works well for countries with a single PTT administration, but as telecom markets around the world become deregulated, there are sure to be changes in the point-code structures. In the United States, where many telecom providers exist, the ANSI specification defines a 24-bit point-code structure illustrated in Figure 3-4.

Bellcore manages the address space of the ANSI format network identifiers. Large SS7 networks have unique network identifiers, while smaller networks must share the network IDs 1 through 4. The smallest networks share the network ID 5. The cluster field is used to identify smaller networks, or provide summarization in large networks. The last field identifies individual members of the cluster or network. STPs usually have a member code value of 0 in ANSI SS7 networks. This is similar to routers being assigned a 0.1 address in an IP subnet.

Figure 3-4   *ANSI Point-Code Structure Used for SS7 Networks in the United States*

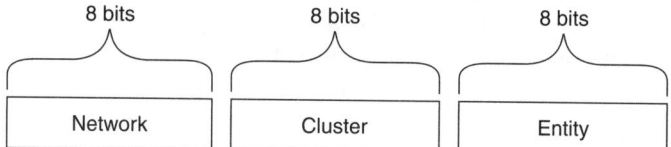

Subsystem Numbers

Messages can be routed to an SS7 node using a point code, but there must be a mechanism to identify the destination database or service within the node. This is necessary because each node may have multiple databases, application interfaces, or user parts. The *subsystem number* identifies a service within the node, just like a TCP or UDP port identifies a service within an IP host.

Subsystem numbers are currently 8 bits, but they may be expanded to accommodate more services in the future. A few well-known subsystem numbers are currently reserved for ISUP, management functions, and cellular internetworking (for example, Home and Visitor Location Registers, Mobile Switching Center, Equipment Identification Register, and so on). Most of the subsystem numbers are available for use in database applications.

Signaling Link Codes

Signaling link codes, which have significance only within a given signaling point, are logical addresses that identify physical interfaces. Whereas IP networks assign a different IP address to every interface, SS7 networks assign a single point code to the node as a whole. A node may have multiple point codes, but they are not tied to a physical interface. There must be another mechanism to specify individual interfaces within a signaling point. All of the links that connect to a given destination form a link set, and the links within the link set are identified by signaling link codes.

Circuit Identification Codes

SS7 networks support signaling traffic on a separate network from the voice trunks. The CIC provides the necessary information for a signaling message to uniquely identify a specific voice trunk or bearer channel associated with a call. The format for the CIC is not standardized, but carriers have made arrangements to ensure consistent interpretation. As SS7 facilities migrate to ATM, VPI/VCI values will provide this function.

Protocols

A picture is worth a thousand words, so here in a nutshell is the organization of the SS7 protocol suite. (See Figure 3-5.)

Figure 3-5   *Architecture of the SS7 Protocol Suite*

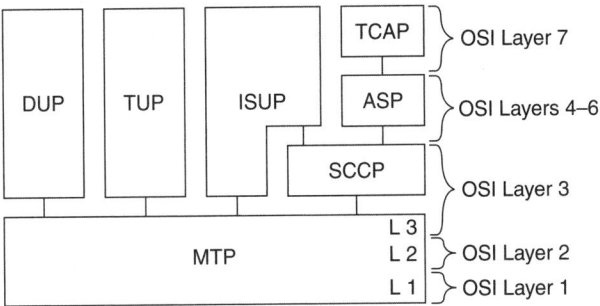

This section explores the functions and structure of the following protocols:

- Message Transfer Part (MTP) Levels 1, 2, and 3
- Telephone User Part (TUP) and Data User Part (DUP)
- ISDN User Part (ISUP)
- Signaling Connection Control Part (SCCP)
- Application Service Part (ASP)
- Transaction Capabilities Application Part (TCAP)

It is important to note a convention in this book relating to protocol header diagrams. Most people with a data networking background are accustomed to reading illustrations of protocol headers from left to right. The assumption is that the bits of the protocol header fields are physically transmitted in the order that we read them—from left to right. Diagrams in the SS7 standards are often illustrated with the first transmitted header fields on the right side of the diagram, which is confusing if you do not expect it. In this book, all of the SS7 headers have been drawn as they would be presented in a data networking book.

It is also important to note a fundamental difference between SS7 and IP network protocols. IP datagrams are composed of a header and an opaque data field, which is filled by an intelligent user of the network (such as a computer application). SS7 messages contain data as an integral part of the message structure; most of the data that passes through the network is precategorized into message types and parameters. There is no clear delineation between a header and a payload in an SS7 message—the functions are intermingled. SS7 is designed to hide the network complexity from subscribers, so it contains the end-user intelligence within the protocol definition—hence the intelligent network.

NOTE   IP datagrams have a payload encapsulated in a header. SS7 messages do not have an explicit payload. SS7 data is structured into predefined message types and parameters, so all of the information is in the header.

You can interpret the entire SS7 message as if it were a header; that is, you can stratify message fields by function into headers for the different protocol layers. Although some of these headers really contain the message data, this conceptual framework may be more accessible for people with a TCP/IP networking background. The following sections use this approach.

MTP Level 1

MTP Level 1 (MTP L1) provides the functionality of OSI Layer 1, including electrical or optical transmission characteristics. In the United States, ANSI and Bellcore have specified a 56-kbps DS-0A or V.35 for MTP L1. Other countries use a 64-kbps DS-0. Over time, DS-1 and SONET facilities will carry ATM-based SS7 messages.

MTP Level 2

MTP Level 2 (MTP L2) provides the functionality of OSI Layer 2, including link error detection/correction and message sequencing between two nodes. All SS7 messages are encapsulated in a header that provides these functions. If there are no messages to send, then a blank keepalive message is sent with the MTP L2 encapsulation. This blank keep-alive message, which is called a Fill-In Signal Unit (FISU), is illustrated in Figure 3-6.

Figure 3-6 *FISU Is a Null Message Encapsulated in an MTP L2 Header*

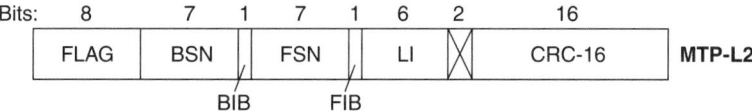

Table 3-1 summarizes the function of each field.

Table 3-1 *Fields of the MTP L2 Header*

Field Name	Function
Flag	A pattern of {01111110} to identify the beginning of the message
BSN	Backward sequence number, identifies the last valid sequence number received
BIB	Backward indicator bit, set to the opposite of the Forward Indicator Bit (FIB) to indicate an MTP L2 error
FSN	Forward sequence number, identifies the last valid sequence number transmitted
FIB	Forward indicator bit, set equal the BIB when acknowledging a retransmission
LI	Length indicator, identifies FISU (LI=0), link status signal unit (LSSU) (LI=1 or 2), or message signal unit (MSU) (LI=3+)
FCS	Frame check sum, uses CRC-16 to detect transmission errors

The BIB and FIB bits are used together during error detection and correction. During normal operation, the BIB and FIB bits have the same value. When a node detects an error, a message is sent back to the sender with the BIB bit toggled, so that the BIB and FIB bits have different values. The BSN in this error notification contains the last valid sequence number received. When the sender gets the error notification, it retransmits all of the messages with a sequence greater than the BSN. Upon receipt of the retransmitted messages, the receiver toggles the FIB bit as an acknowledgment back to the sender. At this point, the FIB and BIB are equal again, so transmission continues as normal.

A link may be unusable even if it does not show signs of errors (for example, invalid CRC-16 or toggled FIB/BIB values). For example, a node may have a functioning MTP L2 while the higher layers are experiencing a failure. In this case, the node sends a Link Status Signal Unit (LSSU) across the link as shown in Figure 3-7.

Figure 3-7   *Link Status Signal Unit (LSSU) Indicates Congestion; Upper-Layer Errors*

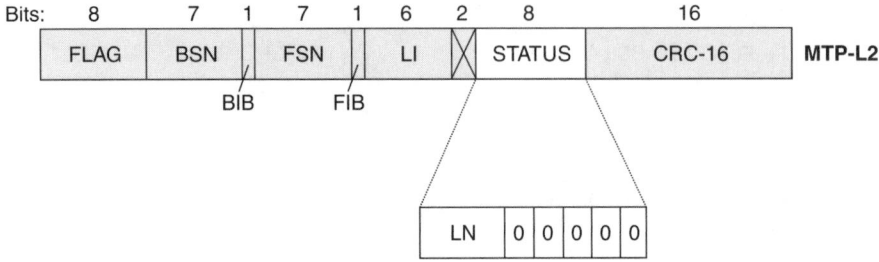

Table 3-2 summarizes the link notification (LN) types that are encoded in the three most significant bits of the status field. The remaining five bits are set to {0}.

Table 3-2   *LSSU Notification Types*

Notification Types	Function
SIB	Status indicator busy, node that transmitted the message is congested
SIPO	Status indicator processor Outage, cannot communicate with MTP-L3
SIO	SI out of alignment, received message that violated length or density of 1
SIOS	SI out of service, cannot send MTP L3 messages for various reasons
SIN	Status indicator normal, self-testing commenced, cannot send MTP-L3
SIE	Status indicator emergency, quick self-testing commenced, no MTP-L3

It is important to note that the LSSU messages are only sent over the link to which they refer. This implies that the messages are only used when MTP-L2 is functional, but other problems may be present. The LSSU is not intended to report conditions of complete link failure. Such a function requires the use of an alternate link layer connection, which is beyond the scope of MTP-L2. MTP-L3 provides notification and rerouting in the case of complete link failures.

MTP Level 3

MTP Level 3 (MTP-L3) provides the functionality of OSI Layer 3, including network-wide addressing, routing, and management of multiple links. MTP-L3 also identifies the higher-layer user part to which a message should be passed upon arrival at the destination point code. The international SS7 specification of MTP-L3 is in ITU-T Recommendations Q.704 to Q.707. ANSI T1.111.4 to T1.111.7 and Bellcore TR-NWT-000246 document the standard implementations for the United States.

Message Signal Units

MTP-L3 messages are passed as Message Signal Units (MSUs). Figure 3-8 illustrates an MSU, which encapsulates higher-layer information from the user parts.

Figure 3-8   *MSU Includes SIO and SIF Fields Encapsulated in an MTP-L2 Header*

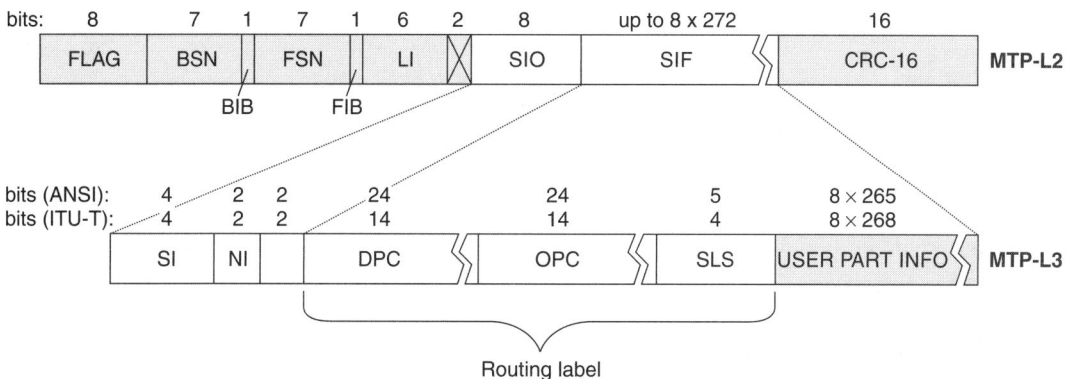

The key elements of the Message Signal Unit are the Service Information Octet (SIO) and the routing label within the Service Information Field (SIF). The routing label contains the source and destination point codes, as well as the *signaling link selection (SLS)*. The SLS identifies a logical link within a link-set, which connects the next hop signaling point. Point codes are assigned to a signaling point as a whole, as opposed to specific link interfaces, so a link must be specified for communication between two signaling points that share multiple links. The SLS field provides this functionality.

The SIO provides three pieces of information:

- Service Indicator (SI)—the user part for which the MSU is destined
- Whether the MSU uses national or international SS7 point codes and protocols
- The national SS7 protocol version, or priority in the ANSI/Bellcore SS7 network

MTP-L3 employs the decision process for each MSU shown in Figure 3-9.

Figure 3-9   *Processing of an MTP-L3 MSU*

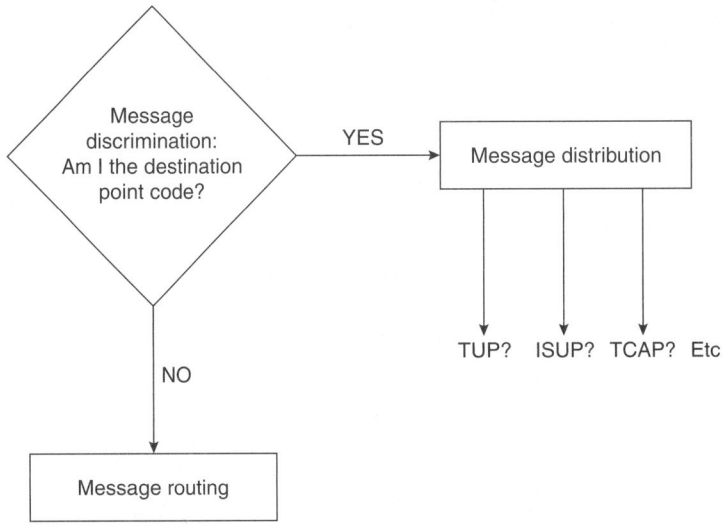

MTP-L3 first performs a message discrimination function on the MSU. The signaling point compares its own point code with the destination point code from the routing label of the MSU. If they are the same, the SI from the SIO is examined to determine which user part in the local signaling point should receive the MSU. The message distribution function then sends the message to the appropriate user part. If they are different, then the MSU is sent to the message routing function to reach the next hop signaling point.

SS7 Message Routing

When the routing function of MTP-L3 receives an MSU, the destination point code is compared with the local point code routing table. The matching entry specifies a link set across which the message should be forwarded. The Signaling Link Selector (SLS) field from the routing label identifies which link of the link set should be used.

If you have a data networking background, you will not be impressed with the routing technology used in SS7 networks. Point-code routing tables are manually defined in every signaling point, but they may be dynamically altered by network events such as link failures. In essence, MTP messages provide dynamic fault tolerance through rerouting, but not dynamic distribution of initial routing information.

Each switch is initially configured with a set of prioritized routes to reach every destination. The system is more reliable as the number of alternate routes for each destination increases. The routing goal is to generate efficient paths with low latency, so routes that result in fewer hops are preferred. From the perspective of an SSP, routes for different link types are administratively defined in the following order:

1   F link, if destination is directly attached

2   E link, to reach the destination local STP

3   A link, to reach the local STP

From the perspective of an STP, routes are preferred in the following order:

1   A link or E link, if destination is directly attached

2   B link, to reach the destination local STP

3   D link, to reach the higher-tier STP associated with the destination

4   D link, to reach the local higher-tier STP

Figures 3-10 and 3-11 illustrate these guidelines.

Figure 3-10   *Order of Preferred Routes from an SSP Perspective*

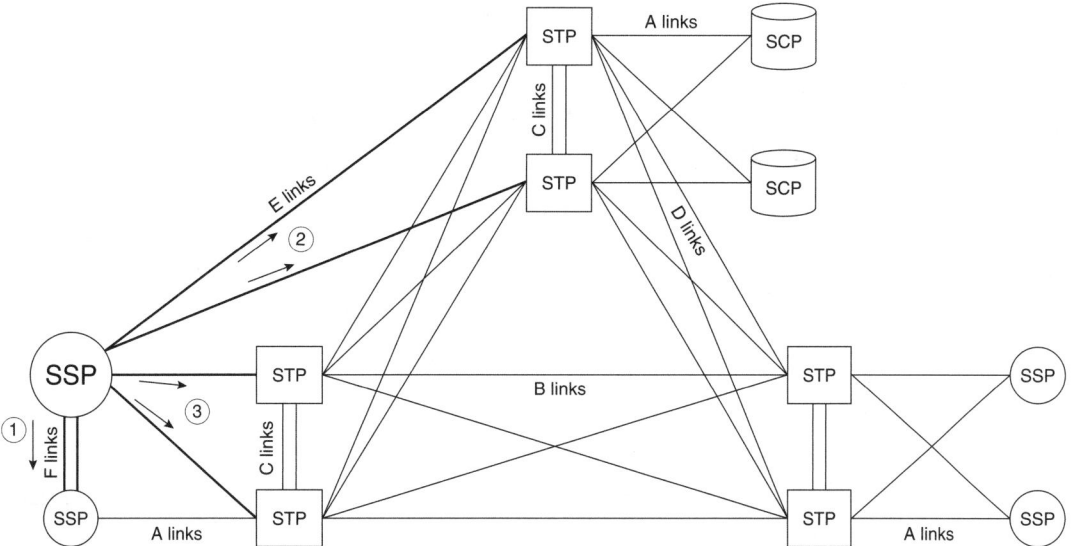

Figure 3-11   *Order of Preferred Routes from an STP Perspective*

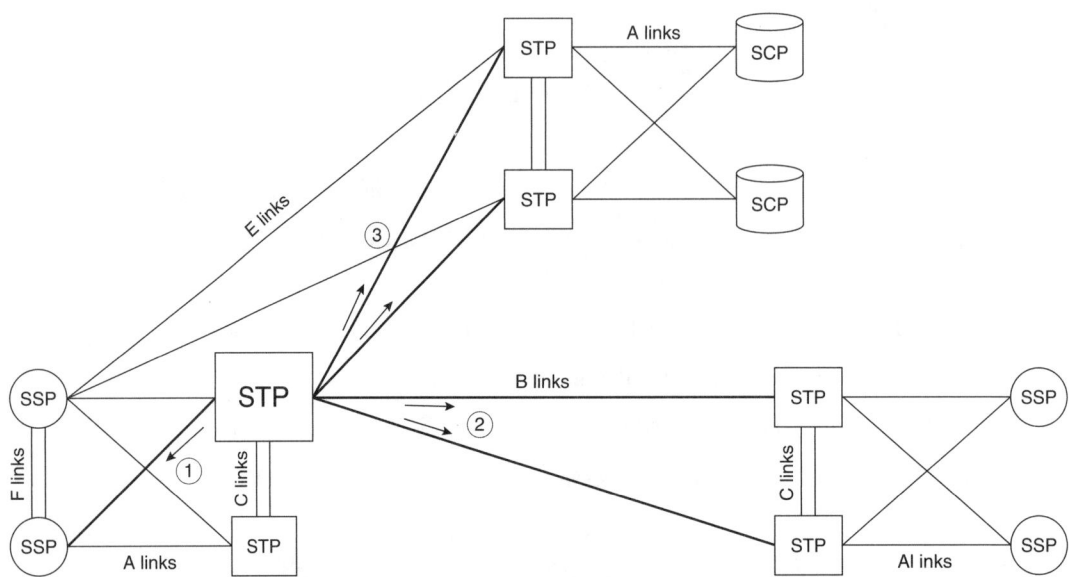

In a normal steady state, all of the programmed routes are available, and messages flow according to the primary routes. If any link becomes congested or fails, or if MTP-L3 is unable to send messages to the higher-layer user part, then the affected links are dynamically removed from the routing tables of the affected signaling points. When the problems are corrected, the routes are dynamically restored.

This dynamic behavior is enabled by management messages exchanged between neighbor signaling points. The management functions fall into three categories:

- Link
- Traffic
- Route

Link management is concerned with the status of individual links on a signaling point, and is responsible for activating, deactivating, and restoring links based on input from MTP-L2 messages. Link management also triggers traffic management functions.

Traffic management enables signaling points to notify each other about the availability of links, and make routing adjustments in response. Traffic management issues change-over and change-back messages in response to link-management messages on adjacent links in the link set. A receiving signaling point reacts to such messages by altering its routing tables to exclude or include the links in question. (See Figure 3-12.) All buffered messages are retransmitted back to the last acknowledged sequence number, so that no messages are lost in the routing change. In the event that the message buffer memory is lost, then the normal link-testing procedures are shortened so that the link operation can be restored more quickly.

Figure 3-12   *Traffic Management Affects Link Selection for Message Forwarding to Adjacent Nodes*

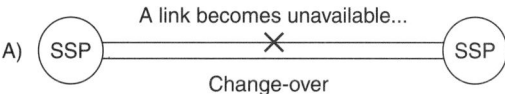

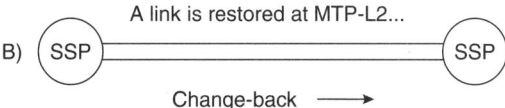

Traffic management does not affect which next-hop signaling point is used. If all of the links to an adjacent signaling point become unavailable, then route-management functions are responsible for redirecting traffic to a different signaling point.

Route management enables the path through signaling points to change based on topology changes or congestion conditions. When a signaling point loses all links to a destination (see Figure 3-13A), it advertises this fact to its neighbors with a transfer-prohibited (TFP) message. The neighbors must then find an alternate signaling point to reach the intended destination (in other words, use a backup route). When the links are restored and the destination becomes available again (see Figure 3-13B), the signaling point sends a transfer-allowed (TFA) message to each of its neighbors. The primary routes to the destination are then restored in each of the neighbors.

TUP and DUP

Though TUP is widely used outside the United States, it is being replaced by ISUP as subscribers request additional calling features. *TUP* provides basic call setup and teardown, with limited additional features. If you are interested in the details of TUP, consult the ITU-T Recommendations Q.721 to Q.725. DUP is also being replaced by ISUP. Consult ITU-T Recommendations Q.741 and X.61 for more information about DUP.

Figure 3-13   *Route Management Affects Signaling-Point Selection for Message Forwarding*

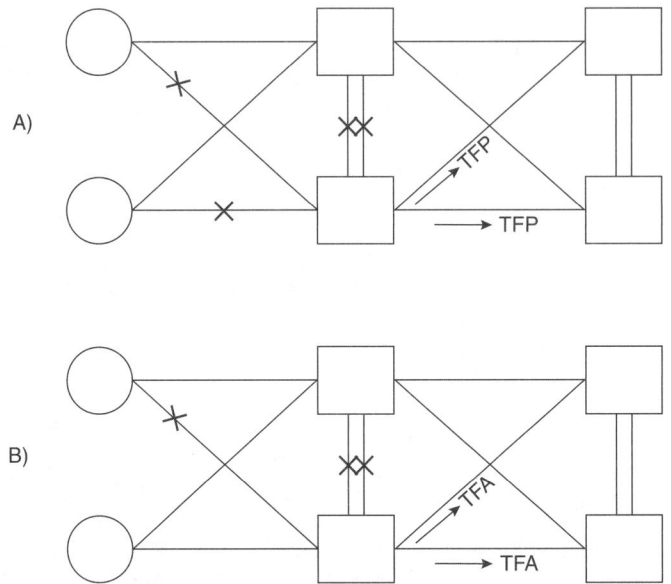

ISUP

ISUP performs all basic and supplementary services related to bearer-channel circuits. Bearer channels are currently either data or voice, but other types will be supported in the future. If you have spent time troubleshooting ISDN problems in data networks, then you should be familiar with the types of messages in ITU-T Recommendation Q.931, such as connection requests, connections, call progress, disconnects, and so on. The ISUP protocol is essentially a superset of the ISDN Q.931 protocol.

ISUP messages may be sent between signaling points using either the pass-along method or the end-to-end method. The end-to-end method requires the services of SCCP, but it is not currently implemented in SS7 networks. The pass-along method requires that all intermediate signaling points interpret the message before forwarding, which is less efficient than the end-to-end method. The pass-along method must also be forwarded along the same path as the call-setup message, so any signaling-link outages that occur after a call setup will block further transmission of ISUP status or informational messages. The end-to-end method does not have this problem, because end-to-end ISUP messages can follow any route independent of other messages associated with the call.

ISUP Message Format

Figure 3-14 illustrates the structure of the ISUP fields in the SS7 message.

Figure 3-14   *ISUP Header Fields*

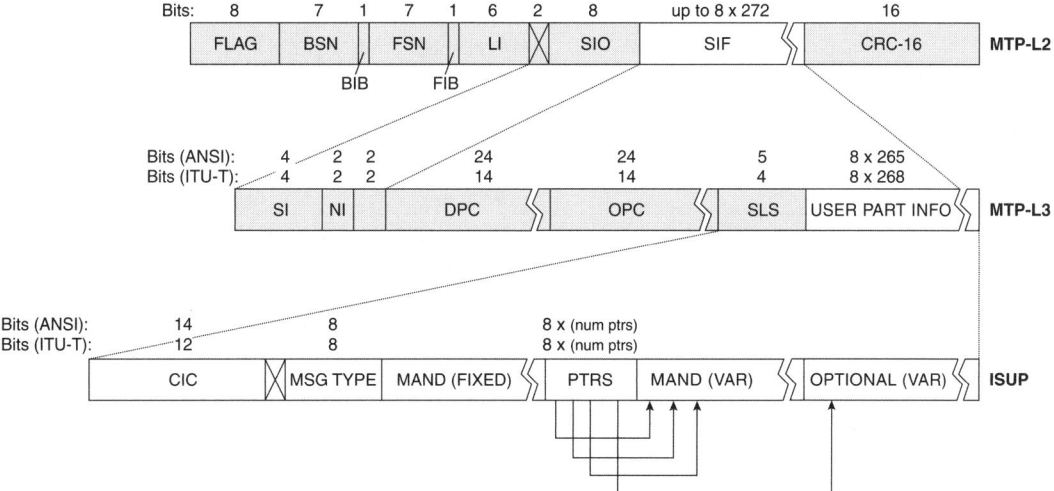

The CIC specifies the facilities to be used for the voice or data-bearer channels. At present, there is not a standard for allocating information in this field, but carriers have made implementation agreements to ensure interoperability.

The message type code, which is the first byte after the CIC, determines the format for the remainder of the ISUP message. All ISUP messages are constructed from a pool of predefined parameters, and each message type uses a specific set of these predefined parameters. There are nearly 50 ISUP message types currently defined. Table 3-3 summarizes the functions of some of these message types.

Table 3-3   *Selected ISUP Message Types*

ISUP Message Type		Function/Meaning
PAM	Pass along message	Used as a wrapper to pass other message types to distant signaling points
IAM	Initial address message	Used to establish a call; many parameters possible
EXM	Exit message	Indicates that an IAM is leaving the local network via a gateway STP
ACM	Address complete message	Digits received at far end (alerting in progress); okay to provide ring-back tone
CPG	Call progress message	Indicates call-related events (such as forwarding), relays ISDN cause codes

continues

Table 3-3   *Selected ISUP Message Types (Continued)*

ISUP Message Type		Function/Meaning
ANM	Answer message	Called party answered the call; okay to connect the audio path
CON	Connect	Not used by ANSI/Bellcore; indicates that audio path is connected for ITU-T
INR	Information request	During an active call, request calling party ID, charge information, and so on
INF	Information	Provides the information requested in an INR message
FAC	Facility	Requests/replies for remote operations; enable call features (call waiting, and so on)
REL	Release	Indicates that either party disconnected; need RLC to release the circuit
RLC	Release complete	Acknowledges that distant party disconnected; circuit released
CCR	Continuity check request	Requests a loopback test of the bearer channel before the IAM is sent
COT	Continuity check	Results of the loopback test reported to requester
CRM	Circuit reservation message	Requests for voice trunk in non-ISDN portion of network during call setup
CRA	Circuit reservation acknowledge	Indicates that voice trunk has been reserved; ready for use following ANM
SUS	Suspend	Non-ISDN endpoint went on-hook during call; REL message usually follows
RES	Resume	Non-ISDN endpoint went back off-hook before disconnected timer expired

In addition to the message types identified in the table, there are messages for managing circuit facilities, such as blocking and unblocking individual circuits or circuit groups, resetting circuits, and so on. There are also messages for billing instructions, diagnostics, and a variety of other purposes. Travis Russell's book, *Signaling System #7*, Second Edition, contains a detailed description of each of the message types used in ANSI networks; for ITU-T networks, consult the ITU-T Recommendations Q.761 to Q.764, and Q.766.

The ISUP message parameters carry the data associated with each message type, and are classified into three categories:

- Mandatory fixed
- Mandatory variable
- Optional variable

Immediately following the message type in the ISUP header are the mandatory fixed parameters. For a given message type, the fields can be easily parsed because the field lengths are known. Because the other parameter types have a variable length, the next fields contain pointers to each of the mandatory variable parameters, and the beginning of the optional variable parameters. Each of the mandatory variable parameters is encoded as an 8-bit length field and a variable-length data field. The optional variable parameters are encoded as a tuple of 8-bit parameter name, 8-bit parameter length, and a variable-length data field.

Some parameters are used by most of the message types, while others are used for only a specific message type. Table 3-4 indicates a sampling of the parameters that may appear in an IAM message type.

Table 3-4   *Message Parameters of an ISUP IAM*

ISUP Message Parameter	Function/Meaning
Nature of connection indicators	Indicates the presence of satellite hps, echo cancellers, and so on
Forward call indicators	Pass-along versus SCCP; ISDN end-to-end preference, and so on
Calling party's category	Indicates special priority for emergency calls, language of operator, and so on
User service information	Identifies the type of bearer traffic for ISDN (for example, ITU-T codecs, data, and so on)
Called party number	The dialed digits, or Local Routing Number (LRN) for ported numbers
Access transport	Indicates the level of congestion in the originating switch
Business group	Identifies a group (for example, a Centrex customer), and the features associated with that group
Call reference	Provides a unique tracking ID, and the point code of the assigning node
Calling party number	The phone number of the originating party
Carrier identification/selection	Can be manually picked by dialing 1010xxx before the number in the United States
Charge number	Indicates the ANI of the calling or called party for billing purposes

continues

Table 3-4 *Message Parameters of an ISUP IAM (Continued)*

ISUP Message Parameter	Function/Meaning
Generic digits	A container for subscriber information such as account number or PIN
Generic name	An ASCII name to be used for Caller-ID devices
Hop counter	Used like the time to live (TTL) field in the IP header to recover from routing loops
Original called number	Holds dialed digits when called party changes (call forwarded/redirected)
Precedence	In military networks: Routine, Priority, Immediate, Flash, or Flash Override
Redirecting number	The most recent phone number from which the call was forwarded
Redirection information	The reason and number of times the call has been redirected
Remote ops/service activation	Triggers features in remote switches, and used for phone booth functions
Special processing request	May be required for calls originating in a PBX that require translation

For the IAM type, the first five fields are required and the rest of the fields are optional. The point here is not to comprehensively document parameter options; more options are available for the IAM type and other message types. The point is to provide a sampling of the information that is contained in various parameters. As you can see, these fields contain the core information that must be transmitted by ISUP SS7 messages.

ISUP Example

In addition to understanding the fields and message types used by ISUP, it is important to understand the dynamic sequence of ISUP transactions. Consider a simple call session, without Local Number Portability, 800 service, or other issues that require database lookups. In Figure 3-15, time progresses down the page, and the arrows indicate ISUP message transfers between signaling points.

Figure 3-15   *Example ISUP Transactions for Call Setup and Teardown*

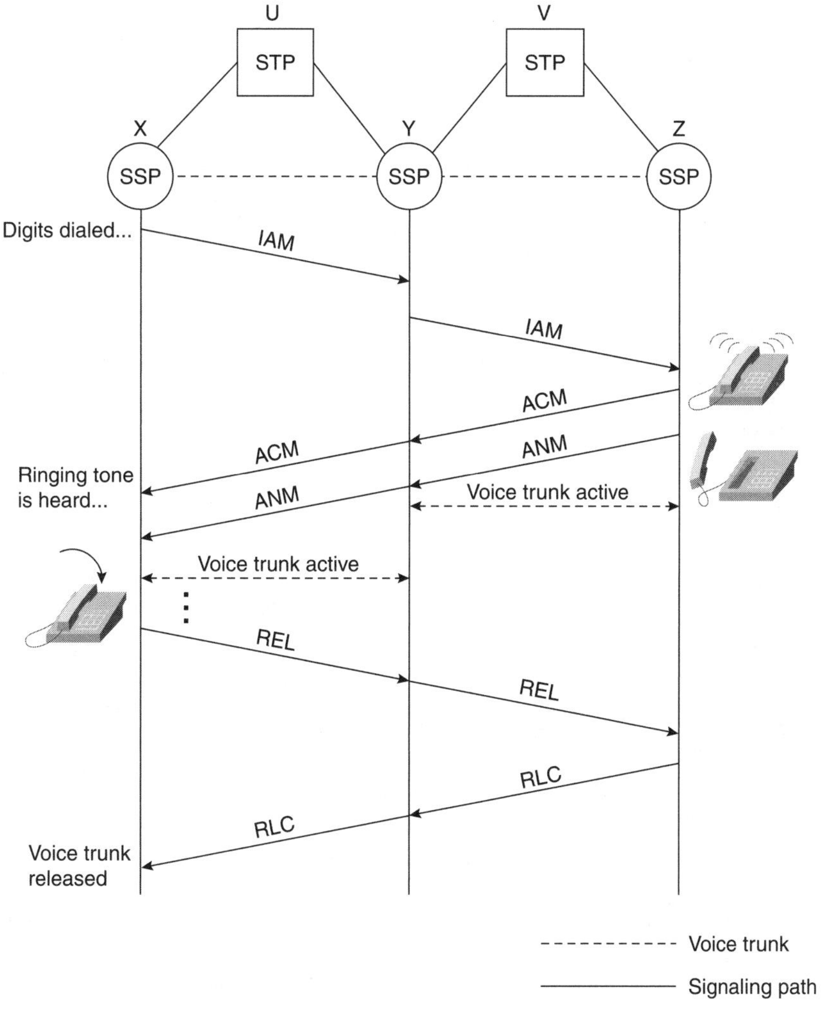

In this scenario, there is no direct trunk {XZ} from the originating phone switch to the terminating phone switch. As such, the end-to-end audio path must be pieced together from multiple circuit pieces: {XY} and {YZ}. These pieces must be established in sequence using ISUP messages. The circuit setup and teardown messages must be exchanged between SSP peers, but STPs may be in the signaling path between SSPs. The IAM messages are encapsulated in PAMs for transit through the intermediate STPs. This step is not illustrated in the preceding diagram for the sake of clarity. You can visualize this additional step as a PAM tunnel through which each arrow passes whenever the message must traverse an STP.

After the calling party finishes dialing the digits, SSP X uses its local call-routing table to determine which trunk should carry the voice circuit—trunk {XY} in this case. SSP X creates an IAM message to reserve the trunk, and determines the next-hop signaling point to which the message should be forwarded—STP U in this case. Because the next hop-signaling point is an STP, which does not interpret call-setup or teardown requests, the IAM is encapsulated in a PAM. STP U interprets the PAM, and forwards the message to SSP Y.

SSP Y determines that the circuit specified in the CIC is available, and reserves the circuit. Upon successfully reserving the circuit, Y sends an ACM back along the signaling path (encapsulated in a PAM for transmission through U) to inform X that its IAM message reached the correct destination and is being processed. Y examines its call-routing tables, and determines that the call should be connected via trunk {YZ}. Y then generates an IAM message destined for Z, and sends the message via V (using a PAM). V repeats the process of U to send the message to Z. This process of reserving voice trunks continues for as many hops as necessary to form an end-to-end audio path.

The destination SSP, Z in this case, receives the IAM message and recognizes that it is the destination SSP. If the phone line is busy, Z sends a REL message to Y, which is relayed to X. The disconnection is acknowledged in an RLC message sent by X and forwarded through Y to Z.

If the desired phone line is not busy, Z sends an ACM message to the previous SSP and sends a ringing signal to the phone line. When the phone line is answered, Z sends an ANM message to Y, who in turn sends an ANM message to X. Each SSP that receives the ANM connects the reserved circuits in a process called audio cut-through. When the ANM reaches the originating SSP, the entire audio path should be cut through, and the call commences.

During the course of the active call, additional ISUP messages may be exchanged between the end SSPs using the PAM method. Such ISUP messages may contain information requests, billing information, and so on. When either party disconnects, the local SSP sends an REL message along the signaling path, which is forwarded to the opposite-end SSP. The opposite SSP then acknowledges the disconnection with an RLC message. Each SSP in the path that receives the RLC message releases the associated circuit and forwards the message to the signaling point. When the RLC reaches the SSP that initiated the REL message, each of the circuit pieces should be released and available for reuse.

SCCP

The *SCCP* provides functions similar to OSI Layers 3-4, but the correlation between the SS7 stack and the OSI stack begins to deteriorate in this range. There are provisions for connection-oriented and connectionless services from SCCP, but at present only the connectionless services are implemented in SS7 networks. As additional applications are defined for SS7 networks, the connection-oriented services may be required.

The fields identified in the SCCP portion of a message header are illustrated in Figure 3-16.

Figure 3-16 *SCCP Header Fields*

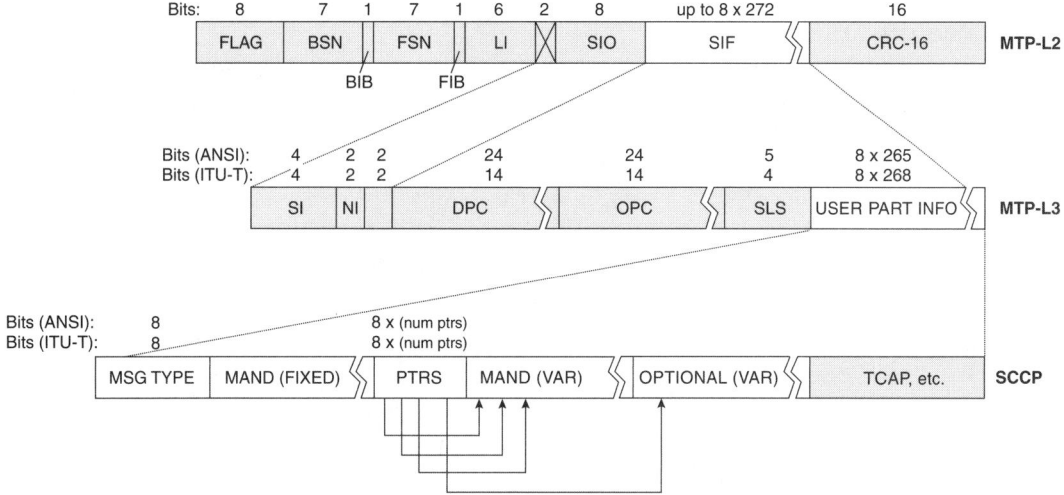

The header structure for SCCP is similar to that used for ISUP, where the parameters are categorized as mandatory fixed, mandatory variable, and optional variable. The calling-party address and called-party address parameters contain fields for the telephone number (global title), point code, and subsystem number, which are used in the Global Title Translation process.

SCCP provides functions that build on MTP-L3, including:

- End-to-end routing
- Global title translation user part flow control

End-to-End Routing

SCCP enables the user parts (such as TCAP) of nonadjacent signaling points to communicate with each other directly. MTP-L3 cannot provide this functionality for a couple of reasons. Signaling points usually know the point codes of immediately adjacent nodes, but they may not know how to reach all point codes in the network. They have more robust routing tables for telephone number addresses. A message that must traverse multiple hops to reach a database needs to use the telephone number address (Global Title digits) to point to the appropriate next-hop signaling point.

In addition, user parts like TCAP do not exclusively use point codes for addressing, but MTP-L3 can only route based on point codes. SCCP provides a bridge between telephone number (Global Title digits) and subsystem addresses provided by user parts like TCAP, and the point codes required by MTP-L3. This function is called Global Title Translation, and is provided by some STPs in the network.

Global Title Translation

What happens when an SSP needs to contact a database associated with a distant SCP? Consider the example of a subscriber placing a call to an 800, 888, or 900 number in the United States. These leading digits identify special services that do not follow a geographic hierarchy, as opposed to normal area codes that specify a particular area to route the call. As a result, these calls cannot be routed according to a summarized call-routing table. Imagine if millions of computers in the Internet required host routes in the global Border Gateway Protocol (BGP) routing tables! Obviously this is not a practical approach.

To solve this problem, carriers maintain centralized databases to map between the special services numbers and actual routable numbers. The databases are located behind SCPs, and are accessed via TCAP messages sent to the SCPs. So how does an end office in the carrier network know how to find such a database? The answer is, they often do not! The end office can route the message to an STP that presumably has more knowledge of database locations. If the local STP does not know about the specific database, then it can route the message, based on the dialed digits, to a higher-tier STP that may know about the database. This process continues until the message reaches an STP that is able to perform the Global Title Translation function. The STP examines the address fields of the SCCP header (most likely the Global Title, and perhaps a subsystem number), and provides the destination point code (and the subsystem number if this was not already available). Figure 3-17 summarizes this process.

User Part Flow Control

SCCP is responsible for regulating traffic flow between peer user parts in different nodes. MTP manages congestion for links and nodes, and SCCP is responsible for flow control at a higher layer. The network operates more efficiently when these functions are separated. For example, a node may have ample processing power and available links to transmit ISUP traffic, but access to a database via TCAP may be slow. In this case, the node can send messages to slow the receipt of TCAP traffic without impacting the ISUP traffic. In the absence of the SCCP flow control, MTP flow control would signal its neighbors to slow the transmission of all traffic types.

Figure 3-17   *Messages for SCP Databases Require Global Title Translation Services of SCCP*

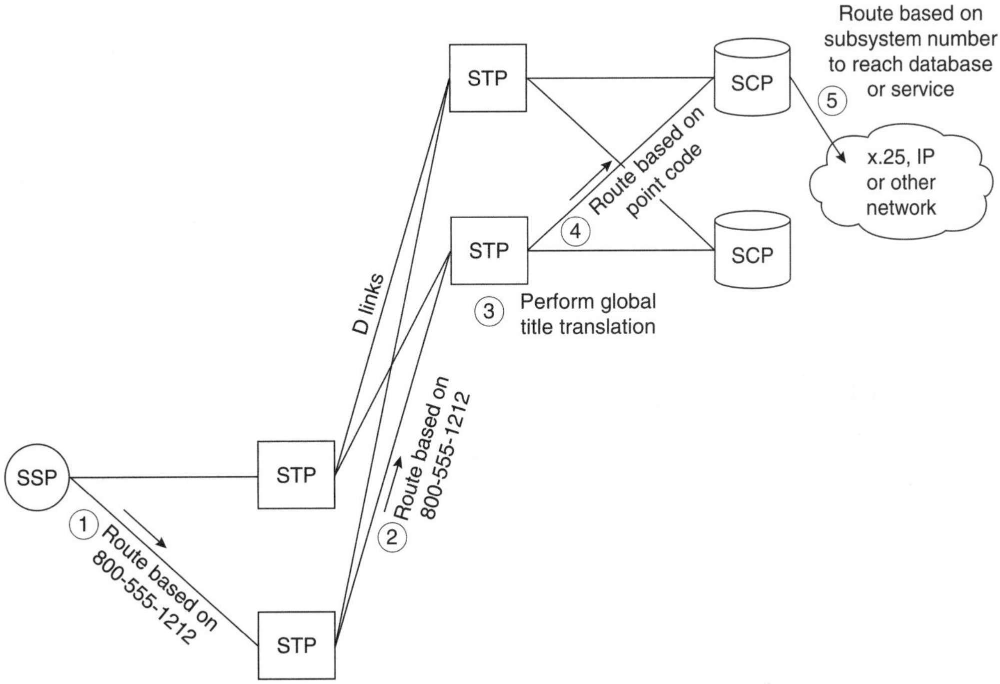

ASP

The *ASP* will build on the connection-oriented services of SCCP and provide session and presentation services to TCAP and other application user parts. These services may be required for connection-oriented applications that manage complex sessions. At present, no SS7 applications use the connection-oriented services of SCCP, so ASP is not used.

TCAP

TCAP provides communication between application interfaces in different signaling points. TCAP messages are used to access databases and invoke procedures or services in remote nodes. The most common example of a service requiring TCAP is the toll-free 800 service. TCAP messages are used to request information from an 800 number database, and to respond with the local routing number for the requesting node. Another example is Call Return, where a calling party is automatically connected with a busy destination when it becomes available. TCAP messages pass instructions to the remote phone switch to enable this service.

TCAP does not itself provide any network features. It is a communication protocol with a predefined format to transport functions and variables with specified data types. The end signaling points that communicate via TCAP messages must support whatever data types and functions are passed via TCAP.

TCAP message format is versatile and extensible. It is the protocol of choice for non-circuit-related transactions. As the number of applications available for the AIN increase, the amount of TCAP traffic in the network will also increase. Eventually, TCAP messages will be the predominant traffic in SS7 networks.

TCAP Message Format

Figure 3-18 illustrates the structure of a TCAP message.

Figure 3-18   *TCAP Message Format*

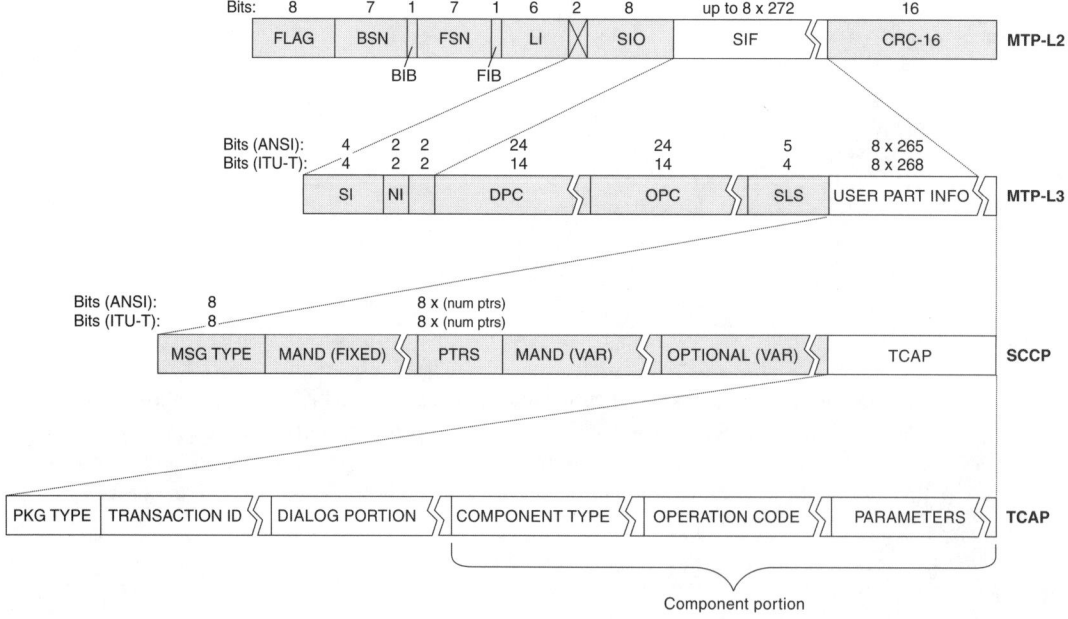

Component portion

The Transaction Portion provides information about the state of the TCAP transaction. This includes whether or not a response is expected, and whether or not the message is part of a sequence. This information is coded as the Package Type and Transaction ID. Table 3-5 summarizes the Package Types defined for TCAP messages.

Table 3-5   *Package Types for TCAP Messages*

TCAP Package Type	Function/Purpose
Unidirectional	Single message with no response expected
Query with permission	Accesses a database; reply may be conversation or response
Query without permission	Accesses a database; reply may only be a conversation
Conversation with permission	Continues a dialog; replay may be a conversation or response
Conversation without permission	Continues a dialog; reply may only be a conversation
Response	Ends a dialog after providing a response (peer must give Permission)
Abort	Cancels the transaction because of protocol errors or user request

Figure 3-19 illustrates several examples of TCAP transactions that use the preceding package types.

The Transaction ID associates multiple TCAP messages with the correct communication thread. For example, an SCP that maintains several simultaneous communication sessions with different requesting nodes uses a unique Transaction ID to identify each session. The Transaction ID is separately assigned in each direction of a dialog, and has significance only to the signaling point that assigned the ID.

Figure 3-19 *Sample TCAP Transactions Using Different TCAP Package Types*

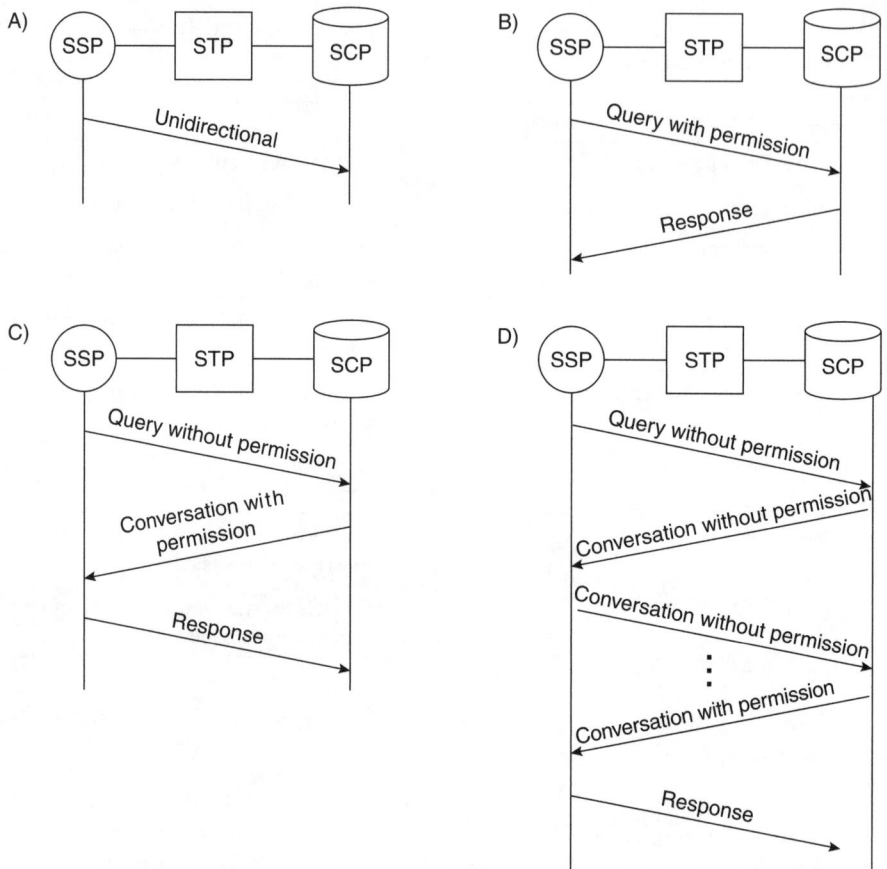

The Dialog Portion is optional and provides information as indicated in Table 3-6.

Table 3-6 *Fields Within the Optional Dialog Portion of a TCAP Message*

Part of Dialog Portion	Function/Meaning
Protocol version	Which TCAP formats are supported (for example, 1996 or 2000 ANSI T1.114, and so on)
Application context	Used by the end applications to associate state information, and so on
User Information	May contain any type of information provided by the user application
Security context	Determines format of information in the confidentiality part
Confidentiality	Includes type of encryption algorithm and information to encrypt/decrypt a message

The Component Portion contains the primary data of the TCAP message. The Component Portion can be further subdivided into the following parts:

- Component Type
- Operation Codes
- Parameters

The Component Type values, summarized in Table 3-7, indicate whether the TCAP message is a remote operation request or response, and whether additional requests or responses follow:

Table 3-7   *Component Types for TCAP Messages*

TCAP Component Types	Function/Meaning
Invoke (last)	Requests an operation to be performed in a remote node; last request of the transaction
Invoke (not last)	Requests an operation to be performed in a remote node; more requests follow
Return Result (last)	Response to an Invoke with the results of the remote operation; last request of transaction
Return Result (not last)	Response to an Invoke with the results of the remote operation; more requests follow
Return error	Returns a code indicating the type of application error relating to a previous Invoke
Reject	Returns a code indicating a problem with the syntax of the previous Invoke

The Operation Codes identify what actions or functions are to be performed by the receiving node. The Operation Codes are organized into families of similar operations. The first byte of the Operation Code identifies the family, and the second byte identifies the operation within the family. Table 3-8 summarizes the Operation Codes that are defined in ANSI T1.114 as revised in the year 2000.

Table 3-8   *Remote Operations Supported by TCAP (ANSI T1.114)*

TCAP Operation Codes	Function/Meaning
Parameter Family:	
Provide value	Requests the values of the variables in the Parameter fields
Set value	Asks the remote application to set the Parameter variables

continues

Table 3-8 *Remote Operations Supported by TCAP (ANSI T1.114) (Continued)*

TCAP Operation Codes	Function/Meaning
Charging family:	
Bill call	Generates a billing record
Provide instructions family:	
Start	Starts running a script of service instructions
Assist	An assisting node requests a script of service instructions
Connection control family:	
Connect	Establishes a call connection
Temporary connect	Establishes a short-term call connection
Disconnect	Ends a call connection
Forward disconnect	Ends call connections established with Temporary Connect
Caller interaction family:	
Play announcement	Plays for the caller an announcement specified in the parameters
Play announcement and collect digits	Same as above, but accepts input from the caller
Indicate information waiting	Tells another application: "inform me when you are ready to send"
Indicate information provided	Tells another application: "tell me when you have sent everything"
Send notification family:	
When party free	Informs the requester when the party becomes available
Network management family:	
Automatic code gap	Used for congestion control to inhibit other codes for some time
Procedural family:	
Temporary handover	No longer supported in the year 2000 version of ANSI t1.114
Report assist termination	An assisting node indicates that the assist is over
Security	Pass parameters for authentication/ authorization

Table 3-8   *Remote Operations Supported by TCAP (ANSI T1.114) (Continued)*

TCAP Operation Codes	Function/Meaning
Operation control family:	
Cancel	Used to cancel a previously specified operation
Report event family:	
Voice message available	Signals from voice-mail systems switch to subscribers switch
Voice message retrieved	Signals from subscribers switch to clear voice-mail indicator
Miscellaneous family:	
Queue call	Adds a call request to this list (for call-return feature)
Dequeue call	Removes a call from the request list

TCAP Parameters provide a method for passing data between nodes. Each Operation Code references a specific set of Parameters, which encode the variables used in the operation. The Operation Codes and Parameters must be used together in TCAP messages to perform useful functions or services. Table 3-9 summarizes the TCAP Parameters that are available for the different operations:

Table 3-9   *TCAP Parameters Used in Conjunction with Remote Operations (ANSI T1.114)*

TCAP Parameters	Function/Meaning
Timestamp	Indicates when an event occurred (locate time and GMT offset)
Automatic code gap indicators	Why, how often, and how long to suppress transmission
Standard announcement	Values include: busy, reorder, ringing, disconnected number, and so on
Customized announcement	Enables a carrier to implement nonstandard announcements
Digits	Includes context: billing number versus calling party versus called party, and so on
Standard user error code	Indicates a problem with an operation because of a subscriber action

continues

Table 3-9   *TCAP Parameters Used in Conjunction with Remote Operations (ANSI T1.114) (Continued)*

TCAP Parameters	Function/Meaning
Problem data	Indicates a problem with the format/value of a transmitted parameter
SCCP calling-party address	Discontinued in year 2000 version of ANSI t1.114
Transaction ID	Discontinued in year 2000 version of ANSI t1.114
Package type	Discontinued in year 2000 version of ANSI t1.114
Service key	Indicates which parameter to search when accessing a database record
Call forwarding status	Indicates type of call forwarding (busy/no answer/immediate) and status
Originating restrictions	Calling-party limitations related to a business group (for example, Centrex)
Terminating restrictions	Called-party limitations related to a business group (Centrex)
Directory number to line service type mapping	Line service types include: single line, hunt group; pay phone, PBX, unassigned, out-of-service, and so on
Duration	How long a function/service lasts (for example, call return, forward, and so on)
Returned data	Return of data that caused a problem
Bearer capability requested	Types: {3.1 kHz, 7 kHz, or 15 kHz audio; video; data} at 64 to 1920 kbps
Bearer capability supported	Indicates whether bearer request is supported, authorized, and available
Reference ID	Identifies a transaction
Business group parameter	Identifies a business group (for example, a Centrex customer) and group information
Signaling networks identifier	Identifies the Network ID and Cluster ID fields of ANSI point codes
Generic name	Names for calling/called/redirected parties and caller ID blocking status
Message waiting indicator type	Urgent versus Normal messages, number of waiting messages, and so on

Table 3-9 *TCAP Parameters Used in Conjunction with Remote Operations (ANSI T1.114) (Continued)*

TCAP Parameters	Function/Meaning
Look ahead for busy response	Determines whether a busy destination can be preempted
Circuit identification code	Identifies the physical path between CO switches
Precedence identifier	Flash, flash override, immediate, priority, routine, and so on
Call reference	Used in secure networks (such as the military) to keep a record of each call
Authorization	A password or login ID
Integrity	Used to verify that information is not changed in transit
Sequence number	Identifies messages in order and counteracts message replays
Key exchange	Used to exchange cryptographic keys

Subscriber Interface to SS7 Networks

The ISDN Basic Rate Interface (BRI) or Primary Rate Interface (PRI) provide subscriber access to SS7 networks. Subscribers (for example, businesses and individuals) do not have direct access to SS7 networks for reasons of security and network stability. ISDN provides the network functionality required by subscribers, without revealing the circuit vendor SS7 network topology and addressing. This indirect access also protects SS7 signaling points from poorly configured subscriber devices (for example, routers and PBXs) or malicious attacks, which could compromise the high availability requirements of the network.

The message format for the signaling D channel is specified in ITU-T Recommendation Q.921 for the link layer and Q.931 for the network layer. The Q.931 messages correspond to ISUP messages, because ISUP is designed to internetwork with ISDN. Figure 3-20 indicates the flow of signaling for the ISDN and SS7 portions of the network for a simplified call session.

Figure 3-20 *Call Setup and Teardown Signaling Across ISDN and SS7 Networks*

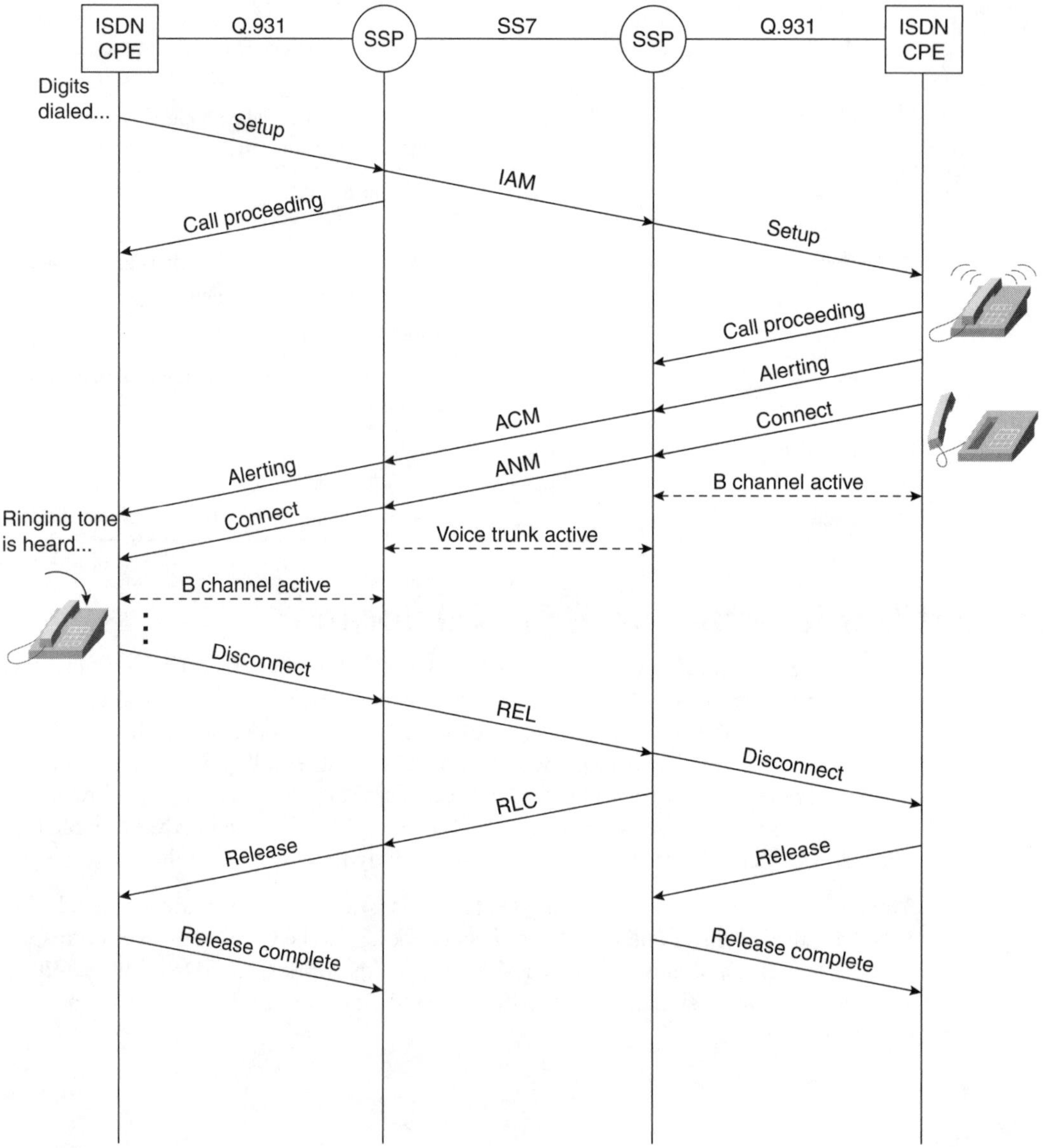

Summary

This chapter has examined the devices that reside in SS7 networks, the manner in which they are connected, the addressing required to reach each entity, and the messages exchanged between them. The SS7 message structure is very detailed, because most events or transactions in the network have been associated with specific message types with pre-identified variables. The "Intelligent Network" is built to understand the specific requirements of the end-user applications.

There are many details of SS7 protocols, particularly ISUP and TCAP, that have not been addressed in this chapter, because a full description of the various options requires a whole book. Travis Russell's book, *Signaling System #7*, Second Edition, provides good coverage of the North American (ANSI and Bellcore) implementations of various SS7 messages. About the best way to learn the details of the international implementations, or specific national variants, is to read the original specifications. Table 3-10 summarizes the international standards and the country-specific standards for the United States:

Table 3-10 *SS7 Protocol Specifications*

SS7 Layer	ANSI Standard	ITU-T Recommendation
MTP-L2	T1.111.2–T1.111.3	Q.701–Q.703
MTP-l3	T1.111.4–T1.11.7	Q.704–Q.707
SCCP	T1.112	Q.711–Q.714, Q.716
TUP	-	Q.721–Q.725
ISUP	T1.113	Q.761–Q.764, Q.766
TCAP	T1.114	Q.771–Q.775
OMAP		Q.750–Q.755

CHAPTER 4

Call Routing and Dial Plans

Just like data networks, voice networks must have a way to identify and locate network users. IP addresses uniquely identify destinations in the Internet, and telephone numbers uniquely identify destinations in the Public Switched Telephone Network (PSTN). Internet users can find each other because routers maintain forwarding tables for network destinations. Similarly, PSTN users can find each other because telephone switches maintain forwarding tables for telephone numbers.

Because the Internet is packet-switched and the PSTN is circuit-switched, there are substantial differences in how routing is handled in the different networks. Each IP packet in a communication session must be independently routed in the Internet. Routers may cache forwarding decisions for packets in a given flow, but there is still a routing process that examines each packet. In the circuit-switched PSTN, call routing is important to establish a call connection but is not needed after the connection is established. For the duration of a session, audio information follows the circuit path established at call setup time.

While circuit switching requires fewer route-processing resources than packet switching, it is not as resilient to network topology changes. In a packet-switching network, a data session can continue uninterrupted while packets are rerouted around a failed path. If a PBX loses a trunk connection to the PSTN, all active calls on the trunk are aborted.

Dial Plans

A *dial plan*, also called a *numbering plan*, describes the addressing and routing aspects of a telephony network. The plan identifies telephone number blocks associated with each site or region, and it guides the routing behavior of all phone switches in the network. Generally, this plan is documented as a directory of site or region telephone numbers or number prefixes.

International Public Numbering Plan

The International Telecommunications Union, Telecommunication Standardization Sector (ITU-T) leads the effort to standardize telephone dialing around the globe. The ITU-T recommendation E.164 provides the framework for telephony interworking among all of the countries of the globe. The document also provides suggestions to assist each country in developing its national numbering plan. The format for international telephone numbers is specified in Figure 4-1.

Figure 4-1   *Format for International Telephone Numbers*

According to a CCITT[1] recommendation from 1964, international numbers should not exceed 12 digits. Country codes are explicitly defined with a regional hierarchy, where each country is assigned a one-, two-, or three-digit code based on the expected number requirements. For example, a country or region with a well-developed communications infrastructure and many telephone subscribers is assigned a one-digit country code (CC), so that 11 digits are available for internal allocation. A country with few subscribers or an undeveloped communications infrastructure is assigned a three-digit CC, because the country does not need more than nine digits for internal allocation. The longer country codes enable the numbering plan to accommodate more countries. The variable-length country code allows conservation of the numbering space. This concept is similar to the original allocation of Class-A, Class-B, and Class-C IP address blocks in the public Internet.

The *National Destination Code (NDC)*, defined in E.160, characterizes a "numbering area within a country (or group of countries included in one integrated numbering plan)." For example, the NDC in the North American Numbering Plan is a three-digit area code. People in North America simply refer to the NDC as the *area code*.

The *Subscriber Number (SN)*, also defined in E.160, is the number typically included in the local directory of the numbering area. This is the number that subscribers within the same numbering area have historically used to call each other. Some metropolitan areas are now associated with many NDCs, so the SN must also be used with the NDC even for local calls. For example, subscribers in some metropolitan areas of the United States must dial an area code and local number for all calls (ten digits plus the trunk prefix 1).

Annex A of recommendation E.164, which provides a detailed listing of country codes for the international numbering plan, is included in Appendix A, List of ITU-T Recommendation E.164 Assigned Country Codes.

---

1. The Consultative Committee on International Telegraphy and Telephony (CCITT) is the former name of the Telecommunications Standardization Sector (ITU-T) of the International Telecommunication Union (ITU).

North American Numbering Plan

The North American Numbering Plan (NANP) encompasses all of the United States of America and its territories, Canada, Mexico, and most of the Caribbean islands. The numbering plan is consistent across all of these countries, and uses the international country code of 1 per recommendation E.164. The format of these numbers is shown in Figure 4-2.

Figure 4-2   *North American Numbering Plan Convention*

NXX - XXX - XXXX

Note that in the plan, N can be any number from 2 through 9, and X can be any number from 0 through 9. The first three digits form the area code, which subdivides the numbering plan into geographic regions and non-geographic services. Examples of non-geographic services in North America include toll-free 800 numbers, and premium services such as 976 numbers that incur additional per-minute charges. The next three digits identify the central office within the area. Multiple prefixes may be associated with a single central office. All 80 of the N9X area codes are reserved for future expansion of the area code field. These digits will indicate the presence of additional area code digits.

Unfortunately, the area codes are not geographically distributed in such a way as to allow summarized call routing. You can imagine, for example, that all 2XX and 3XX area codes could refer to a single region like the east coast of the United States. If this were the case, then the central office from which the call originated would only need to examine the first (and maybe the second) digit of the dialed number. However, the actual area code assignment does not allow this degree of summarization. As an example, the area code 213 is used in Southern California, while 212 is used in New York, on the opposite side of the continent! In fact, the 21X numbers represent eight different U.S. states and Canadian territories, spread across the continent! It seems that the area code assignment could not have been more poorly designed with respect to geography and routing. From an end-user's perspective, this distribution is challenging for telephone subscribers trying to associate a geographic region with a telephone prefix.

Why Is the NANP Not Hierarchical?

To understand the seemingly poor allocation of area codes in the North American Numbering Plan (NANP), you must think back to the days before dual tone multi-frequency (DTMF) tones. Prior to using DTMF tones to represent dialed digits, phones had rotary dials that generated a series of on-off voltage pulses to represent each digit. Remember how dialing a 9 or a 0 used to take longer than dialing a 1 or 2? It was quite annoying when you were in a hurry.

Well, the designers of the NANP considered this and tried to allocate area codes such that the most commonly dialed numbers required the least amount of time. As a result, the metropolitan areas of North America (that is, the places with the most telephones) were assigned the area codes with the smallest numbers (and therefore the smallest dialing delays). New York received 212, Los Angeles received 213, and Chicago received 312. Alaska's 907 area code was the slowest to dial in the early days of the public telephone network. Requiring 26 on-off digit pulses, it took five times longer than dialing the New York area code, which required only five on-off pulses. With the advent of DTMF tones, the underlying design constraint vanished, but the public numbering scheme is entrenched and not likely to change soon (until VoIP is omnipresent and everyone has a URL for voice services!).

For more information about the North American Numbering Plan, go to www.nanpa.com.

Private Numbering Plans

Organizations of all sizes use private dialing plans. A company with two offices might use two-digit extensions to reach employees at either location. Companies with 100,000+ employees around the globe may use a seven-digit dialing plan to uniquely identify all locations and individuals. Implicit in such plans is the existence of private switching equipment and facilities to implement the plan. In some cases, an organization may contract with a public telephone company to create a virtual private dialing network. Centrex service provides this functionality, but on a limited geographic scale. In any case, the private voice network is a distinct entity from the Public Switched Telephone Network (PSTN). As such, the numbering plan must address the routing of calls between the private network and the PSTN.

The primary business drivers for creating a private dialing plan should be:

1 Simplify telephone communication between members of the organization.

2 Reduce telephony expenses for the organization.

To see how a private numbering plan can simplify telephone communication, consider a small international company with an office in Japan and an office in the U.S. Without a private numbering plan, it is awkward for employees in each office to contact each other through the PSTN. (See Figure 4-3.) Employees in the U.S. might dial 9-011-81-3-3501-xxxx to reach employees in Japan. Employees in Japan must also dial a long string of digits.

Figure 4-3 *Long Dialed Strings Required to Call Between Offices Using the PSTN*

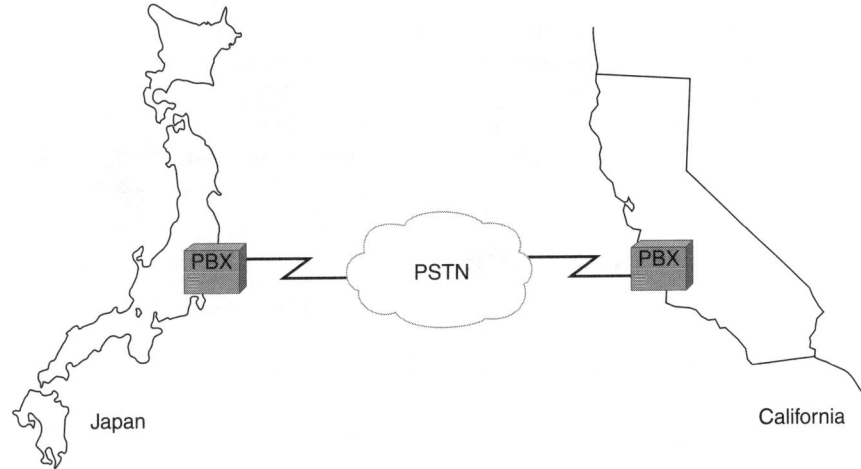

With a private numbering plan, and a private voice network, these long digit strings can be reduced to two or three digits! For example, the Japan office might have extensions 5xx and the U.S. office might have extensions 6xx. (See Figure 4-4.) Not only is this easier for the employees to remember, but it is more convenient to dial, as well. This concept of simplicity extends for organizations of any size. The largest global corporations can operate comfortably with a seven- or eight-digit dial plan, which is more convenient than the E.164 addressing of the PSTN.

Figure 4-4 *Private Voice Network and Dialing Plan Enables Simplified Dialing Between Offices*

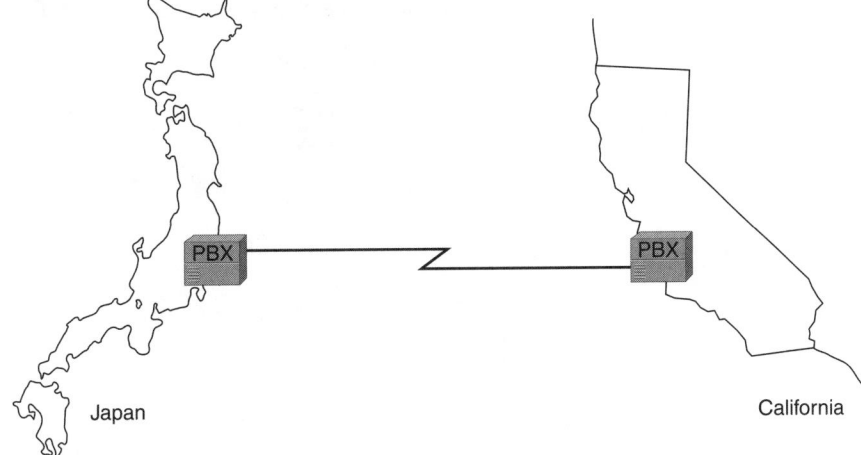

Private numbering plans do not directly reduce telephony expenses, but they are closely related to the private equipment and circuits that do reduce expenses. The majority of private dialing plans require private facilities to route calls between sites. The fixed cost of private circuits and equipment is less than the cost of usage-based PSTN connections, so an implementation of a private dialing plan will generally save money compared to a PSTN-based dialing plan. It is true that private circuits can be used between sites without using a private dialing plan, but the benefit of simplicity might as well be used when it is an option.

Dial Plan Implementations

A dial plan indicates how numbers are assigned to different sites and end users, but it does not indicate how calls will route from the origin to the destination. The following techniques are most commonly used to implement a dial plan within telephone switching equipment:

- TAC codes
- True digit routing
- Speed dialing

TAC Codes

The expression *TAC code* is somewhat redundant because TAC is an abbreviation for *Trunk Access Code*. A TAC code is a number sequence that identifies a trunk (or trunk group) to be used for outbound calling from a traditional telephone switch. The TAC code has significance within the local phone switch only. TAC codes enable the call originator to decide how the call should be routed through the phone switch. For example, consider a small voice network with three remote sites and a central site as depicted in Figure 4-5.

Figure 4-5 *Small Voice Network Using TAC Codes to Implement Dial Plan*

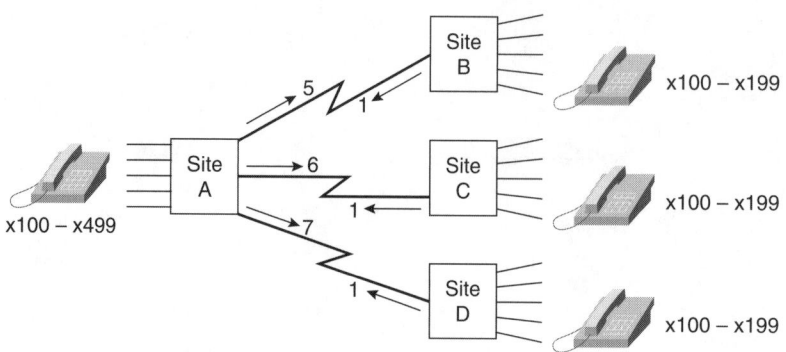

Users at all sites can dial three-digit extensions to reach other users at the local site. To call between sites, users dial a TAC code to connect to the phone switch at the remote site. After receiving a second dial tone from the remote phone switch, users can then dial a three-digit extension as if they were located at the remote site. Users may again enter a TAC code to receive dial tone from a third remote phone switch that is connected to the second phone switch. In this manner, users can hop from phone switch to phone switch until they reach the destination site, and then dial a local extension on the phone switch at the destination site.

Users from Site A must dial 5 to reach Site B, 6 to reach Site C, and 7 to reach Site D. In each case, the users hear a secondary dial tone from the telephone switch at the remote site. The users then dial phone extensions at the remote site as if their phones are directly connected to the remote phone switch. It is more complicated for remote site users to call other remote sites. Users must first dial a 1 to reach the central site, receive a secondary dial tone, and then dial a 5, 6, or 7 to reach the desired remote site. After a third dial tone, the users can then dial the three-digit extension at the remote site if they are local to the site.

Table 4-1 describes the dialing plan for the network.

Table 4-1   *Dial Plan for Sample Network*

Destinations	Dialed Numbers
From Site A:	
Local Site	100 to 499
Site B	5100 to 5199
Site C	6100 to 6199
Site D	7100 to 7199
From Sites B, C, or D:	
Local Site	100 to 199
Site A	1100 to 1499
Site B	15100 to 15199
Site C	16100 to 16199
Site D	17100 to 17199

The dial plan in Table 4-1 is a little confusing, because each site does not have a unique address. Also notice that the dial plan includes numbers of variable length. The essence of the difficulty is that the address changes with the call originating point. In other words, the phone number for a given site depends on the site from which you are calling! In fact, each directory listing defines a calling path, not a destination. A *phone number* in this network is a hop-by-hop description of how the call proceeds from the origin to the destination.

This approach does not scale well as the number of sites and the topological complexity of the voice network increase. Consider a voice network with up to five hops between sites. Users at these distant sites may dial five digits just to reach the destination phone switch, and then dial additional digits to reach the desired extension. In many cases, a single digit TAC code is not feasible in a telephone switch because there are more than seven private trunks going to remote offices. Remember that 0, 1, and 9 are generally in use as leading digits, so this leaves only seven digits to assign as single-digit TAC codes. In the case of two-digit TAC codes, the voice network with five hops requires ten digits plus the extension at the remote site! Users might as well dial via the PSTN in these cases.

From a different perspective, consider the difficulty of this type of dialing plan for employees that travel from site to site. The dialing plan is not consistent between sites, so traveling employees must ask others for help, or refer to a site-specific directory to call other sites. Remember that one of the primary goals of a private voice network is to simplify telephone communications for members of the organization. In this scenario, employees cannot use the phone without asking for help! What happened?

Digit Routing

The TAC code implementation described in the preceding section is usually associated with low-end telephone switching systems (for example, key systems) that do not support digit routing. That is, the phone switches do not decide which trunks to use based on the dialed digits. You may argue that the TAC code is effectively a routing decision, but a TAC code is really an address or label for the trunk group. You generally cannot assign multiple TAC codes to the same trunk group in traditional phone switches (but you can on Cisco routers), so you cannot route a variety of digit patterns over the same trunk using TAC codes. With true digit routing, you can specify a destination trunk for each configured digit pattern. This is analogous to an IP routing table, where wildcard digits in a telephone number pattern are equivalent to don't care bits in an IP routing entry.

It is easy to create a consistent dial plan for a voice network that performs true digit routing. You can associate a globally unique number range (within your private network) to each site, and ensure that members of your organization can use the phone system at any site in a consistent manner. With true digit routing, there is no need to have a variable length dial plan. You must still consider the physical topology of the trunk connections between sites, so that call routing tables may be summarized. This topic is further explored in Chapter 14, "Establishing an Integrated Dialing Plan."

It is important to note that PBX routing tables are static. That is, the routing entries must be manually configured on each PBX. Proprietary solutions may exist to dynamically update call routing tables (which requires Common Channel Signaling to allow interswitch communication on a data channel), but this scenario is not common. Most PBXs do support *Least Cost Routing (LCR)*, which is similar to IP policy routing within Cisco routers. Information other than the dialed destination can affect how the call is routed. The most common implementation of LCR enables calls to be routed to different trunks based on the time of day. This feature is primarily used for trunks with usage-based fees (for example, trunks to the PSTN). Some circuit vendors offer rate plans that vary with the time of day, so it may be cheaper to use vendor A for daytime business calls, vendor B for night and evening calls, and vendor C for weekend calls. All three trunks are always available, but the call routing is established such that the least-cost paths are preferred at a given time of day. The more expensive paths are reserved for overflow during periods of heavy call volume.

Speed Dialing

You can think of speed dialing as a patch to an ailing dialing plan. There are other valid uses for speed dialing, but for now just consider this perspective. Consider a voice network with low-end switches that are not capable of digit routing. In some cases, users must traverse multiple phone switches to reach a remote site. The dial plan looks different from every site, and numbers can be of variable length. Speed dialing codes can be overlaid on this TAC code network to create a uniform dialing plan.

First, you assign a unique number to each site. Then from each site, establish a speed dial code to every other site using the unique numbers just identified. The speed dial code to each site should resolve to the string of TAC codes required to reach that site.

Consider the voice network illustrated in Figure 4-5, and the dial plan described in Table 4-1. Notice that to reach Site D, users must dial 7100 from some sites, and 17100 from other sites. Though this is a very simple example, some networks might have more than ten prefixes associated with the same site, depending on the source of the call. To resolve this problem, overlay globally unique speed dial codes for each site in the network as shown in Table 4-2.

Table 4-2   *Speed Dial Codes Assigned with Global Significance for Each Site*

Site Name	Unique Identifier
Site A	#4
Site B	#5
Site C	#6
Site D	#7

Each switch will have the speed dial codes implemented in a different way, as illustrated in Table 4-3. Note that the actual digit string may require pause digits (such as commas) so that the phone switch at each hop is ready to receive the next digits.

Table 4-3   *Speed Dial Implementation in the Switches at Each Site*

Calling Destination	Associated Speed Dial (from any site)	Actual Digits Dialed by the Phone Switch at Site . . .			
		Site A	Site B	Site C	Side D
Site A	#4	—	1	1	1
Site B	#5	5	—	15	15
Site C	#6	6	16	—	16
Site D	#7	7	17	17	—

As you can see, traveling users can now dial the same digit string from any office to reach any other office. The speed dial function provides a layer of addressing on top of the TAC codes, which frees travelers from knowing the locally significant TAC codes. This strategy is limited by the number of system speed dials that each switch can accommodate. Usually, phone switches can accommodate hundreds of system speed dials, so you should consider a routed voice network before this limitation becomes an issue.

Cisco Router Dial Peers

Cisco devices implement dial plans with *dial peers*. A dial peer is a logical construct that represents a static call routing entry. Instead of creating a single-line syntax for the call routing statement, Cisco has left the dial-peer entity as a block of statements that are easier to use and understand than a single-line statement with many optional parameters.

Dial-Peer Functions

Dial peers perform three main tasks:

- Identify which calls are routed
- Identify where calls are routed
- Identify any configurable parameters for the calls

Each dial peer includes a destination pattern that represents which calls should be processed according to that dial peer. The destination pattern is a string of explicit and/or wildcard digits that identify one or more dialed strings (phone numbers). A single digit wildcard is represented by the full-stop character ".". For example, the string "3..." represents any four-digit number that begins with the number three. The use of wildcards greatly reduces the amount of call routing entries required for a well-designed dial plan. Variable-length wildcards (as opposed to single-digit wildcards) will be discussed shortly.

After a dialed digit string is associated with a specific dial peer (via the destination pattern), the call is routed to the next hop via a session target. The format of the session target varies with each flavor of Voice over X (VoX). VoFR dial peers route calls to a serial interface and Data Link Connection Identifier (DLCI). VoATM dial peers route calls to a serial interface, Virtual Path Identifier (VPI), and Virtual Channel Identifier (VCI). Finally, VoIP calls are routed to an IP address. VoIP may be used over any link layer, but some people confuse VoIP over frame relay with VoFR. VoIP may cross frame relay links, but the session target of a VoIP dial peer is always an IP address. Similarly, VoIP over ATM is different from VoATM, and the type of dial peer reflects this difference.

When the call reaches the terminating router (the last hop of the VoX network), the call is routed to a physical voice port on the router. If a POTS phone is attached to the router, then the call routing is complete. If the router connects to a key system or PBX, the call may be routed across the traditional voice network before completion.

Other dial-peer configuration elements are optional and vary for different VoX technologies. The most commonly used parameters include codecs and voice activity detection (VAD). Other examples include Interactive Voice Response (IVR) applications, SNMP traps, IP precedence and RSVP for VoIP.

Dial-Peer Types

There are two categories of dial peers:

* Dial peers facing the traditional voice network
* Dial peers facing the data network

Dial peers that face the voice network are called *plain old telephone system (POTS)* dial peers. POTS dial peers route calls to specific voice ports on the router—they do not route calls to session targets. These dial peers are always associated with calls routing out of the data network and onto traditional voice switching equipment or telephones.

There are different types of dial peers, depending on the flavor of VoX, for the dial peers that face the data network. For example, a VoIP dial peer is used with VoIP, a VoFR dial peer with VoFR, and so on. Having different dial-peer types enables the router to expect different syntax for the session target.

Consider a call from phone A to phone D in the simple network illustrated in Figure 4-6:

Figure 4-6   *Simple Voice/Data Network*

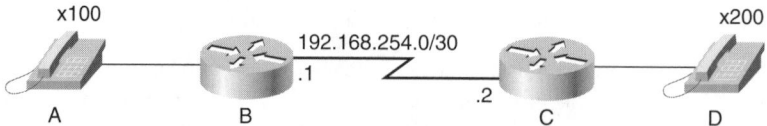

Phone A is identified by extension 100 and phone D is identified by extension 200. When
a user dials 200 from phone A, router B receives the digits. A VoX dial peer in router B must
match 200 in a destination pattern, and specify an appropriate session target to get the call
over to router C. A POTS dial peer in router C must then match 200 in a destination pattern,
and have a voice port specified for sending the call via the appropriate voice module to
phone D. No additional dial peers are required to establish a two-way audio path from
phone A to phone D. However, if calls must be initiated from phone D to phone A, then
additional dial peers are required. Router C would need a VoX dial peer matching 100 and
router B would need a POTS dial peer matching 100. Example 4-1 shows excerpts of the
dial-peer configurations for router B, and Example 4-2 shows excerpts on the dial-peer
configurations for router C.

NOTE   All Cisco router output is shown as it actually appears onscreen.

Example 4-1   *Dial-Peer Configurations for Router B*

```
dial-peer voice 1 pots
  destination-pattern 100
  port 1/1/1
!
dial-peer voice 2 voip
  destination-pattern 2..
  session target ipv4:192.168.254.2
!
```

Example 4-2   *Dial-Peer Configurations for Router C.*

```
dial-peer voice 1 pots
  destination-pattern 200
  port 1/1/1
!
dial-peer voice 2 voip
  destination-pattern 1..
  session target ipv4:192.168.254.1
!
```

Examples 4-1 and 4-2 demonstrate very simple examples of dial peers. Chapter 17,
"Establishing Network-Wide Calling Capability," explores dial peers in detail, along with
numerous topics that relate to the dialing plan and establishing end-to-end calling
connectivity.

Digit Manipulation

When implementing a dial plan, sometimes it is convenient to manipulate the digit string representing the called destination. For example, suppose a PBX must route the digits 5432 across a tie line, but the circuit drops. It would be nice if the PBX could use the PSTN as an alternate path to complete the call. The PSTN address of the destination is 1 408 555 5432. In order for the PBX to use the PSTN, it must prepend the digits 1 408 555 to the digits already being routed. Most PBXs support this feature. Cisco router dial peers also support this feature using the **prefix** command.

There are three mechanisms to manipulate the routed digit string with Cisco routers:

- Prepend digits to the routed digit string
- Remove leading digits from the routed digit string
- Translate digits of the routed digit string

How these mechanisms are implemented with Cisco IOS syntax, and the implications of various implementations, are described in detail in Chapter 17.

Variable-Length Dial Plans

Sometimes you do not have the luxury to start fresh when making a dial plan. What happens if you inherit a voice network where 5 is the prefix for one site, and 55 is the prefix for another site? You can create dial peers with the destination properties as indicated in Table 4-4.

Table 4-4 *Overlapping Digit Ranges Require Many Extra Dial Peers*

Site Name	Destination Pattern
Site A	50..
Site A	51..
Site A	52..
Site A	53..
Site A	54..
Site B	55...
Site A	56..
Site A	57..
Site A	58..
Site A	59..

As long as Site A does not use extensions that match "55.." or "....", this dial plan will work. The reason for not having the "...." destination pattern will be explained shortly. It is somewhat awkward that nine times as many dial peers are required for Site A because of the single instance of digit overlap with Site B. Eight extra dial peers representing the site may not seem like a problem, but consider when these dial peers must be separately configured for each of six analog voice ports on a small router. Because of the single instance of digit overlap, 54 extra dial peers on the router are required. You will have ample time to consider the problem while you are manually entering the dial-peer configurations. The job is somewhat easier if you use a text editor and copy the dial-peer configurations to the router (using TFTP). Do you then want to manage or troubleshoot a router configuration with 54 extra dial-peer blocks for each destination pattern?

Let's assume that you can overcome the awkwardness of the extra dial-peer configurations. But what happens if Site A uses extensions in the range of 500 to 599? The good news is that the dial peers pointing to Site A can be simplified to a single entry by using "5..." for the destination pattern. The bad news is that the dial plan will not work. You are faced with "5..." going to site A, and "55..." going to site B. If someone wants to call site B and dials 55-123, the router will match the "5..." dial peer first and send the call to 5512 at Site A. The last dialed digit is ignored because a dial peer already matched before the router received the last digit.

You may be thinking, "What about longest match lookup?" The longest match lookup does not apply to wildcard digits, so it seems that the "55..." dial peer should match better than the "5..." dial peer. However, the "5..." dial peer is matched before the router even receives the last digit of 55123, so the "55..." can never be matched in this scenario. In general, any matching four-digit destination pattern will obscure a five-digit destination pattern. This is the reason that the "...." dial peer cannot be used when there is a five-digit destination pattern.

It may seem that this is an intractable problem, but there is a solution with variable length wildcards. Cisco uses the T character at the end of a destination pattern to indicate that one or more wildcard digits follow. Destination patterns with the trailing T character cannot match a dialed digit string until the inter-digit timer has expired. Consider what happens with the default setting of 10 seconds for the inter-digit timer. After the router receives each digit of a dialed string, it resets the inter-digit timer. When the router receives the last digit, 10 seconds pass and the inter-digit timer expires. At this point, the dialed string is eligible to match destination patterns that end with a T. The inter-digit timer is normally shortened when using the T feature in destination patterns. Otherwise, 10 seconds will be added to the setup time for each call.

Consider a dial plan for the preceding scenario that uses the T wildcard to solve several problems, as shown in Table 4-5.

Table 4-5   *Simplified Dial Plan Using the Variable-Length Wildcard T*

Site Name	Destination Pattern
Site A	5..T
Site B	55..T

The most obvious advantage of this dial plan is that it is much shorter than the original plan. The less obvious but more significant advantage is that this plan works even if Site A uses extensions from 500 to 599.

Let's take a moment to review how this dial plan works. Consider that you dial 55123 to reach a user at Site B. After the router receives the fourth digit, it does not match the 5..T dial peer because the inter-digit timer has not expired. When the last digit arrives, and the inter-digit timer expires, the router compares the dial peers and matches 55..T because this pattern matches the most non-wildcard digits.

Now imagine that you dial 5511 to reach a user at Site A. After the router receives the fourth digit, it waits for more digits because of the trailing T in the destination patterns. After the inter-digit timeout expires, the router matches the dialed digits to the 5..T dial peer and sends the call to Site A. Even though more digits are explicitly matched for the 55..T destination pattern, this pattern is not matched because it expects at least five digits. This highlights an important point in the dial plan above. Just using 5T and 55T for destination patterns does not solve the problem, because some calls destined for Site A would be sent to Site B. For example 5511 should be sent to Site A, but it matches 55T pattern better than the 5T pattern.

The preceding example demonstrates the importance of understanding how a technology works to avoid using it incorrectly. In many areas of voice/data networking, simple Cisco IOS syntax belies an underlying design complexity. A router may not behave the way you want because it is doing precisely what you configured it to do! It is not enough to configure a feature with correct syntax—you must also configure the feature with parameters that make sense in your network environment.

Summary

This chapter has reviewed traditional dial plans and the methods to implement them. This chapter has also introduced dial peers, which Cisco uses to implement dial plans. Several features of dial peers, and the mechanics of destination pattern matching have been explored. Chapter 14 provides more detail for designing a dial plan to encompass Cisco routers and traditional telephone switches. Dial peers are given further treatment in Chapter 17. The chapter also discusses Cisco-specific technologies and configurations that affect the dialing plan, including connection modes (for example, trunk and PLAR), digit manipulation, call routing with H.323 gatekeepers, and other considerations for establishing end-to-end calling connectivity.

CHAPTER 5

Defining and Measuring Voice Quality

The definition and measurement of voice quality is a challenge that has been examined from many perspectives. It is still an active area of research in the International Telecommunications Union (Study Group 12, ITU-T). Efforts have included the precise characterization of physical waveform transmission, subjective listening tests, and psychophysical modeling. These efforts have produced numerous recommendations for circuit transmission and equipment performance, and the measurement and characterization of voice quality. The most recent research is focused on speech quality for systems using the new low bit-rate codecs (such as G.723.1 and G.729), and systems that integrate VoIP with the Public Switched Telephone Network (PSTN).

This chapter explores the following topics:

- Variables that affect voice quality
- Subjective speech quality measurement
- Objective speech quality measurement

Variables that Affect Voice Quality

There are many possible ways to group and account for the variables that affect voice quality, of which the approach taken here is just one. Table 5-1 summarizes the variables, each of which is defined in this section.

Table 5-1   *Summary of Variables that Affect Voice Quality*

Endpoint Variables	Network Variables
Background noise at sender and receiver	Circuit noise
Input and output signal level	Frequency-dependent distortions
Amplitude clipping	Delay and jitter
Quantization distortion	Talker and listener echo
Codec distortion	Random bit errors
Temporal clipping (VAD)	Burst errors (Packet Loss)
Multiple talkers	Quantization/codec distortion

Background Noise

Background noise at both the sending and receiving ends of an audio stream may have a significant impact on the voice quality perceived by a listener. Examples of background noise include a noisy office, a busy street, or a computer data center with numerous equipment fans and air conditioning. The effects of background noise at the listening side are generally outside the scope of network planning and design, because the network does not contribute to this problem. Background noise at the sending (talking) side is a significant consideration, because it affects the operation of codecs and voice-activity detection (VAD) systems.

Signal Level

Signal level is important at numerous points along the audio path, including the input and output, intermediate analog paths, and A/D or D/A conversion points (A/D is analog/digital). The *signal level* refers to the audio volume, the analog electrical voltage or current, the pulse code modulation (PCM) sample level in a digital byte, or whatever represents the audio level in a given medium. Generally speaking, the signal level remains constant when it is converted to digital form. However, network elements may add "digital padding" that reduces the signal level, or other signal processing may affect the level when in the digital domain. In the analog domain, signals become attenuated as a function of transmission distance. Longer transmission paths weaken the signal strength. Intermediate relays or regeneration devices have the unwanted side effect of amplifying the accumulated circuit noise along with the desired signal. If signal levels are too low or too high at any point along the audio path, then the signal becomes distorted (that is, audio information may be lost).

Amplitude Clipping

Amplitude clipping occurs when a signal level is too large to be accurately represented in some device or transmission medium. The signal is rounded down to the level that may be transmitted, which causes a distortion of the original waveform. Figure 5-1 illustrates this concept.

The waveform on the left side of Figure 5-1 is within the amplitude limits of some part of the network. As the waveform moves to a different part of the network with less ability to accommodate loud signals, the original waveform is "clipped" to fit within the restricted envelope of transmission.

Figure 5-1   *Amplitude Clipping Changes the Shape of a Signal*

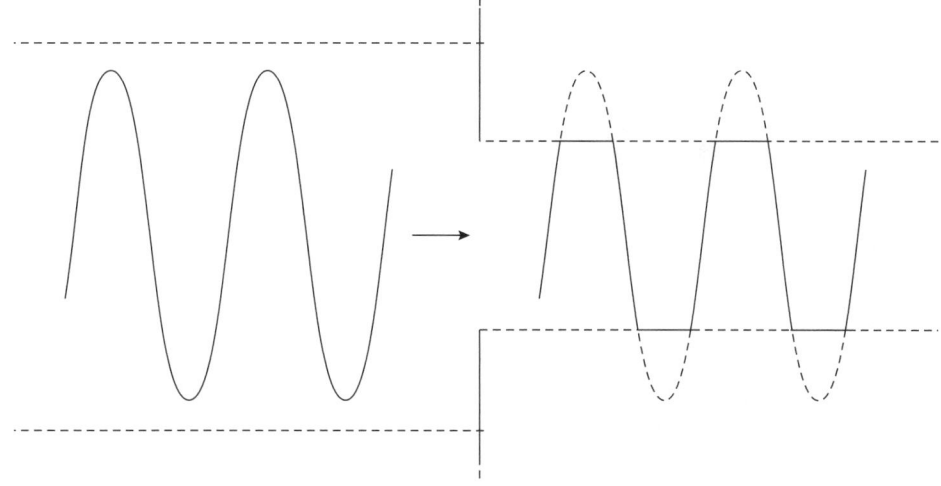

Quantization Distortion

Quantization distortion is the effect of converting an analog signal that varies continuously with respect to time and amplitude into a digital signal that changes at discrete times to discrete amplitudes. Chapter 6, "Voice Digitization and Coding" explores this concept in more detail (see Figure 6-10). For networks that employ low bit-rate codecs (such as many VoIP networks), the effects of quantization distortion are negligible compared to other impairments.

Codec Distortion

Codec distortion occurs because many low bit-rate speech-coding algorithms employ a lossy compression scheme. This means that the listening side does not receive all of the original signal information. Codec distortion affects both speech signals and nonspeech signals such as dual tone multifrequency (DTMF) and multifrequency (MF) tones.

The effects of codec distortion are dependent on other variables, including most of the variables presented in this section. Therefore, the impact of codec distortion in a system should not be considered until other impairments have been accurately characterized. Chapter 6 explores the properties of the speech codecs that are commonly used in VoIP systems.

Temporal Clipping

Temporal clipping (that is, clipping with respect to time) is introduced by VAD systems, which are designed to save bandwidth and eliminate background noise during periods of silence in a conversation. When a speaker begins talking, VAD systems require a finite amount of time to change from a silence-suppression mode to a speech-transmission mode. The beginning of words or sentences may be lost during this time. Chapter 18, "Resolving Voice Quality Issues," explores the topic of VAD in more detail (see Figure 18-3).

Multiple Talkers

Multiple talkers can affect a telephony system in several ways. Low bit-rate speech coders model the signal patterns of a single talker, so they may not provide optimal voice quality when multiple people speak from a single location (for example, a speakerphone or multiple telephones on an analog line). Audio conferences that have multiple simultaneous speakers from different locations have similar problems. Note that *hoot-n-holler*, or always active, audio connections also use a multipoint configuration that may be affected by low bit-rate speech codecs.

Aside from issues with the quality of voice coding, echo cancellation may not function correctly when the parties on two or more ends of a connection speak simultaneously. The nonlinear processor function of an echo-canceller, which is responsible for a significant amount of echo reduction, is deactivated when both parties speak simultaneously. This fundamental behavior of a nonlinear processor cannot be changed. The relevance of these effects for a given environment must be considered as part of the voice quality evaluation in your network environment.

Circuit Noise

Circuit noise is primarily a concern for analog telephony circuits in the PSTN. Analog circuits that transport a desired signal may introduce additional unwanted signals, such as random electrical noise, cross-talk or mutual inductance between adjacent wires, and clicks and pops from electrical-current spikes during switching. Circuit noise may be a significant factor for long-haul analog circuits because the desired signal may be very weak when noise is introduced. As a result, the signal-to-noise ratio (SNR) may be very low for such circuits. Bit-errors may be considered the digital version of noise.

Frequency-Dependent Distortions

Frequency-dependent distortions occur because analog wires have different electrical-transmission properties for signals of different frequencies. For example, an electrical signal travels slightly faster through a wire in the middle frequency range than at higher or lower frequencies. As a result, different frequency components of the same speech sample reach the destination at different times. This phenomenon is called *group delay distortion*. Similar effects cause frequency-dependent attenuation across a circuit, and other time- or amplitude-skewing phenomena. High-speed fax and modem transmission must consider the effects of these phenomena, but speech quality is not significantly impacted.

Delay and Jitter

Delay and *jitter* are prominent factors in packet voice networks. Delay may be a consideration for any long-distance communication, but packet voice networks introduce the additional delays of low bit-rate codecs, queuing, and packet formation. Packet voice networks must also consider the effects of variable delay, or jitter, because the end-to-end connection is not a synchronous serial stream, as it is for digital circuit-switched networks. These subjects are discussed in Chapter 7, "Quality of Service Criteria for Packet Telephony."

Echo

Echo is the result of speech signals from one direction reflecting or leaking into the opposite direction. Talker echo occurs when the speech signal travels toward the destination and is reflected or leaked into the return audio path at a point near the destination. This reflected or leaked signal reaches the ears of the talker, who hears an echo of his or her own voice. If the echo signal is reflected or leaked again, it becomes listener echo for the remote party. Because a reflected signal is usually weaker than the original signal, talker echo is more common than listener echo. Chapter 13, "Delay Budgets and Loss Plans," discusses echo in more detail, in the context of delay budgeting and loss plans. Figure 5-2 illustrates the two types of echo:

Figure 5-2 *Talker Echo Versus Listener Echo*

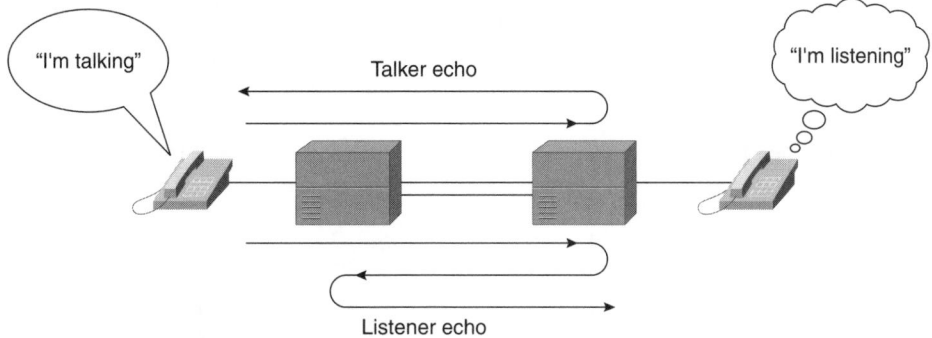

The degree to which an echo is annoying is related to the delay and the signal level of the echo signal. Chapter 13 explores these concepts.

TIP	Remember that if you hear your own echo, the signal is being reflected by the opposite end of the network.

Random Bit Errors

Random bit errors occur in digital transmissions because of faulty wiring, malfunctioning equipment, weak signal levels, or for various other reasons. Bit errors are characterized by occasional, nonperiodic changes to the transmitted signal (for example, 0 replaced with 1), and are usually measured in terms of bit error rate (BER). If the BER of a circuit is 10^{-6}, it means that one out of every million bits is transmitted incorrectly. In traditional telephony networks, digitized voice signals are resilient to bit errors, because each bit represents such a small part of the information stream, and changes to a few bits do not significantly change the output signal. Bit errors have a more significant impact on low bit-rate speech codecs, but the effect is still mild for a low BER.

In packet networks, a single bit error corrupts an entire packet. Bit errors are usually detected with cyclic redundancy check (CRC) algorithms that confirm the data integrity of the packet. Given that entire VoIP packets, VoFR frames, or VoATM cells are discarded when there is a single bit error, you should try to resolve any persistent bit error problems in your network before deploying VoX technologies.

NOTE	For VoIP networks, the CRC field of the user datagram protocol (UDP) header is responsible for detecting bit errors that may occur from software processing in the receiving station. The CRC field in the UDP header is not generally required for correcting bit errors that occur across a transmission line, because the link-layer header usually includes a CRC field for this purpose. As such, it is generally safe to disable the UDP checksums when using Compressed Real-time Transport Protocol (CRTP), which is also known as RTP Header Compression. Removing UDP checksums reduces the CRTP header from 4 bytes to 2 bytes, which is a significant improvement in header efficiency for VoIP. Chapter 10, "Review of IP Features for Voice/Data Integration," and Chapter 15, "Enabling Network-Wide Quality of Service," discuss CRTP in detail. Chapter 11, "VoIP Transport and Signaling Protocols," discusses RTP and the protocol stack for VoIP audio packets.

Burst Errors

Burst errors occur when adjacent bits in a digital stream are corrupted. In packet networks, burst errors are less destructive than bit errors because only the packets with the cluster of errors need to be retransmitted. Random bit errors are more distributed, so more packets are affected and must be retransmitted. In a voice network, the opposite behavior is observed; that is, burst errors are more destructive than random bit errors. A voice stream is not badly affected by a low rate of random signal changes that are spread over time, but any clustering of errors causes a pronounced effect. The effects of burst errors on low bit-rate codecs are magnified, because each bit of a compressed voice stream represents more information. A loss of consecutive meaningful bits can affect a noticeable portion of the output audio stream.

There are certainly other factors that contribute to the voice quality perceived by a listener, but this section has addressed the dominant factors. Note that codec performance, which may be the largest impairment observed in a VoIP network, is highly dependent on a number of variables. These variables are explored further in Chapter 6, which individually considers each of the common ITU speech codecs.

Subjective Speech Quality Measurement

Subjective speech quality measurement is the most reliable and respected approach for measuring voice quality. This approach empirically determines the measured voice quality of a codec or system through the use of listener or conversational tests with real humans. A large number of people, acting as the experimental subjects, listen to audio samples and provide their feedback in the form of a category ranking. The responses from many people to different audio samples and test scenarios are statistically evaluated to determine the mean response of the group. This mean response reflects the performance of the system under test, and the effects of various factors (such as background noise, multiple talkers, low signal levels, and so on) may be individually quantified.

This section explores the three most prevalent methods of subjective testing that are advocated by the ITU:

- Mean Opinion Score (MOS)
- Comparison Mean Opinion Score (CMOS)
- Degradation Mean Opinion Score (DMOS)

Mean Opinion Score

A *Mean Opinion Score (MOS)* is the result of an absolute category ranking (ACR) test. In the ACR test, subjects listen to groups of speech samples and indicate the level of speech quality they perceive for each sample, according to the Listening Quality Scale or the Listening Effort Scale as listed in Table 5-2.

Table 5-2 *Rating Scales for MOS*

MOS Score	Listening Quality Scale	Listening Effort Scale
5	Excellent	Complete relaxation possible; no effort required
4	Good	Attention necessary; no appreciable effort required
3	Fair	Moderate effort required
2	Poor	Considerable effort required
1	Bad	No meaning understood with any feasible effort

Most ACR tests utilize a Listening Quality Scale, which is the approach generally recommended by the ITU. If you see a codec or a system rated with an MOS score, you can assume that the result refers to a Listening Quality Scale unless indicated otherwise. The Listening Effort Scale is suitable when the testing goal is to measure the conversational performance (as opposed to the one-way perception of speech quality) of a system.

Of the subjective testing options available, results of the ACR method will most closely reflect the normal experience of the users of a VoIP system.

Comparison Mean Opinion Score

A *Comparison Mean Opinion Score (CMOS)* is the result of a comparison category ranking (CCR) test. In a CCR test, the subjects are presented with pairs of samples, and they must decide which sample is better and by how much. Each pair of samples is composed of a reference control and an experimental variable, played in a random order. The reference is a good quality sample, such as a standard G.711 codec output or a linear 16-bit PCM recording sampled at 8000 Hz. The subjects assign a category ranking, as listed in Table 5-3, to describe how the second sample compares to the first sample.

Table 5-3 *Rating Scale for CMOS*

CMOS Score	Quality of the Second Compared to Quality of the First
3	Much better
2	Better
1	Slightly better
0	About the same
−1	Slightly worse
−2	Worse
−3	Much worse

The CCR test is a very sensitive measure of the relative performance of a codec or system. Any audio impairments that are introduced by the codec or system are easier to identify in the context of a good comparison sample. This test is well suited to determine which is the better of two scenarios, but it yields a pessimistic assessment of low bit-rate codecs or VoIP systems. In a side-by-side comparison, listeners perceive a substantial difference between low bit-rate codecs and a reference toll-quality sample. In normal listening, however, as in the case of a normal telephone call, listeners are less aware of a difference in the low bit-rate codec.

Degradation Mean Opinion Score

A *Degradation Mean Opinion Score (DMOS)* is the result of a degradation category ranking (DCR) test. In a DCR test, the listeners are presented with two speech samples, but they are explicitly told that the second sample is of a lower quality than the first sample. The listeners must indicate how bad they think the second sample is compared to the first, using a DMOS score as described in Table 5-4.

Table 5-4   *Rating Scale for DMOS*

DMOS Score	Observation of Degradation
5	Degradation is inaudible
4	Degradation is audible but not annoying
3	Degradation is slightly annoying
2	Degradation is annoying
1	Degradation is very annoying

This method is useful for quantifying the effects of various factors on a codec performance, using the best-case scenario for the codec as the reference point. For example, the various codecs being considered for G.729 were compared on the basis of DCR tests. Each codec was tested for its ability to operate in the presence of background noise.

You can find more information about the category ranking tests presented here in ITU Recommendations P.800 ("Methods for subjective determination of transmission quality"), and P.830 ("Subjective performance assessment of telephone-band and wide-band digital codecs").

For real examples of these subjective testing methods in use, read the September 1997 issue of *IEEE Communications Magazine*. It contains numerous articles that characterize the G.729 codec, and reports on global experiments of the types described previously.

Objective Speech Quality Measurement

While the subjective testing methods are reliable and respected, they are also time-consuming and expensive. It would be desirable to have a machine-based automatic assessment of voice quality that accurately reflects the results of a subjective test without incurring the time and expense. This area, known as objective speech quality measurement, is actively being researched.

The objective method of speech quality measurement that has gained acceptance and popularity through the ITU is Perceptual Speech Quality Measurement.

Perceptual Speech Quality Measurement

The Perceptual Speech Quality Measurement (PSQM) model, specified in ITU Recommendation P.861, yields results consistent with a subjective test of a codec under certain conditions, but is not verified for many conditions present in a live network. The ITU selected the PSQM model out of many choices, as it most closely matches the results of subjective tests. The following sections explore two aspects of PSQM:

- What are valid uses of PSQM?
- How does PSQM work?

Applicability

PSQM is ideally suited for measuring codec performance in a laboratory, and can be tuned for analysis of speech quality in a VoIP network (after capturing sound samples), but is difficult to implement for real-time network evaluations.

Table 5-5 summarizes the conditions for which PSQM is and is not applicable.

Table 5-5   *Applicability of PSQM for Different Voice-Testing Scenarios*

Proven Accuracy for . . .	Unknown accuracy for . . .	Poor accuracy for . . .
Speech input levels	Listening levels	Delay
Talker dependencies	Multiple simultaneous talkers	
Multiple bit-rates	Background noise at sending side	
Transcodings	Music	
Dropped codec frames	Temporal clipping (from VAD)	
	Amplitude clipping (input gain)	

The original publication of P.861 indicates that PSQM has not been evaluated for use with channel errors (such as random bit errors, burst errors, or dropped frames), but the forthcoming update to Annex I of P.861 addresses the issue of dropped frames (including missing codec samples and dropped packets). The updated Annex I has not been published as of this writing, so it is not discussed further here.

The PSQM algorithm specifically adds noise during the processing to simulate a normal telephony environment. If you apply the PSQM model to a real network, the model should be adjusted to remove this portion of the processing from the input or reference signal. If you record the output signal directly from the wire, then the PSQM algorithm still needs to add noise at the receiving side to simulate a normal listening environment.

Before applying the PSQM algorithm, the input and output audio streams must be adjusted such that there is no delay or difference in loudness between the samples. Some PC-compatible software implementations require a recorded sample of the input and the output (for example, .wav files), which must be processed before the PSQM algorithm is applied. Any PSQM products that claim applicability for measuring live VoIP networks must have automated features to adjust the time and signal levels prior to sending the samples to the PSQM algorithm. Also, be sure to check that the variables may be tuned to remove or reduce the noise simulation included as part of the PSQM algorithm. You should verify the details of the product operation before you make any purchases to ensure that it generates results that are applicable to your environment.

NOTE   The ITU is working on a draft of Recommendation P.862, which specifies Perceptual Evaluation of Speech Quality (PESQ). PESQ performs well for predicting speech quality in a wide variety of applications, including VoIP in real networks. If PESQ is approved by the ITU without delay, it should be available as of February 2001. When P.862 is standardized, it will replace P.861 PSQM.

Operation

Figure 5-3 illustrates the basic process of the PSQM method.

Both the reference (original) waveform and the processed waveform (for example, codec output, or treated VoIP network output) are modified to simulate the physical aspects of the human ear as a sound pressure sensor. The signal is frequency-filtered as if it passed from the outer to the inner ear, with a simulated noise component added to reflect normal listening conditions. The strength of each frequency component is then adjusted to reflect the critical bands, or sensitivity regions, of the basilar membrane. The *basilar membrane* is the actual microphone inside the cochlea of the inner ear to which nerves are attached. Figure 5-4 illustrates a cross section of a human ear, and how the PSQM model simulates the physical properties of hearing.

Figure 5-3   *PSQM Algorithm*

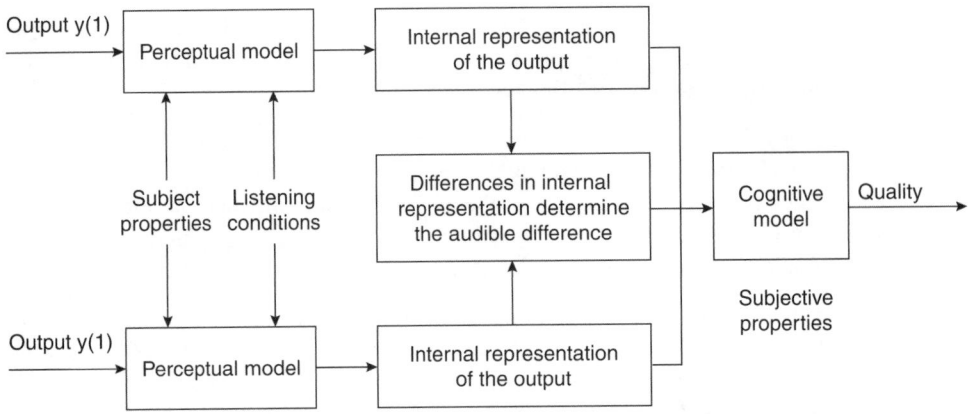

Figure 5-4   *PSQM Model Simulates the Physical Properties of a Human Ear*

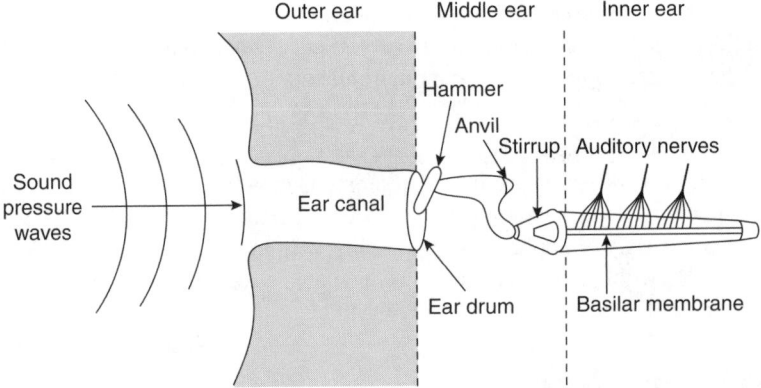

The physical shape of the basilar membrane is not straight, as depicted in Figure 5-4. It is actually rolled within a snail- or cinnamon roll-shaped organ called the cochlea.

After the two signals have passed through the physical model of the ear, they are then compared in the context of a cognitive model, which simulates a human brain's interpretation of the sounds. For example, our brains are more sensitive to extra sounds added to an audio signal than to parts of the signal that are unexpectedly removed. Our brains can mask the missing sounds with the expected sounds, similar to how an audio codec can guess what the next sample should be when a frame is dropped. This and other processes are considered to yield an objective quality scale rating. This objective rating may then be transformed into one of several subjective quality measures.

Speech Quality Estimation for Planning Purposes

Several speech quality models have been developed to address network design and planning needs. Whereas the objective listening measurements are designed for testing a codec, or testing an existing network, the methods discussed here are useful to estimate the voice quality in advance of building the network, based on an analysis of the network design components. For example, it is desirable to know how the customers of a national phone service will respond to a different audio codec, an increase in signal delay, or numerous other factors.

The two models discussed here are closely related:

- The Equipment Impairment Factor method
- The E-model

Equipment Impairment Factor Method

The Equipment Impairment Factor (EIF) method of estimating speech quality is described in ITU Recommendation G.113 (Transmission Impairments). This model is a simplification of the E-Model developed by the European Telecommunications Standards Institute (ETSI). The basic problem addressed by the model is that various transmission impairments (factors that degrade audio perception) are measured in different dimensions, so how can these separate and independent measurements be combined to yield a single scalar value? For example, if you know how delay affects sound quality, and you know how quantization distortion affects sound quality, how can you guess the combined effect of these factors?

The foundational premise of this model is that the separate impairments can be transformed to a scale of psychological factors that are additive. The sum of these psychological factors is a single scalar value that represents all of the impairments, and this value may be converted to a subjective test score (for example, MOS) to determine the likely effect on listeners.

The EIF method is calculated as follows:

$$I_{nc} + I_{lr} + I_q + I_{dte} + I_{dd} + I_e = I_{tot}$$

$$I_{tot} - A = I_{cpif}$$

Table 5-6 describes the variables used in this approach.

Table 5-6 *Variables Used in the EIF Method of Quality Estimation*

Impairment	Caused By...
I_{nc}	Circuit noise
I_{lr}	Nonoptimal Overall Loudness Rating (OLR); (discussed in Chapter 13)
I_q	Quantization distortion from A/D and D/A conversion (via PCM process)
I_{dte}	Talker echo (discussed in Chapter 13)
I_{dd}	Delay (that is, one-way transit delay)
I_e	Special equipment (such as non-waveform, low bit-rate codecs, packet network effects, and so on)
I_{tot}	Total effect of all impairments
A	Expectation Factor: reduced quality expectation of end users because of some other benefit
I_{cpif}	Calculated Planning Impairment Factor: indicates the expected level of user satisfaction

Each of the psychological factors, or impairment variables, listed in the table is mapped from a physically measurable property (see Tables 5-9 through 5-15 at the end of this section). The sum of these variables is the total impairment I_{tot}. In the absence of any extenuating customer expectations, this value represents the level of satisfaction that customers will have with the service. I_{tot} should be modified by the expectation factor A, which accounts for lowered user expectations to yield the calculated planning impairment factor, I_{cpif}.

Table 5-7 relates the I_{cpif} values to a conventional category rating. You can roughly translate these values to the MOS scores 1 through 5.

Table 5-7 *Relationship Between I_{cpif} and Speech Quality; Also Correlates with MOS*

Upper Limit for I_{cpif}	Speech Communication Quality
5	Very good
10	Good
20	Adequate
30	Limiting case
45	Exceptional limiting case
55	Customers likely to vehemently complain or switch to a different network provider

Expectation Factor

The *expectation factor*, A, represents any reduced quality expectations that customers may have because they are gaining some other benefit from the system. For example, wireless subscribers are not tied to a phone at a desk, so they are more flexible in accepting a lower level of signal quality. Similarly, people in remote areas without phone service are tolerant of huge delays from multiple satellite hops. In some cases, international calling access is not taken for granted, in which case the users often have lesser expectations of speech quality. In each of these cases, the A value quantifies the amount of degraded service that customers accept in exchange for another benefit.

As part of a network design, you can estimate an A value for the network to offset absolute performance that is less than toll quality. You must make a reasonable estimate of A based on interviews with users or other data you have gathered, or the network you design will not yield the desired level of customer satisfaction. In other words, if you select an A value that is too large, then you are overestimating the tolerance of users and you risk designing a network that does not meet the users' expectations. Table 5-8 illustrates the maximum recommended values for A in several circumstances.

Table 5-8   *Maximum Values of Expectation Factor A for Given Situations*

Advantage that Customer Gains with the Communication System	A_{max}
Conventional wire-bound access (no advantage)	0
Mobility allowed within a building	5
Mobility within a geographic area or a vehicle	10
PSTN access from hard-to-reach locations (for example, via multihop satellite)	20

The concept of expectation factor may be extended with caution to VoIP networks. In terms of feature improvements, a VoIP system may enable customers to use new multiservice applications (for example, "click to dial" from a web page), and in some cases may even simplify the operation of traditional telephony services. Consider an international toll-bypass scenario, for example. Instead of dialing an international phone number, reaching an auto-attendant, and dialing the extension of a person in the office, you may dial a number from a private dial plan and reach the person directly via single-stage dialing. The convenience of not remembering a long number and not waiting for the two-stage dialing might make you more tolerant of slightly degraded voice quality.

The VoIP network may also be favored for economic reasons. People that are accountable for the costs of international calls will very much appreciate the reduced cost of the VoIP network. This person may also be more tolerant of reduced voice quality in exchange for the monetary savings and the ability to place international calls more frequently. It must be noted that this effect is not significant for people who are not accountable for or aware of the costs of the telecommunications infrastructure.

When determining a value for A, consider Table 5-8 as a reference, and ask yourself a few hypothetical questions that explore the trade-off between the benefits of the service and the impairments that would be accepted. In the case of a VoX network, consider how much service degradation from the baseline PSTN service is acceptable in exchange for the cost savings, new applications, or other benefits of the VoX service that are tangible to the end users. The following questions demonstrate the idea:

- How much delay or echo will you accept to save $<X> per month?
- How much codec degradation is acceptable for the ability to place calls from a web page?

After you answer these questions, you can examine the impairment values associated with the real-world measures, and assign a number for A. Remember that the impairment factors are additive, so your assessment of A based on a comparison to a single variable (that is, just echo, or just delay) tends to discount the real quality that would arise from a given situation. In other words, if you think you can tolerate 200 ms of delay in exchange for some cost or feature benefit, do not forget to consider that some delay, distortion, and other negative effects may be present along with the delay. In the end, your customers (internal or external) will confirm or deny your estimate of A, because their level of satisfaction with the actual service is what the EIF method attempts to measure. The expect factor is a calibration tool to match the EIF method to a real environment, and you should adjust the value based on feedback from your customers.

Impairment Values

The following tables summarize the mappings of various tangible measurements to the scale of psychological factors, as measured by impairment values. All impairment values are measured in terms of eif units, or equipment impairment factor units. These tables are directly reported from ITU Recommendation G.113, including Appendix I, which was updated in December of 1998.

Circuit Noise

The amount of voice quality impairment introduced by circuit noise at the receiving end of the circuit is presented in Table 5-9.

Table 5-9   *EIF Equivalents for Circuit Noise (N_c)*

N_c (dBm0)	I_{nc} (eif)
< –60	0
–60	4
–50	15
–40	30

Overall Loudness Rating

The amount of voice quality impairment introduced by the overall loudness rating (OLR) of the circuit is presented in Table 5-10. The OLR value, which relates to the gain or attenuation for different parts of the circuit, is discussed in more detail in Chapter 13 of this book.

Table 5-10   *EIF Equivalents for OLR*

OLR (dB)	I_{lr} (eif)
5 to 10	0
15	7
20	14
25	21

Quantization Distortion

Quantization Distortion, the amount of voice quality impairment introduced by quantization distortion, as measured in quantization distortion units (qdu), is presented in Table 5-11. Note that this impairment only reflects the analog to digital conversion of a G.711 PCM process. Any additional processing, such as required for low bit-rate codecs, is not considered by this measure.

Table 5-11   *EIF Equivalents for Quantization Distortion*

qdu	I_q (eif)
≤4	0
6	2
8	7
10	11
15	20
20	28

Residual Talker Echo Loudness Rating

The *residual talker echo loudness rating (residual TELR or RTELR)* describes the speech quality effects of a talker's own voice being reflected back to the talker. The residual TELR is the difference between the observed signal strength of the echo (TELR) and the maximum acceptable echo signal level for a given delay (TELR$_c$). The relationship between the echo level and the delay of the echo is based on Figure 1 of ITU Recommendation G.131, which is reprinted in this book as Figure 13-7.

For example, consider an echo of the talker's voice that reaches the talker with a TELR of 40 decibels (dB), and is delayed by 180 ms. According to Figure 13-7, an echo delayed by 180 ms has a $TELR_c$ of about 52 dB (based on the top curve). Applying the formula for residual echo:

$$RTELR = (TELR) - (TELR_c)$$

yields –12 dB, which correlates with an impairment factor of about 44 eif (see Table 5-12).

Table 5-12   *EIF Equivalents for Residual Talker Echo (TELR-TELR$_c$)*

RTELR (dB)	I$_{dte}$ (eif)
15	0
10	3
5	8
0	17
–5	30
–10	40
–15	50

One-Way Delay

The amount of voice quality impairment introduced by the one-way delay of the circuit is presented in Table 5-13. Note that after a point, additional delay does not significantly degrade the quality of the conversation, because the real-time character has already been lost.

Table 5-13   *EIF Equivalents for One-Way Delay (T$_a$)*

T$_a$ (ms)	I$_{dd}$ (eif)
150	0
200	3
250	10
300	15
400	25
500	30
600	35
800	40
>800	40

Speech Codec

The amount of voice quality impairment introduced by the use of a low bit-rate codec is presented in Table 5-14. These values, which apply to error-free operation of a single coding and decoding process, have been derived from subjective listening tests for each of the codecs. The properties of these codecs are explored in more detail in Chapter 6.

Table 5-14   *EIF Equivalents for Various Speech Codecs*

Reference	Codec Type	Bit Rate (kbps)	I_e (eif)
G.726	AD-PCM	40	2
G.726	AD-PCM	32	7
G.726	AD-PCM	24	25
G.726	AD-PCM	16	50
G.728	LD-CELP	16	7
G.729	CS-ACELP	8	10
G.729A + B	CS-ACELP	8	11
G.723.1	ACELP	5.3	19
G.723.1	MP-MLQ	6.3	15

Table 5-15 presents the performance for the G.729A CS-ACELP and G.723.1 ACELP low bit-rate codecs for various levels of packet loss in a network. These values are especially applicable to VoIP systems, but the experiment has not been sufficiently replicated to qualify as a solid characterization of the codec performance.

Table 5-15   *EIF Equivalents for Various Speech Codecs in the Presence of Packet Loss*

% Packet Loss	I_e [G.729A + VAD (8 kbps)]	I_e [G.723.1 + VAD (6.3 kbps)]
0	11	15
0.5	13	17
1	15	19
1.5	17	22
2	19	24
3	23	27
4	26	32
8	36	41
16	49	55

If your network requires tandem encoding (that is, multiple compression/decompression cycles for the same audio path), simply add one instance of the impairment factor for each encoding (for example, four codec cycles of 32 kbps G.726 yields a combined I_e of 28 eif).

E-Model

The E-model, upon which the Equipment Impairment Factor method is based, is a more robust and complex model of transmission impairments. The E-model is described in ETSI (EG 201 050), and has been incorporated into ITU standards as G.107.

Functionality

The E-model is based on the notion that psychological factors on a psychological scale are additive. Whereas the EIF method produces an I_{cpif} value to represent the sum of all transmission impairments, the E-model produces an R-value (illustrated in Figure 5-5).

Figure 5-5   *R-Value Is the Output Measurement of the E-Model*

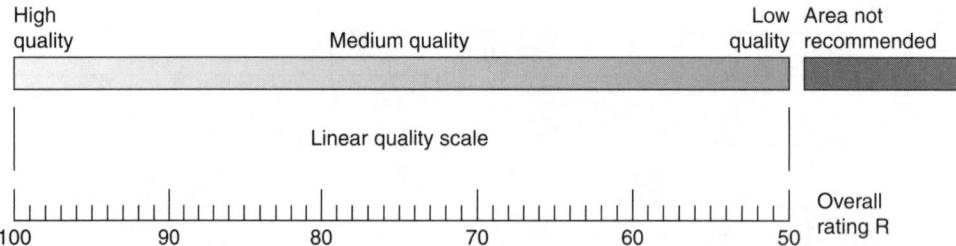

ITU-T Recommendation G.109 provides a mapping between the R-values and the categorical ratings that are commonly associated with subjective speech quality tests. This mapping is described in Table 5-16:

Table 5-16   *R-Values Translated to Categorical Speech Quality Estimations*

R-Value Range	Quality Category	User Satisfaction
$90 \leq R < 100$	Best	Very satisfied
$80 \leq R < 90$	High	Satisfied
$70 \leq R < 80$	Medium	Some users dissatisfied
$60 \leq R < 70$	Low	Many users dissatisfied
$50 \leq R < 60$	Poor	Nearly all users dissatisfied

The E-model considers numerous effects in addition to the impairments considered by the EIF model. These effects include room noise, side-tone masking (signal transmitted from mouthpiece to earphone that provides desired feedback to the talker, and masks low-delay echoes), send and receive loudness ratings (discussed in Chapter 13), and various other factors. Figure 5-6 illustrates the fundamental variables that contribute to the E-model calculation.

Figure 5-6 *E-Model Reference Diagram*

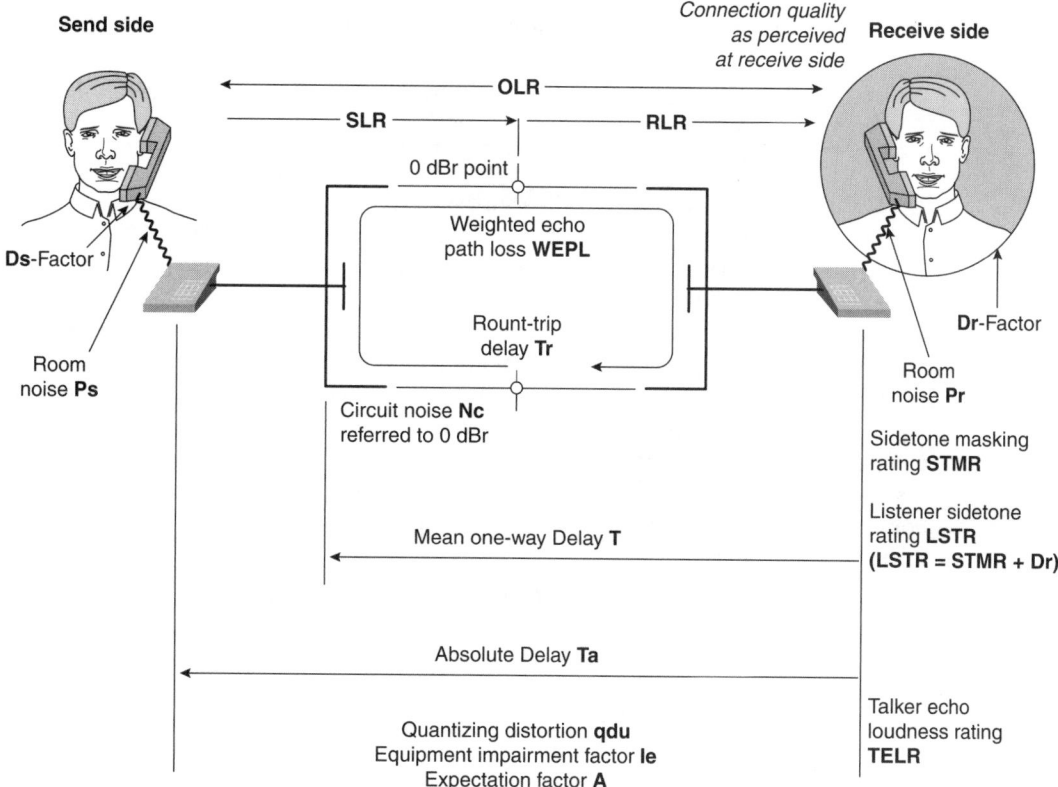

These variables are grouped by impairment type and represented in a summarized equation to determine the R-value:

$$R_o - I_s - I_d - I_e + A = R$$

Table 5-17 describes the variables used in this approach.

Table 5-17 *Calculation of the R-Value, as Used in the E-Model*

Impairment	Caused By . . .
R_o	Noise floor (room noise at receive and send sides, circuit noise)
I_s	Simultaneous factors (excessive loudness, sidetone, quantizing distortion)
I_d	Delayed factors (talker echo, listener echo, absolute delay)
I_e	Special equipment (non-waveform low bit-rate codecs, packet network effects, and so on)
A	Advantage, or Expectation Factor: reduced expectation of end-users, because of another benefit
R	Calculated Planning Impairment Factor: indicates the expected level of user satisfaction

The I_e values for the low bit-rate codecs are the same as indicated in Table 5-14. This is not surprising because the results published in ITU Recommendation G.113 Annex I and ETSI EG-201-050 are based on the same experiments. Each of the other E-model impairment components is a nontrivial function of multiple variables. The fully expanded equation for R, in terms of the fundamental variables, would be a frightful sight. Practical application of the E-model requires a computer program to perform the calculation in terms of the fundamental variables. The EIF method, by contrast, has been pre-calculated into lookup tables. This enables you to examine various network design scenarios without performing complex calculations. Given a computer application that implements the E-model, and assuming that you understand and can determine the values for the input to the E-model, you will have a more accurate estimate of speech quality by using the E-model than by using the EIF method.

Information to purchase a computer implementation of the E-model is available from the ETSI at the following URL:

www.etsi.org/stq/presentations/emodel.htm

Relationship to MOS

Once you have determined the R-value for a given network, you can convert this to an equivalent result of a subjective speech quality test. Figure 5-7 illustrates the relationship between the R-values of the E-model and the MOS scores of a subjective listening test. The MOS score and R-values for several network scenarios are superimposed on this diagram as a reference.

Figure 5-7   *Relationship Between R-Values and MOS Scores*

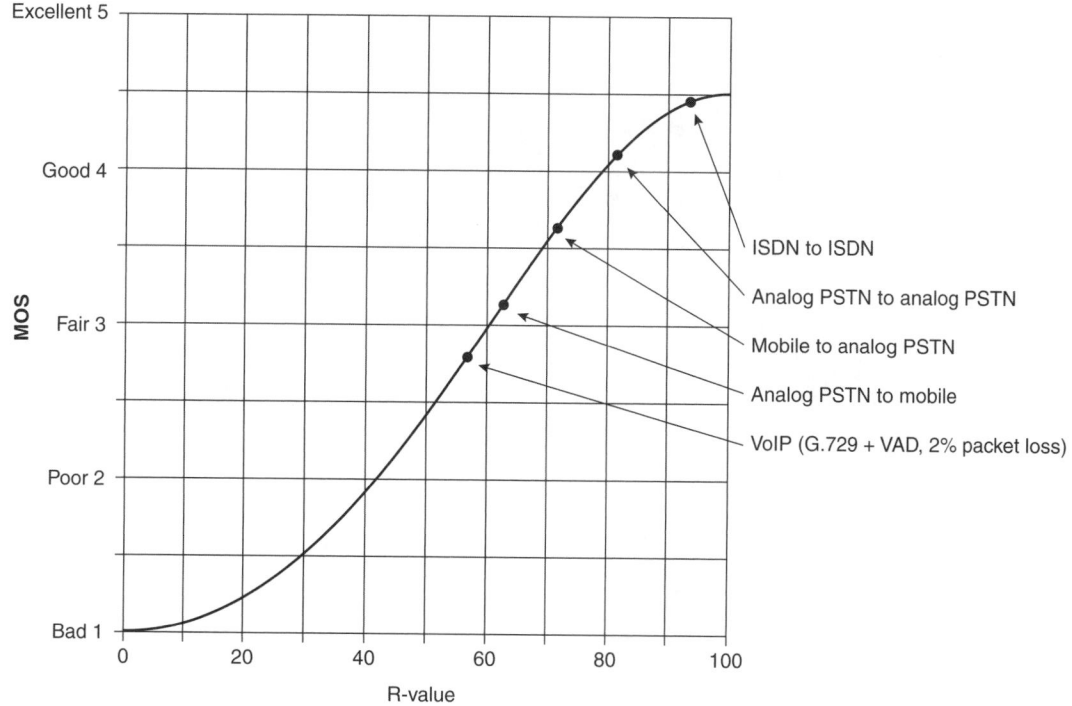

Summary

This chapter has explored the factors that contribute to speech quality perception, the measuring techniques used to quantify speech quality, and estimating techniques to aid in the design of a network.

It is likely that many of the transmission impairments discussed in this chapter are unfamiliar to you. Most of these topics are described in some detail in various chapters of this book. Codecs and quantization are examined in Chapter 6 and delay and echo are examined in Chapter 13. Temporal and amplitude clipping are discussed further in Chapter 18 and Chapter 7 explores packet voice issues such as packet loss, delay, and jitter. Other points are sprinkled throughout the book, although an attempt has been made to present the wide array of information in an organized manner.

CHAPTER 6

Voice Digitization and Coding

This chapter provides a light technical background to help you understand how different speech codecs work. Following an exploration of the various codec types and performance criteria, each of the common codecs used in VoX networks is examined. After reading this chapter, you should be able to choose an appropriate speech codec based on the requirements of your specific network environment. This chapter is organized into the following sections:

- Analog versus digital signals
- Digitizing an analog signal
- Speech-coding algorithms
- Criteria for codec selection
- Comparison of selected codecs

Analog Versus Digital Signals

Before exploring the conversion of signals between analog and digital forms, you should understand the inherent differences between these signal types. You should also understand the merits of each signal type so that you can appreciate why the conversion process is required.

Continuous Versus Discreet

Analog signals are continuously variable within a given range. An analog signal that varies over time may have a curve as shown in Figure 6-1.

Figure 6-1 *Analog Signals Can Have Any Value Along the Y-Axis*

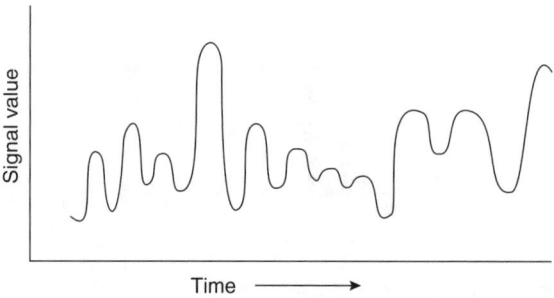

Digital signals have discreet values within a given range. A digital signal that varies over time has a curve with characteristic straight lines and discontinuities, as shown in Figure 6-2.

Figure 6-2 *Digital Signals Can Only Have Specified Values Along the Y-Axis*

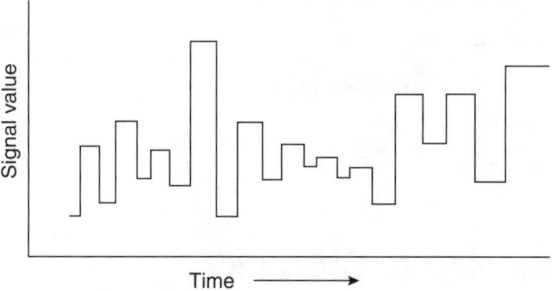

To put this difference succinctly, analog signals are continuous and digital signals are discreet. While analog and digital signals can be represented in many forms, consider an electric potential (that is, voltage) that varies with time as the representation for the rest of this discussion.

Encoding Values in the Signal

An analog electrical signal is usually derived from a transducer that converts the signal from one physical form to another, without changing its waveform appearance. For example, a telephone mouthpiece converts a changing air pressure (sound) signal into a changing electrical voltage signal. For sound, conversion to electrical form is convenient because electrical signals can be transmitted much farther than pressure waves in air. Figure 6-3 illustrates the relationship between an information source (air pressure) and an analog signal (voltage) that represents the information source.

Figure 6-3   *An Analog Electrical Signal Maps Directly to the Sound Source at Every Instant*

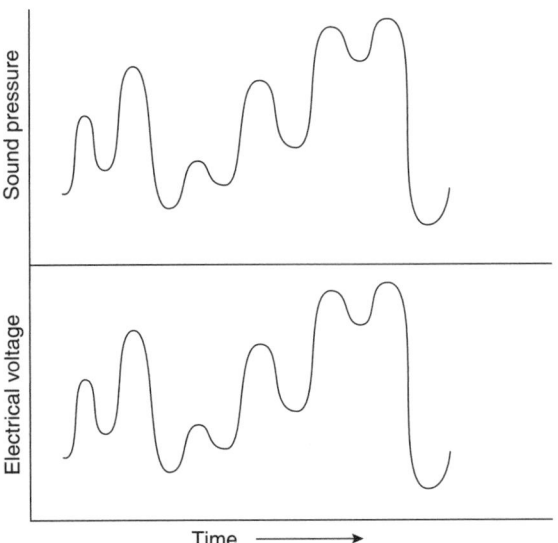

While the value of an analog signal at any instant reflects the value of the information source, the value of a binary digital signal at any instant reflects one of two values: 0 or 1. Digital systems are not required to have only two signaling states, but the binary system is by far the most prevalent on planet Earth. Instead of relying on the instantaneous value of the signal to encode the information source, binary digital signals rely on a series of signal values to represent a single instant of the information source. Figure 6-4 illustrates the relationship between an information source and a binary digital signal that represents the source.

So how is a digital signal actually represented on an electrical wire? In the most basic scheme, 0 and 1 are each assigned a range of voltage values. Consider an implementation with a voltage range of 0 to 5volts (V). Any voltage from 0 to 2.5V corresponds to a logical state of 0 and any voltage from 2.5 to 5V corresponds to a logical state of 1. (This example is highly simplified to suit our present discussion.) The encoded information is resilient to small variations or noise in the physical representation. While the actual waveform of the voltage on the wire may look somewhat irregular, the symbolic meaning of this signal is a crisp digital signal. (See Figure 6-5.)

Figure 6-4   *Digital Signals Represent the Information Source as a Series of Binary-Encoded Values*

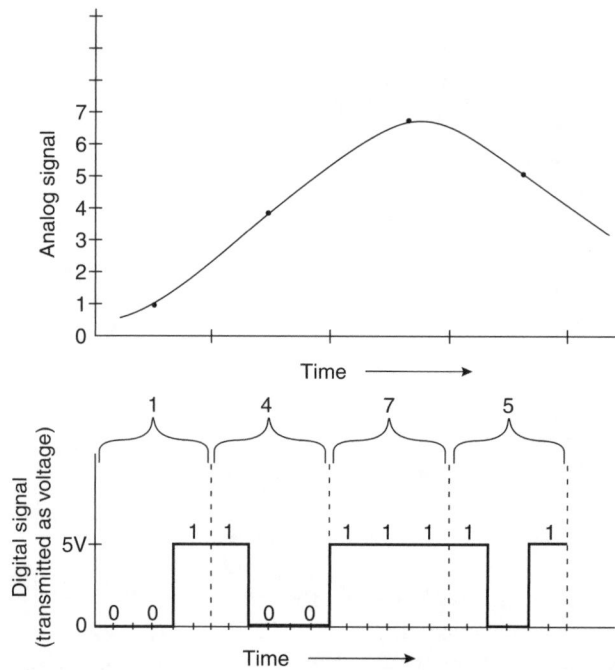

Figure 6-5   *Digital Signals Are Resilient to Small Variations in the Physical Representation*

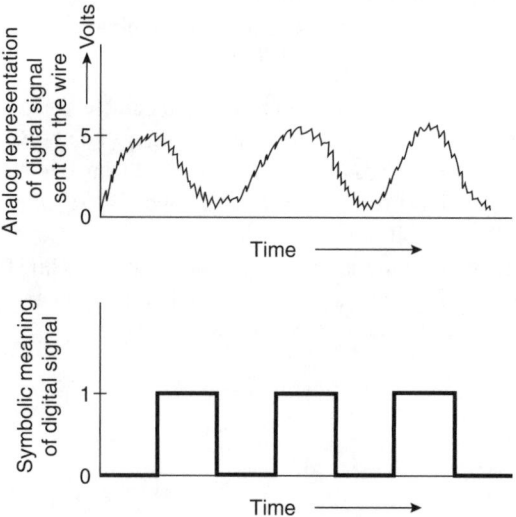

Transmission, Replication, and Storage

Analog and binary digital signal representations have important consequences for information transmission, replication, and storage. A digital signal can tolerate small signal changes while maintaining the integrity of the encoded data. Any change in an analog signal implies a change in the encoded information.

Consider an analog electrical signal that carries audio information. Because of electrical resistance in the wire, the voltage decreases as the length of the wire increases. As a result of this decrease, the audio level interpreted at the receiving end is too low. This problem may be remedied by amplifying the voltage at various points along the wire path. Unfortunately, analog amplifiers boost the entire input signal, including any noise introduced in the path. The receiving end may hear a large amount of background noise that obscures the actual signal. The signal-to-noise ratio (SNR) suffers in this scenario. Figure 6-6 illustrates the problem.

Figure 6-6 *Analog Amplifiers Boost the Intended Signal and Noise, Effectively Lowering the SNR*

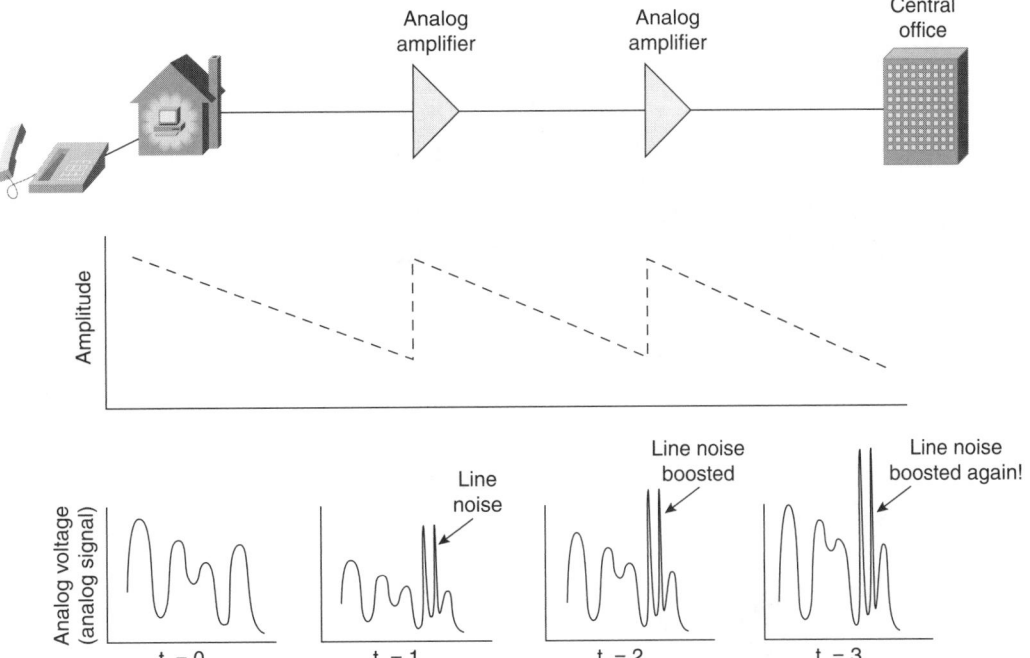

Now consider a digital electrical signal that carries the same audio information. The voltage of the digital signal is still affected by resistance, but there is not a problem with degradation of the signal. Instead of boosting the level of the voltage waveform, a digital repeater can interpret, and regenerate a clean version of the signal. With this method, there is no accumulation of errors as the signal propagates. This process is summarized in Figure 6-7.

Figure 6-7 *Digital Repeaters Propagate Digital Signals Without Accumulation of Errors*

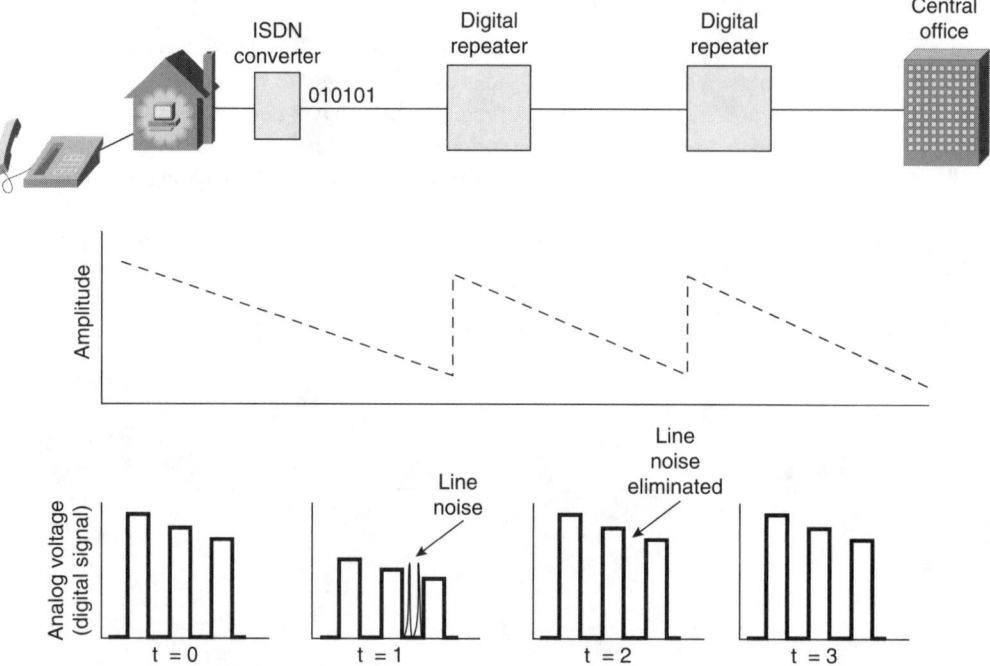

There are analog solutions to the transmission noise problem, such as using electrically balanced signals, but analog signals have other shortcomings. Analog signals lose quality when they are replicated or stored. Digital signals are inherently well suited to replication and storage without alteration. In general, digital signals are reliable for transmission, processing, replication, and storage, while analog signals are often required to interact with the physical world.

Digitizing an Analog Signal

Analog signals are continuous in two dimensions: time and value. In order to digitize an analog signal, these two dimensions must be made discrete. Sampling is the process of making an analog signal discreet with respect to time, and quantizing is the process of making a signal discreet with respect to the encoded value.

Digital Sampling

Figure 6-8 illustrates the process of sampling an analog signal. A clock source provides a time reference to take a snapshot of the analog signal at fixed time intervals. According to the Nyquist Theorem, the sampling frequency must be at least twice as high as the highest input frequency. For example, an analog signal with a component that varies at 1000 Hz must be sampled at 2000 Hz or more to be accurately represented.

Figure 6-8 *Analog Signal Is Sampled by Recording Its Value at Fixed Time Intervals*

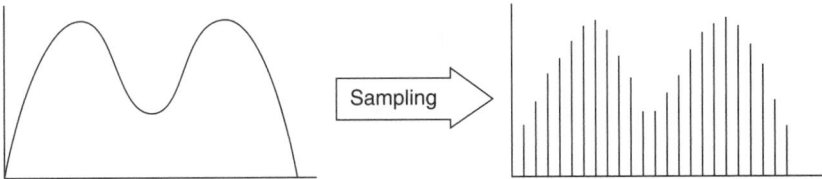

While humans can hear frequencies as high as 20 kHz, most of the information conveyed in speech does not exceed 4 kHz. Analog telephone signals are filtered prior to sampling so that most of the signal lies between 300 and 3400 Hz. This signal is sampled at 8000 Hz so that frequencies up to 4000 Hz may be recorded. Every 125 microseconds (1/8000th of a second), the value of the analog telephone signal is passed to the quantizing function.

Quantizing

Consider the output of the sampling function as illustrated in Figure 6-9.

Figure 6-9 *Sampled Signal Prior to Quantizing*

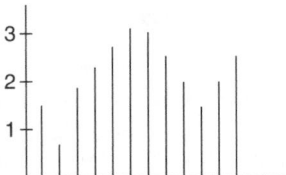

Notice that each of the sampled values does not lie within a set of predefined discreet values—in this case, the set of integers {0,1,2,3}. Quantization is the process of rounding these sampled values to the nearest predefined discreet value. This enables the value of the pulse to be represented as a binary bit-stream instead of in raw analog format. The quantization process must consider two important variables:

- Number of quantization levels
- Distribution of quantization levels

The number of quantization levels is a trade-off between the required signal quality and the bit rate of the digitized output. The digital signal more closely resembles the analog signal as the number of quantization levels increases. (See Figure 6-10.) However, the added signal resolution requires that more information is encoded. In other words, the number of bits per sample must increase, which increases the bit rate of the digitized output.

Figure 6-10 *Digital Signal Quality Degrades as the Number of Quantization Levels Decreases*

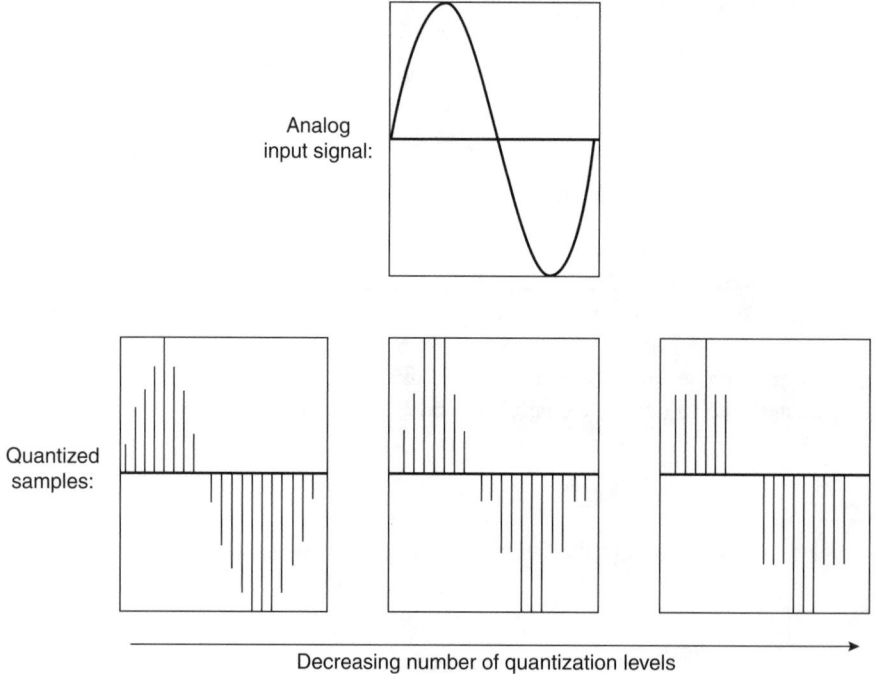

Analog input signal:

Quantized samples:

Decreasing number of quantization levels

The distribution of quantization levels indicates the digital resolution at different ranges of the analog signal value. In the simplest case, a linear distribution of quantized values results in equal signal quality for all value ranges. If the available bandwidth is limited, then creative distribution of the quantization levels may optimize signal quality for desired applications. For example, public telephone networks concentrate more quantization levels of the audio signal around quiet levels, and sacrifice resolution for loud signal values. This is a good trade-off for voice traffic, because the perceived voice quality does not suffer much from the loss of resolution for loud noises. Figure 6-11 illustrates the concept of nonlinear quantization levels.

Figure 6-11 *Nonlinear Distribution of Quantization Levels Increases Quality for a Given Bit Rate*

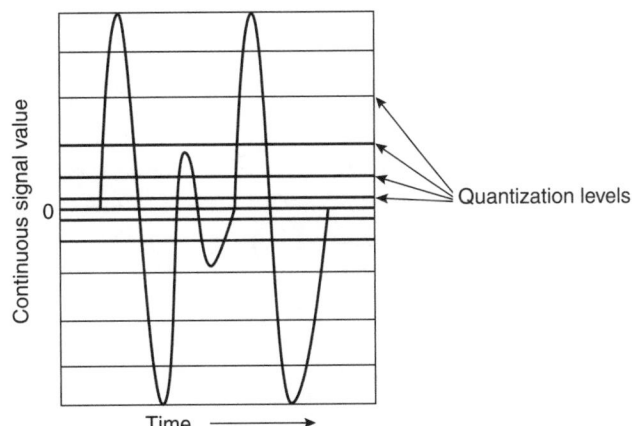

Speech-Coding Algorithms

The field of speech coding encompasses more than the digitization of analog speech signals. The focus of research is to develop audio codecs that provide better speech quality with a lower bit rate, delay, and implementation complexity.

The word *codec* is derived from a combination of *coder* and *decoder*. The coder function is the process of encoding a digitized signal into a more efficient form for transmission or storage, while the decoder part is the process of restoring the coded signal to the original form. (See Figure 6-12.) Low bit-rate codecs are *lossy*, which means that signal quality is reduced by successive codec cycles.

Figure 6-12 *Codecs Are Comprised of Coder and Decoder Functions*

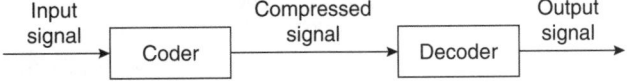

Speech-coding algorithms can be categorized as follows:

*   Waveform codecs
*   Source codecs
*   Hybrid codecs

Figure 6-13 illustrates the range of bit rate requirements and audio quality for the different approaches to audio encoding. The following sections provide an overview of these codec types.

Figure 6-13 *Bit Rate Versus Audio Quality for Different Audio Codec Types*

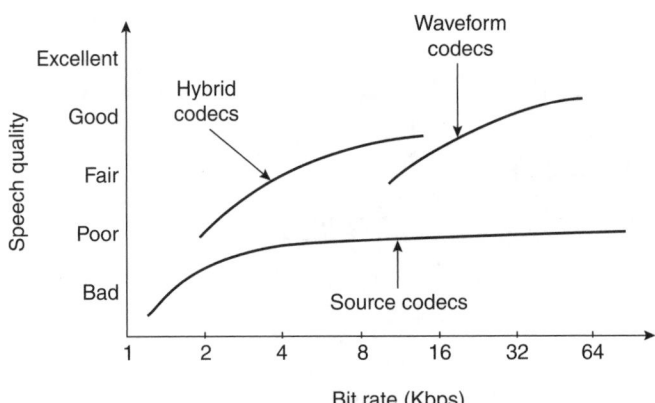

Waveform Codecs

Waveform codecs reconstruct an input signal without modeling the process that created the input signal. The output signal re-creates the shape of the input waveform, regardless of whether the input is speech, music, or random noise. A benefit of this approach is that few assumptions are made about the type of input, so the codec can replicate sounds from many sources. The cost of this feature is that the codec is not optimized for low bit-rate coding of specific input types, such as speech. Waveform codecs are the least complex of the codec types.

The pulse code modulation (PCM) codec, specified in ITU-T Recommendation G.711, is a waveform codec. The analog speech signal is filtered to remove high- and low-frequency components, and sampled at 8000 times per second. The sampled value is quantized to one of 256 values, which are represented in 8 bits. The resultant bit rate of the G.711 codec is 64 kbps, which determines the size of a DS-0. The value of each sample is encoded using one of two coding laws: mu-law or A-law. This refers to the distribution of quantization levels as described in a preceding section. Both the mu-law and the A-law emphasize signal quality in the quiet audio ranges, at the expense of signal quality in the loud audio ranges. This technique is often called companding, which is short for compressing and expanding. The mu-law is used in the United States, while the A-law is used in most other countries. Figure 6-14 illustrates the similarity between the mu-law and the A-law encoding schemes. Only the absolute values of the audio level are plotted because the positive and negative values are symmetrically coded.

TIP	Because loud signals have less resolution in G.711, dual tone multi-frequency (DTMF) signals may be unrecognizable if the audio level is too loud.

Figure 6-14 *Audio Levels Corresponding to Bit Values for A-law and Mu-Law Companding*

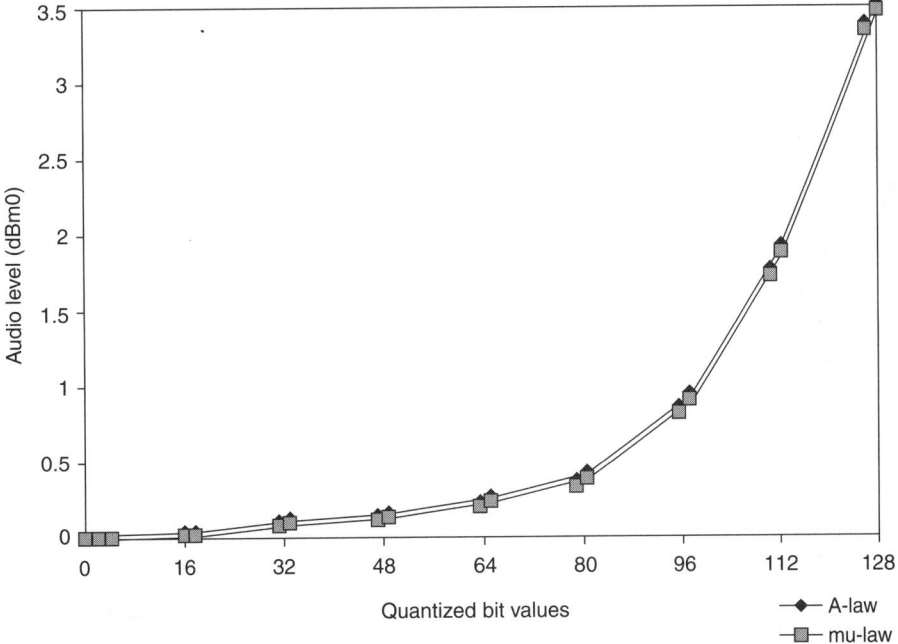

The mu-law is slightly more sensitive to differences in quiet audio signals than the A-law. Figure 6-15, which shows the audio signal encoding for the first 64 quantization levels, illustrates this fact. Consider an audio signal that varies between 0 and 0.025 dBm0 (see Table 13-2 for a definition of variations of the decibel (dB) measurement unit); the A-law provides roughly 16 quantization levels in this range, whereas the mu-law provides roughly 24 quantization levels.

Figure 6-15 *Mu-Law Is Slightly More Sensitive than A-Law for Quiet Audio Signals*

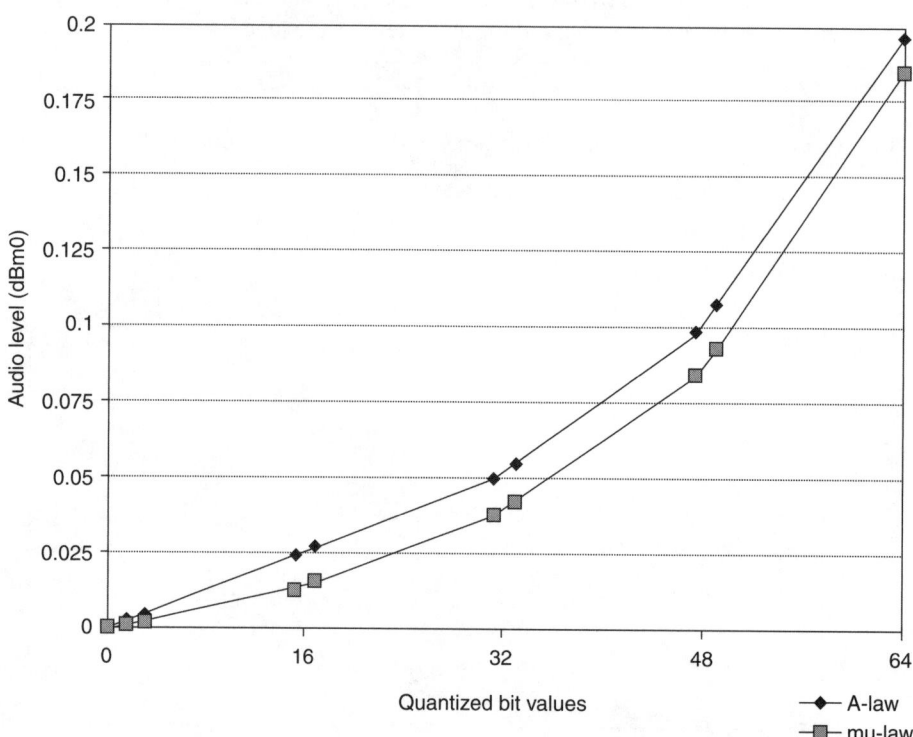

The adaptive differential pulse code modulation (AD-PCM) codec, specified in ITU-T Recommendation G.726, is a more advanced waveform codec. Instead of transmitting the actual PCM values of the waveform, the AD-PCM codec transmits an error signal that is the difference between the actual input and an estimated input. If the estimated input is reasonably close to the actual input, the error signal should have a smaller magnitude and variation than the original input. This is how AD-PCM provides near toll-quality speech at sub-PCM bit rates. The following equation summarizes the coder process:

$$(original\_input) - (estimated\_input) = (error\_signal)$$

where the estimated input is purely a function of successive error signal samples. The coder uses successive values of its own output to predict the current input. The decoder also uses this information to make an identical prediction of the current input. Because the prediction formula changes based on characteristics of the input signal, the Differential PCM scheme is called AD-PCM. Rearranging terms of the previous equation leads to the following equation:

$$(error\_signal) + (estimated\_input) = (original\_input)$$

which describes the decoder process. Since the decoder derives the estimated input in the same manner as the coder, the output of the decoder should match the original input of the coder.

The error signal is quantized before it is transmitted to the decoder. Recommendation G.726 specifies four different bit rates that correspond to the number of bits used in the quantization of the error signal. Table 6-1 summarizes the bit rates and number of bits used to quantize the error signal.

Table 6-1   *Bits Per Sample and Number of Quantization Levels for G.726 AD-PCM*

Bit Rate	Bits Per Sample of Error Signal	Number of Quantization Levels
40 kbps	5	31
32 kbps	4	15
24 kbps	3	7
16 kbps	2	4

It is clear that the quantized error signal rapidly loses quality as the bit rate of the AD-PCM coder decreases. It is not practical to make an AD-PCM coder that operates below 16 kbps, because there is too much quantization noise of the error signal. Because the error signal is also used to derive the estimated input signal, there is not much room for compression below an error signal with only four states.

Figure 6-16, reprinted with permission from ITU-T Recommendation G.726, illustrates a simplified block diagram of the AD-PCM coder and decoder. This diagram includes the quantizing function, and shows more of the input estimation function.

Both the PCM and AD-PCM codecs operate in the time domain. Examples of frequency-domain codec techniques include Sub-Band Coding (SBC) and Adaptive Transform Coding (ATC). These techniques can yield toll-quality speech signals with about the same bit rates as AD-PCM, but there is more flexibility to allocate bit resolution to frequency bands with high perceptual value.

Figure 6-16   *Simplified Block Diagram of ITU-T G.726 Codec (AD-PCM)*

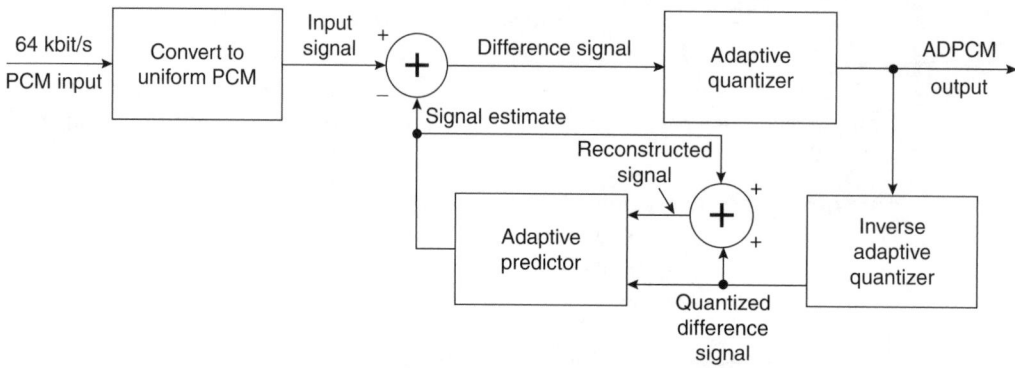

a) Encoder

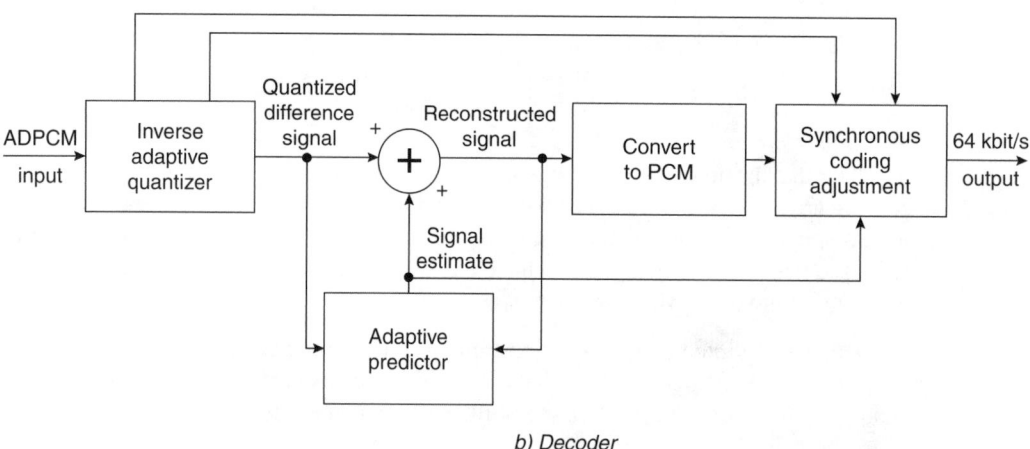

b) Decoder

Source Codecs

Source codecs are designed with a philosophy that is fundamentally different from waveform codecs. Source codecs are designed for specific input types (for example, human speech), and make use of this input assumption to model the signal source. Speech source codecs attempt to replicate the physical process of sound creation. During speech, an excitation signal from the lungs and vocal chords is filtered by the vocal tract (that is, the throat, tongue, nasal cavity, and lips). For unvoiced sounds, turbulent air leaving the lungs produces a hissing sound that is shaped by the vocal tract. Vocal chords are not involved in the production of unvoiced sounds. The unvoiced signal is similar to white noise, with energy in many frequency bands. For voiced sounds, vocal chords open and close at different frequencies that modulate air passing through them. The modulated signal has a triangular waveform that makes a buzzing sound. This waveform is also composed of many frequency components, so there is ample source material to be shaped into words and speech by the vocal tract. Figure 6-17 illustrates the sound creation process for voiced and unvoiced sounds.

Figure 6-17   *Signal from Lungs and Vocal Chords Excites a Vocal Tract Filter*

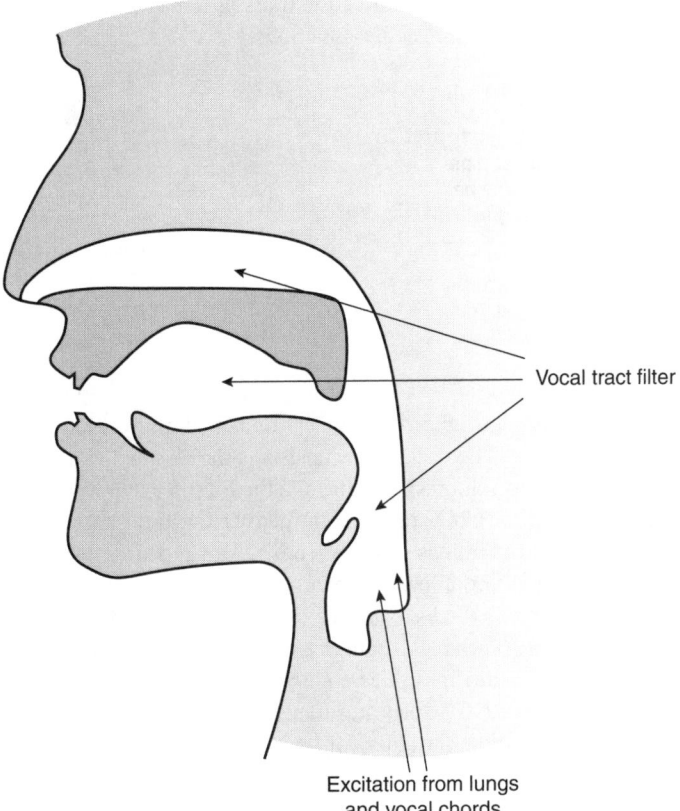

Vocal tract filter

Excitation from lungs
and vocal chords

Speech source coders emulate the function of the excitation signal and the vocal tract filter. The audio samples that enter the coder are grouped into frames, and these frames are analyzed to determine both the type of excitation signal and the shape of the filter. The type of excitation signal is often encoded in a single bit, indicating either a voiced or an unvoiced excitation. For unvoiced excitations, the decoder can use white noise (a random signal) for the excitation signal, so the coder only needs to identify that the excitation is unvoiced. For voiced excitations, the coder determines the pulse frequency of the vocal chord modulation.

The vocal tract filter is an algebraic function of signal frequency. Some frequencies are emphasized by the function, while others are muted, depending on the values of the coefficients in the algebraic equation. For each group of samples that is analyzed, a set of coefficients is determined that yield the best match for the vocal tract filter. Most filter models use at least a 10th order linear equation (hence the term linear prediction). The coefficients of the linear equation are updated for every frame, so the shape of the vocal tract filter changes every 5 to 30 ms or so. The frame size can vary for each specific codec. The linear equation coefficients, a single bit for the type of excitation source, and possibly the frequency of the voiced excitation, are transmitted for every frame. Figure 6-18 summarizes the speech source codec functions.

Figure 6-18 *Components of a Speech Source Codec*

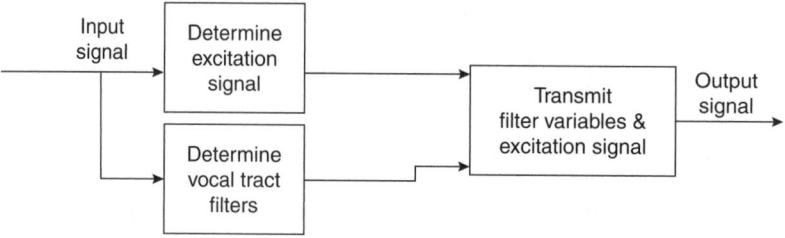

An important concept introduced in this section is that of grouping samples into frames for analysis and encoding. The decoder reconstructs the original signal on a frame-by-frame basis by passing the excitation signal through the filter for that frame. The coder determines the value of the filter variables for each frame by examining the samples in the current frame. The coder also examines samples from before and after the current frame to improve the quality of the filter variables for the current frame. The window of samples that occur after the current frame is the look-ahead. The specifications for a codec are often summarized by several variables, including the frame size and the look-ahead. These values are important because they introduce an algorithmic delay to the system in which the codecs are used. Figure 6-19 illustrates the frame structure, and the window of samples used to determine the filter variables for the frame.

Figure 6-19   *Relationship Between the Frame of Samples, Window of Analysis, and the Look-Ahead*

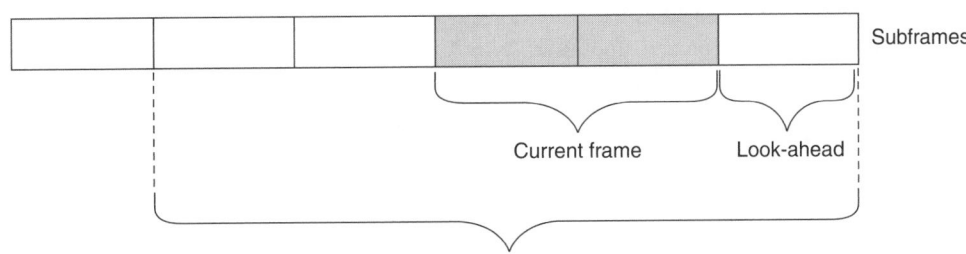

Speech source coders yield very low bit-rate signals but have limited potential for voice quality. They have been most extensively used by the military for secure communication applications. Hybrid codecs have mostly replaced source codecs, because higher-quality speech throughput can be achieved with similar bit rates.

Hybrid Codecs

Hybrid codecs provide better quality speech than source codecs, with lower bit rates than waveform codecs. To achieve this performance, hybrid codecs use a combination of source modeling and waveform analysis. These algorithms tend to be fairly complex.

The most common hybrid codecs operate in the time domain using linear prediction analysis-by-synthesis (LPAS) techniques. Like source codecs, LPAS codecs model an excitation signal and a filter. The filter component is similar to that modeled in source codecs, but the encoding of the excitation signal is more sophisticated. There are three main strategies for encoding the excitation signal:

- Multi-Pulse Excitation (MPE)
- Regular Pulse Excitation (RPE)
- Code-Excited Linear Prediction (CELP)

Each of these techniques generates the excitation signal in different ways, but they all process a variety of excitation signals through the filter to see which excitation produces the best match of the original waveform. Once the best match is obtained, the codec transmits the filter variables and information about the excitation signal. The representation of the excitation signal is different for MPE, RPE, and CELP codecs.

Multi-Pulse Excitation

The MPE model encodes the excitation signal as a series of non-zero pulses that may vary in temporal position and amplitude. Typically, this excitation signal is determined for subframes, instead of for the whole frame. Figure 6-20 clarifies this concept.

Figure 6-20 *MPE Enables Each Pulse to Vary in Position and Amplitude*

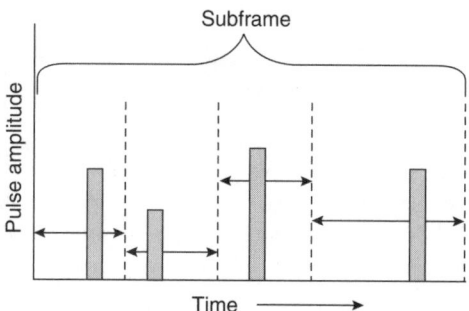

The codec algorithm determines the number of pulses that can float within the subframe, which is usually approximately 5 ms. Often the subframe is divided into smaller time intervals, and a single pulse may be located within each of these time intervals. The last time interval in a subframe is often larger than the other time intervals. In this scenario, the codec separately calculates the optimal position and amplitude for each pulse. Typically, there are four to six pulses within a 5-ms subframe. The output of the coder includes the position and amplitude of each of the pulses in the excitation signal.

The ITU-T Recommendation G.723.1 operates at two different bit rates: 5.3 kbps and 6.3 kbps. The 6.3-kbps codec uses a version of the MPE algorithm called Multi-Pulse Maximum Likelihood Quantization (MP-MLQ).

Regular Pulse Excitation

Like MPE, RPE represents the excitation signal as a series of pulses. Instead of specifying the position and amplitude of each pulse, only the amplitude of each pulse is specified. A small amount of information encodes the offset of the first pulse within the subframe, and all of the remaining pulses follow at a fixed time interval. Compared to the MPE method, the RPE method reduces the number of bits required to represent a given number of pulses. RPE reallocates the bits saved in this manner to provide a greater number of pulses within a subframe of the excitation signal. A typical RPE codec may use 10 to 12 pulses per subframe. Figure 6-21 illustrates the RPE method of encoding the excitation signal.

Figure 6-21   *RPE Provides More Pulses, but with Fixed Positions*

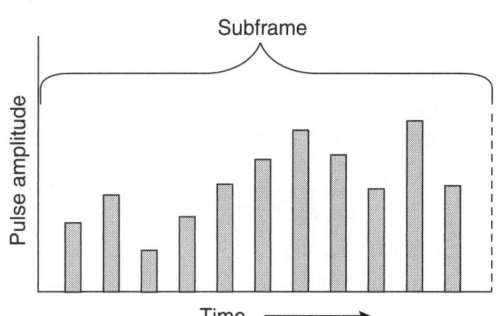

An RPE codec operating at 13 kbps is currently used in the GSM standard for wireless telephony.

CELP

The MPE and the RPE coders transmit information about each of the pulses as separate pieces of information. CELP uses a different approach to encode the pulses. A code book identifies many different combinations of pulse amplitudes and positions, and each of these combinations is represented by an index into the code book. Both the coder and the decoder reference the same code book. For each subframe, CELP coders transmit the bit value of the code-book index, corresponding to the excitation signal that produces the best match of the original input signal. The decoder uses the index to identify the excitation signal from its own copy of the code book. Figure 6-22 illustrates the CELP method of encoding the excitation signal.

Figure 6-22   *CELP Represents Excitation as a Code-Book Index*

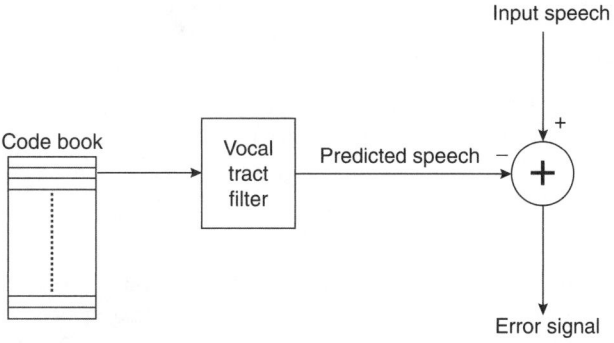

The code-book approach enables a large amount of information to be transmitted in very few bits. A trade-off of this approach is that identifying the best code-book index for each subframe is very processor intensive and may require a large amount of time. Imagine a code book with 1000 entries. Each of these entries must be processed through the vocal tract filter, while the output is compared with the original input signal until a suitable match is identified. This process must be repeated for every subframe—approximately every 5 ms!

The performance of CELP codecs is very much related to the number of entries in the code books, the content of the code books, and the efficiency of the code-book searching algorithms. To simplify the search process, some code books have entries for the pulse positions only; the amplitude of these pulses must be determined separately. Some CELP implementations use simplified code books with no amplitude information and only a few pulses, so that algebraic techniques may be employed to simplify the code book search. These encoding methods are called Algebraic CELP, or ACELP.

Many different codecs belong to the CELP class, including the ITU-T Recommendation G.728 Low-Delay CELP (LD-CELP) at 16 kbps, and G.729 Conjugate-Structure ACELP (CS-ACELP) at 8 kbps. G.729 Annex A uses CS-ACELP with a few processing shortcuts, and G.723.1 uses ACELP when operating in the 5.3-kbps output mode. The U.S. Federal Standard 1016 (FS-1016) also employs CELP in a 4.8-kbps coded signal, used in conjunction with secure telephony applications.

Criteria for Codec Selection

Now that you have read more than you probably wanted to know about analog/digital conversion and speech codecs, it is time to consider choosing among the available options. How should you decide which audio codecs are appropriate for your applications?

Speech codecs are generally measured by five performance characteristics:

- Coded bit rate
- Algorithmic delay
- Processing complexity
- Speech quality
- Performance for non-speech signals

Coded Bit Rate

The bit rate of the coder output is a key measure of a codec's performance. Codec research continues so that speech signals can be represented with ever-decreasing bit rates. Over the years, toll-quality speech has been reduced from 64 kbps, to 32 kbps, and down to 16 kbps. As of 1996, the ITU-T recommended several codecs with near toll-quality speech at or below a peak rate of 8 kbps. As of 2000, the ITU-T is investigating near toll-quality speech at or below a peak rate of 4 kbps.

Many codecs support silence suppression and comfort noise to further reduce bandwidth requirements. Each party in a two-way conversation does not speak more than 40 percent of the time on average. In a conference with N people, each person will speak less than 1/N of the time on average. If the codec can surrender bandwidth when a speaker is not talking, then the effective bit rate of the coder is reduced by at least a factor of two. It is important that the decoder inserts a low-level noise signal into the output audio path during periods when it receives no information from the coder. Otherwise, the sound of complete silence is disconcerting to the listeners, who may think that the connection is lost. The inserted noise is called comfort noise.

If bandwidth is expensive or not available in your network, then the bit rate of the coder output is a crucial factor for you to consider. You may have to sacrifice speech quality or pay more for hardware to support lower bit-rate codecs, depending on your network environment. Oftentimes it is possible to use low bit-rate codecs and maintain good voice quality in the network.

Algorithmic Delay

All but the simplest coding algorithms examine groups of samples, called frames, to determine coefficients for the predictor filters. Many coders examine samples from adjacent frames to improve the filter quality for a given frame. These processes can add substantial delay to the audio path. The algorithmic delay for a speech codec is a function of two variables:

- Frame size
- Look-ahead

To understand how these variables relate to the algorithmic delay, consider the end-to-end process of coding and decoding. For this example, consider a generic coder that uses a frame size of 30 ms (240 samples at 8000 samples/sec), and a look-ahead of 7.5 ms (60 samples at 8000 samples/sec):

1 At t=0 ms, the coder receives the first sample of a frame.

2 At t=30 ms, the coder receives the last sample of a frame.

3 At t=37.5 ms, the coder receives the last sample of the look-ahead window, and begins to process the frame.

It should be clear that the algorithmic delay of the coder is the sum of the frame size and the look-ahead. You can think of this as inbound serialization delay within the codec. The coder incurs additional delay from processing the frame to determine the filter coefficients and excitation signal (code-book lookup for CELP codecs), but this delay is a function of codec complexity and computing power of the digital signal processor (DSP).

What about the algorithmic delay from the decoder? The input to the decoder requires fewer bits than the coder input, so there is less serialization delay of the coded signal entering the decoder. The actual amount of delay depends on the bit rate of the coded signal. The decoder does not need to wait until all of the information is received before it begins to reconstruct the original input signal. It can create the filter before the excitation signal arrives, or it can determine the excitation signal before the filter coefficients arrive. Because of these factors, the algorithmic delay for the decoder is more difficult to calculate, but is usually smaller than that for the coder. The processing delay of the decoder must still be considered, but this relates to the complexity of the codec and the computing power of the DSP.

Delay is often a concern when designing packet voice networks. WAN-transmission delays, tandeming, and serialization delay on slow links all conspire to break the delay budget for real-time conversations. Large codec delays can make the difference between acceptable and unacceptable delays. If multiple codec cycles cannot be avoided, then it is wise to avoid codecs with high algorithmic delays. Examples of situations when multiple codec cycles cannot be avoided include:

- Calls between remote sites that tandem through a central-site private branch exchange (PBX) to route calls or to capture call detail records (CDR) for accounting purposes

- Calls between remote sites that tandem through a central-site PBX when transparent common channel signaling (CCS) is used from the central site to remote offices

- Call transfers between sites

- Multipoint conferencing through an MCU

Processing Complexity

The processing delay of a given codec is very dependent on the processor architecture and speed. For any hardware or software platform, the processing delay of a codec is correlated with the processing complexity. It is common to compare the complexity of different speech codecs in terms of instructions per second required for real-time speech processing. The performance is characterized in terms of millions of instructions per second (MIPS). The number of instructions per CPU clock cycle will vary on different architectures, but the same basic instructions must be performed on any platform. For a particular platform, the MIPS value can be roughly converted to processing delay by considering the CPU clock rate and the number of instructions performed in a single CPU clock cycle. This estimate is rough, because it does not account for other processes competing for CPU resources.

Codec complexity can also be measured in terms of the memory requirements for the implementation. For example, the programmed instruction set of any hardware-based codec must be stored in ROM, and codecs that use a code-book lookup must store each of the code-book patterns in ROM. While the codec is operating, RAM is required to store temporary values and perform calculations.

All of the processing complexity issues for codecs relate to the amount of physical resources required to implement a codec. As codecs become more complex, they require more expensive processors, more memory, and consume more power. These issues affect the economic feasibility of the codec for widespread deployment. Codec complexity is especially important for mobile devices (such as wireless telephones), because battery life is reduced when more power is consumed.

Another consideration for a codec selection is whether it has been specified for implementation with integer math operations or floating-point math operations. This is a concern if you plan to implement software telephony terminals (for example, PC telephone applications). Real-time voice processing may be a burden on desktop PCs, especially when other applications are active. Desktop computers are much more efficient at floating-point math operations, so a floating-point codec implementation is often a requirement for desktop PC deployment of speech codecs.

Speech Quality

Speech quality is the most difficult codec characteristic to quantify. There are many factors that can be considered, and there is no obvious formula to relate a codec's performance on different tests. Chapter 5, "Defining and Measuring Voice Quality," examines various issues associated with speech quality testing. Most referenced codec comparisons are based on a simple test of each codec under ideal conditions, such as a clean input signal, with no frame loss or errors between the coder and decoder. A more robust testing process might consider the effects of the following factors, both singly and in combinations:

- Codec frame loss or errors
- Background noise in the source signal
- Multiple simultaneous speakers
- Non-speech sound sources, such as music
- Language of speaker
- Multiple codec cycles (for example, tandem encoding)

You should pay close attention to codec comparison tests that mimic aspects of your networking environment. For example, if your network requires common channel signaling (CCS)- or PBX-based call routing, then you should focus on speech quality for multiple codec cycles. If you must transfer calls between sites, you should also make sure to use a codec that is robust to multiple codec cycles. If your telephone users work in a noisy environment (such as a factory floor, or noisy office), then you should consider tests that examine background noise at the sender side. If you require inbound customer service calls, and callers hear music on hold, then it is important that the codec does not badly distort the music. Do not forget that each codec is affected differently by packet loss or errors in the data network.

It is important to note that many codecs have been formally tested for a limited number of languages, such as English, French, and Japanese. If your environment requires support for languages with very different characteristics (for example, different phonetic sounds or inflections), it is a good idea to perform a simple proof-of-concept test with the language in question. Make sure to test silence-suppression options. Two routers, two telephones, and a few hours of time with the representative speakers can identify any serious codec issues early in the project.

Performance for Non-speech Signals

Many environments demand that DTMF tones, fax signals, and modem signals cross the voice network. It is a serious oversight to plan the network for speech-only requirements and lose nonspeech performance. For example, tandem encodings of a low bit-rate codec may produce acceptable voice quality, but DTMF performance may be unreliable. In this scenario, voice-mail systems and call-center applications become unreliable. Some codecs have special provisions to pass DTMF tones as out-of-band signals, and some hardware implementations add this functionality to codecs that do not otherwise support this feature.

When out-of-band DTMF signaling is not possible, you must optimize the network to transport these signals. Parameters to optimize include (but are not limited to):

- Input gain of analog signals
- Silence suppression options associated with voice activity detection (VAD)
- Jitter buffers (and end-to-end quality of service [QoS])

Fax calls may represent a larger proportion of your telephone bill than voice calls. Indeed, more than half of the calls on voice trunks between the United States and Japan are fax calls. Not all codecs support fax traffic, and among the codecs that do, the data transfer rate may be compromised. Be sure to consider the fax capabilities of any candidate codecs if it is an important requirement for your environment.

Some people want to pass modem signals across a voice/data network. There are applications where this is appropriate for service provider environments, but modem over VoX can generally be avoided in enterprise networks. Consider the following three possible scenarios for modem signaling in your voice network:

- Both modems are within the private network
- Originating modem is within the private network, destination is in the Public Switched Telephone Network (PSTN)
- Originating modem is in the PSTN, destination modem is in the private network

If both end devices in your network communicate via modems, then surely they support EIA/TIA-232 serial connections. Cisco routers can locally terminate the serial signals and transparently tunnel them across an IP backbone. Cisco calls this technique async tunneling, which is short for asynchronous serial tunneling across IP.

Modems within your network may take advantage of tail-end hop off for toll avoidance when calling to arbitrary numbers in the PSTN. If the devices with modems also have IP connections, then you can use remote modem banks (such as a Cisco AS5300 or 2511) in conjunction with client software that emulates a locally attached modem on a virtual serial port. The traffic is then passed as a telnet session to the access server, and the access server performs the outbound dialing. If the devices with modems do not support IP, then you can use async tunneling in conjunction with outbound modem pools.

You might have regional offices providing local modem access to customers. In this case, your private voice network can relay modem calls from the PSTN to centralized devices with attached modems. If the central devices in your network support IP, then inbound calls should be converted to telnet sessions at the access server in each location. If the central devices do not support IP, then consider async tunneling from the access servers to the centralized servers.

For any of the modem designs, consider this: You are expending effort to make modem signals function across a VoX network, or to make serial signals function across an async tunneling solution, or both. This effort may be better spent supporting IP in the systems that currently require modem signals.

Comparison of Selected Codecs

Figure 6-23, reprinted from an article by Richard V. Cox in the September 1997 issue of *IEEE Communications Magazine*[1], shows the speech quality and bit-rate requirements for many different speech codecs. Note how actual codec implementations align with the theoretical bit rate and quality ranges that were identified in Figure 6-13.

Figure 6-23 *Bit Rate Versus Speech Quality for a Variety of Codecs*

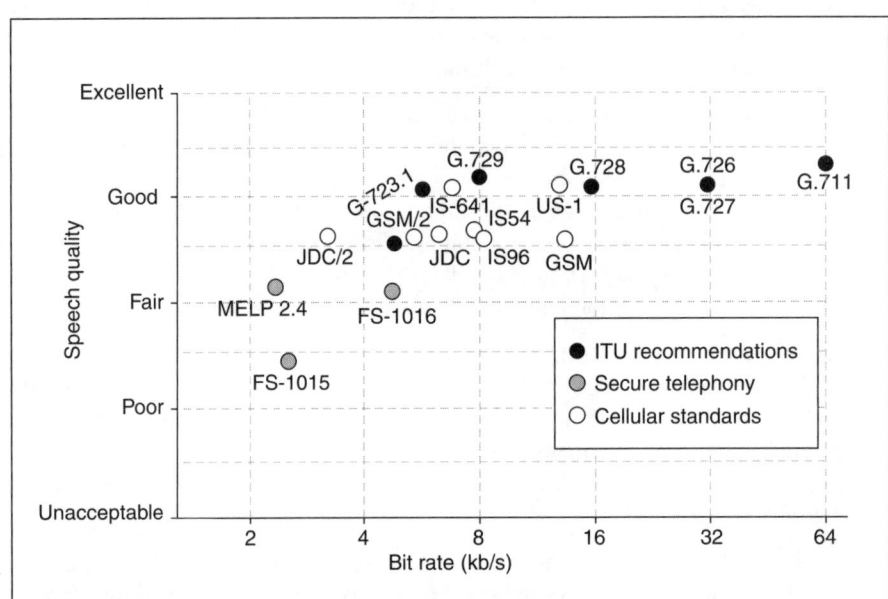

Table 6-2 summarizes the performance characteristics for a variety of codecs that are commonly used in VoX networks.

Table 6-2 *Performance Characteristics for Speech Codecs Used in Integrated Voice/Data Networks*

Codec	Bit Rate (kbps)	Frame Size[2] (ms)	Look-Ahead[3] (ms)	Process-ing[3] (MIPS)	RAM[3] (words)	Speech Quality[4] (MOS)
G.711 (PCM)	64	0.125	0	> 0.5	>100	4.10
G.726 (AD-PCM)	16/24/32/ 40	0.125	0	2	>100	3.85
G.728 (LD-CELP)	16	0.625	0	_[5]	_[5]	3.85
G.729 (CS-ACELP)	8	10	5	20	2700	3.92

Table 6-2 *Performance Characteristics for Speech Codecs Used in Integrated Voice/Data Networks (Continued)*

Codec	Bit Rate (kbps)	Frame Size[2] (ms)	Look-Ahead[3] (ms)	Processing[3] (MIPS)	RAM[3] (words)	Speech Quality[4] (MOS)
G.729A (CS-ACELP)	8	10	5	10.5	2000	3.7
G.723.1 (MP-MLQ)	6.3	30	7.5	14.6	2200	3.9
G.723.1 (ACELP)	5.3	30	7.5	16	2200	3.65
GSM Full-Rate (RPE-LTP)	13	20	0	_[5]	_[5]	3.5
GSM Half-Rate (VCELP)	5.6	20	0	_[5]	_[5]	3.5

2. Included in original ITU-T recommendations.

3. Reported by Richard V. Cox and Peter Kroon in IEEE Communications Magazine, December 1996.

4. Reported by Perkins, Evans, Pascal, and Thorpe in IEEE Communications Magazine, September 1997; also (2) above.

5. Information could not be located as of press time.

As a familiar reference point regarding speech quality, note that the GSM cellular standard produces speech with a 3.5-mean opinion score (MOS) rating. If all else is designed well in the VoX network, then the best-case voice quality for any of the listed codecs is better than the best-case quality for the GSM cellular standard.

The speech-quality measurements summarized in Table 6-2 are misleading, because they reflect a best-case ideal scenario, which may be remarkably different from the environment in which you plan to use the codecs. Your environment most likely has some or all of the elements described in the preceding section, such as background noise, tandem encodings, and packet loss. Each codec responds differently to these elements. Unfortunately, not all of the codecs have been formally tested in the same experiment for these characteristics, so there is only anecdotal evidence to support any comparison claims. In his *IEEE Communications Magazine* article from December 1997, Cox states that "the overall performance of the three coders [G.729, G.723.1, G.729A] was similar. It seemed that the G.723.1 and G.729A coders were slightly less robust for background noises and tandem conditions [than the G.729 coder]."

That being said, the G.729 codec may serve as a reference point, because it has been formally tested under a variety of adverse conditions. The Speech Quality Experts Group (SQEG) of the ITU-T conducted a range of experiments in laboratories around the globe to test the subjective performance of the G.729 codec in the following scenarios:

- High levels and different types of background noise
- Tandem encoding with itself, G.726 AD-PCM, and cellular codecs
- Degraded transmission paths resulting in codec frame loss and errors

The results of the G.729 subjective testing are reported in the December 1997 issue of *IEEE Communications Magazine*. Various data from this study are included here, with implications extended for voice/data network environments.

Effects of Background Noise

In Figure 6-24, it is clear that G.729 does not perform as well amidst background noise as does G.726. This result is expected, because G.729 employs elements of speech prediction that assume the input source is speech, whereas G.726 is a waveform coder. Background noise violates the assumptions of the predictive model, but it does not affect waveform coders. At first glance it appears that G.726 actually performs better with background babble than with no noise, but this is not really the case. The Comparison MOS (CMOS) scores reflect that listeners in the experiment perceived less of a difference between the reference and the encoded signal when the reference was already degraded.

Note that in this experiment, G.726 is subjectively rated better than G.729 (even without noise), but the MOS scores in Table 6-2 indicate that G.729 is relatively better. Indeed, another SQEG experiment indicates that the average MOS score is higher for G.729 than for G.726, but the study also indicates that there is no statistical difference between the sample groups. It is common in nonacademic material to focus on averages and neglect statistical information. This practice simplifies the presentation of some information, but in cases like this it can be misleading.

Figure 6-24 *Effects of Background Noise on Speech Quality for Several Codec Scenarios*

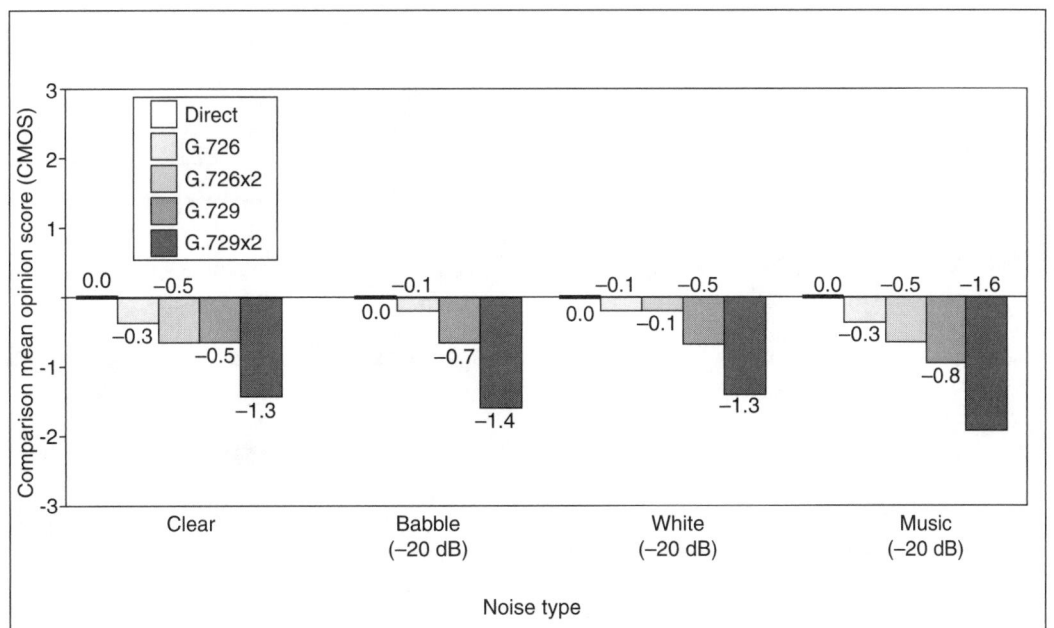

Effects of Tandem Encoding

The ITU-T specified a requirement and an objective with respect to tandem speech encoding for the G.729 candidate codecs. The requirement was that a double encoding must provide speech quality at least as good as four codec cycles of G.726, with the objective that triple encoding should meet this goal. As Figures 6-25 and 6-26 indicate, the final G.729 codec meets the requirement, but does not quite meet the objective.

Figure 6-25 *G.729 Speech Quality Meets Performance Goals for Double Encoding Scenarios*

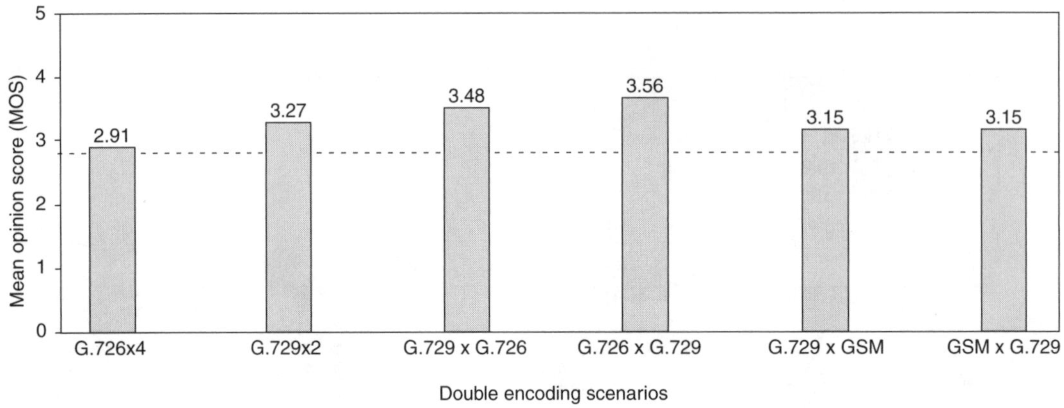

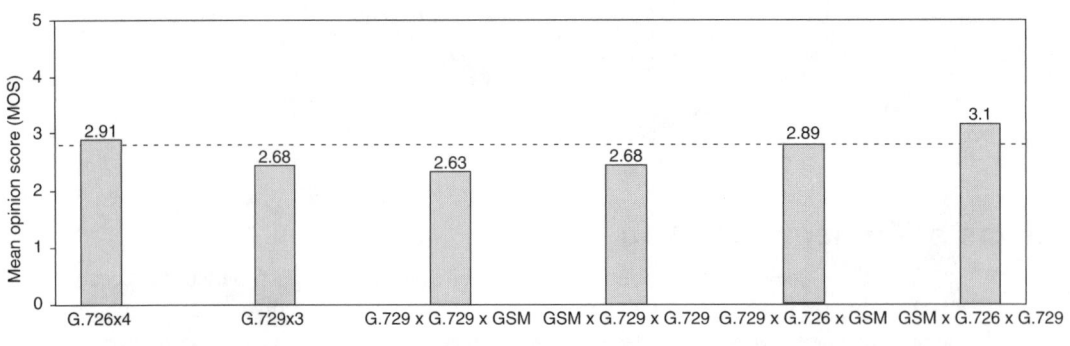

Figure 6-26 *G.729 Speech Quality Does Not Meet Performance Goals for Triple Encoding Scenarios*

Consider this if you must design your network such that triple or quadruple encodings are required (such as call transfer between sites with centralized voice mail or CCS). Also remember that anecdotal evidence indicates that G.729A and G.723.1 perform slightly worse, so your only real option for three or more tandem encodings is G.726 or G.711.

Effects of Frame Loss

Figure 6-27, reprinted from the SQEG study, shows the effects of random- and burst-frame erasures on G.729 speech quality (for clean input signals). Singly encoded G.729 is resilient to random- and burst-frame erasures (for example, lost packets) in the absence of other impairments. Up to 3 percent of random-frame erasures are tolerable for doubly encoded G.729.

Figure 6-27   *Effects of Random- and Burst-Frame Drops on G.279 Encoded Speech*

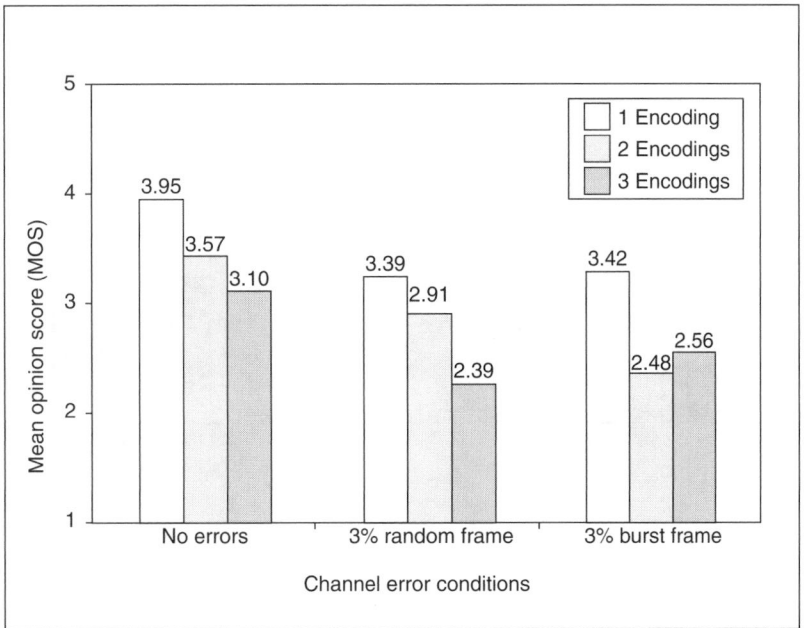

Burst-frame drops are more damaging to speech quality, and cannot be tolerated when the audio path has more than a single encoding of G.729. This implies that you must be careful when using multiple codec frames per packet. While packing multiple frames into a packet improves bandwidth efficiency, every lost packet results in a substantial frame-burst error that reduces speech quality to an unacceptable level. If your network has any problems with packet loss, then it is not advisable to place multiple frames in the same packet.

Figure 6-28 demonstrates that G.729 performs poorly when there is background noise in the input signal, and any type of lost frames between the coder and decoder. In all practicality, you cannot change the amount of background noise on either end of a call. You can, however, monitor your network and improve QoS to ensure that there is a low degree of packet loss. For real-time traffic, late is the same as lost, so your network QoS strategy must be solid.

Figure 6-28   *Background Noise and Frame Erasures Result in Poor Speech Quality for G.729*

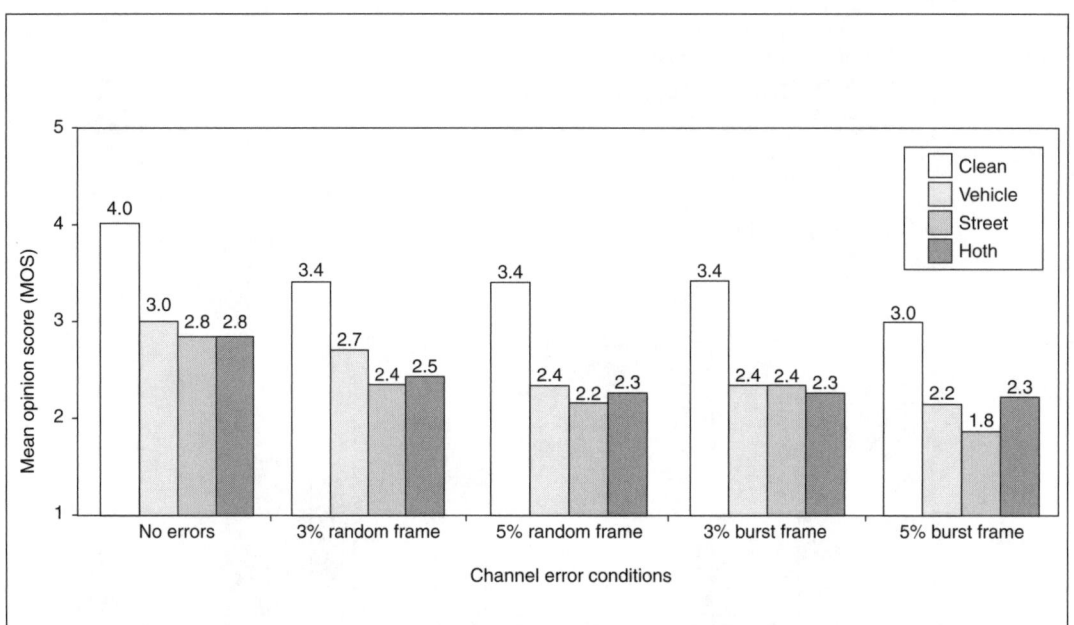

Summary

This chapter has presented a lot of information that you do not require on a day-to-day basis as a network engineer. Amidst all the detail, it is important that you do not miss a few key points:

* Noisy environments affect the low bit-rate codecs more than G.726 and G.711.

* Do not use low bit-rate codecs if more than two codec cycles are required.

* If you have a suboptimal QoS implementation or error-prone WAN links, do not use multiple codec frames per packet with low bit-rate codecs.

You can refer to Table 6-2 for general codec characteristics. The Frame Relay Forum supports the G.729 and G.729 Recommendations for low bit-rate codecs, so these are the best choices for multivendor VoFR environments. G.729A does not support faxes, so you must use G.729 in conjunction with G.729A for this purpose. The VoIP Forum supports G.723.1, because it first had a floating-point specification (in Annex B) that enables software implementations of desktop telephony. The delay of G.723.1 may be too high for conferencing scenarios if transmission delay is already near a problem threshold. G.729

also includes a floating-point specification in Annex C, so the choice between G.723.1 and G.729 is more difficult.

If you experience quality problems with any of the low bit-rate codecs, review this chapter for the factors that may contribute to the problems. Try removing the silence suppression scheme, or VAD. If you cannot isolate and remedy the problems, then your recourse is to use a higher bit-rate codec. G.726 is the codec of choice in these scenarios. You should not need to use G.711, but it is still more efficient than traditional TDM if you have idle voice channels.

References

[1]Cox, Richard V. "Three New Speech Coders from the ITU Cover a Range of Applications" *IEEE Communications Magazine*. September 1997: 40–47.

[2]Included in original ITU-T recommendations.

[3]Cox, Richard V. and Kroon, Peter. "Low Bit-Rate Coders for Multimedia Communication". *IEEE Communications Magazine*. December 1996: 34–41.

[4]Perkins, Mark E. et al. "Characterizing the Subjective Performance of the ITU-T 8 kb/s Speech Coding Algorithm- ITU-T G.729". *IEEE Communications Magazine*. September 1997: 74–81.

PART II

Packet Voice and Data Networks

This part of the book explores the technologies that bring voice and data networks together. The technologies include quality of service (QoS) in data networks, and audio transport and call signaling protocols for Frame Relay, ATM, and IP.

Chapter 7 explores the characteristics of a data network that are required to support packet telephony and real-time network applications in general. This chapter forms a basis for understanding the QoS requirements that are an integral part of voice/data network integration.

Chapter 8 explores the functions of clear-channel T-1/E-1, Frame Relay, and ATM technologies that facilitate the integration of voice and data services. The chapter first develops a baseline QoS profile of clear-channel T-1/E-1 circuits and considers the downside of TDM technology. This section is followed by an examination of the Frame Relay Forum (FRF) implementation agreements that relate to voice services, including VoFR and VoIP over Frame Relay. The chapter concludes with a review of ATM adaptation layers and ATM classes of service (CoS), in the context of VoATM and ATM-CES services.

Chapter 9 builds on the foundation provided in Chapter 8 to examine the design considerations for voice data integration across a WAN. The chapter provides recommendations for VoFR and VoIP over Frame Relay, and provides a limited review of VoATM and VoIP over ATM. Finally, the chapter explores the use of clear-channel T-1/E-1 circuits for VoFR and VoATM, using private Frame Relay or ATM encapsulation.

Chapter 10 examines IP QoS technologies from a conceptual standpoint, highlighting the technologies that are appropriate for VoIP applications.

Chapter 11 explores VoIP audio transport using RTP and RTCP, and call signaling based on H.323 or SIP. The chapter also provides a framework for understanding the relationship between traditional telephony protocols and the VoIP transport and signaling protocols.

CHAPTER 7

Quality of Service Criteria for Packet Telephony

Packet networks must be optimized to support the quality of service (QoS) requirements of toll-quality voice transmission. Without optimization, packet networks introduce variable delays and real-time information loss for a variety of reasons. These effects degrade voice quality for calls placed through the network. This chapter examines the basic criteria that define QoS, and the QoS requirements to which packet voice networks must adhere to ensure good voice quality.

The following categories define QoS in packet networks:

- Reliability
- Delay
- Delay variation
- Bandwidth

To support packet telephony applications, and real-time applications in general, a packet network must provide high reliability, low delay, low delay variation, and sufficient bandwidth for the identified applications. Note that a packet network need not provide such performance for all network applications. The following sections examine each of these QoS categories, and consider the problems and solutions associated with meeting the QoS requirements of packet telephony.

Reliability

Real-time protocols have much stricter requirements for reliability than normal data protocols (such as Hypertext Transfer Protocol [HTTP], File Transfer Protocol [FTP], Simple Mail Transfer Protocol [SMTP], Telnet, and so on) because retransmission is not an option. Any information that is lost and retransmitted arrives too late and out of context to be useful at the receiving end. Telephony applications are especially sensitive to this condition. Imagine that during a phone conversation, you do not hear the first part of a word. You do not benefit from hearing this word fragment inserted at a subsequent point in the conversation.

Because real-time network applications cannot use packets that arrive late, sensible implementations save bandwidth and processing load by not retransmitting lost packets.

For IP networks, the reliable service of TCP is not appropriate for real-time applications because TCP uses retransmission to ensure reliability. This is one of the reasons that the Real-Time Transfer Protocol (RTP), which is the standard audio transmission protocol for all popular Voice over IP (VoIP) implementations, is based on User Datagram Protocol (UDP) instead of TCP.

One method to increase reliability without requiring packet retransmission is to use Forward Error Correction (FEC). With this technique, important parts of an information stream are sent redundantly through the network. The idea is that if a packet with some part of the data stream is lost, another packet with the same information will likely reach the destination. Introducing additional redundancy increases the reliability of the information transfer. FEC provides increased reliability at the expense of bandwidth because extra copies of information are transmitted.

There are two types of reliability to consider for telephony applications:

- Reliability within a call session
- Reliability between call sessions

Reliability Within a Call Session

Within a call session, audio streams must successfully traverse the network with minimal information loss. The time scale for this reliability measure is the duration of the conversation. During this interval, network reliability greatly affects voice quality. Figure 7-1 shows the decrease in voice quality following successive packet loss in a network. Each codec algorithm will have a different loss tolerance characteristic, but the general behavior of each is similar to that depicted for the G.729 algorithm.

Figure 7-1 *Voice Quality Degrades with the Loss of Successive Codec Frames*

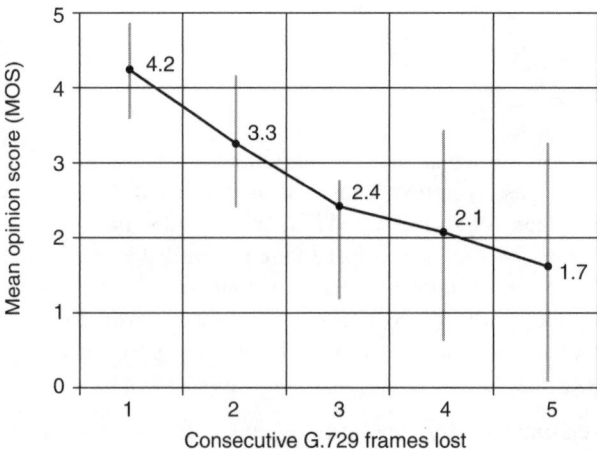

Data from "G.729 Error Recovery for Internet Telephony" by Jonathan D. Rosenberg.
Full paper available at http://www.cs.columbia.edu/~jdrosen/e6880/index.html

Note that Figure 7-1 depicts a scenario where codec frames are lost because of burst errors in the network connection, as opposed to random bit errors. *Burst errors* typically occur when multiple codec frames are placed in a single packet which is subsequently lost, or when multiple consecutive packets are lost. For example, a router may unintentionally drop consecutive voice packets when a congested interface buffer overflows. Codecs are generally less sensitive to a low frequency of random bit errors at the input of a decoder. Note that random bit errors that reach the decoder are generally the result of software problems at the receiving station, because bit errors caused during network transit are detected by link-layer Cyclic Redundancy Check (CRC) algorithms. Packets with detected CRC errors are discarded before they are sent to the decoder.

Reliability Between Call Sessions

Reliability between call sessions is related to *Grade of Service (GoS)*. GoS indicates the fraction of calls that are successfully completed in a timely fashion. Call Completion Rate (CCR) is another name for this reliability measurement in telephony networks. CCR accounts for the effects of packet network reliability, individual voice hardware components such as voice domain specific part (DSP) chips in the routers, and traditional voice network elements.

The network must provide long-term reliability to ensure a high GoS. In an unreliable network, GoS is adversely affected when call setup and teardown messages are lost. A lost signal for call setup may result in an unsuccessful call attempt. A lost signal for call teardown may cause a trunk to remain unavailable when it is no longer in use, which reduces the trunk resources available for other calls. Fortunately, call setup and teardown messages are not as time sensitive as the audio stream during the call, so lost messages may be retransmitted to improve GoS. In fact, it is desirable to use a reliable transmission protocol for call setup and teardown messages.

Designing reliable networks is outside the scope of this book, but the subject is fully explored in *Top-Down Network Design*, by Priscilla Openheimer (Cisco Press).

Here is a summary of points to consider when designing a network for reliability:

- Use reliable components—cables, patch panels, routers and switches, and so on.
- Where possible, build redundancy and fail-over capability into the system using techniques such as dynamic routing, Spanning Tree for switched LAN environments, Hot-Standby Router Protocol (HSRP), and so forth.
- Implement a network management program so you can react quickly to network outages and degraded service, and respond proactively to network utilization trends.

Delay

Across a network with excessive delay, we might have a conversation such as the following:

> You: "Please repeat what you said. Over."
>
> Me: "I said, 'What did you say?' I was talking too. Over."

In a normal conversation, each party takes a turn to speak while others listen. When the speaker is silent for a certain period of time, another person may speak. If nobody else speaks, the original speaker may continue. When this behavior is mapped to a telephone conversation with excessive delay, the effect is like a traffic light that shows green to cars entering an intersection from all directions. All parties begin to speak at the same time, and then all stop speaking when they hear others speaking. After a suitable pause, all begin to speak again, only to stop when they hear that all others are speaking again as well. For most people, 250 ms is about the threshold for acceptable delay to prevent speech collisions. People who are accustomed to international calling via satellite paths will have a higher tolerance for delay, a fact which designers of international packet voice networks should appreciate.

It is important to minimize delay in voice networks not only to avoid speech collisions, but also to mitigate unwanted audio signal reflections (echoes). The degree to which echoes are annoying in a telephone conversation is based on the loudness of the echo and the delay of the echo. When you reduce the end-to-end delay in your network, any echo that might be present is less annoying to the users. Chapter 13, "Delay Budgets and Loss Plans," discusses echoes and the relationship between delay and echo in detail.

Sources of Delay

Before you can minimize delay in a network, you must understand the most significant sources of delay. Figure 7-2 traces the audio signal through the network and indicates the major points at which the signal is delayed. These points introduce the following sources of delay:

- Codec processing
- Packet formation
- Interface queuing
- Serialization
- WAN cloud transmission and buffering
- WAN egress serialization
- Playout buffer

Figure 7-2   *Sources of Delay in the Audio Transmission Path*

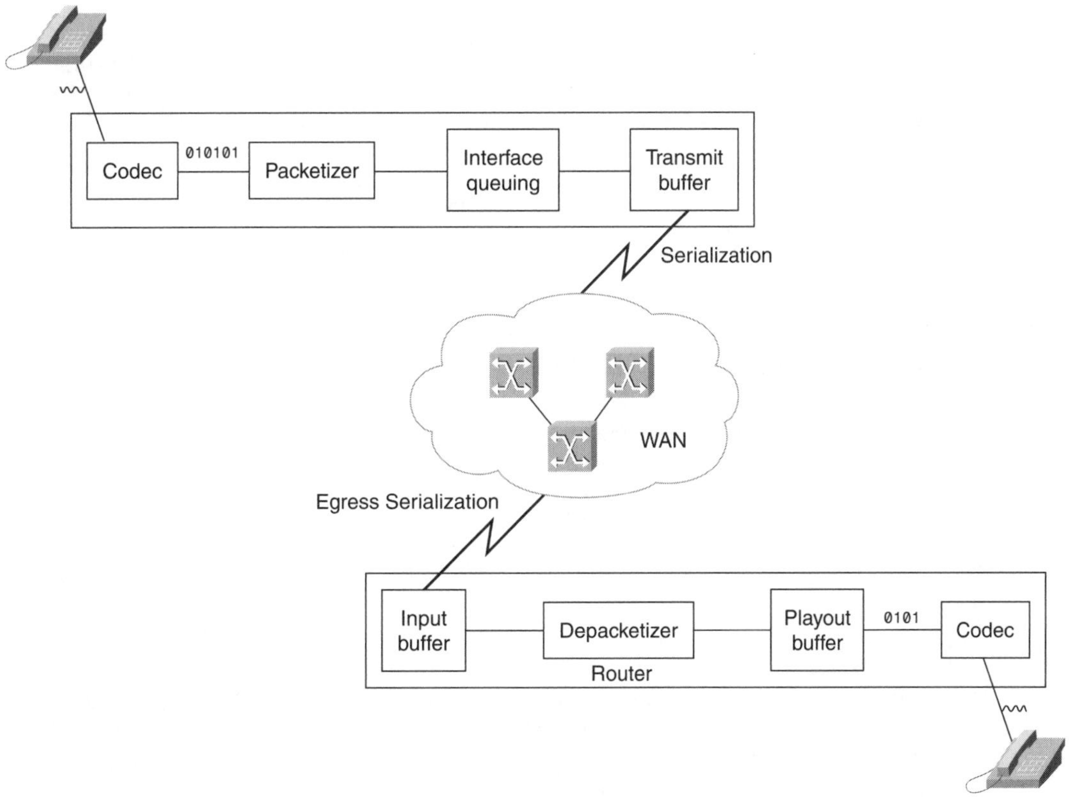

Codec Processing

The first substantial delay occurs when a codec converts the audio signal from an analog voltage to a digitized and compressed representation. Chapter 5, "Defining and Measuring Voice Quality," explores the delay properties of various codecs. In general, the audio codecs with lower bit rates have higher delays. A notable exception is the G.728 Low-Delay Code-Excited Linear Prediction (LD-CELP) algorithm, which yields a 16-kbps bit rate with less than 1 ms of delay.

Packet Formation

Codec frames (which are the output of the coder) are then placed into RTP/UDP/IP packets (for VoIP), Frame Relay frames (for Voice over Frame Relay [VoFR]), or ATM cells (for Voice over ATM [VoATM]). When a single codec frame is transmitted in each packet, frame, or cell, the packet formation delay is not a significant source of delay. However, if multiple codec frames are grouped into a single packet, frame, or cell, then the first codec frame of the group must wait while additional codec frames are generated to complete the packet. You should be aware of this if you increase the number of codec frames per [packet | frame | cell] to reduce the bandwidth consumption of headers. Chapter 17, "Establishing Network-Wide Calling Capability," shows how to change the size of the codec payload used by Cisco routers.

Note that the receiving station must remove the packet, frame, or cell headers from the codec frames, which is an additional (but minor) delay component.

Interface Queuing

After the codec frames are formed into packets and are ready for transmission, they might wait a substantial amount of time in a logical interface queuing buffer. While packets wait in the queuing buffer, an administrative policy arbitrates the order in which packets are transmitted. To reduce the delay experienced by voice packets, the queuing policy must move voice packets to the front of the logical interface queue. Chapter 10, "Review of IP Features for Voice/Data Integration," and Chapter 15, "Enabling Network-Wide Quality of Service," explore the queuing methods available in Cisco IOS.

Serialization

Even if voice packets are moved to the front of the logical interface queue, they can still experience delay in the physical transmission buffer. If a voice packet reaches the buffer after another packet begins transmission, the voice packet must wait until transmission of the other packet is complete. Figure 7-3 illustrates this concept. If the other packet is large, or if the interface transmission rate is low, then a significant amount of time might pass before the last bit of the other packet is transmitted. The time that a voice packet must wait for the other packet to transmit bit by bit is called the *serialization delay*.

The amount of serialization delay experienced by a voice packet in the transmission buffer depends on the length of the preceding packet, how much of the preceding packet has been transmitted when the voice packet arrives, and the transmission rate of the interface. Clearly, larger packets or lower clocking speeds will require more time for the serial transmission. You can determine the maximum serialization delay caused by a packet in mid-transmission by using the following formula:

$$serialization\_delay = \frac{(transmitted\_packet\_length)}{(interface\_clocking\_rate)}$$

Figure 7-3   *Voice Packet Must Wait for Another Packet in Mid-Transmission*

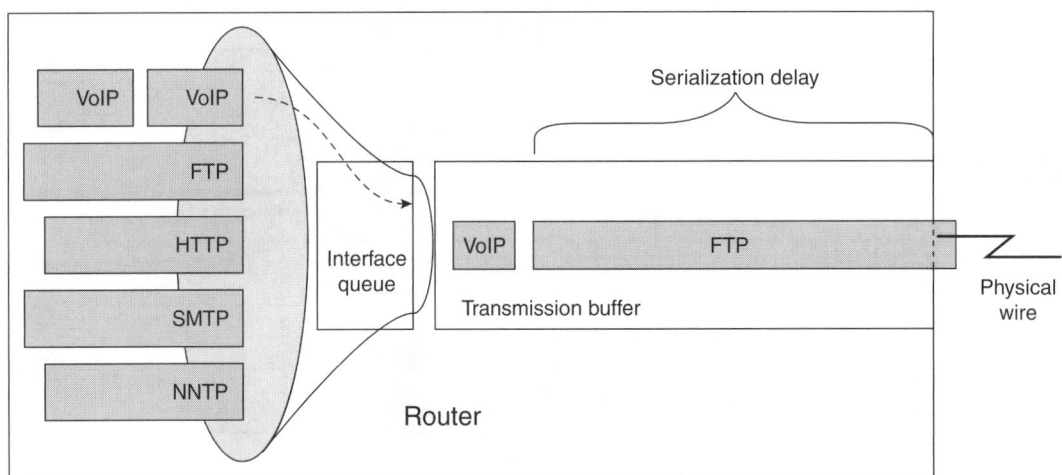

Figure 7-4 summarizes the serialization delay that results from a variety of packet sizes for a variety of interface transmission rates. Note that you should avoid the fragment size and interface clocking rate combinations shown in gray. The values above and to the right in the figure yield a serialization delay that is unacceptably large, and the values below and to the left yield excessive bandwidth overhead from fragment headers. Link fragmentation and interleaving (LFI) are discussed in Chapter 8, "WAN Protocols for Integrated Voice and Data Services," Chapter 9, "Design Considerations for WAN Protocols," Chapter 10, and Chapter 15.

WAN Cloud Transmission and Buffering

After the packet passes the physical interface, it is officially in the WAN cloud. The cloud is composed of numerous packet switches (each of which buffer the packets), or cell switches (which create a virtual end-to-end wire path more predictable delay), or a combination of switch types. The WAN cloud is often the most significant contribution to the overall delay budget because of the distances across which the packets must be transmitted. A case study following this section examines the transmission delay component of a WAN cloud. For all entities except service providers, the WAN cloud may be abstracted to a delay component and a delay variation component.

Figure 7-4 *Serialization Delay—Resulting from Various Fragment Sizes and Effective Clocking Rates*

Packet or frame fragment size (bytes)

		40	70	80	160	320	480	640	960	1200	1600
Effective clocking rate (kbps)	32	10	17.5	20	40	80	120	160	240	300	400
	56	5.7	10	11.4	22.9	45.7	68.6	91.4	137.1	171.4	228.6
	64	5	8.8	10	20	40	60	80	120	150	200
	128	2.5	4.4	5	10	20	30	40	60	75	100
	256	1.3	2.2	2.5	5	10	15	20	30	37.5	50
	384	0.8	1.5	1.7	3.3	6.7	10	13.3	20	25	33.3
	512	0.6	1.1	1.3	2.5	5	7.5	10	15	18.8	25
	768	0.4	0.7	0.8	1.7	3.3	5	6.7	10	12.5	16.7
	960	0.3	0.6	0.7	1.3	2.7	4	5.3	8	10	13.3
	1536	0.2	0.4	0.4	0.8	1.7	2.5	3.3	5	6.3	8.3
	1920	0.2	0.3	0.3	0.7	1.3	2	2.7	4	5	6.7

☐ Acceptable serialization delay

▨ Too much serialization delay (above right) or too much frame fragment overhead (below left)

WAN Egress Serialization

Just as serialization delay is a factor for packets entering the WAN cloud, it is also a factor for packets leaving the WAN cloud. This delay factor is called the *WAN egress serialization delay*, and is controlled by the access switch in the carrier network at the far end of the connection. WAN egress serialization delay is important to consider for VoFR and VoIP over Frame Relay. It can also be a significant source of jitter for VoFR or VoIP over Frame Relay.

Playout Buffer

When a [packet | frame | cell] reaches the destination router, the headers are removed and the codec frames are placed into a playout buffer. Because the codec frames arrive via the data network in a bursty manner, the playout buffer must be large enough to ensure that the codec frames can be played out smoothly to the decoder. Otherwise, the decoder cannot generate a continuous audio stream, which reduces the voice quality of the signal. The number of codec frames in the playout buffer changes constantly, but the buffer should never be completely full or completely empty. The amount of delay introduced by the playout buffer at a given time depends on the number of codec frames that are in the buffer at the time.

Minimizing Delay

Overall delay is not usually a design concern unless the delay introduced by the WAN cloud is sizeable. If you must reduce the overall delay for telephone conversations across the VoX network, then focus on the following design elements:

- Work with the circuit vendor to manually optimize the physical transmission path of circuits through the vendor cloud. Auto-provisioned circuits often follow suboptimal physical paths based on trunk availability at the time of provisioning. If possible, define the optimized path as a preferred path so that it will be restored following an outage.

- On all routers in your network that might experience congestion (not just voice/data routers), employ a queuing policy that prioritizes voice traffic ahead of other traffic (to reduce queuing delay). To achieve this goal with VoIP, you must use priority queuing, low latency queuing (LLQ), or IP RTP Priority with weighted-fair queuing (WFQ), or class-based weighted-fair queuing (CB-WFQ). Chapter 10 and Chapter 15 discuss these options. To achieve this goal with VoFR or VoATM, you must configure parameters that are specific to Frame Relay or ATM technologies. Chapter 8 and Chapter 9 discuss these options. Make sure that you have provisioned a sufficient amount of bandwidth so that prioritized voice traffic queues do not starve data traffic queues.

- To reduce serialization delay, use LFI technologies such as FRF.12 and ML-PPP fragment/interleave on all routers with low-speed interfaces in your network—not just on voice/data routers. Using a fragment size of 80 bytes for every 64 kbps of transmission rate ensures that serialization delay does not exceed 10 ms for the fragment. Chapters 8, 9, 10 and 15 discuss LFI technologies in detail.

- Select a codec that introduces minimal delay. Different hardware vendors may support a limited set of codecs, but Cisco routers support a wide range of codecs standardized by the International Telecommunications Union (ITU). Be mindful of other trade-offs associated with the selected codec, such as digital signal processor (DSP) resource requirements, voice quality, performance for tandem encodings (if applicable in your network), and bandwidth. Chapter 6 discusses these trade-offs in detail.

- If the size of the playout buffer is statically configured, you can reduce it to minimize playout delay. You should only consider this option when the network has a small delay variation, such as when using clear-channel T-1/E-1 circuits with a high transmission delay. In general, it is not a good idea to use this approach when you have Frame Relay circuits, because the end-to-end delay is not consistent. Cisco routers dynamically adjust the size of the playout buffer based on current delay and jitter characteristics, so you do not need to adjust playout buffers in Cisco routers.

TIP	Remember that some actions to reduce delay for voice traffic may adversely affect performance for other traffic types, or may compromise other aspects of voice quality. Carefully consider the effects of codec selection, packet fragmenting, and playout buffer tuning. **Do not consider any issue in isolation.**

Case Study: Transmission Delay

LANs and network end-devices currently operate at speeds that can easily support retransmission of dropped packets in the telephone audio path. However, physical limitations may prevent this capability in the WAN for some time. An example will clearly demonstrate the problem:

The distance between San Francisco, USA and Sydney, Australia is about 11,922 km following the shortest path on the surface of the earth. Light travels at roughly 299,792,458 meters per second in a vacuum. Suppose now that the following events occur:

1 San Francisco transmits a light signal to Sydney, which is lost en route.

2 Sydney detects the loss of the expected signal at the earliest possible moment (that is, 39.76 ms after San Francisco sent the first part of the signal).

3 Sydney instantly sends a retransmission request to San Francisco, where it is received 79.53 ms after the original transmission.

4 San Francisco instantly retransmits the light signal when it receives the request. The retransmitted signal is received in Sydney 119.3 ms after the original signal was sent.

Now, consider the following facts:

• Light does not travel through fiber as fast as it travels in a vacuum.

• The optical fiber path between San Francisco and Sydney does not precisely follow the shortest path distance.

• A receiver cannot detect a lost signal immediately after the minimal expected arrival time, and cannot instantly process transmissions or retransmission requests.

• Regeneration and switching components along the fiber path introduce substantial delays.

• San Francisco and Sydney are not the most widely separated cities that require telephone communication.

While the speed of light in a vacuum yields transmission latencies of 3.33 ms per 1000 km, real fiber optics allow 5 ms per 1000 km, and telecom carriers use a figure of 6 to 9 ms per 1000 km to account for a variety of facts including those previously listed.

Delay Variation

Delay variation, or *jitter*, is a more serious concern for packet voice networks than absolute delay. A phone conversation with delay may be awkward, but the audio information is still intelligible. Jitter can render an audio stream completely unrecognizable. The following sections explore jitter from several perspectives:

- What is jitter?
- Playout buffers
- Sources of jitter
- Minimizing jitter

What Is Jitter?

The concept of jitter is illustrated in Figure 7-5. The top half of the diagram shows the time spacing between voice packets at the sender when they are first transmitted. The bottom half of the diagram shows the time spacing at the receiver after the packets have experienced variable delays while transiting the network. If all packets experienced the same amount of delay through the network, then the time spacing, or interpacket difference D_1 would equal D_3, and D_2 would equal D_4. As you can see, VoX_1 and VoX_2 are much closer together at the receiver side than they were at the sender side. This happens because VoX_2 experienced less delay than VoX_1 while transiting the network. Similarly, VoX_2 and VoX_3 are farther apart at the receiver side than at the sender side, because VoX_3 experienced more delay than VoX_2 while transiting the network.

Figure 7-5   *Jitter Is Caused When Packets Experience Unequal Delays when Transiting a Network*

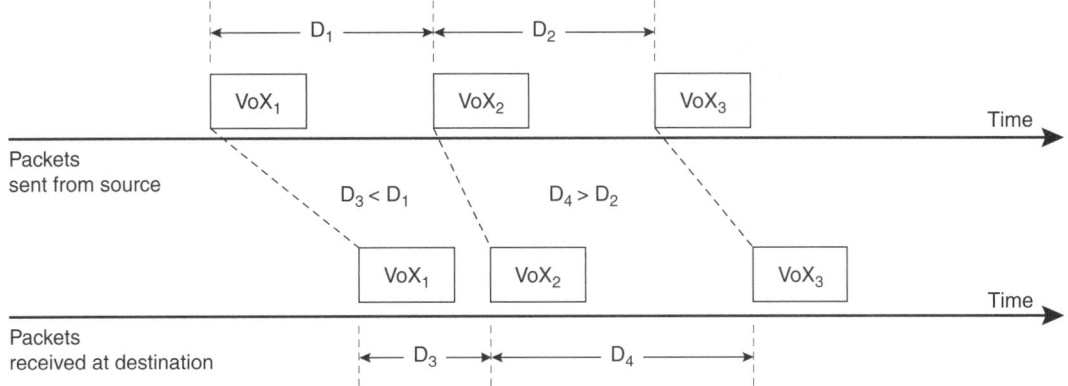

Voice quality is extremely dependent on the timing with which sound samples are played out to the listener. If the timing between codec frames at the sender is different from the timing between codec frames at the receiver, then the receiver will not hear an accurate representation of the original sound. To get a better feeling for the impact of jitter on an audio stream, imagine listening to an audiocassette tape or vinyl record that is played at constantly changing speeds. In a more updated example, imagine the sound of an audio CD that is played while alternating between pause and fast-forward search mode. The garbled sound is characteristic of jitter.

Playout Buffers

To help combat the effects of jitter, all packet voice systems (and packet audio systems in general) use playout buffers, which are also known as *dejitter buffers*. Sometimes you will hear people shorten the name to jitter buffers. The idea is that the buffer stores a supply of codec frames for a brief amount of time to ensure that it can play out the codec frames at a constant rate. The number of codec frames in the buffer shrinks when there are hiccups in the network (that is, when no voice packets arrive from the network), and the buffer grows when a burst of voice packets arrive. Even though the number of codec frames in the playout buffer is always changing, codec frames are drained from the buffer at a constant rate. As long as the buffer is never completely empty or full, codec frames continue to be played out at a constant rate, which ensures an accurate re-creation of the audio signal.

Increasing the size of the playout buffer (to accommodate more codec frames) makes it more resilient to jitter, but the time required to buffer the additional codec frames introduces more delay into the system. If you have ever listened to streaming audio from a web site (such as Real Audio™ or Microsoft Media-Player™), then you have noticed that you must wait 5, 10, 15, or more seconds before the sound begins. These are not real-time systems, so they can afford to buffer sound for a longer period of time. The extra time ensures that you always hear a constant stream of sound in spite of the bursty nature in which the packets arrive. For packet telephony, sound can be buffered for a few hundred milliseconds at most (generally not more than 100 ms) to maintain the characteristics of real-time communication. Because the playout buffers are so small, jitter is a major design concern for packet telephony.

Figure 7-6 illustrates how jitter in the network can disrupt the playout of the audio signal. In Figure 7-6a, the playout buffer completely drains, and the audio stream is replaced by an abrupt silence. This situation is called a playout buffer underrun. In Figure 7-6b, the playout buffer completely fills and newly arriving packets are discarded. The audio samples before and after the discarded packets are played out with no time lapse to represent the dropped packets. This situation is called a playout buffer overrun. Because overruns usually result in the loss of several adjacent codec samples, they are especially damaging for low bit-rate codecs, such as G.723.1 and G.729.

Figure 7-6   *Excessive Jitter Disrupts the Smooth Playout of the Audio Signal*

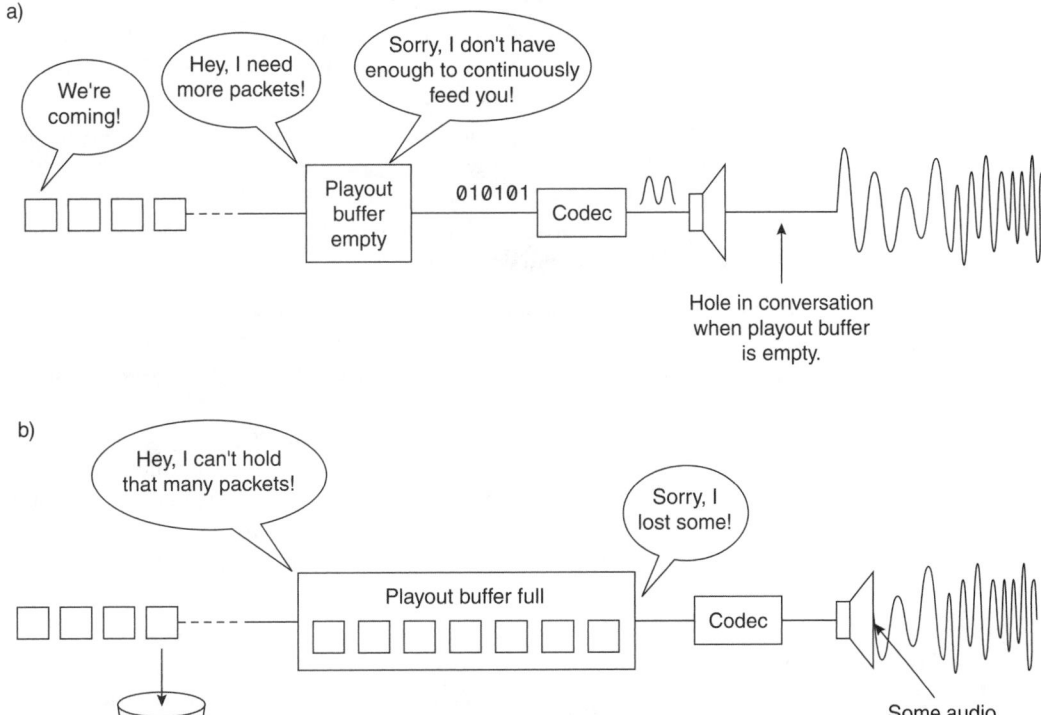

Because playout buffers can only eliminate a minimal amount of jitter for packet telephony systems, you must design a network that introduces very little jitter for packets in transit. To accomplish this goal, you must understand the points in the network where jitter is introduced.

Sources of Jitter

Jitter is an inherent characteristic of packet network systems, because there is no end-to-end synchronous transmission like in circuit-switched networks. Jitter occurs at every point in a packet network where interface buffering occurs, both in private networks and public networks (such as in a circuit vendor Frame Relay cloud). The following points in the audio transmission path can introduce jitter:

- Interface queuing
- Serialization
- WAN cloud buffering and egress serialization

Interface Queuing

Buffering is required to accommodate the bursty nature of data networks. Interface queues are buffers that absorb packet bursts and transmit them when an interface is no longer congested. When an interface can transmit packets faster than sources are trying to send packets to the interface, packets do not need to wait in a buffer. If more packets are offered to an interface than it can transmit in a given time, the packets are stored in a buffer until the interface is ready to transmit them. Large buffers accommodate more bursty traffic and reduce the amount of packets dropped from buffer overflows, but they also introduce sizable delays and jitter. Every packet switch has at least an input buffer and an output buffer that contribute to the end-to-end delay and jitter.

If no queuing policies are implemented that give preferential treatment to voice packets, then voice packets may experience a lot of delay while waiting in interface queues for other packets to transmit. Because an interface queue may be empty or full or anywhere in between when voice packets arrive, the voice packets may wait anywhere from no time to several seconds before transmission. Each interface queue imposes this delay variation, so packets that must cross several packet switches might experience an enormous delay variation in transit. It should be clear that the amount of jitter caused by interface buffering far outstrips the ability of a real-time playout buffer to accommodate the jitter. For this reason, queuing policies are essential to move voice packets to the front of all queues.

Serialization

Serialization delay, as already described in a preceding section in the context of absolute delay, is a critical consideration for low-speed interfaces. The amount of serialization delay that a voice packet experiences in a transmission buffer is variable, and bounded by the largest packet size in the network. A voice packet that is moved to the front of an interface queue may be instantly transmitted if no other packets are in mid-transmission, or it may have to wait in a transmission buffer behind a 1500-byte data packet that has just begun transmitting. If the interface is transmitting at 64 kbps, then the voice packet must wait 188 ms! Note that a packet telephony playout buffer can experience an underrun condition just by the variable serialization delay of a single interface. A typical audio path crosses at least a few interfaces that can introduce this much variable delay.

The solution to this problem is to break up the large packets into fragments, and enable the voice packets to be interleaved between the fragments of a single large packet. This technique is generally called LFI, and is discussed later in the section, "Minimizing Jitter."

WAN Cloud Buffering and Egress Serialization

Just as you must consider interface buffers and serialization delay in the parts of the network that you manage, you must also consider these factors in the parts of the network managed by your circuit vendor. If you have clear-channel circuits (that is, full or fractional T-1/E-1), then you do not need to worry about buffering or serialization in the carrier network, because there is a synchronous serial stream of information across the circuit with a fixed and constant delay. However, if you have Frame Relay circuits, then the carrier is multiplexing your traffic along with numerous other customers, and your traffic is likely to wait in various buffers as it crosses the carrier network. If you have ATM circuits, you are in a better position to control these factors because you can order circuits that meet specific delay and jitter requirements. Frame Relay offers no guarantees with respect to delay or jitter. These topics are discussed in detail in Chapters 8 and 9.

Minimizing Jitter

From a design perspective, use several strategies to minimize and manage jitter:

- Implement a queuing policy that prioritizes voice traffic ahead of other data traffic. This eliminates the variable interface buffer delay, but you must still deal with the serialization delay and variations in how different hardware platforms service the transmission buffers (see the section "Dual FIFO Transmit Buffers," in Chapter 10).

- To minimize variable serialization delay, decrease the maximum packet size using LFI technologies as appropriate for the effective clocking rate of the interface. Note that traffic shaping (which is most commonly used for Frame Relay) reduces the effective clocking rate below the actual clocking rate. For VoFR and VoIP over Frame Relay, traffic shaping should reduce the effective clocking rate to the Committed Information Rate (CIR) of the permanent-virtual circuit (PVC). Be aware that fragment headers introduce a slight amount of additional overhead bandwidth. Chapters 8, 9, 10, and 15 discuss these technologies.

- Avoid parallel transmission paths with different delay characteristics. Packets arriving from streams with different latencies may burden the jitter buffers and cause buffer overflows. Chapter 10 explores the design considerations for parallel transmission paths.

- Increase the length of playout buffers to accommodate high delay variation. A high overall delay is much better than an audio stream with jitter, but you should conform to the ITU-T G.114 Recommendations for one-way delay (see Chapter 13, "Delay Budgets and Loss Plans"). Note that Cisco routers use a dynamic playout buffer depth that automatically responds to delay and jitter characteristics, so you do not need to adjust the buffer depth for Cisco routers.

Bandwidth

Capacity planning for networks that carry real-time traffic is somewhat different than capacity planning for traditional data-only networks. Though bandwidth requirements are still based on peak traffic rates, the intervals over which the peak rates are measured must be shorter. Consider a network that is designed for a busy-hour traffic rate of 200 kbps average. It may seem that a 256-kbps WAN circuit would accommodate the traffic load just fine. Now consider that throughout the hour, the traffic level may repeatedly reach 300 kbps for busy-minute intervals, followed by light usage for some time. In this scenario, users may or may not complain of sluggish network performance. They will definitely complain about poor voice performance because they have high expectations of voice quality and availability. During times of high network utilization, buffers overflow, and voice quality suffers as voice packets are dropped or delayed.

Economic considerations are often at the heart of decisions to increase bandwidth on WAN circuits. One approach to avoiding bandwidth upgrades is to optimize the data throughput efficiency by prioritizing traffic, minimizing routing updates, and decreasing the amount of packet overhead. Though advanced router configurations can be a great tool to stave off bandwidth upgrades, the cost of supporting complex router configurations should be considered as well. In some cases, the money saved by delaying bandwidth upgrades may be spent on additional resources to design and maintain the complex network. In general, compare the total cost of each strategy to make informed decisions. When bandwidth costs are very high (such as with international circuits), complex router configurations are easily justified. For a clear channel circuit (fractional T1/E1) across town, perhaps additional bandwidth may be less expensive than supporting routers with complex configurations. Do not think that complexity can or should always be avoided. Consider all factors when making a decision.

Chapter 12 explores bandwidth and capacity-planning issues in detail.

Minimizing Bandwidth Usage

The following steps will optimize voice and data throughput for a given amount of network bandwidth:

- Use a voice codec with a large compression ratio. Examples include G.729 (8 kbps) and G.723.1 (6.3 kbps or 5.3 kbps).
- Minimize the size of headers that encapsulate data.
- Reserve bandwidth for real-time and critical applications, so that the network gracefully degrades during periods of congestion.
- Monitor the network and project utilization trends to help plan bandwidth upgrades. Consider the lead times associated with circuit installations and plan accordingly.

Summary

It is clear that all aspects of a network cannot be simultaneously improved. You must balance the network design for data throughput, overall delay, jitter, and reliability. There are not many rules in this arena—the priorities and requirements of a given environment will dictate the appropriate compromises.

In general, jitter must be reduced as much as possible throughout the network, and eliminated with playout buffers at the receiving end. You can control jitter at the expense of either bandwidth or delay. LFI technologies effectively reduce jitter from serialization delays, but decrease the bandwidth efficiency of circuits that already have limited bandwidth. Large playout buffers reduce end-to-end jitter from any source, but add to the overall delay.

When you select a voice codec, you must choose whether to minimize delay, bandwidth usage, or processing load. You can make this decision in conjunction with your method of controlling jitter. For example, to offset the increased bandwidth of LFI techniques that control jitter, you can use a low bit-rate codec. These decisions and their consequences are for you, the network designer, to contemplate.

CHAPTER 8

WAN Protocols for Integrated Voice and Data Services

Introduction

This chapter explores features of the following mature WAN technologies that provide integrated transport for voice and data networks:

- Clear-channel T-1/E-1 circuits

- Frame Relay

- Asynchronous transfer mode (ATM)

While there are a variety of other WAN services offered by data circuit vendors today, including Switched Multimegabit Data Service (SMDS), X.25, xDSL, data over cable, SONET, and Dense Wave-Division Multiplexing (DWDM), these technologies do not provide integral support for voice services (with the exception of voice over digital subscriber line [DSL]). Rather, these link-layer technologies might support packet voice in the form of Voice over IP (VoIP), which is introduced in Chapter 10, "Review of IP Features for Voice/Data Integration," and Chapter 11, "VoIP Transport and Signaling Protocols."

This chapter is not intended to be a thorough reference on WAN technologies for data networks. Basic familiarity with T-1/E-1, ISDN, Frame Relay, and ATM is assumed. If you find that this review is too cursory, then the references at the end of this chapter can provide you with more background material. In addition, the "Internetworking Technology Overview," which is available on Cisco Connection Online (CCO), is a great starting point for learning more about these subjects.

This chapter is primarily focused on the features of WAN protocols that support integrated voice and data networks. Chapter 9, "Design Considerations for WAN Protocols," builds on the concepts presented in this chapter to highlight design considerations and implementation techniques for packet telephony across a WAN.

NOTE   ISDN protocols are specifically excluded from this chapter. The voice services of ISDN are part of traditional voice networks, and are explored in Chapter 1, "The State of Voice Communications," and Chapter 2, "Enterprise Telephony Signaling." The data services of ISDN (with PPP encapsulation) may be used as a link layer for VoIP. Chapter 10 and Chapter 15, "Enabling Network-Wide QoS," consider VoIP issues that relate to PPP encapsulation.

Clear-Channel T-1/E-1 Circuits

Clear-channel T-1/E-1 data circuits evolved directly from the digital facilities used to aggregate voice calls in the Public Switched Telephone Network (PSTN). These facilities provide a framing structure that contains 8-bit samples from many voice channels. These voice channels are separated into different timeslots, hence the term, time-division multiplexing (TDM). Instead of using each of the channels on the digital facility for a voice conversation, the circuit vendor may provide channels to the customer to transport any data. Clear-channel T-1 data circuits typically use the Extended Superframe (ESF) framing pattern, and the binary 8-zero substitution (B8ZS) line coding, while E-1 data circuits typically use cyclic redundancy check-4 (CRC-4) multiframes and high-density bipolar-3 (HDB3) line coding. The details of these framing and line-coding techniques are outside the scope of this book, but you can find detailed information in the book *Cisco WAN Quick Start*, which is available from Cisco Press. This and other references are available at the end of the chapter.

Circuit vendors provision clear-channel TDM circuits for full-time use from one customer location to another. A channel service unit (CSU) at each customer location can rearrange and direct individual channels from the digital facility to different end devices. The device that performs this function is sometimes called an Add Drop Multiplexer (ADM). The channels may be grouped to provide a single larger bandwidth facility, in multiples of 64 kbps. After a CSU processes the channels, a data service unit (DSU) translates data from one or more selected channels into a single serial data stream. The serial output connects to an end device, such as a router. It is very common to have the CSU and DSU functions combined into a single device, aptly called a CSU/DSU.

Voice/data integration is not a new concept for leased-line users. Traditionally, a CSU at the customer location separates channels of the incoming digital facility into two or more groups. One group feeds a CSU/DSU that connects to a data router, and the other group feeds a connection to a private branch exchange (PBX). The router sees a leased-line connection to a remote router, and the PBX sees a tie-line connection to a remote PBX. Figure 8-1 illustrates this scenario.

Figure 8-1 *Application of TDM for Voice and Data Traffic*

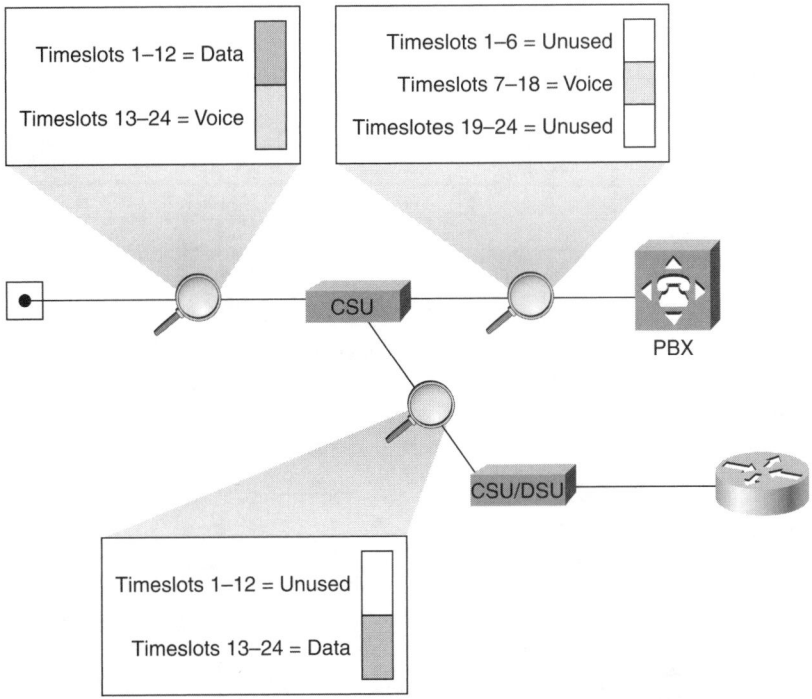

While the CSU may flexibly allocate channels to voice or data, the allocation is fairly static. If 12 channels of a 24-channel T1 circuit are mapped to a PBX, then only 12 channels are available for data, even if all of the voice channels are idle.

Some CSU manufacturers[1] have added flexibility to this system by allowing you to create multiple channel maps, which can change automatically based on the time of day. In this scenario, a T1 CSU might be programmed to use 20 voice channels and 4 data channels during the daytime, but use only 2 voice channels and 22 data channels at night. (See Figure 8-2.) This plan would accommodate heavy telephone use during the business day, and would enable nightly bulk file transfers when telephony needs are small. While this channel-mapping system is somewhat flexible, it does not provide for optimized dynamic use of the available bandwidth.

---

1. Larscom manufactures a CSU/DSU called the Split-T™, which offers dynamic channel maps that change with the time of day.

Figure 8-2 *CSU/DSU May Have Alternate Channel Maps for Night and Day to Accommodate Varying Traffic Needs Between Voice and Data*

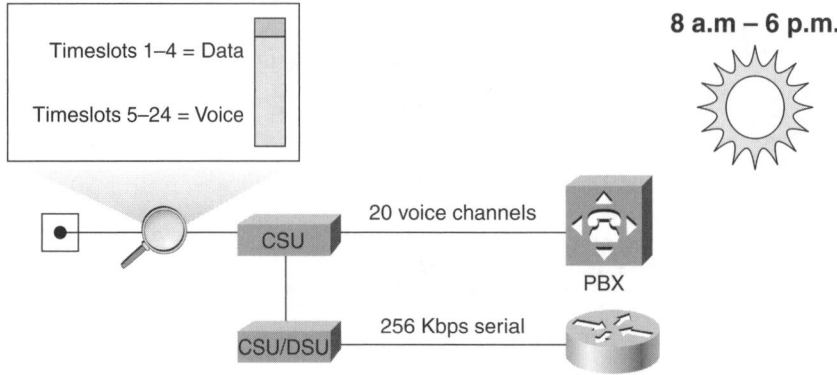

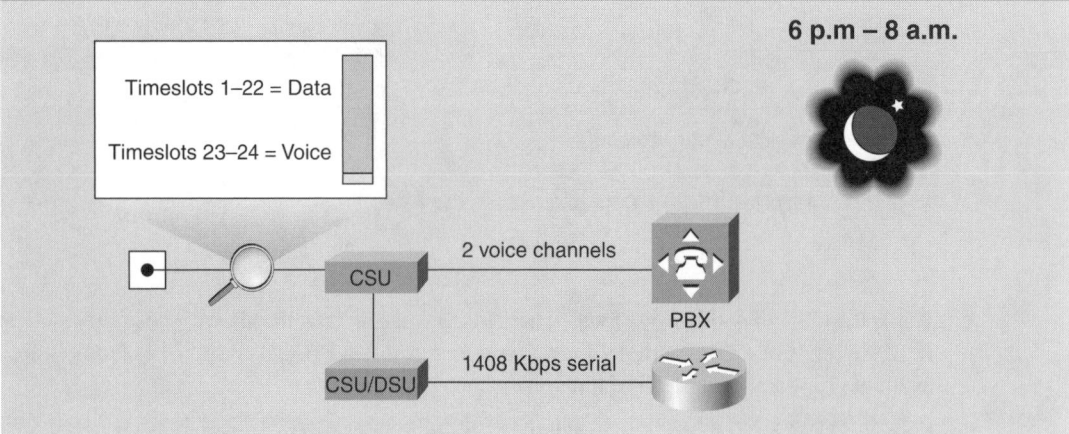

NOTE	A CSU/DSU makes the number of channels allocated in a T-1/E-1 transparent to a V.35 serial interface. As long as a CSU/DSU with time-varying channel maps is attached to a Cisco router via a serial interface, the changing channel maps are transparent to the router. That is, a router might have a 256-kbps serial interface during the day and a 1408-kbps serial interface at night, with no configuration change to the router (assuming the channel map changes in the CSU/DSU).

Quality of Service Baseline for Clear-Channel TDM Circuits

Clear-channel circuits are the basis of the old public telephony network and PBX tie-line networks. Because people have become accustomed to the voice quality achieved with this technology, the network performance of clear-channel TDM is the standard by which new network systems are compared. To facilitate a comparison with other technologies, the remainder of this section develops a baseline picture of clear-channel circuits with respect to the following quality of service (QoS) characteristics:

- Reliability
- Delay
- Delay variation
- Bandwidth

Clear-channel circuits offer excellent performance with respect to delay and delay variation. Transmission delay accounts for almost all of the delay associated with clear-channel circuits. Transmission delay is a function of circuit distance, but clear-channel circuits offer the lowest possible delay to connect endpoints separated by a given distance. Because clear-channel circuits are provisioned with dedicated end-to-end facilities, a provider network has no oversubscribed links. This means that any voice traffic that enters the provider network will be transported across the network without experiencing congestion, and without incurring variable delays that change the timing relationship between adjacent voice samples.

While the basic hardware and technology of clear-channel TDM circuits are reliable, the lack of redundancy support reduces the overall reliability of the technology. If a digital facility fails during an active conversation, then the call cannot be automatically rerouted to another facility.

TDM allocation of voice or data channels does not efficiently utilize available bandwidth. Data throughput may be congested when bandwidth is available in idle voice channels, or voice calls may be dropped when data channels are underutilized. When the price of WAN bandwidth is at a premium, this is a serious concern. The bandwidth issue is a significant (but not the only) business driver to embrace more advanced voice/data integration technologies. Chapter 9 explores advanced uses of clear-channel circuits to leverage the strengths and overcome the weaknesses of clear-channel TDM circuit technology.

In summary, clear-channel TDM circuits exhibit the following QoS characteristics:

- Reliable components, but not robust in the case of link failures during active calls
- Excellent performance for delay and delay variation
- Inefficient use of available bandwidth

Frame Relay

This section reviews Frame Relay from a traditional data perspective, and then focuses on the extensions to Frame Relay that permit real-time voice communications. The following two sections explore these topics:

- Overview of Frame Relay
- Frame Relay and voice traffic

NOTE   If you are not familiar with Frame Relay as a WAN technology for data transport, and you want more information than provided here, you can learn more about it from the sources listed at the end of this chapter.

Overview of Frame Relay

Instead of using groups of TDM channels to form circuits, Frame Relay uses virtual circuits (VCs) that are not bound to the TDM channels of T1/E1/J1/Y1 facilities. Each data stream is encapsulated in Frame Relay frames, which include a data-link connection identifier (DLCI) field to identify the VC. Frames from a given virtual circuit may ride on any or all of the channels of the TDM circuit. Figure 8-3 illustrates this concept.

Figure 8-3   *Frame Relay VCs Are Independent of the Physical Layer TDM Channel Assignments*

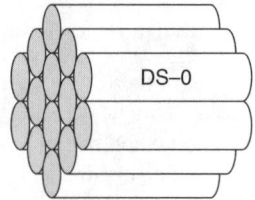

Each TDM channel assigned to a specific service

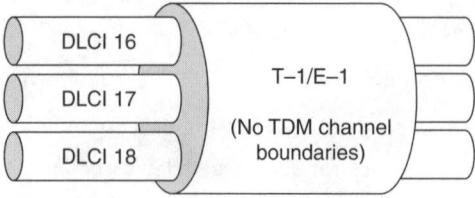

Virtual circuits are independent of TDM Channels

Frame Relay supports variable bandwidth requirements for each VC. A carrier assigns a committed information rate (CIR) for a VC, which is a guarantee to the customer to provide at least the stated amount of bandwidth for the VC. The carrier also enables the customer to send traffic in excess of the CIR, which may or may not be transported (depending on the level of congestion in the carrier network). The traffic-bursting capability of VCs enables customers to dynamically allocate bandwidth between sites without regard to a fixed TDM channel allocation. Because multiple virtual circuits can share the same TDM channels, and because all customers do not simultaneously use their virtual circuits at full capacity, circuit vendors can oversubscribe core network trunks to some extent without adversely impacting customers. Because of the reduced need for core network facilities, circuit vendors can offer reduced prices for Frame Relay circuits compared to clear-channel circuits. Both customers and circuit vendors benefit from the statistical multiplexing of data traffic.

Customers have traditionally connected to a provider Frame Relay network cloud via a clear-channel TDM circuit, but recent enhancements to the Frame Relay standards have enabled a variety of physical layer interfaces (see FRF.14). A router or Frame Relay access device (FRAD) at the customer location communicates with the carrier Frame Relay switch (usually in a central office, or CO) to exchange data and control information. This type of connection is called a User-Network Interface (UNI). The Frame Relay protocol between a customer and a provider across the UNI is called the Local Management Interface (LMI). The LMI provides status information about the UNI connection between the customer premises equipment (CPE) and Frame Relay switch, and includes information about the VCs that are terminated in the router or FRAD.

Sometimes a virtual circuit must cross the networks of multiple circuit vendors—perhaps a local carrier and a long-distance carrier, or perhaps between carriers in different countries. The point where these networks meet and exchange data and control information is called the Network-to-Network Interface (NNI). It is possible for a vendor with a large Frame Relay network to maintain multiple NNI connections within its own network. UNI and NNI interfaces, as well as the relationship between LMI and VCs, are depicted in Figure 8-4.

Because transport facilities are not dedicated throughout the network, a Frame Relay network must have a mechanism to inform the sender or the receiver when transport facilities are limited. In practice, a switch detects congestion by counting the number of frames waiting in a buffer. Frame Relay switches can send Explicit Congestion Notification messages to the source or destination of traffic experiencing congestion. Notifications sent to the source are called Backward Explicit Congestion Notifications (BECNs), and messages sent to the destination are called Forward Explicit Congestion Notifications (FECNs). FECNs and BECNs are each identified by a single bit in the Frame Relay header of normal user traffic, so there is no need to have frames dedicated to congestion notification.

Figure 8-4 *Locations of UNI and NNI Interfaces in Frame Relay Networks, and Relationship Between LMI and VCs*

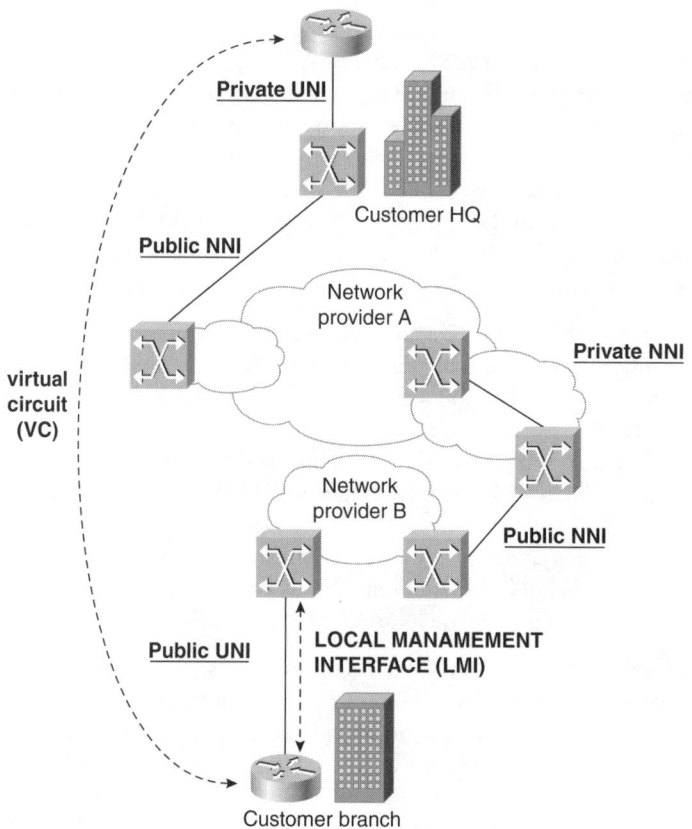

Frame Relay switches send congestion notifications so that routers or FRADs can regulate the rate at which they offer traffic to the network. Cisco routers can use FECN and BECN messages to influence traffic-shaping and queuing processes for a dynamic and optimal use of available bandwidth. The FECN and BECN response features in Cisco IOS are useful for data-only networks, but networks with real-time traffic such as telephony should not use these features. Chapter 9 explores this design consideration in detail.

To ensure a minimal quality of service, Frame Relay provides a bandwidth guarantee in the form of a CIR, but it does not provide any guarantees with respect to delay or delay variation[2]. Because circuit vendors have not deployed Frame Relay services with latency

---

2. The Service level definitions of FRF.13 include a measure for delay. Widespread adoption of FRF.13 should enable delay guarantees from circuit vendors; however, delay variation is still an unresolved issue.

guarantees, they might use large buffers in their frame switches to avoid dropping frames during periods of congestion. This practice helps them meet their CIR guarantee while still enabling them to maintain highly oversubscribed and cost-efficient networks. Data network applications can accommodate the delay incurred by the large switch buffers, but the delay and jitter are unacceptable for telephony applications. Until the widespread adoption of service level agreements (SLAs) based on FRF.13, you are at the mercy of the Frame Relay provider to provide acceptable service for voice traffic.

NOTE   Instead of using native Frame Relay networks, some carriers support Frame Relay services using FRF.5 Frame-ATM Network Interworking, which transports Frame Relay frames across the provider ATM backbone. In such cases, the carrier can identify the ATM VCs that transport Frame Relay traffic, and transmit the ATM VCs with low priority (because Frame Relay provides no latency guarantees). Therefore, an ATM core network does not necessarily improve the end-to-end performance for Frame Relay VCs.

When traffic on a permanent virtual circuit (PVC) exceeds the CIR, the provider may set a Discard Eligible (DE) bit in the frame headers of your traffic. Frame Relay switches in a provider network will discard these frames before other frames during times of congestion. A key point is that the DE bit is set in the provider network irrespective of whether the frames contain voice or data traffic. The voice and data traffic appears the same to the carrier because it is all within a single PVC. As soon as you exceed the CIR by any amount, all of your traffic is equally subject to some amount of discard. In other words, you cannot transmit voice traffic within the CIR of a PVC, and then burst data traffic on the same PVC.

When the American National Standards Institute (ANSI) and the International Telecommunications Union-Telecommunications (ITU-T) Services Sector standardized Frame Relay by 1991, voice traffic was not a consideration. The technology was created to transport bursty data traffic that in general is not sensitive to delay-file transfers, e-mail, news, and so on. The mechanisms that give Frame Relay its efficiency for data networks cause severe performance problems for real-time voice applications. Sizable delay can be introduced by frame buffering. Worse yet, frame buffering and the serialization of variably sized frames introduce jitter (variable delay).

NOTE

Across an international Frame Relay circuit between Bogota, Colombia and San Jose, California, USA, I was accustomed to a small-packet ping time of 200 to 300 ms during periods of low network utilization. During periods of high network utilization, the ping time would soar to 2000 ms or more. Buffering in the circuit vendor Frame Relay switches is the culprit.

Since 1991, the Frame Relay Forum (FRF) has published a series of Implementation Agreements (IAs) that extend the functionality of Frame Relay networks and provide a consolidated standard reference for vendor interoperability. Table 8-1 lists the FRF IAs published as of this writing.

Table 8-1 *Frame Relay Forum IAs*

Document	Description
FRF.1.2	UNI; references ANSI T1.617 and ITU-T Q.933; describes customer connection to a provider via a LMI
FRF.2.2	NNI; enables Frame Relay VCs to cross multiple provider networks
FRF.3.2	Multiprotocol Encapsulation; provides a network-layer protocol identification (NLPID) field to identify the frame payload
FRF.4.1	Switched Virtual Circuit (SVC); enables short-lived VCs that can be associated with different endpoints
FRF.5	Frame Relay/ATM PVC Network Interworking; enables transit of Frame Relay frames across an ATM network
FRF.6	Frame Relay Service Customer Network Management
FRF.7	Frame Relay PVC Multicast Service and Protocol Description
FRF.8.1	Frame Relay/ATM PVC Service Interworking; enables ATM endpoints to communicate with Frame Relay endpoints
FRF.9	Data Compression over Frame Relay; enables payload compression using a negotiable algorithm; support for ANSI X3.241-1994 (LZS) data compression is mandatory
FRF.10	Frame Relay NNI Interface SVC; enables switched VCs to cross network provider boundaries
FRF.11	Voice over Frame Relay (VoFR); provides subchannels within a PVC for separate voice calls, and a method to interleave VoFR frames between large frame fragments
FRF.12	Frame Relay Fragmentation; includes end-to-end and UNI methods for fragmenting large frames and interleaving small time-sensitive frames between the fragments
FRF.13	Service Level Definitions; includes delay as a service level parameter

Table 8-1   *Frame Relay Forum IAs (Continued)*

Document	Description
FRF.14	Physical Layer Interface; includes T-1/E-1, T-3/E-3, HSSI, SONET, and others
FRF.15	End-to-End Multilink Frame Relay; describes sharing multiple VCs for a single logical connection
FRF.16	Multilink Frame Relay UNI/NNI; provides an IMUX or inverse multiplexing function for multiple physical circuits to share a single Frame Relay LMI connection
FRF.17	Frame Relay Privacy; describes link-layer encryption methods and interaction with FRF.9 compression, FRF.11 voice, and FRF.12 fragment/interleave services
FRF.18	Network-to-Network FR/ATM SVC; Service Interworking

Frame Relay and Voice Traffic

Figure 8-5 illustrates the relationship between different Frame Relay protocols for voice services. Note that VoFR is associated with FRF.11, and VoIP over Frame Relay is associated with FRF.12.

Figure 8-5   *Protocol Architecture for Frame Relay Services that Support Telephony*

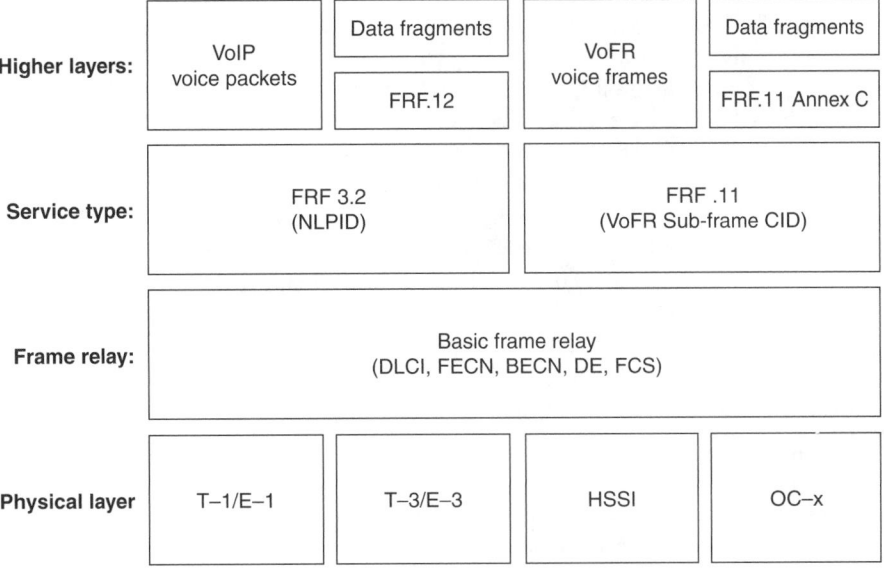

Although Figure 8-5 only lists four examples, Frame Relay may use any of the physical layers specified in FRF.14. The basic Frame Relay header contains the DLCI for the VC, congestion notification bits, and a discard eligible bit, while the trailer contains a frame check sequence.

If a VC transports any VoFR voice frames, then all frames are encapsulated within FRF.11 VoFR subframes. Voice frames are directly encapsulated in a VoFR subframe, while other data in the PVC is fragmented according to FRF.11 Annex C, which inserts an FRF.12 fragment header within the VoFR subframe.

If a VC is used for VoIP over Frame Relay, then all frames are encapsulated in FRF.3.2 multiprotocol over Frame Relay headers. Data packets are fragmented and prepended with a FRF.12 fragment header, while VoIP packets are carried directly in the FRF.3.1 header with no fragmentation. Because FRF.12 requires ordered delivery of the fragments, it would not be possible to interleave VoIP packets between fragments of large frames if VoIP packets had FRF.12 headers. Note that the treatment of VoIP packets with FRF.12 has not been standardized, but Cisco has developed the solution presented here, which is not in conflict with any of the FRF implementation agreements.

VoFR

FRF.11 provides a standard way for hardware vendors to transmit VoFR frames on a VC, and also to transmit data frames on the same VC. This is achieved with a VoFR subheader that includes a subchannel identifier (CID) to distinguish voice frames from data frames.

Figure 8-6 illustrates the format of a VoFR frame that uses FRF.11 encapsulation. All Frame Relay frames begin with a 1-byte flag with the bits {01111110}. The main Frame Relay header contains a 10-bit DLCI, the FECN and BECN bits, and a DE bit. In the VoFR subframe header, the extension indicator (EI) and length indicator (LI) bits signal the presence of additional header bytes. The VoFR sub-CID is used to distinguish between voice and data subchannels that share the PVC. You may have heard this address called a sub-DLCI. If the CID is greater than 63, then the EI bit must be set so that an extra byte is present to encode the rest of the CID value. The EI bit must also be set to identify a nondefault payload type. For VoFR frames, the payload type of the subframe is {0000} for voice samples (which is the default), {0001} for dialed digits, {0010} for signaling bits, {0011} for fax relay, and {0100} for silence information descriptors. The payload length field is only present if there are two or more subframes within a frame. The last subframe in a frame does not have a payload length field.

NOTE   In Figures 8-6 through 8-9, bits are transmitted from left to right (just as you would read them), from the top rows to the bottom rows.

Figure 8-6 *VoFR Frame Using FRF.11 Subframe Encapsulation*

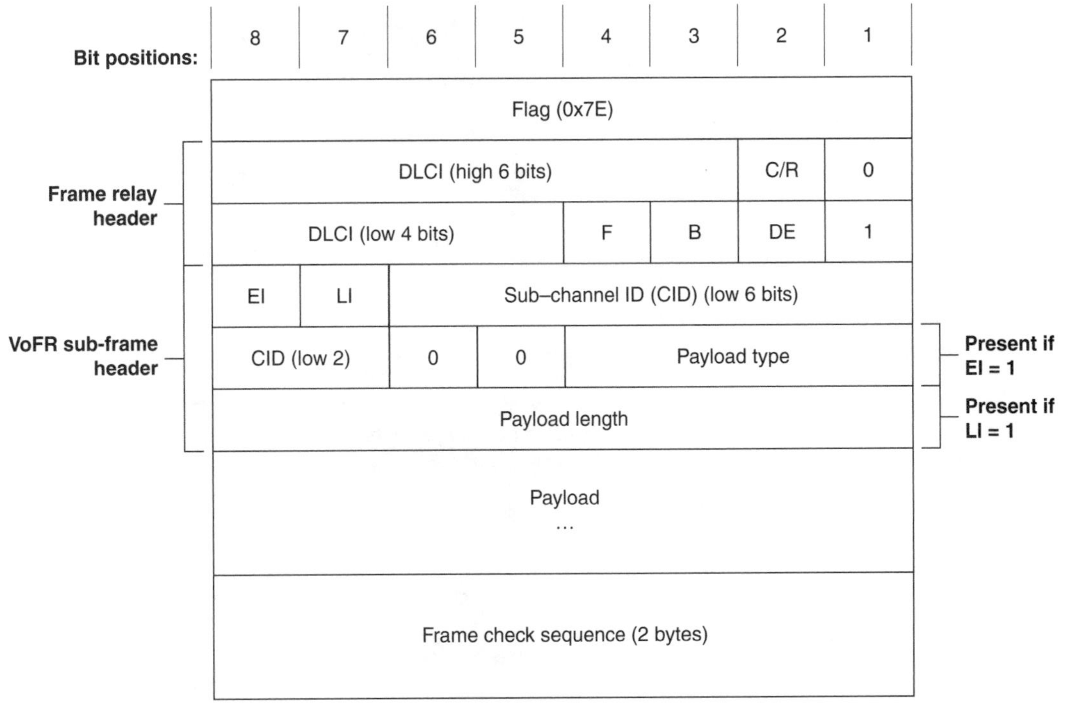

Data traffic that shares a VC with VoFR traffic still uses the FRF.11 subframe header, but also uses the FRF.11 Annex C format for data as illustrated in Figure 8-7. The flag and the basic Frame Relay header are the same as for voice frames, but the short version of the VoFR subframe header is used (with a CID that identifies data traffic). Per FRF.11 Annex C, an FRF.12 fragment header is included within the VoFR subframe. The payload is a fragmented data frame.

When VoFR and data frames share the same PVC, Cisco routers recognize the voice frames and give them transmission priority over the data fragments, which reduces delay and jitter.

Figure 8-7 *Data Frame Using FRF.11 Annex C Encapsulation*

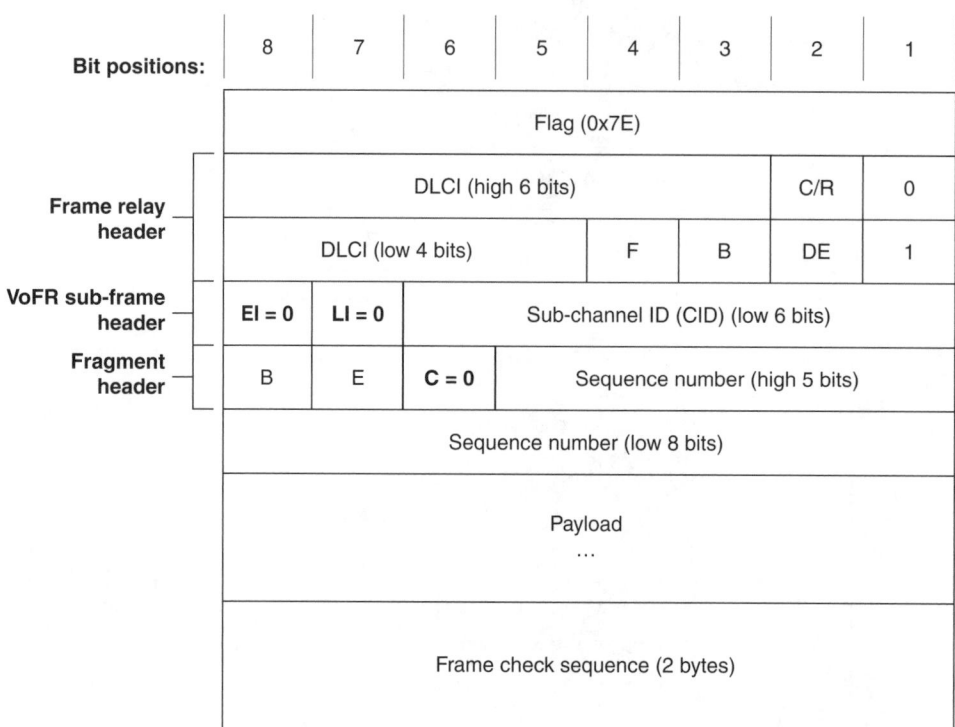

VoIP over Frame Relay

FRF.12 provides a link-layer fragment/interleave (LFI) method that enables Frame Relay networks to behave similar to cell relay networks. With FRF.12, any small frames that have real-time requirements, such as VoIP packets, can be interleaved between fragments of larger data frames. When large frames are fragmented to an appropriate size, the variable delay associated with the frame serialization is reduced.

Figure 8-8 illustrates the frame format of a data frame that has been fragmented and encapsulated according to FRF.12 End-to-End. Note that the network layer protocol identification (NLPID) for FRF.12 fragments is {0xB1}. The standard assignments of NLPIDs are available in ISO TR 9577. The B bit (for beginning) is set in the first data fragment of a larger frame. Similarly, the E bit (for ending) is set in the last data fragment of a larger frame. Note that if B and E are both set, the fragmentation header is prepended to an unfragmented payload. Cisco routers can accept such frames, but will never generate them. The sequence number is required to ensure ordered receipt of the fragments prior to reassembly.

Figure 8-8 *Data Frame Using FRF.12 Fragment Encapsulation*

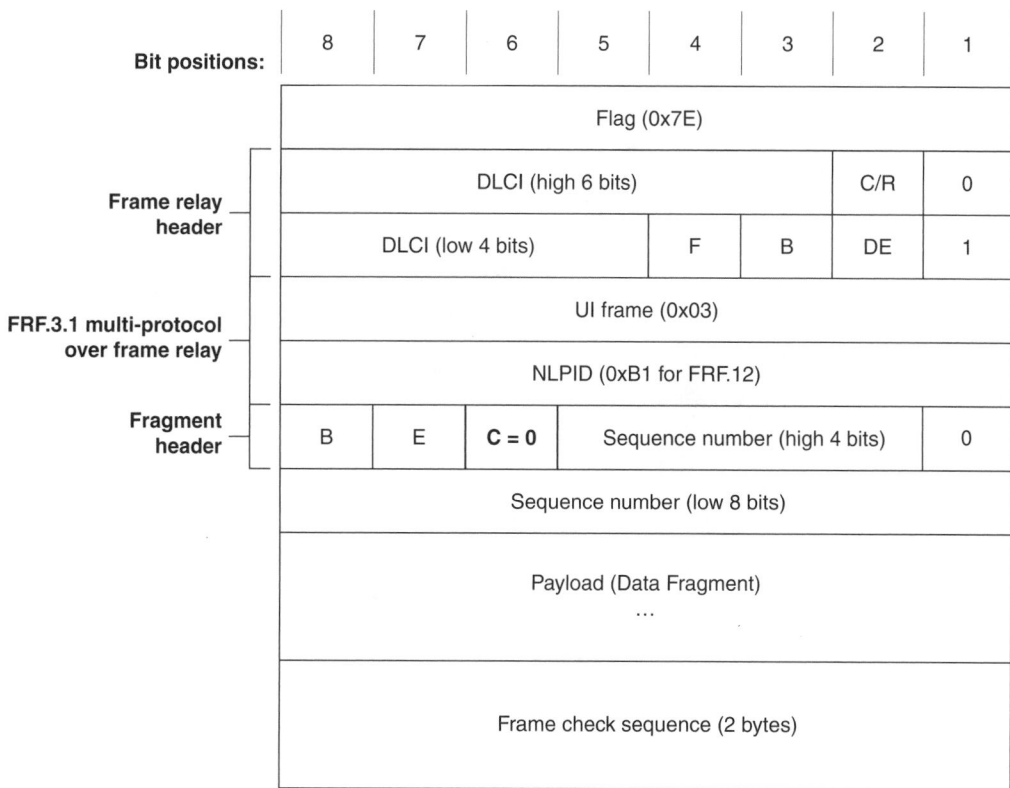

It may seem odd at first, but VoIP packets do not use FRF.12 fragment headers. The reason for this, as mentioned in a preceding paragraph, is that FRF.12 fragments must be delivered in the proper order (as determined by sequence numbers in the FRF.12 fragment header). VoIP packets use a different NLPID than FRF.12 fragments, so VoIP packets can be interleaved between fragments of larger frames without violating the sequencing rule of FRF.12. If VoIP used an FRF.12 fragment header, then VoIP packets interleaved between data fragments would cause the fragment sequence numbers to be out of order, which would violate the requirements of FRF.12.

VoIP packets are encapsulated as would be any other IP packet using the FRF.3.2 multiprotocol over Frame Relay encapsulation. (See Figure 8-9.) The NLPID for IPv4 is {0xCC}. Again, ISO TR 9577 contains the standard assignments of all NLPID values. Note that the frame format of Figure 8-9 applies to VoIP packets whether or not Routing Update Protocol (RTP) header compression is used (see Chapter 11 for VoIP details).

Figure 8-9   *VoIP Frames Are Not Fragmented and Do Not Use FRF.12 Encapsulation*

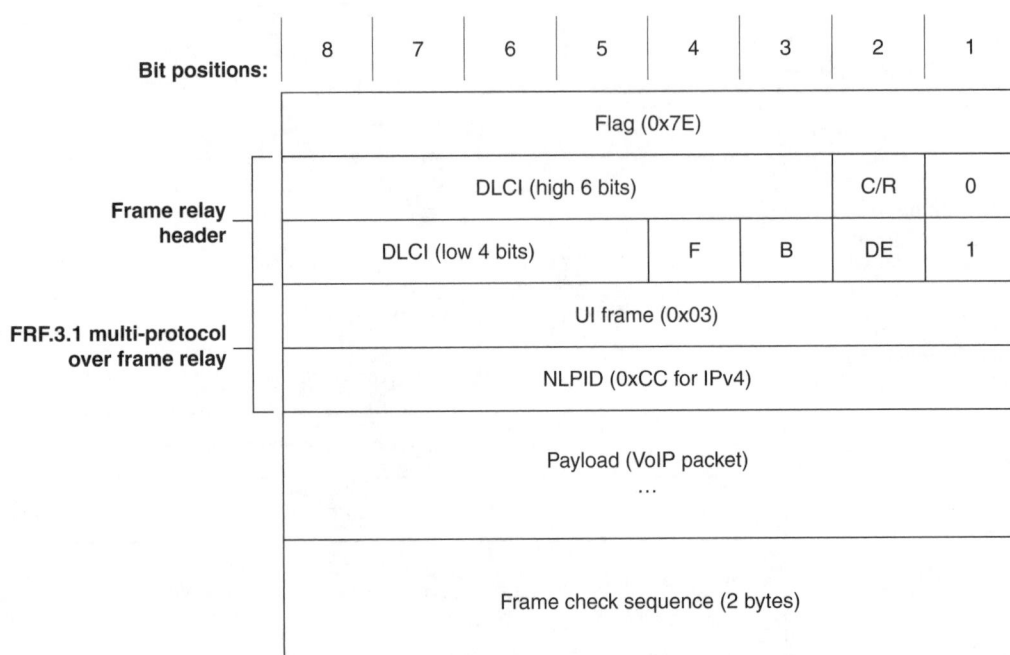

ATM

ATM technology was designed from the beginning to create an integrated multiservice network:

- Cell-relay technology is ideally suited for coexistence of applications with a variety of service requirements. The small fixed cell size enables voice, video, and other real-time applications to meet performance goals, even when interspersed with bulk file transfers and other high-throughput traffic. Frame-based services have had to incorporate fragment and interleave extensions to emulate the behavior of fixed size cell services for real-time applications.

- The QoS features associated with the ATM Adaptation Layers (AAL) enable traffic prioritization and policing at the link layer. These QoS policies may be implemented solely in the ATM protocols, or they may support prioritization policies of upper-layer protocols. These policies enable performance guarantees in terms of cell loss, cell delay, and cell-delay variation. This is precisely the type of network control required for telephony applications.

There are many features and dimensions to ATM technology, but this book will focus on a few key elements that are most necessary to understand voice/data integration issues. This section provides a high-level overview of the elements of ATM technology, followed by a discussion of AAL and QoS classifications. These QoS classifications will then be mapped to applications recommended by the standards bodies. The following sections discuss these topics:

- Overview of ATM
- AAL
- AAL and QoS

Chapter 9 explores current industry practices for ATM from a hardware and network service offering perspective, and clarifies key issues for VoATM.

NOTE   Although ATM provides a multilayer protocol stack with network-wide addressing, for the purposes of this book we will consider ATM as a link-layer (Open System Interconnection [OSI] layer 2) WAN protocol.

Overview of ATM

The ATM protocol space is divided into Control, Management, and User Planes. The Control Plane is responsible for ATM addressing and routing, and all issues associated with virtual connections. This plane enables ATM to support SVCs. The Management Plane monitors the User Plane and Control Plane, ensures that data flows meet performance contracts, and performs a variety of network management tasks. These functions are outside the scope of this book. Figure 8-10 provides an overview of the User Plane protocol layers associated with ATM:

ATM cells may ride over many physical layer technologies, including copper, fiber, and wireless. Each link between ATM switches may use a different physical layer without affecting the upper layers. For the purpose of designing or evaluating a voice/data network, we do not need to be concerned with the mechanisms of ATM transport across the various physical media.

The ATM layer uses a fixed-size 53-byte cell. The fixed size virtually eliminates cell-delay variation introduced by serialization delay—but jitter may still enter the system from other sources. The fixed cell size also enables hardware vendors to create ATM switching hardware that operates efficiently at high cell-switching rates. Figure 8-11 illustrates the simple format of an ATM UNI cell.

Figure 8-10   *ATM User Plane Protocol Stack*

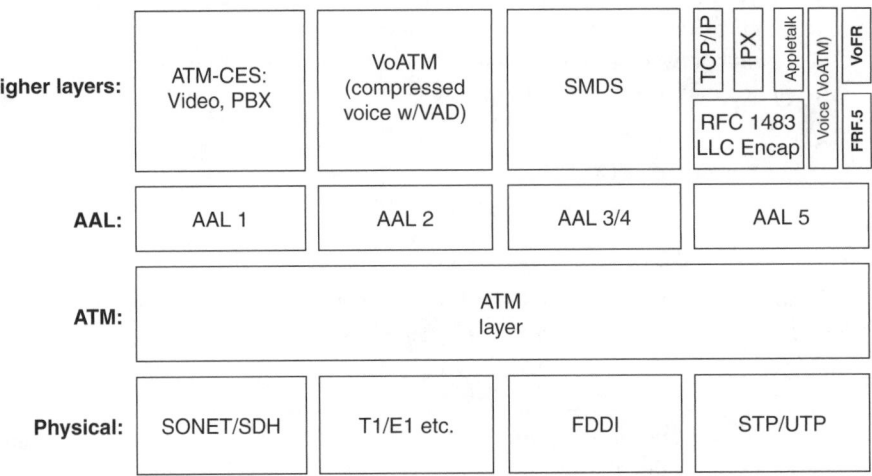

NOTE   An ATM NNI cell is very similar to a UNI cell, except that the Generic Flow Control (GFC) field from a UNI cell is removed, and the virtual path identifier/virtual channel identifier (VPI/VCI) fields are expanded to accommodate a greater number of VCs.

Figure 8-11   *Format of an ATM UNI Cell*

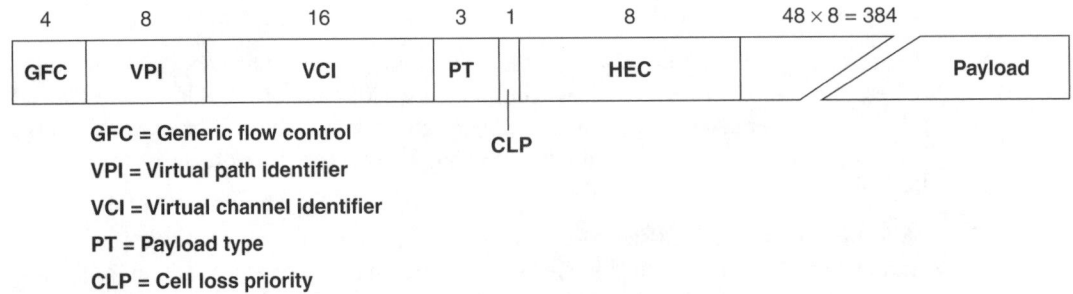

The GFC field in the ATM UNI cell is normally set to all zeros, indicating an uncontrolled flow. This field can be used to prioritize multiple ATM traffic flows entering a single congested interface. This function is similar to the function of IP precedence bits. Because the GFC field is not present in the NNI cell, this field is not passed across an ATM network.

The GFC field may be used within a switch to help prioritize among inbound connections contending for a congested outbound trunk.

The VPI/VCI fields identify the virtual path and the virtual channel of the virtual circuit. Figure 8-12 presents a hypothetical use of virtual paths and virtual channels to connect routers and PBXs across an ATM network. Each site has DS–3 access to the network provider ATM cloud. A separate virtual path connects each site. Within each virtual path, a separate virtual channel maps to different endpoints within a site (such as a router and a PBX). Note that the diagram depicts logical connections, not physical connections:

Figure 8-12 *Possible Application of VPI/VCI Values*

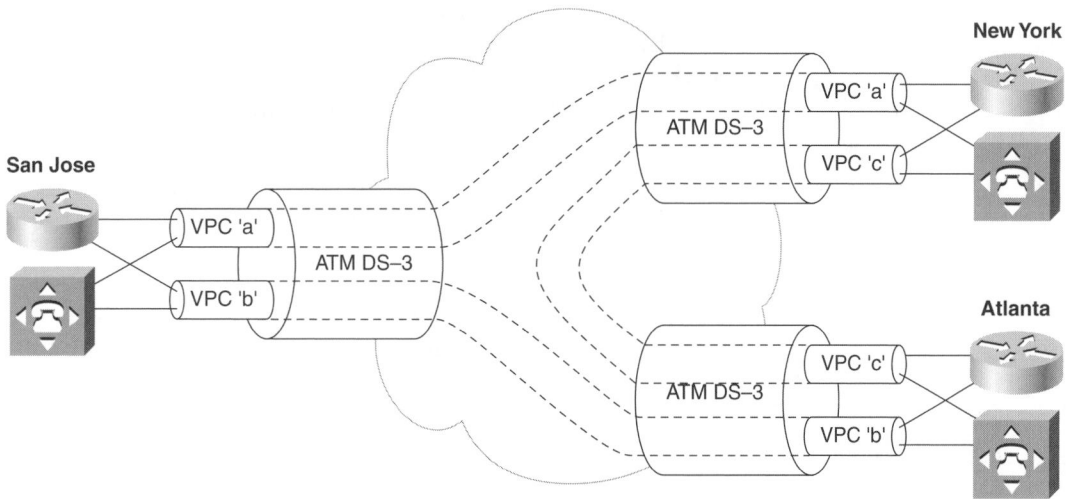

The Payload Type (PT) field of the ATM cell encodes multiple pieces of information. The first bit indicates whether the cell is a user data cell or a management cell. For user cells, the next bit is the Explicit Forward Congestion Indication (EFCI) bit. This is analogous to the FECN bit of Frame Relay. There is no analogous BECN functionality in ATM. The last bit for user cells is an AAL Indication bit, which may be used differently by different AALs. AAL5 uses this bit to mark cells that encode the end of a datagram. This simplifies the logic and hardware required to reassemble a datagram from cells. For management cells, the last 2 PT bits encode the type of management cells, including:

- End-to-end Operations, Administration, and Maintenance (OAM)
- Segment OAM
- Resource management

The Cell Loss Priority (CLP) bit has a similar function to the DE bit in a Frame Relay header. That is, a cell with CLP=1 may be discarded to maintain the service quality for

CLP=0 cells. When a network service provider documents cell-loss ratios, average delay, or cell-delay variation for a given class of service, the type of traffic should be identified as the CLP=0, CLP=1, or CLP={0 or 1} flows.

The 1-byte Header Error Control (HEC) field detects any single and many multiple-bit errors in the ATM cell header. If any errors are detected with this process, then the cell is discarded.

ATM Adaptation Layers

Referring to Figure 8-10, we move up the protocol stack of the User Plane. The AAL enables the network to have different characteristics for different application types. A very appealing feature of ATM is that these different network characteristics are all provided within a single framework. The hardware-switching function of ATM is streamlined in the 5-byte ATM header, and the differentiated services are provided in the AAL header within the payload portion of each cell.

The initial AAL types correspond with the four classes of service identified by the ITU-T in the I.362 Recommendation. These classes are summarized in Table 8-2.

Table 8-2 *ITU-T–Defined Service Classes from I.362*

Service Class	Constant Bit-Rate Required?	End-to-End Timing Required?	Connection-Oriented?
Class A	Yes	Yes	Yes
Class B	No	Yes	Yes
Class C	No	No	Yes
Class D	No	No	No

Class A service is for applications with the most stringent performance requirements. This service is similar to that provided by clear-channel TDM circuits, so it is sometimes called ATM Circuit Emulation Service (ATM-CES). This service class provides a constant bandwidth, with a high quality of service, while preserving end-to-end timing integrity. Timing is important for some applications, such as uncompressed audio/video streams or PBX common-channel signaling. Any application with a predeterminable constant bandwidth consumption that requires good QoS is a candidate for Class A service. Network providers may refer to this service as Constant Bit Rate (CBR) service.

Class B service is similar to Class A, except that there may not be a continuous traffic stream. For example, compressed real-time video or audio connections may require end-to-end clock synchronization (which implies small delay and delay variation), but these connections may come and go. There is no need to reserve bandwidth for a videoconference that is not in progress. The bandwidth requirement may vary even within an audio or video session, because of voice activity detection, or a compressed video image with high- and low-motion segments. These are examples of applications that generate a variable bit rate but require a high QoS.

Distinguishing Class B service from Class A service enables a network to use bandwidth more efficiently. A Class B application may have pauses and gaps, during which other applications can make use of the bandwidth. If this class did not exist, then a Class A service would be used with a constant reserved bandwidth equal to the application peak rate. Some of the reserved bandwidth would remain idle during periods of nonpeak utilization. Network providers may refer to the Class B service as Variable Bit Rate–real time (VBR-rt) service.

Class C service does not provide the end-to-end timing that is provided by Class A and Class B services, but it is still well suited for connection-oriented applications. This service may be used in an ATM backbone that transports X.25 or Frame Relay.

Class D service offers the minimum performance guarantees among services with a specified QoS. Connectionless applications with no real-time requirements or end-to-end timing requirements may still need a guaranteed amount of throughput or some bounds for delay. IP traffic, or SMDS services transported across an ATM backbone are examples of this service class. Both of the Class C and Class D services may be called Variable Bit Rate– non real time (VBR-nrt) by network providers.

The original AAL1 through AAL4 definitions correspond with the Class A through Class D services. AAL3 and AAL4 have subsequently been combined to form AAL3/4. This AAL is primarily used to transport SMDS traffic across an ATM backbone. AAL5 was subsequently added to provide a streamlined and easy-to-use AAL, hence the nickname SEAL, or Simple Efficient Adaptation Layer. This has become the default AAL for applications that do not require CBR service.

From a voice/data integration perspective, the primary ATM adaptation layers are:

- AAL1
- AAL2
- AAL5

The most common application of AAL 1 is for connecting PBXs or video-conferencing equipment via emulated circuits (ATM-CES). The end equipment sees this connection as a clear-channel TDM circuit. The CBR service (as opposed to the VBR-rt service) is required when PBXs use common channel signaling (CCS). The data signals on the control channel may require the end-to-end timing consistency of a synchronous serial connection, so the CBR service ensures that the signals receive the highest QoS. Note that AAL1 CBR service is the least bandwidth-efficient ATM service, because bandwidth is reserved even if it is not used for user traffic.

The ATM Forum recommends AAL2 for narrowband (T-1/E-1 or lower bandwidth) trunking applications, according to af-vtoa-0113-000, which was published in February

1999. In other words, AAL2 is generally recommended for VoATM in the WAN, where multiple voice channels must be supported between user locations. If you have an ATM WAN and you want to use Voice over ATM (VoATM) as opposed to VoIP over ATM, then AAL2 is technically your best option.

AAL5 has been an interim solution for VoATM before the general deployment of AAL2. The ATM Forum also recommends AAL5 for VoATM to native ATM endpoints, according to af-vtoa-0083-001, which was published in February 1999. This Voice over ATM to the Desktop specification mandates the G.711 codec, so the specification is primarily applicable to LAN environments. AAL5 is also appropriate for VoIP over ATM, provided QoS guarantees are available. AAL2 may be more appropriate for VoIP if the circuit vendor does not offer suitable guarantees with respect to delay and delay variation for AAL5.

AAL and QoS

The AAL selected for a VC does not fully specify the QoS characteristics for the VC. The QoS is defined in terms of the following QoS parameters:

- CLR = Cell Loss Ratio
- PIR = Peak Information Rate (cells/second)
- SIR = Sustained Information Rate (cells/second)
- MIR = Minimum Information Rate (cells/second)
- MBS = Maximum Burst Size (cells)
- CDVT = Cell Delay Variation Tolerance (micro-seconds)

Table 8-3 shows the relationship between the service type a network provider might specify, the AAL type associated with this service, and the QoS parameters associated with this service.

Table 8-3 *Relationship Between ATM Service Names, AAL Type, and QoS Parameters*

Service Name	AAL	QoS Parameters Defined
CBR	AAL1	CLR, PIR, CDVT
VBR-rt	AAL5	CLR, PIR, CDVT, SIR, MBS
VBR-nrt	AAL5	CLR, PIR, CDVT, SIR, MBS
ABR	AAL5	MIR, PIR
UBR	AAL5	none

It is important to note that many network providers do not support all service types. Of particular importance to VoATM, many providers do not offer a VBR-rt service (based on AAL2). CBR service is the only reliable VoATM solution if VBR-rt service is not available.

A VBR-nrt service may be acceptable if the CDVT and MBS are sufficiently small. Be aware that AAL2 services are emerging in the marketplace.

Summary

We have focused on clear-channel T-1/E-1 circuits, ISDN, Frame Relay, and ATM as the WAN protocols for integrated voice/data transport. Clear-channel T-1/E-1 circuits provide excellent QoS, but TDM is inherently inefficient. Frame relay makes efficient use of bandwidth, but it lacks formal QoS definitions. ATM offers formal QoS definitions, utilizes bandwidth better than TDM circuits, but has more bandwidth overhead than Frame Relay. Chapter 9 examines these trade-offs and shows how several technologies may be fused to provide an improved voice/data network design.

Additional Reading

Black, U. *Sonet and T1: Architectures for Digital Transport Networks.* Boston: Prentice Hall, 1997.

Buckwalter, J. *Frame Relay: Technology and Practice.* Boston: Addison-Wesley, 1999.

Cisco Systems. *Cisco IOS Wide Area Networking Solutions.* Indianapolis: Cisco Press, 1998.

Kessler, G. *ISDN: Concepts, Facilities, and Services.* San Francisco: McGraw-Hill, 1993.

McCarty, R. *Cisco WAN Quick Start.* Indianapolis: Cisco Press, 2000.

McDysan, D. *ATM: Theory and Application.* San Francisco: McGraw-Hill, 1994.

Design Considerations for WAN Protocols

Designing WAN networks can be challenging at times because you, the network manager, do not have control over all elements in the network. You cannot eliminate transmission delays between distant offices. In many cases, you cannot optimize equipment configurations, such as buffer depths, in the service provider network. You must do the best you can to improve performance through the network provider cloud, and rely on tuning your own network elements to make up the difference.

Recall from Chapter 7, "Quality of Service Criteria for Packet Telephony," that the quality of service (QoS) goals for a packet telephony network are to maximize reliability, minimize delay and jitter, and minimize bandwidth requirements. This chapter addresses the design considerations and tools that help meet these goals for the following voice/data WAN technologies that were discussed in Chapter 8, "WAN Protocols for Integrated Voice and Data Services":

- Frame Relay
- ATM
- T-1/E-1 Circuits

Frame Relay

Most of the design concerns that relate to Frame Relay and QoS (whether for VoFR or VoIP over Frame Relay) can be categorized as follows:

- Physical layer reliability
- Committed information rate (CIR) versus port speed
- Discard eligible (DE) bit
- Traffic shaping
- Frame Relay fragmentation and interleaving
- Separate virtual connections (VCs) for voice and data
- Adjustments in the provider network

Physical Layer Reliability

Frame Relay technology assumes that the underlying physical layer protocol has a low error rate. However, not all of the contemporary physical layer technologies have low error rates. For example, clean copper wire and fiber optics have low error rates, but microwave and satellite transmissions can have high error rates on rainy days. To maintain low error rates for VoFR and VoIP over Frame Relay, select appropriate physical layer technologies with resistance to weather conditions. You do not always have a choice, especially for international circuits, but you should at least inquire about alternatives.

You can order redundant access circuits and VCs to provide path redundancy. Load-balancing or dynamic utilization of a redundant circuit must be accomplished with an upper-layer protocol. Data protocols such as IP provide this service, but VoFR does not have any standard provisions for load-balancing or dynamic utilization of redundant Frame Relay circuits. On Cisco routers, you can configure redundant dial peers pointing to each VC on the separate access circuits, but any active calls on a VC will fail if the VC fails. Chapter 17, "Establishing Network-Wide Calling Capability," discusses dial peers in detail.

CIR Versus Port Speed

The bandwidth available for a Frame Relay circuit is described in terms of a port speed and a CIR. Figure 9-1 highlights an end-to-end Frame Relay connection and illustrates the relationship between the port speed and the CIR for a Frame Relay circuit.

Figure 9-1   *Relationship Between Frame Relay Port Speed and CIR*

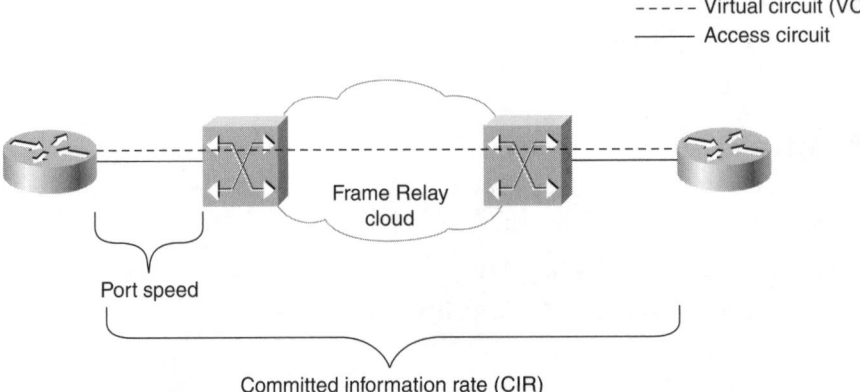

The port speed refers to the clocking rate of the access interface, which is the clear-channel circuit (such as T-1/E-1, HSSI, T-3/E-3) that connects from a router at the customer location to a physical port on a Frame Relay switch in the provider network. The Frame Relay switch is generally located in a central office (CO) or point-of-presence (POP) that is near the customer location, but this is not always the case.

The CIR refers to the end-to-end bandwidth that the carrier is committed to provide for a VC, which is independent of the clocking rate of the physical ports through which the VC is connected. It is common to have multiple VCs flow through a single access port on the carrier Frame Relay switch to the customer location. For example, each of the remote sites is typically connected to a single central site in a hub-and-spoke topology. In such cases, the central site may have a single T-1/E-1 circuit that has many VCs to remote locations.

Unlike time-division multiplexing (TDM) in which individual timeslots must be statically mapped to different locations, Frame Relay VCs are not tied to the timeslot boundaries. The data-link connection identifier (DLCI) in the Frame Relay header determines the VC with which the frame is associated.

Because the VCs are not tied to individual timeslots, the bandwidth that can be allocated to each VC is flexible. The CIR provides a lower bound for the allocated bandwidth, but additional bandwidth (up to the port speed) may be allocated, depending on the level of congestion in the carrier network. Bandwidth usage that exceeds the CIR is referred to as *burst traffic*, and it is common to hear the expression *bursting above CIR*.

Frame Relay customers may be inclined to push data across the provider network in excess of the CIR, which provides more bandwidth at no additional cost. This is one of the main reasons that network managers use Frame Relay circuits instead of clear-channel circuits.

Some network managers carry the idea of economy a little too far and provision several VCs on a Frame Relay port with a combined CIR that exceeds the port speed. They may think that they are saving money on the access circuit. Such designs are contrary to sound logical thinking, because the fundamental design dictates that the customer will never get full use of the committed bandwidth they are purchasing. How can a carrier commit to offering you something that is not physically possible to provide? The key is that it can offer it and take your money for it, but it cannot provide it.

Such flawed designs aside, the fiscal and bandwidth economies of Frame Relay come at the expense of QoS. When a carrier network becomes congested, it buffers frames in interface queues, which reduces the number of dropped frames but increases the amount of delay and jitter. Traffic that exceeds the CIR for a VC is likely to encounter congestion, so bursting above the CIR increases the amount of delay and jitter for the frames in transit. The "bursting" strategy of Frame Relay works when high throughput is the goal, but the strategy fails when real-time voice traffic is introduced. To improve the quality of service for voice traffic crossing a Frame Relay network, *it is critical that traffic does not exceed the CIR on any VC that carries voice frames*.

There are at least three ways to ensure that voice traffic does not exceed the CIR:

- Order CIR from the network provider equal to the port speed.
- Use traffic shaping on the router so that the router does not allow traffic to enter the provider network in excess of the CIR.
- Order separate VCs for data and voice, limit the voice VC to its CIR, and allow the data VC to burst above its CIR.

Ordering a CIR equal to the port speed is appropriate for remote offices with a single VC on a router interface. If you can only have a 64 kbps CIR for a VC that carries voice traffic, then there is no advantage to having a port speed that is larger than 64 kbps. There is little reason to buy a full T-1 port speed that is only a few dollars more, because you get zero benefit out of the added port speed. However, if you plan to upgrade the bandwidth of the VC at some point, it may be simpler to order the higher port speed at the outset and then have a software-only change to increase your CIR when you are ready.

If you have multiple VCs terminated on a single router interface in your network, then you need to use traffic shaping, which is discussed in a following section. Using separate VCs for voice and data is also discussed in a following section.

Discard Eligible Bit

Some people advocate the use of the discard eligible (DE) bit to improve voice quality. This strategy sets the DE bit on data frames only so that data frames will be dropped during congestion instead of voice frames. Voice quality is improved because the probability of dropping voice frames is reduced. While this reasoning is logical, it is also more magnanimous than the typical business would like to be.

If you employ this strategy, the circuit vendor's congested Frame Relay switch will politely discard your data marked with the DE bit and pass your voice frames. You will get less than the CIR you purchase because most of your DE traffic will be dropped. The circuit vendor's other customers will be happy with the amount of data they can burst above their CIR. Your users will complain of poor data network throughput.

Traffic Shaping

The idea of traffic shaping is to transmit frames at a regulated rate, so as not to exceed some bandwidth threshold. In the case of Frame Relay, traffic shaping is intended to let the router retain control of when to buffer or drop frames, when the traffic load exceeds the CIR. If traffic shaping is not used, then the network provider can randomly drop or delay frames that exceed the CIR. When the provider imposes this policy on your traffic, it nullifies any other policies that you have carefully crafted. You can think of traffic shaping as a method to maintain your queuing policies across the WAN. The following section explores this concept in more detail.

Queuing Policy and Loss-Prone WANs

For this discussion, consider a WAN link to be two routers and the WAN circuit between them, as illustrated in Figure 9-2:

Figure 9-2   *WAN Link Composed of a Circuit that Connects Two Routers*

From a queuing perspective, the WAN link can be modeled as a queuing policy enforced by the router, connected to a queuing policy enforced by the WAN. Figure 9-3 illustrates this concept:

Figure 9-3   *WAN Link Modeled as Two Queuing Policies Cascaded Together*

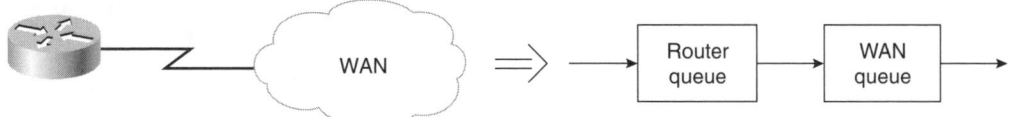

Queuing policies have a cascading effect—filters applied one after the other in succession. All of the queuing stages in an end-to-end traffic flow, whether they are intentional or not, combine to create an effective queuing policy that applies to the end-to-end connection. You must ensure that the intended queuing policies that you create via router configurations are not masked by unintentional policies caused by WAN circuit conditions, intermediate routers, or even other parts of the same router configuration.

If you implement a queuing policy on an outbound WAN interface of a router, the network provider may process traffic in such a way that the router on the opposite end of the link sees a different policy. Consider the following scenario:

1 A WAN interface on a router is configured with a priority queue through which voice traffic is always forwarded ahead of data traffic. During periods of congestion, all voice traffic (up to the circuit capacity) is passed, while data traffic may "starve" in a queue waiting for bandwidth.

2 Meanwhile, during congestion in the provider network, frames sent in excess of the CIR are dropped. From instant to instant, the frames that exceed the CIR are random, so the frames dropped by the provider are random. Many of the dropped frames may be voice frames.

3 To the receiving router, the original priority queuing policy is completely masked! The data stream that arrives at the receiving side does not appear to have voice traffic preferred over data traffic, because voice and data frames have been randomly

dropped. Conceptually, this is the same behavior as a first-in, first-out (FIFO) queue that overflows and drops frames. In fact, most Frame Relay switches in the provider network use FIFO frame queues.

The effective queuing policy for the end-to-end traffic flow is reduced to a FIFO queue, as illustrated in Figure 9-4.

Figure 9-4 *Priority Queue Cascaded with a FIFO Queue Reduces to a FIFO Queue.*

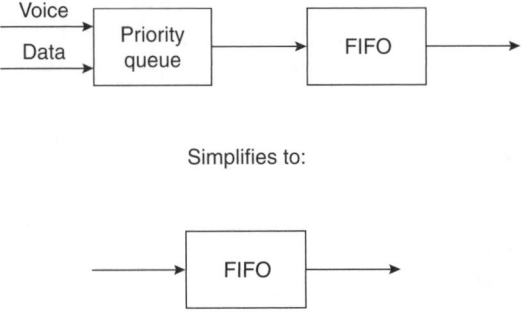

FIFO queues are the simplest queues to implement—they only buffer frames and do not need to distinguish between frame types. They offer the least utility in the face of congestion, because there is no consideration for traffic type—there is a single buffer in which all traffic waits. If the buffer completely fills during periods of congestion, all subsequent traffic is dropped, regardless of traffic type. This treatment obscures any previous queuing policies on the data stream, including priority queuing. FIFO queuing cannot provide any distinct classes of service (CoS) in the face of congestion.

Voice traffic should always be prioritized ahead of data traffic, no matter how much congestion is in the network. Priority queuing for voice traffic ensures that voice will always have the best treatment in the queue. Because voice/data VCs require priority queuing to prefer voice, it follows that voice/data VCs cannot be used in excess of the CIR for the VC. This principle holds for voice-only VCs as well. Although there is no need to prioritize voice frames ahead of data frames on such VCs, the voice frames must not be dropped by the network.

This section has referred to priority treatment of voice traffic in a generic way, but there are several queuing mechanisms to achieve priority queuing treatment for voice. Specific queuing techniques are explored in Chapter 10, "Review of IP Features for Voice/Data Integration," and Chapter 15, "Enabling Network-Wide Quality of Service."

You might have heard the Frame Relay traffic shaping (FRTS) and generic traffic shaping (GTS) algorithms described as token bucket algorithms. Before discussing specific traffic-shaping parameters, the token bucket concept is reviewed here. After an explanation of the traffic-shaping parameters, the specific concerns of real-time traffic are explored. These topics are discussed in the following sections:

- Token bucket concept
- Traffic-shaping parameters
- Traffic shaping and real-time traffic

NOTE   FRTS and GTS have identical algorithms, but they operate at different parts of the transmission path. FRTS is applied at the VC level, whereas GTS is applied at the interface or subinterface level. If you have a single VC for each subinterface, there is little functional difference between them.

Token Bucket Concept

The *token bucket concept*, which is illustrated in Figure 9-5, is a metaphor for one method of controlling the rate of traffic passing a given point in a network. The idea is that frames cannot be transmitted unless they have a token. The tokens are held in a bucket and are immediately given to any frames that are awaiting transmission.

If all the tokens are used up from the bucket, then frames cannot be transmitted until tokens become available. Tokens are added to the bucket at a constant rate, which is equal to the long-term rate at which the frames can be transmitted. If there are no frames to transmit at a given time, then tokens begin accumulating in the bucket. When the bucket is full of tokens, the additional tokens are discarded. You can think of this as "use it or lose it" permission to transmit frames. The number of tokens that the bucket can hold (in other words, the size of the bucket) represents the maximum number of frames that can be sent in a burst of traffic. Following such a burst, the frames must wait until tokens become available.

Figure 9-5 *Token Bucket Used for Traffic Shaping*

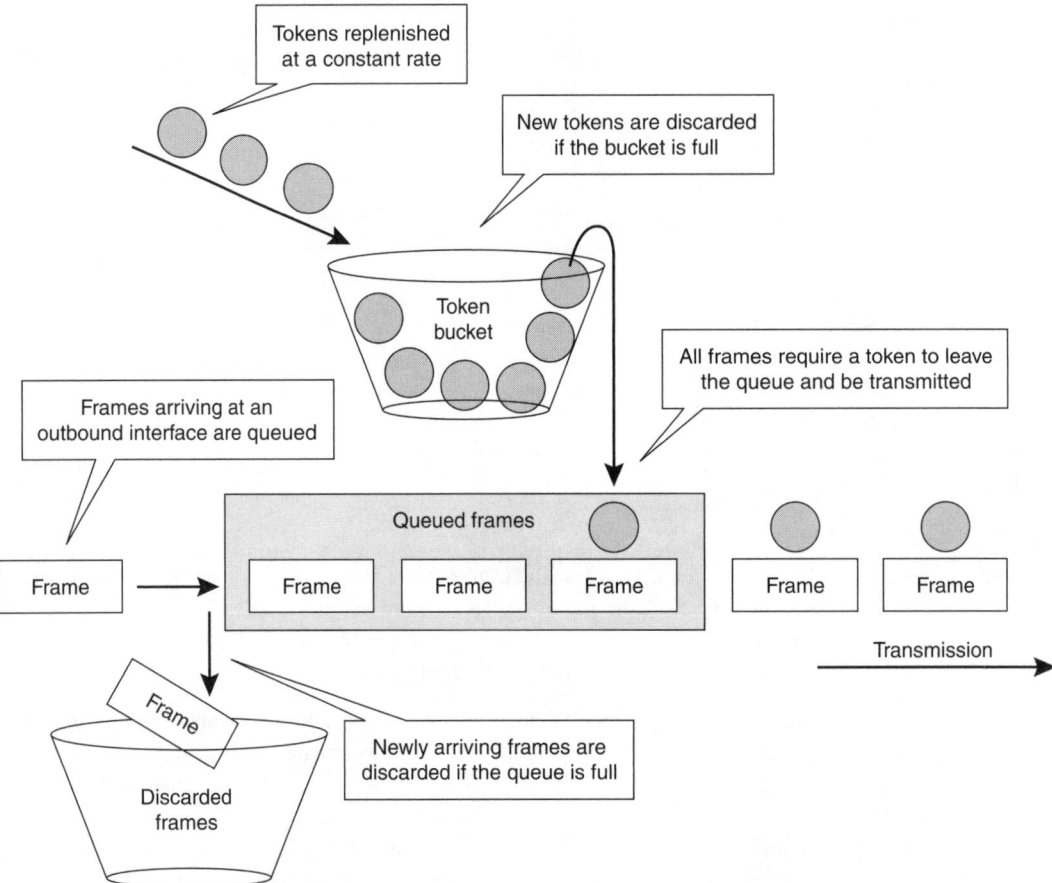

The token bucket control mechanism can be applied to traffic-shaping functions and traffic-policing functions. For traffic-shaping functions, as in Figure 9-5, frames are placed in a queue if the bucket runs out of tokens. Traffic shaping accommodates bursts of traffic, but dampens its burstiness. Traffic policing is more harsh because frames are discarded when the token bucket runs out of tokens. Committed Access Rate (CAR) is a Cisco router feature that implements traffic policing.

Traffic-Shaping Parameters

For FRTS and GTS, each token in the bucket represents a single bit instead of an entire frame. The size of the token bucket represents the committed burst size (B_c), and is measured in bits. The rate at which the bucket is filled represents the CIR, and is measured in kbps. The amount of time required to transmit B_c bits at the rate of CIR is called the *committed time interval (Tc)*. The formula that relates these three variables is:

$$T_c = \frac{B_C}{CIR}$$

At this point, the analogy to the token bucket begins to break down. The way that FRTS and GTS really work is that the bucket is filled with tokens, and then a burst of bits (equal to B_c), as opposed to whole frames, is transmitted until the supply of tokens is exhausted. The bits are then blocked from transmission until the token bucket is filled, and then another burst of bits is transmitted until the bucket is emptied again.

It may be more clear to abandon the metaphor and directly explain the meaning of the traffic-shaping parameters. The *CIR* is the average rate of traffic that the carrier commits to transporting on a macroscopic time scale (that is, over several time intervals that span a few seconds or longer). B_c is the actual number of bits that the carrier commits to transport on a microscopic time scale (within a single time interval, typically a fraction of a second). T_c is the amount of time it takes to transmit B_c bits at the committed rate.

The CIR and B_c values are explicitly defined in most cases, and T_c is implicitly defined by the other two variables. For example, a carrier commits to transporting 64 kbps across a VC. When you configure a router for traffic shaping on this VC, you define the CIR = 64000 bits/sec, and you can select any value for B_c, based on what you want T_c to be. For normal data applications, the value of T_c is not significant, but you must pay close attention to this value when real-time voice frames are involved. The following section discusses suitable values for T_c and B_c when voice frames are present.

Committed burst (B_c) does not refer to traffic that exceeds the CIR. Bursting above CIR is an engineering slang expression that really describes *excess burst (B_e)*. B_e is the number of bits in excess of B_c that may be transmitted in a time interval, or within 1 whole second (which can be many time intervals). B_c relates to traffic within the CIR on a microscopic time frame, and B_e relates to traffic that exceeds the CIR on a microscopic time frame.

The traffic-shaping process in a Cisco router can respond to the backward explicit congestion notification (BECN) bit in the Frame Relay header of received frames. When the router receives frames with the BECN bit set, it decreases the amount of traffic that it lets flow to the VC. The configured cir value actually represents the amount of bandwidth that you hope to achieve on a sustained basis, which can be larger than the actual CIR. The configured mincir value represents the minimum rate at which the router should transmit when it receives BECNs. The traffic-shaping algorithm uses the configured cir value for the sustained traffic rate until BECNs are received, and then the mincir value is used for the sustained traffic rate.

Traffic Shaping and Real-Time Traffic

Recall that traffic should never exceed the CIR on VCs that transport voice frames. Because the B_e value relates to traffic above the CIR, you should always set $B_e = 0$ for VCs that carry voice traffic.

Data-only networks can take advantage of the BECN response feature of traffic shaping to optimize throughput, but this feature causes delay and jitter problems for VoFR and VoIP over Frame Relay. The QoS penalty is more significant than any increased throughput for voice traffic. When a router receives a BECN, there has already been congestion at some point in the Frame Relay cloud, so frames from the VC are already being delayed. Even though the router can decrease the transmission rate, the damage to voice quality has already been done. It would be better for the router to send traffic at a lower rate and avoid the congestion conditions. When voice frames are present on a VC, you should disable the BECN response feature, and set mincir and cir equal to the actual CIR of the VC.

B_c and T_c should be chosen to minimize delay and jitter introduced by the traffic-shaping process. To understand how traffic shaping relates to delay and jitter, consider the mechanics of how traffic shaping works. The router is allowed to transmit B_c number of bits within the time interval of T_c. This rate is equal to the CIR. Within each time interval, though, there is no requirement for how fast or how slow the router transmits the bits.

As illustrated in Figure 9-6, the router transmits B_c number of bits at the actual clocking rate of the interface (which is the Frame Relay port speed), and then stops transmission until the T_c is expired. The router then transmits another B_c bits at the interface clocking rate, and waits idle until the next T_c expires. This process yields the stop-and-go transmission behavior illustrated in Figure 9-6.

Figure 9-6 *Stop-and-Go Transmission Behavior of Traffic Shaping*

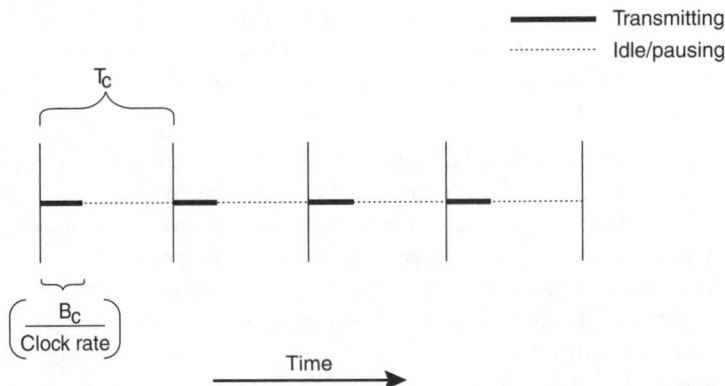

The thick line represents the time when the router is transmitting at the full clock rate, and the dotted line represents the time that the router is pausing, or throttling the transmission. The pausing time, which introduces delay and jitter, consumes a larger proportion of the time interval when the port speed is much larger than the CIR. Three factors can increase the length of the pause cycle, and therefore increase the delay and jitter:

- High Frame Relay port speed
- Low CIR
- Large T_c

When you are at the stage of designing the traffic-shaping parameters, the Frame Relay port speed and CIR have already been determined. Therefore, you must reduce the T_c to reduce the delay and jitter.

In Cisco routers, you do not explicitly configure T_c. Instead, you configure B_c, which implicitly (in conjunction with the CIR) determines the time interval. As a rough guideline, the time interval should not exceed 10 ms for VCs that carry voice traffic. Rearranging the equation stated earlier, and using a value of 10 ms for T_c, yields the following formula for B_c:

$$Bc \leq (0.010) \times CIR$$

To simplify matters, you can configure B_c to the minimum value that the router will allow. If you are running older versions of Cisco IOS, the value of B_c may not be configurable to a small enough value to achieve the 10-ms goal for T_c. You should be running current IOS versions to take advantage of various new voice features, so in practice this will not be a problem.

There is an important and nontrivial interaction between traffic shaping and fragmentation. Because a given fragment does not necessarily align within a single time interval of transmission, the transmission may be paused within a fragment that precedes a voice frame, or even during the voice frame itself. Rather than delving into the details of this complex interaction that determines the effective serialization delay, just try to minimize the pause interval by reducing B_c. In no case should the value of B_c be larger than the frame fragment size. Frame Relay fragmentation is discussed in the following section.

Frame Relay Fragmentation and Interleaving

The following sections explore these aspects of Frame Relay fragmentation and interleaving:

- Why is fragmentation necessary?
- Selecting a fragment size
- FRF.12 User-Network Interface (UNI) versus end-to-end
- Fragmentation or traffic shaping first?

Why Is Fragmentation Necessary?

Even when voice frames are always queued ahead of data frames, and traffic is shaped to the CIR to preserve this queuing policy across the WAN cloud, there may still be a problem with delay and jitter. Consider the following scenario:

1 A voice queue is empty, and a data frame is ready for transmission.

2 After the first few bits of the data frame have started transmitting, a voice frame arrives.

3 The data frame happens to be part of an FTP session, and is 1500 bytes long. The circuit has a clocking rate equivalent to 128 kbps. It will take:

$$\frac{(1500\ bytes) \times (8\ bits/byte)}{(128,000\ bits/sec)} = 93.75\ ms$$

for the data frame to finish transmitting before the voice frame can be sent!

This is quite unacceptable performance—not only is it a lot of delay, but all of the delay is subject to variation. This type of delay is called serialization delay, or blocking delay. During this time, the playout buffer at the receiving end is most likely drained and the underrun causes a discontinuity in the played-out voice signal.

The solution to this problem is to decrease the size of the frames that may be in mid-transmission when voice frames arrive. Link fragmentation and interleaving provides this function. Refer to Chapter 8 for a discussion of FRF.11 Annex C fragmentation for VoFR, and FRF.12 fragmentation for VoIP.

Fragmentation is worthless if voice frames cannot be interleaved between the fragments. The objective of fragmenting frames is to reduce the serialization delay that a voice frame may experience. If a data frame arrives at an interface for transmission before a voice frame, it is first broken into fragments, and then each fragment is queued for transmission. As soon as a voice frame arrives, it is placed immediately next in line for transmission, after the fragment that is currently transmitting.

Selecting a Fragment Size

Because the goal of fragmenting frames is to decrease the serialization delay encountered by voice frames, it follows that the target fragment size should be based on the target serialization delay. You can determine the maximum serialization delay caused by a fragment using the following formula:

$$serialization\_delay = \frac{fragment\_size}{effective\_clock\_rate}$$

An arbitrary guideline for the maximum serialization delay is 10 ms.

In the absence of traffic shaping, the effective clock rate is simply the clocking rate of the physical interface, which is equal to the Frame Relay port speed. An interface with traffic shaping rapidly alternates between periods of transmission and pausing, which lowers the effective clock rate to the committed information rate (CIR) configured in the traffic-shaping process. Because traffic shaping is mandatory for VoIP over Frame Relay (unless the CIR = port speed), and for VoFR in all cases, then the effective clocking rate is always equal to the CIR.

Rearranging terms and substituting variables in the preceding equation yields the following formula for the fragment size:

$$fragment\_size = (0.010\sec) \times CIR$$

A simple rule of thumb based on this formula is 80 bytes of fragment size for every 64 kbps of CIR. Thus, a VC with 384 kbps of CIR would need a fragment size of $6 \times 80 = 480$ bytes.

TIP   The Frame Relay fragment size should increase by 80 bytes for every 64 kbps of CIR on a VC.

When there are multiple VCs on a single router interface, such as at the head end (central site) of a hub-and-spoke network, then each VC should be independently configured with the fragmentation and traffic-shaping requirements for the VC. Figure 9-7 illustrates a hub-and-spoke Frame Relay network in which each VC has a different CIR.

Because all of the VCs share the same Frame Relay port at the CO, it may seem that the large fragment size of one VC could cause serialization delay for another VC that uses a smaller fragment size. For example, a 960-byte fragment going to site A (based on 768 kbps CIR) could conceivably cause a long serialization delay for voice frames going to site D, because that VC only uses a fragment size of 70 bytes. However, the port speed at the CO is clocking at 1536 kbps (excluding the 8-kbps framing), so a 960-byte fragment introduces only 10 ms of serialization delay. If you also consider the effects of traffic shaping on each VC, then the 960-byte fragment might be split across two separate time intervals. In this case, the pause period increases the serialization delay by 5 ms, to a total of 15 ms. As you can see, there is not a problem with multiple VCs with different CIRs on a Frame Relay port.

Figure 9-7   *Different CIR Values for Each VC in a Hub-and-Spoke Frame Relay Network*

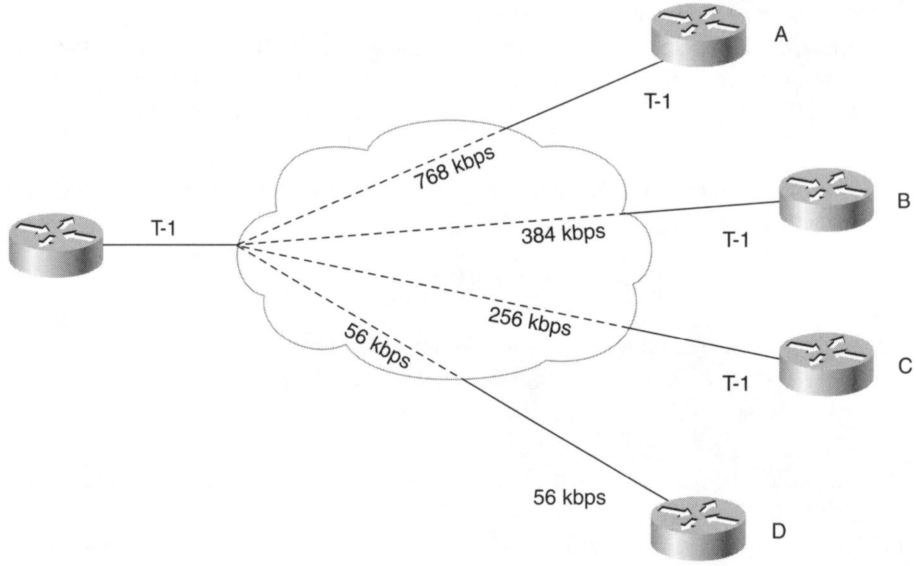

A more serious concern is the additive serialization delay of multiple VCs. For example, if there are 20 VCs that each have a CIR of 64 kbps, then each of the VCs contributes 10 ms of serialization delay (in a worst case from being split across two traffic-shaping time intervals). If the VCs are serviced in a round-robin fashion, then a voice frame waiting in one of the VCs can wait for $19 \times 10 = 190$ ms! The solution to this problem is the "dual FIFO transmission buffer," which creates a priority queue at the transmit buffer to prefer voice frames from one VC ahead of data frames from another VC. See Chapter 10 for a discussion of dual FIFO transmit buffers.

FRF.12 UNI Versus End-to-End

When you need to send VoIP packets and data packets across the same Frame Relay port (even if there are different VCs), there are two ways that FRF.12 frame fragments can be arranged:

- FRF.12 UNI: fragment headers before the normal Frame Relay header
- FRF.12 end-to-end: fragment headers within the payload of the normal Frame Relay header

In the first scenario, FRF.12 is acting as a UNI protocol—the circuit provider must interpret the FRF.12 header and reconstruct the original frame. By removing the fragmentation at the ingress to the provider network, the bandwidth overhead associated with the extra fragment headers is reduced. Because serialization delay is only an issue on circuits with slow clocking rates, providers typically do not need to use fragmented frames on the trunk circuits between their Frame Relay switches. The frame can again be fragmented at the egress switch for the access circuit to the customer equipment at the destination.

The benefit of FRF.12 UNI fragmenting to you, as a customer of the circuit vendor, is that you have more efficient use of the CIR that you purchase. Imagine that you have voice traffic interspersed with bulk data transfers. Without fragmentation, the data frames have 1500 bytes in the payload and 7 bytes in headers: 1 byte for the flag, 2 bytes for the Frame Relay header, 2 bytes for the FRF 3.1 header for multiprotocol encapsulation, and a 2-byte checksum trailer. When that 1500-byte payload is divided into 19 fragments of 80 bytes each (60 bytes in the last one), you have $19 \times 7 = 133$ bytes of header information. But that is not all. Each fragment also has a 2-byte fragment header, so the overhead is really $19 \times 9 = 171$ bytes. That is about 11.4 percent overhead added by the fragmentation process.

If most of your data traffic is large frames, then the fragmentation process consumes

$$\frac{171 \; bytes}{(1500 \; bytes + 171 \; bytes)} \approx 10.2\%$$

of your bandwidth. By using FRF.12 as a UNI protocol, this extra overhead is only on the access link, and the provider core network is not burdened with the extra traffic. The provider can pass this bandwidth efficiency on to you by not counting the FRF.12 UNI header overhead as traffic contributing to your CIR. In other words, the carrier can measure the CIR as the bandwidth you consume across its backbone—not what you consume across the access circuit. For a 64-kbps VC, you would receive an extra 6.5 kbps of throughput, which amounts to an extra G.723 call that can be supported across the VC! To realize the bandwidth savings, you must have a port speed that is higher than the CIR, so that the CIR of the unfragmented payload and the added FRF.12 UNI headers can be transmitted across the access circuit.

What happens when your Frame Relay circuit vendor does not support FRF.12 but you need to use it? You can use FRF.12 end-to-end fragmenting. When the fragment headers are moved within the payload of the normal frame header, only the end devices need to understand the fragmenting protocol. Of course, every fragment must have the original Frame Relay header. The intermediate Frame Relay switches can operate on the normal Frame Relay header, and do not need to see the fragment headers. As of this writing, Cisco routers only support end-to-end FRF.12, because the FRF.12 UNI fragmenting service is not generally available from Frame Relay circuit vendors.

It is important to note that fragmenting large data frames does nothing to improve voice quality if voice frames cannot be interleaved within the data frame fragments. This implies that the queuing policy (which prefers voice ahead of data) must act on the frame fragments, not the whole frames. As of this writing, Cisco routers support queuing of FRF.12 fragments for the following queuing technologies:

- Weighted-fair queuing (WFQ)
- Class-based weighted-fair queuing (CB-WFQ), and low latency queuing (LLQ)
- IP RTP Priority

NOTE   Note that the traditional priority queuing feature in Cisco IOS does not support queuing of FRF.12 fragments. As a result, priority queuing is not suitable for VoIP on low-speed Frame Relay interfaces.

Fragmentation or Traffic Shaping First?

The order in which fragmentation and traffic shaping occur in a router can have a real impact on your network if you do not plan carefully. Consider a data flow that is first traffic shaped to a CIR of 64 Kbps, and then fragmented to 80-byte fragments (remember 80 bytes per 64 kbps of effective clocking rate). For 1500-byte data frames, the fragmentation process introduces about 10.2 percent extra overhead (the preceding section details this calculation), which translates to about 6 kbps. It may seem that you are sending only 64 kbps of traffic to the network, but in fact you are sending $64 + 6 = 70$ kbps. Because you are sending 70 kbps of data across a VC with a 64-kbps CIR, the carrier may randomly drop or delay

$$\frac{6 \ kbps}{70 \ kbps} \approx 8.6\%$$

of the traffic that you transmit across the network. This high of a frame loss definitely results in poor audio quality.

Now consider that the frames are first fragmented, and then traffic shaped to the CIR of 64 kbps. In this case, there will be no problems, because the overhead of the fragment headers is accounted for in the traffic-shaping process.

Separate VCs for Voice and Data

If you combine voice and data on a single PVC, then you must purchase a CIR equal to the Frame Relay port speed, or you must use traffic shaping to throttle your transmission rate. If you purchase a CIR equal to the port speed, you are effectively purchasing a leased line with the risk of increased delay and delay variation. If you are considering this option, compare circuit prices for clear-channel TDM circuits and Frame Relay circuits with a CIR equal to the port speed. If the prices are similar, order the clear-channel TDM circuit instead. Remember that a key benefit of Frame Relay networks is the ability to send data bursts in excess of CIR for a minimal price. If you are combining voice and data in a single PVC, you sacrifice this benefit.

If you separate voice and data onto separate PVCs, then you can realize the benefit of bursting over the CIR on the data PVC while keeping traffic within the CIR on the voice PVC. To employ this strategy, order PVC for voice with a CIR that accommodates the peak voice traffic, and order a second PVC for data, with a CIR as appropriate.

For example, imagine that you have two locations, each with an E-1 access circuit into a full E-1 port in the local Frame Relay switch. You have a single PVC of 768 kbps for voice and data traffic between the two locations. If you instead order a voice PVC with 128-kbps CIR (to accommodate 10 VoIP calls using G.729 compression and CRTP (see Chapter 10), and a data PVC with 512-kbps CIR, then you can enjoy the benefits of bursting up to full E-1 capacity on the data PVC. You still pay for 768 kbps of CIR, but you can take advantage of extra bandwidth for no additional price. There may be price differences between a single PVC with 768 kbps CIR and two PVCs with a total of 768 kbps CIR, but the concept remains the same.

NOTE You should be aware that there are significant differences between circuit vendors with respect to how they handle traffic bursts above CIR. Some providers do not even offer a CIR, and pass all traffic as bursting traffic. Others offer a CIR, but in practice allow minimal traffic above the CIR.

To use separate VCs for voice and data, there must be some mechanism to sort the traffic and control which frames flow over which VC. This is a simple task for VoFR on Cisco routers, because you can use dial peers to map a VC to voice traffic, and use a serial interface or subinterface to map a VC to data traffic. For VoIP, however, the task is not so simple.

VoIP packets and regular data packets follow the same IP routing rules. Normal IP routing protocols are not sufficient to make the two traffic types route over different links, but there are a number of techniques you can use to send VoIP packets on one VC while data packets flow on another VC:

- You can use policy routing to identify VoIP packets and direct them to a different subinterface (which corresponds to a different VC), but this approach is not scalable. The configuration is a more complex version static routing, and you give up the benefits of dynamic routing.

- There is a feature in Cisco IOS called Priority DLCI groups (see Chapter 15), which enables you to send identified traffic classes over different VCs. For example, VoIP packets can be mapped to the high-priority VC, while all other packets are mapped to the normal-priority VC. The beauty of this approach is that both VCs are in the same IP subnet, so there are no strange requirements for IP routing. Unfortunately, this feature is not supported in conjunction with FRF.12 fragmentation, so you cannot effectively use it with VoIP. By the time you read this, it will be worth checking whether the feature is available in conjunction with FRF.12.

- Careful planning of IP address assignments, along with a minimal use of route filter lists, allows the use of normal IP routing protocols to steer VoIP packets over one VC while data packets use a different VC. This method requires a routing protocol that can use variable length subnet masks (VLSM). The following section provides a description of this method.

TIP   When using separate VCs for voice and data, remember to enable fragmenting and interleaving (FRF.11 Annex C for VoFR, FRF.12 for VoIP) on all data and voice VCs to reduce jitter for the voice PVC.

Routing VoIP and Data Packets over Different VCs

It is desirable to have separate VCs for VoIP and data traffic so that data traffic can burst above the CIR without causing delay or jitter for the voice traffic. For large networks, a scalable approach is required to route VoIP traffic onto a different VC than the data traffic. Policy routing is not a scalable approach because of the detailed configuration requirements that change from router to router, and the lack of support for dynamic rerouting in the case of link failures.

The key to using normal routing protocols to treat VoIP packets and data packets independently is to have a single IP address block that identifies the source and destination addresses of all VoIP flows. For example, you can allocate the address block {192.168.254.0/24}, which includes 256 addresses, to be used for VoIP endpoints. You can assign a single one of these IP addresses to a loopback interface on each VoIP gateway, using a 255.255.255.255 subnet mask. Note that you can have multiple loopback addresses on a router, so you should not have any conflicts if you need to use another IP address on a loopback interface for a different function. Just make sure that you configure the router to use the correct loopback interface for VoIP traffic. You now have a concise way to refer to all VoIP traffic flows using only IP address information, which enables a standard IP routing protocol to distinguish VoIP packets from data packets.

To capitalize on this distinction, you need to create two simple IP access lists that can be reused on every router. The first list identifies only the VoIP addresses, and the second list identifies all other addresses. Using the address block created for VoIP addresses in the preceding paragraph, your access lists would look like this:

```
access-list 1 permit 192.168.254.0 0.0.0.255
access-list 2 deny 192.168.254.0 0.0.0.255
access-list 2 permit any
```

To steer all VoIP traffic to a voice VC, simply apply access-list 1 as an inbound route filter on the voice VC, and apply access-list 2 as an inbound route filter on the data VC. For both EIGRP and OSPF, you can configure the inbound route filters in the router configuration mode as follows:

```
distribute-list 1 in serial 1/0:0.1
distribute-list 2 in serial 1/0:0.2
```

For the remote site routers in a hub-and-spoke topology, these five configuration lines are all that is necessary. Note that the configuration is identical for all remote site routers. For the central site, the same access lists are required, but the two distribute-list entries must be replicated in the router configuration mode for each remote site.

With these minimal additions to the configuration, dynamic IP routing protocols can still be used, while VoIP traffic is steered differently than data traffic. You may need to incorporate variations on this theme, such as a floating static route to point VoIP packets to a different VC when the voice VC fails. A *floating static route* is simply a static route that has a higher administrative distance than a dynamic routing protocol, so that the static route is used as a backup when the dynamic route is not available. Enough information has been provided here for you to experiment with variations on your own.

Note that the routing protocol must support VLSM and routing filters. Also note that this approach does not work when desktop PCs or arbitrary IP endpoints are used as H.323 terminals. It can work with IP telephones, provided that they are in separate subnets from the computers. Ideally, the IP telephones should all be in contiguous subnets that can be aggregated into a single routing entry, such as {10.10.0.0 255.255.0.0}, but this is not necessary.

Adjustments in the Provider Network

There are two aspects of a provider Frame Relay network that you should seek to optimize for the transport of voice traffic:

- WAN switch buffer sizes
- Queuing from the egress WAN switch

You may or may not have luck working with your provider, depending on how flexible it is and how large of a customer you are.

WAN Switch Buffer Sizes

Considering that every frame buffer in the physical transmission path introduces a variable delay component, you should seek to minimize the number of buffers and the size of each buffer in the transmission path. Work with your network provider to ensure that your VCs follow optimal switching paths using the minimum number of frame switches so that your traffic encounters fewer queues. Ask your provider to reduce the per-VC buffer depth for all of your VCs that carry voice traffic. This will reduce the delay and jitter for your traffic, but it will increase the likelihood that your traffic is dropped. Dropping voice frames that would otherwise be buffered for a long time is not a problem, because the frames would arrive at the destination too late to be useful.

Queuing from the Egress WAN Switch

Whenever you order multiple VCs over a single Frame Relay port and access circuit, the issue of egress queuing becomes important. When frames from multiple VCs arrive at the egress port on the WAN switch nearest the destination, frames from one of the VCs must wait while frames from the other source are transmitted. This is bad if the waiting VC carries VoIP or VoFR traffic. If your network provider uses Cisco WAN switches, ask it to enable a feature called *DLCI prioritization*. With this feature, traffic from several VCs can be prioritized such that frames from a voice VC are transmitted before frames from a data VC on the outgoing port.

Summary of Frame Relay Recommendations

Table 9-1 summarizes the Frame Relay design recommendations that were discussed in the preceding sections.

Table 9-1 *Summary of Frame Relay Design Recommendations*

Category	Recommendation
Physical layer reliability	Avoid microwave and satellite links, which can have high error rates during bad weather.
	Use redundant access circuits and VCs to increase resiliency against link failures. Active VoFR calls will be dropped when a link fails, but VoIP calls can be dynamically rerouted to another link.

Table 9-1 *Summary of Frame Relay Design Recommendations (Continued)*

Category	Recommendation
CIR versus port speed	Do not exceed the CIR on VCs with voice frames (whether VoFR or VoIP).
	If only one VC is associated with a port, do not waste money on a port speed that is higher than the CIR.
	Do not let the aggregate CIR of multiple VCs on a port exceed the port speed.
Discard eligible (DE) bit	Do not set the DE bit unless you are willing to donate your bandwidth to other customers of your network provider.
Traffic shaping	Disable BECN response; set mincir and cir equal to the actual CIR.
	Set $B_e = 0$.
	Arbitrary goal for T_c is 10 ms.
	Set $B_c = (0.01) \times \text{CIR}$ to achieve $T_c = 10$ ms.
	If traffic shaping happens before fragmentation, fragment headers are not included in the traffic-shaping process. This causes the router to transmit traffic in excess of the actual CIR.
	To solve the problem of traffic shaping not accounting for fragment headers, decrease the configured cir and mincir below the actual CIR, such that when added with the overhead of the fragment headers, the traffic does not exceed the real CIR.
Fragmentation/ interleaving	Use the CIR, not the port speed, to determine the fragment size.
	The rule of thumb is to add 80 bytes of fragment size per 64 kbps of CIR on the VC.
	Independently assign the fragment size for each VC.
	Use FRF.11 Annex C for VoFR, and FRF.12 for VoIP.
	Use FRF.12 UNI fragmenting for VoIP if it becomes available.
	Do not mix VoFR and VoIP on the same VC. VoIP frames will be stuck behind queued data frames.
	If you must mix VoFR and VoIP on the same physical interface, the VoFR frames in one VC will always have strict priority ahead of VoIP frames in another VC. VoIP frames can be prioritized ahead of data frames within a VC, but the dual FIFO transmit buffer always prefers fragmented frames over unfragmented frames. VoIP frames are unfragmented, and therefore, not preferred.

continues

Table 9-1   *Summary of Frame Relay Design Recommendations (Continued)*

Category	Recommendation
Separate VCs for voice and data	A single VC for voice and data is the most simple, but you cannot let data traffic burst above the CIR.
	Separate VCs for voice and data enable the voice traffic to stay within the CIR while the data traffic can burst above the CIR.
	Separate VCs for voice and data is easy to implement for VoFR, but is a little more work for VoIP.
	The most scalable solution to use separate VCs for VoIP and data is to assign all VoIP gateways in a summarizable IP address range and use route filters to steer traffic between VCs with a dynamic routing protocol (EIGRP or OSPF).
Adjustments in the provider net	Ask the network provider to reduce the per-VC buffers at the ingress and egress of the network.
	Ask the provider for DLCI Prioritization on the egress WAN switch near the destination.

ATM Circuits

You get what you pay for when it comes to cell delay variation and cell loss in ATM networks. Most circuit vendors offer a constant bit rate (CBR), a variable bit rate (VBR-nRT), and an unspecified bit rate (UBR) service. As of this writing, very few vendors offer a VBR-rt service, though this area may see rapid growth. The CBR service is typically on AAL1, while the VBR-nrt and UBR services are AAL5. Emerging VBR-RT services use AAL2 or AAL 5.

Cisco routers support VoATM using AAL5, and AAL2 is available for the MC3810 as of IOS 12.1(2)T. Enhanced feature support for AAL2 on the MC3810 and availability for other platforms is on its way. Cisco routers and ATM switches can also use CBR for circuit emulation services (ATM-CES), which emulates a synchronous TDM circuit across the ATM cloud. ATM-CES is commonly used to provide transparent tie-line connections between PBXs, but the ATM-CES function should be considered as a separate technology from VoATM. Unlike VoATM, which incorporates some knowledge of the voice payload, the ATM-CES service provides a generic and opaque pipe with a high quality of service. A router or switch using ATM-CES only passes information to the fixed endpoints, as opposed to interpreting call signaling and digits, and routing calls.

VBR-nRT is the best small-scale VoATM option that is generally available from many circuit vendors. Fortunately, the performance targets for the VBR-nRT services are often quite acceptable for telephony applications. For example, one large regional Bell operating company (RBOC)—an incumbent local exchange carrier in the United States—offers a fractional T1 VBR-nRT service with a cell delay variation tolerance (CDVT) equal to 6 ms.

A playout buffer of 10 ms can accommodate the delay variation introduced by these links (but you must still account for serialization delays and other sources of jitter within the routers).

Be very careful before jumping into a migration plan though, because some vendors do not provision multiple service classes on circuits below T1 access speeds. This means that you cannot purchase 384 kbps of VBR-nRT service for voice traffic, and have 1152 kbps for UBR data traffic. Do not lose hope prematurely—just make sure to ask your circuit vendor about the exact details of the ATM services they offer. Ask for written verification of the QoS parameters described in Chapter 8, and make sure that multiple service classes can be provisioned on a single access circuit.

In addition to pure ATM services, many circuit vendors offer Frame Relay to ATM service interworking (based on FRF.8.1). This technology helps you migrate away from Frame Relay to ATM, or include Frame Relay links in an ATM WAN when ATM is not supported at all remote locations. You can migrate the central site of a hub-and-spoke Frame Relay WAN to ATM, and the carrier provides the conversion for the remote sites that still have Frame Relay. Remote sites can then be converted one at a time to ATM services. This is a nice migration path if you want to have an integrated voice/data/video network with robust support for QoS in the WAN. If you want the integrated services now, but public ATM support for fractional T-1/E-1 is not available, consider clear-channel circuits as a temporary alternative. If you run VoATM on top of the leased lines, you can have the equipment and network ready for when your circuit provider offers the ATM services you want.

VoX over Clear-Channel T-1/E-1 Circuits

The traditional TDM approach to using clear-channel circuits for voice/data integration is now considered an inefficient use of WAN bandwidth. However, clear-channel circuits do provide excellent performance to minimize delay variation. The new approach to using these circuits combines the best features of clear-channel circuits and other protocols to create very attractive voice/data integration options. VoX technologies may be used in conjunction with the following WAN technologies over clear-channel T-1/E-1 circuits:

- Private Frame Relay over clear-channel T-1/E-1
- Private ATM over clear-channel T-1/E-1

Private Frame Relay over Clear-Channel T-1/E-1

To use VoFR on a clear-channel circuit, you must configure the routers to provide Frame Relay encapsulation across the clear-channel circuit, instead of the normal High-Level Data Link Control (HDLC) or Point-to-Point Protocol (PPP) encapsulation. One of the routers must be configured to act as a Frame Relay switch and provide the Frame Relay DCE functionality. This router advertises the configured VCs to the Frame Relay DTE router via the Local Management Interface (LMI). Do not confuse the serial connection DCE and DTE with Frame Relay DCE and DTE. In a lab environment where two routers are connected back to back, one of the routers must be configured as the DCE to provide physical clocking to the other router. This is different from the Frame Relay DCE, which identifies the network side of the UNI for Frame Relay.

In a typical real-world scenario using clear-channel circuits, both routers will be configured as serial DTE devices that receive clocking from the carrier or external CSU/DSU. However, one of the routers must be configured to act as the Frame Relay DCE. If you have a central site, configure the routers at this site as the Frame Relay DCE end of the circuit. This will enable you to perform Frame Relay switching between remote sites if this is desirable in your network.

Because you are using a clear-channel circuit, you do not have to worry about exceeding the CIR for the PVCs you create, and you do not have to worry about traffic shaping (except that VoFR software in Cisco IOS requires traffic shaping to enable the transfer of voice frames). You only need to configure a single PVC across the circuit for voice and data. There are situations in which you may want to have multiple PVCs from a remote site. For example, you may want to terminate voice traffic on a small voice router (also known as a multiaccess concentrator), and offload the data traffic to another router via Frame Relay switching. Make sure you have valid design motives and assumptions before heading down this path.

Because serialization delay is an issue for any WAN technology, you still need to use FRF.11 Annex C fragmentation and interleaving as appropriate for the CIR (which should be set to the full clocking rate) of the interface. Deciding on the fragment size is less complex than for public Frame Relay circuits, because the clocking rate of the interfaces on either end of the circuit are the same.

Private ATM over Clear-Channel T-1/E-1

VoATM should be used with clear-channel circuits only when you want to incorporate video or another ATM-CES service along with voice and data. In this case, you can use the same clear-channel circuit to multiplex all of these traffic types. If you only have voice and data services on the circuit, then the cell overhead of ATM is excessive for a clear-channel circuit. (See Figure 9-8.) You already have good performance for delay variation in the WAN because you have a clear-channel circuit. You need appropriate queuing techniques to ensure that end-to-end delay variation remains low, but you do not need any of the mechanisms of ATM for a private circuit.

TIP	Only use VoATM over a clear-channel circuit when you also need to run video or another ATM-CES service.

Figure 9-8 *Headers Consume 43.4 Percent of a VoATM Cell*

ATM header	Voice header	Voice payload	PAD	AAL5 trailer
5 bytes	4 bytes	~30 bytes	6 bytes	8 bytes

$$\frac{23}{53} = 43.4\% \text{ Overhead}$$

The preceding paragraph is directed to narrow-band VoATM deployments for most companies. There is definitely a large niche for VoATM over private clear-channel circuits, but this mainly applies to very large enterprise environments. In this case, a company might have multiple sites with large Frame Relay or ATM WAN switches. The switches would be connected via clear-channel T-1/E-1 or T-3/E-3 trunks. Such a network environment is really a model of a circuit vendor network and is beyond the scope of this book.

Summary

Good voice quality can be supported over Frame Relay, ATM, or clear-channel T-1/E-1 circuits. ATM provides explicit service guarantees, and clear-channel circuits have inherently good performance for delay variation. Frame Relay circuits can be challenging because of the lack of service guarantees for frame loss rates, delay, and delay variation. Hybrid solutions that employ VoFR or VoATM over clear-channel circuits combine the best features of these link-layer technologies into an attractive package. However, cost may still be a restrictive issue for using clear-channel circuits.

Chapter 8 and Chapter 9, "Design Considerations for WAN Protocols," have explored voice/data integration at the link layer (OSI layer 2). An issue with link layer voice/data integration is that devices at every hop must be aware of the voice and data applications. As the size of the network grows, managing the separate voice and data relationships at every link can become unwieldy. For small networks, a hub-and-spoke VoFR solution may be convenient. For larger networks, the scalability of layer 3 dial peers and centralized call routing (via H.323 gatekeepers, SIP proxy servers and registrars, or media gateway controllers) makes VoIP an attractive solution. QoS for VoIP is introduced in Chapter 10 and Chapter 11, "VoIP Transport and Signaling Protocols," explores the transport and signaling aspects of VoIP.

CHAPTER 10

Review of IP Features for Voice/Data Integration

This chapter describes many IP features that improve Quality of Service (QoS) for VoIP. You can think of these features as the "data" side of VoIP. Chapter 11, "VoIP Transport and Signaling Protocols," explores the voice side of VoIP, which includes audio transport and call-signaling issues. This chapter is organized into the following sections:

- Managing reliability
- Managing bandwidth, delay, and jitter
- Policy routing to load-share links with different latencies

Managing Reliability

A reliable network should be built from reliable components, including the routers and the WAN links that connect remote sites. Beyond this, the network layer design should create a system that is more reliable than the component link-layer connections and hardware. From a layer 3 perspective, a reliable network accurately routes traffic to the proper destination, and quickly converges following topology changes such as link failures. Routing stability contributes to overall network reliability. Routing tables should experience as few changes as possible, because frequent changes in routing tables can cause routing loops, dropped packets, and excessive processing load on the routers in the network.

In general, follow these guidelines to create a reliable network:

- Create a stable routing environment
- Provision redundant physical paths, and design the routing to use the redundant paths

The preceding points are relevant for any network layer protocol, but layer 3 protocols other than IP are outside the scope of this book.

Creating a Stable Routing Environment

A stable routing environment is resilient to topology changes such as WAN link failures and flapping links. A *flapping link layer connection* is a serial link that frequently changes state between up and down, and can cause frequent changes in the routing table of all routers that learn routes via that link. This can include many routers—not just the routers directly attached to the flapping link. The precious CPU cycles of the router are wasted if they must recalculate routes every time a link flaps. Frequent topology changes also increase the risk that the routers in the network have an inconsistent view of the network; this can lead to routing loops. For these reasons, it is important to control routing such that a flapping link in one part of the network does not cause all of the routers to be burdened with route changes. Only those routers that truly require the information should be aware of the topology change. Imagine what would happen if every router in the Internet updated its routing tables every time there was a flapping link anywhere on the planet!

Route summarization is the primary method of making a routing environment resilient to flapping links. When contiguous IP subnets are advertised as part of a larger address block, the summary route is available to other routers even if some of the subnets are unstable. Consider a typical routed LAN with a hub-and-spoke WAN (shown in Figure 10-1):

Figure 10-1   *Route Summarization Stabilizes Routing in this Environment*

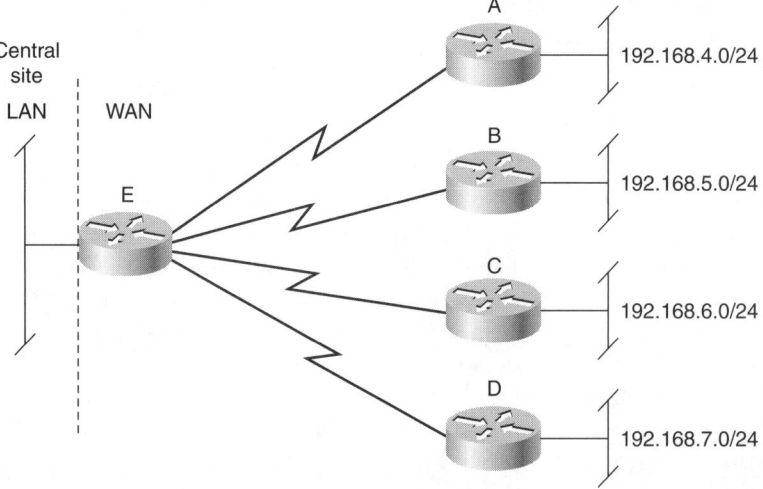

If the central site WAN router advertises four separate subnets to the central site routers, then each of these routes is subject to flapping when the associated serial link flaps. If the central site WAN router advertises only a summary route (for example, 192.168.4.0 255.255.252.0), then only the routers on either end of a flapping link will be affected. It is important to note that in this scenario, the central site WAN router passes only summarized routes to the LAN and to each of the remote sites that comprise the summarized address block. This functions correctly because routers use the longest routing-prefix match when finding a route to a destination. This means that router A in Figure 10-1 will have the following routes (not considering the WAN interface subnets):

192.168.4.0 /24	!for the local LAN subnet
192.168.4.0 /22	!summary address for all four WAN sites

Abbreviated Subnet Mask Notation

If you are not already familiar with the abbreviated subnet mask notation, it is easy to understand. Subnet masks are traditionally represented with the dotted decimal notation used for IP addresses, such as 255.255.255.0, which explicitly identifies the 32-bit subnet mask value. Subnet masks may also be represented with the abbreviated form /xx, where x is the number of leftmost bits that are set to 1 in a 32-bit IPv4 subnet mask. For example, 255.255.0.0 is abbreviated to /16, and 255.255.255.252 is abbreviated to /30. The subnet mask notation applies not only to logical IP subnets, but also to summarized IP routing entries.

A prerequisite to this routing plan is that the routing protocol must understand variable-length subnet masks (VLSM). Otherwise, route summarization is not possible. Without subnet mask information, the routing scheme appears to be two identical routes, and router A cannot forward traffic to routers B, C, or D. Examples of interior routing protocols that are suitable for this task include EIGRP, OSPF, IS-IS, and RIPv2. You should avoid RIPv1 and IGRP because these protocols are not capable of using VLSM.

NOTE   Generally, route summarization is used in a large routing environment. The example of Figure 10-1 illustrates the methodology of route summarization, but the size of the network in the example does not justify summarization. It would be better in this example to have distinct routes for each remote LAN, so you can tell at a glance from any router if a specific site were unreachable.

The routing environment must converge quickly following topology changes, or network reliability may suffer. A slowly converging network may experience routing loops that cause some subnets to be unreachable. Link-state protocols such as OSPF and IS-IS converge quickly, as does EIGRP with the DUAL algorithm. For a detailed discussion of routing protocols, see *CCIE Professional Development: Routing TCP/IP* by Jeff Doyle (Cisco Press 1998).

Redundant Physical Paths

Implicit in the discussion of routing around link failures and topology changes is the existence of an alternate physical path. Consider a variety of failure scenarios, including:

*   A simple WAN circuit failure
*   A router failure
*   A site failure

To plan for a single WAN circuit failure, it is sufficient to provision redundant circuits between a single router at each site, as shown in Figure 10-2.

Figure 10-2   *Redundant WAN Circuits Protect Against a Single Circuit Failure*

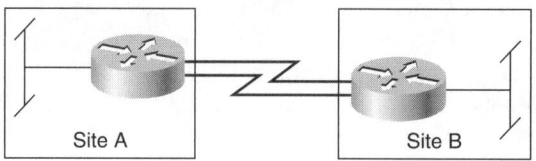

A more thorough redundancy plan also considers the failure of a key router, such as a central site router in a hub-and-spoke configuration, as shown in Figure 10-3.

Figure 10-3   *Redundant WAN Circuits and Central Site Routers Offer Added Protection*

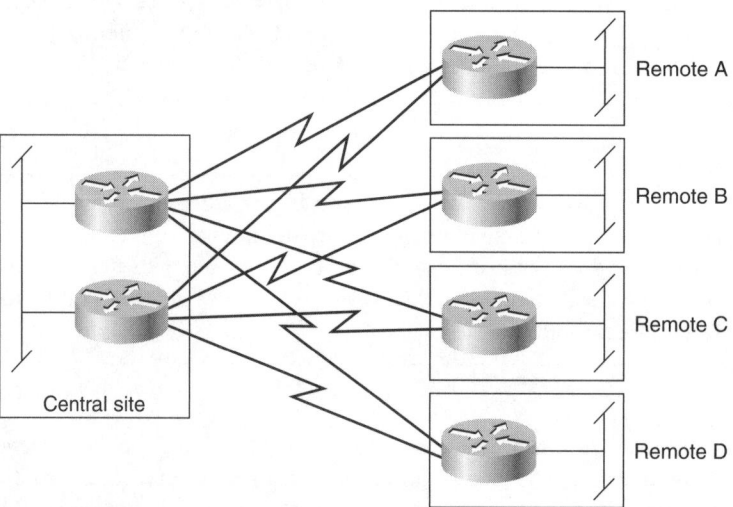

In general, if you use redundant WAN circuits to connect remote sites to a central site, consider having each of the redundant connections terminated on independent routers at the central site. If there are users on the LAN directly attached to the central site WAN routers, then you should use the Hot Standby Router Protocol (HSRP) to provide a more reliable default gateway for these users. (See Figure 10-4.) All of the hosts on the subnet should use the HSRP address for the default gateway. The HSRP protocol running between the Ethernet interfaces of the WAN routers determines which interface actually responds to the HSRP address. If either of the WAN routers fails, then the users will transparently use the alternate router as the default gateway, even though they are only configured with a single IP address for the default gateway.

Figure 10-4   *HSRP Is Recommended when Users and Redundant WAN Routers Are on the Same IP Subnet*

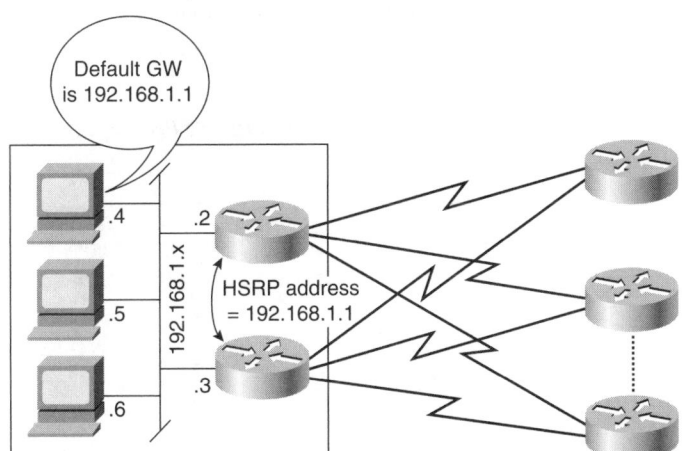

Two medium-size routers might not cost much more than a single large router with similar interfaces. If you have dual T1/E1s to each site, then you can load-balance traffic across each of the circuits. If you are using a primary/backup scenario (such as Frame Relay with ISDN backup) with many sites, then you might be concerned about loading one central site router to capacity while another sits idle. The design shown in Figure 10-5 may have the weakness just described:

Figure 10-5   *One Central Site Router Handles All Primary Circuits, While Another Handles All Backup Circuits*

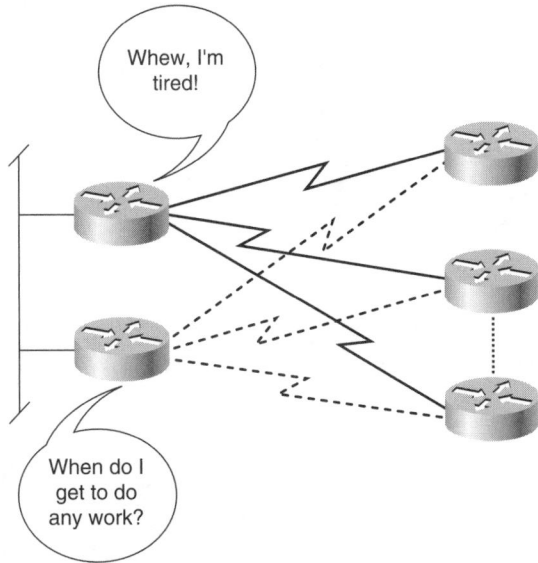

It is desirable to have balanced resources in each router pair at the central site, because either of these routers may be called upon to carry double the load when the other router fails. The design shown in Figure 10-6 can balance the processing and resource load of two central site routers.

Figure 10-6 *Two Symmetrically Configured Central Site Routers Handle Primary Connections for Some Remote Sites, and Redundant Connections for Other Sites*

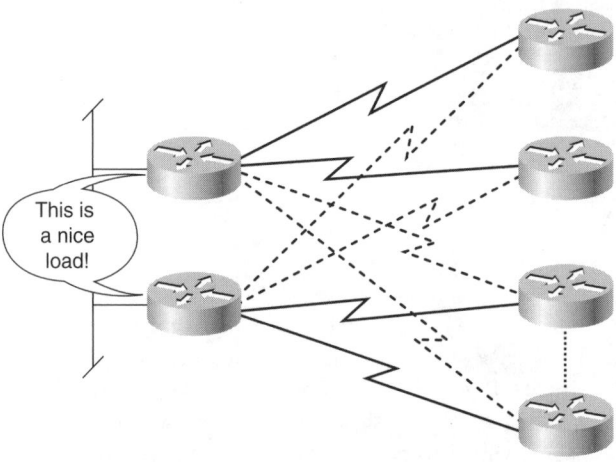

Note that this design ensures that if either of the central site routers fails, then the other will carry all traffic. Also note that during normal operation, each router carries a similar processing load, so resources are equitably distributed between the routers.

This concept can be easily extended to provide site redundancy in addition to router redundancy. Instead of placing both routers on a single rack at a central site, you can provide site redundancy of various magnitudes:

- Different racks and electrical circuits
- Different rooms
- Different buildings at your central campus
- Different continents

The redundant routers each require a connection to the networked resources (such as the central servers), which becomes more complex as the magnitude of site redundancy increases.

The level of redundancy that makes sense for your environment depends on a number of factors, such as:

- How much does downtime cost you? In other words, what is the opportunity cost of not having network communication? Remember that both voice and data services will be lost in the case of an integrated network failure. What happens to your organization if your customers cannot call you?

- What is the likelihood and duration of each failure scenario? A WAN link can take hours to fix, a router might take days to replace, and a site can take years to build.

- Are your voice and data services prepared to leverage a given degree of redundancy? If you lose your central site, do you have mirrored PBXs, voice mail, unified messaging, and various data servers at another site, or are you out of business?

- What is your bottom-line budget for the infrastructure project? If you find yourself with a minimal budget for redundancy but face dire consequences in a voice or data failure scenario, perhaps it is time to make a presentation to the board, your boss, or whoever approves the budget.

This reliability discussion is a fundamental subject, but it has been reviewed here to ensure that you do not deploy VoIP over a questionable IP network. Telephone users have high expectations of availability, and complain vigorously when they lose phone service. You will look bad and achieve high visibility in your company if you deploy VoIP over an ill-designed IP network.

Managing Bandwidth, Delay, and Jitter

This section introduces QOS technology areas that relate to bandwidth optimization and real-time traffic prioritization in an IP environment. These technologies are essential for meeting the bandwidth, delay, and jitter performance requirements of VoIP:

- Resource Reservation Protocol (RSVP)
- Queuing policies
- Traffic policing and shaping (to enforce queuing policies)
- Header compression
- Fragmentation and interleaving
- Dual First-In First-Out (FIFO) transmit buffers
- Mapping IP QoS requirements to Asynchronous Transfer Mode (ATM) service classes

Multiprotocol Networks

If you have multiple network protocols running in a large network, then each protocol must be made to run as efficiently as possible. Your objective is to reduce the bandwidth overhead associated with routing updates and service advertisements, so that sufficient bandwidth remains for voice traffic and actual user data traffic. In addition, you must use a link-layer fragment and interleaving method, because not all network layer protocols have fragmentation mechanisms. Network and link-layer fragmentation methods are discussed later in this chapter.

IPX Routing Information Protocol (RIP) and Service Advertising Protocol (SAP) advertisements are notorious for periodic information flooding that can temporarily consume all of the available bandwidth on a link. Other protocols exhibit similar behavior. While the details of bandwidth management in a multiprotocol network are outside the scope of this book, the following list is a starting point for your research into these topics:

- Use access lists on Cisco routers to block IPX SAP and RIP advertisements from where they are not needed, to reduce periodic traffic bursts that can completely consume the available bandwidth.

- Use access lists on Cisco routers to block AppleTalk zone and AURP updates from where they are not needed, for the same reasons as blocking IPX SAP and RIP advertisements.

- Use EIGRP for IPX and AppleTalk routing across WAN links so that full periodic routing table updates are replaced by occasional event-triggered routing changes.

- Consider static routes for remote sites with a single path to the core network because the overhead of a dynamic routing protocol is not necessary in this situation.

- Only advertise DECnet areas and nodes that are used. Beware that the default behavior of DECnet on Cisco routers is to send frequent reachability updates about all of the 1024 node numbers in an area, even if the nodes do not exist!

- Avoid bridging across routers, especially across WANs with limited bandwidth. Use Media Access Control (MAC) address and type field filters (for example, access lists and access expressions on Cisco routers) to reduce unnecessary traffic if you must bridge (as opposed to route) traffic across a WAN.

For detailed information on these topics, consult the excellent documentation available at Cisco Connection Online, in the Network Protocols Configuration Guides and Command References, Volumes 2 and 3.

Resource Reservation Protocol

RFC 2210 identifies two requirements to provide QoS for real-time traffic in the Internet:

- Routers along a traffic path must have mechanisms to control the QoS given to the packets.
- There must be a way for applications to inform the routers of their QoS requirements.

In order for the routers to control the QoS delivered to traffic flows, applications must specify the type of QoS they require. There are two primary types of QoS guarantees that the user can seek from the network:

- Controlled Load
- Guaranteed QoS

The Controlled Load service, specified in RFC 2211, is for applications that are sensitive to highly loaded or congested network conditions. With Controlled Load service, applications experience end-to-end performance similar to a network that is not loaded. This does not mean that the network appears to be idle; each packet experiences delay as it would in a partially utilized (but not congested) network.

Guaranteed QoS, specified in RFC 2212, provides specified bounds for delay and bandwidth. Packets that receive this service will not experience more than a maximal end-to-end queuing delay determined for the flow, as long as they do not exceed the specified bandwidth. This means that each router must have a queuing implementation that can give priority to packets requiring this service.

Resource Reservation Protocol (RSVP), specified in RFC 2205, is a standards-track method for applications to request QoS guarantees from the network. Like Internet Control Message Protocol (ICMP) or Internet Group Management Protocol (IGMP), RSVP is a signaling protocol that operates directly over IP (that is, it does not require UDP or TCP). RSVP enables routers to dynamically allocate bandwidth for specified flows that require special service. It is designed to work with multicast or unicast traffic, and uses the underlying routing protocols to determine the next hops toward the destination. Instead of the sender specifying the requirements for the reservation, each receiver specifies its own requirements to receive the stream. This enables multiple receivers to request different QoS levels from the same sender. This functionality is useful if receivers can pay for different QoS levels, or if receivers have different levels of available bandwidth. VoIP implementations mostly use unicast RSVP reservations, because most calls are of a point-to-point nature. Conference calls implemented with multicasting require multicast RSVP reservations.

If you are interested in the details of RSVP reservation setup, you should read the RFCs. The following summary refers to Figure 10-7, which illustrates the basic flow of an RSVP reservation setup:

1 The sending application transmits a PATH message toward the unicast or multicast destination (via the default gateway). The PATH message contains the Tspec, which specifies the bandwidth characteristics of the flow.

2 The router caches the information from the PATH message for later use, and forwards the PATH message toward the destination. Every RSVP-capable router in the IP path gleans the flow characteristics from the PATH message, and remembers the previous RSVP-capable router. This will later be used to direct RSVP messages back to the sending application.

3 The final router delivers the PATH message to the receiver, which replies with an RESV message. This message is the actual request for network resources. The RESV message flows back along the path of RSVP-capable routers that was identified with the previous PATH command. The RESV message is still unicast in a multicast reservation, and stops at the point where multiple leaf nodes originate (that is, the nearest branch in the multicast tree).

4 Upon receiving the RESV message, each router checks that it has sufficient bandwidth to make the reservation, and that the receiver is authorized to make the reservation. If both checks succeed, then the router reserves the queuing resources, and passes the RESV message to the next hop RSVP-capable router.

5 When the original sender receives the RESV message, the reservation is complete and the sender begins to transmit data.

NOTE   If a router receives an RESV message and there is not sufficient bandwidth, or the receiver is not authorized, then the router will send an error notification to the receiver that initiated the RESV message.

The senders and the receivers periodically retransmit the PATH and RESV messages so the reservation can track changes in the underlying network topology. The reservation is removed if the PATH and RESV messages are not periodically updated.

Figure 10-7 *RSVP Reservation Establishment Process*

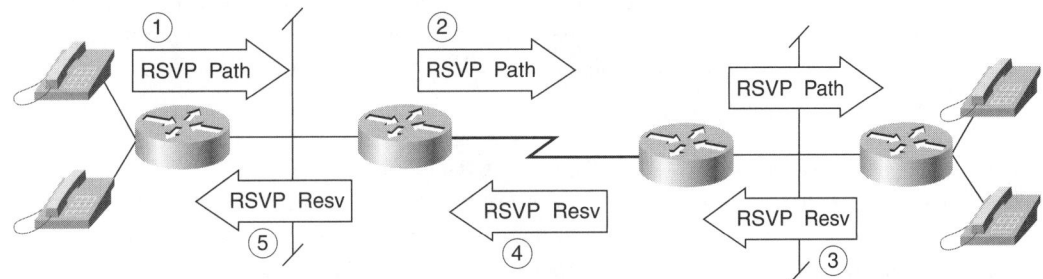

RSVP can accommodate multiple senders in a multicast session with a single reservation. The following reservation styles indicate whether there are one or more senders, and whether or not the senders are explicitly identified:

- Fixed Filter
- Shared Explicit
- Wildcard

The Fixed Filter reservation style is appropriate when there is a single sender for a unicast or multicast session. The Shared Explicit reservation style is appropriate for multicast sessions with multiple senders who are explicitly identified. The Wildcard reservation style enables any host to act as a sender and transmit using the reserved bandwidth for a multicast session.

The Shared Explicit and Wildcard reservation styles are designed to accommodate multiple senders, but not simultaneously. Each RSVP reservation (whether it is Fixed, Shared Explicit, or Wildcard) reserves bandwidth for a single source to actively send at a given time. As such, multicast sessions should implement some sort of a microphone-passing control feature to prevent multiple active senders from exceeding the bandwidth reservation. If multiple senders must transmit simultaneously, then there should be a separate reservation for each simultaneous transmitter.

For a normal unicast VoIP call with only two parties, you should use a Fixed Filter reservation. VoIP audio conferences (based on multicast traffic flows) fit the intended model of the Shared Explicit or Wildcard reservation styles. Each audio conference may have multiple speakers (that is, senders), but only one is generally active at a given time. A single RSVP reservation (for example, Shared Explicit or Wildcard) can accommodate the entire conference for any number of participants, as long as there is only one active speaker at a time. For audio conferences in which anyone is authorized to speak and multiple parties may speak at the same time, you can implement multiple RSVP reservations of the Wildcard style. If you want to accommodate two simultaneous speakers, then you need two Wildcard reservations. You would need three Wildcard reservations to support three simultaneous speakers, and so on.

NOTE There is a caveat concerning the use of RSVP with VoIP. Since each reservation requires a source and destination IP address and UDP port to define the reserved flow, an RSVP reservation cannot be established until after the VoIP call setup identifies the UDP port numbers used for the call. In H.323 networks, for example, an RSVP reservation cannot be attempted until after the H.245 media control negotiation. At this point, the call has already been connected via H.225.0 call control (see Chapter 11). In this situation, the call setup may succeed when there is not enough bandwidth available for a successful reservation, which leads to a call with poor voice quality (if the audio path is established without the reservation). Alternatively, the audio path may not be established, even though the call-setup signaling is already complete. In either case, RSVP is not an acceptable method of providing connection admission control (CAC). Calls that exceed the bandwidth allotment are still connected, possibly to the detriment of the voice quality of other active calls.

If RSVP is not a useful CAC mechanism for VoIP, then it should at least ensure good QoS treatment. While RSVP reservations do ensure very favorable treatment from a Weighted Fair Queuing (WFQ) process, WFQ + RSVP is not sufficient to ensure strict queuing priority for VoIP packets. To ensure adequate QoS treatment for VoIP packets, you should use the IP RTP Priority feature in conjunction with WFQ, or the Low Latency Queuing (LLQ) feature in conjunction with Class-Based WFQ (CB-WFQ). These features are conceptually explored later in this chapter, and examined from an implementation perspective in Chapter 15, "Enabling Network-Wide Quality of Service."

In summary, RSVP is not an adequate CAC or QoS mechanism for VoIP as of this writing, so it is of questionable value in real network implementations. However, future protocol advancements and developments within Cisco IOS will make RSVP a useful CAC mechanism. CAC will become increasingly important as VoIP endpoints expand beyond Cisco routers to include arbitrary endpoints in an enterprise network.

Consult the RFCs for more information about RSVP, or check with the RSVP Working Group of the Internet Engineering Task Force (IETF). The Information Science Institute (ISI) of the University of Southern California has a leading role in RSVP development.

Queuing Policies

Every router interface has a queue to hold packets awaiting transmission. You have a lot of control over what happens to queued packets. This is good, because output interface queues are a crucial part of your network from a QoS perspective. Any QoS initiatives in your network should begin by optimizing the interface-queuing policies. A large part of IP network tuning for voice/data integration is related to queuing policies.

Queuing policies have historically developed to address two core issues:

- Provide required QoS for identified applications
- Provide an equitable distribution of bandwidth resources

The first goal is focused on managing delay and delay variation for selected applications. The second goal is focused on overall fairness to applications sharing the bandwidth. These design goals do not appear to be complementary. By giving low latency and jitter to a given application, other applications may suffer. If the queuing algorithm distributes bandwidth fairly, then high-priority applications may experience excessive delay or delay variation. Early solutions to the above goals addressed one issue or the other, but not both.

Queuing algorithms have addressed the preceding issues from two technical perspectives:

- Manage the queue depth
- Schedule the order of packet delivery

Algorithms such as Random Early Detection (RED) and Weighted RED (WRED) actively manage the interface queue depth (that is, the number of packets in the queue), so that the queue is not continuously full. These algorithms are also called congestion-avoidance mechanisms. A queue that is full in the steady state is useless because any bursts of traffic are dropped. It is better to select which traffic to drop than to drop whatever packets arrive next because the packets that arrive next may be high priority. For example, a router may unknowingly drop VoIP packets if an interface buffer is too full to accommodate the packets.

With the exception of WRED, the queuing techniques in this section are classified as packet schedulers. Packet schedulers control the order in which packets leave an interface, based on administratively defined policies. The most relevant queuing policy for VoIP is to make sure that VoIP packets are moved to the front of the queue so they are not delayed by other packet types. Another common queuing policy is to equitably divide the available bandwidth among each of the traffic flows or classes of applications. While older queuing techniques are designed to achieve only one of these policies, Cisco has developed new queuing techniques that implement both of these policies at the same time.

Cisco has long provided the following three queuing techniques:

- FIFO queuing
- Priority queuing
- Custom queuing

More recent additions to Cisco's queuing arsenal include:

- WFQ
- WRED

Cisco's queuing technology has matured with the addition of these features:

- CB-WFQ
- RTP Prioritization
- Low latency queuing (LLQ)

The following sections discuss these technologies from a conceptual perspective. Chapter 15 shows how to implement these technologies in your network using Cisco IOS.

FIFO Queuing

The most basic queuing technique is FIFO. A *FIFO queue* is a simple buffer that holds outbound packets until the transmitting interface can send them. Packets are sent out of the interface in the order in which they arrived in the buffer as shown in Figure 10-8.

Figure 10-8   *FIFO Queuing Does Not Change the Order of Packets in Queue*

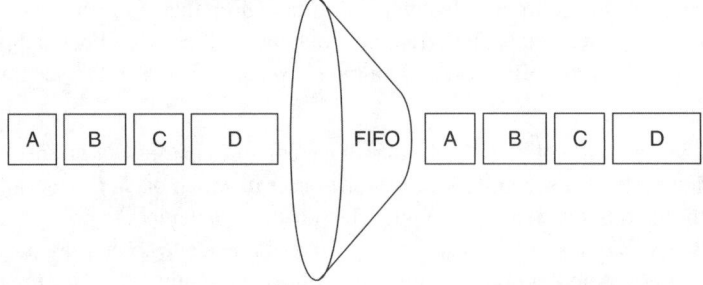

This queuing technique provides neither QoS for given flows, nor equitable bandwidth distribution between flows sharing a link. During periods of congestion, the buffer fills and packets are dropped without regard for the packet type or associated application requirements. This is bad for VoIP. FIFO queues do not treat all traffic flows equally or fairly either, even though they drop packets independently of packet characteristics. Suppose that N packets are dropped from the end of a queue in a given time period. The problem is that some flows may only contain N packets in that time window, so the whole flow could be destroyed. N packets might only represent 1 percent of another flow during that same time window. So FIFO queues are biased against flows with small or occasional bandwidth requirements. This is another reason that FIFO is not a good queuing strategy for interfaces that pass VoIP traffic.

Priority Queuing

Priority queuing is a simple approach to offering preferential treatment to identified packets. This is the "brute force" method of ensuring that designated packets get the best treatment possible. Packets arriving at an interface for transmission are separated into four queues: low, normal, medium, and high priority. The output from these four queues feeds an interface transmission buffer, as indicated in Figure 10-9.

Figure 10-9   *Four Levels of Prioritized Traffic Feed the Transmission Buffer*

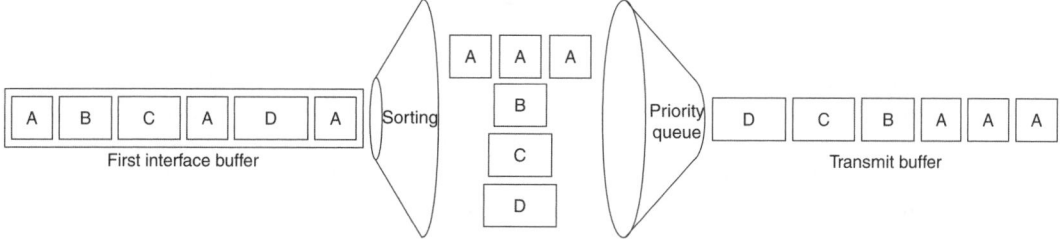

Packets are always serviced from the higher-priority queues first. If packets are waiting in the high-priority queue, they will be sent to the transmitting buffer. If the high-priority queue is empty, then any packets in the medium-priority queue are sent to the buffer. If the high-priority queue and the medium-priority queue are empty, then packets from the normal queue are sent to the transmission buffer, and so on.

Priority queuing meets the QoS requirements of VoIP, but it leaves much to be desired for equitable bandwidth distribution for the remaining traffic. High-priority traffic incurs the least possible latency and jitter with this queuing technique, but there are no provisions for distributing bandwidth among traffic with equal priorities. Within a given priority, the traffic is FIFO queued. A more significant limitation is that if any of the queues has a constant stream of traffic, then the lower-priority queues are completely starved of bandwidth, as shown in Figure 10-10.

Figure 10-10   *Constant Stream of Traffic in a Given Queue Will Stop Lower-Priority Queues from Being Serviced*

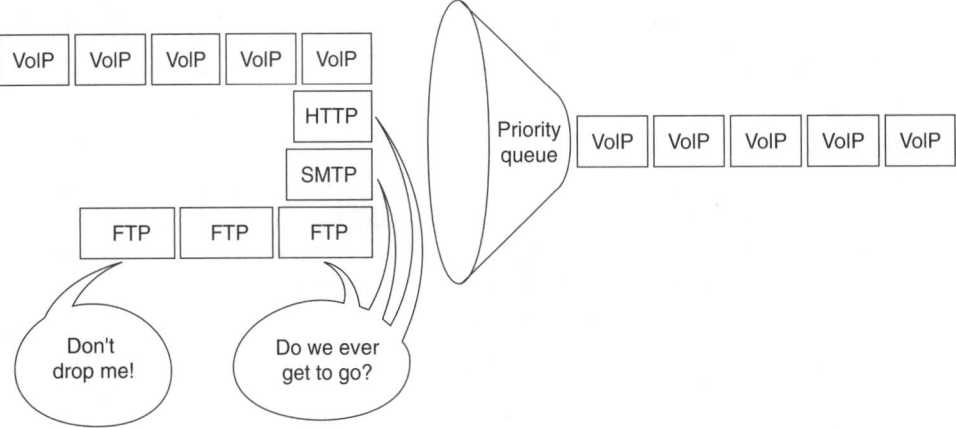

In general, priority queuing is not recommended for VoIP, but it is useful when you must deal with multiple types of high-priority traffic. If you have VoIP and Systems Network Architecture (SNA) traffic on the same link for example, you need to ensure that VoIP packets are always placed at the front of the queue, but SNA packets should be right behind VoIP but ahead of normal data traffic. As of this writing, LLQ and WFQ with IP RTP Priority are unable to meet these objectives. Priority queuing can also meet the queuing needs of VoIP mixed with real-time video traffic. Chapter 15 provides configuration examples for VoIP mixed with SNA, and clearly defines the extension for VoIP with SNA and real-time video traffic.

NOTE   While priority queuing is still useful when multiple real-time traffic types are present, it is not supported in conjunction with FRF.12 Frame Relay fragmentation. As a result, you cannot effectively mix multiple real-time traffic types on low-speed Frame Relay links.

Custom Queuing

Custom queuing is a manually configured fair queuing algorithm. Traffic is sorted into separate queues, and each queue is serviced in a round-robin fashion to ensure that no queue is starved. Figure 10-11 illustrates the custom-queue structure:

Figure 10-11   *Custom-Queue Structure*

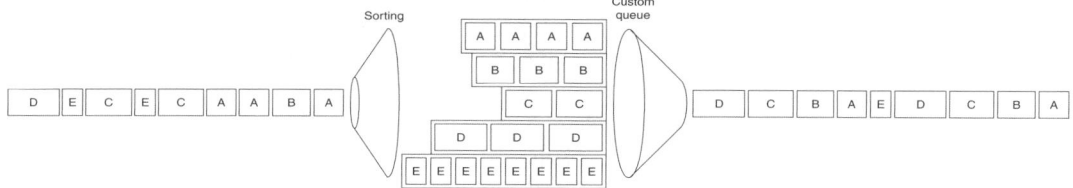

You must manually configure:

- What traffic is associated with each of the queues
- How many packets can wait in each queue
- How much bandwidth is allocated to each queue

It can be difficult to configure the bandwidth allocation for each of the queues. Instead of directly configuring a bandwidth allocation, you must define the number of bytes to be transmitted from each queue when it is serviced. The relative number of bytes assigned to each queue identifies the percentage of bandwidth allocated for that queue.

Although the transmitting capacity of each queue is specified in bytes, the queue actually transmits packets. The queue will transmit packets until the byte-count limit is reached, and then it will finish the packet that is in midtransmission. This means that if the byte count is set to 3050, and there are three IP packets of 1500 bytes each, the queue will transmit all three packets, for a total of 4500 bytes! You must be careful when determining the byte-count values for each queue, or else the actual bandwidth allocation may be very different from what you have planned. This can be quite difficult, especially since some protocols like IPX dynamically adjust the frame size depending on the link speed. You can find more information about custom-queuing design on Cisco Connection Online (CCO).

Custom queuing addresses the issue of equitable bandwidth distribution, but it is not well suited to provide QoS to specified traffic flows. Because each of the queues is serviced in a round-robin fashion, there is no queue with higher priority than any other (except the system queue for router keepalives, and so on). Some queues may have higher throughput than others, but no queue can be given special treatment with respect to latency or jitter. This makes custom queuing a poor choice for VoIP.

Weighted Fair Queuing

Weighted Fair Queuing (WFQ) works so well that it has become the default queuing method on Cisco router interfaces at or below T1/E1 speeds. Conceptually, it is quite similar to custom queuing except that it does not require any configuration. WFQ creates a separate queue for each traffic flow (for example, source/destination IP address and TCP/UDP port), and uses a reasonable default value for the queue depth. You have the option to configure the queue depth, which is applied to every flow.

The weighted part of WFQ comes into play when used with IP precedence bits and Resource Reservation Protocol (RSVP). In the absence of RSVP or IP precedence, WFQ provides equal bandwidth to all flows. This is a special case of the rule that WFQ provides an equal amount of bandwidth to all flows with the same IP precedence or RSVP status. Between flows of different priority levels, WFQ allocates bandwidth based on the weight associated with the flow. WFQ uses the following formula to assign weights to flows with different IP precedence bit values:

$$weight = \frac{4096}{\left(1 + IP\_precedence\right)}$$

For packets with active RSVP reservations, WFQ uses this formula:

$$weight = \frac{\left(highest\_BW\_reservation\right)}{\left(BW\_reservation\_for\_this\_flow\right)}$$

How do these weight values translate to bandwidth allocation? Bandwidth is allocated in proportion to the inverse of the weight values. Consider a simple system with three flows:

1 IP precedence = 0

2 IP precedence = 1

3 IP precedence = 3

Table 10-1 summarizes the calculations:

Table 10-1   *Calculating WFQ Bandwidth Allocation Based on IP Precedence Values*

Flow	Weight	Inverse of Weight	Simple Ratio	Bandwidth Percentage
IP precedence = 0	4096		1	14.3%
IP precedence = 1	2048		2	28.6%
IP precedence = 3	1024		4	57.1%

You may have observed that the simplified ratio of bandwidth for a flow is (1 + IP precedence). So why go to the trouble of including the magic number 4096 in the weight formulas, which makes the computation more unwieldy? It appears that this value cancels out, so it has no use. Consider now that RSVP flows can coexist with IP precedence flows. The nature of an RSVP reservation is such that the router is obliged to service this request, even at the expense of flows with high IP precedence. That magic number 4096 becomes the simplified bandwidth ratio for the biggest RSVP flow when compared to IP precedence flows. There must be another mechanism to police the amount of bandwidth admitted for the RSVP flows, because WFQ on a link with few flows yields an unreasonable amount of bandwidth to the RSVP flows.

Consider now a busy link servicing 4096 normal-priority flows (or 820 high-precedence VoIP calls) and a single RSVP flow. The RSVP flow is allocated one half of the bandwidth, and the other flows share the remaining bandwidth. In this contrived case, WFQ cannot satisfy an RSVP request for more than 50 percent of the bandwidth.

WFQ provides an equitable distribution of bandwidth, enables higher-priority traffic to have a higher-bandwidth allocation, and is automatically configured in most cases. WFQ provides much better service for low-bandwidth flows than FIFO queuing. If many flows are present, fair queuing does not service any flow often enough to maintain the low latency and jitter required for VoIP. WFQ must be supplemented with IP RTP Priority to provide the necessary QoS treatment for voice traffic.

Weighted Random Early Detection

During periods of congestion, a router that implements RED randomly discards packets that are queued for transmission on an interface. At first thought, the idea of discarding random packets may seem ludicrous—doesn't this have the same effect as letting the buffers overflow in a FIFO queue? Why bother with a feature that performs such a silly function? On closer inspection, however, RED is seen to be a beautiful way to increase data throughput in a congested network.

To understand how RED manages bandwidth, take a step back and review several features of TCP that relate to bandwidth management:

- Sliding windows
- Receiver window advertisement versus congestion window
- Congestion window behavior following packet loss
- Congestion window behavior following successful packet transmissions

Because TCP provides a guaranteed delivery service, there is an implicit requirement that each transmitted packet be acknowledged by the receiver. If the sender waits for each packet acknowledgment from the receiver before sending another packet, then transmission takes a large amount of time (that is, the number of packets multiplied by round-trip latency). In a more efficient design, the sender transmits a block of N packets and waits for the acknowledgment of each of these packets, before sending another N packets. The size of the block N is the window size. The data throughput is on the order of N times faster than in the single packet acknowledgment scenario. This protocol still causes the sender to wait for all of the acknowledgments in the block before sending additional data. The protocol is improved when the block becomes a sliding window of N packets that moves continuously as acknowledgments are received. This is the sliding-window mechanism, which enables the transmission time of an acknowledged data stream to be minimally affected by the latency of the network.

NOTE   Lost TCP acknowledgments are not a problem, because a subsequent acknowledgment will implicitly include the lost acknowledgment. This is because TCP receivers acknowledge the total number of ordered bytes they have received in a session, not each individual packet. An acknowledgment indicates that all packets have been successfully received up to the specified point in the information stream.

In the standard TCP implementation, both the sender and the receiver control the data transfer rate by adjusting the size of the window described in the preceding paragraphs. The receiver advertises the maximum window size it can accept, which is effectively the size of its input packet buffer. The sender uses this as the maximum window size, but may use a smaller window based on its assessment of network congestion. The sender must regulate the congestion-window size such that data transmission is: (1) quickly throttled during network congestion; (2) quickly resumed following relief from congestion; (3) controlled enough that the network does not become quickly overloaded again, causing a cycle of congestion and idleness.

The sender regulates the congestion-window size based on TCP packet acknowledgments from the receiver. When data transfer begins, the congestion window (measured in bytes) is set to the size of a single packet. Every acknowledged segment increases the congestion window by the size of the acknowledged packet. In this way, the congestion window doubles every round-trip transmission period: One acknowledged packet increases the congestion window to two packets; two packets are sent and acknowledged, which increases the window size to 4; the acknowledgment of the next four packets increases the congestion window size to 8, and so on. At a certain point, the sender changes its behavior, such that the congestion window size increases by only one segment when all of the packets in the current window size have been acknowledged. This slows the increase of the congestion window size from an exponential to a linear function as the traffic volume approaches the level where congestion is expected. Figure 10-12 illustrates how the TCP window size grows over time.

Figure 10-12 *TCP Congestion Window Size Grows when All Packet Acknowledgments Are Received*

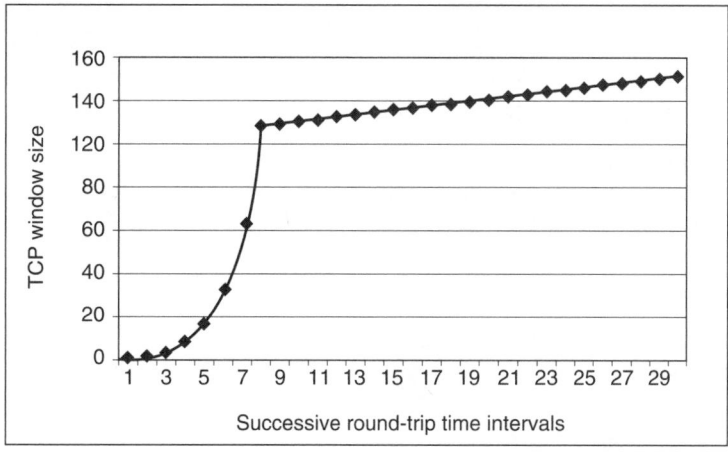

The congestion window continues to increase until it is equal to the maximum window size of the receiver, or until the sender does not receive the expected acknowledgments. When the sender does not receive packet acknowledgments, the assumption is that the network is congested. At this point, the sender throttles back the congestion window size to one segment. In addition, the cross-over point from the exponential to the linear growth of the window is set at one half of the congestion window size just prior to the throttling. That is, if the congestion window had grown to 17,000 bytes when congestion occurred, then the cross-over point would be set to 8500 bytes, and the congestion window would be reset to the size of a single packet. This process is called the TCP slow-start mechanism. The entire process is visually summarized in Figure 10-13.

Figure 10-13 *TCP Congestion Window Size Responds to the State of Network Congestion*

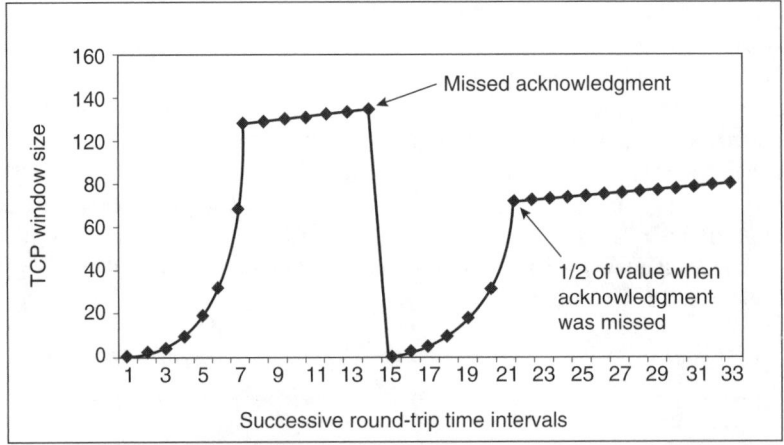

The preceding TCP discussion and more is detailed in RFC 2581. Stevens and Comer offer additional detail, as do the references in RFC 2581.

The point of this diversion into TCP is to provide the prerequisites to understand RED. Allow one more paragraph to examine TCP from the perspective of a router, and then, at last, the point of RED will be clear.

Now, imagine that a router passes traffic from enough hosts to reach a congestion level on a given link. It is a fair assumption that much of this traffic will be TCP traffic because HTTP, SMTP, FTP, telnet, and numerous other protocols use TCP as the transport layer protocol. When the router becomes so congested that its buffers overflow and it drops packets, many of the TCP sessions will move into the slow-start phase and throttle back the data-transfer rate. The router will then recover from congestion and empty its buffers; this is indeed the expectation of the TCP design. Unfortunately, most of the TCP senders use one of a few implementations, so that the behavior of numerous TCP senders will be synchronized in the face of network congestion. The senders will throttle back traffic in near unison, and then increase the traffic rate in near unison until the router again drops packets. From the perspective of a router, the amount of traffic originating from all of the TCP senders over time is illustrated in Figure 10-14.

Figure 10-14   *TCP Traffic Load when Subject to Network Congestion Through a Router*

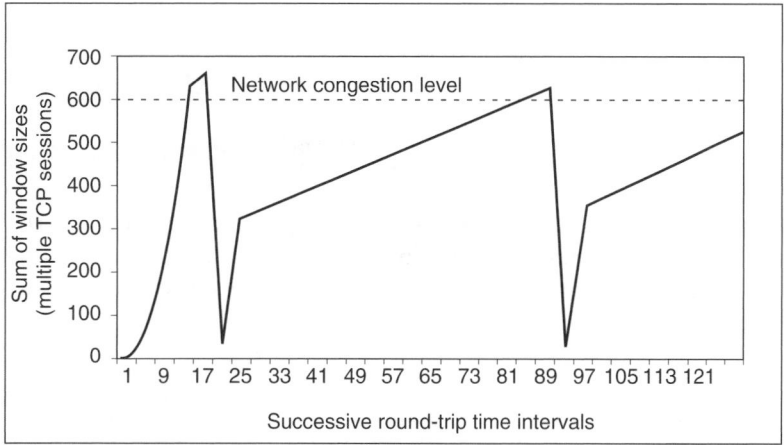

Note how the traffic rate oscillates over time. This is the effect of many TCP sessions synchronized in their congestion-control mechanisms. You may have heard this called *global synchronization* of TCP sessions. Consider that the overall network throughput, in bytes, is measured as the area under the curve in Figure 10-14. It is clear that during the times when traffic is throttled back, the network is underutilized. RED is designed to maximize network throughput (which is the area under the curve) by reducing the oscillation of the synchronized TCP sessions. Ideally, RED would cause the traffic rate over time to look like Figure 10-15.

Figure 10-15 *Uniform Network Throughput Is the Goal of RED*

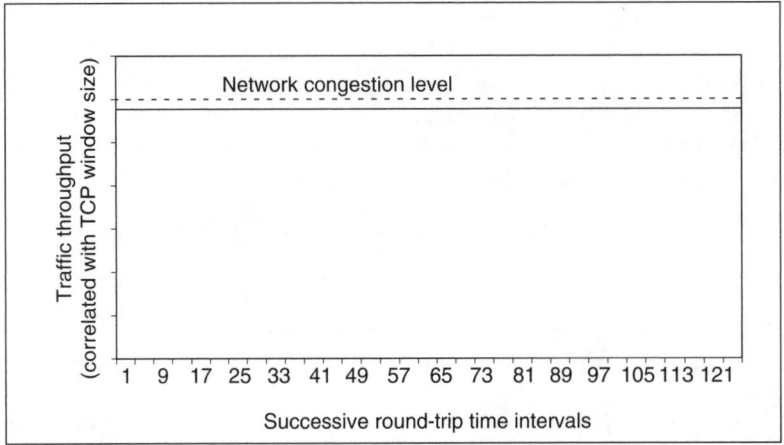

RED dampens the synchronized TCP oscillations by causing individual TCP sessions to enter the slow-start phase at different times. When the individual TCP sessions are allowed to rise and fall out of phase, the summation of these sessions yields a more uniform aggregate traffic flow. Figure 10-16 clarifies this concept.

Figure 10-16 *When TCP Slow-Starts Are Not Synchronized, Aggregate Throughput Is Increased*

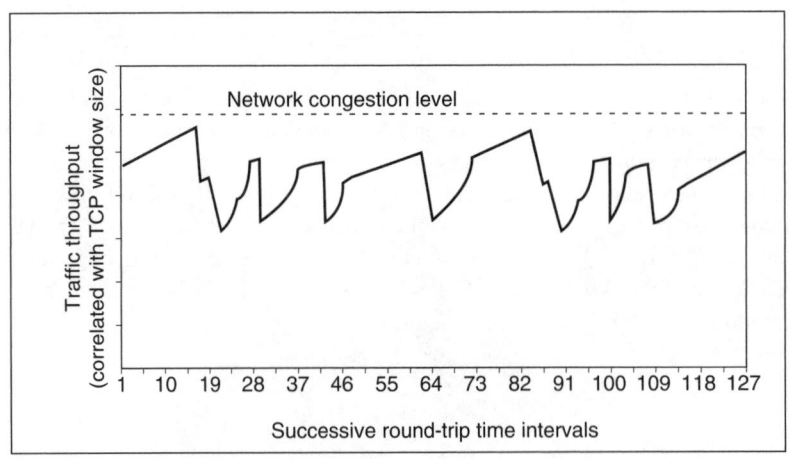

RED is a form of active queue management. Instead of passively waiting until the buffers fill and enabling all subsequent traffic to be dropped, RED progressively drops packets as soon as the buffers begin to fill. The name Random Early Detection reflects that packets in a buffer are randomly dropped based upon early detection of congestion. Below a minimum buffer threshold, no packets are discarded. Above the maximum buffer threshold, all packets are discarded. Between the minimum and the maximum, the probability of a packet being discarded increases linearly from 0 to 100 percent. It is important to note that the recorded buffer depth compared against the threshold values is a time-averaged value, not an instantaneous value. This means that if the queue has been full for a while, it is more likely to drop packets than if it had been empty and suddenly received a burst of traffic. Figure 10-17 illustrates the difference between congestive discarding on an interface not using RED and an interface using RED.

Figure 10-17 *RED Softens the Boundary Between Transmitted and Congestive Discarded Traffic*

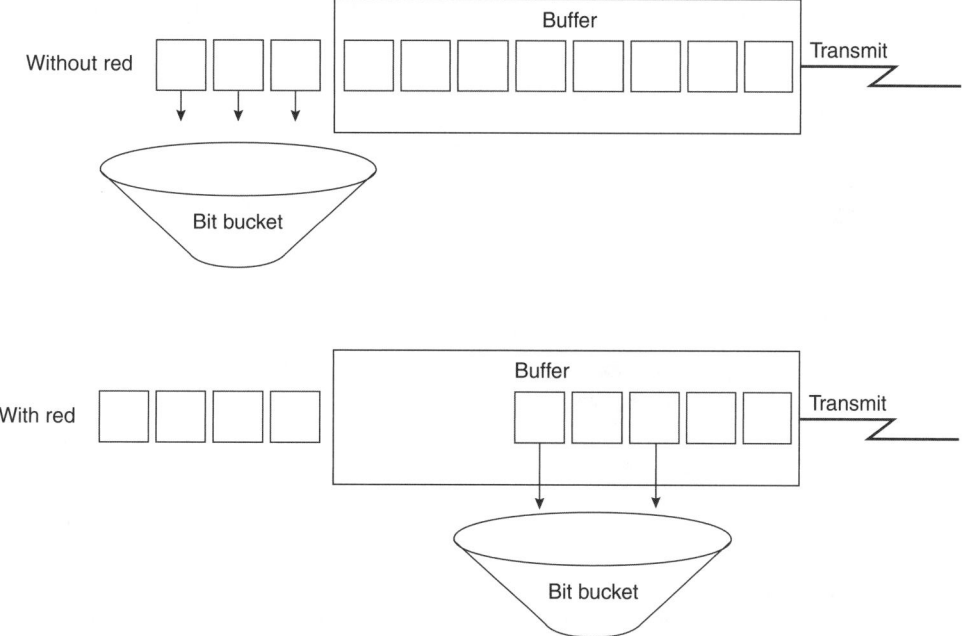

What about the W in WRED? Weighted Random Early Detection is Cisco's implementation of RED that takes into account the type of traffic. First, traffic is classified by IP precedence value, and then a separate minimum buffer threshold is assigned to each traffic class. Traffic with an RSVP reservation is treated above the highest IP precedence value. The default setting for the minimum buffer threshold increases as IP precedence increases, so packets with higher IP precedence will not be dropped as often as packets with lower IP precedence. This is one reason that it is important to set the IP precedence bits to a high value for VoIP packets.

Cisco also offers a flow-based WRED, which uses source/destination IP addresses and TCP/UDP port numbers to differentiate traffic. The idea is to introduce fairness among flows in a manner similar to WFQ. In normal WRED, packets are discarded independent of whether or not they are from a high-bandwidth or a low-bandwidth conversation. As a result, a larger percentage of traffic from low-bandwidth conversations can be discarded by WRED. Flow-based WRED provides a more equitable treatment for each of the flows, so that low-bandwidth flows have better performance.

Unlike RED, which purely manages queue depth, WRED also has some characteristics of a scheduling algorithm. Instead of explicitly stating which packets will go next, WRED selects which packets will not go next. Most scheduling algorithms are additive in nature, where the final packet order is the result of each packet being explicitly placed in order. WRED starts with a random ordering of packets, and removes packets such that the desired packet ordering is approached. This subtractive process offers a very limited scheduling functionality. The additive process offers a much finer control, but the subtractive process uses far fewer system resources. Consider the two processes illustrated in Figure 10-18.

Figure 10-18 *Additive Versus Subtractive Packet Ordering*

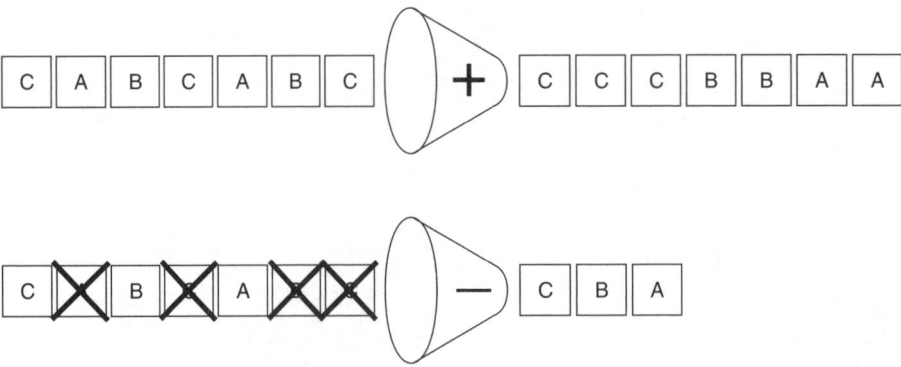

Whereas the additive-ordering mechanism must actively move (or at least store a pointer for) each packet into a new reordered buffer, the subtractive mechanism merely discards packets that violate the ordering rules. Each packet requires less processing and less buffer resources when using the subtractive ordering mechanism. WRED is the primary queuing technique for high-bandwidth interfaces (greater than T1/E1).

RED can manage queue depth for all types of traffic, but RED will only maximize throughput for traffic that responds to congestion, such as standard TCP implementations. The workings of TCP windowing were belabored in this section to instill a deep understanding of the types of traffic that will respond well to RED. For more information about other benefits, subtleties, and considerations associated with RED, read RFC 2309, titled "Recommendations on Queue Management and Congestion Avoidance in the

Internet." Information about the latest research and real-world findings for RED can be found at the following URL:

www.aciri.org/floyd/red.html

Class-Based Weighted Fair Queuing

Class-Based Weighted Fair Queuing (CB-WFQ) incorporates Custom Queuing ideas into the format of Weighted Fair Queuing (WFQ). This reworking has created a number of improvements over each of the older queuing techniques. The maximum number of custom queues (now called classes) is increased from 16 to 64. There is still great flexibility for assigning traffic to each of the classes. Each class can use the standard tail-drop method of queue-depth management (that is, passively enable the queues to fill and overflow during congestion), or WRED can be configured independently for each class. With CB-WFQ, you can directly and independently specify the amount of bandwidth you want allocated to each class, and CB-WFQ adjusts internal parameters to make this happen.

With WFQ, it is difficult to precisely specify the amount of bandwidth allocated for a flow. The problem is that the actual bandwidth per flow depends on the number of flows, which can constantly change. The weight parameter influences bandwidth allocation in WFQ, but there are only six weights that can be specified (IP precedence 0 to 5), plus one per RSVP flow. Since WFQ is a fair-queuing algorithm, an adjustment to any flow or IP precedence level affects all other flows and precedence levels. This greatly adds to the complexity of bandwidth management with WFQ.

CB-WFQ addresses the problem of bandwidth allocation to individual classes using a custom queuing concept. In custom queuing, individual queues are configured with a byte-count value that controls the amount of bandwidth used by each queue. The CB-WFQ implementation is more refined because you directly specify the amount of bandwidth you want allocated to each class. The algorithm adjusts the weight assigned to the class based on the bandwidth assignments for each class and the overall bandwidth available for the link.

As an overall recommendation for IP, you should use one of two queuing techniques for low-bandwidth interfaces, depending upon your needs:

- WFQ
- CB-WFQ

Both of these queuing techniques provide equitable bandwidth distribution and must be used with a mechanism to prioritize VoIP traffic. WFQ requires IP RTP Priority, and CB-WFQ requires a prioritized traffic class. Note that CB-WFQ with a prioritized class is called LLQ. You can decide which technique to use based on your bandwidth allocation requirements and the level of configuration complexity you are willing to experience. WFQ requires almost no configuration, but CB-WFQ is somewhat of an advanced IOS configuration.

RTP Prioritization

Up to this point, each of the queuing techniques has been discussed from a single-stage queuing perspective. That is, the queuing model for the interface looks like Figure 10-19.

Figure 10-19 *Single-Stage Queuing Model Can Provide Either QoS or Equitable BW Distribution*

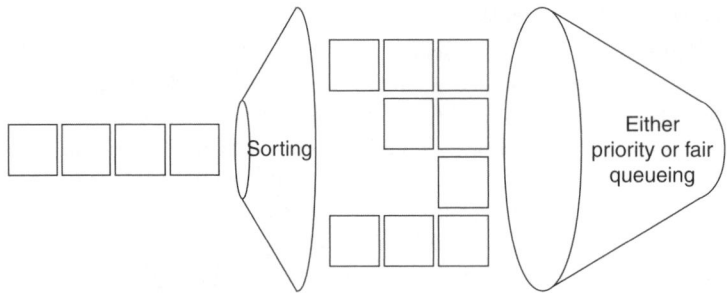

To meet the conflicting requirements for flow-specific QoS and equitable bandwidth for all flows, a multistage queuing model is useful. (See Figure 10-20.) The first-stage queue identifies the high-priority traffic that cannot tolerate delay and jitter. This traffic is sent directly to the transmitting buffers. The remaining traffic passes through the second queue, which provides equitable treatment to the various data flows.

For VoIP, this multistage queuing model is implemented with the IP RTP Priority feature. When this feature is enabled, all RTP traffic using specified UDP ports is separated in the first-stage queue and sent directly to the transmitting buffer. The remaining traffic uses WFQ or CB-WFQ to equitably allocate bandwidth to traffic flows or classes. You should note that RTP prioritization provides low delay and jitter for the audio path of the VoIP conversation, but the call setup, teardown, and any other signaling messages must still traverse the second-stage queue. For busy interfaces with many flows, CB-WFQ improves the performance for call-signaling messages. The next chapter will explore the packet details for the VoIP audio path and signaling messages. For now, just know that VoIP call signaling does not use RTP.

Traffic Policing and Shaping

The queuing policies discussed in the previous sections make a large assumption. The assumption is that no traffic will be lost in the WAN between adjacent routers. For clear channel circuits, this might be a realistic assumption, because low bit-error rates rarely result in corrupted packets. But what about Frame Relay, the most popular data transport? The common practice with Frame Relay is to push as much traffic across a PVC as possible, exceeding the committed rate, and hope the carrier does not drop too much of it.

Figure 10-20   *Multistage Queuing Model Provides Both QoS and Equitable BW Distribution*

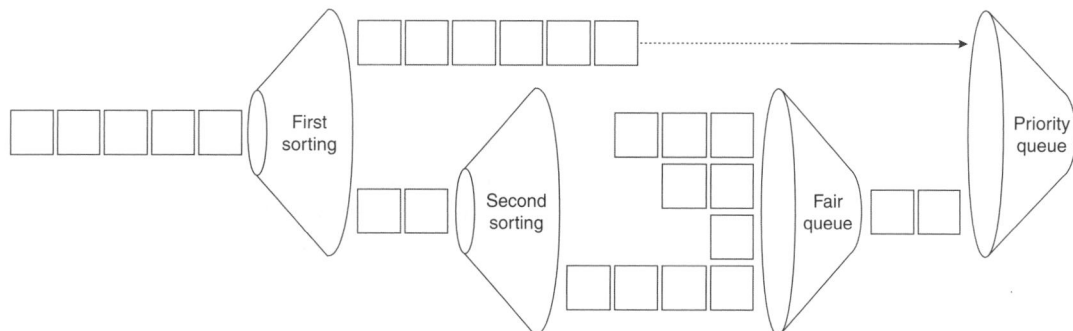

This practice does not work with VoIP. If you must transmit loss-sensitive traffic across a Frame Relay network (for example, DLSW, VoIP), then you should regulate the volume of your traffic output. Otherwise, the carrier will regulate your traffic in a less accommodating way (that is, by randomly dropping traffic when you exceed the committed information rate). The carrier does not care whether dropped frames are VoIP, SNA, or normal data. You must be responsible for the traffic you send to the carrier, and you must decide what traffic should be dropped or delayed. This is the role of traffic shaping and policing on the router.

Traffic shaping and policing can be used for other functions, such as regulating bandwidth used by specific applications. For low-bandwidth interfaces (that is, T1/E1 or less), CB-WFQ is a better mechanism to enforce bandwidth allocation between applications. This chapter focuses on policing and traffic shaping for overall bandwidth regulation of Frame Relay links.

Traffic policing and traffic shaping both classify packets and identify violations in the same manner. The distinction between policing and shaping is in the treatment of packets that violate the bandwidth or rate limits. Traffic policers discard violating traffic, or at least lower the IP precedence or set a DE bit for Frame Relay. Traffic shapers queue the traffic to avoid exceeding the contracted rates.

NOTE   Traffic shaping and policing operate independently in each direction of transmission. That is, the operation of traffic shaping or policing in one router does not require any support from the router on the opposite end of the link. Because most WAN circuits offer symmetrical bandwidth and performance characteristics, the traffic shaping and policing configurations are usually consistent in both directions of transmission. If you have circuits with asymmetrical bandwidth, it is completely acceptable to have different traffic shaping and policing parameters on each end of a link.

Among the policing and shaping features implemented by Cisco are:

- Committed Access Rate (CAR)
- Generic Traffic Shaping (GTS)
- Frame Relay Traffic Shaping (FRTS)

CAR ensures that the identified traffic will not exceed a long-term average rate. CAR allows bursting within a time interval up to a configured amount, and excess bursting over a series of time intervals up to a configured amount. The excess-bursting feature enables CAR to avoid dropping excess packets before they can be classified. Like RED, this feature is a form of queue-depth management.

GTS and FRTS are very similar. The underlying technology is the same, but they are implemented in different parts of the traffic path. GTS is implemented on an interface or a subinterface, whereas FRTS is implemented on each PVC. If you have a single PVC configured on each subinterface, they have almost the same effect.

GTS and FRTS have different queuing options available. With FRTS, you can use priority queuing or custom queuing to control which traffic is queued (and WFQ as of later IOS releases). With GTS, you can use WFQ to control which traffic is queued. Based on the queuing differences, it makes more sense to use GTS for VoIP, unless WFQ is supported for FRTS in the version of IOS that you are using. Chapter 15 explores FRTS and GTS in more detail, including specific implementation recommendations.

NOTE   Carriers should not drop your frames when you use traffic shaping to limit traffic to the committed information rate (CIR). However, Frame Relay does not have any delay guarantees, so the carrier may buffer your traffic for an intolerable amount of time when you are transmitting at or below the CIR. In this case, you need a stricter Service Level Agreement (SLA) that encourages the carrier to fix the problem, or you need a new carrier.

Header Compression

The basic concept of header compression is to reduce the bandwidth used for packet overhead and increase the amount of bandwidth available for actual data. Header compression techniques are link-layer protocols. They are typically used between WAN interfaces on routers—not by the end systems. For the feature to be useful, every low-bandwidth interface along the path should have the feature enabled. Interfaces that do not use this feature may become bandwidth bottlenecks for the end-to-end path.

Packet overhead is not much of a concern for large packets, but consider what a typical telnet packet looks like on the wire, as shown in Figure 10-21.

Figure 10-21   *Typical Telnet Packet with 1 Byte of Data and 40 Bytes of Overhead*

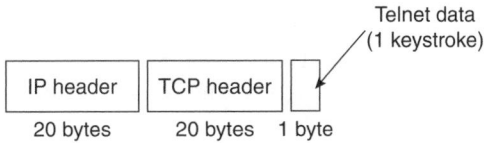

Now imagine that a busy link may have many traffic flows that look like this. Packet headers can consume a large amount of bandwidth, which effectively reduces data throughput for the link. Cisco routers can use two types of header compression:

* TCP/IP header compression
* Compressed Real-Time Transport Protocol (CRTP)

TCP/IP Header Compression

In RFC 1144, Van Jacobson proposed a technique called TCP/IP header compression to reduce the amount of bandwidth allocated to TCP/IP headers in small packets. Figure 10-22 illustrates a typical telnet packet when TCP/IP header compression is used.

Figure 10-22   *With TCP/IP Header Compression, the Packet Overhead Is Drastically Reduced*

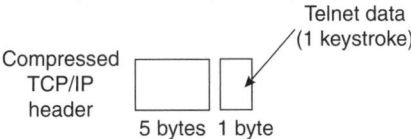

How can the TCP/IP header be compressed from 40 bytes to 5 bytes? There are three main observations that make it possible:

* About half of the TCP/IP header remains constant for the life of a connection.
* Some fields that do change during the life of the connection do not change often.
* Some large fields that change every packet change in a small or predictable way.

The key to header compression is that the receiver remembers the state of each active TCP connection. If the receiver caches the fields that do not change, then the sender only needs to transmit the changing fields. The receiver can determine the IP total length field by examining the link-layer header, so the sender does not need to send this field either. The sender skips the checksums, and lets the receiver recalculate them. These steps have reduced the headers from 40 bytes to 16 bytes. Some of the remaining fields change infrequently during the session. These fields can be identified on a packet-by-packet basis with a bit-mask (an extra piece of control information from the sender to the receiver), and only the changed values need to be sent. This process saves an extra 6 bytes per packet on average.

Some of the remaining fields change with every packet, but their changes exhibit autocorrelation. That is, the value of a field in one packet is likely to be close to the value of that field in the next or previous packet. Only the differences between adjacent packets of this type are sent, because the differences are much smaller than the actual field values. The receiver can determine the actual values by caching the previous values of the fields and adding the difference from the current transmission. For example, the 32-bit sequence number in the TCP header increases only by the size of the preceding packet payload. At a maximum, this can be a 16-bit number (that is, a 64,000-byte packet), but usually this value will change by not more than 11 bits (that is, a 1500-byte packet). If the sender encodes the difference in a 16-bit field instead of the actual value in a 32-bit field, 2 bytes are saved from this field alone.

Compressed Real-Time Transport Protocol

Compressed Real-Time Transport Protocol (CRTP) leverages many of the techniques used in TCP/IP header compression. The receiver caches the constant fields and the state of changing fields, so that the sender only needs to transmit the changed fields or the differences of changed fields. The sender adds a hash of the source/destination information in the IP, UDP, and RTP headers, and from this creates a context identifier field. This field enables the receiver to associate the packet with the correct IP/UDP/RTP stream. An uncompressed VoIP packet is shown in Figure 10-23.

Figure 10-23   *VoIP Packet with Codec Data Payload, RTP Header, UDP Header, and IP Header*

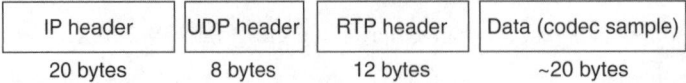

IP header	UDP header	RTP header	Data (codec sample)
20 bytes	8 bytes	12 bytes	~20 bytes

This protocol stack is examined in more detail in Chapter 11. Figure 10-24 shows a VoIP packet that uses the CRTP.

Figure 10-24 *VoIP Packet After CRTP*

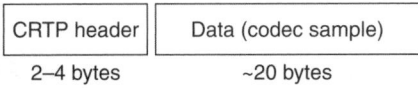

Consider the queuing implications of CRTP. To make accurate bandwidth allocations, the router should use CRTP before the queuing processes. That way, RSVP reservations for VoIP reflect the actual amount of bandwidth required, and RTP prioritization can accurately set the maximum bandwidth for VoIP allowed through the priority queue. But if the IP/UDP/RTP header on a VoIP packet is mostly reduced to a context identifier, then how would the router identify this flow for WFQ, RTP prioritization, or RSVP? The CRTP context identifier can identify the flow, which is sufficient for WFQ and RTP prioritization.

RSVP is a more complicated case, because not every router on a path may implement RSVP, and not every link may use CRTP. Consider Figure 10-25. Router A reserves a 10 kbps for a VoIP call to router C, based on a G.729 codec and CRTP. Router B does not understand RSVP, so router C becomes the next RSVP hop. The link between B and C does not use CRTP. Each call now requires a full 24 kbps (G.729 codec without CRTP) from A to C, but the reservation is only for 10 kbps. In the more general case where receivers (not routers) request the bandwidth reservation, they cannot make assumptions about CRTP on each intermediate link. A possible solution in this case could be that the routers allocate less bandwidth than the reservation dictates, and use CRTP on the link.

Figure 10-25 *In this Case, RSVP Reservation Does Not Accommodate Bandwidth Needs of VoIP Call*

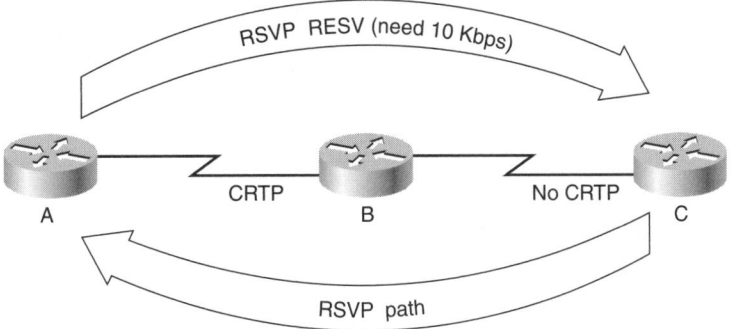

Given that there are many unresolved issues with respect to CRTP before interface queuing, the CRTP feature is currently implemented after interface queuing in Cisco routers. This means that you must be careful with the following features when using CRTP:

- RSVP
- IP RTP Priority

RSVP cannot adjust for the lesser-bandwidth requirements of CRTP when making bandwidth reservations for VoIP. In practice, 24 kbps is reserved for a single G.729 conversation (8 kbps data, 16 kbps headers). Unfortunately, two G.729 conversations using CRTP (each conversation requires only 9.6 kbps) cannot share the 24-kbps reservation. RSVP will make a separate reservation for each conversation, so 48 kbps would be reserved for the two conversations. The unused bandwidth is distributed among the remaining flows according to the weight values, but additional RSVP reservations may be refused even though bandwidth is available.

The workaround for this situation is to increase the configured bandwidth statement on the router interface or subinterface. For example, if you have a 64-kbps link and you want to reserve bandwidth for four VoIP calls, you might configure the interface bandwidth to be 120 kbps. In this way, you can make four RSVP reservations that total 96 kbps, which leaves 24 kbps for other data in a fair queuing scheme. This has the same effect as if RSVP considered CRTP and accurately reserved approximately 40 kbps, leaving 24 kbps for the other flows. Just be careful that you do not oversubscribe the real bandwidth needed on the link.

The IP RTP Priority command is very strict about bandwidth allocation. If you attempt to send more prioritized traffic than you have allocated for IP RTP Priority, then the packets will be dropped. So when you configure RTP prioritization, make sure you allocate bandwidth for VoIP as if CRTP is not used. This may be tricky when you want to have, say, ten VoIP calls across a 128-kbps link. Without header compression, you would need 160 kbps for these calls (plus a few kbps padding for system traffic such as keepalives, and so on). You cannot configure RTP prioritization in excess of the interface bandwidth. Again, the workaround is to increase the configured bandwidth on the interface. Remember to be thorough when you plan your real bandwidth requirements.

Fragmentation and Interleaving

A large amount of this chapter is dedicated to queuing. The key issues revolve around providing low latency and jitter for VoIP packets while servicing other data packets in a fair and equitable manner. Even if VoIP packets are always sent to the front of the queue, there is still the issue of serialization delay. That is, a large packet may be on its way out of the physical interface when a VoIP packet is sent to the front of the queue. In a normal worst-case scenario, serialization delay can cause the VoIP packet to wait as much as:

$$serialization\_delay = \frac{(1500\ bytes) \times (8\ bits\ /\ byte)}{(64,000\ bits\ /\ second)} = 187.5\ ms$$

The solution to this issue is to fragment large packets such that they will never cause a VoIP packet to wait more than a predefined amount of time. Of course, the VoIP packets must be allowed to transmit in between the fragments of the larger packets, or there would be no point in fragmenting. A standard goal for serialization delay is around 10 ms. This equates to a fragment size of 80 bytes for every 64 kbps of the clocking rate for the interface. The fragmentation and interleaving can be accomplished at multiple levels:

- Network-Layer Fragmentation/Interleaving (NFI)
- Link-Layer Fragmentation/Interleaving (LFI)

Link-Layer Versus Network-Layer Fragmentation/Interleaving

Consider the header implications of fragmentation. Whenever you fragment a packet at a given protocol layer, the headers associated with that protocol layer must be replicated in every fragment. For Frame Relay or Point-to-Point Protocol (PPP), this means an extra few bytes must be transmitted for each fragment. Now consider IP fragmentation. If you decrease the IP maximum transmission unit (MTU) to cause IP fragmentation, then each fragment must have a 20-byte IP header added. In addition, each fragment still has a link-layer header! It should be clear that decreasing the IP MTU is a bad idea unless there is no alternative. Before FRF.12 provided a standard Frame Relay fragmentation method, decreasing the IP MTU was the only option for improving voice quality on slow Frame Relay links. Data throughput suffered horribly.

Link-Layer Fragmentation/Interleaving Options

The LFI option that you use depends on the type of WAN link you have. You may have multiple types in your IP network because these are link-layer technologies. The two basic options for VoIP are:

- Frame Relay FRF.12
- Multilink PPP

Frame Relay FRF.12

If you have Frame Relay circuits, then you should use pure FRF.12 end-to-end
fragmentation/interleaving. Though Cisco also supports FRF.11 Annex C and another
proprietary option, these options are designed for VoFR and do not preserve QoS for VoIP
packets across the link. There are various caveats if you must use VoFR and VoIP on the
same Frame Relay circuit, but in general you should avoid the situation entirely.

Frame fragmentation size is based on the clocking rate of the physical interface. An
interface clocking rate—not the CIR—is what regulates the serialization delay. (Traffic
shaping bends this rule, and is discussed later in the chapter.) Beware that there are multiple
physical interfaces that you should examine. Consider the scenario depicted in Figure
10-26.

Figure 10-26   *Frame Relay Fragmentation Requires Knowledge of Physical Path of Each PVC*

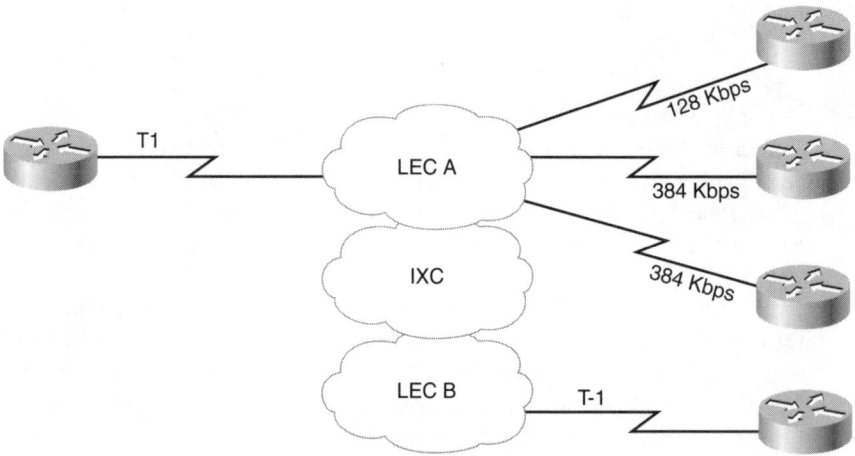

The central site is connected to a full T1 Frame Relay port on the LEC A Frame Relay
switch. Several remote sites are connected via 384-kbps access circuits to the LEC A Frame
Relay switch. One remote site connects to the LEC A Frame Relay switch via a 128-kbps-
access circuit. The last remote site is connected to the LEC B Frame Relay switch via a full
T1 access circuit. All remote sites have a PVC back to the central site. The remote site
connected to LEC B must pass its PVC through an IXC to reach the central site. The CIR
for these PVCs does not matter, because fragmentation is only based on clocking rates.
How should the fragment size be configured for each PVC?

The simplest approach would be to only consider the local access rate associated with each PVC. This would yield the following fragmentation recommendations:

- No fragmentation from the central site to the remote sites.
- The sites with 384-kbps access should use 480 bytes as the fragment size.
- The site with 128-kbps access should use 160 bytes as the fragment size.
- The last site with full T1 access should use no fragmentation.

After implementing the previously mentioned scheme, all of the remote sites report horrible voice quality. People at the central site do not seem to complain, so your coworkers think that some people are just overly sensitive. If you suspect that there is something more to the problem, then you are right. For each PVC, the remote-site access rate is also important. If you do not fragment at the central site, then the large frames will cause serialization delay at the remote end when they leave the carrier switch for the remote site router. Considering the remote access rates for each PVC yields the following recommendations:

- The sites with 384-kbps access should use 480-byte fragments.
- The site with 128-kbps access should use 160-byte fragments.
- The remote site with T1 access does not need fragmentation.
- The central site sets the fragmentation for each PVC to match the fragment size of the remote site.

After adjusting the fragment sizes according to this scheme, everything seems fine except for one site. Calls to and from the last remote site have poor voice quality. This does not seem to be a fragmentation issue, because both sites have full T1 access circuits. But wait a minute . . . Because the CIR is only 128 kbps (which should not matter), the IXC provisioned this circuit with a 256-kbps port speed. Your sites interface to the local exchange carrier network at full T1 rates, but the NNI hand-offs between the local exchange carriers and the interexchange carrier are provisioned at 256-kbps access rates! None of the information given to you by the circuit vendors reflected the NNI hand-off information. You discovered this when talking about a different problem to a technician from the IXC. The moral of this story is that you do not always know what you think you know. It never hurts to ask questions. Just to be clear, the Frame Relay fragment size should reflect the slowest access rate of any part of the physical path that the PVC follows.

NOTE   The preceding discussion of clock rate and fragment size ignores a critical factor in real Frame Relay networks. When a Frame Relay PVC has a CIR less than the port speed, you must use traffic shaping to prevent traffic bursts above the CIR. When you implement traffic shaping, you are simulating a lower clocking rate from the interface, so the fragment size should be based on the simulated clocking rate imposed by traffic shaping.

Contrary to the statement at the beginning of this section, you should look at the CIR to determine an appropriate fragment size (that is, 80 bytes per 64 kbps of bandwidth) if traffic shaping is implemented. The example in the preceding section (which begins with a misleading recommendation) is developed so that you really understand how different network parameters relate to the fragment size.

Multilink PPP

Multilink PPP (ML-PPP) is not as devious as Frame Relay. Generally, PPP is used over a permanent time-division multiplexing (TDM) circuit or a switched ISDN circuit. These circuit types have a uniform bandwidth allocation along the full physical path, so what you see on your local interface is what you get, end to end.

To enable fragmentation/interleaving on PPP links, Cisco has modified the fragmentation feature of the RFC 1990 ML-PPP. ML-PPP provides fragmentation at the sending end, and buffers at the receiving end, for reassembling fragments. The original concept was to facilitate PPP bonding across multiple physical links. When multiple physical links are bonded in an ML-PPP connection, fragments from slower physical links arrive later than fragments from faster physical links. The reassembly buffers enable the receiver to wait for fragments that arrive out of order. Cisco has extended this feature to enable VoIP packets to be interleaved between the fragments at the sending end. Instead of a slow physical link causing some fragments on a bonded channel to arrive late, VoIP packets may cause some fragments to arrive late. At this point, reassembly and processing is according to the ML-PPP standard.

Dual FIFO Transmit Buffers

Even if VoIP packets are sent to the front of the queue, and even if data packets are fragmented to reduce serialization delay, there is still a source of serialization delay that can damage the quality of a VoIP conversation. This section also applies to VoFR.

Consider a Frame Relay interface with multiple PVCs. The typical scenario is a central site router in a hub-and-spoke Frame Relay network. Each PVC is configured under a separate subinterface and has its own queues. Imagine that a VoIP packet is forwarded past other packets within the PVC queue to the physical interface transmission buffer. But there are many data-frame fragments waiting in the physical transmission buffer!

As Figure 10-27 illustrates, the VoIP packet is prioritized over traffic in its PVC, but there are many PVCs on the physical interface that can send frames to the transmit buffer. Though the frames in the buffer are fragmented, there may be many of them. If there are 20 PVCs on the interface, then a VoIP frame might have to wait for 19 frame fragments before it is transmitted. This can cause a horrible delay for the VoIP frame.

The solution to this problem is a dual-queue transmission buffer. (See Figure 10-28.) Each queue is a simple FIFO queue, but one of the queues always has transmission priority. The physical interface transmission queue is essentially a priority queue in this scenario. VoIP packets and Frame Relay Local Management Interface (LMI) messages are always sent over the high-priority queue, while all other frame fragments are sent over the normal-priority queue.

Numerous queuing techniques and related technologies have been discussed in this chapter. An illustration might help put all of the components in perspective. The overall queuing structure for an interface might look like the example shown in Figure 10-29.

Figure 10-27   *Data Fragments from Different PVCs Block VoIP Frame Transmission*

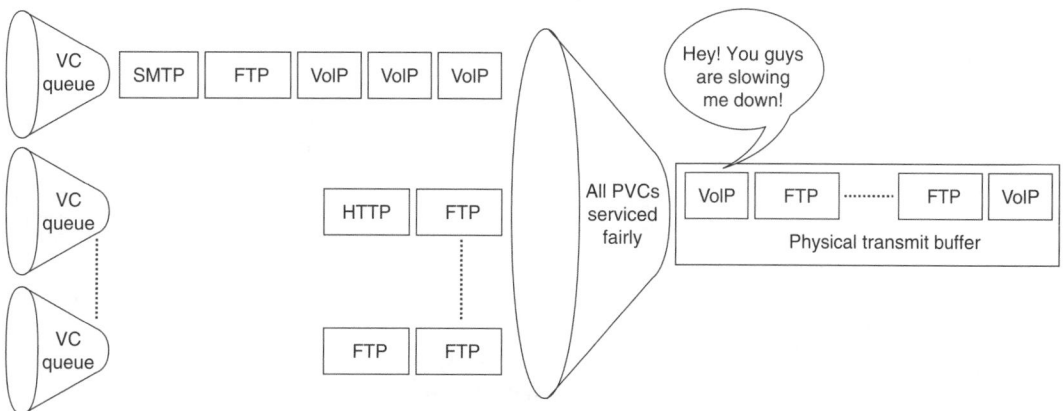

Figure 10-28   *Amidst Traffic from Multiple PVCs, Priority Queuing at the Physical Interface Transmission Level Maintains QoS for VoIP Packets*

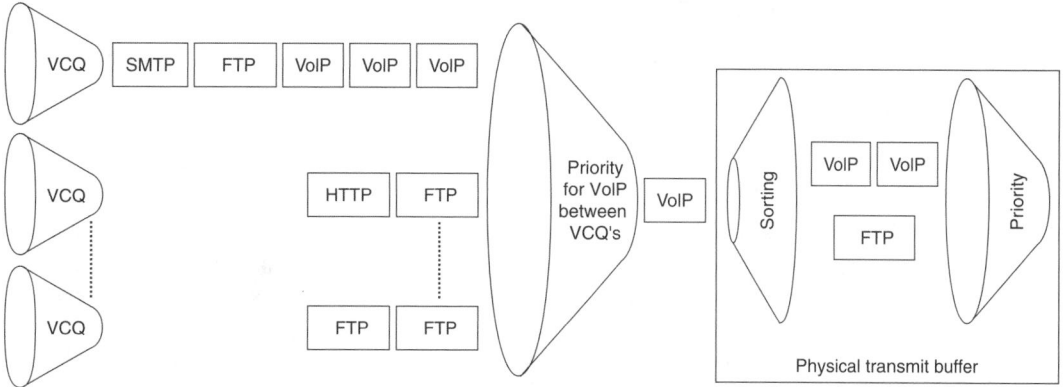

Figure 10-29 *Example Queuing Structure for a Single Physical Interface*

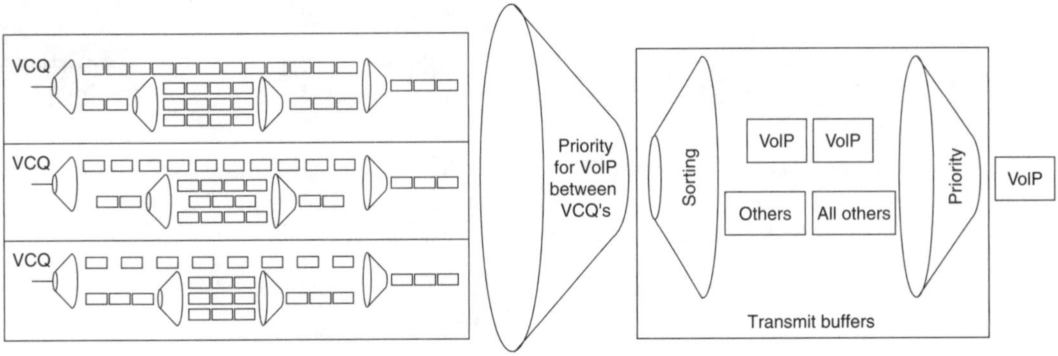

Mapping IP QoS Requirements to ATM Service Classes

Much of this chapter is dedicated to preserving good QoS for VoIP. The tools to achieve this are centered on the router interface. There comes a time when traffic leaves your router interface, enters the carrier network, and you no longer have control over QoS . . . Or do you? ATM extends QoS into the WAN in a tangible and reliable way. You can order virtual circuits (VCs) with very specific performance requirements that ensure good treatment for VoIP packets. But how do you get only the VoIP packets into a constant bit rate virtual circuit (CBR VC), while the rest of the traffic uses the unspecified bit rate VC (UBR VC)? You do not want all of your traffic in the CBR circuit because it is expensive, and because it could introduce serialization delay for VoIP packets stuck behind data packets in the CBR VC. ATM QoS is designed to offer different levels of service between different types of VCs, but there are no provisions for interleaving VoIP in between fragments of the same VC. This means that VoIP packets must be on different VCs than data to provide good QoS.

Until recently, different VCs had to be configured as separate ATM subinterfaces. This required a separate IP subnet for each VC. On Cisco routers, policy routing is the only way to route VoIP packets over one path while data packets use a different path. Policy routing does not integrate well with standard routing plans, because it is difficult to manage rerouting and redundancy in failure scenarios.

ATM VC Bundles address this issue by enabling multiple VCs to be bundled for a single network-layer adjacency. That is, you can configure a single IP subnet to use multiple VCs, and direct traffic to the different VCs based on queuing decisions and QoS requirements. You can assign traffic to different VCs based on a number of criteria. For VoIP, a good approach is to mark the VoIP packets with high IP precedence and forward the high-precedence packets into a CBR VC. This behavior is analogous to the data-link connection identifier (DLCI) prioritization feature available for Frame Relay, in which priority queuing sorts traffic into different PVCs.

As of this writing, ATM VC Bundles can only be configured on ATM DS-3 interfaces, using the PA-A3+ port adapter module on the 7200 and 7500 series Cisco routers. This means you must have two sites that are large enough to require DS-3 bandwidth. You cannot use it to provide QoS to typical remote sites. Think of it as a WAN backbone technology, or a technology to help ISPs support QoS for VoIP.

Policy Routing to Load-Share Links with Different Latencies

This section addresses a challenge that multinational organizations must face. Consider a company with offices around the world, including countries with limited telecommunications infrastructures. Some countries have a single terrestrial fiber path for access in or out of the country. In some cases, international circuit vendors share a single fiber path for communication with these countries. Some countries do not have any terrestrial fiber facilities for external communication! Many of these countries do have satellite-based facilities, though these suffer from high delay.

If you have supported networks with sites in such countries, you are familiar with the headaches of frequent outages—you do not want to have pager duty for these sites! The redundancy options that the carriers provide can be surprisingly limited. For example, the circuit vendor may offer an ISDN circuit solution as a backup to an international Frame Relay link. Unfortunately, all ISDN calls from the country may be switched across the same fiber facility as the Frame Relay circuit. This redundancy helps for problems in the local loop, but a problem at any part of the fiber path impairs the primary and backup circuits for the site.

In many countries, the most reliable solution is a terrestrial primary circuit, and a satellite backup circuit. If you have diverse local loops for these circuits, then the entire physical paths are often diverse. The switching office with the satellite base station is usually different from the switching office with the international terrestrial connection. The problem with this solution is that international bandwidth is often too expensive to leave as an idle backup. If you can use ISDN over a satellite path, this may provide the desired physical redundancy at a lower price. Otherwise, it would be nice to load-share traffic across both links.

At last we come to the heart of the matter: The terrestrial circuit may have a round-trip latency of 280 ms, while the satellite circuit has a round-trip latency of 600 ms. So how can these facilities be load-shared? If they are bonded with ML PPP, the router requires large buffers to accommodate the PPP frames that may arrive out of sequence. Higher bandwidth facilities exacerbate this problem. Another approach is to use separate IP subnets for each link, and rely on routing to isolate traffic between the flows.

When parallel equal-cost routing links exist, Cisco caches routing entries to specific destination hosts instead of to destination networks. In our scenario, this causes all traffic within a flow to use the same latency path. For our present scenario, consider the following physical path permutations that may yield different round-trip latencies:

- Outbound terrestrial, inbound terrestrial (lowest latency)
- Outbound terrestrial, inbound satellite
- Outbound satellite, inbound terrestrial
- Outbound satellite, inbound satellite (highest latency)

Caching routes based on destination address solves the issue of consistency within a flow, but the flow may be randomly cached to any one of the latency paths. What we would really like is to specify the path used by different types of traffic (that is, make routing decisions based on latency requirements of the traffic).

Cisco routers provide this functionality with the Policy Routing feature. To enable policy routing, you first create a policy map that identifies traffic by a variety of characteristics and applies some action to that matching traffic. For example, you can specify that VoIP always uses the lowest-latency path (this requires policy routing on the routers on both sides of the load-shared links). You can create a backup policy to use the next available path if the least-latency path is unavailable. You might then assign FTP, SMTP, News, and other bulk traffic to use the high-latency path, and direct telnet, HTTP, and DLSW to use the low-latency path. Be sure to include a default action that routes traffic to the high-latency path. You can fine-tune the policy if users of specific applications complain about latency issues.

Another key use for policy routing is the ability to set IP precedence bits. You may be interested in this technique to identify key applications for your organization, and improve their performance through routers that use WFQ. You do not need to do this with VoIP, because the IP precedence is set in dial-peer statements that map phone numbers to IP addresses.

Summary

A glance at the table of contents for this chapter may help you mentally organize all of the disparate technologies covered here. The unifying theme is that VoIP has specific needs in terms of:

- Reliability
- Bandwidth
- Delay
- Delay variation

All of the technologies presented here address at least one of these goals, and some of the technologies address multiple goals. Aside from providing the required service for VoIP, traditional data applications still have varying requirements. It is important to have a flexible architecture that can accommodate changing application requirements. The overall IP network design must provide fair treatment for all of the traffic types while meeting the stringent QoS needs of VoIP.

Additional Reading

Comer, Douglas. *Internetworking with TCP/IP, Volume I: Principles, Protocols, and Architecture.* New York: Prentice Hall, 2000.

Stevens, W. Richard. *TCP/IP Illustrated, Volume 1: The Protocols.* Boston: Addison-Wesley, 1994.

CHAPTER 11

VoIP Transport and Signaling Protocols

The protocols associated with VoIP can be logically divided into those supporting the audio path transport, and those supporting the call signaling and control functions. The protocols that manage the audio path transport provide timing information to assure consistent audio playout at the receiving side, and quality of service (QoS) performance feedback regarding the underlying network. The call signaling and control functions provide call setup and teardown, addressing and routing, informational and supplementary services, and methods to interwork with other signaling types.

This chapter explores Real-Time Transport Protocol (RTP) and RTP Control Protocol (RTCP), as they are the universally accepted VoIP audio path protocols. In addition to providing a technical review of the H.323, Session Initiation Protocol (SIP), and Media Gateway Control Protocol (MGCP)/Megaco/H.248 signaling protocols, this chapter also attempts to provide a high-level framework for understanding how these signaling protocols complement and compete with each other. Because research and standards for the integration of the Public Switched Telephone Network (PSTN) and the Internet are growing and evolving, this chapter concludes with pointers to current information about these efforts.

This chapter is organized into the following sections:

- Relationship between VoIP and PSTN protocols
- VoIP audio path: RTP/RTCP
- VoIP signaling: H.323
- VoIP signaling: SIP
- Scaling VoIP/PSTN gateways: MGCP, Megaco, and H.248
- Areas of standards research

Relationship Between VoIP and PSTN Protocols

Figure 11-1 is a view of the protocols, reference points, and interfaces related to VoIP and the PSTN from a functional perspective. The intent of this figure is to give you a holistic understanding of how the protocols fit together, and to highlight areas of overlapping standards.

Figure 11-1   *Architecture for Integrated PSTN and Internet Telephony*

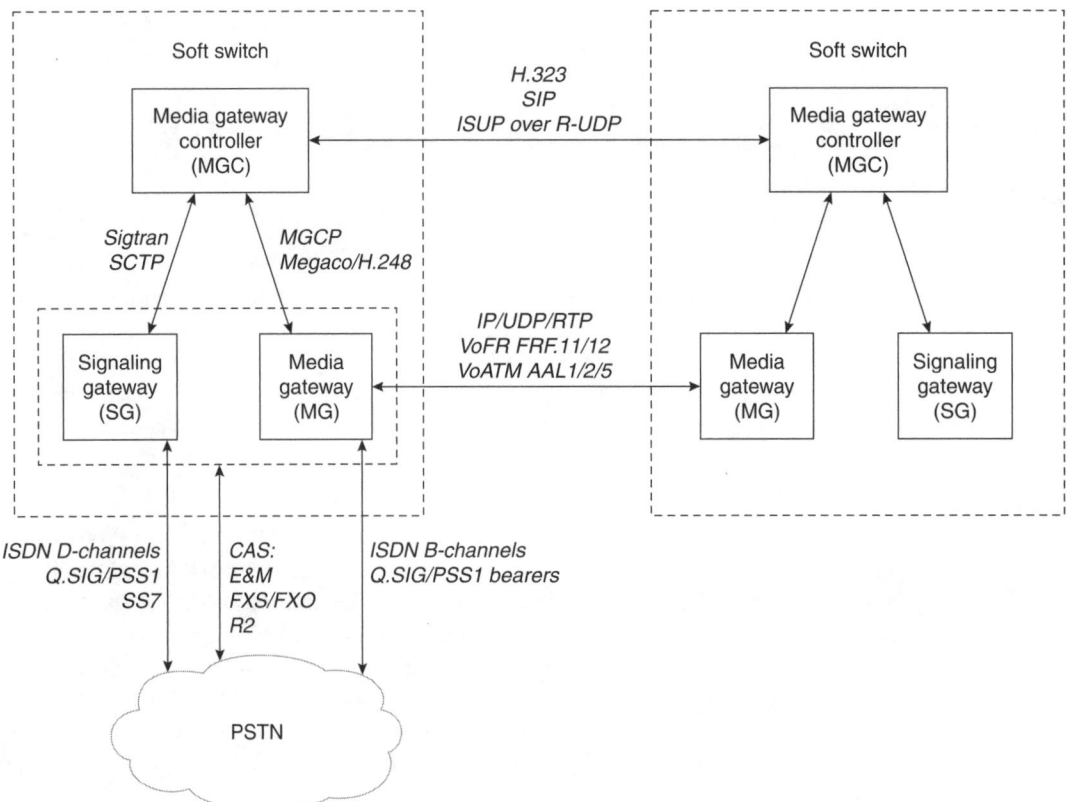

The International Telecommunications Union (ITU) and the Internet Engineering Task Force (IETF) are working from different perspectives toward a common goal of a converged PSTN and Internet infrastructure. The ITU efforts represent a conceptual extension of circuit-switched models to include operation over packet-based networks. The IETF efforts represent an extension of packet-based network applications and infrastructures to meet real-time performance requirements. In the coming years, interoperation between the IETF paradigm for VoIP, the ITU paradigm for VoIP, and the traditional PSTN will be of paramount importance.

VoIP Audio Path: RTP/RTCP

VoIP packets are composed of one or more speech codec samples or frames (see Chapter 6, "Voice Digitization and Coding") encapsulated in IP/UDP/RTP headers. VoIP uses UDP as the transport layer protocol because the retransmission facilities of TCP are not needed.

Recall that for real-time applications, retransmitted packets arrive too late to be used by the receiver. UDP provides the framing and application multiplexing services for VoIP (via UDP port numbers), and RTP provides the additional services required for real-time data transport.

UDP port selection for RTP sessions depends on the type of call signaling. In an H.323 environment, H.225.0 signaling determines which UDP ports will carry the RTP traffic. In a SIP environment, a SIP message sender indicates (via a session description) the UDP ports on which it will receive the RTP stream.

Figure 11-2 illustrates an example VoIP packet, with the RTP header shown in detail.

Figure 11-2 *VoIP Packet with RTP Header Emphasized*

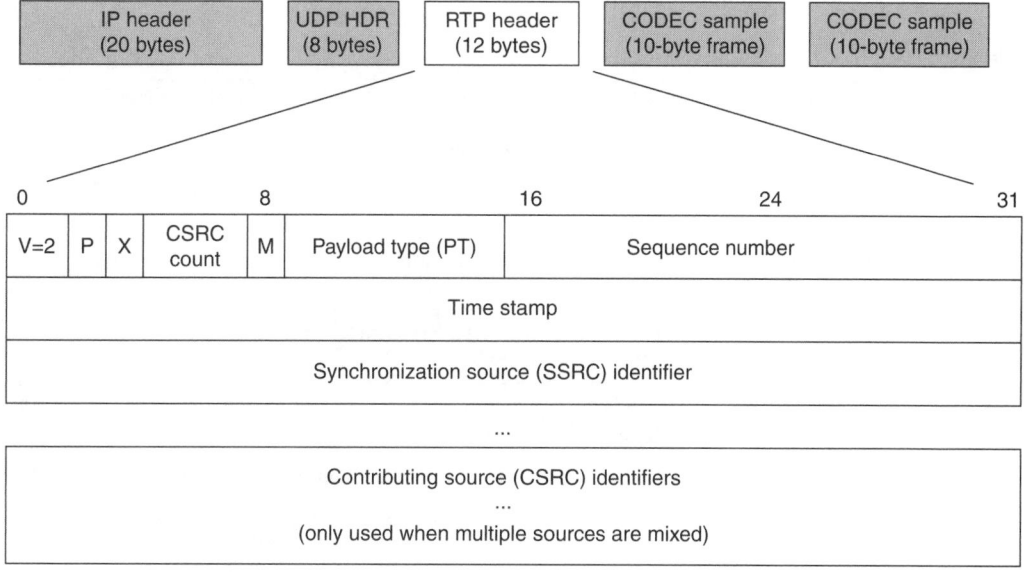

A glance at the preceding figure is enough to see that VoIP transport is not efficient. Twice as many bits are allocated to headers as to the actual payload. There are mechanisms to vastly improve the bandwidth efficiency of VoIP, but we will first explore the functionality that is provided by RTP. The following sections examine these topics:

- Real-Time Transport Protocol (RTP)
- Real-Time Control Protocol (RTCP)
- Improving RTP bandwidth efficiency

Real-Time Transport Protocol

Real-Time Transport Protocol (RTP) provides the following services:

- Distinguishes between multiple senders in an RTP multicast stream
- Preserves the timing relationship between packets
- Enables timing synchronization between media streams
- Sequences the data to identify lost packets
- Identifies media types
- Does *not* provide or ensure QoS

These services are explored here in the context of the RTP header fields, which are summarized in Table 11-1.

Table 11-1   *Summary Definitions of RTP Header Fields*

RTP Header Field	Function or Purpose
Version (V)	Specifies the version of RTP; for RFC 1889–compliant RTP, V=2.
Padding (P)	Indicates presence/absence of padding bytes for fixed block-size encryption algorithms.
Extension (X)	Identifies whether a single variable-length header extension follows the fixed 12-byte header.
CSRC Count (CC)	Indicates the number of CSRC header fields that follow the fixed 12-byte header.
Marker (M)	Depends on application; identifies the beginning of a "speech burst" for VoIP applications.
Payload Type (PT)	Identifies the encoded media (that is, the different audio codecs for VoIP).
Sequence Number	Enables receiver to detect packet loss; begins with random number, increments by 1 each packet.
Time Stamp	Enables correct timing of playout; increments by 1 for each codec sample interval.
SSRC	Sending Source: unique random identifier for each sender in a given multicast RTP session.
CSRC	Contributing Sources: for VoIP, indicates all the SSRCs that are mixed together in a conference.

The only value of the 2-bit V field that is consistent with current standard practice is V=2, which reflects RTP as defined in RFC 1889. The P-bit indicates the presence or absence of padding bytes at the end of the payload. If P=1, the last octet of the payload indicates how many padding bytes have been added to make the RTP packet end on some byte boundary (such as for RTP over Asynchronous Transfer Mode [ATM], or for encrypting the payload with block-encryption). The X-bit enables RTP to be flexible for experimental uses by indicating the presence of an extra variable-length header.

Distinguishing Between Multiple Senders

The 32-bit SSRC identifies the sending source of the media stream. An SSRC value is randomly assigned for each sender at the beginning of each media-stream session. The SSRC is useful to distinguish between senders within a single media stream, but it cannot be used to identify a particular sender between sessions, or to correlate multiple media streams from the same sender. An RTCP sender description header provides this functionality with the CNAME field.

The 32-bit CSRC fields, which are optionally appended to the 12-byte fixed RTP header, contain the SSRC identifiers for each of the senders that contribute to a composite media stream. When a multicast conference unit (MCU) mixes the media of several sources (for example, a VoIP conference bridge), the MCU sends RTP packets with its own SSRC in the SSRC field, and the SSRC of each sender is placed into separate CSRC fields. The 4-bit CC field identifies the number of CSRC fields that follow the 12-byte fixed RTP header. Up to 16 simultaneous senders may be identified via CSRC fields.

Note that extensive use of the CSRC fields can potentially reduce the effectiveness of RTP header compression because each CSRC is a 32-bit random number that may change frequently. Because each party generally speaks for at least a few seconds at a time, however, the CSRC field will remain constant for at least 50 to 100 packets, which allows considerable bandwidth savings via stateful compression techniques.

Timing Preservation and Synchronization

The *marker*, or *M-bit*, identifies the beginning of a talk-spurt following a period of silence, which is significant in the context of maintaining the de-jitter buffer (also known as playout buffer). Slight differences between the sampling clock of the sender's coder and the receiver's decoder can cause the receiver's playout buffer to slowly drain or fill. For example, a codec that nominally operates at 8000 samples per second may actually send out 8001 samples per second. If the receiver's codec actually operates at the nominal rate of 8000 samples per second, then an extra sample is left in the playout buffer every second. Over a period of time, these extra samples cause the playout buffer to fill. The playout buffer is designed to stay half-full to accommodate either lulls or bursts of received packets. If a burst of packets reaches a full playout buffer, then some of the samples will be lost. Figure 11-3 illustrates this concept.

Figure 11-3 *Playout Buffers Affected by Differences Between Send and Receive Sampling Clocks*

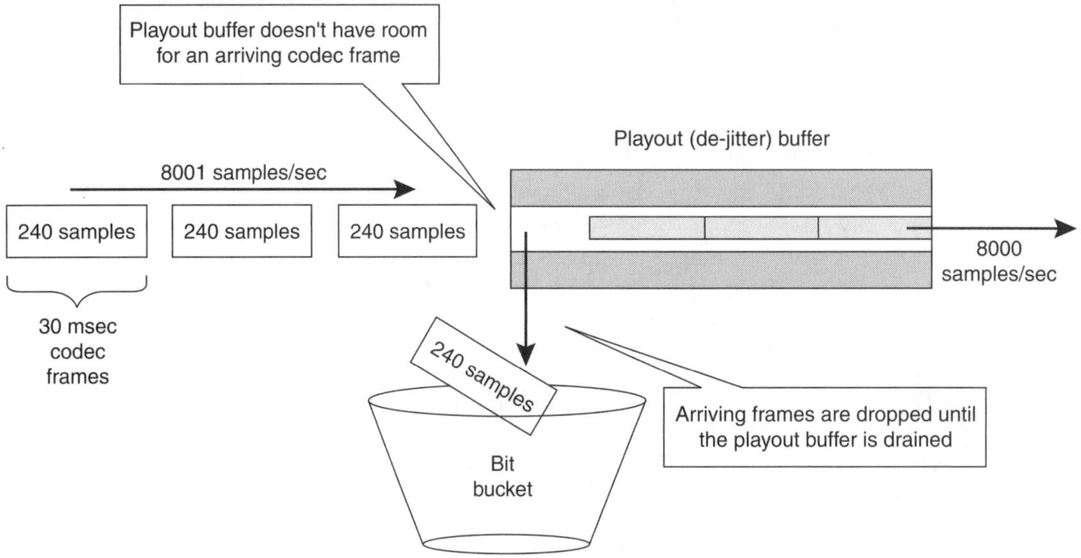

During periods of speech, a playout buffer cannot be adjusted without speeding up or slowing down the playout of sound, which would distort the speech signals and impact voice quality. During periods of silence (assuming that voice activity detection, or VAD, is used), a playout buffer can be adjusted to the optimal half-full position without impacting voice quality because people are not sensitive to small differences in the length of a speech pause. The playout buffer can steal time from a pause to play out extra samples that have accumulated, or add time to a pause to enable incoming samples to refill a drained buffer.

So how does the playout buffer relate to the M-bit? M=1 signifies that a silent period has just finished, so setting the M-bit provides notification at the RTP layer about an opportunity to adjust the playout buffers. Without the M-bit, a playout buffer can only be adjusted by inspecting the audio payload, which requires interaction with the codec. The M-bit provides a simpler method for the receiver to know when to adjust the playout buffer.

The time-stamp field of RTP headers enables the media source to specify the precise timing that a receiver should use when playing out successive packets in the media stream. Each tick of the RTP time stamp represents the amount of time for a single codec sample. Consider a source that transmits G.711 mu-law codec samples. If the source transmits exactly 160 samples in each RTP packet, then the time-stamp field increments by 160 ticks in each RTP packet. If silence suppression (VAD) is used, then the time-stamp field for the next RTP packet with active speech is set as if the transmissions never stopped. In other words, the time stamps continue incrementing even when the coder is suppressing transmission.

Because the time-stamp field begins at a random number when each RTP session begins, the time stamp only provides relative time information. In other words, you can compute differences between time intervals and synchronize multiple sessions using the time-stamp field, but you cannot relate events to real-world time with the time-stamp field. With RTP alone, you can synchronize an audio stream to the moving lips in a video image, but you need RTCP to relate the timing information to real-world events. RTCP provides a correlation between RTP time stamps and real time via a Network Time Protocol (NTP) time stamp in the RTCP sender report.

Packet Loss Detection

RTP sequence numbers are not used for retransmission, but they do enable a receiver to track packet loss. The packet loss statistics, along with other QoS information, are relayed back to the sender via RTCP receiver reports or sender reports.

Media Identification

For VoIP, the RTP payload type should reflect the audio codec that is used. However, both SIP and H.323 have alternate mechanisms for identifying the media stream. Because H.323 clients and gateways negotiate the codec type during the H.245 capabilities exchange, they know how to interpret the data in the RTP payload. Similarly, SIP user agents negotiate the codec selection through the session description in INVITE and 200 OK messages.

The RTP payload type is still important, because it is used by the Session Description Protocol (SDP) to identify common codecs.

RTP Payload Type and SDP

The SDP indicates common media types (such as audio codecs) via references to RTP payload types, as in the following example:

    m=audio 20736 RTP/AVP 8 0 4 2 15 18

In this example, the sender indicates that it supports the codecs identified by the RTP payload types 8, 0, 4, 2, 15, and 18 from the RTP Audio/Video Profile (draft-ietf-avt-profile-new-08.txt). Table 11-2 identifies the codecs represented by these payload types. See Chapter 6 for a discussion of the different codecs.

Table 11-2 *Mapping Between RTP Payload Types and Common Codecs (Per IETF)*

Codec Description	RTP PT
G.711 (PCM A-law)	8
G.711 (PCM mu-law)	0

continues

Table 11-2 *Mapping Between RTP Payload Types and Common Codecs (Per IETF) (Continued)*

Codec Description	RTP PT
G.723.1 all options (ACELP, MP-MLQ, Annex A)	4
G.726 (AD-PCM 16 kbps, 24 kbps, 32 kbps)	2
G.728 (LD-CELP)	15
G.729 all options (CS-ACELP, Annex A, Annex B)	18

For codecs that are not included in the RTP Audio/Video Profile, SDP allows codecs to be assigned a dynamic RTP payload type from the range 96 to 127. Because codecs assigned to RTP payload types in this manner have not been fully specified, SDP must provide additional information about the codec, as in the following example:

    m=audio 20864 RTP/AVP 97
    a=rtpmap:97 L16/8000

Here, SDP has indicated that the RTP payload type should be 97, which is from the dynamic range and not associated with a specific codec. The details of the codec are provided in the rtpmap statement as a 16-bit linear PCM codec with 8000 Hz sampling rate. The general form for rtpmap advertisements using SDP is:

    a=rtpmap:<PT> <codec_name>/<sampling_rate>[/<options>]

If a codec can operate at multiple bit-rates or with different options (such as with or without VAD), then it is a good idea that the codec name reflects these rates and options to avoid ambiguity. For example, G729D6.4 or G729E11.8 could be appropriate names for G.729 Annex D operating at 6.4 kbps and G.729 Annex E operating at 11.8 kbps, respectively. The sampling rate field should not change for multiple versions of a codec that provide different levels of compression. For example, most telephone-grade speech codecs have a sampling rate of 8000 Hz, which is independent of the bit rate of the compressed bit stream. For VoIP, the options field should always identify the number of audio channels, and it should specifically be avoided as a means of adding codec-specific parameters. For more information on these session descriptions, refer to RFC 2327.

Nonstandard Standards

Each static RTP payload-type definition in the audio/video profile should be specific enough that a receiver can decode the RTP payload based on knowledge of the PT field. In practice, this is not the case because of variations in how vendors implement codecs. For example, a Cisco router may be configured for G.723.1 with or without Annex A VAD, and at either 5.3 kbps or 6.3 kbps. The RTP payload definition for G.723.1 assumes that all options are supported, so there is no mechanism for a Cisco router to advertise a configured subset of these options (for example, only G.723.1 at 6.3 kbps without Annex A).

While ITU Recommendation G.723.1 requires that all options be supported (and Cisco routers do support all options), it is inevitable that someone will configure a router without enabling all four variations of the G.723.1 codec. If the router advertises the G.723.1 capability to other vendors in these cases, other vendors may send a media stream that the Cisco router is not configured to support. When configuring a Cisco router for integration with other vendors, make sure that if you plan to support any version of a G.723.1, G.729, or G.726 codec, that you enable all of the versions.

Table 11-3 identifies the codec options that Cisco routers support, and the resulting RTP payload types that the router sets in a SIP INVITE message, as of IOS 12.1(1)T.

Table 11-3   *Mapping of RTP Payload Types to Various Codecs for Cisco IOS 12.1(1)T*

Cisco Name	Codec Description	RTP PT
g711alaw	G.711 (PCM A-law 64 kbps)	8
g711ulaw	G.711 (PCM mu-law 64 kbps)	0
g723ar53	G.723 (ACELP 5.3 kbps) with Annex A VAD	65535
g723ar63	G.723 (MP-MLQ 6.3 kbps) with Annex A VAD	65535
g723r53	G.723 (ACELP 5.3 kbps)	65535
g723r63	G.723 (MP-MLQ 6.3 kbps)	4
g726r16	G.726 (AD-PCM 16 kbps)	2
g726r24	G.726 (AD-PCM 24 kbps)	65535
g726r32	G.726 (AD-PCM 32 kbps)	65535
g728	G.728 (LD-CELP)	15
g729br8	G.729 or G.729A (CS-ACELP) with Annex B VAD	65535
g729r8	G.729 or G.729A (CS-ACELP)	18

Note that the 65535 value is not a valid RTP payload type. Cisco routers use this value to represent codecs that are not supported for the given application. In Table 11-3, for example, the codecs listed with 65535 are supported in the hardware but are not supported by the SIP software. The 65535 acts as a placeholder in the SIP INVITE message to indicate that there is a codec but it is not one of the supported codecs.

Real-Time Control Protocol

The *RTP Control Protocol (RTCP)* supplements RTP by handling the administrative and reporting aspects of an RTP multicast conference. RTCP is specified in RFC 1889 as part of RTP. Even though RTCP is designed to scale for large conferences, it is useful in a simple point-to-point VoIP call to provide QoS feedback from the receiver to the sender in each direction.

For large multicast conferences, the bandwidth of RTP media streams tends to remain constant because only a few people can speak at a time, even if thousands of people are listening. RTCP control information is sent from each participant to every other participant, so scalability is a big issue. If each participant sends a 100-byte packet every second, then a conference with 10,000 people causes each participant to receive 1 Mbps of control information. RTCP addresses this problem by transmitting packets less often as the number of detected conference participants increases. Figure 11-4 illustrates this concept. The RTCP algorithm limits control bandwidth to approximately 5 percent of the bandwidth in the media stream by default, although applications can adjust this amount as necessary.

Figure 11-4 *RTCP Limits Control Bandwidth as the Number of Multicast Participants Increases*

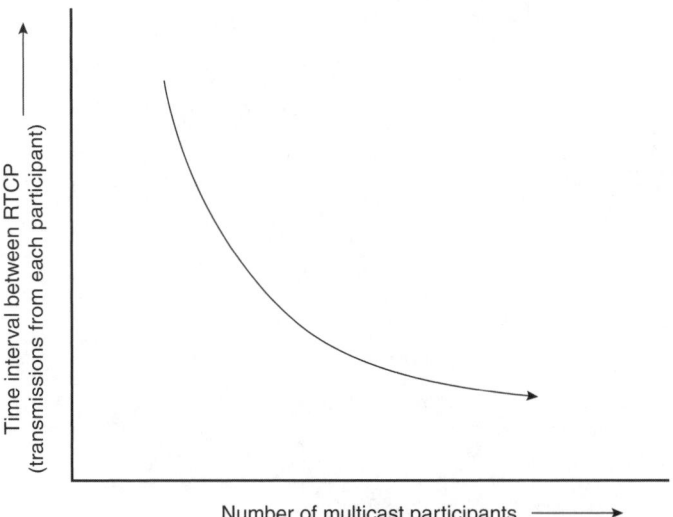

The specific functions that RTCP performs are explored here in the context of the five RTCP message types:

- Sender report (SR) and receiver report (RR)
- Source description (SDES)
- Disconnection (BYE)
- Application-specific (APP)

Sender Report and Receiver Report

Sources of an RTP media stream transmit sender reports (SRs) to all multicast participants. Nonsource participants transmit receiver reports (RRs) to all other multicast participants. Both SRs and RRs contain a reception report section, but the SR also contains a sender information section. Figure 11-5 illustrates the format of an RTCP SR packet.

Figure 11-5 *RTCP SR*

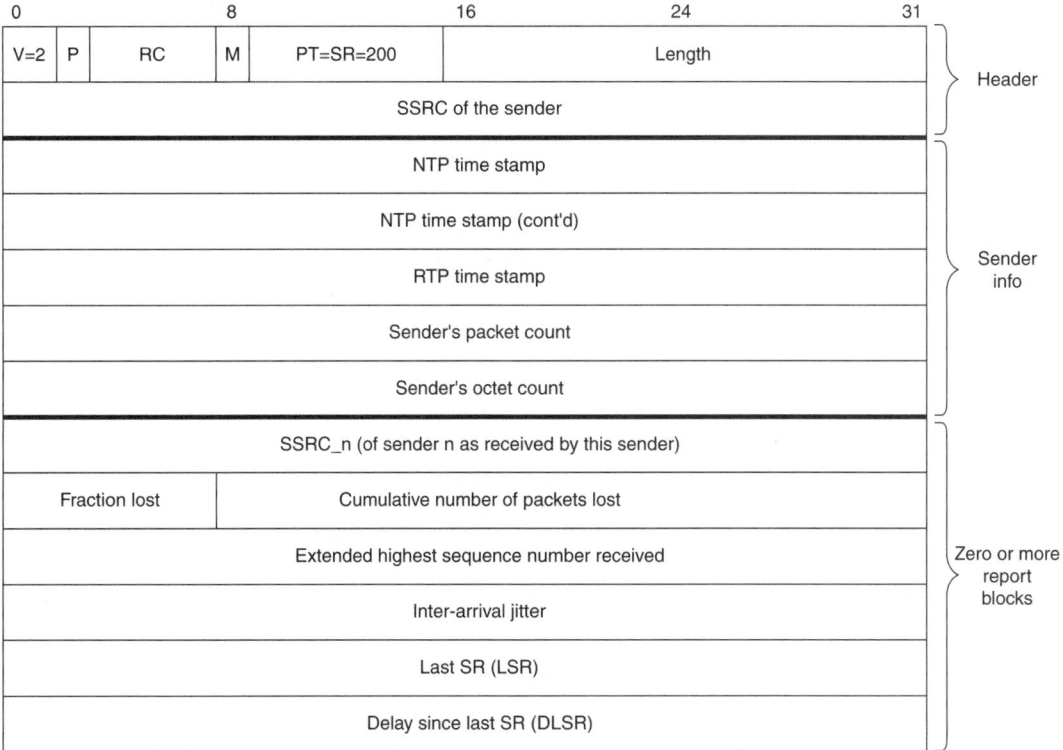

Note that an SR is a combination of RTCP sender information and an RTCP reception report regarding every other sender from which this sender receives media streams. An RR provides the same information, except the sender information is excluded because no media streams are sent. In a point-to-point VoIP conversation, each endpoint acts as a sender, so both endpoints create SRs. Each endpoint learns how the other perceived the transport quality via the reception report section of received SRs.

The contents of each field in the RTCP SR are summarized in Table 11-4.

Table 11-4 *Fields of the RTCP SR*

RTCP Header Field	Function or Purpose
Version (V)	Specifies the version of RTP; for RFC 1889–compliant RTP, V=2.
Padding (P)	Indicates presence/absence of padding bytes.
Reception Report Count (RC)	Indicates the number of reception report blocks that follow the sender information.
Packet Type (PT)	Identifies the packet as an RTCP SR with PT=200 (RR uses PT=201).
Length	Length of the RTCP sender report; equals the number of 32-bit words minus 1.
SSRC	Sending source identification of the RTCP packet sender.
NTP Time Stamp	Provides the real-world time that the packet is transmitted.
RTP Time Stamp	Enables the RTP time stamps to be correlated with real-world time via NTP.
Sender's Packet Count	Total number of packets sent in the RTP media stream.
Sender's Byte Count	Total number of bytes sent in the RTP media stream.
SSRC_n	SSRC identification of the sender about whom this reception report block applies.
Fraction Lost	Number of RTP packets lost divided by the RTP packets sent (since last SR/RR).
Cumulative Packets Lost	Number of RTP packets lost since the beginning of the session.
Extended Sequence Number Received	Highest sequence number received from sender (extra digits to prevent wrapping).
Interarrival Jitter (J)	D= difference between interpacket times at sender and receiver; J= deviation of D.
Last SR (LSR) Time Stamp	NTP time stamp (32-bit version) in the last SR packet received from the sender.
Delay Since Last SR (DLSR)	Time difference between receiving the last SR and sending this reception report.

The RR is identical to the SR except that the packet type PT=201, and the sender information section (that is, time stamps and packets/bytes sent) is eliminated.

The RTCP fields in SRs and RRs give media senders important QoS feedback from the receivers. In addition, each receiver can determine if its reception quality is consistent with other receivers, or whether local problems may be adversely impacting its reception quality. Specifically, senders can learn the following network statistics:

- Round-trip transit time (RTT)
- Packet loss rate
- Jitter

Media senders calculate the RTT by noting when RR packets are received (say, NTP time stamp A) and using the LSR and DLSR fields. A sender calculates the RTT as the difference between when it sent an SR to receivers and received an RR back from the receivers, accounting for the turnaround time at the receiver. This is expressed in the following formula:

$$RTT = (LSR - A) - DLSR$$

All participants in the session learn about packet-loss rates in the network by examining the RTCP RRs. The fraction lost shows the loss rate over the most recent time interval, and the cumulative packets lost allows each participant to know how chronic the problem is without needing to remember and track data.

WARNING You may want to skip this section if you have a faint heart for math, but read on if you are a techno-masochist! Actually, it is not that bad if you stay with it.

The jitter is calculated at each receiver by noting when RTP media packets arrive, and using the value of the RTP time-stamp field contained in those packets. The receiver first calculates the transit time for each received packet. The difference in transit times between any two adjacent packets is calculated according to the following formula:

$$D(i, j) = (R_j - S_j) - (R_i - S_i)$$

The variables are defined as:

- $D(i,j)$ is the difference in transit times between adjacent packets i and j
- R_j is the time when packet j was received
- S_j is the time when packet j was sent (determined from the RTP time stamp)
- R_i is the time when packet i was received
- S_i is the time when packet i was sent (determined from the RTP time stamp)

Each inbound RTP media packet causes a new calculation of the transit time difference between the current received packet i and the previous received packet i–1. Instead of writing this transit time difference as D(i–1,i), consider the simpler syntax D_i.

According to RFC 1889, the jitter (J_i) up to and including packet i is calculated with the following equation:

$$J_i = J_i - 1 + \left(\frac{D_i - J_i - 1}{16} \right)$$

This formula is written in a recursive form because it simplifies the calculation for computers, but it can also be written as a series sum, which is more intuitive to understand. J is the time-weighted average of the transit delay differences (D_i), with more recent measurements of D_i contributing more significantly to the average:

$$J_i = \left(\frac{15^0}{16^1} \right) \times D_i + \left(\frac{15^1}{16^2} \right) \times D_i - 1 + \left(\frac{15^2}{16^3} \right) \times D_i - 2 + \left(\frac{15^3}{16^4} \right) \times D_i - 3 + \dots$$

or more concisely as:

$$J_i = \frac{1}{16} \times \sum_{n-0}^{i} \left(\frac{15}{16} \right)^n D_{i-n}$$

Note that the value 16 in the denominator of the jitter equation (RFC 1889 form) is a magic number. The magic number (hereafter called M) controls the degree to which the jitter measure is affected by current versus previous measures of D_i. For small values of M, the jitter measure is weighted toward recent measures of D_i. This causes the jitter measure to change frequently with the arrival of new data, and reflect the most recent network conditions. For large values of M, the jitter measure is weighted toward previous measures of D_i. This tends to smooth the effects of transient spikes in successive jitter measurements, and show long-term averages of D_i. Figure 11-6 illustrates successive measures of D_i and J_i for a network with a random one-way delay between 60 and 250 ms. J_i is graphed for various values of M to demonstrate how increasing M yields a smoother curve.

Figure 11-6   *Time Weighting of the Jitter Measure Is Affected by the Magic Number M*

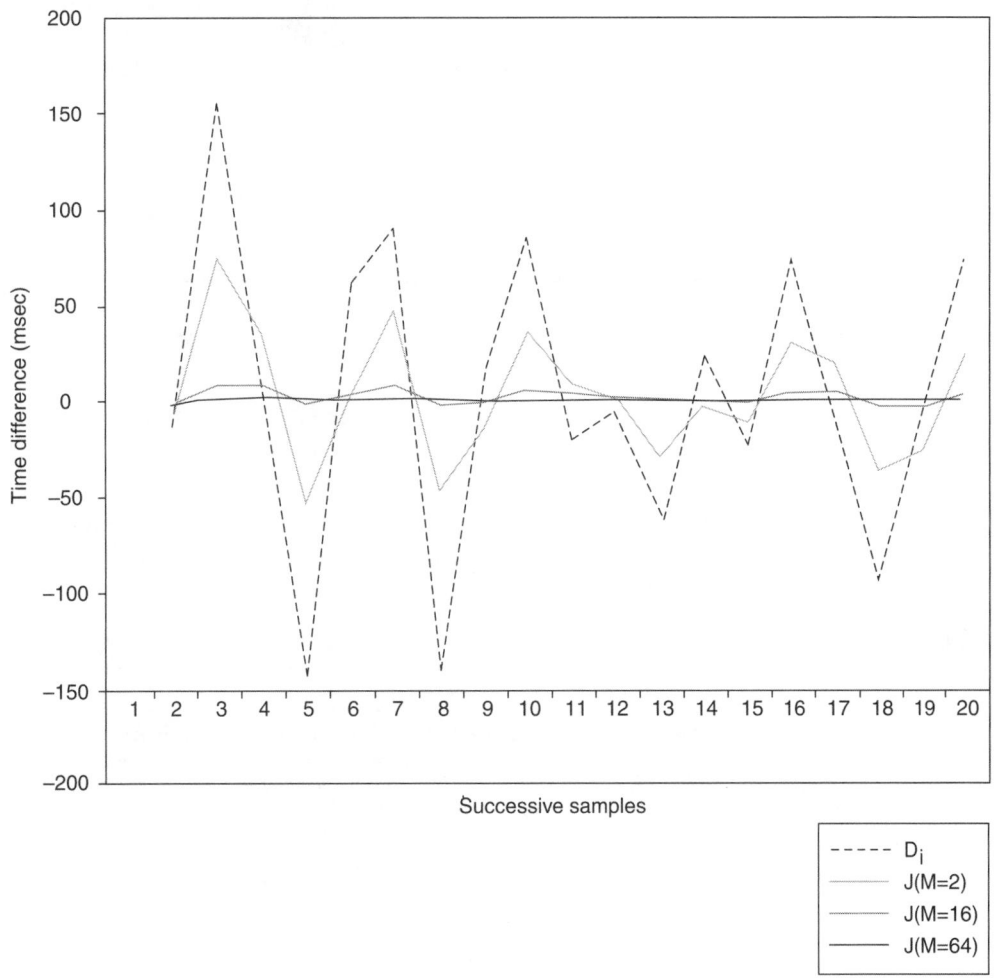

In RFC 1889, the value M=16 was chosen as a compromise to enable a smooth and averaged representation of J over time, while still enabling J to respond to current network conditions.

You have two options now:

- Let your mind rest, because the math part is over!
- Chuckle to yourself that it was easy, and deride the author for his simplicity.

Source Description

The source description (SDES) provides information about each RTP media sender in a multicast session. Only the CNAME element is mandatory, so that the real-world identity of each sender is clearly defined. Figure 11-7 illustrates the format of an RTCP source description packet:

Figure 11-7 *RTCP SDES*

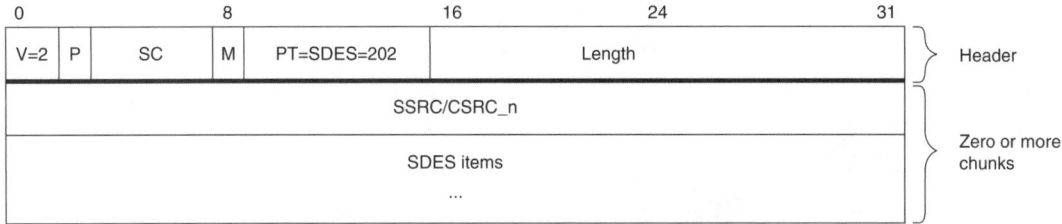

Each host usually sends a single SDES item, which relates to its own SSRC identification, in a source description RTCP packet. A mixing device (for example, a VoIP conference bridge or an MCU) sends multiple SDES item blocks (each with a different CSRC) in one SDES RTCP packet. Table 11-5 describes the elements that form an SDES item block.

Table 11-5 *Elements of a SDES*

Element	Description
CNAME	<user>@<host-name> (reflects the application host, which may be different than the e-mail host).
NAME	Actual name, as opposed to a login ID.
EMAIL	E-mail address of the sender.
PHONE	Telephone number of the sender, in full E.164 format (for example, +1 408 555 1212).
LOC	Geographic location of the sender.
TOOL	If generated by an application or utility, the name and version of such entity.
NOTE	Free-form text for transient messages. Not to be used routinely, as it wastes RTCP bandwidth.
PRIV	Experimental or application-specific extensions.

Disconnection

When participants disconnect from an RTP multimedia conference, they send an RTCP Disconnection (BYE) message, so that each participant can keep track of the total number of participants. This is important because each participant rate-limits its RTCP transmissions based on its knowledge of the total number of participants.

Without BYE messages, the perceived number of multicast participants continues to rise as various listeners join and leave. Eventually, the perceived group size is so large that hosts rarely transmit RTCP traffic. In such cases, newcomers are not able to synchronize the media streams or identify sources. Figure 11-8 illustrates the format of an RTCP disconnection packet.

Figure 11-8   *RTCP BYE*

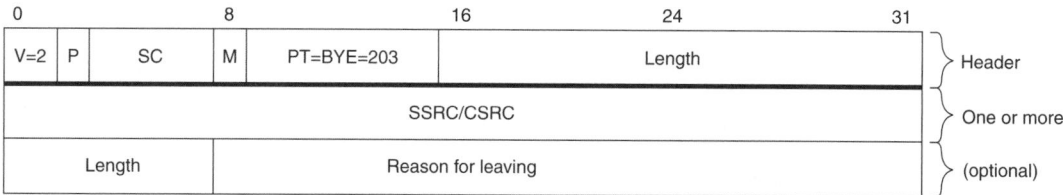

Application-Specific

Application-specific (APP) RTCP packets enable experimentation and extensions to the protocol, without requiring new packet types to be registered with a payload/packet type. Figure 11-9 illustrates the format of an RTCP APP packet:

Figure 11-9   *RTCP APP*

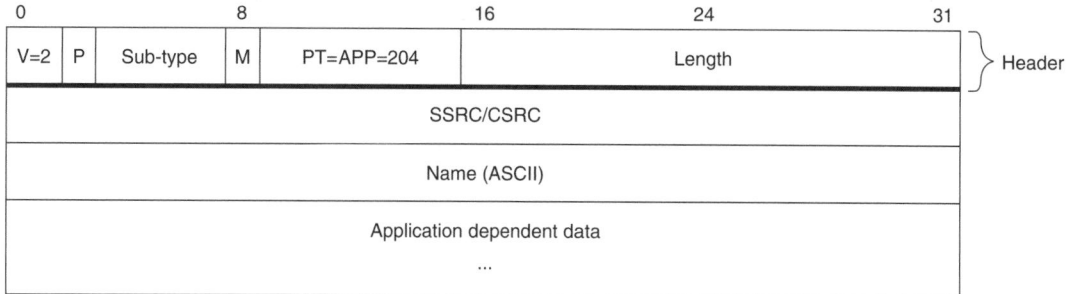

Compound RTCP Packets

Each of the five RTCP packet types just described falls on even 32-bit word boundaries. These RTCP packets may be stacked together to form a compound packet or meta-packet, all of which is transported in a UDP payload. RTCP meta-packets help reduce the IP/UDP overhead associated with the RTCP data. Except for the following rules, RTCP meta-packets may occur in any order:

- The first RTCP packet in the meta-packet must be an RR or SR. If a large meta-packet is fragmented into multiple UDP payloads, each fragment must begin with an RR or SR (empty RR or SR packets are acceptable if there is no additional data).
- Each meta-packet must contain an SDES with CNAME.
- If a BYE packet is present in the meta-packet, it should be in the last position.

Figure 11-10 illustrates these rules and the structure of the RTCP meta-packet.

Figure 11-10 *RTCP Meta-packet*

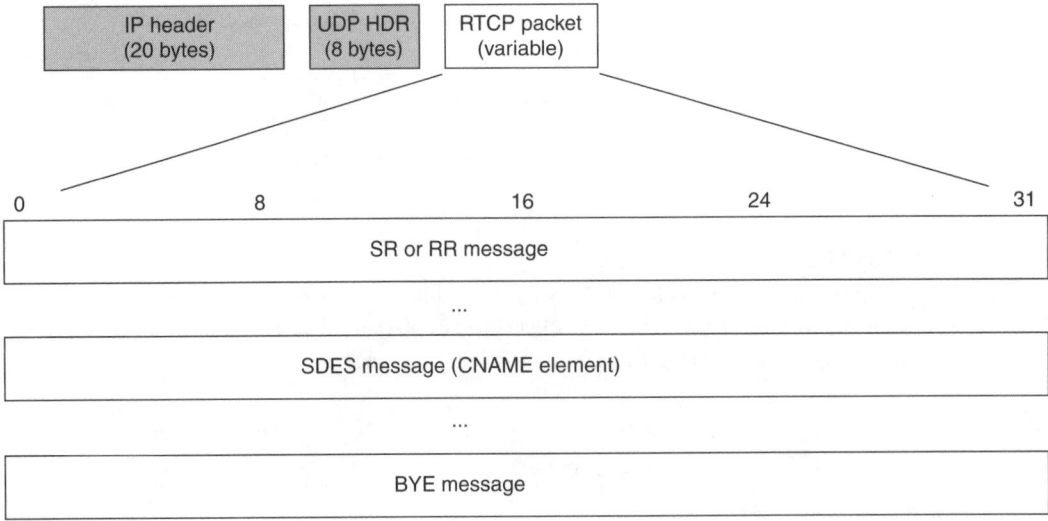

Improving RTP Bandwidth Efficiency

Bandwidth efficiency is a major issue with RTP audio streams because the IP/UDP/RTP headers consume a large portion of the available bandwidth, thus reducing the effective bandwidth for the audio payload (and other traffic on the link). The solution to this problem is to implement a header compression scheme.

Compressed RTP

Compressed RTP (CRTP), which is specified in RFC 2508, is based on the principles of TCP header compression (RFC 1144). CRTP reduces the 40 bytes of IP/UDP/RTP headers to 4 bytes if UDP checksums are enabled, or only 2 bytes if UDP checksums are disabled. The bandwidth savings are possible because many header fields do not change for each packet; some fields change in a predictable manner, and some fields that change in small increments enable differential encoding. Chapter 10, "Review of IP Features for Voice/Data Integration," discusses these topics in more detail for TCP header compression.

RTP header compression requires that the sender and receiver maintain shared-state information for each RTP context. A unique RTP context is defined by a combination of source/destination IP addresses, source/destination UDP ports, and the RTP SSRC. The shared-state information for each context includes an uncompressed RTP packet, and any negotiated delta parameters that describe how certain fields change from packet to packet. The sender then removes the IP/UDP/RTP header and affixes a CRTP header, which includes an RTP context identifier (CID). The CID enables the receiver to search its table of RTP contexts, and reconstruct the original RTP packet based on the context information and the residual information encoded in the CRTP header. Depending on the number of concurrent RTP contexts that two hosts expect to maintain, they can negotiate an 8-bit or a 16-bit CID. This puts an effective limit of 65,535 concurrent RTP contexts between any two machines (that have a lot of processing power!).

Because RTP header compression relies on shared-state information between the sender and receiver, it is important to consider what happens when the sender and receiver lose the shared state, or fall out of sync with each other. The receiver must inform the sender that it lost the context information, and the sender must reply by sending a full RTP packet so the receiver can renew the context. During the time that the receiver is waiting to reestablish the RTP context (which is at least twice the link delay), the receiver must discard all of the CRTP packets that arrive. For this reason, CRTP is not desirable on links with excessive delay. For example, a full second of speech may be lost on a satellite link each time a CRTP receiver loses the RTP context. This may also be an issue for Tunneling Multiplexed CRTP (TCRTP), which is discussed shortly. IETF development efforts are in progress to make CRTP more robust to the loss of shared state, which will improve performance on links with excessive delay.

Tunneling Multiplexed CRTP

Consider a scenario where a large number of RTP streams pass between two routers on opposite sides of a network, as is the case between VoIP/PSTN gateway POPs in a provider network, or between two corporate sites in a private intranet. Figure 11-11 illustrates the scenario when RTP header compression is not used. Using RTP header compression across this path would nearly triple the effective bandwidth (compare one G.729 call at 24 kbps without header compression to three calls totaling 26.4 kbps with header compression), which is a big motivation to implement it.

Figure 11-11   *Large Number of RTP Streams Pass Through IP Cloud Between Routers*

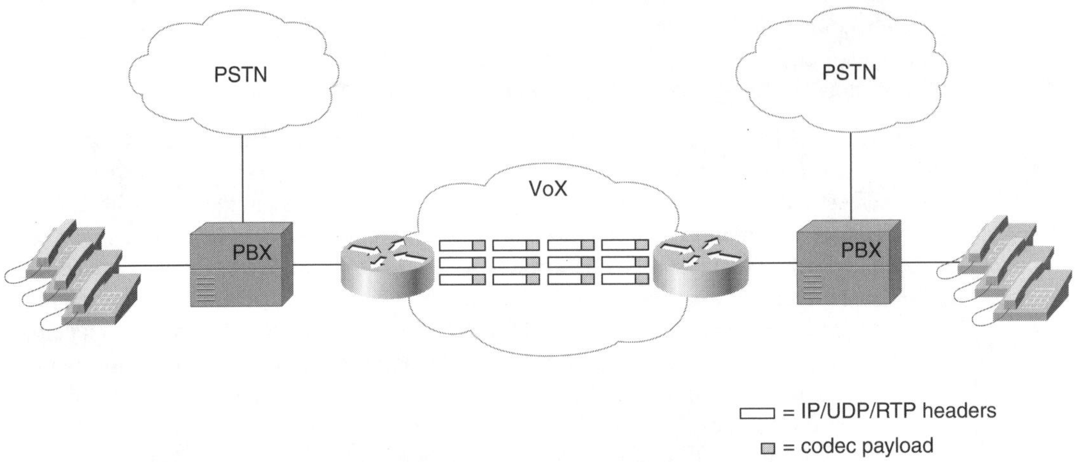

☐ = IP/UDP/RTP headers
▫ = codec payload

While CRTP is a good tool to make RTP bandwidth-efficient, it requires implementation on a link-by-link basis to realize the bandwidth efficiency. This is neither efficient nor practical for a high-speed IP backbone. The question is, how can IP/UDP/RTP headers be compressed, but somehow pass across the network transparently without link-by-link processing? The answer, according to the most recent IETF draft as of this writing, is Tunneling Multiplexed CRTP (TCRTP).

TCRTP, as defined in draft-ietf-avt-tcrtp-00.txt, is an amalgamation of several existing protocols with new extensions:

- RFC 2508, Compressing IP/UDP/RTP Headers for Low-Speed Serial Links (CRTP)
- <koren-avt-crtp-enhance-01.txt>, Enhancements to IP/UDP/RTP Header Compression
- <draft-ietf-pppext-pppmux-00.txt>, PPP Multiplexed Frame Option
- RFC 2661, Layer 2 Tunneling Protocol (L2TP)
- <draft-ietf-l2tpext-l2tphc-01.txt>, L2TP Header Compression (L2TPHC)

The following process describes how TCRTP can be used to realize bandwidth savings for multiple RTP streams across an IP network, without requiring CRTP on every link. Note that this process applies between two routers that either terminate large numbers of VoIP calls, or act as aggregator routers for connection to a high-speed backbone:

Step 1   Each RTP stream is compressed into CRTP packets according to RFC 2508.

Step 2   Apply a PPP header to each packet.

Step 3   Multiplex the separate PPP frames into a single PPP frame with multiple CRTP packets.

Figure 11-12 illustrates steps 1 through 3.

Figure 11-12   *RTP Stream Is Compressed Via CRTP and Encapsulated Via PPP Multiplexing*

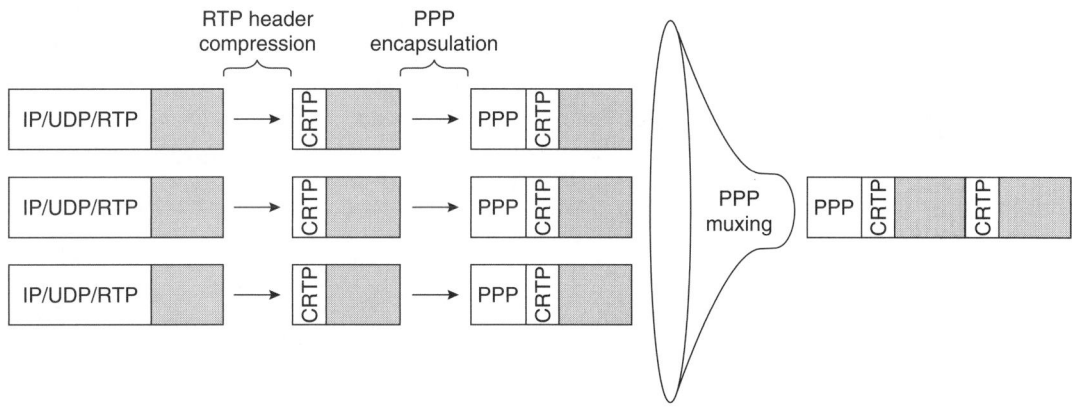

The multiplexed PPP frame, which contains multiple CRTP packets, is then processed as follows:

Step 4   Encapsulate the muxed PPP frame in a 16-byte L2TP header and a 20-byte IP header.

Step 5   Apply L2TP header compression, which reduces the L2TP header to 1 byte.

Step 6   Forward the new IP datagram across the IP backbone.

Figure 11-13 illustrates steps 4 through 6.

Figure 11-13   *PPP Frame Is Forwarded Via an L2TP Tunnel with L2TP Header Compression*

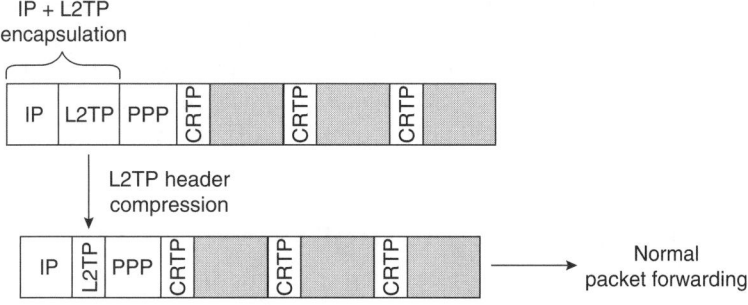

At the receiving end of the tunnel, these steps are applied in reverse to restore the original RTP media streams. Who needs encryption when the codec payload is hiding under so many headers? Actually, computers are good at sorting through these headers, so the codec data is still vulnerable to snooping, which enables anonymous parties to eavesdrop on conversations.

TCRTP does provide a good opportunity for network-based encryption of VoIP. Endpoints do not need to implement or understand encryption, as long as the connections between the endpoints and the entryways to the L2TP tunnel are trusted. With this solution, companies can direct their interoffice voice traffic through ISPs that provide QoS-enabled virtual private networks (VPNs). (See Figure 11-14.) This concept represents the next WAN cost-cutting step in the evolution of the corporate communications infrastructure, and a significant opportunity for enterprises and service providers alike.

Figure 11-14 *QoS-Enabled VPNs Provide Secure Transit for VoIP Across an ISP Backbone*

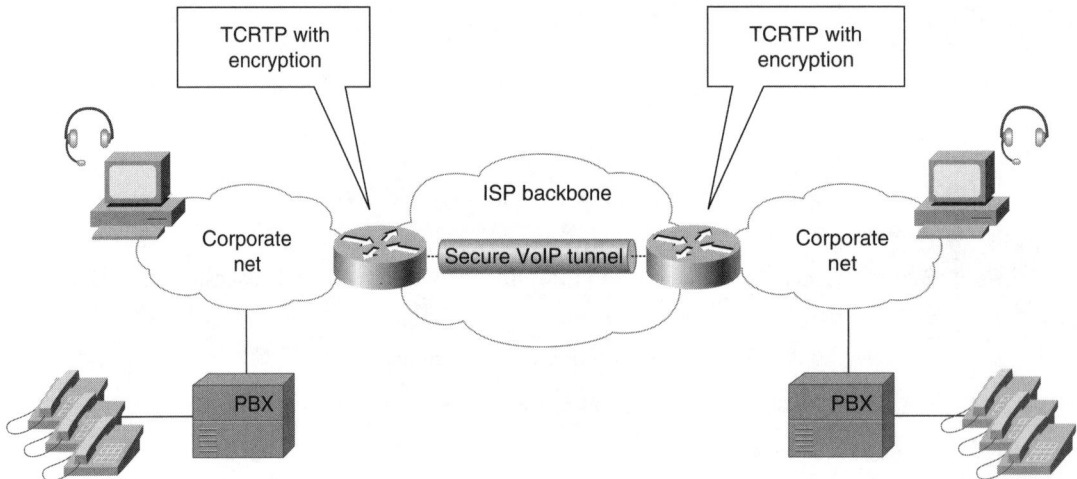

Recall that CRTP is sensitive to large delay times across a link. TCRTP increases the potential delay time for the link tunnel that CRTP crosses. The efforts to make CRTP more resilient to a loss of shared state will also help TCRTP performance. It is also important to note that the PPP multiplexing process used in TCRTP must not wait to completely fill a frame if there is insufficient traffic, because this would add delay and jitter to the CRTP packets. You can find the latest developments with TCRTP at the IETF web site.

VoIP Signaling: H.323 Paradigm

ITU Recommendation H.323, Packet-Based Multimedia Communication Systems, is the most mature set of standards for multiparty multimedia communications. H.323 is a container document that refers to protocols and message formats described in other standard documents, and explains how the various protocols interact with defined system elements in a common framework. The ITU recommendations in Table 11-6 are an integral part of the H.323 signaling specifications.

Table 11-6 *ITU-T Recommendations that Support H.323 Signaling Functions*

ITU Recommendation	Title
H.225.0	Call Signaling Protocols and Media Stream Packetization for Packet-Based Multimedia Communication Systems
H.235	Security and Encryption for H-Series Multimedia Terminals
H.245	Control Protocol for Multimedia Communication
H.450.x	Supplemental Services for H.323
T.120 series	Data Protocols for Multimedia Conferencing

In addition to the signaling functions, the H.323 framework incorporates a variety of media formats and application structures, as indicated in Table 11-7.

Table 11-7 *ITU-T–Endorsed Media Formats for H.323*

Media	Formats
Audio	G.711, G.722, G.723.1, G.728, G.729, GSM, ISO/IEC 11172-3, and ISO/IEC 13818-3
Video	H.261, H.262, H.263
Data Protocols	T.120 series

This chapter explores the parts of H.323 that relate to VoIP services. The H.235 security components are not discussed here, although security is an important issue. The sections that follow explore the H.323 framework from three perspectives:

- System components
- Addressing
- Protocols

System Components

H.323 communications occur between the following system components, which in some cases are separate physical devices, and in other cases are software elements that may reside on the same platform:

- Terminal
- Multipoint Control Unit (MCU)

- Gateway
- Gatekeeper

Terminal

You can think of an H.323 terminal as a telephone on steroids, with optional support for interactive video and data-sharing applications. Terminals have packet-based interfaces and are directly operated by end users.

Figure 11-15 illustrates the functional elements of an H.323 terminal. The H.225.0 Layer provides logical framing, sequencing, and error detection for transmission and reception of media and control messages. In a VoIP network, this is IP/UDP/RTP for the audio payload, and either IP/UDP or IP/TCP for control messages. H.323 endpoints must support audio codecs, but support for video codecs and data applications is optional. The System Control Unit provides all of the call-related and media-related signaling functions. H.225.0 RAS manages registration, admission, and status signaling between the endpoint and a gatekeeper. This function is not used in systems without a gatekeeper. H.225.0 Call Control manages call setup and teardown between the endpoints (or proxies), and establishes the H.245 media control channel. H.245 media control negotiates codec, QoS, and other media options, establishes RTP sessions, and monitors transmission quality.

Multipoint Control Unit

A *Multipoint Control Unit (MCU)* is a combination of two fundamental system components that enable multipoint communications:

- Multipoint Controller (MC)
- Multipoint Processor (MP)

The MC provides control of the media channels, such as negotiating codecs and establishing unicast and multicast RTP sessions via H.245 signaling. When an endpoint (such as a terminal or a gateway) joins a conference, it must establish an H.245 connection with the MC. The H.245 connection procedures include a master-slave determination sequence to negotiate which device acts as the MC when multiple devices have the MC functionality. A conference cannot have more than one MC.

The MP sends and receives media streams (for example, audio samples in RTP packets) to and from the conference participants. The MP may convert media between different formats (such as G.711 audio to G.723.1 audio), and it may combine media from multiple sources (for example, mix audio from multiple sources). The exact functions of the MP depend on where it is located in the network, and the type of conference that it is processing.

Figure 11-15   *Functional Elements of an H.323 Terminal*

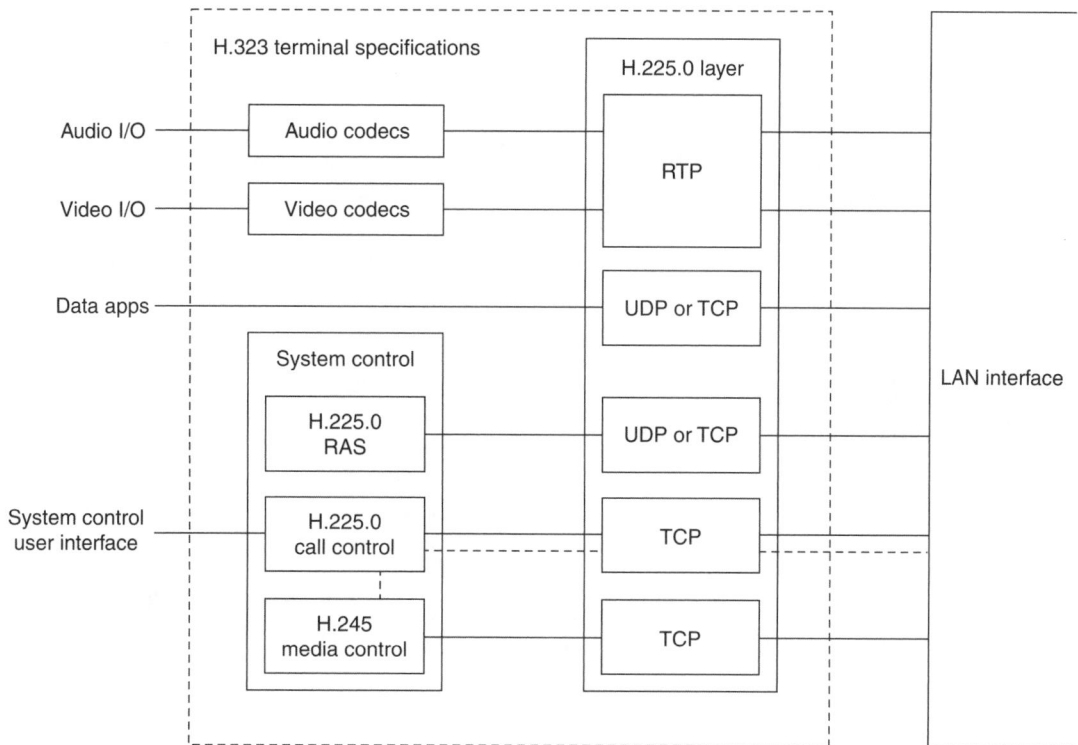

Figure 11-16 illustrates where the MC and MP functions may be located in an H.323 network. Given that a single MC may be active for a conference, all of these devices cannot simultaneously provide the MC and MP functions. Note that as of H.323v3, the possibility of multiple MPs being controlled by a single MC is not explored. All published versions of H.323 assume that an MP is located with the MC, which implies that a single MP is used in a conference. Several conferences, each with an active MCU, may be connected via an MCU that acts as an endpoint in one of the conferences.

Any terminal, gateway, or gatekeeper with MC functionality can support ad hoc conferences (such as a third person added to a two-party call). Gateways and gatekeepers may include both MC and MP functionality, which is a special case of an MCU colocated with the gateway or gatekeeper. Terminals can contain some of the functions of an MP, such as codec translation and mixing, but terminals never retransmit a received media stream. By definition, a device that performs such a function is an MP, which is part of an MCU.

Figure 11-16 *Distributed MP and MC Functions Enable a Variety of Conference Types*

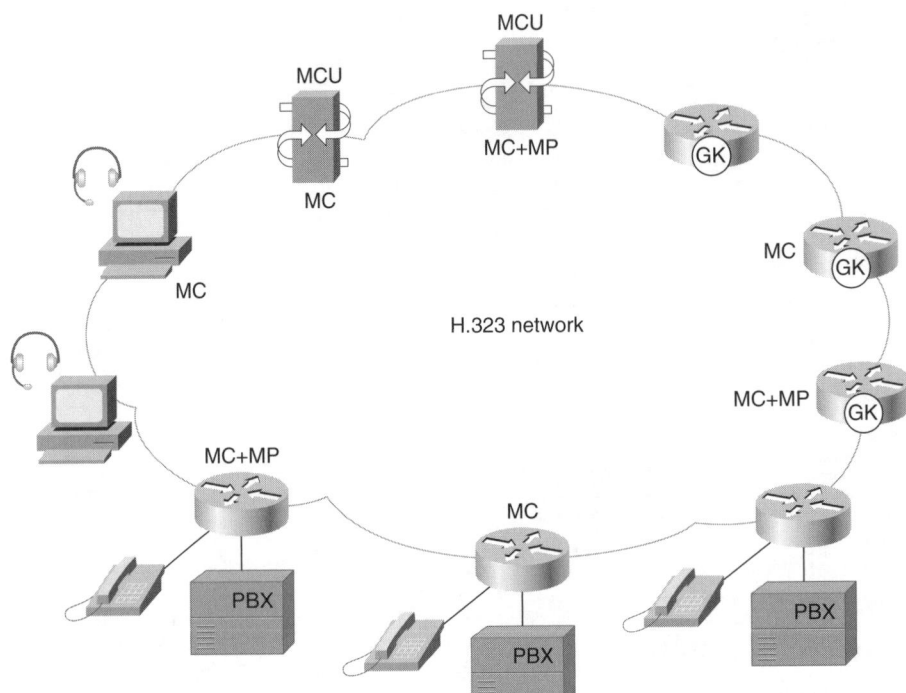

The MCU functionality is explored here in the context of different conference types. Multipoint conferences can be conceptually divided into the following scenarios:

- Centralized unicast
- Centralized multicast
- Decentralized multicast
- Mixed

Figure 11-17 illustrates a centralized unicast audio conference. In this example, the MC and the MP are colocated in an MCU. All terminals and gateways involved in the conference establish bidirectional H.245 media control sessions with the MC, as indicated by the dashed arrows. All terminals and gateways send a media stream to the MP, as indicated by the solid arrow. The MP mixes the audio from all sources, and sends the mixed audio stream back out to each source separately. When mixing the audio, the MP filters out the participant contribution. The MP may also translate the codec format to support endpoints with different capabilities. The send and receive media streams are two separate connections, but they are illustrated with a single bidirectional arrow to simplify the drawing.

Figure 11-17   *Centralized Unicast Conference—MC and MP Combined in MCU*

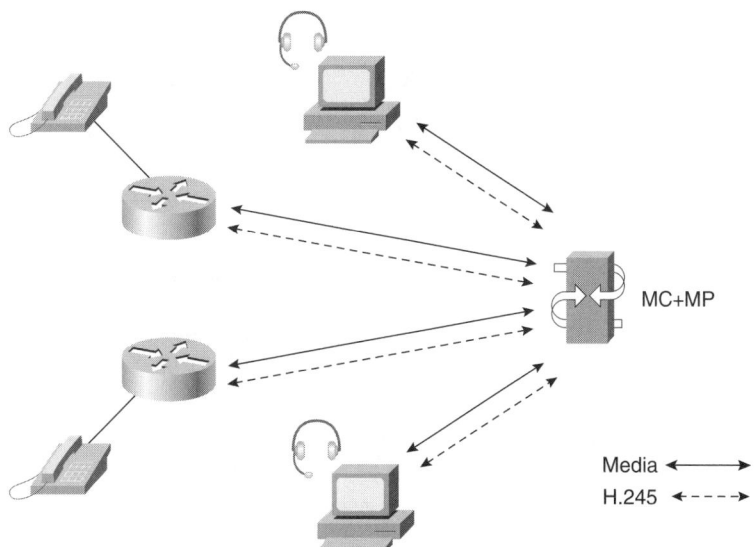

Figure 11-18 illustrates a centralized multicast audio conference. In this example, the MC and the MP are colocated in the MCU. As before, all terminals and gateways involved in the conference establish bidirectional H.245 media control sessions with the MC. Also as before, each conference participant sends a unicast media stream to the MP, as illustrated by the solid arrow. Notice now that the MP does not send a unicast stream back to each participant. After mixing the audio and performing any required codec translations, the MP sends a single copy of the media stream to the multicast group, which is received by each conference participant. The MP may send several multicast streams, with different bandwidth requirements and administrative scopes, to accommodate sites with different bandwidth capabilities.

Figure 11-19 illustrates a decentralized multicast conference. In this example, the MCU only acts as an MC, and does not provide the MP functionality. A gateway or a gatekeeper can also provide the MC function, as indicated in Figure 11-16. As before, all terminals and gateways involved in the conference establish bidirectional H.245 media control sessions with the MC. Each endpoint now sends its media stream to the multicast group, where each participant receives it. The MCU does not need to join the multicast group. In this example, there is no need for a centralized MP function, because each participant directly receives the audio stream from every other participant. Endpoints with decentralized conference capabilities must be able to mix the audio streams from each source, understand all codec formats in use, and present a single audio stream to the user.

Figure 11-18 *Centralized Multicast Conference—MC and MP Combined in MCU*

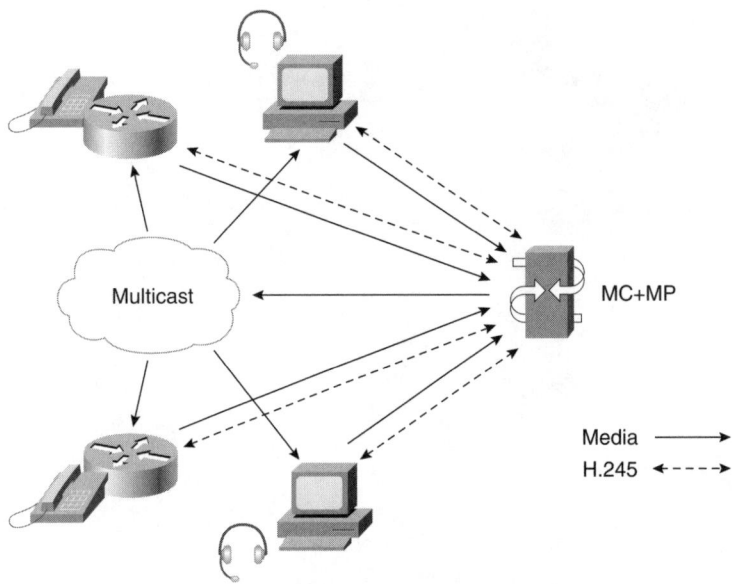

Figure 11-19 *Decentralized Multicast Conference—MCU only Provides MC Functions*

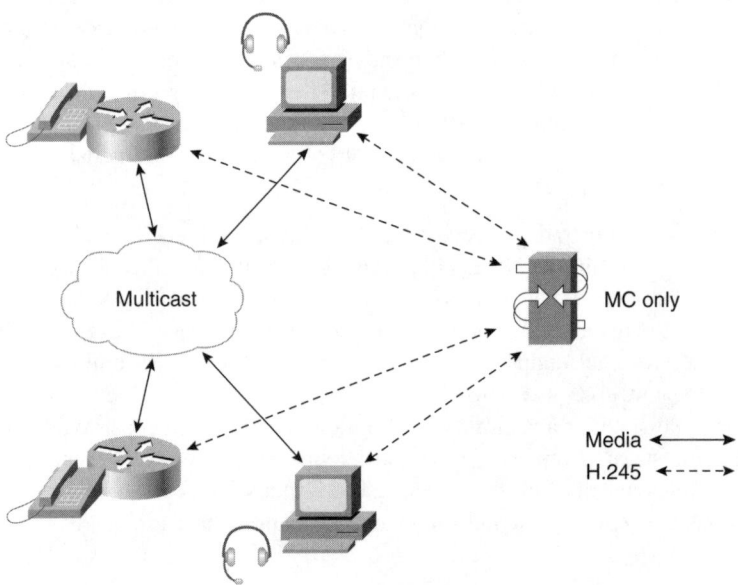

Figure 11-20 illustrates a mixed conference that includes each of the types already discussed, bridged by a central MCU. Every participant establishes a bidirectional H.245 session with the MC, but a variety of methods is used to transmit the audio paths. Notice now that the MCU joins the multicast group for the decentralized multimedia portion of the conference (via the MP) to enable communication between all conference participants. The MCU is an effective tool to provide access to multicast conferences for hosts that do not support multicast.

Figure 11-20 *Mixed Multicast Conference—MCU Bridges All Conference Types*

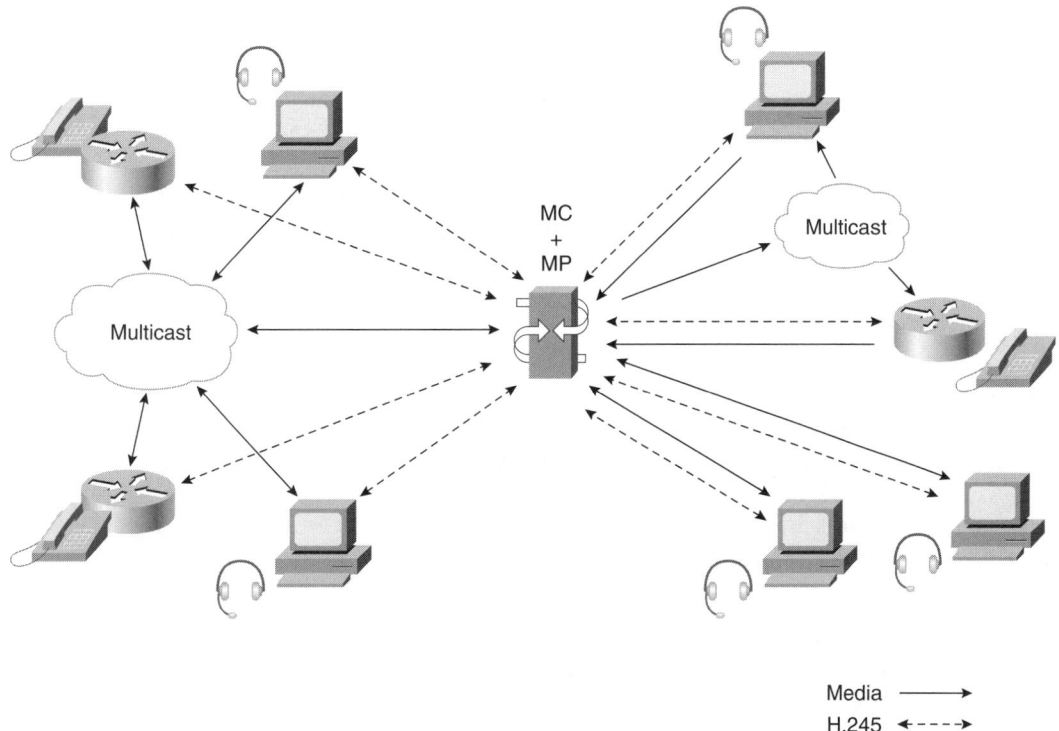

Gateway

Gateways provide interworking with non-H.323 technologies, such as H.320 ISDN video conferencing, or traditional telephone networks. An example of an H.323 gateway is a Cisco router with voice interfaces. A telephone in the PSTN may connect through the Cisco gateway, and appear to the H.323 network as an H.323 endpoint (albeit limited to audio capabilities). Conversely, an H.323 endpoint may place a call to the PSTN through the

Cisco gateway, and the call appears to originate from a telephone subscriber. Figure 11-21 illustrates the logical structure of an H.323 gateway:

Figure 11-21 *Logical Structure of an H.323 Gateway*

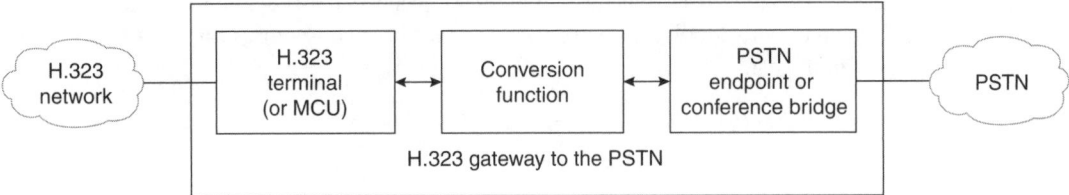

Note that gateways manage (1) the call-signaling conversion, (2) the media-signaling conversion, and (3) the media conversion when connecting an H.323 network with a different network type. In order to allow VoIP/PSTN gateways to economically scale to large traffic volumes, both the IETF and the ITU are dividing the functional components of a gateway and defining standard interactions between the functional components. These efforts are summarized in the section, "Scaling VoIP/PSTN Gateways: The Soft Switch," later in this chapter.

Gatekeeper

As its name implies, an H.323 gatekeeper controls an H.323 zone. Just as a gatekeeper in a castle can regulate who passes in or out, an H.323 gatekeeper regulates which endpoints within its zone can initiate or receive calls. An H.323 gatekeeper can also regulate how calls may proceed, by either enabling direct communication between endpoints, or acting as an intermediary to relay call signaling.

An H.323 zone is an administratively defined group of devices that are controlled by a gatekeeper. H.323 version 3 (published September 1999) specifically addresses the issue of gatekeeper redundancy within a zone, but does not discuss load balancing for multiple gatekeepers within a zone. As of this writing, H.323 allows one active gatekeeper within a zone at a given time. Chapter 17, "Establishing Network-Wide Calling Capability," discusses gatekeeper redundancy designs.

Gatekeepers are not a mandatory requirement for H.323 networks. The H.323 recommendations specify that when gatekeepers are present, they must perform the following mandatory functions for endpoints:

- Address translation
- Admissions and bandwidth control

Note that a gatekeeper must provide these mandatory services only for endpoints within the gatekeeper zone that have registered with the gatekeeper.

Address Translation

The gatekeeper converts H.323 or E.164 aliases into network addresses and transport service access point (TSAP) identifiers. For example, a gatekeeper may receive a call request from a terminal for jane@company.com or +1-408-555-1212. The gateway must convert these address forms to an IP address (such as 192.168.254.1), and a TCP or UDP port number (such as TCP port 1720 for H.225.0 connection establishment).

Admissions and Bandwidth Control

In admissions control, the gatekeeper authorizes terminals, gateways, and MCUs to place calls in the network through the H.225.0 RAS channel. Admissions control is the A part of RAS. The gatekeeper issues admission confirm (ACF) or admission reject (ARJ) messages in response to admission request (ARQ) messages from endpoints. The decision may be based on criteria not specified within H.323, or a less complex system may simply accept all requests. In response to bandwidth requests (BRQ) from endpoints, a gatekeeper sends bandwidth confirm (BCF) or bandwidth reject (BRJ) messages. Just as in the case of admission control, bandwidth control may be based on criteria beyond H.323, or on a simple all-accepting policy. RAS messages and functions are discussed in the "Protocols" section later in this chapter.

Optional Gatekeeper Functions

Some of the useful applications for gatekeepers in an H.323 network are listed here. Note that these items are not mandatory gatekeeper functions, but they offer compelling reasons to use a gatekeeper:

- Gatekeepers provide a centralized mechanism to manage dial plans and call routing in a VoIP network. Without gatekeepers, each VoIP gateway must maintain call-routing information (dial peers) for every other destination, unless a non-H.323 method of call routing is implemented.

- Gatekeepers provide access to authentication, authorization, and accounting (AAA) functions that are essential for security and billing systems. The back-end interaction between gatekeepers and other systems for AAA functions is not within the scope of H.323.

- Gatekeepers provide a centralized point for policy-based resource allocation. For example, a policy server may instruct a gatekeeper to restrict calls based on destination, bandwidth availability, user privilege, time of day, and so forth.

- Gatekeepers facilitate third-party call control, which is essential in call-center environments and other specialized calling applications. For example, an autodialer in an outbound call center may initiate calls to targeted customers, and connect a call-center agent after a customer answers the phone.

For these reasons, you should consider gatekeepers a required part of all but the most basic VoIP installations that use H.323.

Addressing

H.323 employs a naming scheme that is independent of the underlying network technology, and also identifies specific address requirements for H.323 over IP, the de facto standard network protocol. The following sections discuss addressing in H.323/IP networks:

- Network addresses and transport service access point (TSAP) identifiers
- H.323 aliases
- Alias-naming conventions for interzone communication
- Determining network addresses and TSAP identifiers

Network Addresses and TSAP Identifiers

Establishing communication with any H.323 device requires knowledge of its network address and a TSAP identifier. For IP networks, the network address is an IP address, and the TSAP identifier is a TCP or UDP port number.

All H.323 entities must have at least one network address (most commonly an IP address), but may have multiple network addresses for the sake of redundancy (that is, a separate address for each physical interface). Cisco routers do not require multiple addresses for redundancy, because a logically defined loopback interface enables communication through any active physical interface.

H.323 Aliases

Given that network addresses and TSAP identifiers are not easy for humans to remember, H.323 provides user-friendly H.323 aliases to identify endpoints and multiparty conferences. (A conference alias resolves to the network address and TSAP identifier of the MC for the conference.) Note that gatekeepers and MP devices do not use H.323 aliases because they are not directly callable.

Why not just use DNS names instead of H.323 aliases? Well, H.323 is designed for use with any network layer, and can operate independently of IP. Instead of relying on a network-dependent name resolution, H.323 specifies that gatekeepers resolve aliases into network addresses and TSAP identifiers (gatekeepers obtain this information when endpoints register with them).

H.323 aliases may take several forms:

- Alphanumeric strings: Bob, bob@host.com, host.com, arbitrary-string
- E.164 addresses: +1-408-555-1212, 5551212, 4199

Alias-Naming Conventions for Interzone Communication

H.323 aliases have significance within a single zone. To reach endpoints in a different zone, the name of the zone should be embedded in H.323 aliases. For large H.323 implementations, it is important to establish a sensible alias-naming convention such as:

user@zone_name

where user is an e-mail ID, or any other personal identifier used in an organization, and the zone_name matches the DNS domain name where the gatekeeper resides. This recommendation is consistent with the informational Appendix IV of H.225.0 (February 1998). Note that the complete string user@zone_name is the H.323 alias. The naming convention presented here enables you to use DNS to overcome the interzone communication weakness of H.323.

NOTE   You should read the following paragraph again after you understand the sections about gatekeeper discovery via DNS and the H.225.0 RAS protocols.

You may have many gatekeepers (for different H.323 zones) in the same DNS domain if your DNS domains are large. This is an acceptable design (and the most simple to ensure consistent H.323 aliases), but you should be aware of a shortcoming of this approach. Every time a gatekeeper is unable to locally resolve an alias, it sends a query to all of the gatekeepers in the DNS domain specified by the H.323 alias. If all of the gatekeepers are in a single DNS domain, then each gatekeeper is forced to process location requests (LRQ) for every H.323 zone. Most of the LRQ traffic that each gatekeeper receives will be for nonlocal endpoints. Figure 11-22 illustrates this problem.

If your gatekeepers are unable to process all of the extra traffic, you may need to impose an extra layer of DNS hierarchy, only to be used by H.323 gatekeepers, to prevent overloading the gatekeepers. For example, if your company has a single large domain called company.com, you can create zone1.company.com, zone2.company.com, or any other names that match your organization. Assign each gatekeeper to a different new zone, but do not change the existing DNS registration of the endpoints. In other words, all of the endpoints should remain in the company.com DNS domain, while the gatekeepers are each in a different DNS subdomain of company.com. Each H.323 zone (which is identified by a DNS subdomain of the main company domain) should have alternate gatekeepers for fault tolerance.

Figure 11-22 *LRQ Messages Flooded to All Gatekeepers in a Large DNS Domain*

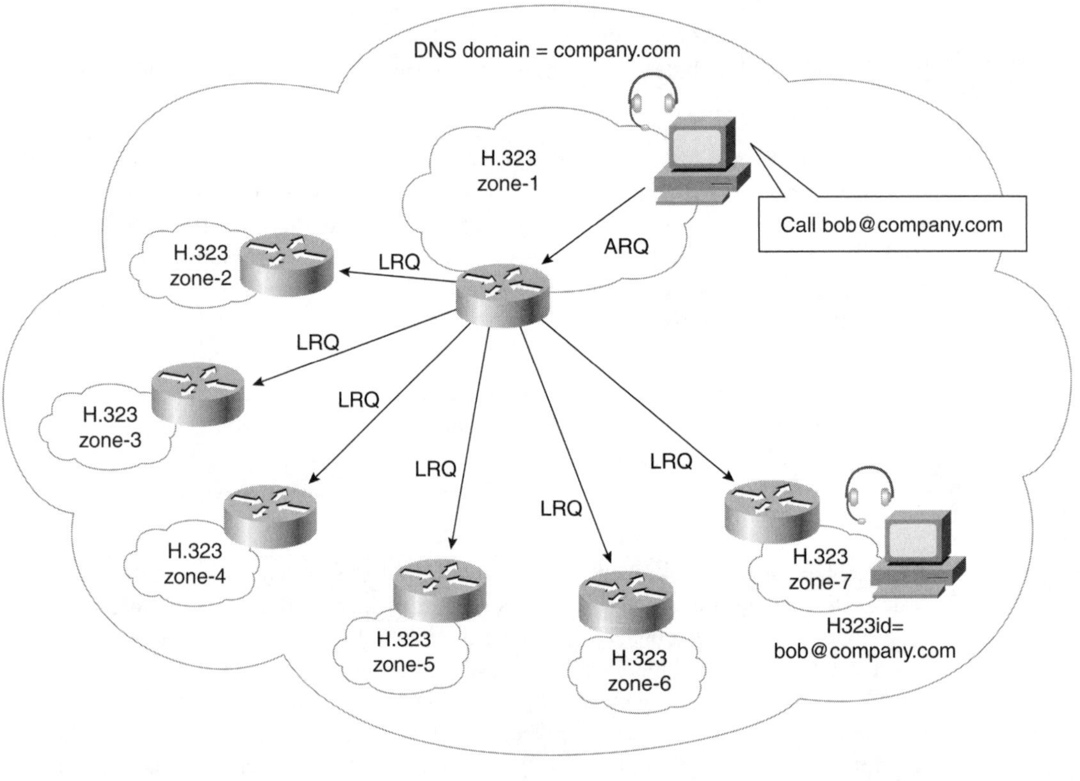

This strategy results in each endpoint having different e-mail addresses and H.323 aliases. For example, a user may have an e-mail address of user@company.com, and an H.323 alias of user@zoneX.company.com. If this is not acceptable for your network, then you can upgrade your gatekeepers to accommodate the extra LRQ traffic and processing, or introduce another application that resolves user@company.com to the proper H.323 zone name. Such an application is beyond the present scope of H.323 and this book.

With the solutions described here, each local gatekeeper is able to identify the appropriate gatekeeper and request an alias resolution for endpoints in different zones.

Determining Network Addresses and TSAP Identifiers

The following sections answer three high-level questions while exploring related issues along the way:

- When an H.323 endpoint first connects to a network, how does it learn the network address and TSAP identifier to discover its gatekeeper?

- How does an endpoint learn the TSAP identifier for gatekeeper RAS services?

- How does an endpoint learn the network address of a called destination, and determine the appropriate TSAP identifier for H.225.0 call control, H.245 media control, and general media streams?

Gatekeeper discovery is an important aspect of an H.323 network design, because it determines how endpoints are associated with gatekeepers. In other words, the gatekeeper discovery process shapes the boundaries of H.323 zones. There are three general strategies by which endpoints can discover the network address and TSAP identifiers for a gatekeeper: (1) preconfiguration, (2) multicast, and (3) DNS.

Gatekeeper Discovery: Preconfigured

An endpoint may be preconfigured with the IP address of the gatekeeper. Gatekeeper discovery is not normally required in these cases, but endpoints may still send gatekeeper request (GRQ) messages to negotiate encryption services for the H.225.0 RAS connection. The well-known TSAP identifier for GRQ messages is UDP port 1718.

Gatekeeper Discovery: Multicast

Multicast enabled endpoints that are not preconfigured with the gatekeeper IP address can send GRQ messages to the following well-known DNS name or IP multicast group address:

gatekeeper.mcast.net   224.0.1.41

As an experiment, try a DNS lookup on these items. You will find both the A and PTR records. The well-known TSAP identifier for gatekeeper discovery (GRQ) messages is still UDP port 1718.

Gatekeeper Discovery: DNS

Endpoints can use DNS in several ways to discover a gatekeeper:

- SRV records
- TXT records

Note that these processes are relevant for (1) a terminal seeking a gatekeeper for registration, and (2) a gatekeeper seeking another gatekeeper to process an interzone LRQ.

SRV Records   A DNS server responds to an SRV record by returning a list of host names (resolvable via A records) and required TCP/UDP ports to contact the service. An endpoint may query a DNS server for an SRV record corresponding with the gatekeeper discovery service. Several variations of the implementation are possible. The endpoint can issue the SRV query using its own domain, which implies that the gateway and gatekeeper are in the same domain. This can be a problem for some designs. (Refer to "Alias-Naming Conventions for Interzone Communication" earlier in this chapter). The endpoint can also be configured with a domain name for the gatekeeper, which essentially tells the endpoint to which zone it belongs. Both of these methods leverage the strength of SRV records; that is, the IP address and UDP port for gatekeeper discovery may be centrally changed for maintenance, administrative, or security purposes without reconfiguring each client.

TXT Records   If you have not implemented a version of DNS that supports SRV records, you can use TXT records to perform a similar function. A DNS server responds to a TXT query by returning a list of all TXT records for the requested domain. You can create a TXT record for each gatekeeper in a domain with the following recommended syntax:

> ras [< gk id>@]<domain name >[:<portnum>] [<priority>]

Even if you are using the TXT records for other purposes, the keyword ras in the first position enables the H.323 client to filter out undesired TXT records. Following this syntax enables an H.323 endpoint to discover the gatekeeper in a manner analogous to the SRV records.

Design Considerations when Using DNS with H.323

NOTE   You should read this section again after you have a thorough understanding of the H.225.0 RAS protocols. These protocols are described in a following section.

Both the SRV and TXT methods of gatekeeper discovery introduce new H.323 behavior worth noting:

If multiple gatekeepers are in the same DNS domain, then endpoints may randomly register with any gatekeeper (which identifies an H.323 zone) that is within the DNS domain. In such cases, different H.323 zones exist only to limit the number of users per gatekeeper. Presumably, the gatekeepers are configured to reject endpoint registration requests when they have reached their processing limit. For this design to function correctly, each of the H.323 zones (that is, gatekeepers) within a DNS domain should have consistent policies and gateway access privileges. All endpoints will have an H.323 alias of the form user@domain.com, and the actual H.323 zone with which an endpoint is registered is irrelevant (except when it comes time to troubleshoot problems!).

Whenever a gatekeeper receives a request for an H.323 alias in a different zone, the gatekeeper sends an LRQ to the gatekeeper of the destination H.323 zone. The DNS solutions described here determine the destination H.323 zone by looking at the domain name specified in the H.323 alias of the destination. If multiple gatekeepers are located in the DNS domain specified by the H.323 alias, then the DNS domain name does not uniquely map to an H.323 zone. A gatekeeper trying to resolve an alias from a different zone must then send an LRQ to each of the gatekeepers in the DNS domain specified by the H.323 alias. The correct gatekeeper will respond with an LCF, but every other gatekeeper in the domain must process the query and return an LRJ. If there are many gatekeepers in a single domain, the extra LRQ/LRJ messages can become a legitimate concern.

Gatekeeper RAS

After H.323 endpoints have discovered (that is, determined the network address of) a local gatekeeper, they must exchange H.225.0 RAS messages with the gatekeeper. The well-known TSAP identifier for gatekeeper RAS communications is UDP port 1719.

Endpoints first send registration request (RRQ) messages to the gatekeeper on UDP port 1719. This registration enables the gatekeeper to associate the H.323 alias of an endpoint with its network address and TSAP identifier for H.225.0 call control. Additional RAS messages occur periodically and in response to certain events. Most RAS communications are initiated by the endpoints to UDP port 1719 on the gatekeeper. (The gatekeeper initiates some RAS transactions.)

H.225.0 Call Control

When endpoints initiate a call-connection request, they must determine the network address and TSAP identifier of the destination. Endpoints may discover this information "out of band" (for example, via an e-mail message), which is outside the scope of H.323. Endpoints may also initiate a connection based on an H.323 alias. In this case, it is the responsibility of the gatekeeper to resolve the alias to a network address and TSAP identifier.

The default TSAP identifier for all H.225.0 call control channels is TCP port 1720. An endpoint may advertise a different TSAP identifier in its gatekeeper registration message, which is transparent to other endpoints that initiate calls to H.323 aliases. Endpoints that initiate calls to IP addresses and TCP port numbers must learn the nondefault port number via an out-of-band method.

H.245 Media Control

Well-known network address and TSAP identifiers for H.245 media control channels are not necessary because the endpoints and MCUs that need to establish H.245 channels are already communicating via an H.225.0 call control channel. The network addresses for H.245 communication are the same as for the existing H.225.0 control channel, and the TSAP addresses for H.245 are negotiated over the call control channel.

Media Streams: RTP/RTCP

Well-known network address and TSAP identifiers for the media channels (i.e., RTP/RTCP) are not necessary or desirable because an endpoint or MCU may have many active sessions, and each session may require a different application or decoding function. It would be cumbersome to identify a fixed set of TSAP identifiers for each of the many possible applications, with an arbitrary number of ports available for each application type.

H.323 endpoints use the H.245 media control channel to negotiate a dynamic mapping between the TSAP identifier and the application type, and to establish the media session. In other words, the H.245 media control channel determines the UDP port numbers that are used for the RTP and RTCP sessions. The H.245 media control channel also determines the RTP payload type for the media session. The RTP payload type may also be modified at the application layer of the endpoint, such as for transport of DTMF tones or comfort noise between packets of a specified codec type.

In summary, Table 11-8 describes how an endpoint learns the destination network address and TSAP identifiers for the different layers of H.323 communications.

Table 11-8   *How H.323 Endpoints Determine Other Network Addresses and TSAP Identifiers*

Endpoint Request	How Network Address Is Learned	How TSAP Is Learned
Gatekeeper Discovery via GRQ messages	gatekeeper.mcast.net = 224.0.1.41	Well-known (UDP port 1718)
	DNS query for SRV or TXT records	
	Statically configured	
Gatekeeper Communications (RAS)	gatekeeper.mcast.net = 224.0.1.41	Well-known (UDP port 1719)
	DNS query for SRV or TXT records	
	Statically configured	
H.225.0 Call Requests	H.323 alias resolved by gatekeeper	H.323 alias resolution, or well-known (TCP port 1720)
	Known via non-H.323 method	
H.245 Media Control Channels	Same destination as H.225.0 call request	Dynamic TCP port learned via H.225.0 negotiation
RTP/RTCP Media Channels	Specified in the H.245 logical channel setup	Dynamic UDP ports learned via H.245 negotiation

Protocols

The H.323 protocol suite provides multiparty, multimedia, real-time communications services over an existing QoS-enabled network. The H.323 services are bundled into user applications that include mandatory audio capabilities, and optional video and data-sharing capabilities. Figure 11-23 illustrates the H.323 protocol stack. Note that H.235, which is not included in this illustration, provides secure and authenticated transmission services for various protocols.

Figure 11-23 *H.323 Protocol Stack*

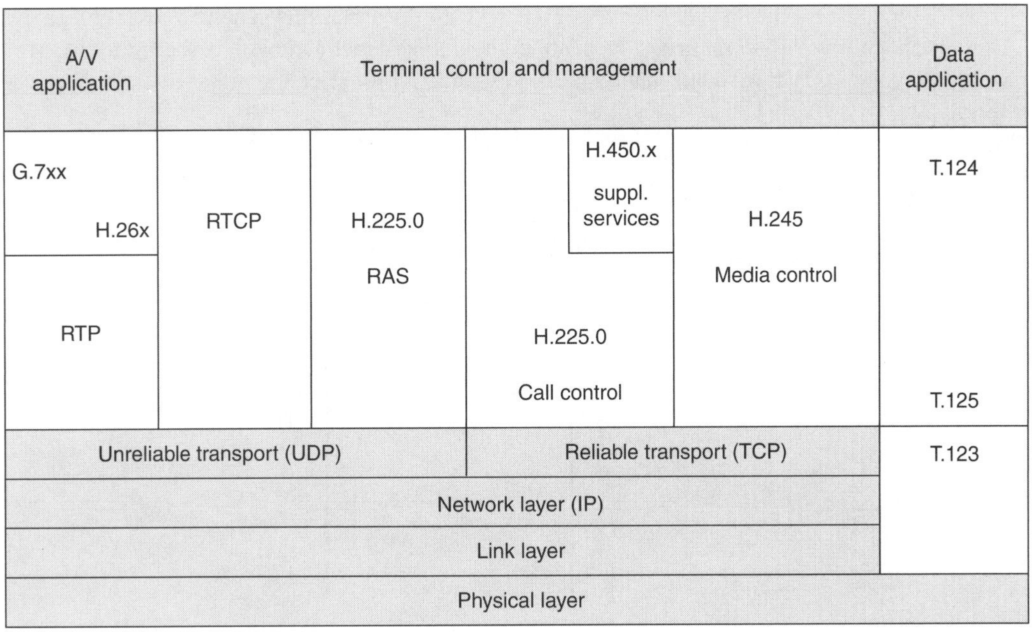

The following sections examine message exchanges for the H.323 protocols that relate to VoIP:

- Gatekeeper discovery and RAS (H.225.0)
- H.225.0 call control
- H.450.x supplementary services
- H.245 media control

Gatekeeper Discovery and RAS (H.225.0)

ITU Recommendation H.225.0 defines the interactions between an H.323 terminal and an H.323 gatekeeper. These interactions include an endpoint discovering a gatekeeper, and the RAS signaling between an endpoint and a gatekeeper. Note that RAS is an abbreviation of registration, admission, and status. A gatekeeper also provides location services as part of the RAS functions, which may be requested by either local endpoints in the same zone, or other gatekeepers in different zones.

Most of the RAS-related messages follow a common structure. An endpoint requests a service or action from the gatekeeper, and the gatekeeper responds with a confirmation or rejection of the service or action. Figure 11-24 illustrates this generic transaction process. Each of the RAS messages is identified by a three-letter acronym, of the form *RQ for requests, *CF for confirmation messages, and *RJ for rejection messages.

Figure 11-24   *Generic Format of Message Exchanges Used for H.225.0 RAS Signaling*

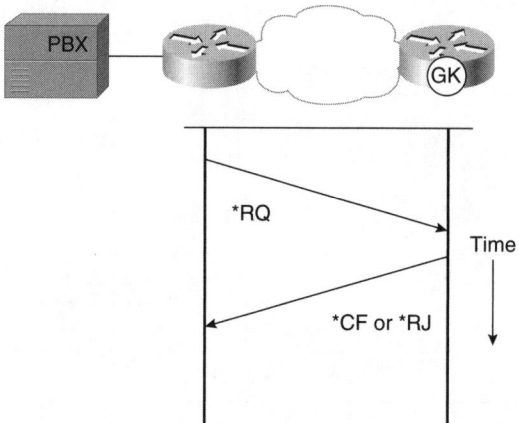

The * character in the generic message name is replaced with a specific letter to represent different services, as discussed in the following sections:

- Gateway discovery
- Registration (R) and unregistration (U)
- Location (L)
- Admission (A) and bandwidth

After all of the RAS message types have been defined, a short section provides several examples of H.225.0 RAS message exchanges.

Gateway Discovery

The "Addressing" section within the H.323 portion of this chapter already explored in detail the various methods by which an endpoint may learn the network address or TSAP identifier for a gatekeeper. This section focuses on the actual H.225.0 messages that are exchanged between endpoints and gatekeepers: GRQ, gateway confirm (GCF), and gateway reject (GRJ).

The GRQ message, sent by an endpoint when it is searching for a gatekeeper, provides information about the endpoint. Among other items, the endpoint provides the following information to the gatekeeper:

- Zero or more H.323 aliases to identify the endpoint
- IP address and port number on which it expects to receive H.225.0 RAS messages
- Whether it is a terminal, gateway, or MCU
- Encryption capabilities (optional)
- Vendor identification (optional)

The GCF message, returned by a gatekeeper to an endpoint in response to a GRQ, indicates that the endpoint may proceed with registration. Among other items, the gatekeeper provides the following information to the endpoint:

- H.323 gatekeeper identification
- IP address and port number on which it expects to receive an RRQ
- Zero or more alternate gatekeepers (that is, IP addresses and UDP ports) to be used for registration in the event that this gatekeeper fails
- Mode of encryption chosen from the endpoint capabilities (optional)

The GRJ message, returned by a gatekeeper to an endpoint in response to a GRQ, indicates that the endpoint should find a different gatekeeper. Among other items, the gatekeeper provides the following information in the GRJ:

- H.323 gatekeeper identification
- Reason for rejecting the gatekeeper discovery message
- Information about other gatekeepers to query (optional)

Registration and Unregistration

An endpoint that receives a GCF message from a gatekeeper proceeds to register with that gatekeeper. If an endpoint is preconfigured with the RAS contact information of the gatekeeper, the endpoint may bypass the GRQ message and initiate contact using this registration sequence. The registration messages are registration request (RRQ), registration confirm (RCF), and registration reject (RRJ). The unregister messages are unregistration request (URQ), unregistration confirm (UCF), and unregistration reject (URJ).

The RRQ message, sent by an endpoint when it registers with a gatekeeper, provides information about the endpoint. Among other items, the endpoint provides the following information to the gatekeeper:

- Zero or more H.323 aliases to identify the endpoint
- One or more IP-address/TCP-port number pairs on which it expects to receive inbound calls (that is, the H.225.0 call control channel that uses Q.931 messages)
- One or more IP-address/UDP-port number pairs on which it expects to receive RAS messages
- Whether it is a terminal, gateway, or MCU
- Time to live (TTL) of the registration (enables gatekeeper to age out the registration if the endpoint becomes inactive)
- Encryption capabilities (optional)
- Vendor identification (optional)

The RCF message, sent by a gatekeeper to an endpoint to confirm registration, provides information about the gatekeeper. Among other items, the gatekeeper provides the following information to the endpoint:

- H.323 gatekeeper identification
- One or more IP-address/port-number pairs on which the gatekeeper expects to receive calls (that is, H.225.0 call setup messages)
- Zero or more alternate gatekeepers (identified by IP addresses and UDP ports) to be used for registration in the event that this gatekeeper fails
- Confirmation of the H.323 aliases for the endpoint
- Confirmation of the TTL for the endpoint registration
- Pregranted ARQ (optional); gatekeeper authorizes the endpoint to initiate calls without using the ARQ/ACF sequence, which reduces the time of the call setup

The RRJ message, sent by a gatekeeper to an endpoint to reject the registration, provides the following information:

- H.323 gatekeeper identification
- Reason for rejecting the gatekeeper registration
- Information about other gatekeepers to query (optional)

The URQ message may be sent by an endpoint or a gatekeeper. When sent by an endpoint, the URQ informs the gatekeeper of H.323 aliases that the endpoint is no longer using. When sent by a gatekeeper, the URQ informs the endpoint that it may no longer use the specified aliases. If all of the aliases are unregistered, the endpoint is no longer associated with the gatekeeper. The URQ message includes the following items:

- List of H.323 aliases that are no longer registered

- One or more IP-address/port-number pairs for the endpoint that are no longer used

- Reason why the gatekeeper initiated the URQ, if applicable

The UCF message may be sent by an endpoint or a gatekeeper. There is no significant information in the UCF, aside from sequence numbers, and optional data integrity checks and encryption fields.

The URJ message indicates failure of the URQ. The most likely reason for this message is that a gatekeeper receives a URQ from an endpoint that is not registered with the gatekeeper.

Location

Location messages are used to resolve H.323 aliases into network addresses and TSAP identifiers. Endpoints send location requests to their local gatekeeper, and gatekeepers send location requests to gatekeepers in other zones when they are not able to locally resolve an alias.

Gatekeepers are able to process local requests because they learn about all H.323 aliases in their zone via endpoint RRQ messages. If a gatekeeper does not recognize an H.323 alias, then the alias either does not exist or belongs to a different zone. Gatekeepers may use a scantily defined method of interzone location to resolve aliases from different zones (see the sidebar, "H.323 Scalability" later in this chapter), or they may simply send a reject message to the requesting endpoint.

The basic location messages are LRQ, LCF, and LRJ.

The LRQ message sent to a gatekeeper contains the following information:

- One or more H.323 aliases to be resolved into network addresses and TSAP identifiers

- The sender of this LRQ; may be an endpoint or a gatekeeper

- The address to which the LCF should be sent, which may be different than the LRQ sender address (for example, a gatekeeper forwarding an LRQ to a gatekeeper in a different zone may indicate that the original requester should receive the LCF)

The LCF response from the gatekeeper, which indicates a successful resolution of the H.323 alias, contains the following information for each alias in the LRQ:

- The IP address and TCP port for initiating calls to the destination (that is, the H.225.0 call control channel that uses Q.931 messages)

- The IP address and UDP port for H.225.0 RAS messages to the destination

- A list of other aliases for the destination endpoint

- Additional information to be used by gateways, such as extra phone numbers to dial or phone extension information (for example, a gateway can reach the endpoint by dialing 555-1212, and then dialing extension 1234)

The LRJ response from the gatekeeper, which indicates a failure to resolve the H.323 alias, contains the following information:

- Reason for rejecting the LRQ
- Information about other gatekeepers to query (optional)

H.323 Scalability

One of the weaknesses of H.323 is the lack of a robust method for gatekeepers to determine the appropriate H.323 zone for nonlocal aliases. Though not required, H.323 recommends that alias names be structured similar to DNS names so that DNS methods may be used to identify the remote H.323 zone and choose an appropriate gatekeeper for location requests.

Using this method, a gatekeeper sends an LRQ message to each gatekeeper that is in the same DNS domain (based on the actual DNS host name of the gatekeeper) as indicated by the H.323 alias. For example, an endpoint with the alias bob@company.com is presumably controlled by a gatekeeper in the DNS domain company.com (for example, a gatekeeper named gk1.company.com). This works well if the H.323 zone allocation matches the DNS domain allocation.

The problem with this approach, as already described in the "H.323 Addressing" section, is that the existing layout of DNS domains may not be compatible with the required layout of H.323 zones. Many DNS infrastructures are based on a single large domain, which works because DNS is a stateless service that can scale to large numbers of users. H.323 is a stateful service, which places a greater load on centralized gatekeepers that maintain information about each registered endpoint. DNS may rely on several servers to answer for a domain, using well-defined interactions between servers to maintain synchronization. H.323 lacks the facilities for multiple local gatekeepers to load-share endpoint requests and maintain synchronized state. Synchronization is more difficult between gatekeepers than between DNS servers because of the real-time state information each gatekeeper contains, but this problem is not insurmountable. H.323 should evolve (Note: author's speculation here) to support multiple gatekeepers that load-share within a zone.

The interzone communication problem is a result of the LAN-centric framework of H.323. The first version of H.323 only provided for local zone communication, and assumed that all nonlocal communication would be achieved through gateways to H.320 ISDN networks. Though the H.323 title has changed to indicate a broader scope (that is, packet-based networks in general), the H.323 technical specifications are still attempting to crawl out from under the original LAN framework.

Admission and Bandwidth

When a gatekeeper is present in the network, endpoints must register with the gatekeeper. In order for an endpoint to initiate a call or receive a call, it must ask permission from the gatekeeper. The gatekeeper may admit or refuse the call, based upon criteria beyond the scope of H.323 (such as an AAA or policy server). Alternatively, a basic gatekeeper may indiscriminately admit all inbound and outbound calls. If a zone contains gateways (for example, to POTS or H.320 ISDN networks), then some sort of admission control is highly desirable to manage the expenses incurred by outbound calls to the PSTN from the gateway.

The gatekeeper may impose endpoint restrictions based on general ability to send or receive calls (which is called *admission control*), or based on bandwidth usage quotas (which is called *bandwidth control*. The H.225 RAS messages that convey this information are the following: ARQ, ACF, ARJ, BRQ, BCF, and BRJ.

The ARQ message is sent by an endpoint to a gatekeeper when it receives an inbound call request, or when it desires to place a call. The ARQ includes the following information:

- H.323 gatekeeper identification
- Bandwidth requested for the call (that is, only the codec bandwidth excluding headers)
- Whether the call is point-to-point, one-to-many, many-to-one, or many-to-many
- Request H.225.0 call control either direct between endpoints or gatekeeper-routed
- Source and destination H.323 alias (which may also be E.164 numbers); if the endpoint is receiving a call, the endpoint sends the ARQ with its own address as the destination
- Source and destination IP address and TCP port for H.225.0 call control. (Note: for outbound calls routed through the gatekeeper, this value should not be the well-known TCP port 1720 because multiple endpoints need to share the gatekeeper for outbound call relay. Inbound calls may be destined for TCP port 1720 on an endpoint.)
- Whether the calling party is an active MC for a multiparty call
- Any QoS reservation capabilities (such as RSVP) of the endpoint sending the ARQ

The ACF message is sent by the gatekeeper to an endpoint, to authorize an inbound or outbound call request. The ACF includes the following information:

- H.323 gatekeeper identification
- Bandwidth allowed for the call, which may be less than requested
- Whether H.225.0 call control is direct between endpoints or gatekeeper-routed
- If call is outbound, whether the destination is a terminal, gateway, or MCU
- If call is outbound, the network address and TSAP identifier to use for H.225.0 call control

- For outbound calls via a gateway, any extra information required to complete the call
- Whether the gatekeeper or an endpoint controls QoS reservations

The ARJ message may be sent by a gatekeeper because the endpoint is not registered with it, the registration has expired, or for other security/policy reasons. ARJ messages include the following information:

- Reason for rejecting the admission request
- Information about other gatekeepers to query (optional)

The BRQ message is sent by an endpoint to a gatekeeper when the media requirements for the call change. For example, an audio conference may convert to a video conference, or endpoints may negotiate a new codec during the call to improve voice quality. If such changes require a different amount of bandwidth than allowed in the ACF message, then a BRQ is necessary. The BRQ includes the following information:

- H.323 gatekeeper identification
- A reference to the call that requires more (or less) bandwidth
- Whether the call is point-to-point, one-to-many, many-to-one, or many-to-many
- New bandwidth required (for codec only—not considering headers)

The BCF message is sent by a gatekeeper to confirm a bandwidth change request. The message confirms the new amount of allowed bandwidth.

The BRJ message is sent by a gatekeeper to deny a bandwidth change request. In response to valid BRQs, the message confirms the previous amount of allowed bandwidth. The message may also be sent when an unregistered endpoint (or a registered endpoint with no active calls) erroneously sends a BRQ.

Disengage

The call disconnection messages are important when H.225.0 call control channels are not routed through the gatekeeper. A disconnect message from an endpoint informs the gatekeeper that a previously admitted call is finished. The gatekeeper must know this information to keep an accurate record of the available bandwidth in the zone, and to know if endpoints may receive calls. The disengage messages are disengage request (DRQ), disengage confirm (DCF), and disengage reject (DRJ).

The DRQ message, sent by an endpoint to the gatekeeper, includes the following elements:

- The H.323 gatekeeper identification
- Call ID or other reference for the finished call
- The reason the call was disengaged

The DCF message acknowledges a DRQ.

The DRJ message is sent by a gatekeeper if it receives a DCF from an unregistered endpoint, or an endpoint with no active calls.

Resource Availability

The resource availability messages enable load balancing between gateways in an H.323 zone. The gatekeeper knows to stop sending calls to a gateway when the gateway sends a message indicating that its resources are nearly consumed. For the definitions included here, the gateway is assumed to be a VoIP gateway connected to the PSTN or a private phone switch. The two messages are resource availability indication (RAI) and resource availability confirmation (RAC).

The RAI message, sent by a gateway to a gatekeeper, includes the following elements:

- How many call channels are currently available
- How much bandwidth is required for each channel
- An optional warning message indicating that resources are nearly exhausted

The RAC message is sent by the gatekeeper and acknowledges receipt of the RAI.

Information

Endpoints and gatekeepers use the RAS information messages as a keepalive mechanism. There are four message types that slightly stray from the standard *RQ/*CF/*RJ sequence: information request (IRQ), information response (IRR), information acknowledge (IACK), and information negative acknowledge (INAK).

When a gatekeeper sends an IRQ message to an endpoint, the endpoint must respond with an IRR. This is sort of a ping test from the gatekeeper to the endpoint. Endpoints may negotiate during the initial registration to have the gatekeeper acknowledge the IRR messages (with an IACK or INAK message), and then the endpoints can send unsolicited IRRs. This constitutes a ping test from the endpoint to the gatekeeper.

The IRQ message from a gatekeeper to an endpoint includes the IP address and UDP port to which the IRR response should be sent. This mechanism enables the gatekeeper to periodically poll the endpoints and have them send information to a data-gathering or monitoring station. You may be able to take advantage of this feature in your network to augment the information gathered via SNMP or call detail records on routers. This feature enables you to account for traffic between H.323 endpoints that does not cross a Cisco VoIP gateway.

The IRR message includes the following information about each active call for a polled endpoint:

- Type of media streams in use (such as audio, video, or data sharing)
- RTP/RTCP session information, such as CNAME, SSRC, and UDP port numbers
- IP addresses and TCP ports for H.225.0 call control and H.245 media control channels
- Whether the call is point-to-point, one-to-many, many-to-one, or many-to-many
- The bandwidth used by the media streams
- Whether the H.225.0 call control is directly between endpoints or via gatekeepers

The IACK and INAK messages do not contain significant information because they are primarily available for the endpoints to ping the gatekeeper. There is no use for these messages from a data-polling or information-gathering perspective. Of course, vendors may introduce proprietary solutions that make more use of these messages.

Miscellaneous

Several RAS messages do not adhere to the standard *RQ/*CF/*RJ message sequence. These include:

- The non-standard message (NSM), which is included for protocol extensibility
- The unknown message response (XRS), sent by all H.323 devices in response to messages they do not understand
- The request in progress (RIP) message, for when a device cannot reply to a message request before the configured timeout periods (note that H.225.0 RAS messages use unreliable transport, so request messages have timeout periods and retry counters)

The timeout periods and retry counters for various H.225.0 RAS requests are listed in Table 11-9. RIP messages reset the timeout and retry counters for these request types to prevent the request from failing.

Table 11-9 *H.225.0 RAS Request Timers and Retry Counters*

RAS Message	Timeout (sec)	Retry Count
GRQ	5	2
RRQ	3	2
URQ	3	1
ARQ	3	2
BRQ	3	2
IRQ	3	1
IRR	5	2

Table 11-9 *H.225.0 RAS Request Timers and Retry Counters (Continued)*

RAS Message	Timeout (sec)	Retry Count
DRQ	3	2
LRQ	5	2
RAI	3	2

Summary of H.225.0 RAS Messages

Most of the RAS messages follow the standard request/confirm/reject sequence. These messages are summarized in Table 11-10.

Table 11-10 *Standard H.225.0 RAS Messages*

Functional Area	Request	Confirm	Reject
Gatekeeper discovery	GRQ	GCF	GRJ
Registration with gatekeeper	RRQ	RCF	RRJ
Unregistration with gatekeeper	URQ	UCF	URJ
Location of endpoints in a different zone	LRQ	LCF	LRJ
Admission control via gatekeeper	ARQ	ACF	ARJ
Bandwidth control via gatekeeper	BRQ	BCF	BRJ
Disengage an active call	DRQ	DCF	DRJ

The H.225.0 RAS messages that do not follow the standard message sequence are listed in Table 11-11.

Table 11-11 *H.225.0 RAS Messages that Use Different Message Sequences*

Functional Area	RAS Message
Keepalives between endpoint and GK	IRQ/IRR/IACK/INAK
Nonstandard message	NSM
Unknown message response	XRS
Request in progress (to reset timeouts)	RIP

Example H.225.0 RAS Message Exchange

Figure 11-25 illustrates a typical RAS exchange between endpoints and gatekeepers, when endpoints first connect to a network and when they initiate calls. In the first phase of communication, the endpoint attempts to locate a gatekeeper with a GRQ message.

A gatekeeper replies with a GCF, indicating how the endpoint should register with the gateway. The endpoint then sends to the gatekeeper an RRQ message that contains information about the endpoint such as H.323 aliases, and IP address and TCP ports for inbound calls. The gatekeeper accepts the registration with an RCF message, which tells the endpoints how to contact the gatekeeper for gatekeeper-routed H.225.0 call control.

When an endpoint is ready to initiate a call, it sends an ARQ to the gatekeeper requesting permission to make the call. Since the destination is in a remote zone, the gatekeeper issues an LRQ to the gatekeeper in the destination zone, which it has determined through means not mandated in H.323. The remote gatekeeper replies to the local gatekeeper with an LCF containing the IP address and TCP port of the destination. The local gatekeeper performs an authentication screen (or applies some other policy, or no policy at all), and then admits the endpoint with an ACF message. The address information that the gatekeeper learned via the LRQ is sent with the ACF.

The endpoint then initiates the H.225.0 call control channel directly to the destination endpoint, which causes the destination to issue an ARQ message to its local gatekeeper. The gatekeeper admits the call with an ACF message. At this point, the H.225.0 call control channel is established, and after negotiation, the endpoints open an H.245 media control channel. In the media control channel, the endpoints negotiate UDP ports for the RTP audio stream, and then the audio path is established. When the call is completed, each endpoint sends a DRQ to its local gatekeeper, which gatekeepers acknowledge with DCF messages.

Call Control

The call control (H.225.0) channel is a reliable channel over which call setup, teardown, and supplementary service messages are exchanged. By default, endpoints respond to TCP port 1720 for inbound call requests. Endpoints may receive calls on a different TCP port, and advertise this port to a gatekeeper for H.323 alias resolution. In networks that do not use a gatekeeper, the H.225.0 call control channel is the first step in the process of placing a call. For networks that do use a gatekeeper, the endpoints must have permission from the gatekeeper (via an ACF message) to issue H.225.0 setup requests.

Figure 11-25 *Typical H.225.0 RAS Exchange Between Endpoints and Gatekeepers*

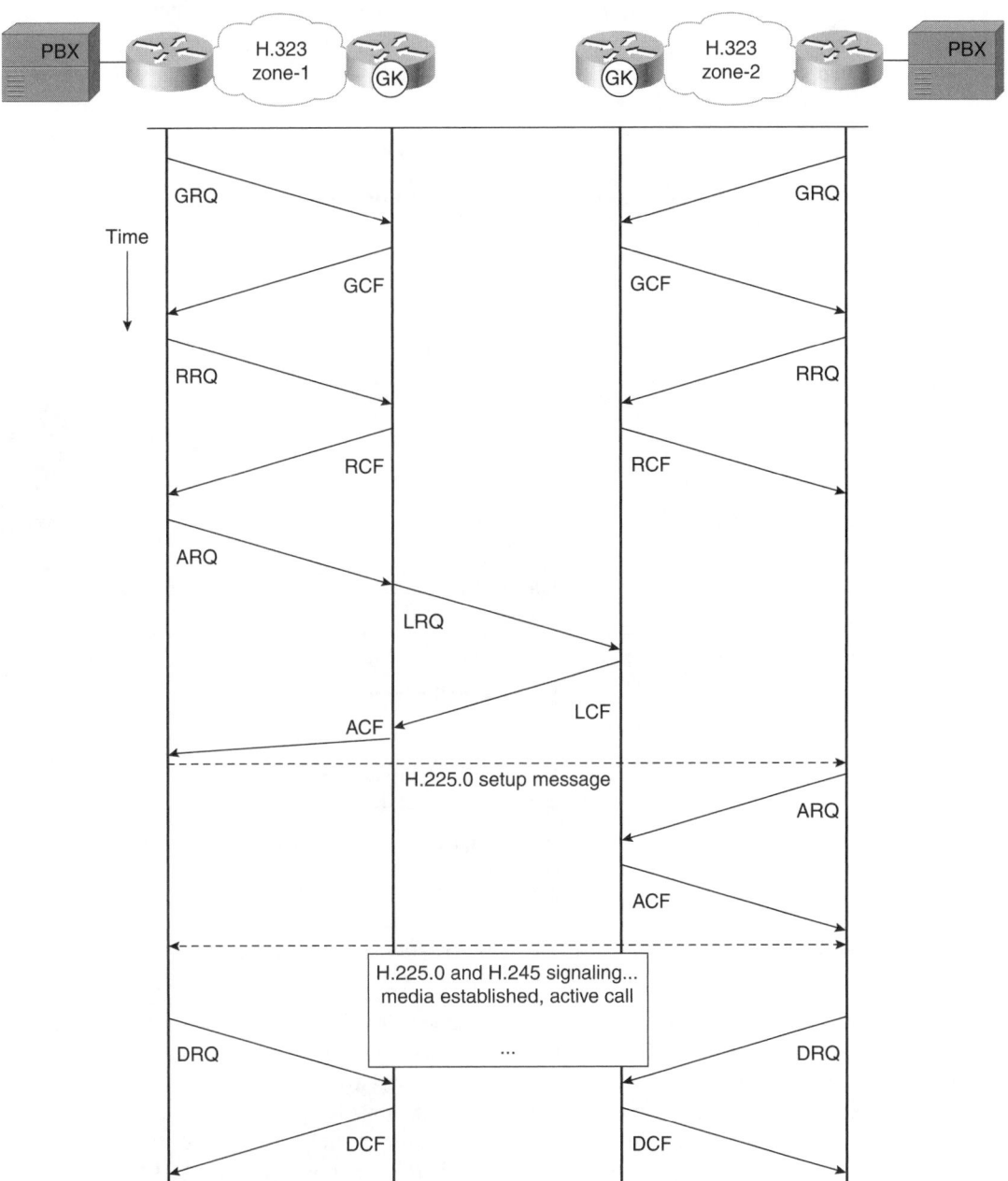

Comparison of H.225.0 and Q.931 Messages

The message syntax for H.225.0 call control is directly borrowed from ITU-T Recommendations Q.931 and Q.932, though some messages have been removed and some processes simplified. Table 11-12 summarizes the Q.931 and Q.932 messages that are used for call control in H.225.0.

Table 11-12   *Q.931/Q.932 Messages Borrowed for Call Control in H.225.0*

Q.931/Q.932 Message Type	Description or Function
ALERTING	The remote party is being actively signaled.
CALL PROCEEDING	All call-setup information has been received; no more call-setup information accepted.
CONNECT	The remote party is accepting the call.
USER INFORMATION	Provides miscellaneous information to deliver proprietary features.
PROGRESS	Sent by a gateway to provide status on calls to the PSTN; optional for terminals.
RELEASE COMPLETE	Simplifies the disconnect/release/release-complete sequence; ISDN cause codes.
SETUP	Initiates a call session; may include fastStart elements to bypass H.245.
SETUP ACKNOWLEDGE	Acknowledges receipt of a setup request.
STATUS	Used for RAS information messages.
STATUS INQUIRY	Used for RAS information messages.
FACILITY	Reroutes a call through a gatekeeper; requests H.450 supplementary services.
NOTIFY	Provides miscellaneous information (for example, user suspended)

Aside from the fact that H.225.0 does not use some Q.931 messages, there are other differences.

H.225.0 streamlines the cumbersome exchanges that Q.931 uses for call-connect and disconnect sequences. Q.931 assumes a low-latency circuit, so serial exchanges are not an issue for call-setup times. H.225.0 is more pressured to complete a call quickly because the longer delays in packet-based networks erode the time budget for call setup and teardown. H.225.0 eliminates the call-connect acknowledgment, and simplifies the disconnect/release/ release-complete sequence to a single release complete message. For supplementary services, H.225.0 uses few of the Q.932 messages, and instead focuses on the offerings of H.450.x supplementary services.

H.225.0 structures all messages according to Abstract Syntax Notation One (ASN.1) packed encoding rules (PER) specified in ITU-T Recommendation X.691. Q.931 messages in an ISDN network have formatted headers that are similar to TCP/IP protocols. Table 11-13 shows the translation between the Q.931 cause code information elements and the H.225.0 ReleaseCompleteReason values, to illustrate how Q.931 information elements (IEs) map to ASN.1 variable names.

Table 11-13   *Mapping Between H.225.0 Release Reason Messages and Q.931 Cause Codes*

Value of H.225.0 ReleaseCompleteReason	Q.931 Cause Code for Call Clearing
NoBandwidth	34—No circuit/channel available
GatekeeperResources	47—Resource unavailable
UnreachableDestination	3—No route to destination
DestinationRejection	16—Normal call clearing
InvalidRevision	88—Incompatible destination
NoPermission	111—Interworking, unspecified
UnreachableGatekeeper	38—Network out of order
GatewayResources	42—Switching equipment congestion
BadFormatAddress	28 —Invalid number format
AdaptiveBusy	41—Temporary Failure
InConf	17—User busy
UndefinedReason	31—Normal, unspecified
FacilityCallDeflection	16—Normal call clearing
SecurityDenied	31—Normal, unspecified
CalledPartyNotRegistered	20—Subscriber absent
CallerNotRegistered	31—Normal, unspecified

Direct-Routed Versus Gatekeeper-Routed Calls

The H.225.0 call control channel may be directly routed between endpoints in a single TCP session, or the call control may be routed through one or more gatekeepers with separate TCP sessions for each leg of the communication. The decision ultimately rests with the gatekeeper for each endpoint. The primary reason that a gatekeeper may wish to intercept the call control channel is to provide proxy/security services for an endpoint, or to enable supplementary call services or multiparty conference capabilities.

Figures 11-26 through 11-28 illustrate some of the possibilities for how the H.225.0 call control channel may be routed.

Figure 11-26   *Call Control Directly Routed Between Endpoints*

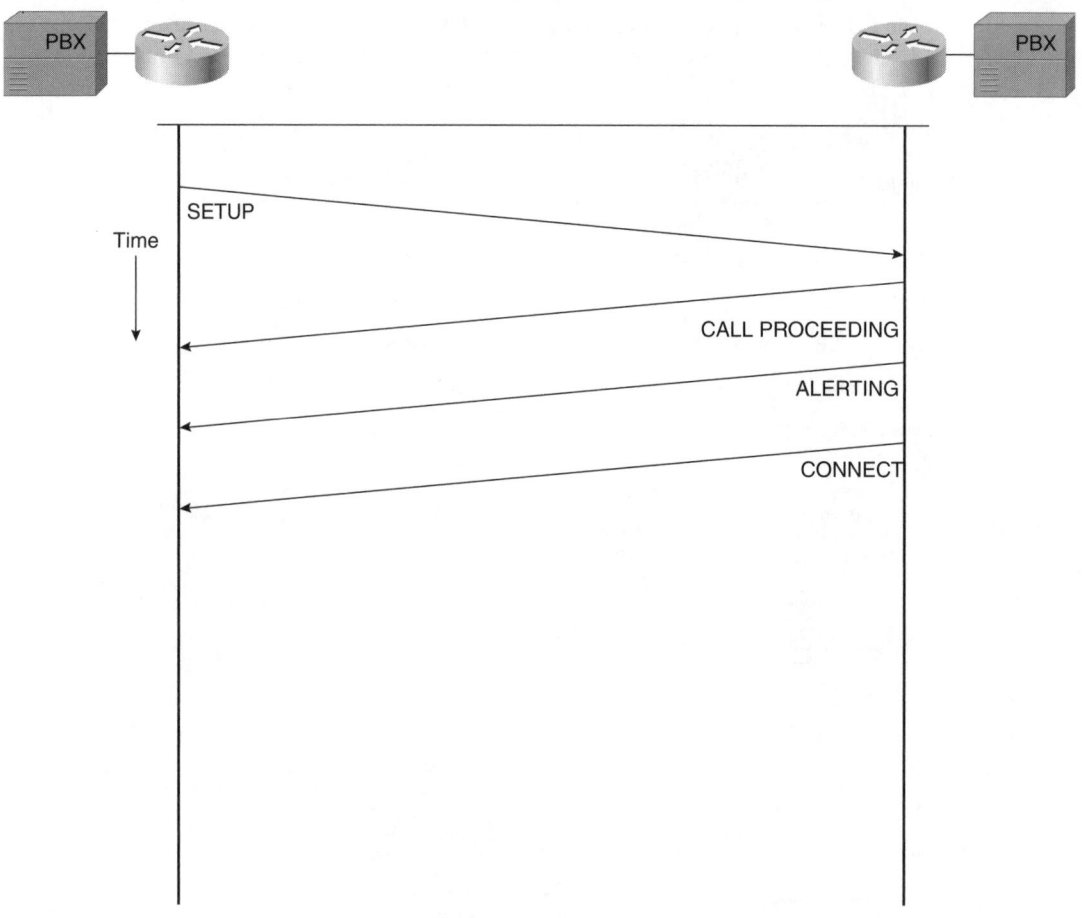

Figure 11-27 *Call Control Routed Through a Single Gatekeeper*

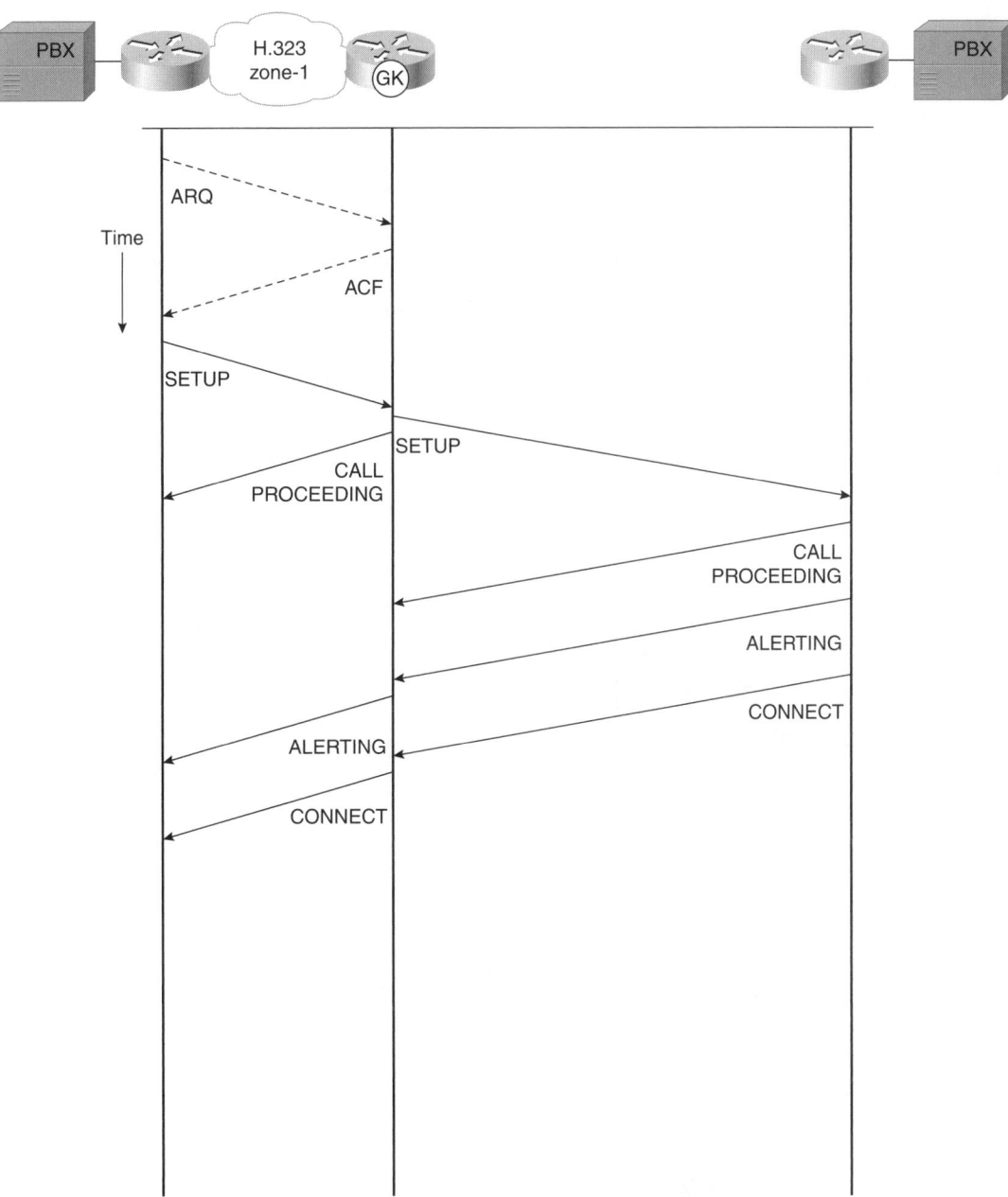

Figure 11-28   *Call Control Routed Through Two Gatekeepers*

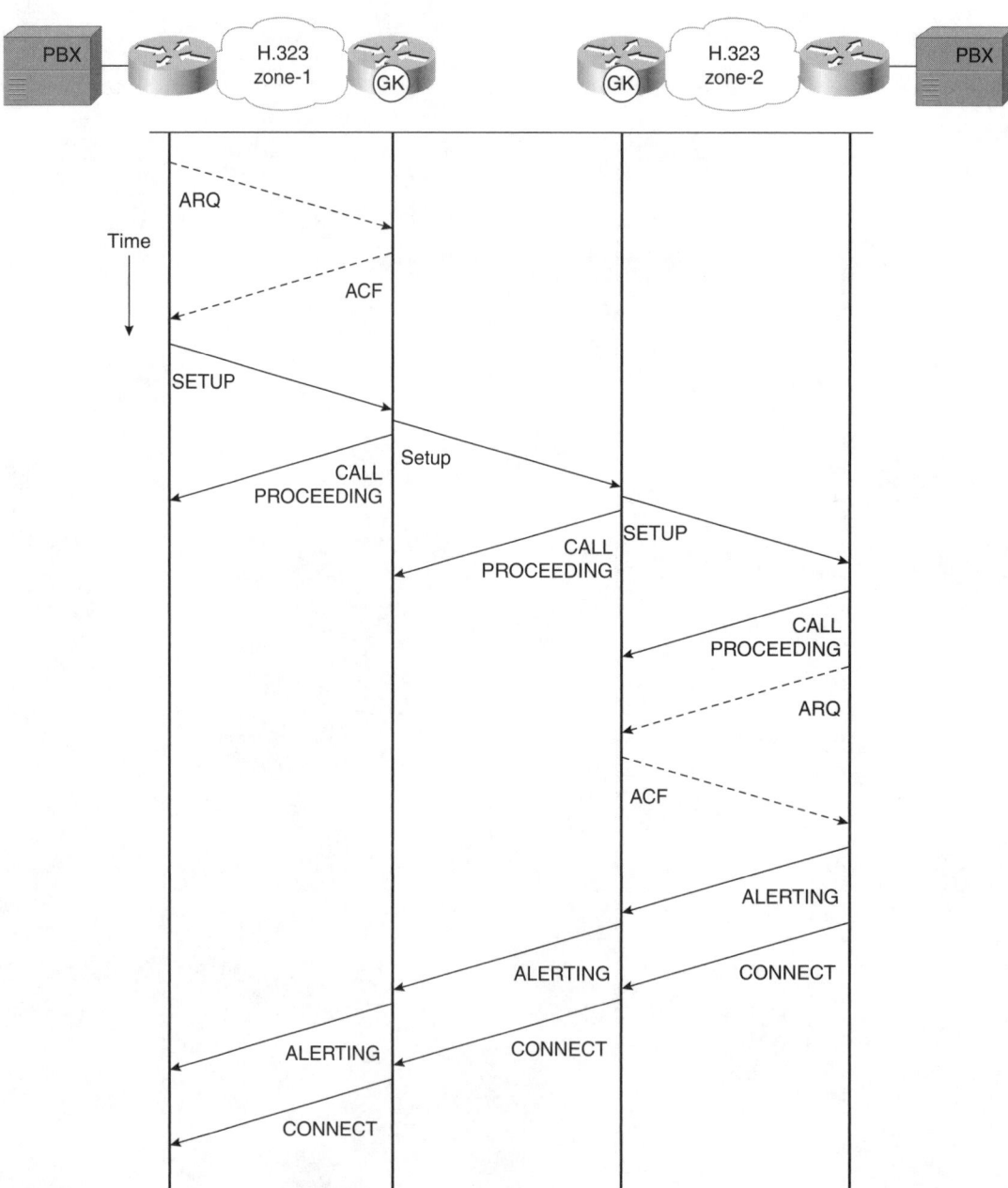

Supplementary Services (H.450.x)

The H.450.x supplementary services provide advanced calling features for H.323 networks. H.450.1 specifies the framework for how supplementary services should be designed, and the other recommendations in H.450.x identify specific supplementary services that have been implemented according to the methods of H.450.1.

H.450.1 adds a number of message types (specified in ASN.1 syntax, of course) that are transmitted over the reliable channel provided by H.225.0 call control. These messages are organized in a structure borrowed from SS7 TCAP component types (see Table 3-7 in Chapter 3), and provide the similar functionality. Table 11-14 illustrates the H.323 supplementary services that are either published or about to be published as of this writing:

Table 11-14 *H.323 Supplementary Services*

Recommendation	Description of Supplementary Service
H.450.1	Generic functional protocol for the support of supplementary services in H.323
H.450.2	Call-transfer supplementary service for H.323
H.450.3	Call-diversion supplementary service for H.323
H.450.4	Call-hold supplementary service for H.323
H.450.5	Call-park and call-pickup supplementary services for H.323
H.450.6	Call-waiting supplementary service for H.323
H.450.7	Message waiting–indication supplementary service for H.323
H.450.8	Name identification services

Media Control

The media control (H.245) channel is dynamically established over a reliable TCP connection, based on parameters in the H.225.0 call control (Q.931) CONNECT message. Although the TCP ports are different for the H.245 and the H.225.0 connections[1], the endpoints are the same. For multiparty conferences (all types), each party has a single H.245 connection to the MC. The messages used for H.245 media control are organized into four classes:

- Request
- Response
- Command
- Indication

---

1. Except in the case of H.245 fast-start procedures, where the H.245 logical channel is tunneled through the H.225.0 call control channel.

Most of the interesting transactions in H.245 media control are sequences of request/ response, or request/response/indication messages. The command message class enables an endpoint to request a transaction during an active call, and to perform maintenance functions.

The following sequence of events occurs over the H.245 media control channel:

- Endpoint capabilities exchange
- Master-slave determination
- Logical channel establishment for media streams

Capabilities Exchange

Before endpoints can establish any media sessions, they must negotiate a common set of media formats that all parties can use. H.323 provides a robust mechanism to exchange media capabilities, including support for complex expressions like the following:

```
{
[G.711 and H.261 and T.120] or
[(G.723.1 or G.729 or G.726) and T.120] or
[H.263]
}
```

Note that this capability is far more advanced than the functionality offered by the session description protocol (SDP), which is used with SIP. H.323 is limited, however, by its explicit representation of each codec type (only ITU and a few European standard audio codecs are supported), and a single extension field (that is, the NonStandardParameter) to describe additional codecs. SDP offers more flexibility in this regard. For VoIP networks, the codec capabilities set is a simple list of supported audio codecs, so the robust capability expressions of H.323 are not a significantly useful feature. Flexibility in expressing capability sets may become more important as VoIP networks evolve into true multimedia networks.

VoIP endpoints exchange the following information as part of the transport capabilities and user input capabilities negotiations:

- Supported RTP payload types (which refer to standard codecs)
- Whether or not RSVP is supported (QoSCapabilities element)
- What types of media channels are supported (such as IP/UDP)
- If RSVP is supported, what parameters are supported (RSVPParameters element)
- If RSVP is supported, which type of reservations are supported (guaranteed service versus controlled-load service)
- Whether or not DTMF relay is supported (for tones during an active call)

- Whether or not "hook-flash" relay is supported (for accessing features in remote phone switches)

H.245 provides explicit representation for the audio codecs listed in Table 11-15. Other codecs must be represented using a nonStandardParameter.

Table 11-15 *Audio Codecs Explicitly Supported by H.245 Media Control*

H.245-Supported Audio Codecs			
g711Alaw64k	g722-56k	g729	is13818AudioCapability
g711Alaw56k	g722-48k	g729AnnexA	gsmFullRate
g711Ulaw64k	g7231	g729wAnnexB	gsmHalfRate
g711Ulaw56k	g7231AnnexC	g729AnnexAwAnnexB	gsmEnhancedFullRate
g722-64k	g728	is11172AudioCapability	silenceSuppression

Master-Slave Determination

One of the endpoints must take charge of the H.245 connection and assert decision-making authority, or else problems may occur with conflicting session establishments, and so forth. H.245 media control uses a master-slave determination sequence to decide which endpoint is better poised to control the media establishment. Generally speaking, the endpoint with more media capabilities asserts authority. An MCU with MC support, and MP support for audio, video, and data is the most capable device in the network. For endpoints with similar capabilities, it does not matter which end becomes the master, as long as a decision is made. The point is to avoid having two sides try to control the session at the same time.

Logical Channel Establishment

The logical channel establishment phase of H.245 media control is when the RTP and RTCP sessions are initiated for the media streams. Independent connections are established in each direction. An H.245 openLogicalChannel message initiates the media stream session, using the following parameters:

- UDP port numbers for RTP and RTCP sessions
- Media format (that is, audio codec, video codec, or T.120 series data format)
- QoS mechanism (that is, RSVP information)
- Whether or not DTMF and hook-flash relay are supported

Figure 11-29 illustrates the H.245 process for establishing a media stream. Note that RSVP reservation establishment is an integral part of the process. An endpoint can specify that no media is transmitted until the RSVP reservation is complete by setting the flowControlToZero element in the OpenLogicalChannelAck message. The endpoint sends an H.245 command message to enable the media to flow (that is, restore FlowControl to an unrestricted state) after the RSVP reservation is established.

Figure 11-29 *Media Stream Established via H.245 Media Control Messages*

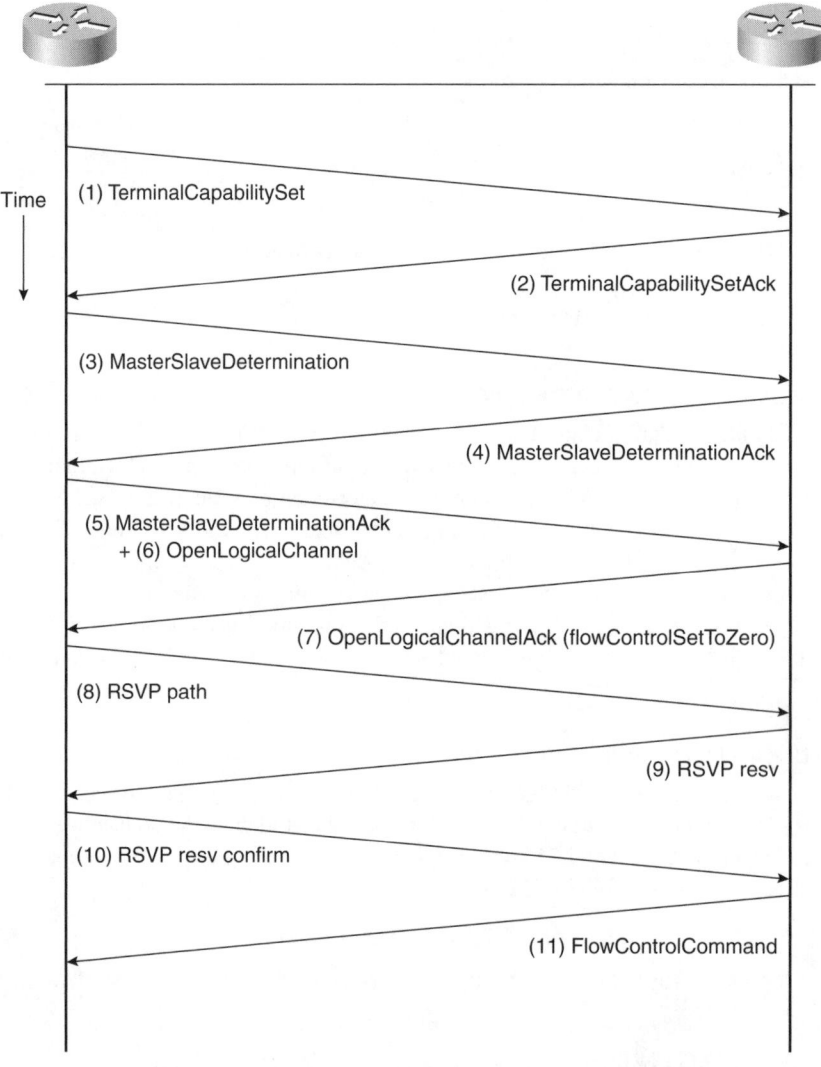

At this point, the media stream is established and functioning as described in "VoIP Audio Path: RTP/RTCP" earlier in this chapter.

Fast-Start Procedures and H.245 Tunneling

Because the original H.323v1 specification is designed for a LAN environment, it does not consider the possibility of transmission delays between signaling entities. Many round-trip communications are not a problem in a LAN environment because the cumulative delay of these transactions is negligible. The basic protocol design becomes a problem when it is implemented across a WAN, as demonstrated in the following example.

When a calling endpoint receives an H.225.0 connect message, the called party has already accepted the connection. In VoIP networks, the users at each endpoint (which are most likely telephones) expect to have an active audio path and may begin speaking. However, the audio path cannot be built until the H.245 negotiations are complete. This requires at least three to five round-trip communications (see Figure 11-29), and more if there are any parameters that require renegotiation. If there is a 150-ms one-way delay between the endpoints, then the H.245 negotiations may require 1500 ms of time before the audio channel can be established (for example, 150-ms one-way delay × 2 for round-trip × 5 round-trips). This does not include any processing time in intermediate gatekeepers. A result of the H.245 negotiation latency is that the first words of the called and calling parties may not be passed across the active connection because the audio path is not yet built. This is not an acceptable condition for most telephone users.

H.323v2 introduces a new model for media negotiation to remedy the audio-path problem and make H.323 more robust to network delays. The idea is to bypass the normal H.245 media negotiation process and pass the OpenLogicalChannel H.245 message in the initial H.225.0 SETUP message. The called endpoint can respond to the OpenLogicalChannel message with an OpenLogicalChannelAck in the H.225.0 CONNECT message. As soon as the H.225.0 connection is established (that is, the calling endpoint receives the H.225.0 CONNECT), both endpoints are ready to transmit and receive media streams.

Subsequent H.245 messages may be tunneled through the H.225.0 connection, or a separate TCP session may be established for the H.245 channel. Either party can abort the fast-start procedure and resort to the normal H.245 negotiation in the event that H.245 features are required that are not supported by the fast-connect procedure.

VoIP Signaling: SIP Paradigm

The Session Initiation Protocol (SIP), which is specified in RFC 2543, is an IETF standard. As of this writing, an updated version of RFC 2543 dubbed "RFC 2543bis" is being submitted as an Internet Draft, and will most likely be the standard by the time you read this.

As stated in the abstract of the SIP RFC, "The Session Initiation Protocol (SIP) is an application-layer control (signaling) protocol for creating, modifying, and terminating sessions with one or more participants. These sessions include Internet multimedia conferences, Internet telephone calls and multimedia distribution . . .."

SIP is just one of the protocols that form the IETF architecture for scalable, real-time, multiparty multimedia communication. Some of the prominent protocols (excluding QoS-related efforts) in this architecture are listed here:

- RTP and RTCP, specified in RFC 1889, provide real-time delivery of media.

- The Real-Time Streaming Protocol (RTSP), specified in RFC 2326, provides on-demand delivery of real-time data.

- The Session Description Protocol (SDP), specified in RFC 2327, provides a standardized description format for exchanging media capabilities (such as speech codecs for VoIP). The Session Announcement Protocol (SAP), which is still a draft standard, provides an advertisement method targeted for multicast sessions (such as Session Directory (SDR) for the MBONE).

Because this book is focused on voice/data integration, only the protocols that are relevant to a VoIP deployment are explored. These protocols include RTP/RTCP, which are covered earlier in this chapter; SIP, which provides the VoIP call signaling; and SDP, which provides a format for exchanging speech codec capabilities. RTSP may be relevant in some circumstances (for example, to play recorded announcements), but it is not a core part of VoIP and not discussed here. The following sections explore various aspects of the SIP model:

- Attributes of SIP
- System components
- Addressing
- Server location
- Message structure
- SIP operation

Attributes of SIP

SIP is designed as a long-term solution for Internet telephony and multimedia conferencing. Many considerations have gone into the protocol development to ensure that the protocol is a viable platform for future Internet-based communications:

- **Simplicity**—Unlike most Internet and telephony protocols, SIP uses plain-text messages that are human-readable. In addition, existing standards such as HTTP 1.1 and "mailto:" formats are followed. This makes the protocol relatively simple to troubleshoot and integrate with other applications.

- **Efficiency**—The high protocol overhead of SIP has little impact on communication efficiency because signaling functions consume little bandwidth relative to media streams. SIP is very efficient in terms of call setup time, because all information required for call establishment is included in the initial message.

- **Scalability**—Servers do not maintain state information about UDP-based SIP sessions that they process, so a single server can efficiently handle many clients. Message-routing loops, which may consume extensive network resources, become more common as networks grow. SIP detects and prevents message-routing loops, which improves performance in large networks.

- **Flexibility**—Because SIP uses SDP to negotiate codecs, any codec can be used that is registered with the Internet Assigned Numbers Authority (IANA). Contrast this with H.323, where the codecs are explicitly defined as part of the slow-changing standard, and all other codecs must share a generic field for "nonstandard codecs."

- **Support for Mobility**—The SIP communication model revolves around users that may move from terminal to terminal (for example, phones and computers), as opposed to the terminals themselves. The protocol provides robust support for proxying and redirection, so that the users have the option of providing or hiding their true location.

- **User Programmability**—In addition to native support for traditional telephony features (for example, call forwarding, transfer, hold, conference, and so on), SIP can take advantage of the Call Processing Language (CPL). This enables users to provide complex rules to a server regarding who can reach them at different times, different locations, and with what media types. H.323 systems can also take advantage of CPL. Tools such as SIP "servlets" and SIP common gateway interface (CGI) extensions are currently being standardized, which will facilitate the development of SIP-enabled applications.

- **Extensibility**—The protocol creators recognize that they cannot foresee all of the protocol requirements, so they created an architecture that is modular and flexible. This enables incremental improvements and extensions to the protocol, while ensuring smooth operation with older versions. This also allows unused protocol options to be gracefully retired, which will keep the protocol from becoming unwieldy.

System Components

Figure 11-30 illustrates a network with the following SIP components:

- **User Agents** (UA) are the endpoint applications that send and receive SIP requests on behalf of users (for example, people or automated systems). User Agent Clients (UAC) send SIP requests for the calling party, and User Agent Servers (UAS) receive requests for the called party. Each user may have multiple user agents. For example, you may have separate user agents for your work phone, home phone, mobile phone, and multimedia-enabled computer. A SIP address is associated with each user agent.

- **Proxy Servers** are applications that receive SIP requests from clients, and initiate new requests on behalf of the clients toward the destination user agents. You can think of proxy servers as SIP routers that forward call signaling messages toward the destination. This behavior is analogous to gatekeeper routed signaling (GKRS) in

H.323. It is also similar to SMTP mail gateways, except that the messages must be forwarded in real time. The information that a proxy server uses to direct SIP requests is beyond the scope of the SIP specification (candidates include finger, whois, or new protocols from the ENUM and Instant Messaging and Presence Protocol (IMPP) working groups of the IETF—see references in Table 11-22). SIP proxy servers may have local knowledge of user agents from a colocated SIP registrar. A proxy server may know several alternatives for reaching a user agent, and can attempt each of these alternatives in a forking process that may be sequential or parallel. Depending on how the SIP proxy is configured, SIP responses can flow through proxy servers in the reverse direction of SIP requests, or they can flow directly to the original sender of the SIP Invite message. Proxy servers can also provide a redirect address to the requesting client instead of forwarding the SIP request.

- **Registrars** accept registrations from clients that indicate the addresses at which they may be reached. The registrar functionality is often combined with a proxy or redirect server, but it is a separate logical process and is officially outside the scope of SIP. For example, a SIP registrar may be a software extension to an LDAP database that contains a directory of users.

Figure 11-30 *SIP Client and Server System Components*

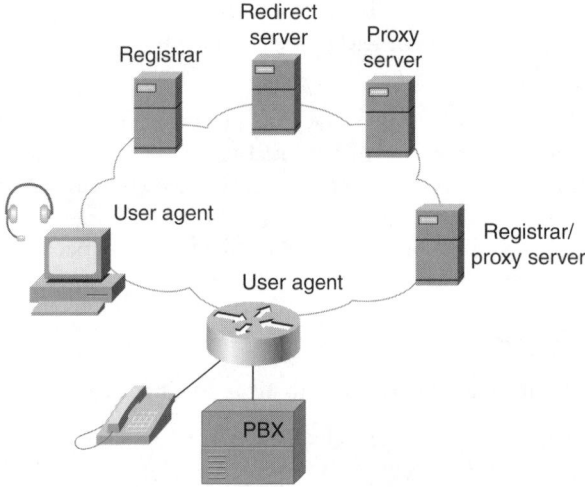

Addressing

Although proxy servers, redirect servers, and registrars may be involved with a SIP transaction, only users and user agents have SIP addresses. SIP servers (such as proxy, redirect, registrar) are only identified by IP addresses and TCP/UDP ports. By default, SIP servers listen on TCP and UDP port 5060, but they may use any port number.

The next three sections explore the following address-related topics:

- SIP address syntax
- SIP support for E.164 addresses
- Telephone URLs for E.164 addresses

SIP Address Syntax

The syntax of a SIP URL is modeled after RFC 2396, titled "Uniform Resource Identifiers (URI): Generic Syntax." For a complete description of the SIP URL syntax, see Figure 3 of RFC 2543. A basic SIP URL has the following format:

```
"sip:" [ user [ ":" password ] "@" ] ( hostname ¦ IP-address ) [ : port ]
```

Examples of valid SIP URLs include:

- sip:company.com
- sip:bob@company.com
- sip:bob@192.168.1.1
- sip:bob:secret@company.com
- sip:bob:secret@company.com:5060
- sip:bob@192.168.1.1:5060

SIP URLs may also include parameters and header information, with the following syntax appended to the basic SIP URL:

```
[ ";" param "=" value ] [ "?" 1st_header "=" value [ "&" other_headers "=" value ] ]
```

A SIP URL may have multiple parameters and header fields, as indicated in the following examples:

- sip:bob@company.com;transport=udp
- sip:bob@company.com;transport=udp;user=ip
- sip:bob@company.com;transport=tcp;user=ip?subject=test%20TCP%20call
- sip:bob@company.com?subject=test%20UDP%20call&body=abcdefgh

Note that the %20 in the above URLs is the encoded value for a space character.

SIP Support for E.164 Addresses

SIP distinguishes E.164 endpoints (telephones) from regular IP endpoints using the user parameter in a SIP URL. Many places where SIP URLs are normally used (for example, the To, From, and Request-URI headers) do not allow extended SIP URL parameters or headers, but the "user" parameter is an exception to this rule to allow ubiquitous support for E.164 endpoints.

The following examples illustrate SIP addresses for E.164 endpoints:

- sip:+1-408-555-1212@voip-gw.company.com;user=phone
- sip:+14085551212@192.168.1.1;user=phone
- sip:4199@192.168.1.1:5060;user=phone

The following examples illustrate SIP addresses that are generally not associated with E.164 endpoints:

- sip:+1-408-555-1212@voip-gw.company.com
- sip:4199@voip-gw.company.com
- sip:4199@192.168.1.1:5060;user=ip

You will not usually see the user=ip option because it is the default in SIP URLs. A SIP URL that contains user=ip never refers to an E.164 number. It is possible that an implementation does not support the user= option, in which case the first two preceding examples can refer to E.164 addresses. Such a scenario represents a nonstandard implementation.

Telephone URLs for E.164 Addresses

There is a working draft specification of telephony URLS (draft-antti-telephony-url-12.txt) which provides three alternatives to the SIP URL: tel, fax, and modem. In addition to encoding the basic numbers, these URLs can also indicate the capabilities of the associated devices or special calling sequences. For example, a modem URL can indicate supported protocols and the number of data bits, parity, and stopbits. The following examples illustrate several variations of a tel URL:

- tel:555-1212
- tel:+14085551212;postd=w1234
- tel:+18005551212;postd=ppppp1p4085551212pp123456789#

The first example indicates a local telephone number, which assumes that the user is familiar with the context in which the number should be used. The dash character embedded in the string of digits has no functional meaning; it may be included to improve the readability of the phone number. The second example indicates an international number (the # key indicates that an E.164 international country code follows), with a post-dial instruction (indicated by postd=). In this case, the dialing agent should wait for a secondary dial tone after the original number is dialed, and then enter the extension 1234.

The third example indicates how a dialing agent may use a calling card service. After dialing the toll-free number of the calling card service, the agent pauses for 5 seconds (as indicated by ppppp). By this time, an automated attendant reads a menu of options, and the calling agent enters 1. After pausing for one second, during which the autoattendant asks for the destination number, the calling agent enters 4085551212, and then pauses for 2 more seconds. During this time, the autoattendant asks for a calling card number and PIN, which the calling agent provides as 123456789#. The phone rings again at this point, which is the ring-back tone from the called party (that is, 4085551212). The user of the tel URL hears the ringing tone of the final destination, after all of the preceding steps are complete. Note that this use of the telephone URL may be a flagrant security violation, because the calling card PIN is included in clear text. Using the telephone URL in this manner requires that it not be shared with anyone, nor included in any type of document to which other parties have access.

SIP URLs that encode telephone numbers can take advantage of the features described here, as long as the option ;user=phone is included.

NOTE   As of this writing, Cisco routers only recognize sip: URLS in conjunction with SIP. They do not recognize or generate tel: URLs.

Support for Mobility

Consider the following example of Jane Doe, who is a user with the generic e-mail and SIP address of jdoe@company.com. She may be contacted at specific devices with the following SIP addresses:

- sip:jdoe@jdoe-pc.company.com
- sip:+14085551212@voip-gw.company.com;user=phone
- tel:+1-650-555-1212

As Jane Doe moves from her PC at work, to her mobile phone, to her home telephone, she can update the SIP registrar for jdoe@company.com with the preferred SIP address to forward her calls. The SIP registrar can communicate with the SIP proxy server so that any requests that arrive for jdoe@company.com are proxied to the device of Jane's choice. Alternatively, Jane may leave jdoe@company.com pointing to her PC, and configure her PC to act as a SIP proxy server that forwards her calls.

Server Location

A common scenario for SIP clients is to use a local proxy server as the next-hop delivery point for all outbound SIP requests. In order for SIP clients to use local proxy servers, they must be able to locate them. The SIP URL of the called party is usually determined from an out-of-band method (for example, known through a directory, a previous communication, an e-mail message, or another method), but the local proxy server that relays the SIP request must be learned by some other means. Note that DNS generally has a prominent role in SIP call routing, because most SIP URLs include DNS names that must be resolved.

In order for proxy servers to properly route inbound SIP requests, they can use information from a SIP registrar. The registrar relies on updates from the user agents, which implies that the user agents need to know how to reach a SIP registrar. The following two sections explore how SIP clients locate SIP proxy/relay servers and SIP registrars.

Finding a Proxy/Redirect Server

The base specification for SIP (RFC 2543) does not provide a method for UA clients to automatically learn about local proxy or redirect servers. Although UA clients do not need to use local servers (because calling party UA clients can communicate directly with the called party UA server or called party proxy server), a local proxy server may be required to get through a firewall or for other reasons.

Annex D of RFC 2543 does provide a method for UA clients to dynamically locate SIP servers, given a minimal amount of information (such as the DNS domain name of the local SIP server). The process takes advantage of the new SRV resource record type in DNS, which is specified in RFC 2782 (formerly RFC 2052). Figure 11-31 illustrates how a UA client with minimal information may use DNS to locate a proxy server.

The UA client initiates a DNS query for the SRV record with the service type sip and the appropriate DNS domain name.

The DNS server responds with the host name and TCP/UDP port of the SIP server.

The UA client then queries the DNS server for the A record of the SIP server host name.

The DNS server responds with the IP address of the SIP server.

The benefit of the DNS-based approach to UA client configuration, as opposed to hard-coding the information in each client, is that you can add or remove SIP servers as necessary without needing to update each client. For stationary UA clients, location of the proxy server is practically automatic. For mobile UA clients that can connect to different DNS domains, the SIP proxy cannot be located until the DNS domain name is manually updated in the SIP client configuration. Note that the process is not as simple as copying the user's domain into the SIP client configuration, because the local SIP proxy may be in a different domain than the client.

An IETF work in progress (draft-ietf-sip-dhcp-01.txt) describes a method for UA clients to obtain the DNS domain name of the SIP server via a DHCP option (the DHCP option code for the SIP server domain is not specified as of this writing).

Another option that does not require new standards is to use the TFTP server (66) option of DHCP, and have the UA client download a configuration file that contains the DNS domain name, or the IP address and TCP port of the SIP server. This option is very practical as it is available today and it enables SIP UA clients to be completely portable.

Figure 11-31 *UA Client Determines the IP Address and TCP/UDP Port of Proxy Server Via DNS*

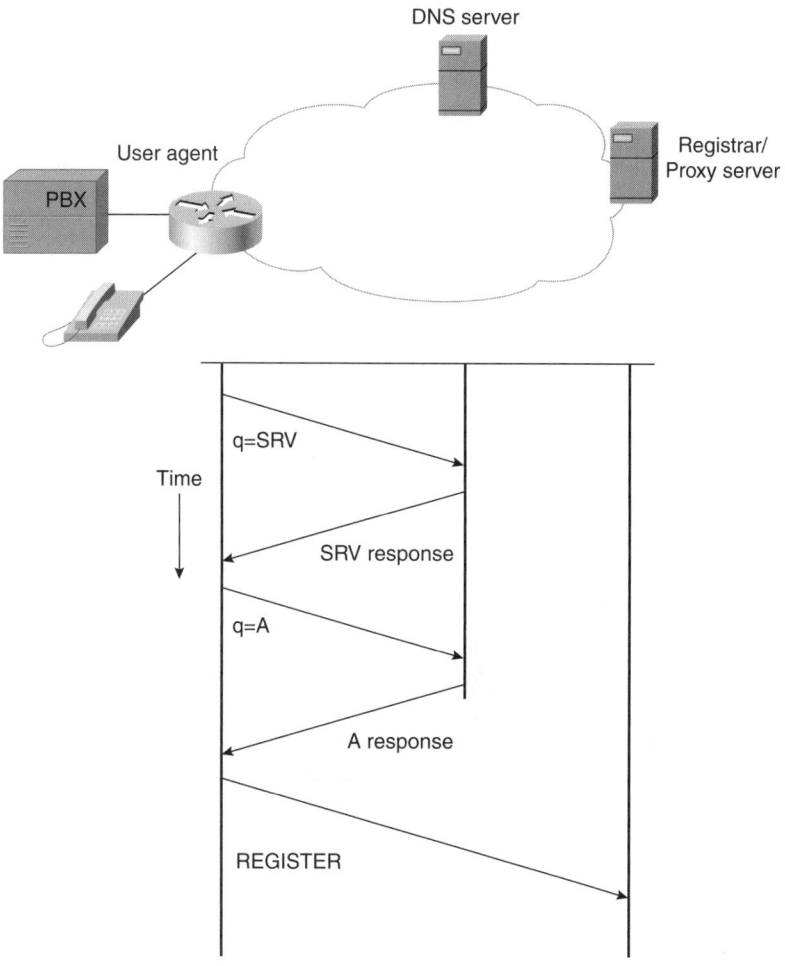

SIP clients default to using TCP/UDP port 5060 to reach a SIP server, but will use whatever port is specified in a SIP URL, returned by a DNS SRV query, or configured via TFTP at boot-up time.

Finding a Registrar

SIP user agents can either be statically configured with the location of a SIP registrar, or they can use multicast to dynamically find a SIP registrar. (See Figure 11-32.) The well-known multicast address for U.S. clients to register with a SIP registrar is 224.0.1.75. There is also a well-known DNS name for this address, which is sip.mcast.net.

Figure 11-32   *SIP User Agent Locates a SIP Registrar Via the Well-Known Multicast Address*

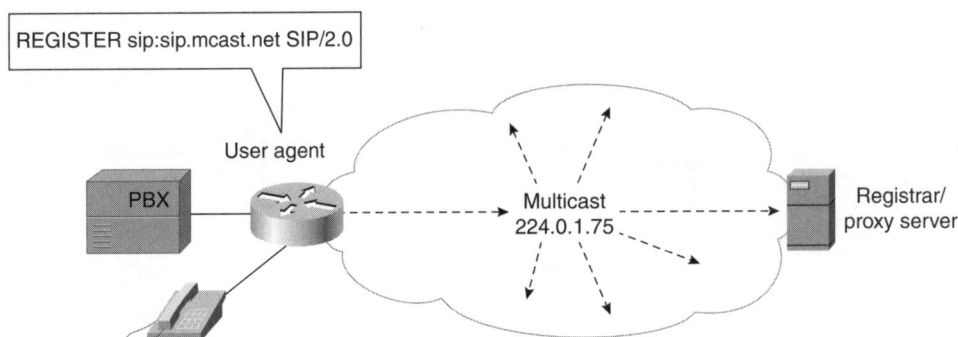

If you use the multicast method to locate registrars, then you must be sure to limit the scope of the multicast address such that SIP registration requests never leave your administrative domain (unless you want your clients registering to someone else's SIP registrars!). To limit the scope of the multicast address, you can use access lists at multicast border routers, or reduce the size of the TTL field in the IP header based on the diameter of your network. For more information about multicast, read Beau Williamson's book titled *Developing IP Multicast Networks, Vol. 1*.

It is interesting to note that SIP user agents within your network may listen to the SIP registrar multicast address to learn about the presence of other user agents. This technique can be an efficient mechanism for user agents to develop full-mesh reachability within an administrative domain in the absence of a local proxy server. However, this method may become processor-intensive for clients when there are a large number of clients in the multicast domain.

Message Structure

There are three parts to a SIP message:

- Start line
- Headers
- Body

The start line indicates the purpose of the message, the headers provide the details of the message, and the optional body provides added details that do not fit in the headers. The next three sections explore these message parts.

Start Line

The format of the start line depends on whether the message is a request or a response. All SIP messages are either requests or responses.

SIP Requests

The format of the start line for SIP requests is as follows:

<Method> <Request-URI> <SIP version>

Where <Method> is one of the SIP request types identified in Table 11-16, <Request-URI> is the SIP URL (or other type of URL) of the entity that should receive the message (for example, a proxy server or the called party UAS), and <SIP version> is currently SIP/2.0. Examples include:

- INVITE sip:jdoe@company.com SIP/2.0

- ACK sip:+14085551212@192.168.1.1;user=phone SIP/2.0

- BYE tel:+1-408-555-1212;postd=p4199 SIP/2.0

Clients send SIP requests to communicate with servers. There are six types of SIP requests, also called SIP methods, which are identified in RFC 2543. An IETF work in progress identifies two additional methods, which are included here. Table 11-16 summarizes how each of these methods is used. New methods may be added as the need arises.

Table 11-16   *Request Types Sent by SIP Clients (* Denotes IEFT Work in Progress)*

Method	Purpose
INVITE	Initiates a VoIP call; in general, invites the called party or parties to join a session.
ACK	Acknowledges a SIP response.
OPTIONS	Queries a UA server for its capabilities; server response should include the SIP methods it supports.
BYE	UA clients (either called party or calling party) signal their desire to release a call.
CANCEL	Cancels a pending request (for example, proxy aborts parallel UAS searches after one successful response).
REGISTER	UA clients register the address in the To: header with a registrar; enables proxy to find UA.
PRACK *	UA clients request reliable delivery of informational (1xx) responses.

continues

Table 11-16 *Request Types Sent by SIP Clients (* Denotes IEFT Work in Progress) (Continued)*

Method	Purpose
INFO *	Transmits call signals during an active call (for example, ISUP or Q.SIG message tunneling).
SUBSCRIBE *	UA clients request presence/availability updates about other users from a SIP registrar, whenever the user changes registration information. (Associated with the IMPP working group of the IETF.)
NOTIFY *	Instant updates from a registrar to a UA client about users that have changed registration information. UA clients must first SUBSCRIBE to receive NOTIFY updates about a given user.

The PRACK and the INFO methods, which are works in progress as of this writing, facilitate the interworking of SIP with circuit-switched telephony protocols.

The PRACK method (draft-ietf-sip-100rel-NN.txt), which is an abbreviation of progress acknowledgment, enables UA clients to specify reliable delivery from the SIP server for informational (that is, 1xx) responses. The 1xx responses in SIP correspond with call progress messages in ISDN, SS7 ISUP, and other telephony protocols. Traditional telephony protocols may not operate correctly if call progress messages are dropped or received out of order, so these messages must pass through a SIP cloud reliably and in the proper order. A PRACK request alerts the SIP server that reliable and ordered delivery is required.

Future integration of RSVP with SIP will also require use of the PRACK method, because reservations should be established at the earliest time to ensure that an audio path is available when the call is completed. The earliest time to establish the RSVP reservation is when the source and destination IP address and port information are available, which is upon receipt of the 183 Session Progress response that precedes a 200 OK response. Without the PRACK method, the 183 Session Progress might not be received before the 200 OK message, in which case the reservation might not be established by the time that both parties expect to hear each other. SIP 183 and 200 responses are discussed in the following section. You might want to come back and read this paragraph after you understand the normal sequence of SIP message exchanges.

The INFO method (draft-ietf-sip-info-method-NN.txt) transmits signaling information during the course of an active session without impacting the current session. RFC 2543 only provides signaling during an active call when some characteristic of the session changes. The INFO method is useful for tunneling midcall signaling information from circuit-switched protocols through a SIP cloud. For example, Q.SIG or SS7 ISUP/TCAP messages may be required for supplementary services during an active conversation. The SIP INFO method enables these messages to be forwarded through a SIP cloud without affecting the state of the SIP session. The body of the INFO method is encoded in MIME format (RFCs 2045-2049) so that it can be used for a variety of midcall signaling needs.

SIP Responses

The format of the start line for SIP responses is as follows:

<SIP version> <Status Code> <Reason Phrase>

Where <SIP version> is currently SIP/2.0, and <Status Code> and <Reason Phrase> are set to one of the pairs listed in Table 11-18. Examples include:

- SIP/2.0 404 Not Found
- SIP/2.0 180 Ringing
- SIP/2.0 200 OK

Servers respond to client requests with one or more responses. The standardized SIP responses are coded with a three-digit response code and a textual description following the format of HTTP version 1.1. (See RFC 2616.) The responses are organized into six categories, which are identified by the first digit of the response code. (See Table 11-17.) The first five categories are identical to HTTP/1.1.

Table 11-17 *SIP Response Categories*

Code	SIP Response Category	Description
1xx	Informational	Provide status (for example, call-progress information).
2xx	Success	Requested action was received, understood, and accepted.
3xx	Redirection	Client must take additional action to complete the request.
4xx	Request Failure	Request is invalid on this particular server (might be successful elsewhere).
5xx	Server Failure	Request may be valid, but this particular server failed for other reasons.
6xx	Global Failures	Request will fail everywhere (do not try any other servers).

Many SIP/2.0 response codes within each category are identical to the corresponding HTTP/1.1 response codes. SIP codes in a given category that do not match existing HTTP codes generally use the range x80 to x99, while new HTTP response codes will be assigned below x80. This consideration enables SIP and HTTP to adopt each other's new codes and maintain consistency. Response code consistency is important because SIP and HTTP are evolving to share the same server application components (for example, parsers, error handling, and so forth).

SIP introduces the 6xx category of codes to distinguish between error responses that would occur on any server and error responses that are unique to a given server. For example, a UA server may decline a client request because it is busy (which is an error response for a given server), but the client needs to know whether it should pursue the request elsewhere. The called user may wish to be unreachable from any source (do not disturb on a global setting), so the UA server can inform the client of this state with the 600 busy everywhere response. The client then knows to stop sending INVITE requests to other UA servers for the user.

If a client receives a SIP response code that it does not recognize, it treats the response as an x00 response for the given category. This behavior ensures backward compatibility with older SIP clients, while allowing extensions to the SIP response codes.

The SIP response codes for SIP/2.0 are listed in Table 11-18.

Table 11-18   *SIP Response Codes (* Denotes IEFT Work in Progress)*

Code	Response Description	Code	Response Description
100	Trying	411	Length Required
180	Ringing	413	Request Entity Too Large
181	Call Is Being Forwarded	414	Request-URI Too Large
182	Queued	415	Unsupported Media Type
183	Session Progress *	420	Bad Extension
		480	Temporarily Not Available
200	OK	481	Call Leg or Transaction Does Not Exist
		482	Loop Detected
300	Multiple Choices	483	Too Many Hops
301	Moved Permanently	484	Address Incomplete
302	Moved Temporarily	485	Ambiguous
303	See Other	486	Busy Here
305	Use Proxy	487	Request Terminated
380	Alternative Service	488	Not Acceptable Here
400	Bad Request	500	Internal Server Error
401	Unauthorized	501	Not Implemented
402	Payment Required	502	Bad Gateway

Table 11-18 *SIP Response Codes (* Denotes IEFT Work in Progress) (Continued)*

Code	Response Description	Code	Response Description
403	Forbidden	503	Service Unavailable
404	Not Found	504	Gateway Timeout
405	Method Not Allowed	505	SIP Version Not Supported
406	Not Acceptable		
407	Proxy Authentication Required	600	Busy Everywhere
408	Request Timed Out	603	Decline
409	Conflict	604	Does Not Exist Anywhere
410	Gone	606	Not Acceptable

The SIP response codes in the 1xx range are provisional responses, which means that the server will make additional responses to the client request. All other responses from a server are final for a given SIP request. If the request is an INVITE method from a client, then the client must send an ACK method to acknowledge the final response from the server.

SIP Headers

Headers in SIP messages perform the same function as fields in a normal protocol header. That is, each SIP header represents a variable value that is transported across the network. Some SIP headers are mandatory in every message, and others are used depending on the type of request or response. The general format for SIP headers is:

< Header Name>:   <Header Value>
<Continuation of Header Value>

Where the header name is one of the items listed in Table 11-19, and the header value is one or more lines of information. Leading white spaces identify multiline header continuations. A PGP encryption key is an example of a header value that requires multiple lines. Single line examples include:

- From: sip:102@2.0.0.1
- User-Agent: Cisco VoIP Gateway/ IOS 12.x/ SIP enabled
- Content-Type: application/sdp

The order in which SIP headers appear in a message is not important, with two exceptions:

- Via headers appear in the order that SIP responses should flow back through proxy servers to get to the calling party UA.
- Hop-by-Hop headers (that is, headers that should be processed by proxy servers) should appear before End-to-End headers (such as headers for the calling and called party UA).

Aside from these restrictions, headers should be arranged in order of the functional groups.

SIP header types are logically organized into four groups, as identified in Table 11-19. Though it is not a requirement, the headers should appear in SIP messages in the order of these groups (that is, general headers, followed by request headers, followed by response headers, followed by entity headers).

Table 11-19 *SIP Header Elements (* Denotes IEFT Work in Progress)*

General	Request	Response	Entity
Accept	Accept-Contact *	Allow	Content-Encoding
Accept-Encoding	Authorization	Proxy-Authenticate	Content-Length
Accept-Language	Contact	Retry-After	Content-Type
Call-ID	Hide	Rseq *	
Contact	Max-Forwards	Server	
CSeq	Organization	Unsupported	
Date	Priority	Warning	
Encryption	Proxy-Authorization	WWW-Authenticate	
Expires	Proxy-Require		
From	RAck *		
Record-Route	Reject-Contact *		
Session-Expires *	Request-Disposition *		
Supported *	Require		
Time Stamp	Response Key		
To	Route		
Via	Subject		
	User-Agent		

Header Extensions

New headers may be added to SIP as the need arises. The Require, Proxy-Require, Supported, and Unsupported headers enable new SIP headers to be added without causing problems to older clients and servers. These headers contain information about client or server functions that must be understood to process the extension headers. If a server does not understand one of the required functions, it returns a response indicating that the feature is not supported. Clients and servers can share information with each other about which features are supported, so they can agree on a common set of supported functions.

Examples of headers that provide support for new SIP header types include:

- Require: com.cisco.inband-alerting
- Support: org.ietf.sip.100rel

Note that new functions or extensions are named according to a reverse-ordered DNS name, and may be registered with the Internet Assigned Numbers Authority (IANA). Organizations that choose not to register the functions can include them under their own administration (such as in the Cisco example).

NOTE   As of IOS 12.1(3)T, Cisco no longer uses the inband-alerting function because a more standard method using the 183 Session Progress response is now available. However, the Cisco example still highlights the way in which new functions may be incorporated in the absence of a standard way of achieving a given goal within the SIP standards.

Header Name Abbreviations

It is desirable to avoid fragmentation for SIP messages, so the message should be small enough to fit within the maximum transmission unit (MTU) of the network. Several SIP header names may be abbreviated to reduce the byte-count of the message and avoid fragmentation. All SIP servers must be able to interpret any combination of abbreviated and normal header names. Table 11-20 lists the header names that may be abbreviated.

Table 11-20   *Header Names that May Be Abbreviated to Reduce the SIP Message Byte-Count*

Header Name (Normal)	Header Name (Compact)
Call-ID	i
Contact	m
Content-Encoding	e
Content-Length	l
Content-Type	c
From	f
Subject	s
To	t
Via	v

Body of SIP Messages

The contents of a message body vary depending on the type of SIP request or response. For SIP requests, the BYE method never includes a body, while the INVITE, ACK, and OPTIONS methods encode the body according to SDP. For SIP responses, the code range 1xx may include advisory information about the request, the 2xx range contains the negotiated session description, the 3xx may contain information about alternative services or destinations to fulfill the request, and the 4xx to 6xx range may contain human-readable information about the failure.

The following section provides information about the SDP encoding

Session Description Protocol

Session description protocol (SDP) is designed to completely identify all attributes of a session, including media, administrative, and scheduling information. This multipurpose protocol is used by SIP, and is available for other applications such as the MBONE session directory.

Unlike SIP headers, the order of SDP attributes is strictly specified. The ordering is enforced to minimize the size and complexity of the protocol parser. Table 11-21 identifies the attributes that may be specified with SDP.

Table 11-21 *SDP Attribute Types and Values (* Denotes Optional Lines)*

SDP Type	Value
Session Description	
v=	Protocol version
o=	Owner/creator and session identifier
s=	Session name
i=	* Session information
u=	* URI of description
e=	* E-mail address
p=	* Phone number
c=	* Connection information—not required if included in all media
b=	* Bandwidth information
<TIME_DESCR>	One or more Time Descriptions (see below)
z=	* Time zone adjustments
k=	* Encryption key
a=	* Zero or more session attribute lines

Table 11-21   *SDP Attribute Types and Values (* Denotes Optional Lines) (Continued)*

SDP Type	Value
<MEDIA_DESCR>	* Zero or more Media Descriptions (see below)
Time Description	
t=	Time the session is active
r=	* Zero or more repeat times
Media Description	
m=	Media name and transport address
i=	* Media title
c=	* Connection information—optional if included at session level
b=	* Bandwidth information
k=	* Encryption key
a=	* Zero or more media attribute lines

For more information about any of the SIP methods, responses, or headers, consult RFC 2543 and the IETF drafts associated with the SIP working group. (See Table 11-22 at the end of this chapter for the URL of various IETF working groups.) For more information about SDP formats, consult RFC 2327.

SIP Operation

This section provides examples of simple SIP transactions. An excellent work in progress from the IETF SIP working group (draft-ietf-sip-call-flows-NN.txt) contains numerous examples of success and failure scenarios. The document includes summary diagrams, detailed explanations, and actual SIP messages.

Figures 11-33 through 11-37 illustrate the following successful SIP transactions:

- Direct SIP call between IP endpoints
- Direct SIP call between VoIP routers acting as SIP/ISDN gateways
- New registration by a SIP client
- Updated registration by a SIP client
- Redirect server, proxy server, and VoIP gateway

Figure 11-33 *Direct SIP Call Between IP Endpoints*

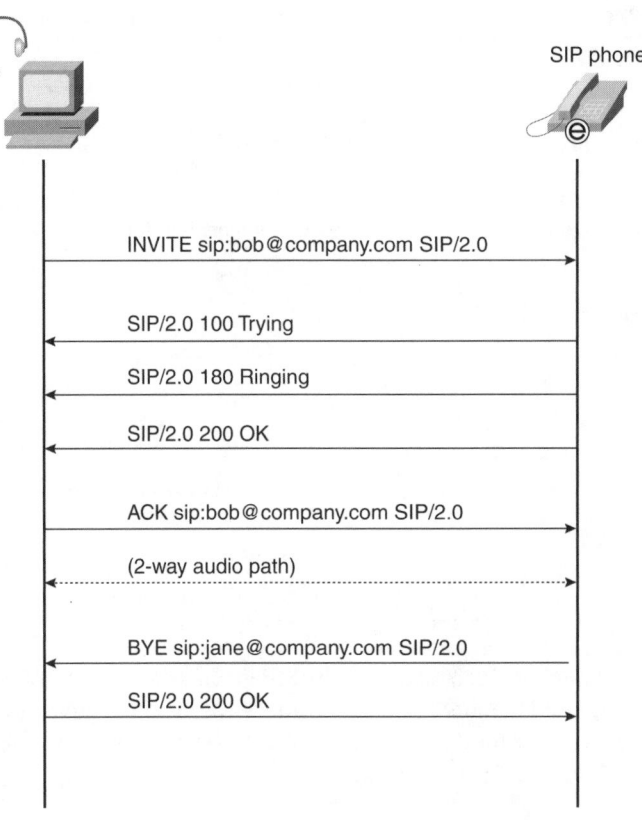

Figure 11-34 *Direct SIP Call Between VoIP Gateways*

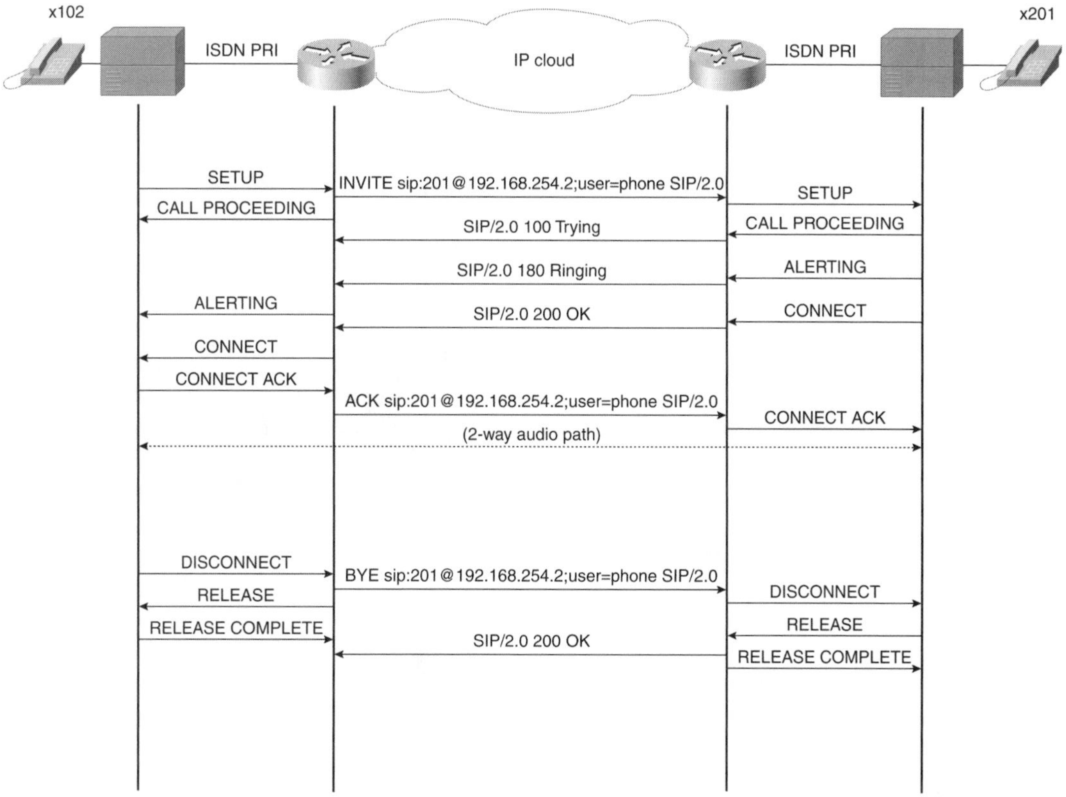

Figure 11-35 *Client Registers with SIP Registrar for the First Time Since Power-On*

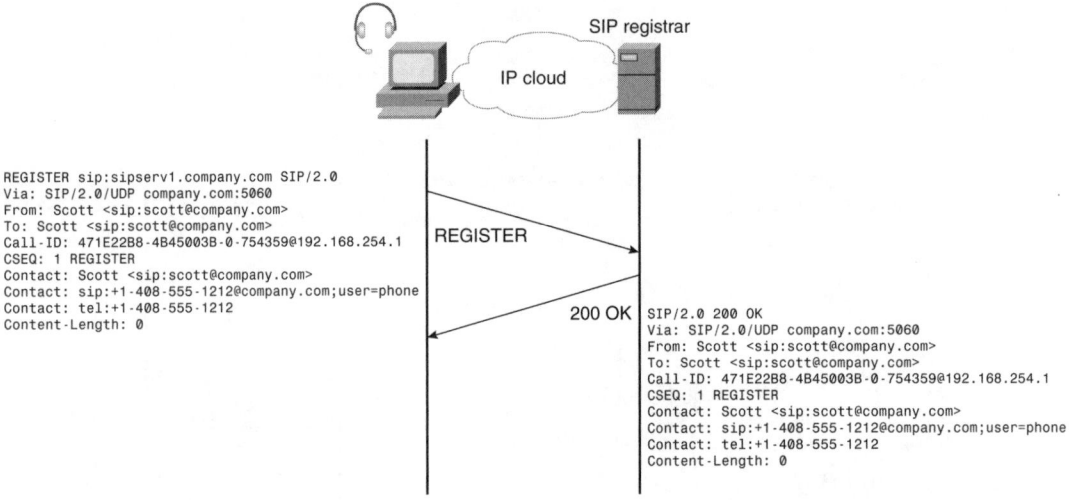

```
REGISTER sip:sipserv1.company.com SIP/2.0
Via: SIP/2.0/UDP company.com:5060
From: Scott <sip:scott@company.com>
To: Scott <sip:scott@company.com>
Call-ID: 471E22B8-4B45003B-0-754359@192.168.254.1
CSEQ: 1 REGISTER
Contact: Scott <sip:scott@company.com>
Contact: sip:+1-408-555-1212@company.com;user=phone
Contact: tel:+1-408-555-1212
Content-Length: 0
```
REGISTER

200 OK
```
SIP/2.0 200 OK
Via: SIP/2.0/UDP company.com:5060
From: Scott <sip:scott@company.com>
To: Scott <sip:scott@company.com>
Call-ID: 471E22B8-4B45003B-0-754359@192.168.254.1
CSEQ: 1 REGISTER
Contact: Scott <sip:scott@company.com>
Contact: sip:+1-408-555-1212@company.com;user=phone
Contact: tel:+1-408-555-1212
Content-Length: 0
```

Figure 11-36 *Client Updates Contact Information with the SIP Registrar*

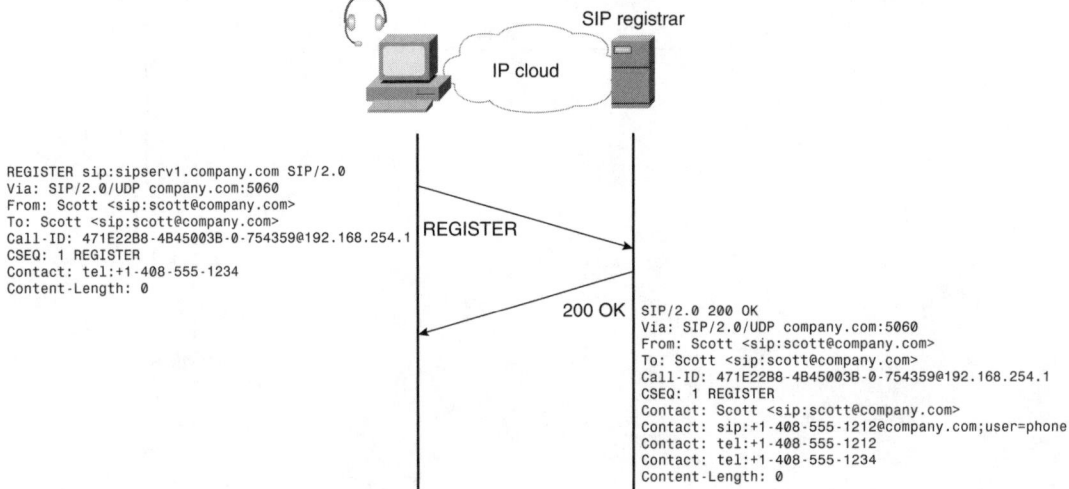

```
REGISTER sip:sipserv1.company.com SIP/2.0
Via: SIP/2.0/UDP company.com:5060
From: Scott <sip:scott@company.com>
To: Scott <sip:scott@company.com>
Call-ID: 471E22B8-4B45003B-0-754359@192.168.254.1
CSEQ: 1 REGISTER
Contact: tel:+1-408-555-1234
Content-Length: 0
```
REGISTER

200 OK
```
SIP/2.0 200 OK
Via: SIP/2.0/UDP company.com:5060
From: Scott <sip:scott@company.com>
To: Scott <sip:scott@company.com>
Call-ID: 471E22B8-4B45003B-0-754359@192.168.254.1
CSEQ: 1 REGISTER
Contact: Scott <sip:scott@company.com>
Contact: sip:+1-408-555-1212@company.com;user=phone
Contact: tel:+1-408-555-1212
Contact: tel:+1-408-555-1234
Content-Length: 0
```

Figure 11-37 *UA Client Redirected to a Proxy Server; VoIP Router Acts as SIP/ISDN Gateway*

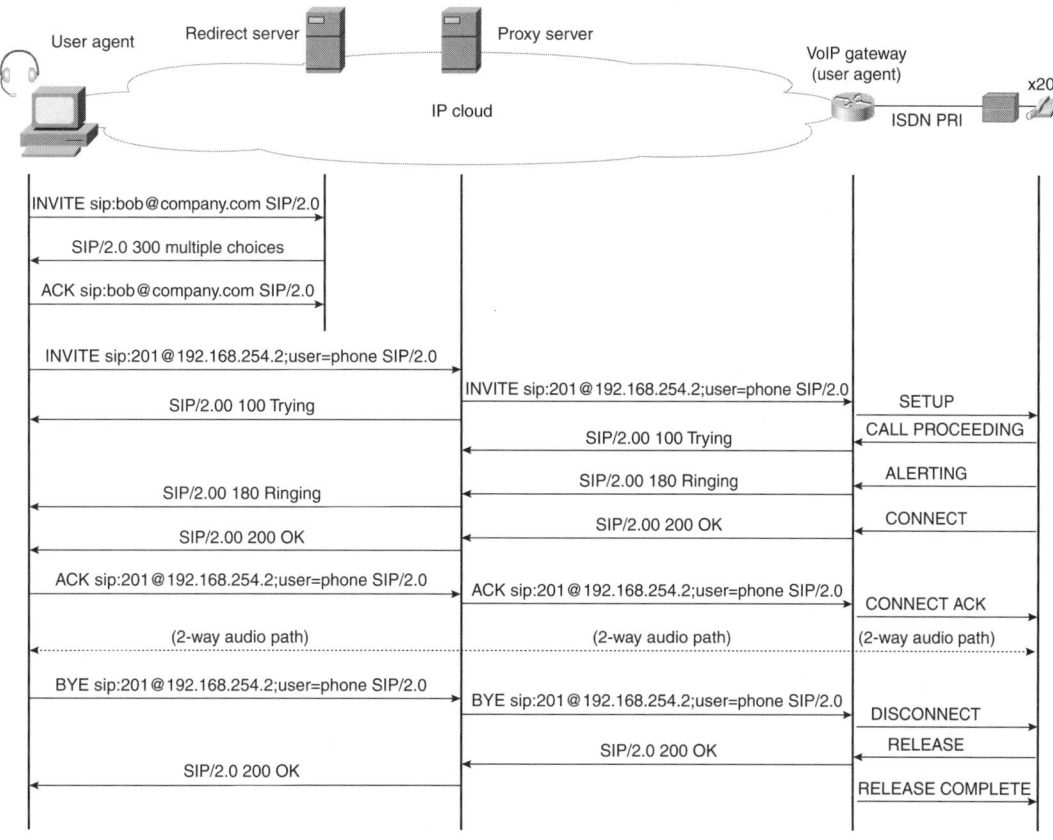

Examples 11-1 through 11-7 show the actual SIP messages that are exchanged between VoIP gateways in the scenario illustrated in Example 11-1. Each example illustrates a separate SIP message either sent or received by the router acting as the UA client.

Example 11-1 *SIP UA Client Sends an INVITE Message*

```
INVITE sip:201@192.168.254.2;user=phone SIP/2.0
Via: SIP/2.0/UDP  2.0.0.1:52341
From: sip:102@2.0.0.1
To: <sip:201@192.168.254.2;user=phone>
Date: Tue, 18 Apr 2000 11:50:53 PST
Call-ID: 471E22B8-4B45003B-0-754360@192.168.254.1
Cisco-Guid: 1193157304-1262813241-0-7677160
Require: com.cisco.inband-alerting
```

continues

Example 11-1 *SIP UA Client Sends an INVITE Message (Continued)*

```
User-Agent: Cisco VoIP Gateway/ IOS 12.x/ SIP enabled
CSeq: 100 INVITE
Content-Type: application/sdp
Content-Length: 117

v=0
o=CiscoSystemsSIPUserAgent 62 9015 IN IP4 2.0.0.1
s=SIP Call
c=IN IP4 2.0.0.1
m=audio 20902 RTP/AVP 65535 0
```

Example 11-2 *SIP UA Client Receives the Informational Response 100 Trying*

```
SIP/2.0 100 Trying
Via: SIP/2.0/UDP  2.0.0.1:52341
From: sip:102@2.0.0.1
To: <sip:201@192.168.254.2;user=phone>;tag=753D44-23F4
Date: Tue, 18 Apr 2000 19:50:53 UTC
Call-ID: 471E22B8-4B45003B-0-754360@192.168.254.1
Server: Cisco VoIP Gateway/ IOS 12.x/ SIP enabled
CSeq: 100 INVITE
Content-Length: 0
```

Example 11-3 *SIP UA Client Receives the Informational Response 180 Ringing*

```
SIP/2.0 180 Ringing
Via: SIP/2.0/UDP  2.0.0.1:52341
From: sip:102@2.0.0.1
To: <sip:201@192.168.254.2;user=phone>;tag=753D44-23F4
Date: Tue, 18 Apr 2000 19:50:53 UTC
Call-ID: 471E22B8-4B45003B-0-754360@192.168.254.1
Server: Cisco VoIP Gateway/ IOS 12.x/ SIP enabled
Content-Type: application/sdp
CSeq: 100 INVITE
Content-Length: 112

v=0
o=CiscoSystemsSIPUserAgent 154 1334 IN IP4 2.0.0.2
s=SIP Call
c=IN IP4 2.0.0.2
m=audio 20736 RTP/AVP 0
```

Example 11-4 *SIP UA Client Receives the Successful Response 200 OK to the INVITE Request*

```
SIP/2.0 200 OK
Via: SIP/2.0/UDP  2.0.0.1:52341
From: sip:102@2.0.0.1
To: <sip:201@192.168.254.2;user=phone>;tag=753D44-23F4
Date: Tue, 18 Apr 2000 19:50:53 UTC
Call-ID: 471E22B8-4B45003B-0-754360@192.168.254.1
```

Example 11-4 *SIP UA Client Receives the Successful Response 200 OK to the INVITE Request (Continued)*

```
Server: Cisco VoIP Gateway/ IOS 12.x/ SIP enabled
Content-Type: application/sdp
CSeq: 100 INVITE
Content-Length: 113

v=0
o=CiscoSystemsSIPUserAgent 6942 6672 IN IP4 2.0.0.2
s=SIP Call
c=IN IP4 2.0.0.2
m=audio 20736 RTP/AVP 0
```

Example 11-5 *SIP UA Client Sends the ACK Message to Acknowledge the Call Completion*

```
ACK sip:201@192.168.254.2;user=phone SIP/2.0
Via: SIP/2.0/UDP  2.0.0.1:52341
From: sip:102@2.0.0.1
To: <sip:201@192.168.254.2;user=phone>;tag=753D44-23F4
Date: Tue, 18 Apr 2000 11:50:53 PST
Call-ID: 471E22B8-4B45003B-0-754360@192.168.254.1
Content-Type: application/sdp
Content-Length: 112
CSeq: 100 ACK

v=0
o=CiscoSystemsSIPUserAgent 5509 356 IN IP4 2.0.0.1
s=SIP Call
c=IN IP4 2.0.0.1
m=audio 20902 RTP/AVP 0
```

Example 11-6 *SIP UA Client Sends the BYE Message to Terminate the Conversation*

```
BYE sip:201@192.168.254.2;user=phone SIP/2.0
Via: SIP/2.0/UDP  2.0.0.1:52341
From: sip:102@2.0.0.1
To: <sip:201@192.168.254.2;user=phone>;tag=753D44-23F4
Date: Tue, 18 Apr 2000 11:50:53 PST
Call-ID: 471E22B8-4B45003B-0-754360@192.168.254.1
User-Agent: Cisco VoIP Gateway/ IOS 12.x/ SIP enabled
CSeq: 101 BYE
Content-Length: 0
```

Example 11-7 *SIP UA Client Receives a Successful Response 200 OK to the BYE Request*

```
SIP/2.0 200 OK
Via: SIP/2.0/UDP  2.0.0.1:52341
From: sip:102@2.0.0.1
To: <sip:201@192.168.254.2;user=phone>;tag=753D44-23F4
Date: Tue, 18 Apr 2000 19:51:13 UTC
Call-ID: 471E22B8-4B45003B-0-754360@192.168.254.1
Server: Cisco VoIP Gateway/ IOS 12.x/ SIP enabled
Content-Length: 0
CSeq: 101 BYE
```

Scaling VoIP/PSTN Gateways: The Soft Switch

If you refer back to Figure 11-1, you will notice that a logical soft switch embodies the media gateway controller, signaling gateway, and media gateway functions. These three functions have traditionally been combined in a single monolithic platform, offered by a few manufacturers to the public telephony providers. Technological advancement in these platforms, as embodied by new service offerings, has not kept pace with the computer and data communications industries. Competition in this industry has not flourished because public telephone providers have enormous investments in the monolithic platforms, and they cannot afford to replace entire systems. As such, the telephone providers are at the mercy of their chosen monolithic switch vendor to provide software and hardware upgrades that facilitate new services.

One of the goals of decomposing the signaling gateway, media gateway, and media gateway controller functions into separate logical entities is to create competitive opportunities for smaller companies and to foster technical innovation. The key to realizing this vision is to ensure that all communications between the logical entities is standardized. Standard protocols ensure that public telephony providers can independently choose components that meet their specific needs, with the comfort of knowing that all parts function together in a harmonious fashion. This concept has led to the enormous success and technical evolution of the public Internet, and will be responsible for technical advancement in the public telephony networks in the coming years.

A key protocol that facilitates the soft switch model is the MGCP. As of this writing, the version of the protocol that is endorsed by the International Softswitch Consortium is MGCPv1.0. This version of the protocol is documented in RFC 2705, and is the only version that has progressed beyond a draft state as of this writing. By the time you read these words, there will most likely be an RFC with the keyword Megaco in the title. The text of this document should be identical to ITU-T Recommendation H.248.

History of Megaco and H.248

Figure 11-38 illustrates the genesis of the Megaco/H.248 protocol. It began as the Simple Gateway Control Protocol version 1.0 (SGCP1.0), developed at Telcordia Technologies (formerly Bellcore). SGCP version 1.0 and version 1.1 became IETF drafts. The development of SGCP was then fused with the parallel development of IP Device Control (IPDC) by Level3 Communications (which was based on the RADIUS and DIAMETER protocols). The combined effort was known as MGCPv0.1, and several vendors (including Cisco) have developed products based on this protocol. The IETF draft that specifies MGCPv0.1 is expired and no longer available from the IETF web site. However, you can still find the most recent version of the MGCPv0.1 draft at Henning Schulzrinne's SIP web site at the following URL:

www.cs.columbia.edu/~hgs/sip/drafts/draft-huitema-megaco-mgcp-v0r1-05.txt

When the protocol incorporated additional changes, it became known as MGCPv1.0, and was officially published as RFC 2705. As of this writing, numerous vendors have products nearly ready for market that use MGCP version 1.0 (including Cisco). By the time you read this, the products will be widely available.

As the evolution of MGCP continued, it was renamed Megaco Protocol. You may hear people refer to this latest development as MEGACOP. The Megaco Protocol represents the mature stage of the protocol, with consistent standardization between the IETF and the ITU. The ITU version is known as H.248, but the RFC number with which the protocol will be standardized in the IETF is not available as this book goes to press.

Figure 11-38 *Relationship Between SGCP, IPDC, MCGP, Megaco, and H.248.*

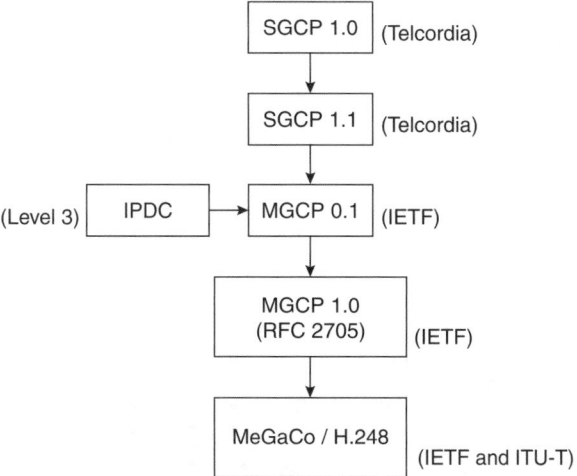

MGCP, Megaco, and H.248 are well suited for large service provider environments, where it becomes unwieldy to independently manage each VoIP gateway as a separate entity. The Cisco Call Manager product family (commonly known as the Architecture for Voice, Video, and Integrated Data, or AVVID) can also use MGCP to maintain centralized control of the gateways via a GUI.

The primary focus of this book is integrating packet voice technologies with traditional enterprise telephone networks. Scalability issues for public telephony service providers are beyond the scope of this book, as is the Cisco Call Manager family of applications. As such, the details of MGCP and Megaco/H.248 are not provided here.

Areas of Standards Research

The ITU-T and the IETF are the leading organizations that are developing protocols for Internet telephony and interoperation with the PSTN. Other vendor coalitions and regional standards bodies are helping to shape the standards and ensure interoperable implementations.

ITU-T

In addition to its work with the H.323 specifications, the ITU-T is actively exploring issues related to VoIP gateways, under Question 21 of Study Group 15: "Transport Network Equipment for Interconnecting GSTN and IP Networks." (The general switched telephone network (GSTN) is synonymous with PSTN.) The ITU-T refers to VoIP gateways as TIGINs, which is an abbreviation of the title of Question 21. The study group is specifically chartered to answer the following questions:

- What overall functionality should TIGIN possess?
- What interfaces within GSTN and IP interface points should TIGIN possess?
- What protocols and Internet interworking functions are to be supported by TIGIN?
- What control and operational interfaces need to be specified?
- What should be recommended for TIGIN in the areas of level offset, echo return loss, and background noise?
- What should be recommended in TIGIN functionality to ensure minimal end-to-end delay?
- What are the effects of placing TIGINs in tandem and what should be recommended to minimize the impact of these effects?
- What degradation is there when low bit-rate coders and other nonlinearities are present in connections incorporating TIGIN, and what should be recommended to minimize the impact of these degradations?
- What tests should be included to guarantee acceptable behavior with voiceband data signals, signaling tones, call-processing tones, speech, and so forth?
- What hardware and software tools are needed to support testing of TIGIN?
- What is the impact of evolving terminal equipment such as modems, fax, wireless, and multimedia terminals on TIGIN?

The recommendations of Study Group 15 will be included in ITU-T Recommendation G.799.1, which is not published as of this writing but may be published before you read this. ITU-T work related to Media Gateway Control, which is coordinated with the IETF Megaco efforts, is published under ITU-T H.248.

The ITU is also beginning the Y-series of recommendations for Internet Protocol (IP) related issues. Of most relevance to voice/data integration will be the Y.1100 series recommendations that pertain to Services and Applications (including Multimedia), and the Y.1500 series recommendations that pertain to Quality of Service and Network Performance.

You can find more up-to-date information about these and other ITU-T standards efforts at:

www.itu.int/ITU-T/

IETF

Table 11-22 lists URLs for various working groups of the IETF that have developed or are currently developing protocols related to Internet telephony. Working groups dedicated to QoS issues are not included here, though the work of the QoS groups is foundational for the Internet telephony applications.

Table 11-22 *IETF Working Groups Related to Internet Telephony and Integration with the PSTN*

Name	Working Group Description	URL for Additional Information
AVT	Audio/Video Transport (RTP)	www.ietf.org/html.charters/avt-charter.html
ENUM	Telephone Number Mapping (E.164 to IP)	www.ietf.org/html.charters/enum-charter.html
FAX	Internet Fax	www.ietf.org/html.charters/fax-charter.html
IMPP	Instant Messaging and Presence Protocol	www.ietf.org/html.charters/impp-charter.html
IPTEL	IP Telephony (TRIP, also known as Telephony BGP)	www.ietf.org/html.charters/iptel-charter.html
PINT	PSTN and Internet Interworking	www.ietf.org/html.charters/pint-charter.html
MEGACO	Media Gateway Control	www.ietf.org/html.charters/megaco-charter.html
MMUSIC	Multiparty Multimedia Session Control	www.ietf.org/html.charters/mmusic-charter.html
SPIRITS	Service in the PSTN/IN Requesting Internet Service	www.ietf.org/html.charters/spirits-charter.html
SIGTRAN	Signal Translation (Q.931 and SS7 over IP)	www.ietf.org/html.charters/sigtran-charter.html
SIP	Session Initiation Protocol	www.ietf.org/html.charters/sip-charter.html

Other Organizations

In addition to the IETF and the ITU, there are numerous vendor coalitions and regional organizations making efforts to standardize Internet telephony and its interaction with the PSTN. The largest regional effort is the European Telecommunication Standards Institute (ETSI) project TIPHON, also known as Telecommunications and Internet Protocol Harmonization over Networks. You can read more about the TIPHON project at the following URL:

webapp.etsi.org/tbhomepage/TBDetails.asp?TB_ID=291&TB_NAME=TIPHON

Over 150 product vendors and other organizations are part of the International Multimedia Teleconferencing Consortium (IMTC), which sponsors the Conferencing over IP (CoIP) activity group. You can read more about this group at the following URL:

www.imtc.org/act_coip.htm

The Softswitch Consortium, which comprises 140 member companies as of this writing, is dedicated to international industry consensus and interoperability of soft switch devices and protocols. The group does not develop standards, but advocates standards from the IETF and the ITU-T. As of this writing, the Softswitch Consortium advocates H.323, SIP, MGCP1.0 (RFC 2705), RTP, RTSP, and SDP. You can find more updated information about the Softswitch Consortium at:

www.softswitch.org/

The SIP Forum was created just as this book went to press. Headquartered in Sweden, the group is focused on international development and industry consolidation around SIP and related protocols. You can find more information about the SIP Forum at:

www.sipforum.org/

PART III

Voice/Data Integration: Methodology, Planning, and Design

This part of the book focuses on the planning and design considerations that come before the implementation phase of an integration project.

Chapter 12 discusses the early phases of a voice/data integration project, which include information discovery, analysis, and planning. This chapter emphasizes how to select a VoX technology (for example, VoFR, VoATM, or VoIP), and how to plan trunk and bandwidth requirements for your network.

Chapter 13 considers delay budgets and loss plans across traditional and packet voice networks. The concepts presented in this chapter enable you to actively plan and design your network for specific delay and signal loss requirements.

Chapter 14 is focused on creating an integrated dialing plan that spans traditional and packet voice networks. The chapter explores several approaches, and considers various criteria upon which you can base your numbering plan and call routing strategy.

CHAPTER 12

Initial Network Planning and Design

If you live (or at least work) in the real world, then the success of your voice/data integration project(s) will be judged by more than whether or not the technical solution is eventually achieved. The path to that solution, in terms of time and money, is critical. If you have a cavalier approach to the initial planning phases, there is an increased likelihood that you will be surprised later in the project. And I can tell you from experience that the surprise is not usually good!

Most organizations want to save time and money. For non-technical project managers, this may translate to a reduction in discovery, analysis, and planning phases: "Let's not waste any time—we needed this done last week and we are paying by the hour!"

As a technical project manager, it is your job to resist the intuitive—albeit wrong—reaction of cutting corners on the initial phases. The extra time you spend at the beginning of a project is well rewarded by an easier implementation. The implementation phase is the wrong time to discover fundamental flaws with the design, incompatible interfaces, unsupported features, and so on. It can be very expensive and awkward to correct such problems when a project is far along the implementation path. According to an old adage, "A stitch in time saves nine." This may be updated for our purposes to, "A dollar spent on planning and design, in implementation, will save nine."

Before you place an order for new hardware, there are a number of project steps that you must complete:

- Gathering requirements and expectations for voice services
- Gathering telephony interface and signaling information
- Selecting a VoX technology
- Planning trunk and bandwidth requirements
- Selecting hardware platforms
- Reviewing proposed solutions in terms of requirements

Gathering Requirements and Expectations for Voice Services

It is important that you work with all concerned parties at the beginning of the project to determine the requirements for the project and the measures of success. Specifically, you must address the issues of calling patterns, voice-mail services, voice applications such as call centers and ACD groups, and the voice quality expectations of all concerned parties.

To understand why calling patterns are a concern, consider the following scenario:

> You call the main telephone number of Acme Corporation, and the receptionist transfers you to a person in sales. When you speak to the person in sales, you realize that you really need to speak to someone in marketing. Nobody answers the telephone when you are transferred to marketing, so you are automatically forwarded to voice mail.

This is a fairly normal business communication process, and companies expect their voice systems to accommodate these types of transactions. It is very likely that an integrated voice/data network would perform poorly when placed in this environment. Some may claim that the technology is not yet mature, but it is more commonly a problem with the design.

The inherent problem in this case is that the company may have departments in different locations. This means that every time a call is transferred between departments, it crosses a PBX/router interface and incurs another tandem encoding. Voice quality rapidly degrades as the signal undergoes coding/decoding cycles—current low bit-rate codecs tolerate a maximum of two encoding cycles in real networks. The previous call scenario may require four encodings. Now imagine that the person placing the call is using a mobile telephone; another low bit-rate codec is in the audio path. The best solution in this case is to use a G.726 or G.711 codec, which greatly increases the bandwidth consumption on the network, but preserves voice quality during tandem encodings.

Many network designers would not even consider this issue before implementing the network. The integrated network would be installed, and preliminary tests would indicate that voice quality is good. But they would forget to test call transfers between sites. After about a month, end users complain bitterly.

The point of the preceding story is to "think outside the box" when designing these networks. Do not assume you understand all of the requirements ahead of time. Talk in detail with the end users of the network to understand how they will use it. The project will be more successful if you understand the requirements, voice your concerns in a timely fashion, and address them properly. Among other issues, be sure to address voice mail from the earliest phases of the project. This is almost always a show-stopper issue if there are problems, so get it right the first time. If a centralized voice-mail system is used, you generally cannot use low bit-rate codecs and preserve good voice quality. If you are selling the project based on 8-kbps calls, you better rework your strategy.

In general, be wary of situations that require tandem encoding. Common examples include centralized call accounting, centralized voice-mail systems, and proprietary PBX features supported via transparent common channel signaling (CCS). Possible solutions include using higher bit-rate codecs, and possibly using Q.SIG instead of transparent CCS.

Here is one last thought with respect to voice/data network designs that can cause problems. Some corporations have a hierarchical data network design, based on the classic concept of a corporate headquarters, regional hubs, and satellite offices. All is well in the data-only world, with regional e-mail hubs and data centers. But this design may introduce problems for company-wide, real-time applications. Consider what happens if users in a satellite office call users in a distant satellite office. The audio path must traverse four WAN circuits:

- Originating satellite office to originating regional hub
- Originating regional hub to corporate headquarters
- Corporate headquarters to destination regional hub
- Destination regional hub to destination satellite office

The combined effect of transmission delays and variable queuing/serialization delays can severely impact voice quality. Even though the data network is well designed, it is not designed well for the addition of voice traffic. There are at least three solutions to this problem:

- Collapse the hierarchy to a hub-and-spoke topology from the corporate headquarters.
- Add extra circuits from satellite offices to corporate headquarters.
- Install circuits between offices with identified high-traffic patterns.

Each of these solutions has technical, logistical, and economic implications that are nontrivial. There are no easy fixes for these types of problems, but you are in a better position to manage them if you identify them early in the process.

You have read some of the ways your project can go awry. Hopefully, you will not repeat the mistakes presented here. Think through the consequences of your design decisions, and talk with others about issues of concern.

Gathering Telephony Trunk and Signaling Information

Early on in the project, you must evaluate your role. If you are working with a strong telecom department that has specific ideas about how to do things, then you might not want to dictate designs and requirements to them. If you alienate these folks, then your job will be more difficult. On the other hand, some organizations very badly need someone to take charge and figure out what needs to be done. These extremes are important to identify because it affects how you gather the required telephony information.

If you have a strong telecom department, you can rely on them to provide the information you need, such as what type of PBX ports will be connected to the router, and what signaling types to use. Make sure to provide feedback to them on key issues, such as how to divide number blocks for the address plan.

Be prepared to make decisions if you have a lot of unanswered questions, or you get responses such as, "We can do either," or "What do you want to do?" This is a more common scenario when you are working with telecom technicians who are not responsible for the whole network. They usually program the basic switch options using information provided to them, and leave many options in default settings. In these cases, you can choose which of the available PBX ports to use, how to provision the signaling, who provides clocking, and so on.

Refer to Chapter 2, "Enterprise Telephony Signaling," for a detailed discussion of the traditional telephony signaling types. From a project-planning perspective, you can gather the required information in phases:

- Type of equipment and physical interface connecting to the router
- Software configuration options for interface connecting to the router

It is usually easy to identify at an early stage whether a router will connect to POTS telephones, a key system (KSU), a private branch exchange (PBX), or a voice trunk provided by a carrier. It may be more onerous to determine what interfaces are available on the phone switches at each site, such as analog station cards or trunk cards. If your telecom contacts are competent, then you can work with them to determine the information you need. At least try to determine whether analog or digital interfaces will be used for routers connecting to phone switches or carrier-provided voice circuits. Make sure the telecom contacts know that proprietary digital phone sets cannot be connected to the voice ports on the router. A channel bank can interface to such phones, and connect to serial interfaces on the router for circuit emulation. Table 12-1 summarizes the types of interfaces that you may connect to Cisco multiservice routers.

Table 12-1   *Traditional Telephony Interfaces, and Corresponding Cisco Router Voice Interfaces*

If the PBX or other interface is a . . .	Then connect to this Cisco voice interface:
POTS telephone (residential phone)	FXS
Fax	FXS
Carrier provided: analog loop start/ground start (1 MB,and so on)	FXO
Carrier provided: digital T1/E1—CAS (DID, both-way, and so on)	Digital T1/E1
Carrier provided: digital T1/E1—PRI (to support E911, and so on)	Digital T1/E1—PRI

Table 12-1 *Traditional Telephony Interfaces, and Corresponding Cisco Router Voice Interfaces (Continued)*

If the PBX or other interface is a . . .	Then connect to this Cisco voice interface:
PBX/Key: analog station card (normally for fax or POTS phone)	FXO
PBX/Key: analog trunk card (normally for loop start/ground start to CO)	FXS
PBX/Key: analog E&M tie line (normally to remote PBX via CO)	E&M
PBX/Key: digital T1/E1—CAS or CCS	Digital T1/E1
PBX/Key: digital T1/E1—PRI	Digital T1/E1—PRI
Vendor-specific business set (proprietary digital phone)	none
Proprietary digital phone via telco channel bank (or other CSU)	Non-voice T1/E1 (use CES or PBX)

Often, you will have to ask questions of people who have no idea what you are talking about. When you try to find a more technical contact, you might get responses such as, "Our phone switch has been running fine for the last five years. I think the company that installed it went out of business." In these situations, your best bet is to partner with a PBX service company that has experience with the specific model of PBX or key system. In the absence of such partners, you might have to read many manuals. Worse yet, you might have to solve the enigma black box. If you are working with an ancient and questionable phone switch, it may be less expensive to purchase a new one than to spend a lot of time or money to connect it to a router. You can burn hour after hour troubleshooting, only to determine that the old phone switch is not behaving properly. "It seemed so close! It was working yesterday . . . " On the other hand, make sure you have configured everything properly (and reset interfaces) before you blame an old phone switch.

TIP   If you are considering a new phone switch, it might not be a bad time to look at the Cisco Call Manager. The solution supports traditional calling features and new applications such as voice-mail/e-mail integration, using native IP telephones and simple GUI web interfaces for configuration.

Assuming you can work with the telecom contacts, and the existing phone switches seem functional, then you can proceed with the data collection. This is easier to manage if you complete a form for each site (or router). Using a form ensures that you do not forget to ask for key pieces of information, and provides written documentation of the project progress.

If problems arise during the subsequent implementation, this form may help identify what went wrong.

You are likely to have problems if you are not involved in the form-completion process. It is interesting to note that no matter how detailed, simple, or precise you make the telecom information form, you will still receive baffling results from some sources. Even though it seems like a good place to save time, your time is well spent if you work with each contact to complete the form. Your project will stay on track if you schedule time to work with each contact for this purpose. If you make each telecom contact responsible for completing the form, you will have several weeks of silence from some (or many) sources, followed by a form with blank spots and vague answers to multiple-choice questions. Do not ask how— it just happens.

Making Early Estimates

You may be pressured for cost estimates and budgetary approvals before you have enough information to develop an accurate bill of materials. If this is the case, you can determine budgetary pricing (but not an accurate bill of materials) before you know the exact PBX interfaces with which the routers must connect. You still need to know the basic router platforms, which VoX technology will be used, the number of telephony interfaces required, and whether the interfaces are analog or digital. Because gathering the exact PBX interface information is often time-consuming, you can hasten the budget-approval process by pricing the analog hardware with arbitrary analog voice interface (for example, FXS). The equipment order should not be placed until the actual bill of materials is ready—after the PBX interface information has been gathered. You must take pains to ensure that nobody places an equipment order based on the budgetary bill of materials. I have seen it happen for 50 routers.

Selecting a VoX Technology

There are at least two ways to decide whether VoFR, VoATM, or VoIP is appropriate for your network: (1) compare the relative merits and shortcomings of each technology and weigh these factors based on their importance in your network, or (2) just pick VoIP.

If you choose the more thought-intensive approach, you should consider the following criteria for the decision:

- Reliability
- Scalability
- Quality of Service
- Cost and Complexity
- Feature Support
- Existing WAN Environment

VoFR, VoATM, and VoIP are compared against each of these criteria in the following subsections.

Reliability

Because both VoFR and VoATM are link-layer technologies, they are sensitive to circuit failures. Redundant circuits increase the chance of successful call connections, but any active VoFR or VoATM calls are terminated when a circuit fails. VoIP performs better in this respect because it operates at the network layer. IP packets may be rapidly rerouted around a failed circuit, without causing active VoIP calls to be dropped.

While VoIP is resilient to circuit failures, it is sensitive to routing problems and configuration errors. Both the signaling and audio portions of VoIP rely on the existing routing protocols in the IP network. If a new device that falsely advertises routes is added to the network, then valid destinations may become unreachable. Any routing problems in the network may impact VoIP connections, even if the problems are not caused by VoIP routers. VoFR and VoATM are less likely to be affected by changes in unrelated parts of the network.

If your IP network is stable, then VoIP offers the best overall reliability.

Scalability

The main scalability issue for enterprises with VoX technologies is the management of dial peers and call routing. There are two aspects to managing dial peers that must be considered as networks grow:

- End-to-End Versus Hop-by-Hop Peering
- Number of Dial Peers per Router

End-to-End Versus Hop-by-Hop Peering

Even with default dial peers, VoFR and VoATM require more configuration and maintenance than VoIP. VoFR and VoATM dial peers must be configured at every router along a call path, whereas VoIP only requires the end routers associated with the call to have dial peers. VoIP is simpler in this respect because it builds on the services offered by IP routing protocols that are already a part of the network.

The preceding discussion assumes that PVCs are used for ATM, which is not the most scalable option. The ATM PNNI protocol can operate with E.164-based ATM addresses when creating SVCs, which allows dynamic call routing. However, this approach does not appear to be making significant advances in the market. Most companies that use ATM in the WAN have PVCs; few companies use SVCs between sites over carrier-provided Permanent Virtual Paths (PVPs). Companies can implement an E.164-based SVC solution between their own sites, but generally these networks are isolated from other companies and the PSTN as a whole. Because the technology is not ubiquitous, scalability is limited by market adoption.

Number of Dial Peers per Router

For large networks, it is not feasible to statically configure dial peers in each router. It is difficult to manage the consistency of dial-peer configurations across multiple boxes, the router configuration memory is limited, and pattern searches become inefficient as the number of dial peers increase. Hub-and-spoke networks can extensively use default call routing, but the central site routers may still be burdened. Hierarchical networks can distribute the dial peers, but still require maintenance of the dial peers in many different routers.

For VoFR and VoATM, the hierarchical approach (of which the hub-and-spoke design is a subset) enables call-routing summarization, and is the best option to scale. VoIP can take advantage of H.323 gatekeepers or SIP proxy servers, which enable dial peers to be hierarchical without forcing the VoIP signaling and audio paths across the same hierarchy. The signaling and audio paths of the call are still optimized according to IP routing, so there is no performance degradation for centralizing the dial-peer databases (other than the delay for the lookup request). The ENUM Working Group of the Internet Engineering Task Force (Transport Area) is currently defining a distributed database standard that enables mapping between E.164 telephone numbers (hence the name ENUM) and URLs, followed by a DNS resolution to an IP address. The ENUM telephone number mapping, and the Telephony Routing over IP (TRIP) protocol, will enable VoIP–call-routing scale to the entire Internet.

Quality of Service

Frame Relay offers rudimentary mechanisms to provide quality-of-service assurances. The Committed Information Rate (CIR) provides a working bandwidth guarantee, assuming the carrier does not oversubscribe its backbone too much. However, there is no guarantee for delay or delay variation. During periods of network congestion, latency across a Frame Relay PVC may increase by a factor of 20 or more (based on personal observation of the author). A consequence of this behavior is that enterprises are not empowered to provide end-to-end QoS for VoFR. You can ensure that your equipment is configured properly to enable the best performance for VoFR, but if you have an uncooperative carrier, then voice quality may suffer. Be wary of situations where VoFR traffic must cross multiple carriers' Frame Relay networks, because there is less accountability for poor performance. If you pursue a VoFR solution, you must closely monitor your frame relay provider to ensure that you are receiving the contracted CIR with a reasonable latency.

ATM offers a clear and compelling quality-of-service solution. QoS is a pillar of ATM network design, offering guarantees for bandwidth, delay, and delay variation. ATM is an excellent technology to provide real-time quality of service along with standard traffic requirements. Both VoATM and VoIP can take advantage of the QoS features of ATM.

Current IP QoS solutions meet the needs of VoIP in the enterprise. It is important to realize, however, that end-to-end QoS in an IP network relies heavily on link-layer QoS. It does not matter how high the IP precedence field is set if the packet is stuck in a congested Frame Relay network. For this reason, you must be careful when selecting a link layer for the WAN. The best options are currently ATM or leased lines. In the LAN, excess bandwidth has traditionally been the best form of QoS, but IEEE 802.1p and the RSVP Subnet Bandwidth Manager (SBM) standards now provide other options.

QoS options for the Internet are rapidly evolving. Internet telephony service providers (ITSPs) now offer VoIP-enabled backbones for their customers, but the contracts between service providers are still developing. Clearinghouse and settlement services allow ITSPs to significantly extend the reach of their QoS network, which enables subscribers to place native VoIP calls to more destinations.

Cost and Complexity

VoFR, VoATM, and VoIP all have similar requirements for interfacing with traditional telephony equipment. The differences in cost and complexity are mainly attributed to assuring QoS.

Frame Relay is an economical WAN technology for voice, provided that QoS requirements can be met. Cisco hardware options are available for small installations, and products can scale to large enterprise deployments. For companies that want to switch to VoIP, Cisco products offer a software-only upgrade path from VoFR solutions to VoIP solutions. The conceptual issues for Frame Relay QoS are somewhat challenging, but the actual router configurations are less difficult.

ATM for voice applications is more expensive than Frame Relay, but you get what you pay for. The built-in QoS guarantees across the WAN reduce the likelihood of stumbling blocks during the implementation phase. If the routers are configured correctly and the network is designed properly (that is, there are minimal tandem codecs), then VoATM quality should be good.

VoIP solutions require more router configuration commands than VoFR or VoATM solutions. In addition to configuring link-layer QoS (that is, FRF.12 fragmentation or ATM CoS parameters), VoIP requires network and transport layer QoS options such as RSVP, special queuing techniques, IP precedence, WRED, and so on. While these features require additional experience from a design and implementation perspective, they offer flexibility beyond what VoFR or VoATM can provide. A unified VoIP network can span heterogeneous link-layer technologies.

Feature Support

It is important to consider not only the traditional PBX features, but also new features and applications that are emerging as communication technologies advance.

Traditional Telephony Features

There are few inherent differences between VoFR, VoATM, and VoIP with respect to telephony feature support. Integrated voice and data networks in general support fewer telephony features than proprietary single-vendor telecom environments. Integrated voice/data networks often sacrifice some features across the WAN in favor of reducing toll costs. If your company already uses PBX equipment from a variety of vendors, many features are not available regardless of voice/data integration.

Emerging MultiService Applications

While VoFR and VoATM will remain as technologies for integrating legacy voice networks, VoIP is developing as a native end-to-end solution. Traditional telephony features are supported in hardware and software versions of IP telephones, and multiservice applications are being integrated with these products. Companies that use VoIP to integrate their legacy voice networks with their data networks will be positioned to take advantage of new multimedia applications and communications tools. There is a clear, long-term, strategic advantage to using VoIP for voice/data integration.

Existing WAN Environment

ATM, ISDN, and clear channel TDM facilities provide good performance for VoX technologies. Because these services are circuit-switched technologies, they ensure consistent delay characteristics, which is important for real-time traffic. Frame Relay can work well for real-time traffic, but it is a risky proposition. You have no assurances that performance will remain good for VoFR or VoIP across Frame Relay.

Consideration of the existing WAN environment was very important before VoIP supported FRF.12 and hardware options matured. Still, your WAN environment should heavily influence your selection of a VoX technology. The following WAN types are considered here:

- Frame Relay
- ATM
- Clear Channel TDM
- ISDN

Frame Relay

When this book was conceived, VoFR was the only reasonable option for networks with a Frame Relay WAN. Since Cisco has incorporated support for FRF.12 fragment/interleaving into VoIP platforms, this advantage has disappeared. VoIP can now provide the same level of QoS as VoFR across frame relay networks.

ATM

VoATM and VoIP are available for networks with an ATM WAN. There is no difference in quality of service between VoATM and VoIP over ATM, but there is an important bandwidth and efficiency consideration. If IP RTP header compression is not available for ATM interfaces, then VoATM is more bandwidth-efficient than VoIP across an ATM network. This is because 40 bytes of IP/UDP/RTP header information are included with the data in each VoIP packet, which means that at least two ATM cells are required to transmit each VoIP packet. VoATM encapsulates the voice coder output directly in a single ATM cell.

Another bandwidth issue arises because ATM cells carry a fixed 48-byte payload (minus 1- or 2- byte AAL headers). If the transported data does not fill the cell, then the additional payload space is padded. Considering that a typical VoIP packet (with two G.729 samples) is 60 bytes long without header compression, then it must be segmented into two ATM cells. The second cell carries about 12 to 14 bytes of data, with more than 40 padded bytes! This yields an ATM payload efficiency of 62.5 percent for a VoIP packet. VoIP does support a configurable number of codec samples per packet, and ATM payload efficiency climbs to 94 percent when VoIP is properly tuned. For example, five samples of G.729 at 10 bytes each, along with 40 bytes of IP/RTP/UDP header, yield 90 bytes of data in two ATM cells. Using the G.723.1 codec with VoIP, which would ostensibly save bandwidth, results in an ATM payload efficiency of only 73 percent. Because G.723.1 uses a 30-ms frame, placing multiple frames into a packet to improve the ATM payload efficiency is not feasible because of the additional packetizing delay incurred.

You must address the ATM payload efficiency issue for both VoIP and VoATM, or you might waste much of your WAN bandwidth, support fewer simultaneous calls, and telephony users will experience reduced Grade of Service (GoS).

Leased-Line TDM

For TDM circuits (for example, T1/E1/J1/Y1), any VoX option may be used. Private ATM across leased lines is usually not a good option, because ATM cell headers consume much of the bandwidth. You should only consider VoATM on these circuits if you also have applications such as video using ATM-CES. VoFR was a good option when VoIP hardware options were limited, but now there is no compelling reason to use it. VoIP is a good option because it has low overhead (when using RTP header compression), requires fewer dial peers, and is flexible to integrate with other WAN technologies. On low-bandwidth TDM circuits, VoIP requires Frame Relay or multilink PPP encapsulation to provide fragment/interleaving.

If other parts of your network use a given VoX technology, you should match that technology on leased-line TDM circuits. This will allow you to keep an integrated dial plan with compatible dial peers. When call passing between VoX technologies is available, this will not be necessary. By the time you read these passages, it may already be available.

ISDN

Many companies use ISDN as a backup solution to their primary frame relay, ATM, or clear channel circuits. In some countries—Japan for example—permanent ISDN connections are available. The only VoX technology that is reasonable for these environments is VoIP, which can run with PPP encapsulation. VoIP is a very attractive option when redundancy is required, because ISDN can economically provide fault tolerance. VoFR and VoATM are not compatible with ISDN.

Table 12-2 summarizes the attributes of VoFR, VoATM, and VoIP with respect to the criteria discussed in the preceding sections.

Table 12-2 *General VoX Attributes*

	Vox Technology		
Attributes	**VoFR**	**VoATM**	**VoIP**
Reliability	OK	OK	Good
Scalability	Poor	OK	Good
Quality of Service	Poor	Good	Good
Cost	Good	OK	Good
Complexity	Good	OK	Poor
Support of Telephony Features	OK	OK	Good
Emerging Applications	Poor	OK	Good

Planning Voice Trunk and Bandwidth Requirements

The object of telecom traffic planning is to determine an optimal number of voice trunks to a destination, such that a certain call success rate is achieved during peak traffic intervals. The standard models used in the telecom industry are statistical models developed by A.K. Erlang at the beginning of the 20th century:

- Erlang B
- Extended Erlang B
- Erlang C

Model Assumptions and Applicability

Each of these models assumes that time between received call attempts is random with a Poisson distribution. These models do not apply to environments that receive spikes of call traffic, such as radio call-in contests, or ticketing vendors when concerts come to town. Each of the models differs with respect to how calls are handled when the trunks in question are busy.

The *Erlang B* model is appropriate when there is an overflow path for busy trunks. For example, a PBX may reroute calls to the PSTN if the VoX trunks are all busy. This example assumes that the remote location has Direct Inward Dial (DID) trunks to facilitate direct PSTN rerouting, or else functionality is compromised (for example, a call destined for a specific person may reach an operator when routed via the PSTN). Another example is a PBX with standard tie lines as a backup to the VoX trunks.

The *Extended Erlang B* model is appropriate when there is no overflow path, and the caller hears a busy tone when the desired VoX trunks are busy. This scenario is common when a site PBX has VoX trunks for interoffice dialing, and no alternate routes through the PSTN (that is, remote sites do not have DID and operator intervention is not acceptable). This model accounts for the fact that many users will immediately redial when a call fails, which increases the amount of incoming traffic.

The *Erlang C* model is appropriate if calls are placed in a queue when the VoX trunks are busy. This model is applicable to call centers, which strive to maintain high utilization of call center agents and trunk facilities. Call centers are outside the scope of this book.

Using the Models

The Erlang models require that you provide some of the variables to solve for an unknown variable. Table 12-3 provides definitions for the variables and measurement units that are commonly associated with these models.

Table 12-3   *Definition of Common Terms for Telecom Trunk Planning*

Term	Definition
Erlang	A measure of call volume equal to 1 hour of aggregate traffic.
	Three calls of 20-minute duration yield 1 Erlang of call traffic.
Centi-Call Seconds (CCS)	100 seconds of calling traffic. 36 CCS = 1 Erlang.
	(Not to be confused with Common Channel Signaling CCS.)
Lines	The number of provisioned voice trunks that carry traffic.
	Each analog port is 1 line; a full T-1 CAS port is 24 lines.
Busy Hour Traffic (BHT)	Amount of call traffic (in Erlangs) that must be supported during a peak-traffic reference hour. Use high estimates for conservative trunk planning.
Blocking	Percentage of calls that cannot be accommodated because of busy trunks.
	A typical blocking design goal is 1 to 3 percent.
Recall Factor	When there is no overflow path for blocked calls, this is the percentage of calls that are immediately retried (for example, the end user redials the destination).

To determine the optimal number of Lines, the Erlang B model requires the Busy Hour Traffic (BHT), measured in Erlangs, and the Blocking fraction for calls attempted during the busy hour. The blocking fraction is a measure of Grade of Service (GoS). The Extended Erlang B requires the same input and the Recall Factor, which indicates how many people redial after hearing a busy tone.

The Erlang C model operates with slightly different variables. Instead of using the BHT measure, the model uses the number of calls per hour and the average call length. Instead of measuring a blocking factor, the model considers how long the callers must wait before speaking with an agent. Table 12-4 summarizes the form and application for each model type.

Table 12-4   *Applicability and Required Information for the Erlang Trunk Planning Models*

Model	Equation Form	Response When VoX Trunks Are Busy
Erlang B	Lines = f(BHT,Blocking)	Overflow to standard trunks or PSTN
Extended Erlang B	Lines = f(BHT,Blocking,Recall)	Terminate the call (user hears busy tone)
Erlang C	Lines = f(CallsPerHour,Duration,WaitTime)	Call added to a waiting queue (ACD system)

The equations to solve these models are not pretty, so network planners use reference tables that contain presolved values for the different traffic models. A few years ago, it would have been appropriate to include such a table as an appendix to this book. Now, there are numerous online tools that perform the calculation for you. Search the Web for Erlang calculator.

Adjusting the Models for VoX

The way these models apply to real networks is different for VoX networks than for traditional telecom networks. In traditional voice networks, each remote location is reachable via dedicated tie lines. There is no sharing between the lines (tandem switching is excluded for the moment to make a point). In VoX networks, the lines for all remote sites are pooled and connected to a router. Instead of having two lines to each of five different locations, ten lines are all connected to a router, which can appropriately direct the traffic. Figure 12-1 illustrates the difference between tie-line connections in traditional versus VoX networks:

The difference between independent and pooled lines affects the total number of lines required during peak loads. Consider a company with 2 lines dedicated to 50 different offices. A third call to a given office will fail, even if there are 98 idle lines! In a VoX network, all 100 lines could be provisioned for calls to any of the offices. A traditional network may require 3 lines to each office, a total of 150 lines, to accommodate the occasional peak. In the VoX environment, 100 lines may be more than sufficient to meet the total traffic requirements. The assumption here is that the peak traffic load to every destination does not occur at the same time. The ability to reduce the number of lines per site as more sites are added *(statistical multiplexing)* is a hidden benefit of integrated voice/data networks. The companies that benefit most are those with high traffic between many sites.

Figure 12-1 *Independent Tie Lines for Traditional Networks; Pooled Tie Lines for VoX Networks*

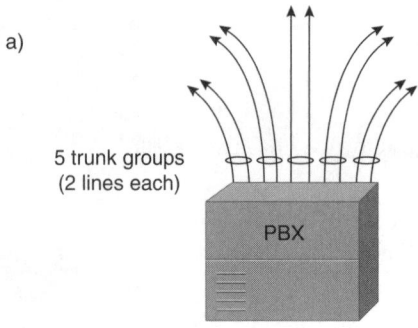

a)

5 trunk groups
(2 lines each)

PBX

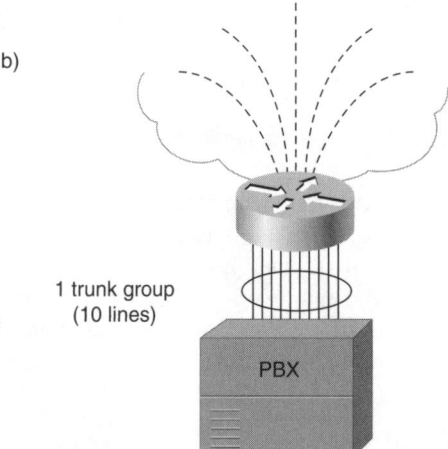

b)

1 trunk group
(10 lines)

PBX

There is one concern caused by the pooled line strategy. Consider a hub-and-spoke network, where each of five remote PBXs have three lines connecting to a router, and the central site PBX has ten lines connecting to a router (taking advantage of statistical multiplexing). The first three calls between the central site and a remote site proceed normally, but all successive calls are routed in a suboptimal fashion. Figure 12-2 illustrates what happens for every call when the remote lines are busy:

1 The central PBX receives a call for the remote site and forwards it to the router, because there are free lines.

2 The central router accepts the call from the PBX, receives the digits, and attempts to establish the call with the remote router identified by the VoX dial peer.

3 Because the remote router does not have a free voice port (that is, they all are busy), it rejects the call setup request.

4 To prevent dropping the call, the central router should have an alternate dial peer pointing back to the PBX. The same digits cannot be sent back to the PBX because a routing loop would occur between the PBX and the router, which would seize all of the lines. The dial peer that points back to the PBX should add a prefix such as 91555 to the dialed digits, such that the PBX completes the call through the PSTN.

5 The PBX completes the call from the router to the PSTN. The call now occupies two lines between the router and PBX for the duration of the call.

Figure 12-2 *The Hairpin, Trombone, or Boomerang Effect When All Lines at a Remote Site Are Busy*

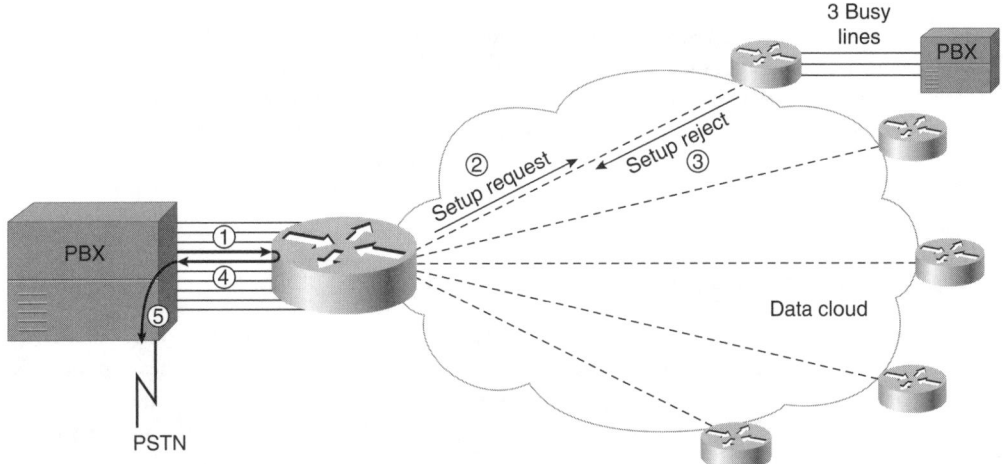

All calls that exceed the planned VoX capacity must exit the central PBX to the router, and immediately return to the PBX before routing to the PSTN. This situation is called a *hairpin*, *trombone*, or *boomerang*. It is undesirable because it uses two lines between the router and PBX for each call. There is no performance degradation from multiple codec cycles, because calls between local voice ports on a Cisco router are not compressed. But the wasted lines are an efficiency concern.

The solution to this problem is to have more communication between the router and the PBX, such that the path can be dynamically optimized (for example, cut the router out of the loop). This is a common feature between PBXs from the same vendor, but it has not historically been supported between vendors. QSIG is designed to fill this gap—to provide a standard telephony signaling protocol for vendor interoperability. QSIG must be supported in the PBX and in the router to take advantage of interoperable signaling.

Using the trunk or PLAR-OPX connection modes on Cisco routers is another way to solve this problem. The local router is able to refuse connection requests from the PBX when it knows the status of the remote VoX sites (via the PLAR-OPX or trunk signaling). This solution comes at the expense of dedicating voice ports on the router to specific remote destinations, which may not be the most efficient use of the voice ports.

Back to the trunk-planning issue. For VoX networks, the Erlang models should not be applied separately for traffic to each remote site. Rather, apply the models to the total traffic volume to all sites during the combined busy hour. Keep in mind that the busy hour for the combined traffic to all sites may not match the busy hour to any specific site. Applying the Erlang models to the pooled traffic (as opposed to independently for each site) yields a fewer number of required lines, in harmony with the statistical multiplexing advantage. This does not account for the hairpin effect, where two lines are required between the router and PBX for each call that is rerouted to the PSTN. To rigorously account for the hairpin effect, the Erlang traffic models should be modified.

In practice, you can observe the traffic that reroutes to the PSTN during the combined busy hour (for example, on a Cisco router, show dial peer for the peer that matches rerouted traffic, or review the call detail records), and perform an Erlang calculation on this traffic to determine the number of additional lines required for hairpinning. An alternative method is to make an educated guess about the number of extra lines required for traffic rerouted to the PSTN during the combined busy hour.

Converting Number of Trunks to Bandwidth

The Erlang calculations tell you how many voice ports you need on the router and PBX, but you must still determine the amount of bandwidth that each call consumes. This varies depending on the flavor of VoX and the codec. ATM efficiency is variable depending on the payload size. Refer to the section "Selecting a VoX Technology" in this chapter for a discussion of ATM payload efficiency.

The bandwidth calculations are not included here for every combination of codec type, samples per frame, VoX technology, and WAN transport. Instead, tools are provided to help you calculate these values yourself. You can calculate the overall bandwidth per the following equation:

$$(actual\_bandwidth) = (codec\_bandwidth) \times \frac{(payload\_length + encapsulation\_length)}{(payload\_length)}$$

This equation provides the amount of bandwidth required for each call, including the encapsulation overhead. The codec bandwidth values are provided in Table 12-5.

Table 12-5   *Bandwidth Requirements Per Call for Different Codecs*

Codec	Bandwidth (kbps)
G.711	64
G.723.1	6.3/5.3
G.726	16/24/32/40
G.728	16
G.729	8
G.729A	8

The configurable payload length must be an integer multiple of the codec sample size. This controls how many codec samples are placed in each cell, frame, or packet. Because the default values used in Cisco IOS may change, they are not provided here. You should adjust the default value if you need to:

- Increase ATM payload efficiency
- Decrease encapsulation overhead
- Reduce the effects of high cell/frame/packet loss rates

Table 12-6 summarizes the header lengths for various VoIP implementations. Add the number of bytes in the link-layer header to the number of bytes in whichever VoIP packet option you are using (for example, IP/UDP/RTP, CRTP with UDP checksums, CRTP without UDP checksums) to determine the total number of overhead bytes.

Table 12-6   *Header Length (Bytes) for VoIP over Different WAN Technologies*

WAN Technology	Link Layer	IP/UDP/RTP	CRTP (UDP Checksums)	CRTP (No UDP Checksums)
HDLC	6-8	40	4	2
ML-PPP	7-9	40	4	2
Frame Relay	4	40	4	2
FRF.11 Annex C	9	40	4	2
FRF.12	8	40	4	2
ATM-AAL1	6-12	40	4	2
ATM-AAL5	13-18	40	4	2

ATM header requirements actually vary with the VoIP packet size. For all data segmented into AAL5, each cell introduces a 5-byte header, with the final cell requiring an 8-byte trailer. VoIP packets that fit into a single ATM cell payload require 5 + 8 bytes of ATM headers, and VoIP packets that fit into two ATM cell payloads require 5 + 5 + 8 bytes of ATM headers. This does not include any padding that is necessary to fill the payload field. The values in Table 12-6 assume that the IP header and codec data fit within one ATM cell when CRTP is used, and within two ATM cells when CRTP is not used.

Table 12-7 summarizes the header lengths for various VoFR implementations.

Table 12-7 *Header Length for VoFR in Different Configurations*

	Overhead (Bytes)
FRF.11 (Annex C fragmentation)	9
FRF.11 (FRF.12 fragmentation)	8
Cisco proprietary (voice-encap method)	6

VoATM is currently supported on the Cisco MC3810 router using AAL5 and AAL2. In addition to the 5-byte ATM header, there is a 4-byte VoATM header before the codec data. The ATM header lengths (for VoATM and VoIP) do not consider the payload padding, which increases the effective size of the header. You cannot determine the effective header length until you choose the payload size. Be sure to add the payload pad to the header length before calculating the required bandwidth.

Selecting Hardware to Meet Requirements

The surest way to make a book obsolete before it is published is to refer to the capabilities of specific hardware models. That being said, traditional telephony interfaces are available for the following Cisco routers as of this writing:

- 1750 Modular Access Router
- MC3810 Multi-access Concentrator
- 2600 series Modular Access Routers
- 3600 series Modular Access Routers
- AS-5300, AS-5800, and Access-Path Solutions
- 7200VXR series Core Routers
- 7500 series Core Routers

High-end ATM switches are not included here because the services they offer for voice are usually of the ATM-CES variety as opposed to VoATM. The distinction is made because the ATM-CES service provides a T1/E1 type of service, with no telephony intelligence required.

Small-scale implementations can support up to 4 analog ports (FXS/FXO/E&M) or 48 to 60 digital ports (2 T1/E1) in the 2600 series Modular Access Routers. The 3600 series offers up to three times the port density of the 2600 series, and the 7200 and 7500 routers provide higher density aggregation. The Access Server router line (for example, AS-5300, and so on) provides high-density T1/E1 telephony connections for VoIP, with value-adds like SS7 adjuncts and Interactive Voice Response (IVR).

As of this writing, there are various hardware caveats for supporting transparent pass-through of common channel signaling (CCS) and interpreted QSIG. For current hardware support and feature comparisons, you should look at Cisco Connection Online (CCO): www.cisco.com/. If you have not spent a lot of time there already, you are missing a truly incredible amount of free documentation. Cisco deserves a lot of credit for maintaining and constantly updating a wide range of product and technology information.

Reviewing Proposed Solutions in Terms of Requirements

After you have spent time developing the high-level integrated network design (that is, selecting the VoX technology, interfaces between routers and phone switches, bandwidth and trunk requirements, and hardware platforms), you must take a step back and verify whether you have met the design goals that were initially identified. Presumably, you have been mindful of the design goals at all phases of the early design, but it is a worthwhile task to review the requirements again before you commit to an equipment purchase.

CHAPTER 13

Delay Budgets and Loss Plans

The previous chapter explored the issues that must be addressed before phone switch or router equipment is ordered. Following the order of this equipment, there is usually a lead time before the equipment arrives. If the project is scheduled well, this coincides with the lead time for any required circuit upgrades. If you are not already aware, international circuit upgrades may take many months, which requires that these orders are placed as soon as possible.

The equipment and circuit order lead times are an excellent time to finish the design and planning phases of the integration project. In addition to the software-configurable voice interface options (for example, loop start versus ground start, E&M wink versus immediate, and so on) that may not have been finalized before the equipment order, the following design elements must be addressed:

- Delay budgets
- Loss plans
- Dial plans

This chapter examines the delay budget and loss plan, while the next chapter is dedicated to dial plan issues. The delay budget and the loss plan are considered together in this chapter because these are the two major components that affect echo perception. A primary motivation for minimizing delay and implementing a loss plan is to make echoes less annoying.

Delay Budgets

Calculating the delay budget is the process of accounting for each delay component in the network, and ensuring that the total delay is within a defined limit. The limit that you decide on may vary depending on the circumstances in your network, such as satellite hops, the presence of echo problems, tandem encoding requirements, the cost of bandwidth, and so on. As various factors conspire to drive the end-to-end delay higher, you should expend more effort to reduce the delay. For example, an end-to-end delay of 70 ms may not require much attention, but it is worth considerable effort to reduce a 400-ms delay.

Maximum One-Way Delays

The ITU-T has conducted numerous studies to determine how much delay is acceptable in various types of telephone conversations. ITU-T Recommendation G.114 provides general guidelines for delay budgeting, including a summary of studies that contributed to these guidelines. Table 13-1 summarizes the maximum delay recommendations from G.114.

Table 13-1 *One-Way Delay Considerations from ITU-T Recommendation G.114*

One-Way Delays	Acceptable Conditions
0 to 150 ms	Acceptable for most user applications.
150 to 400 ms	Acceptable provided the impact to applications is considered.
400 ms +	Unacceptable for general planning; may be required in certain situations.

The ITU-T recommends that delay should be minimized even within the 0- to 150-ms interval to improve performance for real-time transactions. Transmission paths that include a satellite hop usually conform to the 150- to 400-ms interval. The ITU-T recognizes that certain calls may not conform to the 400-ms maximum delay, such as calls with multiple satellite hops, mobile networks, and/or VoX networks. Examples include two mobile endpoints separated by a satellite link, or an off-net call from a VoX network to a mobile user in the PSTN.

Country-specific recommendations may be more stringent than the ITU-T recommendations, because intracountry calls span a smaller distance and require less transmission time than global calls. In practice, consider 150 ms as the one-way delay limit for intracountry calls, 200 ms for international calls over terrestrial facilities, and 400 ms for calls with a satellite hop. The presence of multiple satellite links may require leniency with these limits. The best guideline is to consider the past experience and expectations of the network users.

Delay Components

In a VoX network, the following elements contribute to the one-way delay time:

- Coding/decoding delays
- Per-link delays
- Playout buffer delays

Coding/Decoding Delays

The *coding/decoding delays* are dependent on the choice of codec algorithm (as described in Chapter 6, "Voice Digitization and Coding"). In general, lower bit-rate codecs introduce more delay into the system. Multiple coding/decoding cycles (also referred to as tandem encoding) can substantially increase the network delay. Tandem encoding also reduces voice quality, so you should avoid it as much as possible.

If you must reduce delay in a system at any cost, then you can use a high bit-rate codec implementation (for example, G.711 or G.726) that introduces less than 2 ms of delay. The downside of this option is that additional bandwidth is required for each call. The price of bandwidth is usually at a premium for high-latency circuits, so high bit-rate codecs are often an impractical solution to the delay problem. The G.728 (LD-CELP) algorithm, which offers 16-kbps compression with 3- to 5-ms delay and good voice quality, is a good compromise for this application.

Per-Link Delays

The following delay components are introduced for each WAN link in the audio path:

- Interface queuing
- Ingress/egress serialization delays
- WAN cloud delays

The *interface queuing delay* is managed with the use of priority queuing for voice packets/frames/cells. Beware of physical interfaces with multiple frame relay PVCs. In these cases, you must ensure that voice traffic on a PVC is not waiting behind data from adjacent PVCs. Cisco's support for voice prioritization across PVCs is dependent on link fragmentation. Unfragmented frames usually carry voice or other small real-time payloads, so they are transmitted ahead of fragmented frames, which presumably carry bulk data traffic. If no fragmentation is configured, then VoFR frames and VoIP frames cannot be queued ahead of data on other PVCs.

The *ingress/egress serialization delay* is managed by using appropriate fragment/interleave technologies. Note that serialization delay can be minimized at the expense of bandwidth (that is, reduced payload efficiency). Even if the minimum clocking rate across the PVC does not merit fragmentation/interleaving, you should still consider how this impacts the interface queuing as described in the preceding paragraph.

The *WAN cloud delay* may be unmanageable if you cannot influence the network design of your carrier, or the laws of physics that dictate transmission rates. If you have influence over your circuit provider, you should ask it to optimize the physical transmission path of your high-latency circuits. This can reduce the round-trip latency for international circuits by 100 ms or more! Also, you should ask for DLCI prioritization when using separate frame relay PVCs for voice and data traffic. This reduces the interface queuing delay at the egress of the carrier's network.

The per-link delays are additive for every WAN circuit in the audio path. In certain circumstances, reducing the number of WAN links in the audio path may reduce the per-link delays. Consider a hierarchical network that is not distributed across a wide geography. The hierarchy may have been introduced to enable the routing protocol to scale for a large number of remote offices. Calls between adjacent sites may tandem through two regional hub sites and a central site, which requires four WAN links in the audio path. The network delay may be reduced if the remote offices connect directly to a central site, instead of through a regional hub site. This concept is illustrated in Figure 13-1.

Figure 13-1 *Collapsing the WAN Hierarchy to Reduce Latency Between Remote Sites*

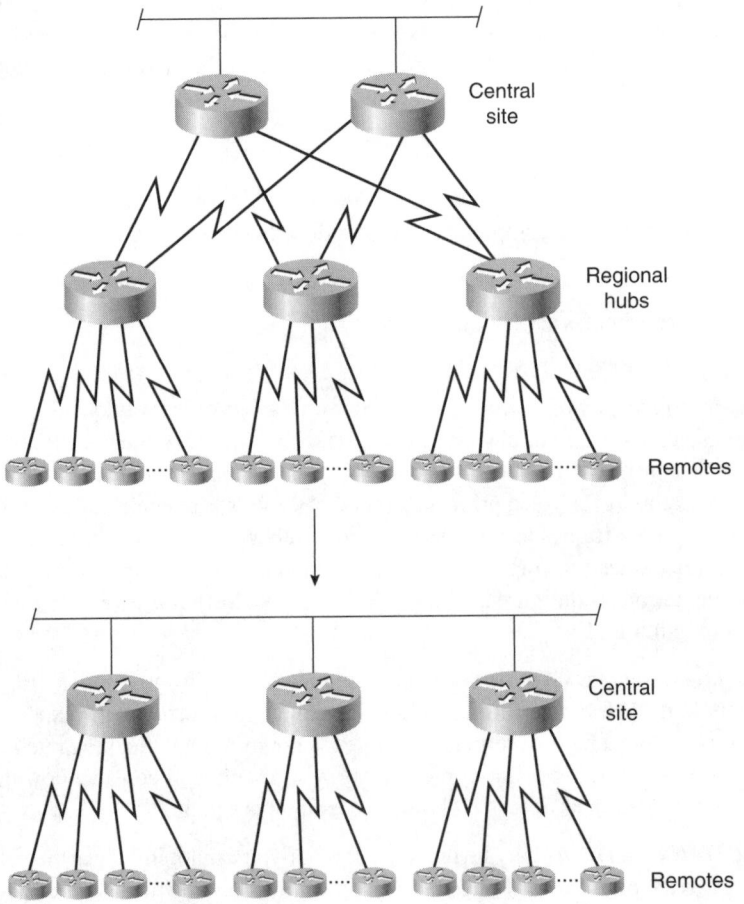

Reducing the WAN hierarchy seems to conflict with routing design guidelines for large networks, but the two design concepts can be reconciled. By segregating WAN routers from backbone routers at the central site, extra WAN links may be eliminated while the logical routing hierarchy is preserved. This requires that the WAN routers only connect to the backbone via the backbone routers, so that route summarization and query boundaries can be located at two levels within the network. (See Figure 13-2.) Bear in mind that collapsing a layer of the WAN hierarchy is only applicable to networks that span a small geographic distance. Delay may not be an issue in such networks, so these design considerations may be moot. On the other hand, if each WAN circuit introduces a delay of 20 ms or more, then it may be worth eliminating two WAN circuit hops.

Figure 13-2   *Reconciling Delay Requirements with Routing Scalability Requirements*

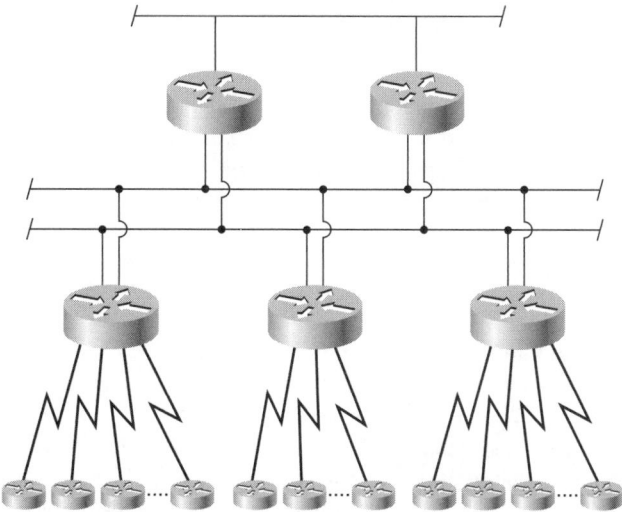

When designing hierarchical voice/data networks that span large distances, follow commonsense best practices. For example, calls from London to Amsterdam should not tandem through New York City. When selecting a hub site for North America, Chicago or Ottawa are better choices than San Francisco or New York, because they are more centrally located. This means that the delay to reach the end offices is more evenly distributed. Similarly, Singapore and Hong Kong are better hub-site choices for the Asia-Pacific region than Sydney or Melbourne. Of course, the geographical presence of your organization may be an overriding factor for these decisions.

Playout Buffer Delays

The *playout buffer*, also known as the *de-jitter buffer*, enables the receiving end to play an audio stream in a smooth fashion, despite the fact that audio information arrives in bursts. The playout buffer should be large enough to accommodate the interarrival time variation of the received audio samples. If jitter in the network can be minimized, then the size of the de-jitter buffer can be decreased. This reduces the overall delay time.

You can reduce jitter in the network by using synchronous WAN links, such as clear channel TDM or ATM-CES, and by reducing fragment sizes. Using synchronous WAN links avoids the variable delays associated with buffers in carrier WAN switches. Reducing fragment sizes in voice/data routers decreases the amount of variable serialization delay.

There are two components to the playout buffer:

- Maximum buffer depth
- Nominal buffer depth

During normal operation, the playout buffer should be half full (that is, the nominal buffer depth). The buffer can fill to absorb bursts of traffic (up to the maximum buffer depth), and drain to cover the gaps in traffic flow.

In the Cisco MC3810, the maximum buffer depth and the nominal buffer depths are configurable. In other platforms, the size of the de-jitter buffer is dynamically managed to optimize performance. Simply minimizing jitter in the network will reduce the depth of the de-jitter buffer in these platforms.

Loss Planning

It is very important to manage signal levels throughout each audio path in the network. If the signal level is too low, then it may be too quiet at the destination. The signal can be boosted at the receiving side, but because quiet signals have a poor signal-to-noise ratio, this introduces excessive noise. If the signal level is too high, audio echoes may be present when extra signal energy is reflected at various points in the network. In addition, the signal may be distorted by amplitude clipping (see Chapter 5, "Defining and Measuring Voice Quality," and Chapter 18, "Resolving Voice Quality Issues"). If the right balance of signal levels is not maintained at each point in the network, then voice quality will suffer. Even worse, certain applications that rely on DTMF tones, such as PSTN hop-off or voice mail, may not function at all.

Voice networks are designed to have a certain amount of end-to-end signal loss. That is, the power of the electrical signal is specifically designed to decrease as the signal follows the audio path. If the physical properties of the connection (such as the long-distance cables) do not naturally generate the expected signal loss, then additional signal loss is inserted at various points along the audio path.

The following points are explored in the next sections:

- Why insert signal loss?
- Definition of loss planning terms
- Loss requirements for a single audio path
- Compromises for multiple audio paths

Why Insert Signal Loss?

It may seem odd to intentionally insert loss in the network, but there are at least two good reasons to do it:

- Maintain consistent audio levels
- Reduce signal reflections

Maintain Consistent Audio Levels

Consider what would happen to audio levels in the absence of intentionally inserted losses. The audio level for each conversation would vary depending on the distance and equipment between the end points. A call across town would be much louder than a call across the country or an international call. Telephones would require a volume knob to adjust the level for each call. The design philosophy in the original Bell network was to keep the end points simple, and place the intelligence in the network. In keeping with this philosophy, loss is intentionally inserted in audio paths, so that a fixed end-to-end loss range is defined for all paths in the public phone network. This allows the volume level to remain nearly constant for each call without requiring adjustment at the end points for each call.

Analog networks use variable-network loss plans. Signal loss in analog networks naturally varies based on audio path distance, so a variable amount of loss is inserted such that the end-to-end loss meets the design guidelines. Digital networks use a simpler fixed-network loss plan, because there is no natural signal loss across the digital portions of the network. By inserting fixed loss amounts at specified points in the network, digital networks are designed with the same end-to-end loss levels as analog networks. Because of the similar loss levels, calls between analog and digital networks have the same audio level.

This is all good in theory, but in practice you have probably experienced calls with low-volume levels, and high amounts of noise. This is because real networks are not always designed and implemented well, and conflicting design goals may call for compromises. Sometimes a fixed loss plan is applied to analog networks because it is simpler to manage than a variable loss plan. Fixed loss plans are not appropriate for analog networks that cover a distance greater than 1,500 km, per ITU-T Recommendation G.171.

It is clearly desirable to maintain consistent audio levels for all calls, but why should this goal be achieved by inserting loss instead of gain? For example, why not bring all calls up to the loudest volume, instead of reducing some calls to a quieter volume? The answer is related to network stability. If there is a positive gain from one end of a connection to another, imagine what would happen to echoes on the line. As the echoes bounced back and forth, they would get louder and louder, until they overloaded the equipment in the signal path. This situation produces feedback just like when a microphone is placed close to a loudspeaker. To avoid this, there must be an end-to-end loss for each audio path, so echoes will be dampened as they bounce back and forth. Preferably, they should be dampened to the point that they are inaudible after a single bounce.

Reduce Signal Reflections

Telephone users hear echoes of themselves or of the distant party when signals are reflected in the analog audio path. If the cause of the signal reflection cannot be remedied, echoes can be made less annoying in two ways:

1 Reduce the delay time of the reflected signals.

2 Reduce the signal level of the reflected signals.

Voice networks are designed with an end-to-end loss to help reduce the level of reflected signals. At first it seems that the desired signals are attenuated as much as the reflected signals. Consider though, that a reflected signal crosses the audio path twice, whereas the desired signals cross the audio path once. This means that reflected signals are attenuated twice as much as the desired signals, assuming that the loss plan is symmetrical. Figure 13-3 illustrates this concept.

Figure 13-3 *Reflected Signals Are Attenuated More than Desired Signals Because of the Loss Plan*

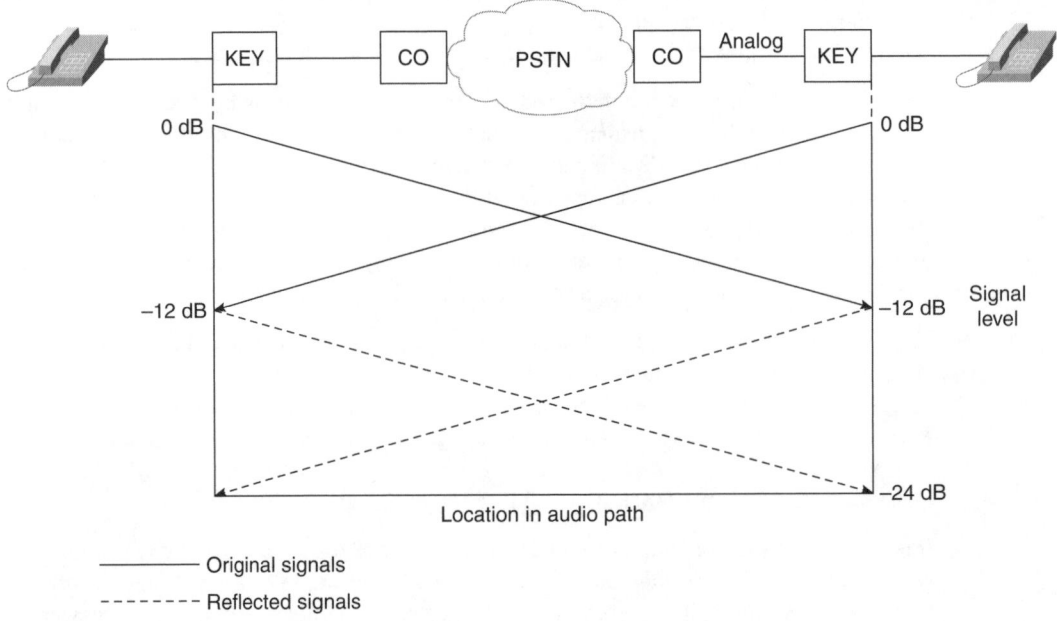

Actually, the amount of attenuation for the reflected signal depends on the point in the audio path at which the signal is reflected. If the signal is reflected at the far end of the audio path (near the remote party), then the reflected signal is twice as attenuated as the signal that originates from the remote party. Signals that are reflected near the source are not attenuated as much. Fortunately, reflections that occur close to the source have a low delay time, so they are masked by the *sidetone* of the original signal. The sidetone, which is the signal fed from the microphone directly to the earpiece, is present so speakers can hear themselves and gauge how well their voice is being carried in the network.

Loss Planning Terms

Many telecom guides discuss signal levels without explicitly stating what values are measured. You are expected to understand what quantities are reported, either through the context or through a footnote that may be accurate if not understandable. Terms such as relative levels, loudness ratings, and loss are similarly obscure, so it can be difficult to understand exactly what quantity is measured. These quantities may be reported with different variants of decibel units, such as dB, dBm, dBm0, and dBr, which further complicates matters. This section contains an explanation of the decibel system, and defines key terms used in loss planning.

Decibels

Decibels are not true units of measure in the sense of meters, seconds, and grams. The decibel unit is a relative rating that compares two measurements, or one measurement to a predefined standard value. A simple ratio provides the same type of comparison, but what happens if the compared signals are different by many orders of magnitude? Ratios quickly become difficult to work with because the numbers can be very large or very small. The decibel system solves this problem by applying the logarithm function to the ratios, which translates the wide range of possible values to a smaller number range that is more tangible.

For example, humans can detect sounds at pressures as small as 0.00002 Newtons/meter^2, but the hearing pain threshold does not occur until around 20 Newtons/meter^2. The decibel system condenses this wide range of possible values, to the more manageable range of 0 to 120 dB. The formula to achieve this translation is:

$$SPL = 10 \times \log\left(\frac{p^2}{p_0^2}\right) = 20 \times \log\left(\frac{p}{p_0}\right)$$

where SPL is the sound pressure level in decibels, $p_0 = 2 \times 10^{-5}$ Newtons/meter^2 is the reference pressure (0 dB), and p is the actual pressure exerted by the measured sound. For every tenfold increase in pressure, the SPL increases by 20 dB. Similarly, a 6-dB increase in SPL corresponds to a doubling of the actual pressure, and a 6-dB decrease in SPL corresponds to a halving of the actual pressure.

Because the dB unit is applicable to many types of signals, it is not always obvious what quantities are represented. Context clues or a special notation is required to discriminate the meaning of a given dB measurement, which can indicate an absolute or relative value, and which can apply to different physical quantities such as sound pressure, electrical power, voltage, or current. Table 13-2 lists variants of dB units that appear in telecommunications references. These variants are discussed in more detail in ITU-T Recommendations G.100 and G.101.

Table 13-2 *Variants of dB Measures Used in Telecommunications*

Unit	Usage
dBM	Absolute electrical power level with respect to 1 watt.
dBm	Absolute electrical power level with respect to 1 milliwatt.
dBr	Relative electrical power level with respect to a 0 dBr reference point.
dBm0	Absolute electrical power level for a test signal at the 0 dBr reference point: dBm0 + dBr = dBm for a 1,020-Hz sinusoidal test signal.
dBV	Absolute voltage level with respect to 1 volt.
dBu	Absolute voltage level with respect to 0.775 volts.
dBrs	Relative sound power level with respect to another measured 0dBrs point.
dB	Ambiguous (interpret from context).

Relative electrical power level (that is, gain or loss) is the most commonly cited dB variant in telecom loss planning. If a document indicates a certain dB gain or loss, the relative electrical power level is generally assumed. If one point is defined as the 0-dBr-reference point, then the dBr value of the other point is equal to the power gain. Power gain, measured in dB units, is calculated according to the following equation:

$$Power\_Gain = 10 \times \log\left(\frac{P_a}{P_b}\right) = 10 \times \log\left(\frac{V_a^2 / Z_a}{V_b^2 / Z_b}\right) = 20 \times \log\left(\left|\frac{V_a}{V_b}\right| \times \sqrt{\frac{Z_b}{Z_a}}\right)$$

where P_a and P_b are measures of electrical power at different reference points, V_a and V_b are measures of voltage, and Z_a and Z_b are impedances that can be purely resistive or frequency dependent. Since impedance may vary with signal frequency, power gain is usually measured with a reference signal of 1020 Hz per ITU-T Recommendation G.100. This ensures that different power measurements are made under comparable conditions.

Note the value of 10 in the electrical power gain equation, where there is a value of 20 in the sound pressure level and voltage equations. The power gain equation is different because power is related to the square of voltage ($P = V^2/Z$). There is no exponential factor of 2 to extract from the logarithmic expression of power. As a result of this difference, a 6-dB difference in sound pressure level or voltage level corresponds with a doubling of pressure or voltage, but only a 3-dB power gain corresponds to a doubling of power. This is an important point to remember.

TIP	A 3-dB power gain doubles the power. A 6-dB voltage gain doubles the voltage. A 6-dB increase in sound pressure level doubles the sound pressure.

Loss and Loudness Rating Terms

Table 13-3 provides a summary definition of selected terms that describe signal loss between specific points in the network.

Table 13-3 *Summary Definitions of Loss Planning Terms*

	Loss Planning Terms	**Summary Definitions**
SLR	Send Loudness Rating	The loudness loss between the speaking subscriber's mouth and an electric interface in the network.
RLR	Receive Loudness Rating	The loudness loss between an electric interface in the network and the listening subscriber's ear.
CLR	Circuit Loudness Rating	The power loss between two electrical interfaces in a circuit connection.
OLR	Overall Loudness Rating	The loudness loss between the speaking subscriber's mouth and the listening subscriber's ear via a circuit connection.
TELR	Talker Echo Loudness Rating	The loudness loss of a speaker's voice that is reflected in the circuit and returns to the speaker's ear as a delayed echo.
L_{hybrid}	Return Loss at Hybrid	The power loss of an electrical signal that is reflected at a hybrid because of an impedance mismatch.
L_{canc}	Loss at Echo Canceller	The power loss of an echo signal passing through an echo canceller.
L_{nlp}	Loss at Nonlinear Processor	The power loss of the residual echo (echo canceller output) passing through the nonlinear processor, or "noise gate."
A_{com}	Combined Loss	$A_{com} = L_{canc} + L_{nlp} + L_{hybrid}$

Figure 13-4 illustrates the reference points for the loudness rating variables.

Figure 13-4   *Reference Points for Loudness Rating Variables*

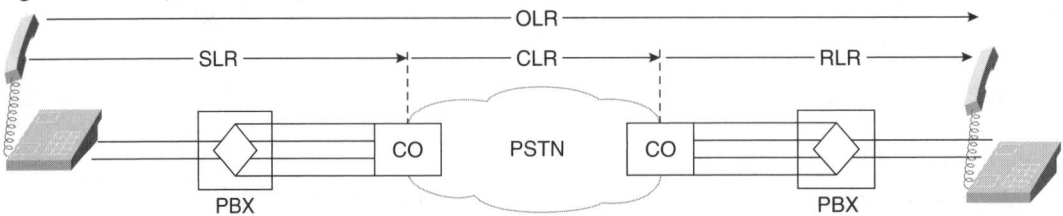

Unlike most dB values, in which the compared quantities have the same units of measure, the SLR and RLR are a mixture of sound pressure level and electrical voltage gain measurements. For the purpose of loss planning, you can just consider the SLR and RLR in terms of an electrical power gain or loss up to the point of conversion from electricity to sound.

The TELR value depends on where the signal reflection occurs, and can be a function of most of the loss planning terms described in Table 13-3. The two-wire/four-wire junctions (also known as "hybrids") are generally responsible for signal reflections in the audio path. Hybrids that are distant from the speaker cause a given echo level to be more annoying because of the increased delay. The most likely trouble spots include the remote CO if the distant local loop is two-wire, or the remote PBX if the distant local loop is four-wire (such as E&M or digital). You can estimate the TELR that will result from likely reflection points by using the following formula:

$$TELR = A_{com} + \sum (SLR, RLR, CLR)$$

Note that the SLR, RLR, and CLR components that are applicable depend on the path through which the reflected signal travels. For most scenarios, this expression can be simplified to twice the value of the OLR.

The hybrid loss is primarily a function of the impedances on either end of the hybrid, as follows:

$$L_{hybrid} \approx 20 \times \log \left| \frac{Z_a + Z_b}{Z_a - Z_b} \right|$$

If the impedance values are closely matched on either end of the hybrid, then the hybrid loss value is very large. An ideal hybrid with perfectly matched impedance will cause infinite loss for reflected signals; in other words, there is no reflection. In a real-world example, if the impedance at one end is 600 ohms and the other end is 610 ohms, then the reflected signal loses nearly 42 dB of power. If there is a significant impedance mismatch, such as 600 ohms versus 3000 ohms, then the reflected signal only loses 3.5 dB of power.

An impedance mismatch may arise when a wire does not have good electrical contact at a hybrid junction point, or the equipment may have been configured incorrectly.

According to ITU-T Recommendation G.165, echo cancellers require at least 6 dB of power loss in the echo signal to operate properly. Given that the hybrid reflection introduces enough loss to meet this requirement, a G.165-compliant echo canceller introduces at least 18 to 26 dB of loss (L_{canc}) in the reflected signal for a single-speaker condition. If both parties are speaking at the same time, then the echo canceller introduces a loss of only 8 to 16 dB. Echo cancellers achieve the higher end of the loss range when the echo signal is louder. Note that echoes may not be cancelled for the first 500 ms of speech, when the echo canceller is in "learning mode." Remember this behavior when troubleshooting echo problems that primarily occur at the beginning of a conversation.

Assuming the echo canceller sufficiently reduces the reflected signal level, a nonlinear processor eliminates low-level residual noise. The device acts as a noise gate that blocks the signal when it is not above a certain threshold. Because original speech signals should be much louder than reflected speech or background noise, low-level signals indicate that no desirable signal is present. The noise gate lets the signal through when there is desirable speech, and blocks the signal when there is only low-level noise. Residual echoes or background noise cannot be blocked when there is also a desirable speech signal present, because the composite signal is above the threshold. As a result, the nonlinear processor is deactivated when both parties speak at the same time. When the nonlinear processor is active, at least 35 dB of loss (L_{nlp}) is added to the reflected signal.

Figure 13-5 graphically depicts the losses that an echo signal incurs because of reflection, echo cancellers, and nonlinear processing.

Figure 13-5 *Echo Signal Loses Power from Reflection, Echo Canceller, and Nonlinear Processing*

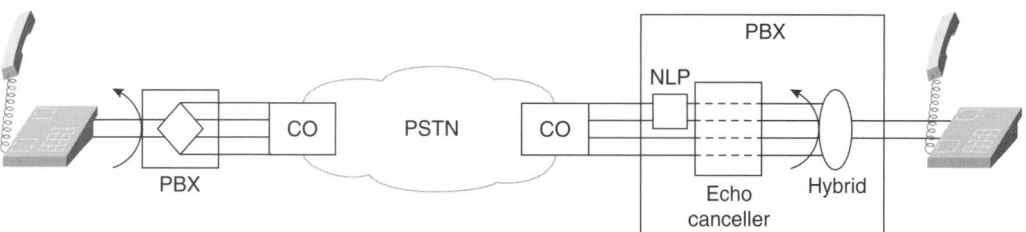

End-to-End Path Loss Requirements

ITU-T G.111 recommends an overall loudness rating (OLR) of 8 to 12 dB, but recognizes that an OLR up to 21 dB may be required in some cases (for example, with long-distance analog connections). Most network planners follow this recommendation, aiming for a 12-dB end-to-end loss. What is the logic behind this recommendation? The following section answers this question.

Theoretical Motivation

The primary reason for having end-to-end loss is to combat echo, so it is sensible to tailor the loss plan based on the echo characteristics of your network. A constant level of "talker echo" becomes more annoying as the delay time of the echo increases. To keep echoes below the threshold of annoyance, the signal level of the echoes must be reduced as the echo delay increases. This means that you can design your end-to-end loss plan based on the expected audio path delay times in your network. To help guide you in this respect, ITU-T Recommendation G.131 contains the graph shown in Figure 13-6.

Figure 13-6   *Threshold for Echo Annoyance, Defined by Echo Delay Time and Echo Level*

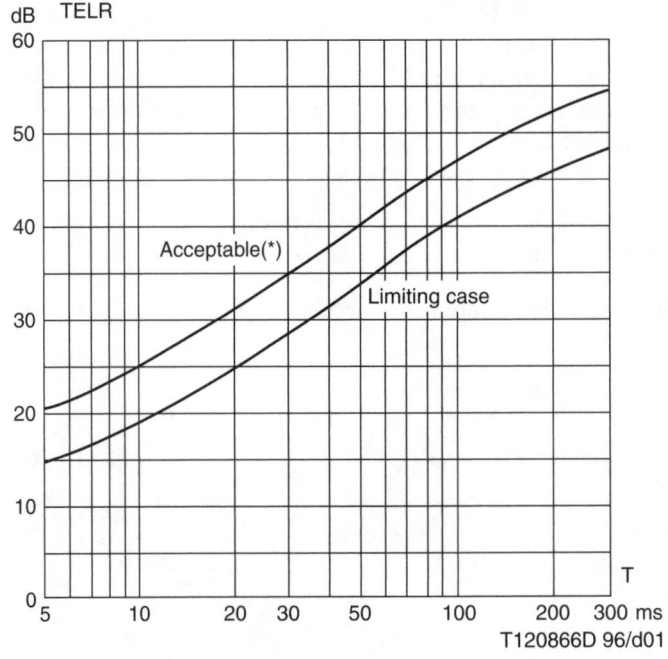

T120866D 96/d01

TELR	Talker Echo Loudness Rating
T	Mean one-way transmission time
(*)	The Acceptable curve is equivalent to the curve with 1% probability of encountering objectionable echo.

The upper line on the graph represents the threshold where 1 percent of the test subjects were annoyed by the echo. Above and to the left of this line, the combination of echo delay and echo level is acceptable. Below and to the right of this line, the combination of echo delay and echo level is objectionable. Recall that as the TELR value increases, the echoes become quieter. The following subsections apply this delay-level relationship to determine end-to-end loss requirements for a variety of design scenarios.

Traditional Network Example

Consider a voice network without echo cancellers that uses a 12-dB end-to-end loss plan. If a talker's echo is reflected from the far side of the circuit, the loss plan introduces 24 dB of loss to the echo signal (12 dB in each direction). Considering the average reflection loss at a good hybrid (L_{hybrid}) is approximately 15 dB, the TELR is 39 dB for this scenario. Looking at the graph, this TELR allows 50 ms of delay at the threshold of echo annoyance. Calls with more than 50 ms of end-to-end delay will produce an objectionable level of echo in this network. Now consider that there is an impedance mismatch at a hybrid, and L_{hybrid} is only 4 dB. Now the TELR value drops to 28 dB, which only allows 15 ms of delay before the echoes are objectionable. This is a pretty small delay budget!

The preceding examples did not include echo cancellers, which ITU-T Recommendation G.131 indicates should be present for all circuits with a one-way delay in excess of 25 ms. If this condition is met, then the TELR is greatly lowered, which allows greater echo delay times.

VoX Network Example

Now consider a real scenario for the VoX network illustrated in Figure 13-7. The goal is to design an end-to-end loss requirement that is suitable for calls from San Francisco, California, USA to Buenos Aires, Argentina.

Routers at each location are attached via a 256-kbps fractional T1/E1 (clear-channel TDM), with a one-way latency of 140 ms (terrestrial fiber). Each router provides tie trunks to a local PBX, and the dial plan enables lines from one PBX to call lines on the other PBX. The G.723.1 codec is used to compress the voice, which introduces 67.5 ms of delay. VoIP is implemented on the routers, with RTP header compression and appropriate QoS considerations. The multilink PPP fragment size is set to 320 bits on the WAN link, which yields a variable serialization delay of 10 ms. Add another 5 to 10 ms of delay for miscellaneous factors such as encapsulation time, queuing behind other active voice calls, and so on.

Figure 13-7   *Determining End-to-End Loss Requirements for a VoX Network*

In this scenario, we have approximately 225 ms of one-way delay. Consulting the graph in Figure 13-6, the TELR value must be approximately 53 dB to keep talker echo from becoming objectionable. With a good hybrid termination (L_{hybrid} = 15 dB) but no echo canceller, the end-to-end loss must introduce the remaining 38 dB of signal loss for the reflected signals. This means a one-way loss of 19 dB. With bad hybrid connections, this could easily jump to 25 dB of loss required in each direction. It is likely that the audio level will be too quiet with this much loss inserted, so another option should be explored.

Echo cancellers in the routers are activated at each end of the circuit. Note that the echo canceller in Buenos Aires reduces the echo levels perceived in San Francisco, and vice versa. Planning for the possibility of both parties speaking simultaneously, the effects of nonlinear processing should not be considered. Recall that the goal is to achieve a 53-dB

TELR, using a combination of hybrid loss, echo cancellation, and the end-to-end loss plan. With reasonable values of L_{hybrid} = 15 dB and L_{canc} = 12 dB (reduced performance because of doubletalk), the end-to-end loss plan must provide 26 dB of roundtrip loss. This is a 13-dB loss in each direction, which seems very reasonable.

Now consider the same example with a marginal hybrid termination that introduces only 6 dB of reflection loss. This is just enough loss in the echo signal for the echo canceller to be effective. If the echo canceller introduces 16 dB of loss, then the loss plan must introduce 15.5 dB of loss in each direction. If the standard loss plan of 12 dB is used in this case, people may complain about echo problems. If the two-wire/four-wire hybrid is located in the PBX (that is, there is a four-wire connection from router to PBX), swapping cards in the PBX may not fix the hybrid termination problem because all of the cards may be performing at the marginally acceptable level. There are three solutions to this problem:

1   Use the router for the hybrid connection by changing the router/PBX interface to a two-wire connection (FXO/FXS). This will reduce some functionality, such as direct dialing of extensions between the PBXs. Chapter 16, "Establishing Router-PBX Connectivity," discusses router-PBX connectivity and interface types.

2   Modify the end-to-end loss plan such that 15.5 dB of loss is introduced in each direction of the audio path. The audio levels will be slightly quieter, but direct dialing is preserved.

3   Continue with the 12-dB one-way loss plan, and accept that echo performance in the network is at a marginal level. With TELR = 46 dB, the echo performance lies on the lower line of the graph, which represents worst-case planning for exceptional and unavoidable cases.

It should be clear that more severe cases are common. For example, consider the same network with a satellite link instead of a terrestrial fiber connection. The 140-ms WAN latency jumps to 250+ ms, which pushes the end-to-end delay to around 315 ms. Factor in tail-end hop-off functionality, with calls to wireless network subscribers, and the delay is well over 500 ms. Fortunately, the TELR requirements do not radically increase for these marginal cases of extreme delay, because the TELR must already be so high that the echo signal is essentially gone.

PSTN Hop-Off Example

For high-delay connections, the most threatening problem is tail-end hop-off to long-haul PSTN connections. For example, consider a call from the U.S. that traverses a VoIP network, and hops off to the PSTN in India. (See Figure 13-8.) There is a 25-ms delay on the analog portion of the call in India, which does not require an echo canceller per ITU-T G.131. The router can cancel echoes within 32 ms of when the signals leave the router, but the echoes may not return for 50 ms. As a result, this echo signal propagates back through the VoIP network, and reaches the talker in the U.S. with a large delay and magnitude. No echo canceller has affected the signal; only the reflection loss L_{hybrid} and the loss plan can provide the TELR requirement.

Figure 13-8 *Loss Planning Is Difficult with Long-Haul VoX Networks and Long PSTN Hop-Offs*

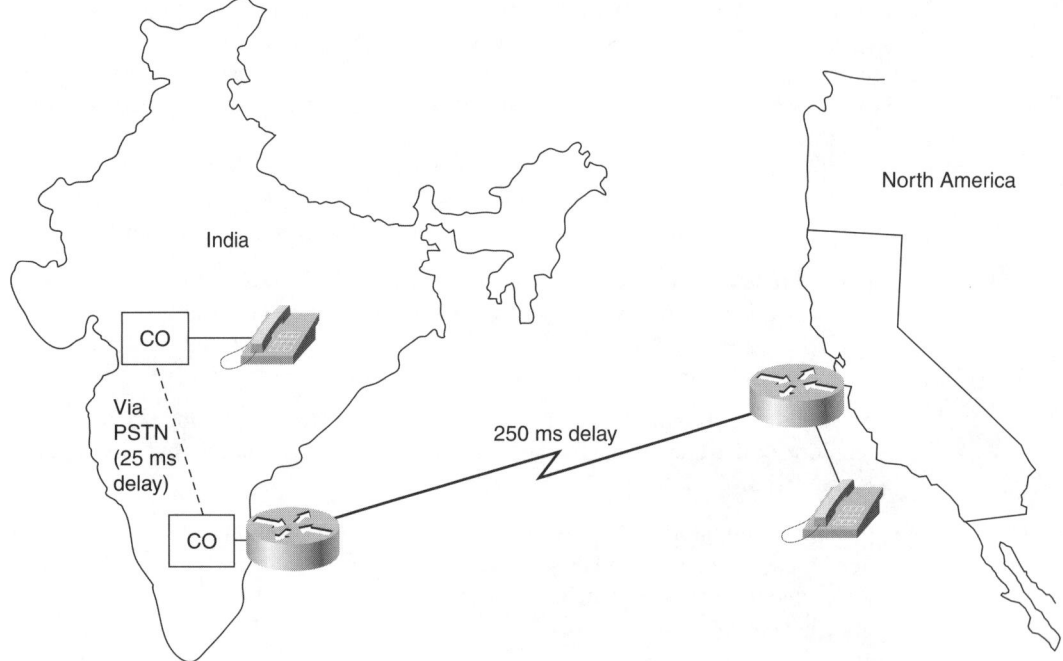

With an optimistic 250-ms one-way delay for the VoIP portion of the network, and another 25 ms for the analog portion of the network in India, the echo may return to the talker in the U.S. with a 550-ms delay! The hybrid at the far end of the analog hop in India provides 15 dB of reflection loss in a good case, and the in-country PSTN provides about 12 dB of loss in each direction. With a TELR goal around 60 dB, the VoIP network must introduce an additional 10.5 dB of loss in each direction. Now the one-way loss is around 20.5 dB, which is noticeably quiet. It is interesting to note that this scenario is very close to the worst-case end-to-end loss suggested by the ITU-T in G.111. We will not even consider the case of a bad hybrid termination in the PSTN. Here, the tough compromise is tolerating echoes, or tolerating a very quiet connection. If you must call from a noisy environment, such as an air-conditioned data center or a noisy office, you should learn to speak while ignoring your own echoes.

Bidirectional PSTN Hop-Off Example

There are some cases in which the object is not to defeat echo, but to maintain adequate audio levels. When a VoX network provides toll-bypass between two PSTN segments, the OLR is almost always too large for the end-to-end connection. A glance at the diagram shown in Figure 13-9 should make this clear:

Figure 13-9 *Excessive Loss when a VoX Network Connects Two PSTN Segments*

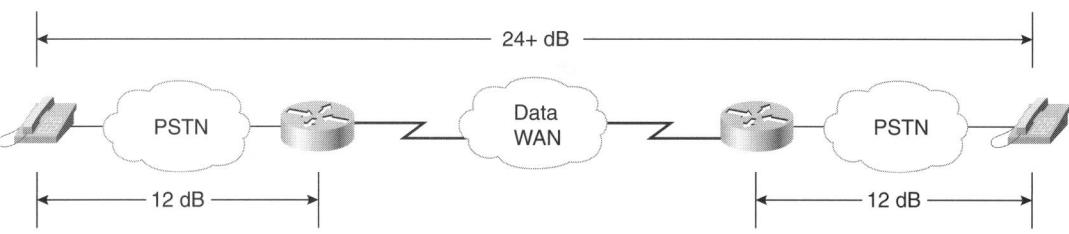

Most public loss plans provide at least 8 to 12 dB of loss for a connection. Because two PSTN segments are attached via a VoX segment, the end-to-end audio path experiences the signal loss of each PSTN connection in addition to any loss from the VoX part of the network. Even if the VoX segment introduces no loss, the end-to-end connection experiences twice as much loss as a normal PSTN connection.

In this scenario, the VoX network must provide signal gain to increase the OLR to an acceptable level. It is important to ensure that no gain is inserted to a signal path that also transmits higher level inputs. For example, do not apply gain to an interface if calls of local origin may also route through the interface. A high gain applied to a call with normal audio levels may overload the attached PBX or PSTN equipment.

Distribution of Loss Within an Audio Path

For planning purposes, it is not enough to know how much end-to-end signal loss should occur along an audio path. It is also important to know how the loss is distributed throughout the audio path, and what considerations affect the placement of loss pads. For example, should loss be evenly distributed along the audio path? Should loss be placed nearer the speaker or nearer the listener? How does the location of a two-wire/four-wire hybrid affect the placement of loss pads? The key to answering these questions is to remember that loss plans are intended to reduce echoes, so the distribution of loss should help achieve this goal.

In Principle

Talker echo is the most common type of echo problem, so the focus of this discussion is how to distribute loss such that talker echo is minimized (and TELR is increased). Recall that talker echo is the result of signal reflection at a hybrid on the remote side of the network. To be more specific, signal reflection occurs on the two-wire side of the hybrid, but signal leakage occurs on the four-wire side of the hybrid (from the transmit pair to the receive pair). Figure 13-10, which details the components around the hybrid at the remote (relative to the talker) side of the network, is an important reference for the discussion that follows.

Figure 13-10   *R and T Loss Pads Relative to Echo Canceller and Two-Wire/Four-Wire Hybrid*

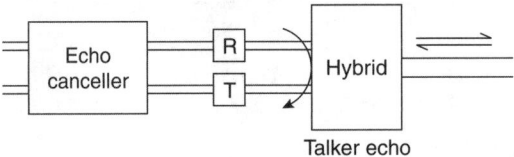

Talker echo

In the diagram, voice signals from the talker proceed along the transmit portion (top-two wires) of the four-wire circuit, and most of the signal energy proceeds through the hybrid into the two-wire portion of the circuit. Some of the signal energy leaks through the hybrid to the receive portion (bottom-two wires) of the four-wire circuit. This energy constitutes the echo signal. The R and T loss pads represent the software configurable loss that may be inserted into each direction of the circuit. The R refers to the receive side of the two-wire connection, and the T refers to the transmit side of the two-wire connection. Assume that both ends of the audio path have a similar design with similar values for R and T.

Recall that the goal of this discussion is to distribute loss in such a way that minimizes talker echo. In the preceding diagram, this amounts to optimizing the values for R and T. Because echo cancellers require at least 6-dB loss in echo signals to operate, the following equation must be valid:

$$R + T + L_{hybrid} \geq 6 \, dB$$

To make the system more resilient to impedance mismatches at the hybrid, R and T alone should be able to provide the minimum 6-dB loss. If T provides all of the loss, then desired voice signals are attenuated as much as the undesired reflections, which is confusing for the echo canceller. If R provides all of the loss, then reflected signals are quieter than the inbound desired voice signals, and the echo canceller performs well. Talker echo is reduced when the echo canceller performs well, so the loss should be concentrated at R.

The distribution of loss between R and T is essentially the same question as how to distribute loss along the entire audio path. The end-to-end loss is concentrated at the listener side when R provides all of the loss, and at the talker side when T provides all the loss. The preceding discussion clearly indicates that loss should be concentrated after the echo canceller but before the remote-end hybrid, near the listener side. Note that other portions of the analog network provide natural loss, but these loss components are not readily configurable.

The remote hybrid may be located in a central office (CO), a private branch exchange (PBX), or a router. When the hybrid is in a CO, the R and T values are standardized as part of the national loss plan. Consistent with the preceding discussion, every country sets R to be much larger than T. Most countries set T equal to zero, with the Netherlands, Norway, New Zealand, and the United Kingdom as notable exceptions. When the hybrid is in a PBX or a router, the R and T values are the input and output loss pads on the four-wire interface (for example, analog E&M or digital).

In Practice

The following examples represent a variety of scenarios for distributing loss in both traditional and VoX networks. In all of the diagrams that follow, a single line represents a pair of wires. That is, a single line represents a two-wire connection, and two lines represent a four-wire connection.

The most basic type of end-to-end connection is two POTS phones connected via a PSTN. (See Figure 13-11.) The circuit vendor manages the loss plan in this scenario. Key systems, which enable multiple telephones to share a fewer number of analog lines, are an extension of this design.

Figure 13-11   *POTS Phones and Key Systems Connected Via a PSTN*

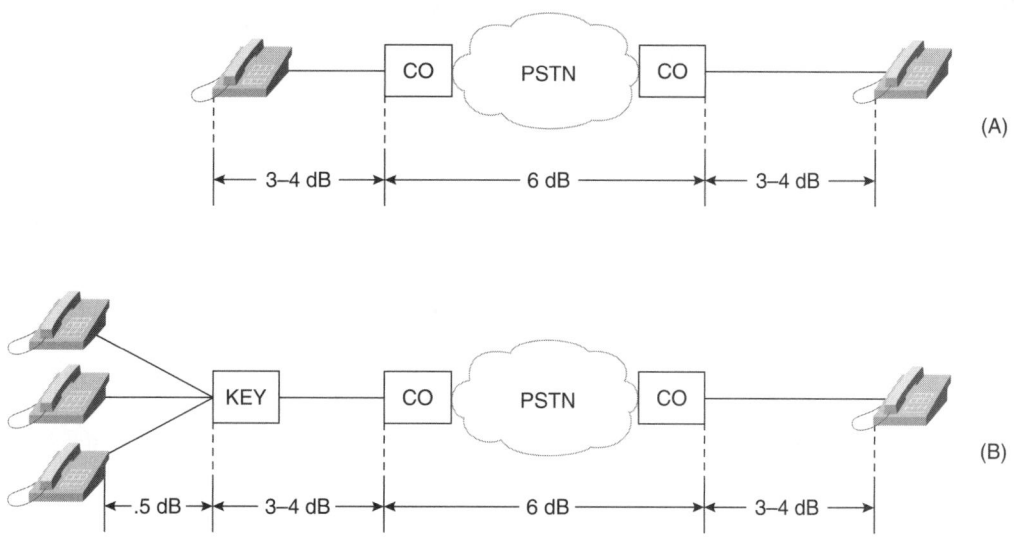

PBXs support more users, and usually have digital (T1/E1) connections to a CO. (See Figure 13-12.) There is no signal loss along the digital path from the CO to the PBX, so a loss pad must be inserted to simulate the loss of an analog local loop. An average analog loop has 4 dB of line loss, whereas the average line from a PBX to an analog phone has 1 dB of line loss. The loss pad, provided by the CO or the PBX, must provide the 3-dB difference. If the CO does not insert more loss for digital trunks than for analog trunks, then the PBX must insert the 3-dB loss pad.

Figure 13-12   *Loss Plan for a PBX with a Digital Connection to a PSTN*

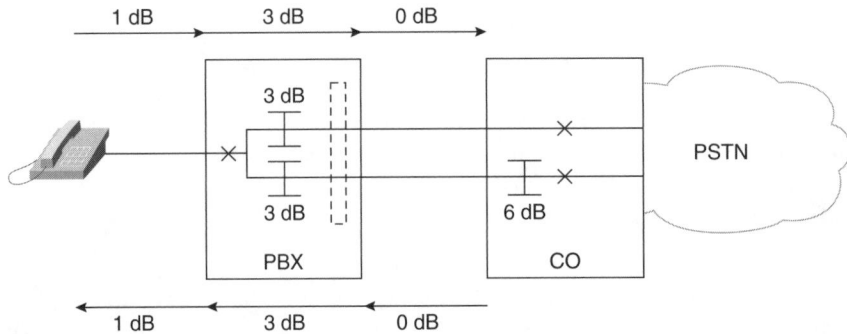

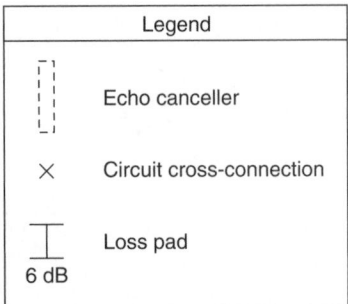

Note that the preceding diagram only illustrates the near end of the connection. This is for simplicity, because the loss requirements up to the point of connection to the PSTN are independent of the far end of the connection. Assuming that the CO does not provide extra loss padding for digital connections, the private network must provide loss (from the phone set to the point of PSTN connection) that is analogous to the 4-dB line loss of an analog loop.

Tail-end hop-off applications require tandem PBX connections to reach the PSTN. (See Figure 13-13.) It is highly desirable that tandem PBX connections use four-wire facilities, so that only the originating/terminating exchange requires a two-wire/four-wire hybrid. Each hybrid introduces a possible path for echoes, so the number of hybrids should be minimized. The two-wire portion of the connection may be extended beyond the originating/terminating PBX (for example, moved to a tandem PBX), but the connection should not alternate between two-wire and four-wire circuits.

Figure 13-13 *Originating/Terminating PBXs Insert Loss Pads, but Tandem PBXs Do Not*

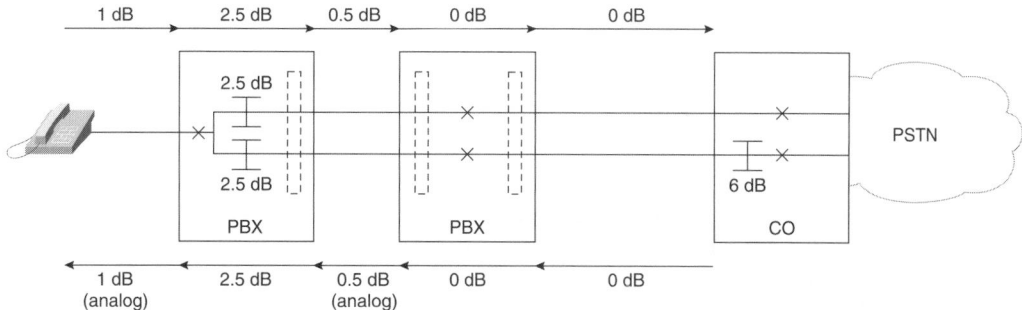

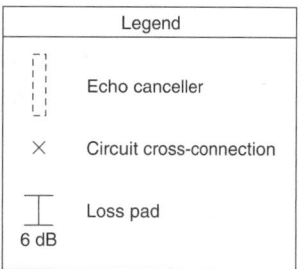

As indicated in the figure, the originating/terminating PBXs insert all of the loss required from the private network. Note that the required loss pad may be smaller if the tandem circuits are analog. Tandem PBXs should not insert loss, unless the conversion from four-wire to two-wire facilities occurs in the tandem PBX. In such cases, the tandem PBX must insert loss to ensure that the echo canceller functions properly (that is, "R" and "T" provide at least 6-dB loss). The loss pad in the originating/terminating PBX must be adjusted accordingly.

The preceding examples involve traditional voice networks. Consider now the variety of configurations when traditional voice networks are mixed with VoX networks. In the simplest VoX scenario, shown in Figure 13-14, the router does not need to insert loss.

Figure 13-14 *No Loss Pad Required when Router Connected to PSTN Via Analog Local Loop*

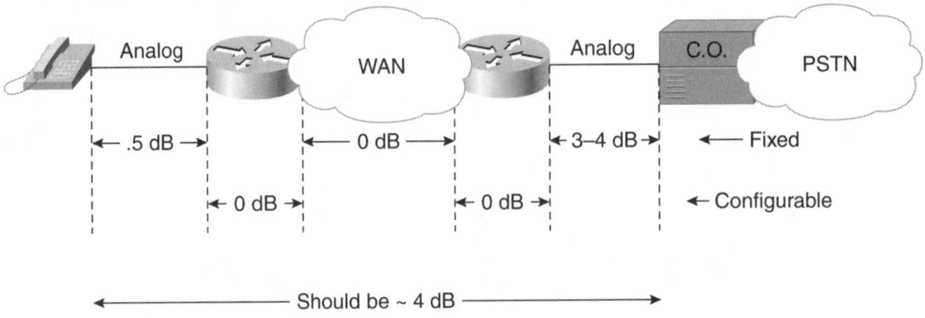

It is important to note that Cisco routers by default insert a 3-dB loss pad in both directions for Foreign Exchange Station (FXS) voice ports. The configuration of the router indicates a 0dB pad, but this is a relative level that corresponds to the 3 dB of implicit loss. For example, an interface configured for 3 dB of loss will actually exhibit 6 dB of loss. In Figure 13-14, the input gain of the router's FXS port should be configured to +3 dB to offset the implicit loss, because the analog local loop naturally provides the 3-dB loss. The output signal can only be attenuated (not boosted) in Cisco routers, so someone using a telephone attached to the router may hear a slightly quieter signal in this scenario.

There is a caveat to removing the implicit 3-dB loss pads for FXS interfaces. Consider that the output of the coder is a four-wire signal, while the FXS port is two-wire. This means that a hybrid must be present, so there is a potential for talker echo. In the unlikely event that the hybrid in the router does not perform well, the default 3-dB pads on the interface provide a safety net to activate the echo canceller. You should be aware that you are removing this safety net if you remove the 3-dB loss pad. Fortunately, it is easy to remedy the situation if talker echo is a problem. Remember that the remote party (PSTN connection) will experience talker echo if signals are reflected from this hybrid.

The network configuration shown in Figure 13-15 is a common Off-Premise Extension (OPX) solution for VoX networks.

In this scenario, the PBX should act as a tandem PBX (that is, refrain from inserting loss), and the terminating router should provide 3 dB of loss padding (default for FXS interfaces). The connection between the router and PBX is typically so short that cable loss for analog connections is negligible. Verify this fact in your network before making the assumption.

The design shown in Figure 13-16 is common when all sites have a PBX, or at least a key system with configurable loss pads.

Figure 13-15 *Loss Plan for OPX Solutions in a VoX Network*

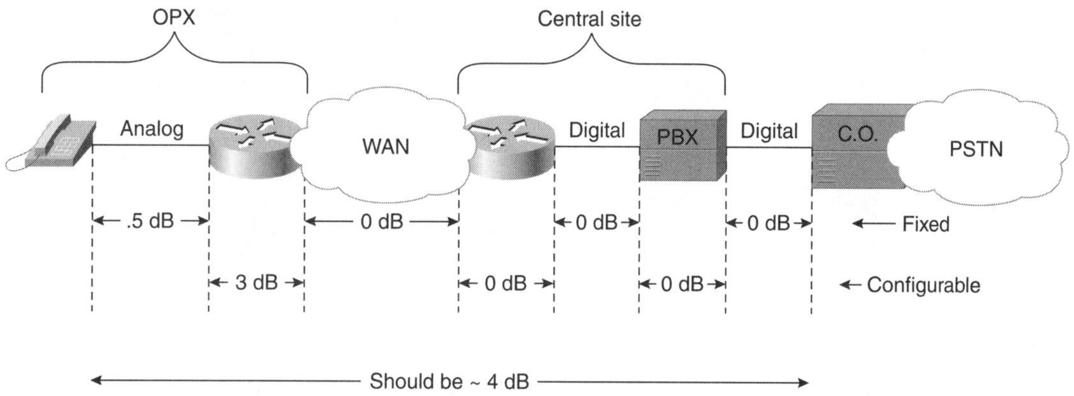

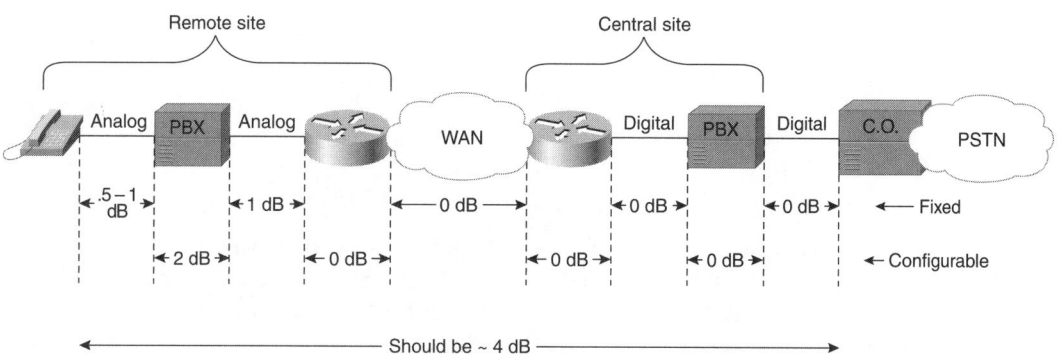

Figure 13-16 *Loss Plan when Routers Provide Tie-Line Replacement for PBXs*

In this scenario, the routers act as tandem PBXs. No router should insert loss, unless it contains a two-wire/four-wire hybrid (for example, an FXS/FXO port on the terminating side of the connection). If a router contains a hybrid, then it must provide enough loss to activate the echo cancellers. The default input/output loss of 3 dB for FXS ports provides a 6-dB reduction of echo signals, which meets the echo canceller requirements. For FXO ports, the loss must be manually configured.

Note that when multiple audio paths (in other words, more than two termination points) are involved, the optimum settings cannot be applied to every audio path. The next section explores several examples where compromise is required for multiple audio paths.

Compromises for Multiple Audio Paths

Each of the last three examples involves a connection to the PSTN, but the most common use of private voice networks is for internal calling. Consider a more realistic network design that must balance the loss requirements for internal calls and calls to the PSTN as seen in Figure 13-17.

Figure 13-17   *Compromise Between Connections with Different Loss Requirements*

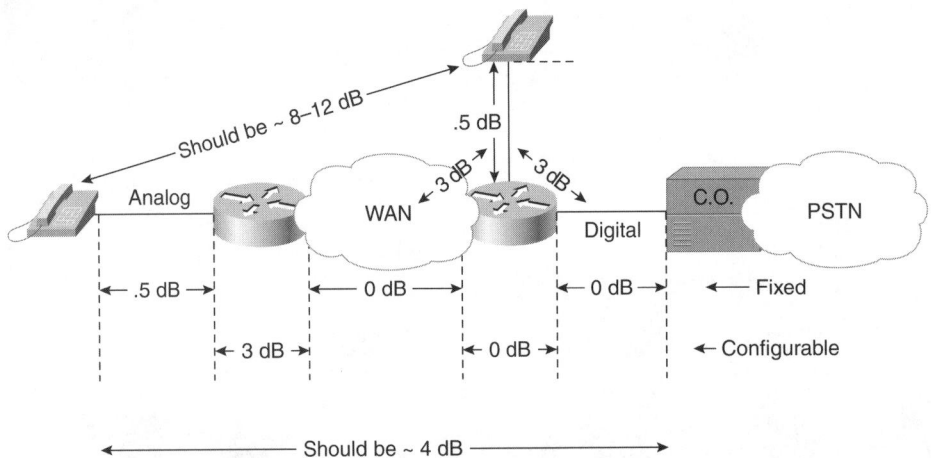

In this example, the default 3-dB loss for FXS interfaces provides the standard loss for calls to the PSTN, but calls between phones in the private network only have a 6-dB end-to-end loss. If additional loss is added for the sake of internal calls, then calls to the PSTN will also experience this added loss. It may be better to let the loudness be a little high for internal calls than to make the PSTN calls too quiet. You should decide based on the relative amount of calls for each type, such that most of the callers have acceptable audio levels. Recall that ITU-T Recommendation G.111 advocates 8- to 12-dB loss, but it also indicates that a value around 5 dB is optimal in the absence of echo. Given the good hybrids, echo cancellers, and nonlinear processors within the routers, echo is not a problem in router-only VoX networks, even when network delay is high.

If the connection to the PSTN is analog, then the 3-dB pad should still be used for the FXS interfaces, even though this exceeds the targeted loss. If you remove the 3-dB pad in this case, calls within the network will be quite loud, and the risk of echo is greater for calls to the PSTN.

Calls from small remote sites to a larger central site often have the design shown in Figure 13-18.

Figure 13-18   *Loss Plan for Calls from VoX OPX Lines to PBX Extensions*

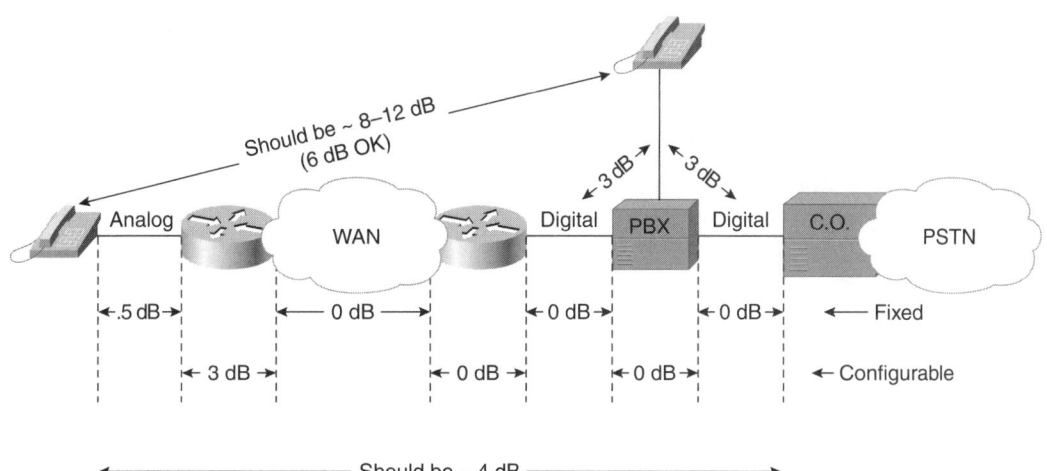

This is a slight variation of the previous configuration. The only difference from a loss planning perspective is that the router connected to the PBX acts like a tandem PBX and does not insert loss. The PBX balances the loss requirements for different types of connections. This is actually a good design because PBXs can provide a feature called *pad switching*, where the loss pad for a given voice port depends on the type of connection using that port. If the PBX acts as a tandem switch (for example, the call originates in a remote PBX or router and the tandem PBX passes the call to the PSTN) for a given call, then the PBX can switch in the loss pad. If a call originates or terminates on the PBX, then the PBX can switch out (or bypass) the loss pad.

In this last scenario, the routers play a minimal role in managing the loss plan. Because no calls originate or terminate on the routers, they usually act as tandem switches and insert no loss. The PBXs must manage the loss for each type of connection, based on the principles described in this chapter. For more detailed guidance on loss planning principles for private networks, consult ITU-T Recommendation G.171, and EIA/TIA-464-B. ITU-T Recommendations G.111 and G.121 provide additional insight for loss planning concepts, in the context of national and international public networks. ITU-T Recommendations G.100 and G.101 provide good background material to help make sense of the other recommendations.

Summary

This chapter has considered delay and loss as separate subjects, but has attempted to show the important ways in which these variables interact. While developing a delay budget and designing a loss plan are ostensibly separate activities, you are well advised to consider them part of the same exercise. Any decision you make with respect to one may have a significant impact on the other. If you recognize this relationship from the beginning, you can use it to your advantage when designing an integrated network.

CHAPTER 14

Establishing an Integrated Dialing Plan

The integrated dialing plan describes connectivity between all phone stations in the voice and data networks. It considers functions in the traditional telephone switches as well as the multiservice routers. Most organizations do not have a document that they call the *dial plan*, but they generally have a directory of phone number prefixes for each site and, if you are fortunate, a written description of the routing methodology. In many cases, the only reference to the routing methodology may be in the actual phone switch configurations.

The integrated dialing plan document that you create or modify is not meant for archiving. It should be updated as necessary and reflect the real state of your network. Make sure to document the plan such that another person can understand your design decisions and expand the plan as the organization grows.

This chapter explores two key components of the dialing plan that you must define:

- Numbering plan
- Routing plan

Create a Numbering Plan

Remember that the numbering plan should be easy to use by everyone—not just by engineers. You should strive for absolute simplicity and elegance. This may increase the complexity of configuring and maintaining the routers and phone switches, but your users will appreciate it. They may not stop to admire the simplicity of the dial plan they use, but this means you have done your job well.

Prefix Assignment Strategies

Organizations approach numbering plan design with a variety of strategies. Unfortunately, many organizations let the numbering plan "design itself." This method may work for small networks, but as the network grows, a complete and awkward redesign may be required.

For those organizations that take a more active role in the evolution of the numbering plan, most efforts can be categorized as follows:

- Maximize call-routing summarization
- Minimize number translation between private network and PSTN
- Use a hybrid approach

You must assess which strategy is appropriate for your environment. For example, you may align the numbering plan with PSTN assignments where possible because you want to avoid complicated number translations. On the other hand, you may not be happy about hundreds of routing entries in your phone switches and routers, so a hierarchical plan might look good to you. If your voice network has many locations and a topology that permits, default routing might enable you to maintain easy number translations and small routing tables in many of your PBXs and routers. More important than the actual strategy you choose is that you plan carefully and consider the implications of your decision in your environment.

Maximizing Geographic Summarization

If there are many sites in your organization, you may be interested in keeping the PBX routing tables as short as possible. A hierarchical numbering scheme will help you achieve this goal. The hierarchy should generally follow the topology of your network. The danger of this approach is that your organizational structure and network topology may radically change such that summarization is no longer possible. If your network topology changes that much, you will be making so many changes that you might as well revisit the dial plan. In other words, it is usually worth the risk to have the dial-plan hierarchy follow your network topology.

Figure 14-1 illustrates a simple example of a hierarchical voice network. Notice that the dial-plan hierarchy only applies to the site prefix. The phone extensions assigned within a site are irrelevant to call routing between sites. This concept is completely analogous to data routing in an IP environment. That is, IP routing tables only contain entries for IP subnets, and the arrangement of hosts within each subnet is irrelevant to IP routing between subnets.

If a user at Site C calls "22-123" to reach a user at Site F, the switches at Sites C and A know where to route the call after the first digit. The hierarchical addressing improves call processing performance, and more significantly, it reduces the number of routing entries by an order of ten for every digit that is summarized.

What happens to the call-routing summarization if Site C orders a tie line to Site F? Now calls from Site C with a destination pattern of "22..." should use the new leased line, while all other calls to "2...." should use the connection via Site A. This is not a problem. The point is, you can make variations on the basic hierarchical structure to accommodate your particular environment. It is common to have some specific routing entries to augment the summary routes, because many networks do not have a strictly hierarchical topology.

Figure 14-1   *Simple Hierarchical Network*

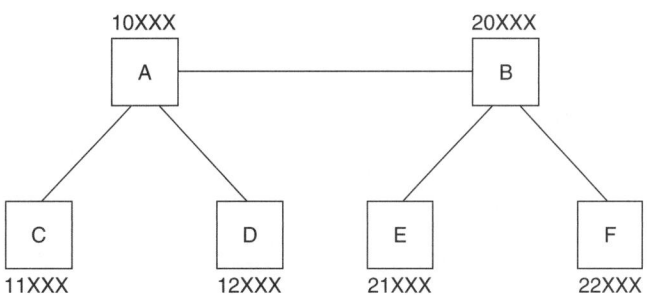

You may want to increase the reliability of your voice network by offering alternate paths to complete a call. For example, you may provision a private circuit as the primary path to complete a call between sites, with a PSTN connection as a secondary path. In order to use a PSTN connection as a secondary call path, there must be a mechanism to translate the internal phone number to a number that can be routed across the PSTN. When you use a hierarchical addressing plan, you will usually have to remove all of the site prefix digits and replace them with the appropriate string for dialing via the PSTN.

Minimizing Number Translation

To minimize number translations in site PBXs, private dialing plans must be designed to integrate with the PSTN telephone numbers assigned to the site. If direct inward dial (DID) number blocks are used, make sure the private extension range assigned to the site matches the DID blocks. Also, it is a good idea to associate site prefixes in the private numbering plan with local PSTN prefixes. This reduces the complexity of number translation procedures when routing calls between the private network and the PSTN.

You do not have much flexibility when you order a block of DID numbers for a site. Overlapping DID blocks at different sites is not a concern, because site prefixes ensure that the private numbers are unique. In most cases, the numbers assigned in the DID block represent the extensions in a site, so these digits are not considered for call routing between sites.

You have almost no flexibility with local prefixes, regional codes, and country codes of the PSTN numbers at your sites. You can order your voice circuits from a different CO to get a different local prefix for a site, or you can order FX lines to get a number in a different area code. You would not want to make either of these changes just to improve the dialing plan. When you design a voice network with many sites, there are bound to be instances where locations in different areas share the same PSTN number prefix. (See Figure 14-2.) In such cases, you must be creative to resolve the conflict. Considering that the overall goal of this numbering strategy is to reduce complications of number translations, try to assign a private site prefix that preserves as many digits of the PSTN number as possible, from right to left.

This ensures that you will only have a one-to-one translation of the far-left digits when converting between public and private numbers. Any other arrangement adds to the complexity of number translation and may not be supported on all phone switches in your network.

Figure 14-2   *Private Numbering Plan Complicated by Overlapping PSTN Local Prefixes*

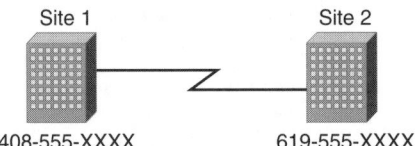

Compare the translation procedures required in a hierarchical dial plan with those required for the PSTN matching plan. In the hierarchical plan, all digits of the private site prefix must be stripped, and then replaced with a PSTN dial-string prefix. When the site prefix is aligned with the local PSTN prefix, no digits need to be stripped, and fewer digits need to be added to complete the PSTN dial string. For example, a hierarchical network might need to translate "112-1234" into "1-408-555-1234". This operation requires removal of the first three digits of the dialed string, and an addition of seven digits. For a network designed to follow the PSTN, the private dialed string would be "555-1234", so the translation procedure would only involve the addition of four digits to form the PSTN dial string.

The difficulty of this numbering-plan approach is that it does not scale well. If there are N sites in the network, then each phone switch will have approximately N routing entries. Default routing, described in the next section, provides some relief to this problem.

Using a Hybrid Approach

If your voice network has a hierarchical topology, then you may be able to align your private site prefixes with PSTN prefixes, and keep the routing tables small. The key to this balance is using default call routing. That is, every switch maintains routes for the calling prefixes in the downstream switches, and a default route pointing to the upstream switch. This concept applies to routers with dial peers just as well as to phone switches with programmed routing entries. Consider the network topology in Figure 14-3.

Figure 14-3 *Hierarchical Voice Network Topology Permits Route Summarization*

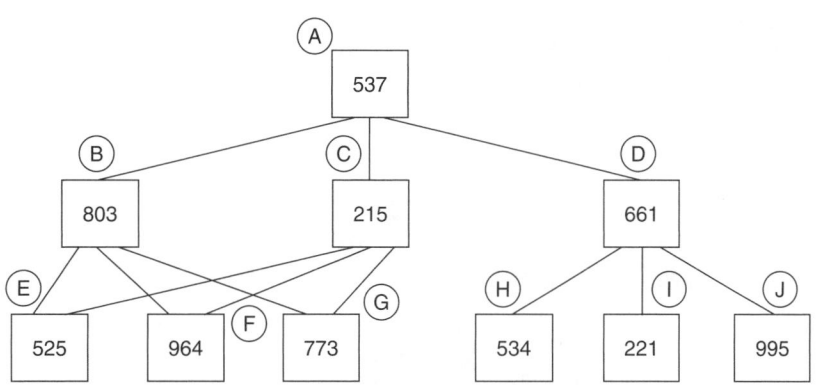

In this topology, switch A maintains a complete routing table. Switch D, however, only maintains routes for Sites H, I, J, and its own Site D. Any other destinations are reachable via a default route to switch A. The routing table of switch D is enumerated in Table 14-1.

Table 14-1 *Call-Routing Table for Switch D in Figure 14-3*

Dial String	Next Hop
661....	Local
534....	Site H
221....	Site I
995....	Site J
....	Site A

The leaf switches H, I, and J have a single upstream connection, so their routing tables consist of local site prefixes and a single default route to site D. The leaf switches E, F, and G have redundant connections to upstream neighbors. The concept of default route summarization is still valid in this context, with a slight modification. These leaf switches have a default route pointing to Sites B and C, with an optional preference assigned to one of the upstream neighbors. In addition, these leaf switches may have explicit routes for the immediately upstream neighbors to optimize call routing between these adjacent sites. For example, switch E has an explicit route for "215...." pointing to Site C. This prevents the call from unnecessarily crossing Sites B and A. Switch E also has an explicit route for "803...." pointing to Site B for similar reasons.

Choosing a Scale for the Numbering Plan

One of the first steps of a numbering-plan design is deciding the number of digits to use. Some small companies may survive with a two-digit dialing plan. Many large corporations use seven-digit dialing plans. It can be very traumatic for your organization to undergo complete renumbering, so make sure you reserve plenty of numbers for growth. There are two types of growth that you must accommodate:

- Additional sites
- Additional people at each site

To accommodate additional sites, reserve enough digits to represent the maximum number of sites that you envision for the network—think five or more years ahead. This may be a difficult proposition if your company is rapidly expanding, but do your best. You are aided by the fact that each digit increases by tenfold the number of sites you can support. You should be able to provide an estimate within an order of ten! If your network already has 50+ sites, do not do your company the disservice of using a two-digit prefix, because somebody will curse you in a few years.

As you do for prefixes, assign enough digits to the site extension to represent the maximum number of people that you envision at any site. If you know that each of your offices will never grow beyond 100 people, then you can allocate just two digits to represent the extensions in the office. If an office does grow larger, then you can assign additional prefixes to the office at that time. The risk is that the only available prefixes will damage the route summarization plan. Alternatively, you can assign three or four digits to each office, most of which will never outgrow this numbering space. The problem with this strategy is that you may waste quite a few numbers, and use more digits in the dialing plan than your company really needs.

In a large organization, there may be a substantial variation in the number of people per site. The central campus may have 30,000 people or more, while some remote offices may have as few as 30, or even 3 people! How can you assign a fixed number of digits to accommodate this variation? The answer is, do not limit yourself to using a fixed number of digits for all sites. Just as with the original Class A/B/C networks allocated for IP addresses, you can vary the boundary between site addressing and extension addressing. Another way to think of this is to create a fixed number of digits for the site extensions, and then let some large sites use contiguous ranges of site prefixes.

Consider this scenario: You have 50 remote sites with fewer than 60 people and a growing central site with 800 people. A four-digit dial plan might be sufficient for this network, using a two-digit site prefix and a two-digit site extension. You assign a unique prefix to each remote site, while you save three contiguous blocks of ten prefixes for the central site. Table 14-2 summarizes the plan.

Table 14-2 *Dial Plan Demonstrating Contiguous Blocks of Site Prefixes*

Dial String	Associated Site
01..	Remote 1
02..	Remote 2
Etc.	Etc.
50..	Remote 50
70.. to 99..	Central Site

This allows up to 3000 extensions at the central site, while each remote site can grow up to 100 extensions. You might want to reserve certain numbers such as 911, so take these prefixes into account when you estimate the amount of extensions available. In addition to the 50 remote sites allocated here, the plan can support another 19 remote sites. If any of the remote sites require more extensions in the future, it does not matter whether the additional prefixes are contiguous. Summarization is not possible unless ten prefixes are used within the same site, according to the traditional rules of routing summarization.

New features of Cisco IOS enable the creation of summarized dial peers, even if noncontiguous blocks of addresses are used. For example, if "01..", "02..", and "08.." are all associated with the same site, these prefixes can be summarized into a single Cisco dial peer with the following syntax for the destination pattern: "0[128]..". This syntax follows the regular expression syntax familiar on UNIX systems. Chapter 17, "Establishing Network-Wide Calling Capability" explores the expanded dial-peer syntax available with Cisco IOS.

A Case Study

You should keep summarization in mind even when it does not appear to be the primary design focus. Imagine that you are designing the dial plan for a simple hub-and-spoke voice network with four remote sites and a single central site. A phone switch vendor suggests the following number allocation for a three-digit plan as shown in Table 14-3.

Table 14-3 *Number Allocation in a Small Hub-and-Spoke Voice Network*

Site	Number Range
Central	100 to 299
Remote 1	300 to 349
Remote 2	350 to 399
Remote 3	400 to 449
Remote 4	450 to 499

This seems like a fine plan. You will never have more than 50 people at a remote site, so it conserves the numbering space well. You also need to reserve number ranges for two new sites. You agree to the plan and the project starts.

When you begin implementing this plan, you learn a lesson about summarization on digit boundaries. You learn this lesson while configuring dial peers on the central site router. Instead of using a single dial peer pointing to each remote site, you must create five dial peers for each remote site. To reach the first remote site, for example, you must create the following set of destination patterns: {"30." "31." "32." "33." "34."}. The second remote site uses the following set of destination patterns: {"35." "36." "37." "38." "39."}.

You are not too concerned, because the central router only requires 20 patterns (5 patterns per site, multiplied by 4 remote sites) to reach the remote offices. But then you realize that each remote site has a similar problem. When configuring the plain old telephone service (POTS) dial peers at each remote site, you must again specify a set of destination patterns. But you must configure a separate POTS dial peer for each of the six physical ports! So now you must configure five POTS dial peers for each of six voice ports (for example, analog E&M ports to a small PBX), for a total of 30 local dial peers at each remote site. There would have been six local dial peers if the plan had been designed better.

Actually, there is a solution for the POTS dial peer problem at the remote sites. Remember that the router will select the dial peer that matches the most explicit digits of a destination pattern. Using the first remote site as an example, you can use "3.." as the destination pattern for the POTS dial peer associated with each voice port. Then you rely on the longest-match lookup to route calls to the second remote site with the following VoX destination patterns: {"35." "36." "37." "38." "39."}. Be aware that if the VoX dial peers become unavailable (for example, WAN failure), then these calls are redirected back to the PBX on another local voice port because the "3.." dial peer will match! Where 35 dial peers had been required to distinguish local calls from calls to the second remote site, now only 10 dial peers are required. Additional dial peers are still required to reach the central and other remote sites.

After this experience, you decide to redesign the numbering plan, as shown in Table 14-4.

Table 14-4 *Better Number Allocation in a Small Hub-and-Spoke Voice Network*

Site	Number Range
Central	100 to 299
Remote 1	300 to 399
Remote 2	400 to 499
Remote 3	500 to 599
Remote 4	600 to 699

Your central site router now requires only 4 dial peers instead of 20 dial peers to reach the remote sites—a fivefold reduction. In addition, each remote site only requires 6 POTS dial peers with no tricks to route calls properly.

The proliferation of dial peers does not seem like much of a problem in this network because it is small, but consider this problem in a large network. If each remote site uses 24 or 30 voice ports instead of only 6, you must configure over 100 local POTS dial peers for each router. If there are 100 remote sites, then you must configure 500 extra dial peers because of poor dial-plan summarization! Now the bad design becomes practically impossible.

The overall problem here is that the uniqueness of a site prefix is compromised to represent more sites in fewer prefix digits. The numbering plan recommended by the phone switch vendor can accommodate the central site and up to 14 remote sites, seemingly with a single prefix digit. Because a single-decimal digit can accommodate only 10 values, some information must be borrowed from the local extension digits to encode all of the sites. In fact, the number of prefix digits is a noninteger value between 1 and 2 in this case. This is a reasonable solution if you want to minimize the number of dialed digits, but represent more sites. Just be aware that from a call-routing perspective, you are really dealing with a 2-digit dial-peer structure that can accommodate 100 sites. Accordingly, you should expect more complexity when dealing with the dial plan.

Note that recent changes to Cisco's dial-peer implementation make your job of designing the integrated dial plan easier. You now have the flexibility to create dial peers that reference multiple prefixes with a single pattern. As long as you can work with Cisco IOS after 12.1(1)T, you can take advantage of dial-peer features that sidestep the problem described in the preceding paragraphs. See Chapter 17 for more information about the extended syntax for destination patterns in Cisco dial peers.

Creating a Routing Plan

A key decision for the integrated voice/data network design is where to locate the call routing intelligence. There are few formal guidelines, but the parties involved may have strong opinions. For example, a telecom manager may not like the idea of placing the call-routing intelligence into Cisco routers. The data manager may think it is a great idea. Resolving these conflicts is outside the scope of this book. Instead, the focus here is to highlight design practices based on technical merits.

Opposite Ends of a Spectrum

You must decide on a specific strategy for distributing the call-routing intelligence between phone switches and multiservice routers. Before making an arbitrary decision, you should understand the variety of solutions that are possible. This allows you to weigh the merits of various scenarios and make an informed decision.

Consider the variety of solutions as a spectrum, as illustrated in Figure 14-4.

Figure 14-4 *Possibilities for Distributing Routing Intelligence*

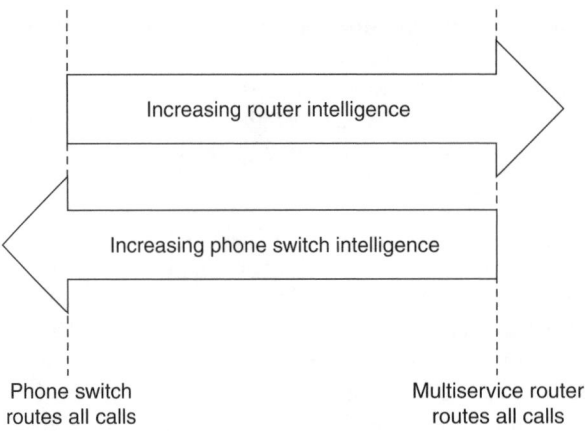

On one end of the spectrum, the phone switches maintain all of the call-routing intelligence for the network. In this scenario, the multiservice routers are not involved in routing each call. Instead, the routers provide transparent connections from remote stations or switches to a central PBX that routes the calls. The routers provide transport between fixed destinations, and the equipment on either end of the transport peer directly with each other. For example, Cisco routers might replace carrier-provided OPX or FXS circuits. Figure 14-5 illustrates this scenario.

Figure 14-5 *Call-Routing Intelligence Based in Traditional Telephony Equipment*

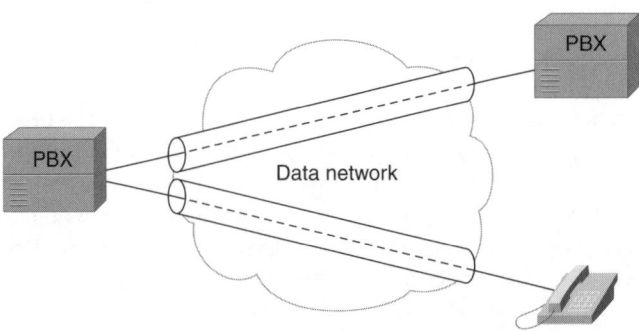

On the other end of the spectrum, the multiservice routers contain all of the call-routing intelligence. In this scenario, the primary job of the phone switches is to provide connections for the end stations. The phone switches may provide connections and call routing to the PSTN, but the multiservice routers control the internal voice traffic. The phone switches may also provide additional calling features, voice mail, and auto-attendant functions, but these services are mostly restricted to the local site. The phone switches at each site peer with a multiservice router at the same site, so there is no direct communication between phone switches at different locations. Figure 14-6 illustrates this scenario.

Figure 14-6   *Call-Routing Intelligence Based in Multiservice Routers*

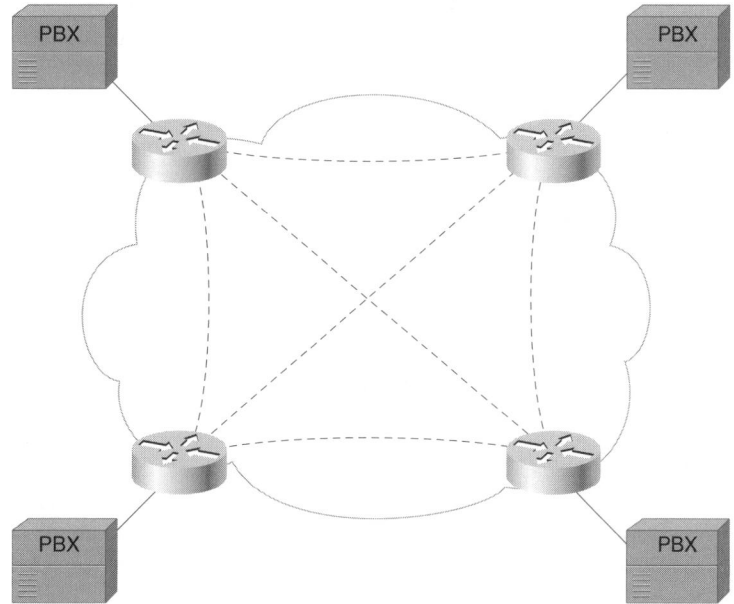

It is important to note that your network may not have a uniform design. Some sites may completely leverage the routers for call-routing intelligence, while others might use the routers purely as a transport for signaling between remote phone switches. Still other sites may be somewhere between the two ends of the spectrum. The next few sections explore the advantages and disadvantages associated with each end of the spectrum. You should leverage the strengths of each approach to efficiently and economically meet your needs.

Leveraging Strengths of the Router

Multiservice routers bring the following benefits to your traditional telephony network:

- Simplified tie-line topology
- Bandwidth efficiency and economy
- Migration toward multiservice applications

These topics are addressed in the following sections.

Simplified Tie-Line Topology

Consider a voice network with a partially meshed tie-line topology, as shown in Figure 14-7.

Figure 14-7 *Partially Meshed Voice Tie-Line Topology*

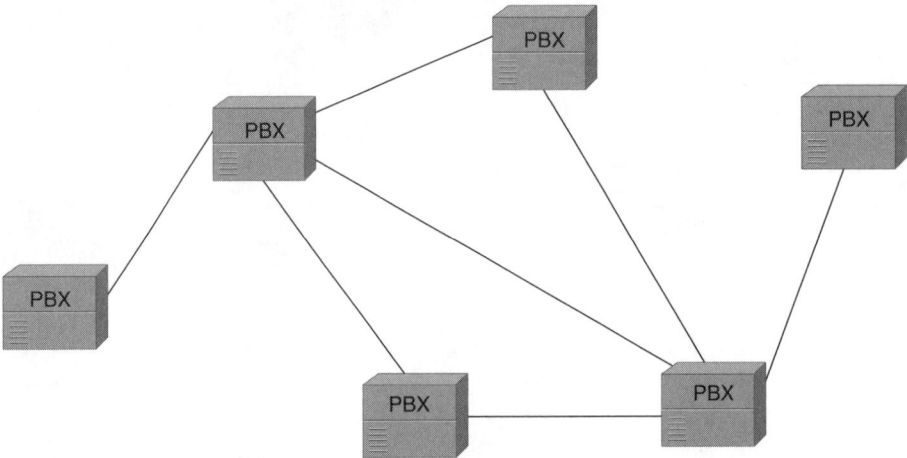

Consider the administration for all of these voice circuits in addition to the data circuits. Also consider the call-routing table maintenance—how multiple phone switches along a path must be configured to route calls between remote locations. Now imagine how this network can look when integrated with the data network as shown in Figure 14-8.

You may be thinking, "Sure it looks cleaner from the phone switch perspective, but isn't the complication just shifted to the routers?" In some flavors of VoX this is basically true, but think about VoIP. Instead of explicitly identifying a call route in every call-routing hop to reach a remote destination, you merely specify an IP address on the other side of the IP cloud! You can leverage the IP-routing infrastructure to reduce the number of call-routing hops. You can also increase the reliability of any call-routing hop because IP can dynamically reroute around failures. Have you ever heard of traditional tie-line backups that do not disrupt the calls in progress? This is a very compelling technical argument for using multiservice routers for call routing.

Figure 14-8   *Fully Meshed Virtual Tie-Lines in a Voice/Data Network*

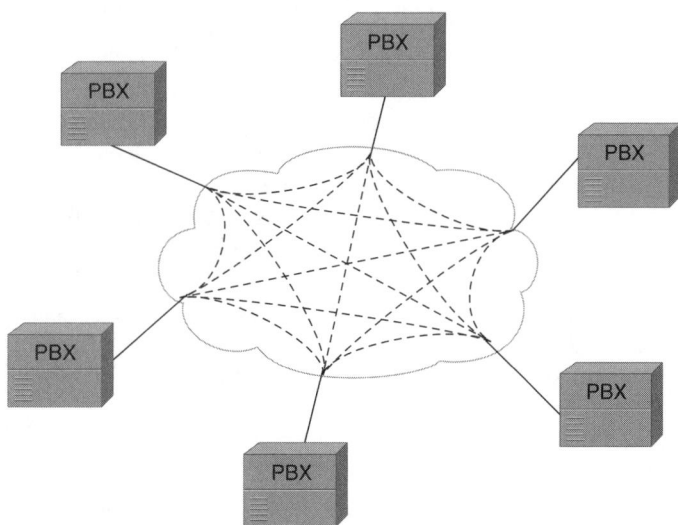

Bandwidth Efficiency and Economy

Multiservice routers offer efficiency and economy for intersite telephony networks. That is, the routers help reduce bandwidth usage and recurring circuit fees for telephone connectivity between sites. The routers achieve this feat via two mechanisms:

- Voice compression
- Intelligent bandwidth sharing for voice and data over WAN links

Voice compression introduces a dramatic reduction in WAN bandwidth requirements for voice. The voice signal can be compressed eight times or more with little reduction in voice quality, provided certain design caveats are addressed. Though some PBX manufacturers offer proprietary voice-compression algorithms, or even support for the standards-based ADPCM, Cisco routers offer a variety of standards-based compression options that give you flexibility to choose the best technology for your environment. These options range from a full duplex 64 kbps per voice channel using a G.711 codec, down to simplex 5.3 kbps per voice channel using the G.723.1 codec with voice activity detection (VAD) and silence suppression.

Routers are uniquely positioned to offer another major benefit. Routers can intelligently share bandwidth between voice and data traffic with the granularity of individual packets. Not considering the benefit of voice compression, a router can pass a single voice channel and approximately 64 kbps of data across a 128-kbps leased-line circuit. When there are no voice calls, the router can use the full 128 kbps for data traffic. Even better, the router can extract additional bandwidth for data from the silent portions of active voice calls.

Phone switches must reserve a duplex 64-kbps stream for the duration of the call, whether or not useful information is being transmitted in this stream. Routers can release the potential bandwidth from the silent parts of the conversation that occur in each direction. For example, while you are listening to another party speak during a conversation, the router can send extra data across the link because there is no audio information to send from your side. When you begin speaking, the router transmits your speech, and the remote router can send extra data because the other party is listening to you. This functionality is called *voice activity detection (VAD)* with silence suppression. This concept alone nearly doubles the efficiency of voice conversations through a router versus a traditional phone switch. In order for a phone switch to match this performance (in terms of bandwidth sharing at the packet level), it must become a router!

Migration Toward Multiservice Applications

New applications are rapidly evolving that allow multiple users to communicate via real-time audio and video teleconferences with file sharing, screen sharing, and other data applications. Most of these applications revolve around the ITU-T recommendation H.323 and related H-series recommendations, or the IETF-sponsored Session Initiation Protocol (SIP) and related protocols. IP is the common network protocol for these developments, though no network layer protocol is mandated in H.323.

Multiservice routers can act as gateways between traditional telephony systems and the new breed of communication terminals. While the end stations attached to a traditional PBX cannot participate in a videoconference, they can join the audio portion of the conference via a router acting as an H.323 or SIP gateway. Routers help bridge the gap between current communication practices (such as traditional telephony) and future communication practices (such as H.323 or SIP applications).

If you want to integrate your traditional telephony systems with emerging H.323 or SIP-based applications, then your multiservice routers must be involved with call routing. Incidentally, you must use VoIP, or have other routers that can interwork between your VoX and VoIP, to allow access to the H.323 multipoint conferencing units.

Leveraging Strengths of the Existing Phone Switch

Traditional phone systems are not well suited for wide area networking, but you should take advantage of the following functions that they provide:

- Phone station aggregation
- Advanced calling features
- Secure access to the PSTN

When integrating your voice and data networks, the primary use of a traditional phone switch is to provide connections to the phone stations. Presumably, you have an investment in your current phone switch and the attached phones, and you do not want to throw away this investment. You can continue to use your existing phones, though some of the functionality may change when you merge the voice and data networks. For example, if you switch from common channel signaling (CCS) to channel associated signaling (CAS), you may lose proprietary phone switch functions such as message-waiting lights.

The phone switches also provide useful features such as call forwarding, music on hold, transfer, conference calling, and so on. Review Chapter 1, "The State of Voice Communications," for a description of various calling features. Voice mail and auto-attendant functions are often associated with phone switches. They may be part of a hybrid key system unit (KSU), or another piece of hardware may provide these functions. In any case, voice mail and auto-attendant features are most likely a part of your traditional telephony environment, and you should take advantage of them in your integrated voice and data network.

Phone switches often have robust functions for regulating call access. Phone stations connected to a switch may be divided into different groups, and different levels of calling privileges may be assigned to each group. These features are useful to limit the abuse of your phone system policies. For example, you may not want anyone in the PSTN to receive dial tone from your phone switch, and then place calls to other countries or 1-900-SEX-CALL. You probably do not want anyone from the PSTN to have access to your private trunk lines either, unless they have a password. Similarly, you can restrict access from phones in common areas such as the lobby or lunchroom. It is possible to completely restrict calls to certain numbers using routers, but in general you cannot use routers to restrict calling on a per-user basis.

It is important to note that VoIP is evolving rapidly, and will soon be in a position to offer more robust security and policy services than traditional phone switches. Policy and access servers in an IP network promise to provide as much granularity for policy control as you are prepared to develop.

Additional Dial-Plan Considerations

It is crucial that you consider how voice quality is affected by your dial-plan decision. Because it controls the physical path that the audio channel follows, the dial plan affects the audio signal in several ways:

- Gain or loss
- Delay and jitter
- Echo
- Codec distortion

All of these factors affect voice quality. The first three items must be addressed in any telephony environment (well, maybe not jitter). Chapter 5, "Defining and Measuring Voice Quality," and Chapter 18, "Resolving Voice Quality Issues," explore the voice quality implications of these factors. The last item, codec distortion, is of the utmost importance for an integrated voice and data network.

When designing the dial plan, you should be primarily concerned with two key parts of the audio path. These parts are the analog portions of the audio path, and the codec conversion points. The analog portions of the audio path are subject to echoes, quietness, and distortion from various sources. The coder/decoder function may greatly reduce voice quality if it is applied multiple times to the same signal. These trouble spots occur mostly at the interface between the routers and the phone switches. Your design goal should be to minimize the number of times that the audio path crosses these interfaces.

TIP   When designing the dial plan, minimize the number of times that a call crosses the interface between a router and a phone switch.

The audio path remains digitized within the router network, so delay, jitter, and packet loss are the only factors that impact voice quality when the call traverses the router network. These three factors are managed as part of a solid network design, with proper consideration for QoS requirements.

You should be mindful of call routing through a data network that traverses numerous WAN circuits, because the cumulative delay may exceed desirable levels. Even in a hub-and-spoke frame relay network, voice calls between remote sites may experience excessive delay because of tandem routing through the central site. In these scenarios, it may be a good idea to order a voice-only PVC directly between remote sites that have justifiable voice traffic. (See Figure 14-9.) The frame relay port is already established, and normal data traffic still routes through the central site, but the separate PVC for voice can greatly improve voice quality.

Following are two common examples where the dial-plan design might adversely affect voice quality:

- Call detail reporting (CDR) from a central PBX
- Common channel signaling (CCS)

Figure 14-9   *Using a Dedicated PVC Between Remote Sites to Reduce Delay for Voice Calls*

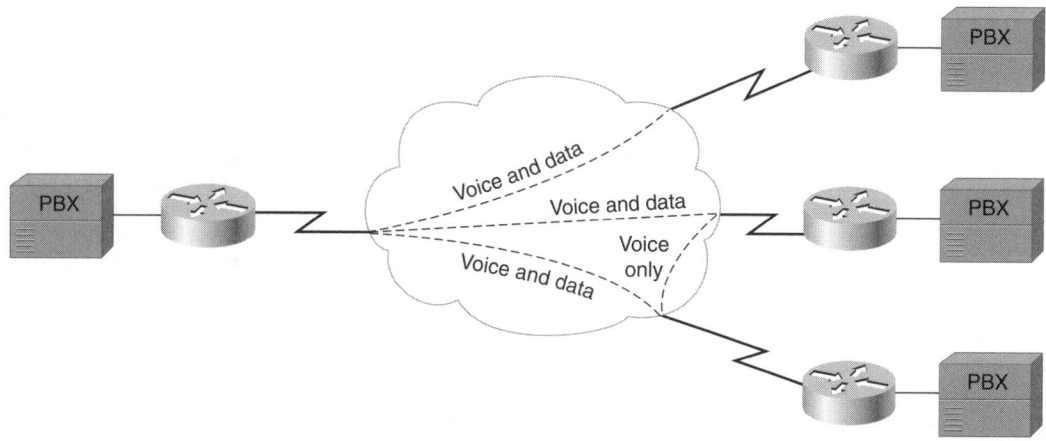

Some voice network administrators need accurate CDR features for departmental bill-back procedures, or for whatever reason. Since they are not familiar with SNMP, or the call detail reporting features of Cisco routers, they might insist that tandem calls route through the PBX whenever possible. In Figure 14-10, the PBX in the central site performs the tandem call routing:

Figure 14-10   *Call Routing Through the Central Site PBX to Maintain Call Detail Reporting (CDR)*

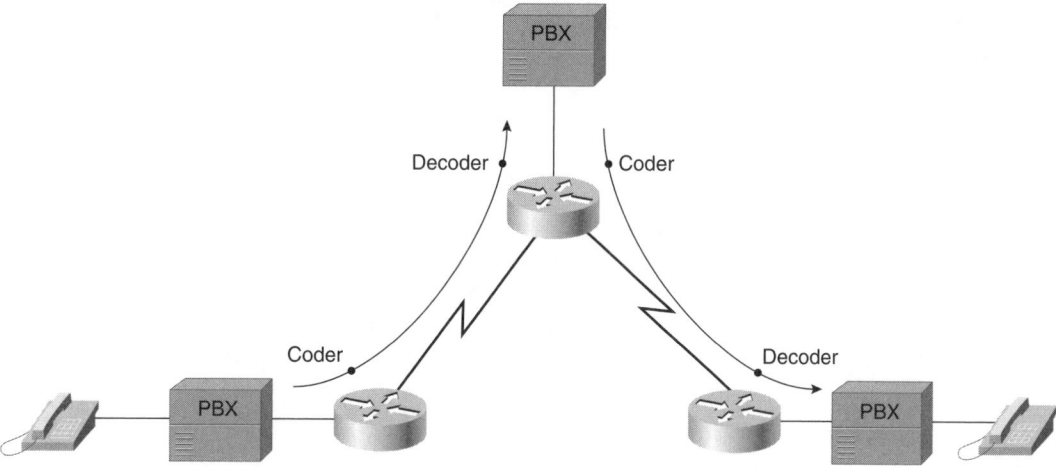

Follow the audio signal as it is compressed at the first router and decompressed at the central router for transit to the PBX. After the PBX routes the call back to the router, the signal is again compressed, and decompressed at the destination site router. This is a simple case of a call directly between two sites, with no transfers or rerouting for voice mail. All calls between sites will have questionable voice quality if a low bit-rate codec (such as G.729, G.723.1) is used in this scenario. Refer back to Chapter 6, "Voice Digitization and Coding," to see how different codec algorithms perform under multiple coding/decoding cycles.

Now consider an improved dial plan, where the router at the central site performs the tandem routing. In Figure 14-11, the central site router does not rely on the PBX to route calls, so the router does not have to decompress and recompress the voice signal. The audio quality is much better for calls between sites because there are fewer compression/decompression cycles.

Figure 14-11   *Voice Quality Improves when Central Site Router Performs Tandem Call Routing*

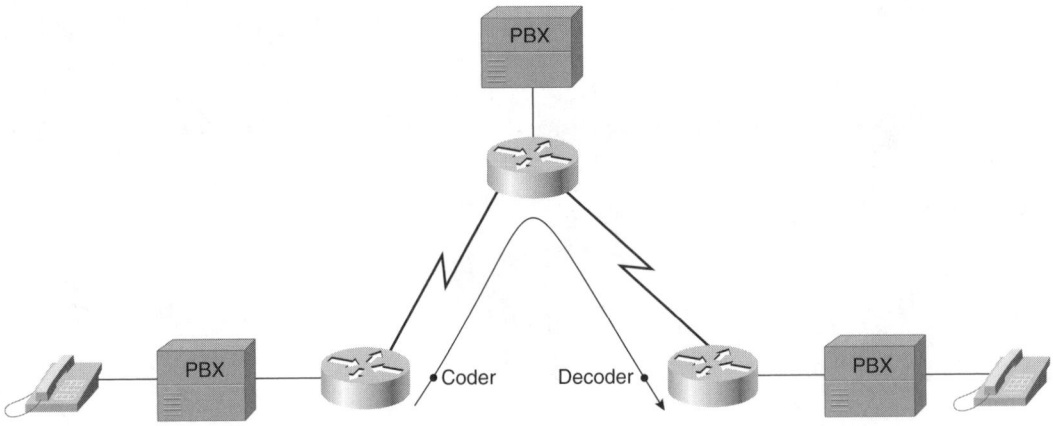

Tandem call routing through a PBX can also be a problem because of common channel signaling (CCS). Consider a voice network where the routers transparently pass a CCS signaling channel between phone switches, and forward all voice calls along a fixed path between the phone switches. In Figure 14-12, it is clear that all calls that tandem through the central site PBX must incur the penalty of double coding/decoding.

Figure 14-12   *Tandem Routing Through CCS Links Causes Multiple Coder/Decoder Cycles*

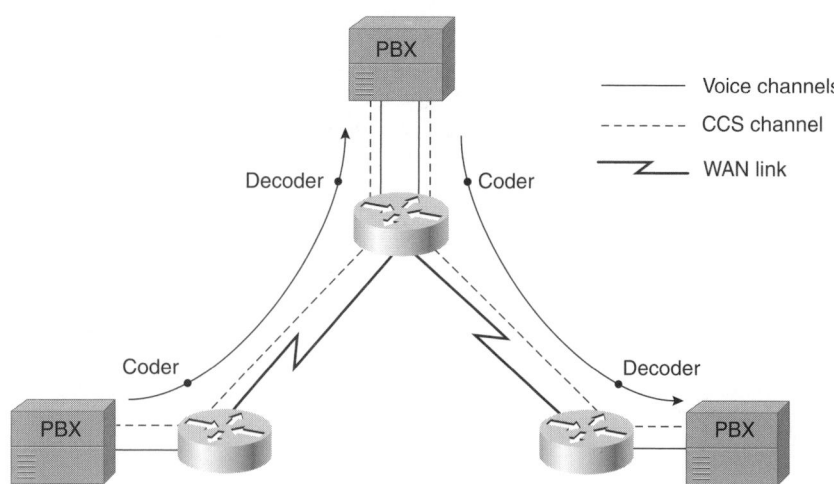

Voice quality is barely acceptable in this scenario, but what happens if the call must be transferred, or forwarded to a central site voice mail? Centralized voice mail is one of the primary reasons that companies want to maintain a CCS network. Any calls between sites that must forward to voice mail will require three coder/decoder cycles! In practice, this is unacceptable for low bit-rate codecs, despite what published results may indicate. In this case, you have no real choice but to use a high bit-rate codec like G.711 or G.726.

Common channel signaling will not cause voice quality problems if the router can directly peer with the PBX and understand the CCS messages. This is because the router can then make a routing decision without requiring the decompression/recompression of the audio signal. Most often, the router cannot peer with the PBX because there are proprietary CCS signaling methods and technology licensing issues between the vendors. A notable exception is NEC Fusion signaling, which is the result of a collaboration between Cisco and NEC. QSIG offers a standards-based signaling approach that resolves the vendor interoperability issue and facilitates multivendor CCS networks.

QSIG is standardized in a series of documents from the European Computer Manufacturers Association (ECMA). You can download the specifications from the ECMA web site:

www.ecma.ch/

You can learn more about QSIG from the ISDN PBX Network Specification (IPNS) Forum at the following URL:

www.qsig.ie/

To get you started, Chapter 2, "Enterprise Telephony Signaling," provides an overview of QSIG signaling and the various supplemental services that have been standardized.

Summary

To summarize the key point from a dial plan perspective, you should ensure that routers make routing decisions for tandem calls. If you involve a PBX to make a tandem routing decision (when calls are just passing through the site), then voice quality will suffer. This is the most crucial point of designing a call routing plan that integrates routers and traditional phone switches. You will experience fewer problems down the road if you heed this advice.

If you have read this book in order, you are now armed with most of the information you need to avoid the major pitfalls of voice/data network design. Of course, you will still suffer somewhat as you discover design points on your own. But that is one of the beauties of our profession; there is an unending stream of opportunity to expand our knowledge!

PART IV

Implementation and Cisco Router Configuration

The following chapters present the Cisco router configurations required to implement integrated voice and data networks. The preceding chapters in this book have developed the conceptual background that relates to the material in these chapters.

Chapter 15 describes how to configure Cisco routers to use the quality of service (QoS) features that were introduced at a conceptual level in Chapter 10. These features include congestion avoidance, queuing techniques, resource reservation, traffic shaping and policing, and fragmentation/interleaving techniques.

Chapter 16 illustrates both the minimal and the optional voice-port configurations to establish connectivity between a Cisco router and a variety of traditional telephony equipment, including key systems, PBXs, and Central Office (CO) phone switches. The configuration elements explored in this chapter are closely related to the material discussed in Chapter 2. Appendixes B and C support the maintenance and troubleshooting discussions of this chapter.

Chapter 17 considers the end-to-end calling path through a VoX network, which includes dial-peer issues, call routing, connection modes (for example, PLAR, PLAR-OPX, trunk, tie line), and session protocols. In addition, VoIP scalability with H.323 is given careful consideration. Appendix D supports the maintenance and troubleshooting discussions of this chapter.

Chapter 18 addresses voice quality issues that may arise after end-to-end calling connectivity is established. The chapter classifies different types of voice quality problems and offers solutions to correct these problems. Related areas such as inconsistent DTMF digit recognition are also covered.

CHAPTER 15

Enabling Network-Wide Quality of Service

A quality of service (QoS)–enabled infrastructure consistently provides end-to-end transmission with low delay, jitter, and packet-loss characteristics for defined traffic types and bandwidth requirements. Even though QoS mechanisms are only required for the paths that transport voice or other real-time traffic, developing a QoS plan for your entire network positions your organization for ubiquitous use of VoIP and real-time multiservice applications.

Enabling network-wide QoS is the process of knitting together disparate technologies to achieve the common goal of managing reliability, delay, and jitter. As the network architect, you must have the vision for how the QoS tools work together to meet these goals. Chapter 11, "VoIP Transport and Signaling Protocols," helps you develop that vision by exploring IP QoS mechanisms at a conceptual level, while this chapter is focused on Cisco router implementation of the following technologies:

- Congestion avoidance
- Congestion management
- IP precedence
- Resource Reservation Protocol (RSVP)
- Link fragmentation/interleaving
- Traffic shaping and policing
- Header compression

This chapter does not—nor does it intend to—provide exhaustive coverage of QoS configuration options. The scope of this book is too wide to permit that level of detail. If you need more information about any of the topics described in this chapter, consult the Quality of Service Solutions Configuration Guide and Command Reference sections of Cisco Connection Online (CCO), which you can find starting from the documentation home page:

www.cisco.com/univercd/home/home.htm

Congestion Avoidance

Senders of TCP traffic flows respond to network congestion conditions by reducing the number of packets offered to the network. This TCP host behavior, which is related to dampening, negative feedback, or control theory in other technology areas, was proposed by Van Jacobson to enhance the overall stability of TCP/IP networks. Chapter 10, "Review of IP Features for Voice/Data Integration," provides a detailed examination of TCP behavior in congested networks.

Core network routers can use Random Early Detection (RED) or Weighted RED (WRED) to exploit the self-regulating transmission behavior of TCP hosts by randomly discarding occasional (nonadjacent) packets before router queues become full. Whereas RED provides equal drop probabilities for all packets at a given queue depth threshold, WRED allows different packet drop probabilities and thresholds for different classes of traffic (for example, different applications). The conceptual underpinnings of RED and WRED are explored in detail in Chapter 10.

RED and WRED fill the QoS niche for high bandwidth links (that is, greater than E-1) at the core of a network, where other queuing techniques cannot operate. Both RED and WRED exhibit scalable performance as packet throughput increases, because they have modest CPU and buffer requirements. In addition, the congestion-avoidance algorithms are more effective at optimizing bandwidth utilization when there are large numbers of TCP flows. Though RED and WRED are ideally suited for high bandwidth links in lieu of other queuing techniques, you can also use them within the framework of class-based weighted-fair queuing, which is discussed later in this chapter.

If VoIP packets cross the core of your network, then you should use WRED on all core router interfaces that have the potential to be congested. Otherwise, VoIP packets may be dropped because of full interface buffers. To ensure that VoIP traffic receives the best treatment from WRED, you should set the IP precedence value to 5 for all VoIP packets. Remember that WRED drops packets with less frequency as the IP precedence value increases.

You can enable WRED on a router interface with the command shown in Example 15-1.

Example 15-1 *Configuring Weighted Random Early Detection (WRED)*

```
r2#conf t
Enter configuration commands, one per line.  End with CNTL/Z.
r2 (config)#interface serial0
r2 (config-if)#random-detect
r2 (config-if)#random-detect exponential-weighting-constant 10
r2 (config-if)#^Z
r2#
```

Note that WRED may also be used on subinterfaces, virtual circuits, and different traffic classes in CB-WFQ. The probability of a WRED packet drop when the queue is at the maximum threshold is provided by the following equation:

$$P = \left(\frac{1}{2^C} \right)$$

where C is the exponential weighting constant. The default value of 9 has been carefully selected by Cisco, based on empirical research of traffic performance with RED in the Internet. Unless you have performed studies in your network that indicate another value should be used, you should not tune this parameter.

You can monitor the performance of WRED with the command in Example 15-2.

Example 15-2 *Verifying Operation of Weighted Random Early Detection (WRED)*

```
r2#show queueing random-detect
Current random-detect configuration:
  Serial0
    Queueing strategy: random early detection (WRED)
    Exp-weight-constant: 9 (1/512)
    Mean queue depth: 0

    Class   Random      Tail    Minimum     Maximum     Mark
            drop        drop    threshold   threshold   probability
      0       0           0        20          40        1/10
      1       0           0        22          40        1/10
      2       0           0        24          40        1/10
      3       0           0        26          40        1/10
      4       0           0        28          40        1/10
      5       0           0        31          40        1/10
      6       0           0        33          40        1/10
      7       0           0        35          40        1/10
    rsvp      0           0        37          40        1/10

r2#
```

Although the default values are carefully selected for most cases, you can adjust the minimum and maximum queue-depth thresholds for each WRED process, as well as the discard probability when the queue depth is at the maximum threshold level. Consider for example, that you use Resource Reservation Protocol (RSVP) or IP precedence in conjunction with VoIP. Because VoIP is UDP-based, senders do not throttle transmission in response to packet drops. Using RED on such traffic flows is pointless. Actually, it is worse than pointless—it is counterproductive. You can effectively disable WRED for such flows, while still preserving WRED for other flow types, with the commands found in Example 15-3.

Example 15-3 *Tuning Performance for Weighted Random Early Detection (WRED)*

```
r2#conf t
Enter configuration commands, one per line.  End with CNTL/Z.
r2 (config-if)#random-detect precedence 5 100 101 65536
r2 (config-if)#random-detect precedence rsvp 100 101 65536
r2 (config-if)#^Z
r2#
```

The effect of this change is that for RSVP or critical (5) IP precedence flows, 100 packets must be queued before WRED drops are possible, and then the WRED drop probability is only 0.0015 percent. If you do not have memory resource constraints in your routers, then you can set the threshold queue depths as high as 4096, which further reduces the effective WRED drop rate for these flows.

RED concepts are documented in RFC 2309, and the following URL is an excellent repository of RED research:

> www.aciri.org/floyd/red.html

Congestion Management

When more packets are supplied to an interface than the interface can transmit in a given amount of time, some of the packets must wait. Queuing strategies sort the waiting packets according to various rules, such as first-come first-served, strict preference for certain traffic types, or equal sharing of bandwidth for different traffic flows. Newer queuing techniques are a hybrid of these basic types that combine the best features of each. These powerful new congestion management tools come at the expense of the increased configuration complexity.

The following queuing techniques are demonstrated in this section:

- First-in first-out (FIFO) queuing
- Priority queuing
- Custom queuing
- Flow-based weighted-fair queuing (WFQ)
- IP RTP Priority
- Class-based weighted-fair queuing (CB-WFQ)

FIFO Queuing

On high-bandwidth interfaces, FIFO queuing is the default. Some people also refer to this queuing type as first-come first-served (FCFS). On serial interfaces operating at an E1 rate or lower, disabling the default WFQ enables FIFO queuing as shown in Example 15-4.

Example 15-4 *Configuring FIFO Queuing*

```
r2#conf t
Enter configuration commands, one per line.  End with CNTL/Z.
r2(config)#interface serial0
r2(config-if)#no fair-queue
r2(config-if)#^Z
r2#
```

You can examine the status of the FIFO queue with the command found in Example 15-5.

As indicated in the preceding example, the outbound FIFO queue can hold 40 packets, but there are currently no packets in the queue. The inbound FIFO queue can hold 75 packets,

Example 15-5 *Verifying the Operation of FIFO Queuing*

```
r2#show interface serial0
Serial0 is up, line protocol is up
  Hardware is HD64570
  Internet address is 1.1.1.1/24
  MTU 1500 bytes, BW 1544 Kbit, DLY 20000 usec, rely 255/255, load 1/255
  Encapsulation HDLC, loopback not set, keepalive set (10 sec)
  Last input 00:00:08, output 00:00:03, output hang never
  Last clearing of "show interface" counters never
  Queueing strategy: fifo
  Output queue 0/40, 0 drops; input queue 0/75, 0 drops
  5 minute input rate 0 bits/sec, 0 packets/sec
  5 minute output rate 0 bits/sec, 0 packets/sec
     516 packets input, 31410 bytes, 0 no buffer
     Received 516 broadcasts, 0 runts, 0 giants, 0 throttles
     0 input errors, 0 CRC, 0 frame, 0 overrun, 0 ignored, 0 abort
     664 packets output, 40026 bytes, 0 underruns
     0 output errors, 0 collisions, 8 interface resets
     0 output buffer failures, 0 output buffers swapped out
     0 carrier transitions
     DCD=up  DSR=up  DTR=up  RTS=up  CTS=up
r2#
```

but there are no packets presently in the queue. No packets have been dropped, which indicates that this interface has not experienced congestion.

FIFO queuing is not desirable as a standalone method to manage interface congestion. If configuration simplicity is required, WFQ is a better choice for low-speed links. FIFO queuing should be used with WRED for high-speed links.

Priority Queuing

Priority queuing is applicable to serial interfaces that operate at line rates up to and including E1 (2.048 Mbps). As indicated in Chapter 10, *priority queuing* satisfies the queuing requirements for voice traffic, but each queue can starve queues of lower priority. That is, low-priority queues may never be allowed to transmit packets if the higher-priority queues always have traffic to transmit.

In general, you should use one of the newer queuing techniques such as IP RTP Priority or low latency queuing (LLQ) to ensure that VoIP packets get high-priority treatment. However, the traditional priority queuing is more flexible if you have multiple types of high-priority traffic. For example, if you have VoIP and Systems Network Architecture (SNA) traffic flowing across the same links, then you can set VoIP packets to have high priority, and assign SNA traffic to medium priority. This way, SNA is still prioritized ahead of all data traffic, but it does not impair voice quality.

Priority queuing is also appropriate when mixing VoIP traffic with real-time video-conferencing traffic. You can ensure that VoIP receives the best service, and that IP video-conferencing (IPVC) traffic is prioritized ahead of regular data traffic without impacting VoIP traffic. If you have the challenging requirements of VoIP, video-conferencing, and

SNA traffic over the same link, you can set the default queuing priority to low so that you have three different queues for higher-priority treatment. VoIP should always be in the high priority queue, but you can experiment with the order in which SNA and video traffic are assigned to the medium and normal queues.

TIP	Use priority queuing when mixing VoIP with SNA, video-conferencing, or other real-time applications.

The following steps are required to enable priority queuing on an interface:

Step 1   Identify traffic types for each of the four priority queues.

Step 2   Assign a maximum queue depth to each of the priority queues.

Step 3   Assign the priority queues to an interface.

Traffic is assigned to one of four priority queues (high, medium, normal, low) based on network protocol, packet size, originating interface, or an access list that identifies specific addresses or higher-layer protocols. Queue depths are independently assigned to each queue, so you can regulate whether packets are delayed or dropped during congestion. Because packets in the lower-priority queues must wait more often, the lower-priority queues can accommodate more packets by default.

Example 15-6 classifies DLSW traffic as medium priority, VoIP traffic as high priority, and all other traffic as normal priority. Note that access list 102, which is not shown here, matches the VoIP traffic. VoIP packets that originate on Cisco routers use UDP port numbers in the range 16,384 to 16,384 + 4N, where N is the number of voice calls that the router can support. The queue depth is explicitly set to the default value of 20 packets for the high queue, 40 packets for the medium queue, 60 packets for the normal queue, and 80 packets for the low queue. The priority group is then applied to an interface.

Example 15-6   *Configuring Priority Queuing*

```
r2#conf t
Enter configuration commands, one per line.  End with CNTL/Z.
r2(config)#priority-list 1 protocol dlsw medium
r2(config)#priority-list 1 protocol ip high list 102
r2(config)#priority-list 1 default normal
r2(config)#priority-list 1 queue-limit 20 40 60 80
r2(config)#interface serial0
r2(config-if)#priority-group 1
r2(config-if)#^Z
r2#
```

The following commands enable you to verify how traffic is sorted into the queues and monitor the number of packets in each queue as shown in Example 15-7.

Example 15-7   *Verifying Configuration and Operation of Priority Queues*

```
r2#show queueing priority
Current priority queue configuration:

List   Queue  Args
1      medium protocol dlsw
1      high   protocol ip          list 102
r2#
r2#show interface s0
Serial0 is up, line protocol is up
  Hardware is HD64570
  Internet address is 1.1.1.1/24
  MTU 1500 bytes, BW 1544 Kbit, DLY 20000 usec, rely 255/255, load 1/255
  Encapsulation HDLC, loopback not set, keepalive set (10 sec)
  Last input 00:00:03, output 00:00:08, output hang never
  Last clearing of "show interface" counters never
  Input queue: 0/75/0 (size/max/drops); Total output drops: 0
  Queueing strategy: priority-list 1
  Output queue (queue priority: size/max/drops):
     high: 0/20/0, medium: 0/40/0, normal: 0/60/0, low: 0/80/0
  5 minute input rate 0 bits/sec, 0 packets/sec
  5 minute output rate 0 bits/sec, 0 packets/sec
     670 packets input, 40386 bytes, 0 no buffer
     Received 670 broadcasts, 0 runts, 0 giants, 0 throttles
     0 input errors, 0 CRC, 0 frame, 0 overrun, 0 ignored, 0 abort
     864 packets output, 51612 bytes, 0 underruns
     0 output errors, 0 collisions, 9 interface resets
     0 output buffer failures, 0 output buffers swapped out
     0 carrier transitions
     DCD=up  DSR=up  DTR=up  RTS=up  CTS=up
r2#
```

If you have multiple virtual circuits on a router interface (or subinterface), you can apply a separate priority group to each virtual circuit (VC), as opposed to the interface as a whole. You must first assign the priority group to a map class. The map class must then be applied to a VC as seen in Example 15-8.

Example 15-8   *Priority Queuing at the VC Level*

```
r2#conf t
Enter configuration commands, one per line.  End with CNTL/Z.
r2(config)#map-class frame-relay Prioritize
r2(config-map-class)#frame-relay priority-group 1
r2(config-map-class)#exit
r2(config)#interface serial1
r2(config-if)#frame-relay interface-dlci 16
r2(config-fr-dlci)#class Prioritize
r2(config-fr-dlci)#^Z
r2#
```

You can also send traffic from each queue in a priority group to a different VC. For example, you can direct traffic from the high queue to data-link connection identifier (DLCI) 16 and direct the medium, normal, and low queues to DLCI 17. All the PVCs in the priority DLCI group share the same network layer addressing, which simplifies routing (that is, no policy routing required). Each of the PVCs in the priority DLCI group must be associated with the interface, but you only need to provide DLCI-to-network-address mapping for the DLCI associated with the high-priority traffic. The other PVCs on the (sub)interface are implicitly mapped to the same network addresses shown in Example 15-9.

Example 15-9   *Sending Traffic from Each Queue in a Priority Group to Different VCs*

```
r2#conf t
Enter configuration commands, one per line.  End with CNTL/Z.
r2(config)#interface serial0
r2(config-if)#ip address 2.2.2.1 255.255.255.0
r2(config-if)#frame-relay interface-dlci 16
r2(config-if)#frame-relay interface-dlci 17
r2(config-if)#frame-relay map ip 2.2.2.2 16 broadcast
r2(config-if)#frame-relay priority-dlci-group 1 16 17 17 17
r2(config-if)#^Z
r2#
```

Note that priority DLCI groups do not treat any traffic in a preferential manner. The name implies a prioritization, but in effect, packets are only classified and separated into different VCs. The priority DLCI group feature only provides prioritization if the WAN can provide differential treatment for the different VCs.

TIP   You cannot use priority queuing in conjunction with FRF.12 Frame Relay fragmentation and interleaving, which means the priority queuing is not appropriate for low-speed Frame Relay links. In this situation, you should use LLQ (which is available on a per-VC basis as of IOS 12.1(2)T).

Custom Queuing

Like priority queuing, custom queuing is applicable to serial interfaces that operate at line rates up to and including E1 (2.048 Mbps). *Custom queuing* is a form of fair queuing that enables flexible bandwidth distribution between defined traffic classes, without starving any of the traffic classes. Fair queuing strategies are not well suited for voice or other jitter-sensitive traffic, because queued voice packets incur a variable delay while waiting for each of the queues to be serviced. The adverse impact on voice and jitter-sensitive traffic is exacerbated when the number of queues or the number of bytes accepted from each queue increases.

TIP   You should not use custom queuing on interfaces that transmit VoIP or other jitter-sensitive traffic. CB-WFQ with IP RTP Priority or LLQ is the recommended method to maintain VoIP prioritization and enable arbitrary bandwidth allocation for different traffic classes.

The queues are serviced in round-robin fashion, with each queue allowed to transmit the configured number of bytes before passing control to the next queue. If the allotted byte-count is consumed in midtransmission of a packet, the queue is allowed to finish transmission of the packet. For example, if a queue that contains two 1500-byte packets is configured to transmit 1501 bytes, then both packets are transmitted (for a total of 3000 bytes). You must consider the effect of packet sizes when configuring byte-counts to ensure that bandwidth is distributed the way you expect.

In the following configuration example, traffic is divided into three groups, based on access list matches. Bandwidth is assigned according to the ratio of 3000:4500:3000, which is equivalent to 28.5 percent for the first and third groups, and 43 percent for the second group. Traffic that does not match access lists 101 or 102 is treated in the default queue. Because this queue may contain a large percentage of the traffic, the default queue depth is increased to accommodate the extra packets as seen in Example 15-10.

Example 15-10   *Configuring Custom Queuing*

```
r2#conf t
Enter configuration commands, one per line.  End with CNTL/Z.
r2(config)#queue-list 1 protocol ip 1 list 101
r2(config)#queue-list 1 protocol ip 2 list 102
r2(config)#queue-list 1 default 3
r2(config)#queue-list 1 queue 1 byte-count 3000 limit 100
r2(config)#queue-list 1 queue 2 byte-count 4500 limit 100
r2(config)#queue-list 1 queue 3 byte-count 3000 limit 1000
r2(config)#interface serial0
r2(config-if)#custom-queue-list 1
r2(config-if)#^Z
r2#
```

The questionable assumption for bandwidth ratio calculations is that each queue reaches its byte-count limit at the end of a transmitted packet. The actual bandwidth ratios may be drastically different if this assumption is false. For this reason, custom queuing is considered by some to be a mystical art.

You can use the following commands to see how packets are classified into each queue, how many packets have been dropped, and to assess the current level of congestion in each of the queues seen in Example 15-11.

Example 15-11 *Verifying the Configuration and Operation of Custom Queuing*

```
r2#show queueing custom
Current custom queue configuration:

List   Queue   Args
1      3       default
1      1       protocol ip         list 101
1      2       protocol ip         list 102
1      1       byte-count 3000 limit 100
1      2       byte-count 4500 limit 10
1      3       byte-count 3000 limit 1000
r2#
r2#sh interface serial0
Serial0 is up, line protocol is up
  Hardware is HD64570
  Internet address is 1.1.1.1/24
  MTU 1500 bytes, BW 1544 Kbit, DLY 20000 usec, rely 255/255, load 1/255
  Encapsulation HDLC, loopback not set, keepalive set (10 sec)
  Last input 00:00:08, output 00:00:04, output hang never
  Last clearing of "show interface" counters never
  Input queue: 0/75/0 (size/max/drops); Total output drops: 0
  Queueing strategy: custom-list 1
  Output queues: (queue #: size/max/drops)
      0: 0/20/0 1: 0/100/0 2: 0/10/0 3: 0/1000/0 4: 0/20/0
      5: 0/20/0 6: 0/20/0 7: 0/20/0 8: 0/20/0 9: 0/20/0
      10: 0/20/0 11: 0/20/0 12: 0/20/0 13: 0/20/0 14: 0/20/0
      15: 0/20/0 16: 0/20/0
  5 minute input rate 0 bits/sec, 0 packets/sec
  5 minute output rate 0 bits/sec, 0 packets/sec
      873 packets input, 52218 bytes, 0 no buffer
      Received 873 broadcasts, 0 runts, 0 giants, 0 throttles
      0 input errors, 0 CRC, 0 frame, 0 overrun, 0 ignored, 0 abort
      1131 packets output, 66994 bytes, 0 underruns
      0 output errors, 0 collisions, 12 interface resets
      0 output buffer failures, 0 output buffers swapped out
      0 carrier transitions
      DCD=up  DSR=up  DTR=up  RTS=up  CTS=up
r2#
```

As indicated in the preceding example, this interface has not experienced any congestion. No packets have been dropped from any of the 16 configurable queues (only 3 configured in this case), and there are currently no packets awaiting transmission.

Custom queuing is also available on a per-VC basis, just like priority queuing.

Flow-Based Weighted-Fair Queuing

Weighted fair queuing (WFQ) is designed to provide equal treatment to all traffic flows. Recall that a flow is defined by source/destination addresses and port numbers. FIFO queuing may seem to offer fair treatment, but it enables flows with high packet volumes (that is, FTP sessions) to consume a disproportionate amount of the interface bandwidth. Flow-based WFQ solves this problem by establishing a separate queue for each traffic flow, and transmitting some traffic from each queue in a round-robin fashion. In this way, flows with high packet volumes do not block transmission of flows with fewer packets, such as telnet sessions or other interactive applications.

TIP   If you want to use WFQ for interfaces that pass VoIP traffic, then you must also configure IP RTP Priority to ensure adequate performance for VoIP packets.

Unlike priority or custom queuing, WFQ is refreshingly easy to configure. Because WFQ is the default for interfaces at E1 rates or less, you can reap the queuing benefits with no configuration at all! If the default configurations for WFQ do not meet your needs, you can tune them with the command as shown in Example 15-12.

Example 15-12   *Configuring WFQ Parameters*

```
r2#conf t
Enter configuration commands, one per line.  End with CNTL/Z.
r2(config)#in s0
r2(config-if)#fair-queue 64 256 1
r2(config-if)#^Z
r2#
```

The first parameter specifies the queue depth for each traffic flow, or conversation. You can allocate up to 4096 packets per conversation queue. The second parameter specifies the maximum number of queues available (up to 4096) to sort conversations. The final parameter is the number of queues that can be reserved by RSVP. Keep in mind that extra queue capacity consumes system memory, so it is not generally a good idea to maximize these parameters. Enabling WFQ on a single interface, with the maximum queue depth and number of conversation queues, consumes about 1 MB of RAM on an idle 2500 series router as seen in Example 15-13.

Example 15-13   *Memory Consumption of Queuing Processes*

```
r2#conf t
Enter configuration commands, one per line.  End with CNTL/Z.
r2(config-if)#no fair-queue
r2(config-if)#^Z
r2#show processor memory
Total: 18194004, Used: 2058248, Free: 16135756

r2#conf t
Enter configuration commands, one per line.  End with CNTL/Z.
```

continues

Example 15-13 *Memory Consumption of Queuing Processes (Continued)*

```
r2(config-if)#fair-queue
r2(config-if)#^Z
r2#show processor memory
Total: 18194004, Used: 2063656, Free: 16130348

r2#conf t
Enter configuration commands, one per line.  End with CNTL/Z.
r2(config-if)#fair-queue 4096 4096 1000
r2(config-if)#^Z
r2#show processor memory
Total: 18194004, Used: 3039152, Free: 15154852
```

During actual congestion conditions, the router will not have enough memory to manage these queues. Consider that 16 million packets may be queued with maximal fair-queue settings, which corresponds to at least 1 GB of RAM! This many packets cannot be realistically driven to an interface that would use WFQ, but the point remains that you should use reasonable settings for queue depth and number of conversations.

You can verify the configuration and operation of WFQ with the commands in Example 15-14.

Example 15-14 *Verifying Configuration and Operation of WFQ*

```
r2#sh queueing fair
Current fair queue configuration:

  Interface         Discard      Dynamic        Reserved
                    threshold    queue count    queue count
  Serial0           64           256            1
  Serial1           64           256            0

r2#
r2#sh queue Serial0
  Input queue: 0/75/0 (size/max/drops); Total output drops: 0
  Queueing strategy: weighted fair
  Output queue: 0/1000/64/0 (size/max total/threshold/drops)
     Conversations  0/1/256 (active/max active/max total)
     Reserved Conversations 0/1 (allocated/max allocated)
r2#
```

For 7500 series routers with VIP cards, you can also use the **show interfaces fair-queue** command to verify the operation of distributed WFQ.

IP RTP Priority

Although flow-based WFQ is a good queuing mechanism for data traffic in general, it is not well suited to VoIP or other jitter-sensitive traffic. As the number of conversations increases, VoIP packets must wait longer and longer while each of the queues is serviced in a round-robin fashion. A better arrangement would enable priority queuing treatment for the VoIP flows, while other data flows receive the normal WFQ treatment. This is exactly the functionality provided by the IP RTP Priority feature available in Cisco IOS. You may have also heard this feature described as priority-queuing weighted-fair queuing (PQ-WFQ).

In its early version, this feature was implemented with the **ip rtp reserve** command at the interface configuration level. As of IOS 12.0(5)T, a more robust version is available using the command shown in Example 15-15.

Example 15-15   *Configuring IP RTP Priority in Conjunction with WFQ*

```
r2#conf t
Enter configuration commands, one per line.  End with CNTL/Z.
r2(config)#interface serial0
r2(config-if)#ip rtp priority 16384 100 120
r2(config-if)#^Z
r2#
```

The first parameter in the command is the UDP port number for the beginning of the range to prioritize. Cisco routers use 16384 as the start of the RTP range for VoIP audio packets. Other vendors may use a different number range. The second parameter specifies the number of UDP ports to prioritize after the starting port. In the preceding example, UDP ports 16,384 through 16,483 are treated in the priority queue. This port range is appropriate for a router that supports up to 25 simultaneous calls. Note that you should prioritize ports in the range 16,384 to 16,384 + 4N, where N is the number of simultaneous calls. The final parameter is the maximum amount of bandwidth, in kbps, allowed for the priority queue. The bandwidth parameter ensures that the priority queue does not starve the other conversation queues in the WFQ scheme.

When packets in the priority queue exceed the configured bandwidth allotment, they are dropped. You cannot control which packets are dropped when the priority bandwidth is exceeded, so all active VoIP calls may experience reduced voice quality when the priority bandwidth is exceeded. Consider a link with 48 kbps allocated for IP RTP priority and four active calls using G.729 and RTP header compression (around 11 kbps per call). Voice quality is fine because these four calls do not consume more than 48 kbps. As soon as a fifth call is initiated, the total prioritized bandwidth exceeds the allotment by nearly 7 kbps. On average, each of the five calls will lose 1.4 kbps worth of traffic, so the voice quality will noticeably degrade for all active calls.

The solution to this problem is to use RSVP or another mechanism for connection admission control (CAC). If you use H.323 for VoIP call signaling, then you can ensure that an audio path is not built unless an RSVP reservation is successful. Chapter 16, "Establishing Router-PBX Connectivity," discusses the use of RSVP in conjunction with VoIP call setup on Cisco routers.

TIP   For IP RTP Priority, configure bandwidth to reflect RTP/TCP header compression, but do not consider Layer 2 headers. However, you must consider Layer 2 headers when allocating bandwidth for LLQ.

Make sure that you include all the UDP ports used for RTP in your environment. You can empirically determine the port numbers in use with the **debug ip packet detail** command, filtered through a UDP port-restricted access list. Beware that many active calls will yield a large amount of output and may cause a router crash. You can also get port information from **show ip cache flow** if you have configured **ip route-cache flow** at the interface level. Alternatively, you can give priority treatment to all UDP ports in the range 16,384 to 32,768, which is the range that Cisco routers may use for VoIP.

TIP   If you must determine the UDP ports that another vendor uses for VoIP calls, and you are concerned about crashing a Cisco router with the **debug ip packet** output, then you can use an external protocol analyzer to capture the traffic. Before you expend this much effort, however, you should consult the documentation and support resources of the other vendor.

Note that the **ip rtp priority** command only provides prioritization for even-numbered UDP ports with RTP traffic flows. RTCP control packets and TCP-based call setup messages do not receive priority treatment with the PQ-WFQ feature. If you want to provide priority queuing treatment to non-RTP packets, then use the priority class feature of CB-WFQ. To preserve voice quality on very low-speed links, however, only audio packets should receive priority treatment (that is, the behavior of **ip rtp priority** is desired).

To monitor the operation of the IP RTP Priority feature, use the **debug priority** command.

Class-Based Weighted-Fair Queuing

Class-based weighted-fair queuing (CB-WFQ) is a very robust queuing model that combines the best elements of priority, custom, and WFQ along with WRED. CB-WFQ is more complex to configure than other queuing types, because the underlying queuing model is more complex and full-featured. This complexity gives you the freedom to sort traffic classes according to a variety of characteristics and apply independent queuing policies to each of the classes.

You can directly assign bandwidth allowances to different classes, as opposed to the archaic byte-counts required in custom queuing. You can specify one or multiple classes to have high-priority queuing treatment, without limiting the other classes to the priority queuing structure. You can use WFQ to have multiple conversation queues within a class, while still imposing a bandwidth limitation for the class as a whole. Aside from the queuing type and bandwidth allowances for each class, you can also specify WRED for each class. This way, you can use WRED where it is sensible, and adjust parameters (congestion thresholds and drop probabilities) based on the characteristics of each traffic class. The flexibility provided by CB-WFQ is a real asset to network designers.

There are three main steps in the process of implementing CB-WFQ:

Step 1   Sort traffic into classes.

Step 2   Apply policies to classes.

Step 3   Assign a service policy to an interface.

Sorting Traffic into Classes

A class of traffic is identified by a class map. All the traffic assigned to a given class map should have the same QoS and policy requirements. After you create a class map, you can assign it traffic based on the inbound interface, the protocol type (for example, IPX, AppleTalk, DECnet, and so on), or an access list. You will probably use the access list option most often, as in the configuration example found in Example 15-16.

Example 15-16 *Sorting Traffic into Classes for CB-WFQ*

```
r2#conf t
Enter configuration commands, one per line.  End with CNTL/Z.
r2(config)#class-map Voice
r2(config-cmap)#match access-group 101
r2(config-cmap)#exit
r2(config)#class-map WebSurfing
r2(config-cmap)#match access-group 102
r2(config-cmap)#exit
r2(config)#class-map ServerBackUps
r2(config-cmap)#match access-group 103
r2(config-cmap)#^Z
r2#
```

With a little imagination, you can use this traffic classification scheme to implement complex policies. Suppose you want to allocate 128 kbps for VoIP calls within your company, and 64 kbps for off-net calls. You can configure your VoIP routers with multiple loopback interfaces, and point VoIP dial peers to different loopback interfaces depending on the call type. For example, off-net calls point to Loopback-1, and on-net calls point to Loopback-2. You can then sort the calls based on destination IP address (using access lists) and associate the calls with the On-Net or the Off-Net classes.

Applying Policies to Classes

After traffic is sorted into classes, you must define the traffic policies that apply to each class. You can also define policies for the default class of traffic that does not belong to existing classes. The collection of traffic classes and the policies that apply to them is called a *service policy*. The service policy must be applied to a router interface to take effect. The following policy options are configurable for each class:

- Minimum bandwidth during periods of congestion
- FIFO queue depth for defined classes
- Tail-drop or WRED behavior during congestion
- Congestion thresholds and drop probabilities for WRED classes
- Priority treatment for the class as a whole, which is called LLQ
- FIFO or WFQ behavior for the default class
- Number of WFQ conversations for the default class

Basic Class Policy

A minimal policy configuration for each class is the bandwidth assigned to the class during periods of congestion. Configuring the class bandwidth assigns a FIFO queue with a default depth of 64 packets, which is the maximum. WRED is disabled by default, so the FIFO queue exhibits tail-drop behavior during congestion. The commands found in Example 15-17 provide a minimal policy configuration for a class.

Example 15-17 *Configuring a Class for Specified Bandwidth, Queue Size, and a Tail-Drop Policy*

```
r2#conf t
Enter configuration commands, one per line.  End with CNTL/Z.
r2(config)#policy-map RemoteOffices
r2(config-pmap)#class ServerBackUps
r2(config-pmap-c)#bandwidth 256
r2(config-pmap-c)#queue-limit 64
r2(config-pmap-c)#^Z
r2#
```

Bandwidth is specified in kbps, and the queue limit is specified in number of packets. In the preceding example, the queue limit is explicitly set to the default value.

WRED Class Policy

The following commands configure a class for a FIFO queue with a depth of 64 packets and WRED drop during periods of congestion. Note that each class may be configured with different packet drop probabilities and congestion thresholds as seen in Example 15-18.

Example 15-18   *Configuring a Class for Specified Bandwidth and a WRED Drop Policy*

```
r2#conf t
Enter configuration commands, one per line.  End with CNTL/Z.
r2(config)#policy-map RemoteOffices
r2(config-pmap)#class WebSurfing
r2(config-pmap-c)#bandwidth 256
r2(config-pmap-c)#random-detect
r2(config-pmap-c)#random-detect exponential-weighting-constant 10
r2(config-pmap-c)#random-detect precedence 0   20   40   10
r2(config-pmap-c)#^Z
r2#
```

Priority Class Policy

VoIP traffic should be assigned to its own class, and it should receive priority queuing treatment akin to the IP RTP Priority feature. The priority class feature was originally called PQ-CBWFQ, but since that acronym pushes the bounds of absurdity, the feature is now documented with the more manageable name of low latency queuing (LLQ). The configuration in Example 15-19 configures LLQ for the Voice class.

Example 15-19   *Configuring a Class for Priority Queuing Treatment*

```
r2#conf t
Enter configuration commands, one per line.  End with CNTL/Z.
r2(config)#policy-map RemoteOffices
r2(config-pmap)#class Voice
r2(config-pmap-c)#priority 256
r2(config-pmap-c)#queue-limit 32
r2(config-pmap-c)#^Z
r2#
```

Multiple classes may be assigned to the priority queue, which gives you the flexibility to allocate bandwidth to different classes within the priority queue. Considering a previous example, you might allocate some bandwidth for an off-net VoIP class and some for an on-net VoIP class. Note that bandwidth is configured in the priority command, so you should not configure the regular bandwidth statement for the class. When planning the bandwidth allocations, you must account for link-layer headers, such as Frame Relay, HDLC, or PPP. For ATM, consider the padding bytes in the cell payload, but not the ATM header.

TIP	For CB-WFQ priority classes (LLQ), configure bandwidth to reflect RTP/TCP header compression and Layer 2 headers. However, do not consider Layer 2 headers when allocating bandwidth for IP RTP Priority.

The queue limit in the preceding configuration is reduced to 32 packets to combat jitter. Unless RTP header compression is implemented, VoIP packets are approximately 60 bytes (with various assumptions). At the default queue-depth of 64 packets, a VoIP packet in the priority queue may experience up to 20 ms of variable queuing delay at a T1 clocking rate or up to 480 ms at a 64 kbps clocking rate! The policy map in the preceding example will be applied to a T1 interface, so the queue has been reduced to yield an arbitrary value of 10 ms for the queuing delay.

Queuing-delay problems in the priority queue may also occur when the RTP Priority feature is used with flow-based WFQ. The default queue depth for WFQ, which is 64 packets, is applied to the RTP Priority queue. For interfaces with a low clocking rate, the default queue depth introduces an excessive amount of variable delay for the priority queue. Unfortunately, the only way to combat this problem is to decrease the queue size for all WFQ conversations or to implement the more complex CB-WFQ.

If you have very low-speed interfaces, then using CB-WFQ priority classes for voice may not be a good idea. The only way to classify voice packets into a class is by matching a range of UDP ports from 16,384 to 32,767 (assuming that the VoIP packets are generated by Cisco routers). The problem is that for every even UDP port used by RTP audio packets, there is an adjacent odd UDP port used by RTCP control packets. The priority class feature of CB-WFQ will put the RTP and RTCP packets in the priority queue, so the audio packets are forced to wait longer because of the control packets. Using the **ip rtp priority** command at the interface configuration mode, along with CB-WFQ for nonvoice traffic, ensures that only the RTP audio packets are in the priority queue. The IP RTP Priority approach is your best option to preserve voice quality for VoIP across very low-speed interfaces.

Default Class Policy

After you have associated policies with the explicitly defined classes, you can associate default policies with the remaining traffic that does not match any of the classes. A potential problem with this approach is that hundreds of traffic flows may share the default class, which has a FIFO queue depth of 64 packets. Fortunately, the default class can operate in WFQ mode, which allows up to 4096 conversations with a maximum queue depth of 64 packets for each conversation. The following commands configure a default class shown in Example 15-20.

Example 15-20 *Configuring a Default Class to Set Policies for Unspecified Traffic*

```
r2#conf t
Enter configuration commands, one per line.  End with CNTL/Z.
r2(config)#policy-map RemoteOffices
r2(config-pmap)#class class-default
r2(config-pmap-c)#fair-queue 512
r2(config-pmap-c)#queue-limit 64
r2(config-pmap-c)#^Z
r2#
```

TIP
You must explicitly name the default class as class-default. The ? help system in the router does not identify this as an option—you must know this specific name to trigger the default class operation.

All the class policies that have been applied are summarized in the configuration display found in Example 15-21.

Example 15-21 *Summary of Class-Map and Policy-Map Configurations*

```
r2#show running-config
Building configuration...
<only CB-WFQ commands shown here>
!
class-map Voice
  match access-group 101
class-map WebSurfing
  match access-group 102
class-map ServerBackUps
  match access-group 103
!
policy-map RemoteOffices
  class Voice
    priority 256
    queue-limit 32
  class ServerBackUps
    bandwidth 256
  class WebSurfing
    bandwidth 256
    random-detect
    random-detect exponential-weighting-constant 10
    random-detect precedence 0   20    40    10
  class class-default
    fair-queue 512
!
```

Note that the **queue-limit 64** command does not show because it is the default for each class. If you want to compare the performance for several policy configurations, you can create multiple policy maps that use the same classes, but different policy parameters. Then, you can alternate interface queuing policies just by changing which policy map is applied to the router interface.

Assigning a Service Policy to an Interface

The command shown in Example 15-22 applies the service policy, which is a collection of classes and associated policies, to a serial interface. Beginning in IOS 12.1(2)T, you can also apply the service policy (and hence the LLQ feature) to Frame Relay VCs.

Example 15-22 *Applying a Policy Map to a Router Interface*

```
r2#conf t
Enter configuration commands, one per line.  End with CNTL/Z.
r2(config)#interface serial0
r2(config-if)#service-policy output RemoteOffices
r2(config-if)#^Z
r2#
```

The configuration of the service policy can be verified with the command found in Example 15-23.

Example 15-23 *Verifying Configuration of a Service Policy*

```
r2#show policy-map RemoteOffices
  Policy Map RemoteOffices
   Weighted Fair Queueing
     Class Voice
       Strict Priority
       Bandwidth 256 (kbps) Max Threshold 32 (packets)
     Class ServerBackUps
       Bandwidth 256 (kbps) Max Threshold 64 (packets)
     Class WebSurfing
       Bandwidth 256 (kbps)
       exponential weight 10
       class     min-threshold    max-threshold    mark-probability
       ----------------------------------------------------------

       0         20               40               1/10
       1         -                -                1/10
       2         -                -                1/10
       3         -                -                1/10
       4         -                -                1/10
       5         -                -                1/10
       6         -                -                1/10
       7         -                -                1/10
       rsvp      -                -                1/10

     Class class-default
       Flow based Fair Queueing Max Threshold 64 (packets)
r2#
```

Note that for the WRED class, only the IP precedence = 0 category displays a minimum and maximum queue-depth threshold. Since this command reflects the configured state of the router, the output accurately indicates that the other categories are not explicitly configured (that is, default settings are in effect).

When the service policy is applied to a router interface, you can monitor the queuing performance and verify the policy parameters that are actually running on the interface as shown in Example 15-24.

Example 15-24 *Verifying Operation of a Service Policy on an Interface*

```
r2#sh policy interface serial0
 Serial1  output : RemoteOffices
  Weighted Fair Queueing
    Class Voice
      Strict Priority
      Output Queue: Conversation 521
        Bandwidth 256 (kbps) Packets Matched 0 Max Threshold 32 (packets)
        (discards/tail drops) 0/0
    Class ServerBackUps
      Output Queue: Conversation 522
        Bandwidth 256 (kbps) Packets Matched 0 Max Threshold 64 (packets)
        (discards/tail drops) 0/0
    Class WebSurfing
      Output Queue: Conversation 523
        Bandwidth 256 (kbps) Packets Matched 0
        mean queue depth: 0
        drops: class  random    tail      min-th    max-th    mark-prob
                 0      0         0         20        40        1/10
                 1      0         0         22        40        1/10
                 2      0         0         24        40        1/10
                 3      0         0         26        40        1/10
                 4      0         0         28        40        1/10
                 5      0         0         30        40        1/10
                 6      0         0         32        40        1/10
                 7      0         0         34        40        1/10
               rsvp     0         0         36        40        1/10
    Class class-default
      Flow Based Fair Queueing
      Maximum Number of Hashed Queues 512  Max Threshold 64 (packets)
 r2#
```

Note that in this output, the queue-depth thresholds for WRED reflect the default configuration settings in addition to the manually configured settings. You can also determine from this output which classes are congested and how many packets are dropped because of full queues versus the WRED process.

IP Precedence

The IP precedence bits are the three high-order bits in the type of service (TOS) field of the IP header. The three bits provide eight levels of traffic priority as indicated in Table 15-1.

Table 15-1 *IP Precedence Bit Values*

IP Precedence	Bit Value	Priority
0	000	Routine
1	001	Priority

continues

Table 15-1 *IP Precedence Bit Values (Continued)*

IP Precedence	Bit Value	Priority
2	010	Immediate
3	011	Flash
4	100	Flash-override
5	101	Critical
6	110	Internet
7	111	Network

IP precedence values of 6 and 7 are assigned to routing protocols, control messages, and traffic that is essential for network operation. For user data including VoIP, the highest IP precedence value that may be assigned is 5. By default, IP packets use the Routine precedence setting {0}.

IP precedence bits affect the behavior of WFQ and WRED by default. Increasing the IP precedence increases the amount of bandwidth for a flow in WFQ, and it decreases the probability of WRED packet drops for the flow. CB-WFQ also considers IP precedence for per-class WRED and WFQ in the default class.

There are at least three ways to set IP precedence values in Cisco routers:

* Route maps
* Dial peers
* RSVP

You can set IP precedence bits (and override any pre-existing values) for any desired traffic types with a route map. Example 15-25 sets IP precedence in a route map (for all packets that match access list 101) and applies the route map via policy routing on an interface.

Example 15-25 *Setting IP Precedence Bits Using a Policy Route Map*

```
r2#conf t
Enter configuration commands, one per line.  End with CNTL/Z.
r2(config)#route-map SetPrecedence permit 10
r2(config-route-map)#match ip address 101
r2(config-route-map)#set ip precedence critical
r2(config-route-map)#exit
r2(config)#interface serial0
r2(config-if)#ip policy route-map SetPrecedence
r2(config-if)#ip route-cache policy
r2(config-if)#^Z
r2#
```

You can use policy routing to set IP precedence bits for traffic crossing an interface, while still using a dynamic routing protocol to propagate normal route information. The **debug**

ip policy command shows you which route map entry is matched for traffic that crosses the policy routing interface.

If you are using RSVP, you can modify IP precedence bits for packets based on whether or not the traffic flows conform to the reservation. If the traffic flow is within the bandwidth reservation, then the IP precedence may be set high. Routers in the path that are RSVP-unaware may provide better treatment to packets with high IP precedence values. If the traffic flow exceeds the reserved bandwidth, then RSVP may reduce the IP precedence value to remove the preferential treatment. This may be the case for a VoIP packet in which the IP precedence is set high in a dial peer. The nonconforming packets can be reduced to routine IP precedence, which yields normal treatment. The commands found in Example 15-26 modify IP precedence bits, assuming that RSVP is already configured.

Example 15-26 *Setting IP Precedence Bits Based on RSVP Reservation Conformity*

```
r2#conf t
Enter configuration commands, one per line.  End with CNTL/Z.
r2(config)#interface serial0
r2(config-if)#ip rsvp precedence conform 5
r2(config-if)#ip rsvp precedence exceed 0
r2(config-if)#^Z
r2#
```

It is normal for RTP prioritization to drop traffic in excess of the configured RTP bandwidth, so this policing feature of RSVP is not normally required for VoIP. It may be useful if you use RSVP for other traffic types, though.

The most common way to set IP precedence bits for VoIP is with the dial-peer configuration commands as seen in Example 15-27.

Example 15-27 *Setting IP Precedence Bits Using a VoIP Dial Peer*

```
r2#conf t
Enter configuration commands, one per line.  End with CNTL/Z.
r2(config)#dial-peer voice 1 voip
r2(config-dial-peer)#ip precedence 5
r2(config-dial-peer)#^Z
r2#
```

If you are only modifying IP precedence for VoIP packets, using dial peers is the preferred implementation. You should have RTP prioritization (or priority classes for CB-WFQ) configured at all the bandwidth bottlenecks in your network. As such, the IP precedence values for VoIP packet do not matter for WFQ weighting. The primary value of setting the precedence bits for VoIP is to influence the behavior of WRED on high-bandwidth interfaces. The goal is to minimize or eliminate WRED packet drops for VoIP flows.

RSVP

If you enable some form of priority queuing for VoIP at all the bandwidth bottlenecks in your network, and if all your VoIP traffic originates on Cisco routers that you control, then you do not need to use RSVP to maintain voice quality. Because you are in control of all the VoIP packet sources, you can accurately scope the amount of bandwidth that is allowed priority treatment. RSVP may be useful if you want to reserve occasional bandwidth for other applications (which can also be done with CB-WFQ), set IP precedence based on reservation conformity, or if you must connect with networking devices from other vendors that rely on RSVP to prioritize voice.

If you have H.323 terminals, software-based IP telephones, or other VoIP devices in your network, then you should use RSVP as a part of CAC to limit bandwidth usage. For example, RSVP can be negotiated as part of the H.245 media negotiation phase of an H.323 call setup. If the RSVP reservation fails (for example, because there is no available bandwidth), then the audio path of the H.323 call is not established.

The default behavior of interfaces in Cisco routers is to ignore RSVP signaling. The command found in Example 15-28 enables an interface to respond to RSVP signaling, and take appropriate actions to implement a reservation.

Example 15-28   *Setting RSVP Bandwidth Limitations and Enabling RSVP Processing on an Interface*

```
r2#conf t
Enter configuration commands, one per line.  End with CNTL/Z.
r2(config)#interface serial0
r2(config-if)#ip rsvp bandwidth 240 24
r2(config-if)#^Z
r2#
```

The first parameter defines the amount of bandwidth (kbps) available for the aggregate of RSVP flows through the interface, and the second parameter defines the maximum bandwidth (kbps) allowed per flow. The example configuration allows a maximum flow size of 24 kbps, corresponding to a G.729 VoIP call (8-kbps payload) without RTP header compression (16-kbps overhead). Ten simultaneous calls are supported before the aggregate RSVP limit for the interface is reached.

RSVP and RTP Header Compression

It is important to note that RSVP does not consider the effects of RTP header compression, so you must always configure RSVP as if you are not implementing RTP header compression. If you configure a maximum flow size of 10-kbps, no RSVP reservations will be made for VoIP calls, because RSVP sees each flow before the RTP header compression is applied. Consider an interface with 384-kbps bandwidth and support for 24 VoIP calls. Considering RTP header compression, the VoIP calls can be supported with approximately

240-kbps bandwidth. From the perspective of RSVP, 576 kbps must be reserved for VoIP calls (24 calls × 24 kbps/call). RSVP will not allow this because it exceeds the configured interface bandwidth. The workaround is to falsely state the interface bandwidth at a higher value (that is, 768 kbps), but you must be careful not to overcommit the link. Remember to consider other queuing processes such as CB-WFQ and link-layer headers.

RSVP and the NetFlow Route Cache

You can improve the performance of RSVP when used in conjunction with NetFlow switching, by enabling the configuration elements found in Example 15-29.

Example 15-29 *Improving Performance for RSVP with NetFlow Route-Cache*

```
r2#conf t
Enter configuration commands, one per line.  End with CNTL/Z.
r2(config)#ip flow-cache feature-accelerate
r2(config)#interface serial0
r2(config-if)#ip route-cache flow
r2(config-if)#ip rsvp flow-assist
r2(config-if)#^Z
r2#
```

RSVP Security Concerns

It is a good idea to consider the security implications of enabling RSVP on a router interface. You should regulate which hosts are allowed to make bandwidth reservations to prevent anonymous bandwidth hogs from degrading performance for everyone. If you do not regulate RSVP reservations, you open another hole in your network for denial-of-service attacks. You can restrict (via an access list) which hosts are allowed to make RSVP reservations, using the configuration shown in Example 15-30.

Example 15-30 *Controlling Which Hosts Are Allowed to Make RSVP Reservations Via ACL 199*

```
r2#conf t
Enter configuration commands, one per line.  End with CNTL/Z.
r2(config)#interface serial0
r2(config-if)#ip rsvp neighbor 199
r2(config-if)#^Z
r2#
```

If you are only configuring RSVP for the sake of voice quality, then you should only permit your voice routers in the access list. Microsoft NetMeeting clients (or other H.323 clients) may also need to be included. If you are not concerned about CPU overhead, you can further limit this access to UDP ports 16384 through 32767 (assuming only Cisco routers initiate VoIP calls).

Monitoring RSVP Configuration and Performance

You can monitor many aspects of RSVP processing with the following commands found in Example 15-31.

Example 15-31   *Variety of Commands to Verify Operation of RSVP*

```
r2#sh ip rsvp ?
  atm-peak-rate-limit  RSVP peak rate limit
  host                 RSVP Endpoint Senders and Receivers
  installed            RSVP installed reservations
  interface            RSVP interface information
  neighbor             RSVP neighbor information
  precedence           RSVP precedence/TOS settings
  request              RSVP Reservations Upstream
  reservation          RSVP Reservation Requests from Downstream
  sbm                  RSVP SBM information
  sender               RSVP Path State information
  temp-psb             RSVP PATH Requests awaiting Policy decisions
  temp-rsb             RSVP Reservation Requests awaiting Policy decisions
  tos                  RSVP precedence/TOS settings

r2#
```

Most of the options are self-explanatory if you are familiar with the basic operation of RSVP.

The Subnet Bandwidth Manager (SBM) option is implemented as of Cisco IOS 12.0(5)T, and refers to the SBM protocol. The basic idea is to provide a single source of admission control for RSVP on IEEE 802 interfaces (such as ethernet). Without a single point of admission control, multiple routers may grant RSVP reservations that exceed the available bandwidth for the media.

The SBM technology is being standardized by the Internet Engineering Task Force (IETF). The latest working draft (as of this writing) is draft-ietf-issll-is802-sbm-10.txt. You can find a more current copy of the draft (or maybe an RFC by the time you read this) by searching the IETF web site for SBM.

Link Fragmentation/Interleaving

The goal of *link fragmentation/interleaving (LFI)* is to reduce the serialization delay associated with large packets in midtransmission. Without LFI, high-priority voice packets at the front of a queue are still delayed if a large data packet has already begun transmission. For 1500-byte data packets on a 56-kbps link, this delay can be 214 ms! This section addresses link-based fragment/interleave methods, because network layer solutions (such as decreasing the MTU for IP and all network layer protocols) are horribly inefficient and should be treated as a last resort.

The LFI methods you can use depend on the link-layer protocol:

- Frame Relay
- Multilink PPP
- ATM

Frame Relay

There are three LFI options for Frame Relay:

- Cisco proprietary
- FRF.11 Annex C
- FRF.12 end-to-end

Cisco Proprietary

The Cisco-proprietary fragmentation method applies to VoFR implementations (as opposed to VoIP over Frame Relay) and should only be used when you must connect to MC3810 routers running Cisco IOS 12.0(3)T or older. For an MC3810 that runs this older IOS software, the Cisco-proprietary fragmentation is the only option, and it is configured with the commands shown in Example 15-32.

Example 15-32   *Configuring Cisco-Proprietary Fragmentation on MC3810 Before IOS 12.0(4)T*

```
r2#conf t
Enter configuration commands, one per line.  End with CNTL/Z.
r2(config)#interface serial0:0
r2(config-if)#bandwidth 256
r2(config-if)#frame-relay interface-dlci 16 voice-encap 320
r2(config-if)#^Z
r2#
```

The bandwidth command is not required, but it is included to emphasize that the fragment size should be 80 bytes for every 64 kbps of clocking rate. In this case, a 256-kbps clocking rate requires a 320-byte fragment size. If the CIR is less than the port speed and you have configured frame relay traffic shaping, then the fragment size should match the configured value for B_c. Traffic shaping is discussed in a following section.

TIP   When using frame relay fragmentation in conjunction with traffic shaping, set the fragment size equal to the committed burst size. Beware that fragment size is configured in bytes, and B_c is configured in bits.

An MC3810 running with IOS 12.0(3)T or older only supports FIFO queuing for the data traffic on VoFR PVCs. Beginning in IOS 12.0(4)T, there are two ways to enable the Cisco-proprietary fragmentation while enabling WFQ, custom, or priority queuing for data on the same VoFR PVC:

- voice-encap style
- cisco vofr style

The original VoFR implementation fragmented the data before queuing, which made the IP address and TCP/UDP port information unavailable for the queuing function. This is why FIFO queuing was the only method available. To make the IP address and TCP/UDP port information available for fancy queuing (that is, WFQ, custom, priority), the fragmentation must happen after the queuing process. In other words, there must be no fragmentation before queuing. The command to achieve this behavior is [**no**] **frag-pre-queuing**.

After configuring [**no**] **frag-pre-queuing**, you can configure WFQ, custom queuing, or priority queuing as normal. That is, you can configure the fancy queuing at the (sub)interface level, or at the VC level with a frame relay map class. (See Example 15-33.)

Example 15-33 **voice-encap** *Style of Cisco-Proprietary Fragmentation with WFQ Support*

```
r2#conf t
Enter configuration commands, one per line.  End with CNTL/Z.
r2(config)#interface serial0:0
r2(config-if)#no frag-pre-queuing
r2(config-if)#fair-queue 64 256 0
r2(config-if)#frame-relay interface-dlci 16 voice-encap 320
r2(config-if-dlci)#^Z
r2#
```

The **voice-encap** style of configuring VoFR and Cisco-proprietary data fragmentation (refer to Example 15-33) will not be supported in future versions of IOS. For all voice platforms (MC3810, 2600, 3600, 7200, and so on) beginning in IOS 12.0(4)T, the **vofr cisco** configuration is recommended to implement VoFR with Cisco-proprietary fragmentation as shown in Example 15-34.

Example 15-34 **vofr cisco** *Style of Cisco-Proprietary Fragmentation with WFQ Support*

```
r2#conf t
Enter configuration commands, one per line.  End with CNTL/Z.
r2(config)#interface serial0:0
r2(config-if)#frame-relay traffic-shaping
r2(config-if)#frame-relay interface-dlci 16
r2(config-if-dlci)#vofr cisco
r2(config-if-dlci)#class TraffShape
r2(config-if-dlci)#exit
r2(config-if)#exit
r2(config)#map-class frame-relay TraffShape
r2(config-map-class)#frame-relay fragment 320
r2(config-map-class)#frame-relay voice-bandwidth 120000
r2(config-map-class)#frame-relay fair-queue 64 256 0
r2(config-map-class)#^Z
r2#
```

There are a few key parts to this configuration:

- Traffic shaping is mandatory, as is the frame relay map class.

- If a frame relay fragment size is not specified, then no data will be transmitted. This is important to remember for full T1/E1 interfaces, where fragmentation would not otherwise be required. In such cases, specify the maximum value of 1600 bytes. In general, the fragment size should equal the committed burst size (see the discussion of traffic shaping later in this chapter).

- The **frame-relay voice-bandwidth** command is required to activate voice transmission. The parameter specifies a limit on the bandwidth allocated for voice, to ensure that the prioritized voice traffic does not monopolize the interface. The command also ensures that the voice quality of active calls is not degraded by additional calls that would exceed the available bandwidth (that is, additional calls are rejected).

- You can configure WFQ, custom, or priority queuing in the map class. There is no need to configure the [**no**] **frag-pre-queuing** command in this configuration, because the behavior is implicitly included in the new syntax.

- Do not forget to specify the standard Frame Relay traffic-shaping parameters, which are not shown in this configuration example. The appropriate values for frame relay traffic-shaping parameters are discussed later in this chapter.

Remember that the examples in this section only apply to Cisco proprietary fragmentation for VoFR implementations.

FRF.11 Annex C

FRF.11 Annex C is the standards-compliant implementation of data fragmentation for VoFR PVCs. According to FRF.11 Annex C, all data frames must have a fragment header, regardless of size. VoFR frames do not have the fragment headers.

FRF.11 Annex C is the recommended method of configuring VoFR, except for the following cases that require the Cisco-proprietary method:

- Remote router is a Cisco MC3810 with IOS 12.03(T) or earlier. (Upgrade it!)

- Router acts as a tandem voice switch—for example, when a router must process VoFR calls that do not originate or terminate on the router (which is quite common).

Example 15-35 illustrates the configuration of VoFR using the FRF.11 Annex C method of fragmenting data frames:

Example 15-35   *Standards-Based VoFR Using FRF.11 Annex C Fragmentation with WFQ Support*

```
r2#conf t
Enter configuration commands, one per line.  End with CNTL/Z.
r2(config)#interface serial0:0
r2(config-if)#frame-relay traffic-shaping
r2(config-if)#frame-relay interface-dlci 16
r2(config-if-dlci)#vofr data 4
r2(config-if-dlci)#class TraffShape
r2(config-if-dlci)#exit
r2(config-if)#exit
r2(config)#map-class frame-relay TraffShape
r2(config-map-class)#frame-relay fragment 320
r2(config-map-class)#frame-relay voice-bandwidth 120000
r2(config-map-class)#frame-relay fair-queue 64 256 0
r2(config-map-class)#^Z
r2#
```

Note that this configuration is identical to the **vofr cisco** style of configuration, with the exception of the **vofr** command in the DLCI configuration mode. This configuration applies to all Cisco voice platforms that support VoFR, including MC3810, 2600, 3600, and 7200 series routers. The **vofr data** parameter specifies which VoFR subchannel is used for data traffic. The subchannel may need to be changed when integrating with other vendors' VoFR equipment.

FRF.12 End-to-End

The FRF.12 Implementation Agreement specifies an end-to-end fragmentation method and a User-Network Interface (UNI) fragmentation method. As of this writing, Cisco routers do not support the UNI method because it must also be supported in the circuit vendor's frame relay switches. The UNI method is more bandwidth-efficient in the circuit vendor's backbone, but the end-to-end method does not require support from the circuit vendor.

The FRF.12 end-to-end fragmentation is recommended for all PVCs that do not have VoFR traffic but require fragmentation. The following scenarios are examples where FRF.12 fragmentation is appropriate:

- PVCs with VoIP traffic
- Data-only PVCs on the same interface as a VoFR PVC
- Data-only PVCs on the same interface as any PVC with VoIP traffic

FRF.12 fragmentation is configured with the commands shown in Example 15-36.

Example 15-36   *Configuring FRF.12 Frame Relay Fragmentation with Fancy Queuing Support*

```
r2#conf t
Enter configuration commands, one per line.  End with CNTL/Z.
r2(config)#interface serial0:0
r2(config-if)#frame-relay traffic-shaping
r2(config-if)#frame-relay interface-dlci 16
r2(config-if-dlci)#class TraffShape
r2(config-if-dlci)#exit
r2(config-if)#exit
r2(config)#map-class frame-relay TraffShape
r2(config-map-class)#frame-relay fragment 320
r2(config-map-class)#frame-relay fair-queue 64 256 0
r2(config-map-class)#^Z
r2#
```

This example is similar to the FRF.11 Annex C configuration, except that the elements for VoFR have been removed (that is, the **vofr** and **frame-relay voice-bandwidth** commands). As of Cisco IOS 12.07(T), WFQ is the only queuing option supported with FRF.12 fragmentation.

Unlike the FRF.11 Annex C fragmentation, in which all data frames are fragmented, only data frames that are larger than the fragment size are fragmented in FRF.12. This has important implications for the operation of the Dual FIFO Transmit Buffers. The "Dual FIFO Transmit Buffers" section in Chapter 10 includes the simplified statement that "VoIP packets and LMI messages use the high-priority transmit buffer, while all other traffic uses the regular transmit buffer." Actually, Cisco routers place unfragmented frames in the high-priority buffer, and fragmented frames in the regular buffers.

A serious consequence of this behavior is that VoIP frames are fragmented if they are larger than the FRF.12 fragment size. In such cases, VoIP frames are placed in the normal transmit buffer, where they may incur excessive delay from data in other PVCs. *It is critical that the FRF.12 fragment size is larger than VoIP packets.* For very low-speed interfaces, you must increase the fragment size or reduce the VoIP payload size to ensure adequate handling of VoIP packets.

TIP   It is critical that the FRF.12 fragment size is larger than VoIP packets.

Another serious consequence of the FRF.12 fragmentation behavior is that non-VoIP packets may be placed in the high-priority transmit buffer. For example, Telnet packets are usually smaller than the fragment size. A large number of Telnet sessions through an interface may cause voice-quality problems. You should be aware of a few other issues associated with FRF.12 fragmentation:

- Per the Implementation Agreement, Local Management Interface (LMI) messages are not fragmented. Excessive LMI traffic can adversely impact voice quality.

- As of this writing, not all router platforms support FRF.12 (such as, the 2500 series). Make sure that VoIP traffic does not pass through such routers attached to low-speed frame relay links.

You can monitor the performance of frame relay fragmentation with the commands found in Example 15-37.

Example 15-37 *Monitoring Performance of Frame Relay Fragmentation*

```
r2#show frame-relay fragment
interface      dlci  frag-type     frag-size  in-frag     out-frag    dropped-frag
Serial0:0      16    VoFR-cisco    80         1261        1298        0
Serial0:0      17    VoFR          80         0           243         0
Serial0:0      18    end-to-end    80         0           0           0

r2# show frame-relay fragment interface Serial0:0 16
  fragment-size 80                    fragment type end-to-end
  in fragmented pkts 0                out fragmented pkts 0
  in fragmented bytes 0               out fragmented bytes 0
  in un-fragmented pkts 0             out un-fragmented pkts 0
  in un-fragmented bytes 0            out un-fragmented bytes 0
  in assembled pkts 0                 out pre-fragmented pkts 0
  in assembled bytes 0               out pre-fragmented bytes
  in dropped reassembling pkts 0      out dropped fragmenting pkts 0
  in timeouts 0
  in out-of-sequence fragments 0
  in fragments with unexpected B bit set 0
  out interleaved packets 0
```

Multilink PPP

Multilink PPP (ML-PPP) is the encapsulation of choice for leased lines and ISDN when VoIP traffic must be supported. The original intent for ML-PPP fragmentation, as described in RFC 1990 (which supercedes RFC 1717), is to support multilink bundles that include physical channels with different transmission rates. Without fragmentation, bonded links with different transmission rates (for example, a V.34 modem line bonded with an ISDN B-channel) will cause packets to be received out of order. With ML-PPP fragmentation, traffic can be better distributed between paths that have different transmission rates. Unordered fragments may be resequenced by ML-PPP, so network protocols reap the benefits of higher aggregate bandwidth without the burden of unordered packet receipt. A larger discrepancy between transmission rates on physical channels requires a larger buffer to resequence the out-of-order fragments.

Cisco has built upon this technology to support an entirely different goal. Because RFC 1990 enables unordered receipt of ML-PPP fragments, and not all packets must be fragmented, ML-PPP is an excellent framework to support interleaving of small real-time packets between fragments of larger data packets. VoIP packets can be sent between fragments of large data packets, and the receiver can reorder and reassemble the data fragments without a problem.

For ISDN Basic Rate Interfaces (BRIs) or Primary Rate Interfaces (PRIs), and for dialer interfaces, the commands shown in Example 15-38 implement ML-PPP fragment/interleaving.

Example 15-38   *Configuring ML-PPP Fragment/Interleaving for Dialer Interfaces*

```
r2#conf t
Enter configuration commands, one per line.  End with CNTL/Z.
r2(config)#interface bri0
r2(config-if)#rotary-group 8
r2(config-if)#exit
r2(config)#interface Dialer8
r2(config-if)#ip address 5.5.5.1 255.255.255.0
r2(config-if)#ppp multilink
r2(config-if)#ppp fragmentation
r2(config-if)#ppp multilink fragment-delay 10
r2(config-if)#ppp multilink interleave
r2(config-if)#fair-queue 64 256 0
r2(config-if)#ip rtp reserve 16384 16383 64
r2(config-if)#^Z
r2#
```

For leased lines, you must configure a virtual-template interface, which is dynamically applied to a serial interface as a virtual-access interface. For information about virtual templates and virtual-access interfaces, consult the Dial Solutions Configuration Guide on CCO. The commands shown in Example 15-39 enable ML-PPP fragment/interleaving for a serial interface:

Example 15-39   *Configuring ML-PPP Fragment/Interleaving for Serial Interfaces*

```
r2#conf t
Enter configuration commands, one per line.  End with CNTL/Z.
r2(config)#interface serial0
r2(config-if)#encapsulation ppp
r2(config-if)#ppp multilink
r2(config-if)#exit
r2(config)#interface virtual-template1
r2(config-if)#ip address 5.5.5.1 255.255.255.0
r2(config-if)#ppp multilink
r2(config-if)#ppp fragmentation
r2(config-if)#ppp multilink fragment-delay 10
r2(config-if)#fair-queue 64 256 0
r2(config-if)#ppp multilink interleave
r2(config-if)#ip rtp reserve 16384 16383 64
r2(config-if)#exit
r2(config)# multilink virtual-template 1
r2(config)#^Z
r2#
```

First, the serial interface is minimally configured for ML-PPP. A virtual-template interface is then configured with the normal interface commands (such as network protocol information), in addition to the special ML-PPP commands. The virtual-template interface configuration is then dynamically applied to the serial interface with the **multilink virtual-template** global command.

The commands in bold print are explicitly required to implement the fragment/interleave function for ML-PPP. The parameter for the fragment-delay configuration is the number of milliseconds of serialization delay that a fragment will generate. The router uses the interface bandwidth and this parameter to adjust the size of fragments. WFQ is not the default for virtual-template interfaces. If you do not enable WFQ (or CB-WFQ), the ML-PPP fragmentation function is not activated. RTP prioritization must be implemented to create the high-priority queue for VoIP packets. Without this configuration, there is no way to interleave the VoIP packets between the ML-PPP fragments.

If you do not explicitly configure a form of WFQ on the virtual template interface, the output of the **show interface virtual-access** reminds you that ML-PPP fragmentation will not function properly as seen in Example 15-40.

Example 15-40 *Verifying Application of Virtual-Template Configuration to the Serial Interface*

```
r1#show interface virtual-access 1
Virtual-Access1 is up, line protocol is up
  Hardware is Virtual Access interface
  Internet address is 5.5.5.2/24
  MTU 1500 bytes, BW 1544 Kbit, DLY 100000 usec,
     reliability 255/255, txload 1/255, rxload 1/255
  Encapsulation PPP, loopback not set
  Keepalive set (10 sec)
  DTR is pulsed for 5 seconds on reset
  LCP Open, multilink Open
  Open: IPCP
  NOTE: Multilink interleaving is configured but inactive
        because queuing strategy is not fair-queueing
  Last input 00:00:14, output never, output hang never
  Last clearing of "show interface" counters 00:00:22
  Queueing strategy: fifo

  <output truncated>
r1#
```

It is important to configure a shut and no shut on the serial interface following any changes to the virtual template configuration. The original virtual template configuration stays active on the serial interface until the virtual access interface is reset.

You can monitor the performance of the ML-PPP link, including fragmentation errors, with the command found in Example 15-41.

Example 15-41 *Monitoring Performance of ML-PPP Fragmentation*

```
r1#show ppp multilink

Virtual-Access1, bundle name is r2
  0 lost fragments, 0 reordered, 0 unassigned, sequence 0x5/0x5 rcvd/sent
  0 discarded, 0 lost received, 1/255 load
  Member links: 1 (max not set, min not set)
    Serial0  1930 weight
```

ATM

There is nothing to configure with respect to fragmentation in ATM networks. The technology natively breaks traffic into 53-byte cells. However, there is a bandwidth efficiency issue because the cells are of a fixed length. Assuming CRTP (RTP header compression) is supported on ATM interfaces, a VoIP packet may be 22 bytes long. Because voice traffic cannot wait for additional packets to fill the payload, the unfilled portion of the ATM cell is padded and 53 bytes are transmitted. It is important to tune the size of VoIP packets such that an ATM cell is optimally filled. The best way to achieve this is to tune the codec payload size in the dial-peer or voice-class codec configuration mode (see Chapter 17, "Establishing Network-Wide Calling Capability"). The cell payload size should also be tuned for native VoATM implementations.

Traffic Shaping and Policing

Traffic shaping is important when a router can transmit data faster than the link-layer connection can support. This situation is common in frame relay and ATM networks, because a router can send traffic into the cloud at the port access speed, which usually exceeds the end-to-end committed rate for the virtual circuit (VC). When a router sends data in excess of the committed rate, the circuit provider may randomly drop frames or cells to keep traffic within the contracted bandwidth allowances. Because frames or cells are randomly dropped in the WAN cloud, any queuing policies implemented in routers are nullified. For example, a VoIP packet may be prioritized ahead of data in a router queue, but this service is wasted if the VoIP packet is dropped in the WAN cloud.

Some people have the misconception that voice should be transmitted within the committed rate, while data should be allowed to burst above the committed rate for a VC. If voice and data traffic share the same VC, this idea is completely wrong. The committed rate applies to all traffic on a VC, no matter how you sort it. If you send voice traffic at the committed rate, then any additional data traffic puts the voice traffic at risk of being dropped. The following rules always apply:

- If any part of a VC is used for voice or real-time traffic, then you must not exceed the committed rate for the VC.

- If you want to allow data traffic to burst above the committed rate, then you must put the data traffic in a separate VC.

Whereas traffic shaping places extra traffic in a queue, *traffic policing* either discards the traffic or rewrites the IP precedence/ToS bits. Although traffic policing can be used to drop packets that exceed the committed rate, it causes lost data and retransmissions. Traffic policing is a useful tool to enforce policies, but it is not critical to implement for the sake of preserving voice quality. Traffic shaping is a gentler tool to manage transmission rates, because the queued traffic can still reach its destination. For more information about traffic policing on Cisco routers, search for CAR or Committed Access Rate on CCO.

You can configure two types of traffic shaping on Cisco routers:

- Frame relay traffic shaping (FRTS)
- Generic traffic shaping (GTS)

Frame Relay Traffic Shaping

There are three steps to configuring Frame Relay traffic shaping (FRTS):

1 Create a Frame Relay map class and define the traffic-shaping parameters.

2 Assign the Frame Relay map class to a VC.

3 Enable FRTS on the interface that contains the VC.

TIP   When the CIR is equal to the port speed, you do not need to configure FRTS (except in the case of VoFR, which may still require traffic shaping).

Defining the Traffic-Shaping Parameters

Most of the work required to implement FRTS is defining the parameters within the Frame Relay map class as shown in Example 15-42.

Example 15-42   *Defining Traffic-Shaping Parameters in a Frame Relay Map Class*

```
r2#conf t
Enter configuration commands, one per line.  End with CNTL/Z.
r2(config)#map-class frame-relay TraffShape
r2(config-map-class)#frame-relay fair-queue
r2(config-map-class)#no frame-relay adaptive-shaping
r2(config-map-class)#frame-relay mincir out 128000
r2(config-map-class)#frame-relay cir out 128000
r2(config-map-class)#frame-relay be out 0
r2(config-map-class)#frame-relay bc out 1280
r2(config-map-class)#frame-relay fragment 160
r2(config-map-class)#^Z
r2#
```

By default, FRTS enables FIFO queuing for the VC. You should activate the more desirable WFQ with the **frame-relay fair-queue** command in the map class.

In consideration of voice quality, there are a few rules you should follow when setting the traffic shaping parameters:

1 Disable Frame Relay adaptive shaping.

2 Set mincir and cir equal to the contracted CIR from the circuit vendor. If Frame Relay fragmentation is also used, then set mincir and cir a little lower than the actual CIR to account for fragment headers.

3 Set B_e equal to zero.

4 Set B_c according to the following formula:,

$$B_C = CIR * \left(\frac{T_C}{1000} \right)$$

where T_c (in ms) should simulate the desired serialization delay (explained in more detail shortly). A reasonable value for T_c is 10 ms.

5 Enable Frame Relay fragmentation and interleaving, setting the fragment size equal to B_c. Note that the fragment parameter is configured in bytes, and the B_c parameter is configured in bits.

Frame Relay adaptive shaping should be disabled because it does not improve performance for voice traffic. By the time a BECN or FECN is received, voice quality has already been degraded by congestion in the WAN. You must take a more proactive approach by limiting traffic to the CIR, which should prevent FECNs and BECNs. In older Cisco IOS (versions 11.2 and 11.3), adaptive shaping is disabled by configuring [**no**] **frame-relay becn-response-enable** in the map class.

The mincir and cir are set to different values only if used with adaptive shaping. The mincir value represents the real CIR contracted with the vendor, and the cir value represents a higher amount of traffic that you hope to transmit on a sustained basis. When BECNs are received, the transmission rate is reduced from the configured cir value to the mincir value. Because you are disabling adaptive shaping, you should set cir equal to mincir to ensure that you do not burst above the actual CIR. If voice and data share a single VC (and you have no data-only VCs), you should order the circuit with a CIR equal to the port speed. If you do not, you are paying for a higher port speed than you can use.

The bc value defaults to 1/8 of the configured CIR, which yields a time interval T_c of 125 ms for a single transmit/pause cycle (see Chapter 8, "WAN Protocols for Integrated Voice and Data Services," for a review of FRTS principles, including T_c, B_c, B_e, and CIR). This is completely unacceptable for voice traffic. The value of T_c for a Frame Relay VC should be selected in a similar manner as the serialization delay for clear channel circuits. Recall that a serialization delay of 10 ms is the design goal behind Cisco's recommendation of 80 bytes of fragment size per 64 kbps of bandwidth. In keeping with this delay target, the value of T_c should be set to 10 ms. Using this value for T_c, the B_c value should equal 1 percent of the CIR.

Note that you can set B_c to an even smaller value, but there is little benefit unless you also decrease the Frame Relay fragment size. Decreasing the fragment size incurs significantly more overhead from fragment headers, so it is not recommended to reduce the fragment size below 80 bytes per 64 kbps of CIR.

TIP	Set B_c to $1/100^{th}$ of the configured CIR, and set the Frame Relay fragment size equal to the committed burst size. Beware that fragment size is configured in bytes, and B_c is configured in bits.

Engineers commonly use the term burst in reference to traffic above CIR, so the meanings of committed burst (B_c) and excess burst (B_e) have become obscured. B_c refers to the number of bits within CIR that are transmitted in an interval, and B_e refers to the number of bits above the CIR that are transmitted in an interval. In other words, B_c is committed traffic, and B_e is bursting traffic. With these definitions, it is clear that B_e should be 0 for all VCs that have voice traffic, because bursting above CIR is not allowed.

Enabling Frame Relay Traffic Shaping on an Interface

After you have defined the traffic-shaping parameters in a Frame Relay map class, you must apply the map class in one of three places:

- VC
- Sub-interface
- Major interface

The router searches in this order when deciding which map class to apply if there are multiple map classes assigned. You can take advantage of this behavior to simplify the configuration of routers with many sub-interfaces or VCs. For example, if most of the VCs on an interface have the same CIR and remote port speed (this last element is critical to fragmentation issues), then you can apply the map class to the major interface (instead of to each sub-interface or VC). If just a few sites have different characteristics, then you can apply a different map class to these sub-interfaces or VCs. Example 15-43 shows the configuration of a map class for a specific VC.

Example 15-43   *Assigning a Frame Relay Map Class to a VC and Enabling Frame Relay Traffic Shaping*

```
r2#conf t
Enter configuration commands, one per line.  End with CNTL/Z.
r2(config)#interface serial0
r2(config-if)#frame-relay traffic-shaping
r2(config-if)#frame-relay interface-dlci 16
r2(config-fr-dlci)#class TraffShape
r2(config-fr-dlci)#^Z
r2#
```

The **frame-relay traffic-shaping** command is always configured on the major interface only. If you want to associate a map class with the major interface or a sub-interface, then use the frame-relay class configuration at the interface or sub-interface level.

Verifying Operation and Monitoring Performance

To verify the configuration of FRTS, use the command shown in Example 15-44.

Example 15-44 *Verifying Configuration of Frame Relay Traffic Shaping*

```
r2#show traffic-shape

Interface   Se0
         Access Target   Byte   Sustain   Excess    Interval  Increment Adapt
VC       List   Rate     Limit  bits/int  bits/int  (ms)      (bytes)   Active
16              128000   160    1280      0         10        160       -
r2#
```

The port speed for this example (not shown in the output) is 1536 kbps, excluding the T1 framing. With CIR at 128 kbps, and B_c set according to the formula in the preceding section, the interface transmission should repeat the following cycle:

1 Transmit 160 bytes at the full T-1 line rate for 0.833 ms.

2 Pause for 9.167 ms.

We explicitly designed this behavior, because we set B_c such that the transmission and pause duration would exactly equal 10 ms (by setting T_c=10 in the equation for B_c). The Frame Relay fragment size should be set equal to B_c so that a single fragment is transmitted in the time interval T_c.

You can monitor traffic-shaping performance as illustrated in Example 15-45.

Example 15-45 *Monitoring Performance and Operation of Frame Relay Traffic Shaping*

```
r2#show traffic-shape statistics
         Access Queue            Packets   Bytes     Packets   Bytes     Shaping
I/F      List   Depth                                Delayed   Delayed   Active
Se0             14               1212      1518044   1110      1391304   yes
```

From this output, it is clear that traffic shaping is active, and that the potential traffic load is exceeding the CIR, because packets are in queue.

Circuit vendors do not have the contractual right to drop any of your traffic as long as you limit your traffic rate to the CIR. In reality, you may still experience problems with certain vendors because of over-subscription. Carriers knowingly provision more committed bandwidth across trunks than they can support, because not all customers use their full committed bandwidth at the same time. You may not experience frame drops, but you may very likely see increased delay and jitter through the Frame Relay cloud when the provider network is congested. The solution to this problem is to track performance for your circuits and hold vendors to service level agreements (SLA). It is important to prenegotiate SLAs with your circuit vendors that provide monetary penalties and give you the opportunity to end a contract for unacceptable circuit performance. This is your only real tool to combat WAN QoS issues, because no router configuration in your network can fix problems in your provider network.

Generic Traffic Shaping

Generic traffic shaping (GTS) is conceptually very similar to FRTS. You must define the target bit rate, which is analogous to CIR, and the committed bits per interval, which is analogous to B_c. You should set the committed bits per interval value according to the same formula used for B_c. You must also define the excess bits per interval, according to the same rules used for B_e. Finally, you must define a queue depth for packets that are delayed from transmission by the GTS process. Example 15-46 commands configure GTS.

Example 15-46 *Configuring GTS*

```
r2#conf t
Enter configuration commands, one per line.  End with CNTL/Z.
R2(config)#interface serial0
r2(config-if)#traffic-shape rate 128000 1280 0 512
r2(config-if)#^Z
r2#
```

In practice, GTS is used for Frame Relay and ATM interfaces. It is not common to use GTS on other interface types, because the committed bandwidth is usually synonymous with the port speed (for example, 128 kbps for ISDN BRI, 1536 kbps for T1, and so on). Aside from ATM and Frame Relay interfaces, you can use GTS if you need to constrain bandwidth utilization for some other reason. For example, you may want to place a rate limit on traffic that is tunneled through another network, or limit the bandwidth of certain applications using an access list with GTS. If your goal is to limit bandwidth for specific applications, you should consider a standard queuing technique as your first option (for example, CB-WFQ).

You can verify the configuration of GTS with the same command used for FRTS as shown in Example 15-47.

Example 15-47 *Verifying Configuration of GTS*

```
r2#show traffic-shape serial0

Interface   Se0
        Access Target   Byte    Sustain   Excess    Interval  Increment Adapt
VC      List   Rate     Limit   bits/int  bits/int  (ms)      (bytes)   Active
-              128000   160     1280      0         10        160       -
r2#
```

Note that in the first column, there is no VC specified, because this is not FRTS. GTS applies to the interface or sub-interface as a whole.

You can monitor the performance of GTS with the same command used for FRTS as shown in Example 15-48.

Example 15-48 *Monitoring Performance and Operation of GTS*

```
r2#show traffic-shape statistics
           Access Queue    Packets   Bytes     Packets   Bytes     Shaping
I/F        List   Depth                        Delayed   Delayed   Active
Se0               6        590       782320    536       716906    yes
r2#
```

Header Compression

Header compression is most useful for applications that generate small data payloads, because the protocol headers of such applications consume a significant percentage of available bandwidth. Real-time applications typically generate small payloads, because they cannot tolerate the delay incurred when filling the payload. Target applications for header compression include Telnet and most RTP applications. Table 15-2 shows the bandwidth efficiency improvements that header compression can have for specific applications.

Table 15-2 *Header Compression Reduces Protocol Overhead and Increases Bandwidth Efficiency*

	Bandwidth Consumed by Headers Without Header Compression	Bandwidth Consumed by Headers With Header Compression
VoIP call	66.7%	9.1%
Telnet session	97.6%	66.7%
FTP session	2.6%	1.3%

There are two types of header compression available in Cisco routers:

- TCP header compression
- RTP header compression

When TCP header compression is enabled, it applies to all TCP flows. There is no mechanism to restrict its function to specific application types. To reap the bandwidth savings of TCP header compression for Telnet flows, you must also compress TCP/IP headers for other traffic types including FTP and HTTP. Header compression for bulk transfers yields little bandwidth savings, but may consume significant CPU resources in your routers.

RTP header compression yields significant bandwidth savings for most applications, so it should almost always be implemented when RTP traffic is present. If the predominant RTP traffic in your network is VoIP, then you should definitely implement RTP header compression.

The commands shown in Example 15-49 implement both TCP and RTP header compression.

Example 15-49   *Configuring TCP and RTP Header Compression*

```
r2#conf t
Enter configuration commands, one per line.  End with CNTL/Z.
r2(config)#interface serial1
r2(config-if)#ip tcp header-compression
r2(config-if)#ip tcp compression-connections 96
r2(config-if)#ip rtp header-compression
r2(config-if)#ip rtp compression-connections 96
r2(config-if)#^Z
r2#
```

The compression-connections parameters indicate the maximum number of connections that may be compressed, after which additional connections are not compressed. This command is important to limit the number of packets that are process-switched in software versions before IOS 12.0(7)T. Without this command, excessive router CPU resources may be allocated to header compression functions. The value of the **compression-connections** command when header compression is fast-switched is less clear.

You can use the command shown in Example 15-50 to monitor the performance of TCP header compression.

Example 15-50   *Monitoring Performance of TCP Header Compression*

```
r1#sh ip tcp header-compression
TCP/IP header compression statistics:
  Interface Serial0:
    Rcvd:    188 total, 186 compressed, 0 errors
             0 dropped, 0 buffer copies, 0 buffer failures
    Sent:    51 total, 43 compressed,
             1306 bytes saved, 420 bytes sent
             4.10 efficiency improvement factor
    Connect: 128 rx slots, 128 tx slots, 2 long searches, 2 misses
             96% hit ratio, five minute miss rate 0 misses/sec, 0 max

r1#
```

Most of the traffic in the preceding example is Telnet traffic, so almost all the packets are compressed. A similar command is used to monitor performance of RTP header compression as shown in Example 15-51.

Example 15-51 *Performance of RTP Header Compression*

```
r2#sh ip rtp header-compression
RTP/UDP/IP header compression statistics:
Interface Serial2/0/2:0:
    Rcvd:    1218808 total, 1218315 compressed, 0 errors
             0 dropped, 35322 buffer copies, 0 buffer failures
    Sent:    1098239 total, 1097762 compressed,
             39467877 bytes saved, 178710363 bytes sent
             1.22 efficiency improvement factor
    Connect: 16 rx slots, 16 tx slots, 127415 long searches, 449 misses
             99% hit ratio, five minute miss rate 0 misses/sec, 0 max

r2#
```

The efficiency improvement factor shown in Example 15-51 indicates the average VoIP packet size reduction, according to the following formula:

All VoIP traffic across the interface from which the example output was captured uses a G.711 audio codec with 160-byte payloads. Before RTP header compression, each packet is 200 bytes, and after RTP header compression, each packet is 164 bytes. As you can see, 200 divided by 164 yields an efficiency improvement factor of 1.22, which is reported in Example 15-51.

You can clear the header-compression statistics counters with the **clear ip tcp header-compression** and **clear ip rtp header-compression** commands.

The primary argument against header compression is that packets must be process-switched when header compression is applied. In other words, the router CPU must handle each packet, which takes more time and effort than the normal fast-switching process. The packet throughput of routers is significantly reduced if packets must be process-switched as opposed to fast-switched. Beginning in Cisco IOS 12.0(7)T, both RTP and TCP headers are compressed in the fast-switching or Cisco Express Forwarding (CEF) path. IOS 12.1(2)T introduces additional enhancements that enable three or four times as many concurrent CRTP sessions, using the CEF switching path. There is now little argument against implementing RTP and TCP header compression.

LAN Considerations in Brief

- All the technologies explored in this chapter, with the exception of WRED, are applied in the WAN portion of your network. Just as your WAN links may be congested, so your LAN connections may be congested.

- Many network designers simply add bandwidth in the LAN to overcome QoS issues, but you should develop a more comprehensive QoS plan for your campus environments. Specifically, you should implement the IEEE 802.1p CoS bits in the tags that switches prepend to Ethernet frames. Cisco switches use these tags to implement a WRED-like feature at the link layer to ensure that VoIP packets are not dropped because of congested switch port buffers.

- You should pay close attention to the hardware and software architecture of the Ethernet switches in your LANs. Cisco switches are carefully designed to efficiently buffer and queue Ethernet frames when there is contention for a single port (such as the port attached to a router or server), whereas other vendors may inadequately address port contention. Many vendors market the total capacity of a switch, which measures the back-plane capacity in the absence of port contention. The total capacity measurement does not reflect traffic patterns in most real networks, so be sure to consider how your switches actually perform in your environment.

Summary

Remember that your network-wide QoS plan is only as good as the weakest element. At this point, you should understand each of the points that need to be addressed. This chapter includes examples of a variety of QoS technologies that are appropriate for the parts of your network that are most likely to be the performance bottlenecks. You can explore Cisco Connection Online for additional examples of QoS in ATM backbones and Ethernet Campus backbones.

CHAPTER 16

Establishing Router-PBX Connectivity

Most of this chapter is focused on commands that affect the operation of the voice ports on Cisco routers. In the case of digital voice ports, you must attend to other configuration elements as well, including controller interfaces and serial interfaces for the D-channel of Integrated Services Digital Network (ISDN), Q.SIG, and transparent common channel signaling (CCS) connections. The various connection modes that you can configure on the voice port of a Cisco router (for example, PLAR, PLAR-OPX, trunk, and tie) are discussed in Chapter 17, "Establishing Network-Wide Calling Capability," as these concepts relate to end-to-end voice connectivity. The **debug vpm signal** command is explored in detail in Appendix C.

This chapter is organized into the following sections:

- Selecting voice-port hardware for Cisco routers
- Basic analog voice-port configuration
- Basic digital voice-port configuration
- Tuning voice-port parameters
- Maintenance and troubleshooting commands

A variety of voice-signaling concepts are briefly mentioned in this chapter, in the process of demonstrating Cisco router configurations. If you are unfamiliar with any of the signaling concepts that are mentioned in this chapter, refer back to Chapter 2, "Enterprise Telephony Signaling," for a more detailed explanation.

Selecting Voice-Port Hardware for Cisco Routers

The first step in establishing connectivity between a router and a phone switch (or other traditional telephony device) is to ensure hardware compatibility. You must survey the existing phone switches (PBXs or key systems), and determine the card types that your phone switches support and that you have currently available. When considering the cards that are available in the existing phone switches, it is common practice to include the cards for tie lines and OPX lines that will be disconnected as a result of the voice/data integration project.

As of this writing, the following Cisco router and switch families support voice interfaces:

- 1750 series2600 series
- 3600 series
- MC3810
- Catalyst 3500, 4000 and 6000 series
- AS5300 and AS5800 series
- 7100 series
- 7200 series
- 7500 series

These router and switch families provide broad coverage to support the following types of voice hardware:

- Analog FXS
- Analog FXO
- Analog E&M
- Digital BRI
- Digital T-1/E-1/PRI

NOTE   Not all router and switch families support all types of voice interfaces. For example, the Cisco 1750 branch router only supports analog interfaces, and the AS5300 and AS5800 only support digital T-1/E-1/PRI interfaces. Make sure to check the current product catalog or configuration tool available at Cisco Connection Online (CCO).

Analog FXS ports act as the central office (CO) side of the analog loop-start and ground-start trunks, as described in Chapter 2. You can connect the FXS ports of a Cisco router to individual telephony terminals such as fax machines or residential-style telephones. You can also connect FXS ports to the two-wire analog loop-start or ground-start trunk ports of a phone switch (that is, the same ports on the phone switch that you would normally attach to the CO).

Analog FXO ports act as the customer premises equipment (CPE) side of the analog loop-start and ground-start trunks, as described in Chapter 2. You can connect the FXO ports of a Cisco router anywhere that you would normally connect a telephone or fax machine—that is, to the analog station ports on a phone switch, or to a loop-start or ground-start trunk from a provider network.

NOTE	If you are considering an FXO daughter card for a 1700/2600/3600 series router (such as Cisco part numbers VIC-2FXO or VIC-2FXO-EU), you should order the updated version of the card that supports battery-reversal for loop-start answer supervision. The new product numbers are VIC-2FXO-M1 for North America and VIC-2FXO-M2 for Europe. See Chapter 2 for more details on loop-start answer supervision.

Analog E&M ports act as the CO side of analog E&M connections. The analog E&M ports can emulate any type of E&M circuit except E&M Type IV. All useful applications of analog E&M ports involve a local connection between a router and a phone switch. If you have an odd reason to connect a router to an E&M tie line through a CO, you should be aware that E&M Type I circuits cannot operate back-to-back, so the router acting as the CO side of the connection cannot connect to the actual CO. You can connect E&M Types II, III, and V to a tie line from the CO (assuming the appropriate type is supported by the circuit vendor), but it should be emphasized that this is not a normal mode of operation and is discouraged.

Digital Basic Rate Interface (BRI) voice ports provide ISDN user-side signaling as of this writing but will also provide ISDN network-side signaling by the time you read this. The BRI voice port with network-side signaling enables an ISDN telephone terminal or PBX to connect to the router just as it would connect to an ISDN circuit going to a CO. ISDN telephones have access to numerous calling features because of the advanced signaling available with ISDN and SS7 networks.

Digital T-1/E-1 voice ports support all of the various signaling types through software configuration, so hardware selection is simple. If you know you have a digital connection in a PBX or from a CO, then your only hardware choice is a digital T-1/E-1. If you have specific software signaling requirements, you may want to do a little more research because different Cisco router platforms and IOS software versions provide differing levels of signaling support. For example, routers with older IOS versions cannot act as the CO side of an ISDN PRI connection. In addition, E&M feature group D (FGD) support (which provides calling party number) is available in different hardware platforms beginning in different IOS releases. Software-based signaling considerations may steer you to a specific router platform if you need certain features before they are available in other platforms (for example, AS5300 for support of FGD). Subsequent software releases should provide similar signaling support on all hardware platforms.

NOTE	A digital connection between a router and a PBX requires a cross-over T-1/E-1 cable. In other words, the transmit pair from the router must be connected to the receive pair of the PBX, and the transmit pair of the PBX must be connected to the receive pair of the router. For T-1/E-1 connections that use RJ-45 jacks on both ends of the connection, pins 1 and 2

from the router side must end up at pins 4 and 5 on the PBX side and vice versa. For E-1 connections that use twin BNC cables, the transmit cable of the router must be connected to the receive cable of the PBX and vice versa. Follow these principles for other wiring configurations. You can determine whether the cables are connected correctly by checking the output of **show controller** [**t1** | **e1**] on the router.

Ensuring hardware compatibility is a simple process, but it should be done before the router voice ports are ordered. This may seem like unnecessary advice, but there are cases of voice/data projects that began with a mass order for routers with identical voice ports, only to discover later that many ports need to be replaced with a different type. To make matters worse, the data portion of such networks are often installed and in operation before the voice incompatibilities are discovered. As a result, extra site visits and downtime for the production network are required to fix what should have been done correctly at the beginning of the project.

Basic Analog Voice-Port Configuration

The minimal voice-port configurations depend on the type of hardware. FXS/FXO ports have similar configuration elements because they represent opposite ends of the same type of connection. E&M ports have a different set of requirements and in general require more configuring to ensure correct operation with a phone switch.

FXS/FXO

To enable basic operation of an FXS/FXO port, you must select either loop-start or ground-start signaling as a minimal configuration. Loop-start signaling is the default for FXS and FXO ports, so you do not need to configure anything on the voice ports in many situations. For example, connecting a plain old telephone or fax machine to an FXS port of a Cisco router requires no voice-port configuration. Neither is voice-port configuration required when connecting an FXO port to an analog station (telephone) port on a phone switch.

When using an FXS port on a router to emulate a CO connection to a key system or PBX, you can most likely use the default loop-start signaling. However, if your phone switch expects ground-start signaling from the CO, then you must configure the FXS port on the router as indicated in Example 16-1.

Example 16-1 *Configuring an FXS or FXO Port for Loop-Start or Ground-Start Signaling*

```
voice-gw2#conf t
Enter configuration commands, one per line.  End with CNTL/Z.
voice-gw2(config)#voice-port 1/1/1
voice-gw2(config-voiceport)#signal ?
  groundStart  Ground Start
```

Example 16-1 *Configuring an FXS or FXO Port for Loop-Start or Ground-Start Signaling (Continued)*

```
  loopStart    Loop Start

voice-gw2(config-voiceport)#signal groundStart
voice-gw2(config-voiceport)#^Z
voice-gw2#
```

You can also configure FXO ports for ground-start signaling, but this is generally used when you connect the router directly to the Public Switched Telephone Network (PSTN) via the CO. Refer to Chapter 2 for information about loop-start and ground-start signaling. Additional configuration options for FXO and FXS ports are included later in this chapter.

E&M

To enable basic operation of an analog E&M port, you must ensure that two configuration options match in the router and the phone switch:

- Circuit type
- Number of audio path wires

You can configure the E&M circuit type as illustrated in Example 16-2. Many PBX technicians may not know which E&M type they are using if you ask them, but E&M Type I is by far the most common in the United States. Outside of the United States, E&M Type V is very common, but Nortel equipment often uses E&M Type II. It is unlikely that you will see E&M Type III in use because it was primarily used when COs were connected via analog lines. Note that Cisco routers do not support E&M Type IV, but you can use E&M Type II on the router if the phone switch expects E&M Type IV. Refer back to Chapter 2 for the operational details of the different E&M circuit types.

Example 16-2 *Configuring the E&M Circuit Type for a Voice Port*

```
voice-gw1#conf t
Enter configuration commands, one per line.  End with CNTL/Z.
voice-gw1(config)#voice-port 1/1/1
voice-gw1(config-voiceport)#type ?
  1  E&M type I
  2  E&M type II
  3  E&M type III
  5  E&M type V

voice-gw1(config-voiceport)#type 5
voice-gw1(config-voiceport)#^Z
voice-gw1#
```

As illustrated in Example 16-3, you must also define whether the audio path uses two or four wires. Either option is acceptable, but the router and PBX must agree. Note that this configuration option is only relevant for analog E&M connections. Digital E&M connections use the ABCD bits for signaling, and the audio path is always four-wire (regardless of how the router is configured for this option) because T-1/E-1 circuits transmit and receive on separate wire pairs.

Example 16-3   *Configuring the E&M Circuit to Use Two Wires or Four Wires for the Audio Path*

```
voice-gw1#conf t
Enter configuration commands, one per line.  End with CNTL/Z.
voice-gw1(config)#voice-port 1/1/1
voice-gw1(config-voiceport)#operation ?
  2-wire  2-wire operation
  4-wire  4-wire operation

voice-gw1(config-voiceport)#operation 4-wire
voice-gw1(config-voiceport)#^Z
voice-gw1#
```

If you do not have access to the PBX configuration, you can guess if the PBX is configured for two-wire or four-wire audio by counting the total number of wires used for each E&M connection. Most likely, the wires will be visible on a punch-down block or cross-connect panel.

You can assume only two wires are used for E&M signaling in the United States, because E&M Type I is the norm. If you know that the circuit is either E&M Type I or Type V, you can generally assume that only two signaling wires are connected (but beware of extra unused wires that are connected!). Therefore, an E&M connection with four total wires definitely uses only a two-wire audio path, and an E&M connection with six total wires most likely uses a four-wire audio path (if E&M Type I or Type V is used). If you know that the connection is E&M Type II or Type IV (such as, back-to-back connections between Nortel PBXs), then you know that four wires are used for the signaling. In this case, an E&M connection with six total wires uses a two-wire audio path, and a connection with all eight wires uses a four-wire audio path. It is possible that all eight wires are connected to the PBX when not all of the wires are used. In this case, you need a voltmeter to understand the wiring.

If it is not already apparent to you, the physical wiring is often the most difficult part of working with analog E&M circuits. If you did not understand the preceding paragraph, then you should review the E&M circuit types as presented in Chapter 2.

Basic Digital Voice-Port Configuration

There are three parts of a router configuration that are required to enable digital voice ports:

- Card Type
- Controllers
- Voice Ports

On the Cisco 7100, 7200, and 7500 series routers, you must first define which card type is used for each physical module (for example, a Port Adapter Module). When you define the card types as either T-1 or E-1, then controller t1 or controller e1 interfaces are dynamically created in the router configuration. With the Cisco 2600 and 3600 series routers, you must explicitly order the hardware to support either T-1 or E-1. You may then configure the controller t1/e1 to assign which DS-0s are used for which type of signaling, such as channel-associated signaling (CAS), Primary Rate Interface (PRI), common channel signaling (CCS), and so forth. Assigning DS-0s to a specific signaling type dynamically creates a voice port. You may then configure the voice port with parameters as for an analog voice port. The following sections provide more detail on these configuration steps.

NOTE   You can also consider digital signal processor (DSP) interfaces (such as dspfarm on the 7200/7500 series, or voice-card on the 2600/3600 series) to be part of the voice-port configuration. You must define the *codec complexity* for these DSP interfaces, which determines whether the DSP resources can support many calls with low-complexity codecs or fewer calls with high-complexity codecs. Because codecs are now part of dial-peer configurations, the DSP interfaces are discussed in Chapter 17, which considers end-to-end calling connectivity and dial-peer issues.

Card Type T1/E1

The first step to enable a voice port for the Cisco 7100, 7200, and 7500 series routers is to define whether it will use T-1 or E-1 signaling. Example 16-4 demonstrates the card-type configuration on a Cisco 7206 VXR router, which has PA-2VXC cards in slots 3 and 5. The configuration in Example 16-4 creates four controller configuration blocks:

- Controller t1 3/0
- Controller t1 3/1
- Controller e1 5/0
- Controller e1 5/1

Example 16-4   *Defining a Digital Voice Port to Use T-1 or E-1 Signaling, Which Creates a Controller t1 or Controller e1*

```
voip-gw3#conf t
Enter configuration commands, one per line.  End with CNTL/Z.
voip-gw3(config)#card type ?
  e1  E1
  t1  T1

voip-gw3(config)#card type t1 ?
  <0-6>  Card slot number

voip-gw3(config)#card type t1 3
voip-gw3(config)#card type e1 5
voip-gw3(config)#^Z
voip-gw3#
```

While you can configure each physical module to support T-1 or E-1 independently, all of the voice ports on a physical module share the same type.

T-1/E-1 Controllers

There are different configuration requirements for the voice ports and the T-1/E-1 controllers on Cisco routers, depending on which signaling method you use. The different signaling methods can be grouped into three classes:

- CAS
- PRI and Q.SIG
- Transparent CCS

CAS

To activate a digital voice interface that uses CAS, you must configure a ds0-group as part of the controller [t1 | e1] configuration. Example 16-5 demonstrates the variety of CAS types that are available on most Cisco routers (for example, MC3810, 2600 series, 3600 series, 7200 series, 7500 series). Note that the router can act as the CO or the CPE side of CAS connections. The configuration in Example 16-5 dynamically creates voice-port 3/0:0.

Example 16-5 *Configuring a Controller T1 for CAS Signaling, Which Creates a Voice Port*

```
voip-gw1#conf t
Enter configuration commands, one per line.  End with CNTL/Z.
voip-gw1(config)#controller t1 3/0
voip-gw1(config-controller)#ds0-group 0 timeslots 1-24 type ?
  e&m-delay-dial      E & M Delay Dial
  e&m-immediate-start E & M Immediate Start
  e&m-wink-start      E & M Wink Start
  fxo-ground-start    FXO Ground Start
  fxo-loop-start      FXO Loop Start
  fxs-ground-start    FXS Ground Start
  fxs-loop-start      FXS Loop Start
  e&m-melcas-immed    E & M MELCAS Immediate Start
  e&m-melcas-wink     E & M MELCAS Wink Start
  e&m-melcas-delay    E & M MELCAS Delay Start
  fxo-melcas          FXO MELCAS
  fxs-melcas          FXS MELCAS

voip-gw1(config-controller)#ds0-group 0 timeslots 1-24 type fxo-loop-start
voip-gw1(config-controller)#^Z
voip-gw1#
```

Line-Side Versus Trunk-Side CAS Protocols

You may hear CAS protocols described as line-side or trunk-side. These labels are from the perspective of a phone switch in a CO as illustrated in Figure 16-1. *Line-side* refers to subscriber connections (for example, from a local exchange carrier (LEC) phone switch to a subscriber's PBX), and *trunk-side* refers to connections between circuit vendor switches (for example, from a LEC phone switch to an Inter-Exchange Carrier (IXC) phone switch).

Figure 16-1   *Line-Side Versus Trunk-Side Signaling*

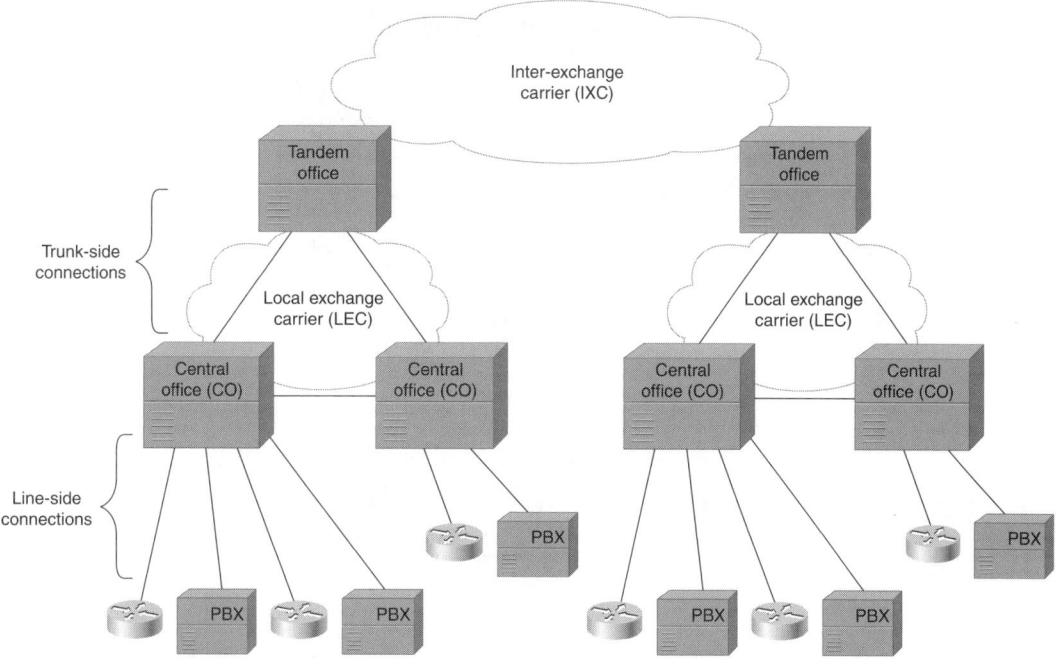

In North America, subscribers can have a long-distance provider (that is, an IXC) predetermined for all outbound calls. This way, subscribers can dial any E.164 number directly without first dialing an access code to reach the long-distance provider. An IXC can only offer this convenience to subscribers if the IXC has E&M FGD (or ISDN/SST) trunk connections to the LEC. An IXC must also have FGD connections to an LEC if it wants to offer the 1010-xxx long-distance provider codes for North American subscribers to access their network. If an IXC does not have FGD (or ISDN/SST) trunk connections to the LEC, subscribers can only access the long-distance network using a calling card scenario. In other words, subscribers call the long-distance provider (hopefully via a toll-free phone number), enter a calling card and PIN number, receive a secondary dial tone, and then dial final destination.

Enterprises may also need E&M FGD connections to a circuit provider if they want to receive ANI with inbound calls from the PSTN. This service is important for call centers and toll-free phone number services.

Cisco AS5300 and AS5800 routers support trunk-side CAS to accommodate service-provider environments and connections to the PSTN. Example 16-6 demonstrates an E&M FGD trunk configured to accept the ANI for inbound calls. Cisco AS5X00 routers can receive and interpret the calling party ANI for inbound calls, but they cannot generate the ANI for outbound calls using FGD. Also note that as of IOS 12.1(1)T, ANI collection for FGD is only supported with MF signaling. Example 16-6 illustrates that when DTMF digits are used across the trunk, the ANI configuration option is not available.

Example 16-6 *Configuring E&M FGD to Recognize ANI in Addition to DNIS (Requires MF Tones)*

```
voip-gw5#conf t
Enter configuration commands, one per line.  End with CNTL/Z.
voip-gw1(config)#controller t1 3
voip-gw1(config-controller)#ds0-group 0 timeslots 1-24 type ?
  e&m-fgb              E & M Type II FGB
  e&m-fgd              E & M Type II FGD
  e&m-immediate-start  E & M Immediate Start
  fgd-eana             FGD Exchange Access North American
  fgd-os               FGD Operator Services
  fxs-ground-start     FXS Ground Start
  fxs-loop-start       FXS Loop Start
  none                 Null Signaling for External Call Control
  r1-itu               R1 ITU
  r1-modified          R1 MODIFIED
  r1-turkey            R1 Signaling for Turkey
  sas-ground-start     SAS Ground Start
  sas-loop-start       SAS Loop Start
  <cr>

voip-gw1(config-controller)#ds0-group 0 timeslots 1-24 type e&m-fgd ?
dtmf     DTMF tone signaling
mf       MF tone signaling
  service  Specify the type of service
  <cr>

voip-gw1(config-controller)#ds0-group 0 timeslots 1-24 type e&m-fgd dtmf ?
  dnis     DNIS addr info provisioned
  service  Specify the type of service
  <cr>
```

Example 16-6   *Configuring E&M FGD to Recognize ANI in Addition to DNIS (Requires MF Tones) (Continued)*

```
voip-gw1(config-controller)#ds0-group 0 timeslots 1-24 type e&m-fgd mf ?
  ani-dnis  ANI/DNIS addr info provisioned
  dnis      DNIS addr info provisioned
  service   Specify the type of service
  <cr>

voip-gw1(config-controller)#ds0-group 0 timeslots 1-24 type e&m-fgd mf ani-dnis
voip-gw1(config-controller)#^Z
voip-gw1#
```

You can also collect ANI information using FGB trunks, as long as the router is configured to know the delimiting character between the ANI and DNIS. Example 16-7 illustrates how to configure a router to accept ANI and DNIS information on an E&M FGB trunk that uses DTMF digit transmission. You must configure a signaling class, which is later applied to the ds0-group using the command **cas-custom X**, where X is the number of the ds0-group.

Example 16-7   *Configuring E&M FGB to Recognize ANI in Addition to DNIS (Using Delimiter)*

```
voip-gw1#conf t
Enter configuration commands, one per line.  End with CNTL/Z.
voip-gw1(config)#signaling-class cas ?
  WORD  Signaling class name

voip-gw1(config)#signaling-class cas ANI*DNIS
voip-gw1(config-sig-class)#profile incoming ?
  WORD  Setting template for profile

voip-gw1(config-sig-class)#profile incoming S<*a<*d<*n
voip-gw1(config-sig-class)#exit
voip-gw1(config)#
voip-gw1(config)#controller t1 3
voip-gw1(config-controller)#ds0-group 0 timeslots 1-24 type e&m-fgb dtmf dnis
voip-gw1(config-controller)#cas-custom 0
voip-gw1(config-ctrl-cas)#class ANI*DNIS
voip-gw1(config-ctrl-cas)#^Z
voip-gw1#
```

Within the signaling-class configuration mode, you must define a template that instructs the tone detector how to process the inbound digits of received calls. Table 16-1 defines the syntax that is used to define the template shown in Example 16-7. You can use this feature to collect ANI on FGB trunks as of IOS 12.1(1)T on Cisco AS5X00 routers.

Table 16-1 *Syntax for signaling-class cas Profiles*

Character	Meaning
S	Start listening for tones
<*	Expect * as a delimiter character
a	Interpret all subsequent digits as ANI (until a nonnumeric digit is received)
<*	Expect * as a delimiter character
d	Interpret all subsequent digits as DNIS (until a nonnumeric digit is received)
<*	Expect * as a delimiter character
n	Process the ANI and DNIS information

PRI and Q.SIG

To activate a digital voice interface that uses ISDN PRI signaling, you must configure a pri-group as part of the controller [t1 | e1] configuration and configure the PRI options under the serial interface that is also generated by the controller [t1 | e1]. When controller t1 3/1 is configured in Example 16-8, the following configuration elements are dynamically created:

- Serial 3/1:23
- Voice-port 3/1:23

Note that on the AS5300 and AS5800 platforms, the serial interface and voice port are identified with a ":D" for D-channel, instead of the ":23" (for T-1) or ":15" (for E-1) on other platforms. At a minimum, you must configure the PRI options as specified in Example 16-8.

Example 16-8 *Creating a T-1 PRI Voice Port*

```
voip-gw1#conf t
Enter configuration commands, one per line.  End with CNTL/Z.
voip-gw1(config)#controller t1 3/1
voip-gw1(config-controller)#pri-group timeslots 1-24
voip-gw1(config-controller)#exit
voip-gw1(config)#interface serial 3/1:23
voip-gw1(config-if)#isdn protocol-emulate ?
  network  ISDN protocol emulation network side
  user     ISDN protocol emulation user side (default)

voip-gw1(config-if)#isdn protocol-emulate network
voip-gw1(config-if)#isdn switch-type ?
  primary-4ess   AT&T 4ESS switch type for the U.S.
  primary-5ess   AT&T 5ESS switch type for the U.S.
```

Example 16-8   *Creating a T-1 PRI Voice Port (Continued)*

```
primary-dms100  Northern Telecom switch type for North America
primary-net5    NET5 switch type for UK, Europe and Asia
primary-ni      National ISDN Switch type for North America
primary-ntt     Japan switch type
primary-qsig    QSIG switch type
primary-ts014   Australia switch type

voip-gw1(config-if)#isdn switch-type primary-ni
voip-gw1(config-if)#isdn incoming-voice ?
  data   Incoming voice calls will be handled as data.
  modem  Incoming voice calls will be handled as modems.
  voice  Incoming voice calls will be handled as voice.

voip-gw1(config-if)#isdn incoming-voice voice
voip-gw1(config-if)#^Z
voip-gw1#
```

When the router PRI voice port connects to the PSTN, you must configure the ISDN switch type to match the phone switch in the CO, just as you would for a data connection. The router acts as the user side of the ISDN connection in this scenario. When you connect the router PRI voice port to a PBX, you must then configure the router to emulate the CO side of the ISDN connection (in other words, the network side). In this scenario, you may configure the ISDN switch type for whatever protocol that the PBX supports. Finally, you must specify that incoming ISDN calls that have the bearer type "voice" are to be processed by the voice module. This option is the default for digital voice ports, but general-purpose T-1/E-1 ports treat incoming voice calls as dial-up modem connections by default.

Example 16-9 illustrates other PRI options that you may configure on the router. By default, the router expects to receive the dialed digits of inbound calls *en bloc*, which means all at once. If the phone switch attached to the router sends digits one at a time in separate messages, you should configure the router for isdn overlap receiving. You can configure the router to send any ISDN cause code to the attached phone switch when the router cannot complete a call. You should ensure that the phone switch understands whatever cause code you send to it, so that it can reroute failed calls. When some phone switches deliver calls to a router, they require Q.931 ALERTING messages from the router in order to generate ring-back tone to the calling party. You can configure the router to send ALERTING messages in response to inbound calls from a phone switch with the **isdn send-alerting** command. The **isdn sending-complete** command is required in some places to comply with local ISDN standards (such as in Taiwan or Hong Kong). You can configure Q.SIG support by setting the ISDN switch type as basic-qsig for BRI or primary-qsig for PRI.

Example 16-9 *Configuration Options for a T-1 PRI Voice Port*

```
voip-gw1#conf t
Enter configuration commands, one per line.  End with CNTL/Z.
voip-gw1(config)#interface serial 3/1:23
voip-gw1(config-if)#isdn ?
  T309-enable             Enable T309 timer
  all-incoming-calls-v120 Answer all incoming calls as V.120
  answer1                 Specify Called Party number and subaddress
  answer2                 Specify Called Party number and subaddress
  bchan-number-order      Specify bchannel starting number order
  bind-l2                 Bind Layer 2 protocol to signaling interface
  bind-l3                 Bind Layer 3 protocol to signaling interface
  caller                  Specify incoming telephone number to be verified
  calling-number          Specify Calling Number included for outgoing calls
  disconnect-cause        Specify cause code to return in call rejection to the
                          switch
  fast-rollover-delay     Delay between fastrollover dials
  incoming-voice          Specify options for incoming calls.
  map                     Specify E.164 address to numbering plan/type mapping
  network-failure-cause   Specify cause code sent to pbx when there is a
                          failure in the network
  not-end-to-end          Specify speed when calls received are not isdn end to
                          end
  outgoing-voice          Specify information transfer capability for voice
                          calls
  overlap-receiving       Specify if the interface will do Overlap Receiving
  protocol-emulate        Protocol (L2/L3) emulation network/user side
  rlm-group               Specify the RLM group for this PRI
  send-alerting           Specify if Alerting message to be sent out before
                          Connect message
  sending-complete        Specify if Sending Complete included in outgoing
                          SETUP message
  service                 Set the specified interface or B channel to the
                          specified state.
  switch-type             Select the Interface ISDN switch type
  tei-negotiation         Set when ISDN TEI negotiation should occur
  unit_test               Corsair Unit test call

voip-gw1(config-if)#^Z
voip-gw1#
```

Transparent CCS

Transparent CCS is required when PBXs must communicate with a proprietary CCS protocol across a VoX network. For example, you may have a Siemens PBX network that communicates via the CorNet-N protocol or a Nortel PBX network that communicates via MCDN. NEC, Lucent, and other phone switch vendors also have proprietary CCS protocols. Cisco routers cannot communicate using these proprietary protocols (except in the case of NEC Fusion), but they can provide a transparent connection between the PBXs across a VoX network. Even though the signaling channel cannot be compressed, the bearer channels can still benefit from voice compression, voice activity detection (VAD), and sharing bandwidth with data traffic when the voice calls are idle.

Figure 16-2 illustrates the signaling relationships between the routers and PBXs when transparent CCS is used.

Figure 16-2   *Relationship Between Routers and PBXs in Transparent CCS Operation*

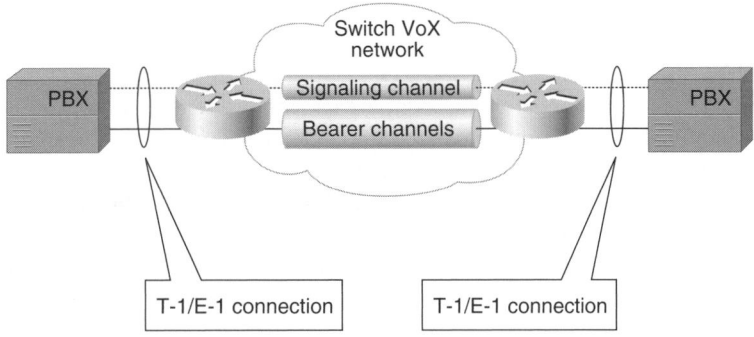

As of this writing, Cisco routers can transparently pass the CCS data channel in two ways:

- TDM cross-connect
- Frame forwarding

For the time-division multiplexing (TDM) cross-connect method, the routers pass the D-channel information across the network without interpreting the contents of the DS-0. For the frame-forwarding method, the routers pass the High-Level Data Link Control (HDLC)-encapsulated CCS messages in Frame Relay frames without interpreting the contents of the messages. In both cases, the bearer channels are passed across the VoX network using the "trunk" connection mode on the router voice ports. Trunk connections are explored in more detail in Chapter 17, but a configuration example is included in a following section to provide a complete configuration for transparent CCS support.

As of this writing, transparent CCS is only supported on the Cisco MC3810. By the time you read this, the TDM cross-connect method should be available on many platforms, and an IP equivalent for the FRF.11 frame-forwarding method may also be available for VoIP. The following examples have been configured on MC3810 routers that run IOS 12.0(7)XK1.

NOTE   Transparent CCS support for VoIP is available as of IOS 12.1(2)XD and 12.1(3)T. While these IOS images are not available as of this writing, you can learn more about these features by searching the "New Features and Release Notes" section of the IOS 12.1 documentation on Cisco's web site. You can also find information about a new type of T-CCS support by searching for the keywords clear-channel codec.

TDM Cross-Connect

The TDM cross-connect method requires a leased line (that is, a clear-channel T-1/E-1 circuit) WAN connection between the routers. The benefit of this approach is that you can support arbitrary CCS protocols, even if they are based on a serial bit-stream as opposed to HDLC messages. Because the entire DS-0 must be passed across the network, this method is not the most bandwidth-efficient way to handle transparent CCS. When no signaling activity is present on the D-channel, the entire DS-0 is still allocated for voice-signaling traffic, and the bandwidth is not available for data traffic or active voice calls.

Example 16-10 illustrates the configuration required for the TDM cross-connect method of transparent CCS. In this example, the router cross-connects timeslot 24 of the T-1 between the router and the PBX with timeslot 24 of the T-1 data circuit for the WAN. The remote router is similarly configured. Note that the router receives clocking from the T-1 leased line and provides this clocking to the PBX. The PBXs on each side of the CCS connection are indirectly driven by the same clock (that is, the clock for T-1 for the WAN circuit), which makes the synchronous serial connection possible.

Example 16-10   *Configuring Transparent CCS Using TDM Cross-Connect*

```
vofr-gw1#conf t
Enter configuration commands, one per line.  End with CNTL/Z.
vofr-gw1(config)#controller t1 0
vofr-gw1(config-controller)#framing esf
vofr-gw1(config-controller)#linecode b8zs
vofr-gw1(config-controller)#clock source line
vofr-gw1(config-controller)#channel-group 0 timeslots 1-23
vofr-gw1(config-controller)#tdm-group 3 timeslots 24
vofr-gw1(config-controller)#exit
vofr-gw1(config)#controller t1 1
vofr-gw1(config-controller)#framing esf
vofr-gw1(config-controller)#linecode b8zs
vofr-gw1(config-controller)#clock source internal
vofr-gw1(config-controller)#mode ccs ?
  cross-connect      cross-connect the CCS channel
  frame-forwarding   CCS frame-forwarding
  <cr>

vofr-gw1(config-controller)#mode ccs cross-connect
vofr-gw1(config-controller)#ds0-group 0 timeslots 1-23 type ?
  e&m-delay-dial       E & M Delay Dial
```

Example 16-10 *Configuring Transparent CCS Using TDM Cross-Connect (Continued)*

```
  e&m-immediate-start  E & M Immediate Start
  e&m-wink-start       E & M Wink Start
  ext-sig              External Signaling
  fxo-ground-start     FXO Ground Start
  fxo-loop-start       FXO Loop Start
  fxs-ground-start     FXS Ground Start
  fxs-loop-start       FXS Loop Start

vofr-gw1(config-controller)#ds0-group 0 timeslots 1-23 type ext-sig
vofr-gw1(config-controller)#tdm-group 4 timeslots 24
vofr-gw1(config-controller)#exit
vofr-gw1(config)#cross-connect ?
  <0-31>  Cross-connect ID

vofr-gw1(config)#cross-connect 9 t1 0 3 t1 1 4
vofr-gw1(config)#^Z
vofr-gw1#
```

The configuration for controller t1 0 is the same as for a normal data circuit, except that one of the DS-0s (timeslot 24) is separately allocated for the CCSs. The controller t1 1 is configured to provide clocking to the PBX and to use the CCS cross-connect mode for voice signaling. The voice-bearer channels (timeslots 1 through 23) must be configured to use external signaling, which tells the router to let the PBX passively provide any necessary signaling. The signaling channel is configured as a separate tdm-group so it can be cross connected with a DS-0 from the WAN circuit. The last configuration line in Example 16-10 shows the actual cross-connect configuration, where tdm-group 3 of controller t1 0 is cross-connected with tdm-group 4 of controller t1 1.

FRF.11 Frame Forwarding

The FRF.11 frame-forwarding method requires a Frame Relay PVC between the routers. This approach supports CCS protocols that use HDLC encapsulation, but it does not support CCS protocols that require a generic serial bit-stream. Fortunately, all common CCS protocols use HDLC encapsulation, so this is not an issue in most networks. Each HDLC message on the CCS signaling channel is encapsulated in a Frame Relay header and sent across the Frame Relay network to the remote site. The frame-forwarding method is a very efficient way to handle transparent CCS because bandwidth is only consumed in the Frame Relay network when there are CCS messages to transmit.

If you have a clear channel T-1/E-1 WAN circuit between routers, you can still take advantage of the bandwidth savings of FRF.11 frame forwarding by using Frame Relay encapsulation on the routers. To use Frame Relay encapsulation over a clear channel T-1/E-1 WAN circuit, you must configure one of the routers with the global command **frame-relay switching** and the serial interface command **frame-relay intf-type dce**. Whatever data-link connection identifiers (DLCIs) you define on the DCE router will appear on the other router with a normal Frame Relay configuration.

Example 16-11 illustrates the configuration required for the FRF.11 frame-forwarding method of transparent CCS. All of the timeslots on the WAN circuit are allocated for the data circuit because there is no need to monopolize a DS-0 for the CCS signaling traffic.

Example 16-11 *Configuring Transparent CCS Using FRF.11 Frame Forwarding*

```
vofr-gw1#conf t
Enter configuration commands, one per line.  End with CNTL/Z.
vofr-gw1(config)#controller t1 0
vofr-gw1(config-controller)#framing esf
vofr-gw1(config-controller)#linecode b8zs
vofr-gw1(config-controller)#clock source line
vofr-gw1(config-controller)#channel-group 0 timeslots 1-24
vofr-gw1(config-controller)#exit
vofr-gw1(config)#controller t1 1
vofr-gw1(config-controller)#framing esf
vofr-gw1(config-controller)#linecode b8zs
vofr-gw1(config-controller)#clock source internal
vofr-gw1(config-controller)#mode ccs frame-forwarding
vofr-gw1(config-controller)#ds0-group 0 timeslots 1-23 type ext-sig
vofr-gw1(config-controller)#exit
vofr-gw1(config)#interface serial 1:23
vofr-gw1(config-if)#ccs encap frf11
vofr-gw1(config-if)#ccs connect ?
  Serial  Serial

vofr-gw1(config-if)#ccs connect serial 0:0 ?
  <16-1007>  Frame relay DLCI
  <cr>

vofr-gw1(config-if)#ccs connect serial 0:0 16 ?
  <5-255>  Frame relay CID
  <cr>

vofr-gw1(config-if)#ccs connect serial 0:0 16 254
vofr-gw1(config-if)#no cdp enable
vofr-gw1(config-if)#no keepalive
vofr-gw1(config-if)#^Z
vofr-gw1#
```

The bearer channels on the voice T-1 (timeslots 1 through 23) are configured for external signaling, just as in the case of TDM cross-connect. However, the signaling mode is now ccs frame-forwarding, and there is no TDM-group defined on controller t1 1 for the signaling channel. Instead, the signaling channel is configured on a serial interface (serial 1:23) just as in the case of a PRI circuit. The **ccs encap frf11** command tells the router to encapsulate the signaling messages in a Frame Relay header. The **ccs connect** command tells the router to forward the frames out of a specific serial interface, PVC, and subframe channel. Finally, the router must be configured to suppress keepalive and Cisco Discovery

Protocol (CDP) packets on the signaling channel, which would otherwise disrupt the signaling between the PBXs.

Bearer-Channel Connections

Cisco routers pass the bearer channels (that is, the DS-0s that are used for the voice audio path) across the VoX network using a trunk connection. The trunk connection mode and other connection modes are discussed in Chapter 17. Example 16-12 is included here to show the configuration elements that complete either of the transparent CCS examples described in the preceding sections (TDM cross-connect or FRF.11 frame forwarding).

Example 16-12 *Configuring a Trunk Connection for the Bearer Channels of the CCS Trunk*

```
vofr-gw1#conf t
Enter configuration commands, one per line.  End with CNTL/Z.
vofr-gw1(config)#voice-port 1:0
vofr-gw1(config-voiceport)#connection trunk 1002
vofr-gw1(config-voiceport)#exit
vofr-gw1(config)#dial-peer voice 1001 pots
vofr-gw1(config-dial-peer)#destination-pattern 1001
vofr-gw1(config-dial-peer)#port 1:0
vofr-gw1(config)#dial-peer voice 1002 vofr
vofr-gw1(config-dial-peer)#destination-pattern 1002
vofr-gw1(config-dial-peer)#session target serial 0:0 16
vofr-gw1(config-dial-peer)#^Z
vofr-gw1#
```

As soon as the trunk connection is configured on the router voice port, the router establishes a call to the destination specified in the trunk configuration (1002 in Example 16-12). The voice port that represents the bearer channels on the other router should be configured with a trunk connection to 1001, followed by the keyword answer-mode (which makes the router act as the slave of the master-slave trunk relationship).

Chapter 17 discusses the features that you can add to the dial-peer configurations, such as support for specific codecs, voice-activity detection, and so forth.

Digital Voice Ports

There is no mandatory configuration on digital voice-ports because all of the mandatory signaling options are specified as part of the controller [t1 | e1] or ISDN D-channel interface configurations. The following section discusses parameters that you may tune as part of an analog or digital voice-port configuration. Note that some of these parameters, such as the timing for E&M signaling, may be required to establish basic connectivity with a phone switch that uses nonstandard parameters.

Tuning Voice-Port Parameters

While not usually required, there are many auxiliary commands that can enhance the signaling operation or voice quality of calls through voice port. In some cases, such as E&M signaling, you may need to adjust timers just to establish basic connectivity between a router and a PBX. The following topics are explored in this section:

- Signal timing and timeouts
- ABCD bit values
- Answer and disconnect signaling
- Ringing cadence and automatic answering
- Digit representation
- Call progress tones
- Companding
- Input and output voice levels
- Echo cancellation and nonlinear processing
- Busyout-monitor

Signal Timing and Timeouts

Example 16-13 illustrates the voice-port timing options that are available for different interface types (such as E&M, FXS, FXO) and hardware platforms. Note that you will not see this exact output on a router because it is a composite of options available on different interfaces. The different options have all been combined here so you can see at a glance what the various options are.

Example 16-13 *Configuring Signaling Timers for Various Signaling Methods*

```
voice-gw1#conf t
Enter configuration commands, one per line.  End with CNTL/Z.
voice-gw1(config)#voice-port 4/1:0
voice-gw1(config-voiceport)#timing ?
  clear-wait       time of inactive seizure signal to declare call cleared in
                   milliseconds
  delay-duration   Max delay signal duration for delay dial signalling in
                   milliseconds
  delay-start      Timing of generation of delay start sig from detect
                   incoming seizure in milliseconds
  guard-out        a time window after call is disconnected that no outgoing
                   call is allowed
  hookflash-in     Hookflash input duration in milliseconds (FXS only)
  hookflash-out    Hookflash output duration in milliseconds (FXO only)
  wink-duration    Max wink duration for wink start signaling in milliseconds
  wink-wait        Max wink wait for wink start signaling in milliseconds
```

Example 16-13   *Configuring Signaling Timers for Various Signaling Methods (Continued)*

```
voice-gw1(config-voiceport)#^Z
voice-gw1#
```

Example 16-14 illustrates the different voice-port timeouts options that are available. Again, you will not see this exact output on a router because it is a composite of commands available of different types of voice interfaces.

Example 16-14   *Configuring Timeout Values for Various Signaling Parameters*

```
voice-gw1#conf t
Enter configuration commands, one per line.  End with CNTL/Z.
voice-gw1(config)#voice-port 4/1:0
voice-gw1(config-voiceport)#timeouts ?
  call-disconnect  Call Disconnect Timeout after Destination Hangs Up in seconds
  initial          Initial Timeout duration in seconds
  interdigit       Interdigit Timeout duration in seconds
  ringing          Ringing no answer timeout duration in seconds
  wait-release     Wait release timeout duration in seconds

voice-gw1(config-voiceport)#^Z
voice-gw1#
```

The command-line help options illustrated in Example 16-13 and Example 16-14 are fairly explanatory for each of the timing and timeout options, assuming that you are familiar with the basic operation of the signaling types. Review Chapter 2 for information about E&M wink-start and delay-start operation.

ABCD Bit Values

The default behavior of the transmit and receive ABCD bit patterns is dictated by the type of digital signaling (refer to Examples 16-5 and 16-6) that is used on the router voice port. There are two router configuration approaches to modify the default-signaling behavior to suit the nonstandard needs of an attached phone switch:

- Define/ignore
- Condition

The **define** and **ignore** voice-port commands are useful if you have well-defined but nonstandard requirements for a variant of E&M signaling. You can explicitly define arbitrary bit patterns to represent the on-hook and off-hook states, but you cannot attribute any other meaning to the signaling states. Because the ABCD bits for digital loop-start and ground-start represent more than just a simple on-hook and off-hook state, the **define** and **ignore** voice-port commands are not appropriate for digital loop-start or ground-start signaling.

Example 16-15 illustrates the configuration to convert a standard International Telecommunications Union (ITU) or Bellcore implementation of digital E&M signaling to the Mercury Exchange Limited CAS (MELCAS) version of E&M signaling (which is used in the United Kingdom). Configuring a standard E&M wink-start trunk in conjunction with the commands in Example 16-15 yields an E&M MELCAS wink-start trunk. Similarly, configuring a standard E&M immediate-start trunk with the commands of Example 16-15 yields an E&M MELCAS immediate-start trunk.

Example 16-15   *Defining Arbitrary On-Hook and Off-Hook ABCD Bit Patterns for E&M Signaling*

```
dent-gw1#conf t
Enter configuration commands, one per line.  End with CNTL/Z.
dent-gw1(config)#voice-port 4/1:0
dent-gw1(config-voiceport)#define ?
  Rx-bits  Define Rx Signaling bits
  Tx-bits  Define Tx Signaling bits

dent-gw1(config-voiceport)#define rx-bits ?
  idle   Define Rx Idle byte
  seize  Define Rx Seize byte
  <cr>

dent-gw1(config-voiceport)#define rx-bits idle ?
  0000  Define Rx pattern ABCD = 0000
  0001  Define Rx pattern ABCD = 0001
  0010  Define Rx pattern ABCD = 0010
  0011  Define Rx pattern ABCD = 0011
  0100  Define Rx pattern ABCD = 0100
  0101  Define Rx pattern ABCD = 0101
  0110  Define Rx pattern ABCD = 0110
  0111  Define Rx pattern ABCD = 0111
  1000  Define Rx pattern ABCD = 1000
  1001  Define Rx pattern ABCD = 1001
  1010  Define Rx pattern ABCD = 1010
  1011  Define Rx pattern ABCD = 1011
  1100  Define Rx pattern ABCD = 1100
  1101  Define Rx pattern ABCD = 1101
  1110  Define Rx pattern ABCD = 1110
  1111  Define Rx pattern ABCD = 1111

dent-gw1(config-voiceport)#define rx-bits idle 1101
dent-gw1(config-voiceport)#define rx-bits seize 0101
dent-gw1(config-voiceport)#define tx-bits idle 1101
dent-gw1(config-voiceport)#define tx-bits seize 0101
dent-gw1(config-voiceport)#^Z
dent-gw1#
```

You may need to modify which ABCD bits are considered for a modified version of E&M signaling. For example, a local E&M implementation may require that the on-hook/off-hook status be provided on the D-bit, while the other bits are unimportant. Example 16-16 demonstrates how to configure this functionality for an E&M signaling variant.

Example 16-16   *Controlling the Inbound ABCD Bits that the Router Examines for E&M Signaling*

```
dent-gw1#conf t
Enter configuration commands, one per line.  End with CNTL/Z.
dent-gw1(config)#voice-port 4/1:0
dent-gw1(config-voiceport)#ignore ?
  rx-a-bit  Ignore Rx A bit
  rx-b-bit  Ignore Rx B bit
  rx-c-bit  Ignore Rx C bit
  rx-d-bit  Ignore Rx D bit

dent-gw1(config-voiceport)#ignore rx-a-bit
dent-gw1(config-voiceport)#ignore rx-b-bit
dent-gw1(config-voiceport)#ignore rx-c-bit
dent-gw1(config-voiceport)#no ignore rx-d-bit
dent-gw1(config-voiceport)#^Z
dent-gw1#
```

Unlike the **voice-port** command that statically defines a bit representation for on-hook and off-hook states, the **condition** command manipulates the ABCD bits in predetermined ways, irrespective of the represented signaling states. In other words, the **condition** command can invert or preserve ABCD bit values on a bit-by-bit basis, no matter whether the bits represent on-hook/off-hook, ringing, or some other function. As a result, the **condition** command can be useful for variants of any signaling type—not just E&M variants. Specifically, the **condition** command is useful for loop-start and ground-start signaling variants. Example 16-17 illustrates a digital loop-start variant created by inverting the A and B bits.

Example 16-17   *Manipulating the ABCD Bit Values in Conjunction with Any Digital Signaling Type*

```
dent-gw1#conf t
Enter configuration commands, one per line.  End with CNTL/Z.
dent-gw1(config)#voice-port 4/1:0
dent-gw1(config-voiceport)#condition ?
  rx-a-bit  Condition Rx A bit
  rx-b-bit  Condition Rx B bit
  rx-c-bit  Condition Rx C bit
  rx-d-bit  Condition Rx D bit
  tx-a-bit  Condition Tx A bit
  tx-b-bit  Condition Tx B bit
  tx-c-bit  Condition Tx C bit
  tx-d-bit  Condition Tx D bit

dent-gw1(config-voiceport)#condition rx-a-bit ?
  invert  Condition Rx A Bit Inverted
  off     Condition Rx A Bit OFF
  on      Condition Rx A Bit ON

dent-gw1(config-voiceport)#condition rx-a-bit invert
dent-gw1(config-voiceport)#condition rx-b-bit invert
```

continues

Example 16-17 *Manipulating the ABCD Bit Values in Conjunction with Any Digital Signaling Type (Continued)*

```
dent-gw1(config-voiceport)#condition rx-c-bit off
dent-gw1(config-voiceport)#condition rx-d-bit on
dent-gw1(config-voiceport)#condition tx-a-bit invert
dent-gw1(config-voiceport)#condition tx-b-bit invert
dent-gw1(config-voiceport)#condition tx-c-bit off
dent-gw1(config-voiceport)#condition tx-d-bit on
dent-gw1(config-voiceport)#^Z
dent-gw1#
```

Answer and Disconnect Signaling

This section addresses several features of Cisco IOS that control how a router responds to answer and disconnect signaling from a phone switch or telephone:

- Battery-reversal
- Supervisory-disconnect
- Disconnect-ack
- Auto-cut-through

Battery-reversal is a form of answer and disconnect supervision that is used in conjunction with loop-start signaling. Figures 2-7 and 2-8 and the surrounding text in Chapter 2 discuss the operation of battery-reversal for answer and disconnect supervision. In summary, the phone switch changes the battery from the ring wire to the tip wire when the called party answers the call. As soon as the distant party disconnects, the battery switches back to the ring wire. The **battery-reversal** command illustrated in Example 16-18 is only applicable to FXO ports.

Example 16-18 *Configuring an FXO Port to Interpret Battery-Reversal as a Form of Answer and Disconnect Supervision*

```
voice-gw1#conf t
Enter configuration commands, one per line.  End with CNTL/Z.
voice-gw1(config)#voice-port 1/1/1
voice-gw1(config-voiceport)#battery-reversal
voice-gw1(config-voiceport)#^Z
voice-gw1#
```

The battery-reversal command is available as of IOS 12.0(7)XK and 12.1(2)T. Note that the VIC-2FXO (North America) and VIC-2FXO-EU (Europe) cards for the 1700/2600/3600 series routers do not have hardware support for this feature. Battery-reversal is supported for the newer versions of the FXO VIC cards, which are VIC-2FXO-M1 (North America) and VIC-2FXO-M2 (Europe). The FXO analog personality modules used in the MC3810 router do not require a hardware upgrade to support this feature.

Power denial is another form of disconnect supervision used in conjunction with loop-start signaling. The CO may remove battery power from the circuit for 350 ms, which informs the attached CPE that the remote party has disconnected. Disconnect supervision is important for billing purposes, and it is also important to efficiently utilize a voice port on a router. When inbound calls to a router are abandoned before the router answers, the voice port may not be available until a timer expires. This means that other inbound or outbound calls cannot use the port during this period. The CO may deny battery on the circuit to notify the router when inbound calls are abandoned, so that the router can immediately release the port for other calls. Example 16-19 illustrates how to configure an FXO port on a router to interpret power denial as a form of disconnect supervision.

Example 16-19 *Configuring an FXO Port to Interpret Power Denial from the CO as Disconnect Supervision*

```
voice-gw1#conf t
Enter configuration commands, one per line.  End with CNTL/Z.
voice-gw1(config-voiceport)#voice-port 1/0/0
voice-gw1(config-voiceport)#supervisory disconnect
voice-gw1(config-voiceport)#^Z
voice-gw1#
```

When a PBX terminates a loop-start connection to a CO, the PBX must wait a period of time before placing additional calls on the port (to ensure that the CO is ready for another call). The PBX can release the port for additional calls if the CO can acknowledge when the PBX disconnects on a loop-start trunk. Example 16-20 illustrates the configuration of an FXS port on a Cisco router (which acts as the CO) to provide disconnect acknowledgment, so that the attached PBX can release the voice port and make it available for additional calls.

Example 16-20 *Configuring an FXS Port to Deny Power to CPE in Response to CPE Disconnection*

```
voice-gw1#conf t
Enter configuration commands, one per line.  End with CNTL/Z.
voice-gw1(config)#voice-port 1/1/1
voice-gw1(config-voiceport)#disconnect-ack
voice-gw1(config-voiceport)#^Z
voice-gw1#
```

The **auto-cut-through** command, illustrated in Example 16-21, is used when a PBX that is attached to the router does not respond to trunk seizure requests. When a router delivers a call to a PBX via an E&M connection, the router initiates a trunk seizure (that is, it goes off-hook) by sending a signal on the E-lead. The correct response from the PBX depends on whether immediate-start, wink-start, or delay-start is used. In any case, the PBX must send a signal on the M-lead when it wants to indicate an off-hook condition back to the router. If the PBX does not send signals on the M-lead for some reason, the router can be configured to proceed as if all is well. This feature is important to enable operation in some environments, but the pitfall of this approach is that the router will always complete the call, regardless of whether or not the PBX is ready to receive it.

Example 16-21 *Configuring an E&M Port to Function Even If the PBX Does Not Send M-Lead Signals*

```
voice-gw5#conf t
Enter configuration commands, one per line.  End with CNTL/Z.
voice-gw5(config)#voice-port 1/1/1
voice-gw5(config-voiceport)#auto-cut-through
voice-gw5(config-voiceport)#^Z
voice-gw5#
```

Ringing Cadence and Automatic Answering

You can adjust how FXO ports respond to a ringing tone from a phone switch and how FXS ports provide ringings to attached telephones, fax machines, or phone switches. By default, an FXO port answers a call after the first ring. Consider an example in which you have a standard telephone connected in parallel to the same phone circuit as the FXO port (for example, in the same manner as two residential phones connected to the same loop-start circuit). You might want the opportunity to answer the telephone within a certain number of rings and let the FXO port accept the call otherwise. This is similar to how a telephone answering machine works in a residential setting. To provide a similar function, you might configure the FXO port to forward calls to another telephone number or to a distant answering machine. Example 16-22 demonstrates how to make the FXO port wait for four rings before answering the call.

Example 16-22 *Configuring the Number of Rings Before an FXO Port Answers an Inbound Call*

```
voice-gw1#conf t
Enter configuration commands, one per line.  End with CNTL/Z.
voice-gw1(config)#voice-port 1/0/0
voice-gw1(config-voiceport)#ring number ?
  <1-10>  The number of rings detected before closing loop

voice-gw1(config-voiceport)#ring number 4
voice-gw1(config-voiceport)#^Z
voice-gw1#
```

Most telephone ringing signals are composed of alternate periods of ringing and silence. The pattern of ringing and silent periods is called the *ringing cadence*. With FXS ports on Cisco routers, you can adjust the frequency of the signal during the ringing periods, and you can also adjust the ringing cadence. Example 16-23 illustrates how to adjust both of these parameters.

Example 16-23 *Defining the Ringing Patterns Provided by an FXS Interface*

```
voice-gw1#conf t
Enter configuration commands, one per line.  End with CNTL/Z.
voice-gw1(config)#voice-port 1/1/0
voice-gw1(config-voiceport)#ring ?
```

Example 16-23 *Defining the Ringing Patterns Provided by an FXS Interface (Continued)*

```
  cadence     Ringing cadence on/off durations
  frequency   The ring  frequency to be used in the FXS interface

r2(config-voiceport)#ring frequency ?
  25  ring frequency 25 Hertz
  50  ring frequency 50 Hertz

r2(config-voiceport)#ring frequency 50
voice-gw1(config-voiceport)#ring cadence ?
  define     User Defined Cadence
  pattern01  2sec on 4sec off
  pattern02  1sec on 4sec off
  pattern03  1.5sec on 3.5sec off
  pattern04  1sec on 2sec off
  pattern05  1sec on 5sec off
  pattern06  1sec on 3sec off
  pattern07  .8sec on 3.2sec off
  pattern08  1.5sec on 3sec off
  pattern09  1.2sec on 3.7sec off
  pattern10  1.2sec on 4.7sec off
  pattern11  .4sec on .2sec off .4sec on 2sec off
  pattern12  .4sec on .2sec off .4sec on 2.6sec off

voice-gw1(config-voiceport)#ring cadence define ?
  <1-50>  unit of 100 milliseconds

voice-gw1(config-voiceport)#ring cadence define 4 2 2 3
voice-gw1(config-voiceport)#^Z
voice-gw1#
```

If you do not want to use one of the standard ringing cadences that are predefined, you can manually define an arbitrary ringing cadence. As a point of interest, the ringing cadence and frequency defined in Example 16-23 produces a sound that is quite similar to a chirping cricket. You can experiment with these commands to create distinctive ringing tones, but as of IOS 12.1(2)T, you cannot apply different ringing tones in response to different called or calling party numbers.

Digit Representation

You can configure a voice port to send dialed digits using pulse tones, MF tones (as used for analog trunks between circuit provider phone switches), or DTMF tones. You also can adjust how DTMF tones or digit pulses are transmitted. Example 16-24 illustrates how to configure a method other than the default DTMF digit transmission.

Example 16-24 *Defining How Digits Are Transmitted Out of a Router Voice Port*

```
voice-gw1#conf t
Enter configuration commands, one per line.  End with CNTL/Z.
voice-gw1(config)#voice-port 1/0/0
voice-gw1(config-voiceport)#dial-type ?
  dtmf   touch-tone dialer
  mf     mf-tone dialer
  pulse  pulse dialer

voice-gw1(config-voiceport)#dial-type pulse
voice-gw1(config-voiceport)#^Z
voice-gw1#
```

The default parameters for pulse dialing are appropriate for North America, but you can adjust them to suit the requirements of a given country. Example 16-25 illustrates how to change the pulse configuration for operation in Japan, which requires 20 pulses per second (PPS), as opposed to 10 PPS in North America. You can also adjust the duty cycle of each pulse, which is the percent of time that each pulse is on-hook versus off-hook (refer to Figure 2-1), and the gap between pulsed digits.

Example 16-25 *Adjusting the Transmission of Pulsed Digits from FXO and E&M Ports*

```
r2#conf t
Enter configuration commands, one per line.  End with CNTL/Z.
r2(config)#voice-port 1/0/0
r2(config-voiceport)#timing pulse ?
  <10-20>  pulses per second

r2(config-voiceport)#timing pulse 20
r2(config-voiceport)#timing percentbreak ?
  <20-80>  percent

r2(config-voiceport)#timing percentbreak 60
r2(config-voiceport)#timing pulse-inter-digit ?
  <100-1000>  milliseconds

r2(config-voiceport)#timing pulse-inter-digit 200
r2(config-voiceport)#^Z
r2#
```

For DTMF digit transmission, you can configure the amount of time that each DTMF tone is played and the period of time between each digit transmission, as illustrated in Example 16-26.

Example 16-26 *Adjusting the Transmission of DTMF Digits from FXO and E&M Ports*

```
r2#conf t
Enter configuration commands, one per line.  End with CNTL/Z.
r2(config)#voice-port 1/0/0
r2(config-voiceport)#timing digit ?
  <50-500>  milliseconds

r2(config-voiceport)#timing digit 100
r2(config-voiceport)#timing inter-digit ?
  <50-500>  milliseconds

r2(config-voiceport)#timing inter-digit 100
r2(config-voiceport)#^Z
r2#
```

Call Progress Tones

There are two types of progress tones that you should consider when configuring the voice ports on your routers:

- Standard call progress tones
- Cisco-specific confirmation tones for PLAR connections

You should configure analog voice ports to generate or understand the call progress tones that are appropriate for the country, so that users hear the audio tones to which they are accustomed (such as busy, reorder, and other conditions). Call progress tones may be more important if you have phone switches or other automated equipment attached to the router because the functionality of these devices may depend on the appropriate progress tones. Example 16-27 demonstrates the variety of country-specific progress tones that Cisco routers support. By the time you read this, there are sure to be more countries supported.

Example 16-27 *Country-Specific Options for Call Progress Tones*

```
voice-gw1#conf t
Enter configuration commands, one per line.  End with CNTL/Z.
voice-gw1(config)#voice-port 4/1:0
voice-gw1(config-voiceport)#cptone ?
  locale   2 letter ISO-3166 country code

AR Argentina      IS Iceland       PT Portugal
AU Australia      IN India         RU Russian Federation
AT Austria        ID Indonesia     SG Singapore
BE Belgium        IE Ireland       SK Slovakia
BR Brazil         IL Israel        SI Slovenia
CA Canada         IT Italy         ZA South Africa
```

continues

Example 16-27 *Country-Specific Options for Call Progress Tones (Continued)*

```
CN China              JP Japan              ES Spain
CO Colombia           KR Korea Republic     SE Sweden
CY Cyprus             LU Luxembourg         CH Switzerland
CZ Czech Republic     MY Malaysia           TW Taiwan
DK Denmark            MX Mexico             TH Thailand
FI Finland            NL Netherlands        TR Turkey
FR France             NZ New Zealand        GB United Kingdom
DE Germany            NO Norway             US United States
GR Greece             PE Peru               VE Venezuela
HK Hong Kong          PH Philippines
HU Hungary

voice-gw1(config-voiceport)#cptone br
voice-gw1(config-voiceport)#^Z
voice-gw1#
```

For PLAR and PLAR-OPX connections, Cisco routers introduce another type of call progress tone. The router provides a two-beep confirmation tone to let you know that a dial peer matched for the PLAR connection, and the call is being established. This confirmation tone is useful when you are building the network and you want to verify correct operation, but you can disable the tone when the network is in normal operation. If you do not disable the confirmation tones, then users may be confused by the extra noises to which they are not accustomed. Example 16-28 illustrates how to disable the two-beep confirmation tone.

Example 16-28 *Disabling the Two Beeps that Are Heard When Using a PLAR Connection*

```
voice-gw1#conf t
Enter configuration commands, one per line.  End with CNTL/Z.
voice-gw1(config)#voice-port 5/1:0
voice-gw1(config-voiceport)#connection plar-opx 1111
voice-gw1(config-voiceport)#no voice confirmation-tone
voice-gw1(config-voiceport)#^Z
voice-gw1#
```

Companding

The companding type defines how the 16-bit linear PCM sample is compressed using a nonlinear representation of signal levels. (See Chapter 6, "Voice Digitization and Coding.") Recall that mu-law is common in North America and Japan, and A-law is used in most other places. The Cisco IOS router images that are derived from the MC3810 software (such as IOS 12.0(7)XK and 12.1(2)T) include an option to change the compand-type for each voice port. Example 16-29 illustrates this option, which you should avoid.

Example 16-29 *Configuring an FXS or FXO Port for A-Law or mu-Law Companding (Old Method)*

```
r2#conf t
Enter configuration commands, one per line.  End with CNTL/Z.
r2(config)#voice-port 1/0/0
r2(config-voiceport)#compand-type ?
  a-law  A-law
  u-law  u-law

r2(config-voiceport)#compand-type a-law
r2(config-voiceport)#^Z
r2#
```

While the type of companding is important for G.711 codecs, you should use the newer
configuration method that specifies the companding as part of the codec definition.
Example 16-30 illustrates the preferred method of adjusting the companding type.

Example 16-30 *Preferred Method of Setting the compand-type for G.711 Codecs*

```
r2#conf t
Enter configuration commands, one per line.  End with CNTL/Z.
r2(config)#dial-peer voice 111 voip
r2(config-dial-peer)#codec ?
  g711alaw  G.711 A Law 64000 bps
  g711ulaw  G.711 u Law 64000 bps
  <etc.>
r2(config-dial-peer)#codec g711alaw
r2(config-dial-peer)#^Z
r2#
```

Conversion Between mu-Law and A-Law

The following excerpt is from section 3.4 of the International Telecommunication Union
Telecommunication (ITU-T) Recommendation G.711:

> Digital paths between countries which have adopted different encoding laws should
> carry signals encoded in accordance with the A-law. Where both countries have adopted
> the same law, that law should be used on digital paths between them. Any necessary
> conversion will be done by the countries using the mu-law.

In the context of Cisco routers, this means you should use codec g711alaw for dial peers
that connect to countries using the A-law, whether or not the local country uses mu-law or
A-law. For dial peers that connect to countries using the mu-law, the dial peer should follow
the convention of the local country (that is, A-law if the local country uses A-law, or mu-
law if the local country uses mu-law). For example, a router in the United States should use
A-law for G.711-encoded calls to Europe, mu-law for domestic calls, and mu-law for calls
to Japan.

Input and Output Voice Levels

You can adjust the audio level for sound signals entering and leaving a voice port, as illustrated in Example 16-31. You may need to tune the audio-levels if the audio path is too loud or too quiet, or you may need to tune the audio levels to help control echo problems. In general, you should develop a loss plan before making arbitrary audio-level adjustments. Any adjustments you make that deviate from the loss plan should be to resolve specific issues with voice quality, DTMF tone recognition, and so on. Chapter 13, "Delay Budgets and Loss Plans," discusses loss planning, and Chapter 18, "Resolving Voice Quality Issues," addresses voice quality issues that relate to audio level and echo control.

Example 16-31 *Adjusting the Audio Levels Entering and Leaving a Voice Port*

```
voip-gw1#conf t
Enter configuration commands, one per line.  End with CNTL/Z.
voip-gw1(config)#voice-port 1/1/1
voip-gw1(config-voiceport)#input gain ?
  <-6 - 14>  gain in db

voip-gw1(config-voiceport)#input gain -3
voip-gw1(config-voiceport)#output attenuation ?
  <0-14>  attenuation in db

voip-gw1(config-voiceport)#output attenuation 3
voip-gw1(config-voiceport)#^Z
voip-gw1#
```

Echo Cancellation and Nonlinear Processing

You can enable or disable echo cancellation and nonlinear processing on a per voice-port basis, as illustrated in Example 16-32. Note that you may need to tune the input gain and output attenuation on various voice ports to resolve echo problems in the audio path. Chapter 13 provides additional background for echo control, and Chapter 18 explores specific strategies for controlling audio path echoes.

Example 16-32 *Increasing Echo-Cancel Coverage and Nonlinear Processing for Long Tail Circuits*

```
voip-gw3#conf t
Enter configuration commands, one per line.  End with CNTL/Z.
voip-gw3(config)#voice-port 1/1/1
voip-gw3(config-voiceport)#echo-cancel enable
voip-gw3(config-voiceport)#echo-cancel coverage ?
  16  16 milliseconds echo canceller coverage
  24  24 milliseconds echo canceller coverage
  32  32 milliseconds echo canceller coverage
  8   8 milliseconds echo canceller coverage

voip-gw3(config-voiceport)#echo-cancel coverage 32
voip-gw3(config-voiceport)#non-linear
voip-gw3(config-voiceport)#^Z
voip-gw3#
```

busyout monitor

You can configure a router's voice port to reject incoming calls when a required network path is unavailable. This feature solves a black hole problem that can occur because of limited signaling between a router and a PBX. In the black hole failure scenario, the router accepts calls from the PBX and is subsequently unable to complete the call because the WAN circuit or a remote router is unavailable. The PBX cannot reroute the call because the call is successfully completed from its perspective. The router can hair-pin the call back to the PBX on a different voice port, but this does not efficiently utilize the voice ports, and it may not be an option when there are no more free voice ports. The **busyout monitor** commands enable the router to reject calls from a PBX when network interfaces are unavailable, so the PBX can reroute the call (or forward to voice mail, and so forth). If multiple network interfaces are available to cross the VoX network, the router can monitor all of the interfaces and only cause the voice port to be busied out when all of the paths are unavailable. Example 16-33 illustrates this configuration.

Example 16-33 *Automatically Disabling a Voice Port When the Required Network Interfaces Are Down*

```
voip-gw1#conf t
Enter configuration commands, one per line.  End with CNTL/Z.
voip-gw1(config)#voice-port 1/0/0
voip-gw1(config-voiceport)#busyout monitor interface serial 1/0:0.16
voip-gw1(config-voiceport)#busyout monitor interface serial 1/1:0.21
voip-gw1(config-voiceport)#^Z
voip-gw1#
```

One problem with the **busyout monitor** command, which also plagues the **backup-interface** command for dial-on-demand routing, is that Frame Relay interfaces do not always go down when the remote side of the connection fails. If a Frame Relay permanent virtual circuit (PVC) crosses multiple provider networks—in other words, if there is a Network-to-Network Interface (NNI) involved—then failure conditions at the remote location may not be transmitted through the NNI connection. Because the PVC is still active in the Frame Relay network of the local provider, the router incorrectly learns that the PVC is still active. The router attempts to transmit data through the PVC, but all data is lost because the end-to-end connection is not available. The impact for voice services is that the **busyout monitor** interface does not cause the voice port to be busied out because the network interface still appears to be active. As such, a PBX may forward calls to the router which are subsequently black holed.

The solution to this problem (which is applicable both to the **busyout monitor** voice-port command and the **backup-interface** dial-on-demand command) is a proprietary Frame Relay enhancement developed by Cisco. If you have Cisco routers with IOS 12.0(5)T or higher on both ends of a PVC, you can configure the routers to exchange end-to-end keepalive messages that determine the true availability of the PVC. With this feature enabled, the router will show the PVC as inactive when the end-to-end connection is unavailable, even if Local Management Interface (LMI) messages indicate that the PVC is active. As illustrated in Example 16-34, you must first configure a Frame Relay map class (which you should already have to enable QoS features) with the **end-to-end keepalive** command and apply the map class to the PVC.

Example 16-34 *Configuring Frame Relay PVCs to Shut Down When Remote Connectivity Fails*

```
voip-gw1#conf t
Enter configuration commands, one per line.  End with CNTL/Z.
voip-gw1(config)#map-class frame-relay voip-test
voip-gw1(config-map-class)#frame-relay end-to-end keepalive mode bidirectional
voip-gw1(config-map-class)#exit
voip-gw1(config)#interface s1/0:0.16 point-to-point
voip-gw1(config-if)#frame-relay interface-dlci 16
voip-gw1(config-fr-dlci)#class voip-test
voip-gw1(config-fr-dlci)#exit
voip-gw1(config)#interface s1/0:0.21 point-to-point
voip-gw1(config-if)#frame-relay interface-dlci 21
voip-gw1(config-fr-dlci)#class voip-test
voip-gw1(config-fr-dlci)#^Z
voip-gw12#
```

NOTE   You can also use the PLAR, PLAR-OPX, and trunk connection modes on a voice port to resolve the black hole call routing problem. Chapter 17 discusses the various connection modes that Cisco supports on voice ports. If you need to use a normal switched connection mode, then the **busyout monitor** command may be an important part of the overall network design.

Maintenance and Troubleshooting Commands

The following Cisco router commands and monitoring features are explored in this section:

- show controller [t1 | e1]
- show ISDN status
- show voice port
- debug vpm signal

SNMP Voice-Port Monitoring

You can configure a router to send SNMP traps when a voice port becomes unavailable, as illustrated in Example 16-35. Note that the router must already be configured to send SNMP traps to a server.

Example 16-35 *Enabling SNMP Traps When the Voice Port Is Down*

```
voice-gw2#conf t
Enter configuration commands, one per line.  End with CNTL/Z.
voice-gw2(config)#voice-port  1/0/0
voice-gw2(config-voiceport)#snmp trap ?
  link-status  Allow SNMP LINKUP and LINKDOWN traps
voice-gw2(config-voiceport)#snmp trap link-status
voice-gw2(config-voiceport)#^Z
voice-gw2#
```

show controller [t1 | e1]

You can use the same **show controller** command to examine digital voice ports as you would use to verify the operation of a T-1/E-1 data interface with an internal channel service unit/digital service unit (CSU/DSU). This should be one of your first diagnostic steps when troubleshooting the failed operation or new installation of a digital voice port. From the output illustrated in Example 16-36, you can determine at a glance how the T-1/E-1 interface is configured for framing, line coding, and clocking. You also can determine whether the devices are synchronized across the T-1/E-1 connection, whether there are cyclic redundancy check (CRC) errors (which may indicate poor cabling or hardware errors), whether there are frame slips (which indicate clocking problems), or whether there are other framing or line-coding problems.

Example 16-36 *Verifying the Configuration and Operation of a Digital T-1/E-1 Controller*

```
voice-gw2#show controller t1 4/1
T1 4/1 is up.
  Applique type is Channelized T1
  Cablelength is short 110
  No alarms detected.
  Framing is ESF, FDL is ansi & att, Line Code is B8ZS, Clock Source is Internal.
  Active xconns: 0
  Data in current interval (332 seconds elapsed):
     0 Line Code Violations, 0 Path Code Violations
     0 Slip Secs, 0 Fr Loss Secs, 0 Line Err Secs, 0 Degraded Mins
     0 Errored Secs, 0 Bursty Err Secs, 0 Severely Err Secs, 0 Unavail Secs
voice-gw2#
```

show isdn status

For voice PRI and BRI connections, you have the same **show** and **debug** commands available as for data ISDN connections. Example 16-37 shows the output of **show isdn status** for a BRI voice port that is communicating properly on the D-channel, with no active calls on the B-channels. You should see the keyword MULTIPLE_FRAME_ ESTABLISHED as part of the Layer 2 status to verify correct configuration of the D-channel.

Example 16-37 *Verifying the Operation of an ISDN Interface*

```
voice-gw2#show isdn status
Global ISDN Switchtype = basic-5ess
ISDN BRI0/0 interface
        dsl 0, interface ISDN Switchtype = basic-5ess
    Layer 1 Status:
        ACTIVE
    Layer 2 Status:
        TEI = 104, Ces = 1, SAPI = 0, State = MULTIPLE_FRAME_ESTABLISHED
        TEI 104, ces = 1, state = 8(established)
            spid1 configured, no LDN, spid1 NOT sent, spid1 valid
            Endpoint ID Info: epsf = 1, usid = 0, tid = 68
    Layer 3 Status:
        0 Active Layer 3 Call(s)
    Activated dsl 0 CCBs = 0
    The Free Channel Mask:  0x80000003
voice-gw2#
```

If you do not see the MULTIPLE_FRAME_ESTABLISHED keyword, there may be a
physical-layer or configuration problem. Example 16-38 demonstrates an ISDN interface
that is down because of cabling problems. Note the keyword DEACTIVATED in the layer
1 status, which informs you that there is a physical-layer problem. Before tracing cables,
make sure to check that you do not have the controller [t1 | e1] configured with shutdown,
which can also cause the output shown in Example 16-38. If layer 1 status is ACTIVE, then
you should verify that you have correctly entered the SPIDS and ISDN switch type for the
port. Note that the keyword TEI_ASSIGNED in the Layer 2 status is an indication that the
router is not communicating properly on the D-channel with the ISDN switch.

Example 16-38 *Verifying the Configuration and Operation of a Digital T-1/E-1 Controller*

```
voice-gw2#show isdn status
Global ISDN Switchtype = basic-5ess
ISDN BRI0/0 interface
        dsl 0, interface ISDN Switchtype = basic-5ess
    Layer 1 Status:
        DEACTIVATED
    Layer 2 Status:
        TEI = 104, Ces = 1, SAPI = 0, State = TEI_ASSIGNED
        TEI 104, ces = 1, state = 8(established)
            spid1 configured, no LDN, spid1 NOT sent, spid1 valid
            Endpoint ID Info: epsf = 1, usid = 0, tid = 68
    Layer 3 Status:
        0 Active Layer 3 Call(s)
    Activated dsl 0 CCBs = 0
    The Free Channel Mask:  0x80000003
    Total Allocated ISDN CCBs = 0
voice-gw2#
```

show voice port

You can get an overview of the configuration and operational status of all of the voice ports on a router, or you can see detailed configuration and status about a specific voice port. Example 16-39 demonstrates the **show voice port summary** output for a 3640 router with a single voice network module with two VIC daughter cards (that is, VIC-2FXS and VIC-2FXO-M1). Voice port 1/1/1 is on-hook and receiving an inbound call, while voice-port 1/1/0 is hosting an active call. You cannot distinguish from this output whether port 1/1/0 has an active call or is simply off-hook. You can use the **show call active voice** command to view what active calls are currently active in a router.

Example 16-39 *Overview of Current Voice-Port Configuration and Operational Status*

```
voice-gw2#show voice port summary
                                  IN       OUT
PORT   CH SIG-TYPE   ADMIN OPER STATUS   STATUS   EC
====== == ========== ===== ==== ======== ======== ==
1/0/0  -- fxo-ls     up    dorm idle     on-hook  y
1/0/1  -- fxo-ls     up    dorm idle     on-hook  y
1/1/0  -- fxs-ls     up    up   off-hook idle     y
1/1/1  -- fxs-ls     up    up   on-hook  ringing  y

voice-gw2#
```

Example 16-40 illustrates the output of the detailed version of the **show voice port** command. Note that you can see all of the timing and timeout parameters for this port, as well as the gain/loss settings, connection mode, music-threshold (which relates to VAD), and numerous other parameters. This command is very useful when troubleshooting router-PBX connectivity issues and you want to verify configuration operations at a glance. Note that most of the configuration information included here is not visible in the router running-config because most default options are not displayed in the **show running-config** output.

You may note in this particular output that the music-threshold has been decreased to –50 decibels (dB)—from the default –38 dB—to reduce the amount of VAD silence suppression in a noisy environment. Also note that the input gain has been decreased as much as possible to –6 dB, which compensates for very loud audio signals from an attached phone switch. The echo cancel coverage has been increased from the default 8 ms to the maximum value of 32 ms to accommodate longer delays in a tail-end hop-off circuit. More information about controlling echoes and tuning voice quality is included in Chapter 18.

Example 16-40 *Detail of Current Voice-Port Configuration and Operational Status*

```
voice-gw4#show voice port 4/1:0

recEive and transMit Slot is 4, Sub-unit is 1, Port is 0
 Type of VoicePort is E&M
 Operation State is DORMANT
 Administrative State is UP
 The Last Interface Down Failure Cause is Administrative Shutdown
```

continues

Example 16-40 *Detail of Current Voice-Port Configuration and Operational Status (Continued)*

```
Description is not set
Noise Regeneration is enabled
Non Linear Processing is enabled
Music On Hold Threshold is Set to -50 dBm
In Gain is Set to -6 dB
Out Attenuation is Set to 0 dB
Echo Cancellation is enabled
Echo Cancel Coverage is set to 32 ms
Connection Mode is normal
Connection Number is not set
Initial Time Out is set to 10 s
Interdigit Time Out is set to 10 s
Call-Disconnect Time Out is set to 60 s
Region Tone is set for US

Analog Info Follows:
Currently processing Voice
Maintenance Mode Set to None (not in mtc mode)
Number of signaling protocol errors are 0
Impedance is set to 600r Ohm

Voice card specific Info Follows:
Signal Type is wink-start
Operation Type is 2-wire
E&M Type is 1
Dial Type is dtmf
In Seizure is inactive
Out Seizure is inactive
Digit Duration Timing is set to 100 ms
InterDigit Duration Timing is set to 100 ms
Pulse Rate Timing is set to 10 pulses/second
InterDigit Pulse Duration Timing is set to 500 ms
Clear Wait Duration Timing is set to 400 ms
Wink Wait Duration Timing is set to 200 ms
Wink Duration Timing is set to 200 ms
Delay Start Timing is set to 300 ms
Delay Duration Timing is set to 2000 ms
Dial Pulse Min. Delay is set to 140 ms
voice-gw4#
```

debug vpm signal

The **debug vpm signal** command is one of the most important troubleshooting tools when you have problems establishing connectivity between a router and a phone switch. See Appendix C, "Debug VPM Signal," for a discussion of the **debug vpm signal** output.

Summary and Related Topics

This chapter has explored the minimal configurations for analog and digital voice ports, as well as the various voice-port parameters that may be tuned. You can refer back to Chapter 2 for detailed coverage of topics that are briefly mentioned here. Several **show** commands have been explored in this chapter, while the **debug vpm signal** command is explored in Appendix C. The **debug** command is allocated more space in the appendix because it is a critical command to help understand and troubleshoot failure scenarios, and it is quite poorly documented in other sources. Connection modes such as PLAR, PLAR-OPX, and trunk are discussed as part of end-to-end calling connectivity in Chapter 17. Voice-port configurations that relate to voice-quality tuning are described in more detail (with other voice-quality issues) in Chapter 18.

Establishing Network-Wide Calling Capability

After you have established connectivity between a router and a PBX, you must incorporate that single connection into the integrated voice/data network. Beyond the issue of correctly interpreting on-hook/off-hook conditions and accepting digits on each individual voice port, you must ensure end-to-end voice connectivity. In other words, you must ensure that the phone switches and individual phones that connect to the VoX network can establish a connection to any required destination through the VoX network. This connectivity depends on correct call routing through the VoX network, compatible interactions between the routers and PBXs on either end of the connection, and correct end-to-end signaling of required features such as DTMF digits and hook-flash. The features described in this chapter are the glue that binds the disparate technologies used in traditional voice and data networks. This part of the network design is the core of the integration project.

The goal of this chapter is to provide the tools to establish whatever types of voice connections are required across your voice/data network. Voice quality issues are treated separately in Chapter 18, "Resolving Voice Quality Issues." This chapter explores the following topics:

- Dial peers
- Tandem call routing
- Connection modes
- Session protocols
- VoX dial-peer options
- VoIP scaling: H.323
- VoIP scaling: Session Initiation Protocol (SIP)
- Telephone Routing over IP (TRIP): the future of VoIP call routing
- Additional references

NOTE	I often use the word router to describe what is more appropriately termed a voice gateway, because many Cisco routers also implement a voice gateway function. It should be noted that a voice gateway can be implemented as a stand-alone function, independent of a data routing function.

Dial Peers

The following sections explore how the source and destination phone numbers and data network addresses are determined for each call:

- Call legs and dial peers
- Destination patterns and digit matching
- Session targets

Call Legs and Dial Peers

Consider the simple VoX network depicted in Figure 17-1. When user A initiates a call to user B, how do the two routers process the call? The answer to this question requires an understanding of call legs and dial peers.

Figure 17-1 *Simple VoX Scenario with Call Proceeding from User A to User B*

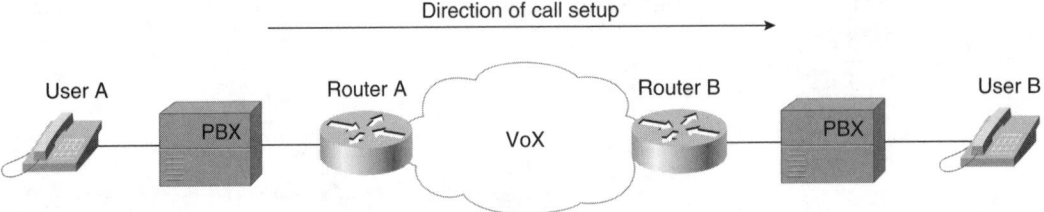

There are four router-based perspectives from which the call connection illustrated in Figure 17-1 may be examined:

- Inbound to router A
- Outbound from router A
- Inbound to router B
- Outbound from router B

Each of these router-based perspectives is known as a call leg. You can think of a call leg as a logical link in the end-to-end phone connection. Establishing an end-to-end call connection requires that each of the four call legs be identified through some means and gathered together to form a single connection. The inbound and outbound labels for the call legs reflect the direction of travel for the call-setup signaling. In other words, a call from user A to user B uses different logical call legs than a call from user B to user A. It is possible for calls from B to A to have different configuration parameters than calls from A to B. Figure 17-2 illustrates the concept of call legs and an end-to-end connection.

Figure 17-2   *Relationship Between Call Legs and an End-to-End Connection*

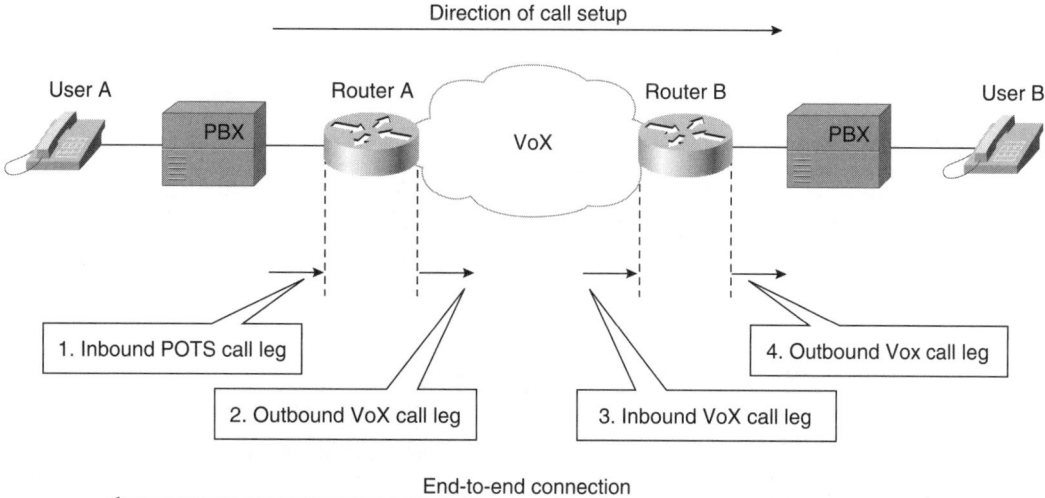

Call legs are controlled in the routers via dial peers. Just as there are four call legs associated with each call (or more for tandem switching VoFR or VoATM), there are four dial peers that provide configuration control for the connection[1]. The dotted vertical lines in Figure 17-2 illustrate the points at which dial peers affect a call. Inbound and outbound call legs must be joined in a router via the appropriate selection of dial peers. Table 17-1 summarizes the different types of dial peers that control inbound and outbound call legs from both voice ports and network connections. Note that routers do not originate or terminate calls.

Table 17-1   *Four Types of Dial Peers that Control Four Types of Call Legs*

Dial Peer Type	Description
Inbound POTS	Calls entering a router via a voice port
Outbound VoX	Calls leaving a router via a network connection
Inbound VoX	Calls entering a router via a network connection
Outbound POTS	Calls leaving a router via a voice port

1. If both ends of the connection are terminated in the same router, only two POTS dial peers control the call.

All calls that are processed by a router are associated with an inbound dial peer when the call enters the router and an outbound dial peer when the call leaves the router. This is true whether the call enters the router from a voice port or a network connection.

A common practice that obscures the operation of dial peers is that a single configured dial peer is often applied to both inbound and outbound call legs. This is efficient when the call legs are intended to behave symmetrically, but you should be aware that calls associated with a voice port or a network connection may use one dial peer for inbound calls and a different dial peer for outbound calls. This flexibility is important in some voice applications.

Dial-Peer Matching

Table 17-2 summarizes the different mechanisms to select dial peers for inbound and outbound call legs. These mechanisms are explored in the following sections:

- Outbound call legs
- Inbound call legs

Table 17-2   *Mechanisms to Associate Dial Peers with Call Legs*

Outbound Call Legs	Inbound Call Legs
Destination pattern	Incoming called number
Numbering type	Answer address
Preference	Destination pattern
	Voice port

Outbound Call Legs

Outbound call legs are matched with available VoX or POTS dial peers in order of the following criteria:

1. Numbering type
2. Destination pattern
3. Dial-peer type (POTS or VoX)
4. Preference
5. Order of configuration

Numbering Type

Called and calling party information elements in Q.931 call-setup messages specify a 3-bit numbering type and a 4-bit numbering-plan identification. Table 17-3 lists the numbering types defined in Q.931. Because the H.225.0 call-control signaling is derived from Q.931, this information field is available for all VoIP calls that use the default H.323 session protocol (session protocol cisco). The numbering-plan identification (that is, the four least-significant bits marked as x in Table 17-3) is set to E.164, which corresponds to the binary value 0001. The most-significant bit is an extension bit that is always set to 1 for calling and called party numbers. Hence, an unknown numbering type from the E.164 numbering plan corresponds with a hexadecimal value of 0x81.

The binary representation of this octet from the Q.931 header is included here because you will see information relating to numbering type in some of the VoIP debugging output on Cisco routers. Among the output of **debug voip ccapi inout** (see Appendix D, "Debug VoIP CCAPI inout"), the numbering type and numbering-plan identification are indicated for calling and called parties as called_oct3 and calling_oct3. This is because these fields represent the third octet of the called and calling party information element in the Q.931 setup message. This octet for the called party is also labeled as the numbering_type in the debugging output. Appendix D provides a fairly detailed analysis of the output of **debug voip ccapi inout** for a normal call setup and completion.

Table 17-3   *Q.931 Number Types Used for Destination Patterns and Translation Rules*

Type of Number	Binary Value	Description
Unknown	x000xxxx	No information is available
International Number	x001xxxx	Per E.164 (with country code)
National Number	x010xxxx	Per E.164 (without country code)
Network Specific Number	x011xxxx	Admin/service number (for example, operator)
Subscriber Number	x100xxxx	Per E.164 (without country or national code)
	x101xxxx	Unassigned
Abbreviated Number	x110xxxx	Formatted per a private numbering plan
Reserved for Extension	x111xxxx	Available for proprietary usage in interim

You can control outbound dial-peer selection by specifying that a given dial peer is only associated with certain types of numbers. An example of where you might want to take advantage of this field is to provide different levels of voice quality for domestic and international voice calls. A dial peer for international calls may specify a low bit-rate codec with voice activity detection (VAD) enabled to maximize bandwidth savings on the expensive international links, while a dial peer for domestic calls may use less aggressive bandwidth-saving techniques to allow the highest voice quality.

The numbering types associated with the calling and called party numbers are defined either by an ISDN/SS7 network, or by translation rules configured in Cisco routers. For calls that originate on non-ISDN voice ports, the default numbering type is unknown. Translation rules are discussed later in this chapter in the section, "Destination Patterns and Digit Manipulation." Example 17-1 illustrates the configuration of a numbering-type restriction for an outgoing dial peer. In order for the dial peer to match the outbound call leg, the numbering type configured in the outgoing dial peer must match the numbering type associated with the called party number (DNIS). Note that you may specify a numbering type for outbound POTS and VoX dial peers.

Example 17-1   *Configuring a Numbering Type (Per Q.931 and I.330)*

```
voice-gw3#conf t
Enter configuration commands, one per line.  End with CNTL/Z.
voice-gw3(config)#dial-peer voice 200 voip
voice-gw3(config-dial-peer)#numbering-type ?
  abbreviated    The numbering type is abbreviated
  international  The numbering type is international
  national       The numbering type is national
  network        The numbering type is network
  reserved       The numbering type is reserved
  subscriber     The numbering type is subscriber
  unknown        The numbering type is unknown

voice-gw3(config-dial-peer)#numbering-type international
voice-gw3(config-dial-peer)#^Z
voice-gw3#
```

An otherwise matching dial peer (for inbound or outbound call legs) will not match if the numbering type for the dial peer does not match the numbering type associated with the call request. Example 17-2 illustrates the output from the router console, which notifies you when a dial peer does not match for this reason.

Example 17-2   *Console Output When a Dial Peer Fails to Match Because of Numbering Type*

```
voice-gw3#
00:34:21: %CALL_CONTROL-6-NUMBERING_TYPE_NO_MATCH: The called number numbering type
did not match The event for the callid 4 is being discarded.
voice-gw3#
```

Destination Pattern

The most basic and commonly used method to associate an outbound call leg with a dial peer is the destination pattern. A destination pattern may be as simple as an explicit telephone number or as complex as a UNIX-style regular expression. Example 17-3 illustrates the configuration of a destination pattern that matches any 11-digit telephone number that begins with 1408555.

Example 17-3   *Configuring a Destination Pattern to Match the Called Phone Number*

```
voice-gw3#conf t
Enter configuration commands, one per line.  End with CNTL/Z.
voice-gw3(config)#dial-peer voice 200 voip
voice-gw3(config-dial-peer)#destination-pattern +1408555....
voice-gw3(config-dial-peer)#^Z
voice-gw3#
```

If the numbering types are equal or not assigned for the dial peers, then inbound and outbound call legs are associated with the dial peer that explicitly matches the most digits (excluding wildcard digits) of the destination pattern. For example, if the called number is 4199, then a pattern of {4199} is the most explicit match, {41..} may be the next most specific, and {4...} may be the next choice. This behavior is analogous to IP routing with variable-length subnet masks (VLSM), where routes are selected based on the most specific (that is, the longest IP subnet mask) routing entry that matches.

The + sign in the first position indicates that the number string is compatible with the E.164 syntax for international numbers (country code is present, no special prefix digits). It is not proper to use the + sign as the leading digit in conjunction with a private numbering plan. If you also use the numbering-type parameter, then the + sign should only be used when the numbering type is set to international. A + sign located anywhere other than the leading position in a number pattern is defined according to regular expression pattern-matching rules (that is, one or more occurrences of the previous character or pattern). Destination patterns are explored in more detail later in this chapter.

Dial-Peer Type

If a POTS dial peer and a VoX dial peer share the same numbering type and destination pattern, then the POTS dial peer is always selected first. This behavior is sensible for most applications, but you can avoid any potential conflicts in your network if you are aware of this behavior. If you need to prioritize a VoX dial peer ahead of a POTS dial peer, then make sure the destination pattern in the VoX dial peer includes more specific digits than the POTS dial peer.

Preference

If a set of dial peers is configured with the same numbering type (or none at all), the same number of matching digits in the destination pattern, and the same dial-peer type (POTS or VoX), you can configure preference values to specify the order in which the dial peers are matched. You may associate a preference with both inbound and outbound dial peers, and with POTS or VoX dial peers. The preference values range from 0 to 10, with 0 being the most preferred. Unfortunately, 0 is the default preference value. If you want a single dial peer to be prioritized ahead of all others, then you must explicitly configure a lower preference on all of the other dial peers that are otherwise equal. Example 17-4 illustrates the configuration of a preference value on a dial peer. The configuration is the same for all types of dial peers.

Example 17-4 *Configuring a Dial-Peer Preference and* **huntstop** *to Control Selection of Dial Peers*

```
voice-gw3#conf t
Enter configuration commands, one per line.  End with CNTL/Z.
voice-gw3(config)#dial-peer voice 200 voip
voice-gw3(config-dial-peer)#preference ?
  <0-10>  Preference order

voice-gw3(config-dial-peer)#preference 5
voice-gw3(config-dial-peer)#huntstop
voice-gw3(config-dial-peer)#^Z
voice-gw3#
```

The most common reason to use preference values is to control the behavior of hunt groups. It is common to associate a number of physical voice ports with the same destination phone numbers, so that any one of the available voice ports may accept calls. When a router receives a call for one of the destinations, it hunts through the list of available voice ports until it finds one that is available. The method to configure this behavior is to create a separate POTS dial peer for each voice port, using the same destination pattern. To force the hunt group to use voice ports in a specified order, you can assign a separate preference to each of the dial peers in the hunt group.

The **huntstop** command is also demonstrated in Example 17-6. A router stops hunting for alternate dial peers as soon as it checks a dial peer configured with this directive. You can use this command to prevent call-routing loops. Consider, for example, that when a call reaches the destination router, there are no POTS dial peers available. In a VoIP network, the call would die because there is no tandem call routing (discussed in a following section). In a VoFR or VoATM network, however, the call may follow a default dial peer and bounce around the network wasting resources. In general, you should only use the **huntstop** command when you control the order of dial-peer selection with the **preference** command. In such cases, **huntstop** should only be associated with the least preferred dial peer in the hunt group.

Configuration Order

If all other criteria are equal for several outbound dial peers, then dial peers are matched in the order in which they were configured. This is why dial peers are not automatically rearranged in ascending numeric order. The dial peers that appear first in a configuration will match a call leg first if all other attributes are equal. If you want dial peers to be neatly arranged in your configuration, the easiest way to achieve this is to edit the dial peers offline (that is, rearrange them to your liking) and copy them into the configuration. You must first remove the old dial peers for this to work.

Inbound Call Legs

Inbound call legs are matched with available VoX or POTS dial peers in order of the following criteria:

1 Dial-peer type (POTS or VoX)

2 Incoming called number

3 Answer address

4 Destination pattern

5 Voice port (for POTS dial peers only)

6 Order of configuration

7 Default null dial peer

Dial-Peer Type

A router knows whether a call arrives via a voice port or via the network. Incoming calls on voice ports must be matched against POTS dial peers, and incoming calls from the network must be matched against VoX dial peers.

Incoming Called Number

Inbound call legs may be associated with dial peers based on the DNIS. Example 17-5 illustrates the configuration of an **incoming called-number** to enable this method of inbound dial-peer selection. You can only associate a single DNIS with each dial peer.

Example 17-5 *Configuring Inbound Dial-Peer Selection Based on the DNIS*

```
pri-gw#conf t
Enter configuration commands, one per line.  End with CNTL/Z.
pri-gw(config)#dial-peer voice 100 voip
pri-gw(config-dial-peer)#incoming called-number 5671212
pri-gw(config-dial-peer)#^Z
pri-gw#
```

Call setup messages from ISDN voice ports contain the DNIS, so you can use the **incoming called-number** command to select an inbound POTS dial peer based on the DNIS. For non-ISDN voice ports, a POTS dial peer is assigned as soon as the voice port is seized, which is before the router can collect the digits of the called number. For this reason, the router cannot use the **incoming called-number** to associate inbound POTS dial peers with the DNIS for non-ISDN voice ports.

TIP

You can only select an inbound POTS dial peer based on the called party number DNIS when the call arrives via an ISDN port.

Answer Address

If no dial-peers are configured with a matching **incoming called-number**, then inbound call legs may be associated with dial peers based on the calling party number. Example 17-6 illustrates the configuration of an **answer-address** to enable this method of inbound dial-peer selection.

Example 17-6 *Configuring Inbound Dial-Peer Selection Based on Calling Party Number*

```
r2#conf t
Enter configuration commands, one per line.  End with CNTL/Z.
r2(config)#dial-peer voice 10 pots
r2(config-dial-peer)#answer-address 5551234
r2(config-dial-peer)#^Z
r2#
```

Destination Pattern

If no dial peers are configured with an **incoming called-number** that matches the DNIS, and if no dial peers are configured with an **answer-address** that matches the calling party number, then dial peers are searched for a destination pattern that matches the calling party number. The **destination-pattern** and **answer-address** criteria are only useful if a calling party number is present in the incoming call request (for example, ANI from ISDN setup; caller ID from analog phase-shift keying; ANI from E&M feature group B (FGB); calling number from H.225.0 call setup, and so forth). The **destination-pattern** command is most commonly used to associate inbound calls from the network with VoX dial peers. Example 17-7 illustrates configuration of a destination pattern. The same dial peer may also be used for outbound calls.

Example 17-7 *Using the **destination-pattern** to Match an Inbound Dial Peer*

```
r2#conf t
Enter configuration commands, one per line.  End with CNTL/Z.
r2(config)#dial-peer voice 200 voip
r2(config-dial-peer)#destination-pattern 555....
r2(config-dial-peer)#^Z
r2#
```

When multiple destination patterns match the calling party number for an inbound call leg, then the same pattern-matching rules apply as for outbound call legs. The dial peer with the most explicitly matching digits (excluding wildcards) in the destination pattern is selected.

Voice Port

If no other dial peers have an **incoming called-number** that matches the DNIS, and if no other dial peers have an **answer-address** or **destination-pattern** that matches the calling party number, then a dial peer may be selected based on the originating voice port. The originating voice port is the most common method to associate an inbound call leg with a POTS dial peer (for calls that originate on non-ISDN voice ports). Example 17-8 illustrates a dial peer configured to match calls that arrive from voice port 1/0/0.

Example 17-8 *Configuring Inbound Dial-Peer Selection Based on the Originating Voice Port*

```
r2#conf t
Enter configuration commands, one per line.  End with CNTL/Z.
r2(config)#dial-peer voice 10 pots
r2(config-dial-peer)#port 1/0/0
r2(config-dial-peer)#^Z
r2#
```

Configuration Order

If an inbound call leg is assigned to a dial peer based on the voice port, and multiple POTS dial peers refer to the same voice port, then the first such dial peer is associated with the inbound call leg. This situation is common when multiple destination patterns are reachable via the same voice port.

In IOS releases prior to 12.1(4)T, the inbound call leg may not be properly associated with a POTS dial peer if the first POTS dial peer that refers to the voice port is in a shutdown state. In this situation, the null dial peer may be associated with the incoming call instead. Refer to the configuration in Example 17-9 to clarify the issue. Calls arriving on port 1/1/0 try to match against dial peer 200 even though it is shut down. The null fdial peer is associated with the inbound call leg, even though dial peer 201 is available. If dial peer 200 is deleted, then dial peer 201 is assigned to the inbound call leg. This issue is documented with the Bug ID CSCds05420.

Example 17-9 *Two POTS Dial Peers Associated with a Single Voice Port*

```
dial-peer voice 200 pots
  shutdown
  destination-pattern 20.
  port 1/1/0
!
dial-peer voice 201 pots
  destination-pattern 20.
  port 1/1/0
```

With the configuration illustrated in Example 17-9, the calls arriving on port 1/1/0 try to match against dial peer 200 although it is shut down. The null dial peer is associated with the inbound call leg, even though dial peer 201 is available. If dial peer 200 is deleted, then dial peer 201 is assigned to the inbound call leg. Again, this behavior is present as late as IOS 12.1(1)T, but it may be resolved in more current IOS versions. Fortunately, it is simple to verify and work around this behavior if you suspect it is causing problems for you.

Default null Dial Peer

If no dial peers match the inbound POTS or VoX call leg, then the call leg is associated with the default null dial peer (dial peer 0). The null dial peer has the default attributes for features such as VAD, codec, direct inward dial, and so forth. These defaults include VAD enabled, G.729r8 codec, DTMF relay disabled, direct-inward-dial disabled, and any other options that you would see after configuring a dial peer without specifying additional commands. The exact values for all parameters are subject to change in different versions of Cisco IOS. A calling party number is not associated with the call unless it is provided via an ISDN voice port or it is included in an inbound H.225.0 call setup message.

Destination Patterns and Digit Manipulation

If you are responsible for implementing a dial plan on Cisco routers, it is imperative that you understand (1) how destination patterns work for POTS and VoX dial peers, and (2) what commands are used to manipulate digits of the called and calling party numbers. The following sections discuss these topics:

- Destination patterns
- Prefix, forward digits, and digit strip
- Number expansion
- Translation rules
- Verifying dial-plan behavior

Pattern Matching

This section explores the following aspects of pattern matching for destination patterns:

- Basic pattern matching
- Advanced pattern matching
- Variable-length patterns and termination characters
- Differences between POTS and VoX dial peers

Basic Pattern Matching

A destination pattern is a string of digits or wildcard characters (and optional regular expression characters) that represents one or more telephone numbers. A destination pattern enables a dial peer to be associated with a call leg based on the calling or called party number. The most simple destination patterns explicitly match a single telephone number, such as:

- 14085551212
- 5551212
- 1212

Note that *telephone number* is broadly defined as a single destination within a numbering plan that may be represented by any number of digits between 1 and 32. A more flexible dial destination pattern uses the "." character as a wildcard digit to represent any single digit. A destination pattern can use wildcard digits to represent multiple phone numbers, such as:

```
1408555....
555....
1...
```

In the first case, the pattern matches any number with 11 digits or more that begins with 1408555. As long as the remaining four digits are present in the number, it does not matter what they are because the wildcard digits will match any numbers. If a 10-digit number is entered that begins with 1408555, the dial peer will not match and the call will time out (or inbound call legs will be associated with the "null" dial peer).

You can use a destination pattern with all wildcards (for example, ".......") to concisely represent all other telephone numbers, but you should make sure that you have defined more specific destination patterns for numbers that you want to match different dial peers. If you are not careful with your numbering-plan design and implementation, you may have problems using a default destination pattern like this, because misrouted calls can bounce around your network and create call routing loops that waste resources. Call routing loops are less of a problem in VoIP networks because tandem call routing is not supported, but you can still cause call routing loops between a router and a PBX. For example, if an incorrect number is dialed or all of the available voice ports are busy at a given destination, a default dial peer pointing to a PBX may send a call back to the PBX from which the router received the call. In this scenario, you can watch the call consume all available voice ports between the router and the PBX. You must also plan carefully when using default dial peers in conjunction with variable-length dial plans (which are discussed in a following section).

TIP	If you are using VoFR or VoATM, it is a good idea to use the **huntstop** feature on POTS dial peers to prevent calls from unintentionally tandem routing through the default dial peer when all of the voice ports are busy. This is less of a problem with VoIP because tandem call routing is not supported, but you should still be careful of call routing loops between a router and a PBX.

Advanced Pattern Matching

As of IOS 12.0(7)XR2, 12.0(7)XK, and 12.1(1)T, Cisco supports the use of UNIX-style regular expressions in the destination-pattern syntax. Table 17-4 illustrates the special characters that are available. Note that the % symbol is used instead of the standard * symbol for pattern repetition, to avoid confusion with the * key that is used on the telephone keypad. Standard regular-expression syntax solves this problem by using the \ key to escape the special behavior of symbol characters (for example, to represent an actual * in the telephone number with a *), but this behavior is not supported as of IOS 12.1(1)T. Just remember to use the % symbol instead of the * symbol when a wildcard is intended in destination patterns that support regular-expression syntax.

Table 17-4   *Special Characters Used in Dial-Peer Matching*

Symbol	Description
%	Indicates zero or more occurrences of previous character or pattern (like * in regular expressions)
+	Indicates one or more occurrences of previous character or pattern
?	Indicates exactly zero or one occurrence of the previous character or pattern.
.	Matches any single character
[ ]	Matches a single occurrence of any character within [ ]
( )	Identifies all characters within ( ) as a single pattern

The [ ] symbols are very useful to reduce the number of dial peers required in many situations. Consider a 4-digit numbering plan that assigns blocks of 50 numbers to each of 10 sites. Prior to the regular-expression syntax for destination patterns, you would need five dial peers (each with a different destination pattern) to represent the numbers associated with each site, such as:

    10..
    11..
    12..
    13..
    14..

With the regular-expression syntax, you can represent all of the these destination patterns as:

        1[0-4]..

Consistent with the standard regular-expression syntax, you can enumerate each character within the square brackets separated by a comma, or you can indicate a contiguous range of characters with a dash. The following examples highlight the different methods of using the [ ] symbol:

        [1,2,3,4,5,6,7,8,9]...
        [1-9]...
        [1,3-7,9]...

The first two examples match any four-digit string that starts with any non-zero digit. The last example matches any four-digit string that starts with any digit except 0, 2, or 8. Note that all destination patterns may also use the character set [*#ABCD] from extended DTMF dial pads.

TIP

If you have not configured regular expressions for other features on Cisco routers (for example, Border Gateway Protocol (BGP) as-path access lists, or X.25 call routing), then you may feel like the object of a cruel joke the first time you want to configure a ? within the regular expression. Every time you type ? from the command line, the router offers you help. But it does not tell you how to avoid its help! The trick is to enter the control sequence <Ctrl-V>, followed by the ? character, to bypass the command-line help and actually enter a ? in the configuration.

Variable-Length Patterns and Termination Characters

The PSTN/ISDN numbering plan (specified in ITU Recommendation E.164) is a variable-length-numbering plan that you use every day. When you make international calls, you dial an international access code, followed by a country code, a regional code used within the destination country, and the local subscriber number. For calls within a country, you dial the regional code (such as the area code within North America) and the local subscriber number. For calls within a given region, you only need to dial the local subscriber number. Similar conventions exist in private networks, where calls within a campus may require only the local site extension, and calls between campuses may require a site prefix and a local extension.

These examples highlight the fact that you cannot always avoid a variable-length-dialing plan. Even if you manage to keep your network on a fixed-length dialing plan, what happens when you mix the public dialing plan with your private dialing plan, or you merge with another company that has a different number of digits in its dialing plan? At some point, you will most likely need to work with a variable-length-dialing plan.

Destination patterns require a special mechanism to work with variable-length dialing plans. To understand why, consider the following example illustrated in Figure 17-3. In addition to calling between the extensions in each office, the New York office would like to use tail-end hop-off to make local calls in San Jose via the VoIP network. Similarly, the San Jose office would like to make local calls to New York City via the VoIP network.

Figure 17-3 *Network with Variable-Length Dialing Plan*

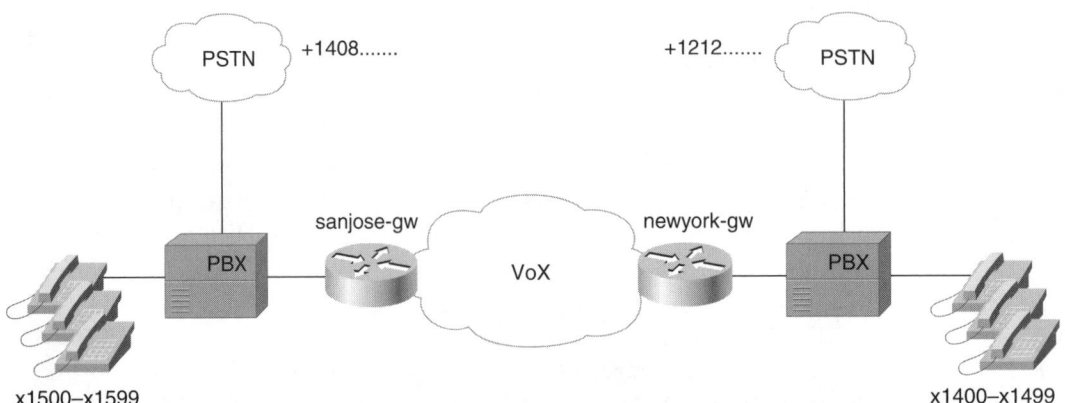

Using fixed-length dial peers, the router in New York might be configured as illustrated in Example 17-10. The idea is for the New York router to pass calls across the VoIP network that are directed to the 15xx extensions or to the public phone numbers in the 408 area code around San Jose.

Example 17-10 *Fixed-Length Dial Peers for a Small Network*

```
dial-peer voice 1400 pots
 destination-pattern 14..
 prefix 14
 port 2/1:0

dial-peer voice 1212 pots
 destination-pattern 1212.......
 prefix 91212
 port 2/1:0
!
dial-peer voice 1500 voip
 destination-pattern 15..
 session target ipv4:192.168.254.45
!
dial-peer voice 1408 voip
 destination-pattern 1408.......
 session target ipv4:192.168.254.45
```

Calls from New York to the x1500-x1599 extensions in San Jose succeed, but tail-end hop-off calls to San Jose never succeed with this configuration. Instead, the hop-off calls to San Jose are always directed to the user with extension x1408 in New York. This configuration fails because it assumes a fixed-length-dialing plan. The 1400 POTS dial peer always matches before enough digits are collected to match the 1408 VoIP dial peer.

This type of dialing plan can only work if there is a way to keep collecting digits and suppress the dial-peer matching process until all of the digits have been collected. This is exactly the function of the variable-length dialing plan feature for destination patterns. The T character in a destination pattern indicates that more digits may follow, and the pattern should not match until the interdigit timeout expires or the user dials the termination character. By default, the interdigit timeout is 10 seconds, which implies that dial peers ending with a T will not match for 10 seconds after the last number is dialed. To reduce the call-setup time, you can decrease the interdigit timer under the voice-port configuration. Users can also dial a termination character (which is # by default) to immediately signal the end of digit input.

If you have applications that require the # character to be used for other purposes, you can define a different character to be the termination character. For example, if you have a PBX that expects the calling party address to be passed with the called party address and separated by the # character, you do not want the router to interpret # as the end of dialed digits. You might define the * symbol to be the terminating character in this network, but make sure you are not also using the * for invoking features from the PBX (for example, *79, *40).

To correct the router configuration in Example 17-10 to take advantage of the variable-length dialing plan feature for destination patterns, simply add a T character to the end of the destination pattern in POTS dial peer 1400.

Differences Between POTS and VoX Dial Peers

Destination patterns function differently for outbound POTS and VoX dial peers. Both types of dial peers match digit strings in the same manner, but they differ in how they process the digits after a dial peer is matched. When a digit string matches an outgoing VoX dial peer, all of the digits that match the destination pattern are forwarded as part of the called number (including the explicit-matched and wildcard-matched digits). Outgoing POTS dial peers remove the leading digits that explicitly match a destination pattern, and only forward the digits that match the wildcard pattern.

Consider the configuration example shown in Example 17-11. If the VoIP dial peer matches the called number 101 for an outbound call leg, then all three digits are forwarded to the destination. If the POTS dial peer matches a called number of 201 for an outbound call leg, then the explicitly matching digits 20 are removed, and only the final digit 1 is sent out of the voice port to the attached phone switch. The next section explores the different methods of modifying what digits are transmitted for outbound POTS dial peers.

Example 17-11   *Example Configurations of POTS and VoX Destination Patterns*

```
dial-peer voice 1 pots
 destination-pattern 20.
 port 1/1/1
!
dial-peer voice 2 voip
 destination-pattern 10.
 session target ipv4:192.168.254.1
!
```

The destination patterns for POTS dial peers were a little different on the early versions of the Cisco MC3810. If you wanted to explicitly match some number of digits and pass the remaining digits to the PBX, you only configured the destination pattern with the explicitly matching digits (i.e., no wildcard "." digits). Any digits that followed the explicitly matched pattern would be forwarded to the PBX, subject to the control of the **forward-digits** command (which is described in the following section). So, instead of a destination pattern of "555....", you would use a pattern of "555" to match any number of the form 555-xxxx.

Prefix, Forward Digits, and Digit Strip

The default digit-stripping behavior of POTS dial-peers is suitable for many applications. For example, if you have destination patterns that explicitly define a site phone number prefix and use wildcards for the local extensions, then only the extension digits are passed to the PBX. Because users within the site dial each other using only the local extensions, the behavior of the router is consistent with the behavior of the local users.

In some cases you need to provide more or fewer digits to the PBX, depending on the routing scheme used within the PBX. For example, if you must send a call from a router to a PBX that acts as a tandem switch, then the PBX needs to know the destination site prefix in addition to the extension number. In general, you must collaborate with the PBX support personnel to ensure that the router sends the number of digits that the PBX expects, and vice-versa. Depending on your hardware platform and the version of IOS you are running, there are three voice-port commands to manipulate the leading digits of the phone number:

- **prefix**
- **forward-digits**
- **digit-strip**

The **prefix** command is supported on every platform. It is easy to understand and usually gets the job done. Example 17-12 illustrates the configuration of prefix digits to restore the digits that were stripped by the destination pattern matching.

Example 17-12 *Using* **prefix** *to Restore the Digits that Were Stripped by the* **destination-pattern**

```
r2#conf t
Enter configuration commands, one per line.  End with CNTL/Z.
r2(config)#dial-peer voice 555 pots
r2(config-dial-peer)#destination-pattern 555....
r2(config-dial-peer)#prefix 555
r2(config-dial-peer)#port 1/0/0
r2(config-dial-peer)#^Z
r2#
```

TIP

Sometimes a router transmits digits before a PBX or phone switch is ready to receive them. This mostly happens when E&M immediate-start signaling is used. The call setup usually times out in such cases, and the user hears a long silence followed eventually by a busy signal.

This problem can be corrected by inserting a pause before the router sends digits to the phone switch. You can use a comma as the first character of the number string in the **prefix** command to represent a 1-sec pause. For example, "prefix ,555" causes a router to wait 1 sec, then send 555, then send the wildcard digits from the destination pattern. Occasionally, you may need to use two commas at the front of a prefix number string (to represent a 2-sec pause).

The **forward-digits** command was first supported on the Cisco MC3810, and it has migrated to other platforms (for example, 2600/3600/7200) in the IOS 12.0XK train. With the **forward-digits** command, you can specify the number of digits that you want forwarded to the PBX, you can use the keyword **all** to mimic the behavior of VoX dial peers, or you can use the keyword **none** to block all digit transmission to the PBX. Example 17-13 demonstrates this configuration.

Example 17-13 *Using* **forward-digits all** *to Restore Digits that Were Stripped by the* **destination pattern**

```
mc3810-gw#conf t
Enter configuration commands, one per line.  End with CNTL/Z.
mc3810-gw(config)#dial-peer voice 555 pots
mc3810-gw(config-dial-peer)#destination-pattern 555....
mc3810-gw(config-dial-peer)#forward-digits all
mc3810-gw(config-dial-peer)#port 1/6
mc3810-gw(config-dial-peer)#^Z
mc3810-gw#
```

The **digit-strip** command is available as of IOS 12.1(1)T, and provides a similar functionality to **forward-digits all** and **forward-digits none**. There is no option with the **digit-strip** command to control the number of digits that are stripped—it is all or nothing. To emulate the behavior of **forward-digits all**, you can configure **no digit-strip** on the POTS dial peer as illustrated in Example 17-14.

Example 17-14 *Using* **no digit-strip** *to Restore Digits that Were Stripped by the* **destination pattern**

```
r2#conf t
Enter configuration commands, one per line.  End with CNTL/Z.
r2(config)#dial-peer voice 555 pots
r2(config-dial-peer)#destination-pattern 555....
r2(config-dial-peer)#no digit-strip
r2(config-dial-peer)#port 1/0/0
r2(config-dial-peer)#^Z
r2#
```

Pattern Substitutions

Aside from the methods of adding and stripping digits at the voice port, there are two methods to add, remove, or substitute digits at a global or dial-peer level:

- Number expansion
- Translation rules

Number Expansion

Number expansion is useful if you enable calls to reroute through the Public Switched Telephone Network (PSTN). For example, the users may dial only four- or five-digit extensions to reach users in another office via a private network. If calls fail through the private network, then they may be retried through the public network. If a router cannot complete a call through the VoX network, then it can send the call back to the PBX for transmission to the PSTN (that is, "hairpin" the call).

The public phone network does not understand four- or five-digit private extensions, so interoffice calls cannot be rerouted through the PSTN without additional processing. Many PBXs support digit prepending to facilitate different policies, such as prepending a 1010XXX code to specify a long-distance carrier, or adding the appropriate country, regional, and city prefix codes to the interoffice extensions. However, you do not want to rely on the PBX to provide this functionality, because the PBX may already have a defined route for the abbreviated numbers. If the router hairpins an extension number back to the PBX, the PBX may determine that the best route is back through the VoX network. To avoid this call-routing loop (and immediate seizure of all available voice ports), you should configure the routers in your network to perform number expansion to convert the interoffice extensions into public routable phone numbers. The PBX can then recognize that calls beginning with a 9 should be routed to the PSTN, and there is no chance of a call-routing loop. A failure in the VoX network will be transparent to users if you configure the network to support PSTN rerouting.

The biggest consequence of configuring number expansion for all numbers is that your destination patterns no longer match the interoffice extensions. Instead, your destination patterns match the public-routable phone numbers that you have expanded. This is because the number expansion is performed before an inbound or outbound dial peer is matched.

Example 17-15 illustrates how an interoffice extension does not match a destination pattern that expects a public-routable number. In Example 17-16, the number expansion is configured, and the **show dialplan number** command verifies that the number expansion is applied and that a dial peer now matches the number.

Example 17-15 *Interoffice Extensions Do Not Match Destination Patterns in Dial Peers*

```
r2#conf t
Enter configuration commands, one per line.  End with CNTL/Z.
r2(config)#dial-peer voice 1408
r2(config-dial-peer)#destination-pattern 1408555....
r2(config-dial-peer)#^Z
r2#
r2#show dialplan number 51212
Macro Exp.: 51212
No match, result=-1

r2#
```

Example 17-16 *Interoffice Extension Is Mapped to the Expanded Number to Match a Dial Peer*

```
r2#conf t
Enter configuration commands, one per line.  End with CNTL/Z.
r2(config)#num-exp 5.... 1408555....
r2(config-dial-peer)#^Z
r2#
r2#show dialplan number 51212
Macro Exp.: 14085551212

VoiceOverIpPeer1408
        information type = voice,
        tag = 1408, destination-pattern = `1408555....',
        <et cetera>

r2#
```

Number expansion is also useful when joining the voice networks of two merged companies. If there are any site-prefix overlaps, you can create a new dial plan for the site prefixes, and map the old site prefixes to the new site prefixes using a number expansion. While the **translation-rule** commands are a more powerful method to achieve this and other digit manipulation goals, the number-expansion method works well too. If you must run a version of IOS that does not support translation rules (for example, pre-IOS 12.0(7)XR2, 12.0(7)XK1, 12.1(1)T), or if you are experiencing the bugs present in the early implementations of translation rules, then the number expansion is a fine alternative.

Translation Rules

One of the problems with the number-expansion mechanism is that it operates on every call. There is no way to selectively enable it or disable it. The new translation-rule mechanism enables you to define a set of substitution operations as a translation rule, and selectively apply the translation rule in several ways:

- To all inbound call legs from the network
- To all inbound call legs from a specified voice port
- To all outbound call legs matching a specified dial peer

Example 17-17 illustrates the configuration of a translation rule. You can define numerous translation rules, and up to ten rules within each translation rule. Translation rules, which support regular expressions, are actually more robust than the number-expansion method of digit manipulation. However, the regular-expression functionality (as of IOS 12.1(1)T) is not robust with respect to string substitutions, meta-characters between explicit digits, and support for multiple pattern substitutions within a single expression.

Example 17-17   *Configuring a Translation Rule*

```
r2#conf t
Enter configuration commands, one per line.  End with CNTL/Z.
r2(config)#translation-rule 2
r2(config-translate)#rule 1 408555.... 1408555
r2(config-translate)#rule 2 555.... 1408555
r2(config-translate)#rule 3 5.... 1408555
r2(config-translate)#^Z
r2#
```

The translation rule is applied to all calls arriving from the network in Example 17-18, and to all calls arriving on a voice port in Example 17-19.

Example 17-18   *Applying the Translation Rule to All Inbound Call Legs from the Network*

```
r2#conf t
Enter configuration commands, one per line.  End with CNTL/Z.
r2(config)#voip-incoming translation-rule 2 ?
  called   called party number will required translate
  calling  calling party number will required translate

r2(config)#voip-incoming translation-rule 2 calling
r2(config)#^Z
r2#
```

Example 17-19   *Applying the Translation Rule to All Inbound Call Legs from a Specified Voice Port*

```
r2#conf t
Enter configuration commands, one per line.  End with CNTL/Z.
r2(config)#voice-port 1/0/0
r2(config-voiceport)#translate ?
```

Example 17-19 *Applying the Translation Rule to All Inbound Call Legs from a Specified Voice Port (Continued)*

```
 called    called party number will required translate
 calling   calling party number will required translate

r2(config-voiceport)#translate called ?
  <1-2147483647>  Translation rule TAG

r2(config-voiceport)#translate called 2
r2(config-voiceport)#^Z
r2#
```

Example 17-20 illustrates the translation rule applied to an outgoing call leg that matches a specific voice port. Notice the error message from the console after the translation rule has been applied to the dial peer. This message appears because the dial peer is already configured with a prefix, and the **translate-outgoing** dial-peer command cannot be used at the same time as the **prefix** command on a given dial peer. This is sensible because both commands change the called number on the outbound call leg, and there would be confusion as to which command has precedence. The router does not accept the **translate-outgoing** command until the prefix is removed.

Example 17-20 *Applying the Translation Rule to All Outbound Call Legs that Match a Dial Peer*

```
r2#conf t
Enter configuration commands, one per line.  End with CNTL/Z.
r2(config)#dial-peer voice 11 pots
r2(config-dial-peer)#translate-outgoing ?
  called    called party number will required translate
  calling   calling party number will required translate

r2(config-dial-peer)#translate-outgoing calling ?
  <1-2147483647>  Translation rule TAG

r2(config-dial-peer)#translate-outgoing calling 2
r2(config-dial-peer)#^Z
r2#
Mar  1 01:31:12.019: Delete prefix then setup translation
01:31:13: %SYS-5-CONFIG_I: Configured from console by console
r2#
```

Verifying Dial-Plan Behavior

Aside from the debugging commands that show you more than you probably want to know about a call, the following two commands are very useful to diagnose problems with dial-peer matching and pattern substitutions:

- **show dialplan number**
- **test translation-rule**

show dialplan number

The **show dialplan number** command is one of the most useful commands when you are troubleshooting a new network installation. You can determine whether number expansions are processed (via the **Macro Exp** output), the number of digits that matched the destination pattern, and many configurable attributes of the dial peer. You can also see the operational status and performance of the dial peer in terms of call failures and completions, and the reasons for call failures. Example 17-21 illustrates the output of the **show dialplan number** command.

Example 17-21 *Show Information About the Dial Peer that Matches a Given Telephone Number*

```
r2#show dialplan number 51212
Macro Exp.: 14085551212

VoiceOverIpPeer1408
        information type = voice,
        tag = 1408, destination-pattern = `1408555....',
        answer-address = `', preference=0,
        numbering Type = `unknown'
        group = 1408, Admin state is up, Operation state is up,
        incoming called-number = `', connections/maximum = 0/unlimited,
        application associated:
        type = voip, session-target = `ipv4:192.168.254.1',
        technology prefix:
        settle-call = disabled
        ip precedence = 0, UDP checksum = disabled,
        session-protocol = cisco,
        session-transport = udp, req-qos = best-effort,
        acc-qos = best-effort,
        fax-rate = voice,   payload size =  20 bytes
        codec = g729r8,   payload size =  20 bytes,
        Playout: Mode adaptive,
        Expect factor = 10,
        Max Redirects = 1, Icpif = 30,signaling-type = cas,
        CLID Restrict = disabled
        VAD = enabled, Poor QOV Trap = disabled,
        Connect Time = 0, Charged Units = 0,
        Successful Calls = 0, Failed Calls = 0,
        Accepted Calls = 0, Refused Calls = 0,
        Last Disconnect Cause is "",
        Last Disconnect Text is "",
        Last Setup Time = 0.
Matched: 14085551212   Digits: 7
Target: ipv4:192.168.254.1

r2#
```

test translation-rule

Example 17-22 demonstrates how you can verify the operation of the translation rules that you configure. In this example, different input digit strings are compared against the translation rule that was configured in Example 17-17. As you can see, the translation rule changes all forms of the same destination number to the international form (which simplifies the dial-peer configuration).

Example 17-22 *Verifying Operation of the Translation Rules for Different Input Digit Strings*

```
r2#test translation-rule 2 51212 ?
  abbreviated    The numbering type is abbreviated
  international  The numbering type is international
  national       The numbering type is national
  network        The numbering type is network
  reserved       The numbering type is reserved
  subscriber     The numbering type is subscriber
  unknown        The numbering type is unknown

r2#test translation-rule 2 51212 unknown
r2#
Mar  1 00:47:49.298: The replace number 14085551212
r2#
r2#test translation-rule 2 5551212 unknown
r2#
Mar  1 00:49:26.982: The replace number 14085551212
r2#
r2#test translation-rule 2 4085551212 unknown
r2#
Mar  1 00:49:35.246: The replace number 14085551212
r2#
r2#test translation-rule 2 1212 unknown
r2#
Mar  1 00:52:04.534: Input number 1212 can't match any translation rules
r2#
```

Session Targets

If the dialed digits match a destination pattern in a VoX dial peer, then the session protocol (discussed later in this chapter) establishes a connection to the session target for that dial peer. The format of the session target depends on the type of VoX, and on the session protocol. The following session-target formats are supported as of this writing:

- VoFR
- VoATM
- IPv4
- DNS
- RAS
- SIP server

For VoFR, the session target identifies a serial interface and a data-link connection identifier (DLCI) number to which the call should be directed. For VoATM, the session target identifies a serial interface and a virtual path identifier/virtual connection identifier (VPI/VCI) pair. A VoIP session target can point directly to the called destination via IP address or DNS host name, or the session target may point to an H.323 gatekeeper (using RAS signaling) or a SIP proxy server. The keyword **ras** in the session target indicates that an ARQ message should be sent to an H.323 gatekeeper, which will respond with the destination IP address and TCP port in an ACF message. Calls cannot be established using **ras** as the session target until the router is configured as an H.323 gateway, and an H.323 gatekeeper is configured to resolve the destination E.164 alias. The keyword **sip-server** may only be used when the router is configured as a SIP user agent (UA) with a SIP proxy/registrar server identified. Example 17-23 illustrates the configuration of these various session targets. Note that the rest of the VoX dial-peer configuration elements (such as the destination pattern) have been excluded for clarity.

Example 17-23 *Configuring the Different Types of Session Targets on Cisco Routers*

```
voice-gw4#conf t
Enter configuration commands, one per line.  End with CNTL/Z.
voice-gw4(config)#dial-peer voice 6 vofr
voice-gw4(config-dial-peer)#session target serial 1 16
voice-gw4(config-dial-peer)#exit
voice-gw4(config)#dial-peer voice 7 voatm
voice-gw4(config-dial-peer)#session target atm0 pvc 1/20
voice-gw4(config-dial-peer)#exit
voice-gw4(config)#dial-peer voice 8 voip
voice-gw4(config-dial-peer)#session target ipv4:192.168.254.1
voice-gw4(config-dial-peer)#exit
voice-gw4(config)#dial-peer voice 9 voip
voice-gw4(config-dial-peer)#session target dns:voice-gw2.company.com
voice-gw4(config-dial-peer)#exit
voice-gw4(config)#dial-peer voice 10 voip
voice-gw4(config-dial-peer)#session target ras
voice-gw4(config-dial-peer)#exit
voice-gw4(config)#dial-peer voice 11 voip
voice-gw4(config-dial-peer)#session target sip-server
voice-gw4(config-dial-peer)#^Z
voice-gw4#
```

Tandem Call Routing

Tandem call routing in the context of Cisco routers can be succinctly defined as receiving an inbound call leg on a VoX dial peer, and connecting it with an outbound call leg on another VoX dial peer. In other words, a Cisco router that does not originate or terminate a call, but processes it using dial peers, is a tandem call router. A normal IP router that passes VoIP packets is not considered a tandem call router because it does not examine the digits and make a routing decision using a dial peer. A normal IP router simply forwards VoIP packets according to the path specified for the destination IP address.

VoFR and VoATM

Link-layer VoX technologies (for example, VoFR and VoATM) require tandem call routing for economy and scalability. Without tandem call routing, VoFR and VoATM networks require a full mesh of virtual circuits to provide any-to-any calling connectivity. Aside from the burden of establishing a full mesh of virtual circuits, each router would also require at least one dial peer for every destination in the network, which is impractical for large networks.

With tandem call routing, economical network designs (for example, hub and spoke) are possible, and significantly fewer dial peers are required. A central tandem call router is configured with knowledge of the whole network, but remote sites only need a summary route that points all calls to the tandem router. The tandem router then initiates a call-setup request to the actual destination (or the next-hop tandem router), and connects the inbound network call leg with the outbound network call leg. Router B in Figure 17-4 acts as a tandem router for calls from user A to user C. Note that the PBX attached to router B is not involved in the tandem call routing.

Figure 17-4 *Tandem Call Router Joins Two Network Call Legs*

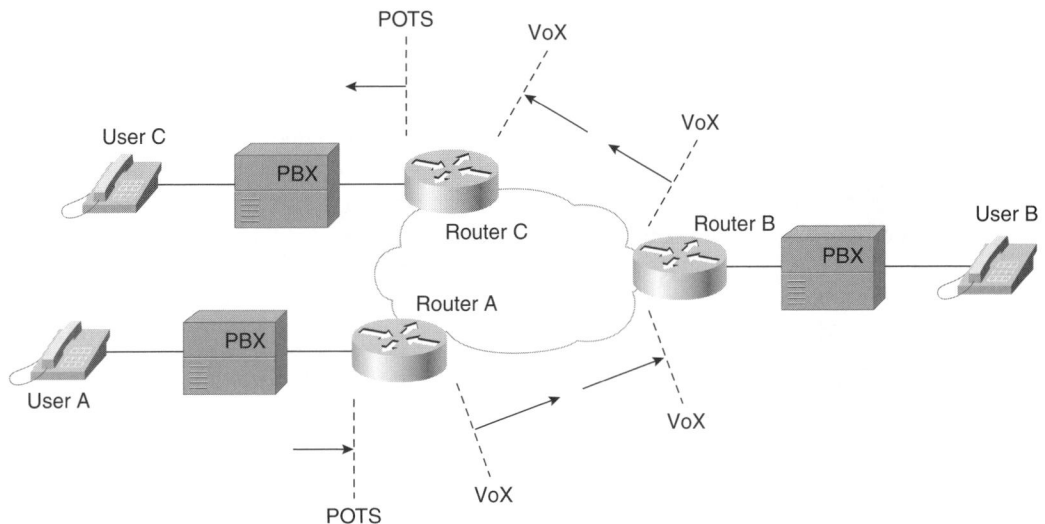

Tandem call routing introduces the possibility that many different VoX dial peers will interact. Some mechanism is required to ensure that the configuration options of different VoX dial peers are compatible. A strictly compliant FRF.11 VoFR call must be manually configured on both ends to use the same call parameters. There is no standard for a dynamic negotiation-based method to ensure parameter compatibility (such as codec, VAD, and so forth), but Cisco has implemented a Q.931-like proprietary method to dynamically negotiate call parameters. You can take advantage of these features by using the cisco-switched session protocol (described later in this chapter), which is the default for VoFR dial peers. You can tandem switch between VoFR and VoATM dial peers, which is a convenient method of uniting a dial plan across disparate link-layer VoX technologies.

VoIP

Network-layer VoX technologies (such as VoIP) do not require tandem call routing, because the network layer already provides any-to-any connectivity. There are times, however, when the functionality of tandem call routing is useful. Consider a VoIP network implemented over a hub-and-spoke topology. It would certainly be convenient to have a central router that knows all the destinations, and then configure each of the remote sites with a default dial peer pointing to the central router. Cisco does not implement true tandem call routing for VoIP because there are more robust methods of managing dial peers in VoIP networks. Specifically, H.323 gatekeepers and SIP proxy servers provide this functionality. Using these services to implement a scalable VoIP dial plan is described later in this chapter.

Connection Modes

Connection modes define the services that VoX and POTS call legs provide when establishing a connection between voice ports (or other endpoints such as H.323 terminals). For example, the connection mode specifies whether the same endpoints are connected in a fixed and constant manner for all calls, or whether the endpoints may connect to any destination. The connection mode also specifies what voice-port signaling is passed across the connection (for example, hookflash), which devices interpret DTMF digits, and how voice ports respond to remote busy/no-answer conditions. The dialing plan for the integrated network is critically affected by your selection of connection modes, because the connection mode determines how the call-routing intelligence is distributed between the routers and phone switches.

For each voice port on a Cisco router, you must choose one of these five connection modes:

- Switched (normal)
- Private Line Automatic Ring-down (PLAR)
- PLAR for Off-Premise Extensions (PLAR-OPX)
- Tie line
- Trunk

Switched (Normal)

If you do not configure a connection mode on a voice port, then the default connection mode enables normal switching operation. That is, inbound calls on the voice port may connect to any destination that a user dials, provided that a dial peer matches the dialed number. The normal connection mode is associated with integrated dialing plans that favor call-routing intelligence in the router and minimal call-routing intelligence in the external phone switches. In such cases, the routers have dial peers for every possible destination, or at least default dial peers to reach routers that know more destinations.

When a voice port that operates in a normal connection mode receives an off-hook indication, it waits to receive dialed digits that specify where the call should be connected. After the digits have been collected, the router compares the received digits with the configured dial peers until there is a match. A call connection is then established between the voice port and the destination indicated by the matched dial peer.

The normal connection mode makes efficient use of voice ports, and is a good choice as long as the services associated with a trunk connection are not required (for example, hookflash relay, or centralized voice mail for OPX lines). To understand the efficiency of the normal connection mode, consider the example of a traditional hub-and-spoke voice network with ten remote sites, as illustrated in Figure 17-5. Each of the remote offices has four analog E&M tie lines that connect to the central site, which terminate in two T-1 circuits. The remote offices mostly call the central site, but sometimes they call each other. Calls between offices must be relayed through the central site, which consumes two voice channels at the central site.

Figure 17-5   *Traditional Interoffice Voice Connectivity*

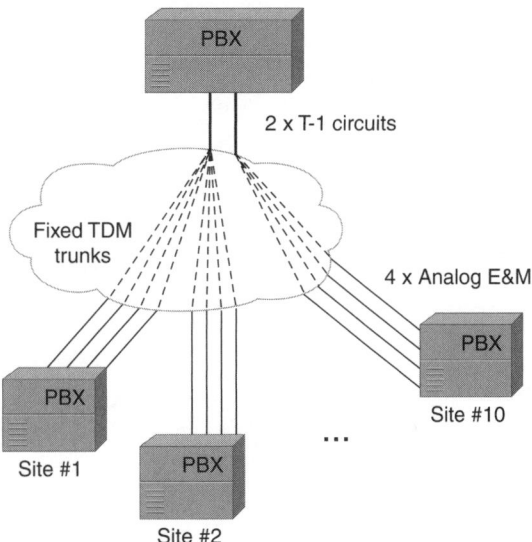

Now consider a VoX network that replaces the circuit connections in the traditional network. At the remote sites, the four analog E&M connections are locally terminated in a router. At the central site, only one T-1 circuit is needed between the router and the PBX. Why is this? There is an assumption here that every remote site will not simultaneously use all four lines to call the central site. This assumption is based on the fact that sometimes the remote sites call each other, and sometimes the lines are idle. But wait! When the remote sites call each other, aren't two voice ports at the central site consumed? If you place the call-routing intelligence in the routers, then the central site PBX is not required to make a call-routing decision, so calls can route directly through the VoX network without touching a voice port on the PBX at the central site. As for the assumption of idle time on the line, this is dependent on individual networks. If you have 100 people at a remote office sharing 4 lines out of a PBX, chances are there will be little idle time on the lines, so you cannot oversubscribe the voice ports at the central site as much.

The VoX network just described is essentially a private switched telephone network. Each office connects to the VoX network cloud just as it would connect to the public switched telephone network (PSTN). Any site can call any other site, and there are no dedicated connections between any offices. Figure 17-6 illustrates this concept. This model is based on the use of the normal switched connection mode on all voice ports in the VoX network.

Figure 17-6   *VoX Network Acts as a Private Switched Telephone Network*

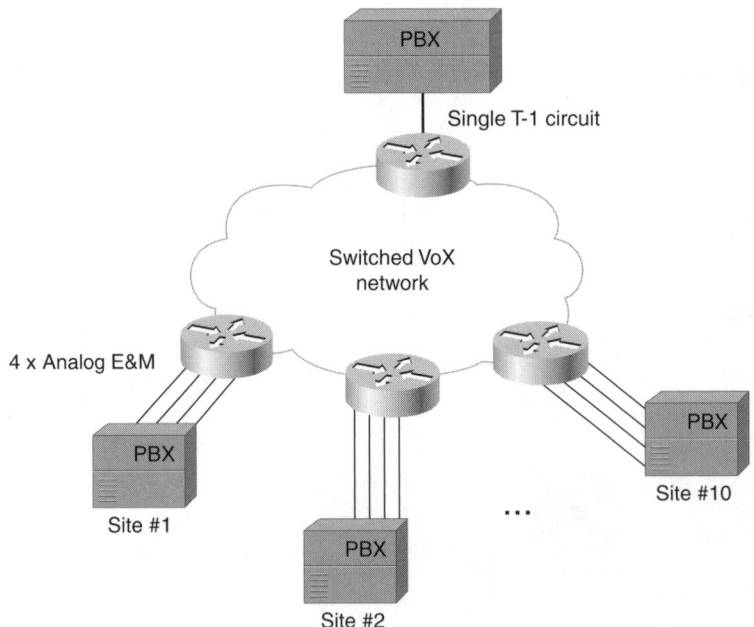

Private Line Automatic Ring-Down

When a user goes off-hook (in other words, picks up the phone) on a voice port configured for private line automatic ring-down (PLAR), a predetermined destination number is automatically dialed. The user immediately hears a ring-back tone if the predetermined destination is a phone. If you only want users to call one destination, this is the easiest way to do it. For example, you may have a courtesy telephone outside the front door of your office building, so after-hours visitors can contact the security department or an operator. The phone is configured with a PLAR connection to (1) make the experience easier for the end user, and (2) avoid fraudulent use of the telephone for other purposes.

You configure a PLAR connection in the voice-port configuration mode, as illustrated in Example 17-24. You must specify the destination phone number to which the call should automatically connect.

Example 17-24 *Configuring a PLAR Connection*

```
voice-gw1#conf t
Enter configuration commands, one per line.  End with CNTL/Z.
voice-gw1(config)#voice-port 1/0/1
voice-gw1(config-voiceport)#connection plar +14085551234
voice-gw1(config)#^Z
voice-gw1#
```

The phone number that you configure in the **connection plar** command is treated the same as if the user dialed the number. In other words, the number is compared against a list of locally configured dial peers, and a switched call connection is established with the destination specified in the matching dial peer. PLAR connections operate identically to normal switched connections, except for the fact that the dialed phone number is predetermined.

PLAR is also used to provide a replacement for off-premise extension (OPX) lines. Recall that OPX lines enable phones at different locations to appear as if they are directly and locally attached to a centralized phone switch (PBX). When users at a remote office go off-hook, they hear dial tone from the PBX at the central site. When the PBX sends a ringing signal to one of the lines, the phone at the remote office rings. An OPX line is essentially a tunnel through a circuit vendor network for all signaling and audio path information between the phone and the PBX.

Using Cisco routers, you can configure a PLAR connection to act as an OPX tunnel between a remote phone and a central PBX. This approach is conceptually similar to sending IP traffic through a generic routing encapsulation (GRE) tunnel. You must have an IP address at both ends of a GRE tunnel, and you must also have phone numbers at both ends of a PLAR connection. The IP addresses of the tunnel endpoints are unrelated to the IP addresses of the traffic flowing through the GRE tunnel, and the phone numbers of the

PLAR connection endpoints are unrelated to the phone numbers that may be dialed and accessed through the OPX tunnel. Figure 17-7 illustrates the OPX tunnel concept.

Figure 17-7 *PLAR Connection Acts as an OPX Tunnel, Connecting Remote Phones to a Central PBX*

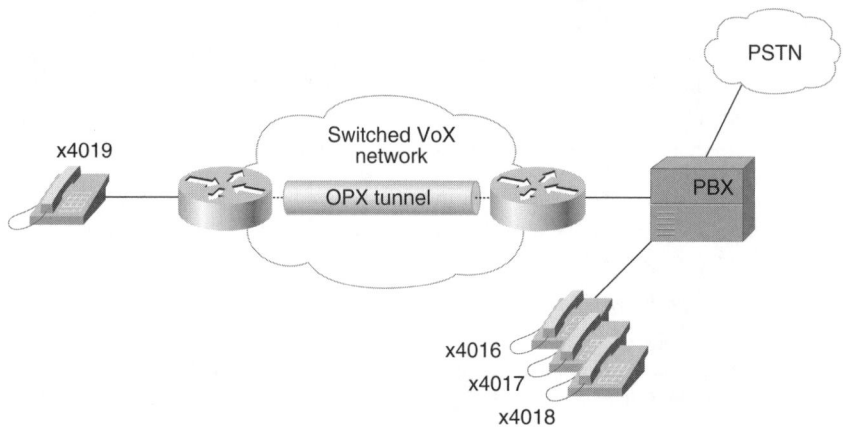

When a voice port on a remote site router detects an off-hook condition (in other words, a user picks up the phone to make a call), the router initiates a call to the voice port on the central site router. The voice port on the central site router automatically answers the call, and the PBX attached to the central router voice port detects the off-hook condition. The PBX responds by sending a dial tone on the line, but by this time the connection is established between the central and remote router voice ports. The dial tone passes through the active audio path of the PLAR connection all the way back to the original user that picked up the phone at the remote office. Users immediately hear this dial tone (from the central PBX) when they pick up a phone at a remote site.

When the users dial a destination phone number, the digits are passed through the OPX tunnel and interpreted by the central PBX. The remote site router does not interpret the digits because it has already completed the call (from its perspective) and any subsequent signaling is treated as in-band audio information. The remote router may intercept user-dialed digits and relay them to the opposite end of the PLAR connection, where the central site router cleanly regenerates the DTMF tones for the central PBX. The remote router only intercepts the user-dialed digits when the VoX dial peer (associated with the PLAR connection) is configured with a form of DTMF relay.

It is important to note that PLAR connections configured for OPX applications do not transmit any voice-port signals across the connection. Specifically, hookflash (to invoke features) and stutter dial tones (as message-waiting indicators) are not transmitted across the PLAR connection. You should use a trunk connection if you need these features.

As of IOS 12.1(1)T, Cisco routers support a hookflash-relay feature that is independent of the connection mode. This feature is available when the remote site uses an FXS port, the central site uses an FXO port, and an H.245-based DTMF relay is configured on the VoX dial peer. When the phone at the remote site sends the hookflash signal (a brief transition from off-hook to on-hook to off-hook), the remote router sends a ! character in the same manner as a DTMF digit relayed through the H.245 channel. You can use hookflash across a PLAR connection using the hookflash feature, but stutter dial tone is still not supported for PLAR connections.

Another important design point is that PLAR connections are ephemeral. That is, they last only as long as a given call connection. Between calls, all of the network resources and voice ports are released, so a given voice port at the central site may accept PLAR connections from many different remote sites. For networks in which the central site router or PBX voice ports are a scarce commodity, the ability to oversubscribe OPX lines may be important. For example, 100 remote sites may be configured to have PLAR connections to a single oversubscribed T-1 voice port at the central site. The PBX only allows inbound calls from the VoX network on this T-1 (which appears to be 24 telephones), and routes outbound calls to the router via a different T-1 (which appears to be a tie line to another PBX). The PBX sends the destination digits for calls to the phones via the second T-1, and the router uses a normal switched connection to reach the desired phone. Figure 17-8 illustrates this scenario, which also highlights that voice network designs do not need to be symmetrical.

Remember this design feature (the ability of PLAR to oversubscribe OPX lines) when contemplating the choice of trunk connections or PLAR connections for OPX-replacement scenarios. Trunk connections are statically associated with both endpoints, which prevents oversubscription. Trunk connections are described in a following section.

PLAR for Off-Premise Extensions

PLAR and PLAR for Off-Premise Extensions (PLAR-OPX) connections are very similar, but a crucial difference gives each of these connection modes a defined niche for voice applications. The difference lies in the behavior of a voice port during an inbound call. Look at Figure 17-7, and consider what happens when the central PBX must deliver a call to a remote phone. The voice port on the central site router detects a ringing tone from the PBX, and automatically goes off-hook to answer the call. When the central router goes off-hook on the voice port, the PLAR connection is stimulated to call the remote router voice port. The remote router voice port then sends ringing tone to the phone.

Figure 17-8 *Using PLAR to Oversubscribe OPX Lines*

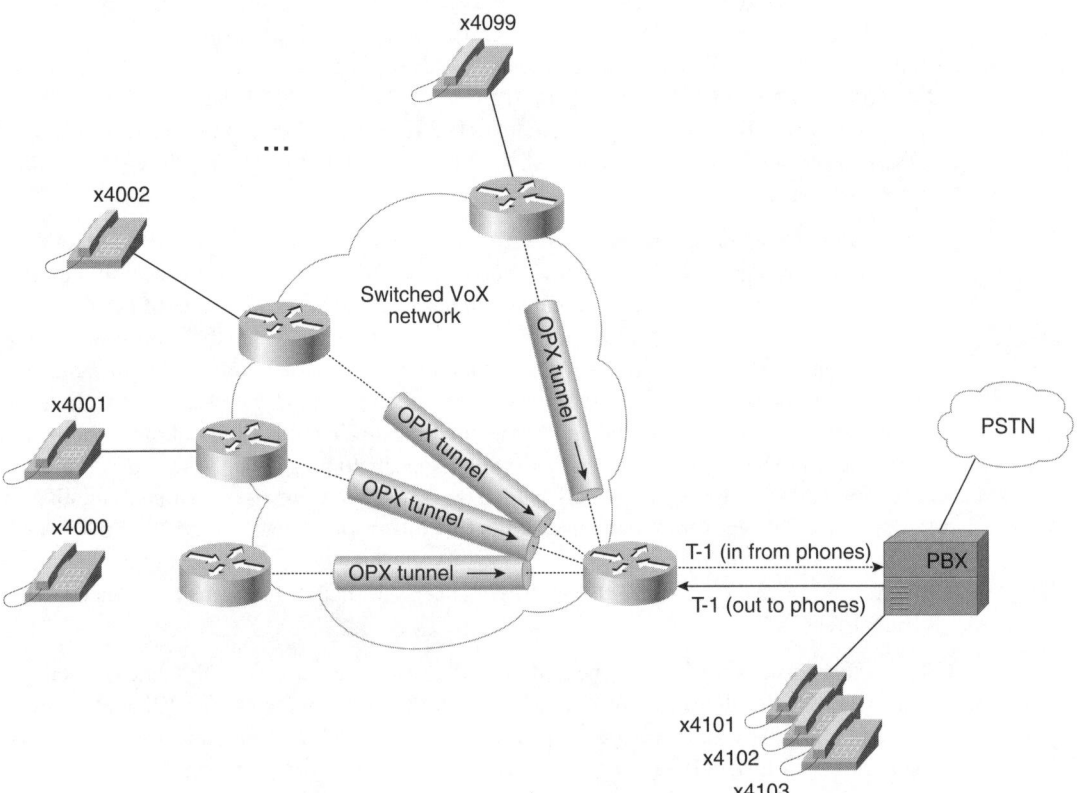

What happens if the remote phone is busy or nobody answers? The router at the central site has already gone off-hook in response to the ringing tone from the PBX, so the call is completed as far as the PBX is concerned. The PBX cannot redirect the call to a voice-mail system because the call is already connected. However, the call dies in the VoX network because there is nowhere to complete the call. This black hole effect occurs because the central site router answers the call from the PBX before it knows if the remote phone will answer. This is the limitation of PLAR, which is illustrated in Figure 17-9.

Figure 17-9 *PLAR Causes Black Hole in the VoX Network; PBX Cannot Redirect Calls*

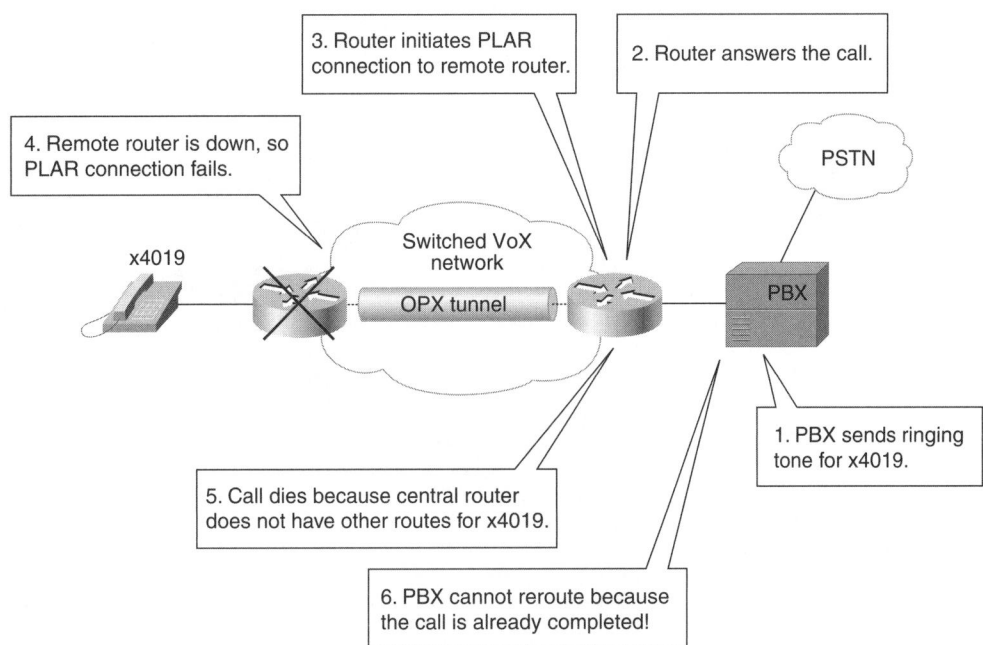

PLAR-OPX connections resolve the black hole problem by not immediately answering an inbound call from the PBX. When the central router analog or digital FXO port receives ringing tone from the PBX, a PLAR connection is initiated to the remote router without going off-hook on the local voice port. The remote router sends ringing tone to its directly attached phone, while the central router waits for a response. If a user answers the phone, then the remote router sends a signal to the central router. The central router then answers the call from the PBX, and the end-to-end connection is established. If the phone at the remote site is already in use, or if nobody answers the phone after a predetermined number of rings, then the central site router rejects the call from the PBX. This key feature enables the PBX at the central site to reroute the call to another extension, or forward the call to a personal voice mailbox. Even if the central site router never rejects the PBX connection request, the PBX can reroute the call to a voice mailbox after some number of rings, because the router will not answer the call from the PBX until the destination answers first. Figure 17-10 illustrates the benefits of PLAR-OPX.

Figure 17-10 *PLAR-OPX Enables a PBX to Redirect Busy/Unanswered Calls to Voice Mail*

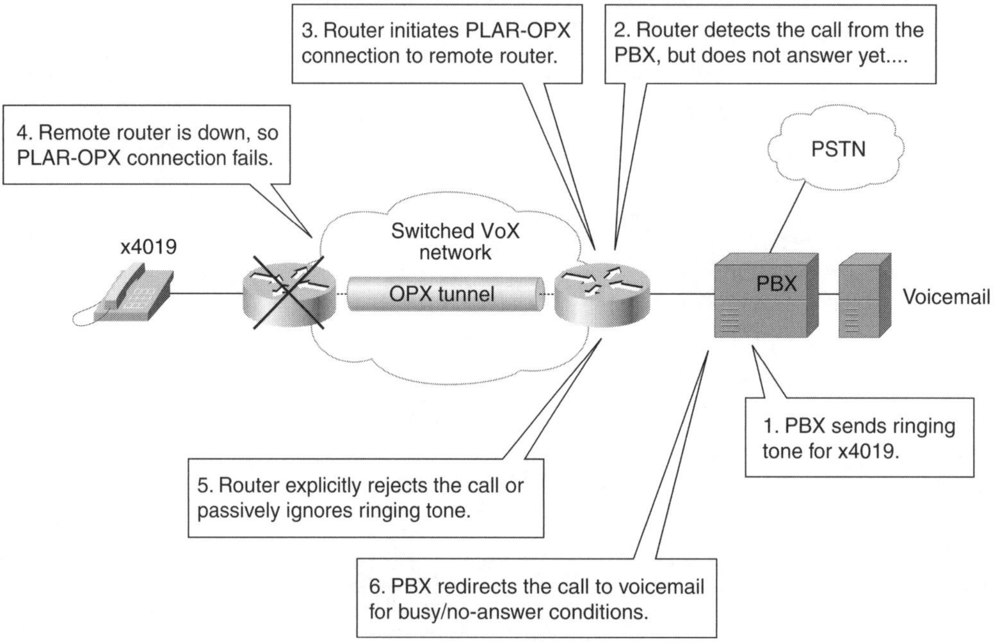

Consider the design scenarios where PLAR-OPX is useful, and it should make sense to you that the PLAR-OPX functionality is only available for FXO ports. PLAR-OPX connections are only useful on voice ports that act as a proxy for a single remote phone. Because FXO is the only type of voice port that acts as a proxy for an individual telephone, no other voice port needs the services of PLAR-OPX connections.

It is normal to have both PLAR and PLAR-OPX connections in a VoX network. A typical VoX network that provides support for OPX lines uses PLAR connections on the remote router FXS ports (which connect to individual telephones), and PLAR-OPX connections on the central router FXO ports (which connect to a PBX). Example 17-25 illustrates the configuration of a PLAR-OPX connection on a voice port.

Example 17-25 *Configuring a PLAR-OPX Connection*

```
voice-gw1#conf t
Enter configuration commands, one per line.  End with CNTL/Z.
voice-gw1(config)#voice-port 1/0/1
voice-gw1(config-voiceport)#connection plar-opx +14085551234
voice-gw1(config)#^Z
voice-gw1#
```

Tie Line

The tie-line connection mode is positioned as a replacement for traditional tie lines. Using tie-line connections, you can associate a router voice port at one location with a voice port across the VoX network, which provides a virtual connection between the PBXs on either end.

The tie-line connection mode is very similar to the PLAR connection mode. Both tie lines and PLAR connections force calls arriving on a voice port to route to a specific VoX destination based on a preconfigured phone number, but they differ in how they handle digits that are subsequently dialed by the originating user or phone switch. PLAR connections immediately connect to the destination when the voice port goes off-hook, and any digits dialed by the user are passed in-band after the connection is established. The PBX at the far end of the PLAR connection receives the user-dialed digits through the audio path of the established PLAR connection. With tie-line connections, the voice port waits for the user or phone switch to send digits, and then initiates a connection based on the preconfigured destination and the digits dialed by the user. The destination phone number of the connection request includes the preconfigured digits concatenated with the user-dialed digits. At the receiving end of the tie-line connection, a POTS dial peer matches the preconfigured digits, and the user-dialed digits are played out to the voice port as excess digits. The PBX receives the excess digits (which generally correspond with a local extension in the PBX), and the PBX routes the call to the final endpoint.

In summary, the main difference between PLAR connections and tie-line connections is that PLAR passes the user-dialed digits in-band through the audio path to the PBX, and tie-line connections pass the digits out of band to the PBX. The PLAR method exposes the DTMF signals to voice quality degradation as they cross the audio path, while the tie-line method relays the DTMF signals as part of a call-setup message, where they are played out by the router directly attached to the PBX. With the general availability of DTMF-relay commands, the tie-line connection mode no longer has a significant advantage over the PLAR connection mode. The method that you use to route calls is a matter of personal preference. Example 17-26 illustrates the configuration of a tie-line connection.

Example 17-26 *Configuring a Tie-Line Connection*

```
voice-gw1#conf t
Enter configuration commands, one per line.  End with CNTL/Z.
voice-gw1(config)#voice-port 1/0/1
voice-gw1(config-voiceport)#connection tie-line 1408555
voice-gw1(config)#^Z
voice-gw1#
```

Trunk

Unlike the four connection modes discussed in the preceding sections, a trunk connection is a permanent call. In other words, a trunk connection between voice ports is active whether or not any calls are using the connection. Trunk connections are established as soon as the voice ports are configured and activated. As long as the voice port signaling is correctly configured for the voice ports on either end of the trunk connection, the routers can suppress transmission of voice packets while the trunks are idle. This is an important feature for bandwidth savings, and it operates independently of VAD. Without this feature, each trunk consumes bandwidth whether or not calls are present, which is similar to the inefficient operation of TDM trunks.

To understand why trunk connections are useful, consider a problem that occurs with other connection modes. The voice port on a VoX router must accept a trunk seizure from a PBX to receive the digits of the destination and complete the call. From the perspective of the PBX, the call is completed as soon as the router accepts the trunk seizure. If the router cannot forward calls to the destination (for example, a busy remote router, an intermediate network failure, or some other reason), then the PBX cannot reroute the call to another trunk because it has already delivered the call to the VoX router. Such calls may die in the VoX network, or the local VoX router may hair-pin such calls back to the PBX using a different voice-port. Though the hairpin technique works (see Chapter 12, "Initial Network Planning and Design"), it consumes extra voice ports that may not be available at peak traffic loads.

Trunk connections solve the problem of a PBX delivering a call to a VoX network that cannot complete the call. While PLAR-OPX connections offer this same benefit, they are only useful when the remote destination is an individual phone, fax machine, or a simple key system. Trunk connections offer this benefit when the remote destination is another phone switch that receives digits and routes calls (for example, a PBX or hybrid key system). Refer to Figure 17-11 for the description that follows.

Whatever signaling state (for example, on-hook or off-hook) that a voice port on a VoX router receives, it proxies across the trunk connection in real time, where it is regenerated by the remote router voice port to the remote PBX. This mechanism can relay arbitrary signaling that is composed of on-hook and off-hook sequences, from E&M wink-start to hookflash. In this way, the PBXs on either end of the VoX network are truly exchanging signals with each other, through the proxy mechanism of the trunk connection. The VoX routers do not interpret the signaling, and do not establish or disconnect any calls, because the trunk connection is always an open channel. Contrast this behavior with all of the other connection types, where a VoX router interprets the voice-port signaling and the voice ports on either end of the connection operate independently.

Note that trunk connections are designed to pass on-hook/off-hook signaling across the trunk, but they are not intended for common channel signaling (CCS) methods or for relaying DTMF tones (although DTMF relay may be used in conjunction with trunk connections). Because hookflash signals are composed of on-hook/off-hook transitions, hookflash is natively supported by trunk connections.

Figure 17-11   *Voice Ports Proxy the Call Setup and Teardown Signaling Across Trunk Connections*

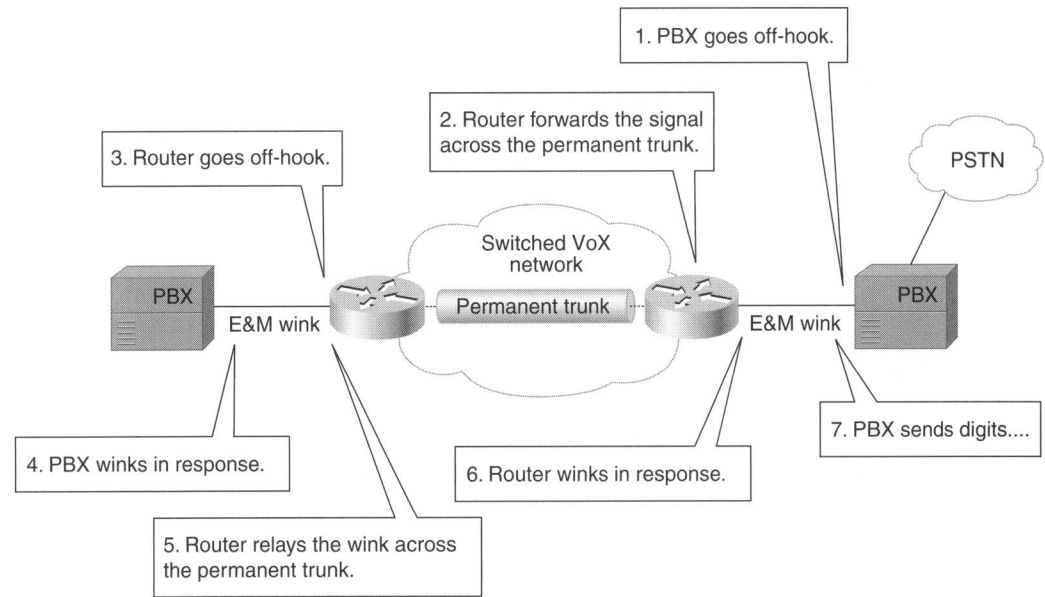

So, how do trunk connections solve the problem of a PBX delivering a call to a VoX network that cannot complete the call? When trunk connections are used, the VoX network is not responsible for accepting calls from the PBX. The remote PBX accepts the call, and the signaling to achieve this is proxied through the trunk connection. If a remote PBX does not accept a trunk seizure from a local PBX, then the local PBX can reroute calls to a different trunk.

Since the phone switches on either end of a trunk connection essentially communicate with each other (through the proxy mechanism), the voice ports on either end of a trunk connection must be of complementary technologies. For example, an E&M port may have a trunk connection to another E&M port, provided that the same type of signaling (such as Type I or Type V) is used. An FXS port may have a trunk connection to a remote FXO port. Note that an E&M port cannot have a trunk connection to an FXS or FXO port, and trunk connections do not work between two FXS ports or two FXO ports. In general, if you can connect two voice ports in a back-to-back fashion (or through a tie-line circuit), then you can configure a trunk connection between them.

Example 17-27 demonstrates the configuration of a trunk connection on the two different routers in Figure 17-11. When the voice port is activated, a connection is immediately established to the destination identified in a matching dial peer. Note that voice-gw2 is configured with the keyword **answer-mode**, which indicates that this voice port should act as the slave of the master/slave relationship and passively wait for a trunk connection request from the remote router. This is important so that both routers do not try to act as the master and block each other while initiating connection requests.

Example 17-27 *Configuring a Trunk Connection*

```
voice-gw1#conf t
Enter configuration commands, one per line.  End with CNTL/Z.
voice-gw1(config)#voice-port 1/0/1
voice-gw1(config-voiceport)#connection trunk 2222
voice-gw1(config)#^Z
voice-gw1#

voice-gw2#conf t
Enter configuration commands, one per line.  End with CNTL/Z.
voice-gw2(config)#voice-port 2/1:0
voice-gw2(config-voiceport)#connection trunk 1111 answer-mode
voice-gw2(config)#^Z
voice-gw2#
```

You can configure various timing and signaling parameters of the trunk connection using the **voice class permanent** commands, as illustrated in Example 17-28. If you have nonstandard signaling for on-hook/off-hook conditions, or odd patterns for the ABCD signaling bits, then you need to adjust the **voice class permanent** parameters. You may also wish to explicitly define timeout parameters for the trunk connection, so that idle trunks stop sending voice packets after an explicitly defined time interval, and inactive trunks attempt to reinitiate the connection at defined time intervals.

Example 17-28 *Configuring Trunk Signaling and Timing Parameters Under* **voice class permanent**

```
voice-gw2#conf t
Enter configuration commands, one per line.  End with CNTL/Z.
voice-gw2(config)#voice class permanent 1
voice-gw2(config-class)#signal ?
  keepalive  Set the keepalive signaling packet interval for permanent calls
  pattern    Set the signal pattern (ABCD bit-pattern) for permanent calls
  sequence   specify the sequence of signaling bit pattern
  timing     Set the timer value associated with call states for permanent
             calls

voice-gw2(config-class)#signal keepalive ?
  <1-65535>  Time in seconds

voice-gw2(config-class)#signal pattern ?
  idle  Idle (on-hook) state of the call
  oos   Out of service state of the call

voice-gw2(config-class)#signal pattern idle ?
  receive   Signal pattern (ABCD bits) from the data network side (to PBX)
  transmit  Signal pattern (ABCD bits) to the data network side (from PBX)

voice-gw2(config-class)#signal pattern oos ?
  receive   Signal pattern (ABCD bits) from the data network side (to PBX)
```

Example 17-28 *Configuring Trunk Signaling and Timing Parameters Under* **voice class permanent** *(Continued)*

```
     transmit  Signal pattern (ABCD bits) to the data network side (from PBX)

voice-gw2(config-class)#signal sequence oos ?
  both       send idle followed by oos to the PBX
  idle-only  only send idle pattern  to the PBX
  no-action  no idle-oos pattern are sent to the PBX
  oos-only   only send oos pattern  to the PBX

voice-gw2(config-class)#signal timing ?
  idle  idle (on-hook) state of the call
  oos   Out of service state of the call

voice-gw2(config-class)#signal timing idle ?
  suppress-voice  Shut down voice traffic once existing of idle state exceeds
                  configured time

voice-gw2(config-class)#signal timing oos ?
  restart         Set signaling packet timeout period to trigger reinitializing
                  a permanent call connection
  slave-standby   Set timeout period for slave ports to return to the standby
                  state for permanent calls
  suppress-all    Shut down both signal and voice traffic once existence of
                  transmit oos state exceeds configured time (oos indication
                  from PBX)
  suppress-voice  Shut down voice traffic once existence of transmit oos state
                  exceeds configured time (oos indication from PBX)
  timeout         Set timeout period to assert receive oos pattern to PBX on
                  loss of signaling packets

voice-gw2(config-class)#^Z
voice-gw2#
```

After you have configured the signaling and timing parameters in a voice class, you need to apply the voice class to a voice port that has been configured as a trunk (see Example 17-29).

Example 17-29 *Applying the Trunk Signaling and Timing Parameters to a Voice Port*

```
voice-gw2#conf t
Enter configuration commands, one per line.  End with CNTL/Z.
voice-gw2(config)#voice-port 2/1:0
voice-gw2(config-voiceport)#voice-class permanent 1
voice-gw2(config-voiceport)#^Z
voice-gw2#
```

Session Protocols

Whereas a connection mode defines how VoX and POTS call legs are used in a network design, a session protocol defines the underlying call signaling used by the VoX call legs.

Among other things, the session protocol defines the structure of headers, and the types of communication channels required for call control and media control. The session protocol is the focus of vendor interoperability, because the bit-orders and message sequences must be compatible for equipment from different vendors to interoperate.

Depending on your hardware platform, and whether you are configuring VoFR, VoATM, or VoIP dial peers, you have a subset of the following choices for a session protocol:

- Cisco
- Cisco-switched
- FRF11-trunk
- AAL2-trunk
- SIPv2

The session protocol that you choose depends on several factors including the flavor of VoX in your network, whether vendor interoperability is important for you, whether you need tandem call routing, and what release of Cisco IOS software you can run in your network. Table 17-5 summarizes the characteristics of the different session protocols.

Table 17-5   *Session Protocols for VoX Dial Peers of Cisco Routers*

Session Protocol	VoX Support	Tandem Routing?	Related Standard	Minimum IOS
Cisco	VoIP	No	ITU H.323	11.3(1)T
Cisco-switched	VoFR, VoATM	Yes	Proprietary	12.0(3)XG
FRF11-trunk	VoFR	Yes	FRF.11	12.0(3)XG
AAL2-trunk	VoATM	Yes	ATM Forum	12.1(1)XA
SIPv2	VoIP	No	IETF SIP	12.1(3)T

Cisco introduced the proprietary Cisco-switched session protocol to address the shortcomings of the FRF.11 standard. As described earlier in this chapter, FRF.11 requires that both endpoints be manually configured with the correct call parameters (such as codecs, VAD, and so on). There is no FRF.11 support for dynamic negotiation of these parameters, which is not a problem when the endpoints are fixed (for example, a point-to-point trunk connection). However, if a source can call different destinations, and some of these destinations use different call parameters, the static FRF.11 method does not work. Cisco added a Q.931-like signaling protocol to the FRF.11 standard to enable endpoints to negotiate capabilities, which facilitates switched VoFR calls.

NOTE   Although Table 17-5 indicates that SIP is not supported until IOS 12.1(3)T, you can experiment with earlier IOS releases that provide limited support for SIP.

VoX Dial-Peer Options

Various features that relate to the call connection are configured within VoX dial peers. These topics are explored in the following sections:

- Signal processing
- Voice quality enhancement
- Voice quality measurement

Signal Processing

Signal processing encompasses the codec functions and related technologies, such as VAD and silence suppression, comfort noise, and DTMF relay.

- Digital signal processor (DSP) resources
- Configuring codec options

DSP Resources

Cisco routers with digital (T-1/E-1) voice ports allow flexible allocation of DSP resources. Recall that the DSP chips perform the operations required for the codec functions. These operations include analog to digital (A/D) and digital to analog (D/A) conversion, low bit-rate speech codec conversions, and detection of DTMF and other tones. Each codec type requires a different amount of CPU resources from a DSP, so the number of calls that a given DSP chip can support depends on the type of codec configured. More DSPs are required to process high-complexity codecs, so you must limit the number of high-complexity codecs when DSP resources are limited.

In practice, it is convenient to order a router with sufficient DSP resources so that all calls can use high-complexity, low bit-rate codecs. For example, a router with two E-1 voice ports may have 60 simultaneous calls. If each DSP chip processes 2 calls that use high-complexity codecs or 4 calls that use medium-complexity codecs (this is a very hardware-dependent factor), then you should have 30 DSP chips allocated for the 2 E-1 voice ports. This approach enables you to focus on more critical design constraints in the network, and use low bit-rate codecs whenever appropriate.

Whether or not you have limited DSP resources in a router with digital voice ports, you must configure the DSPs to allow high-, medium-, or low-complexity codecs. If you have no resource constraints, then configure all DSPs to allow high-complexity codecs. If DSPs are limited in a tight-budget network, then you can restrict the use of high-complexity codecs. Ironically, conserving money on the one-time cost of DSP chips may cause more money to be spent on a recurring basis for bandwidth, because calls cannot be compressed as much with fewer DSPs. Before purchasing a router with minimal DSP resources, you should consider this factor in the context of your environment, and ask yourself: Is bandwidth expensive? Can we use low bit-rate codecs?

Example 17-30 illustrates the DSP configuration for a Cisco 7200 series router, and Example 17-31 illustrates the DSP configuration for a Cisco 2600/3600 series router with digital voice ports.

Example 17-30 *Configuring the DSPs for Codec Performance in a Cisco 7200 Series Router*

```
voice-gw2#conf t
Enter configuration commands, one per line.  End with CNTL/Z.
voice-gw2(config)#dspint DSPfarm 4/0
voice-gw2(config-dspfarm)#codec ?
  high  High Complexity: 2 channels of any mix of codec
  med   Medium Complexity: 4 channels of g711/g726/g729a/fax

voice-gw2(config-dspfarm)#codec high ?
  <0-30>  List of DSPs to configure
  <cr>

voice-gw2(config-dspfarm)#codec high 0-30
voice-gw2(config-dspfarm)#^Z
voice-gw2#
```

Example 17-31 *Configuring the DSPs for Codec Performance in a Cisco 2600/3600 Series Router*

```
voice-gw3#conf t
Enter configuration commands, one per line.  End with CNTL/Z.
voice-gw3(config)#voice-card 1
westwood-es-gw(config-voicec)#codec complexity ?
  high    Set codec complexity high.  High complexity, lower call density.
  medium  Set codec complexity medium.  Mid range complexity and call density.
  <cr>

voice-gw3(config-voicec)#codec complexity high
voice-gw3(config-voicec)#^Z
voice-gw3#
```

Configuring Codec Options

A VoX dial peer can be configured to use a single codec type or a defined group of codecs. Using a defined group of codecs gives you more flexibility when designing a dial plan, because you do not need to worry as much about mismatched codec capabilities. Consider the network illustrated in Figure 17-12. Each of the three remote sites is configured to support a different codec type: One site prefers the best voice quality possible, G.711; one site frequently transfers calls to other sites, G.726; and one site prefers to reduce bandwidth consumption, G.723.1.

Figure 17-12 *Network with Multiple Codec Requirements*

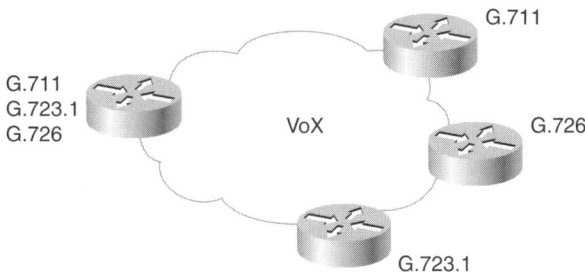

If you configure each VoX dial peer with a single codec, then the remote sites cannot communicate with each other. Furthermore, the central site requires a separate dial peer for each remote site. If you centralize routing intelligence in an H.323 gatekeeper or a SIP proxy server, then you still need multiple dial peers, with a different codec specified in each one. You must also match the correct phone number destination with the codec for a given dial peer, which increases the likelihood of configuration errors. In summary, you should use a defined group of codecs for each dial peer unless you use the same codec throughout your network.

You define a group of codecs using the **voice class** configuration commands, as illustrated in Example 17-32. You may have multiple codec groups configured on the same router. Note that there is not a separate entry for G.729 and G.729A. When the DSP is configured for high complexity, the G.729 codec is used, and when the DSP is configured for medium complexity, the G.729A codec is used. This decision is independent of whether the Annex B VAD function is enabled.

Example 17-32 *Defining a Group of Codecs that Will Be Applied to a VoX Dial Peer*

```
voice-gw3#conf t
Enter configuration commands, one per line.  End with CNTL/Z.
voice-gw3(config)#voice class codec 1
voice-gw3(config-class)#codec preference ?
  <1-12>  Priority order (1 = Highest)

voice-gw3(config-class)#codec preference 5 ?
  g711alaw  G.711 A Law 64000 bps
  g711ulaw  G.711 u Law 64000 bps
  g723ar53  G.723.1 ANNEX-A 5300 bps
  g723ar63  G.723.1 ANNEX-A 6300 bps
  g723r53   G.723.1 5300 bps
  g723r63   G.723.1 6300 bps
  g726r16   G.726 16000 bps
  g726r24   G.726 24000 bps
  g726r32   G.726 32000 bps
  g728      G.728 16000 bps
  g729br8   G.729 ANNEX-B 8000 bps
```

continues

Example 17-32 *Defining a Group of Codecs that Will Be Applied to a VoX Dial Peer (Continued)*

```
  g729r8    G.729 8000 bps

voice-gw3(config-class)#codec preference 5 g723ar53 bytes 40
voice-gw3(config-class)#codec preference 6 g723ar63 bytes 48
voice-gw3(config-class)#codec preference 7 g729br8 bytes 50
voice-gw3(config-class)# ^Z
voice-gw1#
```

Note that each codec in the voice class can be optionally configured with a payload size (via the parameter after the keyword "bytes"). Increasing the payload size makes the transmission more efficient (by reducing the bandwidth required for headers), but it also increases the packet-formation delay. The first codec frame in a packet cannot be transmitted until the subsequent codec frames are created and included in the packet. This also causes jitter in the network, because the first codec frame in a packet is delayed longer than the last codec frame in a packet.

After you have defined the codec group, you can apply it to a VoX dial peer as indicated in Example 17-33. Note that the first dial peer uses the **voice-class** command to assign the group of codecs, and the second dial peer uses a single codec. Also note that VAD is not assigned with the first dial peer, because each of the codecs in the group incorporates a VAD function. Because the G.726 codec does not have a built-in VAD function, VAD is enabled for the second dial peer.

Example 17-33 *Applying a Single Codec or a Group of Codecs to a Dial Peer*

```
voice-gw3#conf t
Enter configuration commands, one per line.  End with CNTL/Z.
voice-gw3(config)#dial-peer voice 1 voip
voice-gw3(config-dial-peer)#no vad
voice-gw3(config-dial-peer)#voice-class codec 1
voice-gw3(config-dial-peer)#exit
voice-gw3(config)#dial-peer voice 2 voip
voice-gw3(config-dial-peer)#vad
voice-gw3(config-dial-peer)#codec g726r24
voice-gw3(config-dial-peer)#^Z
voice-gw3#
```

When VAD is enabled on a VoX dial peer, the corresponding voice port at the receiving side should be configured with comfort noise so that the listener does not hear dead silence when the talker pauses. Without comfort noise, listeners may misinterpret the silence and think that the line has been disconnected. Fortunately, comfort noise is enabled by default for all voice ports, so you do not need to configure anything to enable this feature.

Cisco routers can be configured to locally interpret inbound DTMF tones, transmit the signals out of band across the network, and replicate them at the far end. When DTMF relay is enabled, the DSP chips are responsible for detecting the DTMF tones, and regenerating them at the far end. For VoFR, you enable DTMF relay as a VoFR dial-peer command. For VoIP, you have several options, as indicated in Example 17-34.

Example 17-34 *Configuring DTMF Relay to Preserve Quality of DTMF Tones in a VoIP Network*

```
voice-gw1#conf t
Enter configuration commands, one per line.  End with CNTL/Z.
voice-gw1(config)#dial-peer voice 1 voip
voice-gw1(config-dial-peer)#dtmf-relay ?
  cisco-rtp          Cisco Proprietary RTP
  h245-alphanumeric  DTMF Relay via H245 Alphanumeric IE
  h245-signal        DTMF Relay via H245 Signal IE

voice-gw1(config-dial-peer)#dtmf-relay cisco-rtp
voice-gw1(config-dial-peer)#^Z
voice-gw1#
```

The H.245 alphanumeric method passes the tone information but not the duration that the tone is played. The receiving end regenerates a 100-ms tone regardless of the length that the tone is played at the sending side. The H.245 signal method transmits the tone and duration it was played, so that the receiving end can faithfully reproduce the original signal. However, the H.245 media control channel uses dynamic TCP ports (negotiated in the H.225.0 call-control channel), so it is not practical to provide QoS for these packets. As a result, the DTMF tones may be delayed in transit the same as any nonprioritized data traffic. The Cisco–RTP method addresses this problem by sending the DTMF tones as a proprietary Application extension of the RTCP header. Because RTCP uses the odd-numbered port that is one larger than the RTP port of the voice payload, it is easy to provide the same level of QoS to these packets as to the voice packets. Chapter 18 discusses these options in more detail, in the section entitled "DTMF Problems."

Your choice of DTMF-relay methods has several implications that may not seem obvious. As of IOS 12.1(1)T, Cisco routers support hookflash relay, H.323v2 fast-start procedures for call setup, and H.245 tunneling through the H.225.0 call-control channel. These features are all implicitly tied to the choice of DTMF relay for a given dial peer. The hookflash-relay function, which is only available for hookflashes originating on FXS ports relayed to FXO ports, requires that one of the H.245 DTMF-relay options be used. If you use the Cisco-RTP method of DTMF relay, then hookflash relay will not work. Similarly, the H.323v2 fast-start procedures for call setup are triggered by the configuration of H.245 DTMF relay. If you use the Cisco-RTP method of DTMF relay, then you cannot take advantage of H.323v2 fast-start. Finally, H.245 tunneling through the H.225.0 call-control channel is triggered by the configuration of an H.245 DTMF-relay method. In summary, you should use one of the standard H.245 methods of DTMF relay if you base your VoIP network on H.323.

If your VoIP network is based on SIP, then your only option for DTMF relay is Cisco-RTP.

Voice Quality Enhancement

There are several VoX dial-peer features that can improve the QoS experienced by the voice packets or improve the performance of the codecs in response to error conditions. Example 17-35 illustrates two features that help improve codec performance.

Example 17-35 *Improving Codec Performance in VoIP and VoFR Networks*

```
voice-gw1#conf t
Enter configuration commands, one per line.  End with CNTL/Z.
voice-gw1(config)#dial-peer voice 1 voip
voice-gw1(config-dial-peer)#ip udp checksum
voice-gw1(config)#dial-peer voice 2 vofr
voice-gw1(config-dial-peer)#sequence-numbers
voice-gw1(config)#^Z
voice-gw1#
```

Though UDP checksums double the size of compressed RTP headers (from 2 bytes to 4 bytes), they should only be disabled after careful consideration because they perform an important function. UDP checksums detect corrupted data in the codec payload, whereas the IP checksum only covers the IP header. The UDP checksum functions as a backup to the link layer checksum mechanism. If your network has more than a trace amount of errors, then you should enable UDP checksums so that corrupted codec frames may be discarded. The codec can mask discarded packets, with little reduction in voice quality, by sending duplicate or interpolated samples. Voice quality suffers more when the codec processes corrupted frames and generates bad output.

The sequence-numbers configuration is not applicable to VoIP, because the RTP header of VoIP packets provides this service all of the time. However, sequence numbers are optional for some types of VoFR payloads. Several annexes to the FRF.11.1 specification indicate that sequence numbers are mandatory for the following payload types:

- G.711 PCM
- G.726 AD-PCM
- DTMF tones
- Fax payloads

Sequence numbers are optional for the following VoFR payload types:

- G.728 LD-CELP
- G.729 CS-ACELP
- G.723.1 ACELP or MP-MPLQ

If you can afford the bandwidth incurred by one extra byte per packet, then you should leave sequence numbers enabled in the VoFR dial peer to improve codec performance. The sequence numbers help the codec mask missing or unordered frames, which generally improves voice quality.

For VoIP networks, you can improve the QoS experienced by each voice packet using IP precedence and Resource Reservation Protocol (RSVP). The IP precedence bits (from the type of service [ToS] field of the IP header) influence queuing priority in both edge and core routers. Edge routers may use the IP precedence values to adjust weights in a weighted-fair queuing (WFQ) scheme (which is actually a suboptimal method of QoS for VoIP at the network edge). Core routers that run weighted random early detection (WRED) drop fewer packets when IP precedence bits are set. RSVP reservations provide explicit queuing preference on a dynamic and session-specific basis.

Example 17-36 demonstrates the configuration of IP precedence assignments and RSVP reservations as part of a VoX dial-peer configuration. The **req-qos** command is used to request the RSVP reservation. The **req-qos** configuration triggers an RSVP PATH message to be generated whenever the dial peer is used for an outbound call leg. The PATH messages propagate toward the destination, alerting each RSVP-aware router in the path that a reservation is coming. The destination replies with an RESV message, which propagates back toward the origin of the PATH message. Each router that receives the RESV message activates the reservation if it is accepted. The **acc-qos** command causes the router to generate a Simple Network Management Protocol (SNMP) trap whenever the RSVP reservation fails, which is usually because of bandwidth constraints.

Example 17-36 *Configuring IP Precedence and RSVP to Improve QoS for VoIP*

```
voice-gw1#conf t
Enter configuration commands, one per line.  End with CNTL/Z.
voice-gw1(config)#dial-peer voice 1000 voip
voice-gw1(config-dial-peer)#ip precedence 5
voice-gw1(config-dial-peer)#req-qos ?
  best-effort       Best Effort
  controlled-load   Controlled Load
  guaranteed-delay  Guaranteed Delay

voice-gw1(config-dial-peer)#req-qos guaranteed-delay
voice-gw1(config-dial-peer)#acc-qos guaranteed-delay
voice-gw1(config)#^Z
voice-gw1#
```

Note that you must have SNMP otherwise enabled on your router before the traps generated from the **acc-qos** command are sent to an SNMP server. The next section describes the minimal SNMP configurations to achieve this goal.

Voice Quality Monitoring

Cisco routers support voice quality measurement and monitoring via the Equipment Impairment Factor (EIF) method, which is described in Chapter 5, "Defining and Measuring Voice Quality." The router automatically calculates the value of I_{tot} based on input from the DSP and the received RTCP packets (which implies that the feature is only available for VoIP). You may configure the expectation factor associated with a dial peer, which indicates the degree to which users will accept degraded voice quality in exchange for another benefit (for example, mobility or economy). The value of the expect factor is subtracted from the I_{tot} value to yield the I_{cpif}.

NOTE   In older IOS versions, the expect factor defaults to 10, but newer IOS images use a default value of zero to reflect user expectations of normal toll-quality voice.

You may configure a threshold for the calculated planning impairment factor (I_{cpif}), which indicates your voice quality design goal or service level agreement. All calls that exhibit a larger impairment value will generate an SNMP trap to alert the network monitoring staff. Example 17-37 illustrates the commands required to enable monitoring via the Equipment Impairment Factor method.

Example 17-37   *Configuring Parameters of the EIF Method for Voice Quality Measurement*

```
voice-gw1#conf t
Enter configuration commands, one per line.  End with CNTL/Z.
voice-gw1(config)#dial-peer voice 1 voip
voice-gw(config-dial-peer)#expect-factor ?
  <0-20>  Range of Expect Factor

voice-gw(config-dial-peer)#expect-factor 5
voice-gw(config-dial-peer)#icpif ?
  <0-55>  Range of Icpif

voice-gw(config-dial-peer)#icpif 20
voice-gw(config-dial-peer)#^Z
voice-gw#
```

In practice, you want the generation of SNMP traps to be correlated with user experiences. That is, you do not want to receive constant traps when users are satisfied, and you do not want to miss traps when users are unhappy. To achieve this balance, you need to adjust the expect factor to mirror the real expectations of the users in your network, and the I_{cpif} to mirror your service level goals (which may change over time). The default settings are a good place to start, but you should fine-tune these values for your network over time.

Though the preceding commands cause SNMP traps to be generated, a router must be configured to send the traps to an SNMP server (such as a network management workstation running HP Openview). As demonstrated in Example 17-38, the router must be given the IP address of an SNMP server, and voice-related traps must be specifically enabled at the global configuration level and on a per dial-peer basis.

Example 17-38 *Enabling SNMP Traps for Poor Voice Quality to Be Sent to a Network Management Workstation*

```
voice-gw1#conf t
Enter configuration commands, one per line.  End with CNTL/Z.
voice-gw1(config)#snmp-server host 1.1.1.1 traps version 3 public
voice-gw1(config)#snmp-server enable traps voice poor-qov
voice-gw1(config)#dial-peer voice 1000 voip
voice-gw1(config-dial-peer)#snmp enable peer-trap poor-qov
voice-gw1(config)#^Z
voice-gw1#
```

Note that other options are available for SNMP configuration, but these are the minimal required configuration elements. You should not use the passwords public and private for the read and write SNMP community strings unless you want to simplify the job of a network hacker. To improve network security, you should also restrict (via access lists) the hosts from which routers will accept SNMP queries.

VoIP Scaling: H.323

The H.323 protocol suite is the most mature and feature-filled set of standards for VoIP. In addition to the basic call and media services offered by H.225.0 and H.245, Cisco routers support the H.235 security mechanisms and several of the H.450.x supplemental services (for example, call transfer and call forwarding). You can configure a Cisco gatekeeper (via the AAA feature set) to use a radius server for authentication and authorization of endpoints (for registration and call admission). The "New Feature Release Notes" for Cisco IOS 12.1(1)T provide a good starting point for the advanced features of H.323v2:

> www.cisco.com/univercd/cc/td/doc/product/software/ios121/121newft/121t/121t1/ h323v2p2.htm

The sections that follow are focused on the call-routing aspects of H.323, and how to exploit H.323 features to make VoIP call routing more scalable and manageable. A final section addresses the H.323v2 fast connect procedure and the tunneling of H.245 media setup messages within the H.225.0 call-control channel.

Intrazone Alias Resolution and Call Routing

Without an H.323 gatekeeper, each H.323 gateway must be configured with a separate VoIP dial peer for every E.164 number prefix in the zone. For large zones, this can amount to hundreds or thousands of dial peers, which is not acceptable.

This problem does not usually appear in VoFR networks because VoFR enables tandem call routing (described earlier in this chapter). Each remote VoFR router simply points all nonlocal calls to a central router that knows about more destinations. The central router then relays the call to the next hop router or the destination. You cannot apply this dial-plan design directly to a VoIP network, because an intermediate VoIP router cannot relay the call (via dial peers) to the next hop router or the destination. In other words, Cisco routers do not support tandem call routing for VoIP. An H.323 gateway provides the same functionality and more, so there is no real need to have true tandem call routing for VoIP.

NOTE   Do not confuse VoIP tandem call routing with generic IP packet routing; any router can act as an intermediate hop for IP packets, which may happen to be VoIP packets. In such cases, the generic IP routers are forwarding packets based on IP destination, not based on the destination E.164 phone number. Tandem call routing occurs when a voice-enabled router receives an inbound call, examines the destination phone number, and routes the call to another router via an outbound dial peer. Refer to the "Tandem Call Routing" section in this chapter for more explanation.

Example 17-39 illustrates the minimal commands required to enable an H.323 gatekeeper. Note that a router running the gatekeeper software cannot also be used as a gateway. In other words, a router with voice interfaces cannot be used as the gatekeeper. This limitation should be resolved by IOS 12.1(3)T, which may be available by the time you read this. You should check the gatekeeper documentation for new software releases on CCO to verify the current status of combined gatekeeper and gateway functionality.

Example 17-39   *Basic Commands to Enable an H.323 Gatekeeper*

```
zone-gk1#conf t
Enter configuration commands, one per line.  End with CNTL/Z.
zone-gk1(config)#gatekeeper
zone-gk1(config-gk)#zone local zone-gk1 company.com 192.168.254.99
zone-gk1(config-gk)#no shut
zone-gk1(config-gk)#^Z
zone-gk1#
```

After you enable a gatekeeper, you must ensure that the gatekeeper learns about all of the endpoints in its zone, and knows how to reach endpoints in other zones. You can configure this functionality in two ways, as described in the following sections:

- Statically configured gatekeepers
- Dynamic endpoint registration

Figure 17-13 illustrates the network topology that applies to the configuration examples in the next two sections.

Figure 17-13 *H.323 Network Topology for the Configuration Examples that Follow*

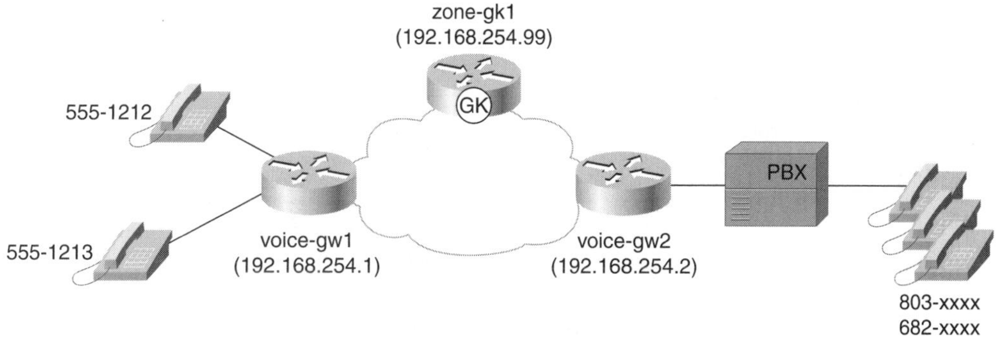

Statically Configured Gatekeepers

While it is better to have H.323 endpoints in a zone dynamically register with a gatekeeper (which is discussed in the following section), there are times that dynamic registration is not used. For example, some administrations may not have any gatekeepers with which the local endpoints can register. In order for these endpoints to be reachable from other zones, the gatekeepers in other zones must be statically configured with information about the unaffiliated endpoints.

Example 17-40 illustrates how to configure a static H.323 alias. You must specify an IP address to reach the endpoint, and identify whether the endpoint is an H.323 terminal, gateway, or MCU. You can optionally define E.164 and H.323 aliases for the endpoint, and the TCP ports used to reach the endpoints for RAS (port 1719 by default) and inbound call signaling (port 1720 by default).

Example 17-40 *Statically Associating IP Addresses with E.164 and H.323 Aliases of VoIP Gateways*

```
zone-gk1#conf t
Enter configuration commands, one per line.  End with CNTL/Z.
zone-gk1(config)#gatekeeper
zone-gk1(config-gk)#alias static 192.168.254.10 1720 gkid zone-gk1 ?
  e164      E.164 address of the associated static endpoint
  gateway   Static endpoint is a Gateway
  h323id    H.323-ID of the associated static endpoint
  mcu       Static endpoint is an MCU
  ras       Configure RAS signaling IP address of the associated static endpoint
  terminal  Static endpoint is an H.323 terminal
  <cr>

zone-gk1(config-gk)#alias static 192.168.254.10 1720 gkid zone-gk1 gateway voip e164
5551212 e164 5551213 h323id voice-gw1
zone-gk1(config-gk)#^Z
zone-gk1#
```

You can also configure a gatekeeper with the range of E.164 phone numbers (identified by prefixes) that are associated with each gateway, as illustrated in Example 17-41.

Example 17-41 *Statically Associating E.164 Prefixes with Specific Gateways*

```
zone-gk1#conf t
Enter configuration commands, one per line.  End with CNTL/Z.
zone-gk1(config)#gatekeeper
zone-gk1(config-gk)#zone prefix zone-gk1 803.... gw-priority ?
  <0-10>  Priority level from 0 to 10.  Where 10 is the highest priority and 0
          means never use the following gateway(s) for this zone prefix

zone-gk1(config-gk)#zone prefix zone-gk1 803.... gw-priority 5 voice-gw2
zone-gk1(config-gk)#zone prefix zone-gk1 803.... gw-priority 0 voice-gw1
zone-gk1(config-gk)#zone prefix zone-gk1 682.... gw-priority 5 voice-gw2
zone-gk1(config-gk)#zone prefix zone-gk1 682.... gw-priority 0 voice-gw1
zone-gk1(config-gk)#^Z
zone-gk1#
```

You must be careful when statically assigning prefixes, because the feature is really designed to associate an E.164 prefix with an entire zone (not individual gateways). That is, once a prefix has been associated with a zone, the gatekeeper may send calls for the prefix to any gateway in the zone. This load-sharing behavior is acceptable if you are an ISP with ten gateways at a VoIP point of presence (POP), all of which are used to access the PSTN. In such cases, each POP is configured as its own H.323 zone, and call routing between sites uses H.323 interzone routing. If you are an enterprise with a single VoIP gateway at each of 20 different sites, then the load-sharing nature of the **zone prefix** command is not good. You do not want a call to be randomly routed to any remote office—you want a call to go to the correct location.

As an enterprise, what you really need is an association between an E.164 prefix and a specific gateway. You can achieve this by creating a separate H.323 zone with a single gateway for each remote site, but this is an awful lot of work for a dubious design. Alternatively, you can use the gw-priority clause of the **zone prefix** command to block certain gateways from receiving calls for a given prefix. This is the approach used in Example 17-41.

The double entries for each prefix in Example 17-41 highlight a severe limitation of the **zone prefix** approach. Each gateway in a zone must be explicitly identified if you want to prevent calls from hunting to it (by setting the gw-priority to zero). If there are N gateways in a zone, then you must configure at least N-1 entries for every E.164 prefix to prevent incorrectly routed calls. If there are 50 prefixes in your network distributed among 50 different sites, then you would have $50 \times 49 = 2450$ lines of **zone prefix** commands!

The **zone prefix** commands are obviously not a scalable solution for VoIP call routing in an enterprise. Basically, there is no scalable way to statically configure VoIP call routing within a zone. You need the services of an H.323 gatekeeper that dynamically learns about call routes from its registered endpoints.

<table><tr><td>TIP</td><td>If you do decide to use the **zone prefix** commands for routing within a local zone, you should be aware that gatekeepers only accept E.164 alias registrations when the alias matches one of the zone prefixes configured for the same zone. In other words, if you configure a gatekeeper with zone prefixes and you also want it to accept E.164 registrations for an alias of "5551212", then you better have a zone prefix for the same zone that matches "555...." or something similar. Otherwise, the gatekeeper will reject the registration with a message like the following:

```
value RasMessage ::= registrationReject :
  {
    requestSeqNum 010805,
    protocolIdentifier { 0 0 8 2250 0 2 },
    rejectReason invalidAlias : NULL,
    gatekeeperIdentifier "zone-gk1"
  }
```
</td></tr></table>

Dynamic Endpoint Registration

Individual endpoints in an H.323 zone must register with a gatekeeper if one is available. Among other things, the registration process enables the gatekeeper to associate E.164 and H.323 aliases with the appropriate IP address and TCP ports for each endpoint. The gatekeeper maintains current knowledge of the endpoints in a zone because endpoints must periodically refresh their registration.

After you have configured the basic commands to enable a Cisco gatekeeper, it is ready to respond to gateway registration requests—RRQ messages—and build a database of endpoints in the zone. This section is focused on how to make the Cisco VoIP gateways register with the gatekeeper and share call-routing information.

Example 17-42 demonstrates the commands that enable a VoIP router to participate in an H.323 zone. The gateway global configuration enables the VoIP router to act as an H.323 gateway. The **h323-gateway** interface commands bind an IP address to the gateway, specify an H.323 alias, and identify the gatekeeper with which the gateway should register.

Example 17-42 *Basic Configuration of an H.323 Gateway*

```
voice-gw1#conf t
Enter configuration commands, one per line.  End with CNTL/Z.
voice-gw1(config)#gateway
```

continues

Example 17-42 *Basic Configuration of an H.323 Gateway (Continued)*

```
voice-gw1(config-gateway)#exit
voice-gw1(config)#interface loopback0
voice-gw1(config-if)#ip address 192.168.254.1 255.255.255.255
voice-gw1(config-if)#h323-gateway voip interface
voice-gw1(config-if)#h323-gateway voip id zone-gk1 ipaddr 192.168.254.99
voice-gw1(config-if)#h323-gateway voip h323-id voice-gw1.company.com
voice-gw1(config-if)#^Z
voice-gw1#
```

E.164 Alias Registration

With the basic H.323 gateway configuration described in the preceding section, the gateway only registers its H.323 alias with the gatekeeper. The gateway registers specific E.164 aliases when you configure POTS dial peers on the gateway with the **register e164** command, as illustrated in Example 17-43. Note that the **register e164** command is enabled by default, but gateways only advertise POTS dial peers that have fully qualified E.164 destination patterns. In other words, any wildcard digits in the destination pattern prevent the address from being registered with the gatekeeper. In most cases, the E.164 autoregistration function is only useful for routers with analog FXS ports. Note the response from the router in Example 17-43, when E.164 registration is configured with a destination pattern that uses wildcard digits.

Example 17-43 *H.323 Gateway Configured to Register Complete E.164 Aliases with the Gatekeeper*

```
voice-gw1#conf t
Enter configuration commands, one per line.  End with CNTL/Z.
voice-gw1(config)#dial-peer voice 1 pots
voice-gw1(config-dial-pee)#destination-pattern 5551212
voice-gw1(config-dial-pee)#register e164
voice-gw1(config-dial-pee)#exit
voice-gw1(config)#dial-peer voice 2 pots
voice-gw1(config-dial-pee)#destination-pattern 5551213
voice-gw1(config-dial-pee)#exit
voice-gw1(config)#dial-peer voice 3 pots
voice-gw1(config-dial-pee)#destination-pattern 555....
voice-gw1(config-dial-peer)#register e164
ERROR-register-e164: Dial-peer destination-pattern is not a full E.164 number
voice-gw1(config-dial-pee)#^Z
voice-gw1#
```

Tech Prefix: Normal Application

While the E.164 alias registration is useful, it most likely excludes many of the call-routing entries in your network. Just about every voice port that is connected to a PBX or key system uses wildcard digits in the POTS dial peers, so you need some way to register these call-routing entries with the gatekeeper. The solution to this problem is what Cisco calls technology prefixes. This section first describes the common application of technology prefixes, and then describes how you can use them to let gateways register E.164 prefixes for normal call routing.

Cisco documentation positions the **tech-prefix** command as a tool to route calls based on technology type. For example, say you have an H.323 network that spans North America, but your only gateway to an H.320 ISDN videoconferencing network is located in San Francisco. Calls from your H.323 network to any H.320 endpoints must be routed via the gateway in San Francisco, because the H.323-H.320 gateway provides the technology-interworking function. You must somehow override the normal call-routing mechanism based on destination phone numbers, and route the call based on a more important criterion, which is technology type. The **tech-prefix** command enables this exact functionality.

Using the **tech-prefix** command, you can steer a call from H.323 endpoints in New York to H.320 endpoints in New York via the gateway in San Francisco. Without the tech prefix, the call would route based on destination number through a local H.323 VoIP gateway. If the call passed through the H.323 VoIP gateway, it would fail because the necessary H.323-H.320 interworking is not provided. Thus, the **tech-prefix** command can play a vital role in your network.

To use tech-prefix call routing, you must first define a tech prefix for each communication technology. For example, 1# is associated with calls to the PSTN or a traditional voice network, and 2# is associated with calls to H.320 endpoints. After you establish this convention, you configure all VoIP gateways to advertise the 1# tech prefix (as illustrated in Example 17-44), and configure the H.320 gateways to advertise the 2# tech prefix.

Example 17-44   *H.323 VoIP Gateway Advertising 1# Tech Prefix for Voice Endpoints*

```
voice-gw2#conf t
Enter configuration commands, one per line.  End with CNTL/Z.
voice-gw2(config)#interface loopback0
voice-gw2(config-if)#h323-gateway voip tech-prefix 1#
voice-gw2(config-if)#^Z
voice-gw2#
```

Now, users must be educated to dial the appropriate technology prefix before the actual destination number. For example, users must dial 2# and the destination number when they want to reach an H.320 endpoint. The call then routes through the H.323 network based on the 2# tech prefix to an H.320 gateway, where the 2# is removed before placing the H.320 call.

Given the inconvenience of training users to dial the tech prefixes, you can configure the routers to make the tech prefixes mostly transparent to the users. For example, if most of your H.323 calls are VoIP, then you can configure the gatekeeper to use the tech prefix for

VoIP (for example, 1#) as the default. This way, users that do not dial the tech prefixes will reach the correct VoIP destinations, and only the users that make calls to different types of networks are burdened with the tech-prefix dialing. Example 17-45 demonstrates the configuration required on the gatekeeper to achieve this goal.

Example 17-45 *Gatekeeper Configured to Treat Calls of Unknown Type as VoIP Calls*

```
zone-gk1#conf t
Enter configuration commands, one per line.  End with CNTL/Z.
zone-gk1(config)#gatekeeper
zone-gk1(config-gk)#gw-type-prefix 1# default-technology
zone-gk1(config-gk)#^Z
zone-gk1#
```

If you know that certain phone numbers are associated with H.320 endpoints, then you can configure the VoIP dial peer in a gateway to add the 2# prefix, so users do not have to dial it. Example 17-46 illustrates this configuration.

Example 17-46 *Gateway Configured to Prepend a Tech Prefix When the Endpoint Technology Is Known*

```
voice-gw1#conf t
Enter configuration commands, one per line.  End with CNTL/Z.
voice-gw1(config)#dial-peer voice 2125551234 voip
voice-gw1(config-dial-peer)#destination-pattern +12125551234
voice-gw1(config-dial-peer)#tech-prefix 2#
voice-gw1(config-dial-peer)#^Z
voice-gw1#
```

There is no configuration option for tech prefixes in POTS dial peers; when routing calls based on tech prefixes, you must remember to include the tech prefix in the destination patterns of POTS dial peers. Example 17-47 illustrates how to configure an H.323 gateway (which connects to a network with a different technology) to remove the tech prefix and dial the original number.

Example 17-47 *Gateway Configured to Strip the Tech Prefix and Dial the Original Number*

```
voice-gw4#conf t
Enter configuration commands, one per line.  End with CNTL/Z.
voice-gw4(config)#dial-peer voice 2 pots
voice-gw4(config-dial-peer)#destination-pattern 2#..........
voice-gw4(config-dial-peer)#^Z
voice-gw4#
```

Tech Prefix: E.164 Prefix Registration

Though tech prefixes are used by convention to distinguish the technology type of destination endpoints, there is no reason that they cannot be used for other purposes. The tech prefix is just an arbitrary group of digits that have precedence for call routing. From this perspective, you can view the tech prefix as a site-specific phone number prefix in a private dialing plan, an area code in a national public dialing plan, or a country code and regional prefix in an international public dialing plan.

Example 17-48 illustrates how you might use the tech prefix to represent a three-digit site code in a private dialing plan. In this example, the gateway is configured to register two different site codes with the gatekeeper (refer back to the network diagram in Figure 17-13). Note that the configurations under the loopback interface trigger the prefix registration, and the dial peers are only used for inbound calls. This is in contrast to the E.164 alias registration, where the dial peers actually trigger the registration.

Example 17-48 *H.323 Gateway Configured to Register an E.164 Prefix with the Gatekeeper*

```
voice-gw2#conf t
Enter configuration commands, one per line.  End with CNTL/Z.
voice-gw2(config)#interface loopback0
voice-gw2(config-if)#h323-gateway voip tech-prefix 803
voice-gw2(config-if)#h323-gateway voip tech-prefix 682
voice-gw2(config-if)#exit
voice-gw2(config)#dial-peer voice 682 pots
voice-gw2(config-dial-peer)#destination-pattern 682....
voice-gw2(config-dial-peer)#port 1/1:0
voice-gw2(config-dial-peer)#exit
voice-gw2(config)#dial-peer voice 803 pots
voice-gw2(config-dial-peer)#destination-pattern 803....
voice-gw2(config-dial-peer)#port 1/1:0
voice-gw2(config-dial-peer)# ^Z
voice-gw2#
```

Example 17-49 shows part of the ASN.1 syntax of a registration request (RRQ) message for both an E.164 alias registration and a tech-prefix registration. You can see on the left that E.164 aliases are registered as part of the EndpointAlias structure, and the tech prefix is registered as part of the GatewayInfo structure on the right. Knowing how E.164 aliases and prefixes are encoded in the registration message can help you more quickly identify problems that may arise with respect to call routing and registration. You can view this output by using the debugging commands shown in Example 17-53.

Example 17-49 *Comparison of Gateway Registration Messages: E.164 Alias Versus Tech Prefix*

```
RRQ for an E.164 Alias               RRQ for a Tech-Prefix
endpointType                         endpointType
    {                                    {
    gateway                              gateway
        {                                    {
        protocol                             protocol
            {                                    {
            voice :                              voice :
                {                                    {
                supportedPrefixes                    supportedPrefixes
                    {                                    {
                    }                                        {
                }                                            prefix e164 : "682"
            }                                            },
        },                                               {
        mc FALSE,                                            prefix e164 : "803"
        undefinedNode FALSE                              }
    },                                               }
    gatekeeperIdentifier "zone-gk1",             }
    endpointAlias                            }
    {                                    },
        e164 : "5551212",                mc FALSE,
        e164 : "5551213",                undefinedNode FALSE
        h323-ID : "voice-gw1.company.com"    },
    }                                    gatekeeperIdentifier "zone-gk1",
                                         endpointAlias
                                         {
                                             h323-ID : "voice-gw2.company.com"
                                         }
```

Verifying Registration of E.164 Aliases and Prefixes

After you have configured a gateway to advertise E.164 aliases or prefixes (that is, registered them with a gatekeeper), you can verify that the registration is successful from either the gateway or the gatekeeper. Example 17-50 illustrates the output of the **show gateway** command on the H.323 gateway.

Example 17-50 *Verifying E.164 and H.323 Alias Registration from the Gateway*

```
voice-gw1#show gateway
 Gateway voice-gw1.company.com is registered to Gatekeeper zone-gk1

 Alias list (CLI configured)
  E164-ID 5551212
  E164-ID 5551213
  H323-ID voice-gw1.company.com
 Alias list (last RCF)
  E164-ID 5551212
  E164-ID 5551213
  H323-ID voice-gw1.company.com

 H323 resource thresholding is Disabled
voice-gw1#
```

You can see all of the endpoints and specific E.164 aliases associated with a gatekeeper using the **show gatekeeper endpoints** command illustrated in Example 17-51. Each endpoint is identified by a line that begins with the IP address and TCP port for H.225.0 call-setup messages. All of the E.164 and H.323 aliases for the endpoint are listed on the indented lines that follow.

Example 17-51 *Verifying E.164 and H.323 Alias Registration on the Gatekeeper*

```
zone-gk1#show gatekeeper endpoints
                    GATEKEEPER ENDPOINT REGISTRATION
                    ================================
CallSignalAddr  Port  RASSignalAddr   Port  Zone Name      Type    F
---------------  -----  ---------------  -----  ---------      ----    --
192.168.254.1   1720  192.168.254.1   2027  zone-gk1       VOIP-GW
    E164-ID: 5551212
    E164-ID: 5551213
    H323-ID: voice-gw1.company.com
192.168.254.2   1720  192.168.254.2   1602  zone-gk1       VOIP-GW
    H323-ID: voice-gw2.company.com
Total number of active registrations = 2

zone-gk1#
```

To see the E.164 prefixes that are registered with a gatekeeper as tech prefixes, use the **show gatekeeper gw-type-prefix** command illustrated in Example 17-52. The registered tech prefixes are listed one at a time, along with the H.323 zones and gateways within each zone that use the tech prefix. When you are using the tech prefixes as site prefixes, then you may have many entries for tech prefixes, but only one or a few gateways listed under each tech prefix. The asterisk character after each tech prefix represents any number of wildcard digits.

Example 17-52 *Verifying E.164 Prefix Registration on the Gatekeeper*

```
zone-gk1#show gatekeeper gw-type-prefix
GATEWAY TYPE PREFIX TABLE
=========================
Prefix: 682*
  Zone zone-gk1 master gateway list:
    192.168.254.2:1720 voice-gw2.company.com

Prefix: 803*
  Zone campus-gk2 master gateway list:
    192.168.254.2:1720 voice-gw2.company.com

zone-gk1#
```

You can view the ASN.1-formatted RAS messages sent and received by a gateway (for example, registration requests and confirmations), by using the debug commands illustrated in Example 17-53. You can use these debug commands to see the output shown in Example 17-49.

Example 17-53 *Debugging RAS Messages and Viewing the Details in ASN.1 Syntax*

```
voice-gw1#terminal monitor
voice-gw1#debug ras
H.323 RAS Messages debugging is on
voice-gw1#debug h225 asn1
H.225 ASN1 Messages debugging is on
voice-gw1#
```

Do not use these debug commands on a VoIP router that processes many calls, because a large amount of output is generated and you may disable the router. You can track the basic RAS message exchanges without using the H.225.0 ASN.1 debug, but you will not see the details of which aliases are being registered or why registrations may fail.

Interzone Alias Resolution and Call Routing

The preceding sections have addressed the call-routing requirements within a single zone, but large VoIP networks may need to have many H.323 zones. Because each zone can only have a single active gatekeeper, additional zones are required when a gatekeeper cannot process all of the zone traffic (for example, RAS messages for all registered endpoints, gatekeeper-routed calls, location requests, and so forth).

A standard method to provide interzone alias resolution and call routing in an H.323 network has been established as this book goes to press. The first two versions of H.323 did not address the problem, but H.323v3 incorporates interzone support through H.225.0 Annex G, Communication Between Administrative Domains. H.225.0 Annex G, which was standardized in May 2000, provides a model for address resolution, access authorization, and usage reporting between domains (zones).

In the interest of enabling large VoIP networks for customers who needed it prior to a standardized method, Cisco developed a proprietary solution for H.323 interzone alias resolution based on RAS location messages (such as LRQ, LCF, LRJ). The following description refers to the numbered steps in Figure 17-14. The first four steps describe the interzone alias resolution, but the entire resolution and call-setup process is illustrated for perspective. When a gatekeeper receives an admission request (ARQ) for a nonlocal E.164 alias (step 1), it looks for a match in a configured list of zone prefix entries for all of the remote zones. When it finds a match, it sends an LRQ message to the remote gatekeeper associated with the matched entry (step 2). When the remote gatekeeper receives the LRQ, it resolves the E.164 alias to an IP address and TCP port of the gateway (using its endpoint registration database), and returns this information to the requesting gatekeeper in an LCF message (step 3). The local gatekeeper then provides this information to the original requesting endpoint in an ACF message (step 4). The requesting endpoint can then initiate the H.225.0 call-control channel (either directly or routed through the gatekeeper) (step 5), but the destination endpoint must still submit an ARQ to its gatekeeper for authorization and accounting purposes (step 6). After the destination endpoint receives an ACF from its gatekeeper (step 7), it continues with the normal call-setup process (step 8).

Figure 17-14 *Interzone Alias Resolution and Call-Admission Using Location RAS Messages*

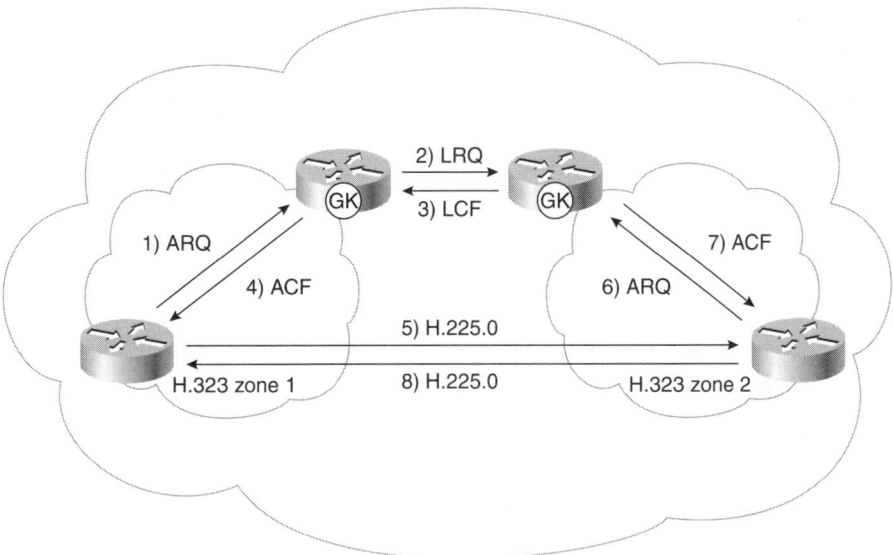

To implement this method of interzone alias resolution, each gatekeeper is statically configured with the IP address and H.323 gatekeeper ID of every other gatekeeper. Then, each nonlocal E.164 prefix is associated with one of the remote gatekeepers. Example 17-54 illustrates this configuration. The last zone prefix entry is a wildcard entry, which sends all unknown prefixes to the newyork H.323 zone.

Example 17-54 *Gatekeeper Statically Configured with Remote Zones for E.164 Prefixes*

```
zone-gk1#conf t
Enter configuration commands, one per line.  End with CNTL/Z.
zone-gk1(config)#gatekeeper
zone-gk1(config-gk)#zone remote sanfrancisco company.com 192.168.253.1
zone-gk1(config-gk)#zone remote tokyo company.com 192.168.253.2
zone-gk1(config-gk)#zone remote newyork company.com 192.168.253.3
zone-gk1(config-gk)#zone prefix sanfrancisco 1415.......
zone-gk1(config-gk)#zone prefix sanfrancisco 1650.......
zone-gk1(config-gk)#zone prefix tokyo 8103........
zone-gk1(config-gk)#zone prefix newyork *
zone-gk1(config-gk)#^Z
zone-gk1#
```

This approach quickly becomes unmanageable when there are many H.323 zones. To help alleviate this problem, Cisco introduces a directory gatekeeper or super-gatekeeper. The idea is that one or a few gatekeepers are configured with complete knowledge of the network, and the rest of the gatekeepers only need to have a default zone prefix pointing to the directory gatekeeper. Example 17-55 illustrates the simplified configuration for most gatekeepers in the network.

Example 17-55   *Gatekeeper Configured to Query a Directory Gatekeeper for Nonlocal Destinations*

```
zone-gk1#conf t
Enter configuration commands, one per line.  End with CNTL/Z.
zone-gk1(config)#gatekeeper
zone-gk1(config-gk)#zone local zone-gk1 company.com 192.168.254.99
zone-gk1(config-gk)#zone remote super-gk company.com 192.168.1.1
zone-gk1(config-gk)#zone prefix super-gk *
zone-gk1(config-gk)#^Z
zone-gk1#
```

The directory gatekeeper is configured with a zone remote entry for each gatekeeper in the network, and one or more zone prefix entries for each remote gatekeeper. In addition, the directory gatekeeper must be configured to forward the LRQ requests that it receives from each gatekeeper to the appropriate destination gatekeeper. The destination gatekeeper can bypass the directory gatekeeper and directly reply to the requesting gatekeeper with an LCF or an LRJ. This way, the directory gatekeeper is minimally involved in the call processing and can handle requests from more gatekeepers. Example 17-56 illustrates the configuration of the directory gatekeeper.

Example 17-56   *Directory Gatekeeper Knows All Zone Prefixes and Forwards Location Requests*

```
zone-gk1#conf t
Enter configuration commands, one per line.  End with CNTL/Z.
zone-gk1(config)#gatekeeper
zone-gk1(config-gk)#zone local super-gk company.com 192.168.1.1
zone-gk1(config-gk)#zone remote a company.com 192.168.250.1
zone-gk1(config-gk)#zone remote b company.com 192.168.250.2
zone-gk1(config-gk)#zone remote c company.com 192.168.250.3
    <snip>
zone-gk1(config-gk)#zone remote z company.com 192.168.250.26
zone-gk1(config-gk)#zone prefix a 1408.......
zone-gk1(config-gk)#zone prefix b 1650.......
zone-gk1(config-gk)#zone prefix c 1415.......
    <snip>
zone-gk1(config-gk)#zone prefix z 1212.......
zone-gk1(config-gk)#lrq forward-queries
zone-gk1(config-gk)#^Z
zone-gk1#
```

Note that the example of the directory gatekeeper described here is a simple two-tier gatekeeper model. That is, all of the tier-1 gatekeepers send LRQs to one, or maybe a few, tier-2 directory gatekeepers. The model easily extends to include more tiers to enable a larger-scale call-routing plan. For example, 100 tier-1 gatekeepers may use the services of a single tier-2 directory gatekeeper. The tier-2 directory gatekeeper has zone prefixes for all of the tier-1 gatekeepers that use its services, and a default zone prefix pointing to a tier-3 gatekeeper. The tier-2 directory gatekeeper may be one out of 100 tier-2 directory gatekeepers that use the services of a tier-3 directory gatekeeper.

Additional tiers in the hierarchy can enable the number of H.323 zones to grow many orders of magnitude. The main limitation arises from lengthy call-setup times when the LRQ message must be forwarded up and down the directory-gatekeeper hierarchy, as illustrated in Figure 17-15. For an N-tiered hierarchical model, the LRQ message is sent $2 \times (N - 1)$ times. This number, multiplied by the transmission latency from one directory gatekeeper to the next, indicates the additional call-setup delay introduced by the gatekeeper hierarchy.

Figure 17-15   *Hierarchical Gatekeeper Network Incurs High Latency for Responses to LRQs*

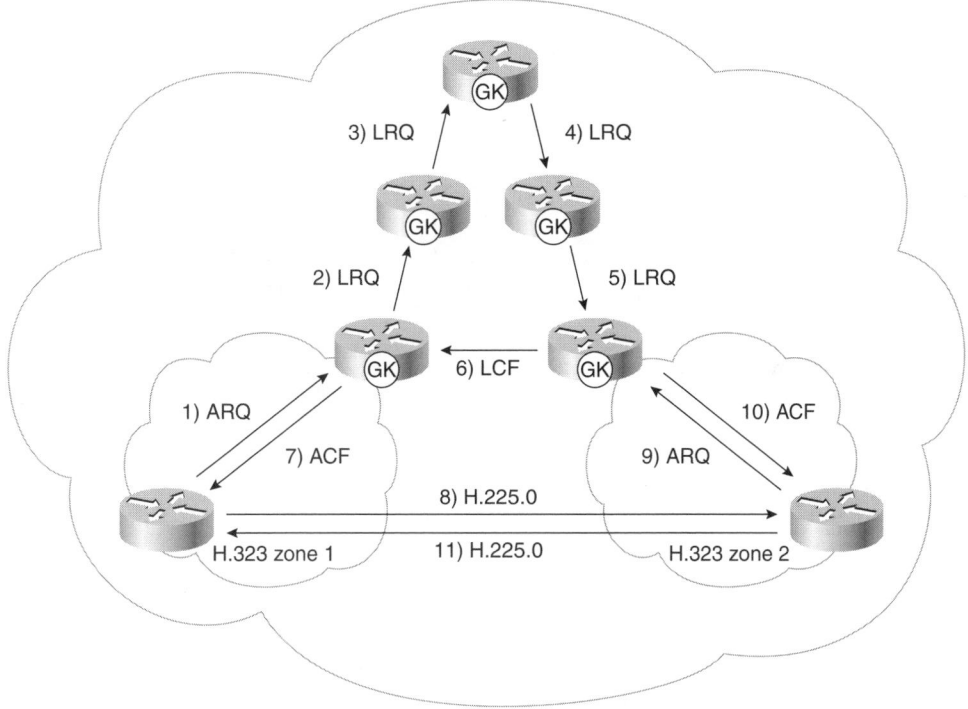

In order for the hierarchical-gatekeeper approach to truly scale well, the numbering-plan hierarchy must follow the gatekeeper hierarchy. Figure 17-16 illustrates a hierarchical phone number allocation model for a ten-digit dial plan. This example plan includes a four-tiered hierarchy, and you can see that an LRQ message may be forwarded five times (that is, six total LRQ messages) before the destination gatekeeper responds with an LCF or an LRJ.

Figure 17-16 *Directory Gatekeeper Hierarchy for a Ten-Digit Dial Plan*

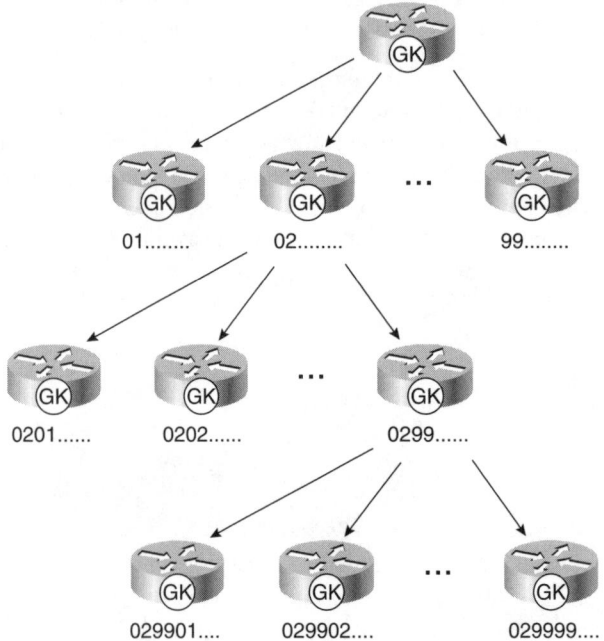

If you know the transmission latency for messages between different tiers of the hierarchy, and the longest call-setup times that your network design can tolerate, then you can determine the maximum depth of the hierarchy. After you have determined the depth of the hierarchy, then you can calculate the maximum size of your network based on the number of gatekeepers in each tier of the hierarchy.

Reducing Call-Setup Delays

As described in Chapter 11, "VoIP Transport and Signaling Protocols," H.323v2 provides a more efficient method of call setup than the method provided in H.323v1. Instead of waiting for the establishment of the H.245 media control channel, an endpoint using the fast-connect procedure sends all of the media-setup requirements within the first call-setup message over the H.225.0 call-control channel. This enables a media channel (for example, RTP session) to be established in as little as one round-trip transaction. Subsequent H.245 media-control signaling may also be tunneled within the H.225.0 call-control channel, which reduces the number of TCP sockets required for a call. A separate H.245 media-control channel may be established later if additional services are required that are not supported by H.245 tunneling.

These features are enabled by default in Cisco routers as of IOS 12.1(1)T, but you must be aware of their interaction with a seemingly unrelated command. The H.245 tunneling is disabled if you do not use one of the standard H.245 methods of DTMF relay on a dial peer (for example, h245-alphanumeric or h245-signal).

VoIP Scaling: SIP

SIP is designed to be a scalable protocol for establishing Internet telephony connections and multiparty multimedia conferences in general. SIP is still in its infancy, but industry support is quickly coalescing around this promising protocol.

As of this writing, Cisco routers can be configured as SIP user agents, but an external server must provide the SIP proxy server and registrar functions. This area is rapidly developing, so you should check CCO to learn about the latest status of SIP-related products. This section focuses on the SIP user agent available as of IOS 12.1(1)T.

Example 17-57 illustrates the minimal configuration required to enable a SIP user agent. The **sip-ua** global command enables the SIP user-agent function on the VoIP gateway, and the **sip-server** command informs the gateway how to register with the SIP registrar and how to route outbound proxied calls through the SIP proxy server.

Example 17-57 *Enabling a Cisco Router to Act as a SIP User Agent and Use the SIP Session Protocol*

```
r2#conf t
Enter configuration commands, one per line.  End with CNTL/Z.
r2(config)#sip-ua
r2(config-sip-ua)#sip-server ipv4:192.168.254.1
r2(config-sip-ua)#exit
r2(config)#dial-peer voice 100 voip
r2(config-dial-peer)#session protocol sipv2
r2(config-dial-peer)#session target sip-server
r2(config-dial-peer)#^Z
r2#
```

As part of the dial-peer configuration, the SIP session protocol is identified for the call-setup process. The call is either routed directly via a session target to an IP address, or proxy routed through the SIP proxy server if the session target uses the keyword **sip-server**. Using the **sip-server** command is a more scalable approach, because only a default dial peer is needed for all calls. The VoIP gateway configurations are easier to manage, and changes to the dial plan may be centrally administered on the SIP proxy servers.

Example 17-58 illustrates the various timers and retry intervals that may be adjusted. If your network has high transmission delays between the calling and called endpoints, then you may need to increase the timers to prevent call failures. Increasing the timers also increases call-setup times when packets are dropped, because retransmissions occur less often.

Example 17-58 *Adjusting SIP Timers, Retry Intervals, and Redirects*

```
r2#conf t
Enter configuration commands, one per line.  End with CNTL/Z.
r2(config)#sip-ua
r2(config-sip-ua)#?
SIP UA configuration commands:
  default         Set a command to its defaults
  exit            Exit from sip-ua configuration mode
  inband-alerting Specify an Inband-alerting SIP header
  no              Negate a command or set its defaults
  retry           Change default retries for each SIP Method
  sip-server      Configure a SIP Server Interface
  timers          SIP Signaling Timers Configuration
  transport       Enable SIP UA transport for TCP/UDP

r2(config-sip-ua)#timers ?
  200-wait-ack    Timer for waiting for an ACK to a 200 response
  bye-wait-200    Timer for waiting for a 200 response to a BYE request
  invite-wait-100 Timer for waiting for a 100 response to an INVITE request
  invite-wait-180 Timer for waiting for a 180 response to an INVITE request
  invite-wait-200 Timer for waiting for a 200 response to an INVITE request

r2(config-sip-ua)#timers invite-wait-100 ?
  <100-1000>  invite-wait-100 timer value in msec

r2(config-sip-ua)#retry ?
  bye       BYE retry value
  cancel    CANCEL retry value
  invite    INVITE retry value
  response  Response Methods retry value

r2(config-sip-ua)#retry invite ?
  <1-10>  Number of retries (1-10)

r2(config-sip-ua)#exit
r2(config)#dial-peer voice 100 voip
r2(config-dial-peer)#max-redirects 3
r2(config-dial-peer)#^Z
r2#
```

You can view the SIP user agent statistics as demonstrated in Example 17-59. A glance at this output shows you whether call setups are failing or not, and you can quickly see when errors are recurring.

Example 17-59   *Viewing SIP Statistics for Call Completion and Failures*

```
r2#sh sip-ua status
SIP User Agent Status
SIP User Agent for UDP : ENABLED
SIP User Agent for TCP : ENABLED

SIP Statistics

SIP Call Origination counters
call_origination_attempt_counter  2 sip_recd_3xx_counter          0
sip_invite_wait100_tm_counter     0 sip_invite_wait180_tm_counter 0
sip_invite_wait200_tm_counter     0 sip_drop_msgs_counter         0
sip_retx_invite_to_rs_counter     0 sip_retx_invite_to_gw_counter 0
sip_calls_redirected_counter      0 sip_subsqnt_redirect_counter  0
sip_exceeded_max_redirect_counter 0 sip_invite_to_rs_counter      2
sip_invite_to_gw_counter          0 sip_fail_invite_counter       0

SIP Call Termination counters
sip_recd_invite_counter           5 sip_send_200_counter          1
sip_fail_200_counter              0

SIP Socket Statistics for UDP
sip_open_socket_counter           0 sip_open_conn_counter         2
sip_close_conn_counter            2 udpsock_close_connect_counter 2

r2#
```

There are various SIP debugging commands you can use to diagnose call-setup problems in real time. Example 17-60 shows the output of the **debug ccsip messages** command for a normal call-setup and disconnect sequence.

Note the media capabilities exchange that occurs in the body of the SIP messages, using the media descriptor (m =) option of SDP. The INVITE message indicates support for six different codec types (corresponding with the RTP payload types from the audio/video profile). The destination picks one of the codecs and indicates the selection in the "180 Ringing" and 200 OK response messages. The call originator sends an ACK message that confirms the codec selection.

Example 17-60   *Viewing Actual SIP Messages of a Normal Call Sequence*

```
r2#deb ccsip ?
  all       Enable all SIP debugging traces
  calls     Enable CCSIP SPI calls debugging trace
  error     Enable SIP error debugging trace
  events    Enable SIP events debugging trace
  messages  Enable CCSIP SPI messages debugging trace
  states    Enable CCSIP SPI states debugging trace
```

continues

Example 17-60 *Viewing Actual SIP Messages of a Normal Call Sequence (Continued)*

```
r2#deb ccsip messages
SIP Call messages tracing is enabled
r2#
May  9 16:01:19.620:
Send:
 INVITE sip:102@192.168.254.1;user=phone SIP/2.0
Via: SIP/2.0/UDP  2.0.0.2:53395
From: sip:201@2.0.0.2
To: <sip:102@192.168.254.1;user=phone>
Date: Tue, 09 May 2000 16:01:19 UTC
Call-ID: B49B48C5-A0F50014-0-1BDC54@192.168.254.2
Cisco-Guid: 3030075589-2700410898-0-1819176
Require: com.cisco.inband-alerting
User-Agent: Cisco VoIP Gateway/ IOS 12.x/ SIP enabled
CSeq: 100 INVITE
Content-Type: application/sdp
Content-Length: 161

v=0
o=CiscoSystemsSIPUserAgent 8501 9061 IN IP4 2.0.0.2
s=SIP Call
c=IN IP4 2.0.0.2
m=audio 20316 RTP/AVP 8 0 4 2 15 18

May  9 16:01:19.636: Received :
SIP/2.0 100 Trying
Via: SIP/2.0/UDP  2.0.0.2:53395
From: sip:201@2.0.0.2
To: <sip:102@192.168.254.1;user=phone>;tag=1BE17C-13E3
Date: Sun, 28 Feb 1993 16:30:27 PST
Call-ID: B49B48C5-A0F50014-0-1BDC54@192.168.254.2
Server: Cisco VoIP Gateway/ IOS 12.x/ SIP enabled
CSeq: 100 INVITE
Content-Length: 0


May  9 16:01:19.644: Received :
SIP/2.0 180 Ringing
Via: SIP/2.0/UDP  2.0.0.2:53395
From: sip:201@2.0.0.2
To: <sip:102@192.168.254.1;user=phone>;tag=1BE17C-13E3
Date: Sun, 28 Feb 1993 16:30:27 PST
Call-ID: B49B48C5-A0F50014-0-1BDC54@192.168.254.2
Server: Cisco VoIP Gateway/ IOS 12.x/ SIP enabled
Content-Type: application/sdp
CSeq: 100 INVITE
Content-Length: 113

v=0
o=CiscoSystemsSIPUserAgent 8877 4896 IN IP4 2.0.0.1
s=SIP Call
```

Example 17-60 *Viewing Actual SIP Messages of a Normal Call Sequence (Continued)*

```
c=IN IP4 2.0.0.1
m=audio 20098 RTP/AVP 0


May  9 16:01:30.112: Received :
SIP/2.0 200 OK
Via: SIP/2.0/UDP  2.0.0.2:53395
From: sip:201@2.0.0.2
To: <sip:102@192.168.254.1;user=phone>;tag=1BE17C-13E3
Date: Sun, 28 Feb 1993 16:30:27 PST
Call-ID: B49B48C5-A0F50014-0-1BDC54@192.168.254.2
Server: Cisco VoIP Gateway/ IOS 12.x/ SIP enabled
Content-Type: application/sdp
CSeq: 100 INVITE
Content-Length: 112


v=0
o=CiscoSystemsSIPUserAgent 133 3181 IN IP4 2.0.0.1
s=SIP Call
c=IN IP4 2.0.0.1
m=audio 20098 RTP/AVP 0


May  9 16:01:30.116:
Send:
 ACK sip:102@192.168.254.1;user=phone SIP/2.0
Via: SIP/2.0/UDP  2.0.0.2:53395
From: sip:201@2.0.0.2
To: <sip:102@192.168.254.1;user=phone>;tag=1BE17C-13E3
Date: Tue, 09 May 2000 16:01:19 UTC
Call-ID: B49B48C5-A0F50014-0-1BDC54@192.168.254.2
Content-Type: application/sdp
Content-Length: 113
CSeq: 100 ACK


v=0
o=CiscoSystemsSIPUserAgent 2502 4328 IN IP4 2.0.0.2
s=SIP Call
c=IN IP4 2.0.0.2
m=audio 20316 RTP/AVP 0


May  9 16:01:36.032: Received :
BYE sip:201@2.0.0.2;user=phone SIP/2.0
Via: SIP/2.0/UDP  2.0.0.1:5060
From: <sip:102@192.168.254.1;user=phone>;tag=1BE17C-13E3
To: sip:201@2.0.0.2
Date: Sun, 28 Feb 1993 16:30:37 PST
Call-ID: B49B48C5-A0F50014-0-1BDC54@192.168.254.2
User-Agent: Cisco VoIP Gateway/ IOS 12.x/ SIP enabled
CSeq: 101 BYE
Content-Length: 0


May  9 16:01:36.036:
```

continues

Example 17-60 *Viewing Actual SIP Messages of a Normal Call Sequence (Continued)*

```
Send:
 SIP/2.0 200 OK
Via: SIP/2.0/UDP  2.0.0.1:5060
From: <sip:102@192.168.254.1;user=phone>;tag=1BE17C-13E3
To: sip:201@2.0.0.2
Date: Tue, 09 May 2000 16:01:36 UTC
Call-ID: B49B48C5-A0F50014-0-1BDC54@192.168.254.2
Server: Cisco VoIP Gateway/ IOS 12.x/ SIP enabled
Content-Length: 0
CSeq: 101 BYE

r2#
```

TRIP: The Future of VoIP Call Routing

The Telephone Routing over IP (TRIP) protocol, described in draft-ietf-iptel-trip-01.txt, is currently under development within the Internet Engineering Task Force (IETF). TRIP is independent of call-signaling protocols such as SIP or H.323, so it can be used by any VoIP call-signaling protocol. In an H.323 framework, TRIP could replace the interzone gatekeeper communications. Alternatively, interzone gatekeeper communication may continue to be used within an organization, while TRIP is used to exchange call-routing information with other service providers. In a SIP framework, proxy servers may implement TRIP to exchange reachability information, or the proxy servers may communicate with a separate device that is dedicated for TRIP.

The TRIP protocol is closely related to earlier efforts known as Telephone Border Gateway Protocol (TBGP). TRIP is indeed modeled after BGP-4 as the interdomain policy and routing requirements are very similar for telephone numbers and IP addresses. TRIP improves upon the scalability of BGP-4 by not requiring a full-mesh peering for internal neighbors within an autonomous system. Instead of requiring full-mesh internal topologies, TRIP uses a link-state flooding mechanism to announce topology changes, similar to OSPF and IS-IS. By the time you read this, the detailed IETF draft document will have been updated, so you should look for further developments from the IP Telephony working group in the Transport Area of the IETF.

Additional References

The "New Feature Release Notes" section of the CCO is an excellent source of information, and a good starting point to learn about new technologies and features supported in Cisco routers. The following links are general points of entry to read about new features for different IOS 12.x releases:

www.cisco.com/univercd/cc/td/doc/product/software/ios120/120newft/index.htm
www.cisco.com/univercd/cc/td/doc/product/software/ios121/121newft/index.htm

You can browse through these directories, though it may be somewhat overwhelming if you do not know what you are looking for. If you are looking for specific features, it is easy to lose focus and find other interesting features along the way.

Table 17-6 lists a sampling of links that are recommended reading for voice-related IOS features. The location of all of these items is indicated as subdirectories of the following URL:

www.cisco.com/univercd/cc/td/doc/product/software/

Table 17-6 *Sampling of Online Documentation for Voice-Related IOS Features*

Description	URL Location
VoFR using FRF.11 and FRF.12	ios120/120newft/120t/120t4/120tvofr/index.htm
Update for FRF.11 and FRF.12	os120/120newft/120limit/120xk/1207xk/vofr_6x.htm
VoATM on Cisco 3600 series	ios120/120newft/120limit/120xk/1207xk/voatm_6x.htm
VoATM and AAL-2 trunking (MC3810)	ios121/121newft/121limit/121x/121xa/121xa_1/aal2_fm.htm
VoIP for Cisco 3600 series routers	ios113ed/113t/113t_1/voip/index.htm
VoIP for Cisco 7200 series (T1/ E1 voice)	ios120/120newft/120limit/120xe/120xe5/t1_vo_xe.htm
Class-based weighted-fair queuing	ios120/120newft/120t/120t5/cbwfq.htm
Low latency queuing (PC-CBWFQ)	ios120/120newft/120t/120t7/pqcbwfq.htm
QoS for VPNs (VoIP and encryption)	ios120/120newft/120limit/120xe/120xe5_3/qosvpn.htm
New commands in IOS 12.0(7)XK	ios120/120newft/120limit/120xk/1207xk/cref_7xk.htm
Dial-peer enhancements in IOS 12.1(1)T	ios121/121newft/121t/121t1/dt0390s7.htm

continues

Table 17-6   *Sampling of Online Documentation for Voice-Related IOS Features (Continued)*

Description	URL Location
CCS enhancements for MC3810	ios120/120newft/120limit/120xk/1207xk/tccs_7xk.htm
Q.SIG support	ios120/120newft/120limit/120xk/1207xk/qsig_7xk.htm
Voice-port testing enhancements	ios120/120newft/120limit/120xk/1207xk/testvpfm.htm
H.323v2 Gateway	ios120/120newft/120t/120t5/h323v2.htm
H.323v2 Gatekeeper	ios120/120newft/120t/120t5/mcmenh.htm
Advanced H.323v2 features	ios121/121newft/121t/121t1/h323v2p2.htm
SIP user agent for VoIP routers	ios121/121newft/121t/121t1/0251clmb.htm
Example SIP call flows	software/ios121/121newft/121t/121t1/sipcf.htm

There are many more gems of information in the various directories of the new feature release notes, but the documents listed in Table 17-6 will keep you busy for a while. Looking through these documents will point you to as many additional references as you care to spend time researching.

CHAPTER 18

Resolving Voice Quality Issues

Voice quality issues can be related to most aspects of your integrated voice/data network, from PBX tuning, to data network QoS, to codec selection, to network topology, and so on. You must be able to isolate the aspects of the network that are causing voice quality problems, and decide how to fix them (often at the expense of other network design goals). It is also important to identify when you have met the voice quality goals established for your environment.

Chapter 5, "Defining and Measuring Voice Quality," explores the definition and measurement of voice quality. This chapter is intended to be a practical guide to resolving voice quality issues that you may encounter while integrating voice and data networks. This chapter specifically addresses the following issues:

- Goal-setting and expectations
- Clipped speech
- Quiet or loud speech
- Long delays
- Echo problems
- DTMF problems
- Problems with music on hold
- Garbled/distorted/unintelligible speech

Goal-Setting and Expectations

One of the first steps in resolving issues with voice quality is to properly set expectations at the start of a voice/data integration project. It is important that all parties involved in the project have a consistent view of the project goals with respect to economy, functionality, and voice quality. There are trade-offs associated with these goals:

- You can save bandwidth and maintain good voice quality, at the expense of calling flexibility (intersite transfers and centralized voice mail not allowed).
- You can save bandwidth and maintain calling flexibility, at the expense of voice quality.

- You can maintain calling flexibility and good voice quality, at the expense of bandwidth.

Another way to look at these trade-offs is that you can optimize only two of the following three elements in your network: bandwidth, voice quality, and calling flexibility.

By ensuring that all parties understand the trade-offs between the project goals, you can have an active role in shaping their expectations. With this level of understanding in place at the start of a project, you will greatly increase customer satisfaction with the project, and ensure that any voice quality (or economy, or functionality) issues that do arise are not the result of misinformed expectations.

With that said, it is time to explore common voice quality problems and their solutions.

Clipped Speech

Speech may be clipped with respect to time and amplitude, as illustrated in Figure 18-1. Nontechnical listeners (that is, users who report the problems) cannot generally articulate problems with amplitude clipping, so the topic is discussed in the section, "Garbled/ Distorted/Unintelligible Speech," later in this chapter. This section focuses on problems with temporally clipped speech.

Figure 18-1 *Temporal and Amplitude Clipping of Audio Signals*

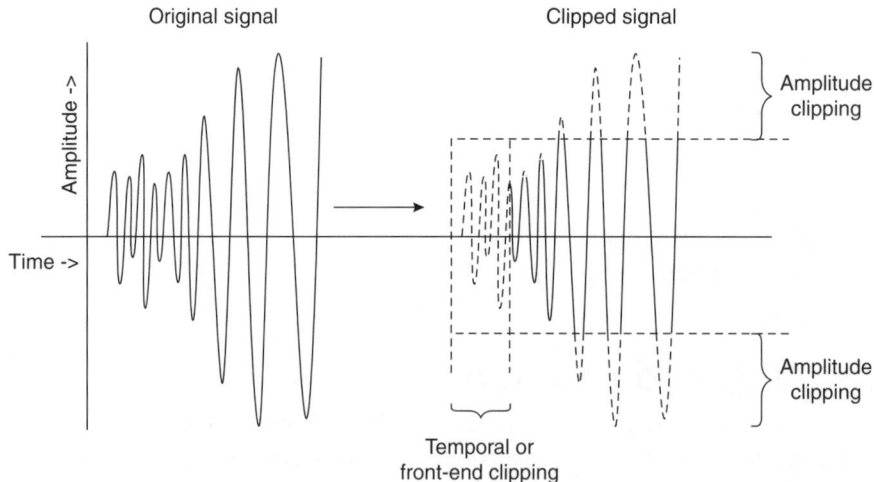

An example of clipped speech in a conversation is hearing "Lo, my name is Scott," instead of "Hello, my name is Scott." Whenever you encounter problems with temporally clipped speech, your first action (that is, the "quick fix") should be to disable Voice Activity Detection (VAD). You can disable VAD on Cisco routers in the dial-peer configuration mode, as indicated in Example 18-1.

Example 18-1 *Disabling VAD on a Cisco Router*

```
voice-gw#configure terminal
Enter configuration commands, one per line.  End with CNTL/Z.
voice-gw(config)#dial-peer voice 1000 voip
voice-gw(config-dial-peer)#no vad
voice-gw(config-dial-peer)#^Z
voice-gw#
```

VAD is designed to reduce bandwidth consumption by transmitting the voice information only when there are active speech signals. In other words, information from your side is only transmitted when you speak, and bandwidth is saved when you are quiet (that is, when you pause for thought or listen to the other party). A typical conversation includes alternating periods of speech activity and silence. Figure 18-2 illustrates three variables that affect VAD performance:

- Background noise threshold
- Suppression/transmission switching time
- Silence recognition time

Figure 18-2 *Factors that Affect VAD Performance*

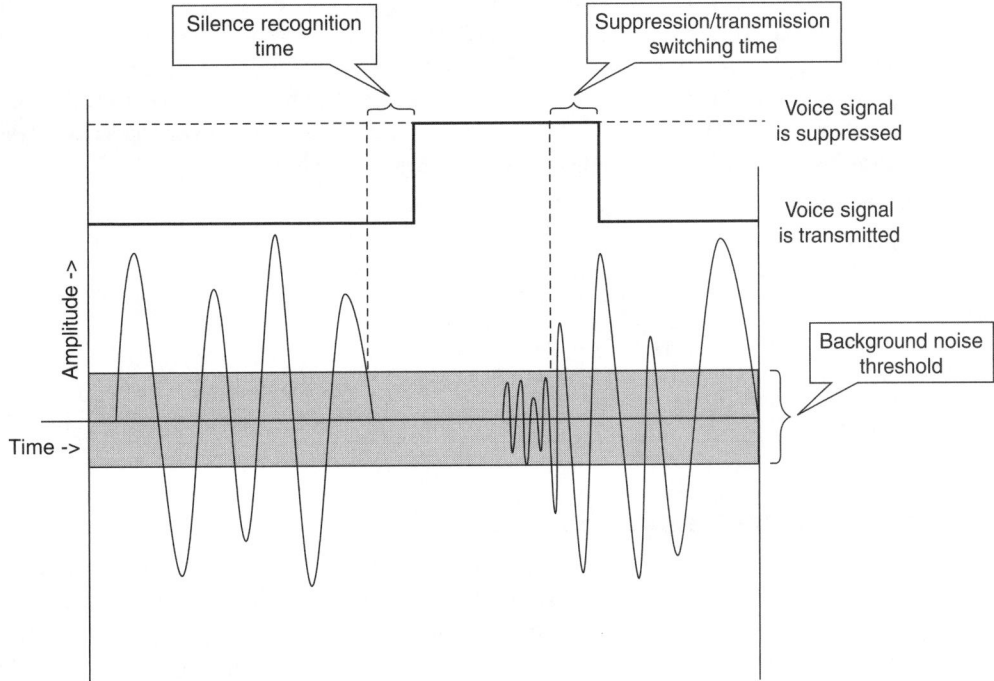

Background Noise Threshold

The background noise threshold sets a level (in dBm units— see Chapter 13, "Delay Budgets and Loss Plans") such that quieter signals are treated as noise (that is, ignored) and louder signals are treated as active speech signals (that is, transmitted). The noise threshold is usually set at a level slightly below quiet speech. In noisy environments such as data centers and call centers, the background noise may be louder than quiet speech signals. For VAD to work in such cases, the noise threshold must be raised above the level of the background noise. Consequently, intended but quiet voice signals are treated as background noise, so speakers in the noisy environment must speak loudly. When the background noise is highly variable, you have several design options with respect to VAD:

- Disable VAD (and lose bandwidth savings) to maximize voice quality.

- Set VAD for the highest background noise levels (to save the most bandwidth), which requires speakers to talk loudly at all times.

- Set VAD for normal background noise levels, and accept that there will be no bandwidth savings when high background noise is present.

In Cisco IOS, the default noise threshold (also called music threshold) is –38 decibels (dB). This means that any signals below the –38 dB level are treated as noise (in other words, they are not transmitted), while any signals that are louder than this level are treated as speech activity (in other words, they are transmitted). If you experience VAD clipping in the quiet parts of conversations, try setting the VAD noise threshold (music threshold) to a larger negative value than the –38 dB default. If you have a lot of background noise, you want to save bandwidth, and you do not mind talking loudly, then set the VAD noise threshold to a smaller negative number. Example 18-2 demonstrates adjusting the VAD noise threshold to stop VAD from blocking quiet speech in a low-noise environment.

Example 18-2 *Adjusting the Noise Threshold for VAD*

```
voice-gw#conf t
Enter configuration commands, one per line.  End with CNTL/Z.
voice-gw(config)#voice-port 1/0/0
voice-gw(config-voiceport)#music-threshold ?
  WORD  Enter a number b/w (-70 to -30)
voice-gw(config-voiceport)#music-threshold -50
voice-gw(config-voiceport)#^Z
voice-gw#
```

Suppression/Transmission Switching Time

The amount of front-end speech clipping is related to the time required to switch from a silence-suppression mode to a voice-transmission mode. When voice activity triggers transmission, the leading edge of the voice signal may be lost while the system returns to transmit mode. This component of VAD is generally a function of a specific hardware or software design; it is not generally a configurable component.

When short periods of silence trigger the silence-suppression mode, voice signals are more frequently affected by the suppression/transmission switching time. For example, silence between spoken phrases, or even between spoken words, can result in the front-end clipping of most spoken words. The best way to reduce the ill effects of the suppression/transmission switching time is to enter the suppression mode less frequently.

Silence Recognition Time

You can increase the duration of silence that triggers silence suppression to avoid triggering the silence suppression too often. With this adjustment, the silence mode is only triggered during longer pauses in speech, which reduces the frequency of front-end speech clipping during normal speech.

Example 18-3 demonstrates how to increase the silence recognition time with the **voice vad-time** command, which reduces the number of words that are affected by front-end speech clipping.

Example 18-3 *Reducing Front-End Speech Clipping that Occurs in the Middle of Spoken Sentences*

```
voice-gw#conf t
Enter configuration commands, one per line.  End with CNTL/Z.
voice-gw(config)#voice vad-time ?
  <250-65536>  milliseconds

voice-gw(config)#voice vad-time 2000
voice-gw(config)#^Z
voice-gw#
```

Codecs with Integrated VAD

The International Telecommunications Union (ITU-T) has standardized several VAD implementations in conjunction with low bit-rate codecs. These VAD implementations require less processing and introduce less delay than traditional VAD implementations, because the VAD operations are performed in parallel with the coder/decoder functions. Cisco IOS supports the following ITU-T standards for VAD in conjunction with low bit-rate codec processing:

- G.723.1 Annex A
- G.729 Annex B

Example 18-4 demonstrates the configuration of the codecs with built-in VAD support.

Example 18-4 *Configuring Codecs with Built-In VAD Functionality*

```
voice-gw#conf t
Enter configuration commands, one per line.  End with CNTL/Z.
voice-gw(config)#voice class codec 10
voice-gw(config-class)#codec preference ?
  <1-12>  Priority order (1 = Highest)
```

continues

Example 18-4 *Configuring Codecs with Built-In VAD Functionality (Continued)*

```
voice-gw(config-class)#codec preference 1 ?
  g711alaw  G.711 A Law 64000 bps
  g711ulaw  G.711 u Law 64000 bps
  g723ar53  G.723.1 ANNEX-A 5300 bps
  g723ar63  G.723.1 ANNEX-A 6300 bps
  g723r53   G.723.1 5300 bps
  g723r63   G.723.1 6300 bps
  g726r16   G.726 16000 bps
  g726r24   G.726 24000 bps
  g726r32   G.726 32000 bps
  g728      G.728 16000 bps
  g729br8   G.729 ANNEX-B 8000 bps
  g729r8    G.729 8000 bps

voice-gw(config-class)#codec preference 1 g723ar53
voice-gw(config-class)#codec preference 2 g723ar63
voice-gw(config-class)#codec preference 3 g729br8
voice-gw(config-class)#exit
voice-gw(config)#dial-peer voice 1000 voip
voice-gw(config-dial-peer)#voice-class codec 10
voice-gw(config-dial-peer)#^Z
voice-gw#
```

If you have problems from speech clipping while using one of the VAD-enabled ITU-T codecs, then change to a version of the codec without VAD.

Quiet or Loud Speech

Aside from problems associated with individual telephones (which you should rule out as a first troubleshooting step), network-related issues may cause the audio levels to be too loud or too quiet for some connections. Some problems are caused by poor adjustment of the network (that is, improper gain/loss settings on voice interfaces), while other problems are more of a fundamental challenge.

For example, many traditional phone networks have problems with call transfers between sites. Each time the call is transferred, the signal level becomes quieter and quieter. This is because the physical path that the audio signal traverses is not always optimized after a call transfer. After several intersite transfers, the overall audio path is composed of three or more separate audio paths glued together, with signal loss accumulating from each audio path. The audio path can be optimized through vendor-proprietary methods or with the use of Q.SIG signaling. The standard Q.SIG method, defined in ECMA-175 Path Replacement Additional Network Feature, allows the audio path to be optimized directly between the new endpoints. The original endpoints that no longer participate in an active call can be pruned out of the audio path.

The following sections are focused on the measurement and adjustment of audio signal levels at the voice interfaces in the network. There is no assumption here that you have the assistance of a PBX technician to make measurements or adjustments in phone switches. However, it should be clear that such assistance is useful, and nearly essential if PBX configurations are the source of problems.

Measuring Audio Levels

After you have isolated call paths that have problems with signal levels, you can roughly measure the sound levels without dedicated testing equipment. Ideally, you should use a dedicated testing device that generates a 1004-Hz sine wave at 0 dBm for the audio source signal, and a separate external unit in the place of a telephone to measure the output signal. In practice, the source signal can be a DTMF tone generated by the * key on an analog residential-style telephone. The tone should continue to be generated as long as you press the key. If you use a proprietary digital phone (associated with a PBX) to generate the test signal, verify that the PBX does not play out a DTMF tone of short duration. The measuring instrument at the destination side of the audio path can be a remotely monitored Cisco router. Figure 18-3 illustrates a test measurement scenario using a POTS phone to generate the test signal and a Cisco router to measure the signal.

Figure 18-3   *Using DTMF Tones and Cisco Routers to Measure Audio Levels*

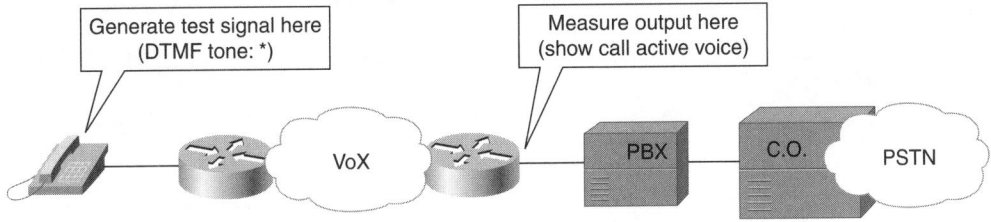

Based on the principles described in Chapter 13, you can determine reasonable signal levels at various points along the audio paths in your network. In most scenarios, the signal level entering the router (either from a directly attached phone, or via PBX to a phone) should be around –3 dB or –4 dB for a DTMF test tone. The signal level leaving a router (to a directly attached phone or via a PBX to a phone) should be between –6 dB and –12 dB, though you may need to compromise with –18 dB or more (that is, when PSTN hop-on or hop-off is part of the audio path). Do not forget to factor in the signal loss for parts of the audio path that are not included in your test.

Example 18-5 demonstrates the measurement of input and output signal levels at a voice port on a Cisco router. Note that VAD and echo-cancellation have been disabled to allow a clear measurement of the signal levels. If possible, ask the PBX technician to remove echo cancellers from the audio path during the tests.

Example 18-5   *Measurement of Input and Output Signal Levels at a Voice Port on a Cisco Router*

```
voice-gw#conf t
Enter configuration commands, one per line.  End with CNTL/Z.
voice-gw(config)#voice-port 1/0/1
voice-gw(config-voiceport)#no non-linear
voice-gw(config-voiceport)#no echo-cancel enable
voice-gw(config-voiceport)#exit
voice-gw(config)#dial-peer voice 200 voip
voice-gw(config-dial-peer)#no vad
voice-gw(config-dial-peer)#^Z
voice-gw#sh call active voice brief
<ID>: <start>hs.<index> +<connect> pid:<peer_id> <dir> <addr> <state>
  dur hh:mm:ss tx:<packets>/<bytes> rx:<packets>/<bytes> <state>
 IP <ip>:<udp> rtt:<time>ms pl:<play>/<gap>ms lost:<lost>/<early>/<late>
  delay:<last>/<min>/<max>ms <codec>
 FR <protocol> [int dlci cid] vad:<y/n> dtmf:<y/n> seq:<y/n>
  sig:<on/off> <codec> (payload size)
 Tele <int>: tx:<tot>/<v>/<fax>ms <codec> noise:<l> acom:<l> i/o:<l>/<l> dBm

23    : 305104hs.1 +436 pid:2 Answer 102 active
 dur 00:00:14 tx:543/4128 rx:561/17292
 Tele 1/0/1:18: tx:13420/4470/0ms g723r53 noise:0 acom:20  i/0:-4/-70 dBm

23    : 305361hs.1 +179 pid:200 Originate 201 active
 dur 00:00:14 tx:561/10560 rx:543/10860
 IP 192.168.254.2:16840 rtt:3ms pl:4750/0ms lost:51064/0/0 delay:130/70/130ms
g723r53

voice-gw#
```

NOTE   As of IOS 12.0(7)XK, Cisco offers excellent support for generating test signals on the 3810, 2600, and 3600 series routers, which obviates the need to use external telephones to generate DTMF tones as test signals. The new feature in Cisco IOS is easier to manage and more accurate than the old hack with external telephones.

You can learn all about this new testing method in the IOS 12.0(7)XK New Features Release Notes, available on Cisco Connection Online (CCO). Look for a document titled Voice Port Testing Enhancements in Cisco 2600 and 3600 Series Routers and MC3810 Series Concentrators.

Adjusting Audio Levels

Cisco routers enable you to adjust audio levels at four points in a two-way audio path. The signal level may be modified at the ingress or egress point in each direction, as illustrated in Figure 18-4.

Figure 18-4 *Reference Points Where Audio Signal Levels May Be Adjusted*

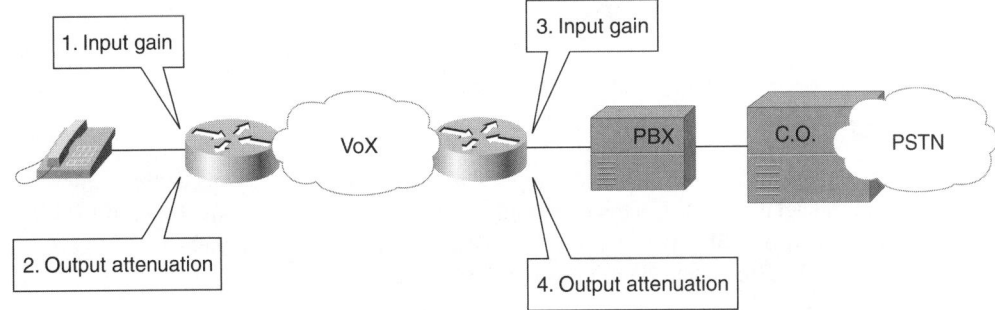

The ingress adjustment is referred to as the *input gain*, while the egress adjustment is referred to as the *output attenuation*. To protect public network resources, you generally cannot amplify the outbound signal. In other words, output attenuation cannot be set to negative values. Thus, if the audio path is too quiet, your only option is to increase the input gain setting. Always keep in mind the direction of signal travel, and realize that to increase the signal level (that is, audio volume) heard from a local router, you must make the configuration change on the remote router at the source of the audio signal.

If the audio path is too loud (in other words, there is not enough loss), then you must ensure that the proper amount of loss is configured at the ingress and egress of the connection. Consider the following guidelines:

- If you hear your own echoes while speaking from the local side, then increase the outbound attenuation at the remote router.

- If the remote party hears distorted speech such as buzzing or amplitude clipping, and even if they do not think the signal is too loud, then decrease the input gain at the local router.

Example 18-6 demonstrates 3 dB of loss introduced at the ingress and egress of a voice port on a voice port of a Cisco router.

Example 18-6 *Ingress and Egress Loss of 3 dB Introduced on a Cisco Voice Port*

```
voice-gw#conf t
Enter configuration commands, one per line.  End with CNTL/Z.
voice-gw(config)#voice-port 4/1:0
voice-gw(config-voiceport)#input gain ?
  <-6 to +14>  gain in db
```

continues

Example 18-6   *Ingress and Egress Loss of 3 dB Introduced on a Cisco Voice Port (Continued)*

```
voice-gw(config-voiceport)#input gain -3
voice-gw(config-voiceport)#
voice-gw(config-voiceport)#output attenuation ?
  <0-14>  attenuation in db

voice-gw(config-voiceport)#output attenuation 3
voice-gw(config-voiceport)#^Z
voice-gw#
```

Long Delays

For a given audio path, there is a minimal amount of delay that you cannot eliminate. This minimal delay is based on the time required for the electrical or optical signals to propagate across a wire or fiber path, or the time required for an electromagnetic wave to propagate through the atmosphere in microwave or satellite transmissions.

You can control or influence the following elements in your network to reduce the overall delay across an audio path:

- Network topology
- Path optimization on call transfer
- Quality of service
- Codec selection

Network Topology

You should review your network topology to ensure that calls follow a reasonable route. In particular, avoid hub-and-spoke designs that span large geographic distances. Calls between cities on one side of a country should not cross through a hub site on the opposite side of the country. If you have clout with your circuit vendor, you can examine the topology of its network, and work with it to optimize inefficient transport paths for circuits with long delay. Also beware of circuit vendors that heavily oversubscribe packet/frame/cell–based services in their backbones.

Path Optimization on Call Transfer

Most multivendor voice/data networks do not support path optimization after call transfer unless Q.SIG is implemented. It should be obvious that when multiple audio paths are glued together from inefficient call transfers, the negative effects of delay (and coder/decoder cycles) are cumulative. The solution to this source of delay is to eliminate intersite call transfers (which may shorten your future with the company), or implement Q.SIG in your network. Chances are good that some equipment in your network does not support Q.SIG. In such cases, you have the option of migrating to vendors that support open standards, or committing your network to a proprietary solution of a single vendor(if they have one).

Quality of Service

Numerous chapters of this book discuss various aspects of quality of service (QoS). In essence, you must ensure that voice packets are prioritized ahead of data packets at every bandwidth bottleneck in the network, which means any part of the network where traffic is queued (including in the carrier network). In addition, you must ensure that all interfaces with low clocking rates (that is, fractional T-1/E-1) employ a form of interleaving voice packets (or frames or cells) between fragments of data packets in a queue.

When you address these issues in your network, you also resolve problems with jitter (also known as delay variation). Reducing jitter enables jitter buffers to be smaller, which reduces the absolute delay in the network.

Codec Selection

Most low bit-rate speech codecs introduce a significant amount of audio path delay because of sampling windows and complex processing. A notable exception is the G.728 LD-CELP algorithm, which yields a good quality 16-kbps audio stream with minimal delay. Chapter 6, "Voice Digitization and Coding," discusses the details of why these codecs introduce delay. Table 18-1 summarizes the characteristics that affect delay for each codec. Refer back to Table 6-2 for additional codec characteristics and notes relevant to the quantities reported here.

Table 18-1 *Codec Characteristics that Affect Audio Path Delay*

Codec	Bit Rate (kbps)	Frame Size (ms)	Look-Ahead (ms)	Processing (mips)[1]
G.711 (PCM)	64	0.125	0	> 0.5
G.726 (AD-PCM)	16/24/32/40	0.125	0	2
G.728 (LD-CELP)	16	0.625	0	
G.729 (CS-ACELP)	8	10	5	20
G.729A (CS-ACELP)	8	10	5	10.5
G.723.1 (MP-MLQ)	6.3	30	7.5	14.6
G.723.1 (ACELP)	5.3	30	7.5	16

continues

Table 18-1 *Codec Characteristics that Affect Audio Path Delay (Continued)*

Codec	Bit Rate (kbps)	Frame Size (ms)	Look-Ahead (ms)	Processing (mips)[1]
GSM Full-Rate (RPE-LTP)	13	20	0	
GSM Half-Rate (VCELP)	5.6	20	0	

1. mips=millions of instructions per second

To get an idea of how the codec processing requirements translate to actual delay times, you must consider the performance of the digital signal processor (DSP) chip on which the codec is implemented. As of this writing, a Texas Instruments TMS320VC549 DSP chip can operate at up to 120 mips, so a codec that requires 20 mips of processing power can process 1 sec of speech in 167 ms of computing time. This translates to 1.67 ms for a 10-ms codec sample. It should be clear that with the powerful DSPs that are currently available (and getting faster and cheaper), that processing delay is becoming a nonissue.

You can roughly estimate the audio path delay introduced by the codec with the following formula:

$$\text{Delay}_{codec} \approx (2 \times \text{Frame\_Size}) + \text{Look\_Ahead}$$

Echo Problems

In some circumstances, you can hear reflections of your own speech when speaking via a telephone connection. The reflections of your own voice can be very annoying, to the point that you cannot speak properly or hear words spoken by the remote party. The degree to which these signal reflections are annoying is a function of two variables:

- Delay of the reflected signal
- Audio level of the reflected signal

Echoes that map above and to the left of the curves in Figure 18-5 are acceptable, while echoes below and to the right are likely to be annoying. In other words, echoes are more annoying when they are louder or more delayed. Figure 18-5, which is identical to Figure 13-7 in this book, is reprinted from Figure 1 of ITU-T Recommendation G.131 ("Control of Talker Echo").

Figure 18-5   *Relationship Between Delay and Signal Strength for Talker Echoes*

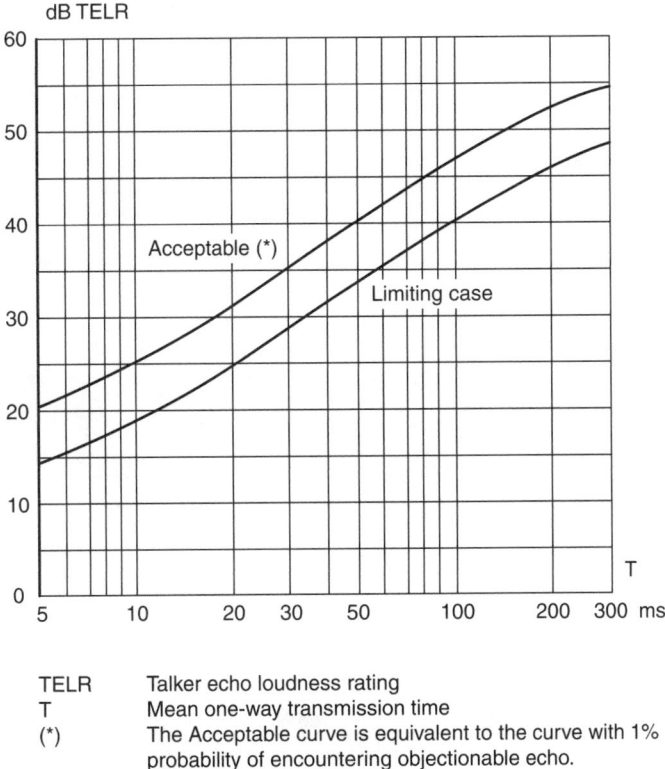

TELR	Talker echo loudness rating
T	Mean one-way transmission time
(*)	The Acceptable curve is equivalent to the curve with 1% probability of encountering objectionable echo.

You can address echo problems from the perspective of delay and from the perspective of the loss plan. You may have heard these perspectives described as "long echo" versus "loud echo." The idea is that you can identify which factor contributes most to the problem, and focus your resources on improving that factor. Refer to the "Quiet or Loud Speech" section earlier in this chapter for more information about adjusting the loss plan, and the "Long Delays" section for more information about reducing delay. Chapter 13 provides detailed coverage of both of these topics from a conceptual perspective.

There is one issue that is worth exploring here. You may have a situation where PBXs introduce signal reflections, but the echoes are not annoying to users because of low circuit delays. In Example 18-6, the echo maps fairly low, but to the left, it is still above the curve. As soon as you replace the traditional audio path with a VoX network using low bit-rate codecs, the echoes suddenly become noticeable and annoying because of the extra delay introduced (the echo moves to the right in Example 18-6). It can be difficult to convince a nontechnical or semitechnical person that the PBX is part of the problem. They may say, "We had no problems before you added the router, so the PBX is not the problem."

How can you reduce the signal reflection, which occurs within the PBX, if you do not have the cooperation of the people who manage the PBX equipment? There is a nice design trick to solve this problem. Figure 18-6 illustrates the audio path details in a typical scenario with echoes caused by a PBX:

Figure 18-6   *Signal Reflections Caused by Two-Wire/Four-Wire Hybrid in a PBX*

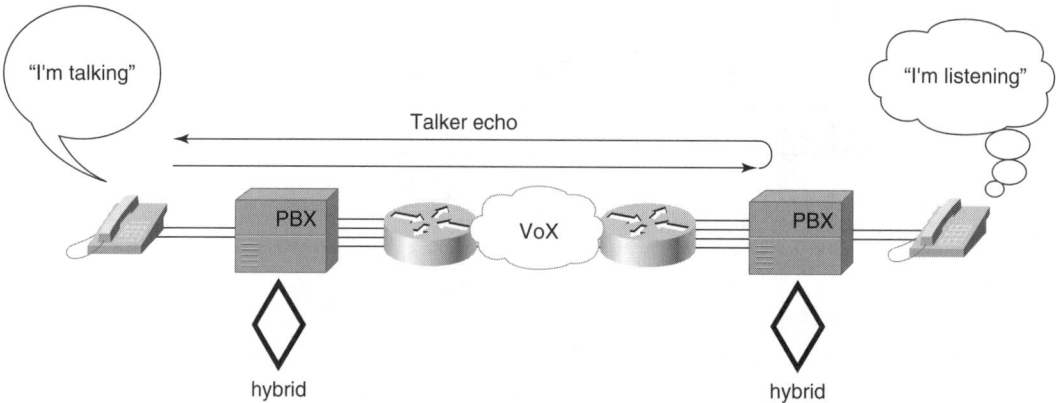

If you address the problem by reducing the VoX delay (by using a higher bit-rate codec) you lose the economy of bandwidth savings. The PBX folks may not be cooperative to resolve signal reflections within their own system, so you cannot reduce the audio level of reflected signals. You can, however, control the location of the two-wire/four-wire hybrid, which is the point where echo is typically generated. By placing the hybrid in a Cisco router, you can bypass the bad hybrid in the PBX. Any potential echoes will be caused at the hybrid in the router, which is designed well enough to minimize reflections. Figure 18-7 illustrates moving the hybrid from the PBX to the Cisco router:

So, how exactly do you move the hybrid from the PBX to the router? You replace the four-wire audio interface (analog four-wire E&M or any digital interface) from the router to the PBX with a two-wire interface (analog FXS/FXO, or analog two-wire E&M). This way, a hybrid in the router merges the audio paths for each direction into a bidirectional audio transmission over a single wire pair to the PBX. The PBX no longer performs the hybrid function, so the PBX does not generate echoes.

The analog E&M voice cards are nice to work with in this scenario, because the choice of two-wire or four-wire audio path is a software configuration option. If you have digital voice cards, you must physically replace them with analog cards that support much lower call density. While this is not a good solution for a full-scale deployment, it is a good proof of concept to show dissenters that the PBX is indeed causing the echo.

Figure 18-7 *Relocating the Two-Wire/Four-Wire Hybrid from the PBX to a Cisco Router*

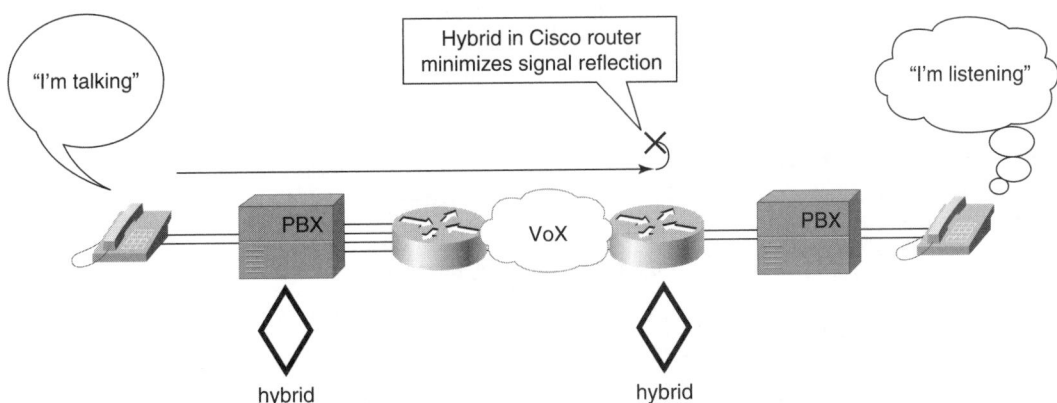

DTMF Problems

DTMF signals are an essential part of most telephony environments. DTMF tones enable people to interact via telephone with voice-mail units, autoattendants, and computer systems in general (that is, input or retrieve information from a database, such as schedules and reservations, academic grade reporting, or customer support information). Even if these features do not seem important for a given environment, you may need DTMF tones for simple call completion in some scenarios (such as a call across a VoX network to a PBX, and then dialing 9 for an outside line). Given the importance of DTMF tones, you should test DTMF functionality at the same time as testing voice quality.

Most of the ITU-T low bit-rate codecs are designed for speech, and do not handle DTMF tones very well. It is common, especially in applications with tandem encodings (that is, multiple coder/decoder cycles), for voice quality to be acceptable while DTMF tones fail. For example, a remote voice-mail unit may not recognize any DTMF tones to navigate the system, or it may interpret numbers incorrectly (for instance, it might confuse 8 with 2). You have several options for addressing problems with in-band DTMF digit transmission:

- Enable a DTMF relay function for out-of-band transmission
- Ensure appropriate gain/loss settings
- Reduce the number of tandem coder/decoder cycles required in the network design
- Use a waveform codec that is not customized for speech

DTMF Relay

The best solution for dealing with DTMF issues is to enable a DTMF relay function. With this feature, Cisco routers locally interpret the in-band DTMF tones (before codec processing), transmit the digit information in an out-of-band channel, and regenerate the DTMF tones at the destination. Figure 18-8 illustrates this process:

Figure 18-8 *DTMF Tones Locally Interpreted by Routers Eliminate In-Band Signal Degeneration*

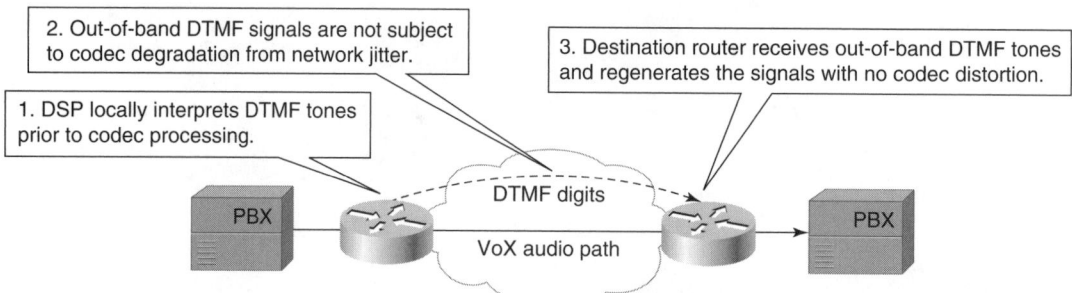

The chief benefit of this approach is that low bit-rate codecs may be used without impacting DTMF performance, because the DTMF tones are not distorted by multiple coder/decoder cycles.

Example 18-7 illustrates the three methods of VoIP DTMF relay that Cisco routers support, in addition to the VoFR DTMF relay:

- H.245-alphanumeric
- H.245-signal
- Cisco-RTP
- FRF.11 Annex A

Example 18-7 *Configuration of DTMF Relay Methods*

```
voice-gw#conf t
Enter configuration commands, one per line.  End with CNTL/Z.
voice-gw(config)#dial-peer voice 1000 voip
voice-gw(config-dial-peer)#dtmf-relay ?
  cisco-rtp          Cisco Proprietary RTP
  h245-alphanumeric  DTMF Relay via H245 Alphanumeric IE
  h245-signal        DTMF Relay via H245 Signal IE

voice-gw(config-dial-peer)#dtmf-relay cisco-rtp
voice-gw(config-dial-peer)#exit
voice-gw(config)#dial-peer voice 2000 vofr
voice-gw(config-dial-peer)#dtmf-relay
voice-gw(config-dial-peer)#^Z
voice-gw#
```

When deciding which to use, you must answer the following questions for your environment:

- Is the duration of each DTMF pulse significant for the application?
- Is the timing between DTMF pulses significant for the application?
- Is H.323v2 vendor interoperability important for the application?

H.245-Alphanumeric

The H.245-alphanumeric method of DTMF relay, which is the default method for implementations compliant with H.323v2, sends the digits [0-9,*,#,A-D] one at a time encapsulated in H.245 alphanumeric UserInputIndication messages. The receiving gateway plays each DTMF tone for 100 ms, regardless of how long the tone is played at the originating side. This DTMF relay method is the most efficient method for VoIP, but it is not well suited for some applications.

Because the digits are always out-pulsed for a constant duration, the H.245-alphanumeric method should not be used for applications where the duration of each DTMF pulse is important. For example, calling-card applications often interpret a long input of the # key as a signal to terminate the current call and place another call on the same calling card account.

Because H.245 packets are not normally configured with the same priority as RTP voice packets, H.245 messages are subject to the same delays experienced by other data applications. As such, this DTMF relay method should be avoided for applications that have strict timing requirements between pulses. For example, some networked voice-mail systems communicate via a series of DTMF pulses.

In spite of these limitations, the H.245-alphanumeric method may be your only DTMF relay option when working in a multivendor H.323v2 environment.

H.245-Signal

The H.245-signal method of DTMF relay, which is an optional method for implementations compliant with H.323v2, sends each digit [0-9,*,#,A-D], along with the tone duration, encapsulated in H.245 signal UserInputIndication messages. The tone duration is initially specified as 400 ms in the signal UserInputIndication message, and is subsequently refined with signalUpdate messages. If the originating gateway is still receiving the same DTMF tone within 50 ms of when the duration signal expires, the gateway sends a signalUpdate message with a 1000-ms continuation of the tone duration. This process continues until the originating gateway detects the end of the DTMF tone. When the gateway detects the end of the tone, it sends a signalUpdate message with the actual time signaled in the last tone duration interval.

While this DTMF relay method preserves the duration of each tone, it does not preserve the timing relationship between tones by default. This is because the relayed digits are transported in H.245 over TCP, which is not normally treated like voice traffic. Because the TCP port numbers for H.245 are dynamically assigned as part of the H.225 call setup, you cannot provide better QoS for H.245 packets before the fact. After TCP ports are established for H.245 sessions, Resource Reservation Protocol (RSVP) can dynamically reserve bandwidth for better treatment of the H.245 messages. In such cases, the RSVP reservation must not override the strict prioritization for RTP voice packets.

Cisco-RTP

Cisco has created a proprietary DTMF relay method to sidestep the timing problems associated with the H.245 methods. Instead of implementing fancy QoS for H.245, the Cisco-RTP solution encodes the digits directly in RTP packets so that the same QoS associated with voice traffic is applied to the DTMF tones. While this solution is elegant, it is not part of the H.323v2 standard, so it is not suited for multivendor H.323v2 deployments.

NOTE   The Internet Engineering Task Force (IETF) has recently published RFC 2833, titled "RTP Payload for DTMF Digits, Telephony Tones, and Telephony Signals." By the time you read this, Cisco routers might have a new DTMF relay option (or modification of the existing option) to be in full conformance with the new standard.

FRF.11 Annex A

For VoFR networks, DTMF relay is standardized in FRF.11 Annex A. This DTMF relay method preserves the signal level (loudness) of each tone, the duration that each tone is played, and the timing between tones. When a tone is played, a VoFR frame (with the same priority as voice traffic) is sent every 20 ms, which contains information about the current 20-ms interval, and the two previous 20-ms intervals. With this moving window, all of the DTMF information is relayed three times, which improves the reliability of the transmission.

Gain/Loss Settings

While gain/loss settings may not seem highly relevant to DTMF transmission, they are often at the heart of in-band DTMF problems. Increasing the audio level via input gain adjustments, which is often required to improve voice quality, can actually cause degraded performance for DTMF tones.

The issue arises because of the companding process in the analog-to-digital (A/D) conversion of the audio stream. As illustrated in Figure 18-9, the audio stream is finely encoded in the quiet audio levels, but coarsely encoded at loud audio levels. The horizontal lines represent the quantizing levels, to which the sampled signal must be approximated when it is converted to digital form. Review Chapter 6 for the details of A/D conversion of the audio signal.

Figure 18-9   *Companding in A/D Conversion Reduces Signal Quality at High Audio Levels*

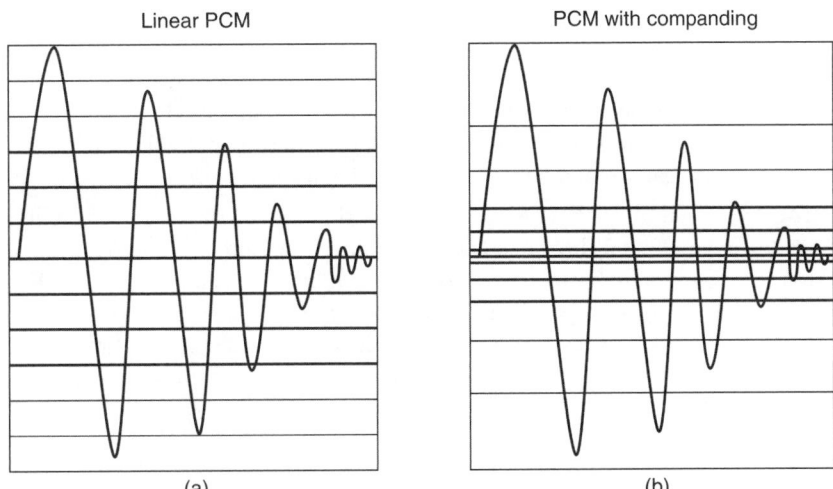

Linear PCM

PCM with companding

(a)

(b)

The logarithmic distribution of quantizing levels is consistent with the physical design of our ears, which are logarithmic sensors of sound pressure. A companded signal efficiently transmits the information that is most psycho-acoustically relevant to humans. A consequence of the logarithmic distribution is that nonhuman sensors (which have more linear sensitivity) cannot discern signals at the higher audio end of the encoding range. This explains why the audio level may seem acceptable for humans, but unacceptable for DTMF sensing devices.

The essence of this discussion is that gain settings should be balanced between human listening requirements and DTMF requirements. If users are not complaining of audio level problems, but DTMF problems are present, then decrease the input gain from sources that have failed DTMF tone transmission. You may also need to decrease the output attenuation at the egress router. For more information, refer back to the section, "Quiet or Loud Speech," earlier in this chapter.

Audio Levels and DTMF

I once received a user request to increase the audio level for VoX calls between a site in San Jose, USA, and an office in Argentina. The system had been operating fine for months, but I needed to move the San Jose end of the connection to a new building, which required a connection to a different PBX. I saw no cause for concern after hearing the user request, so I increased the input gain by +5 dB on both sides of the link. I reasoned that this would improve the audio level for people on both sides of the link to Peru, and I was correct. They told me that the sound level was much better, and I thought nothing more of the problem for several days.

I was eventually informed that all voice-mail messages from Argentina had failed for the last few days. People who sent networked voice-mail messages were not aware that the actual message transmission failed at a later time. The unsent voice-mail messages caused at least one disagreement between high-level managers.

The voice-mail transmissions failed because the voice-mail server was configured to send messages via the VoX link, and DTMF digit transmission failed across the VoX link when I increased the gain. I resolved an obvious problem (quiet audio) with the changes I made, but introduced a worse problem (voice-mail failure) in the process. After tuning the gain down to +2 dB, the audio level was still acceptable and the DTMF functionality was restored. Shortly after that occasion, I was compelled to learn about companding, and the relationship between audio level and digital signal quality.

Coder/Decoder Cycles

As discussed elsewhere in this book, the performance of low bit-rate codecs degrades considerably for tandem encoding applications. If you can modify the network topology to eliminate some coder/decoder cycles, then you can greatly improve the performance of in-band DTMF tones. Ideas for reducing coder/decoder cycles include the following:

- Place call-routing intelligence in routers instead of PBXs.
- Eliminate central PBX call accounting by enabling router-based call-detail reporting.
- Use distributed voice mail (that is, a voice-mail unit at each site instead of centralized voice mail).

Codec Selection

If you are unable to take advantage of DTMF relay tools, you have optimized the gain/loss settings, and you cannot modify the network topology to reduce the number of coder/decoder cycles, then you can resort to changing the codec to improve DTMF performance.

You will achieve much better in-band DTMF performance with codecs that are based on the waveform encoding, which make no assumptions about the input audio source. The low bit-rate codecs are optimized for speech, so they try to interpret DTMF tones as human sounds. It is not surprising that these codecs do not perform well for DTMF input. You can use the G.726 AD-PCM codec to economize on bandwidth, or resort to the G.711 PCM codec for maximum voice quality and in-band DTMF performance.

Problems with Music on Hold

Most organizations are concerned about the sound quality of music on hold with respect to inbound calls from their customers. If overall voice quality is acceptable, but you experience problems with music on hold, then you should focus on two aspects of the network design:

- Codec selection
- VAD

Musical sounds may be degraded by low bit-rate speech codecs, for the same reasons that DTMF tones are degraded by speech codecs. Music with little vocal material is most adversely affected. You can experiment with different low bit-rate codecs to see if one accommodates your musical material. To ensure the highest music quality, you may need to use a waveform codec (which is not biased for speech signals), such as the G.732 AD-PCM at 24 or 32 kbps.

VAD is often the source of problems with musical sound quality. Whereas low bit-rate codecs can make music sound mushy, VAD can make the music sound choppy or fade in and out. The solution to this problem is to disable VAD, or to lower the music threshold (to a larger negative number) as described in the "Clipped Speech" section earlier in this chapter.

Garbled/Distorted/Unintelligible Speech

This is a catch-all category of problems that users may report with respect to speech quality. Most users describe voice quality problems in a nontechnical way, such as fuzzy, buzzy, tinny, choppy, sounds like underwater, sounds mixed up, and so forth. You must translate these descriptions into potential problem areas to investigate. If a user is unable to describe the voice quality problem (or describes the problem too creatively), you may need to hear the problem yourself. In many cases, it is a good idea to hear the problem yourself to ensure an accurate diagnosis. Over time, you can recognize different types of voice quality problems just by listening.

If you recognize that a voice quality problem exists, but are unsure about what may be causing the problem, you should investigate the following areas:

- Is the audio codec appropriate for the calling environment?
- Is the gain/loss plan reasonably tuned?
- Are too many calls passing across a link with limited bandwidth?
- Is QoS optimized for voice traffic across the data network?

Codec Selection

Low bit-rate codecs are designed for specific applications. The low bit-rate speech codecs standardized by the ITU (G.723.1, G.729, and G.729A) are designed for speech signals—not music or modem tones—with a maximum of three tandem encodings. In the presence of other impairments that are common in voice/data networks (such as delay, jitter, background noise, suboptimal audio levels, and so on), low bit-rate ITU speech codecs should never incur more than two tandem encodings. In some environments, more than a single coder/decoder cycle may be unacceptable.

In terms of network design with routers and PBXs, an audio path should cross router-PBX junctions as few times as possible. Figure 18-10 illustrates what is acceptable and what is not when using low bit-rate codecs. The number of router-PBX junctions for an audio path increases when you maintain centralized voice mail or centralized call-accounting features in a PBX. Every time a call is transferred to another site, an additional coder/decoder cycle is added to the audio path, because the original endpoints cannot be pruned out of the audio path. With low bit-rate codecs, you should not transfer calls between sites more than once. This also implies that transferred calls cannot be redirected to a centralized voice-mail system.

In practice, if you answer yes to either of the following questions, then you should not use a low bit-rate codec in your voice network:

- Do you have centralized voice mail or call accounting?
- Do you need to transfer calls between sites?

You may find that the G.726 AD-PCM (40, 32, or 16 kbps) codec is a good compromise between the low bit-rate codecs (>8 kbps) and the G.711 PCM standard (64 kbps). The AD-PCM codecs are bandwidth-efficient when compared with G.711, and they are more tolerant of coder/decoder cycles (up to four) than the low bit-rate codecs. You may also consider G.726 if your network is prone to bursty errors (that is, loss of multiple adjacent packets), because the low bit-rate codecs perform badly in these circumstances.

Figure 18-10 *Do Not Employ More Than Two Coder/Decoder Cycles in a Voice/Data Network*

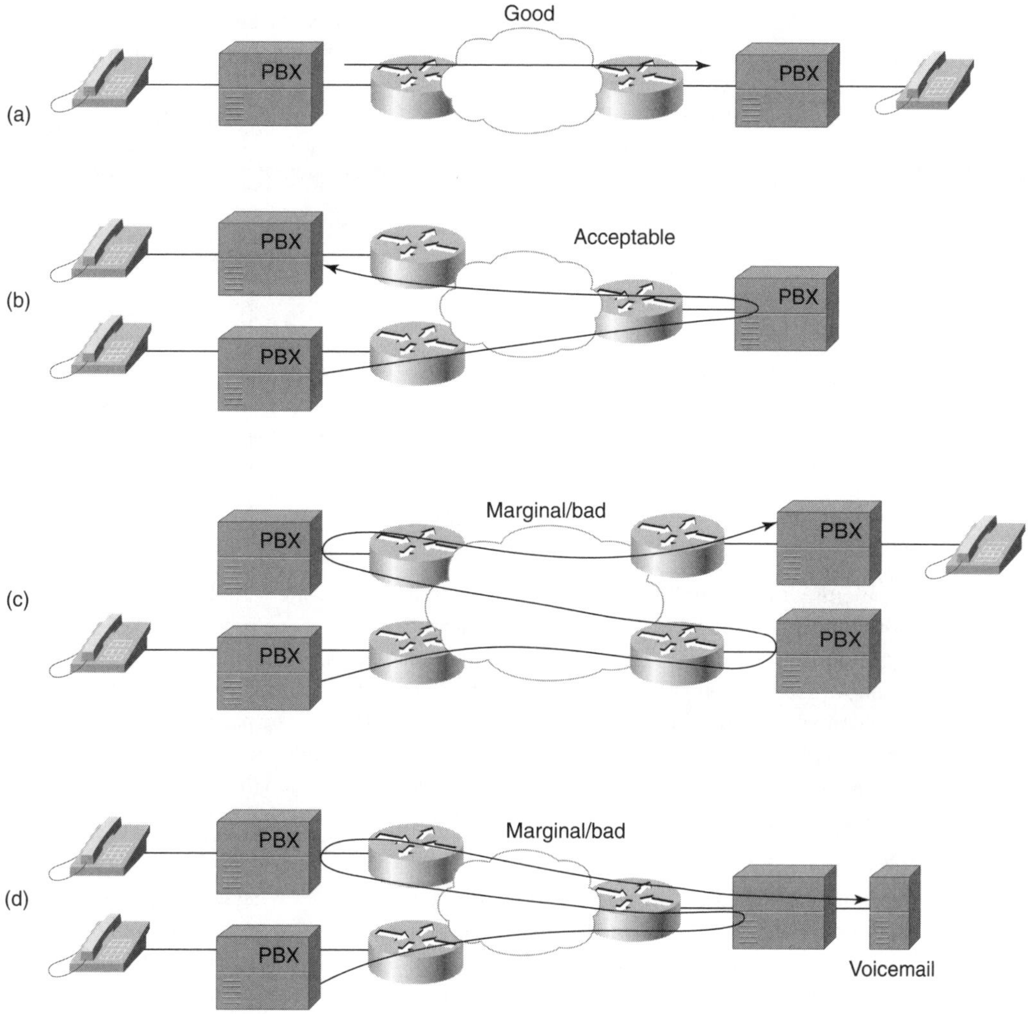

Gain/Loss Settings

The gain/loss plan, which has already been discussed in the context of quiet or loud speech, is included here because it may be responsible for distortion of the audio signal. Recall from an earlier part of this chapter that audio signals may be clipped with respect to time and amplitude. The amplitude-clipping effects are the subjects of this section.

Amplitude clipping occurs when the audio signal levels exceed the functional range of some component in an audio path. For example, an improperly configured analog voice port on a Cisco router may transmit excessively loud signals (that is, electrical signals with high voltage) to a PBX. The PBX, which is not equipped to deal with signals outside of a defined range, cannot accurately propagate the signal. The waveform is clipped, as if with scissors, to the maximal level that the PBX can accommodate. Figure 18-11 illustrates this process.

Figure 18-11 *Audio Signal Amplitude Is Clipped When an Element in the Audio Path Is Overloaded*

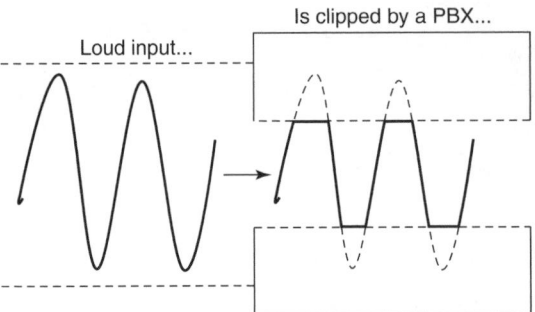

Problems with gain or loss settings can sometimes be identified as a loud output audio level with buzzing sounds. You may be familiar with this sound as a blown speaker in a stereo system, or the sound of a cheap audio speaker (such as a police radio, or a drive-through window at a fast-food restaurant). The buzzing sound is caused by high-frequency components introduced at the cusps in the waveform (that is, the points at the beginning and end of a clipped section of the waveform). Note that clipping can occur in both the analog domain (in other words, excessive electrical voltage levels) and the digital domain (in other words, PCM samples set at the maximum digital value).

Problems with the audio level gain/loss plan may not be so obvious. The level may be in an acceptable range at the output, but it is important to consider what happens along the entire audio path. For example, a signal that is too loud at one point may be subsequently attenuated to an acceptable level, as illustrated in Figure 18-12. In such cases, the amplitude of the audio signal is clipped at an intermediate point in the audio path. Because of the subsequent attenuation, the audio level at the output provides no evidence of the clipping. Other types of distortion may even conceal the characteristic clips in the waveform shape. Unless you have a device to visually examine the time-domain waveform, you would not be able to see the clipping, but you may hear the buzzing sound at a normal signal level.

Figure 18-12 *Audio Signal Amplitude Is Clipped at an Intermediate Point in the Audio Path*

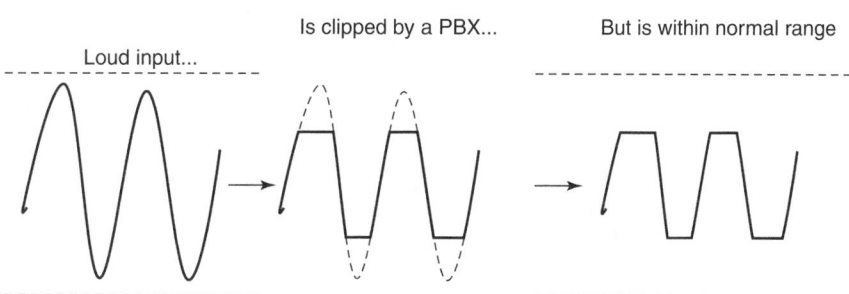

Amplitude clipping may not be so severe as to cause buzzing sounds, but it may still contribute to degraded speech quality. The G.711 codec reproduces sounds less accurately at the loud end of the acceptable range because there are fewer quantizing levels (see Chapter 6). The companding process of G.711 is included in many speech codecs, so this effect is not limited to the G.711 codec. To diagnose such problems, check for signal levels that stay near the high end of the acceptable range of the router or PBX interface. If there are multiple router or PBX interfaces in the audio path, you should check for potential amplitude clipping at each interface. Use dedicated test equipment or the DTMF tones and Cisco router output as described earlier in this chapter for this purpose.

Number of Simultaneous Calls

The number of simultaneous calls that a low-bandwidth link can support is really a part of the overall QoS plan for the network, but it is treated separately here to bring attention to this often overlooked issue. You must address two questions in your network with respect to the number of voice calls across links with limited bandwidth:

- If a link has enough bandwidth to support four active calls, what happens when someone places a fifth call?

- Even if there is enough bandwidth for N number of compressed calls, are there other QoS concerns?

Consider the question of a fifth call across a network that can only support four calls. All five calls will be placed in the high-priority voice queue, and some traffic will be dropped because there is only enough bandwidth to support four simultaneous calls. The problem is that some packets, frames, or cells will be dropped from each of the voice calls, so the voice quality is degraded for all voice calls.

There needs to be a way to prevent a fifth call from starting when there are four active calls, to protect the voice quality of the four active calls. You must implement some form of call admission control (CAC) to meet this objective. RSVP and policy-management servers are evolving to meet this need in a robust, flexible, and scalable way, but Example 18-8 demonstrates a simple solution that is available as of this writing. The **max-conn** dial-peer command puts a hard limit on the number of calls that can be used for a given dial peer, and it can be applied to both VoX and POTS dial peers.

Example 18-8   *Using the **max-conn** Dial-Peer Command to Limit the Number of Voice Calls to a Destination*

```
voice-gw#conf t
Enter configuration commands, one per line.  End with CNTL/Z.
voice-gw(config)#dial-peer voice 100 voip
voice-gw(config-dial-peer)#max-conn ?
  <1-2147483647>  Maximum connections, negation sets to unlimited

voice-gw(config-dial-peer)#max-conn 4
voice-gw(config-dial-peer)#^Z
voice-gw#
```

Aside from bandwidth, there is another concern related to many simultaneous calls on a low-bandwidth link. Consider a 64-kbps clear-channel serial link, with six simultaneous VoIP calls using RTP header compression and the G.723.1 codec (at 5.3 kbps). There does not seem to be a problem with this scenario at first glance, because there is enough bandwidth for all six of the active calls. However, there is only one queue for high-priority traffic on the voice interface, so packets from all six voice calls share the same queue. A VoIP packet from one of the calls might have to wait for the transmission of a VoIP packet from each of the other five calls.

The minimum codec payload size for G.723.1 (at 5.3 kbps) is a single codec frame of 20 bytes, which represents 30 ms of the speech signal. The codec payload is encapsulated in a compressed RTP header that uses 2 bytes, assuming that UDP checksums have been disabled in the dial-peer configuration (UDP checksums would require an additional 2 bytes in the CRTP header). The 22-byte packet incurs 2.75 ms of serialization delay, which is the lowest delay possible for this codec. So, voice packets from each of the six active calls on the 64-kbps link may incur a queuing delay of five times the 2.75 serialization delay, or a total of 13.75 ms.

The queuing delay in this scenario is quite acceptable, but it highlights an important consideration. If you decided to increase the codec payload size to reduce the packet overhead (which seems like a good idea from a bandwidth perspective), you would increase the queuing delay for each call beyond an acceptable range. For example, placing two codec frames in each payload would increase the queuing delay to 27.5 ms. This variable queuing delay (caused by VoIP packets competing with each other) is in addition to the packet formation delay caused by multiple codec frames in a single payload. While 27.5 ms might be acceptable for absolute delay, it pushes the bounds of acceptability from a jitter perspective.

Network-Wide QoS

Without restating several of the chapters in this book, the following points should be reviewed in your network:

- Is packet loss a factor in any part of the audio path?
- Are voice packets consistently routed across a single path?
- Are voice packets prioritized ahead of data packets at all bandwidth bottlenecks?
- Are fragment sizes properly set for all links affected by low clocking rates?
- Are voice packets interleaved between data fragments?
- Is the Frame Relay network designed well? Are traffic shaping parameters configured correctly?
- Are the ATM class of service (CoS) parameters correctly configured?
- Have voice codecs been tuned to optimize the ATM cell-payload efficiency?
- Is your carrier meeting the service level agreement (SLA) requirements?
- Do you enforce the SLA requirements with your carrier?

What happens if you have reviewed each of the topics in this chapter, you feel comfortable that your network is designed and configured correctly, you have verified acceptable WAN circuit performance, and you are still having voice quality problems? You may have discovered a bona fide bug! It is possible that you are experiencing a software bug or a hardware/DSP problem in the router, but this is the source of problems much less often than configuration or design issues.

List of ITU-T Recommendation E.164 Assigned Coundtry Codes

(Position on 1 March 1999)

Annex to ITU Operational Bulletin

No. 687 – 1.III.1999

ITU-T

TELECOMMUNICATION

STANDARDIZATION SECTOR

OF ITU

COMPLEMENT TO ITU-T RECOMMENDATION E.164 (05/1997)

Geneva, 1999

Note by the TSB

1 This List of ITU-T Recommendation E.164 assigned country codes replaces the previous one published as Annex to the ITU Operational Bulletin No. 658 of 15 December 1997. Since then, various new assignments have been made, and they have been published in the ITU Operational Bulletin up to No. 683 of 1 January 1999.

2 This List includes:

— A list of ITU-T Recommendation E.164 assigned country codes—numerical order

— A list of ITU-T Recommendation E.164 assigned country codes—alphabetical order

3 This list will be updated by numbered series of amendments published in the ITU Operational Bulletin. Furthermore, the information contained in this Annex is also available on the ITU home page www.itu.int/itudoc/itu-t/ob-lists, and can be consulted by subscribers by remote access.

4 Please address any comments, suggestions, or modifications concerning this publication to the Director of the TSB:

Tel:	+41 22 730 58 87
Fax:	+41 22 730 58 53
Telex:	421000 uit ch
E-mail:	john.tar@itu.int

5 The designations employed and the presentation of material in this list do not imply the expression of any opinion whatsoever on the part of the ITU concerning the legal status of any country or geographical area, or of its authorities.

List of ITU-T Recommendation E.164 Assigned Country Codes—Numerical Order

Country Code	Country, Geographical Area, or Global Service	Note
0	Reserved	a
1	Anguilla	b
1	Antigua and Barbuda	b
1	Bahamas (Commonwealth of the)	b
1	Barbados	b
1	Bermuda	b
1	British Virgin Islands	b
1	Canada	b
1	Cayman Islands	b
1	Dominica (Commonwealth of)	b
1	Dominican Republic	b
1	Grenada	b
1	Guam	b

Country Code	Country, Geographical Area, or Global Service	Note
1	Jamaica	b
1	Montserrat	b
1	Northern Mariana Islands (Commonwealth of the)	b
1	Puerto Rico	b
1	Saint Kitts and Nevis	b
1	Saint Lucia	b
1	Saint Vincent and the Grenadines	b
1	Trinidad and Tobago	b
1	Turks and Caicos Islands	b
1	United States of America	b
1	United States Virgin Islands	b
20	Egypt (Arab Republic of)	
210	Spare code	
211	Spare code	
212	Morocco (Kingdom of)	
213	Algeria (People's Democratic Republic of)	
214	Spare code	
215	Spare code	
216	Tunisia	
217	Spare code	
218	Libya (Socialist People's Libyan Arab Jamahiriya)	
219	Spare code	
220	Gambia (Republic of)	
221	Senegal (Republic of)	
222	Mauritania (Islamic Republic of)	
223	Mali (Republic of)	
224	Guinea (Republic of)	
225	Côte d'Ivoire (Republic of)	
226	Burkina Faso	
227	Niger (Republic of the)	

continues

Country Code	Country, Geographical Area, or Global Service	Note
228	Togolese Republic	
229	Benin (Republic of)	
230	Mauritius (Republic of)	
231	Liberia (Republic of)	
232	Sierra Leone	
233	Ghana	
234	Nigeria (Federal Republic of)	
235	Chad (Republic of)	
236	Central African Republic	
237	Cameroon (Republic of)	
238	Cape Verde (Republic of)	
239	Sao Tome and Principe (Democratic Republic of)	
240	Equatorial Guinea (Republic of)	
241	Gabonese Republic	
242	Congo (Republic of the)	
243	Democratic Republic of the Congo	
244	Angola (Republic of)	
245	Guinea-Bissau (Republic of)	
246	Diego Garcia	
247	Ascension	
248	Seychelles (Republic of)	
249	Sudan (Republic of the)	
250	Rwandese Republic	
251	Ethiopia (Federal Democratic Republic of)	
252	Somali Democratic Republic	
253	Djibouti (Republic of)	
254	Kenya (Republic of)	
255	Tanzania (United Republic of)	
256	Uganda (Republic of)	
257	Burundi (Republic of)	

Country Code	Country, Geographical Area, or Global Service	Note
258	Mozambique (Republic of)	
259	Spare code	
260	Zambia (Republic of)	
261	Madagascar (Republic of)	
262	Reunion (French Department of)	
263	Zimbabwe (Republic of)	
264	Namibia (Republic of)	
265	Malawi	
266	Lesotho (Kingdom of)	
267	Botswana (Republic of)	
268	Swaziland (Kingdom of)	
269	Comoros (Islamic Federal Republic of the)	c
269	Mayotte (Collectivité territoriale de la République française)	c
27	South Africa (Republic of)	
280	Spare code	m
281	Spare code	m
282	Spare code	m
283	Spare code	m
284	Spare code	m
285	Spare code	m
286	Spare code	m
287	Spare code	m
288	Spare code	m
289	Spare code	m
290	Saint Helena	
291	Eritrea	
292	Spare code	
293	Spare code	
294	Spare code	
295	Spare code	

continues

Country Code	Country, Geographical Area, or Global Service	Note
296	Spare code	
297	Aruba	
298	Faroe Islands (Denmark)	
299	Greenland (Denmark)	
30	Greece	
31	Netherlands (Kingdom of the)	
32	Belgium	
33	France	
34	Spain	
350	Gibraltar	
351	Portugal	
352	Luxembourg	
353	Ireland	
354	Iceland	
355	Albania (Republic of)	
356	Malta	
357	Cyprus (Republic of)	
358	Finland	
359	Bulgaria (Republic of)	
36	Hungary (Republic of)	
370	Lithuania (Republic of)	
371	Latvia (Republic of)	
372	Estonia (Republic of)	
373	Moldova (Republic of)	
374	Armenia (Republic of)	
375	Belarus (Republic of)	
376	Andorra (Principality of)	
377	Monaco (Principality of)	
378	San Marino (Republic of)	
379	Vatican City State	f

Country Code	Country, Geographical Area, or Global Service	Note
380	Ukraine	
381	Yugoslavia (Federal Republic of)	
382	Spare code	
383	Spare code	
384	Spare code	
385	Croatia (Republic of)	
386	Slovenia (Republic of)	
387	Bosnia and Herzegovina (Republic of)	
388	Reserved—for European Telephony Numbering Space (ETNS) trial	
389	The Former Yugoslav Republic of Macedonia	
39	Italy	
39	Vatican City State	
40	Romania	
41	Switzerland (Confederation of)	
420	Czech Republic	
421	Slovak Republic	
422	Spare code	
423	Liechtenstein (Principality of)	
424	Spare code	
425	Spare code	
426	Spare code	
427	Spare code	
428	Spare code	
429	Spare code	
43	Austria	
44	United Kingdom of Great Britain and Northern Ireland	
45	Denmark	
46	Sweden	
47	Norway	

continues

Country Code	Country, Geographical Area, or Global Service	Note
48	Poland (Republic of)	
49	Germany (Federal Republic of)	
500	Falkland Islands (Malvinas)	
501	Belize	
502	Guatemala (Republic of)	
503	El Salvador (Republic of)	
504	Honduras (Republic of)	
505	Nicaragua	
506	Costa Rica	
507	Panama (Republic of)	
508	Saint Pierre and Miquelon (Collectivité territoriale de la République française)	
509	Haiti (Republic of)	
51	Peru	
52	Mexico	
53	Cuba	
54	Argentine Republic	
55	Brazil (Federative Republic of)	
56	Chile	
57	Colombia (Republic of)	
58	Venezuela (Republic of)	
590	Guadeloupe (French Department of)	
591	Bolivia (Republic of)	
592	Guyana	
593	Ecuador	
594	Guiana (French Department of)	
595	Paraguay (Republic of)	
596	Martinique (French Department of)	
597	Suriname (Republic of)	
598	Uruguay (Eastern Republic of)	

Country Code	Country, Geographical Area, or Global Service	Note
599	Netherlands Antilles	
60	Malaysia	
61	Australia	I
62	Indonesia (Republic of)	
63	Philippines (Republic of the)	
64	New Zealand	
65	Singapore (Republic of)	
66	Thailand	
670	Spare code	
671	Spare code	
672	Australian External Territories	g
673	Brunei Darussalam	
674	Nauru (Republic of)	
675	Papua New Guinea	
676	Tonga (Kingdom of)	
677	Solomon Islands	
678	Vanuatu (Republic of)	
679	Fiji (Republic of)	
680	Palau (Republic of)	
681	Wallis and Futuna (Territoire français d'outre-mer)	
682	Cook Islands	
683	Niue	
684	American Samoa	
685	Western Samoa (Independent State of)	
686	Kiribati (Republic of)	
687	New Caledonia (Territoire français d'outre-mer)	
688	Tuvalu	
689	French Polynesia (Territoire français d'outre-mer)	
690	Tokelau	
691	Micronesia (Federated States of)	

continues

Country Code	Country, Geographical Area, or Global Service	Note
692	Marshall Islands (Republic of the)	
693	Spare code	
694	Spare code	
695	Spare code	
696	Spare code	
697	Spare code	
698	Spare code	
699	Spare code	
7	Kazakstan (Republic of)	b
7	Russian Federation	b
7	Tajikistan (Republic of)	b
800	International Freephone Service	
801	Spare code	d
802	Spare code	d
803	Spare code	d
804	Spare code	d
805	Spare code	d
806	Spare code	d
807	Spare code	d
808	Reserved for International Shared Cost Service (ISCS)	
809	Spare code	d
81	Japan	
82	Korea (Republic of)	
830	Spare code	m
831	Spare code	m
832	Spare code	m
833	Spare code	m
834	Spare code	m
835	Spare code	m
836	Spare code	m

Country Code	Country, Geographical Area, or Global Service	Note
837	Spare code	m
838	Spare code	m
839	Spare code	m
84	Vietnam (Socialist Republic of)	
850	Democratic People's Republic of Korea	
851	Spare code	
852	Hong Kong	
853	Macau	
854	Spare code	
855	Cambodia (Kingdom of)	
856	Lao People's Democratic Republic	
857	Spare code	
858	Spare code	
859	Spare code	
86	China (People's Republic of)	
870	Inmarsat SNAC	
871	Inmarsat (Atlantic Ocean-East)	
872	Inmarsat (Pacific Ocean)	
873	Inmarsat (Indian Ocean)	
874	Inmarsat (Atlantic Ocean-West)	
875	Reserved—Maritime Mobile Service Applications	
876	Reserved—Maritime Mobile Service Applications	
877	Reserved—Maritime Mobile Service Applications	
878	Reserved—Universal Personal Telecommunication (UPT) Service	e
879	Reserved for national purposes	
880	Bangladesh (People's Republic of)	
881	Global Mobile Satellite System (GMSS), shared code	k
882	International Networks, shared code	j
883	Spare code	

continues

Country Code	Country, Geographical Area, or Global Service	Note
884	Spare code	
885	Spare code	
886	Reserved	
887	Spare code	
888	Reserved for future global service	
889	Spare code	
890	Spare code	m
891	Spare code	m
892	Spare code	m
893	Spare code	m
894	Spare code	m
895	Spare code	m
896	Spare code	m
897	Spare code	m
898	Spare code	m
899	Spare code	m
90	Turkey	
91	India (Republic of)	
92	Pakistan (Islamic Republic of)	
93	Afghanistan (Islamic State of)	
94	Sri Lanka (Democratic Socialist Republic of)	
95	Myanmar (Union of)	
960	Maldives (Republic of)	
961	Lebanon	
962	Jordan (Hashemite Kingdom of)	
963	Syrian Arab Republic	
964	Iraq (Republic of)	
965	Kuwait (State of)	
966	Saudi Arabia (Kingdom of)	
967	Yemen (Republic of)	

Country Code	Country, Geographical Area, or Global Service	Note
968	Oman (Sultanate of)	
969	Reserved—reservation currently under investigation	
970	Reserved	l
971	United Arab Emirates	h
972	Israel (State of)	
973	Bahrain (State of)	
974	Qatar (State of)	
975	Bhutan (Kingdom of)	
976	Mongolia	
977	Nepal	
978	Spare code	
979	Reserved for the International Premium Rate Service (IPRS)	
98	Iran (Islamic Republic of)	
990	Spare code	
991	Spare code	
992	Tajikistan (Republic of)	f
993	Turkmenistan	
994	Azerbaijani Republic	
995	Georgia	
996	Kyrgyz Republic	
997	Spare code	
998	Uzbekistan (Republic of)	
999	Spare code	

List of ITU-T Recommendation E.164 Assigned Country Codes—Alphabetical Order

Country Code	Country, Geographical Area, or Global Service	Note
93	Afghanistan (Islamic State of)	
355	Albania (Republic of)	
213	Algeria (People's Democratic Republic of)	
684	American Samoa	
376	Andorra (Principality of)	
244	Angola (Republic of)	
1	Anguilla	b
1	Antigua and Barbuda	b
54	Argentine Republic	
374	Armenia (Republic of)	
297	Aruba	
247	Ascension	
61	Australia	i
672	Australian External Territories	g
43	Austria	
994	Azerbaijani Republic	
1	Bahamas (Commonwealth of the)	b
973	Bahrain (State of)	
880	Bangladesh (People's Republic of)	
1	Barbados	b
375	Belarus (Republic of)	
32	Belgium	
501	Belize	
229	Benin (Republic of)	
1	Bermuda	b
975	Bhutan (Kingdom of)	
591	Bolivia (Republic of)	
387	Bosnia and Herzegovina (Republic of)	

Country Code	Country, Geographical Area, or Global Service	Note
267	Botswana (Republic of)	
55	Brazil (Federative Republic of)	
1	British Virgin Islands	b
673	Brunei Darussalam	
359	Bulgaria (Republic of)	
226	Burkina Faso	
257	Burundi (Republic of)	
855	Cambodia (Kingdom of)	
237	Cameroon (Republic of)	
1	Canada	b
238	Cape Verde (Republic of)	
1	Cayman Islands	b
236	Central African Republic	
235	Chad (Republic of)	
56	Chile	
86	China (People's Republic of)	
57	Colombia (Republic of)	
269	Comoros (Islamic Federal Republic of the)	c
242	Congo (Republic of the)	
682	Cook Islands	
506	Costa Rica	
225	Côte d'Ivoire (Republic of)	
385	Croatia (Republic of)	
53	Cuba	
357	Cyprus (Republic of)	
420	Czech Republic	
850	Democratic People's Republic of Korea	
243	Democratic Republic of the Congo	
45	Denmark	
246	Diego Garcia	

continues

Country Code	Country, Geographical Area, or Global Service	Note
253	Djibouti (Republic of)	
1	Dominica (Commonwealth of)	b
1	Dominican Republic	b
593	Ecuador	
20	Egypt (Arab Republic of)	
503	El Salvador (Republic of)	
240	Equatorial Guinea (Republic of)	
291	Eritrea	
372	Estonia (Republic of)	
251	Ethiopia (Federal Democratic Republic of)	
500	Falkland Islands (Malvinas)	
298	Faroe Islands (Denmark)	
679	Fiji (Republic of)	
358	Finland	
33	France	
689	French Polynesia (Territoire français d'outre-mer)	
241	Gabonese Republic	
220	Gambia (Republic of)	
995	Georgia	
49	Germany (Federal Republic of)	
233	Ghana	
350	Gibraltar	
881	Global Mobile Satellite System (GMSS), shared code	k
30	Greece	
299	Greenland (Denmark)	
1	Grenada	b
590	Guadeloupe (French Department of)	
1	Guam	b
502	Guatemala (Republic of)	

Country Code	Country, Geographical Area, or Global Service	Note
594	Guiana (French Department of)	
224	Guinea (Republic of)	
245	Guinea-Bissau (Republic of)	
592	Guyana	
509	Haiti (Republic of)	
504	Honduras (Republic of)	
852	Hong Kong	
36	Hungary (Republic of)	
354	Iceland	
91	India (Republic of)	
62	Indonesia (Republic of)	
871	Inmarsat (Atlantic Ocean-East)	
874	Inmarsat (Atlantic Ocean-West)	
873	Inmarsat (Indian Ocean)	
872	Inmarsat (Pacific Ocean)	
870	Inmarsat SNAC	
800	International Freephone Service	
882	International Networks, shared code	j
98	Iran (Islamic Republic of)	
964	Iraq (Republic of)	
353	Ireland	
972	Israel (State of)	
39	Italy	
1	Jamaica	b
81	Japan	
962	Jordan (Hashemite Kingdom of)	
7	Kazakstan (Republic of)	b
254	Kenya (Republic of)	
686	Kiribati (Republic of)	
82	Korea (Republic of)	

continues

Country Code	Country, Geographical Area, or Global Service	Note
965	Kuwait (State of)	
996	Kyrgyz Republic	
856	Lao People's Democratic Republic	
371	Latvia (Republic of)	
961	Lebanon	
266	Lesotho (Kingdom of)	
231	Liberia (Republic of)	
218	Libya (Socialist People's Libyan Arab Jamahiriya)	
423	Liechtenstein (Principality of)	
370	Lithuania (Republic of)	
352	Luxembourg	
853	Macau	
261	Madagascar (Republic of)	
265	Malawi	
60	Malaysia	
960	Maldives (Republic of)	
223	Mali (Republic of)	
356	Malta	
692	Marshall Islands (Republic of the)	
596	Martinique (French Department of)	
222	Mauritania (Islamic Republic of)	
230	Mauritius (Republic of)	
269	Mayotte (Collectivité territoriale de la République française)	c
52	Mexico	
691	Micronesia (Federated States of)	
373	Moldova (Republic of)	
377	Monaco (Principality of)	
976	Mongolia	
1	Montserrat	b

Country Code	Country, Geographical Area, or Global Service	Note
212	Morocco (Kingdom of)	
258	Mozambique (Republic of)	
95	Myanmar (Union of)	
264	Namibia (Republic of)	
674	Nauru (Republic of)	
977	Nepal	
31	Netherlands (Kingdom of the)	
599	Netherlands Antilles	
687	New Caledonia (Territoire français d'outre-mer)	
64	New Zealand	
505	Nicaragua	
227	Niger (Republic of the)	
234	Nigeria (Federal Republic of)	
683	Niue	
1	Northern Mariana Islands (Commonwealth of the)	b
47	Norway	
968	Oman (Sultanate of)	
92	Pakistan (Islamic Republic of)	
680	Palau (Republic of)	
507	Panama (Republic of)	
675	Papua New Guinea	
595	Paraguay (Republic of)	
51	Peru	
63	Philippines (Republic of the)	
48	Poland (Republic of)	
351	Portugal	
1	Puerto Rico	b
974	Qatar (State of)	
262	Reunion (French Department of)	

continues

Country Code	Country, Geographical Area, or Global Service	Note
40	Romania	
7	Russian Federation	b
250	Rwandese Republic	
290	Saint Helena	
1	Saint Kitts and Nevis	b
1	Saint Lucia	b
508	Saint Pierre and Miquelon (Collectivité territoriale de la République française)	
1	Saint Vincent and the Grenadines	b
378	San Marino (Republic of)	
239	Sao Tome and Principe (Democratic Republic of)	
966	Saudi Arabia (Kingdom of)	
221	Senegal (Republic of)	
248	Seychelles (Republic of)	
232	Sierra Leone	
65	Singapore (Republic of)	
421	Slovak Republic	
386	Slovenia (Republic of)	
677	Solomon Islands	
252	Somali Democratic Republic	
27	South Africa (Republic of)	
34	Spain	
94	Sri Lanka (Democratic Socialist Republic of)	
249	Sudan (Republic of the)	
597	Suriname (Republic of)	
268	Swaziland (Kingdom of)	
46	Sweden	
41	Switzerland (Confederation of)	
963	Syrian Arab Republic	

Country Code	Country, Geographical Area, or Global Service	Note
7	Tajikistan (Republic of)	b
992	Tajikistan (Republic of)	f
255	Tanzania (United Republic of)	
66	Thailand	
389	The Former Yugoslav Republic of Macedonia	
228	Togolese Republic	
690	Tokelau	
676	Tonga (Kingdom of)	
1	Trinidad and Tobago	b
216	Tunisia	
90	Turkey	
993	Turkmenistan	
1	Turks and Caicos Islands	b
688	Tuvalu	
256	Uganda (Republic of)	
380	Ukraine	
971	United Arab Emirates	h
44	United Kingdom of Great Britain and Northern Ireland	
1	United States of America	b
1	United States Virgin Islands	b
598	Uruguay (Eastern Republic of)	
998	Uzbekistan (Republic of)	
678	Vanuatu (Republic of)	
379	Vatican City State	f
39	Vatican City State	
58	Venezuela (Republic of)	
84	Vietnam (Socialist Republic of)	
681	Wallis and Futuna (Territoire français d'outre-mer)	
685	Western Samoa (Independent State of)	

continues

Country Code	Country, Geographical Area, or Global Service	Note
967	Yemen (Republic of)	
381	Yugoslavia (Federal Republic of)	
260	Zambia (Republic of)	
263	Zimbabwe (Republic of)	
0	Reserved	a
886	Reserved	
970	Reserved	l
388	Reserved—for ETNS (European Telephony Numbering Space) trial	
875	Reserved—Maritime Mobile Service Applications	
876	Reserved—Maritime Mobile Service Applications	
877	Reserved—Maritime Mobile Service Applications	
969	Reserved—reservation currently under investigation	
878	Reserved—Universal Personal Telecommunication (UPT) Service	e
888	Reserved for future global service	
808	Reserved for International Shared Cost Service (ISCS)	
879	Reserved for national purposes	
979	Reserved for the International Premium Rate Service (IPRS)	
210	Spare code	
211	Spare code	
214	Spare code	
215	Spare code	
217	Spare code	
219	Spare code	
259	Spare code	
280	Spare code	m

Country Code	Country, Geographical Area, or Global Service	Note
281	Spare code	m
282	Spare code	m
283	Spare code	m
284	Spare code	m
285	Spare code	m
286	Spare code	m
287	Spare code	m
288	Spare code	m
289	Spare code	m
292	Spare code	
293	Spare code	
294	Spare code	
295	Spare code	
296	Spare code	
382	Spare code	
383	Spare code	
384	Spare code	
422	Spare code	
424	Spare code	
425	Spare code	
426	Spare code	
427	Spare code	
428	Spare code	
429	Spare code	
670	Spare code	
671	Spare code	
693	Spare code	
694	Spare code	
695	Spare code	
696	Spare code	

continues

Country Code	Country, Geographical Area, or Global Service	Note
697	Spare code	
698	Spare code	
699	Spare code	
801	Spare code	d
802	Spare code	d
803	Spare code	d
804	Spare code	d
805	Spare code	d
806	Spare code	d
807	Spare code	d
809	Spare code	d
830	Spare code	m
831	Spare code	m
832	Spare code	m
833	Spare code	m
834	Spare code	m
835	Spare code	m
836	Spare code	m
837	Spare code	m
838	Spare code	m
839	Spare code	m
851	Spare code	
854	Spare code	
857	Spare code	
858	Spare code	
859	Spare code	
883	Spare code	
884	Spare code	
885	Spare code	
887	Spare code	

Country Code	Country, Geographical Area, or Global Service	Note
889	Spare code	
890	Spare code	m
891	Spare code	m
892	Spare code	m
893	Spare code	m
894	Spare code	m
895	Spare code	m
896	Spare code	m
897	Spare code	m
898	Spare code	m
899	Spare code	m
978	Spare code	
990	Spare code	
991	Spare code	
997	Spare code	
999	Spare code	

Notes Common to Numerical and Alphabetical Lists of ITU-T Recommendation E.164 Assigned Country Codes

Note:

a   Assignment of all 0XX codes will be feasible after 31 December 2000. Assignment of some of these codes may be possible as soon as 1 January 1997; this question is currently under study.

b   Integrated numbering plan.

c   Code shared between Mayotte Island and Comoros (Islamic Federal Republic of the).

d   Will be allocated, only after all three-digit codes from groups of ten are exhausted.

e   ITU-T Study Group 2, at its meeting in May 1996, has agreed that E.164 country code '878' is reserved for future use by the Universal Personal Telecommunication (UPT) Service. The purpose of this announcement is to recommend that administrations and

Recognized Operating Agencies (ROAs) not use this country code for national purposes, for example, testing.

f   Reserved for future use.

g   Including Australian Antarctic Territory Bases, Christmas Island, and Norfolk Island.

h   U.A.E.: Abu Dhabi, Ajman, Dubai, Fujeirah, Ras Al Khaimah, Sharjah, Umm Al Qaiwain.

i   Including Cocos-Keeling Islands.

j   Associated with shared country code 882, the following two-digit identification code reservations or assignments have been made for the international networks of:

Applicant	Network	Country Code and Identification Code	Status
British Telecommunications plc	Global Office Application	+882 10	Assigned
Singapore Telecommunications Pte Ltd (ST)	Asia Pacific Mobile Telecommunications (APMT)	+882 11	Reserved
MCI	HyperStream International (HSI) Data Network	+882 12	Reserved
Telespazio S.p.A.	EMS Regional Mobile Satellite System	+882 13	Assigned
GTE	GTE International Networks	+882 14	Reserved
Telstra	ITERRA Digital Network	+882 15	Reserved
United Arab Emirates Administration	Thuraya RMSS Network	+882 16	Reserved
AT&T	AT&T International ATM Network	+882 17	Reserved
Teledesic	Teledesic Global Network	+882 18	Reserved
Telecom Italia	Telecom Italia Global Network	+882 19	Reserved

Applicant	Network	Country Code and Identification Code	Status
Asia Cellular Satellite (ACeS)	Garuda Mobile Telecommunication Satellite System	+882 20	Reserved
Ameritech	Ameritech's Gateway Global Service, Inc. (AGGSI) Network	+882 21	Reserved
Cable & Wireless plc	Cable & Wireless Global Network	+882 22	Assigned
Sita-Equant Joint Venture	Sita-Equant Network	+882 23	Reserved
Telia AB	Telia multinational ATM Network	+882 24	Reserved
Constellation Communications, Inc.	Constellation System	+882 25	Reserved

k   Associated with shared country code 881, the following one-digit identification codes have been made for the GMSS networks:

Network	Country Code and Identification Code	Status
ICO Global Communications	+881 0 and +881 1	Reserved
Iridium	+881 6 and +881 7	Assigned
Globalstar	+881 8 and +881 9	Reserved

l   Reserved for the Palestinian Authority.

m   Reserved for E.164 country code expansion.

Spare Country Codes of the List of ITU-T Recommendation E.164

Spare codes that may be allocated as country codes or global service codes:

Table A-1 *Spare Codes with a Note*

280,	281,	282,	283,	284,	285,	286,	287,	288,	289
801,	802,	803,	804,	805,	806,	807,	809		
830,	831,	832,	833,	834,	835,	836,	837,	838,	839
890,	891,	892,	893,	894,	895,	896,	897,	898,	899

Table A-2 *Spare Codes Without a Note*

210,	211,	214,	215,	217,	219			
259								
292,	293,	294,	295,	296				
382,	383,	384						
422,	424,	425,	426,	427,	428,	429		
670,	671,	693,	694,	695,	696,	697,	698,	699
851,	854,	857,	858,	859				
883,	884,	885,	887,	889				
978								
990,	991,	997,	999					

Amendments

Amendment No.	Operational Bulletin No.	Country
1		
2		
3		
4		
5		
6		
7		
8		
9		
10		
11		
12		
13		
14		
15		
16		
17		
18		
19		
20		
21		
22		
23		
24		
25		
26		
27		
28		
29		
30		

ISDN Cause Codes

ITU-T Recommendation Q.850 defines the ISDN cause codes that are used in Recommendation Q.931. Recommendation H.225, which is used for H.323 call setup, is based in part on Recommendation Q.931, and Cisco's proprietary call session application is also based in part on Q.931 message exchanges. As a result of these relationships, you will see ISDN cause codes in the following settings:

- ISDN interfaces (BRI and PRI)
- Q.SIG
- H.225 call establishment in H.323 networks
- Cisco-proprietary call session application

Note that in **show** and **debug** commands, Cisco routers generally display the 7-bit hexadecimal representation of ISDN cause codes, even if the number is not preceded with the characters 0x. The 8-bit hexadecimal representation is different because the most significant bit is always set to 1 in the Q.931 cause code fields.

Table B-1   *Normal Events*

8-Bit Hex	7-Bit Hex	Dec	ISDN Cause Code
0x81	0x01	1	Unallocated (unassigned) number
0x82	0x02	2	No route to specified transit network
0x83	0x03	3	No route to destination
0x86	0x06	6	Channel unacceptable
0x87	0x07	7	Call awarded and being delivered in an established channel
0x90	0x10	16	Normal call clearing
0x91	0x11	17	User busy
0x92	0x12	18	No user responding
0x93	0x13	19	No answer from user (user alerted)
0x95	0x15	21	Call rejected
0x96	0x16	22	Number changed

continues

Table B-1   *Normal Events (Continued)*

8-Bit Hex	7-Bit Hex	Dec	ISDN Cause Code
0x9A	0x1A	26	Nonselected user clearing
0x9B	0x1B	27	Destination out of order
0x9C	0x1C	28	Invalid number format
0x9D	0x1D	29	Facility rejected
0x9E	0x1E	30	Response to status inquiry
0x9F	0x1F	31	Normal unspecified

Table B-2   *Network Congestion*

8-Bit Hex	7-Bit Hex	Dec	ISDN Cause Code
0xA2	0x22	34	No channel available
0xA3	0x23	35	Call queued (AT&T)
0xA6	0x26	38	Network out of order
0xA9	0x29	41	Temporary failure
0xAA	0x2A	42	Switching equipment congestion
0xAB	0x2B	43	User information discarded
0xAC	0x2C	44	Requested channel not available
0xAD	0x2D	45	Preempted
0xAF	0x2F	47	Resources unavailable, unspecified

Table B-3   *Service or Option Not Available*

8-Bit Hex	7-Bit Hex	Dec	ISDN Cause Code
0xB1	0x31	49	Quality of service unavailable
0xB2	0x32	50	Requested facility not subscribed
0xB4	0x34	52	Outgoing calls barred (AT&T)
0xB6	0x36	54	Incoming calls barred
0xB9	0x39	57	Bearer capability not authorized
0xBA	0x3A	58	Bearer capability not now available
0xBF	0x3F	63	Service or option not available, unspecified

Table B-4 *Service or Option Not Implemented*

8-Bit Hex	7-Bit Hex	Dec	ISDN Cause Code
0xC1	0x41	65	Bearer capability not implemented
0xC2	0x42	66	Channel type not implemented
0xC5	0x45	69	Requested facility not implemented
0xC6	0x46	70	Only restricted digital information bearer capability is available
0xCF	0x4F	79	Service not implemented, unspecified

Table B-5 *Invalid Message*

8-Bit Hex	7-Bit Hex	Dec	ISDN Cause Code
0xD1	0x51	81	Invalid call reference value
0xD2	0x52	82	Channel does not exist
0xD3	0x53	83	Suspended call exists, but this call ID does not
0xD4	0x54	84	Call ID in use
0xD5	0x55	85	Invalid digit value for number, or no call suspended
0xD6	0x56	86	Call with requested ID is cleared
0xD8	0x58	88	Incompatible destination
0xDB	0x5B	91	Invalid transit network selection
0xDF	0x5F	95	Invalid message, unspecified

Table B-6 *Protocol Error and Interworking*

8-Bit Hex	7-Bit Hex	Dec	ISDN Cause Code
0xE0	0x60	96	Mandatory information element missing
0xE1	0x61	97	Message type nonexistent or not implemented
0xE2	0x62	98	Message not compatible with call state
0xE3	0x63	99	Information element not implemented
0xE4	0x64	100	Invalid information element contents
0xE5	0x65	101	Message not compatible with call state
0xE6	0x66	102	Recovery on timer expiry (timer 0)
0xEF	0x6F	111	Protocol error, unspecified
0xFF	0x7F	127	Interworking, unspecified

Debug VPM Signal

If you are having problems establishing connectivity between a router and a PBX, you can discover much about the problem using the **debug vpm signal** command. As with many of the Cisco debugging commands, there is a lot of powerful information to be gleaned, but you must really understand the underlying protocols to make use of it. Chapter 2, "Enterprise Telephony Signaling," discusses the voice-signaling protocols in sufficient depth to provide you with the necessary background knowledge.

Beyond the basic voice-signaling knowledge, you need to become familiar with the Cisco-specific keywords and organization of the debugging output. Voice support in Cisco IOS is actually divided into different functional layers like the OSI-model, so that the physical operation of the voice port may be abstracted from the call-processing software. The names of the different voice-debugging commands reflect this functional layer separation:

- **debug vpm signal** (voice-port module debugging)
- **debug vpm spi** (session-protocol debugging)
- **debug ccapi inout** (call connection application debugging)

It is no small achievement if you can follow the output of the voice-debugging commands and understand the underlying processes. The **debug vpm signal** command is considered in this appendix, and Appendix D, "Debug VoIP CCAPI inout," explores the **debug voip ccapi inout** command. This book does not explore the **debug vpm spi** command because from a field implementation and troubleshooting perspective, the information is similar to the output of **debug voip ccapi inout**.

You will notice that for both analog and digital calls, the router displays Q.931-style messages relating to call setup and teardown, such as SETUP ACK, PROCEEDING, and CONNECT. This is because Cisco routers use a proprietary call session application based on Q.931. The router internal software states reflect the different stages of a Q.931 call establishment and teardown, but these states are an abstraction from the actual voice-port signaling. In other words, the Q.931-style messages that the router displays are part of an internal call-control mechanism, but the actual voice port signaling may be different depending on the type of voice port.

The syntax of the output for **debug vpm signal** varies between IOS releases, but more recent (and easy-to-follow) output begins the majority of lines with the following syntax:

```
<timestamp> [<voice-port>, <current-state>, <received-event>]
```

In older IOS releases, the "received-event" is listed as a cryptic number, but more recently the actual event name from the software code is listed in the debugging output. Table C-1 provides a translation between the cryptic numbering in the older IOS releases and the received events, which are called *HTSP events*. The name HTSP is an abbreviation of Host Telephony Service Provider, which refers to the part of Cisco IOS software that handles voice-port signaling on the 2600 and 3600 series router platforms.

Table C-1 *HTSP Event Codes Shown in* **debug vpm signal**

Code	HTSP Event Name	Meaning
-1	E_HTSP_ERROR	Error in router signaling module
0	E_HTSP_INIT	Voice port is initializing
1	E_HTSP_INSERVE	Voice port is in service
2	E_HTSP_IF_INSERVICE	Voice port activated ("no shutdown")
3	E_HTSP_IF_OOS	Out of service ("shutdown")
4	E_HTSP_IF_OOS_CONF	Voice port acknowledges OOS state
5	E_HTSP_SETUP_REQ	Router receives a call SETUP request
6	E_HTSP_CONNECT	Both parties connected
7	E_HTSP_RELEASE_REQ	Call disconnection initiated
8	E_HTSP_SETUP_ACK	Router acknowledges SETUP request
9	E_HTSP_PRE_CONN_DISC	Disconnect before call established
10	E_HTSP_PROCEEDING	Call proceeding (not yet connected)
11	E_HTSP_VOICE_CUT_THROUGH	Audio path created for call progress
12	E_HTSP_LOOPBACK	Audio path is looped
13	E_HTSP_GO_UP	Part of activation (follows Code 2)
14	E_HTSP_GO_TRUNK	Like 13, but for trunk connections
15	E_HTSP_TRUNK_UP	Trunk connection is up
16	E_HTSP_TRUNK_DOWN	Trunk connection is down
17	E_HTSP_TRUNKED	Trunk connection is active
18	E_HTSP_LINE_UP	T-1/E-1 controller is up
19	E_HTSP_LINE_DOWN	T-1/E-1 controller is down
20	E_DSP_PULSE_DIALING_DONE	Router finished sending pulse digits
21	E_DSP_DIALING_DONE	Router finished sending DTMF digits

Table C-1 *HTSP Event Codes Shown in* **debug vpm signal** (Continued)

Code	HTSP Event Name	Meaning
22	E_DSP_INTERFACE_INFO	Indicates FXS, FXO, or E&M
23	E_DSP_RESTART_IND	Restart indicator
24	E_DSP_SEND_SIG_STATUS_0000	Router receives ABCD bits = "0000"
25	E_DSP_SEND_SIG_STATUS_0001	Router receives ABCD bits = "0001"
26	E_DSP_SEND_SIG_STATUS_0010	Router receives ABCD bits = "0010"
27	E_DSP_SEND_SIG_STATUS_0011	Router receives ABCD bits = "0011"
28	E_DSP_SEND_SIG_STATUS_0100	…
29	E_DSP_SEND_SIG_STATUS_0101	…
30	E_DSP_SEND_SIG_STATUS_0110	…
31	E_DSP_SEND_SIG_STATUS_0111	…
32	E_DSP_SEND_SIG_STATUS_1000	…
33	E_DSP_SEND_SIG_STATUS_1001	…
34	E_DSP_SEND_SIG_STATUS_1010	…
35	E_DSP_SEND_SIG_STATUS_1011	…
36	E_DSP_SEND_SIG_STATUS_1100	…
37	E_DSP_SEND_SIG_STATUS_1101	…
38	E_DSP_SEND_SIG_STATUS_1110	Router receives ABCD bits = 1110
39	E_DSP_SEND_SIG_STATUS_1111	Router receives ABCD bits = 1111
40	E_DSP_SUP_DISCONNECT	Supervisory disconnect
41	E_HTSP_EVENT_TIMER	Track various timing/timeout values (such as E&M wink timers, and so on)
42	E_HTSP_EVENT_TIMER2	
43	E_HTSP_RESET	The voice-hardware module is reset
44	E_HTSP_HOOKFLASH	Router receives a hook-flash signal
45	E_HTSP_BUSYOUT	Voice port has been busied out
46	E_HTSP_OUT_BUSYOUT	
47	E_HTSP_EVENT_COUNT	Last HTSP event in a multipart message

To facilitate a discussion of the different events, line numbers are added to the debugging output in Examples C-1 through C-4. Example C-1 illustrates a successful call from a normal analog telephone attached to an analog FXS port. Lines 3 and 4 of the output are generated when the phone goes off-hook. The voice port is initially in the on-hook state and receives an off-hook signal (ABCD=1100) from the remote side. The voice port does not actually receive the ABCD bits from the remote side because this is an analog connection; the voice DSPs in the router simulate the ABCD states so that the same call-processing software may be used for analog and digital calls.

Line 5 indicates that the voice port is in an off-hook state when it is notified that the call is proceeding (after the digits have been dialed). Line 6 shows that the audio path is established from the remote side back to the calling party, to facilitate ring-back and other progress tones. After the called party answers the phone, line 7 indicates that the connection is established. After the conversation is completed, line 9 shows that the actively connected voice port receives a RELEASE REQUEST from the remote side. Lines 14 through 16 show that the voice port is held in the off-hook state for 3 seconds following the end of the call to prevent another inbound call from seizing the port before it is ready for a new call. Line 17 shows the ABCD bits returned to a normal idle state, where the voice port is ready for another inbound or outbound call.

Example C-1   *Successful Phone Call Initiated from an Analog FXS Port*

```
Line#   Debugging Output
1       voice-gw2#debug vpm signal
2       Voice Port Module signaling debugging is enabled
3       Mar  1 00:36:31.211: [1/1/0, FXSLS_ONHOOK, E_DSP_SIG_1100]
        fxsls_onhook_offhook htsp_setup_ind
4       Mar  1 00:36:31.215: [1/1/0, FXSLS_WAIT_SETUP_ACK, E_HTSP_SETUP_ACK]
5       Mar  1 00:36:41.415: [1/1/0, FXSLS_OFFHOOK, E_HTSP_PROCEEDING]
        htsp_alert_notify
6       Mar  1 00:36:41.451: [1/1/0, FXSLS_OFFHOOK, E_HTSP_VOICE_CUT_THROUGH]
7       Mar  1 00:36:52.983: [1/1/0, FXSLS_OFFHOOK, E_HTSP_CONNECT]
        fxsls_offhook_connect
8       Mar  1 00:36:52.983: [1/1/0] set signal state = 0x6 timestamp = 0
9       Mar  1 00:37:11.415: [1/1/0, FXSLS_CONNECT, E_HTSP_RELEASE_REQ]
        fxsls_connect_disc
10      Mar  1 00:37:11.415: htsp_timer_stop
11      Mar  1 00:37:11.415: [1/1/0] set signal state = 0xC timestamp = 0
12      Mar  1 00:37:11.419: [1/1/0] set signal state = 0x4 timestamp = 750
13      Mar  1 00:37:11.419: htsp_timer - 950 msec
14      Mar  1 00:37:12.371: [1/1/0, FXSLS_CPC, E_HTSP_EVENT_TIMER] fxsls_cpc_timer
15      Mar  1 00:37:12.371: htsp_timer - 30000 msec
16      Mar  1 00:37:12.371: [1/1/0, FXSLS_WAIT_ONHOOK, E_DSP_SIG_1100]
17      Mar  1 00:37:17.407: [1/1/0, FXSLS_WAIT_ONHOOK, E_DSP_SIG_0100]
        fxsls_waitonhook_onhook
18      Mar  1 00:37:17.407: htsp_timer_stop htsp_report_onhook_sig
```

Example C-2 illustrates an inbound call on a digital port configured for E&M wink-start, when the called party across the VoX network does not answer the phone. In this example, the cryptic HTSP event code numbers are highlighted (refer to Table C-1 to translate these numbers). The signaling state of the voice port is also coded in an obscure number format, which is different for each voice-signaling type and hardware platform, and is also subject to change between IOS versions. You can still learn much about the voice-port signaling without knowing these states.

Line 1 shows that the voice port receives an off-hook indication (ABCD=1100) when the attached telephone switch seizes the trunk. Line 2 shows the SETUP ACK from the router, and line 3 shows the PROCEEDING message after the phone switch passes the DTMF digits. Note that these debugging messages refer to software-based call events (based on Q.931) that are independent of the physical voice-port signaling mechanisms. Line 4 shows the audio path established to transmit call-progress tones (for example, ring-back), after which no further signaling occurs for nearly a minute. During this time, the phone is ringing at the destination across the VoX network, but nobody answers the phone.

Eventually the calling party tires of listening to the phone ring and disconnects. In line 5, the router receives an on-hook signal from the attached phone switch and starts a timer to verify that the on-hook signal is intentional. Line 6 shows the timer expiring after 480 ms, and line 7 shows the router still receiving an on-hook state (ABCD=0000). Line 8 shows the router recognizing a RELEASE REQUEST signal and starting a 400-ms timer. Line 9 shows the timer expiring, after which the trunk is released and ready for another call.

Example C-2 *Inbound Call on E&M Wink-Start Port; No Answer from the Far Side of VoX Network*

Line#	Debugging Output
1	May 29 16:06:36.702 UTC: htsp_process_event: [4/1:0(1), 1.4 , 36] em_onhook_offhookem_onhookem_offhookem_onhookhtsp_setup_ind
2	May 29 16:06:36.706 UTC: htsp_process_event: [4/1:0(1), 1.7 , 8]
3	May 29 16:06:38.110 UTC: htsp_process_event: [4/1:0(1), 1.7 , 10] htsp_alert_notify
4	May 29 16:06:38.702 UTC: htsp_process_event: [4/1:0(1), 1.7 , 11]
5	May 29 16:07:17.490 UTC: htsp_process_event: [4/1:0(1), 1.7 , 24] em_offhook_onhookem_stop_timers em_start_timer: 480 ms
6	May 29 16:07:17.970 UTC: htsp_process_event: [4/1:0(1), 1.8 , 41] em_delay_onhookpersistexpiryem_stop_timers em_start_timer: 600 ms
7	May 29 16:07:17.970 UTC: htsp_process_event: [4/1:0(1), 1.5 , 24] em_onhookpersist_onhook
8	May 29 16:07:17.970 UTC: htsp_process_event: [4/1:0(1), 1.6 , 7] em_onhook_discem_start_timer: 400 ms em_onhook
9	May 29 16:07:18.370 UTC: htsp_process_event: [4/1:0(1), 1.3 , 41] em_clr_timeout em_stop_timers

Example C-3 illustrates a failed call attempt initiated from a phone attached to an analog FXS port. The call fails because the router does not know how to reach the destination dialed by the user. Line 1 shows the voice port receiving an off-hook indication from the attached phone (ABCD=1100, refer to Figure 2-25), and line 2 shows the internal software-based call event that is similar to a Q.931 SETUP ACK message. Remember that these software-based call events are abstracted from the details of the physical voice-port signaling, and apply to all voice-port types. After the user dials the digits, lines 3 and 4 show that the router initiates a call disconnection before the connection has been established. The router provides a hexadecimal ISDN cause code (cause=1C) that indicates an invalid number format (see Appendix B, "ISDN Cause Codes," for a list of standard ISDN cause codes).

When the user hangs up the phone and the circuit loop is broken, line 5 shows that the router receives the idle indication (ABCD=0100). Lines 6 and 7 show the router starting a 600-ms timer (to verify whether the user is disconnecting or sending a hook-flash signal), after which the router recognizes in RELEASE REQUEST in line 8. Line 9 shows that the router stops the timer, and the voice port is left in the idle state.

Example C-3   *Failed Phone Call Initiated from an FXS Port; No Matching Outbound Dial Peer*

Line#	Debugging Output
1	Mar 1 01:08:07.014: [1/1/0, FXSLS_ONHOOK, E_DSP_SIG_1100] fxsls_onhook_offhook htsp_setup_ind
2	Mar 1 01:08:07.018: [1/1/0, FXSLS_WAIT_SETUP_ACK, E_HTSP_SETUP_ACK]
3	Mar 1 01:08:15.406: htsp_pre_connect_disconnect, cdb = 61D03CB4 cause = 1C
4	Mar 1 01:08:15.410: [1/1/0, FXSLS_OFFHOOK, E_HTSP_PRE_CONN_DISC]
5	Mar 1 01:08:23.402: [1/1/0, FXSLS_OFFHOOK, E_DSP_SIG_0100] fxsls_offhook_onhook
6	Mar 1 01:08:23.406: htsp_timer - 600 msec
7	Mar 1 01:08:24.006: [1/1/0, FXSLS_OFFHOOK, E_HTSP_EVENT_TIMER] fxsls_offhook_timer
8	Mar 1 01:08:24.006: [1/1/0, FXSLS_ONHOOK, E_HTSP_RELEASE_REQ] fxsls_onhook_release
9	Mar 1 01:08:24.006: htsp_timer_stop

Example C-4 illustrates an inbound call attempt via a digital E&M wink-start port. The router uses an H.323 gatekeeper to determine the VoIP destination address, but the call fails in this case because the gatekeeper is unable to resolve the E.164 address into an IP address and destination port. Line 1 shows that the router receives a trunk-seizure request (ABCD=1100), and line 2 shows the SETUP ACK (which is an internal software state for non-ISDN voice ports). Lines 3 through 5 show the router disconnecting before the call connection is completed, just as in Example C-3. This time, however, the ISDN cause code is 15 (encoded in 7-bit hexadecimal, see Appendix B), which indicates that the call is rejected. In this case, the router has a matching outbound dial peer for the call (that is, pointing to the gatekeeper), but the gatekeeper rejects the call (with an ARJ message) because it is unable to resolve the E.164 address.

Line 6 shows that the router receives an idle seizure indication from the attached phone switch (for example, the phone switch releases the trunk), after which the router starts a 480-ms timer to verify that the idle seizure request is intentional. Line 7 shows the timer expiring after 480 ms, and line 8 shows the router still receiving an on-hook state (ABCD=0000). Line 9 shows the router recognizing a RELEASE REQUEST signal and starting a 400-ms timer. Line 10 shows the timer expiring, after which the trunk is released and ready for another call.

Example C-4 *Inbound Call on E&M Wink-Start Port; Gatekeeper Cannot Resolve the
E.164 Destination*

Line#	Debugging Output
1	May 29 16:21:37.882 UTC: htsp_process_event: [4/1:0(2), 1.4 , 36] em_onhook_offhookem_onhookem_offhookem_onhookhtsp_setup_ind
2	May 29 16:21:37.882 UTC: htsp_process_event: [4/1:0(2), 1.7 , 8]
3	May 29 16:21:39.282 UTC: htsp_process_event: [4/1:0(2), 1.7 , 10]
4	May 29 16:21:39.302 UTC: htsp_pre_connect_disc, cdb = 61E7F9F4 cause = 15
5	May 29 16:21:39.302 UTC: htsp_process_event: [4/1:0(2), 1.7 , 9]
6	May 29 16:21:54.698 UTC: htsp_process_event: [4/1:0(2), 1.7 , 24] em_offhook_onhookem_stop_timers em_start_timer: 480 ms
7	May 29 16:21:55.178 UTC: htsp_process_event: [4/1:0(2), 1.8 , 41] em_delay_onhookpersistexpiryem_stop_timers em_start_timer: 600 ms
8	May 29 16:21:55.178 UTC: htsp_process_event: [4/1:0(2), 1.5 , 24] em_onhookpersist_onhook
9	May 29 16:21:55.178 UTC: htsp_process_event: [4/1:0(2), 1.6 , 7] em_onhook_discem_start_timer: 400 ms em_onhook
10	May 29 16:21:55.578 UTC: htsp_process_event: [4/1:0(2), 1.3 , 41] em_clr_timeout em_stop_timers

Debug VoIP CCAPI inout

As indicated in Appendix C, "Debug VPM Signal," the voice support in Cisco IOS is actually divided into different functional layers like the OSI model. This approach allows the physical operation of the voice port to be abstracted from the call-processing software. Appendix C explores the output of **debug vpm signal**, and the output of the **debug voip ccapi inout** command is explored here. This appendix is divided into the following example scenarios:

- Successful VoIP call setup and termination
- Failed VoIP call setup 1: H.323 gatekeeper problems
- Failed VoIP call setup 2: missing dial peer
- Failed VoIP call setup 3: codec negotiation failure

TIP

Because many of the telephony signaling processes are time-sensitive, it can be important to have a detailed record of the time sequence of events displayed in debugging (and logged) output. You can enable timestamps with resolution down to the millisecond with the following command on Cisco IOS devices (in global configuration mode):

```
voice-gw1#conf t
Enter configuration commands, one per line.  End with CNTL/Z.
voice-gw1(config)#service timestamps debug datetime msec
voice-gw1(config)#service timestamps log datetime msec
voice-gw1(config)#^Z
voice-gw1#
```

Successful VoIP Call Setup and Termination

The basic process within each router is that an inbound call leg is joined with an outbound call leg to form a call. Both the inbound and outbound call legs must be associated with dial peers, which are the points of administrative control that define the properties of the call legs.

Examples D-1 and D-2 illustrate the output of **debug voip ccapi inout** for a successful call setup and disconnect sequence. Example D-1 illustrates the output from the originating VoIP gateway, and Example D-2 illustrates the output for the same call from the perspective of the destination VoIP gateway. The originating side has a T1 interface to a PBX, with E&M wink-start signaling, and the destination has an FXS interface attached to a key system (which appears to the VoIP gateway just like an individual phone). However, the details of the physical interface type are abstracted from the Call Control Application Programming Interface (CCAPI), so the interface types are irrelevant for the **debug voip ccapi inout** command.

Many details are provided in this debugging output, but you do not generally need to know every detail to solve a given problem. The nature of the problem can help guide you to specific parts of the debugging output for more detailed examination. The following descriptions provide a fairly uniform level of detail for the different parts of the debugging output.

Calling VoIP Gateway

In Example D-1, line 5 shows the initial call processing that occurs when a voice port goes off-hook and the router prepares to handle an outbound call request. The vdbPtr uniquely identifies the call leg, but it is actually a pointer to a memory location that stores information about the call leg; a shorter callID value is a more practical identifier for the call leg. The callInfo structure stores the calling and called party numbers, along with the number types as defined in the Q.931 specification (such as national or international—see Table 17-3 in Chapter 17, "Establishing Network-Wide Calling Capability"). Line 6 shows the dial peer (peer_tag) that is associated with the inbound call leg, which, in this case, is dial peer 1. Also note that the destination pattern of the dial peer for the inbound call leg is reported as "calling=...." in line 5 (four wildcard digits, in this case). You can examine the running configuration of the gateway to determine whether dial peer 1 is a POTS or VoIP dial peer.

Disregard the callID value that is reported in line 6 because the variable is not yet initialized for the current call. Line 9 shows the callID assigned to the inbound call leg, which is encoded in decimal as 772. Line 11 shows a pointer being assigned to the memory location that will store the outbound call leg information. Note that in this line, the callID for the inbound call leg is reported in hexadecimal as 0x304, which is numerically equivalent to decimal 772. The characters 0x always indicate that the number is written in hexadecimal form, but hexadecimal numbers are occasionally reported without the 0x characters.

Line 12 shows the acknowledgment from the lower software layer (the session application) to proceed with the call setup. Line 13 shows the router generating an audio tone (which, in this case, is a dial tone) to the voice port. Table D-1 illustrates the different tone types that the router generates, along with the numeric value reported in the debugging output. Note that the values are in hexadecimal, even though they are not preceded by 0x. Each tone type is identified by setting a single bit in the 8-bit tone type variable.

Table D-1   *Tones Generated by the Router and Corresponding Numeric Values in Debugging Output*

Numeric Value	Tone Type
0x01	Ringback tone
0x02	Fax tone
0x04	Busy signal
0x08	Dial tone
0x10	Out-of-service tone
0x20	Confirmation tone (two beeps)
0x40	Disconnect tone
0x80	Alarm for phone left off-hook

Beginning in line 14, the call-processing software enters a control loop for collecting digits. Each iteration of the loop collects a digit and checks the dial peers for a match. If there is no dial peer match, then the loop is repeated.

Lines 14 through 25 show the first iteration of the loop. In both lines 14 and 19, you can see the digit 4 dialed by the user. Line 14 marks the start of a received tone, such as when a number button is pressed by the calling party. Line 19 marks the end of the received tone, such as when a number button is released by the calling party, and it indicates the duration of the tone as 100 ms.

If you compare the timestamps between lines 14 and 19, you will see that only 52 ms have elapsed, but the discrepancy is related to the time that it takes the router to process the incoming signal through the different software layers. The debugging output does not show the start of the digit tone until it has played long enough (around 50 ms) to be recognized as a specific tone, as opposed to a spurious noise signal. If you note the timestamp when the router provides the dial tone, you will see that this is approximately 108 ms before the received tone is completed. The quick response to the dial tone, combined with the fact that the tone duration is exactly 100 ms, provides a clue that the source of the tone is a machine (such as a PBX) instead of a human pressing a key. Alternatively, the source of the digit may be an electronic phone that generates a constant-length DTMF tone, no matter how long the user presses a key.

Lines 20 through 24 indicate processing by the lower software layers, and line 25 shows the result of the dial peer check. In this case, result=1 indicates that no dial peer matches the digit sequence, so the digit collection loop must begin again. A result=0 would indicate that a dial peer is matched, which would trigger an exit from the digit collection loop.

Lines 26 through 37 show another iteration of the digit collection loop. The user dialed the digit 3 for 110 ms, and the cumulative digit sequence {43} fails to match a dial peer, as shown in line 37. Lines 38 through 49 show a third iteration of the digit collection loop, which yields the digit 5 pressed for 100 ms. Again, the cumulative digit sequence {435} fails to match a dial peer. In the fourth iteration of the digit collection loop, as shown in lines 50 through 61, the digit 6 is pressed for 100 ms. Line 61 shows that the cumulative digit sequence {4356} matches a dial peer (result=0), and the digit collection loop is terminated.

Line 62 shows a prioritized list of dial peers that match the dialed digit sequence. Dial peer 4000 is a VoIP dial peer that is configured with a destination pattern of {4...}. Dial peer 1 is a POTS dial peer configured with a destination pattern of {....}. Line 63 shows the number of digits that explicitly match the destination pattern of the preferred dial peer, along with the prefix digits that are configured for the dial peer. Because VoIP dial peers do not strip the explicitly matched digits of a destination pattern, there is no need to use prefix digits in this case (hence, the empty field). The encapType(2) indicates that this is a VoIP call leg. Other encapType values include (0) for no encapsulation type, and (1) for voice (such as for a POTS call leg).

Line 64 indicates the call proceeding message from the call control application to the lower software layers. If the originating voice port were an ISDN PRI, the Q.931 CALL PROCEEDING message would be sent over the D channel from the VoIP gateway to the PBX. Line 65 shows the request to establish the outbound call leg, which marks the first signals sent by the router across the IP cloud to establish the call. Aside from the callID and the outbound dial peer, the line 65 also shows the mode of the call, which, in this case, is a normal switched call. Table D-2 identifies the different call modes that apply for VoIP.

Table D-2   *VoIP Call Modes and Associated Numeric Values*

Value	VoIP Call Mode
0	Normal switched call
1	Trunk connection
2	RTP loopback connection
3	Uncompressed loopback
4	Compressed loopback

If you read Chapter 17, you should understand the difference between the normal switched mode and the trunk connection mode. The loopback modes are available for diagnostic functions and are activated with special keywords in the session target:

```
Loopback:rtp
Loopback:uncompressed
Loopback:compressed
```

Figure D-1 illustrates the point at which the audio path is looped for each of the loopback types:

Figure D-1 *Audio Loopback Points for VoIP Diagnostics*

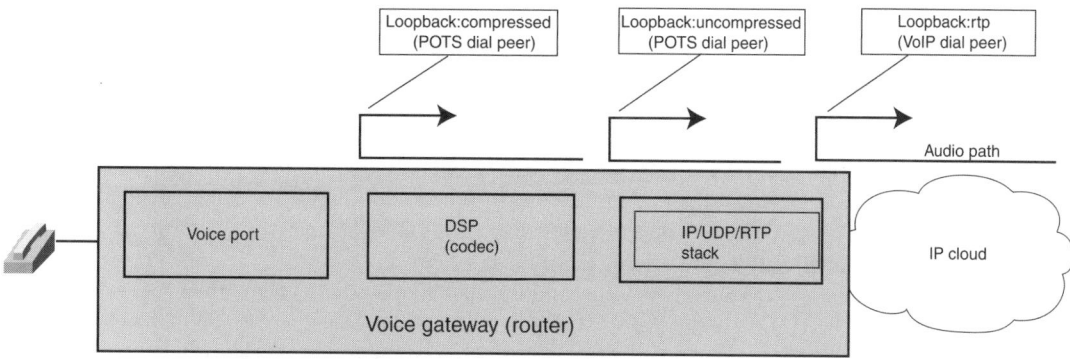

The next significant debugging output is in line 82, where the callID 0x305 is assigned for the outbound call leg. The cc_api_call_alert in line 83 is a progress alert received from the destination VoIP gateway by the outbound call leg of the local VoIP gateway. This alert message is forwarded to the inbound call leg, as shown by the ccCallAlert in line 88. The prog_ind=0x8 shows that a progress indicator has been received in-band as part of the audio path. If the **debug vpm signal** command was also active, you would see that the receive audio path has already been established (for the specific purpose of receiving in-band audio signals from the remote equipment). A prog_ind=0x0 would indicate an out-of-band message, such as through D-channel signaling on an ISDN PRI interface, or through the Q.931-style signals during the H.225.0 call setup across the IP cloud. The sig_ind=0x1 in line 88 indicates that the progress signal is a ring-back tone from the remote side. Table D-3 lists other common progress indicators that may be received. Taken together, the values in lines 83 and 88 indicate that the remote equipment has provided a ringback tone within the active audio path.

Table D-3 *Progress Indicators Shown in Debugging Output*

Signal Indicator	Type of Received Signal
0x0	Dial tone
0x1	Ringback tone
0x2	Intercept tone
0x3	Network congestion tone
0x4	Busy signal
0x5	Confirmation tone (two beeps)

continues

Table D-3 *Progress Indicators Shown in Debugging Output (Continued)*

Signal Indicator	Type of Received Signal
0x6	Answer tone
0x7	Call waiting tone
0x8	Alarm for phone left off-hook
0x9	Preemption (barge-in) tone

Line 89 shows the start of the process to join the inbound and outbound call legs. Notice that the call leg construct and the process of joining call legs is a flexible mechanism to permit not only point-to-point calls, but also multipoint conference calls, with the capability for individual call legs to join or leave the conference. In line 89, the confID (conference identification) is assigned, and the call legs that are joined to the conference are identified. Lines 90 and 91 show the details of the call legs being joined, such as which memory location pointers are involved. Note that the lines with cc_api_bridge_done all contain similar output, but from the perspective of each voice interface and call leg in the conference.

The capability exchange occurs in lines 92 through 125. In this process, the local and remote voice gateways inform each other of their capability to support different codec, fax, VAD, and modem options. These options are determined by the hardware/software support and the IOS configuration of the voice gateway on a per-dial-peer basis.

The codec capabilities set is expressed as a hexadecimal number. Each bit in the binary form of the number is associated with a single codec. Table D-4 shows the codecs for each bit position, identified with hexadecimal numbers as in the debugging output. Older IOS versions do not support all these codec options, and there may be additional codec options by the time you read this. Summing the hexadecimal values of each codec in an arbitrary set yields a compact representation of all codecs in the set. For example, a dial peer that is configured to support G.711 mu-law, A-law, G.728, and GSM full rate (via the **voice-class codec** configuration) would have a codec capability set of 0x0483. Similarly, fax rate capabilities are represented by the values shown in Table D-5, and VAD capabilities are represented by the values in Table D-6.

Table D-4 *Components of a Codec Capability Set*

Value	Codec Capabilities
0x0001	g711ulaw
0x0002	g711alaw
0x0004	g729r8
0x0008	g729ar8
0x0010	g726r16

Table D-4 *Components of a Codec Capability Set (Continued)*

Value	Codec Capabilities
0x0020	g726r24
0x0040	g726r32
0x0080	g728
0x0100	g723r63
0x0200	g723r53
0x0400	gsmfr
0x0800	g729br8
0x1000	g729abr8
0x2000	g723ar63
0x4000	g723ar53

Table D-5 *Fax Rate Capabilities*

Value	Fax Rate Capabilities
0x0001	Disabled
0x0002	Voice (maximum allowed by audio codec)
0x0004	14400 bps
0x0008	9600 bps
0x0010	7200 bps
0x0020	4800 bps
0x0040	2400 bps
0x0080	12000 bps

Table D-6 *Voice Activity Detection (VAD) Capabilities*

Value	VAD Capabilities
0x0001	Disabled
0x0002	Enabled

The two basic processes of the capabilities exchange are the capabilities indication (cc_api_caps_ind) and the capabilities acknowledgment (cc_api_caps_ack). You can determine which call leg is performing the indication or acknowledgment from the dstVdbPtr parameter. For the point-to-point call in this example, there are two dstVdbPtr values:

dstVdbPtr=0x624B86C4 (assigned to the local gateway in line 5)
dstVdbPtr=0x621B7D58 (assigned for the remote gateway in line 78)

You should ignore the first capabilities indication values stated in lines 92 through 94 because they do not change when you change the configuration of the remote voice gateway. In lines 100 through 102, the local gateway advertises the G.726r32 codec with an 80-byte payload and is VAD-enabled, as well as the maximum fax rate allowed by the voice codec. Line 103 shows the buffer depth values assigned for the dynamic audio playout buffer. In lines 104 through 106, the lower software layer (the session application) acknowledges the capabilities stated by the CCAPI. Lines 107 through 113 contain the same information as lines 100 through 106, which may be the result of duplicate debugging printf statements in different parts of the IOS software code.

Lines 114 through 116 contain the acknowledgment from the remote gateway for the codec capabilities advertised by the local gateway, which implies that the capabilities negotiation has been successful. Lines 119 through 121 contain the same information as lines 114 through 116, which again may be the result of duplicate printf statements in the IOS software code. Lines 124 and 125 are duplicates from the CCAPI to the lower-layer session application, which indicate that the codec negotiation has been successful.

Between lines 125 and 127, there is nearly a 32-second pause in the debugging output. During this period, the calling party is hearing ringback tone, and the phone is ringing for the called party. This is an indication that the remote voice port is most likely an FXS port because other types of voice ports (such as an E&M connection to a PBX) would answer the call sooner.

Lines 127 through 133 show the call connection process when the called party answers the ringing phone. In line 133, the list of alternate matching dial peers is flushed because a call has been successfully established to the current dial peer. Recall that the list of matching dial peers was displayed in line 62.

Between lines 133 and 135, there is again a significant pause in the debugging output. This pause marks the period when there are no state changes because the call is in an active steady-state condition. After a conversation that lasts nearly 23 seconds, the call is disconnected by the local gateway (that is, the calling party). Line 135 indicates that the calling party disconnected first (note the value of the vdbPtr and the callID), and cause=0x10 is the reason for the disconnection. This value is an ISDN cause code, which translates to normal call clearing. If you check the output of **show dial-peer** for the appropriate VoIP dial peer, you will see this text listed as the reason for the last disconnect. Consult Appendix B, "ISDN Cause Codes," for a detailed listing of the ISDN cause codes defined in ITU Q.850 and referenced in Q.931. The ISDN cause codes are stated in the debugging output in 7-bit hexadecimal form.

Lines 136 through 160 show the software state changes for the session application during the call termination, the removal of the inbound and outbound call legs from the conference (lines 142 and 143), and the teardown of the conference with the specified confID.

Example D-1 *Successful Call Completion from the Perspective of the Originating VoIP Gateway*

Line Number	Cisco IOS Debugging Output
1	`voice-gw2#deb voip ccapi inout`
2	`voip ccAPI function enter/exit debugging is on`
3	`voice-gw2#term mon`
4	`voice-gw2#`
5	`Jul 28 12:12:00.848 UTC: cc_api_call_setup_ind (vdbPtr=0x624B86C4, callInfo={called=,called_oct3=0x8●,calling=....,calling_oct3=0xEA,calle d_oct3a=0x0,`
6	`        fdest=0 peer_tag=1},callID=0x62472490)`
7	`Jul 28 12:12:00.848 UTC: cc_api_call_setup_ind type 1 , prot 0`
8	`Jul 28 12:12:00.848 UTC: cc_process_call_setup_ind (event=0x625967EC) handed call to app "SESSION"`
9	`Jul 28 12:12:00.848 UTC: sess_appl: ev(23=CC_EV_CALL_SETUP_IND), cid(772), disp(0)`
10	`Jul 28 12:12:00.848 UTC: sess_appl: ev(SSA_EV_CALL_SETUP_IND), cid(772), disp(0)`
11	`Jul 28 12:12:00.848 UTC: ccCallSetContext (callID=0x304, context=0x626D5E9C)`
12	`Jul 28 12:12:00.848 UTC: ccCallSetupAck (callID=0x304)`
13	`Jul 28 12:12:00.848 UTC: ccGenerateTone (callID=0x304 tone=8)`
14	`Jul 28 12:12:01.904 UTC: cc_api_call_digit_begin (vdbPtr=0x624B86C4, callID=0x304, digit=4, flags=0x1, timestamp=0xA4F5FA87, expiration=0x0)`
15	`Jul 28 12:12:01.908 UTC: sess_appl: ev(10=CC_EV_CALL_DIGIT_BEGIN), cid(772), disp(0)`
16	`Jul 28 12:12:01.908 UTC: cid(772)st(SSA_CS_MAPPING)ev(SSA_EV_DIGIT_BEGIN)`
17	`oldst(SSA_CS_MAPPING)cfid(-1)csize(0)in(1)fDest(0)`
18	`Jul 28 12:12:01.908 UTC: ssaIgnore cid(772), st(SSA_CS_MAPPING),oldst(0), ev(10)`
19	`Jul 28 12:12:01.956 UTC: cc_api_call_digit (vdbPtr=0x624B86C4, callID=0x304, digit=4, duration=100,tag 0, callparty 0 )`
20	`Jul 28 12:12:01.956 UTC: sess_appl: ev(9=CC_EV_CALL_DIGIT), cid(772), disp(0)`
21	`Jul 28 12:12:01.956 UTC: cid(772)st(SSA_CS_MAPPING)ev(SSA_EV_CALL_DIGIT)`
22	`oldst(SSA_CS_MAPPING)cfid(-1)csize(0)in(1)fDest(0)`
23	`Jul 28 12:12:01.956 UTC: ssaDigit`
24	`Jul 28 12:12:01.956 UTC: ssaDigit, callinfo , digit 4, tag 0,callparty 0`
25	`Jul 28 12:12:01.956 UTC: ssaDigit, calling ....,result 1`
26	`Jul 28 12:12:02.044 UTC: cc_api_call_digit_begin (vdbPtr=0x624B86C4, callID=0x304, digit=3, flags=0x1, timestamp=0xA4F5FA87, expiration=0x0)`
27	`Jul 28 12:12:02.048 UTC: sess_appl: ev(10=CC_EV_CALL_DIGIT_BEGIN), cid(772), disp(0)`
28	`Jul 28 12:12:02.048 UTC: cid(772)st(SSA_CS_MAPPING)ev(SSA_EV_DIGIT_BEGIN)`
29	`oldst(SSA_CS_MAPPING)cfid(-1)csize(0)in(1)fDest(0)`

continues

Example D-1 *Successful Call Completion from the Perspective of the Originating VoIP Gateway (Continued)*

```
30      Jul 28 12:12:02.048 UTC: ssaIgnore cid(772), st(SSA_CS_MAPPING),oldst(0),
        ev(10)
31      Jul 28 12:12:02.104 UTC: cc_api_call_digit (vdbPtr=0x624B86C4,
        callID=0x304, digit=3, duration=110,tag 0, callparty 0 )
32      Jul 28 12:12:02.108 UTC: sess_appl: ev(9=CC_EV_CALL_DIGIT), cid(772),
        disp(0)
33      Jul 28 12:12:02.108 UTC: cid(772)st(SSA_CS_MAPPING)ev(SSA_EV_CALL_DIGIT)
34      oldst(SSA_CS_MAPPING)cfid(-1)csize(0)in(1)fDest(0)
35      Jul 28 12:12:02.108 UTC: ssaDigit
36      Jul 28 12:12:02.108 UTC: ssaDigit, callinfo , digit 43, tag 0,callparty 0
37      Jul 28 12:12:02.108 UTC: ssaDigit, calling ....,result 1
38      Jul 28 12:12:02.196 UTC: cc_api_call_digit_begin (vdbPtr=0x624B86C4,
        callID=0x304, digit=5, flags=0x1, timestamp=0xA4F5FA87, expiration=0x0)
39      Jul 28 12:12:02.196 UTC: sess_appl: ev(10=CC_EV_CALL_DIGIT_BEGIN),
        cid(772), disp(0)
40      Jul 28 12:12:02.196 UTC:
        cid(772)st(SSA_CS_MAPPING)ev(SSA_EV_DIGIT_BEGIN)
41      oldst(SSA_CS_MAPPING)cfid(-1)csize(0)in(1)fDest(0)
42      Jul 28 12:12:02.196 UTC: ssaIgnore cid(772), st(SSA_CS_MAPPING),oldst(0),
        ev(10)
43      Jul 28 12:12:02.248 UTC: cc_api_call_digit (vdbPtr=0x624B86C4,
        callID=0x304, digit=5, duration=100,tag 0, callparty 0 )
44      Jul 28 12:12:02.248 UTC: sess_appl: ev(9=CC_EV_CALL_DIGIT), cid(772),
        disp(0)
45      Jul 28 12:12:02.248 UTC: cid(772)st(SSA_CS_MAPPING)ev(SSA_EV_CALL_DIGIT)
46      oldst(SSA_CS_MAPPING)cfid(-1)csize(0)in(1)fDest(0)
47      Jul 28 12:12:02.248 UTC: ssaDigit
48      Jul 28 12:12:02.248 UTC: ssaDigit, callinfo , digit 435, tag 0,callparty 0
49      Jul 28 12:12:02.248 UTC: ssaDigit, calling ....,result 1
50      Jul 28 12:12:02.336 UTC: cc_api_call_digit_begin (vdbPtr=0x624B86C4,
        callID=0x304, digit=6, flags=0x1, timestamp=0xA4F5FA87, expiration=0x0)
51      Jul 28 12:12:02.336 UTC: sess_appl: ev(10=CC_EV_CALL_DIGIT_BEGIN),
        cid(772), disp(0)
52      Jul 28 12:12:02.336 UTC:
        cid(772)st(SSA_CS_MAPPING)ev(SSA_EV_DIGIT_BEGIN)
53      oldst(SSA_CS_MAPPING)cfid(-1)csize(0)in(1)fDest(0)
54      Jul 28 12:12:02.336 UTC: ssaIgnore cid(772), st(SSA_CS_MAPPING),oldst(0),
        ev(10)
55      Jul 28 12:12:02.388 UTC: cc_api_call_digit (vdbPtr=0x624B86C4,
        callID=0x304, digit=6, duration=100,tag 0, callparty 0 )
56      Jul 28 12:12:02.388 UTC: sess_appl: ev(9=CC_EV_CALL_DIGIT), cid(772),
        disp(0)
57      Jul 28 12:12:02.388 UTC: cid(772)st(SSA_CS_MAPPING)ev(SSA_EV_CALL_DIGIT)
58      oldst(SSA_CS_MAPPING)cfid(-1)csize(0)in(1)fDest(0)
59      Jul 28 12:12:02.388 UTC: ssaDigit
60      Jul 28 12:12:02.388 UTC: ssaDigit, callinfo , digit 4356, tag 0,callparty
        0
61      Jul 28 12:12:02.388 UTC: ssaDigit, calling ....,result 0
62      Jul 28 12:12:02.388 UTC: ssaSetupPeer cid(772) peer list:  tag(4000)
        called number (4356)  tag(1) called number (4356)
63      Jul 28 12:12:02.388 UTC: ssaSetupPeer cid(772), destPat(4356),
        matched(1), prefix(), peer(6266E184), peer->encapType (2)
64      Jul 28 12:12:02.388 UTC: ccCallProceeding (callID=0x304, prog_ind=0x0)
65      Jul 28 12:12:02.388 UTC: ccCallSetupRequest (Inbound call = 0x304,
        outbound peer =4000, dest=, params=0x626D5EB0 mode=0, *callID=0x6259E100)
```

Example D-1 *Successful Call Completion from the Perspective of the Originating VoIP Gateway (Continued)*

```
66      Jul 28 12:12:02.388 UTC: ccCallSetupRequest numbering_type 0x81
67      Jul 28 12:12:02.388 UTC: callingNumber=...., calledNumber=4356,
        redirectNumber=
68      Jul 28 12:12:02.388 UTC: accountNumber=, pinNumber=
69      Jul 28 12:12:02.388 UTC: finalDestFlag=0,
        guid=153f.1d20.13f9.02b3.0000.0000.1428.75c4
70      Jul 28 12:12:02.388 UTC: peer_tag=1
71      Jul 28 12:12:02.388 UTC:  dest_pat 4...
72      Jul 28 12:12:02.388 UTC: digit_strip_checking: dest_pat4...
73      Jul 28 12:12:02.388 UTC:  strip 1, peer_string 4...
74      Jul 28 12:12:02.388 UTC: callingNumber=...., calledNumber=4356,
        redirectNumber=
75      Jul 28 12:12:02.388 UTC: accountNumber=, pinNumber=
76      Jul 28 12:12:02.388 UTC: finalDestFlag=0,
        guid=153f.1d20.13f9.02b3.0000.0000.1428.75c4
77      Jul 28 12:12:02.388 UTC: peer_tag=4000
78      Jul 28 12:12:02.388 UTC: ccIFCallSetupRequest: (vdbPtr=0x621B7D58, dest=,
        callParams={called=4356,called_oct3=0x81,calling=....,calling_oct3=0xEA
        ,fdest=0, voice_peer_tag=4000},mode=0x0) vdbPtr type = 1
79      Jul 28 12:12:02.388 UTC: ccIFCallSetupRequest: (vdbPtr=0x621B7D58, dest=,
        callParams={called=4356, called_oct3 0x81,
80              calling=....,calling_oct3 0xEA,fdest=0, voice_peer_tag=4000},
        mode=0x0)
81      Jul 28 12:12:02.388 UTC: ccSaveDialpeerTag (callID=0x304, dialpeer_tag=
82      Jul 28 12:12:02.388 UTC: ccCallSetContext (callID=0x305,
        context=0x626AA6B8)
83      Jul 28 12:12:02.828 UTC: cc_api_call_alert(vdbPtr=0x621B7D58,
        callID=0x305, prog_ind=0x8, sig_ind=0x1)
84      Jul 28 12:12:02.828 UTC: sess_appl: ev(7=CC_EV_CALL_ALERT), cid(773),
        disp(0)
85      Jul 28 12:12:02.828 UTC:
        cid(773)st(SSA_CS_CALL_SETTING)ev(SSA_EV_CALL_ALERT)
86      oldst(SSA_CS_MAPPING)cfid(-1)csize(0)in(0)fDest(0)
87      Jul 28 12:12:02.828 UTC: -
        cid2(772)st2(SSA_CS_CALL_SETTING)oldst2(SSA_CS_MAPPING)
88      Jul 28 12:12:02.828 UTC: ccCallAlert (callID=0x304, prog_ind=0x8,
        sig_ind=0x1)
89      Jul 28 12:12:02.828 UTC: ccConferenceCreate (confID=0x6259E360,
        callID1=0x304, callID2=0x305, tag=0x0)
90      Jul 28 12:12:02.828 UTC: cc_api_bridge_done (confID=0x157,
        srcIF=0x621B7D58, srcCallID=0x305, dstCallID=0x304, disposition=0,
        tag=0x0)
91      Jul 28 12:12:02.828 UTC: cc_api_bridge_done (confID=0x157,
        srcIF=0x624B86C4, srcCallID=0x304, dstCallID=0x305, disposition=0,
        tag=0x0)
92      Jul 28 12:12:02.828 UTC: cc_api_caps_ind (dstVdbPtr=0x621B7D58,
        dstCallId=0x305, srcCallId=0x304,
93          caps={codec=0x887F, fax_rate=0x7F, vad=0x3, modem=0x61B8C5C0
94              codec_bytes=0, signal_type=3})
95      Jul 28 12:12:02.828 UTC: cc_api_caps_ind (Playout: mode 0, initial
        38464,min 24811, max 38168)
96      Jul 28 12:12:02.828 UTC: sess_appl: ev(28=CC_EV_CONF_CREATE_DONE),
        cid(772), disp(0)
```

continues

Example D-1 *Successful Call Completion from the Perspective of the Originating VoIP Gateway (Continued)*

```
97     Jul 28 12:12:02.828 UTC:
       cid(772)st(SSA_CS_CONFERENCING_ALERT)ev(SSA_EV_CONF_CREATE_DONE)
98     oldst(SSA_CS_MAPPING)cfid(343)csize(0)in(1)fDest(0)
99     Jul 28 12:12:02.828 UTC: -
       cid2(773)st2(SSA_CS_CONFERENCING_ALERT)oldst2(SSA_CS_CALL_SETTING)
100    Jul 28 12:12:03.332 UTC: cc_api_caps_ind (dstVdbPtr=0x624B86C4,
       dstCallId=0x304, srcCallId=0x305,
101        caps={codec=0x40, fax_rate=0x2, vad=0x2, modem=0x2
102            codec_bytes=80, signal_type=2})
103    Jul 28 12:12:03.332 UTC: cc_api_caps_ind (Playout: mode 1, initial 60,min
       4, max 200)
104    Jul 28 12:12:03.332 UTC: cc_api_caps_ack (dstVdbPtr=0x624B86C4,
       dstCallId=0x304, srcCallId=0x305,
105        caps={codec=0x40, fax_rate=0x2, vad=0x2, modem=0x2
106            codec_bytes=80, signal_type=2})
107    Jul 28 12:12:03.336 UTC: cc_api_caps_ind (dstVdbPtr=0x624B86C4,
       dstCallId=0x304, srcCallId=0x305,
108        caps={codec=0x40, fax_rate=0x2, vad=0x2, modem=0x2
109            codec_bytes=80, signal_type=2})
110    Jul 28 12:12:03.336 UTC: cc_api_caps_ind (Playout: mode 1, initial 60,min
       4, max 200)
111    Jul 28 12:12:03.336 UTC: cc_api_caps_ack (dstVdbPtr=0x624B86C4,
       dstCallId=0x304, srcCallId=0x305,
112        caps={codec=0x40, fax_rate=0x2, vad=0x2, modem=0x2
113            codec_bytes=80, signal_type=2})
114    Jul 28 12:12:03.336 UTC: cc_api_caps_ack (dstVdbPtr=0x621B7D58,
       dstCallId=0x305, srcCallId=0x304,
115        caps={codec=0x40, fax_rate=0x2, vad=0x2, modem=0x2
116            codec_bytes=80, signal_type=2})
117    Jul 28 12:12:03.336 UTC: cc_api_voice_mode_event , callID=0x304
118    Jul 28 12:12:03.336 UTC: Call Pointer =626D5E9C
119    Jul 28 12:12:03.336 UTC: cc_api_caps_ack (dstVdbPtr=0x621B7D58,
       dstCallId=0x305, srcCallId=0x304,
120        caps={codec=0x40, fax_rate=0x2, vad=0x2, modem=0x2
121            codec_bytes=80, signal_type=2})
122    Jul 28 12:12:03.336 UTC: cc_api_voice_mode_event , callID=0x304
123    Jul 28 12:12:03.336 UTC: Call Pointer =626D5E9C
124    Jul 28 12:12:03.336 UTC: sess_appl: ev(37=CC_EV_VOICE_MODE_DONE),
       cid(772), disp(0)
125    Jul 28 12:12:03.336 UTC: sess_appl: ev(37=CC_EV_VOICE_MODE_DONE),
       cid(772), disp(0)
126    voice-gw2#
127    Jul 28 12:12:35.112 UTC: cc_api_call_connected(vdbPtr=0x621B7D58,
       callID=0x305)
128    Jul 28 12:12:35.112 UTC: sess_appl: ev(8=CC_EV_CALL_CONNECTED), cid(773),
       disp(0)
129    Jul 28 12:12:35.112 UTC:
       cid(773)st(SSA_CS_CONFERENCED_ALERT)ev(SSA_EV_CALL_CONNECTED)
130    oldst(SSA_CS_CALL_SETTING)cfid(343)csize(0)in(0)fDest(0)
131    Jul 28 12:12:35.112 UTC: -
       cid2(772)st2(SSA_CS_CONFERENCED_ALERT)oldst2(SSA_CS_CONFERENCING_ALERT)
132    Jul 28 12:12:35.112 UTC: ccCallConnect (callID=0x304)
133    Jul 28 12:12:35.112 UTC: ssaFlushPeerTagQueue cid(772) peer list:  tag(1)
       called number (4356)
```

Example D-1 *Successful Call Completion from the Perspective of the Originating VoIP Gateway (Continued)*

```
134     voice-gw2#
135     Jul 28 12:12:58.124 UTC: cc_api_call_disconnected(vdbPtr=0x624B86C4,
        callID=0x304, cause=0x10)
136     Jul 28 12:12:58.124 UTC: sess_appl: ev(12=CC_EV_CALL_DISCONNECTED),
        cid(772), disp(0)
137     Jul 28 12:12:58.124 UTC:
        cid(772)st(SSA_CS_ACTIVE)ev(SSA_EV_CALL_DISCONNECTED)
138     oldst(SSA_CS_CONFERENCING_ALERT)cfid(343)csize(0)in(1)fDest(0)
139     Jul 28 12:12:58.124 UTC: -
        cid2(773)st2(SSA_CS_ACTIVE)oldst2(SSA_CS_CONFERENCED_ALERT)
140     Jul 28 12:12:58.124 UTC: ssa: Disconnected cid(772) state(5) cause(0x10)
141     Jul 28 12:12:58.124 UTC: ccConferenceDestroy (confID=0x157, tag=0x0)
142     Jul 28 12:12:58.124 UTC: cc_api_bridge_drop_done (confID=0x157,
        srcIF=0x621B7D58, srcCallID=0x305, dstCallID=0x304, disposition=0
        tag=0x0)
143     Jul 28 12:12:58.124 UTC: cc_api_bridge_drop_done (confID=0x157,
        srcIF=0x624B86C4, srcCallID=0x304, dstCallID=0x305, disposition=0
        tag=0x0)
144     Jul 28 12:12:58.124 UTC: sess_appl: ev(29=CC_EV_CONF_DESTROY_DONE),
        cid(772), disp(0)
145     Jul 28 12:12:58.124 UTC:
        cid(772)st(SSA_CS_CONF_DESTROYING)ev(SSA_EV_CONF_DESTROY_DONE)
146     oldst(SSA_CS_ACTIVE)cfid(-1)csize(0)in(1)fDest(0)
147     Jul 28 12:12:58.124 UTC: -
        cid2(773)st2(SSA_CS_CONF_DESTROYING)oldst2(SSA_CS_CONFERENCED_ALERT)
148     Jul 28 12:12:58.124 UTC: ccCallDisconnect (callID=0x304, cause=0x10
        tag=0x0)
149     Jul 28 12:12:58.124 UTC: ccCallDisconnect (callID=0x305, cause=0x10
        tag=0x0)
150     Jul 28 12:12:58.136 UTC: cc_api_call_disconnect_done(vdbPtr=0x621B7D58,
        callID=0x305, disp=0, tag=0x0)
151     Jul 28 12:12:58.136 UTC: sess_appl: ev(13=CC_EV_CALL_DISCONNECT_DONE),
        cid(773), disp(0)
152     Jul 28 12:12:58.136 UTC:
        cid(773)st(SSA_CS_DISCONNECTING)ev(SSA_EV_CALL_DISCONNECT_DONE)
153     oldst(SSA_CS_CONFERENCED_ALERT)cfid(-1)csize(0)in(0)fDest(0)
154     Jul 28 12:12:58.136 UTC: -
        cid2(772)st2(SSA_CS_DISCONNECTING)oldst2(SSA_CS_CONF_DESTROYING)
155     Jul 28 12:12:58.924 UTC: cc_api_call_feature: (vdbPtr=0x624B86C4,
        callID=0x304,feature_ind.type=5
156     Jul 28 12:12:58.924 UTC: cc_api_call_disconnect_done(vdbPtr=0x624B86C4,
        callID=0x304, disp=0, tag=0x0)
157     Jul 28 12:12:58.924 UTC: sess_appl: ev(27=CC_EV_CALL_FEATURE), cid(772),
        disp(0)
158     Jul 28 12:12:58.924 UTC: sess_appl: ev(13=CC_EV_CALL_DISCONNECT_DONE),
        cid(772), disp(0)
159     Jul 28 12:12:58.924 UTC:
        cid(772)st(SSA_CS_DISCONNECTING)ev(SSA_EV_CALL_DISCONNECT_DONE)
160     oldst(SSA_CS_CONF_DESTROYING)cfid(-1)csize(1)in(1)fDest(0)
161     voice-gw2#
```

Called VoIP Gateway

Example D-2 shows the debugging output of **debug voip ccapi inout** for the same call, from the perspective of the destination VoIP gateway. Note that the command **terminal monitor** is issued from privileged exec mode, so the debugging output is displayed to the virtual terminal (Telnet connection).

Line 5 shows the inbound call setup request. The called party number is immediately available in this case because the originating VoIP gateway collected all the dialed digits and sent them as part of the setup request to this gateway. Again, disregard the CallID value reported in line 5 because it has not been initialized for the current call. Line 8 shows the callID assignment for the current call. Note the field fdest=1 in line 5, which indicates that this VoIP gateway is the final destination of the call. Looking back at Example D-1, you can see fdest=0 on the VoIP gateway that originates the call setup.

The calling party number is generally set to the destination pattern of the dial peer that matches the inbound call leg on the originating VoIP gateway. In the present example, the calling party number field is empty because the matching inbound POTS dial peer at the ingress to the VoIP network did not have any explicitly defined digits. The matching destination pattern was {....}, which represents four wildcard digits. Example D-6 does show a nonempty calling party number in the setup messages on the called VoIP gateway because the inbound POTS dial peer on the originating gateway has a destination pattern of {9}. Because there is no calling party number in the call setup request, the inbound call leg does not match any of the VoIP dial peers configured on the router. The peer_tag=0 indicates that the inbound call leg matches the null dial peer.

NOTE   The debugging output in Example D-2 reveals an interesting anomaly because the null dial peer should be associated with the g729r8 codec (see Chapter 17). Note that the discussion of lines 38 through 49 will reveal a different codec advertisement, which is in fact consistent with the actual router configuration (not shown here).

The calling party field in line 5 should really be set to {....} in this case, and the inbound VoIP dial peer with a destination pattern of {....} should match. The codec negotiation actually proceeds as would be expected based on such a match, which casts doubt on the accuracy of the null dial peer match shown in line 5. The empty calling party field and the matching peer_tag=0 in line 5 is not consistent with the expected inbound dial peer match based on the configuration of the gateway, or the actual behavior of the gateway during the codec negotiation.

The calling VoIP gateway in this example is a Cisco 7206 running IOS 12.0(7)XK1, and the called VoIP gateway is a Cisco 2611 running IOS 12.0(7)T1 because of memory constraints. You should not encounter this mild anomaly (which is noticeable only in the debugging output) when you run up-to-date IOS images.

Line 10 shows the ordered list of dial peers that match the outbound call leg (dial peers 4356, 1000, and 1). Because the call arrived via the IP network, the outbound call leg must be a POTS dial peer (because tandem call routing is not supported with VoIP as of IOS 12.1(2)T; see Chapter 17 for an explanation of tandem call routing). Line 12 shows that the call is using mode=0, which means that it is a normal switched call (as opposed to a trunk call or an audio loopback test; see Table D-2).

Line 17 shows the request for the outbound POTS call leg to be joined to the call, line 18 shows a CallID being assigned to the outbound call leg, and line 19 shows the response back to the originating VoIP gateway that the call is proceeding. The prog_ind=0x0 informs you that the response is part of the H.225.0 call signaling (similar to a Q.931 PROGRESS message), as opposed to an in-band audio signal. Remember that prog_ind=0x8 identifies in-band audio signals.

Although line 19 shows the CCAPI software sending a progress message to the originating VoIP gateway, lines 20 and 21 show the CCAPI software receiving a progress message from the lower software layers (the session application). The session application is acting on behalf of the physical voice interface that is associated with the outbound POTS call leg. This process is similar to the link-by-link progress messages that occur in an ISDN Q.931 or an H.225.0 call setup. The difference is that the signaling happens at the interface between the different software layers (session application and CCAPI), not between different physical boxes. The concept is the same, though, because call setup signals still pass between two separate entities.

Line 22 shows the CCAPI software receiving (from the session application) an audible ringback tone, as evidenced by the prog_ind=0x8 and the sig_ind=0x1 (from Table D-1). Line 28 shows the gateway flushing out the alternate dial peer list because the current dial peer appears to be connecting successfully. If the call processing with the current dial peer fails after this point, the router cannot try alternate dial peers to complete the call. In line 29, the CCAPI software forwards the audible ringback tone to the originating VoIP gateway. You can distinguish between whether the CCAPI is sending something or receiving a signal by noting the CallID associated with the signal, and having an idea of the intended direction of the signal. For example, you should expect the ringback tone to be heading from the called gateway toward the calling gateway. You can find when the CallID values are assigned by looking for lines that begin with ccCallSetContext, such as lines 8 and 18 in Example D-2.

Line 30 shows the creation of a conference to which the inbound and outbound call legs will be joined, line 31 shows the inbound VoIP call leg joining the conference, and line 32 shows the outbound POTS call leg joining the conference. Lines 33 through 35 show the first capabilities indication message that you can generally disregard.

Lines 38 through 40 show the codec capabilities advertisement from the originating VoIP gateway (note the SrcCallID), and lines 41 through 43 show the local gateway acknowledging these capabilities back to the originating VoIP gateway. This first advertisement identifies the g711ulaw codec with 160-byte packets (see Tables D-4 through D-6).

Lines 44 through 46 show another codec capabilities advertisement from the originating VoIP gateway, and lines 47 through 49 show the local gateway acknowledging these capabilities back to the originating VoIP gateway. This advertisement identifies the g726r32 codec with 160-byte packets.

Lines 50 through 52 show the originating VoIP gateway acknowledging the acknowledgment (completing a three-way handshake) for the g711ulaw codec, and lines 53 through 55 show the same process for the second codec (g726r32). To summarize the codec negotiation, the originating gateway offered two different codecs to the destination gateway, both of which were acknowledged by the called gateway. The originating gateway then acknowledged the responses of the called gateway, so both gateways acknowledged the capabilities of each other.

At this point, the originating gateway selects one of the codecs that both gateways support (the one with the lowest preference configured in the voice class on the originating VoIP gateway) to proceed with the call. If you could examine the configuration of the calling VoIP gateway, you would see that the g726r32 codec is the most preferred codec in the voice class that is applied to the outbound VoIP dial peer for this call.

The long lapse in output between lines 53 and 57 (as indicated by the timestamps) is the period during which a ringing alert is sent to the called party. As was mentioned in the previous section, the long lapse at this stage indicates that the voice port is most likely an FXS port because other physical port types would respond sooner.

Line 57 shows the called party answering the call, in the form of a message from the session application to the CCAPI. The CCAPI, in turn, passes the message as an H.225.0 CONNECT message to the originating VoIP gateway in line 60. Again, you can determine whether signals are entering or leaving the CCAPI software by knowing the direction that the signals should be traveling and by paying attention to the callID values associated with the lines in the debugging output. In this case, the CONNECT message should be traveling from the called party to the calling party when the called party answers the phone.

Line 61 shows the alternate dial peer list being flushed, but it is already empty because it was flushed at an earlier stage in the call setup. At this point, the call is active and the parties communicate for approximately 23 seconds (as determined by the difference between timestamps in lines 60 and 63).

The call disconnection is initiated by the calling VoIP gateway, as shown in line 63. You can verify this because the inbound VoIP call leg (identified by the callID), as opposed to the outbound POTS call leg, is disconnected in line 63. The call is disconnected with cause=0x10 as the reason, which you can see from Appendix B indicates a normal call clearing. The remainder of the output mirrors the disconnect sequence described for Example D-1.

Example D-2 *Successful Call Completion from the Perspective of the Destination VoIP Gateway*

Line Number	Cisco IOS Debugging Output
1	voice-gw3#**terminal monitor**
2	voice-gw3#**debug voip ccapi inout**
3	voip ccAPI function enter/exit debugging is on
4	voice-gw3#
5	Jul 28 12:12:02.793 UTC: cc_api_call_setup_ind (vdbPtr=0x8167E948, callInfo={called=4356, calling=, fdest=1 peer_tag=0}, callID=0x817851E8)
6	Jul 28 12:12:02.797 UTC: cc_process_call_setup_ind (event=0x8170F2A8) handed call to app "SESSION"
7	Jul 28 12:12:02.797 UTC: sess_appl: ev(19=CC_EV_CALL_SETUP_IND), cid(388), disp(0)
8	Jul 28 12:12:02.797 UTC: ccCallSetContext (callID=0x184, context=0x817A5020)
9	Jul 28 12:12:02.801 UTC: ssaCallSetupInd finalDest cllng(), clled(4356)
10	Jul 28 12:12:02.801 UTC: ssaSetupPeer cid(388) peer list: tag(4356) tag(1000) tag(1)
11	Jul 28 12:12:02.801 UTC: ssaSetupPeer cid(388), destPat(4356), matched(4), prefix(), peer(817E2EA8)
12	Jul 28 12:12:02.801 UTC: ccCallSetupRequest (peer=0x817E2EA8, dest=, params=0x817A5034 mode=0, *callID=0x817142C8)
13	Jul 28 12:12:02.801 UTC: callingNumber=, calledNumber=4356, redirectNumber=
14	Jul 28 12:12:02.805 UTC: accountNumber=, finalDestFlag=1,
15	guid=153f.1d20.13f9.02b3.0000.0000.1428.75c4
16	Jul 28 12:12:02.805 UTC: peer_tag=4356
17	Jul 28 12:12:02.805 UTC: ccIFCallSetupRequest: (vdbPtr=0x8170BAEC, dest=, callParams={called=4356, calling=, fdest=1, voice_peer_tag=4356}, mode=0x0)
18	Jul 28 12:12:02.805 UTC: ccCallSetContext (callID=0x185, context=0x817A396C)
19	Jul 28 12:12:02.805 UTC: ccCallProceeding (callID=0x184, prog_ind=0x0)
20	Jul 28 12:12:02.809 UTC: cc_api_call_proceeding(vdbPtr=0x8170BAEC, callID=0x185,
21	prog_ind=0x0)
22	Jul 28 12:12:02.813 UTC: cc_api_call_alert(vdbPtr=0x8170BAEC, callID=0x185, prog_ind=0x8, sig_ind=0x1)
23	Jul 28 12:12:02.813 UTC: sess_appl: ev(17=CC_EV_CALL_PROCEEDING), cid(389), disp(0)
24	Jul 28 12:12:02.813 UTC: ssa: cid(389)st(1)oldst(0)cfid(-1)csize(0)in(0)fDest(0)-cid2(388)st2(1)oldst2(0)
25	Jul 28 12:12:02.813 UTC: ssaIgnore cid(389), st(1),oldst(1), ev(17)
26	Jul 28 12:12:02.813 UTC: sess_appl: ev(7=CC_EV_CALL_ALERT), cid(389), disp(0)
27	Jul 28 12:12:02.813 UTC: ssa: cid(389)st(1)oldst(1)cfid(-1)csize(0)in(0)fDest(0)-cid2(388)st2(1)oldst2(0)
28	Jul 28 12:12:02.817 UTC: ssaFlushPeerTagQueue cid(388) peer list: tag(1000) tag(1)
29	Jul 28 12:12:02.817 UTC: ccCallAlert (callID=0x184, prog_ind=0x8, sig_ind=0x1)
30	Jul 28 12:12:02.817 UTC: ccConferenceCreate (confID=0x81714318, callID1=0x184, callID2=0x185, tag=0x0)

continues

Example D-2 *Successful Call Completion from the Perspective of the Destination VoIP Gateway (Continued)*

```
31      Jul 28 12:12:02.817 UTC: cc_api_bridge_done (confID=0xA8,
        srcIF=0x8167E948, srcCallID=0x184, dstCallID=0x185, disposition=0,
        tag=0x0)
32      Jul 28 12:12:02.825 UTC: cc_api_bridge_done (confID=0xA8,
        srcIF=0x8170BAEC, srcCallID=0x185, dstCallID=0x184, disposition=0,
        tag=0x0)
33      Jul 28 12:12:02.829 UTC: cc_api_caps_ind (dstVdbPtr=0x8167E948,
        dstCallId=0x184, srcCallId=0x185,
34          caps={codec=0x887F, fax_rate=0x7F, vad=0x3, modem=0x0
35              codec_bytes=0, signal_type=3})
36      Jul 28 12:12:02.829 UTC: sess_appl: ev(23=CC_EV_CONF_CREATE_DONE),
        cid(388), disp(0)
37      Jul 28 12:12:02.829 UTC: ssa:
        cid(388)st(3)oldst(0)cfid(168)csize(0)in(1)fDest(1)-
        cid2(389)st2(3)oldst2(1)
38      Jul 28 12:12:03.122 UTC: cc_api_caps_ind (dstVdbPtr=0x8170BAEC,
        dstCallId=0x185, srcCallId=0x184,
39          caps={codec=0x1, fax_rate=0x2, vad=0x2, modem=0x1
40              codec_bytes=160, signal_type=0})
41      Jul 28 12:12:03.122 UTC: cc_api_caps_ack (dstVdbPtr=0x8170BAEC,
        dstCallId=0x185, srcCallId=0x184,
42          caps={codec=0x1, fax_rate=0x2, vad=0x2, modem=0x1
43              codec_bytes=160, signal_type=0})
44      Jul 28 12:12:03.122 UTC: cc_api_caps_ind (dstVdbPtr=0x8170BAEC,
        dstCallId=0x185, srcCallId=0x184,
45          caps={codec=0x40, fax_rate=0x2, vad=0x2, modem=0x1
46              codec_bytes=160, signal_type=0})
47      Jul 28 12:12:03.126 UTC: cc_api_caps_ack (dstVdbPtr=0x8170BAEC,
        dstCallId=0x185, srcCallId=0x184,
48          caps={codec=0x40, fax_rate=0x2, vad=0x2, modem=0x1
49              codec_bytes=160, signal_type=0})
50      Jul 28 12:12:03.142 UTC: cc_api_caps_ack (dstVdbPtr=0x8167E948,
        dstCallId=0x184, srcCallId=0x185,
51          caps={codec=0x1, fax_rate=0x2, vad=0x2, modem=0x1
52              codec_bytes=160, signal_type=0})
53      Jul 28 12:12:03.142 UTC: cc_api_caps_ack (dstVdbPtr=0x8167E948,
        dstCallId=0x184, srcCallId=0x185,
54          caps={codec=0x40, fax_rate=0x2, vad=0x2, modem=0x1
55              codec_bytes=160, signal_type=0})
56      voice-gw3#
57      Jul 28 12:12:35.094 UTC: cc_api_call_connected(vdbPtr=0x8170BAEC,
        callID=0x185)
58      Jul 28 12:12:35.094 UTC: sess_appl: ev(8=CC_EV_CALL_CONNECTED),
        cid(389), disp(0)
59      Jul 28 12:12:35.098 UTC: ssa:
        cid(389)st(4)oldst(1)cfid(168)csize(0)in(0)fDest(0)-
        cid2(388)st2(4)oldst2(3)
60      Jul 28 12:12:35.098 UTC: ccCallConnect (callID=0x184)
61      Jul 28 12:12:35.098 UTC: ssaFlushPeerTagQueue cid(388) peer list: (empty)
62      voice-gw3#
63      Jul 28 12:12:58.132 UTC: cc_api_call_disconnected(vdbPtr=0x0,
        callID=0x184, cause=0x10)
64      Jul 28 12:12:58.136 UTC: sess_appl: ev(12=CC_EV_CALL_DISCONNECTED),
        cid(388), disp(0)
```

Example D-2   *Successful Call Completion from the Perspective of the Destination VoIP Gateway (Continued)*

```
65    Jul 28 12:12:58.136 UTC: ssa:
      cid(388)st(5)oldst(3)cfid(168)csize(0)in(1)fDest(1)-
      cid2(389)st2(5)oldst2(4)
66    Jul 28 12:12:58.136 UTC: ssa: Disconnected cid(388) state(5) cause(0x10)
67    Jul 28 12:12:58.136 UTC: ccConferenceDestroy (confID=0xA8, tag=0x0)
68    Jul 28 12:12:58.136 UTC: cc_api_bridge_done (confID=0xA8,
      srcIF=0x8167E948, srcCallID=0x184, dstCallID=0x185, disposition=0
      tag=0x0)
69    Jul 28 12:12:58.140 UTC: cc_api_bridge_done (confID=0xA8,
      srcIF=0x8170BAEC, srcCallID=0x185, dstCallID=0x184, disposition=0
      tag=0x0)
70    Jul 28 12:12:58.144 UTC: sess_appl: ev(24=CC_EV_CONF_DESTROY_DONE),
      cid(388), disp(0)
71    Jul 28 12:12:58.144 UTC: ssa: cid(388)st(6)oldst(5)cfid(-
      1)csize(0)in(1)fDest(1)-cid2(389)st2(6)oldst2(4)
72    Jul 28 12:12:58.144 UTC: ccCallDisconnect (callID=0x184, cause=0x10
      tag=0x0)
73    Jul 28 12:12:58.144 UTC: ccCallDisconnect (callID=0x185, cause=0x10
      tag=0x0)
74    Jul 28 12:12:58.192 UTC: cc_api_call_disconnect_done(vdbPtr=0x0,
      callID=0x184, disp=0, tag=0x0)
75    Jul 28 12:12:58.196 UTC: sess_appl: ev(13=CC_EV_CALL_DISCONNECT_DONE),
      cid(388), disp(0)
76    voice-gw3#
77    Jul 28 12:12:58.196 UTC: ssa: cid(388)st(7)oldst(6)cfid(-
      1)csize(0)in(1)fDest(1)-cid2(389)st2(7)oldst2(4)
78    Jul 28 12:12:58.505 UTC: cc_api_call_disconnect_done(vdbPtr=0x8170BAEC,
      callID=0x185, disp=0, tag=0x8178800C)
79    Jul 28 12:12:58.505 UTC: sess_appl: ev(13=CC_EV_CALL_DISCONNECT_DONE),
      cid(389), disp(0)
80    Jul 28 12:12:58.505 UTC: ssa: cid(389)st(7)oldst(4)cfid(-
      1)csize(1)in(0)fDest(0)
81    voice-gw3#
```

Failed VoIP Call Setup 1: H.323 Gatekeeper Problems

In this scenario, VoIP gateways are configured to ask a gatekeeper to resolve phone numbers to IP addresses, instead of manually configuring each gateway with the mapping for every destination phone number. Review Chapter 17 for the details of configuring H.323 functionality.

The call setup in Example D-3 begins just as in the case of Example D-1, with a memory pointer allocated for the call and a dial peer selected for the inbound call leg in lines 3 and 4. The dial peer is selected based on the voice port from which the call is initiated. In this case, the POTS dial peer 9 matches because it is the first dial peer configured with the voice port from which the call arrives. The destination pattern for this dial peer is 9 and is assigned as the calling party number.

The call setup process continues normally, with the assignment of a valid CallID for the inbound call leg in line 9, and the dial tone provided to the calling party in line 11. The digit collection loop occurs in lines 12 through 59, and the list of dial peers that match the outbound call leg in shown in line 60. The VoIP dial peer 8000 is the only matching dial peer, which is configured in the voice gateway to point to an H.323 gatekeeper (via the **session target ras** command). You cannot determine this information by examining the debugging output, but you would have known this information by examining the configuration of the voice gateway.

Continuing with the call setup, the setup request is sent to the remote VoIP gateway (actually the H.323 gatekeeper, in this case) in lines 77 and 78. The CallID for the outbound call leg is assigned in line 80, and then a problem appears. The call setup is halted in line 81, with cause=0x15 as the only indication of a problem. Consulting Appendix B, you can see the reason listed as call rejected. Because you already know from examining the router configuration that the dial peer points to an H.323 gatekeeper, you should now know that the gatekeeper is not accepting the call request. This is the heart of what the **debug voip ccapi inout** command can tell you in this case, and you can further isolate the problem as follows:

- Verify that the VoIP gateway is registered with the H.323 gatekeeper using the **show gateway** command on the VoIP gateway.

- Verify the running configuration of the H.323 gatekeeper.

- Verify that the gatekeeper knows how to resolve the E.164 destination pattern (via the **show gatekeeper endpoints** and **show gatekeeper gw-type-prefix** commands).

- Examine the transactions between the VoIP gateway and the gatekeeper using **debug h225 asn1** together with the **debug h323 ras** command.

In this case, examination of the H.323 gatekeeper would reveal that the number 8999 is not registered as an E.164 alias with the gatekeeper. Neither does the gatekeeper have a registered gw-type-prefix that is equal to {8}, {89}, {899}, or {8999}. The problem is therefore isolated to the gatekeeper, and the exact reason is that the gatekeeper does not have a route to complete the call.

The remainder of the output for the **debug voip ccapi inout** command includes the normal information associated with a call disconnection, as in the case of Example D-1.

Example D-3 **debug voip ccapi inout** *for Failed VoIP Call Setup (H.323 Gatekeeper Problems)*

Line Number	Cisco IOS Debugging Output
1	voice-gw2#debug voip ccapi inout
2	voice-gw2#
3	Aug 15 16:41:45.790 UTC: cc_api_call_setup_ind (vdbPtr=0x624F79D8, callInfo={called=,called_oct3=0x81,calling=9,calling_oct3=0x7B,called_oct3a=0x0,
4	fdest=0 peer_tag=9},callID=0x627106E4)
5	Aug 15 16:41:45.790 UTC: cc_api_call_setup_ind type 1 , prot 0

Example D-3 **debug voip ccapi inout** *for Failed VoIP Call Setup (H.323 Gatekeeper Problems) (Continued)*

6	Aug 15 16:41:45.790 UTC: cc_process_call_setup_ind (event=0x625D66A4) handed call to app "SESSION"
7	Aug 15 16:41:45.790 UTC: sess_appl: ev(23=CC_EV_CALL_SETUP_IND), cid(6241), disp(0)
8	Aug 15 16:41:45.790 UTC: sess_appl: ev(SSA_EV_CALL_SETUP_IND), cid(6241), disp(0)
9	Aug 15 16:41:45.790 UTC: ccCallSetContext (callID=0x1861, context=0x628AB2D8)
10	Aug 15 16:41:45.790 UTC: ccCallSetupAck (callID=0x1861)
11	Aug 15 16:41:45.790 UTC: ccGenerateTone (callID=0x1861 tone=8)
12	Aug 15 16:41:46.850 UTC: cc_api_call_digit_begin (vdbPtr=0x624F79D8, callID=0x1861, digit=8, flags=0x1, timestamp=0x22FFBB89, expiration=0x0)
13	Aug 15 16:41:46.850 UTC: sess_appl: ev(10=CC_EV_CALL_DIGIT_BEGIN), cid(6241), disp(0)
14	Aug 15 16:41:46.850 UTC: cid(6241)st(SSA_CS_MAPPING)ev(SSA_EV_DIGIT_BEGIN)
15	oldst(SSA_CS_MAPPING)cfid(-1)csize(0)in(1)fDest(0)
16	Aug 15 16:41:46.850 UTC: ssaIgnore cid(6241), st(SSA_CS_MAPPING),oldst(0), ev(10)
17	Aug 15 16:41:46.910 UTC: cc_api_call_digit (vdbPtr=0x624F79D8, callID=0x1861, digit=8, duration=110,tag 0, callparty 0)
18	Aug 15 16:41:46.910 UTC: sess_appl: ev(9=CC_EV_CALL_DIGIT), cid(6241), disp(0)
19	Aug 15 16:41:46.910 UTC: cid(6241)st(SSA_CS_MAPPING)ev(SSA_EV_CALL_DIGIT)
20	oldst(SSA_CS_MAPPING)cfid(-1)csize(0)in(1)fDest(0)
21	Aug 15 16:41:46.910 UTC: ssaDigit
22	Aug 15 16:41:46.910 UTC: ssaDigit, callinfo , digit 8, tag 0,callparty 0
23	Aug 15 16:41:46.910 UTC: ssaDigit, calling 9,result 1
24	Aug 15 16:41:46.998 UTC: cc_api_call_digit_begin (vdbPtr=0x624F79D8, callID=0x1861, digit=9, flags=0x1, timestamp=0x22FFBB89, expiration=0x0)
25	Aug 15 16:41:46.998 UTC: sess_appl: ev(10=CC_EV_CALL_DIGIT_BEGIN), cid(6241), disp(0)
26	Aug 15 16:41:46.998 UTC: cid(6241)st(SSA_CS_MAPPING)ev(SSA_EV_DIGIT_BEGIN)
27	oldst(SSA_CS_MAPPING)cfid(-1)csize(0)in(1)fDest(0)
28	Aug 15 16:41:46.998 UTC: ssaIgnore cid(6241), st(SSA_CS_MAPPING),oldst(0), ev(10)
29	Aug 15 16:41:47.038 UTC: cc_api_call_digit (vdbPtr=0x624F79D8, callID=0x1861, digit=9, duration=90,tag 0, callparty 0)
30	Aug 15 16:41:47.038 UTC: sess_appl: ev(9=CC_EV_CALL_DIGIT), cid(6241), disp(0)
31	Aug 15 16:41:47.038 UTC: cid(6241)st(SSA_CS_MAPPING)ev(SSA_EV_CALL_DIGIT)
32	oldst(SSA_CS_MAPPING)cfid(-1)csize(0)in(1)fDest(0)
33	Aug 15 16:41:47.038 UTC: ssaDigit
34	Aug 15 16:41:47.038 UTC: ssaDigit, callinfo , digit 89, tag 0,callparty 0
35	Aug 15 16:41:47.038 UTC: ssaDigit, calling 9,result 1
36	Aug 15 16:41:47.138 UTC: cc_api_call_digit_begin (vdbPtr=0x624F79D8, callID=0x1861, digit=9, flags=0x1, timestamp=0x22FFBB89, expiration=0x0)
37	Aug 15 16:41:47.138 UTC: sess_appl: ev(10=CC_EV_CALL_DIGIT_BEGIN), cid(6241), disp(0)

continues

Example D-3 **debug voip ccapi inout** *for Failed VoIP Call Setup (H.323 Gatekeeper Problems) (Continued)*

```
38      Aug 15 16:41:47.138 UTC:
        cid(6241)st(SSA_CS_MAPPING)ev(SSA_EV_DIGIT_BEGIN)
39      oldst(SSA_CS_MAPPING)cfid(-1)csize(0)in(1)fDest(0)
40      Aug 15 16:41:47.138 UTC: ssaIgnore cid(6241),
        st(SSA_CS_MAPPING),oldst(0), ev(10)
41      Aug 15 16:41:47.190 UTC: cc_api_call_digit (vdbPtr=0x624F79D8,
        callID=0x1861, digit=9, duration=100,tag 0, callparty 0 )
42      Aug 15 16:41:47.190 UTC: sess_appl: ev(9=CC_EV_CALL_DIGIT), cid(6241),
        disp(0)
43      Aug 15 16:41:47.190 UTC:
        cid(6241)st(SSA_CS_MAPPING)ev(SSA_EV_CALL_DIGIT)
44      oldst(SSA_CS_MAPPING)cfid(-1)csize(0)in(1)fDest(0)
45      Aug 15 16:41:47.190 UTC: ssaDigit
46      Aug 15 16:41:47.190 UTC: ssaDigit, callinfo , digit 899, tag 0,callparty
        0
47      Aug 15 16:41:47.190 UTC: ssaDigit, calling 9,result 1
48      Aug 15 16:41:47.278 UTC: cc_api_call_digit_begin (vdbPtr=0x624F79D8,
        callID=0x1861, digit=9, flags=0x1, timestamp=0x22FFBB89,
        expiration=0x0)
49      Aug 15 16:41:47.278 UTC: sess_appl: ev(10=CC_EV_CALL_DIGIT_BEGIN),
        cid(6241), disp(0)
50      Aug 15 16:41:47.278 UTC:
        cid(6241)st(SSA_CS_MAPPING)ev(SSA_EV_DIGIT_BEGIN)
51      oldst(SSA_CS_MAPPING)cfid(-1)csize(0)in(1)fDest(0)
52      Aug 15 16:41:47.278 UTC: ssaIgnore cid(6241),
        st(SSA_CS_MAPPING),oldst(0), ev(10)
53      Aug 15 16:41:47.338 UTC: cc_api_call_digit (vdbPtr=0x624F79D8,
        callID=0x1861, digit=9, duration=110,tag 0, callparty 0 )
54      Aug 15 16:41:47.338 UTC: sess_appl: ev(9=CC_EV_CALL_DIGIT), cid(6241),
        disp(0)
55      Aug 15 16:41:47.338 UTC:
        cid(6241)st(SSA_CS_MAPPING)ev(SSA_EV_CALL_DIGIT)
56      oldst(SSA_CS_MAPPING)cfid(-1)csize(0)in(1)fDest(0)
57      Aug 15 16:41:47.338 UTC: ssaDigit
58      Aug 15 16:41:47.338 UTC: ssaDigit, callinfo , digit 8999, tag
        0,callparty 0
59      Aug 15 16:41:47.338 UTC: ssaDigit, calling 9,result 0
60      Aug 15 16:41:47.338 UTC: ssaSetupPeer cid(6241) peer list:  tag(8000)
        called number (8999)
61      Aug 15 16:41:47.338 UTC: ssaSetupPeer cid(6241), destPat(8999),
        matched(1), prefix(), peer(626B5DA8), peer->encapType (2)
62      Aug 15 16:41:47.338 UTC: ccCallProceeding (callID=0x1861, prog_ind=0x0)
63      Aug 15 16:41:47.338 UTC: ccCallSetupRequest (Inbound call = 0x1861,
        outbound peer =8000, dest=, params=0x628AB2EC mode=0,
        *callID=0x625DF678)
64      Aug 15 16:41:47.338 UTC: ccCallSetupRequest numbering_type 0x81
65      Aug 15 16:41:47.338 UTC: callingNumber=9, calledNumber=8999,
        redirectNumber=
66      Aug 15 16:41:47.338 UTC: accountNumber=, pinNumber=
67      Aug 15 16:41:47.342 UTC: finalDestFlag=0,
        guid=5a94.457f.2f4a.20db.0000.0000.161c.d364
68      Aug 15 16:41:47.342 UTC: peer_tag=9
69      Aug 15 16:41:47.342 UTC: dest_pat 8...
70      Aug 15 16:41:47.342 UTC: digit_strip_checking: dest_pat8...
71      Aug 15 16:41:47.342 UTC:  strip 1, peer_string 8...
```

Example D-3   **debug voip ccapi inout** *for Failed VoIP Call Setup (H.323 Gatekeeper Problems) (Continued)*

```
72        Aug 15 16:41:47.342 UTC: callingNumber=9, calledNumber=8999,
          redirectNumber=
73        Aug 15 16:41:47.342 UTC: accountNumber=, pinNumber=
74        Aug 15 16:41:47.342 UTC: finalDestFlag=0,
          guid=5a94.457f.2f4a.20db.0000.0000.161c.d364
75        Aug 15 16:41:47.342 UTC: peer_tag=8000
76        Aug 15 16:41:47.342 UTC: ccIFCallSetupRequest: (vdbPtr=0x621F3DB8,
          dest=,
          callParams={called=8999,called_oct3=0x81,calling=9,calling_oct3=0x7B,f
          dest=0, voice_peer_tag=8000},mode=0x0) vdbPtr type = 1
77        Aug 15 16:41:47.342 UTC: ccIFCallSetupRequest: (vdbPtr=0x621F3DB8,
          dest=, callParams={called=8999, called_oct3 0x81,
78              calling=9,calling_oct3 0x7B,fdest=0, voice_peer_tag=8000},
          mode=0x0)
79        Aug 15 16:41:47.342 UTC: ccSaveDialpeerTag (callID=0x1861,
          dialpeer_tag=
80        Aug 15 16:41:47.342 UTC: ccCallSetContext (callID=0x1862,
          context=0x628A0478)
81        Aug 15 16:41:47.346 UTC: cc_api_call_disconnected(vdbPtr=0x621F3DB8,
          callID=0x1862, cause=0x15)
82        Aug 15 16:41:47.346 UTC: sess_appl: ev(12=CC_EV_CALL_DISCONNECTED),
          cid(6242), disp(0)
83        Aug 15 16:41:47.346 UTC:
          cid(6242)st(SSA_CS_CALL_SETTING)ev(SSA_EV_CALL_DISCONNECTED)
84        oldst(SSA_CS_MAPPING)cfid(-1)csize(0)in(0)fDest(0)
85        Aug 15 16:41:47.350 UTC: -
          cid2(6241)st2(SSA_CS_CALL_SETTING)oldst2(SSA_CS_MAPPING)
86        Aug 15 16:41:47.350 UTC: ssa: Disconnected cid(6242) state(1)
          cause(0x15)
87        Aug 15 16:41:47.350 UTC: ccCallDisconnect (callID=0x1862, cause=0x15
          tag=0x0)
88        Aug 15 16:41:47.350 UTC: ccCallDisconnect (callID=0x1861, cause=0x15
          tag=0x0)
89        Aug 15 16:41:47.350 UTC: cc_api_call_disconnect_done(vdbPtr=0x621F3DB8,
          callID=0x1862, disp=0, tag=0x0)
90        Aug 15 16:41:47.350 UTC: sess_appl: ev(13=CC_EV_CALL_DISCONNECT_DONE),
          cid(6242), disp(0)
91        Aug 15 16:41:47.350 UTC:
          cid(6242)st(SSA_CS_DISCONNECTING)ev(SSA_EV_CALL_DISCONNECT_DONE)
92        oldst(SSA_CS_CALL_SETTING)cfid(-1)csize(0)in(0)fDest(0)
93        Aug 15 16:41:47.350 UTC: -
          cid2(6241)st2(SSA_CS_DISCONNECTING)oldst2(SSA_CS_MAPPING)
94        Aug 15 16:41:57.870 UTC: cc_api_call_disconnect_done(vdbPtr=0x624F79D8,
          callID=0x1861, disp=0, tag=0x0)
95        Aug 15 16:41:57.870 UTC: sess_appl: ev(13=CC_EV_CALL_DISCONNECT_DONE),
          cid(6241), disp(0)
96        Aug 15 16:41:57.870 UTC:
          cid(6241)st(SSA_CS_DISCONNECTING)ev(SSA_EV_CALL_DISCONNECT_DONE)
97        oldst(SSA_CS_MAPPING)cfid(-1)csize(1)in(1)fDest(0)
98        voice-gw2#
```

Failed VoIP Call Setup 2: Missing Dial Peer

In this scenario, the voice gateway assigns an inbound call leg but fails to assign an outbound call leg because it does not have a dial peer with a destination pattern that matches the called party number.

Just as in Examples D-1 and D-3, the call setup process in Example D-4 begins with a memory pointer assignment and a dial-peer selection for the inbound call leg (shown in lines 3 though 6). The CallID for the inbound call leg is assigned in line 11, and the voice gateway provides a dial tone (as seen in line 13) to the calling party. The digit collection loop begins in line 14 and is quickly curtailed. After the first digit 8 is dialed (beginning in line 14 and ending in line 23), line 28 shows that no dial peers match in the router. Actually, tag 0 indicates that the null dial peer is matched, which is not acceptable to complete an outbound call leg. Line 29 shows the result=1, which indicates that the digit sequence does not match a dial peer. If there were a possibility for other dial peers to match, the voice gateway would continue in the digit collection loop. However, no other dial peers begin with {8} or a wildcard {.}, so the gateway immediately abandons the call.

Lines 30 and 31 are duplicate messages that show the call disconnection, with cause=0x1C as the reason. The 7-bit hexadecimal value of the ISDN cause code, as provided in Appendix B, is listed as invalid number format. Lines 35 through 40 show the remainder of the call abandonment. As an added confirmation that the problem is related to a lack of a dial peer for the outbound call leg, the output of **show dialplan number** is provided in lines 42 through 44.

Example D-4 **debug voip ccapi inout** *for Failed VoIP Call Setup (Missing Dial Peer)*

Line Number	Cisco IOS Debugging Output
1	voice-gw2#**debug voip ccapi inout**
2	voice-gw2#
3	Aug 15 16:47:36.638 UTC: cc_api_call_setup_ind (vdbPtr=0x624F79D8,
4	
5	callInfo={called=,called_oct3=0x81,calling=9,calling_oct3=0x0,called_oct3a=0x0,
6	fdest=0 peer_tag=9},callID=0x627106E4)
7	Aug 15 16:47:36.638 UTC: cc_api_call_setup_ind type 1 , prot 0
8	Aug 15 16:47:36.638 UTC: cc_process_call_setup_ind (event=0x625D88C4) handed call to app SESSION
9	Aug 15 16:47:36.638 UTC: sess_appl: ev(23=CC_EV_CALL_SETUP_IND), cid(6243), disp(0)
10	Aug 15 16:47:36.638 UTC: sess_appl: ev(SSA_EV_CALL_SETUP_IND), cid(6243), disp(0)
11	Aug 15 16:47:36.638 UTC: ccCallSetContext (callID=0x1863, context=0x628AB2D8)
12	Aug 15 16:47:36.638 UTC: ccCallSetupAck (callID=0x1863)
13	Aug 15 16:47:36.638 UTC: ccGenerateTone (callID=0x1863 tone=8)
14	Aug 15 16:47:37.658 UTC: cc_api_call_digit_begin (vdbPtr=0x624F79D8, callID=0x1863,
15	
16	digit=8, flags=0x1, timestamp=0x9D67ECD1, expiration=0x0)

Example D-4 **debug voip ccapi inout** *for Failed VoIP Call Setup (Missing Dial Peer) (Continued)*

```
17        Aug 15 16:47:37.658 UTC: sess_appl: ev(10=CC_EV_CALL_DIGIT_BEGIN),
          cid(6243), disp(0)
18        Aug 15 16:47:37.658 UTC:
          cid(6243)st(SSA_CS_MAPPING)ev(SSA_EV_DIGIT_BEGIN)
19        oldst(SSA_CS_MAPPING)cfid(-1)csize(0)in(1)fDest(0)
20        Aug 15 16:47:37.658 UTC: ssaIgnore cid(6243),
          st(SSA_CS_MAPPING),oldst(0), ev(10)
21        Aug 15 16:47:37.698 UTC: cc_api_call_digit (vdbPtr=0x624F79D8,
          callID=0x1863, digit=8,
22
23        duration=90,tag 0, callparty 0 )
24        Aug 15 16:47:37.698 UTC: sess_appl: ev(9=CC_EV_CALL_DIGIT), cid(6243),
          disp(0)
25        Aug 15 16:47:37.698 UTC:
          cid(6243)st(SSA_CS_MAPPING)ev(SSA_EV_CALL_DIGIT)
26        oldst(SSA_CS_MAPPING)cfid(-1)csize(0)in(1)fDest(0)
27        Aug 15 16:47:37.698 UTC: ssaDigit
28        Aug 15 16:47:37.698 UTC: ssaDigit, callinfo , digit 8, tag 0,callparty 0
29        Aug 15 16:47:37.698 UTC: ssaDigit, calling 9,result -1
30        Aug 15 16:47:37.698 UTC: ccCallDisconnect (callID=0x1863, cause=0x1C
          tag=0x0)
31        Aug 15 16:47:37.698 UTC: ccCallDisconnect (callID=0x1863, cause=0x1C
          tag=0x0)
32        voice-gw2#
33        voice-gw2#
34        voice-gw2#
35        Aug 15 16:47:48.090 UTC: cc_api_call_disconnect_done(vdbPtr=0x624F79D8,
          callID=0x1863,
36
37        disp=0, tag=0x6278E3AC)
38        Aug 15 16:47:48.090 UTC: sess_appl: ev(13=CC_EV_CALL_DISCONNECT_DONE),
          cid(6243), disp(0)
39        Aug 15 16:47:48.090 UTC:
          cid(6243)st(SSA_CS_DISCONNECTING)ev(SSA_EV_CALL_DISCONNECT_DONE)
40        oldst(SSA_CS_MAPPING)cfid(-1)csize(0)in(1)fDest(0)
41        voice-gw2#
42        voice-gw2#show dialplan number 8999
43        Macro Exp.: 8999
44        No match, result=-1
45
46        voice-gw2#
```

Failed VoIP Call Setup 3: Codec Negotiation Failure

The problem in this scenario is subtler than the two previous failure scenarios. A quick
examination of the debugging output does not reveal anything that is immediately wrong,
other than an early call disconnection. The ISDN cause code associated with the
disconnection does not indicate any problems because the call is ended with cause=0x10 or
normal call clearing. However, closer examination of the codec negotiation sequence and
comparison with the configuration that is running in the gateway points to the problem.

Calling VoIP Gateway

Once again, the call setup in Example D-5 begins with a memory pointer allocated for the call and a dial peer selected for the inbound call leg in lines 3 and 4. The POTS dial peer 9 matches because it is the first dial peer configured with the voice port from which the call arrives. The destination pattern for this dial peer is 9 and is assigned as the calling party number.

The call proceeds as expected until lines 90 through 98. The capabilities indication in lines 90 through 93 is part of a normal successful call setup process, but the first capabilities indication message is generally ignored in favor of the actual capabilities indication that follows from the local gateway. In this case, there is no capabilities indication from the local gateway before the call is disconnected in line 98. To really see what went wrong, you must examine the debugging output from the other end of the connection. For now, you have at least isolated the problem to the capabilities exchange because the initial caps_ind message is followed by a disconnect message before any additional caps_ind or caps_ack messages follow. Lines 99 through 121 show the remainder of the normal call disconnection process.

Note that in line 98, cause=0x10 is listed as the reason for the call disconnect. This value indicates a normal call clearing and does not provide any indication that there is a problem. Recall that H.323 relies on H.225.0 for the call setup and teardown, while H.245 provides the media establishment (see Chapter 11, "VoIP Transport and Signaling Protocols"). H.225.0 draws heavily from Q.931, which in turn uses the ISDN cause codes from Q.850. In this case, the H.225 call setup proceeds normally, but the problem is with the H.245 media negotiation (that is, the codec negotiation). At the H.225.0 layer, the call is successful, but the end-to-end audio path is never established because the H.245 media establishment fails. Remember this fact when a **show dial-peer** on the voice gateway indicates that all calls have completed with a normal call clearing, but you know that calls are failing.

Example D-5 **debug voip ccapi inout** *on the Calling VoIP Gateway (Codec Negotiation Failure)*

Line Number	Cisco IOS Debugging Output
1	voice-gw2#**debug voip ccapi inout**
2	voice-gw2#
3	Aug 15 17:13:27.190 UTC: cc_api_call_setup_ind (vdbPtr=0x624F79D8, callInfo={called=,called_oct3=0x81,calling=9,calling_oct3=0x0,called_oct3a=0x0,
4	fdest=0 peer_tag=9},callID=0x627106E4)
5	Aug 15 17:13:27.190 UTC: cc_api_call_setup_ind type 1 , prot 0
6	Aug 15 17:13:27.190 UTC: cc_process_call_setup_ind (event=0x625D586C) handed call to app "SESSION"
7	Aug 15 17:13:27.190 UTC: sess_appl: ev(23=CC_EV_CALL_SETUP_IND), cid(6258), disp(0)
8	Aug 15 17:13:27.190 UTC: sess_appl: ev(SSA_EV_CALL_SETUP_IND), cid(6258), disp(0)
9	Aug 15 17:13:27.190 UTC: ccCallSetContext (callID=0x1872, context=0x62749E58)
10	Aug 15 17:13:27.190 UTC: ccCallSetupAck (callID=0x1872)
11	Aug 15 17:13:27.190 UTC: ccGenerateTone (callID=0x1872 tone=8)

Example D-5 **debug voip ccapi inout** *on the Calling VoIP Gateway (Codec Negotiation Failure) (Continued)*

12	Aug 15 17:13:28.250 UTC: cc_api_call_digit_begin (vdbPtr=0x624F79D8, callID=0x1872, digit=4, flags=0x1, timestamp=0xDACFC519, expiration=0x0)
13	Aug 15 17:13:28.250 UTC: sess_appl: ev(10=CC_EV_CALL_DIGIT_BEGIN), cid(6258), disp(0)
14	Aug 15 17:13:28.250 UTC: cid(6258)st(SSA_CS_MAPPING)ev(SSA_EV_DIGIT_BEGIN)
15	oldst(SSA_CS_MAPPING)cfid(-1)csize(0)in(1)fDest(0)
16	Aug 15 17:13:28.250 UTC: ssaIgnore cid(6258), st(SSA_CS_MAPPING),oldst(0), ev(10)
17	Aug 15 17:13:28.298 UTC: cc_api_call_digit (vdbPtr=0x624F79D8, callID=0x1872, digit=4, duration=100,tag 0, callparty 0)
18	Aug 15 17:13:28.298 UTC: sess_appl: ev(9=CC_EV_CALL_DIGIT), cid(6258), disp(0)
19	Aug 15 17:13:28.298 UTC: cid(6258)st(SSA_CS_MAPPING)ev(SSA_EV_CALL_DIGIT)
20	oldst(SSA_CS_MAPPING)cfid(-1)csize(0)in(1)fDest(0)
21	Aug 15 17:13:28.298 UTC: ssaDigit
22	Aug 15 17:13:28.298 UTC: ssaDigit, callinfo , digit 4, tag 0,callparty 0
23	Aug 15 17:13:28.298 UTC: ssaDigit, calling 9,result 1
24	Aug 15 17:13:28.390 UTC: cc_api_call_digit_begin (vdbPtr=0x624F79D8, callID=0x1872, digit=3, flags=0x1, timestamp=0xDACFC519, expiration=0x0)
25	Aug 15 17:13:28.390 UTC: sess_appl: ev(10=CC_EV_CALL_DIGIT_BEGIN), cid(6258), disp(0)
26	Aug 15 17:13:28.390 UTC: cid(6258)st(SSA_CS_MAPPING)ev(SSA_EV_DIGIT_BEGIN)
27	oldst(SSA_CS_MAPPING)cfid(-1)csize(0)in(1)fDest(0)
28	Aug 15 17:13:28.390 UTC: ssaIgnore cid(6258), st(SSA_CS_MAPPING),oldst(0), ev(10)
29	Aug 15 17:13:28.450 UTC: cc_api_call_digit (vdbPtr=0x624F79D8, callID=0x1872, digit=3, duration=110,tag 0, callparty 0)
30	Aug 15 17:13:28.450 UTC: sess_appl: ev(9=CC_EV_CALL_DIGIT), cid(6258), disp(0)
31	Aug 15 17:13:28.450 UTC: cid(6258)st(SSA_CS_MAPPING)ev(SSA_EV_CALL_DIGIT)
32	oldst(SSA_CS_MAPPING)cfid(-1)csize(0)in(1)fDest(0)
33	Aug 15 17:13:28.450 UTC: ssaDigit
34	Aug 15 17:13:28.450 UTC: ssaDigit, callinfo , digit 43, tag 0,callparty 0
35	Aug 15 17:13:28.450 UTC: ssaDigit, calling 9,result 1
36	Aug 15 17:13:28.538 UTC: cc_api_call_digit_begin (vdbPtr=0x624F79D8, callID=0x1872, digit=5, flags=0x1, timestamp=0xDACFC519, expiration=0x0)
37	Aug 15 17:13:28.538 UTC: sess_appl: ev(10=CC_EV_CALL_DIGIT_BEGIN), cid(6258), disp(0)
38	Aug 15 17:13:28.538 UTC: cid(6258)st(SSA_CS_MAPPING)ev(SSA_EV_DIGIT_BEGIN)
39	oldst(SSA_CS_MAPPING)cfid(-1)csize(0)in(1)fDest(0)
40	Aug 15 17:13:28.538 UTC: ssaIgnore cid(6258), st(SSA_CS_MAPPING),oldst(0), ev(10)
41	Aug 15 17:13:28.590 UTC: cc_api_call_digit (vdbPtr=0x624F79D8, callID=0x1872, digit=5, duration=100,tag 0, callparty 0)
42	Aug 15 17:13:28.590 UTC: sess_appl: ev(9=CC_EV_CALL_DIGIT), cid(6258), disp(0)

continues

Example D-5 **debug voip ccapi inout** *on the Calling VoIP Gateway (Codec Negotiation Failure) (Continued)*

```
43      Aug 15 17:13:28.590 UTC:
        cid(6258)st(SSA_CS_MAPPING)ev(SSA_EV_CALL_DIGIT)
44      oldst(SSA_CS_MAPPING)cfid(-1)csize(0)in(1)fDest(0)
45      Aug 15 17:13:28.590 UTC: ssaDigit
46      Aug 15 17:13:28.590 UTC: ssaDigit, callinfo , digit 435, tag 0,callparty
        0
47      Aug 15 17:13:28.590 UTC: ssaDigit, calling 9,result 1
48      Aug 15 17:13:28.678 UTC: cc_api_call_digit_begin (vdbPtr=0x624F79D8,
        callID=0x1872, digit=6, flags=0x1, timestamp=0xDACFC519,
        expiration=0x0)
49      Aug 15 17:13:28.678 UTC: sess_appl: ev(10=CC_EV_CALL_DIGIT_BEGIN),
        cid(6258), disp(0)
50      Aug 15 17:13:28.678 UTC:
        cid(6258)st(SSA_CS_MAPPING)ev(SSA_EV_DIGIT_BEGIN)
51      oldst(SSA_CS_MAPPING)cfid(-1)csize(0)in(1)fDest(0)
52      Aug 15 17:13:28.678 UTC: ssaIgnore cid(6258),
        st(SSA_CS_MAPPING),oldst(0), ev(10)
53      Aug 15 17:13:28.738 UTC: cc_api_call_digit (vdbPtr=0x624F79D8,
        callID=0x1872, digit=6, duration=110,tag 0, callparty 0 )
54      Aug 15 17:13:28.738 UTC: sess_appl: ev(9=CC_EV_CALL_DIGIT), cid(6258),
        disp(0)
55      Aug 15 17:13:28.738 UTC:
        cid(6258)st(SSA_CS_MAPPING)ev(SSA_EV_CALL_DIGIT)
56      oldst(SSA_CS_MAPPING)cfid(-1)csize(0)in(1)fDest(0)
57      Aug 15 17:13:28.738 UTC: ssaDigit
58      Aug 15 17:13:28.738 UTC: ssaDigit, callinfo , digit 4356, tag
        0,callparty 0
59      Aug 15 17:13:28.738 UTC: ssaDigit, calling 9,result 0
60      Aug 15 17:13:28.738 UTC: ssaSetupPeer cid(6258) peer list:  tag(4000)
        called number (4356)
61      Aug 15 17:13:28.738 UTC: ssaSetupPeer cid(6258), destPat(4356),
        matched(1), prefix(), peer(626B0088), peer->encapType (2)
62      Aug 15 17:13:28.738 UTC: ccCallProceeding (callID=0x1872, prog_ind=0x0)
63      Aug 15 17:13:28.738 UTC: ccCallSetupRequest (Inbound call = 0x1872,
        outbound peer =4000, dest=, params=0x62749E6C mode=0,
        *callID=0x625DF678)
64      Aug 15 17:13:28.738 UTC: ccCallSetupRequest numbering_type 0x81
65      Aug 15 17:13:28.738 UTC: callingNumber=9, calledNumber=4356,
        redirectNumber=
66      Aug 15 17:13:28.738 UTC: accountNumber=, pinNumber=
67      Aug 15 17:13:28.738 UTC: finalDestFlag=0,
        guid=5a94.457f.2f4a.20ef.0000.0000.1639.d6bc
68      Aug 15 17:13:28.738 UTC: peer_tag=9
69      Aug 15 17:13:28.738 UTC:  dest_pat 4...
70      Aug 15 17:13:28.738 UTC: digit_strip_checking: dest_pat4...
71      Aug 15 17:13:28.738 UTC:  strip 1, peer_string 4...
72      Aug 15 17:13:28.738 UTC: callingNumber=9, calledNumber=4356,
        redirectNumber=
73      Aug 15 17:13:28.738 UTC: accountNumber=, pinNumber=
74      Aug 15 17:13:28.738 UTC: finalDestFlag=0,
        guid=5a94.457f.2f4a.20ef.0000.0000.1639.d6bc
75      Aug 15 17:13:28.738 UTC: peer_tag=4000
```

Example D-5 **debug voip ccapi inout** *on the Calling VoIP Gateway (Codec Negotiation Failure) (Continued)*

```
76        Aug 15 17:13:28.738 UTC: ccIFCallSetupRequest: (vdbPtr=0x621F3DB8,
          dest=,
          callParams={called=4356,called_oct3=0x81,calling=9,calling_oct3=0x0,fd
          est=0, voice_peer_tag=4000},mode=0x0) vdbPtr type = 1
77        Aug 15 17:13:28.738 UTC: ccIFCallSetupRequest: (vdbPtr=0x621F3DB8,
          dest=, callParams={called=4356, called_oct3 0x81,
78               calling=9,calling_oct3 0x0,fdest=0, voice_peer_tag=4000},
          mode=0x0)
79        Aug 15 17:13:28.738 UTC: ccSaveDialpeerTag (callID=0x1872,
          dialpeer_tag=
80        Aug 15 17:13:28.738 UTC: ccCallSetContext (callID=0x1873,
          context=0x6249D1B8)
81        Aug 15 17:13:28.922 UTC: cc_api_call_alert(vdbPtr=0x621F3DB8,
          callID=0x1873, prog_ind=0x8, sig_ind=0x1)
82        Aug 15 17:13:28.922 UTC: sess_appl: ev(7=CC_EV_CALL_ALERT), cid(6259),
          disp(0)
83        Aug 15 17:13:28.922 UTC:
          cid(6259)st(SSA_CS_CALL_SETTING)ev(SSA_EV_CALL_ALERT)
84        oldst(SSA_CS_MAPPING)cfid(-1)csize(0)in(0)fDest(0)
85        Aug 15 17:13:28.922 UTC: -
          cid2(6258)st2(SSA_CS_CALL_SETTING)oldst2(SSA_CS_MAPPING)
86        Aug 15 17:13:28.922 UTC: ccCallAlert (callID=0x1872, prog_ind=0x8,
          sig_ind=0x1)
87        Aug 15 17:13:28.922 UTC: ccConferenceCreate (confID=0x625DF8D8,
          callID1=0x1872, callID2=0x1873, tag=0x0)
88        Aug 15 17:13:28.922 UTC: cc_api_bridge_done (confID=0xB08,
          srcIF=0x621F3DB8, srcCallID=0x1873, dstCallID=0x1872, disposition=0,
          tag=0x0)
89        Aug 15 17:13:28.922 UTC: cc_api_bridge_done (confID=0xB08,
          srcIF=0x624F79D8, srcCallID=0x1872, dstCallID=0x1873, disposition=0,
          tag=0x0)
90        Aug 15 17:13:28.922 UTC: cc_api_caps_ind (dstVdbPtr=0x621F3DB8,
          dstCallId=0x1873, srcCallId=0x1872,
91             caps={codec=0x887F, fax_rate=0x7F, vad=0x3, modem=0x62705770
92                  codec_bytes=0, signal_type=3})
93        Aug 15 17:13:28.922 UTC: cc_api_caps_ind (Playout: mode 0, initial
          7768,min 24815, max 7468)
94        Aug 15 17:13:28.922 UTC: sess_appl: ev(28=CC_EV_CONF_CREATE_DONE),
          cid(6258), disp(0)
95        Aug 15 17:13:28.922 UTC:
          cid(6258)st(SSA_CS_CONFERENCING_ALERT)ev(SSA_EV_CONF_CREATE_DONE)
96        oldst(SSA_CS_MAPPING)cfid(2824)csize(0)in(1)fDest(0)
97        Aug 15 17:13:28.922 UTC: -
          cid2(6259)st2(SSA_CS_CONFERENCING_ALERT)oldst2(SSA_CS_CALL_SETTING)
98        Aug 15 17:13:28.998 UTC: cc_api_call_disconnected(vdbPtr=0x621F3DB8,
          callID=0x1873, cause=0x10)
99        Aug 15 17:13:28.998 UTC: sess_appl: ev(12=CC_EV_CALL_DISCONNECTED),
          cid(6259), disp(0)
100       Aug 15 17:13:28.998 UTC:
          cid(6259)st(SSA_CS_CONFERENCED_ALERT)ev(SSA_EV_CALL_DISCONNECTED)
101       oldst(SSA_CS_CALL_SETTING)cfid(2824)csize(0)in(0)fDest(0)
102       Aug 15 17:13:28.998 UTC: -
          cid2(6258)st2(SSA_CS_CONFERENCED_ALERT)oldst2(SSA_CS_CONFERENCING_ALER
          T)
103       Aug 15 17:13:28.998 UTC: ssaDisconnectedAlert: redirect_numbers(0)
104       Aug 15 17:13:28.998 UTC: ccConferenceDestroy (confID=0xB08, tag=0x0)
```

continues

Example D-5 **debug voip ccapi inout** *on the Calling VoIP Gateway (Codec Negotiation Failure) (Continued)*

```
105    Aug 15 17:13:28.998 UTC: cc_api_bridge_drop_done (confID=0xB08,
       srcIF=0x621F3DB8, srcCallID=0x1873, dstCallID=0x1872, disposition=0
       tag=0x0)
106    Aug 15 17:13:28.998 UTC: cc_api_bridge_drop_done (confID=0xB08,
       srcIF=0x624F79D8, srcCallID=0x1872, dstCallID=0x1873, disposition=0
       tag=0x0)
107    Aug 15 17:13:28.998 UTC: sess_appl: ev(29=CC_EV_CONF_DESTROY_DONE),
       cid(6258), disp(0)
108    Aug 15 17:13:28.998 UTC:
       cid(6258)st(SSA_CS_CONF_DESTROYING)ev(SSA_EV_CONF_DESTROY_DONE)
109    oldst(SSA_CS_CONFERENCING_ALERT)cfid(2824)csize(0)in(1)fDest(0)
110    Aug 15 17:13:28.998 UTC: -
       cid2(6259)st2(SSA_CS_CONF_DESTROYING)oldst2(SSA_CS_CONFERENCED_ALERT)
111    Aug 15 17:13:28.998 UTC: ccCallDisconnect (callID=0x1872, cause=0x10
       tag=0x0)
112    Aug 15 17:13:28.998 UTC: ccCallDisconnect (callID=0x1873, cause=0x10
       tag=0x0)
113    Aug 15 17:13:29.006 UTC: cc_api_call_disconnect_done(vdbPtr=0x621F3DB8,
       callID=0x1873, disp=0, tag=0x0)
114    Aug 15 17:13:29.006 UTC: sess_appl: ev(13=CC_EV_CALL_DISCONNECT_DONE),
       cid(6259), disp(0)
115    Aug 15 17:13:29.006 UTC:
       cid(6259)st(SSA_CS_DISCONNECTING)ev(SSA_EV_CALL_DISCONNECT_DONE)
116    oldst(SSA_CS_CONFERENCED_ALERT)cfid(-1)csize(0)in(0)fDest(0)
117    Aug 15 17:13:29.006 UTC: -
       cid2(6258)st2(SSA_CS_DISCONNECTING)oldst2(SSA_CS_CONF_DESTROYING)
118    Aug 15 17:13:42.574 UTC: cc_api_call_disconnect_done(vdbPtr=0x624F79D8,
       callID=0x1872, disp=0, tag=0x0)
119    Aug 15 17:13:42.574 UTC: sess_appl: ev(13=CC_EV_CALL_DISCONNECT_DONE),
       cid(6258), disp(0)
120    Aug 15 17:13:42.574 UTC:
       cid(6258)st(SSA_CS_DISCONNECTING)ev(SSA_EV_CALL_DISCONNECT_DONE)
121    oldst(SSA_CS_CONF_DESTROYING)cfid(-1)csize(1)in(1)fDest(0)
122    voice-gw2#
```

Called VoIP Gateway

Example D-6 shows the same call failure of Example D-5, from the perspective of the called VoIP gateway. Lines 3 through 30 contain the normal information of a successful call setup, to the point of the media negotiation (also known as the H.245 negotiation or the capabilities exchange).

In lines 34 through 36, you can see that the remote VoIP advertises only the codec capabilities set of 0x4. Consulting Table D-4, the codec type 0x4 (which is the same as 0x0004) represents the g729r8 codec. This codec type is the default codec used for dial peers, and is also the codec associated with the null (tag 0) dial peer. In lines 37 through 49, the inbound VoIP call leg (note the dstVdbPtr values) of the local gateway acknowledges the capabilities advertisement from the remote VoIP gateway. In lines 40 through 42, the outbound POTS call leg of the local gateway receives the capabilities advertisement.

The configurations of the voice gateways are not shown here, but you would observe that the local gateway (the called gateway, in this example) is not configured to support the g729r8 codec. The local gateway is configured to support only the g711ulaw codec. When the H.245 media negotiation is incapable of establishing a media channel that both endpoints can understand, the call is disconnected in line 45. Lines 46 through 61 contain the normal information of a call disconnection sequence. The key information to derive from this debugging output is the codec capability set that the remote gateway advertises, which you can compare with the running configuration of the local gateway.

Again, the ISDN cause code in line 45 (cause=0x10) does not reveal a problem associated with the disconnection. This is because the call is successful at the H.225.0 layer (which generates the Q.850 cause code values). Your observation of the router configuration, along with examination of the debugging output to determine which codecs are being advertised by the remote side, will lead to the diagnosis of a codec negotiation failure.

TIP   The most common source of codec negotiation failure is a configuration oversight on one of the voice gateways, or a problem with old IOS versions that is resolved in 12.0(7)XK. In the case of an oversight, there is most likely a missing **codec** or **voice-class** statement in the VoIP dial peer, so the default codec of g729r8 is used for one end of the codec negotiation. Beware that an oversight in both routers may cause calls to succeed using the g729r8 codec, when you expect another codec to be used.

With IOS versions prior to 12.0(7)XK, the VoIP dial peers can lose **voice-class** statements when the router is reloaded. The startup configuration appears to be correct, but the running configuration will not show the **voice-class** line in the dial peer configuration. This problem arises when the gateway reads the startup configuration file after booting and processes the configuration elements in the order in which they appear in the configuration file. Because the dial peer blocks appear in the configuration before the voice class blocks (in IOS versions prior to 12.0[7]XK), the **voice-class** statements in the dial peer blocks refer to voice classes that have not yet been defined in the configuration (because that part of the startup configuration file has not yet been read). The gateway silently removes the undefined references to voice class blocks from the running configuration. This problem is corrected in 12.0(7)XK and beyond by putting the voice class blocks at the beginning of the configuration and the dial peer blocks at the end of the configuration.

Example D-6   **debug voip ccapi inout** *on the Called VoIP Gateway (Codec Negotiation Failure)*

Line Number	Cisco IOS Debugging Output
1	`voice-gw1#debug voip ccapi inout`
2	`voice-gw1#`

continues

Example D-6 *debug voip ccapi inout on the Called VoIP Gateway (Codec Negotiation Failure) (Continued)*

3	Aug 15 17:13:28.886 UTC: cc_api_call_setup_ind (vdbPtr=0x8167E948, callInfo={called=4356, calling=9, fdest=1 peer_tag=9}, callID=0x817A1B74)
4	Aug 15 17:13:28.890 UTC: cc_process_call_setup_ind (event=0x8170FB48) handed call to app "SESSION"
5	Aug 15 17:13:28.894 UTC: sess_appl: ev(19=CC_EV_CALL_SETUP_IND), cid(1538), disp(0)
6	Aug 15 17:13:28.894 UTC: ccCallSetContext (callID=0x602, context=0x8177DC0C)
7	Aug 15 17:13:28.894 UTC: ssaCallSetupInd finalDest cllng(9), clled(4356)
8	Aug 15 17:13:28.894 UTC: ssaSetupPeer cid(1538) peer list: tag(4356) tag(1000) tag(1)
9	Aug 15 17:13:28.894 UTC: ssaSetupPeer cid(1538), destPat(4356), matched(4), prefix(), peer(817E2EA8)
10	Aug 15 17:13:28.898 UTC: ccCallSetupRequest (peer=0x817E2EA8, dest=, params=0x8177DC20 mode=0, *callID=0x817142C8)
11	Aug 15 17:13:28.898 UTC: callingNumber=9, calledNumber=4356, redirectNumber=
12	Aug 15 17:13:28.898 UTC: accountNumber=, finalDestFlag=1,
13	guid=5a94.457f.2f4a.20ef.0000.0000.1639.d6bc
14	Aug 15 17:13:28.898 UTC: peer_tag=4356
15	Aug 15 17:13:28.898 UTC: ccIFCallSetupRequest: (vdbPtr=0x8170BAEC, dest=, callParams={called=4356, calling=9, fdest=1, voice_peer_tag=4356}, mode=0x0)
16	Aug 15 17:13:28.898 UTC: ccCallSetContext (callID=0x603, context=0x81783EAC)
17	Aug 15 17:13:28.898 UTC: ccCallProceeding (callID=0x602, prog_ind=0x0)
18	Aug 15 17:13:28.906 UTC: cc_api_call_proceeding(vdbPtr=0x8170BAEC, callID=0x603,
19	prog_ind=0x0)
20	Aug 15 17:13:28.906 UTC: cc_api_call_alert(vdbPtr=0x8170BAEC, callID=0x603, prog_ind=0x8, sig_ind=0x1)
21	Aug 15 17:13:28.906 UTC: sess_appl: ev(17=CC_EV_CALL_PROCEEDING), cid(1539), disp(0)
22	Aug 15 17:13:28.906 UTC: ssa: cid(1539)st(1)oldst(0)cfid(-1)csize(0)in(0)fDest(0)-cid2(1538)st2(1)oldst2(0)
23	Aug 15 17:13:28.906 UTC: ssaIgnore cid(1539), st(1),oldst(1), ev(17)
24	Aug 15 17:13:28.910 UTC: sess_appl: ev(7=CC_EV_CALL_ALERT), cid(1539), disp(0)
25	Aug 15 17:13:28.910 UTC: ssa: cid(1539)st(1)oldst(1)cfid(-1)csize(0)in(0)fDest(0)-cid2(1538)st2(1)oldst2(0)
26	Aug 15 17:13:28.910 UTC: ssaFlushPeerTagQueue cid(1538) peer list: tag(1000) tag(1)
27	Aug 15 17:13:28.910 UTC: ccCallAlert (callID=0x602, prog_ind=0x8, sig_ind=0x1)
28	Aug 15 17:13:28.910 UTC: ccConferenceCreate (confID=0x81714318, callID1=0x602, callID2=0x603, tag=0x0)
29	Aug 15 17:13:28.910 UTC: cc_api_bridge_done (confID=0x277, srcIF=0x8167E948, srcCallID=0x602, dstCallID=0x603, disposition=0, tag=0x0)
30	Aug 15 17:13:28.922 UTC: cc_api_bridge_done (confID=0x277, srcIF=0x8170BAEC, srcCallID=0x603, dstCallID=0x602, disposition=0, tag=0x0)
31	Aug 15 17:13:28.922 UTC: cc_api_caps_ind (dstVdbPtr=0x8167E948, dstCallId=0x602, srcCallId=0x603,

Example D-6   **debug voip ccapi inout** *on the Called VoIP Gateway (Codec Negotiation Failure) (Continued)*

```
32              caps={codec=0x887F, fax_rate=0x7F, vad=0x3, modem=0x0
33                  codec_bytes=0, signal_type=3})
34          Aug 15 17:13:28.922 UTC: cc_api_caps_ind (dstVdbPtr=0x8170BAEC,
            dstCallId=0x603, srcCallId=0x602,
35              caps={codec=0x4, fax_rate=0x2, vad=0x2, modem=0x1
36                  codec_bytes=20, signal_type=0})
37          Aug 15 17:13:28.922 UTC: cc_api_caps_ack (dstVdbPtr=0x8170BAEC,
            dstCallId=0x603, srcCallId=0x602,
38              caps={codec=0x4, fax_rate=0x2, vad=0x2, modem=0x1
39                  codec_bytes=20, signal_type=0})
40          Aug 15 17:13:28.926 UTC: cc_api_caps_ack (dstVdbPtr=0x8167E948,
            dstCallId=0x602, srcCallId=0x603,
41              caps={codec=0x4, fax_rate=0x2, vad=0x2, modem=0x1
42                  codec_bytes=20, signal_type=0})
43          Aug 15 17:13:28.926 UTC: sess_appl: ev(23=CC_EV_CONF_CREATE_DONE),
            cid(1538), disp(0)
44          Aug 15 17:13:28.926 UTC: ssa:
            cid(1538)st(3)oldst(0)cfid(631)csize(0)in(1)fDest(1)-
            cid2(1539)st2(3)oldst2(1)
45          Aug 15 17:13:29.010 UTC: cc_api_call_disconnected(vdbPtr=0x0,
            callID=0x602, cause=0x10)
46          Aug 15 17:13:29.022 UTC: sess_appl: ev(12=CC_EV_CALL_DISCONNECTED),
            cid(1538), disp(0)
47          Aug 15 17:13:29.022 UTC: ssa:
            cid(1538)st(4)oldst(3)cfid(631)csize(0)in(1)fDest(1)-
            cid2(1539)st2(4)oldst2(1)
48          Aug 15 17:13:29.022 UTC: ssa: Disconnected cid(1538) state(4)
            cause(0x10)
49          Aug 15 17:13:29.022 UTC: ccConferenceDestroy (confID=0x277, tag=0x0)
50          Aug 15 17:13:29.022 UTC: cc_api_bridge_done (confID=0x277,
            srcIF=0x8167E948, srcCallID=0x602, dstCallID=0x603, disposition=0
            tag=0x0)
51          Aug 15 17:13:29.034 UTC: cc_api_bridge_done (confID=0x277,
            srcIF=0x8170BAEC, srcCallID=0x603, dstCallID=0x602, disposition=0
            tag=0x0)
52          Aug 15 17:13:29.034 UTC: sess_appl: ev(24=CC_EV_CONF_DESTROY_DONE),
            cid(1538), disp(0)
53          Aug 15 17:13:29.038 UTC: ssa: cid(1538)st(6)oldst(4)cfid(-
            1)csize(0)in(1)fDest(1)-cid2(1539)st2(6)oldst2(1)
54          Aug 15 17:13:29.038 UTC: ccCallDisconnect (callID=0x602, cause=0x10
            tag=0x0)
55          Aug 15 17:13:29.038 UTC: ccCallDisconnect (callID=0x603, cause=0x10
            tag=0x0)
56          Aug 15 17:13:29.066 UTC: cc_api_call_disconnect_done(vdbPtr=0x0,
            callID=0x602, disp=0, tag=0x0)
57          Aug 15 17:13:29.070 UTC: sess_appl: ev(13=CC_EV_CALL_DISCONNECT_DONE),
            cid(1538), disp(0)
58          Aug 15 17:13:29.070 UTC: ssa: cid(1538)st(7)oldst(6)cfid(-
            1)csize(0)in(1)fDest(1)-cid2(1539)st2(7)oldst2(1)
59          Aug 15 17:13:29.074 UTC: cc_api_call_disconnect_done(vdbPtr=0x8170BAEC,
            callID=0x603, disp=0, tag=0x817A28FC)
60          Aug 15 17:13:29.074 UTC: sess_appl: ev(13=CC_EV_CALL_DISCONNECT_DONE),
            cid(1539), disp(0)
61          Aug 15 17:13:29.074 UTC: ssa: cid(1539)st(7)oldst(1)cfid(-
            1)csize(1)in(0)fDest(0)
62          voice-gw1#
```

E

F

J-K

L

M

S

T

CCIE Professional Development

Cisco LAN Switching

Kennedy Clark, CCIE; Kevin Hamilton, CCIE

1-57870-094-9 • AVAILABLE NOW

This volume provides an in-depth analysis of Cisco LAN switching technologies, architectures, and deployments, including unique coverage of Catalyst network design essentials. Network designs and configuration examples are incorporated throughout to demonstrate the principles and enable easy translation of the material into practice in production networks.

Advanced IP Network Design

Alvaro Retana, CCIE; Don Slice, CCIE; and Russ White, CCIE

1-57870-097-3 • AVAILABLE NOW

Network engineers and managers can use these case studies, which highlight various network design goals, to explore issues including protocol choice, network stability, and growth. This book also includes theoretical discussion on advanced design topics.

Large-Scale IP Network Solutions

Khalid Raza, CCIE; and Mark Turner

1-57870-084-1 • AVAILABLE NOW

Network engineers can find solutions as their IP networks grow in size and complexity. Examine all the major IP protocols in-depth and learn about scalability, migration planning, network management, and security for large-scale networks.

Routing TCP/IP, Volume I

Jeff Doyle, CCIE

1-57870-041-8 • AVAILABLE NOW

This book takes the reader from a basic understanding of routers and routing protocols through a detailed examination of each of the IP interior routing protocols. Learn techniques for designing networks that maximize the efficiency of the protocol being used. Exercises and review questions provide core study for the CCIE Routing and Switching exam.

Cisco Press

www.ciscopress.com

Cisco Career Certifications

Cisco CCNA Exam #640-507 Certification Guide

Wendell Odom, CCIE

0-7357-0971-8 • AVAILABLE NOW

Although it's only the first step in Cisco Career Certification, the Cisco Certified Network Associate (CCNA) exam is a difficult test. Your first attempt at becoming Cisco certified requires a lot of study and confidence in your networking knowledge. When you're ready to test your skills, complete your knowledge of the exam topics, and prepare for exam day, you need the preparation tools found in *Cisco CCNA Exam #640-507 Certification Guide* from Cisco Press.

CCDA Exam Certification Guide

Anthony Bruno, CCIE & Jacqueline Kim

0-7357-0074-5 • AVAILABLE NOW

CCDA Exam Certification Guide is a comprehensive study tool for DCN Exam #640-441. Written by a CCIE and a CCDA, and reviewed by Cisco technical experts, *CCDA Exam Certification Guide* will help you understand and master the exam objectives. In this solid review on the design areas of the DCN exam, you'll learn to design a network that meets a customer's requirements for perfomance, security, capacity, and scalability.

Interconnecting Cisco Network Devices

Edited by Steve McQuerry

1-57870-111-2 • AVAILABLE NOW

Based on the Cisco course taught worldwide, *Interconnecting Cisco Network Devices* teaches you how to configure Cisco switches and routers in multi-protocol internetworks. ICND is the primary course recommended by Cisco Systems for CCNA #640-507 preparation. If you are pursuing CCNA certification, this book is an excellent starting point for your study.

Designing Cisco Networks

Edited by Diane Teare

1-57870-105-8 • AVAILABLE NOW

Based on the Cisco Systems instructor-led and self-study course available worldwide, *Designing Cisco Networks* will help you understand how to analyze and solve existing network problems while building a framework that supports the functionality, performance, and scalability required from any given environment. Self-assessment through exercises and chapter-ending tests starts you down the path for attaining your CCDA certification.

Cisco Press   **www.ciscopress.com**

Cisco Press Solutions

Enhanced IP Services for Cisco Networks
Donald C. Lee, CCIE

1-57870-106-6 • AVAILABLE NOW

This is a guide to improving your network's capabilities by understanding the new enabling and advanced Cisco IOS services that build more scalable, intelligent, and secure networks. Learn the technical details necessary to deploy Quality of Service, VPN technologies, IPsec, the IOS firewall and IOS Intrusion Detection. These services will allow you to extend the network to new frontiers securely, protect your network from attacks, and increase the sophistication of network services.

Developing IP Multicast Networks, Volume I
Beau Williamson, CCIE

1-57870-077-9 • AVAILABLE NOW

This book provides a solid foundation of IP multicast concepts and explains how to design and deploy the networks that will support appplications such as audio and video conferencing, distance-learning, and data replication. Includes an in-depth discussion of the PIM protocol used in Cisco routers and detailed coverage of the rules that control the creation and maintenance of Cisco mroute state entries.

Designing Network Security
Merike Kaeo

1-57870-043-4 • AVAILABLE NOW

Designing Network Security is a practical guide designed to help you understand the fundamentals of securing your corporate infrastructure. This book takes a comprehensive look at underlying security technologies, the process of creating a security policy, and the practical requirements necessary to implement a corporate security policy.

Cisco Press

www.ciscopress.com

Cisco Press Solutions

EIGRP Network Design Solutions

Ivan Pepelnjak, CCIE

1-57870-165-1 • AVAILABLE NOW

EIGRP Network Design Solutions uses case studies and real-world configuration examples to help you gain an in-depth understanding of the issues involved in designing, deploying, and managing EIGRP-based networks. This book details proper designs that can be used to build large and scalable EIGRP-based networks and documents possible ways each EIGRP feature can be used in network design, implmentation, troubleshooting, and monitoring.

Top-Down Network Design

Priscilla Oppenheimer

1-57870-069-8 • AVAILABLE NOW

Building reliable, secure, and manageable networks is every network professional's goal. This practical guide teaches you a systematic method for network design that can be applied to campus LANs, remote-access networks, WAN links, and large-scale internetworks. Learn how to analyze business and technical requirements, examine traffic flow and Quality of Service requirements, and select protocols and technologies based on performance goals.

Cisco IOS Releases: The Complete Reference

Mack M. Coulibaly

1-57870-179-1 • AVAILABLE NOW

Cisco IOS Releases: The Complete Reference is the first comprehensive guide to the more than three dozen types of Cisco IOS releases being used today on enterprise and service provider networks. It details the release process and its numbering and naming conventions, as well as when, where, and how to use the various releases. A complete map of Cisco IOS software releases and their relationships to one another, in addition to insights into decoding information contained within the software, make this book an indispensable resource for any network professional.

Cisco Press

Cisco Press Solutions

Residential Broadband, Second Edition
George Abe

1-57870-177-5 • AVAILABLE NOW

This book will answer basic questions of residential broadband networks such as: Why do we need high speed networks at home? How will high speed residential services be delivered to the home? How do regulatory or commercial factors affect this technology? Explore such networking topics as xDSL, cable, and wireless.

Internetworking Technologies Handbook, Second Edition
Kevin Downes, CCIE, Merilee Ford, H. Kim Lew, Steve Spanier, Tim Stevenson

1-57870-102-3 • AVAILABLE NOW

This comprehensive reference provides a foundation for understanding and implementing contemporary internetworking technologies, providing you with the necessary information needed to make rational networking decisions. Master terms, concepts, technologies, and devices that are used in the internetworking industry today. You also learn how to incorporate networking technologies into a LAN/WAN environment, as well as how to apply the OSI reference model to categorize protocols, technologies, and devices.

OpenCable Architecture
Michael Adams

1-57870-135-X • AVAILABLE NOW

Whether you're a television, data communications, or telecommunications professional, or simply an interested business person, this book will help you understand the technical and business issues surrounding interactive television services. It will also provide you with an inside look at the combined efforts of the cable, data, and consumer electronics industries' efforts to develop those new services.

Performance and Fault Management
Paul Della Maggiora, Christopher Elliott, Robert Pavone, Kent Phelps, James Thompson

1-57870-180-5 • AVAILABLE NOW

This book is a comprehensive guide to designing and implementing effective strategies for monitoring performance levels and correctng problems in Cisco networks. It provides an overview of router and LAN switch operations to help you understand how to manage such devices, as well as guidance on the essential MIBs, traps, syslog messages, and show commands for managing Cisco routers and switches.

Cisco Press   **www.ciscopress.com**

Cisco Press Fundamentals

IP Routing Primer
Robert Wright, CCIE
1-57870-108-2 • AVAILABLE NOW

Learn how IP routing behaves in a Cisco router environment. In addition to teaching the core fundamentals, this book enhances your ability to troubleshoot IP routing problems yourself, often eliminating the need to call for additional technical support. The information is presented in an approachable, workbook-type format with dozens of detailed illustrations and real-life scenarios integrated throughout.

Cisco Router Configuration
Allan Leinwand, Bruce Pinsky, Mark Culpepper
1-57870-022-1 • AVAILABLE NOW

An example-oriented and chronological approach helps you implement and administer your internetworking devices. Starting with the configuration devices "out of the box;" this book moves to configuring Cisco IOS for the three most popular networking protocols today: TCP/IP, AppleTalk, and Novell Interwork Packet Exchange (IPX). You also learn basic administrative and management configuration, including access control with TACACS+ and RADIUS, network management with SNMP, logging of messages, and time control with NTP.

IP Routing Fundamentals
Mark A. Sportack
1-57870-071-x • AVAILABLE NOW

This comprehensive guide provides essential background information on routing in IP networks for network professionals who are deploying and maintaining LANs and WANs daily. Explore the mechanics of routers, routing protocols, network interfaces, and operating systems.

Cisco Press

www.ciscopress.com

Cisco Press Fundamentals

Internet Routing Architectures, Second Edition

Sam Halabi with Danny McPherson

1-57870-233-x • AVAILABLE NOW

This book explores the ins and outs of interdomain routing network design with emphasis on BGP-4 (Border Gateway Protocol Version 4)--the de facto interdomain routing protocol. You will have all the information you need to make knowledgeable routing decisions for Internet connectivity in your environment.

Voice over IP Fundamentals

Jonathan Davidson and James Peters

1-57870-168-6 • AVAILABLE NOW

Voice over IP (VoIP), which integrates voice and data transmission, is quickly becoming an important factor in network communications. It promises lower operational costs, greater flexibility, and a variety of enhanced applications. This book provides a thorough introduction to this new technology to help experts in both the data and telephone industries plan for the new networks.

For the latest on Cisco Press resources and Certification and

Training guides, or for information on publishing opportunities, visit

www.ciscopress.com

Hey, you've got enough worries.

Don't let IT training be one of them.

Get on the fast track to IT training at InformIT,
your total Information Technology training network.

 | **www.informit.com** |

■ Hundreds of timely articles on dozens of topics ■ Discounts on IT books from all our publishing partners, including Cisco Press ■ Free, unabridged books from the InformIT Free Library ■ "Expert Q&A"—our live, online chat with IT experts ■ Faster, easier certification and training from our Web- or classroom-based training programs ■ Current IT news ■ Software downloads ■ Career-enhancing resources

Cost Accounting

Cost Accounting

Lester E. Heitger, Ph.D., C.P.A.
Graduate School of Business
Indiana University

Serge Matulich, Ph.D., C.P.A.
Roy E. Crummer Graduate School of Business
Rollins College

McGraw-Hill Book Company
New York   St. Louis   San Francisco   Auckland   Bogotá   Hamburg
Johannesburg   London   Madrid   Mexico   Montreal   New Delhi
Panama   Paris   São Paulo   Singapore   Sydney   Tokyo   Toronto

COST ACCOUNTING

1 2 3 4 5 6 7 8 9 0   DOCDOC   8 9 8 7 6 5 4

ISBN 0-07-027991-8

This book was set in Caledonia by Progressive Typographers, Inc.
The editors were Jim DeVoe, Michael Elia, and Peggy Rehberger;
the designer was Merrill Haber;
the production supervisor was Charles Hess.
The drawings were done by J & R Services, Inc.
R. R. Donnelley & Sons Company was printer and binder.

Library of Congress Cataloging in Publication Data

Heitger, Lester E.
      Cost accounting.

      Includes index.
      1. Cost accounting.   I. Matulich, Serge.
II. Title.
HF5686.C8H385   1985   657′.42   84-14342
ISBN 0-07-027991-8

Material from Uniform CPA Examination Questions and Unofficial Answers, Copyright © 1960, 1961, 1962, 1963, 1964, 1965, 1966, 1967, 1968, 1969, 1970, 1971, 1972, 1973, 1974, 1975, 1976, 1977, 1978, 1979, 1980, 1981, 1982, 1983 by the American Institute of Certified Public Accountants, Inc., is reprinted (or adapted) with permission.

Material from the Certificate in Management Accounting Examinations Copyright © 1972, 1973, 1974, 1975, 1976, 1977, 1978, 1979, 1980, 1981, 1982 by the National Association of Accountants, is reprinted (or adapted) with permission.

CONTENTS

PREFACE

There was a time when only students majoring in accounting would consider taking an accounting course beyond those required for all business majors. Now many students and instructors recognize the value of more advanced accounting courses for nonaccounting students. Finance majors often take intermediate accounting and cost accounting, either as required courses or as electives. Students majoring in management, marketing, production, information systems, and other areas find that a course in cost accounting is especially useful.

This book was written to satisfy the needs of accounting majors and nonaccounting students who desire a strong background in cost accounting concepts and procedures and in the managerial reporting process. It is suitable for schools that cover undergraduate or graduate cost accounting courses in either one or two semesters or quarters. The book is intended for students who have obtained a minimum of one semester of financial accounting as a background.

The book covers a range of material that is sufficiently comprehensive to accommodate various course objectives. We have tried to achieve a careful balance between conceptual and technical material based on the philosophy that future managers need a solid grasp of managerial and cost accounting concepts to use cost accounting data effectively in making business decisions.

ORGANIZATION OF THE BOOK

The book is divided into seven major parts. It covers cost accounting for both manufacturing and nonmanufacturing businesses and activities. Part One, Fundamental Cost Accounting Concepts, introduces students to the cost accounting environment, the basic concepts of costs and cost flows, cost behavior, and decision making using cost-volume-profit relationships. Part Two, Product Costing, introduces students to the accounting systems used to accumulate product costs in manufacturing operations—job order costing and process costing. Part Three, Planning and Control, covers the development of a complete master budget, introduces flexible budgeting, and discusses the concepts of control through standard costing and analysis of variances.

With a background in product costing, planning, and control, students are ready to proceed to Part Four, Managerial Uses of Cost Data. Included here are relevant costs and alternative choice decisions, variable costing, decentralized operations, and segment performance measurement and reporting. The part ends with chapters on inventory management and control and the use of cost data in pricing decisions. Part Five, Long Range Planning, takes students through a comprehensive coverage of capital budgeting and also covers planning for not-for-profit operations.

For instructors who want thorough coverage of several important cost accounting areas, Part Six, In-Depth Cost Accounting Topics, includes extensive discussions on accounting for the cost of materials, labor, and manufacturing overhead. Also included in this part are chapters on joint products and by-products and on mix and yield variances in a standard costing system. The book concludes with Part Seven, Tools for Managerial Analysis, which covers quantitative concepts commonly used in cost analysis and decision making. A chapter on basic statistics, probability, and sampling reviews these concepts with a special emphasis on business management. Regression and correlation analysis, a powerful managerial tool, is covered thoroughly in Chapter 24. A comprehensive coverage of learning curve analysis is included in the last chapter, which also includes basic linear programming concepts.

The book concludes with an appendix on the time value of money, allowing students to review compound interest concepts. The appendix is accompanied by a set of compound interest tables. The book also includes a table of random numbers, a normal curve table, and learning curve tables, all suitable for use with the quantitative chapters. A very complete glossary of all key terms introduced in the book is included, with chapter references to guide the student to the chapter where each term was first used. The glossary is followed by a section of key figures for all exercises and problems for which a single numeric answer can be provided. Students may use the key figures to determine if they have obtained the correct solution to their assignments.

SPECIAL FEATURES OF THE BOOK

The book is comprehensive and flexible. The material is organized in an order that we consider logical for class presentation. But cost accounting courses can be structured in many different ways. Therefore the material was written to permit maximum flexibility. After Chapter 4, many chapters can be covered in a variety of sequences without loss of continuity. This permits instructors a wide choice of topics to suit individual course goals.

Numerous learning aids are included throughout the book. Marginal notes focus the students' attention or emphasize important concepts or topics in the chapters. The wide margins allow students to insert their own marginal notes as they deem necessary. Many examples and figures illustrate key concepts. All new terms are printed in **boldface** type and are clearly defined when they are introduced in the text. The use of appropriate headings throughout each chapter helps students perceive the organization of topics and guides their study of the material.

A comprehensive summary at the end of each chapter reinforces important material and provides a quick review of the entire chapter. The summary is followed by a list of important terms introduced in the chapter. Each key term is referenced to the page number where it is first used, an innovation that we first used in our *Financial* and *Managerial* books and that is now widely copied because students find it so useful. We purposely omit definitions at the end of the chapter so that students will look for unfamiliar terms in their appropriate context. Of course, they may also refer to the glossary for any term, without having to guess in which chapter it was first introduced.

END-OF-CHAPTER MATERIAL

Questions at the end of each chapter address important issues or concepts and require thought and insight rather than mere repetition of what the chapter stated. The exercises and problems at the end of each chapter are generally arranged in the same sequence as the chapter material, and they cover all topics in the chapter. To the extent possible, the exercises and problems are also arranged in the order of difficulty, with the shorter and easier problems occurring first, and the more demanding ones found in the later part of the chapter. The exercises are generally short and relatively simple, typically covering a single topic or concept. The problems are longer and more challenging, usually integrating several topics or concepts. At the end of each chapter, we have also included one or two cases covering more complex topics that require analysis; these often integrate ideas from earlier chapters. Questions, exercises, problems, and cases all include materials from the CPA and the CMA examinations in addition to original items developed by the authors.

Far more end-of-chapter material is provided than can possibly be covered in any one course, adding flexibility in problem selection and the ability to suit many course goals in both graduate and undergraduate programs. One of the important features of the exercises and problems is their thorough coordination with chapter material, thus enabling students to obtain guidance from the chapter when attempting a solution. In addition, the questions, exercises, problems, and cases range over a wide variety of topics, present students with interesting situations, and offer a variety of learning experiences. To enhance the students' comprehension, we avoid using strange or artificial products and situations and instead describe goods and services to which students can relate because they are easily visualized and understood. All questions, exercises, problems, and cases and their solutions, with the exception of professional examination material, have been designed by the authors and are thoroughly compatible with the text material. Solutions have been prepared by the authors and checked carefully for accuracy by two accountants. Professional examination material has been carefully selected and edited to fit the book.

One of the most valuabe features of this book is the very complete set of student and instructor supplements that accompanies the text. Each supplement has been developed and written by the authors to ensure complete integration with the text. Below we discuss supplements available to students and to instructors.

STUDENT SUPPLEMENTS

A *Study Guide* is available that provides guidance and practice for each chapter of the book. It is designed to give students a maximum learning experience with a minimum of effort, focusing on the important aspects of each chapter and reinforcing chapter material by means of objective and practical exercises and self-tests. For each chapter in the text, the *Study Guide* contains a set of learning objectives, comments on the salient aspects of the chapter, a complete sentence outline of the chapter, objective questions for study and self-testing, and exercises that cover the chapter topics. To minimize the time lost in learning to solve new problems, students are given suggestions on how to approach the problem and what steps to take in arriving at the correct solution. Solutions explaining the steps needed to arrive at answers, or the logic of a particular solution are provided for all *Study Guide* materials.

Two *Practice Sets* are available with the book and may be used to strengthen the knowledge of materials studied in the text. One practice set covers the product cost cycle in a manufacturing operation using a job order cost system; the other presents a profit planning and performance measurement problem. The profit planning practice set encompasses budgeting, standard costs, performance reports, and cost volume profit analysis. The job order practice set is available in computerized form only. It will be available for use on Apple II+ and IIe, as well as IBM(PC) microcomputers. Either or both practice sets may be assigned, or they may be alternated for different terms. The practice sets contain all forms necessary for a complete solution. A separate *Solutions Manual* for both practice sets is available to adopters.

INSTRUCTOR'S SUPPLEMENTS

Four separate items are available to the instructor to help with planning the course, making assignments, teaching, testing, and grading materials. The first is a complete *Solutions Manual,* which contains solutions to all questions, exercises, problems, and cases. A very comprehensive *Instructors' Resource Manual* provides invaluable help for users of the textbook. Included is information that helps instructors plan course assignments, preview the chapter, and prepare lectures and class materials. Important features of this supplement include a problem-topic grid that provides a complete cross-reference between exercises, problems, and cases and the topics covered in the chapter. The *Instructors' Resource Manual* also contains a complete set of lecture notes with suitable illustrations and examples, most of which are also available on teaching transparencies designed for use with the lecture notes.

A comprehensive book of *Examination Questions* includes a large number of objective questions, both conceptual and numeric, and numerous test problems, all with complete solutions. Appropriate professional examination material is included, in addition to the materials prepared by the authors. All examination material also indicates the time required to solve each problem.

An instructor can easily devise an unlimited number of different tests to suit any class situation using this supplement.

A complete set of overhead transparencies actually makes up two instructor supplements. One is a set of solutions to appropriate exercises, problems, and cases for use in class discussion of homework assignments. The other is a set of teaching transparencies developed specifically to supplement the instructor's class lectures.

The combination of textbook, student supplements, and instructor's supplements is unique among cost accounting textbooks that are currently published. The entire package makes the book flexible and adaptable to many classroom situations.

ACKNOWLEDGMENTS

The authors are grateful to many professors, students, and others who have provided us with help and guidance in the preparation of this book. We wish to offer special thanks to Mr. Arunkhumar and Professor Louis Geller, who were especially helpful with checking the accuracy of end-of-chapter materials as well as examination problems and *Study Guide* exercises. Reviews provided by William F. Bentz, University of Oklahoma; Louis Geller, Queens College; Gardner M. Jones, Michigan State University; Rajabali Kiani, California State University; Lawrence Klein, University of Wyoming; Pekin Ogan, Indiana University; Grover L. Porter, Western Kentucky University; John Tabor, Loyola University of Chicago; Joseph Techavichit, University of Nevada; John T. Wheeler, University of California, Berkeley; and Barbara Vidulich, Northeastern University helped the authors immensely in orienting the book toward potential users. The editorial staff of McGraw-Hill whose help was invaluable in the preparation of the book includes Marjorie Singer, Mike Elia, Jim DeVoe, Peggy Rehberger, Mel Haber, and Dennis Conroy. Members of the authors' immediate families contributed a great deal in work, suggestions, patience, and understanding. Without the help of the people listed above, we could not have completed the books and supplements, nor could we have made the necessary corrections and improvements embodied in the final package. Of course, any errors are the sole responsibility of the authors.

Lester E. Heitger

Serge Matulich

Cost Accounting

PART ONE
Fundamental Cost Accounting Concepts

All organizations can be described by accounting information, which is used to measure performance and financial status. Managers are the internal users of accounting information. They use it to decide how to operate the organization — to plan and control its activities. External users also need accounting information to make decisions about an organization. Stockholders use it to decide if they want to buy or sell ownership in the organization; bond holders and other creditors decide if they want to lend to it; and government agencies use it to regulate the organization's behavior.

Much of the accounting information used for this sort of decision making is data about costs. Cost accounting data are used by managers to monitor activities, evaluate performance, make decisions, and obtain answers to the many problems that managers must solve daily. How much did the promotional program for the new product cost? Was the construction cost of the new plant within the budget? Did the wheel bearing division achieve its target profit? Did the 8-horsepower garden tractor cost more to manufacture than the $640 estimated by management? There is no limit to the number of questions addressed by detailed cost accounting data.

To use cost data, managers must know what it means. They must understand the nature of costs and cost accounting terminology. The study of cost accounting starts with an introduction to the environment of cost accounting, which is covered in Chapter 1. Chapter 2 presents many fundamental cost accounting concepts and discusses how cost information is measured so that it reflects the way it is related to business activities. Chapter 3 discusses the way costs behave, the way they change as the volume of activity changes, and illustrates the impact of cost behavior on management planning and decision making.

CHAPTER 1
The Cost Accounting Environment

Business managers need information on the cost of making products, providing services, marketing products, and many other business activities. The climate of our current economy demands that managers be **accountable** for the results of their decisions. How will profits be affected if a manufacturing process is changed? Should an auto manufacturer make the windshields for its cars or buy them from a glass manufacturer? To increase production, should additional employees be hired or should employees work overtime? Will expanding the manufacturing plant be less costly if started now while unemployment is high and labor is plentiful, or later when the economy is stronger but interest rates are lower? Should the Navy develop its own mathematics training program for its personnel or hire professional instructors? Will the purchase and operation of a computer provide better and more timely information for a hospital's needs than use of a computer service company?

Managers of both profit-seeking and not-for-profit organizations depend heavily on accounting information to make informed decisions on issues like these. Cost data are particularly necessary, because any activity of an organization can be described by its cost. This text explores and analyzes the many different types of costs and explains and illustrates the use of various cost data in managing organizations effectively.

THE NEED FOR ACCOUNTING DATA

Accounting information has always been vital in the management of organizations. When organizations and the climate in which they operated were simple, they produced little accounting information. For example, prior to the Industrial Revolution, artisans and traders needed relatively simple data to operate profitably. As business grew and became more complex, the accounting information needed to measure and describe the organization also became more voluminous and complex. Eventually, with the advent of partnerships, joint ventures, and corporations, two distinct users of an organization's accounting information emerged: those who managed the business and those who had an interest because they were owners or creditors. A natural division in accounting occurred, with one branch serving the internal needs of managers and another serving the needs of those outside of the business.

Managers must report on their stewardship responsibilities

Financial and Managerial Accounting

Accounting information is provided in reports designed to suit the information needs of users. **Financial accounting** reports such as income statements, balance sheets, and statements of changes in financial position are intended primarily for external users who need a periodic overview of the operations and financial position of an organization. Naturally such reports also serve managers, but not really in the day-to-day management of a business. The primary function of financial accounting is to provide accounting information to external users.

Managerial accounting reports are designed to satisfy the specific information needs of the organization's management. Such reports provide detailed accounting data that are essential for the effective and efficient management of an organization's resources.

Financial reports are general and satisfy GAAP

In contrast to financial accounting reports, which are general, managerial accounting reports contain specific information, such as the cost of manufacturing a particular product or the planned expenditure for a television advertising program. Financial reports are issued annually or quarterly; managerial reports are prepared monthly, weekly, or even daily. Often financial accounting reports are audited to ensure accuracy of information and compliance with generally accepted accounting principles. On the other hand, managers require timely information and are often willing to sacrifice some accuracy in order to get data quickly. Managers sometimes rely on immediate estimates rather than waiting for actual and precise data.

Managerial reports are specific, frequent, and must satisfy management needs

Cost Accounting

Managers of both profit-seeking businesses and not-for-profit organizations need detailed accounting data to monitor daily operations, control costs, and evaluate performance. The information most useful for these managerial functions is cost accounting data. **Cost accounting** is the process of determining the cost of producing some product, providing some service, or undertaking some activity. Managers therefore depend heavily on cost accountants, who are trained to accumulate cost information and report it to managers in the form best suited for decision making.

Cost accounting is a process that provides cost data

Managers have always been interested in the cost of products and activities. However, the field of cost accounting really developed when it became necessary to measure the cost of making specific products in a complex manufacturing activity. For a merchant who bought cloth at one price and sold it at another price, the cost of merchandise was known and did not pose serious measurement problems. The craftsman who hired an apprentice to perform unskilled labor while learning a trade was not faced with serious problems of measuring labor costs. But as products required a variety of materials, many types of labor, and resources such as machinery and clerical staff of an entire factory, specific techniques had to be developed to measure product costs.

Cost accounting developed relatively late as a separate field of accounting. It was incorporated in the double-entry accounting system even later, only near the end of the nineteenth century. This was the point in the

Industrial Revolution when manufacturing activities dictated a need for detailed measurements of manufacturing costs.

Cost accounting is needed for all organizations, not just manufacturing

Cost accounting developed originally in manufacturing businesses to satisfy management's need for product cost information. For this reason, we tend to associate cost accounting with manufacturing operations. Cost accounting information, however, is useful for all types of activities in all types of organizations.

Planning and Control

Managers need cost accounting information to plan and control the operations of the organization. **Planning** is the process of setting goals, determining what resources are needed, and deciding how best to use them to achieve the goals. Although many types of information are useful for planning, cost accounting information is designed especially for this purpose. Costs are measurable and verifiable dollar amounts of objectives, activities, and programs that are intended to satisfy organizational goals.

Control is the day-to-day management function intended to ensure that operations accomplish what was planned. To control operations, managers compare actual performance with planned performance. Deviations from the plans are investigated to determine the cause and to decide how to adjust for it if necessary.

Figure 1-1 illustrates the planning, control, and performance measurement process. At the top are the major goals of the organization, established at the highest level of decision making, for example, by the board of directors. An example of such goals is to provide a fair return to investors by manufacturing products in the major appliance industry. To achieve these goals, top managers set specific objectives to guide the organization. One such objective may be to produce refrigerators, ranges, and dishwashers. To satisfy the objectives, detailed plans are developed with the help of accounting information. These plans consist of budgets that describe the amounts of material and labor to be used for making each product, decisions on product pricing, and marketing strategies. Operations are guided by managers in accordance with the detailed plans, and as results are achieved their costs are measured by accountants. The costs accumulated during operations make up the data needed for preparing accounting reports.

The managerial reports prepared from the cost data form a feedback loop and provide managers with information on how the specific plans of the organization are being met. Managers can compare actual performance with planned operations, and if actual performance deviates from the plans, managers use the information to control performance by making adjustments in operations. The financial reports prepared from the cost data also form a feedback loop. They enable managers to determine whether the specific objectives of the organization are being satisfied. If they are not, the information is used to control operations by changing the plans. Of course, both financial and managerial reports are used at all levels of the organization, but the detailed managerial reports are more relevant for controlling operations at lower levels, whereas the more general financial reports are most suitable for higher-level policy setting.

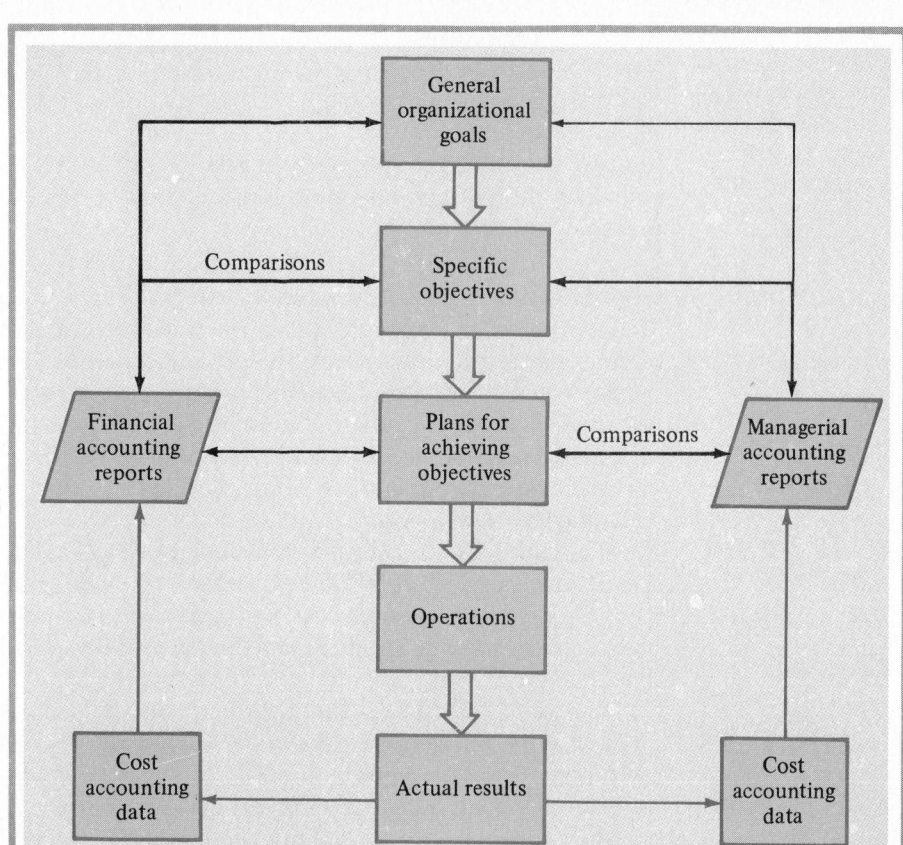

Figure 1-1. Cost accounting data and accounting reports enable managers to perform the planning and control functions. Cost accounting information provides feedback to managers so that they can compare actual results and planned objectives to determine if plans are being satisfied and if objectives are being met. Control is achieved by taking action to prevent operations from deviating significantly from plans. The heaviest lines show the most important feedback loops needed for control. All information is used internally, but some is less useful for control purposes, as indicated by the lighter feedback loops, which are more relevant for planning.

The Cost Accounting Data Base

What is the relationship of cost accounting to financial and managerial accounting? Cost accounting is the process of determining costs that become the information in financial and managerial reports. Typically, managerial accounting reports are quite detailed. Examples are the weekly product cost reports for the production of 10-inch bread knives, a weekly report on the difference between the actual and expected labor cost of producing 2-horsepower circular saws, and the monthly reports on the cost of selling a product. In financial accounting reports, cost accounting data are summarized into

Figure 1-2. The cost accounting data base is the foundation on which financial and managerial accounting reports are built.

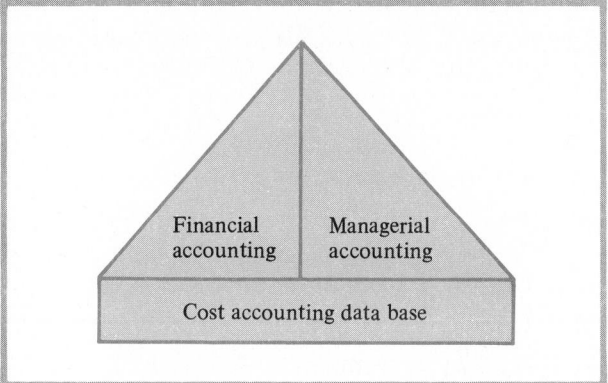

aggregate figures that describe the cost of activities for some particular time period. The cost of goods sold in the income statement is a summary of the cost of all products sold during the accounting period covered by the report. As Figure 1-2 shows, cost accounting provides a **data base** for both financial and managerial accounting reports, but the two types of reports have different purposes. The **cost accounting data base** is the data foundation that supports financial and managerial accounting activities.

DECISION MAKING

To understand how cost accounting information helps managers make decisions, it is important for you to appreciate the steps taken in making decisions. All of us are faced daily with many decisions, some so routine and insignificant that we think little of either the decision or the process we go through to reach it. You decide what clothes to wear, what to eat for breakfast, and which television program to watch. Each of these activities requires a decision, but you probably recall few factors that influenced the decision or little information that helped you to decide. Typically, people tend to remember only the more important decisions, such as the purchase of a new car or the selection of a job.

Decision making is a part of all activities

The same situation occurs in business. Managers make many decisions each day. Some have a greater impact than others and therefore require more careful analysis. Routine decisions often receive little analysis or attention. More complex decisions that require committing a large amount of resources, such as the building of a new production plant or the development of a new product line, often are evaluated using very complex analysis models. The more impact the decision has on organizational goals, the greater the need to analyze it carefully and systematically. Managers should understand well the decision-making process and the information used in the analysis in order to make decisions efficiently and to achieve the desired results from them.

Many researchers have analyzed the decision-making process and proposed and developed a body of knowledge known as **decision theory**, which is the body of knowledge that describes the decision-making process. According to decision theory, the decision process can be segmented into a series of specific steps that can be applied to any decision to analyze problems logically.

Decision-Making Process

Probably no two people make decisions in exactly the same way. However, most people agree that the decision-making process includes the following general steps:

1. Defining the problem
2. Identifying alternatives
3. Accumulating relevant information
4. Making the decision

To avoid wasting time in the decision-making process, problems must first be defined

Defining the Problem. All of the activities in the decision-making process depend on the problem definition. Managers must be able to identify clearly the specific problem at hand; if they cannot do so, they may spend considerable time and resources identifying alternatives and gathering information that are not pertinent to solving the problem. Let's look at a specific situation to see how the decision-making process works.

Various line managers of the Ace Water Heater Corporation have reported production costs that are greater than planned. Top management is interested in identifying the specific problem causing the higher costs and in taking corrective action. Bruce Jones, the production supervisor, noticed that his department was charged significantly more than usual for the cost of steel used in the production of hot water heaters. He informed Jane Williams, the plant manager, who assumed that the purchasing agent was not diligent in securing the raw materials at the lowest prices. An analysis of purchasing activities, however, showed that the cost increase resulted from a switch to a specially treated steel. Believing that the steel requirements were changed unnecessarily, Williams tried to determine who made the decision. Further investigation showed that the material change was initiated by design engineers when sales personnel reported that the less costly material deteriorated too quickly. The specially treated steel was necessary to make the product more durable and therefore more attractive when compared with competing products.

What is actually the problem in this situation? It is not the action of the purchasing agent, design department, or sales personnel. The problem is the cost of a specific material. The decision to substitute a higher-cost steel without investigating its effect on the overall cost of the product may have resulted in a product that is better but that cannot be competitively priced. Complex problems sometimes require extensive analysis before a clear problem definition is reached.

Identifying Alternatives.   Having defined the problem, what is the next step in the decision-making process? There is more than one feasible solution to most problems. To make the most effective decision, managers should identify all potentially practical solutions. In this phase of decision making, managers should use their ingenuity. Daring and creativity are assets when identifying alternatives, and there is no need to be cautious or inhibited since the alternatives are evaluated at a later phase.

The idea stage of decision making requires innovation

Let us return to the problem of high material costs faced by the management of the Ace Water Heater Company. Jane Williams would like to achieve the company's planned costs for the production of water heaters without impairing market position. Several different managers suggested possible solutions. One suggested a complete testing of the specially treated steel to see if the change is actually warranted. Another suggestion called for a product price increase accompanied by a special advertising program to extol the qualities of the higher-grade production materials. A third alternative is to use the original steel for construction but add a special protective treatment near the end of the production process. A fourth calls for reducing the cost of the insulation and outer casing of the heater to offset the higher steel cost. None of these alternatives can be accepted or rejected until they are evaluated, and they cannot be evaluated until the relevant information is obtained and analyzed.

Accumulating Relevant Information.   Decision makers rely on various types of information to assist them in selecting among alternatives. Some information may be subjective and some objective; some may be internal to the organization and some may be external. Some information may be based on past costs or events and some on management's expectations about future costs or events.

Only relevant information bears on a decision

Whatever the nature of the information, it must be useful to the decision maker. Only information that affects the decision should be accumulated; information that does not should be discarded. With the tremendous data processing capabilities of today's computers, decision makers often are flooded with huge quantities of data. This "information overload" can be avoided by carefully selecting only information that is relevant.

Information reduces the risk of incorrect action in the decision-making process

Information should increase the decision maker's knowledge about the problem at hand, or reduce the risk of reaching an incorrect decision. For example, Ace Water Heater Company is evaluating alternative protective treatments for its water heater tanks. Jones, the production supervisor, is aware of four different treatments that may work, but each would have to be tested for effectiveness. If one of the treatments meets the necessary criteria, the others could be discarded. But which is the most suitable alternative? How can more information help to reach a decision with the least cost or risk of making a mistake?

Without further information, Jones has a 25 percent chance of guessing which treatment is suitable. By random selection, he may have to test two, three, or all four treatments before finding the acceptable one. When he is informed that one of the treatments is not compatible with steel, this information increases the chance of guessing correctly to one-third and reduces the risk of incurring a high testing cost. Subsequently, Jones finds out that another of the available treatments was tested last year by another department and did not meet specifications. This additional information reduces the risk of error to 50 percent, since only two treatments remain to be tested. When Jones learns that one of the two treatments is not compatible with copper casings, this information is not relevant to the decision at hand. You can see that relevant information increased the knowledge of the situation and reduced the risk of selecting the wrong treatment for testing. When a treatment is finally selected, its cost becomes part of the information of this alternative. In our water heater example, cost data are prepared for each of the proposed alternatives to obtain information about the economic consequences of each proposed alternative.

Making the Decision. It may appear that once the problem is defined, the alternatives are identified, and relevant information is selected, it is obvious what to do. Sometimes this is the case. In the water heater example, managers may decide, on the basis of cost data and analysis of marketing strategies, to use treated steel and increase the price of the water heaters. But solutions to complex problems are seldom so simple in practice. Often, no single variable dominates the decision, but rather several important decision criteria interact. For example, in deciding on the location for a new store, a company may consider traffic patterns, potential customers living in the vicinity, availability of an adequate labor force, the cost of the location, the location of competing and complementary businesses, and other variables. Some locations may rank high for some variables and low for others.

Many firms use decision models to solve problems. **A decision model** is a verbal or mathematical description of the way that a decision is made. Decision models are suitable for making decisions in situations where the same problem recurs frequently. Most decision models typically use only objective information. For example, a manager may decide to buy lubricating

Figure 1-3. Decision making can be reduced to several general steps. Although they may overlap in the process of reaching a decision, it is helpful to visualize them as distinct parts of the process. The diagram shows that prior to taking action, additional alternatives may have to be identified or the problem may have to be redefined.

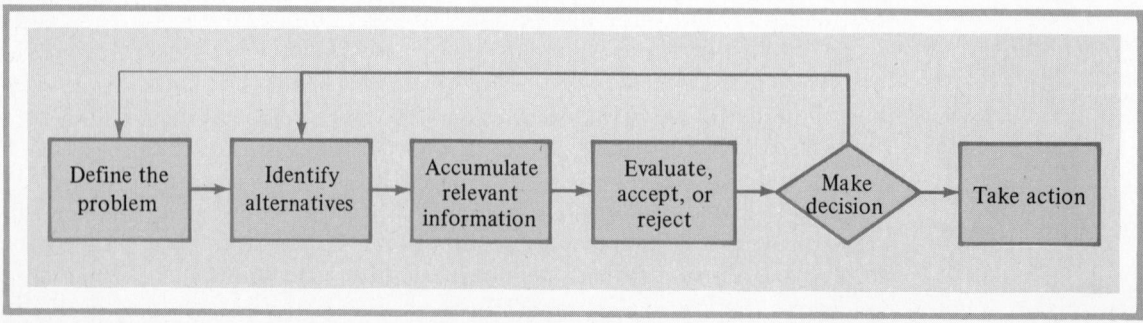

oil whenever the supply of oil is down to 5 gallons. The decision model may be: "Order 50 gallons of lubricating oil when 5 gallons are left in inventory." Other variables may be included in the decision model, such as the cost of placing the order or the time required to receive delivery. Additional variables make the decision model more complex. Whether simple or complex, the model is used as an "automatic pilot" device, enabling managers to spend their time making the more difficult decisions that rely on subjective information. In the final analysis, the **quality** of a decision is high if the decision leads toward the achievement of the organization's goals. The decision process illustrated in Figure 1-3 is the same whether or not a precise decision model is used.

A decision model is an automatic pilot—it helps to reach the decision but does not provide it

THE ROLE OF ACCOUNTING INFORMATION IN DECISION MAKING

When a manager selects one alternative from among several to solve a particular problem, he incurs a risk. There is the possibility the alternative selected will not solve the problem or that another alternative would have solved the problem better. This is especially true when the decision process includes subjective information. In the water heater example, Williams runs the risk that the advertising campaign will not convince potential customers that the product is worth the increased price, and the company will not achieve its expected sales and profit from the product. Information about advertising is often subjective. No one can state precisely that a given quantity of advertising will attract a specific number of customers. It is therefore preferable to use objective information whenever possible.

Unlike subjective information, accounting information is quantitative and verifiable, and is therefore very effective in giving credibility to decision makers. Managers use both subjective and objective information and the decision-making techniques available to them to make the most effective decisions possible. But because they are accountable for their decisions, they prefer objective information such as accounting data for use in decision making.

Objectivity is a valuable trait of accounting information

To illustrate, over the last two years Modesto Furniture Company has been experiencing regular increases in the cost of all its wood furniture products. Dave Keller, an experienced production supervisor, states that the higher product costs are due to increased lumber costs and a decline in productivity. A detailed cost analysis from the accounting department shows that the lumber costs increased an average of 7 percent per year over the last two years. On the other hand, during the same time period, production labor costs increased by 42 percent, and most of that increase, specifically 34 percent, was due to declining labor productivity.

Clearly, Dave Keller is correct about the causes of the cost increases. But as a manager would you rather have the subjective evaluation of the production supervisor or the more quantitative data presented by the cost accountant? Surely you prefer the accounting report, because it not only indicates the primary cause of the cost increases, but also measures the magnitude of the increases for each production resource. With the cost data, managers can map strategy more effectively, solve problems more quickly, and in general make better use of their managerial skills and talents.

Accounting Information Characteristics

For accounting information to be useful it must be:

1. Relevant
2. Timely
3. Accurate

Relevance.   Information is relevant when it has a bearing on the problem at hand. Relevance is therefore the most important characteristic of accounting information. Accounting information is relevant when it is useful in evaluating problems, measuring performance, and making decisions. Relevance is essential to both external and internal accounting reports, but has special significance to internal, or managerial, reporting. Managerial reports are not bounded by the rules and traditions of external reports. Managers have substantial freedom to secure precisely the type, amount, and timing of information necessary to accomplish their objectives. The primary limitation on internal reporting is the cost of preparing such reports.

The cost of information must be less than the benefits it provides

The cost of any management accounting report is justified only if the benefits derived from the information are greater than the costs of providing the information.

Timeliness.   Accounting information must be current. Many types of information lose value very rapidly, and financial information is particularly sensitive to the passage of time.

Knowing yesterday's market price of a company's stock may enable an investor to decide whether or not to invest in the business. If the market price information is a week old, the investor's decision may not be made wisely. Similarly, a department store manager may find daily sales information very useful in assessing the value of advertising programs as long as the sales information is reported on a timely basis. If the information is a month old when received, it may be of little value.

Approximate information now is better than accurate information too late

Internal accounting information must be timely because it is used to monitor and control daily operations. Sometimes immediate but approximate information is more useful than precise but late information.

Accuracy.   Even the most timely information is of no value if it is not accurate. Relevant and timely information must be accurate to be of use to decision makers. It is important, however, to distinguish between accuracy and precision. A report stating that the company produced 100,000 units last month may be accurate, although the precise number is 100,163 units. In this case precision may be unnecessary and accuracy is certainly good enough—after all, the difference between precision and accuracy is less than .2 percent

Precision and accuracy are not the same thing

(163/100,163). Accounting **data** and **information**[1] should be accurate to the extent allowed by the methods of measurement, and by the standards used to produce information.

In addition to relevance, timeliness, and accuracy, accounting information must also be understandable, objective, and free from bias.

Cost Accounting Activities

Systems are organized processes

A cost accounting system is a set of systematic processes and procedures used to measure, record, and report cost accounting data. There are four distinct activities in any cost accounting system:

Parts of the cost accounting system

1. Cost measuring
2. Cost recording
3. Cost analyzing
4. Cost reporting

Cost Measuring. The cost accountant accumulates the data needed to determine the cost of some specific product or activity. To enable the accountant to perform this activity, almost everyone in an organization must provide information about their work. Data on hours worked, units produced, and materials used all help the accountant measure the cost of operating the business.

Cost Recording. Most cost accounting systems are an integral part of a firm's double-entry accounting system, which requires recording costs in the journal and posting them to the ledger. The source of information for the system is the raw data produced by the firm's employees. The accountant converts hours worked or materials used into dollar figures that represent the cost of labor or materials, and the dollar amounts are recorded in the accounting system.

Cost Analyzing. Because accountants develop the cost data, they are in the best position to analyze costs for solving problems, planning operations, or providing advice to managers. Meaningful cost analysis depends upon an understanding of the cost measurement methods. The cost accounting system can generate huge amounts of information, but it is meaningful only to the manager who analyzes it thoroughly. Identifying trends in costs or the relationships between changes in costs and changes in the volume of business may provide valuable information to help a manager select the best course of action. Often it is up to the accountant to show managers how to analyze cost data and how to interpret and use accounting information.

---

[1] **Information** consists of data that have been put together into a usable form. The term **data** is used to describe the raw material or building blocks of an information system. In this book we do not adhere to strict definitions of data and information. Usually we use **data** to mean accumulated or recorded costs. **Information** describes specific reports or cost analyses. You should be aware of the more specific meanings of the terms when studying other subjects.

Cost Reporting.   Costs are reported in detail in internal reports and in aggregate in external financial statements. Reporting is the process of communicating with decision makers by disseminating relevant information to them. The entire cost accounting system is geared toward producing relevant and accurate information that can be communicated on a timely basis to those who need it.

Factors Affecting Cost Accounting Systems

A cost system should be designed to suit the organization

Many factors determine how complex the cost accounting system will be and how much data it will generate:

1. Size of the firm
2. Type of production process
3. Number of different products produced by the firm
4. Management's attitude toward cost information
5. External variables such as laws and regulations

Size of the Firm.   The amount of cost data necessary to manage a firm depends on its size. Managing a firm in which five people manufacture molded plastic flowerpots requires less cost data than managing a firm that manufactures the same item but employs 200 workers. In addition, the process of measuring costs is more complex in the larger firm, because its size makes it difficult to trace costs to specific products or activities. In general, the volume of cost data and the complexity of the cost system increase with firm size.

Type of Production Process.   In the simplest cases, the accountant measures the cost of materials, labor, and other resources used in making the product and assigns those costs to the product. To illustrate, the labor cost of a product is determined by the amount of time employees work on the product, and by their wage rate. When a worker's labor time can be identified with a specific product, accountants are able to assign the costs of that labor to the product. However, some production processes are complex, making it difficult to trace the cost of specific labor or specific material to a particular product. For example, if a worker requires 8 hours to produce 100 ten-gallon molded flowerpots, it is easy to assign a portion of his hourly wage to each pot. On the other hand if a worker requires 8 hours to operate a machine that produces 50 ten-gallon pots, 100 twelve-inch pot bases, and 200 five-gallon pots, assigning his wage and the machine depreciation to each item is not as simple. The more complex the production process, the more difficult it is to measure the cost of specific products, and the more sophisticated the cost accounting system must be.

Number of Different Products Produced.   If a firm produces only one product, all manufacturing costs can be assigned to it. When a firm produces several different products, however, accountants must distribute the manufacturing costs among the products. Some manufacturing costs, such as the cost of materials, are clearly related to specific products; but other costs of production, such as energy costs and property taxes, are not so clearly identified with specific products. Usually the number of costs not identifiable with specific products increases with the number of products produced.

Management's Attitude toward Cost Information.   Whether large or small, every manufacturing firm needs some minimum measure of its product cost to satisfy state and federal taxing authorities when it files tax returns. There is, however, a tremendous difference between the bare minimum requirement for cost data to satisfy external reporting needs and the amount of cost data developed in firms using extensive managerial reporting systems. The difference between the minimum and optimum cost system is determined by management's attitude toward cost information. Cost information is not free; it should be produced only when the value of the information is greater than the cost of preparing it.

External Variables.   Regulatory agencies such as the Internal Revenue Service, the Federal Trade Commission, and the Securities and Exchange Commission are having a growing influence on the frequency, detail, and structure of cost data shown in external reports. In addition to satisfying the needs of management, cost accounting systems must report information required by numerous laws and regulations.

EXTERNAL ORGANIZATIONS AND THE COST DATA BASE

External forces impose obligations on businesses

The kind and amount of cost data generated by a business for external reporting is, of course, influenced by the requirements of regulatory agencies. For example, businesses with certain types of federal government contracts are required to prepare cost data for the contracts in prescribed ways. Very large businesses must report information to the Federal Trade Commission. In general, the federal government influences the volume, detail, and form of a firm's cost data base.

Federal Trade Commission

The Federal Trade Commission (FTC) affects a firm's cost accounting system by enforcing the Robinson-Patman Act and through its lines of business reporting requirements.

The Robinson-Patman Act.   A firm that must comply with the Robinson-Patman Act may not charge more to one customer than to another for the same product. Discriminatory pricing of products of equal grade and quantity when such pricing would reduce competition is prohibited by the Robinson-Patman Act. According to the act, the only way a firm can discriminate in its pricing policy is by showing that:

1. The price difference is due to changing market conditions, or
2. The price difference was established to match the price difference of competitors, or
3. The price difference is caused directly by cost differences for the selling firm in manufacturing and distributing the product for different customers

When businesses base their pricing on the third case, the government requires them to support the price differences with detailed cost information.

Lines of Business Reporting. The FTC has the power to require large businesses to provide revenue and cost data by business segment rather than just company totals. Business segments may be defined according to the geographic markets served, such as foreign and domestic, or western, eastern, and southern United States; or by product lines, such as large appliances, automotive, and financial services. Business segments also are called lines of business and are categorized by a general classification chart provided by the FTC. The purpose of segmental or lines of business reporting is to gather business data that may be useful in identifying and eliminating unfair restraint of trade.

As a firm grows and reaches the size for which segmental reporting is required, it may find it necessary to restructure its cost accounting system to comply with FTC classifications. The cost of gathering and reporting segmental data frequently is a point of disagreement between the FTC and the reporting firms.

Internal Revenue Service

The Internal Revenue Service (IRS) is responsible for ensuring that individuals and organizations pay their legal share of federal income tax. Basically the IRS allows firms to use generally accepted accounting principles (GAAP) in determining taxable income. But the Internal Revenue Code does establish certain rules and procedures that affect costs. For instance the Code defines product costs, sets depreciation guidelines, encourages consistency in the use of alternative accounting procedures, and requires the use of last in, first out (LIFO) inventory valuation for book purposes if it is used for tax purposes.

Securities and Exchange Commission

The Securities and Exchange Commission (SEC) is responsible for ensuring that the financial statements published by publicly held corporations are fair representations of financial position. Like the IRS, the SEC relies heavily on the accounting profession's generally accepted accounting principles. In addition the SEC issues accounting pronouncements whenever it feels that some change in accounting practice is necessary to present a correct picture of the economic situation of businesses. Some SEC rules relate to cost accounting activities.

Cost Accounting Standards Board

Each year the federal government spends huge amounts of money purchasing goods and services from the private sector. Some items, such as computer hardware and food supplies for military personnel, are readily available in the market. Potential suppliers of such goods may submit bids when the government advertises the need for them.

Many items, such as nuclear submarines and jet fighter airplanes, must be produced by businesses to conform to specifications established by the government. Typically, such goods require developmental work prior to actual production; often it is difficult to estimate accurately what the cost of development and production will be. As a result government contracts with manufacturers often provide for payment of these costs plus a reasonable profit. In theory, such contracts seem very logical, but in practice much controversy can arise over what costs should be included as the basis for what the government should pay.

To minimize the potential for cost abuses in these kinds of negotiated contracts between manufacturers and the government, Congress created the **Cost Accounting Standards Board (CASB)** in 1970. Basically, the Board was created to ensure that the government pays a fair price. Specifically the CASB established the following objectives:

1. Uniformity: Achieve like costs under like circumstances
2. Consistency: Consistent practices within a firm over time
3. Comparability: Similarity of information and practices among different firms
4. Neutrality: Fairness with neither bias or prejudice to either contracting party

To achieve these objectives the CASB issued cost accounting standards. In 1980 the CASB went out of existence because Congress decided to terminate its funding. By this time it had issued 19 standards on those areas of cost accounting most relevant to negotiated government contracts.[2] Although the CASB no longer exists, its standards remain in force.

Financial Accounting Standards Board

The Financial Accounting Standards Board (FASB) is a professional rule-making body that establishes standards for financial reporting. All publicly held corporations must prepare their external accounting reports in accordance with FASB standards. Because cost accounting information is part of the external financial statements of most organizations, FASB pronouncements have a direct impact on the cost accounting systems of firms.

---

[2] A more detailed discussion of CASB objectives and standards may be found in *Cumulative Progress Report to the Congress 1971–1980*, Cost Accounting Standards Board, November, 1980.

THE CERTIFICATE IN MANAGEMENT ACCOUNTING

Recognition of professional competence is an essential part of an accountant's professional development. In public accounting a practitioner strives to become a **Certified Public Accountant (CPA).** To become a CPA, a candidate must pass a rigorous two-and-a-half day examination. In many states an applicant must also have a college degree and must work some minimum amount of time in public accounting in addition to passing the CPA examination before becoming eligible for certification.

The CMA — symbol of professional status

Management accounting is somewhat different from public accounting; in some states only people working in public accounting may take the CPA examination. To provide a measure of managerial accounting competence, the National Association of Accountants, through its Institute of Management Accounting, offers a **Certificate in Management Accounting (CMA).** An applicant earns this certificate by passing a rigorous five-part, two-and-a-half day examination and by meeting work experience requirements. The format of the CMA examination is similar to that of the CPA test, but the questions refer to a firm's internal reporting activities and management information needs. Both examinations are offered twice a year.

SUMMARY

Accounting information is required for making decisions in both business and nonbusiness organizations. Information is provided to users outside business organizations in the form of **financial accounting** reports. **Managerial accounting** is the internal reporting of accounting information for use by the business firm's managers. Both financial and managerial accounting reports include cost accounting information. **Cost accounting** is the process of measuring the cost of products and activities, especially in manufacturing operations where it is essential to measure the detailed cost of manufactured products.

Cost accounting provides management with the data necessary for effective planning and control. **Planning** is the process of setting goals and deciding how resources are to be used to achieve them. **Control** is the day-to-day management of operations to ensure that the plans are carried out. Control includes the measurement and evaluation of performance, and the investigation of deviations from plans. The **cost accounting data base** is the collection of cost data that enables management to develop plans and to control operations.

Decision making is a logical and systematic process comprising several steps: **defining the problem, identifying alternatives, accumulating relevant information,** and **making the decision.** A formal description of the way a decision is made is called a **decision model.**

The role of information, especially accounting information, is to increase knowledge and decrease the risk of making an incorrect decision. The information should be relevant, timely, and accurate. **Relevance** means that accounting data must satisfy the specific information needs of the user. **Timeliness** describes the need for accounting information to be current, since it tends to lose its value with the passage of time. **Accuracy** is the correctness of accounting information.

A **cost accounting system** is the set of practices and procedures used to accumulate, record, and report cost accounting information. Cost accounting activities include **cost measuring, cost recording, cost analyzing,** and **cost reporting.** The system should provide information whose benefit is greater than the cost of the information. The size and complexity of the cost accounting system in any organization depends on the size of the firm, the type of product, the variety of products, the attitude of management toward cost information, and external variables. The major external variables are government agencies and regulatory bodies.

Several government agencies influence the type of cost accounting data that businesses must gather. In particular the **Federal Trade Commission (FTC),** the **Internal Revenue Service (IRS),** and the **Securities and Exchange Commission (SEC)** enforce regulations that specify the manner in which some costs must be reported.

The **Cost Accounting Standards Board (CASB)** was created by Congress to establish standards and procedures for negotiated federal government contracts. Although the CASB no longer exists, its standards are still in force, and they make it necessary for many organizations to accumulate and maintain large amounts of cost accounting data.

Although the responsibility of the **Financial Accounting Standards Board (FASB)** is to create guidelines for financial reporting, it has an impact on the way that cost data are accumulated since aggregate totals appear on financial statements.

Recognition of professional excellence in cost accounting is obtained by qualifying for the **Certificate in Management Accounting (CMA).** The certificate is earned by having the necessary amount of qualified work experience and by passing a rigorous examination, similar in format to the CPA test.

KEY TERMS   Many new terms commonly used in business and accounting are introduced throughout this book. They are shown in **boldface** type and are usually defined when they are first introduced. Many of them are used and explained later in the book. You should become familiar with the terms in the list that follows. The italic numbers in parentheses indicate the pages where the terms first appear.

accuracy *(12)*
Certificate in Management Accounting (CMA) *(18)*
certified public accountant (CPA) *(18)*
control *(5)*
cost accounting *(4)*
cost accounting data base *(7)*
Cost Accounting Standards Board (CASB) *(17)*
cost accounting system *(13)*

cost analyzing *(13)*
cost measuring *(13)*
cost recording *(13)*
cost reporting *(14)*
data *(13)*
data base *(7)*
decision model *(10)*
decision theory *(7)*
Federal Trade Commission (FTC) *(15)*
financial accounting *(4)*

Financial Accounting Standards Board (FASB) *(17)*
information *(13)*
Internal Revenue Service (IRS) *(16)*
managerial accounting *(4)*
planning *(5)*
relevance *(12)*
Securities and Exchange Commission (SEC) *(16)*
timeliness *(12)*

QUESTIONS

1. Managers responsible for the stewardship of resources are accountable to owners and creditors who provided these resources. In laymen's terms, accounting may be defined as reporting by managers on the way they have discharged their responsibility. How does cost accounting fit into this definition? What is cost accounting? Is it inconsistent with reporting by management to external users of information?

2. Explain how the cost accounting data base supports internal reporting and how it affects external reporting. What types of information do you see as belonging in the cost accounting data base?

3. Planning and control are described in the chapter as functions of management that benefit from the use of cost data. Not all planning and control depends on cost data, however. Describe the process of planning and control required when the following activities are undertaken.
   a. A trip from Denver to New York City by airline for a 2-week vacation.
   b. Construction of a float for the homecoming parade.
   c. Moving from home into a dormitory room for the next year at college.

4. Managers are responsible for reporting accounting information to external users in accordance with generally accepted accounting principles. A company that owns an executive jet airplane, for example, must report the cost of the airplane, accumulated depreciation, and the method of depreciation used. A manager of the company would not be satisfied with only this information about the airplane. What other information does the manager need that is of little interest to external users of accounting reports?

EXERCISES

Ex. 1-1
The Decision-Making Process

You have been enrolled in college for two semesters and are now seriously considering majoring in accounting. You are aware, however, that this is an important decision that should not be made lightly.

REQUIRED

Prepare a report on the procedure that you should undertake to make your decision. Include in your report each of the steps used in the decision-making process.

Ex. 1-2
Relevant Information for a Business

Billie Brown's uncle has been operating a candy booth in a shopping mall for some years and has lived very comfortably on its income. Recently he died and left the business to Billie as her inheritance. Billie has just been laid off from her job as an assembly worker for an automobile manufacturer and would like to operate the candy booth, but she knows little about business. She comes to you and asks you to tell her what kind of information she might want to collect in order to operate her new business successfully.

REQUIRED

Respond to Billie's request emphasizing the purpose of the information that she may need.

Ex. 1-3
Information on
Decision
Alternatives

Michael recently won $50,000 in a state lottery. He wants to invest the money and is looking at several alternatives.

a. The first is an apartment house that is about 8 years old and is fully occupied. It is managed by a real estate firm. The buyer could assume the current mortgage, which would require about $46,000 cash payment plus monthly payments on the mortgage.

b. One of Michael's acquaintances is vice president of a small company that wants to expand its operations. He indicates that for $50,000 Michael could acquire about 30 percent of the company's stock. The vice president owns about 5 percent of the company and the rest is owned by three other individuals.

c. A realtor has shown Michael a 50-acre plot of land selling at $1,000 per acre. It consists of slightly rolling ground with a brook running through one corner. About 60 percent of the land has a variety of trees growing on it; the rest is grassland.

REQUIRED

Discuss what kind of information Michael should accumulate on each possible investment in order to decide which is most appropriate for him.

PROBLEMS

P. 1-1
Decision-Making
Alternatives

Mrs. Willow is retired and receives $450 per month in Social Security benefits. She supplements her income by baking delicious home-made pies and sells them for $3.00 each. She spends about 60 hours per month on pie-baking and feels that this is as much as she wants to work. Although she sells 300 pies per month, she would like to earn more money. Recently, Mrs. Willow's church offered to hire her for 40 hours per month at $4.00 per hour to maintain church records. If she takes the job she feels she would have to give up baking pies, and she is reluctant to do without the pie income. A friend suggests to her to keep good records of her baking expenses to determine how much she earns. In a month of record keeping Mrs. Willow collects the following data, which she feels represent an average month for her:

Grocery store receipts	$1,000
Utilities	110
Gasoline	45
Repairs and maintenance of car and appliances	25
Miscellaneous expenses	35

About 20 percent of the grocery bill represents items consumed by Mrs. Willow, and the rest consists of pie ingredients and supplies. She estimates that her utility bill would be only $90 if she did not bake pies. About half of the gasoline and maintenance costs can be attributed to her baking activities. The miscellaneous items are all personal.

REQUIRED

Evaluate Mrs. Willow's pie-baking business and advise her if she should continue to bake or accept the church job.

P. 1-2
Identifying
Relevant
Information

John Simmons has just purchased a record store from a friend who is retiring. When he took over the store he prepared an inventory of the merchandise, showing the original and replacement cost and the original and current selling price of each category of recordings.

		Per Unit			
	Quantity	Original Cost	Repl. Cost	Original Price	Current Price
Long-playing record albums	8,000	$5.50	$6.00	$7.00	$8.00
45 RPM records	5,000	2.20	1.20	3.00	2.00
Cassette tapes	6,000	4.00	4.50	8.00	8.00
8-track tapes	3,000	6.00	5.00	9.00	8.00

Simmons examined the data and made the following observations:

a. Record albums' prices have increased faster than their costs and should be pushed as the most profitable item.
b. 45 RPM record prices have dropped sharply. These records are now selling below original cost and clearly should be dropped from the product line.
c. The cost of cassette tapes has increased but the selling price remained the same. Should this item be discontinued?
d. The price of 8-track tapes has declined by a smaller percentage than the decline in cost. This looks like a good item to sell.
e. What problems may occur if a product line is dropped?

REQUIRED   Respond to each of Simmons's observations and questions and discuss any observations of your own.

P. 1-3
Basing Decisions on
Cost Accounting
Data

Bill Spencer designed and built a lovely wooden rocking horse for his grandson's first birthday. A neighbor saw the finished horse and stated that a safe, sturdy, basic toy of such quality could easily be sold for $30 each. Mr. Spencer, who is retired and likes to work with this woodworking equipment, is now thinking of building more rocking horses to sell directly from his home. He puts together the following list of materials:

Head	2 bd ft
Body	4 " "
Legs	1 " "
Rockers	3 " "
Dowels	3 lin ft @ $.10 per ft
Glue and screws	$.70 per horse
Varnish	$2.00 per horse

Spencer can buy lumber at $.80 per board foot. His woodworking tools cost $4,500 and can be expected to last 10 years with normal use. He spent 7 hours designing and building his grandson's rocking horse, but he estimates that if he works on batches of 50 horses at a time he will be able to finish a batch in a month with a total of 150 hours of work. Being realistic, he decides to allocate $100 per month for workshop depreciation and $15.00 per month for utilities. He does not want to work more than about 150 hours per month, and also estimates that demand for the horses would not be much more than 50 per month.

Spencer has just received an offer to work as a school crossing guard. The job requires about 150 hours per month and pays $4.00 per hour. Spencer would prefer to work at home but cannot afford to do so if he can earn more by working as a school crossing guard.

REQUIRED

a.   Calculate the hourly earnings for Spencer if he builds rocking horses.
b.   What other considerations are relevant to his decision?

P. 1-4
Identifying
Relevant
Accounting
Information

For many years Walter's Department Store has made all local deliveries by using a delivery service. The cost of the service averages $.30 per pound this year for the 600,000 pounds of merchandise delivered. The delivery service company plans to raise the rate by 20 percent for next year. The management of the department store is not pleased with the rate increase and is thinking of starting the store's own delivery service.

The following data have been gathered. An affiliated store in another city currently spends $.27 a pound for local deliveries. Two new delivery trucks would cost $80,000 each, have a delivery capacity of 500,000 pounds each per year, and would have a salvage value of $5,000 each at the end of five years. Other truck costs would average $.02 per pound for insurance, $.08 for gas and oil, $.03 for maintenance, and $.10 for personnel. Other costs associated with loading, storing, and delivering merchandise would amount to $.08 a pound. If the trucks had been purchased last year, they would have cost only $65,000 each.

REQUIRED

a.   Determine the cost per pound of deliveries if the store starts using its own trucks. Should the store accept this alternative?
b.   Would your answer to part *a* change if deliveries for the next year were 800,000 pounds instead of 600,000 pounds?
c.   What items of data did you choose to ignore in your analysis of parts *a* and *b*? Why?

CHAPTER 2
Cost Flows and Concepts

What costs should be provided to managers? There are many different kinds of costs and many ways they can be reported. Different costs serve different purposes. A manager may need a variety of cost reports for making decisions and evaluations. This chapter introduces basic cost concepts and terminology that you need in order to understand the role of cost accounting in the accounting system. Topics covered include how each cost is determined, when it is used, and how and when it is reported to managers and to external users of accounting information.

THE CONCEPT OF COST

Perhaps no other accounting term is used more frequently in everyday conversation than cost. People worry about increases in the cost of living, the cost of food, the cost of buying or renting a house, the cost of utilities and transportation, and the cost of vacations or other leisure activities. The term cost, however, may have different meanings to different people. Most people measure costs in dollars, but costs can also be measured as the time needed to accomplish a task, the energy expended to construct a product, or the opportunities lost by choosing one course of action over several available alternatives. But it is not enough to say that costs are measured in dollars. The term *cost* has many different meanings, and accountants must provide managers with a clear understanding of what types of costs are reported.

Cost defined

Cost is the amount of resource given up in exchange for some good or service. The resource given up is usually cash, but if not, it is still expressed in dollars. For example, if a manufacturing company acquires a new production machine in exchange for a delivery truck no longer needed, the new equipment is valued at the fair value of the truck given up.

The cost of purchased products

Determining costs can be simple. For example, the cost of new walnut desks for the office can be obtained by contacting various office supply companies. Similarly, you may determine the cost of typing a 100-page report by finding that the rate for typing service is $1.50 per page. In these cases, the cost of the product or service is merely its purchase price, or the value of the asset given up.

The cost of manufactured products

In some cases, however, determining the costs of products and activities is not easy. For example, if a company decides to manufacture walnut desks instead of buying them, measuring their cost is much more complex because the cost of all resources used in the production of the desks must be included

24

in the cost of the desks. Materials such as lumber, adhesives, and finishing compounds; the labor cost of cutting, assembling, and finishing the desks; and the cost of the necessary plant and production equipment used in making the desks all must be included in the measurement of the desks' cost. Similarly, if the 100-page report is typed by company personnel, what is its cost? Is it the typist's salary? What part of the salary? What about the cost of the typewriter, supplies, and maintenance? Other costs might be included in the cost of typing the report, such as a portion of the typist's health insurance cost that is paid by the company. The typist needs office space and utilities — all of which have a cost. Should these costs be added to the cost of the typed report?

Just what is included in a report on the cost of a product depends on the purpose of the report. For external reporting purposes accountants include all costs of producing the product or providing the service. But as you will learn later, a manager may want only some specific costs included for certain purposes, and others for other purposes. There are many different types of cost accounting reports that serve different management needs. To measure costs accurately and to satisfy managers' needs for specific types of cost reports, the particular product or business activity whose cost is to be reported must be carefully described or defined.

Defining Cost Objectives

Cost objectives are essential to determining cost

The first step in determining the cost of any product or activity is to define precisely the cost objective. A **cost objective** is any product, activity, or project whose cost is to be measured. For example, to find the cost of walnut office desks you must carefully describe the desk you need. The dealer may have desks of different sizes, made of solid walnut or walnut veneer, with or without full-suspension drawers, and with other variations in features, sizes, and quality. When the cost objective is a manufactured product, it must be defined clearly enough for the accountant to include all of the costs of producing the product, including manufacturing costs such as utilities, depreciation, insurance, and maintenance.

The cost objective is **not** the cost itself; rather the cost objective is the product or activity whose cost is to be measured. The more specifically and clearly the cost objectives are defined, the more accurate the resulting cost data that are reported and used to make many different decisions.

In a manufacturing firm, the primary cost objectives are products. What is the cost of making a refrigerator or a dinette table? Even in a manufacturing firm, however, products are not the only cost objectives of interest to managers. Many different costs influence decisions, and managers require cost information about all aspects of business. Typical cost objectives other than products include the cost of advertising, the cost of distributing products, the cost of computer services, the cost of operating the typing pool, and the cost of operating a division. The point is that a cost objective must be carefully defined before its cost can be measured.

To understand what we mean by a particular cost objective, we must agree on the parameters that define it. For example, if the cost objective is the marketing of a particular product, what are the parameters? Are they

1. Only the sales commission on the product?
2. Sales commission plus a portion of sales salaries?
3. Sales commissions, sales salaries, and advertising for the product?
4. Sales commissions, sales salaries, product advertising, and a portion of indirect costs such as clerical costs, office space and equipment costs, and computer service costs in the marketing department?

Any of these may define the cost objective for marketing a product. Which one to use depends on management's objectives in measuring and reporting marketing costs. The cost objective must be clearly defined so that accountants can accumulate the cost data representing the objective, and so that managers who use the cost information will know what it represents.

We begin our discussion of cost accounting concepts and procedures with tangible products such as chairs, radios, or baseball bats, because it is easy for you to visualize the production activities and their corresponding costs as the product moves through the manufacturing process. Although the cost of services and other activities may not be as easy to visualize, they must be measured, accumulated, and accounted for as well.

Manufacturing Cost Elements

There are three major types of costs incurred in manufacturing products. These are called **cost elements** and include:

Product cost elements

1. Direct materials
2. Direct labor
3. Manufacturing overhead

Material identified with specific products

Direct materials are the raw materials that are specifically identified with the production of a particular product. Direct materials become a part of the product, such as the handle of an axe, the wood in a table, or the steel in an automobile. For many products direct material is the largest manufacturing cost element.

Some materials may be used in the manufacturing process but do not become part of the product. For example, the masking tape used in painting a product is discarded when painting is complete. There are some raw materials that become part of the product but their cost is so insignificant in comparison with the total cost of manufacturing that accountants do not identify them as direct materials. An example is the cost of staples used to fasten upholstery to a piece of furniture. It is not possible nor economically feasible to identify these kinds of raw material costs with individual products. Such raw materials are called **indirect materials** and are accounted for as manufacturing overhead.

Labor identified with specific products

Direct labor is the cost of labor that can be identified specifically with the production of a particular product and that contributes directly to the completion of the product. The cost of employees assembling the parts of an automobile as it moves along the assembly line is direct labor. Similarly, the cost of an employee welding a steel beam to a column for a bridge, and the cost of a carpenter nailing together the framing of a house are also classified as direct labor. Some products require a significant amount of direct labor with correspondingly high direct labor costs.

Not all manufacturing labor can be identified readily with specific products. For example, employees who carry materials from storage to a work station and employees who repair and maintain the plant and production equipment are a necessary part of the production process, but their cost is not accounted for as direct labor because it cannot be identified with specific products. This **indirect labor** is part of manufacturing overhead cost.

Indirect costs of manufacturing

Manufacturing overhead (MOH) consists of all manufacturing costs other than direct materials and direct labor. It contains all of the indirect costs in the manufacturing process. Indirect manufacturing costs are necessary production costs that cannot be identified with specific products.

Manufacturing overhead costs are classified according to the nature of the product and the type of production process. The two most common classifications are indirect material and indirect labor. Other manufacturing overhead costs are the costs of operating the production facilities. They are called **occupancy costs** or **capacity costs** and include:

1. Building and equipment lease and rental costs
2. Depreciation of buildings and machinery
3. Heat, light, and power costs
4. Maintenance costs
5. Insurance and taxes on manufacturing facilities
6. Property taxes on production facilities

Other typical manufacturing overhead costs include employee fringe benefits, such as health insurance, vacation pay, and pension benefits; supervisory salaries for manufacturing personnel; and inventory handling costs. Although manufacturing overhead costs are indirect costs of production and by their very nature are not directly identifiable with specific products, they are **necessary** manufacturing costs and accountants must be able to assign them to products just as they assign the direct costs. In Chapter 4 we discuss the process of assigning overhead costs to products.

Manufacturing overhead also is called factory overhead, manufacturing burden, factory burden, or simply burden or overhead. All of these terms mean the same thing, and they are used interchangeably. Nevertheless, manufacturing overhead, sometimes abbreviated MOH, is most common and is used throughout this text. Furthermore, the term *burden* is a misnomer and implies an unnecessary drag on the organization, whereas overhead costs are essential to the production process.

In addition to direct materials, direct labor, and manufacturing overhead, other terms are sometimes used to describe manufacturing costs. Direct materials and direct labor together are called **prime costs,** because they can be traced directly to the finished product. Also, prime costs often receive the primary attention of management in its effort to control costs. Direct labor and manufacturing overhead together are called **conversion cost** because together they are costs of converting raw materials into finished products.

None of the three basic cost elements is generally more important than the others. Nevertheless, one cost may be much higher than others, depending on the type of product manufactured and the way it is produced. One product may require more costly material or less skilled labor than another.

COST FLOWS AND THEIR RELATIONSHIP TO PRODUCTS

Manufacturing a product can be thought of as the physical flow of materials, labor, and overhead through the production process. Engineers and production personnel are responsible for ensuring the smooth and efficient flow of these resources. Managerial accountants measure the flow, express it as a series of costs, and report the costs to managers in a relevant and timely manner.

Cost flows closely parallel production flows

The flow of product costs parallels the physical flow of the product through the production process. The relationship between production activity and product costs is clear for direct material costs and direct labor costs, but not so easy to determine for indirect manufacturing costs. The measurement of product costs is guided by the **matching principle,** which requires the matching of expenses with the related revenues. Production costs are assigned to products; when a product is sold, the cost assigned to it becomes an expense that is matched with the revenue generated by the sale.

Cost Flow Example

Visualize the production of a simple product such as a sledgehammer. A worker picks up a wooden handle and inserts it in the hole of the hammer's head. The worker then drives a wedge into a slot to tighten the fit and keep the handle and head from separating. You see that three raw materials, the head, the handle, and the wedge, and a certain amount of labor are required to produce a finished sledgehammer. With the addition of the labor, the three materials flow together to make up the finished product. Each of the materials, and the labor, has a specific cost.

When the hammerhead is joined to the handle, the sledgehammer's cost is the total of the two separate material costs. When the wedge is added, the cost of the hammer increases by the cost of the wedge. At the same time, the cost of labor further increases the cost of the hammer. The flow of product costs parallels the physical flow of the materials and labor through the production process. Of course, each of these production activities increases the value of the hammer. The increased value will be realized when the product is sold.

Production supervisors are interested in controlling production flows. Are enough handles available? Is the quality of the product satisfactory? Is the amount of time spent on assembly excessive?

Accountants, on the other hand, are interested in determining and reporting the production costs, so that managers will know the economic consequences of the decisions they make. As the sledgehammer takes shape, or flows through the production process, its costs flow through the cost accounting process. But while the costs of material and labor flow through the process as materials and labor are added, the indirect costs of production also become part of the cost flow. It is through these cost data that managers evaluate how well they are managing their resources.

Manufacturing Inventories

The business of service firms is to sell services. They have little or no inventory that they hold for resale to customers. The business of merchandising firms is to acquire products and sell them to customers. The business of manufacturing firms is to manufacture products and sell them. Therefore, inventories are prominent in merchandising and manufacturing firms, but not in service firms.

A merchandising firm may have many different classifications of inventory and many items within each inventory classification, but all inventory items are ready for sale. They do not require any major modifications, although assembly and other services may be performed to increase their salability.

Manufacturing firms have three major categories of inventory:

The three categories of manufacturing inventories

1. Raw materials
2. Work in process
3. Finished goods

The basic materials of the production process

Raw Materials.   The basic inputs that are converted into final products are called **raw materials.** Raw materials are not necessarily the most basic resources, such as lumber and iron ore. Instead they may be a partially manufactured product that a company is processing further. For example, pig iron is the raw material of the forging company that makes sledgehammer heads and sells them to the sledgehammer manufacturer. The final product of the forge, the finished hammerhead, is the raw material of the sledgehammer manufacturer who buys the heads, wood handles, and wedges used in the manufacture of the hammers. A manufacturer making a single product may have a large number of raw materials; one with a diversified product line may have thousands of different kinds of raw materials in inventory. Most raw materials are used as direct material. A small portion is indirect material.

Partially completed products

Work in Process.   Unfinished products that are in the process of being converted into final products, such as the sledgehammer with head and handle joined but not yet wedged, are called **work in process.** Many different items can be in work in process simultaneously. For example, a baker can have a variety of breads, cakes, and doughnuts in process at any given time, and an automobile manufacturer has many cars in various stages of production simultaneously.

Products ready for sale

Finished Goods. Products ready for sale, such as the completed sledgehammers, are called **finished goods.** In a manufacturing firm, finished goods inventory is similar to the merchandise inventory in a merchandising firm. In a multiple-product manufacturing firm, there are many different items in finished goods inventory.

THE PRODUCT COSTING CYCLE ILLUSTRATED

To determine the costs of a manufactured product, accountants rely on the flow of production activities as a basis for gathering cost data. Let's take a closer look at both the production and costing processes and see how the different production stages are monitored by the accountant. Figure 2-1 illustrates the flow of production activity and the parallel flow of the costs of those activities. The physical flow of products is shown at the bottom and the corresponding flow of costs through the ledger accounts is depicted at the top.

Figure 2-1. The physical flow of products through the production process is paralleled by the flow of costs through the ledger accounts. The matching concept guides accountants in assigning costs to products.

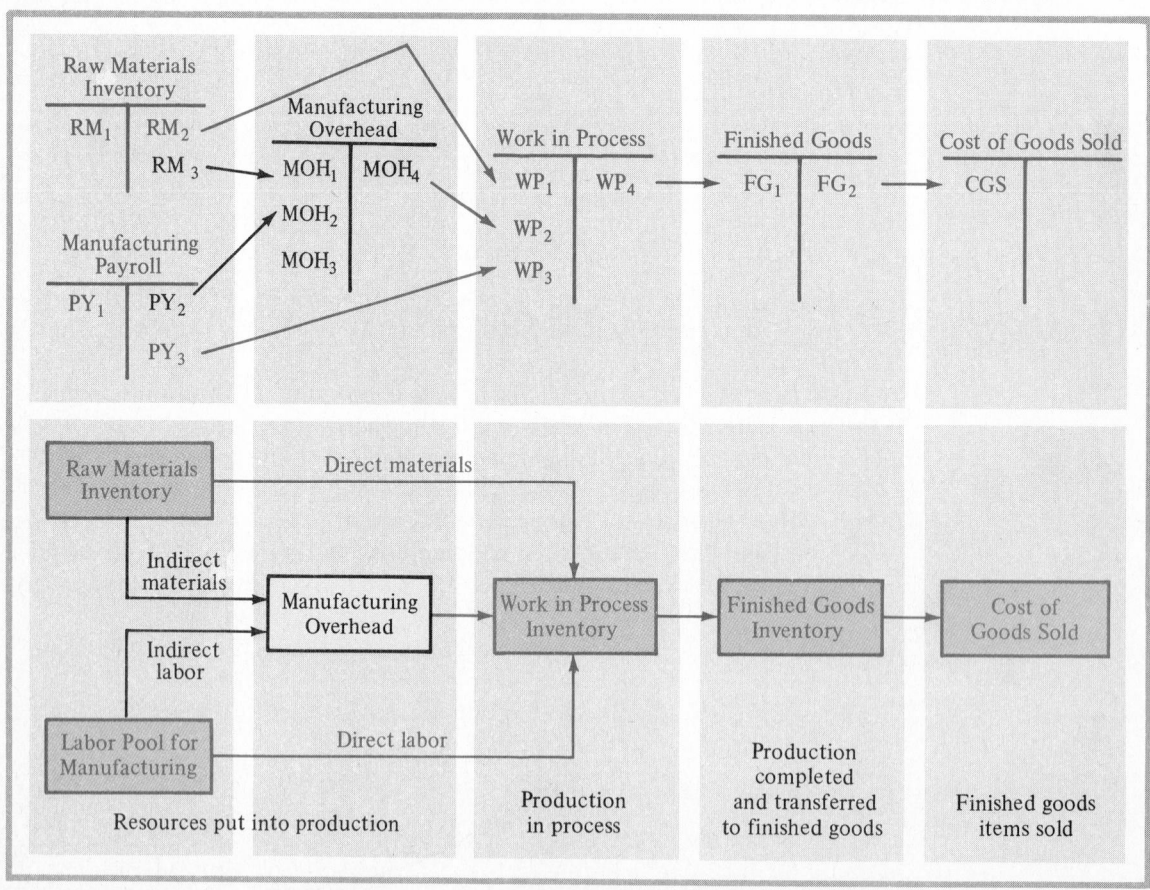

Purchases of raw materials are recorded in the Raw Materials Inventory account with a debit, represented by RM_1 in Figure 2-1. As raw materials are transferred to production, a similar transfer of costs occurs in the accounting records. Raw materials are used either as direct materials or as indirect materials. The cost of direct materials is recorded with a debit to Work in Process Inventory, WP_1, and a credit to Raw Materials Inventory, RM_2. The cost of indirect materials is recorded with a debit to Manufacturing Overhead, MOH_1, and a credit to Raw Materials Inventory, RM_3. Indirect materials cannot be assigned to the product directly so they become part of manufacturing overhead costs, which are assigned to products in a separate step.

Manufacturing payroll represents the cost of labor; it is accounted for in a manner similar to materials. The cost of production employees' wages during the period is charged to Manufacturing Payroll with the entry PY_1. The portion of this labor that cannot be identified directly with the products is indirect labor; indirect labor is removed from the Manufacturing Payroll account with the credit PY_2 and transferred to Manufacturing Overhead with the debit MOH_2. The labor cost of employees whose time can be identified with specific products is called direct labor; this cost is assigned directly to Work in Process Inventory with the debit WP_3 and removed from the Manufacturing Payroll account with the credit PY_3.

The debits to Manufacturing Overhead for indirect labor and indirect material are only a part of total MOH for most firms, usually a small part. The greater portion of MOH consists of numerous other costs incurred in the manufacturing process, such as factory depreciation, taxes, insurance, maintenance, and utilities. All of these other overhead items are represented by the debit MOH_3. Total manufacturing overhead cost is charged to production with a debit to Work in Process Inventory, WP_2, and a credit to Manufacturing Overhead, MOH_4. With this entry, the indirect materials and indirect labor, as well as other indirect manufacturing costs, all become part of the cost of manufactured products.

The Work in Process account contains manufacturing costs for all products currently in production. When the product is transferred from work in process inventory to finished goods inventory, the cost associated with producing it is transferred from the Work in Process Inventory account to the Finished Goods Inventory account. In Figure 2-1 the entry is represented by a debit to Finished Goods, FG_1, and a credit to Work in Process, WP_4.

You should be aware that both Work in Process Inventory and Finished Goods Inventory contain some costs, such as payroll, utilities, depreciation, and property taxes, that appear as expenses in the income statement of a nonmanufacturing firm. In nonmanufacturing businesses, these items are expensed because they have been consumed. In a manufacturing firm, however, these costs enhance the value of the product on hand. Direct labor and production facilities convert raw materials into goods that are more valuable than the raw materials from which they are made. This enhancement in value is not realized, however, until the product is sold. Since all of the costs that flow into production increase the value of the product, the costs are said to be inventoriable. **Inventoriable costs** are costs that legitimately can be made a

Costs that can be added to manufactured products

part of a manufactured product's cost rather than becoming an expense of the period in which the product was made.

The sale of the product is the final step in the product cost flow cycle. It is the event that causes the product cost to be transferred from the asset account Finished Goods to the expense account Cost of Goods Sold. The cost transfer is dictated by the matching principle, which requires matching expenses with associated revenues. The product cost is matched with the revenue generated from the sale of the product. This is accomplished by debiting Cost of Goods Sold, CGS, and crediting Finished Goods Inventory, FG_2, as shown in Figure 2-1. Regardless of how simple or complex the production process, the basic cost flow is the same as the one just described.

COST CONCEPTS

In addition to the basic concepts of cost flows, there are several other fundamental cost concepts that are essential to your understanding and appreciation of cost accounting.

Costs vs. Expenses

Cost is the amount given up for the resource

In daily conversation the terms *cost* and *expense* often are used interchangeably. But in accounting each term has a distinct meaning.

Cost is the amount of resource given up for some product or service. **Expense** is the amount of resource used during some specific accounting period.

Expense is the amount of resource used during the period

To illustrate, a one-year maintenance contract on office typewriters is purchased on October 1 for $1,800. The **cost** of the contract **is the $1,800 paid** for the maintenance service. At the end of the year, however, only three months of the service have been used up. The **expense** for the year **is $450** $(3/12 \times \$1,800)$. Similarly, equipment purchased on January 3 has a cost of $80,000. The depreciation expense for the year is $16,000 if the equipment has a useful life of 5 years and no salvage value and if straight-line depreciation is used. Notice that expense is a **timing concept** dictated by the matching principle, whereas cost is a **valuation concept.**

Product Costs and Period Costs

You may have noticed while studying product cost flows in a manufacturing firm that direct labor costs and overhead costs such as plant depreciation, utilities, and property taxes are recorded in Work in Process Inventory, which is an asset account. The cost of completed products is transferred to Finished Goods Inventory, also an asset account. These costs of producing the product do not become expenses until the product is sold. However, depreciation, utilities, and property taxes on the office building, as well as office personnel salaries, are recorded as expenses in the period in which they are incurred.

Accountants make a distinction between the cost of manufactured products and the costs incurred in nonmanufacturing activities. **Product costs** are recorded and carried as assets at the time products are made; they become expenses only when the product is sold. **Period costs** are costs of goods and services that are recorded as expenses in the period in which they are consumed.

To make a clear distinction between product and period costs, we look at the way these costs are reported in the income statements of the three basic types of businesses: service firms, merchandising firms, and manufacturing firms.

Service Firms.   Dentists, physicians, lawyers, certified public accountants, realtors, hairstylists, and carpet cleaning companies are all examples of businesses that generate revenues by selling services rather than products. The income statements of service firms have no product costs — only period costs. The only deductions from revenue are operating expenses, which are costs that expired during the current accounting period and must be matched with the current period's revenues. Figure 2-2 illustrates a simple income statement of a service business.

Service firms have no product cost

Figure 2-2. The income statement for a service firm has no product cost. Operating expenses are deducted from revenue to find net income.

Janice Stallings Real Estate Company
Income Statement
For the Year Ended December 31, 1985

Revenue from commissions		$264,000
Operating expenses:		
Advertising	$26,000	
Depreciation on furniture and equipment	9,400	
Salaries for clerical staff	29,700	
Salaries and commissions for sales staff	96,400	
Legal expenses	8,200	
Office rent	15,000	
Supplies	5,100	
Insurance	3,900	
Utilities	6,200	
Miscellaneous expenses	3,100	
Total operating expenses		203,000
Net income		$ 61,000

Merchandising Firms.   Department stores, drug stores, gift shops, and grocery stores are common examples of merchandising businesses. The income statement of the Corner Drug Store, shown in Figure 2-3, is used to illustrate the distinction between product costs and period costs of a merchandising firm. Like all merchandising firms, the drug store must first buy products before it can resell them to customers. The cost of the merchandise is called **product cost,** and the goods the firm buys are called **merchandise inventory,** whose cost is recorded as an asset until the goods are sold. When products are sold the product cost becomes an expense called **cost of goods sold.** The product costs include all direct and indirect costs incurred by the manufacturer to make the product, but the merchandising firm pays all these costs as part of the purchase price of the goods.

At the end of an accounting period, the cost of unsold products remains recorded as an asset because the goods not sold have future economic value. The cost of the ending merchandise inventory appears in the current assets section of the balance sheet. The cost of the sold goods becomes an expense in accordance with the matching principle. The revenue from the sale of a product is reported in the income statement, and the corresponding cost of that product is reported as an expense in the same period on the income statement.

Figure 2-3. A merchandising firm buys products that it sells to customers for a profit. The cost of the merchandise becomes an expense when the product is sold. The difference between sales revenue and product expense is called gross margin.

Corner Drug Store
Income Statement
For the Year Ended December 31, 1985

Sales			$253,100
Less cost of goods sold:			
Beginning inventory 1/1/85		$ 92,000	
Purchases	$173,000		
Less purchase returns	(11,400)		
Add freight-in	3,100		
Net purchases		164,700	
Goods available for sale		256,700	
Less ending inventory 12/31/85		104,800	
Cost of goods sold			151,900
Gross margin			101,200
Less operating expenses:			
Salaries		34,200	
Commissions		2,900	
Advertising		2,400	
Building depreciation		8,400	
Equipment rent		7,200	
Supplies		1,300	
Insurance		2,700	
Utilities		7,200	66,300
Net income			$ 34,900

Gross margin is computed for merchandising firms

The revenue account in a merchandising firm is called Sales. Revenue is generated by the sale of products; therefore the cost of the products sold should be matched with the sales revenue. The difference between sales revenue and cost of goods sold is called **gross margin.** Gross margin is the excess of the selling price over the cost of the product. For example, if a product sells for $15 and costs $9, the gross margin is $6.

The period costs of merchandising firms are the operating expenses deducted from gross margin. The operating expenses of most merchandising firms are similar to those of service firms. Differences in operating expenses occur because of the varying nature of operating activities of businesses. For instance, a merchandising firm has inventory handling expenses and usually more advertising expenses than a service firm.

Manufacturing Firms. Like merchandising firms, manufacturing firms have a product cost that is subtracted from sales revenue to arrive at gross margin. Figure 2-4 illustrates the income statement of a manufacturing business. Product cost of a merchandising firm is simply the invoice price paid for the product and recorded as an asset. In a manufacturing firm, however, the product cost must be calculated. These calculations, which can be complex, are the subject of Chapters 4, 5, and 6.

Figure 2-4. An income statement for a manufacturing business. The cost of goods manufactured figure is provided in a separate schedule. Manufacturing firms convert raw materials into finished products using labor and production facilities.

Marlin Manufacturing Company
Income Statement
For the Year Ended December 31, 1985

Sales		$929,600
Less cost of goods sold:		
Beginning finished goods inventory 1/1/85	$ 91,250	
Add cost of goods manufactured in 1985 (see Fig. 2-5)	587,200	
Total goods available for sale	678,450	
Less ending finished goods inventory 12/31/85	123,700	
Cost of goods sold		554,750
Gross margin		374,850
Less operating expenses:		
Sales salaries	48,100	
Sales commissions	46,450	
Advertising	18,400	
Administrative salaries	91,250	
Depreciation of office facilities	36,000	
Depreciation of office equipment	32,000	
Insurance	4,400	
Property taxes	9,000	
Office supplies	4,300	
Utilities	13,200	
Total operating expenses		303,100
Net income		$ 71,750

A manufacturing company purchases resources that are used to create salable products. The flow of costs from raw materials through finished goods to cost of goods sold is more difficult to identify than the product cost flow of a merchandising firm. In particular, the indirect costs of production are not as easy to trace through the production process. In a manufacturing firm the accountant measures the indirect costs and assigns them to the manufactured products. Although this is a complex process, it is necessary in order to develop accurate product costs for internal and external users of accounting information.

The cost of manufactured products

The period costs of a manufacturing firm are operating expenses similar to those of a merchandising or service firm. In a manufacturing firm all operating expenses are nonmanufacturing costs such as marketing and administrative expenses. All manufacturing costs appear as cost of goods sold if the product is sold, as finished goods inventory if the product is completed but not sold, or as ending work in process if the product is not yet completed.

Computing cost of goods sold

The Schedule of Cost of Goods Manufactured

The computation of cost of goods sold is shown in Figure 2-4. Adding the beginning finished goods inventory and the cost of goods manufactured during the period yields the cost of goods available for sale. If all finished units were sold, the cost of goods available for sale and the cost of goods sold would be the same for the period. In most cases, however, some units are not sold and remain in ending finished goods inventory. The cost of these unsold units is subtracted from the goods available for sale to determine the cost of goods sold. A major component of this calculation is the cost of goods manufactured; this is $587,200 in our example. How was this figure obtained? It is not an account balance. It is calculated in the schedule of cost of goods manufactured that accompanies the income statement of a manufacturing business.

Computing cost of goods manufactured

The schedule of **cost of goods manufactured** identifies the cost of products transferred from work in process inventory to finished goods inventory during the period. It summarizes the flow of product costs through the work in process account for a specified period of time. The example in Figure 2-5 covers the calendar year 1985. Sometimes the statement covers time periods other than a year, such as a month or a quarter.

Figure 2-5. A cost of goods manufactured schedule summarizes the total manufacturing cost for the period, the cost of units completed during the period, and the beginning and ending balances in work in process inventory.

Marlin Manufacturing Company
Schedule of Cost of Goods Manufactured
For the Year Ended December 31, 1985

Beginning work in process inventory 1/1/85			$107,400
Direct materials		$159,100	
Direct labor		184,900	
Manufacturing overhead:			
Indirect materials	$ 9,580		
Indirect labor	21,620		
Depreciation, manufacturing plant	52,000		
Depreciation, plant equipment	48,000		
Salaries, production supervisors	92,800		
Insurance, manufacturing plant	14,300		
Property taxes, manufacturing plant	17,900		
Utilities, manufacturing plant	32,700	288,900	
Total manufacturing cost for 1985			632,900
Total manufacturing cost in production for 1985			740,300
Less ending work in process inventory 12/31/85			153,100
Cost of goods manufactured 1985			$587,200

Figure 2-6 illustrates how the resources available to the manufacturing company are combined during the period to yield the data reported in the income statement and the schedule of cost of goods manufactured. The basic form of the cost of goods manufactured computation and the computation of cost of goods sold are quite similar. One major distinction is that cost of goods

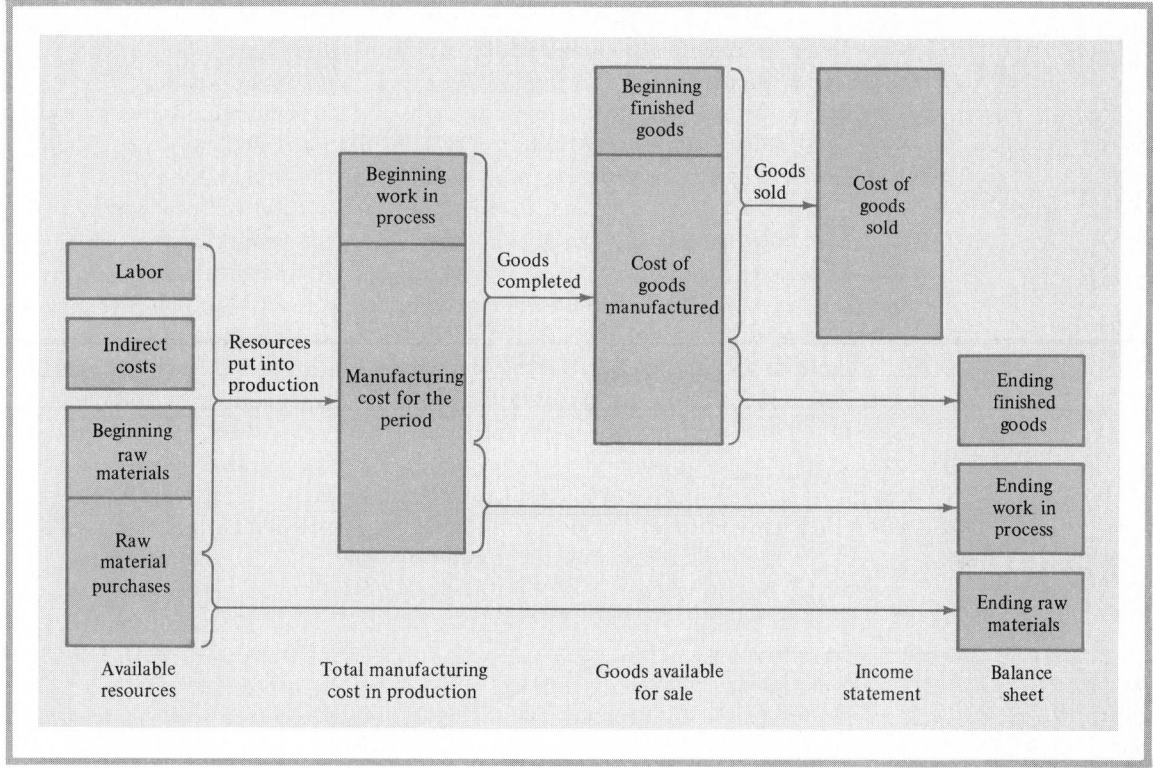

Figure 2-6. Costs flow through the accounting records as production takes place. The firm starts the accounting period with some production resources, including the beginning inventories of raw materials, work in process, and finished goods. Part of the resources flow from one level to the next, and part remains as ending inventory.

sold is computed using the Finished Goods Inventory account, whereas cost of goods manufactured is computed using work in process inventory.

To obtain cost of goods sold, the following format is used:

	Cost of finished goods at beginning of period
Add	Finished goods acquired during the period
	Total finished goods available for sale
Less	Finished goods left in inventory at end of period
	Cost of goods sold during the period

The above calculation is illustrated in the left half of Figure 2-6. The basic cost of goods manufactured calculation is similar. It is illustrated in the center of Figure 2-6. The calculation starts with work in process on hand at the beginning of the period, to which is added the manufacturing costs incurred during the period. From the sum of the two, the ending work in process is deducted to yield cost of goods manufactured.

	Cost of work in process inventory at beginning of period
Add	Manufacturing costs incurred during period
	Total manufacturing cost in production during the period
Less	Work in process inventory at the end of period
	Cost of products completed during the period

Again we emphasize that cost of goods sold is computed using the Finished Goods Inventory account, and cost of goods manufactured is computed using the Work in Process Inventory account. The cost of goods manufactured schedule starts with the beginning work in process, consisting of goods that were started in the manufacturing process in the previous period but were not completed. To this amount is added the production costs for the period, which is all of the direct materials, direct labor, and manufacturing overhead charged to production during the current accounting period. The result is identified in the cost of goods manufactured schedule as **total manufacturing costs** of the period, illustrated in the left half of Figure 2-6.

The total manufacturing cost of the period plus the beginning work in process inventory together represent the **total manufacturing costs in production** during the period. The ending work in process inventory is subtracted from total manufacturing costs in production to obtain the cost of products that have been completed and transferred to finished goods inventory during the accounting period. This final number is called **cost of goods manufactured.**

Do not confuse **cost of goods manufactured** with **total manufacturing cost** for the period. Cost of goods manufactured describes the cost of the goods actually transferred to finished goods from work in process during the period. The total manufacturing cost of the current period does not include any work in process from the preceding period. The two costs are identical only when the beginning and ending work in process inventory costs are the same.

Figure 2-6 also shows the three levels of manufacturing company inventories: raw materials, work in process, and finished goods. Some of each inventory is available at the beginning of the accounting period, and some is left at the end of the accounting period. The ending balances of these inventories are reported in the balance sheet.

The Significance of Product Cost

Variations in product cost have a significant impact on net income in both manufacturing and merchandising firms. To illustrate, a condensed income statement is presented below.

Sales	$2,000
Cost of goods sold	1,200
Gross margin	800
Operating expenses	500
Net income	$ 300

Now assume that the product cost increases by 20 percent, or $240 ($1,200 × .20). All other costs and revenues remain the same. In this case the new income statement is:

Sales	$2,000
Cost of goods sold	1,440
Gross margin	560
Operating expenses	500
Net income	$ 60

Impact of changing costs

A 20 percent increase in the product cost caused gross margin to decline by 30 percent ($800 − $560)/$800. However, the really significant change is the 80 percent decline in net income ($300 − $60)/$300. You see that a relatively small change in product cost can cause a very significant change in net income.

Control Accounts

A **control account** is used to summarize the individual balances in a set of accounts of a particular type. For example, the accounts receivable control account contains the sum of the balances of all individual accounts receivable from customers, and the accounts payable control account contains the sum of all the individual accounts payable to suppliers. All control accounts are supported by detailed subsidiary accounts that are maintained in a **subsidiary ledger.** The total of the individual balances in the subsidiary ledger is the balance in the general ledger control account. For example, a company has the following balances in its individual accounts receivable:

Jones Company	Brown Company	Smith Company
1,200	800	900

Grubbs Company	Metzger Company
1,700	700

The total of these individual accounts receivable is $5,300. Rather than maintain these separate accounts in the general ledger, the $5,300 total is recorded in a single account called Accounts Receivable Control. The control account is in the general ledger, and the individual accounts are maintained separately in the subsidiary ledger for that control account.

Control accounts simplify the cost reporting process

Control accounts are particularly useful in cost accounting. They are maintained for raw materials, work in process, finished goods, and manufacturing overhead. Control accounts streamline the recording and reporting of cost flows, and provide a convenient source for locating cost totals.

Unit Costs

It is not very meaningful to managers to compare the total cost of producing, for instance, 1,000 units in May with the cost of producing 1,400 units in June. A more useful comparison is the cost of one unit produced in May and the cost of one produced in June.

The **unit cost** is the cost of producing one unit of product or providing one unit of service. Unit costs are used to compare production costs from one month to the next, to provide data for setting product prices, to help evaluate management performance, and to help managers decide whether to keep producing the product or service or buy it from a supplier. Some examples of unit costs are:

- $.30 to manufacture one 60-watt light bulb
- $32.62 to produce a pair of leather cowboy boots
- $7.84 to process each sales invoice
- $8.85 to perform one hour of lifeguard duty

Unit costs are averages

Unit costs are calculated by dividing the total manufacturing cost for the product by the number of units produced. This yields an average unit cost of making the product during the time period in question. The unit cost of the product may have been higher or lower in prior periods, and may be more or less in future periods. A few production processes such as construction of a bridge, a dam, or a ship result in a single unit of product, but most unit costs represent averaging to some degree.

Periodic and Perpetual Inventories

In manufacturing operations the cost of inventories is a large proportion of current assets. A company may use either a periodic inventory system or a perpetual inventory system for keeping track of inventory costs.

Periodic inventory systems are used by many merchandising firms. In a **periodic inventory system** the beginning inventory balance is carried in the inventory account. All purchases of inventory are recorded in a separate purchases account. Sales of inventory are not recorded during the accounting period. Instead, at the end of the period total net purchases are added to beginning inventory to find the total inventory available for sale during the period. Ending inventory is subtracted from total inventory available to determine the amount of inventory sold.

The merchandising firm in Figure 2-3 uses a periodic inventory system. Such systems are suitable when it is impractical to keep track of the cost of each item in inventory or to write off the cost at the time of sale. In a periodic inventory system, the cost of goods sold can be computed only after a physical count of inventory is taken to find the ending inventory figure. The units in ending inventory can be valued by one of several valuation methods, such as first in, first out (FIFO); last in, first out (LIFO); or weighted average. The disadvantage of periodic inventory systems is the inability to have timely information about the cost of products used or sold until the accounting period is over. For this reason, manufacturing firms typically do not use a periodic inventory system, except perhaps for finished goods inventory.

In a **perpetual inventory system,** both additions to inventory and uses of inventory are recorded continuously to keep the inventory account perpetually up-to-date. Inventory acquisitions are recorded as increases in the inventory account and sales of merchandise or uses of raw materials are deducted from the inventory accounts. Either FIFO, LIFO, moving average, or specific identification are used for costing inventory in a perpetual system.

A perpetual inventory system is most useful in a manufacturing firm because it enables recording the flow of costs from Raw Materials Inventory to Work in Process Inventory to Finished Goods Inventory as the physical flow of production occurs.

Unlike a periodic system, a perpetual inventory system allows accountants to prepare timely manufacturing cost reports. Also, because the accounting records contain information on each purchase and use of raw materials as well as on the flow of production costs through the production process, a perpetual inventory system provides better internal control over inventory shortages caused by inefficiencies or theft. At the end of the period, a physical inventory count is taken, and the data obtained are compared with the data in the accounting records. Any differences can be reconciled, and management can attempt to identify their cause.

In a periodic inventory system, the ending inventory cost determined by the physical count is subtracted from the cost of total available inventory. The entire difference is assumed to be the amount of inventory used. Any losses for spoilage, breakage, or theft are buried in the computation of inventory used.

Controllable Costs

A **controllable cost** is one over which a manager has control because he has the authority to make decisions that affect the cost. Since a manager can control a cost, that cost is a yardstick for reporting management performance. For example, a production supervisor has some control over the amount of labor used to manufacture a product. Therefore one of the criteria for evaluating the supervisor is the cost of labor used to produce the product, which can be compared with the expected labor cost for that amount of production.

Controllable costs are useful in management reporting

Controllable costs are used to evaluate managers' performance over time and to compare the performance among managers. Actual controllable costs can be compared with expected costs, and if differences occur managers can take appropriate actions. They can focus their attention on controllable costs to make their decisions. It is therefore useful to separate controllable costs from other costs over which a manager has no control, because managerial performance is often used as a basis for promotions, pay raises, and the allocation of resources among business units.

To be sure, there are many factors that influence what a particular cost will be. Consequently, identifying responsibility for every cost in the firm is not simple, particularly at lower levels in the organization's management structure where several managers may have some influence over a cost. Therefore, in practice a controllable cost often is defined as a cost over which a manager has **primary** influence or control.

Cost Behavior

Cost behavior describes the way costs change with respect to some measure of activity such as the dollars of sales, the number of units produced, the quantity of resource used in production, or merely the passage of time. Usually, cost behavior is measured by comparing the amount of cost with the level of activity for a number of different activity levels. For example, the accountant accumulates utility cost and the number of direct labor hours worked on a monthly basis. By comparing the change in the monthly utility cost with the change in the monthly number of direct labor hours worked, the accountant can learn something about the cost behavior pattern of utility costs.

Variable costs change proportionately with the volume of activity

Costs that vary directly, or proportionately, with activity are called **variable costs** or **directly variable costs.** For example, if the production of a steel desk requires 3 hours of direct labor time at $8 per hour, direct labor is a variable cost of $24 per unit. If 300 desks are manufactured in April, the total variable cost of direct labor is $7,200.

Fixed costs remain constant

A cost that does not change with the activity level is called a **fixed cost.** For example, the cost of leasing the building used in the production of the desks is $2,800 a month. The cost is fixed because it does not change as the volume of production changes. The $2,800 monthly charge must be paid whether 1,000 desks, 300 desks, or no desks are produced.

Cost behavior is used in management accounting reports for the purpose of management planning and decision making. For example, in evaluating a possible new contract to produce a large number of units each month, managers are interested in knowing which production costs will vary directly with the number of additional units produced and which costs will remain constant and unaffected by additional production. Similarly, many variable costs, such as direct materials and direct labor, are controllable by production supervisors and as such are key costs in performance reports.

Common Costs

Costs are incurred to satisfy cost objectives, and the more specifically the accountant can identify a cost with a specific cost objective, the better a manager can evaluate performance or determine how well objectives have been satisfied. It is not always possible, however, to identify a cost specifically with a single cost objective. For example, installing separate electric meters enables managers to identify electric power costs for each production department. Variations in the amount of power used by the departments can be measured, and power costs can be included in the performance report of each department manager. If, on the other hand, only one electric meter is used for the entire plant, the cost of the resource is shared by all the production departments and cannot be clearly identified with individual departments. Costs that are shared by two or more cost objectives are called **common costs.**

Often it is necessary to assign part of a common cost to each cost objective benefiting from it. For example, the Internal Revenue Service requires that the product cost used in determining a company's taxable income include all necessary costs of production, both direct and indirect. Therefore costs common to more than one product must be assigned to the various products to determine product cost for reporting net income.

Assigning a common cost to objectives that benefit from the cost is called **cost allocation.** Sometimes cost allocation is simple and logical. For example, the laboratory supervisor may keep accurate records of the time spent on each project. Then the cost of the supervisor can be allocated to the several projects in proportion to the time spent on each. There should be a logical and reasonable basis for allocating costs to cost objectives.

Common costs are assigned to cost objectives by cost allocation

SUMMARY

Cost is the amount of resource given up in exchange for some good or service. It is easier to measure the cost of a purchased product or service than the cost of a product or service produced within the organization. **A cost objective** is a product, service, or activity whose cost is to be measured.

Managers of manufacturing firms need detailed cost information. The **product cost** of manufactured products consists of **direct materials, direct labor,** and **manufacturing overhead.** Direct materials and direct labor are identifiable directly with products and together are referred to as **prime costs.** Manufacturing overhead (**MOH**) includes indirect materials, indirect labor, and all occupancy and capacity costs, such as plant depreciation, insurance, plant taxes, and utilities for manufacturing operations. Manufacturing overhead and direct labor together are called **conversion costs,** because together they convert raw materials into finished products. Prime costs are direct manufacturing costs and overhead is an indirect manufacturing cost.

Manufacturing firms have three categories of inventories. **Raw materials** are the basic ingredients of manufactured products. **Work in process** consists of partially completed products. **Finished goods** are manufactured products ready for sale, similar to merchandise inventory in a merchandising firm.

The physical flow of products through the manufacturing process is paralleled by a flow of costs through the firm's general ledger accounts. As resources are added to the products, their value increases. The costs of the resources used are recorded first in the Work in Process account. When products are completed their costs are transferred to the Finished Goods Inventory account. All production costs are **inventoriable,** which means they are charged to inventory accounts that are assets. The costs remain in the inventory accounts until the goods are sold, at which time the product cost becomes an expense. The expense is matched with the revenue from the sale of the product, satisfying the **matching principle.**

Cost is the amount of resource given up for some good or service. **Expense** is the amount of resource used during a particular accounting period. For some items, cost and expense are the same because the resource is used in the period in which it is purchased. Some items, such as fixed assets, benefit many periods, and their annual expense is different from their cost. **Product costs** are costs of acquiring or producing products, and are recorded as assets. **Period costs** are nonmanufacturing expenses.

The **cost of goods manufactured schedule** is a summary of manufacturing costs incurred during the accounting period. The schedule starts with beginning work in process; then current period production costs are added, and ending work in process is subtracted. The result is called **cost of goods manufactured,** and is the total cost of products transferred to finished goods during the accounting period.

Cost of goods sold is the product expense for the period resulting from the sale of products. In a manufacturing business, cost of goods sold is computed by adding cost of goods manufactured to the beginning finished goods inventory, then subtracting the ending finished goods inventory.

Control accounts are general ledger accounts used to summarize the balances of individual accounts such as Accounts Receivable, Accounts Payable, Raw Materials, Work in Process, and Finished Goods. All control accounts are supported by **subsidiary ledgers** that provide the necessary detail not found in the control accounts.

The **unit cost** of manufactured products is an **average** cost of each unit of product manufactured in a specific **time period** or production run.

A **perpetual inventory** system is used to maintain a continuous record of all inventory transactions and is essential in manufacturing operations to provide timely cost data for managerial accounting reports. In a **periodic inventory** system the amount of resource used or sold is recorded at the end of the period when an inventory count is taken to see how much inventory is left. Cost of goods sold is determined by subtracting the ending inventory from the total goods available. Periodic inventory systems are suitable for many merchandising operations.

A **controllable cost** is one over which a manager has direct control and the authority to make decisions that affect the cost. Controllable costs are useful in evaluating the performance of managers. **Cost behavior** describes the change in a particular cost with respect to the change in some activity, such as units of production, dollars of sales, or number of direct labor hours worked. **Variable costs** change proportionately with the level of activity. **Fixed costs** remain constant at all levels of activity.

Common costs are costs that benefit more than one cost objective. **Cost allocation** is the process of assigning common costs to cost objectives in a systematic manner. Cost allocation must be reasonable and logical in order to result in relevant internal and external accounting reports.

KEY TERMS

capacity costs *(27)*
common costs *(42)*
control account *(39)*
controllable cost *(41)*
conversion cost *(28)*
cost *(32)*
cost allocation *(43)*
cost behavior *(42)*
cost of goods manufactured *(36)*
cost of goods sold *(33)*
cost objective *(25)*

direct labor *(26)*
direct materials *(26)*
expense *(32)*
finished goods *(30)*
fixed cost *(42)*
indirect costs *(27)*
indirect labor *(27)*
indirect material *(26)*
inventoriable cost *(31)*
manufacturing overhead *(27)*
matching principle *(28)*

occupancy costs   *(27)*
overhead   *(27)*
period costs   *(33)*
periodic inventory system   *(40)*
perpetual inventory system   *(41)*
prime costs   *(27)*

product costs   *(32)*
raw materials   *(29)*
subsidiary ledger   *(39)*
unit cost   *(40)*
variable costs   *(42)*
work in process   *(29)*

QUESTIONS

1. Discuss some of the reasons why costs are useful to all types of organizations. How is cost information used by managers?

2. Discuss the difference in inventories in service, merchandising, and manufacturing firms. What type of inventory system is most useful in a manufacturing business?

3. Accounting information is a representation of events that occur in business operations. Visualize the process of manufacturing cedar chests and describe the way the process is reflected by the accounting system in the information it provides to managers. Consider both the direct and indirect materials, and direct and indirect labor needed to produce the product.

4. "I just bought a very expensive car," explains George. "The reason it is expensive is because it has a large amount of optional equipment such as a stereo tape player, a deluxe air conditioner, and a leather interior. But the cost of operation is low."

   An accountant says, "The cost of this equipment is high, but the equipment is not very expensive. Fuel consumption is only 8 gallons per hour, maintenance is needed only once a year, and it can be operated by a single individual who earns $10 per hour."

   What do the two people mean by the terms *expensive* and *cost?* In what sense is George's concept of expense correct? Include in your discussion a definition of cost and expense.

5. "The concept of product costs and period costs is simple. Product costs are assets and period costs are expenses." In what way is this statement correct, and in what way is it incorrect? Elaborate on the statement using a more precise description of product costs and period costs.

6. (AICPA) You were requested to deliver personally your auditor's report to the board of directors of Sebal Manufacturing Corporation and answer questions posed about the financial statements. While reading the statements, one director asked, "What are the precise meanings of the terms *cost* and *expense?* These terms sometimes seem to identify similar items and other times seem to identify dissimilar items."

   a. Explain the meanings of the terms (1) *cost* and (2) *expense* as used in financial reporting in conformity with generally accepted accounting principles. In your explanation discuss the distinguishing characteristics of the terms and their similarities and interrelationships.

   b. Classify each of the following items as a cost, expense, or other category and explain how the classification of each may change:
      1. Cost of goods sold
      2. Depreciation expense for plant machinery
      3. Work in process

c. The terms *period cost* and *product cost* are sometimes used to describe certain items in financial statements. Define these terms and distinguish between them. To what types of items does each apply?

EXERCISES

Ex. 2-1
Computing Net
Income

Below are selected financial data of Americo Company for 2 consecutive years.

	1984	1985
Operating expenses	$ 90,000	$110,000
Beginning finished goods	18,000	36,000
Sales	348,000	390,000
Ending finished goods	36,000	47,000
Cost of goods manufactured	222,000	264,000

REQUIRED   Prepare income statements for both years.

Ex. 2-2
Changing Product
Costs

Below is the condensed income statement of the Ajax Company.

Ajax Company
Income Statement

Sales (15,000 units)	$300,000
Cost of goods sold	240,000
Gross margin	60,000
Operating expenses	30,000
Net income	$ 30,000

The cost of the units sold is broken down as follows:

Direct material: $8
Direct labor: $5
Manufacturing overhead: $3

REQUIRED   Determine the percentage change in net income caused by each of the following **independent** situations:

a. Direct materials cost rises by 20 percent.
b. Direct labor costs rises by 20 percent.
c. Manufacturing overhead cost increases by 20 percent.
d. Selling price increases by 20 percent.
e. Both selling price and **all** product costs increase by 20 percent.

Ex. 2-3
Cost of Goods
Manufactured and
the Income
Statement

Below are general ledger account balances of the Arch-A-Tech Engineering Products Company for the year ended December 31, 1985. Any beginning inventory balances were taken from the company's general ledger on January 1, 1985.

Administrative salaries	$ 600,000
Advertising	150,000
Beginning finished goods inventory 1/1/85	150,000
Beginning work in process inventory 1/1/85	95,000
Delivery expense for finished products	14,000
Direct labor	520,000
Direct materials	506,000
Employee fringe benefits (60% factory employees)	180,000
Ending finished goods inventory	180,000
Ending work in process inventory	100,000
Factory fire insurance	11,000
Factory property tax	26,000
Factory supervision	135,000
Indirect labor	65,000
Indirect materials	42,000
Office equipment depreciation	5,000
Office fire insurance	4,500
Production equipment depreciation	32,000
Sales	3,125,000
Sales returns and allowances	64,000
Sales salaries	200,000

REQUIRED

a. Prepare a schedule of cost of goods manufactured.
b. Prepare an income statement.

Ex. 2-4
Cost of Goods
Manufactured

Following are 1985 year-end account balances and inventory data for the Candle Company.

Ending finished goods inventory 12/31/85	$ 57,100
Indirect labor	7,900
Cash	43,211
Accounts receivable	12,210
Direct labor	79,350
Depreciation, building (70% manufacturing)	40,000
Rent, office equipment	3,200
Property tax (70% manufacturing)	9,000
Utilities (80% manufacturing)	26,000
Ending work in process inventory 12/31/85	32,400
Investments	126,000
Direct material	82,000
Miscellaneous factory costs	8,900
Fire insurance, building (70% manufacturing)	10,800
Fire insurance, finished goods inventory	3,400
Beginning work in process inventory 1/1/85	37,300
Beginning finished goods inventory 1/1/85	31,750
Salaries, sales personnel	73,400
Salaries, factory supervision	51,900

a. Prepare a schedule of cost of goods manufactured.
b. Prepare a schedule of cost of goods sold.

Ex. 2-5
Identifying Fixed
and Variable Costs

Below is a list of cost accounts for a manufacturing business.

a. Depreciation, production plant
b. Direct materials
c. Plant maintenance
d. Depreciation, production equipment
e. Electricity for the production plant
f. Heating costs for the production plant
g. Direct labor
h. Indirect labor
i. Property taxes for the production plant
j. Plant fire insurance
k. Patent royalty on each unit produced
l. Payroll taxes on production employees

REQUIRED

For each of the costs listed, indicate whether the cost would most likely be fixed or vary with the number of units produced.

Ex. 2-6
Identifying Product
and Period Costs

Below is a list of accounts used by Omicron Manufacturing Company:

a. Administrative salaries
b. Advertising
c. Indirect materials
d. Direct labor
e. Property taxes on the office facilities
f. Depreciation on the office building
g. Maintenance contract on hydraulic presses
h. Insurance on the production plant
i. Sales commissions
j. Depreciation on manufacturing equipment
k. Direct materials
l. Fire insurance on finished goods inventory
m. Fire insurance on raw materials inventory
n. Storage and handling costs on raw materials inventory
o. Sales salaries
p. Lease cost for a computer used solely for production scheduling
q. Operating costs of office personnel cafeteria
r. Operating costs for factory first aid room

REQUIRED

For each of the accounts listed above indicate if it is most likely classified as a product cost or a period cost.

Ex. 2-7
Identifying Cost
Categories

Below is a list of costs for a manufacturing company.

a. Sales commissions
b. Depreciation, production plant
c. Indirect labor
d. Depreciation, office equipment
e. Property taxes, sales office
f. Rent on manufacturing equipment

   g.   Fire insurance on production plant
   h.   Fire insurance on finished goods inventory
   i.   Utilities, production plant
   j.   Direct labor
   k.   Indirect material
   l.   President's salary
   m.   Direct material
   n.   Payroll taxes, office employees
   o.   Payroll taxes, factory employees

REQUIRED   For each cost listed, indicate whether it should be classified as fixed or variable **and** as product or period cost.

Ex. 2-8
Determining
Missing Data

Below are partial data from four **independent** income statements. Blanks represent missing data.

	Situation			
	W	X	Y	Z
Sales	$90,000	$60,000	$110,000	$ ____
Beginning finished goods	12,000	7,000		
Beginning work in process	9,000	5,000	15,000	14,000
Direct materials	22,000	16,000	19,000	13,000
Direct labor		21,000	18,000	29,000
Manufacturing overhead	17,000	19,000		18,000
Ending work in process	18,000	9,000	9,000	
Cost of goods manufactured	57,000		65,000	67,000
Ending finished goods	19,000		11,000	21,000
Costs of goods sold		39,000	84,000	73,000
Gross margin				24,000
Operating expenses		23,000		
Net income	$ 9,000	$ ____	$ (6,000)	$ 7,000

REQUIRED   Fill in the missing data for each situation.

Ex. 2-9
Assigning Fixed
Costs

Betty Chung plans to open a photography studio in the concourse of a closed mall shopping center. She will specialize in children's pictures. The revenue from each sale will be $15 and the cost of photographic supplies used in taking and developing the portraits will be $5 per sale. The mall shop rents for $600 per month. All utility costs are included in the rent. Betty expects she will sell 125 children's portraits per month, but she thinks the sales level could range between 80 and 150 portraits per month.

REQUIRED   a.   If Betty's expected sales level is achieved, what is the cost per sale of the monthly rent?
   b.   Compute the cost per sale of the monthly rent if the lowest level of sales is achieved, and also if the highest level of sales is achieved.
   c.   If Betty sells 140 portraits per month, what will be her monthly profit?

Ex. 2-10
Interpreting
Financial Data

Below is the 1985 income statement of Svensen, Incorporated. Svensen is a manufacturing company that makes and sells a single product. During 1985 the company
manufactured 98,000 units and sold 100,000 units. Beginning work in process inventory on January 1, 1985 was $59,000 and work in process inventory on December 31,
1985 was $66,400.

Svensen, Incorporated
Income Statement
For the Year Ended December 31, 1985

Sales		$660,000
Less cost of goods sold:		
Beginning finished goods inventory 1/1/85	$ 56,000	
Add cost of goods manufactured in 1985	345,000	
Total goods available for sale	401,000	
Less ending finished goods inventory 12/31/85	48,000	
Cost of goods sold		353,000
Gross margin		307,000
Less operating expenses:		
Sales salaries and commissions	88,000	
Administrative salaries	73,000	
Depreciation of office buildings and equipment	44,000	
Insurance	5,500	
Property taxes	7,000	
Office supplies	4,500	
Utilities	7,000	
Total operating expenses		229,000
Net income		$ 78,000

REQUIRED   Use the data presented above to respond to the following questions and requirements.

a.   Compute the change in finished goods inventory from the beginning to the
     end of the accounting period.
b.   Compute the total manufacturing costs incurred during the period.
c.   Compute the cost per unit of sales salaries and commissions.
d.   What was the product expense as a percentage of total expenses for 1985?
e.   Compute the average unit cost of goods manufactured during the period.

PROBLEMS

P. 2-1
Understanding
Manufacturing
Income Statements

Below is the income statement of the Bolinski Company. It was prepared by a new
accountant who has had no experience with manufacturing businesses. The owner of
the company is certain that there are a number of errors in the statement, and you are
called in to analyze the statement and supporting accounting records.

Bolinski Company
Income Statement
For the Year Ended December 31, 1985

Sales		$968,000
Less cost of goods sold:		
Beginning work in process inventory 1/1/85	$ 56,200	
Add raw materials purchases for 1985	289,300	
Total goods available for sale	345,500	
Less ending raw materials inventory 12/31/85	43,700	301,800
Gross margin		666,200
Less operating expenses:		
Sales salaries	56,900	
Sales commissions	36,700	
Depreciation of office facilities	32,000	
Depreciation of office equipment	14,600	
Insurance (60% on production facilities)	12,000	
Office supplies	6,400	
Utilities (75% for manufacturing operations)	27,600	
Total operating expenses		186,200
Net income		$480,000

Your analysis of the data indicates that all of the account balances used in the income statement are correct. In addition, you find that the following accounts did not appear in any of the company's financial reports:

Finished goods inventory 1/1/85	$107,500
Advertising	26,700
Administrative salaries	106,000
Depreciation, production machinery	44,000
Maintenance contract on production equipment	22,000
Maintenance contract on office computer	14,400
Finished goods inventory 12/31/85	98,000

You compute that the cost of goods manufactured in 1985 was $519,900.

REQUIRED   Prepare a new income statement in good form for the Bolinski Company using the additional data.

P. 2-2
Using Fixed and
Variable Costs in
Analysis

The Soft Shoe Dance Studio is a well-established company with many loyal customers. Two years ago the company moved into a large new facility with a significant amount of excess space. The owners of the studio are considering expanding the number of dance classes, but before doing so, they have hired an accountant to analyze their accounting data. The accountant has prepared an analysis of cost behavior patterns showing the costs that varied with the number of student-hours taught and the costs that remained constant. The costs for the last year are presented below in two categories. During the year, 15,000 student-hours were taught and revenue totaled $96,000.

Costs that did not change with volume of hours taught:

Depreciation of studio	$ 8,000
Depreciation of furniture and fixtures	2,500
Utilities	2,400
Advertising	5,000
Administrative salaries	26,000
Property taxes	4,100

Costs that varied with number of hours taught:

Instructor salaries	$21,000
Supplies	4,500
Utilities	3,000

The company is considering two alternatives that should help it to increase income in the current year:

1. Adopt an advertising campaign that will cost $6,000 and should increase student-hours by one-third.
2. Lower prices by $2 per student-hour, which should double the number of student-hours taught.

REQUIRED

a. Compute the revenue per student-hour taught last year.
b. Compute net income for last year.
c. Compute net income per student-hour taught.
d. Calculate the effect of adopting the advertising campaign.
e. Calculate the effect of lowering the price of lessons.

P. 2-3
Cost of Goods Manufactured and the Income Statement

Below are account balances of Donavon Products as of December 31, except for beginning inventory amounts on January 1, which are so indicated. All accounts have normal balances.

Administrative salaries	$139,300
Advertising	39,000
Beginning finished goods 1/1	76,900
Beginning work in process 1/1	56,700
Depreciation, factory	34,000
Depreciation, office	21,500
Depreciation, factory equipment	56,000
Direct labor	117,100
Direct material	224,500
Ending finished goods	94,000
Ending work in process	63,800
Fire insurance (70% production plant)	8,900
Indirect labor	19,400
Indirect material	9,000
Miscellaneous office expense	6,200
Property taxes (60% production plant)	15,600
Raw materials inventory	87,700
Rent, office equipment	11,400
Sales	890,000
Sales commissions	35,600

Sales returns and allowances	$ 16,800
Sales salaries	74,500
Utilities (80% production plant)	38,200

a.   Prepare a cost of goods manufactured schedule in good form.

b.   Prepare an income statement in good form.

The Wilsons have always enjoyed their hobby of seashore art. They use shells, driftwood, and other items from the beach and make decorative art forms of various types. After much evaluation, they decided to move to the Gulf Coast of Florida and open a shop where they will make and sell their art work. The Wilsons started their business, called Beach Art, in January, and the following transactions and events occurred.

January 5   Invested $50,000 in the new business.

6   Leased a shop for $15,000 per year. Sixty percent of the building space is used for producing art works and 40 percent is used for sales space.

8   Purchased various production equipment for $12,000 cash. The equipment has a useful life of 5 years with no salvage value. Straight-line depreciation is used.

15   Purchased cash register, display cases, and other sales and administrative equipment costing $35,000, paying $5,000 down and giving a $30,000 note payable. The salvage value is estimated as $5,000 and the useful life is 6 years.

During the rest of the calendar year:

Direct materials costing $28,000 were purchased.
Office supplies costing $1,400 were purchased.
Utilities expenses of $2,500 were paid.
Insurance expenses were $3,000 for the year.
Property taxes were $1,500.
Part-time sales help cost $4,200.
Part-time manufacturing labor was $3,100.
Sales totaled $85,100.

At year-end:

Office supplies costing $600 were on hand.
Direct materials was $4,600.
Finished goods inventory at cost was $5,100.
Ending work in process on December 31 cost $2,200.

During the year, Mr. Wilson worked 1,600 hours and Mrs. Wilson worked 1,900 hours. They estimated that Mr. Wilson's time was spent 60 percent selling and 40 percent manufacturing products. Mrs. Wilson's time was spent 30 percent selling and 70 percent manufacturing.

a. Prepare a cost of goods manufactured schedule and an income statement for the Wilson's business.
b. Repeat part *a* assuming the Wilsons pay themselves $7 per hour for manufacturing activities and $5 per hour for selling activities. Assume the same year-end cost for work in process and finished goods inventory.
c. Assuming the Wilsons pay themselves no wages, what was their average hourly earnings for the time they worked during the year?

P. 2-5
Income Statement
for a Merchandising
Business

Mary Waltz has been a comic book collector for many years and recently decided to use her hobby to supplement the income from her regular job as a telephone installer. On April 1, she rented a small shop on Main Street for $210 per month and invested $2,500 cash and $12,000 of comic books as inventory to open the Comic Shoppe. On April 2 she purchased a $3,500 cash register with a $1,000 down payment and a note payable for the balance. The cash register has a 5-year useful life and $500 salvage value. During the rest of the calendar year the following occurred:

Purchased supplies costing $760.
Comic book sales totaled $31,700.
Purchased comics costing $14,200.
Paid $7,700 in salaries to sales help when Mary is working at her regular job.
Incurred advertising expense of $550.
Paid utility bills of $1,180.
Mary worked 798 hours at the shop.
Paid $900 for a one-year fire insurance policy starting on August 1.

At year-end:

Supplies inventory is $290.
Comic book inventory at cost is $13,300.
Interest accrued on cash register note is $200.

a. Prepare an income statement for the Comic Shoppe.
b. Compute the amount Mary earned per hour worked.
c. Assuming sales are for cash and all expenses were paid during the year, compute the year-end cash balance of the business.
d. Prepare a year-end balance sheet for the Comic Shoppe.

P. 2-6
Interpreting Cost of
Goods
Manufactured Data

The Verde Valley Company manufactures pressure valves that it sells through a national chain of department stores. The 1985 cost of goods manufactured schedule for the company is on page 55. During 1985 the company transferred 135,000 units from work in process inventory to finished goods inventory, and sold 130,000 units. The Raw Materials Inventory account balance on December 31, 1985, was $57,300, and $133,800 of raw materials were purchased during 1985.

Use the data presented below to answer the following questions and requirements:

a. What was the amount of change in the Work in Process Inventory account from the beginning of the accounting period to the end?
b. Determine the total amount of manufacturing cost incurred in the current accounting period.
c. Compute the average unit cost of pressure valves manufactured in 1985.
d. What percentage of manufacturing labor was direct labor?
e. Compute the balance in the Raw Materials Inventory account on 1/1/85.

Verde Valley Company
Schedule of Cost of Goods Manufactured
For the Year Ended December 31, 1985

Beginning work in process inventory 1/1/85		$117,200
Direct materials	$146,100	
Direct labor	123,000	
Manufacturing overhead:		
Indirect materials	$11,200	
Indirect labor	14,000	
Depreciation, plant and equipment	41,000	
Salaries, production supervisors	73,400	
Insurance, manufacturing plant	11,700	
Property taxes, manufacturing plant	9,800	
Utilities, manufacturing plant	19,500	180,600
Total manufacturing cost for 1985		449,700
Total manufacturing cost in production for 1985		566,900
Less ending work in process inventory 12/31/85		94,400
Cost of goods manufactured 1985		$472,500

P. 2-7
Understanding Financial Data of a Manufacturing Firm

Below are the income statement and cost of goods manufactured schedule of Wallace Company. The statements were prepared by Kevin, the new accountant recently hired by the firm. Kevin has worked for three years as the accountant for a retailing operation, but this is his first accounting job with a manufacturing business.

Wallace Company
Income Statement
December 31, 1985

Sales		$856,000
Less cost of goods sold:		
Beginning raw materials inventory 1/1/85	$ 46,000	
Add raw materials purchased during 1985	214,000	
Total goods available for sale	260,000	
Less ending finished goods inventory 12/31/85	109,500	
Cost of goods sold		150,500
Gross margin		705,500
Less operating expenses:		
Sales salaries and commissions	84,300	
Advertising	9,200	
Administrative salaries	77,100	
Production supervisors' salaries	56,000	
Depreciation, office and office equipment	21,000	
Depreciation, production plant and equipment	44,000	
Fire and casualty insurance, office	5,700	
Property taxes, office	6,000	
Office supplies	3,300	
Utilities (70% factory)	42,000	
Total operating expenses		348,600
Net income		$356,900

Wallace Company
Schedule of Cost of Goods Manufactured
For the Year Ended December 31, 1985

Beginning finished goods inventory 1/1/85			$ 91,300
Direct materials		$138,900	
Direct labor		201,700	
Manufacturing overhead:			
Indirect materials	$ 7,800		
Indirect labor	12,600		
Insurance, manufacturing plant	14,300		
Advertising	9,200		
Property taxes, manufacturing plant	17,900		
Maintenance on office computer equipment	8,000	69,800	
Total manufacturing cost for 1985			410,400
Total manufacturing cost in production for 1985			501,700
Less ending work in process inventory 12/31/85			128,300
Cost of goods manufactured 1985			$373,400

The president of the company realized immediately that this year's financial statements were not entirely correct. The president called you and asked you to evaluate the statements and make any necessary corrections. Your analysis indicates that all of the accounts used in the statements had their correct titles and balances. In addition, the Work in Process account on January 1, 1985, had a balance of $42,000, and the Finished Goods account on January 1, 1985, had a balance of $91,300.

REQUIRED   Prepare the income statement and cost of goods manufactured schedule in good form for the Wallace Company.

P. 2-8
Allocating Common
Costs to Cost
Objectives

Destin Management Services is a consulting business that provides customers with specialized computer programming and systems analysis skills. Most customers secure the services of Destin personnel because the management consulting firm can provide skilled people on short notice and when the demand for the skill is satisfied the consultant moves on to other assignments.

An important activity at Destin is costing the services it provides to clients so that the fees it charges are adequate to cover cost and provide the firm with a reasonable profit. The firm has about $30,000 a month in overhead costs. Included are the costs of managerial personnel who schedule and supervise engagements, the costs of operating the firm's office, and other overhead costs, such as educational expenses for employees.

Rather than arbitrarily assign costs to contracts, the management of the consulting firm has decided to allocate the overhead costs based on the number of hours personnel spent working on the various contracts during the month. Below is a schedule of the hours that each employee spent on contracts during the month. A normal work month is 173 hours; however, most employees are not able to charge all of their work time to contracts. Some time is spent in educational programs and some time is spent unassigned because of scheduling gaps between contracts.

| Employee | Contract Number | | | | | | Total Hours |
	342	344	345	346	348	349	
P. Jones	18	45	32	—	—	45	140
B. Melton	56	19	—	—	—	50	125
M. Morton	—	—	23	67	—	55	145
R. Perry	—	—	—	60	56	34	150
T. Green	12	45	17	23	53	—	150
R. Sangster	—	—	28	37	81	14	160
H. Eckel	24	21	—	33	—	52	130
Totals	110	130	100	220	190	250	1,000

REQUIRED

a. Prepare a schedule indicating how much of the firm's monthly overhead should be charged to each contract, using number of hours worked on each contract as the allocation base.

b. How much would have been allocated to each contract if the overhead costs had been spread evenly over the contracts?

c. Prepare a schedule showing the difference in overhead costs assigned to contracts between the two methods used in parts a and b above.

P. 2-9
Estimating Costs
from Partial Data

Ima Planner built a manufacturing plant in High-Water Canyon just downstream from an earthen dam built in 1896. The company operated successfully at this location for several years, then heavy April rains caused the dam to break on May 1. All was lost in the ensuing flood. Insurance claims on plant and equipment cause no problem, but the company must estimate the cost of the inventory lost in the flood. Most of the inventory records were lost, but the following information has been pieced together:

Finished goods inventory 1/1	$ 55,000
Work in process inventory 1/1	49,000
Raw materials inventory 1/1	46,000
Sales 1/1 through 5/1 are	800,000
Direct labor cost	260,000

Factory overhead averages 35 percent of conversion cost.
Material purchases for the four-month period are $220,000.
Prime costs average 80 percent of cost of goods manufactured.
Gross margin on sales averages 25 percent.
Cost of goods available for sale is estimated at $675,000.

REQUIRED   Use the above data to estimate the May 1 balance in

a. Raw materials inventory.
b. Work in process inventory.
c. Finished goods inventory.

P. 2-10
Understanding
Manufacturing
Financial
Statements

Below are the income statement and schedule of cost of goods manufactured for the Smolden Company.

Smolden Company
Income Statement
For the Year Ended December 31, 1985

Sales		$842,300
Less cost of goods sold:		
Beginning finished goods inventory 1/1/85	$ 82,000	
Add cost of goods manufactured in 1985	456,000	
Total goods available for sale	538,000	
Less ending finished goods inventory 12/31/85	105,900	432,100
Gross margin		410,200
Less operating expenses:		
Sales salaries	62,400	
Sales commissions	39,100	
Advertising	22,400	
Administrative salaries	96,500	
Depreciation of office facilities	28,000	
Depreciation of office equipment	37,000	
Insurance	5,000	
Property taxes	12,600	
Office supplies	6,100	
Utilities	15,600	
Total operating expenses		324,700
Net income		$ 85,500

Smolden Company
Schedule of Cost of Goods Manufactured
For the Year Ending December 31, 1985

Beginning work in process inventory 1/1/85			$ 97,800
Direct materials		$142,500	
Direct labor		161,300	
Manufacturing overhead:			
Indirect materials	$ 8,400		
Indirect labor	12,600		
Depreciation, manufacturing plant	42,000		
Depreciation, plant equipment	41,000		
Salaries, production supervisors	76,600		
Insurance, manufacturing plant	12,300		
Property taxes, manufacturing plant	14,800		
Utilities, manufacturing plant	22,700	230,400	
Total manufacturing cost for 1985			534,200
Total manufacturing cost in production for 1985			632,000
Less ending work in process inventory 12/31/85			176,000
Cost of goods manufactured 1985			$456,000

REQUIRED   Use the financial data for Smolden Company presented above to answer the following questions.

    a.   What was the total manufacturing costs incurred in 1985?

    b.   What was the total building depreciation for 1985?

    c.   Raw materials inventory on January 1, 1985, was $79,300. What was the total inventory balance on January 1, 1985, for Smolden Company?

    d.   The raw materials inventory on December 31, 1985, was $84,600. What was the change in total inventory from the beginning to the end of the accounting period?

    e.   If 114,000 units of product were transferred from work in process to finished goods during the year, what was the average unit cost of the products manufactured in 1985?

    f.   What percentage of the company's total costs incurred in 1985 were product costs?

    g.   If Smolden had been able to sell all of its products, what would have been the cost of goods sold?

    h.   In 1985, 105,000 units were sold. Compute the sales commission expense as a percentage of sales dollars and also on a per unit sold basis.

P. 2-11
Identifying and
Correcting
Financial Reporting
Errors

Filmore Company has just completed its first year of operations as a manufacturer of metal bookshelves. The owner has been so busy planning, managing, and systematizing the new manufacturing operations that he has paid little attention to designing and implementing an adequate accounting system. At year-end the company secretary, who has no accounting training, is asked to prepare an income statement. The result is the following report.

Filmore Company
Yearly Report
December 31, 1985

Sales	$166,000	
Cash	53,000	
		$219,600
Expenses:		
Purchases of materials	66,000	
Purchase of manufacturing equipment	62,000	
Salaries, office personnel	31,000	
Wages, factory employees	58,000	
Rent, equipment	2,200	
Rent, building	14,400	
Office supplies	1,100	
Utilities	6,000	
Commissions	7,700	
Total expenses		248,400
Loss		$ (28,800)

The owner of the company realizes that the statement has some errors in it, and decides to seek professional accounting help. An analysis of the company's data reveals:

Ending raw materials inventory of $24,000.
Ending work in process inventory of $16,320.
Ending finished goods inventory of $19,600.
Ending office supplies of $450.
Manufacturing equipment has a six-year useful life with a $2,000 salvage value.
Straight-line depreciation method is used.
Rented equipment is used in the office.
The building and utilities are used 80 percent for manufacturing activities.
1,375 bookcases are completed in 1985.

REQUIRED
a. Prepare a schedule of cost of goods manufactured.
b. Prepare an income statement in good form.
c. Compute the unit cost of the bookshelves.
d. Compute the unit selling price of the bookshelves.

CASES

Case 2-1
Analysis of
Manufacturing
Financial Data

Surbonia, Ltd., manufactures heating units for electric hot water heaters. Below are a year-end trial balance and other financial data.

Surbonia Ltd.
Trial Balance
December 31, 1985

	Debits	Credits
Cash	$ 146,000	
Accounts receivable	145,000	
Raw materials inventory	115,000	
Work in process inventory	144,000	
Finished goods inventory	154,000	
Building	1,450,000	
Accumulated depreciation, building		$ 510,000
Equipment	210,000	
Accumulated depreciation, equipment		50,000
Investments	62,000	
Accounts payable		165,000
Notes payable		280,000
Mortgage payable		535,000
Capital stock		390,000
Retained earnings		430,000
Dividends on common stock	25,000	
Sales		1,440,000
Sales returns and allowances	22,000	
Cost of goods sold	760,000	
Advertising	25,500	
Sales commissions	84,000	
Depreciation, building	70,000	
Depreciation, equipment	45,000	
Equipment rent	12,500	
Administrative salaries	256,000	
Utilities	74,000	
Totals	$3,800,000	$3,800,000

Surbonia, Ltd.
Manufacturing Overhead
Subsidiary Ledger Balances
December 31, 1985

Indirect materials	$ 24,000
Indirect labor	32,000
Supervisory salaries	103,000
Maintenance	39,000
Depreciation, factory	66,000
Depreciation, equipment	58,000
Factory utilities	47,000
Factory property taxes	16,000
Factory insurance	11,000

The January 1, 1985, inventory balances were $97,500 for raw materials, $119,000 for work in process, and $96,000 for finished goods. During 1985, direct material costs were $256,000 and direct labor costs were $191,000. The company manufactured 25,500 units in 1985 and sold 24,000 units.

REQUIRED

a. Prepare a cost of goods manufactured schedule in good form for Surbonia, Ltd.
b. Prepare an income statement in good accounting form for Surbonia Ltd.
c. Compute the balance in the retained earnings account after the books are closed.
d. Compute the average sales price of units sold in 1985.
e. Compute the average unit cost of the units sold during 1985.
f. Compute the average unit cost of the units transferred from work in process to finished goods during 1985.
g. Compute the amount of raw materials purchased during the accounting period.
h. What percentage of Surbonia's total expenses for the period were product expenses?
i. Explain why direct materials, direct labor, and manufacturing overhead do not appear on the company's trial balance. Was this an error on the part of the accountant?

CHAPTER 3
Cost Behavior and Cost-Volume-Profit Relationships

Accountants classify costs and expenses by business function in financial accounting reports and in many managerial accounting reports. A manufacturing firm, for example, manufactures products and sells them. Manufacturing and selling are two distinct activities, or functions, whose costs are reported separately in the firm's income statement. Aggregating costs into several functional categories, such as manufacturing, selling, and administrative, is satisfactory for external users of income statements. On the other hand, managers need more detailed cost information, and thus they look at labor, material, and overhead costs as three separate manufacturing functions. In some reports these may be further subdivided into even more detail, such as assembly labor and finishing labor, or plant maintenance, inventory handling, and utility costs.

Functional classifications of costs provide managers with valuable information which they use to identify activities that should be analyzed, to determine trends in costs, and to adjust production activities. Reporting specific costs according to their function serves many managerial purposes, but however detailed such reports are, they cannot satisfy all management needs. Therefore accountants also classify costs according to the way they behave with respect to changes in business activity.

Instead of reporting costs of separate activities, accountants measure the way certain costs behave when business activity increases or decreases. For instance, a company's property taxes remain the same when the level of production increases from 100,000 units to 120,000 units per month. But the amount of direct labor and direct material increases with an increase in the number of units manufactured, and of course, their costs also increase. Costs such as property taxes are called **fixed costs** because they do not increase with the production level. Costs such as direct labor and direct material are **variable costs** because they vary directly with changes in production activity. Identifying and reporting costs according to behavior helps managers plan operations, control costs, and make decisions.

COST BEHAVIOR

The cost of an activity may be characterized according to the way it behaves as the volume of activity changes. The **volume of activity,** also called **activity level,** may be measured in many different ways, such as units of output, direct labor hours, or dollars of sales.

If there are many ways to measure the volume of activity, which is the one to use? The measure of activity to use for determining the behavior of costs is the one that provides the most meaningful link between the activity and a cost. A common measure of activity is the number of units of product manufactured. But that is not a good activity measure for a service firm, although it may be ideal for a school bus manufacturer whose products are all identical. Number of clients served or sales dollars billed could be a more meaningful measure of activity for a service firm. For a manufacturing firm that produces several very different products, number of units produced might not be a meaningful measure of activity. A more desirable measure of production activity might be direct labor hours. Another organization may use sales dollars, total payroll cost, or number of employees as activity measures that can be related to costs in order to determine how costs behave.

All costs can be grouped into five general behavior categories:

Typical cost
behavior patterns

1. Fixed costs
2. Variable costs
3. Mixed costs
4. Semivariable costs
5. Semifixed costs

Fixed Costs

Costs that do not change as the volume of activity changes are called **fixed costs.** They remain the same during the accounting period whether the activity level is high or low. Examples are rent for office space, property taxes on land, depreciation of factory buildings, and equipment lease costs. Whether a manufacturer produces few or many goods, fixed costs such as these will remain the same.

Fixed costs do not
change whether
production is high
or low

If a fixed cost is plotted in a graph with the activity level on the horizontal axis and cost on the vertical axis, the fixed cost is represented as a horizontal line as shown in Figure 3-1. The cost (Y) is in dollars, and the activity level (X) may be expressed in any measure of activity, such as hours of work, units manufactured, or tons of materials used. The fixed cost is the dollar amount a in the graph. We can express fixed cost with the equation

$$Y = a$$

The cost Y equals a dollars no matter what the activity level X is. Expressing cost behavior mathematically, as well as graphically, makes it easier to solve many managerial problems.

Although total fixed cost does not change with changes in the volume of activity, the fixed cost **per unit of activity** changes. The greater the activity level, the lower the fixed cost per unit; the lower the activity level, the greater the fixed cost per unit. For example, if annual depreciation on a factory building is $40,000 and 40,000 units are produced, each unit's share of

Figure 3-1. Fixed costs remain constant at all activity levels and therefore plot as a horizontal line. The total fixed cost, *Y*, is represented by *a*.

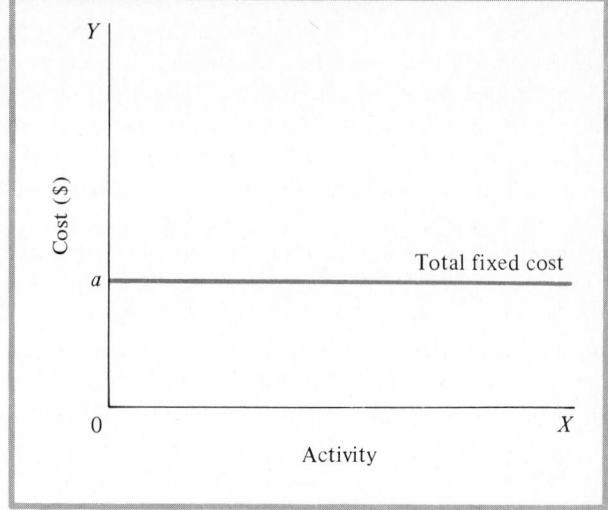

building depreciation is $1. But if only 20,000 units are produced, each unit's share of depreciation is $2. Therefore, in the case of fixed manufacturing costs, it costs less to produce the product when production is high than it does when production is low, because fixed costs can be spread over a greater number of units, and the fixed cost per unit is smaller.

Committed and Discretionary Costs. Just because a cost is fixed does not mean that it cannot be changed. A firm can acquire a new building to increase manufacturing capacity, thus increasing depreciation cost, which is a fixed cost. If the building has to be designed and constructed, it would take some time to make it available for use, so the fixed cost is not increased immediately. If instead the firm leases a completed building, the fixed lease cost increases much sooner. Sometimes managers try to reduce fixed costs, but not all fixed costs can be reduced quickly. Some fixed costs, such as depreciation on an existing building, do not change easily. Such costs are called **committed fixed costs.** Examples are depreciation, property taxes, long-term leases, and pension benefits.

Discretionary fixed costs can be eliminated, but it is difficult to reduce committed fixed costs

On the other hand, some fixed costs can be changed or eliminated in a relatively short time. These are called **discretionary fixed costs.** Examples are research and development costs, administrative salaries, rent on factories or offices, and advertising. For example, if a business cannot use all of its rented office space, it may decide to give up a portion of the space in order to reduce its rent. The cost of rent, which is categorized as a fixed cost, can be reduced at the discretion of management in a relatively short time.

Variable Costs

Costs that change directly and proportionately with the volume of activity are called **variable costs.** Examples of variable costs are direct materials, sales commissions, payroll taxes, and direct labor. For example, if the cost of direct

Figure 3-2. Variable costs change directly with changes in activity, and therefore plot as a straight line sloping upward and to the right from the origin. The ratio of the variable cost, *Y*, to the activity level, *X*, is the rate of increase in the cost caused by the increase in one unit of activity. This ratio determines *b*, the slope of the variable cost line.

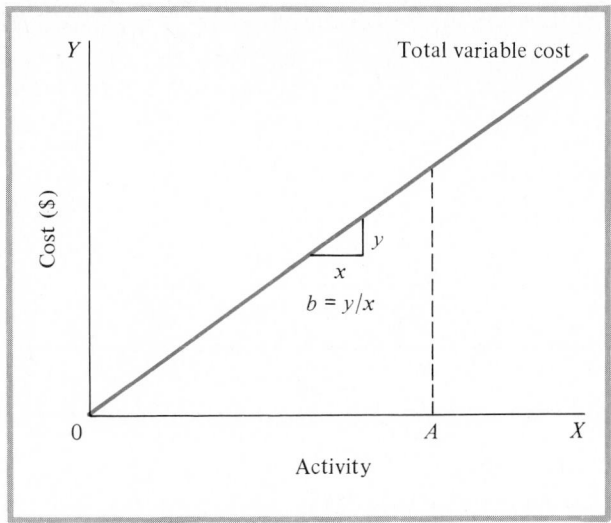

Total variable cost

$b = y/x$

Variable costs change directly with activity. More production means more variable cost

labor required to produce one electronic calculator is $3, then to produce 1,000 calculators, the direct labor cost is $3,000. To produce 1,001 calculators, total direct labor cost is $3,003. For each additional unit built, the total direct labor cost increases by $3, but the cost per unit remains the same.

Figure 3-2 is a graphic representation of a variable cost. It shows the relationship between total variable cost and the level of activity. Total variable cost (Y) appears on the vertical axis; activity (X) is on the horizontal axis. For a specific activity level A, the total variable cost is the vertical distance between the X axis at point A and the variable cost line, as shown by the broken line. Every time activity changes, total variable cost changes in direct proportion. The ratio of total variable cost to activity (Y/X) is a proportional relationship that remains the same for all activity levels.

Equations used to express cost relationships are useful for solving problems

If there is no activity there is no variable cost. That is why the variable cost line starts at the origin where X and Y are both zero. The line slopes upward and to the right. The relationship between activity and variable cost is expressed mathematically by the equation

$$Y = bX$$

where Y = total variable cost
X = the activity level
b = the variable cost per unit of activity

In the calculator example with a direct labor cost of $3 per unit, the total variable cost is

$$Y = \$3X$$

This equation allows us to compute the total variable cost for labor for any number of units produced. If 800 calculators are produced, the total variable labor cost is $2,400 ($3 × 800 units). If production increases to 900 units the total variable labor cost becomes $2,700 ($3 × 900 units), or an increase of $300.

The variable cost per unit is the slope of the total variable cost line, which is the ratio Y/X. It measures the change in total variable cost with changing activity. The larger the variable cost, the steeper the slope of the variable cost line. In the calculator example, the change in total variable cost resulting from the change in production is ($3 × 900) − ($3 × 800) = $300. The unit cost can be calculated as the ratio Y/X. For 800 units of activity, the ratio of $2,400/800 units is $3 per unit, which is b, the slope of the variable cost line. Similarly, the change in activity level and the variable cost of the change can be expressed as the ratio Y/X in order to find variable cost per unit. In this example we have $300/100 units, or $3 per unit.

No matter what the level of activity, the variable cost **per unit** remains the same. Contrast this with fixed cost per unit, which changes if the level of activity changes. Figure 3-3 illustrates the relationship between total fixed costs and fixed cost per unit, and total variable costs and variable cost per unit. In this figure, diagram (a) shows that the fixed costs, building rent and equipment depreciation, remain the same at all levels of activity. On the other hand, fixed cost per unit is not the same if the level of activity changes. Diagram (b) shows that rent is $10 per unit when 1,000 units are produced, and only $5 per unit when activity is 2,000 units. Diagram (c) in Figure 3-3 shows a variable cost with a slope 3/1 for product q and another variable cost with a slope 2/1 for product r. Diagram (d) shows that the variable cost per unit of q and r is $3 and $2 respectively, no matter what the level of activity. Be sure you understand the distinction between total fixed and variable costs and fixed and variable cost per unit.

Manageable or Controllable Costs.   Some variable costs are called **manageable costs** or **controllable costs** because managers are able to exercise some control over the amount of these costs or to decide whether the cost should be incurred. Direct labor is a controllable cost because managers monitor and control the production efficiency of employees. Although many variable costs are controllable by managers, not all of them are. The terms *variable costs* and *controllable costs* are not synonymous.

Some variable costs are not controllable by managers. For example, a company may have to pay a royalty to the government for every ton of coal mined on government land. It is not possible to mine the coal without incurring the royalty cost. A manager cannot control the variable royalty cost as long as coal is being mined.

Some controllable costs do not behave like variable costs. For example, a manager may enter into a one-year leasing arrangement for some automated equipment needed for the manufacture of a product component. Once the lease contract is signed, the cost of the leased equipment becomes fixed for the year, and remains a fixed cost until the contract expires.

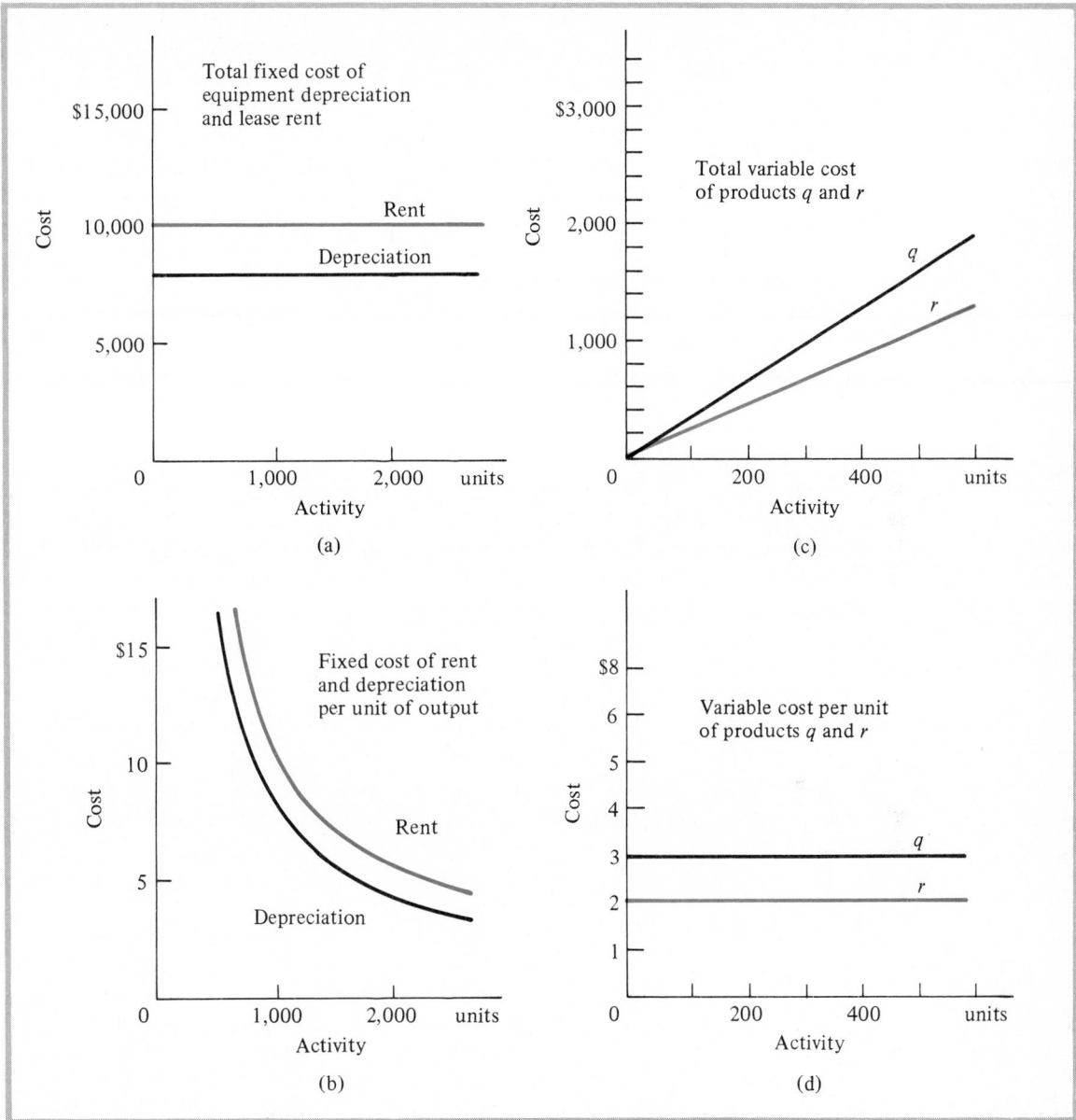

Figure 3-3. Total fixed costs remain the same at all levels of activity, but fixed costs per unit change as activity changes. Total variable costs change as activity changes, but variable costs per unit remain the same regardless of the level of activity.

You can see that the distinction between fixed and variable costs is not always clear. Moreover, there are many costs that are not entirely fixed or entirely variable, but contain components of both types of costs.

Mixed Costs

Mixed costs have both variable and fixed components

Identifying costs as variable or fixed enables managers to make decisions and to evaluate business performance. But some costs do not fit neatly into either of these simple cost behavior patterns. Costs that cannot be described as either variable or fixed, because they contain some of both cost behavior patterns, are called **mixed costs.** Mixed costs can be separated into fixed and variable components to make them easier to analyze. For example, a company's sales representatives are paid a base salary plus a commission on all sales they generate. The compensation cost for sales representatives consists of a fixed portion—the base salary—and a variable portion—the commission.

A mixed cost can be separated into its fixed and variable components, and the behavior of each component can be analyzed and evaluated in the same way as any fixed and variable costs are analyzed.

Figure 3-4 illustrates a mixed cost. The vertical distance between the X axis and the horizontal line is the fixed portion of the cost. The vertical distance between the fixed cost line and the sloping line is the variable portion of the mixed cost.

Since a mixed cost is the sum of a fixed component and a variable component, it can be represented mathematically as the sum of a fixed cost equation and a variable cost equation.

$$\text{Fixed cost:} \quad Y = a$$
$$\text{Variable cost:} \quad Y = bX$$
$$\text{Mixed cost[1]:} \quad Y = a + bX$$

[1] The equation $Y = a + bX$ is the general form of the equation for any straight line. This same equation is used in Chapters 22 and 23 on financial data analysis.

Figure 3-4. Mixed costs contain fixed and variable components that can be separated for managerial purposes. The sum of the fixed cost, a, plus the variable cost, bX, for any level of activity equals the total cost.

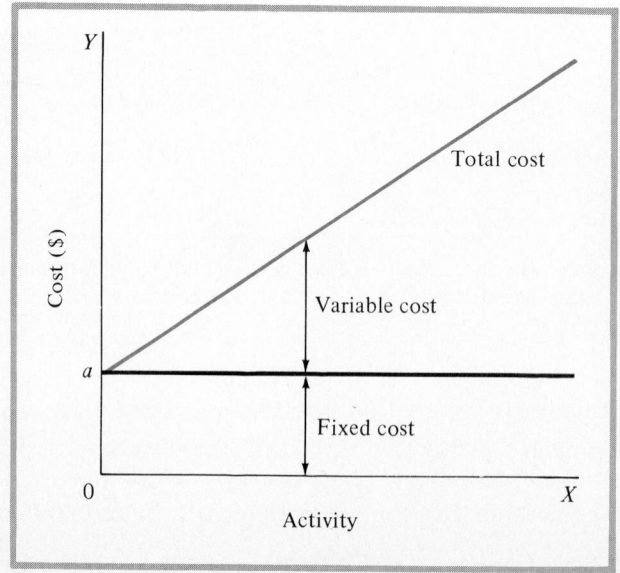

The total mixed cost Y consists of the fixed cost a, which is the same at every level of activity, plus the variable cost bX, which depends on the level of activity X. The values a and b are constants dictated by the nature of the mixed cost.

By substituting values for a and b we can describe a particular mixed cost. For example, a sales representative's base salary is $17,000 and the commission for each unit sold is $125. Then $a = \$17,000$, $b = \$125$, and the mixed cost is expressed mathematically by the equation

$$Y = \$17,000 + \$125X$$

The sales representative's total compensation is the firm's mixed cost. To find the total compensation for an individual, it is only necessary to substitute

Figure 3-5. Mixed costs may be plotted with the variable component either above or below the fixed component. At 38 units of sales, the total cost is $21,750 and the fixed cost is $17,000.

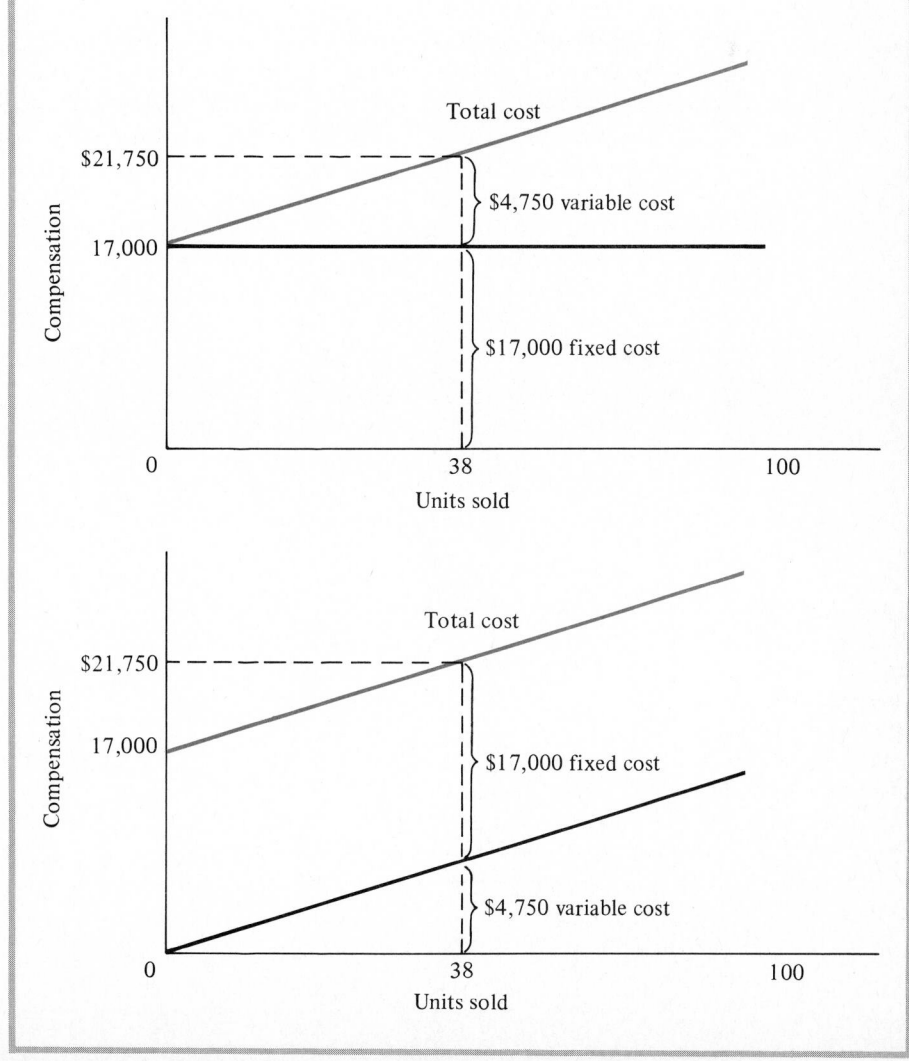

the appropriate value for X, the number of units sold. For a representative who sold 38 units, the firm's mixed cost is

$$Y = a + bX$$
$$= \$17{,}000 + \$125(38)$$
$$= \$17{,}000 + \$4{,}750$$
$$= \$21{,}750$$

Figure 3-5 shows two ways of graphing the sales representatives' compensation cost. Fixed costs and variable costs are the same in both cases, and so is the mixed cost. Either method of illustrating mixed costs may be used, and the method selected depends on the needs of managers when they analyze costs.

Semivariable Costs

Some costs change with activity levels but not proportionally. Instead they change at increasing or decreasing rates throughout the entire range of activity. Such costs are called **semivariable costs** and are illustrated in Figure 3-6. Diagram (a) shows a semivariable cost that increases at an increasing rate as the volume of activity increases. Such costs can get out of hand very quickly; managers must be careful to control them. Fortunately, such costs are relatively rare. An example of an increasing semivariable cost is that of electricity in locations where utilities charge progressively more per kilowatt hour of electricity used, in order to encourage energy conservation.

Semivariable costs plot as curved lines

Diagram (b) in Figure 3-6 shows a semivariable cost that increases at a decreasing rate as the volume of activity increases. This is known as a **learning curve cost** because it is characteristic of labor costs for workers who learn a new task and become increasingly more efficient as they perform it repeatedly.

A learning curve describes improving labor efficiency

For example, a firm producing a batch of calculators for the first time may find that it requires 22 minutes of direct labor to produce each unit. With

Figure 3-6. Semivariable costs may increase at an increasing or decreasing rate. Part (b) depicts a learning curve cost.

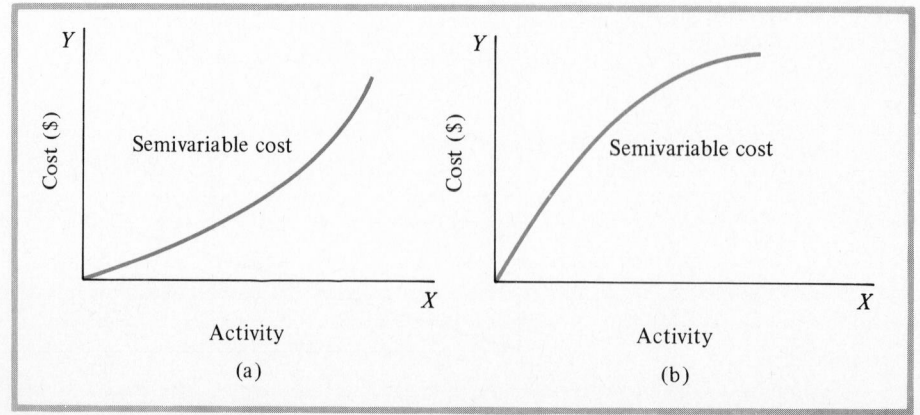

the second batch, the time per calculator may fall to 19 minutes per unit. Eventually, the time may decrease to 16 minutes per calculator and fall no further because there is no further improvement in labor efficiency. Analyzing learning curve costs can be very useful for managers, as you will see in Chapter 25.

Semifixed Costs

Semifixed costs change in steps but remain fixed between changes

Some costs behave like fixed costs only within specific ranges of activity, increasing or decreasing in discrete jumps as activity levels change. Such costs are called **semifixed costs** or **step function costs.** For example, a firm may increase production by adding a night shift or by working overtime without increasing the cost of its production facilities. When maximum capacity is reached within the available facilities, however, increased production can be achieved only by expanding the plant. This expansion causes a jump in the fixed cost of production facilities.

Semifixed costs are illustrated in Figure 3-7, which shows the cost fixed up to point *A*, then increasing at that point and remaining fixed at the higher level until activity level *B* is reached. How much the cost increases and how much activity is necessary to cause a jump in the cost depends on the type of cost and the type of activity.

Semifixed costs cannot be described easily with an equation. Managers typically analyze such costs graphically. For example, if a manager knows that activity during a period will be between points *A* and *B*, as in Figure 3-7, then the semifixed costs can be viewed as a fixed cost for this range of activity.

Cost Behavior Assumptions

There are two assumptions that underlie the concept of cost behavior. They are the relevant range assumption and the time assumption.

The Relevant Range Assumption.   Although it is convenient to view costs as variable, fixed, or mixed, almost no cost exhibits the same pattern of behavior

Figure 3-7. Semifixed costs change in intermittent jumps and are therefore called step function costs. The cost remains fixed for some range of activity but increases above that range.

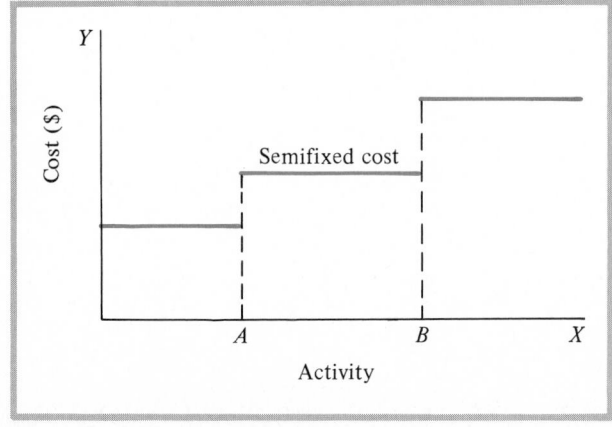

at all ranges of activity. We therefore assume that the cost behavior pattern identified for each cost is correct only for a certain range of activity known as the **relevant range.** Above or below the relevant range of activity, the cost may have a different behavior pattern.

For example, earlier we illustrated the variable cost of labor for producing calculators. What we did not say was that each calculator can be produced with $3 of direct labor only as long as a large enough number of calculators is made on a highly automated production line. To produce only one or two calculators may require making them entirely by hand. In that case direct labor cost could be much higher than $3, perhaps as high as $20 per unit. If 50 or 60 units are produced, it may be possible to divide the manual work among several people, each of whom performs a specific task and therefore works more efficiently; the cost may drop to $10 per unit. At some very high level of production, the variable cost may increase above $3 per unit. It may be necessary to pay overtime to each worker to produce a larger than normal number of units, and the variable labor cost may become $3.50 per unit.

You can see that the variable cost line may not increase proportionately in the entire possible range of activity. Figure 3-8 shows that the variable cost in this example is very steep at low levels of activity, becomes less steep at activity level A, and then again becomes steeper above activity level B.

It is difficult to describe mathematically the variable cost shown here. However, if the level of activity is not expected to be below level A nor above level B, managers may make the assumption that the variable cost component is the straight sloping line within this relevant range and the fixed component is depicted by the horizontal line shown in the figure. These assumptions can

Cost behavior patterns are valid within a relevant range of activity

Figure 3-8. Cost behavior patterns are valid for a given range of activity. The total cost line shows a variety of characteristics, but in the range from A to B, it can be viewed as a mixed cost whose fixed component is depicted by a.

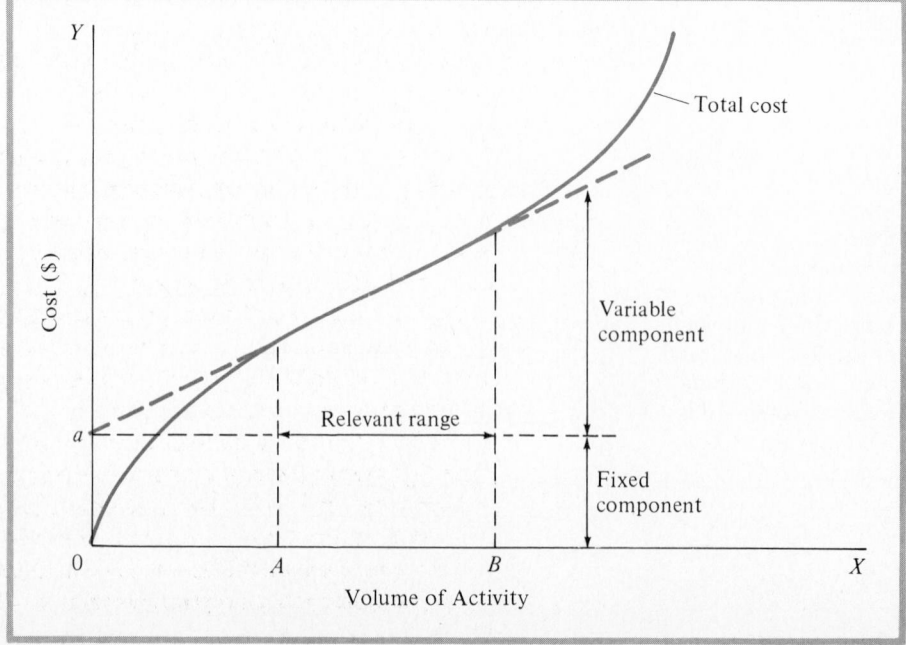

be made because, within the relevant range, the total mixed cost behaves as if it is made up of the fixed and variable cost components depicted in the figure. Therefore the behavior patterns in the relevant range can be used for cost analysis and decision making. Of course if actual activity is below *A* or above *B* the decisions made using the assumed cost patterns may be poor. Managers should be cautious not to project costs and make decisions for one range of activity when using cost behavior patterns based on data from another range of activity.

The Time Assumption.   The second assumption about costs is that a particular cost will fit a particular behavior pattern only for some specific time period, such as a year. Cost behavior may change over time. In the long run any fixed cost may change. A one-year lease is a fixed cost only for a year; it may be higher next year, or it will not exist if the lease is not renewed. Variable costs may change within relatively short periods of time. The cost of direct labor to produce calculators may decline when a single new component is developed that replaces several old components, making it possible to assemble the calculators with less labor.

Over time, cost behavior patterns may change

COST ESTIMATION TECHNIQUES

How do accountants determine the behavior pattern of a cost? Typically, they use historical cost data. Costs and activities of the recent past usually are the best indicators of cost behavior patterns for the present or immediate future. For example, to plot the variable cost of $3 per unit for the direct labor of producing calculators, first it is necessary to obtain some cost data from ledger accounts.

Accountants have several cost estimation techniques they can use in an effort to analyze actual cost data and fit them into one of the cost behavior patterns described earlier. To use these techniques, they must have sufficient cost data for the analysis. Either graphic or mathematical techniques can be used to analyze cost behavior.

The Scatter Diagram

One way to obtain an idea of how actual costs behave is to plot them in a graph and observe the pattern they form. To illustrate, we present a sample of labor costs and corresponding activity levels for the last six months of the past year. The sample is taken from the operation of a single production department of a manufacturing business.

Month	Total Labor Cost	Total Labor Hours
July	$19,000	2,750
August	13,500	1,400
September	18,000	2,000
October	16,500	2,300
November	21,500	3,000
December	15,500	1,600

Figure 3-9. Scatter diagrams can be used to visualize cost behavior patterns. This one shows a mixed cost with a strong linear relationship between costs and activity. Connecting the high and low point in the diagram provides an estimate of the variable cost and fixed cost. The estimate of the total cost of 2,500 hours of labor is $19,000 according to the diagram.

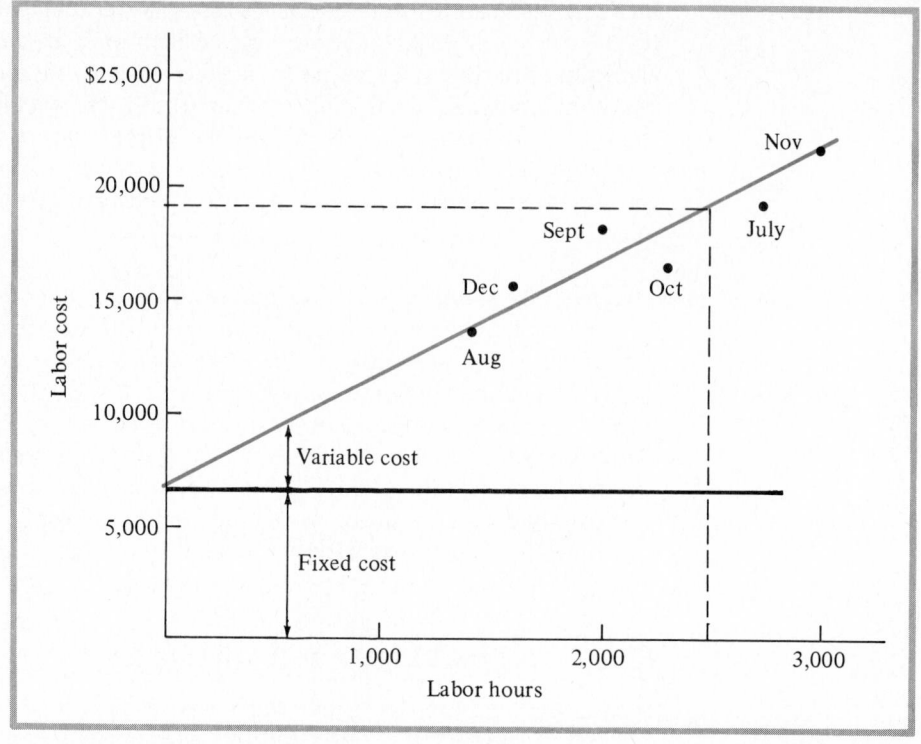

A scatter diagram helps to visualize a cost behavior pattern exhibited by cost and activity data

Plotting the data on a graph with labor costs on the vertical axis and activity level on the horizontal axis, we obtain the diagram illustrated in Figure 3-9. This diagram is called a **scatter diagram,** or **scattergram,** because the plotted data points are scattered across the graph. Observe that the points on the graph form a distinct pattern, indicating a relationship between total cost and total activity, with costs increasing as activity increases.

By drawing a straight line through the points, we obtain an estimate of the fixed portion of these costs where the line intersects the Y axis, and an estimate of the variable portion represented by the slope of the line. In Figure 3-9 the straight line is drawn through the highest and lowest points in the graph. This "high-low" method is only one of several ways of representing this set of data by a straight line. If a more precise estimate is needed, a statistical method of cost estimation called regression analysis may be used.

The High-Low Method

A line through the high and low point in a scattergram defines the slope of the variable cost and the level of fixed costs

The slope of the variable cost line is the ratio of change in cost for each unit change in activity. Using this relationship, we can estimate how much the labor costs in our sample of data changed for each additional hour of labor. The **high-low method** is a simple technique that enables us to find the ratio of cost to activity by looking at the change between the highest and lowest cost and the change between the corresponding activity levels. Dividing the change in cost by the change in labor hours between the highest and lowest points, we obtain the change in cost for each additional unit of labor time. This computation yields the variable cost b in the total cost formula $Y = a + bX$.

The highest cost in the last six months is \$21,500 for November, when 3,000 hours of labor were used. The lowest cost occurred in August, when \$13,500 was paid for 1,400 hours of labor. We calculate b by finding the difference between the highest and lowest cost and dividing by the difference in the hours associated with those costs.

$$b = \frac{\text{Change in cost}}{\text{Change in hours}}$$

$$= \frac{\$21,500 - \$13,500}{3,000 \text{ hr} - 1,400 \text{ hr}}$$

$$= \frac{\$8,000}{1,600 \text{ hr}}$$

$$= \$5 \text{ per hour}$$

The estimate indicates that for every hour of labor used, the labor cost was \$5. Substituting b and either the highest cost and hours worked or the lowest cost and hours worked into the mixed cost formula, we can solve for the fixed cost a. In August, 1,400 hours costing \$13,500 were used. Substituting these values into the total cost equation we get

$$Y = a + bX$$

$$\$13,500 = a + \$5 \text{ per hour} \times 1,400 \text{ hours}$$

$$\$13,500 = a + \$7,000$$

$$a = \$13,500 - \$7,000$$

$$= \$6,500$$

Note that the total cost line in Figure 3-9 intersects the Y axis at \$6,500. Our calculations verify that a straight line drawn through the high and low points yields a fixed cost of \$6,500.

Sometimes the highest cost is not associated with the highest level of activity, or the lowest cost with the lowest level of activity. In such cases, the accountant must decide if the high and low points should be based on the highest and lowest cost or the highest and lowest activity level. The measure selected should be the one that provides the best cost behavior information.

The high-low method provides a simple way of obtaining the fixed cost and variable cost components of a sample of cost data. Once we have those values, we can use them in the cost equation to estimate the labor cost at other levels of activity. For example, if a manager wants to estimate the total cost of 2,500 labor hours, the following computation provides an answer.

$$Y = a + bX$$

$$Y = \$6,500 + \$5(2,500)$$

$$= \$6,500 + \$12,500$$

$$= \$19,000$$

The actual labor cost for 2,500 labor hours might be somewhat higher or lower than $19,000. That is because the straight line drawn through the entire set of cost data is not an exact representation of each point; instead it is a good approximation. In many situations, the labor cost estimate of $19,000 is sufficient for planning future labor needs, for securing necessary cash, or for assessing cost data for a particular period. More precise estimates might not be needed or may cost too much or take too much time for current reporting needs. The high-low method is a quick way of assessing data, and can yield useful estimates in many situations.

The high-low method, while simple to apply, does not give meaningful results if the data do not have a strong linear relationship. A sample of data may not clearly exhibit a linear relationship between costs and activities like the one shown in Figure 3-9.

In Figure 3-10 several scattergrams are shown. Diagram *(a)* shows no discernible relationship between costs and activity levels. It is not logical to attempt to represent the data with a straight or even a curved line. Diagram *(b)* shows that costs and activity seem to be strongly related, but the relationship is not linear. Diagram *(c)* shows a strong linear relationship between costs and activity, but the highest cost is not also the highest activity. In that case the manager must decide whether to apply the high-low method to the highest cost or the highest activity, or use another method of analysis.

A more precise method of estimating fixed and variable costs from cost data is a statistical method called linear regression. It is used to compute the straight line that best fits the data. The computations needed to calculate the

Figure 3-10. Some costs such as those depicted in diagram (a) show no obvious relationship to activity levels. The costs in diagram (b) fall into a learning curve pattern, but if enough points are not plotted the pattern could be mistaken as linear. The dilemma of the high-low method, when the highest cost is not also the highest level of activity, is illustrated in diagram (c). Which line should be used to estimate the fixed and variable components of this mixed cost pattern?

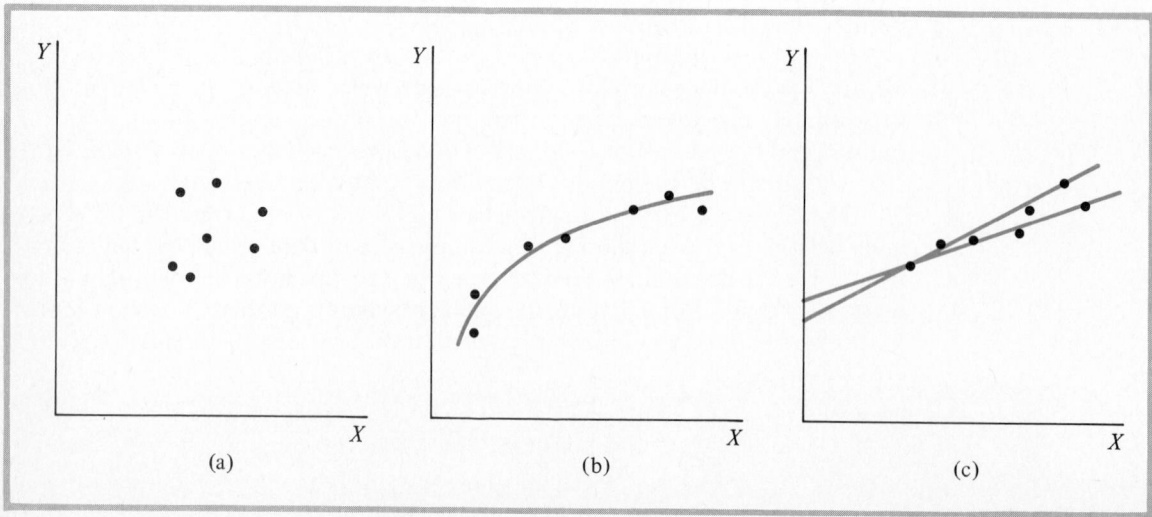

regression line can be fairly complex. When there are many data points, the computation may require a computer. Chapter 24 explains how to make the calculations.

COST-VOLUME-PROFIT RELATIONSHIPS

The economic environment changes constantly. This is the basic reason why it is impossible to predict or to estimate precisely the volume of activity and the quantity of resources needed to conduct business. A major reason for analyzing cost data to determine cost behavior patterns is to provide managers with information that can be used to plan activities, analyze alternative courses of action, and make intelligent decisions in changing economic conditions. **Cost-volume-profit (CVP) analysis** is the systematic examination of the relationships among costs, volume of activity, prices, and profit. CVP analysis is used to determine the break-even point of operations and to make many other analyses for managing not only profit-seeking businesses but not-for-profit organizations as well.

Break-Even Analysis

The activity level at which total costs equal total revenues is called the **break-even point.** At the break-even point of operations, there is neither profit nor loss. Businesses are not particularly interested in operating at the break-even point; investors do not commit resources to operations that promise zero return. But an understanding of break-even analysis helps managers to operate profitably. Moreover, not-for-profit organizations such as cooperatives and foundations try to operate close to the break-even point.

A break-even point need not be defined for an entire firm. A division, a single product, a group of products, a sales region, or any other well-defined cost objective may be used in the analysis.

The break-even point, with zero profit, means that total revenue equals total cost

The basic profit calculation is to deduct from revenues all expenses to arrive at profit. To perform a break-even analysis correctly, the accountant must include all costs associated with the revenue. It is common practice in CVP analysis to assume that all costs become expenses during the period under analysis. Therefore, we do not differentiate between costs and expenses in performing the analysis. For purposes of CVP analysis, profit is revenue minus cost. The calculation of profit is

$$\text{Total revenue} - \text{Total cost} = \text{Profit}$$

and if activity is at the break-even point, profit is zero, giving

$$\text{Total revenue} - \text{Total cost} = 0$$

Graphically, total revenue and total cost are plotted on the Y axis, and units of activity are plotted on the X axis. Therefore we can use Y to mean total revenue and the equation becomes

$$Y = \text{Total cost}$$

For break-even analysis, it is necessary to separate total cost into its fixed and variable components. At the break-even point

$$\text{Total revenue} = \text{Fixed cost} + \text{Variable cost}$$
$$Y = FC + VC$$

Often, however, break-even analysis requires revenue and variable costs to be expressed in unit prices, unit costs, and volume. Revenue is expressed as selling price per unit (S) times the number of units (X) produced and sold, and variable cost is expressed as the variable cost per unit (VC) times the number of units (X) produced and sold. This equation is

$$\text{Total revenue} = \text{Total cost}$$
$$\left(\begin{array}{c} \text{Selling price} \\ \times \text{No. of units} \end{array} \right) = \text{Fixed cost} + \left(\begin{array}{c} \text{Variable cost per} \\ \text{unit} \times \text{No. of units} \end{array} \right)$$
$$S(X) = FC + VC(X)$$

Break-Even Point in Units.   To illustrate the break-even calculation, let's assume that activity is measured as the number of units of a product. Rember Company plans to start manufacturing a new compass. Fixed costs are $20,000 and the variable cost is $6 per compass. The company expects to set selling price at $10 per unit. To find the break-even point, we substitute these values into the equation:

$$S(X) = FC + VC(X)$$
$$\$10 \text{ per unit} \times X = \$20,000 + \$6 \text{ per unit} \times X$$

Solving for X we get

$$\$10X - \$6X = \$20,000$$
$$\$4X = \$20,000$$
$$X = \$20,000 / \$4$$
$$= 5,000 \text{ units}$$

If the company produces and sells 5,000 compasses, it will break even. At this level of activity revenue is $50,000 ($10 × 5,000 units), variable cost is $30,000 ($6 × 5,000 units), and fixed cost is $20,000. Total cost equals total revenue, leaving neither profit nor loss. This mathematical analysis is illustrated graphically in Figure 3-11. The break-even point is shown where the total revenue line crosses the total cost line.

In the graph, the total revenue line starts at zero revenue, that is, at the origin, because when no units are sold there is no revenue. The total revenue line slopes up and to the right with increasing volume of production or sales.[2]

---

[2] Remember that we assume all costs become expenses. That implies that all products made are sold, so we often refer only to production rather than production and sales or sales alone.

Figure 3-11. The cost - volume - profit chart illustrates the CVP relationships for a wide range of activity. It is easy to visualize the effects of a change in one or more of the variables that make up the diagram.

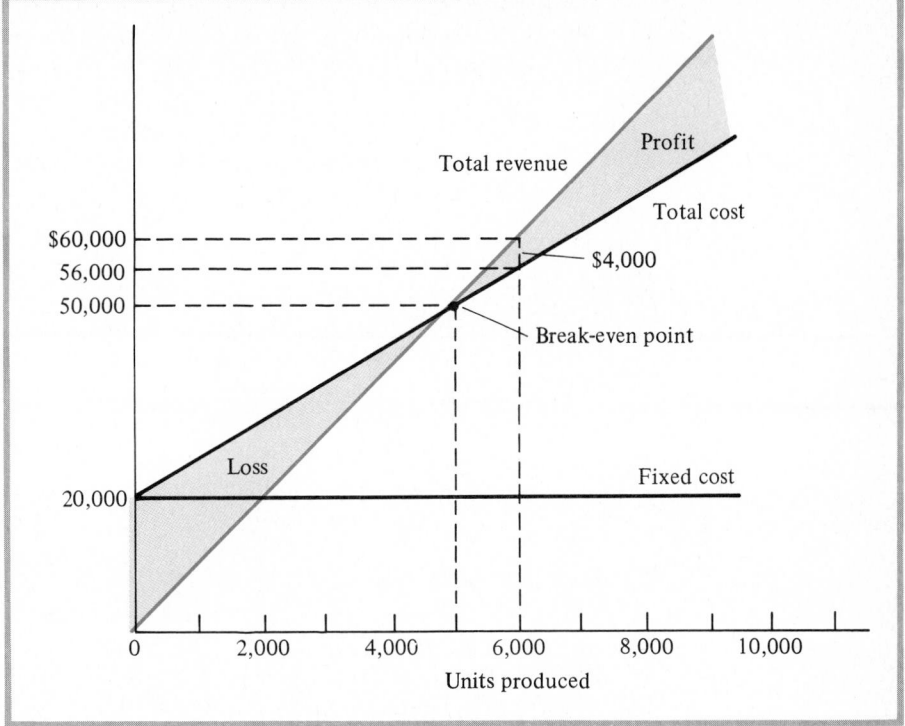

The slope of the total revenue line is $10 per unit. That means that for every unit increase in sales volume, the sales revenue increases by $10, which is the selling price of the compass. The fixed cost is $20,000 and the variable cost is $6 per unit. Therefore, the total cost line starts at $20,000 for zero production, and slopes upward but not as steeply as the revenue line, because the variable cost per unit is less than the selling price per unit.

At 5,000 units total revenue and total cost are equal, as shown by the point where the total revenue and total cost lines intersect. The difference between the total revenue line and the total cost line is the profit or loss that results at levels of activity above or below 5,000 units. For example, if 6,000 units are produced and sold, total revenue is $60,000, total cost is $56,000, and profit is $4,000, as graphically determined in Figure 3-11. This can be verified mathematically by using the basic profit equation

$$\text{Price} \times \text{Units sold} = \text{Fixed cost} + (\text{Variable cost} \times \text{Units sold}) + \text{Profit}$$
$$S(X) = FC + VC(X) + P$$
$$\$10\,(6{,}000 \text{ units}) = \$20{,}000 + \$6\,(6{,}000 \text{ units}) + P$$
$$\$60{,}000 = \$20{,}000 + \$36{,}000 + P$$
$$P = \$60{,}000 - \$56{,}000$$
$$= \$4{,}000$$

The graph in Figure 3-11 is called the **cost-volume-profit diagram** or the **CVP chart**; it is used commonly in CVP analysis. Graphic analyses of CVP relationships have many advantages. Graphs can show what happens over a range of activity, whereas a calculation provides results for only one specific activity level. Graphs can often illustrate complex analysis in an understandable way, especially for individuals who have difficulty analyzing and understanding numeric data.

Contribution Margin

Another way of finding the break-even point is the contribution margin method. **Contribution margin** is the difference between total revenue and total variable cost and is the amount available to cover fixed costs and provide a profit. Contribution margin may be calculated in total or per unit. For a single compass produced by Rember Company the contribution margin is

$$\text{Contribution margin} = \text{Revenue} - \text{Variable cost}$$
$$CM = Y - VC$$
$$= \$10 - \$6$$
$$= \$4$$

Contribution margin, the difference between selling price and variable cost, provides a profit after covering fixed costs

The contribution margin of $4 is the amount that each unit contributes toward covering fixed costs and providing a profit. A certain number of units must be produced and sold just to cover the fixed costs. All units produced above this break-even level contribute their margin toward profit.

Sometimes it is useful to express contribution margin as a percentage of sales. In our example the **contribution margin ratio** is .4, or 40 percent, calculated as $4/$10.

We just found that in the Rember Company example the break-even volume is 5,000 units. This means that if 5,001 units are sold, the profit will be $4, because the 5,001st unit contributes its margin toward profit. We can use the contribution margin per unit to calculate the break-even point by dividing unit contribution margin into fixed costs[3] as follows:

$$\text{Break-even point} = \frac{\text{Fixed cost}}{\text{Contribution margin per unit}}$$
$$= \frac{\$20,000}{\$4/\text{unit}}$$
$$= 5,000 \text{ units}$$

---

[3] This formula can be derived from the basic break-even equation expressed in units of production:

$$S(X) = FC + VC(X)$$
$$FC = S(X) - VC(X)$$

Factoring the right side yields

$$FC = X(S - VC)$$

and the term in parentheses $(S - VC)$ is contribution margin per unit. Then break-even production quantity (X) is

$$X = FC/(S - VC)$$

Figure 3-12. CVP chart showing contribution margin as the difference between the variable cost line and the total revenue line. Below the break-even point, contribution margin is not sufficient to cover fixed cost. The deficiency is shown as the shaded area that represents loss. At 6,000 units of production, contribution margin is $24,000 and profit is $4,000.

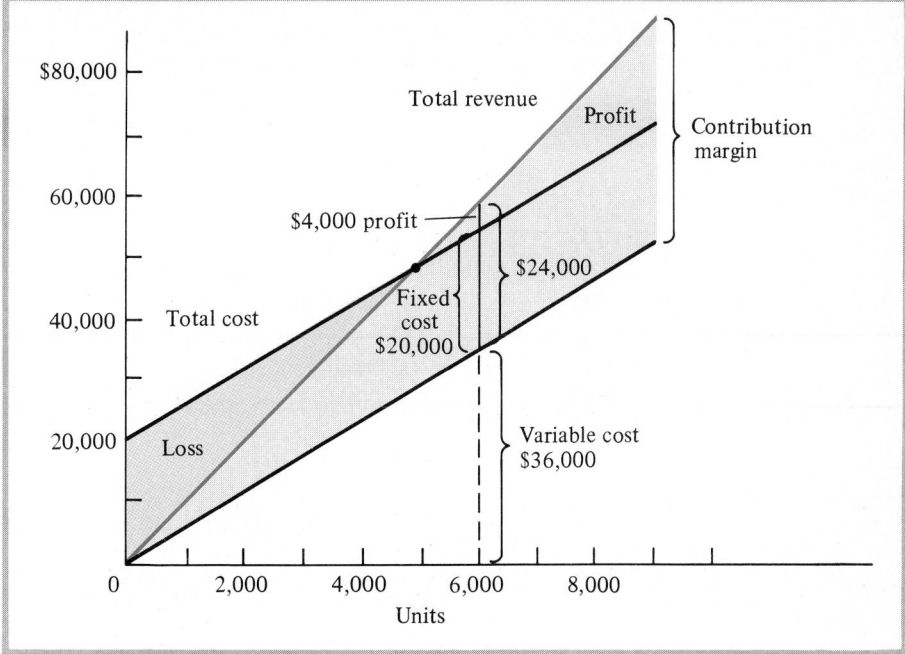

Figure 3-12 shows the break-even point, with contribution margin illustrated by placing the fixed cost above variable cost. The diagram emphasizes that contribution margin covers fixed costs and profit **above** the break-even point, whereas it does not cover all of fixed cost below the break-even point, therefore resulting in losses. When 6,000 units are produced the total contribution margin is $24,000 (6,000 units × $4/unit), of which $20,000 covers fixed cost and $4,000 is profit.

Break-Even Point in Dollars. Sometimes you may need to find the break-even point expressed in revenue rather than units. In such cases, variable cost can be expressed as a percentage of revenue in the break-even equation. With a selling price of $10 per unit and variable cost of $6 per unit, variable cost is 60 percent of selling price. The same break-even equation is used as before, but now there are no units used in it.

$$\text{Revenue} = FC + VC$$
$$Y = \$20{,}000 + .6Y$$

The break-even point occurs when total revenue (Y) is equal to fixed cost plus 60 percent of revenue. Solving for Y, we get

$$Y - .6Y = \$20{,}000$$
$$.4Y = \$20{,}000$$
$$Y = \$20{,}000 / .4$$
$$= \$50{,}000$$

The .4 in the equation is the contribution margin ratio. You can see now that to compute the break-even point in units, you divide fixed cost by contribution margin per unit. To compute the break-even point in dollars, you divide fixed cost by the contribution margin ratio.

CVP Analysis

Managers analyze CVP relationships to determine how changes in fixed costs, variable costs, selling prices, or combinations of these affect profit. CVP analysis also provides information on the volume of activity, cost, or price needed to achieve a target profit or to determine what happens to profits and costs at various levels of activity.

Cost-volume-profit analysis discloses the effect of changes in costs, prices, and volume

We first examine the effects of changes in each CVP component independently of the others. Then we look at the effects of simultaneous changes in several components. In all cases we use the same equation to solve the problems:

$$\text{Revenue} = FC + VC + \text{Profit}$$

Change in Fixed Cost. By definition, fixed costs do not change in the relevant range and during the identified time period. Nevertheless, managers are able to plan future operations to increase or decrease fixed costs if such changes can increase productivity, solve labor problems, or improve operations. CVP analysis enables managers to analyze costs over which they have little or no control, such as an increase in property taxes; this analysis permits managers to evaluate the impact on total profits from changes in fixed costs, such as an increase in operating capacity by investing in new automated equipment.

For example, the management of Rember Company expects that its level of activity next year will allow it to operate without the use of some rented factory space. Eliminating the rent on this space and moving all operations to its own plant will reduce fixed costs by $4,000. The new break-even point is computed by substituting the new fixed cost into the break-even equation.

$$\text{Revenue} = FC + VC$$
$$\$10X = \$16,000 + \$6X$$
$$\$4X = \$16,000$$
$$X = 4,000 \text{ units}$$

Since the contribution margin is $4 per unit, a decrease in fixed cost of $4,000 means that the firm can sell 1,000 fewer units and cover the lower fixed costs. If the company manufactures 6,000 units, profit is

$$\$10(6,000) = \$16,000 + \$6(6,000) + P$$
$$\$60,000 = \$16,000 + \$36,000 + P$$
$$P = \$60,000 - \$52,000$$
$$= \$8,000$$

The change in fixed cost is illustrated as diagram (a) in Figure 3-13. With the decrease in fixed cost and no change in variable cost, total cost decreases, shifting the total cost line downward. This has the effect of shifting the break-even point down along the total revenue line to a lower break-even revenue and break-even volume. The diagram verifies the break-even calculation and also shows the profit generated with 6,000 units of sales.

CVP charts permit visual analysis of a wide range of CVP relationships

Figure 3-13. CVP charts showing how changes in variables used in CVP analysis affect the break-even point. The four charts illustrate: (a) decrease in fixed cost; (b) increase in variable cost; (c) increase in selling price; and (d) volume of production required to meet a target profit.

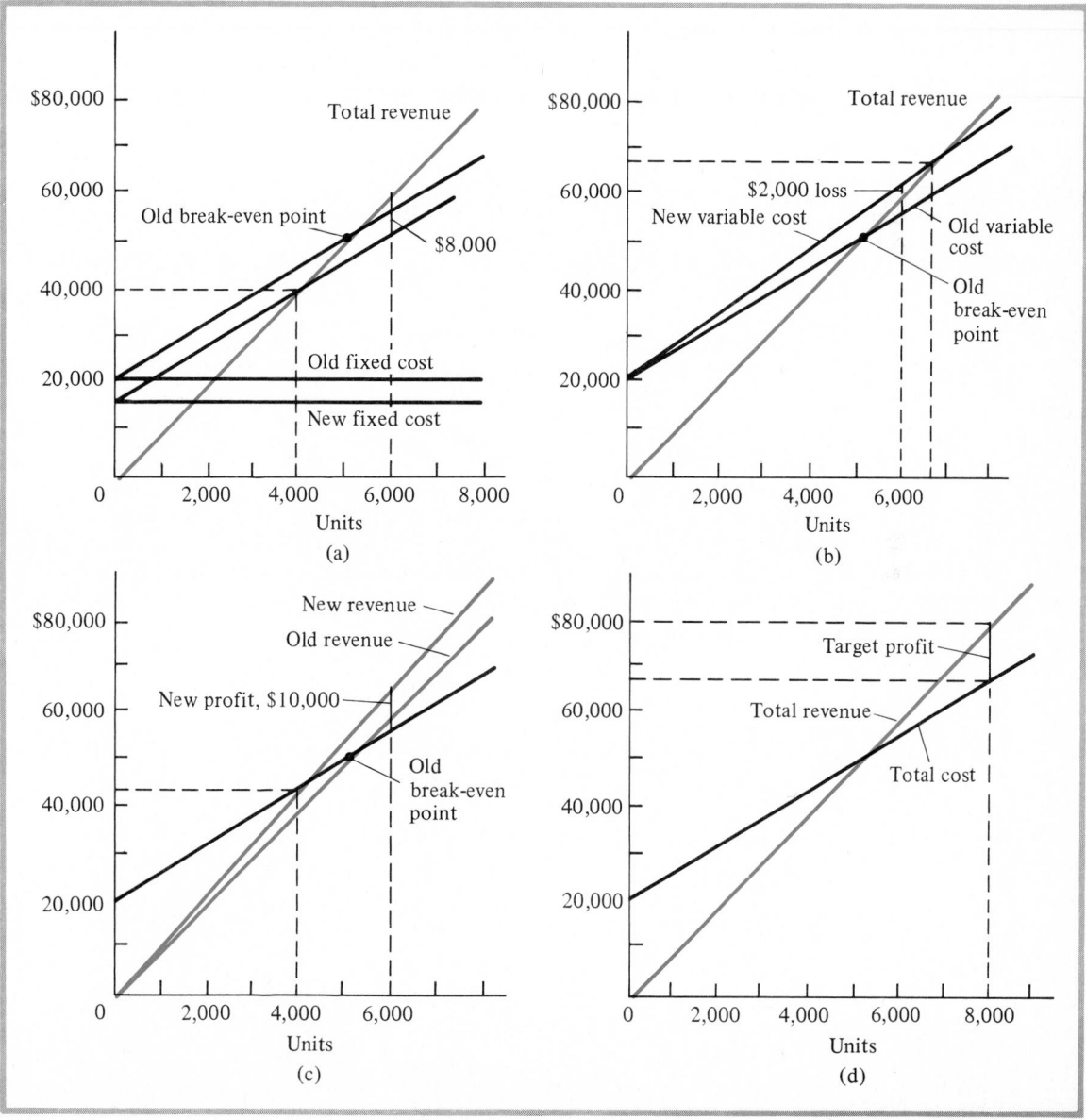

Change in Variable Cost.   Variable costs change for many reasons, such as new labor contracts, increased material costs, higher energy costs, or other variable cost increases or decreases.

Rember Company negotiates a new labor contract requiring an increase in variable cost of $1 per unit. Fixed cost remains the same. The new break-even point is

$$\$10X = \$20,000 + \$7X$$
$$\$10X - \$7X = \$20,000$$
$$\$3X = \$20,000$$
$$X = 6,667 \text{ units}$$

The $1 increase in cost is only 10 percent of the selling price ($1/$10) but it is 25 percent of the old contribution margin ($1/$4), resulting in a 33 percent increase in the break-even point (1,667 units/5,000 units). A lower contribution margin requires more units to cover the fixed cost, resulting in a higher break-even point. If the company produces only 6,000 units it will incur a loss of $2,000. Diagram (b) in Figure 3-13 shows the effect of increasing variable cost. The slope of the total cost line increases, moving the break-even point up the revenue line to 6,667 units and $66,670 of sales revenue. Although we computed only the change in volume, the graph also shows the new break-even revenue and the loss incurred at 6,000 units of production.

Change in Selling Price.   A change in selling price affects the contribution margin. If the selling price increases while costs remain unchanged, the break-even point should decrease. If selling price is raised to $11 per unit, the new break-even point is

$$\$11X = \$20,000 + \$6X$$
$$\$5X = \$20,000$$
$$X = 4,000 \text{ units}$$

To obtain the sales revenue at the break-even point, we merely multiply the number of units by the selling price. With the new selling price the break-even revenue is $44,000. Diagram (c) in Figure 3-13 illustrates the effect of raising the selling price. Note that at 6,000 units and $10 per unit selling price, profit was $4,000; at 6,000 units and $11 per unit selling price, profit is $10,000, or a 250 percent increase, although the price increased only by 10 percent.

Target Net Income.   Managers are not interested simply in breaking even; they usually plan for an activity level that will provide a desired profit. To calculate the level of sales that will produce a desired target profit, it is only necessary to include the target profit in the break-even equation.

For example, if Rember Company wants to earn a $15,000 profit on the sale of its compasses, it can find the number of units needed to achieve this goal with the following equation:

$$\$10X = \$20,000 + \$6X + \$15,000$$
$$\$10X - \$6X = \$20,000 + \$15,000$$
$$\$4X = \$35,000$$
$$X = 8,750 \text{ units}$$

It may not be possible for the company to produce or sell 8,750 units. Demand for the compasses and competition may not permit that sales level. This number of units may be beyond the capacity of the plant, or the level of activity may be beyond the relevant range. Management must evaluate any analysis to determine if it is realistic. In this case management decides that 8,750 units is not realistic, and wants to determine how many units would be required to achieve, not a specific amount of profit, but a profit of 15 percent of sales revenue. This can be solved in terms of dollars by expressing variable cost and target profit as percentages of selling price. You may remember that variable cost is 60 percent of selling price and we want profit to be 15 percent of selling price. The required sales revenue is found as

$$\text{Sales revenue} = FC + VC + \text{Target profit}$$
$$= FC + 60\% \text{ of revenue} + 15\% \text{ of revenue}$$
$$Y = \$20,000 + .6Y + .15Y$$
$$Y - .6Y - .15Y = \$20,000$$
$$.25Y = \$20,000$$
$$Y = \$80,000$$

At a $10 selling price, the number of units required to generate $80,000 of revenue is 8,000 units.

The problem can be solved in units by noting that 15 percent of selling price is $1.50. This means that $1.50 of each unit's revenue is needed for profit and the rest is needed to cover costs. The equation is

$$S(X) = FC + VC(X) + \text{Target profit } (X)$$
$$\$10X = \$20,000 + \$6X + \$1.50X$$
$$\$2.50X = \$20,000$$
$$X = 8,000 \text{ units}$$

Diagram (d) in Figure 3-13 shows that total revenue and total cost can be read on the vertical axis at 8,000 units of activity. Diagrams sometimes lack the precision that can be obtained by means of calculations, and they do not show profit or cost as a percentage of selling price.

*CVP analysis can be
used to examine
simultaneous
changes in several
variables*

Combination Changes.   In practice, more than one CVP variable may change. A CVP analysis must simultaneously include all changes.

Management may decide that by increasing some fixed costs it will be possible to decrease some variable costs. Or it may be necessary to increase selling price to compensate for an unavoidable increase in a fixed or variable cost. An increase in price may cause a decrease in sales volume.

For example, Rember Company is faced with an $.80 per unit increase in labor cost and wants to compensate for this by decreasing its fixed cost. It decides to give up some rented space and move all of its operations into its own plant, reducing fixed cost by $2,000. At the same time, management believes that increasing the selling price of each unit by $.40 will not adversely affect demand for its product, and that a target profit of $9,000 can be maintained. If all of these changes are incorporated in the analysis, the number of units that must be produced and sold is

$$\$10.40X = \$18,000 + \$6.80X + \$9,000$$
$$\$10.40X - \$6.80X = \$18,000 + \$9,000$$
$$\$3.60X = \$27,000$$
$$X = 7,500 \text{ units}$$

The Effect of Taxes

The cost-volume-profit analysis presented so far involves changes in the basic components — fixed costs, variable costs, volume, and profit. A more refined analysis is possible if the basic components are broken down further. For example, Figure 3-14 illustrates a break-even chart with variable costs divided into several parts. The chart also shows income divided into two parts — income after tax and income tax expense. The line showing income tax expense starts at the break-even point because there is no income tax until income is earned.

Our earlier examples do not specifically include income taxes in the analysis. Management can easily determine the effect of taxes.

Income taxes are a percentage of net income. Rember Company is subject to a 30 percent tax rate and management seeks an after-tax profit of $8,400. In order to compute the required sales level to achieve an after-tax profit of $8,400, it is necessary to include the income tax rate in the basic CVP calculations. If the tax rate is 30 percent, then after-tax net income is 70 percent of pretax income. Pretax income is therefore found as

$$\text{Target net income} = \text{Pretax income} \times (1 - \text{Tax rate})$$

$$\text{Pretax income} = \frac{\text{Target net income}}{1 - \text{Tax rate}}$$

$$= \frac{\$8,400}{1 - .30} = \frac{\$8,400}{.70} = \$12,000$$

Figure 3-14. Detailed CVP chart showing the breakdown of variable costs into several components. Note the income tax line that starts at the break-even point.

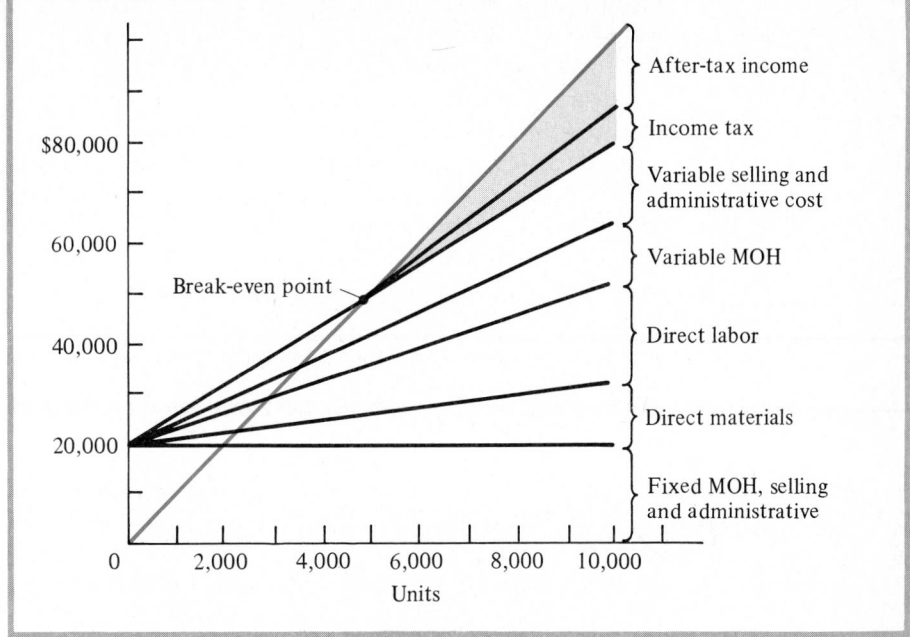

A cost-volume-profit analysis can now be performed to determine the activity level at which this target income will be achieved.

$$\$10X = \$20,000 + \$6X + \$12,000$$

$$X = 8,000 \text{ units}$$

Profit-Volume Chart

A variation of the cost-volume-profit diagram is the **profit-volume chart,** which highlights the break-even point and profitability without showing costs. Figure 3-15 shows a profit-volume chart for the Rember Company data

Figure 3-15. Profit-volume charts depict the break-even point and profit, without reference to costs. This chart illustrates the same situation as the CVP chart in Figures 3-11 and 3-12.

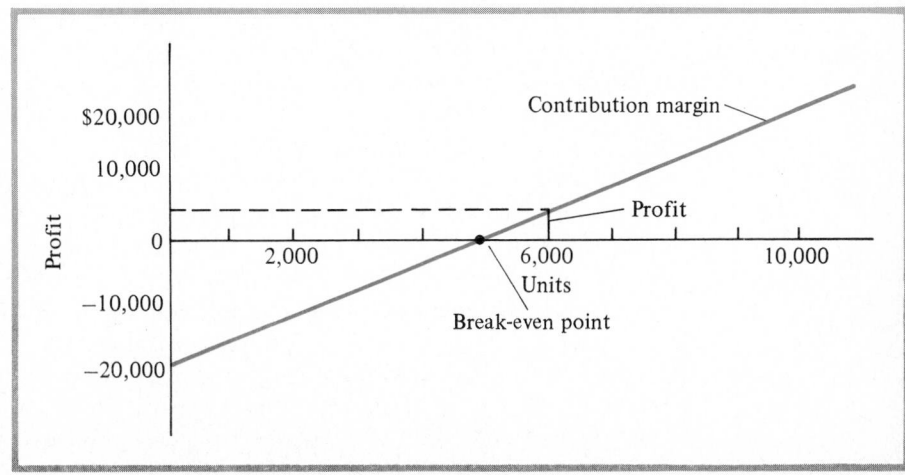

discussed earlier and illustrated in Figure 3-11, with a break-even point of 5,000 units, fixed cost of $20,000, and variable cost of $6 per unit. The horizontal axis represents activity levels and the vertical axis shows the profit in dollars. The vertical axis has negative and positive values, since any activity below the break-even point results in losses.

A profit-volume chart emphasizes the break-even point and profit, without including costs

The profit line is the difference between total revenue and total cost. Where it touches the vertical axis, at zero activity, there is a loss of $20,000, which is the amount of fixed cost incurred in Rember Company's operations. The profit line intercepts the vertical axis at a negative value, which is the fixed cost, as shown by the following calculations:

$$\text{Profit} = \text{Total revenue} - \text{Total cost}$$
$$= (\text{Sales price} \times \text{Units}) - FC - (VC \times \text{Units})$$
$$= (\$10 \times 0) - \$20,000 - (\$6 \times 0)$$
$$= 0 - \$20,000 - 0$$
$$= -\$20,000$$

The same information can be obtained from Figure 3-11 by comparing the vertical distance between the total cost of $20,000 and the total revenue of zero at zero activity. The advantage of the profit-volume chart is that profit and loss information is more readily apparent.

The profit line slopes upward and to the right. The slope of the line is the contribution margin per unit. The higher the contribution margin the steeper the slope.

At the point where the profit line crosses the horizontal axis, profit is zero, and this is, of course, the break-even point. The profit or loss for any activity level may be read directly from the chart. At a volume of 6,000 units the chart shows a profit of $4,000, as computed earlier and shown in Figure 3-12.

Operations Beyond the Relevant Range

As with all CVP diagrams, the profit-volume chart may not be applicable at levels of activity outside the relevant range. CVP analysis is based on the assumption that all costs are either fixed or variable, and this assumption is usually valid in the relevant range. Moreover, accountants assume that both the total revenue and the total cost are straight lines, making possible the type of CVP calculations illustrated in this chapter. On the other hand, economists argue that cost and revenue lines are not straight.

The economists' view of revenue and cost lines is depicted in Figure 3-16, which shows two break-even points, *M* and *N*. The shaded area represents losses. On page 72, we explained why the cost line may be curved as shown in this figure. The revenue line may also curve as shown. At a given level of demand for a product or service, a small volume offered for sale will result in a high price. A larger volume requires a lower price in order to attract buyers. Such economic assumptions are valid for entire markets, but may not hold for a single supplier of goods or services.

Figure 3-16. The economist's view of break-even analysis, with curvilinear costs and revenues. In the relevant range between points *A* and *B*, the straight-line assumptions of the accountant provide valid relationships.

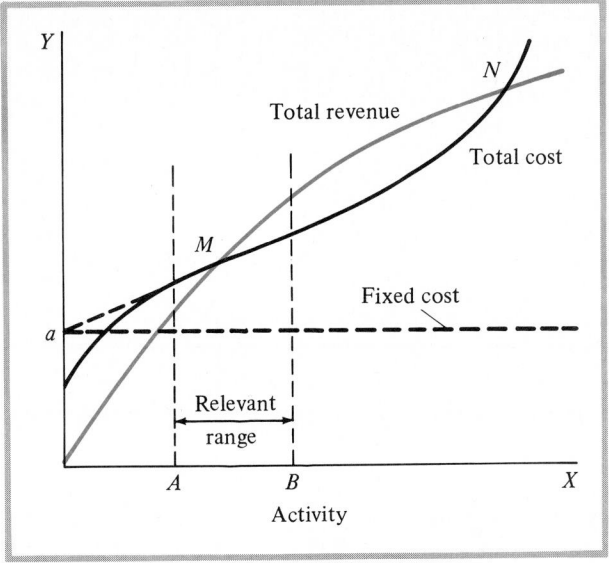

The economic view of CVP differs somewhat from the accounting view

Although the curves in Figure 3-16 may show realistic cost and price behavior, the graph includes activity levels that are outside the relevant range and have little chance of occurring. In the relevant range between the vertical lines *A* and *B* the cost and revenue curves are nearly straight lines. The cost curve can be extended to the vertical axis to provide the intercept *a*, which is assumed to be the fixed cost. Such assumptions typically allow managers to make CVP analyses for managerial control, planning, and decision making.

Margin of Safety Ratio

Risk is measured by the margin of safety ratio

CVP analysis may indicate the degree of risk that management assumes with a given combination of selling price, fixed cost, variable cost, and activity level. The **margin of safety ratio** is a measure of the difference between the actual activity level and the break-even point, expressed as a percentage of sales. The margin of safety ratio is a measure of risk. A large ratio means that the firm is less likely to operate below the break-even point if a decrease in sales occurs.

The margin of safety ratio may be computed in terms of revenue or in terms of activity by expressing sales either in units or in dollars in the following equation:

$$\text{Margin of safety ratio} = \frac{\text{Actual sales} - \text{Break-even sales}}{\text{Actual sales}}$$

As calculated above, the ratio can have values ranging from $-\infty$ to $+1$, with positive values for operations above the break-even point. To illustrate the use of the margin of safety ratio, we refer again to Rember Company's CVP analysis.

The company's managers want to determine the level of operations required to earn a profit of $12,000 before taxes. They also want to know if it would be more profitable to change the method of operations, by automating part of the compass assembly and eliminating some of the direct labor currently required.

The company faces two alternatives: One is to maintain its current production operations; the other is to use the more automated production process. Selling price of the compass is $10 and Rember Company's management has no plans to change the price. Fixed cost is $20,000 at present, and variable cost is $6 per unit.

The company can lease additional equipment for $7,500 per year, which would enable some automatic assembly and would reduce variable cost to $5 per unit. The two alternatives are analyzed below.

ALTERNATIVE 1

$$\text{Revenue} = FC + VC + \text{Target profit}$$
$$\$10X = \$20,000 + \$6X + \$12,000$$
$$\$4X = \$32,000$$

Sales level:	$X = 8,000$ units
Revenue:	$\$10 \times 8,000 = \$80,000$
Break-even point:	$\$20,000/\$4 = 5,000$ units

ALTERNATIVE 2

$$\$10X = \$27,500 + \$5X + \$12,000$$
$$\$5X = \$39,500$$

Sales level:	$X = 7,900$ units
Revenue:	$\$10 \times 8,000 = \$80,000$
Break-even point:	$\$27,500/\$5 = 5,500$ units

With alternative 1, the break-even point is 5,000 units and production of 8,000 units is required to earn the target profit of $12,000. With alternative 2, the break-even point is 5,500 units and only 7,900 units of production are required to earn the target profit. Alternative 2 can earn the target profit with $1,000 less revenue than required by alternative 1. Which is the preferable alternative in terms of risk? To answer this question, we compute the margin of safety ratio for each alternative. The two alternatives are also diagrammed in Figure 3-17.

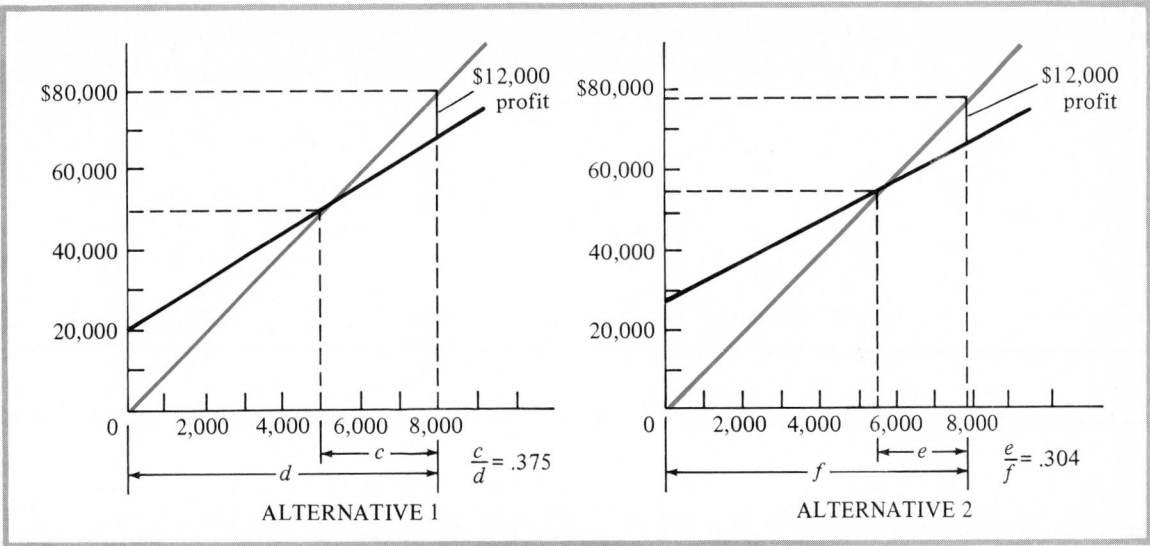

Figure 3-17. The margin of safety can be compared in these two CVP charts. Diagram (a) has a lower fixed cost and a higher variable cost than diagram (b). Profit is the same in both situations, with production of 8,000 units in (a) and 7,900 units in (b), but the break-even point is higher in diagram (b), resulting in a greater degree of risk, indicated by the smaller margin of safety ratio.

ALTERNATIVE 1

$$\text{Margin of safety ratio} = \frac{\text{Actual units} - \text{Break-even units}}{\text{Actual units}}$$

$$= \frac{8,000 - 5,000}{8,000} = .375$$

ALTERNATIVE 2

$$\text{Margin of safety ratio} = \frac{7,900 - 5,500}{7,900} = .304$$

Although the profit in each alternative is $12,000, alternative 2 has a smaller margin of safety ratio. If expected sales do not materialize, the company is more likely to operate at or below the break-even level with alternative 2 than with alternative 1.

In Figure 3-17 the margin of safety for alternative 1 is the ratio of distance c to distance d; for alternative 2 it is the ratio of distance e to distance f.

The interpretation of the margin of safety ratio depends on the specific situation under analysis, on the manager making the decision, and on typical industry experience for the business in question. In general, if the ratio is close to 1, the situation is clearly safe; if it approaches zero, the risk of loss becomes greater.

CVP analysis provides information, not decisions; the decision must be made by the manager

The preceding analysis of margin of safety does not mean that management should adopt alternative 1 and maintain current operations. Alternative 1 is the preferred alternative based on the margin of safety calculation, but there may be many other factors that management must take into account. For example, automating the plant may increase its capacity, and future demand for the company's products may increase beyond present capacity. Labor cost may increase in the future above the current $6 per unit, making alternative 2 more attractive, especially if selling prices are also expected to increase. As usual, CVP analysis may provide much relevant information for decision making, but it does not provide the decision. Managers must combine the CVP information with other information at their disposal in order to arrive at the best decision.

The margin of safety ratio is directly related to contribution margin and the return on sales. For example, with alternative 1 the return on sales is 15 percent ($12,000/$80,000) and the contribution margin is $4 per unit, or 40 percent of sales. If these ratios are known the margin of safety ratio can be computed as

$$\text{Margin of safety ratio} = \frac{\text{Return on sales}}{\text{Contribution margin ratio}}$$
$$= \frac{.15}{.40}$$
$$= .375$$

Similarly, if the margin of safety ratio and contribution margin ratio are known, return on sales can be computed as follows:

$$\text{Return on sales} = \text{Margin of safety ratio} \times \text{Contribution margin ratio}$$
$$= .375 \times .40$$
$$= .15, \text{ or } 15 \text{ percent}$$

MULTIPLE-ACTIVITY CVP ANALYSIS

Until this point, we have used CVP analysis for decisions affecting only one product. However, it is often necessary to evaluate the profitability of a sales region, a sales representative, a group of customers, or the activity of a division. Often such CVP analyses involve two or more products. For multiple products or activities, CVP analysis requires additional computations and also some assumptions that must be satisfied if the results of the analysis are to be meaningful.

To demonstrate CVP analysis for a firm that produces or sells multiple products, we use the following data:

	Product A	Product B	Product C
Sales in units	2,000	3,000	5,000
Selling price per unit	$20	$50	$40
Variable cost per unit	$16	$36	$28
Total fixed cost = $77,000			

From these data it is easy to compute each product's contribution margin, contribution margin ratio, and the sales mix percentage. The **sales mix** percentage is the proportion of each product's sales in units to total sales in units.

	Product A	Product B	Product C
Contribution margin	$4	$14	$12
Contribution margin ratio	20%	28%	30%
Sales mix percentage	20%	30%	50%

In a multiproduct situation, the break-even point is determined by the amount of total sales of all products, in dollars or in units. If sales consist mostly of products with a high contribution margin, a smaller sales revenue is necessary to break even than if sales consist primarily of products with low contribution margins. Therefore the break-even point can be calculated only if some assumption is made about the sales mix of all products. If the sales mix changes, the break-even point usually changes also.

Multiple-product CVP analysis requires computation of the average contribution margin

Typically, each product has a different contribution margin, and it is necessary to reduce the separate contribution margins to a weighted average contribution margin of all products. The average contribution margin is not simply the sum of $4, $14, and $12 divided by 3, because the products are not sold in equal proportions. The contribution margin of product C, which constitutes 50 percent of unit sales, must be weighted more heavily than the contribution margins of products A and B. The weighted average contribution margin, therefore, represents the contribution margins of all separate products with a specific sales mix.

Finding the Average Contribution Margin

There are several ways of finding the average contribution margin or the average contribution margin ratio. Below we illustrate one method.

Product	Units Sold	Sales Mix %	Sales Price	Sales Revenue	Variable Cost	Contribution Margin	CM Ratio
A	2,000	20%	$20	$ 40,000	$ 32,000	$ 8,000	20%
B	3,000	30%	50	150,000	108,000	42,000	28%
C	5,000	50%	40	200,000	140,000	60,000	30%
Total	10,000	100%		$390,000	$280,000	110,000	
Less total fixed cost						77,000	
Profit						$ 33,000	

$$\text{Average contribution margin in dollars} = \frac{\text{Total CM}}{\text{Total units}}$$

$$= \frac{\$110,000}{10,000 \text{ units}} = \$11 \text{ per unit}$$

$$\text{Average contribution margin ratio} = \frac{\text{Total CM}}{\text{Total revenue}}$$

$$= \frac{\$110,000}{\$390,000} = .28205$$

Once the average contribution margin or the contribution margin ratio is found, the CVP analysis proceeds as before. The break-even point can be calculated either in units or in dollars. We divide fixed costs by the average contribution margin per unit to obtain the break-even volume. We divide fixed costs by the average contribution margin ratio to obtain break-even sales revenue.

$$\text{Break-even point in units} = \frac{\text{Fixed cost}}{\text{Average CM/unit}} = \frac{\$77,000}{\$11/\text{unit}} = 7,000 \text{ units}$$

$$\text{Break-even point in dollars} = \frac{\text{Fixed cost}}{\text{Average CM ratio}} = \frac{\$77,000}{.28205} = \$273,000$$

Another way of finding the average contribution margin is to compute the weighted contribution margin for each unit, where the weights consist of the sales mix percentage. In our example the computation is

Product	CM	×	Sales Mix	=	Weighted CM
A	$ 4		.20		$ .80
B	14		.30		4.20
C	12		.50		6.00
Average contribution margin					$11.00

A similar calculation can be performed on sales price and variable cost to obtain averages of these items. The difference between average sales price and average variable cost is the average contribution margin, as shown below.

Product	1 Sales Mix	2 Sales Price	3 Weighted Price (col. 1 × col. 2)	4 Variable Cost	5 Weighted Cost (col. 1 × col. 4)	6 Contribution Margin (col. 3 − col. 5)
A	.20	$20	$ 4.00	$16	$ 3.20	$ .80
B	.30	50	15.00	36	10.80	4.20
C	.50	40	20.00	28	14.00	6.00
Weighted average			$39.00		$28.00	$11.00

The weighted average selling price in column 3 and the weighted average contribution margin in column 6 can be used to calculate the weighted average contribution margin ratio. In our example the contribution margin ratio is

$$\frac{\text{Average CM}}{\text{Average price}} = \frac{\$11}{\$39} = .28205$$

Note that the weighted average sales price, variable cost, and contribution margin are not equal to the price, cost, or margin of any of the three products. These are just averages obtained from the available data.

Individual Product Break-Even Points

The break-even point of 7,000 units is for all three products combined. Production planning and scheduling, however, require break-even data for individual products. The sales mix used to calculate the weighted average contribution margin is now used to extract the individual product break-even points. Total break-even units are multiplied by the individual sales mix percentages to determine the break-even point for individual products. The calculation is as follows:

Product	Total Units	×	Sales Mix	=	Individual Product Break-Even in Units	×	Selling Price	=	Individual Product Break-Even in Dollars
A	7,000		.20		1,400		$20		$ 28,000
B	7,000		.30		2,100		50		105,000
C	7,000		.50		3,500		40		140,000
Totals					7,000				$273,000

The Effect of a Change in Sales Mix

The multiple-activity break-even point depends on a critical assumption: The sales mix is accurate and will not change. For any other sales mix the break-even point may be different.

For example, what is the break-even point if the sales mix of products A and B changes to .40 each, leaving C with 20 percent of total sales? The computation is shown below:

Product	Sales Price	Contribution Margin	Sales Mix	Weighted Contribution Margin	Weighted Sales Price
A	$20	$ 4	.40	$1.60	$ 8.00
B	50	14	.40	5.60	20.00
C	40	12	.20	2.40	8.00
Average contribution margin				$9.60	$36.00

$$\text{Contribution margin ratio} = \frac{\$9.60}{\$36.00} = .2666666$$

$$\text{Break-even in units} = \frac{\$77,000}{\$9.60/\text{unit}} = 8,021 \text{ units}$$

$$\text{Break-even in dollars} = \frac{\$77,000}{.2666666} = \$288,750$$

In this case, the break-even point in units and in sales dollars is higher than before. This should be expected because the sales mix shifted from units that have a high contribution margin to units with a low margin. This means the company is selling more units with a small profit and fewer units with a large profit. Therefore, more units will have to be sold in order to break even. The effect on income is shown below, assuming sales of 10,000 units:

Product	Sales in Units	Sales Price	Revenue	Variable Cost	Contribution Margin
A	4,000	$20	$ 80,000	$ 64,000	$16,000
B	4,000	50	200,000	144,000	56,000
C	2,000	40	80,000	56,000	24,000
	10,000		$360,000	$264,000	96,000
Total fixed cost					77,000
Net income					$19,000

Our discussion of multiple-product CVP analysis is based on the assumption that fixed costs associated with production of the three products cannot be allocated to the three products in any reasonable manner. The fixed cost of $77,000 is assumed to be common for all products in this case. This assumption is valid for many types of fixed costs. It is difficult to identify pension costs, office depreciation and insurance, and some property taxes with specific products.

SUMMARY

Costs may be classified according to their behavior into fixed, variable, mixed, semivariable, and semifixed costs.

Fixed costs remain the same regardless of the level of business activity. Some fixed costs, such as depreciation, cannot be changed easily and are known as **committed fixed costs.** Others, such as research and development, may be changed at management's discretion and are known as **discretionary fixed costs.**

Variable costs change proportionately with the volume of activity. Total variable cost increases as activity increases, but the cost per unit of activity remains the same. Variable costs may be **controllable** or **manageable costs** if managers can decide whether or not the cost will be incurred.

Some costs are made up of both fixed and variable components and are known as **mixed costs.** They can be separated into their component parts when analyzed.

Semivariable costs change with changing activity levels, but not in proportion to the volume of activity. They may change at an increasing rate or a decreasing rate. Semivariable costs that increase at a decreasing rate are called **learning curve costs. Semifixed costs** remain constant in given ranges of activity. Beyond a specific range they increase or decrease to a new level in steps, and are therefore called **step function costs.**

All cost behavior is assumed to be valid only in the **relevant range** of operations and for a specific **time period.** Beyond the relevant range or in a different time period, the behavior of specific costs may change. Managers should be aware of the relevant range and time assumptions when making estimates of costs and cost behavior.

Several cost estimation techniques are available. The **scatter diagram** is used to observe any relationship between costs and activity levels. The **high-low method** is used to estimate fixed costs and variable costs from a sample of actual or estimated cost data. **Regression analysis** is a statistical method that produces more accurate results than the others.

Cost-volume-profit (CVP) analysis enables a manager to see the relationship among costs, volume of activity, and selling price and to determine the **break-even point** of operations. The break-even point can be computed in sales revenue dollars or in units of sales needed to break even. **Cost-volume-profit diagrams** enable managers to analyze graphically CVP relationships.

The break-even point is calculated by dividing fixed cost by the contribution margin. **Contribution margin** is the difference between selling price and variable cost; it measures how much is available from the revenue of each unit of product or service to cover fixed costs and to provide a profit. The **contribution margin ratio** is contribution margin expressed as a percentage of sales. The break-even point in dollars is found by dividing contribution margin into total fixed costs. Break-even in units is obtained by dividing the contribution margin ratio into fixed costs.

In addition to break-even analysis, CVP analysis enables managers to determine the effects of changing costs, prices, or volume of activity, and helps managers decide how much must be produced to earn a target income, before or after income taxes.

The **profit-volume chart** is a variation of a CVP chart designed to highlight the relationship between the break-even point and profit. All CVP relationships are valid only in the relevant range of operations.

The difference between the actual activity level and the break-even point, expressed as a percentage of actual activity, is called the **margin of safety ratio.** This ratio provides an indication of the riskiness of choices facing a manager.

CVP analysis may be applied to multiple activities. The weighted average contribution margin is calculated using the **sales mix** of the products. The average contribution margin is divided into total fixed costs to obtain the break-even point of operations in units. Alternatively, the average contribution margin ratio may be divided into total fixed costs to obtain the break-even point in sales dollars.

Multiproduct break-even analysis is valid only if the sales mix is constant. If the sales mix changes, the break-even point changes also. Multiple-activity CVP analysis is used when fixed costs cannot be assigned to specific activities but apply to all activities jointly.

KEY TERMS

break-even point *(77)*	learning curve cost *(70)*
committed fixed costs *(64)*	manageable costs *(66)*
contribution margin *(80)*	margin of safety ratio *(89)*
contribution margin ratio *(80)*	mixed costs *(68)*
controllable costs *(66)*	profit-volume chart *(87)*
cost-volume-profit(CVP)	relevant range *(72)*
analysis *(77)*	scatter diagram *(74)*
CVP diagram *(80)*	semifixed costs *(71)*
discretionary fixed costs *(64)*	semivariable costs *(70)*
fixed costs *(63)*	step function costs *(71)*
high-low method *(74)*	variable costs *(64)*

QUESTIONS

1. Costs can be classified into several categories according to the way they change with changes in the level of activity. Briefly describe the change that would occur in fixed costs as activity increases. Do the same for variable, mixed, semifixed, and semivariable costs.

2. The high-low method of cost analysis has some weaknesses, but under certain conditions it can be very useful for determining cost behavior. Describe what is accomplished by analyzing costs using the high-low method, and discuss the conditions that should prevail in order to make the analysis reliable.

3. Looking at a CVP chart, a manager says, "According to this chart, 40,000 units of product per year result in a profit of $300,000. After our stock issue is completed we'll have the money to add enough factory space to triple production. Therefore within two years we should be earning a profit of over $1 million." What factors is the manager neglecting to assess?

4. In economic theory, CVP analysis includes fixed costs, variable costs, and a return to investors as items that must be covered in order to break even. In accounting terms, return to investors is part of the profit. Assuming operations in the relevant range, discuss how the analysis changes to accommodate economic theory.

5. "What use is this analysis?" asks a vice president. "With one alternative we make more profit but the margin of safety is low. If the margin of safety is higher, profit declines too. This does not tell me which alternative to select." Discuss the concept of margin of safety and the dilemma faced by the vice president.

6. Discuss the concept of multiproduct CVP analysis and the assumptions underlying the computations of individual product break-even points.

7. (AICPA) An important part of managerial accounting is the analysis of the types of costs that a business entity can incur. These types of costs are generally classified as variable, fixed, and mixed.

a. Define and discuss the identifying characteristics of (1) a variable cost and (2) a fixed cost.

b. With respect to mixed costs, (1) define and discuss the identifying characteristic of a mixed cost and (2) discuss the three basic methods employed to break down a mixed cost into its component parts.

EXERCISES

Ex. 3-1
Graph of Mixed Costs

The handbook for sales representatives of Ablex Corporation states: "Commissions shall be calculated as $20 per unit plus 5 percent of unit selling price for sales of 20 units or less; if more than 20 units are sold, commission for all units sold shall be $20 per unit plus 6 percent of unit selling price. The number of units shall be counted from the first day of each month."

REQUIRED

Draw a graph of commission costs with a total of 40 units on the X axis, assuming that the selling price is $1,200 per unit.

Ex. 3-2
Cost Estimates from Scatter Diagrams

Following are production data accumulated by Lemore Company on the production of aluminum window frame assemblies. The company performs the work on contract and operates in a part of a building that it rents from Mr. Downy. When the company has a large contract for frames, Mr. Downy allows it to use more space in his building and charges more rent. In addition, he charges the company for a prorated portion of building utility costs.

Units Produced	Direct Labor Cost	Facility Cost
80	$1,100	$520
150	1,600	800
120	1,500	570
60	700	500
220	1,750	910
190	1,700	850
140	1,500	600

REQUIRED

Plot the data in a scatter diagram. Use your graph to estimate the direct labor cost and facility cost of producing orders of 100 units and 200 units.

Ex. 3-3
Using Contribution Margin

A small company breaks even if it sells 900 units of product for total revenue of $33,300. Its contribution margin is 46 percent.

REQUIRED. Find the selling price, the variable cost per unit, and the fixed cost.

Ex. 3-4
Simple CVP Relationships

Christy Company is a small entity whose break-even sales occur at $97,520. The selling price of its single product is $42.40 per unit and variable cost is $16.96 per unit. Sales are 3,500 units.

REQUIRED

Calculate the fixed cost, break-even volume, and contribution margin. Also calculate profit on the 3,500 units.

Ex. 3-5
CVP Relationships

Marloff Company's fixed cost is $17,500 per month. Its return on sales is 7 percent, contribution margin is 35 percent, and the company breaks even if it sells 2,500 units per month.

REQUIRED

Calculate the number of units sold, variable cost per unit, and sales revenue and profit for one month.

Ex. 3-6
Simple Break-Even Analysis

Flimmer Company's fixed cost is $301,000. Selling price of its single product is $650 per unit and variable cost is $510 per unit. The company plans a target net income of $70,000.

REQUIRED

Calculate the break-even point and the desired sales level in units.

Ex. 3-7
Break-Even Point in Units and Dollars

Bartock Corporation's fixed cost is $5,940,000 per year. This year it sold 3,200 intelligent computer terminals at $6,500 each. The variable cost is $4,300 per unit.

REQUIRED

Calculate the profit and the break-even point in units and in dollars.

Ex. 3-8 (AICPA)
CVP Analysis

Carey Company sold 100,000 units of its product at $20 per unit. Variable costs are $14 per unit (manufacturing costs of $11 and selling costs of $3). Fixed costs are incurred uniformly throughout the year and amount to $792,000 (manufacturing costs of $500,000 and selling costs of $292,000). There are no beginning or ending inventories. The break-even point for this product is

   a. $3,640,000 or 182,000 units.
   b. $2,600,000 or 130,000 units.
   c. $1,800,000 or 90,000 units.
   d. $1,760,000 or 88,000 units.
   e. none of the above.

The number of units that must be sold to earn a net income of $60,000 for the year before income taxes is

a. 142,000.   b. 132,000.   c. 100,000.   d. 88,000.   e. none of these.

If the income tax rate is 40 percent, the number of units that must be sold to earn an after-tax income of $90,000 is

a. 169,500.   b. 157,000.   c. 144,500.   d. 104,777.   e. none of these.

If labor costs are 50 percent of variable costs and 20 percent of fixed costs, a 10 percent increase in wages and salaries would increase the number of units required to break even (in fraction form) to

a. 807,840/14.7.   b. 831,600/5.78.   c. 807,840/5.3.   d. 831,600/14.28.

Ex. 3-9
Contribution Margin and Margin of Safety Ratio

Data on three departments of Fleda Company are presented below:

	Design	Production	Delivery
Revenue	$42,000	$95,000	$21,000
Fixed cost	$8,000	$15,000	$4,500
Variable cost	$5 per hour	$6 per unit	$.25 per mile
Activity	6,000 hours	11,875 units	70,000 miles

REQUIRED   For each department calculate the contribution margin, break-even volume, and margin of safety ratio.

Ex. 3-10
Using CVP
Relationships

MEMORANDUM

TO: E. J.

FROM: C. M.

Here are the figures you wanted. Last month our net income was $19,200, which represents a 15 percent return on sales. With our fixed cost of $32,000 we break even at 4,000 units per month.

REQUIRED   Use the data in the above memorandum to calculate contribution margin, selling price per unit, variable cost, and margin of safety.

Ex. 3-11
Break-Even
Volume and Margin
of Safety

Wilde Company sold 60,000 units of small transformers for electric trains at $10 per unit in 1985. The variable costs were $4 per unit, and the fixed costs were $300,000.

REQUIRED
a.   Calculate the break-even volume in units.
b.   Compute the break-even volume in dollars.
c.   What does the unit contribution margin show?
d.   What was Wilde Company's margin of safety ratio in 1985?

Ex. 3-12
Profit-Volume
Chart

Flitter Company manufactures small metal-handled brushes that are later attached to glue-bottle covers. The company's fixed cost is $700. The brushes sell for $.10 each and have a variable cost of $.05 per unit.

REQUIRED   Prepare a profit-volume graph for the company, showing break-even volume and the profit that can be expected when 24,000 brushes are produced and sold.

Ex. 3-13
Changing Sales Mix

Data on two chemicals produced by the Solvents Division of Chem-Sol Company are provided below:

	Solvex	Dysolve
Unit selling price	$10	$20
Unit variable cost	7	12
Sales mix	.6	.4
Fixed cost = $29,700		

REQUIRED
a.   Calculate the break-even point in units.
b.   Calculate the break-even point in units if the sales mix is changed to .5 for each product.

Ex. 3-14
Multiple Product
Break-Even
Analysis

Per-unit data on the operations of Flupp Company are provided below. The company produces three products and has a fixed cost of $363,000 per year.

	A	B	C
Selling price	$18	$12	$36
Variable cost	$12	$7	$27
Relative sales mix	.4	.3	.3

REQUIRED

Find the break-even point in units and determine how many units of each product must be sold to earn a net income of $99,000.

Ex. 3-15
Multiple Product
Break-Even Point

Dynatone Tape Company produces two types of blank recording tapes that it distributes through wholesalers or sells directly to large retailers. The following data apply to these products:

Product	Sales Price	Variable Costs	Contribution Margin	Expected % of Units Sold
Cassette	$2.00	$ .60	$1.40	60
Cartridge	3.00	1.10	1.90	40
				100

Fixed costs
Sales personnel	$ 500,000
Advertising and other promotion	2,000,000
Other fixed costs	500,000
Total fixed costs	$3,000,000

REQUIRED

a. Calculate the break-even point for each product in units and in dollars.
b. Calculate the unit volume and sales necessary to achieve a 20 percent return on sales.

Ex. 3-16 (AICPA)
CVP Analysis

Flear Company has a maximum productive capacity of 210,000 units per year. Variable manufacturing costs are $11 per unit. Fixed factory overhead is $360,000 per year. Variable selling expenses are $3 per unit and fixed selling expenses are $252,000 per year. The unit sales price is $20. In 1985 the company produced and sold 150,000 units.

REQUIRED

a. What is the break-even point in dollars?
b. How many units must be sold to earn a net income of $60,000 per year?
c. How many units must be sold to earn a net income of 10 percent of sales?

Ex. 3-17
CVP Analysis with
Income Tax

Filstrup Company's 1985 sales were 22,000 units, an increase of 10 percent over 1984 sales. As a result, 1985 after-tax income was $69,600, 16 percent higher than in 1984. Variable cost remained unchanged at $10 per unit. The company was subject to a 40 percent tax rate in both years.

REQUIRED

Find the company's 1984 tax expense and contribution margin. Also calculate the 1985 contribution margin and the company's fixed cost and selling price per unit.

Ex. 3-18
CVP Chart and
Calculations

Sycamore Flying School owns two training aircraft. It charges $25 per hour for solo and $35 per hour for dual time with an instructor. It pays instructors $10 per hour so all aircraft time is viewed as a single rate for accounting purposes. The company's fixed cost is $800 per month and variable cost of the airplanes is $15 per hour. In October the airplanes were flown a total of 120 billable hours, but in November only 60 hours were charged, due to bad weather that prevented training flights.

REQUIRED

a. Prepare a cost-volume-profit chart showing the break-even point and the amounts earned in October and November.
b. Verify the results shown on your chart with calculations.
c. Calculate the margin of safety for October and November.

Ex. 3-19
Profit-Volume
Charts and
Calculations

Refer to the data in Exercise 3-18 on the operations of Sycamore Flying School.

REQUIRED.   Prepare a profit-volume chart showing the break-even point and the amounts earned in October and November. Verify your chart results with calculations. Calculate the margin of safety for each month.

PROBLEMS

P. 3-1
Simple CVP
Analysis

Marion Company management received the following income statement from the accounting department:

Marion Company
Income Statement
For the Month Ended July 31, 1985

Sales (400 units)		$20,000
Less cost of goods sold:		
Direct labor	$3,200	
Direct materials	2,800	
MOH (40 percent fixed)	2,500	8,500
Gross margin		11,500
Selling and administrative expenses:		
Selling (50 percent fixed)	4,000	
Administrative (80 percent fixed)	2,500	6,500
Income before tax		$ 5,000

Management believes that monthly sales can increase by 20 percent if an advertising campaign costing $1,500 per month is started.

REQUIRED

a. Calculate the present break-even point in units and in dollars.
b. Calculate the break-even point if the advertising campaign is undertaken.
c. Calculate the expected income for next month with the advertising campaign.
d. Calculate the current and expected margin of safety ratio.

P. 3-2
Break-Even
Analysis

Beautique Company sells its merchandise at three boutiques located in department stores. Last month sales were $10,000 and profit was 8 percent of sales. Fixed costs were $1,700.

The locations of the boutiques have become less desirable recently and the merchandise less appealing to the kind of shoppers frequenting the department stores. If the boutiques are eliminated and door-to-door selling is started instead, it is estimated that sales could be increased 25 percent and profit would increase $200 per month. Fixed costs are expected to decrease to $1,000 because operations could be moved to a low-rent facility. Variable costs will also change.

REQUIRED

a. Calculate the break-even point for last month under the old operations.
b. Calculate the break-even point expected with the new method of operations.
c. What level of sales is required with the new operations in order to earn as much profit as last month?
d. Calculate the margin of safety for the old and new methods of operations.

P. 3-3
Scattergram and
Cost Estimation

Televoice Corporation manufactures miniature radio telephones and has collected the following activity, direct labor cost, and maintenance cost data over a period of six months. The company's direct labor cost is $8 per hour. Its production process involves the use of sensitive equipment and instruments that require frequent maintenance and adjustments.

Month	Labor Hours	Units Produced	Maintenance Cost
March	280	140	$1,200
April	495	230	1,090
May	600	300	1,380
June	525	270	1,260
July	258	110	1,320
August	425	190	1,400

REQUIRED

a. Prepare a scatter diagram with costs in dollars on the vertical axis and units produced on the horizontal axis. Include both labor and maintenance cost in the diagram.
b. Examine the scattergram and the data and develop cost equations for each of the two costs of production.
c. Use your cost equations to determine the direct labor and maintenance costs of producing 150 radio telephones during the current month.

P. 3-4
CVP Analysis

Taranto Corporation sells an electronic watch for $40 by mail. The variable cost is $24 per unit and fixed cost is $32,000 per year. The company is subject to a 40 percent income tax rate. Management is evaluating operations and considers making the following changes:

1. Lease a new packaging machine for $4,000 per year, which will reduce variable cost by $1 per unit.
2. Increase selling price 10 percent to counteract an expected 25 percent increase in fixed cost.
3. Reduce fixed cost by 25 percent by moving to a lower rent location. This would have the effect of increasing variable costs by 10 percent.

REQUIRED

a. Calculate the current break-even point in units and dollars.
b. Calculate the unit and dollar sales level that must be maintained with current operations to earn a return on sales of 9 percent after taxes.

c. Calculate the expected after-tax profit for alternative 1 with sales of 3,200 units.
d. Calculate the break-even point for alternative 2.
e. Calculate the break-even point for alternative 3.
f. Calculate the volume of sales needed to earn $15,000 after tax with alternative 3.

**P. 3-5
High-Low Method
and Break-Even
Analysis**

Thistlethorn Carpeting Company installs commercial and residential floor carpeting. One type of carpet that it sells is priced at $15 per square meter, including installation. The company completed six contracts using this type of carpet during the past month and collected the following cost data for each contract.

Job No.	Total Cost	Square Meters
2	$ 7,000	350
5	16,000	1,100
6	9,000	700
9	13,000	1,000
12	17,000	1,600
16	15,000	1,550

The company is now bidding on a 1,200 square meter contract and wants to determine in advance what profit it can expect to earn.

REQUIRED

a. Use the high-low method to estimate the fixed and variable costs of carpet installation.
b. Use your cost estimate to find the break-even point for this type of carpeting contract.
c. Determine the expected profit or loss on the contract being bid.

**P. 3-6
Scattergram,
High-Low Method,
and Cost Estimation**

Department No. 7 of Ribiloff Company processes several products using materials, labor, and machinery. Below are data on 8 weeks of production on one type of staple gun trigger assembly, one of the department's products:

Week	Units Produced	Material Cost	Machine Hours
December 9	132	$ 78	20
December 16	100	60	30
December 23	168	67	41
December 30	300	110	45
January 6	202	97	21
January 13	220	83	44
January 20	251	85	34
January 27	230	100	42

The company estimates that each machine hour costs $2. It wants to use the above data to forecast the cost of production for February, when 1,000 staple gun trigger assemblies are expected to be produced.

REQUIRED

a. Prepare a scatter diagram of units and material costs.
b. Prepare a scatter diagram of units and machine costs.
c. Decide by examining the scatter diagrams which cost can be expected to yield the best forecast of trigger assembly costs, and use the high-low method to estimate the total cost equation.
d. Use your equation to estimate the cost of next month's trigger assembly production.
e. Discuss possible reasons why one cost is a better predictor than the other.

P. 3-7
Multiple Activity Income Statement

Miltrop Company makes two sizes of barrels. The 10-liter barrel sells for $10 and has a variable cost of $7. It constitutes 70 percent of the company's sales. The 20-liter barrel sells for $20 and has a variable cost of $12. It makes up 30 percent of total sales. The company's total fixed costs are $36,000.

REQUIRED

a. Calculate the break-even volume of sales.
b. Calculate the volume of sales needed to earn $9,900 of profit.
c. Prepare an income statement showing contribution margin of each type of barrel with the volume you obtained in part *b*.

P. 3-8
Break-Even Analysis with High-Low Estimation

Pied Piper Company owns a unique process for exterminating rats from cities. Its fees are based on a city's population. The company charges a fee of $15,000 per city plus $1 per person. Below are revenue and operating data for the last six contracts.

City	Operating Cost	Rat Population	Total Revenue
Hummel	$ 70,000	400,000	$ 55,000
Hamilot	125,000	1,500,000	165,000
Himmel	80,000	500,000	85,000
Homily	90,000	1,000,000	130,000
Hamlet	110,000	1,350,000	140,000
Humer	115,000	1,200,000	120,000

The company is negotiating a contract with the city of Hamelin, which has a population of 110,000. The rat population is estimated at 1,100,000. (Hint: A break-even diagram should help you.)

REQUIRED

a. Use the rat population and operating costs with the high-low method to estimate the total cost line for the operation.
b. Use the rat population and revenue with the high-low method to estimate the total revenue line.
c. Calculate the break-even point in units and dollars for the company's operations based on your estimates in parts *a* and *b*.
d. Use the city population and estimate of rat population for Hamelin to determine the expected profit or loss on the contract

P. 3-9
CVP Analysis with
Changing Costs and
Prices

Middling Manufacturing Company has been in operation for three years. At the end of 1985 the company reported the following annual sales and expenses:

Sales		$ 800,000
Variable manufacturing	$360,000	
Fixed manufacturing	300,000	
Variable selling and administrative	120,000	
Fixed selling and administrative	120,000	900,000
Net income (loss)		$(100,000)

Management had targeted a $150,000 net income for the year. For 1986 the company expects variable manufacturing costs to increase by 12 percent and variable selling and administrative costs to increase by 4 percent. Fixed manufacturing costs are expected to increase by $9,000, and fixed selling and administrative costs are expected to increase by $30,000.

Company management believes the company's product may be underpriced and that a 20 percent price increase would have little effect on the number of units sold.

REQUIRED

a. Compute the break-even level of sales for 1985.
b. Compute the level of sales in 1985 that would have provided the company with its target net income.
c. Compute the break-even point for 1986, assuming the expected cost increases occur without a change in selling price.
d. Compute the break-even volume for 1986, assuming both the price and cost increases take place.

P. 3-10 (CMA)
CVP Analysis with
Income Tax

All-Day Candy Company is a wholesale distributor of candy. The company services grocery, convenience, and drug stores in a large metropolitan area.

Small but steady growth in sales has been achieved by the All-Day Candy Company over the past few years while candy prices have been increasing. The company is formulating its plans for the coming fiscal year. Presented below are the data used to project the current year's after-tax net income of $110,400.

Average selling price	$4.00 per box
Average variable costs:	
Cost of candy	$2.00 per box
Selling expenses	.40 per box
Total	$2.40 per box
Annual fixed costs:	
Selling	$160,000
Administrative	280,000
Total	$440,000

Expected annual sales volume (390,000 boxes) $1,560,000

Tax rate 40%

Manufacturers of candy have announced that they will increase prices of their products an average of 15 percent in the coming year due to increases in raw material (sugar, cocoa, peanuts, etc.) and labor costs. All-Day Candy Company expects that all other costs will remain at the same rates or levels as the current year.

REQUIRED

a. What is All-Day Candy Company's break-even point in boxes of candy for the current year?

b. What selling price per box must All-Day Candy Company charge to cover the 15 percent increase in the cost of candy and still maintain the current contribution margin ratio?

c. What volume of sales in dollars must the All-Day Candy Company achieve in the coming year to maintain the same net income after taxes as projected for the current year if the selling price of candy remains at $4.00 per box and the cost of candy increases 15 percent?

P. 3-11 (AICPA)
CVP Analysis

The president of Beth Corporation, which manufactures tape decks and sells them to producers of sound reproduction systems, anticipates a 10 percent wage increase on January 1 of next year to the manufacturing employees (variable labor). He expects no other changes in costs. Overhead will not change as a result of the wage increase. The president has asked you to assist him in developing the information he needs to formulate a reasonable product strategy for next year.

You are satisfied by regression analysis that volume is the primary factor affecting costs and have separated the mixed costs into their fixed and variable components. You also observe that the beginning and ending inventories are never materially different. Current operating capacity is 5,300 units.

Below are the current year data assembled for your analysis:

Current selling price per unit	$ 80.00
Variable cost per unit:	
Material	$ 30.00
Labor	12.00
Overhead	6.00
Total	$ 48.00
Annual volume of sales	5,000 units
Fixed costs	$51,000

REQUIRED

Provide the following information for the president using cost-volume-profit analysis:

a. What increase in the selling price is necessary to cover the 10 percent wage increase and still maintain the current profit-volume-cost ratio?

b. How many tape decks must be sold to maintain the current net income if the sales price remains at $80.00 and the 10 percent wage increase goes into effect?

c. The president believes that an additional $190,000 of machinery (to be depreciated at 10 percent annually) will increase present capacity by 30 percent. If all tape decks produced can be sold at the present price and the wage increase goes into effect, how would the estimated net income before capacity is increased compare with the estimated net income after capacity is increased? Prepare computations of estimated net income **before** and **after** the expansion.

P. 3-12 (AICPA)
CVP Analysis for a
Hospital

The Columbus Hospital operates a general hospital but rents space and beds to separate entities for specialized areas such as pediatrics, maternity, psychiatric, etc. Columbus charges each separate entity for common services to its patients such as meals and laundry and for administrative services such as billings, collections, etc. All uncollectible accounts are charged directly to the entity. Space and bed rentals are fixed for the year.

For the entire year ended June 30, 1985, the pediatrics department at Columbus Hospital charged each patient an average of $65 per day, had a capacity of 60 beds, operated 24 hours per day for 365 days, and had revenue of $1,138,800.

Expenses charged by the hospital to the pediatrics department for the year ended June 30, 1985, were as follows:

	Basis of Allocation	
	Patient Days	Bed Capacity
Dietary	$ 42,952	
Janitorial		$ 12,800
Laundry	28,000	
Laboratory, other than direct charges to patients	47,800	
Pharmacy	33,800	
Repairs and maintenance	5,200	7,140
General administrative services		131,760
Rent		275,320
Billings and collections	40,000	
Bad debt expense	47,000	
Other	18,048	25,980
Totals	$262,800	$453,000

The only personnel directly employed by the pediatrics department are supervising nurses, nurses, and aides. The hospital has minimum personnel requirements based on total annual patient days. Hospital requirements beginning at the minimum, expected level of operation follow.

Annual Patient Days	Aides	Nurses	Supervising Nurses
10,000–14,000	21	11	4
14,001–17,000	22	12	4
17,001–23,725	22	13	4
23,726–25,550	25	14	5
25,551–27,375	26	14	5
27,376–29,200	29	16	6

The staffing levels above represent full-time equivalents, and it should be assumed that the pediatrics department always employs only the minimum number of required full-time equivalent personnel.

Annual salaries for each class of employee follow: supervising nurses—$18,000, nurses—$13,000, and aides—$5,000. Salary expense for the year ended June 30, 1985, for supervising nurses, nurses, and aides was $72,000, $169,000, and $110,000, respectively.

The pediatrics department operated at 100 percent capacity during 111 days for the past year. It is estimated that during 90 of these capacity days, the demand averaged 17 patients more than capacity and even went as high as 20 patients more on some days. The hospital has an additional 20 beds available for rent for the year ending June 30, 1986.

REQUIRED

a. Calculate the **minimum** number of patient days required for the pediatrics department to break even for the year ending June 30, 1986, if the additional 20 beds are not rented. Patient demand is unknown, but assume that revenue per patient day, cost per patient day, cost per bed, and employee salary rates will remain the same as for the year ended June 30, 1985. Present calculations in good form.

b. Assuming for purposes of this problem that patient demand, revenue per patient day, cost per patient day, cost per bed, and employee salary rates for the year ending June 30, 1986, remain the same as for the year ended June 30, 1985, should the pediatrics department rent the additional 20 beds? Show the annual gain or loss from the additional beds. Present calculations in good form.

P. 3-13
Multiple Activity
CVP Analysis

Highridge Roofing Company specializes in small residential roof repairs and replacements. It works with either wood or composition shingles. The company bids on all roof replacement work at a standard price per square foot. Following are data on its replacement operations for the past year.

	Wood	Composition
Installations in square feet	492,000	328,000
Bid price per square foot	$1.60	$1.10
Variable cost per square foot	.90	.75
Fixed cost = $252,000		

The company's price on composition shingles is very competitive. However, management thinks that it could increase the current year's installations to 900,000 square feet, with 65 percent of this in wood shingles, if it lowers its wood shingle bids to $1.50 per square foot. All costs are expected to remain unchanged.

REQUIRED

a. Use the data provided to determine the company's income for the past year, and to estimate its contribution margin.

b. Find the break-even point in units and in dollars for the past year and calculate the margin of safety ratio.

c. Determine the expected income and contribution margin for the current year if management's estimate is correct.

d. Find the expected break-even point in total units and total dollars for the current year and calculate the margin of safety ratio.

e. Find the break-even point for the current year for each product.

f. Discuss the merit of changing to the $1.50 price on wood shingles.

CASES

David Britener is the sole shareholder and president of Britener Lighting, Inc., a small company that manufactures lighting fixtures. At the end of the current year he is examining the following income statement, which details the results of producing and selling the four types of fixtures that the company makes.

Fixture Type	A	B	C	D	Total
Revenue	$81,900	$70,200	$124,800	$78,080	$354,980
Variable expenses	32,760	24,570	56,160	23,400	136,890
Contribution margin	$49,140	$45,630	$ 68,640	$54,680	$218,090
Less fixed expenses:					
Manufacturing				$90,000	
Selling				30,000	
Administrative				50,000	170,000
Income before tax					48,090
Income tax expense (30% of net income)					14,427
Net income after tax					$ 33,663

The owner is not especially satisfied with the net income, since he receives a very small salary from the company and depends on the income for his livelihood. The manager, however, pointed out that the net income is 9.5 percent of sales, which is an excellent return for the company, since it operates in a highly competitive industry. "We are actually very efficient," he says, "and it would be pretty hard to find any place to cut costs." The president thought it may be possible to increase sales and started making calculations. He came up with the following figures:

Total sales = 6,500 units

Product	Unit Price	CM Ratio	Sales Mix
A	$36	.60	.35
B	54	.65	.20
C	64	.55	.30
D	80	.70	.15

"The fixture with the highest contribution margin has the lowest proportion of sales," said the president. "Let's see what we can do about that." He called in the company's sales representative and production supervisor to discuss the problem.

The sales representative pointed out that it would be very difficult to sell more of item D, because of its price. "The competition has similar units selling for less than $80," she said. "To increase sales of D you would have to lower the price to about $75. On the other hand, unit C could stand a slight price increase. Add $1.50 to the price of C and reduce the price of D by $5. That should change the sales mix to 25 percent C and 20 percent D."

The production supervisor said, "If you cut the price of D, you can't expect a cut in cost. The only unit on which we can save something is A. There is a plastic bracket available that we can use in place of the metal one we use now. It's internal so there is no change in appearance, but it can save you $.70 per unit."

The sales representative suggested hiring another representative, but both the president and the manager thought it would cost too much to break open new territory. "We would have to double sales almost, and we are working at 80 percent capacity now. But I have looked into a new advertising campaign that would cost $10,000 per year and should increase sales in our current territory."

"The most you can expect is an increase of 500 units," said the sales representative. "My territory just cannot accept more. I can use the help but $10,000 may be too much for just 500 units of sales."

"We can look into it. To summarize, we seem to have the following options," said the manager, and he started writing on a pad:

Decrease price of D by $5 and increase sales mix to 20 percent.
Increase price of C by $1.50 and decrease sales mix to 25 percent.
Decrease variable cost of A by $.70 with no change in sales mix.
Increase sales by 500 units by increasing fixed cost $10,000.

The decision was made to evaluate the results of the above changes, then meet again to discuss the projections.

REQUIRED

a. Calculate the current break-even point and margin of safety.
b. Calculate the break-even point and margin of safety that can be expected if all of the discussed changes take place.
c. Evaluate the benefit of the advertising campaign.
d. Prepare a projected income statement to reflect the change in prices, sales mix, and volume.
e. Discuss the merits of undertaking the changes.

PART TWO
Product Costing

During the Industrial Revolution, managers experienced a growing need for detailed information about the cost of a variety of increasingly numerous products manufactured in a complex environment. Every dollar spent in production must somehow be assigned to the products made, and attempts to assign costs to products in a rational and systematic manner resulted in the development of cost accounting. Today cost accounting has extended its boundaries to include the measurement of the costs of performing all kinds of services and activities, many of them in the nonmanufacturing area. But the heart of cost accounting systems still lies in the careful measurement and timely reporting of the costs of manufactured products.

We devote the next three chapters to product costing systems. Chapter 4 discusses how product costs are accumulated in a company's accounting records when production takes place in batches or specific lots. Chapters 5 and 6 discuss product costing when production takes place in a continuous flow process. These three chapters are essential to your understanding of many cost accounting concepts covered in the remainder of the book.

CHAPTER 4
Determining Product Costs: Job Order Costing

The schedule of cost of goods manufactured, which you studied in Chapter 2, is a report of all costs used in the manufacture of products during an accounting period. To prepare the schedule, the accountant obtains data from many accounts in the general ledger. But how do the data get into these accounts? In practice, the accountant accumulates the data by carefully monitoring and analyzing the production activities, and by accumulating from many sources information about production and product costs. As production costs are incurred, they are collected and recorded in accounts designed to accumulate the details of cost of goods manufactured.

Product costs are essential components in the performance measurement of manufacturing firms. The analysis of product costs and of the systems used to generate product costs is an essential part of cost accounting. Managers should therefore understand how costs are determined so that they can use cost information effectively in making decisions.

In this chapter we return to the three basic cost elements—direct materials, direct labor, and manufacturing overhead—and look at how the accountant measures and accounts for each, and how each is incorporated in the measurement of product costs. Next we discuss job order costing, one of the two product costing systems, to see how costs of specific products are determined. The chapter concludes by illustrating how cost accounting data are recorded in the company's accounting system.

A CLOSER LOOK AT COST ELEMENTS

To reinforce your understanding of how to measure the costs for a specific product, we expand our discussion of direct materials, direct labor, and manufacturing overhead, paying special attention to how each cost element is measured.

Raw Materials

In most manufacturing businesses, raw materials inventory is a major asset, usually requiring a large investment of capital. Well-managed manufacturing firms carefully plan and control raw materials inventory acquisitions, storage, and distribution to ensure effective use of inventory resources and maintain profitability. The management of and accounting for raw materials inventory

Raw materials inventory is a major investment for manufacturing firms

are covered in Chapter 13. Our interest here is to identify the physical flow of raw materials into the company and through the production process. We can trace the parallel flow of the raw material and its cost as it moves through production to finished products.

Manufacturing firms must account for raw materials acquisition and for raw materials distribution. The **acquisition** process includes the purchase and receipt of raw materials and its movement into the inventory storage area, usually called the storeroom, the stores area, or the stockroom. Inventory acquisition typically involves external transactions with other firms.

Inventory distribution consists of internal transactions within the manufacturing firm. It is the transfer of raw materials into production. The distribution process may sound quite simple, but in large manufacturing companies inventory distribution may be quite complex. The right amount and type of raw material must be supplied to the right production location at the time it is needed.

Figure 4-1 illustrates the process entailed in raw materials acquisitions and describes the common source documents generated in the process. These documents are needed to identify product costs and to provide an audit trail. An **audit trail** is the interrelated evidence consisting of accounting reports, ledger and journal entries, journal memoranda, and source documents used by accountants to trace transactions through the accounting system to their source. A clear audit trail enables accountants to trace transactions if problems arise or if errors are detected, and to test the accuracy and efficiency of the accounting system. Therefore, the proper design and preparation of source documents is a prerequisite to collecting accounting data in a cost accounting system.

The two basic inventory activities, acquisition and distribution

Raw Materials Acquisition.   The first step in the acquisition of raw materials inventory is to identify the need to purchase some raw materials. Whenever a new material is needed or the supply of existing materials is running low, a

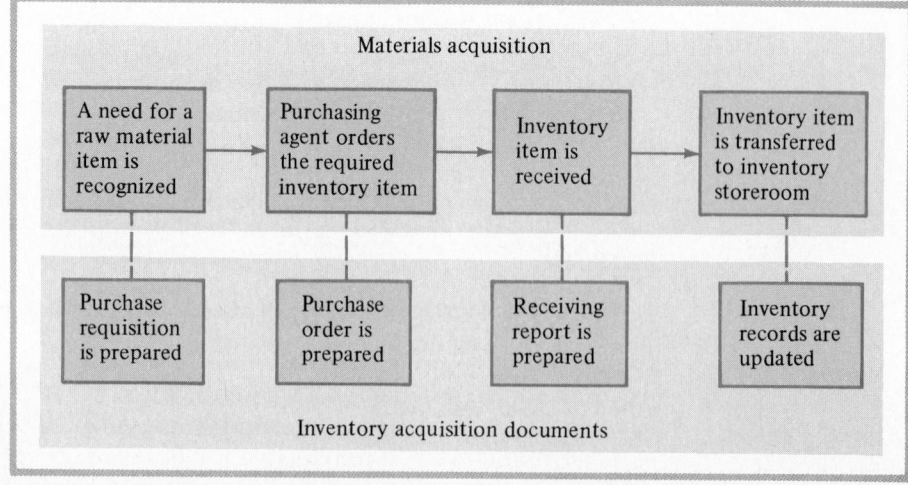

Figure 4-1. Each inventory acquisition activity results in the preparation or updating of a source document. These documents are used to initiate accounting entries and management actions.

purchase requisition is prepared to show that an item of inventory should be bought. This document is sent to the purchasing department, which has the responsibility for acquiring materials and supplies for the organization. The purchasing agent determines the most economical way of fulfilling the purchase request and issues a **purchase order,** a document used to place orders with suppliers. The **purchasing agent** is the person who manages the purchasing activity. In a small business, purchasing may be only one of several responsibilities of the purchasing agent, and in large organizations the purchasing agent may manage a large department. Whatever the size of the firm, the responsibility for purchasing, as for all important activities of an organization, should be clearly defined and understood.

Key documents in inventory acquisition

When the new raw materials arrive, personnel in the receiving department or inventory storeroom compare the materials with the purchase order to ensure that the quantity and quality ordered was received. In large organizations a separate receiving department may exist, and a **receiving report** is prepared when an inventory shipment arrives. This report is used to update inventory and accounts receivable records. In smaller organizations the receiving function may be performed by the inventory storeroom employees.

Raw Materials Inventory Distribution.   Most manufacturers have one or more inventory storerooms located strategically about the plant to provide the most efficient distribution of raw materials to the manufacturing process. The degree of efficiency achieved in the materials distribution process can have a strong influence on the profit of a manufacturing firm. Consequently, many manufacturing businesses invest significant amounts of money in inventory management systems.

A purchase requisition is used for the purchase of materials and a materials requisition is used to put materials into production

Figure 4-2 illustrates inventory distribution cost flows and related accounting activities. **A materials requisition** starts the physical flow of raw materials into the production process and triggers the associated entry for material costs in the company's accounting records. Material requisitions report the type, quantity, and production location of the requisitioned material. Be sure you understand the distinction between a materials requisition and a purchase requisition: A purchase requisition is an inventory acquisition document that initiates the purchasing process, whereas a materials requisition is an inventory distribution document that starts material into production.

A returned materials report is prepared when some of the requisitioned materials are not used in production and are returned to the inventory storeroom. The source documents used for inventory acquisition and distribution are needed to verify raw materials transactions and provide product cost data to enter into the company's accounting records.

Materials requisitions are periodically summarized

Many firms prepare a **materials requisition summary report,** which shows the quantity and cost of materials charged to each product during the time period covered by the summary report. The summary report may be prepared monthly, weekly, or even daily, depending on the information needs of management. The more frequent the summary report, the more timely the product cost information that results from using the data in it.

Figure 4-2. Accountants measure the costs of manufacturing activities and record the costs in ledger accounts. The matching concept guides accountants in assigning costs to products.

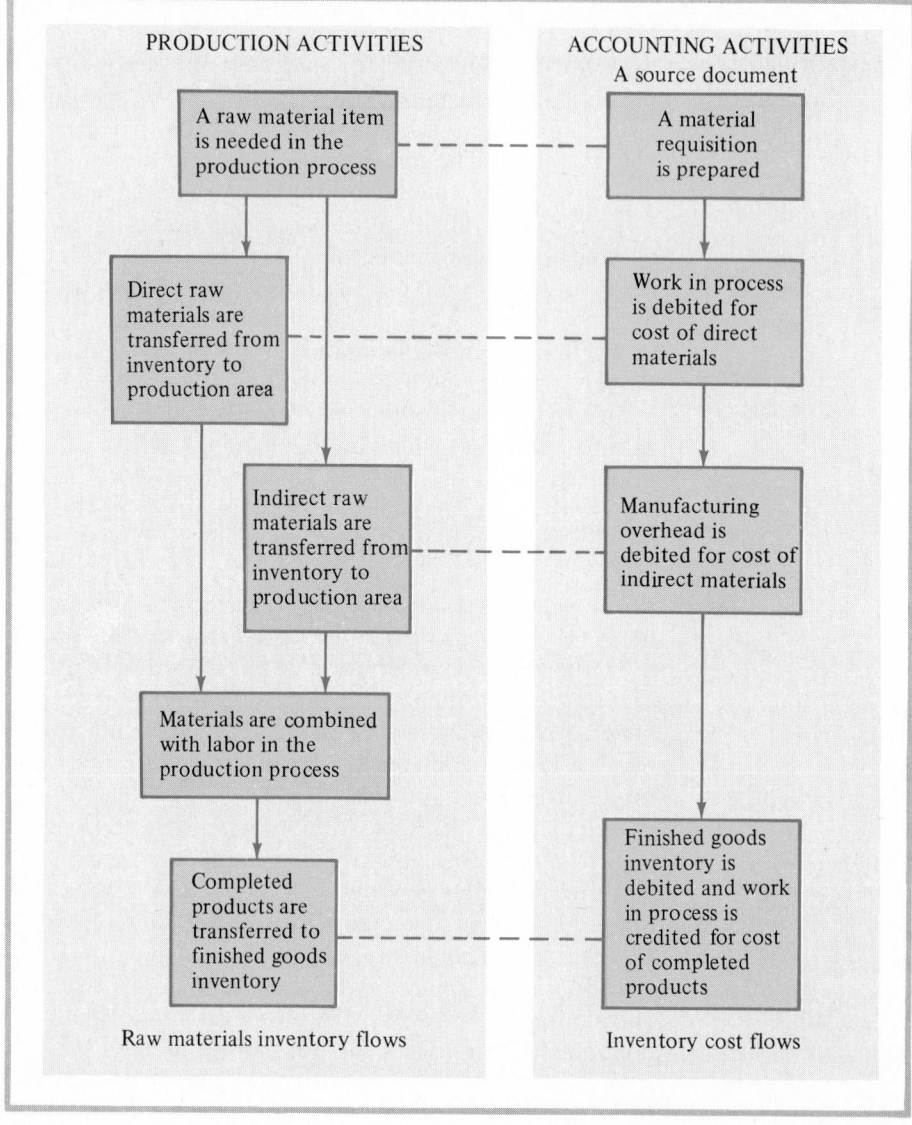

PRODUCTION ACTIVITIES

ACCOUNTING ACTIVITIES
A source document

A raw material item is needed in the production process

A material requisition is prepared

Direct raw materials are transferred from inventory to production area

Work in process is debited for cost of direct materials

Indirect raw materials are transferred from inventory to production area

Manufacturing overhead is debited for cost of indirect materials

Materials are combined with labor in the production process

Completed products are transferred to finished goods inventory

Finished goods inventory is debited and work in process is credited for cost of completed products

Raw materials inventory flows

Inventory cost flows

Labor

Labor costs must be assigned to cost objectives

The second manufacturing cost element is labor. In all businesses, payroll expenses appear in the income statement as deductions from revenue to determine net income. In a manufacturing company, payroll expenses consist of wages paid to production workers and salaries of sales employees, accountants, general administrative people, and other personnel who work in nonmanufacturing activities of the company. Most payroll costs in a manufacturing firm are not reported as payroll expenses, because the majority of workers are employed in the production of products. The wages of production employees are included in the cost of manufactured products and do not become an expense until the product is sold. In order to assign payroll costs to products, the accountant must measure the cost of direct labor, determine the amount of indirect labor, and record the cost of labor in the product cost accounts. Salary expenses, on the other hand, are period costs, and are not assigned to products. They are expensed in the period in which they are incurred regardless of the quantity of products manufactured or sold.

Measuring the Cost of Labor.   The employer's total payroll consists of gross payroll cost plus the cost of employee benefits. **Gross payroll** is the sum of the employees' wage rates times the number of hours worked and the salaries of supervisors and managers. The amount of money employees receive in their paychecks is significantly less than the gross payroll, because various sums are withheld from employees' paychecks to satisfy government obligations, among others. Federal income taxes, FICA taxes, and state and local income taxes are withheld by the employer. In addition, many employees request that part of their earnings be withheld for savings programs, loan payments, union dues, or insurance programs.

Gross payroll is the total payroll before deductions

Even though the employer writes paychecks for much less than the gross payroll, the employer's payroll cost is not reduced. Any payroll deductions must be paid, often immediately, to the federal government, state government, labor unions, insurance companies, or credit unions. In fact, the record keeping needed to manage payrolls is itself a cost that adds to the total cost of labor.

Net pay is the gross payroll minus all payroll deductions

In addition to gross payroll, other labor-related costs that add to the total cost of labor are payroll taxes and employee benefits. The employer incurs obligations to governments in the form of **payroll taxes,** which are part of the cost of employing people. The employer must pay FICA taxes equal to the amount withheld from the employee's checks. In addition, most companies must pay federal and state unemployment taxes on wages earned by employees, and in some states, employers must contribute to a fund that compensates victims of job-related accidents that cause injury or death. Payroll taxes are obligations of the employer and should not be confused with taxes withheld from employee's paychecks to satisfy government requirements. The withheld items are, in effect, paid by employees through deductions, whereas payroll taxes are paid by employers.

In addition to gross payroll, employers incur other labor-related costs

Employee benefits, commonly referred to as **fringe benefits,** are compensation provided to employees in addition to salaries and wages. Common examples are paid vacations and holidays, pension plans, health and life insurance, and recreation and education programs. The cost of payroll taxes and employee benefits may be as large as 35 to 45 percent of gross payroll for many large manufacturing firms. Payroll taxes and employee benefit costs are usually treated as indirect labor costs and are debited to Manufacturing Overhead Control. The problem with this approach is that managers may view gross payroll as the total cost of labor because the other labor costs are buried in overhead and not identified as direct labor. The total cost of payroll is illustrated graphically in Figure 4-3.

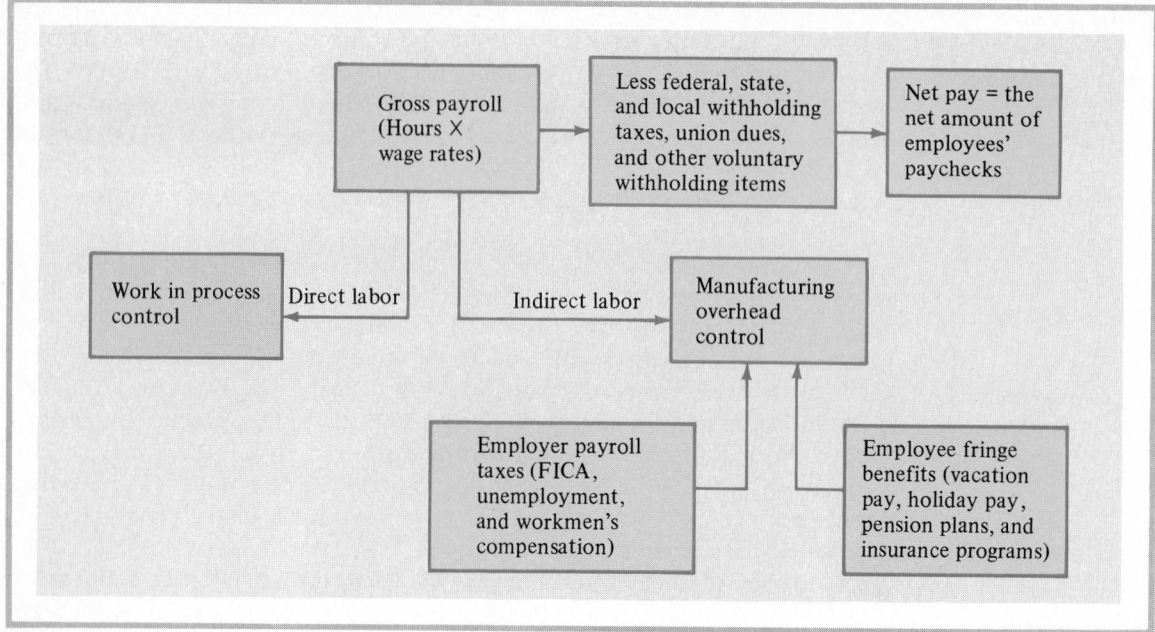

Figure 4-3. Accountants record the cost of labor and withholding items from employee's paychecks. In addition gross payroll must be assigned to specific cost objectives.

Payroll taxes and employee benefits often are significant obligations of the employer

Managers should be aware of the total cost of employee compensation when evaluating performance and making decisions affecting labor. This can be accomplished by providing managers with detailed labor cost reports that identify the portion of labor-related overhead cost. An alternative costing approach is to identify payroll taxes and employee benefit costs with employees and assign those costs as part of the direct labor cost. This approach requires more record keeping, but in some cases the more accurate labor cost data may justify the cost.

Payroll Distribution. Cost accountants must be able to identify the cost of each employee's labor with the specific products produced by the employee. Two documents used to track manufacturing labor costs are daily time tickets and job time tickets. Employees fill out **daily time tickets,** sometimes called **time cards,** at the end of the day, describing all of the job activities performed during the day. Any labor time not identified with specific products is indirect labor and is recorded on the time card so that it can be charged to manufacturing overhead. Another method of tracing labor costs is to use job time tickets. Employees fill out **job time tickets** after completing work on a particular production job. Both daily time tickets and job time tickets can provide accountants with timely detailed labor cost data for product costing and reporting labor costs to managers. Neither of the two methods described is generally preferable to the other. Accountants select the method they believe most efficient for accumulating product cost data.

Identifying labor costs with specific products

The labor distribution report summarizes labor costs for a particular time period, such as a week

Periodically, the time tickets are summarized in a **labor distribution report,** sometimes called a **labor summary** or a **labor recapitulation report.** This report identifies the payroll costs that should be assigned to the various products. Direct labor costs are debited to the Work in Process Control account. Any manufacturing labor identified as indirect is assigned to manufacturing overhead by a debit to the Manufacturing Overhead Control account.

Manufacturing Overhead

Manufacturing overhead costs are all necessary indirect costs of production

In addition to indirect materials and indirect labor, manufacturing overhead costs include factory maintenance, depreciation or lease costs on production plant and equipment, factory utilities, and all other necessary manufacturing costs. By definition, these costs cannot be identified directly with specific products. Nonetheless, they are real and necessary costs of production and often constitute a large part of the cost of manufacturing a product. Managers must monitor and control overhead costs with the same diligence and skill they apply to direct production costs.

Throughout the accounting period, direct costs are assigned to products as they are identified in documents such as material requisitions and daily time cards, and summarized in daily or weekly reports. But if managers are to know the cost of production, indirect costs must also be assigned to products on a timely basis. Unlike direct materials and direct labor, however, manufacturing overhead costs such as factory lighting, equipment maintenance, and factory property taxes cannot be identified directly with specific products. Clearly, such indirect costs are all essential for production. But how much of each overhead cost should be assigned to each product, and how should these overhead costs be accounted for? The accountant must devise a system for measuring and recording the actual overhead costs as they occur and also a system for assigning manufacturing overhead to products as they are made.

Actual overhead costs are recorded as they occur

Measuring and Recording Actual Overhead.   Actual overhead costs are incurred throughout the accounting period. Indirect materials are put into production, indirect labor is used to support production activities, utilities are used, and factory maintenance is performed. Each time an overhead cost is incurred, the **Manufacturing Overhead Control** account is debited and some other account is credited. For example, when indirect material costing $250 is put into production, the journal entry is

	Manufacturing overhead control	250	
	Raw materials inventory control		250

Similarly, indirect labor requires a debit to Manufacturing Overhead Control and a credit to Payroll, the use of electric power requires a debit to Overhead and a credit to Cash, and so on. As the accounting period progresses, the Manufacturing Overhead Control account accumulates a debit balance for the amount of overhead actually incurred.

Manufacturing Overhead Control is used to accumulate actual overhead costs as they occur

Some overhead costs, such as factory property taxes and casualty insurance premiums, are typically paid in advance once or twice a year, and are usually recorded when paid. On the other hand, depreciation on the factory and equipment is typically recorded at the end of the accounting period. Although these costs benefit production throughout the year, they may be recorded before or after production takes place. Therefore, throughout much of the accounting period, the Manufacturing Overhead Control account may contain more or less of the overhead costs that must be assigned to products.

Assigning Overhead Costs to Products.   The accumulation of actual overhead costs is a key function in cost accounting, but it does not accomplish the essential function of assigning overhead costs to specific products. How should overhead costs be assigned to products? One approach is to wait until the end of the accounting period, when all of the overhead costs have been recorded, and assign the total overhead cost to products manufactured during the period.

For example, if total overhead costs for the year were $380,000 and 95,000 units of product were made during the year, overhead cost is $4 per unit ($380,000/95,000 units). The problem with this approach is that overhead costs are assigned too late to be of much use in managing production. Without knowing the total cost of products as they are made, managers have difficulty making decisions about product pricing, contract negotiations, placing or accepting new orders, and employee benefit measurements.

In order to provide managers with timely product cost data, accountants **must** have a systematic means of assigning overhead costs to specific products on a timely basis. The process of assigning overhead costs to products is called **applying overhead.** Accountants apply overhead costs to products as they are manufactured.

Manufacturing overhead rates allow accountants to match overhead costs with products on a timely basis

Since actual overhead cost is not known until the end of the year, and overhead costs cannot be directly identified with products, accountants apply overhead by using a **manufacturing overhead rate,** which is merely a device for assigning overhead costs to products as they are manufactured. An example of an overhead rate is $6 per unit produced. In this case, each unit of output is assigned an overhead cost of $6 regardless of the actual overhead cost incurred while the unit was being made. Another example of an overhead rate is 120 percent of direct labor cost. In this case, for every dollar of direct labor cost assigned to the product, $1.20 of overhead cost is charged to the product. If the direct labor used to produce one unit of the product costs $8, the overhead cost applied to the product is $9.60 ($8.00 × 1.20).

When a company manufactures many different types and models of products, an overhead rate based on units may not be a good way to assign overhead costs to products. For instance, if a company manufactures small pickup trucks and large commercial trucks, overhead applied on the basis of a simple count of units of output would assign too much overhead to each small pickup truck and not enough to each large commercial truck. A more accurate way to match overhead costs with products is to apply overhead costs to each

The overhead rate should be based on a logical activity measure

unit on the basis of some measure of the total overhead costs used to produce each item. If a large truck requires four times as much direct labor as a small truck, it may be reasonable to assume that large trucks also require four times as much overhead as the small ones. In that case, the manufacturing overhead rate may be based on direct labor hours. Other bases for overhead rates may be machine hours or direct labor cost.

The overhead rate is a useful device for charging overhead cost to products as they flow through the production process. But how is the overhead rate determined? The objective is to assign overhead costs to products so that each product receives its fair share of the overhead costs actually incurred. Logically, the amount of overhead charged to each product should be in proportion to the amount of overhead resources used in its production. Because the accountant needs to assign overhead costs to products as soon as production takes place, the overhead rate must be created long before the total amount of actual overhead cost for the period is known. Consequently, accountants must estimate in advance the amount of overhead cost for the accounting period and the amount of production for the period.

Calculating the Overhead Rate.   To determine the overhead rate, the estimated overhead cost is divided by the estimated activity level. For example, total overhead cost for the next year is estimated at $500,000 and total production is estimated as 125,000 units. The overhead rate is $4 per unit ($500,000/125,000 units). The activity level may be estimated as some measure of the next period's production, such as units, labor hours, or machine hours. A similar computation is made if activity is measured in other than units. For example, management estimates that 200,000 direct labor hours will be required for next year's production. The overhead rate is $2.50 per direct labor hour ($500,000/200,000 direct labor hours). The unit of measure used in the overhead rate, such as units of output, direct labor hours, or machine hours, is called the **overhead application base.**

The overhead rate is always stated in terms of some activity

Because the overhead rate is created before the accounting period starts, it is sometimes called the **predetermined overhead rate.** Overhead is charged to products as they are produced by multiplying the predetermined overhead rate by the production quantity as measured by the overhead application base. For example, the overhead rate is $2.50 per direct labor hour, and during the first week of the accounting period 30 direct labor hours are used to make a particular product. The amount of manufacturing overhead for the product is $75 ($2.50 per direct labor hour × 30 direct labor hours).

The overhead cost to be applied to a product is calculated from the predetermined manufacturing overhead rate *and* the actual measure of activity. For this reason the overhead rate must be stated in terms of an activity measure and not just as a dollar amount or percentage. It is not enough to state the overhead rate as $4, $2.50, or 150 percent. Instead, it must be stated as $4 per unit, $2.50 per direct labor hour, or 150 percent of direct labor cost.

Applying Overhead.   Overhead may be applied to products daily, weekly, or at some other time period that satisfies the information needs of management.

Typically, if overhead is applied using direct labor hours as the application base, overhead is applied whenever direct labor costs are assigned to products.

Overhead costs are applied by debiting Work in Process

Although manufacturing overhead is an indirect cost, it is nonetheless a necessary cost of production and must be assigned to products. The application of overhead costs to products increases the product cost account Work in Process Control. For example, to apply $75 of overhead to production the entry is

	Work in process control	75	
	Manufacturing overhead applied		75

The debit to the Work in Process Control account increases the balance in that account and corresponds to the increase in the cost of the product caused by the cost of overhead. But look at the credit side of the entry. When actual overhead costs are recorded, Manufacturing Overhead Control is debited. But when overhead is applied, Manufacturing Overhead Applied is credited. There are two different overhead accounts.

Overhead Accounts. There are two functions in accounting for overhead: One is to measure and record the actual amount of overhead costs as they occur; the other is to assign overhead costs to products on a timely basis. To accomplish these functions efficiently, accountants use two separate overhead accounts to record manufacturing overhead. The **Manufacturing Overhead Control** account is used to record **actual** manufacturing overhead costs. This account is debited when overhead costs are incurred. Over time, the overhead control account continues to accumulate a debit balance.

Manufacturing Overhead Applied is used to accumulate the amount of overhead applied to products during the period.

A second overhead account, called **Manufacturing Overhead Applied,** is used to accumulate the amount of overhead costs **applied** to products by means of the overhead application rate. Whenever overhead is applied to production, the Work in Process Control account is debited and the Manufacturing Overhead Applied account is credited. During the accounting period, this account accumulates a credit balance.

At any point in the accounting period, it is unlikely that the overhead control account and the overhead applied account will have identical balances. The amounts recorded in the overhead applied account are based on estimates, and the amounts recorded in the overhead control account may be recorded early or late in the year, or at erratic time intervals. By the end of the accounting period, however, the two accounts should have similar balances. Any difference is due to estimation error, which is usually small if managers are experienced at making good estimates of costs and production activities. The balances in the two accounts are easily compared at the end of the accounting period to determine the difference between applied overhead and actual overhead.

Underapplied and Overapplied Overhead

If the balance in the applied overhead account is **greater** than the balance in the overhead control account at year-end, overhead is **overapplied**—too much overhead has been assigned to the products. If applied overhead is **less** than overhead control, then overhead is **underapplied**—actual overhead costs exceeded the amount applied to production, so that not enough overhead cost was assigned to the products. Figure 4-4 illustrates the two overhead accounts. Actual overhead of $17,200 is made up of a variety of indirect

Subsidiary MOH Ledger	Control Accounts

Indirect Materials	**Manufacturing Overhead Control**
1,800	1,800
	2,900
	3,500
Indirect Labor	4,000
2,900	5,000
	17,200

Utilities	
3,500	

Maintenance	**Manufacturing Overhead Applied**
4,000	17,000

Plant Depreciation	**Work in Process**
5,000	38,300 | 63,500
	11,600
	MOH 17,000

End of Period Comparison:

Actual manufacturing overhead	$17,200
Applied manufacturing overhead (3,400 direct labor hours × $5 per hr)	17,000
Underapplied overhead	$ 200

Figure 4-4. All actual manufacturing overhead costs are charged to the Manufacturing Overhead Control account and posted both to the control account and individual accounts in the overhead subsidiary ledger. Applied overhead is recorded as a credit in the Manufacturing Overhead Applied account. At the end of the period the control account and the applied account are compared and any difference is underapplied or overapplied overhead.

costs recorded in the control account and in the subsidiary MOH ledger. Applied overhead of $17,000 is calculated by multiplying a $5 overhead rate times 3,400 actual hours of direct labor. The overhead cost of $17,000 is applied to production by debiting the Work in Process account, which also includes direct material and direct labor costs. Most of these costs have been transferred to Finished Goods by the end of the period, and most of the finished goods are usually sold.

The difference between the balances in the two overhead accounts is underapplied overhead. An adjustment is required at the end of the accounting period to assign the $200 difference to products. The adjustment is accomplished by closing the two overhead accounts and assigning the difference to Cost of Goods Sold, as follows:

Manufacturing overhead applied		17,000	
Cost of goods sold		200	
Manufacturing overhead control			17,200
To assign underapplied overhead.			

Small differences between actual and applied overhead are assigned to Cost of Goods Sold

Underapplied overhead is added to Cost of Goods Sold and overapplied overhead is subtracted. This simple method of disposing of underapplied or overapplied overhead is justified for two reasons:

1. The difference between actual and applied overhead is small and is therefore immaterial.
2. Typically, most of the products produced during the year are sold by the end of the year.

Occasionally the difference between applied and actual overhead is large. Perhaps the estimates of overhead costs or of activity levels were wrong, or factors beyond the control of management, such as a strike experienced by the company or a major supplier, forced management to reduce production quantities significantly. What constitutes a large rather than small difference usually is a matter of judgment. Whatever the cause of the large difference between actual and applied overhead, an adjustment should be made at the end of the period so that product accounts will have correct balances before financial statements are prepared.

Large differences between actual and applied overhead are prorated to Work in Process, Finished Goods, and Cost of Goods Sold

If the difference between actual and applied overhead is large at the end of the accounting period, the cost accounting records should be adjusted to reflect the actual cost of manufacturing overhead in the product costs. Product costs are accumulated in Work in Process Control for units still in production, Finished Goods Inventory for completed units, and Cost of Goods Sold, which is the product expense for units sold during the accounting period. Each of these accounts contains manufacturing overhead costs along with direct material costs and direct labor costs.

Figure 4-5. When the difference between applied overhead and actual overhead is large, the difference is prorated to Work in Process, Finished Goods, and Costs of Goods Sold in proportion to the amount of overhead costs that are in these accounts at the time the adjustment is made.

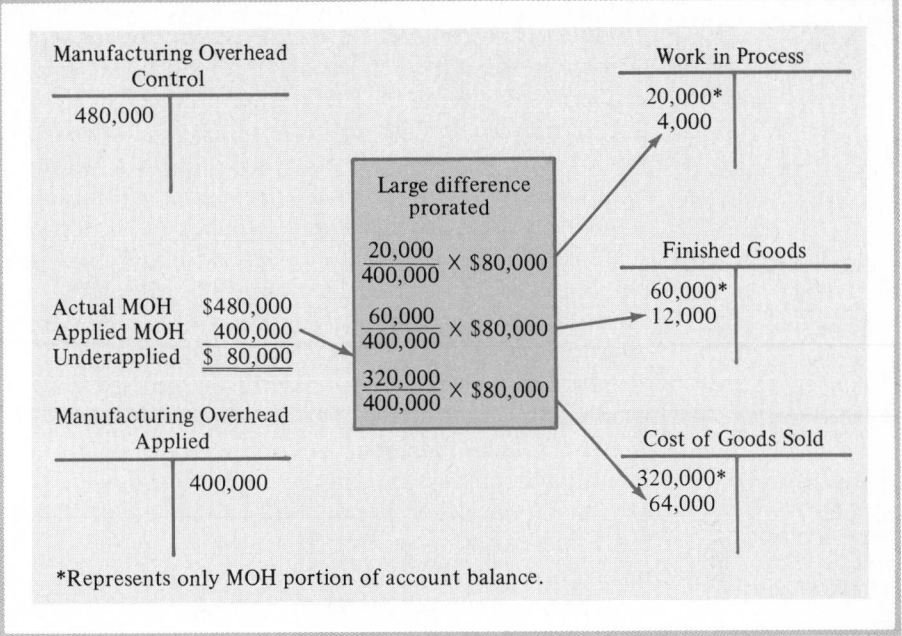

If the actual overhead is significantly different from the amount of overhead assigned to these accounts, the accounts should be adjusted. The difference in overhead costs is allocated to the three accounts in proportion to the amount of overhead cost that remains in each account at the end of the accounting period. For example, Figure 4-5 shows a situation in which applied overhead is $80,000 less than actual overhead. The $80,000 difference is considered by management to be large, so it is allocated to the three product cost accounts in proportion to the amount of overhead that remains in these accounts at year-end. In this case, $4,000 is assigned to Work in Process, $12,000 to Finished Goods, and $64,000 to Cost of Goods Sold.

TYPES OF COST ACCOUNTING SYSTEMS

The preceding discussion of production cost elements is an overview of the cost components of a product costing system. Now we turn to the concepts and procedures necessary to measure the manufacturing cost of specific products. There are two types of product costing systems, job order costing and process costing.

Job order costing is used for batch processing

Job order costing systems are used to accumulate the costs of products manufactured in batches or intermittent production runs, in which the beginning and end of production can be clearly identified. Specialized machinery, personalized items, and custom-made goods are common examples of products that are typically costed using a job order system. Some companies do not sell enough of a product to warrant continuous production runs of all their products. For example, a company may produce several models of lawn mowers in the winter to satisfy the demand for spring and summer sales. It may schedule production in batches of 100 of one model, then 150 of another. In the late summer and fall all production of lawn mowers stops and production of snowmobiles and snow blowers starts, because the snow equipment constitutes most of the fall and winter sales for the company. In this situation it is possible to cost each batch of products using a job order costing system.

Job order production has a clearly identifiable starting point and finishing point. Accountants start accumulating production costs as soon as the job starts. Costs are accumulated until the job is complete, at which time the costs are totaled and unit costs are computed.

Process costing is used for continuous-flow production processes

Process costing is used to measure the cost of manufacturing products produced in continuous-flow production processes. Petroleum products, chemicals, and appliances are produced in a continuous flow without clearly identifiable starting and completion times. Some units are just being started as others units are being completed. The flow of production continues throughout the accounting period. The accountant cannot conveniently wait until production stops to calculate the cost of the product. Therefore, accountants have developed methods for measuring the cost of products manufactured in continuous-flow production processes. Process costing is discussed at length in Chapters 5 and 6.

JOB ORDER COSTING

In a job order costing system, the cost objective is a particular job or production run of a product. Manufacturing costs and other pertinent data are accumulated for each job or production run. These data are recorded on a **job cost sheet,** which is a document used to accumulate production costs and other descriptive data about the job. A job cost sheet is illustrated in Figure 4-6.

Production costs are accumulated on a job cost sheet

The specific information contained on a job cost sheet varies from firm to firm and depends on the types of information needed by managers and the methods used in processing accounting data. Most job cost sheets, however, contain similar information. Typically, job cost sheets are separated into three segments. The top section contains general information about the product, the customer, or the job. The second section is used to accumulate production costs, and the third section contains product cost summary data. Firms using job cost sheets design them for their specific information needs, but the top section typically contains some common elements:

Common types of general information data

1. The date the job was started
2. The date the job was completed
3. A description or part number for the product produced
4. The customer ordering the product
5. The quantity produced
6. A job number

Figure 4-6. A typical job cost sheet form. The top section is general information about the job and product, the middle section is for accumulating actual production costs, and the bottom section is for summarizing production costs when the job is completed.

Job Cost Sheet

Date started _____   Job number _____
Date completed _____   Quantity _____
Product _____   Customer _____

Direct Materials			Direct Labor			Manufacturing Overhead		
Date	Reference	Amount	Date	Reference	Amount	Date	Reference	Amount

Summary of Costs

Item	Total Cost	Unit Cost
Direct materials	_____	_____
Direct labor	_____	_____
Manufacturing overhead	_____	_____
Totals	_____	_____

Actual production costs are accumulated on the job cost sheet

A unique **job number** is assigned to each job and distinguishes it from all other jobs in the company. The job number may be a simple sequential number or one that includes information about the product or the sequence of steps in the production process. Whatever the nature of the information included in the job number, it always provides a unique identification for the job in question.

The middle section of the job cost sheet contains detailed data for each cost element. Direct material, direct labor, and manufacturing overhead data are presented separately, along with dates and other supporting data about the various costs. The date column for each cost element is used to record the day the cost was incurred. The reference column is used to identify the source of the cost data entered in the cost sheet, or to describe some other data, such as the type of raw material used or the number of direct labor hours worked. The reference column can provide a convenient cross-reference to other accounting records, such as inventory records or payroll reports. The amount column shows the cost assigned to the job for a particular item.

A job may have only one entry for each cost element or it may have many entries, depending on the manufacturing process and the company's accounting system. For example, one company may record costs in job cost sheets daily and another company may record costs only once a week. In either case, however, costs are recorded in the job cost sheet until the job is completed, at which time the products are transferred to finished goods inventory. The manufacturing costs of the job are summarized in the bottom section of the job cost sheet and the cost of the completed products is transferred from the Work in Process Control account to the Finished Goods Inventory account.

The bottom section of the job cost sheet summarizes the manufacturing costs for the job. When the job is completed, the accountant sums the costs for

Costs are summarized when the job is completed and unit costs are computed

each cost element and divides the number of units produced into the costs to find unit costs. Usually unit costs are computed for materials, labor, and overhead and for the costs in total. Once the costs are summarized they are transferred to the Finished Goods Inventory Control account. These cost data are used by managers to evaluate production performance, to identify trends in production costs, to evaluate product prices, and to make a variety of other decisions and evaluations.

The Job Cost Sheet Illustrated

Figure 4-7 illustrates a typical job order cost sheet. The cost sheet from the Hallkirk Products Company is for the production of 50 steel machine tables for use with computer terminals and other office equipment.

The reference column provides an audit trail that ties the accounting system together

The top section of the job cost sheet describes the job briefly—the production of 50 machine tables—and shows that the job was started on January 8, 1985, and completed on January 23, 1985. The 50 units manufactured were produced for general stock rather than for a specific customer. This information indicates that the tables are available for sale to any customer. The job number MT24X48-47201 is listed in the upper right corner of the job cost sheet. Like many companies, Hallkirk uses more than a simple sequential job number. The first part of the job number identifies the product

Hallkirk Company
Job Cost Sheet

Date started _____ 1/8/85 _____   Job number _____ MT24X48-47201 _____
Date completed _____ 1/23/85 _____   Quantity _____ 50 _____
Product _____ 24" x 48" machine table _____   Customer _____ general stock _____

Direct Materials			Direct Labor			Manufacturing Overhead		
Date	Reference	Amount	Date	Reference	Amount	Date	Reference	Amount
1/9/85	MRQ4340	$1,550	1/14/85	LD1-14-85	$ 240	1/14/85	LD1-14-85	$ 288
1/11/85	MRQ4347	575	1/21/85	LD1-21-85	960	1/21/85	LD1-21-85	1,152
1/16/85	MRQ4368	425	1/28/85	LD1-28-85	600	1/28/85	LD1-28-85	720
		$2,550			$1,800			$2,160

Summary of Costs

Item	Total Cost	Unit Cost
Direct materials	$2,550	$ 51.00
Direct labor	1,800	36.00
Manufacturing overhead	2,160	43.20
Totals	$6,510	$130.20

Figure 4-7. A completed job cost sheet. When the job is completed, the cost data in the middle section are accumulated and reported in the bottom section of the job cost sheet along with unit costs.

and the second part is the unique job number. MT stands for machine table and 24X48 is the table size. The unique part of the job number, 47201, appears after the hyphen and also on material requisitions, labor reports, and other internal documents that accountants use for product costing and management reporting.

Materials. The product cost section of the job cost sheet shows the costs that were charged to the job during production. The three materials requisitions listed in the materials column of the job cost sheet identify the direct materials charged to this job. The materials requisition data are found on the weekly materials requisition summary report, which is prepared by inventory storeroom employees. This supporting document, shown in Figure 4-8, lists all of the materials requisitions filled during the week, and indicates the job to which each requisition was charged. Requisitions for indirect materials are charged to Manufacturing Overhead Control.

The date the raw materials are issued is shown on the job cost sheet. The materials requisition number is found in the reference column for materials. You can find the first two materials requisitions for Job 47201 in the materials summary report shown in Figure 4-8 and can verify the amount of material cost charged to the job during the first week of production. In some companies, the reference column in the job cost sheet is used to provide descriptive information about the material issued, such as the amount or type of material.

	Hallkirk Company			
	Weekly Summary of Material Requisitions			
	For the Week of January 7-11, 1985			
Requisition No.	Date	Inventory No.	Job No.	Amount
MRQ4334	1/7/85	ST751	DT18X30-47199	$1,960
MRQ4335	1/7/85	ST755	MT18X36-47200	2,360
MRQ4336	1/8/85	WR273	DT18X30-47199	912
MRQ4337	1/8/85	PT104	MT15X30-47194	155
MRQ4338	1/8/85	CM617	MC69464-47195	704
MRQ4339	1/9/85	FC088	MT16X30-47194	220
MRQ4340	1/9/85	ST751	MT24X48-47201	1,550
MRQ4341	1/9/85	ST731	DT18X30-47199	4,285
MRQ4342	1/10/85	WR207	DT18X30-47199	1,344
MRQ4343	1/10/85	PT102	PK29406-47196	900
MRQ4344	1/10/85	FC099	PK29405-47196	160
MRQ4345	1/11/85	CC440	Indirect material	173
MRQ4346	1/11/85	ST755	MT18X36-47200	1,980
MRQ4347	1/11/85	CM620	MT24X48-47201	575
MRQ4348	1/11/85	WR273	MT18X36-47200	605
MRQ4349	1/11/85	PT109	DT18X30-47199	295

Figure 4-8. A summary of material requisitions reports information about material requisitions that have been filled during some particular time period. The report may be prepared monthly, weekly, daily, or for some other time period, depending on the information requirements of management.

Some companies prepare daily summaries for materials requisitions. Computers have made such processing and reporting of cost data very timely and efficient.

Labor. At the end of each work day, each employee fills out daily time tickets that identify the jobs worked on and the number of hours worked on each job during the day. The daily time tickets are summarized weekly in the labor distribution report, illustrated in Figure 4-9. This document lists each job's direct labor cost for the week. At the Hallkirk Company, the weekly labor distribution report is prepared on Monday following the work week. The report in Figure 4-9 is prepared on January 14 for the week ending on January 11. It shows the number of hours worked by each employee on each job, and also the number of labor hours spent on tasks not associated directly with specific jobs. These indirect labor hours are charged to manufacturing overhead. The cost of indirect labor shown in the labor distribution report is charged to the Manufacturing Overhead Control account. The $240 cost of direct labor for Job 47201 is found on the labor distribution report in Figure 4-9 and is reported on the job cost sheet in Figure 4-7 along with the labor distribution report number and date.

The job in Figure 4-7 was completed on January 23, 1985, but the last entry for labor is made on the job cost sheet on January 28, 1985. The work performed on the job between January 21 and 23 does not appear on a labor distribution report until Wednesday, January 28. The job cost sheet cannot be completed until all of the necessary cost data are available.

Figure 4-9. Labor distribution reports summarize labor time and costs for some time period, such as a week.

Hallkirk Company
Labor Distribution Report
For the Week Ended January 11, 1985

Employee	Hours Worked on Job Number						Total	
	47194	47195	47196	47199	47200	47201	MOH	Hours
M. Frank	12	8	14	—	—	—	6	40
J. Fergus	—	24	9	—	—	—	7	40
L. Phillips	—	—	17	15	—	—	—	32
F. Olery	—	18	20	—	—	—	2	40
T. Levy	—	—	—	22	—	—	2	24
K. Chin	—	14	—	19	2	—	5	40
N. Hillman	12	—	—	—	15	10	3	40
R. Rossi	22	—	—	—	8	8	2	40
H. Perez	—	—	—	—	24	12	4	40
Total hours per job	46	64	60	56	49	30	31	336
Wage rate	$8/hr	$8/hr	$8/hr	$8/hr	$8/hr	$8/hr	$8/hr	$8/hr
Labor cost per job	$368	$512	$480	$448	$392	$240	$248	$2,688

Manufacturing Overhead.   The third cost element, manufacturing overhead, is charged to the job using an overhead rate of 120 percent of direct labor cost. In this example, a convenient time to apply overhead to jobs is at the time the direct labor costs are charged to the jobs. The labor cost data are obtained from the weekly labor distribution reports; therefore the report number appears in the manufacturing overhead reference column. The overhead cost for the Hallkirk example is merely the labor cost times 120 percent. When other manufacturing overhead application bases are used, such as machine hours, the accountant obtains overhead application data from a machine utilization report.

Cost Sheet Summary Section.   The manufacturing costs for a job are summarized at the bottom of the job cost sheet when the job is completed. The unit costs computed in this illustration and in other job cost sheets are averages. The $51.00 unit cost for materials, shown in the job cost sheet in Figure 4-7, is the average cost of materials used in each unit for this particular job. Some of the machine tables built may have had a material cost of $49.50 and some $52.00, but the average for the entire job was $51.00. Similarly, the same type of machine table may have been produced earlier in the year with a material cost of $47.75, and future production runs of the same product may yield different unit costs. The difference in material costs can occur because of price changes by suppliers, differences in the efficiency of employees making the product, or random production differences.

Work in Process Control in Job Order Costing

The job cost sheet for any job currently in production is called an open job cost sheet

When the manufacturing process begins for a job, a job cost sheet is started, or opened, by filling in the product information in the top section of the job cost sheet. Once the job cost sheet is started, it is called an **open job cost sheet** until the job is completed and the cost sheet is summarized. When the job is completed, the costs are transferred from the Work in Process Control account to the Finished Goods Inventory account. The journal entry to accomplish the cost transfer for Hallkirk's job number MT24X48-47201 is:

The balance in the Work in Process Control account is equal to the sum of all open job cost sheets

1/28/85	Finished goods inventory control	6,510	
	Work in process control		6,510
	To transfer the cost of Job MT24X48-		
	47201 to finished goods inventory.		

Summarized job cost sheets for completed jobs are called closed job cost sheets

In a job order costing system the balance in the Work in Process Control account at any point in the accounting period is equal to the sum of the balances in all the **open** job cost sheets. Figure 4-10 shows the relationship between open job cost sheets and the Work in Process Control account. A cost sheet that has been summarized and whose costs are transferred to finished goods is a **closed job cost sheet.** Although closed job cost sheets are no longer part of the Work in Process Control account, they still provide managers with cost data for analysis and evaluation.

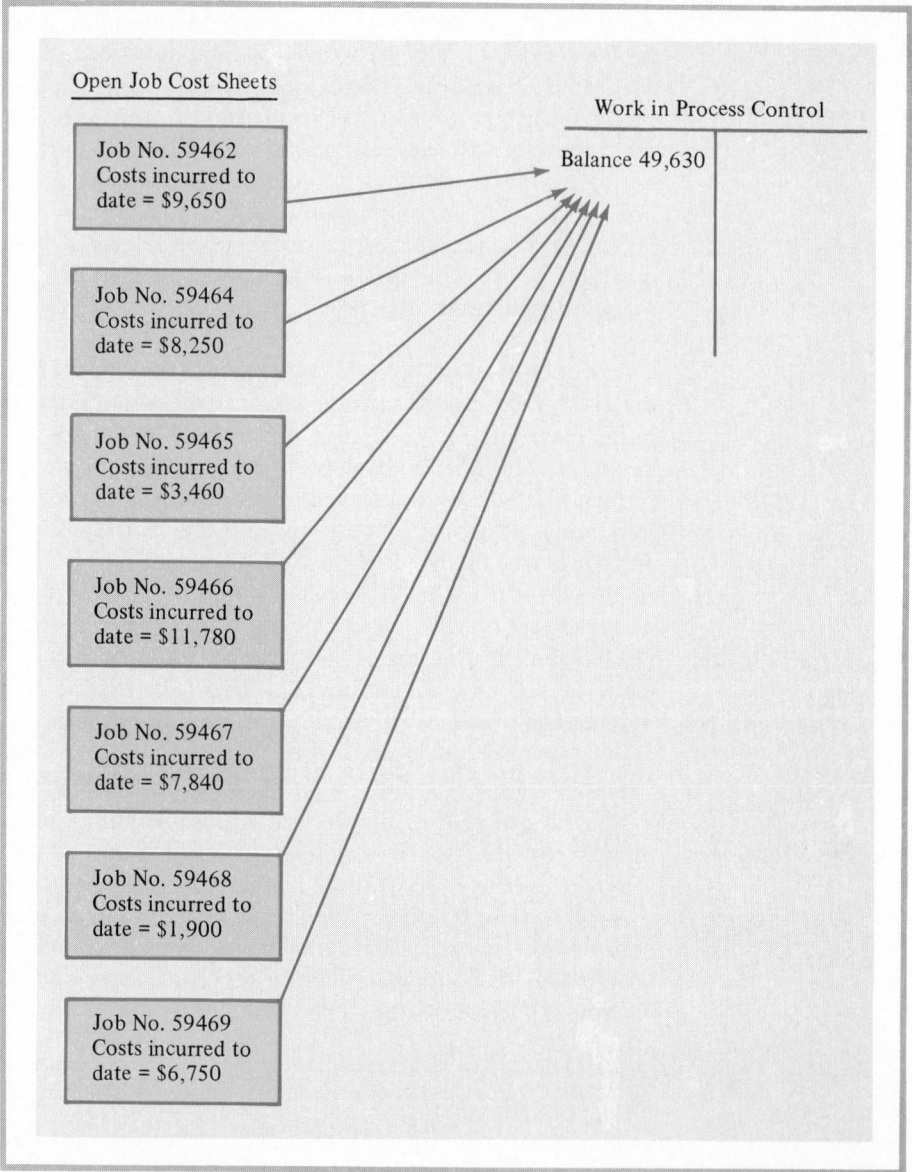

Figure 4-10. The job cost sheets of all jobs currently in production are called open job cost sheets. At any given point in time the sum of costs in all open job cost sheets is equal to the balance in the Work in Process Control account.

Departmental Job Cost Sheets

In some situations, the type of job cost sheet just illustrated does not provide the cost detail needed by management. In such cases it may be necessary to develop a **departmental job cost sheet,** where unit and total costs are accumu-

Departmental job cost sheets provide more detail than a general job cost sheet

lated for each cost element in each production department. Figure 4-11 shows a departmental job cost sheet for Hallkirk's job number MT24X48-47201. This is the same job costed above, except here the production costs are identified with each department.

The Hallkirk Company uses three production departments to manufacture the machine tables. The first department is forming, the second is assembly, and the third is finishing. Most of the raw material is added in the forming department; labor and overhead costs are incurred in all three departments. A departmental job cost sheet provides one matrix of unit and total cost information that many managers can use to evaluate performance and make projections.

The additional detail offered by the departmental job cost sheet enables managers to refine their control and performance evaluation functions beyond what is possible with less detailed job cost sheets. But this refinement has an added cost, because the accountant must expend more time and

Figure 4-11. Departmental job cost sheets provide managers with more detailed production cost data. This additional detail may provide a better basis for monitoring and controlling costs but it also requires additional costs to accumulate the data and prepare the reports.

Hallkirk Company
Job Cost Sheet

Date started	1/8/85			Job number	MT24X48-47201		
Date completed	1/23/85			Quantity	50		
Product	24" x 48" machine table			Customer	general stock		

Department	Direct Materials			Direct Labor			Manufacturing Overhead		
	Date	Reference	Amount	Date	Reference	Amount	Date	Reference	Amount
Forming	1/8/85	MRQ4340	$1,550	1/14/85	1/14/85	$240	1/14/85	LD1-14-85	$288
	1/10/85	MRQ4347	575	1/21/85	1/21/85	520	1/21/85	LD1-21-85	624
			$2,125			$760			$912
Assembly	1/16/85	MRQ4368	$ 425	1/21/85	LD1-21-85	$440	1/21/85	LD1-21-85	$528
Finishing	—	—	—	1/28/85	LD1-28-85	$600	1/28/85	LD1-28-85	$720

	Summary of Costs								
	Direct Material		Direct Labor		Mfg. Overhead		Total		Costs
Department	Total	Unit	Total	Unit	Total	Unit	Total		Unit
Forming	$2,125	$42.50	$ 760	$15.20	$ 912	$18.24	$3,797		$ 75.94
Assembly	425	8.50	440	8.80	528	10.56	1,393		27.86
Finishing	—	—	600	12.00	720	14.40	1,320		26.40
Totals	$2,550	$51.00	$1,800	$36.00	$2,160	$43.20	$6,510		$130.20

resources to provide the additional detail. Managers must therefore ensure that the more detailed information is worth the additional cost.

RECORDING MANUFACTURING COSTS

We illustrate the accumulation and recording of production costs in the accounting system with the following transactions of Parklette Manufacturing Company, which uses job order costing.

a.   Parklette buys $20,000 of 12-gauge steel and $46,000 of 14-gauge galvanized steel on open account.

b.   Direct materials costing $31,350 and indirect materials costing $1,260 are transferred from the inventory storeroom into production.

c.   The weekly payroll for manufacturing activities is $146,000.

d.   A summary of the daily time sheets shows that $131,600 of labor cost can be identified as direct labor.

e.   Additional payroll costs for the week include the company's share of FICA taxes, $9,260; state unemployment taxes, $3,150; and federal unemployment taxes, $950.

f.   A property tax bill of $26,400 on the manufacturing facility is received and paid.

g.   Utility bills for the manufacturing facility in the amount of $9,600 are received and paid.

h.   Manufacturing overhead is applied at the rate of $6.00 per machine hour. During the week 10,200 machine hours are used.

i.   During the week three jobs are completed and transferred to finished goods. The jobs had a combined total cost of $166,700.

j.   Products costing $182,000 are sold for $244,000 on open account.

a.   Bought $20,000 of 12-gauge steel and $46,000 of 14-gauge galvanized steel on open account.

Like most manufacturing companies, Parklette uses a perpetual inventory system. The purchase of materials is recorded as follows:

a.	Raw materials inventory control	66,000	
	Accounts payable		66,000
	Bought $20,000 of 12-gauge steel and		
	$46,000 of 14-gauge steel on account.		

In a perpetual inventory system purchases and uses of inventory items are recorded directly in the Raw Materials Inventory Control account as they occur. A purchases account is not used. The Raw Materials Inventory Control

The cost of manufacturing activities must be entered into the firm's accounting records just like financial accounting activities

account is debited for the amount of the purchase. In addition to the control account for raw materials, the company maintains a subsidiary ledger of raw materials inventory accounts, one for each type of raw material. When the journal entry is posted to the ledger accounts, these individual inventory accounts also must be debited for the purchases of materials. If each transaction is posted to both the control account and the subsidiary accounts, then the subsidiary account balances will total to the Raw Materials Inventory Control account balance. In transaction *a*, the 12-gauge steel account is debited for $20,000 and the 14-gauge galvanized steel account for $46,000.

b.   Direct materials costing $31,350 and indirect materials costing $1,260 are transferred from the inventory storeroom into production.

b.			
	Work in process control	31,350	
	Manufacturing overhead control	1,260	
	Raw materials inventory control		32,610
	Issued direct material and indirect		
	material to production.		

Data from the materials requisition summary report are used to record the journal entry above and to assign direct materials costs to the specific job cost sheets. Most materials are identifiable as direct materials and are charged to Work in Process Control. Indirect materials are charged to the Manufacturing Overhead Control account and are assigned to products as part of overhead when overhead is applied to production.

c.   The weekly payroll for manufacturing activities is $146,000.

c.			
	Payroll	146,000	
	Federal withholding tax payable		28,400
	FICA tax payable		9,260
	State withholding tax payable		7,400
	Union dues payable		1,450
	Insurance premiums payable		3,100
	Cash		96,390
	Paid the weekly payroll and recorded		
	the withholding items.		

The gross payroll is recorded in the Payroll account. This account holds the payroll costs until they are distributed to the appropriate jobs or other cost objectives. Checks are written to employees for $96,390, and $49,610 is withheld from employees' checks for taxes and other requirements. The company must pay the amounts withheld from employee paychecks to the federal and state governments and other organizations such as the employees' labor union. You are not given the information necessary to compute the withholding amounts. Detailed payroll accounting procedures are discussed in Chapter 19. For our current purposes it is necessary only that you understand the nature of withholding items, and the employer's obligation for the gross payroll.

> d. A summary of the daily time sheets shows that $131,600 of labor cost can be identified as direct labor.

The journal entry for transaction c is a financial accounting entry that records the company's payroll obligations in the firm's accounting system. However, this entry does not accomplish the costing requirement of assigning the payroll costs to the proper cost objective. The identification of labor costs with specific products or activities is accomplished with employee time tickets and periodic labor summaries like the labor distribution report. Using the information contained in this report, the cost of direct labor is charged to the Work in Process Control account and entered on the individual job cost sheets. Indirect labor is charged to the Manufacturing Overhead Control account. The credit is to the Payroll account. Transaction c illustrates only manufacturing payroll; therefore, the only division of labor costs in entry d is between direct labor and indirect labor.

d.	Work in process control	131,600	
	Manufacturing overhead control	14,400	
	Payroll		146,000
	To record the distribution of		
	manufacturing labor costs for		
	direct and indirect labor.		

> e. Additional payroll costs for the week include the company's share of FICA taxes, $9,260; state unemployment taxes, $3,150; and federal unemployment taxes, $950.

The gross payroll is only a portion of the total cost of labor. In addition employers must pay payroll taxes and they incur the cost of other employee benefits. These additional payroll costs must be recorded in the company's accounting records, and the costs must be distributed to the appropriate cost objective. Entry e contains several common payroll taxes. Note that these taxes are costs of the company, whereas the taxes withheld from the employees' checks are the costs of the employees.

e.	Manufacturing overhead control	13,360	
	FICA taxes payable		9,260
	State unemployment tax payable		3,150
	Federal unemployment tax payable		950
	Recorded payroll taxes on		
	manufacturing wages.		

Typically, payroll taxes for manufacturing employees are assigned to the Manufacturing Overhead Control account and charged to products as part of the manufacturing overhead applied to production. As with the payroll entry in transaction c, you do not have enough information to compute the amount of taxes. These taxes and their computation are discussed in Chapter 19.

f. A property tax bill of $26,400 on the manufacturing facility is received and paid.

g. Utility bills for the manufacturing facility in the amount of $9,600 are received and paid.

Entries f and g are used to record manufacturing overhead costs incurred during the period. Actual overhead costs are charged to the overhead control account, but no overhead is assigned to the products themselves by entries f and g. This is accomplished in entry h.

f.	Manufacturing overhead control	26,400	
	Cash		26,400
	Paid the property taxes on the		
	manufacturing facilities.		
g.	Manufacturing overhead control	9,600	
	Cash		9,600
	Received and paid the utility		
	bill for the period.		

Accumulating actual overhead costs and applying those overhead costs to products are two distinctly different processes. Entries f and g illustrate the recording of actual overhead costs. In entry h, overhead costs are applied to products based on machine hours.

h. Manufacturing overhead is applied at the rate of $6.00 per machine hour. During the week 10,200 machine hours are used.

h.	Work in process control	61,200	
	Manufacturing overhead applied		61,200
	Applied manufacturing overhead to		
	products using machine hours as the		
	application base.		

i. During the week three jobs are completed and transferred to finished goods. The jobs had a combined total cost of $166,700.

In Chapter 2 you saw that the physical flow of production is closely paralleled by the flow of manufacturing costs through the accounting system.

Therefore, the physical transfer of products from work in process to the finished goods inventory is paralleled by the accounting entry used to record this transfer.

i.	Finished goods inventory	166,700	
	Work in process control		166,700
	Recorded the transfer of units from		
	work in process to finished goods.		

j.   Products costing $182,000 are sold for $244,000 on open account.

In a perpetual inventory system, the product expense is recorded at the time of sale. Entry *j* is a summary entry used to record the sales for the week.

j.	Accounts receivable	244,000	
	Cost of goods sold	182,000	
	Sales		244,000
	Finished goods inventory		182,000
	Recorded the sales of products		
	for the week.		

SUMMARY

A major function of accountants in a manufacturing business is the measurement of product costs. The three cost elements of manufactured products are direct materials, direct labor, and manufacturing overhead. **Direct materials** are raw materials that can be identified directly with the production of a specific product. Raw materials **acquisition** is the purchase and receipt of inventory. **A purchase requisition** tells the purchasing agent an item is needed, a **purchase order** starts the actual purchasing activity, and a **receiving report** identifies the receipt of inventory items. Raw materials **distribution** is the process of transferring inventory items into the production process. A **materials requisition** is used to identify the type and amount of materials transferred into production.

Labor that can be identified with the production of specific products is called **direct labor.** Typically, employees prepare **daily time tickets** or **job time tickets** to record how they spent their work time. Time tickets are summarized on **labor distribution reports** or **labor summary reports.** Accountants record labor costs and assign them to the appropriate cost objectives. Manufacturing labor that can be identified directly with products is **direct labor** and is assigned directly to Work in Process. Labor not identifiable directly with products is called **indirect labor** and is charged to Manufacturing Overhead Control.

Gross payroll is the total payroll for a pay period. Various amounts are withheld from employees' paychecks and are paid as taxes to governments, as fees to labor unions, or as voluntary payments to other organizations. In addition to gross payroll, employers incur other payroll costs, such as payroll taxes and employee benefits which must be assigned to products. Often payroll taxes and other employee benefit costs for manufacturing employees are charged to the manufacturing overhead control account and assigned to products when overhead is applied to production.

Overhead is difficult to associate with specific products, but it is a necessary manufacturing cost that must be assigned to cost objectives to satisfy the matching principle. Typically, overhead is assigned to products by using a predetermined **overhead rate.** The rate is created in advance of production. Manufacturing overhead is then applied to production by multiplying the overhead rate times the actual measures of activity. Overhead is applied by debiting the Work in Process Control account and crediting the **Manufacturing Overhead Applied** account.

Actual overhead costs are accumulated in the **Manufacturing Overhead Control** account. At any point in the accounting period, including year-end, the amounts in the control and applied accounts are not likely to be identical, but should be fairly close. If the control account is larger than the applied account, overhead is said to be **underapplied.** If the reverse is true, overhead is **overapplied.** Small differences between applied and actual overhead are closed to Cost of Goods Sold. Large differences must be allocated between Work in Process, Finished Goods, and Cost of Goods Sold.

The type of product costing system used in manufacturing operations is determined by the nature of the production process. **Job order costing** is used to accumulate the manufacturing costs for products manufactured in batches or intermittent production runs. **Process costing** is used to measure the cost of products manufactured in continuous-flow production processes.

In a job order cost system, product costs are accumulated on a **job cost sheet.** The top portion of the job cost sheet contains general information about the job, including a unique job number. Costs are accumulated in the middle section of the job cost sheet. When the job is completed, the total and unit costs are summarized in the bottom portion of the cost sheet. The cost of the completed job is transferred to Finished Goods Inventory.

Job cost sheets for jobs currently in production are called **open job cost sheets,** and they are the subsidiary ledger for the Work in Process Control account. Job cost sheets for completed jobs are called **closed job cost sheets** and are **no longer** part of work in process.

Departmental job cost sheets provide managers with more detailed information than general job cost sheets. Costs are accumulated for each cost element by production department or activity. The summary of costs section contains unit and total costs classified by departments and by cost elements.

Manufacturing costs must be recorded in the organization's accounting records and posted to the appropriate control accounts and subsidiary ledger accounts. The manufacturing costs must also be assigned to the correct cost objectives.

KEY TERMS   audit trail *(116)*
daily time ticket *(120)*
employee fring benefits *(119)*
gross payroll *(119)*
inventory acquisition *(116)*
inventory distribution *(116)*
job number *(129)*
job order cost sheet *(128)*
job order costing *(127)*
job time ticket *(120)*
labor distribution report *(121)*
manufacturing overhead
   applied *(124)*

manufacturing overhead
   control *(121)*
manufacturing overhead rate *(122)*
materials requisition *(117)*
payroll taxes *(119)*
overapplied overhead *(125)*
underapplied overhead *(125)*
process costing *(128)*
purchase order *(117)*
purchase requisition *(117)*
receiving report *(117)*
returned materials report *(117)*
subsidiary ledger *(125)*

QUESTIONS

1. Last summer, Charlie Greene had a job with a large, successful corporation that produces many electronic products. Charlie spent much of his working time accumulating cost data, using a process costing system, for a production line assembling parts of a ship-to-shore radio-telephone that the company makes. As a result, he also learned something about process costing. A friend of Charlie's father operates a small manufacturing operation, and during a conversation told Charlie that he had just started production on an order of radio-telephones. When he indicated that he accounted for this order using a job order system, Charlie insisted that the method could not be appropriate, or his former employer would have used it too. Explain why one company would use process costing and another job order costing for the same product. Justify each method.

2. A primary function of accounting information is to allow managers to exercise control over operations. Job order costing is a system of accounting for the costs of products, and as such should provide management with the ability to control production. What are some of the control aspects of job order costing systems, and how are they used for control purposes?

3. Accounting is traditionally a historical discipline, reporting on events that have happened in the past, and showing the financial consequence of such events. When accountants apply overhead to products in order to determine product costs, they do not use historical information on overhead costs, although it is available. How can you justify the practice of applying overhead using rates obtained by making estimates of future events?

4. "It does not really matter what sort of overhead application base is used to arrive at an overhead application rate. On the one hand, all overhead must be applied to products, and in a job order system a given quantity of overhead will be applied to all products in a batch, so each product will be assigned the same amount of overhead cost, no matter what the base. On the other hand, the application base is only an estimate anyway, and at the end of the year an adjustment must be made to ensure that the amount applied is the same as the actual amount, so whatever the application rate, products will be assigned the actual cost eventually." Discuss the flaws in the reasoning illustrated by the above statements.

5. (AICPA) What is the rationale supporting the use of process costing instead of job order costing for product costing purposes?

EXERCISES

Ex. 4-1
Journal Entries for a Manufacturing Firm

The following information is selected from the manufacturing operations of Mellon Company, which uses a perpetual inventory system.

a. Materials are purchased on account for $60,000.

b. Materials requisitions are filled for direct materials costing $20,000 and for indirect materials costing $5,000.

c. Weekly machine hours totaled 1,800. Manufacturing overhead is applied at $5 per machine hour.

d. Job 506 is completed. It consists of 60 units, $2,000 direct materials cost, $3,000 direct labor cost, and $6,000 manufacturing overhead cost.

e. Job 506 is sold to a customer for $16,000 cash.

f. The property tax bill for the year in the amount of $10,000 is received; 75 percent is for manufacturing facilities.

REQUIRED   Journalize the above events and transactions.

Ex. 4-2
Computing Underapplied and Overapplied Overhead

The Nikie Products Company uses direct labor hours as the basis for applying overhead to products. Estimated manufacturing overhead costs for 1985 are $200,000, and estimated direct labor hours for the year are 32,000 hours. During 1985, 36,400 actual direct labor hours were worked and the Manufacturing Overhead Control account had a year-end balance of $238,420.

REQUIRED

a. Compute the manufacturing overhead rate for 1985.

b. Compute the amount of applied manufacturing overhead for 1985.

c. Compute the amount of underapplied or overapplied overhead for the year.

d. Compute the actual overhead cost per direct labor hour.

Ex. 4-3
Job Order Cost Sheet

The Holmsted Manufacturing Company manufactures twenty different products in intermittent production runs. A job order costing system is used to accumulate and report product costs. Job number 912 was started on May 18 and completed on May 21. Two hundred steel castings were produced. Materials were issued to the job on May 18 and May 20 in the amounts of $1,460 and $1,220, with materials requisitions no. 6711 and 6788 respectively. The weekly payroll distribution report issued May 22 showed 125 direct labor hours at a cost of $1,100 for Job 912. Manufacturing overhead is applied at the rate of $8.00 per direct labor hour.

REQUIRED   Prepare a job cost sheet in good form for Job number 912.

Ex. 4-4
Job Cost Sheet

Presented below are summaries of materials requisitions and payroll costs for the first week in June for the Nebo Manufacturing Company. Manufacturing overhead is applied to jobs at the rate of $6.50 per direct labor hour. Job number 2271 was started and completed during the first week of June, and 100 units were manufactured.

Direct Labor Summary 6/8				Materials Requisition Summary			
Job Number	Labor Hours	Amount		Date	Job Numbers	Req. No.	Amount
2265	120	$ 960		6/2	2271	15741	$1,640
2268	210	1,685		6/2	2268	15742	860
2270	140	1,050		6/3	2271	15743	945
2271	345	2,898		6/3	2272	15744	1,325
2272	190	1,425		6/3	2273	15745	720
2273	85	765		6/4	2268	15746	415
2274	60	480		6/5	2271	15747	210
				6/5	2274	15748	1,167
				6/6	2272	15749	674
				6/6	2273	15750	860

REQUIRED   Prepare a job cost sheet in good form for Job number 2271.

Ex. 4-5
Job Order Costing and the Work in Process Account

Refer to the data in Exercise 4-4. Jobs 2271 through 2274 were started during the week, but only Job 2271 was completed. All other jobs identified in the payroll summary report were completed during the first week of June.

REQUIRED

a. Prepare job cost sheets for the jobs that are not completed at the end of the week.
b. Determine the balance in the Work in Process Control account at the end of the week.

Ex. 4-6
Computing Underapplied and Overapplied Overhead

Perez Manufacturing Company has been using direct labor hours as its application base for applying overhead to products. The newly hired chief accountant suggested recently that it would require less clerical work if the company would use direct labor cost as its application base.

Budgeted overhead cost for 1985 was $600,000, and budgeted direct labor hours were 100,000. Budgeted direct labor cost was $800,000. The balance in the Manufacturing Overhead Control account at the end of 1985 was $629,000. Actual direct labor hours worked were 104,300 and actual direct labor cost was $893,500.

REQUIRED

a. Using direct labor hours as the overhead application base, calculate the manufacturing overhead rate, the amount of overhead applied in 1985, and the underapplied or overapplied overhead for the year.
b. Using direct labor cost as the overhead application base, compute the manufacturing overhead rate, the overhead applied for 1985, and the underapplied or overapplied overhead for the year.

Ex. 4-7
Departmental Product Cost Information

United Nuclear Products just sold 800 pressure rings, otherwise known as C-rings. C-rings are produced in job-lot batches for special orders and are not carried in general inventory ready for sale. Job production data are presented below.

Job 6113 (800 C-rings)

Production Department	Direct Materials	Direct Labor		Manufacturing Overhead Rate
		Hours	Rate	
Forming	$4,200	140	$6.00 per hour	120% of prime cost
Chemical Treatment	1,000	200	5.00 per hour	120% of prime cost
Pressurizing	200	80	4.00 per hour	$5.00 per direct labor hour
Crating	320	24	5.00 per hour	$5.00 per direct labor hour

REQUIRED   Prepare the summary of costs section of a departmental job cost sheet for this production run of C-rings.

Ex. 4-8
Accounting for
Underapplied or
Overapplied
Overhead

The Digbie Manufacturing Company uses a predetermined manufacturing overhead rate to apply overhead cost to its products. The rate for 1985 was $12.00 per machine hour. Company policy is to assign any underapplied or overapplied overhead to the cost of goods sold account. If underapplied or overapplied overhead is greater than 15 percent of actual overhead, the amount is assigned to work in process, finished goods, and cost of goods sold in proportion to the amount of applied overhead that remains in the three accounts at year-end. At the end of 1985, the following account balances existed:

Manufacturing Overhead Control	$184,000
Manufacturing Overhead Applied	226,000
Work in Process Control (20% is applied MOH)	228,000
Finished Goods Inventory (25% is applied MOH)	91,200
Cost of Goods Sold (25% is applied MOH)	638,400

REQUIRED
a. Calculate the underapplied or overapplied overhead for 1985.
b. Calculate underapplied or overapplied overhead as a percentage of actual manufacturing overhead.
c. Prepare a journal entry to dispose of the underapplied or overapplied overhead in accordance with company policy.
d. Determine the balances in Work in Process, Finished Goods, and Cost of Goods Sold after the journal entry you made in part c.

Ex. 4-9
Departmental Job
Cost Sheet

The Seville Company uses departmental job cost sheets to accumulate the manufacturing costs for the products it produces. Job number 3144, consisting of 100 wall clocks, was started on October 7 and completed on October 18. Overhead is applied at the rate of 80 percent of direct labor cost. Below are weekly data pertaining to Job number 3144.

Week Ending October 11:

Department	Date	Material Requisition No.	Labor Distribution Report Number	Amount
Fabricating	Oct. 7	RQ3323		$2,220
Fabricating	Oct. 11		LD10/11	1,760
Assembly	Oct. 10	RQ3336		3,250
Assembly	Oct. 11		LD10/11	1,910

Week Ending October 18:

Department	Date	Material Requisition No.	Labor Distribution Report Number	Amount
Assembly	Oct. 18		LD10/18	$1,080
Finishing	Oct. 14	RQ3351		625
Finishing	Oct. 18		LD10/18	1,330

REQUIRED   Prepare a departmental job order cost sheet in good form for Job number 3144.

Ex. 4-10
Manufacturing
Overhead Control

Below are selected transactions of the Hopple Street Manufacturing Company.

a. Indirect materials costing $945 are issued to production.
b. Purchased $10,485 of sheet steel on open account.
c. A bill for $375 was received from a firm that repaired the hydraulic metal press on Friday.
d. Sent $6,900 of lumber and $3,340 of cloth from the inventory storeroom to the fabricating department for Job number 5427.
e. Overhead is applied to production at the rate of $7.00 per machine hour. During this week, 2,750 machine hours were clocked.
f. Job 5422 is completed at a cost of $34,960.
g. Received a bill of $1,350 for maintenance work on metal shearing equipment.
h. A utility bill is received for $4,000. Eighty percent of the bill is attributable to the manufacturing activities of the business.
i. Received a bill for $870 for repairs on the word processor.
j. Job 5422 is delivered to the customer and a bill sent for $47,350.
k. Paid the weekly payroll. Gross pay was $29,400; withholding items included $3,760 for federal income tax, $1,740 for FICA taxes, $2,120 for state income tax, and $420 for union dues.
l. Other payroll-related items include the employer's share of FICA taxes, and state and federal unemployment taxes of 2.7 percent and .7 percent of gross pay, respectively.
m. Direct labor is $26,100 of the total payroll. The rest is indirect labor.

REQUIRED

a. Journalize all transactions that affect the Manufacturing Overhead Control account or the Manufacturing Overhead Applied account.
b. Post journal entries to the overhead control account and to the appropriate subsidiary ledger accounts.

Ex. 4-11
Computing
Overhead Account
Balances

Below are partial data for overhead costs and activity levels for three **independent** companies.

	Kayvert	Frummly	Cavenaugh
Budgeted overhead cost	$800,000	$_____	$750,000
Actual overhead cost	$872,000		$743,000
Applied overhead	$857,600	$882,000	_____
Budgeted activity level	250,000 DLH	200,000 DLH	
Actual activity level	_____	196,000 DLH	310,000 DLH
Underapplied or (overapplied) overhead	_____	$(23,400)	$(32,000)

REQUIRED   Find the missing values for each of the companies.

Ex. 4-12
Understanding
Manufacturing
Overhead Costs

In 1985 the Aurielious Company began making Christmas tree stands. Direct material costs average $3.80 per unit and direct labor time averages .4 of an hour per stand at $11 per hour. Manufacturing overhead is applied to products at the rate of $9 per direct labor hour. The expected activity level for the year was 40,000 direct labor hours. During the accounting period, 80,000 units were completed. At the end of the accounting period there were 6,000 units in finished goods inventory and 10,000 units remained in ending work in process inventory. Eighty percent of the labor required to produce the Christmas tree stands has been performed on the units in ending work in process inventory. There were no beginning inventories. At the end of the accounting period the Manufacturing Overhead Control account had a balance of $312,000.

REQUIRED

a. Calculate the balance in the Manufacturing Overhead Applied account at the end of the accounting period.
b. Calculate the amount of applied overhead in the Work in Process Control, the Finished Goods Inventory Control, and the Cost of Goods Sold accounts at the end of the accounting period.
c. Calculate the underapplied or overapplied overhead for the year.
d. Calculate the budgeted manufacturing overhead cost.

PROBLEMS

P. 4-1
Recording Cost
Flows

The R. Jones Manufacturing Company produces office furniture and uses a job order costing system to accumulate product costs. Below are a number of transactions that occurred during the last week of the month.

a. Sent $4,800 of steel and $1,750 of lumber from the inventory storeroom to the fabricating department for Job number 14326.
b. Purchased $12,640 of cold rolled steel on open account.
c. Paid the weekly payroll. Gross pay was $26,700; withholding items included $3,240 for federal income tax, $1,565 for FICA tax, $1,725 for state income tax, and $578 for union dues.
d. Other payroll-related items include the employer's share of FICA taxes, and state and federal unemployment taxes of 2.7 percent and .7 percent of gross pay, respectively.

e. Direct labor is $24,260 of the gross payroll. The rest is indirect labor.
f. Indirect materials in the amount of $945 are issued to production.
g. Overhead is applied to production at the rate of $5.50 per direct labor hour. During this week's pay period, 2,460 direct labor hours were clocked.
h. A bill for $375 was received from a firm that repaired the hydraulic metal press on Tuesday.
i. Job 14322 is completed at a cost of $28,442.
j. Job 14322 is delivered to the customer and a bill sent for $39,880.
k. A utility bill is received for $3,600. Eighty percent of the bill is attributable to the manufacturing activities of the business.

REQUIRED   Prepare journal entries in good form for each of the transactions described above.

P. 4-2
Accounting for
Underapplied and
Overapplied
Overhead

Jefferson Ceramics Company manufactures a variety of products in a single manufacturing plant. Manufacturing overhead is applied to products at the rate of 150 percent of direct labor cost. At the end of the year the overhead control account has a debit balance of $620,000. The company assigns any underapplied or overapplied overhead to cost of goods sold unless applied overhead is more than 20 percent different from actual overhead. In such cases the difference is assigned to work in process, finished goods, and cost of goods sold in proportion to the amount of applied overhead that still remains in each account at year-end. Below is a listing of the amount of **applied overhead** that remained in each account at the end of the accounting year.

Work in process	$ 45,000
Finished goods	90,000
Cost of goods sold	315,000
Total applied overhead	$450,000

REQUIRED
a. Calculate the total underapplied or overapplied overhead for the year.
b. Calculate the distribution of underapplied or overapplied overhead and record the distribution.
c. Calculate the ending balance of applied overhead in work in process, finished goods, and cost of goods sold.

P. 4-3
The Effect of
Overhead on
Product Costs

Starco Music, Inc., manufactures an upright piano that has the following production costs:

Direct labor	$200
Direct materials	450
Manufacturing overhead	150
Total cost	$800

The piano sells for $1,000 yielding a gross margin of $200. During the accounting period just completed, actual manufacturing overhead was 18 percent more than the amount of overhead applied.

REQUIRED
a. What is the actual amount of overhead cost for the piano?
b. What is the percentage change in product cost caused by the underapplied overhead?
c. Compute the actual gross margin for the Starco piano.
d. Compute the percentage change in gross margin caused by the underapplied overhead.

P. 4-4
Computing and
Using Overhead
Rates

A manufacturer of small appliances estimates overhead costs of $500,000 for 1985. Three possible overhead application bases are being considered by management: direct labor hours, direct labor cost, and machine hours. Estimated 1985 activity levels for each of the potential application bases are given below:

Direct labor hours   100,000 hours
Direct labor cost $800,000
Machine hours   80,000 hours

A counter-top oven-broiler manufactured by the company requires 2 direct labor hours, $18.00 of direct labor cost, and 1.2 hours of machine time. The balance in the Manufacturing Overhead Control account was $576,000 on December 31, 1985. During 1985, 120,000 direct labor hours were worked at a cost of $970,000, and 90,000 machine hours were used. There were 10,000 oven broilers manufactured in 1985 requiring 20,000 direct labor hours.

REQUIRED

a. Compute the 1985 manufacturing overhead rate using each of the three potential application bases.
b. Compute the unit cost of manufacturing overhead for the oven-broilers using each of the application bases.
c. Compute the underapplied or overapplied overhead that would have occurred in 1985 using each of the application bases.
d. Assume direct labor hours was used as the application base. Compute the unit cost of overhead using actual overhead cost for the year.

P. 4-5
Analyzing Labor
Costs

The management of Reven Company is negotiating a new labor agreement with its employees. The labor contract that expires at the end of the current year includes the following elements:

Wage rate $6.00 per hour
Paid vacation   2 weeks per year
Paid holidays   10 days per year
Employer contributions to insurance programs $.50 per hour worked

The union for the employees has proposed a new agreement that has the following provisions:

Wage rate $6.30 per hour
Paid vacation   4 weeks per year
Paid holidays   15 days per year
Employer's contribution to life and health insur-
  ance $1.00 per hour worked
Employer's contribution to education and recre-
  ation programs $.50 per hour worked

The union negotiating team refers to the plan as one that provides employees with a very modest wage increase of 5 percent while concentrating on items that affect the employees' quality of life. Employees work five-day weeks and eight hours a day. Reven Company's payroll taxes are 10 percent of gross wages.

REQUIRED

a. Compute the total cost per labor hour worked under the current labor agreement.
b. Compute the total cost per labor hour worked under the union's proposed contract.

c. Compute the change in the total cost per labor hour worked between the two labor contracts.

d. Express the employee benefits as a percentage of gross wages earned under both labor contracts.

P. 4-6
Analyzing
Overhead Costs

Stone Company applies manufacturing overhead at the rate of $9.50 per machine hour. During 1985, 40,000 machine hours were clocked. At the end of 1985, the manufacturing overhead control account had a balance of $352,000. Job number 3213, consisting of 100 microwave ovens, was started and completed during the year. The job required 1,000 machine hours, total direct material of $12,000, and direct labor costs of $10,000.

REQUIRED

a. Compute the underapplied or overapplied overhead for 1985.

b. Compute the per unit costs of the ovens produced in Job number 3213.

c. Compute the overhead rate that would have yielded no underapplied or overapplied overhead in 1985.

d. Compute the total and per unit amount of overhead that would have been charged to the ovens if actual overhead rather than the predetermined overhead rate had been used to assign overhead to the job.

P. 4-7
Accounting for
Payroll

The Bean Blossom String Factory manufactures stringed musical instruments, and uses a job order costing system to measure product costs. Employees prepare daily time tickets identifying the jobs they worked on during the day. Any time not specifically identified with a job is classified as indirect labor and charged to manufacturing overhead. A payroll distribution report is prepared weekly and is the basis for making the payroll journal entries and assigning payroll costs to production. Below is the labor distribution report for the last week in April.

Bean Blossom String Factory
Labor Distribution Report
April 30

Name	Job Number 453	456	457	453	459	460	MOH	Total Hours	Hourly Wage Rate	Total Cost
J. Skorinski	12	8		17		3		40	$7	$ 280.00
P. Lucas	17	12	6				5	40	7	280.00
S. Petersen		15	9	10		2	4	40	8	320.00
J. Yamamoto	8	4	23	4				39	8	312.00
M. McKittrick			6	5	22		7	40	7.50	300.00
F. Johnson		13	10	12			5	40	6.50	260.00
B. Dodd	23				9		8	40	9	360.00
L. Stone				14		21	5	40	7.50	300.00
R. Grubbs				12	7	16	3	38	8	304.00
G. DeSloover	2	6	22	10				40	9	360.00
Totals	62	58	76	84	38	42	37	397		$3,076.00

In addition to gross wages the company must pay FICA taxes, state unemployment taxes of 2 percent, and federal unemployment taxes of .7 percent. Assume that 15 percent of gross wages are withheld from employees' checks for federal income taxes, 5 percent is withheld for state income taxes, and 3 percent is withheld for union dues. For convenience, assume the FICA tax rate is 7 percent.

a. Prepare the journal entry to record the payroll and the payroll taxes.
b. Prepare the journal entry to distribute the payroll to the appropriate cost objectives.
c. Prepare a schedule that identifies the amount of direct labor cost charged to each job for the week.

P. 4-8
Departmental Job
Cost Sheet

The Medix Manufacturing Company manufactures medical equipment for use in hospital emergency rooms. The data below pertain to Order 9100, the production of medical equipment that sells for $5,000 per unit.

Customer: Los Pembert County Hospital
Description: 10 cardiovascular support units
Date started: Feb. 5
Date finished: Feb. 19

	Week Ending 2/12	Week Ending 2/19
Department 1:		
Materials	$5,200	$4,100
Direct labor rate	$5.00 per hour	$5.00 per hour
Labor hours	1,000	800
Manufacturing overhead rate	$6.00 per hour	$6.00 per hour
Department 2:		
Direct labor rate	$4.00 per hour	$4.00 per hour
Labor hours	650	500
Manufacturing overhead rate	$6.00 per hour	$6.00 per hour

a. Prepare a departmental job cost sheet using the above data.
b. What is the percentage gross margin on this job?

P. 4-9
Using Product Cost
Data

Baxter Electronics manufactures a variety of components for the aerospace industry. The company evaluates the price of each product every year according to company policy. The firm attempts to price as low as possible to remain competitive, but not to sell at a nonprofitable price. The desired price for products provides a 35 percent gross margin on sales, although competition sometimes forces less profitable prices. The minimum acceptable gross margin is 25 percent.

One of the company's largest selling products, a turbine temperature gauge, should have its price reevaluated based on production costs of the past year. The current selling price is $100. Below are cost data for the three production runs during the past year.

Job Number	Date Completed	Units Produced	Material	Labor	Overhead	Total Cost
			Material	Labor	Overhead	
6120	3/12	2,000	$ 50,000	$ 60,000	$ 20,000	$130,000
7115	6/1	3,000	80,000	90,000	35,000	205,000
8930	9/3	4,000	100,000	130,000	60,000	290,000
Totals		9,000	$230,000	$280,000	$115,000	$625,000

a. Use the above data to determine what the price should be, based on:
1. The cost of the first production run.
2. Average unit cost for the year.
3. Unit cost of the most recent production run.

b. Do the cost data suggest any significant trends in costs or significant variables that may affect the cost of the product? Explain.

c. Of the prices computed in part *a*, which one would you select? Explain.

P. 4-10
Analyzing the
Effects of Overhead
Costs

The Comstock Cosmetics Company manufactures a complete line of fine cosmetics. A new line of products is designed to satisfy the most discriminating customers. An important item in the new line is an expensive facial cream. In order to keep the price close to that of competitors' products of similar quality, a careful cost analysis was done. The current price is $12.00 per jar, which is 150 percent of the product's estimated manufactured cost. Data accumulated on first-year sales and production costs indicate that overhead costs were significantly higher than estimated. Below are estimated and actual cost data for the production of the cream.

	Unit Cost	
	Original Estimate	Actual Cost
Direct materials	$4.50	$4.30
Direct labor	1.50	1.60
Manufacturing overhead	2.00	3.50
Total cost	$8.00	$9.40

The company estimated first-year sales of the cream of 40,000 jars. Actual sales for the first year were 56,000 jars. Variable costs associated with marketing the product were $78,400.

Analyze the data and determine:

a. The dollar impact on profits of incorrectly estimating overhead costs.

b. The change in gross margin percentage caused by the higher overhead costs.

c. The correct product price based on the original cost/price relationship expressed in the problem.

d. If the price you calculated in part *c* of the problem is used and causes a reduction in sales of the product from the current level to 36,000 units, and the per unit cost of marketing remains the same, should the price be changed or should it remain as is?

P. 4-11
Understanding Cost
Flows

Chun Motor Parts rebuilds automobile generators and sells them to parts stores and automobile repair shops. The company buys the generators from scrap dealers and other suppliers and installs whatever parts and materials are necessary to repair the generators. On January 1, 1985, Chun had no beginning inventories. During 1985, 55,000 generators were started and 47,000 were completed. The company sold 42,000 generators for $53 each with a 90-day guarantee. In 1985, $862,000 of raw materials was charged to production, of which $44,000 was indirect materials. Production payroll cost for the year was $525,000. Direct labor was 90 percent of total payroll. Overhead is applied at the rate of 120 percent of direct labor cost. At the end of 1985, the Work in Process Control account had a balance of $179,600 made up of

$66,000 of direct materials, $49,500 of direct labor, and $64,100 of applied manufacturing overhead. Budgeted overhead for 1985 was $550,000 and actual overhead for 1985 was $576,000.

REQUIRED

a. Calculate the total applied overhead for 1985.
b. Calculate the total amount of production costs charged to Work in Process Control during 1985.
c. Calculate the cost of goods manufactured for 1985.
d. Calculate the average unit cost for each cost element and the average unit cost in total for units completed in 1985.
e. Using the average unit cost of completed units in 1985, calculate the year-end balance in the Finished Goods Inventory Control account.
f. Calculate underapplied or overapplied manufacturing overhead for 1985.

P. 4-12
Departmental Job
Cost Sheet

Jethroe Machine Tool Company manufactures specialized tools and machines to meet the manufacturing and other needs of customers. The special nature of the products the company makes requires careful monitoring of production costs. Therefore, the company uses a departmental job order costing system. Weekly summaries are prepared for labor and materials. Below is the labor distribution summary and the materials requisition summary for the week of February 14–18. Both reports identify the job number and the department for the resources used. Job number 165 was a special order to produce high-grade metric calibrated torque wrenches for the Loomis Company.

Jethroe Machine Tool Company
Labor Distribution Report
For the Week Ending February 18

| | | Hours Charged to Job Number | | | | Assigned | Total |
Employee	Department	163	164	165	166	to MOH	Hours
F. Morgan	Fabricating	—	—	10	28	2	40
B. Evans	Fabricating	—	—	20	16	4	40
A. Brula	Fabricating	—	—	23	13	4	40
M. Wettle	Welding	11	10	15	—	3	39
T. Terry	Welding	—	9	9	17	5	40
P. Johnson	Machining	—	6	5	19	6	36
E. Kafer	Machining	21	—	15	4	—	40
C. Germer	Assembly	—	13	19	—	8	40
L. Hagg	Assembly	12	—	17	4	3	36
C. Hall	Assembly	15	—	—	14	3	32
Total hours		59	38	133	115	38	383

Wage Rates	
Fabricating	$8.00 per hour
Welding	9.00
Machining	9.00
Assembly	7.00

Jethroe Machine Tool Company
Summary of Material Requisitions
For the Week of February 14–18

Date	Materials Requisition Number	Job Number	Department	Amount
2/14	972	165	Fabricating	$ 700
2/14	973	166	Fabricating	3,900
2/15	974	163	Welding	350
2/16	975	164	Assembly	1,130
2/16	976	163	Welding	175
2/17	977	166	Fabricating	2,160
2/17	978	165	Fabricating	950
2/17	979	165	Welding	600
2/18	980	164	Assembly	2,060
2/18	981	165	Assembly	630
2/18	982	MOH	General	210

Overhead is applied to jobs using the following rates:

Fabricating: 75% of direct labor cost
Welding: $6 per direct labor hour
Machining: $6 per direct labor hour
Assembly: $6 per direct labor hour

The four jobs listed were all started during the week and were the only jobs in process during the week. Only Job 165 was completed by the end of the week.

The company's normal gross margin is 30 percent, but on special orders policy is to double the normal gross margin.

REQUIRED

a. Prepare a departmental job cost sheet in good form for Job 165.
b. Compute the amount of the sales invoice to Loomis Company.
c. Assuming that the jobs listed are the only jobs in production, compute the cost of work in process at the end of the week.

P. 4-13 (CMA)
Using
Manufacturing
Overhead Concepts

Baehr Company is a manufacturing company with a fiscal year that runs from July 1 to June 30. The company uses a job order accounting system for its production costs.

A predetermined overhead rate based upon direct labor hours is used to apply overhead to individual jobs. A flexible budget of overhead costs was prepared for the 1984–85 fiscal year as shown below.

Direct labor hours	100,000	120,000	140,000
Variable overhead costs	$325,000	$390,000	$455,000
Fixed overhead costs	216,000	216,000	216,000
Total overhead costs	$541,000	$606,000	$671,000

Although the annual ideal capacity is 150,000 direct labor hours, company officials have determined 120,000 direct labor hours as normal capacity for the year.

The information presented below is for November. Jobs 77-50 and 77-51 were completed during November.

Inventories November 1:

Raw materials and supplies	$ 10,500
Work in process (Job 77-50)	54,000
Finished goods	112,500

Purchases of raw materials and supplies:

Raw materials	$135,000
Supplies	15,000

Materials and supplies requisitioned for production:

Job 77-50	$ 45,000
Job 77-51	37,500
Job 77-52	25,500
Supplies	12,000
Total materials and supplies	$120,000

Factory direct labor hours:

Job 77-50	3,500 DLH
Job 77-51	3,000 DLH
Job 77-52	2,000 DLH

Labor costs:

Direct labor wages	$ 51,000
Indirect labor wages (4,000 hours)	15,000
Supervisory salaries	6,000

Building occupancy costs (heat, light, depreciation, etc.):

Factory facilities	$ 6,500
Sales offices	1,500
Administrative offices	1,000
Total occupancy costs	$ 9,000

Factory equipment costs:

Power	$ 4,000
Repairs and maintenance	1,500
Depreciation	1,500
Other	1,000
Total factory equipment cost	$ 8,000

REQUIRED   Select the best answer for each of these items.

1. The predetermined overhead rate to be used to apply overhead to individual jobs during the current fiscal year is
   a. $3.25 per DLH.   d. $5.41 per DLH.
   b. $4.69 per DLH.   e. some rate other than those shown above.
   c. $5.05 per DLH.

Note: Without prejudice to your answer to item 1 assume the predetermined overhead rate is $4.50 per direct labor hour. Use this amount in answering items 2 through 6.

2. The total cost of Job 77-50 is
   a. $81,750.   d. $146,750.
   b. $135,750.   e. some amount other than those shown above.
   c. $142,750.

3. The factory overhead costs applied to Job 77-52 during November were
   a. $9,000.   d. $8,000.
   b. $47,500.   e. some amount other than those shown here.
   c. $46,500.

4. The total amount of overhead applied to jobs during November was
   a. $29,250.   d. $56,250.
   b. $38,250.   e. some amount other than those shown here.
   c. $47,250.

5. Actual factory overhead incurred during November was
   a. $38,000.   d. $50,500.
   b. $41,500.   e. some amount other than those shown here.
   c. $47,500.

6. At the end of the last fiscal year (June 30), Baehr Company had the following account balances:

Overapplied overhead	$ 1,000
Cost of goods sold	980,000
Work in process inventory	38,000
Finished goods inventory	82,000

   The most common treatment of the overapplied overhead would be to
   a. prorate it between work in process inventory and finished goods inventory.
   b. prorate it between work in process inventory, finished goods inventory, and cost of goods sold.
   c. carry it as a deferred credit on the balance sheet.
   d. carry it as miscellaneous operating revenue on the income statement.
   e. credit it to cost of goods sold.

P. 4-14
Analyzing and Using Manufacturing Overhead Costs

Below are December 31, 1985, account balances of Rovelier Company, a manufacturer of snowmobiles.

Sales salaries	$ 85,400
Advertising	44,000
Raw materials inventory	126,100
Direct materials	325,000

Work in process	$ 73,900
Indirect labor	22,700
Depreciation, factory	31,000
Property taxes (70% production plant)	18,000
Fire insurance (80% production plant)	9,800
Sales commissions	28,500
Administrative salaries	167,200
Finished goods	77,300
Direct labor	293,800
Indirect material	11,600
Utilities (80 percent factory)	45,000
Rent, office equipment	8,700
Depreciation, office	17,400
Depreciation, factory equipment	44,000
Sales	981,700
Miscellaneous office expense	4,300
Sales returns and allowances	36,100

All accounts have normal balances. Beginning work in process was $49,000 and beginning finished goods was $87,300.

Rovelier's 1985 budget called for production of 800 snowmobiles. On average it takes 26 hours of direct labor per snowmobile at a wage rate of $11 per hour. The manufacturing overhead rate is $6 per direct labor hour.

During 1985, 920 snowmobiles were produced. Actual direct labor hours averaged 3 per unit more than expected.

REQUIRED
a. Calculate the total prime cost for 1985.
b. Calculate the balance in the Manufacturing Overhead Control account at December 31, 1985.
c. Calculate the underapplied or overapplied overhead for the year.
d. Calculate the average unit cost of snowmobiles completed during 1985.
e. What percentage of the total product cost is manufacturing overhead?

CASES

Case 4-1
Accounting for Job
Order Costing
Activities

The Waterford Hi-Type Products Company makes office and general-purpose furniture for commercial and institutional customers. Many of the company's products are manufactured as special orders. Some are manufactured for general stock. All production is in job lots, and a job order costing system is used to measure the cost of products. At the end of July, the company had three jobs in production. The production costs to date on these jobs are shown on the open job costs sheets below. Manufacturing overhead is applied to products at the rate of 80 percent of direct labor cost. Overhead is applied at the time direct labor is charged to jobs.

Expected sales for the year are $840,000 and expected annual operating expenses are $156,000. The company has a net investment in assets of $945,000. The July 31 inventory balances are $34,600 in Finished Goods and $27,900 in Raw Materials. During the first week of August the following transactions and events took place:

Aug. 2 Purchased lumber costing $2,600, vinyl covering costing $900, and foam padding costing $700, all from the same supplier.

Aug. 2 Started Job number 8745 to make office lounge chairs for Slater Company. Issued $1,550 of direct material to the job on requisition number MRQ12774.

Aug. 3 Issued $900 of materials to Job number 8743 as reported in MRQ12775.

Aug. 3 Issued $360 of cleaning compound and $175 of lubricating material to the factory maintenance department; MRQ12776.

Aug. 4 Started the production of folding chairs for open stock with Job number 8746. Issued $1,880 of material to production with MRQ12777.

Aug. 5 Completed Job number 8741, the production of 100 bar stools.

Aug. 5 Received property tax bill for $8,500. Eighty percent is for the production facility.

Aug. 6 Completed Job number 8743 which yielded 50 desk chairs.

Aug. 7 The weekly gross manufacturing payroll was $9,200. Federal withholding is 15 percent, state withholding is 4 percent, FICA tax is 7 percent, and other withholding is 3 percent. Employer payroll taxes total 11 percent of gross payroll.

Aug. 7 The weekly labor distribution showed the following direct labor costs. All other labor costs are indirect labor.

Job	Amount
8741	$ 600
8743	1,200
8744	1,800
8745	1,600
8746	2,700

Aug. 7 Sold Job number 8743 on open account for $190 per unit.

OPEN JOB COST SHEETS

Waterford Hi-Type Products
Job Cost Sheet

Date started 7/25/85
Date completed
Product Bar stools
Job number 8741
Quantity
Customer Stock

Direct Materials			Direct Labor			Manufacturing Overhead		
Date	Reference	Amount	Date	Reference	Amount	Date	Reference	Amount
7/25	MRQ12765	$2,100	7/31	LD 7/31	$1,400	7/31	LD 7/31	$1,120
7/29	MRQ12772	800						

Summary of Costs

Item	Total Cost	Unit Cost
Direct materials		
Direct labor		
Manufacturing overhead		
Totals		

Waterford Hi-Type Products
Job Cost Sheet

Date started ___7/29/85___   Job number ___8743___
Date completed _____   Quantity _____
Product ___Desk chairs___   Customer ___Cranston Corp.___

Direct Materials			Direct Labor			Manufacturing Overhead		
Date	Reference	Amount	Date	Reference	Amount	Date	Reference	Amount
7/29	MRQ12770	$2,700	7/31	LD 7/31	$800	7/31	LD 7/31	$640

Summary of Costs

Item	Total Cost	Unit Cost
Direct materials	_____	_____
Direct labor	_____	_____
Manufacturing overhead	_____	_____
Totals	_____	_____

Waterford Hi-Type Products
Job Cost Sheet

Date started ___7/29/85___   Job number ___8744___
Date completed _____   Quantity _____
Product ___Folding chairs___   Customer ___Kramer College___

Direct Materials			Direct Labor			Manufacturing Overhead		
Date	Reference	Amount	Date	Reference	Amount	Date	Reference	Amount
7/29	MRQ12773	$2,100	7/31	LD 7/31	$600	7/31	LD 7/31	$480

Summary of Costs

Item	Total Cost	Unit Cost
Direct materials	_____	_____
Direct labor	_____	_____
Manufacturing overhead	_____	_____
Totals	_____	_____

REQUIRED

a. Compute the July 31 balance in work in process control.
b. Journalize the transactions for the first week of August.
c. Post all necessary data to the appropriate job cost sheet.
d. Complete any job cost sheets for finished jobs.
e. Compute the balance in the work in process account at the end of the first week in August.
f. Compute the total balance in inventory accounts at the end of the first week in August.

g. Compute the gross margin on sales percentage for Job number 8743.

h. Assuming the gross margin on sales percentage on Job number 8743 is standard for the company, compute the expected profit for the year.

i. Based on the data available, discuss the performance of the company.

Case 4-2
Using Cost
Accounting Data

The typing pool of Tuph University's Economics Department employs four secretaries. They type correspondence, examinations, and research manuscripts, and also take dictation, distribute the mail, operate duplicating equipment, and perform other miscellaneous services for faculty members. The workload has been excessive during the past semester, resulting in long waiting times for low-priority work such as manuscripts. The dean would like to request an addition to the budget for another secretary but is not sure the request would be approved, especially since this would also entail buying another typewriter for $1,000. The secretaries receive a salary of $700 per month.

In order to justify the budget request the dean decides to conduct a study of typing pool productivity. Data are collected over a six-week period and yield the following findings:

1. Seventy-five percent of the secretaries' time is devoted to typing and the other 25 percent to other duties such as dictation, duplicating, and mail processing.

2. On the average, each secretary produces 3,750 lines of typing per month.

3. A 33 1/3 percent increase in typing output would be sufficient to satisfy current departmental demands. This could be provided by one new secretary whose duties would be devoted entirely to typing, but it would leave no excess capacity.

4. The nontyping work of the secretaries is performed efficiently and is not expected to change in volume.

During a faculty meeting the dean announces that one of the typing pool secretaries has resigned as of the end of the semester. Since this salary is already part of the departmental budget, a new secretary can be hired. But the dean expresses his doubts about getting budget approval for another position and typewriter and asks the faculty for suggestions.

One of the faculty members suggests not hiring a replacement for the secretary who is leaving. Instead he says the department should obtain word processing equipment for two of the remaining three secretaries. The equipment costs $36,000 but can be leased at $1,150 per month on a four-year lease, at the end of which the department would own the equipment. By leasing the equipment the dean would have to request only $340 per month increase in the budget. The equipment manufacturer claims it is possible to increase productivity fivefold, but a more realistic estimate is a threefold increase in typing capacity for the two secretaries who would be using the equipment. This increase is possible because material once typed with the equipment does not have to be retyped, as it is stored on magnetic discs. In addition, errors are corrected more easily and changes are easily made that often require retyping entire pages when the work is done on a typewriter.

The dean is not sure that three secretaries could handle the entire workload even with a threefold improvement in typing productivity with the new equipment. However, he thinks that the additional budget amount would be approved by the administration. Moreover, if waiting time for manuscripts is reduced he believes that faculty members would become more productive researchers.

a. Determine the salary cost of typing one line of material with the current arrangement.

b. Determine the typing capacity of the typing pool with three secretaries, two of whom use word processing equipment, and assuming that the nontyping workload does not change.

c. Calculate the cost of typing one line of material using the word processing equipment plus one typewriter based on the salaries of three secretaries and the lease payments on the equipment.

d. Recommend to the dean whether to increase the typing pool to five secretaries or acquire word processing equipment.

CHAPTER 5
Process Costing

Process costing is a system for measuring and reporting the cost of manufactured products that are produced in continuous-flow production processes. Most chemicals, petroleum products, and many plastics are costed using process costing. In contrast, job order costing is used to measure the cost of products that are produced in batches or intermittent production runs. With job order costing, costs are totaled and unit costs are computed when the job is completed. In process costing there is no specific time when all units are completed. Instead, as some units are completed, others are being started, and still others are in various stages of production. Regardless of the costing system, managers require timely product cost information. Consequently, accountants must provide periodic reports of product costs in process costing situations.

Common process costing products

In a process costing system, as with job order costing, accountants carefully measure the cost of manufacturing the product; therefore the cost accounting activities closely parallel the production activities. The parallel relationship between production and cost accounting is shown in Figure 5-1.

PROCESS COSTING ACTIVITIES

There are a number of specific steps in creating and operating a process costing system. These steps include:

1. Establish specific process costing centers.
2. Determine the time period to be covered by the product cost reports.
3. Accumulate actual manufacturing costs for each process center for the reporting period.
4. For each process center measure the quantity of product produced during the reporting period.
5. Compute unit costs for each process center using the manufacturing cost and output data gathered in steps 3 and 4.
6. Prepare the product cost reports.

Steps in a process costing system

Figure 5-1. As with all product costing, process costing activities parallel closely the physical production activities. The unit cost of each product is determined by dividing the costs of manufacturing by the quantity of production.

Parallel Flow of Production Activities and the Associated Cost Accounting Activities in a Process Costing System for Each Process Center

Production Activities	Cost Accounting Activities
Resources are used in production:	Costs are measured:
One or more raw materials is put into production.	Raw materials inventory is reduced and work in process is increased by cost of raw materials.
Direct labor is used to change the materials into a finished product.	Cost of direct labor is added to work in process inventory.
Manufacturing overhead costs such as production facilities, indirect materials, indirect labor, maintenance, and electricity are incurred.	Actual manufacturing overhead costs are recorded when incurred. Applied manufacturing overhead costs are added to work in process inventory.
Products are manufactured:	Output is measured in whole units.
Units started in previous period are completed.	Unit costs are computed:
Some units are started and completed during the current period.	The manufacturing costs for the period are divided by the production output to find the unit cost of products manufactured during the period.
Some units are started and only partially completed during the current period.	Accounting reports are prepared:
	Costs and production output data are used to prepare management reports and financial statements.

Establishing Process Costing Centers

The first step in developing a process costing system is to establish specific process costing centers. For each product, the accountant separates the manufacturing operations into specific identifiable production processes or activities. Each production process is called a **process center.** For example, a company makes souvenir metal ashtrays that look like football helmets. The product is manufactured by stamping the ashtrays out of sheet metal, then painting them and packaging them in a gift box. Stamping, painting, and packaging are three separate processes, each of which becomes a process center for which costs are accumulated and output is measured. A process center is distinguished by three characteristics:

Characteristics of process centers

1. Some specific identifiable production activity is performed.
2. The same type and amount of work is performed on all units passing through the process center.
3. Only one type of product passes through each process center.

In process costing, process centers are the focal point for accumulating manufacturing costs and measuring the amount of output. To determine the cost of a product, it is necessary to measure the cost of production in each process center used in making the product. The number of separate process centers necessary to complete a product depends on many factors, such as the type of product, the complexity of the production process, and the management of the manufacturing activities. One type of product may require only two or three process centers to complete; others may require 15 or more process centers. The number of process centers required to manufacture a product determines the amount of cost accounting work that must be done and the volume of cost data supplied to managers, but the cost accounting concepts and activities are similar for both simple and complex process costing situations.

Be careful not to confuse process centers with production departments in job order costing. Production departments are used to manufacture a variety of products from many different jobs, and each product may have significantly different kinds of work performed. In a process center, on the other hand, only one type of product is produced, and identical work is performed on each unit passing through the process center. A production department may have many process centers, each performing specific work on a particular product.

For example, a company makes five different types of computer terminals whose costs are accounted for using a process costing system. All of the terminals require assembly, but each type of terminal requires somewhat different assembly operations. Although all of the terminals are assembled in the assembly department, the company establishes a separate assembly process center for **each** type of computer terminal. The assembly department, then, consists of five process centers. It prepares five cost of production reports. Each report is identified according to the department as well as by product. Therefore, several cost of production reports may be labeled as assembly department reports, and each would identify a different product to show precisely which process center is reported. In addition, each product has process centers in other departments for additional necessary manufacturing activities.

Determining Reporting Intervals

In job order costing, unit costs are computed when the job is completed; with continuous-flow production there is a constant flow of products through the manufacturing process. The convenient starting and completion points found in job order costing do not exist in continuous-flow production. But managers need frequent, detailed cost accounting reports to manage effectively daily operations and plan future production.

Product costs should be timely

Accountants must prepare frequent cost accounting reports. How frequently cost accounting reports should be provided depends on the cost of preparing the reports and the benefits derived from them. Some companies may prepare product cost reports once a month, others once a week, and in some cases reports may be prepared daily. Whatever the reporting interval, the timing of the reports must be determined early so that the necessary cost accounting activities can be planned and accomplished.

Accumulating Manufacturing Costs

Manufacturing costs are accumulated for each process center

Once process cost centers have been clearly identified and cost reporting time intervals established, the manufacturing costs of direct materials, direct labor, and manufacturing overhead are accumulated for each process center for the period. If process centers are clearly defined, material, labor, and overhead costs can be assigned easily to the appropriate process center. Similarly, if the report timing interval is clearly defined and understood, manufacturing costs of one period will not be erroneously included in another reporting period. The actual accumulation of production costs is discussed and illustrated later in this chapter and in Chapter 6.

Measuring Production Output

In a continuous production process, with some units just started, others almost completed, and still others already finished, total manufacturing costs of a process center may be of little value to managers. What often is more informative is the unit cost of production in the process center for the period. But to measure unit costs, first it is necessary to know how many units were produced.

Accountants must measure the amount of output during the period for each process center

In process costing the accountant cannot wait until all units are completed to measure the amount of production output, because production is continuous. During any reporting period some units are started and completed, but usually there are some units in beginning inventory that were partially completed at the beginning of the period and are finished during the current reporting period. In addition, there may be some units started during the period but not completed. The partially completed units in ending inventory have had some work done on them during this reporting period, but they are not yet finished when the reporting period ends.

Output is measured in terms of equivalent whole units

To measure the amount of production, clearly we must include the units started and completed during the reporting period. But what do we do with the units started last period and the units that are only partially completed at the end of this period? Partially completed units cannot logically be treated as whole units, or we would overstate the amount of manufacturing work accomplished during the period. On the other hand, these units cannot be ignored, because some work was done on them and some of the manufacturing costs of the period were incurred in working on them. Ignoring these partially completed units would clearly understate the amount of manufacturing accomplishment for the period. The logical solution is to measure the amount of work done on the partially completed units and express that work effort in terms of whole units of output, which accountants call **equivalent units of production** or **equivalent whole units** or just **equivalent units.** The concept of equivalent units is shown graphically in Figure 5-2.

Figure 5-2 illustrates the measurement of production output for June for a company that manufactures camping trailers. At the beginning of June there were four camping trailers in beginning work in process inventory, already three-fourths complete. During June these trailers in beginning inventory were completed and eight more units were started and completed. In addi-

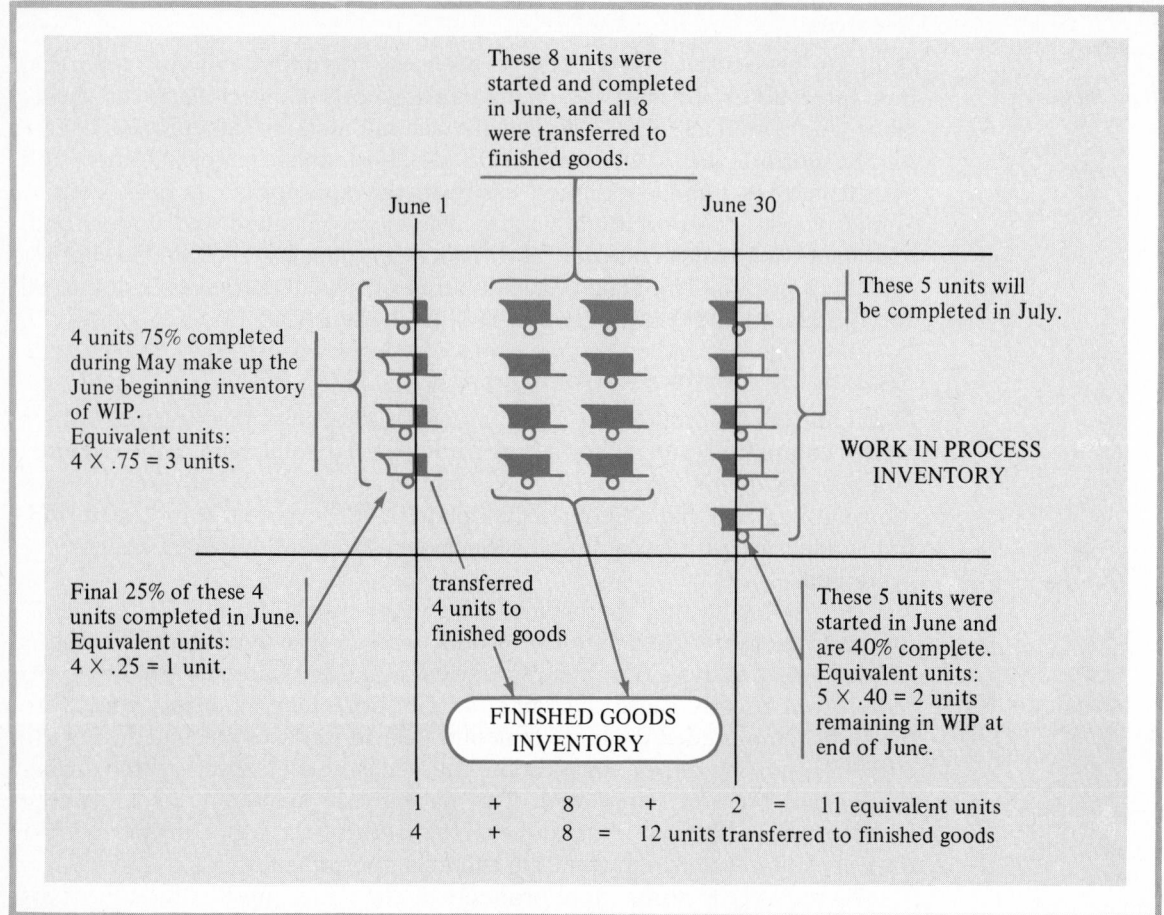

These 8 units were started and completed in June, and all 8 were transferred to finished goods.

June 1

June 30

These 5 units will be completed in July.

4 units 75% completed during May make up the June beginning inventory of WIP. Equivalent units: 4 × .75 = 3 units.

WORK IN PROCESS INVENTORY

Final 25% of these 4 units completed in June. Equivalent units: 4 × .25 = 1 unit.

transferred 4 units to finished goods

These 5 units were started in June and are 40% complete. Equivalent units: 5 × .40 = 2 units remaining in WIP at end of June.

FINISHED GOODS INVENTORY

1 + 8 + 2 = 11 equivalent units
4 + 8 = 12 units transferred to finished goods

Figure 5-2. In process costing the accountant must measure the amount of production for the period in order to compute unit costs. The production quantity for the period includes the completion of beginning work in process inventory, the units started and completed during the period, and the work done on ending work in process inventory.

Equivalent units = Completion of beginning work in process + Units started and completed + Work done on ending work in process

tion, five trailers were started during the month but only partially finished by June 30. The units in ending work in process inventory are 40 percent complete at the end of the month. During June the company did the one-fourth remaining work on the four units in beginning inventory, which is one equivalent unit of work (.25 × four units). The eight units started and completed during the month are already expressed as whole units, and the amount of work done on ending inventory is two equivalent units (five trailers × 40 percent completion). Summing the amount of work during the month, we get 11 equivalent units (1 + 8 + 2).

Computing Unit Costs

The cost per unit of manufacturing a product is determined by dividing the total manufacturing costs of the period by the number of units produced during the period. In a job order costing system, it is easy to measure the unit costs because the calculations are not made until the job is completed. The completion of the job is the key to the measurement of unit costs rather than a specific time interval.

In process costing, unit costs are determined by dividing the total manufacturing costs for the reporting period by the quantity produced during the period to determine the unit cost of manufacturing the product for a **particular reporting period.**

Unit costs are convenient measures of cost and performance. Frequently, managers monitor unit costs for a series of reporting periods, or they compare the company's unit costs with unit costs of other companies in the same industry.

The manufacturing costs for the period are divided by the number of units produced during the period to find unit costs. Typically, unit costs are computed for each of the cost elements. The number of equivalent units used to calculate unit costs for direct materials sometimes is different from the number of equivalent units used to compute unit costs for direct labor or manufacturing overhead. This occurs because units in beginning and ending inventory may not be the same amount complete for all production resources. For example, all materials may be added to a product as soon as it is started into production, but the work necessary to assemble, weld, buff, and otherwise complete the product may not be done right away. Therefore, units in ending work in process may be complete in terms of materials but only partially complete in terms of the conversion process.

Preparing Product Cost Reports

Cost of production report defined

In a process costing system, manufacturing costs are reported periodically using a **cost of production report,** which summarizes the cost and production data for the period for a specific process center. The report includes total manufacturing costs, the production quantity, and unit costs. A cost of production report is somewhat similar to a job order cost sheet, but instead of reporting costs for the job, it reports costs for a specific time period.

An important distinction between a cost of production report and a job order cost sheet is that a cost of production report summarizes the production activity for a single process center. If six process centers are needed to complete the production of a particular product, six cost of production reports provide the detailed cost data associated with the entire production of the product. On the other hand, a job cost sheet contains a summary of all the cost data for the manufacture of a product in a particular job. A comparison of the characteristics of job cost sheets and cost of production reports is presented at the top of the following page:

Item	Job Order Costing	Process Costing
Timing of the report	Prepared when the job is completed	Prepared periodically to satisfy management's information needs
Manufacturing costs to be reported	All production costs for the product	Only production costs for a particular process center
Measurement of the output	Number of units produced with the job	Number of units started and completed during the period, plus the equivalent number of whole units represented by partially completed units

Job order and process costing compared

Notice the difference in the timing of product costs between job order costing and process costing. The job cost sheet is summarized and unit costs of the product are reported only when the job is completed. In process costing, unit product costs are reported periodically as desired by management. Figure 5-3 illustrates the product costing activities for job order costing and process costing.

PROCESS COSTING ILLUSTRATED

A discussion of process costing activities provides some understanding of the nature of process costing, but to achieve a working knowledge of process costing a careful study of process costing examples is necessary. In the illustrations that follow, a variety of process costing manufacturing situations are presented one at a time, and each situation is costed separately so that you can see the effect of each on the costing activity.

Description of the Manufacturing Activities

The Grubbs Manufacturing Company produces several different types of clocks. A popular model is a large kitchen clock manufactured in three process centers. The first process center is molding, where the plastic body of the clock is formed in molds, cooled, and checked for imperfections. In the second process center, finishing, the clock body is trimmed and buffed, and the clock face is sealed with a silicone substance. The last process center is assembly, where the clock mechanisms, which are purchased from a supplier, are installed in the body of the clock. The clocks are also tested and packaged in the last process center before being sent to the finished goods inventory storeroom.

Clocks produced in three process centers.

The company prepares monthly manufacturing cost reports for each of its products. We use April manufacturing data to illustrate cost of production

Figure 5-3. In job order costing, product costs are accumulated for the life of the job and unit costs are computed and reported when the job is completed. In process costing, product costs are measured and reported periodically.

Comparison of Job Order Costing and Process Costing

Job Order Costing System

Beginning of Production		End of Production
Job Is Started	**Job Is in Production**	**Job Is Completed**
A job cost sheet is created.	Costs are incurred and accumulated on the job sheet and recorded in the company's books.	The job cost sheet is summarized and unit costs are computed for the product. Product costs are transferred from the Work in Process Control account to the Finished Goods Control account.

Process Costing System

Beginning of the Reporting Period	During the Reporting Period	End of the Reporting Period
Units already in production are not complete. Manufacturing costs already incurred were recorded in last period.	Units already in production are completed. Additional units are started. Manufacturing costs are accumulated as incurred. Completed units are transferred to the next process center or finished goods. Units started but not completed remain in work in process inventory.	Production quantity is measured for each process center. Costs of production for the period are divided by production quantity to obtain unit costs. Cost of production report is prepared.

reports and process costing activities. A cost of production report is presented for April for each of the three process centers used in manufacturing the kitchen clocks. Manufacturing activities for the kitchen clocks and the parallel flow of manufacturing costs are shown in Figure 5-4.

First Process Center: No Beginning Inventory

Molding Process Center Production Data.   On April 1, there was no beginning work in process inventory in molding, the first process center. During April, 11,000 units were started. By the end of April, 10,000 units had been completed and transferred to the next process center, finishing. The 1,000 units that were in ending inventory at the end of the month had all material added and 70 percent of the labor and overhead cost incurred. When the percentage of completion is the same for labor and overhead, these two cost

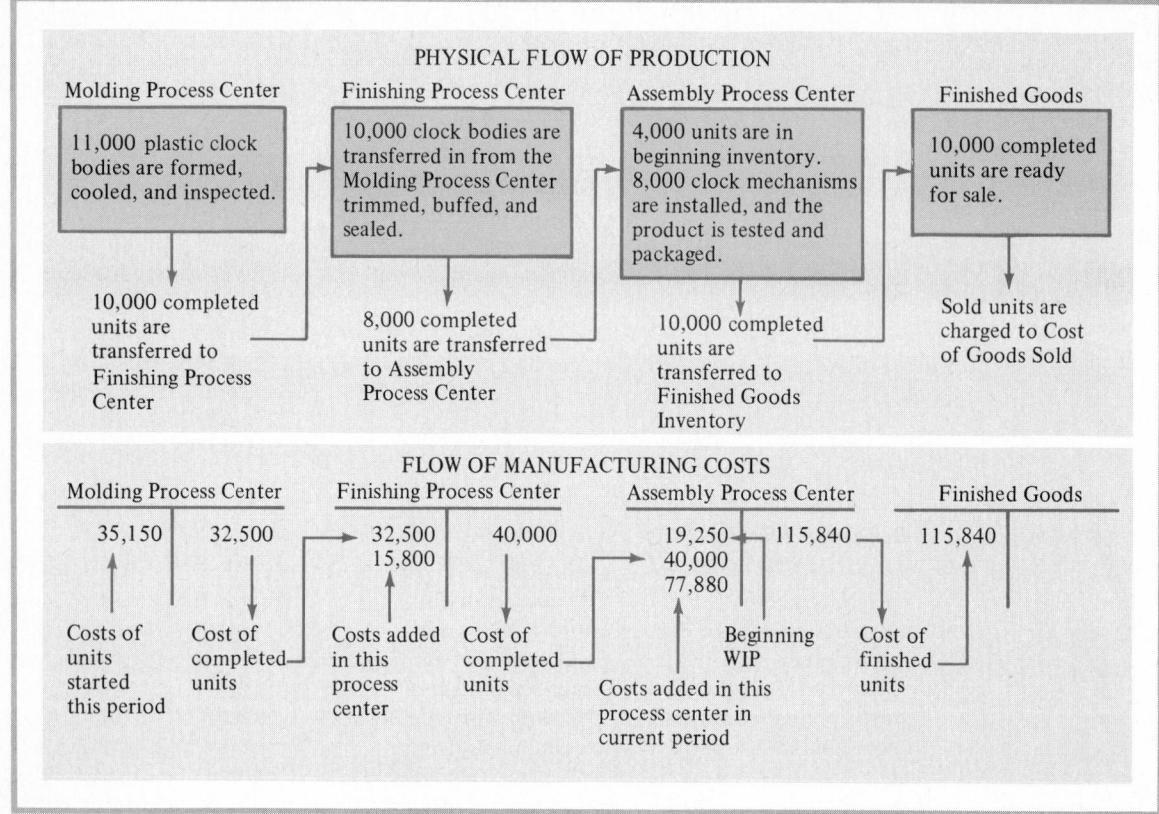

Figure 5-4. Clocks are manufactured in three process centers. Accountants measure the cost of producing the clocks by accumulating production costs in each process center for the period and determining the number of units made each period. The flow of costs through the ledger accounts parallels the flow of products through the manufacturing process.

elements together may be referred to as **conversion.** For example, we could state that the ending work in process inventory is 70 percent converted or conversion is 70 percent complete.

The material cost in April was $13,750, labor cost was $8,560, and applied overhead was $12,840. Using these cost and production data, it is easy to prepare a cost of production report for the process center, as illustrated in Figure 5-5.

Developing the Cost of Production Report.   Using the data above, we can prepare the April cost of production report for the first process center. The title of the report identifies the reporting entity, the type of report, the process center, and the time period covered. The body of the report is divided into several parts. The top portion identifies the physical flow of the units through the process center for the period. The second section reports the total manufacturing costs for the period and the unit costs of production. The next section reports the disposition of the costs. Typically, most units are

Figure 5-5. In the first process center there is no beginning inventory. Costs incurred during the period are divided by the output to find unit costs which are used to cost completed units and units in ending inventory.

Grubbs Manufacturing Company
Cost of Production Report
Kitchen Wall Clocks
Molding Department
April

Units to Account For		Units Accounted For	
Started during the period	11,000	Units transferred out	10,000
		Ending work in process	1,000
Total units to account for	11,000	Total units accounted for	11,000

Costs to Account For	Costs	Equivalent Units	Unit Cost
Direct material	$13,750	11,000	$1.25
Direct labor	8,560	10,700	.80
Manufacturing overhead	12,840	10,700	1.20
Total costs to account for	$35,150		$3.25

Costs Accounted For

Transferred out of the process center:

10,000 units @ $3.25		$32,500

Ending work in process inventory:

Direct material	1,000 units @ 1.25	$1,250	
Direct labor	700 units @ .80	560	
Manufacturing overhead	700 units @ 1.20	840	2,650
Total costs accounted for			$35,150

Schedule of Equivalent Units

	Materials	Conversion
Units started and completed during the period	10,000	10,000
Materials in ending work in process:		
1,000 units with 100% of the material added	1,000	
Conversion of ending work in process:		
1,000 units with 70% conversion		700
Equivalent units of output for the period	11,000	10,700

completed during the period and their costs are transferred out of the process center; the remaining costs are for ending work in process inventory.

Reporting the Flow of Units. The physical flow of units is described at the top of the cost of production report and is used to measure production quantity and to assign costs to units. The **units to account for** section identifies the source of the units worked on during the period in the process center. There are two sources of units, beginning work in process and units started during the period. In the Molding process center, there are no units in beginning inventory.

The **units accounted for** section identifies the disposition of the units worked on during the period in the process center. Most units are completed during the period and transferred to the next process center, or to finished goods if this is the last process center in the production process. In addition to completed units, typically some units are partially completed and are the ending work in process for the period in the process center. The total number of units identified in the units to account for section must equal the total number of units in the units accounted for section. Any lost or spoiled units must be identified. Lost and spoiled units are discussed in Chapter 6.

The data on the physical flow of units are used to measure the production quantity for the period. For example, the amount of production done in April in molding is equal to the 10,000 units started and completed during the period plus the amount of work done on the 1,000 partially completed units in ending work in process. The work done on ending inventory is expressed as equivalent whole units and added to the number of units started and completed during the period. The calculation of equivalent units is presented at the bottom of the report in the **schedule of equivalent units.**

Measuring Unit Costs. The second section of the cost of production report presents the manufacturing costs for the period, reports unit costs, and shows total cost to account for in the process center. This section of the report is called **costs to account for.** Here manufacturing costs are reported and unit costs are computed. The cost data for this section are accumulated throughout the period for each process center. Material requisition summary reports, labor distribution reports, and other source data are used as the basis for identifying costs with specific process centers. Manufacturing costs not identified with specific process centers are charged to manufacturing overhead and are applied to production in each process center using a manufacturing overhead rate. The accumulated costs are reported in the cost of production report in total and are divided by equivalent units to find unit costs. The unit costs are reported in this section of the report and are used below to cost the completed units and the units that are in ending work in process.

Total and per unit production costs are reported

The concept of equivalent units requires special attention to be fully understood. Equivalent units are a measure of the number of whole units of production that includes units started and completed and units partially completed during the period. The computation of equivalent units typically is shown in the cost of production report in a **schedule of equivalent units.** The units started and completed during the period are easy to understand since they are simply whole units of output. But how are partially completed units used in computing equivalent units? For example, in molding, the first process center in the production of kitchen clocks, 11,000 units are started but only 10,000 are completed and transferred to the second process center.

The schedule of equivalent units reports the output of the period

There are 1,000 partially completed clock housings that are in ending work in process inventory in the molding process center at the end of April. All of the material has been added to the ending inventory, but only 70 percent of the conversion has been accomplished. The equivalent units for materials amount to 11,000, and equivalent units for labor and overhead are 10,700. The equivalent units are computed as follows:

<u>Schedule of Equivalent Units</u>

	Materials	Conversion
Units started and completed during the period	10,000	10,000
Materials in ending work in process:		
1,000 units with 100% of the material added	1,000	
Conversion of ending work in process:		
1,000 units with 70% conversion		700
Equivalent units of output for the period	11,000	10,700

Computation of equivalent units

Because there was no beginning work in process inventory, the units completed had to have all of the material added to them during the current period. The units in ending inventory also had all of the material already added to them at the end of the reporting period (the month of April); thus no material will need to be added to those units next month to complete them.

Completed units that are transferred to the second process center are 100 percent complete with respect to all resources—material, labor, and overhead. With no units in beginning inventory in April in the molding process center, the 10,000 units transferred out during the period must have been started and completed during the month. The units in ending inventory, however, are only 70 percent complete in terms of conversion costs—labor and overhead. Therefore, there are 700 (1,000 units × .70) equivalent units of direct labor and manufacturing overhead in ending work in process in the molding process center on April 30.

Why are the equivalent units different for direct materials and conversion costs? Actually, this is quite common in manufacturing activities. Often, material is added at the beginning of a process center and then labor and overhead resources are used to cut, machine, drill, polish, assemble, or in other ways convert the raw material into a finished product. The flow of various resources into production is not always proportional throughout the production process. The important concept here is that the accountant must be able to identify the cost of production resources with the amount of product manufactured so that accurate unit costs are reported.

The manufacturing costs for each cost element are divided by their corresponding equivalent units to determine unit costs. The total unit cost for this process center for April is $3.25, as shown in Figure 5-5. This is an average unit cost for April. A particular unit of product may have cost $3.31 or $3.22 or some other amount. If cost of production reports were prepared weekly instead of monthly, the average unit costs each week might have been something other than the $3.25 average for April. Also, note that unit costs for preceding or following months may be different than for April, depending on resource costs, production efficiencies, or other factors.

Accounting for Manufacturing Costs

The total amount of cost to account for in the molding process center in April is $35,150. This is the **exact** amount that must be accounted for in the next part of the cost of production report. The **costs accounted for** section reports the disposition of the process center's manufacturing costs for the period. In this example, the costs accounted for section shows what happens to the $35,150 of manufacturing costs that were incurred in the molding process center during April.

Costs are transferred out or remain in ending inventory

Costs are accounted for in one of two ways. Most costs are incurred to manufacture units that are completed in the process center and transferred to the next process center or to finished goods. In the molding process center, 10,000 units were completed during the period and transferred to the next process center. The cost assigned to the completed units is $32,500 (10,000 units × $3.25). In this case there was no beginning work in process inventory, so the cost of the units transferred out was merely the number of units completed times the current period's cost of production.

The costs accounted for always must equal the costs to account for

The remaining costs were incurred in the production of the partially completed units that are in ending inventory. There are 1,000 units in ending work in process inventory, but these units are not 100 percent complete. All of the materials have been added to the units, but only 70 percent of the conversion has been completed. Therefore, the cost associated with the units is the number of equivalent units times the unit cost for each of the cost elements. The total of $2,650 is the cost of ending work in process inventory in this process center on April 30. The total of the costs in ending work in process inventory and the costs transferred out is the total cost accounted for and must equal the total cost to account for, in this case $35,150.

Second Process Center: Units Transferred In

Finishing Process Center Production Data.　The second process center is finishing, where the clock bodies are trimmed and buffed and the faces sealed. The 10,000 units transferred out of the first process center are transferred into this second process center. As with the first process center, there is no beginning inventory on April 1. In the finishing process center, 8,000 units are completed during the month and 2,000 units are in ending inventory at the end of the month, with all material added and 40 percent of the conversion completed. The cost of production report for the finishing process center is presented in Figure 5-6.

Costs transferred in from preceding departments

Costs Transferred into a Process Center.　The form and content of the cost of production report for finishing is very similar to the report of the molding process center. The primary difference is that this is the second process center, and in addition to material, labor, and overhead costs, there are costs transferred in from the first process center. The $32,500 cost transferred in is the same amount transferred out of the first process center. The costs assigned to the products remain with the products as they pass from one process center to the next until the units are completed.

In addition to the costs transferred into the process center, other manufacturing costs are incurred in finishing during April. Material costs are $4,000, labor costs $5,280, and overhead $6,600. Each of these costs incurred in the finishing process center is divided by its equivalent units of

Figure 5-6. The costs transferred out of the first process center are transferred into the second process center. In addition to the transferred-in costs, there are additional direct materials, direct labor, and manufacturing overhead costs incurred in this second process center.

Grubbs Manufacturing Company
Cost of Production Report
Kitchen Wall Clocks
Finishing Department
April

Units to Account For		Units Accounted For	
Transferred in during the period	10,000	Units transferred out	8,000
		Ending work in process	2,000
Total units to account for	10,000	Total units accounted for	10,000

Costs to Account For	Costs	Equivalent Units	Unit Cost
Preceding department costs	$32,500	10,000	$3.25
Direct material	4,000	10,000	.40
Direct labor	5,280	8,800	.60
Manufacturing overhead	6,600	8,800	.75
Total costs to account for	$48,380		$5.00

Costs Accounted For

Transferred out of the process center:

8,000 units @ $5.00		$40,000

Ending work in process inventory:

Preceding department cost	2,000 units @	3.25	$6,500	
Direct material	2,000 units @	.40	800	
Direct labor	800 units @	.60	480	
Manufacturing overhead	800 units @	.75	600	8,380
Total costs accounted for				$48,380

Schedule of Equivalent Units

	Materials	Conversion
Units started and completed during the period	8,000	8,000
Materials in ending work in process:		
2,000 units with 100% of the material added	2,000	
Conversion of ending work in process:		
2,000 units with 40% conversion		800
Equivalent units of output for the period	10,000	8,800

production in the finishing process center to find the unit costs **in finishing** in April. We see that after the first process center there are two categories of costs to account for: those costs that are transferred into the process center from preceding process centers, and additional manufacturing costs that are incurred in the current process center.

The computation of equivalent units in finishing is similar to the computation for the molding process center. With no beginning work in process on April 1, the computation is as follows:

	Materials	Conversion
Units started and completed during the period	8,000	8,000
Material in ending work in process:		
2,000 units with 100% of the material added	2,000	
Conversion of ending work in process:		
2,000 units 40% converted		800
Equivalent units of production for the period	10,000	8,800

The total cost to account for is $48,380, which includes $32,500 of costs transferred in from the preceding process center and a total of $15,880 of new costs incurred in this process center. Similarly, the total unit cost of $5.00 includes $3.25 of unit cost transferred in from the molding process center and $1.75 of costs incurred in the finishing process center. The $5.00 unit cost is the average unit cost of manufacturing a unit of product through the first two process centers during April.

Notice that if you want to know the total amount of manufacturing cost incurred during April in the first two process centers, you cannot merely add up the total costs to account for in the two process centers, because some of the manufacturing costs incurred in the first process center have already been transferred to the second process center and therefore appear in both cost of production reports. Summing costs to account for would result in double counting of some of the costs. Instead, the manufacturing costs incurred in each department during the period must be added to find the total manufacturing costs for the period.

Most of the $48,380 total cost to account for is transferred out of finishing to the next process center. $40,000 (8,000 units at $5.00 per unit) are sent to the assembly process center. The remaining $8,380 of cost remains in the ending work in process inventory of the finishing process center on April 30. In addition to the preceding department costs already assigned to the ending inventory, the cost of these units also includes 100 percent of the material cost. But only 40 percent of the conversion has been done on the 2,000 units in ending work in process. Therefore, there are 800 equivalent units of labor and overhead in ending work in process. As always, the cost accounted for equals the cost to account for.

Third Process Center: Beginning Work in Process

Assembly Process Center Production Data.   The final process center in the production of kitchen clocks is assembly, where the clock mechanisms are installed and the clocks are tested and packaged. During April the following production activities occurred in the assembly process center:

- The 8,000 units completed in the finishing process center at a total cost of $40,000 are transferred into assembly.
- Direct material put into production in assembly during April cost $24,400.

- Direct labor cost for the month in assembly was $21,210.
- Applied manufacturing overhead for the month in assembly was $17,010.
- On April 1, there were 4,000 units in beginning work in process inventory in the assembly process center.
- The units in beginning inventory already have all their required material and 25 percent on the necessary conversion.
- The cost of units in beginning inventory is $19,520 of preceding department costs, $12,080 of material costs, $1,790 of labor costs, and $1,390 of overhead costs.
- There were 2,000 units in ending work in process with all materials and 75 percent conversion.

The costs of units in beginning work in process in April are obtained from the ending inventory costs reported in the process center's cost of production report for March. The April assembly process center cost of production report is illustrated in Figure 5-7.

The beginning inventory costs include $19,520 of costs transferred into the assembly process center from preceding departments during March, the previous month. In addition there were direct materials of $12,080, direct labor of $1,790, and applied overhead of $1,390, all of which were incurred in assembly during the previous month. The unit costs of beginning inventory shown in the cost of production report are the unit costs of producing the product during the previous month.

The cost of production report for assembly is somewhat different than the reports for the first two process centers because it contains beginning work in process inventory. The cost of beginning work in process inventory affects the cost to account for section of the report and also the costs accounted for section of the report. In the preceding two process centers, all costs of production were April costs. In the assembly process center there are April production costs, of course, but the beginning work in process consists of March costs. It is unlikely that April unit costs will be identical to March unit costs. Changing costs of raw materials or differing production efficiencies cause some variation in the unit costs of production from one period to the next. Therefore, the accountant must make a cost flow assumption to account for the units transferred out of the process center and the units in ending work in process.

Accountants use either FIFO or average costing to cost production flows

The most common cost flow methods used in costing manufacturing inventories are first in, first out (FIFO) and weighted average. These two inventory methods are the same as used in merchandising operations, but in a manufacturing company the unit costs of inventory are not given on a purchase invoice or an inventory card. Instead, they must be computed from the production data. With first in, first out, the costs of beginning work in process inventory must be identified separately from the costs of current period production, so that cost can be transferred on a FIFO basis. With weighted average, the costs of beginning and ending inventory are averaged together in proportion to the amount of production in beginning inventory and current production. The FIFO inventory method is illustrated in Figure 5-7.

Figure 5-7. The
final process center
is assembly. This
process center has
beginning inventory
on April 1. Because
the unit cost of be-
ginning inventory
typically is different
than the current pe-
riod unit cost of pro-
duction, manage-
ment must use some
cost flow assumption
to cost completed
units and units in
ending inventory.
First in, first out
(FIFO) is used in
this report.

Grubbs Manufacturing Company
Cost of Production Report
Kitchen Wall Clocks
Assembly Department
April

Units to Account For		Units Accounted For	
Beginning work in process	4,000	Units transferred out	10,000
Transferred in during the period	8,000	Ending work in process	2,000
Total units to account for	12,000	Total units accounted for	12,000

Costs to Account For	Costs	Equivalent Units	Unit Cost
Beginning work in process:			
Preceding department costs	$ 19,520	4,000	$ 4.88
Direct material	12,080	4,000	3.02
Direct labor	1,790	1,000	1.79
Manufacturing overhead	1,390	1,000	1.39
Total	34,780		$11.08
Current period production:			
Preceding department costs	40,000	8,000	$ 5.00
Direct material	24,400	8,000	3.05
Direct labor	21,210	10,500	2.02
Manufacturing overhead	17,010	10,500	1.62
Total	102,620		$11.69
Total costs to account for	$137,400		

Costs Accounted For

Transferred out of the process center:

Preceding department cost	4,000 units @ $4.88	$19,520	
Preceding department cost	6,000 units @ 5.00	30,000	
Direct material	4,000 units @ 3.02	12,080	
Direct material	6,000 units @ 3.05	18,300	
Direct labor	1,000 units @ 1.79	1,790	
Direct labor	9,000 units @ 2.02	18,180	
Manufacturing overhead	1,000 units @ 1.39	1,390	
Manufacturing overhead	9,000 units @ 1.62	14,580	$115,840

Ending work in process inventory:

Preceding department cost	2,000 units @ 5.00	10,000	
Direct material	2,000 units @ 3.05	6,100	
Direct labor	1,500 units @ 2.02	3,030	
Manufacturing overhead	1,500 units @ 1.62	2,430	21,560
Total costs accounted for			$137,400

Schedule of Equivalent Units

	Materials	Conversion
Materials added this period to units in beginning inventory	0	
Conversion 25% complete on beginning inventory:		
4,000 units, 75% conversion required to complete		3,000
Units started and completed during the period	6,000	6,000
Materials in ending work in process:		
2,000 units with 100% of the material added	2,000	
Conversion of ending work in process:		
2,000 units with 75% conversion		1,500
Equivalent units of output for the period	8,000	10,500

The units to account for section in Figure 5-7 shows that there is beginning work in process inventory in this process center. The costs to account for section is much larger than in the previous two cost of production reports. This occurs because it is necessary to separate the costs of beginning work in process inventory from the costs of current period production when the FIFO inventory method is used. The beginning inventory costs were incurred during March and include preceding department costs, material costs, and a portion of the necessary conversion costs. The costs incurred during April to complete the beginning work in process are reported as current period production costs, along with the costs of producing the new units transferred into the department during April.

The units in beginning work in process already have 100 percent of the materials completed, and they also include all preceding department costs. The preceding department costs are always 100 percent complete or the units would not yet be in the current process center. Often material is added at the beginning of a process or very early in a process, therefore it is common for beginning work in process to have all materials already added. The conversion of beginning work in process inventory is only 25 percent complete. In other words, beginning work in process requires an additional 75 percent conversion before the units will be complete. The cost of beginning work in process inventory is divided by the equivalent units to find the unit costs.

If FIFO is used to account for product costs, it is necessary to measure separately the equivalent units in beginning work in process and the current period equivalent units. Equivalent units in beginning inventory is the amount of production that was done before the current period started. In this illustration, it is the amount of production done on beginning inventory during March. The equivalent units for the current period is the amount of production performed during the current period, in this case during April. Current period production is comprised of conversion needed to complete the units in beginning inventory, materials and conversion for the units started and completed during the period, and materials and conversion used on units in ending work in process.

Costs of beginning inventory and current period production are identified separately

After the beginning inventory costs are reported, the costs, outputs, and unit costs for current period production are reported. The costs transferred in from the finishing process center are reported first, followed by the April material, labor, and overhead costs incurred in the assembly process center. These costs are determined as before by material requisitions, labor reports, and other documents of the firm.

Calculating Equivalent Units with Beginning Work in Process. To find equivalent units of production for the current period, an additional calculation must be made. In addition to the units started and completed and the work done on ending work in process inventory, the accountant also must add the amount of work done to complete the units in the beginning work in process. The measure of current period equivalent units includes two types of partially completed units, the work done to complete the beginning work in process and the work done on ending work in process by the end of the period. In this process center the computation of current period equivalent units is as follows:

Measuring equivalent units with beginning inventory

Schedule of Equivalent Units		
	Materials	Conversion
Materials added this period to units in beginning inventory	0	
Conversion 25% complete on beginning inventory: 4,000 units, 75% conversion required to complete		3,000
Units started and completed during the period	6,000	6,000
Materials in ending work in process: 2,000 units with 100% of the material added	2,000	
Conversion of ending work in process: 2,000 units with 75% conversion		1,500
Equivalent units of output for the period	8,000	10,500

To measure **current period** equivalent units, we include the equivalent units required to **complete** the beginning work in process and **not** the amount of work that was already done on the units when the period started. For example, in the previous period 25 percent of the conversion work was done on the units in beginning inventory. Therefore the amount of conversion done during the **current period** on the 4,000 units of beginning work in process inventory was 75 percent of 4,000 units, or 3,000 equivalent units.

The number of units started and completed during the period can be computed in two ways. One way is to deduct the ending work in process inventory from the units transferred into the period (8,000 units − 2,000 units = 6,000 units). A second approach is to subtract the number of units in beginning work in process inventory from the number of units transferred out of the department during the period (10,000 units − 4,000 units = 6,000 units). Both methods yield the correct answer.

Accounting for Inventory Cost Flows.   As is often the case, in the assembly process center the unit costs are different for beginning work in process and for the current period. The unit cost information is important from both an accounting and a management point of view. The accountant must select an inventory cost flow method to assign costs to completed units and to units in ending inventory. In addition, managers need the production cost data to manage operations. Cost of production reports provide managers with production quantity and unit cost data that may show cost and efficiency trends. Cost of production reports are valuable management tools, and they provide cost of goods sold data for the income statement and inventory cost data for the balance sheet. However, the report is primarily an internal management document designed to provide timely manufacturing cost data.

The cost accounted for section of the assembly cost of production report looks much different than the previous two cost of production reports discussed. Instead of having a single cost figure for the units transferred out, there is a list of figures under this heading. The units transferred to finished goods were comprised of some partially completed units from beginning work in process and some units started and completed during April. All costs flow through production on a first in, first out (FIFO) basis. Therefore, the first costs transferred out are the beginning inventory costs, followed by the costs required to complete beginning inventory, and finally the costs of units started and completed during the current period.

In total, 10,000 units are transferred to finished goods inventory. It may seem logical to transfer 4,000 units from beginning inventory at the total unit cost of $11.08 and the remaining 6,000 units at the current period production cost of $11.69. However, the beginning inventory was only partially complete. There were 4,000 equivalent units of preceding department costs but only 25 percent of the conversion had been completed. The objective is to transfer out the manufacturing costs of the 10,000 units of product completed during April. Below is a schedule showing the number of equivalent units of cost transferred from beginning inventory and from current period production to finished goods.

Schedule of Units Transferred Out

Cost Element	Equivalent Units from Beginning Work in Process	Equivalent Units from Current Period Production	Total Units Transferred to Finished Goods Inventory
Preceding department cost	4,000	6,000	10,000
Direct material	4,000	6,000	10,000
Direct labor	1,000	9,000	10,000
Manufacturing overhead	1,000	9,000	10,000

The 10,000 completed units transferred to finished goods are, of course, complete and their cost includes all of the cost components from all preceding process centers plus materials, labor, and overhead used in the assembly process center. Using FIFO, the first costs transferred to Finished Goods come from the beginning work in process. Since the beginning work in process is 100 percent complete with respect to preceding department costs and materials, the first 4,000 units of each of those cost components is at the beginning inventory cost. The next 6,000 units of preceding department cost and materials cost must come from current period production.

Costs transferred out using FIFO

Labor and overhead costs are treated in the same way. The first costs are transferred from beginning inventory, followed by current period production costs. However, labor and overhead is only 25 percent complete for beginning inventory. Only 1,000 units of cost for labor and overhead are transferred out from beginning work in process. The remaining 9,000 units of labor and overhead costs come from current period production (3,000 equivalent units to complete beginning inventory and 6,000 units started and completed during the period).

Notice that the total cost to account for includes both the current period manufacturing costs and costs included in beginning work in process. The majority of the costs are accounted for by transferring them to the next process center, and the remaining costs remain in the department at the end of the period in ending work in process inventory. The total cost accounted for always equals the total cost to account for. Sometimes small differences may occur because of rounding unit costs to two or three decimal places. These small rounding differences must be accounted for by adjusting one or more of the numbers in the cost accounted for section of the report. This adjustment process is illustrated later in the chapter.

FIFO costs become averaged in the next process center

Averaging of FIFO Costs.   The total cost transferred out of the process center is $115,840 for 10,000 units. The FIFO inventory method was used to determine the amount of cost to transfer out of the process center for these 10,000 units. But when the units are transferred into finished goods inventory, they are recorded as 10,000 units at a total cost of $115,840. That gives them a cost of $11.584 per unit. Even though FIFO was used to transfer the units out of assembly, the unit cost of $11.584 is used for inventory cost records. You can see that FIFO may be used in individual process centers to transfer units and cost ending inventory, but these costs become somewhat averaged as they pass through process centers to finished goods inventory.

Recording Costs in Process Costing

The discussion of recording manufacturing costs presented in Chapter 4 applies generally to both job order costing and process costing. However, the flow of products from one process center to the next is different than in job order costing and warrants special attention so that you understand how costs are recorded in a process costing system.

As units flow from one process center to the next, the cost of those units flow with them. That means that accountants transfer the cost of units out of one process center and into the next process center. Of course, this is accomplished with journal entries.

To illustrate, 8,000 units were transferred out of the finishing process center and into the assembly process center in April. These units had a cost of $5 each, or $40,000 in total. The entry to record the transfer of costs is as follows:

	Work in process control, finishing	40,000	
	Work in process control, assembly		40,000
	To record the transfer of 8,000 units		
	from assembly to finishing.		

The cost of the units transferred into assembly is only part of the production costs in assembly. In addition, other resources are added, including direct materials, direct labor, and manufacturing overhead. A summary journal entry to record these costs is as follows:

	Work in process control, assembly	62,620	
	Raw materials inventory control		24,400
	Payroll		21,210
	Manufacturing overhead applied		17,010
	To record April production costs incurred		
	in assembly.		

During April, 10,000 units were completed and transferred to finished goods inventory. The entry to record the cost of these units is as follows:

	Finished goods inventory control	115,840	
	Work in process control, assembly		115,840
	To record the transfer of completed units		
	to the finished goods inventory.		

Weighted Average Inventory Method

A common alternative to using FIFO to transfer production costs is the **weighted average inventory method,** sometimes called **average costing.** With the average cost method, accountants compute the weighted average cost of the units in beginning inventory and the units produced during the period. Since the number of equivalent units often is not the same for all cost components, an average cost is computed for each of the cost components. The average cost is used to cost the units transferred out of the process center and to cost the units in ending work in process. The following discussion illustrates the average costing method using **exactly the same cost and production quantity data** used to illustrate FIFO costing in the assembly process center.

Average unit costs are used to cost all units

The function of the cost of production report is the same regardless of whether FIFO or weighted average is used to account for the cost flows. In either case the accountant must provide managers with product cost data for decision making, planning, and performance evaluation, and also for external reporting.

The assembly process center cost of production report using average costing is presented in Figure 5-8. Compare this report with the report using FIFO, presented in Figure 5-7, and notice the similarities and differences discussed below.

The units to account for and the units accounted for sections of the reports are identical for FIFO and weighted average. This is logical because these sections deal with the physical flow of products through the process center, and FIFO and weighted average are accounting concepts that deal with the flow of costs through the process center.

Figure 5-8. An alternative method of costing units is weighted average. With this method, current period and beginning inventory costs are added together and divided by the total equivalent units to find the weighted average unit cost which is then used to cost units.

Grubbs Manufacturing Company
Cost of Production Report
Kitchen Wall Clocks
Assembly Department
April

Units to Account For		Units Accounted For	
Beginning work in process	4,000	Units transferred out	10,000
Transferred in during the period	8,000	Ending work in process	2,000
Total units to account for	12,000	Total units accounted for	12,000

Costs to Account For	Costs	Equivalent Units	Unit Cost
Preceding department costs:			
Beginning work in process	$ 19,520	4,000	$ 4.88
Current period	40,000	8,000	5.00
Total	59,520	12,000	4.96
Direct material:			
Beginning work in process	12,080	4,000	3.02
Current period	24,400	8,000	3.05
Total	36,480	12,000	3.04
Direct labor:			
Beginning work in process	1,790	1,000	1.79
Current period	21,210	10,500	2.02
Total	23,000	11,500	2.00
Manufacturing overhead:			
Beginning work in process	1,390	1,000	1.39
Current period	17,010	10,500	1.62
Total	18,400	11,500	1.60
Total costs to account for	$137,400		$11.60

Costs Accounted For

Transferred out of the process center:

10,000 units @ $11.60 per unit		$116,000

Ending work in process inventory:

Preceding department cost	2,000 units @ $4.96	$9,920	
Direct material	2,000 units @ 3.04	6,080	
Direct labor	1,500 units @ 2.00	3,000	
Manufacturing overhead	1,500 units @ 1.60	2,400	21,400
Total costs accounted for			$137,400

Schedule of Equivalent Units

	Materials	Conversion
Materials added this period to units in beginning inventory	0	
Conversion 25% complete on beginning inventory:		
4,000 units, 75% conversion required to complete		3,000
Units started and completed during the period	6,000	6,000
Materials in ending work in process:		
2,000 units with 100% of the material added	2,000	
Conversion of ending work in process:		
2,000 units with 75% conversion		1,500
Equivalent units of output for the current period	8,000	10,500
Equivalent units in beginning work in process	4,000	1,000
Total units used to compute average unit costs	12,000	11,500

Calculating Weighted Average Unit Costs.   The cost to account for section of this report is different than in the FIFO report. Instead of all the beginning inventory costs being grouped together followed by all of the current period production costs, the costs are grouped according to the type of cost element. That is, the beginning work in process and current period production are grouped together into preceding department costs, materials, labor, and manufacturing overhead.

The forms of the reports are different because they reflect different cost flow assumptions. The emphasis in the FIFO report is on identifying beginning work in process and current period production cost data with the reporting period in which the costs were incurred. Therefore, costs are grouped together by period. With weighted average, the emphasis is on the identification of average costs for each of the cost elements. Therefore, the beginning inventory and current period costs are grouped together for each cost element so that an average cost can be computed easily.

Comparing the data from the FIFO and average inventory reports shows that the costs of beginning inventory and current period production are the same; they are merely grouped differently. The weighted average unit cost for each of the cost elements is computed by adding the cost of beginning inventory to the current period cost to get total cost. This total is then divided by the total number of equivalent units for that cost element. The total number of units is merely the sum of the equivalent units in beginning work in process inventory and the equivalent units in current period production.

It is sometimes said that the number of equivalent units is different for FIFO and weighted average. Actually, what is different is the measure of equivalent units that the accountant uses to compute the average unit cost. Equivalent units are the production output, which does not change with the accountant's choice of inventory cost flows. But with FIFO the equivalent units are separated for product costing, and with weighted average the equivalent units of beginning inventory and the current period are added together to get the total equivalent units for both work in process and current period production. This total is divided into the total cost to obtain average unit cost.

An alternative method of calculating the total number of equivalent units is as follows:

Schedule of Equivalent Units
Used to Compute Average Unit Costs
Assembly Department
April

	Materials	Conversion
Units transferred out during the period	10,000	10,000

Work done on ending work in process:
  Material added: 2,000 units 100% added during April
  Conversion: 2,000 units with 75% conversion
	2,000	1,500

Total equivalent units represented by beginning work in process and current period production (sometimes referred to as weighted average equivalent units)	12,000	11,500

This method yields the total number of equivalent units, but it does not indicate the number of equivalent units in the beginning work in process and the current period production. Although this method of equivalent unit computation provides the production quantity data necessary to compute the average unit costs, it does not provide enough data to compute the unit cost data for beginning work in process and current period production. Some companies find that they require only average cost data, whereas others require more detailed cost reports that provide information about changes in production costs between periods. An example of a cost of production report that reports only the average cost data is presented in Figure 5-9. This is the same as Figure 5-8, but the unit cost data for beginning work in process and current period production have been eliminated.

Comparison of FIFO and Weighted Average Methods

Comparison between FIFO and average costing cost of production reports shows several similarities and differences. First, the total costs to account for is the same for the two types of reports. The type of costing method used does not affect the total amount of cost that the accountant has to deal with, only the way the costs are treated.

Comparing FIFO and average costing

Second, the unit costs for both beginning work in process and current period costs are identical for both the FIFO and average inventory methods. With FIFO, total unit costs are calculated for beginning work in process and also for current period production, and these two totals are maintained separately. With the weighted average method, units costs are computed for each cost element, and the total unit cost for each cost element is also calculated. That is, the total unit cost of each cost element is not the sum of the beginning and current period unit costs; it is obtained by dividing total costs by total equivalent units.

With FIFO, the units transferred out are all of the beginning inventory units with their separate unit costs, plus part of the units from current period production with their separate unit costs. The ending inventory consists only of current period costs. With weighted average costing, units completed during the period and transferred out are costed at the weighted average unit cost. All units remaining in ending work in process inventory at the end of the period are also costed at average cost. However, ending inventory is not completed, and therefore the equivalent units of each cost element must be costed at the average unit cost for that particular cost element rather than the total unit cost used for units transferred out. It is a mistake to transfer units out at the average unit cost and then cost the ending inventory at the current period manufacturing cost. Such mixing of inventory costing methods results in a small difference between the cost to account for and the costs accounted for. There is a temptation to believe that a small rounding error exists when the actual error is more serious.

A careful comparison of Figures 5-7 and 5-8 shows that both reports contain the same types of information and that many of the data are identical on the two reports. The differences are caused by the inventory cost flow assumption used for each report.

Figure 5-9. Some weighted average cost of production reports include only the average unit cost of production.

Grubbs Manufacturing Company
Cost of Production Report
Kitchen Wall Clocks
Assembly Department
April

Units to Account For		Units Accounted For	
Beginning work in process	4,000	Units transferred out	10,000
Transferred in during the period	8,000	Ending work in process	2,000
Total units to account for	12,000	Total units accounted for	12,000

Costs to Account For	Costs	Equivalent Units	Unit Cost
Preceding department costs:			
Beginning work in process	$ 19,520		
Current period	40,000		
Total	59,520	12,000	$ 4.96
Direct material:			
Beginning work in process	12,080		
Current period	24,400		
Total	36,480	12,000	3.04
Direct labor:			
Beginning work in process	1,790		
Current period	21,210		
Total	23,000	11,500	2.00
Manufacturing overhead:			
Beginning work in process	1,390		
Current period	17,010		
Total	18,400	11,500	1.60
Total cost to account for	$137,400		$11.60

Costs Accounted For

Transferred out of the process center:

10,000 units @ $11.60 per unit		$116,000

Ending work in process inventory:

Preceding department cost	2,000 units @	4.96	$9,920
Direct material	2,000 units @	3.04	6,080
Direct labor	1,500 units @	2.00	3,000
Manufacturing overhead	1,500 units @	1.60	2,400

Manufacturing overhead	21,400
Total costs accounted for	$137,400

Schedule of Equivalent Units

	Materials	Conversion
Units started and completed during the period	10,000	10,000
Materials in ending work in process:		
2,000 units with 100% of the material added	2,000	
Conversion of ending work in process:		
2,000 units with 75% conversion		1,500
Equivalent units of output for the period	12,000	11,500

Summary Product Cost Report

With job order costing, a job cost sheet identifies all of the detailed manufacturing cost data for a particular job from the start of production to the completion of the job. However, cost of production reports show detailed cost data only for the process center covered by the report. Costs incurred in previous process centers are merely identified in total as preceding department costs. No detailed breakdown of the composition of those costs is possible without referring to the preceding reports. Also, any costs that are incurred in process centers further along in the production process cannot be reflected in earlier cost of production reports.

Summary product cost reports provide detailed product cost information

To provide managers with an overview of product cost data in a process costing environment, a **summary product cost report** may be prepared. Such a report is illustrated in Figure 5-10.

The unit costs of direct material, direct labor, and manufacturing overhead are summarized for all process centers in the production process. The cost data presented here are the current period unit costs in each of the process centers. Thus, the total amount of unit cost reported here is not identical with the unit cost figure shown in Figure 5-8, which is an average of the beginning work in process and current period costs.

Sometimes cost of production reports combine direct labor and manufacturing overhead costs and report them as conversion costs

Direct Labor and Manufacturing Overhead Combined

In Chapter 2 we defined **conversion** as direct labor and manufacturing overhead taken together. Sometimes in process costing these two costs are combined in the reporting process. The idea is that in some manufacturing operations direct labor and overhead are closely related and should be

Figure 5-10. A summary product cost report provides managers detailed unit product cost data. The unit cost of each cost element and total unit costs are presented for each of the process centers used to manufacture a product.

Grubbs Manufacturing Company
Summary Product Cost Report
Kitchen Wall Clocks
April

Physical Flow	Units			
	Molding	Finishing	Assembly	Total
Beginning inventory	0	0	4,000	4,000
Started or transferred in	11,000	10,000	8,000	—
Ending inventory	1,000	2,000	2,000	5,000
Transferred out	10,000	8,000	10,000	—

Cost Flow	Unit Costs			
	Molding	Finishing	Assembly	Total
Materials	$1.25	$ .40	$3.05	$ 4.70
Labor	.80	.60	2.02	3.42
Manufacturing overhead	1.20	.75	1.62	3.57
Total	$3.25	$1.75	$6.69	$11.69

Figure 5-11. Some cost of production reports combine direct labor and manufacturing overhead costs into conversion costs and report only the combined amount. This does not change the unit cost of the product, but it does reduce the amount of detailed cost data presented to managers.

Grubbs Manufacturing Company
Cost of Production Report
Kitchen Wall Clocks
Assembly Department
April

Units to Account For		Units Accounted For	
Beginning work in process	4,000	Units transferred out	10,000
Transferred in during the period	8,000	Ending work in process	2,000
Total units to account for	12,000	Total units accounted for	12,000

Costs to Account For	Costs	Equivalent Units	Unit Cost
Beginning work in process:			
Preceding department costs	$ 19,520	4,000	$ 4.88
Direct material	12,080	4,000	3.02
Conversion	3,180	1,000	3.18
Total	34,780		$11.08
Current period production:			
Preceding department costs	40,000	8,000	$ 5.00
Direct material	24,400	8,000	3.05
Conversion	38,220	10,500	3.64
Total	102,620		$11.69
Total costs to account for	$137,400		

Costs Accounted For

Transferred out of the process center:			
Preceding department cost	4,000 units @ $4.88	$19,520	
Preceding department cost	6,000 units @ 5.00	30,000	
Direct material	4,000 units @ 3.02	12,080	
Direct material	6,000 units @ 3.05	18,300	
Conversion	1,000 units @ 3.18	3,180	
Conversion	9,000 units @ 3.64	32,760	
			$115,840
Ending work in process inventory:			
Preceding department cost	2,000 units @ 5.00	10,000	
Direct material	2,000 units @ 3.05	6,100	
Conversion	1,500 units @ 3.64	5,460	21,560
Total costs accounted for			$137,400

Schedule of Equivalent Units

	Materials	Conversion
Materials added this period to units in beginning inventory	0	
Conversion 25% complete on beginning inventory		
4,000 units, 75% conversion required to complete		3,000
Units started and completed during the period	6,000	6,000
Materials in ending work in process:		
2,000 units with 100% of the material added	2,000	
Conversion of ending work in process:		
2,000 units with 75% conversion		1,500
Equivalent units of output for the period	8,000	10,500

logically reported together. Of course the main issue is whether or not management needs to have the detail of labor and overhead identified separately. An illustration of a cost of production report with conversion costs reported is shown in Figure 5-11. This report uses the identical data reported in Figure 5-7, except direct labor and overhead total costs and unit costs are combined.

SUMMARY

Process costing is one of the two main types of product costing systems. It is used to accumulate the costs of products manufactured in continuous-flow production processes. Manufacturing activities are separated into specific activities called **process centers,** for which cost data are accumulated. Periodically, cost data are summarized and reported in **cost of production reports.** These reports describe the physical flow of units through the process center during the period and the associated cost flows. Cost data are accumulated for each cost element, and unit costs are determined by dividing the production quantities, called **equivalent units,** into the product costs.

The cost of production report is divided into several sections. The first is the physical flow of production, which includes **units to account for** and **units accounted for.** The second section, **costs to account for,** reports the total and unit costs of production. Costs are identified for each cost element and for costs in total. The third section of the report is called **costs accounted for.** Here the costs are assigned to the units transferred out of the process center and the units that remain in ending work in process. The quantity of production for the period is shown below in the **schedule of equivalent units.**

Since process costing is used to measure product costs for continuous-flow production processes, it is common to have beginning and ending work in process inventories. If the beginning inventory unit cost is different from the unit cost of the current period's production, some inventory cost flow assumption must be used to transfer costs out of the process center and to cost ending inventory. The two common methods are first in, first out (FIFO) and weighted average.

With FIFO, beginning inventory costs are grouped together and current period costs are grouped together. Costs are transferred out using FIFO. Costs and equivalent units are separated for beginning inventory and current production.

Weighted average requires grouping the costs together by cost element so that average costs may be computed easily. For each cost element, beginning inventory costs are totaled and divided by the total number of equivalent units for that cost. The average unit costs are used as the basis for costing inventory and transferring costs through inventory. Unit and total cost data for current period production and beginning inventory are often included in a weighted average cost of production report to provide managers with valuable cost data.

Unlike a job cost sheet, a cost of production report does not include the complete detailed cost data for a product. To obtain such data, a manager must have cost of production reports for all process centers involved in the production of the product, or a summary product cost report must be prepared.

KEY TERMS

cost of production report *(167)*
costs to account for *(172)*
costs accounted for *(173)*
equivalent units *(165)*
process center *(163)*

process costing *(162)*
schedule of equivalent units *(172)*
summary product cost report *(188)*
units to account for *(171)*
units accounted for *(172)*

QUESTIONS

1. "The problem with process costing is that you can never be sure the cost assigned to products is accurate. On the other hand, when a job is completed and job order costing is used, you can be sure that the costs assigned are correct." Discuss this comment in relation to both types of systems.

2. "There is no such thing as FIFO inventory flow in process costing. You may think you are using FIFO, but when you look at those FIFO costs in the next process center they turn out to be average costs." Explain what is meant by this comment.

3. (AICPA) An important concept in process costing is that of equivalent units.

   a. Describe the difference between units placed in process for a period and equivalent units for a period when there is no beginning work in process inventory and the ending work in process inventory is 50 percent complete.
   b. Describe the difference between units completed for a period and equivalent units for a period when there is no beginning work in process inventory and the ending work in process inventory is 50 percent complete.
   c. Describe how equivalent units for a period are used to compute the cost of the ending work in process inventory.

4. (AICPA) Presented below are three independent questions about a typical manufacturing company that uses a process cost accounting system. Your response to each question should be complete, including simple examples or illustrations where appropriate.

   a. Explain the rationale supporting the use of process costing instead of job order costing for product costing purposes.
   b. Define equivalent production (equivalent units produced). Explain the significance and use of equivalent production for product costing purposes.
   c. Explain how the first in, first out (FIFO) method of process costing differs from the weighted average method of process costing.

EXERCISES

Ex. 5-1
Measuring
Equivalent Units:
No Beginning Work
in Process

A plastics manufacturing company uses process costing to measure the production costs of its products. The molding process center is the second process in the manufacture of one of its main products, plastic sailboats. During July, 4,200 boats were started and 3,600 were completed and transferred to the next process center. The 600 units in ending work in process inventory were 100 percent complete in terms of material and half complete in terms of conversion. There were no units in beginning work in process inventory in molding on July 1.

REQUIRED

Compute the number of equivalent units of production in the molding department for each cost element in July.

Ex. 5-2
Process Costing: No
Work in Process

Moogle Company manufactures pipe racks that require three process centers in the manufacturing process. Below are production and cost data for the first process center, shearing.

> Units started during June, 2,000
> Direct material cost in June, $13,200
> Direct labor cost in June, $8,600
> Manufacturing overhead applied in June, $10,400
> No beginning or ending work in process

REQUIRED   Prepare a June cost of production report in good form for the shearing department.

Ex. 5-3
Process Costing: No
Beginning Work in
Process

The TCP Manufacturing Company produces heating controls for waterbeds. The first process center is the molding department. Production cost data for the month of September are presented below.

> Units started during the month, 5,000
> Direct materials cost, $12,600
> Direct labor cost, $9,165
> Manufacturing overhead applied, $10,998
> Beginning work in process, none
> Ending work in process, 1,200 units with all materials and 75 percent conversion

REQUIRED   Prepare a September cost of production report in good form for the molding department.

Ex. 5-4
Measuring Output
in a Process Costing
Environment

B. G. Wip Company manufactures and sells buggy whips as novelty items. A continuous-flow production operation is necessary to satisfy demand. The company is relatively new and the accountant hired last month worked only for a job order manufacturing company before this position. The accountant is familiar with what costs to accumulate as product costs, but is having difficulty determining the amount of output for the month so that unit costs can be computed. Below are some notes the accountant has gathered to help determine the output for the last process center in the manufacturing process.

> 2,000 units were in beginning inventory.
> 9,000 units were transferred in from the preceding process center during the month.
> 7,700 units were completed and transferred to finished goods inventory during the month.
> Both the beginning and ending work in process inventory had all material added. Conversion was 60 percent complete on the beginning work in process inventory but only one-third complete on the ending inventory.

REQUIRED   Prepare a schedule for the new accountant showing the amount of production for the period in the last process center.

Ex. 5-5
Understanding
Weighted Average
Cost of Production
Reports

Below is presented part of the March cost of production report for one process center of the Mabling Manufacturing Corporation. The costs accounted for section is missing from the report, but the rest of the report is complete and correctly prepared. The ending work in process is complete in terms of material and 50 percent complete for conversion.

Mabling Manufacturing Corporation
Cost of Production Report
December

Units to Account For		Units Accounted For	
Beginning work in process	3,000	Units transferred out	10,000
Transferred in this period	9,000	Ending work in process	2,000
Total units to account for	12,000	Total units accounted for	12,000

Costs to Account For	Costs	Equivalent Units	Unit Cost
Direct material:			
Beginning work in process	$ 6,000	3,000	$2.00
Current period	18,720	9,000	2.08
Total	24,720	12,000	2.06
Direct labor:			
Beginning work in process	4,220	2,000	2.11
Current period	19,980	9,000	2.22
Total	24,200	11,000	2.20
Manufacturing overhead:			
Beginning work in process	8,440	2,000	4.22
Current period	39,960	9,000	4.44
Total	48,400	11,000	4.40
Total costs to account for	$97,320		$8.66

REQUIRED   Prepare the costs accounted for section of the cost of production report for the process center in good form, using the average cost inventory method.

Ex. 5-6
Understanding
FIFO Cost of
Production Reports

Refer to the Mabling Manufacturing Corporation data in Exercise 5-5.

REQUIRED.   Prepare the costs accounted for section of the cost of production report for the Mabling Manufacturing Corporation in good form, using the FIFO inventory method.

Ex. 5-7
Computing
Equivalent Units

Below are production flow data for four **independent** situations.

	Process Center			
	1	2	3	4
Beginning work in process in units	3,000	12,000	0	8,000
Percentage complete materials	100	100	100	100
Percentage complete conversion	30	50	0	60
Units transferred in	9,000	60,000	9,000	30,000
Ending work in process in units	4,000	6,000	2,000	5,000
Percentage complete materials	100	100	100	100
Percentage complete conversion	60	90	100	80

REQUIRED   For each situation, compute the current period equivalent units for materials and conversion.

Ex. 5-8
Measuring Output of Several Related Process Centers

Below is a summary of the physical flow of production through three process centers for the production of a pesticide. The data are for manufacturing activities in the month of April.

Process Center 1

Beginning work in process: 1,000 units with all materials and 70% conversion.
Units started: 8,000
Ending work in process: 2,500 units with all materials and 60% conversion.

Process Center 2

Beginning work in process: 1,200 units with all materials and 2/3 conversion.
Ending work in process: 2,000 units with all materials and 2/5 conversion.

Process Center 3

Beginning work in process: 3,000 units with all materials and 80% conversion.
Ending work in process: 1,800 units with all materials and 75% conversion.

REQUIRED   Compute the amount of output for each process center for each cost element for April.

Ex. 5-9
FIFO Cost of Production Report

Gander Products uses a process costing system to accumulate product costs. The fabricating process center is the first process center in the production of bronze lighters. Below are cost data for the process center for the month of November.

Beginning work in process inventory is 8,000 units with all materials and 75 percent conversion.
Beginning inventory costs include $12,000 for materials, $6,000 for labor, and $3,000 for applied overhead.
There were 64,000 units started in November.
Material costs for November were $102,400.
November labor costs were $63,825.
Applied manufacturing overhead was $36,075.
Ending work in process was 14,000 units with all materials and 25 percent conversion.
FIFO inventory method used.

REQUIRED   Prepare a cost of production report in good form for the fabricating process center for November.

Ex. 5-10
Weighted Average Cost of Production Report

Paint-Co manufactures several lines of quality exterior paints. Below are July production data for the mixing department, which is the first process center in the production of a barn roof paint.

Beginning work in process consists of 3,000 gallons of base with all materials added and 50 percent conversion.
Beginning work in process costs include $6,000 of material, $1,095 of labor, and $640 of manufacturing overhead.
Units started during July are 27,000 gallons.
Material costs in July are $48,600.
July labor costs are $30,625.
Overhead costs in July are $14,700.
Ending work in process is 8,000 gallons, with all materials and 50 percent conversion.
Weighted average inventory is used.

REQUIRED   Prepare a July cost of production report in good form for the mixing department.

Ex. 5-11
First Department
FIFO Cost of
Production Report

The Stargel Products Company uses process costing to accumulate product costs for the products it manufactures. The company manufactures many products for outdoor use, including an insect spray that requires three process centers. The first process center is mixing. During January, 6,000 units of output were started. Beginning work in process was 1,000 units with all materials and 2/5 conversion. Ending work in process was 1,500 units with all materials and 2/3 conversion.

Beginning work in process inventory costs were $800 materials, $400 direct labor, and $480 applied overhead. During January, materials cost in mixing was $4,920, direct labor cost was $6,405, and applied manufacturing overhead was $7,625. The company uses the FIFO inventory method to transfer all mfg. costs.

REQUIRED   Prepare a January cost of production report for the mixing process center.

Ex. 5-12
One-Department
Average Costing

Blending is the first process center in the Fender Company's production of an agricultural insecticide. The concentrate, sold in 5-gallon cans, is mixed with water and applied to the soil at time of planting.

During the month of October 1985, 1,200 cans of output were started in the blending process center. October direct material cost in blending was $10,850, direct labor cost was $7,825, and applied overhead was $5,210. Work in process in blending on October 1, 1985, was 300 cans with all material added and one-third conversion. Beginning work in process costs were $2,650 for materials, $575 for direct labor, and $390 for applied overhead. Ending work in process consisted of 500 cans with all materials and 80 percent conversion. In October, 1,000 cans are completed in blending and transferred to the next process center, settling.

Fender Company uses the average cost inventory method, but does not identify current period and beginning inventory costs separately.

REQUIRED   Prepare the October 1985, cost of production report for the blending process center.

Ex. 5-13
Costing Ending
Inventory Using
FIFO

The Fainer Corporation uses the FIFO inventory method to cost production. One of Fainer's products is a metal daisy print wheel for rotary printers used with some computers and word processors. The last process center in the production process is finishing. During the month of July 1985 the following production activity and costs occurred in finishing.

Finishing Department	July
Beginning work in process	2,000 units
Percent complete materials	100 %
Percent complete conversion	25 %
Beginning inventory costs:	
Preceding department	$ 7,000
Direct materials	$ 8,000
Direct labor	$ 3,500
Manufacturing overhead	$ 1,000
Units transferred in this month	9,000 units
Current period costs:	
Transferred in	$33,750
Direct materials	$35,100
Direct labor	$62,080
Manufacturing overhead	$16,975
Ending work in process	4,000 units
Percent complete materials	100 %
Percent complete conversion	80 %

REQUIRED   Compute the cost of work in process inventory in finishing on July 31, 1985.

Ex. 5-14
Two-Department
Process Costing
without Beginning
WIP

Kevlar, Ltd., manufactures a grease-cutting compound that it sells to industrial customers in barrels. The first process center is blending, where the basic materials are combined and mixed to specifications. In the second process center, distilling, additional materials are added to refine the product, and it is distilled and placed in barrels for shipping.

Below are production and cost data for the month of November 1985. There was no beginning work in process for the month in either process center, because the plant was closed the last half of October for annual equipment cleaning and preventive maintenance activities.

In blending, 1,200 barrels of product were started, and 800 units were completed and transferred to distilling. The units in ending work in process had all materials and were one-half converted. During November, in blending direct materials cost was $12,000 and conversion cost was $6,000.

Distilling incurred $3,200 of direct material costs and $3,750 of conversion costs during November. A total of 600 barrels of product were completed and transferred to finished goods and 200 units remained in ending inventory, with all materials and three-fourths conversion.

REQUIRED

Prepare the blending and distilling cost of production reports in good form for the month of November.

Ex. 5-15
Costing Ending
Inventory Using
Average Costing

A diversified consumer products company, Riverton Industries, makes a wide array of winter sports products in its Vail Division. A particularly popular product is its Evergreen downhill ski boot. It is manufactured in a continuous-flow production process accounted for in five process centers. In the last, laminating, the boot-lacing framework is sown and the boots are sealed, checked for defects, and boxed for shipment to customers.

September production and cost data for the Laminating process center are as follows. Beginning work in process was 2,000 units, with materials complete and conversion 25 percent complete. Beginning inventory costs consisted of $34,000 for preceding department costs, $8,000 for direct materials, and $3,275 for conversion. During September, 8,000 units were transferred in from the preceding process center, with a cost of $152,000. September direct materials costs were $40,000 in laminating and conversion costs were $52,725. There were 7,000 units completed and transferred to finished goods during the month. The units in ending inventory had all materials and were one-third converted.

REQUIRED

Compute the cost of ending work in process inventory in laminating on September 30 using weighted average cost flows.

Ex. 5-16
Costing Ending
Inventory Using
FIFO

Refer to the data in Exercise 5-15 on Riverton Industries production of boots.

REQUIRED. Compute the cost of ending work in process inventory in laminating on September 30 using FIFO cost flows.

PROBLEMS

P. 5-1
Process Costing
Journal Entries

Wayland's Ltd. manufactures sporting goods items and uses a process costing system to accumulate product costs. Below are data pertaining to the last process center, packaging, in the manufacture of golf balls.

Units transferred in from the finishing process center, 8,000, with a cost of $18,000.

Beginning work in process, none.

Materials cost for the period, $28,000.

Direct labor cost for the month, $14,000.

Applied manufacturing overhead during the month, $21,000.

Ending work in process, 2,000 units, with all materials and 50 percent conversion.

REQUIRED

a. Prepare summary journal entries to record the input of production resources into this process center.

b. Prepare a journal entry to record the transfer of completed products to finished goods inventory.

c. Compute the cost of ending work in process inventory in packaging at the end of the period.

P. 5-2
Cost of Production Report with Beginning Work in Process

The Mainline Company uses a process costing system to account for manufacturing activities. Assembly is the last process center in the production process. During August, assembly had 4,000 units in beginning work in process inventory and 8,000 units were transferred in from the preceding process center. During the month, 10,000 units were transferred to finished goods. The beginning and ending work in process inventories were complete in terms of materials. The beginning inventory was 25 percent complete in terms of conversion and the ending inventory was 75 percent complete.

Beginning inventory costs included $13,600 for preceding department costs, $4,400 for materials, $1,600 for labor, and $1,000 for manufacturing overhead. During August, $28,800 of cost was transferred in from the preceding process center, material cost of $10,400, labor cost of $15,750, and overhead of $9,975 were incurred. Mainline uses FIFO inventory to account for production costs.

REQUIRED

Prepare the August cost of production report in good form for the assembly department.

P. 5-3
Weighted Average Inventory

Logger Manufacturing Company produces chain saws in a continuous-flow production process. The Hand-Guard Division makes the vinyl-covered aluminum hand-safety guard, which it sells to the assembly division. The second process center in the manufacture of hand guards is molding. This division, like all others in the firm, uses weighted average to account for all inventories.

During November, the division had 10,000 units transferred in from the first process center. The 2,000 units in beginning work in process inventory had all materials and were half converted. The 4,000 units in ending work in process also had all materials and were half converted.

Beginning inventory costs consisted of $6,000 of preceding department cost, $2,100 of material cost, $2,600 of labor cost, and $2,900 of applied manufacturing overhead. Preceding department costs of $32,000 were transferred into the process center during November. Material costs for the month were $11,500 in the second process center, labor costs were $21,000, and overhead was $27,000.

REQUIRED

Prepare the November cost of production report for the process center.

P. 5-4
Two-Department Process Costing Using Weighted Average

The Selma Corporation manufactures several lines of suitcases that are sold in discount department chains in the eastern United States. The Cordwood Division makes molded suitcases in eight different sizes. The "Overnighter," a popular size, is manufactured in a continuous-flow production process requiring two process centers, molding and finishing. The company uses the weighted average inventory method to account for production inventory cost flows. Below are production data for the month of November 1985. There was no beginning inventory in the molding process center at the beginning of November because of extensive equipment maintenance in molding at the end of October.

Molding Process Center

No beginning work in process.
5,000 units started during the month.
4,000 units completed and transferred to finishing.
Ending inventory is complete in terms of material and 60% converted.
Direct material cost in November was $25,000.
November conversion cost was $13,800.

Finishing Process Center

Beginning work in process on November 1 was 2,000 units with all materials and 50% conversion.
Costs in beginning inventory were $15,760 for preceding department costs, $4,300 for materials, and $3,000 for conversion.
Work in process inventory in finishing on November 30 was 1,500 units with all materials and 2/3 conversion.
November materials cost was $8,000 and conversion cost was $14,490.

REQUIRED   Prepare the November cost of production reports in good form for the two process centers.

P. 5-5
Identifying Errors
in a Cost of
Production Report

A manufacturing company recently hired a new employee to account for its manufacturing operations. The first month on the job was quite difficult on the new accountant because he had very little previous accounting experience with a process costing system. Several of the cost of production reports for the month did not balance, and the accountant thought this might be due to rounding of numbers, which is sometimes necessary with the weighted average inventory method. The largest discrepancy occurred in the welding department. The "rounding error" was so large that it was questioned by top management. The cost of production report for the welding department is presented on page 199. You have been hired as a consultant by top management to evaluate the report and determine the errors, if any, in the report.
Your analysis of the supporting data indicates that:

The beginning work in process was complete in terms of materials and 60 percent complete for conversion.
The ending work in process was complete for materials and 25 percent converted.
Ten thousand units were transferred into the process center during the month.
The total cost data reported in the left column of the report are correct.

REQUIRED   a. List any errors that you find in the report.
b. Prepare a new cost of production report for the process center in good form, correcting any errors that you may have detected.

Cost of Production Report

Units to Account For:		Units Accounted For:	
Beginning work in process	5,000	Units transferred out	11,000
Transferred in this period	10,000	Ending work in process	4,000
Total units to account for	15,000	Total units accounted for	15,000

Costs to Account For:	Costs	Equivalent Units	Unit Cost
Preceding department costs:			
Beginning work in process	$ 14,800	5,000	$2.96
Current period	30,200	10,000	3.02
Total	45,000	15,000	3.00
Direct material:			
Beginning work in process	7,000	5,000	1.40
Current period	15,500	10,000	1.55
Total	22,500	15,000	1.60
Direct labor:			
Beginning work in process	6,360	5,000	1.272
Current period	17,640	9,000	1.96
Total	24,000	14,000	1.714
Manufacturing overhead:			
Beginning work in process	3,330	5,000	.666
Current period	11,070	9,000	1.23
Total	14,400	14,000	1.029
Total costs to account for	$105,900		$7.343

Costs Accounted For:

Transferred out of the process center:

       10,000 units @ $7.334 per unit $ 73,430

Ending work in process inventory:

Preceding department cost	4,000 units @	3.02 $12,080	
Direct material	4,000 units @	1.55 6,200	
Direct labor	4,000 units @	1.96 7,840	
Manufacturing overhead	1,000 units @	1.23 1,230	27,350
			100,780
Rounding factor			5,120
Total costs accounted for			$105,900

P. 5-6
Two-Department Process Costing Using FIFO and Average Costing

Hempfield Equipment Company makes lawn sweepers, one product in its line of garden tools and equipment. The frame and body components of the lawn sweeper are cut and shaped in the fabricating department. These parts are sent to the assembly department, where they are bolted and welded together and where the wheel and brush assemblies, which are purchased parts, are installed. The company uses average cost to account for inventory cost flows in the fabricating department and FIFO in assembly. Below are December production and cost data for the two process centers.

Fabricating. Beginning work in process for December was 1,000 units with all materials and one-half complete with respect to conversion. Beginning inventory costs were $11,120 for direct materials and $4,335 for conversion. During December, 6,000 units were started. December material cost in fabricating was $65,880 and December conversion cost was $49,665. Ending work in process for the month was 1,500 units with all materials added and one-third conversion.

Assembly. Beginning inventory consisted of 2,000 units with all materials and 60 percent conversion. Costs in beginning inventory were $40,900 for preceding department costs, $34,500 for materials, and $15,120 for conversion. Current month production costs were $89,100 for materials and $77,945 for conversion. There were 700 units in ending inventory with all materials and 50 percent conversion.

REQUIRED   Prepare the December cost of production reports in good form for the two process centers.

P. 5-7
Understanding
FIFO Inventory
Process Costing
Information

Presented below are March production cost data for the welding process center of Kolb Inc. Units are transferred from welding to assembly.

Beginning work in process, 8,000 units with all materials and 75 percent conversion.

Beginning inventory costs include $48,800 for preceding department costs, $11,200 for materials, $12,900 for labor, and $8,100 for overhead.

40,000 units are transferred into the process center during the month.

Ending work in process for March is 4,000 units with all materials and 25 percent conversion.

Preceding department costs were $248,000 for March.

March material costs were $60,000.

Direct labor costs for March were $78,000.

$50,700 of overhead was applied in welding during the month.

FIFO inventory method is used.

REQUIRED   a.   Prepare the March cost of production report for welding.
   b.   Determine the amount of current period manufacturing cost incurred in welding during March.
   c.   Compute the unit cost for current period preceding department costs that will appear in the March cost of production report for the assembly department.

P. 5-8
Two-Department
Process Costing
Using FIFO

The Purrty-Paint Company makes many different interior and exterior paints for home and commercial use. A popular interior latex paint is manufactured using three process centers. The paint base common to several product lines is produced in the first process center. In the second process center, several agents are added that increase durability, and in the third process center pigments and additional agents are added and the product is packaged in gallon cans. Below are data for the second and third process center. The company uses FIFO inventory valuation.

Process Center 2. Beginning work in process inventory is 2,000 units, with all materials and 75 percent conversion. Ending work in process is 1,000 units with all materials and 40 percent conversion. Beginning inventory costs were $4,800 for preceding department costs, $1,600 for material, $750 for labor, and $1,125 for manufacturing overhead. There were 10,000 units transferred out of process center 2 during October. October costs in process center 2 were $22,140 for preceding department costs, $7,380 for direct material, $4,628 for direct labor, and $6,675 for overhead.

Process Center 3. Beginning work in process consists of 6,000 units one-third converted, and ending work in process is 3,000 units two-thirds converted. Both beginning and ending inventory are complete in terms of material. Beginning inventory costs are $27,420 for preceding department costs, $7,680 for material costs, $3,300 for labor costs, and $3,000 for overhead costs. Costs incurred in process center 3 during October include $13,000 of material cost, $20,280 of direct labor cost, and $18,720 of overhead.

REQUIRED   Prepare cost of production reports in good form for process centers 2 and 3, using FIFO.

P. 5-9
Two-Department
Process Costing
Using Weighted
Average and FIFO

Stewart's makes chemicals for photographic work. A special developer for fine-grain films is manufactured using two process centers. In the first process center chemicals are combined in solution and blended to the proper strength and consistency. In the second process center the chemicals are refined, distilled, and packaged in containers for sale to commercial users. Stewart's uses weighted average inventory for the first process center and FIFO inventory for the second process center. Below are production cost data for the two process centers for July.

Process Center 1

Beginning work in process, 3,000 units with all materials and 2/3 conversion.
Beginning inventory costs are $5,640 for material, $2,840 for labor, and $2,320 for manufacturing overhead.
9,000 units were started in July.
July direct material cost is $18,360.
July direct labor cost is $12,160.
July manufacturing overhead cost is $9,680.
Ending work in process inventory is 4,000 units, 1/2 converted and all materials.

Process Center 2

Beginning work in process, 5,000 units 80 percent converted and all materials.
Beginning inventory costs were $22,500 for preceding department costs, $5,750 for materials, $3,200 for direct labor, and $2,200 for overhead.
Direct materials cost in July is $8,000.
Direct labor cost for July is $6,300.
Manufacturing overhead cost for July is $4,200.
Ending work in process inventory consists of 3,000 units, 1/3 converted with all materials added.

REQUIRED   Prepare cost of production reports in good form for the two process centers.

P. 5-10
Measuring Product
Costs for Two
Periods

On July 1, 1985, the Haymore Company started to manufacture gas valve regulators, a new product for the company. The company purchases rough-cast valve housing from a supplier. In the first process center the valves are machined, drilled, and threaded. The housings are then transferred to the finishing department, where they are polished and fittings are added. Finally the valves are transferred to packaging, where they are tested and packaged for shipment.

Below are production and cost data for the first two months of operations in the first process center, machining. The company uses average costing for production inventory flows.

July

No beginning work in process.
9,000 units started during the month.
Direct materials cost in July was $31,500.
Conversion cost in July was $36,000.
7,000 units are completed and transferred to finishing.
Ending work in process was 2,000 units with all materials and 1/2 conversion.

August

10,000 units are started during August.
Direct material cost in August was $35,600.
Conversion cost in August was $37,200.
8,000 units are completed and transferred to finishing.
Ending work in process was 4,000 units with all materials and 1/4 conversion.

REQUIRED

Prepare the cost of production reports in good form for July and August for the machining department.

P. 5-11 (AICPA)
Process Costing
with Some
Purchased
Inventory

Bisto Corporation manufactures valves and pumps for liquids. On December 1, 1985 Bisto paid $25,000 to the Poplen Company for the patent for its Watertite valve. Bisto planned to carry on Poplen's procedure of having the valve casing and parts cast by an independent foundry and doing the grinding and assembling in its own plant.

Bisto also purchased Poplen's inventory of the valves at 80 percent of its cost to Poplen. The purchased inventory was comprised of the following:

	Units
Raw material (unfinished casings and parts)	1,100
Work in process	
Grinding (25% complete)	800
Assembling (40% complete)	600
Finished valves	900

Poplen's cost accounting system provided the following unit costs:

	Cost per Unit
Raw materials (unfinished casings and parts)	$2.00
Grinding costs	1.00
Assembling costs	2.50

Bisto's cost accounting system accumulated the following costs for the month of December, which do not include cost of the inventory purchased from Poplen:

Raw material purchases (casings and parts for 5,000 units)	$10,500
Grinding costs	2,430
Assembling costs	5,664

Bisto's inventory of Watertite valves at December 31, 1985 follows:

Raw material (unfinished casings and parts)	2,700
Work in process	
Grinding (35% complete)	2,000
Assembling (33 1/3% complete)	300
Finished valves	2,250

No valves were spoiled or lost during the manufacturing process. Bisto uses the process costing method in its accounting system.

REQUIRED

a. Prepare a schedule to compute the equivalent units produced and costs incurred per unit for the month of December 1985.
b. Prepare a schedule of inventories on the FIFO basis as of December 1 and 31, 1985, setting forth by layers the number of units, unit costs and amounts. Show all supporting schedules in good form.

P. 5-12
Two-Period Cost of
Production Reports
Using FIFO
Inventory

The Compass Division of Habor Marine Manufacturing makes an illuminated liquid marine compass. Manufacturing costs are accounted for using a process costing system. The last process center in the production process is assembly, where the compass assembly is installed in the housing, the unit is wired, and the housing is sealed. Production quantity and cost data are presented below for April and May.

Assembly Department	April	May
Beginning work in process	500 units	?
Percent complete materials	100 %	?
Percent complete conversion	60 %	?
Beginning inventory costs:		
Preceding department	$ 8,500	?
Direct materials	$ 1,500	?
Direct labor	$ 1,800	?
Manufacturing overhead	$ 1,200	?
Units transferred in this month	3,000 units	3,400 units
Current period costs:		
Transferred in	$46,500	$51,000
Direct materials	$ 9,600	$11,560
Direct labor	$15,960	$16,500
Manufacturing overhead	$10,640	$10,950
Ending work in process	800 units	1,000 units
Percent complete materials	100 %	100 %
Percent complete conversion	50 %	20 %

REQUIRED   Prepare the cost of production reports in good form for the assembly department of Habor Marine Manufacturing for April and May.

CASES

Blue Water Fishing Supply, Inc., makes a variety of fishing and boating products that it markets nationwide. A recent management analysis of product offerings indicated a need for a top-of-the-line double-tray tackle box. Company product engineers designed the new tackle box, which is manufactured in a two-process-center production system. In the first process center, fabricating, the top and bottom housing of the tackle box is cut and formed from rolled aluminum. The units are buffed and holes are drilled for the hinges and latches that are installed later. In the second process center, assembly, hinges, latches, and tackle box trays are installed. These parts are purchased from vendors.

Management believes the tackle box will sell quite favorably at a retail price of $35 each. The company sells its products to retailers at a discount of 30 percent, and variable marketing costs typically average 8 percent of the company's product revenue. The company's product policy is to earn a minimum gross margin on product sales revenue of 45 percent.

Production of the tackle boxes began on October 1, and below are production quantity and cost data for the first 2 months of production. The company uses the weighted average inventory method to account for production cost flows.

October Production	Fabricating	Assembly
Beginning work in process	0	0
Units started during the month	15,000 units	—
Current period costs:		
Transferred in	—	?
Direct materials	$90,900	$24,600
Conversion	$49,920	$35,200
Units completed and transferred out	12,000 units	8,000 units
Ending work in process	3,000 units	4,000 units
Percent complete materials	100 %	100 %
Percent complete conversion	33 1/3 %	75 %

November Production	Fabricating	Assembly
Units started during the month	9,000 units	—
Current period costs:		
Transferred in	—	?
Direct materials	$53,820	$12,600
Conversion	$36,160	$15,600
Units completed and transferred out	6,000 units	7,000 units
Ending work in process	6,000 units	3,000 units
Percent complete materials	100 %	100 %
Percent complete conversion	66 2/3 %	33 1/3 %

a. Prepare cost of production reports in good form for both process centers for the first 2 months of production.
b. Prepare product cost summary reports for the first 2 months of production.
c. Compute the November percentage gross margin on product sales revenue for the new product. (Assume all units produced are sold.)
d. Compute the required retail sales price to satisfy the company's minimum gross margin requirement.
e. Assuming the maximum competitive retail price for the tackle box is $40, what is your evaluation of the potential for this product?

CHAPTER 6
Process Costing: Spoiled Units and Other Concepts

Process costing poses many interesting challenges for the accountant. For example, sometimes units are spoiled or lost in the production process. In other situations, output measures may change from one kind of measuring unit to another. For example, a product may be measured in pounds in the first process center, change to gallons in the second process center, and change again to cans of paint in the final process center. In general, the more complex the production process, the more difficult it is for accountants to measure product costs.

In this chapter we expand on the concepts of process costing and discuss the methods used to report on the following process costing situations:

1. Changes in the number of units of production as products move from one process center to the next

2. Ending work in process that is only partially complete in terms of direct materials

3. Identifying units that are spoiled or lost in the manufacturing process

4. Distinguishing between normal and abnormal spoilage

5. Spoiled units that have a market value

Each situation has a specific effect on the cost of production report and may also require special journal entries.

To illustrate the process costing topics of this chapter, we use the example of Kleenway Company, which produces a chemical cleaning compound. The product is manufactured in five process centers. The basic chemicals and labor are used in Process Center 1 to start production. In Process Center 2 solvents are added that increase the number of units. In Process Centers 3 through 5, the addition of more cleaning agents increases the number of units, and spoiled units must be accounted for.

Each process center is used to illustrate a specific costing situation that is described in detail when the process center is discussed. The first three process centers have no beginning work in process inventory. This makes it easier to understand the effect of each new situation on the cost of production report, the unit cost of the product, and the necessary journal entries.

CHANGE IN NUMBER OF UNITS FROM ONE PROCESS CENTER TO ANOTHER

It is common for the measure of units to change as they go from one process center to the next

A change in the units of output from one process center to the next may occur for several reasons. For example, in the first several process centers of a bakery, output may be measured in pounds of dough, but the baking department measures output in loaves of bread weighing 1.35 pounds each. In another case, an automobile manufacturer may have many process centers feeding component parts to the final assembly process. One process center produces wheels and output may be 50,000 units. However, five wheels are used for each car, and the 50,000-wheel output eventually becomes 10,000 cars. In a third case a manufacturer adds a diluting solution to a concentrate made in a preceding process center. This causes the quantity of output to triple. Regardless of the manufacturing situation that causes the change in units from one process center to the next, the accountant can easily convert the output units of the prior process center to the output units of the current process center.

Kleenway Company's production of its chemical cleaning compound starts in Process Center 1, where the active ingredients are mixed. Output is measured in gallons. During January, 2,000 gallons were completed and transferred to Process Center 2. The cost accounted for section of the January cost of production report of Process Center 1 is presented in Figure 6-1 with the cost and units transferred out highlighted. The unit cost of production in January in Process Center 1 was $5.00. Therefore, the cost transferred to the next process center was $10,000 (2,000 units × $5.00).

The 2,000 gallons of output transferred out of Process Center 1 went into Process Center 2, where 6,000 gallons of solvent were added to cut the solution to desired strength. The 6,000 gallons of solvent, when added to the

Kleenway Company
Process Center 1
January

Costs Accounted For:				
Transferred out of the process center:				
	2,000 units @ $5.00			$10,000
Ending work in process inventory:				
Direct material	400 units @	2.80	$1,120	
Direct labor	250 units @	1.40	350	
Manufacturing overhead	250 units @	.80	200	1,670
Total costs accounted for				$11,670

Figure 6-1. The cost to account for section of the cost of production report for Process Center 1. The key item in this figure is the number of units and the cost transferred out of the process center. Look carefully at how these data appear in the cost of production report of Process Center 2 shown in Figure 6-2.

2,000 gallons transferred in, yielded 8,000 gallons of product in Process Center 2. The January production costs in this process center were the $10,000 transferred in from the preceding process center, $3,200 for direct materials, $3,800 for direct labor, and $5,700 for overhead. During January, 7,000 gallons of product were completed and transferred to the next process center, and 1,000 gallons were in ending work in process with all materials and 60 percent conversion. The cost of production report for this process center is presented in Figure 6-2.

Figure 6-2. The addition of materials in this process center changed the units transferred in from 2,000 to 8,000. The cost of production report is always expressed in the unit measure used by the process center, regardless of the unit measure used by other process centers.

Kleenway Company
Cost of Production Report
Process Center 2
January

Units to Account For:		Units Accounted For:	
Transferred in during the period	8,000ª	Units transferred out	7,000
		Ending work in process	1,000
Total units to account for	8,000	Total units accounted for	8,000

Costs to Account For:	Costs	Equivalent Units	Unit Cost
Preceding department costs	$10,000	8,000ª	$1.25
Direct material	3,200	8,000	.40
Direct labor	3,800	7,600	.50
Manufacturing overhead	5,700	7,600	.75
Total costs to account for	$22,700		$2.90

Costs Accounted For:

Transferred out of the process center:

7,000 units @ $2.90 .... $20,300

Ending work in process inventory:

Preceding department costs	1,000 units @	1.25	$1,250	
Direct material	1,000 units @	.40	400	
Direct labor	600 units @	.50	300	
Manufacturing overhead	600 units @	.75	450	2,400

Total costs accounted for $22,700

Schedule of Equivalent Units

	Materials	Conversion
Units started and completed during the period	7,000	7,000
Materials in ending work in process:		
1,000 units with 100% of the material added	1,000	
Conversion of ending work in process:		
1,000 units with 60% conversion		600
Equivalent units of output for the period	8,000	7,600

ª 2,000 units are transferred in from Process Center 1, but material added in this process center increases the number of units of output to 8,000.

Production is always reported in the output units of the process center

The units transferred in are expressed as 8,000 gallons. We know that only 2,000 gallons were transferred into the second process center. Then how can the report state that 8,000 gallons were transferred in? The answer lies in the rule that all units in a cost of production report are expressed in output units of the process center covered by the report. Given the production requirements, it takes 1 gallon of input from Process Center 1 to yield 4 gallons of output in Process Center 2. Because units must be measured in output units of the process center, the 2,000 units transferred in are reported as 8,000 units, which is the number of output units they will yield.

The change in the output units affects not only the physical units in the units to account for section of the cost of production report, but also the unit cost of the units transferred in. The $10,000 total cost transferred in from the preceding center is not affected by the change in the units, but the unit cost transferred in changes from $5.00 per unit to $1.25 per unit ($10,000/8,000 units rather than $10,000/2,000 units).

Once the units transferred into the process center have been converted to output units, equivalent units can be calculated and unit costs computed as before. The cost of each cost element incurred in this process center during the month is divided by its equivalent units to find unit costs. The total cost for a completed unit is $2.90, as shown in Figure 6-2. During January, 7,000 units at $2.90 a unit, or $20,300, was transferred out of the second process center into Process Center 3. The remaining $2,400 of cost to account for is ending work in process.

EQUIVALENT UNITS FOR PARTIALLY COMPLETE MATERIAL

In some manufacturing situations, all of the material used in a process center is not added at the beginning of production. Instead some of the material is added late in the production process or throughout production. For example, in the manufacture of chocolate candy, cocoa, milk, and sugar are gradually combined and slowly stirred in the mixing process. At any point in time some of the units have only a portion of the total material they will receive in that process center. In situations such as this, accountants must measure the equivalent units of production for materials in the same manner that equivalent units are measured for conversion. Of course the units transferred out must have 100 percent of the material required for that process center, but the units in beginning and ending work in process may be only partially complete in terms of materials.

To illustrate, we continue the example of the Kleenway Company. The 7,000 units from Process Center 2 are transferred into Process Center 3, where a curing agent is added throughout the curing process. This curing agent does **not** increase the number of units in production. Five thousand gallons are completed and transferred out. The 2,000 units in ending inventory have 30 percent of the conversion done and 75 percent of the material added. The equivalent units for the period are computed as follows:

Schedule of Equivalent Units

	Materials	Conversion
Units started and completed during the period	5,000	5,000
Units in ending work in process: 2,000		
With 75% of the material added	1,500	
With 30% conversion		600
Equivalent units of output for the period	6,500	5,600

The equivalent units calculated above are used to compute unit cost for the month. The 6,500 equivalent units of material are divided into the January material cost of $5,200 in the process center. Similarly, the conver-

Figure 6-3. When materials are partially complete in work in process inventory, the computation of equivalent units for materials includes material required to complete beginning work in process, units started and completed during the period, and material added to ending work in process.

Kleenway Company
Cost of Production Report
Process Center 3
January

Units to Account For:		Units Accounted For:	
Transferred in during the period	7,000	Units transferred out	5,000
		Ending work in process	2,000
Total units to account for	7,000	Total units accounted for	7,000

Costs to Account For:	Costs	Equivalent Units	Unit Cost
Preceding department costs	$20,300	7,000	$2.90
Direct material	5,200	6,500	.80
Direct labor	4,200	5,600	.75
Manufacturing overhead	2,800	5,600	.50
Total costs to account for	$32,500		$4.95

Costs Accounted For:

Transferred out of the process center:

5,000 units @ $4.95		$24,750

Ending work in process inventory:

Preceding department costs	2,000 units @ 2.90	$5,800	
Direct material	1,500 units @ .80	1,200	
Direct labor	600 units @ .75	450	
Manufacturing overhead	600 units @ .50	300	7,750
Total costs accounted for			$32,500

Schedule of Equivalent Units

	Materials	Conversion
Units started and completed during the period	5,000	5,000
Materials in ending work in process:		
2,000 units with 75% of the material added	1,500	
Conversion of ending work in process:		
2,000 units with 30% conversion		600
Equivalent units of output for the period	6,500	5,600

sion equivalent units of 5,600 are divided into the labor and overhead cost of $4,200 and $2,800, respectively. The results are reported in Figure 6-3, which shows the cost of production report for January for the third process center.

Many variations of the partial material situation can occur. For example, material may not be added to units until immediately before they are transferred to the next process center. In that case the units transferred out of the process center would have 100 percent of the material costs from the current process center assigned to them. The ending work in process inventory would have no material costs. In all of these production situations, the accountant must ascertain the physical flow of the production activity and compute unit costs accordingly.

SPOILED AND LOST UNITS

Spoiled and lost units may be normal or abnormal

A common occurrence in manufacturing processes is the loss or spoilage of some of the product. The terms *lost units* and *spoiled units* often are used interchangeably, although there are production situations where one seems more appropriate than the other. For example, **lost units** is more descriptive if gallons of a solution evaporate or disappear, whereas **spoiled units** is the better term if units are inspected and fail to meet quality control standards. Losses or spoilage often cannot be avoided. For instance, human error may cause a hole to be drilled in the wrong place on a motor mount plate. Good parts may be discarded inadvertently with scrap material; some compound may be left too long in the curing process; or a machine may go out of adjustment and perform unacceptable work on products. Regardless of the cause of the spoiled or lost units, the accountant must identify the loss, measure its cost, and account for it in the proper way.

Normal Spoilage

Normal spoilage occurs in the normal production process

Often the spoilage that occurs in manufacturing products cannot be avoided given the production environment. That is, given the quality of the materials and labor used to produce the product and the efficiency of the production machinery, some spoilage will occur in the normal course of operations. Such spoilage is called **normal spoilage** or **normal lost units.** The skill level of the employees, human errors, malfunctions of equipment, and random factors combine to cause some normal spoilage.

The cost of normal spoilage is assigned to the good units that are produced

Although managers try to avoid all spoilage, they know that good units cannot be produced without production problems that cause some spoiled units. In effect, the cost of spoiled units is like any other manufacturing cost, such as machine maintenance or property taxes on the manufacturing facilities. Because some spoiled units are an unavoidable part of many manufacturing processes, the cost of such spoilage is included as part of the manufacturing cost of good units. The accountant must measure the cost of the spoiled units and assign the cost to the good units.

There are two approaches to accounting for the cost of normal spoilage. One is to absorb the cost of the spoiled units into the cost of the good units without specifically identifying it as spoilage cost. The other approach is to isolate and identify the total cost of spoiled units separately and show how much the spoilage cost increased the cost of the good units.

Spoiled Units Not Separately Identified.   We continue the example of the Kleenway Company to illustrate the first accounting alternative of absorbing the cost of spoiled units into the good units without identifying separately the cost of spoiled units. The 5,000 gallons that were transferred out of Process Center 3 at a cost of $24,750, or $4.95 per gallon, are transferred into Process Center 4, where the product is tested for purity and strength. The testing takes place before any material is added in this process center and before any conversion takes place.[1] Any product not meeting purity and strength specifications is discarded, because reprocessing costs are higher than the value of the product.

During the current month, 500 gallons of product did not satisfy the quality criteria and were discarded. The cost of the spoiled units must be included in the cost of the 4,500 gallons that passed the inspection. Production costs during the month in the fourth process center included $5,850 of materials, $3,440 of labor, and $1,720 of applied overhead. There were 3,500 units transferred to the next process center, and the ending work in process inventory of 1,000 units has all materials added and 80 percent of conversion. Figure 6-4 presents the cost of production report for Process Center 4 with the cost of spoiled units **not** identified separately.

The units to account for section of the cost of production report identifies all 5,000 units transferred into Process Center 4. The process center must account for all these units and their cost, although 500 of the units are discarded. These 500 lost units are accounted for by showing them in the units accounted for section of the report, which also shows 3,500 units transferred out and 1,000 units in ending inventory.

The $24,750 cost of the 5,000 units transferred in must also be accounted for by Process Center 4. This cost was incurred for all 5,000 units, but now it is assigned to 4,500 units only. Consequently, the $4.95 unit cost transferred out of Process Center 3 becomes $5.50 per unit ($24,750/4,500 gallons) in Process Center 4, where the 500 lost units occurred. Dividing the total cost transferred in by the number of units passing inspection spreads the cost of spoilage over the good units without identifying separately either the total cost of spoilage or the increase in unit costs caused by spoilage.

The total cost of spoiled units is $2,475 ($4.95 per unit × 500 lost units). The good units share this cost equally, which increases their cost by $.55 per gallon ($2,475/4,500 gallons). Both the increase in unit cost and the total cost of the spoiled units can be computed from the information in the cost of production report in Figure 6-4 and the report of the preceding process center, but neither report provides this information directly. For that reason,

---

[1] The cost of testing for quality control is typically treated as an overhead cost. The actual cost of testing is recorded in Manufacturing Overhead Control. The overhead application rate used for allocating overhead to production includes quality control costs.

Figure 6-4. Spoiled units are common in many production processes. The cost of normal spoilage is spread over the good units. In this illustration the cost of spoiled units is not identified separately; instead it is buried in the cost of the good units that remain in production.

Kleenway Company
Cost of Production Report
Process Center 4
January

Units to Account For:		Units Accounted For:	
		Units transferred out	3,500
		Ending work in process	1,000
Transferred in during the period	5,000	Spoiled units	500
Total units to account for	5,000	Total units accounted for	5,000

Costs to Account For:	Costs	Equivalent Units	Unit Cost
Preceding department costs	$24,750	4,500[a]	$5.50
Direct material	5,850	4,500	1.30
Direct labor	3,440	4,300	.80
Manufacturing overhead	1,720	4,300	.40
Total costs to account for	$35,760		$8.00

Costs Accounted For:

Transferred out of the process center:

3,500 units @ $8.00			$28,000

Ending work in process inventory:

Preceding department costs	1,000 units @ 5.50	$5,500	
Direct material	1,000 units @ 1.30	1,300	
Direct labor	800 units @ .80	640	
Manufacturing overhead	800 units @ .40	320	7,760
Total costs accounted for			$35,760

Schedule of Equivalent Units

	Materials	Conversion
Units started and completed during the period	3,500	3,500
Ending work in process: 1,000 units		
With 100% of materials	1,000	
With 80% of conversion		800
Equivalent units of output for the period	4,500	4,300

[a] 5,000 units are transferred in from Process Center 3, but 500 units are spoiled before any material is added or any conversion work is done on them in Process Center 4.

the spoiled unit costs are said to be **buried** with this type of reporting treatment.

In this example, the product spoilage is isolated early in Process Center 4, before any production occurs. Therefore, the cost of all materials added and the cost of conversion in the process center are applied to the 4,500 good units. Equivalent units are calculated for materials and labor as if the spoiled units never existed. When spoiled units are not included in the computation of equivalent units, spoilage costs are **not** to be identified separately. The computation of equivalent units is as follows:

Schedule of Equivalent Units		
	Materials	Conversion
Units started and completed during the period	3,500	3,500
Ending work in process: 1,000 units		
With 100% of the material added	1,000	
With 80% conversion		800
Equivalent units of output for the period	4,500	4,300

Spoilage information may not be worth the cost of identifying separately

When the cost of spoilage is not identified separately, it is absorbed into the cost of good units. The increase in unit costs caused by the spoilage and the total cost of the spoilage are not reported. The units transferred out and units in ending work in process include some spoilage cost, but the amount is not identified. This reporting method is used when the value of spoilage cost information does not warrant the cost of separate reporting. Spoilage costs may be relatively small, or nothing can be done to reduce spoilage, so reporting this cost serves no purpose. In other cases, however, managers need to have spoilage cost data identified separately so that spoilage can be monitored and controlled.

Separately Identified Spoiled Units Cost.   Accountants measure and report the cost of spoiled units by doing the following:

1. Determine the cost of one spoiled unit.
2. Multiply the cost of one spoiled unit by the number of units spoiled during the reporting period.
3. Prorate the total spoilage over the number of good units.

Cost of one spoiled unit

Total cost of spoiled units

The first step is to determine the **cost of one spoiled unit,** which is merely the cost to get the unit to the point in the production process where the spoilage or loss is identified. In Process Center 4 the cost of a spoiled unit is the cost transferred into the process center, because the loss is identified in an inspection process at the beginning of Process Center 4. Therefore, the cost of one spoiled unit is $4.95 ($24,750/5,000 units), the unit cost transferred out of Process Center 3 and into Process Center 4. The **total cost of spoilage** is the number of units lost or spoiled times the cost of one unit. In this illustration the total is $2,475 (500 units × $4.95).

When the cost of spoilage is identified separately, spoiled units and good units are combined to measure unit costs. That is, spoiled units are included in the calculation of equivalent units, which are then divided into costs to find unit costs. It is necessary to include spoiled units in the cost calculations so that their cost can be reported in the cost of production report. Production resources are added to all units in production until the spoiled units are identified. Therefore, the cost of making spoiled units is the same as the cost of making good units before the spoilage is discovered. Then the spoiled units are separated and work continues on the good units only. When the production of spoiled units stops, their cost is allocated to the good units that continue in the production process.

The total cost of spoilage is assigned to the good units that have made it beyond the point where the spoilage occurred. Often it is difficult to determine precisely where the loss occurred, and therefore spoilage is spread over all of the good units that have passed beyond the point where the loss was identified. Frequently spoilage is identified at an inspection point or some other quality control procedure even though it may have occurred somewhere else in the manufacturing process.

We illustrate separate reporting of spoiled unit costs by using the same production data from Process Center 4, but this time the cost of spoiled units is reported separately. The cost of production report is presented in Figure 6-5. Except for the separately identified spoiled units cost, this report is the same as Figure 6-4.

In Process Center 4, the spoiled units were identified before any material was added or conversion done in the process center. Therefore, spoiled units are used to calculate equivalent units only for preceding department costs. The calculations of equivalent units for materials and conversion do not include spoiled units in Process Center 4 because those resources were not added to spoiled units in this process center. The calculation of equivalent units is as follows:

Schedule of Equivalent Units			
	Materials	Conversion	Preceding Dept.
Units started and completed this period	3,500	3,500	3,500
Ending work in process: 1,000 units			
With 100% of the material added	1,000		
With 80% conversion		800	
With 100% preceding department			1,000
Equivalent units in spoiled units[a]	0	0	500
Equivalent units of output this period	4,500	4,300	5,000

[a] 500 units are identified as spoiled before any material is added or any conversion is done on them. Therefore only the preceding department costs apply to the spoiled units.

The equivalent units for each cost element are divided into their respective production costs to find unit costs. The only difference between the unit costs reported in Figure 6-4 and those reported in Figure 6-5 is preceding department costs. Because spoiled units are included in the computation of unit costs when spoilage costs are reported separately, the unit cost is $4.95 here rather than the $5.50 reported in Figure 6-4. The $4.95 is the cost of all units — both good and spoiled — transferred into Process Center 4. The total cost of the 500 spoiled units is $2,475 ($4.95 × 500 units). This amount is shown in the cost of production report between the costs to account for section of the report and the cost accounted for section.

Figure 6-5. If a separate spoiled unit cost is identified, spoiled units are treated as good units in computing equivalent units in order to measure the cost of the spoiled units. Then the cost is separated and spread over the cost of the good units.

Kleenway Company
Cost of Production Report
Process Center 4
January

Units to Account For:		Units Accounted For:	
Transferred in during the period	5,000	Units transferred out	3,500
		Ending work in process	1,000
		Spoiled units	500
Total units to account for	5,000	Total units accounted for	5,000

Costs to Account For:	Costs	Equivalent Units	Unit Cost
Preceding department costs	$24,750	5,000	$4.95
Direct material	5,850	4,500	1.30
Direct labor	3,440	4,300	.80
Manufactured overhead	1,720	4,300	.40
Total costs to account for	$35,760		7.45

Spoiled unit cost: 500 units @ $4.95 = $2,475
Spoiled unit cost prorated over good units: $2,475/4,500 units =   .55
$8.00

Costs Accounted For:

Transferred out of the process center:
3,500 units @ $8.00 $28,000

Ending work in process inventory:

Preceding department costs	1,000 units @	4.95	$4,950
Spoiled unit cost	1,000 units @	.55	550
Direct material	1,000 units @	1.30	1,300
Direct labor	800 units @	.80	640
Manufacturing overhead	800 units @	.40	320	7,760

Total costs accounted for $35,760

Schedule of Equivalent Units

	Materials	Conversion	Preceding Dept.
Units started and completed during the period	3,500	3,500	3,500
Ending work in process: 1,000 units			1,000
With 100% of materials	1,000		
With 80% of conversion		800	
Spoiled units[a]	0	0	500[a]
Equivalent units of output for the period	4,500	4,300	5,000[a]

[a] 500 units are lost before any material is added or any conversion is done on the units. Therefore only the preceding department costs were complete before the units were lost.

Next, the total spoilage cost is assigned to the good units. In Process Center 4, all of the units—those transferred out and units in ending inventory—have passed beyond the point where the loss occurred. The total spoilage cost of $2,475 is divided by the 4,500 good units to get $.55, which is the amount of increase in the unit cost of each good unit caused by spoilage. This increase in unit costs often is called the **prorated spoilage cost** or **prorated lost units costs.** Be careful not to confuse this with the cost of one spoiled unit. The cost of one spoiled unit is the unit cost of production to the point in the production process where spoilage is identified, whereas the prorated spoilage cost is the increase in the cost of good units caused by spoilage costs.

The $.55 spoilage cost is added to the unit cost of good units and is included in the costs transferred out of the process center and in the costs of units in ending work in process inventory.

The major difference between the two reports in Figure 6-4 and Figure 6-5 is the separate reporting of spoilage cost. An important issue is whether reporting spoilage costs separately provides benefits that warrant the additional reporting costs. As with all managerial accounting information, managers must make the decision based on cost-benefit relationships. Often spoiled units data are important enough to identify and report separately. Managers use the data to identify unusual production inefficiencies or undesirable trends in the amount of spoilage. Spoilage cost data are useful in determining where to concentrate quality control programs and whether to pay bonuses for outstanding management performance. These and other managerial decisions may be aided, at least in part, by detailed spoiled units cost data.

Spoilage During Processing

Spoilage may be identified at any point in the production process

It is common in manufacturing processes to detect spoilage during the manufacturing process, after some material and labor have been added to production. In such cases any costs incurred in the production of the spoiled units must be included in their costs and assigned to the good units that are manufactured. To illustrate, we continue the previous example.

In Process Center 5, the product is filtered and packaged in 1-gallon containers before transfer to the finished goods inventory. Just before the containers are sealed, their contents go through a final inspection. Any that do not meet standards are discarded. During January, 400 units were rejected. The cost of production report for Process Center 5 is presented in Figure 6-6.

Process Center 5 had beginning work in process of 1,500 units, and 3,500 units were transferred in from Process Center 4. Of the 5,000 units to account for during the month, 4,000 units passed inspection and were transferred to finished goods inventory and 400 units were inspected and did not pass. The remaining 600 units did not yet reach the inspection point and are in ending work in process inventory.

Costs in beginning work in process were $11,700 of preceding department costs, $1,485 of direct material cost, $576 of direct labor cost, and $324 of applied overhead. January production costs in Process Center 5 were $28,000 transferred in from Process Center 4, $3,815 of materials, $2,124 of

Kleenway Company
Cost of Production Report
Process Center 5
January

Units to Account For:		Units Accounted For:	
Beginning work in process	1,500	Units transferred out	4,000
Transferred in during the period	3,500	Ending work in process	600
		Spoiled units	400
Total units to account for	5,000	Total units accounted for	5,000

Costs to Account For:	Costs	Equivalent Units	Unit Cost
Preceding department costs:			
Beginning work in process	$11,700	1,500	$ 7.80
Current period	28,000	3,500	8.00
Total	39,700	5,000	7.94
Direct material:			
Beginning work in process	1,485	1,500	.99
Current period	3,815	3,500	1.09
Total	5,300	5,000	1.06
Direct labor:			
Beginning work in process	576	900	.64
Current period	2,124	3,600	.59
Total	2,700	4,500	.60
Manufacturing overhead:			
Beginning work in process	324	900	.36
Current period	1,476	3,600	.41
Total	1,800	4,500	.40
Total costs to account for	$49,500		10.00

Spoiled unit cost: 400 units @ $10.00 = $4,000
Spoiled unit cost prorated over good units: $4,000/4,000 units   1.00
Total unit cost $11.00

Costs Accounted For:

Transferred out of the process center:

	4,000 units @ $11.00			$44,000
Ending work in process inventory				
Preceding department costs	600 units @	7.94	$4,764	
Direct material	600 units @	1.06	636	
Direct labor	100 units @	.60	60	
Manufacturing overhead	100 units @	.40	40	5,500
Total costs accounted for				$49,500

Schedule of Equivalent Units

	Materials	Conversion	Preceding Dept.
Beginning work in process: 1,500 units			
Required to complete: 0% of materials			
Required to complete: 40% of conversion		600	
Units started and completed during the period	2,500	2,500	2,500
Ending work in process: 600 units			600
With 100% of materials	600		
With 1/6 of conversion		100	
Spoiled units[a]	400	400	400
Equivalent units of output for the period	3,500	3,600	3,500
Equivalent units in beginning work in process	1,500	900	1,500
Total units used to compute average unit costs	5,000	4,500	5,000

[a] Spoiled units occur at the end of production at inspection after all material has been added and all conversion has taken place.

labor, and $1,476 of applied overhead. The company uses weighted average to cost production flows. The cost to account for section reports total unit cost of $10, obtained by adding the average unit cost for each cost element. Before the unit costs can be calculated, however, it is necessary to compute equivalent units.

The units in beginning inventory had all materials added and 60 percent of the conversion completed. The ending inventory has all materials added and 1/6 of the necessary conversion completed. Of course, all of the lost units were 100 percent complete in terms of all cost elements, or they would not have made it to the final inspection point.

To prepare the cost of production report, we first compute the equivalent units and then compute the unit costs. If a separate spoiled unit cost is required, the amount of work done on the spoiled units is included in the computation of equivalent units so that the cost of a spoiled unit can be determined. The computation of equivalent units for this process center is presented below:

Schedule of Equivalent Units

	Materials	Conversion	Preceding Dept.
Beginning work in process: 1,500 units			
Required to complete: 0% of materials			
Required to complete: 40% of conversion		600	
Units started and completed during the period	2,500	2,500	2,500
Ending work in process: 600 units			600
With 100% of materials	600		
With 1/6 of conversion		100	
Spoiled units[a]	400	400	400
Equivalent units of output for the period	3,500	3,600	3,500
Equivalent units in beginning work in process	1,500	900	1,500
Total units used to compute average unit costs	5,000	4,500	5,000

[a] Spoiled units occur at the end of production at inspection after all material has been added and all conversion has taken place.

Unlike Process Center 4, Process Center 5 has spoiled units included in the computation of equivalent units for both materials and conversion. This is done because the spoiled units were not identified in this process center until the end of the production process, after all materials had been added and all conversion had taken place. Therefore, the spoilage cost is $10.00 per unit, the cost to get each unit to the end of the production process in Process Center 5. The total cost of the 400 spoiled units is $4,000 ($10.00 per unit × 400 units).

The total cost of spoilage is shared by the good units that have passed the point where the spoilage is identified. In this case, that is all of the units that made it through the inspection process during the period and were transferred to finished goods. Why was none of the spoilage cost assigned to the units in ending work in process inventory? The answer is that none of those units have been completed and inspected yet. If this month's experience is typical, about 1 out of 11 of the units in ending inventory will not pass inspection when they are finally completed. In other words, some of the units in ending inventory probably will be included in spoiled units next month, but the exact number is not known until the units are completed and inspected during the next period.

Spoiled Units with Salvage Value

Sometimes units that do not satisfy normal quality requirements can be sold, usually for a lower price than regular quality products. The revenue from the sale of these units can reduce, or in some cases eliminate altogether, the loss from spoiled units.

Salvage value reduces the cost of spoiled units

Let us assume that the **normal** lost units that occurred in Process Center 5 and shown in Figure 6-6 can be sold for $6.00 each. Then the **net cost of lost units** is $1,600 ($4,000 − $2,400). The net cost of lost units is the difference between the cost of the spoiled units and the revenue realized from the sale of the units. The cost of production report in Figure 6-6 now must report normal lost units with a salvage value of $6 per spoiled unit. This is shown below with all other data the same as in Figure 6-6. The only difference is that here we assume the spoiled units can be sold for $6 each and in Figure 6-6 the spoiled units have no value and are discarded.

Cost to account for	$49,500	$10.00
Revenue from the sale of spoiled units	(2,400)	
Total costs to account for	$47,100	

Net spoiled unit cost: 400 units × ($10.00 − $6.00) = $1,600

Prorated spoiled unit cost: $1,600/4,000 units =		.40
		$10.40

Costs Accounted For:

Transferred out of the process center:

4,000 units @ $10.40		$41,600

Ending work in process inventory:

Preceding department costs	600 units @	7.94	$4,764	
Direct material	600 units @	1.06	636	
Direct labor	100 units @	.60	60	
Manufacturing overhead	100 units @	.40	40	5,500
Total costs accounted for				$47,100

The revenue realized from the spoiled units is, in effect, a cost reduction. The spoiled units did not really cost $10.00 per unit, but rather $10.00 minus the $6.00 realized from their sale. The $4 net cost of the lost units is assigned to the good units. The result is that the amount of spoiled unit cost assigned to each good unit is $.40 rather than the $1.00 reported in Figure 6-6 when there was no salvage value for the spoiled units. The cost saving realized by the sale of the spoiled units is recorded with the following journal entry:

	Cash	2,400	
	Work in process control		2,400
	To record the sale of spoiled units		
	from Process Center 5.		

If the units are first transferred to a spoiled units inventory and sold sometime later, the entries are:

	Spoiled units inventory	2,400	
	Work in process control		2,400
	To record the transfer of spoiled units		
	to inventory from Process Center 5.		
	Cash	2,400	
	Spoiled units inventory		2,400
	To record the sale of spoiled units.		

Abnormal Spoiled Units

Normal spoilage is usually unavoidable and is an expected part of the manufacturing process. Occasionally, however, unusual spoilage may occur that is not normal. For example, during a power outage a company's backup power system fails, resulting in the loss of several hundred metal casings that are undergoing heat treatment. As another example, a small earthen dam used to store cooling water breaks and causes a small flood that destroys all the units in the ground floor fabricating department.

Abnormal spoilage is not expected

The cost of **abnormal spoilage** is not treated as a cost of production and assigned to the units produced. Instead, these costs are removed from manufacturing costs and expensed in the period in which they occur.

Abnormal spoilage costs are not assigned to good production but are charged to loss for the period

To illustrate the concept of abnormal spoiled units, we return to Process Center 5 and again use the January production data. This time, however, we assume that spoiled units are not normally incurred in this process center. The 400 spoiled units that were identified at the end of production are all abnormal spoilage. The cost of the spoiled units should be identified, removed from the cost of production in Process Center 5, and recorded as an abnormal spoilage loss. The cost of production report for Process Center 5 with the spoilage appears in Figure 6-7.

The difference between Figure 6-7 and Figure 6-6 is that in Figure 6-7 the spoiled units are treated as abnormal spoilage. In both cases, the accountant measures the cost of lost units. With abnormal spoilage, however, the spoilage cost is **not** prorated to the good units. Instead, the spoilage cost is taken out of production costs and recorded as a loss of the period, because abnormal spoilage is, by definition, not a normal cost of production and as

Figure 6-7. This process cost report shows the disposition of abnormal spoiled units. Their cost is taken out of production and charged to a loss account.

Kleenway Company
Cost of Production Report
Process Center 5
January

Units to Account For:		Units Accounted For:	
Beginning work in process	1,500	Units transferred out	4,000
Transferred in during the period	3,500	Ending work in process	600
		Spoiled units	400
Total units to account for	5,000	Total units accounted for	5,000

Costs to Account For:	Costs	Equivalent Units	Unit Cost
Preceding department costs:			
Beginning work in process	$11,700	1,500	$ 7.80
Current period	28,000	3,500	8.00
Total	39,700	5,000	7.94
Direct material:			
Beginning work in process	1,485	1,500	.99
Current period	3,815	3,500	1.09
Total	5,300	5,000	1.06
Direct labor:			
Beginning work in process	576	900	.64
Current period	2,124	3,600	.59
Total	2,700	4,500	.60
Manufacturing overhead:			
Beginning work in process	324	900	.36
Current period	1,476	3,600	.41
Total	1,800	4,500	.40
Total	49,500		$10.00

Less abnormal spoilage cost 400 units
× $10.00   (4,000)

Total costs to account for	$45,500

Costs Accounted For:

Transferred out of the process center:

4,000 units @ $10.00				$40,000

Ending work in process inventory:

Preceding department costs	600 units @	7.94	$4,764	
Direct material	600 units @	1.06	636	
Direct labor	100 units @	.60	60	
Manufacturing overhead	100 units @	.40	40	5,500
Total costs accounted for				45,500

Schedule of Equivalent Units

	Materials	Conversion	Preceding Dept.
Beginning work in process: 1,500 units			
Required to complete: 0% of materials			
Required to complete: 40% of conversion		600	
Units started and completed during the period	2,500	2,500	2,500
Ending work in process: 600 units			600
With 100% of materials	600		
With 1/6 of conversion		100	
Spoiled units[a]	400	400	400
Equivalent units of output for the period	3,500	3,600	3,500
Equivalent units in beginnins work in process	1,500	900	1,500
Total units used to compute average unit costs	5,000	4,500	5,000

[a] Spoiled units occur at the end of production at inspection after all material has been added and all conversion has taken place. Lost units are not normal to the production process.

221

such should not be included in the cost of good products. The journal entry to transfer the abnormal spoilage costs from production to a loss account is shown below:

Recording abnormal spoilage

	Abnormal spoiled unit loss	4,000	
	Work in process control		4,000
	To record the transfer of abnormal		
	spoiled unit cost from Process Center		
	5 to a loss account.		

This journal entry transfers the cost of spoiled units out of the Work in Process Control account, and the cost of production report for the process center also must reflect the reduction in production costs. The $4,000 abnormal spoilage cost is subtracted from the total costs to account for to arrive at an adjusted total costs to account for. Since no spoiled unit cost is assigned to the good units, the total costs to account for and the total costs accounted for are equal after the abnormal spoiled units cost is removed from production.

An alternative treatment of abnormal spoilage on the cost of production report is to leave it in the costs to account for section and then add the total cost of spoiled units in the cost accounted for section. Neither approach is generally better than the other, although the first method discussed illustrates the fact that abnormal spoilage costs are removed from production.

Sale of Abnormal Spoiled Units.   Accounting for the sale of abnormal spoiled units is a simple and logical process. The receipt of cash is recorded, abnormal spoiled unit loss is recognized, and the total cost of the spoiled units is removed from the process center where the loss occurred. To illustrate, we assume the 400 spoiled units that occurred in Process Center 5 are abnormal spoilage and that the units can be sold for $6.00 each.

The journal entry to record the sale of spoiled units must reflect the amount received from the sale and the loss charged for the abnormal spoilage.

	Cash	2,400	
	Abnormal spoilage loss	1,600	
	Work in process control		4,000
	To record the sale of spoiled units from		
	Process Center 5.		

Whether or not abnormal spoiled units have a salvage value, the cost of production report may be prepared as shown in Figure 6-7 although managers may want to see in the report the amount realized from the sale of the spoiled units. In that case the abnormal spoilage may be reported as follows:

Total cost to account for	$49,500
Revenue from the sale of spoiled units	(2,400)
Abnormal spoiled unit cost	(1,600)
Total cost to account for	$45,500

As before, $4,000 is deducted from total cost to account for, but now the amount is split between abnormal spoiled units cost and the salvage value received for the sale of the spoiled units.

SUMMARY

In a process costing environment, when the unit of measure changes from one process center to the next, accountants report units in each cost of production report in terms of output units of the process center for which the report is prepared. Units reported in gallons in one process center may be reported in pounds in the next process center.

Sometimes material is added throughout the manufacturing activity in a process center, and units in ending work in process inventory do not have all material added at the end of the accounting period. The equivalent units of production must be computed for material, recognizing the amount of material needed to complete beginning work in process and the partial completion of the units in ending work in process. The computation is the same as used in computing equivalent units for conversion.

Spoiled or lost units are products that do not satisfy quality control requirements. Normal spoiled units are spoilage that cannot be avoided, given the manufacturing environment. The cost of such units is part of the normal and necessary cost of manufacturing good units. Spoilage cost can be buried in the cost of the good units or reported separately in the cost of production report. Spoilage cost should be reported separately if the value of the information exceeds the cost of reporting it.

The cost of one spoiled unit is the cost to get the unit to the point in the production process where the loss is identified. The total cost of spoiled units is the number of lost or spoiled units times the cost of one spoiled unit. The total cost of the spoiled units is reported and that amount is then prorated over the cost of the units that have passed beyond the point where the loss occurred.

To report spoilage that occurs during the processing activity in a process center, the lost units are included in the computation of equivalent units.

Sometimes spoiled units have some value, which has the effect of reducing the net cost of the loss. The actual cost of spoiled units is the total cost of the loss less any amount received for the sale of the bad units.

Occasionally, abnormal spoilage or abnormal lost units occur. The cost of such spoilage is not included in the manufacturing cost of the good products, but instead is treated as an expense of the period. The cost of abnormal spoilage is removed from the Work in Process Inventory account and charged to a loss account.

KEY TERMS
abnormal spoilage *(220)*
cost of one spoiled unit *(213)*
net cost of lost units *(219)*
normal lost units *(210)*

normal spoilage *(210)*
prorated lost units cost *(216)*
prorated spoilage cost *(216)*
total cost of spoilage *(213)*

QUESTIONS

1. Silversheen Paperboard Company manufactures large cardboard containers used for shipping appliances and equipment. The manufacturing process starts with scrap newspaper, rags, paperboard, and other waste products, which are pulverized and treated in acid baths in large vats. The resulting pulp is then dried and pressed into continuous sheets of heavy brown paper. The rolls of paper are mounted on machines that corrugate, cut, and glue the paper into large sheets of cardboard that are then formed into containers by folding, gluing, and stapling. Assuming that the company uses four process centers, discuss how the manufacturing process should be divided among the process centers and describe the unit measures that each process center should use to measure its output.

2. (AICPA) Define normal spoilage and abnormal spoilage. Explain how normal spoilage costs and abnormal spoilage costs should be reported for management purposes.

3. Microgiant Corporation produces a large variety of household products, such as utensils, paper and plastic dishes, and disposable cutlery. Most production is in a process costing environment. The company has no system for reporting spoilage; it simply assigns all costs to good units leaving a process center. Recently the company hired a new controller, and gave him instructions to develop a policy for reporting all spoilage to management. You are the new controller. What are some of the items you may want to consider in developing the new policy?

EXERCISES

Ex. 6-1
Computing
Equivalent Units

Below are production quantity data for a process center.

Beginning work in process	4,000 units 3/4 material, 1/2 conversion
Units transferred in	16,000 units
Ending work in process	6,000 units 2/3 material, 1/4 conversion

REQUIRED   Compute the equivalent units of production for materials and conversion.

Ex. 6-2
Process Costing
with Materials
Partially Completed

A grain mixture is added evenly throughout production in the first process center of a feed manufacturer. There was no beginning work in process on June 1, and 20,000 tons of output were started during the month. Ending work in process is 3,000 units with 60 percent materials and 50 percent conversion. June production costs are $3,290,000 materials, $481,000 labor, and $333,000 overhead.

REQUIRED   Prepare a June cost of production report in good form for the first process center.

Ex. 6-3
Change in Units from One Process Center to the Next

A company manufactures newsprint in three process centers. Material added at the beginning of production in the second process center triples the number of units transferred into the process center. During February, the first process center transferred out 5,000 units at a total cost of $27,000.

There was no beginning inventory in process center 2 on February 1. Material added at the beginning of production in process center 2 cost $13,500 and tripled the number of units transferred in. February labor cost in the process center was $16,380, and overhead was $12,600. Ending work in process contained 6,000 units with all material and 60 percent conversion.

REQUIRED   Prepare the February cost of production report in good form for the second process center.

Ex. 6-4
Computing Equivalent Units for a Variety of Situations

Below are data on five independent manufacturing situations:

	Situation				
	A	B	C	D	E
Beginning work in process	0	1,000	2,000	5,000	2,500
Percentage complete, materials	—	20	30	100	80
Percentage complete, conversion	—	60	10	90	80
Units transferred in	7,500	9,000	6,500	12,000	8,000
Ending work in process	1,500	2,000	500	4,000	2,500
Percentage complete, materials	100	35	40	90	70
Percentage complete, conversion	70	40	55	80	40

REQUIRED   Compute the current period equivalent units for materials and conversion for each of the **independent** situations described above.

Ex. 6-5
Process Costing with Partially Completed Materials

Blending is the second process center in the production of a blacktop sealer. Material is blended into the base mixture throughout processing in the blending department. During January, 10,000 gallons of product are transferred in from the first process center. Ending work in process for January is 1,000 units, with 75 percent materials and 80 percent conversion. There was no beginning work in process in January. January production costs for blending were $42,900 for materials, $31,850 for labor, $25,480 for manufacturing overhead, and $38,000 of transferred-in costs.

REQUIRED   Prepare the January cost of production report in good form for the blending department.

Ex. 6-6
Journal Entries for Salvage Value of Spoilage

The machining process center identified 2,000 spoiled units in the inspection process at the end of production in the process center. The spoiled units cost $7.75 each. Machining activities are very difficult, requiring skill and concentration by employees. Any spoilage that occurs in this process center is considered normal since some employee error and random errors are bound to occur. Another company has agreed to buy the spoiled units for $4.20 each.

REQUIRED   Prepare any necessary journal entries associated with the lost units.

Ex. 6-7
Recording the Sale of Abnormal Spoilage

Refer to the data in Exercise 6-6. Assume that any spoilage is considered abnormal in the machining process center.

REQUIRED.   Record any necessary journal entries associated with the spoiled units.

Ex. 6-8
Recording
Abnormal Spoilage
REQUIRED

Refer to Exercise 6-6. Assume that there is no market for the spoiled units and they are just discarded with other waste materials.

Record the recognition of the spoiled units.

Ex. 6-9
Computing Spoiled
Unit Cost

During September, 10,000 units were transferred into the finishing process center at a total cost of $465,000. The units are buffed and painted in finishing before transfer to the finished goods inventory. Additional manufacturing costs added in finishing during September amounted to $4.80 per unit. Units are inspected right before they are transferred to finished goods. Any unit not passing inspection is sold to a salvage company for $8.50 each. In September, 500 units were rejected at inspection. There was no beginning or ending work in process inventory in finishing during September.

REQUIRED

a. Compute the total cost of the spoiled units.
b. Compute the per unit net cost of the spoiled units.
c. If there was no beginning inventory in September, compute the prorated share of spoiled unit cost assigned to each good unit.

Ex. 6-10
Normal Spoilage at
the Beginning of
Production

The last department in the manufacture of open-face spinning reels is packaging. Units transferred into this process center are tested before they are sealed in plastic and boxed along with a guarantee and instructions. Units not passing inspection are assumed to be normal spoilage and are junked, since the cost of reworking the units is prohibitive. During March, 10,000 units were transferred into packaging, of which 1,000 did not pass inspection. The costs for March were $45,000 transferred in, $2,700 materials, $3,400 direct labor, and $2,550 manufacturing overhead. On March 31, 2,000 units remained in ending inventory, with all materials and 75 percent conversion. There was no beginning work in process in March. Management's policy is not to identify a separate spoiled unit cost.

REQUIRED

Prepare the March cost of production report in good form for the packaging process center.

Ex. 6-11
Normal Spoilage
with a Separate
Spoiled Unit Cost

Refer to Exercise 6-10. Assume that the policy of management is to identify and report a separate spoiled unit cost.

REQUIRED.   Prepare the March cost of production report in good form for the packaging process center.

Ex. 6-12
Cost of Production
Report with
Normal Spoilage

The first process center in the manufacture of wallboard sealer is mixing. The mixed compound is tested before it is transferred to the next process. Some of the product does not satisfy adhesive requirements and is discarded. Such spoilage is typically small and is part of the normal manufacturing process. During November, 5,000 units were started and 4,500 units were completed and transferred to the next process center. There are 300 units in ending work in process, with all material and two-thirds conversion. Material costs for November were $70,000, labor costs $24,500, and overhead costs $39,200. There was no beginning inventory in November. The management of the company has a policy of identifying all lost unit costs separately.

REQUIRED

Prepare the November cost of production report in good form for the first process center.

Ex. 6-13
Normal Spoilage without a Separate Spoiled Unit Cost

Refer to Exercise 6-12. Assume that management policy is **not** to identify a separate spoiled unit cost.

REQUIRED.   Prepare the November cost of production report in good form for the first process center.

Ex. 6-14
Partial Materials and a Change in Output Units

DKS Industries produces a variety of herbicides and other agricultural supplies. A liquid broadleaf weed control product is manufactured in three process centers. Units transferred out of Process Center 1 triple in quantity with the material added in the second process center. During November, 6,000 units were transferred out of the first process center at a cost of $6.75 per unit.

November manufacturing costs in Process Center 2 were $11,200 for direct materials, $19,200 for direct labor, and $24,000 for manufacturing overhead. There was no beginning work in process inventory in the process center on November 1, and the ending inventory consisted of 5,000 units with 1/5 materials and 3/5 conversion.

REQUIRED

Prepare the November cost of production report in good form for the second process center.

Ex. 6-15
Interpreting Spoiled Units Journal Entries

Below is the April journal entry to record the spoiled units in the finishing process center. Sixty percent of the April spoilage is normal.

	Spoiled goods inventory	4,200	
	Abnormal spoilage loss	2,400	
	Work in process control, finishing		6,600
	To record the transfer of 800 spoiled units		
	from finishing to spoiled goods.		

REQUIRED

a.   What, if anything, was the per unit salvage value of the spoiled units?
b.   Calculate the total number of spoiled units.
c.   Calculate the number of abnormal spoiled units.
d.   Calculate the total cost of all spoiled units.
e.   Calculate the net cost of all normal spoiled units.
f.   If 5,000 good units were manufactured during the month, how much did spoiled units increase the unit cost of good units?

PROBLEMS

P. 6-1
Change in the Number of Units During Processing

The Lochniff Manufacturing Company produces various snack food items that are packaged in cases and sold to wholesale food distributors. One product is manufactured in two process centers. The basic dough is produced in the first center and transferred to the second process center, where additional material is added and the product is baked and packaged. The material added at the beginning of the second process center doubles the number of units transferred in from the first center. Below are relevant production data for December. The company uses the FIFO inventory method.

<u>Process Center 1:</u>

8,000 units transferred out at a cost of $7.40 per unit.

<u>Process Center 2:</u>

Beginning work in process of 2,000 units with all material and 80% conversion. Preceding department cost of $7,100, material cost of $3,600, labor cost of $2,400, and overhead of $2,800.

During December the following costs were incurred in the process center: materials $30,400, labor $22,320, and overhead $25,632.

Ending work in process was 5,000 units with all materials and 60% conversion.

REQUIRED   Prepare the December cost of production report for Process Center 2.

P. 6-2
Process Costing
with Partially
Complete Material

The Vitlea Company produces insecticides for home use. In the final process center in the production of their flying insect spray, material is added throughout the process. During February the following production occurred:

Beginning work in process was 1,000 units with 75 percent materials and 60 percent conversion.
Beginning work in process costs were $1,600 transferred in, $1,125 for direct materials, $660 for direct labor, and $330 for manufacturing overhead.
5,000 units were transferred in during February at a cost of $8,500.
February production costs included:
   Direct materials $9,500
   Direct labor $5,022
   Manufacturing overhead $2,511
Ending work in process was 1,500 units with 2/3 materials and 1/2 conversion.

REQUIRED   Prepare the February cost of production report in good form.

P. 6-3
Computing Spoiled
Unit Costs

A company manufactures a solution used in tanning leather products. The solution requires four manufacturing processes accomplished in four separate process centers. At the end of production in the third process center, the solution is tested for strength and stability. Solution that does not satisfy quality control measures is discarded. Discarded solution is accounted for as normal spoilage.

During one month, 500 units of solution failed to pass the quality control inspection. The cost of units transferred into the process center was $4.60 per unit. Additional cost incurred in the process center during the month was $1.20 per unit.

REQUIRED   Compute the total cost of normal spoilage assuming:

a. All spoilage is normal in this process center.
b. Normal spoilage in the process center does not exceed 200 units per month.
c. All spoilage is normal and can be sold for $2.50 per unit.
d. Normal spoilage for the month does not exceed 200 units and all spoiled units can be sold for $2.50 each.

P. 6-4
Normal Spoiled Units at the Beginning of Processing

Craftison, Inc., makes and sells bilge pumps. In the final assembly process necessary fittings and valves are added to the main pump unit, and the pump is packaged. The pumps are each tested as they enter the assembly department. Any unit that does not generate the standard level of pressure is discarded, and the substandard units are treated as normal lost units. October production and cost data for assembly are presented below.

Beginning work in process 3,000 units with all materials and 2/3 conversion.
Beginning work in process cost:
  Preceding department $36,120
  Direct materials $14,760
  Direct labor $3,880
  Manufacturing overhead $5,940
Current period manufacturing costs:
  9,000 units transferred into assembly during October
  Preceding department costs $109,080
  Direct materials $40,240
  Direct labor $12,120
  Manufacturing overhead $18,060
Ending work in process consists of 4,000 units with all materials and 1/4 conversion.
1,000 units are lost at the beginning of production before any material is added or any conversion takes place in assembly.
Weighted average inventory is used.

REQUIRED Prepare the cost of production report for the assembly department, identifying a separate lost unit cost.

P. 6-5
Normal Spoiled Units at the End of Production

An important product of the Stone Mountain Company is its Downhome Fudge, which it manufactures and sells in 5-pound boxes to candy shops and other specialty stores that sell quality candy. The manufacture of high-quality fudge is a special art that requires careful attention and skill. If the fudge is cooked too long it hardens in the pots and does not have the proper texture. If it is cooked too little it does not harden properly. Each 5-pound box of fudge is tested for quality in the last process center, cooking, before it is sealed and shipped to customers. Any fudge not passing inspection is given to employees free of charge and is treated as normal spoilage.

On May 1 there were 2,000 units of beginning work in process inventory in the cooking department with all materials added and 3/4 of the conversion. During the month 8,000 units were transferred in and 2,000 units remained in work in process at month-end with all materials and 1/2 conversion. Of the units completed during May, 1,000 were rejected in the inspection process. The company policy is to report a separate lost unit cost to monitor the production efficiency of employees. The weighted average inventory method is used to account for all inventories. Below are May cost data for cooking:

Beginning work in process inventory costs:
  Preceding department costs $12,020
  Direct materials $3,840
  Direct labor $2,550
  Manufacturing overhead $3,450

Current period costs:
  Preceding department costs $48,480
  Direct materials $16,160
  Direct labor $13,650
  Manufacturing overhead $18,150

REQUIRED Prepare the May cost of production report for the cooking department in good form.

P. 6-6 (CMA)
Understanding
Process Costing
Data with Spoiled
Units

JC Company employs a process cost system. A unit of product passes through three departments—molding, assembly, and finishing—before it is completed. The following activity took place in the finishing department during May:

	Units
Work in process inventory, May 1	1,400
Units transferred in from the assembly department	14,000
Units spoiled	700
Units transferred out to finished goods inventory	11,200

Raw material is added at the beginning of processing in the finishing department without changing the number of units being processed. The work in process inventory was 70 percent complete as to conversion on May 1 and 40 percent complete as to conversion on May 31. All spoilage was discovered at final inspection before the units were transferred to finished goods; 560 of the units spoiled were within the limit considered normal. JC Company employs the weighted average costing method. The equivalent units and the current costs per equivalent unit of production for each cost factor are as follows:

	Equivalent Units	Current Costs per Equivalent Unit
Cost of prior departments	15,400	$5.00
Raw material	15,400	1.00
Conversion cost	13,300	3.00
Total cost		$9.00

REQUIRED   Respond to the following multiple choice questions:

1. The cost of production transferred to the finished goods inventory is
    a. $100,800.   b. $105,840.   c. $107,100.   d. $102,060.
    e. some amount other than those given above.

2. The cost assigned to work in process inventory on May 31 is
    a. $28,000.   b. $31,000.   c. $25,200.   d. $30,240.
    e. some amount other than those given above.

3. If the total costs of prior departments included in the work in process inventory of the finishing department on May 1 amounted to $6,300, the total cost transferred in from the assembly department to the finishing department during May is
    a. $70,000.   b. $62,300.   c. $70,700.   d. $63,700.
    e. some amount other than those given above.

4. The cost associated with the abnormal spoilage is
    a. $6,300.   b. $1,260.   c. $560.   d. $840.
    e. some amount other than those given above.

5. The cost associated with abnormal spoilage ordinarily would be
    a. charged to inventory.
    b. charged to a material variance account.
    c. charged to retained earnings.
    d. charged to manufacturing overhead.
    e. charged to a special loss account.

P. 6-7 (CMA)
Understanding
Process Costing
Data

The McCullick Company uses a process costing system to account for the production of its product, Glookal. The two production processes are mixing and refining. During the month of July the following production occurred in refining:

	Units
Transferred in from mixing	9,000
Transferred to finished goods	7,000
Beginning work in process	2,500
Units spoiled	1,000

There is no change in the number of units from the beginning to the end of production. Spoiled units occur at the end of production after all production is complete. Material is added at the beginning of production in refining. Work in process inventory on July 1 was 60 percent converted and ending inventory was 80 percent converted. Normal spoilage does not exceed 10 percent of completed units. The company uses the weighted average inventory method.

Unit costs for the month of July were:

	Unit Cost
Preceding department costs	$6.00
Materials costs	1.40
Conversion costs	1.10
Total unit cost	$8.50

REQUIRED

a. Compute the number of units in ending inventory on July 1.
b. Compute the total equivalent units of production used to compute unit costs with average costing.
c. Compute the total cost of spoiled units.
d. If the current period conversion cost in refining was $9,420, what was the cost of conversion in beginning inventory?
e. What is the number of abnormal spoiled units?
f. Compute the cost of abnormal spoilage.
g. Record any necessary journal entries associated with spoiled units.
h. What was the cost of Glookal transferred to finished goods during July?

P. 6-8 (CMA)
Process Costing
without a Separate
Spoiled Unit Cost

West Corporation is a divisionalized manufacturing company. A product called Aggregate is manufactured in one department of the California Division. Aggregate is transferred upon completion to the Utah Division at a predetermined price, where it is used in the manufacture of other products.

The raw material is added at the beginning of the process. Labor and overhead are added continuously throughout the process. Shrinkage of 10 to 14 percent, all occurring at the beginning of the process, is considered normal. In the California Division all departmental overhead is charged to the departments and divisional overhead is allocated to the departments on the basis of direct labor hours. The divisional overhead rate is $2 per direct labor hour.

The following information relates to production during November.

- Work in process, November 1 (4,000 pounds—75% converted)

Raw material	$22,800
Direct labor @ $5.00 per hour	$24,650
Departmental overhead	$12,000
Divisional overhead	$ 9,860

- Raw material:

Inventory, November 1, 2,000 pounds	$10,000
Purchases, November 3, 10,000 pounds	$51,000
Purchases, November 18, 10,000 pounds	$51,500
Released to production during November, 16,000 pounds	

- Direct labor costs @ $5.00 per hour, $103,350
- Direct departmental overhead costs, $52,000
- Transferred to Utah Division, 15,000 pounds
- Work in process, November 30, 3,000 pounds, 33 1/3% converted.

The FIFO method is used for materials inventory valuation and the weighted average method is used for work in process inventories. A separate cost for shrinkage is not required.

REQUIRED   Prepare a cost of production report for the department of California Division producing Aggregate for November that presents:

1. The equivalent units of production by cost factor of Aggregate (e.g., raw material, direct labor, and overhead).
2. The equivalent unit costs for each cost factor of Aggregate.
3. The cost of Aggregate transferred to the Utah Division.
4. The cost of abnormal shrinkage, if any.
5. The cost of the work in process inventory at November 30.

P. 6-9
Normal and
Abnormal Spoiled
Units with Salvage
Value

The lubricating compound produced by Rogets Manufacturing must pass a final quality control inspection before transfer to the finished goods inventory. Although quality standards are quite high, the manufacturing activity is well managed and employees are highly skilled. As a result the company does not expect to experience more than 150 units of spoilage in any particular month. Any amount greater than 150 units in a month is treated as abnormal spoilage. Company policy dictates the reporting of a separate spoiled unit cost.

During August, 3,000 units were in beginning work in process in the last process center with all material and 2/3 conversion. A total of 5,000 units were transferred in from the preceding process center. Ending work in process inventory was 2,500 units complete in terms of material and one-fifth converted. During August, 400 units were rejected at inspection. The rejected units were sold for $3.40 per unit. August production costs included:

Beginning work in process:
  Preceding department costs $12,300
  Direct material costs $4,350
  Direct labor costs $4,680
  Manufacturing overhead costs $4,000

Current period production costs:
Preceding department costs $21,300
Direct material costs $7,650
Direct labor costs $10,320
Manufacturing overhead costs $8,000

The company uses the weighted average inventory method.

REQUIRED

a. Prepare the August cost of production report for the process center.
b. Record the transactions associated with the spoiled units.

P.6-10
Measuring Spoiled
Unit Costs

Painting is the fifth process center in the manufacture of 15-horsepower outboard motors. The transferred-in cost in July was $316, and the transferred-out cost was $342. During July, 8,000 units were transferred into painting. A quality control check in the department shows that 150 of the outboard motors have serious flaws and cannot be sold to the dealers.

REQUIRED

Compute the total cost of normal spoiled units assuming:

a. All spoilage is normal and the units are lost at the beginning of production in painting.
b. All spoilage is normal and the units are lost at the end of production in painting.
c. All spoilage is normal, the units are lost at the beginning of production in painting, and the spoiled units can be sold to a job shop for $125 each.
d. The units are lost at the end of the production process in painting and normal spoilage does not exceed 60 units a month in this process center.
e. The units are lost at the beginning of the production process in painting, normal spoilage does not exceed 60 units per month, and the spoiled units may be sold to a job shop for $125 each.

P. 6-11 (AICPA)
Two Department
Spoilage, Separate
Spoilage Cost

The Dexter Production Company manufactures a single product. Its operations are a continuing process carried on in two departments—machining and finishing. In the production process, materials are added to the product in each department **without increasing the number of units produced.**

For the month of June, the company records indicated the following production statistics for each department.

	Machining Department	Finishing Department
Units in process, June 1	0	0
Units transferred from preceding department	0	60,000
Units started in production	80,000	0
Units completed and transferred out	60,000	50,000
Units in process, June 30[a]	20,000	8,000
Units spoiled in production	0	2,000

[a] Percent of completion of units in process at June 30:

Materials	100%	100%
Labor	50%	70%
Overhead	25%	70%

The units spoiled in production had no scrap value and were 50 percent complete as to material, labor, and overhead. The company's policy is to treat the cost of spoiled units in production as a separate element of cost **in the department in which the spoilage occurs.**

Cost records showed the following charges for the month of June:

	Machining Department	Finishing Department
Materials	$240,000	$ 88,500
Labor	140,000	141,500
Overhead	65,000	25,700

REQUIRED   For both the machining and finishing departments, prepare in good form the following reports for the month of June:

1.   Quantity of production report.
2.   Cost of production report, using the following columnar headings:

Machining Department		Finishing Department	
Cost	Per Unit	Cost	Per Unit

Round all computations to the nearest cent.

P. 6-12 (CMA)
Process Costing
with Normal and
Abnormal Spoilage

Ranka Company manufactures high-quality leather products. The company's profits have declined during the past nine months. Ranka has used unit cost data that were developed eighteen months ago in planning and controlling its operations. In an attempt to isolate the causes of poor profit performance, management is investigating the manufacturing operations of each of its products.

One of Ranka's main products is fine leather belts. The belts are produced in a single, continuous process in the Bluett Plant. During the process leather strips are sewn, punched, and dyed. Buckles are attached by rivets when the belts are 70 percent complete as to direct labor and overhead (conversion costs). The belts then enter a final finishing stage to conclude the process. Labor and overhead are applied continuously during the process.

The leather belts are inspected twice during the process: (1) right before the buckles are attached (70 percent point in the process) and (2) at the conclusion of the finishing stage (100 percent point in the process). Ranka uses the weighted average method to calculate its unit costs.

The leather belts produced at the Bluett Plant wholesale for $9.95 each. Management wants to compare the current manufacturing costs per unit with the prices that exist on the market for leather belts. Top management has asked the Bluett Plant to submit data on the cost of manufacturing the leather belts for the month of October. These cost data will be used to evaluate whether modifications in the production process should be initiated or whether an increase in the selling price of the belts is justified. The cost per equivalent unit that is being used for planning and controlling purposes is $5.35 per unit.

The work in process inventory consisted of 400 partially completed units on October 1. The belts were 25 percent complete as to conversion costs. The costs included in the inventory on October 1 were as follows:

Leather strips	$1,000
Conversion costs	300
Total cost	$1,300

During October, 7,600 leather strips were placed in production. A total of 6,800 good leather belts were completed. A total of 300 belts were identified as defective at the two inspection points—100 at the first inspection point (before buckle is attached) and 200 at the final inspection point (after finishing). This quantity of defective belts was considered normal. In addition, 200 belts were removed from the production line when the process was 40 percent complete as to conversion costs because they had been damaged as a result of a malfunction during the sewing operation. This malfunction was considered an unusual occurrence, and consequently, the spoilage was classified as abnormal. Defective (spoiled) units are not reprocessed and have zero salvage value. The work in process inventory on October 31 consisted of 700 belts that were 50 percent complete as to conversion costs.

The costs charged to production during October were as follows:

Leather strips	$20,600
Buckles	4,550
Conversion costs	20,700
Total cost	$45,850

REQUIRED   In order to provide cost data regarding the manufacture of leather belts in the Bluett Plant to the top management of Ranka Company, determine for the month of October

    a. The equivalent units for each factor of production.

    b. The cost per equivalent whole unit for each factor of production.

    c. The assignment of total production costs to the work in process inventory and to goods transferred out.

    d. The average unit cost of the 6,800 good leather belts completed and transferred to finished goods.

    e. Explain the difference between normal and abnormal spoilage.

CASES

Case 6-1
Analyzing Process
Costing Data

As a member of the internal audit staff of a large manufacturing company, you have been sent to audit the cost of production reports of the assembly process center used in the production of color picture tubes. After several days of work on the reports and supporting documents for the first six months of the year, you identify the following items:

- In August, 10,000 picture tubes were manufactured at a cost of $48 per unit ($24 preceding department cost, $14 materials, and $10 conversion).
- During August, 2,000 tubes were faulty at final inspection and discarded although they could have been sold for $8 each as scrap.
- It is unusual in this process center to have more than 500 spoiled units in a month.
- Both beginning and ending work in process inventory had 2,000 units with 80 percent materials and 60 percent conversion.

- The faulty picture tubes were treated as good units in preparing the cost of production report. It showed that 12,000 tubes were transferred to finished goods at a cost of $48 each.
- $26,400 of assembly direct labor costs were charged to the wrong production department by mistake.
- Company policy calls for a separate lost units cost.
- Average costing is used.
- The new accountant who has responsibility for preparing the assembly cost of production report seems very unhappy with the time he is spending helping you find audit evidence.

REQUIRED

a. Prepare a schedule showing the total unit cost before any spoiled units adjustment.
b. Calculate the total cost of spoiled units.
c. Calculate the normal cost of spoiled units.
d. Prepare any necessary journal entry to record spoiled units, assuming the spoiled units were not sold.
e. Calculate the total cost to account for before any spoiled unit adjustments.
f. Calculate the affect of not selling the spoiled units on the unit cost of good units.
g. Record any necessary journal entries for spoiled units assuming the units had been sold for scrap.
h. Comment on the new accountant's performance and attitude.

PART THREE
Planning and Control

The complex business environment facing business managers today dictates systematic planning and an effective system of monitoring and controlling activities. Effective managers plan every phase of business operations and ensure, by means of well-developed control systems, that plans are carried out. Managers in large organizations achieve goals by assigning responsibility to subordinates and by monitoring activities in all segments of the business with performance reporting systems. Many commonly used performance reports are presented in this section of the book.

For most organizations, planning is accomplished primarily with the company's budgeting system. Chapter 7 introduces the concepts of budgeting and shows how an initial product sales estimate is developed into a comprehensive budget and how actual results are compared with budget data in performance reports. Chapter 8 discusses standard costs and their role in measuring performance. Chapter 9 extends the discussion of budgeting to flexible budgets, which are prepared for a range of possible activity levels.

CHAPTER 7
Fundamental Budgeting Concepts

Much of the discussion in the first six chapters of this book is devoted to measuring, interpreting, analyzing, and reporting actual costs, sometimes called historical costs. Actual costs are of great interest to managers, investors, lenders, and others, because they are identifiable, measurable, and verifiable. They did in fact occur, and often people believe that costs of the immediate past are the best indicator of costs in the near future. Yet by themselves, actual costs do not provide a complete picture of the success of a firm or a measure of how well it succeeded in achieving its goals. To increase the value of actual cost data, firms often compare actual costs with expected costs to determine how well the firm performed.

The purpose of this chapter is to introduce the basic framework of budgeting, define significant budgeting terms, and illustrate the nature of the formal budgeting process. We emphasize budgeting for a business, but the concepts discussed are applicable to nonbusiness organizations as well.

CHARACTERISTICS OF BUDGETS

Definition of a budget

A **budget** is a comprehensive, formal plan, expressed in quantitative terms, describing the expected operations of a business over some future time period. A budget: (1) deals with a specific entity; (2) covers a future time period; and (3) is quantitative.

Budget Entity

A budget must apply to a specific, clearly defined entity

A budget may cover only a small part of an operation, such as revenues for a department or expenses for a project, or it may cover all aspects of all operations for an entity. A budget must be identified with a clearly defined accounting entity. For budgeting purposes, a **budget entity** consists of a part of an organization, such as a department or division; a specific function, such as marketing or accounting; or an identifiable activity, such as a construction project or an employee education program. The budget entity must be carefully defined before the budget is prepared. For example, the budget for the engineering design of a wind-driven generator is illustrated in Figure 7-1. Note that the budget covers only the activity of designing the generator. It does not include building a prototype, testing it, tooling to manufacture the generators, nor marketing them. The budget would be different if the budget entity included building a prototype generator. If the firm wishes to budget more than the design, the budget entity is different and the firm must determine in advance just what this budget entity is.

Figure 7-1. A simple budget. Most organizations find it necessary to do some budgeting, although the budgeting process may be quite informal.

Spinfast Company
Budget for Designing a
Wind-Driven Generator
For the Quarter Ending June 30, 1985

Research salaries	$12,600
Designer salaries	9,800
Drafting	3,600
Materials and supplies	450
Office overhead	5,000
Total	$31,450

Future Time Period

Budgets are estimates of future economic events

Budgets are projections, or forecasts, covering some period of time in the future. Unless the time period is clearly specified, the budget data may be of little value. The time period may be long or short, depending on the information needs and planning needs of management and on the nature and function of the activity budgeted. Whether the budget covers a month, a year, or 10 years, the time period should be clearly stated.

Typically, the shorter the time period covered by the budget, the more detailed the budget. Managers need detailed, timely budgets to schedule production, plan for labor requirements, manage inventory, and provide liquidity. For many firms, quarterly budgets provide adequate detail.

Important areas such as the management of cash resources may require weekly or daily budgets to help managers make effective decisions. Short-range budgets make possible quicker detection of problems and responses to them. They also allow managers to make adjustments when necessary in order to manage scarce resources properly.

Long-term budgets may be prepared for 2, 5, 10, or more years in the future. For example, electric utilities must prepare budgets for long-range sales of electric power as a basis for constructing adequate power-generating facilities.

Quantitative Budgets

Plans are expressed in quantitative measures

Budgets may contain significant qualitative descriptions of the programs and activities in addition to the quantitative data. From an accounting point of view, however, the primary consideration is the quantitative description of the activities covered by the budget. A budget is most useful when all plans are reduced to the common measure of money and units of output and input.

PURPOSES OF BUDGETING

Budgeting serves a variety of important purposes for an organization. Budgeting:

1. Requires periodic planning
2. Fosters coordination, cooperation, and communication

3. Forces managers to quantify their plans
4. Establishes a framework for evaluating performance
5. Creates an awareness of the cost of operating a business
6. Satisfies legal and contractual requirements
7. Orients activities toward organizational goals

There are many reasons for budgeting

Periodic Planning

Few intended objectives are achieved without planning. In personal life, even simple activities such as a family outing requires some small amount of planning to ensure that food and other necessary picnic supplies are available. More complex activities such as a two-week vacation to Hawaii require significantly more planning to ensure that travel and accommodation arrangements are made. In business, planning is even more essential, because many people are involved in managing and operating the business. Planning is necessary to coordinate the efforts of all to achieve company goals. Furthermore, planning is necessary to ensure the effective and efficient use of scarce resources. Budgeting provides a framework that specifies measurable periodic objectives for each phase of planning.

Budgets should help to achieve organizational goals

Periodic budgets do not ensure success; the plan also must be executed. But budgets do guide operations, and serve as a standard for comparing planned activities with actual results.

Coordination, Cooperation, and Communication

If members of an organization acted independently of the others, each free to develop and execute individual plans, there would be little chance of achieving organizational goals. The organization's budget is the means of integrating the plans of everyone in the organization. The budgeting process is an excellent vehicle for the exchange of ideas and coordination of plans among all parts of the organization. The need to coordinate the plans of various organizational segments fosters communication among managers, and requires cooperation among organizational units when the budgeting process discloses possible problems. The budget helps to detect problems that may emerge during operations and provides the basis for solving these problems or avoiding them before they occur.

Quantification

Organizations typically have managers with many diverse skills that together form the means for achieving organizational goals. Top managers may find it difficult to evaluate and monitor such diverse activities as engineering, manufacturing, marketing, product research, and accounting. Each of these functional areas provides essential services, and each provides different benefits for the organization. A budget supplies the common denominator for evaluating all activities and the allocation and use of company resources. Activities, operations, and the use of resources planned for the budget period are expressed in monetary terms in the budget.

Quantifying the budget enables managers to compare the costs and benefits of their projects to evaluate the most appropriate allocation of resources. Measuring costs and benefits in quantitative terms may not be easy. For example, the benefits of an advertising campaign may be increased sales and an improved company image. The cost of the campaign may be measured easily, but it is difficult to estimate the specific amount of additional sales revenue resulting from the advertising. It is even more difficult to quantify the improvement in the company image, and what that means in terms of increased sales revenue.

Performance Evaluation

Budgets are used to evaluate performance

Since budgets are management's estimates of future operations, they also serve as realistic estimates of acceptable performance by the management of the budget entity. Managerial performance may be appraised by comparing actual performance with expected performance as expressed in the budget. Managers like to know what is expected of them; the budget supplies this information and gives managers the basis for monitoring their own performance.

Cost Awareness

Accounting managers and finance managers tend to be aware of the cost implications of decisions and activities. Other managers would have little concern about costs if the budget did not focus their attention on the cost of their operations. Marketing managers think about sales; production supervisors concentrate on output of products; engineers may be preoccupied with product design. It is easy for many people to overlook costs and cost-benefit relationships. At budgeting time, however, managers who are responsible for their budgets must think in terms of costs and benefits as they evaluate projects and activities. This cost awareness provides the common language among the various functional areas of an organization.

Legal and Contractual Requirements

Many not-for-profit organizations are required to prepare periodic budgets. A local fire department may consider its budget too much trouble, but it cannot ignore it. Many agencies would simply go out of existence if they decided one year not to submit a budget. Although most businesses have no legal budgeting requirements, many enter into contractual agreements that require them to prepare budgets. Loan agreements or licensing arrangements may require companies to submit periodic budgets to the entity providing loan funds or operating licenses.

Goal Orientation

Resource allocation decisions should be based on the organization's goals and objectives. It is not always easy to relate general organizational goals to specific projects and activities. The reason is that many organizations have nonoperational goals. For example, the following organizational goals are not operational:

Earn a satisfactory profit each year

Maintain an adequate growth rate

Maintain sufficient liquidity

The terms **satisfactory, adequate,** and **sufficient** do not have specific meanings. Goals such as the ones listed above are not operational because they cannot be achieved by means of specific operations.

Operational goals, on the other hand, are stated in terms that permit achievement by means of operations whose results can be measured. The following are operational goals:

Earn a return of 14 percent on capital

Maintain a sales growth rate of 10 percent per year

Maintain a current ratio of 1.8 or greater

Organizational goals and objectives should be stated formally

Goal-oriented budgeting can be based only on operational goals. The first step toward effective budgeting is to formalize the goals of the organization. Starting at the top, general organizational goals should be clearly stated in writing, even if they are not operational. Next, each major unit of the organization should develop specific operational goals that indicate how they contribute to the organization's goals. Divisions of each organizational unit must do the same.

FUNCTIONS OF BUDGETING

Budgeting serves two primary functions: planning future operations and activities, and controlling those operations and activities.

Planning

To many people, budgeting is synonymous with planning. The formal **planning** process encompasses the entire range of budget preparation activities from initial ideas through the final stages of budget development. If planning is carried out carefully, it establishes the framework for controlling the resulting plans.

Control

In the control phase of budgeting, actual results are compared with budgets to evaluate performance

Controlling encompasses comparing actual results with the budgeted expectations, evaluating the differences, and taking necessary action to adjust for differences. Actual results and budgeted expectations can be compared only after some actual accounting data are available. For example, when January actual cost data are available they can be compared with the January budgeted cost data to measure any differences. Such comparisons are often prepared in **budget performance reports,** which show performance based on both budgeted and actual data and the differences between them.

The term *control* does not refer merely to reducing cost. It refers to monitoring performance and taking corrective actions when actual results differ from expectations. The budget acts as a gauge against which managers measure actual costs and revenues. Revenues cannot be generated without incurring costs. The idea is to optimize costs rather than minimize them. If an additional dollar of costs increases the return on investment, that cost should be incurred; if the additional cost increases revenue by an amount that is too small to increase return, that cost should not be incurred. The budget helps managers to optimize costs and to ensure the highest possible return on each dollar spent.

THE MASTER BUDGET

The **master budget** is the final product of the entire planning function of the budgeting process. It is the end result of all budgets combined into a single plan that describes the firm's operations for the next accounting period. Because the intent of business organizations is to earn a profit, the master budget is sometimes referred to as a **profit plan.** What exactly comprises a master budget depends on the type and size of the business. However it is structured, the master budget represents the organization's overall plan for the budget period.

The total budget package is a plan for successful operations

The discussion that follows focuses on a manufacturing firm, but many of the concepts pertain to all types of organizations. The basic components of the manufacturing firm's master budget are presented in two major categories: the operating budget and the financial budget, as shown in Figure 7-2. The components fit together to make up the detailed operating and financial plan for the organization's next accounting period.

Figure 7-2. Typical master budget for a manufacturing firm. Master budgets for other types of organizations also include an operating budget and a financial budget, although the components of each may vary. For example, a merchandising firm does not prepare a production budget.

The Master Budget

Operating Budgets	Financial Budgets
Sales budget	Capital expenditure budget
Ending inventory budgets	Cash budget
Production budgets:	Budgeted balance sheet
Direct materials budget	Budgeted statement of changes
Direct labor budget	in financial position
Manufacturing overhead budget	Other budgets as required
Cost of goods manufactured budget	
Cost of goods sold budget	
Selling expense budget	
Administrative expense budget	
Budgeted net income	

The **operating budget** includes budgeted revenues, production costs, and operating expenses, which result in budgeted net income. The **financial budget** includes the budgeted balance sheet, plans for capital projects, and detailed plans on cash inflows and outflows, including borrowing and investing plans. A major portion of the financial budget is determined by the operating budget and the beginning balance sheet.

Even for a small organization, the master budget can be a voluminous document. The simple example we provide indicates the size and complexity of the master budget. The example shows a **fixed budget,** also called a **static budget,** which means that the budget is prepared for a specific level of activity. Flexible budgets, which cover several possible activity levels, are discussed in Chapter 9.

The master budget in our example is the 1986 budget for Castone Corporation, a manufacturer of precast concrete beams and columns used in the construction of bridges, overpasses, causeways, and highway ramps. These products are manufactured in the factory and delivered to construction sites. The company produces concrete beams and columns of a standard size and shape for inventory, and for special orders, using a job order cost system. Highway construction in the company's geographic market takes place primarily in spring, summer, and early fall, with less activity during the winter. Although the demand for the company's products declines during the winter, the company operates year-round, with excess winter production used to build inventory.

Resources are required for production

The company cannot predict the exact proportion of beams and columns that will be demanded, because builders use the beams and columns in two different ways, as illustrated in Figure 7-3. Normal construction requires two columns and one beam spaced 20 to 30 feet apart, depending on the engineering design. Highways designed to carry heavy loads require three columns with one beam.

Production of Castone Corporation's columns and beams requires labor and two raw materials. The resources and costs used to produce the columns and beams are presented in the table at the top of the next page.

Figure 7-3. Two products used in highway construction whose manufacture is to be budgeted for a one-year period. The steel-reinforced concrete beam may be placed on two concrete columns or it may require three columns for heavy loads. The budgets in this chapter are for the production of these two simple products. Imagine the budgets that are needed for a much more complex manufacturing situation.

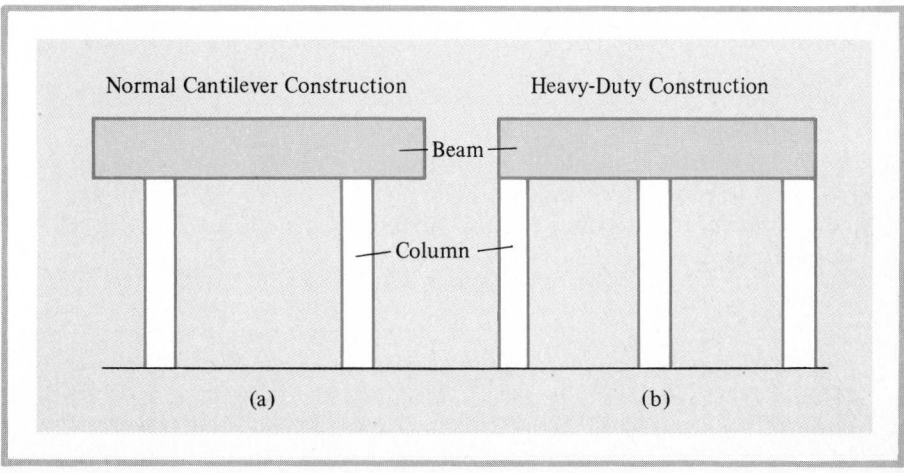

		Product	
Resource	Cost	Column	Beam
Reinforcing steel	$.30/lb	200 lb	500 lb
Concrete	$50/cu yd	.5 cu yd	2 cu yd
Direct labor	$12/hr	2 hr	5 hr

The Operating Budget

The operating budget consists of many separate budgets

The **operating budget** is a plan of the expected revenues and expenses from normal operations and activities. For profit-seeking firms, revenues and expenses make up the income statement. The operating budget includes detailed budgets for all of the income statement components, such as sales, production, marketing, and administration.

Sales Budget. The **sales budget** is management's estimate of sales volume and sales revenue. It is the first budget to be prepared because the estimates in the other budgets are based on the sales estimates. Production, marketing, administrative, inventory, personnel, and other budgets are all affected by the amount of expected sales revenue. Many factors are incorporated in the sales budget, such as economic conditions, pricing decisions, competitor actions, industry conditions, and marketing programs. To develop the most reliable sales budget possible, firms employ experts and spend considerable resources in sales forecasting.

The sales budget is prepared first

Castone Corporation makes its sales projections on the basis of highway department construction plans and highway designs, estimating the proportion of precast concrete beams and columns that will be ordered from the company. The sales budget is based on the expected sales and the unit selling price of the products. The 1986 sales budget, prepared in units and dollars, is illustrated in Figure 7-4. This sales budget is composed of quarterly sales

Castone Corporation
Sales Budget
For the Year Ending December 31, 1986

	Columns		Beams		Total	
	Units	Revenue	Units	Revenue	Units	Revenue
Selling price		$260		$600		
First quarter	10,000	$ 2,600,000	4,000	$ 2,400,000	14,000	$ 5,000,000
Second quarter	15,000	3,900,000	6,000	3,600,000	21,000	7,500,000
Third quarter	18,000	4,680,000	7,000	4,200,000	25,000	8,880,000
Fourth quarter	12,000	3,120,000	5,000	3,000,000	17,000	6,120,000
Total	55,000	$14,300,000	22,000	$13,200,000	77,000	$27,500,000

Figure 7-4. Sales budget prepared by quarters in units and in dollars. The seasonal fluctuations in the quarterly amounts would be hidden if only annual figures were presented.

estimates. Some firms prepare sales budgets of shorter duration, such as monthly. The time interval of the budget should meet management's planning and control needs.

Ending Inventory Budget.   Inventories often comprise a large portion of the current assets of manufacturing companies. Management must determine the optimum level of ending inventories for raw materials, work in process, and finished goods. The availability of materials, delivery times, inventory ordering and carrying costs, the cost of running out of inventory, and other variables affect inventory level decisions.

Inventories must be carefully budgeted

The **ending inventory budget** for finished goods, illustrated in Figure 7-5, shows how much ending inventory the company expects to have on hand each quarter, based on management's inventory policy. Castone operates in a somewhat seasonal market, as reflected in its sales budget. To satisfy demand for its products, Castone maintains inventories of columns and beams at the end of each quarter equal to 10 percent of next quarter's budgeted sales. Second quarter sales are expected to be 15,000 columns and 6,000 beams, so the ending inventory for the first quarter is budgeted at 1,500 columns and 600 beams. Note that the ending inventory of finished goods at the end of the fourth quarter requires an estimate of sales for the first quarter of 1987.

Figure 7-5. The quarterly budget for ending finished goods inventory is determined by expected sales levels and desired supplies of each inventory item.

Castone Corporation
Budgeted Quarterly Ending Finished Goods Inventory
For the Year Ending December 31, 1986

	Quarter			
	1	2	3	4
Columns	1,500	1,800	1,200	1,100
Beams	600	700	500	450

Production Quantity Budget.   The production quantity budget is the starting point for developing the entire set of production budgets. It becomes part of the **production budget,** which consists of budgets for production quantities, direct materials, direct labor, and manufacturing overhead. The raw materials ending inventory budget also emerges as a result of planning production quantities.

Production quantities are calculated with the help of sales and inventory budgets

The **production quantity budget** indicates the number of units of each product to be produced. It includes information from the sales budget and finished goods ending inventory budget. Planned production includes the units expected to be sold during the period plus the units needed in finished goods ending inventory at the end of the period. However, any beginning inventory reduces the total production requirement for the period.

The quarterly production quantity budget of Castone Corporation is illustrated in Figure 7-6. The inventory of beams and columns at the **beginning** of the first quarter must be estimated, because the master budget is prepared well before the end of the current accounting period. Actual data for

Castone Corporation
Production Quantity Budget
For the Year Ending December 31, 1986

Figure 7-6. The production quantity budget is prepared from information on beginning and ending inventory requirements and quarterly sales estimates. This budget is the primary determinant of the amounts in all the other production budgets.

Columns	1	2	3	4	Total
		Quarter			
Budgeted sales in units	10,000	15,000	18,000	12,000	55,000
Required ending inventory	1,500	1,800	1,200	1,100	1,100
Total requirements	11,500	16,800	19,200	13,100	56,100
Less beginning inventory	1,000	1,500	1,800	1,200	1,000
Budgeted production	10,500	15,300	17,400	11,900	55,100
Beams					
Budgeted sales in units	4,000	6,000	7,000	5,000	22,000
Required ending inventory	600	700	500	450	450
Total requirements	4,600	6,700	7,500	5,450	22,450
Less beginning inventory	400	600	700	500	400
Budgeted production	4,200	6,100	6,800	4,950	22,050

the end of the current year are not available yet. Estimates of finished goods inventories at the end of the current year are available from the 1985 budget. Here you see that the 1986 budget requires estimates of 1985 production.

The beginning inventory for each quarter is the ending inventory of the previous quarter, shown in the finished goods inventory budget in Figure 7-5. For example, required production of concrete beams for the second quarter is calculated as follows:

Budgeted second quarter sales of beams	6,000 units
Add required ending finished goods inventory	700
Total	6,700
Less beginning inventory (ending inventory of first quarter)	600
Budgeted production quantity for second quarter	6,100 units

Raw Materials Ending Inventory Budget.   Sometimes it is possible to prepare the ending inventory budget for raw materials at the same time as for finished goods. If the level of ending inventory depends on the production quantity budget, as it does in our example, the production quantity budget must be prepared before the **raw materials ending inventory budget.** Castone Corporation's policy is to have sufficient reinforcing steel on hand at the end of one quarter to meet 20 percent of the next quarter's production. This policy is based, in part, on delivery time for reinforcing steel. There is no ending inventory of concrete because the company uses ready-mix concrete obtained from a local vendor as needed.

The budget in Figure 7-7 shows the number of pounds of steel required in ending inventory at the end of each quarter. For the first quarter's ending

Another inventory budget

Castone Corporation
Budgeted Raw Materials Ending Inventory
For the Year Ending December 31, 1986

	Quarter			
Columns	1	2	3	4
Next quarter's production in units	15,300	17,400	11,900	11,500[a]
× pounds of steel per column	200	200	200	200
Steel required, pounds	3,060,000	3,480,000	2,380,000	2,300,000
Beams				
Next quarter's production in units	6,100	6,800	4,950	4,650[a]
× pounds of steel per beam	500	500	500	500
Steel required, pounds	3,050,000	3,400,000	2,475,000	2,325,000
Total steel required, pounds	6,110,000	6,880,000	4,855,000	4,625,000
× required percentage	.20	.20	.20	.20
Ending inventory of steel, pounds	1,222,000	1,376,000	971,000	925,000

[a] Estimated for first quarter of 1987.

Figure 7-7. Raw materials inventory levels are budgeted from estimated production. The quantities must comply with company policy on minimum levels of inventories. Excessive inventories tie up capital without producing revenue.

inventory requirement, the second quarter's budgeted production is used to calculate the total steel requirement for both columns and beams. Twenty percent of this is then budgeted for ending inventory in the first quarter. Here again it is necessary to estimate production requirements for the first quarter of 1987 in order to plan ending inventory of steel for the last quarter of 1986. This ending inventory budget is expressed in units, but when the 925,000 pounds of steel are shown in the budgeted balance sheet, they will be shown at estimated cost in dollars.

Direct Materials Budget. The raw materials ending inventory budget in Figure 7-7 reflects factors such as the time required to receive materials after placing an order and the cost of ordering and carrying the inventory. The **direct materials budget** describes the amount of direct material expected to be used during the budget period. Because in our illustration all raw materials are used in production as direct materials, the direct materials budget, shown in Figure 7-8, is based on the raw materials ending inventory budget and on the production quantity budget. The direct materials budget reflects the cost of direct materials that will be required for each quarter's production. Knowing the necessary lead times for ordering materials is important for planning production in each period. The budget in Figure 7-8 shows the number of pounds of steel and the number of cubic yards of concrete that will be required each quarter, and it also shows the cost of these materials. These costs are used in other budgets needed for financial planning.

Castone Corporation
Direct Materials Budget
For the Year Ending December 31, 1986

Reinforcing Steel in Pounds	Quarter 1	2	3	4	Total
Required for columns	2,100,000	3,060,000	3,480,000	2,380,000	11,020,000
Required for beams	2,100,000	3,050,000	3,400,000	2,475,000	11,025,000
Ending inventory required	1,222,000	1,376,000	971,000	925,000	925,000
Total requirements	5,422,000	7,486,000	7,851,000	5,780,000	22,970,000
Less beginning inventory	840,000	1,222,000	1,376,000	971,000	840,000
Current period purchases	4,582,000	6,264,000	6,475,000	4,809,000	22,130,000
× Cost per pound	$.30	$.30	$.30	$.30	$.30
Cost of steel purchases	$1,374,600	$1,879,200	$1,942,500	$1,442,700	$ 6,639,000
Concrete in cubic yards					
Required for columns	5,250	7,650	8,700	5,950	27,550
Required for beams	8,400	12,200	13,600	9,900	44,100
Total requirements	13,650	19,850	22,300	15,850	71,650
× Cost per cubic yard	$50	$50	$50	$50	$50
Cost of concrete purchases	682,500	992,500	1,115,000	792,500	3,582,500
Total materials cost	$2,057,100	$2,871,700	$3,057,500	$2,235,200	$10,221,500

Figure 7-8. The direct materials budget is a plan for purchasing materials for use in production. It is based on required beginning and ending inventory levels and production during each quarter. The budget for concrete is simpler than the one for reinforcing steel because concrete cannot be stored in inventory. Material quantity purchased is converted to dollars by multiplying by the purchase price for each raw material. The dollar amounts are used in the cash budget to plan cash payments.

The figures in the direct materials budget require some explanation, as they are obtained from calculations that are not all shown in the budget. For example, the steel requirement for the first quarter is computed as follows:

First quarter budgeted production of columns from Figure 7-6	10,500 units
Pounds of steel required for each column	× 200 lb per unit
Total steel required for columns	2,100,000
First quarter budgeted production of beams from Figure 7-6	4,200 units
Pounds of steel required for each beam	× 500 lb per unit
Total steel required for beams	2,100,000
Required ending inventory of steel from Figure 7-7	1,222,000
Total	5,422,000 lb
Less beginning inventory of steel as budgeted in current period and reported in 1985 budgeted balance sheet	840,000
Total steel requirement	4,582,000 lb
Budgeted cost of steel per pound	× $.30
Total cost of steel required for first quarter	$1,374,600

As you can see, the amount of raw material needed for each quarter is obtained by multiplying the number of units to be produced by the amount of material needed for each unit. The calculation shown is for reinforcing steel only. A similar calculation must be made for concrete requirements. Note that the calculation for concrete is somewhat simpler than that for steel, because there are no beginning and ending inventories of concrete.

First quarter budgeted production of columns (from Figure 7-6)	10,500 units
Cubic yards of concrete for each column	× .5 yd per unit
Concrete required for columns	5,250 cu yd
First quarter budgeted production of beams (from Figure 7-6)	4,200 units
Cubic yards of concrete for each beam	× 2 yd per unit
Concrete required for beams	8,400 cu yd
Total concrete required for the quarter	13,650 cu yd
Cost of concrete per cubic yard	× $50
Total cost of concrete required in first quarter	$682,500

Combining the cost of steel and concrete yields the total direct material cost for both columns and beams for the first quarter. Each subsequent quarter's direct material cost is calculated in a similar way.

Direct Labor Budget. The **direct labor budget** identifies the quantity and cost of direct labor needed for the budget period. This budget is essential for production planning and for planning personnel resources. Firms must plan for any changes in labor requirements resulting from changes in the mix of products sold or resulting from cyclical sales and production patterns. Managing fluctuations in materials needs is easier than managing labor. Typically, it is easier to acquire more or less material as necessary than it is to hire or terminate qualified personnel. Labor relations must be considered, as well as contractual obligations with labor unions. A firm that simply dismisses workers when production slows down may quickly develop labor difficulties. Consequently, labor requirements must be planned very carefully with the direct labor budget.

Budgeted production determines the need for direct labor

The direct labor budget in Figure 7-9 is prepared directly from the production quantity budget in Figure 7-6. The budgeted quantities of columns and beams are multiplied by the required number of hours of labor needed for each product. Two hours of direct labor are budgeted for each column and 5 hours for each beam. The total hours required in each quarter are multiplied by the labor rate to obtain the total cost of direct labor for each quarter and for the entire year. These figures are used to plan personnel hiring, and also to prepare financial budgets. In this example we assume a single labor rate and ignore many complicating factors. The primary purpose here is to illustrate the basic budgeting concepts.

Castone Corporation
Direct Labor Budget
For the Year Ending December 31, 1986

Columns	Quarter				Total
	1	2	3	4	
Budgeted production in units	10,500	15,300	17,400	11,900	55,100
× hours per unit	2	2	2	2	2
Hours required	21,000	30,600	34,800	23,800	110,200
Beams					
Budgeted production in units	4,200	6,100	6,800	4,950	22,050
× hours per unit	5	5	5	5	5
Hours required	21,000	30,500	34,000	24,750	110,250
Total hours required	42,000	61,100	68,800	48,550	220,450
× hourly rate	$12	$12	$12	$12	$12
Total direct labor cost	$504,000	$733,200	$825,600	$582,600	$2,645,400

Figure 7-9. The direct labor budget is an extension of the production quantity budget in Figure 7-6. Production quantities are multiplied by each product's labor requirement.

Manufacturing Overhead Budget. The **manufacturing overhead budget** is a schedule showing the expected amounts of variable overhead cost and fixed overhead cost that will be incurred during the budget period. Manufacturing overhead consists of both fixed and variable cost components. Variable overhead costs fluctuate proportionately with the volume of production, while fixed overhead costs remain constant. Variable overhead costs such as indirect labor and indirect materials cannot be related directly to the production of specific products, although these overhead costs vary with the volume of production. For example, past experience may indicate that for every hour of direct labor, or for every unit of output produced, a certain amount of variable overhead cost is incurred.

Castone Corporation uses direct labor hours as its measure of activity for budgeting variable overhead costs. The budgeted variable overhead costs are based on the following estimated figures:

Cost	Amount per Direct Labor Hour
Indirect materials	$ .60
Indirect labor	2.70
Labor fringe benefits	4.10
Payroll tax	1.00
Utilities	1.80
Maintenance	.80
Total	$11.00 per labor hour

Using these estimates, the company decides to apply $11 of variable overhead to product cost for each hour of direct labor.

The manufacturing overhead budget shown in Figure 7-10 identifies variable overhead and fixed overhead costs for each quarter's production and for the year. For example, production budgeted for the first quarter requires 42,000 hours of direct labor. Experience indicates that 42,000 hours of direct labor will result in using $25,200 of indirect materials (42,000 hr × $.60). Similarly, budgeted indirect labor is $113,400 for the first quarter, calculated as $2.70 × 42,000 direct labor hours. Other variable overhead costs are budgeted in the same manner.

The overhead budget often requires numerous calculations

Castone Corporation
Manufacturing Overhead Budget
For the Year Ending December 31, 1986

	Quarter				
Variable Overhead	1	2	3	4	Total
Indirect materials	$ 25,200	$ 36,660	$ 41,280	$ 29,130	$ 132,270
Indirect labor	113,400	164,970	185,760	131,085	595,215
Labor fringe benefits	172,200	250,510	282,080	199,055	903,845
Payroll taxes	42,000	61,100	68,800	48,550	220,450
Utilities	75,600	109,980	123,840	87,390	396,810
Maintenance	33,600	48,880	55,040	38,840	176,360
Total variable overhead	462,000	672,100	756,800	534,050	2,424,950
Fixed Overhead					
Supervision	27,000	27,000	27,000	27,000	108,000
Depreciation	300,000	300,000	300,000	300,000	1,200,000
Maintenance	78,000	78,000	78,000	78,000	312,000
Insurance	21,625	21,625	21,625	21,625	86,500
Property taxes	124,500	124,500	124,500	124,500	498,000
Total fixed overhead	551,125	551,125	551,125	551,125	2,204,500
Total overhead	$1,013,125	$1,223,225	$1,307,925	$1,085,175	$4,629,450

Figure 7-10. The manufacturing overhead budget is divided into variable and fixed costs. The total overhead for the year is divided by the overhead application base to calculate the overhead rate.

The estimate of fixed overhead cost is based on past experience adjusted for anticipated changes. In the overhead budget, fixed costs are shown for individual items such as supervision, depreciation, and other costs, and the total amounts to $551,125 per quarter. The amounts in the manufacturing overhead budget are used in financial budgeting, and also to plan operations and to control the various resources described in the budget. Notice that the overhead budget includes depreciation, which is a fixed cost that does not involve cash payments.

The manufacturing overhead budget completes the entire production budget, which consists of four separate budgets shown in Figures 7-6, 7-8, 7-9, and 7-10. It is now possible to calculate the budgeted unit costs of the products. The unit cost of products is used to prepare the cost of goods sold budget. Using direct labor hours as the measure of activity, we divide total annual overhead cost by total annual direct labor hours to obtain overhead cost per direct labor hour.

$$\frac{\text{Total overhead cost}}{\text{Total direct labor hours}} = \frac{\$4,629,450}{220,450 \text{ hours}} = \$21 \text{ per DLH}$$

Each concrete column requires 2 direct labor hours, so we assign $42 of overhead to the cost of each column (2 hr × $21 per DLH). In addition to overhead, each product requires direct material and direct labor. A schedule of budgeted production costs for each product is shown below:

Resource	Columns		Beams	
Reinforcing steel @ $.30 per pound	200 lb	$ 60	500 lb	$150
Concrete @ $50 per cubic yard	.5 cu yd	25	2 cu yd	100
Direct labor @ $12 per hour	2 hr	24	5 hr	60
Overhead @ $21 per DLH	2 hr	42	5 hr	105
Total cost per unit		$151		$415

Cost of Goods Manufactured Budget. The **cost of goods manufactured budget** summarizes the budgeted cost of production. In most manufacturing operations there is some beginning work in process as well as some ending work in process, and the cost of finished goods produced during a period is found by adding the period's production to the beginning work in process and deducting the ending work in process. The resulting figure is then added to the inventory of finished goods and is also used to calculate cost of goods sold.

Castone Corporation
Budgeted Cost of Goods Manufactured
For the Year Ending December 31, 1986

	Quarter				
	1	2	3	4	Total
Direct materials:					
Reinforcing steel	$1,260,000	$1,833,000	$2,064,000	$1,456,500	$ 6,613,500
Concrete	682,500	992,500	1,115,000	792,500	3,582,500
Total direct materials	1,942,500	2,825,500	3,179,000	2,249,000	10,196,000
Direct labor	504,000	733,200	825,600	582,600	2,645,400
Manufacturing overhead	882,000	1,283,100	1,444,800	1,019,550	4,629,450
Cost of goods manufactured	$3,328,500	$4,841,800	$5,449,400	$3,851,150	$17,470,850

Figure 7-11. The cost of goods manufactured budget includes the three basic manufacturing costs — direct materials, direct labor, and overhead. The budget shown here is condensed; it can be made more detailed by showing costs for each product separately.

Castone Corporation does not have any work in process at the beginning or end of its accounting period, so its cost of goods manufactured budget is fairly simple. Figure 7-11 illustrates this budget for each quarter and for the year. Included in the figures are the budgeted costs of direct materials, direct labor, and manufacturing overhead. The figures used are obtained from other budgets already prepared. For example, cost of goods manufactured for the first quarter is calculated as follows:

First Quarter Cost of Goods Manufactured

Direct materials:		
Cost of reinforcing steel required for columns (From Figure 7-7)	3,060,000 lb	
Reinforcing steel required for beams (From Figure 7-7)	3,050,000	
Total steel required	6,110,000	
Cost per pound	× $.30	
Cost of steel		$1,260,000
Cost of concrete required for columns and beams (From Figure 7-8)		682,500
Total direct materials		1,942,500
Direct labor (From Figure 7-9)		504,000
Manufacturing overhead (From Figure 7-10)		1,012,875
Cost of goods manufactured		$3,328,500

Cost of Goods Sold Budget. The **cost of goods sold budget** identifies the amount of product expense associated with the budgeted sales for the period. Typically, the units sold during one period are taken from beginning finished goods inventory and from current period production. Some current period production usually remains in ending inventory at the end of the period.

Cost of goods sold budgets combine data from many other budgets

Castone Corporation's cost of goods sold budget is shown in Figure 7-12. It shows a beginning inventory of 1,000 columns costing $145 each and 400 beams costing $400 each. The number of units was estimated earlier and shown in Figure 7-6. The cost of these units must be estimated because the actual cost of production for the 1985 production period will not be known until the period is over, and the 1986 budget must be completed before then. A good place to obtain these cost estimates is from the 1985 budget, with adjustments for any known cost differences.

In our illustration each product cost is computed separately, with totals provided. The beginning inventory and budgeted production are added together to arrive at goods available for sale. Then the budgeted ending inventory is deducted to arrive at budgeted cost of goods sold. The separate figures for the two products are combined to obtain the totals that will be used in the budgeted income statement. The ending inventory figures come from the budgeted finished goods ending inventory in Figure 7-5. The cost of goods manufactured total for each quarter can be found in Figure 7-11.

Castone Corporation
Cost of Goods Sold Budget
For the Year Ending December 31, 1986

First Quarter	Columns		Beams		Total	Year Total
Beginning inventory	1,000		400			
× unit cost	$145	$ 145,000	$400	$ 160,000	$ 305,000	$ 305,000
Production	10,500		4,200			
× unit cost	$151	1,585,500	$415	1,743,000	3,328,500	3,328,500
Goods available		1,730,500		1,903,000	3,633,500	
Less ending inventory	1,500		600			
× unit cost	$151	226,500	$415	249,000	475,500	
Cost of goods sold		$1,504,000		$1,654,000	$ 3,158,000	

Second Quarter						
Beginning inventory	1,500		600			
× unit cost	$151	$ 226,500	$415	$ 249,000	$ 475,500	
Production	15,300		6,100			
× unit cost	$151	2,310,300	$415	2,531,500	4,841,800	4,841,800
Goods available		2,536,800		2,780,500	5,317,300	
Less ending inventory	1,800		700			
× unit cost	$151	271,800	$415	290,500	562,300	
Cost of goods sold		$2,265,000		$2,490,000	$ 4,755,000	

Third Quarter						
Beginning inventory	1,800		700			
× unit cost	$151	$ 271,800	$415	$ 290,500	$ 562,300	
Production	17,400		6,800			
× unit cost	$151	2,627,400	$415	2,822,000	5,449,400	5,449,400
Goods available		2,899,200		3,112,500	6,011,700	
Less ending inventory	1,200		500			
× unit cost	$151	181,200	$415	207,500	388,700	
Cost of goods sold		$2,718,000		$2,905,000	$ 5,623,000	

Fourth Quarter						
Beginning inventory	1,200		500			
× unit cost	$151	$ 181,200	$415	$ 207,500	$ 388,700	
Production	11,900		4,950			
× unit cost	$151	1,796,900	$415	2,054,250	3,851,150	3,851,150
Goods available		1,978,100		2,261,750	4,239,850	
Less ending inventory	1,100		450			
× unit cost	$151	166,100	$415	186,750	352,850	(352,850)
Cost of goods sold		$1,812,000		$2,075,000	$ 3,887,000	$17,423,000

Figure 7-12. The cost of goods sold budget is derived from the cost of beginning inventory and the budgeted costs of production for the period. A FIFO inventory flow is assumed. The totals from the cost of goods manufactured budget are used in the last two columns of this budget.

Selling Expense Budget. The **selling expense budget** shows the detail of variable and fixed selling expenses that must be incurred in the process of marketing the company's products. The marketing effort is the important determinant of sales volume. Consequently, the selling expense budget should be prepared at least in part during the early stages in the budgeting process when the sales budget is prepared. Those marketing costs that are variable will depend directly on the volume of anticipated sales, while the fixed costs remain stable regardless of the sales volume. The selling expense budget is presented in Figure 7-13.

Figure 7-13. In the selling expense budget variable costs fluctuate with the level of sales. Fixed costs are assumed to be spread evenly over the four quarters.

Castone Corporation
Selling Expense Budget
For the Year Ending December 31, 1986

| | Quarter | | | | |
	1	2	3	4	Total
Variable Selling Expenses					
Commissions	$125,000	$187,500	$222,000	$153,000	$ 687,500
Clerical	4,550	6,820	8,070	5,560	25,000
Supplies	1,270	1,910	2,260	1,560	7,000
Travel	43,800	65,700	77,900	53,600	241,000
Total variable	174,620	261,930	310,230	213,720	960,500
Fixed Selling Expenses					
Salaries	53,125	53,125	53,125	53,125	212,500
Clerical	12,500	12,500	12,500	12,500	50,000
Advertising	40,000	40,000	40,000	40,000	160,000
Entertainment	17,500	17,500	17,500	17,500	70,000
Insurance	11,250	11,250	11,250	11,250	45,000
Maintenance	23,750	23,750	23,750	23,750	95,000
Supplies	2,500	2,500	2,500	2,500	10,000
Property tax	10,500	10,500	10,500	10,500	42,000
Depreciation	45,000	45,000	45,000	45,000	180,000
Total fixed	216,125	216,125	216,125	216,125	864,500
Total expenses	$390,745	$478,055	$526,355	$429,845	$1,825,000

Administrative Expense Budget. The **administrative expense budget,** shown in Figure 7-14, includes the cost of nonmanufacturing administrative activities. Typically, this budget contains many fixed costs over which managers may have no control. Costs such as mortgage payments and property taxes cannot be changed or eliminated easily. They are known as **committed fixed costs.** But not all fixed costs are beyond the control of managers. Some fixed costs are discretionary. **Discretionary fixed costs** are costs that are avoidable at the discretion of management, such as research and development, but if they are incurred they do not vary with the activity level. Therefore, the fixed costs in the administrative expense budget are not merely a list of items that cannot be planned. The budget is used to decide which fixed costs are to be

Castone Corporation
Administrative Expense Budget
For the Year Ending December 31, 1986

| | Quarter | | | | |
	1	2	3	4	Total
Administrative salaries	$176,650	$176,650	$176,650	$176,650	$ 706,600
Clerical salaries	15,250	15,250	15,250	15,250	61,000
Insurance	20,000	20,000	20,000	20,000	80,000
Maintenance	27,500	27,500	27,500	27,500	110,000
Office supplies	10,000	10,000	10,000	10,000	40,000
Property taxes	17,500	17,500	17,500	17,500	70,000
Depreciation	52,500	52,500	52,500	52,500	210,000
Utilities	55,000	55,000	55,000	55,000	220,000
Total	$374,400	$374,400	$374,400	$374,400	$1,497,600

Figure 7-14. In this administrative expense budget, expenses are assumed to be spread equally over all four quarters, but in some cases they may vary throughout the year. A budget should reflect the expected cost behavior.

incurred in the future, and it also shows those to which the firm is already committed.

The administrative expense budget sometimes includes various financing expenses, such as mortgage and bond interest. In our example, debt service expenses are not included in this budget because the company prepares a separate schedule to determine interest expense.

Budgeted Income Statement.   The **budgeted income statement** reflects the revenues and expenses expected from the budgeted operations of the period. It is one of the more eagerly awaited budgets because it shows expected net income from normal operations. It is the major component of the organization's profit objective and as such should reflect the vast majority of the firm's activities for the budget period.

Nonoperating items should be budgeted when possible

Sometimes a firm expects to have nonoperating items that affect net income, such as interest on investments and gains or losses from the sale of fixed assets. Usually these nonoperating items are relatively small, but should be included in the budgeted income statement.

The final operating budget item in the income statement is budgeted income tax expense. Income taxes are levied on actual income rather than on budgeted income, but the tax should nevertheless be estimated and included in the statement, for it is another business expense that requires planning.

The budgeted income statement in Figure 7-15 contains data from many previously prepared budgets, as indicated. Interest expense comes from the debt service budget shown later in Figure 7-20, where it is discussed in connection with the financial budget. The budgeted income tax can be estimated and in this example is based on a 40 percent income tax rate.

Figure 7-15. The budgeted income statement is the culmination of the operating budget and is a key document in the profit plan. If budgeted net income is unsatisfactory, management may revise its plans and prepare new budgets.

Castone Corporation
Budgeted Income Statement
For the Year Ending December 31, 1986

Sales[a]		$27,500,000
Less cost of goods sold[b]		
Beginning finished goods inventory	$ 305,000	
Add cost of goods manufactured	17,470,850	
Goods available for sale	17,775,850	
Less ending finished goods inventory	352,850	
Cost of goods sold		17,423,000
Gross margin		10,077,000
Selling expenses[c]	1,825,000	
Administrative expenses[d]	1,497,600	
Interest expense[e]	1,928,800	5,21,400
Income before tax		4,825,600
Income tax		1,930,240
Net income after tax		$ 2,895,360

[a] From sales budget, Figure 7-4
[b] From cost of goods sold budget, Figure 7-12
[c] From selling expense budget, Figure 7-13
[d] From administrative expense budget, Figure 7-14
[e] From debt service budget, Figure 7-20

If the budgeted net income is not acceptable, management may have to revise some or all of the budgets in an effort to generate a satisfactory profit plan. This, of course, could require an enormous amount of time and resources. But if, for example, budgeted income is lower than required to make debt payments or to satisfy contractual agreements, the firm needs to develop a new plan that is satisfactory. Budget revisions are an important part of the budgeting process, but at this point in your study of budgeting we concentrate on the development of the initial master budget.

The budgeted income statement is the final product of the operating budget

The Financial Budget

Financing and investing activities are included in the financial budget

Although there are some differences between the operating budgets of manufacturing and nonmanufacturing organizations, their financial budgets are very similar. **Financial budgets** cover the financing and investing activities of the firm.

Capital investment decisions usually involve large amounts of resources

The Capital Expenditure Budget.   Capital budgeting refers to planning the acquisition of plant and equipment and other major assets, projects, or activities. For example, employee education programs and pension plans may be part of capital budgets. The **capital expenditure budget** is a plan of future investments in fixed assets and often includes amounts for large expenditures that have a long-term impact on the organization and the achievement of its goals. Typically, capital expenditure projects have useful lives far beyond one accounting period. Consequently the budgets for these projects require careful planning, analysis, and evaluation. Like other budgets, capital expen-

Castone Corporation
Capital Expenditure Budget
For the Year Ending December 31, 1986

	Quarter				
	1	2	3	4	Total
Office furniture and equipment	—	$ 25,000	—	$ 9,000	$ 34,000
Manufacturing equipment	—	400,000	$900,000	2,000,000	3,300,000
Total capital expenditures	—	$425,000	$900,000	$2,009,000	$3,334,000
Amount to be financed	—	$300,000	$650,000	—	$ 950,000

Figure 7-16. The capital expenditure budget reflects the company's long-range plans for investment in fixed assets. A full discussion of capital budgeting is left for later chapters.

diture budgets are evaluated within the context of organizational goals and objectives. A number of techniques have been developed for capital budgeting purposes. These are discussed in Chapters 15 and 16.

Castone Corporation's capital expenditure budget is illustrated in Figure 7-16. It shows planned expenditures for office equipment and for manufacturing equipment, with a major expenditure planned for the last quarter of the period to replace existing equipment. This budget also indicates the amounts of financing that the company plans to use with its equipment acquisitions.

Cash Budget. All organizations require adequate liquidity, which means the ability to pay debts when they come due. Meeting cash obligations is not as simple as it may appear. Profitability and liquidity are related, but they do not go hand in hand. Many firms experience their most critical liquidity problems when they shift from break-even operations to a profitable position. At that time growing inventories, receivables, payables, and capacity costs may create serious cash shortages.

Planning cash flows is crucial for all types of organizations

The **cash budget** is a plan for managing expected cash requirements. It includes all estimated cash inflows and outflows during the budget period, with special attention to the timing of the cash flows. A good starting point for developing the cash budget is cash from operations, consisting of net income adjusted for noncash items such as depreciation. All nonoperating cash flows are also included, and sometimes these amounts are quite significant. Purchase of land, repayment of bonds, sale of long-term investments, and treasury stock transactions are some examples of nonoperating items that affect the cash budget. The amount of net income and the amount of net cash flows may be quite different for an accounting period because of the nonoperating items or changes in working capital.

The 1986 cash budget in Figure 7-17 shows a first-quarter beginning balance that is estimated, possibly as part of the 1985 budget. The data for this budget are taken from many of the operating and financial budgets already illustrated. Here the timing of cash flows is carefully planned. For example, sales revenues are expected to be collected part in the quarter in which the

Castone Corporation
Cash Budget
For the Year Ending December 31, 1986

Cash Receipts	Quarter				Total
	1	2	3	4	
Beginning balance	$ 60,000	$ 188,340	$ 244,660	$1,786,400	$ 60,000
Collection of accounts[a]	1,090,000	1,000,000	1,500,000	1,776,000	5,366,000
Current sales[b]	4,000,000	6,000,000	7,104,000	4,896,000	22,000,000
New notes (Figure 7-15)		300,000	650,000		950,000
Total receipts	5,150,000	7,488,340	9,498,660	8,458,400	28,376,000
Cash Disbursements					
Payments on account[c]	190,000	205,710	287,170	305,750	988,630
Material purchases[d]	1,851,390	2,584,530	2,751,750	2,011,707	9,199,377
Payroll	504,000	733,200	825,600	582,600	2,645,400
Manufacturing overhead	713,125	923,225	1,007,925	785,175	3,429,450
Selling	345,745	433,055	481,355	384,845	1,645,000
Administrative	321,900	321,900	321,900	321,900	1,287,600
Interest (Figure 7-20)	471,000	476,500	492,500	488,800	1,928,800
Principal (Figure 7-20)	154,500	158,000	161,500	165,200	639,200
Capital investment (Figure 7-15)		425,000	900,000	2,009,000	3,334,000
Taxes	410,000	482,560	482,560	482,560	1,857,680
Dividends		500,000		500,000	1,000,000
Total disbursements	4,961,660	7,243,680	7,712,260	8,037,537	27,955,137
Ending balance	$ 188,340	$ 244,660	1,786,400	$ 420,863	$ 420,863

[a] .2 of previous quarter's sales
[b] .8 of current quarter's sales
[c] .1 of previous quarter's purchases
[d] .9 of current quarter's purchases

Figure 7-17. The cash budget is critical for most businesses. This one is prepared on a quarterly basis, but many firms prepare monthly or weekly cash budgets that are much more elaborate.

sale was made and part in the following quarter. The $1,090,000 collection in the first quarter is the accounts receivable balance at the end of the 1985 operating period. Similarly, the disbursement of $190,000 is for payment of the estimated accounts payable at the end of 1985.

Castone Corporation expects to pay for 90 percent of its material purchases in the quarter of purchase, and the other 10 percent in the following quarter. Therefore the accounts payable balance at the end of each quarter consists of 10 percent of material purchases for the quarter. We assume that labor is paid for in the quarter the cost is incurred. The cost of labor is taken directly from the direct labor budget in Figure 7-9.

The amounts for manufacturing overhead, selling expenses, and administrative expenses come from budgets for these items, but you will note that the figures are somewhat different. For example, Figure 7-10 shows $1,013,125 of manufacturing overhead budgeted for the first quarter, but the cash budget shows a planned cash payment of only $713,125 for this item. The difference occurs because budgeted overhead cost includes depreciation, which does not result in a cash payment. The first quarter's cash outflow for manufacturing overhead is obtained as follows:

Budgeted manufacturing overhead	$1,013,125
Less budgeted depreciation	300,000
Budgeted cash outflow	$ 713,125

Similarly, noncash items such as depreciation are subtracted from budgeted cost for selling and administration costs to calculate the budgeted cash outflow for those items. Note that mortgage principal and mortgage and note interest are included as separate items in the cash budget. These are scheduled separately in our example and shown later in Figure 7-20. In any case, debt repayment is not a part of any of the operating budgets, and may require separate financial budgets.

The cash flow for capital expenditures and the planned inflow from borrowing for capital projects are taken from the capital expenditure budget. Income taxes are paid quarterly in equal amounts but always in the quarter following the earning of income. Consequently, the cash budget shows the last quarterly tax of the previous year paid in the first quarter of the budget period.

Budgeted financial statements are called pro forma statements

Budgeted Balance Sheet.   In a number of the budgets illustrated, data were required that represent ending balances of the current operating period. The budget for the next accounting period is prepared well before the current period has ended, so the balance sheet for the end of the current period is not yet available. Therefore it must be estimated. The 1986 **budgeted balance sheet** is derived from the 1985 budgeted balance sheet and from the expected changes in account balances reflected in the operating and financial budgets.

The budgeted statement of financial position is more than a collection of residual balances resulting from other budget estimates. It can disclose undesirable projected balances and financial ratios that may cause management to revise the entire budget. For example, lending institutions may require a firm to maintain a certain minimum current ratio or debt/equity ratio as a condition of a loan contract. If the budgeted balance sheet is not acceptable, the budget must be revised.

The budgeted income statement ties together the beginning and ending balance sheets for the 1986 budget period of Castone Corporation. The budgeted balance sheets at the end of 1985 and 1986 are shown in Figure 7-18. The change in the account balances from one balance sheet to the next can be traced in the other budgets. For example, the cash budget starts with the cash balance from the 1985 balance sheet; it shows all receipts and disbursements to arrive at the cash balance which appears in the 1986 budgeted balance sheet. Also shown in the cash budget are the scheduled collection of beginning receivables and payment of beginning accounts payable. The beginning balances of accounts receivable and accounts payable are

Figure 7-18. The budgeted balance sheet of the previous period is the basis for preparing the budgeted balance sheet for the budget year. The 1986 budget is prepared before 1985 is over. Therefore the actual 1985 balance sheet is not yet available. The 1986 budgeted balance sheet is used to identify relationships and ratios resulting from the entire profit plan. If some relationships are not satisfactory, the entire budget may have to be revised.

Castone Corporation
Budgeted Balance Sheet
For the Years Ending December 31, 1985, and 1986

	1985	1986
Current assets		
Cash (Figure 7-17)	$ 60,000	$ 420,863
Accounts receivable (Figure 7-4)[a]	1,090,000	1,224,000
Raw materials inventory (Figure 7-7)[b]	252,000	277,530
Finished goods inventory (Figure 7-12)	305,000	352,850
Supplies	12,000	14,000
Total current assets	1,719,000	2,289,243
Fixed assets		
Land	1,260,000	1,260,000
Buildings	17,000,000	17,000,000
Less accumulated depreciation	(6,800,000)	(7,325,000)
Equipment	17,700,000	21,000,000
Less accumulated depreciation	(6,200,000)	(7,160,000)
Furniture and fixtures	980,000	1,014,000
Less accumulated depreciation	(343,000)	(448,000)
Total fixed assets	23,597,000	25,341,000
Total assets	$25,316,000	$27,630,243
Current liabilities		
Accounts payable (Figure 7-8)[c]	$ 190,000	$ 225,523
Income taxes payable	410,000	482,560
Other taxes payable	150,000	150,000
Total current liabilities	750,000	858,083
Long-term debt		
Mortgage payable, 9%	8,800,000	8,160,800
Notes payable	8,350,000	9,300,000
Total long-term debt	17,150,000	17,460,800
Total liabilities	17,900,000	18,318,883
Capital		
Common stock	4,000,000	4,000,000
Retained earnings	3,416,000	5,311,360
Total capital	7,416,000	9,311,360
Total liabilities and capital	$25,316,000	$27,630,243

[a] .8 of 4th quarter sales
[b] 925,100 lb steel × $.30 for 1986
[c] .1 of 4th quarter purchases

shown in the 1985 budgeted balance sheet. The ending balances of these accounts, shown in the 1986 balance sheet, result from the way that collections of sales revenue and payments for material purchases are budgeted in the last quarter, as shown in the cash budget and derived from the sales budget and direct materials budget.

Changes in fixed asset accounts are derived from planned purchases shown in the capital expenditures budget and from depreciation shown in the manufacturing overhead, selling, and administrative expense budgets. Other balance sheet account changes are determined by analyzing various budgets to identify their impact on assets, liabilities, and capital. The decrease in the mortgage payable and the increase in notes payable from 1985 to 1986 are detailed in the cash budget and planned in the debt service and capital expenditure budgets. The change in retained earnings comes from the budgeted income statement and from dividends planned in the cash budget.

Budgeted Statement of Changes in Financial Position. The last element in the master budget is the **budgeted statement of changes in financial position,** which shows the expected change in funds resulting from the financing and investing activities planned for the budget year. The statement of changes is derived from the two budgeted balance sheets, the budgeted income statement, and other budgets. This statement, illustrated in Figure 7-19, is prepared with funds defined as working capital. It may also be prepared with funds defined as cash, depending on the preference of management. The budgeted statement of changes is a useful tool in the financial planning process and completes the master budget.

Funds can be defined in more than one way for preparing the funds flow statement

Figure 7-19. The budgeted statement of changes in financial position reports the expected financing and investing activities of the firm.

Castone Corporation
Budgeted Statement of Changes in Financial Position
For the Year Ending December 31, 1986

Sources of Working Capital

From operations		
Net income	$2,895,360	
Add depreciation	1,590,000	
Total from operations		$4,485,360
Other sources		
New long-term debt		950,000
Total sources of working capital		$5,435,360

Uses of Working Capital

Purchase of fixed assets	$3,334,000	
Repayment of long-term debt	639,200	
Payment of dividends	1,000,000	
Increase in working capital	462,160	
Total uses of working capital		$5,435,360

Change in Working Capital

Increase in cash	$ 360,863
Increase in accounts receivable	134,000
Increase in raw materials	25,530
Increase in finished goods	47,850
Increase in supplies	2,000
Increase in accounts payable	(35,523)
Increase in income taxes payable	(72,560)
Increase in working capital	$ 462,160

Other Budgets

As indicated previously, many preliminary budgets are prepared during the budgeting process, some of which are combined into the final budgets illustrated here. Managers may prepare budgets for any purpose that requires careful and detailed planning. For example, Castone Corporation has several categories of long-term debts that require control to ensure that they are managed and repaid as required. The company therefore prepares a debt service budget to plan the payment of interest and repayment of principal. This budget is illustrated in Figure 7-20. It is derived from interest payment schedules and mortgage amortization schedules prepared for each individual note. Many other similar budgets may be prepared for a variety of purposes.

Castone Corporation
Debt Service Budget
For the Year Ending December 31, 1986

	Quarter				Total
	1	2	3	4	
Mortgage beginning balance	$8,800,000	$8,645,500	$8,487,500	$8,326,000	$8,160,800
Mortgage installment	375,000	375,000	375,000	375,000	1,500,000
Mortgage interest	220,500	217,000	213,500	209,800	860,800
Principal reduction	154,500	158,000	161,500	165,200	639,200
Mortage ending balance	$8,645,500	$8,487,500	$8,326,000	$8,160,800	$8,160,800
Notes payable beginning balance	$8,350,000	$8,350,000	$8,650,000	$9,300,000	$8,350,000
New notes	—	300,000	650,000	—	950,000
Notes payable ending balance	8,350,000	8,650,000	9,300,000	9,300,000	9,300,000
Interest on notes	250,500	259,500	279,000	279,000	1,068,000
Total interest	$ 471,000	$ 476,500	$ 492,500	$ 488,800	$1,928,800

Figure 7-20. Before the profit plan can be prepared, preliminary work may be needed to prepare budgets that provide figures for the master budget. This preliminary debt service budget provides data for the cash budget.

Graphic Illustration of the Master Budget

The Castone Corporation master budget is a small, uncomplicated example of a profit plan. Nevertheless, it consists of many budgets and the plan requires many computations. It should be obvious that for a more complex organization, the master budget is a document with many schedules and supporting data, often consisting of hundreds of pages.

Now that you have examined the details of the master budget, look at the diagram in Figure 7-21, which illustrates the steps in the development of the master budget for a manufacturing firm. Note the relationship among the various budgets and how they are classified into operating and financial functions. The operating budget is essentially composed of income statement items: revenues, cost of production, cost of goods sold, and operating expenses. The financial budget consists primarily of balance sheet items.

Figure 7-21. The master budget is usually developed in a sequential process in which information from one budget is input for another budget. Some of the budgets, however, may be relatively independent of others. The capital expenditure budget is an example.

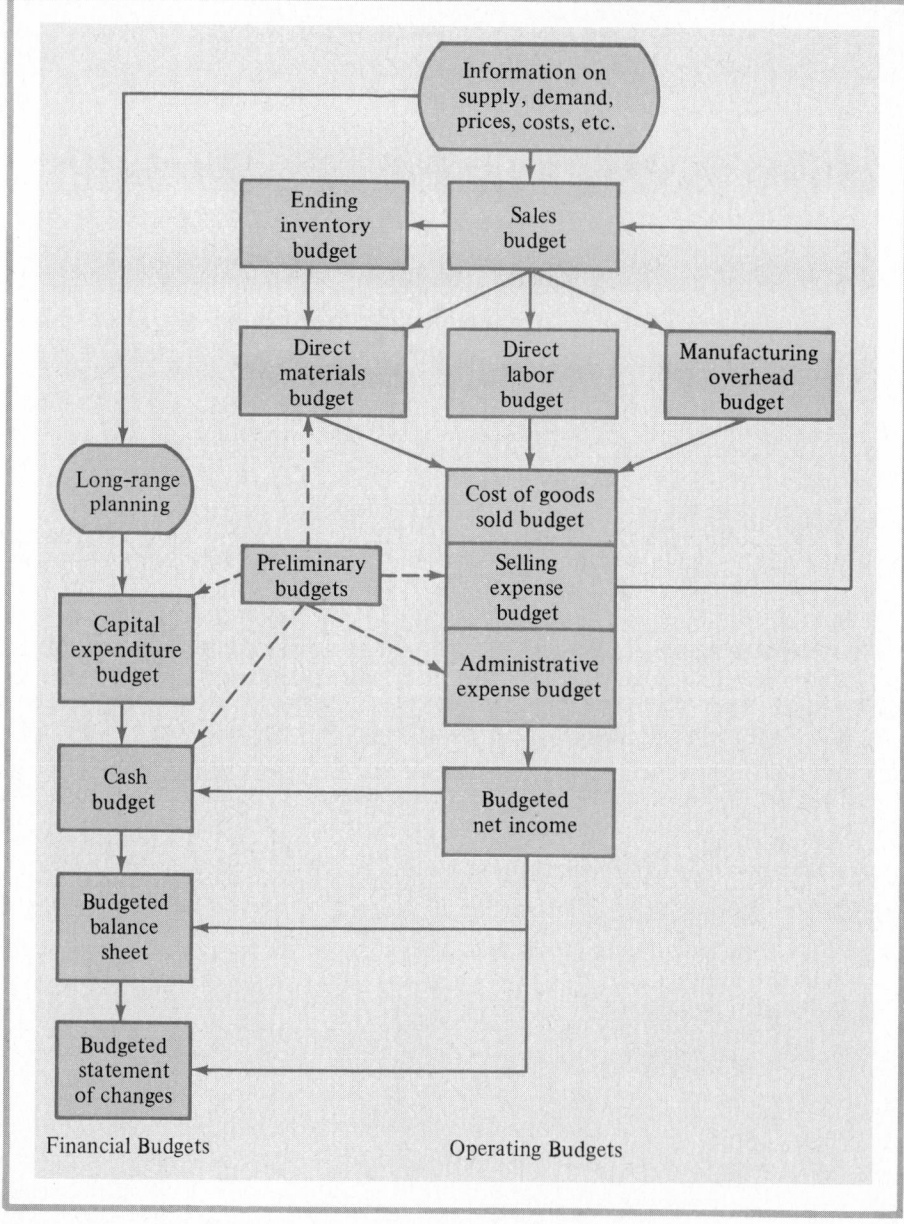

CONTROL THROUGH BUDGETING

Performance reports are used to compare actual results with budgets

An important part of the control function of budgeting is the comparison of budgeted data with actual operating results. The comparisons are presented in periodic **performance reports,** which show both budgeted and actual data as well as an analysis of any differences. Performance reports may be prepared as frequently as desired, but remember that information has a cost. The more information and the more frequently it is provided, the greater the cost. Consequently, performance reports should be prepared only when the value of the information provided is greater than its cost.

Performance Evaluation

Castone Corporation prepares quarterly budgets and quarterly performance reports. In Figure 7-22 we illustrate a performance report for manufacturing overhead for the first quarter of the 1986 budget period. The report is based on budgeted costs taken from the 1986 manufacturing overhead budget in Figure 7-10 and actual manufacturing overhead cost data accumulated during the first quarter of 1986. The last column in the report shows the difference between budgeted and actual amounts. These differences are called **variances** because they show the variation between budgeted and actual results. If actual costs are less than budgeted, the variance is favorable, indicated in the report by parentheses and the F behind the variance. If actual costs are more than expected the variance is unfavorable, indicated by U. In practice the F and U are usually not shown because the parentheses are well understood. You may view the amounts in parentheses as credits and amounts without them as debits. Thus debits are expenses in excess of budgeted amounts and credits are reductions in expenses.

During the first quarter of 1986, actual production by Castone Corporation was 10,600 concrete columns and 4,350 concrete beams. Costs incurred in the first quarter production of columns and beams are accumulated in

Figure 7-22. A manufacturing overhead quarterly performance report. Detailed timely performance reports provide managers with a framework for identifying potential problem areas. The variances show how budgeted and actual performance compare, and focus attention on areas that should be investigated.

Castone Corporation
Manufacturing Overhead Performance Report
For the Quarter Ended March 31, 1986

Variable Overhead	Budgeted	Actual	Variance	
Indirect materials	$ 25,200	$ 27,800	$ 2,600	U
Indirect labor	113,400	118,000	4,600	U
Labor fringe benefits	172,200	179,800	7,600	U
Payroll taxes	42,000	43,600	1,600	U
Utilities	75,600	78,400	2,800	U
Maintenance	33,600	30,900	(2,700)	F
Total variable overhead	462,000	478,500	16,500	U
Fixed Overhead				
Supervision	27,000	26,400	(600)	F
Depreciation	300,000	300,000	0	
Maintenance	78,000	78,950	950	U
Insurance	21,625	21,275	(350)	F
Property taxes	124,500	127,000	2,500	U
Total fixed overhead	551,125	553,625	2,500	U
Total overhead	$1,013,125	$1,032,125	$19,000	U

ledger accounts and are reported in the middle column of the performance report in Figure 7-22. The actual costs are compared with the first quarter planned overhead costs found in Figure 7-10 and shown in the budgeted column in Figure 7-22. Actual and budgeted costs are compared for each account and in total. Most of the variances are unfavorable, but the total variance of $19,000 is only about 1.2 percent of budgeted overhead cost. An analysis of individual variances is necessary to determine if any problems need investigating and to decide if corrective action should be taken.

The unfavorable variances in variable overhead are due, partly at least, to the fact that production was greater than budgeted. The sales budget in Figure 7-4 shows that first quarter sales were planned at 10,000 columns and 4,000 beams. Given this expected sales level, the production quantity budget in Figure 7-6 required production of 10,500 columns and 4,200 beams. Because of a stronger than expected demand, the company produced 100 more columns and 150 more beams than planned. When actual production is greater than budgeted production, costs can be expected to be greater also.

Variable maintenance costs show a favorable variance. This in itself may not be especially good. It is possible that needed maintenance was not performed, due to the increased production, but maintenance not performed in one period could cause problems later. Future breakdowns may cause loss of production if time is lost to make repairs that the maintenance might have prevented. Of course, it is possible that the maintenance was performed efficiently, resulting in lower cost. Meaningful interpretation of variances requires a good understanding of operations.

Fixed overhead variances are quite small and only two are unfavorable. The property tax variance may be beyond management's control, as it probably occurred due to an increase in the tax rate. The unfavorable fixed maintenance variance should be examined in light of the favorable variable maintenance variance. It is especially important that the details of variances are presented in performance reports. A small total variance could be caused by very large individual variances that offset one another, and it is the individual variances that need to be investigated.

Performance reporting alone does not make a control system. The reports must be used to focus attention on problems and on performance. Employees will strive to attain budget objectives if performance evaluation is tied to the company's reward structure. Favorable employee performance should be rewarded by means of pay raises, promotions, bonuses, and other incentives that indicate management's appreciation for efficiency in operations.

Participative Budgeting

Most budgeting experts agree that budgets should not be imposed by top-level management but instead should be prepared with the active participation of middle- and lower-level managers who are responsible for their individual budgets. **Participative budgeting** does not mean that managers can choose their budgets; it means that managers with budget responsibility have an opportunity to explain and defend their respective proposals.

Human Behavior and Budgets

Budgets should not be imposed

It is difficult to discuss the control aspects of budgeting without mentioning behavioral implications. Budget control is based on the concept that managers should be held responsible for the activities they manage. Performance reports reflect the degree of achievement of plans as embodied in the budget. However, there can be a variety of human reactions even to the most carefully prepared performance reports. To minimize adverse behavioral problems, care should be taken to develop and administer budgets appropriately. Budgets should not be used as a hammer to demand unattainable performance from employees. The best safeguard against unrealistic budgets is participative budgeting.

THE BUDGET REVIEW PROCESS

The budget is a plan for allocating the use of scarce resources of the organization. If the allocation process is to be logical, budget requests must be reviewed, coordinated, and evaluated to ensure that resources are used in their most efficient way to satisfy organizational goals. The **budget review process** is the systematic evaluation of budget proposals.

In the early stages of planning, the review of plans and budget proposals may not be very formal. Budget decisions may be made by one or a few individuals at lower managerial levels. Next, a higher level of management evaluates budget proposals, discusses them, suggests revisions, and coordinates the various proposals into a single budget. Eventually the budgets developed in this manner reach a level of management that contains a budget review committee. Here the budgets are subjected to a more formal evaluation and may have to satisfy clearly defined criteria.

The budget review process determines the allocation of resources

The budget review varies with different organizations. For large firms budgets may be reviewed at successive levels of management, each level approving a larger segment of the firm's overall budget. Eventually the entire master budget is subject to review. If the process has been thorough and carefully executed, the master budget is more likely to satisfy desired management goals. The basic review process is relatively similar in most firms. It is illustrated in Figure 7-23.

SUMMARY

A **budget** is a comprehensive quantitative plan for the utilization of an entity's resources for some specific time period. The **budget entity** must be carefully defined to ensure that the specific activity, project, or function is represented by the budget. The amount of detail provided in the budget is determined by the information needs of the user. Budgets force periodic planning, improve coordination and communication, and require quantification of plans. In addition, a budget provides a performance measurement framework, creates cost awareness, and promotes goal orientation.

Planning and control are the two basic functions of budgeting. **Planning** involves the entire budget development process. **Control** is exercised by

Figure 7-23. The budget review process starts at the lowest level of management. Budgets work their way up to top management where they are integrated into a master budget.

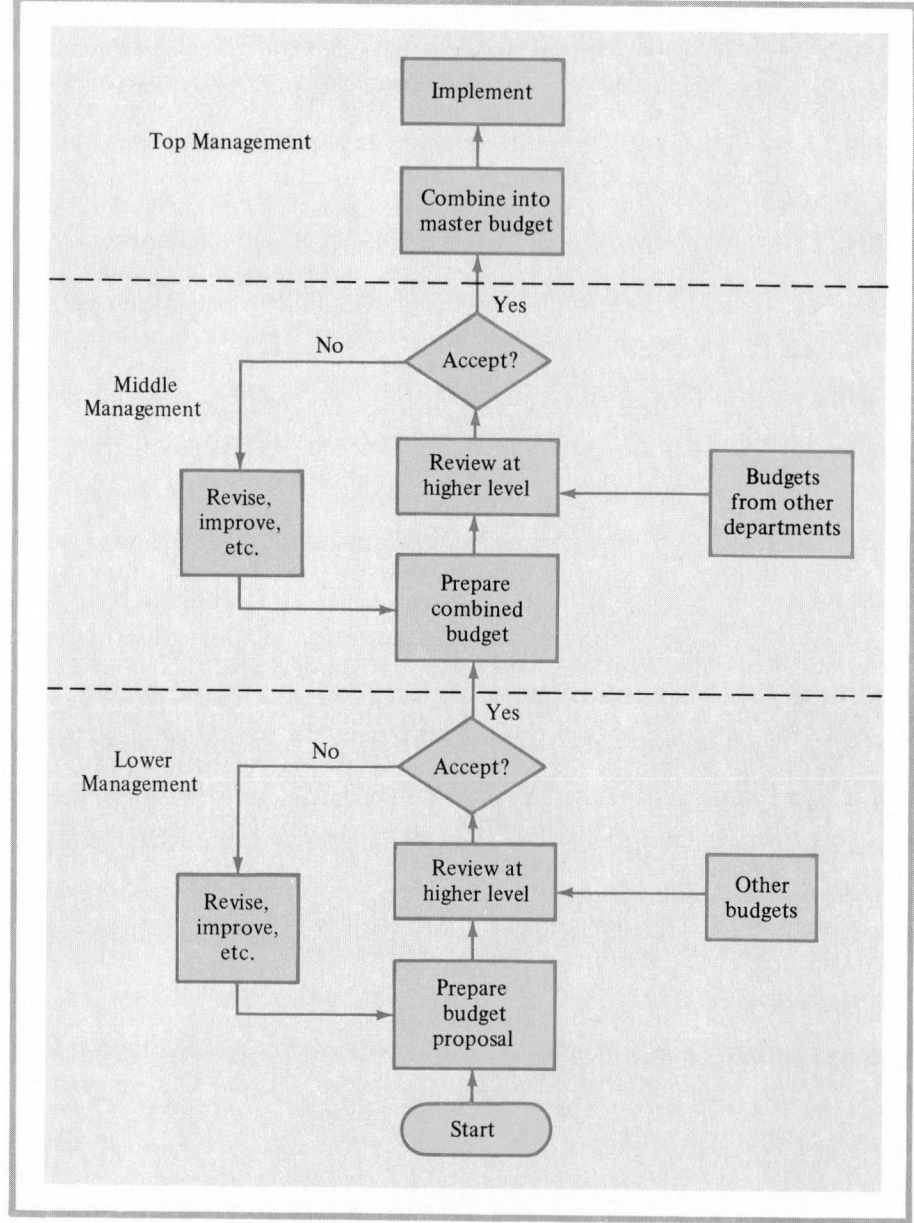

comparing actual results with budgeted data. The reporting process alone does not ensure control; it merely provides performance measures. Control should involve tying budget performance to the organization's reward structure.

The total budget package for an organization is called the **master budget.** It includes the operating budget and the financial budget. The **operating budget** describes the expected results of future operations of the organization. For a manufacturing firm it includes budgeted sales, inventories, materials, direct labor, manufacturing overhead, cost of goods manufactured, cost of goods sold, administrative expenses, marketing expenses, and net income. The **financial budget** includes budgeted capital expenditures, cash flows, balance sheets, and changes in financial position. In addition, many special budgets may be prepared to suit the needs of management and provide help in preparing the operating and financial budgets.

      Participative budgeting refers to the active involvement of all levels of management in the budgeting process. Budgets should not be imposed but rather should be developed with the input of managers who have budget responsibility. Budgets should never be used purely as pressure devices.

KEY TERMS

administrative expense
  budget *(257)*
budget *(239)*
budget entity *(239)*
budget performance report *(244)*
budget review process *(269)*
budgeted balance sheet *(262)*
budgeted income statement *(258)*
budgeted statement of changes in
  financial position *(264)*
capital expenditure budget *(259)*
cash budget *(260)*
committed fixed costs *(257)*
control *(243)*
cost of goods manufactured
  budget *(254)*
cost of goods sold budget *(255)*
direct labor budget *(251)*
direct materials budget *(249)*

discretionary fixed costs *(257)*
ending inventory budget *(247)*
financial budget *(244)*
fixed budget *(245)*
manufacturing overhead
  budget *(252)*
master budget *(244)*
operating budget *(244)*
operational goals *(243)*
participative budgeting *(268)*
planning *(243)*
productive budget *(247)*
production quantity budget *(247)*
profit plan *(244)*
raw materials budget *(248)*
sales budget *(246)*
selling expense budget *(257)*
static budget *(245)*
variance *(267)*

QUESTIONS

1. The controller of Umble Company was talking with a vice president of Yorik Corporation. "With a small firm like mine, it's hard enough to take care of the day-to-day operations without having to spend large amounts of time planning for the future. We have some idea of what will happen next year, but we cannot afford to devote our resources to prepare formal budgets." "I disagree," said the vice president. "We don't put much time into budgeting, but even a poor budget is better than none at all. But I think planning beyond a year ahead is a waste of time. No one can make predictions that far in advance." Evaluate the comments of the two individuals.

2. A company that manufactures small appliances develops a comprehensive profit plan each year and depends heavily on the forecasts of its sales personnel for the data needed to prepare the sales budget. Now the company is planning to start manufacturing electronic games. How will the sales forecast be made when the sales personnel have no experience with the new products?

3. "Everybody does some padding in their budgets, so it is not wise to approve budgets in the amount originally requested. In good times we cut requests about 5 percent. When the economy is in bad shape we may cut 10 or 15 percent. But whatever the cuts, to be fair we cut each budget the same percentage." Comment on the soundness of this policy and its effect on the overall budget.

4. Fred, the marketing manager, was recently overheard saying, "I hate this time of year. It's budget time again. I always put off preparing my budget because I hate pushing around those funny-money numbers. Every year it's the same. I go down there and tell them what I need to sell their product, and they end up giving me about half of what I need. No wonder I don't like to play their budget game." Comment on the sales manager's attitude about budgeting and its possible impact on his job performance.

EXERCISES

Ex. 7-1
Sales and Cash Receipts Budgets

Sales of *Art Reproduction* magazine published by Artists Publishing Company are expected to be 80,000 copies in the first quarter, and are expected to increase by 10 percent each successive quarter of 1986. The magazine sells for $4 per copy, but the company plans to increase the price to $4.50 per copy starting with the July issue. All sales are on open account. The company expects to collect 80 percent of all accounts in the quarter of sale and the balance in the following quarter. The accounts receivable balance on December 31, 1985, is $62,000.

REQUIRED
a. Prepare an annual sales budget by quarters.
b. Prepare a schedule of quarterly cash collections.

Ex. 7-2
Sales and Cash Receipts Budgets

Microbit Company has just developed a new microswitch that will be marketed for the first time in January 1986. The initial selling price of the switch is $1.20 each but the company plans to increase the price by 5 percent on July 1. The following quarterly sales of the switch are expected:

| First quarter | 9,000 units | Third quarter | 17,500 units |
| Second quarter | 12,000 | Fourth quarter | 15,000 |

The company sells 10 percent of its products for cash and 90 percent on open account. It collects 80 percent of its receivables in the quarter of sales, and the remainder in the following quarter.

REQUIRED
a. Prepare a quarterly sales budget.
b. Prepare a schedule of cash collections for each quarter.

Ex. 7-3
Inventory Purchase Budget

Megafry Ovens, Inc. is planning its purchases of microwave ovens inventory for the coming calendar year. Demand is seasonal, with relatively high sales in summer when air-conditioning costs are high, and also during the holiday season. Because of model changes at the end of each year, the company plans to have no more than 500 units on hand at the end of the calendar year. For other quarters it must plan on an ending inventory of 40 percent of next quarter's budgeted sales. Following are sales projections for the budget period:

| First quarter | 2,500 units | Third quarter | 3,000 units |
| Second quarter | 3,500 | Fourth quarter | 4,500 |

Beginning inventory for the budget year is expected to be 400 units.

REQUIRED   Prepare a purchase quantity budget for microwave ovens for the coming budget year.

Ex. 7-4
Production and
Overhead Budgets

Minibilt Company plans to manufacture a new line of electric pencil sharpeners. Production is scheduled to start in June and the following sales are expected:

June	300	August	800
July	600	September	900

There is no beginning inventory and desired ending inventory each month is 25 percent of next month's sales. Each unit requires 4 hours of labor. Estimated variable overhead per direct labor hour is

Indirect materials	$1.15
Indirect labor	1.05
Fringe benefits	3.20
Payroll taxes	2.70
Utilities	1.65

Annual fixed overhead consists of depreciation, $40,800; maintenance, $93,000; and other manufacturing overhead, $112,200, allocated equally to each month.

REQUIRED

a. Prepare a production quantity budget in units for June, July, and August.
b. Prepare a manufacturing overhead budget for each of the 3 months.

Ex. 7-5
Direct Labor
Budget

Next year Soozan Company expects to sell 20,000 Klein bottles. Its ending inventory of Klein bottles is expected to be 1,500 units this year and the company plans to have an ending inventory next year of 3,500 units. Each unit requires 100 grams of material. Labor time per unit is as follows:

Forming	2.6 hours at $11 per hour
Finishing	1.1 hours at 13 per hour
Testing	.3 hours at 9 per hour

REQUIRED

Prepare a direct labor budget for the coming year.

Ex. 7-6
Direct Materials
Budget

Refer to Soozan Company's production of Klein bottles in Exercise 7-5. The material used to produce the bottles costs $1.72 per gram.

REQUIRED.   Prepare a direct materials budget for next year.

Ex. 7-7
Direct Labor
Budget

Rocos Speaker Company manufactures speakers for stereo systems. Below are budgeted production quantity data for two sizes of speakers to be produced in 1986 and direct labor requirements for each speaker:

Budgeted Quarterly Production in Units

Quarter	1	2	3	4
13" woofer	9,000	12,000	11,000	10,000
4" tweeter	15,000	18,000	16,000	17,000

Labor requirements at $8 per hour

13" woofer	.6 hours
4" tweeter	.4 hours

REQUIRED

Prepare a direct labor budget by quarters for the company.

Ex. 7-8
Direct Materials
Use Budget

Octobus Toy Company's sales budget calls for sales of 46,000 eight-wheel toy buses in November. Ending inventory of finished buses is expected to consist of 6,300 units at the end of October. The company's policy is to have an ending inventory each month equal to 15 percent of budgeted sales volume that month.

The assembly department of the company is planning its November production. Assembly is the last process in the manufacture of the buses and requires .2 hours of labor per unit. The department uses the following materials per unit of production:

Plastic molded body	1 @	$2.16 each
Wheels	8 @	.06 each
Axles	4 @	.02 each

REQUIRED　Prepare a materials use budget for November.

Ex. 7-9
Direct Labor
Budget

Refer to Octobus Toy Company's production of toy buses in Exercise 7-8. The company pays $7.20 per hour for direct labor in the assembly department.

REQUIRED.　Prepare a direct labor budget for November.

Ex. 7-10
Direct Materials
Purchases Budget

The assembly department of Octobus Toy Company has budgeted production of 36,000 eight-wheel toy buses for July. Raw materials on hand at the end of June are expected to consist of

Plastic molded bodies	8,000
Wheels	20,000
Axles	9,000

Ending inventory at the end of July should be sufficient to produce 5,000 units. Assembly requires the following raw materials per unit of production:

Plastic molded bodies	1 at	$2.16 each
Wheels	8 at	.06 each
Axles	4 at	.02 each

REQUIRED　Prepare a direct materials purchases budget for July for the assembly department.

Ex. 7-11
Manufacturing
Overhead Budget
and Rate

Bill Bezglave has been toying with the idea of manufacturing two novelty items that he invented. He plans to use his garage for production space and to hire part-time help. In order to budget his overhead costs for the coming year he prepares the following estimates:

	Budgeted Sales per Unit	Labor Requirement per Unit
Exploding tennis balls	12,000	.3 hours
Dissolving ballpoint pens	41,000	.2 hours
Overhead		
Fixed:		
Depreciation of garage	$400 per year	
Utilities	120	
Property tax	70	
Variable:		
Indirect materials	$.10 per direct labor hour	
Utilities	.15 per direct labor hour	

REQUIRED
a. Prepare a manufacturing overhead budget.
b. Calculate the manufacturing overhead rate using direct labor hours as the application base.

Ex. 7-12
Cost of Goods Sold Budget

The following analysis of budgeted production costs has been prepared by the controller of Flitt Company. The company manufactures three sizes of lamp shades.

Budgeted Production for March

	Small	Medium	Large	Total
Direct materials	$ 3,600	$ 4,100	$ 6,500	$14,200
Direct labor	4,600	5,100	5,800	15,500
Manufacturing overhead	13,800	15,300	17,400	46,500
Total manufacturing cost	$22,000	$24,500	$29,700	$76,200
Budgeted production in units	2,000	1,750	1,800	5,550
Budgeted beginning inventory in units on March 1	400	300	300	1,000
Budgeted ending inventory, March 31	450	400	300	1,150

No change in costs is expected over the first three months of the year.

REQUIRED Prepare a cost of goods sold budget for March.

Ex. 7-13
Selling Expense Budget

TDY Corporation expects to sell 1,600 electronic memory typewriters during the coming budget year at $3,950 each. Based on past experience, its sales representatives will average 300 miles of travel for each unit of sales. There are five representatives, all of whom use their own cars, for which they are compensated $.22 per mile. They earn a salary of $1,000 per month plus a commission of 5 percent of sales. They spend about $15 per unit of sales on phone calls, and charge the company an average of $70 per day for meals and lodging while traveling. Sales representatives typically travel 220 days per year. Clerical costs needed to support the selling function amount to $62,000 per year and other selling expenses are $7,000 per month.

REQUIRED Prepare an annual selling expense budget for next year's sales of typewriters.

Ex. 7-14
Cash Receipts Budget

Alister Company is preparing its cash receipts budget for the months of February, March, and April. It makes all sales on account and typically experiences collections as follows: 10 percent of sales are collected in the month of sale, 60 percent in the month after the sale, 20 percent 2 months after the sale, and 8 percent 3 months after the sale. It experiences uncollectible accounts of about 2 percent of sales. On January 31, the company's balance of accounts receivable was $226,500 and its allowance for doubtful accounts was $1,500. Sales for the past 3 months and sales projections for the next 3 months are as follows:

November	$410,000
December	340,000
January	360,000
February	390,000
March	400,000
April	420,000

REQUIRED Prepare a budget of cash receipts for February, March, and April.

Ex. 7-15 (AICPA)
Cash Budgets

The following information was available from Montero Corporation's books:

1985	Purchases	Sales
January	$42,000	$72,000
February	48,000	66,000
March	36,000	60,000
April	54,000	78,000

Collections from customers are normally 70 percent in the month of sale, 20 percent in the month following the sale, and 9 percent in the second month following the sale. The balance is expected to be uncollectible. Montero takes full advantage of the 2 percent discount allowed on purchases paid for by the tenth of the following month. Purchases for May are budgeted at $60,000, and sales for May are forecasted at $66,000. Cash disbursements for expenses are expected to be $14,400 for the month of May. Montero's cash balance at May 1 was $22,000.

REQUIRED   Prepare the following schedules:

a.   Expected cash collections during May.
b.   Expected cash disbursements during May.
c.   Expected cash balance at May 31.

PROBLEMS

P. 7-1
Ending Raw
Materials Inventory
Budget

The following production quantity budget has just been received by the materials manager of Tubula Furniture Company:

Production Quantity Budget for Chair Model 7D
For Four Quarters Ending December 31

	Quarter			
	1	2	3	4
Budgeted sales in units	6,000	8,000	9,000	7,000
Desired ending inventory	1,000	1,500	2,000	1,800
Total requirement	7,000	9,500	11,000	8,800
Less beginning inventory	800	1,000	1,500	2,000
Budgeted production	6,200	8,500	9,500	6,800

Chair Model 7D requires the following materials and ending inventories:

Material	Quantity	Required Ending Inventory at End of Previous Quarter
Metal tubing	10 ft	20%
Plywood	2.5 sq ft	10%
Vinyl	12 sq ft	20%
Foam padding	2 lb	50%

The percentages in the above schedule indicate how much of each quarter's material requirement should be in the ending inventory of the previous quarter. Beginning inventories are expected to be as follows:

Metal tubing	11,000 ft
Plywood	1,800 sq ft
Vinyl	15,000 sq ft
Foam padding	5,000 lb

REQUIRED Prepare a budget of raw materials ending inventory for the first three quarters of the budget year.

P. 7-2
Sales and
Production Budgets

Eberleek Sealants, Inc., makes a roof sealer that it sells in 5-gallon cans for $45 per can. The company's budget committee is reviewing the budget for the next year. The sales manager has submitted a budget with a sales estimate of 3,600 units, divided into quarters as follows:

First quarter	1,000 units
Second quarter	1,100
Third quarter	800
Fourth quarter	700

The production manager indicates that operating capacity is 900 units per quarter. To produce more than 900 units requires additional costs. Production cost is $30 per unit and there would be a 20 percent increase in cost for units in excess of 900 per quarter. The production manager is evaluated on the cost of production, while the sales manager is evaluated on the basis of sales revenue. The sales manager claims that if he had only 900 units to sell in each of the first two quarters, the unsatisfied customers would switch to new products and sales in each of the last two quarters would be 50 units less than estimated.

REQUIRED Prepare sales and production budgets to determine how production should be scheduled and resolve the conflict between the sales manager and the production manager.

P. 7-3
Production, Labor,
and Materials
Budgets

Septimus Company expects to sell 37,500 left-handed key cases in each of the next 2 years. At the end of the current year it expects to have an ending inventory of 3,825 units. Its policy is to have an ending inventory equal to 15 percent of next period's sales. Each unit requires .15 hours of direct labor costing $6.20 per hour, and the following direct materials:

Vinyl	12 sq in @	$2.16 per sq ft
Clips	6 @	.30 per dozen
Snaps	2 @	5.00 per box of 1,000

The company charges overhead at $5 per direct labor hour. It sets selling price at total unit cost plus 100 percent.

REQUIRED
a. Prepare a production quantity budget for the year.
b. Prepare a direct labor budget.
c. Prepare a direct materials budget.
d. Determine the selling price per unit.

P. 7-4
Cash Receipts and Disbursements Budget

Seaflat Company plans to start production of outdoor molded flowerpots in July. Production and sales for the first 4-month production run are budgeted as follows:

Month	Budgeted Production	Budgeted Sales
July	750	500
August	800	600
September	900	800
October	850	1,000

Each unit requires $6 of direct materials. The company plans to have an ending inventory of materials each month equal to 50 percent of next month's production requirement. Eighty percent of material purchases are paid in the month of purchase and the remaining 20 percent in the following month.

Selling price of the product is $12 per unit. Twenty percent of sales are expected to be for cash. Twenty-five percent of credit sales are expected to be collected in the month of sale, and 75 percent the following month.

REQUIRED

a. Prepare a material purchases budget for July, August, and September.
b. Determine the cash requirements for payment of material purchases.
c. Determine the amount of cash that will be generated by sales revenue in July, August, and September.

P. 7-5
Budgeted Income Statement

Below is the income statement of Fradle Company:

Fradle Company
Income Statement
For the Year Ending December 31, 1985

Sales		$500,000
Less cost of goods sold		
Direct materials	$120,000	
Direct labor	150,000	
Manufacturing overhead		
Variable	36,000	
Fixed	64,000	370,000
Gross margin		130,000
Selling expenses		
Variable	$30,000	
Fixed	23,000	53,000
Administrative expenses		
Variable	25,000	
Fixed	15,000	40,000	93,000
Income before tax		37,000
Income tax expense		11,100
Net income		$ 25,900

The company expects 1986 operations to change as follows:

   a. Sales volume will increase 15 percent.
   b. Direct material cost will increase 10 percent.
   c. Direct labor cost will increase 6 percent; direct labor volume per unit will decrease 10 percent.
   d. Variable manufacturing overhead is expected to be 20 percent of material cost.
   e. Fixed manufacturing overhead will increase by $10,000.
   f. Selling and administrative variable expenses will be 20 percent greater than in 1985.
   g. Selling and administrative fixed expenses will increase by 10 percent.
   h. The tax rate will remain at 30 percent.

REQUIRED

   a. Prepare a budgeted income statement for the year ending December 31, 1986, reflecting the above changes, and assuming no change in selling prices.
   b. Calculate the pretax return on sales with the expected changes.
   c. Calculate the percentage increase in selling price that would be necessary if the company wants to earn a pretax return on sales of 10 percent.

P. 7-6
Budgets and
Performance
Reporting

Production of Hoppington Company's electronic desk calculators is budgeted as follows for the first 4 months of 1986:

January	6,000 units	March	8,000 units
February	7,000	April	7,500

The ending inventory of calculators on December 31, 1985, is expected to be 2,000 units. The desired ending inventory of finished goods each month is 40 percent of next month's expected sales. Each calculator requires 5 hours of direct labor costing $9 per hour. Fixed overhead of $1,879,200 per year is allocated equally to each month. Estimated variable overhead per direct labor hour is

Indirect materials	$ .50
Indirect labor	1.20
Fringe benefits	1.70
Payroll taxes	.60
Other expenses	1.10

By the end of January, the company had produced 7,000 units using 35,350 hours of labor. Actual overhead was as follows:

Indirect materials	$ 17,200
Indirect labor	40,000
Fringe benefits	60,000
Payroll taxes	21,300
Other expenses	36,100
Fixed overhead	160,000

REQUIRED

   a. Prepare a monthly production quantity budget for the first quarter of 1986.
   b. Prepare a monthly direct labor budget for the first quarter.
   c. Prepare a monthly manufacturing overhead budget for the first quarter.
   d. Prepare a budget performance report for labor and overhead for January.

P. 7-7
Analysis of
Budgeted Sales and
Income

Banglouder Company has recently developed a semiautomatic nail gun designed to compete with existing guns in the market. The New Products Committee is meeting to determine the potential of the new nail gun and to plan production for the next 3 years.

The sales manager wants the gun priced at $60 each to undercut competition. Market penetration is expected to be slow at first but should increase rapidly as users recognize the gun's advantages. The sales manager believes that sales should be 1,000 units in the first year, 2,000 in the second year, and 2,500 in subsequent years.

The production manager says that variable cost of the gun is $50 each and the company cannot afford to sell its products for a 17 percent contribution margin. He thinks the price of the gun should be at least $80 each, but admits that at this price sales would probably be 10 percent less than estimated by the sales manager.

The sales manager points out that the gun is not a primary revenue item. His research indicates that for each gun sold the company can expect to sell 20 cartons of nails per year. The nails sell for $10 per carton and have a variable cost of $4. Fixed cost is $250,000 per year.

REQUIRED

Prepare a schedule of budgeted sales and income for the first three years under each of the pricing options and decide which price should be charged for the nail gun.

P. 7-8
Comprehensive
Manufacturing
Budget

Plastine Corporation has been developing new plastic materials for use in the space program under a government research grant. The company recently succeeded in perfecting two new sheet plastics and plans to go into production in 1986. Sales of the lightweight rigid plastic PR17 are expected to be 60,000 square meters. The flexible resilient plastic PF19 is expected to have total sales of 25,000 square meters. Selling prices for the two plastics are expected to be

PR17 $10 per sq m
PF19 $16 per sq m

Production will start in January 1986 after tooling is completed, and there will be no beginning inventories. The company wants the finished goods ending inventory to be 20 percent of estimated 1986 sales. Ending raw materials inventory should be 10 percent of the periods budgeted use. Estimated cost and material data for the two plastics are given below.

Production Requirements per Square Meter

Product	Direct Materials			Direct Labor	
	Polymers	Inert Filler	Catalyst	Blending	Curing
PR17	2 kg	4 kg	10 g	.1 hr	.1 hr
PF19	4 kg	8 kg	4 g	.2 hr	.1 hr

Material Costs		Labor Costs	
Polymer	$.90 per kg	Blending	$10 per hr
Inert filler	.40 per kg	Curing	8 per hr
Catalyst	.20 per g		

	Other Costs		
	Manufacturing Overhead	Selling	Administrative
Variable	$2 per direct labor hour	5% of sales	2% of sales
Fixed	$93,600	$40,000	$60,000

REQUIRED Prepare the following budgets and schedules for the 1986 operating year.

    a. Sales budget
    b. Production quantity budget
    c. Materials use budget
    d. Materials purchases budget
    e. Direct labor budget
    f. Manufacturing overhead rate based on direct labor cost
    g. Schedule of product costs per unit
    h. Cost of goods sold budget
    i. Selling and administrative expense budget
    j. Budgeted income statement

P. 7-9 (AICPA)
Comprehensive
Sales and
Production Budget

The Scarborough Corporation manufactures and sells two products, Thingone and Thingtwo. In July 1985, Scarborough's budget department gathered the following data in order to project sales and budget requirements for 1986.

1986 Projected Sales:

Product	Units	Price
Thingone	60,000	$ 70
Thingtwo	40,000	$100

1986 Inventories — in Units:

Product	Expected January 1, 1986	Desired December 31, 1986
Thingone	20,000	25,000
Thingtwo	8,000	9,000

In order to produce one unit of Thingone and Thingtwo, the following raw materials are used:

Raw Material	Unit	Amount Used per Unit Thingone	Thingtwo
A	lb	4	5
B	lb	2	3
C	each		1

Projected data for 1986 with respect to raw materials are as follows:

Raw Material	Anticipated Purchase Price	Expected Inventories January 1, 1986	Desired Inventories December 31, 1986
A	$8	32,000 lb	36,000 lb
B	$5	29,000 lb	32,000 lb
C	$3	6,000 each	7,000 each

Projected direct labor requirements for 1986 and rates are as follows:

Product	Hours per Unit	Rate per Hour
Thingone	2	$3
Thingtwo	3	$4

Overhead is applied at the rate of $2 per direct labor hour.

REQUIRED   Based upon the above projections and budget requirements for 1986 for Thingone and Thingtwo, prepare the following budgets for 1986:

a. Sales budget (in dollars).
b. Production budget (in units).
c. Raw materials purchase budget (in quantities).
d. Raw materials purchase budget (in dollars).
e. Direct labor budget (in dollars).
f. Budgeted finished goods inventory at December 31, 1986 (in dollars).

P. 7-10 (AICPA)
Cash Requirements
Budget

The Loading Company is planning to construct a two-unit facility for the loading of iron ore into ships. On or before January 1, 1986, the stockholders will invest $100,000 in the company's capital stock to provide its initial working capital. To finance the construction program (the total planned cost of which is $1,800,000), the company will obtain a commitment from a lending organization for a loan of $1,800,000. This loan is to be secured by a 10-year mortgage note bearing interest at 5 percent per year on the unpaid balance. The principal amount of the loan is to be repaid in equal semiannual installments of $100,000 beginning June 30, 1987.

Inasmuch as the proceeds of the loan will only be required as construction work progresses, the company has agreed to pay a commitment fee beginning January 1, 1986 equal to 1 percent per year on the unused portion of the loan commitment. This fee is payable at the time amounts are "drawn-down," except at the time of the first "draw-down."

Work on the construction of the facility will commence in the fall of 1985. The first payment to the contractor will be due on January 1, 1986, at which time the commitment and loan agreement will become effective and the company will make its first "draw-down," for payment to the contractor, in the amount of $800,000. As construction progresses, additional payments will be made to the contractors by "drawing-down" the remaining loan proceeds as follows (it is assumed that payment to the contractors will be made on the same dates as the loan proceeds are "drawn-down"):

April 1, 1986	$500,000
July 1, 1986	300,000
December 31, 1986	100,000
April 1, 1987	100,000

Because of weather conditions, the facility can operate only from April 1 through November 30 of each year. The construction program will permit the completion of the first of the two plant units (capable of handling 5,000,000 tons) in time for its use during the 1986 shipping season. The second unit (capable of handling an additional 3,000,000 tons) will be completed in time for the 1987 season. It is expected that 5,000,000 tons will be handled by the facility during the 1986 season; thereafter, the tonnage handled is expected to increase in each subsequent year by 300,000 tons until a level of 6,500,000 tons is reached.

The company's revenues will be derived by charging the consignees of the ore for its services at a fixed rate per ton loaded. Billing terms will be net, ten days. Based upon past experience with similar facilities elsewhere, it is expected that the Loading Company's operating profit should average $.04 per ton before charges for interest, finance charges, and depreciation of $.03 per ton.

REQUIRED   Prepare a cash forecast for each of three calendar years starting with 1986 to demonstrate the sufficiency of cash, to be obtained from (1) the sale of capital stock, (2) "draw-downs" on the loan, and (3) the amount to be produced by the operating facility, to cover payments to the contractor and on the debt principal and interest.

P. 7-11 (AICPA)
Comprehensive
Budgeted Income
Statement for a
Service Firm

Ruidoso Ski Lodge operates a ski shop, restaurant, and lodge during the 120-day ski season from November 15 to March 15. The proprietor is considering changing his operations and keeping the lodge open all year.

Results of the operations for the year ended March 15, 1985 were as follows:

	Ski Shop		Restaurant		Lodge	
	Amount	Percent	Amount	Percent	Amount	Percent
Revenue	$27,000	100%	$40,000	100%	$108,000	100%
Costs:						
Costs of goods sold	14,850	55	24,000	60		
Supplies	1,350	5	4,000	10	7,560	7
Utilities	270	1	1,200	3	2,160	2
Salaries	1,620	6	12,000	30	32,400	30
Insurance	810	3	800	2	9,720	9
Property taxes on building	540	2	1,600	4	6,480	6
Depreciation	1,080	4	2,000	5	28,080	26
Total costs	20,520	76	45,600	114	86,400	80
Net income or (loss)	$ 6,480	24%	$ (5,600)	(14)%	$ 21,600	20%

1. The lodge has 100 rooms and the rate from November 15 to March 15 is $10 per day for one or two persons. The occupancy rate from November 15 to March 15 is 90 percent.
2. Ski shop and restaurant sales vary in direct proportion to room occupancy.
3. For the ski shop and restaurant, cost of goods sold, supplies, and utilities vary in direct proportion to sales. For the lodge, supplies and utilities vary in direct proportion to room occupancy.
4. The ski shop, restaurant, and lodge are located in the same building. Depreciation on the building is charged to the lodge. The ski shop and restaurant are charged with depreciation only on equipment. The full cost of the restaurant equipment became fully depreciated on March 15, 1985 but the equipment has a remaining useful life of 3 years. The equipment can be sold for $1,200 but will be worthless in 3 years. All depreciation is computed by the straight-line method.

5. Insurance premiums are for annual coverage for public liability and fire insurance on the building and equipment. All building insurance is charged to the lodge.
6. Salaries are the minimum necessary to keep each facility open and are for the ski season only, except for the lodge security guard, who is paid $5,400 per year.

Two alternatives are being considered for the future operation of Ruidoso Ski Lodge:

1. The proprietor believes that during the ski season the restaurant should be closed because "it does not have enough revenue to cover its out-of-pocket costs." It is estimated that lodge occupancy would drop to 80 percent of capacity if the restaurant were closed during the ski season. The space utilized by the restaurant would be used as a lounge for lodge guests.
2. The proprietor is considering keeping the lodge open from March 15 to November 15. The ski shop would be converted into a gift shop if the lodge should be operated during this period, with conversion costs of $1,000 in March and $1,000 in November each year. It is estimated that revenues from the gift shop would be the same per room occupied as revenues from the ski shop, that variable costs would be in the same ratio to revenues, and that all other costs would be the same for the gift shop as for the ski shop. The occupancy rate of the lodge at a room rate of $7 per day is estimated at 50 percent during the period from March 15 to November 15 whether or not the restaurant is operated.

REQUIRED   (Ignore income taxes and use 30 days per month for computational purposes.)

a. Prepare a projected income statement for the ski shop and lodge from November 15, 1985, to March 15, 1986, assuming the restaurant is closed during this period and all facilities are closed during the remainder of the year.
b. Assume that all facilities will continue to be operated during the 4 month period of November 15 to March 15 of each year.
   1. Assume that the lodge is operated during the 8 months from March 15 to November 15. Prepare an analysis which indicates the projected marginal income or loss of operating the gift shop and lodge during this 8-month period.
   2. Compute the minimum room rate required from March 1985 to November 1986 to allow the lodge to break even.

CASES

Case 7-1
Comprehensive
Operating Budget

Dulledge Cutlery Company manufactures fine cutlery. Currently it is planning its production of three types of knives. Following are expected sales for the year and beginning inventory data based on FIFO:

	Sales Price	Sales in Units	Units in Beginning Inventory	Unit Cost
9" slicer	$8.50	10,000	0	0
7" chopper	8.00	15,000	1,500	$5.30
5" paring	5.00	18,000	2,000	3.05

Production Requirements

	Direct Materials				Direct Labor		
Product	Blade Steel	Wood Handle	Molded Handle	Brass Rivets	Forging $10/hour	Assembly $8/hour	Finishing $9/hour
9" slicer	7 oz	1	—	3	.08 hr	.1 hr	.2 hr
7" chopper	6 oz	1		3	.06 hr	.1 hr	.2 hr
5" paring	3 oz		1	2	.03 hr	.08 hr	.1 hr

Material Costs:

Blade steel	$.09 per oz
Wood handle	.38 each
Molded handle	.19 each
Brass rivets	.02 each

Manufacturing Overhead:

Variable	$1.97/DLH
Fixed	$29,750

Selling expense: Variable = 4% of sales; fixed = $20,000
Administrative expense: Variable = 3% of sales; fixed = $15,000

At the end of each month, the company wants an ending inventory in units equal to 15 percent of that month's sales in units. The company is subject to an income tax rate of 30 percent.

REQUIRED Prepare the following budgets and schedules:

    a. Sales budget.
    b. Production quantity budget.
    c. Materials use budget.
    d. Material purchases budget.
    e. Direct labor budget.
    f. Schedule of manufacturing overhead rates.
    g. Schedule of product costs per unit.
    h. Cost of goods sold budget.
    i. Selling and administrative budget.
    j. Budgeted income statement.

CHAPTER 8
Standard Costs

Budgeting is a system of planning and controlling an organization's operations by expressing expected results for each part of the organization in a set of budgets. Actual results are accumulated and are compared periodically with budget data to determine how well each part of the organization is achieving goals. Another management planning and control system that provides a framework for even more timely and detailed performance measurement than budgets is a standard cost system. **Standard costs** are carefully predetermined costs. They are management's expectations of costs to be incurred for making a product or providing some service.

The term **standard** has found its way into our everyday conversations, and its use gives us some hint of what standard costs are in business. For example, you hear sports announcers and television commercials using the term "standard of excellence." A grade point average of 3.0 is often used as a standard for admitting students to graduate school or some other academic program. Similarly, par in a game of golf and emission control criteria for automobiles sold in California are examples of standards that influence decisions or serve as criteria for performance appraisal. The use of standards in measuring performance in business is much the same.

The purpose of this chapter is to introduce standard costs, explain their function, and show how a standard cost system operates. In addition, we illustrate standard cost performance reports commonly used in business.

STANDARD COSTS DEFINED

Standard costs are predetermined costs used as performance criteria

Standard costs are carefully predetermined costs of resources required to make some product or provide some service. Standard costs are used most frequently in connection with manufacturing activities, although they can be used with nonmanufacturing operations as well. Both job order costing systems and process costing accounting systems can be used with a standard cost system.

For example, management created the following standard costs for the production of an oak coffee table:

Resource	Quantity	Cost of Resource
Oak lumber	12 bd ft	$ 1.50 per bd ft
Varnish	.25 gal	16.00 per gal
Direct labor	2.5 hr	10.00 per hr
Manufacturing overhead	2.5 hr	6.00 per direct labor hr

This schedule identifies both the expected quantity and cost of the resources needed to make the oak coffee tables. The standard cost of one coffee table is computed easily by multiplying the resource quantities by their respective costs as follows:

Resource	Quantity	Cost of Resource	Total
Oak lumber	12 bd ft	$ 1.50 per bd ft	$18.00
Varnish	.25 gal	16.00 per gal	4.00
Direct labor	2.5 hr	10.00 per hr	25.00
Overhead	2.5 hr	6.00 per DLH	15.00
Standard cost of one coffee table			$62.00

The standard costs and quantities are the basis for preparing standard cost performance reports. Actual production costs are accumulated for the reporting period and compared with the standards. How standards are set and how they are used to measure performance is discussed in the rest of this chapter.

THE REASONS FOR USING STANDARDS

Businesses have many reasons for using standard costs, including:

1. Cost control
2. Pricing decisions
3. Performance appraisal
4. Cost awareness
5. Management by objective

Cost Control

Standards are used to control costs

Cost control does not refer merely to minimizing costs. It means identifying a cost with its related benefits and ensuring that the cost is justified given the benefits derived. Standard costs provide a very useful framework for cost control.

The cost of a single unit of output is often used to explain a standard, such as $62 for one oak coffee table. In this way the standard can be used to evaluate the cost of manufacturing any number of units. It becomes easy to compare actual costs with standard costs as frequently as necessary, whether monthly, weekly, daily, for a single work shift, or some other period. It is necessary only to measure the amount of output and the actual cost of the production activity of the period.

Standard costs make it possible to compare actual costs with expected costs on a timely basis. With timely performance reporting, managers can take action quickly to correct problems as they arise. Without standard costs, unnecessary costs could go undetected until considerable losses are incurred.

Pricing Decisions

The cost of a product is related in some way to its selling price. In some types of markets, such as agricultural commodities, the seller often does not influence the price but has to accept the market price that prevails—a perfectly competitive market—whether or not that price covers the cost of production. The decision for a producer in such a market is whether or not to produce the commodity.

Most products, however, do not sell in a perfectly competitive market. Sellers often have some control over prices. To obtain more control over prices, sellers frequently try to differentiate their product from competing products in the market and try to convince buyers that their products are in some ways superior and worth their price.

When product prices are based in some way on product costs, standard costs are often used instead of actual costs to arrive at the price. Standard costs reflect the expected cost of a product, whereas actual cost may include production efficiencies or inefficiencies that cannot be anticipated when the pricing decisions are made.

Performance Appraisal

When standards are established for performance evaluation, they provide measurements that can be applied uniformly to all personnel being evaluated. For example, the standard amount of labor time required to produce the oak coffee tables may be used to evaluate the efficiency of employees working on the tables. Similarly, the supervisor may be evaluated on how close his entire crew comes to achieving standards, and the purchasing agent is appraised on how close the cost of purchased materials is to the standard cost.

Standards help managers to evaluate performance

Evaluating employee performance is a difficult task, involving many different variables, some of which may be quite subjective and therefore difficult or inappropriate to use. Standards can provide an objective means of evaluation. If standards are to work well, the people being evaluated must have a clear understanding of them and how they are used. In addition, employees should be provided with timely reports on their performance. The availability of standards makes timely reporting possible and easy.

Cost Awareness

Many employees have little awareness of the cost of business activities. They are concerned primarily with such things as increasing production, improving employee morale, or reducing absenteeism. Although these are important goals, there are costs to achieving them. Employees who are unaware of costs will fail to relate costs to business activities. Standard costs and standard cost performance reports often inform employees about the cost implications of their actions. When people are aware of costs they may make efforts at effective cost control.

Management by Objective (MBO)

A simple yet powerful business concept, **management by objective** means that specific objectives are established for each business activity and the manager responsible for that activity works to achieve the objectives. When an activity falls within acceptable performance levels, little managerial action is necessary other than routine supervision. When performance varies significantly from acceptable levels, the manager tries to correct the problem by taking whatever action is necessary. A standard cost system facilitates MBO because it provides a quick reference for identifying and reporting differences between standard and actual performance. A standard cost system is helpful in achieving desired objectives because it makes possible a fast response to problems.

Managers attend to deviations from plans

TYPES OF STANDARDS

Standards are classified into three types. They are

1. Ideal standards
2. Basic standards
3. Currently attainable standards

Ideal Standards

Standards that can be achieved only under perfect operating conditions are called **ideal standards.** They may be attainable if there is no idle time, no shortages, no breakdowns, and no errors—in other words, if perfect conditions prevail. Such standards are also called **theoretical standards** or **engineering standards.** Conditions that satisfy ideal standards are extremely rare, but the standards may nevertheless be useful as measures of optimum performance. No one is expected to achieve ideal standards but rather to come as close to them as possible. Sometimes ideal standards are used as a basis for setting realistic performance measures.

Basic Standards

Basic standards provide a framework for comparing performance over a period of years. They are sometimes called long-range standards because once created they are not changed for a number of years. Basic standards are helpful in determining trends in performance. In rapidly changing environments, however, they tend to lose their value in this respect. In an economy where prices change quickly and technological innovation frequently requires changes in the methods of production, few businesses find basic standards useful.

Currently Attainable Standards

The most commonly used standards are known as **currently attainable standards.** They represent benchmarks of efficient production in the current operating environment. Currently attainable standards allow for usual production problems, such as down time for maintenance, employee errors, or occasional inventory shortages. Such standards represent desirable performance because they tend to be realistic and are most likely to be acceptable to employees. There is no doubt that standards operate best when they are viewed as attainable and realistic by those whose performance is measured against the standard.

THE STANDARD COST SYSTEM

A standard cost system consists of three basic activities. They include: (1) standard setting, (2) accumulation of actual costs, and (3) variance analysis.

Standard Setting

The first step in establishing a standard cost system is the creation of standards to be used for performance evaluation. In establishing standards, keep in mind that poorly conceived standards result in inappropriate measures of performance and may cause serious problems with employee acceptance of the system.

Standard-setting practices vary among firms. Some use simple techniques applied by an individual; others use sophisticated methods based on engineering and management science principles.

The Standards-Setting Committee.   Because many factors affect the setting of standards, commonly they are set by a **standards committee** made up of a representative cross section of all the departments of an organization affected by standards. The standards committee establishes and monitors standards for the firm and is responsible for changing and updating the standards when necessary. The controller or some other member of the accounting department is usually a key member of the standards committee.

Scientific Standards Setting.   Many methods exist for determining what the quantity and cost of inputs should be for a specific type of activity. **Time and motion studies** consist of observing, measuring, and tabulating in detail the movements and time required to perform a task. **Simulation studies** use models of the activity or operation for which standards are to be established. Many business models are mathematical formulas that can be used with a computer repeatedly to simulate an activity, varying the parameters of the model to estimate acceptable standards. Another approach involves **pilot projects** whereby a small amount of product is made to provide some production data that can be used to establish standards. In such situations, **learning curve analysis** may be required to determine expected production costs under full-scale operating conditions. Learning curves are mathematical models that describe the decreasing labor time and cost that are experienced as a new task is learned. Chapter 25 covers learning curve analysis.

Establishing standards is a scientific process

Past Experience.   The immediate past is often an excellent indicator of what can be expected in the near future. Past results are real and verifiable, and often are very valuable in setting standards. Managers may give heavy weight to past experience in setting standards for future production.

Other Inputs.   Few management decisions are made without considering the effects on employees, customers, government regulations, and other factors. Standard setting is no exception. Employees and labor unions are keenly interested in standards that affect labor productivity and often dispute labor standards established by managers. Because disputes over standards may cause strikes or other labor actions, management should work closely with labor to establish realistic and attainable standards. Clearly, the environment in which the firm operates is bound to have an effect on the standards that are established.

Accumulation of Actual Costs

After standards are established, actual cost data are accumulated and compared with standards in performance reports. Actual manufacturing costs are accumulated using either a job order system or a process cost system as discussed in Chapters 4, 5, and 6.

Actual costs are needed for comparison with standard costs

Accumulating actual costs is the main function of cost accounting. The use of a standard cost system does not mean that actual costs do not have to be measured. Instead, a standard cost system provides a means for getting more information from the cost data than is possible with just actual costs. A standard cost system provides guidance in determining the type of cost data needed and the form in which the data should be reported.

Variance Analysis

A **variance** is the difference between an actual cost and its corresponding standard cost. Variances are typically expressed in dollars and in sufficient detail to permit cost analysis and control. For example, it cost $298 to make five oak coffee tables. The standard cost of one coffee table is $62. Therefore the standard cost of five tables is $310 (5 units × $62 per unit). The actual cost of making the five coffee tables is $12 less than standard cost ($310 standard cost − $298 actual cost). Because the actual cost is less than standard cost, the variance is favorable. The tables were produced for less cost than expected. The difference between the actual cost and the standard cost is the total variance for the production of the five oak coffee tables.

Exactly why did the $12 favorable variance occur? Perhaps the material cost less than expected, or less than the expected amount of labor was used to make the tables. In many cases the total variance is the result of a number of variables all occurring at the same time. To help managers determine the cause of variances, and to help them to control costs, accountants separate the total variance into a number of more specific variances and report the information to management. A performance report showing variances may help managers decide, for example, to reduce labor time on its coffee tables by substituting a varnish that can be sprayed for the varnish now used that must be brushed.

THE ANALYSIS OF VARIANCES

Variance analysis is a systematic process of comparing actual costs and standard costs, identifying variances, and interpreting the source of each variance. If actual costs are more than standard costs, an **unfavorable variance** occurs. If actual costs are less than standard costs, a **favorable variance** is reported.

When actual results are compared with standards, it is unlikely that actual costs and quantities of materials and labor required for production will be precisely the same as standard costs and quantities. Even when small variances occur, it is necessary to analyze them carefully. A small total variance may be made up of significant individual variances. For example, the $12 favorable total variance for the production of five coffee tables may include a $50 favorable variance from buying oak lumber at a lower than standard price and a $38 unfavorable variance caused by inefficient use of labor. By analyzing the total variance carefully, managers may be able to improve performance by continuing activities that result in favorable variances and modifying other activities to eliminate or reduce unfavorable variances. A systematic evaluation of variances gives managers useful detailed information for monitoring and improving performance. Variance analysis attempts to answer these two questions:

Variance analysis addresses two questions

1. What is the difference between actual costs and standard costs?
2. Why did the difference occur?

To answer the first question we must calculate variances. The calculations are made using both actual and standard cost and quantity data. The second question is the more important one to answer because it addresses the causes of variances and focuses on the solutions to the problems that caused them. The second question is also the more difficult to answer. Sometimes variances result from complex interactions of human and physical variables. For example, the $38 unfavorable labor variance that occurred in producing the oak coffee tables may have occurred for one of the following reasons:

1. The purchasing agent bought number two grade oak lumber instead of number one grade, which is normally used. The poorer-quality lumber cost less and provided a favorable material variance, but with some knots and a rougher finish it took longer for workers to complete the tables. This resulted in the $38 unfavorable labor variance.

2. A second possibility is that the production supervisor was new and did not know how to coordinate efficiently the production activities in making the coffee tables.

3. A third possibility is that a new employee was hired who required some on-the-job training. His performance in making these five tables was much poorer than it would be with an experienced employee.

In the first situation, the unfavorable labor variance was caused by a decision related to material purchases. The variances caused by the second and third situations will correct themselves as the new employees gain experience. In each case, calculating the variance is a simple matter; determining the exact cause of the variances or the most appropriate course of action is more difficult. In practice, managerial experience and an understanding of production activities are used to interpret variances and determine appropriate courses of action. To provide that skill and understanding, the company may have a policy of assigning accountants to specific locations in the plant so that they gain needed experience and a knowledge of the operating characteristics of the business. Such a policy may contribute to more meaningful accounting information as the accountants become familiar with specific production activities and information needs.

Variances may be favorable or unfavorable, and they occur for many reasons

Computation of Variances

Variances are computed for all of the three basic cost elements of manufacturing — direct labor, direct materials, and manufacturing overhead. The computations of labor and material variances are very similar and are covered in detail in this chapter. Overhead variances are more complex and can be computed in several different ways. In this chapter we only mention total overhead variances; we cover manufacturing overhead variance analysis in Chapter 9.

Standards allow comparison of actual costs with desired costs on a timely basis

To derive the greatest benefit from the timely performance information, variances should be isolated and reported as early as possible. This usually means computing the variances as soon as actual cost data have been accumulated and compared with standards. Once computed, the variances are reported in dollar amounts, indicating whether they are favorable or unfavorable. A variance is not complete without an amount and a designation as favorable or unfavorable. If the variance is unfavorable, managers may attach a significantly different weight to it than if the same size variance is favorable. An unfavorable variance is a cost, whereas a favorable variance is a cost saving. Therefore a company may have a policy of investigating unfavorable variances greater than $500 and favorable variances greater than $2,000.

To illustrate variance analysis we use the example of Hy-Tension Concrete Company and its production of concrete arches and columns. April production data are used to illustrate the computation and reporting of variances. This example is used throughout the rest of the chapter.

Bill of Materials

It is common to prepare a list of standard materials used to manufacture a product. Such a list is called a **bill of materials** and shows the standard quantity of material that the product requires. An example of a bill of materials for Hy-Tension Concrete Company's concrete arches is shown in Figure 8-1. For products requiring many components, the bill of materials can be a complex document, describing in detail each part, the quantity required, and other information.

Figure 8-1. The bill of materials describes each component of a product and its standard quantity.

Bill of Materials		
Product: Concrete arch	**Standard lot:** 200 units	
Material	**Quantity**	**Description**
#6 Re-bar	6 each	Curved, top and bottom
#8 Re-bar	4 each	Curved, top and bottom
#8 Re-bar	2 each	
#4 Re-bar	25 each	Spreader tie @ 16" centers
Concrete	2 cubic yd	3000#/square inch. Mix design 2B

Setting Labor Standards

Once standards are established for labor, a company may prepare a list of standard operations, such as illustrated in Figure 8-2. Such a form shows the amount of standard time allotted to specific operations and is used in scheduling various production tasks.

Many manufacturing operations require setup time, which is the time needed to make possible the start of a task. Setup time usually does not change, whether the subsequent task is to be performed a few times or many times. For example, a certain amount of time is needed to set up equipment to bend reinforcing steel into a specific shape. If the equipment is used to bend 100 steel bars, the setup cost per unit is greater than if several thousand units are produced. Because setup cost per unit can vary, it is usually not included in the standard direct labor cost of the product. Instead, setup time is included in manufacturing overhead.

Setup costs are often treated as overhead

Calculation of Total Variances

Variances are computed for April by comparing actual April production with the standard costs of the products. The standard costs of the products are presented in Figure 8-3.

Figure 8-2. The list of standard operations is similar to a bill of materials but it describes labor instead. The standard amount of time allotted to each task is shown.

Hy-Tension Concrete Company **List of Standard Operations**			
Part: Horizontal bent bar for arches		**ID:** RB8–4	
Material: #8 Reinforcing steel		**Standard quantity:** 400	

Operation	Standard Time in Minutes		Description
	Setup	Per Unit	
30	12	.4	Cut to length
40	9	1.2	90 degree bend, each end
50	11	2.5	30 degree bends, 4 each bar
60	—	.2	Move to conveyor

Actual cost data for April are presented in Figure 8-4. During April the company completed 1,000 arches and 1,500 columns. Using the standard costs from Figure 8-3 and the actual costs from Figure 8-4, it is easy to

Hy-Tension Concrete Company
Standard Costs for Concrete Arches and Columns

	Input Cost	Arches		Columns	
		Input Quantity	Output Cost	Input Quantity	Output Cost
Reinforcing steel	$ .30/lb	400 lb	$120	220 lb	$ 66
Concrete	50.00/cu yd	2 cu yd	100	.6 cu yd	30
Direct labor	10.00/hr	4.5 hr	45	2.1 hr	21
Total prime cost			265		117
Manufacturing overhead	20.00/hr	4.5 hr	90	2.1 hr	42
Total cost			$355		$159

Figure 8-3. Standards are established for each resource used in production. They provide managers with a timely basis for evaluating performance and determining whether production is deviating from standards. This company makes two products, each using two materials and one type of labor.

Figure 8-4. Actual costs of production are accumulated in the cost accounting system so that they can be compared with standards. These are actual costs of products whose standard costs are described in Figure 8-3.

Hy-Tension Concrete Company
Actual Production Cost for April

	Arches		Columns	
	Resource	Cost	Resource	Cost
Reinforcing steel	420,000 lb	$117,600	352,500 lb	$ 98,700
Concrete	1,985 cu yd	101,235	870 cu yd	44,370
Direct labor	4,600 hr	47,150	3,000 hr	30,770
Manufacturing overhead		93,600		57,400
Total April production costs		$359,585		$231,240
Units produced	1,000		1,500	

Steel purchased: 2,000 tons, $1,120,000

compute the total variance for both products. The total variance is as shown below:

Total variance = Total standard cost − Total actual cost

= (Units produced × Unit standard cost) − Actual cost

Concrete Arches:		
1,000 units × $355 per unit	$355,000	
Actual cost	359,585	
Total variance for arches		$4,585 U
Concrete Columns:		
1,500 units × $159 per unit	238,500	
Actual cost	231,240	
Total variance for columns		7,260 F
Total variance for April production		$2,675 F

According to the standards, 1,000 arches **should** cost $355,000, but they actually cost $359,585, so there is a $4,585 unfavorable variance for the arches. Similarly, 1,500 columns should cost $238,500, but they actually cost $231,240, so the variance of $7,260 is favorable. But these are total variances, and management needs much more detailed information. The details are provided by calculating separate variances for materials, labor, and overhead. In this chapter we concentrate on detailed material and labor variances, and compute only the total overhead variance.

Favorable variances mean actual costs are lower than standard

Typically, two variances are calculated for each prime resource used in production: one for the quantity of resource used, and one for the cost of the resource. The cost variances measure if the price paid for materials or the wage rate paid for labor was more or less than standard. The quantity variances measure if the amounts of materials or labor used were more or less than standard. By separating the total variance into component parts, managers can determine precisely the areas in which production was more or less costly than expected.

A total variance can be broken down into several components

DIRECT MATERIAL VARIANCES

Material variances are isolated as soon as actual cost data are available. Often the material price variance can be identified when material is purchased. Sometimes it is calculated only when the material is used.

Material Price Variance

The **material price variance** measures the difference between the actual cost of material and the standard cost expected to be paid for the material. If the actual cost is greater than the standard cost, the variance is unfavorable. A favorable variance occurs if the actual cost is less than the standard cost. The computation of the material price variance is

Formula for material price variance

$$\text{Material price variance} = \left(\begin{array}{c} \text{Actual quantity} \\ \times \text{Standard price} \\ \text{per unit} \end{array} \right) - \left(\begin{array}{c} \text{Actual quantity} \\ \times \text{Actual price} \\ \text{per unit} \end{array} \right)$$

Note that in both multiplications the actual quantity of material is multiplied by the price per unit of material. In one case the actual price is used and in the other the standard price. This makes sense because we want to isolate the variance caused by paying more or less than standard for material. The formula can be shortened as follows:

$$\text{Material price variance} = \left(\begin{array}{c} \text{Standard price per unit} \\ - \text{Actual price per unit} \end{array} \right) \times \text{Actual quantity}$$

or

$$\text{Material price variance} = \text{Difference in price} \times \text{Actual quantity}$$

Figure 8-3 shows the standard price of the two materials used by Hy-Tension Concrete Company. Figure 8-4 shows the actual quantities of materials purchased and the quantity used. As is often the case, the quantity used during the period is not identical to the quantity purchased. Because variances should be measured as soon as feasible, the material price variance is calculated at the time of purchase whenever possible. In the case of reinforcing steel, the company may acquire sufficient steel for several months' production at one time, or it may acquire steel several times a month at various prices. In either case it is not necessary to wait until production data are available to calculate the price variance for steel. On the other hand, the company acquires ready-mixed concrete as needed for production, because ready-mixed concrete cannot be stored; it must be used within a few hours of mixing. Consequently the price variance of concrete can be computed only when production takes place.

Price Variance for Materials Purchases.   To calculate the price variance for reinforcing steel we use the quantity of steel purchased in April, rather than the quantity used. The company purchased 2,000 tons of steel in April for $1,120,000. At 2,000 pounds per ton, the April purchase amounts to 4,000,000 pounds of steel costing $.28 per pound. The price variance of steel is favorable, because the standard price is $.30 per pound and the actual cost is $.28 per pound. The amount of price variance is computed using the formula presented earlier:

$$\begin{matrix} \text{Material price variance} \\ \text{Reinforcing steel} \end{matrix} = \begin{pmatrix} \text{Actual quantity} \\ \text{purchased} \times \\ \text{Standard price} \end{pmatrix} - \begin{pmatrix} \text{Actual quantity} \\ \text{purchased} \times \\ \text{Actual price} \end{pmatrix}$$

$$= 4,000,000 \text{ lb} \times \$.30 - \$1,120,000$$

$$= \$1,200,000 - \$1,120,000$$

$$= \$80,000 \text{ F}$$

A graph of the material price variance is illustrated in Figure 8-5, which shows the cost of reinforcing steel on the vertical axis and the quantity purchased on the horizontal axis. The entire colored rectangle in the figure is the total standard cost of 2,000 tons of steel; and the cross-hatched area at the top is the favorable price variance, which is the portion of the standard cost that was not incurred when the steel was purchased.

Not all material variances can be isolated at the time of purchase. Sometimes a material price variance occurs because one raw material is substituted

Figure 8-5. Two thousand tons of steel, shown on the horizontal axis, has a standard price of $600 per ton shown on the vertical axis. The colored rectangle defined by these figures is the total standard cost of steel. The actual cost is less than standard. The cross-hatched rectangle at the top of the diagram shows the favorable price variance as the portion of the standard cost that was not incurred. It is the difference between the total standard and total actual costs.

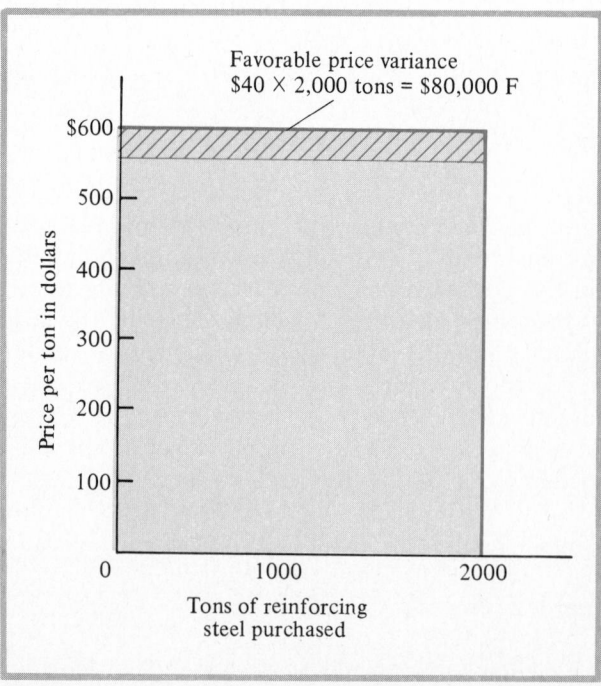

Favorable price variance
$40 × 2,000 tons = $80,000 F

for another whose standard cost is different. This is also called a **material substitution variance.** For example, the company runs out of one size of reinforcing steel because of a truckers' strike. Rather than stop production and idle workers and production facilities, it is more economical to substitute a larger size of steel reinforcing that has a higher standard cost. Consequently the price of steel used in production is higher than the standard price for reinforcing steel because of the material substitution. As you see, there can be two types of material price variances. One occurs because the resource is purchased for an amount different than standard and the other occurs because one material is substituted for another of a different standard cost.

One material may be substituted for another

Price Variance of Material Used.   If material is purchased as it is used, the actual quantity used in production is the quantity used to compute the material price variance. In our example, concrete is purchased as needed for production. Figure 8-4 provides actual data for concrete used in arches and columns; the standards are found in Figure 8-3. The following material price variance calculations for concrete used in arches can be made only after production takes place.

$$\begin{aligned} \text{Material price variance} \atop \text{Concrete for arches} &= \left(\begin{array}{c} \text{Actual quantity} \\ \text{used} \times \\ \text{Standard price} \end{array}\right) - \left(\begin{array}{c} \text{Actual quantity} \\ \text{used} \times \\ \text{Actual price} \end{array}\right) \end{aligned}$$

$$= 1{,}985 \text{ cu yd} \times \$50 - \$101{,}235$$
$$= \$99{,}250 - \$101{,}235$$
$$= \$1{,}985 \text{ U}$$

The variance is unfavorable because more was paid for concrete than the standard price. A similar calculation for concrete columns is shown below:

$$\begin{aligned} \text{Material price variance} \atop \text{Concrete for columns} \quad &= 870 \text{ cu yd} \times \$50 - \$44{,}370 \\ &= \$43{,}500 - \$44{,}370 \\ &= \$870 \text{ U} \end{aligned}$$

The material price variance is calculated the same whether it is for materials purchased or for materials used. Only the timing of the calculation may differ.

Material Quantity Variance

The **material quantity variance** measures the difference between the actual quantity of material used and the standard quantity that should have been used to produce the output. It is also called the **material use variance.** If more than the standard quantity of material is used, the variance is unfavorable. A favorable variance results from using less than the standard quantity of material.

The formula for the computation of the material quantity variance is:

$$\text{Material quantity variance} = \begin{pmatrix} \text{Standard quantity} \\ \times \text{ Standard price} \end{pmatrix} - \begin{pmatrix} \text{Actual quantity} \\ \times \text{ Standard price} \end{pmatrix}$$

Formula for material quantity variance

The formula can be shortened as follows:

$$\text{Material quantity variance} = \begin{pmatrix} \text{Standard quantity} \\ - \text{ Actual quantity} \end{pmatrix} \times \text{Standard price}$$

The standard quantity is the amount of material that should be used for the amount of output produced. For example, 1,000 arches were produced in April. There are two materials used in production—reinforcing steel and concrete. The standard quantity of reinforcing steel is 400 lb for each arch, or 400,000 lb in total. The actual quantity used was 420,000 lb. Clearly the material quantity variance for the production of arches is unfavorable. It is calculated below:

$$\text{Material quantity variance} = \begin{pmatrix} 400,000 \text{ lb} \\ \times \$.30/\text{lb} \end{pmatrix} - \begin{pmatrix} 420,000 \text{ lb} \\ \times \$.30/\text{lb} \end{pmatrix}$$
$$= \$120,000 - \$126,000$$
$$= \$6,000 \text{ U}$$

or

$$\text{Material quantity variance} = (400,000 \text{ lb} - 420,000 \text{ lb}) \times \$.30 \text{ lb}$$
$$= \$6,000 \text{ U}$$

The standard quantity of concrete used to produce the 1,000 arches was 2,000 cubic yards (1,000 arches × 2 cu yd). The actual quantity used was 1,985 cu yd, so the concrete material quantity variance for the production of arches was favorable. The dollar amount of the variance is computed as follows:

$$\text{Material quantity variance} = \begin{pmatrix} 2,000 \text{ cu yd} \\ - 1,985 \text{ cu yd} \end{pmatrix} \times \$50 \text{ cu yd}$$
$$= \$750 \text{ F}$$

The company has a favorable material quantity variance for concrete because it used less than the standard quantity of concrete. The steel and concrete material variances for the company's other product—concrete columns—are computed in the same way. We omit these calculations here but the variances are shown later in the chapter in the summary variance reports.

As soon as the material quantity variances are isolated, they can be recorded in the books of account. The journal entries to record the variances are discussed later in the chapter.

Figure 8-6. The direct material price variance measures the difference between the standard and actual price at the actual quantity. The quantity variance measures the difference between the standard and actual quantity at the standard price. These two variances together make up the total material variance.

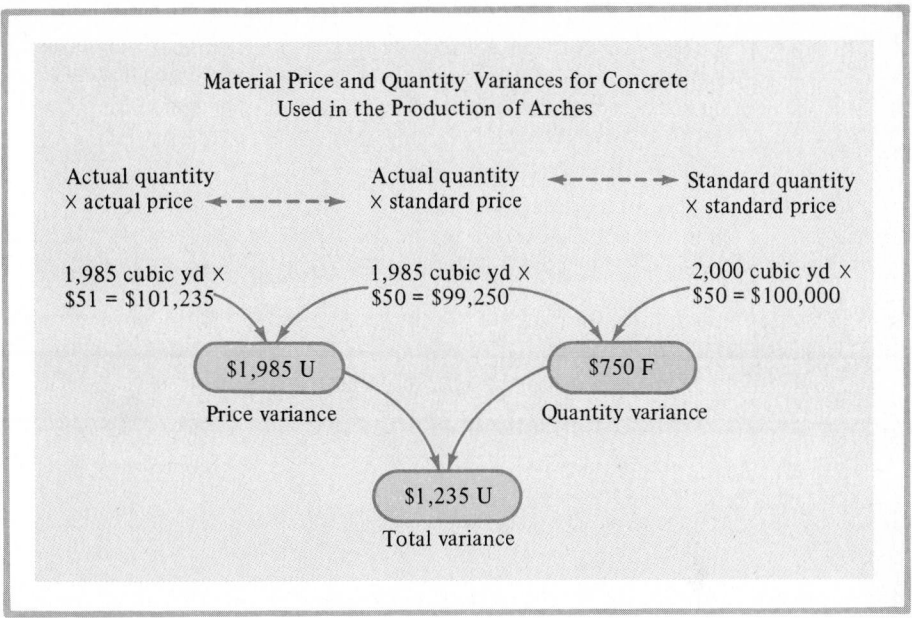

Material Price and Quantity Variances for Concrete
Used in the Production of Arches

Actual quantity × actual price ← - - - - - → Actual quantity × standard price ← - - - - - → Standard quantity × standard price

1,985 cubic yd × $51 = $101,235

1,985 cubic yd × $50 = $99,250

2,000 cubic yd × $50 = $100,000

$1,985 U
Price variance

$750 F
Quantity variance

$1,235 U
Total variance

Graphic Solution of Variances

Graphic analysis helps to visualize variances

A diagram of the calculation of the material price variance and the material quantity variance for concrete used in the construction of arches is shown in Figure 8-6. Note that the two variances together result in an overall unfavorable variance of $1,235 for concrete used in the construction of arches.

The material price and quantity variances incurred in making arches are also illustrated graphically in Figure 8-7. Diagram (a) is for reinforcing steel, and diagram (b) is for concrete. The cost of material is plotted on the vertical axis and the quantity on the horizontal axis. The colored area indicates the total standard cost of steel and concrete. In the case of steel, the price variance has already been isolated, and the diagram shows only the unfavorable quantity variance. The white rectangle at the right in diagram (a) is the cost of the material used in excess of standard.

In the diagram for concrete, the colored area is the total standard cost of concrete for 1,000 arches. The cross-hatched rectangle at the right shows the favorable material quantity variance resulting from using less concrete than standard to make the arches. The price of the concrete, however, was more than standard, and the unfavorable price variance is shown on top of the diagram as the white portion that extends above the standard cost.

Responsibility for Material Variances

Typically, the purchasing agent is responsible for material price variances, whereas production personnel are responsible for material quantity variances. However, this is not always the case, and each situation must be examined carefully to determine actual responsibility. For example, the purchasing agent may obtain materials at what seems like a favorable price,

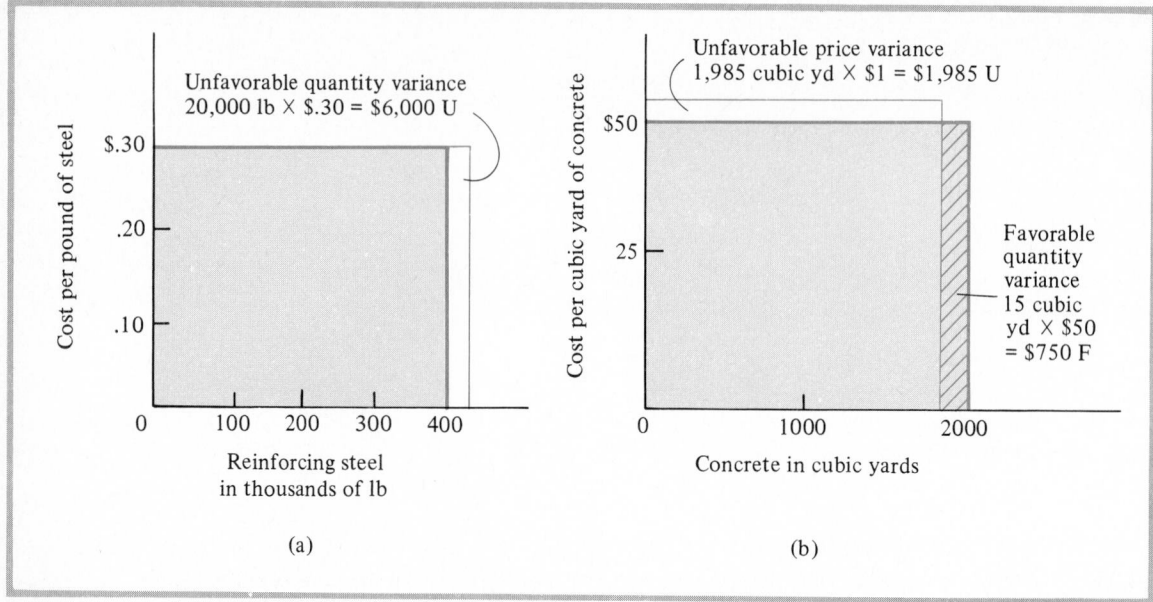

Figure 8-7. The colored areas are total standard costs. In part (a), the quantity of steel used was greater than standard, resulting in the unfavorable variance shown by the white rectangle. The actual quantity of concrete used, shown in part (b), was less than standard, resulting in the favorable variance shown as the cross-hatched rectangle. This part of the standard cost was not incurred. But the price paid for the concrete was greater than standard, resulting in the unfavorable variance at the top of the diagram.

but the quality is inferior. Using this inferior material may result in more than a normal amount of waste and therefore an unfavorable quantity variance. In some cases, shortages of required materials may result in substituting a more expensive material in order to maintain production on schedule. The result is an unfavorable price variance.

All variances need not be investigated

Unfavorable variances are not necessarily bad. A manager may decide that an unfavorable quantity variance on inferior material may be more than offset by the favorable price variance. Substituting a more costly material may be a good decision, despite an unfavorable price variance, if the alternative is a delay in production that costs more than the materials used. Trading a favorable price variance for an unfavorable quantity variance is often a wise decision. Variance evaluations must be made in the light of such situations.

DIRECT LABOR VARIANCES

Labor variances are calculated in the same way as material variances. Labor variances can be isolated after the data on labor time and cost are accumulated. The **labor rate variance** and the **labor efficiency variance** are calculated using standard and actual labor rates and hours.

Labor Rate Variance

The **labor rate variance** is caused by paying workers more or less than the standard rate for labor. It is calculated as the difference between the standard labor rate and the actual rate times the actual hours worked. The formula is as follows:

$$\text{Labor rate variance} = \left(\begin{array}{c}\text{Actual hours} \times \\ \text{Standard rate}\end{array}\right) - \left(\begin{array}{c}\text{Actual hours} \times \\ \text{Actual rate}\end{array}\right)$$

Note that in both multiplications the actual hours worked are multiplied by the standard rate and the actual rate. This is logical because we want to isolate the variance due to the difference in labor rates. The formula can be shortened as follows:

Labor rate variance = (Standard rate − Actual rate) × Actual hours

Using the example of April production by Hy-Tension Concrete Company, we calculate the labor rate variance for the production of concrete arches and columns. The standard labor rate is $10 per hour.

Production of 1,000 arches required 4,600 hours of labor time at a total cost of $47,150. This amounts to $10.25 per hour actually paid for labor ($47,150/4,600 hours). The labor rate variance is unfavorable because the actual rate is greater than the standard rate. To calculate the labor rate variance we multiply the difference between the actual rate and the standard rate by the actual labor hours worked.

Labor rate variance for arches:

$$
\begin{aligned}
\text{Labor rate variance} &= \text{(Standard rate} - \text{Actual rate)} \times \text{Actual hours} \\
&= (\$10.00 - \$10.25) \times 4{,}600 \text{ hr} \\
&= \$1{,}150 \text{ U}
\end{aligned}
$$

A similar calculation is made for columns. Production of 1,500 columns required 3,000 hours costing $30,770. In this case the labor rate is $10.256667 per hour, calculated as $30,770/3,000 hours. Rather than working with a long decimal fraction that may result in having to round numbers, we simply use the first form of the labor rate formula without the actual rate per hour.

Labor Rate Variance for Columns:	
Actual hours × standard rate	
3,000 hours × $10 per hour	$30,000
Actual hours × actual rate	30,770
Labor rate variance for columns	$ 770 U

Labor Efficiency Variance

Comparing the amount of time spent on a product with the expected amount of time for making the product provides a measure of labor efficiency. The **labor efficiency variance** is caused by using more or less labor than standard for the output produced. If the time worked is less than standard, labor has been used efficiently and the labor efficiency variance is favorable. An unfavorable labor efficiency variance occurs when more than the standard amount of labor time is used in production.

The total standard hours that should have been used during the period cannot be determined without knowing the quantity of production for the period. In our example, 1,000 concrete arches and 1,500 concrete columns were produced in April. The standard quantity of labor for each arch is 4.5 hours; the standard for each column is 2.1 hours. Consequently, the standard number of labor hours for April production is calculated as follows:

$$\text{Standard labor quantity} = \text{Units produced} \times \text{Standard hours per unit}$$

Arches:

$$\text{Standard labor quantity} = 1,000 \text{ arches} \times 4.5 \text{ hr per arch}$$
$$= 4,500 \text{ hr for arches}$$

Columns:

$$\text{Standard labor quantity} = 1,500 \text{ columns} \times 2.1 \text{ hr per column}$$
$$= 3,150 \text{ hr for columns}$$

The labor efficiency variance is now computed using this formula:

Formula for labor efficiency variance

$$\text{Labor efficiency variance} = \left(\begin{array}{c}\text{Standard hours} \\ \times \text{ Standard rate}\end{array}\right) - \left(\begin{array}{c}\text{Actual hours} \times \\ \text{Standard rate}\end{array}\right)$$

The calculation of the variance for arches and columns is shown below using the shortened version of the formula:

$$\text{Labor efficiency variance} = \text{Difference in hours} \times \text{Standard rate}$$

Concrete arches:

$$\text{Labor efficiency variance} = (4,500 \text{ hr} - 4,600 \text{ hr}) \times \$10/\text{hr}$$
$$= -100 \text{ hr} \times \$10/\text{hr}$$
$$= \$1,000 \text{ U}$$

Concrete columns:

$$\text{Labor efficiency variance} = (3,150 \text{ hr} - 3,000 \text{ hr}) \times \$10/\text{hr}$$
$$= 150 \text{ hr} \times \$10/\text{hr}$$
$$= \$1,500 \text{ F}$$

Graphic Presentation

The diagram in Figure 8-8 shows the relationship between the cost and quantity of labor and the resulting variances for the production of concrete arches. In this case both variances are unfavorable, resulting in a $2,150 total unfavorable labor variance for arches.

Figure 8-9 illustrates graphically the same labor variances shown in Figure 8-8. Diagram (a) in Figure 8-9 shows the labor variances for concrete arches, and diagram (b) illustrates the labor variances for concrete columns. In diagram (a) for arches, the colored area is the total standard cost of labor for

Figure 8-8. The same computations are made for labor variances as for materials shown in Figure 8-6, although the names of the labor variances are somewhat different.

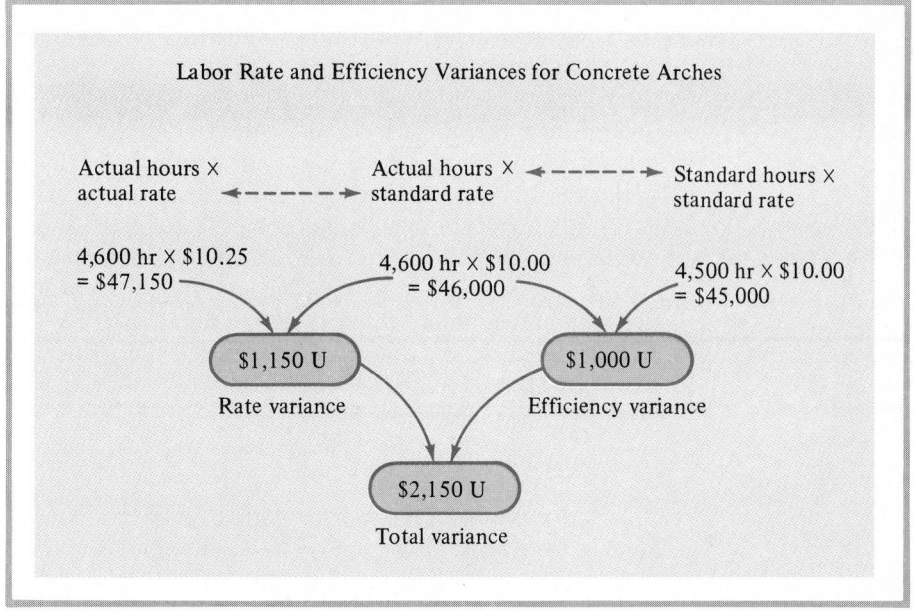

Figure 8-9. The colored area in part (a) of the figure is the total standard cost of labor for arches. Both the actual quantity and actual rate were above standard, resulting in the additional costs shown by the narrow rectangles at the top and side of the diagram. In part (b), the rate variance is unfavorable. But actual hours were less than standard, resulting in the favorable variance shown as the cross-hatched portion of the standard costs which was not incurred.

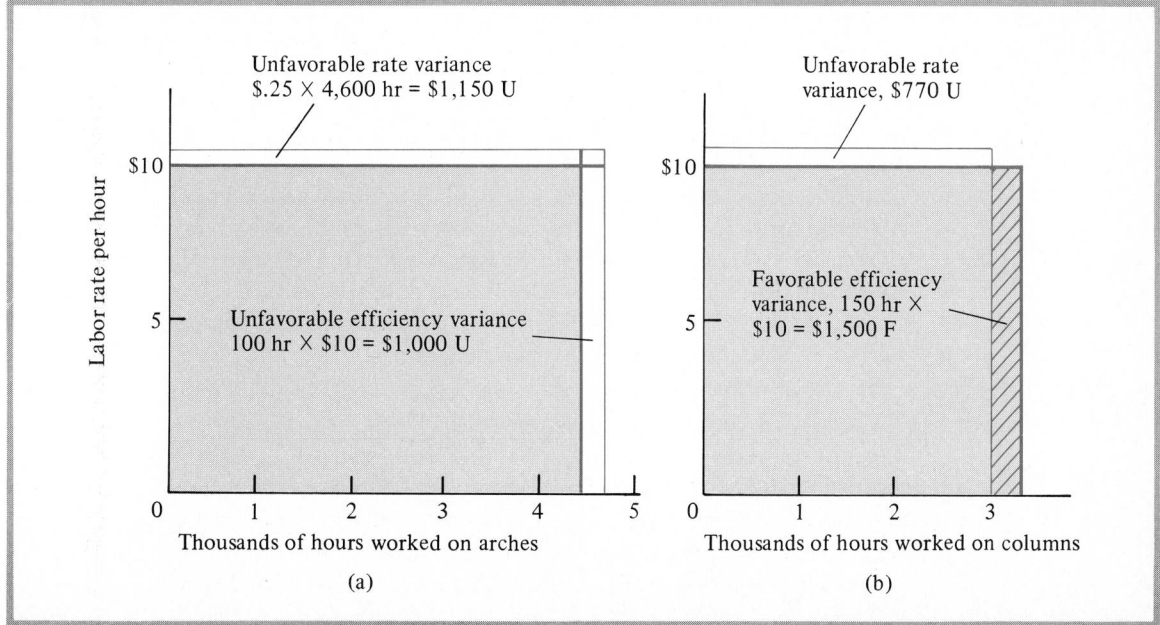

producing 1,000 arches. On the top and right side of the standard cost rectangle are the unfavorable variances. Note the joint unfavorable rate and efficiency variance in the upper right corner of the diagram. This portion of the labor variance is caused by the combined effect of the labor rate being higher than the standard rate and the amount of labor hours used being greater than the standard number of hours. Although this is a **combined variance,** it is usually viewed as part of the rate variance.

The colored portion of diagram (b) is the total standard cost of labor for producing 1,500 concrete columns. The white rectangle on top is the unfavorable rate variance, showing the amount paid for labor in excess of standard due to a higher than standard labor rate. The cross-hatched rectangle at the right is the favorable efficiency variance, which is the amount of standard cost saved by using fewer than the standard number of hours to produce the product.

Responsibility for Labor Variances

Production managers have little control over the rates paid to employees once labor rates are established. Often, however, managers can affect the amounts of high-cost labor and low-cost labor used in production. This mix of labor resources affects the labor rate variance. Usually production managers have some influence over the amount of labor hours used. Skill in managing labor resources can mean the difference between favorable or unfavorable labor efficiency variances. Therefore, production supervisors are generally responsible for labor efficiency variances for workers under their control.

Care must be taken in evaluating unfavorable labor variances to determine the cause. Labor rate variances may occur if workers earning a high wage rate work on jobs requiring lower-paid employees. Labor efficiency variances may occur from equipment down time which leaves workers idle, from faulty materials, fatigue, and other factors.

ACCOUNTING FOR VARIANCES

Variances are recorded in ledger accounts

Variances are identified and recorded as soon as possible so that managers can evaluate performance and quickly take any necessary corrective actions. Material price variances typically are recorded as soon as materials are purchased, and material quantity variances are recorded when material is used and the difference between actual and standard quantities can be measured. Below we illustrate the journal entries to record material and labor variances calculated in the previous examples.

Recording Material Variances

The purchase of raw material at less than standard price resulted in a favorable material price variance. Favorable variances are recorded as credits, because they are, in effect, reductions of expenses, while unfavorable variances are like additional expenses and are recorded as debits. The entry to record the purchase of 2,000 tons of reinforcing steel at $.28 per pound is:

	Raw materials inventory control	1,200,000	
	Materials price variance		80,000
	Accounts payable		1,120,000
	Purchased reinforcing steel.		
	Actual 4,000,000 × $.28 = $1,120,000		
	Standard 4,000,000 × $.30 = $1,200,000		

The material is recorded in inventory at the standard cost and the difference between the amount owed and the standard cost is recorded in a variance account. A separate variance account may be used for each type of material, or a single account may be used, depending on the information needs of management, and on the cost of gathering the additional detail.

The purchase of concrete takes place during production and is recorded in the Work in Process Control account, again at standard cost. Concrete used for the construction of arches is recorded as follows:

	Work in process control	99,250	
	Materials price variance	1,985	
	Accounts payable		101,235
	Purchased concrete for arches.		
	Actual 1,985 cu yd × $51 = $101,235		
	Standard 1,985 cu yd × $50 = $99,250		

The steel used in the production of concrete arches resulted in an unfavorable quantity variance. The entry to transfer steel from raw materials inventory into production is recorded as follows:

	Work in process inventory control	120,000	
	Material quantity variance	6,000	
	Raw materials inventory control		126,000
	Reinforcing steel used for arches.		
	Actual 420,000 lb × $.30 = $126,000		
	Standard 400,000 lb × $.30 = $120,000		

Sometimes it is possible to determine both the labor rate variance and the labor efficiency variance at the time the payroll is distributed to production. If that is the case with the production of arches, the entry is:

	Work in process inventory control	45,000	
	Labor rate variance	1,150	
	Labor efficiency variance	1,000	
	Payroll		47,150
	Labor hours used for production of arches.		
	Actual 4,600 hr × $10.25 = $47,150		
	Standard 4,500 hr × $10 = $45,000		

If the efficiency variance cannot be determined at the time labor cost is charged to production, the following entries would be made **in place of the entry above:**

	Work in process inventory control	46,000	
	Labor rate variance	1,150	
	Payroll		47,150
	Actual 4,600 hr × $10.25 = $47,150		
	Standard 4,600 hr × $10.00 = $46,000		

Later, when the efficiency variances are obtained, the entry to transfer the labor portion of work in process to finished goods is:

	Finished goods inventory control	45,000	
	Labor efficiency variance	1,000	
	Work in process inventory control		46,000
	Actual 4,600 hr × $10.00 = $46,000		
	Standard 4,500 hr × $10.00 = $45,000		

Note again that in all cases inventories are recorded at the standard cost, and variances are accumulated in separate accounts for later reporting and disposition.

REPORTING OF VARIANCES

Variances may be reported to management in a variety of ways, with the content, format, and timing of the reports varying among firms. As with all managerial information, variance reports should suit the needs of managers and should be cost-benefit justified.

Performance reports bring variances to managers' attention

We illustrate variance reporting for Hy-Tension Concrete Company's April production of concrete arches and columns. Figure 8-10 is a performance report for material variances. A similar performance report for labor variances is shown in Figure 8-11.

Figure 8-10. This is a typical performance report showing variances for materials. Many forms are possible for the report, as long as it is logical and understandable and serves the needs of managers.

Hy-Tension Concrete Company
Performance Report — Direct Materials
For the Month Ended April 30

Material Price Variance:

Material	Actual Quantity @ Actual Price	Actual Quantity @ Standard Price	Variance	Total Variance
Arches				
Reinforcing steel	$117,600	$126,000	$8,400 F	
Concrete	101,235	99,250	1,985 U	$ 6,415 F
Columns				
Reinforcing steel	98,700	105,750	7,050 F	
Concrete	44,370	43,500	870 U	6,180 F
Total price variance				12,595 F

Material Quantity Variance:

Material	Actual Quantity @ Standard Price	Standard Quantity @ Standard Price	Variance	
Arches				
Reinforcing steel	$126,000	$120,000	$6,000 U	
Concrete	99,250	100,000	750 F	5,250 U
Columns				
Reinforcing steel	105,750	99,000	6,750 U	
Concrete	43,500	45,000	1,500 F	5,250 U
Total quantity variance				10,500 U
Total variance				$ 2,095 F

Figure 8-11. The labor performance report shows variances that can be investigated by managers to determine where problems are occurring and how they should be solved.

Hy-Tension Concrete Company
Performance Report — Direct Labor
For the Month Ended April 30

Labor Rate Variance:

Product	Actual Hours @ Actual Rate	Actual Hours @ Standard Rate	Variance	Total Variance
Arches	$47,150	$46,000	$1,150 U	
Columns	30,770	30,000	770 U	$1,920 U

Labor Efficiency Variance:

Product	Actual Hours @ Standard Rate	Standard Hours @ Standard Rate	Variance	
Arches	$46,000	$45,000	$1,000 U	
Columns	30,000	31,500	1,500 F	500 F
Total labor variance				$1,420 U

Figure 8-12. Manufacturing overhead is usually analyzed in detail. This report shows only total overhead variances. The detailed variances are discussed in the next chapter.

Hy-Tension Concrete Company
Schedule of Manufacturing Overhead Variances
For the Month Ended April 30

Product	Standard Hours	MOH Rate	Standard Overhead	Actual Overhead	MOH Variance
Arches	4,500 DLH	$20/DLH	$90,000	$93,600	$3,600 U
Columns	3,150	20	63,000	57,400	5,600 F
Total manufacturing overhead variance for April					$2,000 F

A detailed analysis of manufacturing overhead is presented in Chapter 9. For now, we merely compute the total manufacturing overhead variance, which is merely the difference between the actual cost of overhead and the expected cost of overhead as required by standards. Actual overhead cost is given in Figure 8-4, on page 296.

The standard amount of overhead cost is computed by multiplying the standard number of direct labor hours times the manufacturing overhead rate. The overhead rate is $20 per hour as shown in Figure 8-3 on page 295. The standard number of hours was calculated earlier for the labor efficiency variance calculation and is the number of units produced times the number of standard labor hours per unit. Multiplying the standard labor hours times the manufacturing overhead rate yields the standard applied overhead for each product. The actual overhead is compared with the standard overhead for each product to find the overhead variances for each product. For arches the overhead variance is $3,600 unfavorable and for columns it is $5,600 favorable. The total manufacturing overhead variance for both concrete arches and columns is presented in Figure 8-12.

Material, labor, and overhead variances are summarized in a summary report

The variance information in the three variance reports may be summarized in a comprehensive report such as the one illustrated in Figure 8-13. Some detail is lost in such a report, but a large amount of information is concentrated in one place and identified with specific products.

Figure 8-13. This report summarizes all variances for each product. It provides an overview of production performance for materials, labor, and overhead, but is not as detailed as the reports for each separate resource.

Hy-Tension Concrete Company
Product Variance Analysis Report
For the Month Ended April 30

Variance	Arches	Columns	Total
Material price variance	$6,415 F	$6,180 F	$12,595 F
Material quantity variance	5,250 U	5,250 U	10,500 U
Total material variance	1,165 F	70 U	2,095 F
Labor rate variance	1,150 U	770 U	1,920 U
Labor efficiency variance	1,000 U	1,500 F	500 F
Total labor variance	2,150 U	730 F	1,420 U
Manufacturing overhead variance	3,600 U	5,600 F	2,000 F
Total variance	$4,585 U	$7,260 F	$ 2,675 F

Disposition of Variances

Generally accepted accounting principles require reporting of actual inventory costs in financial statements. Standard costs used internally therefore cannot be used for external reporting unless the standard costs are so close to actual costs that the difference is not material. When variances are small enough not to cause material distortions in the financial statements, variance accounts may be closed into cost of goods sold in the income statement. An example of such an entry using hypothetical year-end figures is as follows.

	Cost of goods sold	4,200	
	Material price variance	3,800	
	Labor efficiency variance	1,700	
	Material quantity variance		5,100
	Labor rate variance		4,600
	To transfer year-end material and labor		
	variances to cost of goods sold.		

Variance accounts must be closed to inventories or cost of goods sold

When the balances in variance accounts are large, they should be transferred into the accounts that are affected by the variances to adjust those accounts to actual costs. Material variances typically affect all inventory accounts and cost of goods sold, so a large balance in the material price variance account should be assigned to Raw Materials Inventory Control, Work in Process Control, Finished Goods Inventory Control, and Cost of Goods Sold. On the other hand, labor and overhead variances typically do not affect the raw materials account but they do affect the cost of work in process, finished goods, and cost of goods sold.

A logical question is how are large variances assigned to the inventory and cost of goods sold accounts? Usually, large variances are assigned to the inventory accounts and cost of goods sold in proportion to the amount of resource cost in each account at the end of the period. For example, during the year, $200,000 of direct labor costs has been charged to production. At year-end the total direct labor unfavorable variance is $40,000, consisting of $23,000 unfavorable rate variance and $17,000 unfavorable efficiency variance. Management believes this amount is significant. Of the $200,000 of direct labor charged to production during the year, $30,000 remains in Work in Process at year-end, $50,000 in Finished Goods Inventory, and $120,000 in Cost of Goods Sold. The allocation of the $40,000 of direct labor variance is as follows:

Work in process control	($30,000/$200,000) × $40,000 =	$ 6,000
Finished goods inventory	($50,000/$200,000) × $40,000 =	10,000
Cost of goods sold	($120,000/$200,000) × $40,000 =	24,000
Total		$40,000

The large variances are transferred to the three accounts that contain direct labor costs, as follows:

	Work in process control	6,000	
	Finished goods inventory control	10,000	
	Cost of goods sold	24,000	
	Labor rate variance		23,000
	Labor efficiency variance		17,000
	To distribute significant labor variances		
	to the appropriate affected accounts.		

Large material variances are closed to inventory accounts and cost of goods sold in the same manner. Material price variances, however, affect the Raw Materials Inventory Control account as well as other inventories.

When all variance accounts are closed by entries such as the above, the inventory and cost of goods sold accounts reflect actual costs.

STANDARD COSTS AND PROCESS COSTING

The discussion and illustrations in this chapter apply equally to job order costing systems and process costing systems. However, one element of process costing — the measurement of output — warrants some special attention.

In order to compute the standard quantity of material in calculating material quantity variances or the standard number of direct labor hours in calculating labor efficiency variances, it is necessary to multiply the per unit standard quantity of each resource times the production output of the period. In the main example in this chapter, production output was 1,000 concrete arches and 1,500 concrete columns. Both of these outputs are completed units.

In a process costing system, not all of the output for a period is completed. Some work is done to complete units in beginning work in process inventory, some work is done on partially complete units in ending work in process inventory. To calculate the total amount of production for the period, we must find equivalent units of production for each resource. To illustrate the measurement of output in a standard cost process costing system, we use the following example:

Resource	Standards per Unit of Output	
	Std. Quantity	Std. Price
Paint base	.90 gal	$4 per gal
Pigments	.20 lb	8 per lb
Direct labor	.15 hr	9 per hr

Production Quantity for July

Beginning inventory, 2,000 units with:
90 percent of paint base
40 percent of pigments
60 percent of labor
Started during the period: 6,000 units
Ending work in process inventory, 3,000 units with:
70 percent of base paint
20 percent of pigments
50 percent of labor

Actual Production for July

Resource	Quantity Used	Actual Unit Cost	Total Cost
Paint base	5,100 gal	$4.25 per gal	$21,675
Pigments	940 lb	8.10 per gal	7,614
Direct labor	890 hr	8.70 per hr	7,743

Price and Rate Variances

The material price variances and the labor rate variance can be found directly from the data given without computing the equivalent units of production. For example, the material price variances are:

$$\text{Price variance, paint base} = (\$4.00 - \$4.25) \times 5,100 \text{ gal}$$
$$= \$1,275 \text{ U}$$
$$\text{Price variance, pigments} = (\$8.00 - \$8.10) \times 940 \text{ lb}$$
$$= \$94 \text{ U}$$

Similarly, the labor rate variance is:

$$\text{Labor rate variance} = (\$9.00 - \$8.70) \times 890 \text{ hr}$$
$$= \$267 \text{ F}$$

Quantity and Efficiency Variances

Equivalent units must be calculated in order to measure variances in a process costing system

The material quantity variance and the labor efficiency variance cannot be computed until we measure the production output for the period. In a process costing system, this means computing the equivalent units for each of the resources used in production. As discussed in Chapters 5 and 6, equivalent units are merely the production quantity for some period of time. The schedule of equivalent units for our example is as follows:

Schedule of Equivalent Units

	Paint Base	Pigments	Direct Labor
Beginning work in process: 2,000 units			
Required to complete: 10% of paint base	200		
Required to complete: 60% of coloring		1,200	
Required to complete: 40% of direct labor			800
Units started and completed during the period	3,000	3,000	3,000
Ending work in process: 3,000 units			
With 70% of paint base	2,100		
With 20% of coloring		600	
With 50% of direct labor			1,500
Equivalent units of output for the period	5,300	4,800	5,300

The standard quantities of materials and the standard number of direct labor hours are computed below:

Resource	Standard Quantity per Unit	Equivalent Units	Total Standard Quantity
Paint base	.90 gal	5,300	4,770 gal
Coloring	.20 lb	4,800	960 lb
Direct labor	.15 hr	5,300	795 hr

Using the standard quantities calculated above, the material quantity variances and the labor rate variances are:

$$\text{Quantity variance, paint base} = (4,770 \text{ gal} - 5,100 \text{ gal}) \times \$4.00$$
$$= \$1,320 \text{ U}$$
$$\text{Quantity variance, coloring} = (960 \text{ lb} - 940 \text{ lb}) \times \$8.00$$
$$= \$160 \text{ F}$$
$$\text{Labor rate variance} = (795 \text{ hr} - 950 \text{ hr}) \times \$9.00$$
$$= \$1,395 \text{ U}$$

The only difference between computing variances for process costing and for job order costing is the need to calculate equivalent units for each resource in process costing before the material quantity variances or labor efficiency variances can be computed. All other standard costing procedures are the same with both systems.

SUMMARY

Standard costs are carefully predetermined costs. They are convenient measures of performance usually expressed in terms of cost per unit. A standard consists of two parts, a quantity and a cost. Standards are used for cost control, pricing decisions, performance appraisal, cost awareness, and management by objective. **Ideal standards** are very tight, reflecting a production utopia. **Basic standards** are created for use over a period of several years. **Currently attainable standards** are the most widely used. They reflect desirable performance given normal production problems.

There are three basic activities in a standard cost system. They are **standard setting, accumulating actual costs,** and **variance analysis.** Standard setting is an important and difficult task involving many variables. Standards are usually set by a **standards committee** with representation from all parts of the organization affected by the standards. Inputs from engineering and technological studies assist the committee in setting standards. Management's desires in setting standards are tempered by the environment, particularly employees and labor unions. Standards must be revised frequently to remain current if they are to be useful for performance evaluation.

Variance analysis is the systematic evaluation of variances to provide managers with useful information. Variance analysis is performed for all three types of manufacturing cost elements—direct materials, direct labor, and manufacturing overhead. Variance analysis answers two questions: What is the amount of the variance? Why did the variance occur? The first question is answered by performing computations on data gathered in the standard cost system. The answer to the second question requires more subjective evaluations of the operations and cost data.

A variance is expressed in dollar amounts and is identified as favorable or unfavorable. **Favorable variances** mean that actual costs or quantities are less than standard. **Unfavorable variances** mean that actual costs or quantities are greater than standard. Most firms incorporate their standard cost system into their formal accounting system. Costs are recorded at standard, and any difference is recorded in a variance account. Unfavorable variances have debit balances and favorable variances have credit balances.

A material price variance occurs when the actual price of materials is different from the standard price. **A material quantity variance** results from using more or less than the standard amount of materials. The **labor rate variance** occurs because the actual labor rate was different than the standard labor rate. The **labor efficiency variance** occurs because the number of actual direct labor hours worked was more or less than standard.

Once computed, variances should be reported so as to provide management with a maximum amount of useful information. Variance reports should be tailored to the information requirements of management, and many formats are possible.

Technically, only actual costs may be reported in external financial statements. However, if variances are not material, standard costs may be used for the financial statements, because they closely approximate actual costs. Any minor variance is closed to Cost of Goods Sold. If variances are large, the affected inventory accounts must be adjusted to reflect actual costs.

Standard costs are used with both job order costing systems and process costing systems. With process costing, the accountant must first measure the equivalent units of production before computing material quantity variances and labor rate variances.

KEY TERMS

basic standards *(289)*
bill of materials *(293)*
currently attainable standards *(289)*
engineering standards *(289)*
favorable variance *(292)*
ideal standards *(289)*
labor efficiency variance *(303)*
labor rate variance *(302)*
management by objective *(288)*
material price variance *(297)*

material quantity variance *(299)*
material substitution variance *(299)*
material use variance *(299)*
standard cost *(286)*
standard setting *(290)*
standards committee *(290)*
theoretical standards *(289)*
unfavorable variance *(292)*
variance analysis *(292)*

QUESTIONS

1. Harry says, "Standards should be established that are just high enough so that they cannot be achieved. This causes unfavorable variances, which are an inducement to strive continuously toward better performance." "I disagree," replies George. "Standards should be established that are low enough to result in favorable variances most of the time. This gives people a feeling of satisfaction at having done a good job, and satisfied people perform better than those frustrated by the inability to reach the standards." Comment on these two statements.

2. A manufacturing company uses skilled labor in one of its production processes in which a special rush order is in the process of production. A small accidental fire in the production facility required the hospitalization of most of the skilled production workers when highly toxic chemical fumes were released by one of the materials that burned. At the same time a group of semiskilled workers producing an entirely different product in another department was completely idled as a result of a lack of materials caused by a transportation strike. In order to complete the special order in time, the company put the semiskilled workers on its production. Without the needed skill, the special order resulted in a high unfavorable labor efficiency variance. The overall labor variance, however, was highly favorable because the semiskilled workers are paid less than the skilled workers. Observing the large rate and efficiency variances, a manager commented, "Either the standards are wrong, or we are paying too much for skilled labor, or both." Discuss this comment and the situation that elicited it.

3. (AICPA) Standard costing procedures are widely used in manufacturing operations and, more recently, have become common in many nonmanufacturing operations. Define standard costs. Distinguish between basic and current standards. What are the advantages of a standard cost system?

EXERCISES

Ex. 8-1
Direct Material
Variances

Marjorie Company has established a standard of 30 feet of 28-gauge wire for the manufacture of each circuit board. The standard cost of the wire is $30 per 1,000-foot roll. During September, 16,000 circuit boards were wired using a total of 475 rolls of wire that cost $32 per roll.

REQUIRED   Compute material price and quantity variances.

Ex. 8-2
Direct Labor Variances

Similite Company established the following direct labor standards for lathe operators who produce wooden lamp bases:

Standard labor rate $9 per hr
Standard labor time   .4 hr per lamp base

During July, the lathe operators produced 8,000 lamp bases in 3,100 hours at a cost of $28,830.

REQUIRED   Compute the direct labor variances for Similite Company.

Ex. 8-3
Direct Material Variances

The son-in-law of Hynesite Company's president prepared the following material standards for the production of 2-liter Erlenmeyer flasks:

Standard material price/flask $1.00 per unit
Standard material quantity/flask   200 grams
Standard production run   1,100 units

At the end of the first production run, 1,000 units were produced with 220,000 grams of material costing $1,250.

REQUIRED   Compute the material variances for the production run.

Ex. 8-4
Graph of Material Variances

Refer to the data of Hynesite Company in Exercise 8-3 for the production of Erlenmeyer flasks.

REQUIRED   Prepare a graph of material price and quantity variances for the data, similar to Figure 8-5.

Ex. 8-5
Direct Labor Variances

Following are standards developed by Beckview Company for its proposed design department, which is to complete the design for a new line of folding outdoor furniture.

Standard salary rate $10 per hr
Standard hours to complete design   11,000 hr

After experiencing some difficulty hiring the needed personnel, the company managed to obtain five designers whose actual cost and output were as follows:

Actual salary rate $11.50 per hr
Actual hours required to complete design   10,000 hr

REQUIRED   Compute the direct labor variances.

Ex. 8-6
Graph of Labor Variances

Refer to the data for Beckview Company's labor standards in Exercise 8-5.

REQUIRED.   Use the data provided to prepare a graph of labor variances similar to the one in Figure 8-9 in the chapter.

Ex. 8-7
Material Variances and Journal Entries

Arista Company has established the following material standards for production of magnet-actuated switches:

Material	Units	Unit Cost
Glass tubing	3 in	$.04/in
Spring contacts	2 in	$.15/in

Purchases of raw materials in April are as follows:

| Glass tubing | 1,000 ft | $ 504.00 |
| Spring contact stock | 1,000 ft | 1,680.00 |

April production required 405 feet of glass tubing and 235 feet of spring contact materials in order to produce 1,500 switches.

REQUIRED
a. Compute the material variances for Arista Company.
b. Journalize the purchase of materials and the transfer of materials into production.

Ex. 8-8
Material
Performance
Report

Refer to the data on Arista Company's production of magnetic switches in Exercise 8-7.

REQUIRED. Prepare a materials performance report for April, similar to the report in Figure 8-10 in the chapter.

Ex. 8-9
Labor Variances
and Journal Entries

Arista Company has budgeted the following labor standards for the production of its magnetic switches:

	Units	Cost
Glass tubing preparation	25 per hr	$8 per hr
Spring contact preparation	40 per hr	6 per hr
Assembly and sealing	30 per hr	7 per hr

April production of 1,500 switches required the following amounts of labor:

Glass tubing preparation	65 hr	$495
Spring contact preparation	40 hr	232
Assembly and sealing	46 hr	322

REQUIRED
a. Compute the labor variances for Arista Company.
b. Prepare the journal entry to record the labor cost of production.

Ex. 8-10
Labor Performance
Report
REQUIRED

Refer to the labor data on Arista Company's production of magnetic switches in Exercise 8-9.

Prepare a labor performance report for April, similar to the report in Figure 8-11 in the chapter.

Ex. 8-11
Disposition of
Variances

An analysis of three accounts of Pollie Company indicates that the ending balances consist of the following amounts of direct labor and direct materials:

	Work in Process	Finished Goods	Cost of Goods Sold
Direct materials	$120,000	$180,000	$ 900,000
Direct labor	283,200	590,000	1,486,800

The ledger further indicates the following account balances for variances and raw materials:

	Debit	Credit
Raw materials inventory	$300,000	
Labor rate variance	140,000	
Labor efficiency variance	160,000	
Material price variance		$120,000
Material quantity variance	50,000	

Company policy is to allocate variances to the Inventory and Cost of Goods Sold accounts if they exceed $25,000.

REQUIRED   Prepare the journal entry to allocate the variances to the appropriate accounts.

Ex. 8-12
Interpreting Journal Entries

Following are journal entries that were recorded to assign direct materials and direct labor to production for one week:

	Work in process, labor	55,890	
	Labor rate variance	1,280	
	Labor efficiency variance		1,650
	Payroll		55,520
	Work in process, materials	47,300	
	Material quantity variance		1,960
	Raw materials inventory		45,340

REQUIRED
a.   What is the standard cost of labor?
b.   Is the labor rate variance favorable or unfavorable?
c.   What is the actual cost of labor?
d.   Was the total labor variance favorable or unfavorable?
e.   What is the standard cost of the standard quantity of material?
f.   What is the standard cost of materials used?
g.   Is the material variance favorable or unfavorable?

Ex. 8-13 (AICPA)
Basic Standard Cost Variances

Armando Corporation manufactures a product with the following standard costs:

Direct materials—20 yards @ $1.35 per yard	$27
Direct labor—4 hours @ $9.00 per hour	36
Factory overhead—applied at 5/6 of direct labor cost	30
Total standard cost per unit of output	$93

Standards are based on normal monthly production of 2,400 direct labor hours for 600 units of output. The following information pertains to July activities:

Units produced in July	500
Direct materials purchased: 18,000 yards @ $1.38 per yard	$24,840
Direct materials used: 9,500 yards	
Direct labor: 2,100 hours @ $9.15 per hour	19,215
Actual factory overhead	16,650

REQUIRED   Prepare the following schedules for July, indicating whether each variance is favorable or unfavorable.

    a. Material price variance based on purchases.
    b. Material quantity variance.
    c. Labor rate variance.
    d. Labor efficiency variance.
    e. Total manufacturing overhead variance.

PROBLEMS

P. 8-1
Direct Labor and
Material Variances

Signell Corporation manufactures small motors for use in servomechanisms. It has established the following labor and material standards for each motor armature:

Labor	1.2 hr	$7 per hr
Copper wire	600 ft	$1.20 per unit
Core	1	$ .70 per unit

The following production data are accumulated for May:

Wire purchased	20,000,000 ft @ $.0016 per ft
Cores purchased	50,000 @ $.75 each
Armatures produced	20,000
Wire used	12,180,000 ft
Cores used	20,400
Labor used	25,000 hr @ $7.05 per hr

REQUIRED   Calculate the labor and material variances.

P. 8-2
Labor and Material
Variances

Hovell and Schakk Construction Company builds custom-designed homes and uses a standard cost system for a number of construction costs. The standard for spraying 1,000 square feet of acoustical ceilings is as follows:

Labor	1.25 hr @ $11.00 per hr
Materials	24 lb @ $.60 per lb

Actual data on the home currently under construction are as follows:

Ceiling area	3,800 sq ft
Labor	4.5 hr, $55
Materials	90 lb, $60

REQUIRED

    a. Compute the labor and material variances.
    b. Prepare journal entries to record the variances.

P. 8-3
Identifying and
Interpreting
Variances

Below is a condensed trial balance of Phandelle Company at the end of its fiscal year. The company is subject to a 40 percent income tax rate.

Phandelle Company
Trial Balance
September 30

Cash	$ 310,000	
Accounts receivable	400,000	
Inventory	850,000	
Plant and equipment	2,500,000	
Accumulated depreciation		$1,110,000
Accounts payable		200,000
Bonds payable		600,000
Common stock		500,000
Retained earnings		1,050,000
Sales		4,250,000
Cost of goods sold	2,210,000	
Selling expenses	550,000	
Administrative expenses	720,000	
Material price variance		30,000
Material quantity variance	90,000	
Labor rate variance		10,000
Labor efficiency variance	120,000	
Totals	$7,750,000	$7,750,000

REQUIRED

a. Compute the standard cost of the products sold.
b. Compute the actual cost of the products sold.
c. Prepare an income statement for the fiscal year.
d. Compute the standard and actual cost of goods sold as a percentage of sales.

P. 8-4
Material and Labor
Variances

Hovell and Schakk Construction Company uses two types of labor to install wallpaper in its custom-designed homes. Below are standards for wallpaper installations:

Vinyl-coated paper cost	$ .40 per sq ft of paper
Metallic paper cost	$1.00 per sq ft of paper
Wallpaper paste	$1.00 per 100 sq ft of wall
Standard paper quantity	110 percent of wall area
Journeyman labor cost	$7.00 per hr
Apprentice labor cost	$4.50 per hr
Journeyman labor time	2 hr per 100 sq ft of wall
Apprentice labor time	3 hr per 100 sq ft of wall

The home currently under construction required the following quantities and costs for wallpaper installations:

Vinyl paper	1,000 sq ft of wall area
Metallic paper	600 sq ft of wall area
Materials used:	
Vinyl paper	1,160 sq ft, $450
Metallic paper	630 sq ft, $650
Wallpaper paste	$19
Journeyman labor	34 hr, $238
Apprentice labor	52 hr, $240

REQUIRED

a.   Compute the labor and material variances.
b.   Prepare journal entries to record the cost of construction and the variances.

P. 8-5
Variances for a
Service Business

Chemi-Gro Company performs lawn-spraying services using two types of materials. Greenway is a chemical fertilizer and Greenban is a combination of fertilizer and weed killer. The company has established the following labor and material standards for its services.

Labor per 1,000 square feet of lawn:	.2 hr @ $6.80/hr
Greenway per 1,000 square feet of lawn:	3 gal @ $2.60/gal
Greenban per 1,000 square feet of lawn:	4 gal @ $2.50/gal

Each spraying job requires some setup time regardless of lawn size. The average setup time per job is estimated at .5 hour for travel and .25 hour for setting up and putting away equipment on each job. Following are data on spraying performed in August:

	Greenway	Greenban
No. of lawns sprayed	452	316
Total square feet of lawn	3,600,000	2,800,000
Total hours of labor time	1,140	760
Total labor cost	$7,923	$4,978
Total gallons of materials used	10,100	11,000
Total material cost	$25,800	$28,000

REQUIRED

a.   Compute the material variances.
b.   Compute the labor variances.

P. 8-6
Variance Analysis
and Unit Standard
Costs

Phil Johnson's Extravagant Haberdashery sells a variety of custom-tailored clothing items. One of the more profitable products is a cashmere sport coat that sells for $650. Following are production standards for the coat:

Cashmere wool cloth	3 yd @ $24/yd	$ 72
Silk lining	2 yd @ 9/yd	18
Direct labor	9 hr @ 15.00/hr	135
MOH applied at $5/DLH		45

During the past week 10 coats were produced and sold, and the following costs were incurred:

Cashmere wool cloth	29 yd @ $25/yd	$ 725
Silk lining	22 yd @ 8/yd	176
Direct labor	98 hr @ 15.50/hr	1,519
Actual MOH		500
Total cost		$2,920

REQUIRED

a.   Compute the standard cost of one sport coat.
b.   Compute the actual cost of one coat made last week.
c.   Compute the material price and quantity variances.
d.   Compute the labor rate and efficiency variances.

P. 8-7
Recording and
Disposing of
Variances

Alonzo Company produces a variety of products using a process costing system with standard costs. It accumulates variances in a separate variance account for each resource used in production. At the end of each month it disposes of all variances by allocating them to work in process, finished goods, and cost of goods sold if the total variance is 5 percent or more of standard direct cost of a product. If the total variance is less than 5 percent of standard cost, all variances are transferred to cost of goods sold. Below is a summary variance report for one of the company's products:

Alonzo Company
Summary Variance Report
Work in Process for Lotion FAP-8
For the Month Ended June 30

Resource	Standard Direct Cost	Rate or Price Variance	Efficiency or Quantity Variance	Actual Cost
Processing labor	$ 7,500	$122 U	$ 89 F	$ 7,533
Packaging labor	1,680	18 F	65 U	1,727
Component F8	19,000	280 F	12 F	18,708
Component P8	11,300	600 U	572 F	11,328
Packaging material	1,200	65 U	27 U	1,292
Total	$40,680			$40,588

By the end of June, 90 percent of the work in process has been completed and 85 percent of the finished goods has been sold.

REQUIRED

a. Prepare journal entries to record the cost of each resource put into production.
b. Journalize the transfer of work in process to finished goods.
c. Journalize the disposition of variances at the end of June.

P. 8-8
Prime Cost
Variance Analysis

The following production standards have been established by Plastine Corporation for the manufacture of its two newly developed sheet plastics:

Resource	Cost	Rigid PR17 Quantity per sq m	Flexible PF19 Quantity per sq m
Polymers	$ .90/kg	2 kg	4 kg
Inert fillers	.40/kg	4 kg	8 kg
Catalyst	.20/g	10 g	4 g
Blending labor	10.00/hr	.1 hr	.2 hr
Curing labor	8.00/hr	.1 hr	.1 hr

February production consisted of 7,200 square meters of rigid plastic PR17 and 3,000 square meters of flexible plastic PF19. The following costs were incurred in production:

Resource	Cost	Rigid PR17 Quantity	Flexible PF19 Quantity
Polymers	$24,288	14,100 kg	12,300 kg
Inert filler	20,592	29,000 kg	23,800 kg
Catalyst	16,095	75,000 g	12,000 g
Blending labor	14,637	710 hr	725 hr
Curing labor	7,347	600 hr	330 hr

REQUIRED   From the information provided above, develop and present in good form the following calculations and reports for February:

    a. Computation of the actual unit cost of resources.
    b. Performance report for direct materials.
    c. Performance report for direct labor.
    d. Product variance analysis report for prime costs.
    e. Computation of the direct product cost per square meter.

P. 8-9
Disposition of
Variances

A selected portion of Falloway Company's trial balance is provided below prior to closing the books. Company policy is to distribute any variance to cost of goods sold if it is less than 3 percent of sales. If a variance is 3 or more percent of sales it is allocated to the inventory accounts and cost of goods sold.

Falloway Company
Trial Balance
December 31

Raw materials	$40,000	
Work in process	25,000	
Finished goods	20,000	
Sales		$130,000
Cost of goods sold	80,000	
Material price variance		4,000
Material quantity variance	6,100	
Labor rate variance	5,800	
Labor efficiency variance		1,200
Manufacturing overhead variance	0	

An analysis of account balances reveals that they contain the following proportion of product costs:

	WIP	Finished Goods	CGS
Direct materials	.40	.10	.35
Direct labor	.12	.25	.15
Manufacturing overhead	.48	.65	.50

REQUIRED   Prepare journal entries to dispose of variance account balances in order to convert product accounts to actual cost.

P. 8-10 (AICPA)
Complete Variance
Analysis

Ross Shirts, Inc., manufactures short- and long-sleeve men's shirts for large stores. Ross produces a single quality shirt in lots to each customer's order and attaches the store's label to each. The standard costs for a dozen long-sleeve shirts are:

Direct materials	24 yards @ $ .55	$13.20
Direct labor	3 hours @ $2.45	7.35
Manufacturing overhead	3 hours @ $2.00	6.00
Standard cost per dozen		$26.55

During October Ross worked on three orders for long-sleeve shirts. Job cost records for the month disclose the following:

Lot	Units in Lot	Material Used	Hours Worked
30	1,000 dozen	24,100 yards	2,980
31	1,700 dozen	40,440 yards	5,130
32	1,200 dozen	28,825 yards	2,890

The following information is also available:

1. Ross purchased 95,000 yards of material during the month at a cost of $53,200. The material price variance is recorded when goods are purchased and all inventories are carried at standard cost.
2. Direct labor incurred amounted to $27,500 during October. According to payroll records, production employees were paid $2.50 per hour.
3. Overhead is applied on the basis of direct labor hours. Manufacturing overhead totaling $22,800 was incurred during October.
4. A total of $288,000 was budgeted for overhead for the year based on estimated production at the plant's normal capacity of 48,000 dozen shirts per year. Overhead is 40 percent fixed and 60 percent variable at this level of production.
5. There was no work in process at October 1. During October, lots 30 and 31 were completed and all material was issued for lot 32 and it was 80 percent completed as to labor.

REQUIRED

a. Prepare a schedule computing the standard cost for October of lots 30, 31, and 32.
b. Prepare a schedule computing the material price variance for October and indicate whether the variance is favorable or unfavorable.
c. Prepare schedules computing (and indicating whether the variances are favorable or unfavorable) for each lot produced during October the:
   1. Material quantity variance in yards.
   2. Labor efficiency variance in hours.
   3. Labor rate variance in dollars.
d. Prepare a schedule showing the total manufacturing overhead variance.

P. 8-11 (AICPA)
Standard Cost
Process Costing

Melody Corporation is a manufacturing company that produces a single product known as "Jupiter." Melody uses the first in, first out (FIFO) process costing method for both financial statement and internal management reporting.

In analyzing production results, standard costs are used, whereas actual costs are used for financial statement reporting. The standards, which are based upon equivalent units of production, are as follows:

Raw material per unit	1 pound at $10 per pound
Direct labor per unit	2 hours at $4 per hour
Factory overhead per unit	2 hours at $1.25 per hour

Budgeted factory overhead for standard hours allowed for April production is $30,000.

Data for the month of April are presented below:

- The beginning inventory consisted of 2,500 units which were 100 percent complete as to raw material and 40 percent complete as to direct labor and factory overhead.
- An additional 10,000 units were started during the month.
- The ending inventory consisted of 2,000 units which were 100 percent complete as to raw material and 40 percent complete as to direct labor and factory overhead.
- Costs applicable to April production are as follows:

	Actual Cost	Standard Cost
Raw material used (11,000 pounds)	$121,000	$100,000
Direct labor (25,000 hours actually worked)	105,575	82,400
Factory overhead	31,930	25,750

REQUIRED

a. For each element of production for April (raw material, direct labor, and factory overhead) compute the following:
1. Equivalent units of production.
2. Cost per equivalent unit of production at actual and at standard.
Show supporting computations in good form.

b. Prepare a schedule analyzing for April production the following variances as either favorable or unfavorable:
1. Total materials.
2. Materials price.
3. Materials quantity.
4. Total labor.
5. Labor rate.
6. Labor efficiency.
7. Total factory overhead.

CASES

Opake Products Corporation fabricates a variety of products from sheet plastics. One of its divisions uses clear plastics to mold windshields and canopies for boats, airplanes, and gliders. The process involves marking appropriate patterns on the sheet plastic, cutting them into individual pieces, and heating the material until it is flexible enough to be draped in either a positive or negative mold to form the appropriate shape. The process is performed primarily by the manual labor of the department's 17 employees.

The company uses a job order cost system with the following standard costs:

Operation	No. of Employees	Wage Rate	Boat Windshield	Airlane Windshield	Glider Canopy
Pattern	4	$7.00/hr	6 min	12 min	15 min
Cutting	4	6.00	9	15	18
Molding	9	8.00	18	30	42
Material @ $1.20/sq ft			10 sq ft	23 sq ft	30 sq ft
MOH per unit			$4.00	$7.00	$10.00
Annual production in units			20,000	6,000	8,000

In addition to performing the standard tasks listed above, employees also need a certain amount of time to set up equipment, prepare the materials, clean up the work area, and perform other miscellaneous duties. Each worker works 40 hours per week for 48 weeks of the year. The remaining four weeks consist of unpaid holidays and paid vacation. Of the total time worked, employees spend the following approximate proportions on direct production and other duties:

	Direct Production	Other Duties
Pattern	68%	32%
Cutting	90	10
Molding	84	16

The company's share of various payroll taxes amounts to 12 percent of gross payroll. The company is now negotiating with the employee's union for a new contract. The union is asking for a 10 percent wage increase and the following changes in fringe benefits, all to be paid by the company:

	Current Benefits	Proposed Benefits
Paid vacation	10 days/yr	15 days/yr
Medical insurance	$400/yr	$480/yr
Dental insurance	0	$120/yr

In addition, the union is asking for the following production standards for labor on the three products made by the department:

Operation	Boat Windshield	Airplane Windshield	Glider Canopy
Pattern	6 min	12 min	18 min
Cutting	12	15	21
Molding	18	33	42

Company negotiators point out that the above standards represent almost 5 percent additional labor time for production. This would require either producing fewer products or hiring more workers. The union claims, however, that only one more worker would have to be hired to perform some of the setup and other production tasks that the production workers now do. The union would provide a new employee at only $5.50 per hour because his duties would not involve any of the fabricating operations. However, he would be entitled to all the benefits that other workers have. If the new standards, wage rates, and additional employee are used by the company, manufacturing overhead on the three products is expected to be: Boat windshield, $4.20; airplane windshield, $7.35; and glider canopy, $10.50. These figures do not include the gross pay of the new employee, which would be considered direct labor.

During the labor negotiations the company was approached by a representative of a robot manufacturer. The representative indicates that his company could supply automatic digital-controlled equipment that would perform most of the labor operations in the department more precisely and faster than the current manual process. The new equipment would design cutting patterns with a minimum of waste material, cut them automatically, and heat them uniformly for automatic molding using the company's present molds.

The automatic equipment would increase manufacturing overhead on each unit of product by 50 percent above the current overhead rate. It would require a labor force of only 4 employees to operate the equipment. The employees would have to have the same fringe benefits now requested by the union, but since they would be more highly trained, they would receive a higher salary. If the company were to acquire the new equipment, the following standards could be established for the products:

Operation	No. of Employees	Wage Rate	Boat Windshield	Airplane Windshield	Glider Canopy
Pattern	1	$8	3 min	3 min	3 min
Cutting	1	7	3	6	6
Molding	2	9	4	8	9
Materials @ $1.20/sq ft			9.5 sq ft	22 sq ft	28 sq ft

Management is concerned about the labor negotiations. It is faced with a competitive market situation, with profit margins being squeezed close to 30 percent of sales. Total sales of the three products are $1,600,000 per year, and there is no possibility of raising prices without losing a significant share of the market. If profit margin goes below 30 percent, the company would lose money on the department's operation.

REQUIRED

a. Compute the current standard cost of each product and the total cost of production.

b. Compute the standard cost of each product and total production cost based on the new standards proposed by the labor union.

c. Compute the expected product cost and total cost of production if the automated equipment is acquired.

d. Compute the total hourly cost of labor for each fabricating process using your costs in *a* and *b* above for the current situation and the union proposal.

e. Compute the gross margin and gross margin percentage that the company now has, and also for each of the two alternatives available to the company.

f. Discuss the company's alternatives and decide which one the company should adopt.

Case 8-2
Determining
Standard Costs for
Budgeting Purposes

CPC Corporation manufactures large-diameter concrete pipe for use in storm drains and sewers. It has operated for a number of years at the same location, and demand for its products has grown steadily because of product quality and the company's reputation for reliable production and timely delivery on contracts. The company has been turning down orders due to limited production capacity, which it cannot expand due to lack of space. Management is sure that if the company could increase production by several times, all of its products could be sold.

The company is presently negotiating a large order for its 36-inch-diameter storm drain pipe. Present capacity is 500 units per day, limited by the fact that there is space enough to work with 500 molds and each pipe casting requires one day of curing time before it can be removed from the mold. Additional curing time then takes place for six days in a curing yard whose capacity is also limited, but which can accommodate production of about 1,600 units per day.

Production of 500 units requires 15 employees working 8 hours a day at $8 per hour. Each pipe requires 6 cubic feet of concrete costing $11 per cubic foot. Overhead is estimated at $5 per direct labor hour. The selling price per unit is to be determined by contract negotiations, and management feels the company can be competitive at $95 per unit. Administrative expenses are $75,000 per month and the company is subject to a 30 percent tax rate.

In order to decide how to bid on the 36-inch pipe contract, the company's vice president for production started to investigate the possibility of increasing production by changing the production process. Two possibilities emerged that may enable the company to increase production. Both warrant investigating because the contract under consideration is very large and could keep the company busy most of the year even if production capacity were increased fourfold. Whatever portion of the pipe order CPC Corporation cannot produce will be lost to competitors.

One alternative is to switch production to a steam curing process. Curing time would be reduced to about 6 hours and would permit the company to employ its 500 molds three times in each 24-hour period. However, to handle the steam equipment and higher production volume the labor force would have to be increased from 15 to 54 employees who would work in three shifts of 18 employees each. The second shift would have to be paid $11 per hour and the third shift $14 per hour. In addition, the cost of steam is expected to be $504 per day, and the lease cost of the steam generating equipment would add $2 per direct labor hour to overhead cost.

The second alternative would also triple daily production, and would require operating three shifts of 16 employees each. No new equipment would be required. Instead, the company would add to its concrete a newly developed chemical additive that causes extremely rapid curing. The cost of the chemical would be $4.40 per unit of product. The same labor rates would be incurred as with steam curing, but the overhead rate would remain at $5 per direct labor hour. In all cases the company would operate 20 days per month.

Neither of the proposed alternatives is expected to increase the $75,000 monthly administrative expense.

REQUIRED

a. Calculate the standard cost of the product with the current production process.
b. Calculate the standard cost of the product using the steam curing process.
c. Calculate the standard cost of the product using the chemical additive process.
d. Calculate the expected net income after tax with each production process.
e. Calculate the after-tax return on sales for each production process.
f. Discuss which alternative the company should adopt.

CHAPTER 9
Flexible Budgeting and Manufacturing Overhead Variance Analysis

Thus far we have discussed two tools used by managers for dealing with uncertainty: budgeting, which is a detailed and structured approach to planning and controlling operations; and standard costing, which is a mechanism for analyzing deviations from expected performance. As unpredictable events occur, causing performance to deviate from expectations, managers look to the budgets as early warning systems for information about how significant the deviation is and how to correct it.

The budgets illustrated in Chapter 7 help managers to plan for an expected level of operations. Essentially, the budget is fixed at some expected level of activity. Such budgets are useful when the expected level of activity can be predicted with some degree of accuracy. However, in some situations, managers are not able to predict activity levels accurately, thus a fixed budget is not very useful. In such situations managers can prepare a flexible budget that enables them to plan for a range of possible levels of activity. Flexible budgets are also useful in analyzing manufacturing overhead variances. To set the stage for a discussion of flexible budgets, we first present some aspects of fixed budgeting.

FIXED BUDGETS

Fixed budgets are prepared for only one level of activity

A **fixed budget,** sometimes called a **static budget,** is prepared for a single level of activity. The master budget and its component parts shown in Chapter 7 are fixed budgets. The activity level used by Castone Corporation in preparing its budget was 55,100 concrete columns and 22,050 concrete beams. This volume of production was translated into the resources necessary to manufacture, administer, and market the budgeted quantity of each product. The fixed budget was also used late in Chapter 7 to measure performance, as illustrated with the manufacturing overhead budget performance report in Figure 7-22.

Fixed budgets are common in business. They provide managers with information for planning and controlling daily activities and special projects, such as shown in Figure 9-1, which illustrates a fixed budget for the marketing activities of Barton's Department Store. The budget is based on expected sales of $500,000 — the expected activity for the budget period. The costs in the sales budget are obtained from the following estimates of variable and fixed marketing costs:

Variable Costs	Cost per Sales Dollar
Sales commissions	$.05
Clerical	.02
Supplies	.02
Travel	.03
Distribution	.06
Royalties	.03

Fixed Costs	Amount
Sales salaries	$52,000
Advertising	27,000
Entertainment	12,000
Maintenance	9,000
Depreciation	8,000
Supplies	4,000
Insurance	3,500
Property taxes	2,500

Figure 9-1. This is a fixed budget for the marketing department of a department store. Although we used cost behavior data to help prepare this budget, it is a fixed budget because it covers only one level of activity.

Barton's Department Store
Marketing Budget
For the Year Ending December 31, 1986

Variable Costs	Amount
Sales commissions	$ 25,000
Clerical	10,000
Supplies	10,000
Travel	15,000
Distribution	30,000
Royalties	15,000
Total variable costs	105,000

Fixed Costs	
Sales salaries	52,000
Advertising	27,000
Entertainment	12,000
Maintenance	9,000
Depreciation	8,000
Supplies	4,000
Insurance	3,500
Property taxes	2,500
Total fixed costs	118,000
Total budgeted marketing costs	$223,000

Actual activity may differ significantly from the budgeted level of activity. An economic downturn, an unexpected strike, an escalation in interest rates, or a very large new order may cause actual activity to be much different than expected. In such cases, a fixed budget may not provide a good basis for

Figure 9-2. The fixed budget performance report shows an unfavorable variance, but the marketing costs were incurred at an activity level that was 20 percent higher than the budgeted activity level.

Barton's Department Store
Marketing Performance Report
For the Year Ended December 31, 1986

Variable Costs	Budget	Actual	Variance	
Sales commissions	$ 25,000	$ 31,100	$ 6,100	U
Clerical	10,000	12,250	2,250	U
Supplies	10,000	14,700	4,700	U
Travel	15,000	16,350	1,350	U
Distribution	30,000	31,400	1,400	U
Royalties	15,000	18,400	3,400	U
Total variable costs	105,000	124,200	19,200	U
Fixed Costs				
Sales salaries	52,000	52,200	200	U
Advertising	27,000	26,500	(500)	F
Entertainment	12,000	12,200	200	U
Maintenance	9,000	9,700	700	U
Depreciation	8,000	8,000	—	
Supplies	4,000	4,100	100	U
Insurance	3,500	3,500	—	
Property taxes	2,500	2,500		
Total fixed costs	118,000	118,700	700	U
Total budgeted marketing costs	$223,000	$242,900	$19,900	U

Actual results are compared with the budgeted costs in the fixed budget

measuring performance or for managing the change in the activity level. For example, Figure 9-2 illustrates an annual performance report for the marketing activity of the department store. During 1986, actual sales were $600,000 and actual marketing costs are presented in the performance report.

The report indicates a total unfavorable variance of $19,900, or about 9 percent above the budget. In this situation it is difficult to determine if the report provides valuable information about the performance of managers. The variance is 9 percent unfavorable, but the level of sales was $600,000 instead of $500,000, or 20 percent higher than expected. If the actual level of activity is close to the expected level of activity, the resulting budget performance report can provide useful information to managers. However, in some cases, such as this one, the actual level of activity differs significantly from the budgeted level. In such cases it is difficult to evaluate performance with a fixed budget, because some costs remain constant but others change with the level of activity.

For example, insurance expense is expected to be the same regardless of sales level. But if sales are greater than expected, expenses such as sales commissions are also expected to be greater. Therefore, to determine what the costs should have been at $600,000 of sales, it is necessary to know how various costs behave. Then, using the expected costs for the actual level of activity, it is possible to compare actual costs with expectations in the performance report.

FLEXIBLE BUDGETS

Flexible budgets cover a range of activity

Flexible budgets, also called **dynamic budgets,** are prepared for more than one level of activity. For example, a company may prepare a flexible budget with production levels of 5,000, 6,000, and 7,000 units — a range of activities most likely to embrace the actual activity level. Initially, managers plan for the acquisition and use of resources based on their best estimate of the volume of activity. But as the budget year progresses, the flexible budget can be used to alter plans if activity deviates from budget expectations. In addition, when budget performance reports are prepared in a flexible budgeting system, managers do not have to rely on a budget for a single level of activity. Instead, actual results are compared with a flexible budget prepared for the exact level of activity achieved. Therefore the resulting performance reports are much better indicators of how much actual costs varied from expected costs.

Actual results are compared with a budget at the actual level of activity

Characteristics of Flexible Budgets

Flexible budgets have a number of characteristics that distinguish them from fixed budgets and make them desirable for many organizations. Flexible budgets

1. Cover a range of activity
2. Are dynamic
3. Facilitate performance measurement

Flexible Budgets Cover a Range of Activity.   Forecasts of future events, whether sports, games, weather, or business, always involve some uncertainty. Business managers regularly deal with uncertainties. Sales may vary because of general economic conditions, changes in customer preferences, or competitor actions. Production may fall below expected levels because of employee absenteeism, inventory shortages caused by a truckers' strike, or damaged equipment caused by a fire.

Managers can modify their plans easily with flexible budgets

Managers must be ready to modify their plans to incorporate unexpected events or changes in the level of activities. Fortunately, flexible budgets can give managers information about the expected operations and financial position at various levels of operations. A flexible budget does not reduce the likelihood of fluctuations in the level of activity, but it increases a manager's ability to understand fluctuations and cope with them.

Some organizations experience stable operations with a steady or highly predictable level of activity. For instance, a company may experience a steady sales growth of 5 percent a year for 5 consecutive years. In such cases, a fixed budget may provide managers with all the data necessary to manage the organization effectively.

Other organizations may experience widely fluctuating levels of activity, with rapid or cyclical growth. For example, businesses such as tourism are strongly influenced by weather conditions, the general health of the economy, international currency exchange rates, and the cost of transportation.

Flexible budgets are prepared within the firm's relevant range of activity

A key determination in flexible budgeting is the range of activity covered by the budget. Managers require information about a range of possible realizable activity levels. They do not want to analyze budget data for activity levels that have little or no chance of occurring. Therefore, the flexible budget should cover only the possible range of activity, with special emphasis on the level of activity that is most useful for planning the acquisition and use of resources.

Flexible Budgets Are Dynamic.   Flexible budgets allow managers to adjust budget estimates on a timely basis. When the flexible budget is initially prepared, the analysis of cost behavior patterns provides the data needed for modifying the budget if the actual volume of activity makes modifications necessary. The greater the fluctuation in activity, the more useful is flexible budgeting as a dynamic management tool.

Flexible budgets provide a good framework for measuring performance

Flexible Budgets Facilitate Performance Measurement.   An important element of budgeting is control of operations. Figure 9-2 is a typical performance report used in a fixed budgeting system. The budgeted costs are based on $500,000 of sales. The actual costs resulted from sales of $600,000. A higher volume of activity would suggest higher costs. But how much higher should costs be, given that some are fixed and some are variable? To answer this question of "how much more," we use a flexible budget performance report. The actual costs shown in the report are compared with a flexible budget, whose costs are based on the actual sales level of $600,000 using the cost behavior patterns described earlier in the chapter. In effect, flexible budgets answer the question, "What should costs have been given the volume of activity achieved?"

To illustrate the use of flexible budget performance reports based on the actual sales level of $600,000, we return to the data for the department store example discussed earlier. The fixed budget performance report in Figure 9-2 shows an unfavorable total variance of $19,900, or about 9 percent above budget, and individual variances of up to 47 percent occur for certain accounts. Some managers might immediately suspect unfavorable marketing performance. But would such an evaluation be logical? Remember that the budget shown in Figure 9-1 and used in the performance report in Figure 9-2 is based on expected sales of $500,000. Actual sales for the year were $600,000. Although the marketing costs did exceed budget amounts by 9 percent, perhaps the additional costs were warranted given the higher level of sales. Such thoughts are mere speculation until a budget is prepared at the level of activity actually achieved. Figure 9-3 presents a performance report based on a flexible budget. That is, instead of using a budget fixed at $500,000 of sales, the budget is adjusted to fit the $600,000 sales level.

The flexible budget prepared for the actual activity level is based on the cost data presented on page 331. For example, the $30,000 of sales commissions is computed by multiplying $600,000 of sales times .05, the sales commission per dollar of sales. Similarly, clerical costs are $12,000 ($600,000 × .02). The fixed costs are the same for both the fixed and the flexible budget.

Figure 9-3. Here the actual costs are compared with a budget based on the actual sales level of $600,000. The result is a performance report that has a net favorable variance instead of a net unfavorable variance as occurred with the fixed budget report.

Barton's Department Store
Flexible Budget Marketing Performance Report
For the Year Ended December 31, 1986

Variable Costs for $600,000 of Sales	Budget	Actual	Variance
Sales commissions	$ 30,000	$ 31,100	$ 1,100 U
Clerical	12,000	12,250	250 U
Supplies	12,000	14,700	2,700 U
Travel	18,000	16,350	(1,650) F
Distribution	36,000	31,400	(4,600) F
Royalties	18,000	18,400	400 U
Total variable costs	126,000	124,200	(1,800) F
Fixed Costs			
Sales Salaries	52,000	52,200	200 U
Advertising	27,000	26,500	(500) F
Entertainment	12,000	12,200	200 U
Maintenance	9,000	9,700	700 U
Depreciation	8,000	8,000	—
Supplies	4,000	4,100	100 U
Insurance	3,500	3,500	—
Property taxes	2,500	2,500	—
Total fixed costs	118,000	118,700	700 U
Total budgeted marketing costs	$244,000	$242,900	$(1,100) F

As expected, the variable costs in the flexible budget are 20 percent higher than in the fixed budget. As a result some of the unfavorable variances reported in Figure 9-2 become favorable and the remaining unfavorable variances are much smaller. Of course the fixed costs are identical in the two reports. The total variance with the flexible budget is slightly favorable instead of 9 percent unfavorable. In this case, if the fixed budget performance report had been used to evaluate marketing activities, an incorrect conclusion might have been reached. The flexible budget provides data on the quality of performance given the actual level of activity.

FLEXIBLE BUDGETING ILLUSTRATED

To illustrate how to develop a flexible budget and how to prepare the budget performance report, we use the example of a graduate student dormitory cafeteria. The cafeteria serves meals to dormitory residents, faculty, and nonresident students. Residents of the dormitory may purchase a contract for all their meals or they may purchase one of several options whereby only some meals are eaten in the cafeteria. Because of the variety of options open to dormitory residents, combined with cafeteria use by nonresidents, the cafeteria experiences significant fluctuations in the number of meals served during the year. To help plan labor, supply, and other costs, the managers of the cafeteria use a flexible budgeting system.

Steps in the Flexible Budgeting Process

The steps in developing a flexible budget are:

1. Determine the range of activity.
2. Determine the cost behavior pattern for each cost in the budget.
3. Select the activity levels to be budgeted.
4. Use the cost behavior pattern data to prepare the budget for the selected activity levels.
5. At the end of the period, prepare another budget at the actual level of activity and compare it with actual results to measure performance.

The first step is to determine the relevant range

Step 1.   The initial step in flexible budgeting is to determine the range of activity the budget will cover. This is an important step for two reasons. First, managers are primarily interested in planning for activity levels that have a reasonable chance of occurring. Second, a basic assumption of cost behavior patterns is that they hold true for a relevant range of activity. Cost behavior may be different outside the **relevant range.** For example, depreciation of $14,000 on the cafeteria equipment may be correct for an activity level of 60,000 meals or less, but above that level additional needed equipment would increase depreciation expense. Therefore, the activity levels for the flexible budget should fall within the relevant range for the cost behavior patterns used in preparing the budget.

Cost data must be analyzed

Step 2.   The major feature of flexible budgets is that budgeted costs and revenues are different for each of the different levels of activity. But exactly how do these costs and revenues change with respect to changes in the volume of activity? The determination of cost behavior patterns requires careful analysis of past cost and activity data, as illustrated in Chapter 5. More sophisticated analysis techniques are discussed in the last part of this book.

In the cafeteria example, the number of meals served is used as the measure of activity. Other activity measures are possible, such as dollar amount of sales. Management should select the activity measure that is closely related to the costs being analyzed.

Thirteen cost categories are identified for the cafeteria. Each cost is analyzed using the high-low method, or some other technique, to determine the cost behavior pattern. Some costs are found to be entirely fixed, some entirely variable, and some are mixed costs, having both fixed and variable components. Figure 9-4 presents the cost patterns for the 1985–86 school year. The time period is important. Cost behavior patterns hold only for a period of time. In the future a cost may behave differently than it does now.

Administrative salaries and clerical wages are completely fixed and are constant for all levels of activity. The wages of kitchen employees have a fixed component of $32,000 and a variable component of $.30 per meal. Depreciation and computer service costs are entirely fixed. All other costs have a fixed and a variable component, except food cost, which is entirely variable. The amount of variable cost per meal can be computed by adding the variable costs of the individual accounts presented in Figure 9-4.

Figure 9-4. Cost behavior data are used to prepare the flexible budget for the Graduate Dorm Cafeteria.

Graduate Dorm Cafeteria
Schedule of Expected Cost Behavior Patterns
For the 1985–86 School Year

Cost	Amount of Fixed Cost	Variable Cost per Meal
Administrative salaries	$40,000	—
Clerical wages	8,000	—
Kitchen employee wages	32,000	$ .30
Depreciation, building	28,000	—
Depreciation, equipment	14,000	—
Utilities	6,000	.15
Food costs	—	1.50
Kitchen supplies	4,000	.25
Maintenance	16,000	.05
Employee benefits	8,000	.03
Uniform and linen cleaning	3,000	.02
Computer services	2,000	—
Miscellaneous	2,000	.04

Select the activity levels for the budget

Step 3. A budget is prepared for the highest and lowest activity levels selected within the relevant range. In addition, one or more activity levels are budgeted within the flexible budget range. Once cost behavior patterns are identified, it is easy to prepare budgets for several activity levels. Typically, the level of activity that is most likely to occur serves as the focal point for securing resources and planning their use. The cafeteria in our example uses three activity levels—30,000, 40,000, and 50,000 meals—for its flexible budget.

Step 4. The cost data from Figure 9-4 are used to prepare the flexible budget presented in Figure 9-5. The fixed and variable cost components are separated in this figure to highlight the composition of each cost at each activity level.

The variable costs at each activity level are determined by multiplying the variable part of each cost by the respective activity level. For example, kitchen employee wages have a fixed component of $32,000 and a variable component of $.30 per meal. At 30,000 meals the variable cost is $9,000, obtained as $.30 × 30,000 meals. At 40,000 meals, the variable cost is $.30 × 40,000 meals, and the fixed cost is the same no matter how many meals are served. The fixed and variable amounts are entered into the budget for each activity level. Each fixed and each variable cost column is then totaled. As expected, the fixed cost column totals are the same for all activity levels, and the variable cost totals increase proportionately with the level of activity.

Usually, flexible budgets are not presented with fixed and variable components separated as in Figure 9-5. Instead, the components are combined into one amount. For example, for 30,000 meals, kitchen employee wages are

Graduate Dorm Cafeteria
Flexible Budget
For the 1985–86 School Year

	30,000 Meals		40,000 Meals		50,000 Meals	
Cost	Fixed	Variable	Fixed	Variable	Fixed	Variable
Administrative salaries	$ 40,000	$ 0	$ 40,000	$ 0	$ 40,000	$ 0
Clerical wages	8,000	0	8,000	0	8,000	0
Kitchen employee wages	32,000	9,000	32,000	12,000	32,000	15,000
Depreciation, building	28,000	0	28,000	0	28,000	0
Depreciation, equipment	14,000	0	14,000	0	14,000	0
Utilities	6,000	4,500	6,000	6,000	6,000	7,500
Food costs	0	45,000	0	60,000	0	75,000
Kitchen supplies	4,000	7,500	4,000	10,000	4,000	12,500
Maintenance	16,000	1,500	16,000	2,000	16,000	2,500
Employee benefits	8,000	900	8,000	1,200	8,000	1,500
Uniform and linen cleaning	3,000	600	3,000	800	3,000	1,000
Computer services	2,000	0	2,000	0	2,000	0
Miscellaneous	2,000	1,200	2,000	1,600	2,000	2,000
Totals	$163,000	$70,200	$163,000	$93,600	$163,000	$117,000

Figure 9-5. Fixed and variable costs are computed for each cost for each of the selected activity levels. Notice that total fixed cost remains the same for all levels of activity.

budgeted at $41,000 ($32,000 fixed + $9,000 variable), and for 40,000 meals, this cost is budgeted at $44,000 ($32,000 fixed and $12,000 variable). The budget in Figure 9-6 is made up by combining the fixed and variable parts from Figure 9-5.

Figure 9-6. Typically, the fixed and variable costs are combined in the budget report.

Graduate Dorm Cafeteria
Flexible Budget
For the 1985–86 School Year

Cost	30,000 Meals	40,000 Meals	50,000 Meals
Administrative salaries	$ 40,000	$ 40,000	$ 40,000
Clerical wages	8,000	8,000	8,000
Kitchen employee wages	41,000	44,000	47,000
Depreciation, building	28,000	28,000	28,000
Depreciation, equipment	14,000	14,000	14,000
Utilities	10,500	12,000	13,500
Food costs	45,000	60,000	75,000
Kitchen supplies	11,500	14,000	16,500
Maintenance	17,500	18,000	18,500
Employee benefits	8,900	9,200	9,500
Uniform and linen cleaning	3,600	3,800	4,000
Computer services	2,000	2,000	2,000
Miscellaneous	3,200	3,600	4,000
Totals	$233,200	$256,600	$280,000

Control through performance reporting is a major benefit of flexible budgeting

Step 5.   Probably the most significant contribution of flexible budgeting comes in step 5, when actual results are compared with a budget based on the level of activity that occurred. Instead of measuring performance against a budget that is only an approximation of the activity level achieved, performance is measured against a budget that represents what should have been accomplished at the actual level of activity.

By the end of the budget period, actual activity in the cafeteria was 44,000 meals, and actual costs totaled $272,830. If these actual costs are compared with the budgeted costs for 40,000 meals or for 50,000 meals, the resulting variances would not be reliable indicators of performance. A better measure of the cafeteria's performance is to prepare another budget at the 44,000-meal level of activity, again using the cost behavior data presented in Figure 9-4. This budget is prepared **after** the accounting period is over, because the actual activity level is not known until the end of the period. The flexible budget performance report for the cafeteria is illustrated in Figure 9-7.

Figure 9-7. None of the selected activity levels occurred, so a new budget at the actual level of activity is prepared. This is what costs should have been, given that 44,000 meals were actually served during the period. Actual costs are compared with this budget in the performance report.

Graduate Dorm Cafeteria
Flexible Budget Performance Report
For the 1985–86 School Year

Cost	Budget Based on 44,000 Meals	Actual Cost	Variance	
Administrative salaries	$ 40,000	$ 41,000	$ 1,000	U
Clerical wages	8,000	8,000	—	
Kitchen employee wages	45,200	43,800	(1,400)	F
Depreciation, building	28,000	28,000	—	
Depreciation, equipment	14,000	15,400	1,400	U
Utilities	12,600	13,300	700	U
Food costs	66,000	70,500	4,500	U
Kitchen supplies	15,000	13,600	(1,400)	F
Maintenance	18,200	19,900	1,700	U
Employee benefits	9,320	9,230	(90)	F
Uniform and linen cleaning	3,880	3,700	(180)	F
Computer services	2,000	2,000	—	
Miscellaneous	3,760	4,400	640	U
Totals	$265,960	$272,830	$ 6,870	U

The actual costs are compared with the budgeted costs at the activity level of 44,000 meals. Differences between actual and budgeted costs are shown in the variance column and identified as favorable or unfavorable. The total variance of $6,870 unfavorable is only 2.6 percent of the budgeted costs for the activity level achieved. If the budget performance report had been based on the budget at 40,000 meals, the total variance would have been $16,230 unfavorable, and if the budget for 50,000 meals had been used for the comparison, the variance would have been $7,170 favorable. Neither of these latter two comparisons provides management with very good performance information, because they are based on comparisons of actual costs that resulted from one activity level and expected costs from another level of activity.

BUDGETING AND MANUFACTURING OVERHEAD

Flexible budgeting is particularly useful in planning and controlling overhead costs

Flexible budgets are used for planning and controlling all kinds of business activities, but they are particularly useful in developing manufacturing overhead rates and in analyzing overhead variances. Flexible budgets allow managers to see the effect of different activity levels on the overhead rate and resulting product costs. Armed with this information, managers may be able to adjust production levels or accept special orders to improve their competitive position or modify their prices.

We use the Frostless Freezer Company to illustrate the development of a manufacturing overhead rate from a flexible budget. The same example is used to illustrate manufacturing overhead variance analysis. The Frostless Freezer Company manufactures small home freezers for use in vacation homes or other places where space is limited or a larger freezer is not necessary. Production of each freezer requires 4 direct labor hours. Direct labor hours are used as the basis for applying manufacturing overhead to production. The company manufactures only enough units for the current year's demand, because annual model changes are necessary to meet competition. Management estimates freezer production and sales of 2,000 units with a possible sales range from 1,500 to 2,500 units. The range of activity, measured in terms of direct labor hours, is 6,000 DLH (1,500 units × 4 hours) to 10,000 DLH (2,500 units × 4 hours).

After establishing the range of activity, it is necessary to determine the cost behavior patterns of the overhead costs. Figure 9-8 presents expected cost data for the Frostless Freezer Company. Using these data, budgets can be

Figure 9-8. Manufacturing overhead cost behavior data used to prepare the overhead flexible budget for the Frostless Freezer Company.

Frostless Freezer Company
Manufacturing Overhead
Expected Cost Behavior Patterns
For the Year 1986

Cost	Fixed Cost	Variable Cost
Indirect materials	—	$ .30
Indirect labor	—	.60
Factory supplies	$ 3,000	.30
Supervision	22,000	—
Maintenance	3,000	.50
Insurance	2,500	.05
Property taxes	3,500	—
Utilities	1,000	.75
Depreciation, equipment	6,000	—
Lease expense on plant	7,000	—
Total	$48,000	$2.50

prepared for any level of activity within the relevant range desired by management. In our example, three activity levels are budgeted at 6,000, 8,000, and 10,000 direct labor hours. It is possible to develop budgets for more levels of activity, but for our purposes three are enough.

The flexible budget for the three selected levels of activity is presented in Figure 9-9. Note that overhead costs are separated into fixed and variable components. This allows us to see easily the change in each cost from one activity level to another. Also, managers can see the amount of fixed and variable overhead cost at each activity level. This information is useful in planning activities and, as you will see later in the chapter, it is useful in measuring overhead variances.

Fixed and variable overhead costs are separated to highlight how they are affected by changes in activity

Frostless Freezer Company
Manufacturing Overhead Flexible Budget
For the Year 1986

| | Activity Level (Direct Labor Hours) | | | | | |
| | 6,000 | | 8,000 | | 10,000 | |
Cost	Fixed	Variable	Fixed	Variable	Fixed	Variable
Indirect materials	—	$ 1,800	—	$ 2,400	—	$ 3,000
Indirect labor	—	3,600	—	4,800	—	6,000
Factory supplies	$ 3,000	1,800	$ 3,000	2,400	$ 3,000	3,000
Supervision	22,000	—	22,000	—	22,000	—
Maintenance	3,000	3,000	3,000	4,000	3,000	5,000
Insurance	2,500	300	2,500	400	2,500	500
Property taxes	3,500	—	3,500	—	3,500	—
Utilities	1,000	4,500	1,000	6,000	1,000	7,500
Depreciation, equipment	6,000	—	6,000	—	6,000	—
Plant lease expense	7,000	—	7,000	—	7,000	—
Total	$48,000	$15,000	$48,000	$20,000	$48,000	$25,000
Total MOH cost	$48,000	$15,000	$48,000	$20,000	$48,000	$25,000
Divided by DLH	÷ 6,000	÷ 6,000	÷ 8,000	÷ 8,000	÷ 10,000	÷ 10,000
Manufacturing overhead per DLH	$8/DLH	$2.50/DLH	$6/DLH	$2.50/DLH	$4.80/DLH	$2.50/DLH
Manufacturing overhead rate	$10.50/DLH		$8.50/DLH		$7.30/DLH	

Figure 9-9. The total fixed overhead cost is constant for all three activity levels, but the cost per direct labor hour declines at higher activity levels. The variable cost is the same per direct labor hour for all activity levels, but the total variable overhead costs increases with the volume of activity.

Separating the fixed and variable costs also highlights their impact on the manufacturing overhead rate at different levels of activity. The overhead rate at each of the three budgeted levels of activity is shown on the bottom line of Figure 9-9. This rate is computed by dividing the total overhead cost by the volume of activity for each activity level. The overhead rate includes a fixed component and a variable component. The two parts are calculated in Figure 9-9 and added together to make up the overhead rate for each level of activity.

In Figure 9-9, you can see that the variable manufacturing overhead rate is the same at all activity levels; the fixed rate changes with changes in activity. The fixed part spreads the fixed manufacturing overhead costs evenly over the units produced. By definition, fixed costs do not change with the level of activity, so the success of this fixed cost allocation depends heavily on management's estimate of the activity level. If the estimate of the activity level is too high, not all of the fixed cost will be assigned to production. If the estimate of activity is too low, too much fixed overhead will be assigned to production.

The variable part of the overhead rate assigns to production the overhead costs that increase with the volume of activity. These are indirect variable costs; they cannot be identified directly with specific products, but they vary with the level of activity. Whatever activity level is estimated, the same amount of variable overhead will be assigned per unit of production.

Total fixed overhead remains constant throughout the relevant range

Some important cost and activity relationships are worthy of comment. The **total** amount of fixed overhead cost is the same for all levels of activity, but the amount of fixed **overhead per direct labor hour** declines from $8.00 per hour at 6,000 direct labor hours to $4.80 per hour at 10,000 direct labor hours. Also, the **total** amount of variable overhead increases proportionately with the level of activity, but the amount of variable **overhead per direct labor hour** is $2.50, the same for all activity levels. Figure 9-10 illustrates graphically the relationship between total and per unit fixed costs and variable costs as the level of activity changes.

Fixed cost per unit declines as the volume of activity increases

The total manufacturing overhead rate for any particular level of activity is the sum of the fixed and variable overhead rates per direct labor hour. Because the variable overhead is $2.50 at all levels of activity, the difference in overhead rates between any two levels of activity is caused by the amount of fixed overhead per unit at each level of activity.

The manufacturing overhead rate is based on normal capacity

Usually the manufacturing overhead rate is based on **normal capacity,** which is the expected activity level for the period assuming normal operating conditions. The management of the Frostless Freezer Company expects to sell 2,000 freezers during the coming year. Therefore, the normal capacity for the company is 8,000 direct labor hours (2,000 freezers × 4 direct labor hours per freezer), and the rate used to apply overhead to production during the accounting period is $8.50 per direct labor hour.

Identifying the normal capacity is essential in developing the manufacturing overhead rate. To illustrate, let's assume for the moment that the actual capacity is 6,000 direct labor hours instead of 8,000 as estimated by management. That means the overhead cost of the freezers should be $42.00 per unit ($10.50 per direct labor hour × 4 hours per unit). However, the amount of overhead applied to freezers was $34.00 ($8.50 per direct labor hour × 4 hours per unit), because the overhead rate is based on the incorrect capacity of 8,000 direct labor hours. The $8.00 difference between the amount of overhead that should have been applied to freezers and the amount that was applied is an understatement of overhead costs of about 19 percent ($8.00/ $42.00).

A flexible budget enables us to analyze the effect on product cost of different levels of activity. If a fixed budget is used, this type of information and analysis is not readily available.

Figure 9-10. A comparison of total cost and the per unit cost of fixed overhead and variable overhead. The fixed overhead cost in diagram (a) remains the same for all activity levels, but the fixed cost per unit, shown in diagram (b), declines as activity increases. The variable overhead cost in diagram (c) increases with increasing activity, but the variable cost per unit remains the same, as shown in diagram (d).

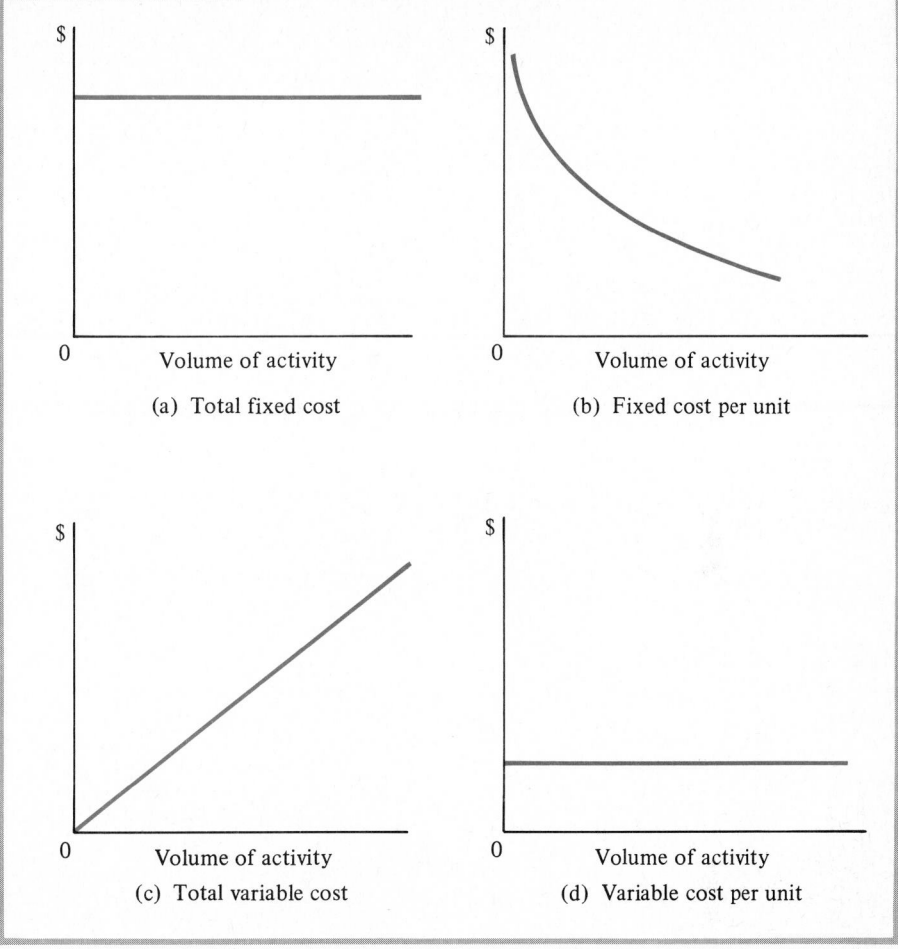

(a) Total fixed cost

(b) Fixed cost per unit

(c) Total variable cost

(d) Variable cost per unit

MANUFACTURING OVERHEAD VARIANCE ANALYSIS

Manufacturing overhead variances are somewhat more complex to analyze than prime cost variances. Overhead costs are indirect costs and contain both fixed and variable components. In contrast, direct material costs and direct labor costs vary directly with production; they do not contain a fixed component. If the actual activity level is different than expected, it is easy to measure and understand the impact on direct costs. With overhead, however, if the actual volume of activity turns out to be different than expected, it is more difficult to determine the effect on total overhead cost and on the unit cost of products. The purpose of **manufacturing overhead variance analysis** is the same as for other types of variance analysis: to determine the amount that actual cost differs from standard and to determine why the variance occurred.

To illustrate manufacturing overhead variance analysis, we continue with the example of the Frostless Freezer Company. The following additional data are provided:

1.   Actual production for the year was 1,800 freezers.

2.   Actual manufacturing overhead cost was $65,500.

3.   Actual direct labor hours worked was 7,400.

Analyzing the difference between actual and standard manufacturing overhead costs

The total overhead variance is the difference between the amount of overhead applied to production during the period and the amount of actual overhead cost incurred during the period. Actual overhead costs are recorded in the Manufacturing Overhead Control account as they are incurred. The balance in the account at year-end for the Frostless Freezer Company is $65,500. Applied overhead in a standard cost system is based on standards and the amount of production during the period. In this example, applied overhead for the period is determined as follows:

$$\text{Applied overhead} = \text{Actual output} \times \text{Standard overhead cost}$$
$$= \text{Actual output} \times \text{Standard hours per unit of output} \times \text{Manufacturing overhead rate}$$
$$= \$1,800 \text{ units} \times 4 \text{ DLH} \times \$8.50 \text{ per DLH}$$
$$= \$61,200$$

The total overhead variance is computed as follows:

Actual overhead	$65,500
Applied overhead	61,200
Overhead variance	$ 4,300 Unfavorable

The total overhead variance can be diagramed as follows:

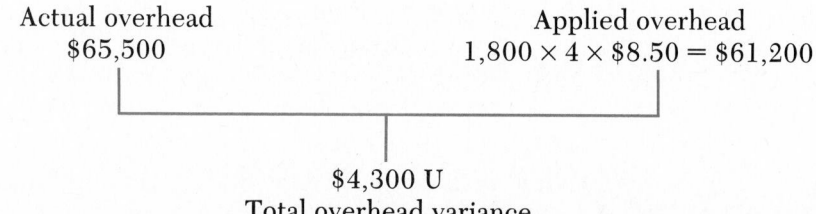

Actual overhead   Applied overhead
$65,500   1,800 × 4 × $8.50 = $61,200

$4,300 U
Total overhead variance

Total overhead variance

In practice, the total overhead variance can be determined by comparing the debit balance in the Manufacturing Overhead Control account, which is where actual overhead costs are recorded, with the credit balance in the Manufacturing Overhead Applied account. At the end of the period these account balances for the Frostless Freezer Company are as follows:

MOH Control	MOH Applied
65,500	61,200

The total overhead variance provides some general information about overhead costs. But often managers require detailed information about what caused the overhead variance. Just as the total material and labor variances are separated into detailed variances, so typically are overhead variances.

Manufacturing overhead variances can be analyzed in detail

Manufacturing overhead variance analysis is the detailed analysis of overhead variances. There are a number of different ways to analyze overhead variances, each serving somewhat different information needs of management. Typically, managers will select one of the overhead analysis methods. Below we discuss two methods of variance analysis; two other methods are presented in the appendix to the chapter.

The Difference Between Budgeted, Actual, and Standard Hours. One of the most common measures of activity and for applying manufacturing overhead to production is direct labor hours (DLH). In analyzing overhead variances, direct labor hours are used in three different ways to measure activity.

Budgeted direct labor hours are estimated before the accounting period started. They are the basis for determining the overhead rate and in particular the amount of fixed overhead assigned to products for each direct labor hour worked. **Actual hours** are the number of direct labor hours actually worked during the period. Actual hours cannot be determined until the period is over.

Measures of activity

Standard direct labor hours are the number of direct labor hours that should have been worked given the amount of output produced. Standard hours cannot be computed until the output has been measured.

Two-Variance Method

The **two-variance method** is used to isolate two components from the total manufacturing overhead variance: the component that is controllable by management — the controllable variance — and the component that is caused by operating at an activity level different than the budgeted volume of activity — the volume variance. Separating the total overhead variance into two parts provides managers with information about the cause of the overhead variance that a single variance cannot supply. The **controllable variance** results from comparing actual overhead cost of production with the overhead cost that should have been incurred for the actual volume of production. The cost that should have been incurred is the expected overhead cost at the actual volume of production as measured with a flexible budget.

The volume variance deals with fixed overhead costs

The same flexible budget cost is used with the volume variance. The **volume variance** results from comparing the overhead costs that should have been incurred for the actual production with the standard overhead cost that was applied. The computation of these two overhead variances can be shown graphically as follows:

Actual MOH	Flexible budget based on the actual amount of output	Applied MOH

Controllable variance

Volume variance

Total variance

Actual overhead is found in the Manufacturing Overhead Control account

The actual overhead cost is found in the Manufacturing Overhead Control account in the general ledger. The applied overhead cost is found in the Manufacturing Overhead Applied account in the general ledger. It is calculated as the standard hours per unit times the number of units produced times the overhead rate. The flexible budget based on output is computed by multiplying the output times the variable overhead cost per unit and then adding the fixed overhead component. This is the amount of overhead the company should have incurred given the level of production. The comparison of this flexible budget with actual overhead cost yields the controllable variance. The comparison of this flexible budget with applied overhead cost gives us the volume variance.

To illustrate the two-variance method, we return to the Frostless Freezer example, in which actual manufacturing overhead for the period was $65,500. Applied overhead was based on 1,800 units of output, times 4 standard hours per freezer, times the overhead rate of $8.50 per direct labor hour, or $61,200 ($1,800 units × 4 DLH × $8.50 per DLH).

What overhead costs should have been given the number of units produced

A flexible budget based on output, in this example, is a budget for 1,800 units of production. The actual output was 1,800 units, but the Frostless Freezer Company measures activity in terms of direct labor hours. The standard for each freezer is 4 direct labor hours. Therefore, a flexible budget based on outputs means that 1,800 units of output require 7,200 direct labor hours (1,800 units × 4 hours per units). Using the variable and fixed cost data in Figure 9-8 on page 340, we find the total budgeted cost for this level of output is $66,000 as shown below.

Flexible budget based on actual output of 1,800 units	(Standard hours × Variable overhead cost per hour) + Fixed overhead costs	
Variable cost	7,200 hr × $2.50/hr	= $18,000
Fixed cost		48,000
Flexible budget based on the actual amount of production		$66,000

Substituting the data into the two-variance analysis gives the following:

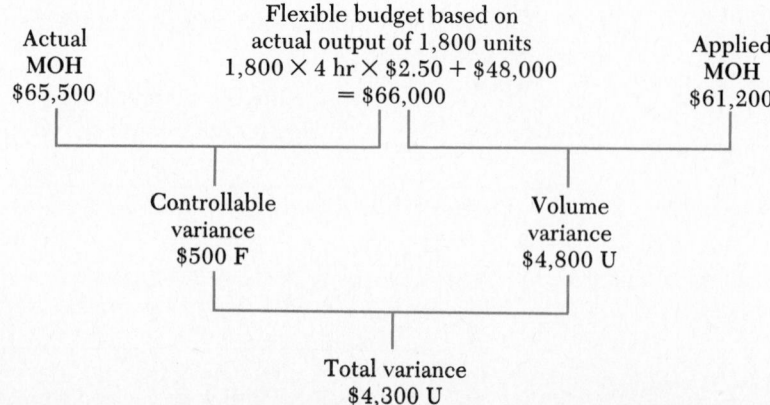

| Actual MOH $65,500 | Flexible budget based on actual output of 1,800 units 1,800 × 4 hr × $2.50 + $48,000 = $66,000 | Applied MOH $61,200 |

Controllable variance $500 F   Volume variance $4,800 U

Total variance $4,300 U

Comparing the actual overhead with the flexible budget based on the amount of output yields a variance of $500. In this case the variance is favorable, because actual overhead is less than the budget. The company spent $500 less on manufacturing overhead than was budgeted for the 1,800 units. The budget tells us what overhead costs should have been for the amount of production. If actual costs are less, the variance is favorable. The flexible budget is a benchmark, or standard of excellence, for a particular level of activity, and managers have a significant amount of control over any variances from that budget. For example, by effectively scheduling manufacturing labor, a production manager can reduce labor-related overhead costs such as payroll taxes, pension contributions, and insurance premiums. The **controllable variance** isolates the difference between the amount that should have been spent on overhead for the level of output achieved and the amount that actually was spent on overhead.

Controllable variance described

A volume variance occurs when the amount of actual output is different from the budgeted amount of output. In our example, the budget was based on 2,000 units, so 8,000 hours were budgeted. For the 1,800 units produced, the activity level is 7,200 direct labor hours (1,800 units × 4 DLH). Therefore, a volume variance occurred because the number of standard direct labor hours is different from the 8,000 budgeted hours. Remember that the standard direct labor hours is the number of labor hours at standard required to make the units produced.

Variance caused by operating at an activity level different than expected

The volume variance deals with the fixed part of the manufacturing overhead rate. In our illustration, the fixed part of the overhead rate is $6.00 per direct labor hour at the normal capacity level of activity. If 2,000 units are manufactured requiring 8,000 direct labor hours, the entire $48,000 of fixed overhead will be applied to production. However, if the company falls short of the normal capacity, not all of the $48,000 of fixed costs are allocated to production. With 7,200 standard direct labor hours for the period, the amount of fixed overhead assigned to production was $43,200 (7,200 direct labor hours × $6.00 per hour fixed overhead rate). Actual fixed overhead was $48,000. Therefore, actual fixed overhead was $4,800 more ($48,000 − $43,200) than the amount of overhead applied.

Another way of looking at the volume variance is to remember that fixed overhead costs are spread evenly over the output. In this example the company expected to spread the $48,000 of fixed overhead cost over 8,000 direct labor hours. But actual activity was only 7,200 labor hours. As a result the company fell 800 hours short of the expected activity level of 8,000. With a fixed overhead rate of $6.00 per direct labor hour, the volume variance is $4,800 unfavorable (800 hours × $6.00 per hour). The variance is unfavorable because the fixed manufacturing overhead must be absorbed by a smaller number of units of output, resulting in a higher cost per unit. In effect, the cost of manufacturing overhead is higher than the expected $24.00 per unit, because the fixed part of the overhead cost is shared by fewer units.

The rule in determining whether a volume variance is favorable or unfavorable is as follows: If the actual output is less than the budgeted output, the volume variance is unfavorable. If the actual output is greater than the budgeted output, the volume variance is favorable.

Three-Variance Method

The **three-variance method** is similar to the two-variance method except that the controllable variance is separated further into two parts, called a spending variance and an efficiency variance. The **spending variance** results from spending more or less than the expected amount for overhead. The expected amount is determined by a flexible budget based on inputs—in this case the actual number of direct labor hours worked. The manufacturing overhead **efficiency variance** results from using more or fewer direct labor hours than standard. The efficiency variance is computed by multiplying the variable manufacturing overhead rate by the difference between the actual and standard hours. A comparison of a flexible budget based on actual hours worked and a flexible budget based on standard hours also yields the efficiency variance. The **volume variance** is the same in the three-variance method as it is in the two-variance method. It measures the amount of variance caused by using the production facilities at above or below the expected level. The three-variance method can be computed using the following graphic approach:

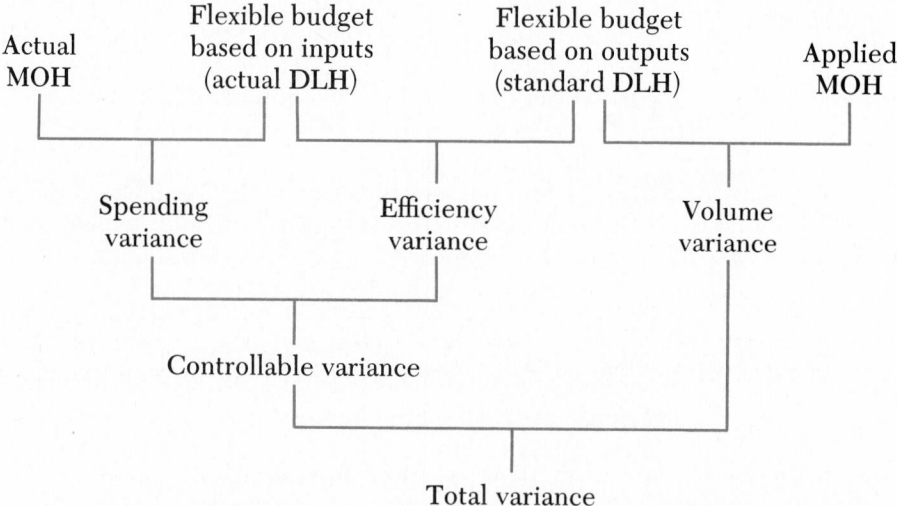

What overhead costs should have been, given the number of direct labor hours actually worked

A flexible budget based on inputs merely means a budget based on the number of actual direct labor hours worked rather than the standard direct labor hours. If another overhead application base were used, such as machine hours, the budget would be based on the number of actual machine hours worked. The flexible budget based on actual direct labor hours worked is computed as follows:

Flexible budget based on inputs = (Actual hours × Variable overhead cost per labor hour) + Fixed overhead cost

Variable cost	7,400 hours × $2.50/hr = $18,500
Fixed cost	48,000
Flexible budget based on actual inputs (DLH)	$66,500

A flexible budget based on outputs (standard direct labor hours) is $66,000, which was computed earlier for the two-variance analysis; therefore all the data are available to prepare the three-variance analysis. Substituting the data into the graphic approach we can compute the three variances, which we then discuss below.

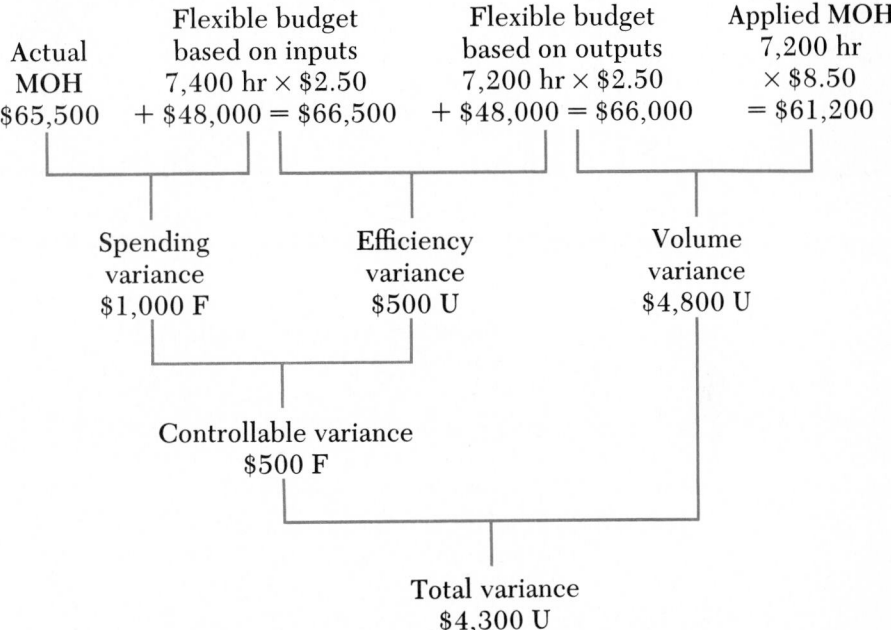

First notice that the total overhead variance is $4,300 unfavorable, the same as with the two-variance analysis presented earlier. The total overhead variance is the difference between the standard overhead cost (applied overhead in a standard cost system) and the overhead cost actually incurred (the balance in the Manufacturing Overhead Control account). The total variance is not changed by the method of overhead variance analysis used. It is merely divided into different types of variances to facilitate management's analysis and evaluation of the variances.

The **spending variance** addresses the issue of how much should have been spent on overhead given the number of direct labor hours actually used. In this example, based on the number of actual labor hours worked, total overhead cost should have been $66,500, but instead it was $65,500. The difference of $1,000 is favorable, because the company spent less than it should have for the level of activity. The idea is that the variable part of overhead is affected by the number of labor hours actually worked. The **actual** overhead cost and the budget based on the **actual** hours worked are compared to find the spending variance. This variance results from spending more or less for overhead than expected given the actual number of labor hours worked.

The **efficiency variance** is caused by using more or fewer direct labor hours than standard. The efficiency variance is the difference between a budget based on actual hours worked and a budget based on standard hours.

We spent more or less than we should have for manufacturing overhead

The efficiency variance measures the overhead variance caused by using more or less direct labor hours than standard

Both of these budgets include the fixed overhead of $48,000. Therefore any difference between them is the variable overhead. The budget based on inputs is the variable overhead rate of $2.50 per labor hour times the **actual direct labor hours** worked, and the budget based on outputs is the variable overhead rate times the **standard direct labor hours.** The difference between the two budgets can be found easily as the difference between the actual hours worked and the standard hours multiplied by the variable manufacturing overhead rate. In this case the efficiency variance is

$$(7,400 \text{ actual hr} - 7,200 \text{ standard hr}) \times \$2.50 \text{ per DLH} = \$500 \text{ U}$$

This efficiency variance is unfavorable because the company used more labor hours than standard to make the products. As a result, some variable overhead costs were incurred that were not expected. If the number of actual direct labor hours is less than the number of standard hours, the efficiency variance is favorable; if the number of actual direct labor hours is greater than standard, the efficiency variance is unfavorable.

Other measures of volume variance

The volume variance of $4,800 unfavorable is identical to the volume variance isolated in the two-variance approach discussed earlier. The terms **capacity variance** and **denominator variance** are sometimes used to describe the volume variance or a similar type of variance that deals with the fixed overhead cost. Capacity variance is used in an alternate method of overhead analysis discussed in the appendix to this chapter.

When the spending, efficiency, and volume variances are combined, they sum to $4,300 unfavorable, which is the total overhead variance. Regardless of the overhead variance analysis method used or the number of individual variances isolated, the sum of all individual variances must equal the total variance for the period. Different variance analysis methods are used to help managers analyze overhead variance in ways that provide information useful in planning and controlling manufacturing overhead costs.

SUMMARY

Flexible budgets and standard costs are tools that assist managers in dealing with uncertainty. **Fixed budgets,** sometimes called **static budgets,** are prepared for a single level of activity. Such budgets often provide managers with valuable information for planning and controlling activities. When activity levels are hard to predict, it may be necessary to prepare a flexible budget.

Flexible budgets, sometimes called **dynamic budgets,** are prepared for more than one level of activity. Flexible budgets cover a range of activity, are dynamic, and facilitate performance measurement. The range of activity should include all levels of activity that have some likelihood of occurring. The activity levels included in the budget should all be within the relevant range of the cost behavior patterns for the costs used in the budget.

With a flexible budgeting system, performance reports compare actual results with a budget at the actual level of activity. Such comparisons typically are more useful in assessing performance than fixed budget reports. Steps in the flexible budgeting process include determining the activity range of the budget, identifying cost behavior patterns, selecting activity levels for the budget, preparing the flexible budget, and comparing actual results with a budget based on the actual level of activity.

Flexible budgets are especially helpful in planning overhead costs and measuring overhead variances in a standard cost system. Of major value is the ability to separate the fixed and variable components of the manufacturing overhead rate. These two components are affected differently when the actual level of activity is different from the expected level of activity.

The **total manufacturing overhead** variance is the difference between the actual manufacturing overhead and the applied manufacturing overhead. In a standard cost system, applied manufacturing overhead is determined by the amount of output and the standard amount of overhead per unit of output. Usually the amount of overhead per unit of output is expressed as an overhead rate.

There are several ways to analyze manufacturing overhead variances. The **two-variance approach** separates the total overhead variance into a controllable variance and a volume variance. The **controllable variance** is the difference between actual overhead and a flexible budget based on the amount of output. The variance is called controllable because the flexible budget is a standard of performance. The **volume variance** measures the amount of overhead variance that occurs because the actual level of activity is different from the budgeted level of activity, which is usually the normal capacity.

In the **three-variance approach** the controllable variance is separated further into a spending variance and an overhead efficiency variance. The **spending variance** is a comparison of the actual manufacturing overhead cost with a budget based on actual amount of inputs. Inputs are usually measured in terms of some overhead application base such as direct labor hours or machine hours. The manufacturing overhead **efficiency variance** is the difference between the actual direct labor hours and the standard direct labor hours multiplied by the **variable** part of the manufacturing overhead rate.

KEY TERMS

actual hours *(345)*
budgeted hours *(345)*
capacity variance *(350)*, *(352)*
controllable variance *(345)*, *(347)*
dynamic budget *(333)*
efficiency variance *(348)*, *(349)*
fixed budget *(330)*
fixed efficiency variance *(354)*
flexible budget *(333)*

relevant range *(336)*
spending variance *(348)*
standard hours *(345)*
static budget *(330)*
three-variance method *(348)*
two-variance method *(345)*
variable efficiency variance *(354)*
volume variance *(345)*

APPENDIX: OTHER OVERHEAD VARIANCE ANALYSIS APPROACHES

This appendix presents two additional methods of analyzing manufacturing overhead variance: an alternative three-variance method and a four-variance method. Other methods can also be used, none of which is generally superior or more preferred by managers than the others. Instead managers select a method based on the nature of the company's overhead cost or just managerial preference.

Alternate Three-Variance Method

This alternate approach to the three-variance method of analyzing overhead variances provides managers with a somewhat different measure of the efficiency variance and the variance associated with fixed overhead costs. The **spending variance** is the same for both three-variance methods. It is the difference between actual overhead and an overhead budget based on inputs.

The **efficiency variance** in this alternative three-variance method measures the amount of overhead variance, both fixed and variable, that can be attributed to using more or fewer labor hours than standard. As with the other three-variance method, the efficiency variance is the difference between the actual hours worked and the standard hours worked. But in this alternate variance analysis method, we multiply the difference by the **total manufacturing overhead rate** rather than just the variable part of the overhead rate.

In our example, the total overhead rate is $8.50 per direct labor hour. For 1,800 units produced, 7,200 hours are budgeted and 7,400 direct labor hours were used. The variance is $1,700 unfavorable, calculated as (7,200 standard hours − 7,400 actual hours) × $8.50 per hour. The efficiency variance is unfavorable because the actual number of direct labor hours worked was more than the standard number of hours for the output produced.

Capacity variance is similar to the volume variance

The **capacity variance** is similar to the volume variance. It attempts to measure the amount of variance that occurs because the actual activity level was different from the budgeted activity level. The costs of manufacturing production facilities such as plant and equipment are called capacity costs. Many of these production facility costs are fixed. If actual production output equals the expected level, then the fixed resources invested are being used to achieve the expected (budgeted) output. If actual output falls below the expected level, then the production resources are being underutilized and the capacity or volume variance is unfavorable. If, on the other hand, actual output exceeds the budgeted level, the production facilities are being utilized better than expected and the resulting capacity or volume variance is favorable.

Capacity variance is measured on inputs and volume variance is measured on outputs

Both the capacity variance and the volume variance discussed earlier are favorable or unfavorable depending on whether the actual level of activity is more or less than the budgeted level of activity. The difference between the two variances lies in the way actual activity is measured. With the **capacity variance**, actual activity is measured with inputs, in this example the number of **actual direct labor hours**. With the **volume variance**, actual activity is measured in terms of outputs, in this example the number of units multiplied by four **standard direct labor hours.** The capacity variance is computed as follows for our example.

Actual hours	7,400 hours
Normal capacity (budgeted hours)	8,000
Difference	600
Fixed overhead rate	$6/hour
Capacity variance	$3,600 unfavorable

The capacity variance is unfavorable because the actual activity level was less than budgeted. In effect, the production facility was not used as effectively as expected. The dollar amount of capacity variance depends on how much the actual volume of activity is above or below the expected level and on the size of the fixed part of the overhead rate. Because fewer than the expected number of units were made during the period, the actual cost of fixed overhead was somewhat higher than $6 per direct labor hour.

Combining all three variances yields a total variance of $4,300 unfavorable ($1,000 F spending + $1,700 U efficiency + $3,600 U capacity).

This three-variance method can be diagramed as follows:

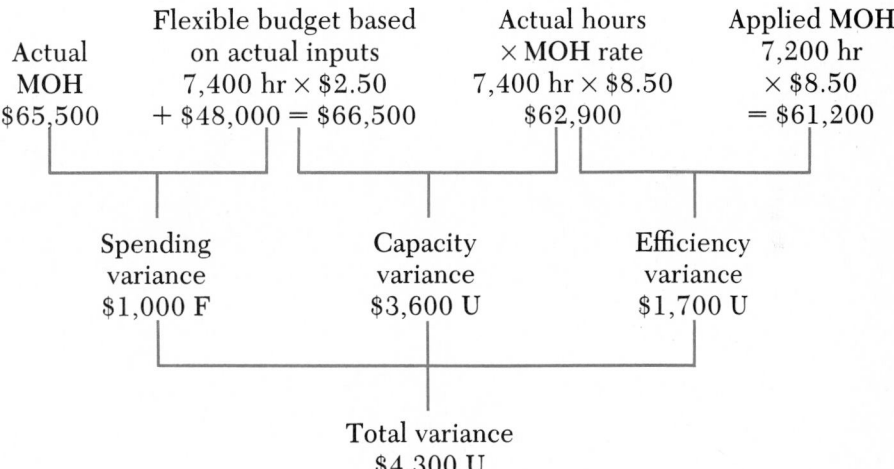

The above approach to computing the overhead variances for this analysis method is somewhat mechanical, but after using the approach a few times, it is easy to relate the process to the variances. For example, the flexible budget based on inputs and the actual hours times the overhead rate both contain the same amount of variable manufacturing overhead. However, the flexible budget includes all of the fixed overhead cost and the actual hours times the overhead rate contains fixed overhead equal to the fixed part of the overhead rate times the actual hours. Therefore, the difference between these two numbers yields the capacity variance just as our earlier calculation did.

The Four-Variance Method

The four-variance method is similar to the three-variance method presented earlier in the chapter, except that the efficiency variance is separated into a variable efficiency variance and a fixed efficiency variance. The four variances are the spending variance, the variable efficiency variance, the fixed efficiency variance, and the capacity variance. This method may also be viewed as an extension of the two-variance method. The controllable variance in the two-variance method is divided into a spending variance and a variable efficiency variance. The volume variance in the two-variance method is divided into a fixed efficiency variance and a capacity variance. The spending variance and the capacity variance also are identical to the ones just computed in the alternative three-variance method.

The spending variance and variable efficiency variance total to the controllable variance in the two-variance analysis

The **variable efficiency variance** measures the amount of overhead variance attributable to using more or fewer hours of labor than standard, and is computed by multiplying the **variable** part of the overhead rate times the difference between the standard and actual hours. In our example the variable efficiency variance is $500 unfavorable, or (7,200 standard hours − 7,400 actual hours) × $2.50 variable overhead rate. Because variable costs change with the level of activity, the variable efficiency variance often is thought of as a controllable cost.

The capacity variance and the fixed efficiency variance total to the volume variance in the two-variance method

The **fixed efficiency variance** is computed by multiplying the **fixed** part of the overhead rate times the difference between the standard and actual labor hours. The fixed efficiency variance is $1,200 unfavorable, or (7,200 standard hours − 7,400 actual hours) × $6.00 fixed overhead rate. The fixed part of the overhead rate is an allocation of fixed overhead cost, so these costs do not change with the activity level. Consequently, this variance typically is not thought of as controllable.

The diagram for the four-variance approach is similar to the three-variance diagram on page 349, but the volume variance is further divided into two parts.

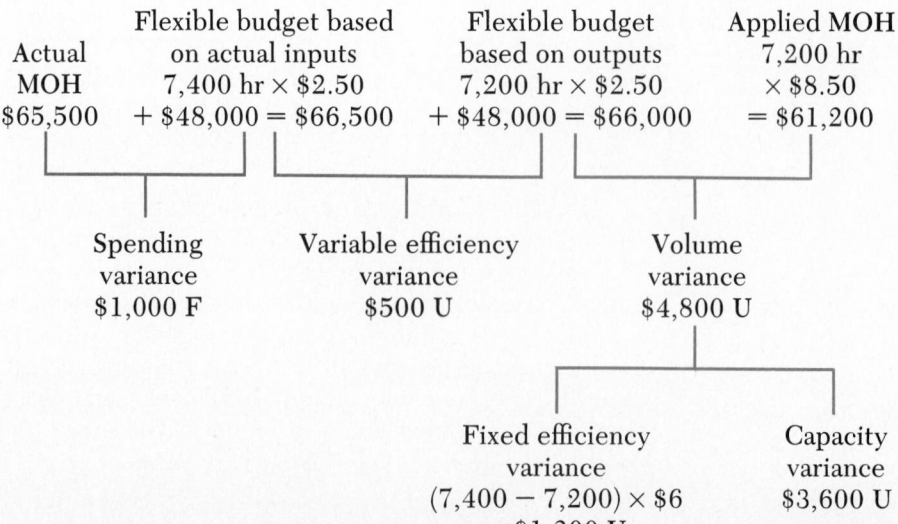

The volume variance that results in this diagram is separated into the fixed efficiency variance and the capacity variance. The capacity variance may be computed as in the alternative three-variance analysis, or it is obtained as the difference between the volume variance and its fixed efficiency variance component.

QUESTIONS

1. "Here's an example of futility and waste," says James. "Martin's firm prepares elaborate flexible budgets for several possible levels of activity on a quarterly basis. When the quarter is over, Martin prepares a report to management comparing actual and budgeted activity. But he doesn't use any of the budgets the company prepared. He prepares an entirely new budget to fit his department's output. So his firm wasted time and money to prepare budgets which are never used, and his managers get a comparison with a budget that he makes up to suit his department after the quarter is over." Discuss James's criticism of Martin's budgeting and reporting activities.

2. "A budget is nothing more than a set of standards used for comparing actual and planned performance. Therefore a flexible budget and standard costs are really one and the same thing." Evaluate this comment. Discuss the primary purposes of flexible budgets and standard costs, and indicate the different functions that each accomplishes.

3. (AICPA) Meyer Company's cost accounting department has prepared a factory overhead variance analysis report using the two-variance method. The plant manager of Meyer Company is interested in understanding the managerial usefulness of this report. What are the purposes of a factory overhead variance analysis report? Identify and explain the underlying assumptions associated with the two-variance method. Discuss the significance of each variance.

EXERCISES

Ex. 9-1
Flexible Budget for a Merchandising Firm

The management of Sea and Sand Gift Shop has decided to use a flexible budgeting system to plan activities and control costs. Tourist business is affected greatly by weather, the price of gasoline, and the economy in general. During the last accounting period cost behavior data have been accumulated and are presented below.

Item	Fixed	Variable
Salaries	$35,000	—
Commissions	—	$.10 per sales dollar
Store rent	6,000	.03
Equipment rent	1,500	—
Advertising	2,800	—
Utilities	1,800	.02
Cost of goods sold	—	.35
Maintenance	2,400	—
Employee benefits	3,500	.04
Property taxes	1,600	.02
Insurance	1,400	.01

REQUIRED

Prepare a flexible budget for the gift shop using sales levels of $100,000, $125,000, and $150,000.

Ex. 9-2
Flexible Budget
Performance
Report

Refer to the budget and cost behavior data presented in Exercise 9-1 for the Sea and Sand Gift Shop. During the current year the shop had sales of $143,000 and incurred the following costs.

	Actual
Salaries	$33,400
Commissions	14,850
Store rent	10,290
Equipment rent	1,600
Advertising	3,300
Utilities	4,880
Cost of goods sold	46,980
Maintenance	2,200
Employee benefits	8,930
Property taxes	4,565
Insurance	2,850

REQUIRED   Prepare a flexible budget performance report for the year.

Ex. 9-3
Identifying the
Direction of
Overhead Variances

Following are budgeted, actual, and standard labor hours for three separate manufacturing firms that use direct labor hours as the basis for applying overhead to production.

	Company		
	X	Y	Z
Budgeted hours	25,000	10,000	50,000
Actual hours	26,000	9,800	49,800
Standard hours	25,500	10,000	49,500

REQUIRED   For each firm determine the direction (favorable or unfavorable) of the manufacturing overhead efficiency variance, volume variance, and labor efficiency variance.

Ex. 9-4
Flexible Budget for
a Service Business

Three-C Computer Service sells computer processing services and related support services. Company management uses a fixed budgeting system for planning and control purposes, because of the belief that computer operations are primarily fixed cost–oriented. However, recently management has been evaluating the possibility of using a flexible budgeting system. Cost behavior data have been prepared during the last several months and are presented below.

	Fixed	Variable
Advertising	$ 4,000	—
Salaries	42,000	—
Wages	14,000	$.12 per sales dollar
Supplies	1,000	.08
Equipment rent	34,000	.02
Building rent	12,000	.03
Building maintenance	4,800	—
Equipment maintenance	7,000	.02
Insurance	4,200	—
Utilities	3,000	.03

REQUIRED

    a. Prepare a flexible budget for Three-C Computer Service at sales levels of $175,000, $200,000, and $225,000.

    b. Compute the break-even level of activity for the company.

Ex. 9-5
Understanding
Overhead Cost
Relationships

During 1985 the Deloide Company had the following manufacturing overhead variances:

Spending	$5,100 U
Efficiency	2,800 F
Volume	4,000 F

The manufacturing overhead rate for 1985 is $12 per direct labor hour, of which $4 per hour is variable cost. In 1985 Deloide had actual overhead costs of $124,300, and standard direct labor hours for the year were 10,500.

REQUIRED

From the above data compute:

    a. The fixed part of the overhead rate.

    b. Budgeted direct labor hours.

    c. Actual direct labor hours.

    d. Applied manufacturing overhead.

    e. The total amount of fixed overhead cost.

Ex. 9-6
Two-Variance
Overhead Analysis

The Freestone Company uses machine hours as the basis for applying overhead to products. The company's 1985 overhead budget was $200,000, of which $110,000 was fixed overhead cost. The budget was based on an expected activity level of 40,000 machine hours, which is Freestone's normal capacity. During 1985 the company manufactured 9,600 units using 41,000 actual machine hours. The standard number of machine hours required for the units produced is 38,400. Actual manufacturing overhead for 1985 was $196,700.

REQUIRED

Prepare a two-variance overhead analysis.

Ex. 9-7
Three-Variance
Overhead Analysis

Refer to the overhead data for the Freestone Company presented in Exercise 9-6.

REQUIRED.   Use the three-variance approach to analyze the overhead variance for 1985.

Ex. 9-8
The Impact of
Overhead Costs

A manufacturing company applies manufacturing overhead to production at the rate of $10 per direct labor hour. The overhead rate is based on a total overhead budget of $1,200,000, $900,000 of which is fixed cost. The company has been using 120,000 direct labor hours as its normal capacity for establishing its overhead rate.

    During the current year, actual overhead cost was $1,125,000 for 90,000 actual direct labor hours. For the past several years the firm's activity level has been around 90,000 direct labor hours rather than the 120,000 used as the measure of normal capacity. Several key managers feel that competition and the economy in general have had a permanent effect on the company's normal capacity, and that consequently 90,000 direct labor hours should be used as the firm's normal capacity in establishing the overhead rate.

    The company has a government contract for the production of a tank stabilizer bar. The contract calls for a price equal to actual manufacturing cost plus 40 percent. The completed job included prime costs of $120,000 and required 8,000 direct labor hours.

a. Determine the fixed and variable components of the company's current manufacturing overhead rate.
b. Compute the manufacturing overhead rate if the company's correct normal capacity is 90,000 direct labor hours.
c. Compute the price of the government contract using the new normal capacity of 90,000 direct labor hours.

Ex. 9-9°
Identifying
Favorable and
Unfavorable
Variances

A manufacturing business uses direct labor hours as the base for applying manufacturing overhead costs to products. The company has five manufacturing plants, each with its own overhead rate. Below are individual plant data for budgeted, standard, and actual direct labor hours.

			Plant		
	A	B	C	D	E
Budgeted hours	10,000	20,000	40,000	35,000	12,000
Actual hours	11,000	19,500	40,000	33,800	11,200
Standard hours	10,000	19,500	40,600	36,000	11,800

REQUIRED

For **each** plant determine the direction (favorable or unfavorable) of the variable efficiency variance, volume variance, capacity variance, and labor efficiency variance.

Ex. 9-10 (AICPA)
Understanding
Overhead Variance
Relationships

Strayer Company, which uses a fully integrated standard cost system, had budgeted the following sales and costs for 1985:

Unit sales	20,000
Sales	$200,000
Total production costs at standard cost	130,000
Gross margin	70,000
Beginning inventories	None
Ending inventories	None

At the end of 1985 Strayer Company reported production and sales of 19,200 units. Total factory overhead incurred was exactly equal to budgeted factory overhead for 1985 and there was underapplied total factory overhead of $2,000 at December 31, 1985. Factory overhead is applied to the work in process inventory on the basis of standard direct labor hours allowed for units produced. Also, there was a favorable direct labor efficiency variance, but no direct labor rate variance and no raw-material variances for 1985.

REQUIRED

Explain why factory overhead was underapplied by $2,000, and being as specific as the data permit, indicate which overhead variances may have been affected. Strayer uses a three-variance method of analyzing the total factory overhead variance: The three variances are (1) spending variance, (2) efficiency variance, and (3) volume variance.

° Exercises marked with an asterisk are based on information in the appendix of this chapter.

Ex. 9-11°
Four-Variance
Method of
Overhead Variance
Analysis

A manufacturing company uses a standard costing system for its manufacturing opera-tions. During the year, the company produced 3,000 units of output using 8,600 direct labor hours. Standards call for 3 direct labor hours per unit. Direct labor hours are used as the base for applying overhead to products.

The overhead rate is based on a total overhead budget of $84,000 and expected production at the normal capacity level of 3,500 units of output. Budgeted fixed cost for the year was $31,500. Actual overhead cost for the year was $70,800.

REQUIRED   Prepare a four-variance analysis of overhead for the company.

Ex. 9-12 (AICPA)
Analyzing
Overhead Costs

Armando Corporation manufactures a product with the following standard cost:

Direct materials—20 yards @ $1.35 per yard	$27
Direct labor—4 hours @ $9.00 per hour	36
Factory overhead—applied at five-sixths of direct labor. Ratio of variable costs to fixed costs: 2 to 1	30
Total standard cost per unit of output	$93

Standards are based on normal monthly production involving 2,400 direct labor hours (600 units of output).

The following information pertains to the month of July:

Direct materials purchased—18,000 yards @ $1.38 per yard	$24,840
Direct materials used—9,500 yards	
Direct labor—2,100 hours @ $9.15 per hour	19,215
Actual factory overhead	16,650

500 units of the product were actually produced in July.

REQUIRED

a. Prepare the following schedules computing:
   1. Variable factory overhead rate per direct labor hour.
   2. Total fixed factory overhead based on normal activity.
b. Prepare the following schedules for the month of July, indicating whether each variance is favorable or unfavorable:
   1. Controllable factory overhead variance.
   2. Volume factory overhead variance.

Ex. 9-13 (CMA)
Overhead Variances

King Company estimates that it will operate its manufacturing facilities at 800,000 direct labor hours for the year. The estimate for total budgeted overhead is $2,000,000. The standard variable overhead rate is estimated to be $2 per direct labor hour, or $6 per unit. The actual data for the year are presented below:

Actual finished units	250,000
Actual direct labor hours	764,000
Actual variable overhead	$1,610,000
Actual fixed overhead	$392,000

° Exercises marked with an asterisk are based on information in the appendix of this chapter.

REQUIRED   Respond to the following questions by selecting the best answer.

1. The variable overhead spending variance for the year is
   a. $2,000 F.   b. $10,000 U.   c. $82,00 U.   d. $110,000 U.
   e. some response other than those shown above.

2. The variable overhead efficiency variance for the year is
   a. $28,000 U.   b. $100,000 U.   c. $110,000 U.
   d. determined from information other than that given above.
   e. some response other than those shown above.

3. The fixed overhead spending variance for the year is
   a. $8,000 F.   b. $10,000 U.   c. $17,000 U.   d. $74,000 U.
   e. some amount other than those shown above.

4. The fixed overhead volume variance for the year is
   a. $7,000 U.   b. $25,000 U.   c. $41,667 U.   d. $18,000 F.
   e. some amount other than those shown above.

PROBLEMS

P. 9-1
Flexible Budget for a Drugstore

The following cost behavior data pertain to the Cedartown Drugstore. The owner of the store uses flexible budgets to plan activities and measure results. Several new stores have been built recently nearby and the owner is uncertain what the effect will be on sales.

	Fixed Cost	Variable Cost per Sales Dollar
Advertising	$ 8,000	—
Wages and commissions	22,000	$.06
Building lease cost	7,200	.02
Supplies	1,200	.02
Equipment depreciation	600	—
Utilities	600	.03
Maintenance	3,000	.03
Product cost	—	.40

REQUIRED   Prepare a flexible budget for the Cedartown Drugstore using sales of $60,000, $80,000, and $100,000.

P. 9-2
Manufacturing Overhead Flexible Budget

Parklen Products manufactures several different small home appliances. Company management has selected direct labor hours as the application base for manufacturing overhead. The company uses a flexible budget to plan and control all costs, including overhead costs. Below are estimated overhead cost behavior data for 1986. Variable costs are expressed in terms of cost per direct labor hour. Product sales fluctuate with economic trends in the country. In 1986 management expects to operate between 20,000 and 30,000 direct labor hours.

	Fixed Costs	Variable Costs
Indirect material	$ 2,000	$ .10
Indirect labor	6,000	.25
Factory utilities	15,000	.20
Factory insurance	12,000	—
Factory property taxes	18,000	—
Maintenance	6,000	.15
Depreciation, manufacturing equipment	10,000	—
Depreciation, manufacturing plant	20,000	—
Employee benefits	4,000	.40
First aid room	6,000	.05
Cafeteria for the manufacturing plant	4,000	.05
Manufacturing supervisory salaries	40,000	—

REQUIRED

a. Prepare a flexible budget using 20,000, 25,000, and 30,000 direct labor hours as the selected activity levels.
b. Compute the overhead rate assuming 25,000 is the normal capacity.

P. 9-3
Two-Variance Method of Overhead Variance Analysis

The Borsch Company uses machine hours as the basis for applying manufacturing overhead to production. The variable part of the manufacturing overhead rate is $3 per machine hour. Budgeted fixed overhead cost for 1985 is $80,000, and the company's normal capacity is 20,000 machine hours per year. During 1985 actual overhead cost was $140,400, and actual machine hours were 19,800. Standard machine hours for the amount of output produced were 20,400.

REQUIRED   Prepare a two-variance overhead analysis.

P. 9-4
Three-Variance Method of Overhead Variance Analysis

Blanchart Ltd., is a manufacturing business that produces and sells automobile parts for several different automobile manufacturers. Blanchart applies overhead at the rate of $9 per direct labor hour to all products it makes. The company uses 100,000 direct labor hours as its estimate of normal capacity in setting its overhead rate. Estimated fixed overhead cost for 1985 is $700,000.

At the end of 1985 the Manufacturing Overhead Control account had a balance of $963,000. During the year actual direct labor hours were 112,400, and standard direct labor hours for the output produced are 109,200.

REQUIRED   Prepare a three-variance overhead analysis isolating the spending, efficiency, and volume variances.

P. 9-5
Flexible Budget Performance Report

The Huddle Hotel uses a flexible budgeting system for planning and control. Below are flexible budget data for the fiscal year just completed. In addition, actual results of operations are presented.

	Budget		Actual Results
Revenue	$600,000	$900,000	$800,000
Employee wages	150,000	180,000	164,000
Supervisory salaries	95,000	95,000	92,000
Depreciation, building and furniture	40,000	40,000	40,000
Rent on equipment	22,000	28,000	23,000
Maintenance	18,000	21,000	14,000
Linen service	30,000	45,000	42,000
Property taxes	14,000	14,000	17,000
Insurance	31,000	34,000	37,000
Advertising and promotion	85,000	85,000	76,000
Utilities	54,000	69,000	70,000
Supplies	12,000	15,000	10,000
Miscellaneous	32,000	47,000	42,000
Total expenses	583,000	673,000	627,000
Net income	$ 17,000	$227,000	$173,000

REQUIRED   Prepare a performance report in good form for the hotel.

P. 9-6
Understanding
Overhead Variance
Relationships

The Commerce Manufacturing Company applies overhead at the rate of $3 per standard direct labor hour. Variable overhead accounts for $2 of the overhead rate. The budgeted activity level is 25,000 direct labor hours. The company uses the three-variance method to analyze overhead variances. For the year just completed the overhead variances are:

Spending variance	$1,000 Unfavorable
Efficiency variance	4,000 Unfavorable
Volume variance	1,000 Favorable

REQUIRED   Use the above data to compute:

a.   Standard hours.
b.   Actual hours worked.
c.   Applied overhead.
d.   Actual overhead.

P. 9-7°
Four-Variance
Method of
Overhead Variance
Analysis

Overton Company uses the four-variance method of analyzing overhead variances. Budgeted manufacturing overhead for 1985 is $400,000, of which $250,000 is fixed overhead. The company bases its overhead rate on a normal capacity of 50,000 direct labor hours. On December 31, Overton Company had a balance of $384,000 in its Manufacturing Overhead Control account. During the year, 47,800 actual hours were worked, and standard hours for the amount of output produced were 47,000.

REQUIRED   Prepare a four-variance analysis of overhead.

P. 9-8 (AICPA)
Flexible Budgeting
and Performance
Reports

Department A is one of 15 departments in the plant and is involved in the production of all of the six products manufactured. The department is highly mechanized and as a result its output is measured in direct machine hours. Variable (flexible) budgets are utilized throughout the factory in planning and controlling costs, but here the focus is

° Problems marked with an asterisk are based on information in the appendix of this chapter.

upon the application of variable budgets only in Department A. The following data covering a time span of approximately 6 months were taken from the various budgets, accounting records, and performance reports (only representative items and amounts are utilized here):

- On March 15, 1985 the following variable budget was approved for the department; it will be used throughout the 1986 fiscal year which begins July 1, 1985. This variable budget was developed through the cooperative efforts of the department manager, his supervisor and certain staff members from the budget department.

1986 Flexible Budget — Department A

Controllable Costs	Fixed Amount per Month	Variable Rate per Direct Machine Hour
Employee salaries	$ 9,000	
Indirect wages	18,000	$.07
Indirect materials		.09
Other costs	6,000	.03
Totals	$33,000	$.19

- On May 5, 1985 the annual sales plan and the production budget were completed. In order to continue preparation of the annual profit plan (which was detailed by month) the production budget was translated to planned activity for each of the factory departments. The planned activity for Department A was:

	For the 12 Months Ending June 30, 1986				
	Year	July	Aug.	Sept.	Etc.
Planned output in direct machine hours	325,000	22,000	25,000	29,000	249,000

- On August 31, 1985 the manager of Department A was informed that his planned output for September had been revised to 34,000 direct machine hours. He expressed some doubt as to whether this volume could be attained.
- At the end of September 1985 the accounting records provided the following data for the month for the department:

Actual output in direct machine hours	33,000
Actual controllable costs incurred:	
Employee salaries	$ 9,300
Indirect wages	20,500
Indirect materials	2,850
Other costs	7,510
Total	$40,160

REQUIRED   The requirements relate primarily to the potential uses of the variable budget for the period March through September 1985.

a.   What activity base is utilized as a measure of volume in the budget for this department? How should one determine the range of the activity base to which the variable rates per direct machine hour are relevant? Explain.

b.   The high-low point method was utilized in developing this variable budget. Using indirect wage costs as an example, illustrate and explain how this method would be applied in determining the fixed and variable components of indirect wage costs for this department. Assume that the high-low budget values for indirect wages are $19,400 at 20,000 direct machine hours and $20,100 at 30,000 direct machine hours.

c.   Explain and illustrate how the variable budget should be utilized:
1.   In budgeting costs when the annual sales plan and production budget are completed (about May 5, 1985 or shortly thereafter).
2.   In budgeting a cost revision based upon a revised production budget (about August 31, 1985 or shortly thereafter).
3.   In preparing a cost performance report for September 1985.

P. 9-9°
Manufacturing
Overhead Variance
Relationships

Hyte II Manufacturing produces high-speed printers for stand-alone word processing systems. The printers require 10 direct labor hours to produce. The company uses a standard cost system to account for production costs, and overhead is applied to production at the rate of $5 per direct labor hour.

The 1985 production budget called for the manufacture and sale of 2,000 printers. Budgeted fixed overhead costs were $60,000. During 1985, 1,900 printers were actually produced. At year-end, the company's accountant computed the following overhead variances using one of the three variance methods.

Spending variance	$ 3,600 F
Efficiency variance	10,000 U
Capacity variance	3,000 U

REQUIRED   Using the above data compute:

a.   Budgeted direct labor hours.
b.   Standard direct labor hours.
c.   The amount of applied overhead.
d.   The balance in the Manufacturing Overhead Control account at the end of 1985.
e.   The actual direct labor hours worked.
f.   The amount of overhead cost that should have been incurred given the number of units produced.

P. 9-10°
Understanding
Four-Variance
Overhead
Relationships

Rafer Company manufactures control panels for hard-rock drilling machines. It takes 5 direct labor hours at standard to produce one control panel. Overhead is applied to products at the rate of $9 per direct labor hour. The variable part of the overhead rate is $5 per hour. Total fixed manufacturing overhead cost is $200,000.

The two-variance method of overhead variance analysis yields a $2,000 favorable controllable variance and a $16,000 unfavorable volume variance. The management of Rafer Company would like to have a four-variance analysis of the 1985 overhead variance, but the current company accountant is only familiar with the two-variance approach. During 1985, actual direct labor hours exceeded standard by 1,200.

° Problems marked with an asterisk are based on information in the appendix of this chapter.

REQUIRED   Using the data presented above compute:

a. The budgeted number of units to be produced.
b. The budgeted number of direct labor hours.
c. The standard direct labor hours.
d. The amount of applied overhead in 1985.
e. The amount of actual overhead in 1985.
f. The actual direct labor hours.
g. The spending, variable efficiency, fixed efficiency, and capacity variances.

P. 9-11 (AICPA)   Ross Shirts, Inc., manufactures short- and long-sleeve men's shirts for large stores.
Comprehensive   Ross produces a single quality shirt in lots to each customer's order and attaches the
Variance Analysis   store's label to each. The standard costs for a dozen long-sleeve shirts are:
Problem with
Two-Variance
Overhead Analysis

Direct materials	24 yd @ $ .55	$13.20
Direct labor	3 hr @ $2.45	7.35
Manufacturing overhead	3 hr @ $2.00	6.00
Standard cost per dozen		$26.55

During October, Ross worked on three orders for long-sleeve shirts. Job cost records for the month disclose the following:

The following information is also available:

Lot	Units in Lot	Material Used	Hours Worked
30	1,000 doz	24,100 yd	2,980
31	1,700 doz	40,440 yd	5,130
32	1,200 doz	28,825 yd	2,890

1. Ross purchased 95,000 yards of material during the month at a cost of $53,200. The materials price variance is recorded when goods are purchased, and all inventories are carried at standard cost.
2. Direct labor incurred amounted to $27,500 during October. According to payroll records, production employees were paid $2.50 per hour.
3. Overhead is applied on the basis of direct labor hours. Manufacturing overhead totaling $22,800 was incurred during October.
4. A total of $288,000 was budgeted for overhead for the year based on estimated production at the plant's normal capacity of 48,000 dozen shirts per year. Overhead is 40 percent fixed and 60 percent variable at this level of production.
5. There was no work in process at October 1. During October lots 30 and 31 were completed and all material was issued for lot 32 and it was 80 percent completed as to labor.

REQUIRED   a. Prepare a schedule computing the standard cost for October of lots 30, 31, and 32.
b. Prepare a schedule computing the materials price variance for October and indicate whether the variance is favorable or unfavorable.

c. Prepare schedules computing (and indicating whether the variances are favorable or unfavorable) for each lot produced during October the:
   1. Materials quantity variance in yards.
   2. Labor efficiency variance in hours.
   3. Labor rate variance in dollars.

d. Prepare a schedule computing the manufacturing overhead controllable and volume variances for October and indicate whether the variances are favorable or unfavorable.

CASES

Case 9-1
Flexible Budget
Analysis for a
Manufacturing
Business

Lazy-Day Company makes motor homes that sell for $24,500 each. Careful analysis of production, marketing, and distribution data indicates that direct material costs are $8,800 per unit, and direct labor costs are $4,500 per unit. Each motor home requires 450 direct labor hours. Fixed costs for the year are $80,000 for property taxes, $75,000 for insurance, $105,000 building depreciation, and $130,000 of equipment depreciation. Many costs contain both fixed and variable components. The chief accountant of Lazy-Day prepared the following flexible budget for the company's mixed costs:

Direct labor hours	80,000	100,000
Indirect material	$120,000	$140,000
Indirect labor	180,000	220,000
Maintenance	240,000	250,000
Utilities	200,000	230,000
Production supervision	270,000	275,000
Miscellaneous	110,000	125,000
Administration	440,000	450,000
Marketing and distribution	360,000	400,000

The chief executive of Lazy-Day Company believes there is $200,000 of discretionary fixed costs in the total budget that can be eliminated without loss of product quality or customer service. In addition he thinks total variable costs can be trimmed by about 10 percent.

REQUIRED

a. Prepare a schedule showing the cost behavior patterns for the mixed costs.
b. Prepare a flexible budget for Lazy-Day Company using activity levels of 200, 250, and 300 motor homes.
c. During the year, 280 motor homes were produced and sold yielding a profit of $678,000. Using the flexible budget data, determine the total variance from expected profit at that level.
d. Compute the variance as a percentage of total expected costs.
e. At the current level of expected costs, how many units must the company sell to break even?
f. Assuming the chief executive officer's cost-cutting plan can be achieved, what will be the new expected break-even level?
g. Assuming the chief executive officer's cost-cutting plan can be achieved, what would be the expected profit at production and sales of 220 units?

PART FOUR
Managerial Uses of Cost Data

The detailed cost data described in the first part of this book provide managers with information they need for making the many decisions intended to achieve organizational goals. Effective use of these cost data enable managers to operate the business efficiently. This part of the book consists of five chapters that deal specifically with the use of cost accounting data for making decisions and measuring the effectiveness of those decisions by evaluating business performance.

Chapter 10 extends the cost-volume-profit concepts in Chapter 3 to the analysis of decisions that involve alternative choices of action. The key is to determine which costs are relevant for such decisions. Chapter 11 continues the theme of using relevant costs for specific business analysis purposes, such as measuring the performance of business segments. Chapter 12 continues the concept of reporting performance of business segments by looking at product profitability reports of a company's divisions. In Chapter 13 we examine the way inventory cost data are used to manage inventories efficiently by determining when and how much inventory to order. Chapter 14 discusses the many factors, including cost data, that enter into the determination of product prices.

CHAPTER 10
Relevant Costs and Alternative Choice Decisions

A key question for accountants is, "What accounting information do managers need?" Specifically, what manufacturing cost data are needed to help managers measure efficiency, determine production priorities, and make resource allocation decisions? What marketing cost data and sales reports are needed to provide information for setting delivery schedules, determining sales priorities, and making pricing decisions? You cannot design a management accounting information system without first addressing these kinds of questions.

Chapter 1 emphasized that accounting information must be relevant to the decision or evaluation at hand. Relevance refers primarily to the usefulness of information in making decisions. Since different individuals make decisions differently, there is no universal measure of relevance for all accounting information. Many types of accounting information, however, are generally useful to managers in analyzing common business decisions such as whether to make or buy a product or whether to raise the price of a product. This chapter presents the concept of relevant costs and relates it to decision making. Some common business decisions are used to illustrate how to identify relevant costs and how to use them in decision making.

We start by defining relevant costs and then we discuss how they are used in choosing between alternative courses of action. Decisions involving two alternatives are discussed first, followed by a discussion of three-alternative decisions.

RELEVANT COSTS

All accounting information is useful at some time to one or more managers. But most accounting information systems generate so much data that managers must choose what is relevant to the decision or evaluation at hand. Typically, cost data are among the variables needed in making decisions. But, as you have learned in previous chapters, there are many different types of costs. Some costs are classified according to their behavior pattern, such as fixed or variable. Other costs are classified by function, such as manufacturing or administrative. Still others have different classifications, such as controllable and noncontrollable. Managers must learn what costs are useful in making each of the decisions their jobs require. Such costs are called **relevant costs,** because they relate to the decision or evaluation the manager is making. Most people attribute two important characteristics to relevant costs:

Characteristics of relevant costs

1. They are expected future costs.
2. They differ between decision alternatives.

Expected future costs

Expected future cost means that the cost is expected to occur during the time period covered by the decision. For instance, a sales manager developing a sales plan should consider salaries, commission rates, travel costs, and other marketing costs that are expected to occur during the period. Historical costs are relevant to the decision only if they are expected to continue into the future. Often, past costs are used in decision making, but only because they are surrogates for the actual costs that will be incurred in the immediate future.

Differ between decision alternatives

In order to be relevant, costs must differ between decision alternatives. Otherwise they have no impact on choosing between the alternatives. For example, a store manager is evaluating two types of cash registers for use in a department store. Each register can be operated by sales employees earning $5 per hour. Clearly, then, the wage rate of the employees is not a relevant cost in evaluating which cash register to use. This does not imply that the wage rate of employees is never a relevant cost, but rather that it is not relevant in deciding between these two types of cash registers. If, however, one type of cash register requires a skilled operator costing $8 per hour, then the wage rate is different between the two alternatives and this information is relevant to the decision.

Costs that differ between alternatives are called **differential costs** or **incremental costs**. The differential cost in the case mentioned above is $3 per hour ($8 per hour − $5 per hour).

ALTERNATIVE CHOICE DECISIONS

Decisions involving two or more courses of action

In many business situations there is more than one approach to achieving a goal. Many management decisions involve selecting the course of action deemed most appropriate for the situation. **Alternative choice decisions** are decisions that require the decision maker to choose between two or more courses of action. A decision involving more than two alternatives is called a **multiple-alternative decision.**

Examples of alternative choice decisions

There are many different kinds of alternative choice decisions in business. Some examples are:

1. Should the company buy its own computer or continue using a computer service company?
2. Should the company manufacture valves necessary for the production of a new line of dishwashers or should it buy them?
3. Should product prices be raised to compensate for higher manufacturing costs?
4. Should the company accept a special order for a product at a price below the normal selling price?
5. Should the old machine tool manufacturing plant be replaced with a more energy-efficient plant?

TWO-ALTERNATIVE DECISIONS

Many business decisions are two-alternative decisions. For example, a manager evaluating the purchase of one of two different copying machines is making a two-alternative decision. Many decisions are so routine that we do not notice that they are two-alternative decisions. For instance, a quality control supervisor evaluates a variety of data to decide whether the system is in control or should be adjusted. One of the alternatives is to do nothing; the other is to adjust the system. Many business decisions include the alternative to maintain the current situation and take no action.

To illustrate several important concepts in analyzing alternative choice decisions, we use an example of a new company that plans to manufacture ornate ceramic planters. The Earthen Company is evaluating two methods of manufacturing the planters. One method is primarily manual, with only a small amount of leased equipment necessary. The other production method is significantly more automated and requires leasing a large automated baking kiln and several other pieces of equipment. Both production methods require the same size and quality of manufacturing facility, and each will yield an identical product that will sell for $10 each. Figure 10-1 presents the fixed and variable costs for each of the two possible production methods.

Figure 10-1. Estimated fixed and variable cost data for the production of planters using each of the two production methods being evaluated.

Earthen Company
Expected Production Costs for Planters
Two Alternate Production Methods

	Manual	Automated	Differential
Fixed costs:			
Occupancy costs	$ 6,000	$ 6,000	—
Equipment lease	8,000	32,000	$24,000
Insurance and taxes	1,000	7,000	6,000
Total	$15,000	$45,000	$30,000
Variable costs:			
Labor	$3.00/unit	$2.00/unit	$1.00/unit
Material	2.00	1.50	.50
Others	1.00	.50	.50
Total	$6.00/unit	$4.00/unit	$2.00/unit

Notice that all of the costs listed in Figure 10-1 are expected future costs associated with the manufacture of the planters. However, not all of the costs are differential costs. That is, not all of the costs make a difference in deciding between the two production methods. For example, the occupancy costs are the same for both alternatives. Since the occupancy cost is identical for each method, it is not a relevant cost in choosing between the two alternatives under consideration. However, this occupancy cost may be useful for some other decisions and evaluations that a manager may make. Clearly, the fixed cost of the automated method is much higher than the fixed cost of the manual method. But the variable costs are higher with the manual method. With this trade-off between fixed and variable costs, which of the two alternatives should management choose?

If the decision is based solely on profit, management will select the method that yields the higher net income. But which method is that? Some simple calculations at different sales levels can provide some answers. If Earthen Company makes 7,000 units and sells them for $10 each, it will generate $13,000 of income with the manual method and a $3,000 loss with the automated production method, determined as follows:

Comparative income measures

	Manual		Automated
Sales (7,000 units × $10)	$70,000		$70,000
Less fixed costs	(15,000)		(45,000)
Variable costs ($6 × 7,000)	(42,000)	($4 × 7,000)	(28,000)
Income (loss)	$13,000		$(3,000)

Now let us assume 17,000 units are produced and sold. The results are as follows:

	Manual		Automated
Sales (17,000 units × 10)	$170,000		$170,000
Less fixed costs	(15,000)		(45,000)
Variable costs ($6 × 17,000)	(102,000)	($4 × 17,000)	(68,000)
Income	$ 53,000		$ 57,000

Merely comparing the results of the computations indicates that the manual method is more profitable at 7,000 units, but the automated method yields a larger profit at 17,000 units. Although this analysis indicates which method of production should be used for these two levels of activity, it does not provide a general solution to the decision of selecting the appropriate manufacturing method for all activity levels. This is accomplished by computing the cost indifference point.

The Cost Indifference Point

A general solution approach to two alternative decisions

A general solution to selecting the appropriate production method for all levels of activity is possible by using the relevant costs. The manual production method has lower fixed costs but higher variable costs than the automated method. Eventually, the lower fixed costs of the manual method are more than offset by its higher variable costs. The key question is, "At what activity level does the lower fixed cost of the manual method exactly offset the higher variable cost of that method?" This activity level is called the **cost indifference point.** It is the activity level at which the total cost is identical for the two alternatives. The cost indifference point is computed easily by setting the cost formulas for the two production methods equal to each other, as shown below:

The activity level at which the total cost is identical for the two alternatives

Total cost of manual method = Total cost of automated method

Total fixed cost of manual method + Total variable cost of manual method = Total fixed cost of automated method + Total variable cost of automated method

$$\$15,000 + \$6X = \$45,000 + \$4X$$

$$\$2X = \$30,000$$

$$X = 15,000 \text{ units}$$

The cost indifference point in this example is 15,000 units. That means that at 15,000 units, the two methods have identical total costs, produce identical sales revenue, and yield identical profits. Therefore, from a profit point of view alone, the manager is indifferent between the two production methods at 15,000 units of activity. Of course many other factors besides profit may enter into the decision. However, often the cost indifference point is an important element in the decision process.

It is easy to verify the cost indifference point merely by computing profit for each production method at the cost indifference point and for activity levels just above and just below the indifference point. Figure 10-2 presents revenue and cost data for the cost indifference point and at activity levels just above and below it.

Figure 10-2. Estimated net income is computed for each of the production methods at three levels of activity: the cost indifference point and activity levels just above and just below the cost indifference point. The data show that our interpretation of the production strategy is correct.

Earthen Company
Expected Production Costs for Planters
Several Activity Levels

	Manual Production Method		
Activity level in units	14,900	15,000	15,100
Sales	$149,000	$150,000	$151,000
Less fixed costs	(15,000)	(15,000)	(15,000)
Variable costs	(89,400)	(90,000)	(90,600)
Profit	$ 44,600	$ 45,000	$ 45,400

	Automated Production Method		
Activity level in units	14,900	15,000	15,100
Sales	$149,000	$150,000	$151,000
Less fixed costs	(45,000)	(45,000)	(45,000)
Variable costs	(59,600)	(60,000)	60,400)
Profit	$ 44,400	$ 45,000	$ 45,600

As expected, at the cost indifference activity level of 15,000 units the two production methods yield identical net incomes. At activity levels below the cost indifference point, the lower fixed cost of the manual method makes it the more profitable alternative, and above the cost indifference point, the automatic system is more profitable. Notice that the amount of revenue is identical for either production method at any given level of activity. The difference in profit is caused by the difference in the cost of each of the alternatives at each activity level, because the two alternatives have different cost functions. Therefore, the concept of cost indifference points can be used by all types of organizations whether they are profit-seeking or not. Universities, government organizations, and other not-for-profit organizations can use cost indifference points in analyzing alternative choice decisions.

The cost indifference point can be computed using the differential costs of the two alternatives. The computation is as follows:

Cost indifference point calculated using differential costs

$$\text{Cost indifference point} = \frac{\text{Differential fixed costs}}{\text{Differential variable costs}}$$

$$= \frac{\$45,000 - \$15,000}{\$6 \text{ per unit} - \$4 \text{ per unit}}$$

$$= \frac{\$30,000}{\$2 \text{ per unit}}$$

$$= 15,000 \text{ units}$$

Graphic Analysis. A graphic presentation of the cost indifference point is shown in Figure 10-3. The fixed and total cost lines are shown for both the manual and automated methods. Because of the higher fixed cost for the automated method, its total cost line starts much higher than the total cost line for the manual method. However, the lower variable cost of the automated method eventually offsets the higher fixed cost at the cost indifference point of 15,000. This graph illustrates an important assumption necessary when using cost indifference points. The analysis assumes a linear relationship between the costs and the activity levels. Of course, the relevant range concept discussed in Chapter 3 in connection with cost behavior patterns is also important. If the analysis incorporates activity levels beyond the relevant range, the results should be viewed with caution.

It is easy to see cost indifference points with graphs

Figure 10-3 illustrates a graphic solution to finding the cost indifference point utilizing total cost data for the two alternatives. A similar graphic analysis is possible using the differential fixed and differential variable costs, as shown in Figure 10-4.

The differential fixed cost is $30,000 ($45,000 − $15,000). The differential variable cost is $2 per unit ($6 − $4). The indifference point occurs where the differential fixed cost is equal to the total differential variable cost. Either the total cost approach or the differential cost approach yields the same answer.

Break-Even Point and Cost Indifference Point Compared

The cost behavior concepts discussed in Chapter 3 are essential in understanding the analysis of cost indifference points. Both break-even analysis and indifference point analysis draw heavily on the relationship between fixed and variable costs, but the two analyses address different issues. Break-even analysis determines the level of activity at which total costs equal total

Figure 10-3. This graph shows that the lower fixed cost of the manual production method eventually is offset by its higher variable cost. Therefore, at activity levels above the cost indifference point of 15,000 units, the automated method has a lower total production cost.

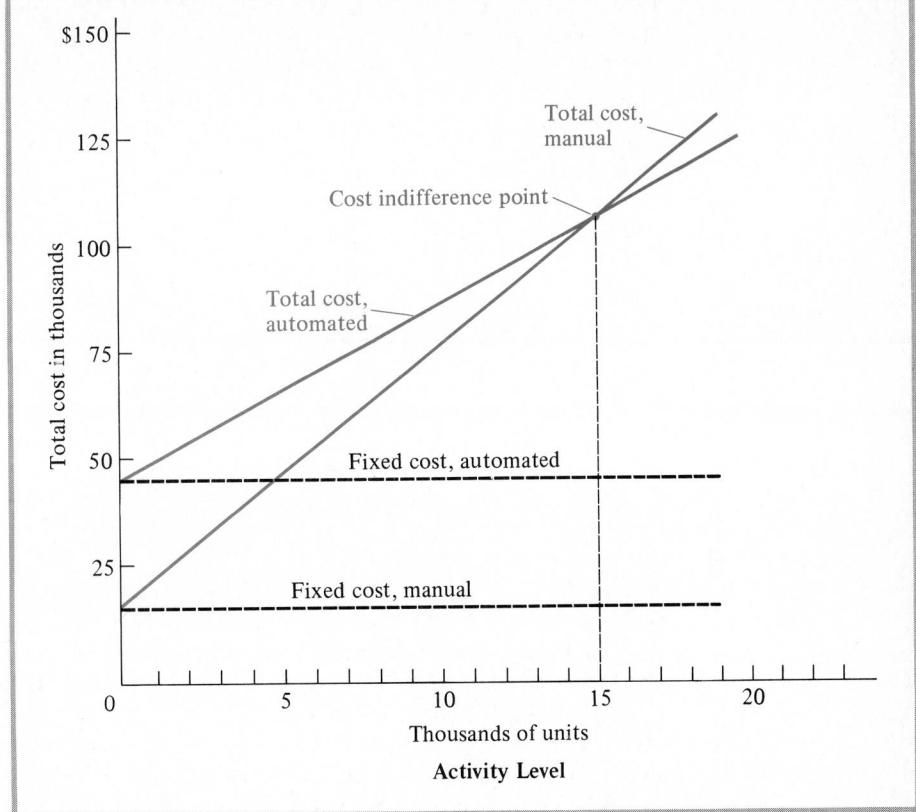

Figure 10-4. Using differential costs instead of total costs, we see that the difference in fixed costs is eventually offset by the difference in variable costs. As before, the trade-off between fixed and variable costs cancels at 15,000 units, which is the cost indifference point.

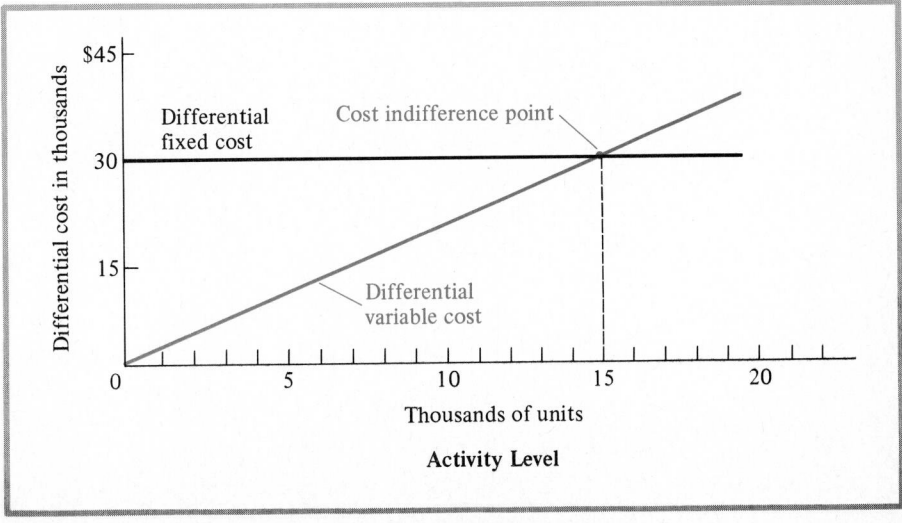

revenue for a particular production and sales alternative. Cost indifference point analysis identifies the activity level at which the total costs of two alternatives are equal. In the Earthen Company example, there is one cost indifference point and two break-even points, one for each of the production alternatives. The break-even points are computed as follows:

$$\text{Selling price} \times \text{Units} = \text{Fixed costs} + \text{Variable cost} \times \text{Units}$$

Break-even, manual method:

$$\$10X = \$15,000 + \$6X$$
$$\$4X = \$15,000$$
$$X = 3,750 \text{ units}$$

Break-even, automated method:

$$\$10X = \$45,000 + \$4X$$
$$\$6X = \$45,000$$
$$X = 7,500 \text{ units}$$

The two break-even points and the cost indifference point are graphed in Figure 10-5. The graph shows clearly that each break-even point is determined by the intersection of the **total revenue line** and **one of the total cost lines.** The indifference point is determined by the intersection of the **two total cost lines.** The two analyses provide different but complementary information. The cost indifference point indicates that at activity levels higher than 15,000 units, such as 16,000 units, the automated method should be used. But this production method has a higher break-even point and a lower margin of safety ratio than the manual method, as shown by the calculations below.

$$\text{Margin of safety ratio} = \frac{\text{Actual sales} - \text{Break-even sales}}{\text{Actual sales}}$$

Margin of safety, manual method:

$$\text{Margin of safety} = \frac{16,000 \text{ units} - 3,750 \text{ units}}{16,000 \text{ units}}$$
$$= \frac{12,250 \text{ units}}{16,000 \text{ units}}$$
$$= .766$$

Margin of safety, automated method:

$$\text{Margin of safety} = \frac{16,000 \text{ units} - 7,500 \text{ units}}{16,000 \text{ units}}$$
$$= \frac{8,500 \text{ units}}{16,000 \text{ units}}$$
$$= .531$$

Figure 10-5. This figure is similar to Figure 10-3 except that we have added the revenue line, which allows us to find the break-even point for both the manual and the automated production methods. The graph shows the relationship of the cost indifference point and the break-even points.

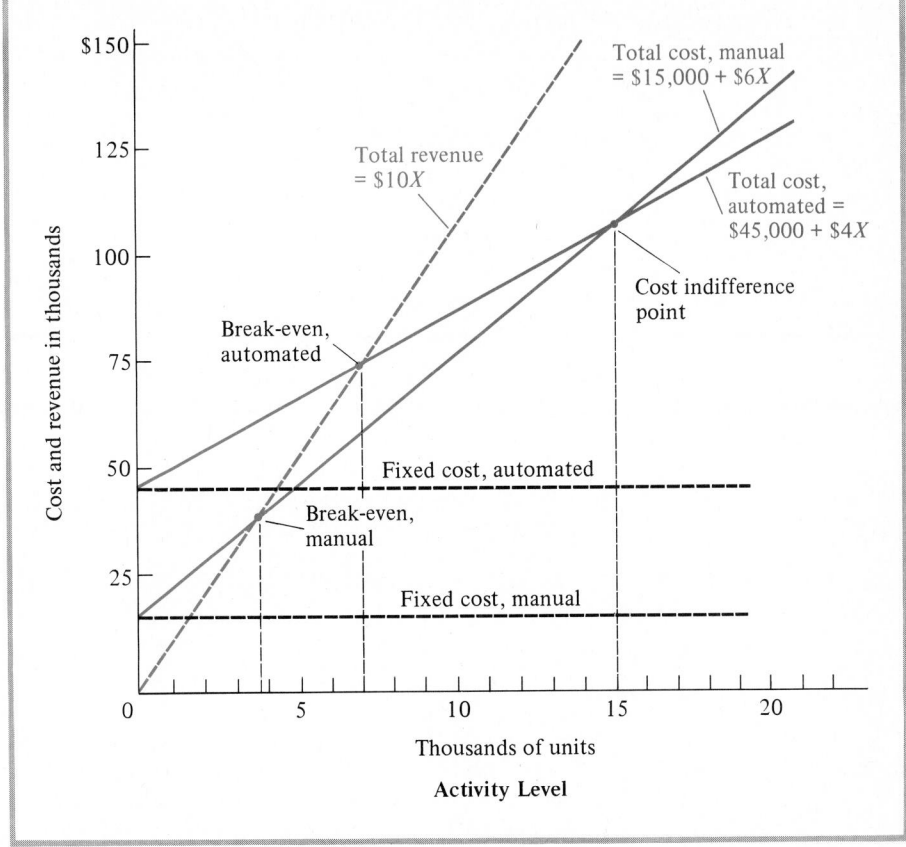

The manager must decide whether the higher profit provided by the automated method warrants the higher risk implied by the method's break-even point and margin of safety. Cost data seldom provide managers with a clear-cut decision. Instead, cost data must be assimilated with other relevant information to reach the best possible decision.

USING RELEVANT COSTS

Relevant costs and cost indifference point analysis can be applied effectively to many types of alternative choice decisions, such as choosing between alternative marketing programs, determining whether to manufacture a part or buy it, and selecting the best production method for a new product.

Managers may use special orders to utilize excess capacity or take advantage of special situations

Special Order Decisions

The dynamic nature of business makes management a challenging experience. Each business opportunity must be evaluated on its own merit in light of its special characteristics. For example, special orders, or one-time orders, typically are evaluated differently than recurring orders. Special orders are evaluated on the basis of costs relevant to the specific situation and the goals and objectives of the company.

To illustrate, the Blu-Sky Canoe Company manufactures white-water canoes and other types of canoes. The company is operating at about 70 percent of capacity. High interest rates and a sluggish economy have caused sales to lag somewhat from expected levels. A national organization of youth camps offers to buy one hundred 17-foot shallow draft canoes at $450 each for use in its camps around the country. The normal price of the canoes is $600 each. The marketing manager for the canoe company asks the accountant to prepare cost data for the proposed order. The following cost estimates are provided:

	Total Cost	Unit Cost
Direct materials	$25,000	$250
Direct labor	9,000	90
MOH (70% is allocated fixed MOH)	10,000	100
Selling and administrative (40% fixed)	7,000	70
Totals	$51,000	$510

Identifying Relevant Costs. It appears from the cost data that the special order should not be accepted. The offered price is $450 per canoe and the estimated unit cost to produce and distribute is $510. It looks as if the order would result in a loss of $60 per canoe, or a total of $6,000.

But in this example 70 percent of the manufacturing overhead cost is fixed and 40 percent of the selling and administrative cost is fixed. These fixed costs will occur whether or not the special order is accepted. Plant and equipment depreciation, insurance, property taxes, and some basic maintenance functions are some examples of costs that in large part exist whether or not the special order is accepted. Therefore, allocating a portion of these costs to the special order may cloud the analysis of the decision.

Because the fixed costs are identical for both alternatives, they are not relevant to the decision. The decision to accept or reject the special order should rest only on relevant costs. A more logical method of analyzing this special order decision is to include only the differential costs and differential revenues in the analysis, as follows:

Differential revenue (100 canoes @ $450)		$45,000
Differential costs:		
Direct materials	$25,000	
Direct labor	9,000	
Variable MOH (30% of $10,000)	3,000	
Variable selling and admin. (60% of $7,000)	4,200	41,200
Addition to the company's profit		$ 3,800

The differential costs used in the analysis are direct materials, direct labor, and the **variable** portion of overhead and **variable** selling and administrative costs. The amount of differential overhead costs is only 30 percent of the total overhead cost, and the amount of differential selling and administrative costs is 60 percent of that cost.

Using differential costs and differential revenue in the special order analysis shows a net increase in profit of $3,800, or $38 per canoe. Therefore, the relevant cost and revenue data suggest the order should be accepted.

Other Factors in Special Order Decisions.   In the above example, the company has enough excess capacity to produce the units for the special order. If the production or distribution capacity is not available, additional fixed costs may have to be incurred to satisfy the requirements of the special order. In that situation, the additional fixed costs would be differential costs and would be relevant in the analysis.

Factors other than profit or cost may enter into a decision

Factors other than profit may influence the decision. Cost data and accounting information are only part of the information managers use in reaching intelligent, informed decisions. Sometimes special order decisions are particularly sensitive. For example, if regular customers learn that some other customers are buying products for less than normal prices, the regular customers may demand the same price or buy elsewhere. Also, a special order customer may attempt to become a regular customer and expect the special price to continue. In addition to customer attitude problems, the Robinson-Patman Act serves as another barrier to special order pricing. This law prohibits price differentiation among customers unless the price differences can be justified by differences in the cost of producing or distributing the product.

Make-Buy Decisions

A common business decision is a make-buy decision, in which a manager chooses between buying an item and manufacturing it. Sometimes the item is a part used in the production of a larger or more complete product. For instance, automobile manufacturers may buy windshields for the cars they produce or they may manufacture the windshields themselves. Make-buy decisions are not limited to tangible items like windshields. Often managers must evaluate the best way of designing a new manufacturing plant or providing computer services for the company. Personnel of the firm may perform the work, or the services may be purchased from outside consultants. Regardless of the type of product or service involved in the make-buy decision, relevant costs are essential in the analysis.

To illustrate, Typomatic, Ltd., manufactures word processing systems. An essential element of the system is the printer. The management of Typomatic must decide whether to buy the printers it supplies as part of its word processing system or to manufacture them. The company expects to need 4,000 printers during the coming year. Typomatic sells the printers to its customers for $5,000 each. The company can buy the printers from a reliable supplier for $4,000 each. Typomatic has just built a new plant and has enough excess capacity to produce the printers in its manufacturing facilities. Estimated cost data for producing the printers are shown in Figure 10-6.

Figure 10-6. The total production cost of making the printers for the word processing systems. This is the traditional full-cost way of measuring the cost of manufacturing a product.

Typomatic, Ltd.
Estimated Costs to Produce Printers

	Units	Unit Cost	Total Cost
Direct materials	4,000	$1,400	$ 5,600,000
Direct labor	4,000	1,200	4,800,000
Variable MOH	4,000	600	2,400,000
Direct fixed cost	4,000	400	1,600,000
Allocated fixed MOH	4,000	800	3,200,000
Totals		$4,400	$17,600,000

Analysis of the Data. A glance at the data indicates the printers should be purchased. After all, the purchase cost is $4,000 per unit, and the cost to manufacture is $4,400 per unit. However, not all of the costs identified in the schedule of estimated costs are relevant to this make-buy decision. All of the variable costs are relevant because they will not occur if the printers are purchased. The direct fixed costs are for lease and depreciation costs on equipment that will need to be acquired if Typomatic manufactures the printers. Therefore, these costs are also relevant to the make-buy decision. However, the allocated fixed overhead costs are not relevant. The company will incur these costs whether or not it manufactures the printers. Such costs are called **sunk costs** because they have already been incurred and cannot be changed in the short run. In this case they are primarily capacity costs—the costs of providing the production facilities. As noted earlier, Typomatic currently has some excess capacity. If Typomatic buys the printers, the fixed overhead costs that would have been allocated to the printers will be absorbed by the other products the company produces.

Sunk costs have already been incurred and cannot be changed in the short run

Eliminating the allocated fixed overhead costs from the analysis leaves relevant unit costs of $3,600.

$$\text{Unit manufacturing cost after eliminating allocated fixed MOH} = \frac{\$17,600,000 - \$3,200,000}{4,000 \text{ units}}$$

$$= \$3,600 \text{ per unit}$$

Comparing this amount with the $4,000 purchase cost indicates that the units should be manufactured. By doing so the company can save $400 per printer, or an estimated $1,600,000 for the year ($400 per unit × 4,000 units).

Not all production capacity costs can be evaluated in the same way. In the analysis above, capacity costs are ignored in the make-buy analysis, because they are not differential between the two alternatives. The costs exist for both alternatives. If, however, there is an alternative use for the space, then these costs should be included in the analysis. Let us assume, for example, that Typomatic can lease the excess space to another company and that the rental income and reduction in costs associated with the space would result in a cost saving of $2,200,000. If Typomatic manufactures the printers, it cannot also rent the space. Therefore, it would lose the revenue and cost savings of $2,200,000. This is the opportunity cost of using the space to make printers when the space could also be rented. **Opportunity cost** is the benefit given up by rejecting one alternative and accepting another. It is the benefit given up of the best alternative not selected.

Opportunity costs are relevant in making decisions

Given the opportunity cost of the space, the printers should be purchased. The analysis in Figure 10-7 shows that the relevant cost in the production of the printers is $4,150 per unit. Therefore, the company would earn $600,000 more by purchasing the printers.

Figure 10-7. If there is an alternate use for the production facilities, the value of the alternate use should be incorporated in the analysis of the make-buy decision.

Typomatic, Ltd.
Estimated Costs to Produce Printers

	Units	Unit Cost	Total Cost
Direct materials	4,000	$1,400	$ 5,600,000
Direct labor	4,000	1,200	4,800,000
Variable MOH	4,000	600	2,400,000
Direct fixed cost	4,000	400	1,600,000
Opportunity cost for production space	4,000	550	2,200,000
Totals		$4,150	$16,600,000

Pricing Decisions

A very interesting alternative choice decision is pricing. Virtually all organizations have to establish prices for new products or services and revise prices of current products or services. Even not-for-profit organizations often must make pricing decisions. For example, universities must periodically reevaluate tuition rates, dormitory fees, and other university-related fees. Likewise, state parks and other governmental units may charge for the use of facilities such as swimming pools and tennis courts or for services such as swimming lessons or golf course fees. But the most frequent pricing decisions are made by managers in profit-seeking businesses. With inflation, changing economic conditions, competitor pressures, and other factors, many business managers find pricing decisions to be among the most important they make. Pricing decisions are so interesting and important that we devote all of Chapter 14 to them. Here we introduce relevant accounting information as it relates to pricing.

Many types of organizations must make pricing decisions

Pricing decisions are fascinating because they involve so many factors, some of which are not accounting variables, but which eventually affect accounting measurements. For example, how customer buying habits change after a price increase is not an accounting variable, but the accountant measures the results in the form of sales and profit.

Typically, a decision to change a price has an impact on the number of units sold, the total sales revenue for the product, and the profitability of the product. Managers attempt to increase the profitability of a product by raising its price, although the price increase may cause sales volume to decline. Sometimes a firm changes its prices to respond to a competitor's price change. Whatever the reason for changing prices, managers are concerned about the effect of the change on sales and profitability.

The effect on demand of changing prices

In spite of the many economic models available for evaluating pricing decisions, it is difficult to predict the precise impact of a pricing change. As a general rule, a price increase causes a decline in the number of units of product demanded; a price decrease has just the opposite effect. If the increase in price and the decrease in demand result in an increase in total revenue, the demand for the product is said to be **inelastic.** If an increase in price and decrease in the units demanded result in a decrease in the total revenue, demand for the product is said to be **elastic.** The degree of **demand elasticity** is an important consideration in pricing decisions. For example, cigarettes, liquor, and food products are generally considered demand inelastic. When coffee and sugar prices rose dramatically, consumers still used about the same amount of each product. Often state or federal governments will levy taxes on tobacco or liquor products because customers consume about the same amount of the products even if the price increases. Such consumer behavior makes it easy for the taxing authority to determine the amount of tax that will be collected, and the tax does not reduce significantly suppliers' profits by decreasing demand.

A problem with pricing is that it is difficult to measure, or in some cases even estimate, the demand elasticity of many products. Managers need some useful guidelines to help them with pricing decisions. Often it is difficult to estimate the impact on sales of raising the price of products such as television sets from $520 to $575. One aid in making pricing decisions is the price indifference point.

Price Indifference Point.   The **price indifference point** is the level of sales with the new selling price that provides the identical profit achieved with the old selling price and old unit sales volume. In other words, if a company was selling 5,000 units of a product at $8 per unit and earning a $12,000 profit, how many units would the company have to sell at the new price of $10 per unit to earn that same $12,000 profit?

Price indifference point defined

The Country Products Company is used to illustrate the computation and use of price indifference points. The company sells redwood mixing bowls at a

Figure 10-8.   A condensed income statement for the Country Products Company.

Country Products Company
Income Statement
For the Year Ended December 31, 1985

Sales	12,000 units @ $12	$144,000
Less variable costs	12,000 units @ $8	96,000
Fixed costs		30,000
Net income		$ 18,000

current price of $12. Figure 10-8 presents a condensed income statement for the year just completed.

The company is contemplating raising the price to $14 per bowl, which the marketing manager believes is more in line with competitor prices. There is some disagreement on the precise impact of the proposed higher price. Management is willing to increase the price if profit will not decline from the 1985 level. The question is, how much can unit sales decline without profits falling below the 1985 level? The solution is found by utilizing cost-volume-profit concepts presented in Chapter 3. Essentially, the problem is to achieve a target profit with the proposed selling price, when the target profit is the same as profit with the current price.

Price indifference point:

$$(\text{New selling price})(\text{Units sold}) = \begin{array}{l} (\text{Variable cost})(\text{Units sold}) \\ + \text{Fixed costs} + \text{Profit at the} \\ \text{old price and volume} \end{array}$$

$$\$14X = \$8X + \$30{,}000 + \$18{,}000$$
$$\$6X = \$48{,}000$$
$$X = 8{,}000 \text{ units}$$

To verify that at the new price the firm will earn $18,000 of income, we prepare an income statement at the price indifference point of 8,000 units.

Revenue	8,000 units @ $14 per unit	$112,000
Less variable cost	8,000 units @ $8 per unit	(64,000)
Fixed cost		(30,000)
Net income		$ 18,000

Interpreting Price Indifference Points. The price indifference point of 8,000 units in this illustration means that with the new price of $14 per unit, sales can fall from the current level of 12,000 units all the way to 8,000 units and the company will still earn as much profit as with the current $12 price and 12,000 unit of sales. At sales above the price indifference point, the company will earn more than $18,000.

Should the price be changed?

This kind of pricing information often is very helpful. It may be difficult to determine the exact impact of the $2 increase in the price of the wood bowls, but it may be relatively easy to say that sales will not decline to 8,000 units. Usually it is easier to evaluate a range of activity than to make a precise estimate of the change in activity expected from a price change. Of course, managers utilize information other than the price indifference point and evaluate many variables in making pricing decisions. Competitor actions, government regulations, public image, and other factors may be important.

Graphic Analysis of Pricing Decisions. As with other analyses discussed in this chapter, it may be useful to look at a graphic analysis of the price

Figure 10-9.
Graphic analysis of the price indifference point. The higher contribution margin with the new price allows the firm to earn the target net income with fewer units sold. However, some former customers may no longer buy the product. The trade-off is whether the benefit of the higher price will be more than offset by the lower number of units sold.

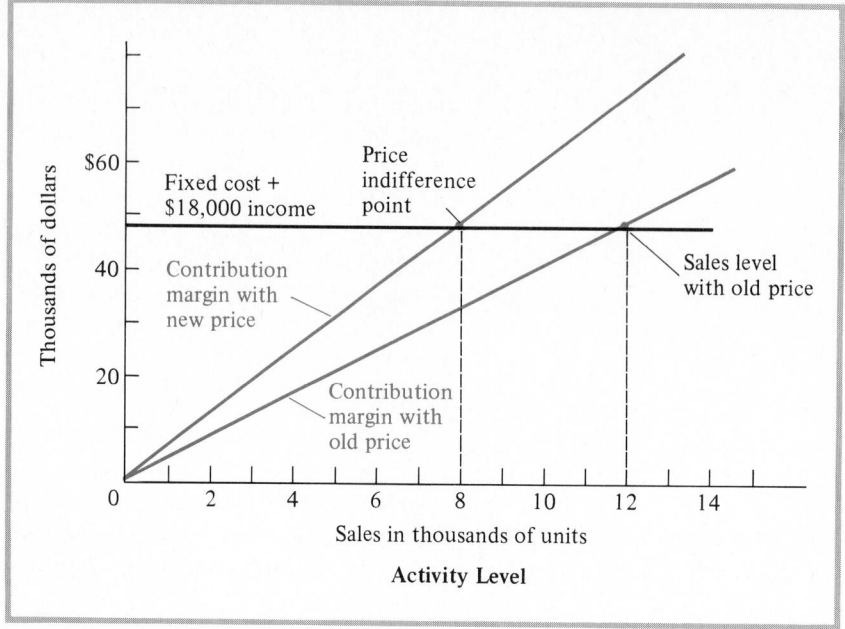

indifference point. The horizontal line in Figure 10-9 is the fixed cost plus the profit at the current price and sales level. The lower sloped line is the contribution margin with the old price. It starts at the origin of the graph and slopes up and to the right at the rate of $4 per bowl, which is the original selling price of $12 minus the variable cost of $8. The steeper-sloped line is the contribution margin with the new price. It starts at the origin and slopes up at the rate of $6 per bowl, the new price of $14 minus the variable cost of $8.

The old contribution margin line crosses the fixed cost and profit line at 12,000 units of sales. The new contribution margin line crosses the fixed cost and profit line at a lower activity level because each sale contributes more toward covering fixed costs and achieving a desired level of profit.

The price indifference point does not yield an obvious pricing decision. Instead it gives managers additional data to assist in the pricing decision. Also, the pricing decision has no impact on a cost indifference point. If we were evaluating a price change for a production situation with two alternative methods of production, the pricing decision would be made independently of the decision of what production method to use. Since the pricing decision does not impact on the cost, it does not affect the cost indifference point.

MULTIPLE-ALTERNATIVE DECISIONS

Multiple-alternative decision analysis involves more than two alternatives

Often managers are faced with a decision that involves evaluating many alternatives. For instance, a company evaluating the purchase of a new computer system may have 10 or more different computer systems to evaluate in making the selection. Each system may have somewhat different capabilities, different purchase costs, different operating costs, and other differences that are evaluated in making the decision.

Multiple alternatives complicate the decision process. The decision maker must accumulate more information, making the computations, analyses, and interpretation of the relevant information more complex.

Information overload means all information cannot be assimilated

How does a manager evaluate a large number of decision alternatives? Often managers attempt to simplify multiple-alternative decisions by systematically eliminating alternatives until only the two or three best alternatives remain. To begin, the manager eliminates all alternatives that are clearly inferior. After the number of alternatives has been reduced, then relevant information should be gathered for those remaining to be evaluated in the final analysis.

Analyzing Costs with Multiple Alternatives

The cost analysis for multiple alternatives is very similar to that of two-alternative decisions. Cost indifference points and break-even points can be computed, and a variety of other cost-volume-profit analyses can be made. However, the amount of cost analysis in the evaluation and the complexity of the analysis is typically much greater with multiple alternatives.

The cost analysis is more complex with multiple alternatives

Most likely, there is more than one cost indifference point with multiple alternatives. Remember that the cost indifference point is defined as the activity level where the total costs of **two** alternatives are identical. With multiple alternatives costs are compared for **each pair** of alternatives in the set of multiple alternatives.

The analysis of multiple alternatives is illustrated with the example of the Quik-Kopy Company, a copying service that is evaluating three new copying machines for use in its business. Each of the copying machine alternatives has different characteristics and different costs. Data for the alternatives are presented in Figure 10-10.

Figure 10-10. Fixed and variable costs are presented for each of the three alternatives. The cost indifference points are computed by comparing costs for each **pair** of alternatives.

Quik-Kopy Company
Cost Analysis of Three Copying Machines

	Alternatives		
	A	B	C
	Normal Copy	Fast Copy	Lightning Copy
Monthly fixed costs:			
Equipment lease	$ 500	$ 900	$1,600
Maintenance contract	200	400	600
Building lease	500	500	500
Other occupancy costs	300	300	300
Total	$1,500	$2,100	$3,000
Variable costs per 1,000 copies:			
Contract cost	$25	$20	$10
Labor	20	15	5
Supplies	20	10	10
Total	$65	$45	$25

Each machine can be leased at a monthly charge plus a charge for the number of copies made during the month. Also, each machine requires a maintenance agreement that covers all labor and materials associated with machine breakdowns or necessary adjustments. The difference in labor costs per copy results from the different copying speeds of the machines.

The computation of the cost indifference point for any pair of alternatives is identical to the procedure described earlier in the chapter, only here we must identify which two alternatives are to be compared. For instance, the cost indifference point for alternatives A and B is computed as follows:

AB cost indifference point:

$$\text{Total cost of } A = \text{Total cost of } B$$
$$\$1,500 + \$65X = \$2,100 + \$45X$$
$$\$20X = \$600$$
$$X = 30, \text{ or } 30,000 \text{ copies}$$

This cost indifference point provides managers with the same kind of information obtained in the two-alternative analysis. That is, 30,000 copies is the activity level at which the total cost of copying is the same for both alternative A (Normal Copy) and alternative B (Fast Copy). In this case, however, there are two other cost indifference points: the AC cost indifference point and the BC cost indifference point. Each provides similar information. Each cost indifference point is the activity level at which the cost is identical for the two alternatives being evaluated. For this illustration the AC and BC cost indifference points are:

AC cost indifference point:

$$\text{Total cost of } A = \text{Total cost of } C$$
$$\$1,500 + \$65X = \$3,000 + \$25X$$
$$\$40X = \$1,500$$
$$X = 37.5, \text{ or } 37,500 \text{ copies}$$

BC cost indifference point:

$$\text{Total cost of } B = \text{Total cost of } C$$
$$\$2,100 + \$45X = \$3,000 + \$25X$$
$$\$20X = \$900$$
$$X = 45, \text{ or } 45,000 \text{ copies}$$

Interpreting the Cost Indifference Points.   Having computed the three cost indifference points, we need to remind ourselves of the definition of cost indifference points to help us understand how they are used in the cost analysis of **three-alternative decisions.** In the two-alternative analysis, it is easy to see that at activity levels below the cost indifference point, the alternative with the lower fixed cost and higher variable cost yields the lower total cost; just the reverse is true for activity levels above the cost indifference point. But how should three cost indifference points be used in the analysis? Each cost indifference point must be analyzed and the appropriate course of action identified. After the three cost indifference points are computed, it is possible to develop a plan for selecting the best alternative for all levels of activity. Again, we note that the selection based on cost indifference points is based solely on costs. Other variables may play a key role in the final decision analysis. In the copying company example, the cost indifference point comparisons and courses of action are:

The set of cost indifference points must be interpreted together

    AB indifference point:
      0 to 30,000 copies use *A* and above 30,000 copies use *B*

    AC indifference point:
      0 to 37,500 copies use *A* and above 37,500 copies use *C*

    BC indifference point:
      0 to 45,000 copies use *B* and above 45,000 copies use *C*

Because of its low fixed cost, method *A* is preferred to either *B* or *C* at low volumes of activity. A different copying machine is chosen at 30,000 copies when compared with *B* and at 37,500 copies when compared with *C*. Since the switch to *B* is made at a lower activity level than *C*, management should select copying method *B* above 30,000 units. The next activity level encountered in our computations of cost indifference points is 37,500, but that is the *AC* cost indifference point, and above 30,000 copies the company would not use *A* but *B*. Therefore the appropriate comparison is the *BC* cost indifference point, which is 45,000 copies. The decision is to use *B* below 45,000 copies and *C* above 45,000 copies. In effect, the *AC* cost indifference point of 37,500 copies is irrelevant, because at that level of activity the company should use machine *B*. Therefore, the comparison of *A* with *C* is not appropriate. Instead, machine *B* should be compared with machine *C*. Combining the analysis just described, we have the following:

    0 to 30,000 copies use copying machine *A*
    30,000 to 45,000 copies use copying machine *B*
    Above 45,000 copies use copying machine *C*

The analysis process is really quite simple: Select the alternative that provides the lowest total cost for all levels of activity. The strategy described above does **not** identify the appropriate decision for the company. It merely describes the most cost-effective course of action at various levels of activity. The managers of Quik-Kopy Company must determine the expected level of activity and make their decision accordingly.

The objective is to minimize costs at all levels of activity

Graphic Analysis of Multiple Alternatives. Graphic analysis is especially helpful in understanding the cost relationships of multiple alternatives. Figure 10-11 shows the cost data and cost indifference points for the copying machine example. The total cost line of each alternative is presented and each cost indifference point is identified. Remember that the strategy is to choose the alternative that provides the lowest total cost at each level of activity. The lowest cost for all levels of activity is identified with a colored line. It starts at zero copies with method A because A has the lowest fixed cost and therefore the lowest total cost at low levels of activity. The lowest cost alternative is the total cost line for method A until we reach the AB cost indifference point. Above this level of 30,000 copies, method B becomes the lowest cost alternative, and the green line follows the total cost line of alternative B. When the BC indifference point is reached at 45,000 copies, C becomes the lowest cost alternative. Notice that the decision path follows the lowest possible cost at all

Figure 10-11. The dark green line shows the lowest cost alternative at all levels of activity in the relevant range. The intersection of any two total cost lines is one of the cost indifference points. The AC cost indifference point is not relevant to the decision, because alternative B is already in use before the AC indifference point is encountered.

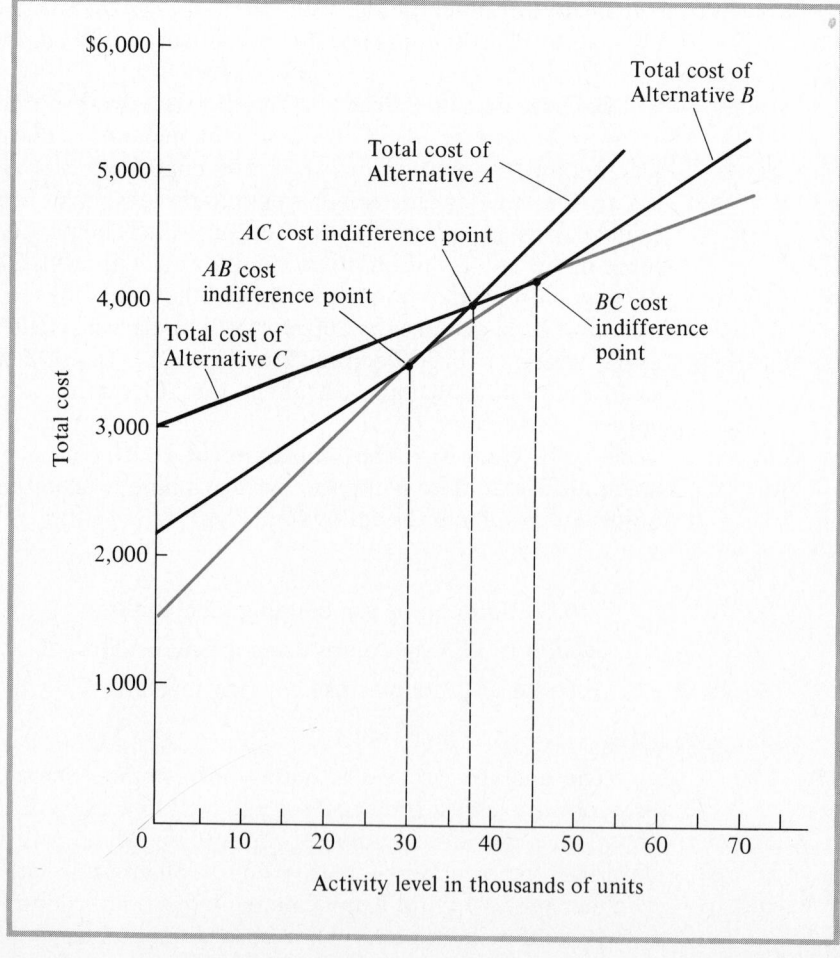

levels of activity and that the *AC* cost indifference point does not fall on the decision path and is therefore not relevant to the decision.

The preceding example illustrates the cost analysis of a three-alternative decision. Of course, more than three alternatives may be evaluated. The analysis process is similar except that the complexity grows rapidly. For example, it is possible to have six cost indifference points with four alternatives and ten indifference points with five alternatives. The possible number of separate cost indifference points for multiple alternatives is $n(n-1)/2$ where n equals the number of alternatives.

SUMMARY   **Alternative choice decisions** are decisions in which a person or organization must choose between two or more courses of action. An important part of the decision-making process is the selection of relevant information. Many kinds of information may be useful in reaching an appropriate decision, but nearly always some cost data are useful. **Relevant costs** are expected future costs that are different between decision alternatives. Costs that differ between alternatives are also referred to as **differential costs** or **incremental costs.**

Two-alternative decisions involve selecting the best course of action from two alternatives. The **cost indifference point** is the activity level at which the costs of two alternatives are identical. It is computed by setting the cost formula for two alternatives equal to each other or by dividing the differential variable cost into the differential fixed cost. The cost indifference point does not yield a decision, but rather provides cost data for the analysis. The decision maker must still select the expected level of activity for the period and incorporate any relevant data in making the decision.

Break-even points and cost indifference points provide managers with different types of cost information. Break-even analysis utilizes cost and revenue data to determine the zero profit level of activity. Cost indifference analysis identifies the activity level at which the total costs of two alternatives are equal. The two analyses provide complementary information.

A sunk cost is a cost that has already been incurred and cannot be changed. Therefore, such costs are seldom relevant costs in evaluating decision alternatives. An **opportunity cost** is the benefit given up by rejecting one alternative and selecting another.

If a price increase results in an increase in total revenue, the demand for the product is **inelastic.** If a price increase results in a decrease in the total revenue, the product is said to have **elastic** demand.

Decisions involving two courses of action are called **two-alternative decisions.** Common examples include special order decisions, make-buy decisions, and pricing decisions. **Special order decisions** occur when a firm has the opportunity to secure a one-time or infrequent order at a price below the normal selling price. **Make-buy decisions** involve choosing between producing a product or service internally and buying it from an outside source. **Pricing decisions** involve choosing between the current price of a product or service and setting a new price. All of the above decisions require the decision maker to identify and accumulate relevant costs. Pricing decisions are facilitated by computing a **price indifference point,** which is the activity level with a new selling price that provides the same profit as the old price and activity level.

Multiple-alternative decisions involve three or more courses of action. The decision maker must identify and assimilate relevant information. If the decision maker receives more information than can be used, information overload may occur. Typically, cost indifference points are useful in multiple-alternative analysis. **Three-alternative decisions** may have three cost indifference points. The indifference points are interpreted by choosing the alternative that yields the lowest cost at all levels of activity. Graphic analysis of multiple alternatives is very helpful. More than three alternatives can have many cost indifference points.

KEY TERMS

alternative choice decisions *(370)*
cost indifference point *(372)*
differential costs *(370)*
elastic demand *(382)*
incremental cost *(370)*
inelastic demand *(382)*
make-buy decisions *(379)*
multiple-alternative decisions *(370, 384)*

opportunity cost *(381)*
price indifference point *(382)*
pricing decisions *(381)*
relevant costs *(369)*
special order decisions *(377)*
sunk cost *(380)*
three-alternative decisions *(387)*
two-alternative decisions *(371)*

QUESTIONS

1. Mike, who manages the stringing department of the Zither Manufacturing Company, is arguing with his supervisor about replacing the automatic wire-winding machine bought 2 years ago with a more efficient model that is now on the market. "You're telling me that the cost of this machine should not enter into the decision because it is a sunk cost. Well, I have the opportunity to recover that cost by using the machine for another three years, instead of selling the machine practically for scrap. You can't convince me that the opportunity cost is not relevant. My mistake was in not using accelerated depreciation on the machine, so its remaining cost will result in too big a loss if we replace the machine now." Comment on Mike's concepts of cost and the way they affect the decision to replace the existing machine. What factors should be considered in the decision?

2. A restaurant keeps two sets of menus on hand. One includes breakfasts and lunches, the other is for dinners. However, many of the dinners are identical to the lunches, except that their price is higher. What sort of information might management evaluate in order to establish two sets of prices for identical meals? What quantitative information is relevant for making the pricing decision? What qualitative data are used? How do costs affect the decision to establish two sets of prices?

3. Last year when Ineptus Company had excess capacity in the production of its golf umbrellas, it accepted a special order from Taekem Company for 50,000 umbrellas at $3 below its normal selling price. Normal capacity is 120,000 units and the normal selling price is $14 per unit. The company is now operating near full capacity at an average of 100,000 units per month. Taekem Company has just indicated that it would like to buy the umbrellas on a regular basis at 25,000 units

per month at the same price it paid last year. How could Ineptus justify selling the umbrellas at less than the normal price? Should the company accept Taekem's offer? What justification can management provide to Taekem for wanting its regular price for the umbrellas?

EXERCISES

Ex. 10-1
Cost Indifference Point

City Services must open a new sanitary disposal site, because the current site is nearly full. A major feature of the new disposal site will be a trash compaction facility. A number of options have been proposed, and the evaluation has been narrowed to two options. The two trash compaction systems are the Scruncher and the Cruncher. The latter is a larger system that requires higher fixed costs, but is more efficient to operate. Cost data for the two alternatives are presented below:

Fixed Costs	Scruncher	Cruncher
Annual depreciation	$12,000	$30,000
Hydraulic maintenance contract	5,000	9,000
Insurance and miscellaneous maintenance	3,000	2,000
Variable Costs per Ton Processed		
Labor	$.18	$.06
Fuel	.05	.03
Supplies and other variable costs	.02	.01

REQUIRED

a. Compute the cost indifference point.
b. If the city expects to process 130,000 tons of trash next year at the new site, which trash compactor should be purchased?

Ex. 10-2
Computing a Price Indifference Point

Following are cost and sales data for the sale of hot dogs at a corner vending stand in a large city.

Current price	$.85
Variable costs	.40
Current annual sales level	60,000 hot dogs
Fixed cost per year	$10,000

The owner of the stand is evaluating the possibility of raising the hot dog price to $1.00.

REQUIRED

a. Compute the current profit of the stand.
b. Compute the price indifference point.

Ex. 10-3
Make-Buy Decision

The Mello-Tone Radio Company currently produces and sells many different types of radios and is planning to begin production of clock radios. The cost accounting department and production engineers have prepared cost estimates for the production of the clock radios. One unresolved issue is whether to manufacture the clocks for the radios or purchase them. Cost estimates for clock production are presented below:

Direct materials	$2.50
Direct labor	1.25
Applied variable overhead	.50
Applied fixed overhead	1.50
Total cost	$5.75

A clock manufacturer has offered to sell Mello-Tone the clocks for $5.00 each. Currently Mello-Tone is operating at 60 percent of plant capacity and could easily accommodate the clock production space needs. The company expects to produce and sell 50,000 clock radios next year.

REQUIRED

a. Determine if Mello-Tone should manufacture or purchase the clocks.
b. If the management of Mello-Tone chose the opposite decision than you did for part *a*, what would be the cost of the incorrect decision?

Ex. 10-4
Make-Buy Decision
with Opportunity
Cost

Refer to the Mello-Tone Radio Company data presented in Exercise 10-3. Assume that all the data are the same as presented except that the space used for the production of clocks could be rented to another company for $2,500 a month.

REQUIRED

a. Analyze the data and determine if the clocks should be purchased or manufactured.
b. If the management of Mello-Tone chose the opposite decision than you did for part *a*, what is the cost of the incorrect decision?

Ex. 10-5
Special Order
Decisions

The Denval Company is evaluating an opportunity to sell 1,000 heavy-duty life rafts to the United States Coast Guard. The unit price on the special order is $175, which is $65 per unit lower than the normal price. Cost data associated with the production and distribution of the rafts are presented below:

Direct materials	$ 70.00
Direct labor	45.00
Manufacturing overhead (30 percent variable)	60.00
Marketing (60 percent variable)	15.00
Distribution (80 percent variable)	10.00
Administrative (all fixed)	15.00
Total product-related costs	$215.00

Eighty percent of the variable marketing cost is commissions. Field sales personnel are paid a 3 percent sales commission. If the special order is accepted, the sales commission will apply. Because of a decline in recreational sales, Denval can fill the order without additional capacity.

REQUIRED

a. Determine if the special order should be accepted and show supporting computations.
b. What is the effect of your decision in *a* on total net income?

Ex. 10-6
Break-Even Point
and Cost
Indifference Point

Martinez Cleaners has experienced significant growth at its two downtown locations. Management is thinking about opening a new store in a large new shopping mall that is opening soon. Two types of cleaning systems are being evaluated. One is highly automated and requires a minimal amount of cleaning labor. The other is a more conventional system that requires a good deal of manual work. Cost data for the two alternatives are listed below. Variable costs are expressed in terms of cost per 100 pounds of cleaning. Average revenue per 100 pounds is $60.

Annual Fixed Cost	Conventional	Automatic
Depreciation on equipment	$8,000	$22,000
Maintenance and insurance	2,000	6,000
Variable Cost per 100 Pounds of Cleaning		
Labor	$20.00	$ 5.00
Supplies	8.00	10.00
Other	4.00	2.00

REQUIRED

a. Compute the cost indifference point for the two alternatives.
b. Using only the cost indifference point data, describe the course of action that should be taken.
c. Compute the break-even point for each of the alternatives.

Ex. 10-7
Identifying
Relevant Cost Data

Following are partially complete data from the analysis of four different **independent** alternative choice decisions. Each situation is an analysis of a two-alternative decision.

	Situation			
	A	B	C	D
Variable cost of alternative 1	$20	$10	$40	$5
Fixed cost of alternative 1	$20,000	$15,000		$6,000
Variable cost of alternative 2	$14	$19	$25	
Fixed cost of alternative 2	$41,000		$62,000	$3,000
Cost indifference point in units		1,000	3,000	1,000
Expected activity level in units	4,000	800	4,200	900
Alternative chosen based on cost				

REQUIRED

Provide the missing data.

Ex. 10-8
Price Indifference
Point Analysis

Bently Pharmaceuticals currently sells its multiple vitamins for $5 per bottle and sells 200,000 bottles a year. At that price the company realizes a profit on the product of $50,000. Fixed cost associated with the product is $250,000. Bently management is thinking about increasing the price of the vitamins to $6 per bottle. If the price is not increased, management believes the current sales and profit levels will be maintained.

REQUIRED

a. Compute the variable cost of a bottle of vitamins.
b. Compute the price indifference point for the price increase.
c. If Bently management implements the price increase and sales decline to 115,000 units, what is the impact on company profits?

Ex. 10-9
Make-Buy Decision
with Opportunity
Cost

Shippley Company makes inboard-outboard engines for boats. Currently the company makes all parts for the engines, but recently Shippley received an offer to supply the engine blocks used to make the engines for a price of $190 each. Current year production data for production of the engine blocks are as follows:

Units produced	2,000
Total costs:	
Direct materials	$145,000
Direct labor	165,000
Manufacturing overhead (30% variable)	200,000
Total manufacturing costs	$510,000

Unit cost of engine blocks ($510,000/2,000 units) = $255

If engine blocks are purchased, all of the variable costs can be eliminated and 20 percent of the fixed overhead cost can be eliminated. The space used to produce the engine blocks can be leased to another company for $60,000 a year. Additional fixed cost of $15,000 will be incurred if the facilities are leased. In addition, eight employees would lose their jobs. The company expects to make 2,500 engines during the next year. The production capacity is enough to handle the increase in output without any increase in fixed costs.

REQUIRED   Compute the change in profit for Shippley if they accept the offer and buy the engine blocks.

Ex. 10-10
Multiple-Alternative Decision

A manufacturer of air-conditioning systems plans to install a new coil-winding machine in the fall. Several machine tool companies have prepared preliminary design proposals. Each machine has attractive features, and all can produce the quality coils required. A major element in the analysis is cost. Estimated production cost data for the three alternatives are presented below. Variable costs are expressed in terms of cost per 100 feet of coil.

Variable Costs	Die-Master	Tool-Town	Ready-Tool
Direct materials	$22.00	$23.00	$25.00
Direct labor	12.00	8.00	4.00
Variable overhead	8.00	6.00	3.00
Annual Fixed Costs			
Equipment depreciation	$15,000	$25,000	$50,000
Maintenance and insurance	4,000	8,000	15,000

REQUIRED
a. Compute all of the cost indifference points for the three alternatives.
b. Graph the cost lines for the three alternatives. Draw a heavy dark line along the lowest cost-path of the three alternatives.
c. Describe the most cost-effective course of action at all levels of activity.

PROBLEMS

P. 10-1
Two-Alternative Graphic Analysis

Woodbine Family Theme Park is a large family resort that includes an amusement park, a water park, a family campground, and a golf resort. The management of the park is skilled and confident at operating all of the resort facilities, but an area of concern is security. Woodbine management has had little experience in planning and operating security systems. The current security system is operated by the company that constructed the park, but the last of the construction activities is nearly complete and the current security force will be leaving soon.

Woodbine has two plans under evaluation. One alternative is to hire a private security force from a national security firm. The charge for the service would be an annual fixed fee of $400,000 plus $35 per patrol hour. If Woodbine develops its own security system, the costs are expected to be:

Annual Fixed Cost	
Depreciation, equipment	$450,000
Supervision	120,000
Occupancy costs	100,000

Variable Cost per Patrol Hour	
Labor	$13.00
Gasoline	4.00
Other variable costs	3.00

Management estimates 1,500,000 park visitors during the first season of operations. National statistics indicates there should be 1 patrol hour per 100 park visitors to maintain adequate security.

REQUIRED

a. Carefully graph the total cost lines of the two alternatives.
b. Compute the cost indifference point.
c. Describe the appropriate course of action suggested by the cost indifference point for all activity levels.
d. Compute the total cost for security at the expected level of activity using the most cost-effective course of action.
e. Compute the cost of not selecting the correct alternative, assuming the expected activity level occurs.

P. 10-2
Special Order
Decisions

McPhail Company sells office furniture and supplies. Recently the business manager of a school system offered to buy 100 oak bookcases for school libraries at $200 each. The normal price of the bookshelves is $290. The bookcases are purchased unfinished from the manufacturer. Company employees stain and seal the bookcases before they are sold to customers. This year sales have been slow because of high interest rates and a sluggish economy. The sales manager asks the chief accountant to prepare cost data relevant to the analysis. The accountant prepares the following:

Cost of unfinished bookshelves	$130.00
Finishing material	24.00
Finishing labor	25.00
Applied overhead for finishing activity	20.00
Sales commissions	29.00
Administrative costs	29.00
Total cost	$257.00

The accountant provides the following explanation of the cost data:

1. About 20 percent of the applied overhead is variable cost.
2. Sales commissions are 10 percent of the selling price.
3. To help assess the profitability of products, management assigns administrative costs to products at the rate of 10 percent of selling price. Ten percent of the administrative costs are variable.

REQUIRED

a. Determine if the special order should be accepted assuming sales commissions must be paid on the sale.

b. Determine the impact on total profit of accepting the special order using the assumption in part *a*.

c. Determine if the special order should be accepted assuming a special 4 percent sales commission will be paid on this sale.

d. Determine the impact on total profit of accepting the special order using the assumption in part *c*.

P. 10-3
Price Indifference
Point with a Price
Reduction

Pro-Dog Company has the concession contract at several baseball stadiums around the state. They sell hot dogs for $1.25 each. The food cost of the hot dogs is $.40 each. Vendors are paid a commission for each hot dog sold. The commission and other variable costs associated with selling the hot dogs in $.30 each. The fixed costs associated with operating the business are $110,000 a year. Last year the company sold 260,000 hot dogs at baseball games.

The management of Pro-Dog is not pleased with the level of sales and profit last season. An alternative being considered is to lower the price of hot dogs to $1.10. During the upcoming season management expects the food costs to increase 10 percent, but all other costs are expected to remain the same.

REQUIRED

a. Compute the price indifference point for the new price using last year's cost data.

b. Compute the price indifference point using the expected cost changes in the analysis.

c. If the price is lowered to $1.10 and sales increase to 320,000 units, what is the impact on profits?

P. 10-4
Two-Alternative
Cost Analysis

Leadlow University, a college of 12,000 students, uses a computer to process all student grades and to prepare student grade reports. The current term grades are added to a student master file that is loaded on tape. The updated master file tape is printed and the most current student record is filed, so that administrators and others may have access to current student records. Requests for student records data are processed manually. The appropriate data are copied and sent to the student, prospective employer, or other authorized people. The average number of inquiries for each student record has been rising from 2.2 per year 5 years ago to 3.5 per year last year. Increased competition for jobs is one reason for the increase in the use of student records, but there are probably other causes as well. The dean of student affairs thinks the request for student records will level off at about 3.5 requests per student per year.

The rapidly rising cost of manually processing requests for student data has caused the university to evaluate data base management systems for managing student records. All student records could be loaded on the system and information requests could be satisfied easily and quickly. The alternatives have been narrowed to Maxi-Data and Data-Tron. Both systems are excellent and can easily satisfy the university's needs. Below are cost data for the two systems, including the lease of a separate computer for the data base system.

Annual Fixed Costs	Maxi-Data	Data-Tron
Lease cost	$24,000	$15,000
Maintenance cost	4,000	3,000
Insurance cost	3,000	2,000
Occupancy costs	16,000	16,000

Variable Cost per Inquiry

Labor cost	$1.50	$1.80
Supply cost	.40	.45
Other variable costs	.30	.20

REQUIRED

a. Determine which data base system is most cost-effective for the university.

b. If the average number of student requests increases to 4.5 per year, which of the two systems should be used?

c. If the university selects the data base management system you selected in part *a* and actual information requests average 4.5 per student, what is the cost of the decision?

P. 10-5
Break-Even Point
and Cost
Indifference Point

In January, Peguales Company will start production of a new 2-horsepower outboard motor for use on canoes and as trolling motors. A major unresolved issue is the type of production operation that will be used in manufacturing the motors. The production manager favors a highly automated system that minimizes the number of manual assembly operations. This system has a much higher initial cost and higher maintenance cost. But it is a very efficient system that has low labor cost and efficient use of raw materials. The chief financial officer of Peguales prefers a more modest initial investment that requires much more manual assembly of the outboard motors. She believes it is wise to see how well the 2-horsepower outboards sell before committing a significant amount of resources to the company's manufacturing facilities. The motors will sell for $300 each. Below are estimated cost data for the two production alternatives:

	Assembly Method	
Annual Fixed Costs	**Manual**	**Automated**
Equipment depreciation	$ 30,000	$210,000
Occupancy cost	40,000	50,000
Insurance	3,000	10,000
Property taxes	7,000	10,000
Marketing and administrative	70,000	70,000
Total fixed cost	$150,000	$350,000
Variable Costs		
Direct materials	$120	$110
Direct labor	50	30
Variable overhead	30	35
Marketing, distribution, and administrative	25	25
	$225	$200

REQUIRED

a. Compute the cost indifference point for the two assembly alternatives.

b. Compute the break-even point for both alternatives.

c. If expected sales of the 2-horsepower motors are 6,000 units, what assembly method would you recommend?

d. If management decides to raise the motor price 10 percent, what impact does this decision have on the cost indifference point you computed in part *a*?

P. 10-6
Make-Buy Decision

The Verde Company manufactures air-moving systems for office and commercial use. Their MJ80 fan is popular for high-velocity air requirements such as in paint-drying operations. Since the MJ80's introduction 3 years ago, Verde Company has purchased the 20-horsepower electric motor used in production. In 1983 the motors cost $185, but prices have increased steadily and they cost $220 by the end of 1985. Recent information from the vendor indicates the price will increase 10 percent early in 1986. During 1985, Verde Company used 4,000 electric motors, and the company expects to use the same number in 1986.

Early in 1985, management asked the production engineering and accounting departments to prepare cost estimates for manufacturing the electric motor. The resulting cost data are reported below:

Direct materials	$100 per motor
Direct labor	60
Variable manufacturing overhead	10
Allocated fixed overhead	40
Discretionary fixed overhead associated with the motors	30
Total per unit cost of production	$240

The allocated fixed overhead costs are mostly capacity costs, such as plant depreciation and utilities. This discretionary fixed overhead consists of costs for new equipment and other fixed cost resources necessary to manufacture the motors. Management expects the direct materials and variable overhead costs to increase 20 percent in 1985. Direct labor costs will increase 15 percent due to a new union agreement. Other costs are expected to be the same as estimated. Verde Company has enough production space to manufacture the electric motors.

REQUIRED

a. Determine if Verde Company should make or buy the motors.
b. If the company can rent the current excess production space for $60,000 a year, should the motors be produced?

P. 10-7
Comprehensive
Pricing Analysis

The Par-More miniature golf course is located in a prime recreational location in Florida. It contains three 18-hole miniature golf courses that attract a good flow of customers most of the year. In addition to offering a quality facility, management awards free soft drinks and other small prizes for a hole-in-one or posting very low scores. The current price for a round of golf is $.80. The variable cost of operating the facility during 1985 was $.15 a round. Fixed cost for the year was $195,000. Net income for 1985 was $65,000 on sales of $320,000. Significant increases in both fixed and variable costs have eroded Par-More's income over the last several years, and management expects a 20 percent increase in both fixed and variable costs in 1986. To offset the impact of the cost increases, management is contemplating a price increase of $.20 a round for golf.

REQUIRED

a. Compute the number of rounds of golf sold in 1985.
b. If the price is not increased in 1986, what is the expected net income assuming the same volume of activity?
c. Compute the price indifference point for the new golf price.
d. Compute the break-even level for 1985.
e. Compute the break-even point for 1986 (1) with the price increase and (2) without the price increase.

f.   If the price increase will decrease the number of rounds of golf sold by 20 percent, should it be implemented?

g.   Compute the required level of activity in 1986 to achieve the 1985 net income, assuming the price increase.

P. 10-8
Cost Indifference
Point and Price
Indifference Point

Cortez Company is evaluating two methods of producing a new product that it plans to market next year. The product will require construction of a new production facility. Plan 1 uses sophisticated metal forming, shearing, and drilling machines in the production process. Plan 1 relies on skilled labor with many more manual operations. Plan 2 requires a much heavier commitment of fixed costs, but it has a lower variable production cost. Management expects to sell 25,000 units of the new product the first year of production, at a price of $80 a unit. Below are estimated cost data for the two production plans:

Variable Costs	Plan 1	Plan 2
Direct materials	$20	$22
Direct labor	17	8
Variable overhead	8	5
Variable marketing, distribution, and admin.	5	5
Annual Fixed Costs		
Depreciation, equipment	$70,000	$200,000
Depreciation, production facilities	90,000	120,000
Other fixed overhead	20,000	30,000
Marketing, distribution, and administration	90,000	90,000

REQUIRED

a.   Compute the break-even point for the two alternatives.

b.   Compute the cost indifference point.

c.   Compute the net income for the first year given the expected sales level and the more cost-effective production method.

d.   Compute the price indifference point for a $20 increase in the price of the product.

P. 10-9
Multiple-
Alternative Analysis

The Industrial Metals Mining Company has just purchased an underground copper mine in northern Michigan. A major issue in acquiring the mine was a plan to open a drive that has not been worked for many years. New mining equipment must be purchased to work the new drive. An important piece of equipment is a rock drill. The equipment is used to drill holes 8 feet deep in the hard rock where the copper ore is found. These holes are loaded with blasting powder and electric blasting caps to shoot down the copper ore. The ore is hauled to a smelter for refining.

The selection has been narrowed to three alternatives. Each seems to be capable of drilling the required holes, but each has somewhat different costs. The hand drill requires a lot of hard work and a great deal of labor time, but it does not cost much. The buggy drill is mounted on wheels and is much easier to use. The automatic drill is mounted on a mobile platform and is capable of drilling eight holes at a time. This drill is very fast, freeing personnel to work on other jobs. Below are cost data pertaining to the three alternatives.

	Drilling Method		
Variable Costs per 10 Holes	Hand Drill	Buggy Drill	Automatic
Labor cost	$50	$30	$10
Supplies and bit sharpening	7	7	15
Other variable costs	3	3	3
Annual Fixed Cost			
Depreciation	$3,600	$10,000	$25,000
Maintenance	800	1,500	5,000
Insurance	400	1,000	3,000
Miscellaneous	200	1,500	2,000

REQUIRED

a. Compute all of the cost indifference points for the three alternatives.
b. Describe the course of action that should be taken at all levels of activity.
c. Are all of the indifference points relevant to the analysis?
d. If management selects the hand drill and actual activity during the first year is 22,000 holes, what is the cost of making that decision?

P. 10-10 (AICPA)
Make-Buy Decision
Analysis

When you had completed your audit of The Scoopa Company, management asked for your assistance in arriving at a decision whether to continue manufacturing a part or to buy it from an outside supplier. The part, which is named Faktron, is a component used in some of the finished products of the company.

From your audit working papers and from further investigation you develop the following data as being typical of the company's operations:

1. The annual requirement for Faktrons is 5,000 units. The lowest quotation from a supplier was $8.00 per unit.
2. Faktrons have been manufactured in the precision machinery department. If Faktrons are purchased from an outside supplier, certain machinery will be sold and would realize its book value.
3. Following are the total costs of the precision machinery department during the year under audit when 5,000 Faktrons were made:

Materials	$67,500
Direct labor	50,000
Indirect labor	20,000
Light and heat	5,500
Power	3,000
Depreciation	10,000
Property taxes and insurance	8,000
Payroll taxes and other benefits	9,800
Other	5,000

4. The following precision machinery department costs apply to the manufacture of Faktrons: material, $17,500; direct labor, $28,000; indirect labor, $6,000; power, $300, other, $500. The sale of the equipment used for Faktrons would reduce the following costs by the amounts indicated: depreciation, $2,000; property taxes and insurance, $1,000.

5. The following additional precision machinery department costs would be incurred if Faktrons were purchased from an outside supplier: freight, $.50 per unit; indirect labor for receiving, materials handling, inspection, etc., $5,000. The cost of the purchased Faktrons would be considered a precision machinery department cost.

REQUIRED

a. Prepare a schedule showing a comparison of the total costs of the precision machinery department (1) when Faktrons are made, and (2) when Faktrons are bought from an outside supplier.

b. Discuss the considerations in addition to the cost factors that you would bring to the attention of management in assisting them to arrive at a decision whether to make or buy Faktrons. Include in your discussion the considerations that might be applied to the evaluation of the outside supplier.

P. 10-11 (AICPA)
Decision Analysis

The management of the Southern Cottonseed Company has engaged you to assist in the development of information to be used for managerial decisions.

The company has the capacity to process 20,000 tons of cottonseed per year. The yield of a ton of cottonseed is as follows:

Product	Average Yield per Ton of Cottonseed	Average Selling Price per Trade Unit
Oil	300 lb	$ .15 per lb
Meal	600 lb	50.00 per ton
Hulls	800 lb	20.00 per ton
Lint	100 lb	3.00 per cwt
Waste	200 lb	

A special marketing study revealed that the company can expect to sell its entire output for the coming year at the listed average selling prices.

You have determined the company's costs to be as follows:

Processing Costs

Variable: $9 per ton of cottonseed put into process
Fixed: $108,000 per year

Marketing Costs

All variable: $20 per ton sold

Administrative Costs

All fixed: $90,000 per year

From the above information you prepared and submitted to management a detailed report on the company's break-even point. In view of conditions in the cottonseed market, management told you that they would also like to know the average maximum amount that the company can afford to pay for a ton of cottonseed.

Management has defined the average maximum amount that the company can afford to pay for a ton of cottonseed as the amount that would result in the company's having losses no greater when operating than when closed down under the existing cost and revenue structure. Management states that you are to assume that the fixed costs shown in your break-even point report will continue unchanged even when the operations are shut down.

a. Compute the average maximum amount that the company can afford to pay for a ton of cottonseed.

b. You also plan to mention to management the factors, other than the costs that entered into your computation, that they should consider in deciding whether to shut down the plant. Discuss these additional factors.

c. The stockholders consider the minimum satisfactory return on their investment in the business to be 25 percent before corporate income taxes. The stockholders' equity in the company is $968,000. Compute the maximum average amount that the company can pay for a ton of cottonseed to realize the minimum satisfactory return on the stockholders' investment in the business.

P. 10-12 (CMA)
Three-Alternative
Analysis

Valbec Company manufactures and distributes toy dollhouses. The toy industry is a seasonal business. Therefore, a large portion of Valbec's sales occur in the late summer and fall.

The projected sales in units for 1985 are shown in the schedule below. With a sales price of $10 per unit, the total sales revenue for 1985 is projected at $1.2 million. Valbec scheduled its production in the past so that finished goods inventory at the end of each month, exclusive of a safety stock of 4,000 dollhouses, would equal the next month's sales. One-half hour of direct labor time is required to produce each dollhouse under normal operating conditions. Using the production schedule followed in the past, the total direct labor hours by month that would be required to meet the 1985 sales estimate are also shown in the schedule below.

Valbec Company
Projected Sales and Planned Production
For the Year Ending December 31, 1985

	Projected Sales (in units)	Direct Labor Hours Required[a]
January	8,000	4,000
February	8,000	4,000
March	8,000	4,000
April	8,000	4,000
May	8,000	5,000
June	10,000	6,000
July	12,000	6,000
August	12,000	6,500
September	13,000	6,500
October	13,000	6,000
November	12,000	4,000
December	8,000	4,000[b]
Total	120,000 units	60,000 hours

[a] This schedule does not incorporate any additional direct labor hours resulting from inefficiencies.
[b] Sales for January 1986 are projected at 8,000 units.

The production schedule followed in the past requires the scheduling of overtime hours for any production over 8,000 units (4,000 direct labor hours) in one month. While the use of overtime is feasible, the Valbec management has decided that it should consider two other possible alternatives: (1) Hire temporary help from an agency during the peak months, or (2) expand its labor force and adopt a level production schedule. The use of a second shift was not considered because management believed the community would not support this alternative.

Factory employees are paid $6.00 per hour for regular time; the fringe benefits average 20 percent of regular pay. For hours worked in excess of 4,000 hours per month, employees receive time and one-half; however, fringe benefits only average 10 percent on these additional wages. Past experience has shown that when overtime is required, labor inefficiencies do occur during overtime at the rate of 5 percent of overtime hours; this 5 percent inefficiency was not included in the direct labor hour estimates presented in the schedule.

Rather than pay overtime to its regular labor force, Valbec could hire temporary employees when production exceeds 8,000 units per month. The temporary workers can be hired through an agency at the same labor rate of $6.00 per hour, but there would be no fringe benefit costs. Management estimates that the temporary workers would require 25 percent more time than the regular employees to produce the dollhouses.

If Valbec goes to a level production schedule, the labor force would be expanded. However, no overtime would be required. The same labor rate of $6.00 per hour and fringe benefit rate of 20 percent would apply.

The manufacturing facilities have the capacity to produce 18,000 dollhouses per month. On-site storage facilities for completed units are adequate. The estimated annual cost of carrying inventory is $1 per unit. Valbec is subject to a 40 percent income tax rate.

REQUIRED

a. Prepare an analysis that compares the costs associated with each of Valbec Company's three alternatives:
   1. Schedule overtime hours.
   2. Hire temporary workers.
   3. Expand labor force and schedule level production.
b. Identify and discuss briefly the noncost factors and the factors that are difficult to cost that Valbec Company should consider in conjunction with the cost analysis prepared in requirement *a* before a final decision is made on the three alternatives.

CASES

Case 10-1
Comprehensive
Decision Analysis

Steno-Pool, Inc., offers typing services to the general public. The company is known for quality services, delivered on time, with a spirit of cooperation in satisfying customer needs. Currently the company employs 25 typists, three supervisors, and a general manager. All work is done on late-model electric typewriters that have a cost of $36,000 and a book value of $20,000. The company charges $1.25 per typed page. Typists average 10 typed pages per hour. Variable costs for paper, ribbons, and other supplies average $.12 per page. Typists work 40 hours a week and 50 weeks per year. Their wage rate, including payroll taxes and employee benefits, is $7 per hour. During 1985, the company had the following results:

Steno-Pool, Inc.
Income Statement
For the Year Ended December 31, 1985

Revenue		$625,000
Operating expenses:		
Typist wages	$350,000	
Salaries	95,000	
Supplies	60,000	
Depreciation, typewriters	9,000	
Depreciation, facilities	12,000	
Utilities	10,000	
Property taxes	6,000	
Miscellaneous	8,000	
Total operating expenses		550,000
Net income		$ 75,000

The owners of Steno-Pool are not pleased with the firm's 1985 profit. Costs are expected to increase in 1986, but because of competition, the general manager sees no way to increase prices without some decline in sales volume. In spite of the general manager's opinion, the owners are contemplating raising prices to $1.40 per page accompanied by an extensive $10,000 advertising campaign.

All costs except typist wages and supplies are considered fixed costs. With no change in operations, wages and supply costs are expected to increase 10 percent in 1986. In addition, salaries are expected to increase 15 percent and utilities and miscellaneous expenses are expected to rise 20 percent in 1986.

A management consulting firm hired by the owners suggested the company switch all of its work to word processors. Because of time saved in all revision work and the extra speed of the electronic system, operators will average 20 pages per hour. With operators working two shifts, the number of word processing input stations could be held to seven and the total lease cost of the new equipment would be $24,000 per year. Word processing operators would need to be hired at a cost of $12 per hour including employee benefits, and all typists would be terminated. Variable costs for paper, printer ribbons, and other supplies would average $.15 per page. The old typewriters can be sold for $10,000.

REQUIRED

a. Compute the 1986 expected profit if no changes are made.
b. Compute the price indifference point in 1986 for the proposed price increase.
c. If sales fall to 400,000 pages per year, should the price be increased?
d. At the 1985 level of sales, what would be the effect on net income of changing to word processing in 1986?
e. Assume the used typewriters are given to a charity. At what activity level is Steno-Pool indifferent between the current typing system and the proposed word processing system?
f. Discuss nonfinancial factors you might include in your evaluation.

CHAPTER 11
The Contribution Approach and Variable Costing

Contribution margin is the difference between revenue and variable costs. To find contribution margin per unit, we subtract the variable cost of making, selling, and distributing a unit of product from its sales revenue. Contribution margin is used to cover fixed costs and provide a profit. This concept is quite useful in computing break-even points, in performing cost-volume-profit analyses as in Chapter 3, and in evaluating decisions as in Chapter 10.

In this chapter we use contribution margin to measure the performance of business components, such as divisions and product lines. In the second part of the chapter we use contribution margin in variable costing, which is a way of measuring and reporting the cost of products.

THE CONTRIBUTION APPROACH COMPARED WITH ABSORPTION COSTING

All production costs—fixed and variable, direct and indirect—are included in the product cost

Absorption costing, also called **full costing,** is the generally accepted method of measuring and reporting product costs. In absorption costing, all necessary costs of production—both direct and indirect, fixed and variable—are assigned to the product. The Internal Revenue Service, as well as most other authoritative bodies, require full costing for reporting product costs in external financial statements. For internal reporting purposes there are no such reporting restrictions. A firm uses whatever product costing method it feels best serves its management information needs.

The contribution approach highlights the costs that change with the volume of activity

In contrast to absorption costing, many firms use the **contribution approach** to costing, whereby only variable costs of production are assigned to products. All variable costs are deducted from revenue to arrive at the total contribution margin. Fixed expenses are deducted from the contribution margin to determine the contribution to the firm's profit made by a particular segment or product.

Both absorption costing and the contribution approach provide managers with useful financial information. But each method of reporting supplies different types of information. The full costing approach classifies costs into traditional functions, such as product costs and operating expenses. Full cost financial statements are useful because classifying cost by function provides a familiar frame of reference understandable to the business and investing community.

Advocates of contribution approach reporting argue that it is more useful than full costing for making some types of managerial decisions. For example: A product's sales volume is expected to decline next year by 20 percent, from 10,000 units to 8,000 units. With full costing data, it is difficult to look at the current period's income statement and use it to evaluate the impact of the expected sales decline on profit; a portion of the product cost data reported in the income statement is allocated fixed costs, which will not change with the level of sales. If, however, contribution data were used to report current period income, the income statement would be more useful for the analysis. It would identify all costs as fixed or variable. The major advantage of using contribution approach reports is that they enable managers to identify the effect on profits from changing levels of activity.

We now discuss several common types of contribution reports to illustrate how they are used in evaluating the performance of business segments.

THE CONTRIBUTION APPROACH TO SEGMENTAL REPORTING

Financial accounting is devoted to reporting income and financial position for an entire business. But most businesses find it necessary to determine the performance of business segments, such as divisions, departments, or product lines. Accountants can, and often do, prepare income statements for separate business segments. Many managers find that for planning, control, and decision making, the contribution margin approach makes such reports quite useful.

There are many different types of segmental contribution reports. But they are all based on the same concept—reporting the contribution of a particular segment or activity of the firm toward (1) covering fixed costs and (2) providing a profit. Three common types of contribution reports are:

*Common types of
segmental
contribution reports*

1. A divisional contribution report
2. A product contribution report
3. A sales region contribution report

Divisional Contribution Report

A **divisional contribution report** identifies the total contribution margin provided by each division of a company. **Contribution margin** is the difference between revenue and variable costs. This same concept is discussed in Chapter 3 in connection with cost-volume-profit analysis, except there contribution margin was typically used in reference to a single product; here we use it to refer to the total dollar amount of contribution margin for each division.

Colefield Business Products is used to illustrate contribution reports. The company manufactures products in three different divisions. The contribution margin provided by each of its divisions is one measure of the effectiveness of the production and marketing strategies in each division. Figure 11-1

Figure 11-1. Divisional sales and cost data for the Colefield Business Products Company. Costs must be divided into fixed and variable costs in order to prepare the divisional contribution report.

Colefield Business Products
Divisional Sales and Cost Data
For the Year Ended December 31, 1985

	Division		
	Calculators	Furniture	Typewriters
Units sold	26,000	4,000	10,000
Average unit sales price	$50	$650	$320
Average unit variable costs:			
Manufacturing	20	300	146
Marketing	3	50	32
Distribution	2	40	10
Administrative	2	10	12
Fixed costs directly identifiable with divisions:			
Manufacturing	$280,000	$400,000	$390,000
Marketing	80,000	95,000	115,000
Distribution	50,000	110,000	95,000
Administrative	140,000	160,000	175,000
Corporate expenses not identifiable with specific divisions			380,000

presents cost and revenue data for the three manufacturing divisions. From these data the divisional contribution report is prepared, as shown in Figure 11-2.

Manufacturing contribution margin defined

For each division, **manufacturing contribution margin,** shown on the third line of the report in Figure 11-2, is the difference between the sales revenue of products and the **variable costs of making the products.** This number is useful to managers in evaluating special orders for which some or all of the normal variable marketing and administration costs can be eliminated. By separating the manufacturing variable costs in the report from the nonmanufacturing variable costs, it is easier for managers to evaluate special situations without requiring additional information. Nonmanufacturing variable costs of selling and distributing the products include sales commissions, shipping costs, and some of the costs of processing sales orders. These costs are subtracted from the manufacturing contribution margin to determine the **contribution margin.**

Variable nonmanufacturing costs are deducted from manufacturing contribution margin to find the contribution margin

Each division's fixed expenses are deducted from its contribution margin to yield the division's contribution to the company. This **division contribution margin,** also called **divisional contribution margin,** is the amount each division contributes toward covering corporate expenses and providing the net income of the corporation. Corporate expenses include general administrative expenses and any expenses that cannot be identified with individual divisions. Each of the three divisions of Colefield Business Products contributes some division contribution margin to cover the company's corporate expenses and provide an income. The smallest contribution is provided by the calculator division, with $48,000. The largest contribution is the $425,000 of the typewriter division.

Colefield Business Products
Divisional Contribution Report
For the Year Ended December 31, 1985

	Division			Company Total
	Calculators	Furniture	Typewriters	
Sales	$1,300,000	$2,600,000	$3,200,000	$7,100,000
Less variable manufacturing expenses	520,000	1,200,000	1,460,000	3,180,000
Manufacturing contribution margin	780,000	1,400,000	1,740,000	3,920,000
Less other variable expenses:				
Variable marketing	78,000	200,000	320,000	598,000
Variable distribution	52,000	160,000	100,000	312,000
Variable administrative	52,000	40,000	120,000	212,000
Total	182,000	400,000	540,000	1,122,000
Contribution margin	598,000	1,000,000	1,200,000	2,798,000
Less divisional fixed expenses:				
Fixed manufacturing	280,000	400,000	390,000	1,070,000
Fixed marketing	80,000	95,000	115,000	290,000
Fixed distribution	50,000	110,000	95,000	255,000
Fixed administrative	140,000	160,000	175,000	475,000
Total fixed expenses	550,000	765,000	775,000	2,090,000
Divisional contribution	$ 48,000	$ 235,000	$ 425,000	708,000
Corporate expenses				380,000
Net income				$ 328,000

Figure 11-2. A divisional contribution report identifies the total contribution margin provided by specific divisions of the company. Divisional contribution reports highlight the costs that change with the volume of activity. This type of information is helpful to managers in evaluating many types of business decisions.

The absolute dollar amount of contribution provided by each division is not always the best way of comparing divisions. For example, in this illustration the largest and smallest contribution margins are provided by the divisions with the largest and smallest amount of sales respectively. It may be more meaningful to express the contribution of each division in a common measure, such as the amount of contribution per dollar of sales revenue. For this example, the computations are as follows:

Contribution per sales dollar

	Division		
	Calculators	Furniture	Typewriters
Contribution	$48,000	$235,000	$425,000
Sales	$1,300,000	$2,600,000	$3,200,000
Contribution per sales dollar	$.037	$.09	$.133

From this analysis we see that the typewriter division generates the most contribution per dollar of sales. Furthermore, we can see also that the difference between the calculator and typewriter divisions is not as great as the contribution data alone indicate. Based only on the total divisional contribution margins, it appeared that the typewriter division provided nearly nine times as much contribution ($425,000/$48,000) as the calculator division. But based on contribution per dollar of sales, we see that the typewriter division is only about three and a half times ($.133/$.037) as effective as the calculator division in generating contribution margin for the company. A more important point is that all three divisions did provide some contribution to the firm's overall profit.

The $380,000 of corporate expenses are not included in the divisional analysis. If, however, Colefield management has a policy of allocating corporate expenses to divisions based on the dollar volume of sales in each division, the following divisional income would result.

Contribution with allocated corporate expenses

| | Division | | | |
	Calculators	Furniture	Typewriters	Total
Divisional contribution	$ 48,000	$235,000	$425,000	$708,000
Less corporate expenses allocated on the division's total sales percentage[a]	(69,577)	(139,155)	(171,268)	(380,000)
Divisional profit (loss)	$ (21,577)	$ 95,845	$253,732	$328,000

[a] Allocation of corporate expenses:
  Calculator Division: ($1,300,000/$7,100,000) × $380,000 = $ 69,577
  Furniture Division: (2,600,000/ 7,100,000) × 380,000 = 139,155
  Typewriter Division: (3,200,000/ 7,100,000) × 380,000 = 171,268

This analysis indicates that the calculator division lost $21,577 while the other divisions earned a profit. The result might seem to indicate that Colefield should eliminate the calculator division. But the divisional contribution statement in Figure 11-2 shows that the calculator division did contribute something to overall corporate profit. If the company eliminated this division, the other two divisions would have to absorb all of the corporate expenses themselves and perhaps, in the short run, even some of the calculator division's fixed costs. The result would be as follows:

| | Division | | |
	Furniture	Typewriters	Total
Divisional contribution	$235,000	$425,000	$660,000
Less corporate expenses allocated on the division's total sales percentage[a]	(170,345)	(209,655)	(380,000)
Divisional profit	$ 64,655	$215,345	$280,000

[a] Without the calculator division, total sales are $5,800,000 ($7,100,000 − $1,300,000), so the allocation of corporate expenses is:
  Furniture Division: ($2,600,000/$5,800,000) × $380,000 = $170,345
  Typewriter Division: (3,200,000/ 5,800,000) × 380,000 = 209,655

The corporate expenses previously allocated to the calculator division are now allocated to the two remaining divisions, lowering the profits of each division and the profit of the corporation. You can see that the divisional contribution statement provides valuable information that would not be evident without the contribution approach.

Product Contribution Report

Measuring the contribution of individual products

A **product contribution report** is similar to a divisional contribution report except that it presents the contribution provided by individual products of a firm. The report may show information about a single product, all the products of a particular division, or some other combination of products. The product contribution report enables managers to evaluate whether a specific product or group of products is contributing a sufficient amount to the firm's net income.

Most product contribution reports present the manufacturing contribution margin and the contribution margin for each product. The manufacturing contribution is computed by deducting all of the variable costs of manufacturing the product from the sales revenue. Then the contribution margin is found by subtracting all variable nonmanufacturing costs, such as variable selling and administrative costs. The detailed cost data in the product contribution reports help managers establish prices, prepare marketing strategies, schedule production, and discontinue product lines.

We illustrate a product contribution report with the Typewriter Division of Colefield Business Products. Some of the data necessary for the report are available in Figure 11-1. Other data needed for the report are presented in Figure 11-3. Two products are manufactured in the Typewriter Division of Colefield Business Products. The price and sales quantity of each of the two products are given in Figure 11-3, along with the variable and fixed costs associated with the production, sales, and administration of the products. The data for the typewriter division that appeared in the divisional contribution report in Figure 11-2 can be derived from the division's product cost data in Figure 11-3. For example, the 4,000 electric and 6,000 manual typewriters make up the 10,000 units sold that appears in the divisional statement. The product price of $320 appearing in the divisional statement is the weighted average price of the two typerwriters [$500 × (4,000/10,000) + $200 × (6,000/10,000)]. Each of the variable costs is an average weighted by the number of units sold (4,000 electric typewriters and 6,000 manual typewriters).

The product contribution report and the divisional contribution report have similar formats but a different cost objective

The product contribution report is illustrated in Figure 11-4. The variable manufacturing costs of each product are subtracted from the sales revenue to determine the manufacturing contribution margin. As with divisional statements, variable operating expenses of products are deducted to find the product contribution margin. Next, the fixed expenses identifiable with specific products are subtracted to find the total contribution of each product. The product contribution is the amount that each product contributes toward covering the fixed expenses of the division and then providing the divisional contribution.

Figure 11-3. Cost, price, and sales data for the two products made in the typewriter division of Colefield Business Products. These data are necessary to prepare the product contribution report for the typewriter division. As with the divisional report, costs must be identified as fixed or variable.

Colefield Business Products
Typewriter Division
Product Sales and Cost Data
For the Year Ended December 31, 1985

| | Product | | Division Expenses[a] |
	Electric Typewriter	Manual Typewriter	
Sales in units	4,000	6,000	
Sales price	$500	$200	
Unit variable costs:			
Manufacturing	230	90	
Marketing	50	20	
Distribution	10	10	
Administrative	15	10	
Fixed costs directly identifiable with products:			
Manufacturing	$180,000	$120,000	$ 90,000
Marketing	25,000	25,000	65,000
Distribution	20,000	15,000	60,000
Administrative	50,000	40,000	85,000
Total divisional expenses			$300,000

[a] Fixed expenses identifiable with the division but not with specific products.

Figure 11-4. The product contribution report shows the amount of total contribution margin provided by each of the products. Some of the fixed expenses associated with the typewriter division cannot be identified with specific products, and they are subtracted from the total contribution margin of the two products to find divisional contribution, which coincides with the amount shown in the divisional contribution report.

Colefield Business Products
Typewriter Division
Product Contribution Report
For the Year Ended December 31, 1985

| | Product | | Division Totals |
	Electric Typewriter	Manual Typewriter	
Sales	$2,000,000	$1,200,000	$3,200,000
Less variable manufacturing expenses	920,000	540,000	1,460,000
Manufacturing contribution margin	1,080,000	660,000	1,740,000
Less other variable expenses:			
Variable marketing	200,000	120,000	320,000
Variable distribution	40,000	60,000	100,000
Variable administrative	60,000	60,000	120,000
Total variable expenses	300,000	240,000	540,000
Contribution margin	780,000	420,000	1,200,000
Less fixed direct expenses:			
Fixed manufacturing	180,000	120,000	300,000
Fixed marketing	25,000	25,000	50,000
Fixed distribution	20,000	15,000	35,000
Fixed administrative	50,000	40,000	90,000
Total fixed direct expenses	275,000	200,000	475,000
Product contribution	$ 505,000	$ 220,000	725,000
Less fixed divisional expenses[a]			300,000
Divisional contribution			$ 425,000

[a] Divisional fixed expenses not identifiable with products include $90,000 manufacturing, $65,000 marketing, $60,000 distribution, and $85,000 administrative.

The contribution of the electric typewriters is more than twice that of the manual typewriters ($505,000 vs. $220,000). That comparison, however, must be evaluated in light of the volume of sales for the two products. Sales volume for electric typewriters was $2,000,000 and for manual typewriters it was $1,200,000. If the contribution margin is expressed as contribution per sales dollar, the results are as follows:

Product contribution per sales dollar

	Product	
	Electric	Manual
Contribution	$505,000	$220,000
Sales	$2,000,000	$1,200,000
Contribution per dollar of sales	$.253	$.183

The electric typewriters' total contribution margin was 130 percent higher [($505,000 − $220,000)/$220,000] than the manual typewriters' total contribution margin. But the contribution margin per dollar of sales was only 38 percent higher [($.253 − $.183)/$.183]. When there is a significant difference in volume of sales between the products, it may be useful to convert the data to a common measure, such as contribution margin per dollar of sales.

The total product contribution of the two typewriters is $725,000. This is **not** the amount that appears in the divisional contribution report for the typewriter division. The difference results from the fact that not all of the divisional expenses can be identified with the individual products. Some of the expenses are identifiable with the division but not with specific products. The total of these divisional fixed expenses is $300,000, which is deducted from the $725,000 total product contribution to arrive at the $425,000 of divisional contribution that appears in the divisional report. The composition of the $300,000 cost is described in the footnote at the end of the product contribution statement. Similar product contribution statements can also be prepared for the calculator and furniture divisions.

Sales Region Contribution Report

Contribution by sales regions

A **sales region contribution report** shows the amount of contribution margin each sales region provides toward covering fixed costs and earning a profit. Marketing, administration, and distribution costs may vary significantly from one sales region to another, and other factors may vary as well and affect the contribution provided by sales regions. For example, product prices in one sales region may have to be lower than in other regions because of local competition, local regulations, and other factors. Without regional sales data and contribution reports, poor or outstanding sales performances might go unnoticed. However, a sales region contribution report may indicate sales regions that are not contributing anything to corporate profits even though the product contribution report may show that the product in all regions combined has a positive contribution margin.

We illustrate a sales region contribution report using the Typewriter Division of the Colefield Business Products Company. The company divides its sales activities into north and south regions. Sales, marketing, and distribution data necessary for the sales region report are shown in Figure 11-5.

Figure 11-5. The sales quantity and cost data by sales region are necessary data for the preparation of the sales region contribution report.

Colefield Business Products
Typewriter Division
Schedule of Regional Sales and Cost Data
For the Year Ended December 31, 1985

	Electric Typewriter	Manual Typewriter
Sales in units:		
Northern region	2,500	3,500
Southern region	1,500	2,500
Marketing costs per unit:		
Northern region	$53.00	$18.00
Southern region	45.00	22.80
Distribution costs per unit:		
Northern region	$ 6.40	$ 6.00
Southern region	16.00	15.60

The typewriter division manufacturing plant is located in the northern sales region, where the market for the products is largest. To encourage sales and to reduce the impact of heavy competition for electric typewriters in the northern sales region, management pays an $8 higher commission to dealers in the northern region. This dealer incentive is reflected in the higher marketing cost for electric typewriters in the northern region ($53 vs. $45). To penetrate the southern market with the manual typewriter, the company has entered into a joint marketing agreement with a business machines company selling compatible products. This marketing agreement is reflected in the $4.80 per unit higher variable marketing cost for the manual typewriter in the southern sales region ($22.80 vs. $18). Distribution costs are much higher in the southern region for both products, because of the greater shipping distance from the manufacturing plant.

Sales region reports may be prepared in many forms

The sales and cost data from Figures 11-5 and 11-3 are used to prepare the sales region contribution statement presented in Figure 11-6. Notice that there are $500,000 in fixed costs not directly identifiable with specific sales regions. For example, all $390,000 of the fixed manufacturing costs are assigned to the division as a whole. Manufacturing facilities are used to produce the products that are sold in both of the regions, and as such should not be assigned to individual sales regions.

As with division and product contribution margins, the sales region contribution margin can be expressed in terms of some common measure, such as sales dollars. The northern region contributes $.308 per sales dollar ($600,000/$1,950,000), and the southern region contributes $.26 per sales

Figure 11-6. The sales region contribution report emphasizes the contribution margin provided by each of the company's sales regions. Differing marketing, distribution, and administrative costs between sales regions can cause a significant difference in the contribution margin of the products sold in those regions.

Colefield Business Products
Typewriter Division
Sales Region Contribution Report
For the Year Ended December 31, 1985

| | Region | | Division |
	Northern	Southern	Totals
Sales	$1,950,000	$1,250,000	$3,200,000
Less variable manufacturing expenses	890,000	570,000	1,460,000
Manufacturing contribution margin	1,060,000	680,000	1,740,000
Less other variable expenses:			
Variable marketing	195,500	124,500	320,000
Variable distribution	37,000	63,000	100,000
Variable administrative	72,500	47,500	120,000
Total variable expenses	305,000	235,000	540,000
Contribution margin	755,000	445,000	1,200,000
Less fixed direct expenses:			
Fixed marketing	20,000	45,000	65,000
Fixed distribution	35,000	45,000	80,000
Fixed administrative	100,000	30,000	130,000
Total fixed direct expenses	155,000	120,000	275,000
Region contribution	$ 600,000	$ 325,000	925,000
Less fixed divisional expenses not assignable to regions[a]			500,000
Divisional contribution			$ 425,000

[a] Divisional fixed expenses not assignable to sales regions include $390,000 manufacturing, $50,000 marketing, $15,000 distribution, and $45,000 administrative.

dollar ($325,000/$1,250,000). With a large amount of fixed divisional expense in this analysis, the contribution per sales dollar from each region may be of less value than in the earlier analyses.

THE CONTRIBUTION APPROACH TO PRODUCT COSTING

The contribution approach just used to illustrate segmental reporting also can be applied specifically to measuring and reporting the cost of manufactured products. Until now, virtually all of the discussion of product costing presented in this book has dealt with absorption (full) costing. Now we discuss and illustrate variable costing, which is the contribution approach applied to product costing.

Variable Costing

Variable costing, also referred to as **direct costing,** assigns only the variable cost of manufacturing to the product. Included are direct materials, direct labor, and the **variable** part of manufacturing overhead. With variable costing, fixed manufacturing overhead costs are not part of the manufacturing overhead rate; rather, they are expensed in the period incurred, together with all nonmanufacturing expenses. Although the term *direct costing* is frequently used for this approach, the term *variable costing* more accurately describes the process, because **indirect variable** overhead costs are included in the product cost.

Variable costing and direct costing are the same thing

There are two major differences between income statements based on **absorption costing** and income statements based on variable costing. One difference is the type of manufacturing costs that are assigned to products with the two methods. The second is the kind of information reported on the income statements.

Type of Costs Assigned to Products. The main issue between absorption costing and variable costing centers on which costs should be inventoried, that is, assigned to products. Variable costing advocates maintain a cost should be inventoried only if incurring the cost now means the cost will not be incurred later. For instance, if an employee assembles a chair now, it eliminates the need to assemble the same chair in the future. On the other hand, fixed capacity costs, such as depreciation on plant and equipment, typically are not avoidable in the future because of current period production. Therefore, with variable costing, fixed capacity costs are not assigned to production.

Only the variable costs of manufacturing are assigned to the product

Absorption costing advocates believe that all necessary costs of production, direct and indirect, fixed and variable, should be assigned to the products. Therefore, fixed capacity costs are included in product cost using absorption costing.

Type of Information Reported in the Income Statement. In addition to different product costs resulting from absorption and variable costing, the nature of the information reported in the income statements using absorption costing or variable costing also differs. Absorption costing income statements report costs by function. Costs of the manufacturing function are subtracted from sales to obtain gross margin. The costs of selling and administrative functions are deducted from gross margin to calculate operating income. Costs of financing and other functions are deducted from operating income to arrive at net income.

Using variable costing, cost behavior rather than business function is the key in developing the income statement. The variable costs of products sold are deducted from sales to find the manufacturing contribution margin. Next, variable nonmanufacturing costs are deducted to arrive at the total contribution margin. Finally, all of the fixed costs are deducted to find the net income for the period.

Variable costing highlights the costs that change with the volume of activity

There is a major difference between the two income statements in the type of information provided to managers. With variable costing, managers can evaluate readily the impact of possible changes in the volume of activity, because variable and fixed costs are reported separately.

ABSORPTION AND VARIABLE COSTING ILLUSTRATED

Constant prices and costs are used in the first example

To illustrate the similarities and differences between absorption costing and variable costing, we use the example of Mullett Manufacturing Company. Production, sales, and cost data for 4 years are presented in Figure 11-7. In this example, the selling price and all of the cost data, both fixed and variable, are the same for each of the 4 years. In reality, it is unlikely that costs and selling prices would not change at all in 4 years. However, this assumption makes it easier to explain variable costing and to demonstrate the differences and similarities between the two costing methods. The constant cost and price assumption is relaxed later in the chapter.

Figure 11-7. Sales quantity and price data and production quantity and cost data for 4 years. The costs and price do not change during the 4-year period in order to illustrate and discuss more clearly the similarities and differences between absorption costing and variable costing.

Mullett Manufacturing Company
Production, Sales, and Cost Data
Years 1 through 4

	Year			
	1	2	3	4
Sales in units	8,000	9,000	13,000	10,000
Production in units	10,000	12,000	10,000	8,000
Beginning inventory in units	0	2,000	5,000	2,000
Direct materials per unit	$ 6	$ 6	$ 6	$ 6
Direct labor per unit	3	3	3	3
Variable MOH per unit	2	2	2	2
Fixed MOH	50,000	50,000	50,000	50,000
Variable selling and administrative cost per unit	3	3	3	3
Fixed selling and administrative	30,000	30,000	30,000	30,000
Sales price per unit	25	25	25	25

The logical first step in preparing either an absorption costing or a variable costing income statement is to compute the unit product cost for both absorption costing and variable costing. The computation of product costs is presented in Figure 11-8. The cost data used in the computations are obtained from Figure 11-7.

The product cost with variable costing includes all variable manufacturing costs, direct material, direct labor, and **variable** manufacturing overhead. For each of the 4 years in this example the product cost is $11 using variable costing.

With absorption costing, part of fixed overhead cost is assigned to each unit of product

The product cost using absorption costing is the variable manufacturing costs **plus** a portion of the fixed manufacturing overhead assigned to the product. The amount of fixed overhead assigned to each unit is based on the overhead application rate, which is determined from the budgeted amount of total manufacturing overhead divided by the normal capacity. Mullett Manufacturing has $50,000 of budgeted fixed overhead for each of the 4 years in the example. The normal capacity is 10,000 units per year. Therefore, the

Figure 11-8. Product costs with variable costing include only the variable manufacturing costs; all fixed manufacturing costs are expensed during the period. With absorption costing, a portion of the fixed manufacturing overhead cost is allocated to each unit of product.

Mullett Manufacturing Company
Unit Production Cost Data
Years 1 through 4

	Year			
	1	2	3	4
Variable manufacturing costs:				
Direct materials	$ 6	$ 6	$ 6	$ 6
Direct labor	3	3	3	3
Variable MOH	2	2	2	2
Product cost using variable costing	11	11	11	11
Add prorated fixed MOH cost	5	5	5	5
Product cost using absorption costing	$16	$16	$16	$16

amount of fixed overhead assigned to each unit is $5 ($50,000/10,000 units). Adding the $5 of fixed overhead cost to the $11 of variable manufacturing cost yields a product cost of $16 per unit with absorption costing.

In this example the unit cost is identical for all 4 years. If the cost data varied from year to year, the unit costs would be different, but the computation of the unit cost would be the same as just illustrated.

Absorption Costing Income Statement

With the product costs determined, it is now possible to prepare the income statements for all 4 years for both absorption and variable costing. The income statements for both costing methods are presented in Figure 11-9, with absorption costing presented first. The sales revenue for each year is determined by multiplying the units sold by the selling price of $25 per unit. Cost of goods sold is the number of units sold times the absorption costing product cost.

Selling and administrative costs are subtracted from gross margin to find net income. Variable selling and administrative expense is equal to $3 per unit times the number of units sold. Fixed selling and administrative expense is $30,000 each year.

Computation of underapplied and overapplied manufacturing overhead

In years 1 and 3, actual production equaled normal capacity of 10,000 units. Therefore, there was no underapplied or overapplied overhead. However, in year 2, actual production was 12,000 units, which is 2,000 more than the normal capacity. The amount of **fixed** manufacturing overhead applied to production during the year was $60,000 ($5 per unit of fixed overhead times 12,000 units). Actual fixed overhead was $50,000, so overhead was overapplied by $10,000. In effect, $10,000 too much fixed overhead was applied to production. In year 4, just the reverse is true. Actual production of 8,000 is 2,000 units below the normal capacity of 10,000 units. Applied **fixed** overhead was $40,000 ($5 per unit times 8,000 units). Overhead is underapplied by $10,000. Overapplied and underapplied overhead is small enough to assign to cost of good sold for the period.

Mullett Manufacturing Company
Absorption Costing Income Statements
For Years 1 through 4

	Year			
	1	2	3	4
Sales	$200,000	$225,000	$325,000	$250,000
Cost of goods sold	128,000	144,000	208,000	160,000
Gross margin	72,000	81,000	117,000	90,000
Variable selling and administrative	24,000	27,000	39,000	30,000
Fixed selling and administrative	30,000	30,000	30,000	30,000
Underapplied (overapplied) overhead	—	(10,000)	—	10,000
Total operating expenses	54,000	47,000	69,000	70,000
Net income	$ 18,000	$ 34,000	$ 48,000	$ 20,000

Mullett Manufacturing Company
Variable Costing Income Statements
For Years 1 through 4

	Year			
	1	2	3	4
Sales	$200,000	$225,000	$325,000	$250,000
Variable product cost	88,000	99,000	143,000	110,000
Manufacturing contribution margin	112,000	126,000	182,000	140,000
Variable selling and administrative	24,000	27,000	39,000	30,000
Contribution margin	88,000	99,000	143,000	110,000
Fixed manufacturing overhead	50,000	50,000	50,000	50,000
Fixed selling and administrative	30,000	30,000	30,000	30,000
Total fixed cost	80,000	80,000	80,000	80,000
Net income	$ 8,000	$ 19,000	$ 63,000	$ 30,000

Figure 11-9. Absorption costing expenses manufacturing costs as the products are sold. With variable costing, variable manufacturing costs are expensed when the product is sold, but fixed manufacturing costs are expensed in the period the cost is incurred. The difference in net income for any year between the two methods is caused by the fixed overhead carried in the beginning and ending inventories with absorption costing.

Variable Costing Income Statement

The variable costing income statements appear at the bottom of Figure 11-9. Notice that sales revenue reported is the same in any given year for both absorption and variable costing. However, except for the first line, the variable costing income statement is much different from the absorption costing income statement. In addition, the net income figure for any particular year differs between absorption costing and variable costing.

First we subtract variable product expense from sales revenue to find the

Variable product expense is deducted from revenue first

manufacturing contribution margin. This is merely the difference between sales revenue and the variable manufacturing cost of the products **sold.** In this example, the variable product cost is $11 per unit and the selling price is $25. Therefore, the manufacturing contribution margin is $14 per unit ($25 − $11), and the total manufacturing contribution margin in any particular year is the number of units sold times $14 per unit. In year 1, for example, the total manufacturing contribution margin is $112,000 ($14 per unit times 8,000 units sold). It is important to remember that the product expense reported on either the absorption or the variable costing income statement is based on the number of units **sold,** not the number of units produced.

Next the variable nonmanufacturing expenses are subtracted to find the contribution margin

All other variable expenses, in this case variable selling and administrative expenses, are subtracted from the manufacturing contribution margin to determine the **contribution margin.** This is the same type of contribution margin discussed in Chapter 3 in connection with cost-volume-profit analysis, but here we are dealing with the total contribution margin from all units sold during the period. In this case the total variable cost is $14 ($11 of variable product cost + $3 of variable selling and administrative cost). The unit contribution margin is $11 ($25 selling price − $14 total variable cost). The total contribution margin for any particular year is $11 per unit times the number of units **sold.**

Next all fixed expenses are subtracted from the contribution margin to determine net income. Notice that fixed expenses include selling and administrative costs **and** fixed manufacturing overhead costs. With variable costing, fixed overhead costs do not become part of the product cost; instead, they are expensed in the period in which they occur, along with all nonmanufacturing expenses.

Absorption and Variable Costing Compared

You can see that for any of the 4 years, the two types of income statements report different amounts of income. The **sole reason** for the difference in reported net income between the two methods is this: Fixed overhead cost is included in the product cost with absorption costing; fixed overhead cost is a period expense with variable costing.

The reason for the difference in net income

With absorption costing, the fixed overhead cost is assigned to the product during production and becomes part of the product cost. The product cost becomes an expense when the product is sold. If some units are not sold, their product cost, including their share of fixed overhead cost, appears in the ending inventory for the period.

With variable costing, however, all fixed manufacturing overhead is expensed in the period in which it is incurred. None appears in ending inventory, regardless of how many units are sold. In other words, absorption costing treats fixed overhead as an asset, whereas variable costing treats it as an expense.

To illustrate the concept of inventory costs with both absorption and variable costing, Figure 11-10 presents a schedule of beginning and ending inventories for both costing methods. Both the physical quantities and the associated costs are presented for the 4-year period.

Figure 11-10. The number of units in inventory at any point in time is a physical measure and is the same for absorption costing or variable costing. The difference in the cost of beginning and ending inventory between absorption costing and variable costing is due entirely to the fixed overhead cost that is assigned to absorption costing units but not to variable costing units.

Mullett Manufacturing Company
Schedule of Beginning and Ending Inventory
Under Absorption Costing and Variable Costing

Absorption Costing				
	Year			
	1	2	3	4
Beginning inventory:				
Number of units	0	2,000	5,000	2,000
Unit cost	—	$16	$16	$16
Total cost	—	$32,000	$80,000	$32,000
Ending inventory:				
Number of units	2,000	5,000	2,000	0
Unit cost	$16	$16	$16	—
Total cost	$32,000	$80,000	$32,000	—
Variable Costing				
	Year			
	1	2	3	4
Beginning inventory:				
Number of units	0	2,000	5,000	2,000
Unit cost	—	$11	$11	$11
Total cost	—	$22,000	$55,000	$22,000
Ending inventory:				
Number of units	2,000	5,000	2,000	0
Unit cost	$11	$11	$11	—
Total cost	$22,000	$55,000	$22,000	—

The physical quantity of beginning and ending inventory is the same for either method. The choice of absorption costing or variable costing is an accounting decision that does not affect the physical flow of inventory. For any quantity of inventory, the absorption costing method shows a $5 per unit higher cost because of the fixed manufacturing overhead cost. All other components of the product cost are identical for the two methods.

Reconciling Net Income

To understand the difference in net income between the two methods, it is necessary to recall that product costs are assets until the product is sold. With absorption costing, the ending inventory includes some fixed overhead cost ($5 per unit in our example). This fixed overhead is part of the cost of ending inventory, which appears in the balance sheet at the end of the period. The cost of this inventory, including the fixed manufacturing overhead, is expensed in a later period when the product is sold.

Conversely, with variable costing all fixed manufacturing overhead costs are expensed in the period in which they occur. No fixed manufacturing overhead costs are assigned to products and therefore, no fixed overhead costs are included in ending inventory. As a result, fixed manufacturing overhead costs are **not** carried from period to period through beginning and ending inventories when variable costing is used.

Fixed overhead is carried from one accounting period to the next in beginning inventory and in ending inventory

For any given year, the difference in net income between absorption costing and variable costing is caused **entirely** by the fixed overhead cost that is transferred from one accounting period to another through beginning and ending inventories with absorption costing. This concept is illustrated in Figure 11-11, which reconciles the difference in net income between the two methods for each of the 4 years.

Mullett Manufacturing Company
Schedule of Fixed Overhead Costs Included in
Beginning and Ending Inventory Under Absorption Costing

	Year			
	1	2	3	4
Fixed MOH transferred into the period in beginning inventory	0	2,000 units @ $5 = $10,000	5,000 units @ $5 = $25,000	2,000 units @ $5 = $10,000
Fixed MOH transferred out of the period in ending inventory	2,000 units @ $5 = $10,000	5,000 units @ $5 = $25,000	2,000 units @ $5 = $10,000	0
Causes absorption costing net income to be	$10,000 higher	$15,000 higher	$15,000 lower	$10,000 lower

Figure 11-11. The difference in net income for any particular year between absorption costing and variable costing is caused by the fixed manufacturing overhead that is carried from one accounting period to the next through inventory. Fixed overhead expenses included in ending inventory are transferred out of the period, thus reducing expenses and net income. Fixed manufacturing overhead expenses included in beginning inventory increase period expenses and reduce net income.

In year 1 there is no beginning inventory, so no fixed overhead is transferred into the period through beginning inventory. However, at the end of the year there are 2,000 units in ending inventory, and with absorption costing each unit has $5 of fixed overhead assigned to it. With absorption costing, the amount of fixed overhead expensed during the period was 8,000 units sold times the $5 per unit fixed overhead cost, or $40,000. All $50,000 of the fixed overhead cost was expensed using variable costing. The $10,000 lower fixed expense with absorption costing explains the $10,000 higher net income with absorption costing in year 1.

In year 2, the $10,000 of fixed overhead cost transferred into the period through beginning inventory is expensed when the products are sold. If there were no ending work in process for the year, net income would be $10,000 lower than with variable costing. But in this case, there are 5,000 units of ending inventory, as shown in Figure 11-10. Those units contain $25,000 ($5 per unit times 5,000 units) of fixed manufacturing overhead cost. The net effect is that $10,000 of fixed overhead costs are transferred into the period, thus lowering net income by that amount; but $25,000 of fixed manufacturing overhead is transferred out of the period through ending inventory, thereby raising the net income by that amount. The result is that year 2 absorption costing net income is $15,000 higher ($25,000 − $10,000) than variable costing net income.

In year 3, the process is reversed because the ending inventory is smaller than the beginning inventory. The $25,000 of fixed overhead cost in beginning inventory is expensed in year 3, and only $10,000 of fixed manufacturing overhead is transferred out of the period in ending inventory. The net effect is absorption costing income that is $15,000 lower than variable costing income. Finally, in year 4 there is no ending inventory, so the $10,000 of fixed overhead transferred into the period in beginning inventory reduces net income by that amount, but no fixed overhead is transferred out of the period through ending inventory. The result is a $10,000 lower net income for absorption costing.

The total net income of the 4-year period is identical in this example:

| Year | Net Income | |
	Absorption	Variable
1	$ 18,000	$ 8,000
2	34,000	19,000
3	48,000	63,000
4	20,000	30,000
Total	$120,000	$120,000

Conditions for total net income to be the same for the two costing methods

For any group of reporting periods, such as the 4 years in this example, the **total** net income is identical for absorption costing and variable costing **if there is no beginning inventory in the first period and no ending inventory in the last period.** This is the case for Mullett Manufacturing Company. Furthermore, if the amount of fixed manufacturing overhead in the first period beginning inventory is the same as the amount of fixed overhead in the last period ending inventory, the total net income over the periods is the same for absorption costing and variable costing.

In any particular year, absorption and variable costing will yield the same net income if there is no beginning and ending inventory, or if the amount of fixed overhead in beginning inventory is the same as the amount of fixed overhead in ending inventory.

Absorption and Variable Costing with Varying Price and Costs

In the second example, prices and costs vary from one year to the next

The Mullett Manufacturing Company example contains the simplifying assumption that costs and selling price remain unchanged. This makes it easier to explain and to understand the differences between the two costing concepts. But it is unrealistic to assume that prices, costs, and volume of activity will remain constant. Now we show an example with the selling price and costs changing from one year to the next. The purpose of this illustration is to demonstrate that despite changing costs and changing prices, the difference in net income reported for absorption costing and the net income reported for

Figure 11-12. This second example uses a more realistic situation in which price, fixed costs, and variable costs change from year to year. The concepts, procedures, and cost relationships are the same as with the first example. The production and sales quantities are identical for both examples.

Mullett II Manufacturing Company
Production, Sales, and Cost Data
Years 1 through 4

	Year			
	1	2	3	4
Sales in units	8,000	9,000	13,000	10,000
Production in units	10,000	12,000	10,000	8,000
Beginning inventory in units	0	2,000	5,000	2,000
Direct materials per unit	$ 6	$ 6	$ 7	$ 8
Direct labor per unit	3	4	4	5
Variable MOH per unit	2	2	3	4
Fixed MOH	50,000	60,000	70,000	80,000
Variable selling and administrative cost per unit	3	3	4	5
Fixed selling and administrative cost	30,000	35,000	40,000	50,000
Sales price per unit	25	27	30	35

variable costing is the result of fixed manufacturing overhead costs carried from one reporting period to another through beginning and ending inventories with the absorption costing method.

Figure 11-12 presents product, sales, and cost data for the Mullett II Manufacturing Company. The production and sales quantity data for each of the 4 years are identical to the first example. However, the selling price increases each year, and the fixed and variable costs increase throughout the 4 years. Of particular importance is the fixed manufacturing overhead cost that increases by $10,000 each year, from $50,000 in year 1 to $80,000 in year 4. With a normal capacity of 50,000 units a year, the fixed manufacturing overhead cost per unit increases each year. The impact of this becomes clear as you study the illustration.

Figure 11-13. In this example, the variable product costs increase each year. With absorption costing, the amount of fixed overhead cost assigned to units increases each year because the total amount of fixed overhead increased each year.

Mullett II Manufacturing Company
Unit Product Cost Data
Years 1 through 4

	Year			
	1	2	3	4
Variable manufacturing costs:				
Direct materials	$ 6	$ 6	$ 7	$ 8
Direct labor	3	4	4	5
Variable MOH	2	2	3	4
Product cost using variable costing	11	12	14	17
Add prorated fixed MOH cost	5	6	7	8
Product cost using absorption costing	$16	$18	$21	$25

As with the first illustration, the first step is to determine the product cost per unit for each year for both absorption and variable costing as shown in Figure 11-13. This figure is similar to Figure 11-8, but here the schedule reflects the change in product cost over the 4-year period. The variable product cost in year 1 is $11 just as in the first example, but it increases to $12 in year 2, $14 in year 3, and $17 in year 4. Similarly, the fixed manufacturing overhead cost is $5 per unit in year 1, but increases by $1 each year as the total amount of fixed overhead increases by $10,000 a year.

The data from Figures 11-12 and 11-13 are used to prepare the absorption costing and variable costing income statements presented in Figure 11-14. The process of preparing these income statements is the same as discussed with the first example, but we must be careful in determining the total product expense reported in the income statements for absorption costing and variable costing. In the earlier example, the product cost per unit is the same for all 4 years. The total product expense reported in the income statement is found merely by multiplying the units sold by the product cost

Figure 11-14. The computation of net income for both variable costing and absorption costing is the same as in the first example (Figure 11-10) except that the costs are changing each period. In particular, we must be cautious of measuring the product expense. To help with this measurement we prepare a new schedule, shown in Figure 11-15.

Mullett II Manufacturing Company
Absorption Costing Income Statement
For Years 1 through 4

	Year 1	2	3	4
Sales	$200,000	$243,000	$390,000	$350,000
Cost of goods sold	128,000	158,000	258,000	242,000
Gross margin	72,000	85,000	132,000	108,000
Variable selling and administrative	24,000	27,000	52,000	50,000
Fixed selling and administrative	30,000	35,000	40,000	50,000
Underapplied (overapplied) overhead	—	(12,000)	—	16,000
Total operating expenses	54,000	50,000	92,000	116,000
Net income	$ 18,000	$ 35,000	$ 40,000	$ (8,000)

Mullett II Manufacturing Company
Variable Costing Income Statement
For Years 1 through 4

	Year 1	2	3	4
Sales	$200,000	$243,000	$390,000	$350,000
Variable product cost	88,000	106,000	172,000	164,000
Manufacturing contribution margin	112,000	137,000	218,000	186,000
Variable selling and administrative	24,000	27,000	52,000	50,000
Contribution margin	88,000	110,000	166,000	136,000
Fixed manufacturing overhead	50,000	60,000	70,000	80,000
Fixed selling and administrative	30,000	35,000	40,000	50,000
Total fixed cost	80,000	95,000	110,000	130,000
Net income	$ 8,000	$ 15,000	$ 56,000	$ 6,000

per unit. In the Mullett II example, both absorption and variable costing product costs change from year to year. Therefore, to find the total product expense reported in the income statements, we must know how many of the sold units are from the beginning inventory and how many are from the current year's production. For this example we assume a first in, first out (FIFO) cost flow. The computation of product expense for each year for both absorption and variable costing is presented in Figure 11-15. This type of schedule was not prepared for the first example because of the constant cost.

Mullett II Manufacturing Company
Schedule of Product Expense Using Absorption Costing
Years 1 through 4

Year	Product Expense from Beginning Inventory		Current Year Production	Total Product Expense
1	0		8,000 units @ $16	$128,000
2	2,000 units @ $16	+	7,000 units @ 18	158,000
3	5,000 units @ 18	+	8,000 units @ 21	258,000
4	2,000 units @ 21	+	8,000 units @ 25	242,000

Mullett II Manufacturing Company
Schedule of Product Expense Using Variable Costing
Years 1 through 4

Year	Product Expense from Beginning Inventory		Current Year Production	Total Product Expense
1	0		8,000 units @ $11	$ 88,000
2	2,000 units @ $11	+	7,000 units @ 12	106,000
3	5,000 units @ 12	+	8,000 units @ 14	172,000
4	2,000 units @ 14	+	8,000 units @ 17	164,000

Figure 11-15. This schedule shows the computation of product expense for both variable costing and absorption costing. Because the cost of beginning inventory each period is different from the current period product cost, it is necessary to use FIFO or some other inventory flow assumption to compute the annual product expense and ending inventory cost.

As with the first example, the difference in net income is caused entirely by fixed overhead included in inventory costs

The inventory flow and associated product costs are presented in Figure 11-16, and the difference in net income for each year is reconciled in Figure 11-17. The major difference between this and the earlier example is that the amount of fixed overhead cost per unit changes from year to year, so merely knowing the number of units in beginning and ending inventory does not explain the difference in income. Instead we must know the amount of fixed overhead included in inventory.

Figure 11-16. This schedule of beginning and ending inventory costs reflects not only the change in the number of units in inventory, but also the change in the cost of units over time.

Mullett II Manufacturing Company
Schedule of Beginning and Ending Inventory
Under Absorption Costing and Variable Costing

Absorption Costing

	Year			
	1	2	3	4
Beginning inventory:				
Number of units	0	2,000	5,000	2,000
Unit cost	—	$16	$18	$21
Total cost	—	$32,000	$90,000	$42,000
Ending inventory:				
Number of units	2,000	5,000	2,000	0
Unit cost	$16	$18	$21	—
Total cost	$32,000	$90,000	$42,000	—

Variable Costing

	Year			
	1	2	3	4
Beginning inventory:				
Number of units	0	2,000	5,000	2,000
Unit cost	—	$11	$12	$14
Total cost	—	$22,000	$60,000	$28,000
Ending inventory:				
Number of units	2,000	5,000	2,000	0
Unit cost	$11	$12	$14	—
Total cost	$22,000	$60,000	$28,000	—

Mullett II Manufacturing Company
Schedule of Fixed Overhead Costs Included in
Beginning and Ending Inventory Under Absorption Costing

	Year			
	1	2	3	4
Fixed MOH transferred into the period in beginning inventory	0	2,000 units @ $5 = $10,000	5,000 units @ $6 = $30,000	2,000 units @ $7 = $14,000
Fixed MOH transferred out of the period in ending inventory	2,000 units @ $5 = $10,000	5,000 units @ $6 = $30,000	2,000 units @ $7 = $14,000	0
Causes absorption costing net income to be	$10,000 higher	$20,000 higher	$16,000 lower	$14,000 lower

Figure 11-17. The total difference in reported income between the absorption costing and variable costing methods is caused by the fixed overhead that is transferred from one period to the next through inventory. This difference can be computed by finding the amount of fixed manufacturing overhead that is included in the product cost of beginning and ending inventory.

SUMMARY   Most accounting reports are based on the concept of **absorption costing,** also called **full costing,** which requires that products are assigned all costs of production, both direct and indirect, fixed and variable. An alternative method of reporting is the **contribution approach,** in which the emphasis is on the cost behavior patterns rather than functional cost classifications. **Divisional, product,** and **sales region contribution reports** are common.

Contribution reports emphasize cost behavior. Variable manufacturing costs are subtracted from sales revenue to find the **manufacturing contribution margin.** All other variable costs are then deducted to determine the **contribution margin.** All fixed costs are subtracted from the contribution margin to arrive at the divisional, product, or sales region contribution. Often managers find it useful to convert the total contribution to some common measure, such as contribution per dollar of sales.

The contribution approach may be used for product costing in addition to reporting on the performance of various business segments. **Variable costing,** also called **direct costing,** assigns to products only the variable manufacturing costs, including direct materials, direct labor, and **variable** manufacturing overhead. All fixed costs, including fixed manufacturing overhead, are expensed in the period in which incurred. The main issues are which costs should be inventoried, and what information should be reported on the income statement.

Differences in net income between absorption and variable costing methods in any particular year are caused by the fixed manufacturing overhead cost carried from one period to the next through beginning and ending inventory. If there are no beginning and ending inventories, the reported net income is identical but the type of information presented in the income statements is different.

KEY TERMS   absorption costing *(405)*
contribution approach *(405, 414)*
contribution margin *(405)*
direct costing *(414)*
divisional contribution report *(406)*
full costing *(405)*

manufacturing contribution
  margin *(407)*
product contribution report *(410)*
sales region contribution
  report *(412)*
variable costing *(414)*

QUESTIONS   1. Distinguish between contribution margin and manufacturing contribution margin. What information does each provide to management?

2. Kliptite Company's industrial products division manufactures an automatic nailing and stapling gun used in the construction industry. Its fastener division manufactures various types of fasteners, including the nails and staples used in the gun. Looking at the latest product contribution statement, the newly hired vice president of production says, "Looks like we should discontinue production of the Rapid-Klip nail gun. Its contribution margin is only eight percent. After allocating its fair share of fixed costs to it, the product will show a loss." The production

manager is upset. He argues that discontinuing the gun will cause a decline in overall company profit. "Nonsense," says the vice president. "If you eliminate a product that loses money, you can only improve profits." Discuss the vice president's comments. Discuss the reasons why the production manager might be right.

3. (AICPA) Although direct costing is not a current generally accepted method of costing inventory for external reporting, it is useful for internal reporting purposes. Describe the difference between direct costing and the current generally accepted method of costing inventory for external reporting. Describe how a direct costing structure facilitates calculation of the contribution margin and the break-even point.

EXERCISES

Ex. 11-1
Contribution
Measures

Maxwella Department Store uses the contribution approach to report performance for each of its three departments. Below are summarized data for the year just completed.

	Division		
	Sporting Goods	Women's Clothing	Home Appliances
Sales	$200,000	$400,000	$800,000
Variable costs	80,000	160,000	500,000
Contribution margin	120,000	240,000	300,000
Fixed expenses	40,000	140,000	140,000
Contribution	$ 80,000	$100,000	$160,000

Corporate expenses not identifiable with divisions are $200,000.

REQUIRED

a. Compute the corporate net income for the period.
b. For each division compute the contribution per sales dollar.

Ex. 11-2
Product
Contribution
Report

The Consumer Division of the Electric Products Company makes two models of hot water heaters. Both the 80-gallon and the 55-gallon models are excellent products. Some customers prefer the added capacity of the 80-gallon model, but it is slightly less energy-efficient. Product cost and sales data are presented below for the fiscal year ended June 30.

	Product		
	80-Gallon	55-Gallon	Total
Sales in units	500	300	
Sales price	$ 400	$ 260	
Unit variable costs:			
Manufacturing	180	110	
Other variable costs	40	25	
Fixed costs directly identifiable with products:			
Manufacturing	42,000	20,000	$62,000
Other fixed costs	26,000	8,000	34,000
Total divisional expenses			26,000

REQUIRED   Prepare a product contribution statement for the Consumer Division of the Electric Products Company.

Ex. 11-3
Sales Region
Contribution
Statement

Refer to the data in Exercise 11-2 for the Consumer Division of the Electric Products Company. The following data are pertinent to the development of a sales region contribution statement.

	Region	
	Eastern	Western
Sales in units:		
80-gallon	400	100
55-gallon	120	180
Other variable costs:		
80-gallon	$35.00	$60.00
55-gallon	17.50	30.00
Fixed costs:		
Other fixed costs	$18,000	$16,000
Fixed costs not identifiable with sales regions:		
Manufacturing	$62,000	
Others	6,000	
Divisional expenses	20,000	

REQUIRED   Prepare a sales region contribution statement in good form for the Consumer Division of the Electric Products Company.

Ex. 11-4
Variable Costing
Income Statement

Following are 1985 operating data for the Northside Iron Works.

Units manufactured	60,000
Normal capacity	60,000
Selling price	$40
Variable costs:	
Direct materials	8
Direct labor	5
Manufacturing overhead	4
Selling and administrative	3
Fixed costs:	
Manufacturing overhead	$300,000
Selling and administrative	120,000
Units sold	55,000
No beginning inventory	

REQUIRED   Prepare a variable costing income statement in good form for Northside Iron Works.

Ex. 11-5
Absorption Costing
Income Statement

Refer to the Northside Iron Works operating data presented in Exercise 11-4.

REQUIRED.   Prepare an absorption costing income statement in good form for Northside Iron Works.

Ex. 11-6
Understanding
Absorption and
Variable Costing
Data

The Medfore Company uses absorption costing for all of its external financial statements and variable costing to provide management with useful planning and control data. The following data were collected for the current year:

	Units	Variable Unit Cost	Absorption Unit Cost
Beginning inventory	6,000	$10	$14
Ending inventory	9,000	11	16
Normal capacity	30,000		
Underapplied or overapplied overhead = 0			

REQUIRED   Determine:

   a.   The cost of ending inventory using variable costing.
   b.   The cost of ending inventory using absorption costing.
   c.   The number of units sold.
   d.   The difference in net income between the two product costing methods.

Ex. 11-7
Variable Costing
with Beginning
Inventory

Tepco, Inc., manufactures garbage disposals. During 1985, 22,000 units were manufactured and 19,000 units were sold. The price of the garbage disposal is $90. Variable manufacturing costs were $28 for materials, $16 for labor, and $8 for variable manufacturing overhead. Variable selling and administrative costs were $6 per unit sold, and fixed selling and administrative costs were $325,000. Budgeted and actual fixed manufacturing overhead was $200,000. Normal capacity is 20,000 units. Beginning inventory on January 1, 1985, was 5,000 units with a variable product cost of $48 per unit. Tepco uses the FIFO inventory method.

REQUIRED   Prepare a variable costing income statement in good form for Tepco, Inc.

Ex. 11-8
Absorption Costing
with Beginning
Inventory

Refer to the data in Exercise 11-7 for Tepco, Inc. Beginning inventory using absorption costing has a unit cost of $57.

REQUIRED.   Prepare an absorption costing income statement in good form for Tepco, Inc.

Ex. 11-9
Variable and
Absorption Costing
Income Statements

Largen Company manufactured 60,000 metal bookcases during 1985. Prime cost was $22 per unit, variable overhead $6 per unit, and variable selling and administrative cost $3 per unit. Budgeted and actual fixed overhead cost was $300,000 and fixed selling and administrative cost was $220,000. During 1985, 55,000 units were sold for $50 each. Beginning inventory was 6,000 units, with variable manufacturing costs of $25 and applied fixed overhead of $4 per unit. Normal capacity is 60,000 bookcases a year. The FIFO inventory method is used.

REQUIRED

   a.   Prepare a variable costing income statement in good form for the Largen Company.
   b.   Prepare an absorption costing income statement in good form for the Largen Company. Underapplied or overapplied MOH is assigned to cost of goods sold.

Ex. 11-10 (AICPA)
CVP Analysis with
Direct and
Absorption Costing

The following data relate to a year's budgeted activity for Patsy Corporation, a single-product company:

	Units
Beginning inventory	30,000
Production	120,000
Goods available	150,000
Sales	110,000
Ending inventory	40,000

	Per Unit
Selling price	$5.00
Variable manufacturing costs	1.00
Variable selling costs	2.00
Fixed manufacturing costs, based on 100,000 units	.25
Fixed selling costs, based on 100,000 units	.65

Total fixed costs remain unchanged within the relevant range of 25,000 units to total capacity of 160,000 units.

REQUIRED

Respond to the following multiple-choice questions:

1. The projected annual break-even sales in units for Patsy Corporation is
   a. 30,000.   b. 37,143.   c. 45,000   d. 50,000.
2. The projected net income for Patsy Corporation for the year under direct (variable) costing is
   a. $110,000.   b. $127,500.   c. $130,000.   d. $150,000.
3. If all the variances are charged to cost of goods sold, the projected net income for Patsy Corporation for the year under absorption costing is
   a. $122,500.   b. $127,500.   c. $130,000.   d. $132,500.
4. A special order is received to purchase 10,000 units to be used in an unrelated market. Given the original data, what price per unit should be charged on this order to increase Patsy Corporation's net income by $5,000?
   a. $3.50.   b. $4.40.   c. $5.00.   d. $6.50.
5. Concerning the data for Patsy Corporation, assume selling price increases by 20 percent, variable manufacturing costs increase by 10 percent, variable selling costs remain the same, and total fixed costs increase to $104,400. How many units must now be sold to generate a profit equal to 10 percent of the contribution margin?
   a. 36,000.   b. 40,000.   c. 43,320.   d. 45,390.

Ex. 11-11 (AICPA)
Absorption and
Direct Costing
Income Statements

Flear Company has a maximum productive capacity of 210,000 units per year. Normal capacity is regarded as 180,000 units per year. Standard variable manufacturing costs are $11 per unit. Fixed factory overhead is $360,000 per year. Variable selling expenses are $3 per unit and fixed selling expenses are $252,000 per year. The unit sales price is $20.

The operating results of 1985 are: sales, 150,000 units; production, 160,000 units; beginning inventory, 10,000 units; and net unfavorable variance for standard variable manufacturing costs, $40,000. All variances are written off as addition to or deductions from standard cost of goods sold.

a. Prepare formal income statements for 1985 using
   1. Absorption costing.
   2. Variable costing.
b. Briefly describe the reasons for the difference in net income between the two income statements.

PROBLEMS

P. 11-1
Divisional
Contribution
Statement

The Auto-Parts Corporation makes a variety of automobile parts that it sells to major automobile manufacturers. The company's operations are separated into three divisions. Sales and cost data for the divisions are presented below:

Auto-Parts Corporation
Divisional Sales and Cost Data
For the Year Ended December 31, 1985

	Division		
	Windshields	Bumpers	Generators
Units sold	10,000	16,000	8,000
Average unit sales price	$120	$100	$60
Average unit variable costs:			
Manufacturing	55	48	25
Marketing	6	5	3
Distribution	10	7	3
Administrative	2	2	2
Fixed costs directly identifiable with divisions:			
Manufacturing	$190,000	$150,000	$100,000
Marketing	70,000	85,000	25,000
Distribution	80,000	50,000	45,000
Administrative	90,000	100,000	60,000
Corporate expenses not identifiable with specific divisions			230,000

Prepare a divisional contribution statement in good form for the Auto-Parts Corporation.

P. 11-2
Product
Contribution
Statement

The Home Products Company Appliance Division manufactures washing machines and dryers. The company uses contribution reports to assist in measuring performance for division and products. Below are sales and cost data for the two products produced in the Appliance Division.

Home Products
Appliance Division
Product Sales and Cost Data
For the Year Ended December 31, 1985

	Product		Division Expenses[a]
	Washing Machines	Drying Machines	
Sales in units	2,000	3,000	
Sales price	$350	$250	
Unit variable costs:			
Manufacturing	150	110	
Marketing	40	25	
Distribution	30	20	
Administrative	15	10	
Fixed costs directly identifiable with products:			
Manufacturing	$80,000	$ 60,000	$ 40,000
Marketing	20,000	20,000	30,000
Distribution	30,000	25,000	40,000
Administration	30,000	20,000	45,000
Total divisional expenses			$155,000

[a] Fixed expenses identifiable with the division but not with specific products.

REQUIRED   Prepare a product contribution report in good form for the appliance division.

P. 11-3
Sales Region
Contribution
Report

Refer to the data in Problem 11-2 for the Appliance Division of the Home Products Company. Variable manufacturing costs and variable administrative costs are the same for both regions. The following data are pertinent to the development of a sales region contribution statement.

	Region		Divisional Costs
	Northern	Southern	
Sales in units:			
Washing machines	1,000	1,000	
Drying machines	1,200	1,800	
Variable costs:			
Marketing:			
Washing machines	$ 45.00	$ 35.00	
Drying machines	32.50	20.00	
Distribution:			
Washing machines	36.00	24.00	
Drying machines	27.50	15.00	
Fixed costs:			
Marketing	15,000	25,000	
Distribution	20,000	35,000	
Administrative	20,000	20,000	
Fixed costs not identifiable with regions:			
Manufacturing			$180,000
Marketing			30,000
Distribution			40,000
Administrative			55,000
Total fixed costs not identifiable with regions:			$305,000

REQUIRED   Prepare a sales region contribution report in good form for the Appliance Division of the Home Products Company.

P. 11-4
Analyzing Variable
Costing Data

Below is the 1985 variable costing income statement for the Monford Company. The company's normal capacity is 20,000 units a year. Beginning inventory was 6,000 units at a variable cost of $25 per unit. Ending inventory was 8,000 units.

Monford Company
Variable Costing Income Statement
For the Year Ended December 31, 1985

Sales ($55 × 21,000 units)		$1,155,000
Less variable manufacturing expense		570,000
Manufacturing contribution margin		585,000
Less variable selling and administrative expense		126,000
Contribution margin		459,000
Less fixed expenses:		
Manufacturing overhead	$160,000	
Selling and administrative	120,000	280,000
Net income		$ 179,000

REQUIRED

a. Compute the number of units manufactured in 1985.
b. Prepare a product cost schedule for 1985 for both variable and absorption costing.
c. Prepare an absorption costing income statement for 1985 in good form. Assume that fixed overhead cost per unit in beginning inventory is the same as in 1985.

P. 11-5
Product
Contribution for a
Merchandising
Firm

The Delvin Pool Products Company sells a variety of chemicals, equipment, and recreational supplies for home swimming pools. The company purchases all of its products from wholesalers or factory representatives. Company management recently decided to separate operations into four divisions: chemicals, plumbing equipment, pool cleaning equipment, and recreational supplies. Divisional and product contribution statements are prepared for all divisions.

The pool cleaning equipment division sells three products, the Whizzo, the Whammo, and the Whacco. They sell for $300, $200, and $120 respectively. The products cost Delvin $150, $120, and $75 respectively. Sales commissions are the only variable selling costs and are 10 percent of selling price. Variable administrative cost is $4 per unit for processing the sales order. Variable distribution cost includes packaging, delivery, and setup and is $25 per unit on the Whizzo, $20 on the Whammo, and $10 for the Whacco. Fixed marketing costs for the products are primarily product advertising costs, which are $12,000 for the Whizzo, $6,000 for the Whammo, and $5,000 for the Whacco. All other fixed costs associated with the products are $4,000, $3,000, and $3,000 respectively. 1985 sales were 400 Whizzos, 800 Whammos, and 700 Whaccos. Divisional expenses not identifiable with specific products amount to $19,000.

REQUIRED

Prepare a product contribution statement for the Pool Cleaning Equipment Division of The Delvin Pool Products Company.

P. 11-6
Understanding
Absorption and
Variable Costing
Data

Following are selected data of the Howthorne Company.

	Units	Prime Cost	Applied Overhead
Beginning Inventory	12,000	$25/unit	$15/unit ($6 variable)
Ending inventory	8,000	$28/unit	$18/unit ($7 variable)
Normal capacity	40,000		

Underapplied overhead = $33,000 (all fixed overhead and assignable to cost of goods sold)

REQUIRED

Use the above data to determine:

a. The total amount of fixed overhead during the current year.
b. The difference in net income between absorption and variable costing for the year.
c. The number of units produced during the period.
d. The number of units sold during the period.
e. The cost of ending inventory using variable costing.

P. 11-7
Identifying
Absorption and
Variable Costing
Information

A partial list of sales and cost data is presented below for the Creede Manufacturing Company.

Sales (18,000 units)	$630,000
Manufacturing costs for the units produced:	
Prime cost	252,000
Variable MOH	84,000
Fixed MOH	100,000
Operating expenses:	
Variable selling expense	54,000
Fixed selling expense	45,000
Fixed administrative	90,000

During the year, 21,000 units were produced, which is 1,000 more than normal capacity. There were 4,000 units in beginning inventory, with a variable manufacturing cost of $15 per unit. Fixed MOH included in the beginning inventory was $4.50 per unit.

REQUIRED

From the above data, determine:

a. The number of units in ending inventory.
b. The cost of ending inventory using absorption costing.
c. The cost of ending inventory using variable costing.
d. The company's gross margin on sales percentage.
e. The company's contribution margin as a percentage of sales.
f. The company's total manufacturing contribution margin.
g. The difference in net income between the two costing methods.

P. 11-8
Understanding
Absorption and
Variable Costing
Data

Folgens Chemical Company manufactures a rust inhibitor that it sells to commercial customers in 50-gallon drums. Following are 2 years of production, sales, and cost data.

	Year 2	Year 3
Sales in units	40,000	55,000
Production in units	50,000	55,000
Unit selling price	$75	$80
Variable costs:		
Prime cost	$1,750,000	$2,090,000
Variable MOH	200,000	275,000
Selling expense	280,000	440,000
Fixed costs:		
Manufacturing overhead	500,000	600,000
Selling expense	200,000	225,000
Administrative expense	400,000	430,000

The beginning inventory in year 2 is 12,000 units, with variable manufacturing costs of $37 per unit. The fixed manufacturing overhead costs in year 1 were $500,000, and normal capacity is 50,000 units (50-gallon drums) a year. FIFO inventory is used.

REQUIRED

a. Prepare a schedule of product costs for absorption and variable costing for both years.
b. Compute the cost of ending inventory for year 3 using absorption costing.
c. Compute the difference in net income between absorption and variable costing for year 2 and year 3.
d. Prepare an absorption costing income statement in good form for year 3.

P. 11-9
Three-Year
Absorption and
Variable Costing

McCarver Company uses absorption costing for all external reporting requirements, but recently some top managers have expressed an interest in using variable costing for internal reporting purposes. Following are production, sales, and cost data for the past 3 years. Normal capacity is 5,000 units a year.

	1983	1984	1985
Sales in units	4,000	5,000	6,000
Production in units	5,000	6,000	4,000
Beginning inventory in units	0	1,000	2,000
Direct materials per unit	$ 10	$ 10	$ 10
Direct labor per unit	8	8	8
Variable MOH per unit	3	3	3
Fixed MOH	75,000	75,000	75,000
Variable selling and administrative per unit	6	6	6
Fixed selling and administrative	50,000	50,000	50,000
Sales price per unit	60	60	60

REQUIRED
a. Prepare a schedule of product costs for the 3 years for both variable costing and absorption costing.
b. Prepare a schedule of variable and absorption costing net income for the 3 years.
c. Prepare a schedule to reconcile the difference in annual income between the two methods.

P. 11-10
Absorption and Variable Costing with Changing Costs

Following are data from the Flagston Company. Management uses both absorption and variable costing income statements.

Flagston Company
Schedule of Sales, Production, and Cost Data

	Year			
	1	2	3	4
Sales in units	12,000	16,000	18,000	14,000
Production in units	17,000	18,000	12,000	13,000
Beginning inventory in units	0	5,000	7,000	1,000
Direct materials per unit	$ 5	$ 6	$ 7	$ 7
Direct labor per unit	6	7	9	10
Variable MOH per unit	3	3	4	5
Fixed MOH	90,000	105,000	120,000	120,000
Variable selling and administrative per unit	4	5	6	6
Fixed selling and administrative	50,000	60,000	80,000	90,000
Sales price per unit	40	45	50	52

The company assigns fixed overhead based on expected production of 15,000 units a year.

REQUIRED
a. Prepare a schedule of product costs for each year for both variable and absorption costing.
b. Prepare a schedule of product expenses for each of the years using both absorption and variable costing.
c. Prepare a schedule of net income for both absorption and variable costing.
d. Prepare a schedule to reconcile the difference in net income between the two methods.

P. 11-11 (AICPA)
Absorption and Direct Costing

Management of Bicent Company uses the following unit costs for the one product it manufactures:

	Projected Cost per Unit
Direct material (all variable)	$30.00
Direct labor (all variable)	19.00
Manufacturing overhead:	
Variable cost	6.00
Fixed cost (based on 10,000 units per month)	5.00
Selling, general, and administrative:	
Variable cost	4.00
Fixed cost (based on 10,000 units per month)	2.80

The projected selling price is $80 per unit. The fixed costs remain fixed within the relevant range of 4,000 to 16,000 units of production.

Management has also projected the following data for the month of June 1985:

	Units
Beginning inventory	2,000
Production	9,000
Available	11,000
Sales	7,500
Ending inventory	3,500

REQUIRED

Prepare projected income statements for June 1985 for management purposes under each of the following product costing methods:

a. Absorption costing with all variances charged to cost of goods sold each month.
b. Direct (variable) costing.

Supporting schedules calculating inventoriable production costs per unit should be presented in good form. **Ignore income taxes.**

P. 11-12(CMA)
Product
Contribution
Report

Pralina Products Company is a regional firm that has three major product lines — cereals, breakfast bars, and dog food. The income statement for the year ended April 30, 1985, is shown at the top of the next page. The statement was prepared by product line using absorption (full) costing. Explanatory data related to the items presented in the income statement appear in the adjoining column.

Other Data

1. **Cost of sales.** The company's inventories of raw materials and finished products do not vary significantly from year to year. The inventories at April 30, 1985, were essentially identical to those at April 30, 1984.

   Factory overhead was applied to products at 120 percent of direct labor dollars. The factory overhead costs for the 1984–85 fiscal year were as follows:

Variable indirect labor and supplies	$ 15,000
Variable employee benefits on factory labor	30,000
Supervisory salaries and related benefits	35,000
Plant occupancy costs	100,000
Total factory overhead	$180,000

   There was no overapplied or underapplied overhead at year-end.

2. **Advertising.** The company has been unable to determine any direct causal relationship between the level of sales volume and the level of advertising expenditures. However, because management believes advertising is necessary, an annual advertising program is implemented for each product line. Each product line is advertised independently of the others.

Pralina Products Company
Income Statement
For the Year Ended April 30, 1985
(000 omitted)

	Cereals	Breakfast Bars	Dog Food	Total
Sales in pounds	2,000	500	500	3,000
Revenue from sales	$1,000	$400	$200	$1,600
Cost of sales:				
Raw materials	330	160	100	590
Direct labor	90	40	20	150
Factory overhead	108	48	24	180
Total cost of sales	528	248	144	920
Gross margin	472	152	56	680
Operating expenses:				
Selling expenses:				
Advertising	50	30	20	100
Commissions	50	40	20	110
Salaries and related benefits	30	20	10	60
Total selling expenses	130	90	50	270
General and administrative expenses:				
Licenses	50	20	15	85
Salaries and related benefits	60	25	15	100
Total general and administrative expenses	110	45	30	185
Total operating expenses	240	135	80	455
Operating income before taxes	$ 232	$ 17	$ (24)	$ 225

3. **Commissions.** Sales commissions are paid to the sales force at the rates of 5 percent of sales on the cereals and 10 percent on the breakfast bars and dog food.
4. **Licenses.** Various licenses are required for each product line. These are renewed annually for each product line.
5. **Salaries and related benefits.** Sales and general and administrative personnel devote time and effort to all product lines. Their salaries and wages are allocated on the basis of management's estimates of time spent on each product line.

REQUIRED

a. The controller of Pralina Products Company has recommended that the company do a cost-volume-profit (CVP) analysis of its operations. As a first step, the controller has requested that you prepare a revised income statement for Pralina Products Company that employs a product contribution margin format, which will be useful in CVP analysis. The statement should show the profit contribution for each product line and the net income before taxes for the company as a whole.
b. What effect, if any, would there be on net income before taxes determined in requirement a if the inventories as of April 30, 1985, had increased significantly over the inventory levels of April 30, 1984? Explain your answer.

P. 11-13(AICPA)
Product
Contribution
Analysis

The Marcia Company, your client, has asked your assistance in determining an economical sales and production mix of its products for 1985. The company manufactures a line of dolls and a doll dress sewing kit.

The company's sales department provides the following data:

Item	Estimated Demand for 1985 (Units)	Established Net Price (Units)
Laurie	50,000	$5.20
Debbie	42,000	2.40
Sarah	35,000	8.50
Kathy	40,000	4.00
Sewing kit	325,000	3.00

To promote sales of the sewing kit, there is a 15 percent reduction in the established net price for a kit purchased at the same time that a Marcia Company doll is purchased.

From accounting records you develop the following data:

1. The production standards per unit:

Item	Material	Labor
Laurie	$1.40	$ .80
Debbie	.70	.50
Sarah	2.69	1.40
Kathy	1.00	1.00
Sewing kit	.60	.40

2. The labor rate of $2.00 per hour is expected to continue without change in 1985. The plant has an effective capacity of 130,000 labor hours per year on a single-shift basis. Present equipment can produce all of the products.
3. The total fixed costs for 1985 will be $100,000. Variable costs will be equivalent to 50 percent of direct labor cost.
4. The company has a small inventory of its products that can be ignored.

REQUIRED

a. Prepare a schedule computing the contribution to profit of a unit of each product.
b. Prepare a schedule computing the contribution to profit of a unit of each product per labor dollar expended on the product.
c. Prepare a schedule computing the total labor hours required to produce the estimated sales units for 1985. Indicate the item and number of units that you would recommend be increased (or decreased) in production to attain the company's effective productive capacity.
d. Without regard to your answer in c, assume that the estimated sales units for 1985 would require 12,000 labor hours in excess of the company's effective productive capacity. Discuss the possible methods of providing the missing capacity. Include in your discussion all factors that must be taken into consideration in evaluating the methods of providing the missing capacity.

CASES

Mancos Lake Manufacturing Company is a third-generation, family-owned business that makes saddles for horses. The company has used traditional absorption costing income statements for both external and internal use since it was formed. Several managers have learned of variable costing from journal articles and professional seminars. Fred comments, "We have been dramatically overstating our net income for years by using absorption costing. Our actual net income would be much lower, but we keep putting that fixed manufacturing overhead in the product cost and it ends up in the ending inventory when it should be an expense." Sandra disagrees. She says, "How can variable costing be an acceptable costing method if it gives a different net income than what we have always used?" Jim comments, "I think you are both missing the point. For our purposes, we aren't concerned with the net income figure. What we really need from variable costing is a better understanding of the nature of our costs and the impact of changing activity levels on our performance." Ralph Mancos, current company president, is somewhat confused by the discussion of variable costing. He says, "You can't all be right about this subject. Have you got any data to support your points? Quite frankly, I'm not very interested in switching to a new costing method. I understand what we currently have and I am pretty comfortable with it." To cast some light on the subject, the chief accountant has developed some production, sales, and cost data for the last 3 years of operations. All manufacturing overhead costs are fixed unless indicated otherwise, and the company uses FIFO inventory valuation.

	1983	1984	1985
Normal capacity (in units)	20,000	20,000	20,000
Units produced	20,000	22,000	25,000
Units sold	18,000	20,000	26,000
Selling price per unit	$ 180	$ 190	$ 195
Costs:			
Direct materials	1,100,000	1,276,000	1,500,000
Direct labor	400,000	462,000	575,000
Production supervision	345,000	408,200	420,000
Office salaries	190,000	220,000	240,000
Depreciation, production plant and equipment	340,000	340,000	360,000
Depreciation, office	180,000	180,000	180,000
Property taxes, 70% production facilities	100,000	100,000	100,000
Insurance, production facilities	40,000	42,000	45,500
Insurance, office	14,000	15,000	16,000
Indirect labor (80% variable)	45,000	55,000	70,000
Indirect material (100% variable)	40,000	44,000	50,000
Selling expense (40% variable)	157,500	180,000	228,000
Administrative expenses	156,000	190,000	210,000
Utilities, 80% production facilities (50% variable)	90,000	104,500	131,250
Total costs	$3,202,500	$3,608,500	$4,125,250
Beginning inventory (units)	6,000		
Unit cost ($40 fixed overhead)	$120		

REQUIRED

a. Discuss in some detail the comments made by Fred, Sandra, and Jim.

b. Prepare a product cost schedule for both absorption and variable costing including all 3 years of data.

c. Prepare a schedule of beginning and ending inventory quantities for each of the 3 years.

d. Prepare a schedule of net income for both absorption costing and variable costing including each of the 3 years.

e. Is Fred's comment about the effect of variable costing on the company's income correct? Prepare a schedule reconciling the difference in net income between absorption costing and variable costing for each of the 3 years.

f. Compute the cost of ending inventory in 1985 using both absorption costing and variable costing.

g. Respond to the comments of President Mancos about using a new product costing system.

CHAPTER 12
Decentralized Operations and Segmental Reporting

All but the smallest and simplest of organizations find that dividing the organization into segments can enhance the efficiency and effectiveness of managing the business. By assigning decision authority to managers of business segments and holding those managers responsible for the results of their decisions, many firms find a marked improvement in business performance over centralized operations. Of course, the assignment of responsibility and authority to segment managers requires the development of a system for measuring and reporting the performance of business segments.

This chapter is devoted to the measurement of performance by various segments of a business. We begin by discussing the nature of decentralized operations and the concept of responsibility accounting. Next we discuss and illustrate the more common methods of measuring the performance of business segments. Finally we present key issues in measuring transactions that occur between business segments.

DECENTRALIZED OPERATIONS

In many small businesses, one person does virtually all of the planning and makes all of the important decisions. As the business grows, it becomes more difficult and less efficient for one person to perform all the management functions. For example, the owner of a growing drugstore business initially employs a pharmacist and three salesclerks. The owner makes all purchasing, pricing, advertising, inventory, and personnel decisions. When the owner opens new stores in different locations around the state, a manager must be hired for each of the stores. Some of the inventory, personnel, and pricing decisions now must be made by the store managers if the decisions are to be timely. The store managers are given the authority to make these decisions, and with the authority comes responsibility, which means the managers are held accountable for their decisions.

The assignment of authority and responsibility to subordinates is called delegation

Assigning decision authority and responsibility to subordinates is called **delegation.** As organizations grow, decision making can become inefficient if top managers do not delegate some of the management process to subordinates. Separating an organization into manageable units increases the efficiency of the organization and yet provides proper control over operations. Separating the organization into managerial segments is called **decentralization.** These segments of the business are called **responsibility centers** because the managers of each segment are held responsible for the performance of the segment.

Managers of decentralized operations are delegated the authority to make decisions for their part of the business, and they are also held responsible for their performance. The term **responsibility accounting** refers to the accounting process that reports how well managers meet their responsibilities. Typically, responsibility is expressed in terms of measurable variables such as a desired profit level for the division or achievement of budgets or standard costs.

Accounting system that reports how well managers meet their responsibility

RESPONSIBILITY ACCOUNTING

In many respects, accounting is oriented toward measuring the performance of managers of an organization. But in this chapter we are particularly interested in measuring performance, which is more than simply reporting financial data. Responsibility accounting rests on the premise that managers should be held accountable for their performance and the performance of the people and resources they manage. This concept guides accountants in accumulating and reporting accounting information by areas of responsibility. Effective responsibility accounting reports must embody a number of assumptions, including:

Assumptions of responsibility accounting systems

1. Managers are held responsible for the activities over which they exercise control.
2. Managers strive to achieve the goals and objectives that have been established for them and their part of the organization.
3. Managers participate in establishing the goals against which their performance will be measured.
4. Goals are attainable with efficient and effective performance.[1]
5. Performance reports and feedback are timely.
6. The role of responsibility accounting in the company's reward structure is clearly stated.

Reporting the performance of business segment managers is an essential part of controlling the operations of decentralized organizations. Some of the specific benefits that may be achieved with decentralization are:

Benefits of decentralization

1. Organizations are separated into units of manageable size.
2. Decisions are made at a level where managers are most knowledgeable about the problems involved and the decisions that must be made.

---

[1] The terms **effectiveness** and **efficiency** describe different measures of performance. Effectiveness refers to how well a specific goal was met. Efficiency measures whether or not the goal was met within the expected cost. If the goal was to sell 100 units of a product in 1 month and 106 units are sold, the firm was **effective** in meeting its sales quota. If the goal was to have a selling cost of $35 per unit but the actual cost was $46 per unit, the firm was not **efficient** in its selling activities.

3. Decisions are made on a timely basis.

4. The morale and job satisfaction levels of managers are higher because of their active participation in the management process.

5. Managers of business segments have an opportunity to gain valuable managerial skills that provide the organization with a pool of potential top managers.

6. Managers are motivated to act in a manner that is most beneficial to the firm.

TYPES OF RESPONSIBILITY CENTERS

There are several common classifications of **responsibility centers.** Included are **cost centers, profit centers,** and **investment centers.**

The type of responsibility center used to measure the performance of each part of a decentralized organization depends on the objectives of management and the nature of each particular segment. For example, a service department that supports production activities has some control over its costs, but it has no control over the firm's revenue. As a result, the service department is limited to cost responsibility; there is no attempt to measure profit generated by the department because it produces no revenues.

On the other hand, a department that sells goods to customers is responsible for both costs and revenues. The performance report for each responsibility center should be designed to measure the success of each segment in accordance with the way the segment is expected to contribute to the goals of the organization.

Cost Centers

A **cost center** is a business segment that incurs costs but does not generate profits. The manager of a cost center is held responsible for the costs incurred in his or her segment. Cost center managers have control over costs but not over revenues. Cost centers are the most common type of responsibility center, because virtually every segment of an organization incurs costs but many segments do not generate revenues. For example, a company has five different divisions, each making and selling different types of products. Each division incurs costs and generates revenues and can be treated as a profit center if management desires. Within each division, however, the business segments incur costs but do not generate their own revenues. Manufacturing plants, production departments, a single production line, or even an individual production employee can be identified as a cost center. Profit-seeking and not-for-profit organizations can use cost centers for performance measurement.

Cost centers are the most common type of responsibility center

In a business, all parts of the firm contribute in some way to generating revenue and earning an adequate income. But for some parts of a firm, it is difficult, if not impossible, to measure that contribution. To illustrate, the inventory storeroom and materials-handling personnel of a manufacturing business provide an essential service. Nevertheless, it is difficult to measure the precise impact that materials-handling operations have on the firm's profits. Therefore, this activity is treated as a cost center — cost is the only logical basis for responsibility reporting in this case.

Identifying Costs with Cost Centers.   In order to report on the performance of a cost center, it is first necessary to determine what costs should be included in the report. It is reasonable to expect cost center managers to accept responsibility for the costs over which they or their subordinates have control. It is not reasonable for them to be responsible for costs over which they have no control. The criterion for performance reporting is that all costs **controllable** by the management of the cost center should be reported. If the performance of a production supervisor, for example, is based on overtime costs incurred because of unrealistic delivery dates quoted by the company's sales staff, the performance measurement may be quite meaningless. There is no simple solution to the issue of what costs to charge to a manager.

To help provide some guidelines for accountants, the Committee on Cost Concepts and Standards of the American Accounting Association formulated the following:

What costs should be included in the report for a cost center?

1.   The person having authority over both the acquisition and the use of the service should be charged with the cost of such service.

2.   The persons that can significantly influence the amount of cost through their own action may be charged with such costs.

3.   Persons who cannot significantly influence the amount of cost through their own direct action may be charged with those elements with which the management desires them to be concerned, so that they will help to influence those who are responsible.[2]

These guidelines help accountants decide which costs to assign to cost centers. The guidelines also provide support when a manager asks why a particular cost is assigned to his cost center. But the guidelines do not specifically identify how costs should be assigned to cost centers in order to motivate managers to perform in a way that is most beneficial to the firm as a whole. Costs should be charged to business segments so that they encourage employees to achieve company goals. To emphasize this need, the Committee on Cost Concepts and Standards stated:

The basis of measurement used in providing cost data for control is often a matter of management discretion and an important consideration in motivation. Different bases may significantly affect the way in which different individuals are motivated. For this reason, the basis of measurement selected should be consistent with the type of motivation desired. For example, different types of motivation may result when maintenance costs are charged to a responsibility center on the basis of: (1) a rate per maintenance labor hour, (2) a rate per job, or (3) a single amount per month.[3]

[2] "Committee on Cost Concepts and Standards," *Accounting Review*, April 1956, p. 189.
[3] Ibid.

The Importance of Cost Centers. Cost responsibility is common in organizations and is the basis for a significant portion of managerial accounting reports. Job cost sheets, discussed in Chapter 4, and cost of production reports, presented in Chapters 5 and 6, are used for product costing purposes. However, the information in these reports is also the basis for evaluating managers' cost performance. In addition, standard cost variances and budget variances typically are part of cost center responsibility reports.

Figure 12-1 illustrates one type of cost center responsibility report. It presents a monthly budget performance report for the assembly department of Lentrelle Company. Included in the report are costs that top management believes are relevant in measuring the performance of departmental managers and in motivating managers to meet company goals. Costs such as depreciation on plant and equipment are not included in the report because these costs are not useful in evaluating or motivating assembly department managers.

Figure 12-1. Most organizations prepare many different types of cost reports. This is a budget performance report for the assembly department of the Lentrelle Company. Actual November costs are compared with budgeted costs for the month, and variances are reported. Other types of reports may show only the actual cost of making a product or providing a service.

Lentrelle Company
Assembly Department
Monthly Budget Performance Report
November 1985

	Budgeted	Actual	Variance
Direct materials	$124,000	$132,000	$ 8,000
Direct labor	95,000	92,600	(2,400)
Manufacturing overhead:			
Indirect labor	12,000	11,200	(800)
Indirect materials	14,000	17,700	3,700
Fire insurance	3,500	3,500	—
Property taxes	4,000	4,900	900
Maintenance	6,000	11,800	5,800
Supervisory salaries	44,000	48,300	4,300
Equipment repair	9,000	4,100	(4,900)
Utilities	10,000	13,400	3,400
Totals	$321,500	$339,500	$18,000

Profit Centers

Inherent in a company's profit goal is the amount of profit provided by each part of the business. **A profit center** is a business segment that incurs costs and also generates revenues. The manager of a profit center is held responsible for both costs and revenues. Sometimes a profit center is characterized as a business within a business. The main objective of the business—earning a profit—is also the main objective of the profit center manager. Ideally, if each profit center optimizes its profits, the profit of the entire firm is optimized. In practice, however, the actions of one business segment may not be in complete harmony with the interests or actions of all other segments of the business. For example, aggressive sales policies of the sales division manager may result in an inefficient production schedule that causes overall profits of the business to suffer.

Responsibility for both costs and revenues

Identifying Profit Centers.   Management must exercise some caution in designating a business segment as a profit center. Profit responsibility implies control over both costs and revenues. If a segment manager does not have significant control over either of these, the resulting performance report has little chance of providing useful information. The following criteria should help to avoid irrelevant or misleading information for evaluating a profit center.

Criteria for establishing profit centers

1.   The organization must have two or more segments for which separate measures of revenue and expense are obtained.

2.   The management of these units must have considerable control over the segment's expenses and revenues. (Presumably, authority to influence profit must accompany any true responsibility for the size of the profit.)

3.   Each segment's profit must be calculated and reported regularly to top management, and the results of this calculation must be considered by top management as part of its evaluation of the segment's performance.[4]

Preparing Profit Center Reports.   Measuring income for a profit center is similar to measuring income for a business. The costs incurred in the profit center are deducted from the revenues of the center to find net income. One difficulty in measuring profit center performance is that not all of the firm's revenues and costs are specifically identifiable with a profit center. For instance, the costs of research and development, corporate administration, and corporate services may be difficult to identify directly with each profit center of the firm. Such costs may be allocated to profit centers. But if the allocations are made arbitrarily, the resulting profit figures may be of little use for either measuring performance or controlling costs of the profit center. A more meaningful way of highlighting the performance of a profit center is by reporting its income before deducting any allocated corporate costs. The danger of this approach is that the corporate costs are not identified with any segment of the company; furthermore, managers may think of these corporate costs as costs that are not controllable by anyone.

To illustrate profit center reporting, we use the example of Amfield Home Heating Systems. Figure 12-2 presents sales and cost data for the three divisional profit centers of the company, and Figure 12-3 reports the income for each division as well as the expenses and income for the company. The **division income statement** is the performance report for the three profit centers used in the illustration. The profit center report illustrated in Figure 12-3 includes only costs and revenues that are identifiable with each profit center. All corporate costs are reported separately; they are not allocated to the profit centers.

[4] John Mauriel and Robert Anthony, "Misevaluation of Investment Center Performance," *Harvard Business Review*, March–April 1966, p. 99.

Figure 12-2. Data on sales quantity, sales price, production costs, and operating costs are presented for the three divisions of Amfield Home Heating Systems. In addition to division costs, $500,000 of corporate expenses are not specifically identifiable with divisions. These data are used to prepare the division income report shown in Figure 12-3.

Amfield Home Heating Systems
Division Sales and Cost Data
For the Year Ended December 31, 1985

| | Division | | |
	Water Heaters	Water Softeners	Furnaces
Units sold	10,000	5,000	8,000
Average unit sales price	$232	$300	$900
Average unit manufacturing cost:			
Direct materials	$68	$110	$340
Direct labor	47	60	160
Manufacturing overhead	57	55	200
Operating expenses:			
Marketing	$106,000	$125,000	$320,000
Distribution	54,000	46,000	210,000
Administrative	156,000	110,000	460,000
Corporate expenses not directly identifiable with divisions			$500,000

Figure 12-3. A division income statement shows the amount of income provided by each of the divisions. Notice that the corporate expenses must be subtracted from the sum of the division incomes to find the income for the entire corporation.

Amfield Home Heating Systems
Division Income Statement
For the Year Ended December 31, 1985

| | Division | | | Company Total |
	Water Heaters	Water Softeners	Furnaces	
Sales	$2,320,000	$1,500,000	$7,200,000	$11,020,000
Less cost of goods sold	1,720,000	1,125,000	5,600,000	8,445,000
Gross margin	600,000	375,000	1,600,000	2,575,000
Less operating expenses:				
Marketing	106,000	125,000	320,000	551,000
Distribution	54,000	46,000	210,000	310,000
Administrative	156,000	110,000	460,000	726,000
Total operating expenses	316,000	281,000	990,000	1,587,000
Division income	$ 284,000	$ 94,000	$ 610,000	988,000
Corporate expenses				500,000
Net income				$ 488,000

Figure 12-4 presents a division income statement for Amfield with corporate costs allocated to the three profit centers. The corporate costs should be allocated to the profit centers using the matching concept. Here the corporate costs are allocated to divisions based on the dollar volume of sales.

The allocations are computed as follows:

*Allocation of
corporate costs
based on sales*

Allocated costs = (Sales of division/Total company sales) × Corporate costs

Allocation to the Water Heater Division:
($2,320,000/$11,020,000) × $500,000 = $105,263

Allocation to the Water Softener Division:
($1,500,000/$11,020,000) × $500,000 = $68,058

Allocation to the Furnace Division:
($7,200,000/$11,020,000) × $500,000 = $326,679

Amfield Home Heating Systems
Division Income Statement
For the Year Ended December 31, 1985

	Division			
	Water Heaters	Water Softeners	Furnaces	Company Total
Sales	$2,320,000	$1,500,000	$7,200,000	$11,020,000
Less cost of goods sold	1,720,000	1,125,000	5,600,000	8,445,000
Gross margin	600,000	375,000	1,600,000	2,575,000
Less operating expenses:				
Marketing	106,000	125,000	320,000	551,000
Distribution	54,000	46,000	210,000	310,000
Administrative	156,000	110,000	460,000	726,000
Total operating expenses	316,000	281,000	990,000	1,587,000
Division income	284,000	94,000	610,000	988,000
Allocated corporate expenses	105,263	68,058	326,679	500,000
Net income	$ 178,737	$ 25,942	$ 283,321	$ 488,000

Figure 12-4. This division income statement is similar to the one in Figure 12-3, except that here we allocate the corporate expenses to the division before arriving at divisional net income. The corporate expenses are allocated in proportion to each division's sales. The allocated expenses are shown in the last line before net income. Some accountants believe this type of cost allocation is inappropriate in reporting divisional net income.

The data show that the Water Softener Division provided only $25,942 in income for the company. We must be careful not to misinterpret this information. If the Water Softener Division were not operating, the other divisions would have to absorb the corporate expenses allocated to the water softeners. In addition, if the company did not produce the low-profit water softeners, its sales of other products might suffer, because customers often prefer to deal with a company that offers a full complement of products.

Other types of profit center reports may be used. The profitability of specific products and the profitability of sales regions are two common types

Figure 12-5. Detailed cost data for the two products made in the Water Heater Division of Amfield Home Heating Systems. These data are necessary to prepare the product profitability statement shown in Figure 12-6. The data in this figure relate directly to the data for the division shown in Figure 12-2.

Amfield Home Heating Systems
Water Heater Division
Product Sales and Cost Data
For the Year Ended December 31, 1985

	Product		Division Expenses
	40-Gallon	55-Gallon	
Units sold	6,000	4,000	
Unit sales price	$200	$280	
Average unit manufacturing cost:			
Direct materials	$60	$80	
Direct labor	45	50	
Manufacturing overhead	55	60	
Operating expenses:			
Marketing	$30,000	$36,000	$ 40,000
Distribution	26,000	18,000	10,000
Administrative	40,000	36,000	80,000
Total divisional expenses			$130,000

of profit center reports. To illustrate, Figure 12-5 presents data necessary for preparing a product profitability report for the two products of the Water Heater Division of Amfield Home Heating Systems. The report for the two products manufactured in the division is presented in Figure 12-6. The division expenses not identifiable with specific products are reported separately. It is possible to allocate those expenses to the two products in a manner similar to the allocation of corporate expenses in the division profit center reports shown in Figure 12-4.

Profit center reports may be based on product or sales region profit

Figure 12-6. Using the sales and cost data from Figure 12-5, we prepare a product profitability statement for the two products manufactured by the Water Heater Division. Some expenses of the division cannot be assigned to specific products.

Amfield Home Heating Systems
Water Heater Division
Product Profitability Statement
For the Year Ended December 31, 1985

	Product		Totals
	40-Gallon	55-Gallon	
Sales	$1,200,000	$1,120,000	$2,320,000
Less cost of goods sold	960,000	760,000	1,720,000
Gross margin	240,000	360,000	600,000
Less operating expenses:			
Marketing	30,000	36,000	66,000
Distribution	26,000	18,000	44,000
Administrative	40,000	36,000	76,000
Total operating expenses	96,000	90,000	186,000
Product profit	$ 144,000	$ 270,000	414,000
Divisional expenses			130,000
Net income			$ 284,000

Investment Centers

The amount of income earned by a profit center usually is closely related to the amount of resources available to that segment of the business. The more resources available, the larger the income. If company management is evaluating the performance of several profit centers with different amounts of resources available to them, the total amount of income earned by each profit center may not be a logical base for comparison. A better basis for evaluation may be the amount of income earned per dollar of resource invested.

When a business segment is evaluated on the amount of income per dollar of resource invested, the business segment is called an **investment center.** Investment center analysis provides a common base for comparing the performance of large and small business segments.

The evaluation of investment centers is based simply on the return on invested resources. Return is computed as follows:

$$\text{Return on investment} = \frac{\text{Investment center earnings}}{\text{Investment center assets}}$$

For example, if an investment center had annual earnings of $80,000 and assets of $500,000, the return on investment is computed as follows:

Earnings per dollar of investment

$$\text{Return on investment} = \frac{\$80,000}{\$500,000} = .16, \text{ or } 16 \text{ percent}$$

The problems of isolating revenues and expenses are the same for investment centers as for other types of responsibility centers. An added challenge is determining the appropriate investment base because it forms the basis for comparing a segment's performance over time as well as across segments. Some common investment bases are:

Common investment bases used in computing ROI

1. **Total gross assets,** which are all of the assets of the segment without regard to any contra-asset accounts, such as Accumulated Depreciation or Allowance for Doubtful Accounts.

2. **Total net assets** include all assets of the investment center less any contra-asset accounts.

3. **Total net assets employed** include the net assets that generate the investment center's income. Excluded from this investment base are such items as land held for investment, securities of other businesses, and other assets not used in the investment center's normal business operations.

4. **Stockholders' equity** measures the return to investors and includes contributed capital as well as earnings retained in the business. This investment base is applicable only to subsidiaries that are operated as investment centers by the parent company.

5. **Other bases** are possible, including working capital, gross fixed assets, net fixed assets, or any other investment base that management thinks is logical for the situation.

We use the example of the Miderfield Company to illustrate the computation of return on investment using each of these investment bases. Miderfield Company is a wholly-owned subsidiary of the Medwack Company and is operated as a division of the parent company. **Return on investment (ROI)** is used as the measure of performance for all divisions of the parent company. The trial balance for the Miderfield Company is presented in Figure 12-7.

Miderfield Company's sales for the period are $1,250,000, and the total expenses are $950,000, so the income for the period is $300,000. To find the return on investment, the $300,000 income is divided by the investment base. But what investment base should be used? No single investment base is generally more logical or acceptable than any of the others. In practice, management must select the investment base it believes does the best job of measuring the performance of its divisions. For purposes of illustration, we present the computation of ROI for each of the five different investment bases.

Figure 12-7. Trial balance of Miderfield Company, which is a wholly-owned subsidiary of Medwack Company. The data in this trial balance are used to calculate return on investment using a variety of investment bases.

Miderfield Company
Trial Balance
June 30, 1985

	Debits	Credits
Cash	$ 230,000	
Investment in marketable securities	30,000	
Accounts receivable	165,000	
Inventory	225,000	
Land held for investment	500,000	
Prepaid expenses	50,000	
Building	1,200,000	
Accumulated depreciation, building		$ 650,000
Equipment	600,000	
Accumulated depreciation, equipment		350,000
Accounts payable		175,000
Notes payable		120,000
Taxes payable		105,000
Mortgage payable		300,000
Capital stock		400,000
Paid-in capital in excess of par		160,000
Retained earnings		440,000
Sales		1,250,000
Cost of goods sold	600,000	
Advertising	110,000	
Sales salaries and commissions	75,000	
Administrative salaries	85,000	
Office insurance	20,000	
Office property taxes	12,000	
Office utilities	18,000	
Office maintenance	30,000	
Totals	$3,950,000	$3,950,000

Total Gross Assets. An investment base that is easy to understand and use is total gross assets. All asset accounts are used in this investment base without deducting any contra-asset accounts, such as Accumulated Depreciation or Allowance for Doubtful Accounts. In this example, total gross assets are $3,000,000, which is computed by adding the cost of the eight asset accounts in the June 30 trial balance. The return on investment using this asset base is:

Total gross assets:

$$\text{ROI} = \text{Net income/Investment base}$$
$$= \$300,000/\$3,000,000$$
$$= .10, \text{ or } 10 \text{ percent}$$

Total Net Assets. If an investment center has production facilities that have a significant amount of depreciation, the book value of the total assets may be much smaller than their cost. Is the appropriate measure of investment the original cost or the depreciated cost of the asset? Managers may choose net assets as the investment base on the assumption that book value is the investment for the current period.

Total net assets are obtained by deducting contra-asset account balances from total gross assets

The net asset investment base is computed by subtracting all contra-asset account balances from total assets. For Miderfield Company, total net assets are $2,000,000 ($3,000,000 of total gross assets − $1,000,000 of accumulated depreciation). The rate of return on this investment base is:

Total net assets:

$$\text{ROI} = \$300,000/\$2,000,000 = .15, \text{ or } 15 \text{ percent}$$

Assets Employed. Rate of return on investment is a measure of how efficiently managers used resources to generate earnings. The measure should reflect the amount of resources available for use in earning the income. Occasionally a division may have some assets that are not used in operations. For example, Miderfield Company holds some land as a long-term investment. The land is expected to appreciate approximately 20 percent a year. The only value of the land to Miderfield is its investment value. This land asset is not a resource used by the division to generate income from its normal operations. The account Investment in Marketable Securities, on the other hand, is a short-term investment and as such it is part of the normal working capital of the division.

Assets not used to generate operating income are deducted from the investment base

Assets employed can be used either as gross assets or net assets. In either case, any assets not employed in the normal operations of the division are deducted from the asset base. For total gross assets employed, the computation is as follows:

Total gross productive assets:

$$\text{ROI} = \$300,000/(\$3,000,000 - \$500,000)$$
$$= \$300,000/\$2,500,000$$
$$= .12, \text{ or } 12 \text{ percent}$$

The computation for net assets employed is:

Total net productive assets:

$$\text{ROI} = \$300,000/(\$2,000,000 - \$500,000)$$
$$= \$300,000/\$1,500,000$$
$$= .20, \text{ or } 20 \text{ percent}$$

Stockholders' Equity.   Some business segments are not merely divisions of a firm; instead, each segment is a separate legal entity which issues stock that is owned by the parent company. In such organizations, a logical and easy-to-understand measure of performance is return on stockholders' equity. This is a common method of measuring performance for the firm as a whole, and is also a logical measure of performance for divisions that are separate corporations. Of course, a limiting factor of this investment base is that each division so evaluated must be accounted for as a branch or a subsidiary corporation of the parent. Therefore, many decentralized companies cannot use stockholders' equity as an investment base.

Stockholders' equity is the owners' investment in the firm and includes the original investment plus any retained earnings. In the trial balance of Miderfield Company, owners' equity includes $400,000 of capital stock, $160,000 of paid-in capital in excess of par, and $440,000 of retained earnings. But is the sum of these accounts the appropriate amount to use as the investment base? The earnings of $300,000 for the period, less any dividends paid, will be added to the Retained Earnings account at the end of the period when the books are closed. Should the beginning owners' equity balance be used as the investment base, the ending owners' balance, or some other amount?

One of three approaches is commonly used to determine the appropriate investment base for owners' equity. One approach is to use the beginning balance only, another is to use only the ending balance, and the third is to use the average of the beginning and ending balances in owners' equity. Management must select the investment base that it believes best fits the situation. For example, a division issues a large quantity of stock late in the year to the parent company. The money received from the sale was not available for earning income during most of the year. If the ending balance in owners' equity is used as the investment base, there may be a significant distortion in the division's performance measure.

Beginning balance, ending balance, or average owners' equity may be used to calculate return on investment

We illustrate each of the three different approaches to using owners' equity as the investment base. For the illustration, we assume that all of the earnings are retained in the business.

Beginning balance of owners' equity:

$$\text{ROI} = \$300,000/\$1,000,000 = .30, \text{ or } 30 \text{ percent}$$

Ending balance of owners' equity:

$$\text{ROI} = \$300,000/(\$1,000,000 + \$300,000)$$
$$= \$300,000/\$1,300,000$$
$$= .231, \text{ or } 23.1 \text{ percent}$$

Average balance of owners' equity:

$$ROI = \$300,000/[(\$1,000,000 + \$1,300,000)/2]$$
$$= \$300,000/\$1,150,000$$
$$= .261, \text{ or } 26.1 \text{ percent}$$

Other Bases. The choice of an investment base for computing return on investment is a managerial decision. ROI analyses are not used in external reporting; nor are they constrained by generally accepted accounting principles. As a result, any asset base may be used in ROI analysis to satisfy the information needs of managers. The investment bases already discussed are commonly used, but other investment bases are possible.

Working capital is sometimes used as an investment base. In our example, working capital is $420,000. It is computed as the total current assets of $700,000 less the current liabilities of $280,000 (Accounts Payable and Taxes Payable). The return on investment using working capital as the investment base is:

Working capital:

$$ROI = \$300,000/\$420,000 = .714, \text{ or } 71.4 \text{ percent}$$

Return on the current market value of the assets

When inflation rates are high, historical costs may not be good measures of current values. If one division of a company is much older than the others, balance sheet costs may not be comparable for measuring ROI. The use of **market values** or **estimated market values** for assets or owners' equity accounts is an attempt to convert historical balance sheet data to a more useful common measure for evaluating performance. For the Miderfield Company, we assume that the estimated market value of the division's stock is $1,800,000. The ROI using this current market value is:

Market value of assets:

$$ROI = \$300,000/\$1,800,000 = .167, \text{ or } 16.7 \text{ percent}$$

Sometimes the management of a manufacturing company is keenly interested in the return on the investment in productive plant and equipment. In that case, use of **gross fixed assets** or **net fixed assets** as the investment base for computing return on investment may be appropriate. In this example, the computations are as follows:

Gross fixed assets:

$$ROI = \$300,000/\$1,800,000 = .167, \text{ or } 16.7 \text{ percent}$$

Net fixed assets:

$$ROI = \$300,000/\$800,000 = .375, \text{ or } 37.5 \text{ percent}$$

Residual Income Centers

A modification of the profit center and investment center approaches is called the residual income center approach. With **residual income,** management establishes a target level of income or a target rate of return for the profit center. Any income in excess of the target level of income is the **residual income.** Division managers are evaluated on the amount of their division's residual income.

For example, the target level of return for the Miderfield division is 6 percent on gross assets. The target income is then $180,000 (.06 × $3,000,000 of total gross assets). The computation of residual income is:

$$\text{Residual income} = \text{Actual net income} - \text{Target net income}$$
$$= \$300,000 - \$180,000 = \$120,000$$

Advocates of the residual income approach contend that it overcomes the problem of trying to compare profits from divisions of unequal size. If the absolute profit is the primary measure of performance, large divisions have a better chance of achieving a more favorable profit evaluation than smaller divisions. With residual income, the target income is established based on management criteria that typically include essential variables such as the amount of resources invested in each division. However, even with the residual income approach, large divisions may have an advantage over smaller divisions.

To illustrate, look at the following data summarized for three divisions of a decentralized company.

| | Division | | |
	Blue	Green	Red
Total gross assets	$2,000,000	$1,000,000	$200,000
Net income	400,000	200,000	40,000
Return on gross assets	20%	20%	20%
Target income (15% of gross assets)	$300,000	$150,000	$30,000
Residual income	100,000	50,000	10,000

All three divisions earned 20 percent on their total gross assets. The target income used in the computation of residual income is 15 percent of gross assets for each division. As a result, the largest division has the highest target income. The net income of the Blue division is 10 times larger than that of the Red division, which has only one tenth the gross assets of the Blue division. However, when the target income is subtracted from the total income to compute residual income, the largest division still has a significantly higher residual income.

TRANSFER PRICING

One of the primary obstacles to measuring segment performance meaningfully is the transfer of goods and services between segments of a company. If each segment deals only with organizations external to the company, all transactions would be normal business transactions, sometimes called "arm's-length transactions," and the prices of the goods and services transferred would be determined by the market. But in many decentralized firms, much business is transacted between segments of the firm. It is common for the output of one segment of the firm to be a raw material of another segment. For example, the automobile windshields of the glass division and the automobile frames of the body division are both raw materials for the assembly division. In some cases all of the output of one division is "bought" by one or more divisions of the same company. In other cases, only a portion of a segment's output may be sold to another segment of the company, and the remaining amount is sold in the outside market. Whatever the case, the selling segment and buying segment must be able to determine a logical price for the goods or services. The price for such goods or services is called a **transfer price.** The need to set transfer prices for decentralized operations poses the following dilemma in divisional performance measurement:

Business transactions between segments of the same firm

> If a divisionalized company could arrange its affairs so that its divisions had no dealings of any kind with each other, it would have removed one of the principal complexities of divisional profit measurement. It would also, however, have lost a valuable feature of decentralization, namely the capacity to enjoy the fruits of division of labor and of specialization while simultaneously benefiting from integration to a greater or lesser degree. The fact that a divisionalized company is more than the sum of its parts is evidenced through the intricate pattern of interdivisional relationships which can establish itself within a large decentralized company.[5]

A transfer price is the amount charged for goods or services transferred between segments of the same firm

A **transfer price,** sometimes called an **internal charge** or a **charge back,** is the amount charged for the goods or services one part of a business provides for another. The necessity to determine transfer prices arises not only because of the amount of business transacted between segments of the same firm but also because the transfer prices are an essential element of the progress and performance evaluation of the firm's segments.

The significance of transfer prices depends on the amount of business transacted between segments of the firm

The impact of transfer prices on the evaluation of segment performance depends largely on the amount of business transacted between the segments. If the divisions of the firm buy and sell large amounts of goods and services from one another, the transfer pricing system will have a significant influence on the measurements of performance. If, however, few goods and services are transferred between segments, the transfer pricing system has little impact on segment performance measurement.

Types of Transfer Pricing Systems

Many factors determine what transfer price should be used. Some of the common types of transfer prices are:

1. Market price
2. Modified market price

[5] Davis Solomons, *Divisional Performance: Measurement and Control,* Financial Executives Research Foundation, New York, 1965, p. 160.

3. Actual cost

Common transfer pricing methods

4. Standard cost
5. Modified cost
6. Negotiated price
7. Target profit
8. Other transfer prices

Market Price.   The most commonly advocated type of transfer price is **market price,** which is the amount charged for the good or service in the open market. Supporters of the market price maintain that it is most logical because it is determined by parties dealing at arm's length in the market place for the product or service. When market price is used to charge for internal transfers, it is the most objective measure of the value of the goods and services transferred. The market price is thought to be the one that would exist if the division providing the good or service were in fact a separate business. It is the price the selling division receives when selling to external customers, and it is the amount the buying division must pay when it purchases from external vendors.

Although widely supported as a logical transfer pricing method, market price does have some disadvantages. Some products and services provided by one division for another do not have a readily determinable market price. For example, computer circuit boards produced by one division of a company are made specifically for the production of a computer assembled in another division. No outside market exists for this specialized product, although similar types of computer circuit boards are produced by other companies. Similarly, marketing and computer services provided by one division of the company may be unique and not available in the market place. Specialized services or products differentiate the internal product from those offered in the external market, and an appropriate modification of the market price transfer pricing method should be used, as described below, to reflect the special nature of the product or service.

Not all products and services have an external market price

Modified Market Price.   A market price implies that the parties participating in the transaction operate in a typical business environment, incurring normal business expenses, and providing usual customer support and services. In some situations, a major part of the operation of the firm is the marketing and distribution of the product or service. If one division of a company is required to purchase a product or service from another division, the selling division may have little or no marketing and distribution cost. If the selling division receives the market price for the item, but does not have to incur the substantial marketing and distribution expense of others selling in the same market, is the transfer price fair? Many accountants and managers maintain that in this type of situation, the selling division reaps all of the benefits of being an integrated business, and the buying division none. It follows that the performance of the selling division has a distinct advantage over the performance of the buying division. This problem may be resolved by using a **modified market transfer price.**

Market price may be modified to make it into a suitable transfer price

The market price can be modified in whatever way management thinks is logical. The market price may be reduced to reflect the lower marketing and distribution cost of the selling division. The reduction depends on the particular situation, but the resulting transfer price should provide a fair measure of performance for both the buying and the selling division.

Sometimes there is no market price for the specific product or service traded between two divisions. In such cases management may be able to identify a market price for a similar product or service that does trade in the open market.

For instance, a division manufactures a heat regulator valve used in heat pumps by the assembly division. The heat regulator valve is designed to meet the specific needs of one particular product, and all valves are provided by the valve division of the company. No outside market is available for the regulator valve, but several competitors have similar valves that trade in the open market. These similar valves are made of a somewhat inferior material; therefore, management uses a transfer price that is somewhat higher than the market price of the similar valves.

Cost-based transfer prices

Actual Cost. A commonly used alternative to a market-based transfer price is **actual cost,** sometimes called **historical cost.** This transfer price is based on the actual cost of making the product or providing the service. The buying division is charged the actual cost of the product or service. Two reasons for using an actual cost transfer price are: It is definitely determinable and it is readily available. The use of actual cost eliminates the need to determine a market price for a product or service that is unique or specialized. Another advantage is that transfer prices based on actual costs are easy to understand and administer. All types of organizations accumulate costs for most of their activities. Therefore, even not-for-profit organizations can use actual cost in transferring goods and services between segments.

There are many ways to measure cost

If actual cost is to be used as the transfer price, the next question is, what should that actual cost be? Should it be variable product cost, full product cost, or full product cost plus a prorated share of administrative and marketing costs? Or should some other measure of the actual cost be used as the transfer price? Many firms use the most conventional measure of actual cost, which is full product cost, including all direct and indirect costs of manufacturing both fixed and variable. However, any other measure of actual cost can be used if it satisfies the information needs of managers for monitoring and controlling operations.

Although an actual cost transfer price is easy to use and understand, it has potentially serious flaws if used to measure segment performance. The selling division transfers its costs to the buying divisions. Any production or administration inefficiencies in the division are merely transferred to the other divisions. With actual cost transfer prices, there is little incentive on the part of the selling division to be efficient. In addition, with actual cost transfer prices, the selling division cannot earn a profit. If all costs are transferred to buying divisions, the selling division will break even. A way of circumventing the problem of measuring performance when cost-based transfer prices are used is to establish predetermined or expected costs for the goods and services provided by the selling divisions.

Standard Cost. With a **standard cost transfer price,** carefully predetermined standard costs are used to price the transfer of goods and services between segments of the business. Any variances from standard, favorable or unfavorable, are reported in the selling division's performance report. The variances are used in evaluating the selling division, and the use of standard costs as the transfer price ensures that any efficiencies or inefficiencies generated in the selling division are not transferred to the buying divisions.

Advantages of standard cost transfer prices

The primary disadvantage of a standard cost transfer price is that if all products are sold to other divisions within the firm, the "profit" of the selling division is limited to the net favorable variance for the reporting period. If the net variance for the period is unfavorable, the selling division will incur a loss. Later in this section we discuss methods of modifying cost-based transfer prices so that they can operate in a profit center environment.

Modified Cost. Sometimes it is necessary to modify cost-based transfer prices to satisfy the reporting objectives of management. For example, a company may like the ease of using a cost-based transfer price, and yet may want to use profit center performance measurement for all of its operating divisions. To use cost-based transfer prices for measuring profits, the company uses a **cost-plus transfer price** based on actual cost plus a markup. A 20 percent markup, for example, provides the selling division with a normal margin on the sale of the product. The actual profit of the selling division will depend on the amount of product sold and the division's efficiency in administering operations. The product margin may be expressed as a percentage of cost such as described above, or it can be a fixed amount over cost, such as $5 per unit.

Management can use any cost base for computing transfer prices. Actual cost is a common base for a cost-plus transfer price; this method is popular for pricing government contracts. Standard costs also can be used. For instance, a transfer price of standard cost plus 15 percent means that the expected cost of the product plus 15 percent of the standard cost is the amount charged the buying division. Any variances, whether favorable or unfavorable, are charged to the producing division.

A special case of cost-based transfer pricing

Sometimes, to satisfy specific management goals, only a portion of the total cost is used in the transfer price. When only a portion of the total cost is charged for the good or service, the firm is using a **partial-cost transfer price.** This may seem illogical, but for certain services it may be appropriate in achieving the company's goal. For example, when a company acquires a new computer, it is common to have some excess capacity initially. To encourage managers to use the computer, the computer services division may charge only a portion of the total actual cost for services. Fixed costs such as equipment depreciation and insurance may be ignored in determining the charge for computer services. In the long run, partial-cost pricing seldom produces a logical transfer price. In the case of computer services, it often leads to rapid expansion of the demand for computer use, and soon additional computer resources must be acquired. Also, the use of partial-cost transfer prices leads managers to believe that the actual cost of the product or service is less than it really is. This may lead to inappropriate resource allocation decisions.

Negotiated Price. **A negotiated transfer price** is determined by bargaining between the buyer and the seller. A negotiated transfer price suggests an arm's-length transaction similar to that encountered when dealing with entities external to the firm. This type of transfer price certainly sounds logical and fair, and often it is. However, for the system to work, the buying and selling divisions must have the ability to deal outside the firm if the internal negotiation process does not succeed. If the buying and selling divisions must deal solely with each other, a bilateral monopoly exists. Economic analysis indicates that a bilateral monopoly is indeterminate, which means that no logical economic solution can be reached, and in this case no transfer price is negotiated. In such situations, top management may step in and dictate a transfer price, which, in effect, means the transfer price is not negotiated at all. A negotiated transfer price works well only when (1) the two parties involved can deal with both internal and outside customers and suppliers, and (2) there is no management policy that hinders the negotiation process or dealings with external parties.

Target Profit. Sometimes transfer prices are designed specifically to provide divisions with a target profit. If no market price is available, a transfer price intended to provide a target profit may be a logical alternative. Often a **target profit transfer price** is based upon some cost measure plus some desired profit level. A target profit can be thought of as a special case of a cost-plus transfer price, with the emphasis on providing a profit. For example, the transfer price might be standard product cost plus 20 percent. The 20 percent provides revenue to cover nonmanufacturing costs of the division plus a profit. Any cost variances are assigned to the selling division. There are a number of variations of target profit transfer prices. To illustrate several common situations, we use the following data for a manufacturing division of a decentralized business.

	Cost	
	Standard	Actual
Production quantity	—	1,000
Manufacturing expenses	$105,000	$115,000
Operating expense	35,000	40,000

The company's policy is to set transfer prices at a gross margin on sales of 30 percent of standard product cost. The transfer price is computed by calculating the total revenue necessary to achieve the target profit, and then dividing the total revenue by the number of units manufactured to find the transfer price per unit.

$$\text{Total revenue (TR)} = \text{Target profit} + \text{Product standard cost}$$
$$\text{TR} = .3\text{TR} + \$105,000$$
$$.7\text{TR} = \$105,000$$
$$\text{TR} = \$150,000$$

With total revenue of $150,000, the division's profit objective is achieved. Since 1,000 units were produced, the unit transfer price is $150, obtained as follows:

$$\text{Unit transfer price} = \text{Total revenue}/\text{Units produced}$$
$$= \$150,000/1,000 \text{ units}$$
$$= \$150 \text{ per unit}$$

In this example, the producing division incurred unfavorable variances for both manufacturing and operating activities. These unfavorable variances are charged against the selling division's profit. The division realized a loss of $5,000 ($150,000 of revenue − $155,000 total actual expense). If the division could transfer the unfavorable variances to other divisions, the transfer price would be $15 per unit higher ($15,000 of unfavorable variance/1,000 units) and the revenue would be $15,000 higher, resulting in a division profit of $10,000 ($165,000 of revenue − $155,000 of actual costs).

Some businesses do not use standard costs or choose not to use standards in setting transfer prices. The transfer price may be based on gross margin on sales of 20 percent of actual product cost. Again, the first step is to compute the amount of total revenue necessary to achieve the target profit.

$$\text{Total revenue (TR)} = \text{Target profit} + \text{Actual product cost}$$
$$\text{TR} = .2\text{TR} + \$115,000$$
$$.8\text{TR} = \$115,000$$
$$\text{TR} = \$143,750$$

And the unit transfer price is:

$$\text{Unit transfer price} = \text{Total revenue}/\text{Units produced}$$
$$= \$143,750/1,000 \text{ units}$$
$$= \$143.75 \text{ per unit}$$

The computation of a target profit transfer price is complicated somewhat if the selling division sells part of its products to outside customers. For instance, in our example let's say that 800 units are sold in the outside market and 200 units are sold to another division of the company. The company's transfer price is based on a gross margin of 30 percent of standard product cost. The division sells the units to customers outside the firm for $155 each.

Earlier we computed the total target revenue of $150,000. That has not changed, but some of the revenue will come from external sales. In this case, external sales provide $124,000 of the total revenue, and the remaining revenue is generated by sales to other divisions of the company. The amount required from internal sales is merely the total required revenue less revenue provided by external sales.

$$\text{External sales revenue} = \text{Selling price} \times \text{Units sold}$$
$$= \$155 \times 800 \text{ units}$$
$$= \$124,000$$
$$\text{Required internal revenue} = \text{Total target revenue} - \text{External sales}$$
$$= \$150,000 - \$124,000$$
$$= \$26,000$$

The transfer price for units sold to other divisions within the firm is computed by dividing the total required internal revenue by the units sold internally.

$$\text{Unit transfer price} = \$26,000/200 \text{ units}$$
$$= \$130 \text{ per unit}$$

Other Transfer Prices. Some firms develop sophisticated mathematical models for transfer pricing. Any method is acceptable as long as it meets the information needs of management. As with all transfer prices, the system should be readily understandable by all participants and should be easy to administer.

Transfer Pricing Illustrated

With the exception of a target profit transfer price, we have only discussed the characteristics, benefits, and problems of some of the more commonly used transfer prices. Now we look at a simple example that illustrates the use of various transfer pricing methods.

Fetzer Company is a decentralized company that manufactures air conditioners. There are several manufacturing divisions producing component parts for the assembly division. The compressors manufactured in the compressor division can be sold in the open market for $280 each. Here are recent cost data for this division:

Item	Standard Cost	Actual Cost
Direct materials	$120	$126
Direct labor	50	54
Variable MOH	20	18
Applied fixed MOH	30	30

The simplest transfer price to use in this case is the market price of $280 per unit. However, management believes that the market price should be reduced by 15 percent to compensate for the lack of marketing costs and the low distribution costs. The transfer price is

$$\text{Transfer price} = \text{Market price} - 15 \text{ percent of market price}$$
$$= \$280 - (\$280 \times .15) = \$280 - \$42 = \$238$$

If the standard cost of production is used as the transfer price, merely adding the standard costs of $120, $50, $20, and $30 yields a standard cost of $220. An actual cost transfer price is found by adding the actual cost of production. The resulting $228 transfer price includes a net unfavorable variance of $8.

Modified cost transfer prices can be developed using either standard or actual costs. A transfer price based on standard cost plus 20 percent is computed as follows:

$$\text{Transfer price} = \text{Standard cost} + 20 \text{ percent of standard cost}$$
$$= \$220 + (\$220 \times .20) = \$220 + \$44 = \$264$$

A transfer price based on actual cost plus 10 percent is:

$$\text{Transfer price} = \text{Actual cost} + 10 \text{ percent of actual cost}$$
$$= \$228 + (\$228 \times .10) = \$228 + \$22.80 = \$250.80$$

Many other modified cost transfer prices can be used. For example, a transfer price of variable standard cost is

$$\text{Transfer price} = \text{Direct materials} + \text{Direct labor} + \text{Variable overhead}$$
$$= \$120 + \$50 + \$20 = \$190$$

And a transfer price of actual prime cost is

$$\text{Transfer price} = \text{Actual direct material} + \text{Direct labor}$$
$$= \$126 + \$54 = \$180$$

COSTING NONMANUFACTURING ACTIVITIES

Many managers think primarily of manufacturing activities when the term *cost accounting* is used. There are two reasons why that is true. First, because managers needed information about the cost of manufacturing various products, the concept of detailed cost measurement was first developed in manufacturing operations. Second, many nonmanufacturing activities do not lend themselves well to detailed unit cost measurement. The output of most manufacturing activities is a single product or a group of homogeneous products and the production activity is systematic and repetitive. Many of the

Unit costs may be computed for nonmanufacturing activities

cost reports prepared for manufacturing activities provide detailed unit cost data. When nonmanufacturing activities are homogeneous and repetitive it is possible to compute and present unit costs of services in reports similar to product cost reports.

The process of costing nonmanufacturing activities is similar to product costing. The first step is to define carefully the cost objective. Typically, this is somewhat more difficult with nonmanufacturing activities because the activity is less tangible and observable than manufacturing a specific unit of product. The cost objective should include a careful definition of the physical unit of measure. For example, a company's objective is to measure the cost of its telephone marketing activity. The company may want to know the average cost of making one call or it may want to measure the cost of 1 hour of telephone marketing. Another alternative is to measure the marketing cost per unit of product sold. Whatever management's information objective, it must be carefully defined so that (1) accountants can measure the cost accurately, and (2) users of the information can understand it.

After the cost objective is clearly defined and the unit of output carefully specified, costs can be assigned to the activity. As with manufactured products, direct costs are assigned to the activity first. Typically, direct costs are the same as prime product costs: costs of materials that are directly identifiable with the cost objective and costs of direct labor. Next, indirect costs associated with the activity are assigned to it. Indirect costs for nonmanufacturing activities are overhead costs similar to manufacturing overhead. Overhead costs for nonmanufacturing activities are necessary costs of providing the service or activity that is being costed. There are many names for such overhead costs. **Administrative overhead, office overhead, corporate overhead, division overhead, marketing overhead,** and **operating overhead** are but a few names for nonmanufacturing overhead costs.

Indirect costs of nonmanufacturing activities must be assigned

As with manufacturing overhead, a logical method of assigning indirect costs must be used. Typically, overhead rates are used to assign indirect costs to activities, and the overhead application bases used are similar to those used with manufacturing overhead. Direct labor hours, direct labor costs, units of output, and prime costs are some common application bases. But any application base may be used if it satisfies the matching principle, is understood by managers, and is easy to administer.

The Melsher Company is used to illustrate the costing of nonmanufacturing activities. The company sells a variety of consumer goods, primarily through mail-order and telephone sales. Telephone sales are written on order forms and sent to the order processing department. Mail-order sales are accumulated from the daily mail and sent to order processing. Each day, order processing processes the mail orders and telephone sales of the previous day.

The management of Melsher Company wants to compute detailed unit costs for the order processing department activity. The unit of measure in the computation is the number of orders processed. At the top of the next page are activity and cost data for April for the order processing department.

Sales orders processed	12,000
Total direct labor cost (2,400 DLH)	$16,320
Direct materials: 12,300 sales invoice forms used	3,600
Indirect materials and supplies	1,500
Indirect labor	3,400
Depreciation on departmental office and equipment	5,900
Utilities	5,000
Supervision	4,800
Miscellaneous departmental costs	1,200

The costs associated with the preparation of the 12,000 sales orders in April include the order processing department's direct materials and direct labor costs as well as some necessary indirect costs of processing the orders. These cost and activity data are used to prepare the detailed unit cost report for the activity presented in Figure 12-8.

Figure 12-8. Total and unit cost data used as standards for a nonmanufacturing activity. These data are used to measure performance and to calculate variances for processing sales orders.

Melsher Company
Order Processing Costs
April

	Total Cost	Unit Cost
Direct costs:		
Direct materials, forms	$ 3,600	$ .30
Direct labor	16,320	1.36
Total direct costs	19,920	1.66
Indirect costs:		
Indirect materials and supplies	1,500	
Depreciation on office and equipment	5,900	
Utilities	5,000	
Indirect labor	3,400	
Supervision	4,800	
Miscellaneous	2,200	
Total indirect costs	22,800	1.90
Total cost	$42,720	$3.56

The cost report for the order processing department looks similar to product cost reports discussed earlier. The direct costs of processing the orders are identified first, followed by all of the indirect costs. The unit cost of $3.56 is the average cost of processing an order in the department during April. As with product costs, this is an average cost for the time period covered by the report. Any particular order might have cost more or less than the unit cost of $3.56. Similarly, in other months the average unit cost of processing an order might well be different than $3.56.

Standard Costs for Nonmanufacturing Activities

The $3.56 unit cost for processing an order is based on actual costs accumulated for the activity. From the data it is not possible to determine if the

Actual costs are compared with expected costs

performance of the department was favorable, unfavorable, or as expected. To prepare performance reports and compute variances, it is first necessary to determine standard costs. The following standard cost data pertain to the order processing activity:

Direct material: one invoice per order @ $.26 per invoice

Direct labor: 10 minutes to process one order @ $7.00 per hour

Indirect costs: applied at the rate of $12 per direct labor hour

It is easy to prepare a standard cost variance analysis report for the order processing department using the standard costs and the actual cost data. The standard cost variance report for order processing is shown in Figure 12-9.

Figure 12-9.   Performance report for a nonmanufacturing activity. Variances are calculated for direct and indirect costs. Such performance measures are possible for repetitive activities.

Melsher Company
Order Processing Department
Variance Analysis Report for April

Direct materials:		
Material price variance	(12,300 forms × $.26) − $3,600	$ 402 U
Material quantity variance	(12,000 forms − 12,300 forms) × $.26	78 U
Total material variance		480 U
Direct labor:		
Labor rate variance	($7.00 − $6.80) × 2,400 DLH	480 F
Labor efficiency variance	(2,000 hr − 2,400 hr) × $7 hr	2,800 U
Total labor variance		2,320 U
Indirect costs:		
Standard indirect costs	2,000 DLH × $12 per DLH	24,000
Actual indirect costs		22,800
Indirect cost variance		1,200 F
Total variance for April		$ 1,600 U

The computation of variances for the Melsher Company example is the same as discussed in Chapter 8. Direct cost variances are reported first. The material price variance for invoice forms is computed by subtracting the standard cost of the actual number of invoice forms used from the actual cost of the actual number of invoices used. The variance of $402 is unfavorable, because the actual cost of forms (the number of forms purchased times their actual price) is greater than the standard cost (the number of forms purchased times their standard price).

The material quantity variance is unfavorable because 12,300 forms were used in processing 12,000 sales orders during the month. This is 300 more forms than standard. The variance is $78, computed by multiplying the 300 extra forms used times their standard cost of $.26 each.

The labor rate variance is favorable, because the actual labor rate of $6.80 was $.20 per hour less than the standard rate of $7.00 per hour. The actual labor rate is computed by dividing the total direct labor hours into the total direct labor cost ($16,320/2,400 hr). The labor rate variance is $480, which is the $.20 per hour difference between the standard and actual labor rates times the 2,400 actual hours worked.

The labor efficiency variance is $2,800 unfavorable, calculated as follows: The standard number of hours for the number of invoices processed is 2,000. This is computed by multiplying the processing time per invoice (1/6 of an hour) by the 12,000 total orders processed during April. The actual hours worked were 2,400, or 400 more than standard. With a standard labor rate of $7 per hour, the labor efficiency variance is $2,800 unfavorable.

The indirect costs are applied at a predetermined overhead rate of $12 per direct labor hour. Remember that in a standard cost system, overhead is applied on the standard hours, not actual hours. Therefore, the applied indirect cost in this example is $24,000 (2,000 standard hours × $12 per hours).

The actual indirect costs given in the data are used in the actual cost report. Since actual cost is less than the amount applied at standard, the indirect cost variance is favorable. Combining the direct materials variances, the direct labor variances, and the indirect cost variance, we get a net unfavorable variance of $1,600.

Evaluating results of operations requires managerial skill

Managers must understand the operations of the order processing department in order to interpret the variance information presented in this report. The relatively large unfavorable labor efficiency variance during the month may be upsetting. Perhaps the variance was expected because a large number of new employees were hired in the department recently, and managers expect low productivity initially and increased productivity in the near future. As with all variance reports, the interpretation of the information requires skill and a knowledge of personnel and other factors involved in the operation.

SUMMARY

The decision-making process can become difficult and inefficient as organizations grow. To minimize this problem, many organizations separate their operations into more manageable units. This process is called **decentralization.** Managers of decentralized organizations have decision authority over the activities in their part of the organization, and they are held responsible for the decisions they make. The process of assigning decision authority and responsibility to subordinates is called **delegation. Responsibility accounting** is reporting on the performance of responsibility center managers. Responsibility accounting rests on the premise that managers should be held accountable for their management actions and there should be a mechanism for reporting management performance.

The three main types of responsibility centers are cost centers, profit centers, and investment centers. In a **cost center,** managers are held responsible for the costs incurred in their segment of the business. To measure the performance of cost center managers requires identifying controllable costs for the cost center. **Controllable costs** are those over which the responsibility center manager has control or a significant amount of decision authority.

Profit center managers are held responsible for both costs and revenues. Each profit center is in effect a business within a business. In theory, each profit center maximizing its profits should lead to the company as a whole maximizing its profits. In practice, there may be some conflict of interest between the specific goals of individual profit centers and the corporation as a whole.

Investment centers use return on investment to measure the performance of responsibility center managers. The profit of the investment center is divided by the amount of investment in the center to compute the return on investment. An appropriate investment base should be used for computing the return. Common investment bases are **total gross assets, net assets, net assets employed,** and **stockholders' equity.**

A variation of profit center and investment center analysis is **residual income analysis.** A target net income is determined in total dollar amounts or as a percentage. Any income in excess of the target is residual income.

The amount charged for goods and services transferred between divisions is called a **transfer price.** The most commonly advocated transfer price is **market price,** which is the amount paid for the good or service in the open market. **Modified market price** is the market price of the item adjusted for the production and sales situation, such as lower marketing and distribution costs. **Actual cost** transfer prices are based on the actual cost of manufacturing the product or providing the service. A **standard cost** transfer price is based on expected or standard costs and eliminates the problem of transferring inefficiencies from one division to another. Any of the cost bases can be adjusted to meet the reporting needs of the organization. **Modified cost** transfer prices can be based on either standard costs or actual costs. A **negotiated** transfer price means the two parties bargain to determine the amount charged for the goods or services sold between the divisions. This method works best if both the buying and the selling divisions have the ability and authority to deal outside the firm. A **target profit** transfer price is based on management's expectations for the profit of the division. Often the target profit transfer price is based on standard costs, so that inefficient operations become the responsibility of the selling division.

Nonmanufacturing activities include service and merchandising operations as well as the nonmanufacturing activities of manufacturing firms. For systematic, repetitive nonmanufacturing activities with a homogeneous output, it is possible to compute detailed unit costs similar to product costs. Both actual cost and standard cost reports can be prepared for such activities.

KEY TERMS

actual cost transfer price *(460)*

assets employed *(454)*

controllable cost *(446)*

cost center *(445)*

cost-plus transfer price *(461)*

decentralization *(443)*

delegation *(443)*

division income statement *(448)*

investment center *(445)*

market price transfer price *(459)*

modified cost transfer price *(461)*

modified market transfer price *(459)*

negotiated transfer price *(462)*

net assets *(454)*
nonmanufacturing activities *(465)*
partial-cost transfer price *(461)*
profit center *(445)*
residual income *(456)*
responsibility accounting *(444)*

responsibility center *(445)*
standard cost transfer price *(461)*
stockholders' equity *(455)*
target profit transfer price *(462)*
total gross assets *(454)*
transfer price *(458)*

QUESTIONS

1. A manufacturing company makes a variety of consumer products in several production departments. The manufacturing division has been evaluated as a cost center and the marketing division has been evaluated as a profit center. The manager of the manufacturing division suggests that each of the three manufacturing departments should be evaluated as a separate profit center and that a transfer pricing system should be implemented for the transfer of work in process from one department to the next and to finished goods. The marketing manager is concerned that this will be detrimental to him and his department because his profits will become smaller. The supervisor of the first production department is agreeable to the change if the transfer price is based on full product cost. On the other hand, the production supervisor of the third department in the manufacturing division argues that the transfer prices should be based on standard costs. Discuss the merits of making the change and the advantages and disadvantages of each transfer price suggested.

2. Until recently, the computer services of Kriptix Company have been a free good because management wanted to encourage various departments to automate as much of their data processing as possible. Now the proposal has been made to use market price less 5 percent to charge for computer services. The market price is readily obtainable, and managers believe that it is a fair transfer price. Reducing the charges by 5 percent would discourage users of computer services from going to external vendors. An operating department manager has just learned that his data processing requirements will cost about $10,000 per month. He informs the manager of the computer center that he can satisfy his data requirements by using clerical labor to produce the data manually at a cost of $7,600. A manager of a profit center says he will stop using the computer and do without the data generated in the past, because the cost of the data exceed the value to his department. "My profits may decrease somewhat without those data," he says, "but they would decrease much more if I am charged for using the computer." In both cases the variable cost of producing the data by the computer center is $2,000 per month. Discuss the problems created by changing to a transfer price and the way they may be resolved.

EXERCISES

Ex. 12-1
Return on
Investment

The table saw division of Mitchell Products Company had the following revenue, cost, and asset data for the year 1985:

Sales	$ 800,000
Prime costs	340,000
Overhead	160,000
Operating expenses	100,000
Total gross assets	2,000,000
Contra-asset accounts	800,000
Land held for investment	200,000

There are no beginning and ending inventories.

REQUIRED Compute the return on investment for the table saw division using as the investment base:

    a. Total gross assets.
    b. Net assets.
    c. Net assets employed.

Ex. 12-2
Residual Income

Refer to the 1985 operating data for the table saw division of the Mitchell Products Company presented in Exercise 12-1.

REQUIRED Compute the residual income for the table saw division using a target income of:

    a. $140,000.
    b. 15 percent of sales.
    c. 9 percent of gross assets employed.

Ex. 12-3
Measuring Segment
Performance

The Calligan division of Megton Company operates as an investment center. Below are balance sheet data and operating data for the year just completed.

Current assets	$ 50,000
Fixed assets (gross)	450,000
Accumulated depreciation	100,000
Current liabilities	30,000
Long-term liabilities	240,000
Sales	600,000
Product expense	350,000
Operating expenses	190,000

REQUIRED Compute the return on investment using as the investment base:

    a. Net assets.
    b. Gross assets.
    c. Net fixed assets.

Ex. 12-4
Return on Owners'
Equity

The Miser Company uses return on owners' equity as a measure of performance. During the past year the company had sales of $800,000 and total expenses of $600,000. The balance in owners' equity at the beginning of the year was $400,000.

REQUIRED Compute the return on owners' equity using:

    a. The beginning balance of owners' equity.
    b. The ending balance of owners' equity.
    c. The average balance of owners' equity.

Ex. 12-5
Alternative
Performance
Measurement
Methods

The year-end trial balance of the Plannif Company is presented below. The company operates on the calendar year.

Plannif Company
Trial Balance
December 31, 1985

	Debit	Credit
Cash	$ 7,000	
Accounts receivable	12,000	
Inventory	21,000	
Building	60,000	
Accumulated depreciation, building		$ 20,000
Accounts payable		5,000
Mortgage payable		15,000
Capital stock		12,000
Retained earnings		38,000
Sales		75,000
Cost of goods sold	31,000	
Advertising	4,000	
Sales salaries and commissions	10,000	
Administrative salaries	15,000	
Office operation expense	4,000	
Miscellaneous expense	1,000	
Totals	$165,000	$165,000

REQUIRED   Compute the return on investment for the Plannif Company using as the investment base:

a.   Total gross assets.
b.   Total net assets.
c.   Beginning owners' equity.
d.   Ending owners' equity.

Ex. 12-6
Working Backward
from ROI Data

The music box division of Musical Life, Ltd., reported a 1985 income of $50,000. In its annual performance report, the division showed a return on gross assets of 8 percent. The division had accumulated depreciation of $275,000 at the end of the year.

REQUIRED

a.   Compute the amount of gross assets for the music box division.
b.   Compute the division's return on net assets.

Ex. 12-7
Computing
Transfer Prices

The disk division of the Business Products Corporation sells all of its output to the retail sales division of the company. The only product of the disk division is floppy disks used in word processors and computers. The disks are sold in boxes of 10 disks. The retail sales division sells the floppy disks for $95 per box. Below are production and cost data from the disk division for the production of disks during 1985.

Boxes of disks manufactured	50,000
Prime costs	$1,400,000
Manufacturing overhead (20 percent variable)	800,000
Operating expenses (40 percent variable)	750,000

REQUIRED   Compute the transfer price for a box of disks using:

    a. Full product cost.
    b. Variable product cost.
    c. Total cost.
    d. Total variable cost.
    e. Full product cost plus 20 percent.

Ex. 12-8
Target Profit and
Modified Market
Transfer Prices

Refer to the cost data found in Exercise 12-7 for the production of disks in the disk division of the Business Products Corporation.

REQUIRED

    a. Compute the transfer price for a box of disks based on a target profit of 12 percent of total costs.
    b. Compute the transfer price for a box of disks based on a final market sales price less 25 percent for marketing and distribution costs incurred in the retail sales division.
    c. Compute the net income for the disk division using each of the transfer prices computed above.

Ex. 12-9
Costing Service
Activities

Car-Shine, Inc., provides a car-waxing service for all types of cars. The company charges $80 for its professional car-wax job. Each car receives a thorough wash before being cleaned and waxed. The cleaning compound and the paste wax are accounted for as direct materials. All other materials, such as water and buffing pads, are treated as indirect charges. All labor is direct labor except for the shift supervisor's salary. Below are cost data for the month of April, when 300 cars were waxed.

Supervisor's salary	$ 1,500
Employee wages	11,520
Cleaning compound	1,140
Paste wax	1,725
Depreciation on equipment	1,050
Utilities (including water)	1,800
Building lease cost	900
Buffing pads	750
Miscellaneous	450

In addition to the operating costs listed above, the company must pay a franchise fee of 10 percent of gross revenue to the national chain that advertises and provides other support.

REQUIRED

    a. Prepare a detailed report for the cost of waxing cars during April.
    b. Compute the company's profit for April.

Ex. 12-10 (CMA)
Discussion of
Business Segment
Characteristics

Elwood Bank is a large municipal bank with several branch offices. The bank has a computer department that handles all data processing for the bank's operations. In addition, the bank acts as a service bureau by selling its expertise in systems development and excess machine time to several small business firms.

    The computer department currently is treated as a cost center of the bank. The manager of the computer department prepares an expense budget annually for approval by senior bank officials. Monthly operating reports compare actual and budgeted expenses. Revenues from the department's service bureau activities are treated as "other income" by the bank and are not reflected in the computer department's operating reports. The costs of serving these clients are included in departmental reports, however.

The manager of the computer department has proposed that the bank management convert the computer department to a profit or investment center.

REQUIRED

a. Describe the characteristics that differentiate (1) a cost center, (2) a profit center, and (3) an investment center from each other.

b. Would the manager of the computer department be likely to conduct the operations of the department differently if the department were classified as a profit center or an investment center rather than as a cost center? Explain your answer.

PROBLEMS

P. 12-1
Ranking Division
Performance

The Fairfield Appliance Corporation manufactures a variety of home appliances and sells them through large department store chains. The company is a decentralized operation with four divisions. Summarized financial data are presented below for the divisions.

Division	Income	Gross Assets	Net Assets
Refrigerator	$300,000	$4,000,000	$2,200,000
Small appliance	140,000	1,300,000	1,000,000
Air conditioners	350,000	3,000,000	2,800,000
Ranges	150,000	3,000,000	1,050,000

REQUIRED

Rank the four divisions based on total net income, ROI on gross assets, ROI on net assets, and residual income. Use a target income of 12 percent of net assets in computing residual income.

P. 12-2
Working Backward
from ROI

The Morton Company's income for the year is $200,000. Its return on investment is 12.5 percent on gross assets, 16 percent on net assets, and 20 percent on net assets employed. The company has a residual income of ($25,000). The only contra-asset accounts the company has are accumulated depreciation accounts.

REQUIRED

Compute:

a. The company's gross assets.
b. The company's total amount of accumulated depreciation.
c. The amount of assets not employed in the business.
d. The target income used in computing residual income.

P. 12-3
Ranking Division
Performance

The Pizzen Manufacturing Company operates with three divisions. Below are financial data for the three divisions for the fiscal year ended June 30.

	Division		
	X	Y	Z
Sales	$ 60,000	$400,000	$150,000
Cost of goods sold	25,000	240,000	70,000
Operating expenses	20,000	100,000	60,000
Current assets	20,000	80,000	50,000
Land held for investment	80,000	—	—
Fixed assets (gross)	100,000	500,000	120,000
Accumulated depreciation	10,000	350,000	60,000
Current liabilities	15,000	40,000	10,000
Long-term liabilities	—	25,000	15,000

REQUIRED

a. Compute net income for each division.
b. Compute ROI using gross assets.
c. Compute ROI using net assets.
d. Compute ROI using gross assets employed.
e. Compute residual income using a target income of 15 percent of net assets employed.
f. Compute income as a percentage of sales.
g. Prepare a chart ranking the divisions for each of the performance measures.

P. 12-4
The Effect of Asset Base on Performance Measurement

The Stichler Auto Parts Company produces automobile parts for all of the major United States automobile manufacturers. For 35 years, the company has operated a manufacturing plant in southeast Michigan to minimize shipping costs and service its clients efficiently. Demand for products in the late 1960s caused the company to build an additional manufacturing plant. The dispersion of the automobile industry in the last 20 years and favorable state tax incentives caused the company management to build the new plant in the South.

The company operates the two plants as separate investment centers. The management of each plant is evaluated on performance, and year-end bonuses are based primarily on the divisional performance reports. Recently the company has had trouble keeping managers at the newer plant, because bonuses have been very small compared with the Michigan plant. Below are data for the two divisions for the year just completed.

	Division	
	Michigan	Southern
Sales	$8,000,000	$8,000,000
Manufacturing expenses	4,500,000	4,800,000
Marketing and distribution expenses	1,200,000	1,500,000
Administrative expenses	1,600,000	1,100,000
Current assets	1,000,000	1,000,000
Buildings	2,500,000	9,000,000
Accumulated depreciation, buildings	2,200,000	2,500,000
Equipment	6,000,000	8,000,000
Accumulated depreciation, equipment	3,300,000	3,000,000

The higher depreciation charges at the Southern plant are partially offset by lower taxes and other costs.

REQUIRED
- a. Compute the net income for the two divisions.
- b. Compute the return on investment for both divisions using gross assets.
- c. Compute the return on investment for both divisions using net assets.
- d. Comment on the company's division performance measures and its problem with retaining managerial personnel at its Southern plant.

P. 12-5
Divisional
Performance
Measurement

The Peddleworth Corporation is a decentralized firm with three operating divisions. The performance of each division's management is compared using investment center analysis. Salary increases and other benefits are assigned primarily on the relative performance of division managers as reflected by the investment center analysis. Following are data for the three divisions for the year just completed.

	Division		
	A	B	C
Sales	$ 900,000	$400,000	$150,000
Product expense	400,000	250,000	70,000
Operating expenses	350,000	80,000	50,000
Gross assets	1,200,000	800,000	300,000
Net assets	800,000	700,000	100,000
Assets not employed in normal operations	—	300,000	

REQUIRED
- a. Compute the net income for each of the three divisions.
- b. Compute the income for each division as a percentage of sales.
- c. Compute the ROI for each division using gross assets as the investment base.
- d. Compute the ROI for each division using net assets as the investment base.
- e. Compute the ROI for each division using gross assets employed as the investment base.
- f. Compute the ROI for each division using net assets employed as the investment base.
- g. Compute the residual income for each division using a target income of 10 percent of gross assets employed.
- h. Prepare a schedule ranking the divisions for each of the performance measures in parts a through g.
- i. Interpret the results of your analysis.

P. 12-6 (AICPA)
Evaluating a Sales
Region Income
Reporting System

In recent years distribution expenses of the Avey Company have increased more than other expenditures. For more effective control, the company plans to provide each local manager with an income statement for his territory showing monthly and year-to-date amounts for the current and the previous year. Each sales office is supervised by a local manager; sales orders are forwarded to the main office and filled from a central warehouse; billing and collections are also centrally processed. Expenses are first classified by function and then allocated to each territory in the following ways:

Function	Basis
Sales salaries	Actual
Other selling expenses	Relative sales dollars
Warehousing	Relative sales dollars
Packing and shipping	Weight of package
Billing and collections	Number of billings
General administration	Equally

<table>
<tr><td>REQUIRED</td><td>a.</td><td>1.</td><td>Explain responsibility accounting and the classification of revenues and expenses under this concept.</td></tr>
</table>

REQUIRED

a. 1. Explain responsibility accounting and the classification of revenues and expenses under this concept.

2. What are the objectives of profit analysis by sales territories in income statements?

b. 1. Discuss the effectiveness of Avey Company's comparative income statements by sales territories as a tool for planning and control. Include in your answer additional factors that should be considered and changes that might be desirable for effective planning by management and evaluation of the local sales managers.

2. Compare the degree of control that can be achieved over production costs and distribution costs and explain why the degree of control differs.

3. Criticize Avey Company's allocation and/or inclusion of (a) other selling expenses, (b) warehousing expense and (c) general administration expense.

P. 12-7
Return on Owners'
Equity with Stock
Transactions

The Camdon Company experienced the following stock transactions during 1985:

Feb. 1: Issued 2,000 shares for $100 each
May 1: Issued 1,000 shares for $120 each
July 1: Issued 1,500 shares for $120 each
Oct. 1: Issued 2,000 shares for $150 each

On January 1, 1985, the company's stock records showed that the company had 20,000 shares of $10 par value common stock issued and outstanding. The shares traded in the market on January 1, 1985, for $98 per share. The general ledger showed that the 20,000 shares had additional paid-in capital of $800,000. Retained Earnings on December 31, 1985, had a credit balance of $500,000 before closing entries.

On December 31, 1985, the stock is trading in the market for $155 per share. The company has no preferred stock. During 1985, Camdon Company earned $400,000.

REQUIRED   Compute the return on owners' equity using:

a. The beginning balance in owners' equity.
b. The ending balance in owners' equity.
c. The average balance in owners' equity using a monthly average for your calculations.

P. 12-8 (CMA)
Transfer Price
Analysis

MBR Inc., consists of three divisions which formerly were three independent manufacturing companies. Bader Corporation and Roach Company merged in 1984 and the merged corporation acquired Mitchell Co. in 1985. The name of the corporation was subsequently changed to MBR Inc., and each company became a separate division retaining the name of its former company.

The three divisions have operated as if they were still independent companies. Each division has its own sales force and production facilities. Each division's management is responsible for sales, cost of operations, acquisition and financing of divisional assets, and working capital management. The corporate management of MBR evaluates the performance of the divisions and division managements on the basis of return on investment.

Mitchell division has just been awarded a contract for a product which uses a component that is manufactured by the Roach division as well as by outside suppliers. Mitchell used a cost figure of $3.80 for the component manufactured by Roach in preparing its bid for the new product. This cost figure was supplied by Roach in response to Mitchell's request for the average variable cost of the component, and represents the standard variable manufacturing cost and variable selling and distribution expense.

Roach has an active sales force that is continually soliciting new prospects. Roach's regular selling price for the component Mitchell needs for the new product is $6.50. Sales of this component are expected to increase. However, the Roach management has indicated that it could supply Mitchell with the required quantities of the component at the regular selling price less variable selling and distribution expenses. Mitchell's management has responded by offering to pay standard variable manufacturing cost plus 20 percent.

The two divisions have been unable to agree on a transfer price. Corporate management has never established a transfer price policy because interdivision transactions have never occurred. As a compromise, the corporate vice president of finance has suggested a price equal to the standard full manufacturing cost (i.e., no selling and distribution expenses) plus a 15 percent markup. This price has also been rejected by the two division managers, because each considered it grossly unfair.

The unit cost structure for the Roach component and the three suggested prices are shown below.

Regular selling price	$6.50
Standard variable manufacturing cost	$3.20
Standard fixed manufacturing cost	1.20
Variable selling and distribution expenses	.60
Regular selling price less variable selling and distribution expenses ($6.50 − $.60)	$5.90
Variable manufacturing plus 20% ($3.20 × 1.20)	$3.84
Standard full manufacturing cost plus 15% ($4.40 × 1.15)	$5.06

REQUIRED

a. Discuss the effect each of the three proposed prices might have on the Roach division management's attitude toward intracompany business.
b. Is the negotiation of a price between the Mitchell and Roach divisions a satisfactory method to solve the transfer price problem? Explain your answer.
c. Should the corporate management of MBR Inc., become involved in this transfer price controversy? Explain your answer.

P. 12-9
The Creation and Use of Transfer Prices

The compressor division of the General Refrigeration Company makes refrigerator compressors that are sold primarily to the refrigerator division of the company for use in production of its products. Last year the compressor division sold 30 percent of its output in the outside market for $55 each. The rest of the production was sold to the refrigerator division. Normal marketing and distribution costs for the compressor industry average 15 percent of selling price.

During 1985, the compressor division produced 10,000 units with the following total standard costs:

Direct materials	$180,000
Direct labor	120,000
Manufacturing overhead	100,000
Total production cost variances	60,000 unfavorable
Operating expenses:	
Marketing and distribution	20,000
Administrative	80,000

Management expects an 8 percent increase in the market price of the compressors in 1986. Also, the standard costs will increase by 10 percent to reflect expected changes in resource costs and a newly negotiated labor contract. With the new standard costs, the management of the compressor division believe the average variance from standard costs will be 4 percent unfavorable. No changes are expected in marketing and distribution expenses or administrative expenses. Production and sales quantities are expected to be the same.

REQUIRED   Compute the required transfer price for the compressors for each of the following **independent** assumptions: The transfer price should

   a. be based on 1985 standard product cost.
   b. be based on 1985 actual product cost.
   c. be based on 1986 standard product cost.
   d. be based on 1986 expected actual product cost.
   e. be based on 1986 market price.
   f. be based on 1986 market price modified for lower marketing and distribution costs.
   g. provide a 6 percent profit on 1986 expected total costs.
   h. prepare a schedule showing the compressor division's net income for each of the 1986 base transfer pricing alternatives.

P. 12-10
Comparing Various
Transfer Prices

The Tree-Life Corporation manufactures and sells many different types of Christmas decorations. Some of the products are sold by the company's retail division, which operates a chain of retail stores in 20 states. There are five different manufacturing divisions that produce the products for the retail division and for sales to department stores, discount stores, and other customers. A major product of the company is artificial Christmas trees, the sole product of the tree division. During the 1985–1986 fiscal year, the tree division made 20,000 trees. A total of 8,000 trees were sold through the retail division, and the remainder were sold to other customers for $40 per tree.

The tree division, like all divisions of the firm, operates as a decentralized investment center. Cost data for the 1985–1986 fiscal year are presented below.

Direct materials	$280,000
Direct labor	160,000
Manufacturing overhead	140,000
Administrative	80,000
Marketing and distribution	60,000

1. Compute the transfer price for the sale of trees to the retail division based on:
   a. Full product cost.
   b. Market price less 15 percent for lower marketing and distribution costs.
   c. Total cost transfer price.
   d. A target profit of 8 percent of total cost.
   e. Market price.
2. Compute the tree division's net income for the 1985–1986 fiscal year using each of the transfer prices computed above.

CASES

Case 12-1
Transfer Pricing of Services

Big State University has a large centralized computer facility that serves many of the computer needs of the campus. Additional computer services are provided by several minicomputers and computer service companies. People who use the university's central computer are not charged for the services. Instead, the computer center costs are charged to the Administrative Overhead account. Recently this treatment of computer cost has been questioned on a variety of grounds. One criticism is that the costs are understated for research, student record keeping, and other administrative and academic activities. In addition, the analysis of alternative computer resources for new computer needs is impossible, because it appears that the central computer facility is free.

The university's new treasurer has suggested that all computer users should be charged for their use of computer resources, and he suggests that an appropriate transfer price be created for computer resources. The treasurer proposes that a single transfer price can be used for all of the services provided by Central Computer Services. The director of the computer facility states that due to the broad nature of the center's services and the varying demands of its many users, a single transfer price would not do a good job of assigning computer charges to the appropriate cost objective. The treasurer thinks that any good measure of resource use will assign "about the same amount of computer charges to any particular user." To start the process of creating the transfer pricing system and determining who is correct about the transfer price, the university controller has provided the following data for the central computer facility for the 1985–1986 academic year.

Big State University
Central Computer Services Operating Costs
1985–1986

Computer operators' salaries	$ 120,000
Systems analysts' salaries	250,000
Computer programmers' salaries	150,000
Supervisory salaries	130,000
Clerical salaries	60,000
Computer supplies	220,000
Office supplies	10,000
Depreciation	100,000
Lease expense on equipment	350,000
Utilities	80,000
Miscellaneous	30,000
Total central computer services cost	$1,500,000

During the year, Central Computer Services experienced the following activity:

Core hours of time	6,000
Pages of printed output	12,000,000
Punched cards processed	8,000,000
Disk storage (thousands of characters)	200,000
Tape drive hours	20,000
Terminal connect hours	400,000

Student records used the following computer services during the year:

Core hours of time	300
Pages of printed output	560,000
Punched cards processed	80,000
Disk storage (thousands of characters)	40,000
Tape drive hours	220
Terminal connect hours	30,000

The college of engineering used the following computer services during the year:

Core hours of time	1,800
Pages of printed output	240,000
Punched cards processed	10,000
Disk storage (thousands of characters)	80,000
Tape drive hours	400
Terminal connect hours	90,000

REQUIRED

a. Compute the transfer price for Central Computer Services using:
1. Core hours.
2. Pages of print.
3. Punched cards processed.
4. Disk storage.
5. Tape hours.
6. Terminal connect hours.
b. Compute the computer services charge to student records using each of the transfer prices computed above.
c. Compute the computer service charge to the college of engineering using each of the transfer prices computed above.
d. Comment on the logic of using a single transfer price for all of computer services.
e. Suggest a way of assigning computer service costs to users in a more equitable fashion. Provide as much detail as possible in your suggested approach.

CHAPTER 13
Inventory Management

Manufacturing and merchandising companies cannot operate without working capital. Often the largest component of working capital is inventory. Because the investment in inventories is large, it is necessary to manage it as efficiently as possible. Manufacturing operations usually are the most complex to manage because of the variety of inventories that they have. But in any type of business, managers must decide what inventory to buy, the best quantity to purchase, and the best time to place orders. They must also plan the most efficient way of storing, handling, and using inventory.

In this chapter we discuss inventory planning and control. We first discuss how to determine the optimum size of inventory orders and the optimum timing for placing those orders.

INVENTORY PLANNING AND CONTROL

All assets have economic value and require some planning and control to ensure that they are used to achieve the organization's goals. For example, manufacturing operations are scheduled to make the best use of production facilities such as factory buildings and machinery. Information processing is planned to make the best use of computer equipment. Cash must be managed carefully to ensure that enough is on hand to make all necessary disbursements, to maintain liquidity, and to prevent theft, loss, or excess cash balances. Clearly, some assets require more management than others. For example, less effort is required to manage patents or licenses than to manage cash, temporary investments, and inventories.

Two characteristics of inventories

There are two characteristics of inventory that make it necessary to manage it very carefully: Inventory is a large investment, and it is constantly circulating. Unlike buildings and equipment, inventory is continuously being used or sold and must be replaced. Consequently, inventory management is a continuous activity of managers.

The Nature of Inventory Management

Inventory produces earnings only when it is sold. In a manufacturing firm, the generation of profits from inventory can be a lengthy process; raw materials must first be converted to finished goods before they can be sold. Because the money invested in inventories does not earn revenue until the sale takes place, it is important to determine the optimum levels of inventory for all inventory items.

The purpose of inventory management

The purpose of inventory management is to keep production and sales activities moving smoothly without interruptions caused by inventory shortages, and to do so at the lowest possible inventory cost. This involves balancing the cost of acquiring and carrying inventory with the cost of not having enough when it is needed. The balance is achieved at the optimum size of inventory orders and the optimum time for placing the orders. As we show shortly, the quantity of inventory on hand and the frequency and size of inventory orders are directly related to inventory costs.

Inventory Costs

In addition to the actual purchase price of inventory, there are many other costs associated with buying, storing, and using goods. If a firm runs out of inventory, it may suffer lost sales or idle production facilities. Inventory costs can be categorized into ordering costs, carrying costs, and stockout costs. Following are some examples of costs in each category:

There is a cost to ordering inventory and keeping it on hand

Inventory ordering costs:
Cost of acquiring recent price quotations
Cost of preparing and approving purchase orders
Cost of receiving shipments and checking against purchase orders

Inventory carrying costs:
Cost of funds invested in inventory
Cost of heat, light, power, and depreciation on inventory storage facilities
Cost of handling inventory
Cost of inventory insurance
Cost of inventory taxes
Cost of obsolescence, spoilage, deterioration, and theft

Inventory shortage costs:
Cost of lost sales
Cost of inefficient production
Cost of substituting more expensive materials
Penalty for late completion or delivery of products

Inventory **ordering costs** and inventory **carrying costs** are used to compute the optimum size inventory order, which we explain and illustrate below. Inventory **shortage costs** are used in determining the optimum reorder point for inventory.

ECONOMIC ORDER QUANTITY (EOQ)

The order size for a specific inventory item that results in the lowest total inventory cost for a period is called the **economic order quantity (EOQ)**, sometimes called the **optimum order quantity.** Total inventory cost consists of inventory ordering costs and inventory carrying costs. A separate EOQ is computed for each different item in inventory.

The EOQ occurs when the cost of ordering inventory equals the cost of carrying inventory

The economic order quantity is the order size that incurs the lowest total cost for inventory. This minimum cost occurs when the size of an inventory order is large enough so that the cost of ordering that quantity of inventory is equal to the cost of carrying it. The cost of carrying inventory **increases** as the quantity ordered gets larger. The cost of ordering inventory **decreases** as the quantity ordered gets larger. These inventory cost relationships are illustrated in Figure 13-1.

The costs of insurance, storage, and other carrying costs are larger when large amounts of inventory are carried rather than small amounts of inventory. On the other hand, many costs of ordering are the same whether 200 or 5,000 units are ordered. With the large order, the ordering cost per unit is smaller. If small orders are placed, the company carries fewer units in inventory on the average and therefore has a lower carrying cost. But small orders mean more orders must be placed during the year, increasing the total cost of ordering inventory.

If we add the cost of ordering and the cost of carrying any given quantity of inventory, we obtain the total cost of inventory for that order size. Figure 13-1 depicts the total inventory cost of all possible order sizes. This curve has its lowest point directly above the intersection of the ordering cost and carrying cost curves. Any point other than the EOQ yields a higher total inventory cost.

Figure 13-1. Inventory ordering and inventory carrying costs. As the order size increases, the total inventory ordering cost decreases and the total inventory carrying cost increases. The minimum total cost is the economic order quantity. It occurs at the point where total ordering cost equals total carrying cost.

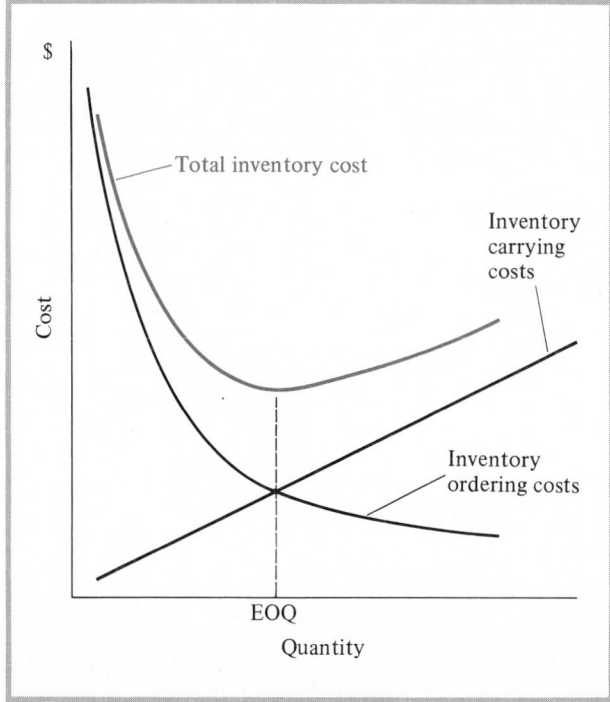

The EOQ Formula

There are several methods for finding the EOQ. The trial-and-error method, which can be quite time-consuming, involves computing the total inventory cost for various order sizes until one is found that approximates the EOQ. Graphing the inventory ordering and carrying costs can provide an estimate of the EOQ. However, management decisions should be based on EOQs that are more precise than is usually possible using the graphic method. A more precise and less time-consuming method is to use a formula to compute the EOQ. The economic order quantity is computed using the following variables:

A = quantity of inventory in units required for the period

P = cost of placing one order

U = unit cost of each item

I = inventory carrying costs expressed as a percentage of unit cost

The economic order quantity model minimizes inventory costs

These variables can be used to derive the total ordering costs and total carrying costs, whose sum may be minimized using calculus[1] to derive the following mathematical model:

$$EOQ = \sqrt{\frac{2AP}{UI}}$$

The EOQ is computed for each item in inventory for some specific time period. Typically, EOQs are computed for the year. That is, we use expected demand, price, ordering cost, and carrying cost data for the year to determine the EOQ. If none of these costs change from year to year, the EOQ will remain

---

[1] The EOQ formula is derived as follows:

$$\text{Total carrying cost} = \text{Average inventory on hand} \times \text{Unit cost} \times \text{Carrying rate}$$

$$= \frac{EOQ}{2} \times UI$$

$$\text{Total ordering cost} = \text{Number of orders} \times \text{Cost of placing an order}$$

$$= \frac{A}{EOQ} \times P$$

Total cost:

$$C = \frac{EOQ}{2} \times UI + \frac{A}{EOQ} \times P$$

$$\frac{d\,C}{d\,EOQ} = \frac{UI}{2} - \frac{AP}{EOQ^2}$$

Set the derivative equal to zero:

$$\frac{UI}{2} - \frac{AP}{EOQ^2} = 0$$

$$EOQ^2 = \frac{2AP}{UI}$$

$$EOQ = \sqrt{\frac{2AP}{UI}}$$

the same. Of course, most of the time costs do change and therefore the EOQ will change.

The economic order quantity model is a mathematical equation that describes the relationship between ordering costs and carrying costs for inventory in terms of order size. The model rests on several assumptions:

The EOQ model is based on several assumptions

1. The demand is constant and is known.
2. Ordering costs are constant and are known.
3. Carrying costs are constant and are known.
4. Production and inventory carrying capacity is unlimited.

Despite these somewhat restrictive assumptions, the model can provide managers with information for planning inventory and making ordering decisions. Most of the variables can be estimated and the model results in EOQs that are well within the production and inventory carrying capacity of the firm.

To illustrate how to calculate the economic order quantity, we use the example of Unisafe Security Systems Company, which offers security devices for homes and businesses. The company is open 5 days per week except for a 2-week period during the holiday season. Its business year is therefore 250 working days. One of its products is an electronic burglar alarm with the following data:

Average daily demand	40 units
Selling price	$200/unit
Cost	$125/unit
Ordering cost	$200/order
Carrying cost	20 percent of unit cost

Using these data, it is easy to calculate the economic order quantity. The quantity required for the year (*A*) is 40 units a day times 250 days, or 10,000 units. The cost of placing one order (*P*) is $200. The carrying cost (*I*) is 20 percent of the $125 per unit cost (*U*). Substituting these values into the EOQ model, we get

$$\text{EOQ} = \sqrt{\frac{2 \times \text{Total units} \times \text{Ordering cost in \$}}{\text{Unit cost in \$} \times \text{Carrying rate}}}$$

$$\text{EOQ} = \sqrt{\frac{(2)(10,000 \text{ units})(\$200)}{(\$125 \text{ per unit})(.2)}}$$

$$= \sqrt{\frac{\$4,000,000 \text{ units}}{\$25}}$$

$$= \sqrt{160,000 \text{ units}}$$

$$= 400 \text{ units}$$

The economic order quantity is 400 units. This is the order size that minimizes the total inventory cost for this particular inventory item. Total inventory cost for the year for this item is merely the carrying cost plus the ordering cost. In this example the total ordering cost is $200 times the number of orders placed. Carrying cost is 20 percent of the cost of the average amount of inventory for the period. The number of orders placed during the year can be determined by dividing the EOQ into the number of units required for the period:

$$\text{Number of orders} = \frac{A}{\text{EOQ}}$$

$$= \frac{10{,}000 \text{ units per year}}{400 \text{ units per order}}$$

$$= 25 \text{ orders per year}$$

The cost of ordering inventory

$$\text{Total ordering cost} = \frac{A}{\text{EOQ}} \times P$$

$$= \frac{(10{,}000 \text{ units per year})(\$200 \text{ per order})}{400 \text{ units per order}}$$

$$= \$5{,}000 \text{ per year}$$

Carrying cost is a function of the average amount of inventory on hand multiplied by the carrying cost rate. With the simple assumption that inventory is used evenly throughout the year and is ordered and delivered just as the item is about to run out, the average inventory on hand is determined by dividing the order size by 2. The inventory carrying cost can be expressed as

$$\text{Average inventory} = \frac{\text{EOQ}}{2}$$

$$= \frac{400 \text{ units}}{2}$$

$$= 200 \text{ units}$$

The cost of carrying inventory

$$\text{Carrying cost} = \frac{\text{EOQ}}{2} \times UI$$

$$= \frac{400 \text{ units} \times (\$125 \text{ per unit})(.2)}{2}$$

$$= \$5{,}000$$

Total Cost of Managing Inventory

As expected, at the EOQ, the cost of ordering for the period is equal to the cost of carrying the inventory for the period. By combining the carrying and ordering cost we can determine the total inventory cost for the period at the EOQ:

The total cost of ordering and carrying inventory does not include the purchase price

$$\text{Total inventory cost} = \frac{AP}{\text{EOQ}} + \frac{\text{EOQ}}{2} \times UI$$

$$= \$5,000 + \$5,000 = \$10,000$$

Note that $10,000 is the cost of ordering and carrying inventory and does not include its purchase cost.

Rather than looking specifically at the cost of ordering and the cost of carrying the economic order quantity, we can determine the cost of ordering and carrying any quantity of inventory (Q) by using:

$$\text{Total inventory cost} = \frac{AP}{Q} + \frac{Q}{2} \times UI$$

Clearly, if Q is greater or smaller than the EOQ, the total inventory cost should be larger than $10,000 because the minimum cost of $10,000 can occur only at the EOQ. For example, if the order size is 420 units, inventory cost is:

$$\text{Total inventory cost} = \frac{(10,000)(\$200)}{420} + \frac{420}{2} \times (\$125)(.2)$$

$$= \$4,761.90 + (210)(\$25)$$

$$= \$10,011.90$$

Similarly, if the order size is less than 400 units, total inventory cost is more than $10,000. For example, ordering 390 units at a time produces an inventory cost of $10,003.21. The lowest possible inventory cost the company can achieve for this item is $10,000. Order sizes near the EOQ yield inventory costs near the minimum cost because the total cost curve is relatively flat at its minimum point. As order sizes deviate significantly from the EOQ, total inventory cost rises rapidly. For example, for an order size either double or half of the EOQ, the total inventory cost is $12,500 — 25 percent greater than the optimum inventory cost.

Cost Estimation and Model Sensitivity

It can be difficult to make precise estimates of the values of the variables used in computing the economic order quantity. Total demand may fluctuate significantly from year to year; carrying costs, such as interest, may be hard to estimate; and ordering costs may change. To determine the effect of incorrect estimates, managers may compute the EOQ with different values for each of the variables used. By comparing the EOQs resulting from the computations, it may be possible to determine how sensitive the EOQ model is to changes in the value of the variables.

For example, Unisafe Company is not sure that demand for the alarm system is 40 units per day, but management is confident that it is at least 30 units and not more than 50 units a day. Substituting these as extreme values into the EOQ model enables us to see what effect different estimates in demand have on the economic order quantity.

Demand of 30 units per day:

$$A = 30 \text{ units per day} \times 250 \text{ days} = 7{,}500 \text{ units}$$

$$EOQ = \sqrt{\frac{(2)(7{,}500 \text{ units})(\$200)}{(\$125 \text{ per unit})(.2)}}$$

$$= 346.4 \text{ units}$$

Demand of 50 units per day:

$$A = 50 \text{ units per day} \times 250 \text{ days} = 12{,}500 \text{ units}$$

$$EOQ = \sqrt{\frac{(2)(12{,}500 \text{ units})(\$200)}{(\$125 \text{ per unit})(.2)}}$$

$$= 447.2 \text{ units}$$

From these computations, management knows that the optimum order size may vary from about 346 units to about 447 units. But what impact do differences in demand estimates have on inventory cost? If any of the estimates used in computing the EOQ turn out to be inaccurate, the EOQ will be incorrect and inventory cost will be higher than optimal.

Making a wrong estimate has a cost

Cost of Estimation Error.   What is the cost of the error — that is, the cost of incorrectly estimating demand — if actual demand turns out to be 30 units per day after the company has already placed orders for 400 units — which is the EOQ for an expected demand of 40 units per day? We simply calculate total inventory cost for a demand of 30 units per day using the EOQ of 346 units, and we do the same for the 400-unit order, and then we look at the difference between these two total costs.

$$\text{Total inventory cost} = \frac{AP}{Q} + \frac{Q}{2} \times UI$$

At 346 units/order:

$$\text{Total inventory cost} = \frac{(7{,}500)(\$200)}{346} + \frac{346}{2} \times (\$125)(.2)$$

$$= \$4{,}335.26 + \$4{,}325.00$$

$$= \$8{,}660.26$$

At 400 units/order:

$$\text{Total inventory cost} = \frac{(7{,}500)(\$200)}{400} + \frac{400}{2} \times (\$125)(.2)$$

$$= \$3{,}750 + \$5{,}000$$

$$= \$8{,}750$$

The total cost of inventory using the correct EOQ for demand of 30 units per day is $8,660.26. The total cost of inventory using the EOQ for demand of 40 units a day when demand is actually 30 units per day is $8,750. The difference in total inventory cost of $89.74 is the cost of incorrectly estimating demand. Evidently the model is not very sensitive to errors in estimating demand. A similar sensitivity analysis for actual demand of 50 units per day yields a $70 cost for estimating demand incorrectly.

Evaluating the cost of estimation error in terms of percentage of inventory cost, we find:

$$\text{Percentage error} = \frac{\text{Cost difference}}{\text{Optimum cost}}$$

$$= \frac{\$89.74}{\$8,660.26} = .0104, \text{ or } 1.04 \text{ percent}$$

A 25 percent error in estimating demand (40 units + or − 10 units) causes a 1 percent increase in total cost of inventory. Thus, in this example inventory costs are rather insensitive to errors in daily demand estimates of 25 percent or less.

Sensitivity of Carrying Cost. The sensitivity of other variables can be tested as well. For example, if the carrying cost of inventory is expected to range from 15 to 25 percent, what is the effect on the EOQ? We substitute into the EOQ model, leaving other variables unchanged from their values in the original example.

Some estimates are more sensitive than others and affect cost to a greater extent

15 percent carrying cost

$$\text{EOQ} = \sqrt{\frac{(2)(10,000 \text{ units})(\$200)}{(\$125 \text{ per unit})(.15)}}$$

$$= 461.9 = 462 \text{ units}$$

25 percent carrying cost:

$$\text{EOQ} = \sqrt{\frac{(2)(10,000 \text{ units})(\$200)}{(\$125 \text{ per unit})(.25)}}$$

$$= 357.8 = 358 \text{ units}$$

As before, we can determine the cost of incorrectly estimating the value of one of the variables in the EOQ model. For instance, suppose that the actual inventory carrying cost is 25 percent rather than the original estimate of 20 percent. For a 25 percent carrying cost, the EOQ is 358 units, whereas management used the 400-unit EOQ estimated for a 20 percent carrying cost. Total inventory costs for both actual and estimated carrying costs and their corresponding EOQs are:

At 358 units/order:

$$\text{Total inventory cost} = \frac{(10,000)(\$200)}{358} + \frac{358}{2} \times (\$125)(.25)$$

$$= \$11,180.34$$

At 400 units/order:

$$\text{Total inventory cost} = \frac{(10{,}000)(\$200)}{400} + \frac{400}{2} \times (\$125)(.25)$$

$$= \$11{,}250.00$$

The difference in total inventory cost of $69.66 is the additional inventory cost incurred by using an inventory order quantity that resulted from an inaccurate estimate of inventory carrying cost. Here again, the model is not very sensitive to errors in estimation. In the previous example, you saw that the cost of estimation error was only 1.04 percent of total inventory cost. In this second cost of estimation error example, actual carrying cost of 25 percent is 20 percent higher than the estimated carrying cost of 20 percent. But the resulting additional cost of using the wrong carrying cost estimate is only .6 percent, as calculated below:

$$\text{Percentage error} = \frac{\text{Cost difference}}{\text{Optimal cost}}$$

$$= \frac{\$69.66}{\$11{,}180.34} = .0062, \text{ or } .62 \text{ percent}$$

When EOQ model sensitivity is low, as in this case, managers cannot justify spending significant amounts of time and money refining their estimates of carrying costs and demand. For some inventories, however, the EOQ model may be very sensitive to estimation errors. In such cases managers may incur significant unnecessary inventory costs and should generally try to make accurate estimates of the values of the EOQ variables.

EOQ and Not-for-Profit Organizations

In the preceding EOQ example, the alarm system selling price of $200 was given, but it was not used in any of the computations. The primary reason for including the selling price is to distinguish it from the purchase price, or cost of the product. If the product consisted of raw materials that are not sold but are used in production, the EOQ computations could still be performed. Economic order quantity computations are based on cost and quantity data only. Consequently, EOQ analysis is applicable to all types of organizations interested in optimizing resources invested in inventory.

EOQ computations include only costs, not selling price

For example, a municipal government uses a centralized purchasing and inventory system. Office supplies for all city facilities are handled through this centralized system. One supply item is letterhead stationery for use by various city offices. The following data pertain to this inventory item:

A	Annual use	7,200 reams
U	Purchase price	$5/ream
P	Ordering cost	$90/order
I	Carrying cost	18 percent of purchase price

Solving for the optimum order size yields 1,200 reams per order, as follows:

$$EOQ = \sqrt{\frac{2AP}{UI}}$$

$$= \sqrt{\frac{(2)(7,200 \text{ reams})(\$90)}{(\$5 \text{ per ream})(.18)}}$$

$$= 1,200 \text{ reams}$$

Orders per year: 7,200 reams/1,200 reams = 6 orders

The municipal government can minimize its inventory cost for stationery by placing six orders a year of 1,200 reams each. The same type of sensitivity analysis can be performed as demonstrated earlier to determine the effect of errors in making estimates of the various EOQ variables.

Determining Optimum Production Lots

The EOQ model may be used to plan production

The EOQ model can be used in job order costing situations to determine the optimum size production run. The model is the same, except we substitute setup costs for ordering costs and unit cost of production for unit purchase price. To illustrate, we assume a firm manufactures products in job lots and this year expects to sell 10,000 units of its 27-gallon cooler. The unit manufacturing cost of the cooler is $10. Setup costs of $625 include labor for making machine settings, installing the new dies, and other costs of setting up the production run of the coolers. The cost of storing and handling units is estimated at 20 percent of production cost. In this case the variables needed to compute the optimum production run are:

A = 10,000 units demanded during the year
U = production cost is $10 per unit
P = cost of setting up the production run is $625 per run
I = inventory carrying cost is 20% of production cost

$$\text{Optimum size production run} = \sqrt{\frac{2AP}{UI}}$$

$$= \sqrt{\frac{2(10,000 \text{ units})(\$625)}{(\$10 \text{ per unit})(.20)}}$$

$$= 2,500 \text{ units}$$

The number of job runs during the year will be:

$$\text{Number of job runs} = \frac{\text{Total demand}}{\text{Optimum size production run}}$$

$$= \frac{10{,}000 \text{ units}}{2{,}500 \text{ units per run}}$$

$$= 4 \text{ production runs}$$

THE REORDER POINT

Inventory is ordered when the quantity on hand declines to a predetermined level

The economic order quantity tells management how many units to order to achieve the minimum total inventory cost for a particular inventory item, but the EOQ does not provide information about when the order should be placed. The **reorder point** is the inventory level at which a new order is placed for some specific inventory item. For example, if a company orders 5-horse-power electric motors whenever the number of motors in inventory declines to 50, then 50 is the reorder point for the motors.

Orders must be placed ahead of time to allow for delivery time

If a firm can buy and receive inventory items instantly, its reorder point is zero; there is no need to place a new order until there are no units left in inventory. In this case, inventory purchases and use would appear as shown in Figure 13-2 for the Unisafe Security Systems Company's burglar alarms. As soon as the company runs out of inventory, it orders the EOQ of 400 units and receives the goods instantly. The quantity of inventory on hand immediately increases to 400 units and declines at the rate of 40 units per day until zero is again reached. Then the cycle starts anew.

Unfortunately, most firms cannot get instant deliveries on orders. Some time is required between the time the order is placed and the time inventory is received. This time period is called **lead time,** sometimes abbreviated **LT.** If

Figure 13-2. The quantity of inventory on hand declines at the rate of 40 units per day. When it reaches zero, the economic order quantity is acquired, increasing the number of units to 400. This diagram assumes instant delivery of goods.

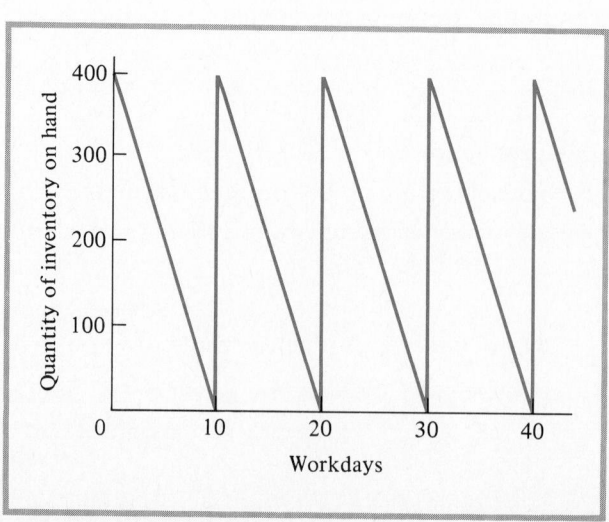

the lead time is known and daily demand is known, the reorder point is easy to determine. Daily demand is merely multiplied by the lead time to compute the **demand during lead time.** The Unisafe Security Systems Company example has a lead time for alarm orders of 3 days, and a daily demand of 40 units. The demand during lead time, or **lead time demand,** is 3×40 units, or 120 units. If the company expects to receive a new shipment of alarms just as the inventory reaches zero, it should place an order when the inventory level reaches 120 units. The inventory flow and timing of inventory orders are shown graphically in Figure 13-3. A new order is placed at an inventory level of 120 alarms 3 days before inventory reaches zero.

A certain quantity will be demanded during lead time

Stockouts and Safety Stock

Although the preceding discussion includes lead time and lead time demand in the analysis of the reorder point, it assumes that both the demand and lead time are known and constant. Often, one or the other of these fluctuate and is not known with certainty. Demand in particular is difficult to predict, as it often fluctuates from day to day. Delivery of inventory is affected by the supplier's own inventory levels and operating efficiency, as well as variations in delivery schedules of shippers.

When there is uncertainty about lead time and demand, the analysis of the inventory reorder point is complicated. A firm must consider the possibility of running out of inventory, a situation known as a **stockout,** which typically has a cost. With merchandise inventory or finished goods inventory, **stockout costs** are likely to be lost sales, customer ill will, or the loss of customers altogether. Raw material inventory stockouts may cause expensive start-up costs, a switch to more expensive raw materials, or penalty costs for late delivery or completion of contracted goods. Often it is difficult to estimate stockout costs due to their uncertainty, but they are very real costs nevertheless.

Stockouts can be costly; they can be avoided by carrying a safety stock, which also has a cost

Figure 13-3. If demand is 40 units per day and it takes 3 days to receive goods, an order is placed when there are 120 units on hand. The lead time of 3 days assures delivery of new inventory when the goods on hand are all sold.

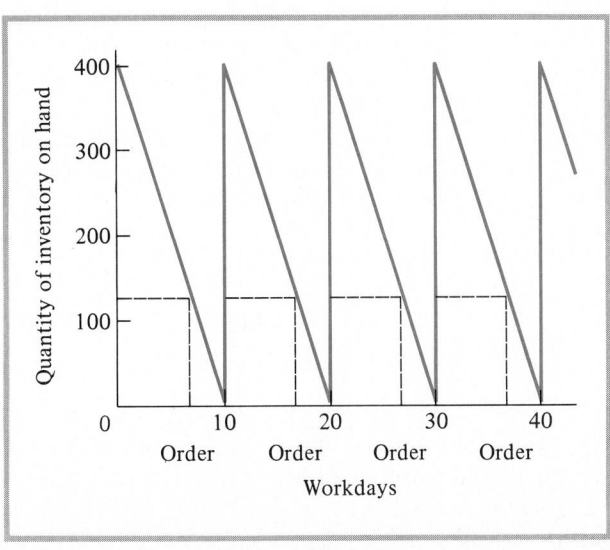

In an effort to avoid stockout costs, firms sometimes carry a **safety stock,** which is an additional amount of inventory above what is needed to satisfy average demand. Safety stocks are used to avoid stockouts and the interruptions in normal operations due to stockouts. If safety stocks are established arbitrarily, they may be very costly.

For example, Unisafe may establish a safety stock of 40 alarms, or 1 day's demand, to guard against heavy demand or late deliveries. The firm places an order when the inventory level reaches 160 units, which is average demand of 40 units × 3 days' lead time plus the safety stock of 40 units. Keeping the additional 40 units on hand at all times will increase the company's carrying cost as follows:

$$40 \text{ units} \times \$125 \text{ per unit} \times .2 = \$1,000$$

The total inventory cost of this particular item is $10,000 without the safety stock; therefore the total cost with a 40-unit safety stock is $11,000 — the 1-day safety stock increases total inventory costs by 10 percent. Perhaps $1,000 does not sound like a large amount to ensure that sales are not lost, but when the same safety stock policy is used on all inventory items the cost can add up to a significant amount indeed.

The cost of carrying safety stock should be less than expected stockout cost

The optimum inventory strategy is to increase safety stock as long as the cost of carrying additional inventory is less than the expected cost of stockouts. The analysis of optimum safety stock requires statistical techniques based on probabilities, as we discuss below.

Probabilities and Optimal Safety Stock

To determine the expected cost of a stockout, management must assign some probability to the occurrence of the stockout. Such probabilities are subjective and depend on the experience and judgments of managers.

To evaluate whether a safety stock of 40 alarms warrants the $1,000 additional carrying cost, it is necessary to compare this cost with the expected cost of a stockout. The **expected cost** of a stockout is the cost of the stockout multiplied by the probability of the stockout occurring. For example, management believes that the probability of a 1-day stockout is .20, or 20 percent if there is no safety stock. If a stockout occurs, the company loses 1 day's sales, which is a loss of $3,000 of contribution margin.[2] This lost contribution margin of $3,000 is the stockout cost. The **expected** stockout cost is the stockout cost times the probability of the stockout occurring, computed as follows:

$$\text{Expected stockout cost} = \text{Stockout cost} \times \text{Probability of occurrence}$$
$$= \$3,000 \times .20$$
$$= \$600$$

The expected cost of the stockout is less than the cost of carrying 40 units of safety stock. Therefore, safety stock should be reduced to the point where its carrying cost is $600. The optimal safety stock is

---

[2] Contribution margin is selling price less variable cost. In this case it is the selling price of $200 less the variable cost of $125 multiplied by 40 units.

Safety stock in units × Cost per unit
$$\times \text{ Carrying cost} = \$600$$

Safety stock in units × \$125 per unit × .20 = \$600

Safety stock in units = \$600/(\$125 per unit × .20)
$$= 24 \text{ units}$$

Instead of the 40 units that management arbitrarily selected, the company should carry only 24 units as safety stock.

In this example, management's estimate of a 20 percent probability of a stockout implies that there is an 80 percent probability that a stockout will not occur. Management may believe, however, that there is a 20 percent probability that a 1-day stockout will occur, but that there is an 8 percent chance that the stockout will last a second day. In this case the probability that a stockout will not occur is only 72 percent. When expected cost of a stockout is calculated, it is important to include in the calculations probabilities that add up to 100 percent. The computation of stockout cost with both a 20 percent and an 8 percent probability is

$$
\begin{array}{rl}
\$3,000 \times .20 = & \$600 \\
3,000 \times .08 = & 240 \\
0 \times .72 = & \underline{\quad 0} \\
\text{Expected stockout cost} & \underline{\underline{\$840}}
\end{array}
$$

Notice that the .72 probability of a stockout not occurring has no cost since there are no lost sales.

SUMMARY

Inventory is a major asset in many firms and must be carefully monitored and controlled. Inventory management requires the analysis of inventory **ordering costs, carrying costs,** and **shortage costs.**

The **economic order quantity (EOQ)** is the inventory order size that results in the lowest inventory cost for the period. It occurs when inventory ordering cost equals inventory carrying cost. The EOQ model may be used to minimize total inventory cost. Estimation of model variables may be difficult. If a range of values exists for some variable, the extreme values may be substituted into the model to determine their impact on the EOQ. The cost of incorrect estimates can be computed and the sensitivity of the model can be measured.

The **reorder point** is the inventory level at which a new order should be placed. Most firms place orders before the inventory level reaches zero to avoid shortages during lead time. **Lead time** is the time between placing an order and receiving it. The amount of inventory used or demanded during lead time is called **lead time demand.** When lead time demand is known, the reorder point is the inventory level equal to lead time demand.

If demand and lead time are not known, the reorder point may be difficult to determine. There is a possibility of a **stockout,** or running out of inventory.

This situation results in **stockout costs,** which occur because of lost production, lost sales, or production inefficiencies. Stockouts may be avoided by maintaining an additional amount of inventory on hand, called **safety stock.** Carrying safety stocks adds to the total cost of inventory. A sophisticated inventory analysis may require the use of probabilities and statistical inference.

KEY TERMS

carrying cost *(484)*
economic order quantity
 (EOQ) *(484)*
lead time *(494)*
lead time demand *(495)*
ordering costs *(484)*

reorder point *(494)*
safety stock *(496)*
shortage costs *(484)*
stockout *(495)*
stockout costs *(495)*

QUESTIONS

1. Inventory management procedures that use purchase prices, ordering costs, quantity demanded, and carrying costs can be used to manage assets other than inventories. A pension fund trustee must keep a certain amount of cash on hand to pay pensions, and this money is unproductive because it is not invested. A mail-order house uses postage meters that must be taken to the post office periodically for refilling. Describe the variables you would use to determine the economic quantity of money that should be available to the trustee. What variables would you use to describe the economic quantity of postage to put into the meters at any one time?

2. (AICPA) Define and discuss the economic order quantity (EOQ), including the assumptions and accounting data used therein.

3. (AICPA) Why do manufacturing firms maintain merchandise and materials inventories? Your answer should state the reasons for physical stocks of goods rather than the accounting significance of inventories. What factors should be considered in computing

   a. Optimum investment in inventory. Identify both those costs that do and those that normally do not explicitly appear on formal accounting records.
   b. Economic order quantity.
   c. Minimum stock reorder point.

4. (AICPA) Describe the advantages and disadvantages to a manufacturer obtained from stabilizing production of a durable seasonal product.

EXERCISES

Ex. 13-1
Economic Order
Quantity

Baylee Company estimates that demand for its size B rechargeable batteries is 25,000 per year. The cost of the batteries is $2.40 each and the cost of placing an order is $180. Inventory carrying costs are 15 percent of unit cost.

REQUIRED

a. Compute the economic order quantity.

b. How many orders a year will the company place if it orders the economic order quantity?

Ex. 13-2
EOQ and Changing Demand

Last year Dayle Company sold 183,750 cordless telephones by mail order at $57.50 each. Management estimates that if the selling price does not change, demand for the telephones will increase 20 percent in the current year. Each telephone costs $25. It costs $400 to place an order and inventory carrying cost per phone is $2.50.

REQUIRED

Calculate the economic order quantity and the number of times orders will have to be placed during the year.

Ex. 13-3
Economic Order Quantity

Smithers operates a small truck stop on Highway 37. He usually sells 2 million gallons of diesel fuel per year. The current cost of the fuel is $.96 per gallon. Ordering cost is $288 per order and carrying cost is 12 percent of purchase price.

REQUIRED

Calculate the economic order quantity and the number of orders that should be placed each year.

Ex. 13-4
EOQ and Inventory Cost

Alladin Carpet Company sells 800 Oriental carpets per year. Each carpet costs $2,000 and sells for $3,600. Carrying cost of the inventory is 18 percent of unit cost and the cost of placing each order to acquire more inventory is $900.

REQUIRED

a. Compute the economic order size.

b. Compute the total cost of inventory.

Ex. 13-5
Reorder Point

The demand for Lukkie Company's toy tractor is 60,000 units per year. The company operates its store 300 days per year and keeps a safety stock equal to 3 days' demand. It takes 10 days to receive an order and the economic order quantity is 9,000 units.

REQUIRED

Compute the reorder point for the toy.

Ex. 13-6
Applying EOQ to Financial Investments

Casey manages a trust fund for a widow who needs an income of $40,000 a year from the fund. She has instructed him to invest the money in securities that can be liquidated on short notice. Casey is to withdraw sufficient money from the fund to provide her with her annual needs, and send her money as often as is most economical.

The trust fund earns 10 percent interest per year. Each time Casey withdraws money from the fund a cost of $31.25 is incurred.

REQUIRED

a. Determine how much money Casey should withdraw from the fund each time in order to satisfy the needs of his client.

b. How often will Casey have to send money to his client?

Ex. 13-7
Determining Demand for a Product

Belden Company sells a variety of industrial products. The economic order size for its V-belts is 5,000 units. Placing an order costs $180, carrying inventory costs 15 percent of unit cost, and each item costs $2.40.

REQUIRED

Calculate the demand for V-belts for Belden Company.

Ex. 13-8
Sensitivity of Demand Error

Pet World estimates that demand for its exotic parrot food is 36,000 boxes per year. Each box costs $3.75 and sells for $4.25. Carrying costs for inventory are 10 percent of cost and the cost of placing an order is $200. Realizing that the estimate of demand may vary by as much as 6,000 boxes, the store's manager wants to know the cost of estimating demand incorrectly.

REQUIRED

a. Calculate the EOQ for demand of 36,000 and 30,000.
b. Determine the cost of using demand of 36,000 when actual demand is 30,000 units.

Ex. 13-9
Error in Demand
Estimate

Alladin Carpets sells Oriental carpets. It estimates the demand for its carpets at 900 units. Each carpet costs $1,500 and has a carrying cost of 18 percent of cost. Ordering costs are $800. The store may experience demand fluctuations of as much as 100 carpets above or below estimated demand.

REQUIRED

a. Compute the EOQ for demand of 1,000 and 900 carpets.
b. Determine the cost of estimating demand incorrectly if actual demand is 1,000 units.

Ex. 13-10
EOQ and
Estimation Error

Tuphe University Book Store expects to sell 33,000 volumes of a paperback book entitled *How to Become a CPA Without Studying Accounting*. The cost of the book is $3.75, and the cost of placing an order for books is $200. The bookstore manager believes that the cost of carrying inventory is 10 percent of book cost, but the actual cost is 15 percent of book cost.

REQUIRED

a. Compute the EOQ using both a 10 percent and a 15 percent carrying cost.
b. Determine the cost of estimating carrying cost incorrectly, assuming 15 percent is correct.

Ex. 13-11
Error in Carrying
Cost Estimate

Flying Digits Inc., sells computer terminals. It estimates the demand for its terminals at 1,200 units and inventory carrying costs at 12 percent of cost. Each terminal costs $1,500. Ordering costs are $750 per order. Actual inventory carrying cost is 18 percent of product cost.

REQUIRED

a. Compute the EOQ with carrying costs of 12 percent and 18 percent.
b. Determine the cost of estimating carrying cost incorrectly.

Ex. 13-12
Effect of Estimation
Errors

Francine Company sells executive furniture in a large metropolitan area. The company estimates that demand for its Loafwell model executive chair is 3,000 units per year and carrying cost is 12 percent of unit cost. Each chair costs $1,800. Ordering cost is $600. Actual demand for the chairs is 2,600 units and actual carrying cost is 16 percent of unit cost.

REQUIRED

a. Compute the EOQ with management's estimates and also for actual data.
b. Determine the cost of management's estimation errors.

Ex. 13-13
Effect of Error in
Cost Estimate

Voltair Company sells low-voltage electric motors for use in robots and servomechanisms. The company made the following estimates for next year's operations:

Expected selling price	$163
Expected unit cost	108
Expected annual demand	42,000 units
Inventory carrying cost	15 percent of cost
Cost of placing an order	$260

Actual cost of the motors next year will be $120 per unit.

REQUIRED

a. Compute the economic order quantity for the motors, with management's estimates and also with the correct cost.
b. Calculate the cost of estimating unit cost of the motors incorrectly.

Ex. 13-14
Effect of Two
Errors in Estimate

Voltair Company sells low-voltage electric motors for use in robots and servomechanisms. The company made the following estimates for next year's operations:

Expected selling price	$163
Expected unit cost	108
Expected annual demand	42,000 units
Inventory carrying cost	15 percent of cost
Cost of placing an order	$260

Actual cost of the motors next year will be $120 per unit, and actual demand is 40,000 units.

REQUIRED

a. Compute the economic order quantity for the motors, with the correct cost and demand and also using management's estimates.
b. Determine how many orders the company should place during the year to minimize inventory cost.
c. Determine the effect of estimating unit cost and demand incorrectly.

Ex. 13-15
Optimal Safety
Stock

Bolero Company estimates that demand for its electronic chess sets is 12 units per day. Carrying cost is 18 percent of inventory cost. Management estimates that the probability of a 1-day stockout is 30 percent. Each net costs $200 and sells for $350.

REQUIRED

Compute the optimal safety stock for the chess sets.

Ex. 13-16
Cost of Incorrect
Safety Stock

The demand for Loraine Company's room ionizer is estimated at 200 units per day. The unit selling price is $92 and unit cost is $80. The owner of the company likes to keep a safety stock of 400 units on hand. He says, "I estimate the chance of a one-day stockout is 25 percent and the chance of being out of stock for two days is about 10 percent without a safety stock. With daily sales of $18,400, I cannot afford a stockout." The cost of carrying units in inventory is 15 percent of product cost.

REQUIRED

a. Compute the expected stockout cost and determine the cost of carrying excess safety stock.
b. Compute the optimal safety stock for the ionizer.

PROBLEMS

P. 13-1
Economic Order
Quantity, Inventory
Cost, and Reorder
Point

Lucasso Company sells 30,000 blank cassette recording tapes per year. Each tape costs $2.50. The cost of placing one order for the tapes is $200 and the carrying cost of the inventory is 15 percent of purchase price. Tapes can be ordered only in boxes of 100 each. The company operates 300 days per year, and keeps a safety stock of 150 tapes. Lead time for an order is 5 days.

REQUIRED

a. Compute the economic order quantity for the tapes.
b. Determine the total cost of inventory if the economic order quantity could be ordered.
c. Determine the number of orders per year and the total cost of inventory for the company.
d. Compute the reorder point for the cassette tapes.

P. 13-2
Analysis of
Inventory

Marlo Company consistently uses 1,000 gallons of styrene per month in the manufacture of several of its products. The material costs $9 per gallon, and inventory carrying cost is 14 percent of product cost. Ordering cost is $90 per order and lead time is 15 days. The company operates 273 days per year. It maintains a 3-day supply of safety stock.

REQUIRED

a. Compute the EOQ for styrene.
b. Determine the total inventory cost at the EOQ without the safety stock.
c. Determine the expected lead time demand.
d. Determine the reorder point for styrene.
e. Compute the cost of providing the safety stock.
f. Compute total inventory cost with the safety stock.

P. 13-3
EOQ and Changing
Demand

Pocks Company uses 6,750 gallons of epoxy resin each year for the manufacture of impregnated memory boards. The cost of the resin is $15 per gallon, and carrying cost is 18 percent of product cost. The cost of placing orders is $50.

The company has always ordered the economic order quantity of epoxy, placing 14 orders per year. Management now expects demand for the memory boards to increase 50 percent next year.

REQUIRED

a. Compute the EOQ for the current year.
b. Compute the total cost of inventory at this year's EOQ.
c. Compute the EOQ for next year and determine the effect of the change in demand on the EOQ.
d. Compute the total cost of inventory at next year's EOQ.
e. What would be the total inventory cost if the company continued to place orders at the old EOQ next year?

P. 13-4
EOQ and Cost of
Inventory

Dayle Company's deluxe cordless telephone sells for $79.95 and costs $40 each. Last year the company sold 85,000 units. The supplier recently announced a price increase of $5 per unit, and management of Dayle estimates that as a result of a selling price increase to $89.95, the demand for the telephone this year will decline 10 percent. It costs $400 to place an order and the carrying cost of the deluxe telephones is 12 percent of cost. The supplier has indicated that due to increased processing costs, it will accept orders only in round lots of 1,000 units at the quoted $45 price. An additional charge of $50 per order is made on any fractional orders.

REQUIRED

a. Compute the economic order quantity.
b. Compute the total cost of inventory if the EOQ is ordered.
c. Compute the total cost of inventory if each order is rounded to the nearest round lot of 1,000 units.
d. What order size should the company place?

P. 13-5
EOQ with FIFO
and LIFO Valuation

Bunda Motorcycle Company estimates that demand for its Cheepo Sprint model motorcycle will be 1,200 units during 1985. Inventory carrying costs are estimated at 12 percent of product cost, and inventory ordering costs are $750 per order. Each motorcycle costs $1,500 and sells for $1,950. The company has 90 units on hand at the beginning of the year, costing a total of $130,500. Company policy is to determine the economic order quantity at the beginning of the year and to order this quantity whenever 20 units remain on hand. Following are weekly sales data taken from the company's sales journal for the first quarter of 1985:

Jan. 1– 5	9 units	Feb. 3– 9	15	Mar. 3– 9	19
6–12	13	10–16	19	10–16	21
13–19	18	17–23	12	17–23	20
20–26	18	24– 2	14	24–30	10
29– 2	12				

On March 1, 1985, the company's supplier announced a price increase of $60 per unit. The company uses a perpetual inventory system.

REQUIRED

a. Compute the economic order quantity for the motorcycles.
b. Calculate sales, gross margin, cost of goods sold, and ending inventory assuming that FIFO inventory valuation is used.
c. Calculate sales, gross margin, cost of goods sold, and ending inventory assuming that LIFO inventory valuation is used.

P. 13-6
EOQ for a Not-for-Profit Organization

Dementia County's demand for computer paper is 7,000 cartons per year. The cost of each carton is $70 and carrying cost is $3.50 per carton. A price increase of $10 per carton has recently been announced that will take effect next year. The county budget for next year also includes an increase in carrying costs to $6.40 per carton. In addition, a study of the demand for computer printouts indicates that the county will use 7,200 cartons of paper next year. It costs $10 to place an order for paper and the county usually orders 300 cartons when it has 250 cartons left on hand. Lead time is 5 days. The maximum number of cartons used in any one day is 35. The county operates its computer 250 days per year.

REQUIRED

a. Compute the economic order quantity for the current budget year.
b. Determine the total cost of inventory at the EOQ.
c. Find the reorder point, safety stock, and reorder point with safety stock.
d. Determine the total cost of inventory at the EOQ with safety stock.
e. Determine the county's actual safety stock and its cost of inventory with the county's present ordering policy.
f. Determine the EOQ for the next budget year.
g. Determine the total cost of inventory at the EOQ with safety stock.

P. 13-7
EOQ and Changing Prices

Patrick Gobrach operates a small mail-order business. He has arranged to have credit card companies include advertisements and order forms for his products with their monthly bills to customers. One of his more popular items is an electronic clock/radio/calendar that sells for $89.95. Demand for the product has been 15,000 units per year. The cost per unit is $64, ordering cost is $80 per order, and inventory carrying cost is 15 percent of cost.

The supplier of the product has announced a price decrease to $60 per unit for next year for orders in lots of 500 units. The price per unit on broken lots is $66. However, ordering cost is expected to increase by $10 per order next year due to increases in postage, phone, and other expenses. Patrick estimates that if he reduces his selling price to $85.95, demand should increase by 20 percent. Any smaller decrease in price probably would not affect demand appreciably.

REQUIRED

a. Compute the EOQ for the current year.
b. Compute total inventory cost at the current EOQ.
c. Compute the EOQ for next year.
d. Compute the inventory cost at next year's EOQ.
e. Determine the additional cost of ordering in lots of 500 units or in broken lots.
f. Discuss the strategy that Patrick should adopt for making inventory decisions.

P. 13-8
Inventory Analysis
with Expected
Stockout Cost

During May and June when the local high schools and colleges hold a lot of parties, Fleener's experiences a demand for evening gowns of 1,200 units per month. Its gowns' average price is $120 each and their average cost is $50. Inventory carrying cost is 16 percent of inventory cost. Ordering cost is $100 per order. Lead time for ordering gowns is 4 days and lead time demand is 200 gowns. The store's owner, Mrs. Fleener, estimates that there is a 40 percent chance that an order will be a day late and a 20 percent chance that it may be 2 days late. To avoid a stockout, the owner likes to carry a safety stock.

REQUIRED

a. Determine the EOQ for evening gowns.
b. Determine the total inventory cost at the EOQ.
c. Determine the expected stockout cost.
d. Determine the optimal safety stock of evening gowns.
e. Compute the reorder point with the safety stock.
f. Compute total inventory cost with the safety stock.

CASES

Case 13-1 (CMA)
Estimation of
Inventory Model
Parameters

Evans Inc., is a large wholesale distributor that deals exclusively in baby shoes. Due to the substantial costs related to ordering and storing the shoes, the company has decided to employ the economic order quantity method (EOQ) to help determine the optimum quantities of shoes to order from the different manufacturers. The EOQ formula is

$$EOQ = \sqrt{\frac{2AP}{UI}}$$

where EOQ = optimum number of units per purchase order
        A = annual demand
        U = purchase price per unit
        P = cost of placing an order
        I = the annual cost of storage per dollar of investment in inventory

Before Evans Inc., can employ the EOQ model, they need to develop values for two of the cost parameters—ordering costs (P) and storage costs (I). As a starting point, management has decided to develop the values for the two cost parameters by using cost data from the most recent fiscal year, 1985.

The company placed 4,000 purchase orders during 1985. The largest number of orders placed during any 1 month was 400 orders in June and the smallest number of orders placed was 250 in December. Selected cost data for these 2 months and the year for the purchasing, accounts payable, and warehousing operations appear at the top of the next page.

The purchasing department is responsible for placing all orders. The costs listed for the accounts payable department relate only to the processing of purchase orders for payment. The warehouse costs reflect two operations—receiving and shipping. The receiving clerks inspect all incoming shipments and place the orders in storage. The shipping clerks are responsible for processing all sales orders to retailers.

	Costs for High Activity Month (June: 400 orders)	Costs for Low Activity Month (December: 250 orders)	Annual Costs
Purchasing department			
Purchasing manager	$ 1,750	$ 1,750	$ 21,000
Buyers	2,500	1,900	28,500
Clerks	2,000	1,100	20,600
Supplies	275	150	2,500
Accounts payable dept.			
Clerks	2,000	1,500	21,500
Supplies	125	75	1,100
Data processing	2,600	2,300	30,000
Warehouse			
Supervisor	1,250	1,250	15,000
Receiving clerks	2,300	1,800	23,300
Receiving supplies	50	25	500
Shipping clerks	3,800	3,500	44,000
Shipping supplies	1,350	1,200	15,200
Freight out	1,600	1,300	16,800
Total costs	$21,600	$17,850	$240,000

The company leases space in a public warehouse. The rental fee is priced according to the square feet occupied during a month. The annual charges during 1985 totaled $34,500. Annual insurance and property taxes on the shoes stored in the warehouse amounted to $5,700 and $7,300 respectively. The company pays 8 percent a year for a small amount of short-term seasonal bank debt. Long-term capital investments are expected to produce a rate of return of 12 percent after taxes. The effective tax rate is 40 percent.

The inventory balances tend to fluctuate during the year depending upon the demand for baby shoes. Selected data on inventory balances are shown below.

Inventory, January 1, 1985	$160,000
Inventory, December 31, 1985	120,000
Highest inventory balance (June)	220,000
Lowest inventory balance (December)	120,000
Average monthly inventory	190,000

The boxes in which the baby shoes are stored are all approximately the same size. Consequently, the shoes all occupy about the same amount of storage space in the warehouse.

REQUIRED

a. Using the 1985 data, determine estimated values appropriate for
   1. P—cost of placing an order.
   2. I—the annual cost of storage per dollar of investment in inventory.
b. Should Evans Inc., use the cost parameters developed solely from the historical data in the employment of the EOQ model? Explain your answer.

CHAPTER 14
Cost Data and Pricing Decisions

Most organizations, whether they are profit-oriented firms or not-for-profit entities, must establish prices for their goods and services. Pricing is an important activity that requires an understanding of relevant concepts as well as an ability to apply those concepts in the complex economic environment of business. In this chapter we discuss the economic framework and accounting concepts used in establishing prices for the products and services sold by an organization.

The pricing decision is one of the more interesting that managers must make. **Pricing** refers to the assignment of a selling price to a product or service provided by a firm. Sometimes the term **price** refers to the **purchase price** of some resource acquired by a firm, but this is more precisely a **cost** to the purchasing firm. In this chapter we discuss **selling price,** which is the amount charged customers for some product or service.

Selling price is the amount charged customers for some product or service

Pricing activities are more extensive than many people realize. It is easy to visualize the need to price each product in a store, but all organizations that provide a service for a fee or sell products must decide on the amount to charge for **each** service or product. A construction firm must decide how much to bid on a building contract. A physician must establish a price for examinations, X-rays, and other services. When people decide whether to accept jobs that pay specific salaries, they are pricing their services. The Postal Service, a not-for-profit organization, sets prices on mail services, and local governments establish prices for marriage licenses.

Once a price is established for a product or service, the pricing decision is not over. Prices must be continuously reevaluated to ensure that they reflect management's pricing objectives in light of current costs, market conditions, and competitor actions. Some prices may remain in effect for a year or more; others may change rapidly. Stamp and coin dealers change some prices daily. Automobile manufacturers may change prices several times a year. Pricing decisions are dynamic and a part of a necessary, continuing activity.

In the first part of the chapter, we discuss the nature of pricing decisions and of the entities that set prices. We introduce the economic framework in which pricing decisions take place so that you understand the reasons behind pricing decisions. The basic economic concepts play a role in production and pricing decisions discussed in the second part of the chapter, in which we illustrate specific pricing models commonly used by businesses.

THE ECONOMICS OF PRICING

Pricing decisions may be influenced by internal factors, such as costs and profit objectives, and by external factors, such as competitors' pricing actions or regulatory pricing guidelines. Some factors that may influence pricing decisions include

Factors influencing pricing decisions

Cost data	Public image
Revenue and profit objectives	Government influence
Type of product or service	Competitor actions
Type of industry	Type of market
Management style	Economic trends

How do the above factors interact and result in a pricing decision? The answer depends on the individual making the decision. Each decision maker incorporates pricing variables into the decision process in a different way. One person may weigh economic trends and industry averages heavily and may ignore government pressure for price restraint. Another may use government pricing guidelines as the primary variable in establishing new prices. Whatever the decision style of the individual, many pricing decisions are couched, at least in part, in the general framework of economic pricing theory. The discussion that follows is an overview of pricing, but it is only a brief presentation of the economic theory underlying pricing decisions.

The way prices are established depends on the market in which goods are traded. Economists describe several types of markets, including:

1. Perfectly competitive markets
2. Monopolistic competition
3. Oligopoly
4. Monopoly

Perfectly Competitive Markets

A market is **perfectly competitive** if it satisfies the following characteristics:

1. The goods traded are homogeneous, which means that the product of one seller is identical, in the opinion of the buyers, to the products of other sellers.

2. Market participants, whether buyers or sellers, cannot individually influence the market price of the products by their actions.

Assumptions underlying perfectly competitive markets

3. There is freedom of entry and exit, which means that anyone may enter or leave the market at any time by offering or withholding resources.

4. Market participants have complete and perfect knowledge of prices and resource costs.

Very few products have perfectly competitive markets if all four characteristics are strictly interpreted. However, if the last two conditions are slightly relaxed, a number of products may be classified as trading in perfectly competitive markets. Such a classification is useful for analyzing prices and pricing decisions. The stock market is viewed by some economists as being nearly perfectly competitive. Probably the most notable products selling in almost perfectly competitive markets are farm commodities such as corn, wheat, cotton, cattle, and hogs.

Supply is the amount that suppliers in aggregate are willing to sell at each market price

Demand is the amount that buyers in aggregate are willing to buy at each market price

The prices in perfectly competitive markets are determined by supply and demand. **Supply** is the total amount of product all suppliers are willing to sell at each possible selling price. **Demand** is the total amount all buyers are willing to purchase at each possible price. Figure 14-1 shows the supply and demand schedules for corn. These schedules are the amount of product that sellers are willing to supply and that buyers are willing to buy at specific prices. At a price of $200 a metric ton, suppliers are willing to produce 180,000 metric tons of corn; at $190 a ton, they will produce only 170,000 metric tons. At lower prices even less corn will be produced.

Figure 14-1. Supply and demand schedules for a commodity that trades in a perfectly competitive market. At higher prices demand is small but supply is large. At lower prices demand is large but supply is small because fewer suppliers find it economically feasible to produce the commodity.

Supply and Demand Schedules for Corn

Price per Metric Ton	Quantity Supplied in Thousands of Tons	Quantity Demanded in Thousands of Tons
$200	180	60
190	170	70
180	156	84
170	135	100
160	120	120
150	88	140
140	65	165
130	43	190

The demand for a product is inversely affected by price, which means that as the price increases, demand for the product decreases. For example, the demand schedule in Figure 14-1 shows that at $200 per metric ton, purchasers are willing to buy only 60,000 tons of corn. At $190 per ton, they are willing to buy 70,000 tons. As the price declines, demand increases because buyers are willing to acquire more corn at lower prices.

Supply and demand curves are graphs of supply and demand functions

The supply and demand schedules may be graphed as shown in Figure 14-2. The supply schedule slopes up and to the right, showing a willingness on the part of sellers to supply greater quantities at higher prices. The graph of the supply schedule is called a **supply curve**. The demand schedule may be graphed in the form of a **demand curve,** which slopes down and to the right as shown in Figure 14-2, indicating an increase in demand as the price of a product declines.

Market equilibrium occurs when the quantity supplied and demanded is equal at a particular price

The only point where the buyers and sellers are in total agreement is where the two curves intersect. The point of intersection, called the **market equilibrium,** yields the price P— $160 a metric ton in this example — and the quantity purchased Q—120,000 metric tons of corn.

Figure 14-2. Supply and demand curves plotted from the data in Figure 14-1. Market equilibrium occurs where the curves intersect. At that price, supply is sufficient to satisfy all demand because suppliers and buyers agree on both price and quantity.

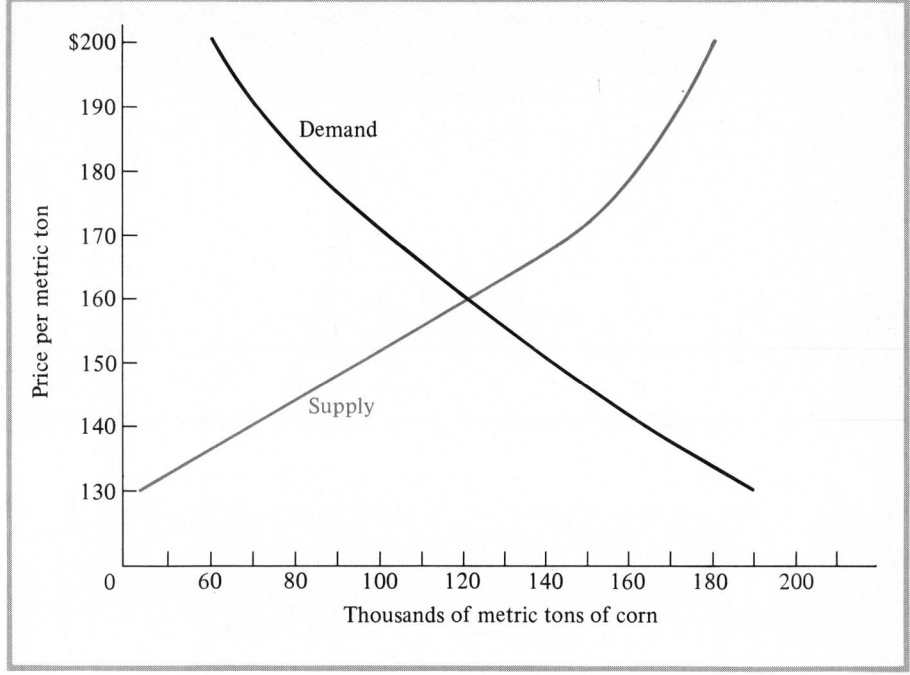

The $160 price and 120,000-ton quantity are determined by all participants in the market. By definition, no single buyer or seller can influence the market. If a seller attempts to charge more than $160 for a ton of corn, the purchaser will buy from someone else. A lower price than $160 makes no sense because individual suppliers can sell their entire supply at the market price in a perfectly competitive market. Therefore, the demand curve for an **individual** supplier in a perfectly competitive market is a horizontal straight line at the selling price. This demand curve is illustrated in Figure 14-5, discussed later. Note the difference between the demand curve for an **individual** seller, and the demand curve in Figure 14-2 for **all** sellers in the market.

In a perfectly competitive market, a supplier cannot influence the price of the product

Since individual suppliers cannot influence the price of a product, their only decision is to decide how much to produce. Using the selling price and production data, each supplier must determine the optimum amount to produce and sell, which is the production level where profit is greatest. To illustrate, Figure 14-3 presents cost data for a supplier with 200 acres available for corn production.

The supplier has certain fixed costs, such as property taxes, and some variable production costs, such as seed and fertilizer. The corn yield can be varied by planting different amounts of the acreage, thereby using more or less fertilizer, labor, and seed and by using varying amounts of labor, fertilizer, and herbicides per acre cultivated. The cost data for various levels of production appear in Figure 14-3. The **marginal cost** is the amount of cost increase caused by a unit increase in output. For example, if production

Marginal cost is the additional cost of producing one more unit

Figure 14-3. An individual producer decides on the best course of action by evaluating the market price and production costs. This production schedule shows that marginal cost declines from zero to 5 metric tons and then increases as production increases.

Schedule of Production Costs for a
Single Producer of Corn

Metric Tons Produced	Total Cost	Marginal Cost
0	$ 100	$ —
1	190	90
2	260	70
3	320	60
4	370	50
5	418	48
6	470	52
7	535	65
8	615	80
9	715	100
10	840	125
11	995	155
12	1,195	200
13	1,455	260
14	1,785	330

Marginal revenue is the additional revenue from selling one more unit

increases from 7 metric tons to 8 metric tons, total cost increases from $535 to $615 per ton, or an increase of $80. The $80 marginal cost applies only to the 8-ton production level. At other production levels the marginal cost is different. The optimum strategy is to produce at the level where marginal cost equals marginal revenue. **Marginal revenue** is the additional revenue obtained by selling one additional unit of product. In a perfectly competitive

Figure 14-4. This schedule shows that profit increases up to 11 metric tons of production, then declines above that level. At this level of production, marginal cost equals marginal revenue and profit is maximized.

Schedule of Revenue, Costs, and Net Income
Single Producer of Corn

Metric Tons Produced	Total Revenue	Total Cost	Net Income
0	$ 0	$ 100	$(100)
1	160	190	(30)
2	320	260	60
3	480	320	160
4	640	370	270
5	800	418	382
6	960	470	490
7	1,120	535	585
8	1,280	615	665
9	1,440	715	725
10	1,600	845	755
11	1,760	995	765
12	1,920	1,195	725
13	2,080	1,455	625
14	2,240	1,785	455

market, marginal revenue is equal to price, so the optimal strategy is to produce at the level where marginal cost equals price. Beyond this point the next metric ton of corn produced will cost more to produce than the revenue it will bring in the market. This strategy is illustrated graphically in Figure 14-5 and is verified by the schedule in Figure 14-4, which shows revenue, cost, and net income.

In Figure 14-5 the marginal cost line crosses the $160 price line at just above 11 metric tons of corn. At this quantity, net income is greatest, as shown in Figure 14-4. Production of less than 11 tons or more than 11 tons yields less net income. Note that this illustration is an example of economic theory that works in aggregate terms. For the individual producer, it is often very difficult to know the marginal revenue and marginal cost. The price of many commodities changes frequently as a result of weather conditions, political atmosphere, changes in supply and demand, and other factors.

Monopolistic Competition, Monopoly, and Oligopoly

Most products are not sold in perfectly competitive markets because they do not satisfy the homogeneity characteristic of perfect competition. Businesses make an effort to differentiate their products from the products of other

Figure 14-5. In a perfectly competitive market, an individual producer's marginal revenue is the selling price, which plots as a horizontal line. To maximize profit, the producer should continue to supply the product until marginal revenue equals marginal cost.

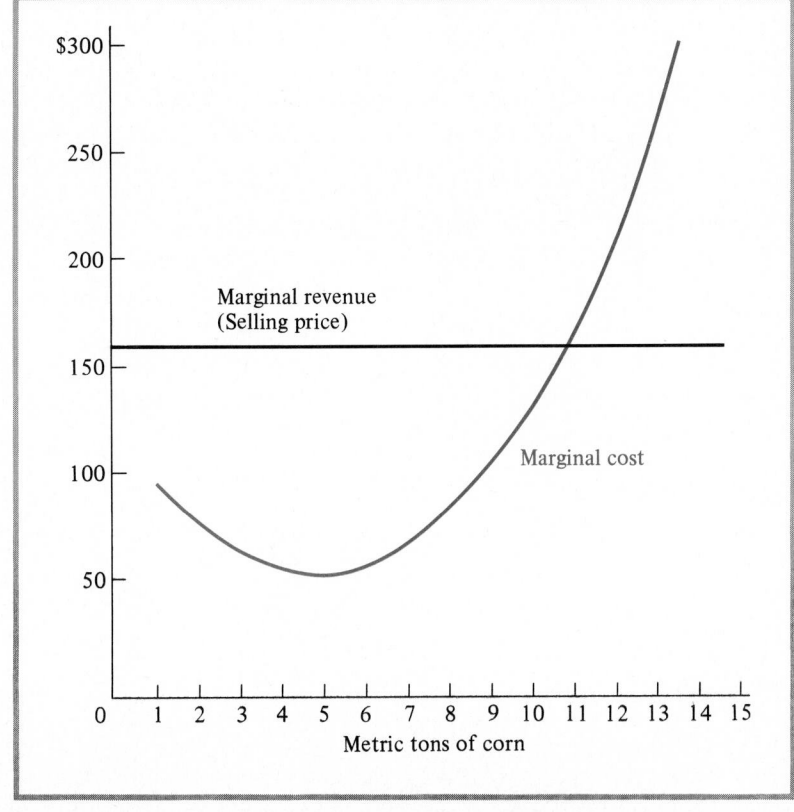

Every producer tries to get some monopolistic characteristics into his competing products

companies. They do so by patenting unique features of their products or by making their product function or perform differently than competing products. In addition, companies advertise their products claiming they are bigger, better, faster, prettier, more practical, easier to use, more colorful, easier to pay for, and so forth. Such differentiation creates a somewhat different type of market and pricing framework, including monopolistic competition, monopoly, and oligopoly.

Monopolistic competition occurs when there are many sellers of similar, but not identical, products in the market. No single seller is able to exercise a perceptible influence over the market price of the similar products. Breakfast cereals, appliances, and furniture are examples of monopolistic competition. **Monopoly** occurs when a firm is the sole supplier of some product. There are no competing products in the market. Electric utilities, telephone companies, and gas utilities are common examples. An **oligopoly** exists when several large sellers dominate a market and compete against one another. The automobile industry and the steel industry are examples of oligopolies.

Monopolistic Competition.   The economic solution to the product pricing decision in other than perfectly competitive markets rests on the same principle of maximizing net income that is achieved when marginal revenue equals marginal cost. The difference between a perfectly competitive market and other types of markets is the shape of the revenue curves. In a perfectly competitive market, a single seller faces a horizontal demand curve. That means the firm can sell as many units of product as it chooses at the market price. The horizontal demand curve is also the marginal revenue curve. Each additional unit of sales adds the same amount to total revenue as the last unit sold. In other types of markets, **each** supplier faces a downward-sloping demand curve similar to the **aggregate** demand curve in a perfectly competitive market.

Individual demand curves in other than perfectly competitive markets slope downward

Figure 14-6.   The demand for a product in monopolistic competition increases as the price declines. To increase unit sales, the supplier must reduce prices. In this example, as total revenue increases, marginal revenue declines.

Schedule of Demand, Total Revenue, and Marginal Revenue

Price	Quantity Demanded	Total Revenue	Marginal Revenue
$1,200	0	$ 0	$ 0
1,100	1	1,100	1,100
1,000	2	2,000	900
900	3	2,700	700
800	4	3,200	500
700	5	3,500	300
600	6	3,600	100
500	7	3,500	(100)
400	8	3,200	(300)
300	9	2,700	(500)
200	10	2,000	(700)
100	11	1,100	(900)

The downward-sloping demand curve occurs because the firm attempts to differentiate its product from competing brands. Differentiation may take place by providing different features for the product, such as a different appearance, more functions, or less complicated controls, and by advertising in order to build brand loyalty and make the product's existence known to a large number of consumers. For example, one automatic dishwasher costs more than another, but it is quieter. A buyer may be willing to pay the higher price in order to obtain less noise, but if the price is much higher, the customer may forgo quiet operation in order to save money. Consequently, there is a range of price variation within which customers will not switch from one product to another. As the price increases, some, but not all, customers may switch to other products, reducing the amount demanded. If the price is decreased, some competitor's customers will be attracted.

The following examples illustrate the general pricing model for monopolistic competition. The quantity and revenue data in Figure 14-6 are used to derive the demand curve facing the individual producer. The quantity demanded by purchasers varies inversely with the product price. Higher prices mean few units are purchased, and low prices result in more units being purchased. The total revenue column in Figure 14-6 is merely the selling price times the number of units demanded at each price. Marginal revenue is the amount added to total revenue by the sale of one additional unit.

The data in Figure 14-6 are graphed in Figure 14-7. Total revenue starts at zero and rises to a peak of $3,600 at six units. Marginal revenue is $1,100 at one unit and declines throughout because selling price must be lowered to generate more demand for the product. The demand curve shows how many units will be sold at a given price.

As with perfectly competitive markets, the supplier sells the product as long as the marginal revenue is greater than the marginal cost. Figure 14-8 shows the production cost data for the firm at each level of activity. The total cost and marginal cost data are graphed in Figure 14-9.

The marginal revenue and marginal cost curves are combined in Figure 14-10, where the vertical scale is changed to accentuate the slope of the curves. At $500 per unit, four units of product will be sold, and at this price and volume, net income is maximized. If the producer raises or lowers the price, net income decreases. Using the cost and revenue data in Figures 14-6 and 14-8, the producer can set the optimal selling price.

Monopoly.   If a business is the only producer of a product for which there is a demand, it controls the price for the product. This does not mean that it can set any price, for at some high price level there will be no demand for its product. If the product satisfies a basic need for which demand is high, a very high price may be commanded. If the product is something that people can easily do without, a high price will drive customers away.

When prices are high relative to production costs, profits are also high, and this attracts other producers into the market, destroying the monopoly. In the case of some products, such as utility services, it is more economical and efficient to have one large producer provide the service than to have many

Figure 14-7. The data in Figure 14-6 are plotted here showing the downward-sloping demand curve, marginal revenue, and the total revenue curve. The revenue curve starts to decline when marginal revenue reaches zero.

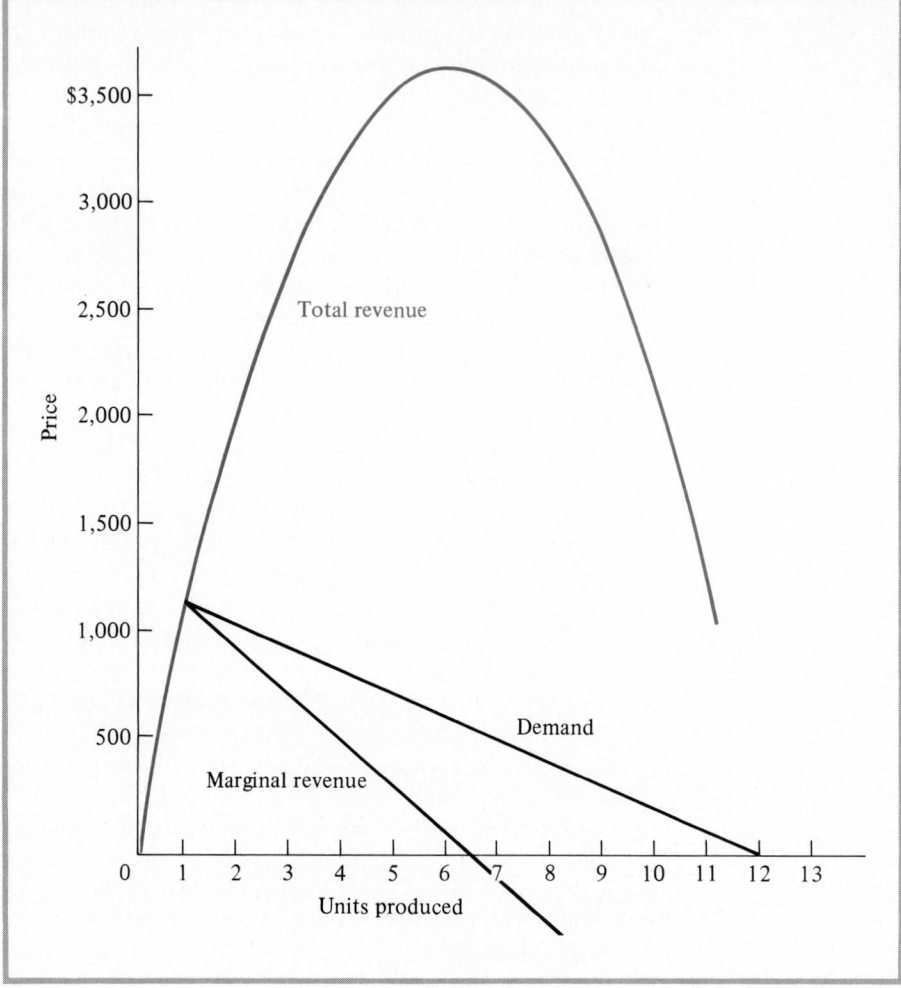

Figure 14-8. Schedule of production costs and marginal cost for a product that sells in monopolistic competition. Marginal cost is the difference in total cost between any two levels of production.

Schedule of Production, Total Cost, and Marginal Cost

Quantity Produced	Total Cost	Marginal Cost
0	$1,000	—
1	1,300	$ 300
2	1,600	300
3	2,000	400
4	2,500	500
5	3,100	600
6	3,800	700
7	4,600	800
8	5,500	900
9	6,500	1,000
10	7,600	1,100
11	8,800	1,200

Figure 14-9. Graph of production costs shown in Figure 14-8. The marginal cost curve is increasing because the total cost curve is increasing at an increasing rate.

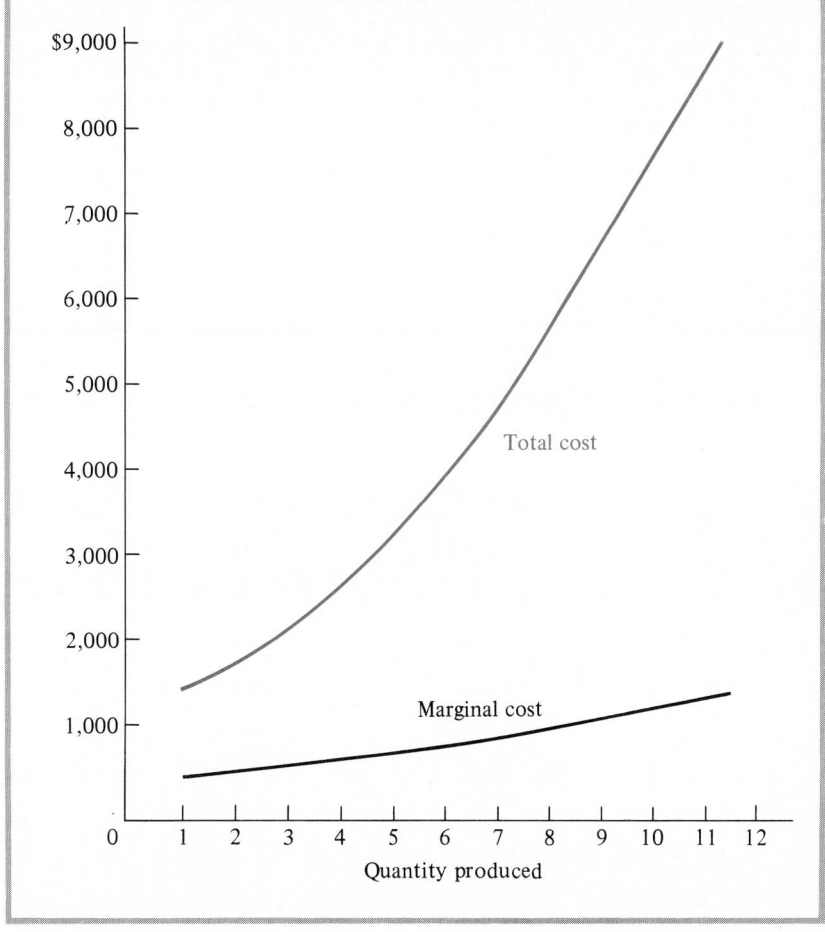

A monopoly must submit to regulation

small, inefficient producers. Consequently, monopoly power may be granted to a single producer in exchange for some guarantee that prices will be reasonable. Reasonable prices are usually ensured by setting a legal ceiling beyond which prices may not be raised or by having a regulatory body establish prices.

Once the price has been set for a monopoly, the firm's pricing decision is the same as under monopolistic competition. The demand curve is downward-sloping because there is some substitution possible among products offered by monopolies. Customers may choose to heat their homes using electric power, natural gas, a wood-burning fireplace, or a combination of all three. If long-distance telephone rates are high, telephone users will forgo calling long-distance and may use the mail instead. A monopoly is usually able to maintain its prices at the highest possible level allowed by law, and in such cases it only needs to decide how much to produce, just as in a perfectly competitive market. But monopoly status usually carries with it the obligation for the business to satisfy demand completely given the established price. In exchange for price control and requirements to satisfy demand, monopolies are guaranteed prices that produce a reasonable profit.

Figure 14-10. Marginal cost plotted in Figure 14-7 and marginal revenue plotted in Figure 14-9 are combined here to show the production level that maximizes profit. The vertical scale is changed to accentuate the slopes of the curves.

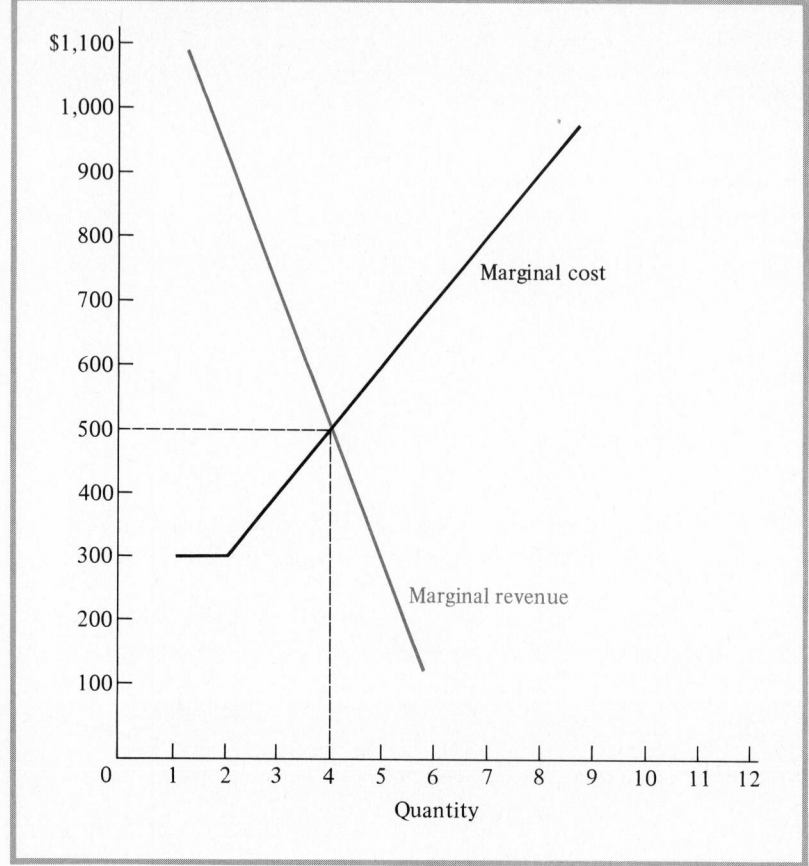

Given the constraints under which they operate, monopolies must monitor and control their costs carefully. As production and operating costs increase and profit margins decline, monopolies request price increases from their regulatory agencies, and must justify such price increases by providing adequate cost data as supporting evidence. In theory, the pricing of products or services provided by monopolies ensures a fair price and efficient operation. In practice, however, much waste may occur if costs are allowed to proliferate, and if rate-setting agencies automatically approve price increases without careful scrutiny of costs and their appropriateness.

Oligopoly. An oligopoly market consists of several large suppliers, any one of which is large enough to affect the market price. As a result, the demand curve of one firm may be directly affected by the pricing actions of other sellers in the market. For example, if one producer of aluminum lowers the price, the demand for other producers' aluminum declines when buyers shift to the lower-priced producer. The result is that the demand curve for an oligopolistic firm may undergo sharp changes when going from one price to

An oligopoly is a group of relatively large firms that together dominate a market

Figure 14-11. A kinked demand curve for a company that competes in an oligopolistic market. A price change by one firm may have a dramatic impact on the demand of competing firms.

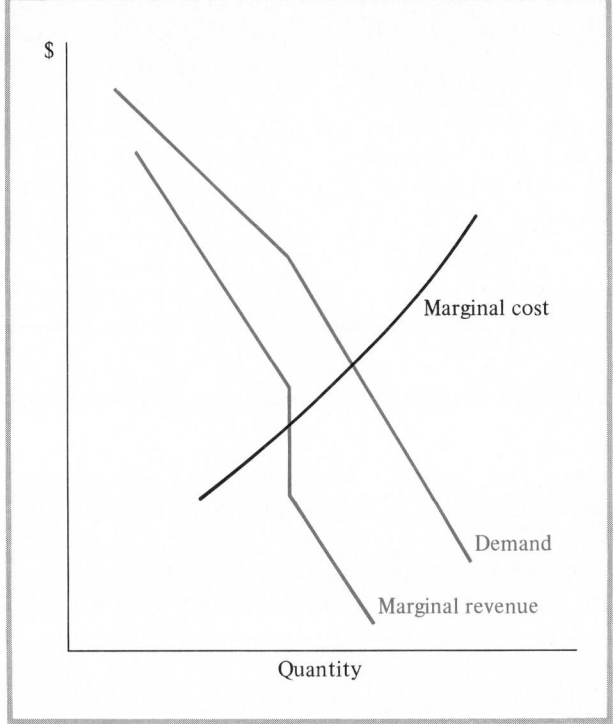

another, resulting in the **kinked demand curve** illustrated in Figure 14-11. There are various solutions to determining price in oligopolistic markets, depending upon the nature of the firms in the market, their relationship to one another, and the attitude of each firm's management about pricing. **Price leaders** in effect establish the price, and the **price followers** merely adopt the price set by the leader. With this approach, a price follower is confronted with a horizontal demand curve, as in perfectly competitive markets. The problem for the price leader is to set prices at the level that will maximize its profits considering that the price followers will be trying to sell all they can at the same price.

Oligopolies have a price leader and price followers

Elasticity of Demand

When individual firms face a downward-sloping demand curve, the shape of the curve often determines the pricing policy to be adopted. A downward-sloping demand curve means that a higher price makes the goods less desirable to customers and a lower price makes them more desirable. At any point on the demand curve for an individual supplier, the quantity and the price together will produce a specific amount of revenue. If the price is increased, the quantity demanded will decrease, but the total revenue with the new price and quantity may be more or less than with the old price and quantity.

Demand elasticity determines the change in revenue from a change in price

If a price increase and a corresponding decrease in quantity produce an increase in total revenue, the demand for the product is said to be **inelastic.** If the price increase results in a decrease in total revenue, demand is said to be **elastic.** Demand elasticity is measured by the ratio of the percentage change in quantity to the percentage change in price. For example, a product sells for $100 and at this price the quantity demanded is 100 units. Total revenue in this case will be $10,000. At a price of $101 per unit, only 99 units will be demanded, and at a price of $99 per unit, 101 units are demanded. In this price and quantity range, demand elasticity is 1, computed as follows:

$$\text{Demand elasticity} = \frac{\text{Percentage change in quantity}}{\text{Percentage change in price}}$$

$$= \frac{1/100}{\$1/\$100} = 1$$

If demand is elastic, revenue is increased by lowering the price

When demand elasticity is 1, a small change in price will produce a change in quantity just large enough to leave total revenue unchanged. When demand elasticity is greater than 1, demand is **elastic** and a **decrease** in price increases total revenue. When demand elasticity is less than 1, demand is **inelastic** and an **increase** in price increases total revenue. For example, a product has the demand curve shown in Figure 14-12. At $10 per unit the quantity demanded is 10 units and total revenue is $100, shown by the shaded area in the figure. If the price is increased to $11.40, only 9 units will be demanded, but total revenue will increase to $102.60. At this point on the demand curve, demand elasticity is less than 1, computed as follows:

$$\text{Demand elasticity} = \frac{1/10}{\$1.4/\$10} = .71$$

Because demand is inelastic, prices can be increased in order to increase total revenue. The area in Figure 14-12 enclosed with the dashed lines is the total revenue with the new price. The revenue lost, shown by the small vertical rectangle on the right, is less than the revenue gained, shown by the small horizontal rectangle at the top. An increase in total revenue does not always mean an increase in profit. Profits may decline if the marginal cost of production is greater than the marginal revenue earned by selling additional units.

For example, demand for a $10 product is 20 units and demand elasticity is greater than 1, which means that a decrease in price should increase total revenue. When price is reduced by $1.20, demand increases by 4 units. Variable cost of production is $5 per unit and fixed cost is $50. In this case, a decrease in price increases revenue but does not increase profit:

	Old Price		New Price	
Revenue	$10 × 20 units	$200	$8.80 × 24 units	$211.20
Variable cost	$5 × 20 units	(100)	$5.00 × 24 units	(120.00)
Fixed cost		(50)		(50.00)
Profit		$ 50		$ 41.20

Figure 14-12. The effect of demand elasticity can be seen by comparing the total revenue at two different prices. When demand is inelastic, an increase in price causes an increase in total revenue. The additional revenue represented by the rectangle added at the top is more than the lost revenue represented by the smaller rectangle on the right.

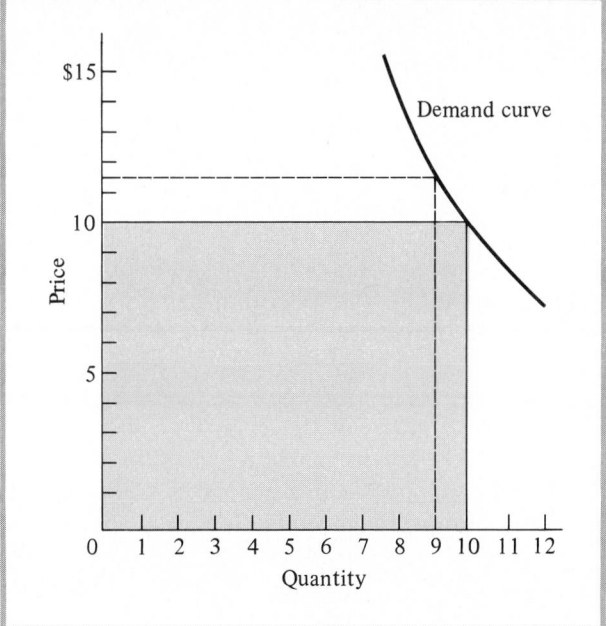

When producers attempt to differentiate their products, they are really trying to make the demand for the product less elastic. Some products, such as tobacco and electric power, have very inelastic demand. Tobacco products trade in competitive markets and an individual producer cannot easily increase the price, because consumers would switch to other brands. But if prices are increased on all tobacco products, demand decreases very slightly. For this reason, taxes placed on products such as tobacco and liquor have no appreciable effect on demand. For this reason also, producers in monopoly markets have controlled prices. An electric utility could establish exorbitant prices for electric power before the demand for power would become elastic.

Demand elasticity is an essential element in pricing decisions. When a new product is developed, the producer may use the strategy of price skimming or one of market penetration, depending on the elasticity of demand.

Price skimming is the strategy of setting very high prices while the product is new and production quantity is small. This strategy takes advantage of those customers who will pay a high price to be the first with a new product. At this stage in the product's life, demand is very inelastic. Products such as ball-point pens and electronic watches have gone through a period of price skimming. When the ball-point pen was invented the unit price was about *Pricing strategies on* $15, and some early electronic watches sold for more than $1,000 each. Price *new products* skimming sometimes is used to recover initial research and development costs before increased competition forces prices lower.

Market penetration is a strategy of setting prices quite low in order to develop a strong customer base before other producers come in with competing products, or because other producers are already well established. Introductory offers on new food products and free samples are attempts at market penetration. Another example is the bargain price for charter membership at a new racquet club. Members joining the club after the charter offer expires pay a higher price.

Some Modifying Variables

The economic models just discussed are useful to managers in making pricing decisions, but the models are only basic frameworks. They are based on theories that apply to aggregate market situations and assume that businesses attempt to maximize profits. Many variables affect the pricing of any particular product. Some key variables that have a modifying effect on economic models are profit satisfaction, government influence, model limitations, and inferior goods.

Profit Satisfaction.   One of the primary assumptions in economic theory is that managers attempt to maximize profits. Without such an assumption, many types of economic analysis are impossible, but in the modern environment of business, profit maximization may not be possible. Even the word *profit* elicits unfavorable comments from some people, and the term *profit maximization* sometimes has the connotation of unwarranted or excessive profits. Economists argue that excessive profits cannot last long because new resources would flow into the market to take advantage of the high profits, thus increasing supply and forcing down prices and profits.

Satisfactory profits may be less than maximum profits

Unfavorable public sentiment toward excessive profits and direct intervention by governmental agencies have led firms from a goal of profit maximization to a more tempered description of profit objectives. The terms **satisfactory profit** and **target profit** describe a level of profits that provides a reasonable return on invested capital, but not an excessive return. Some people maintain that the goal of management historically has been to earn a satisfactory profit in light of the business and social environment within which the firm operates. Target profit levels may reflect the maximum profit the firm strives to achieve, given the constraints of the business environment, and such profit objectives may result in a product price somewhat different from the price suggested by economic models.

Government Influence.   Some firms sell products whose prices are directly or indirectly affected by federal, state, or local governments. During the late 1970s, most energy products, such as gas and oil sold by national firms, had prices established by federal government agencies, or the firms had to seek approval for any product price increase. Electric utilities typically must secure approval for rate increases from some state agency or rate-setting organizations. Sometimes local government agencies also must approve changes in utility rates. In some states hospital price increases must be sanctioned by an agency of the state.

Governments may affect pricing decisions in many different ways

The list of products and services whose prices are affected by one or more agencies of government is lengthy. Often it is the business firm that wants to maintain government price controls. For example, in the early 1980s, the trucking industry vigorously opposed deregulation for fear of competition moving into the industry. When airline industry regulation was substantially reduced in the late 1970s, a large number of small independent airlines established routes at reduced prices, taking considerable business from the previously regulated major airlines, and causing some of the airlines to sustain substantial losses. The key issue here is that businesses are part of a total economic environment in which government plays an important role. The intelligent manager stays abreast of government actions affecting the operation of the business, including those actions affecting pricing decisions.

Modeling Limitations

Models should be good representations of the item or activity modeled

A model is an abstract representation of something in the real world. Models are useful because they allow us to cut away irrelevant details and get at the fundamental issues of the subject being modeled. But modeling has some serious limitations. A model must be a good representation of the item or activity being modeled. The most sophisticated model can be totally useless if care is not taken to ensure a proper fit with the subject. This limitation holds for pricing models as well as for other types of models.

An additional modeling limitation is that of gathering relevant and accurate data for use in the model. Pricing models require cost and revenue data that are projections of the future. Revenue data require estimation of consumer behavior with changing prices. Any projection is difficult and risky, but estimates resting primarily on the actions of others are even more difficult than internal projections. The economic models described earlier in this chapter require a knowledge of supply and demand functions in order to set optimal prices. Because the exact form of these functions is usually not known, managers often set prices that are more or less than optimal. A wide variety of prices may therefore exist for similar goods in markets that are characterized by monopolistic competition, and even in markets that approach perfect competition.

Giffen's paradox

Inferior Goods. Not all supply and demand situations can be described satisfactorily by the general economic models already discussed. Various special cases occur. One is referred to as **inferior goods,** or Giffen's paradox. An inferior good is a product whose quantity demanded varies directly with changes in price for the product. A price increase causes an increase in the quantity demanded, and a price decrease causes a decline in the quantity demanded. No class of products can be generally classified as inferior goods, but some products occasionally seem to possess such demand characteristics.

One plausible explanation for the inferior goods effect is the adage "You get what you pay for." Many consumers equate quality and price; high-priced items are assumed to be high-quality items. Although such a relationship is often true, it is by no means universally true. There are numerous cases of firms that raised the price of a product significantly without changing the product, and they experienced a sharp increase in the number of units sold. One case involved a service firm that was having trouble selling its services. As a desperation measure the firm tripled its service rates, and sales volume increased 400 percent.

PRICING MODELS IN BUSINESS

Armed with the knowledge of general economic relationships described by the economic models, managers must make pricing decisions for specific products. Typically, managers select specific product pricing models that they feel will convert a general economic model into a model usable for pricing individual products. Some of the more common pricing models are discussed below.

Cost-Based Pricing Models

Many pricing models are based on cost relationships. For example, a merchant may set prices by adding 50 percent to the cost paid for the merchandise. A university may estimate its total operating cost for the coming academic year and set tuition rates by dividing estimated student enrollments into the total estimated cost.

Cost is an important variable in making pricing decisions

Prices based on costs are popular because they are easy to use and easy to understand. Prices can be explained easily to management and governmental agencies if necessary. Cost data are readily available from the accounting system, and little if any additional data need be gathered and assimilated to utilize cost-based pricing models. In addition, cost-based models are intuitively logical to many people. It seems reasonable that there should be a direct relationship between the cost of a product or service and the price charged. Although the cost-price relationship does not always exist, economic theory tells us that it should exist over the long run.

Cost-Plus Models

A very simple and widely used cost-based pricing model is referred to as cost-plus. With **cost-plus,** a certain amount or percentage is added to the product cost to determine its selling price. The obvious question is, Which cost should be used? The term *cost* can refer to a variety of possible costs, such as full cost, variable cost, standard cost, and others. Any cost-plus model must clearly identify the cost to be used.

Price may be set at cost plus some amount or percentage

Product cost is a common cost-plus pricing model. For example, Hawkeye Hardware prices all products at cost plus 60 percent. The following products just received are priced below.

Product	Invoice Cost	Markup (60%)	Selling Price
Hammers	$ 5.00	$3.00	$ 8.00
Saws	7.50	4.50	12.00
Drills	16.25	9.75	26.00
Pipe wrenches	6.25	3.75	10.00

The same type of calculations can be used to price a manufactured product, except that the manager cannot merely refer to an invoice for the cost of the product. Instead, the manager must use the firm's accounting records to determine the manufacturing cost of the product. To illustrate, below are the summarized data from a job cost sheet for the production of 150 power mowers. The manufacturer sells these mowers to dealers for product cost plus 40 percent.

Resource	Total Cost	Units Produced	Unit Cost
Direct materials	$18,900	150	$126
Direct labor	10,500	150	70
Applied overhead	12,600	150	84
Total manufacturing cost	$42,000		$280

$$\text{Selling price per unit} = \$280 + .4(\$280) = \$392$$

When product cost is used as the basis for pricing, the addition to cost, or markup, must cover all operating expenses and generate a satisfactory profit. Often, managers must experiment with the values used in the pricing model until a satisfactory level of profit is achieved.

There are many variations of cost-plus models

Total Cost.   A total cost pricing model includes both product costs and operating costs. This is a common approach to pricing government contracts. For example, a contract may establish a price of total cost plus 15 percent. The cost part of the price allows the firm to recover all costs associated with the contract, and the 15 percent is the profit on the contract.

Total cost pricing models are popular for government contracts because the government frequently purchases goods or services for which there is no other ready market. For example, nuclear submarines and anti-aircraft guns cannot be sold to the general public. Frequently, it is impossible to predict accurately the cost of such specialized products. If a price were to be established when the contract is signed, it could be much too high, in order to allow for unknown production problems, or it could be much too low, causing the manufacturer to suffer a loss. The purpose of total cost–based contracts is to provide a fair price and a fair profit that are advantageous to both parties.

A difficulty with total cost pricing is the measurement of total cost. If the producing firm manufactures only a single product for the purchaser, the costing problem is simple, but most firms produce a variety of products for different customers. For example, Boeing Corporation produces aircraft for the federal government and it sells a variety of products to private-sector customers.

We illustrate cost-plus pricing with the example of General Tektonics Corporation, which has a government contract to produce an earthquake-forecasting device. The contract price is total cost plus 12 percent. Total cost is defined as manufacturing cost plus 30 percent of the firm's administrative costs. Production data for the contract and administrative costs for the company are presented at the top of the next page.

Manufacturing costs:

Direct materials	$ 660,000
Direct labor	980,000
Applied overhead	1,460,000
Total administrative costs	2,400,000

The contract price for the device is computed as follows:

Manufacturing cost	$3,100,000
Allocated administrative costs ($2,400,000 × .3)	720,000
Total contract cost	3,820,000
Add .12 contract profit	458,400
Contract price	$4,278,400

Standard cost pricing models isolate efficiencies and inefficiencies of the manufacturing firm

Standard Cost. Actual cost pricing provides a difficult managerial dilemma —the higher the cost, the greater is the profit. In many cases this means that more profit can be earned with inefficient than with efficient operations. For example, if a contract price is set at total cost plus 20 percent, $3 million of total cost yields a profit of $600,000. However, if more inefficient operations yield a total cost of $4 million, the contract profit rises to $800,000. There is a double incentive to assign unnecessary or unwarranted costs to contracts. First, the costs are covered by the contract rather than by other activities of the firm, making the other activities more profitable. Second, these extra costs raise the profit on the cost-plus contract. Even contracts using fixed fees, such as total cost plus $100,000 or product cost plus $250,000, provide little incentive for cost control when cost coverage is a basic part of the contract.

Standard costs provide a framework for eliminating the problem of rewarding inefficiency. Standard cost pricing models place the burden of production efficiency on the manufacturer. The price to the buyer reflects only costs from efficient operations plus the agreed-upon profit. Even standards are not always successful, however, because it is difficult to establish standards for new and complicated products and activities. An example of a standard cost-plus pricing system is presented below. The pricing model is standard manufacturing cost plus 75 percent.

	Unit Cost		
Resource	Standard Cost	Actual Cost	Variance
Direct materials	$13	$12	$(1) F
Direct labor	18	24	6 U
Applied overhead	12	16	4 U
Total	$43	$52	$9 U

Price = $43 + .75($43) = $75.25

If the model were actual manufacturing cost plus 75 percent, the price would be $91 ($52 + .75 × $52). The difference of $15.75 is 21 percent higher than the price based on standard costs. When using standard cost pricing models, variances must be monitored carefully to ensure that prices reflect realistic production costs. If large variances persist, the pricing model may have to be modified.

Contribution Approach Pricing Models. Another approach to cost-plus pricing is **contribution approach pricing,** but this approach is significantly different from full cost pricing. As with other applications of the contribution approach in managerial accounting, we are concerned with identifying all costs that vary with the product or service being priced. Fixed costs are **not** allocated to the product, service, or contract.

The contribution approach to pricing depends on variable costs

The contribution approach is appealing for a variety of reasons. One is the ease of seeing the relationship between prices and costs that vary directly with sales. Cost allocations that may be complicated or that may be based on questionable causal relationships are not necessary with the contribution approach. The contribution pricing method appeals to some customers who are suspicious of allocated fixed costs. Often a customer would rather pay some multiple of variable costs than a much smaller percentage of a cost figure that includes fixed cost allocations. Whatever the reasons, many products are priced using the contribution approach.

A simple example follows. Rydless Machinery Company manufactures a small riding lawn mower as one of its many products. It sets selling prices at variable cost plus 125 percent of variable cost. Variable cost data for the mower are presented below:

Resource	Unit Variable Cost
Direct materials	$ 80
Direct labor	50
Variable MOH	70
Variable selling expense	35
Variable administrative expense	5
Total variable cost	$240

$$\text{Selling price} = \$240 + 1.25(\$240) = \$540$$

The contribution approach to pricing ignores fixed costs in the pricing model. Consequently, there is some danger of overlooking fixed costs altogether. Although fixed costs are not assigned to cost objectives under the contribution approach, they must be taken into account in determining the amount to be added to variable costs to arrive at the price. The amount added must provide enough revenue to cover all of the fixed costs plus a satisfactory profit. Fixed costs are important in the contribution approach to pricing, but they are treated in a different manner than with full cost pricing models.

Target Profits

Target profits are satisfactory profits

Earlier we discussed the concept of **satisfactory profits.** Satisfactory profit levels are **target profits** that managers use as a general guide for establishing prices or as the prime pricing variable, as in utility rate setting. Targets may be established as specific dollar amounts, such as $2,300,000, or in relation to other variables, such as 10 percent of sales or 15 percent return on net assets, as discussed in Chapter 12. Once the target profit is determined, prices are computed by dividing the expected activity level into the target profit.

To illustrate target-profit pricing, assume three attorneys who have just formed a partnership are trying to determine an appropriate hourly fee for their services. They estimate they will incur the following expenses during the coming year:

Secretarial salaries	$30,000
Building and equipment lease	14,000
Utility expenses	7,000
Other expenses	24,000
Total	$75,000

In addition to the above expenses, each of the attorneys wants to earn $35,000 the first year. The three attorneys together expect a total of 3,000 hours of billable time during the year. The rate required to cover all expenses and reach the target profit is calculated as follows:

Total expenses	$ 75,000
Target profit (3 × $35,000)	105,000
Total	$180,000/3,000 hours = $60 per hour

The partners must now examine the $60 per hour price to determine whether it is feasible. If competing firms charge much less, the attorneys may have to lower their profit expectations; on the other hand, they may find $60 to be so low that potential clients stay away, thinking that such low-priced services cannot be very good. The latter situation is an example of Giffen's paradox, discussed earlier in the chapter.

Special Orders

Each special order should be evaluated individually

All business opportunities cannot be evaluated in the same way. The specific characteristics of each opportunity must be examined when evaluating the situation. For example, a one-time **special order** may provide a company with an opportunity to utilize some excess capacity. The selling price of the units in the special order may be different from the normal selling price, but that does not necessarily mean the order should be rejected. Instead, it should be evaluated carefully to see how it impacts on total company profit and other company goals.

To illustrate, we again use Rydless Machinery Company, which produces a variety of parts for the automobile industry. The normal selling price for its automobile generator is $72 each. Recently, an outboard motor manufacturer offered to buy 2,000 generators for $55 per unit.

Rydless currently has excess capacity, and the generators could be produced without incurring any additional fixed costs. This would be a one-time order. The outboard motor manufacturer normally produces its own generators, but new production equipment is being installed in the production facility, causing a temporary interruption in production. The following cost estimates were prepared for the production of the 2,000 units.

Cost Item	Total Cost	Unit Cost
Direct materials	$ 60,000	$30
Direct labor	20,000	10
Manufacturing overhead (60% fixed)	30,000	15
Selling and administrative (80% fixed)	20,000	10
Total	$130,000	$65

Some data are not relevant in evaluating special orders

A quick evaluation of the unit cost data indicates that the company would lose $20,000 (2,000 units × $10 per unit) if the special order is accepted at $55 per unit. But fixed overhead cost and fixed selling and administrative costs are irrelevant to this decision because they will be incurred whether the order is accepted or rejected. A more relevant analysis is to identify those costs that would occur only if the project is accepted:

Cost Item	Unit Cost
Direct materials	$30
Direct labor	10
Variable overhead (40% of $15)	6
Variable selling and administrative (20% of $10)	2
Total	$48

Accepting the order would provide a $7 per unit contribution margin ($55 selling price − $48 variable cost). Therefore, the special order would increase company profit by $14,000 (2,000 units × $7 per unit).

Managers may need to evaluate other factors in making special order pricing decisions. A major concern is the effect on regular customers. If regular customers are paying more for the same products and services, they may demand price reductions or stop buying from the firm. Another problem is that some special order customers may decide to become regular customers, and changes in the price may become necessary. The Robinson-Patman Act, discussed in Chapter 1, serves as another obstacle to special order pricing. This law states that price differentiation between customers is illegal unless the price difference can be justified by cost differences.

Loss Leader Pricing

Loss leaders attract customers who buy normally priced products

An old merchandising joke states "We lose a little on every unit we sell, but we make it up in volume." It does not require any business experience to realize that such a merchandising policy quickly leads to disaster. However, the policy of selling a product at a small loss may be an effective approach in some circumstances. For example, most grocery stores offer weekly specials on certain items that are temporarily priced well below normal prices, perhaps even below cost. Products priced below cost are called **loss leaders,** and their function is to attract customers to the store. Hopefully, customers will purchase enough regularly priced merchandise along with the loss leaders to warrant the low prices on special products. Of course, some people purchase only the specially priced items, but in aggregate, customers usually buy a satisfactory mix of products.

Not all businesses are capable of using loss leader pricing. Ideally, the business should sell a large variety of products that customers purchase on a regular basis. Firms selling expensive products, such as appliances and automobiles, typically are not able to use loss leaders. Most people do not buy one car below dealer cost and several more at the regular price. A form of loss leader pricing is attempted when dealers or manufacturers offer popular options such as power steering, power brakes, or air conditioning well below regular prices. The intent is to attract customers by the low prices on desirable options and induce them to buy the automobile.

SUMMARY

Pricing refers to the assignment of selling price to products or services. Pricing decisions are necessary in all profit-oriented organizations and in many not-for-profit organizations. Many factors affect prices, but pricing decisions are made within the framework of general economic models. The type of pricing model used depends on the type of market in which products are traded.

A **perfectly competitive market** is characterized by homogeneous products, free mobility of resources, and perfect information among participants, none of whom can influence market prices. Prices are determined by supply and demand. **Supply** is the total aggregate quantity of goods or services that suppliers are willing to provide at each possible price. The graph of a supply function is called a **supply curve. Demand** is the total aggregate quantity of goods or services that purchasers are willing to buy at each possible price. The graph of a demand function is called a **demand curve.** The **market equilibrium** point is the price and quantity at which supply equals demand; it is the intersection of the supply and demand curves.

In a perfectly competitive market, individual suppliers face a horizontal demand curve at the market price and can sell as many units of product as they choose at that price. The quantity a supplier will provide is determined by the firm's cost schedule. Each firm maximizes its net income if it sells its products until the marginal cost of supplying the last unit equals the marginal revenue. **Marginal cost** is the amount of cost increase caused by a unit increase in output. **Marginal revenue** is the amount of increase in revenue caused by the sale of one additional unit. In a perfectly competitive market, marginal revenue is the selling price.

Monopolistic competition, monopoly, and oligopoly are three other market types. **Monopolistic competition** occurs where there are many sellers of similar, but not identical, products, and no single seller can influence market prices. **Monopoly** exists when a firm is the sole supplier of a product. **Oligopoly** results when several large sellers dominate a market and compete with one another. The pricing decision in each of these three markets is to maximize profits at the level of sales where marginal cost equals marginal revenue. The individual seller faces a downward-sloping demand curve rather than a horizontal one. Therefore, to increase the volume of sales, a seller must lower the price. Oligopolies may face a **kinked demand curve.** A price decrease by one firm causes a sharp drop in the quantity demanded from other firms. Prices are often set by the **price leader,** and the same price is charged by the remaining firms, which are **price followers.**

At any point on the demand curve, demand for a product may be elastic or inelastic. **Demand elasticity** is measured as the ratio of percentage change in quantity to the percentage change in price along the demand curve. If an increase in price creates more revenue at the new quantity, demand is **inelastic** and demand elasticity is less than 1. If an increase in price creates less revenue, demand is **elastic** and demand elasticity is greater than 1. **Price skimming** is the strategy of setting high prices on a new product when demand for it is inelastic. New products with elastic demand may benefit from a strategy of **market penetration** pricing, which means setting below normal prices to establish a broad customer base.

Most firms do not maximize profits in the strict sense. Instead, firms strive to earn a satisfactory profit that yields a desirable return on capital. Government influence or control affects some pricing decisions. Economic models have limitations because they are abstract representations of the real world. If the model is a poor representation or the data used are inaccurate or inappropriate, the model is of little value. Additionally, the demand for some products does not take the form of a typical demand curve in economics. With **inferior goods,** the quantity demanded decreases as price decreases.

We select specific models for making pricing decisions. **Cost-plus** models use the cost plus an amount or percentage to arrive at the selling price. The cost base may be the product cost, total cost, or standard cost. Total costs are often used in government cost-plus contracts. Standard costs are popular pricing models because the buyer is not charged for seller inefficiencies.

Contribution approach pricing uses only variable costs in establishing prices. Fixed costs do not enter directly into the price, but they must be covered by the price before profits can be realized. **Target profits** can be expressed in dollar amounts or as return on investment, but the target profit measure must be converted to expected sales quantities and mix to establish prices.

In setting prices for **special orders,** managers may choose to sell below full cost as long as variable costs are covered. Caution must be exercised to guard against antagonizing regular customers or violating the law. Some businesses may entice customers into their stores by offering **loss leaders** at very low prices, perhaps even below cost. Customers usually purchase enough regularly priced merchandise to make the loss leaders worthwhile.

KEY TERMS

contribution approach pricing *(525)*	monopolistic competition *(512)*
cost-plus pricing *(522)*	monopoly *(512)*
demand *(508)*	oligopoly *(512)*
demand curve *(508)*	perfectly competitive market *(507)*
demand elasticity *(517)*	price follower *(517)*
elastic demand *(518)*	price leader *(517)*
inelastic demand *(518)*	price skimming *(519)*
inferior goods *(521)*	pricing *(506)*
kinked demand curve *(517)*	purchase price *(506)*
loss leader *(528)*	selling price *(506)*
marginal cost *(509)*	special order *(526)*
marginal revenue *(510)*	supply *(508)*
market equilibrium *(508)*	supply curve *(508)*
market penetration *(519)*	target profit pricing *(520)*

QUESTIONS

1. Datrix Company manufactures electronic games and has recently been faced with stiff competition. The company has changed prices on several of its popular products several times during the past year and has redesigned several products to differentiate them from the competition. The company's managers are trying to plan a strategy to maintain or improve the current profit position. "If we make some revisions in the programming of our games we should be able to sell them at a slightly higher price," said the vice president. "No, I think we can make a lot more money by lowering the price," the sales manager replied. "It will take more than just programming changes to make our products look significantly different from the competition," the production manager commented. What dictates whether an increased or decreased price will produce more profits? What sort of data should the management collect in order to determine in advance what effect a change in price will have on profits? How will product differentiation affect demand?

2. Pifflin Company has just completed development of a new data coupler that promises to make data transmission between computers much more efficient and error-free than existing devices. Production has started on the coupler and the first 5,000 units will be available for distribution within 2 weeks. Management is meeting for the purpose of discussing a pricing policy on the coupler. "Competing couplers sell for $400 each. In order to introduce our product to the market we should price it at less than $350," says Jones. "Production cost will be $240 per unit," replies Smith. "Given the features the coupler has, we should price it above $500." Discuss the two pricing strategies and comment on the merit of each.

EXERCISES

Ex. 14-1
Supply and
Demand Graphic
Analysis

Below are data of the supply and demand functions obtained by Pitchwell Sandals Company for its beach sandals:

| Price | Thousands of Pairs | |
per Pair	Demand	Supply
$30	6	37
25	8	
21		30
20	13	
18	18	
16	20	26
14		24
12	29	21
11	34	
10	40	17
7	5	
6		8

REQUIRED

Graph the supply and demand curve using the available data. Label the equilibrium point and show the market price and quantity demanded.

Ex. 14-2
Interpreting Supply
and Demand
Functions

A polymer extrusion can be manufactured by using either chemical X or chemical Y as one of its components. There is a limited demand for the extrusion and limited other uses for the two chemicals. The demand schedule for the two chemicals is therefore the same, but their supply schedules differ, as shown below:

| Chemicals X and Y | | Chemical X | | Chemical Y | |
Price	Demand	Price	Supply	Price	Supply
$25	20	$24	90	$15	108
20	26	16	70	13	90
15	36	13	60	12	70
10	50	5	30	9	28
5	71	4	20	8	10
2	90				

REQUIRED

a. Diagram the supply and demand functions of the two chemicals.
b. Use your diagram to determine which chemical is easier to manufacture.

Ex. 14-3
Determining
Market
Equilibrium and
Elasticity

The supply and demand functions for soybeans are provided below.

| Price | Millions of Bushels | |
per Bu.	Supply	Demand
$6.60	20	70
7.00	31	60
7.30	40	49
7.90	55	37
8.20	60	30
8.70	70	18

REQUIRED
a.   Compute the market equilibrium.
b.   Find the elasticity of demand at the equilibrium point if the quantity demanded is 100,000 bushels less than the equilibrium quantity.

Ex. 14-4
Optimal Production
Strategy

Digby Company mines a mineral ore whose output sells in a perfectly competitive market at $18 per ton. Production cost data, as collected by management, appear below:

Production in Tons	Total Production Cost	Marginal Cost	Production in Tons	Total Production Cost	Marginal Cost
300	$3,950	—	1,100	$10,600	$1,500
500	4,800	$ 850	1,200	12,400	1,800
700	5,700	900	1,300	14,800	2,400
800	6,700	1,000	1,400	17,800	3,000
900	7,800	1,100	1,500	21,000	3,200
1,000	9,100	1,300			

REQUIRED
a.   Determine the optimum production strategy for the company.
b.   Compute net income at the optimum strategy.
c.   Compute net income at a production level of 1,400 tons.

Ex. 14-5
Elasticity of
Demand

Marthaller Company has determined that its new electronic pocket checkers game has the following demand schedule:

Demand	22	23	24	25	26	27	28	29
Price	$91	$88	$85	$80	$76	$73	$70	$68

REQUIRED
a.   Determine the elasticity of demand at each price.
b.   Decide at what price the product should be sold in order to maximize total revenue.

Ex. 14-6
Cost-Plus Product
Pricing

The Jabber Wok Company prices its woks at full product cost plus 80 percent. It produces two sizes of woks. Following are data on its products.

	Large Wok	Small Wok
Units produced	10,000	12,000
Direct materials	$16,000	$16,200
Direct labor	12,000	12,000
Manufacturing overhead	18,000	18,000
Marketing expense	6,000	7,200
Administrative expense	3,000	3,600

REQUIRED   Use the data above to determine the selling price of each product.

Ex. 14-7
Pricing Legal
Services

Florite Pen Company has a policy of letting employees use the company's legal department when they need personal legal services. The legal services are viewed as a fringe benefit, so the company wants to charge employees only enough to cover the actual cost of the service they require. The following data have been accumulated on time and direct costs of the services used by employees during the last 6 months:

Services provided	550 hours
Salary rate	$22 per hour
Materials and supplies	$1,320
Secretarial costs	$1,980

The company estimates that indirect costs are 25 percent of direct costs.

REQUIRED

a. What should the company charge if recovery of direct costs is the objective?
b. What should the company charge if it wants to recover the full cost of the services?

Ex. 14-8
Target Profit
Product Pricing

Jimmy took a woodworking course as a senior in high school and decided to spend the summer after graduation making wooden hobbyhorses in order to earn money for college expenses. He expected to be able to make 50 horses per month and to earn at least $600 per month. By the end of the first month of summer he had built 40 horses and decided that it was not possible to do more in 1 month. But all 40 horses sold easily at $30 each, and Jimmy had a waiting list of customers. However, he felt that for a month's work he had not earned very much money, so he went through his receipts of materials, accumulated some data, and made some time estimates to come up with the following figures:

Cost of lumber	$ 615
Paint	480
Glue, screws, and miscellaneous	240
Cost of tools and equipment	1,800
Expected useful life of tools and equipment	5 years

Jimmy estimates that of the materials purchased he had used 2/3 for the horses sold and still had 1/3 left for future production.

REQUIRED   Determine the selling price that Jimmy should charge in order to achieve his target profit.

Ex. 14-9
Special Order
Pricing

Cuttwell Manufacturing Company manufactures gasoline motors for chain saws. Its 4.5-cu-in engine sells for $230 and has variable production costs of $175 per unit, a distributor's commission of $14 per unit, and variable distribution costs of $15 per unit. Fixed manufacturing costs associated with this engine are $120,000. Sales are normally 9,500 units a year.

The company has been approached by a new manufacturer of powered hang gliders who offers to pay $190 per unit for a special order of 1,500 engines to be used on hang gliders. The order would require adding some overtime for direct labor, because the labor force is fully employed on regular orders. The company estimates that 1,000 hours of overtime would be used at a cost of $4 per hour in excess of the normal labor rate. The commission and distribution costs would not be incurred on this order.

REQUIRED

a. Decide if the order should be accepted and support your decision with calculations.
b. If the regional distribution representative for the engine insists that his commission must be paid, should the order be accepted?

Ex. 14-10
Cost-Plus Pricing
Strategies

Bukalin Company produces office safes which are sold to dealers. The company uses a standard cost system and has collected the following data on its model TS1824 safe:

	Actual Cost	Standard Cost
Direct materials	$95	$92
Direct labor	39	34
Variable MOH	26	23
Allocated fixed MOH	30	35
Units produced	2,000	

The manager wants to explore several product pricing strategies.

Use the above data to compute the price of the products if the pricing strategy is to charge

REQUIRED

a. Variable product cost plus 90 percent.
b. Standard variable cost plus 90 percent.
c. Prime cost plus 115 percent.

Ex. 14-11
Pricing Analysis

Betty has just finished her sophomore year of college and has received an offer for a summer job at $760 per month with a department store. An alternative is to offer diving lessons to children in the nearby tennis club swimming pool. The pool would be available to Betty 2 hours a day 20 days per month for a fee of $200 per month. Betty plans to give 1-hour lessons to groups of eight children per lesson. Betty would prefer working outdoors but she needs all the money she can earn for her next year in college.

REQUIRED

a. Determine the price Betty would have to charge each student per lesson in order to earn as much as she would working for the department store.
b. Determine how large a group of students Betty would have to have if she is informed that the maximum charge for 1-hour lessons is $2 per student.

Ex. 14-12
Special Order
Pricing

Gorman Manufacturing Company's electric motor division manufactures compressor motors for the compressor division. The motors are transferred to the compressor division at $155 per unit, which includes direct cost of $90 per unit, indirect manufacturing cost of $35, and a markup to cover administrative costs of $320,000, of which 10 percent is variable. Normal production is 8,000 units per year.

The company has been approached by a manufacturer of electric-powered lawn mowers who offers to pay $143 per unit for a special order of 1,000 motors. The order would require a one-time investment of $8,000 for leasing extra space and equipment to complete the order.

REQUIRED

a. Decide if the order should be accepted and support your decision with calculations.
b. If the special order also requires $7.50 per unit for shipping the motors, should the order be accepted?

PROBLEMS

A Canadian farmer produces rapeseed on a large farm. The market price for rapeseed is $340 per metric ton. Following is the farmer's production cost schedule:

P. 14-1
Graphic Analysis in
Perfect
Competition

Metric Tons Produced	Total Cost	Marginal Cost/Ton	Metric Tons Produced	Total Cost	Marginal Cost/Ton
0	$ 400,000	—	7,000	$1,640,000	$140
1,000	700,000	$300	8,400	1,920,000	200
2,000	940,000	240	9,400	2,180,000	260
3,000	1,120,000	180	10,000	2,384,000	260
4,000	1,260,000	140	10,600	2,648,000	440
6,000	1,500,000	120	11,000	2,888,000	600

REQUIRED

a. How much rapeseed should the farmer produce?
b. What is the farmer's net income at the optimum level of production?
c. Graph the marginal cost and marginal revenue to verify your solution.

P. 14-2
Graphing Supply
and Demand

Below are price, supply, and demand data for two ores, both of which are used to refine a rare earth element. Buyers can use either ore to refine the desired element, but the concentration of the element in one type of ore is different from that in the other.

Price	Supply for Ore A	Supply for Ore B	Demand for Ores A and B
$ 5			940
7	100		780
8	220		730
10	400	120	620
15	700	400	400
20	920	560	260
25	1,100	700	160
30		800	100

REQUIRED

a. Develop a graph of the supply and demand curves for the two ores.
b. Use your diagram to determine market equilibrium for the two ores and discuss which ore is more concentrated and which one is easier for suppliers to provide.

P. 14-3
Equilibrium Supply
and Demand

A chemical used in small quantities in the production of certain medicines has the following supply and demand function:

Price	Demand	Price	Supply
$26	18 kg	$24	120 kg
22	30	19	100
18	42	14	76
14	60	10	51
10	80	7	30
5	110	6	10

REQUIRED

a. Compute the equilibrium point for the chemical.
b. Verify your equilibrium point with a graphic solution.

P. 14-4
Optimal Decision in Monopolistic Competition

Flotewell Craft, Inc., builds hovercraft in a market characterized by monopolistic competition. The company has collected the following price, demand, and production cost data for medium-sized hovercraft:

Price	Demand	Total Cost	Price	Demand	Total Cost
$25,000	0	$18,000	$7,000	7	$ 52,250
20,000	1	20,000	6,000	8	60,750
15,000	2	23,000	5,111	9	71,750
12,667	3	27,000	4,200	10	84,750
10,750	4	32,000	3,273	11	100,750
9,200	5	38,000	2,250	12	121,750
8,000	6	45,000			

REQUIRED

a. Compute total revenue, marginal revenue, marginal cost, and net income at all levels of production.
b. Determine the optimal strategy for the company.
c. Determine demand elasticity at optimum production and discuss the producer's strategy based on your findings.
d. Graph the total revenue, marginal revenue, demand, and marginal cost to verify your conclusions.

P. 14-5
Cost-Plus Product Pricing

The Slikke Paint Company prices its products at full product cost plus 75 percent. Following are data on three of the company's products.

	Exterior Paint	Interior Paint	Undercoat
Gallons produced	100,000	70,000	90,000
Direct materials	$200,000	$119,000	$135,000
Direct labor	100,000	63,000	81,000
Manufacturing overhead	100,000	75,600	97,200
Marketing expense	160,400	75,400	109,800
Administrative expense	85,000	46,000	59,000

REQUIRED

Use the data above to determine the selling price of each product and compute the net income from selling all of the three products produced.

P. 14-6
Analysis of Selling Price for a New Product

Innovation, Inc., has recently developed a new camera that produces instant holographic pictures. The camera is expected to have a limited appeal in the consumer hobby market. The product pricing committee is meeting to determine the potential of the new camera and to determine its selling price.

The sales manager wants the camera priced at $60 each to be appealing to as wide a market as possible. Market penetration is expected to be slow at first but should increase as users start appreciating the camera's features. The sales manager believes that sales should be 1,000 units in the first year, 2,000 in the second year, and 2,400 per year in subsequent years.

The production manager says that variable cost of the camera is $50 each and the company cannot afford to sell its products for a 17 percent contribution margin. He thinks the price of the camera should be at least $90 each, but admits that at this price sales would probably be 10 percent less than estimated by the sales manager.

The sales manager points out that the camera is not a primary revenue item. For each camera sold, the company can expect to sell 20 rolls of film per year. The film sells for $10 per roll and has a variable cost of $3. Fixed cost is $300,000 per year.

REQUIRED   Prepare a schedule of expected sales and income for the first 3 years under each of the pricing options and decide which price should be charged for the camera.

P. 14-7
Setting Prices for a
Financial
Institution

The Snobelt Savings and Loan Company has several sources of money. Passbook savings accounts cost 6 percent interest per year. Savings certificates cost 9 percent per year. Money market certificates cost 12 percent per year. In addition, the company sometimes buys money from a federal lending organization at 15 percent per year when demand for loans is greater than can be met from deposits by the public. The S & L must maintain reserves that earn 8.4 percent interest per year. It makes home loans for its primary source of income. All of its outstanding loans are long-term and earn an average interest rate of 12 percent per year. Following are data on the company's deposits and loans at the end of June.

Liabilities:

Passbook accounts	$ 3,500,000
Savings certificates	5,200,000
Money market certificates	4,600,000
Federal loans	1,700,000
Assets	
Reserves	2,450,000
Home loans	12,150,000

The board of directors meets monthly to determine the home loan interest rate that should be charged during the next month. During July, the company expects to obtain $2,000,000 of new deposits, which will earn interest at the average rate paid in June. Principal payments on home loans in the amount of $1,800,000 will be collected. The principal collected consists of old loans whose average interest rate is 6 percent per year. The company expects loan demand of $4,000,000 and will obtain $200,000 of federal loans to have the needed funds available for home loans. Target profit for July is set at $34,400. There is no need to change the amount of reserves.

REQUIRED
a. Compute the company's average interest cost for June.
b. Compute the company's average interest income for June.
c. Compute the interest rate the company must charge in July for home loans in order to earn the target income.

P. 14-8 (CMA)
Economic Pricing
Analysis

The wholesale meat industry in the western region of the United States is characterized by a very large number of firms, with no one firm dominating the market. The Perry Wholesale Meat Company is interested in expanding its production of ground beef because of available capacity and the rapid growth of franchise hamburger outlets in its market area. The regional trade association has estimated the ground beef demand function for the region to be $P = \$2.00 - \$.02Q$ (where P = price per pound and Q = number of truckload lots of 30,000 pounds each).

The Perry management has found that it can sell all of the ground beef that it can produce at $.99 per pound. The controller's office has estimated the total costs, including a normal return on investment, for various levels of production as shown at the top of the next page.

Company's Ground Beef Production (in pounds)	Company's Total Estimated Production Costs Including a Normal Return on Investment (in dollars)
120,000	$120,000
150,000	149,000
180,000	178,200
210,000	207,900
240,000	238,000

Each production level requires a slightly larger investment than the next smaller production level.

REQUIRED

a. What selling price should the Perry Wholesale Meat Company charge for the ground beef? Explain your answer.

b. What level of production will maximize total return on investment for the Perry Wholesale Meat Company? Explain your answer.

c. What pricing and output strategy would the Perry Wholesale Meat Company use if it were the exclusive distributor of ground beef in the western region of the United States? Explain your answer.

P. 14-9 (CMA)
Analysis of Pricing
Alternatives

Stac Industries is a multiproduct company with several manufacturing plants. The Clinton Plant manufactures and distributes two household cleaning and polishing compounds—regular and heavy-duty—under the Cleen-Brite label. The forecasted operating results for the first 6 months of 1986, when 100,000 cases of each compound are expected to be manufactured and sold, are presented in the following statement.

Cleen-Brite Compounds—Clinton Plant
Forecasted Results of Operations
For the 6-Month Period Ending June 30, 1986
(000 omitted)

	Regular	Heavy-Duty	Total
Sales	$2,000	$3,000	$5,000
Cost of sales	1,600	1,900	3,500
Gross profit	400	1,100	1,500
Selling and administrative expenses:			
Variable	400	700	1,100
Fixed[a]	240	360	600
Total selling and administrative expenses	640	1,060	1,700
Income (loss) before taxes	$ (240)	$ 40	$ (200)

[a] The fixed selling and administrative expenses are allocated between the two products on the basis of dollar sales volume on the internal reports.

The regular compound sold for $20 a case and the heavy-duty sold for $30 a case during the first 6 months of 1986. The manufacturing costs by case of product are presented in the following schedule. Each product is manufactured on a separate production line. Annual normal manufacturing capacity is 200,000 cases of each product. However, the plant is capable of producing 250,000 cases of regular compound and 350,000 cases of heavy-duty compound annually.

	Cost per Case	
	Regular	Heavy-Duty
Raw materials	$ 7.00	$ 8.00
Direct labor	4.00	4.00
Variable manufacturing overhead	1.00	2.00
Fixed manufacturing overhead[a]	4.00	5.00
Total manufacturing cost	$16.00	$19.00
Variable selling and administrative costs	$ 4.00	$ 7.00

[a] Depreciation charges are 50 percent of the fixed manufacturing overhead of each line.

The schedule below reflects the consensus of top management regarding the price/volume alternatives for the Cleen-Brite products for the last 6 months of 1986. These are essentially the same alternatives management had during the first 6 months of 1986.

Regular Compound		Heavy-Duty Compound	
Alternative Prices (per case)	Sales Volume (in cases)	Alternative Prices (per case)	Sales Volume (in cases)
$18	120,000	$25	175,000
20	100,000	27	140,000
21	90,000	30	100,000
22	80,000	32	55,000
23	50,000	35	35,000

Top management believes the loss for the first 6 months reflects a tight profit margin caused by intense competition. Management also believes that many companies will be forced out of this market by next year and profits should improve.

REQUIRED

a. What unit selling price should Stac Industries select for each of the Cleen-Brite compounds (regular and heavy-duty) for the remaining 6 months of 1986? Support your selection with appropriate calculations.

b. Without prejudice to your answer to requirement a, assume the optimum price/volume alternatives for the last 6 months were a selling price of $23 and volume level of 50,000 cases for the regular compound and a selling price of $35 and volume of 35,000 cases for the heavy-duty compound.

  1. Should Stac Industries consider closing down its operations until 1987 in order to minimize its losses? Support your answer with appropriate calculations.

  2. Identify and discuss the qualitative factors that should be considered in deciding whether the Clinton Plant should be closed down during the last 6 months of 1986.

P. 14-10 (AICPA)
Pricing
Government
Contracts

Graystone Electronics Corporation's sole activity in 1985 was a federal government fixed-price incentive contract awarded in January 1985. The corporation's prior government contracts were cost-plus-fixed-fee or firm fixed-price contracts that were completed by December 1984.

Provisions of the fixed-price incentive contract include the following:

1. Graystone is to construct eight identical digital computers, deliveries to be made between July 1985 and June 1986.
2. The total contract target price is $780,000, which includes a target cost of $700,000. The total adjusted price cannot exceed a ceiling of $810,000.
3. The incentive clause states:

"The total adjusted price (final contract price) shall be established by adding to the total adjusted cost (final negotiated cost) an allowance for profit determined as follows:

When the Total Adjusted Cost Is:	The Allowance for Profit Is:
Equal to the total target cost	Total target profit.
Greater than the total target cost	Total target profit less 20% of the amount by which the total adjusted cost exceeds the total target cost.
Less than the total target cost	Total target profit plus 20% of the amount by which the total adjusted cost is less than the total target cost."

The following information is available at December 31, 1985:

1. Costs accumulated on the contract:

Direct materials	$170,000
Direct labor	192,000
Overhead	240,000
Total	$602,000

2. The estimated costs to complete the contract:

Direct materials	$ 30,000
Direct labor	48,000
Overhead	60,000
Total	$138,000

3. Past experience indicates that 1 percent of the gross amount of accumulated overhead charges will be disallowed by government auditors as contract costs. No provision has been made for this disallowance.
4. In addition to the estimated 1 percent disallowance in part 3, the following 1985 costs will probably be disallowed:

   a. Depreciation on excess equipment, $1,000. The equipment was sold in January 1986.

   b. Special nonrecurring recruiting costs, $4,000.

5. The corporation failed to take cash discounts totaling $2,000 in 1985. Lost discounts are credited to costs when found by government auditors. The corporation treats cash discounts, when taken, as a reduction of costs.

6. All costs that will probably be disallowed have been treated consistently as period costs by the corporation. Estimated allowable costs have been consistently allocated equally to identical units being manufactured under a contract.

7. Five computers were delivered in 1985 and billed at the target price. Progress payments of $75,000 were received for each computer delivered.

REQUIRED

   a. Prepare a schedule computing the estimated total adjusted price (estimated final contract price) for the fixed-price incentive contract.

   b. Prepare a schedule computing the work in process inventory at estimated cost at December 31, 1985.

   c. Assume that the estimated total adjusted price determined in part *a* was $800,000. Prepare a schedule computing the estimated total amount receivable from the federal government at December 31, 1985 for the computers that were delivered.

CASES

Case 14-1
Developing
Standards for Price
Setting

Chemigreen Company performs lawn-spraying services using two types of materials. Hygreen is a chemical fertilizer and Banweed is a combination of fertilizer and weed killer. The company has been using the chemicals for 3 months and has collected the following data on its operations for the quarter:

	Hygreen	Banweed
Number of lawns sprayed	450	340
Total square feet of lawn	4,130,000	3,850,000
Total hours of labor time	1,276	1,110
Total labor cost	$8,932	$7,437
Total gallons of materials used	12,390	15,400
Total material cost	$22,302	$30,030
Miles driven	4,500	3,400
Administrative expense	$21,800	$21,953

Each spraying job requires some setup time regardless of lawn size. The average setup time per job is estimated at .5 hour for travel, .25 hour for setting up the equipment at the beginning of a job, and .25 hour at the end of each job for cleaning up and putting away equipment. The company estimates that its trucks cost $.60 per mile to operate, including depreciation.

The company believes it has accumulated enough data to establish a standard cost system so that it can use standard costs for bidding on jobs. The data are representative of normal operations for one quarter. The company wants to bid on jobs on the basis of square feet of lawn plus a standard fixed amount for truck and setup expenses. It wants to establish a price per 1,000 square feet of lawn to include standard cost of direct material and labor plus a percentage to cover administrative expenses, and a profit. Management has established a target net income of $60,000 per year and wants to set prices at standard direct cost plus a percentage to achieve the target income.

Most of the company's work involves small residential lawns, but it has been asked to bid on two relatively large jobs. The first is a 21,000-square-foot lawn to be sprayed with Banweed. The second job is a special order for the Mason Country Club, which has offered to have the company spray Hygreen on 900,000 square feet of golf course for $10,000. The company estimates that if it accepts the job it will have to pay some overtime and will incur some additional administrative expenses. These additional costs are expected to total $2,000. The job will require 3 days to complete. The country club has indicated that if it is satisfied with the results, it plans to use the company's services on a regular basis at a price to be negotiated.

REQUIRED

a. Use the available data to establish standard costs and quantities for labor and materials.
b. Determine the direct fixed cost of truck and setup costs.
c. Determine what percentage markup should be added to direct costs in order to achieve the desired target profit.
d. Develop a formula for the price to be used in bidding on spraying jobs.
e. What should be the bid on the 21,000-square-foot job?
f. Decide whether the company should accept the country club offer. Support your decision with figures.

PART FIVE
Long-Range Planning

Managing a successful business requires careful planning of all phases of operations. The short-term planning process for organizations are the budgeting and standard cost systems discussed and illustrated in Chapters 7–9. But in addition to plans that cover day-to-day business operations, it is also necessary to develop effective long-term goals. The decisions managers make today have the potential of affecting a business for many years. To a large degree, effective long-range planning is essential to ensure future business success.

This part of the book is devoted to the long-range planning of organizations. Chapters 15 and 16 deal with the process of identifying, evaluating, and financing investments in fixed assets and long-range projects of the organization. Chapter 15 introduces the topic of capital budgeting and the procedures used to evaluate investment projects. Chapter 16 extends the discussion to include special investment issues such as strategies for the optimal use of limited resources and the impact of taxes on investment decisions. Chapter 17 focuses specifically on the planning and budgeting that take place in not-for-profit organizations and discusses the way government actions influence business decisions.

CHAPTER 15
Capital Budgeting

The productive resources of a business organization usually include a large amount of fixed assets that provide benefits to the organization for many years. Planning the acquisition and replacement of these assets and other major resources is a management function called capital budgeting. **Capital budgeting** is the process of identifying, evaluating, planning, and financing major investment projects of an organization.

Examples of capital budgeting projects include construction of new plants, remodeling of old facilities, acquisition of equipment, introduction of a new product, or purchase of a subsidiary company. Capital budgeting decisions have a long-range impact; such decisions made now determine to a large degree the future success of an organization. Several characteristics differentiate capital budgeting from most other parts of a master budget: Capital projects usually are long-term commitments; they involve relatively large amounts of funds; and they affect long-term policy of a business.

In this chapter we discuss the principles of capital budgeting and describe several methods of evaluating capital budgeting projects. We start with a description of the projects' characteristics, and a discussion of the capital budgeting process. Additional capital budgeting concepts are discussed in Chapter 16.

CHARACTERISTICS OF CAPITAL PROJECTS

Capital projects typically are expected to have useful lives of 2 years or more; many investments, such as buildings, last longer and provide benefits for 20 or more years. Once an investment in a project is made, it may be difficult for a company to extricate itself from the project without incurring substantial losses. Moreover, the longer the life of the project, the more difficult it is to predict its future revenues, expenses, and cost savings. Planning capital projects usually requires many estimates.

Capital projects are large, long-term commitments

It is not unusual for capital investment projects to cost many times the annual income of the business. It may take a long time for a project to start producing a return on the resources invested in it. For example, it takes 5 to 10 years to construct a power plant for an electric utility and it does not earn revenue until it is in operation.

Capital budgeting decisions are long-term policy decisions. Therefore they should satisfy organizational policies about company growth, market share, social responsibility, and others. A capital project may move the company in a different direction from its present course. For example, the decision to acquire a subsidiary may cause the company to shift its emphasis to a new industry, one with which present management may not be entirely familiar. A decision made today to build a new headquarters building in a new location may not affect employees and their families until 2 years later when they have to consider moving to the new location with the company. Meanwhile the company must evaluate the possibility of financing the purchase of new homes, selling employees' old homes, paying for moving costs, and losing employees who chose not to move.

THE CAPITAL BUDGETING PROCESS

Businesses typically have more investment opportunities than they have funds to invest. With many investment alternatives of varying degrees of potential, businesses need systematic methods for identifying and evaluating capital projects. The methods may vary among firms, but they generally include the following activities:

Activities in the capital budgeting process

1. Identify potential capital projects.
2. Estimate project costs and benefits.
3. Evaluate the proposed projects.
4. Develop the capital expenditure budget.
5. Reevaluate projects that are accepted.

Project Identification

Investment proposals may originate at many levels and in any segment of an organization. Some proposals, such as acquisition of a subsidiary or construction of a new plant, usually originate at the highest managerial levels. Others, such as replacement of existing equipment or purchase of new equipment, may occur in segments that need the equipment. New technological developments may prompt a manager to request a new item such as a precision drill press because it may provide the company with a competitive advantage or make operations more efficient.

Estimating the Costs and Benefits of a Project

Estimating benefits and costs requires long-range predictions

A major determinant of project acceptance is the benefit derived from the proposed project and the cost associated with it. Both benefits and costs require estimates of future events. Often, such estimates are difficult to make, particularly for projects with long lives. Over the past few years prices and technology have changed rapidly, which doesn't provide a very helpful base of past history to use in predicting future events. Construction costs have nearly doubled in the past 5 years. Many plant projects will provide benefits for 20 or 30 years, yet estimates of benefits must be made at the time the project is evaluated.

The benefits of capital projects may be in the form of either income or cost savings. Some projects provide a return on investment in the form of income and cash flow. Others provide cost savings through the efficiency they effect. Other benefits are intangible, such as improved employee morale, an improved corporate image, or social benefits. Whatever the future benefits, they must be estimated for the life of the project. A capital project's salvage value at the end of its useful life is also a benefit that must be estimated and included in the evaluation of the project.

Project Evaluation

Evaluating capital investment projects requires systematic procedures and relevant data about a set of diverse projects with differing project lives, costs, and benefits. A number of evaluation methods exist, each with advantages and disadvantages, as we show in this chapter and the next.

Development of the Capital Expenditure Budget

The capital expenditure budget is part of the master budget

The **capital expenditure budget,** or just **capital budget,** is the company's plan for capital investments for the period. The budget contains all capital investment projects that have been approved for the budget period. The total amount of the capital expenditure budget is the sum of all the individual projects. In addition to a listing of the projects and the amount of investment in each, the budget may provide descriptive data about each project. A simple capital budget is discussed in Chapter 7 and illustrated in Figure 7-16. You may remember from that chapter that the capital budget affects other budgets, such as the cash budget and budgeted financial statements.

The capital budget results from the process of evaluating and accepting various capital projects that fit the firm's goals. However, the evaluation process does not result in an automatic acceptance or rejection of a project. Project evaluation seldom provides a clear-cut decision. Instead, managers must use the information provided by the evaluation process to determine which investment proposals best meet the goals of the firm.

More than economic factors enter into capital budgeting decisions

Many factors affect capital budgeting decisions. For instance, managers may need to decide on the amount of resources to be committed to new projects and must set priorities among them. In addition to the cost and benefits of each project, managers must analyze other variables. For example, rejecting all of the proposals of a particular department or division may lower its morale and operating efficiencies. As another example, automating a function that is currently performed manually may be highly desirable from an economic point of view, but may result in an overall decline in morale and productivity as some employees lose their jobs and others start doubting the stability of their own positions.

Project Reevaluation

After capital projects are accepted, they should be reevaluated periodically to determine if they are meeting corporate objectives. A problem with capital projects is that once they are committed they are difficult or impossible to eliminate. Nevertheless, a reevaluation helps managers to learn something about the accuracy of estimates made for the project, and to improve estimates on future projects. A reevaluation may indicate the need for scrapping the project to eliminate a mistake and free invested funds for better purposes.

Project Evaluation Methods

Methods for evaluating capital projects range from simple to complex. Although there are a number of evaluation methods, they can be classified into two general categories: those that rely on the time value of money, called discounted cash flow methods, and those that do not.

1. Discounted cash flow methods
   a. Internal rate of return
   b. Net present value
   c. Profitability index
2. Other methods
   a. Payback
   b. Payback reciprocal
   c. Accounting rate of return

DISCOUNTED CASH FLOW METHODS

The value of a dollar today is greater than the value of a dollar some time in the future. The difference in the value is interest, which is the cost of money to the borrower and a return to the lender. Interest is the reward for waiting for money. Alternatively, it is the price paid for having someone else's money to use now. If a company can invest $1,000 today to earn 10 percent interest, the investment will accumulate to $1,100 a year from now. If that amount remains invested at 10 percent it will grow to $1,210 by the end of 2 years. The **present value** of $1,210 two years from now at 10 percent interest is $1,000.

The concept of **time value of money** is obviously significant in capital budgeting. Money must be invested in a capital project today so that it will produce income or cost savings in the future. The investment should not be larger than the present value of the future cash receipts or cash savings. In other words, we should not pay more for a project than we expect to get in return. Future returns from the investment must be measured in terms of their present value using compound interest concepts.

Discounted cash flow project evaluation methods depend on the time value of money

Discounted cash flow (DCF) is a method of using time value of money concepts to evaluate capital budgeting projects. All cash inflows and outflows associated with a project are discounted to their present value. The internal rate of return (IRR) method is used to find the interest rate earned by a specific capital project. The net present value method (NPV) is used to find the difference between the present value of cash inflows and the present value of cash outflows for a particular capital project using an interest rate selected by management. Later we discuss how management selects an interest rate.

In the following discussion of project evaluation methods, we assume a knowledge of time value of money concepts. If you are not comfortable with the use of these concepts, we urge you to study the appendix at the end of this book (page 897).

Discounted Cash Flow Assumptions

The analysis of most capital budgeting situations requires some simplifying assumptions. These simplifications become part of the estimates that must be made. One such simplification deals with the timing of cash flows associated with a project. It is commonly assumed in project evaluation that the cash inflows from a project occur at the end of each period. It is possible to use other assumptions about the timing of cash flows, but the end-of-period assumption is acceptable for most evaluations.

Cash flows are assumed to occur at the end of the year

Another assumption is that management is able to determine its **cost of capital,** which is the cost of funds obtained from investors. The cost of capital is typically expressed as an interest rate, and theoretically can be computed as the weighted average of the rates paid to various investors.

The cost of capital is estimated

In practice, the computation of the cost of capital is difficult because the debt and equity amounts may change during the year and because either the book values or market values may be used to measure debt and equity. The computation of the cost of capital is discussed later in this chapter.

A third assumption implicit in discounted cash flow methods is that the interest rate used is relevant for the life of the project. This assumption implies that future cash flows from the project can be reinvested at the interest rate used in evaluating the project. Future interest rates may be different from those used now, but it is generally impractical to predict changes in interest rates. The discounted cash flow methods are discussed and illustrated below.

An interest rate must be selected

Internal Rate of Return

Typically, a project produces both cash outflows and cash inflows. The outflow usually occurs when the project is acquired. The cash inflows occur as the project provides future benefits in the form of income or cost reductions. The outflows may be viewed as the investment and the inflow as return on the investment. The **internal rate of return (IRR)** is the interest rate that discounts an investment's future cash flows to the present so that the present value of those cash flows exactly equals the cost of the investment. The IRR is, in fact, the interest rate that is earned on the investment. If all cash flows of the investment are discounted to the present using the IRR, the present values of the cash inflows and outflows are equal.

IRR is the interest rate that sets a project's cash inflows equal to its cash outflows

The internal rate of return is computed from the project's cash inflows and outflows. Once the IRR is found, it is compared with the minimum rate of return that management deems acceptable for capital investment projects. The minimum rate is typically the firm's cost of capital.

To illustrate computation of the internal rate of return, we examine a capital project that Marlin Corporation wishes to evaluate. The company wants to determine whether it should acquire an automatic assembly machine for $49,000. The machine would eliminate some assembly now performed manually. The machine will provide estimated annual savings of $13,000 for the next 6 years, at which point it will be disposed of with no salvage value.

The cost of the project includes all costs necessary to put the project into operation. After adding freight, installation, taxes, discounts, and any other costs necessary to acquire the machine, we find the total cash outflow to be $50,553. Similarly, the $13,000 annual saving includes all cost savings such as labor, taxes, and maintenance.

Computing the Internal Rate of Return.   The evaluation process consists of finding the interest rate that will set the present value of the six $13,000 cash inflows equal to the present value of the $50,553 cash outflow. The outflow occurs at the time the project is acquired, so its present value is $50,553. The inflows, or in this case the cash savings, are an annuity because they are the same in each period. The problem can be diagramed as follows:

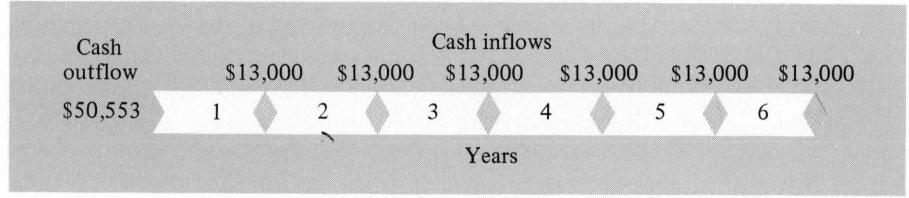

Find the unknown interest rate and you have the IRR

We need to find the interest rate i at which the present value of an annuity of six $13,000 cash receipts, called **rents,** is equal to $50,553. The following equation can be set up:

$$\text{Present value (PV) of annuity} = \text{Rent} \times f(i = ?, n = 6)$$

where f is the present value factor for an annuity of 6 rents and an unknown interest rate. By solving for f and looking it up in a present value of annuity table, we can determine the interest rate.

$$\$50,553 = \$13,000 \times f$$
$$f = \$50,553/\$13,000$$
$$= 3.88869$$

Using the value of f, which is a present value of annuity factor, we look in the present value of annuity table for 6 periods. In the 14 percent column we find the factor 3.88867; therefore the IRR in this example is 14 percent.

What if the investment had a cost of $50,000 instead of $50,553? The analysis is the same, but we get a different present value factor.

$$\text{Present value (PV) of annuity} = \text{Rent} \times f(i = ?, n = 6)$$
$$\$50,000 = \$13,000 \times f$$
$$f = \$50,000/\$13,000$$
$$= 3.84615$$

In this case, the value of f cannot be found in the present value of annuity table. In the 6-period row and the 14 percent column we find the factor 3.88867, and in the 15 percent column we find 3.78448. Therefore the appropriate interest rate is somewhere between 14 and 15 percent.

Compound interest tables that show fractional interest rates would provide a closer approximation. Managers may be satisfied with the 14 to 15 percent figure. If more precision is desired, interpolation may be used to estimate the rate more closely, as follows:

	Annuity Factors		
	At 14%	Computed	At 15%
Annuity factor	3.88867	3.84615	3.78448
Difference		.04252	.06167
Total difference		.10419	

A calculator lets you avoid interpolation

The difference between the annuity factors for 14 and 15 percent is .10419, with the computed annuity factor for the proposed project lying somewhere in between. By finding the difference between the given values and the computed factor we see that the computed value is .04252/.10419, or 41 percent greater than 14 percent. Therefore the computed percentage rate is 14.41 percent. Alternatively, the computed value is .06167/.10419, or .59 smaller than 15 percent, which provides the same answer.

Even more precise interest rates can be obtained by computers or even by small calculators. The actual interest rate in this case is 14.4028 percent, which is far more precise than necessary for evaluating most projects.

Projects with Nonuniform Cash Flows. Not all projects yield uniform cash flows such as those described above. For example, the assembly machine costing $50,000 may be expected to provide greater savings during its early life when it is relatively new. Later, when the machine requires more maintenance and becomes less precise, it can be expected to produce smaller cash savings. For example, management may estimate that the cash savings from using the machine will be as shown at the top of the next page.

When cash flows are not uniform, it is not possible to use annuity tables to find the IRR. Instead, trial and error can be used. This is a tedious process when performed manually, but is easily done by a computer. It involves selecting an interest rate and using it to discount each individual cash saving to

Year	Cash Saving
1	$15,000
2	15,000
3	13,000
4	12,000
5	12,000
6	10,000

Trial and error must be used with nonuniform cash flows

its present value. If the sum of the present values is greater than the cost of the equipment, the IRR is greater than the interest rate selected. A slightly higher interest rate is then used and the process is repeated until the appropriate rate is found.

For example, if the above six cash flows are discounted to the present at 14.5 percent, they yield a total present value of $50,719, computed as follows:

Year	Discount Factor	×	Cash Saving	=	PV of Cash Saving
1	.87336		$15,000		$13,100.40
2	.76276		15,000		11,441.40
3	.66617		13,000		8,660.21
4	.58181		12,000		6,981.72
5	.50813		12,000		6,097.56
6	.44378		10,000		4,437.80
Present value of cash savings					50,719.09
Present value of cash outflow					50,000.00
Difference					$ 719.09

The present value of the cash inflows is $719 greater than the $50,000 cost, so the internal rate of return must be greater than 14.5 percent. Using 15 percent and discounting each cash flow produces the following results:

Year	Discount Factor	×	Cash Saving	=	PV of Cash Saving
1	.86957		$15,000		$13,043.55
2	.75614		15,000		11,342.10
3	.65752		13,000		8,547.76
4	.57175		12,000		6,861.00
5	.49718		12,000		5,966.16
6	.43233		10,000		4,323.30
Present value of cash savings					50,083.87
Present value of cash outflow					50,000.00
Difference					$ 83.87

Using 15 percent, the present value of the six cash savings is $83.87 greater than the present value of the cash outflow. This means that the IRR is higher than 15 percent, but only a little higher. In fact, if the same process is carried out using 15.1 percent, the present value of the future cash savings is $49,958, or $46 below the cost of the project. Therefore the IRR is between 15 and 15.1 percent. A computer can easily be instructed to start with some low interest rate and repeat the computations while increasing the rate by a small increment until the correct rate is found.

Interpreting the Internal Rate of Return.   The preceding computation indicates that the new equipment provides a return of 15.1 percent. Management may now compare this return with other capital projects, and rank the projects according to their returns. The highest return indicates the most favorable project.

Whether the project should be accepted cannot be determined solely by its IRR ranking among all the firm's capital projects. The return of 15.1 percent may be less than the cost that Marlin Corporation pays for its capital. Management must therefore estimate the cost of capital, and should accept only those projects whose internal rate of return is greater than that cost.

By relying on the time value of money, the IRR method offers a realistic project evaluation. The key variable in the evaluation of a project is its expected cash flows. Notice that with the IRR method, accounting income and depreciation on the proposed project play no role in the analysis except to the extent they affect cash flows.

We assume future cash flows can be reinvested at the project's IRR

An essential assumption of IRR is that future cash inflows from a project can be reinvested at the project's IRR. Some people believe it is unrealistic to expect that cash flows from high-yielding projects can be invested at the same high yield. Another criticism is that comparing the IRR for various projects does not take into account how long those projects will provide that yield. A project yielding 18 percent for 3 years may not be as desirable as one yielding 16 percent for 15 years, because the return from the 18 percent project may have to be reinvested at less than 16 percent for the remaining 12 years. As usual, the IRR method provides information to managers, but it does not provide the decision.

Net Present Value

NPV is the difference between the present value of a project's cash inflows and outflows, discounted at the cost of capital

The **net present value method (NPV)** of evaluating a capital project involves discounting all the project's cash flows to their present value using a target rate of interest, which is usually the firm's cost of capital. The method is used to find the net present value of the project, which is the difference between the present value of cash inflows and the present value of cash outflows.

To illustrate the net present value method, we return to Marlin Corporation's evaluation of an assembly machine costing $50,000 and yielding estimated cash savings of $13,000 per year for 6 years. The company's management has decided that 14 percent is the target rate for capital projects.

When the cash flows are uniform, they can be evaluated as an annuity whose future cash flows are discounted to the present using the acceptable interest rate. The net present value is found as follows:

$$\text{Present value of annuity} = \text{Rent} \times f(n = 6, i = 14\%)$$
$$PV = \$13,000 \times 3.88867$$
$$= \$50,552.71$$

Net present value computations with uniform cash flows

Present value of cash savings	$50,552.71
Less present value of cash outflows	50,000.00
Net present value	$ 552.71

The positive net present value of $552.71 means that acquiring the equipment is acceptable if the cost of capital is 14 percent. A positive net present value means the project earns more than the minimum acceptable interest rate.

If the cost of capital in this example is 16 percent, the net present value of the project is negative, computed as follows:

Present value of cash savings	$13,000 × 3.68474 = $47,901.62
Present value of cash outflows	50,000.00
Net present value	$ (2,098.38)

A negative net present value means the project is not acceptable

If the net present value of the project is negative, the project is not acceptable because its rate of return will be less than the minimum acceptable rate. The results just shown are not unexpected. From the previous IRR calculations on page 551, we know that the internal rate of return on the project is 14.4 percent. Evaluating the project using a lower interest rate must yield a positive net present value. Using a rate higher than 14.4 percent yields a negative net present value.

Projects with Nonuniform Cash Flows.   When the cash flows are not uniform, the net present value is found simply by discounting each individual cash flow at the target interest rate. With a 14 percent interest rate, the nonuniform cash flow example shown earlier is evaluated as follows:

Year	Discount Factor	× Cash Saving	= PV of Cash Saving
1	.87719	$15,000	$13,157.85
2	.76947	15,000	11,542.05
3	.67497	13,000	8,774.61
4	.59208	12,000	7,104.96
5	.51937	12,000	6,232.44
6	.45559	10,000	4,555.90
Present value of cash savings			51,367.81
Present value of cash outflow			50,000.00
Net present value			$ 1,367.81

As expected, the net present value is positive. From the IRR computation we know that the project yields slightly more than 15 percent.

Interpreting the Net Present Value. A positive net present value indicates that the present value of the cash inflows from the project exceeds the present value of the cash outflows of the project. The net present value is the present value of the return on the project in excess of the target return. A negative net present value results when the present value of the cash inflows from the project is less than the present value of the cash outflows. This means the present value of the returns from the project is not enough to satisfy the target rate of return. The comparison of cash flows is always made in terms of present values. In the preceding example, the total amount of cash inflow was $77,000, but the $51,367.81 present value of the cash inflows was used to evaluate the project.

The NPV method assumes all cash inflows are reinvested at the cost of capital

The net present value method depends on the time value of money. It is a way of evaluating a capital investment project using its estimated cash inflows and outflows over its life. The computation of net present value rests on the assumption that all cash inflows from a project are reinvested at the firm's target rate of return. But if the target rate of return is the minimum acceptable rate, some projects will earn more than the minimum, and the firm's **average** rate of return will be higher than the minimum. Therefore the assumption underlying the net present value method is not quite realistic. A business must earn more than the cost of capital in order to remain competitive.

Projects with Salvage Value. If a capital project has a salvage value, the money obtained from disposal of the investment is a cash inflow in addition to the other income or cost savings provided by the project. The cash inflow from the salvage value should be included in the IRR or NPV evaluations. The salvage value is merely added to the last year's cash inflows. This poses no problem with the NPV method. But if the addition of the salvage value makes the cash inflows from the project uneven, then the trial-and-error method must be used to find the IRR for the project. For long-lived projects and high discount rates, even a large salvage value may have only a small effect on the NPV and the IRR, because the present value of the salvage value is very small. Nevertheless, if a salvage value is estimated, it should be included in the computation.

Salvage value is a cash inflow and should be used to find NPV

Profitability Index

If net present value is used to evaluate capital budgeting projects, all projects with positive net present values are acceptable and all projects with negative net present values are unacceptable. If a company has limited money to invest in capital projects, how does it select from among those with positive net present values? It might seem logical to accept the projects with the largest net present value first and continue to fund projects in that order until the available investment funds are exhausted. But this is not necessarily the best approach to assigning investment funds to projects, as we show below with two projects that have the following cash flows:

Year	Small Project	Large Project
0	$(35,000)	$(105,000)
1	15,000	45,000
2	15,000	45,000
3	15,000	45,000
4	15,000	45,000

The cash flows of the larger project are exactly three times those of the smaller project. Using a 15 percent target rate of return, the net present values of the two projects are $7,825 and $23,475 respectively. Using just NPV as our evaluation method, it appears that the larger project is more attractive and should be funded first. Logically, we know that the one project is merely three times as big in all respects. The return per dollar of investment is the same for both projects.

The profitability index enables us to compare different size investments

To adjust for the discrepancy in size, it is possible to compute a **profitability index (PI),** which is the ratio of the present value of the cash inflows to the present value of the cash outflows. In the above example, the profitability indexes are

$$\text{Profitability index} = \frac{\text{Present value of cash inflows}}{\text{Present value of cash outflows}}$$

$$\text{Small project:} \quad = \frac{\$42,825}{\$35,000} = 1.22$$

$$\text{Large project:} \quad = \frac{\$128,475}{\$105,000} = 1.22$$

The profitability index converts the net present values of unequal size projects to comparable figures. The profitability index is smaller than 1.0 if the net present value is negative and it is greater than 1.0 if the NPV is positive. The higher the profitability index, the more desirable the project.

OTHER CAPITAL PROJECT EVALUATION METHODS

The payback method and the accounting rate of return method do not depend on compound interest concepts. These methods are simpler to use than the discounted cash flow methods, but with high interest rates and capital costs, the results of the analysis are not always dependable.

Payback

Payback—how soon do we get our money back?

When confronted with a long-term investment, a manager may ask, "How soon will the project pay back the money invested in it?" The **payback** method is a simple computation that answers this question. Also referred to as the **payout** method, it is used to determine how long it takes for a project to return the original investment.

To illustrate the payback method, we use the example of Farley Company, which is planning to acquire equipment costing $66,000 and having a useful life of 10 years. With estimated cash savings from using the equipment of $16,500 per year, it is clear that the first 4 years will produce cash savings of $66,000 ($16,500 × 4). Therefore it will require 4 years for the machine to return the original investment. The computation is easily performed as follows:

$$\text{Payback period} = \frac{\text{Initial cost}}{\text{Annual cash inflows}}$$

$$= \frac{\$66,000}{\$16,500 \text{ per year}} = 4 \text{ years}$$

With nonuniform cash flows, computation of the payback period is somewhat different, although the concept is the same. For example, the cash flows on the investment are expected to be as follows:

Year	Cash Saving		Year	Cash Saving
1	$19,000		6	$12,000
2	18,000		7	9,000
3	17,000		8	7,000
4	16,000		9	6,000
5	14,000		10	4,000

To find the payback period, it is necessary only to add up the cash savings until the investment is recovered. The first 3 years have total cash savings of $54,000, which is $12,000 short of the original investment. Of the $16,000 cash savings in the fourth year, the first $12,000 are needed to recover the investment. Therefore, $54,000 from the first 3 years plus $12,000/$16,000 from the fourth year is required. The payback period is 3 years and 9 months in this case.

Interpreting the Payback. Managers may have in mind a maximum payback period beyond which a project is unacceptable. Up to the maximum period, projects may be accepted in order of shortest payback period. Cash flows occurring in the distant future are more uncertain than those in the near future and managers may therefore view payback as a measure of risk. A short payback indicates a less risky project than a longer payback. Payback is supported by the concept that cash in the present is more valuable than cash in the future.

The payback method ignores the time value of cash flows

A disadvantage of payback is that it does not take into account the time value of money. For example, two projects, each costing $50,000, have the following cash flows:

Year	Project A	Project B
1	$25,000	$10,000
2	20,000	15,000
3	10,000	25,000
4	10,000	25,000
5	10,000	10,000
6	10,000	10,000
7	0	10,000
8	0	10,000
9	0	10,000

Project B has a payback of 3 years, so the payback method favors project A with a payback of less than 3 years. In terms of time value of money, project B is preferable. If the cash flows are discounted at 12 percent, project A has a net present value of $12,479 and project B has a net present value of $21,517. Looking only at the payback data may be misleading because it **ignores the cash flows beyond the payback period.** In this example, project A provides $30,000 of cash flows after the payback period, while project B provides an additional $75,000, but these cash flows are not used in the payback evaluation.

Bailout

A logical extension of the payback method is the bailout concept. **Bailout** is a method of determining how quickly an investment can be recovered from both its cash flows and its salvage value. Payback is used to evaluate only the cash flows from an investment, because the salvage value is typically recovered beyond the payback period. Bailout, on the other hand, is based on the assumption that a capital project has a salvage value at any time management wants to terminate the investment.

Bailout is payback that includes salvage value

For example, Farley Company's evaluation of equipment costing $66,000 includes ten $16,500 inflows (in the form of cash savings) and no salvage value. However, at the end of the first year the company could certainly sell the machine for some amount, even if salvage value is zero at the end of 10 years. In this case management estimates the following salvage values for the machine:

Year	Cash Saving	Salvage Value	Total Salvage + Cash Savings
1	$16,500	$35,000	$ 51,500
2	16,500	24,000	57,000
3	16,500	16,500	66,000
4	16,500	9,000	75,000
5	16,500	6,000	88,500
6	16,500	2,000	101,000
7	16,500	1,000	116,500
8	16,500	700	132,200
9	16,500	200	148,500
10	16,500	0	165,000

By the end of 3 years, the total cash savings of $49,500 plus the salvage value of $16,500 enable the company to recover the entire investment. The cost recovery of 3 years can only be achieved by terminating the project. Payback assumes the continuation of the project until the payback period has been reached. Bailout provides additional information that may enable management to decide if the risk of undertaking a project is warranted.

Payback Reciprocal

Payback reciprocal is an estimate of the internal rate of return

The payback period may be used to approximate the internal rate of return of a project. This is done by computing the **payback reciprocal,** which is 1 divided by the payback period. The payback reciprocal is a reasonable estimate of the internal rate of return only if the life of the project is at least double the payback period. Even then, the estimate is always greater than the actual internal rate of return.

For example, Farley Company's $66,000 project, which yields $16,500 per year, has a payback of 4 years and a life of 10 years. The payback reciprocal is

$$\text{Payback reciprocal} = \frac{1}{\text{Payback}} = \frac{1}{4} = .25, \text{ or } 25 \text{ percent}$$

The internal rate of return on this project is 21.4 percent. As the life of a project increases, the payback reciprocal approaches closer and closer to the internal rate of return. This is illustrated in Figure 15-1, which shows the payback reciprocal for this project and the internal rate of return for the same project with varying lengths of life. From the figure you can see that the payback reciprocal is a poor estimate if the project life is less than double the payback period. With longer lives, the payback reciprocal is a reasonably good estimate of the IRR and one that is easy to compute.

The payback reciprocal should be used only with uniform cash flows. Regardless of the payback period and length of project life, nonuniform cash flows may cause the payback reciprocal to be a very poor estimate of the IRR. As a rough estimator of the IRR under some circumstances, the payback reciprocal can be a useful managerial tool, but it is important to understand its limitations.

Accounting Rate of Return

The **accounting rate of return (ARR)** method of evaluating a capital project is based on the traditional concepts of accounting income and return on investment. A project is evaluated by computing a rate of return on investment using accounting measures of income, with net income obtained by deducting project expenses from project revenues. Remember that accounting income and expenses are **not** cash flows as used with discounted cash flow methods. The formula for the accounting rate of return is

$$\text{ARR} = \frac{\text{Incremental income from the project}}{\text{Project investment cost}}$$

Figure 15-1. Relation of payback reciprocal for a 4-year payback period and internal rate of return for projects with varying lives. When project life exceeds double the payback period, the payback reciprocal provides a reasonable estimate of IRR.

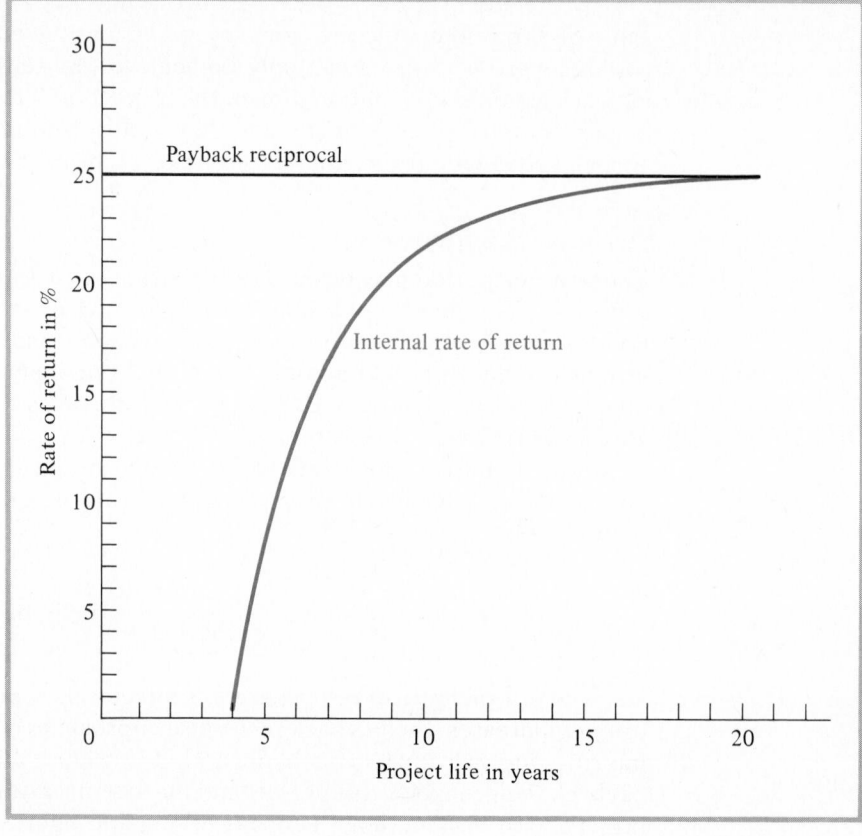

For example, Marlin Corporation is evaluating the possibility of introducing a new product suggested by one of its managers. The project requires an investment of $50,000 including design, promotion, and new equipment. The project is expected to yield $15,000 of additional revenue per year and to incur operating expenses of $4,000 per year in addition to $3,000 annual depreciation. Given these figures, incremental income is computed as follows:

Accounting rate of return is based on revenues less expenses

Revenue		$15,000
Less operating expenses	$4,000	
Depreciation expense	3,000	7,000
Incremental income		$ 8,000

The capital budgeting evaluation methods discussed previously depend on cash flows rather than income; consequently, depreciation does not enter into the evaluations. With ARR, accounting income is the primary element of the analysis, and depreciation is used to determine income. The accounting rate of return is computed as follows:

$$ARR = \frac{\$8,000}{\$50,000} = .16, \text{ or } 16 \text{ percent}$$

Some managers believe that the actual cost of the investment should not be used in the calculation of the ARR. Instead the average cost for the life of the project should be used. As time passes and assets depreciate, the book value declines. The argument is that book value represents the investment. The average book value is obtained by adding the beginning and ending value and dividing by two. In this example, the average investment is ($50,000 + $0)/2, or $25,000. Using this figure as the investment base, the computation is:

$$\text{ARR} = \frac{\$8,000}{\$25,000} = .32, \text{ or } 32 \text{ percent}$$

Although there is a significant difference in the accounting rate of return depending on the investment base, this does not mean that one or the other computation is wrong. Managers should use the investment base they deem most appropriate for making the evaluation. The controversy over investment bases is the same as discussed in Chapter 12 on evaluation of segment performance. A variety of investment bases is possible, each with some advantages and disadvantages.

Using the ARR. The accounting rate of return may be used to rank capital projects so that funds can be allocated to projects with the highest returns. Funds may thus be allocated until exhausted, or a limit may be set on some minimum ARR, such as 20 percent, below which a project is unacceptable. The accounting rate of return is easy for managers to understand because it closely parallels traditional concepts of income analysis and investment return. However, the accounting rate of return method is weak in that it does not use the time value of money nor the timing and duration of cash flows.

ARR ignores the timing and duration of cash flows

ESTIMATING THE COST OF CAPITAL

A business must pay for the use of money in the form of interest or dividends. Businesses obtain funds from many sources, each with a different cost. Interest and dividend rates vary for bonds, mortgages, notes payable, preferred stock, and common stock. Theoretically, the cost of capital can be computed as the weighted average of the rates paid to various investors. For many firms, however, the cost of capital may be difficult to compute because the cost of borrowing or the cost of equity funds may change with changes in the economy, government actions, and changes in the risk of various types of investments. Consequently, the cost of capital can only be estimated. Estimation methods vary and can be very complex. We present only the basic concepts of computing the weighted average cost of capital for a firm.

Companies are generally capitalized with common stock, preferred stock, and long-term debt. In return for the capital provided by investors, companies pay dividends to shareholders and interest to creditors. Given the amount of the dividends and interest, and many other variables, such as the amount of earnings, state of the economy, and tax rates, investors place a value

No matter what the source of capital, it has a cost

on the equity and debt instruments of a company. To estimate the cost of capital, it is necessary to relate the market value and yield of the debt and equity instruments. The following example illustrates the process.

Cost of Common Stock

Harmon Corporation has outstanding 50,000 shares of no-par common stock which trades in the stock market at $40 per share. The company currently pays a cash dividend of $6 per share annually. The cost of common stock to the company is expressed as a percentage rate, computed as follows:

$$\text{Cost of common stock} = \frac{\text{Dividend per share}}{\text{Market price per share}}$$

$$= \frac{\$6}{\$40}$$

$$= .15, \text{ or } 15 \text{ percent}$$

Notice that the computation is nothing more than the company's dividend yield expressed as a percentage. This percentage is the current rate investors demand for providing the company with equity capital. Because the amount of earnings and the company's dividend policy may change, the figure above is also subject to change. In addition, the cost of funds depends on investor expectations about company performance and dividend policy, their knowledge about the company's earnings and the amount retained for expansion and potential future dividends, and their evaluation of investment risk. As investor expectations and evaluations change, the dividend yield changes also.

The cost of stock is its yield to the investor

Cost of Preferred Stock

Another variable used in the computation of a firm's cost of capital is the cost of preferred stock, which is also the stock's dividend yield. Typically, a company pays the required preferred dividend, which usually does not change over the life of the preferred stock. Therefore the preferred dividend yield is usually more stable than the common dividend yield. The preferred dividend yield does change, however, when changes in interest rates cause the price of preferred stock to move up and down.

Harmon Corporation has outstanding 10,000 shares of $9 preferred stock which currently trades in the market at $90 per share. The cost of the preferred stock is

$$\text{Cost of preferred stock} = \frac{\text{Preferred dividend per share}}{\text{Market price of preferred share}}$$

$$= \frac{\$9}{\$90}$$

$$= .10, \text{ or } 10 \text{ percent}$$

Cost of Long-Term Debt

Companies typically have many types of long-term debt with different costs. Except for differences in interest rates, the cost of each is computed the same way. Interest is a tax-deductible expense; its actual cost is less than the interest rate paid. Therefore the company's tax rate must be included in the computation of the cost of long-term debt.

The cost of debt is reduced by income taxes

We assume only one type of long-term debt for Harmon Corporation. It has outstanding $1 million of 12 percent bonds which trade in the market at their face value. The company is subject to a 35 percent tax rate. Its true interest cost is therefore

$$\text{True interest cost} = \text{Interest rate} \times (1 - \text{tax rate})$$

$$.12(1 - .35) = .078, \text{ or } 7.8 \text{ percent}$$

In all cases, the market value of the debt rather than the book value should be used, so that the interest rate computed is the company's actual cost of borrowing rather than the coupon rate of the bonds. Similar calculations may be made for other types of debt, such as mortgages, notes, and leases.

Weighted Average Cost of Capital

We are now ready to compute the weighted average cost of capital for Harmon Company. To do so, we need to know what proportion of its capitalization is debt, preferred, and common equity. We already gave the amounts for common and preferred stock. To compute the cost of capital we multiply each cost times the percentage weight of each type of capitalization.

Type of Capitalization	Market Value	Proportion ×	Cost =	Weighted Cost
Long-term debt	$1,000,000	10/39	.078	.0200
Preferred stock	900,000	9/39	.100	.0231
Common stock	2,000,000	20/39	.150	.0769
Total capitalization	$3,900,000		Cost of capital	.1200

Problems immediately become apparent. For many types of securities, there is no market price from which the cost of capital can be computed. The relative proportion of long-term debt and equity capitalization may not remain the same over time. Changes in company policy, government action, state of the economy, and risk perception of investors all tend to change the relationships that affect the cost of capital. Still, managers can obtain some approximation of the cost of capital in order to use the estimate for capital budgeting purposes.

SUMMARY   The process of evaluating, planning, and financing major long-term investment projects is called **capital budgeting.** Capital projects typically require large commitments of resources and have a significant impact on the long-range success of an organization. A systematic method of budgeting capital projects includes project identification, estimation of costs and benefits, project evaluation, budget development, and reevaluation of accepted projects. Projects should be selected on the basis of decision criteria that are compatible with organizational goals.

Discounted cash flow (DCF) methods of project evaluation depend on the **time value of money.** These methods include the internal rate of return, net present value, and profitability index.

The **internal rate of return (IRR)** is the interest rate earned by a project. It is the rate that discounts the cash inflows from the project to a **present value (PV)** that is equal to the present value of the cash outflows. If the IRR is higher than the cost of capital, the project is acceptable. The **cost of capital** is the amount a company must pay for the use of money, usually in terms of an interest rate.

The **net present value (NPV)** method is used to discount all cash flows from a project to the present using the cost of capital. If the NPV is positive, the project is acceptable. Projects with nonuniform cash flows are easier to evaluate using the net present value method than the internal rate of return method, because the latter requires trial-and-error estimation.

The **profitability index (PI)** is an extension of the NPV method. It is used to convert the NPV computations to a measure of net present value per dollar of investment, so that projects of different sizes can be easily compared.

Project evaluation methods that do not depend on the time value of money include payback, payback reciprocal, and the accounting rate of return. The **payback** method measures how quickly the original investment is recovered. It is easy to compute but it ignores any cash flows beyond the payback period. An extension of payback is the concept of **bailout,** which is a measure of how quickly the investment can be recovered if the project is terminated. The cash inflows from the project and also the proceeds of disposal are used in the computation. The **payback reciprocal** is a rough approximation of the internal rate of return and is computed as 1/payback period. For the payback reciprocal to be a reasonable estimate of the IRR, the cash flows must be uniform and the life of the project must be at least double the payback period.

The **accounting rate of return (ARR)** method is based on accounting concepts of income measurement and investment base to compute a rate of return. The timing of cash flows is ignored, as is the time value of money. Net income is divided by the cost of the investment or by the average investment cost. Unlike other evaluation methods which depend on cash flows rather than income, depreciation is included in the computation of income with the ARR method.

To use the project evaluation methods effectively, it is necessary to have some idea of the cost of capital, but measuring the cost of capital can be complex. Typically, market values and yields of common stock, preferred stock, and long-term debt are used in the computation. In the case of debt, the after-tax interest cost should be used. When the cost of each individual source of funds is established, a weighted average cost for the entire organization is computed.

KEY TERMS

accounting rate of return (ARR) *(559)*
bailout *(558)*
capital budgeting *(545)*
capital expenditure budget *(547)*
cost of capital *(549)*
discounted cash flow (DCF) *(548)*

internal rate of return (IRR) *(549)*
net present value (NPV) *(553)*
payback *(556)*
payback reciprocal *(559)*
present value (PV) *(548)*
profitability index (PI) *(556)*
time value of money *(548)*

QUESTIONS

1. Smith just completed the evaluation of two proposed capital projects for the production department. He reports that using the estimated cost of capital of 15 percent, the robot welder has a net present value of $7,500 and an initial cost of $100,000, whereas the automated spraying equipment has a net present value of $4,800 and a cost of $60,000. Johnson is looking at the figures and asks Smith, "Does this mean that we are going to earn $7,500 a year from the welder and $4,800 a year from the sprayer? That's only 7.5 and 8 percent return on investment." Explain to Johnson what is wrong with his interpretation and what the figures mean.

2. (AICPA) The quantitative techniques employed for capital budgeting decisions depend largely upon accounting data. Cost of capital is an important concept in capital budgeting. Distinguish between capital budgeting and budgeting for operations. Define the term "cost of capital" and explain how it is used in capital budgeting.

3. (AICPA) Three quantitative methods used in making capital budgeting decisions are payback period, accounting rate of return, and discounted cash flows. Two variations of the discounted cash flow method are the internal rate of return method and the net present value method. Discuss the merits of each method, and compare the two variations of the discounted cash flow method.

EXERCISES

Ex. 15-1
Internal Rate of
Return

Rubix Company is evaluating a proposal to acquire a new high-speed punch press requested by one of its shop supervisors. The cost of the punch press is $20,587. In addition, the company would have to pay a 5 percent sales tax on the purchase and spend $1,000 for installation. The machine has a 7-year life and is capable of speeding up production sufficiently to save $5,600 per year. It has no salvage value. The supervisor requesting the punch press has been informed that the company cannot fund any investment whose internal rate of return is less than 15 percent.

REQUIRED

Compute the internal rate of return on the new equipment and determine if it should be acquired.

Ex. 15-2
Internal Rate of Return

Ribbley Corporation's sales division manager recently requested the acquisition of a new intelligent terminal for use by his division. The terminal costs $21,000. The sales tax is 5 percent, and connecting the terminal to the central computer would require a $650 expenditure. The terminal has a useful life of 6 years with no salvage value. The sales division manager estimates that its acquisition would result in a cost saving of $6,000 per year during the life of the terminal. The company evaluates capital projects using the internal rate of return, and rejects any projects whose IRR is less than 16 percent.

REQUIRED

Compute the internal rate of return on the terminal and determine if it should be acquired.

Ex. 15-3
Interpolation of Internal Rate of Return

Milyna Company is planning to install digital control units on its horizontal milling machines. The cost of the project is estimated at $40,500 and should provide an annual cash saving of $9,200 for the next 8 years, at the end of which the units will have no salvage value. The company wants to know the internal rate of return on the project before proceeding with it.

REQUIRED

Compute the internal rate of return rounded to one decimal place.

Ex. 15-4
IRR with Nonuniform Cash Flows

A taxicab costing $10,520 is expected to last 3 years and have the following revenues and expenses, including depreciation expense of $2,740 per year:

Year	Revenue	Operating Expense
1	$45,000	$40,740
2	44,000	42,740
3	42,000	43,240

At the end of 3 years the taxi will be sold for its salvage value of $2,300.

REQUIRED

Find the internal rate of return for the taxicab. For simplicity assume that all cash inflows occur at the end of each year and ignore any tax effects.

Ex. 15-5
Net Present Value and Profitability Index

Lonnex Company is evaluating a proposal to acquire a new high-precision vertical mill for one of its production plants. The cost of the mill is $39,500. In addition the company would have to pay a 6 percent sales tax on the purchase and spend $1,250 for installation. The machine has a 9-year life and is expected to save $9,000 per year. It has no salvage value. The company generally funds investment proposals if they have a positive net present value assuming a 16 percent cost of capital.

REQUIRED

a. Compute the net present value on the new equipment and determine if it should be acquired.
b. Compute the profitability index.

Ex. 15-6
NPV and
Nonuniform Cash
Flows

A taxicab costing $8,500 is expected to last 4 years and have the following revenues and expenses:

Year	Revenue	Operating Expense	Depreciation Expense
1	$44,000	$39,000	$1,675
2	44,000	40,000	1,675
3	42,000	40,500	1,675
4	41,000	38,800	1,675

Operating expenses do not include depreciation, which is shown separately. At the end of 4 years the taxi will be sold for its salvage value of $1,800. The cost of capital is 25 percent.

REQUIRED Find the net present value of the taxicab. For simplicity, assume that all cash inflows occur at the end of each year and ignore any tax effects.

Ex. 15-7
NPV and IRR for a
Capital Project

Fuddle Company plans to acquire several new theodolites because it believes they can save $3,000 of transit crew time per year. The instruments cost $9,800 and have a useful life of 10 years. Company policy is to give its old instruments to its employees, so salvage value is not relevant. Management likes to evaluate its long-term projects using the net present value method with a 25 percent interest rate, and also the IRR method to find the project's actual yield if the project is acceptable.

REQUIRED Find the net present value of the project at 25 percent and also the internal rate of return if the project is acceptable.

Ex. 15-8
Payback Analysis

Marless Company is evaluating two capital projects whose estimated cash savings are as follows:

Year	Project A	Project B	Year	Project A	Project B
1	$7,500	$9,400	5	$7,500	$7,400
2	7,500	9,000	6	7,500	5,900
3	7,500	8,500	7	0	5,600
4	7,500	8,000	8	0	5,100

Project A costs $31,500 and Project B costs $40,400. Neither project has any salvage value at the end of its useful life.

REQUIRED
a. Compute the payback period on each project.
b. Compute the payback reciprocal.
c. Discuss which project is preferable.

Ex. 15-9
Payback and
Payback Reciprocal

Norene Corporation is evaluating two capital projects with the cash flows shown at the top of p. 568.

The company can adopt only one project. It wants to use a payback analysis to

Year	Project X	Project Y	Year	Project X	Project Y
0	$(76,650)	$(83,300)			
1	19,500	17,000	6	$13,500	$17,000
2	18,000	17,000	7	12,700	17,000
3	17,000	17,000	8	0	17,000
4	15,900	17,000	9	0	17,000
5	15,000	17,000	10	0	17,000

decide which project is preferable. Neither project has any salvage value.

REQUIRED

a.   Compute the payback period on each project.
b.   Discuss which project is preferable.
c.   Compute the payback reciprocal on each project and discuss the reliability of the estimate.

Ex. 15-10
Payback and
Bailout Analysis

Dr. Kuttmore plans to buy a new electroencephalograph (EEG). The equipment costs $26,800, has a 6-year useful life, and has a salvage value of $3,600. A sales tax of 5 percent must be paid on the purchase. Freight and installation charges amount to $720. The doctor uses sum-of-the-years'-digits depreciation on his equipment.

The doctor estimates that he can use the machine to provide tests to 10 patients per month at a net cash inflow of $65 per patient. If he cannot get enough use from the equipment, however, he would probably sell it. He estimates that the market value of the equipment at the end of each year of its life would be its book value using sum-of-the-years'-digits depreciation.

REQUIRED

a.   Compute the payback period on the equipment.
b.   Compute the bailout on the equipment.

Ex. 15-11
Payback, NPV,
and IRR

Following are data on a capital project being evaluated by the management of Balder, Dasche & Company, which uses its cost of capital as a minimum criterion for project evaluation.

Annual cost saving	$12,000
NPV	$-4,323.60
Salvage value	$0
Useful life	15 years
IRR	20 percent

REQUIRED   Find the cost of the project, the payback period, and the firms's cost of capital.

Ex. 15-12
Payback, IRR,
and NPV

Following are data on a capital project with uniform annual cost savings, being evaluated by the management of Tosca Company. The company considers its cost of capital as a minimum acceptable return on projects.

Cost	$101,400
Payback	5.07 years
IRR	19 percent
NPV	$4,924
Salvage value	$0

REQUIRED   Find the project's annual cost savings and useful life, and also the firm's cost of capital.

Ex. 15-13
Accounting Rate
of Return

Orin Company is evaluating the purchase of a warehouse that would be operated as an independent division. The cost of the property is $450,000. The building has an estimated life of 20 years and no salvage value. The land is valued at $10,000. The company uses straight-line depreciation. Revenues are estimated at $125,300 per year and operating expenses at $25,000 per year, not including depreciation. Orin Company requires a minimum accounting rate of return of 17 percent before tax on its investments.

REQUIRED

a. Compute the accounting rate of return using project cost as a base and decide if the project is acceptable.
b. Estimate the internal rate of return on the project by computing the payback reciprocal.

Ex. 15-14
Cost of Capital

The capital and long-term debt structure of Marvle Company appears as follows:

Bonds payable 15 percent, due 1999	$1,000,000
Mortgages 14 percent	700,000
Preferred stock, $10.80, $100 par	1,000,000
Common stock, $10 par	400,000
Retained earnings	750,000

The bonds trade in the market at face value, the preferred stock at $90 per share, and the common stock at $60 per share. The fair value of the mortgages is their face value. The company is subject to an income tax rate of 45 percent. It pays a cash dividend on common stock of $9.60 per share.

REQUIRED   Compute the cost of capital.

PROBLEMS

P. 15-1
Capital Project
Evaluation

Fussco Company is evaluating a proposal to acquire several new drill presses for its production department. The cost of the equipment is $73,400. The equipment has a useful life of 10 years and is expected to produce cost savings of $15,750 per year. There is no salvage value. The company's cost of capital is 16 percent.

REQUIRED

a. Compute the net present value of the project.
b. Compute the profitability index.
c. Compute the internal rate of return.

P. 15-2
Capital Project
Evaluation

Romiss Company is evaluating a proposal to acquire several new lathes for its production department. The cost of the equipment is $68,000. In addition the company would have to pay a 5 percent sales tax on the purchase and spend $2,000 for freight and installation. The equipment has a useful life of 10 years and is expected to produce cost savings of $15,750 per year. There is no salvage value. Company policy is not to fund any capital project whose internal rate of return is below the company's 16 percent cost of capital.

REQUIRED

a. Compute the net present value of the project.
b. Compute the profitability index.
c. Find the internal rate of return to the nearest percent.
d. Compute the payback on the project.
e. Compute the payback reciprocal.

P. 15-3
Payback and
Discounted Cash
Flow Analysis

Mr. and Mrs. Booble are looking for some income property in which to invest their savings. They have located a duplex that is rented for $19,000 per year. The asking price is $85,000. Their lawyer has agreed to handle the legal expenses for 4 percent of the asking price. Various fees and other closing costs to purchase the property are estimated at $2,600.

The owner of the property has provided figures which indicate that annual maintenance for the property is $2,300 and property taxes are $1,400 per year. In addition, $300 of miscellaneous expenses are usually incurred each year. The property has a useful life of 25 years and the buyers plan to use straight-line depreciation. They have decided that they must have a return of at least 14 percent on their investment. The salvage value is small and can be ignored.

REQUIRED

  a. Compute the payback on the investment.
  b. Compute the payback reciprocal.
  c. Find the net present value of the investment.
  d. Compute the profitability index.
  e. Find the internal rate of return rounded to one decimal point.

P. 15-4
Comparison of Two
Long-Term
Alternatives

Mr. Freemore is installing a new swimming pool in his backyard. Among the equipment suggested by the pool contractor is an automatic electrolytic chlorinator that costs $800. It operates by electrolyzing a saline solution, and requires the use of one bag of salt every 3 months. The salt costs $9 per bag, and a year's supply comes with the chlorinator. The power required to operate the chlorinator is estimated to cost $40 per year. The equipment has a useful life of 10 years and no salvage value. The pool contractor recommends it because "it pays for itself in 4 years."

Without the automatic chlorinator it will be necessary for Mr. Freemore to buy chlorine compounds used for pool treatments. The cost of chemical treatments is an average of $200 per year. If he decides to use chemicals instead of the automatic equipment, Mr. Freemore plans to buy a year's supply as soon as the pool is completed.

Mr. Freemore would like to analyze the two alternatives using 15 percent as the relevant interest rate.

REQUIRED

  a. Use discounted cash flows to compare the two alternatives' cost over the 10-year life and determine which is preferable.
  b. Discuss the basis of the contractor's statement about the equipment paying for itself in 4 years.
  c. Recommend which alternative should be selected.

P. 15-5
Payback, NPV, PI,
and IRR Analysis

Hillandale Golf Course employs five people to mow its fairways with rotary 48-inch mowers. New gang-type reel mowers that cut an 8-foot width cost $98,500 and have a 10-year life and a $12,000 salvage value. One of the workers is retiring and if the new mowers are acquired he would not be replaced. Another person could be shifted to a golf-cart maintenance job that was left vacant when a maintenance employee recently quit. Consequently, buying the new mowers could save $26,000 per year in personnel salaries. However, maintenance cost on the new mowers would be $5,400 per year higher than on the old ones. The old mowers can be sold for $7,000.

The golf course manager is reluctant to invest almost $100,000 in new equipment. She is afraid that the golf course may be unable to maintain the 16 percent minimum required return if the money is spent. "If the payback is more than four years I would not recommend the investment," she tells the board of directors. But she agrees to have an analysis performed and obtain a recommendation from the analyst.

REQUIRED
a. Compute the project's payback and payback reciprocal.
b. Find the net present value of the project using the minimum required rate of return.
c. Compute the profitability index.
d. Estimate the internal rate of return on the project to the nearest whole decimal.
e. Recommend whether the project should be accepted.

P. 15-6
Payback, NPV, and IRR

Following are data on two **independent** capital projects being evaluated by the management of two different companies. Neither of the projects has any salvage value.

	Project K	Project L
Cost	?	$120,930
Annual cost saving	$9,600	?
Useful life	8 years	?
Payback	?	4.031 years
IRR	19 percent	20 percent
NPV	$1,182.72	$3,969.00
Cost of capital	?	?

REQUIRED   Find the missing values for each project.

P. 15-7
Evaluation of New Project

Delpat Corporation is negotiating the purchase of a patent on a highly efficient water heater for home and industrial use. The company is operating near capacity and would need a new facility to start production. The estimated cost of the new plant is $6,500,000. The expected useful life is 15 years with an estimated residual value of $2,000,000. The following unit manufacturing costs are expected:

Direct material	$35 per unit
Direct labor	25 per unit
Variable overhead	8 per unit
Variable selling and administrative	12 per unit

The water heaters are expected to sell for $125 each. Because of intense competition, heavy promotional costs are needed to penetrate the market. The company estimates that if it spends $400,000 per year for advertising during the first 2 years and $100,000 per year thereafter, it should be able to sell the following number of units:

Year 1	25,000 units
Year 2	30,000
Years 3–15	60,000 units per year

Other fixed costs, including straight-line depreciation, are expected to be $600,000 per year. The company requires a 28 percent return before taxes on any new ventures. However, it will accept a smaller return if the project has a payback of 4 years or less.

REQUIRED
a. Compute the net present value for the project and determine if the project is acceptable.
b. Compute payback on the project and determine if the project is acceptable.

P. 15-8
Accounting Rate of
Return and
Payback Reciprocal

Hyrise Space Company plans to buy an office building for $875,000. The building has an estimated life of 15 years and a salvage value of $50,000. Of the purchase price, $45,000 is allocated to the land and the remainder to the building. The company plans to use straight-line depreciation. Annual rent revenue from the building is expected to be $400,000 and operating expenses are estimated at $225,000, not including depreciation.

REQUIRED

a. Compute the accounting rate of return using actual cost and average cost as a base.
b. Estimate the internal rate of return by computing the payback reciprocal.

P. 15-9
Cost of Capital and
Project Evaluation

Wormling Company operates several sheet metal fabricating shops. It is capitalized with the following securities:

$500,000 12% bonds trading in the market at $80
60,000 shares $100-par $7 preferred stock trading at $50 per share
20,000 shares $2-par common stock trading at $25 per share

The company is subject to a 40 percent income tax rate. It pays $4.50 of cash dividends on its common stock annually. It is planning to acquire a new sheet metal brake for one of its shops. The equipment costs $75,550 and has a useful life of 8 years and no salvage value. Cost savings from operating the new equipment are estimated at $17,000 per year.

REQUIRED

a. Estimate the firm's cost of capital.
b. Compute the net present value of the new equipment using the cost of capital.
c. Compute the profitability index.
d. Compute the internal rate of return.
e. Compute the payback period.

P. 15-10 (AICPA)
Evaluating
Investment
Alternatives

During your examination of the financial statements of Benjamin Industries, the president requested your assistance in the evaluation of several financial management problems in his home appliances division, which he summarized for you as follows:

1. Management wants to determine the best sales price for a new appliance that has a variable cost of $4 per unit. The sales manager has estimated probabilities of achieving annual sales levels for various selling prices as shown in the following chart:

	Selling Price			
Sales Level (Units)	$ 4	$ 5	$ 6	$ 7
20,000	—	—	20%	80%
30,000	—	10%	40%	20%
40,000	50%	50%	20%	—
50,000	50%	40%	20%	—

2. The division's current profit rate is 5 percent on annual sales of $1,200,000; an investment of $400,000 is needed to finance these sales. The company's basis for measuring divisional success is return on investment.
3. Management is also considering the following two alternative plans submitted by employees for improving operations in the home appliances division:

Green believes that sales volume can be doubled by greater promotional effort, but his method would lower the profit rate to 4 percent of sales and require an additional investment of $100,000.

Gold favors eliminating some unprofitable appliances and improving efficiency by adding $200,000 in capital equipment. His methods would decrease sales volume by 10 percent but improve the profit rate to 7 percent.

4. Black, White, and Gray, three franchised home appliance dealers, have requested short-term financing from the company. The dealers have agreed to repay the loans within 3 years and to pay Benjamin Industries 5 percent of net income for the 3-year period for the use of the funds. The following table summarizes by dealer the financing requested and the total remittances (principal plus 5 percent of net income) expected at the end of each year:

	Black	White	Gray
Financing requested	$ 80,000	$40,000	$30,000
Remittances expected at end of—			
Year 1	$ 10,000	$25,000	$10,000
Year 2	40,000	30,000	15,000
Year 3	70,000	5,000	15,000
Total remittances	$120,000	$60,000	$40,000

Management believes these financing requests should be granted only if the annual pretax return to the company exceeds the target internal rate of 20 percent on investment.

REQUIRED

a. Prepare a schedule computing the expected incremental income for each of the sales prices proposed for the new product. The schedule should include the expected sales levels in units (weighted according to the sales manager's estimated probabilities), the expected total monetary sales, expected variable costs, and the expected incremental income.

b. Prepare schedules computing (1) the company's current rate of return on investment in the home appliances division, and the anticipated rates of return under the alternative suggestions made by (2) Green and (3) Gold.

c. Prepare a schedule to compute the net present value of the investment opportunities of financing Black, White, and Gray. The schedule should determine if the discounted cash flows expected from (1) Black, (2) White, and (3) Gray would be more or less than the amounts of Benjamin Industries' investment in loans to each of the three dealers.

CASES

Case 15-1
Uniform Cash
Flows with Salvage
Value

After working several years as a corporate pilot, Jim Largo saved enough money to buy a used airplane and start the Largo Air Charter Service. He has found two airplanes that would meet his needs and are within his price range.

The first airplane is a twin Spinwell Bison with an asking price of $96,250. Jim estimates that the airplane has a useful life of 12 years and a salvage value of $16,000.

The second airplane is a twin Stallmore Shotput with an asking price of $86,975. This airplane is somewhat older, and Jim estimates it has a useful life of 10 years and a salvage value of $15,000.

Operating costs for both airplanes are similar. If Jim charges competitive rates, he estimates that his net cash inflow from operating the charter service will be $18,000 per year. Jim feels that starting a charter service is feasible only if he can earn a minimum 14 percent return on his airplane investments.

REQUIRED

a. Find the net present value of each airplane.
b. Compute the internal rate of return on each airplane rounded to the nearest whole decimal.
c. Which airplane do you recommend to Jim?

Case 15-2
Cost of Capital and Alternative Investments

Marissa Corporation has the following securities making up its capital structure:

Bonds payable: $5,000,000, 10.68% trading in the market at 60
Bonds payable: $2,500,000, 13.44% trading in the market at 80
Preferred stock: 20,000 shares, $7.75, $100 par, trading in the market at $50 per share
Common stock: 100,000 shares, $10 par, trading in the market at $40 per share
Retained earnings: $3,450,000

The company pays $7.36 of cash dividends on the common stock each year. It is subject to a 30 percent income tax rate. Recently the company's management has been considering expansion by means of acquisition of retail outlets. Two opportunities are available at this time that must be evaluated. Estimated data on the two store locations are provided below:

	Location T	Location S
Asking price	$4,000,000	$3,750,000
Portion allocated to land	220,000	100,000
Estimated salvage value of land and bldg.	400,000	300,000
Estimated useful life	16 years	15 years
Estimated sales revenue	$1,600,000	$1,650,000
Estimated product costs and operating expenses	860,000	920,000

The company uses straight-line depreciation. Depreciation expense is not included in the above figures. The company wants to use several evaluation methods to decide which alternative to select.

REQUIRED

a. Compute the cost of capital.
b. Find the net present value of each project at the cost of capital.
c. Find the internal rate of return for each project.
d. Compute the pretax accounting rate of return using average investment as the base.
e. Compute the payback and payback reciprocal.
f. Discuss which alternative is preferable.

CHAPTER 16
Capital Budgeting: Additional Issues

The capital budgeting evaluation methods discussed in Chapter 15 provide managers with valuable information for analyzing proposed capital projects. In this chapter, we use these evaluation methods as we introduce some additional capital budgeting issues that are often encountered when projects are evaluated and the capital budget is prepared and incorporated in the master budget. Included in this chapter is a discussion of ranking capital investment projects when the number of acceptable projects exceeds the available investment funds; the impact of income taxes on capital budgeting; and the sensitivity of investment projects to changes in the variables used to evaluate the projects. Before proceeding to these topics, however, we discuss briefly some factors other than project evaluation that may influence capital budgeting decisions.

OTHER INFLUENCES ON CAPITAL BUDGETING DECISIONS

The decision to undertake a capital project involves far more than simply determining whether a project satisfies some criteria or ranks higher than another project. Other factors that influence management's evaluation of projects include general economic conditions, company growth policies, the risk of the proposed project, and the availability of investment funds.

Economic Conditions

A strong economy is an inducement to make capital investments

The general state of the economy and changes in economic conditions affect business operations and manager's decision-making outlook. If the economy is slowing down, managers may be reluctant to expand operations with capital investments because a slowdown in the economy may mean a reduction of sales, an increase in idle capacity, and a decrease in earnings. When managers perceive favorable economic conditions, they may expand operations to increase operating capacity, sales, and earnings. In the face of inflation, there may be a tendency to increase productive capacity now to avoid expected increases in the cost of buildings and equipment in the future.

Economic changes do not affect all businesses alike. Leisure, recreation, and luxury services and products typically experience a decline in demand during economic downturns. Basic needs such as food, fuel, and transportation experience fairly stable demand and tend to be relatively unaffected by economic downturns. On the other hand, the demand for basics usually does not increase substantially during economic upturns when leisure and luxury products experience strong demand.

Managers evaluate capital budgeting decisions in light of current economic conditions and their expected effect on the firm. General economic conditions might indicate the need for expansion, but a manager will be reluctant to authorize an addition to a store if sales are declining because a competitor opened a store nearby. A wise manager may authorize construction of a capital project in the face of a decline in economic conditions if it appears that idle capacity will enable the firm to perform some of its own construction and impending high inflation rates dictate spending the funds now rather than later.

A sluggish economy may cause curtailment in capital projects

If tight money conditions and cash shortages loom on the horizon, managers often look to the capital expenditure budget for spending cuts. Many businesses sharply curtail capital expenditures to conserve cash during severe economic downturns.

Growth Policies

Too much growth can lead to unmanageable operations

A prosperous company may have more profitable investment alternatives than it can manage successfully. Rather than accept all potentially profitable projects, a firm should accept as many as it can manage effectively, starting with the most profitable. Some managers find it hard to reject investment proposals that look profitable, especially if they evaluate each proposal independently. However, unmanaged growth can turn potentially profitable investments into unprofitable mistakes. There are many examples of successful firms whose management became overzealous with growth policies and suddenly found themselves facing bankruptcy. Capital budgeting policy should be developed in accordance with a reasonable overall growth policy.

Risk Evaluation

Risk is a natural aspect of business and professional activities. Business risk is the possibility that objectives may not be achieved. A significant element of capital budgeting decisions is the estimate of future cash flows from the capital project. Cash flows are easier to predict for some projects than for others. For example, a contractor specializing in the construction of commercial buildings can predict cash flow for a new contract better than a contractor who is experienced in home construction and is bidding on a commercial building for the first time.

In capital budgeting, risk is usually defined in terms of the potential amount of fluctuation in the cash flows of a project. The greater the possible fluctuation in cash flows, the riskier the project. One of the problems with the capital budgeting evaluation methods discussed in Chapter 15 is that none of them have an explicit adjustment for risk. About the only feature is that most of the models weight earlier cash flows more heavily than later cash flows.

To be acceptable, the more risky projects must offer greater expected returns than less risky projects. Sometimes high-risk, high-return projects are viewed as a separate investment category for which a specific amount of funds is earmarked. Money invested in new high-risk ventures is called **venture capital.** There are many companies that provide funds for such investments to potentially profitable new firms. Investors providing venture capital are willing to accept high risks in exchange for especially high returns if the new firm is successful.

Managers require high return in exchange for high risk

Intuitive Factors

Experience, a good business sense, and intuition are often valuable aids in making capital budgeting decisions. Consequently, the capital budget may reflect decisions based on these kinds of inputs as well as data from the capital budgeting models. Less structured methods of project evaluation, sometimes referred to as "seat-of-the-pants" techniques or "by-gut-and-by-golly" methods, may provide valuable insight into a particular project. There are many managers with good performance records who do not use formal methods of evaluating capital projects.

Capital Rationing

The process of selecting the more desirable projects from many profitable investments is called **capital rationing.** Like any rationing, it is designed to maximize the benefits available from using scarce resources. In the case of capital projects, the scarce resources are investment funds, and the benefits are the returns on the investment. When a company does not have the funds to support all the capital projects that appear acceptable, it will use capital rationing to determine which projects to fund.

There is seldom enough money to fund all available projects

Some projects are **mutually exclusive,** which means that the acceptance of one precludes the acceptance of another. For example, if a proposal to erect an office building on a parcel of land is accepted, the same parcel of land cannot be used to build a production plant. Some projects are **complementary,** which means that the acceptance of one dictates the acceptance of the other. For example, the decision to build a warehouse to store large amounts of inventory may require the purchase of lift trucks to handle the inventory. Still other projects are independent of one another and are simply part of the entire set of alternatives to be evaluated. When several independent or mutually exclusive projects satisfy project acceptance criteria, they may be ranked according to their ability to achieve the firm's goals. We now show how managers evaluate and rank a set of proposed capital investment projects.

EVALUATING MULTIPLE PROJECTS

Evaluating and ranking the acceptability of a number of different projects poses some problems. Difficulties occur because of

1. Unequal project lives
2. Budget constraints

3. Mutually exclusive projects
4. Evaluation methods that produce different rankings
5. Evaluation methods that cannot be used with all projects

Below we discuss some aspects of project ranking.

Project Ranking

To illustrate the ranking issue we use five projects, A through E, shown in Figure 16-1. These projects are evaluated by a company that has $250,000 available for capital investment projects. The company estimates its cost of capital at 15 percent. The five projects are evaluated using the IRR, NPV, PI, and payback methods. The accounting rate of return and payback reciprocal are not used because some of the projects have nonuniform cash flows. The idea is to compare the five projects and determine which are the most desirable.

Figure 16-1. Cash flows and results of project evaluation for five investment projects. Each evaluation method results in a different preference ranking for the five projects.

			Project Cash Flows		
Year	A	B	C	D	E
0	$(50,000)	$(40,900)	$(86,800)	$(115,000)	$(30,000)
1	15,000	20,000	42,000	30,300	7,200
2	15,000	16,000	30,000	30,300	7,200
3	15,000	12,000	28,000	30,300	7,200
4	15,000	10,000	25,000	30,300	7,200
5	15,000			70,000	7,200
6	15,000				7,200
7					7,200
8					7,200
9					7,200
10					7,200

			Project Evaluation		
IRR	19.9%	18.0%	18.2%	17.0%	20.2%
NPV	$6,767	$2,197	$5,110	$6,308	$6,135
PI	1.14	1.05	1.06	1.05	1.20
Payback	3.3	2.4	2.5	3.8	4.2

If the projects are ranked according to each evaluation method the result is the following:

Rank	IRR	NPV	PI	Payback
1	E	A	E	B
2	A	D	A	C
3	C	E	C	A
4	B	C	B and D	D
5	D	B		E

Different project evaluation methods result in different project rankings

The data above indicate that there is no consensus about which is the most desirable and least desirable project. Each evaluation method provides a different project ranking. Project E, which has the highest internal rate of return, ranks third using net present value and last using payback. Project B, with the fastest payback, ranks fourth or fifth using the other methods.

Which ranking is correct? Unfortunately, there is no obvious answer. Each method has advocates who believe that the information provided by that method is most useful for making capital budgeting decisions. Most financial analysts prefer discounted cash flow methods because they are based on the time value of money. But three of the methods employed in this example are discounted cash flow methods, and they yield different rankings. There is no correct answer to the ranking question, only knowledgeable opinions.

Why the Differences in Ranking?

Evaluation method assumptions cause conflicting project rankings

The reason for the differences in ranks is the different sizes and lives of the projects and the assumptions underlying the evaluation methods. The net present value method is based on the assumption that cash flows are reinvested at the cost of capital. The IRR method assumes cash flows are reinvested at the internal rate of return. To illustrate, let us look at two projects ranked according to NPV and IRR, by a company whose cost of capital is 12 percent.

	Project X	Project Y
Cost	$4,833	$3,127
Annual cash inflows	$1,000	$1,000
Life	10 years	5 years
IRR	16%	18%
NPV	$817	$478

Project X ranks higher than project Y using the net present value method, but project Y ranks higher using IRR. To compare the projects over the entire 10-year span of project X, we need to determine the amount to which the cash inflows of project Y will accumulate by the end of the 10-year period. Assuming that the cash inflows from each project can be reinvested at the project's internal rate of return, project Y yields the following future value at the end of 10 years:

Project Y:

Years 1–5: Future value of annuity of $1,000
@ 18% for 5 periods = 7.15421 × $1,000
= $7,154

Years 6–10: Future value of $7,154 invested for
5 periods at 18% = 2.28776 × $7,154
= $16,367

If, however, we assume that at the end of 5 years the funds are reinvested at the cost of capital instead of the IRR, project Y accumulates to a future value of $12,608, computed as follows:

Project Y:

Years 1–5: Future value of annuity of $1,000

@ 18% for 5 periods = 7.15421 × $1,000

= $7,154

Years 6–10: Future value of $7,154 invested for

5 periods at 12% = 1.76234 × $7,154

= $12,608

NPV tends to favor projects with longer lives

IRR tends to favor projects with shorter lives

The key issue is, At what rate can cash inflows be reinvested? The internal rate of return method assumes that all cash inflows are reinvested at the IRR of the project. The net present value method assumes that cash inflows from the project are reinvested at the cost of capital. As a result of these assumptions the IRR method tends to favor projects with shorter lives while the NPV method favors those with longer lives. Again, there is no general solution to the problem. Managers should understand the characteristics of each method and take them into account when making capital investment decisions.

Budget Constraints and Indivisible Projects

The company evaluating the five projects in Figure 16-1 has $250,000 available to invest in capital projects. If the company decides to select projects based on their NPV ranking, the following project ranking results:

Project	Cost	NPV
A	$ 50,000	$6,767
D	115,000	6,308
E	30,000	6,135
C	86,800	5,110
B	40,900	2,197

The optimal combination of projects may include a project that is less acceptable than an excluded project

If the first three projects, A, D, and E, are accepted, $195,000 of the capital budget funds are used up, leaving only $55,000. This is not enough for project C, the next most desirable project. Capital projects are often not divisible into parts. It may not be possible to adopt only part of project C. How should the optimal combination of projects be selected? In a simple situation such as this one, management may use trial and error to select the best combination, which turns out to be all the projects except C. The net present value computation for this combination is shown at top of page 581:

Project	Cost	+ NPV	= PV of Cash Flows
A	$ 50,000	$6,767	$ 56,767
D	115,000	6,308	121,308
E	30,000	6,135	36,135
B	40,900	2,197	43,097
Totals	$235,900		$257,307

Net present value = $257,307 − $235,900 = $21,407

Profitability index = $257,307/$235,900 = 1.091

Using trial and error to select the best combination of projects is not feasible with a large number of project combinations. Quantitative methods such as integer programming or linear programming may be used in such cases. Linear programming is discussed in Chapter 25.

Suppose the company decides to select its projects based on the internal rate of return. The five projects are ranked as follows:

Project	Cost	IRR
E	$ 30,000	20.2%
A	50,000	19.9
C	86,800	18.2
B	40,900	18.0
D	115,000	17.0

The highest percentage return does not necessarily provide the highest total return if all the funds are not invested

Again, trial and error may be used to select the best combination of projects within the $250,000 budget constraint. The weighted average internal rate of return is computed for each feasible combination of projects. The best combination again consists of all projects except C. The calculation of the weighted average return of this group of projects is as follows:

Project	Cost	× IRR	= Return
E	$ 30,000	20.2%	$ 6,060
A	50,000	19.9	9,950
B	40,900	18.2	7,444
D	115,000	17.0	19,550
Totals	$235,900		$43,004

Weighted average return = $43,004/$235,900 = .1823

Another method of computing the weighted average return is to multiply each internal rate of return by the proportion of the investment that yields that rate. The computation is shown at top of page 582:

	Cost/Total	×	Return	=	Weighted Return
E	$ 30,000/$235,900	×	.202	=	.0257
A	50,000/ 235,900	×	.199	=	.0422
B	40,900/ 235,900	×	.182	=	.0315
D	115,000/ 235,900	×	.170	=	.0829
Weighted average yield					.1823

In many cases budget constraints are not as rigid as implied here. If a highly desirable project faces rejection due to insufficient funds, management may decide to allocate more funds to the capital budget. Frequently, funding for capital projects is only decided upon when the projects have been evaluated.

THE IMPACT OF TAXES ON CAPITAL BUDGETING

Income taxes have a significant effect on cash flows from investments and should be taken into account when making capital budgeting decisions. The impact of taxes can be complex and must be carefully analyzed. In addition to federal income taxes, many corporations pay state and city income taxes. Federal and state tax laws also provide various tax incentives to encourage capital investment, business expansion, and increases in employment.

Corporate income taxes are imposed at the rate of 15 percent of the first $25,000 of net income, 18 percent of the next $25,000, and 48 percent of all income above $50,000. But net income for tax purposes is not necessarily accounting income. Companies may choose one accounting method for tax purposes and another for accounting purposes, frequently resulting in deferred charges or credits that affect future cash flows.

Effect of Depreciation on Cash Flow

Depreciation is an expense that does not require the use of cash payments, but it has an effect on cash flows because it is a tax deductible expense. For example, a corporation plans to install a soft-drink vending machine in its employee lounge. The cost of the machine is $2,000. It is expected to generate $8,000 of revenue each year and the cost of the soft drinks sold through the machine is expected to be $6,800 per year. Maintenance and electricity are expected to cost $450 per year. The machine has a useful life of 5 years and no salvage value.

The expected net cash inflow from operating the machine is $750 per year, calculated as follows:

Revenue		$8,000
Less cost of merchandise	$6,800	
Maintenance and power	450	7,250
Net cash inflow before taxes		$ 750

The net cash inflow is not accounting income. It does not include depreciation expense nor income tax expense. Depreciation expense does not reduce the cash flow, but tax expense does. If the corporation is subject to a tax rate of 40 percent, the income tax is

Net cash inflow before taxes	$750
Less depreciation	400
Taxable income	350
Tax rate	.40
Income tax	$140

Depreciation affects cash flow because it reduces taxes

The after-tax cash inflow from the vending machine project is $750 less $140 tax, or $610, which is the net cash flow to be used for evaluating the project. This example illustrates an important point. Depreciation does not require a cash outlay, but it does affect cash flows because of its effect on taxes. For this reason, many companies have used accelerated depreciation to reduce taxes in the early years of a project's life.

Tax Incentives

The main purpose of taxes is to generate revenue to finance government programs and activities. But taxes also are designed to accomplish other purposes—to encourage certain behavior in taxpayers. For example, very high tax rates may be established in some situations, not to generate revenue but to discourage the manufacture or use of undesirable products or activities. High import taxes are examples of taxes that discourage purchase of some foreign products. On the other hand, tax laws can be designed to encourage activities that government views as desirable. These types of tax laws—called **tax incentives**—induce people and organizations to undertake some desired activity in order to reduce their tax burden.

Some taxes are designed to discourage economically undesirable activities

Examples of tax incentives are numerous. Rules on accelerated depreciation and investment tax credits are intended to stimulate capital investment. Tax credits have been available for research and development, increasing the number of employees, rehabilitating old buildings, and installing solar- or wind-powered equipment. Another tax incentive intended to stimulate investment is a preferential tax rate on capital gains. We confine our discussion to tax incentives that affect capital projects.

Some taxes encourage activities that stimulate the economy

Prior to 1981, depreciation for accounting purposes and for tax purposes could be based on any of the generally accepted methods, such as straight-line, double declining balance, or sum-of-the-years'-digits. Businesses often used straight-line depreciation for accounting purposes and an accelerated method for tax purposes. Over the entire life of the project, the same total amount of depreciation is reported with either method. However, with accelerated methods, taxable income is reduced in the early years of an asset's life, creating larger cash flows when their present value is greatest. Accelerated depreciation may be used only for assets acquired prior to 1981.

Accelerated Cost Recovery System (ACRS).   The Economic Recovery Tax Act of 1981 provided changes in the way capital assets are depreciated. The act established the **Accelerated Cost Recovery System (ACRS)**, which classifies all assets into one of five categories, and depending on an asset's classification, allows writing off its cost for tax purposes over periods of either 3, 5, 10, or 15 years. The 3-year class is for motor vehicles and equipment used in research and development. The 5-year class is for most other machinery and equipment. The 10-year class is primarily for public utility property, and the 15-year class is for real estate and other public utility property. Figure 16-2 illustrates the ACRS rates to be used for depreciating assets. Use of these rates is basically mandatory, although some modifications are permitted.

ACRS depreciation is mandatory for tax purposes

The ACRS allows businesses to amortize the cost of fixed assets for tax purposes over a shorter period than the assets' physical lives. That is, businesses can recover the cost of their assets by writing off their cost over a relatively short period for tax purposes rather than over the physical life of the asset. That is why the system is called **cost recovery** rather than depreciation, although it is, in fact, an accelerated depreciation system. This tax incentive makes capital projects attractive by making their net cash inflows larger in the early years.

Investment Tax Credit (ITC).   The **investment tax credit** is a tax incentive that has been provided by Congress on several occasions when the government wanted to stimulate the economy. It is a tax provision that permits

Asset Amortization Schedules in Percent
Under the Accelerated Cost Recovery System

	Equipment Class Life in Years				Real Estate Month Asset Is Placed in Service											
Year	3	5	10	15	1	2	3	4	5	6	7	8	9	10	11	12
1	25	15	8	5	12	11	10	9	8	7	6	5	4	3	2	1
2	38	22	14	10	10	10	11	11	11	11	11	11	11	11	11	12
3	37	21	12	9	9	9	9	9	10	10	10	10	10	10	10	10
4		21	10	8	8	8	8	8	8	8	9	9	9	9	9	9
5		21	10	7	7	7	7	7	7	7	8	8	8	8	8	8
6			10	7	6	6	6	6	7	7	7	7	7	7	7	7
7			9	6	6	6	6	6	6	6	6	6	6	6	6	6
8			9	6	6	6	6	6	6	6	5	6	6	6	6	6
9			9	6	6	6	6	6	5	6	5	5	5	6	6	6
10			9	6	5	6	5	6	5	5	5	5	5	5	6	5
11				6	5	5	5	5	5	5	5	5	5	5	5	5
12				6	5	5	5	5	5	5	5	5	5	5	5	5
13				6	5	5	5	5	5	5	5	5	5	5	5	5
14				6	5	5	5	5	5	5	5	5	5	5	5	5
15				6	5	5	5	5	5	5	5	5	5	5	5	5
16						1	1	2	2	3	3	4	4	4	5

Figure 16-2. Cost recovery rates enacted by the Economic Recovery Tax Act of 1981. The depreciation rate is a specified percentage each year. Each column adds up to 100 percent. Salvage value is not used with ACRS. The 10-year and 15-year classes are for utility property only. Real estate is amortized over 15 years, with the annual percentage depending on the month it was placed in service.

purchasers of equipment and some other qualifying assets to reduce their tax liability in the year of asset purchase by a specified percentage of the equipment's cost. The 1981 tax act modified the investment tax credit available to purchasers of qualified assets. Assets in the 3-year ACRS class have a 6 percent investment credit. Equipment in the 5-, 10-, and 15-year classes qualifies for a 10 percent investment tax credit.

The investment tax credit is a direct tax reduction

The investment credit is a powerful incentive because it causes an immediate reduction in taxes for the tax year in which assets are purchased. For example, a company that buys equipment for $100,000 can reduce its tax liability in the year of purchase by $10,000. If the 10 percent or 6 percent investment tax credit is taken, the asset's cost subject to ACRS amortization must be reduced by one-half of the ITC. In this example, claiming a $10,000 ITC on a $100,000 asset means that only $95,000 of the asset's cost can be written off over 5 years in accordance with the ACRS. The investment credit, in effect, provides a 10 percent discount on the purchase of equipment, making such investments attractive as capital projects.

Alternatively, the company may elect to apply ACRS depreciation on the entire cost of the asset, in which case the investment tax credit is only 8 percent instead of 10 percent. For 3-year assets, the 6 percent ITC is reduced to 4 percent if the entire cost of the asset is amortized using ACRS.

We examine again the $2,000 vending machine investment and include in the analysis the ITC and ACRS depreciation. We assume that the machine is acquired in 1985 and the 10 percent investment tax credit is claimed, so ACRS depreciation in the first year is 15 percent of $1,900. The tax effect is computed as follows:

Net cash inflow before taxes	$ 750
Less cost recovery, 15% of $1,900	285
Taxable income	465
Tax rate	.40
Income tax	186
Less investment credit, 10% of cost	(200)
Income tax saving	$ (14)

Instead of a tax of $140 as computed previously, there is actually a $14 tax saving in the year the vending machine is acquired. This means that the first-year cash inflow is $750 plus the tax saving of $14 for a total first-year inflow of $764.

Comprehensive Example of Tax Effects

To illustrate how taxes affect capital budgeting, we use the following comprehensive example. At the beginning of 1985, Larnet Corporation is planning its capital projects for the 1986 calendar year budget. Included in the plan is the replacement of some old equipment with a new machine to be acquired at the end of 1985. The old equipment was acquired in 1981 for $12,000 and, using ACRS depreciation, its cost will be fully written off for tax purposes at the end of 1985. However, the equipment will have a remaining useful life of 2 years beyond 1985. Its life could be extended for yet another 3 years by investing $5,500 to renovate the machine when its useful life is over. Whether or not the machine is renovated, it would have no salvage value at the end of its current or extended life. The cost of operating the old machine is $10,000 per year, not including depreciation. Larnet Corporation is subject to an effective corporate income tax rate of 30 percent. If the new equipment is acquired the old machine would be sold for $2,000 at the end of 1985.

Evaluating alternative choices of action is complicated by tax laws

The new equipment costs $20,000 and has a useful life of 5 years, at the end of which the machine will have a salvage value of $3,000. For tax purposes, its cost can be amortized over 5 years using ACRS, starting with the year of purchase. The cost of operating the new equipment is $7,000 per year, not including depreciation expense. An investment tax credit of 10 percent of the machine's cost may be taken by the company in the year of acquisition.

The company has the alternative of keeping the existing equipment or disposing of it and acquiring the new machine. It must have the equipment in order to carry on its normal operations. Either the old or the new equipment will result in the same amount of operating revenue, so the least costly alternative should be selected.

All cash flows are assumed to occur at the end of each year. The cash flow on the old machine, including the effect of taxes, may be computed as shown in Figure 16-3, assuming renovation of the machine at the end of 1987:

The tax savings in the schedule are the income taxes that will not have to be paid because the operating and depreciation expense of the equipment are deducted from the company's revenues. In other words, if the company did not have the expenses from this machine, its net income would be higher and its taxes would also be higher. But these expenses reduce the tax so they also reduce the cash outflow from operating the equipment.

Schedule of Costs and Cash Flows on Old Machine

	1985	1986	1987	1988	1989	1990
Operating expense	$10,000	$10,000	$10,000	$10,000	$10,000	$10,000
Depreciation[a]	2,520			1,375	2,090	2,035
Total expense	12,520	10,000	10,000	11,375	12,090	12,035
Tax savings[b]	(3,756)	(3,000)	(3,000)	(3,413)	(3,627)	(3,611)
Depreciation[c]	(2,520)	0	0	(1,375)	(2,090)	(2,035)
Renovation			5,500			
Cash outflow	$ 6,244	$ 7,000	$12,500	$ 6,587	$ 6,373	$ 6,389

[a] 1985 depreciation is the ACRS 5th-year rate of 21% of the original $12,000 cost. The $5,500 renovation is amortized using ACRS 3-year rates.
[b] Total expense × 30% tax rate.
[c] Depreciation was added to operating expense to arrive at total expense so the tax saving can be computed. Now depreciation is deducted from total expense because it is not a cash outflow, in order to arrive at a cash flow figure.

Figure 16-3. Analysis of costs and cash flows for an existing piece of equipment. The decision must be made whether to keep the equipment or replace it with a new machine.

If the old machine is not renovated but is discarded at the end of 1987, the cash flow is the same for 1985 and 1986, and it is $7,000 in 1987. At the end of 1987, the machine would have to be replaced.

If the old equipment is sold at the end of 1985 and the new machine is acquired, an entirely different set of cash flows can be expected. When the new machine is purchased, the cash outflow is affected by the investment credit as well as the sale of the old equipment. The book value of the old equipment will be zero at the end of 1985, so the entire proceeds of the sale are taxed as a gain. The investment credit in this case is 10 percent of the cost of the new equipment.

Cost of new machine at end of 1985		$20,000
Less proceeds from sale of old machine	$2,000	
30 percent tax on gain	(600)	
Net proceeds		(1,400)
Less investment credit of 10% on new machine		(2,000)
Net cash outflow to acquire new machine in 1985		$16,600

The timing of investments can have a strong impact on tax savings

This calculation shows that the net cash outflow required to purchase the new equipment is $16,600 at the end of 1985. By acquiring the new equipment prior to 1986, the company can claim the investment tax credit and can also use ACRS depreciation on the new machine for 1985, although the machine is not really used in 1985. The investment tax credit is an important cash saving. In this example it is assumed to be available at the time the equipment is purchased, but in reality the ITC will become available when the next quarterly tax return is filed early in 1986. The cash flows during the life of the new machine are shown in Figure 16-4.

Note carefully the effect of taxes in Figures 16-3 and 16-4. ACRS depreciation is not a cash outflow, but it is an expense used in computing

Schedule of Costs and Cash Flows on New Machine

	1985	1986	1987	1988	1989	1990
Operating expense	$ 0	$ 7,000	$ 7,000	$ 7,000	$ 7,000	$ 7,000
Depreciation[a]	2,850	4,180	3,990	3,990	3,990	0
Total expense	2,850	11,180	10,990	10,990	10,990	7,000
Tax savings[b]	(855)	(3,354)	(3,297)	(3,297)	(3,297)	(2,100)
Depreciation[c]	(2,850)	(4,180)	(3,990)	(3,990)	(3,990)	0
Gain net of tax[d]						(2,100)
Cash outflow	$ (855)	$ 3,646	$ 3,703	$ 3,703	$ 3,703	$ 2,800

[a] Based on 5-year ACRS applied on $20,000 cost less $2,000 investment tax credit.
[b] .30 of total expense.
[c] Deducted from total expense to arrive at cash flow.
[d] $3,000 salvage value less 30% tax.

Figure 16-4. Analysis of costs and cash flows for a new piece of equipment. The decision must be made whether to acquire the equipment and use it to replace an old machine.

income taxes. In some cases, the gain from sales of assets may be taxed at capital gains rates, which are lower than rates on ordinary income.

Once the cash flows have been determined for both the old and new equipment, the analysis proceeds as before, using any of the capital project evaluation methods already discussed. We now compare the two alternatives using the net present value method with a 15 percent cost of capital.

Either machine will generate the same amount of revenue, so the decision is to determine which machine will have the smaller cash outflow from operations. A $16,600 net cash outflow is required to purchase the new machine, but in 1985, the new machine will produce a net cash inflow of $855 due to the ability to depreciate the machine in the year of acquisition. Therefore the net cash outflow in 1985 for the new machine is $15,745 ($16,600 − $855).

Whether or not the new machine is acquired, the 1985 costs of the old machine will be incurred. Therefore the 1985 cash outflow on the old machine is not relevant in the analysis. Only differential costs and cash flows are included in the comparison of the two machines. Discounting the cash flows to the end of 1985, which is the point in time when one of the alternatives is adopted, we get the following present values for the two machines' cash outflows:

	Cash Outflows			Present Value	
Year	Old Machine	New Machine	PV factor	Old	New
1985		$15,745	1.00000		$15,745
1986	$ 7,000	3,646	.86957	$ 6,087	3,170
1987	12,500	3,703	.75614	9,452	2,800
1988	6,587	3,703	.65752	4,331	2,435
1989	6,373	3,703	.57175	3,644	2,117
1990	6,389	2,800	.49718	3,176	1,392
Present value of cash outflows				$26,690	$27,659

Keeping the old machine and renovating it in 1987 would result in a smaller present value of future cash outflows than acquiring the new machine now. Therefore the old machine should be kept and renovated and the new machine should not be acquired.

SENSITIVITY ANALYSIS OF CAPITAL BUDGETING DECISIONS

Some projects are more sensitive to errors in estimates of variables than others

Capital budgeting decisions are made using estimates of future cash flows, often for many years into the future. Even the best-informed and most talented managers cannot hope to make completely accurate estimates. Economic conditions, competitor actions, managerial turnover, and changes in customer preferences are but a few factors that can cause actual results to differ from estimated results. The fact that actual results differ from estimates does not deter management from making capital budgeting decisions. Many management decisions involve some estimate of future events. What makes capital budgeting estimates so critical is the length of time covered by the estimate and the amount of money involved in the decision.

Because managers cannot avoid errors in making capital budgeting cash flow estimates, they attempt to measure the cost consequences of inaccurate estimates. **Sensitivity analysis** is the process of determining the effect on net present value or the internal rate of return of incorrectly estimating one or more parameters used in the evaluation of the capital project. For example, what is the effect on NPV or IRR of overestimating a project's monthly cash inflow by $100, or what is the effect of underestimating the cost of capital by 2 percent? Usually, sensitivity analysis is performed after the actual cost flows have occurred. However, managers may attempt to measure sensitivity of estimation errors in advance by using several alternative estimates of various parameters. We demonstrate sensitivity analysis by means of the following example.

A piece of equipment costs $9,080, has a useful life of 6 years, no salvage value, and provides estimated cash savings of $2,400 per year. The cost of capital is 12 percent. Based on these estimates, the net present value of the investment is $787 and its internal rate of return is 15 percent.

Sensitivity can be tested for any variable that is estimated

The net present value and the IRR are based on several estimates about the project—expected life, annual cash flow, salvage value, and cost of capital. If one or more of those estimates is wrong, the actual net present value of the project or its actual IRR may be different than calculated. Using sensitivity analysis, managers can measure the effect on net present value or IRR of estimating incorrectly the value of the parameters used in computing NPV and IRR. We look first at the sensitivity of incorrectly estimating the cash inflows.

Sensitivity of Error in Cash Flow

The estimated cash inflow used to compute NPV and IRR is $2,400 per year. Management is concerned that actual cash flows may turn out to be only $2,100 per year. What is the impact of overestimating cash inflows by $300 per year? Using the NPV method the following computation can be made:

Present value of cash savings	$2,100 × 4.11141	$8,634
Present value of cash outflows		9,080
Net present value		$ (446)

The original net present value was $787 and the NPV with the revised cash inflow estimate is $(446). Therefore the impact of the $300 per year difference in cash flows is $1,233. In other words, the difference in estimated cash flows caused a $1,233 difference in the net present value.

The same type of sensitivity analysis can be performed using the internal rate of return rather than the net present value. The calculation is as follows:

IRR with expected cash flows:
$9,080/$2,400 = 3.78333   From PV table, $n = 6$ 15.0 percent

IRR with actual cash flows:
$9,080/$2,100 = 4.32381   By interpolation   10.2 percent
Difference in internal rate of return   4.8 percent

Adopting the project would result in about 4.8 percent less return than expected. This type of analysis, although interesting, does not necessarily tell management how much the estimation error will cost the company.

Cost of Estimation Error

Lost income or unexpected expenses may be the cost of an incorrect estimate

The **cost of estimation error,** sometimes called the **cost of prediction error,** is the cost to the firm of incorrectly estimating the value of one or more parameters used in evaluating a capital budgeting project. There are two types of situations in cost of estimation error analysis. In the first, the firm has no other acceptable projects if the project being analyzed is not accepted. In the second case, the firm has other acceptable projects if the one being evaluated is rejected.

No Other Acceptable Projects.   When a company has no acceptable projects other than the one being analyzed, then management's decision is one of accepting or not accepting the project. The cost analysis is merely a comparison of the cost of accepting the project and the cost of not accepting the project.

Sensitivity analysis tells us that if the cash flows from the project are only $2,100 per year, the best decision is to reject the project. If the project is accepted, a cost is incurred. The cost of estimation error can be computed quite easily as follows:

NPV of optimal decision (do not invest) $ 0
Less NPV of original decision given actual cash flows   (446)
Cost of estimation error $446

Suppose, however, that the error in annual cash savings is $100. That is, instead of the expected $2,400 per year, actual cash flow is only $2,300 per year. Then the net present value of the investment is positive, computed as follows:

Present value of cash savings $2,300 × 4.11141 $9,456
Present value of cash outflows   9,080
Net present value $ 376

Errors in estimate sometimes cost nothing

Because the net present value of the investment is positive with either the $2,400 or the $2,300 cash flow, the decision in both cases is to invest in the project, and the cost of estimation error is zero.

NPV of optimal decision	$376
Less NPV of original decision given correct cash flows	376
Cost of estimation error	$ 0

These calculations express the cost of estimation error in terms of net present value. It is important to remember that NPV is not a gain or income and the cost of estimation error is not a loss in the sense that less income is earned or more expense is paid. NPV is simply the difference between two sets of discounted cash flows and its positive or negative sign indicates that the actual return on the investment is larger or smaller than the cost of capital. The actual return on the investment is the internal rate of return.

With no alternative investment, the cost of estimating the incorrect internal rate of return is the annual return that will not be realized because the IRR is lower than expected. With an expected IRR of 15 percent and an actual IRR of 10.2 percent, the cost of estimation error is

Expected annual return $9,080 × .15	$1,362
Actual annual return $9,080 × .102	926
Cost of estimation error	$ 436

An even simpler calculation is to multiply the cost of the project by the difference between expected and actual IRR. In this case the computation is $9,080 × .048 = $436, which yields the same answer.

Other Alternative Projects.   Sometimes organizations have more acceptable capital investment projects than they can undertake. Therefore, management accepts the more desirable projects first. In such situations, if management accepts one project and turns down another, the cost of estimation error is a comparison of the net present value of the accepted investment with the net present value of the best investment not accepted.

Going back to our original example of the equipment with an estimated NPV of $787, we assume that a comparable item of equipment with an expected NPV of $650 was not accepted. The $650 is the benefit of the best investment opportunity not accepted. This amount is an **opportunity cost,** which is the benefit forgone by rejecting an investment. Management gave up the opportunity of the $650 NPV from the drill press, because another investment promised a net present value of $787. But if the cash flow on the accepted project turns out to be only $2,300 instead of $2,400 per year, its actual NPV is $376. The difference between the NPV on the best project rejected and the actual NPV on the project accepted is the cost of estimation error in this type of analysis. The calculation is as follows:

Net present value of best alternative not accepted	$650
Net present value of accepted project with actual cash inflows of $2,300 per year	376
Cost of estimation error	$274

If the internal rate of return of the best alternative investment is 12 percent, the difference between the alternative investment and the investment with the incorrect IRR is 1.8 percent ($12\% - 10.2\%$). In this case the cost of estimation error is

$$\$9,080 \times .018 = \$163$$

Cost of Estimation Error in Estimate of Life

The life of a project is another area where errors in estimate may occur. For example, instead of the expected 6-year life, the actual life of the project is only 5 years. We find the cost of this error using both the NPV and IRR methods. The net present value of the investment with a 5-year life is:

Present value of cash savings	$2,400 × 3.60478	$8,651
Present value of cash outflow		9,080
Net present value		$ (429)

The optimal decision is not to invest in the project, because the NPV is negative. If the investment is made, based on the 6-year life estimate, and there is no alternative investment, the cost of the prediction error is:

NPV of optimal decision (do not invest)	$ 0
NPV of investing if project life is 5 years	(429)
Cost of estimation error	$429

If an alternative investment with a net present value of $200 exists, the cost of estimation error is a $629 sacrifice of net present value.

The internal rate of return on this investment is 10 percent with a 5-year life — 2 percent less than the cost of capital. The IRR is always less than the cost of capital with a negative NPV and more than the cost of capital with a positive NPV, assuming, of course, that the cost of capital was used to calculate the net present value.

Magnitude of Tolerable Error

To be funded, a project must meet specific acceptance criteria, such as a positive net present value or an IRR greater than the firm's costs of capital. Many acceptable projects will provide expected returns greater than the minimum. In such cases, management may want to know the amount of error that can occur in estimating one of the project's variables and still have the

The magnitude of tolerable errors can be evaluated to determine the chance of exceeding the error

project satisfy the firm's minimum acceptance criteria. For example, the expected net present value of the $9,080 machine investment was $787 with the original project data. One of the estimates was the annual cash inflows of $2,400. Management may ask, "How much can the cash inflows fall below the estimated level of $2,400 per year before the net present value of the project becomes zero?" To find the tolerable error, we calculate the amount of annual cash inflow over the project's life that provides a zero net present value. The difference between this amount and management's estimate of cash inflows is the magnitude of tolerable error given the company's capital investment acceptance criteria.

With a cost of capital of 12 percent, the annual cash inflow that will yield a zero NPV is computed as follows:

$$\$9,080/4.11141 = \$2,208$$

Management can tolerate an estimation error of ($2,400 − $2,208), or $192, in the cash inflows and still satisfy its minimum acceptance criteria with the project.

Alternatively, it is possible to compute the minimum acceptable life of the project by computing the present value factor and looking up the number of periods in the 12 percent column of the present value table.

$$f = \$9,080/\$2,400 = 3.78333$$

This factor occurs between 5 and 6 years, and the number of periods may be estimated by interpolation.

Factor for 12 percent and 6 periods	4.11141	4.11141
Computed factor	3.78333	
Factor for 12 percent and 5 periods		3.60478
Difference	.32808	.50663

The life of the project is 6 less .32808/.50663, or 5.35 years. In this case, management could overestimate the life of the project by .65 years and still find the project acceptable.

SUMMARY

Analyzing capital projects using a variety of analysis methods is only one part of the capital budgeting process. The decision to undertake a project includes many other factors, such as current and expected economic conditions, the company's growth policies, and the risks of the various projects. Some very risky projects with potentially high returns may be good candidates as **venture capital** investments.

When several projects are available and the amount of funds is limited, **capital rationing** may have to be used. Some projects are **complementary**, which means that if one is accepted, some other must be accepted also. Some are **mutually exclusive,** which means that accepting one precludes the acceptance of another. Projects can be ranked to determine which are preferable so that the available funds can be rationed among the most suitable projects.

Ranking projects by different evaluation methods may yield conflicting rankings. Projects ranking high with one method may rank low with another because of differences in size of investment and expected life of projects. Budget constraints may dictate selecting a less desirable project and rejecting a more desirable one because the latter requires more funds than are available.

Income taxes have an impact on capital budgeting because they affect the cash flows from capital projects. Depreciation expense does not require the use of funds, but it does affect the amount of income tax and should therefore be taken into account in project evaluations. Depreciation for accounting purposes differs from depreciation required by the **Accelerated Cost Recovery System (ACRS)** for tax purposes. The ACRS and the **investment tax credit** are **tax incentives** designed to stimulate capital investment. Such incentives should be included in capital project analyses because they often have a large impact on cash flows from the project.

Errors in estimating cash flows, salvage value, and expected lives can be evaluated by means of **sensitivity analysis** of capital budgeting decisions. An analysis may also be made of the **cost of estimation error.** It is possible to determine the magnitude of error that can be tolerated in order for the investment to earn the minimum return.

KEY TERMS

accelerated cost recovery system (ACRS) *(584)*
capital rationing *(577)*
complementary projects *(577)*
cost of estimation error *(590)*

investment tax credit *(584)*
mutually exclusive projects *(577)*
sensitivity analysis *(589)*
tax incentives *(583)*
venture capital *(577)*

QUESTIONS

1. "One of the nice things about using discounted cash flow methods for evaluating capital budgeting projects is not having to worry about such irrelevant items as depreciation and taxes. The only relevant variable is the interest rate," says Joe. "You're wrong," replies Frank. "Depreciation and taxes are just as relevant with discounted cash flow methods as with any other method. If you ignore them, you get answers that are meaningless." Respond to these comments.

2. Congress has often used tax incentives to stimulate the economy, and frequently such incentives have affected the capital investment decisions of businesses. Discuss some reasons why tax incentives have been aimed at capital budgeting. How do the investment tax credit and ACRS affect capital budgeting decisions?

EXERCISES

Ex. 16-1
Payback and NPV Evaluation

Problose Company plans to acquire some new equipment for its research and development department. The cost of the equipment is $90,000. It is estimated to have a useful life of 7 years and a salvage value of $10,000. The company estimates that use of the equipment will produce cash savings of $25,000 per year. Its cost of capital is 20 percent.

REQUIRED

a. Compute the payback on the equipment.
b. Compute the payback reciprocal.
c. Compute the net present value.
d. Compute the profitability index.

Ex. 16-2
NPV, PI, and IRR

Bossney Corporation's marketing manager is proposing the acquisition of portable computer terminals for all sales representatives. The terminals would simplify and speed up order processing and would produce cost savings of $10,000 per year. The cost of the new terminals is $27,000, including training the sales representatives to use the terminals. Each terminal has a useful life of 5 years with no salvage value. The company evaluates capital projects using a 17 percent cost of capital.

REQUIRED

a. Compute the net present value of the terminals.
b. Compute the profitability index.
c. Compute the internal rate of return to the nearest whole percent.

Ex. 16-3
Ranking of Two Projects

Billox Company is evaluating a proposal to acquire a new high-precision vertical mill for one of its production plants. The cost of the mill made by Delta Company is $36,500. The machine has an 8-year useful life and is expected to save $9,000 per year in costs. It has no salvage value. A machine made by Gamma Company costs $38,500 and is expected to save $8,000 per year over its 12-year life. It also has no salvage value. The company's cost of capital is 13 percent.

REQUIRED

a. Compute the net present value of the two alternatives using the cost of capital.
b. Compute the internal rate of return for each machine.
c. Rank the machines in order of preference based on your evaluation with each method and discuss any difference in ranking that you may find.

Ex. 16-4
Project Ranking with Discounted Cash Flows

Pillmor Company is investigating two mutually exclusive capital projects. Project A costs $26,900 and has a useful life of 5 years with no salvage value and an annual cash saving of $10,000. Project B costs $38,000 and has a useful life of 10 years and an annual cash saving of $10,000. The company evaluates capital projects using its 17 percent cost of capital.

REQUIRED

a. Compute the net present value of the two projects.
b. Compute the profitability index.
c. Find the internal rate of return for each project.
d. Rank the projects in order of preference using each of the evaluation methods.

Ex. 16-5
Capital Rationing

Blueburr Company is preparing its capital budget and is evaluating several capital projects to determine which should be funded. The company plans to spend $10,000 on capital projects and has a cost of capital of 16 percent. The available projects have the following costs and internal rates of return:

Project	Cost	IRR
V	$1,000	20.0
W	3,000	18.5
X	2,000	19.0
Y	3,500	17.0
Z	6,800	17.5

The company evaluates projects using the IRR method.

REQUIRED

a. Determine the best combination of investments.
b. Compute the weighted average rate of return on the investment combination.

Ex. 16-6
Capital Budgeting
with Taxes

Malinkrod is investigating the purchase of a small hardware store as an investment. The asking price is $48,000. The store operates in leased space with a nonrenewable lease that expires in 15 years. Annual sales are $50,000 and cost of goods sold is 60 percent of sales. Other operating expenses, not including depreciation, are $7,500 per year. Depreciation is $6,000 per year. Malinkrod's marginal tax rate is 48 percent. He has decided that the investment must earn at least a 16 percent return.

REQUIRED

a. Find the annual net cash inflow after taxes for the investment.
b. Evaluate the investment using the NPV and PI methods.

Ex. 16-7
Evaluation of Tax
Incentives

A taxicab costing $12,000 has a 3-year useful life and a salvage value of $2,000. Expected annual operating revenues and expenses are $55,000 and $47,000 respectively, not including ACRS depreciation expense. The vehicle will be put into service at the beginning of 1985. The company has decided to claim the 4 percent investment tax credit and thus amortize the entire cost of the asset. The cost of capital is 20 percent and the income tax rate is 40 percent.

REQUIRED

Using after-tax cash flows based on the accelerated cost recovery system, find the net present value and profitability index of the investment and decide if the investment should be made.

Ex. 16-8
Tax Incentives and
Capital Budgeting

Hoble Company is evaluating the acquisition of a machine that costs $90,000 and is expected to last 5 years with no salvage value. Operating revenues and expenses each year are expected to be $94,000 and $63,000 respectively, not including ACRS depreciation expense. The machine will be put into service at the beginning of 1985. It qualifies for a 10 percent investment credit, which the company plans to claim. The cost of capital is 18 percent and the income tax rate is 40 percent.

REQUIRED

Using after-tax cash flows based on the accelerated cost recovery system, find the net present value and profitability index of the investment and decide whether the investment should be made.

Ex. 16-9
NPV and Cost of
Prediction Error

Mossley Corporation's marketing manager proposed the acquisition of portable computer terminals for all sales representatives. The terminals would simplify and speed up order processing and would produce cost savings of $10,000 per year. The total cost of the new terminals is $23,000, including tax and delivery charges. There is an additional cost of $4,000 to train the sales representatives to use the terminals. Each terminal has a useful life of 5 years with no salvage value. The company evaluates capital projects using the net present value method with a 17 percent cost of capital.

REQUIRED

    a. Compute the net present value of the terminals and determine if they should be acquired.

    b. Find the sensitivity of error if actual cash savings from using the terminal are $9,000 per year.

    c. Find the cost of prediction error if actual cash savings from using the terminal are $9,000 per year and there is no alternative investment.

Ex. 16-10
NPV and Cost of
Estimation Error

Refer to the data in Exercise 16-9 on the acquisition of computer terminals.

REQUIRED

    a. Compute the net present value of the terminals and determine if they should be acquired.

    b. Find the sensitivity of the estimation error if the actual life of the project is 4 years.

    c. Find the cost of estimation error if the actual life of the terminal is only 4 years and no alternative investment exists.

Ex. 16-11
IRR and Sensitivity
Analysis

Qubex Company is evaluating a proposal to acquire a new high-speed punch press requested by one of its shop supervisors. The cost of the punch press is $22,616 including freight and installation. The machine has a 7-year life and is capable of speeding up production sufficiently to save $5,600 per year. It has no salvage value. The supervisor requesting the punch press has been informed that the company cannot fund any investment whose internal rate of return is less than 15 percent.

REQUIRED

    a. Compute the internal rate of return on the new equipment and determine if it should be acquired.

    b. Compute the sensitivity of prediction error if the actual cash savings are only $5,270 per year.

    c. Find the cost of prediction error if the actual cash savings are only $5,270 and there is an alternative investment with the same cost and an annual return of $3,400.

Ex. 16-12
Sensitivity Analysis
with Interpolation

Refer to the data in Exercise 16-11 for the acquisition of a punch press.

REQUIRED

    a. Compute the internal rate of return on the new equipment and determine if it should be acquired.

    b. Compute the sensitivity of prediction error if the actual life of the equipment is only 6 years.

    c. Compute the cost of prediction error assuming no alternative investment.

Ex. 16-13
NPV and Tolerable
Error

Worley Company is evaluating the acquisition of equipment with a cost of $80,000, no salvage value, and an 8-year life. The expected cash flow from using the equipment is $20,000 per year. The company's cost of capital is 15 percent.

REQUIRED

    a. Compute the net present value of the investment.

    b. Determine the magnitude of error in the estimate of cash inflows that the company can tolerate on the project.

Ex. 16-14
IRR and Tolerable
Error

Vigley Company is evaluating the acquisition of equipment with a cost of $60,000, no salvage value, and an 8-year life. The expected cash flow from using the equipment is $14,260 per year. The company evaluates projects using the IRR method and accepts those whose IRR is at least 15 percent.

a. Compute the internal rate of return on the investment.
b. Determine the magnitude of error in the estimate of cash inflows that the company can tolerate on the project.

PROBLEMS

P. 16-1
NPV and PI for
Several Projects

Barton Company is evaluating several investment projects. The following data are available on each.

	Project P	Project Q	Project R
Life	9 years	6 years	12 years
Cost	$150,000	$165,000	$120,000
Annual savings	35,000	46,500	25,000

The company evaluates projects using the NPV method and the profitability index. The cost of capital is 15 percent.

a. Compute the NPV on each project.
b. Find the profitability index for each project.
c. For each evaluation method rank the projects according to their desirability.

P. 16-2
NPV and PI for
Several Projects

Coburn Company is evaluating several capital projects. The following data are available on each.

	Project K	Project L	Project M	Project N
Life	15 years	12 years	6 years	9 years
Cost	$200,000	$185,000	$80,000	$127,500
Annual savings	40,000	36,000	25,000	30,000

The company evaluates projects using the NPV method and the profitability index. The cost of capital is 17 percent.

a. Compute the NPV on each project.
b. Find the profitability index for each project.
c. For each evaluation method rank the projects according to their desirability.

P. 16-3
Evaluation of
Several Proposals

Gronly owns a small office building that has considerable customer traffic. His cost of capital is 15 percent. It occurred to him that some vending machines in the building might prove profitable. He obtains the cash outflow and inflow data listed at the top of page 599 from companies that are willing to provide and service various combinations of vending machines.

a. Compute the payback on each project.
b. Compute the net present value on each project.
c. Compute the profitability index on each project.
d. Compute the internal rate of return on each project to the nearest whole percentage.
e. Rank the projects in order of preference using each of the evaluation methods.

Year	Vendor A	Vendor B	Vendor C	Vendor D
0	$(64,325)	$(71,130)	$(96,700)	$(85,000)
1	15,000	15,000	19,500	17,500
2	15,000	15,000	19,500	17,500
3	15,000	15,000	19,500	17,500
4	15,000	15,000	19,500	17,500
5	15,000	15,000	19,500	17,500
6	15,000	15,000	19,500	17,500
7	15,000	15,000	19,500	17,500
8	0	15,000	19,500	37,500
9	0	15,000	19,500	0
10	0	21,000	19,500	0
11	0	0	19,500	0

P. 16-4
Using Capital Budgeting Concepts

Following are data on a capital project with equal annual cash savings being evaluated by the management of Schloope Company.

Cost	$101,400
Salvage value	0
Payback	5.07 years
IRR	19 percent
PI	1.14

REQUIRED Find the annual cash savings from the project, its useful life, its net present value, and the company's cost of capital.

P. 16-5
Understanding Capital Project Analysis

Following are data on a capital project being evaluated by the management of Luke Coldenhot Company.

Annual cost saving	$10,000
Salvage value	0
Useful life	16 years
IRR	22 percent
Profitability index	1.12

REQUIRED Find the cost of the project, its net present value, its payback period, and the company's cost of capital.

P. 16-6
Capital Rationing

Belinda Company has total investment funds of $1,350,000. It is evaluating several capital projects to decide which should be funded. The available projects have the following costs and total present values of future cash savings, given in thousands of dollars:

Project	Cost	Present Value of Cash Savings
A	$400	$500
B	200	370
C	620	800
D	210	300
E	100	150
F	80	100

Projects B and F are complementary and if one is adopted the other must be adopted also. The company evaluates projects using net present value and the profitability index. It wants to maximize the net present value and PI of the projects given the limitation on funds. Whatever funds are not used for the capital projects will be invested in corporate bonds yielding 15 percent return per year.

REQUIRED

a. Compute the NPV and PI for each project.
b. Decide what combination of projects should be accepted in order to obtain the maximum NPV and PI.

P. 16-7 (CMA)
Using Alternative
Evaluation Methods

Hazman Company plans to replace an old piece of equipment that is obsolete and is expected to be unreliable under the stress of daily operations. The equipment is fully depreciated, and no salvage value can be realized upon its disposal.

One piece of equipment being considered would provide annual cash savings of $7,000 before income taxes. The equipment would cost $18,000 and have an estimated useful life of 5 years. No salvage value would be used for depreciation purposes because the equipment is expected to have no value at the end of 5 years.

Hazman uses the straight-line depreciation method on all equipment for both book and tax purposes. The company is subject to a 40 percent tax rate. Hazman has an after-tax cost of capital of 14 percent. Assume all operating revenues and expenses occur at the end of the year.

REQUIRED

a. Calculate for Hazman Company's proposed investment in new equipment the after-tax:
    1. payback period.
    2. accounting rate of return.
    3. net present value.
    4. profitability index.
    5. internal rate of return.
b. Identify and discuss the issues Hazman Company should consider when deciding which of the five decision models identified in requirement a it should employ to compare and evaluate alternative capital investment projects.

P. 16-8
Capital Rationing

The following projects are being evaluated by Grummett Company, which has $100,000 available for capital investment. The company's cost of capital is 16 percent. The available projects have the following costs and internal rates of return:

Project	Cost	IRR
A	$10,000	20.0%
B	20,000	18.5
C	20,000	18.0
D	30,000	17.0
E	60,000	17.5

The company evaluates projects using the IRR method. The president says she wants the greatest possible IRR on capital projects. The vice president argues that he would prefer the greatest dollar return even if the IRR is less than optimal.

REQUIRED

a. Determine the best combination of investments.
b. Discuss the merits of your combination and the merits of the president's and vice president's arguments.

P. 16-9
Tax Incentives and
Capital Budgeting

Benboola Company plans to buy a machine costing $140,000 that has an 8-year useful life and a salvage value of $20,000. Expected annual revenues and expenses from the machine are $100,000 and $60,000 respectively, not including depreciation. The machine will be put into service at the beginning of 1986. It qualifies for the 10 percent investment tax credit, which is assumed to be available at the end of the first year of operations. The company uses ACRS 5-year depreciation for tax purposes and straight-line depreciation for accounting purposes. Its cost of capital is 15 percent and its income tax rate is 45 percent. The company accepts projects with a positive net present value only if their payback period is less than 5 years.

REQUIRED

a. Find the after-tax net present value of the investment based on the accelerated cost recovery system.
b. Compute the profitability index.
c. Compute the payback period.
d. Decide whether the investment should be made.

P. 16-10
Tax Incentives and
Project Evaluation

Hollunder Company plans to acquire a piece of equipment needed for a government research project. The equipment costs $17,000, has no salvage value, and is expected to have a life of 3 years. The research contract calls for three annual payments of $50,000 to be paid to the company at the end of each year. The company estimates that research costs, not including depreciation of the equipment, will be $40,000 per year. The project is to start in early 1986. The equipment qualifies for a 6 percent investment tax credit and the company elected to claim only 4 percent. The company's cost of capital is 14 percent and its income tax rate is 40 percent. The company normally does not invest in projects that have a profitability index of less than 1.10 and an internal rate of return of less than 20 percent.

REQUIRED

a. Find the after-tax net present value of the investment based on 3-year ACRS depreciation.
b. Compute the profitability index.
c. Find the internal rate of return on the project.
d. Decide if the project satisfies the company's criteria.

P. 16-11
Capital Project
Sensitivity Analysis

Pigou Plastic Playthings, Inc., plans to acquire new production equipment for $68,480. The equipment has a useful life of 10 years and is expected to produce cost savings of $14,700 per year. There is no salvage value. The company's cost of capital is 16 percent. The plant manager believes that there is a possibility that the cost savings could be as little as $13,700 per year.

REQUIRED

Compute the sensitivity of the $1,000 prediction error in cost savings, and calculate the cost of prediction error assuming no alternative investment, using

a. The net present value of the project.
b. The internal rate of return.

P. 16-12
Capital Project
Sensitivity Analysis

Pigou Plastic Playthings, Inc., plans to acquire new production equipment for $68,480. The equipment has a useful life of 10 years and is expected to produce cost savings of $14,700 per year. There is no salvage value. The company's cost of capital is 16 percent. The plant manager believes that there is a possibility that the life of the project could be as little as 9 years. If this equipment is acquired, an alternative investment with a net present value of $2,000 and an internal rate of return of 16.7 percent will not be accepted.

a. Compute the sensitivity of the 1-year prediction error in project life, using the net present value of the project, and also the cost of prediction error.
b. Compute the sensitivity of the 1-year prediction error in project life, using the internal rate of return method, and also the cost of prediction error.
c. Find the error in annual cost saving that can be tolerated by management given the cost of capital and a 10-year project life.
d. Find the error in project life that can be tolerated by management given the cost of capital.

CASES

Case 16-1 (AICPA)
Investment
Analysis and Cost
of Capital

Niebuhr Corporation is beginning its first capital budgeting program and has retained you to assist the budget committee in the evaluation of a project to expand operations designated as proposed expansion project no. 12 (PEP no. 12).

1. The following capital expenditures are under consideration:

Fire sprinkler system	$　300,000
Landscaping	100,000
Replacement of old machines	600,000
Projects to expand operations (including PEP no. 12)	800,000
Total	$1,800,000

2. The corporation requires no minimum return on the sprinkler system or the landscaping. However, it expects a minimum return of 6 percent on all investments to replace old machinery. It also expects investments in expansion projects to yield a return that will exceed the average cost of the capital required to finance the sprinkler system and the landscaping in addition to the expansion projects.

3. Under proposed expansion project 12 (PEP no. 12) a cash investment of $75,000 will be made 1 year before operations begin. The investment will be depreciated by the sum-of-the-years'-digits method over a 3-year period and is expected to have a salvage value of $15,000. Additional financial data for PEP no. 12 follow:

Time Period	Revenue	Variable Costs	Maintenance, Property Taxes, and Insurance
0–1	$80,000	$35,000	$　8,000
1–2	95,000	41,000	11,000
2–3	60,000	25,000	12,000

The amount of the investment recovered during each of the 3 years can be reinvested immediately at a rate of return approximating 15 percent. Each year's recovery of investment, then, will have been reinvested at 15 percent for an average of 6 months at the end of the year.

4.   The capital structure of Niebuhr Corporation follows:

	Amount	Percentage
Short-term notes at 5% interest	$ 3,500,000	10%
4% cumulative preferred stock, $100 par	1,750,000	5
Common stock	12,250,000	35
Retained earnings	17,500,000	50
Total	$35,000,000	100%

5.   Additional data are summarzied below:

	Current Market Price	Expected Earnings per Share	Expected Dividends per Share
Preferred stock, noncallable	$120	—	$4.00
Common stock	50	$3.20	1.60

The average marginal tax rate for Niebuhr stockholders is estimated to be 25 percent.

6.   Assume that the corporate income tax rate is 50 percent.

7.   The present value of $1.00 due at the end of each year and discounted at 15 percent is:

End of Year	Present Value
2 years before 0	$1.32
1 year before 0	1.15
0	1.00
1 year after 0	.87
2 years after 0	.76
3 years after 0	.665752

8.   The present values of $1.00 earned uniformly throughout the year and discounted at 15 percent follow:

Year	Present Value
0–1	$ .93
1–2	.80
2–3	.69

REQUIRED

a.   Assume that the cutoff rate for considering expansion projects is 15 percent. Prepare a schedule calculating the
  1.   Annual cash flows from operations for PEP no. 12.
  2.   Present value of the net cash flows for PEP no. 12.

b. The budget committee has asked you to check the reasonableness of the cutoff rate. You realize that one of the factors to be considered is an estimate of the average cost of capital to this firm.

Prepare a schedule, supported by computations in good form, to compute the average cost of capital weighted by the percentage of the capital structure that each element represents.

c. 1. Assume that the average cost of capital computed in part *b* is 9 percent. Prepare a schedule to compute the minimum return (in dollars) required on expansion projects to cover the average cost of capital for financing the sprinkler system and the landscaping in addition to expansion projects. Assume that it is necessary to replace the old machines.

2. Assume that the minimum return computed in part *c.*1 is $150,000. Calculate the cutoff rate on expansion projects.

CHAPTER 17
The Not-for-Profit Sector

The **not-for-profit sector** of the economy comprises such entities as federal, state, and local governments, universities, foundations, hospitals, churches, and museums. Such organizations typically provide services, and occasionally products, for the general public or some designated group of society, with the primary intent of serving the public rather than generating a profit. The not-for-profit area is sometimes referred to as the **public sector,** but that term is not sufficiently broad because it includes only public institutions, such as governments, whereas not-for-profit entities include many private organizations as well. Although our discussion focuses primarily on the public sector, much of it also applies to other not-for-profit entities.

The not-for-profit sector is sometimes called the public sector

The relative importance of not-for-profit organizations in the economy has changed dramatically in the last decade. From the formation of our country until 1940, this segment of the economy accounted for one-sixth or less of the nation's total economy. Since that time, however, the growth of not-for-profit economic activity has been staggering, both in its absolute dollar amount and in terms of its relative share of the economy. By far the most dramatic increase has been in governmental activities, with the federal government leading the way. Today government and other not-for-profit activities account for nearly half of all economic activity in this country. With not-for-profit spending in excess of one trillion dollars ($1,000,000,000,000) a year, it is logical that we devote a portion of the book to this part of the economy.

Many of the concepts discussed in this book are applicable to not-for-profit entities. Virtually all of the cost measurement, relevant cost, budgeting, cost analysis, and other concepts presented in earlier chapters are relevant to all types of organizations in managing their operations and measuring their performance, whether or not they are profit-seeking.

The purpose of this chapter is to discuss some accounting and managerial issues that relate specifically to not-for-profit organizations. Special attention is given to the federal government budgeting process, because it accounts for such a large portion of the economy and because it affects the budgeting process of many states, cities, and other not-for-profit organizations.

The significance of the public sector

Since virtually all not-for-profit organizations must prepare budgets, we start this chapter by presenting the characteristics and procedures of budgeting that are unique to the not-for-profit area. We illustrate important basic budgeting concepts, introduced in Chapter 7, as they relate specifically to not-for-profit activities. In addition, an overview is presented of the government financing and expenditure process, referred to as public finance.

There are two reasons for devoting a large portion of the chapter to public finance and governmental budgeting: First, the federal government is responsible for well over half of all not-for-profit expenditures; second, federal government financing and spending decisions have a significant impact on business decisions and activities in the **private sector.** Therefore, this chapter should help you to understand how budgeting in the not-for-profit sector affects planning and decision making in the private sector.

The first part of the chapter deals with budgeting for not-for-profit organizations. Similarities and differences between not-for-profit and private-sector budgeting are examined, and program budgeting is illustrated. Next, we present an overview of the way public finance affects public and private entities. Finally, after discussing the influence of government policies on business, we examine the budgeting system used by the federal government and some state and local governments.

THE BUDGETING PROCESS

The two primary functions of budgeting

The fundamentals of budgeting are identical for profit and not-for-profit organizations. In both cases budgeting plays a vital role in planning, monitoring, and controlling the effective and efficient use of scarce resources.

Revenue Budgets

A key element of all budgets is budgeted revenue. It is the primary determinant of all the expenditures in the rest of the budget. In profit-oriented firms, revenue is a key determinant of profit, which is the primary goal of the firm. In most not-for-profit organizations, however, revenue is not the primary benefit. Instead, revenue is used to finance various activities that generate desired benefits. For example, a city police department's revenue is determined primarily by the amount of money appropriated for the police department by the city council. In addition, some federal and state money may be provided for special programs and activities. The revenue provided for the police department determines, to a large degree, the size of the police force and the quality of its services. The benefits are derived by the citizens in the form of police protection and through community education and service programs offered by the police department.

In addition to revenue appropriated by the city council in a budget, some entities obtain revenue from a variety of other sources. For example, Figure 17-1 shows the revenue budget for the current year and the coming fiscal year for Fairview City. For the 1986–87 fiscal year, the city expects revenue from a number of different sources including taxes, fees for services, government programs, and investments.

The detail in the revenue budget allows the city to evaluate each revenue source separately. Some revenue sources are more susceptible to fluctuations or prediction errors than others. For example, water sales, sewage service fees, and property taxes are less likely to fluctuate significantly with economic

Figure 17-1. This is the revenue budget for a relatively small city, with a variety of income sources. By preparing a detailed revenue budget, city managers can monitor actual revenue receipts and compare them with budgeted amounts. If differences occur between budgeted and actual revenue, city management may be able to adjust spending or change revenue collections.

Fairview City
Budgeted Revenue
For the Fiscal Year 1986–87

	Current Budget 1985–86	Approved Budget 1986–87
Taxes:		
Property tax	$3,600,000	$4,300,000
City sales tax	740,000	790,000
Total taxes	4,340,000	5,090,000
Fees and assessments:		
License fees	26,000	29,000
Recreational fees	43,000	46,000
Water sales	1,267,000	1,592,000
Sewage service	1,811,000	2,165,000
Refuse collection	548,000	599,000
Miscellaneous	45,000	49,000
Total fees and assessments	3,740,000	4,480,000
Other revenues:		
Federal government grants and appropriations	450,000	220,000
Investment income	36,000	30,000
Sale of city property	144,000	—
Total other revenue	630,000	250,000
Total revenue	$8,710,000	$9,820,000

Revenue sources

conditions than city sales tax revenue. Similarly, the likelihood of receiving federal government grants may depend on political attitudes in the nation's capital and on other variables outside the control of city officials.

Like a business, the city must determine the probabilities that projected revenues may be different from actual revenues. Variances could have a serious effect on the operation of city services. City officials may, therefore, attempt to identify a range of possible revenue levels for each revenue classification and establish alternative spending plans for the various levels of revenue. The alternative budgets should identify which programs would be curtailed or eliminated in the event of revenue shortages and which programs would be expanded or added with revenue surpluses.

Expenditure Budgets

Expenditure budgets state how the organization plans to spend its resources during the budget period. As with private industry, the format of the budget and nature of the expenditures are dictated somewhat by the type of organization. The Fairview City budget is separated into 12 functional activities. The summary budget for these activities is presented in Figure 17-2, which shows the current budget year as well as the budget for the next fiscal year.

The summary expenditure budget provides an overview of the resources allocated to each major activity of the city. However, this budget is of little use in planning and controlling daily operations of any one of the activities,

Figure 17-2. The expenditure budget states how the organization plans to spend its resources. It can be prepared at whatever level of detail management deems necessary and cost-effective.

Fairview City
Summary Expenditure Budget
For the Fiscal Year 1986–87

	Current Budget 1985–86	Approved Budget 1986–87
City council	$ 120,000	$ 125,000
City office facilities	460,000	490,000
City transit system	433,000	400,000
Court system	360,000	430,000
Fire department	874,000	982,000
Parks and recreation department	327,000	394,000
Police department	1,288,000	1,392,000
Refuse collection department	736,000	887,000
School	2,745,000	2,990,000
Sewage and treatment plant	563,000	795,000
Streets department	480,000	510,000
Water department	324,000	425,000
Total expenditures	$8,710,000	$9,820,000

Detailed expenditure budgets are needed for monitoring and managing operations

such as the city transit system or the city school system. Instead, detailed operating budgets are required for each activity. Figure 17-3 illustrates the operating budget for the fire department. The total for the current year of $874,000 is the same amount that appears in the summary expenditure budget for the department.

Budgets provide an excellent framework for monitoring and controlling costs of government operations. All too often, however, they are viewed merely as devices for securing resources. Once the budget is approved, there may be a tendency to ignore it and simply use the resources provided by it without any effort to measure the cost-benefit relationships of the activities. In such cases, the benefits of control from the budgeting process are lost. The control aspects are important, however, because resources are scarce and only a limited amount may be available for specific purposes.

Budget Performance Reports

Once approved, the budget becomes an operating plan that must be followed by the governmental unit. For example, if a city council approves $4,200,000 for the parks and recreation department, city management cannot simply decide to use part of the funds for road maintenance. If planning is a worthwhile activity, then comparing actual results with the budget to see whether the plans were carried out is also worthwhile. Such comparisons are made in performance reports prepared by accountants to show how the planned activity was accomplished and how the accomplishment compared with the original plan. Figure 17-4 presents a performance report for the fire department for the 1985–86 fiscal year.

Figure 17-3. To manage the financial matters of the fire department, it is necessary to have more detail than the single number in the summary expenditure budget in Figure 17-2.

Fairview City
Fire Department Budget
For the Fiscal Year 1986–87

	Current Budget 1985–86	Approved Budget 1986–87
Clerical wages	$ 35,000	$ 38,000
Education and training	56,000	52,000
Equipment operating expenses	28,000	32,000
Equipment purchases	120,000	175,000
Firemen's salaries	320,000	355,000
Gasoline	12,000	14,000
Insurance	15,000	15,000
Maintenance, buildings	13,000	18,000
Maintenance, equipment	86,000	67,000
Miscellaneous	22,000	25,000
Payroll taxes and fringe benefits	64,000	77,000
Supervisory salaries	62,000	66,000
Supplies	14,000	15,000
Uniform allowances	6,000	7,000
Uniform cleaning	3,000	4,000
Utilities	18,000	22,000
Total expenditures	$874,000	$982,000

Figure 17-4. A budget performance report can be as useful in the not-for-profit sector as it is for the profit-seeking firm. This example is a fixed budget performance report.

Fairview City
Fire Department Budget Performance Report
For the Fiscal Year 1985–86

	Budget 1985–86	Actual 1985–86	Unfavorable (Favorable) Variance
Clerical wages	$ 35,000	$ 32,500	$ (2,500)
Education and training	56,000	47,000	(9,000)
Equipment operating expenses	28,000	29,700	1,700
Equipment purchases	120,000	144,000	24,000
Firemen's salaries	320,000	316,000	(4,000)
Gasoline	12,000	11,000	(1,000)
Insurance	15,000	14,500	(500)
Maintenance, buildings	13,000	19,200	6,200
Maintenance, equipment	86,000	94,800	8,800
Miscellaneous	22,000	27,300	5,300
Payroll taxes and fringe benefits	64,000	62,700	(1,300)
Supervisory salaries	62,000	67,000	5,000
Supplies	14,000	16,000	2,000
Uniform allowances	6,000	5,400	(600)
Uniform cleaning	3,000	3,200	200
Utilities	18,000	22,600	4,600
Totals	$874,000	$912,900	$38,900

PROGRAM BUDGETING

Line budget defined

The master budget of a business, illustrated in Chapter 7, is developed along functional lines. Business functions such as marketing, manufacturing, and administration are major entities in the master budget. This form of budget is called a **line budget** or **functional budget.** Line budgeting is popular because it closely parallels the lines of responsibility in the organization chart, and it facilitates the performance measurement of managers. The budget for each part of the organization provides a convenient framework for developing performance reports.

The Nature of Program Budgets

For not-for-profit organizations, line budgeting is not always a useful framework for monitoring costs and measuring cost-benefit relationships. A form of budgeting that often provides better information is **program budgeting,** with budgets prepared for programs or outputs of the organization.

Program budgeting identifies costs with outputs or objectives of the organization

The distinguishing characteristic of program budgeting is that the focal point in budget preparation and cost control is the program or goal rather than a functional or organizational unit. For example, a school system may prepare budgets for each school program, such as primary education, secondary education, student enrichment programs, adult education, and athletic programs. The amount of detail in the program depends on management's needs. For instance, the budget for adult education programs may be divided into vocational training programs, cultural enrichment programs, and community safety programs. Later you will see that program budgeting may be instrumental in identifying changes in an organization's structure that would facilitate the achievement of goals. To contrast line and program budgeting, refer to Figure 17-5.

Figure 17-5 shows the current and proposed budgets for the Fairview City police department. The budget at the top is a line budget for the department, and the budget at the bottom is a program budget for the same department. The line budget identifies 17 functional activities of the police department. The program budget is divided into six programs. Costs are identified with programs rather than with functions. As with line budgeting, some costs may not be clearly identifiable with a single program in the budget. Such common costs are allocated to the appropriate programs in a logical manner using cost allocation concepts discussed in Chapters 11, 12, and 20.

In business organizations, most activities are intended to contribute to the firm's profit objective, and the benefits from these activities are measured in the income statement. In not-for-profit organizations, there is typically no common measure of program success. For example, a city government uses a variety of programs to achieve many diverse goals, such as education, fire and police protection, city sanitation, and recreation. Success of the various programs cannot be measured in dollars. Instead, the number of high school diplomas, reduced crime rates, enrollments in recreational programs, or attendance at symphony concerts are measures of success. If resources are to be allocated among various programs in ways that maximize total benefits to

Figure 17-5. A line budget is most commonly used. The cost categories follow the lines of responsibility in the organization chart. A program budget identifies costs by outputs or goals and is very useful in comparing costs and benefits during project evaluations.

Fairview City Police Department
Line Budget
For the Fiscal Year Ending June 30

	Current Budget 1985–86	Proposed Budget 1986–87
Administrative salaries	$ 123,000	$ 132,000
Building maintenance salaries	26,000	28,000
Building maintenance supplies	15,000	16,000
Clerical salaries	36,000	38,000
Crime lab supplies	18,000	22,000
Employee education programs	32,000	28,000
Insurance	25,000	30,000
Miscellaneous expenses	16,000	24,000
Office supplies	21,000	23,000
Payroll taxes and employee benefits	92,000	104,000
Police car and equipment maintenance	82,000	98,000
Police car operation	126,000	183,000
Police car purchases	94,000	66,000
Police officers' salaries	520,000	534,000
Transportation	25,000	22,000
Uniform allowances and cleaning	11,000	13,000
Utilities	26,000	31,000
Total expenditures	$1,288,000	$1,392,000

Fairview City Police Department
Program Budget
For the Fiscal Year Ending June 30

	Current Budget 1985–86	Proposed Budget 1986–87
Community crime prevention programs	$ 89,000	$ 102,000
Drug abuse education program	95,000	115,000
School safety program	48,000	55,000
Criminal investigation	382,000	410,000
Criminal proceedings	110,000	120,000
Community patrol program	564,000	590,000
Totals	$1,288,000	$1,392,000

the citizens of the city, there must be a method of comparing program benefits with program costs. Since benefits are measured for programs rather than for organizational lines, it stands to reason that costs should be identified with programs also, so that direct analyses can be made.

Advantages of Program Budgeting

The primary advantage of using program budgeting is that it facilitates cost-benefit analysis for programs in which benefits are measured in something other than dollars. If benefits are measured for projects, then the costs should be identified for each project as well, so that logical resource alloca-

Why use program budgeting?

tions can be made. For example, the benefit of a late-night police patrol through residential areas is a 20 percent reduction in burglaries, and the cost of the patrols is $200,000 annually. Other benefits and costs are identified specifically for this program. If a program budgeting system were not used, the cost of the late-night patrols would be buried in a line budget among personnel costs, gasoline costs, patrol car operating costs, and others.

Line-Program Budget

A combination **line-program budget** provides cost information by function and also by program. An example of this type of budget presentation is shown in Figure 17-6 using the data from the Fairview City police department budget in Figure 17-5.

Combining line and program budgeting gives the best of both worlds

The program budget is presented in the columns and the line budget appears in the rows. The data presented in the combined line-program budget offer greater detail than either the line budget or the program budget separately. Notice that only the 1985–86 fiscal year is presented in Figure 17-6. Another report is required to present the proposed budget for the 1986–87 fiscal year in a similar format. The combined budget provides cost information on programs and on functions and shows the amount of cost planned for each function of each program.

Fairview City Police Department
Line-Program Budget
For the Fiscal Year 1985–86

	Crime Prevention	Drug Education	School Safety	Criminal Investigation	Criminal Proceedings	Community Patrol	Totals
Administrative salaries	$ 8,000	$ 9,000	$ 3,000	$ 47,000	$ 8,000	$ 48,000	$ 123,000
Building maintenance salaries	2,000	1,500	1,500	11,000	3,000	7,000	26,000
Building maintenance supplies	2,500	1,000	1,000	5,500	2,000	3,000	15,000
Clerical salaries	4,000	1,000	2,000	16,000	7,000	6,000	36,000
Crime lab supplies	500	500	—	12,000	1,000	4,000	18,000
Employee education programs	2,000	3,000	1,500	15,500	3,000	7,000	32,000
Insurance	1,000	1,000	1,000	6,000	2,000	14,000	25,000
Miscellaneous expenses	500	500	500	4,000	3,000	7,500	16,000
Office supplies	500	500	500	6,000	5,000	8,500	21,000
Payroll taxes and employee benefits	7,500	8,500	3,500	27,000	9,500	36,000	92,000
Police car and equipment maintenance	3,000	2,000	2,000	17,000	5,000	53,000	82,000
Police car operation	4,500	3,500	3,000	16,000	6,500	92,500	126,000
Police car purchases	7,000	7,000	7,000	14,000	7,000	52,000	94,000
Police officers' salaries	42,000	52,000	17,000	161,000	38,000	210,000	520,000
Transportation	1,000	2,000	2,500	9,000	6,000	4,500	25,000
Uniform allowances and cleaning	1,000	1,000	1,000	2,500	1,500	4,000	11,000
Utilities	2,000	1,000	1,000	12,500	2,500	7,000	26,000
Totals	$89,000	$95,000	$48,000	$382,000	$110,000	$564,000	$1,288,000

Figure 17-6. A combined line-program budget provides budget information using both approaches. This type of budget provides managers with detailed cost information that may be useful in planning and controlling costs.

PUBLIC FINANCE

Public finance defined

Public finance is the entire area of government economic activity, including resource allocations, income distribution, and the financing of government operations. In total, public finance activities affect both the public and private sectors. In this section we present the fundamentals of governmental budgeting, and discuss the nature of public finance activities and their impact on private-sector business.

A budget is a comprehensive quantitative plan for utilizing the resources of an entity for some period of time. Budgeting is used to allocate scarce resources in a way that optimizes the achievement of organizational goals. To a large degree, federal, state, and local government taxing and expenditure decisions determine resource allocations and income distribution. For example, an increase in Social Security taxes takes money out of the hands of taxpayers, and an increase in Social Security benefits puts money into the hands of recipients. Similarly, increases in tax deductions caused by liberalized depreciation guidelines for new business assets are designed to encourage business investment and increase job opportunities for workers. Most people and businesses are affected by taxing and spending decisions, and members of Congress are aware of the impact their decisions have on individuals, businesses, and the entire economy.

Taxation by Governments

Taxation is a carefully guarded power of governments

The ability to tax is an important power of government. To a large degree, taxing powers determine the influence government has over the economy. The founding fathers of the United States were very cautious in granting taxing powers to the federal government, and the constitution specifically describes the types of taxes that can and cannot be levied. It was not until 1913 that the Sixteenth Amendment was passed, allowing direct taxation of income without apportionment of the tax among the states according to population. In 1917 the first personal income tax law was passed. Even then, the federal income tax only affected relatively few citizens. It was not until World War II that the income tax became broadly based among the population. From the start of the war to the end, the number of income taxpayers increased from 8 million to 60 million.

The Need for a Public Sector

The public sector performs services that cannot be done privately

A logical question might be, Why does the public sector exist and what does it do with the vast wealth of resources it collects? The public sector exists to fill the voids not serviced by the private sector and to ensure that the private sector operates in a way that is acceptable to society. Many government services, such as parks, highways, police protection, national defense, and national archives, are not available from the private sector. The market mechanism does not provide for regulatory agencies, such as the Securities and Exchange Commission, the Federal Energy Regulatory Commission, or the Federal Trade Commission.

Federal government rules and regulations affect virtually every facet of business life, including external accounting requirements, health and safety standards, transportation costs, energy costs, employee taxes, and countless other items. Government activities, rules, and regulations often have an impact on business decisions about investments, number and types of employees to hire, types of products to produce, plant locations, and transportation systems used.

Public Finance Objectives

The basic policy objectives of public finance are

Basic objectives of public finance

1. Allocation
2. Distribution
3. Stabilization

Allocation.   The first policy objective deals with providing socially desirable goods and services not made available through the private sector. **Allocation** policy determines what goods and services should be provided and in what quantity. In the public sector, resource allocations are made primarily through the process of voting. Citizens vote for people to represent them in government, and the representatives in turn vote on projects and proposals in Congress, in state legislatures, and in city councils. Allocation decisions in the aggregate have a tremendous impact on our economy and on society. In the private sector the "voting" is done with dollars. Consumers tell suppliers how to allocate resources by spending on the various products and services supplied by the private sector. Typically, consumers are able to adjust their voting patterns more quickly in the private sector than in the public sector, but the process is quite similar.

What goods and services are provided by the public sector?

Distribution.   The second policy objective addresses the issue of who should receive the economic benefits of society. **Distribution** is the process of collecting taxes and using the money to provide government benefits to citizens. The private sector strongly influences income distribution by providing jobs and by distributing profits to owners. However, the impact of government distribution policies is significant. Graduated income taxes take a larger portion of a wage earner's income as wages increase. FICA taxes are paid to the government by wage earners and distributed to recipients who are not employed or who earn a small amount. Many tax programs are designed to tax people earning higher incomes on the assumption that such people are better able to bear the tax burden. Many expenditures are designed primarily to help lower-income people because they are most in need of the services. Frequently, distribution policy decisions are based on establishing a lower limit on poverty or an upper limit on wealth.

Who receives the benefits of government?

Stabilization.   The objective of stabilization policy is to see that the economy runs smoothly. **Stabilization** is the use of economic theory to smooth out excessive fluctuations in economic activities. Economic theory implies that a

Government tries to maintain a stable economy

stable economy characterized by an acceptable level of growth without widely fluctuating economic conditions is most conducive to high employment, stable prices, and reasonable income levels. To minimize fluctuations and wide swings known as depression, inflation, recession, or booms, the government has two basic instruments that may be used to stabilize the economy. They are fiscal policy and monetary policy.

Fiscal Policy

Congress controls fiscal policy — taxing and spending

Fiscal policy pertains to the taxing and spending actions of government. Although taxing and spending together constitute fiscal policy, Congress seldom specifically ties the two functions together. However, both taxing and spending affect the economy. For instance, during periods of high inflation, Congress may raise taxes to reduce the quantity of money available for the purchase of goods and services. Another possibility is to reduce government spending, thereby keeping money out of the economy.

Fiscal actions may have a dramatic impact on businesses. For instance, a manager may postpone an investment because a special tax break on investments is expected shortly, or a company may buy more automated production equipment to avoid higher payroll taxes and a higher minimum wage. Fiscal decisions can create significant changes in economic conditions, particularly for certain segments of the economy. For example, government energy policies and tax breaks brought boom times to insulating firms during the energy shortages in the late 1970s.

Fiscal policy of the federal government is a powerful economic tool with a strong impact on the economy. It is also difficult to implement quickly because it takes time for Congress to enact new tax legislation or new spending programs. When fast action is needed to stabilize the economy, or to counteract the poor timing of fiscal policy, the government has monetary policy at its disposal.

Monetary Policy

The Federal Reserve Board controls monetary policy

Monetary policy deals with the quantity and the cost of money in the economy. Monetary policy is therefore in the hands of a government central bank called the Federal Reserve System. The Federal Reserve System is governed by the Federal Reserve Board, a body of appointed officials who are largely independent of government control or influence.

The Federal Reserve Board, often referred to as the Fed, may change the money supply in the economy by buying and selling government securities in the market, by raising or lowering the interest rates it charges banks for loans, or by raising or lowering bank reserve requirements. Reserve requirements dictate the amount of funds each member bank must keep on reserve with the Fed. When the requirements are high, the amount of money available to banks is not as great as when reserve requirements are low. The Fed can act very quickly to change the quantity of money and interest rates and thus can use monetary policy to fine-tune the economy as necessary to keep it relatively stable.

When the Federal Reserve Board raises the bank interest rate, its actions almost always mean higher interest rates to businesses and consumers. The result is that the cost of borrowing becomes too high for some people and businesses, and purchases are postponed or eliminated. When interest rates and reserve requirements are high, money becomes hard to borrow, resulting in what is sometimes called a "credit crunch." At such times businesses in the housing, automobile, and major appliance industries may experience sharp declines in sales because their products are usually sold on credit.

THE EFFECT OF GOVERNMENTAL INFLUENCE

Governmental taxing and expenditure activities affect our lives in many ways. We may not be fully aware of the effect of some taxes because most taxes are not paid the way a utility bill or store charge account is paid. Instead, many taxes are somewhat hidden. Gasoline taxes are included in the price of the fuel; sales tax is part of the total cost of the purchase; income taxes and FICA taxes are withheld from paychecks; excise taxes are buried in the purchase price of certain products; and property taxes may be part of house payments. Taxpayers should not lose sight of the taxes they pay to governmental units. Taxes pay for governmental services and, as with other outlays for purchases, there should be justification for the resources spent. Such justification is provided in the form of budgets, which elected officials must approve before tax money can be spent.

The federal government affects our lives in many ways

Some tax laws have a direct measurable effect on citizens. For instance, a $50 per person tax credit has a direct effect on the tax burden of each taxpayer, whereas a tax credit on a new home has no effect on a taxpayer who is not in the market for a new home.

Expenditure legislation, such as Social Security payments and welfare payments, are direct benefits to individuals; but many other expenditures have a more indirect effect on the population. It is easy to see that a monthly Social Security check of $480 provides an annual income of $5,760 to the recipient. It is harder to determine the specific value to individuals of a new missile, the space shuttle, highway construction, or the creation of a new national park in Alaska. But government officials must evaluate the benefits of such programs and compare them with the costs of the programs to make intelligent spending decisions.

Effects on Businesses

Government policies affect businesses as well as individuals. Businesses are subject to many types of taxes in addition to income taxes. In order to continue earning profits, businesses must view taxes and other government assessments as part of the cost of doing business and must pass on these costs to customers in the form of prices. Pricing decisions are therefore influenced by government actions.

Fiscal and monetary policies can be used effectively by governments through their influence on businesses. As interest rates are increased by the

Businesses react quickly to changes in government policy

Fed, businesses curtail borrowing or expansion. When the government wants to stimulate the economy, it may induce expansion by providing tax benefits to businesses, such as the investment credit and rapid depreciation of fixed assets. Businesses react to such policies by shifting resources in directions that will minimize their tax burden or place them in a better competitive position.

In addition to influencing business by means of tax legislation, governments also affect business by demanding many types of reports, the cost of which must also be reflected in the price of products.

Government Demand for Information from Business

In the past 10 years there has been a significant increase in the amount and types of information that businesses must provide to government. Some of this information is summarized and used to report general business conditions. Other information is used to monitor adherence to government rules and regulations. Some is used for research by government staffs or private individuals.

Government information needs require businesses to collect many types of data

The impact on businesses of government requirements for business data is both indirect and direct. The indirect impact occurs when the analysis of business data results in new government rules and regulations that affect the operations of businesses. The direct impact occurs from specific reporting requirements that cause a business to modify the way it gathers and reports information. In most cases government information requirements are for financial data. Sometimes firms must modify their financial information system to satisfy government reporting requirements. Some common effects on a company's information system are a more detailed data base, different data base structure, or different reporting characteristics than the business would have for its own use.

More Detailed Data Base.   Numerous government reporting requirements have caused some businesses to develop a more detailed cost data base than they previously had. For example, during the period of the Economic Stabilization Policy, some companies were unable to get price increase approval from the Price Commission solely because the cost data provided by the companies were not detailed enough to prove that the price increase was cost justified. As a result, many companies started to accumulate more detailed cost data primarily to satisfy future information requirements the government might make.

The Cost Accounting Standards Board developed very specific requirements for reporting costs of government contracts. Some firms found that they had to modify their cost accounting data base and develop a detailed cost data base for nonmanufacturing activities to comply with the CASB reporting requirements. Similar examples can be cited for other governmental organizations, such as the Federal Trade Commission and the Internal Revenue Service, which require detailed reporting.

Different Data Base Structure.   The accounting data base consists of the basic data from which internal and external reports are developed. The structure of the data base—that is, the way data are organized and stored—

is determined by such factors as efficiency of updating the data base, efficiency of retrieving needed data, and reporting requirements. Whenever government requires information that is significantly different from the information normally generated by the business, there is a possibility that the company will have to modify its data base structure to satisfy the new reporting requirement. For example, the Federal Trade Commission requires some large businesses to report revenues and expenses for various categories of business, such as domestic and foreign, or by type of product. These lines of business reports may be different from those used by some businesses for their own reporting purposes.

Different Reporting Characteristics.   The frequency, detail, and format of internal reports are dictated by the information needs of managers, which may change with new government requirements. For example, if very detailed product cost information is needed to justify price increases, a firm may change its cost accounting system and internal cost reporting system to provide managers with necessary cost details on a timely basis. Another example is a need to report salary data by race and sex to ensure compliance with affirmative action programs, although such data are not necessary for costing purposes.

FEDERAL GOVERNMENT BUDGETING

All federal resource allocation (spending) decisions are made by the Congress of the United States. It is often said that Congress controls the purse strings of the nation, but much of the information for congressional decisions is provided by the federal government budgeting process. The federal government budgeting system also strongly influences the budgeting processes and procedures of many state and local governments.

Components of PPBS

In 1965, President Johnson announced the introduction of a new budgeting system in the federal government called **planning, programming, budgeting system** (**PPBS**). It is also identified as PPB. The purpose was to provide a systematic process for developing and analyzing budget proposals and for completing the final budget package. As the title implies, **PPBS** is based on program budgeting, but it encompasses more than just the concept of program budgeting. PPBS includes systematic procedures for the accounting, programming, and evaluation processes. It has been suggested that **PPBS** has five distinguishing features:

1. Program accounting
2. Multiyear costing
3. Detailed description of activities
4. Zero-base budgeting
5. Benefit-cost analysis[1]

[1] Leonard Merewitz and Stephen H. Sosnick, *The Budget's New Clothes* (Chicago: Markam Publishing Company, 1973), pp. 2–108.

Program Accounting

A basic requisite of program budgeting is an ability to attach accounting data to specific programs to show the resources used or budgeted for each objective. The process of accumulating costs by programs is referred to as **program accounting.** It must be capable of accumulating historical costs by program and of developing projected program costs. PPBS requires four types of costs to be accumulated for programs: past costs, current year costs, budget year costs, and future costs. **Past costs** are program costs for the last fiscal year. **Current costs** are program costs for the current fiscal year. **Budget year costs** are proposed program costs for the coming fiscal year, and **future costs** are anticipated expenditures for the program covering 4 or more years in the future.

Multiyear Costing

Multiyear costing is the process of identifying costs with a project for the life of the project rather than just for the next budget year. This is not a new budgeting concept. It has been used for many years by businesses to evaluate capital expenditure projects. The logic for multiyear costing in capital expenditure decisions is that most projects require large outlays benefiting many future periods. However, in conventional budgets, few items in the operating budget are evaluated in light of expected outlays beyond the current budget period. Without multiyear costing, some budget proposals may be accepted with only a small portion of the relevant cost data available for analysis.

Often, government programs have life spans covering many accounting periods. Consequently, it is logical to evaluate projects based on costs and benefits over their entire expected life rather than just for 1 year. Like all long-range estimates, multiyear costing of programs becomes more subjective the longer the estimate. Nevertheless, multiyear costing is often cited as one of the major contributions of PPBS because it gives a better picture of program alternatives. Occasionally a proposed program requires very small expenditures initially, followed by very substantial outlays in later years. For example, the growth in Social Security payments since the start of the program has been tremendous.

Detailed Description of Activities

PPBS is intended to provide uniform systematic data for evaluating ongoing programs and new programs alike by providing a detailed description of each activity. An important attribute of PPBS is the uniform application of systematic procedures throughout the federal government budgeting system. Each program requires six specific steps, resulting in information that helps to implement the program in accordance with the planning, programming, budgeting system.

First, objectives must be established for each program. **Objectives** are the basic goals or desired outcomes of the program. Next, each program must have **targets,** which are specific short-term expectations for the program. Then the program director must identify the **selections made,** which are the specific operating plans of the program. The selections made must be supported by a description of the **alternatives reviewed,** with a discussion of why the alternatives were rejected in favor of the selected plans. **Outputs** are the current benefits or results achieved by the program and should relate directly to the targets. Finally, the detailed descriptions of activities must include a discussion of **effectiveness,** which is the measure of how well targets and objectives were achieved. Figure 17-7 illustrates a hypothetical detailed description of activities for the Maritime Administration of the Department of Commerce.

Figure 17-7. This is a hypothetical set of detailed description of activities for the Maritime Administration.

Maritime Administration
Maritime Readiness
Detailed Description of Activities

Objective:	Maintain a well-rounded maritime capability to provide military support during times of crisis and to provide a strong commerce base for international trade.
Target:	Provide 1,000 new shipbuilding jobs annually for American citizens.
Selection made:	Let $200,000,000 of new contracts to United States shipbuilders for Navy ships.
Alternatives:	Offer a 20 percent wage subsidy to firms training new employees. Develop a government training program to teach shipbuilding skills by repairing older Navy ships.
Output:	A total of 700 new employees received skilled labor classifications in the shipbuilding industry.
Effectiveness:	A total of 1,300 people started company job training program in shipbuilding during the year. Of these, 600 dropped out, were terminated, or required more training before being classified as skilled labor.

Notice that all components of PPBS are included in the description of activities. Outputs are the measurable results of the programs. In this case 700 new skilled laborers were trained. In other programs outputs may be measured in higher reading levels of elementary students, improved grain prices, or many other variables. Effectiveness measures compare the output with input. In this example the inputs and outputs are people in a training program. In other cases they may be measured in dollars; for instance, a job training program may cost $2,458 per graduate.

Zero-Base Budgeting

All budget programs, even existing ones, are reviewed each year under zero-base budgeting

Implemented with PPBS in 1965, **zero-base budgeting** means that each project or program must start the budget evaluation process with no commitment of resources. Instead of the old budget being used as a base, a zero base is assumed, and every item in the budget must be justified on its own merit, not simply because it existed previously. Each project must be proved worthy of funding, or it is rejected regardless of whether it is a new proposal or a program of long standing.

Governments operate on budgets that must be approved prior to the beginning of each fiscal year. Before PPBS, the previous budget was a convenient starting point for a new budget because it consisted of revenues and expenditures that had already been approved once before. The new budget usually was a revision of the old budget, with most of the items increased to allow for a growing economy, rising population, or inflation. Such a budgeting process is generally known as **incremental budgeting** because the new budget consists of the old one with an increment. Budget increments based on the inflation rate, increases in appropriations, a fixed percentage, or any other across-the-board increment to the budget beg the question of a true budget evaluation process. As a result of incremental budgeting, there is a tendency for budgets to become ever larger, and it is difficult to eliminate unsuccessful or inefficient programs once they are included in a budget. Many government budgets are routinely prepared by using the previous budget as a base and modifying the figures to suit expectations.

With zero-base budgeting, it is conceivable, although unlikely, that major program classifications, such as national defense or the space program, could be terminated if they proved to be undesirable. Typically, such major programs are sufficiently important to continue receiving congressional support and funding without substantial modifications. Still, there is a natural appeal to the idea that programs of all sorts and durations should be evaluated annually. Obsolete or ineffective programs should be terminated and resources should be shifted to new justifiable programs. Zero-base budgeting is an alternative to incremental budgeting.

Although it is conceptually attractive, zero-base budgeting is not always easy to apply in practice. Programs currently in operation are hard to eliminate or curtail. They may involve long-term commitments or fixed investments that cannot easily be shifted to other areas. For example, military weapons systems, once developed, have little market value if a new system is developed. Program participants with vested interests in the program can cite prestige, hardship, tradition, or countless other reasons for maintaining the program.

Benefit-Cost Analysis

Benefit-cost analysis integrates the four features of PPBS — program accounting, multiyear costing, detailed description of activities, and zero-base budgeting — into a decision framework. Here the term **decision framework** is used somewhat loosely because often no formal decision model is developed. However, all program proposals are evaluated in terms of benefits and costs. Proposals with the highest benefit-cost ratios are accepted first, and other programs are delayed or canceled. The difficult question is, How are benefit-cost ratios determined?

Although program costs are sometimes difficult to measure, program benefits are even harder to determine for many government projects. How does one compare the value of a program that helps a few people a great deal with a program that helps many people a little? How do the benefits of increased defense spending compare with a 10 million acre national park in

Alaska? What is the benefit-cost ratio of a program that reduces unemployment by 50,000 people and costs the taxpayers $1,900,000,000?

None of the above questions is simple, but they must be answered if government is to achieve policy goals effectively. The entire budgeting system collapses if we arrive at the last step and cannot make sound resource allocation decisions based on solid benefit-cost analyses supported by relevant factual data.

PPBS emphasizes quantitative benefit-cost analysis. Quantitative measures of some sort are frequently available if intuition and persistence are applied. Quantitative analysis does not necessarily mean dollar-for-dollar benefit-cost comparisons. For example, many types of unemployment statistics may be evaluated in considering full-employment programs, and park visitation statistics, population densities, and changing recreational patterns may be cited in developing a case for new park facilities.

The Status of PPBS

Probably no other budgeting phenomenon swept the country, even the world, as PPBS did in the late 1960s and early 1970s. Government officials and others raved about it as the new system that would ensure effective and efficient government. In 1966, California adopted the system and renamed it *programming and budgeting (PAB)*. Many state and local governments rushed to pattern their budgeting system after PPBS, or at least to use some of its features. The rush to PPBS has been referred to as the "PPB epidemic."[2]

Is PPBS accomplishing its goals?

Unfortunately, the planning, programming, budgeting system has not fulfilled all of the great expectations held for it. There have been some successes from time to time in various government agencies with parts of PPBS, but in aggregate the system has not produced as much improvement in government budgeting as was expected. The most common reasons cited for the difficulties with PPBS are costs, government size, government organization, and difficult measurement problems.[3]

PPBS Costs. Any accounting and budgeting system must be benefit-cost justifiable. PPBS, with its intricate detail, devotion to full disclosure of all alternatives, need for justification of currently operating programs, and requirement for quantitative measures in benefit-cost analysis, is very expensive and time-consuming. Some people feel the idea is superior, but the economic realities of operating the system are prohibitive.

Government Size. The federal government is huge and growing larger every year. All private-sector businesses, including General Motors and American Telephone and Telegraph, are dwarfed by the size of the federal government. The coordination of large businesses is very difficult; the coordination of all federal government activity is truly mind-boggling. The major purpose of PPBS was to help coordinate resource allocation decisions, but the sheer size of the federal government may preclude any chance of complete success. A

[2] Ibid., p. 2.

[3] Aaron Wildavsky, *The Politics of the Budgetary Process* (Boston: Little, Brown and Company, 1974), pp. 181–208.

comprehensive plan like PPBS for a small firm would require a lot of work; for the federal government PPBS is a massive undertaking.

Government Organization.   Some programs cut across several organizational units, and some government segments house many different programs, causing critics to argue that government is just not organized in a way that is conducive to program budgeting. Some believe a required feature of PPBS is reorganization along lines that facilitate the process of program accounting and budgeting, but major reorganization of the federal government is a very complex political issue.

Difficult Measurement Problems.   Many of the measurements required in PPBS are very difficult to make. Particularly difficult are long-range cost and benefit estimates. So many different benefit measures are used for the myriad of government programs that it is perplexing to attempt to integrate the benefit-cost analysis of each program into a logical structure for comparing all alternative programs.

The Future of PPBS

Any criticism of PPBS must be tempered by the realization that planning, coordinating, and controlling any organization the size of the federal government is tremendously difficult. Any general criticism can be countered with the question, What system would operate more effectively and efficiently than PPBS? For the near future, it appears that the current system will continue to be used, with only minor modifications from time to time to improve the system or to remedy perceived problems.

SUMMARY   Not-for-profit organizations are an important segment of the economy, with total expenditures exceeding $1 trillion. By far the largest element in the not-for-profit sector is government, particularly the federal government. Budgeting is vital to the effective and efficient utilization of resources in the **public sector.** Most budgeting concepts and procedures are the same regardless of the type of organization.

The **revenue** budget influences the number, size, and quality of programs in not-for-profit organizations, but revenue is not a goal in itself. It is merely the means for operating various programs that in turn provide the desired benefits. The **expenditures** budget is the organization's plan for using the resources at its disposal. Budgets should be prepared in sufficient detail to provide adequate control over the resources of not-for-profit organizations. Typically, control includes timely performance reporting.

Line budgets are prepared using functional lines or the organization structure as the budget framework. Typical categories in a line budget include accounting, maintenance, divisions, and departments. **Program budgets** identify costs and benefits for goals or programs, such as education, crime prevention, or recreation. The primary advantage of program budgeting is the ability to compare the cost of a program with its benefits. Some organizations use both line and program budgeting to take advantage of each system.

Public finance refers to the financing of government activities, resource allocations, and income distribution. Three basic policy objectives in public finance are allocation, distribution, and stabilization. **Allocation** is concerned with the quantity and types of goods and services to be provided. **Distribution** addresses the issue of who should receive the economic benefits of society and in what amount. **Stabilization** actions attempt to keep the economy running smoothly. Stabilization is accomplished by means of fiscal and monetary policies. **Fiscal policy** is implemented by taxing and spending decisions. **Monetary policy** is implemented by the Federal Reserve System, which controls interest rates and bank reserve requirements.

An important element of governmental decision making is its budgeting activity. **Planning, programming, budgeting system (PPBS)** is a program budgeting system with five distinguishing features: program accounting, multiyear costing, detailed description of activities, zero-base budgeting, and benefit-cost analysis. **Program accounting** is a system capable of accumulating costs by program or goal. **Multiyear costing** means identifying costs for the life of the project, not merely for the current budget period. **Detailed description of activities** is the careful delineation of the proposed program's goals, targets, selections, alternatives, output, and effectiveness measures. **Zero-base budgeting** requires all activities to be evaluated each year whether the activity is a newly proposed or an old program. **Benefit-cost analysis** requires all proposals to be evaluated in a quantitative systematic manner.

PPBS has had a dramatic impact but its initial expectations have not been fully realized. Some reasons for the lack of complete success are high cost; the size of the government, which is too large to utilize comprehensive budgeting effectively; the fact that the government is not organized along program lines; and the large number of projects whose benefits are difficult to measure and compare.

KEY TERMS

allocation *(614)*
benefit-cost analysis *(621)*
distribution *(614)*
fiscal policy *(615)*
functional budget *(610)*
incremental budgeting *(621)*
line budget *(610)*
line-program budget *(612)*
monetary policy *(615)*
multiyear costing *(619)*

not-for-profit sector *(605)*
planning, programming, budgeting system (**PPBS**) *(618)*
private sector *(606)*
program accounting *(619)*
program budgeting *(610)*
public finance *(613)*
public sector *(605)*
stabilization *(614)*
zero-base budgeting *(620)*

QUESTIONS

1. Marcus Collin has been a businessman for many years. His primary responsibility for the last 4 years has been preparation of the master budget for the manufacturing firm that employed him. Last month Collin was elected mayor of his city and is now faced with preparing the city budget for the coming fiscal year. He comes to

you and asks for your advice. Explain to Collin the major differences between a manufacturing company budget and a budget for a city. Include in your explanation the differences between line and program budgets and the advantages of each.

2. Polybord Corporation is a small manufacturing firm that produces printed circuit boards which it sells to about a dozen clients who make home computers, electronic games, and other electronic products. Competition is keen, with many small firms operating in the field, because entry into the business is relatively easy and requires little capital. The firm depends heavily on bank financing for its operations. It employs 150 production people. Describe what effect the following government actions might have on the operations of the firm:

   a. The Federal Reserve Board increases bank reserve requirements.
   b. New legislation requires all firms with more than 100 employees to report the amount of tax-free contributions that employees make into company-operated retirement systems. Up to now, only the employer's contribution to such systems had to be reported to the government.
   c. New taxes are imposed on the importation of electronic components from foreign countries.

3. (AICPA) There has been much publicity about zero-based budgeting. The system can be applied in government, not-for-profit, and profit-seeking organizations. Its proponents believe that it is a significant change in the budgeting process for most types of organizations and, thus, leads to more effective use of limited resources. Describe a zero-base budgeting system. Explain how it differs from the traditional budgeting process. Identify its advantages and disadvantages.

EXERCISES

Ex. 17-1
Determining
Program Benefits

The head of the parks and recreation department of a city has proposed a free swimming-lesson program for children between the ages of 3 and 14. The estimated cost of the program is $36,000, primarily composed of instructor salaries. City council, already operating with a tight budget, is not very interested in adding a new service without any source of revenue.

REQUIRED

Develop a presentation to the city council to support the addition of the free swimming classes. Provide specific arguments where possible and develop hypothetical data to support your position.

Ex. 17-2
Identifying Line
and Program
Budget Items

Plainfield school system uses both line and program budgeting in planning and managing its activities. Below is a list of cost categories used by the school system. Some of the items are from the program budget and some are from the line budget.

a. Depreciation, equipment
b. Administrative salaries
c. Textbooks
d. Utilities
e. School supplies
f. Athletic programs
g. Teacher salaries
h. Primary education
i. Secondary education
j. School bus costs
k. Student enrichment
l. Adult education
m. Heating
n. Driver training

REQUIRED

For each of the cost categories, determine if it most likely came from the line budget or the program budget.

Ex. 17-3
Budget
Performance
Report

Below are budgeted and actual 1985–86 data for the Fairview City fire department.

	Approved Budget 1985–86	Actual Costs 1985–86
Clerical wages	$ 38,000	$ 39,400
Education and training	52,000	49,700
Equipment operating expenses	32,000	36,300
Equipment purchases	175,000	164,000
Firemen's salaries	355,000	358,100
Gasoline	14,000	12,200
Insurance	15,000	15,900
Maintenance, buildings	18,000	23,500
Maintenance, equipment	67,000	71,300
Miscellaneous	25,000	29,900
Payroll taxes and fringe benefits	77,000	79,600
Supervisory salaries	66,000	66,000
Supplies	15,000	12,700
Uniform allowances	7,000	7,100
Uniform cleaning	4,000	3,800
Utilities	22,000	24,800
Totals	$982,000	$994,300

REQUIRED   Prepare a performance report in good form for the fire department.

Ex. 17-4
Incremental Budget

The Northfield Community Action Center is a not-for-profit community service program that provides a variety of services to the elderly and needy in the community. Included are free transportation to medical services, inexpensive meals, education programs, and other supportive programs. Below is the budget for the current year.

Northfield Community Action Center
Expenditure Budget
1986

Administrative salaries	$ 75,000
Building maintenance	6,000
Employee wages	82,000
Equipment purchases	5,000
Food costs	18,000
Miscellaneous	6,000
Supplies	4,000
Utilities	15,000
Vehicle maintenance	9,000
Vehicle operating costs	12,000
Total	$232,000

The management of the center expects vehicle operating costs to rise 15 percent in 1987. The average age of the vehicle will be 5 years in 1987, and some major repairs will be necessary. Management expects vehicle maintenance to increase 40 percent. The maintenance employee agreement calls for an 8.5 percent wage increase in 1987, and administrative employees will receive a 9 percent raise. Food costs are expected to increase 12 percent, utility costs 15 percent, and all other costs 8 percent.

REQUIRED

a. Prepare the 1987 expenditure budget for the Northfield Community Action Center.
b. Compute the total percentage change in the budget from the 1986 budget.

Ex. 17-5
Developing a
Program Budget

The Glendale Hospital has always used a line budget for its operations. Recently the board of directors of the hospital has suggested that a program budget might be a better way of planning and controlling the hospital's activities. The hospital controller has decided to prepare a line budget for the current budget year. The budget is presented below, followed by the estimated percentage of each line budget cost that pertains to the six hospital programs defined by the board of directors.

Glendale Hospital
Line Budget
1987

Administrative salaries	$ 150,000
Depreciation, building	120,000
Depreciation, equipment	160,000
Food	250,000
Insurance	80,000
Maintenance	90,000
Medical supplies	125,000
Miscellaneous	50,000
Nursing salaries	240,000
Salaries	140,000
Other supplies	60,000
Utilities	50,000
Totals	$1,515,000

Percentage of Cost Assignable to Each Program

	Medical Surgical	Newborn	Emergency Room	Lab Work	Cafeteria
Administrative salaries	45%	15%	20%	12%	8%
Depreciation, building	50	20	15	10	5
Depreciation, equipment	55	10	15	16	4
Food	60	2	—	—	38
Insurance	58	10	20	10	2
Maintenance	35	10	20	20	15
Medical supplies	60	8	12	20	—
Miscellaneous	30	10	20	25	15
Nursing salaries	65	20	15	—	—
Other salaries	10	5	10	55	20
Supplies	15	5	20	50	10
Utilities	45	10	20	15	10

REQUIRED Prepare a program budget for the Glendale Hospital for 1987.

Ex. 17-6
Combined Line-
Program Budget

Refer to the Glendale Hospital budget data presented in Exercise 17-5.

REQUIRED.   Prepare a combined line-program budget for the hospital for 1987.

Ex. 17-7
Relating
Government
Actions to Public
Finance Objectives

Below are a number of actions and decisions from various branches of the federal government. Each of them is intended to satisfy one of three policy objectives—allocation, distribution, or stabilization.

a. Congress passes a bill to increase the amount of the investment credit on new machinery.
b. The Fed increases the interest rate it charges member banks for loans.
c. The National Parks Service announces the creation of a nationwide campfire program for all parks in the system.
d. Congress increases the FICA tax rate.
e. Congress passes a bill to create jobs for the hard-core unemployed.
f. A new sailing ship is purchased for the Naval Academy.
g. Congress increases medical benefits to the elderly.
h. The President signs a bill to build 50 new strategic bombers.
i. Congress passes a 5 percent income tax surtax to help curtail public spending.
j. Reserve requirements for Federal Reserve member banks are lowered.

REQUIRED   Indicate whether the objective of each action is best classified as allocation, distribution, or stabilization.

PROBLEMS

P. 17-1
Revenue Budget

Below is the 1986 revenue budget for the city of Longsburg.

City of Longsburg
Revenue Budget
1986

Taxes:	
Property taxes	$ 4,000,000
City income taxes	1,400,000
Total city tax revenues	5,400,000
Fees:	
Water and sewer	2,800,000
License fees	350,000
Parking meters	540,000
Parks and recreation fees	130,000
Traffic fines and court cost fees	600,000
Total fees	4,420,000
Other revenues:	
State government appropriations	1,600,000
Federal government grants	2,200,000
Total other revenue	3,800,000
Total revenue for 1986	$13,620,000

The controller of Longsburg is preparing data for the 1987 revenue budget. She has identified the following items: The city income tax rate will remain the same, but the total amount of personal income earned by city residents is expected to increase 15 percent. The city's property tax rate will be raised in 1987 by 8 percent and the assessed valuation of property will increase by 16 percent. More stringent water quality requirements will increase the cost of operating the sewage treatment plant in 1987. In addition, the cost of providing water will increase because of new filtration equipment. In total the water and sewer rate will increase by 18 percent, and the amount of use should increase by 10 percent. License fees are expected to increase about 4 percent, which is the expected increase in city population for 1987. The same is true for parks and recreation fees. The parking meter rate will be raised by 40 percent in 1987, and stricter enforcement of parking violations is expected to increase the traffic fines and court cost fees by 20 percent. A tight state government budget suggests that the state appropriations for various civic programs and services will be reduced about 25 percent. On the other hand, federal government grants are expected to increase by 80 percent to pay for a variety of new programs currently funded and administered by the city.

REQUIRED   Prepare the 1987 revenue budget in good form for the city of Longsburg.

P. 17-2
Revenue Budget for
a University

Townsberg College is a small state-supported college with a current enrollment of 4,000 students. During the current year, the state provided $1,200 per student. Student tuition is $40 per credit hour, and a normal load is 30 credit hours per year. Contributions for the year were $3,200,000. Student fees were $25 per student and room and board charges were $1,400.

In planning for the next academic year, the financial management committee is evaluating the college's revenue sources. The committee expects student enrollments to increase 12 percent because a small private college in the area just closed. In addition, state appropriations are expected to increase 2 percent per student. To offset rising costs, the tuition will be increased by 12.5 percent, and room and board rates will increase 8 percent. Student fees will increase to $40, primarily to cover significant increases in insurance charges for the student health center. Current year contributions are the result of a significant fund drive effort aimed at raising money to make badly needed repairs and improvements. The campaign will not be continued next year and contributions are expected to fall 30 percent from the current year.

REQUIRED   Prepare a revenue budget in good form for Townsberg College for the next year.

P. 17-3
Expenditure Budget

Selville College has always relied on the city police force to provide security services for the college. The university pays the city a fee for the service. The board of trustees of the college believed that this was the most effective and economical method of providing campus security. However, the city charge for the services has been increasing about 15 percent a year for the last 5 years, and there is some concern about the quality of the security provided. The board is seriously evaluating the possibility of starting a university security force. To assist in the evaluation, the board requests a budget for a college security force.

The controller of the college and the security consultant have developed a security force plan and associated costs. Twelve officers will be required during the day shift, another six for the evening shift, and four for the night shift. The base pay for the campus security officers will be $22,500 per year, and an additional 30 percent of base pay will be required to pay for payroll taxes, insurance programs, and other employee benefits. One chief of security and one assistant chief of security must be hired at salaries of $45,000 and $36,000 respectively, plus employee benefits that amount to 40 percent of gross pay. All security officers will be provided a $250 per year uniform allowance. The expected cost for clerical salaries is $26,000 per year plus 20 percent for payroll taxes and employee benefits.

Ten patrol cars will need to be purchased during the first year at a cost of $10,400 each. Operating expenses of the patrol cars are expected to be $3,200 per year per car, and maintenance expenses should be $400 a year per car. Adequate physical facilities can be rented for $1,600 per month, and utilities should average about $450 per month. Office supplies and equipment rental should be $350 per month. Miscellaneous costs are budgeted at $15,000 for the first year.

REQUIRED   Prepare a budget in good form for the proposed security force at Selville College.

P. 17-4 (AICPA)
Public School
Budget

The board of education of the Victoria School District is developing a budget for the school year ending June 30, 1986. The budgeted expenditures follow:

Victoria School District
Budgeted Expenditures
For the Year Ending June 30, 1986

Current operating expenditures:			
Instruction:			
General	$1,401,600		
Vocational training	112,000	$1,513,600	
Pupil service:			
Bus transportation	36,300		
School lunches	51,700	88,000	
Attendance and health service		14,000	
Administration		46,000	
Operation and maintenance of plant		208,000	
Pensions, insurance, etc.		154,000	
Total current operating expenditures			$2,023,600
Other expenditures:			
Capital outlays from revenues		75,000	
Debt service (annual installment and interest on long-term debt)		150,000	
Total other expenditures			225,000
Total budgeted expenditures			$2,248,600

The following data are available:

1. The estimated average daily school enrollment of the school district is 5,000 pupils, including 200 pupils enrolled in a vocational training program.
2. Estimated revenues include equalizing grants-in-aid from the state of $150 per pupil. The grants were established by state law under a plan intended to encourage raising the level of education.
3. The federal government matches 60 percent of state grants-in-aid for pupils enrolled in a vocational training program. In addition the federal government contributes towards the cost of bus transportation and school lunches a maximum of $12 per pupil based on total enrollment within the school district

but not to exceed 6 2/3 percent of the state per-pupil equalization grants-in-aid.

4. Interest on temporary investment of school tax receipts and rents of school facilities is expected to be $75,000 and is earmarked for special equipment acquisitions listed as "Capital outlays from revenues" in the budgeted expenditures. Cost of the special equipment acquisitions will be limited to the amount derived from these miscellaneous receipts.

5. The remaining funds needed to finance the budgeted expenditures of the school district are to be raised from local taxation. An allowance of 9 percent of the local tax levy is necessary for possible tax abatements and losses. The assessed valuation of the property located within the school district is $80,000,000.

REQUIRED

a. Prepare a schedule computing the estimated total funds to be obtained from local taxation for the ensuing school year ending June 30, 1986 for the Victoria School District.

b. Prepare a schedule computing the estimated current operating cost per regular pupil and per vocational pupil to be met by local tax funds. Assume that costs other than instructional costs are assignable on a per capita basis to regular and vocational students.

c. Without prejudice to your solution to part *a*, assume that the estimated total tax levy for the ensuing school year ending June 30, 1986 is $1,092,000. Prepare a schedule computing the estimated tax rate per $100 of assessed valuation of the property within the Victoria School District.

P. 17-5
Special Project
Budget

Tradewinds National Park is located on the Gulf coast and provides fishing, scuba diving, boating, and beach activities to approximately 220,000 visitors a year. In addition, the park is a wildlife sanctuary. All wildlife within the park boundaries is protected. The problem of protecting land species is relatively easy, but the park boundaries include several hundred square miles of marshland and gulf coast waters. In the last several years, poachers have taken a greater and greater toll of exotic birds and alligators. In an effort to eliminate the problem, the superintendent of the park has decided to request funds to patrol the park adequately at all times. The superintendent has asked you to prepare a budget for the patrol program. To assist you in the process, the following data are available.

The patrol activity would require four 21-foot tri-hull power boats costing $18,000 each. In addition, six 18-foot flat-bottom airpowered boats are needed for the marshlands, each costing $13,000. Communications and other equipment for the boats will cost an additional $16,000. The superintendent believes that each patrol boat will need two officers. All ten boats will operate during the night, but only five boats will be necessary to patrol during the day and afternoon shifts. Officers will be paid $14,000 a year, and night shift patrols will be paid a premium of 15 percent of gross pay. The park must pay 10 percent of gross wages for payroll taxes, and other employee benefits amount to 15 percent of gross pay.

Each boat will operate an average of 1,600 hours per year. Operating cost will average $6 per hour. Routine maintenance should average $60 per boat per 200 operating hours. Other boat maintenance costs are expected to average $150 per year for the air boats and $300 per boat for the other boats. Insurance on the boats is $350 per boat per year.

REQUIRED

Prepare a budget for the first year of the patrol program.

P. 17-6 (AICPA)
Developing a
College Budget

DeMars College has asked your assistance with its budget for the 1985–86 academic year. You are supplied with the following data for the current year:

	Lower Division (Freshman — Sophomore)	Upper Division (Junior — Senior)
Average number of students per class	25	20
Average salary of faculty member	$20,000	$20,000
Average number of credit hours carried each year per student	33	30
Enrollment including scholarship students	2,500	1,700
Average faculty teaching load in credit hours per year (10 classes of 3 credit hours)	30	30

1. For 1985–86 lower-division enrollment is expected to increase by 10 percent, while the upper division's enrollment is expected to remain stable. Faculty salaries will be increased by a standard 5 percent, and additional merit increases to be awarded to individual faculty members will be $90,750 for the lower division and $85,000 for the upper division.
2. The current budget is $210,000 for operation and maintenance of plant and equipment; this includes $90,000 for salaries and wages. Experience of the past 3 months suggests that the current budget is realistic, but that expected increases for 1985–86 are 5 percent in salaries and wages and $9,000 in other expenditures for operation and maintenance of plant and equipment.
3. The budget for the remaining expenditures for 1985–86 is as follows:

Administrative and general	$240,000
Library	160,000
Health and recreation	75,000
Athletics	120,000
Insurance and retirement	265,000
Interest	48,000
Capital outlay	300,000

4. The college expects to award 25 tuition-free scholarships to lower-division students and 15 to upper-division students. Tuition is $22 per credit hour and no other fees are charged.
5. Budgeted revenues for 1985–86 are as follows:

Endowments	$2,914,000
Net income from auxiliary services	235,000
Athletics	180,000

The college's remaining source of revenue is an annual support campaign held during the spring.

REQUIRED

a. Prepare a schedule computing for 1985–86 by division (1) the expected enrollment, (2) the total credit hours to be carried, and (3) the number of faculty members needed.
b. Prepare a budget for faculty salaries by division for 1985–86.
c. Prepare a schedule computing the tuition revenue budget by division for 1985–86.

d. Assuming that the faculty salaries budget computed in part *b* was $4,800,000 and that the tuition revenue budget in part *c* was $3,000,000, prepare a schedule computing the amount that must be raised during the annual support campaign in order to cover the 1985–86 expenditures budget.

P. 17-7
Performance
Report

The new city controller has just prepared the following budget performance report for the parks and recreation department. The variances are presented as percentages of budgeted amounts. This reporting format is not the same as the one used during prior years, and the city council would like a performance report for the department that clearly identifies both budget and actual costs and the amount of difference between the two for each cost item.

Parks and Recreation Department
Budget Performance Report
1986–87

	Budget 1986–87	Percentage Variance (Favorable) Unfavorable
Equipment operations	$ 5,000	(4)%
Equipment purchases	12,000	(12)
Grounds and pool chemicals	6,000	6
Instructors' wages	46,000	5
Lifeguards' wages	22,000	12
Maintenance and grounds wages	34,000	(8)
Maintenance supplies	7,000	11
Miscellaneous	12,000	24
Payroll taxes and employee benefits	14,000	5
Recreation supplies	9,000	(10)
Supervisory salaries	35,000	(14)
Uniforms, prizes, and trophies	8,000	9
Utilities	14,000	18
	$224,000	

REQUIRED Prepare a budget performance report in good form for the parks and recreation department identifying the amount of actual cost and budget variance for each cost.

CASES

Case 17-1
Analyzing Budget
Data and Resource
Requirements

Pices Aquarium is a not-for-profit organization devoted to the study of aquatic life and to public education. The aquarium has both indoor and outdoor exhibits and has been growing significantly over the last several years. The 1986 revenue and expenditure budgets for Pices Aquarium are presented on the next page.

In the last 5 years the aquarium has experienced a steady 10 percent growth in visitors each year. In 1986, 500,000 people will visit the aquarium and pay the $2.50 admission fee. Although funds for operating the aquarium are available, it is difficult to raise enough money to maintain properly the displays and other facilities. Saltwater

Pices Aquarium
Revenue Budget
1986

Admission fees	$1,250,000
Sales of food, souvenirs, and other concession items	600,000
Federal government grants	150,000
Public contributions	100,000
Contribution from conservation groups	300,000
Total budgeted revenues	$2,400,000

Pices Aquarium
Expenditure Budget
1986

Administrative and professional salaries	$ 340,000
Employee wages	600,000
Animal food and supplies	800,000
Concession items	240,000
Utilities	160,000
Normal maintenance	120,000
Equipment purchases	80,000
Special repairs and maintenance	60,000
Total budgeted expenditures	$2,400,000

displays are particularly vulnerable to deterioration. A problem facing the aquarium is that the main saltwater display tank needs major repair and maintenance. The project has been postponed for several years because of funding problems. But recent evidence indicates that the project must be done in 1987 or the entire display will have to be closed. The projected cost for the entire project is $410,000.

The only special funding for the project is from the conservation groups that currently provide some support for the aquarium. They have promised to increase their 1987 contributions by $150,000. The rest of the funds will have to be raised by the aquarium through higher admission fees. The management of the aquarium is reluctant to raise the admission fee, because it wants as many people as possible to have the opportunity to visit. However, there is no other way of raising the money to protect the facilities.

Management estimates that the expected 10 percent increase in visitors in 1987 will be reduced by 1 percent for every $.10 increase in the admission price. (A price increase from the current $2.50 to $2.60 would result in a 9 percent increase in visitors in 1987 rather than 10 percent.) Concession sales are expected to increase by 8 percent in 1987. A special campaign by a local radio station is expected to increase public contributions by 25 percent next year. No change is expected in federal government support.

In addition to the major repair of the main saltwater tank, most other costs are expected to increase also. Administrative and professional salaries are scheduled to increase 5 percent, and a labor agreement with other employees provides for an 8 percent wage increase in 1987. There are no plans to change in the number of persons employed at the aquarium. The cost of animal food and supplies has been rising at the rate of 12 percent and is expected to continue at the same rate for the next year.

The cost of concession items will remain at the same level per dollar of concession revenue. A recent utility rate change will increase 1987 utility costs by 18 percent. Normal maintenance costs will be about 5 percent higher in 1987 and special repairs and maintenance on other facilities will remain the same for the next year. Management has decided to reduce the equipment purchases budget by 50 percent to help pay for the cost of the main saltwater tank.

REQUIRED
a. Prepare the 1987 expenditure budget in good form for Pices Aquarium.
b. Compute the required admission fee to cover all normal operating costs and pay for the required maintenance on the main saltwater tank.
c. Prepare the 1987 revenue budget in good form for Pices Aquarium.

PART SIX
In-Depth Cost Accounting Topics

The cost of any manufactured product, no matter how complex, is made up of three basic cost elements — materials, labor, and manufacturing overhead. But accounting for these three cost elements involves complex issues of data collection, measurement, and reporting. And managing the cost elements requires skill in interpreting the accounting information and using it to solve production problems. Managers must decide how to combine materials, labor, and overhead resources to manufacture a variety of products and how to determine if their decisions achieved the desired results.

This part of the book addresses some of the more complex issues of managing manufacturing resources and combining them into finished products. It is an in-depth look at each cost element and the costing of products. Chapter 18 is a discussion of materials management. Chapter 19 looks at labor, with particular emphasis on labor-related costs and problems of identifying these costs with products. Chapter 20 discusses the accounting for and management of manufacturing overhead costs. Some special product costing issues are covered in Chapters 21 and 22. Chapter 21 presents costing and allocation concepts and procedures used when several different products emerge from a single manufacturing process. Chapter 22 extends standard costing to nonmanufacturing operations and also to the measurement of variances for products made with a mix of several material and labor inputs.

CHAPTER 18
Accounting for Materials

Early in your study of cost accounting, you learned that materials play a major role in manufacturing activities. Chapter 4 shows how accountants trace the flow of materials costs as they parallel the physical flow of materials through the production process, and Chapter 8 discusses the analysis of material variances in standard costing. The materials accounting system provides information for accountants and for production, financial and marketing managers, and for internal and external reports. Accounting for materials, however, is more detailed and complex than discussed in earlier chapters.

This chapter offers broad coverage of materials accounting concepts, procedures, and documents involved in materials management. In addition to discussing the basic physical flow of inventory and the parallel flow of accounting data and source documents, a number of special materials concepts are presented, including accounting for scrap, defective units, and inventory adjustments.

THE SIGNIFICANCE OF MATERIALS IN PRODUCTION

Efficient management of materials is essential to the successful operation of manufacturing firms

The purchase, handling, and use of materials must be effectively managed to ensure the efficient use of material resources and their availability when needed in production. Some managers believe that in a manufacturing business the management of material resources is of primary importance in maintaining a competitive edge over other firms.

Material is a major asset and a major product cost for manufacturing businesses. Most manufacturers have large amounts of resources invested in inventories. The management of these resources is the shared responsibility of financial managers, production engineers, and production supervisors. Accountants are expected to provide the information necessary to facilitate the management of materials. To explain the role of accounting information in the management of materials inventory, and the nature of inventory documents, we illustrate and review briefly the basic activities and cost flows associated with materials inventory.

Inventory Activities

Two activities associated with raw materials in a manufacturing firm are inventory acquisition and inventory distribution. **Acquisition** includes all

637

Figure 18-1. Inventory acquisition activities are closely paralleled by the measurement of inventory costs. Key factors in the accounting and inventory control process are the source documents associated with inventory acquisition. Shown here are the major inventory acquisition activities and their associated source documents.

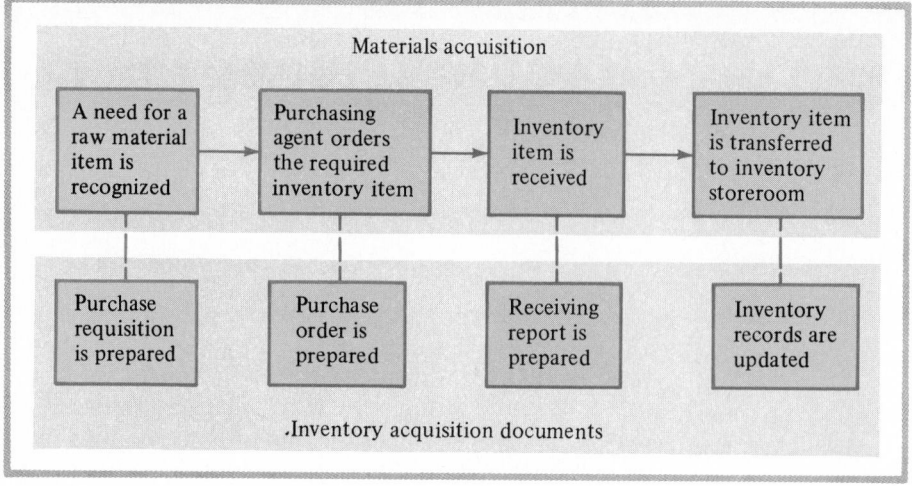

activities necessary to purchase and receive inventory and move it into the inventory storage area, usually referred to as the storeroom or the stores area. **Inventory distribution** includes all activities associated with transferring raw materials into production. The efficient accomplishment of both activities is essential to the successful operation of manufacturing businesses.

Most accounting entries are initiated by some source document, and this is particularly true in accounting for materials in a manufacturing environment. Figure 18-1 illustrates the activities associated with the acquisition of materials and the source documents used in the process. These source documents are essential in identifying product costs and in providing an audit trail. A clear audit trail enables accountants to trace transactions if problems arise or if errors are detected; an audit trail also enables accountants to test the accounting system and verify that it is performing its function properly.

A specific quantity of existing inventory signals the need to order more

Inventory Acquisition.   The first step in inventory acquisition is the determination that some inventory item is needed. The inventory level at which an order is placed is called the **inventory reorder point;** it is established on the basis of the time required to fill and ship an order by a supplier and the number of units used from the time the order is placed until it is delivered. The reorder point is discussed in some detail in Chapter 13.

A **purchase requisition** initiates the purchasing process. It is prepared and sent to the purchasing department, which has the responsibility for acquiring materials and supplies for the organization. Purchase requisitions, like all inventory documents, vary in form and information content from firm to firm, depending on the nature of the business and the information needs of management, but most have a number of common characteristics. Figure 18-2 illustrates a typical purchase requisition.

After receiving the purchase requisition, the purchasing agent determines the most economical way of filling the purchase request and issues a

Figure 18-2. A purchase requisition tells the purchasing department that some item is needed. Data from the requisition provide information needed by the purchasing department to analyze and place the order.

PURCHASE REQUISITION MACGRUDER COMPANY			
Date: 11/22/85			
Source: Stores management			Requisition No. R74982
Quantity	Unit	Description	Part No.
200	Each	5-horsepower electric motors	2344-5HP
50	Rolls	No. 10 wire	1050-10WR
Special instructions:			
Ship motors air freight.			

Ordering and receiving inventory generates several source documents

purchase order, which is a document used to place an order with a supplier. A purchase order is illustrated in Figure 18-3. The **purchasing agent** has the responsibility for managing the purchasing activity. In a small business, the purchasing activity may be only one of several responsibilities of the purchasing agent; in large organizations the purchasing agent may manage a very large department. Whatever the size of the firm, the authority and responsibility for the purchasing function should be clearly defined.

When new materials are received, they are compared with the purchase order to ensure that the quantity and quality are proper and a **receiving report** is prepared. This report is used to update the inventory control account, the balances in specific inventory records, and the accounts payable records. A receiving report is shown in Figure 18-4.

To illustrate accounting for the purchase of materials, we record the purchase of the items shown in the purchase order in Figure 18-3 and the receiving report in Figure 18-4. The journal entry to record the purchase of 200 electric motors and 50 rolls of no. 10 wire is presented below:

	Inventory control	38,250	
	Accounts payable		38,250
	To record the purchase of 200 5-hp		
	electric motors and 50 rolls of		
	no. 10 wire.		

Figure 18-3. A purchase order is used to place an order for materials. It is prepared by the purchasing department and is sent to the vendor supplying the inventory or other purchased items.

MACGRUDER COMPANY	PURCHASE ORDER

Ship to:
 	
    2741 N. Vernon Drive
    Fort Worth, Texas 76149
	P.O. No. P77390
	
	Date: 11/27/85

Vendor:
 	
    Continental Electric
    48470 Venora Blvd.
    Indianapolis, Indiana 47508
	Requisition No. R74982
	
	Requisition Date: 11/22/85
	
	Requisition Source: Stores mgt.

Quantity	Unit	Item: Description	Price	Amount
200	Each	5-horsepower electric motors	$185.00	$37,000
50	Rolls	No. 10 wire	25.00	1,250

Special instructions:

    Ship motors air freight.

The debit of $38,250 is posted to the Inventory Control account in the general ledger, and the individual inventory accounts are posted in the inventory subsidiary ledger. The individual inventory accounts are called **inventory ledger cards, or stores ledger cards.** These documents are used to record the acquisition and use of each inventory item. As you may guess, in a large organization, there can be thousands of inventory ledger cards. Historically, such cards were maintained manually, but now most organizations record detailed inventory data with computers, and inventory status reports sometimes are available instantly on computer terminals. The stores ledger card for the 5-horsepower motors purchased above is presented in Figure 18-5. A similar inventory card is maintained for the no. 10 wire, and it would be posted for the purchase recorded above.

Inventory records are updated as inventory is received and used

The purpose of having a formal, systematic procedure for ordering, receiving, and storing materials inventory is to ensure proper managerial control over these functions. Each procedure and each document is designed to keep track of the materials, fix responsibility for specific functions, prevent errors and losses, and enable proper record keeping, which eventually results in adequate managerial and financial reporting.

Figure 18-4. When items are received, they are counted or measured and compared with the purchase order. Then a receiving report is prepared stating what was received and the quantity.

RECEIVING REPORT MACGRUDER COMPANY			
Date: 12/10/85			Receiving Report No. RP56881
Vendor: Continental Electric			
Quantity	Unit	Part No.	Item: Description
500	Each	2344-5HP	5-horsepower electric motors
50	Rolls	1050-10WR	No. 10 wire

Figure 18-5. Inventory ledger cards are updated when inventory is purchased or used. Often these records are maintained by computers rather than by hand.

INVENTORY LEDGER CARD
MACGRUDER COMPANY

Part No. 2344-5HP

Item: 5-horsepower electric motors

Unit: Each

Inventory Valuation Method: FIFO

Reorder Point: 120 units

Ordered		Received				Issued				Balance		
Date	Quantity	Date	Quantity	Price	Amount	Date	Quantity	Price	Amount	Quantity	Price	Amount
		10/24	150	$180	$27,000					100	$179	$17,900
										150	180	27,000
						11/19	100	$179	$17,900			
							30	180	5,400	120	180	21,600
11/27	200											
		12/10	200	185	37,000					120	180	21,600
										200	185	37,000

Inventory distribution is the process of putting materials into production

Inventory Distribution. Providing the correct inventory items in the right amount for production activities is critical to an efficient manufacturing activity. Ineffective inventory distribution can result in lost production, idle or inefficiently used production facilities, and missed production schedules. The actual management of inventory distribution is the responsibility of production managers and systems engineers, but the measurement of costs associated with the activity is the responsibility of accountants who also use the data in costing production and measuring performance.

Efficient inventory distribution requires careful planning and strategic location of material resources, so that material can be distributed to production activities as efficiently as possible. The storerooms are repositories of raw materials used in the production process, and their location is a primary determinant of the cost of the inventory distribution activity. The process of distributing materials to production can be complex, and the degree of efficiency achieved in materials distribution is often a major determinant of profitability. Consequently, many manufacturing businesses invest significant amounts of money in inventory management systems. Here we are primarily interested in the flow of inventory through the production process and the measurement of the associated costs. Figure 18-6 gives a brief overview of the inventory distribution activities and the associated accounting activities and source documents.

A number of the source documents provided by inventory distribution are used to identify and accumulate inventory cost data. **A materials requisition** starts the physical flow of raw materials into the production process and triggers the associated entry for materials costs in the company's accounting records. Typically, a materials requisition reports the type, quantity, and production location of the requisitioned material. Note the distinction between a materials requisition and a purchase requisition; the latter initiates the purchasing process and the former starts material into production. A materials requisition is illustrated in Figure 18-7.

Materials needed in production are requisitioned

This materials requisition shows the issue of 130 electric motors and 20 rolls of wire to production in the assembly department. FIFO inventory valuation is used, and the cost of all motors is not identical, so two different unit costs are used to determine the amount of materials cost charged to production. The journal entry to record the transfer of these direct materials into production is as follows:

	Work in process control	23,800	
	Inventory control		23,800
	To record the transfer of direct materials		
	into production in the assembly		
	department for Job no. J-8091 per		
	MR22739.		

Figure 18-6. Accounting activities closely parallel inventory and production activities. This diagram shows the inventory and production activities on the left and the corresponding accounting activities on the right.

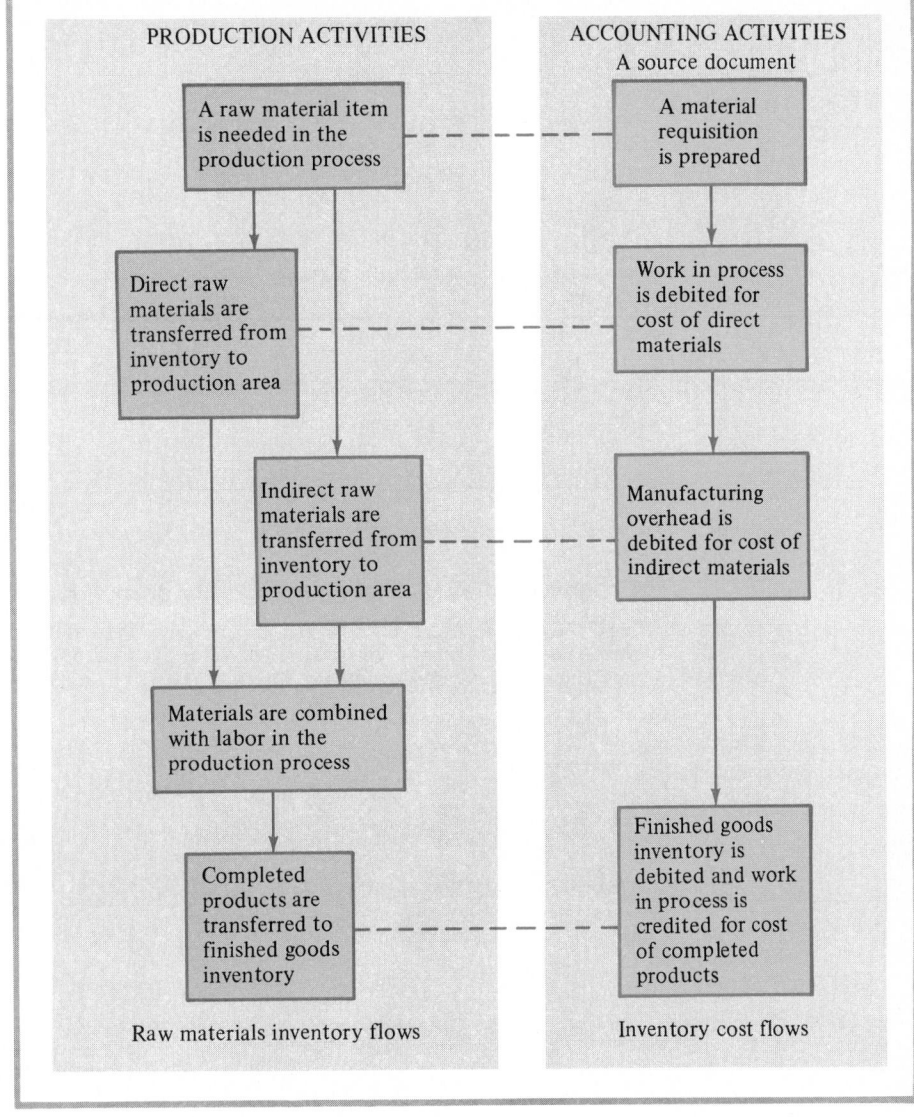

PRODUCTION ACTIVITIES

ACCOUNTING ACTIVITIES
A source document

A raw material item is needed in the production process

A material requisition is prepared

Direct raw materials are transferred from inventory to production area

Work in process is debited for cost of direct materials

Indirect raw materials are transferred from inventory to production area

Manufacturing overhead is debited for cost of indirect materials

Materials are combined with labor in the production process

Completed products are transferred to finished goods inventory

Finished goods inventory is debited and work in process is credited for cost of completed products

Raw materials inventory flows

Inventory cost flows

Periodically, a report may be prepared summarizing materials requisition information for the day, week, month, or some other time period. Figure 18-8 presents a materials requisition summary report.

Sometimes the amount of material issued to production is more than required. Efficient production, less output than expected, or employee errors are but a few reasons why unused production materials may be returned to the inventory storeroom. Returned material must be accounted for properly, so that the inventory records and the amount of materials cost charged to products are correct. **A returned materials report** is prepared when some of

If too much material is issued, some is sent back to inventory

Figure 18-7. A materials requisition is used to start materials into the production process. Storeroom personnel receive the materials requisition and provide the materials for production.

	MATERIALS REQUISITION MACGRUDER COMPANY			
Department: Assembly				
Requisition No. MR22739			Date: 11/19/85	
Job No.	Item: Description	Quantity	Price	Amount
J-8091	5-HP electric motors	100	$179	$17,900
J-8091	5-HP electric motors	30	180	5,400
J-8091	No. 10 wire	20	25	500

the requisitioned material is not used in production and is returned to the inventory storeroom. This document initiates an entry to add the returned material cost to inventory and remove it from work in process. A returned materials report is shown in Figure 18-9.

Figure 18-8. A materials requisition summary report periodically reports the distribution of materials to production. The report may be prepared daily, weekly, monthly, or for some other time period.

	MATERIALS REQUISITION SUMMARY REPORT MACGRUDER COMPANY					
Period: 11/18 – 11/24						
Date of Report: 11/26						
Date	Mat. Req. No.	Department	Job No.	Item	Quantity	Amount
11/18	MR22737	Finishing	J-8077	Paint	5 gal	$ 60
11/19	MR22738	Assembly	J-8092	Fan housings	40	8,000
11/19	MR22739	Assembly	J-8091	Elect. motors	130	23,300
			J-8091	No. 10 wire	20 rolls	500
11/20	MR22740	Welding	MOH Cont.	Welding rods	20 boxes	360
11/21	MR22741	Finishing	J-8075	Lumber	400 ft.	600
11/22	MR22742	Assembly	J-8088	Back panels	120	4,800
11/23	MR22743	Finishing	MOH Cont.	Buffing comp.	500 lb	700
11/23	MR22744	Assembly	J-8091	Compressors	130	58,500

Figure 18-9. If too much material is issued to production, the excess is returned to the inventory storeroom and the return is reported on a returned materials report.

RETURNED MATERIALS REPORT MACGRUDER COMPANY				
Returned from: Assembly Department			**Report No.** RM8173	
Date: 12/17/85				
Job No.	**Item: Description**	**Quantity**	**Price**	**Amount**
J-8091	No. 10 wire	4 rolls	$25	$100

The entry to record the return of the materials to the inventory storeroom is illustrated below:

	Inventory control	100	
	Work in process control		100
	To record the return to inventory of 4		
	rolls of no. 10 wire from Job no. J-8091		
	in the assembly department per RM8173.		

The debit in this entry is posted to the Inventory Control account in the general ledger and also to the individual ledger card for no. 10 wire in the inventory subsidiary ledger. Similarly, the credit is posted to the Work in Process Control account and to the job cost sheet for Job no. J-8091.

The number of transactions involving inventory accounting activities is actually large, but the concepts and procedures are the same as just described. Of course, each company has variations of the process and accounting forms in order to meet specific information needs and characteristics of the company's production process. The procedures and documents used in inventory distribution are designed to help managers safeguard valuable resources, control operations, and make critical decisions that keep the business operating profitably. We now discuss some additional accounting procedures that provide managers with a variety of materials information.

ADDITIONAL CONCEPTS ASSOCIATED WITH INVENTORY ACCOUNTING

Some of the additional concepts essential to the management of materials inventory include accounting for scrap materials, inventory adjustments, materials handling costs, and defective units.

Accounting for Scrap Material

Scrap is material that has economic value but is unusable in normal production activities

Manufacturing processes often generate **scrap material,** which is the salable material resulting from production. Examples are irregular pieces of steel left after parts are sheared from steel sheets, or short pieces of copper tubing left after the production of heating and air-conditioning coils. To be classified as scrap, the material must have two characteristics: First, the scrap is not useful in the normal operations of the business. Second, the scrap must have a market value; otherwise it is merely waste that must be disposed of. A careful distinction must be made between scrap and returned materials. Returned materials are unused raw materials inventory, whereas scrap is not usable in the normal manufacturing activities of the firm.

There are several ways of accounting for scrap material, depending on the relative value of the scrap and management's costing objectives. Three approaches to accounting for scrap are:

Three methods of accounting for scrap material

1. Reduce the cost of the specific products that were produced when the scrap was generated.
2. Reduce the cost of production in general.
3. Record the sale of scrap as miscellaneous revenue.

To illustrate accounting for scrap, we assume that scrap steel with a value of $2,500 is generated during a day's production activities.

Scrap Recorded as a Reduction in Specific Product Cost. Many accountants think that the sale of scrap should be treated as a reduction in the cost of products. The idea is to charge each product with materials costs equal to the total cost of materials used in its production less any savings realized from the sale of scrap that resulted from making the product. The concept is similar to the deposit on a soft drink bottle. If the soft drink cost of 40 cents includes a 10-cent deposit on the bottle, the actual cost of the soft drink is 30 cents. The 10-cent deposit reduces the cost to 30 cents when the empty bottle is returned.

Scrap revenue can reduce the cost of specific products

The matching concept is achieved best if the scrap can be identified with specific products or production activities. The cost saving from the sale of scrap can be credited directly to the specific job or process center. Using the data presented above, the journal entry to record the sale of scrap is:

	Cash (or Accounts receivable)	2,500	
	Work in process control		2,500
	To record the sale of scrap steel resulting		
	from the production of Job no. JO-67584.		

It is possible to identify scrap daily or weekly and accumulate it in a location for scrap inventory. The scrap is then sold at a convenient time when a large enough quantity is accumulated. In such cases, the scrap is recorded first in a scrap inventory account. To illustrate, we assume scrap is recorded daily and sold at the end of each week. On a day when scrap with a $2,500 market value is generated, the entry is

	Scrap inventory	2,500	
	Work in process control		2,500
	To record the scrap inventory resulting		
	from the production of Job no. JO-67584.		

At the end of the week when the scrap is sold, the following entry is made:

	Cash (or Accounts receivable)	12,500	
	Scrap inventory		12,500
	To record the sale of scrap.		

Scrap Recorded as a Reduction of Product Cost in General.   Sometimes it is impossible or economically infeasible to identify scrap with specific products or process centers. In such cases, scrap sales can be used to reduce production costs in general by reducing the Manufacturing Overhead Control account. This is a logical approach when scrap is not directly identifiable with specific products but we want to treat the revenue from its sale as a cost saving. The journal entry for this alternative is:

Scrap revenue can reduce the cost of production in general

	Cash (or Accounts receivable)	2,500	
	Manufacturing overhead control		2,500
	To record the sale of scrap not directly		
	identifiable with specific products.		

If the scrap is recorded first in an inventory account, the entries are as follows:

	Scrap inventory	2,500	
	Manufacturing overhead control		2,500
	To record inventory of scrap not directly		
	identifiable with specific products.		
	Cash (or Accounts receivable)	2,500	
	Scrap inventory		2,500
	To record the sale of scrap.		

Scrap Recorded as Miscellaneous Revenue.   Recording scrap as a miscellaneous revenue does not satisfy the matching principle very well. With this approach, no attempt is made to reduce the cost of products by the amount realized from the sale of scrap. In fact, product cost is not affected in any way. Instead, Cash is debited at the time of sale, and a revenue account is credited. The entry to record the scrap sale as a miscellaneous income item is as follows:

	Cash (or Accounts receivable)	2,500	
	Sale of scrap		2,500
	To record the sale of scrap steel.		

Scrap may be accounted for as miscellaneous sales revenue when its value is relatively small. Any distortion in the cost of the manufactured product is usually not material when scrap is a small portion of total production cost.

Inventory Adjustments

Occasionally it is necessary to adjust the balance in the inventory account to correct for shortages, obsolescence, errors, or losses. The adjustment of inventory does not necessarily reflect inefficient or ineffective accounting, production, or inventory handling. Many adjustments result from normal activities. For example, there are bound to be some differences between the accounting records and the physical amount of inventory when thousands of items are handled every week. An inventory handling and accounting system that eliminates all possible errors would cost too much to operate and may be impossible to design. Below we discuss some of the more common situations requiring adjustments in inventory.

Physical Inventory Counts.

Most organizations take a physical count of their inventory every year even if they use a perpetual inventory system. The inventory count may be a single once-a-year activity or a continuous activity in which different parts of inventory are counted throughout the year. Often the physical inventory count discloses some difference between the amount of inventory on hand and the amount recorded in the accounts. When this occurs, it is necessary to adjust the inventory records. Inventory adjustments may be needed for raw materials and for finished goods. First we discuss raw materials.

Raw materials inventory adjustments are usually relatively small and reflect normal losses, such as breakage, production errors, and evaporation. Small expected shortages are treated as a normal cost of business and are included in product costs as part of manufacturing overhead. For example, if the count of raw materials shows a shortage of $8,500, the entry is:

	Manufacturing overhead control	8,500	
	Raw materials inventory control		8,500
	To record the adjustment in raw materials		
	inventory indicated by physical count.		

The charge to overhead control is posted in the general ledger account and also in the overhead subsidiary ledger account for inventory adjustments.

The credit to the inventory control account is posted to the general ledger account and also to each of the specific raw materials accounts that had incorrect balances in the inventory subsidiary records.

Occasionally, the inventory count reveals more inventory than shown in the accounting records. In this case, the overhead control account is credited and the inventory control account is debited. For instance, if the count shows $4,200 more inventory than is in the records, the entry is:

	Raw materials inventory control	4,200	
	Manufacturing overhead control		4,200
	To record the adjustment in raw materials		
	inventory indicated by physical count.		

Unusual inventory shortages are losses

Sometimes the required inventory adjustment is significantly larger than normally expected. Because overhead costs reflect only normal costs of production, unusually large inventory shortages should not be charged to overhead. Instead they should be charged to a loss account for the period. For example, the physical inventory shows a shortage of $87,200, which is larger than normal. The abnormal inventory shortage is a loss for the period and appears in the income statement. The entry to record this unusual inventory shortage is:

	Loss from abnormal inventory shortage	87,200	
	Raw materials inventory control		87,200
	To record an unusual inventory shortage		
	identified by physical inventory count.		

Inventory differences that occur in finished goods are not part of the production activities. Finished goods inventory carrying costs are not a manufacturing expense; neither is the cost of finished goods inventory shortages. For instance, an inventory count reveals a finished goods inventory shortage of $7,000. The entry to record the loss is:

	Inventory shortage (finished goods)	7,000	
	Finished goods inventory control		7,000
	To record a finished goods inventory		
	shortage disclosed by physical count.		

Adjustments to Lower of Cost or Market

Unrealized declines in inventory values are losses

Inventories are typically recorded at their cost, but if their market value declines below cost, they must be written down to their market value for financial reporting purposes. Typically, such writedowns are accomplished by using an allowance account to record the decline in market value. The allowance account is a contra-asset account similar to the allowance for bad debts. The entry to create or increase such an account is as follows:

	Loss from decline in market		
	value of inventory	9,000	
	Allowance for decline in		
	market value of inventory		9,000
	To reduce inventory to lower of cost or		
	market value.		

Entries such as this one are made before financial statements are prepared. The loss is reported in the income statement as an adjustment to gross margin. If the market value of the inventory increases in a subsequent period, the allowance account is reduced or eliminated and the gain is recorded as a recovery of a previous unrealized loss. For example, in the following year, the market value of finished goods inventory is $7,800 below cost. The $9,000 allowance account is reduced to $7,800 as follows:

	Allowance for decline in market		
	value of inventory	1,200	
	Recovery of unrealized loss		1,200
	To write up the value of inventory		
	previously written down.		

Materials Handling Costs

A separate overhead rate may be used for material handling costs

Materials handling costs are defined as all costs necessary to maintain and operate the inventory storeroom and costs associated with providing raw materials to production. Usually, inventory handling costs are treated as indirect costs of operating a manufacturing operation. Before the year begins, managers estimate the amount of materials handling costs and include them in the overhead budget used for computing the manufacturing overhead rate.

Some managers believe that matching is not achieved by including materials handling costs as part of the general manufacturing overhead rate. Instead, they create a separate materials handling overhead rate and assign materials handling costs to production based on this separate rate. The materials handling application base can be anything that managers think will do a good job of matching the materials handling cost with production. Some common application bases are a percentage of materials cost, a rate per unit of material used, or a rate per materials requisition filled.

ACCOUNTING FOR DEFECTIVE UNITS

Some defective units are common in manufacturing operations

Most manufacturing companies establish quality control standards to maintain satisfactory product quality. Typically, not all production output meets quality control standards, due to occasional employee errors, random errors in the manufacturing process, or a variety of other causes. In most organizations, some unacceptable production is unavoidable. It is part of the normal production process and cannot be eliminated without costly changes in the production equipment, the quality of the employees, or the quality control procedures.

To illustrate accounting for units that do not meet quality control standards, we use the following example:

Job No. 8240	
Total units produced	100
Defective units	10
Normal selling price	$50
Production costs:	
Direct materials	$ 900
Direct labor	1,200
Applied overhead	600
Total cost	$2,700

What is done with the cost of defective units that are not reworked?

Defective units are either discarded, sold for less than normal price, or reworked and sold as normal goods. The disposition of units is determined by the economics of the situation. Units that cannot be economically reworked are discarded or sold, and the rest are reworked. We start by discussing units that cannot be economically reworked.

Defective Units Not Reworked

Units that do not meet standards and cannot be economically reworked fall into two categories: units with no value and units that can be sold at a reduced price.

Units That Cannot Be Sold.   Units with no value are merely discarded. Of the 100 units produced, only 90 are acceptable. The other 10 units are discarded because they have no value. There are two ways to account for this loss. One is to assign all of the loss to the good units that were produced in Job no. 8240. This approach assumes that the cause of the loss is identifiable with the job or the production processes associated with making that particular product.

If all of the cost is assigned to the specific job, no journal entry is necessary to record the cost of the bad units. The total $2,700 manufacturing cost is divided by the 90 good units, resulting in a unit cost of $30.

An alternative approach is to charge the cost of the bad units to all production. The theory is that if the faulty units occurred because of random production errors or some other reason that is not job specific, then the good units in a specific job should not be charged all of the defective unit cost. Instead, all products are made to share this cost by charging overhead control with the cost of the bad units.

This entry reduces the cost in the work in process control account and the job cost sheet for Job no. 8240 by $270, which is the bad units' production cost [($2,700/100 total units) × 10 defective units]. The overhead control account is charged with $270 for defective units. The resulting unit cost of the 90 good units is $27, which is computed as ($2,700 − $270)/90 good units.

	Manufacturing overhead control	270	
	Work in process control		270
	To record the cost of 10 defective units		
	manufactured in Job no. 8240 and assign		
	the cost to all production.		

Sale of Defective Units.   Sometimes defective units can be sold for less than the normal price. For example, assume the 10 bad units in our example can be sold for $10 each. Management must decide whether the cost of the bad units should be assigned to Job no. 8240 or to all production. In this case, however, the revenue from the sale of the bad units may be used to reduce their cost. The cost of the bad units is already recorded in the work in process account for Job no. 8240. Therefore it is only necessary to reduce this cost by the amount of revenue obtained from the sale of the defective units. The defective units are transferred out of work in process into a defective units inventory account at their market value.

Defective units may be sold without reworking

	Defective units inventory	100	
	Work in process control		100
	To reduce cost of Job no. 8240 by the		
	expected revenue from defective units.		

This entry reduces the total cost of Job no. 8240 from $2,700 to $2,600, and the cost of the good units is now $28.89 per unit ($2,600/90).

An alternative approach is to charge the loss to all production. To do this, the cost of the bad units is calculated and removed from Job no. 8240. This cost is then reduced by the expected revenue from the sale of the defective units, and the difference is assigned to overhead. The entry is:

	Defective units inventory	100	
	Manufacturing overhead control	170	
	Work in process control		270
	To remove cost of defective units from		
	Job no. 8240 and assign the cost less		
	sales revenue to all production.		

When the defective units are sold the entry is:

	Cash (or Accounts receivable)	100	
	Defective units inventory		100
	To record the sale of defective units		
	produced in Job no. 8042.		

Defective Units That Are Reworked

Sometimes faulty units can be reworked by adding materials or labor to them until they satisfy quality control requirements and can be sold as normal units. We now assume that the 10 defective units can be reworked by adding $40 of material and $60 of direct labor. In addition, overhead is applied at the rate of 50 percent of direct labor cost.

What is done with the cost of defective units that are reworked?

As before, the choices are to assign costs to the specific job or to costs of production in general. The decision depends on whether the defective production is job specific or the result of general production errors. Assigning the rework costs directly to the job, the entry is:

	Work in process control	150	
	Inventory control		40
	Payroll		60
	Manufacturing overhead applied		50
	To record the cost of reworking defective		
	units produced in Job no. 8240.		

This entry assigns $150 of additional manufacturing cost to Job no. 8240. The total cost is now $2,850 ($2,700 + $150). However, there are now 100 good units. Therefore, the new cost is $28.50 per unit ($2,850/100).

If the defective units are the result of general production errors, the cost of reworking the units is assigned to production in general by charging the overhead control account for the rework costs. The entry is:

	Manufacturing overhead control	150	
	Inventory control		40
	Payroll		60
	Manufacturing overhead applied		50
	To record the cost of reworking defective		
	units produced in Job no. 8240 and assign		
	the costs to all production.		

In this case, all of the cost of reworking the bad units is charged to the overhead control account and is assigned to all units as part of the overhead rate. If reworking defective units is a normal cost of manufacturing for the business, a certain amount of rework cost is included in budgeted overhead when the overhead rate is created. Since none of the rework cost is assigned to Job no. 8240, the total cost in the job cost sheet remains $2,700. However, the number of good units is now 100, so their cost is $27 per unit ($2,700/100).

SUMMARY   Materials are major assets and one of the important costs in manufacturing businesses. Careful management of material resources is an essential aspect of managing manufacturing businesses.

The activities associated with raw materials in a manufacturing firm are inventory acquisition and inventory distribution. **Inventory acquisition** includes purchasing, receiving, and storing inventory. **Inventory distribution** includes all activities associated with transferring raw materials into production.

When some item of inventory is needed, a **purchase requisition** is prepared and sent to the **purchasing agent,** who issues a **purchase order.** When materials are received, a **receiving report** is prepared. The purchase of materials is posted to both the inventory control account and the subsidiary ledger, usually called an **inventory ledger card** or a **stores ledger card.**

A **materials requisition** starts the physical flow of raw materials into production and triggers the entry for materials costs in the accounting records. A **materials requisition summary report** is prepared periodically to summarize the issue of materials during the period. A **returned materials** report is prepared when some of the requisitioned materials are returned to the inventory storeroom.

Salable **scrap material** resulting from the production process can be accounted for in three ways: by reducing the cost of specific products that generated the scrap, by reducing the cost of production in general, or as a miscellaneous revenue.

Occasionally it is necessary to adjust the balance in the inventory account for shortages, obsolescence, or errors. A physical count of the inventory indicates if the actual amount of inventory is different from the inventory records. Small normal differences are treated as adjustments to the overhead control account. Abnormal differences are charged to a loss account that is reported in the income statement.

Inventory shortages in finished goods are not part of the manufacturing activities and are charged to a loss account reported in the income statement. Sometimes an allowance account is used to reduce inventory cost to the lower of cost or market value.

Materials handling costs are the costs of maintaining the inventory storeroom and providing materials to production. These are normal costs of operating a manufacturing activity and are charged to the manufacturing overhead control account. In some cases, a separate overhead account for materials handling is used and costs are assigned using a materials handling overhead rate.

Defective units are unavoidable and are either discarded, sold for less than normal price, or reworked and sold as normal goods. Defective units that cannot be economically reworked are sold for a reduced price or discarded if they have no value. The resulting loss can be assigned to the good units produced in the job or to all products in general.

Sometimes faulty units can be reworked by adding materials or labor to satisfy quality control requirements. The additional manufacturing costs can be assigned to the individual job by debiting Work in Process Control or to all production by debiting Manufacturing Overhead Control.

KEY TERMS

defective units *(651)*
inventory acquisition *(637)*
inventory distribution *(638)*
inventory ledger card *(640)*
materials handling costs *(650)*
materials requisition *(642)*
materials requisition summary
   report *(644)*

purchase order *(639)*
purchase requisition *(638)*
purchasing agent *(639)*
receiving report *(639)*
returned materials report *(643)*
scrap material *(646)*
stores ledger card *(640)*

QUESTIONS

1. "We have streamlined our materials ordering activity to the point of high efficiency. When anyone in the plant notices that some material is getting low, he fills out a purchase order and sends it to the purchasing department for forwarding to the supplier. If time is short, the person making the purchase order may send it to the supplier directly, but usually the purchasing department gets it first. On the delivery end we also save time and money. All deliveries are made directly to the inventory stockroom, where the person receiving the inventory signs for it and posts it to the inventory ledger. Sure there is an occasional foul-up and two people order the same materials, and sometimes the goods on hand don't quite match the inventory cards, but we more than make up for that by saving the cost and bother of making requisitions, receiving reports, and all that other red tape." Comment on the control aspects of this situation.

2. There are several ways of accounting for the sale of scrap material resulting from manufacturing processes. One is to credit the proceeds to the manufacturing overhead account. Another is to reduce the cost of specific products that generated the scrap. A third way is to record the proceeds as a miscellaneous revenue. Discuss the rationale behind each method of handling scrap revenue.

3. "About four percent of our production is defective, and there is no market for defective products. So our choice is either to discard the defective units or rework them. Some require more work than others, but we routinely rework all defective units, because discarding them is pure waste." Discuss the merits of this policy.

EXERCISES

Ex. 18-1
Recording
Inventory
Transactions

Below are purchase, use, and sales data for inventory of a manufacturing business that uses the perpetual inventory system:

a. Purchased raw materials costing $43,600 on open account.
b. Issued direct material costing $17,900 to production.
c. Issued to production indirect materials costing $2,340.
d. Returned $3,600 of direct materials to the storeroom.
e. Completed work in process costing $87,300.
f. Sold finished goods inventory costing $56,500 for $87,200 on open account.

REQUIRED

Prepare the necessary journal entries to record the events described above.

Ex. 18-2
Recording Inventory Adjustments

Mabley Products, Inc., uses a perpetual inventory system to manage and account for both production inventories and finished goods inventory. At the end of each year, a physical count of inventory is taken for the audit and to satisfy management's inventory control requirements. The physical inventory just completed disclosed that the raw materials inventory was overstated by $23,890, and the finished goods inventory was overstated by $13,220.

REQUIRED

a.   Record the necessary adjustment in the inventory account, assuming any inventory shortages in production are normal.
b.   Record the necessary adjustments in the inventory account, assuming the raw materials inventory shortage is abnormal.

Ex. 18-3
Accounting for Scrap Material

The Waverly Corporation manufactures industrial fan housings which it cuts from rolled steel, drills, machines, and welds. The housing is then painted and inspected before it is sent to the finished goods inventory. The fan housings are sold to several different companies that manufacture large air-moving equipment.

During the past week, Waverly started and completed Job number J-9167-4. There were 500 galvanized steel, 56-inch fan housings produced, and in the process $2,600 of galvanized steel scrap was generated.

REQUIRED

Record the sale of the scrap, assuming that it is accounted for as:

a.   A reduction in the cost of Job no. J-9167-4.
b.   A reduction in the cost of all production.
c.   Miscellaneous revenue.

Ex. 18-4
Defective Units Not Reworked

Job no. 7739-D1 was just completed, and the job cost sheet reported the following total costs:

Direct materials	$2,400
Direct labor	2,000
Applied manufacturing overhead	3,000
Total product cost	$7,400

There were 80 units produced, but at inspection six units failed to meet minimum acceptance standards. The bad units have no value and are discarded. The selling price of normal units is $128.00 per unit.

REQUIRED

a.   Compute the unit cost of the good units, assuming the defective production is job specific.
b.   Compute the cost of the good units, assuming the defective production is the result of general production errors.
c.   Prepare a journal entry to account for the defective production using the assumption in part *b*.

Ex. 18-5
Accounting for Defective Units with Economic Value

Refer to the production data for Job no. 7739-D1 presented in Exercise 18-4. Assume that the defective units cannot be economically reworked, but they can be sold for $42.50 per unit.

REQUIRED

a.   Compute the per unit cost of the good units if the defective production is job specific.

b. Compute the cost of the defective units assuming the defective production is random error.

c. Prepare any necessary journal entries to account for the defective production for both the situations described above.

Ex. 18-6
Accounting for
Scrap Materials

McGregor Company is a sheet metal shop that cuts, forms, machines, and finishes metal parts to order for a variety of local customers. In the process of making products, the company generates a significant amount of metal scrap. This scrap is accumulated at the end of each day and sent to the storeroom, where it is weighed and stored until a scrap metal dealer comes to buy it on Friday of each week.

During the first week of May the company collected the following scrap:

	Steel	Copper	Aluminum
Monday	500 lb	100 lb	120 lb
Tuesday	800	140	70
Wednesday	900	180	50
Thursday	600	220	210
Friday	300	160	150

The scrap metal dealer pays for the scrap when he picks it up. Current market rates in tons for scrap are $200 for steel, $800 for copper, and $500 for aluminum.

REQUIRED Prepare a summary journal entry for the scrap assuming:

a. The scrap can be identified directly with specific jobs.

b. The scrap cannot be identified with jobs, but management treats scrap as a reduction in product costs.

c. Management has a policy of treating scrap as miscellaneous income.

Ex. 18-7
Lower of Cost or
Market Inventory
Adjustments

On December 31, 1985, Bulkhurste Department Store has taken a physical count of inventory and determined that the market value of inventory is $36,000 lower than cost. On December 31, 1986, the physical count disclosed that the market value of the store's inventory is $22,000 lower than cost.

REQUIRED

a. Prepare the journal entry to create the allowance account on 12/31/85.

b. Prepare the journal entry to adjust the allowance account on 12/31/86.

Ex. 18-8
Application of
Materials Handling
Costs

A manufacturing company budgets the following costs for its materials handling operations:

Wages, storeroom personnel		$ 86,000
Wages, receiving department		38,000
Supervisory salaries, materials handling		42,000
Employee benefits, materials handling		34,000
Facilities costs, materials handling:		
Depreciation, building	$14,000	
Depreciation, equipment	18,000	
Insurance, building & equipment	5,000	
Insurance, inventory	12,000	
Maintenance	16,000	
Property taxes	6,000	
Utilities	18,000	
Miscellaneous	11,000	
Total material handling cost		100,000
		$300,000

The company estimates that during the coming year, the materials handling activity will fill 15,000 materials requisitions. The estimated cost of the materials to be issued next year is $12,000,000. The storeroom supervisor estimates that the material issued in the 15,000 materials requisitions will weigh 9,000 tons.

REQUIRED Compute a materials handling overhead rate using as an application base:

    a. Number of materials requisitions.
    b. Percentage of material cost.
    c. Cost per pound of material issued.

Ex. 18-9
Defective Units and
Unit Cost

The Evans Company makes air compressors and uses job costing to account for its manufacturing operations. A recent batch of 100 twin cylinder compressors had 20 defective units. The total manufacturing cost of the job was $12,500. Reworking the units would require materials costs of $320 for new valves and fittings, labor costs of $480 for installation and repairs, and overhead costs of 120 percent of direct labor cost.

Most defective units are the result of random production errors that occasionally occur, but sometimes product errors are specific to the job.

REQUIRED Compute the unit cost of the air compressors assuming:

    a. The defective units are due to random production errors.
    b. The defective units are specific to this job.
    c. The defective units are job specific; they are not reworked but are sold as seconds for $50 each.
    d. The defective units result from random production errors; they are not reworked but are sold as seconds for $50 each.

Discuss factors that may enter into management decision to rework or not rework defective units.

Ex. 18-10
Defective Units
Decision Analysis

Claymore Manufacturing Company makes automobile stereo systems in job lots. Production errors occasionally occur, and defective units are reworked if it can be done economically. Otherwise the units are sold as seconds to a company that salvages the usable parts.

Recently the company completed Job no. 447, which includes 200 Whamo-Bam stereos at a cost of $21,000. The systems are sold for $140 each to retail stores. Testing indicates that 50 of the units have faulty speaker assemblies. Reworking the 50 units would incur the following total costs:

Direct materials	$2,000
Direct labor	1,200
Overhead	1,800

The faulty units can be sold to Southside Electronics for $50 each. Eighty percent of the overhead cost is fixed.

REQUIRED Compute unit cost of the good units, assuming the faulty stereos are reworked and:

    a. Defective units are job specific.
    b. Defective units result from random errors.
    c. Prepare a journal entry to record the cost of reworking the defective units, assuming they are the result of random production errors.
    d. Compute the effect on profit of reworking the units.
    e. Should the units be reworked? Support your answer with calculations.

PROBLEMS

P. 18-1
Journalizing
Materials Activities

Overfurd, Inc., uses a perpetual inventory system to account for all inventory transactions. The company is a manufacturing business producing electric cables. Below are selected inventory transactions.

    a. Purchased raw materials costing $67,000 on open account.
    b. Issued $42,400 of material to production, of which $37,200 was for direct materials.
    c. $6,700 of the materials purchased in *a* are defective and are returned to the vendor for credit.
    d. Paid the balance on the purchase in *a*.
    e. Purchased $13,000 of material for cash.
    f. $3,800 of direct materials issued at the end of last month are returned to the inventory storeroom.
    g. Scrap material is sold for $1,400. The company does not treat scrap as a reduction in production cost.

REQUIRED

For each of the events or transactions, prepare the necessary journal entry in good form.

P. 18-2
Understanding
Inventory Cost Data

Below are data relevant to the production of Job number QV1173.

Units produced	200
Direct materials	$5,800
Direct labor	2,300
Manufacturing overhead	2,500

An analysis of the production data indicates a number of additional items as follows:

    a. In addition to the 200 good units, there were 50 defective units produced with the job that were sold for $30 each. The sale of the defective units was recorded as a miscellaneous revenue.
    b. Production materials from the job costing $700 were returned to the storeroom, but no entry was made.
    c. $800 of indirect material for the maintenance department was inadvertently charged to this job as direct materials.
    d. $300 of direct material issued to the job the last week of production was never recorded.

REQUIRED

Analyze the above data and prepare a detailed schedule of the unit cost of the units produced in this job. Include in your analysis any cost differences caused by incorrect entries or omissions as well as the consequences of cost savings from the sale or return of production material.

P. 18-3
Identifying Errors
in Accounting for
Materials

Ristlott Company is a small manufacturing company that uses a perpetual inventory system. Recently the company hired a new accountant who has not worked for a manufacturing company before. In the first week of work, he made the following entries:

a.	Purchases	89,300	
	Accounts payable		89,300
	To record the purchase of raw		
	materials on open account.		
b.	Direct materials	9,000	
	Purchases		9,000
	Issued $9,000 of compound		
	used to lubricate machinery		
	to the maintenance department.		
c.	Inventory control	2,300	
	Scrap revenue		2,300
	To record the sale of scrap		
	materials.		
d.	Returned materials	1,800	
	Work in process control		1,800
	To record the return of unused		
	materials to the storeroom.		
e.	Accounts receivable	56,000	
	Cost of goods sold		34,000
	Profit on sale		22,000
	To record the sale of goods costing		
	$34,000 for revenue of $56,000.		

The description of each event or activity is correct.

REQUIRED Analyze each of the journal entries to determine if it is correct. For any incorrect entry, identify the error and make the necessary correction.

P. 18-4 Accounting for Scrap Materials Alger Company generates copper scrap in its coil manufacturing department. The scrap is gathered and weighed at the end of each work day and sent to the scrap inventory area. At the end of each week, a scrap metal dealer buys the scrap for cash. The company records the sale of scrap as a reduction in production cost; however, there is no way of identifying scrap with specific products. Below are daily scrap data for last week.

Day	Scrap Value
Monday	$1,400
Tuesday	1,100
Wednesday	1,700
Thursday	1,300
Friday	1,200

REQUIRED
a. Record the daily increases in scrap inventory.
b. Record the sale of scrap at the end of the week.

P. 18-5
Using Scrap
Materials
Accounting
Information

FLC Corporation manufactures wooden picnic tables which are sold to department stores and garden stores. Recently the company accepted an offer to make 1,000 picnic tables for the state park system of a midwestern state. The selling price for the state park picnic table contract is prime cost plus 40 percent. The prime cost for producing the picnic tables is $46,000 for direct materials and $24,000 of direct labor.

A certain amount of scrap lumber is produced in the manufacture of picnic tables. The scrap is sold to a charcoal manufacturing company. The scrap generated by the production of the state parks picnic tables was sold for $3,000. Typically, FLC Corporation records scrap as a miscellaneous revenue.

REQUIRED
a. Record the sale of the scrap following FLC Corporation's normal procedure.
b. Record the sale of the scrap so that the individual job receives the benefit of the scrap sale.
c. If FLC follows their normal procedure, what is the per unit price they will receive for the picnic tables?
d. If FLC changed its policy to record the sale of scrap as a reduction in the cost of the individual job, what would be the per unit price of the picnic tables?
e. Compute the percentage decrease in the sales price of the picnic tables if the sale of scrap is assigned to the job.
f. Compute the difference in the total profit that would result from using the two different methods of accounting for the scrap.

P. 18-6
Accounting for
Defective Units
That Are Not
Reworked

Wheatherbee Electronics makes cathode ray tubes (CRTs) for use in home computers, as computer terminals, and in other CRT applications. All tubes are built to rigid specifications. Tubes not passing inspection run a high risk of failure and are discarded with no salvage value.

Most of Wheatherbee's business is special order designed to meet the changing technical needs of its growing number of customers. A recent order for 500 units was produced for a manufacturer of word processors. The tubes are sold for $195 each. The cost data for Job number CRT9742 are as follows:

Direct materials	$32,500
Direct labor	15,000
Manufacturing overhead	25,000
Total cost	$72,500

The cathode ray tubes were inspected at the end of production, and 25 tubes were unacceptable. Since most jobs are somewhat unique at Wheatherbee, management's policy is to assign defective unit production costs to the job.

REQUIRED
a. Compute the unit cost of the good units using the company's policy in accounting for defective unit costs.
b. Record the sale of the good units.
c. Compute the unit cost of the good units, assuming the cost for the defective units is charged to all production.
d. Make any necessary journal entries to account for the cost of the defective units.
e. Record the sale of the good units assuming the treatment of defective unit costs used in part c.

P. 18-7
Defective Units
That Are Not
Reworked

The School Features Company makes briefcases, notebooks, and a number of other school- and business-related products. All products are produced for general stock in job lot production runs. The company's biggest revenue product is its G-40 molded briefcase. It is sold to wholesalers for $36 per unit.

Below is the job cost sheet for the most recent production run of G-40 briefcases.

Job Cost Sheet								

Date started ___4/15/85___   Job number ___JC–5854–G–40___
Date completed _4/26/85_   Quantity_____1,000_____
Product _G–40 briefcase_   Customer_____General stock_____

Direct Materials			Direct Labor			Manufacturing Overhead		
Date	Reference	Amount	Date	Reference	Amount	Date	Reference	Amount
4/15/85	MRQ7961	$ 8,000	4/19/85	LD9874	$ 6,600	4/19/85	LD9874	$ 3,300
4/22/85	MRQ7978	4,000	4/26/85	LD9875	3,000	4/26/85	LD9875	1,500
		$12,000			$ 9,600			$ 4,800

Summary of Costs

Item	Total Cost	Unit Cost
Direct materials	$ 12,000	$ 12.00
Direct labor	9,600	9.60
Manufacturing overhead	4,800	4.80
Totals	$ 26,400	$ 26.40

Briefcases are manufactured with strict quality control procedures. Occasionally, hinges or latches do not meet standards, or there is a flaw in the body of the briefcases. Any cases not satisfying quality control standards are sold as seconds for $10 each. 100 of the 1,000 briefcases produced in Job no. JC-5854-G-40 were faulty and were sold as seconds. The job cost sheet above does not reflect any accounting for the defective units.

REQUIRED

a. Compute the per unit cost of the good units, assuming the cost of the defective units is assigned to the job.

b. Compute the unit cost of the good units, assuming the cost of defective units is charged to all production.

c. Assume the defective units are inventoried and then sold, and the cost of defective units is assigned to the specific job. Record all transactions associated with the identification and sale of the defective units.

d. Assume the costs of defective units are assigned to all production. Record all activities associated with the identification of defective units, the transfer of all units to inventory, and the sale of all units produced from Job no. JC-5854-G-40.

P. 18-8
Accounting for
Defective Units
That Are Reworked

The Heartland Wood Products Company makes a variety of quality wood furniture products. A major item is a solid oak coffee table that sells for $225 per unit. Each unit is carefully inspected upon completion, and any flaws in the table are repaired. Sometimes tables can be repaired simply by rebuffing the table surface. Other times, defective tables may have the finish stripped off and an entire new finish applied.

During May, 1,200 oak coffee tables were manufactured. Production costs for the month were $77,400 for direct materials, $45,000 for direct labor, and $36,000 for applied overhead.

Of the tables produced in May, 80 did not pass inspection for various reasons and had to be reworked. Additional manufacturing costs to rework the defective units were direct materials of $1,800, direct labor of $2,100, and overhead applied as a percentage of direct labor cost.

REQUIRED

a. Compute the unit cost of the tables if the cost of the defective units is charged to all production.
b. Compute the unit cost of the tables if the cost of defective units is charged to the oak coffee tables.
c. Record the cost of reworking the units for both of the situations described above.
d. Record the sale of the coffee tables on open account for each of the situations described in parts a and b.
e. Compute the percentage gross margin on sales for each of the situations described in parts a and b.

P. 18-9
Accounting for
Materials Handling
Costs

The Felles Manufacturing Company budgets the following costs for materials handling activities for the coming year. All personnel costs are for people working in the materials handling activities and all facility costs are for inventory storeroom space and other inventory-related facilities.

Salaries and wages	$ 82,000
Employee benefits	26,000
Maintenance	5,000
Depreciation, building	12,000
Depreciation, equipment	7,000
Utilities	8,000
Property taxes	3,000
Insurance	14,000
Miscellaneous	3,000
Total	$160,000

The company expects to process 8,000 materials requisitions for material costing a total of $8,000,000. The estimated total weight of the material sent to production is 10,000 tons. The expected level of activity for the coming year is 100,000 direct labor hours. The company uses direct labor hours as its manufacturing overhead application base.

The following jobs were started and completed in January. The materials requisition data are presented at the top of the next page:

Job No.	No. of Requisitions	Total Cost of Materials	Total Weight of Materials
42K-2212	22	$18,900	7,800 pounds
67Y-1139	9	42,000	56,000 pounds
17N-3782	14	51,000	16,000 pounds

REQUIRED

a. Compute a separate materials handling application rate using each of the three measures of materials handling activity, materials requisitions, cost of materials, and pounds of materials.

b. Compute the amount the manufacturing overhead rate will increase if the materials handling cost is included in the overhead rate rather than as a separate rate.

c. Compute the amount of materials handling cost assigned to each of the three jobs listed above using **each** of the three materials handling application bases.

d. Based on the information computed in part c, which of the three materials handling application bases is the best?

CASES

Case 18-1
Materials
Accounting and
Defective
Production

Merriweather Outdoor Furniture makes aluminum-frame nylon-fabric patio furniture. The company buys 1-inch aluminum tubing, 2-inch nylon straps, and precut wooden arms for the chairs. The company cuts the aluminum tubing to size, bends it into shape, and welds it. The arms are attached and then the nylon webbing is added. All furniture is made in job lots and is accounted for using a job order costing system. At the beginning of March, Merriweather had the following raw materials inventory:

Aluminum tubing: 4,000 ft at $.15 per foot
Nylon straps: 10,000 yd at $.12 per yard
Wooden arms: 800 at $.32 each

Occasionally some defective units occur in the production of furniture. Usually this is caused by faulty material and is not job specific. Defective units are discarded because the cost of rework is quite high. When defective units are identified, their cost is charged to all production.

At the beginning of March, there were no jobs in process. The company uses a FIFO perpetual inventory system to account for inventory. Manufacturing overhead is applied at the rate of 150 percent of direct labor cost.

During March, the following transactions and events occurred:

Mar. 3   Purchased 3,000 ft of aluminum tubing for $.16 per foot and 6,000 yards of nylon straps for $.14 per yard on open account.

5   Put into production 2,500 ft of aluminum tubing and 4,000 yards of nylon straps to start Job number 32117.

8   Put into production 2,000 ft of aluminum tubing and 3,500 yards of nylon straps to start Job number 32118.

13   Purchased 2,000 wooden arms for $.35 each and 4,000 ft of aluminum tubing for $.18 per foot on open account.

15   Direct labor costs for the first half of March were $800 for Job number 32117 and $600 for Job number 32118.

17   Put into production 1,200 wooden arms for Job number 32117.

21   Put into production 3,000 ft of aluminum tubing and 5,000 yards of nylon straps for Job number 32217.

23   Put into production 2,500 ft of aluminum tubing and 3,000 yards of nylon strap for Job number 32118.

31   Direct labor costs for the last half of March were $400 for Job number 32117 and $700 for Job number 32118.

31   Job number 32117 was completed. There were 600 units produced, but 50 of those did not pass inspection and were discarded.

REQUIRED

a.   Journalize the above transactions in the general journal of the Merriweather Outdoor Furniture.

b.   Create inventory ledger cards for each of the items in raw materials inventory, enter the March beginning balance on the cards, and post the March inventory transactions to the cards, keeping a running balance on each card.

c.   Compute the unit cost of the good units in Job number 32117.

d.   Journalize the cost of faulty units using the firm's policy on defective units.

e.   The new bookkeeper suggests that the firm use a monthly periodic inventory system to account for inventory in an effort to reduce the day-to-day detail work associated with inventory. Comment on the advisability of this suggestion.

CHAPTER 19
Accounting for Labor Costs

The concept of buying labor services and paying for them is certainly not difficult to understand. Labor is used in the production of goods and services and becomes a cost of products produced or services performed. The sale of the products and services produces revenue, part of which must be used to cover the cost of the labor. Despite the conceptual simplicity, labor costs require comprehensive and detailed systems of accounting records. The number of documents, reports, and detailed records is very large and constitutes a major administrative cost and logistics challenge. Most businesses reduce the time and cost of accounting for payroll by using computers to accumulate costs, prepare labor reports, and print paychecks.

Chapters 2, 4, 5, and 6 describe how labor costs are assigned to products. In this chapter we discuss some of the procedures necessary to identify labor costs with cost objectives, maintain payroll records, and record labor costs. Sufficient payroll accounting concepts and procedures are presented to provide a good understanding of how payroll costs are identified and recorded.

IDENTIFYING LABOR COSTS WITH COST OBJECTIVES

Labor costs are identified as manufacturing or nonmanufacturing

Large organizations have many employees who perform a variety of tasks. A key function of payroll accounting is to assign the cost of each employee to an appropriate cost objective so that the cost of operating a business can be properly measured, controlled, monitored, and reported. A first step is to identify payroll costs as either manufacturing or nonmanufacturing. Labor costs for marketing, administration, and other nonmanufacturing functions are expensed in the period the labor is used. All manufacturing labor costs are product costs. They are assigned to products as direct labor or to overhead as indirect labor. When overhead is assigned to products, the indirect labor becomes part of the product cost. These labor costs are expensed as part of cost of goods sold when the product is sold.

Factory workers spend most of their time making products; as a result the cost of most workers is direct labor. Maintenance, materials handling, and other production support personnel provide essential services for manufacturing activities, but their labor cannot be identified with specific products. Their wages are indirect labor costs charged to manufacturing overhead. Indirect labor cost is assigned to products along with all other indirect manufacturing costs when overhead is applied to production.

Measuring labor costs is one function of labor accounting

Assigning labor costs to cost objectives is also a function of labor accounting

Accountants perform two important functions in accounting for labor: One is to measure the amount of payroll cost and the other is to assign those costs to the correct cost objective. In addition to these two activities, accountants record payroll costs in the accounting records and report them to financial and nonfinancial managers.

In order to use labor effectively, managers must know the total cost of labor resources. The total cost of labor includes the wages paid to employees plus payments for employee benefits such as vacation pay, pension plans, and health insurance premiums. The composition of payroll costs is shown graphically in Figure 19-1. You may find it useful to refer to this diagram later in the chapter when we discuss recording payroll costs.

Collecting Labor Cost Data

All nonmanufacturing labor costs are expensed in the period in which they are incurred. Manufacturing labor costs become part of the cost of the manufactured products either as direct labor or as part of the manufacturing overhead costs. Therefore, labor costs must first be identified as manufacturing or nonmanufacturing. Accountants must then distinguish between direct and indirect manufacturing labor.

To differentiate between direct and indirect labor cost, accountants need a method of determining how employees spend their work time. A variety of methods can be used to capture detailed information about employees' labor time. Some companies use sophisticated computer input systems with terminals located in production plants. Other systems are mechanical or manual, with data accumulated and processed by hand. Detailed data are thus col-

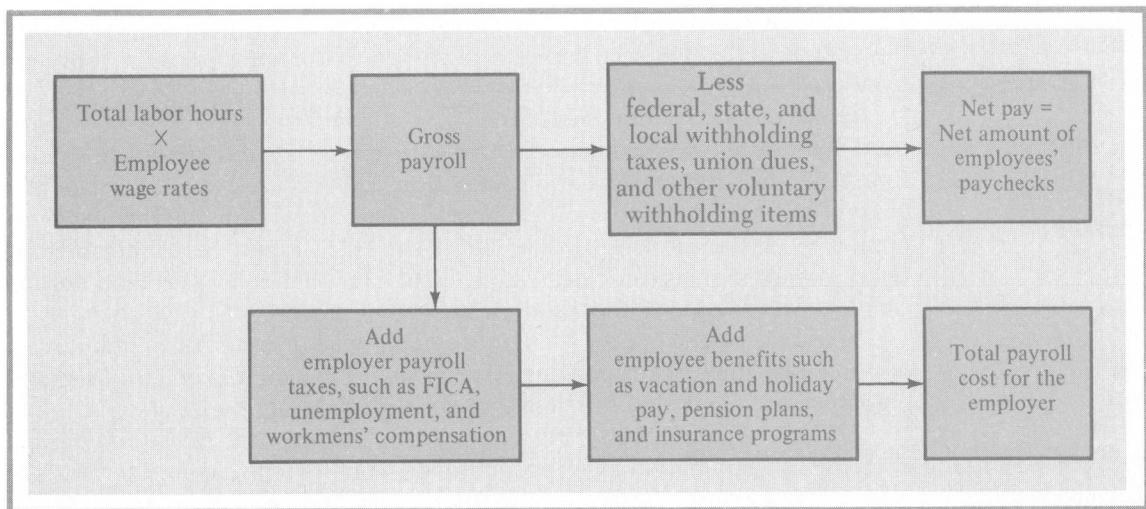

Figure 19-1. Gross payroll is determined from labor time and wage rates. Employees receive less than gross payroll. The employer's cost is more than gross payroll.

Figure 19-2. A daily time ticket is filled out once a day by each employee. It provides the basic labor costs for the accounting system.

DAILY TIME TICKET							
Name Debbie Knox					**Date** 12/19/85		
Department Assembly					**Badge No.** AS59551-F		
Date / **Job**	12/16	12/17	12/18	12/19			**Total**
RC577-56 NY	1.5		2				3.5
RC577-56 RJ	3.0	3.0					6.0
RC579-56 NY	2.0	5.0	4.5	7.5			19.0
Setup	1.5		1.5				3.0
Totals	8.0	8.0	8.0	7.5			31.5
Authorized signature MJ							
Day work rate $7.00/hr		**Piece work rate**			**Total pieces** 86		

lected on the work employees perform and are entered into the cost accounting system so that labor costs can be assigned to the appropriate cost objective.

Labor cost data are collected daily

Labor costs are a function of the labor rate and the amount of labor time used. Labor time for each manufacturing employee is accumulated on a daily time ticket or a job time ticket. **A daily time ticket** is used to accumulate the amount of labor time spent on each product or activity for the day for each employee. A typical daily time ticket is shown in Figure 19-2. **A job time ticket** is used to record each employee's time for each job worked on during the day. An example is illustrated in Figure 19-3.

If daily time tickets are used to accumulate labor use data, an employee has only one time ticket per day. However, if job time tickets are used, an employee has one ticket for each job worked on during the day.

Daily labor data are summarized for reporting purposes

Periodically time tickets are summarized and recorded in the company's records. The summary may be prepared manually or with a computer. Either way, the end result is a summary of labor use and cost data that identifies the amount of labor time and cost assignable to each product and to manufacturing overhead for the time period covered by the summary. The labor sum-

Figure 19-3. A job time ticket is filled out daily by each employee for each job worked on. An employee may have several job time tickets a day. This document is used by some companies to accumulate basic cost data.

JOB TIME TICKET		
Name *Harry Walker*		**Date** *12/18/85*
Department *Machining*		**Badge No.** *MC47439-M*
Part No. *QCM497-36MJ*		
Stop time *11:45 am*	**Operation** *Grind valves*	
Start time *8:00 am*	**Job No.** *991-86172*	**Acct. No.** *994-14441*
	S. L. Jones _____ Authorized signature	

Hours	Pieces	Day work rate	Piece rate
3.75	*120*	*$9:00/hr*	
Hours	**Pieces**	**Day work**	**Piece work**

mary varies by companies; it is commonly called a **labor distribution report** or a **labor recapitulation report.** An example is illustrated in Figure 19-4.

In this report, each employee's labor time is summarized for the entire week. Hours identifiable as direct labor are charged to specific production jobs. All other labor time is charged to manufacturing overhead as indirect labor. As usual, most of the labor cost in this example is direct labor. The direct labor cost for all employees is totaled for each of the jobs and the totals are used to record labor costs.

RECORDING GROSS PAYROLL

Gross payroll is the total earned by employees

Gross payroll is computed by multiplying the number of labor hours worked times the hourly wage rate. It is the amount of wages the company owes employees before withholding income taxes and other items from employees' paychecks. Gross pay is the amount employees earn before any payroll deductions. For example, if an employee works 40 hours a week and earns $8 per hour, $320 is the employee's gross pay for the week. The employee, however, does not receive the entire $320, because some money must be withheld from the paycheck for a number of items discussed below.

Figure 19-4. The labor distribution report is prepared from all daily time tickets or job time tickets accumulated during the week. This source document is used to record labor costs in the accounting records.

Labor Distribution Report For the Week of October 6-12								
			Job Numbers				Indirect	
Employee No.	312	313	315	316	317	318	Labor	Total
Andrews 302	6	5	7	8	9	—	5	40
Bailey 303	12	16	5	—	—	—	8	40
Burton 303	9	14	—	7	2	—	10	42
Messing 304	3	—	16	15	—	—	6	40
Keylor 305	—	—	5	7	15	11	2	40
Total	30	34	33	37	26	11	31	202

Withholding Items

Employees always receive less pay than they earn

Virtually all employees are subject to laws that require **withholding** of money from their paychecks. Most of the withholding items are for federal, state, and sometimes local taxes. Other withholdings, such as union dues, insurance premiums, or savings programs, may be authorized or requested by employees. Withholdings are a major aspect of payroll accounting. For each employee, the accountant must compute and then record the correct amounts of the paycheck and withholdings. The amounts withheld must be properly accounted for, and payments must be made to appropriate organizations such as the federal or state government, labor unions, and insurance companies. By withholding various amounts from employees' pay, employers act as transfer agents for the governments and other organizations to which the withholdings are paid. Below we discuss some of the more common withholding items.

Income Tax Withholdings. Each employee must file a federal government form W-4 with his employer, providing information on the number of dependents claimed for federal income tax purposes. Using this information and federal government guidelines, employers determine how much to withhold from each employee's paycheck for federal income tax. The amount to be withheld for various levels of earnings and for the number of dependents are provided to employers by the Internal Revenue Service in the form of withholding tables. By requiring such withholdings, the government is assured of a steady source of revenue and ensures that citizens with earnings pay their income taxes.

Income tax and FICA tax withholdings are required by law

Social Security Taxes. In 1935 Congress passed the Federal Insurance Contribution Act (FICA), also known as the Social Security Act, which required withholding from employees' pay 1 percent of the first $3,000 of annual earnings, or $30 per year. Agricultural, domestic, federal, state, and municipal workers were exempt from the act. Also exempt were employees of not-for-profit organizations and self-employed persons.

Over the years the act has been amended many times, until now **FICA** covers many more employees and the tax constitutes a significant financial outlay for the majority of American workers. From 1 percent of the first $3,000 earned, the tax has progressed to 7 percent of the first $37,800 earned in 1984 and is scheduled to increase in the years ahead.

The act requires employers to withhold **FICA tax** on the qualified income from each employee. When an employee exceeds the earnings subject to the tax in any one year, the employer stops the withholdings. Consequently, with different employees earning different amounts of wages, employers must keep track of **each** individual's earnings in order to ensure that FICA withholdings do not exceed the maximum.

Employees who work for more than one employer are subject to FICA withholdings from all employers. As a result, more than the maximum amount of tax may be withheld, and the employee may claim a refund when filing the annual federal income tax return.

Other Government-Required Withholdings. Most states and some city governments require withholding of state and local income taxes from employee earnings. Income tax rates vary widely from state to state, from no tax in three states to nearly 20 percent in some. These withholdings add to the cost of processing payrolls, but do not otherwise increase employers' payroll costs.

Employers are accountable to workers for withholdings

By January 31 of each year, employers must provide each employee with a W-2 form, which reports the amount of earnings for the previous calendar year and the amount of withholdings for income and FICA taxes. Copies of this form are also provided to governments to which withholdings are paid and the employee is required to include a copy with annual income tax returns. The amounts withheld from employees are paid periodically to the various governments by the employer throughout the year.

Other Withholdings. Employers may withhold other items from employees' pay as a result of agreements with employees. Included are union dues, group health and life insurance, credit union savings, and car or home mortgage payments. The employer pays these amounts to various recipients on behalf of employees. These amounts are expenses of the employee, but processing the withholdings and maintaining the necessary records add to the employer's cost of accounting for payrolls.

Recording Gross Payroll and Withholdings

Each pay period the employer must determine the amount earned by each employee and the amount to be withheld from each employee's check. For many manufacturing employees, the pay period is a week or 2 weeks. However, bimonthly or monthly pay periods are common also. The gross payroll and withholding items are recorded for each pay period. The actual distribution of payroll costs to products or other cost objectives does not necessarily coincide with the recording of the gross payroll. The distribution of payroll costs to cost objectives is discussed later in the chapter. Below is an example of a journal entry to record the gross payroll and associated withholdings:

Aug. 1	Payroll	40,500	
	Federal withholding tax payable		6,100
	FICA taxes payable		2,835
	State withholding tax payable		2,000
	Union dues payable		240
	Group insurance payable		264
	Cash		29,061
	To record gross payroll for the period		
	ending July 31.		

Net pay is gross pay less withholdings

In this entry, $40,500 is the **gross payroll,** and the cash payment of $29,061 is **net pay.** A journal entry such as this is made at the end of each pay period. The withholding items must be paid to the various recipients soon after the payroll checks are issued. Federal withholding taxes are paid almost immediately to the nearest federal depository — usually a national bank. State government payments vary from state to state, but seldom can a company delay payment beyond the end of a month for withholding items. Payments for other withholding items depend on contractual agreements, tradition, or other factors. Whatever the timing of the payments, it is important to understand that amounts withheld from employees' checks cannot be kept by the employer, but rather must be paid to others.

Withholdings are not the employer's costs but they are the employer's liabilities

The federal and state taxes withheld from employees and all other amounts withheld from employees' checks are **not** costs of the employer. The employer's labor cost is the gross payroll. Withholding items only affect the way that earned wages are distributed to employees by the employer. The employer does have payroll-related taxes and other labor-related costs, discussed below, but none of the withholding items are costs of the employer.

Payroll Control.   For control purposes, many companies maintain a separate payroll bank account. A single check for the total net pay is drawn on the company's regular bank account and is deposited in the payroll account. Individual paychecks are then written on the payroll account and distributed to employees. Payroll checks are usually a different color or size from the company's other checks, and often have a statement attached showing the employee's gross pay and various deductions. Shortly after the payroll is distributed, the payroll checks will be cashed, and if no errors have been made, the payroll bank account should have a small balance equal to the amount maintained in the account to keep it active.

ADDITIONAL PAYROLL COSTS

The gross payroll is the most visible and significant part of labor cost. But there are many other costs associated with labor. Some of these costs can be overlooked easily by managers in planning and controlling production and other activities. Figure 19-1 illustrates a number of labor costs other than

Employers incur payroll costs in addition to wages and salaries

gross payroll that a company incurs. These costs include employer payroll taxes, the cost of employee benefits, and wage incentive plans. Each of these costs and its accounting treatment is discussed below.

Payroll Taxes

Employers are required to pay several types of **payroll taxes,** both federal and state. Such taxes increase the total payroll costs of employers although they do not increase the amount of money received by employees. The exact nature and amount of payroll taxes varies depending on the type of business and state of residence, but common taxes include the employer's share of FICA tax, federal unemployment (FUTA) tax, state unemployment insurance, and workmens' compensation insurance or tax.

FICA Taxes.   The employer's share of FICA tax on wages is equal in amount to the FICA deduction from employees' earnings. The amount deducted from pay for FICA contributions by employees must be matched by employers and the total is paid to the federal government. The FICA tax applies only to a specified earnings base, but over the years both the FICA tax rate and the earnings base have increased significantly and the tax has become a major cost of business. Wages subject to the Social Security tax and the tax rates are shown in the following table:

Payroll taxes have increased over the years

Year	Withholding Rate	Wage Limit	Maximum Withholding	Maximum Total FICA Tax
1981	6.65	$29,700	$1,975.05	$3,950.10
1982	6.70	32,400	2,170.80	4,261.20
1983	6.70	35,700	2,391.90	4,890.90
1984	7.00	37,800	2,532.60[a]	5,178.60
1985	7.05	Automatic cost-of-living adjustments		
1986	7.15	in wage base starting in 1984		
1987	7.15			
1988	7.51			
1989	7.51			
1990	7.65			

[a] .03 percent credit for employees limits maximum withholding to 6.7 percent of wage limit

The last column shows the maximum FICA tax payments per employee each year. It consists of the amount withheld from employees plus the employer's tax.

The employer's share of FICA taxes must be charged to the appropriate cost objective. FICA taxes associated with nonmanufacturing employees are expensed in the period the labor is used. FICA taxes for manufacturing employees become part of the product cost and are expensed when the product is sold. Typically the employer's share of the FICA taxes is charged to the manufacturing overhead control account and assigned to products when overhead is applied to production. Charging payroll taxes to overhead simplifies the accounting procedures but, in effect, buries these payroll costs with indirect manufacturing costs. As a result, this portion of labor cost is not nearly as visible as gross pay.

Employers must file a quarterly FICA tax return together with a payment for any withholdings and taxes not paid previously during the quarter. If an employee has FICA taxes withheld by more than one employer, the employee may get a refund on any amount withheld in excess of the maximum. However, no refund is available to employers, because the employer's share of FICA is a tax on wages regardless of the tax paid by any other employer.

FUTA Tax.   The Federal Unemployment Tax Act (FUTA) created a joint federal and state unemployment compensation program requiring employers to pay an unemployment insurance tax on wages. The **FUTA tax** is a maximum of 3.5 percent of the first $7,000 earned by each employee. Of this amount .8 percent is for the federal government and 2.7 percent is for the state. Some state tax rates are greater than the 2.7 percent minimum required by the federal law and some states apply the tax to a maximum wage of more than $7,000. In addition, some states require employees to contribute a portion of their earnings, in which case the employer withholds the employees' contributions.

FUTA taxes are minimized by keeping a stable work force

The 2.8 percent (or other state rate) is a maximum subject to reduction for employers with a history of stable employment. If an employer keeps its work force employed so that few of its employees apply for unemployment compensation, the state unemployment tax rate for that employer may be reduced to as little as zero. The FUTA tax is payable to the federal government quarterly, unless the amount is less than $100 per year, in which case a single annual payment is made by January 31 of the following year. Payments and reports to states vary but employers must typically file returns quarterly and must report when an employee has been terminated.

Workmen's Compensation Insurance.   Most states require employers to carry insurance to compensate employees for losses caused by occupational accidents or sicknesses. The insurance plan may be operated by the state, a commercial insurer, or the company itself if it has the financial resources to assume its own risk. The total insurance cost is borne by the employer, with no contribution by the employees.

Unemployment taxes and the cost of workmen's compensation typically are charged to manufacturing overhead. Identifying these costs with specific employees is desirable to match costs with products, but it is also more difficult. Advocates of putting the cost in overhead argue that if a direct labor application base is used to apply overhead to production, the matching concept is satisfied. However, managers do not see all of the labor-related costs because some labor costs are reported as overhead costs. Some of the labor costs are buried in the indirect manufacturing costs.

Employer payroll taxes are levied on wages paid, but not on wages accrued. At the end of the month when accrued payroll is recorded, good accounting practice dictates accruing of the payroll taxes as well, but these taxes are not legal liabilities at the time of accrual. For income tax purposes such tax accrual is not permitted and many employers do not record it for accounting purposes either. Any distortion of earnings caused by not recording payroll taxes on accrued earnings at the end of one year is offset by a similar treatment of payroll taxes at the end of the next year. Any part not offset is usually quite small and not material.

Employee Benefits

Employee benefits are a cost of labor borne by the employer

A variety of employee benefits, sometimes called **fringe benefits,** are provided to employees. Common benefits are pension plans, vacation pay, overtime pay, education and training programs, guaranteed annual wage plans, and various types of insurance. The cost of such benefits has grown substantially in the last 20 years. Today employee benefits constitute a significant labor cost in addition to the gross payroll and payroll taxes.

Employee benefits are an essential cost of hiring and maintaining a productive work force. Employers do not provide these benefits without cause. Attractive education programs, vacations, pension plans, and other benefits keep employees motivated and happy and keep other employers from hiring employees away. Management pays for employee benefits because the cost of the programs is more than offset by employee productivity.

Pension Plans.   About 20 years ago it was common for employees to retire after 20, 30, or more years of work and find themselves with little retirement income unless they had the foresight to save a portion of their earnings over their lifetime. Social Security legislation was intended to provide a basic minimum retirement income supplement for people when they retire, but the benefits were not meant to be a comfortable retirement income. More recently many businesses have adopted pension plans that provide a lifetime income to retired employees.

Pension plan accounting is a complex topic, usually covered in advanced financial accounting courses. We can discuss only some of the more important concepts without going into details. We are interested primarily in the assignment of pension fund costs to the correct cost objectives. Determining the cost of a pension plan is an actuarial problem complicated by many factors. The number of employees, their age, the length of time employed, their expected retirement age, and their life expectancy are only some of the factors that determine pension costs. Other factors include expected growth in the number of employees, expected growth in wage rates, expected earnings of the pension fund, and expected cost of administration.

In 1974, Congress passed the Employment Retirement Income Security Act (**ERISA**), which provides standards for pension plan participation, funding, vesting, and management. **Funding** refers to the required contribution to the plan so that sufficient amounts are available for pension payments. **Vesting** refers to employees' rights to pension payments if they terminate their employment prior to retirement. The **vested benefits** portion of the plan cannot be forfeited and must be paid in the form of pension benefits when the employee reaches a specified age. As a result of **ERISA**, many companies had to modify their pension plans and institute stringent record-keeping, reporting, and compliance procedures. **ERISA** is a complex piece of legislation affecting not only pension plans but also health, accident, and death benefit programs. Many employers' pension and other plan costs increased dramatically after passage of the act.

Pension plans may be **contributory,** in which case employees contribute part of their earnings to the retirement plan, and the employer pays a part. Employees' contributions are made by payroll withholdings and they vest immediately. If plans are noncontributory, the employer makes the entire payment into the plan. Employers' contributions may vest immediately or over a period of time, depending on the plan.

Like other employer costs, pension plan costs for manufacturing labor usually are treated as indirect costs charged to the manufacturing overhead control account and the charge to products is made as part of the manufacturing overhead applied. This approach has the advantage of lower accounting costs and convenience, but it reduces the amount of labor cost data available to managers by burying some of the cost in overhead.

Education and Training Programs. Many businesses provide a variety of training and education programs for their employees. Some programs consist of short periods of training for new employees, in order to prepare them for productive work. Comprehensive training programs may be needed when new production facilities are installed or new production processes are started. In addition, employers may provide training for employees moving from one type of work to another, or to update current skills.

Most training and education costs are treated as indirect product costs or period costs, depending on who is trained. In some cases, training program costs may warrant deferral and allocation over several future periods.

Vacation Pay. Vacation pay increases the total cost of labor and can be identified with the time employees perform their work. For example, if an employee earns $5 per hour for 40 hours a week, and is entitled to 2 weeks of paid vacation per year, the company receives 50 weeks' work for 52 weeks' pay. The time worked actually costs $5.20 per hour, calculated as follows:

$$\$5 \text{ per hour} \times 40 \text{ hours} \times 52 \text{ weeks} = \$10,400.00$$
$$\$10,400.00/50 \text{ weeks}/40 \text{ hours} = \$5.20 \text{ per hour}$$

In practice, vacation costs for factory workers are generally charged to overhead. Vacation pay is accrued each pay period by charging overhead or expenses and crediting a liability for vacations. The liability is reduced when an employee on vacation is paid. A similar treatment is accorded to pay for sick leave, paid holidays, military training, or other activities during which employees are absent from work but receive their usual pay. Vacation pay is a period expense for nonmanufacturing employees.

Overtime Pay. Labor agreements and some labor laws require that employers pay a premium for overtime work. **Overtime** is work in excess of a specified number of hours per day or week. Often overtime is considered to be any work over 40 hours per week or any work over 8 hours a day. These measures of overtime may vary, however, from one state to another and from one labor agreement to another. For example, a fire fighter labor agreement may call for employees to be on duty continuously for 24 hours and to be off duty the next 2 days.

A large number of employees are covered by provisions of the Fair Labor Standards Act, which requires a minimum hourly wage and a rate of time-and-a-half for each hour worked in excess of 40 hours per week. Employers may also pay shift premiums for work on the second and third shift of the day.

The method of charging overtime premium to production varies with the reason for the overtime work. For example, a special order is accepted with the knowledge that it could only be completed with overtime work; the cost of the overtime premium should be charged to the order. If overtime is planned for production in general, the overtime premium should be included in the factory overhead rate, so that all work is charged an equal amount of the overtime premium.

Guaranteed Wage Plans.   In some industries, laid-off factory workers receive a guaranteed annual wage, which is a base amount of wages that employees receive under a guaranteed wage plan. Most guaranteed annual wage plans require employers to pay laid-off employees some percentage of their normal pay, such as 65 or 70 percent. Alternatively, the plan may require the employer to pay some amount per hour worked into a guaranteed annual wage fund administered by trustees.

Insurance Programs.   Group life insurance, health and accident insurance, and dental insurance are among the insurance programs provided for employees by many employers. Sometimes the cost of these programs is shared by employees through payroll withholdings. The cost to the employer is typically accounted for as overhead for production employees and as a period cost for nonmanufacturing employees.

Incentive Plans.   Some companies have **incentive plans** intended to stimulate labor efficiency by rewarding employees for productivity above some accepted standard. The plans may be for individual employees, groups of employees, departments, or all employees in the plant. Some plans involve bonuses and others may be based on piece rates for individual work. Incentive payments may be made each pay period or at some other interval. Such payments are accounted for as overhead for production workers, and marketing or administrative expense for other employees.

Incentive plans encourage high labor productivity

Recording Employer Payroll Costs

Employer payroll costs may be recorded at the end of a month, or each time the payroll is paid. To demonstrate the entry, we assume that employer payroll costs are recorded at the same time the payroll is paid. Using our earlier example, the entry on August 1 to record employer payroll costs is

Aug. 1	Payroll	8,852.50	
	FICA taxes payable		2,835.00
	Federal FUTA tax payable		283.50
	State unemployment insurance		
	payable		810.00
	Pension benefits payable		4,200.00
	Group insurance payable		264.00
	Vacation pay payable		460.00
	To record employer payroll cost for the		
	payroll period ending July 31.		

The payroll account accumulates payroll costs until they can be distributed to cost objectives

In the above entry, the FICA tax payable is 7 percent of the $40,500 payroll recorded on page 672. The federal part of FUTA tax is .8 percent of payroll, and the other amounts vary, depending on the company's unemployment experience and agreements with employees.

TOTAL COST OF LABOR

When payroll taxes, employee benefits, and incentive plans are added to gross payroll, it is not uncommon for them to increase total payroll cost by 35 to 40 percent. For example, the following items are typical for a company with a monthly payroll of $10,000 gross pay:

FICA tax 7 percent of $10,000	$ 700.00
FUTA tax .8 percent of $10,000	80.00
State unemployment insurance 2 percent	200.00
Workmen's compensation insurance	100.00
Pension cost 12 percent	1,200.00
Vacation and other time off 7 percent	700.00
Training and education programs	200.00
Guaranteed wage plans 3.5 percent	350.00
Insurance programs 4 percent	400.00
Total additional payroll expenses	$3,930.00

These figures, which do not include incentive or overtime pay, amount to over 39 percent of the gross payroll, not an unusually high percentage.

Identifying the Total Cost of Labor

Total labor cost is much greater than gross payroll

The common accounting practice is to charge virtually all manufacturing payroll taxes and employee benefit costs to overhead. But the managers of some organizations believe it is important to identify and clearly report the total cost of labor with each cost objective. Therefore, employer payroll taxes and employee benefit costs can be identified with each employee and charged to cost objectives along with the gross cost of payroll. For example, Jim

Conners works as a welder in the manufacture of steel bookcases. His wage rate is $10 an hour and during a recent week he spent 34 hours making bookcases and 6 hours cleaning and servicing his welding equipment. In addition to gross wages, Jim's **employer** pays 7 percent of gross wages for FICA taxes, $12 per week for an employee education fund, 2.5 percent for unemployment taxes, 10 percent for a retirement program; also, 8 percent of gross wages is accrued for vacation pay. The computation of total labor cost is:

Gross pay (40 hours × $10 per hour)		$400.00
Other labor costs:		
FICA taxes ($400 × .07)	$28.00	
Education program	12.00	
Unemployment taxes ($400 × .025)	10.00	
Retirement program ($400 × .10)	40.00	
Vacation pay ($400 × .08)	32.00	122.00
Total labor cost		$522.00
Total hourly labor cost ($522.00/40 hr)		$ 13.05 per hr

This total hourly labor cost is used to assign labor cost to the appropriate cost objective. For example, the cost of Jim Conner's work for the week is assigned as follows:

Direct labor charged to work in process:	
34 hours × $13.05 per hour	$443.70
Indirect labor charged to MOH, control	
6 hours × $13.05 per hour	78.30
Total labor cost for Jim Conner	$522.00

PAYROLL ILLUSTRATION

Now we illustrate the journal entries to record the payment of wages to employees for March, and to record withholdings and end-of-month accruals. An entry is made each pay period, which we assume for purposes of our example to be every 2 weeks. In addition to recording gross pay, payroll taxes, and employee benefits, entries are required to accrue the payroll at the end of the month, and to distribute payroll and related costs to production, marketing, and administrative expenses. To illustrate these entries, we assume the following calendar and the situation described below:

March								April						
S	M	T	W	T	F	S		S	M	T	W	T	F	S
		1	2	3	4	5							1	2
6	7	8	9	10	11	12		3	4	5	6	7	8	9
13	14	15	16	17	18	19		10	11	12	13	14	15	16
20	21	22	23	24	25	26		17	18	19	20	21	22	23
27	28	29	30	31				24	25	26	27	28	29	30

1. The payroll is paid every other Monday for the previous 2 weeks. The March 14 payroll of $85,000 and the March 28 payroll of $93,600 are for the following wages and salaries:

	Feb. 28–Mar. 13	Mar. 14–Mar. 27
Direct labor	$36,000	$39,600
Indirect labor	17,000	18,400
Marketing salaries	18,000	21,600
Administrative salaries	14,000	14,000
Total	$85,000	$93,600

2. Payroll taxes and other employer payroll costs are recorded at the end of each month when the payroll is distributed to various accounts. There is no state income tax withholding. In addition to tax and FICA withholdings, the company withholds $15 of union dues from each of its 40 factory workers each pay period and various amounts of group insurance withholdings from all of its employees, based on the number of dependents each has.

3. The company's state unemployment tax rate is 1.9 percent of gross payroll and workmen's compensation is 1 percent of gross payroll. Pension plan cost is $25,000 per month, 50 percent of which is for factory workers and the remainder for the 15 marketing and 9 administrative personnel. Vacation pay is accrued at the rate of 4 percent for factory workers and 5 percent for the marketing and administrative personnel. The company pays $24 per month for health and accident insurance for each of its 64 employees. No employee has exceeded the FICA limit.

4. The accrued payroll for the period March 28–31, which will be paid in April, is for the following wages and salaries:

Direct labor	$ 7,000
Indirect labor	3,150
Marketing salaries	7,500
Administrative salaries	5,250
Total	$22,900

Payroll Accounting

The journal entries to record the March payroll and distribute the costs to the appropriate products or period expense are illustrated and explained below. This example should give you an understanding of the concepts and procedures used in recording the payroll. We have made some simplifying assumptions to reduce the amount of detail. For example, in many companies, salaried employees are paid only once a month whereas factory workers may be paid more frequently.

Recording Gross Payroll.   The entry to record the gross payroll and the associated withholding items and cash payment is

Mar. 14	Payroll	85,000.00	
	Income tax withholdings payable		17,000.00
	FICA taxes payable		5,950.00
	Union dues payable		600.00
	Group insurance payable		578.00
	Cash		60,872.00
	Payroll for period ending March 12.		

Payroll tax liabilities are paid to the government within 3 days of paying wages and salaries

Recording Payment of Federal Income Taxes.   Within 3 banking days of paying the payroll, the income tax withholdings and the employee and employer shares of FICA taxes must be paid to the federal government using Federal Tax Deposit Form 501.[1] The entry to record the payment of federal income tax withholding and FICA taxes payable is presented below:

Mar. 15	Income tax withholdings payable	17,000.00	
	FICA taxes payable	11,900.00	
	Cash		28,900.00
	To record payment of withholdings and		
	employer FICA taxes to the federal		
	government.		

Note that the March 15 payment includes a debit for FICA taxes payable that is larger than the amount withheld on March 14. The employer's share of this tax must be paid whether or not it has been recorded in the company books as a liability.

The gross payroll and withholdings for the second 2-week period of the month are recorded with the following journal entry. It is just like the entry for the first 2-week period, except the amounts are different.

---

[1] Employers with small amounts of withholdings make payments to the government less frequently. Depending on the amount withheld, payments may be due by the 15th of the following month, the end of the following month, or quarterly. The rules are presented in Internal Revenue Service Circular E.

Mar. 28	Payroll	93,600.00	
	Income tax withholdings payable		18,920.00
	FICA taxes payable		6,552.00
	Union dues payable		600.00
	Group insurance payable		578.00
	Cash		66,950.00
	Payroll for period ending March 26.		

Again, the federal taxes are paid shortly after the pay period is over:

Mar. 30	Income tax withholdings payable	18,920.00	
	FICA taxes payable	13,104.00	
	Cash		32,024.00
	To record payment of withholdings and		
	employer FICA taxes to federal		
	government.		

Payroll taxes are not accrued when wages and salaries are accrued

Accruing the Payroll.   At the end of the month the payroll for the last 4 days of the month is accrued and employer payroll costs are recorded. Then the payroll is distributed to cost objectives. The accrual for the last 4 days of March is

Mar. 31	Payroll	22,900.00	
	Accrued payroll		22,900.00
	To accrue payroll for last 4 days		
	of March.		

Recording Payroll Taxes and Employee Benefits.   Some employers record payroll taxes and other payroll costs each time the payroll is paid. Others record these costs only at the end of the month, as we do here. Payroll taxes are levied on amounts actually paid to employees, not on accrued payroll. Tax laws do not require accruing payroll taxes and most companies use the tax rules for accounting purposes as well. The entry below records payroll taxes and employee benefits for the payroll actually paid in March. Therefore the amounts recorded for each of the items are for the two payrolls of the month, not just one of the pay periods.

Mar. 31	Payroll	49,167.80	
	FICA taxes payable		12,502.00
	Federal FUTA tax payable		155.20
	State unemployment insurance		
	payable		368.60
	Workmen's compensation payable		1,786.00
	Pension liability		25,000.00
	Group insurance payable		1,536.00
	Vacation benefits payable		7,820.00
	To record employer payroll taxes and		
	employee benefit costs.		

FICA tax	$178,600 × .07 =	$12,502.00
FUTA tax	19,400 × .008 =	155.20
State unemployment	19,400 × .019 =	368.60
Workmen's compensation	178,600 × .01 =	1,786.00
Group insurance	64 × $24 =	1,536.00
Vacation pay, factory	111,000 × .04 =	4,440.00
Vacation pay, other	67,600 × .05 =	3,380.00

The total amount of payroll taxes and employee benefits is debited to the payroll account, which is a clearing account. **A clearing account, or holding account,** is one in which some cost is recorded until the cost can be distributed to its appropriate cost objective. In this case, the payroll taxes are charged to the payroll account until the accountant determines the amounts that should be charged to each cost objective.

An alternative approach to recording payroll taxes and employee benefits is to record the costs directly to the various cost objectives without using the payroll account. This can be done if at the time of recording payroll taxes and employee benefits, the amounts that should be charged to each cost objective are known.

The $178,600 used to compute the FICA tax and workmen's compensation is the total amount of payroll **paid** in March, and is the sum of the March 14 payroll of $85,000 and the March 28 payroll of $93,600. The **accrued** payroll is not subject to these taxes until it is actually paid. Notice that FUTA tax and state unemployment insurance are computed on only $19,400 of pay. By the end of March many of the employees have earned the maximum limit of $7,000 on which FUTA taxes must be paid. Precise individual pay records must be maintained so that the company knows when each employee reaches the FUTA maximum and the FICA maximum. The factory vacation pay is computed on the amount of direct and indirect labor actually paid in March, and not on the amount accrued. It is possible to record this cost for the accrued payroll as well, but if the difference is not material, the easier approach is usually selected.

The payroll account balance is distributed to cost objectives

Distributing Payroll Costs to Cost Objectives.   The labor costs recorded for March must be assigned to the appropriate cost objectives of the firm. The labor costs of nonmanufacturing personnel are charged to an expense account for the period. Labor costs for manufacturing personnel are charged to products either as direct labor or indirectly as part of manufacturing overhead cost.

The direct labor for the month, both the amount paid and the amount accrued, is now distributed from the payroll account to work in process to become part of product cost. The portion charged to payroll for indirect labor is distributed to overhead, and the remainder is distributed to administrative and marketing expense. Some companies charge work in process, overhead, and various expense accounts directly when the payroll is recorded, instead of going through a payroll account. Payroll is a holding account used for convenience, but there is no requirement to use it. Payroll cost distributions are recorded below.

Mar. 31	Work in process control	82,600.00	
	Manufacturing overhead control	38,550.00	
	Marketing expense control	47,100.00	
	Administrative expense control	33,250.00	
	Payroll		201,500.00
	To distribute March payroll per schedule		

Schedule of March Payroll Distributions

	Mar. 14	Mar. 28	Mar. 31	Total
Direct labor	$36,000	$39,600	$ 7,000	$ 82,600
Indirect labor	17,000	18,400	3,150	38,550
Marketing	18,000	21,600	7,500	47,100
Administrative	14,000	14,000	5,250	33,250
Total	$85,000	$93,600	$22,900	$201,500

The following entry distributes the various employer payroll costs still left in the payroll account. Can you see where the figures come from?

Mar. 31	Factory overhead control	27,239.00	
	Marketing expense control	13,385.30	
	Administrative expense control	8,543.50	
	Payroll		49,167.80
	To distribute employer's payroll costs per		
	schedule		

Schedule of March Payroll Expense Distributions

	MOH	Marketing	Admin.
FICA tax	$ 7,770.00	$ 2,772.00	$1,960.00
FUTA tax	136.00	19.20	
State unemployment	323.00	45.60	
Workmen's comp.	1,110.00	396.00	280.00
Pension cost	12,500.00	7,812.50	4,687.50
Insurance	960.00	360.00	216.00
Vacation	4,440.00	1,980.00	1,400.00
Total	$27,239.00	$13,385.30	$8,543.50

The three FICA tax figures are the employer's portion of this tax. Each is 7 percent of the overhead, marketing, and administrative payroll **paid.** For example, the payroll distribution schedule shows marketing payroll of $18,000 and $21,600 paid on March 14 and March 28. This is a total of $39,600, and 7 percent of this amount is $2,772. Similarly the direct and indirect labor paid is a total of $111,000 and 7 percent of this is $7,770. The employer's FICA tax was already paid to the federal government on March 15 and March 30, together with the employee withholdings, and was charged to Payroll on March 31. Other distributions in the schedule above are computed in a similar way to the FICA tax. These entries and schedules demonstrate the complexity of record keeping necessary for payroll accounting.

Payment of Accrued Payroll.   The April 11 payroll will include 4 days of pay accrued in March on which no withholdings or payroll costs have been accrued or recorded. Below we show only the April 11 payroll entry, which includes payment of the March accrual.

Apr. 11	Payroll	62,700.00	
	Accrued payroll	22,900.00	
	Income tax withholdings payable		17,060.00
	FICA taxes payable		5,992.00
	Union dues payable		600.00
	Group insurance payable		578.00
	Cash		61,370.00
	Payroll for period ending April 9.		

The tax and FICA withholdings in the above entry are for the entire amount paid, which includes both the amount of payroll cost incurred in April and the amount accrued in March. By April 30 the company must file a quarterly return of federal income tax withheld using Form 941. Sometime during April the company also pays the insurance, union dues, and pension liabilities to the appropriate recipients.

SUMMARY   Voluminous and detailed payroll records must be maintained by an employer in order to ensure that correct amounts are paid to employees and charged to appropriate cost objectives and to satisfy all legal requirements. Manufacturing employees accumulate labor time data on **daily time tickets** or **job time tickets.** The information from these tickets is summarized periodically in a **labor distribution report,** which indicates the amount of direct and indirect labor to be charged to production. Direct labor is distributed to products by debiting the work in process account. Indirect labor is charged to Manufacturing Overhead Control. Nonmanufacturing employees' labor time is treated as a period cost.

Gross payroll is the amount actually earned by employees. From this amount, a number of items must be withheld by the employer. **Withholdings** include federal and state income taxes, **FICA taxes,** union dues, insurance premiums, and other items. **Net pay** is the amount actually paid to employees after withholdings. The amounts withheld are paid to federal and state governments, unions, insurance companies, and other recipients.

In addition to gross pay, employers incur other payroll costs, including the employer's share of FICA payroll taxes, federal and state unemployment taxes, workmen's compensation insurance taxes, and a variety of **employee benefits,** also called **fringe benefits.** They include vacation pay, holiday pay, pension plans, education and training programs, overtime pay, guaranteed wage plans, and insurance programs. Pension costs usually constitute large amounts of employee benefits. Under current laws they must be **funded,** which means the employer must make periodic contributions into the plan. Some pension plans are **contributory,** which means that part of the plan is funded by employee withholdings. The portion of the plan that the employee does not forfeit by leaving the employer is called **vested benefits.**

Employers may use a variety of **incentive plans** to promote employee productivity and reward the more productive employees. Altogether, the total cost of payroll taxes and employee benefits may be as much as 40 percent of gross payroll. Some employers compute the actual cost of each employee in order to identify the total cost of labor and assign it to products. Others may assign directly to products only the direct cost consisting of gross payroll, and assign the remainder to manufacturing overhead. Payroll costs may be accumulated in a **clearing account,** or **holding account,** until they can be analyzed and distributed to various cost objectives.

KEY TERMS

clearing account *(683)*
contributory pension plan *(676)*
daily time ticket *(668)*
employee benefits *(675)*
FICA tax *(671)*
fringe benefits *(675)*
funded pension plan *(675)*
FUTA tax *(674)*
gross payroll *(669)*

holding account *(683)*
incentive plans *(677)*
job time ticket *(668)*
labor distribution report *(669)*
labor recapitulation report *(669)*
net pay *(672)*
payroll taxes *(673)*
vested benefits *(675)*
withholdings *(670)*

QUESTIONS

1. Talking to his manager, the new cost accountant said, "For every worker that spends an hour working, we pay a wage and we incur an additional cost for fringe benefits. We know the amount of fringe benefit cost, so if people work directly on a product, the cost of their fringe benefits should be treated as a direct product cost just like their wage." The manager replied, "We always treated fringe benefits as manufacturing overhead, so it must be the right way to do it." Comment on the two treatments, giving reasons for each.

2. Prior to the beginning of an accounting year, a company estimates the annual cost of vacation pay, bonuses, and incentive awards for its employees. It then uses its estimates to assign these costs to production during the year. One manager argues that it does not make sense to estimate costs such as bonuses and incentive pay that depend on results which can only be determined when the accounting period is over. "If we incur a loss, there will be no bonus, but because we planned for profitable operations, the cost of bonuses that don't exist are assigned to products all year." What is the rationale for the treatment used? Comment on the manager's statement.

3. "We cannot afford to have our production workers spend a lot of time on paperwork. At the end of each week, they estimate how much of their 40 hours they put on each job. If they had any overtime, we have the bookkeeping department prorate the overtime cost to the jobs in proportion to the regular time estimates provided by the employees." Comment on this method of collecting labor cost data.

EXERCISES

Ex. 19-1
Recording Payroll
and Payroll Costs

Le Banquet Francaise restaurant employs one manager, two chefs, four waiters, and three helpers. They are paid monthly as follows:

Manager	$3,000
Chef	1,800
Waiter	900
Helper	600

All personnel are entitled to a half month of paid vacation time per year, which the company accrues each month. Income tax withholdings average 20 percent of payroll for federal tax and 5 percent for state tax. All employees except the manager belong to a union whose monthly dues of 2 percent of salary are withheld by the employer. FICA withholdings are 7 percent of pay. The company contributes $18 per month per employee for a group health and accident insurance plan. The waiters receive tips from customers, which they share with the helpers.

REQUIRED

Record the payment of the payroll and the employer's other payroll costs.

Ex. 19-2
Journal Entries for
Payroll and Payroll
Costs

Arbocodiel Company employs five office employees whose monthly pay is as follows:

Arnold	$2,600
Bonser	1,200
Cortie	900
Dilberg	1,500
Elmire	1,800

In addition to the above salaries, Arnold earned a $300 bonus and Elmire a $400 bonus during the first quarter of the year. Income tax withholdings average 22 percent of salary for federal and 2 percent of salary for state income taxes. The FICA rate is 7 percent of the first $38,000 of salary. The company is subject to a total FUTA tax of 3.5 percent of which .8 percent is federal and the remainder is for the state. Only the first $7,000 of each employee's salary is subject to FUTA tax. The monthly pension expense of the company is $840. No bonuses have been earned by any of the employees in April.

REQUIRED

a. Record the April 30 payment of salaries.
b. Record the employer's April payroll costs.

Ex. 19-3
Annual Payroll Cost

Lamson Company employs eight people, whose monthly salaries are as follows:

A	$3,900	E	$2,500
B	3,750	F	1,800
C	3,200	G	1,800
D	2,800	H	1,600

The company pays FICA taxes of 7 percent of the first $38,000 earned by each employee during the year. FUTA federal tax is .8 percent and state unemployment insurance is 2.0 percent of the first $7,000 earned by each employee during the year. Pension cost is 12 percent of pay for all employees but is not paid for the first 12 months of employment. Workmen's compensation is 1 percent of salary. Each employee is entitled to 3 weeks paid vacation per year. The company contributes $21 per month per employee for group insurance. All employees have been with the company more than 2 years except G, who was hired on July 1 of last year.

REQUIRED   Compute the company's total annual payroll cost for this year.

Ex. 19-4
Distributing Payroll Costs

Following are the August payroll data for Sabul Company:

Direct labor	$32,000
Indirect labor	11,500
Marketing salaries	14,000
Administrative salaries	9,800

The FICA tax rate on employees and employers is 7 percent of pay. Workmen's compensation is .06 percent. Only $11,000 of direct labor and $5,000 of indirect labor is subject to FUTA and state unemployment insurance of 1.7 percent. Federal income taxes to be withheld amount to $14,200. There is no state income tax.

REQUIRED

a. Prepare the entries to record the August gross payroll and additional payroll expenses for the month.
b. Prepare the entries to distribute the payroll and additional payroll costs.

Ex. 19-5
Overtime Pay for a Production Department

Harnagle Company employs 10 production workers who are paid $7.50 per hour for first-shift time and a 50 percent overtime premium for any hours worked in excess of 40 per week. Workers on the second shift earn $9.50 per hour and the same percentage overtime premium. Following is the company's labor report for the week of June 8. All time is direct labor. The overtime rate depends on the shift in which an employee works more than 8 hours per day.

Employee	Monday	Tuesday	Wednesday	Thursday	Friday
First Shift					
A	8	8	10	9	7
B			8	8	8
D	8	11	10	8	10
G	8	8	8		
I	9	9	8	10	10
J	8	10	8	8	8
Second Shift					
B	7	8			
C	8	8	9	7	6
E	8	8	8	8	8
F	10	10	10	10	9
G				9	10
H	6	6	6	9	9

REQUIRED

a. Distribute the gross payroll for the week to production assuming that all overtime premiums are charged directly to products.
b. Distribute the gross payroll for the week to production assuming that overtime premiums are shared by all products.

Ex. 19-6
Payroll Costs and Bonus

Marsha's Ceramics has two highly skilled employees who design and produce exquisite ceramic pieces. Each earns a salary of $1,495 per month. Each also gets 1/2 month of paid vacation and a bonus at the end of the year equal to 1 month's pay. The company treats the bonuses and vacation pay as indirect cost. The company deducts 22 percent of salary for federal income tax, 5 percent for state income tax, and 7 percent for FICA tax, and pays 14 percent of gross pay into a pension fund. There is no workmen's compensation or FUTA tax liability.

REQUIRED

a. Record the May payroll.
b. Record the additional payroll costs for May.
c. Record the distribution of the payroll costs.

Ex. 19-7
Bonus Pay and Payroll Costs

Donny Zetti works for Flatone Musical Instruments Company as the only worker in the production department, at a salary of $1,452 per month. He is highly skilled and is therefore entitled to 1 month of paid vacation per year and a bonus of 1 month's pay if the company operates at a profit, which it has done for the past 18 years. The company treats the bonus and vacation pay as indirect cost. The company withholds 20 percent of salary for federal income tax, 3 percent for state income tax, and 7 percent for FICA tax, and pays an additional 15 percent of gross salary into a pension fund. There is no workmen's compensation or FUTA tax liability.

REQUIRED

a. Record the July payroll.
b. Record the additional July payroll costs.
c. Distribute the payroll to production.

Ex. 19-8
Labor Cost of
Production

Michael Angelo is a stonecutter working for Takonite Quarries, Inc. He earns $9 per hour and normally works 40 hours per week. During the first week of May, Michael worked 12 hours cutting marble slabs and 20 hours polishing granite. The remaining 8 hours he spent maintaining the cutting and polishing equipment. For each employee, Michael's employer pays $6 per week for health and accident insurance, $12 a week into a guaranteed annual wage fund, 7 percent FICA tax, and 14 percent into a retirement fund.

REQUIRED

a. Compute the direct labor cost to be assigned to processing marble and granite by Michael.
b. Compute the cost to be assigned to overhead this week for Michael's work.
c. Compute the total hourly cost of employing Michael and total hourly cost of Michael's direct labor if all costs are included in the computations.

PROBLEMS

P. 19-1
Billing Rate for
Labor

George works as a master plumber for Grayson Plumbing Company. His pay is $14.00 per hour and he normally works 40 hours per week. During the second week of May, George worked 31 hours on a construction project and he spent 4 hours on a home repair job. The remaining 5 hours he spent on equipment maintenance, travel between assignments, and deciding what supplies needed to be ordered. The company considers it normal for George to spend 5 hours a week on other than direct labor.

Grayson Plumbing Company pays $7.50 per week for health and accident insurance for each of its employees. Also it pays $10 a week into a guaranteed annual wage fund, 7 percent FICA tax, and 12.5 percent into a retirement fund. In order to cover administrative and other operating expenses the company must charge 180 percent of George's actual direct labor cost for plumbing repairs.

REQUIRED

a. Compute the direct labor cost to be assigned to plumbing repairs and also to the construction job.
b. Compute the cost to be assigned to overhead this week for George's work.
c. Compute the total hourly cost of employing George and total hourly cost of his direct labor if all costs are included in the computations.
d. How much should the company bill the customer for plumbing repairs performed by George?

P. 19-2
Payroll Distribution
Entries

Gnoppe Manufacturing Company has 20 production workers, 10 people in marketing, and 5 in administration. Following are data about the company's payroll for November, which is paid at the end of the month:

Direct labor	$38,000
Indirect labor	17,000
Marketing salaries	21,000
Administrative salaries	14,000

The company withholds 20 percent of salary for federal income taxes, 4 percent for state income taxes, and 7 percent for FICA taxes from each employee. It also withholds $30 of union dues each month from each of its factory workers and $19 for group insurance from each of its employees. None of the payroll is subject to unemployment tax, but workmen's compensation is .7 percent of total pay. Pension plan cost is $10,400 per month, 40 percent of which is for factory workers, 35 percent for the marketing personnel, and 25 percent for administrative personnel. Vacation pay is 6 percent of payroll and is accrued each month. The company pays $19 per month for health and accident insurance for each of its employees. None of the company's employees' pay has exceeded the FICA limit.

REQUIRED Prepare the journal entries to record the payment of the payroll, the employer's additional payroll cost, and the distribution of payroll at the end of November.

P. 19-3
Labor Cost Analysis

Schmidlap Corporation's labor contract calls for an hourly wage of $7 per hour for its production employees. The following data are available about the company's operations:

1. Employees work 8 hours a day 5 days a week and have 2 weeks of paid vacation per year plus 10 paid holidays.
2. Payroll taxes are 7 percent for FICA on the first $36,000 of pay, .8 for FUTA and 2.0 percent for state unemployment insurance on the first $7,000 of pay, and .9 percent for workmen's compensation insurance.
3. The company pays $750 per year into a guaranteed annual wage plan for each employee.
4. On the average, 85 percent of production line time is direct labor and the remainder is indirect.

REQUIRED
a. Compute the total annual labor cost per employee.
b. Determine the total cost per hour worked.
c. Compute the total cost of labor per direct labor hour.

P. 19-4
Overtime and Shift
Premium

Alpha Company employs 13 production workers at $8.00 per hour for first-shift time. Second-shift workers earn $8.80 per hour and third-shift workers earn $9.60 per hour. The company pays a 50 percent overtime premium for any hours worked in excess of 40. Following is the company's labor report for the week of July 11. Indirect labor is 10 percent of all labor time and the remainder is direct. The overtime rate depends on the shift in which an employee works more than 8 hours per day.

Employee	Monday	Tuesday	Wednesday	Thursday	Friday
First Shift					
Baker	8	10	10	10	8
Charlee	8	10	8	—	—
Draper	8	8	8	8	8
Fox	9	8	10	8	10
Gorman	8	—	—	—	4
Haltom	8	8	8	9	8
Second Shift					
Abel	8	8	9	7	9
Echler	8	10	10	10	10
Gorman	—	10	10	10	—
Irwing	—	—	10	9	10
Jules	—	—	8	8	8
Loomis	8	8	8	8	8
Third Shift					
Charlee	—	—	—	8	6
Jules	8	8	—	—	—
King	8	8	8	8	8
Morris	8	9	9	9	9

REQUIRED

a. Compute the amount of gross payroll to be assigned to products and to overhead for the week, assuming that overtime premium is charged directly to products.

b. Compute the amount of gross payroll to be assigned to products and to overhead for the week, assuming that overtime premium is charged to overhead.

P. 19-5
Incentive Plan with
Standard Costs

Dukker Company's three production employees work under an incentive and guaranteed wage plan. Each worker is paid $3 for every rotor blade assembly completed, with a bonus of $2 per unit for any units completed above 20 per day. Each worker is guaranteed $50 per day regardless of the amount of production. The production record for Thursday is provided below:

Worker	Units Assembled
A	23
B	14
C	19

The standard for the rotor assemblies is 20 units per day at $3.00 per unit. The company charges direct labor at standard and any difference between actual and standard labor as a labor rate or efficiency variance. The company pays 7 percent FICA tax, 3.4 percent total FUTA tax, and 1 percent workmen's compensation.

REQUIRED

a. Prepare a direct labor performance report for the day showing the amount of variances for each worker and for the production department.

b. Prepare the journal entry to distribute the day's pay and labor costs to production and overhead.

P. 19-6
Evaluation of Labor
Cost

Cromwill Corporation produces rocket motor assemblies using 40 production workers. It is capable of producing four assemblies per week. Each rocket assembly must sell for 3 times the total production labor cost in order to produce an adequate profit. The company recently negotiated a new labor contract for an hourly wage of $8 per hour for its production employees. The following data have been collected about the company's operations:

1. Payroll taxes are 7 percent for FICA on the first $36,000 of pay, .8 for FUTA and 1.2 percent for state unemployment insurance on the first $7,000 of pay, and .5 percent of gross payroll for workmen's compensation insurance.

2. Employees work 8 hours a day 5 days a week and have 3 weeks of paid vacation per year plus 10 paid holidays.

3. For each week an employee works, the company pays $14 into a guaranteed annual wage plan.

4. On the average, 90 percent of production line time is direct labor and the remainder is indirect.

REQUIRED

a. Compute the total annual labor cost per employee.
b. Determine the total cost per hour worked.
c. Compute the total cost of labor per direct labor hour.
d. Determine the price the company should charge for its rocket motor assemblies.

P. 19-7
Analysis of Labor Costs

The management of Largo Delivery Service is negotiating a new contract with its employees' union. The company has been incurring losses for the past 2 years and believes that it cannot continue in operation much longer unless it can cut its costs. Because labor is its most significant operating cost, it is proposing the following changes from the current contract for each employee:

	Current	Proposed
Wage rate per hour	$7.35	$7.00
Vacation and paid holidays	4 weeks	3 weeks
Pension contribution per week	$22.80	$20.00
Guaranteed wage plan per week	$16.00	$15.00
Training program per year	$150.00	$40.00

Employees work 40 hours per week of which 80 percent is direct delivery labor and 20 percent is indirect. The company pays 7 percent FICA tax, .8 FUTA federal tax on the first $7,000 of pay, no state unemployment tax, and .3 percent workmen's compensation.

REQUIRED

a. Determine the total cost per hour of delivery labor for the current and proposed contracts.
b. Determine the percentage change in each component of total labor cost.
c. Compute the total cost of each hour of direct delivery service under the current and proposed contracts.

P. 19-8
Payroll Journal Entries

Kolsmun Manufacturing Company has 30 production workers, 14 people in marketing, and 6 in administration. Following are data about the company's payroll for March:

1. The payroll is paid every other Monday for the previous 2 weeks. The following wages and salaries were earned for the weeks indicated:

	Mar. 2–14	Mar. 16–28	Mar. 30–31
Direct labor	$ 45,000	$43,600	$ 5,600
Indirect labor	18,500	19,200	2,500
Marketing salaries	26,000	24,800	3,000
Administrative salaries	12,000	12,000	2,100
Total	$101,500	$99,600	$13,200

2. The company withholds 20 percent of salary for income taxes and 7 percent for FICA taxes from each employee. It also withholds $18 of union dues each pay period from each of its factory workers and $12 for group insurance from each of its employees.
3. The company's FUTA tax rate is .8 percent, state unemployment tax rate is 2.1 percent, and workmen's compensation is .8 percent of gross payroll. Pension plan cost is $22,900 per month, 50 percent of which is for factory workers, 30 percent for the marketing personnel, and 20 percent for administrative personnel. Vacation pay is 5 percent of payroll and is accrued each month. The company pays $19 per month for health and accident insurance

for each of its employees. None of the company's employees' pay has exceeded the FICA and FUTA limits.

			March			
S	M	T	W	T	F	S
1	2	3	4	5	6	7
8	9	10	11	12	13	14
15	16	17	18	19	20	21
22	23	24	25	26	27	28
29	30	31				

REQUIRED

Prepare the journal entries to record the payment of the March payrolls, payroll accruals on March 31, employer's payroll costs for March, and March payroll distribution.

CASES

Case 19-1 (AICPA) Analysis of Payroll Withholdings and Taxes

In January 1986 you were examining the financial statements of Lang Manufacturing Company for the year ended December 31, 1985. Lang filed the necessary payroll tax returns for the first three quarters of 1985 and had prepared drafts of the returns scheduled to be filed by January 31, 1986.

The information shown at the top of p. 695 was available from the general ledger, copies and drafts of payroll tax returns, and other sources.

Information from other sources:

1. In August 1985 six laborers were hired to tear down an old warehouse building located on the site where a new warehouse would soon be constructed. The laborers' 1985 wages totaling $1,000 were charged to the land and buildings account. Payroll taxes were not withheld.
2. Included in a 1985 wages expense account is 1 month's salary of $1,400 paid to the president on December 30, 1985 for his 1984 vacation allowance.
3. A gross factory payroll of $1,200 through December 31, 1985 and the related FICA taxes (employer and employee) were accrued on the general ledger at year-end for a portion of the week ending January 4, 1986. Each of the employees included in this payroll earned between $4,000 and $6,000 as a Lang employee in 1985.
4. In December 1985 a contractor was paid $2,300 for making repairs to machinery usually made by company employees and the amount was charged to Wages Expense. No payroll taxes were withheld.

Lang Manufacturing Company
General Ledger

Account	Balance December 31, 1985	Composition of Balance
Wages (various expense accounts)	$121,800	12 monthly entries from payroll summaries.
Payroll taxes expense	9,898	FICA (7% of $102,500) $7,175; state unemployment tax (2.7% of $59,000) $1,593; federal unemployment tax (.8% of $102,500) $820; amounts withheld from employees for FICA tax in October and November and paid to depositary $720.
Employees' payroll taxes withheld	2,145	December income tax $1,530; October through December FICA $980.
Employer's payroll taxes payable	774	December FICA $260, October through December state unemployment tax $199; 1985 federal unemployment tax $410.

Copies of 1984 tax returns:

	Totals for Year	First Three Quarters (Duplicate Copies of Returns)	Last Quarter (Pencil Draft)
Gross wages	$121,800	$95,870	$25,930
Wages taxable for FICA	102,500	88,500	14,000
FICA tax	14,350	12,390	1,960
Income tax withheld	15,740	11,490	4,250
Wages taxable for state unemployment tax	59,000	51,640	7,360
Total state unemployment tax (employer only)	1,593	1,394	199
Total federal unemployment tax — employer only (pencil draft of return for full year)	820		

REQUIRED

a. Prepare a schedule presenting the computation of total taxable wages to be reported on the 1985 payroll tax returns for FICA and for state unemployment taxes.

b. Prepare a schedule presenting the computation of the amounts (to the nearest dollar) that should be paid with each of the year-end payroll tax returns to be filed in January 1986 for (1) FICA taxes and income tax withheld, (2) state unemployment tax, and (3) federal unemployment tax.

c. Prepare a schedule to reconcile the differences between the amounts that should be paid with payroll tax returns to be filed in January 1986 (as computed for b) and the balances shown at December 31, 1985 in the related general ledger liability accounts.

CHAPTER 20
Accounting for Manufacturing Overhead

Product costs consist of three major elements: direct labor, direct materials, and manufacturing overhead. Overhead costs include all necessary costs of production that cannot be classified as either direct materials or direct labor. The types of costs included in the overhead account depend on the type of product manufactured and the kind of manufacturing processes used. A highly automated factory may have a lot of depreciation and lease cost for building and machinery. Another company, making the same product, may use labor-intensive production methods that result in much less depreciation costs in overhead, but more indirect costs associated with labor.

Chapters 2, 4, and 5 describe the way overhead costs are assigned to specific products. These early chapters explain the nature of overhead, how actual overhead costs are accumulated, and how overhead is assigned to products. In this chapter, we build on the earlier material to elaborate on accounting for and controlling overhead costs. We also discuss some of the more complex issues in developing overhead rates and measuring variances in manufacturing environments.

THE NATURE OF OVERHEAD COSTS

Manufacturing costs such as factory depreciation, utilities, maintenance, indirect labor, indirect materials, and payroll taxes are necessary production costs, yet they cannot be identified with specific products. In some cases, overhead costs are larger than direct production costs. For example, a company uses a highly automated production operation to make small steel trays that are sold in resort areas as souvenirs. Sheet steel is fed into cutting machines that automatically align the steel, cut it to size, and send it along a conveyor to the forming machines. The formed trays are placed on a painting line where they are automatically painted and dried in ovens. Decals are attached by machines and the trays are packaged by machine. Little labor is used other than to feed steel to the cutting machines, monitor the equipment, and check product quality. The majority of the product cost is depreciation, maintenance, insurance, and other overhead costs.

Overhead costs cannot be identified with specific products

The Need to Assign Overhead Costs to Products

Managers need to know the costs of making products. Detailed product cost data help managers to control costs, plan production and resource requirements, and measure performance. They also help managers decide which products to emphasize, which to stop producing, and how to set prices. The data used in making these decisions should include all necessary costs of production. If only the direct costs of manufacturing were available, a significant portion of product costs would be missing.

Product costs are also used for external reporting. The income reported to the Internal Revenue Service must be measured using product costs that include both direct and indirect costs of production. The same product cost criteria satisfy the reporting requirements of lenders, the Securities and Exchange Commission, and most other organizations interested in financial information.

Full product costs include overhead costs as well as direct costs

Computation of **full product cost** requires assigning overhead costs to products in addition to direct production costs. But arbitrary assignments of indirect manufacturing costs would violate the matching principle and greatly reduce the value of product cost information. Accountants try to assign overhead costs to products so that the resulting costs satisfy the matching principle, are understandable, and are easy to administer.

Assigning Overhead Costs to Products

The objective in assigning manufacturing overhead costs to products is to measure product costs accurately. Direct materials and direct labor costs are clearly identifiable with the product, so assigning them in a timely fashion is not difficult. But indirect manufacturing costs, which are not clearly identifiable with particular products, nevertheless are essential to successful production; they must be included in the cost of making the products.

Overhead costs should be assigned to products as soon as possible

There are two issues associated with assigning overhead cost to products: One is **when** overhead should be assigned to products, and the other is **how** the costs should be assigned. Accounting for overhead costs would be simplified if accountants could wait until the end of the accounting period to assign overhead costs to products. But this is seldom possible, because managers need the cost information long before the end of the year. As a general rule, information is more valuable when it is new than when it is old. Timeliness is particularly important for managerial reports, because managers must make pricing, production, personnel, and cost control decisions on a daily basis. The accounting system should therefore assign to products all production costs, including manufacturing overhead, as soon as the cost information is available. If direct production costs are charged to products weekly or daily, then typically overhead costs should be assigned at the same time.

Overhead Costs and the Matching Principle

Logically, overhead should be assigned to products in proportion to the amount of overhead resources used in production. But how is this matching of costs accomplished when accounting for overhead? If only one type of product is manufactured, the overhead cost could be assigned to products by merely dividing the total overhead by the number of units manufactured. Many companies, however, manufacture a variety of products and the overhead costs incurred benefit all of them. If a company produces tractors and wheelbarrows, a units-of-output measure would assign too little overhead to tractors and too much to wheelbarrows.

A common measure that assigns the proper proportion of overhead costs to each product is needed. For example, if 3 direct labor hours are required to build a wheelbarrow and 30 hours to build a tractor, assigning overhead on the basis of direct labor hours used allocates overhead costs to products in proportion to the amount of resources used in production. Overhead costs may also be assigned on the basis of direct labor cost, machine hours, or other measures, discussed later in this chapter.

Overhead costs for the coming year are estimated

Manufacturing Overhead Rates. To satisfy the matching principle and to provide timely product cost information, accountants use a predetermined overhead rate to assign overhead costs to products. The rate is based on estimates of the amount of overhead cost for the period and the volume of activity for the period. Typically, the accounting period used is 1 business year.

Estimates are also required because many overhead costs are seasonal or occur only once or twice a year. For example, in northern regions, heating costs are high in the winter and low in the summer. Property taxes may be paid once a year or every 6 months. Casualty insurance premiums may be paid for a full year in advance. Depreciation may be charged to the overhead account only at the end of a year. Because of the sporadic nature of some overhead costs, the balance of the Manufacturing Overhead Control account at the end of January may contain the entire year's insurance cost but no depreciation or property tax cost. To assign this account balance to January production would not make sense. Accountants therefore charge overhead to production based on expected overhead costs and output for the entire accounting year.

MANUFACTURING OVERHEAD RATES

Before the end of one accounting period, managers plan for the next period's operations. These plans are expressed as budgets, some of which show budgeted overhead costs. Costs are estimated for each category of overhead for a given level of anticipated production activity.

Developing the Overhead Rate

A manufacturing overhead rate is based on expected overhead-costs and the expected volume of activity. Because some costs are fixed and others vary with the level of activity, the **budgeted (expected) overhead costs** are based on the expected volume of activity. The **manufacturing overhead rate** is computed by dividing the expected overhead cost by the expected volume of activity. The overhead rate is also called the **budgeted overhead rate** or the **predetermined overhead rate.** The rate is expressed as some amount per unit of activity.

The overhead rate is developed from two estimated figures

$$\text{Manufacturing overhead rate} = \frac{\text{Estimated manufacturing overhead cost}}{\text{Estimated activity level}}$$

Selecting the Level of Activity.   The selection of the appropriate activity level used in computing the manufacturing overhead rate is very important. An inaccurate estimate of the volume of activity can result in assigning incorrect amounts of overhead costs to products.

Some accountants advocate using normal capacity as the activity level on the theory that overhead should reflect production costs at the normal level of activity. Occasional fluctuations in production from year to year should not affect the cost of products in the long run. This long-term view can result in some large differences between applied and actual overhead. Others believe that it is not possible to predict normal capacity over a period of several years and overhead rates should be based on an annual prediction of expected activity. This short-term view usually results in applied overhead and actual overhead that are very similar in amount.

Volume of activity is expressed in some unit measure

The **estimated activity level** is expressed in terms of some measuring unit called the **overhead application base.** Common application bases are direct labor hours, direct labor cost, units of output, and machine hours. The selection of an application base is essential to developing a manufacturing overhead rate that does a good job of matching overhead costs with products.

The application base may be units, hours, or dollars

Selecting the Overhead Application Base

Overhead costs should be assigned to products in proportion to the amount of overhead resources used in making each product. This ensures that the total cost of the product is matched with the revenue earned by selling the product. Such matching not only enables the proper measurement of income, but also provides management with good control over product costs. In addition to satisfying the matching principle, the overhead application base should be selected so that the overhead rate is easy to compute and easy to understand. We now use an example to discuss some common overhead application bases and show how to compute the manufacturing overhead rate using each application base.

A manufacturing company produces 5-cubic-foot wheelbarrows. Each wheelbarrow requires 2 hours of direct labor to produce. The wheelbarrow bowl is formed from sheet steel by a metal press; a pipe frame is bent into shape and welded to the bowl to form the handles, legs, and wheel support. Purchased wheels and tires are then attached.

Production and sales for the coming year are expected to be 15,000 wheelbarrows. Manufacturing overhead for the year is expected to be $138,000.

Direct Labor Hours (DLH).   A popular application base that is easy to understand and apply is direct labor hours. It is used by many manufacturing firms because often it does a good job of matching overhead costs with products. Some overhead costs, such as employer payroll taxes and fringe benefit costs, are related directly to the quantity of labor. Others, such as machinery operating costs and cost of maintaining the equipment operated by direct labor, are also closely related to labor time.

The most commonly used application base

In our example, 30,000 direct labor hours are budgeted for the production of 15,000 wheelbarrows at 2 hours each. With total budgeted overhead of $138,000, the overhead rate is calculated as:

$$\frac{\text{Total budgeted MOH}}{\text{Total budgeted direct labor hours}} = \frac{\$138,000}{30,000 \text{ DLH}} = \$4.60 \text{ per DLH}$$

With this overhead rate, for every hour of direct labor charged to a product, $4.60 of manufacturing overhead cost is also added to the product cost.

In some manufacturing processes, direct labor may not be an appropriate application base. For example, certain chemical processes, such as the production of plastic films, require a relatively small amount of direct labor to operate a large amount of highly automated equipment. Whether the equipment is producing large or small quantities of products, the total amount of direct labor does not change appreciably. In such a situation, an overhead application base other than direct labor hours may do a better job of matching overhead costs with products.

Direct Labor Cost (DLC).   Another direct labor application base is direct labor cost. With this base, a percentage of direct labor cost is added to each product to cover overhead costs. Direct labor cost is popular as an application base because it often satisfies the matching principle, it is easy to understand, and it is easy to apply.

The choice between direct labor hours and direct labor cost often depends on which is the more convenient base. Using the same $138,000 of budgeted overhead cost and a budgeted direct labor cost of $150,000, the calculation of the overhead rate is

$$\frac{\text{Total budgeted MOH}}{\text{Total budgeted direct labor cost}} = \frac{\$138,000}{\$150,000} = .92, \text{ or } 92\% \text{ of DLC}$$

For every dollar of direct labor cost, $.92 is added to the product for overhead.

Units of Production.   If a manufacturer makes only one type of product or all products made are very similar, an overhead rate based on units of production may do a good job of matching overhead costs with products. For example, if the wheelbarrow is the only product made by the company, an overhead rate based on units of production is quite acceptable. With an estimated production of 15,000 units, the overhead rate for our illustration is

$$\frac{\text{Total budgeted MOH}}{\text{Total budgeted units of product}} = \frac{\$138,000}{15,000 \text{ units}} = \$9.20 \text{ per unit}$$

If the company builds 2-cubic-foot garden wheelbarrows as well as its 5-cubic-foot wheelbarrow, an overhead rate based on units of production would assign a disproportionate amount of cost to the smaller product, which requires less materials, labor, and overhead resources. For example, instead of making 15,000 large wheelbarrows, production is planned at 10,000 of the 5-cubic-foot wheelbarrows and 8,000 of the garden wheelbarrows. The small wheelbarrows require 1 direct labor hour per unit compared to 2 hours for the large ones. Dividing the $138,000 of budgeted overhead cost by the 18,000 units of budgeted production yields an overhead rate of $7.67 per unit manufactured. The large wheelbarrow uses more manufacturing overhead resources, yet both are assigned the same overhead cost with a units of production application base.

To alleviate the problem of assigning disproportionate amounts of overhead to products requiring varying amounts of production resources, accountants may weight the amount of overhead charged to products by some measure that will apportion overhead more equitably. We use direct labor hours as a weight to develop an overhead rate based on units of product. For the large and small wheelbarrows, the amount of overhead assigned to each unit is computed as follows:

Sometimes two units of measure make up the application base

	Large	Small
No. of units	10,000	8,000
DLH per unit	2 hr	1 hr
Total hours budgeted	20,000	8,000
Estimated overhead per hour ($138,000/28,000 hr)	$4.93	$4.93
Estimated overhead for each product	$98,571	$39,429
Divide by no. of units	10,000	8,000
Overhead rate per unit	$ 9.86	$ 4.93

Instead of assigning $7.67 of overhead to each wheelbarrow, overhead is assigned at the rate of $9.86 to each 5-cu-ft wheelbarrow and $4.93 to each 2-cu-ft wheelbarrow. The amount of overhead assigned to each product is weighted by the number of labor hours. The weights could also be materials, machine hours, or a combination of several factors.

Machine Hours (MH).   An overhead rate based on machine hours is used when production is performed primarily on machines or when machine-related costs make up a large portion of overhead costs. Machine use data are required for this method. The data may be accumulated manually but some machines have internal clocks or meters that measure the amount of machine use. The cost of data collection is warranted if the result is an overhead rate that does a good job of matching. With an estimated 18,400 machine hours needed to produce the 15,000 large wheelbarrows in our original example, the overhead rate is computed as follows:

$$\frac{\text{Total budgeted MOH}}{\text{Total budgeted machine hours}} = \frac{\$138,000}{18,400 \text{ MH}} = \$7.50 \text{ per MH}$$

Using machine hours as the application base, $7.50 of overhead is charged to production for each machine hour used to produce the wheelbarrows.

Materials Cost. A materials cost application base is logical for situations in which manufacturing overhead costs are related closely to direct materials costs. An example is a drug manufacturing process requiring many specialized materials that result in high materials handling and storage costs. A materials cost overhead rate is expressed as a percentage of direct materials cost. If the direct materials for the contractor's wheelbarrow cost $8 per unit, the total materials cost budgeted for 15,000 units is $120,000, and the overhead rate is:

$$\frac{\text{Total budgeted MOH}}{\text{Total budgeted direct materials cost}} = \frac{\$138,000}{\$120,000} = 1.15, \text{ or } 115\% \text{ of direct materials cost}$$

For every dollar of direct materials used in production, $1.15 of overhead cost is assigned to the product.

Relatively few situations lend themselves to a direct materials application base, compared to the other application bases discussed. Matching problems arise when the relative materials costs vary between products. For example, if one product requires very expensive materials and another uses low-cost materials, a materials cost application base would assign a large amount of overhead cost to the first product and very little overhead cost to the second product, when in fact both products may require a similar amount of overhead resources.

Prime Cost. When several products are manufactured and the proportion of direct labor and direct materials is approximately the same for each product, prime cost may be a suitable allocation base. It is also suitable when there is only one product, as in our example. The prime cost consists of $120,000 of materials cost and $150,000 of direct labor cost. The overhead rate is

$$\frac{\text{Total budgeted MOH}}{\text{Total budgeted prime cost}} = \frac{\$138,000}{\$270,000} = .51, \text{ or } 51\% \text{ of prime cost}$$

For each dollar of prime cost, $.51 cents is charged to production for overhead.

DEPARTMENTAL OVERHEAD RATES

A single overhead rate may not be satisfactory for a complex production environment

Sometimes a single overhead rate for an entire manufacturing plant is satisfactory for applying overhead costs to all products. In other cases, however, a single rate may not be satisfactory. If many different products are made in a plant, a single overhead rate may do a poor job of assigning overhead costs to products. To illustrate, one production department is highly automated with expensive machinery and equipment and relatively little direct labor. Another production department in the same manufacturing plant has labor-intensive operations with small overhead costs. If the products manufactured in the plant use production resources in significantly different proportions, a single overhead rate charges too much overhead cost to some products and too little to others. To avoid this problem, more than one overhead rate may be developed for the manufacturing plant.

A company may develop overhead rates for each department or production activity, for groups of departments with similar characteristics, or for specific products or projects. The number of different manufacturing overhead rates a company may use is limited only by the information needs of managers and the cost of creating and using the rates.

Production and Service Departments

Departments of a manufacturing plant that are directly involved in the production of products are classified as **production departments.** Typical production departments are metal fabricating, machining, assembly, painting, and finishing. Some manufacturing plant departments support the operations of the production departments but are not directly involved in the production of products. They are called **service departments** and include maintenance, inventory storage, toolroom, supply room, and first aid. Service departments provide support essential for production, and their costs, therefore, are part of the total cost of making products. But service department costs cannot be assigned directly to products. Instead, their costs are allocated to production departments and become part of the production department costs that are assigned to products.

Production departments are supported by service departments

Service departments do not work on products directly

Establishing departmental overhead rates is different from establishing a single overhead rate, in several respects. The major difference is that overhead costs must be budgeted for **each department** with a separate overhead rate, rather than for the plant in total. Also the volume of activity must be estimated for each department.

Another difference between developing a single overhead rate and a departmental overhead rate occurs because some overhead costs cannot be identified easily with any one department. They are common to several or all departments in the plant. Insurance, utilities, property taxes, and plant depreciation are all common costs that must be allocated to the various departments in order to develop departmental overhead rates.

Developing Departmental Overhead Rates

Before the accounting period starts, **budget estimates** of all overhead costs are made. Costs identifiable with specific departments are identified directly with them. Budgeted overhead costs common to several departments are allocated to the various departments using appropriate allocation bases. Cost allocations to departments should be based on the matching principle and, when possible, should reflect a causal relationship between the department and the cost.

Each department has a separate budget

For example, heating and air-conditioning costs are closely related to the amount of space heated. These costs may be allocated to departments on the basis of volume of space that each department has. Casualty insurance costs are based on the value of the insured assets, and can be allocated to departments on the same basis. The cost of education and training programs may be allocated to departments in proportion to the number of employees each department has, or the number of employees attending programs.

Allocation bases are used to allocate costs to departments

Number of employees, cubic feet of space, value of assets, and other variables used to allocate common costs to departments are called **allocation bases.** Allocation bases have two purposes. They are used to allocate **budgeted** costs to departments, so that departmental overhead rates can be computed. They also are used later to assign **actual** costs to departments to determine actual overhead costs incurred.

Do not confuse allocation basis with application bases

Be careful not to confuse allocation bases with application bases. The former are used to assign actual or budgeted common costs to departments or other cost objectives, whereas the latter are used to apply overhead costs to products.

DEPARTMENTAL OVERHEAD RATES ILLUSTRATED

To demonstrate the process of developing departmental overhead rates, we use a comprehensive example with which we illustrate

1. Allocation of common costs to departments.
2. Allocation of service department costs to production departments.
3. Computation of overhead rates.
4. Accounting for overhead costs.
5. Allocation of actual overhead to departments.
6. Determining underapplied or overapplied overhead.

Lanco Manufacturing Company operates with three production departments and two service departments. Products are made in the milling, assembly, and finishing departments. The maintenance and inventory departments provide supporting services. The company uses eight overhead cost categories, some of which are common and must be allocated to the five departments. Other costs, such as equipment depreciation and employee benefits, are specifically identified with each department. The total budgeted manufacturing overhead cost for the period, and the allocation bases to be used, are presented in Figure 20-1.

The first step in developing departmental overhead rates is to allocate the budgeted overhead costs in Figure 20-1 to the five departments, using the allocation bases shown in the figure. To allocate the overhead costs to departments, managers must estimate values for each allocation base. Managers estimate how many employees each department will have, how many square feet of space each department will occupy, the value of each department's investment in equipment, and so forth. The budgeted amounts for each

Figure 20-1. Budgeted overhead costs common to all departments, which must be allocated to each department using logical allocation bases.

Lanco Manufacturing Company
Budgeted Manufacturing Overhead Costs
For the Year Ending December 31, 1986

Overhead Cost	Amount	Allocation Base
Indirect labor	$ 60,000	Past indirect labor use
Indirect materials	55,000	Past indirect material use
Heat, light, and power	40,000	Square feet of floor area
Payroll fringe benefits	158,600	Specific identification
Casualty insurance	20,000	Value of investment
Property taxes	30,000	Value of investment
Plant depreciation	80,000	Square feet of floor area
Machinery depreciation	56,400	Specific identification
Total	$500,000	

allocation base are shown in Figure 20-2. The data in Figures 20-1 and 20-2 together are used to determine the amounts of budgeted overhead assigned to each department.

Allocating Overhead Costs to Departments

Common overhead costs are allocated to departments using allocation bases

The amount of budgeted overhead cost allocated to each department is shown in Figure 20-3. The first two costs, indirect labor and indirect materials, are allocated to the five departments on the basis of past use of these resources. The amount used in the past is obtained from accounting records. Indirect labor used last year or the average use for the past several years may be the basis for computing the allocation ratio for indirect labor. Historical data are useful for forecasting only if the current situation is similar to periods from which the data are collected.

Lanco Manufacturing Company
Budgeted Activity Levels and Allocation Bases
For the Year Ending December 31, 1986

Allocation base	Service Departments		Production Departments			Total
	Maintenance	Inventory	Milling	Assembly	Finishing	
Past indirect labor use	4%	5%	35%	40%	16%	100%
Past indirect material use	20%	4%	36%	30%	10%	100%
Square feet of floor area	7,500	2,500	20,000	12,500	7,500	50,000
Estimated fringe benefits	$16,600	$13,000	$70,000	$45,000	$14,000	$158,600
Value of investment	$320,000	$960,000	$960,000	$800,000	$160,000	$3,200,000
Machinery depreciation	$2,000	$800	$23,700	$26,200	$3,700	$56,400
Maintenance hours	460	400	5,500	3,960	1,540	11,860
Material requisitions	500	—	750	800	450	2,500
Machine hours	5,000	3,000	30,000	18,000	10,000	66,000
Direct labor hours	11,000	12,000	61,000	38,000	13,000	135,000
Direct labor cost	$66,000	$80,000	$380,000	$254,000	$100,000	$880,000

Figure 20-2. Each allocation base must be expressed in terms of some estimated activity level. Each department is assigned its share of the activity.

Lanco Manufacturing Company
Schedule of Budgeted Overhead Costs
For the Year Ending December 31, 1986

	Service Departments		Production Departments			Totals from Fig. 20-1
Overhead Cost	Maintenance	Inventory	Milling	Assembly	Finishing	
Indirect labor	$ 2,400	$ 3,000	$ 21,000	$ 24,000	$ 9,600	$ 60,000
Indirect materials	11,000	2,200	19,800	16,500	5,500	55,000
Heat, light, and power	6,000	2,000	16,000	10,000	6,000	40,000
Payroll fringe benefits	16,600	13,000	70,000	45,000	14,000	158,600
Casualty insurance	2,000	6,000	6,000	5,000	1,000	20,000
Property taxes	3,000	9,000	9,000	7,500	1,500	30,000
Plant depreciation	12,000	4,000	32,000	20,000	12,000	80,000
Machinery depreciation	2,000	800	23,700	26,200	3,700	56,400
Total			197,500	154,200	53,300	
Maintenance department cost allocated to producing departments based on estimated maintenance hours required	$55,000		27,500	19,800	7,700	
Inventory department cost allocated to producing departments based on estimated materials requisitions		$40,000	15,000	16,000	9,000	
Total estimated departmental overhead			$240,000	$190,000	$70,000	$500,000
Divided by estimated activity level			30,000 MH	38,000 DLH	$100,000	
Budgeted overhead rate			$8/machine hour	$5/direct labor hr	70 percent of direct labor cost	

Figure 20-3. The budgeted overhead costs in Figure 20-1 and the budgeted activity measures in Figure 20-2 are used to compute the amount of each cost to be assigned to each department. An overhead rate is developed only for production departments.

As an example, the maintenance department historically has used 4 percent of all indirect labor and the milling department has used 35 percent. With utilization ratios expressed as percentages, the $60,000 of budgeted indirect labor cost is allocated as follows:

Department	Budgeted Indirect Labor (See Fig. 20-1)	× Departmental Allocation (See Fig. 20-2)	= Indirect Labor Allocated Cost (See Fig. 20-3)
Maintenance	$60,000	4%	$ 2,400
Inventory	60,000	5	3,000
Milling	60,000	35	21,000
Assembly	60,000	40	24,000
Finishing	60,000	16	9,600
		100%	$60,000

The indirect labor allocation shown in this calculation is how we obtained the first line in Figure 20-3. Budgeted indirect material also is allocated on the basis of past utilization as the allocation base. That allocation appears in the second line of the departmental overhead schedule in the same figure.

The budgeted cost of heat, light, and power is allocated on the basis of budgeted square feet of floor space for each department. The allocation of heat, light, and power cost is as follows:

Department	Heat, Light, and Power Cost	×	Ratio	=	Heat, Light, and Power Allocation
Maintenance	$40,000		7,500/50,000		$ 6,000
Inventory	40,000		2,500/50,000		2,000
Milling	40,000		20,000/50,000		16,000
Assembly	40,000		12,500/50,000		10,000
Finishing	40,000		7,500/50,000		6,000
Totals			50,000/50,000		$40,000

Square feet of floor space are also used to allocate plant depreciation. The $80,000 of budgeted plant depreciation is substituted into the schedule above in place of heat, light, and power cost. Payroll fringe benefits are identified with each department using budgeted payroll cost data for each department.

Casualty insurance premiums and property taxes are based on the estimated value of the assets that are insured and taxed. Therefore, estimated asset values are used to allocate budgeted insurance and property tax costs. Using data in Figure 20-2, you can determine that the maintenance department has 10 percent of the total assets, so it is allocated 10 percent of the insurance and property tax costs. The other departments' allocations are made the same way.

Machinery is identified with each department, so depreciation on machinery is charged to the departments where each machine is located. Depreciation data are found in fixed asset records, and estimated for fixed assets currently owned and any fixed assets that are expected to be acquired during the budget period. In our example, the depreciation data are provided in Figure 20-3.

When all costs have been either identified with departments or allocated to departments, column totals are computed. At this stage in the process, it is not yet possible to compute departmental overhead rates. Because service departments perform no direct production functions, there is no way to charge their costs to products. Therefore, all service department costs must be allocated to the three production departments before departmental overhead rates can be computed.

Allocating Service Department Costs

Service department costs are allocated to producing departments in much the same way we allocated budgeted overhead costs to all five departments. As always, the allocations should be strongly influenced by the matching princi-

Service department costs are allocated to production departments

ple. Lanco Manufacturing Company uses maintenance hours as its measure of the amount of maintenance service performed for each department. The number of materials requisitions filled for each department is used to measure services performed by the inventory department. These two allocation bases —maintenance hours and number of requisitions—are used to distribute maintenance department and inventory department costs to the three production departments.

The method used in this example to allocate service department costs to producing departments is called **direct allocation.** The service department costs are allocated directly to producing departments, without regard to any services provided by one service department for another service department. No service department costs are allocated to other service departments, although the maintenance department performs some service for the inventory department and uses materials requisitions to draw supplies from that department. Direct allocation is based on the assumption that services performed by one service department for another eventually benefit the production departments in proportion to the service department allocation base.

With direct allocation of service department costs, the allocation is based on the proportion of services used by the **production departments only.** Figure 20-2 shows that 11,860 hours of maintenance were used, but only 11,000 of these were used by production departments. Therefore, the proportion of maintenance used by the milling department is calculated as 5,500/11,000, or 50 percent of the maintenance.

When interservice department activities are significant, some cost distortions may occur with direct allocation. Accountants try to minimize such distortions by using **reciprocal allocation,** which is a more precise approach to allocating service department costs, requiring the use of linear algebra. Reciprocal allocation computations are very time-consuming if performed manually, but computers can perform the calculations quickly. Reciprocal allocation is discussed in the appendix at the end of this chapter.

Computing Departmental Overhead Rates

The bottom half of Figure 20-3 shows how allocated service department costs are added to the production department totals to arrive at total budgeted overhead costs in each production department. The three department totals are divided by each production department's budgeted volume of activity to determine the departmental overhead rates. In the milling department, budgeted overhead cost of $240,000 is divided by 30,000 budgeted machine hours, yielding an overhead rate of $8 per machine hour. In the assembly department, the overhead application base is direct labor hours and the rate is $5 per DLH. In the finishing department, the overhead rate is 70 percent of direct labor cost (DLC).

Each production department has its own overhead rate

In this example, the application base is different for each department. It is possible to use the same type of application base for each department and still have separate departmental overhead rates. For example, a company may have departmental overhead rates of $4.60 per DLH, $8.00 per DLH, and $7.40 per DLH for three different production departments. Remember that the overhead rate computations in Figure 20-3 are **all** made with budgeted data before the beginning of the accounting period.

Accounting for Overhead

Once the manufacturing overhead rates have been determined and the accounting period starts, two specific functions are performed in accounting for overhead costs. One is to apply overhead to products as they are produced using the predetermined overhead rate and the actual volume of production. The second function is to record actual manufacturing overhead costs as they are incurred.

Applying Overhead Cost to Production

As production takes place, overhead costs are charged to the products using the overhead rates computed before the accounting period started. For example, $8 of overhead is applied to production for every machine hour worked in the milling department. If Job no. 7194 uses 72 machine hours during the week, $576 is assigned to the job as follows:

Journal entry to apply overhead to production

Feb. 3	Work in process control, milling	576	
	Manufacturing overhead		
	applied, milling		576
	Applied overhead to Job no. 7194.		
	72 machine hours × $8 per hr = $576		

Overhead is applied to products periodically, such as monthly, weekly, or daily. Sophisticated computer systems have greatly enhanced accountants' ability to apply overhead on a timely basis. To illustrate journal entries needed to account for overhead, we assume that Lanco Manufacturing Company applies overhead monthly. Below we present journal entries using hypothetical figures. Each entry is keyed with a small letter so that it may be identified and referred to easily.

a.	Work in process control, milling	20,800	
	MOH applied, milling		20,800
	Applied overhead for 2,600 machine		
	hours. 2,600 MH × $8 = $20,800		
b.	Work in process control, assembly	15,000	
	MOH applied, assembly		15,000
	Applied overhead for 3,000 direct labor		
	hours. 3,000 DLH × $5 = $15,000		
c.	Work in process control, finishing	6,300	
	MOH applied, finishing		6,300
	Applied overhead on basis of $9,000 of		
	direct labor cost. $9,000 × .7 = $6,300		

Notice that each department has an overhead applied account which is used to accumulate the amount of overhead charged to production during the period. If a single overhead rate is used, only one overhead applied account is used to accumulate the overhead charged to production during the period.

Accumulating Actual Overhead Costs. Accountants identify and record actual overhead costs as they occur. Charges are made to the Manufacturing Overhead Control account for indirect labor, indirect materials, factory utilities, and other indirect costs of manufacturing as these costs are identified by the accountant.

Journal entries for actual overhead costs are posted to the Manufacturing Overhead Control account in the general ledger **and** to individual cost accounts in the manufacturing overhead subsidiary ledger. The purpose of the overhead subsidiary ledger is to provide detailed information necessary for cost planning and control. Specific overhead costs such as indirect labor and factory utilities are monitored and evaluated in comparison with budgeted costs. When necessary, managers take action. Energy efficiency programs are implemented, one resource is substituted for another, or other appropriate actions are taken to achieve management goals for overhead and to eliminate serious deviations from the budget. The journal entries shown below illustrate some typical overhead costs.

Actual costs are debited to MOH Control

d.	MOH, indirect labor	5,400	
	Payroll		5,400
	To transfer indirect labor payroll cost		
	to MOH.		
e.	MOH, indirect materials	4,200	
	Raw materials inventory		4,200
	Issued materials to departments.		
f.	MOH, heat, light, and power	3,700	
	Cash		3,700
	Paid utility bill for the month.		
g.	MOH, payroll fringe benefits	15,800	
	Payroll		15,800
	To transfer actual fringe benefits		
	to MOH.		
h.	MOH, casualty insurance	1,800	
	Prepaid insurance		1,800
	Assign expired insurance to overhead.		

i.	MOH, property taxes	2,500	
	Cash		2,500
	Paid property tax.		
j.	MOH, plant depreciation	6,670	
	MOH, machinery depreciation	4,700	
	Accumulated depreciation, plant		6,670
	Accumulated depreciation,		
	machinery		4,700
	To record depreciation on plant and		
	machinery.		

Each of these entries posted to the manufacturing overhead control account is also posted in detail to the overhead subsidiary ledger. The relationship between the control account and the subsidiary ledger is illustrated in Figure 20-4.

Figure 20-4. By recording each overhead cost in a control account and also in a subsidiary account, management achieves a high degree of control.

Subsidiary MOH Ledger

Indirect Labor

d.   5,400

Indirect Materials

e.   4,200

Heat, Light, and Power

f.   3,700

Payroll Fringe Benefits

g.   15,800

Casualty Insurance

h.   1,800

Property Taxes

i.   2,500

Plant Depreciation

j.   6,670

Machinery Depreciation

j.   4,700

Control Accounts

Manufacturing Overhead Control

d.	5,400
e.	4,200
f.	3,700
g.	15,800
h.	1,800
i.	2,500
j.	6,670
j.	4,700

Determining Actual Departmental Overhead Costs

At the end of the accounting period, actual overhead costs are compared with applied overhead costs to find underapplied overhead and overapplied overhead for each department. To accomplish this, we must know the amount of actual overhead in each department.

Some costs, such as depreciation, can be identified with departments as soon as they are recorded. Others, such as heat, light, and power, casualty insurance, and plant depreciation, are not identified with departments at the time of recording. They are allocated to the departments at the end of the accounting period.

Actual overhead is allocated just like budgeted overhead

Allocating Actual Costs to Departments.

The process of allocating actual overhead costs to departments is virtually identical to the process of allocating budgeted overhead. The only difference is that **actual** data are used instead of **budgeted** data. The actual costs recorded in the subsidiary overhead accounts are allocated using allocation measures determined from actual results of operations. For example, maintenance department records will indicate how many actual maintenance hours were used by each production department, and managers will know the actual square footage of floor space used by each department.

Actual overhead costs for the year for Lanco Manufacturing Company are presented in Figure 20-5, and the actual allocation base values are presented in Figure 20-6. You should compare the budgeted data in Figure 20-1 with the actual data in Figure 20-5, and also the budgeted and actual data in Figures 20-2 and 20-6.

The worksheet showing the allocation of actual costs to departments is shown in Figure 20-7. This figure parallels Figure 20-3. The computations are not shown, because they are very similar to those demonstrated for budgeted data, but you may wish to compute the cost allocations for several items to make sure you understand the process. The actual service department costs are allocated to producing departments using direct allocation.

Figure 20-5. Actual overhead costs common to all departments must be allocated to each department. Compare these costs with the budgeted costs in Figure 20-1.

Lanco Manufacturing Company
Actual Manufacturing Overhead Costs
For the Year Ended December 31, 1986

Overhead Cost	Amount	Allocation Base
Indirect labor	$ 66,000	Actual payroll reports
Indirect materials	54,000	Actual materials requisitions
Heat, light, and power	45,000	Square feet of floor area
Payroll fringe benefits	164,000	Actual amounts recorded
Casualty insurance	20,000	Value of investment
Property taxes	35,000	Value of investment
Plant depreciation	80,000	Square feet of floor area
Machinery depreciation	56,000	Specific identification
Total	$520,000	

Lanco Manufacturing Company
Actual Activity Levels and Allocation Bases
For the Year Ended December 31, 1986

| | Service Departments | | Production Departments | | | |
Allocation Base	Maintenance	Inventory	Milling	Assembly	Finishing	Total
Indirect labor use	5.5%	5.0%	36.6%	33.9%	19.0%	100%
Indirect material use	19.2%	4.6%	37.4%	28.0%	10.8%	100%
Square feet of floor area	7,500	2,500	20,000	12,500	7,500	50,000
Actual fringe benefits	$17,652	$12,666	$74,032	$44,000	$15,650	$164,000
Value of investment	$320,000	$960,000	$960,000	$800,000	$160,000	$3,200,000
Machinery depreciation	$2,000	$800	$24,000	$26,000	$3,200	$56,000
Maintenance hours used	500	400	5,760	4,800	1,440	12,900
Materials requisitions used	550	—	960	800	640	2,950
Machine hours used	5,000	3,000	33,000	17,000	10,000	68,000
Direct labor hours used	12,000	12,200	61,800	37,600	13,400	137,000
Direct labor cost used	$71,600	$81,300	$396,000	$246,800	$101,200	$896,900

Figure 20-6. Allocation bases are expressed in terms of activity levels, just as in Figure 20-2. But now the volume of activity is known rather than estimated.

Lanco Manufacturing Company
Schedule of Actual Overhead Costs
For the Year Ended December 31, 1986

| | Service Departments | | Production Departments | | | Totals from Fig. 20-5 |
Overhead Cost	Maintenance	Inventory	Milling	Assembly	Finishing	
Indirect labor	$ 3,630	$ 3,300	$ 24,156	$ 22,374	$12,540	$ 66,000
Indirect materials	10,368	2,484	20,200	15,120	5,828	54,000
Heat, light, and power	6,750	2,250	18,000	11,250	6,750	45,000
Payroll fringe benefits	17,652	12,666	74,032	44,000	15,650	164,000
Casualty insurance	2,000	6,000	6,000	5,000	1,000	20,000
Property taxes	3,500	10,500	10,500	8,750	1,750	35,000
Plant depreciation	12,000	4,000	32,000	20,000	12,000	80,000
Machinery depreciation	2,000	800	24,000	26,000	3,200	56,000
Total			208,888	152,494	58,718	
Maintenance department cost allocated to producing departments based on actual maintenance hours used	$57,900		27,792	23,160	6,948	
Inventory department cost allocated to producing departments based on actual materials requisitions		$42,000	16,800	14,000	11,200	
Total actual departmental overhead			$253,480	$189,654	$76,866	$520,000

Figure 20-7. The same procedure is used to allocate actual departmental overhead costs as was used to allocate budgeted costs. Compare this figure with Figure 20-3.

Determining Underapplied and Overapplied Overhead

At the end of the accounting period, the actual overhead in each department is compared with the applied overhead to determine the amount underapplied or overapplied. Managers may make such comparisons more frequently, such as monthly or quarterly, but an annual comparison is common. In Figure 20-8 we make the comparison for the entire year.

Overapplied overhead makes products appear more costly than they are

The actual overhead cost in the milling department is $253,480 as shown in Figure 20-7. Applied overhead is $264,000, as shown in Figure 20-8. The difference of $10,520 is the amount of overapplied overhead. This means that the amount of overhead cost applied to products in the milling department is too large. The amount applied is 4.15 percent ($10,520/$253,480) more than the actual overhead cost in milling. The **actual** cost of the products produced by the milling department is somewhat lower than the cost recorded.

The actual cost of overhead for the other two departments is somewhat higher than the amount applied to production. In the assembly department, actual overhead is $1,654 more than the applied overhead and in finishing, actual overhead is $6,026 higher than applied overhead, as Figure 20-8 shows. The net result is that total applied overhead is $2,840 more than the total amount of actual overhead.

Figure 20-8 illustrates one of the advantages of departmental cost data as compared with one overall overhead cost figure that results from using a single overhead rate. Total overapplied overhead is $2,840, or .5 percent of actual overhead cost, which is a small variance. But the total variance comprises 4.2 percent overapplied overhead in milling and 7.8 percent underapplied in finishing. Relatively large amounts of underapplied or overapplied overhead in individual departments can result in a small net variance. With departmental overhead, managers can investigate the reasons for any significant discrepancies between applied and actual overhead and can deal with problems that may occur.

Lanco Manufacturing Company
Schedule of Underapplied and Overapplied Overhead
For the Year Ended December 31, 1986

Department	Overhead Rate	Actual Activity	Applied Overhead	Actual Overhead	Underapplied (Overapplied)
Milling	$8/MH	33,000 MH	$264,000	$253,480	$(10,520)
Assembly	$5/DLH	37,600 DLH	188,000	189,654	1,654
Finishing	70% of DLC	$101,200 DLC	70,840	76,866	6,026
Total			$522,840	$520,000	$ (2,840)

Figure 20-8. The difference between applied and actual overhead is either underapplied or overapplied overhead. Some large departmental differences can result in a small net amount; therefore better control may be achieved when overhead costs are separated by individual departments.

Disposition of Underapplied and Overapplied Overhead. At this point in our example, product costs have been charged with applied overhead. Eventually, the actual overhead cost must be reflected in product costs. As discussed and illustrated in Chapter 4, underapplied and overapplied overhead can be disposed of in two ways: If the amount underapplied or overapplied is small, it can be assigned to cost of goods sold. If it is large, it should be assigned to work in process, finished goods, and cost of goods sold in proportion to the amount of overhead remaining in those accounts at the end of the period.

The overhead applied account is closed to the overhead control account

At the end of the accounting period, the Manufacturing Overhead Applied account balance is transferred to the Manufacturing Overhead Control account. This closes the Overhead Applied account and leaves the underapplied or overapplied overhead as the balance in the Manufacturing Overhead Control account. The Overhead Control account is then closed. We illustrate the process below for small amounts of overapplied overhead.

	MOH applied, milling	264,000	
	MOH applied, assembly	188,000	
	MOH applied, finishing	70,840	
	MOH control, milling		264,000
	MOH control, assembly		188,000
	MOH control, finishing		70,840
	To close manufacturing overhead applied		
	accounts.		
	MOH control, milling	10,520	
	MOH control, assembly		1,654
	MOH control, finishing		6,026
	Cost of goods sold		2,840
	To distribute net overapplied overhead to		
	cost of goods sold.		

SUMMARY Manufacturing overhead consists of costs that cannot be identified directly with products but are necessary production costs. Such costs must be assigned to products to measure full product cost. Full product costs provide managers with information for planning and controlling production and measuring performance. In addition, full product costs are required for external reporting purposes.

Manufacturing overhead is assigned to products in order to satisfy the matching principle in accounting. To provide managers with timely product cost information, overhead costs are assigned to products at frequent intervals. Actual overhead cost is recorded by debiting the **manufacturing overhead control** account and posting to both the control account in the general ledger and the appropriate accounts in the subsidiary ledger for overhead.

When Work in Process is debited to record overhead as the product cost, **Manufacturing Overhead Applied** is credited. The balances in the overhead control account and the overhead applied account can be compared to determine underapplied or overapplied overhead.

Manufacturing overhead is typically applied using a predetermined **overhead rate,** which is computed by dividing the **budgeted overhead cost** by the **budgeted activity level.** The activity level selected is called the **overhead application base.** Common bases are direct labor hours, direct labor cost, units of production, machine hours, material cost, or prime cost. Sometimes a single overhead rate is computed for an organization. For more precise overhead costs, **departmental overhead rates** may be computed.

Departmental overhead rates require allocating all overhead costs to departments using some preselected **allocation base.** Allocation bases include such variables as square feet or volume of space for utility costs, value of investment for insurance costs, taxes, and depreciation, number of employees or amount of payroll for employee benefit costs and employer payroll taxes, and other variables that are logically related to overhead costs. Any **service department** cost must be allocated to **production departments** before computing the production departments' overhead rates. **Direct allocation** of service department costs may be used when the amount of services provided by service departments for each other is not substantial. A more accurate allocation of service department costs is obtained by **reciprocal allocation,** which requires using linear algebra to determine how service department costs are allocated among each other.

Departmental cost allocations are made before the accounting period starts, using **budgeted** data to establish departmental overhead rates. At the end of the period, the allocation is again performed using **actual** data to find actual departmental overhead costs. **Actual overhead** is then compared with **applied overhead** to determine the amount of overhead **underapplied** or **overapplied** for each department. At the end of the accounting period, the overhead applied account is closed to the overhead control account and any remaining balance in the control account, consisting of underapplied or overapplied overhead, is assigned to product costs.

KEY TERMS

allocation base *(704)*
application base *(699)*
budgeted activity level *(699)*
budgeted overhead cost *(698)*
budgeted overhead rate *(698)*
departmental overhead rate *(702)*
direct allocation *(708)*
manufacturing overhead
   applied *(709)*
manufacturing overhead
   control *(710)*

overapplied overhead *(714)*
overhead application base *(699)*
overhead rate *(698)*
predetermined overhead rate *(698)*
production department *(703)*
reciprocal allocation *(708)*
service department *(703)*
underapplied overhead *(714)*

APPENDIX: RECIPROCAL ALLOCATION OF SERVICE DEPARTMENT OVERHEAD

When service departments provide substantial amounts of services to other service departments in addition to performing services for production departments, it may be desirable to allocate service department costs among each other as well as among production departments. This approach, called **reciprocal allocation,** often results in a better matching of overhead costs with products.

Reciprocal allocation of overhead can be time-consuming if performed manually, but computers can be used to make the calculations easily. We demonstrate reciprocal cost allocation with the Lanco Manufacturing Company example used in this chapter.

Figure 20-2 shows the amount of maintenance and inventory department services used by all departments. The first step in reciprocal allocation is to convert these services to percentages, as shown in Figure 20-9.

Figure 20-9. Budgeted data from Figure 20-2 converted to percentages for use with reciprocal allocation of overhead.

Department	Total Budgeted Overhead	Budgeted Maintenance Hours	Percent	Budgeted Inventory Requisitions	Percent
Maintenance	$ 55,000	—	—	500	20.0%
Inventory	40,000	460	4.0%		
Milling	198,000	5,500	48.0	750	30.0
Assembly	154,000	3,960	34.6	800	32.0
Finishing	53,000	1,540	13.4	450	18.0
	$500,000	11,460	100.0%	2,500	100.0%

The budget shows that the maintenance department is expected to receive 20 percent of the services provided by the inventory department and the inventory department 4 percent of the services provided by the maintenance department. The total budgeted maintenance department cost (M) can be expressed as $55,000 budgeted for that department plus 20 percent of the inventory department cost. Similarly, the total budgeted inventory department cost (I) can be expressed as $40,000 + 4 percent of the maintenance department cost. Algebraically these costs are

$$M = \$55,000 + .20I$$
$$I = \$40,000 + .04M$$

Substituting the first equation into the second and solving we get the following:

$$I = \$40,000 + .04(\$55,000 + .20I)$$
$$I = \$40,000 + \$2,200 + .008I$$
$$.992I = \$42,200$$
$$I = \$42,200/.992$$
$$= \$42,540$$

Substituting the value of I into the first equation we get

$$M = \$55,000 + .20(\$42,540)$$
$$= \$63,508$$

Now both M and I have been increased to reflect their share of each other's cost. If these larger values are allocated to the three production departments as before, too much cost would be allocated. Instead the percentages used for allocating M and I are those found in Figure 20-9. Inventory department costs are allocated 30 percent to milling, 32 percent to assembly, and 18 percent to finishing. This is a total of 80 percent. The remaining 20 percent has already been allocated in arriving at M. Similarly, maintenance department costs are allocated 48 percent to milling, 34.6 percent to assembly, and 13.4 percent to finishing. The remaining 4 percent has already been allocated in the computation of I.

The allocation of M and I is shown in Figure 20-10. This figure is similar to Figure 20-3 except for the distribution of maintenance and inventory depart-

Lanco Manufacturing Company
Schedule of Budgeted Overhead Costs
For the Year Ending December 31, 1986

	Service Departments		Production Departments			
	Maintenance	Inventory	Milling	Assembly	Finishing	Total from Fig. 20-1
Total overhead costs	$55,000	$40,000	$197,500	$154,200	$53,300	
Inventory department cost allocated to maintenance	8,508					
Maintenance department cost allocated to inventory		2,540				
Maintenance department cost allocated to producing departments	$63,508		48% 30,484	34.6% 21,974	13.4% 8,510	
Inventory department cost allocated to producing departments		$42,540	30% 12,762	32% 13,613	18% 7,657	
Total estimated departmental overhead			$240,746	$189,787	$69,467	$500,000
Total estimated departmental overhead			$240,746	$189,787	$69,467	
Divided by estimated activity level			30,000 MH	38,000 DLH	$100,000	
Budgeted overhead rate			$8.02/machine hour	$4.99/direct labor hr	69.5% of direct labor cost	

Figure 20-10. Allocation of service department costs to production departments based on percentages in Figure 20-9. Note that the $8,508 added to maintenance department cost is 20 percent of *total* inventory department cost of $42,540; the $2,540 added to inventory department cost is 4 percent of *total* maintenance department cost.

ment costs. Note that the total amount of these two service departments' costs allocated to the three production departments is $95,000, which is the total of the two service department costs.

The amount of interservice department costs is small in this example. Nevertheless, reciprocal allocation results in overhead allocation rates that are different from those obtained by direct allocation. For the milling department, the $8 rate computed with direct allocation becomes $8.02 with reciprocal allocation. The other two departments' rates are also different, as you can see by comparing Figures 20-3 and 20-10.

When the differences between direct allocation and reciprocal allocation are as small as in this example, they may be immaterial and the additional work required for reciprocal allocation may not be warranted. If, however, some production departments use substantially more services than others, and some service departments use a large proportion of other service departments' support, the differences between the two allocation methods can be material. In that case, reciprocal cost allocation can produce overhead application rates that result in more accurate product costs than with direct allocation.

QUESTIONS

1. Discuss the difference between service departments and production departments and the way that their overhead costs are allocated to production.

2. Hamlin Company has three service departments and four production departments. The service departments are maintenance, inventory, and computer services. The production departments are machining, fabricating, assembly, and painting. The inventory department receives substantial services from the computer department but the maintenance department does not use any computer services. The assembly department receives very little service from the inventory department because most of the work is performed on components transferred in from other departments. The painting department uses computer services very seldom, while the other production departments make extensive use of the computer department. Discuss how you would allocate service department costs and give reasons for the method you select.

3. How does the use of an overhead control account and overhead applied account help managers to exercise control over overhead costs?

4. (AICPA) Identify three methods or bases used in applying or allocating overhead expenses. What are the advantages and disadvantages of each method?

EXERCISES

Ex. 20-1
Computing
Overhead Rates

The following budget has been prepared by Marston Company for its operations during the next year:

Budgeted costs:

Direct labor		$ 406,780
Direct materials		400,000
Manufacturing overhead		
Indirect labor	$160,000	
Indirect materials	52,000	
Utilities	36,000	
Insurance	45,000	
Labor fringe benefits	98,500	
Depreciation	88,500	480,000
Total		$1,286,780

Other budgeted data:

Machine hours	75,000
Direct labor hours	60,000
Units of output	30,000

REQUIRED   Compute a manufacturing overhead rate based on

a. Direct labor hours.
b. Machine hours.
c. Units of production.
d. Direct labor cost.
e. Direct material cost.
f. Prime cost.

Ex. 20-2
Units of Production
Overhead Rate

Palermo Corporation produces two types of simulated antique rolltop desks. Following are estimated production data for the next accounting period:

	Standard	Executive
No. of units budgeted	4,000	5,000
Direct labor hours per unit	20	24
Direct labor cost per hour	$7.00	$7.00
Direct material cost per unit	$63.00	$93.60
Manufacturing overhead = $540,000		

REQUIRED   Compute an overhead rate per unit of product based on

a. Units weighted by direct labor hours.
b. Units weighted by direct material cost.

Ex. 20-3
Overhead Cost of
Products

Florette Company applies manufacturing overhead using direct labor hours as the application base. In 1985, budgeted overhead was $868,000 and budgeted direct labor was 140,000 hours. The company uses job order costing and recently completed

Job no. 72, which produced 300 units of product and required 480 hours to complete. By the end of the year, the company had used 150,000 direct labor hours and actual overhead was $872,000.

REQUIRED

a. Compute the 1985 overhead rate.
b. Compute the underapplied or overapplied overhead for the year.
c. Determine how much overhead was charged to Job no. 72.
d. Compute the applied overhead cost per unit for the products produced in Job no. 72.

Ex. 20-4
Weighted per Unit
Overhead Rate

Following are data on garden sun umbrellas produced by Shado Company:

	Standard	DeLuxe
No. of units budgeted	24,000	20,000
Direct labor hours per unit	2	3
Direct labor cost per hour	$ 8.00	$ 8.00
Direct material cost per unit	10.00	12.00
Manufacturing overhead = $540,000		

REQUIRED

Compute an overhead rate per unit of product based on units weighted by both direct labor hours and direct material cost.

Ex. 20-5
Overhead Cost of
Products

Memoroot Company uses direct labor cost as a base to apply overhead to production. It budgeted overhead at $704,000 and budgeted direct labor at 137,500 hours for the following year. The average labor rate is $6.40 per hour. In January, the company produced 520 units of product at a labor cost of $78,000. By the end of the year, total labor cost was $865,000 and actual overhead cost was $710,000.

REQUIRED

a. Compute the overhead rate.
b. Determine how much overhead was charged in January.
c. Compute the overhead cost per unit for the products produced in January.
d. Compute the underapplied or overapplied overhead for the year.

Ex. 20-6
Departmental
Overhead
Allocation

Treblinka Manufacturing Company operates with three departments—service, production, and packaging. Following are data on activity for the year just completed and overhead costs incurred during the year:

	Service	Production	Packaging
Number of employees	9	36	15
Asset valuation	$40,000	$560,000	$120,000
Direct labor hours	—	80,000	30,000
Units of product	—	212,000	188,000
Square feet of space	2,000	18,000	5,000

	Overhead Cost	Allocation Base
Supervision	$ 30,000	Number of employees
Administration	240,000	Number of employees
Depreciation	90,000	Asset value
Utilities	45,000	Square feet of space

Service department costs are allocated to the two producing departments on the basis of units of product.

REQUIRED　Prepare a schedule of departmental cost allocation, showing the allocation of all overhead to the production and packaging departments.

Ex. 20-7
Journal Entries for
Overhead

Uppie Company is a small manufacturing operation producing casings for automotive batteries. During July, it manufactured 10,000 units of product and incurred the following manufacturing overhead costs.

a.　Wages and payroll expenses for indirect labor, $8,000.
b.　Indirect materials used, $6,000.
c.　Utility costs, none of which have yet been paid, $1,500.
d.　Depreciation on manufacturing plant and equipment, $3,500.

The company applied manufacturing overhead to products at a rate of $2 per unit. Underapplied or overapplied overhead is assigned to Cost of Goods Sold at the end of each month of operations.

REQUIRED　Prepare journal entries to record actual and applied overhead and to close the overhead accounts at the end of the month.

Ex. 20-8
Departmental
Overhead Journal
Entries

During 1985, Fergun Manufacturing Company produced 12,000 engraved leather book covers, its only product, which it makes on special order from publishers. The company operates with two departments—general services and production. Actual costs in the two departments in 1986 were as follows:

		General Services	Production
a.	Direct labor	—	$25,000
b.	Indirect labor	$3,000	6,000
c.	Direct materials	—	18,000
d.	Indirect materials used	2,000	7,000
e.	Utilities	1,000	3,000
f.	Depreciation	1,500	4,500

Overhead is applied to products at a rate of 120 percent of direct labor cost. Overapplied or underapplied overhead is assigned to Cost of Goods Sold at the end of each year.

REQUIRED　Prepare journal entries to record work in process, actual, and applied overhead and to close the overhead accounts at the end of the year.

Ex. 20-9
Departmental
Overhead Rates

Lobeck Manufacturing Company operates two service departments and two production departments. The following budgeted data are prepared for the quarter ending March 31.

	Service		Production	
	Computer	Maintenance	Fabricating	Assembly
Machine hours budgeted	—	2,400	20,000	6,000
Labor hours budgeted	6,800	8,350	38,400	30,000
Maintenance hours budgeted	470	800	3,750	2,500
Computer CPU time budgeted	2,600	6,000	12,240	5,760
Budgeted total overhead	$31,250	$30,000	$60,750	$158,000

Overhead is allocated to production using machine hours as a base in the fabricating department and labor hours in the assembly department. Computer department costs are allocated to production departments on the basis of budgeted CPU time. Maintenance department costs are allocated to production departments on the basis of budgeted maintenance hours.

REQUIRED   Determine the overhead rate for the two production departments, using direct allocation of service department costs.

PROBLEMS

P. 20-1
Overhead Cost
Computations

Following are data on three jobs completed in August by Gustav Company, which uses a job order cost system. Overhead is applied at the rate of $15 per machine hour in the molding department and $10 per machine hour in the packing department.

	A	B	C
Direct materials cost	$24,000	$12,000	$16,000
Direct labor cost	$6,000	$4,000	$5,000
Molding department machine hours	750	500	620
Packing department machine hours	400	300	300
Units completed	100	200	300

REQUIRED

   a. Compute the amount of manufacturing overhead applied to each job.
   b. Compute the cost of each unit of product.
   c. Compute the percentage of total product cost represented by overhead in each job.

P. 20-2
Units of Production
Overhead Rate

Kulish Company's Wagon Wheel department produces two sizes of wheels for wagons used in making western movies. Following are production data on the two wheels:

	Small	Large
No. of units budgeted	3,000	3,000
Direct labor hours per unit	1.5	2.5
Direct labor cost per hour	$6.00	$6.00
Direct materials cost per unit	$8.00	$11.20
Manufacturing overhead = $60,000		

REQUIRED   Compute an overhead rate per unit of product based on units weighted by

   a. Direct labor hours.
   b. Direct materials cost.
   c. Both direct labor hours and direct materials costs.

P. 20-3
Units of Production Overhead Rates

Garden Phantasy Inc. produces three sizes of garden fountains. Following are production data on the three products:

	Small	Medium	Large
No. of units budgeted	6,000	5,000	4,000
Direct labor cost per hour	$8.00	$8.00	$8.00
Direct material cost per unit	$8.00	$10.00	$12.00
Direct labor hours per unit	3	4	5
Manufacturing overhead = $90,000			

REQUIRED

Compute an overhead rate per unit of product based on units weighted by

a. Direct labor hours.
b. Direct materials cost.
c. Both direct labor hours and direct materials cost.

P. 20-4
Departmental Overhead Journal Entries

Nolyte Manufacturing Company produced 6,000 aluminum windows during 1985. Its operations are carried out with one service department and two production departments. Actual costs in the three departments in 1985 were as follows:

	Supplies	Framing	Glazing
a. Direct labor	—	$25,000	$20,000
b. Indirect labor	$4,000	3,000	6,000
c. Direct materials	—	15,000	18,000
d. Indirect materials	1,000	5,000	7,000
e. Utilities	2,000	4,000	3,000
f. Depreciation	2,000	3,500	4,500

Overhead is applied to products at a rate of 110 percent of direct labor cost. Service department costs are assigned to production departments using direct allocation based on combined cost of direct and indirect materials used. Overapplied or underapplied overhead is assigned to Cost of Goods Sold at the end of each month since all products are sold as soon as they are completed. There was no work in process at the end of the year.

REQUIRED

a. Prepare journal entries to record work in process, actual, and applied overhead and to close the overhead accounts at the end of the year.
b. Compute the total cost of production for 1985 and the cost per unit of product.

P. 20-5
Direct Allocation of Overhead

Brittel Ceramics Company manufactures ceramic components for heat shields used in space vehicles. The company operates with two service departments and three production departments. Below are data on budgeted operations for the coming year:

	Supplies	Maintenance	Molding	Baking	Finishing
Overhead	$80,000	$100,000	$500,000	$400,000	$200,000
Direct materials cost			$12,000	$1,000	$2,000
Direct labor hours			100,000	80,000	60,000
Production in units			462,000	450,000	423,000
Maintenance hours	900	100	600	3,000	1,500

The company allocates supplies department costs on the basis of cost of material used, and maintenance on the basis of maintenance hours of service performed. The overhead rates for the molding and baking departments are based on direct labor hours and the overhead rate for the finishing department is based on units of production.

REQUIRED Allocate the service department costs to production departments using direct allocation and determine the overhead rates for each department.

P. 20-6
Departmental
Overhead Journal
Entries

Cherubino Company operates inventory, production, and finishing departments. Following are data on activity and costs budgeted for the coming year:

	Inventory	Production	Finishing
Number of employees	9	36	15
Asset valuation	$40,000	$560,000	$120,000
Fringe benefits	$900	$4,600	$3,500
Direct labor hours	—	80,000	29,500
Units of product	—	216,000	184,000
Square feet of space	2,000	18,000	5,000

	Overhead Cost	Allocation Base
Supervision	$ 30,000	Number of employees
Administration	240,000	Number of employees
Fringe benefits	9,000	Specific identification
Depreciation	90,000	Asset value
Utilities	45,000	Square feet-of space

Inventory department costs are allocated to the two producing departments on the basis of units of product. The overhead rate is based on direct labor hours. By the end of the year, the following data were obtained on actual costs and activities:

	Inventory	Production	Finishing
Number of employees	9	36	15
Asset valuation	$40,000	$560,000	$120,000
Fringe benefits	$1,600	$5,400	$4,000
Direct labor hours	—	78,000	31,000
Units of product	—	200,000	200,000
Square feet of space	2,000	18,000	5,000

	Overhead Cost	Allocation Base
Supervision	$ 32,000	Number of employees
Administration	244,000	Number of employees
Fringe benefits	11,000	Specific identification
Depreciation	90,000	Asset value
Utilities	50,000	Square feet of space

a. Prepare a schedule of departmental cost allocation for budgeted cost and compute overhead rates for the production and finishing departments.
b. Prepare a schedule of departmental cost allocation for actual costs and show the amount of overapplied or underapplied overhead.
c. Prepare journal entries to record applied and actual overhead costs and close the overhead accounts at the end of the period, with any overapplied or underapplied overhead assigned to cost of goods sold.

P. 20-7
Single and
Departmental
Overhead Rate

Diboly Toy Company uses a single manufacturing overhead rate to assign costs to products. The new cost accountant wants to change to departmental overhead rates, believing that product costs would be more accurate. The vice president of production thinks using more than one overhead rate would be more expensive and would not be any more accurate. To show the vice president what effect departmental rates would have on product costs, the cost accountant obtains data on two recently completed jobs and asks you to prepare a schedule showing the difference in product costs between single and departmental overhead rates. Below are the data on the two jobs:

	Job 16	Job 17
Units produced	100	200
Machining department:		
Machine hours	320	320
Direct material cost	$5,000	$14,000
Direct labor at $10/hr	$3,500	$4,000
Assembly department:		
Direct labor at $10/hr	$600	$4,800
Finishing department:		
Direct labor at $7/hr	$1,050	$2,800

The company applies overhead on the basis of direct labor hours. If departmental overhead rates are used, the cost accountant suggests machine hours for the machining department, direct labor hours for assembly, and direct labor cost for finishing. Following are pertinent overhead data:

	Machining	Assembly	Finishing	Total
Budgeted:				
MOH cost	$1,000,000	$600,000	$400,000	$2,000,000
Direct labor cost	400,000	600,000	175,000	1,175,000
Machine hours	25,000	10,000	30,000	60,000
Direct labor hours	40,000	60,000	25,000	125,000

a. Prepare a schedule showing the product costs, using a single overhead rate.
b. Prepare a schedule of product costs, using departmental overhead rates.
c. Compute the difference between product costs, using the two methods, and discuss your findings.

P. 20-8
Direct Allocation
and Overhead Rates

Molaska Public Service Company is an electric utility serving Molaska County. It generates power and transmits it to customers and, in addition, buys some power from other utilities to meet peak demand. Currently, the company is constructing a new power plant. Operations are divided into three production departments and two service departments. Following are budgeted costs and activities for the coming year.

	Service Departments		Production Departments		
	Accounting	Maintenance	Construction	Generation	Transmission
Budgeted overhead	$60,000	$110,000	$800,000	$500,000	$330,000
Generation in MWH				180,000	
Transmission in MWH					220,000
Direct labor hours			110,000	57,000	36,000
Maintenance hours	1,000	300	1,500	5,500	2,000
Accounting hours	800	4,400	5,600	4,800	5,200

The company allocates service department costs on the basis of hours of service performed, using direct allocation. The overhead rate for the construction department is based on direct labor hours. For the generation and transmission departments, overhead rates are based on megawatt-hours generated and transmitted.

By the end of the year, the company generated 200,000 KWH of power at an overhead cost of $630,000, and transmitted 210,000 MWH at an overhead cost of $365,000.

REQUIRED

a. Allocate the service department costs to production departments using direct allocation and determine the overhead rates for each department.
b. Determine the amount of overapplied or underapplied overhead in the generation and transmission departments.

P. 20-9 (CMA)
Analysis of Cost
Allocation Variables

Bonn Company recently reorganized its computer and data processing activities. The small installations located within the accounting departments at its plants and subsidiaries have been replaced with a single data processing department at corporate headquarters responsible for the operations of a newly acquired large-scale computer system. The new department has been in operation for 2 years and has been regularly producing reliable and timely data for the past 12 months.

Because the department has focused its activities on converting applications to the new system and producing reports for the plant and subsidiary managements, little attention has been devoted to the costs of the department. Now that the department's activities are operating relatively smoothly, company management has requested that the departmental manager recommend a cost accumulation system to facilitate cost control and the development of suitable rates to charge users for service.

For the past 2 years, the department costs have been recorded in one account. The costs have then been allocated to user departments on the basis of computer time used. The schedule on page 728 reports the costs and charging rate for 1985.

The department manager recommends that the department costs be accumulated by five activity centers within the department: systems analysis, programming, data preparation, computer operations (processing), and administration. He then suggests that the costs of the administration activity should be allocated to the other four activity centers before a separate rate for charging users is developed for each of the first four activities.

Data Processing Department
Costs for the Year Ended December 31, 1985

1.	Salaries and benefits	$ 622,600
2.	Supplies	40,000
3.	Equipment maintenance contract	15,000
4.	Insurance	25,000
5.	Heat and air conditioning	36,000
6.	Electricity	50,000
7.	Equipment and furniture depreciation	285,400
8.	Building improvements depreciation	10,000
9.	Building occupancy and security	39,300
10.	Corporate administrative charges	52,700
	Total costs	$1,176,000
	Computer hours for user processing[a]	2,750
	Hourly rate ($1,176,000 ÷ 2,750)	$ 428

[a] Use of available computer hours:

Testing and debugging programs	250
Setup of jobs	500
Processing jobs	2,750
Downtime for maintenance	750
Idle time	742
Total	4,992

The manager made the following observations regarding the charges to the several subsidiary accounts within the department after reviewing the details of the accounts:

1. Salaries and benefits—records the salary and benefit costs of all employees in the department.
2. Supplies—records punch card costs, paper costs for printers, and a small amount for miscellaneous other costs.
3. Equipment maintenance contracts—records charges for maintenance contracts; all equipment is covered by maintenance contracts.
4. Insurance—records cost of insurance covering the equipment and the furniture.
5. Heat and air conditioning—records a charge from the corporate heating and air-conditioning department estimated to be the incremental costs to meet the special needs of the computer department.
6. Electricity—records the charge for electricity based upon a separate meter within the department.
7. Equipment and furniture depreciation—records the depreciation charges for all owned equipment and furniture within the department.
8. Building improvements—records the amortization charges for the building, changes required to provide proper environmental control, and electrical service for the computer equipment.
9. Building occupancy and security—records the computer department's share of the depreciation, maintenance, heat, and security costs of the building; these costs are allocated to the department on the basis of square feet occupied.
10. Corporate administrative charges—records the computer department's share of the corporate administrative costs. They are allocated to the department on the basis of number of employees in the department.

REQUIRED

a. For each of the 10 cost items, state whether or not it should be distributed to the five activity centers, and for each cost item that should be distributed, recommend the basis upon which it should be distributed. Justify your conclusion in each case.

b. Assume the costs of the computer operations (processing) activity will be charged to the user departments on the basis of computer hours. Using the analysis of computer utilization shown as a footnote to the department cost schedule presented in the problem, determine the total number of hours that should be employed to determine the charging rate for computer operations (processing). Justify your answer.

CASES

Case 20-1 (AICPA)
Analyzing the
Impact of Cost
Allocations

Thrift-Shops, Inc. operates a chain of three food stores in a state that recently enacted legislation permitting municipalities within the state to levy an income tax on corporations operating within their respective municipalities. The legislation establishes a uniform tax rate which the municipalities may levy, and regulations which provide that the tax is to be computed on income derived within the taxing municipality after a reasonable and consistent allocation of general overhead expenses. General overhead expenses have not been allocated to individual stores previously and include warehouse, general office, advertising, and delivery expenses.

Each of the municipalities in which Thrift-Shops, Inc. operates a store has levied the corporate income tax as provided by state legislation, and management is considering two plans for allocating general overhead expenses to the stores. The 1985 operating results before general overhead and taxes for each store were as follows:

	Store			
	Ashville	Burns	Clinton	Total
Sales, net	$416,000	$353,600	$270,400	$1,040,000
Less cost of sales	215,700	183,300	140,200	539,200
Gross margin	200,300	170,300	130,200	500,800
Less local operating expenses:				
Fixed	60,800	48,750	50,200	159,750
Variable	54,700	64,220	27,448	146,368
Total	115,500	112,970	77,648	306,118
Income before general overhead and taxes	$ 84,800	$ 57,330	$ 52,552	$ 194,682

General overhead expenses in 1985 were as follows:

Warehousing and delivery expenses:		
Warehouse depreciation	$20,000	
Warehouse operations	30,000	
Delivery expenses	40,000	$ 90,000
Central office expenses:		
Advertising	18,000	
Central office salaries	37,000	
Other central office expenses	28,000	83,000
Total general overhead		$173,000

Additional information includes the following:

1. One-fifth of the warehouse space is used to house the central office and depreciation on this space is included in other central office expenses. Warehouse operating expenses vary with quantity of merchandise sold.
2. Delivery expenses vary with distance and number of deliveries. The distances from the warehouse to each store and the number of deliveries made in 1985 were as follows:

Store	Miles	Number of Deliveries
Ashville	120	140
Burns	200	64
Clinton	100	104

3. All advertising is prepared by the central office and is distributed in the areas in which stores are located.
4. As each store was opened, the fixed portion of central office salaries increased $7,000 and other central office expenses increased $2,500. Basic fixed central office salaries amount to $10,000 and basic fixed other central office expenses amount to $12,000. The remainder of central office salaries and the remainder of other central office expenses vary with sales.

REQUIRED

a. For each of the following plans for allocating general overhead expenses, compute the income of each store that would be subject to the municipal levy on corporation income:

Plan 1. Allocate all general overhead expenses on the basis of sales volume.

Plan 2. First, allocate central office salaries and other central office expenses evenly to warehouse operations and each store. Second, allocate the resulting warehouse operations expenses, warehouse depreciation, and advertising to each store on the basis of sales volume. Third, allocate delivery expenses to each store on the basis of delivery miles times number of deliveries.

b. Management has decided to expand one of the three stores to increase sales by $50,000. The expansion will increase local fixed operating expenses by $7,500 and require 10 additional deliveries from the warehouse. Determine which store management should select for expansion to maximize corporate profits.

CHAPTER 21
Accounting for Joint Products and By-Products

You already know that material, labor, and overhead are combined in production processes to make products such as a wooden coffee table, a metal wastebasket, or a plastic telephone casting. But a single production process can yield more than one product: The smelting of copper yields some silver; the production of beef yields various cuts of beef along with hides; and the refining of crude oil produces gasoline, kerosene, lubricating oils, paraffin, and other petroleum products.

When two or more different products are manufactured in the same production process, a **joint production process** exists. The main products from a joint production process are called **joint products.** Occasionally some products of relatively little value emerge from joint production processes; they are called **by-products.** The purpose of this chapter is to explore the characteristics of joint production processes and to learn how to cost joint products and by-products and to learn how to analyze joint product decisions.

Two or more products can result from the same production process

THE NATURE OF JOINT PRODUCTION ACTIVITIES

Many manufacturing operations produce joint products and by-products. Numerous products in the petroleum, petrochemical, wood products, chemical, and food industries are manufactured in joint production processes. In each industry as well as within each firm, the physical production activity may differ but the flow of production resources is similar for most joint production activities. Figure 21-1 shows a flow diagram for the production of four joint products and two by-products manufactured in four process centers.

In this example, all of the products are indistinguishable during the first two production processes, mixing and cooking. The costs incurred in these two process centers are common to all six products manufactured—these costs are called **joint costs.** The **split-off point** is the point in the production process where the products become identifiable, and as a result of their separate identity, their production costs can be measured separately.

Individual products can be identified at the split-off point

Some joint products are ready for sale once they reach the split-off point. This is the case for joint product A in Figure 21-1. Other joint products require additional processing beyond the split-off point to make them salable or to enhance their economic value. Joint products B, C, and D require

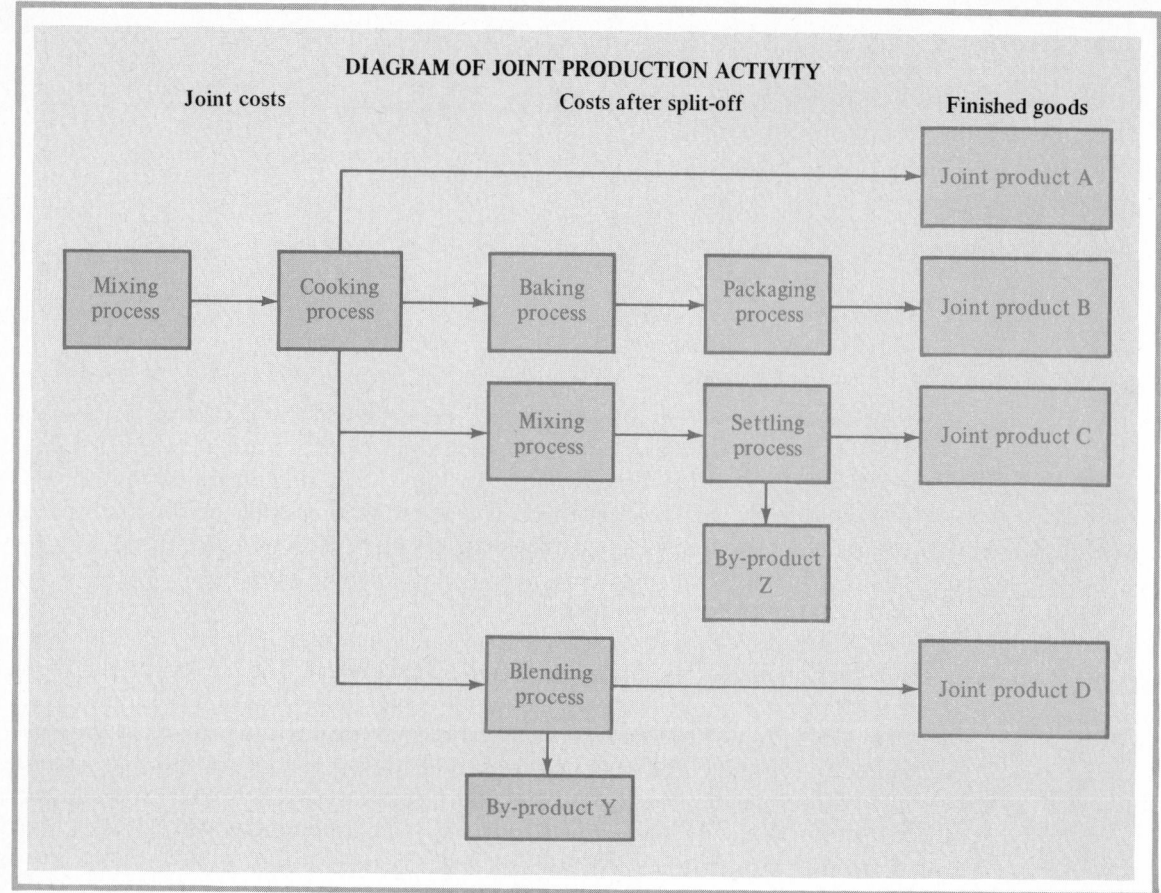

Figure 21-1. Many products can result from a single production process. In the production process diagramed here, no final product is distinguishable in the first two process centers but eventually four joint products and two by-products are produced. In practice, many joint production processes are much more complex than this one.

additional processing. The decision to sell a product at the split-off point or to process it further is analyzed later in the chapter.

In Figure 21-1, there are two by-products that result from the production of the main products. **By-products** result from joint production activities and have a small value relative to the main products manufactured. It is not always simple to determine whether a particular product is a by-product or a joint product. That determination rests on what the accountant defines as a "small relative value." However, a general rule that may be of some use is as follows:

By-product or joint product?

If the value of the product is so small that it has no effect on the decision to produce or not produce the entire product group, it is a **by-product;** if it does affect the decision to produce, it is a **joint product.**

By-products also should be distinguished clearly from scrap materials and returned materials, both of which are discussed in Chapter 18. Scrap is salable material resulting from the production process: Examples are irregular pieces of steel left after shearing parts from steel sheets, pieces of copper tubing generated in producing heating and cooling coils, and scrap lumber resulting from the production of furniture. Scrap is distinguished by two characteristics: First, the scrap is not useful to the company in the normal manufacturing activities. If it were, the material would be returned to the inventory storeroom for later use. Second, scrap must have market value; otherwise the material is merely waste and is thrown away.

Distinction between by-product and scrap

The primary distinction between scrap material and by-products is the way they are produced. Scrap is material whose basic characteristics are unchanged from the time it goes into production except that its size, shape, or quantity is such that it is no longer usable as raw material. By-products, on the other hand, typically are different from the basic raw materials that were put into the production process. A by-product is not merely a fragment of the original material.

The distinction between by-products and scrap is not always clear. As you will see later in the chapter, some methods of accounting for by-products and scrap are the same.

MEASURING JOINT PRODUCT COSTS

The objective of accounting for joint products is to measure the cost of manufacturing each product and to report that information to internal and external users. Like all product cost information, joint product costs are used in financial statements, reports to taxing or other governmental or regulatory authorities, and managerial cost reports.

A major difficulty with measuring joint product costs is that joint costs cannot be identified easily with specific joint products. Nonetheless, in the production of many products, joint costs are significant—sometimes more than half of the total cost of production. They must be assigned to joint products to satisfy full cost reporting standards and they should be allocated in a way that best satisfies the matching principle.

JOINT PRODUCT COSTING ILLUSTRATION

Two steps are necessary in costing joint products:

The two steps in costing joint products

1. Measure the product cost for each joint product after the split-off point, and
2. Allocate the joint costs to joint products.

The first step is essentially the same product costing activities for individual products discussed throughout this book. In this chapter, we concentrate primarily on the allocation of joint costs.

To illustrate joint product costing we use the example of Fairington Industrial Products, a company that makes a variety of wood and metal preservatives. One product group, manufactured in a joint production process, is used in the treatment of high-carbon steel alloys. The four joint products all reduce corrosion and prolong the life of the steel, but each product has different characteristics necessary to satisfy specific environmental requirements such as high or low humidity, extreme temperature fluctuations, and a highly corrosive atmosphere. Production quantity and cost data for the joint products are presented in Figure 21-2.

Figure 21-2. This schedule presents production quantity data with costs after split-off for each joint product and total joint costs for the group of joint products. The total cost of production is the sum of the joint costs and the costs after split-off.

Fairington Industrial Products
Production, Price, and Cost Data
For December 1985

Product	Units Produced	Unit Selling Price	Costs after Split-Off
Z-800	4,000 barrels	$10/barrel	$ 5,000
Z-900	3,000	15	15,000
XZ-880	2,000	25	—
XZ-990	1,000	65	30,000
Totals	10,000 barrels		$50,000

Joint cost = $90,000

Three of the products require additional processing beyond the split-off point before they are sold. Product XZ-880 is sold at split-off without additional processing. During December, 10,000 barrels in total of the four products are manufactured at a total cost of $140,000. Of this amount, $90,000 is a joint cost, which means it is common to all four products and cannot be identified with any specific product. The remaining $50,000 is **cost after split-off,** which can be identified with specific products.

To determine the cost of each product, we must have some logical way of allocating the joint costs to each of them. Ideally, the allocation should be made so that the cost of each product can be matched with the revenue from its sale. But the matching concept may be too difficult to apply in allocating joint cost. Furthermore, a clear cause-and-effect relationship may not exist between the total joint costs and the products that result from incurring those joint costs. Complicating the costing process even more is the fact that there are a number of generally accepted methods of allocating joint costs.

Joint costs are allocated to joint products in a logical manner to satisfy the matching principle

Physical Units Allocation Method

The physical units method allocates the same amount of joint cost to each unit

A common approach to joint cost allocation is the **physical units** method, also known as the **units of output** or **units of production** method. The physical units method is easy to use and understand. The joint costs are allocated equally to each of the units produced. This method is appropriate when the joint products are of relatively equal value and the per unit costs after split-off are similar. In the Fairington example, a total of 10,000 barrels of product were manufactured in December, and joint cost was $90,000. With the physical units method, each barrel of product is assigned $9 ($90,000/ 10,000 barrels) of joint cost. With 4,000 barrels of Z-800 produced, $36,000 ($9 per barrel × 4,000 barrels) of joint cost is assigned to the December production of Z-800. Similarly, $27,000 ($9 × 3,000 barrels) of joint cost is assigned to product Z-900. The joint costs for XZ-880 and XZ-990 are respectively $18,000 ($9 × 2,000 barrels) and $9,000 ($9 × 1,000 barrels). The allocation of the joint cost and the computation of unit product cost are presented in the schedule in Figure 21-3.

Figure 21-3. The physical units joint cost allocation method assigns the same amount of joint cost to each unit of joint product. Total product cost is composed of the allocated joint cost plus the cost after split-off.

Fairington Industrial Products
Schedule of Product Costs Using the Physical Units Allocation Method
December 1985

Product	Joint Costs		Costs after Split-Off		Total Product Cost	
	Total	Per Unit	Total	Per Unit	Total	Per Unit
Z-800	$36,000	$9.00	$ 5,000	$ 1.25	$ 41,000	$10.25
Z-900	27,000	9.00	15,000	5.00	42,000	14.00
XZ-880	18,000	9.00	—	—	18,000	9.00
XZ-990	9,000	9.00	30,000	30.00	39,000	39.00
Totals	$90,000		$50,000		$140,000	

The joint cost per unit is the same for all four joint products with this method; the total cost assigned to each joint product depends on the number of units manufactured during the month. The second pair of columns in the schedule identify the costs after split-off for each product. These costs are easy to identify with the individual products. There is no need to allocate them.

The distinction between identification and allocation is essential to managers who use joint product cost data in making decisions. For example, if the market value of one of the joint products declines significantly, it may be necessary to stop producing it and eliminate most, if not all, of the costs after split-off. But eliminating one of the joint products does not eliminate the joint product costs that are allocated to that product. The allocated joint costs will still be incurred as long as the rest of the joint products are manufactured.

The total product cost for a single joint product is the sum of the joint cost allocated to that product and the cost after split-off of that product. In our example, three of the products have both joint costs and costs after split-off. However, XZ-880 is sold at split-off and has no additional processing costs.

A comparison of product prices presented in Figure 21-2 with the product cost data in Figure 21-3 offers some interesting relationships. For instance, the unit cost of Z-800 is $10.25 per barrel, and the price of that product is $10.00 per barrel. The market dictates that Fairington cannot charge a higher price. Therefore, it appears that the company is selling its largest-volume product for $.25 per barrel less than it costs to make it. The loss per unit is even higher when the analysis includes this product's share of selling, distribution, and administrative costs.

The unit gross margin for product Z-900 is only $1 per barrel ($15 selling price — $14 unit product cost), whereas the unit gross margins for XZ-880 and XZ-990 are $16 and $26, respectively. This is not surprising because the prices of these two products are high compared to the first two. Because the physical units method allocates the same amount of joint cost to all products, the low-priced products will most likely have small or even negative gross margins, and the high-priced products will have high gross margins. Consequently, the physical units method is seldom used when there is a significant difference in the prices of the joint products.

Managers need to know what proportion of a product's cost is joint cost. In this example, total joint costs are 64 percent ($90,000/$140,000) of the total manufacturing costs. As the proportion of joint costs gets larger, it becomes more difficult for managers to use the total product cost data for decision making. It is more difficult because the allocated joint costs are common to all of the joint products rather than identifiable with the specific products. The significance of this issue becomes apparent in the discussion of joint product decision analysis later in the chapter.

Sales Value Allocation Method

The sales value method allocates joint costs in proportion to each product's total sales revenue

The **sales value method** allocates joint costs in proportion to the sales revenue produced by each joint product. The sales revenue contributed by each of the joint products is found by multiplying the number of units of each joint product manufactured times its sales price. Using the data in Figure 21-2, the total sales value is computed as follows:

Product	Quantity Produced	Unit Price	Sales Value
Z-800	4,000 barrels	$10/barrel	$ 40,000
Z-900	3,000	15	45,000
XZ-880	2,000	25	50,000
XZ-990	1,000	65	65,000
		Total sales value	$200,000

Each joint product is assigned joint costs based on its share of the total sales value. For example, Z-800 is allocated $18,000 of joint cost computed as [($40,000/$200,000 of total sales value) × $90,000 of joint cost]. The $18,000 of allocated joint cost is divided by the 4,000 units to find the per unit joint cost of $4.50. Similarly, the joint cost allocated to Z-900 is $20,250 [($45,000/$200,000) × $90,000]. The joint costs allocated to the joint products based on sales value are shown in Figure 21-4.

Comparing the product cost schedule for the sales value method with the product cost schedule for the physical units method provides some interesting information. The joint cost allocations are different, **but** the costs after split-off are the same. It is easy to forget that the costs after split-off do not change just because the method of allocating joint costs is different.

Fairington Industrial Products
Schedule of Product Costs Using the Sales Value Allocation Method
December 1985

Product	Joint Costs Total	Joint Costs Per Unit	Costs after Split-Off Total	Costs after Split-Off Per Unit	Total Product Cost Total	Total Product Cost Per Unit
Z-800	$18,000	$ 4.50	$ 5,000	$ 1.25	$ 23,000	$ 5.75
Z-900	20,250	6.75	15,000	5.00	35,250	11.75
XZ-880	22,500	11.25	—	—	22,500	11.25
XZ-990	29,250	29.25	30,000	30.00	59,250	59.25
Totals	$90,000		$50,000		$140,000	

Figure 21-4. The sales value joint cost allocation method assigns joint costs to products in proportion to the sales revenue each completed product will earn. Notice that costs after split-off are the same as with the physical units method. This is true regardless of the joint cost allocation method used.

Combining the allocated joint costs with the costs after split-off yields the total product cost for each of the joint products. Each joint product has a different unit cost, depending on which method of joint cost allocation is used. Using the sales value method, the cost of Z-800 is 44 percent lower [($10.25 – $5.75)/$10.25] and the cost of XZ-990 is 52 percent higher [($59.25 – $39.00)/$39.00] than with the physical units method. The cost differences for the other two products are not as large.

A logical question is, Which of the two joint cost allocations methods is correct?, or better, Which of the two methods is preferred for allocating joint costs? Neither method is clearly correct or incorrect. Which method is preferred depends on the given production situation and on the reporting needs of management.

Gross Profit Allocation Method

Joint costs can be allocated so that all products have the same percentage gross margin

The **gross profit method,** sometimes called the **gross margin method** or the **constant contribution percentage method,** allocates joint costs so that each of the joint products provides the same **percentage** gross profit. Using the gross profit method, joint costs are allocated so that each of the products has the same percentage gross profit as the whole group. The gross margin for the entire group of joint products is the total sales revenue of all the products less their total production cost. The gross margin percentage is the gross margin divided by the total sales revenue of the products.

The gross profit percentage for the Fairington Industrial Products example is 30 percent [($200,000 − $140,000)/$200,000]. Notice that the $140,000 used in computing the gross profit is the sum of joint costs and costs after split-off. A gross profit of 30 percent means that each product's cost is 70 percent of its selling price. The amount of joint cost to be allocated among the joint products is merely the total product cost minus the cost after split-off.

The total product cost for each product can be computed using either total costs or unit costs. Using total costs the computation is:

Computing total
product costs

Product	Total Sales Value	Product Cost Percentage	Total Product Cost
Z-800	$40,000	70 percent	$ 28,000
Z-900	45,000	70	31,500
XZ-880	50,000	70	35,000
XZ-990	65,000	70	45,500
		Total product cost	$140,000

The total product cost is shown in the schedule of product costs presented in Figure 21-5. The unit cost in this figure is determined by dividing the units produced into the total product cost. For instance, the unit cost of Z-800 is $7.00 ($28,000/4,000 units).

Figure 21-5. The gross profit joint cost allocation method allocates joint costs to products so that each joint product has the same percentage gross margin. The method is based on the total production cost of the group of joint products.

Fairington Industrial Products
Schedule of Product Costs Using the Gross Profit Allocation Method
December 1985

Product	Joint Costs Total	Joint Costs Per Unit	Costs after Split-Off Total	Costs after Split-Off Per Unit	Total Product Costs Total	Total Product Costs Per Unit
Z-800	$23,000	$ 5.75	$ 5,000	$ 1.25	$ 28,000	$ 7.00
Z-900	16,500	5.50	15,000	5.00	31,500	10.50
XZ-880	35,000	17.50	—	—	35,000	17.50
XZ-990	15,500	15.50	30,000	30.00	45,500	45.50
Totals	$90,000		$50,000		$140,000	

Another way of computing the total product cost is to use the unit selling price of the products:

Product	Selling Price	Product Cost Percentage	Unit Product Cost
Z-800	$10/unit	70 percent	$ 7.00
Z-900	15	70	10.50
XZ-880	25	70	17.50
XZ-990	65	70	45.50

To find the total product cost for each product, we multiply the unit cost times the units produced. For example, the total product cost of XZ-990 is $45,500 ($45.50 × 1,000 units).

The allocation of joint cost is a simple subtraction process. We know the total product cost and the cost after split-off for each product. Each product's joint cost is total cost less cost after split-off:

Product	Total Product Cost	Cost after Split-Off	Allocated Joint Cost
Z-800	$28,000	$ 5,000	$23,000
Z-900	31,500	15,000	16,500
XZ-880	35,000	—	35,000
XZ-990	45,500	30,000	15,500
		Total allocated joint cost	$90,000

Computing allocated joint costs

The unit joint cost of each product is computed by dividing each product's allocated joint cost by the number of units manufactured. For instance, the joint cost per unit of Z-900 is $5.50 ($16,500/3,000 units). Study carefully the product cost data in Figure 21-5 for the gross profit method of joint cost allocation and compare the data with the other two joint cost allocation methods already discussed.

Advocates of the gross profit method argue that the method is logical because it parallels management's decision to produce the group of joint products. That is, management evaluates a group of joint products by comparing their total expected revenues and costs. If the decision to produce is made using total costs and total revenues, the assignment of joint costs should be made in the same manner.

Net Realizable Value at Split-Off

Net realizable value is calculated at the split-off point

Another popular method of joint cost allocation is **net realizable value at the point of split-off.** With this method, each product is assigned joint costs in proportion to its net realizable value at the split-off point. **Net realizable value** is the sales value at split-off minus any selling and distribution costs. Many joint products have a ready market at the split-off point, although the market value at split-off is less than the value if processed to completion. Note that net realizable value is merely used to allocate joint costs to products. There is no intent to sell the products at split-off; they will be processed beyond the split-off point to completion.

If there is a readily determinable market value at split-off, the costs to market and distribute the product are estimated and subtracted from the market value to compute the net realizable value at split-off. The four products in our example are assumed to have net realizable values at split-off as follows:

Product	Net Realizable Value at Split-Off
Z-800	$ 20,000
Z-900	18,000
XZ-880	50,000
XZ-990	12,000
Total net realizable value at split-off point	$100,000

Once net realizable value is determined, joint costs are allocated to the joint products in proportion to their net realizable value at split-off as follows:

Product	Percentage of NRV at Split-Off	×	Total Joint Cost	=	Allocated Joint Cost
Z-800	$20,000/$100,000		$90,000		$18,000
Z-900	18,000/ 100,000		90,000		16,200
XZ-880	50,000/ 100,000		90,000		45,000
XZ-990	12,000/ 100,000		90,000		10,800
			Total allocated joint cost		$90,000

The allocated joint costs now are used in the computation of product costs. Figure 21-6 presents the product cost schedule using net realizable value at the split-off point to allocate joint costs.

Figure 21-6. The net relizable value at split-off may be used to allocate joint costs to products even though some or all of the products may be processed further. The assumption is that a market value exists for all joint products at the split-off point.

Fairington Industrial Products
Schedule of Product Costs Using Net Realizable Value at Split-Off
December 1985

Product	Joint Costs		Costs after Split-Off		Total Product Cost	
	Total	Per Unit	Total	Per Unit	Total	Per Unit
Z-800	$18,000	$ 4.50	$ 5,000	$ 1.25	$ 23,000	$ 5.75
Z-900	16,200	5.40	15,000	5.00	31,200	10.40
XZ-880	45,000	22.50	—	—	45,000	22.50
XZ-990	10,800	10.80	30,000	30.00	40,800	40.80
Totals	$90,000		$50,000		$140,000	

Estimated Value at the Split-Off Point

If there is no market value for joint products at split-off, a market value may be estimated.

When joint products have no market value at the split-off point, accountants may estimate market value at split-off. The estimate is made by subtracting a product's costs after split-off from its market value at completion. In the Fairington example, the **estimated market value at split-off** for each product is:

Product	Market Value	Cost after Split-Off	Estimated Market Value at the Split-Off Point
Z-800	$ 40,000	$ 5,000	$ 35,000
Z-900	45,000	15,000	30,000
XZ-880	50,000	—	50,000
XZ-990	65,000	30,000	35,000
Totals	$200,000	$50,000	$150,000

Once the market value is estimated, the joint costs are allocated to products in the same way as with net realizable value.

Product	Portion of Estimated Market Value	×	Total Joint Cost	=	Allocated Joint Cost
Z-800	$35,000/$150,000	×	$90,000	=	$21,000
Z-900	30,000/ 150,000	×	90,000	=	18,000
XZ-880	50,000/ 150,000	×	90,000	=	30,000
XZ-990	35,000/ 150,000	×	90,000	=	21,000
			Total allocated joint cost		$90,000

The product cost schedule for the estimated market value at the split-off point is presented in Figure 21-7.

Figure 21-7. If there is no ready market for some or all of the joint products at split-off, a market value can be estimated by subtracting the costs after split-off from the final market value. These estimated market values are used to allocate joint costs to products.

Fairington Industrial Products
Schedule of Product Costs Using Estimated Value at Split-Off
December 1985

Product	Joint Costs Total	Joint Costs Per Unit	Costs after Split-Off Total	Costs after Split-Off Per Unit	Total Product Cost Total	Total Product Cost Per Unit
Z-800	$21,000	$ 5.25	$ 5,000	$ 1.25	$ 26,000	$ 6.50
Z-900	18,000	6.00	15,000	5.00	33,000	11.00
XZ-880	30,000	15.00	—	—	30,000	15.00
XZ-990	21,000	21.00	30,000	30.00	51,000	51.00
Totals	$90,000		$50,000		$140,000	

The purpose of allocating joint costs using estimated market value at split-off is to eliminate the effects of any value added to joint products by processing beyond the split-off point. We attempt to measure the value added by the joint production costs alone.

The problem with using a market value at split-off is that many joint products do not have a ready value at split-off and estimating their value by deducting costs after split-off may result in wrong or arbitrary values.

Joint Product Inventory Management

The inventory management concepts discussed in Chapters 13 and 18 apply to joint product inventories as well. In addition, joint product inventories provide some additional challenges. A major issue in managing joint product inventory is the maintenance of the desired quantity of inventory for each joint product. If some joint products sell well but others do not, the inventory levels of some joint products may be lower than desired while there are too many units of other joint products manufactured in the same product group. The relative proportion of each joint product is often fixed, so managers cannot merely slow the production of the poorly selling product and increase

The sales mix of joint products may be different from the production mix, leaving inventory management problems

the production of the fast-selling product. With joint products, optimal inventory management methods may be difficult to implement consistently.

Management may attack the joint product inventory issue in a number of ways. Some examples include changing the mix of outputs through research and development activities, additional marketing efforts for the poorer-selling joint products, and a change in the price of the joint products that move slowly.

JOINT PRODUCT DECISIONS

In measuring product costs for joint products, we took special care to separate allocated joint costs from the costs after split-off. This distinction is important as we analyze some joint product decisions. You will see that costs after split-off are the only relevant product costs in evaluating a single product, whereas all product costs are useful in evaluating the entire joint product group.

To illustrate joint product decision making we use the example of Kerrtone Company, a cosmetic manufacturer that makes several different products in joint production processes. Figure 21-8 presents production quantity, cost, and price data for three facial and hand creams the company manufactures in a joint production process.

Figure 21-8. These are production quantity, cost, and price data for a company that makes three joint products.

Kerrtone Company
Schedule of Production and Price Data
January 1985

Product	Quantity Produced	Unit Selling Price	Costs after Split-Off
Tone-1	6,000 jars	$15/jar	$30,000
Tone-2	3,000	20	9,000
Tone-3	1,000	50	11,000
Totals	10,000 jars		$50,000

Joint cost = $100,000

Each of the three products requires some processing beyond the split-off point, although most of the manufacturing cost is joint cost. The products are packaged in 32-ounce jars and sold primarily to cosmetologists. Product cost schedules using both the physical units method and the gross profit method are presented in Figure 21-9. Joint cost decision making is similar using other joint cost allocation methods.

Types of Joint Product Decisions

Decisions may be made about a single joint product or all products in the group

Joint product decisions can be separated into single-product decisions and product group decision. **Single-product decisions** are decisions in which only one of the joint products is evaluated. Examples are decisions to sell at the split-off point or process further and decisions to discontinue selling one

Figure 21-9. The product costs schedules for the three joint products of the Kerrtone Company are prepared from the data in Figure 21-8. The schedule at the top of the figure is based on the physical units method of joint cost allocation; the schedule at the bottom presents product costs using the gross profit method to allocate joint costs.

Kerrtone Company
Schedule of Product Costs
Physical Units Method
January 1985

Product	Joint Costs		Costs after Split-Off		Total Product Cost	
	Total	Per Unit	Total	Per Unit	Total	Per Unit
Tone-1	$ 60,000	$10.00	$30,000	$ 5.00	$ 90,000	$15.00
Tone-2	30,000	10.00	9,000	3.00	39,000	13.00
Tone-3	10,000	10.00	11,000	11.00	21,000	21.00
Totals	$100,000		$50,000		$150,000	

Kerrtone Company
Schedule of Product Costs
Gross Profit Method
January 1985

Product	Joint Costs		Costs after Split-Off		Total Product Cost	
	Total	Per Unit	Total	Per Unit	Total	Per Unit
Tone-1	$ 37,500	$ 6.25	$30,000	$ 5.00	$ 67,500	$ 11.25
Tone-2	36,000	12.00	9,000	3.00	45,000	15.00
Tone-3	26,500	26.50	11,000	11.00	37,500	37.50
Totals	$100,000		$50,000		$150,000	

product in the product group but to continue selling the other joint products. **Product group decisions** are decisions involving all of the products in the joint production process. A decision to stop producing all of the joint products is a common example.

Single-Product Decisions

Single-product decisions are particularly interesting because of the differences in product cost that result from different joint cost allocation methods. A single-product decision is a form of a two-alternative decision with characteristics similar to the two-alternative decisions discussed in Chapter 10.

Sell at Split-Off or Process Further. A common joint product decision is whether to sell a product at the split-off point or process it further. As with all two-alternative decisions, the relevant costs and the relevant revenues are those that differ between the decision alternatives.

Product Tone-1 can be sold at the split-off point for $11 per unit. If it is sold at split-off, all of its costs after split-off can be eliminated. Should the product be sold at split-off or processed further?

Incremental revenues and incremental costs are used in the analysis

Using relevant cost and revenue data, we compare the decrease in cost with the decrease in revenue. The decrease in cost is $5 per unit, or $30,000, and the decrease in revenue is $4 per unit, or $24,000. The decrease in cost is $6,000 greater than the decrease in revenue. Therefore the relevant cost and revenue data indicate the product should be sold at the point of split-off. To process this product beyond split-off costs the company $1 per unit. We can verify this by preparing a gross margin schedule for both alternatives:

	Process after Split-Off	Sell at Split-Off	Difference
Revenue	$200,000	$176,000	$24,000
Less:			
Joint cost	(100,000)	(100,000)	—
Cost after split-off	(50,000)	(20,000)	(30,000)
Gross margin	$ 50,000	$ 56,000	$ (6,000)

Of course there may be variables other than relevant costs and revenues included in the analysis. For example, management may determine that the company must produce the product to completion to maintain a full line of products. Management may decide to continue processing the product beyond the split-off point to avoid reducing its work force.

We have illustrated only hypothetical cost data based on the concept of relevant costs. As we emphasize in Chapter 10 on relevant costs and decision making, relevant economic data are useful in analyzing and making decisions, but seldom are such data the only important variables.

Sometimes it is not possible to eliminate all of the cost after split-off if the decision is made not to process further. Fixed costs and other commitments may preclude eliminating some manufacturing costs, at least in the short run. For example, if 25 percent of the cost after split-off associated with Tone-1 is fixed capacity cost that cannot be eliminated in the forseeable future, should the product be sold at split-off or processed further?

Now the analysis changes a little from the previous example because the relevant cost reduction if the product is sold at split-off is not merely the cost after split-off for the product; the relevant cost after split-off is the amount that can be eliminated if the product is sold at split-off. The cost reduction is $3.75 per unit (the cost after split-off of $5.00 less the 25 percent of the cost that cannot be eliminated). The comparison we have to make then is a $4.00 decline in revenue against a $3.75 decline in cost. The loss of selling after split-off is $.25 a unit, or $1,500 for the 6,000 units. Again, the analysis can be demonstrated by preparing a gross margin schedule:

Analysis of the effect on gross margin

	Process after Split-Off	Sell at Split-Off	Difference
Revenue	$200,000	$176,000	$24,000
Less:			
Joint cost	(100,000)	(100,000)	—
Cost after split-off	(50,000)	(27,500)	(22,500)
Gross margin	$ 50,000	$ 48,500	$ 1,500

In both illustrations, the analysis is made using only costs after split-off. The allocated joint costs and the method of joint cost allocation do not enter into the analysis. The reason is that for single-product decisions, such as whether to sell at split-off or process to completion, allocated joint costs are not relevant. Therefore, the joint cost allocation method used is not relevant to the decision process.

A Change in the Market Price of a Product.   Many products are sold in markets with conditions changing constantly. As market conditions change, managers must decide on the optimum production and sales strategy. For example, competitors' new products dictate that Kerrtone must reduce the price it charges for Tone-3 to $35 per unit. Should the company continue to make and sell the product?

The two product cost schedules in Figure 21-9 yield some confusing data. According to the physical units cost allocation method, it costs $21 to manu-facture the product, yielding a $14 gross margin ($35 – $21) even at the new lower price. However, with the new price of $35, the gross profit joint cost allocation method indicates a negative gross margin of $2.50 per unit ($35.00 – $37.50). The two joint cost allocation methods yield conflicting informa-tion. The reason for the conflict is that the total cost data contain irrelevant information for this single-product decision. As before, the allocated joint costs have no bearing on the analysis and decision. The relevant costs are the costs after split-off and the differential revenue associated with the two alternatives.

For single-product decisions, the relevant costs are costs after split-off

If the company discontinues the sale of Tone-3, it will lose $35,000 in sales revenue ($35 per unit × 1,000 units). It will also have a cost reduction of $11,000 (1,000 units × $11) because the 1,000 units will not be processed beyond the split-off point. Consequently, the company will lose $24,000 of total gross margin if it no longer sells Tone-3. Verifying this analysis:

	Sell All Three Products	Discontinue Production of Tone-3	Difference
Revenue	$185,000	$150,000	$35,000
Less:			
Joint cost	(100,000)	(100,000)	—
Cost after split-off	(50,000)	(39,000)	(11,000)
Gross margin	$ 35,000	$ 11,000	$24,000

The key point here is that the total joint cost of $100,000 is not reduced if Tone-3 is not sold. If Tone-3 is discontinued, the other two joint products must absorb its share of the total joint cost. You can see the importance of identifying the costs that differ between decision alternatives.

Product Group Decisions

Because of the close physical relationship of joint products, many joint product decisions involve the entire group of joint products. Often a major change in the market conditions for one of the joint products affects management's decision to produce or not to produce the entire group. Some product group decisions at first appear to be single-product decisions.

Change in the Market Price of a Product. In the Kerrtone Company example, the selling price decline of $15 per unit for Tone-3 caused a decline in the total gross margin of $15,000 for the 1,000 units produced. We concluded that Tone-3 should still be sold. The relevant data in the analysis are the differential revenue and the differential costs which, in this case, are the costs after split-off for Tone-3.

Now we assume that the price of Tone-3 is the original amount of $50, but because of competition, the price of Tone-1 must be reduced to $6.50 per unit. Should Tone-1 still be sold? The cost after split-off is $5.00 per unit. The revenue from Tone-1 provides $1.50 per unit toward covering joint costs. We analyze the total gross margin data:

	Sell All Three Products	Sell Only Tone-2 and Tone-3	Difference
Revenue	$149,000	$110,000	$39,000
Less:			
Joint cost	(100,000)	(100,000)	—
Cost after split-off	(50,000)	(20,000)	(30,000)
Gross margin	$ (1,000)	$ (10,000)	$ 9,000

Selling all three products provides a negative gross margin. But the loss is smaller than if only Tone-2 and Tone-3 are sold; still, both are loss situations. Based on cost data only, the decision would be to stop producing all of the products.

This situation illustrates an important point: The analysis of the differential revenue and cost data for the lower price of Tone-1 indicates that the company should continue selling all three products. A careful analysis of the total gross margin data for all of the joint products shows a loss for the entire product group. Managers should be cautious when evaluating single-product decisions to be certain that a broader analysis is not warranted.

Target Gross Margins

Is the gross margin large enough to cover all costs and provide a satisfactory profit?

A positive gross margin alone may not be sufficient incentive to manufacture products. Other costs, such as marketing, administration, and distribution, require the gross margin to be large enough to cover all costs and earn a satisfactory profit. For example, given Kerrtone Company's nonmanufacturing costs and profit objectives, it has a policy that the minimum gross margin must be 20 percent for any product.

If competitor actions force the price of Tone-2 to decline from $20 to $15 per unit, while the original prices of the other two products remain unchanged, the new price of $15 reduces the company's revenue by $15,000

($5 per unit × 3,000 units). However, the new price more than covers the $3 per unit cost after split-off. Let us evaluate the effect of the Tone-2 price decline on the gross margin policy of the company.

	Sell All Three Products	Sell Only Tone-1 and Tone-3	Difference
Revenue	$185,000	$140,000	$45,000
Less:			
Joint cost	(100,000)	(100,000)	—
Cost after split-off	(50,000)	(41,000)	(9,000)
Gross margin	$ 35,000	$ (1,000)	$36,000

This analysis shows that continuing the sale of Tone-2 yields $35,000 of total gross margin, which does not satisfy the company's minimum gross margin requirements. If we include the minimum gross margin in the analysis, the correct decision would be to stop producing the group of joint products, as shown below:

Revenue	$185,000
Less:	
Joint costs	(100,000)
Costs after split-off	(50,000)
Required gross margin ($185,000 × .20)	(37,000)
Revenue deficit below the minimum gross margin	$ (2,000)

ACCOUNTING FOR BY-PRODUCTS

Compared to joint products, by-products have relatively little economic value. However, they still must be accounted for along with all other economic events and transactions of an organization. As with joint products, there is more than one way to account for by-products.

By-Products Treated as a Cost Reduction

By-product revenue can be used to reduce the cost of the main product

A logical method of accounting for by-products is to reduce the cost of the main product or group of products by the amount realized from the sale of the by-product. If the by-product occurs after the joint products have split off, the revenue from the sale of the by-product is used to reduce the cost of the joint products from which it is derived. For example, in a manufacturing process that produces a main product and a by-product, 1,000 units of main product were manufactured during January with the following costs:

Direct materials	$23,000
Direct labor	17,000
Manufacturing overhead	15,000
Total product cost	$55,000

Unit cost = $55,000/1,000 units = $55.00 per unit

In addition to the main product, 500 pounds of by-product were manu-factured during the month. The by-product was sold for $4.20 per pound after $850 of additional processing costs. There were no marketing or distri-bution costs associated with the by-product.

The net realizable value of the by-product manufactured in January was $1,250 [(500 pounds × $4.20) − $850]. The total cost saving of $1,250 is spread over the 1,000 units of the main product, yielding a cost reduction of $1.25 per unit ($1,250/1,000 units). Therefore, the January product cost for the main product is $53.75 per unit ($55.00 − $1.25). The same result is achieved using total costs rather than unit costs:

Total cost of main product	$55,000	
Less net revenue from by-product	1,250	
Adjusted cost of main product	$53,750	

Unit cost = $53,750/1,000 = $53.75 per unit

When the by-product splits off from the main product, it is inventoried at its net realizable value. In this example the entry is:

	By-product work in process	1,250	
	Work in process control		1,250
	To record the split-off of by-product		
	at its net realizable value.		

When the additional processing costs for the by-product are incurred, they are also recorded:

	By-product work in process	850	
	Inventory control		300
	Payroll		320
	Manufacturing overhead applied		230
	To record additional processing costs		
	for the by-product.		

Completed units of by-product are transferred to inventory and then sold. The entries to record these activities are as follows:

	By-product inventory	2,100	
	By-product work in process		2,100
	To record the transfer of completed		
	by-products to inventory.		
	Accounts receivable (or Cash)	2,100	
	By-product inventory		2,100
	To record the sale of by-products.		

If the by-product separates from the production process before the split-off point of the main products, the by-product revenue reduces the joint cost, which means that all of the joint products share in the cost reduction.

By-Products Treated as Miscellaneous Income

If the by-product is sold for a small amount, its sale can be treated as miscellaneous income

The easiest method of accounting for by-products is to record their sale as miscellaneous income or other income. The revenue realized from the sale of by-products is reported on the income statement and does not reduce the cost of a main product or a group of joint products. This method is particularly popular if the by-product is sold without further processing and when the value of the by-product is very small. Typically there is no journal entry recorded at the time the by-product separates from the main product, although the physical quantity may be recorded in some inventory records document. When the by-product is sold, the sale is recorded as a miscellaneous revenue or other income item. To illustrate, if 2,000 pounds of a by-product are sold for $2.40 a pound, the entry to record the sale is:

	Accounts receivable (or Cash)	4,800	
	Sale of by-products		4,800
	To record the sale of 2,000 pounds		
	of by-products for $2.40 a pound.		

SUMMARY

In a **joint production process,** two or more products are produced. The main products of joint production processes are called **joint products.** Joint products are indistinguishable in the manufacturing process until the **split-off point,** which is the point in the production process where the products separate. **By-products** are products of relatively small value produced in a joint production process.

Joint costs are manufacturing costs incurred before the split-off point. Joint costs are common to all joint products and are allocated to them to determine total product cost. Many joint products are processed beyond the split-off point. **Costs after split-off** are identifiable with specific products.

The more common methods of allocating joint costs to products include physical units, sales value, gross profit, net realizable value at split-off, and estimated value at the split-off point. The **physical units method,** sometimes called the **units of output** or **units of production method,** allocates the same amount of joint cost to each unit of output. This method can result in some strange product costs when the various joint products have significantly different selling prices. The **sales value method** assigns joint costs to products in proportion to the sales value of the completed product. This method ignores any cost after split-off in the allocation process. The **gross profit method,** also called the **gross margin method** or **constant percentage method,** allocates joint costs so that all products provide the same percentage gross margin. This method parallels the management decision process used in evaluating the production decision for the group of joint products. The **net realizable value at the split-off point method** allocates joint costs in proportion to the sales value at the split-off point. The major problem with this method is that some joint products do not have a market value at the split-off point. The **estimated value at the split-off point method** allocates joint costs in proportion to the estimated market value of the products at the split-off point. The estimated value is determined by subtracting the costs after split-off from the product's total market value.

In addition to costing joint products, managers must carefully monitor joint product inventories. If joint products are sold in proportions different from their production proportions, some inventories may grow large while inventories of other products in the joint product group are smaller than desired.

Joint product decisions can be separated into single-product decisions and product group decisions. **Single-product decisions** are used to evaluate one joint product separately. **Product group decisions** include all of the joint products in the analysis.

Joint product decisions are a form of alternative choice decision, and must be based on relevant cost and revenue data. In general, costs after split-off are the only product costs relevant in evaluating single-product decisions and all product costs are relevant in evaluating decisions about the entire joint product group.

By-products have relatively small economic value. A logical treatment of by-products is to reduce the cost of the main product or products by the amount realized from the sale of the by-product. An individual joint product's cost can be reduced, or the cost of the entire group of joint products, depending on where in the production process the by-product separates from the main product. Another treatment is to record the sale of by-products as miscellaneous or other income.

KEY TERMS

by-product *(731)*
constant percentage method *(737)*
cost after split-off *(734)*
estimated value at split-off
  method *(740)*
gross margin method *(737)*
gross profit method *(737)*
joint cost *(731)*
joint product *(731)*
joint production process *(731)*

net realizable value *(739)*
net realizable value at split-off
  point *(739)*
physical units method *(734)*
product group decisions *(743)*
sales value method *(736)*
single-product decision *(742)*
split-off point *(731)*
units of output method *(734)*
units of production method *(734)*

QUESTIONS   1.   Several methods are available for allocating joint costs to products. One is based on physical output, another on the sales value of the joint products, and a third on their gross margin. Discuss the rationale of each method, together with its advantages and disadvantages.

2. (AICPA) By-products that require no additional processing after the point of separation are often accounted for by assigning to them a value of zero at the point of separation and crediting cost of production as sales are made. Justify the treatment. Discuss its possible shortcomings.

3. (AICPA) Distinguish between the meanings of a joint product and a by-product. Describe and briefly discuss the appropriateness of two acceptable methods of accounting for the by-product in determination of the cost of the joint products. Assuming proper treatment of the by-product costs, describe two acceptable methods of allocating to joint products the cost of the initial producing department.

4. (AICPA) The Harbison Company manufactures two sizes of plate glass which are produced simultaneously in the same manufacturing process. Since the small sheets of plate glass are cut from large sheets that have flaws in them, the joint costs are allocated equally to each good sheet produced, large or small. The difference in after-split-off costs for large and small sheets is material. In 1985, the company decided to increase its efforts to sell the large sheets because they produced a larger gross margin than the small sheets. Accordingly, the amount of the fixed advertising budget devoted to large sheets was increased and the amount devoted to small sheets was decreased. However, no changes in sales prices were made. By midyear the production scheduling department had increased the monthly production of large sheets in order to stay above the minimum inventory level. However, it also had cut back the monthly production of small sheets because the inventory ceiling had been reached. At the end of 1985, the net result of the change in product mix was a decrease of $112,000 in gross margin. Although sales of large sheets had increased 34,500 units, sales of small sheets had decreased 40,200 units. Discuss the propriety of allocating joint costs for general-purpose financial statements on the basis of physical measures, such as weights or units, and relative sales or market value. Identify the mistake that Harbison Company made in deciding to change its product mix and explain why it caused a smaller gross margin for 1985.

EXERCISES

Ex. 21-1
Physical Units and
Gross Profit Joint
Cost Allocation

NWC Company makes natural food supplements, which it distributes through health food stores. A favorite product group is a root and herb supplement. Materials are ground, combined with a natural base fiber compound, and simmered slowly. In the process, the purest base is skimmed off the top and the portion of the compound with the most impurities settles to the bottom. The major portion of each batch remains. Each of these compounds is processed further to enhance its strength, and then packaged. Below are data for a recent batch of the product:

Product	Output in Jars	Sales Price per Jar	Costs after Split-Off
RH-basic	6,000	$ 5.00	$ 9,000
RH-extra	13,000	8.00	26,000
RH-prem	1,000	16.00	5,000

Total joint cost = $50,000

REQUIRED   Prepare a schedule of product costs using:

a. The physical units joint cost allocation method.
b. The gross profit joint cost allocation method.

Ex. 21-2
Net Realizable
Value at Split-Off
Joint Cost
Allocation

RJE-Engine-Aid Company makes gasoline supplements designed to make engines perform more efficiently. A major market for the company's product is the automobile racing industry, but there is a good market among the driving public in general. The company's largest-selling product line is the RJE gas supplement line. The products are sold in cartons of six cans each through a nationwide automobile parts network. Below are November production and price data. Joint cost was $30,000.

	Product		
	R1	R2	R3
Cartons produced	3,000	6,000	1,000
Price per carton	$5.00	$8.00	$14.00
Costs after split-off	$3,000	$12,000	$2,000
Net realizable value at split-off	$3.00	$5.00	$11.00

REQUIRED   Compute the total and per unit joint cost, cost after split-off, and total product cost using:

   a.   Net realizable value at split-off to allocate joint costs.
   b.   Estimated value at the point of split-off to allocate joint costs.

Ex. 21-3
Joint Product
Costing

A plastics manufacturer produces three grades of bulk plastic in a joint production process. Each of the products requires some processing beyond the split-off point. Below are production data for the first week in October.

Product	Pounds Produced	Selling Price	Costs after Split-Off	Net Realizable Value at Split-Off
PL-X	21,000	$1.60	$8,400	$ .70/lb
PL-Y	18,000	2.00	3,600	1.00
PL-Z	11,000	3.00	6,600	1.50

Total joint cost = $66,000

REQUIRED   Prepare a schedule of product costs for the three products using:

   a.   The physical units method of joint cost allocation.
   b.   The sales value method of joint cost allocation.
   c.   The net realizable value at split-off method of joint cost allocation.

Ex. 21-4
Basic Joint Product
Costing

Below are production and sales data for three joint products.

Product	Production Quantity	Selling Price	Cost after Split-Off	Sales Quantity
N1	1,500	$10	$3,000	1,200
M1	2,500	12	—	2,200
Q1	1,000	15	7,000	600

Joint costs = $35,000

REQUIRED   Compute detailed product costs for each of the products using the following to allocate joint costs:

a. Estimated value at split-off.
b. Sales value method.
c. Physical units method.
d. Constant percentage method.

Ex. 21-5
Single Product
Decision Analysis

Par-Tech, Inc., produces industrial cleaning compounds. One product group, especially good as a grease emulsifier, is called the Mol-Tech group. Three Mol-Tech products are produced in a joint production process, each having somewhat different cleaning capabilities. During March, 50,000 gallons of product were produced of which 10 percent was Mol-Tech-1, 30 percent Mol-Tech-2, and 60 percent Mol-Tech-3. Joint cost for the products was $120,000. Mol-Tech-1 is sold at split-off, but Mol-Tech-2 and 3 required $15,000 and $18,000 respectively in additional processing costs beyond the split-off point. The selling prices of the products are $7 per gallon, $4 per gallon, and $3.50 per gallon respectively. The company uses the sales value method of allocating joint costs. If a product is discontinued or not processed beyond the split-off point, 70 percent of costs after split-off can be eliminated.

REQUIRED   Prepare a schedule of product costs for the Mol-Tech products and evaluate each of the **independent** situations described below:

a. Should Mol-Tech-2 be sold at split-off for $3.20 per gallon?
b. Should the company continue to produce and sell Mol-Tech-2 if the selling price declines to $3 per gallon?

Ex. 21-6
Analyzing Standard
Cost Joint and
By-Product Data

Haverly Company makes two chemical solvents used in the production of cleaning compounds. The products are manufactured in a joint production process which also yields a by-product. The standard costs of the two joint products are:

| | Standards per Barrel | |
	Solvene	Solvone
Direct materials	$18.00	$22.00
Direct labor	14.00	16.00
Manufacturing overhead	10.00	12.00
Totals	$42.00	$50.00

The by-product sells for $2 per pound. On the average, 3 pounds of by-product are produced per barrel of main product. Joint costs are 60 percent of the total main-product costs. The physical units method is used to allocate joint costs. The two joint products are priced at 40 percent above standard product cost. In a typical month the company produces 4,000 barrels of Solvene and 6,000 barrels of Solvone.

REQUIRED   a. Compute the expected amount of by-product revenue for the year.
b. If Haverly treated by-product proceeds as a reduction in product cost, by what percentage would the costs of the main products decline?
c. Compute the amount of joint cost allocated to each product.
d. Compute the total sales revenue from the joint products in a typical month.

Ex. 21-7
Joint Product
Decision Analysis

The Maplewood Products Company manufactures three wood treatment products in a joint production process. Each product has certain finish and preservative properties that make it unique and useful for certain wood treatment requirements. Cost, production, and price data are presented below for production of the three products during the month.

Product	Quantity Produced	Sales Price	Cost after Split-Off
FP-Z	1,000	$48	$ 8,000
FP-Y	3,000	14	30,000
FP-X	6,000	10	12,000

Total joint product costs for the month were $62,500. Product cost data prepared by the accounting department are presented below.

Product	Joint Costs	Costs after Split-Off	Total Product Cost
FP-Z	$6.25	$ 8.00	$14.25
FP-Y	6.25	10.00	16.25
FP-X	6.25	2.00	8.25

The cost after split-off of any joint product can be eliminated entirely if Maplewood management decides not to process a product beyond the split-off point.

REQUIRED

Analyze each of the **independent** situations described below:

a. Several managers are very surprised that product FP-Y sells for $2.25 less than it costs to manufacture. Should Maplewood continue to produce and sell the product?

b. If product FP-Y can be sold at the split-off point for $6 per unit, should it be sold at split-off? Show computations.

c. Severe market pressure from a new competitor drives the price of product FP-Y down to $9 per unit. The product can be sold at split-off for $3 per unit. What production and sales policy should the company follow with this new situation?

Ex. 21-8
Joint Product
Decision Analysis

Nevada Synthetics, Inc., manufactures an extensive line of agricultural chemicals. The company has particularly extensive offerings of fertilizers and herbicides. As a general rule, all products are expected to provide a minimum gross margin of 40 percent on sales to be acceptable to the company. Growing competition and a weak agricultural economy over the last several years have caused management to reevaluate some of the company's current products.

Many of the company's products are manufactured in joint production processes. Although there is some variation between product groups, management believes that, on the average, 60 percent of any cost after split-off can be eliminated if a product is no longer processed beyond the split-off point. Also, 80 percent of a product group's manufacturing costs can be eliminated if an entire product group is eliminated.

You have been asked to evaluate the company's Green-Ban herbicide product group. There are three products in the group, and a typical production run yields the following quantities and costs.

Product	Quantity	Joint Cost	Cost after Split-Off	Total Cost	Selling Price
Ban-tron	5,000 tons	$50/ton	$10/ton	$ 60/ton	$ 75/ton
Ban-trap	4,000	50	30	80	90
Ban-plus	1,000	50	60	110	160

REQUIRED   Evaluate each of the **independent** situations presented below:

   a. At the current costs and prices, does the product group satisfy the company's minimum gross margin requirements?
   b. Ban-plus can be sold at split-off for $100 a ton. Should it be sold at split-off or processed further?
   c. What should the company's decision be if competition forces a reduction in the price of Ban-trap to $75 per ton?
   d. What impact would an across-the-board price reduction of 20 percent for all products have on the company's production decision?

Ex. 21-9
By-Products
Recorded as
Miscellaneous
Income

Zolfine Company produces a by-product called Zenfer along with its production of its main petroleum products. Last month the company manufactured 1,000 barrels of Zenfer. The by-product sells for $12 per barrel. Zenfer requires some additional processing costs after it separates from the production of the main products. Additional processing costs for the month were $3,200 of materials, $1,100 of direct labor, and $1,500 of applied overhead. All units produced are sold during the month.

REQUIRED   Record **all** necessary journal entries associated with the production and sale of the by-product, from the point it separates from the production of the main products.

Ex. 21-10
By-Products
Recorded at Net
Realizable Value

SMZ Company makes resins for commercial customers. One production process yields a by-product called EP-404. This by-product sells for $3.00 per gallon and typically requires $1.20 per gallon processing cost after the by-product separates from the production of the main product. Additional processing costs are 50 percent for direct materials, 30 percent for direct labor, and 20 percent for applied overhead. During the past week, 4,000 gallons of EP-404 were manufactured. The company uses the net realizable value method to account for by-product costs.

REQUIRED   Make **all** necessary journal entries associated with the week's production and sale of EP-404.

PROBLEMS

P. 21-1
Joint Product
Costing

Clorotine Chemicals, Inc., makes three distillate chemicals in a joint production process. The company just completed a 10,000-gallon batch of the products that consisted of 1,000 gallons of Clor-O-Rite, 3,000 gallons of Clor-O-Tine, and 6,000 gallons of Clor-O-Foam. The per gallon selling prices of the products are $15, $10, and $6 respectively. The joint products pass through three process centers before they reach the split-off point. Joint costs were $18,000 of direct materials, $7,000 of direct labor, and $10,000 of applied manufacturing overhead. Costs after split-off were $4,300, $5,400, and $12,000 respectively for the three products.

REQUIRED   Prepare a schedule of product costs using the following joint cost allocation methods:

a.   Physical units.
b.   Sales value.
c.   Gross profit.
d.   Estimated value at the point of split-off.

P. 21-2   On July 1, Jacobs Company began production of plant food products which are
Alternative Joint   manufactured in a joint production process. During July, the company produced
Product Costing   150,000 gallons of Fast-Grow, 90,000 gallons of Speed-Grow, and 60,000 gallons of
Methods   Grow-Plus. The three products have various soil and plant nutrients that are designed
to meet various plant and soil requirements. On July 31, the company had ending
inventories of 20,000 gallons of Fast-Grow, 15,000 gallons of Speed-Grow, and
10,000 gallons of Grow-Plus. The products sold for $1.40 a gallon, $3.00 a gallon, and
$3.00 a quart respectively. Fast-Grow is sold at the split-off point, Speed-Grow
required $1.00 per gallon in additional processing costs, and Grow-Plus required
$2.50 per gallon in costs after split-off to complete. Joint cost for July production was
$480,000.

REQUIRED   Prepare a detailed schedule of product costs for the products using:

a.   The physical units method of joint cost allocation.
b.   The gross profit method of joint cost allocation.
c.   The sales value method of joint cost allocation.
d.   Using your product cost data from parts a, b, and c, compute the cost of
     ending inventory with each of the joint costing methods used above.
e.   Using your product cost data from parts a, b, and c, compute the total gross
     margin in July provided by Grow-Plus with each of the joint cost allocation
     methods above.

P. 21-3   Fenton Company makes industrial paints in a joint production process. The three
Analyzing Joint   paints have varying degrees of protection against corrosion, heat stress, and other
Product Cost Data   metal stress. The most protective paint is product A, which sells for $48 per 5-gallon
can. The other two paints sell for much less. Production, cost, and sales data are
presented below.

Product	Quantity Produced	Quantity Sold	Selling Price	Cost after Split-Off
A	1,000	800	$48	$ 8,000
B	3,000	2,900	14	30,000
C	6,000	5,600	10	12,000

Joint cost = $70,000

REQUIRED   a.   Compute the total cost and unit cost for joint cost, cost after split-off, and total
     product cost for each of the three products using the sales value method to
     allocate joint costs.
b.   Compute the total cost and unit cost for joint cost, cost after split-off, and total
     product cost for each of the three products using the gross profit method to
     allocate joint costs. Assume all costs after split-off can be eliminated.

For parts c and d assume **independent** situations.

c.   Should product B be sold at the point of split-off for $3 per unit? Support your
     answer with computations.

d. A sharp decline in the demand for product C causes the price to decline to $4.50 per unit. What should the company's production and sales policy be?

e. Compute the cost of the ending inventory using the sales value method of joint cost allocation. Assume no beginning inventory.

P. 21-4
Joint Product
Costing

The Alpena Baking Company produces cakes, breads, and other baked goods which it sells through grocery stores in the region. The company makes a series of whole-grain breads that all start with the same base. After two processing centers, the output separates into three types of whole wheat bread products. The dough sent out of Process Center 2 is measured in pounds and it takes 1.25 pounds of dough per loaf of bread. During June, 120,000 pounds of dough are transferred out of Process Center 2. Of this output 50 percent is used to make whole wheat bread, 30 percent is used for honey wheat bread, and 20 percent is used for enriched wheat bread. Production costs were:

Joint costs:	
Direct materials	$24,000
Direct labor	15,000
Manufacturing overhead	18,600

Costs after split-off:

	Whole Wheat	Honey Wheat	Enriched Wheat
Direct material	$6,000	$5,500	$5,000
Direct labor	1,400	2,500	1,500
Manufacturing overhead	2,200	3,520	2,140

The three products sell for $1.25, $1.40, and $1.50 respectively.

REQUIRED

a. Compute the cost of each product using the physical units method of joint cost allocation.

b. Compute the cost of each product using the gross profit method of joint cost allocation.

c. Compute the gross margin of each product for each of the joint cost allocation methods used in parts a and b.

P. 21-5
Joint Cost
Allocation: Five
Alternatives

Rosecliff Company manufactures a complete line of cosmetics for men and women. Many of their products are manufactured in joint production processes. One joint product group is composed of cleansing creams and facial creams. The production quantity and cost data for May are presented below along with price data. The products are identified by the company's product code.

Product	Quantity Produced	Unit Selling Price	Cost after Split-Off	Per Unit Sales Value at Split-Off
HK-20	50,000 units	$ 4.00/unit	$55,000	$1.50
HK-30	30,000	5.00	75,000	2.00
HK-40	15,000	9.00	—	9.00
HK-50	5,000	23.00	20,000	6.00

Joint cost = $300,000

All of the products except HK-40 are processed beyond the split-off point. The last column in the chart above shows the market price of each product if it were sold at the split-off point.

REQUIRED   Prepare a schedule of product costs using the following joint cost allocation methods:

   a.   Physical units.
   b.   Sales value.
   c.   Gross profit.
   d.   Net realizable value at split-off.
   e.   Estimated value at the point of split-off.

P. 21-6
Joint Product
Decision with
Target Gross
Margin

Warren Agricultural Products, Inc., manufactures fertilizer and soil treatment products. The company has a policy of requiring a minimum gross margin of 25 percent on all of the joint product groups that it makes. It uses the constant gross margin percentage method as the basis for allocating joint costs. The company makes a series of nitrogen fertilizers in a joint production process. The three products resulting from the production vary somewhat in their nitrogen content and the amount of other soil nutrients. NT10-10 sells for $220 per ton, NT10-20 sells for $260 per ton, and NT10-40 sells for $360 per ton. In a production batch just completed the output was 500 tons, 400 tons, and 100 tons respectively for the three products. Below are product cost data prepared by the accounting department:

Product	Joint Costs		Costs after Split-Off		Total Product Cost	
	Total	Per Unit	Total	Per Unit	Total	Per Unit
NT10-10	$ 70,000	$140.00	$ 7,000	$ 14.00	$ 77,000	$154.00
NT10-20	64,800	162.00	8,000	20.00	72,800	182.00
NT10-40	10,200	102.00	15,000	150.00	25,200	252.00
Totals	$145,000		$30,000		$175,000	

REQUIRED   Analyze each of the following **independent** situations:

   a.   A decline in demand for NT10-10 necessitated a reduction in its price to $200 per ton. What impact does this have on the company's production and sales of nitrogen fertilizers?
   b.   Answer part *a* again assuming the price of NT10-10 falls to $185 per ton.

P. 21-7
Joint Product
Decision Analysis
with Several
Alternatives

Below are product cost data for the production of three distilled chemicals used for industrial applications. The product costs are based on the sales value joint allocation method. TM-J sells for $8 per unit, TM-K for $10 per unit, and TM-X for $24 per unit. Unless otherwise indicated, the costs after split-off can be eliminated if a product is eliminated.

Product	Joint Costs		Costs after Split-Off		Total Product Cost	
	Total	Per Unit	Total	Per Unit	Total	Per Unit
TM-J	$28,000	$ 4.00	$ 7,000	$1.00	$35,000	$ 5.00
TM-K	10,000	5.00	15,000	7.50	25,000	12.50
TM-X	12,000	12.00	8,000	8.00	20,000	20.00
Totals	$50,000		$30,000		$80,000	

Analyze each of the **independent** situations described below:

a. Should the company continue to produce and sell TM-K?

b. New competitor products necessitate the reduction of the price of TM-X to $11 per unit. Should the company continue to produce and sell the product?

c. TM-K can be sold at split-off for $4.00 a unit. Should the company sell at split-off or process further?

d. It appears that to remain competitive, it will be necessary to reduce the price of TM-J from $8 to $5 per unit. What impact should this have on the company's production and sales decisions?

P. 21-8
Alternative
Accounting
Treatment of
By-Products

Tineley Chemicals, Inc. produces Solvoe and Solvine in a joint production process. In addition to these two joint products, a by-product, Solve-X, separates from the main production process shortly before the joint product split-off point. The last batch of this product group yielded 4,000 gallons of Solvoe, 6,000 gallons of Solvine, and 2,000 pounds of Solve-X. The selling price is $6.00 per gallon for Solvoe and $9.00 per gallon for Solvine. The price of the by-product is $2.50 per pound. Joint production costs were direct materials $30,000, direct labor $15,000, and manufacturing overhead $10,000. Solvoe is sold at split-off, and Solvine required $9,000 in additional processing costs after the split-off point. The by-product requires no additional processing costs after separating from the main products, and there is a 10 percent marketing and distribution cost for the by-product. Tineley Chemicals uses the physical units method of accounting for joint costs.

a. Record all necessary journal entries associated with the transfer of by-products to inventory and the sale of the by-products assuming the net realizable value method is used.

b. Record the same events as in part *a* using the miscellaneous income method of accounting for by-products.

c. Compute the unit costs of Solvoe and Solvine using the by-product accounting method from part *a*.

d. Compute the unit costs of Solvoe and Solvine using the by-product accounting method from part *b*.

P. 21-9 (CMA)
Single Product
Decision Analysis

Gossett Chemical Company uses comprehensive annual profit planning procedures to evaluate pricing policies, to finalize production decisions, and to estimate unit costs for its various products. One particular product group involves two joint products and two by-products. This product group is separately analyzed each year to establish appropriate production and marketing policies.

The two joint products—ALCHEM-X and CHEM-P—emerge at the end of processing in department 20. Both chemicals can be sold at this split-off point—ALCHEM-X for $2.50 per unit, and CHEM-P for $3.00 per unit. By-product BY-D20 also emerges at the split-off point in department 20 and is salable without further processing for $.50 per unit. Unit costs of preparing this by-product for market are $.03 for freight and $.12 for packaging.

CHEM-P is sold without further processing, but ALCHEM-X is transferred to department 22 for additional processing into a refined chemical labeled as ALCHEM-XF. No additional raw materials are added in department 22. ALCHEM-XF is sold for $5.00 per unit. By-product BY-D22 is created by the additional processing in department 22, and it can be sold for $.70 per unit. Unit marketing costs for BY-D22 are $.05 for freight and $.15 for packaging.

Gossett Chemical Company accounts for by-product production by crediting the net realizable value of by-products produced to production costs of the main products. The relative sales value method is used to allocate net joint production costs for inventory valuation purposes.

A portion of the 1986 profit plan established in September 1985 is presented below.

Shortly after this budget was compiled the company learned that a chemical which would compete with ALCHEM-XF was to be introduced. The marketing department estimated that this would require a permanent price reduction to $3.50 a unit for the ALCHEM-XF to be sold in present quantities. Gossett must now reevaluate the decision to process ALCHEM-X further.

The market for ALCHEM-X will not be affected by the introduction of this new chemical. Consequently, the quantities of ALCHEM-X that are usually processed into ALCHEM-XF can be sold at the regular price of $2.50 per unit. The costs for marketing ALCHEM-X are estimated to be $105,000. If the further processing is terminated, department 22 will be dismantled and all costs except equipment depreciation, $18,400; supervisory salaries, $21,200; and general overhead, $35,200; will be eliminated.

	Units of Production	
	CHEM-P	ALCHEM-XF
Estimated sales	400,000	210,000
Planned inventory change	−8,000	−6,000
Required production	392,000	204,000
Minimum production based upon joint output ratio	392,000	210,000
By-product output:		
BY-D20		90,000
BY-D22		60,000

	Costs	
Budgeted Production Costs	Department 20	Department 22
Raw material	$160,000	—
Costs transferred from 20[a]	—	$225,000
Hourly direct labor	170,000	120,000
Variable overhead	180,000	140,800
Fixed overhead	247,500	188,000
Total budgeted production costs	$757,500	$673,800

Budgeted Marketing Costs	CHEM-P	ALCHEM-XF
	$196,000	$105,000

[a] The cost transferred to department 22 is calculated as follows:

Sales value of output:		
ALCHEM-X (210,000 × $2.50)	$ 525,000	31%
CHEM-P (392,000 × $3.00)	1,176,000	69
	$1,701,000	100%
Department 20 costs	$ 757,500	
Less by-product (90,000 × $0.35)	31,500	
Net costs	$ 726,000	
ALCHEM-X	31%	$ 225,000, or $1.07 per unit
CHEM-P	69	501,000, or $1.28 per unit
Allocated net costs	100%	$ 726,000

REQUIRED

a. Should Gossett sell ALCHEM-X at the split-off point or continue to process it further in department 22? Prepare a schedule of relevant costs and revenues to support your answer.

b. During discussions of the possible dropping of ALCHEM-XF one person noted that the manufacturing margin for ALCHEM-X would be 57.2 percent [($2.50−$1.07)/$2.50] and 57.3 percent for CHEM-P. The normal markup for products sold in the market with ALCHEM-X is 72 percent. For the CHEM-P portion of the line the markup is 47 percent. He argues that the company's unit costs must be incorrect because the margins differ from the typical rates. Briefly explain why Gossett's rates for the two products are almost identical when "normal" rates are not.

P. 21-10 (AICPA)
Joint Product
Costing

In its three departments Amaco Chemical Company manufactures several products:

- In department 1 the raw materials amanic acid and bonyl hydroxide are used to produce Amanyl, Bonanyl, and Am-Salt. Amanyl is sold to others who use it as a raw material in the manufacture of stimulants. Bonanyl is not salable without further processing. Although Am-Salt is a commercial product for which there is a ready market, Amaco does not sell this product, preferring to submit it to further processing.

- In department 2 Bonanyl is processed into the marketable product, Bonanyl-X. The relationship between Bonanyl used and Bonanyl-X produced has remained constant for several months.

- In department 3 Am-Salt and the raw material colb are used to produce Colbanyl, a liquid propellant that is in great demand. As an inevitable part of this process, Demanyl is also produced. Demanyl was discarded as scrap until discovery of its usefulness as a catalyst in the manufacture of glue; for 2 years Amaco has been able to sell all of its production of Demanyl.

In its financial statements Amaco states inventory at the lower of cost (on the first in, first out basis) or market. Unit costs of the items most recently produced must therefore be computed. Costs allocated to Demanyl are computed so that after allowing for packaging and selling costs of $.04 per pound no profit or loss will be recognized on sales of this product.

Certain data for October 1985 follow:

Raw materials:	Pounds Used	Total Cost
Amanic acid	6,300	$5,670
Bonyl hydroxide	9,100	6,370
Colb	5,600	2,240

Conversion costs (labor and overhead)	Total Cost
Department 1	$33,600
Department 2	3,306
Department 3	22,400

| | Pounds Produced | Inventories, Pounds | | Sales Price per Pound |
Products		September 30	October 31	
Amanyl	3,600			$ 6.65
Bonanyl	2,800	210	110	
Am-Salt	7,600	400	600	6.30
Bonanyl-X	2,755			4.20
Colbanyl	1,400			43.00
Demanyl	9,800			.54

REQUIRED   Prepare for October 1985 the schedules listed below. Supporting computations should be prepared in good form. Round answers to the nearest cent.

  a. Cost per pound of Amanyl, Bonanyl, and Am-Salt produced—relative sales value method.
  b. Cost per pound of Amanyl, Bonanyl, and Am-Salt produced—physical units method.
  c. Cost per pound of Colbanyl produced. Assume that the cost per pound of Am-Salt produced was $3.40 in September 1985 and $3.50 in October 1985.

CASES

Case 21-1
Joint Product
Decision Analysis

Laverty Paint Company manufactures two types of paint in a joint production process. In a typical production run of the paints, 10,000 gallons are produced, 6,000 gallons of Hard-Gloss and 4,000 gallons of Top-Gloss. Joint costs are $60,000 and costs after split-off are $15,000 for Hard-Gloss and $12,000 for Top-Gloss. The products sell for $9.00 and $15.00 respectively.

The company has a policy of only producing products that provide a minimum gross margin on sales of 30 percent. This policy is based on the fact that the company experiences an average cost to market and distribute its products of 20 percent of selling price. About 3/4 of this cost varies with sales. Administrative costs are mostly fixed, but a cost analysis indicates that variable administrative costs average 10 percent of sales.

The company uses the physical units method of joint cost allocation to determine product costs. Recently, the marketing manager came to you, and asked that at the next executive committee meeting you suggest that the company no longer sell Hard-Gloss because the product has only a $.50 gross margin, which is only 5.6 percent of selling price ($.50/$9.00). The marketing manager notes that the marketing and distribution costs alone are 20 percent of selling price, or $1.80 per unit ($9.00 × .20). Any costs after split-off can be eliminated in total if a product is discontinued. Also, the joint costs of any product group can be eliminated if the entire product group is dropped.

REQUIRED   Prepare a complete and detailed analysis of the issues presented by the marketing manager. Determine if you should support the marketing manager's position. Explain all relevant costing concepts necessary to understanding the situation.

CHAPTER 22

Standard Costs Extended: Mix and Yield Variances

The introduction to standard costs in Chapter 8 provides a foundation on the nature and operation of standard cost accounting systems and activities. You learned how standard costs are used in strategic planning, control, and performance measurement. In this chapter, we extend standard costing concepts to production situations not discussed in earlier chapters. We apply standard cost measures to various combinations of production inputs and to some nonmanufacturing activities.

STANDARD COST PERFORMANCE REPORTING

Manufacturing activities are more complex than most of those illustrated in Chapter 8. The more complex the manufacturing process, the more difficult it is to measure product costs. Before we proceed to complex standard costing situations we first briefly review variance reporting with an example that emphasizes the relationships between production inputs and outputs. Then we use this same example to present some new standard costing concepts.

Standard Cost Illustration

Broderick Chemical Company makes industrial solvents and cleaning compounds. One of its products is Hexolene, a grease cutter used to clean machinery, floors, and other surfaces. Four raw materials and three types of labor are used to manufacture Hexolene in batches. The costs are accounted for using a standard cost system. Standards for a typical production run of 1,000 barrels of Hexolene are shown in Figure 22-1 on page 764.

Standard Costs of an Output Unit

The standard cost of a barrel of output is computed by dividing the total standard cost for the entire batch by the expected output. The computations for materials costs are as follows:

Direct Material	Quantity			Input Price	Cost per Barrel
Acetate	10,000 gal/1,000 bbl	= 10 gal/bbl		$2.25/gal	$22.50
Acetone	15,000	/1,000	= 15	1.25	18.75
Ketones	12,000	/1,000	= 12	1.00	12.00
Petroleum distillates	23,000	/1,000	= 23	.75	17.25
Total					$70.50

Figure 22-1. This schedule presents the standard quantities and standard unit costs for the direct materials and direct labor used to make an industrial cleaning fluid. The input data for both labor and materials are expressed as input quantity per 1,000-barrel batch of product.

Broderick Chemical Company
Standard Prime Costs For Hexolene

Materials:

Material	Standard Quantity 1,000- Barrel Batch	Standard Cost per Gallon	Amount
Acetate	10,000 gallons	$2.25	$22,500
Acetone	15,000	1.25	18,750
Ketones	12,000	1.00	12,000
Petroleum distillates	23,000	.75	17,250
Totals	60,000		$70,500

Labor:

Labor Type	Standard Labor Quantity	Standard Labor Rate	Amount
General	600 hours	$ 5.00/hr	$3,000
Semiskilled	350	7.00	2,450
Skilled	250	10.00	2,500
Totals	1,200		$7,950

In this example, direct material inputs are expressed in terms of gallons and outputs are expressed in barrels. Often inputs and outputs are expressed in different units and it is therefore essential to define the inputs in terms of output units. For example, 10,000 gallons of acetate are required per 1,000 barrels of Hexolene output. The relationship between the input — acetate — and the output — 1 barrel of Hexolene — is 10 gallons of input per barrel of output. This mapping of inputs to outputs is essential in measuring material quantity variances and labor efficiency variances and the new variances introduced later in this chapter.

All resource inputs should be defined in terms of output units

The standard cost of direct labor is also defined in terms of output units — that is, labor cost per barrel of output. To measure this cost, the total standard labor cost for the batch of 1,000 barrels is divided by the expected output of 1,000 barrels.

Direct Labor	Hours		Labor Rate	Cost per Barrel
General	600 hr/1,000 bbl = .60 hr/bbl		$ 5	$3.00
Semiskilled	350 /1,000 = .35		7	2.45
Skilled	250 /1,000 = .25		10	2.50
Total				$7.95

The total standard prime cost of Hexolene is $78.45 per barrel ($70.50 for materials and $7.95 for labor). The company has a policy of pricing its industrial products at 200 percent of prime cost. Therefore, the selling price of Hexolene is $156.90 per barrel ($78.45 × 2.00).

Converting all of the components of standard cost data to a common unit of measure, such as 1 barrel of output, makes it easier to analyze how changes in input costs affect output costs. For example, what is the impact on product price of a 20 percent increase in the cost of skilled labor?

The current cost of skilled labor is $10 per hour. A 20 percent increase, or $2 per hour, yields a rate of $12 per hour. One barrel of output requires .25 hour of skilled labor; therefore the $2 per hour increase in the labor rate increases product cost by $.50 per barrel. This means that the selling price of the product will increase by $1 per barrel. Consequently, a 20 percent increase in skilled labor cost increases the product price only .6 percent ($1.00/$156.90) above the old price. In this case, a relatively large increase in the cost of one resource creates a small increase in the price of the product. This analysis is made simple by using standard cost data expressed in a common unit of measure.

Sometimes a significant change in the cost of a production resource has very little effect on the cost of the product

Variance Reports

As you saw in Chapter 8, standard costs are the basis for the measurement and reporting of variances. To analyze variances, we must measure the differences between actual costs and standard costs. How well managers interpret variances and their causes depends a great deal on the content and the amount of detail in the variance reports.

To illustrate standard cost variance reports for the Broderick Chemical Company, we need the data in Figure 22-2, which presents actual materials, labor, and cost data for the production of 1,100 barrels of Hexolene.

Figure 22-2. This schedule shows the actual quantities of materials and labor used to make 1,100 barrels of the product. Also shown are the unit costs paid for each of the material resources used in production.

Broderick Chemical Company
Actual Prime Costs for Hexolene

Materials:

Material	Actual Quantity Used This Batch	Actual Cost per Gallon	Amount
Acetate	11,500 gallons	$2.20	$25,300
Acetone	16,200	1.35	21,870
Ketones	14,200	1.15	16,330
Petroleum distillates	23,500	.70	16,450
Totals	65,400		$79,950

Labor:

Labor Type	Actual Labor Quantity	Actual Amount
General	620 hours	$3,255
Semiskilled	360	2,466
Skilled	300	2,895
Totals	1,280	$8,616

Amount produced: 1,100 barrels

Materials Variances. A materials variance can be separated into a price variance, caused by paying more or less than the standard price for a unit of material, and a quantity variance, caused by using more or less than the standard quantity of material per unit of output. With multiple inputs, price and quantity variances are computed for each of the raw materials.

The **material price variance** is the difference between the standard cost per unit and the actual cost per unit of the raw material times the actual quantity purchased. The **material quantity variance** is the difference between the standard quantity and the actual quantity times the standard cost of the resource.

Material price variance and material quantity variance defined

Figure 22-3. With multiple material inputs, price variances and quantity variances are computed the same as with a single raw material but a separate computation is made for each material.

Broderick Chemical Company
Materials Variance Analysis Report
For Hexolene

Material Price Variance:

Price variance	Standard cost per gallon − Actual cost per gallon × Actual quantity	
Acetate	($2.25 − $2.20) × 11,500 gal	= $ 575 F
Acetone	($1.25 − $1.35) × 16,200 gal	= 1,620 U
Ketones	($1.00 − $1.15) × 14,200 gal	= 2,130 U
Petroleum distillates	($ .75 − $ .70) × 23,500 gal	= 1,175 F

Total material price variance $2,000 U

Material Quantity Variance:

Quantity variance	(Standard quantity − Actual quantity) × Standard cost	
Acetate	(11,000 − 11,500) × $2.25	= $1,125 U
Acetone	(16,500 − 16,200) × $1.25	= 375 F
Ketones	(13,200 − 14,200) × $1.00	= 1,000 U
Petroleum distillates	(25,300 − 23,500) × $ .75	= 1,350 F

Total material quantity variance   400 U

Total materials variance $2,400 U

The material price variance is shown in Figure 22-3. The standard cost per unit of output for each material is obtained from Figure 22-1 and the actual cost per unit of output for each material is found in Figure 22-2. The per unit difference between standard and actual cost is multiplied by the actual amount of material. Actual quantities are found in Figure 22-2.

The material quantity variance shown in Figure 22-3 is calculated by multiplying the standard price per unit of material times the difference between the standard and actual quantity of material. The total actual quantity of each material is found in Figure 22-2. The total standard quantity, however, must be computed by multiplying the standard quantity of material input per unit of output times the quantity of output actually produced. With production of 1,100 barrels, as reported at the bottom of Figure 22-2, the total standard quantity of each of the raw materials is computed as follows:

Material	Input Quantity per Unit of Output	Production Output	Standard Quantity
Acetate	10 gal/bbl	1,100 bbl	11,000 gal
Acetone	15	1,100	16,500
Ketones	12	1,100	13,200
Petroleum distillates	23	1,100	25,300

The standard quantity is sometimes called the **standard quantity allowed** or the **standard quantity earned.** The latter term is more commonly used in connection with the standard quantity of labor.

You can see that the data used in computing the variances reported in Figure 22-3 all come from Figures 22-1 and 22-2. The top part of Figure 22-3 shows the material price variance for each raw material and the net price variance for all of the materials combined. The lower portion of the figure reports the material quantity variances for each of the raw materials and the net variance for the raw materials combined. The final number at the bottom of the report is the net unfavorable materials variance of $2,400 made up of all the price and quantity variances for all of the raw materials.

Labor Variances.   Labor variances are calculated in much the same way as materials variances. The labor rate variance is similar to the material price variance, and the labor efficiency variance is similar to the material quantity variance. In measuring labor performance, most companies identify several labor classifications used to manufacture products. In our example, there are three classifications of labor — skilled, semiskilled, and general — although other labor classifications are possible. For example, a company may have welders, machine operators, maintenance labor, painters, assembly workers, and unskilled laborers. Whatever the classifications, standard cost variances are used to measure the difference between their standard costs and actual costs and the difference between their standard quantities and actual quantities. The more detail provided by the labor classifications, the more detail possible in the standard cost performance report.

The labor rate variance measures the effect on labor cost of paying more or less than the standard rate for labor

The **labor rate variance** is the difference between the standard and actual cost of labor times the actual hours worked. When we say "cost of labor," we are referring to the labor rate. The standard cost, or more precisely the standard rate, is presented in Figure 22-1 and the actual total labor cost data are in Figure 22-2. Unlike the materials cost data, the unit cost of each type of labor is not shown because total labor cost is more meaningful for reporting labor costs. Reporting total labor cost is common because different employees in any particular labor classification may earn different wage rates. Seniority, different jobs within a labor classification, and other factors cause wage differences within a labor classification. Costs for each labor classification are accumulated for the period and the total is reported. Typically the standard cost for a type of labor is the average labor cost for that labor classification. The labor rate variance can be computed using either the total actual labor cost or the average hourly rate of the actual labor cost. To calculate the actual labor rates for the production of 1,100 barrels, we divide the actual labor cost from Figure 22-2 by the actual number of direct labor hours worked given in Figure 22-2:

$$\text{General labor rate} = \$3{,}255/620 \text{ hr} = \$5.25 \text{ per hour}$$
$$\text{Semiskilled labor rate} = 2{,}466/360 = 6.85$$
$$\text{Skilled labor rate} = 2{,}895/300 = 9.65$$

To find the direct labor rate variance, we multiply the actual number of direct labor hours times the difference between the standard labor rate and the actual labor rate. The results are reported in the top half of Figure 22-4.

Figure 22-4.   A labor rate variance and a labor efficiency variance are computed for each of the three classifications of labor. These are then combined to find the total labor rate and labor efficiency variance.

Broderick Chemical Company
Labor Variance Analysis Report
For Hexolene

Labor Rate Variance:

Rate variance	$\dfrac{\text{Standard rate}}{\text{per hour}} - \dfrac{\text{Actual rate}}{\text{per hour}} \times \text{Actual hours}$	
General	($5.00 − $5.25) × 620 hr	= $155 U
Semiskilled	($7.00 − $6.85) × 360 hr	= 54 F
Skilled	($10.00 − $9.65) × 300 hr	= 105 F
Total labor rate variance		$ 4 F

Labor Efficiency Variance:

Efficiency variance	(Standard hours − Actual hours) × Standard rate	
General	(660 hr − 620 hr) × $5/hr	= $200 F
Semiskilled	(385 hr − 360 hr) × $7/hr	= 175 F
Skilled	(275 hr − 300 hr) × $10/hr	= 250 U
Total labor rate efficiency variance		125 F
Total labor variance		$129 F

An alternative approach to calculating the labor rate variance is merely to use the total labor cost data without computing the actual cost per direct labor hour. The computation for general labor is:

$$\text{Labor rate variance} = (\text{Standard rate} \times \text{Actual hours}) - \text{Actual labor cost}$$
$$= (\$5.00 \times 620 \text{ hours}) - \$3{,}255$$
$$= \$3{,}100 - \$3{,}255$$
$$= \$155 \text{ U}$$

The labor efficiency variance is the result of using more or less than the standard number of labor hours to produce the product

As expected, the **labor rate variance** is identical regardless of the computational method used.

To calculate the **labor efficiency variance**, we first have to calculate the standard labor hours that should have been used given the actual quantity produced. Standard hours can be computed only after the production quantity is known. For each labor classification, the standard labor hours per unit of output are multiplied by the amount of output. The computations for the Broderick example are:

General labor   = .60 hour per barrel × 1,100 barrels = 660 hours
Semiskilled labor = .35 hour per barrel × 1,100 barrels = 385 hours
Skilled labor   = .25 hour per barrel × 1,100 barrels = 275 hours

To calculate the labor efficiency variance, the difference between standard direct labor hours and actual direct labor hours is multiplied by the standard direct labor rate for each labor classification. The results are presented in the bottom half of Figure 22-4. The labor rate variances and the labor efficiency variances are combined into the net favorable labor variance of $129 shown at the bottom of the report.

Extending Variance Analysis

More detailed variance analysis may provide managers with useful planning and control information

The variance analysis process just discussed here and in Chapter 8 provides useful information on the performance of the organization. However, if multiple inputs are used in the production of products or services, additional information may be obtained by a further refinement of the variances. Managers can see the economic consequences of varying the combination of inputs in the production process. This refinement is accomplished by separating the material quantity variance and the labor efficiency variance into two parts, called mix and yield variances. The relationship of the mix variances and yield variances to the other variances is illustrated graphically in Figure 22-5.

MIX VARIANCES AND YIELD VARIANCES

Sometimes it is possible to vary the proportion, or mix, of inputs in the production of a product or service without changing the nature or quality of

Figure 22-5. This diagram shows graphically the relationship between the material quantity variance and the material mix and yield variances. Likewise, the labor efficiency variance can be separated into a labor mix variance and a labor yield variance.

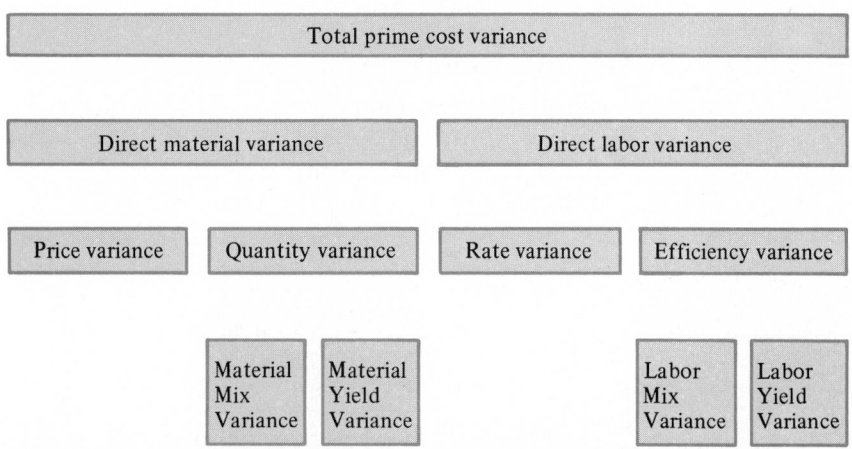

the product. For example, a home builder may be able to use less copper pipe and more plastic pipe in the construction of a house without impairing the reliability or expected life of the plumbing system. Similarly, the builder may use more apprentice carpenters and fewer journeymen carpenters in an effort to control labor costs. Each of these examples may result in mix or yield variances.

There are many reasons for changing the relative proportion of material or labor inputs. Some of them include shortages of a particular resource, attempts by managers to reduce production costs or meet production deadlines, human errors, and random errors. Whatever the reason for changing the relative proportion of inputs, managers often find it useful to measure and report the cost effects of such changes. Mix and yield variances provide the information.

A **mix variance** measures the amount of cost variance caused by using a different proportion of inputs than defined by the standards. For example, the standard proportion or standard mix of labor required to build a particular house is 3 journeymen carpenters and 5 apprentice carpenters. Changing the mix of labor to 2 journeymen carpenters and 6 apprentice carpenters reduces the number of higher-cost carpenters and increases the number of lower-cost carpenters used in the construction. This results in a labor mix variance for the project.

A **yield variance** measures the amount of cost variance caused by using more or fewer total inputs than standard. The use of fewer journeymen and more apprentice carpenters than standard may result in less efficient construction. This reduction in efficiency can be measured as a labor yield variance.

As Figure 22-5 shows, mix and yield variances are components of the material quantity variance and the labor efficiency variance. Therefore the sum of the material mix variance and the material yield variance equals the material quantity variance. Similarly, the sum of the labor mix variance and the labor yield variance equals the labor efficiency variance. It is possible to compute a mix variance and a yield variance for materials but not for labor or for labor but not for materials. Mix and yield variances are measured only when managers believe they provide useful information.

Causes of mix variances

The mix variance results from using a different proportion of inputs than defined by standards

Mix variances and yield variances can be computed for both materials and labor

Mix and Yield Variances for Materials

To illustrate the computation and use of mix and yield variances for materials, we continue with our example of the Broderick Chemical Company. Labor mix and yield variances are discussed later. The unit standard costs for materials are:

Material	Standard Quantity	Standard Input Cost	Standard Material Cost per Barrel
Acetate	10 gal/bbl	$2.25/gal	$22.50/bbl
Acetone	15	1.25	18.75
Ketones	12	1.00	12.00
Petroleum distillates	23	.75	17.25
Total	60		$70.50

The cost of $70.50 per barrel is the standard material cost per unit of output, which is 1 barrel of Hexolene in this example. The standard cost of each raw material is found in Figure 22-1. Each of the raw material inputs has a different standard cost. The **average** cost of a gallon of input, given the standard mix of materials, is $1.175 per gallon ($70.50/60 gallons). The average cost of inputs at the standard quantities and prices is called the **average standard cost** of material inputs. Using the standard costs and quantities it is possible to compute the material mix and yield variances.

The average cost of inputs at the standard mix is called the average standard cost of inputs

Material Mix Variance. The **material mix variance** is a measure of variance caused by using a different mix of material inputs than the standard proportion of materials. A change in the mix of production materials may result from material shortages, changes of input prices, human errors, random errors, or other causes. The objective of measuring a mix variance is to determine the economic consequences of changing the mix of material inputs. Typically, if the mix of inputs is different from standard, some difference can be expected in the final result. Mix and yield variances measure the consequences of such deviations.

We defined the **average standard cost** of material inputs as the average cost of material inputs given the mix of inputs at standard quantities. Any material whose standard cost is higher than the average standard cost is a **high-cost input.** Any material whose standard cost is lower than the average standard cost of material inputs is a **low-cost input.** The mix variance is favorable for a high-cost material input if less than the standard quantity of that material is used in making the product; the mix variance is unfavorable if more than the standard quantity of that material is used. The reverse is true for a low-cost material input: The mix variance is unfavorable if less than the standard quantity of a low-cost input is used; the mix variance is favorable if more than the standard quantity is used.

Identifying high-cost inputs and low-cost inputs

The material mix variance formula is as follows:

Material mix variance = (Standard quantity − Actual quantity) × (Standard cost of a specific material input − Average standard cost of all material inputs)

Calculating the Mix Variance. The material mix variances for the Broderick example are shown in the top half of Figure 22-6. The difference between standard quantity and actual quantity of each material in the mix variance is calculated the same way as the material quantity variance. The standard quantity of each material is merely the amount of material input that **should** be used given the actual amount of production output. For example, the standard quantity of petroleum distillates is 25,300 gallons (23 gallons per barrel times 1,100 barrels). The actual quantity used for each material is shown in Figure 22-2.

The difference between the standard and actual quantities is multiplied by the difference between the standard cost of each material and the average standard cost of all material inputs. We can determine whether a quantity variance is favorable or unfavorable merely by knowing if more or less than

Figure 22-6. The data in Figures 22-1 and 22-2 are used to analyze the material mix variance and the material yield variance. These two variances combined are equal to the material quantity variance shown in Figure 22-3.

Broderick Chemical Company
Material Mix and Yield Variance Analysis
For Hexolene

Mix Variance:

Acetate	$(11,000 - 11,500) \times (\$2.25 - \$1.175)$	= $ 537.50 U
Acetone	$(16,500 - 16,200) \times (\$1.25 - \$1.175)$	= 22.50 F
Ketones	$(13,200 - 14,200) \times (\$1.00 - \$1.175)$	= 175.00 F
Petroleum distillates	$(25,300 - 23,500) \times (\$ .75 - \$1.175)$	= 765.00 U
Total material mix variance:		1,105.00 U

Yield Variance:

65,400 gallons × $1.175/gal	= $76,845	
1,100 barrels × $70.50/bbl	= 77,550	
Total material yield variance		705.00 F
Material quantity variance		$ 400.00 U

the standard quantity is used. To determine if the mix variance is favorable or unfavorable, we must also know if the material is a high-cost or a low-cost material.

To illustrate, Broderick Chemical Company used 500 gallons more of acetate than standard to produce 1,100 barrels of Hexolene. Acetate has a standard cost per unit of $2.25 per gallon, which is nearly twice the average standard cost of material inputs of $1.175 per gallon. Using more than the standard quantity of a high-cost material input is an unfavorable change in the mix of material inputs and therefore produces an unfavorable variance. The amount of the mix variance is determined by two factors: the difference between the standard quantity and the actual quantity and the difference between the standard cost of the specific material input and the average standard cost of all material inputs.

How to determine whether a mix variance is favorable or unfavorable

The second material—acetone—is also a high-cost input because its standard cost is more than the average standard cost of material inputs. However, it is not as costly as acetate. The actual quantity of acetone used was 300 gallons less than standard. Using less than the standard quantity of a high-cost material input results in a favorable mix variance. The favorable mix variance for acetone is less than the unfavorable mix variance for acetate partly because the difference between the standard cost and the average standard cost of material inputs is smaller for acetone than for acetate.

If you use more than the standard quantity of a low-cost material input, the material mix variance is favorable

Ketones and petroleum distillates are both low-cost material inputs. The standard cost of each is less than the average standard cost of material inputs used in production. The mix variance analysis of low-cost material inputs is just the reverse of the analysis of high-cost material inputs. Using more than the standard quantity of low-cost material inputs is favorable; using less is unfavorable. At first the mix variance for low-cost material inputs may seem strange because it is just the reverse of the logic used in analyzing material quantity variances. However, the material mix variance is a component of the material quantity variance. Its function is to isolate and measure the effect of changes in the relative proportion of material used. The other component of the material quantity variance is the yield variance. It deals with the total amount of material used in making products.

The company used 1,000 more gallons of ketones than standard. Using more than the standard quantity of a low-cost material input is a favorable change in the production mix of materials. Therefore, the mix variance for this material is favorable. The $175 favorable mix variance is 1,000 gallons times the $.175 difference between the standard cost of ketones and the average standard cost of material inputs.

The company used 1,800 gallons less of petroleum distillates than the standard quantity for this material. The mix variance of $765 is unfavorable because less than the standard quantity of this low-cost material was used. In effect, we assume that if less of a low-cost material input was used, then more of a high-cost material input must be used to manufacture the same quantity of the product.

An algebraic solution to determining the direction of material mix variances

You may have noticed that if each mix variance computation is made in strict algebraic fashion, all positive outcomes are favorable (F) and all negative results are unfavorable (U) material mix variances. To illustrate:

$$(\text{Standard quantity} - \text{Actual cost}) \times (\text{Standard cost} - \text{Average standard cost})$$

$$\begin{aligned}
\text{Acetate} &= (11,000 - 11,500) \times (\$2.25 - \$1.175) \\
&= (-500) \times (\$1.075) \\
&= -\$537.50 = \$537.50 \text{ U}
\end{aligned}$$

$$\begin{aligned}
\text{Acetone} &= (16,500 - 16,200) \times (\$1.25 - \$1.175) \\
&= (300) \times (\$.075) \\
&= \$22.50 = \$22.50 \text{ F}
\end{aligned}$$

$$\begin{aligned}
\text{Ketones} &= (13,200 - 14,200) \times (\$1.00 - \$1.175) \\
&= (-1,000) \times (-\$.175) \\
&= \$175.00 = \$175.00 \text{ F}
\end{aligned}$$

$$\begin{aligned}
\text{Petroleum distillates} &= (25,300 - 23,500) \times (\$.75 - \$1.175) \\
&= (1,800) \times (-\$.425) \\
&= -\$765.00 = \$765.00 \text{ U}
\end{aligned}$$

This algebraic method of determining if the mix variance is favorable or unfavorable works only if the analysis is structured in the way shown here. If the standard quantities and costs are reversed, the wrong result occurs. Therefore, we recommend this approach only as a means of verifying the correctness of variance calculations.

Material Yield Variance. Yield can be described as the amount of output derived from a certain amount of input. The **material yield variance** is the difference between the expected and actual amount of yield from some actual amount of material inputs. For example, the Broderick Chemical Company expects to get 1 barrel of output from a 60-gallon mix of material inputs. The company used 65,400 gallons of material input as reported in Figure 22-2. Based on the expected yield of 1 barrel of Hexolene per 60 gallons of material, it is easy to determine if the company achieved a favorable yield.

The expected yield from the 65,400 gallons of materials is 1,090 barrels (65,400 gallons/60 gallons per barrel). Actual output was 1,100 barrels, so the company had a favorable yield variance—more output resulted from total material inputs than was expected. But what is the dollar amount of the yield variance? The yield variance can be computed in several ways, all based on standard costs and standard quantities. The method shown in Figure 22-6 is based on the standard cost and quantity of inputs per unit of output.

Yield variance = (Actual quantity of all material inputs × Average standard cost of all material inputs) − (Actual quantity of outputs produced × Standard material cost of output units)

If the standard material cost of the output produced is more than the average standard cost of the material put into production, then the material yield variance is favorable. In effect, more was obtained from the inputs than expected. The material yield variance is unfavorable if the output units at their standard material cost are less than the inputs at their average standard cost.

In the Broderick example, the material yield variance is favorable because the units produced at their standard material cost exceeded the material inputs at their average standard cost. Another way of computing the material yield variance is to compare the expected output of 1,090 barrels from the actual inputs with the actual output of 1,100 barrels. Actual output was 10 barrels more than expected. The standard material cost of a barrel of Hexolene is $70.50. Therefore, the yield variance is $705 favorable (+10 barrels × $70.50). The variance is favorable because more output was produced than expected given the quantity of actual inputs.

Notice that the yield variance does not deal with individual input costs. These are part of the mix variance analysis. By ignoring specific input costs, the yield variance isolates the effect on the quantity variance of the total material quantity used. This way the material mix and the material yield variances together comprise the material quantity variance.

Combining the $705 favorable material yield variance with the $1,105 unfavorable material mix variance provides a net unfavorable materials variance of $400—the material quantity variance computed earlier. The sum of the material mix variance and the material yield variance always equal the material quantity variance for any given set of data.

Understanding Materials Variances. The primary purpose of any variance analysis is to help managers understand the magnitude and causes of deviating from standards. The material price, material mix, and material yield variances help managers isolate the cost effects of decisions about materials purchases and the mix of materials. Managers are interested in determining the cause of the variances and their impact on input costs and output quantity. A change in the mix of materials may result from a shortage of a material or changes in the relative prices of materials, as well as human error, random errors, or other such causes. Whatever the causes, managers must evaluate the available data and determine the most appropriate action.

Mix and Yield Variances for Labor

In some situations, it is possible to modify the relative mix of labor inputs used in the production of a product or a service. For example, a plumbing company may vary the relative amount of apprentice and journeyman labor hours used in installing a septic tank system. Similarly, a manufacturing company may be able to vary the proportion of skilled and semiskilled labor used in production without affecting the quality of the product. Whenever the relative mix of labor can vary from the standard mix, it is possible to measure a labor mix variance and a labor yield variance just as we did for materials. The purpose of isolating labor mix and yield variances is the same as for materials — to provide managers with information about the effects of changing the mix of labor resources.

Mix variances and yield variances for labor are computed in much the same way as for materials

The computation and interpretation of mix and yield variances for labor are similar to those for materials. The first step in the process is to determine the standard costs and standard quantities of labor inputs and the actual number of units produced. The unit standard cost of labor is:

Labor	Hours	Labor Rate	Cost per Barrel
General	.60 hr/bbl	$ 5/hr	$3.00
Semiskilled	.35	7	2.45
Skilled	.25	10	2.50
Total	1.20		$7.95

The standard labor cost for a barrel of output is $7.95, and the standard quantity of labor is 1.20 hours per barrel. If the $7.95 of labor per barrel represents 1.20 hours of labor at the standard mix, then the average standard cost of 1 hour of labor must be $7.95/1.20 hours, or $6.625. The **average standard cost** of labor is measured at the standard mix of labor. Another way of visualizing it is to think of the $6.625 per hour as the weighted average cost of labor using the standard mix of labor. Another way of computing the average standard cost of labor is to use the labor cost and quantity standards shown in Figure 22-1. Dividing the total standard labor cost of $7,950 by the 1,200 total standard labor hours yields the same average standard labor cost of $6.625 per hour.

The labor mix variance and the labor yield variance are reported in Figure 22-7. The standard number of labor hours is determined by multiplying the standard labor hours per barrel times the 1,100 barrels produced. For example, the standard labor hours for general labor is 660 hours (.6 hr per barrel × 1,100 barrels). The standard labor hours for each classification of labor is identical to the standard labor hours used in computing the labor efficiency variances.

Figure 22-7. The labor mix variance and the labor yield variance are similar to the material mix and yield variances. The labor mix variance and the labor yield variance combine to equal the efficiency variance calculated in Figure 22-4.

Broderick Chemical Company
Labor Mix and Yield Variance Analysis
For Hexolene

Mix Variance

General	(660 hr − 620 hr) × ($5 − $6.625)	= $65.000 U	
Semiskilled	(385 hr − 360 hr) × ($7 − $6.625)	= 9.375 F	
Skilled	(275 hr − 300 hr) × ($10 − $6.625)	= 84.375 U	
Total labor rate variance			$140 U

Yield Variance

1,280 hours × $6.625/hr	= $8,480	
1,100 barrels × $7.95/bbl	= 8,745	
Total labor yield variance		265 F
Labor efficiency variance		$125 F

Labor Mix Variance. The **labor mix variance** for general labor is unfavorable because the company used less than the standard amount of low-cost labor. Low-cost labor is labor whose standard cost is lower than the average standard cost of labor. In this example, only general labor is low-cost labor. Semiskilled and skilled labor are both high-cost inputs because each has a standard cost higher than the average standard cost of the labor mix.

The labor mix variance for semiskilled labor is favorable because less than the standard amount of this high-cost labor resource was used.

The mix variance for skilled labor is unfavorable because the company used more than the standard number of hours of this high-cost labor resource.

As with materials, a strict algebraic solution for labor mix variance computations shows that all positive results are favorable mix variances and all negative results are unfavorable.

Labor Yield Variance. The **labor yield variance,** like the material yield variance, is a measure of the variance caused by producing more or fewer units of output than was expected, based on the cost and quantity standards. The labor yield variance is reported at the bottom of Figure 22-7.

The actual labor hours worked are multiplied by the average standard cost of labor. From this amount we subtract the actual amount of output multiplied by the standard labor cost of outputs. In this case, the output units produced at their standard cost are greater than all the labor inputs at their average standard cost. More output was produced than expected given the hours worked, so the variance is favorable.

Another way of computing the labor yield variance is to divide the total actual labor hours worked by the standard labor hours per unit of output, and determine if the actual output is greater than the expected output. In this case, 1.20 hours of labor are required per barrel of output. Therefore, the 1,280 total actual labor hours divided by 1.20 hr/bbl tells us that 1,066.66667 barrels of output should have been produced. Actual output was 1,100 barrels of Hexolene, or 33.33333 barrels more than expected given the number of labor hours worked. The standard labor cost of a barrel of output is $7.95. The labor yield variance is therefore $265 favorable ($7.95 × 33.33333 barrels).

Combining the labor mix variance of $140 U and the labor yield variance of $265 F, results in a net $125 favorable efficiency variance, as reported in Figure 22-4. Any set of labor data results in labor mix and yield variances that are equal in total to the labor efficiency variance. The labor mix variance is the efficiency variance component that isolates the effect of changing the proportion, or mix, of various labor resources. The labor yield variance is the efficiency variance component that isolates the effect of using more or less than the standard quantity of the combination of labor resources.

Interpreting Labor Variances.   In some situations, it is easier to interpret labor mix and yield variances than material mix and yield variances. For example, it may not be clear how a change in the mix of raw materials used in the production of some food products affects the nature or quality of the product. On the other hand, it is easier to visualize that the use of more skilled labor and less general labor should reduce the total number of labor hours worked and perhaps the total labor costs as well. Often an unfavorable labor mix variance results in a favorable labor yield variance because skilled labor is more efficient than unskilled labor. Similarly, a shift to lower-cost labor may result in a favorable labor mix variance but an unfavorable labor yield variance. Many factors may affect the mix of labor used in the production of goods or services. Shortages of certain types of labor, strikes, employee absenteeism, changes in production schedules, attempts to meet deadlines, and a variety of other reasons may cause the mix of labor resources to change from the standard mix.

CONTROL OF NONMANUFACTURING ACTIVITIES

Standard costs can be used in many nonmanufacturing situations

Standard costs are used primarily for planning and controlling manufacturing activities. It is the repetitive nature of manufacturing activities that makes standard costs so useful in monitoring and controlling production costs. But many nonmanufacturing activities can also benefit from standard costs. Here we explore standard costs and performance reports for a marketing activity. Other typical nonmanufacturing activities that may benefit from standards are data processing, personnel, and maintenance services.

Any organization — business or not-for-profit — can create standards for many kinds of nonmanufacturing activities so that comparisons can be made in performance between those standards and actual results. To illustrate standard cost performance reporting for nonmanufacturing activities, we use a retailing business that sells a variety of videocassette recorders and players. Video-World Systems prepares annual sales and cost standards. Data for 1985 are presented in Figure 22-8.

The expected unit sales volumes are based on past experience and planned advertising and promotional activities for the coming year. The variable costs per unit include all variable costs associated with acquiring, storing, marketing, selling, and distributing the products.

Figure 22-8. These are estimated sales, costs, and price data for a merchandising firm that sells four products. The average standard contribution margin is based on the assumption that the expected sales mix does in fact occur.

Video-World Systems
Standard Sales and Cost Data
For the Year 1985

Model	Sales Volume in Units	Price/ Unit	Sales Revenue	Variable Cost/Unit	Contribution Margin/Unit	Total Contribution Margin
VCR-600	500	$ 600	$300,000	$450	$150	$ 75,000
VCR-650	300	700	210,000	530	170	51,000
VCR-750	150	800	120,000	600	200	30,000
VCR-900	50	1,000	50,000	650	350	17,500
Totals	1,000		$680,000			$173,500

Average standard contribution margin = Total contribution margin/Sales units
= $173,500/1,000 units
= $173.50 per unit

The average contribution margin calculated in Figure 22-8 is similar to the average standard cost of material inputs or labor inputs when computing mix variances and yield variances for production activities. The contribution margin for a single product is the difference between the product's selling price and its variable cost. The **average standard contribution margin** for all four products is the average amount of contribution expected from the sale of one unit, given the standard sales mix of products. The average contribution margin is a weighted average if it is based on historical data. It is referred to as the **expected contribution margin** when it is based on standard cost projections in the computation. No single unit of any of the four products has a contribution margin of $173.50, but on the **average,** given the standard sales mix of the four products, $173.50 of contribution margin is generated by each sale.

The expected contribution margin is the average contribution margin at the expected sales mix

The total expected contribution margin of $173,500 is merely the sum of the expected contributions from each of the four products. This total is a key in the computation of marketing standard cost variances, as shown later.

Figure 22-9. Actual results for the retailer show that the company failed to achieve the $173,500 total contribution margin it expected. What caused the unfavorable variance?

Video-World Systems
Actual Sales and Cost Data
For the Year 1985

Model	Sales Volume in Units	Price/ Unit	Sales Revenue	Variable Cost/Unit	Contribution Margin/Unit	Total Contribution Margin
VCR-600	450	$580	$261,000	$440	$140	$ 63,000
VCR-650	320	710	227,200	530	180	57,600
VCR-750	140	760	106,400	590	170	23,800
VCR-900	70	980	68,600	640	340	23,800
Totals	980		$663,200			$168,200

Average actual contribution margin = Total contribution margin/Sales units
= $168,200/980 units
= $171.63 per unit

Actual sales and cost data for 1985 are presented in Figure 22-9. As often happens, the actual costs and actual sales data are somewhat different from what was expected. In the following variance analysis, we measure the difference between expected results—the standards—and actual results; then we prepare a report indicating the cause and significance of each variance.

A key number in Figure 22-9 is the actual total contribution margin of $168,200. The standards called for an expected total contribution margin of $173,500. The actual contribution margin was $5,300 less ($173,500 − $168,200). The difference of $5,300 is the unfavorable total variance. We now analyze the components of this total variance.

The company fell $5,300 short of its expected performance, as measured by its total contribution margin. But a more detailed evaluation of this variance provides insights into what caused it. Because this company is a retailing store, the variances we are about to analyze are often referred to as marketing variances. In this example, we divide the total marketing variance into a contribution margin variance, a sales quantity variance, and a sales mix variance.

Contribution Margin Variance

How much profit did we lose because we did not sell our products at their expected contribution margins?

The **contribution margin variance** is a measure of the amount of variance caused by the actual contribution margin of a product being different from its standard contribution margin. The contribution margin per unit of a product is the difference between the product's sales price and its variable cost per unit. Variable costs include the product's purchase price and the variable portion of selling and distribution expense. The actual contribution margin per unit can vary from the standard because of changes in the sales price, variable costs, or both. The contribution margin variance is computed as follows:

Contribution margin variance = (Standard contribution margin per unit
− Actual contribution margin per unit)
× Actual number of units sold

The contribution margin variances for Video-World Systems are presented at the top of Figure 22-10.

The standard and actual contribution margins per unit for each of the products are shown in Figures 22-8 and 22-9, respectively, and the actual quantity of units sold is shown in Figure 22-9.

The contribution margin variance for product VCR-600 is unfavorable because the company failed to achieve the standard contribution margin of $150 per unit for this product. In this case, the $10 reduction in contribution margin per unit was caused by a $20 per unit decline in price and a $10 per unit decline in variable cost. With 450 VCR-600 units sold, the loss in total contribution margin to the company is $10 per unit times 450 units, or $4,500.

Figure 22-10. These three variances are three of many different variances that can be computed for nonmanufacturing activities. The sales mix was favorable but not enough products were sold to achieve the expected contribution margins.

Video-World Systems
Marketing Variance Analysis Report
For the Year 1985

Contribution Margin Variances:

VCR-600	($150 − $140) × 450 units	= $4,500 U
VCR-650	($170 − $180) × 320 units	= 3,200 F
VCR-750	($200 − $170) × 140 units	= 4,200 U
VCR-900	($350 − $340) × 70 units	= 700 U

Total contribution margin variance $6,200 U

Sales Quantity Variance:

(1,000 total units − 980 total units) × $173.50   =   3,470 U

Sales Mix Variances:

VCR-600	(500 − 450) × ($150 − $173.50)	= $1,175 F
VCR-650	(300 − 320) × ($170 − $173.50)	= 70 U
VCR-750	(150 − 140) × ($200 − $173.50)	= 265 U
VCR-900	(50 − 70) × ($350 − $173.50)	= 3,530 F

Total sales mix variance   4,370 F

Total marketing variance $5,300 U

The contribution margin of the VCR-650 product was $10 greater than expected. With 320 units sold, the contribution margin variance is $3,200 favorable. The contribution margin variances for the VCR-750 units and the VCR-900 units are also unfavorable.

The net contribution margin variance for the year is $6,200 unfavorable. In other words, if the company had achieved its standard contribution margins on all of its products, the total contribution margin of the firm would have been $6,200 greater than actually occurred.

Sales Quantity Variance

The sales quantity variance uses total products regardless of product type to measure the variance

The **sales quantity variance** is a measure of variance caused solely by selling more or fewer units of product. Much like the manufacturing yield variance, the sales quantity variance is blind to which particular type of product is sold from the group of products and to the products' actual contribution margin. This variance is based on total units of all products sold. The difference between the actual total number of units sold and the expected total number of units sold is multiplied by the average standard contribution margin of the mix of all products. The sales quantity variance addresses the very simple question, Did we sell more or fewer total units of product than expected? The sales quantity variance is computed as follows:

Sales quantity variance = (Total expected units of sales − Total actual units of sales) × Average standard contribution margin

The sales quantity variance for Video-World Systems is shown in the middle of Figure 22-10. The sales quantity variance is unfavorable because fewer units were actually sold than expected. The magnitude of the variance is determined by the difference between the standard sales volume multiplied by the average standard contribution margin.

Sales Mix Variance

The **sales mix variance** is a measure of the variance in total contribution margin or profit that results when the proportion of products sold is different than the standard sales mix. Typically, managers prefer to sell higher-profit items rather than lower-profit items. If managers can shift some sales from lower-profit items to higher-profit items, the company can earn a larger profit without increasing the total number of units sold. A **high-profit product** has a contribution margin greater than the average standard contribution margin, and a **low-profit product** has a contribution margin lower than the average standard contribution margin. The average standard contribution margin for our example is $173.50, computed at the bottom of Figure 22-8. As the figure shows, VCR-600 and VCR-650 are low-profit items, and VCR-750 and VCR-900 are high-profit items.

The analysis of sales mix variance is much like production mix variance except here we are trying to maximize profit rather than minimize cost

The logic used to analyze sales mix variances is very similar to that used for material and labor mix variances. However, manufacturing mix variances are intended to help managers control and **minimize cost,** whereas sales mix variances are intended to help managers monitor and **maximize profit.** The sales mix variance is computed as follows:

Sales mix varianc = (Expected unit sales − Actual unit sales) ×
(Expected contribution margin for the product −
Average standard contribution margin of all products)

The individual sales mix variances are calculated as shown at the bottom of Figure 22-10. For VCR-600 units, the sales mix variance is favorable because the company sold less than the standard quantity of this low-profit item. It may be difficult to understand how selling less than the standard quantity of any product can produce a favorable variance. The point to remember is that the sales mix variance measures only the effect of selling a different mix of products than the standard mix; the effect of sales volume is measured by the sales quantity variance discussed above. The sales mix variance is favorable when a high-profit unit is sold instead of a low-profit unit. The sales mix variance for VCR-650 units is unfavorable because the company sold more than the standard amount of a low-profit product.

The VCR-750 units and the VCR-900 units are high-profit products. Because fewer than the standard quantity of VCR-750 units are sold, its sales mix variance is unfavorable. More than the standard quantity of VCR-900 units are sold and this is a high-profit item, so its sales mix variance is favorable. The net sales mix variance is $4,370 favorable, indicating that the total contribution margin for the year is $4,370 higher because of the change in the sales mix.

In our discussion of the manufacturing mix variances, we noted that whether the variance was favorable or unfavorable can be determined by following a strict algebraic solution to the variance equation. All positive outcomes are favorable variances, and all negative outcomes are unfavorable variances. A similar approach can be used for the sales mix variance. The only difference is that the signs for the sales mix variance are **reversed.** That is, for the sales mix variance, positive results are unfavorable variances, and negative results are favorable variances. The reason for the difference is that manufacturing variances deal with costs, which management wants to **minimize,** whereas sales mix variances deal with profits, which management wants to **maximize.**

SUMMARY   Standard costs and standard cost performance reports provide managers with information for planning and controlling manufacturing activities and their costs. When multiple inputs of either materials or labor are used and the input mix varies, analysis of mix and yield variances will provide useful information.

A **material mix variance** measures the cost effect of using a different proportion of material inputs than defined by the standard mix of material inputs. The **material yield variance** measures the cost effect of using more or less total material inputs than the standard quantities. In modifying the mix of material inputs, managers want to increase the relative proportion of low-cost inputs and decrease the relative proportion of high-cost inputs without impairing the nature or quality of the product or service produced. A high-cost or low-cost input is defined in terms of the **average standard cost of inputs,** which is the average cost of all inputs at the standard mix.

The material mix variance is favorable if less than the standard amount of a high-cost input is used or more than the standard amount of a low-cost input is used. The material mix variance is unfavorable if more than the standard amount of a high-cost input is used or less than the standard amount of a low-cost input is used. The standard and actual quantities used in the computation of the material mix variance are the same as those used in the computation of the material quantity variance.

The material yield variance is the difference between the actual amount of material inputs used and the actual amount of output produced, both measured at their standard costs. If the total output at standard cost is greater than the total inputs at their average standard cost, the yield variance is favorable. If the total output at standard cost is less than the inputs at their average standard cost, the yield variance is unfavorable.

The material mix and the material yield variances are components of the material quantity variance. The sum of the mix and yield variances is always equal to the quantity variance.

The **labor mix variance** and the **labor yield variance** are computed just as the material mix and yield variances when there are several classifications of labor. Labor mix and yield variances are components of the labor efficiency variance.

Although standards are used primarily for manufacturing activities, they can also be useful in planning, controlling, and evaluating nonmanufacturing activities. Variance analysis can be particularly useful for marketing activities.

Common marketing variances are contribution margin, sales quantity, and sales mix variances. The **contribution margin variance** measures the effect of selling products at different contribution margins than standard. The **sales quantity variance** measures the effect of selling more or fewer total units than expected, and the **sales mix variance** measures the effect of selling a different product mix than expected. The sales mix variance is favorable if more than the standard quantity of a high-profit product is sold or less than the standard quantity of a low-profit product is sold. The sales mix variance is unfavorable when less than the standard quantity of a high-profit item is sold or more than the standard quantity of a low-profit item is sold. High- or low-profit products are determined by comparing each product's standard contribution margin with the **average standard contribution margin** of all products at the standard sales mix.

KEY TERMS

average standard contribution margin *(778)*
average standard cost of inputs *(771)*
contribution margin variance *(779)*
expected contribution margin *(778)*
high-cost input *(771)*
high-profit product *(781)*
labor efficiency variance *(768)*
labor mix variance *(776)*
labor rate variance *(767)*
labor yield variance *(776)*

low-cost input *(771)*
low-profit product *(781)*
material mix variance *(771)*
material price variance *(766)*
material quantity variance *(766)*
material yield variance *(773)*
mix variance *(770)*
sales mix variance *(781)*
sales quantity variance *(780)*
variance analysis *(770)*
yield variance *(770)*

QUESTIONS

1. A manufacturing company was faced by a shortage of a raw material caused by a strike at the material supplier's plant. In order to complete production, the company substituted another material. The substitute material has a higher cost than the original, but because of its higher quality, should result in fewer rejects. Discuss what kind of variances can be expected as a result of using the substitute material. What decisions might be warranted if the substitute material causes the overall material variance to be favorable or unfavorable?

2. When multiple inputs of labor or material resources are required for the production of a product, the labor efficiency variance and the material quantity variance can each be analyzed into two separate components called mix and yield variances. A quantity or efficiency variance consists of the difference between standard and actual quantity of inputs multiplied by standard resource costs. Describe specifically how these components of the variance are broken down by further analysis and discuss what information is isolated by the mix variance and yield variance.

3. The vice president of marketing was not satisfied with the results of last quarter's sales. He met with the marketing managers and the three regional marketing representatives to discuss the problem and told them: "From now on we'll fix responsibility for sales performance. The regional representatives are responsible for all sales quantity variances. The marketing manager is responsible for sales mix variances, and I'll take responsibility for contribution margin variances. Here are

the new prices. Get those products sold." The vice president had increased most prices to ensure favorable contribution margin variances. By the end of the next quarter, all three regional managers turned in glowing sales quantity variance reports. But the sales mix report showed large unfavorable variances, and although most contribution margin variances were favorable, profit for the quarter was down sharply. Discuss the merits of the vice president's new policy. What may have caused the reported variances?

EXERCISES

Ex. 22-1
Material Price and
Quantity Variances

The Fullerton Company uses three materials in the production of aquariums and terrariums. Material standards and actual results are as follows:

	Per Unit Material Standards	
Resource	Quantity	Price
KL-Silicates	25 pounds	$ .90 per pound
Bonding-Compound	4	2.20
Glazing-Compound	5	3.50
	Actual Results	
Resource	Quantity	Price
KL-Silicates	15,100 pounds	$ .92 per pound
Bonding-Compound	2,640	2.12
Glazing-Compound	3,620	3.36
Actual output = 680 units		

REQUIRED

a. Compute the material price variance.
b. Compute the material quantity variance.

Ex. 22-2
Labor Rate and
Efficiency
Variances

Stably Company uses four classifications of labor in the production of refrigerators. Labor standards are as follows:

Labor Classification	Standard Hours	Labor Rate
Metal work	4 per unit	$8.00 per hour
Electronic components	4	9.50
Assembly	6	7.00
Finishing and painting	3	7.50

August production yielded 450 refrigerators, and the company incurred the following actual labor costs:

Labor Classification	Hours Worked	Total Labor Cost
Metal work	1,940 hours	$15,132
Electronic components	1,650	16,335
Assembly	2,500	18,000
Finishing and painting	1,400	10,640

REQUIRED

a. Compute the labor rate variance for August.
b. Compute the labor efficiency variance for August.

**Ex. 22-3
Simple Mix and
Yield Variances**

A company makes a masonry sealing compound. Material standards for 5,000 gallons of the product follow:

Material	Quantity	Price	Total Cost
C-QM	2,500 gal	$4.00/gal	$10,000
C-QR	1,500	2.00	3,000
C-ZN	1,000	6.00	6,000
Totals	5,000		$19,000

Actual results for the week just ended are presented below:

Amount of product manufactured = 28,000 gallons

Material used:

Material	Quantity	Price	Total Cost
C-QM	16,500 gal	$3.80/gal	$ 62,700
C-QR	8,800	2.30	20,240
C-ZN	4,500	7.00	31,500
Totals	29,800		$114,440

REQUIRED   Compute the material mix and yield variances for the production of the masonry sealing compound.

**Ex. 22-4
Material Price, Mix,
and Yield Variances**

Lemon-Yellow makes a powdered lemonade mix, which it sells in 2-pound cans. The standard material costs are presented below.

Material	Quantity	Price	Cost
Sugar	.90 lb	$ .20/lb	$ .18
Lemon flavoring	.70	1.80	1.26
Ascorbic acid	.08	2.50	.20
Coloring	.12	1.00	.12
Preservatives	.20	.50	.10
Totals	2.00 lb		$1.86

Actual production for the period was 5,000 cans of output. Material use and cost data are presented below.

Material	Quantity	Total Cost
Sugar	4,200 lb	$ 924
Lemon flavoring	3,700	6,105
Ascorbic acid	460	1,288
Coloring	560	504
Preservatives	1,160	638
Totals	10,080 lb	$9,459

REQUIRED   Prepare a variance analysis report isolating the material price, mix, and yield variances for the production of the lemonade product.

Ex. 22-5
Mix and Yield
Variances with
Shrinkage

Livermore Food Products makes an extensive line of canned soups and stews. Livermore's beef stew is manufactured in batches and packaged in 2-pound cans for sale to customers. Materials standards for a typical production batch are presented below. The output from a normal batch of stew is 1,000 pounds. Some shrinkage occurs in the cooking process.

Material	Quantity	Price	Total Cost
Beef	200 lb	$1.60/lb	$ 320
Beef broth	500	.30	150
Potatoes	200	.15	30
Tomatoes	100	.40	40
Sugar	50	.30	15
Spices	50	2.10	105
Totals	1,100 lb		$ 660

During the month, 7,500 cans of stew were manufactured and the following materials costs were incurred:

Material	Quantity	Price	Total Cost
Beef	2,700 lb	$1.75/lb	$ 4,725
Beef broth	8,000	.32	2,560
Potatoes	3,300	.12	396
Tomatoes	1,600	.35	560
Sugar	800	.30	240
Spices	680	2.25	1,530
Totals	17,080 lb		$10,011

REQUIRED

a.   Compute the material price and quantity variances for the production of the stew.
b.   Compute the material mix and yield variances.

Ex. 22-6
Labor Mix and
Yield Variance
Analysis

Medeor Corporation makes modular and mobile homes. The company uses standard costs to monitor and control all of its production activities. Electricians and apprentice electricians install electrical fixtures and appliances. Labor standards for the installation of all electrical items on the Medeor Model are 12 hours of electrician time and 8 hours of apprentice time. Electricians are paid $16 per hour and apprentices are paid $7 per hour.

During the first quarter of 1985, the company made and sold 56 Medeor mobile homes, which was a slight decline from expected sales. As a result, some of the apprentice electricians were laid off during the period, resulting in a higher proportion of electrician labor than standard. There were 810 electrician hours worked on the 56 units and 230 hours of apprentice labor.

REQUIRED

a.   Compute the labor mix and yield variances for the period.
b.   Interpret the variance information you prepared.

Ex. 22-7
Material Mix and Yield Variances

Engine-Kare Company makes engine care products for consumers and commercial users. One product, Noc-Free, is a particularly effective product for freeing sticky valves and for other engine problems. Noc-Free is produced in 10,000-gallon vats, which typically yield 60,000 cans of product. Materials standards for Noc-Free are:

Distillate base	7,000 gallons	$1.40 per gallon
Detergents	1,000	2.50
Emulsifiers	500	3.90
Poly-Mur-4	1,500	6.00

During the last month, Engine-Kare manufactured 240,000 cans of Noc-Free. The materials used in production included:

Distillate base	29,200 gallons	$1.30 per gallon
Detergents	3,800	2.70
Emulsifiers	2,200	4.05
Poly-Mur-4	5,600	5.80

REQUIRED

a. Compute the material price and quantity variances for the month.
b. Compute the material mix and yield variances for the month.

Ex. 22-8
Marketing Variances

An automobile dealer sells three models of automobiles. The dealer has established standards for sales and costs. Standard and actual data for the first quarter of 1985 are:

	Unit Sales		Unit Price		Unit Variable Cost	
Model	Standard	Actual	Standard	Actual	Standard	Actual
Economy	30	21	$ 6,800	$ 6,600	$ 5,700	$ 5,800
Sports-car	12	16	11,600	11,900	9,500	9,600
Full-size	8	17	13,800	13,400	10,900	10,800

REQUIRED

Prepare a detailed analysis of the first-quarter marketing variances identifying the contribution margin variance, the sales quantity variance, and the sales mix variance.

Ex. 22-9
Computing Marketing Variances

Below are estimated summer sales and cost data for the Monarch Ice Cream Company, which sells four ice-cream products from bicycle vendor carts.

Product	Quantity	Price	Cost	Margin	Total Margin
Popsicles	40,000	$.35	$.20	$.15	$ 6,000
Frozen juice bars	30,000	.60	.35	.25	7,500
Fudge-bars	20,000	.40	.20	.20	4,000
Sundaes	10,000	.90	.50	.40	4,000
Totals	100,000				$21,500

Actual sales during the summer were as follows:

Product	Quantity	Price	Cost	Margin	Total Margin
Popsicles	42,000	$.35	$.18	$.17	$ 7,140
Frozen juice bars	35,000	.65	.38	.27	9,450
Fudge-bars	9,000	.40	.21	.19	1,710
Sundaes	12,000	.95	.52	.43	5,160
Totals	98,000				$23,460

REQUIRED

Prepare a detailed analysis of the marketing variances, isolating the contribution margin variance, the sales quantity variance, and the sales mix variance.

Ex. 22-10 (CMA)
Computing
Standard Quantities

Danson Company is a chemical manufacturer that supplies industrial users. The company plans to introduce a new chemical solution and needs to develop a standard product cost for this new solution.

The new chemical solution is made by combining a chemical compound (nyclyn) and a solution (salex), boiling the mixture, adding a second compound (protet), and bottling the resulting solution in 10-liter containers. The initial mix, which is 10 liters in volume, consists of 12 kilograms of nyclyn and 9.6 liters of salex. A 20 percent reduction in volume occurs during the boiling process. The solution is then cooled slightly before 5 kilograms of protet are added; the addition of protet does not affect the total liquid volume.

The purchase prices of the raw materials used in the manufacture of this new chemical solution are as follows.

Nyclyn	$1.30 per kilogram
Salex	1.80 per liter
Protet	2.40 per kilogram

REQUIRED

Determine the standard quantity for each of the raw materials needed to produce a 10-liter container of Danson Company's new chemical solution and the standard materials cost of a 10-liter container of the new product.

PROBLEMS

P. 22-1
Direct Material
Variances

The Madelline Company makes a variety of furniture items. One product, a sofa, has the following materials standards:

Pine lumber	20 board feet	@ $	.80 per board foot
Oak lumber	6 board feet	@	1.50 per board foot
Springs	200 units	@	.30 each
Padding	120 square feet	@	.15 per square foot
Fabric	15 square yards	@	6.00 per square yard

During May, 85 sofas were manufactured, and the following materials costs were incurred:

Item Purchased	Quantity Purchased	Total Cost	Quantity Used
Pine lumber	2,200 bd ft	$1,650	1,780 bd ft
Oak lumber	400 bd ft	660	490 bd ft
Springs	31,000 units	9,300	17,600 units
Padding	6,000 sq ft	1,020	10,800 sq ft
Fabric	—	—	1,300 sq yd

REQUIRED

a. Compute the May material price variance for each of the materials used in the production of the sofas.
b. Compute the May material quantity variance for each of the materials used in the production of sofas.

P. 22-2
Direct Labor
Variances

Luen-Chow Company makes steel shelves, steel furniture, and several other steel products primarily for use in offices and industrial organizations. Standard labor costs for the shelf division are presented below:

Labor Classification	Direct Labor Hours per 20-ft Wall Shelf	Hourly Wage Rate
Cutting labor	1.6 hours	$9.00 per hour
Forming labor	1.2	9.50
Machining labor	2.5	9.40
Assembly labor	3.0	7.00
Painting labor	.8	8.00
Finishing labor	1.3	7.50

During April, the division manufactured 6,000 of the 20-foot wall shelves and incurred the following labor costs:

Labor Classification	Total Labor Hours	Total Labor Cost
Cutting labor	9,400 hours	$ 89,280
Forming labor	7,500	70,500
Machining labor	15,600	149,760
Assembly labor	17,200	125,560
Painting labor	4,400	34,760
Finishing labor	8,300	63,080
Totals	62,400	$532,940

REQUIRED

a. Compute the labor rate variance for April for each classification of labor and in total.
b. Compute the labor efficiency variance for April for each labor classification and in total.

P. 22-3
Material Mix and
Yield Variance with
Shrinkage

The Mercantile Solvents Company makes X-Myer-K, a powerful rust remover. The standard material mix calls for 80 gallons of XZ-Ote at $1.25 per gallon and 20 gallons of XZ-Yte at $4.00 per gallon. A 100-gallon batch of inputs yields 90 gallons of output. The shrinkage is a normal part of the cooking and distilling process. During the past week, the company manufactured 1,350 gallons of X-Myer-K using 1,300 gallons of XZ-Ote at $1.30 per gallon and 240 gallons of XZ-Yte at $3.85 per gallon.

REQUIRED

a. Compute the standard and actual materials cost for the product.
b. Compute the material price variances.
c. Compute the material quantity variances.
d. Compute the material mix and yield variances.

P. 22-4
Labor Mix and
Yield Variances

The Springport Park Department plans to offer free swimming lessons to any children under 14 years of age who want them. The manager of the department estimates that 6,000 children will participate in the lessons. Lessons are offered daily throughout the week to accommodate the schedules of all interested people. The parks department plans to hire 15 full-time instructors to work in the swimming lessons program. The remaining needs will be filled by 25 associate instructors. The park department plans to pay the full-time instructors $2,500 for the summer and the associate instructors $1,500 for the summer.

When the summer arrives, 1,200 more children than expected participated in the free summer swim program. Additional personnel had to be hired to teach all of the students and the average rate paid to instructors was somewhat different than expected. The actual personnel costs and numbers were:

Full-time instructors   22 people at a cost of $2,700 each
Associate instructors   21 people at a cost of $1,400 each

REQUIRED

a. Compute the labor rate variance for each class of instructor and in total.
b. Compute the labor mix and yield variances.
c. Compute the expected and the actual instructor cost per student.

P. 22-5
Materials and Labor Variance Analysis

A very fine plant food, called Flower-Bloom, is made by the Weaver Horticultural Company. The product is manufactured in 50-ton batches and sold in bulk to another company, which packages and distributes the product. The standard prime costs for a typical 50-ton production run of the product are shown below.

Materials	Price / Gallon	Gallons	Total Cost
Potash	$ 2.00	5,000	$10,000
Nitrogen	12.00	3,750	45,000
Phosphoric acid	8.00	1,250	10,000
Inert compounds	.80	5,000	4,000
Totals		15,000	$69,000

Labor	Rate per Hour	Hours	Total Cost
Blending	$ 8.00	160	$1,280
Processing	11.00	240	2,640
Totals		400	$3,920

During March, the company made 250 tons of Flower-Bloom. Actual prime costs of production were:

Materials	Price / Gallon	Gallons	Total Cost
Potash	$ 2.20	28,750	$ 63,250
Nitrogen	11.00	15,000	165,000
Phosphoric acid	9.00	8,750	78,750
Inert compounds	1.10	22,000	24,200
Totals		74,500	$331,200

Labor	Rate per Hour	Hours	Total Cost
Blending	$ 8.40	760	$ 6,384
Processing	11.30	1,150	12,995
Totals		1,910	$19,379

REQUIRED

a. Compute the standard prime cost of a ton of Flower-Bloom.
b. Compute the material price, mix, and yield variances.
c. Compute the labor rate, mix, and yield variances.
d. Compute the material mix variance per ton of product.

P. 22-6
Production Mix and
Yield Variances

The Leebranf Manufacturing Company makes construction and road building supplies. One product, used as a top coat sealer, has the following materials standards for a standard production batch, which consists of 25 tons of top coat:

Petroleum base	20,000 pounds @ $	.12 per pound
Tar	5,000 @	400.00 per ton
Gravel	25,000 @	30.00 per ton
Total inputs	50,000 pounds	

During the past week, the company manufactured 90 tons of top coat sealer and incurred the following materials costs:

Petroleum base	75,000 pounds	@ $ 45 per barrel
Tar	12 tons	@ 410 per ton
Gravel	50 tons	Total cost of $1,600

There are 2,000 pounds in a ton and a barrel of petroleum base weighs 400 pounds.

REQUIRED

a. Compute the standard materials cost per ton of output.
b. Compute the material price variance.
c. Compute the material quantity variance.
d. Compute the material mix and yield variances.

P. 22-7
Unit Standard Costs
and Mix and Yield
Variances

The Kipple Baking Company makes a popular whole-grain bread, which it sells through grocery stores in the region. The bakery uses standard costs to monitor costs and materials use. The materials standards for the whole-grain bread are presented below:

Material	Quantity per 1,000-Loaf Batch	Price per Pound
Whole-grain flour	800 pounds	$ .26
Honey	80	2.20
Milk	400	.40
Yeast	40	3.50
Salt	20	.30
Butter	60	1.80

A recent batch of the whole-grain bread yielded 1,050 loaves of bread and the following actual materials costs were incurred:

Material	Quantity Used	Price per Pound
Whole-grain flour	880 pounds	$ .24
Honey	90	2.35
Milk	410	.42
Yeast	44	3.20
Salt	18	.25
Butter	50	1.70

a. Compute the standard materials cost for a loaf of bread.
b. Compute the actual materials cost for a loaf of bread.
c. Compute the material price variances.
d. Compute the material quantity variances.
e. Compute the material mix and yield variances.

P. 22-8
Marketing Variance
Analysis and
Interpretation

Snyder Marine Sales sells several lines of boats and outboard motors. The owner-manager of the company prepares standard sales and cost data for each product line sold. One line of motors offered by Snyder is available in 4-, 6-, 9.9-, and 15-horsepower models. Expected sales and cost data for the products as prepared by the owner are presented below:

Product	Unit Sales	Price/ Unit	Variable Cost/Unit	Contribution Margin/Unit	Total Contribution Margin
4 hp	10	$ 550	$400	$150	$ 1,500
6 hp	40	750	500	250	10,000
9.9 hp	30	980	650	330	9,900
15 hp	20	1,200	800	400	8,000
Totals	100				$29,400

During the year, Snyder Marine Sales experienced a somewhat different sales mix than expected, but the company sold more motors in total than standard. The actual results for the year were:

Product	Units Sold	Price/ Unit	Variable Cost/Unit	Contribution Margin/Unit	Total Contribution Margin
4 hp	22	$ 540	$410	$130	$ 2,860
6 hp	55	760	520	240	13,200
9.9 hp	12	940	640	300	3,600
15 hp	15	1,250	810	440	6,600
Totals	104				$26,260

a. Prepare a marketing variance analysis report in good form for the outboard motor line.
b. Explain in common language the results of your variance analysis, with special emphasis on the cause of any differences between the expected and actual performance of the product line.

P. 22-9
Marketing Variance
Analysis

Leo decided to open a new bar called Leo's Place near a large college campus. Leo plans to offer only three products: a dark and a light beer on tap and a bottled imported beer. In planning inventory and cash requirements, Leo estimated that beer sales would be 9,000 units a month, split approximately equally between the three products. The two draft beers will be sold for $.75 a glass and the imported beer will be sold for $1.00 a bottle. The variable costs of the three products are expected to be $.30, $.35, and $.70 respectively for the light beer, dark beer, and imported beer. Leo estimates that he will incur monthly wage costs of $1,900, utilities and other occupancy costs of $300 a month, and monthly rent on the facilities of $500.

During the first month of operations, the bar sold only 8,600 units of product, and a much lower dollar sales volume than expected. But Leo still earned a larger profit than planned, based on his original estimates. Actual data showed that all the beer sold for the expected price, but the sales mix was 50 percent light beer, 40 percent dark beer, and only 10 percent for the imported beer. Also, the unit variable costs of the beers were $.29, $.35, and $.75 respectively. All other operating costs were exactly as expected.

REQUIRED

a. Compute the expected amount of monthly profit based on Leo's expectations.
b. Compute the actual profit for the first month of operations at Leo's Place.
c. Explain the positive difference in profit given that the sales level was lower than expected. Use any variance computations and information that will help support your explanation.
d. Assuming the sales mix and variable costs of the first month of operations, determine the sales level in dollars and units that would provide Leo with a monthly profit of $1,000.

P. 22-10 (CMA)
Computing and
Interpreting
Materials Variances

The LAR Chemical Co. manufactures a wide variety of chemical compounds and liquids for industrial uses. The standard mix for producing a single batch of 500 gallons of one liquid is as follows:

Liquid Chemical	Quantity (in gallons)	Cost (per gallon)	Total Cost
Maxan	100	$2.00	$200
Salex	300	.75	225
Cralyn	225	1.00	225
Totals	625		$650

There is a 20 percent loss in liquid volume during processing due to evaporation. The finished liquid is put into 10-gallon bottles for sale. Thus, the standard material cost for a 10-gallon bottle is $13.00.

The actual quantities of raw materials and the respective cost of the materials placed in production during November were as follows:

Liquid Chemical	Quantity (in gallons)	Total Cost
Maxan	8,480	$17,384
Salex	25,200	17,640
Cralyn	18,540	16,686
Totals	52,220	$51,710

REQUIRED A total of 4,000 bottles (40,000 gallons) were produced during November.

a. Calculate the total raw materials variance for the liquid products for the month of November and then further analyze the total variance into a:

1. total material price variance.
2. material mix variance.
3. material yield variance.

b. Explain how LAR Chemical Co. could use each of the three materials variances—price, mix, yield—to help control the cost to manufacture this liquid compound.

CASES

The Markley Division of Rosette Industries manufactures and sells patio chairs. The chairs are manufactured in two versions—a metal model and a plastic model of a lesser quality. The company uses its own sales force to sell the chairs to retail stores and to catalog outlets. Generally, customers purchase both the metal and plastic versions.

Markley Division
Operating Results for the First Quarter

	Actual	Budget	Favorable (Unfavorable) Relative to the Budget
Sales in units:			
Plastic model	60,000	50,000	10,000)
Metal model	20,000	25,000	(5,000)
Sales revenue:			
Plastic model	$630,000	$500,000	$130,000
Metal model	300,000	375,000	(75,000)
Total sales	930,000	875,000	55,000
Less variable costs:			
Manufacturing (at standard):			
Plastic model	480,000	400,000	(80,000)
Metal model	200,000	250,000	50,000
Selling:			
Commissions	46,500	43,750	(2,750)
Bad debt allowance	9,300	8,750	(550)
Total variable costs (except variable manufacturing variances)	735,800	702,500	(33,300)
Contribution margin (except variable manufacturing variances)	194,200	172,500	21,700
Less other costs:			
Variable manufacturing costs variances from standards	49,600	—	(49,600)
Fixed manufacturing costs	49,200	48,000	(1,200)
Fixed selling and admin. costs	38,500	36,000	(2,500)
Corporation offices allocation	18,500	17,500	(1,000)
Total other costs	155,800	101,500	(54,300)
Division operational income	$ 38,400	$ 71,000	$ (32,600)

The chairs are manufactured on two different assembly lines located in adjoining buildings. The division management and sales department occupy the third building on the property. The division management includes a division controller responsible for the division's financial activities and the preparation of reports explaining the differences between actual and budgeted performance. The controller structures these reports such that the sales activities are distinguished from cost factors so that each can be analyzed separately.

The operating results for the first 3 months of the fiscal year as compared to the budget are presented on the facing page.

The budget for the current year was based upon the assumption that Markley Division would maintain its present market share of the estimated total patio chair market (plastic and metal combined). A status report had been sent to corporate management toward the end of the second month indicating that division operating income for the first quarter would probably be about 45 percent below budget; this estimate was just about on target. The division's operating income was below budget even though industry volume for patio chairs increased by 10 percent more than was expected at the time the budget was developed.

The manufacturing activities for the quarter resulted in the production of 55,000 plastic chairs and 22,500 metal chairs. The costs incurred by each manufacturing unit are presented below.

Raw Materials (Stated in Equivalent Finished Chairs):

	Quantity	Price	Plastic Model	Metal Model
Purchases:				
Plastic	60,000	$5.65	$339,000	
Metal	30,000	6.00		$180,000
Use				
Plastic	56,000	5.00	280,000	
Metal	23,000	6.00		138,000
Direct labor:				
9,300 hours @ $6.00 per hour			55,800	
5,600 hours @ $8.00 per hour				44,800
Manufacturing overhead:				
Variable:				
Supplies			43,000	18,000
Power			50,000	15,000
Employee benefits			19,000	12,000
Fixed:				
Supervision			14,000	11,000
Depreciation			12,000	9,000
Property taxes and other items			1,900	1,300

The standard variable manufacturing costs per unit and the budgeted monthly fixed manufacturing costs established for the current year are presented on p. 796.

	Plastic Model	Metal Model
Raw material	$5.00	$ 6.00
Direct labor:		
1/6 hour @ $6.00 per DLH	1.00	
1/4 hour @ $8.00 per DLH		2.00
Variable overhead:		
1/6 hour @ $12.00 per DLH	2.00	
1/4 hour @ $8.00 per DLH		2.00
Standard variable manufacturing cost per unit	$8.00	$10.00
Budgeted fixed costs per month:		
Supervision	$4,500	$3,500
Depreciation	4,000	3,000
Property taxes and other items	600	400
Total budgeted fixed costs for month	$9,100	$6,900

REQUIRED

a. Explain the variance in Markley Division's contribution margin attributable to sales activities by calculating the:

1. total sales price variance.
2. total sales mix variance.
3. sales quantity variance

b. What portion of sales quantity variance, if any, can be attributed to a change in Markley Division's market share?

c. Analyze the variance in Markley Division's variable manufacturing costs ($49,600) in as much detail as the data permit.

d. Based upon your analyses prepared for requirements a, b, and c:

1. Identify the major cause of Markley Division's unfavorable profit performance.
2. Did Markley's management attempt to correct this problem? Explain your answer.
3. What other steps, if any, could Markley's management have taken to improve the division's operating income? Explain your answer.

PART SEVEN
Tools for Managerial Analysis

Cost accounting systems generate a wealth of useful cost data, which can be reported to managers in traditional managerial reports. While managers use the information to make business decisions, managerial accountants and financial analysts constantly look for ways to improve or increase the information content of the reports. In the last three chapters of the book, we look at some of the more powerful tools available to managers for analyzing costs and other types of business and financial data.

Chapter 23 introduces statistical concepts of probability, measures of central tendency, dispersion, and sampling. Chapter 24 covers the topic of regression-correlation, which is one of the most powerful quantitative tools available to managers for making predictions of future costs. The last chapter covers learning curves, which are used to forecast production costs for new products or services, and linear programming, which is used to optimize complex production processes.

CHAPTER 23
Basic Statistics, Probabilities, and Sampling

Cost accounting systems produce a wealth of data that managers use in planning, control, performance evaluation, and decision making. Cost-volume-profit analysis, relevant cost analysis, and other decision evaluation methods presented earlier in this book all depend on cost data from the cost accounting data base. Many managers find, however, that the available data can be even more useful when analyzed with more sophisticated analysis and evaluation techniques. Quantitative analysis methods allow managers to develop information from their cost data base that is not otherwise available. In this chapter, we discuss some basic statistical concepts and techniques available to managers. Other quantitative tools are discussed in the following chapters.

The quantitative tools presented in this chapter have been known for many years, but some of them could be used efficiently only with the widespread use of computers. For example, linear regression analysis, discussed in Chapter 24, requires voluminous, time-consuming manual computations. But with computers, even complex regression analysis problems are performed quickly, leaving time for the manager to evaluate and use the results.

Despite their usefulness, objectivity, and sophistication, quantitative methods do not always provide answers that managers can readily use. Moreover, not all problems lend themselves to quantitative analyses. In this chapter and the next two chapters, we present methods that are **potentially** useful in planning and control activities, and in performance evaluation, analysis, and decision making. Managers proficient with these methods should use them when the methods prove to be fruitful; they should have the courage to ignore them when they are not.

STATISTICS

Many quantitative techniques discussed in this and later chapters are categorized as statistics. Some statistical techniques can be quite complex, but many are simple yet extremely helpful. A **statistic** is a numerical representation or description. Virtually all accounting data and many other types of information are statistics. For example, a person's height is a statistic that partially describes that person. Other statistics about the same person may include weight, age, color of eyes, salary, grade point average, and other types of data.

Statistics are numerical descriptions; everyone uses statistics

Statistics are used as simple surrogates for actual events. Investors use earnings per share as a key measure of management performance, and employers use a student's grade point average as an indicator of expected performance in a new job. Statistics are usually easier to understand and assimilate into a decision than a mass of individual data. Statistics such as earnings per share, price/earnings ratios, and dividend yield are widely used in financial analysis. Those used by managers in the daily operation of a business include inventory turnovers, cash receipts, unit costs of products, and break-even points. Among the most common statistical measures of cost data are measures of central tendency, which represent an average or middle value of some data.

Measures of Central Tendency

Probably the most commonly used statistic is an average. It is a measure of central tendency, describing a middle or central value of a set of data, such as the average number of units produced per hour, or the average hourly pay of production workers. There are several measures of central tendency. To illustrate, we use the data in Figure 23-1, which show the number of gyroscopes assembled by workers in a production department.

There are several types of averages; the mean is the most useful

Mean.   The most commonly used average is the **mean,** usually denoted $\overline{X}$, which is obtained by adding up the values in a set of data and dividing the total by the number of data items in the set. The mean discussed here is more precisely known as the **arithmetic mean** and is sometimes called the **weighted average** or just **average.**

Other means exist, such as the geometric mean and the harmonic mean. These are not relevant for most business analysis, so we refer to the arithmetic mean simply as the mean. The formula for the mean is:

$$\text{Mean} = \frac{x_1 + x_2 + x_3 + \cdots + x_n}{n}$$

or

$$\overline{X} = \frac{\Sigma \, x_i}{n}$$

where x_i = individual value of data elements with $i = 1, 2, \ldots n$
n = the number of data elements
Σ = summation sign indicating that the x_i are added together

Figure 23-1. A sample of production output for workers, used to calculate several statistics about the workers and their work.

Worker	Number of Units Assembled
1	28
2	29
3	14
4	32
5	31
6	29
7	31
8	27
9	31

The mean number of gyroscope assemblies is calculated by substituting into the equation the values of the x_i as follows:

$$\text{Mean} = \frac{28 + 29 + 14 + 32 + 31 + 29 + 31 + 27 + 31}{9}$$

$$= \frac{252}{9}$$

$$= 28$$

The mean indicates that on the average, each worker assembled 28 units. Examination of the data shows that one worker assembled the average number of units and the number assembled ranged from 14 to 32 units. The worker who produced only 14 units worked more slowly than the rest of the group, perhaps because of inexperience. The mean number of gyroscope assemblies produced by the other eight workers is 29.75 but the one low value had a strong enough effect on the mean to reduce it to 28. One of the disadvantages of the mean is that it is influenced by extreme values, such as the 14 in the above example.

Median. A measure of central tendency that is not influenced by extreme values is the median. The **median** is the middle value of a set of data. There is an equal number of values above and below the median. To determine the median, the data are sorted in ascending or descending order. The gyroscope assembly data are sorted as follows:

14   27   28   29   29   31   31   31   32

With nine values in the set of data, the middle one is the fifth item, which has a value of 29. You can see that the median is more representative of the eight experienced workers and indicates their relative performance better than the mean. The median has the disadvantage that it lacks some characteristics needed for more powerful data analyses.

When there is an even number of data in the set, the median is the mean of the two middle values. For example, the median of the following set of six data is 32, computed as $(30 + 34)/2$.

$$19 \quad 24 \quad 30 \quad 34 \quad 35 \quad 37$$

Mode. A third measure of central tendency is the **mode,** which is the value that occurs most frequently in a set of data. In our example of gyroscope assemblies, the value 31 occurs three times. The mode of this set of data is 31; it is determined simply by observing the data. The mode lacks many statistical characteristics found in the mean and its usefulness in statistics is limited. Moreover there may be more than one mode in a set of data, or no mode at all.

The mode is a qualitative measure

The mode is most useful as a qualitative measure; as the most frequently occurring value, it may indicate some useful patterns. For example, the manager of a shoe store is more interested in the most frequently purchased shoe size than in the average or median size. An appliance manufacturer needs to know the most commonly purchased color of appliances in order to produce the proper mix of appliances with the modal color predominant.

Measures of Dispersion

Measures of central tendency by themselves are quite useful to managers but they become more effective when accompanied by some measure of the way data are dispersed about the mean. **Dispersion** refers to the amount of variation of the data about the mean. For example, Figure 23-2 shows the production data for two employees for 8 consecutive days of production in a department of Luna Company.

Each employee produced 480 units in the 8-day period and each has a mean production of 60 units per day. However, the daily output of employee B varied significantly more than that of employee A. The data indicate that employee A will produce close to 60 units each day, whereas employee B's

Figure 23-2. Samples of production data for two workers. B's production fluctuates much more than A's, making it more difficult to estimate how much B will produce next time.

Luna Company
Production Data in Units per Day

Day	Employee A	Employee B
1	61	53
2	64	46
3	58	52
4	60	56
5	56	75
6	62	67
7	57	59
8	62	72
	480	480

$\overline{X} = 480/8 = 60$ units per day

Fluctuation around the mean may be measured as dispersion

daily production is more difficult to predict. A's production ranges from a minimum of 56 units a day to a maximum of 64, according to the sample data. The **range** of production is eight units, computed as $64 - 56$. B's production has a range of 23 units, making it more difficult to predict any one day's output.

The relative dispersion of each employee's output can be seen easily by looking at the data, but mere observation does not provide a numerical measure of the dispersion. The range is one measure of dispersion that is expressed as a numerical value. Even more useful measures of dispersion can be obtained by computing the variance or the standard deviation.

Variance.   The **variance,** usually denoted S^2, is a measure of how much the items in a data set vary about the mean. It is computed as follows:

$$\text{Variance} = S^2 = \frac{\Sigma(x_i - \overline{X})^2}{n - 1}$$

The above equation requires finding the difference between each x and the mean, squaring the differences, and adding them together. Then the sum is divided by the number of data elements less 1. The value $n - 1$ is used because the variance is computed using the mean, which has already been computed from the same data, causing the loss of a **degree of freedom.** If n were used to calculate the variance it would produce a biased statistic. Adjusting for degrees of freedom removes the bias. Any further discussion of degrees of freedom is beyond the scope of this book.

The variance for the production of the two workers in Figure 23-2 is calculated as follows:

A	B
$(61 - 60)^2 = 1$	$(53 - 60)^2 = 49$
$(64 - 60)^2 = 16$	$(46 - 60)^2 = 196$
$(58 - 60)^2 = 4$	$(52 - 60)^2 = 64$
$(60 - 60)^2 = 0$	$(56 - 60)^2 = 16$
$(56 - 60)^2 = 16$	$(75 - 60)^2 = 225$
$(62 - 60)^2 = 4$	$(67 - 60)^2 = 49$
$(57 - 60)^2 = 9$	$(59 - 60)^2 = 1$
$(62 - 60)^2 = \underline{4}$	$(72 - 60)^2 = \underline{144}$
54	744

$S^2 = 54/7 = 7.71$ units $S^2 = 744/7 = 106.29$ units

Standard Deviation.   The relative amount of variance for the production data is much larger for worker B than for worker A. However, because the differences are squared, both numbers are large and rather difficult to interpret. To eliminate this problem, we find the square root of the variance, which yields the **standard deviation,** S. This is a very useful statistic. For the two sets of data, the standard deviation is:

$$S^2 = 7.71 \text{ units} \qquad\qquad S^2 = 106.29 \text{ units}$$
$$S = \sqrt{7.71} \qquad\qquad S = \sqrt{106.29}$$
$$= 2.78 \qquad\qquad = 10.31$$

The calculation of the standard deviation is cumbersome if computed as illustrated. It is calculated more easily using the following formula:

$$S = \sqrt{\frac{n\Sigma x_i^2 - (\Sigma x_i)^2}{n(n-1)}}$$

The derivation of this formula may be found in many statistics books. The formula requires squaring each of the data elements as well as the sum of the data elements, a far easier task than squaring differences between each datum and the mean.

To illustrate use of the formula, we again compute the standard deviation for worker A.

X	X²
61	3,721
64	4,096
58	3,364
60	3,600
56	3,136
62	3,844
57	3,249
62	3,844
480	28,854

$$S = \sqrt{\frac{8(28,854) - 480^2}{8(8-1)}}$$

$$= \sqrt{\frac{230,832 - 230,400}{56}}$$

$$= \sqrt{7.7143}$$

$$= 2.78$$

The standard deviation measures dispersion in understandable terms

The standard deviation has some very useful statistical properties. Under certain conditions, discussed later in the chapter, it is known that approximately 68 percent of a given set of data is found within one standard deviation on each side of the mean. About 95 percent of the data occur within two standard deviations of the mean, and about 99 percent occur within three standard deviations. These characteristics enable managers to use the mean and standard deviation to estimate the probability that certain events will occur. The probability that production output will be at least 600 units per hour or the probability that shortages of certain inventory items will occur can be calculated quite easily.

Sampling Assumptions

The mean and standard deviation discussed above are computed from a sample of data representing the two workers. We selected 8 days of production data from among several weeks of production time required for the gyroscope assembly job. **A sample** is a subset of data collected from the total set of available data. The total set of data from which the sample is taken is called a **population.**

A sample must be representative of a population

The mean and standard deviation of a population are designated as μ and σ. It is not always feasible to find the mean and standard deviation of the entire population. It may be too costly or too time-consuming. A relatively small sample of the total population can provide a timely and accurate estimate of the desired population characteristics.

The sample mean and standard deviation are usually used as estimates of μ and σ. These estimated statistics, computed from a sample, are based on two important assumptions:

1. The sample is representative of the population.
2. The population is normally distributed.

Representative Sample. To provide valid statistics a sample must be a valid representation of the population. Generally the sample is representative if it is sufficiently large, and if it is taken in such a way that its characteristics are most likely to resemble the characteristics of the population. If the 8 days of production data used to measure the mean and standard deviation are not representative of the population of total production for the two workers, the sample statistics may lead to inappropriate actions or decisions.

Normal Distribution. The second assumption underlying the statistics computed from the sample is that the population from which the sample is taken is distributed about the mean in a symmetric, bell-shaped curve such as the one illustrated in Figure 23-3. This curve is called the **normal curve, or normal distribution,** and it has certain mathematical properties that make it especially useful in statistical analyses.

Figure 23-3.   The normal curve, completely defined by the mean and standard deviation of a normal population, can be used to calculate probabilities about any normally distributed population.

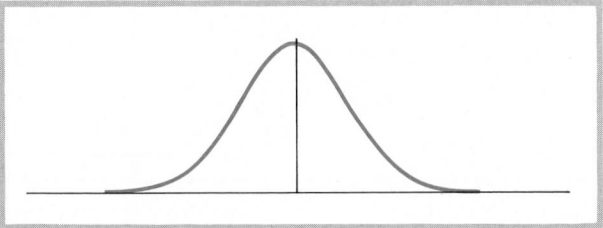

A large number of populations are normally distributed or are close enough to normal to permit the use of the normal curve in data analyses. Many types of business data are normally distributed and yield useful statistics for decision-making purposes.

PROBABILITY

Probability is the chance that something will happen, expressed as a percentage or decimal

One of the great benefits of statistics is that they help managers deal with uncertainty. Managers are constantly faced with the task of making decisions under uncertainty, which means that they must weigh the probability of a favorable or unfavorable event occurring. The use of probabilities in business does not eliminate or reduce the chances of various events occurring, but it does improve management's ability to evaluate situations and make the best possible decisions in the circumstances.

In statistics, **probability** is the relative frequency of the occurrence of events. If the probability of a machine producing a defective part is .03, this means that **in the long run** 3 percent of the parts will be defective. There may be no defective parts next week, or more than 5 percent may be defective tomorrow, but on the average 3 out of 100 parts will be defective.

If the probability is .5 that a coin will fall head up when it is tossed, in the long run half the tosses will result in heads. This does not mean that the next 10 tosses will result in 5 heads and 5 tails. But we can be sure that the probability of a head or tail is .5 because there is no other event that can occur and each of the events has an equal chance of occurring. The probability of an event occurring ranges from 0 to 1. If there is no chance that an event will occur its probability is 0. If it is certain that it will occur its probability is 1. If the probability that an event will occur is .4, then the probability that it will not occur is .6, or 60 percent.

Probability Distributions

If an event has a given probability of occurring, the actual occurrence of the event generates a specific **probability distribution.** A probability distribution shows how the total probability of 1 is distributed among the possible outcomes of an event. The probability distribution can be obtained from the expected frequency of an event occurring. For example the probability distribution of 100 flips of a coin is:

Number of Heads	Expected Frequency	Probability
0	50	.5
1	50	.5

Note that 100 flips of a coin may not produce 50 heads and 50 tails. That is simply what can be **expected** from flipping a coin, because each event has an equal chance of occurring. If we flip two coins simultaneously, for any one flip of the two coins, there are four possible outcomes, each of which is equally probable:

TT   HT   TH   HH

where H and T stand for heads and tails. We can expect to get no heads 1/4 of the time, and one head 1/2 of the time, and two heads 1/4 of the time. The probability distribution is

Number of Heads	Probability
0	.25
1	.50
2	.25

Probability distributions can be developed for many events

If three coins are flipped simultaneously there are eight possible outcomes, each of which has an equal chance of occurring:

TTT   HTT   THT   TTH   HHT   HTH   THH   HHH

We can expect no heads 1/8 of the time, one head 3/8 of the time, two heads 3/8 of the time, and three heads 1/8 of the time. What is the probability distribution if four coins are flipped? There are 16 equally probable events in this case. This and the three previous distributions are diagrammed in Figure 23-4. Notice that as the number of events increases, the probability distribution starts to take on a characteristic symmetrical shape. With a large number of events, the probability distribution often assumes the bell shape similar to the curve in Figure 23-3.

Use of the Normal Curve

The normal curve is described completely by the mean and standard deviation of a normally distributed population. That is, the mathematical equation for the curve is such that with the mean and standard deviation of the population, the height of the curve corresponding to any point and the area under the curve between any two points on the horizontal scale can be calculated. The

Figure 23-4. Probability distributions for flipping coins. As the number of coins is increased, the distribution becomes bell-shaped and symmetric, similar to the normal curve. Any one flip of four coins will rarely result in no head and most of the time will result in two heads.

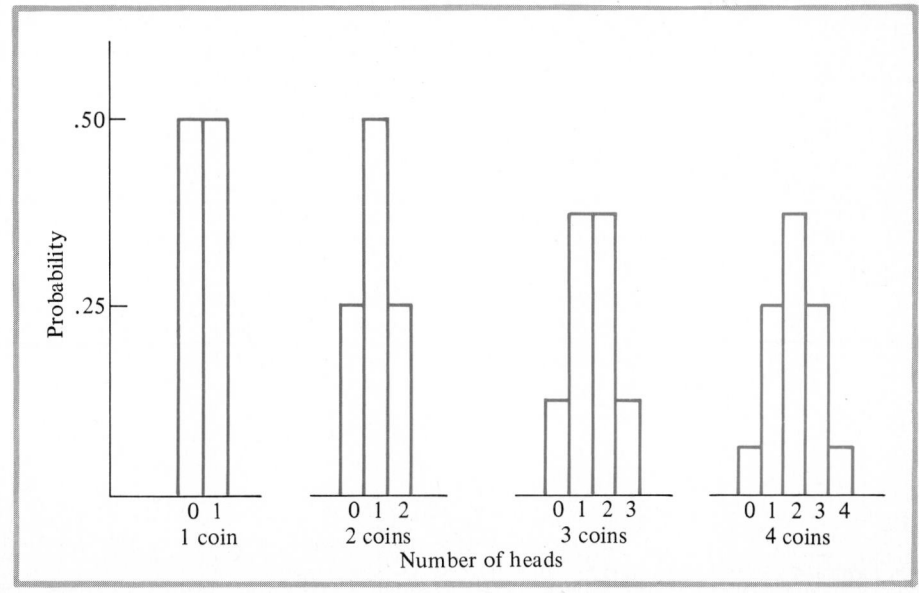

Many populations are normally distributed

area under the normal curve represents the probability of the occurrence of an event that comes from a normally distributed population. The mean of the population occurs on the horizontal scale at the peak of the curve, and the area under the curve on each side of the mean is 50 percent of the total area, representing a 50 percent probability.

It is not necessary to calculate the area, or probability, under the curve because it is available in tables for the standard normal curve. The **standard normal curve** has mean 0 and standard deviation 1; it can be used to develop a table such as Table V on page 914 at the back of the book. The mean and standard deviation of a set of normally distributed data, together with the normal curve table, can be used to find the probabilities of various events occurring.

Table V provides the probabilities as the area under the normal curve between the mean and any point to one side of the mean, with that point measured in standard deviations. For example, to find the area under the curve between the mean and a point 1.74 standard deviations away from the mean, you simply find the row labeled 1.7 and move across to the column labeled .04. This gives a z value of 1.74 and the table indicates that the area between the mean and 1.74 standard deviation away from the mean is .45907, which is a probability of 45.9 percent.

Normal Curve Probabilities.   Examine the two normal curves in Figure 23-5 in order to see how we obtained the 68 percent and 95 percent probabilities mentioned earlier. The first normal curve in the figure shows a shaded area within one standard deviation of the mean. In the normal curve table the area between the mean and one standard deviation is given as .34134. Because the curve is symmetrical, the shaded area on the other side of the mean must be the same. Therefore the total shaded area is .34134 $\times$ 2, or .68268, which is 68.3 percent of the total area.

The area under the normal curve is a measure of probability

The normal curve tells us the probability of events happening if the events are normally distributed

Similarly, the table gives the value .47725 for the area between the mean and two standard deviations. Therefore the total shaded area in the second curve in Figure 23-5 is .95455, or 95.5 percent of the total area. This means that data occur beyond two standard deviations away from the mean less than 5 percent of the time. These relationships hold for all normal populations, no matter what their mean and standard deviation. The normal curve table can also be used to find the probability of an item's being at least as large as some value or at least as small as some value.

Figure 23-5. The shaded areas under these normal curves show the probability of events occurring within one and two standard deviations of the mean. In a normally distributed population, 68 percent of the individual items occur within one standard deviation of the mean and over 95 percent occur within two standard deviations.

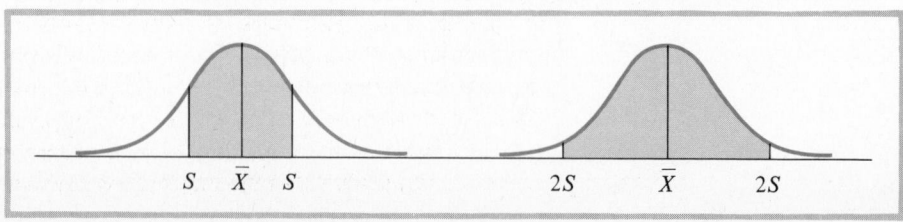

For example, if the two workers' data presented in Figure 23-2 are normally distributed, approximately 68 percent of the time worker A will produce between 57.2 and 62.8 units per day calculated as:

$$\overline{X} \pm S$$

$$60 \pm 2.78$$

On the other hand, 68 percent of the time worker B will produce between 49.7 and 70.3 units, and 95 percent of the time he will produce between 39.4 and 80.6 units per day. This prediction is calculated as follows:

$$\overline{X} \pm 2S$$

$$60 \pm 2(10.31)$$

This kind of information is valuable to a manager in planning production schedules and work assignments. Because of the smaller variance of A's output, the production output of worker A is easier to predict than that of worker B. Similar data can be obtained for entire departments or divisions. Managers can use such data to schedule production runs, plan the availability of raw materials, or establish deadlines for delivery of orders.

Management may wish to know the probability that worker A will produce between 58 and 62 units of product per day. These amounts are two units on either side of the mean. One standard deviation is 2.78 units, so two units is only a portion of one standard deviation. In fact, it is 2/2.78, or .72 standard deviation from the mean. The .72 value in the normal curve table indicates a probability of .26424. This means that there is a 26.4 percent probability that the worker will produce between 60 and 62 units, **or** between 58 and 60 units. Remember, the table measures probabilities only on one side of the mean. To find the probability that the worker will produce between 58 and 62 units, the 26.4 percent is merely doubled to yield 52.8 percent. Slightly more than half the time, worker A will produce between 58 and 62 units of product. The rest of the time he will produce more than 62 units or less than 58 units.

Managers are often more interested in fluctuations in one direction than in another. For example, in order to plan production, a manager may wish to know the probability that worker B will produce at least 54 units of product in a day. This means that we need to know the probability of producing 54 units or more. We already know that the probability of producing more than the mean of 60 units is 50 percent. We need to find the probability of producing between 54 and 60 units. The area under the normal curve that gives the desired probabilities is the shaded area of diagram (a) in Figure 23-6. The standard deviation for worker B is 10.31 and the mean is 60. To find the portion of standard deviation that is needed we solve the following:

$$\frac{x - \overline{X}}{S} = \frac{54 - 60}{10.31}$$

$$= -.58$$

Figure 23-6. Transforming sample statistics to the standard normal form enables the estimation of many probabilities using the normal curve. The shaded areas indicate the probabilities desired for various situations described in the text.

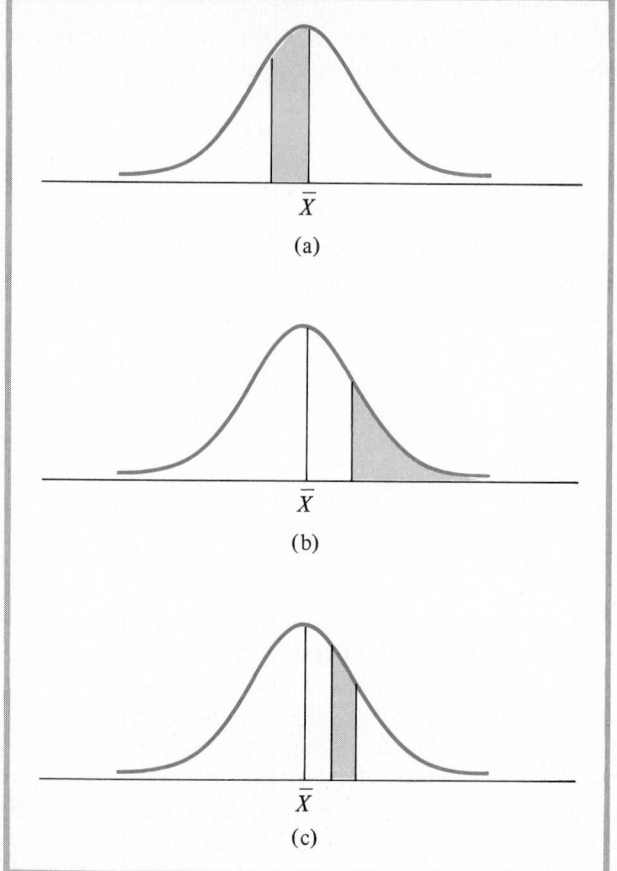

$\overline{X}$

(a)

$\overline{X}$

(b)

$\overline{X}$

(c)

Notice that the answer is negative, which simply means that we are looking for a probability under the left half of the normal curve. Looking at the normal curve table, we find the probability .21904 for .58 standard deviation. This is the probability that the worker will produce between 54 and 60 units. To this we add the probability that he will produce above 60 units, which is .5, and we get .71904. This tells us that 71.9 percent of the days, worker B will produce at least 54 units of product.

Computing z Values. Earlier we said that the standard normal curve table can be used to find probabilities for any normal distribution. This is accomplished by a simple transformation that changes the mean and standard deviation of a set of data into the standard normal mean of 0 and standard deviation of 1. That transformation, already used above, is

Sample statistics are transformed to a standard form for use with the normal curve table

$$z = \frac{x - \overline{X}}{S}$$

The mean, $\overline{X}$, and standard deviation, S, are calculated from the sample data. The value x is a point whose probability we want to estimate. It is located on the horizontal axis of the normal curve. The value z is simply the standard deviation of the data, transformed to a value that can be read as the standard deviation in the normal curve table. If x is greater than the mean, then z is positive, which means that we are looking for a probability under the right half of the normal curve. If z is negative the probability occurs under the left half of the curve. The sign of z is ignored when looking in the table.

The above formula can be used to solve many probability problems. We now look at some additional illustrations of the use of this formula.

Management wants to know what is the maximum daily number of units that worker A will produce 75 percent of the time. Logically we know that 50 percent of the time, the worker will produce less than his mean production quantity of 60 units and 50 percent of the time he will produce more than his mean. To find the most he will produce 75 percent of the time, we need to determine the value above the mean that includes all 50 percent of the area below the mean and 25 percent of the area above the mean. This point on the normal curve includes all 75 percent of the probability and excludes the remaining 25 percent. The problem is illustrated in diagram (b) of Figure 23-6, in which the area to be excluded is shaded. In this problem, we already know the probability and we need to find z and x by using the mean production quantity of 60 units, the standard deviation of 2.78, and the standard normal curve table.

Looking in Table V we find .24857 to be closest to 25 percent. The z for this probability is .67. This means that .67 standard deviations above the mean includes 75 percent of all production outputs. We use this z value and the mean and standard deviation data to find the value of x, which is the maximum production quantity we can expect from worker A 75 percent of the time.

The normal distribution is a versatile tool

$$z = \frac{x - \overline{X}}{S}$$

$$.67 = \frac{x - 60}{2.78}$$

$$.67(2.78) = x - 60$$

$$x = .67(2.78) + 60$$

$$= 61.86 \text{ or } \approx 62$$

The solution tells us that 75 percent of the time, worker A will produce at most 62 units of product per day.

As another illustration of how the standard normal curve table is used to solve problems, we assume management wants to estimate the probability that worker B will produce between 65 and 70 units in any 1 day. This probability is the shaded area under the normal curve in diagram (c) of Figure 23-6. This problem requires finding the area under the curve between the mean and 65 units, and also the area under the curve between the mean and 70 units. When the smaller area is subtracted from the larger, the difference is the probability desired by management.

The mean production quantity of worker B is 60 units with a standard deviation of 10.31 units. Using these statistics, we find z for 65 units is

$$z = \frac{65 - 60}{10.31} = .48$$

This value of z in the normal curve table has a probability of .18438. This is the probability of producing between 60 and 65 units. The area between the mean and 70 units is

$$z = \frac{70 - 60}{10.31} = .97$$

This z value indicates a probability of .33397. This is the probability of producing between 60 and 70 units. The probability of producing between 65 and 70 units is the difference between the two probabilities, which is

$$.33397 - .18438 = .14959, \text{ or 15 percent}$$

MATHEMATICAL EXPECTATION

Sometimes it is not possible to collect the data needed to compute the mean and standard deviation for the purpose of making a decision. In other cases, the data may not be normally distributed and a random sample would not provide the appropriate statistics. Nevertheless, experience or opinion may be helpful in computing useful statistics. In place of the mean, we can calculate the expected value of a variable. The **expected value** of a variable is the weighted average of the variable, where the weights are the probabilities that the variable will occur. The probabilities are obtained by using judgment, previous experience, or past data. Expected value is expressed with the following formula:

Expected value is a form of average

$$\text{Expected value} = \overline{X} = \Sigma(X_i \times P_i)$$

where X_i are the individual events and P_i is the probability of each event occurring. The sum of the probabilities must equal 1.

Expected Value

We already used expected values in Chapter 13 in connection with stockout costs. For example, not having a certain inventory item on hand costs a company $3,000 per day in lost contribution margin. But having too much inventory on hand also involves a cost. Management should weigh the cost of carrying safety stock against the cost of a stockout. If the probability of having a 1-day stockout is 10 percent there is a 90 percent probability that the stockout will not occur, then the **expected cost** of the stockout is only $300, calculated as follows:

$$\text{Cost of stockout} \times \text{Probability of stockout} = \text{Expected cost}$$

$3,000	.10	$300
0	.90	0
	1.00	$300

The delivery of inventory may be erratic, perhaps in this case with as much as 3 days delay. Management may be of the opinion that the probability of a 1-day stockout is .20, the probability of the stockout extending to 2 days is .10, and the probability of it going to 3 days is .04. In this case the expected cost of the stockout is

$$
\begin{aligned}
\$3,000 \times .20 &= \$\ \ 600 \\
3,000 \times .10 &= \ \ \ 300 \\
3,000 \times .04 &= \ \ \ 120 \\
0 \times .66 &= \ \ \ \ \ \ 0 \\
\overline{1.00} \ \ \ \ \ \ &\ \ \ \overline{\$1,020}
\end{aligned}
$$

Note that the probabilities are used as weights by which the variable is multiplied. The probabilities must, of course, sum to 1 in order to include all possible events.

In the above example the expected loss of $1,020 cannot actually occur. This is the average of all losses that will occur over a long period of time if the probabilities used in the calculation are correct.

Expected Standard Deviation

The **expected standard deviation** may be calculated using the following formula:

$$\text{Standard deviation of expected value} = \sqrt{\Sigma[(X_i - \overline{X})^2 \times P_i]}$$

Expected values and expected standard deviations may be used the same way as any other mean and standard deviation

This means that for each event, the expected value, $\overline{X}$, is subtracted from the value of each individual event, the difference is squared, and this product is multiplied by the probability of the event's occurrence. Then these amounts are added together and the square root of the sum is taken. For the 3-day stockout, the standard deviation is

$$
\begin{aligned}
(\ \ \ \ \ \ \ \ 0 - \$1,020)^2 \times .66 &= \$\ \ 686,664 \\
(\$3,000 - 1,020)^2 \times .20 &= \ \ \ 784,080 \\
(\ \ 3,000 - 1,020)^2 \times .10 &= \ \ \ 392,040 \\
(\ \ 3,000 - 1,020)^2 \times .04 &= \ \ \ \underline{156,816} \\
&\ \ \ \ \$2,019,600
\end{aligned}
$$

$$\text{Expected standard deviation} = \sqrt{\$2,019,600} = \$1,421$$

The main problem in using expected values is obtaining the probabilities needed to make the calculations. These are usually subjective opinions and judgments and sometimes are not very accurate. However, even subjective probabilities may yield better results than not making a calculation at all.

SAMPLING

Statistics such as the mean and standard deviation are computed from data in sales invoices, product cost reports, labor use reports, computer utilization studies, and many other sources. Businesses generate huge volumes of data and the analysis of all the available data is not feasible because it would be too costly and time-consuming. Fortunately, good statistics can be obtained by selecting and analyzing a relatively small sample of the data.

The total set of data from which a sample is selected is called a **population** or a **universe.** The population must be carefully defined, such as all students enrolled in a university, all full-time students enrolled in the school of business, all invoices for the year 1985, or all products assembled in May by the assembly department.

Population statistics are estimated from sample statistics

In many cases it is impractical, and sometimes impossible, to examine an entire population in order to obtain statistics about it. A sample of the population may yield very good estimates of population statistics, provided that the sample is selected correctly and is large enough given the characteristics of the population. There are several ways of obtaining representative samples, and statistical techniques exist for determining the appropriate sample size.

Random Sampling

A sample taken in such a way that every element in the population being sampled has an equal chance of being selected is called a **random sample.** This implies that the element of chance must exist in selecting each item for the sample, and it ensures that the sample will be representative of the population. There are a number of ways to select a random sample. We discuss simple random sampling, stratified sampling, and cluster sampling.

A random sample is an unbiased sample

Simple Random Sample.   The simplest form of random sampling involves selection of a sample without any special treatment of the population. To facilitate the selection of random samples, a set of random numbers is used. Random numbers are found in random number tables, such as Table VI at the back of this book, or they can be generated by a computer. If the population to be sampled consists of 900 items and 30 items are needed for a sample, the computer is instructed to generate 30 random numbers ranging from 1 to 900. For example, if three of the random numbers generated by the computer are 485, 23, and 199, then the 485th item, the 23d item, and the 199th item in the population are selected for the sample.

The random numbers used to select the sample must identify each item in the population. For example, if we are analyzing a population of 900 checks numbered from 2651 to 3550, we can use the check numbers to identify the sample. In this case, we would use random number 23 to include check number 2673 in the sample, which is the 23d check in the sequence starting with check number 2651. The desired statistics of the sample are computed from the **value** of the items selected. For example, check number 2673 is for $126.50, which is the variable used to find the mean and standard deviation of the dollar amount of the sample. Or the check may be signed by Mr. Black, which is a variable used to find a mode — the individual in the company who signs checks most often.

To select the numbers from the random number table, we arbitrarily select three columns and any row in order to find 30 three-digit numbers. If one of the numbers selected is beyond the value we need, it is discarded and the next number is selected. For example, if three-digit numbers are to be selected from the table starting with row 7 and column 19 going down, the first few numbers would be

302   195   962   147   34   289   423   664   798

of which the third one would be discarded because it is beyond the range of numbers in our population.

Stratified Sample. In some cases, the population to be sampled can be stratified, or divided, into several categories with specific characteristics; sample design may be improved or the size of the sample may be reduced by selecting a **stratified sample.** For example, a company sells several products to several hundred customers and wants to determine which of its products is the most popular. The firm's customers consist of retailers who purchase relatively small quantities of products at a time, and wholesalers who purchase larger orders. A representative sample of customers is to be tested. Management decides that a random sample of 60 customers is needed to achieve the desired test results. On the other hand, if the population is divided into two categories, it may be possible to improve the quality of the sample information and at the same time reduce the cost by selecting a smaller sample, such as 25 customers from each group.

It is beyond the scope of this book to discuss the mathematics of stratified sampling. You should understand, however, that when a population consists of several strata, such sampling may be appropriate. Deciding on the stratification is often difficult. For example, a sample of invoices may be divided into those with small, medium, and large dollar amounts. Are large invoices those above $5,000 or should $8,000 be considered the cutoff point between medium and large? The answer depends on the specific situation and often on judgment.

Cluster Sample. Sometimes it is not feasible to take a random sample from a population. For example, a farm implement manufacturer is interested in the opinion of farmers in three midwestern states about a new product. It may not be possible for the company to obtain a list of farmers in these states in order to develop a random sample. Even if such a list were available, taking the sample may be too costly. Instead of polling 75 farmers from all the counties of the three states, the company may be able to obtain the same results by polling 100 farmers in 10 different counties.

Stratifying or clustering the population may provide better samples at a lower cost

In this situation, a random sample of 10 counties is selected from the three states. Each county represents a cluster of farmers whose opinions can be obtained. All farmers in the selected counties are polled. **Cluster sampling** may be used in sampling the population of a city. Instead of selecting a random sample of the entire population, a random sample of city blocks may be selected and all members of each block used as the sample.

Nonrandom Sampling

Some methods of sampling do not have the element of chance required for random sampling. Such sampling may be adequate in some situations in which timeliness or simplicity of sample selection are more important than avoiding sample bias. Two methods of nonrandom sampling include systematic sampling and judgmental sampling.

Systematic Sampling.   A simple method of selecting a sample is to select items at fixed intervals, such as every 15th invoice from all invoices available, or every 20th item that comes off an assembly line. This approach to sampling is called **systematic sampling.** The element of randomness is missing, but the sample may nevertheless be representative of the population. In the case of invoices, the sample is sufficiently random because the invoices themselves may be generated in a random manner as customers place orders.

Nonrandom sampling is suitable in some situations

There is a risk that systematic sampling will produce a sample that is biased or not representative of the population. For example, if due to some defect in the assembly line every 10th item is defective, a systematic sample consisting of every 20th item may, by chance, consist only of defective items or only of nondefective ones.

Judgmental Sampling.   **Judgmental sampling** consists of selecting a sample according to someone's judgment about what is appropriate. Such sampling may turn out to be systematic sampling. Judgmental sampling may consist of selecting all sales invoices for out-of-state customers, all checks over $1,000, or all accounts receivable over 30 days past due. Although sometimes effective, judgmental sampling can produce a biased sample. Because there is no scientific method and little random element in judgmental sampling, there is a high risk that the sample will not be reliable. In an effort to reduce this risk, most judgmental samples are larger than would be necessary if random sampling were used, making the cost of the sample higher than necessary.

SAMPLE SIZE

A critical aspect of selecting a sample is the determination of sample size. Previously we pointed out that $\overline{X}$ and S, the mean and standard deviation of the sample, are estimates of μ and σ, the mean and standard deviation of the population. In order for these estimates to be valid, they must be reasonably accurate. Accuracy is generally improved by increasing sample size, but large samples are more costly than small ones. In order to arrive at good estimates without incurring excessive sampling costs, it is necessary to determine the appropriate sample size. The following discussion illustrates how sample size affects statistical estimation and shows the development of a formula for sample size.

Estimating Means

In most business applications, population means and standard deviations are not known. If the sample size is large enough, the sample mean is a reasonably good estimate of the population mean. But there is bound to be some error in the estimate. To understand the nature of the error, it is necessary to discuss the standard error of the mean.

Standard Error of the Mean.   Suppose that we take a sample of production output for a worker over a 5-day period and discover that the mean of this sample is 50 units. In this case $n = 5$. If we take another sample for a different 5-day period, we find the mean to be 48 units. Still more 5-day samples yield means of 55 units, 54 units, 49, 50, and 51 units. Which of these means is the best estimate of the true population mean?

An important statistical theorem, known as the **central limit theorem,** states that if samples of size n are taken from a population whose mean is μ and whose standard deviation is σ, the means of the samples will form a normal distribution whose mean is μ and whose standard deviation is $\sigma/\sqrt{n}$. In the above example, we have seven means, each made up of samples with $n = 5$. What the theorem says is that the mean of these seven means should be equal to the population mean, and the sample means will be dispersed about their mean in such a way that their standard deviation will be equal to the population standard deviation divided by the square root of 5, which is our n. Moreover, the means themselves will be normally distributed. The standard deviation of the sample means is an indication of the error that we can expect in our estimate of the population mean. For this reason the standard deviation of sample means is called the **standard error of the mean,** designated as S_e.

The standard error of the mean is a powerful estimation tool

The above seven sample means have a mean of 51 and a standard error of 2.58 calculated as follows:

$$\overline{X} = \Sigma x_i/n \qquad\qquad S_e = \sqrt{\frac{n\Sigma x_i^2 - (\Sigma x_i)^2}{n(n-1)}}$$

$$= 357/7 \qquad\qquad = \sqrt{\frac{7(18,247) - 357^2}{7(7-1)}}$$

$$= 51 \qquad\qquad = 2.582$$

Note that the formula for the standard deviation is used to compute the standard error of the mean, and that $n = 7$ because there are seven items in our sample of means. But each mean is made up of a sample of 5 days' production. Be careful to differentiate between the number of means and the number of items in each sample.

Substituting S for σ.   The population standard deviation usually is not known, but let us assume that in this case it is 5.75 units. Then we can expect the standard error of the mean for these seven samples with $n = 5$ to be

$$S_e = \sigma/\sqrt{n}$$
$$= 5.75/\sqrt{5}$$
$$= 2.571$$

The population standard deviation is usually not known; we use the sample standard deviation instead

You can see that our 2.582 estimate of the standard error is very close to the actual standard error computed from the known σ. What the above computations tell us is that if the true population mean is 51, we can expect any 5-day sample to be within 2.571 units of the true mean about 68 percent of the time, and within 5.142 units of the true mean 95 percent of the time.

Suppose now that we increase sample size and we take seven 20-day samples instead of seven 5-day samples. We may get the following seven sample means:

$$51, 50, 51, 52, 53, 49, 51$$

The mean of the above means is 51 and the standard error is 1.291 estimated by using the formula for the standard deviation. The above means are made up of samples consisting of 20 items each, and these samples come from the same population as the five-item samples. With a population standard deviation of 5.75 assumed earlier, we can calculate the standard error as follows:

$$S_e = 5.75/\sqrt{20}$$
$$= 1.286$$

Again the 1.291 estimate of the standard error is very close to what we would obtain if we knew the value of σ. Note that the value 1.29 is only half of the previous standard error of 2.57. Clearly with a smaller standard error, any one sample is going to provide a better estimate of the true population mean. But we had to increase the sample size by four times, from 5 to 20 days of data, in order to cut the error in half.

This discussion should give you some idea of the significance that sample size has on estimating the mean of a population. A larger sample provides better estimates. Managers are frequently interested in the magnitude of the error when they make such estimates and with the probability that the error will occur. Typically, managers are interested in a fairly low probability of error as long as the additional cost required to increase the precision of an estimate is not excessive. There is, however, a limit to the benefit obtained from increasing sample size, because the cost of sampling grows much faster than the reduction in estimation error.

Earlier you saw that the probability of a certain event may be found in the normal curve table. Several values of z from the table are frequently used in estimation because they yield the following commonly used probabilities of being correct:

z	Probability
1.64	90 percent
1.96	95 percent
2.33	98 percent
2.58	99 percent

Magnitude of Error

In the above example of 20-day samples, the standard error of the mean is 1.29 and the population mean is 51. Remember that the standard error of the mean is nothing more than the standard deviation of many means. In most cases, only one sample is taken so the standard error cannot be computed, but we know from the central limit theorem that the standard error is the population standard deviation divided by the square root of n, the sample size. With the population standard deviation usually not known, we use S as an estimate.

Previously we used the following equation for finding z values:

$$z = \frac{x - \overline{X}}{S}$$

Estimation error is the difference between the computed mean and the true mean

The z obtained from the above equation can be used to find the probability of a single item, x, being within a certain distance from the sample mean. If we are interested in estimating the true mean of a population from its sample mean and standard deviation, any error in our estimate may be expressed as the difference between the sample mean and population mean. If we want to know the probability of our estimate's being within a certain distance from the true mean—that is, having the error $\overline{X} - \mu$—we can find the z value by dividing this error term by the standard deviation. But now, instead of dividing by the standard deviation, we use the standard error because we are dealing with the sample and population mean rather than with a single value and the sample mean. Consequently, the equation above is now expressed as

$$z = \frac{\overline{X} - \mu}{S/\sqrt{n}}$$

Confidence in the accuracy of an estimate is expressed as a probability

Here we are not interested in solving for a z value, but rather we want to use a z value to estimate how correct our computed mean is. For example, a manager wants to be 95 percent sure that his estimate of the mean is correct; for 95 percent accuracy, we use a z value of 1.96. Remember that the error may be either above or below the mean, so z may be either positive or negative. We restructure the equation above to solve the problem more easily. We transform the equation to isolate the error, which is the top part of the fraction, as follows:

$$\overline{X} - \mu = \text{Error}$$
$$= \pm 1.96 \, S/\sqrt{n}$$

This equation states that if a manager wants to be 95 percent sure that his estimate of a population mean is correct, and he takes a sample of size n which has a standard deviation S, he must be willing to tolerate the amount of error indicated by the equation. For example, a manager takes a sample of the weekly amount of checks written in order to estimate the mean weekly cash outflow for his company. The sample size is 16 weeks, the mean of the sample is $9,800 per week, and the standard deviation is $796. The manager wants to be 95 percent certain that his estimate is correct. How far from the mean might his estimate be? We calculate the error using the above equation and obtain the following:

$$\text{Error} = \pm 1.96(\$796)/\sqrt{16}$$

$$= \pm \$390$$

The manager can be 95 percent certain that his $9,800 estimate of the mean lies within $390 of the true mean of cash outflows. If he wants less risk because cash planning for the company is critical, he can use another z value and find the error that must be tolerated. For example, to estimate the mean at a 99 percent confidence limit, the error is

$$\text{Error} = \pm 2.58(\$796)/\sqrt{16}$$

$$= \pm \$513$$

You can see that one must trade more certainty or less risk for a larger error. If cash planning is critical and the manager wants to be sure that sufficient funds will be available to meet necessary weekly outflows, he must make more cash available. The manager reduces the risk of not having sufficient cash at the cost of having to have a larger amount of an unproductive asset on hand.

Sample Size Formula

Sample size can be found easily if the confidence limit and error magnitude are specified

In the above example, the sample size is 16. If the sample size were larger, the estimate of the mean might be more precise. Sometimes managers may specify the size of error they will tolerate in making estimates and then calculate the sample size that will ensure the error is not exceeded within some level of probability. For example, management is willing to tolerate an error of $300 at the 95 percent level of probability. The error equation can be expressed in terms of n as follows:

$$\text{Error} = \overline{X} - \mu = e$$
$$e = \pm 1.96 \, S/\sqrt{n}$$
$$\sqrt{n} = 1.95 \, S/e$$
$$n = (1.96 \, S/e)^2$$

In this equation, e is the error term for which we simply substitute $300 and solve.

$$n = [1.96(\$796/\$300)]^2$$
$$= 27$$

A 27-week sample of cash outflows would have to be taken in order to be 95 percent certain that the estimate of the mean is within $300 of the true mean of cash flows. To be 99 percent sure that the error is not more than $300, the sample size is:

$$n = [2.58(\$796/\$300)]^2$$
$$= 47$$

The sample size would have to be 47 to increase the certainty and reduce the level of risk. Managers must use judgment to determine whether the reduction of risk warrants the additional cost of increasing the sample size.

A word of caution is necessary at this point. Most of the above discussion pertains to large populations that are normally distributed or nearly so, and we assume that an appropriate method of random sampling is used. In most cases, the sample size should be at least 30 to obtain a reasonable estimate of the mean and standard deviation. For small populations or those not normally distributed, other similar statistical techniques are available. This chapter is not intended to cover the subject exhaustively, but only to give you an idea of some of the more significant and useful tools available to management. Statistical sampling is used for many more decision-making purposes in addition to finding measures of central tendency and dispersion. Some of these are discussed in the following chapters.

SUMMARY

A **statistic** is a numerical description of some characteristic. Statistics are often used as surrogates for actual events and may provide information about the events that cannot be obtained otherwise. Important statistics include measures of central tendency and dispersion. The **mean** is the average of a set of data. The **median** is the middle value of the data, and the **mode** is the most commonly occurring value.

Dispersion refers to the fluctuation of data about the mean. It can be measured as the **range, variance,** or the **standard deviation.** The standard deviation and the mean can be used to estimate the probability of occurrence of certain events. Such probabilities are obtained from a **normal curve** table if the data are normally distributed.

Statistics such as the mean and standard deviation are often estimated from **samples** that represent a **population** or a **universe** of data. A normal population is distributed about the mean symmetrically in a bell-shaped curve whose mathematical properties are very useful in statistical analysis. Many events can be estimated using the normal curve even if the sample comes from a population that is only nearly normal.

When data cannot be collected for statistical estimation, it may be possible to compute the **expected value** of an event by estimating the probabilities that the event will occur. An expected standard deviation may also be computed from such probabilities.

A **random sample** is obtained in such a way that every item in a population has an equal chance of being selected. If the population can be divided into several categories, a **stratified sample** may be taken in order to improve the accuracy of the statistics obtained and reduce the cost of taking the sample. **Cluster sampling** consists of selecting every item from randomly selected segments of a population. **Systematic sampling** involves selecting every nth item from the population. **Judgmental sampling** is based on judgment and lacks the reliability needed for statistical analysis.

The **central limit theorem** may be used to estimate the **sample size** needed to satisfy specific statistical requirements. Sample size is determined by using the **standard error of the estimate,** which is a measure of dispersion for a set of sample means. A large sample produces a smaller estimation error than a small sample, but to reduce the error by one-half requires a sample four times as large.

KEY TERMS

central limit theorem *(817)*
cluster sample *(815)*
dispersion *(802)*
expected standard deviation *(813)*
expected value *(812)*
judgmental sample *(816)*
mean *(800)*
median *(801)*
mode *(802)*
normal curve *(805)*
normal distribution *(805)*
population *(805)*
probability *(806)*

probability distribution *(806)*
random sample *(814)*
range *(803)*
sample *(805)*
sample size *(816)*
standard deviation *(803)*
standard error of the mean *(817)*
standard normal curve *(808)*
statistic *(799)*
stratified sample *(815)*
systematic sample *(816)*
universe *(814)*
variance *(803)*

QUESTIONS

1. A product research organization recently published its findings of the results of mileage tests of several brands of tires. Five tires of each brand were tested and the mileage results of two of the brands were as follows:

	Mileage				
Brand A	26,800	22,300	27,400	24,000	23,500
Brand B	25,600	23,400	21,000	26,000	25,000

Subsequent to the publication of the tests the manufacturers of these two brands of tires each claimed in their advertising that "on the average," its tires held up better than the other brand. Comment on the use of the term *average* by the tire makers. Which average does each have in mind?

2. Geneseed Laboratories, Inc., wants to develop new strains of carrots from seeds bought for that purpose from two different suppliers. The company wants to develop a strain of miniature carrots for use in gourmet delicacies and also a strain of giant carrots for making canned carrot juice. The process involves cultivating carrots from seeds and using the seeds from subsequent generations of plants with the desirable characteristics until the characteristic becomes dominant. To determine which supplier's seeds should be used in the initial planting, Geneseed found that the mean length of carrots from seeds provided by supplier A is 5 inches with a standard deviation of 2.3 inches, whereas the mean length of carrots from seeds provided by supplier B is 5.2 inches with a standard deviation of 1.2 inches. Which supplier's seeds are more likely to produce the desired results? Explain your reasoning. What characteristics other than size may be significant?

3. A boat manufacturer builds boats of the following lengths, in feet: 10, 12, 16, 18, 23, 26, and 35. To plan next year's production, the company decided to hire a surveying firm to determine what size boat the public prefers. When the surveying firm quoted a price of $30,000 for the survey, the company decided to conduct the survey with its own staff. The survey staff visited lake and river resorts and marinas and interviewed boat owners about their preferences. After some time, the surveying staff made the following report: 22 percent of respondents preferred the mean size of the boats, which is 20 feet. Only 14 percent preferred the median size of 18 feet. Forty percent expressed a preference for 16-foot boats, 11 percent preferred boats smaller than 14 feet, and 13 percent preferred boats larger than 26 feet. Which measure of central tendency is most significant to the boat manufacturer? Why? Comment on the reliability of the survey.

EXERCISES

Ex. 23-1
Measures of
Central Tendency

The personnel department of Bledsoe company collected the following biweekly data on worker absenteeism during the current year.

Number of Hours Lost to
Absenteeism in Each Pay Period

56	77	93	55	94
30	85	35	77	17
29	64	84	6	88
43	32	23	45	22
47	10	13	41	9

REQUIRED   Compute the mean, median, and mode for the number of hours of absenteeism.

Ex. 23-2
Mean and
Dispersion

A random sample of 12 days' quality control data from a 6-month population reveals the following frequencies of defective condensers:

Day	Defective Units	Day	Defective Units
7	92	49	65
76	80	35	43
22	60	102	84
19	44	43	75
59	79	6	48
30	68	66	31

REQUIRED   a. Compute the mean number of defective units.
            b. Compute the standard deviation, variance, and range.

Ex. 23-3
Mean and Standard
Deviation

The following random sample was taken from Flamingo Company's data on the weekly cost of machine oil used during a 40-week period:

Sample	Cost	Sample	Cost
1	$230	6	$310
2	180	7	260
3	220	8	340
4	160	9	190
5	300	10	250

REQUIRED   a. Find the mean cost of weekly oil consumption.
            b. Compute the standard deviation, variance, and range.

Ex. 23-4
Normal Curve
Probabilities

Frotula Company's daily cash receipts are normally distributed with a mean of $8,500 and a standard deviation of $500.

REQUIRED

a. Find the probability that daily cash receipts will be between $8,000 and $9,000.
b. Find the probability that daily cash receipts will be greater than $9,000.
c. How much will maximum daily cash receipts be 80 percent of the time?
d. What is the probability that daily cash receipts will be between $9,000 and $9,500?

Ex. 23-5
Expected Value

Gasoline sales by a service station average $1,200 a day on clear days, but only $500 on rainy days. The weather forecast for tomorrow is for a 70 percent chance of thundershowers.

REQUIRED   Compute the expected value of gasoline sales for tomorrow.

Ex. 23-6
Expected Value of a
New Product

Futilla Company has just invested $300,000 in the development of a new product. Management estimates that there is a .75 probability that the product will be successful, in which case the company stands to gain $4,000,000 over the useful life of the product. If the product is not successful, the entire investment will be lost.

REQUIRED   Compute the expected value of the new product.

Ex. 23-7
Expected Value and
Standard Deviation

Bizmark Electric Utility uses a sophisticated model, based on weather predictions, to estimate the probabilities of using various quantities of fuel for electric generation. Following is the latest estimate on fuel use and probabilities:

Tons of Fuel	Probability
125	.10
135	.16
150	.25
160	.25
175	.15
185	.09

REQUIRED   Use the above data to compute the expected tons of fuel that will be used and the standard deviation of the expected value.

Ex. 23-8
Selecting a Random
Sample

Dipple Company produces scientific printing calculators using an assembly line and a process costing system. It operates 200 days per year. The number of units produced each day during last year's production is shown in the table below.

715	660	693	737	792	836	880	770	748	671	627	759
737	528	726	781	660	726	715	814	737	726	726	847
682	649	759	616	770	638	726	451	605	748	737	891
803	759	814	748	748	704	759	550	726	704	781	737
748	660	704	715	671	803	627	682	770	825	682	858
583	726	770	649	770	825	726	770	660	638	814	858
781	671	693	726	737	627	715	693	748	693	748	638
748	814	660	836	682	792	737	792	649	759	693	770
704	737	836	726	726	660	737	561	594	682	660	715
770	671	473	605	759	682	649	759	803	748	748	649
638	660	627	715	737	792	759	682	781	616	759	715
803	715	781	748	814	704	693	671	693	737	748	770
759	704	649	649	781	561	715	748	704	715	671	671
715	605	726	803	638	671	759	693	649	726	726	781
737	704	660	759	737	737	715	770	726	616	737	726
792	748	825	693	660	792	869	726	682	957	704	726
759	704	682	726	781	627	748	847				

REQUIRED   Use the table of random numbers to select a sample of 15 days' production. Use your sample to estimate the mean and standard deviation of daily production of calculators.

Ex. 23-9
Systematic
Sampling

Refer to the data on the production of calculators in Exercise 23-18.

REQUIRED.   Starting anywhere in the first column, select a systematic sample of every 20th item to obtain a sample of 10. Use your sample to estimate the mean and standard deviation of the population.

Ex. 23-10
Estimation Error
and Sample Size

A random sample of 36 cartons of detergent has a mean of 32.40 oz and a standard deviation of 2.3 oz. The contents of the cartons are normally distributed.

REQUIRED
  a. Find the range within which the population mean falls with a 90 percent confidence limit.
  b. Find the sample size needed for a 95 percent confidence interval if the error is to be limited to .60 oz.

PROBLEMS

P. 23-1
Central Tendency
and Dispersion

Vixen Valve Works has been producing a new mechanical gas valve on two automated production lines in a pilot plant. Each production line was acquired from a different manufacturer and both seem to be performing in a satisfactory manner. The company is now ready to build a full-scale plant in which eight production lines will be used to manufacture the valves in a process cost system. In order to determine which of the two production lines to select for its new plant, the company used systematic sampling and tested the entire production for each Thursday of the past 9 weeks. It collected the following data on the number of defective items coming off each of its production lines:

	Defective Units								
Week	1	2	3	4	5	6	7	8	9
Line A	139	171	118	192	130	162	146	180	166
Line B	150	160	146	172	157	169	142	151	175

REQUIRED

a. Find the median number of defective units for each production line.
b. Find the mean number of defective units for each line.
c. Compute the standard deviation of defective units for each production line.
d. Decide which production line should be selected by management for its new plant. Provide reasons for your decision.

P. 23-2
Use of Means and
Standard Deviations

Kratki Tours uses two 70-passenger buses for its organized tours. Daily revenues vary considerably on the Devil's Hole tour and appear to be much more stable on the Thistle Trail tour. The tours last 6 hours each and are priced at $30 per adult and $25 per child. Following are 10 days' revenues that the owner wants analyzed:

Day	Devil's Hole	Thistle Trail	Day	Devil's Hole	Thistle Trail
1	$1,800	$1,650	6	$1,950	$1,500
2	1,350	1,575	7	1,500	1,575
3	1,200	1,500	8	1,050	1,500
4	1,650	1,350	9	900	1,425
5	2,100	1,440	10	1,350	1,485

REQUIRED

a. Compute the mean and standard deviation for daily revenues for each tour.
b. Find the range of revenues for each tour 95.4 percent of the time, assuming a normal distribution.
c. Find the probability that daily revenue for each tour will be below $1,300.

P. 23-3
Expected Cost of
Lost Time

The president of Neverlate Company considers Jonathan to be a very valuable employee, but Jonathan has the bad habit of coming to work late. Based on observations over several months, the president estimates that on any 1 day of the week, Jonathan will be late to work with the following probabilities.

Minutes Late	Probability	Minutes Late	Probability
0	.10	7	.20
1	.01	8	.14
2	.02	9	.10
3	.04	10	.05
4	.06	11	.03
5	.09	12	.01
6	.15		

Jonathan's salary is $30 per hour. Because Jonathan is very productive, the president does not like to complain about his bad habit. He decides to say nothing if the cost to the company is less than $5 per day. But he wants to be 99 percent sure that the cost does not exceed $5 per day on the average. Assume that the data are normally distributed.

REQUIRED   Find the expected number of minutes and expected standard deviation of the 13 items of data. Determine, within the confidence limit desired by the president, the daily cost of Jonathan's tardiness and decide whether the president should discuss the problem with Jonathan.

P. 23-4
Estimation of Mean
by Sampling

Jupiter Corporation collects daily information on the number of differential assemblies produced by its employees. The following data have been collected during the past 200 working days, with each number showing 1 day's production.

550	720	700	700	750	800	750	810	740	740
560	590	680	660	730	700	730	830	720	720
770	720	610	730	710	730	700	660	750	730
690	660	740	810	740	620	720	730	780	680
770	740	670	830	880	710	660	690	730	790
810	730	720	720	710	730	520	720	780	660
450	600	740	630	720	680	640	750	610	770
680	770	820	800	620	740	660	700	710	670
770	660	630	820	720	580	720	770	640	770
690	740	690	620	710	780	670	690	720	730
790	640	750	790	730	740	810	660	830	680
750	800	740	680	640	770	670	470	600	750
680	780	610	790	750	630	660	620	710	730
670	690	730	700	690	800	710	780	740	810
740	700	710	560	710	750	700	640	640	780
690	640	720	670	750	710	600	720	800	630
720	680	950	790	860	790	740	820	690	660
620	740	840	720	780	720	720	750	700	680
770	670	780	640	710	850	850	630	770	710
840	890	730	700	750	750	740	670	720	730

The company wants to obtain an estimate of mean daily production without using the entire population of data.

REQUIRED
a. Select six random samples of five items each and compute the mean of each sample.
b. Compute the mean and standard error of the mean for the six means you found in part a.
c. If management wants to be 90 percent certain that your estimate of the mean is correct, within what range can it expect the true mean to lie?

P. 23-5
Sample Size Needed
to Estimate Mean

Refer to the data in Problem 23-4 for Jupiter Corporation's production of differential assemblies. Management wants to estimate the mean of the population by analyzing a single random sample of 15 items. The population standard deviation is known to be 71.75.

REQUIRED
a. Select a random sample of 15 items from the population and use it to estimate the mean and standard deviation of the population.
b. Compute the magnitude of error that management can expect from the sample mean, using the population standard deviation and a 95 percent confidence limit. Then describe what the error means.

Part Seven Tools for Managerial Analysis

c. Determine what sample size would have to be taken if management wants to be 95 percent certain that its estimate of the population mean does not vary from the true mean by more than 30 units in either direction.

P. 23-6
Statistical Analysis
of Telephone Calls

A random sample of 50 long-distance phone calls was made by Crabbis Company in an effort to determine if restrictions should be placed on long-distance calling. The sample has a mean of 16.3 minutes with a standard deviation of 6.5 minutes.

REQUIRED

a. Determine what percentage of phone calls is longer than 20 minutes in duration.
b. What is the length of phone calls 95 percent of the time?
c. In what range does the population mean of phone calls fall with a 95 percent probability?
d. If management wants to estimate the mean length of phone calls with a 95 percent probability within an error of 1 minute, how large a sample should it take?

P. 23-7 (AICPA)
Using Probabilities
in Budget Estimates

The Wing Manufacturing Corporation produces a chemical compound, product X, which deteriorates and must be discarded if it is not sold by the end of the month during which it is produced. The total variable cost of the manufactured compound, product X, is $50 per unit and its selling price is $80 per unit. Wing can purchase the same compound from a competing company at $80 per unit plus $10 freight per unit. Management has estimated that failure to fill orders would result in the loss of 80 percent of customers placing orders for the compound. Wing has manufactured and sold product X for the past 20 months. Demand for product X has been irregular and at present there is no consistent sales trend. During this period monthly sales have been as follows:

Units Sold per Month	Number of Months
8,000	5
9,000	12
10,000	3

REQUIRED

a. Compute the probability of sales of product X of 8,000, 9,000, or 10,000 units in any month.
b. Compute what the contribution margin would be if 9,000 units of product X were ordered and either 8,000, 9,000, or 10,000 units were manufactured in that same month (with additional units, if necessary, being purchased).
c. Compute the average monthly contribution margin that Wing can expect if 9,000 units of product X are manufactured every month and all sales orders are filled.

CASES

Case 23-1 (AICPA)
Use of Probabilities
to Estimate Profit

Vernon Enterprises designs and manufactures toys. Past experience indicates that the product life cycle of a toy is 3 years. Promotional advertising produces large sales in the early years, but there is a substantial sales decline in the final year of a toy's life.

Consumer demand for new toys placed on the market tends to fall into three classes. About 30 percent of the new toys sell well above expectations, 60 percent sell as anticipated and 10 percent have poor consumer acceptance.

A new toy has been developed. The following sales projections were made by carefully evaluating consumer demand for the new toy:

Consumer Demand for New Toy	Chance of Occurring	Estimated Sales in		
		Year 1	Year 2	Year 3
Above average	30%	$1,200,000	$2,500,000	$600,000
Average	60	700,000	1,700,000	400,000
Below average	10	200,000	900,000	150,000

Variable costs are estimated at 30 percent of the selling price. Special machinery must be purchased at a cost of $860,000 and will be installed in an unused portion of the factory that Vernon has unsuccessfully been trying to rent to someone for several years at $50,000 per year and that has no prospects for future utilization. Fixed expenses (excluding depreciation) of a cash flow nature are estimated at $50,000 per year on the new toy. The new machinery will be depreciated by the sum-of-the-years'-digits method with an estimated salvage value of $110,000 and will be sold at the beginning of the fourth year. Advertising and promotional expenses will be incurred uniformly and will total $100,000 the first year, $150,000 the second year, and $50,000 the third year. These expenses will be deducted as incurred for income tax reporting.

Vernon believes that state and federal income taxes will total 60 percent of income in the foreseeable future and may be assumed to be paid uniformly over the year income is earned.

REQUIRED

a. Prepare a schedule computing the probable sales of this new toy in each of the 3 years, taking into account the probability of above average, average, and below average sales occurring.

b. Assume that the probable sales computed in part *a* are $900,000 in the first year, $1,800,000 in the second year, and $410,000 in the third year. Prepare a schedule computing the probable net income for the new toy in each of the 3 years of its life.

c. Prepare a schedule of net cash flows from sales of the new toy for each of the years involved and from disposition of the machinery purchased. Use the sales data given in part *b*.

d. Assuming a minimum desired rate of return of 10 percent, prepare a schedule of the present value of the net cash flows calculated in part *c*. The following data are relevant:

Year	Present Value of $1.00 Due at the End of Each Year Discounted at 10 Percent	Present Value of $1.00 Earned Uniformly Throughout the Year Discounted at 10 Percent
1	.91	.95
2	.83	.86
3	.75	.78

CHAPTER 24
Regression Analysis and Forecasting

Many of the concepts discussed in this book deal specifically with the relationship between costs and the volume of activity. CVP analysis in Chapter 3, alternative decision analysis in Chapter 10, short-term planning in Chapters 7 and 9, and long-term planning in Chapters 15 and 16 all depend on measuring the relationship between cost data and activities. Such relationships can be measured by methods discussed in this chapter. Statistical techniques that relate costs with other variables include regression, correlation, and trend analysis. These techniques provide data that managers can use to make forecasts for the purpose of planning the future and controlling current operations.

REGRESSION-CORRELATION ANALYSIS

One of the more powerful forecasting and analytic tools available to management is regression-correlation analysis. No other quantitative method has as many applications for cost data analysis and forecasting. **Regression-correlation analysis** is a statistical technique for measuring the nature and strength of the relationship between two or more variables. Past cost data can be analyzed to determine the relationship between specific costs and some measure of activity and to make predictions about future costs and activity levels. Such predictions often are quite accurate and can be used in budgeting, planning, and control.

Regression analysis tests the nature of a relationship

Correlation analysis tests the strength of a relationship

   Regression analysis is used to determine the **nature** of the association between two or more variables. **Correlation analysis** is used to determine the **strength** of the relationship between the variables. We discuss simple linear regression first and multiple linear regression later in the chapter.

Simple Linear Regression

The independent variable causes changes in the dependent variable

Simple linear regression deals with two sets of variables. The **independent variable** is typically derived from historical data, such as volume of production, time required for a certain activity, or number of customers served. The **dependent variable** is derived from historical data whose values depend on the values of the independent variable. For example, daily revenues of a gift shop depend on the number of people visiting the store. A company may use regression-correlation analysis to analyze traffic patterns in a shopping center in order to predict the profit potential of a store location. Here the independent variable is the number of people passing the location and the dependent variable is profit. Profit is the dependent variable because it depends on the number of people and the relationship between them and the revenues generated by those who stop to buy something.

The Regression Line

The linear relationship between the independent variable and the dependent variable is described by a **regression line.** Chapter 3 illustrates a scatter diagram and indicates that a line may be drawn through the scattered points to represent the data. Each datum in the scattergram is one dependent variable associated with a specific independent variable. The scatter diagrams in Figure 24-1 each have a regression line drawn through the data. The dependent variable is plotted on the vertical axis and the independent variable on the horizontal axis.

Figure 24-1. Graphs of two regression lines. Diagram (a) shows a regression line with a positive slope; diagram (b) shows a regression line with a negative slope. The equation of each line can be used to forecast a value of Y for any value of X within a relevant range.

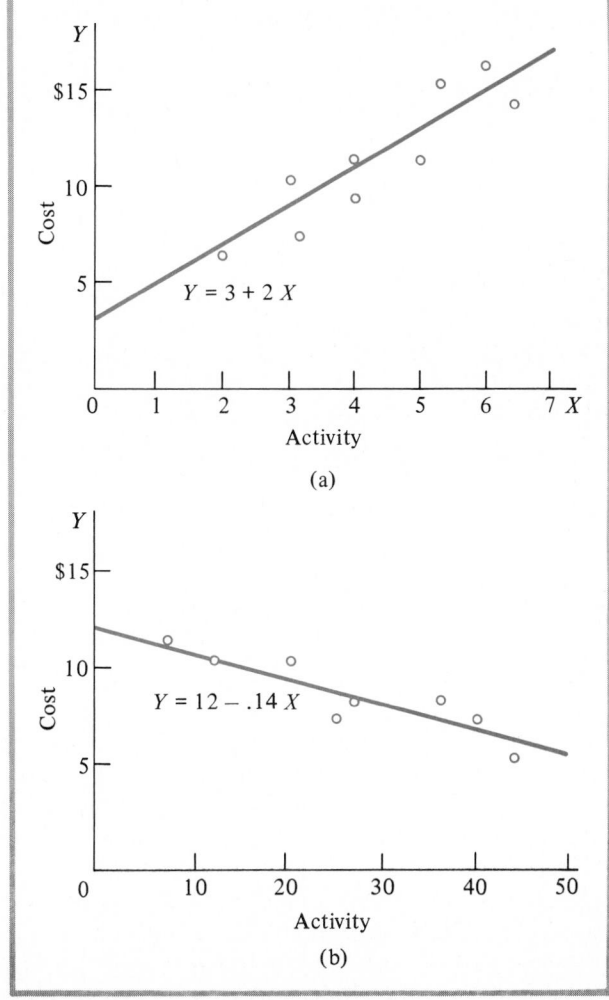

If the value of the dependent variable increases with increasing values of the independent variable, the regression line has a positive slope as in diagram (a). For example, if the dependent variable is production cost and the independent variable is labor time, we expect production costs to increase as more labor time is used.

If the value of the dependent variable decreases with increasing values of the independent variable the regression line has a negative slope as in diagram (b) of Figure 24-1. For example, if the dependent variable is the cost of heating a production facility and the independent variable is the world's supply of crude oil, the relationship illustrated in diagram (b) shows that heating costs decline as the supply of crude oil increases.

Linear regression is a straight-line relationship

The general form of the regression line is described by the traditional equation for a straight line, which is

$$Y_c = a + bX$$

where Y_c = the computed value of the dependent variable obtained from a specific value of the independent variable.

a = the constant or intercept where the regression line crosses the vertical axis. It is the value of Y_c when $X = 0$.

b = the slope of the regression line. It describes the change in the value of Y_c for each unit change in the value of X.

X = the value of the independent variable.

A regression line may slope up or down.

The regression line in diagram (a) of Figure 24-1 is described by the equation $Y_c = \$3 + \$2X$. In this case $a = \$3$, and $b = \$2$. For any value of X, Y is equal to $\$3 + \$2$ times the value of X. In diagram (b), the formula for the line is $\$12 - \$.14X$, which means that for any value of X, Y equals $\$12 - \$.14$ times the value of X. Alternatively, we can say that if X increases by 1 unit, Y decreases by $\$.14$.

Once the regression line is known, it can be used to predict Y for any value of X. For example if X in diagram (b) is 10 the value of Y is expected to be:

$$Y_c = 12 - .14(10)$$
$$= 10.6$$

In Figure 24-1, the values of X and Y are scattered about the regression line; therefore the regression line estimate of Y has some error. The regression line is the best-fitting straight line that can be drawn through the data points. It is the line that minimizes the absolute vertical distance between each data point and the line. In other words, any other straight line drawn through the set of data would leave a larger total vertical distance between the data points and the line.

To find the best-fitting line requires a calculation that minimizes the squared distances between the line and the data points. The distances between the data points and the line are squared to eliminate negative values. For this reason the method of calculating the regression line is called the **least** squares method, and the line is referred to as the **line of best fit** or the **least squares regression line.**

CALCULATING LINEAR REGRESSION

To illustrate the computation and use of regression-correlation analysis, we use the example of Barrows Chemical Company, which produces industrial chemicals. One of its products is manufactured in a process costing system requiring skilled labor and considerable machinery such as centrifuges, mixers, and separators. Figure 24-2 shows a sample of weekly production data for 6 randomly selected weeks. In practice, a sample of six is not large enough to provide a good analysis, but we limit our example to a small sample to simplify the illustration and make it easier to understand the computations.

Figure 24-2. Data for use in performing a simple linear regression analysis. The overhead cost data may be related either to labor hours or to machine hours.

Barrows Chemical Company
Weekly Overhead Cost and Activity Data

Sample Week	Overhead Cost per Week	Labor Hours	Machine Hours
1	$ 2,450	290	225
2	4,000	480	340
3	3,000	340	245
4	4,200	580	415
5	3,700	560	415
6	3,200	420	280
Totals	$20,550	2,670	1,920

The sample consists of overhead costs and two measures of activity, the number of labor hours used and the number of machine hours used. In order to plan and control overhead costs for this product, management wants to relate product costs to some activity measure.

Regression Analysis

In simple linear regression, one independent variable can be related to one dependent variable. The dependent variable in this case is the weekly overhead cost, and the independent variable can be either direct labor hours or machine hours. First we use direct labor hours as the independent variable.

Definition of Variables.   Before we proceed, several terms must be defined.

Variables defined for the regression line

Y_i are the actual values of the dependent variable used in the computation of the regression line. In our example, these are the six weekly overhead costs. For example, Y_1 is $2,450 for week 1 and Y_2 is $4,000 for week 2.

X_i are the actual values of the independent variable. Here labor hours are used, so X_1 is 290 labor hours and X_2 is 480 labor hours.

n is the number of observations used in computing the regression line. In our example $n = 6$.

One of several approaches to computing the regression line is to solve the following set of simultaneous equations:

These complicated-looking equations are easy to work with

$$\Sigma Y_i = na + b\Sigma X_i \qquad (1)$$
$$\Sigma X_i Y_i = a\Sigma X_i + b\Sigma X_i^2 \qquad (2)$$

Despite their appearance, these two equations are easy to solve and require only basic algebra. Below we explain the terms used:

ΣY_i = the total of all observed values of the dependent variable, in this case the sum of weekly overhead costs

ΣX_i = the total of all observed values of the independent variable, in this case the sum of weekly labor hours

$\Sigma X_i Y_i$ = the sum of the products of each pair of X and Y values

ΣX_i^2 = the sum of the squared values of the independent variable

Figure 24-3 shows the computation of each of these expressions. It contains all the data necessary to calculate the regression line equation for our example. In addition, Figure 24-3 contains the values for Y^2, which are not needed to calculate the regression line but are used later. When the numbers are substituted into the two equations, the only unknown variables left are a and b, which are needed to describe the regression line. With two unknown terms and two equations, a solution is possible.

Figure 24-3. Computation of sums required for a linear regression analysis in order to relate overhead costs with labor hours.

Barrows Chemical Company
Data for Regression-Correlation Analysis
Relation between Overhead Cost and Labor Hours

Sample Week	Overhead Cost Y_i	Y_i^2	Labor Hours X_i	X_i^2	$X_i Y_i$
1	$ 2,450	$ 6,002,500	290	84,100	$ 710,500
2	4,000	16,000,000	480	230,400	1,920,000
3	3,000	9,000,000	340	115,600	1,020,000
4	4,200	17,640,000	580	336,400	2,436,000
5	3,700	13,690,000	560	313,600	2,072,000
6	3,200	10,240,000	420	176,400	1,344,000
Totals	$20,550	$72,572,500	2,670	1,256,500	$9,502,500

Solving for a and b. The first step is to substitute the known values from Figure 24-3 into the two equations:

$$\$20,550 = 6a \quad + \quad 2,670b \qquad (1)$$
$$\$9,502,500 = 2,670a + 1,256,500b \qquad (2)$$

We now solve these simultaneous equations by subtraction. The coefficient of a is smaller, so we eliminate a. When each term in equation (1) is multiplied by 445, the coefficients of a in both equations become identical. Subtracting one equation from the other eliminates a, leaving one equation with one unknown. Multiplying equation (1), we get:

$$\$20,550(445) = 6(445)a + 2,670(445)b \qquad (1)$$

Next we subtract equation (1) from equation (2) and solve for b.

$$
\begin{aligned}
\$9,502,500 &= 2,670a + 1,256,500b \qquad &(2)\\
9,144,750 &= 2,670a + 1,188,150b \qquad &(1)\\
\hline
\$\ 357,750 &= \quad 0 \ + \quad 68,350b \\
\end{aligned}
$$
$$b = \$357,750/68,350$$
$$= \$5.234089$$

The value of b is \$5.23, which is the slope of the regression line. It means that for every unit change in X, there is a \$5.23 change in Y. X is the number of labor hours and Y is overhead cost, so we can say that for each additional labor hour, overhead cost increases by \$5.23, the variable part of overhead cost.

Once the value of b is known, it is simple to find the value of a by substituting the value of b into equation (1) or (2). Substituting into (1) we get

$$\$20,550 = 6a + 2,670(\$5.234089)$$
$$6a = \$20,550 - \$13,975.018288$$
$$a = \$6,574.981712/6$$
$$= \$1,095.83$$

The value of a in the regression line equation is the Y intercept and in this example represents the fixed component of overhead costs. The regression line equation is

$$Y_c = \$1,095.83 + \$5.23X$$

This equation says that total cost of overhead is \$1,095.83 plus \$5.23 for each hour worked. Obviously this is only an estimate, but it is a very useful estimate based on past data, and it can help managers to make cost predictions, prepare budgets, or gain a better understanding of costs and their relationship to other variables.

Assumptions Underlying Regression Analysis

You see from the above discussion that regression analysis can be used to isolate the fixed and variable components of cost. Remember the Chapter 3 discussion of cost behavior and the relevant range assumption. It applies to regression analysis as well. The analysis is based on the assumption that the cost and activity data analyzed, and the predictions made from the analysis, fall within the relevant range of operations. In addition, three other assump-

Regression line estimates are valid within a relevant range

tions should be satisfied for regression analysis. They are the assumptions of normality, independence, and constant variance.

Normality.   In the previous chapter, we pointed out that some populations are normally distributed, and many others are close enough to normal to permit use of the normal distribution for estimating probabilities. The normality assumption also applies to regression analysis. For regression analysis to be valid, the data points scattered around the regression line should be normally distributed about the line. In many cases, this assumption holds well. If the normality assumption does not hold, regression analysis may not yield good estimates and predictions.

Independence.   Another assumption underlying regression analysis is that the deviation of any one data point from the regression line is independent of the deviation of any other point. For example, the fact that costs decline in one period as a result of declining activity should not be related to a previous advance in costs due to increasing activity. Costs may rise with increasing activity and tend to remain high, even if the level of activity declines later. The change in costs when activity declines may depend in part on the previous increase in costs when activity increased. Such a situation is called **serial correlation** or **autocorrelation**. A further discussion of serial correlation is beyond the scope of this book. Computer programs exist that can test data for serial correlation in order to determine if the independence assumption is satisfied.

Constant Variance.   The assumption of constant variance means that the data points are scattered uniformly about the regression line. If the points are scattered in a fairly narrow range at one end of the relevant range and in a wide range at the other end, the estimate of b may not be very accurate. A good way to determine if the constant variance assumption holds is to plot a large number of data points and examine the scatter diagram. If they look something like Figure 24-4, the constant variance assumption is not satisfied.

Standard Error of the Estimate

Because the values of a and b are obtained from samples, they are only estimates of the true values of the intercept and slope of the entire population from which the sample is taken. Our data consist of a sample of 6 weeks' production drawn from a 1-year population of production activities. The sample used in regression analysis should, of course, be representative of the population, as discussed in Chapter 23. Remember that we used sample data to estimate the mean and standard deviation of populations, and also the standard error of the mean. For regression analysis, a measure analogous to the standard error can be computed. It is called the **standard error of the estimate** and indicates how far from the regression line the data points are scattered. It is computed from the sample data using the following formula:

The standard error of the estimate measures deviation

$$S_y = \sqrt{\frac{\Sigma Y_i^2 - a\Sigma Y_i - b\Sigma X_i Y_i}{n-2}} \tag{3}$$

Figure 24-4. Linear regression is based on the assumption of a constant variance. The data in this diagram vary more at high values than at low values, hence the constant variance assumption is not satisfied.

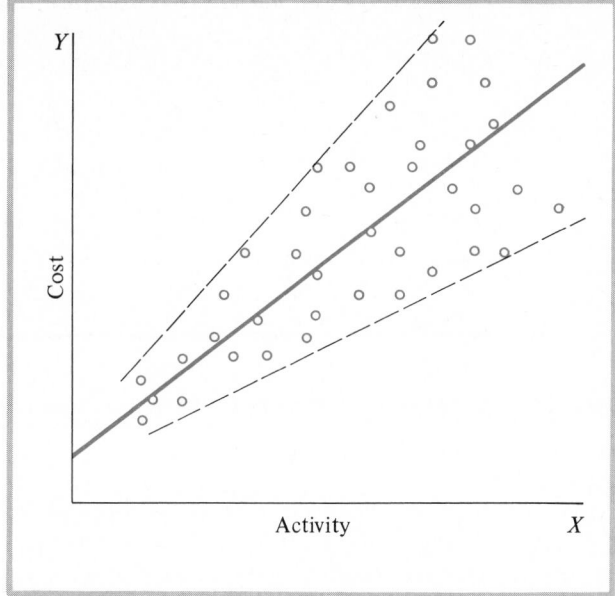

The standard error of the estimate can be used to find the probability of the data points lying within a certain distance from the regression line. For example, if the assumptions of linearity, normality, independence, and constant variance are satisfied, about 68 percent of the time the data points will be within one standard error of the estimate from the regression line; about 95 percent of the time the points will be within two standard errors. Note that the calculation of equation (3) involves dividing by $(n - 2)$. In this case, two degrees of freedom are lost because two values—a and b—are already calculated from the same data and are used in the equation.

We calculate the standard error of the estimate for the data in our illustration.

$$S_y = \sqrt{\frac{\$72{,}572{,}500 - \$1{,}095.83(\$20{,}550) - \$5.234089(\$9{,}502{,}500)}{6 - 2}}$$

$$= \sqrt{\frac{\$316{,}262.78}{4}}$$

$$= \$281.19$$

A manager using the regression line to estimate the cost of overhead at some level of labor activity knows that the estimate will be accurate only within some range. The standard error of the estimate determines this range. The actual overhead cost can be expected to be within $281.19 of the estimate about 68 percent of the time. It will be within $562.38 of the estimate about 95 percent of the time.

A major function of the regression line is in forecasting

To illustrate use of the standard error of the estimate, the regression line $Y_c = \$1,095.83 + \$5.23X$ is used to estimate overhead cost at an activity level of 500 labor hours. The estimated overhead cost is

$$Y_c = \$1,095.83 + \$5.23(500)$$
$$= \$3,710.83$$

Using the standard error of the estimate, it is known that 95 percent of the time, the actual overhead cost will be in the range

$$\$3,710.83 \pm 1.96(\$281.19)$$

or from \$3,159.70 to \$4,261.96. The value 1.96 is the value of z when the desired probability is 95 percent. You can see that the standard error of the estimate can be used in regression analysis just as the standard deviation and standard error of the mean are used in the analysis of means.

CORRELATION ANALYSIS

The regression line describes the relationship between the dependent and independent variables, but it does not say how good the relationship is. Although it is the line of best fit, it is possible that no regression line does a good job of fitting the data. **Correlation analysis** is a statistical technique that measures the strength of the linear relationship between the dependent and the independent variables as described by the regression line.

Coefficient of Correlation

A strong relationship may exist with either positive or negative correlation

One important measure of the strength of regression is called the **coefficient of correlation,** denoted as r. It measures the association between the dependent and independent variables and ranges in value from -1, representing perfect negative correlation, to $+1$, representing perfect positive correlation. **Negative correlation** means that as the independent variable increases, the dependent variable decreases, and vice versa. **Positive correlation** means that as the independent variable increases or decreases, so does the dependent variable. When the value of r is zero, there is no relationship between the variables. Perfect correlation is rare, but values of r near 1 or -1 do occur and indicate strong relationships. Figure 24-5 illustrates the general relationship between r, the regression line, and the data.

One way to find the coefficient of correlation is to solve the following equation:

$$r = \frac{n\Sigma X_i Y_i - (\Sigma X_i)(\Sigma Y_i)}{\sqrt{n\Sigma X_i^2 - (\Sigma X_i)^2} \cdot \sqrt{n\Sigma Y_i^2 - (\Sigma Y_i)^2}} \tag{4}$$

Figure 24-5. When all the data fall on the regression line, correlation is perfect, with values of +1 in diagram (a) and −1 in diagram (b). The more usual situation is illustrated by diagrams (c) and (d), which show less than perfect positive and negative correlation.

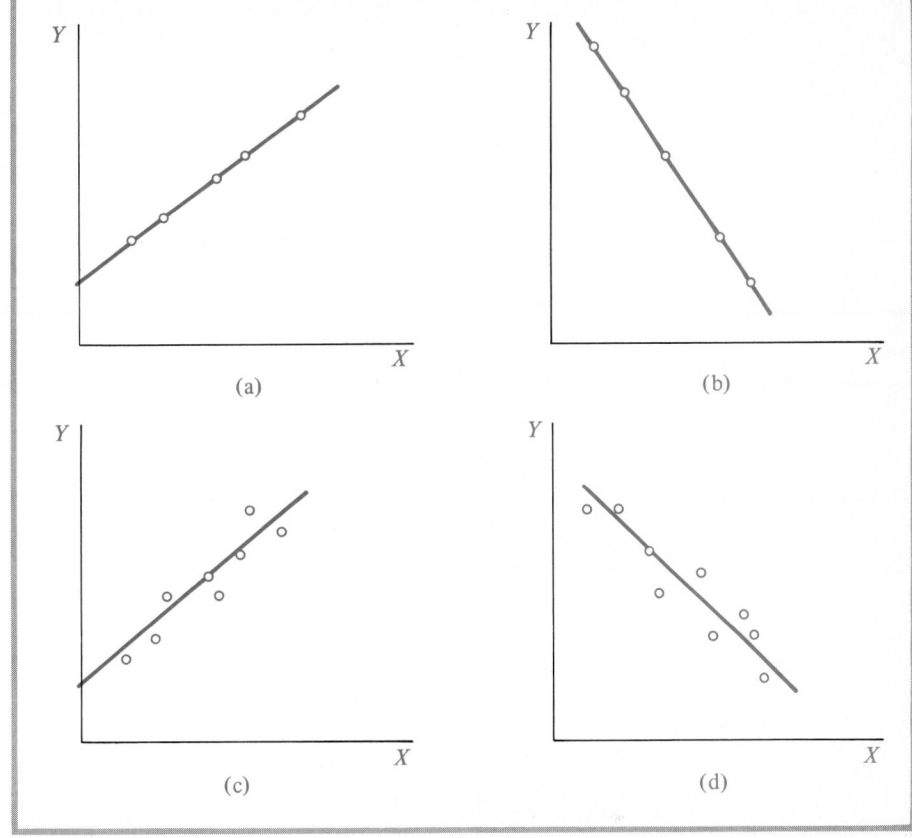

All the data needed for the solution of equation (4) are presented in Figure 24-3. Substituting the required data we get

$$r = \frac{(6)(9{,}502{,}500) - (2{,}670)(20{,}550)}{\sqrt{(6)(1{,}256{,}500) - (2{,}670)^2} \cdot \sqrt{(6)(72{,}572{,}500) - (20{,}550)^2}}$$

$$= \frac{57{,}015{,}000 - 54{,}868{,}500}{\sqrt{7{,}539{,}000 - 7{,}128{,}900} \cdot \sqrt{435{,}435{,}000 - 422{,}302{,}500}}$$

$$= \frac{2{,}146{,}500}{(640.3905)(3{,}623.8791)}$$

$$= .924937$$

An r of .925 indicates a strong positive relationship between weekly overhead costs and the number of labor hours worked. The closer r gets to +1, the stronger the linear relationship between the dependent variable and the independent variable. As r gets closer to 0, it indicates a weak relationship.

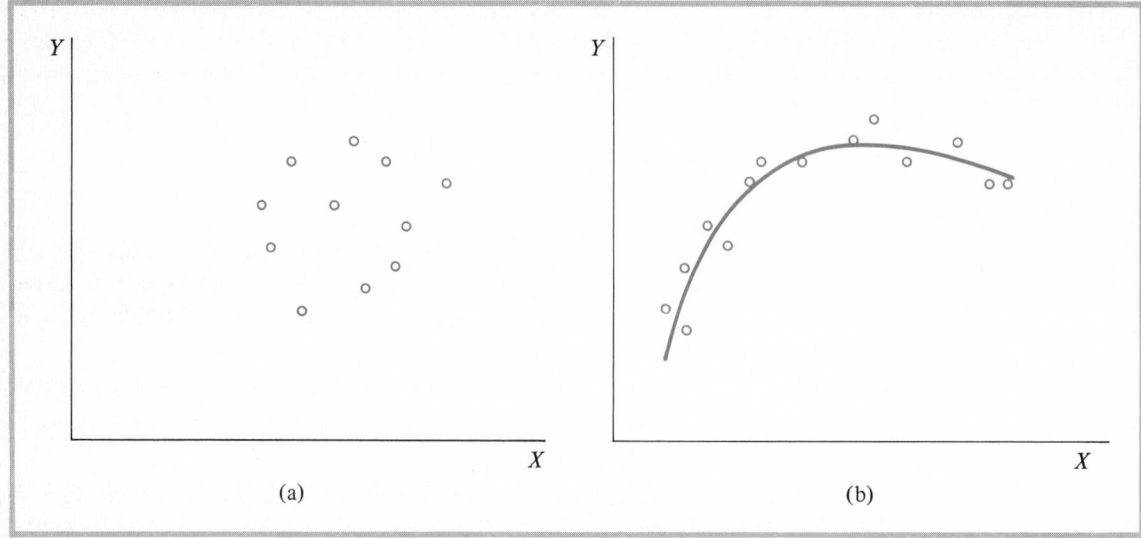

Figure 24-6. The data in diagram (a) are not related. Although a regression line may be computed, the correlation coefficient would be close to 0. Diagram (b) shows data that are strongly related, but the relationship is not linear. An estimate based on linear regression would not give good results.

The sign of r indicates only the direction, not the strength of the relationship. One must be careful in interpreting r; it measures the strength of the **linear** relationship between the dependent and independent variables. It is quite possible for r to be small, indicating a weak linear relationship, when the actual relationship between the variables is quite strong, although it is not linear. Diagram (a) in Figure 24-6 shows two variables whose r is close to 0; the relationship between them is weak. Diagram (b) shows two strongly related variables, but their linear relationship is weak. Simple linear regression analysis looks only for straight-line relationships.

Coefficient of Determination

How does one interpret values of r? An r of .8 does not indicate twice as strong a linear relationship as an r of .4; the larger value indicates a relationship that is four times as strong as the smaller value. To make the interpretation of the coefficient of correlation more meaningful, it can be converted to the coefficient of determination, which is r^2. This eliminates the sign of r and provides a more logical interpretation of the strength of the relationship between the two variables.

Both r and r^2 are measures of goodness of fit

Like r, the **coefficient of determination** is a measure of the goodness of regression line fit. If the fit is good, indicated by a high value for r^2, the relationship between the dependent and independent variables is strong. r^2 is a measure of the degree to which the two variables, X and Y, are related linearly. In the example above

$$r^2 = .924937^2$$
$$= .855509$$
$$= .86$$

Interpreting r^2. Once r has been squared, it is easier to interpret. An r^2 of .80 means twice as strong a relationship as an r^2 of .40 and an r^2 of .90 is three times as strong as an r^2 of .30.

To understand fully the value of r^2 it is first necessary to understand that it is actually a ratio of two variances. Remember that a variance is a measure of fluctuation; in our example, the overhead cost data fluctuate about the regression line. They also fluctuate about the mean of weekly overhead costs. In this case, overhead costs have a mean of $3,425 and a standard deviation of $661.60.

The coefficient of determination tells us how much of the fluctuation of the dependent variable about its mean is caused by fluctuations of the independent variable. The value of .86 for r^2 tells us that 86 percent of the total variation of overhead costs about the mean can be explained by changes in the activity level, as measured by the number of direct labor hours worked.

How this 86 percent value of r^2 is measured is illustrated in Figure 24-7. Diagram (a) in the figure is a plot of the data and the mean overhead cost. The vertical lines show the fluctuation of overhead costs about the mean, as *The coefficient of* measured by the variance. The data also fluctuate about the regression line. *determination is a* Diagram (b) shows the same data and the regression line calculated earlier. *ratio of two* Merely by looking at the two diagrams, you can see that the data fluctuate *variances* much less about the regression line than about the mean. We measure the fluctuation about the regression line as the coefficient of correlation.

The mean and standard deviation give no indication **why** production costs fluctuate from week to week; they merely show the average weekly overhead costs and how much they deviate from their mean. The regression line, on the other hand, relates the costs to the number of labor hours to determine if labor hours cause some of the week-to-week fluctuations in overhead costs. If a relationship exists, we use the coefficient of determination to tell us how much of the variance about the mean is caused by the number of labor hours used. In our example, .86 or 86 percent of the fluctuation in manufacturing overhead costs can be explained by changes in the amount of labor hours used.

Diagram (c) in Figure 24-7 shows both the mean and the regression line, with the vertical lines indicating how the regression line, rather than the data, varies about the mean. Compare all three diagrams and observe the variances shown as the vertical lines. You can see that if the vertical lines in diagram (b) are short, the vertical lines for the same data in diagrams (a) and (c) are similar in length. The coefficient of determination, r^2, is actually the ratio of the variance of the regression line about the mean to the total variance of the actual data about the mean. In other words, r^2 is the ratio of the variance in diagram (c) to the variance in diagram (a). It is expressed mathematically as:

$$r^2 = \frac{\Sigma(Y_c - \overline{Y})/(n-1)}{\Sigma(Y_i - \overline{Y})/(n-1)} \tag{5}$$

The numerator of equation (5) is the variance of the regression line about the mean [diagram (c) in Figure 24-7]; the denominator is the variance of the overhead cost data about the mean [diagram (a) in Figure 24-7]. If the data all fell precisely on the regression line, that is, if $r = 1$, the variance of the

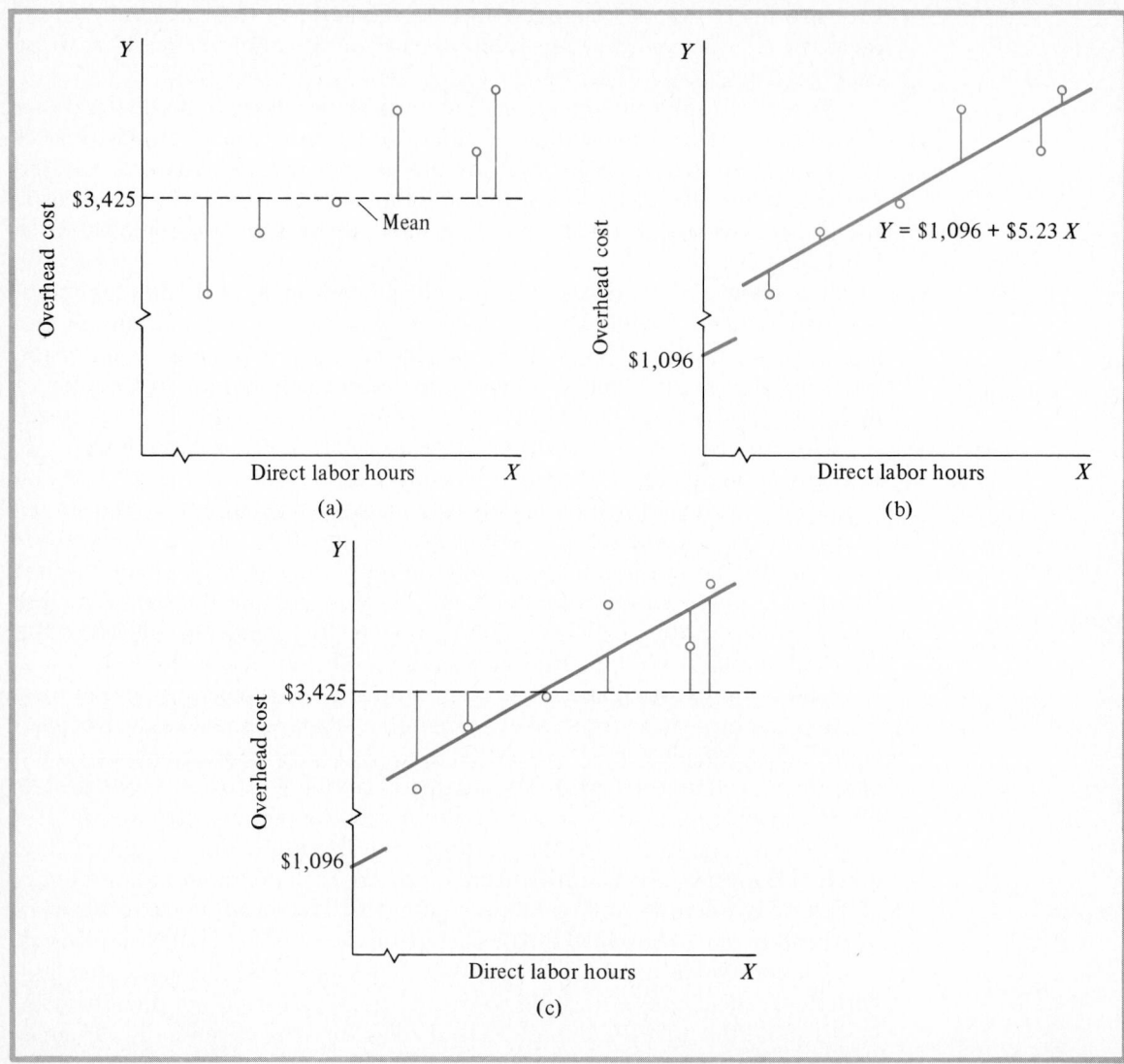

Figure 24-7. Overhead costs are plotted on the vertical axis and direct labor hours on the horizontal axis in each diagram. Diagram (a) shows the variance of costs around their mean. Diagram (b) shows the variance of costs around the regression line. Diagram (c) shows the variance of each estimated cost around the mean. The estimated cost is the value of the regression line at each activity level. The ratio of the variance in diagram (c) to the variance in diagram (a) is the coefficient of determination.

regression line about the mean would be equal to the variance of the data about the mean and the ratio r^2 would be 1. This would mean that all of the costs' fluctuation is caused by the number of labor hours used. In our example, 86 percent of the cost variance is explained by the number of labor hours used and the remainder is due to other factors or random fluctuation.

Now you can see that if r^2 is 90 percent, it indicates a relationship between the dependent and the independent variables that is twice as strong as an r^2 of .45 and three times as strong as an r^2 of .30. In other words, if changes in labor hours influence overhead costs twice as much as changes in machine hours, then r^2 calculated for labor hours and overhead will be twice as large as the r^2 calculated for machine hours and overhead.

The portion of the relationship between the independent and dependent variable that is not explained by r^2 is $(1 - r^2)$; it is called the **coefficient of nondetermination.** With a coefficient of determination of .86 in our example, the coefficient of nondetermination is .14. This portion of the variance is due to other independent variables or it results from random fluctuations in the overhead cost data.

Association Versus Causation

Correlation may be high but spurious

The regression line explains the relationship between the independent and dependent variables; the correlation coefficient explains the strength of that relationship. Although regression-correlation analysis may indicate a strong relationship, it does not prove that changes in the dependent variable are caused by changes in the independent variable.

Many business decisions are influenced by managers' perceptions about the cause-and-effect relationships between activities and costs. Much of responsibility accounting rests on an ability to determine cause-and-effect relationships in business. Regression-correlation analysis measures the nature and association between two variables, usually based on historical data. But association, even if it is strong, does not prove cause-and-effect relationships. Many strong statistical associations exist that certainly suggest causal relationships but do not prove them. Regression-correlation analysis can provide much useful evidence but the manager must determine the ultimate use of the information.

USING LINEAR REGRESSION

Primary uses of regression-correlation analysis are in planning and budgeting. The technique isolates the fixed and variable components of costs and enables managers to use historical data to determine which activity variables have the strongest relationships to cost. These variables can then be used for budgeting and other planning and analysis activities. A separate analysis may be performed on several independent variables to determine which has the strongest effect on cost.

A coefficient of determination of .86 is very good. In practice, an r^2 of .5 is often considered good enough for use by managers. We should note that a lack of strong correlation or negative correlation does not mean a lack of information value. Frequently it is useful to know that the relationship between two variables is weak or nonexistent, particularly if managers previously assumed that there was a strong relationship. When a relationship is disproved, managers can look for other variables to determine if a stronger relationship exists.

Other Independent Variables

To illustrate use of a different independent variable in our analysis, we return to the data presented in Figure 24-2 and this time we use machine hours as the independent variable in a regression analysis. By doing so we can determine if machine hours are more strongly related to overhead costs than labor hours.

Using machine hours, we compute a new regression line and r^2. Figure 24-8 presents the data necessary for the solution. Solving the two simultaneous equations to determine a and b for this regression, we have

$$\Sigma Y_i = na + b\Sigma X_i \qquad (1)$$

$$\Sigma X_i Y_i = a\Sigma X_i + b\Sigma X_i^2 \qquad (2)$$

$$\$20{,}550 = 6a \quad + \quad 1{,}920b \qquad (1)$$

$$\$6{,}820{,}750 = 1{,}920a + 649{,}100b \qquad (2)$$

The multiplier for equation (1) is 1,920/6, or 320, so we get:

$$\$20{,}550(320) = 6(320)a + 1{,}920(320)b \qquad (1)$$

Subtracting the two equations we solve for b:

$$\$6{,}820{,}750 = 1{,}920a + 649{,}100b \qquad (2)$$
$$\underline{6{,}576{,}000 = 1{,}920a + 614{,}400b} \qquad (1)$$
$$\$\ \ 244{,}750 = \qquad 0 + 34{,}700b$$
$$b = \$244{,}750/34{,}700$$
$$= \$7.05331$$

To solve for a we substitute the value of b into equation (1):

$$\$20{,}550 = 6a + \$7.05331(1{,}920)$$
$$6a = \$20{,}550 - 13{,}542.36$$
$$a = 7{,}007.64/6$$
$$= \$1{,}167.94$$

Figure 24-8. Regression computations for relating overhead costs with machine hours. This regression may be compared with the one relating overhead costs with labor hours to determine which relationship provides a better fit.

Barrows Chemical Company
Data for Regression-Correlation Analysis
Relationship between Overhead Cost and Machine Hours

Sample Week	Overhead Cost Y_i	Y_i^2	Machine Hours X_i	X_i^2	$X_i Y_i$
1	$ 2,450	$ 6,002,500	225	50,625	551,250
2	4,000	16,000,000	340	115,600	1,360,000
3	3,000	9,000,000	245	60,025	735,000
4	4,200	17,640,000	415	172,225	1,743,000
5	3,700	13,690,000	415	172,225	1,535,500
6	3,200	10,240,000	280	78,400	896,000
Totals	$20,550	$72,572,500	1,920	649,100	6,820,750

The regression line using machine hours is:

$$Y_c = \$1,167.94 + \$7.05X$$

The standard error of the estimate can now be calculated as before using equation (3):

$$S_y = \sqrt{\frac{\Sigma Y_i^2 - a\Sigma Y_i - b\Sigma X_i Y_i}{n - 2}} \qquad (3)$$

$$S_y = \sqrt{\frac{\$72,572,500 - 1,167.94(\$20,550) - \$7.05331(\$6,820,750)}{6 - 2}}$$

$$= \$340.03$$

A computer performs a complete regression-correlation analysis very quickly

The standard error of the estimate is greater with machine hours than with labor hours. This means that an estimate of production cost based on machine hours is less precise than one based on labor hours. Correlation analysis may indicate why this is the case. To find the value of r and r^2 we use equation (4)

$$r = \frac{n\Sigma X_i Y_i - (\Sigma X_i)(\Sigma Y_i)}{\sqrt{n\Sigma X_i^2 - (\Sigma X_i)^2} \cdot \sqrt{n\Sigma Y_i^2 - (\Sigma Y_i)^2}} \qquad (4)$$

$$r = \frac{(6)(\$6,820,750) - (1,920)(20,550)}{\sqrt{(6)(649,100) - (1,920)^2} \cdot 3,623.8791*}$$

$$= .888096$$

$$r^2 = .788714$$

$$= .79$$

From the above calculation, it is possible to see that machine hours are not as strongly correlated with production costs as labor hours, although the relationship is quite strong. We now discuss how this information is used in making decisions.

Estimating Costs. In our example, labor hours provided the higher coefficient of determination. We therefore use labor hours as the basis for estimating overhead costs for various production levels. We substitute the desired or expected level of activity into the regression equation and solve for the overhead cost. To estimate the overhead cost at 450 labor hours, the following calculation is made:

$$Y_c = \$1,095.83 + \$5.23X$$
$$= \$1,095.83 + \$5.23(450)$$
$$= \$3,449.33$$

---

* Note that this term need not be computed again; it does not change when other independent variables are used with the same dependent variable because it is made up of Y values only.

Earlier we computed the standard error of the estimate of $281.19 for overhead cost and labor hours. This value tells us that about 68 percent of the time, actual cost at 450 hours of labor will be within one standard error of our estimate, or between $3,168.14 and $3,730.52 calculated as

$$\$3,449.33 \pm \$281.19$$

About 95 percent of the time, actual cost will be within two standard errors of our estimate.

Regression and the High-Low Method

In Chapter 3, we used the high-low method to estimate the fixed and variable costs from past data. Regression-correlation analysis allows us to do this with far more precision. The high-low method and regression analysis provide the following estimates of fixed and variable costs, using the production data in Figure 24-2.

Labor Hours	High-Low Method	Regression Line
$b = \dfrac{\$4,200 - \$2,450}{580 \text{ hr} - 290 \text{ hr}} =$	$ 6.03	$ 5.23
$a = \$4,200 - 580(\$6.03444828) =$	700.02	1,095.83
Machine Hours		
$b = \dfrac{\$4,200 - \$2,450}{830 \text{ hr} - 450 \text{ hr}} =$	$ 4.61	$ 3.26
$a = \$4,200 - 830(\$4.6052632) =$	377.63	5,512.14

The high-low method has no goodness-of-fit measure

Which method provides the better estimates? The b values seem reasonably close but the a values differ considerably. Sometimes the high-low method provides reliable cost estimates and sometimes very poor ones. The problem is that the high-low method gives no indication of how good the estimates are. There is no goodness-of-fit measure, such as r^2. One of the real advantages of regression-correlation analysis is the information about the strength of the relationship between two variables.

The computations required in regression-correlation analysis can be made quite easily using small calculators equipped with regression functions. Many computer programs are available for sophisticated regression-correlation analysis. There is no need to make the calculations by hand, but it is valuable to understand how the computations are made.

The regression line and r^2 are typically based on historical data. The use of historical data is warranted only if they are good indicators of future actions or events. Past data are often good indicators of the future, but they are not perfect indicators. If conditions change, past data may be of little value.

Multiple Linear Regression

An extension of simple linear regression is **multiple linear regression,** which involves using one dependent variable and two or more independent variables simultaneously. With simple linear regression, the coefficient of determination indicates the amount of fluctuation about the regression line that can be explained by the independent variable. The rest of the variance is due to other variables or random fluctuations. If other variables can be included in the regression equation, it may be possible to obtain a smaller coefficient of nondetermination and improve the forecast of the dependent variable. In our example of costs and activities, the value of r^2 is high for both labor hours and machine hours. If both labor hours and machine hours could be used at the same time to find the regression line, a stronger r^2 could be obtained than by using each variable independently.

Many independent variables may be used to forecast one dependent variable

Multiple regression is the same two-step process of computing the regression line and then finding the strength of the relationship. The regression line takes the general form:

$$Y_c = a + b_1X_1 + b_2X_2 + b_3X_3 + \cdots + b_nX_n$$

where a is the intercept of the Y axis when **all** X terms have the value zero, and $b_1, \ldots, b_n$ each represent the relationship between the dependent variable and one of the independent variables. Note that each independent variable has its own b coefficient and that the number of terms in the regression line equation depends on the number of independent variables used in the analysis. The strength of the relationship is measured by the **multiple coefficient of determination.**

The computation of multiple regression and multiple r^2 is quite complex and generally is performed by a computer. Multiple regression programs for computers are readily available, however, and managers can easily obtain the a and b values as well as r and r^2 from available data. The following values are obtained from a multiple regression and multiple correlation of the data in Figure 24-2:

$$Y_c = \$1,148.00 + \$10.40X_1 - 7.33X_2$$

$$r^2 = .797$$

If X_1 stands for labor hours and X_2 for machine hours, management can use the above equation to estimate cost of production for a given level of activity using these variables. The high r^2 indicates a good estimate can be made. For example, if 500 labor hours and 350 machine hours are used in production, the estimate of total overhead cost is:

$$Y_c = \$1,148.00 + \$10.40(500) - \$7.33(350)$$
$$= \$1,148.00 + \$5,200.00 - \$2,565.50$$
$$= \$3,782.50$$

The standard error of the estimate can also be computed for multiple regression, allowing the estimate to be stated as $3,782.50 ± one or two standard errors.

Multicolinearity

In addition to the assumptions of normality, independence, and constant variance that apply to simple linear regression, multiple regression depends on the additional assumption of multicolinearity. **Multicolinearity** is a measure of correlation among the **independent** variables of a multiple regression equation. Two independent variables that are highly correlated do not provide as good a multiple regression as two independent variables with low correlation. The problem of multicolinearity can be avoided by combining highly correlated independent variables into one variable, or eliminating all but one of the highly correlated independent variables.

SUMMARY

One of the more powerful managerial tools for analyzing cost relationships is **regression-correlation analysis. Simple linear regression** is used to determine the nature of relationship between a dependent variable and one independent variable. With **multiple regression,** two or more independent variables may be used. **Correlation analysis** is used to test the strength of the relationship between the variables. In cost data analysis, the **dependent variable** is typically a cost and the **independent variables** are usually activity measures. When the regression line has been computed, it can be used to predict the expected or estimated value of the dependent variable for a given level of activity or a given value of the independent variable within the relevant range.

Regression analysis is based on the assumptions that the data being analyzed are normally distributed and independent of one another. In addition, the analysis assumes that the variance of the data is the same at all points of the regression line.

When the regression line is used to make estimates or predictions, the estimate will vary somewhat from actual results. The expected estimation error is measured by computing the **standard error of the estimate.** The standard error of the estimate is used like the standard error of the mean to determine the probability that the actual value lies within some range of the estimated value.

The **coefficient of correlation** is used to measure the strength of the linear relationship described by the regression line. When the coefficient of correlation is squared, the result is the **coefficient of determination.** It explains what percentage of the fluctuation in the data is explained by the relationship between the dependent and independent variable. The remaining variance is due to other factors or random fluctuation.

Regression-correlation analysis does not prove causation. It is possible for two variables to be highly correlated although one does not cause the other. Managers must use judgment to determine whether causation between variables exists.

KEY TERMS coefficient of correlation *(838)*
coefficient of determination *(840)*
coefficient of nondetermination
(843)
correlation analysis *(838)*
dependent variable *(830)*
independent variable *(830)*
least squares regression line *(833)*

line of best fit *(833)*
multicolinearity *(848)*
multiple linear regression *(847)*
negative correlation *(838)*
positive correlation *(838)*
regression analysis *(830)*
simple linear regression *(830)*
standard error of the estimate *(836)*

QUESTIONS 1. During a slack time in the personnel office, a clerk performed a regression-corre-lation analysis between shoe sizes of the company's employees and their salaries, with salaries as the dependent variable. She found that shoe sizes were negatively correlated with salaries, with an r^2 of .64, and she consequently recommended that in order to save money, the company should reject all employment applicants with small shoe sizes. Comment on the nature of the relationship between shoe sizes and salaries. What is the value of the coefficient of correlation? What do you think of the clerk's recommendation?

2. A lumber company executive recently read an article about the use of regression analysis as a tool for analyzing and predicting various operating costs from activity data. He knows that government regulations require each airplane in commercial use to undergo an inspection after every 100 hours of flying. Therefore he reasoned that the cost of these inspections should be highly correlated with the amount of flying time of aircraft. To test his idea, he accumulated inspection cost and flight data on the company's twin-engine executive airplane for the past 24 months and calculated the least square line with cost as the dependent variable and flight time as the independent variable. After obtaining his results, he noticed that the slope of the regression line was negative. He said to his secretary, "This article doesn't make sense. According to the formulas used, the more flying time we put on our airplane, the less it costs to have it inspected." Comment on the executive's findings.

EXERCISES

Ex. 24-1
Interpreting
Regression and
Correlation

The controller of Tixus Company provided the following data to the company's vice president of finance after performing regression-correlation analyses on direct mate-rial costs and direct labor cost, using production quantity as the independent variable.

Regression analysis, production and direct labor cost:

a = $7,450 per month
b = $11.60 per unit
r = .88

Regression analysis, production and direct material cost:

a = $1,485 per month
b = $10.70 per unit
r = .74

Anticipated production next month: 34,500 units

REQUIRED

a. Discuss the meaning of a, b, and r in the above report.
b. Estimate next month's cost of direct materials and direct labor.

Ex. 24-2
Simple Regression
Analysis

The following data on the cost of long-distance telephone calls placed by the sales force during a 5-month period were collected by Robinson Company:

Month	Feb.	Mar.	Apr.	May	June
Telephone cost	$460	$850	$390	$770	$550
Number of orders	360	500	210	480	210

REQUIRED

Perform a regression analysis with number of orders as the independent variable. Develop a cost formula for long-distance calls.

Ex. 24-3
Simple Linear
Regression

Balmer Company's personnel director has accumulated the following data on seven employees' absenteeism record for the past year and the number of years they have worked for the company:

Employee:	A	B	C	D	E	F	G
Days absent:	4	1	9	11	8	15	4
Years employed:	9	10	3	4	7	2	7

REQUIRED

Compute a regression line for the data, using years employed as the independent variable. Discuss briefly the significance of your computation.

Ex. 24-4
Standard Error of
the Estimate

Jimmy operates a small bait shop near a lake that is popular with fishermen. He has collected some data for six weekends on the number of fish caught by his customers and the mean daily temperature and has used linear regression analysis to obtain the following information:

Weekend	Fish Caught Y_i	Y_i^2	Temperature X_i	X_i^2	X_iY_i
1	24	576	91	8,281	2,184
2	16	256	88	7,744	1,408
3	36	1,296	61	3,721	2,196
4	32	1,024	54	2,916	1,728
5	13	169	85	7,225	1,105
6	28	784	77	5,929	2,156
	149	4,105	456	35,816	10,777

$$b = -.47155$$
$$a = 60.67$$

The temperature for the next weekend is forecast to be 70 degrees. Jimmy wants to predict how many fish his customers will catch.

REQUIRED

a. Use the available data to predict the number of fish that will be caught next weekend.
b. Compute the standard error of the estimate and determine within what range Jimmy can expect his prediction to be correct 95 percent of the time.

Ex. 24-5
Correlation
Coefficient

Refer to the data in Exercise 24-4 on the regression of the number of fish caught and mean daily temperature. The temperature for the next weekend is expected to be 80 degrees and the owner wants to predict how many fish his customers will catch.

REQUIRED

a. Use the available data to predict the number of fish that will be caught next weekend.
b. Compute the coefficient of correlation and coefficient of determination and discuss briefly what they indicate.

Ex. 24-6
Scattergram and
Linear Regression

A small machine shop produces a custom-designed gear assembly for a manufacturer on order. The orders vary from two or three assemblies to one or two dozen. Each job requires considerable setup time. The machine shop owner has collected the following data on six orders:

| No. of units | 7 | 13 | 2 | 4 | 18 | 9 |
| Total cost | $200 | $240 | $60 | $140 | $250 | $220 |

The machine shop owner would like to use regression analysis to develop a total cost formula for use in predicting the cost of future orders.

REQUIRED

a. Perform a linear regression on the data with number of units as the independent variable. Develop the cost line and predict the cost of producing 10 units.
b. Draw a scatter diagram with cost on the vertical axis and units on the horizontal axis. Estimate from your diagram the cost of producing 10 units.
c. Discuss the type of relationship disclosed by your analysis and diagram. Which provides a better estimate of production costs?

Ex. 24-7
Linear Regression
and Correlation

Following are data on the cost of operating an earth-moving machine:

| Cost | $230 | $280 | $180 | $300 | $150 |
| Hours of operations | 8 | 10 | 6 | 11 | 5 |

REQUIRED

a. Compute a linear regression line and determine how much it would cost to operate the machine on a 7-hour job.
b. Compute the coefficient of correlation and coefficient of determination.

Ex. 24-8
Estimation with
Multiple Regression

A company that manufactures molded plastic panels for use as trim in various passenger vehicles has developed the following formula for predicting the cost of each 100 square feet of panels:

$$Y = \$147.89 + 153.15X_1 + 98.22X_2 + 79.70X_3 - .23X_4 - .45X_5$$

where X_1 = aircraft
X_2 = passenger rail car
X_3 = passenger road vehicle
X_4 = expected mean daily temperature
X_5 = size of order in hundreds of square feet

If aircraft panels are produced, the value of X_1 is 1 and the values for X_2 and X_3 are 0. Similarly if rail car panels are produced, $X_2 = 1$ and X_1 and X_3 are 0. The company is currently negotiating the following three orders and wants to estimate the cost of each in order to make its proposals:

3,500 square feet of aircraft paneling
7,000 square feet of aircraft paneling
5,000 square feet of railroad car paneling

During the period that the aircraft paneling is to be manufactured, the mean daily temperature is expected to be 74°F. By the time the railroad car paneling is made the temperature is expected to be 82°F.

REQUIRED   Estimate the cost of each order using the multiple regression equation.

Ex. 24-9 (CMA)
Understanding
Regression-
Correlation Data

Brown Company employs 20 salesmen to market its products in well-defined sales territories. The company has analyzed the weekly sales order-getting costs for the past year using regression analysis. The following was derived from the regression analysis:

$$C = \$6{,}000 + \$.50M + \$6.00S$$

where C = weekly sales order-getting costs
M = number of miles driven per week by the sales force
S = number of sales calls completed per week

Standard error of the estimate for C given the values for M and S = 400.

REQUIRED   a. The sales department has estimated that the sales force will drive 10,000 miles and make 500 calls during the first week in July.

  1. Calculate the estimated sales order-getting costs for the week.
  2. What criteria should be met before Brown's sales department relies on the estimate derived in part $a.1.$ above?

b. What does the value for the standard error of the estimate for C (400) mean and how might it be used in cost estimation?

PROBLEMS

P. 24-1
Regression Analysis
and Standard Error

The financial analyst of Doralee Corporation collected the following random sample of data from the population of the company's daily overhead costs and production activity:

Production in units	180	110	150	300	250
Overhead cost	$390	$290	$330	$550	$440

The analyst would like to determine if production activity can be used to predict overhead cost.

REQUIRED   a. Use the data to calculate a regression line with production as the independent variable.
b. Calculate the standard error of the estimate.
c. Use your results to estimate overhead costs for 200 units of production and to develop a range within which actual overhead can be expected to be 95 percent of the time.

P. 24-2
Regression,
Standard Error,
and Correlation

The manager of Flatone Brass Instruments Company believes that its utility costs are strongly correlated with production. He wants to develop a method of predicting utility costs with some reliability. Following are data collected over a 7-month period:

Hundreds of units produced	7	8	5	9	8	3	9
Utility costs (in $100s)	$11	$9	$14	$23	$13	$8	$12

REQUIRED

a. Perform a regression analysis and develop the regression equation with production as the independent variable.
b. Compute the standard error of the estimate.
c. Calculate r and r^2.
d. Estimate utility cost for a production level of 600 units and comment briefly on the value of your estimate.

P. 24-3
Regression-
Correlation
Analysis

The financial analyst of Kloreen Corporation collected the following random sample of data from the population of the company's daily overhead costs and production activity:

Production in units	180	250	150	300	110
Overhead cost	$390	$440	$330	$550	$290

The analyst would like to determine if she can use production activity to predict overhead cost.

REQUIRED

a. Use the data to calculate a regression line with production as the independent variable.
b. Perform a correlation analysis and calculate r and r^2.

P. 24-4
Complete
Regression-
Correlation
Analysis

Skuttle Corporation owns a small subsidiary that manufactures pleasure boats. A random sample of weekly data provided the following figures on production volume and overhead costs.

Production in units	17	23	19	26	18	21
Overhead cost (in $1,000s)	$55	$71	$61	$78	$52	$60

REQUIRED

a. Use the data to calculate a regression line with production quantity as the independent variable.
b. Calculate the standard error of the estimate.
c. Perform a correlation analysis and calculate r and r^2.
d. Use your results to estimate overhead costs for 20 units of production and to develop a range within which actual overhead cost can be expected to be 95 percent of the time.

P. 24-5
Regression Analysis
for Display Space

Pamore & Byless Grocery wanted to determine if the amount of display space allocated to a specific brand of soft drink would have an effect on the amount of that product's sales. In alternate weeks, it allocated 4, 8, and 12 square feet of space to display the soft drink and obtained the following data:

Space	4	8	12	4	12	8
Sales	$510	$670	$720	$540	$690	$660

a. Perform a regression analysis with display space as the independent variable and develop the regression equation.
b. Compute r and r^2 for the data.
c. Discuss your findings briefly and estimate the amount of revenue expected if 8 square feet are allotted to display the product.

P. 24-6
Scattergram and
Cost Estimation by
Regression

Televoice Corporation manufactures miniature radio telephones and has collected the following direct labor hour, production, and maintenance cost data over a period of 6 months. The company's direct labor cost is $8 per hour. Its production process involves the use of sensitive equipment and instruments that require frequent maintenance and adjustments.

Month	Labor Hours	Units Produced	Maintenance Cost
March	280	140	$1,200
April	495	230	1,090
May	600	300	1,380
June	525	270	1,260
July	258	110	1,320
August	425	190	1,400

a. Prepare a scatter diagram with costs in dollars on the vertical axis and units produced on the horizontal axis. Include both labor and maintenance cost in the diagram.
b. Examine the scattergram to determine the amount of cost that is variable. Perform a regression analysis on this cost with units produced as the independent variable. Develop a cost equation but do not perform a correlation analysis.
c. Use your cost equation to determine the direct cost of producing 150 radio telephones during the current month.

P. 24-7
Break-Even Point
and Profit with
Regression Analysis

Pied Piper Company owns a unique process for exterminating rats from cities. Its fees are based on a city's population. The company charges a fee of $15,000 per city plus $1 per person. Below are revenue and operating data for the last six contracts.

City	Operating Cost	Rat Population	Total Revenue
Hummel	$ 70,000	400,000	$ 55,000
Hamilot	125,000	1,500,000	165,000
Himmel	80,000	500,000	85,000
Homily	90,000	1,000,000	130,000
Hamlet	110,000	1,350,000	140,000
Humer	115,000	1,200,000	120,000

The company is negotiating a contract with the city of Hamelin, which has a population of 110,000. The rat population is estimated at 1,100,000. (Hint: A break-even diagram should help you. You can save time by omitting the last three zeros from the data.)

a. Use regression analysis with operating costs as the dependent variable and rat population as the independent variable to develop a formula for the cost line.

b. Use regression analysis with total revenue as the dependent variable and city population as the independent variable to develop a formula for the revenue line.

c. Calculate the break-even point in units and dollars for the company's operations, based on your estimates in parts a and b.

d. Use the city population and estimate of rat population for Hamelin to determine the expected profit or loss on the contract.

P. 24-8
Regression Analysis for a County Government

The board of supervisors of Hyumid County has collected some statistics on interest rates and number of building permits issued in the county in the past 9 years. The supervisors are concerned about the figures because interest rates for 1986 are expected to be 15 percent.

Year	Building Permits	Interest Rates
1977	2,210	8.7
1978	2,040	10.0
1979	2,560	9.1
1980	1,950	11.3
1981	1,740	11.6
1982	1,820	13.9
1983	1,230	16.5
1984	1,040	15.8
1985	1,200	13.8

REQUIRED

a. Perform a regression analysis on the data and develop a regression equation.

b. Compute r and r^2 to determine the strength of the relationship.

c. Compute the expected number of building permits for the current year and discuss briefly your estimate.

P. 24-9 (CMA)
Cash Forecasting with Regression-Correlation

Jackson Company is experiencing cash management problems. In particular, the company has been unable to determine its temporary cash needs on a timely basis. This has increased the cost of borrowing, because Jackson has often been unable to obtain desirable terms. Borrowing in advance would give the company better terms at a lower cost. A review of the cash flows indicates that all factors can be adequately predicted except the expenditures for hourly payroll and certain other expenditures. The cash receipts can be accurately determined because Jackson's customers are all reliable and pay on an identifiable schedule within the 2 calendar months following a sale. The payments for raw materials are similarly predictable because they are all paid in the calendar month subsequent to the purchase. Disbursements for monthly fixed obligations, such as lease payments, salaried personnel, etc., are known well in advance of the payment dates.

In an attempt to forecast cash changes for the next month, the company conducted a statistical analysis of many possible variables that might be suitable as a basis for forecasting the expenditure for payroll and other items. This analysis revealed a high correlation between the advance sales orders received in a month and those expenditures in the next month. The following relationships useful for cash forecasting have been identified:

($N =$ the forecast month)

1. Collections on account: $C_N = .9S_{N-1} + .1S_{N-2}$; where $S =$ sales

2. Disbursements for raw material purchases: $D_N = R_{N-1}$; where $R =$ raw material purchases

3. Monthly fixed obligations: $F_N = \$400,000$

4. Payroll and other expenditures: $P_N = .25A_{N-1} + 70,000$; where $A =$ advance sales orders

Coefficient of correlation	$= .96$
Standard error of the estimate	$= 10,000$
t-statistic for 95% confidence interval[1]	$= 2.07$

[1] t is the statistic for small samples. It is used the same way as z for large samples, as discussed in Chapter 23.

REQUIRED

a. Estimate the change in the cash balance for July using the relationships specified above and the following data:

	Sales (S)	Raw Material Purchases (R)	Advance Sales Orders (A)
April	$1,300,000	$300,000	$1,225,000
May	1,200,000	400,000	1,050,000
June	1,000,000	350,000	1,400,000

b. Revise your estimate of the change in cash to recognize the uncertainty associated with the payroll and other expenditures.
c. How could management use this information to study alternative plans to reduce the short-term borrowing costs?

CASES

Case 24-1
Regression-
Correlation
Analysis and Cost
Prediction

The assembly department of the Walkoff Company makes engine housing requiring the use of materials, labor, and machinery in the production activity. Below are data on 8 weeks of production of engine housings.

Month	Units Produced	Total Production Cost	Machine Hours
December	132	$ 7,800	1,000
December	100	6,000	1,500
December	168	6,700	2,050
December	300	11,000	2,250
January	202	9,700	1,050
January	220	8,300	2,200
January	251	8,500	1,700
January	230	10,000	2,100

The company wants to use the above data to forecast the cost of producing engine housings in February when 1,000 engine housings are expected to be produced.

REQUIRED

a. Perform a complete regression-correlation analysis using total production costs as the dependent variable and units produced as the independent variable.

b. Perform a complete regression-correlation analysis using total production costs as the dependent variable and machine hours as the independent variable.

c. Recommend to management which variables should be used for predicting total production costs. Support your recommendations with a discussion of your findings.

d. Estimate the total production cost for February using the independent variable which you chose. Find the range of estimated total production costs within which you can expect your estimate to occur with a 95 percent probability.

CHAPTER 25
Learning Curves and Linear Programming

The first part of this chapter discusses learning curves, which is a cost analysis tool designed to help managers measure and predict labor costs for new products and procedures that require learning new job skills or activities. In such situations, labor costs tend to decline over time. Learning curve analysis allows managers to measure curvilinear cost behavior for use in planning and control of operations. The second part of the chapter deals with linear programming, a mathematical approach to optimizing production or other activities. Optimization can be achieved either by maximizing objectives such as profit or by minimizing objectives such as cost.

LEARNING CURVES AND COST ANALYSIS

When people perform a new activity that requires some skill, they usually are not very efficient at first, but their performance improves as they repeat the activity. The improvement in efficiency may occur slowly or rapidly. This improvement in work efficiency is a learning effect that can be measured and described mathematically as a hyperbola which is called a **learning curve**. A **learning curve** describes the improvement in efficiency that occurs from learning to perform a task better by repeating the task. The learning curve shows that the effort required to perform a task decreases over time up to some point where no more learning takes place.

Businesses frequently experience the effects of learning when they start producing new products. Managers can use learning curve effects to develop cost estimates, labor requirement estimates, and appropriate product prices. Some products, such as certain toys, games, and fashion goods, have a life cycle of only a year or less; others may have life cycles as short as 3 to 5 years. The labor cost for short-lived products may be characterized by a learning curve during most of the product life. The labor-related cost per unit of such products declines as more units are produced. It would be a mistake for managers to base their decisions on the initial production cost of the product. For example, a company may decide to discontinue production of a product, believing that a satisfactory profit is not possible, when, in fact, declining production costs caused by employee learning will result in a profitable product.

Labor becomes more efficient as a new task is performed repeatedly

Learning Curve Characteristics

The learning curve is an exponential function

While learning is taking place, the labor time required to produce a unit of product declines. For example, 20 hours are required to produce a unit of product for the first time. To produce the second unit may require only 19 hours. The time needed to produce the third unit is even less. The **cumulative** cost of production increases as each additional unit is made, but **not proportionately** with the number of units manufactured. In other words, the per unit cost of production declines while learning occurs. The relationship between total cost and activity is illustrated in Figure 25-1, which shows a learning curve cost plotted as the curve *OA*. Eventually, learning stops and labor costs become directly variable, increasing proportionally with the number of units produced. The total labor cost curve then is a straight line with the slope of the line indicating the cost per unit. When learning stops, the **steady state** is reached. The steady state is illustrated in Figure 25-1 as the *AB* portion of the cost curve.

The precise shape of the learning curve depends on the **learning rate,** which describes the degree of learning or improvement in efficiency. Learning is expressed as a percentage, such as 98 percent, 95 percent, or 90 percent. This means that each time the output doubles, the average cumulative labor cost of the output is equal to the learning curve percentage of the previous labor cost. In other words, when production doubles, the **average** labor cost of the product is a percentage of the cost at the last doubling. For

Average cumulative time applies to all units produced

example, if 20 hours are needed to produce the first unit and 18 hours to produce the second unit, the **cumulative time** to double production is 38 hours, and the **average cumulative time** is 19 hours per unit.

The same concept can be expressed in terms of labor costs. If labor cost is

Figure 25-1. A learning curve is a semivariable cost. As learning takes place, total cost increases at a decreasing rate, as illustrated by the cost *OA*. When the steady state is reached, the cost becomes directly variable, as shown by the straight segment *AB*.

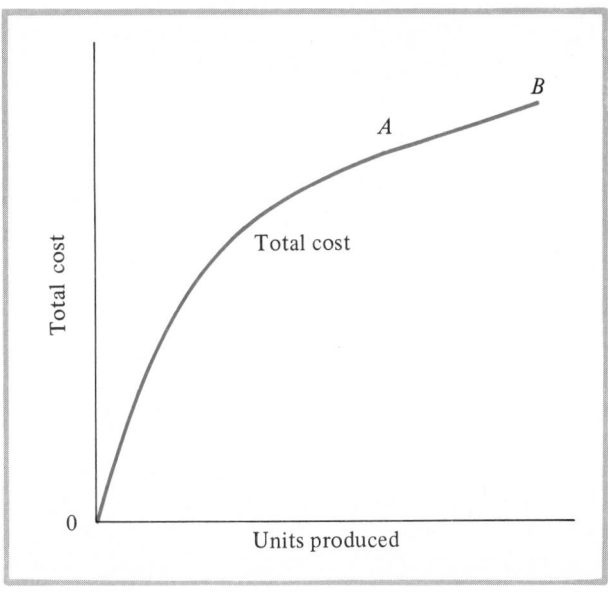

$10 per hour, the cost of labor for producing the first unit is $200 ($10 per hour × 20 hours). The **cumulative cost** of labor for producing the first two units is $380, and the **average cumulative cost** of labor to produce the first two units is $190. In this case the learning rate is 95 percent, measured as the improvement in average cumulative time or cost. Nineteen hours is 95 percent of 20 hours, and $190 is 95 percent of $200. When production doubles again, two more units of product are made, and the time per unit **for all four units** is 95 percent of the time needed for the previous doubling of production, or .95 × 19 hours. This means that by the time four units are made, the average labor time is 18.05 hours or $180.50 of labor cost. With another doubling of production, the average time for **all eight units** produced is 95 percent of 18.05 hours, or 17.1475 hours per unit. The labor cost is 95 percent of $180.50 or $171.475 per unit.

The smaller the learning rate, the faster the learning

The lower the learning curve percentage, the more learning occurs. If our example had an 80 percent learning curve, then doubling production from one to two units would require an average cumulative time for each unit of 16 hours (.80 × 20 hours), or a total of 32 hours for the two units. The first unit required 20 hours, so the time required for the second unit is 12 hours (32 total hours − 20 hours for the first unit). A second doubling to four units would yield an average cumulative time of 12.8 hours (.80 × 16 hours).

Eighty percent is a very high learning rate; such high learning rates occur seldom. The theoretical limit is reached with a 50 percent learning rate. A 50 percent learning curve is impossible, because it means that a doubling in production can be achieved with zero time. If the first unit requires 20 hours to complete and the second requires zero hours, the average for the two units is 10 hours per unit, which is 50 percent of the time required to build the first unit. At the other extreme, a 100 percent learning curve means no learning at all because each doubling in production also requires a doubling in labor time or cost. A 100 percent learning curve represents the steady state.

Learning curves apply to batches as well as to single units.

The learning curve phenomenon applies to batches of units as well as to individual units. For example, the labor cost of the first batch of 100 units of a product is $400 and the learning rate is 90 percent. When production doubles—that is, when 100 more units are made—the average cumulative cost of labor is 90 percent of $400, or $360 per batch. Another doubling of production means 200 more units are built and the average cumulative cost is 90 percent of $360, or 90 percent of 90 percent of $400, which is $324 per batch for all four batches produced. Once the learning rate is known, it can be used to compute the cost of any number of units, such as 235 units or 40 units. Note that learning curves apply to all labor-related costs that change with labor time, such as wages, payroll taxes, and fringe benefits.

Formula for Learning Curves

A valuable feature of learning curve analysis is the ability to express the learning effect in mathematical terms for use in cost analysis and forecasting.

Average Cost Formula. The general form of a learning curve equation for computing the **average cumulative cost** or time of each unit produced is

$$\overline{Y} = aX^b$$

where $\overline{Y}$ = the average time or cost per unit of output for all units produced
a = the time or cost required to produce the first unit or the time or cost per unit of the first batch of units
X = the cumulative number of units or batches produced
b = the learning effect, or learning index

The variable a may be either cost or time, and either for one unit or a batch

The term a may be the cost or time for a single unit or the average time per unit for a batch. The term X is expressed in multiples of batches. Its value is 2^n, where n is the number of doublings. For example, if production has doubled once, two units or batches have been produced and X is 2; if production has doubled twice, four batches have been produced and X is 2^2, or 4; if production has doubled three times, eight batches have been produced and X is 2^3, or 8; and so on. Therefore if the first batch consists of a single unit and X is 8, then 8 units have been produced in three doublings. But if the first batch consists of 5 units and X is 8, then 40 units have been produced. The number of units produced is the number of units in the first batch multiplied by X because X is a multiple of the initial number of units.

To compute the average unit cost of producing 50 units if the first batch consisted of 5 units, X is 10, computed as $50/5$ units. X can also be a figure like .9 or 3.6, representing a fraction of a doubling. For instance, if the cost of producing 32 units is to be found, X is 6.4, computed as $32/5$. This is the same as finding X for the 2.68th doubling because in this case, X is equal to $2^{2.68}$.

The exponent in the cost formula is a constant

The learning index b is the mathematical expression of the rate of learning and is computed by dividing the logarithm of the learning rate by the logarithm of 2. For example, b is $-.3219$ when the learning rate is 80 percent. The logarithm of .80 is $-.2231$ and the logarithm of 2 is .6931, so $b = -.2231/.6931 = -.3219$. It is not necessary to compute the value of b each time because for any given learning rate, b is a constant. The values of b for all learning rates that are likely to be encountered in practice are shown in Figure 25-2. Also included in the figure is d, a variable that is discussed and used in another learning curve formula.

Figure 25-2. Constant values of exponents for various learning rates for use in learning curve formulas.

Values of Exponents for Use in Learning Curve Formulas

Learning Rate	b	d	Learning Rate	b	d	Learning Rate	b	d
.99	−.0145	.9855	.89	−.1681	.8319	.79	−.3401	.6599
.98	−.0291	.9709	.88	−.1844	.8156	.78	−.3585	.6415
.97	−.0439	.9561	.87	−.2009	.7991	.77	−.3771	.6229
.96	−.0589	.9411	.86	−.2176	.7824	.76	−.3959	.6041
.95	−.0740	.9260	.85	−.2345	.7655	.75	−.4150	.5850
.94	−.0893	.9107	.84	−.2515	.7485	.74	−.4344	.5656
.93	−.1047	.8953	.83	−.2688	.7312	.73	−.4540	.5460
.92	−.1203	.8797	.82	−.2863	.7137	.72	−.4739	.5261
.91	−.1361	.8639	.81	−.3040	.6960	.71	−.4941	.5059
.90	−.1520	.8480	.80	−.3219	.6781	.70	−.5146	.4854

Total Cumulative Cost Formula.　The learning curve graphed in Figure 25-1 is the total labor and labor-related costs of production rather than the average cost. The formula for the **total cumulative cost** is given below:

$$Y = aX^d$$

where　Y = the total cumulative labor cost or labor time of producing all units.

　　　a = the labor cost or labor time for the **first** unit or the **first batch** of units.

　　　X = the cumulative number of units produced.

　　　$d = 1 + b$. When 1 is added to b to get the cumulative labor cost, d always becomes a positive number less than 1.

LEARNING CURVES ILLUSTRATED

We now present an illustration to demonstrate the use of learning curves. Belding Electronics Company is bidding on a contract to assemble 20 communication satellites to be placed into orbit around the earth. The satellites, all identical, are intended to form a communication network for worldwide subscription television broadcasting. The assembly process is labor-intensive but the company has assembled electronic equipment in the past and has typically experienced a learning curve of 90 percent for such work.

　　After carefully examining the design and specifications for the satellites, the company estimates that assembly of the first unit will require 10,000 hours at $12 per hour of labor and $100,000 of direct materials. The company applies overhead at the rate of $10 per direct labor hour. The total cost of the first unit is easy to determine, as follows:

Labor cost, 10,000 hours at $12 per hour	$120,000
Direct materials	100,000
Overhead at $10 per direct labor hour	100,000
Total cost of first unit	$320,000

　　To prepare the bid for all 20 units, the company should not simply multiply the cost of the first unit by 20 because labor costs are expected to decline when production efficiencies are realized as a result of learning. The company expects that the steady state will be reached after the fourth doubling in production, that is, after 16 units have been completed.

Computing Labor Cost with Learning Curves

Each doubling of production costs less than the last doubling

With a 90 percent learning curve, each time output doubles the **average cumulative cost** of labor is 90 percent of what it was during the previous doubling. Labor cost for the first unit is $120,000; therefore for the first doubling of production, from one unit to two units, the average cumulative labor cost will be 90 percent of $120,000, or $108,000 per unit. For the

Figure 25-3. A schedule of learning curve costs. With a learning rate of 90 percent, each value in column C is 90 percent of the previous value. Each value in column D is 80 percent of the previous value in column C. In this case, 80 percent is the incremental efficiency constant.

Belding Electronics Company
Schedule of Labor Hours for Satellites
with 90 Percent Learning Curve

Incremental units to double	Cumulative units produced	Average hours per unit		Total hours	
		Cumulative hours	Incremental hours	Cumulative hours	Incremental hours
A	B	C	D	B × C	A × D
	1	10,000 _80%_ 10,000		10,000	10,000
1	2	9,000 _80%_ 8,000		18,000	8,000
2	4	8,100 _80%_ 7,200		32,400	14,400
4	8	7,290	6,480	58,320	25,920

second doubling, from two units to four units, the average cumulative labor cost is $97,200, which is 90 percent of 90 percent, or 81 percent of $120,000. The same computations can be made in terms of time rather than cost, as shown in Figure 25-3.

The average, incremental, and total time needed to produce the first unit is 10,000 hours. Doubling production adds one more unit, shown in column A of Figure 25-3. The average cumulative hours per unit for two units is 9,000, which is 90 percent of the previous figure in column C. Because the average time to make the first two units is 9,000 hours per unit, the second unit must have required 8,000 hours.

Time required to build first two units	18,000 hr
Time required to build first unit	10,000
Incremental time required to build second unit	8,000 hr

The efficiency constant is double the learning rate minus 1

Efficiency Constant. The incremental time of 8,000 hours to build the second satellite is 80 percent of the time required to build the first unit. Eighty percent is the **incremental efficiency constant** achieved with a learning curve of 90 percent. This efficiency measure is a constant that can be computed as follows:

$$\text{Efficiency constant} = 2(\text{learning rate}) - 1$$
$$= 2(.90) - 1$$
$$= .80$$

Computing Labor Hours with Learning Curves. Figure 25-3 shows the **average incremental time** in column D. This is the time required to produce the additional units needed to double production since the last doubling. Each figure in column D is 80 percent of the column C figure for the previous doubling. The second doubling of production requires completion of **two** more units, as shown in column A. The **average time** required to build the four units is 8,100 hours each, but the time required to build the last two units is an average of 7,200 hours per unit, which is 80 percent of the 9,000 cumulative hours shown in column C for the previous doubling.

The data in columns C and D of Figure 25-3 are plotted in Figure 25-4. This figure shows the decline in the cost of producing each additional unit caused by the learning effect. Note how unit costs from 16 to 20 units plot as a straight line rather than a curve because after 16 units, no additional learning occurs, a condition known as the **steady state.**

Total costs are average costs multiplied by units

The total hours in Figure 25-3 are computed by multiplying the average hours per unit by the number of units. If cumulative total hours are desired, the number of units produced, shown in column B, is multiplied by the average cumulative hours per unit in column C. To compute the **total incremental time,** the incremental number of units in column A is multiplied by the average incremental hours per unit in column D. The total of 58,320 in Figure 25-3 is the number of hours required to build all eight units completed with the third doubling. The incremental total of 25,920 hours is the number of hours needed to build the four units produced in the third doubling of production.

The numbers in column C of Figure 25-3 are obtained by starting with the 10,000 hours required to produce the first unit and using the learning rate and the efficiency constant to compute each successive average number of hours. To compute the hours for any doubling, the original hours are multiplied by the learning rate raised to an exponential power equal to the number

Figure 25-4. Diagram of average hours calculated in columns C and D in Figure 25-5. The segments *AB* are straight lines in the steady state.

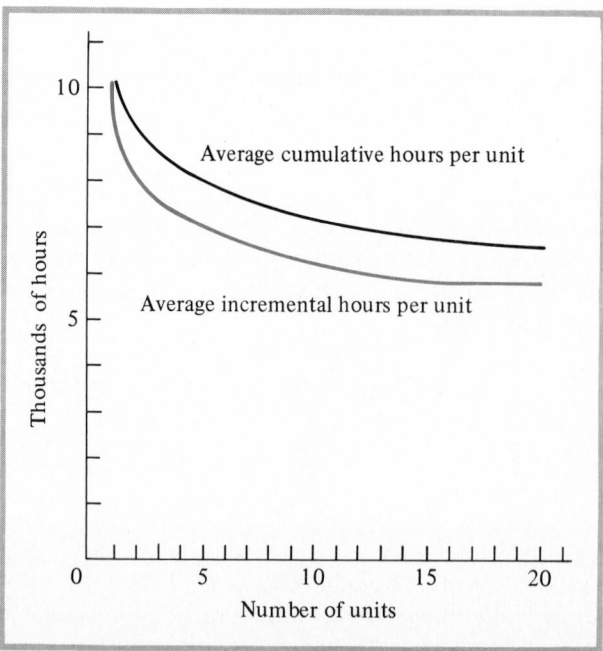

of doublings. The average cumulative hours per unit required for the second doubling are computed as

$$10{,}000 \text{ hours} \times (.90)^2 = 8{,}100 \text{ hours}$$

For the third doubling the number of hours per unit is

$$10{,}000 \text{ hours} \times (.90)^3 = 7{,}290 \text{ hours}$$

With three doublings, eight units are produced so the total time required to produce all eight units is

$$7{,}290 \times 8 = 58{,}320 \text{ hours}$$

Learning curve formulas apply to time as well as to costs

Computing Costs with Learning Curves.   The labor cost of producing the satellites is computed by multiplying the labor hours times the labor rate or by using labor costs instead of labor time in the learning curve computations. The total cost of production is found by adding all three cost elements—labor, materials, and overhead. The cost of producing eight units is:

Labor cost, 58,320 hours at $12 per hour	$ 699,840
Direct materials	800,000
Overhead at $10 per direct labor hour	583,200
Total cost of eight units	$2,083,040

Why should Belding Electronics Company be interested in the total time or cost for producing eight units? In order to bid on the satellite contract, managers need to know the total for all 20 units. There are many reasons for knowing the cost of some number of units less than the total project. The company may need the figures for budgeting purposes, so that it can plan cash flows and the acquisition of resources needed for production. The company also needs figures for less than the entire project for control purposes. By *Learning curve costs are used for control purposes* monitoring the cost of producing each successive unit, managers can determine if their projections were correct and if production is on target. For such purposes, the numbers in Figure 25-3 are somewhat limited. They do not cover production of five, six, or seven units, for instance, yet these activity levels may be important to managers.

Using the Learning Curve Formula.   The cost of producing all 20 satellites or any other number of units can be found by using the general learning curve equation. The equation allows us to compute the average cumulative cost or hours per unit for any number of units. For example, to find the average time per unit for the third doubling, when eight units are completed, the learning curve formula is:

$$\overline{Y} = aX^b$$
$$\overline{Y} = 10{,}000 \text{ hours} \times 8^{-.1520}$$
$$= 7{,}290 \text{ hours per unit}$$

This formula is easily solved using logarithms or a calculator having log functions. The formula can be converted to a linear function by means of logarithms obtained from tables. The transformation to a linear function is

$$ln\ \overline{Y} = ln\ a + b\ ln\ X$$
$$ln\ \overline{Y} = ln\ 10{,}000 \text{ hours} - .1520\ ln\ 8$$
$$= 9.2103404 - .1520(2.0794415)$$
$$= 8.8942653$$
$$\overline{Y} = 7{,}290 \text{ hours per unit}$$

It helps to have a calculator with log functions

The value of $\overline{Y}$ is the antilog of 8.8942653 and may be obtained from tables of natural logarithms or by means of a calculator. Logarithms to the base e, or natural logs, are used here because they are most commonly found on hand calculators. However, logarithms to the base 10, or common logs, may also be used.

The total cumulative hours can be obtained by multiplying the average cumulative hours by the number of units. Alternatively, because we know the time required to produce the first unit, the total cumulative hours can be obtained with the learning curve formula for total hours as follows:

$$Y = aX^d$$
$$Y = 10{,}000 \text{ hours} \times 8^{.848}$$
$$= 58{,}320 \text{ hours}$$

Notice that a in the total cost formula is both the average and total cumulative cost of producing the first unit. Once the average cumulative time per unit is available for the third doubling, the average incremental time per unit for the fourth doubling can be found simply by applying the efficiency constant computed earlier. The incremental time per unit for the fourth doubling is simply 80 percent of the cumulative time per unit for the third doubling, in this case $.80 \times 7{,}290$, or 5,832 hours per unit.

The formulas help in calculations for less than a full doubling

Figure 25-3 verifies that the average cumulative number of hours needed to produce eight satellites is 7,290. The learning curve formula can be used easily for production not shown in the figure. For example, the cumulative average hours required to produce six units is 7,616 hours per unit.

$$\overline{Y} = aX^b$$
$$\overline{Y} = 10{,}000 \text{ hours} \times 6^{-.1520}$$
$$= 7{,}616 \text{ hours per unit}$$

The six units will require a total of 45,695 hours, computed as follows:

$$Y = aX^d$$
$$Y = 10,000 \times 6^{.848}$$
$$= 45,695 \text{ total hours}$$

The total cost of producing six units is:

Labor cost, 45,695 hours at $12 per hour	$ 548,340
Direct materials	600,000
Overhead at $10 per direct labor hour	456,950
Total cost of six units	$1,605,290

The Steady State

In the steady state, no more learning takes place

So far we have not determined the total cost of producing all 20 satellites by Belding Electronics Company. To do so requires that we know how to cost the last four satellites produced, which are made after the learning curve effect stops and the steady state is reached. In our example, the steady state occurs after the fourth doubling of production when 16 units have been completed. Beyond 16 units no more learning takes place and each additional unit completed is expected to require about the same amount of time as the last unit.

Figure 25-5 shows the average and total hours for the production of all 20 satellites. The incremental labor time for producing the last four units is the same as the incremental time of the sixteenth unit. But what is the incremental time required to build the sixteenth unit? This is easily found by calculating the total time needed to build all 16 units and deducting the total time needed for the first 15 units.

$$Y = aX^d$$

Total time for 16 units = $10,000 \times 16^{.848} = 104,977$ hr

Total time for 15 units = $10,000 \times 15^{.848} = $ <u>99,386</u> hr

Incremental time for sixteenth unit   <u>5,591</u>

The sixteenth unit required 5,591 hours and each additional unit above 16 can be expected to take the same amount of time to build. When the steady state is reached, labor hours and associated costs become directly variable. In the steady state, the total cumulative hours increase at a constant rate. But the average cumulative hours are still declining, because the seventeenth unit and subsequent units add fewer hours to total production than the earlier units, so fewer total hours are spread over all units produced.

The learning curve formulas can be used to compute the average hours and the total cumulative hours only up to the steady state. Any production in the steady state must be computed separately.

Figure 25-5. This is the same schedule as in Figure 25-3, but it extends beyond the learning curve into the steady state. The limitation of such schedules is that they do not show costs for partial doublings of production.

Belding Electronics Company
Schedule of Labor Hours for Satellites
with 90 Percent Learning Curve

Incremental units to	Cumulative units produced	Average hours per unit		Total hours	
		Cumulative hours	Incremental hours	Cumulative hours	Incremental hours
A	B	C	D	B × C	A × D
	1	10,000 _80%_	10,000	10,000	10,000
1	2	9,000 _80%_	8,000	18,000	8,000
2	4	8,100	7,200	32,000	14,000
4	8	7,290	6,480	58,320	25,920
8	16	6,561	5,832	104,976	46,656
1	17	6,504	5,591	110,567	5,591
1	18	6,453	5,591	116,158	5,591
1	19	6,408	5,591	121,749	5,591
1	20	6,367	5,591	127,340	5,591

Using the two formulas, we find the average cumulative hours per unit for the fourth doubling, or 16 units, and the total time for the 16 units. Each unit above 16 requires an identical amount of time to produce because the steady state has been reached and no additional learning takes place. Therefore the cost of all 20 units is computed by calculating the cost of the first 16 units with the learning effect and adding on the cost of the last four units in the steady state. The time required for each of the last four units is 5,591 hours, computed above.

$$Y = aX^d$$
$$Y = 10,000 \text{ hours} \times 16^{.848}$$
$$104,977 \text{ total hours}$$

Total cumulative hours for 16 units	= 104,977
Total hours for 4 units: 5,591 × 4 units =	22,364
Total hours for 20 units	127,341

The incremental time of 5,591 hours achieved in the production of the sixteenth unit remains unchanged with each new unit produced. Therefore the time to produce the last four units is 5,591 hours multiplied by 4. Once we have the total hours, the total cost of producing all 20 satellites can be determined. The computation is as follows:

Labor cost, 127,341 hours at $12 per hour	$1,528,092
Direct materials	2,000,000
Overhead at $10 per direct labor hour	1,273,410
Total cost of 20 units	$4,801,502

Most of the learning curve computations discussed above are made with labor hours, but they could just as easily be made with labor costs. Instead of using 10,000 hours for the first unit, $120,000 of labor cost can be used and the final cost data would be identical. In addition, the same procedures apply if production occurs in batches rather than in single units.

Learning Curve Conversion Tables

Learning curve tables save calculation time

The use of learning curves is facilitated by means of learning curve conversion tables, which can be used to compute the average cumulative unit costs, average incremental unit costs, and total cumulative costs for any number of units or batches. Such tables can save time in making computations for a variety of situations with virtually any learning curve.

Average Cumulative Unit Cost Table. Table VII on page 916 shows the conversion factors for computing the average cumulative unit cost or time for a variety of learning curves. Using the table is easy because the factor in the table is nothing more than X^b in the average learning curve formula. It is only necessary to multiply a in the formula, the cost or time for the first batch or unit, by the appropriate factor (f) in the table.

For example, to obtain the average cumulative cost or time for the first six units in the satellite example, the time required to produce the first unit is multiplied by .7616, the 90 percent factor in the table for six units.

$$Y = a(f)$$
$$Y = 10,000 \text{ hours} \times .7616$$
$$= 7,616 \text{ hours}$$

The units in the table may also be batches

This solution is precisely what we obtained previously for six units of production. You should verify that the table will produce our earlier results with 4, 8, and 16 units.

Average Incremental Unit Cost Table. Table VIII on page 917 is used to compute the average incremental unit cost or time with various learning curves. The average incremental unit cost (I) is the difference between the total cost of all units produced and the total cost of all but the last unit produced. We used this approach to find the incremental cost of the sixteenth unit. The formula is easily derived from the total cost formula given earlier:

$$I = aX^d - a(X - 1)^d$$

Earlier in the chapter, to compute the average incremental unit cost for any doubling, we multiplied the average cumulative unit cost of the previous doubling by the efficiency constant. But this method does not permit us to get any of the average incremental unit costs for fractions of a doubling in production. To obtain the average incremental unit cost of the sixth unit we can use the formula above, or simply multiply 6 by the factor in Table VIII. Using the formula we get:

Incremental cost is merely the difference between two total costs

$$I = aX^d - a(X - 1)^d$$
$$= 10{,}000 \text{ hr} \times 6^{.848} - 10{,}000 \times 5^{.848}$$
$$= 6{,}545 \text{ hours}$$

Alternatively, using the table for the computation simply requires multiplying the initial unit cost or time by the factor (f) in the table, as follows:

$$I = a(f)$$
$$= 10{,}000 \times .6545$$
$$= 6{,}545 \text{ hours}$$

Total Cumulative Cost Table.   Table IX on page 918 is used to compute the total cumulative cost or time. The table contains values of X^d and is used the same as the other two tables. The cost or time of the first unit or batch is multiplied by the factor in the table for the appropriate learning curve and number of units desired. The total cumulative time needed to produce six units is 45,695 hours, found by multiplying 4.5695 by 10,000 hours.

Assumptions Underlying Learning Curves

Learning curves can provide much useful information but managers should understand learning curve limitations. Learning curve analysis depends on a number of assumptions that are necessary for a valid analysis.

Suitability Assumption.   The first assumption is that a particular task fits a learning curve situation. Learning curves apply to new tasks or old tasks with new employees. Machines cannot benefit from learning and only people can improve their performance by repeating a task. Learning curve analysis is therefore most useful for labor-intensive tasks.

Continuous Production Assumption.   The learning curve phenomenon occurs when production takes place over a long enough time and a large enough number of units of product. Typically, workers need to repeat a task without significant interruptions such as may occur during a strike, shifting workers to other projects, or material shortages. If major interruptions occur, part of the improvement in skill that has taken place is lost and learning must start again. In such cases, the learning curve may shift or its slope may change. Learning curve analysis assumes that production is continuous and will proceed with little or no interruption.

Interruptions in production may invalidate learning curve computations

Constant Learning Assumption.   Another assumption is that learning is a continuous, uninterrupted process that occurs at a constant rate. This assumption is not always satisfied. Different individuals learn at different rates and often in spurts and jumps rather than continuously. Moreover, learning curves apply to groups of people as well as to individuals, and different groups may learn at different rates. Note that this observation does not violate the assumption that a constant improvement factor applies to each doubling of production. The improvement with the doubling of production has been well documented in practice. But if learning is not continuous and constant, then it is not possible to obtain good measures of learning rates by measuring performance on individual units produced. When learning curves are used for control or performance evaluation, it is probably best to measure performance with batches of products rather than with individual products.

Learning may not always take place at a constant rate

Learning Rate Assumption.   Learning curve analysis also depends on the assumption that the learning rate is known for specific situations and that it applies from the first unit produced. In fact, no single learning rate is generally applicable in any company, industry, or activity. Managers should make careful measurements of production efficiency to determine the appropriate learning rate. When it is necessary to use estimates, they should be based on experience with situations as similar as possible to the situation to which the estimates apply. Measurements should be made over a sufficient amount of production to determine the actual rate.

Steady State Assumption.   Finally, we assume it is known when learning stops and the steady state is reached. Obviously learning cannot continue indefinitely for manual tasks, but it is not always possible to know precisely when the learning effect ends. Typically the timing of the steady state depends on estimates, which should be made on the basis of past experience.

Uses for Learning Curve Analysis

Learning curve analysis has many uses. We have discussed some of them, such as bidding on contracts that involve a new process, product, or procedure. Such contracts often include cancellation clauses which permit one party to cancel production prior to completion of all units. In such cases learning curves are valuable in determining the appropriate compensation. In our example of 20 satellites, the cost of production per unit is quite different if only 15 units are built than if all 20 are completed.

Planning and Control.   Learning curve analysis is useful for planning and control purposes. It can be used to plan working capital needs, the financing and acquisition of resources, and payment of expenses. As workers become more efficient, the rate of production increases resulting in a higher turnover of raw materials and work in process. Learning curve analysis can be used for planning and controlling inventories and scheduling of employees. In addition variance analysis and performance evaluations are facilitated, because standards for learning situations can be made different from standards established for operations that do not involve learning.

LEARNING CURVES WITH PRODUCTION IN BATCHES

The concepts illustrated so far apply to production that starts with a batch of units as well as production that starts with a single unit of product. In addition, however, learning curve analysis can be used to find the cost of partial batches of production and also the cost of the first unit in a batch.

Comprehensive Example

To illustrate the salient issues on learning curve analysis with batches of production, we present a comprehensive example of Lerner Company whose assembly department has just completed assembly of eight music synthesizers. The music synthesizer is a new product and requires assembly of many electronic, mechanical, and electrical components. Assembly of the first batch of eight units required 500 hours of direct labor at a cost of $9 per hour, for a total labor cost of $4,500. This means that the average labor cost per unit in the first batch was $562.50 ($4,500/8 units). Direct materials for each unit cost $850. From past experience with assembly of complex new products, management believes that an 85 percent learning curve will occur for the first four doublings of production.

The company has budgeted production of 150 units, of which 50 are to be completed by the end of the current accounting period, including those already assembled. Management wants to know the direct cost of materials and labor for the current period and for the next period. In addition, management wants to establish a selling price for the synthesizers at 180 percent of prime cost.

Computing Average and Total Cost.   The average cumulative cost per unit for the first 50 units is obtained by using the average cost formula.

$$\overline{Y} = aX^b$$
$$\overline{Y} = \$562.50 \times 6.25^{-.2345}$$
$$= \$366 \text{ per unit}$$

The total cumulative cost is the average cumulative cost per unit times the number of units.

$$\$366 \text{ per unit} \times 50 \text{ units} = \$18,300$$

The same solution is obtained with the total cost formula:

$$Y = aX^d$$
$$= \$4,500 \times 6.25^{.7655}$$
$$= \$18,300$$

Note that a in the total cost formula is not $562.50 but rather $4,500, the total cost of the first batch. When we had only one unit in the first batch, the

Computations with batches require choosing the value of a carefully.

average cumulative cost and the total cumulative cost were the same. When there is more than one unit in the first batch, the average cumulative cost is used in the average cost formula, and the total cumulative cost is used in the total cost formula.

The total direct cost of production for the current year is

Labor cost, $366 × 50 units	$18,300
Direct materials, 50 units × $850	42,500
Total direct cost of first 50 units	$60,800

To construct a schedule of labor costs for various doublings of production, it is convenient to know the value of the efficiency constant.

$$\text{Efficiency constant} = 2(\text{learning rate}) - 1$$
$$= 2(.85) - 1$$
$$= .70$$

The schedule of labor costs for the first 50 units of production is presented in Figure 25-6. The average cumulative cost of each successive doubling is 85 percent of the previous average cumulative cost. The average incremental cost of each doubling is 70 percent of the previous average cumulative cost. Note that the last line in the schedule does not represent a doubling of production. This schedule can be used by management for planning and control of production during the current year. By monitoring actual time and cost of labor at various doublings in production, managers can determine how accurate their estimates are and whether learning is taking place at the estimated 85 percent rate. The schedule can be extended to include all 150 units if management desires.

Figure 25-6. This schedule of learning curve costs is prepared in the same way as a similar schedule of learning curve time. Each cost in column C is 85 percent of the previous cost, because 85 percent is the learning rate. The incremental efficiency constant is 70 percent.

Lerner Company
Assembly Department
Schedule of Labor Costs for Synthesizers
First 50 Units with 85 Percent Learning Curve

Incremental units to double	Cumulative units produced	Average cost per unit		Total cost	
		Cumulative cost	Incremental cost	Cumulative cost	Incremental cost
A	B	C	D	B × C	A × D
	8	$562.50	$562.50	$ 4,500.00	$ 4,500.00
8	16	478.13	393.75	7,650.08	3,150.00
16	32	406.41	334.69	13,005.12	5,355,04
18	50	366.00	294.20	18,300.00	5,295.67

Finding the Cost of the First Unit. The incremental unit cost of the fiftieth unit can be found by using the formula

$$I = aX^d - a(X - 1)^d$$

but this works most easily if we know the cost of the first unit. The cost of the first unit is the average cumulative cost of one-eighth of the first batch, which is one unit. The cost of the first unit is used as the value of a in the incremental cost formula. Note that the incremental cost formula is nothing more than the difference between two total cost formulas. The cost of the first unit is

$$\overline{Y} = \$562.50 \times .125^{-.2345}$$
$$= \$916.00$$

Finding the Cost of a Partial Batch. The formula for I is easily adapted to find the total incremental cost of the last 18 units. This is the total cost of all 50 units less the total cost of the first 32 units. We already have the total cost of all 50 units.

$$I = aX^d - a(X - 18)^d$$
$$I = \$18,300 - \$916.00 \times 32^{.7655}$$
$$= \$18,300 - \$13,004.32$$
$$= \$5,295.68$$

To get the average incremental cost of the last 18 units we simply divide the total incremental cost of $5,295.68 by 18 and get $294.20, the last value in column D of Figure 25-6.

So far the company does not have enough information to establish a price for the product. For this purpose, it needs the total cost of producing all 150 units. If learning stops after four doublings of production the number of units produced during the learning period is 8×2^4, or 128 units. After 128 units are produced, the steady state is reached.

The average cumulative cost per unit for four doublings in production is

$$\overline{Y} = aX^b$$
$$\overline{Y} = \$562.50 \times 16^{-.2345}$$
$$= \$293.60 \text{ per unit}$$

To find the total cumulative cost of 128 units we multiply by the above unit cost.

$$\$293.60 \text{ per unit} \times 128 \text{ units} = \$37,580.80$$

The incremental unit cost of the 128th unit is found as before, using the $916 cost of the first unit and the incremental unit cost formula. The incremental unit cost of the 128th unit should be the unit cost of each additional unit beyond 128, because at this point no more learning takes place.

$$I = aX^d - a(X - 1)^d$$
$$I = \$37{,}580.80 - \$916 \times 127^{.7655}$$
$$= \$37{,}580.80 - \$37{,}355.73$$
$$= \$225.07$$

We can now find the total cost of all 150 units as follows:

Total labor cost of 128 units	\$ 37,580.80
Total labor cost of last 22 units, 22 × \$225.07	4,951.54
Total labor cost of 150 units	42,532.34
Direct materials, 150 × \$850 per unit	127,500.00
Total prime cost	\$170,032.34

Now the price of the product can be established. The prime cost per unit is \$1,133.55, which is \$170,032.34 divided by 150 units. The selling price should be

Prime unit cost	\$1,133.55
Multiply by 180 percent	1.80
Selling price per unit	\$2,040.39

LINEAR PROGRAMMING

Linear programming is a mathematical technique used to optimize production scheduling or other resource allocations. The situation being analyzed is described in a set of linear equations and inequalities, which are solved to obtain an optimum combination of resources. Some uses of linear programming include the design of shipping schedules, blending of materials, scheduling production, or developing resource combinations.

The solution of linear programming problems in practice requires the use of a computer. As a result, it seldom is necessary for managers to know how to solve linear programming problems. They should, however, know what problems are suitable for linear programming and how to set up the problem.

In a linear programming problem, all relationships are linear

The equations used in linear programming form a model that describes in precise mathematical terms the objective of the problem, the variables that represent the resources to be allocated, and the constraints under which those resources can be used. Once the model is developed, the solution is obtained by using one of several mathematical techniques.

Simplex Method

A common linear programming solution technique is called the **simplex method.** It can be used manually for simple problems and with computers to solve complex problems. The simplex method requires expressing the problem as a series of linear equations, which together define a feasible set of solutions. From this feasible set, the simplex method seeks the optimum solution such as the maximum profit or the minimum cost. The simplex method proceeds by finding one feasible solution, then checking if a better solution exists. If a better solution can be found, the first one is discarded. The process continues until the optimum solution is reached.

Computers solve linear programming problems easily and quickly

Manual solution of linear programming problems with the simplex method is time-consuming even with simple problems, but computer programs are available that solve complex problems with many variables. Therefore it is not necessary for you to know the procedure for solving linear programming problems with the simplex method. It is more important to know how to express linear programming problems so that they can be solved with a computer or a sophisticated calculator.

To illustrate linear programming, we use a relatively simple situation. The objective of linear programming is usually either to maximize profit or to minimize cost. We first illustrate profit maximization.

Marbell Company produces two types of marble pedestals, used by museums for displaying exhibits. Each pedestal requires cutting and polishing. The company has available 1,000 hours of cutting capacity and 1,600 hours of polishing capacity per month. The market demand for pedestals is limited to 175 round and 175 square pedestals per month. Data on the two products are provided below.

	Contribution Margin	Cutting Time	Polishing Time
Square pedestal (S)	$40	5 hr	5 hr
Round pedestal (R)	50	5	10

The Objective Function and Constraints. The company wants to maximize the total contribution margin from the two products. Total contribution margin can be expressed with the following formula, which becomes the **objective function** of the linear programming problem:

$$\text{Contribution margin} = \$40\,S + \$50\,R$$

The objective function is either maximized or minimized

The objective function is the mathematical equation that describes the profit to be maximized or the cost to be minimized. In this illustration, we want to maximize the firm's gross margin by producing the optimal mix of the two products, one of which provides $50 per unit in gross margin and the other $40 of gross margin.

The limiting factors in the firm's desire to maximize gross margin are the constraints the firm faces in the production and marketing of its products. The

Constraints are
limitations in
supply and demand

constraints in a linear programming problem are the limits imposed by productive capacity, market demand, supply of materials and labor, or other limiting factors. The constraints within which the company operates must be carefully defined before a solution is possible. All cutting capacity can be used on one product, on the other product, or a combination of both. The same is true for polishing capacity. Given the amount of cutting and polishing capacity and the number of hours required to cut or polish each unit, the constraints are expressed as follows:

Cutting constraint: $5\,S + 5\,R \leq 1{,}000$ hours
Polishing constraint: $5\,S + 10\,R \leq 1{,}600$ hours

These equations mean that the 1,000 hours of cutting capacity can be used making square or round pedestals, each requiring 5 hours per unit. Similarly, there are 1,600 hours of polishing capacity available which can be used to make either product at the rate of 5 hours for square pedestals and 10 hours for round ones. In either case, the total hours available cannot be exceeded.

The limits on the number of units that can be sold also constrain production. These constraints are expressed as follows:

Demand for S: $S \leq 175$ units
Demand for R: $R \leq 175$ units

It is not possible to produce negative amounts of products, so a constraint on negative production is needed. It may seem that such a constraint is so obvious as to be unnecessary. Because the problem is typically solved by a computer, however, these constraints are necessary to prevent solutions that include negative products.

$$S \geq 0 \qquad R \geq 0$$

Graphic Solution.   Simple linear programming problems can be analyzed graphically. Figure 25-7 shows the production quantity of square pedestals on the vertical axis and round pedestals on the horizontal axis. If the company produces only square pedestals it can cut a maximum of 200 units per month. Similarly it can cut only 200 round pedestals if it produces nothing else. These figures are easy to obtain by dividing the 1,000 hours of cutting capacity by the 5 hours required to cut one unit. These two extreme activities are plotted on the axes of the diagram and are connected with a straight line which defines all possible combinations of time spent on square and round pedestal cutting. For example, the combination of 120 square and 80 round pedestals requires 1,000 hours of cutting, located on the constraint line for cutting.

If only square pedestals are produced, a maximum of 320 units can be polished (1,600 hours/5 hours per unit). The maximum polishing capacity for round pedestals is 160 units. If we connect 320 units on the vertical axis and

Figure 25-7. Diagram of a linear programming maximization problem. The feasible space is the shaded area. The constraint on the maximum demand for product *R* has no effect on the solution.

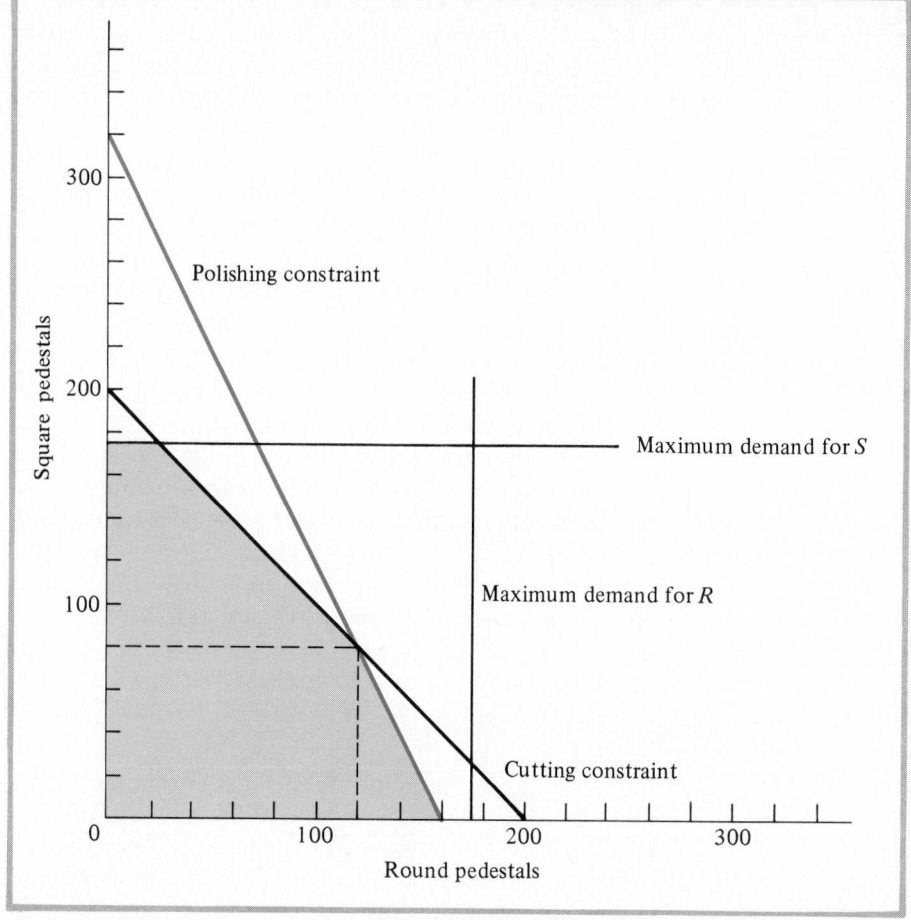

In a two-dimensional problem, the feasible space can be diagramed

160 units on the horizontal axis with a straight line, we get all possible combinations that use all the polishing capacity.

In addition to the constraints on productive capacity, the market constraint must be included in the diagram. The demand for pedestals of either type limits production to 175 units of each type per month. This constraint is shown as the horizontal line at 175 square pedestals and the vertical line at 175 round pedestals.

The lines that describe the four constraints show the limits of production for the two products. The space defined by all the constraint equations combined is called the **feasible solution space** of the linear programming problem, and is shown as the shaded area in Figure 25-7. The optimum solution to the problem must fall within the feasible solution space. Any combination of square and round pedestals that falls in the shaded area in the diagram will not violate the set of constraints. The idea is, of course, to produce that combination that will maximize total contribution margin.

Maximizing Contribution Margin

The round pedestal has a $50 contribution margin and the square pedestal has a $40 contribution margin. But the round pedestal requires more production resources than the square one. The maximum total contribution margin is achieved by some combination of the two products. But what combination is optimum, and how is it determined? To find the maximum contribution margin, we can express the contribution margin of one product in terms of the other and obtain various combinations of products that yield the same contribution margin. One square pedestal has a contribution margin of $40 and one round pedestal has a contribution margin of $50. This means that one round pedestal provides the same contribution margin as 1 1/4 square pedestal. Conversely, one square pedestal has the same contribution margin as 4/5 round pedestal. To obtain the same contribution margin by producing one additional round pedestal, square pedestal production must be reduced by 4/5 unit. In other words, the rate of change in S for one unit of R is $-4/5\ S$, and is the slope of the contribution margin. The contribution margin line is the objective function, and it can be plotted on the diagram. If any part of the line falls within the feasible solution space, that amount of contribution margin can be achieved.

Given the above relationships, we can construct combinations of production quantities that yield identical contribution margins and plot them in the graphic solution. Figure 25-8 shows the feasible solution space. The broken line connecting 100 square and 80 round pedestals is a contribution margin of $4,000 for any combination of products on the line. Following are some such combinations.

Square	+	Round	= Total CM
100	× $40 + 0	× $50 =	$4,000
0	× 40 + 80	× 50 =	4,000
50	× 40 + 40	× 50 =	4,000
25	× 40 + 60	× 50 =	4,000
18.5 ×	40 + 65.2 ×	50 =	4,000

Clearly any combination of products that produces $4,000 of contribution margin is not optimal, but this is only a first solution. The simplex method is an iterative process that starts out with a first solution which can be checked to determine if it is optimal. It then proceeds to another solution, shifting the contribution margin higher but keeping it in the feasible solution space. A larger contribution margin occurs further to the right in Figure 25-8. Eventually, after a sufficient number of iterations, the optimal combination is found.

The contribution margin is maximized at a corner solution

In linear programming problems, the optimal combination of products always occurs at one of the corners within the feasible set of combinations. This becomes evident if you visualize the CM line in Figure 25-8 sliding to the right in the diagram until any further movement would take it out of the feasible solution space. Therefore, in simple problems that can be diagramed in two dimensions, to find the optimal solution it is necessary only to find the

Figure 25-8. Feasible space from Figure 25-8, showing the slope of the contribution margin. The optimal solution is at corner c, which provides the largest possible contribution margin.

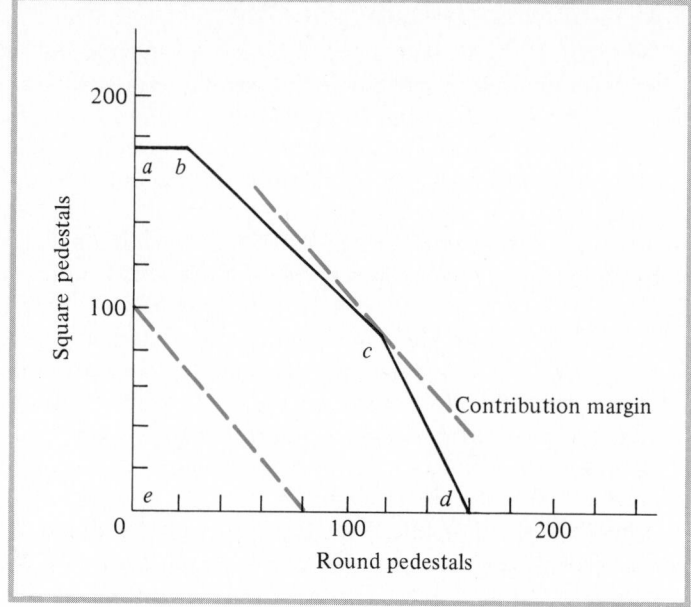

contribution margin at each corner of the feasible solution space. The five corners in the figure provide the following combinations of products:

	Square	+	Round	= Total CM
a.	175 × $40 +		0 × $50 =	$7,000
b.	175 × 40 +		25 × 50 =	8,250
c.	80 × 40 +		120 × 50 =	9,200
d.	0 × 40 +		160 × 50 =	8,000
e.	0 × 40 +		0 × 50 =	0

The optimal production combination consists of 80 square and 120 round pedestals, which occurs at point c in the figure. The broken line intersecting this point on the set of feasible combinations is the contribution margin of $9,200 for any combination of products. A larger contribution margin is not possible without going outside of the feasible set, and the only combination that provides this much contribution margin is at the corner point made up of 80 square and 120 round units.

Occasionally the objective function may have a maximum at two corner points. In that case any combination along the line that connects those two points is optimal. This could happen in our example if the contribution margin line were parallel to the cutting constraint. In most cases however, the optimum is at a corner.

Allocation of Scarce Resources. Looking for the first time at our example, it might appear that the largest total contribution margin can be obtained by producing as many round pedestals as possible, because they have the highest contribution margin. This would be 175 units, the maximum that can be sold. Then any remaining productive capacity could be devoted to square pedestals. Figure 25-8 shows that this would not work. The idea is to maximize contribution margin by maximizing the use of scarce resources, which is productive capacity in this example. Use of productive capacity is maximized by trading cutting of S for cutting of R, or polishing of S for polishing of R. The best combination yields the greatest contribution margin at the corner where the two productive capacity constraints meet.

Linear programming maximizes contribution margin by allocating resources

Sensitivity Analysis of Linear Programming Problems

The solution to the linear programming problem is based on estimates of costs, capacities, and contribution margins. Any of these estimates may be wrong and managers may be interested in knowing the cost of an error in their estimates. If the cost of estimation error is large, new estimation techniques may be warranted.

Sensitivity is tested by changing one variable slightly

To illustrate sensitivity analysis, let us suppose that the estimates of some costs are incorrect, resulting in a contribution margin for round pedestals of only $45 per unit rather than the original estimate of $50. To determine how sensitive the solution is to this estimation error, a new solution can be developed with the correct contribution margin slope. With the new estimate, a round pedestal now provides the same contribution margin as 1 1/9 square pedestals. Alternatively, each square pedestal provides the same contribution margin as 9/10 round pedestal. In effect, the slope of the contribution margin line has changed from $-4/5$ to $-9/10$, expressed as the rate of change in S for one unit of R.

The change in contribution margin slope does not change the constraints nor the production function of the linear programming problem. But the optimal solution may occur at another corner. We can solve for the total contribution margin at each corner and compare with the previous solution.

	Square	+	Round	= Total CM
a.	$175 \times \$40 +$		$0 \times \$45 =$	$7,000
b.	$175 \times 40 +$		$25 \times 45 =$	8,125
c.	$80 \times 40 +$		$120 \times 45 =$	8,600
d.	$0 \times 40 +$		$160 \times 45 =$	7,200
e.	$0 \times 40 +$		$0 \times 45 =$	0

The optimal combination still consists of 80 square and 120 round pedestals. The slope of the contribution margin line (the objective function) did not change sufficiently to warrant changing the product mix. But the optimal solution now provides a contribution margin of $8,600 instead of $9,200. Although the actual contribution earned is $600 less than expected, the production mix of 80 square and 120 round pedestals still produces the highest possible contribution margin, given the objective function and the constraints.

If the error in contribution margin estimate is large enough to change the solution from one corner point to another, then the firm will have produced a nonoptimal mix of products. This situation is illustrated in Figure 25-9, which shows two contribution margins of different slopes, each indicating a different optimal combination of products.

It is possible to determine the size of error that would have to be made in estimating contribution margin before the optimal solution would change from one corner point to another. When the contribution margin slope is equal to the constraint slope between the two points, managers are indifferent between the two corner solutions. Therefore it is only necessary to set one corner solution equal to the other to obtain the indifference contribution margin. A manager may want to know what the contribution margin of round pedestals would have to be in order to be indifferent between producing at point b or point c in Figure 25-9. The contribution margin is found as follows:

$$(80 \times \$40) + (120 \times R) = (175 \times \$40) + (25 \times R)$$
$$(120 \times R) - (25 \times R) = \$7,000 - \$3,200$$
$$95 \times R = \$3,800$$
$$R = \$42.22$$

If the contribution margin of round pedestals declined to $42.22 the company would be indifferent between producing 175 square and 25 round pedestals, 80 square and 120 round pedestals, or any combination between these two that yields the same total contribution margin.

Figure 25-9. If the contribution margin of products changes, the optimal solution may move to another corner. The slope of the total contribution margin is determined by the relative proportion of each product's individual contribution margin.

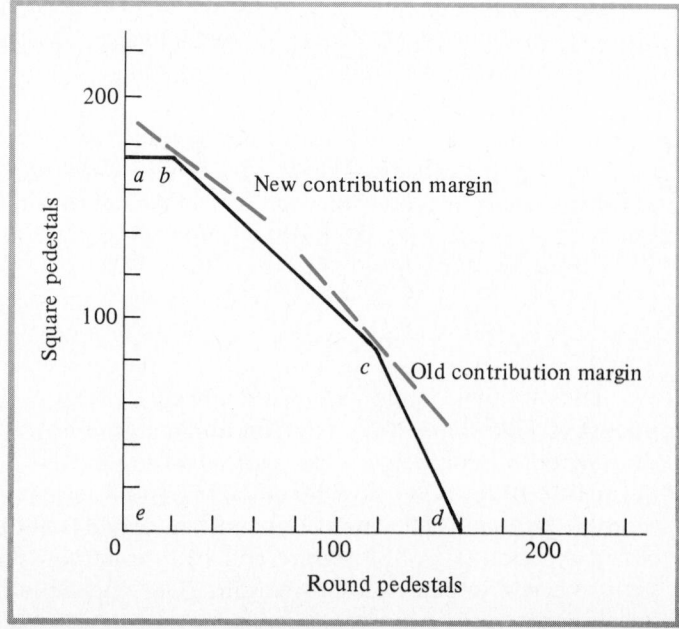

Shadow Prices.   Sensitivity analysis also can be performed on the constraints of the linear programming problem. If the benefits of changing productive capacity are great enough, management will increase capacity. The analysis of increasing productive capacity by one unit results in a shadow price for the resource. **A shadow price** is the opportunity cost of increasing or decreasing a particular resource by one unit. It shows how much the optimal solution would change as a result of relaxing a constraint by one unit. Shadow prices can be computed for any resource. In our example we could compute shadow prices for either production resource.

The shadow price is the contribution margin earned by using one unit of a resource

For example, Marbell Company has 1,000 hours of cutting capacity and 1,600 hours of polishing capacity. If we assume an increase in cutting capacity to 1,001 hours, the additional hour can be used to cut 1/5 of a square pedestal or 1/5 of a round pedestal. Just how much of each resource is used in the production of the optimal mix of products? Square columns require 5 hours of cutting and 5 hours of polishing. Round pedestals require 5 hours of cutting and 10 hours of polishing. Therefore the amount of resource used when 80 square and 120 round pedestals are made is:

$$\text{Cutting:} \quad 80 \times 5 + 120 \times 5 = 1{,}000 \text{ hours}$$
$$\text{Polishing:} \quad 80 \times 5 + 120 \times 10 = 1{,}600 \text{ hours}$$

Both resources are used at their maximum capacity with the optimal solution. Therefore increasing the cutting capacity by 1 hour would leave 1 hour of this resource idle unless production is shifted to free some polishing capacity. Figure 25-10 shows that if cutting capacity increases, production should be shifted from round to square pedestals. This is because for each round unit that is not polished, two square ones can be polished. Although round pedestals produce a greater contribution margin than square ones, two square ones yield more than one round one. In other words, an increase in cutting capacity enables the company to use the idle cutting capacity best by producing square units. However, cutting more square units is of no benefit if they cannot be polished. Therefore if an hour of cutting capacity is made available, production of round units should be decreased to provide polishing capacity for the increased production of square units. Polishing square pedestals is more profitable than polishing round ones.

How do we find the value of 1 hour of cutting capacity? Earlier you saw that 1 round pedestal has to be made for 4/5 square pedestal in order to maintain the same contribution margin. This means that 5 hours of square cutting capacity must become available for each 4 hours of round cutting capacity given up in order to maintain the same contribution margin. But we assume only 1 additional hour of cutting capacity is made available. A square pedestal requires 5 hours of cutting, so only 1/5, or .2, additional square pedestal can be produced with 1 additional hour of cutting capacity. The contribution margin of .2 square pedestal is the same as the contribution margin of .16 round pedestal (.2 × 4/5). But for each round pedestal given up, two square ones can be polished. Therefore giving up .16 of a round pedestal's

If one resource is used to full capacity, adding a second resource changes the optimal combination of products

Figure 25-10. The shadow price of a resource is the amount of contribution margin earned by using one unit of the resource. When cutting capacity is increased, the optimal solution moves to a new combination of products. The loss in contribution margin resulting from making less round pedestals is more than offset by the additional contribution margin gained by making more square pedestals.

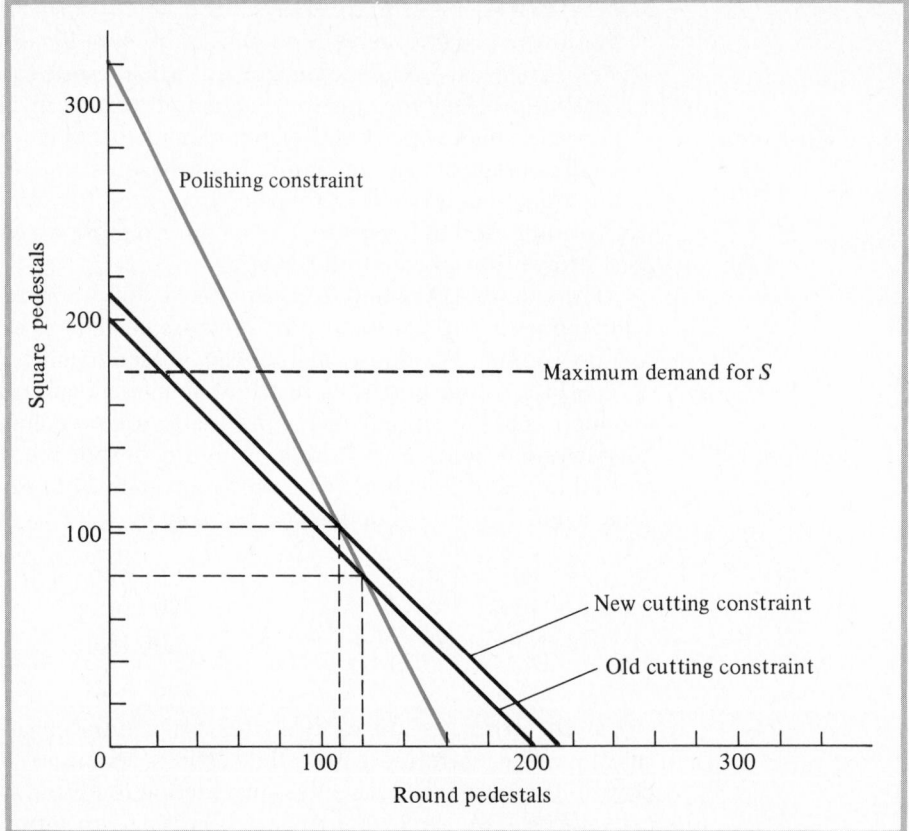

production gains two times the .2 of a square pedestal's production. The relationship can be expressed as follows:

Square pedestal: $+.2 \times 2 = .4$
Round pedestal: $-.16 \times 1 = -.16$

What does this do to the contribution margin? The additional .2 square pedestal increases contribution margin and .16 less round pedestal reduces it, as follows:

$$CM = (.4 \times \$40) + (-.16 \times \$50) = \$8$$

The addition of 1 hour of cutting capacity increases contribution margin by $8, which is the **shadow price** of one unit of cutting capacity. In other words, cutting capacity is worth $8 per hour. A similar computation can be made for polishing capacity. The information provided by shadow prices can be used by managers to plan productive capacity changes.

Minimizing an Objective Function

Sometimes the objective of linear programming is to minimize the objective function, which is usually a cost function. For example, a dietician wants to minimize the cost of providing food services for a school cafeteria but at the same time wants to provide lunches that are well balanced and nutritionally sound. The optimal combination of various foods can be formulated as a linear programming problem and solved by minimizing the cost of the food items while meeting all nutritional requirements. In this situation, the objective function to be minimized is the cost of servings of the various types of foods that the dietician plans to include in the analysis. The constraint equations identify the minimum nutritional requirements for the lunches and any other requirements such as the minimum number of items on the menu.

We assume that eight food items are included in the analysis, identified as $F_1, F_2, \ldots, F_8$. The objective function to be minimized includes the cost per serving of each of the food items as shown below:

Min. cost:

$$\$.4F_1 + \$.2F_2 + \$.1F_3 + \$.5F_4 + \$.1F_5 + \$.3F_6 + \$.6F_7 + \$.2F_8$$

This cost function is to be minimized subject to the nutritional constraints dictated by the school dietician. With linear programming maximization problems, most constraints are "less than or equal to" constraints or just "equal to" constraints. With cost minimization, most constraints are "greater than or equal" constraints. For example, the following three constraint equations express the minimum amount of nutritional value provided by each type of food as a percentage of the federal government's minimum daily requirements.

$$.05F_1 + .10F_2 + .08F_3 + .02F_4 + .08F_5 + .04F_6 + .15F_7 + .08F_8 \geq .25$$

$$.10F_1 + .04F_2 + .03F_3 + .15F_4 + .05F_5 + .08F_6 + .12F_7 + .10F_8 \geq .30$$

$$.20F_1 + .10F_2 + .04F_3 + .22F_4 + .02F_5 + .08F_6 + .14F_7 + .07F_8 \geq .40$$

The first constraint indicates that item F_1 contains 5 percent of some nutrient, such as protein, carbohydrate, or fat; item F_2 contains 10 percent of this same nutrient, and so on. All together, the combination of items selected must provide 25 percent or more of this nutrient in each meal. Similarly, the combination of foods selected must provide at least 30 percent of some other nutrient to each meal, according to the second constraint.

To ensure that there is an adequate variety in the lunches, a constraint is added that minimizes the number of food items that may be included in the lunch. For example, if no less than three food items are to be included in any one meal, the constraint equation is:

$$F_1 + F_2 + F_3 + F_4 + F_5 + F_6 + F_7 + F_8 \geq 3$$

In addition, a constraint is needed for each food item to ensure that it cannot be negative. With the above objective function and the constraint equations, it is a simple matter for a computer to solve this problem. The solution results in an optimal combination of the eight foods resulting in minimum cost lunches that provide the specified nutritional requirements.

SUMMARY

Two quantitative tools available to management are learning curve analysis and linear programming. **Learning curves** describe the improvement in efficiency caused by performing a new task repeatedly. Learning curve analysis is suitable for analyzing labor costs and labor-related costs of production. Learning curves are expressed in terms of learning rates, with lower rates indicating more learning than higher rates. For example, learning is faster with an 80 percent learning curve than with a 90 percent curve. When learning stops, the **steady state** is reached, at which point labor cost or time becomes directly variable.

The learning effect is measured using formulas that determine the **average cumulative cost** of each doubling of production. With an 80 percent learning curve, each time production doubles, the average cost of all units produced is 80 percent of the average cost at the previous doubling. Formulas are also available for computing the **average incremental cost** or time of production and the **total cumulative cost** or time for all units produced. The costs obtained from learning curve analyses apply to batches of products as well as to single units. In addition to formulas, tables are available for computing the average cumulative, incremental, and total cost or time of production.

In order for the learning curve analysis to be valid, the task in question should be subject to learning. Production should be continuous without interruptions, so that relearning does not have to occur. The analysis assumes that learning occurs at a constant rate, that the rate can be estimated with some degree of accuracy, and that it is known when the steady state occurs. Learning curve analysis is useful for planning resource requirements, control of production and resources, setting prices, and bidding on contracts.

Linear programming is a mathematical technique used to optimize business activities by solving a series of linear inequalities. The **objective function** in linear programming may be the minimization of costs or the maximization of profits. The **constraints** of the problem are expressed as inequalities, which define the **feasible solution space.** In simple linear programming problems, a graphic or algebraic solution is possible or the **simplex method** can be used to solve the problem manually, but most linear programming problems are too complex to solve without a computer.

Linear programming problems can be analyzed to determine how sensitive the constraints or resources are to errors in estimation. Analysis yields **shadow prices** for constraints, which are used to find the change in the optimum solution caused by adding or deleting one unit of a particular resource.

KEY TERMS   average cumulative cost or time *(860)*

average incremental cost or time *(863)*

constraint *(877)*

efficiency constant *(863)*

feasible solution space *(878)*

learning curve *(858)*

learning rate *(859)*

linear programming *(875)*

objective function *(876)*

shadow price *(883)*

simplex method *(876)*

steady state *(859)*

total cumulative cost or time *(862)*

total incremental cost or time *(864)*

QUESTIONS

1. "According to this budget, the new inertial navigation unit is going to cost more to produce than its selling price," said the new manager to the production supervisor. The supervisor replied, "That's just for the first 1,000 units, which is at the beginning of the learning curve. The learning rate is estimated at 85 percent and we should reach the steady state at 10,000 units." "I don't like that at all," said the manager, who had only a vague understanding of learning curves. "You see to it that the learning rate is increased to 90 percent and the steady state to no less than 15,000 units." As the production supervisor, respond to the manager's request.

2. For many new products or production processes, some amount of initial production time is required before labor efficiency reaches an acceptable level. During the learning process, the time required for production and the cost of labor are higher than expected for normal production. Management should be aware of the learning curve phenomenon and must be able to use it in planning production of new products. What types of data should a manager collect in order to use learning curves in future planning? What types of decisions might require the use of learning curve computations? In general, what information is obtained from a learning curve analysis?

3. (CMA) The operations of organizations and business enterprises continue to increase in size and complexity. Managers find it more difficult to capture all aspects of a problem as a consequence of the increase in size and complexity of operations. As a result, managers have had to identify, use, and rely upon new tools and techniques to assist in making critical decisions. Linear programming is one tool that managers have employed in their decision-making activities. Explain what linear programming is. Identify and explain the requirements that need to be present in a decision situation to employ linear programming.

EXERCISES

Ex. 25-1
Price Setting with
Learning Curves

The forming department of Brazox Company usually experiences a 90 percent learning curve for the production of new products. The department has just completed 400 units of a new design of molded fiberglass garden sculptures with complex curves, which require manual layup. The time required to produce the batch was 1,400 hours. The steady state is expected after 3,200 units have been completed but the company plans to produce only a total of 2,000 units because it thinks the market for the product is limited to this number. Brazox Company prices its products at 220 percent of direct labor cost rounded to the nearest dollar and it pays $7.80 per hour for direct labor.

REQUIRED   Determine the price per unit of product.

Ex. 25-2
Interpreting a
Labor Schedule
with Learning

Below is a schedule prepared by the manager of Flambaux Company in order to plan the production of a new gear assembly for which the company is negotiating a contract. The schedule is based on past experience with new products of a similar type.

Flambaux Company
Schedule of Labor Costs for Gear Assembly
with Learning Curve

Incremental Units to Double	Cumulative Units Produced	Average Costs per Unit		Total Costs	
		Cumulative Costs	Incremental Costs	Cumulative Costs	Incremental Costs
	1	$50.00	$50.00	$ 50.00	$ 50.00
1	2	45.00	40.00	90.00	40.00
2	4	40.50	36.00	162.00	72.00
4	8	36.46	32.40	291.68	129.60
8	16	32.82	29.16	525.12	233.28
16	32	29.54	26.26	945.28	420.16

REQUIRED

a. Determine the learning rate on which the schedule is based.
b. Briefly describe the significance of each figure in the last line of the schedule.

Ex. 25-3
Learning Curve
Formulas and
Tables

The time required to build the first unit of a product with an 85 percent learning curve effect is 250 hours. A total of 15 units is to be built.

REQUIRED

a. Use the learning curve tables to find the average cumulative time and total cumulative time of the 15 units, and the incremental time of the fifteenth unit.
b. Verify your solutions by use of the learning curve formulas.

Ex. 25-4
Labor Schedule
with Learning
Curve Costs

Botega Company has just completed the first 30 units of a small single-engine airplane of a new design. The average labor cost for the 30 airplanes was $18,000 per unit, with a total labor cost of $540,000. The company plans to build a total of 240 airplanes in the current year. With complex products of this kind, the company usually experiences an 85 percent learning curve.

REQUIRED

a. Prepare a schedule of labor costs similar to Figure 25-6 in the text.
b. Compute the total cost of producing the first 100 airplanes.

Ex. 25-5
Use of Learning
Curve Tables

Palermo Company used 120 hours of direct labor to produce its first simulated antique rolltop desk. The company expects to complete a total of 17 desks this month.

REQUIRED

a. Assume that direct labor for the desk is subject to an 87 percent learning curve. Use the learning curve tables in the chapter to find the average cumulative time and total cumulative time of producing all 17 desks, and also the incremental time for the seventeenth unit.
b. Repeat the requirements in part *a* assuming that direct labor is subject to a 93 percent learning curve.

Ex. 25-6
Learning Curve
Schedule and
Formulas

The time required to complete the first unit of a labor-intensive product was 100 hours. Production is subject to a learning curve with an 80 percent learning rate.

REQUIRED

a. Prepare a labor time schedule similar to Figure 25-3 in the text, for the first three doublings of production. Your schedule should contain four rows of figures rounded to one decimal point.
b. Use the learning curve formulas to verify the average cumulative time and total cumulative time in the last row of your schedule.

Ex. 25-7
Understanding
Learning Curve
Tables

Foom Corporation's electronic toy department has just completed assembly of 15 Android Invasion electronic video games. The direct labor cost of the fifteenth unit was $93.38. The department's manager reports that he has kept track of production carefully since assembly started and has determined that labor for the game is subject to an 87 percent learning curve.

REQUIRED

Use the learning curve tables provided in the textbook to determine the average cumulative cost of the 15 units produced and the total cost of all 15 units.

Ex. 25-8
Use of Learning
Curve Table and
Formula

A team of six technicians required 150 man-hours to assemble the first unit of a new radar receiver. By the time they completed assembly of 18 such receivers, they had worked a total of 1,305 man-hours. A total of 32 receivers are to be completed.

REQUIRED

a. Use the learning curve tables to determine the learning curve for the team of technicians.
b. Compute the average cumulative time that will be required to produce all 32 units.

Ex. 25-9
Setting Up a Linear
Programming
Problem

Sharpell Company's blending department has a capacity of 260 hours per day and its curing department has a capacity of 280 hours per day. The company manufactures two types of sealers. A 10-gallon batch of driveway sealer requires 1 hour of blending and 2 hours of curing. A 10-gallon batch of roof sealer requires 2 hour of blending and 1 hour of curing. The contribution margin of each product is $15 per 10-gallon batch. The demand for roof sealer is 120 gallons per day. The demand for driveway sealer is 200 gallons per day.

REQUIRED

Set up the linear programming problem needed to obtain the optimal combination of products to maximize contribution margin.

Ex. 25-10
Graphic Solution
for a Linear
Programming
Problem

Refer to the data for Sharpell Company's production of sealers in Exercise 25-9.

REQUIRED

a. Diagram the solution to the linear programming problem.
b. Compute the contribution margin at each corner of your feasible set to determine the optimal combination of products.

Ex. 25-11
Interpreting a
Linear
Programming
Diagram

On the next page is the graphic solution for a production problem involving products A and B, which have contribution margins of $30 and $40 respectively. The products are produced in three departments: forming, assembly, and finishing. The diagram indicates daily production and the constraints are in hours. Product A requires 1 hour of forming, 1 hour of assembly, and 2 hours of finishing.

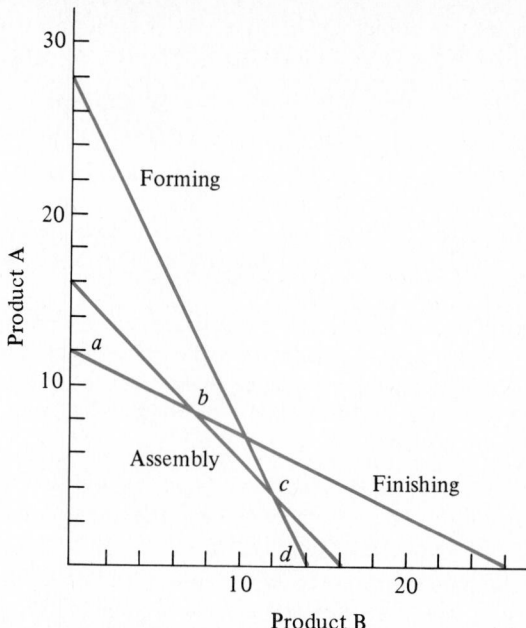

Demand for the two products is changing and the company has to change its prices. Management estimates that the contribution margins will change to $36 for product A and $34 for product B.

REQUIRED

a. Compute the contribution margin at each corner point prior to the change in demand to determine the optimum production of the two products.
b. Compute the contribution margin at each corner point after the change in demand to determine the optimum production of each product.
c. Determine the productive capacity in each department.
d. Decide how much time is required in each department for each unit of product B.

Ex. 25-12
Graphic Solution for Linear Programming Problem

The machining department of Harmell Company has a capacity of 300 hours per week. The assembly department's capacity is 352 hours. The company produces products A and B in these two departments. The following data pertain to each product:

Product	A	B
Contribution margin	$210	$180
Machining	20 hr	10 hr
Assembly	16 hr	22 hr

REQUIRED

a. Diagram the solution to the linear programming problem.
b. Compute the contribution margin at each corner of your feasible set to determine the optimal combination of products.

Ex. 25-13
Shadow Price and
Optimal Production

Farmington Company produces two products in two production departments. The small product requires 1 hour of mixing and 10 hours of curing. The large product requires 2 hours of mixing and 10 hours of curing. The mixing department has 30 hours of capacity and the curing department has 220 hours of capacity. The small product has a contribution margin of $36 and the large product has a contribution margin of $50 per unit.

REQUIRED

a. Diagram the linear programming solution to find the optimal combination of the two products.
b. Compute the contribution margin for each corner in your diagram.
c. Determine the shadow price of 1 hour of mixing capacity.

PROBLEMS

P. 25-1
Interpreting a
Labor Schedule
with Learning
Curve

Flaubert Company has started production of a new lock that requires manual labor to assemble its many parts. The cost of assembling the first lock was $25. The company typically experiences a 90 percent learning curve for assembly of new products at least through the first eight doublings of production.

REQUIRED

a. Prepare a labor schedule, similar to Figure 25-6 in the text, for the first eight doublings of production.
b. Briefly describe the significance of each figure in the bottom line of your schedule.

P. 25-2
Cost Estimation
with Learning
Curve Formulas

The labor cost of assembling a new type of encoding altimeter was $90 for the first unit. The person doing the assembly typically works on new tasks with a 95 percent learning curve and reaches the steady state by the end of six doublings in production.

REQUIRED.   Use the learning curve formulas to compute:

a. Total cost to assemble 50 units.
b. Average cumulative cost to assemble 50 units.
c. Incremental cost of assembling the fiftieth unit.
d. Total cost to reach the steady state.
e. Incremental unit cost of assembly in the steady state.

P. 25-3
Price Setting with
Learning Curve
Costs

Lenco Enterprises has just completed assembly of 500 video recorders of a new design. The company plans production of 7,500 more units during the current period and wants to budget labor and material for the product. The first 500 units required a total of 3,000 hours of direct labor at a total labor-related cost of $24,000. Direct materials cost $100,000 for the units. Based on past experience, the company expects production to be subject to a learning curve of 80 percent with the steady state occurring after four doublings of production. Management sets new product prices at 300 percent of prime cost.

REQUIRED

a. Determine the average cumulative time per unit of producing all 8,000 units.
b. Compute the total prime cost of all 8,000 units and the selling price per unit.

P. 25-4
Using Learning
Curve Formulas

The finishing department of Barbella Furniture Company usually experiences a 96 percent learning curve with new products and typically requires six doublings of production before reaching the steady state. The department has just completed the first 20 units of a new line of Queen Anne love seats in 60 hours of time. Labor cost in the department is $8 per hour.

REQUIRED   Use the learning curve formulas to compute:

a. Total time to produce 1,000 units.
b. Average cumulative time to produce 1,000 units.
c. Incremental time of producing the 1,000th unit.
d. Total time to reach the steady state.

P. 25-5
Learning Curve
Cost Computations

Paraskeva Company is negotiating a contract to produce specialized castings, which require manual labor. The company has already built 15 units as prototypes for approval by the buyer. The cost of the 15 units was $750 total labor and $32.50 per unit for materials. The buyer has accepted the 15 units and wants 465 more units.

The company usually experiences a 90 percent learning curve for new work of this type. It sets prices at 130 percent of prime cost. If the contract is signed, the company expects to complete a total of 90 units, including those already completed, by the end of the current fiscal year. The remaining units will be completed in the following year.

REQUIRED
a. Prepare a labor cost schedule similar to Figure 25-9 in the text.
b. Use the average cost formula and the total cost formula to compute the labor costs of the 90 units scheduled for production in the current year.
c. Determine the contract price that the company should negotiate.

P. 25-6
Learning Curve
Formulas

The assembly department of Sparkette Pottery Company experiences a 92 percent learning curve with new products, and typically requires five doublings of production before reaching the steady state. The department has just completed the first 40 units of a new line of pottery in 100 hours of time. Labor cost in the department is $7 per hour.

REQUIRED   Use the learning curve formulas to compute:

a. Average cumulative time to produce 1,000 units.
b. Total time to produce 1,000 units.
c. Incremental time of producing the 1,000th unit.
d. Total time to reach the steady state.

P. 25-7
Interpreting a
Linear
Programming
Problem

Kleverless Corporation manufactures busts of famous people, using three production processes: casting, curing, and finishing. The company has just developed a large and small bust of Benedict Arnold and wants to decide how many of each size to produce. The large bust is hollow and requires 2 hours of casting time, 1 hour of curing time, and 1 hour of finishing time. The small bust is solid and requires 1 hour of casting time, 2 hours of curing time, and 1 hour of finishing time. The company's controller has established the following linear programming problem to describe the daily production of its large and small Benedict Arnold bust.

$$\text{Contribution margin} = \$19L + \$14S$$

Subject to:

Casting constraint	$2(L) + 1(S) \leq 28$ hr
Curing constraint	$1(L) + 2(S) \leq 24$ hr
Finishing constraint	$1(L) + 1(S) \leq 16$ hr
	$L \geq 0$
	$S \geq 0$

REQUIRED   Discuss the significance of the objective function and the constraints.

P. 25-8
Graphic Solution of Linear Programming Problem

Refer to the data in problem 25-7 on Kleverless Corporation's production of Benedict Arnold busts.

REQUIRED

a. Diagram the solution of the problem and define the feasible set of production.
b. Determine the optimum production combination by computing the total contribution margin at each corner of the feasible set.

P. 25-9
Graphic Solution for Linear Program

Flitoff Company produces chemicals used in a variety of industrial processes. Its distilling department produces two chemicals, Blue-Y and Green-X, which are transferred to the catalyzing department for final processing. Distilling has a capacity of 900 liters per week and catalyzing has a capacity of 1,000 liters per week. Because of scarcity of a raw material, only 200 liters of Blue-Y can be produced per week. Following are data on the production of the two chemicals:

	Blue-Y	Green-X
Contribution margin per liter	$40	$30
Distilling time in hours	2	3
Catalyzing time in hours	4	2

REQUIRED

a. Set up the objective function to maximize contribution margin and the constraints for a linear programming problem to obtain the optimal combination of the two chemicals.
b. Diagram the solution to the linear programming problem.
c. Find the optimal solution by computing the contribution margin at each corner point of your diagram.

P. 25-10
Cost Minimization

A plastic polymer requires two chemical additives, alpha and beta, in order to have dimensional stability, be able to withstand a specified amount of punching shear, and have the required amount of tensile strength. After some experimentation, the manufacturer determined that the following relationships will satisfy the desired characteristics for each 100 kilograms of polymer:

$$3 \text{ alpha} + 2 \text{ beta} \geq 900 \text{ grams}$$
$$\text{alpha} + 2 \text{ beta} \geq 500 \text{ grams}$$
$$1.4 \text{ alpha} + 1.7 \text{ beta} \geq 595 \text{ grams}$$

Within the above constraints, the decision is to use the most economical combination of the two chemicals, given their cost of $4 per gram each.

REQUIRED

a. Diagram the solution to the above linear programming problem.
b. Determine the optimal combination of additives.
c. Determine the optimal combination if the price of beta increases to $6 per gram.

P. 25-11 (CMA)
Optimizing the Use of Production Resources

Leastan Company manufactures a line of carpeting that includes a commercial carpet and a residential carpet. Two grades of fiber—heavy-duty and regular—are used in manufacturing both types of carpeting. The mix of the two grades of fiber differs in each type of carpeting with the commercial grade using a greater amount of heavy-duty fiber.

Leastan will introduce a new line of carpeting in 2 months to replace the current line. The present fiber in stock will not be used in the new line. Management wants to exhaust the present stock of regular and heavy-duty fiber during the last month of production.

Data regarding the current line of commercial and residential carpeting are presented below.

	Commercial	Residential
Selling price per roll	$1,000	$800
Production specifications per roll of carpet:		
Heavy-duty fiber	80 lb	40 lb
Regular fiber	20 lb	40 lb
Direct labor hours	15 hr	15 hr
Standard cost per roll of carpet:		
Heavy-duty fiber ($3/lb)	$240	$120
Regular fiber ($2/lb)	40	80
Direct labor ($10/DLH)	150	150
Variable manufacturing overhead		
(60% of direct labor cost)	90	90
Fixed manufacturing overhead		
(120% of direct labor cost)	180	180
Total standard cost per roll	$700	$620

Leaston has 42,000 pounds of heavy-duty fiber and 24,000 pounds of regular fiber in stock. All fiber not used in the manufacture of the present types of carpeting during the last month of production can be sold as scrap at $.25 a pound.

There are a maximum of 10,500 direct labor hours available during the month. The labor force can work on either type of carpeting.

Sufficient demand exists for the present line of carpeting so that all quantities produced can be sold.

REQUIRED

a. Calculate the number of rolls of commercial carpet and residential carpet Leastan Company must manufacture during the last month of production to exhaust completely the heavy-duty and regular fiber still in stock.

b. Can Leastan Company manufacture these quantities of commercial and residential carpeting during the last month of production? Explain your answer.

c. A member of Leastan Company's cost accounting staff has stated that linear programming should be used to determine the number of rolls of commercial and residential carpeting to manufacture during the last month of production.

1. Explain why linear programming should be used in this application.
2. Formulate the objective and constraint functions so that this application can be solved by linear programming.

P. 25-12 (CMA)
Analysis of Linear
Programming Data

The Frey Company manufactures and sells two products—a toddler bike and a toy high chair. Linear programming is employed to determine the best production and sales mix of bikes and chairs. This approach also allows Frey to speculate on economic changes. For example, management is often interested in knowing how variations in selling prices, resource costs, resource availabilities, and marketing strategies would affect the company's performance.

The demand for bikes and chairs is relatively constant throughout the year. The following economic data pertain to the two products:

	Bike (B)	Chair (C)
Selling price per unit	$12	$10
Variable cost per unit	8	7
Contribution margin per unit	$ 4	$ 3
Raw materials required:		
Wood	1 bd ft	2 bd ft
Plastic	2 lb	1 lb
Direct labor required	2 hr	2 hr

Estimates of the resource quantities available in a nonvacation month during the year are:

Wood	10,000 bd ft
Plastic	10,000 lb
Direct labor	12,000 hr

The graphic formulation of the constraints of the linear programming model that Frey Company has developed for nonvacation months is presented below.

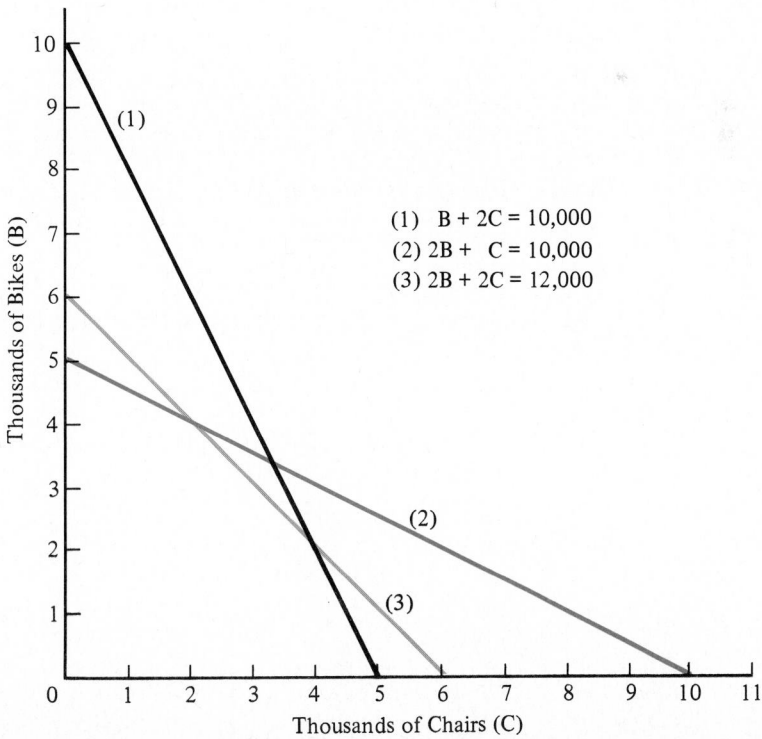

(1) B + 2C = 10,000
(2) 2B + C = 10,000
(3) 2B + 2C = 12,000

The algebraic formulation of the model for the nonvacation months is as follows:

$$\text{Objective function:} \quad \text{MAX } Z = \$4B + \$3C$$

$$\text{Constraints:} \quad B + 2C \leq 10{,}000 \text{ board feet}$$

$$2B + C \leq 10{,}000 \text{ pounds}$$

$$2B + 2C \leq 12{,}000 \text{ direct labor hours}$$

$$B, C \geq 0$$

The results from the linear programming model indicate that Frey Company can maximize its contribution margin (and thus profits) for a nonvacation month by producing and selling 4,000 toddler bikes and 2,000 toy high chairs. This sales mix will yield a total contribution margin of $22,000 in a month.

During the months of June, July, and August the total direct labor hours available are reduced from 12,000 to 10,000 hours per month due to vacations.

REQUIRED

a. What would be the best product mix and maximum total contribution margin when only 10,000 direct labor hours are available during a month?

b. The "shadow price" of a resource is defined as the marginal contribution of a resource or the rate at which profit would increase (decrease) if the amount of resource were increased (decreased). Based upon your solution for part *a*, what is the shadow price on direct labor hours in the original model for a nonvacation month?

c. Competition in the toy market is very strong. Consequently, the prices of the two products tend to fluctuate. Can analysis of data from the linear programming model provide information to management that will indicate when price changes made to meet market conditions will alter the optimum product mix? Explain your answer.

CASES

Case 25-1
Estimating the
Learning Rate

Dortmund Company has been accumulating data on the assembly of components for a new video game it recently developed. Following are data on the performance of one crew working on electronic boards, which are produced in batches of 100.

Batch	Hours	Batch	Hours
1	80.0	6	50.6
2	63.4	7	48.7
3	57.6	8	46.7
4	54.2	9	46.5
5	52.2		

REQUIRED   Estimate the learning rate for the assembly crew.

APPENDIX
Time Value of Money

Money available today is more valuable than money available in the future. The compensation for waiting is the time value of money, called **interest.**

COMPOUND INTEREST

Compound interest occurs when interest earned during the previous period itself earns interest in the next and subsequent periods. If $1,000 is placed into a savings account paying 6 percent interest per year, interest accumulates as follows.

Principal invested in first year	$1,000.00
Interest for first year ($1,000 × .06 × 1)	60.00
Amount available at the end of the first year	1,060.00
Interest for second year ($1,060 × .06 × 1)	63.60
Amount available at the end of second year	$1,123.60

The interest earned in the second year is greater than $60 because it is earned on the principal **plus** the first year's interest. If the savings account pays 6 percent interest compounded quarterly, 1.5 percent interest is added to the account each quarter, as follows:

Principal invested in first year	$1,000.00
Interest for first quarter ($1,000 × .06 × 1 × 1/4)	15.00
Amount available at the end of first quarter	1,015.00
Interest for second quarter ($1,015 × .06 × 1 × 1/4)	15.23
Amount available at the end of second quarter	1,030.23
Interest for third quarter ($1,030.23 × .06 × 1 × 1/4)	15.45
Amount available at the end of third quarter	1,045.68
Interest for fourth quarter ($1,045.68 × .06 × 1 × 1/4)	15.69
Amount available at the end of first year	$1,061.37

With quarterly compounding, the initial investment of $1,000 earned $1.37 more interest in the first year than with annual compounding. To deal with compound interest, we define the following terms:

$P =$ the principal sum that earns interest

$i =$ the interest rate per period

$n =$ the number of periods during which compounding takes place. A period can be any length of time

Future Value of $1

A sum of money invested today at compound interest accumulates to a larger sum called the **amount** or **future value**. The future value of $1,000 invested at 6 percent compounded annually for 2 years is $1,123.60, as shown above. The future value includes the original principal and the accumulated interest.

The future value varies with the interest rate, and compounding frequency, and the number of periods. If we know the future value of a $1 principal investment, we can use it to calculate the future value of any amount invested. For example, at 8 percent interest per period, $1 accumulates as follows:

Future value of $1 at 8% for 1 period = $1.00000 × 1.08 = $1.08000
Future value of $1 at 8% for 2 periods = $1.08000 × 1.08 = $1.16640
Future value of $1 at 8% for 3 periods = $1.16640 × 1.08 = $1.25971

The above table can be diagramed as follows:

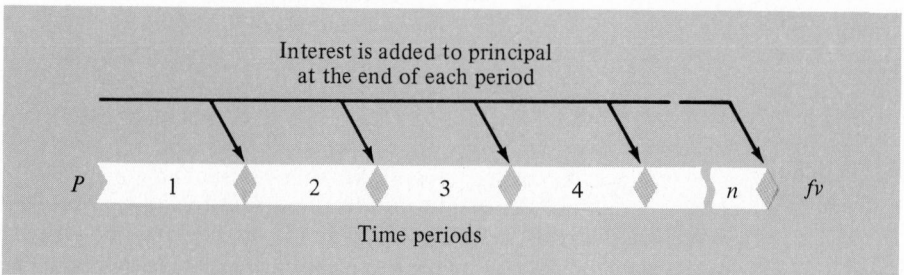

The end of each period is designated by a small diamond. The arrows pointing to the end of each period indicate that payments are made into the investment. The general formula for the future value of $1, with n representing the number of compounding periods is

$$fv = (1 + i)^n$$

Using this formula, future values can be calculated for any interest rate and any number of time periods. Table I on page 906 shows future values of $1 for many interest rates and time periods. To obtain the future value of any principal other than $1, it is only necessary to multiply the principal by the factor found in the table for the future value of $1.

$$fv = P(1 + i)^n$$

or $$fv = Pf$$

where f is the factor in the future value of $1 table, with interest rate i and number of periods n.

Problem 1. Bonzer Company invests $4,000,000 in certificates of deposit that earn 16 percent interest per year, compounded semiannually. What will be the future value of this investment at the end of 5 years when the company plans to use it to build a new plant?

Solution 1. Compounding is semiannual and there are 5 years, so the number of half-year periods is 10. The semiannual interest rate is 1/2 of the 16 percent annual rate, or 8 percent. Using Table I, with $i = 8$ percent and $n = 10$, the factor in the table is 2.15892. Multiplying this factor by the principal investment, we get

$$fv = P \times f(n = 10, i = 8\%)$$
$$= \$4,000,000 \times 2.15892$$
$$= \$8,635,680$$

COMPOUND DISCOUNT

If $1 can be invested at 8 percent today to become $1.08 in the future, then $1 is the **present value** of the future amount of $1.08. The present value of future receipts of money is important in business decision making. Frequently it is necessary to decide how much future receipts are worth today in order to determine whether an investment should be made or how much should be invested. Finding the present value of future receipts involves discounting the future value to the present. **Discounting** is the opposite of compounding. It involves finding the present value of some future amount of money that is assumed to include interest accumulations.

Present Value of $1

Knowing the present value of $1 is useful because it enables you to find the present value of any future payment. Assuming 8 percent interest per period, a table of present values of $1 can be constructed as follows:

Present value of $1 discounted for 1 period at 8% = $1.00000/1.08 = $.92593
Present value of $1 discounted for 2 periods at 8% =   .92593/1.08 = .85734
Present value of $1 discounted for 3 periods at 8% =   .85734/1.08 = .79383

The general formula for the present value of $1 is

$$pv = \frac{1}{(1 + i)^n}$$

Table II on page 908 is constructed from this formula. To find the present value of any future amount, the appropriate factor from the table is multiplied by the amount.

Problem 2. Alpha Company can invest at 16 percent compounded annually. Beta Company can invest at 16 percent compounded semiannually. Each company will need $200,000 four years from now. How much must each invest today?

Solution 2.   With annual compounding $n = 4$ and $i = 16$ percent. With semiannual compounding $n = 8$ and $i = 8$ percent. Using Table II we find the present value factors and multiply by the future value to obtain the present value. For Alpha Company

$$pv = fv \times f(n = 4, i = 16\%)$$
$$= \$200,000 \times .55229$$
$$= \$110,458$$

For Beta Company

$$pv = fv \times f(n = 8, i = 8\%)$$
$$= \$200,000 \times .54027$$
$$= \$108,054$$

The more frequent the compounding, the smaller the present value. Beta Company needs to invest less than Alpha Company because its investment grows faster due to more frequent compounding.

ANNUITIES

An **annuity** is a series of equal payments made at equal time intervals, with compounding or discounting taking place at the time of each payment. Each annuity payment is called a **rent.** There are several different types of annuities, but we discuss only ordinary annuities. In an **ordinary annuity,** each rent is paid or received at the **end** of each period. There are as many rents as there are periods. Installment purchases, long-term bonds, pension plans, and capital budgeting all involve annuities.

Future Value of Annuity of $1

If you open a savings account that compounds interest each month and at the end of each month you deposit $100 in the savings account, your deposits are the rents of an annuity. After 1 year, you will have made 12 deposits of $100 each, or a total of $1,200, but the account will have more than $1,200 in it because each deposit earns interest. If the interest rate is 6 percent a year compounded monthly, your balance is $1,233.56. The **future value of an**

annuity or **amount of annuity** is the sum accumulated in the future from all the rents paid and the interest earned by the rents. The abbreviation **FV** is used as the abbreviation for the future value of an annuity to differentiate it from the lowercase *fv* used for the future value of $1.

To obtain a table of future values of annuities, we assume payments of $1 each period made into a fund that earns 8 percent interest compounded each period. The following diagram illustrates an annuity of four payments of $1, each paid at the end of each period, with interest of 8 percent compounded each period.

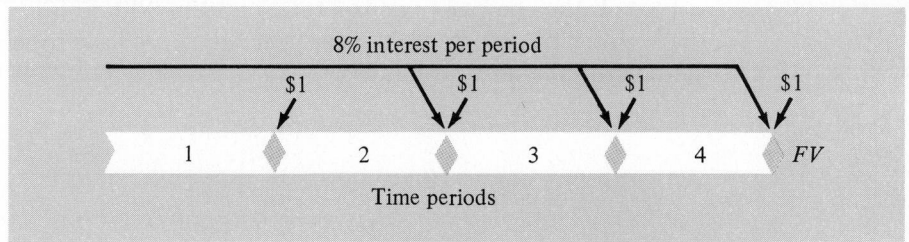

Notice that there are four rents and four periods, and each rent is paid at the end of each period. At the end of the first period, $1 is deposited and earns interest for three periods. The next rent earns interest for two periods, and so on. We want the amount at the end of the fourth period. It can be determined by calculating the future value of each individual $1 deposit as follows:

Future value of $1 at 8% for 3 periods = $1.25971
Future value of $1 at 8% for 2 periods =   1.16640
Future value of $1 at 8% for 1 period =   1.08000
The fourth rent of $1 earns no interest =   1.00000

Total for 4 rents $4.50611

The formula for the future value of an annuity of $1 can be used to produce tables for a variety of periods and interest rates.

$$FV = \frac{(1 + i)^n - 1}{i}$$

Table III on page 910 is derived from this formula. You should know how to use the table to solve annuity problems.

Problem 3. In the beginning of 1985, the directors of Malloy Corporation decided that plant facilities will have to be expanded in a few years. The company plans to invest $50,000 every year, starting on June 30, 1985, into a trust fund that earns 11 percent interest compounded annually. How much money will be in the fund on June 30, 1989, after the last deposit has been made?

Solution 3.   The first deposit is made at the end of the first 1-year period, and there is a total of 5 periods. The last deposit, made on June 30, 1989, earns no interest. The investment is an ordinary annuity, with $n = 5$ and $i = 11$ percent. From Table III we find that the amount of an ordinary annuity of $1 is 6.22780.

$$FV = \text{Rent} \times f(n = 5, \, i = 11\%)$$
$$= \$50{,}000 \times 6.22780$$
$$= \$311{,}390$$

If the company needs a total of $300,000 on June 30, 1989, how much would it have to deposit every year? Here we have to solve for the rent, given the future value, as follows:

$$FV = \text{Rent} \times f(n = 5, \, i = 11\%)$$
$$\$300{,}000 = \text{Rent} \times 6.22780$$
$$\text{Rent} = \$300{,}000 / 6.22780$$
$$= \$48{,}171.10$$

The company has to deposit $48,171 each time in order to accumulate the necessary $300,000 by June 30, 1989.

Present Value of Annuity of $1

The present value of an annuity is the sum that must be invested today at compound interest in order to obtain periodic rents over some future time. Notice that we use the abbreviation *PV* for the present value of an annuity, as differentiated from the lowercase *pv* for the present value of $1. By using the present value of $1, we can obtain a table for the present value of an ordinary annuity of $1. The present value of an annuity of $1 can be illustrated as follows:

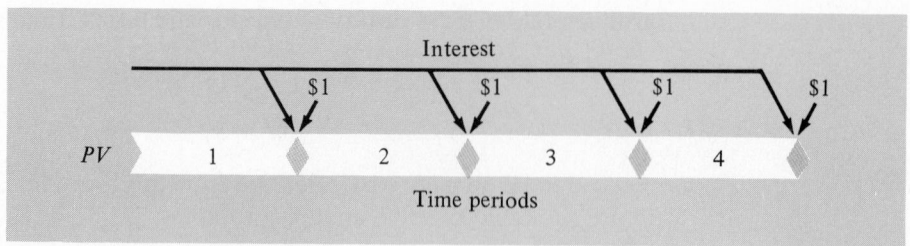

With each rent available at the **end** of each period, when compounding takes place, the number of rents is the same as the number of periods. By discounting each future rent to the present, we find the present value of the entire annuity.

Present value of first $1 discounted for 1 period at 8%   = $ .92593
Present value of second $1 discounted for 2 periods at 8% =   .85734
Present value of third $1 discounted for 3 periods at 8%   =   .79383
Present value of fourth $1 discounted for 4 periods at 8% =   .73503

Present value of annuity of 4 rents at 8% $3.31213

The first rent is worth more than the others because it is received earlier. Table IV on page 912 may be used to solve problems involving the present value of annuities. The formula used to construct Table IV is:

$$PV = \frac{1 - \dfrac{1}{(1 + i)^n}}{i}$$

Problem 4.   Mr. Floryn, the owner of Floryn Corporation, is retiring and wants to use the money from the sale of his company to establish a retirement plan for himself. The plan is to provide an income of $50,000 per year for the rest of his life. An insurance company calculates that his life expectancy is 32 more years and offers an annuity that yields 9 percent compounded annually. How much will the insurance company want now in exchange for the future annuity payments?

Solution 4.   The investment today is the present value of an annuity of $50,000 per year, with $n = 32$ and $i = 9$ percent. In Table IV, we find the factor 10.40624, which is the present value if the rents were $1.

$$PV = \text{Rent} \times f(n = 32, i = 9\%)$$
$$= \$50,000 \times 10.40624$$
$$= \$520,312$$

To assure an income of $50,000 per year, the insurance company must be paid $520,312 today. The first rent will be paid at the end of the first period. What happens if Mr. Floryn lives longer than 32 years?[1]

Solution of Managerial Problems

Many business problems are solved by use of compound interest and present value tables. For example, Barrett Corporation is investigating two possible investments. Project A is the purchase of a mine for $200,000. Net income from the sale of ore is expected to be $48,000 per year for 10 years, at which time the mine will be depleted. The property will then be sold at an estimated price of $60,000. Project B is the purchase of an office building that is leased for 15 years. The lease calls for annual payments of $40,000 at the end of each

---

[1] The insurance company keeps making the payments. Its calculations are based on probabilities. What it pays to those living longer than expected, it makes up from those who die earlier than expected.

of the next 4 years, and annual payments of $45,000 for the remaining life of the lease. The purchase price is $200,000. Barrett Corporation requires a 20 percent return on its investments. Which investment is preferable?

Solution. Project A can be diagramed as follows:

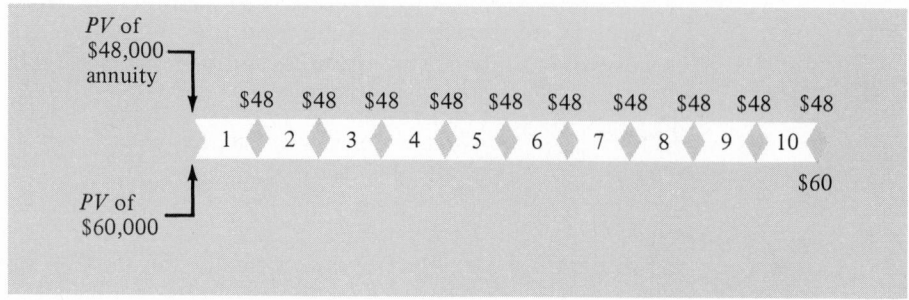

To evaluate the project, we need to find the present value of the future income stream of $48,000 per year plus the present value of the future sales price of $60,000, both discounted to the present at the company's required rate of return of 20 percent.

PV of annuity of $48,000 ($n = 10$, $i = 20\%$) = $48,000 × 4.19247 $201,238.56
pv of $60,000 ($n = 10$, $i = 20\%$) = $60,000 × .16151   9,690.60
Total present value of project A cash inflows $210,929.16

Project B can be diagramed as follows:

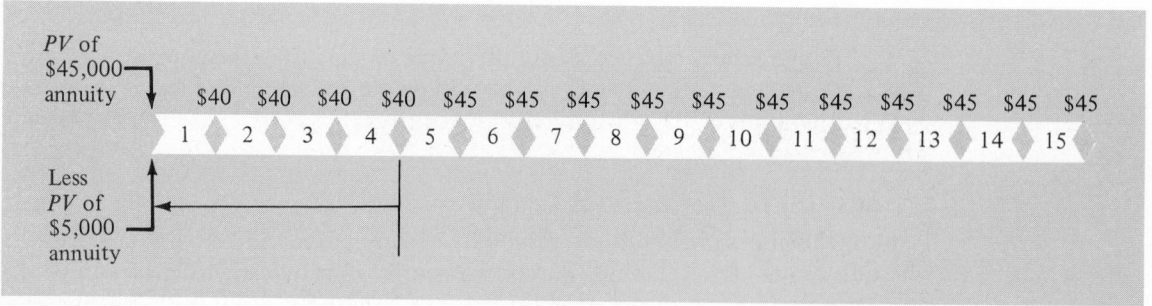

The problem can be broken down into two separate annuities, one with receipts of $45,000 per year for 15 years and the other with payments of $5,000 for 4 years. The present value of the two annuities can be found by computing the present value of an annuity of $45,000 for 15 years at 20 percent minus an annuity of $5,000 for 4 years at 20 percent.

PV of annuity of $45,000 ($n = 15$, $i = 20\%$) = $45,000 × 4.67547 $210,396.15
PV of annuity of $ 5,000 ($n = $ 4, $i = 20\%$) = $ 5,000 × 2.58873   (12,943.65)
Total present value of project B cash inflows $197,452.50

By discounting each project at the company's required rate of return, we find that Project A cash inflows have a present value of $210,929.16 and Project B cash inflows have a present value of $197,452.50. Since the asking price of each project is $200,000, Project B should not be accepted. The value of Project A is greater than the asking price, therefore the company should acquire Project A. By paying less than the present value of the project, the company will obtain a rate of return greater than 20 percent.

Table I
Future Value of $1

n	8%	9%	10%	11%	12%	13%	14%	15%	16%	17%	18%	n
1	1.08000	1.09000	1.10000	1.11000	1.12000	1.13000	1.14000	1.15000	1.16000	1.17000	1.18000	1
2	1.16640	1.18810	1.21000	1.23210	1.25440	1.27690	1.29960	1.32250	1.34560	1.36890	1.39240	2
3	1.25971	1.29503	1.33100	1.36763	1.40493	1.44290	1.48154	1.52087	1.56090	1.60161	1.64303	3
4	1.36049	1.41158	1.46410	1.51807	1.57352	1.63047	1.68896	1.74901	1.81064	1.87389	1.93878	4
5	1.46933	1.53862	1.61051	1.68506	1.76234	1.84244	1.92541	2.01136	2.10034	2.19245	2.28776	5
6	1.58687	1.67710	1.77156	1.87041	1.97382	2.08195	2.19497	2.31306	2.43640	2.56516	2.69955	6
7	1.71382	1.82804	1.94872	2.07616	2.21068	2.35261	2.50227	2.66002	2.82622	3.00124	3.18547	7
8	1.85093	1.99256	2.14359	2.30454	2.47596	2.65844	2.85259	3.05902	3.27841	3.51145	3.75886	8
9	1.99900	2.17189	2.35795	2.55804	2.77308	3.00404	3.25195	3.51788	3.80296	4.10840	4.43545	9
10	2.15892	2.36736	2.59374	2.83942	3.10585	3.39457	3.70722	4.04556	4.41144	4.80683	5.23384	10
11	2.33164	2.58043	2.85312	3.15176	3.47855	3.83586	4.22623	4.65239	5.11726	5.62399	6.17593	11
12	2.51817	2.81266	3.13843	3.49845	3.89598	4.33452	4.81790	5.35025	5.93603	6.58007	7.28759	12
13	2.71962	3.06580	3.45227	3.88328	4.36349	4.89801	5.49241	6.15279	6.88579	7.69868	8.59936	13
14	2.93719	3.34173	3.79750	4.31044	4.88711	5.53475	6.26135	7.07571	7.98752	9.00745	10.14724	14
15	3.17217	3.64248	4.17725	4.78459	5.47357	6.25427	7.13794	8.13706	9.26552	10.53872	11.97375	15
16	3.42594	3.97031	4.59497	5.31089	6.13039	7.06733	8.13725	9.35762	10.74800	12.33030	14.12902	16
17	3.70002	4.32763	5.05447	5.89509	6.86604	7.98608	9.27646	10.76126	12.46768	14.42646	16.67225	17
18	3.99602	4.71712	5.55992	6.54355	7.68997	9.02427	10.57517	12.37545	14.46251	16.87895	19.67325	18
19	4.31570	5.14166	6.11591	7.26334	8.61276	10.19742	12.05569	14.23177	16.77652	19.74838	23.21444	19
20	4.66096	5.60441	6.72750	8.06231	9.64629	11.52309	13.74349	16.36654	19.46076	23.10560	27.39303	20
21	5.03383	6.10881	7.40025	8.94917	10.80385	13.02109	15.66758	18.82152	22.57448	27.03355	32.32378	21
22	5.43654	6.65860	8.14027	9.93357	12.10031	14.71383	17.86104	21.64475	26.18640	31.62925	38.14206	22
23	5.87146	7.25787	8.95430	11.02627	13.55235	16.62663	20.36158	24.89146	30.37622	37.00623	45.00763	23
24	6.34118	7.91108	9.84973	12.23916	15.17863	18.78809	23.21221	28.62518	35.23642	43.29729	53.10901	24
25	6.84848	8.62308	10.83471	13.58546	17.00006	21.23054	26.46192	32.91895	40.87424	50.65783	62.66863	25
26	7.39635	9.39916	11.91818	15.07986	19.04007	23.99051	30.16658	37.85680	47.41412	59.26966	73.94898	26
27	7.98806	10.24508	13.10999	16.73865	21.32488	27.10928	34.38991	43.53531	55.00038	69.34550	87.25980	27
28	8.62711	11.16714	14.42099	18.57990	23.88387	30.63349	39.20449	50.06561	63.80044	81.13423	102.9666	28
29	9.31727	12.17218	15.86309	20.62369	26.74993	34.61584	44.69312	57.57545	74.00851	94.92705	121.5005	29
30	10.06266	13.26768	17.44940	22.89230	29.95992	39.11590	50.95016	66.21177	85.84988	111.0647	143.3706	30
31	10.86767	14.46177	19.19434	25.41045	33.55511	44.20096	58.08318	76.14354	99.58586	129.9456	169.1774	31
32	11.73708	15.76333	21.11378	28.20560	37.58173	49.94709	66.21483	87.56507	115.5196	152.0364	199.6293	32
33	12.67605	17.18203	23.22515	31.30821	42.09153	56.44021	75.48490	100.6998	134.0027	177.8826	235.5626	33
34	13.69013	18.72841	25.54767	34.75212	47.14252	63.77744	86.05279	115.8048	155.4432	208.1226	277.9638	34
35	14.78534	20.41397	28.10244	38.57485	52.79962	72.06851	98.10018	133.1755	180.3141	243.5035	327.9973	35
36	15.96817	22.25123	30.91268	42.81808	59.13557	81.43741	111.8342	153.1519	209.1643	284.8991	387.0368	36
37	17.24563	24.25384	34.00395	47.52807	66.23184	92.02428	127.4910	176.1246	242.6306	333.3319	456.7034	37
38	18.62528	26.43668	37.40434	52.75616	74.17966	103.9874	145.3397	202.5433	281.4515	389.9983	538.9100	38
39	20.11530	28.81598	41.14478	58.55934	83.08122	117.5058	165.6873	232.9248	326.4838	456.2981	635.9139	39
40	21.72452	31.40942	45.25926	65.00087	93.05097	132.7816	188.8835	267.8636	378.7212	533.8687	750.3783	40
41	23.46248	34.23627	49.78518	72.15096	104.2171	150.0432	215.3272	308.0431	439.3165	624.6264	885.4465	41
42	25.33948	37.31753	54.76370	80.08757	116.7231	169.5488	245.4730	354.2495	509.6072	730.8129	1044.827	42
43	27.36664	40.67611	60.24007	88.89720	130.7299	191.5901	279.8392	407.3870	591.1443	855.0511	1232.896	43
44	29.55597	44.33696	66.26408	98.67589	146.4175	216.4968	319.0167	468.4950	685.7274	1000.410	1454.817	44
45	31.92045	48.32729	72.89048	109.5302	163.9876	244.6414	363.6791	538.7693	795.4438	1170.479	1716.684	45
46	34.47409	52.67674	80.17953	121.5786	183.6661	276.4448	414.5941	619.5847	922.7148	1369.461	2025.687	46
47	37.23201	57.41765	88.19749	134.9522	205.7061	312.3826	472.6373	712.5224	1070.349	1602.269	2390.311	47
48	40.21057	62.58524	97.01723	149.7970	230.3908	352.9923	538.8066	819.4007	1241.605	1874.655	2820.567	48
49	43.42742	68.21791	106.7190	166.2746	258.0377	398.8814	614.2395	942.3108	1440.262	2193.346	3328.269	49
50	46.90161	74.35752	117.3909	184.5648	289.0022	450.7359	700.2330	1083.657	1670.704	2566.215	3927.357	50

Table I
Future Value of $1

n	19%	20%	21%	22%	23%	24%	25%	26%	28%	30%	32%	n
1	1.19000	1.20000	1.21000	1.22000	1.23000	1.24000	1.25000	1.26000	1.28000	1.30000	1.32000	1
2	1.41610	1.44000	1.46410	1.48840	1.51290	1.53760	1.56250	1.58760	1.63840	1.69000	1.74240	2
3	1.68516	1.72800	1.77156	1.81585	1.86087	1.90662	1.95312	2.00038	2.09715	2.19700	2.29997	3
4	2.00534	2.07360	2.14359	2.21533	2.28887	2.36421	2.44141	2.52047	2.68435	2.85610	3.03596	4
5	2.38635	2.48832	2.59374	2.70271	2.81531	2.93163	3.05176	3.17580	3.43597	3.71293	4.00746	5
6	2.83976	2.98598	3.13843	3.29730	3.46283	3.63522	3.81470	4.00150	4.39805	4.82681	5.28985	6
7	3.37932	3.58318	3.79750	4.02271	4.25928	4.50767	4.76837	5.04190	5.62950	6.27485	6.98261	7
8	4.02139	4.29982	4.59497	4.90771	5.23891	5.58951	5.96046	6.35279	7.20576	8.15731	9.21704	8
9	4.78545	5.15978	5.55992	5.98740	6.44386	6.93099	7.45058	8.00451	9.22337	10.60450	12.16649	9
10	5.69468	6.19174	6.72750	7.30463	7.92595	8.59443	9.31323	10.08569	11.80592	13.78585	16.05977	10
11	6.77667	7.43008	8.14027	8.91165	9.74891	10.65709	11.64153	12.70796	15.11157	17.92160	21.19890	11
12	8.06424	8.91610	9.84973	10.87221	11.99116	13.21479	14.55192	16.01204	19.34281	23.29809	27.98254	12
13	9.59645	10.69932	11.91818	13.26410	14.74913	16.38634	18.18989	20.17516	24.75880	30.28751	36.93696	13
14	11.41977	12.83918	14.42099	16.18220	18.14143	20.31906	22.73737	25.42071	31.69127	39.37376	48.75678	14
15	13.58953	15.40702	17.44940	19.74229	22.31396	25.19563	28.42171	32.03009	40.56482	51.18589	64.35895	15
16	16.17154	18.48843	21.11378	24.08559	27.44617	31.24259	35.52714	40.35792	51.92297	66.54166	84.95382	16
17	19.24413	22.18611	25.54767	29.38442	33.75879	38.74081	44.40892	50.85097	66.46140	86.50416	112.1390	17
18	22.90052	26.62333	30.91268	35.84899	41.52331	48.03860	55.51115	64.07223	85.07059	112.4554	148.0235	18
19	27.25162	31.94800	37.40434	43.73577	51.07368	59.56786	69.38894	80.73100	108.8904	146.1920	195.3911	19
20	32.42942	38.33760	45.25926	53.35764	62.82062	73.86415	86.73617	101.7211	139.3797	190.0496	257.9162	20
21	38.59101	46.00512	54.76370	65.09632	77.26936	91.59155	108.4202	128.1685	178.4060	247.0645	340.4494	21
22	45.92331	55.20614	66.26408	79.41751	95.04132	113.5735	135.5253	161.4924	228.3596	321.1839	449.3932	22
23	54.64873	66.24737	80.17953	96.88936	116.9008	140.8312	169.4066	203.4804	292.3003	417.5391	593.1990	23
24	65.03199	79.49685	97.01723	118.2050	143.7880	174.6306	211.7582	256.3853	374.1444	542.8008	783.0227	24
25	77.38807	95.39622	117.3909	144.2101	176.8593	216.5420	264.6978	323.0455	478.9049	705.6410	1033.590	25
26	92.09181	114.4755	142.0429	175.9364	217.5369	268.5121	330.8723	407.0373	612.9982	917.3333	1364.339	26
27	109.5893	137.3706	171.8719	214.6424	267.5704	332.9550	413.5903	512.8670	784.6377	1192.533	1800.927	27
28	130.4112	164.8447	207.9651	261.8637	329.1116	412.8642	516.9879	646.2124	1004.336	1550.293	2377.224	28
29	155.1893	197.8136	251.6377	319.4737	404.8072	511.9516	646.2349	814.2276	1285.550	2015.381	3137.935	29
30	184.6753	237.3763	304.4816	389.7579	497.9129	634.8199	807.7936	1025.927	1645.505	2619.996	4142.075	30
31	219.7636	284.8516	368.4228	475.5046	612.4328	787.1767	1009.742	1292.668	2106.246	3405.994	5467.539	31
32	261.5187	341.8219	445.7916	580.1157	753.2924	976.0991	1262.177	1628.761	2695.995	4427.793	7217.151	32
33	311.2073	410.1863	539.4078	707.7411	926.5496	1210.363	1577.722	2052.239	3450.873	5756.130	9526.639	33
34	370.3366	492.2235	652.6834	863.4441	1139.656	1500.850	1972.152	2585.821	4417.118	7482.970	12575.16	34
35	440.7006	590.6682	789.7470	1053.402	1401.777	1861.054	2465.190	3258.135	5653.911	9727.860	16599.22	35
36	524.4337	708.8019	955.5938	1285.150	1724.186	2307.707	3081.488	4105.250	7237.006	12646.22	21910.97	36
37	624.0761	850.5623	1156.269	1567.883	2120.748	2861.557	3851.860	5172.615	9263.367	16440.08	28922.48	37
38	742.6506	1020.675	1399.085	1912.818	2608.520	3548.330	4814.825	6517.495	11857.11	21372.11	38177.67	38
39	883.7542	1224.810	1692.893	2333.638	3208.480	4399.930	6018.531	8212.044	15177.10	27783.74	50394.52	39
40	1051.668	1469.772	2048.400	2847.038	3946.430	5455.913	7523.164	10347.18	19426.69	36118.86	66520.77	40
41	1251.484	1763.726	2478.564	3473.386	4854.110	6765.336	9403.955	13037.44	24866.16	46954.52	87807.41	41
42	1489.266	2116.471	2999.063	4237.531	5970.555	8389.011	11754.94	16427.18	31828.69	61040.88	115905.8	42
43	1772.227	2539.765	3628.866	5169.788	7343.782	10402.37	14693.68	20698.24	40740.72	79353.15	152995.6	43
44	2108.950	3047.718	4390.928	6307.141	9032.852	12898.94	18367.10	26079.78	52148.12	103159.1	201954.2	44
45	2509.651	3657.262	5313.023	7694.712	11110.41	15994.69	22958.87	32860.53	66749.59	134106.8	266579.6	45
46	2986.484	4388.714	6428.757	9387.549	13665.80	19833.42	28698.59	41404.26	85439.48	174338.9	351885.1	46
47	3553.916	5266.457	7778.796	11452.81	16808.94	24593.44	35873.24	52169.37	109362.5	226640.5	464488.3	47
48	4229.160	6319.749	9412.344	13972.43	20674.99	30495.86	44841.55	65733.41	139984.0	294632.7	613124.5	48
49	5032.701	7583.698	11388.94	17046.36	25430.24	37814.87	56051.94	82824.10	179179.6	383022.5	809324.4	49
50	5988.914	9100.438	13780.61	20796.56	31279.20	46890.43	70064.92	104358.4	229349.9	497929.2	1068308.2	50

Table II
Present Value of $1

n	8%	9%	10%	11%	12%	13%	14%	15%	16%	17%	18%	n
1	.92593	.91743	.90909	.90090	.89286	.88496	.87719	.86957	.86207	.85470	.84746	1
2	.85734	.84168	.82645	.81162	.79719	.78315	.76947	.75614	.74316	.73051	.71818	2
3	.79383	.77218	.75131	.73119	.71178	.69305	.67497	.65752	.64066	.62437	.60863	3
4	.73503	.70843	.68301	.65873	.63552	.61332	.59208	.57175	.55229	.53365	.51579	4
5	.68058	.64993	.62092	.59345	.56743	.54276	.51937	.49718	.47611	.45611	.43711	5
6	.63017	.59627	.56447	.53464	.50663	.48032	.45559	.43233	.41044	.38984	.37043	6
7	.58349	.54703	.51316	.48166	.45235	.42506	.39964	.37594	.35383	.33320	.31393	7
8	.54027	.50187	.46651	.43393	.40388	.37616	.35056	.32690	.30503	.28478	.26604	8
9	.50025	.46043	.42410	.39092	.36061	.33288	.30751	.28426	.26295	.24340	.22546	9
10	.46319	.42241	.38554	.35218	.32197	.29459	.26974	.24718	.22668	.20804	.19106	10
11	.42888	.38753	.35049	.31728	.28748	.26070	.23662	.21494	.19542	.17781	.16192	11
12	.39711	.35553	.31863	.28584	.25668	.23071	.20756	.18691	.16846	.15197	.13722	12
13	.36770	.32618	.28966	.25751	.22917	.20416	.18207	.16253	.14523	.12989	.11629	13
14	.34046	.29925	.26333	.23199	.20462	.18068	.15971	.14133	.12520	.11102	.09855	14
15	.31524	.27454	.23939	.20900	.18270	.15989	.14010	.12289	.10793	.09489	.08352	15
16	.29189	.25187	.21763	.18829	.16312	.14150	.12289	.10686	.09304	.08110	.07078	16
17	.27027	.23107	.19784	.16963	.14564	.12522	.10780	.09293	.08021	.06932	.05998	17
18	.25025	.21199	.17986	.15282	.13004	.11081	.09456	.08081	.06914	.05925	.05083	18
19	.23171	.19449	.16351	.13768	.11611	.09806	.08295	.07027	.05961	.05064	.04308	19
20	.21455	.17843	.14864	.12403	.10367	.08678	.07276	.06110	.05139	.04328	.03651	20
21	.19866	.16370	.13513	.11174	.09256	.07680	.06383	.05313	.04430	.03699	.03094	21
22	.18394	.15018	.12285	.10067	.08264	.06796	.05599	.04620	.03819	.03162	.02622	22
23	.17032	.13778	.11168	.09069	.07379	.06014	.04911	.04017	.03292	.02702	.02222	23
24	.15770	.12640	.10153	.08170	.06588	.05323	.04308	.03493	.02838	.02310	.01883	24
25	.14602	.11597	.09230	.07361	.05882	.04710	.03779	.03038	.02447	.01974	.01596	25
26	.13520	.10639	.08391	.06631	.05252	.04168	.03315	.02642	.02109	.01687	.01352	26
27	.12519	.09761	.07628	.05974	.04689	.03689	.02908	.02297	.01818	.01442	.01146	27
28	.11591	.08955	.06934	.05382	.04187	.03264	.02551	.01997	.01567	.01233	.00971	28
29	.10733	.08215	.06304	.04849	.03738	.02889	.02237	.01737	.01351	.01053	.00823	29
30	.09938	.07537	.05731	.04368	.03338	.02557	.01963	.01510	.01165	.00900	.00697	30
31	.09202	.06915	.05210	.03935	.02980	.02262	.01722	.01313	.01004	.00770	.00591	31
32	.08520	.06344	.04736	.03545	.02661	.02002	.01510	.01142	.00866	.00658	.00501	32
33	.07889	.05820	.04306	.03194	.02376	.01772	.01325	.00993	.00746	.00562	.00425	33
34	.07305	.05339	.03914	.02878	.02121	.01568	.01162	.00864	.00643	.00480	.00360	34
35	.06763	.04899	.03558	.02592	.01894	.01388	.01019	.00751	.00555	.00411	.00305	35
36	.06262	.04494	.03235	.02335	.01691	.01228	.00894	.00653	.00478	.00351	.00258	36
37	.05799	.04123	.02941	.02104	.01510	.01087	.00784	.00568	.00412	.00300	.00219	37
38	.05369	.03783	.02673	.01896	.01348	.00962	.00688	.00494	.00355	.00256	.00186	38
39	.04971	.03470	.02430	.01708	.01204	.00851	.00604	.00429	.00306	.00219	.00157	39
40	.04603	.03184	.02209	.01538	.01075	.00753	.00529	.00373	.00264	.00187	.00133	40
41	.04262	.02921	.02009	.01386	.00960	.00666	.00464	.00325	.00228	.00160	.00113	41
42	.03946	.02680	.01826	.01249	.00857	.00590	.00407	.00282	.00196	.00137	.00096	42
43	.03654	.02458	.01660	.01125	.00765	.00522	.00357	.00245	.00169	.00117	.00081	43
44	.03383	.02255	.01509	.01013	.00683	.00462	.00313	.00213	.00146	.00100	.00069	44
45	.03133	.02069	.01372	.00913	.00610	.00409	.00275	.00186	.00126	.00085	.00058	45
46	.02901	.01898	.01247	.00823	.00544	.00362	.00241	.00161	.00108	.00073	.00049	46
47	.02686	.01742	.01134	.00741	.00486	.00320	.00212	.00140	.00093	.00062	.00042	47
48	.02487	.01598	.01031	.00668	.00434	.00283	.00186	.00122	.00081	.00053	.00035	48
49	.02303	.01466	.00937	.00601	.00388	.00251	.00163	.00106	.00069	.00046	.00030	49
50	.02132	.01345	.00852	.00542	.00346	.00222	.00143	.00092	.00060	.00039	.00025	50

Table II
Present Value of $1

n	19%	20%	21%	22%	23%	24%	25%	26%	28%	30%	32%	n
1	.84034	.83333	.82645	.81967	.81301	.80645	.80000	.79365	.78125	.76923	.75758	1
2	.70616	.69444	.68301	.67186	.66098	.65036	.64000	.62988	.61035	.59172	.57392	2
3	.59342	.57870	.56447	.55071	.53738	.52449	.51200	.49991	.47684	.45517	.43479	3
4	.49867	.48225	.46651	.45140	.43690	.42297	.40960	.39675	.37253	.35013	.32939	4
5	.41905	.40188	.38554	.37000	.35520	.34111	.32768	.31488	.29104	.26933	.24953	5
6	.35214	.33490	.31863	.30328	.28878	.27509	.26214	.24991	.22737	.20718	.18904	6
7	.29592	.27908	.26333	.24859	.23478	.22184	.20972	.19834	.17764	.15937	.14321	7
8	.24867	.23257	.21763	.20376	.19088	.17891	.16777	.15741	.13878	.12259	.10849	8
9	.20897	.19381	.17986	.16702	.15519	.14428	.13422	.12493	.10842	.09430	.08219	9
10	.17560	.16151	.14864	.13690	.12617	.11635	.10737	.09915	.08470	.07254	.06227	10
11	.14757	.13459	.12285	.11221	.10258	.09383	.08590	.07869	.06617	.05580	.04717	11
12	.12400	.11216	.10153	.09198	.08339	.07567	.06872	.06245	.05170	.04292	.03574	12
13	.10421	.09346	.08391	.07539	.06780	.06103	.05498	.04957	.04039	.03302	.02707	13
14	.08757	.07789	.06934	.06180	.05512	.04921	.04398	.03934	.03155	.02540	.02051	14
15	.07359	.06491	.05731	.05065	.04481	.03969	.03518	.03122	.02465	.01954	.01554	15
16	.06184	.05409	.04736	.04152	.03643	.03201	.02815	.02478	.01926	.01503	.01177	16
17	.05196	.04507	.03914	.03403	.02962	.02581	.02252	.01967	.01505	.01156	.00892	17
18	.04367	.03756	.03235	.02789	.02408	.02082	.01801	.01561	.01175	.00889	.00676	18
19	.03670	.03130	.02673	.02286	.01958	.01679	.01441	.01239	.00918	.00684	.00512	19
20	.03084	.02608	.02209	.01874	.01592	.01354	.01153	.00983	.00717	.00526	.00388	20
21	.02591	.02174	.01826	.01536	.01294	.01092	.00922	.00780	.00561	.00405	.00294	21
22	.02178	.01811	.01509	.01259	.01052	.00880	.00738	.00619	.00438	.00311	.00223	22
23	.01830	.01509	.01247	.01032	.00855	.00710	.00590	.00491	.00342	.00239	.00169	23
24	.01538	.01258	.01031	.00846	.00695	.00573	.00472	.00390	.00267	.00184	.00128	24
25	.01292	.01048	.00852	.00693	.00565	.00462	.00378	.00310	.00209	.00142	.00097	25
26	.01086	.00874	.00704	.00568	.00460	.00372	.00302	.00246	.00163	.00109	.00073	26
27	.00912	.00728	.00582	.00466	.00374	.00300	.00242	.00195	.00127	.00084	.00056	27
28	.00767	.00607	.00481	.00382	.00304	.00242	.00193	.00155	.00100	.00065	.00042	28
29	.00644	.00506	.00397	.00313	.00247	.00195	.00155	.00123	.00078	.00050	.00032	29
30	.00541	.00421	.00328	.00257	.00201	.00158	.00124	.00097	.00061	.00038	.00024	30
31	.00455	.00351	.00271	.00210	.00163	.00127	.00099	.00077	.00047	.00029	.00018	31
32	.00382	.00293	.00224	.00172	.00133	.00102	.00079	.00061	.00037	.00023	.00014	32
33	.00321	.00244	.00185	.00141	.00108	.00083	.00063	.00049	.00029	.00017	.00010	33
34	.00270	.00203	.00153	.00116	.00088	.00067	.00051	.00039	.00023	.00013	.00008	34
35	.00227	.00169	.00127	.00095	.00071	.00054	.00041	.00031	.00018	.00010	.00006	35
36	.00191	.00141	.00105	.00078	.00058	.00043	.00032	.00024	.00014	.00008	.00005	36
37	.00160	.00118	.00086	.00064	.00047	.00035	.00026	.00019	.00011	.00006	.00003	37
38	.00135	.00098	.00071	.00052	.00038	.00028	.00021	.00015	.00008	.00005	.00003	38
39	.00113	.00082	.00059	.00043	.00031	.00023	.00017	.00012	.00007	.00004	.00002	39
40	.00095	.00068	.00049	.00035	.00025	.00018	.00013	.00010	.00005	.00003	.00002	40
41	.00080	.00057	.00040	.00029	.00021	.00015	.00011	.00008	.00004	.00002	.00001	41
42	.00067	.00047	.00033	.00024	.00017	.00012	.00009	.00006	.00003	.00002	.00001	42
43	.00056	.00039	.00028	.00019	.00014	.00010	.00007	.00005	.00002	.00001	.00001	43
44	.00047	.00033	.00023	.00016	.00011	.00008	.00005	.00004	.00002	.00001	.00000	44
45	.00040	.00027	.00019	.00013	.00009	.00006	.00004	.00003	.00001	.00001	.00000	45
46	.00033	.00023	.00016	.00011	.00007	.00005	.00003	.00002	.00001	.00001	.00000	46
47	.00028	.00019	.00013	.00009	.00006	.00004	.00003	.00002	.00001	.00000	.00000	47
48	.00024	.00016	.00011	.00007	.00005	.00003	.00002	.00002	.00001	.00000	.00000	48
49	.00020	.00013	.00009	.00006	.00004	.00003	.00002	.00001	.00001	.00000	.00000	49
50	.00017	.00011	.00007	.00005	.00003	.00002	.00001	.00001	.00000	.00000	.00000	50

Table III
Future value of Annuity of $1

n	8%	9%	10%	11%	12%	13%	14%	15%	16%	17%	18%	n
1	1.00000	1.00000	1.00000	1.00000	1.00000	1.00000	1.00000	1.00000	1.00000	1.00000	1.00000	1
2	2.08000	2.09000	2.10000	2.11000	2.12000	2.13000	2.14000	2.15000	2.16000	2.17000	2.18000	2
3	3.24640	3.27810	3.31000	3.34210	3.37440	3.40690	3.43960	3.47250	3.50560	3.53890	3.57240	3
4	4.50611	4.57313	4.64100	4.70973	4.77933	4.84980	4.92114	4.99337	5.06650	5.14051	5.21543	4
5	5.86660	5.98471	6.10510	6.22780	6.35285	6.48027	6.61010	6.74238	6.87714	7.01440	7.15421	5
6	7.33593	7.52333	7.71561	7.91286	8.11519	8.32271	8.53552	8.75374	8.97748	9.20685	9.44197	6
7	8.92280	9.20043	9.48717	9.78327	10.08901	10.40466	10.73049	11.06680	11.41387	11.77201	12.14152	7
8	10.63663	11.02847	11.43589	11.85943	12.29969	12.75726	13.23276	13.72682	14.24009	14.77325	15.32700	8
9	12.48756	13.02104	13.57948	14.16397	14.77566	15.41571	16.08535	16.78584	17.51851	18.28471	19.08585	9
10	14.48656	15.19293	15.93742	16.72201	17.54874	18.41975	19.33730	20.30372	21.32147	22.39311	23.52131	10
11	16.64549	17.56029	18.53117	19.56143	20.65458	21.81432	23.04452	24.34928	25.73290	27.19994	28.75514	11
12	18.97713	20.14072	21.38428	22.71319	24.13313	25.65018	27.27075	29.00167	30.85017	32.82393	34.93107	12
13	21.49530	22.95338	24.52271	26.21164	28.02911	29.98470	32.08865	34.35192	36.78620	39.40399	42.21866	13
14	24.21492	26.01919	27.97498	30.09492	32.39260	34.88271	37.58107	40.50471	43.67199	47.10267	50.81802	14
15	27.15211	29.36092	31.77248	34.40536	37.27971	40.41746	43.84241	47.58041	51.65951	56.11013	60.96527	15
16	30.32428	33.00340	35.94973	39.18995	42.75328	46.67173	50.98035	55.71747	60.92503	66.64885	72.93901	16
17	33.75023	36.97370	40.54470	44.50084	48.88367	53.73906	59.11760	65.07509	71.67303	78.97915	87.06804	17
18	37.45024	41.30134	45.59917	50.39594	55.74971	61.72514	68.39407	75.83636	84.14072	93.40561	103.7403	18
19	41.44626	46.01846	51.15909	56.93949	63.43968	70.74941	78.96923	88.21181	98.60323	110.2846	123.4135	19
20	45.76196	51.16012	57.27500	64.20283	72.05244	80.94683	91.02493	102.4436	115.3798	130.0329	146.6280	20
21	50.42292	56.76453	64.00250	72.26514	81.69874	92.46992	104.7684	118.8101	134.8405	153.1385	174.0210	21
22	55.45676	62.87334	71.40275	81.21431	92.50258	105.4910	120.4360	137.6316	157.4150	180.1721	206.3448	22
23	60.89330	69.53194	79.54302	91.14788	104.6029	120.2048	138.2970	159.2764	183.6014	211.8013	244.4869	23
24	66.76476	76.78981	88.49733	102.1742	118.1552	136.8315	158.6586	184.1678	213.9776	248.8076	289.4945	24
25	73.10594	84.70090	98.34706	114.4133	133.3339	155.6196	181.8708	212.7930	249.2140	292.1049	342.6035	25
26	79.95442	93.32398	109.1818	127.9988	150.3339	176.8501	208.3327	245.7120	290.0883	342.7627	405.2721	26
27	87.35077	102.7231	121.0999	143.0786	169.3740	200.8406	238.4993	283.5688	337.5024	402.0323	479.2211	27
28	95.33883	112.9682	134.2099	159.8173	190.6989	227.9499	272.8892	327.1041	392.5028	471.3778	566.4809	28
29	103.9659	124.1354	148.6309	178.3972	214.5828	258.5834	312.0937	377.1697	456.3032	552.5121	669.4475	29
30	113.2832	136.3075	164.4940	199.0209	241.3327	293.1992	356.7869	434.7452	530.3117	647.4391	790.9480	30
31	123.3459	149.5752	181.9434	221.9132	271.2926	332.3151	407.7370	500.9569	616.1616	758.5038	934.3186	31
32	134.2135	164.0370	201.1378	247.3236	304.8477	376.5161	465.8202	577.1005	715.7475	888.4494	1103.496	32
33	145.9506	179.8003	222.2515	275.5292	342.4295	426.4632	532.0350	664.6655	831.2671	1040.486	1303.125	33
34	158.6267	196.9823	245.4767	306.8374	384.5210	482.9034	607.5199	765.3654	965.2698	1218.368	1538.688	34
35	172.3168	215.7108	271.0244	341.5896	431.6635	546.6808	693.5727	881.1702	1120.713	1426.491	1816.652	35
36	187.1022	236.1247	299.1268	380.1644	484.4631	618.7493	791.6729	1014.346	1301.027	1669.995	2144.649	36
37	203.0703	258.3760	330.0395	422.9825	543.5987	700.1867	903.5071	1167.498	1510.191	1954.894	2531.686	37
38	220.3160	282.6298	364.0434	470.5106	609.8305	792.2110	1030.998	1343.622	1752.822	2288.225	2988.389	38
39	238.9412	309.0665	401.4478	523.2667	684.0102	896.1985	1176.338	1546.166	2034.274	2678.224	3527.299	39
40	259.0565	337.8825	442.5926	581.8261	767.0914	1013.704	1342.025	1779.090	2360.757	3134.522	4163.213	40
41	280.7810	369.2919	487.8518	646.8269	860.1424	1146.486	1530.909	2046.954	2739.478	3668.391	4913.591	41
42	304.2435	403.5281	537.6370	718.9779	964.3595	1296.529	1746.236	2354.997	3178.795	4293.017	5799.038	42
43	329.5830	440.8457	592.4007	799.0655	1081.083	1466.078	1991.709	2709.247	3688.402	5023.830	6843.865	43
44	356.9497	481.5218	652.6408	887.9627	1211.813	1657.668	2271.548	3116.633	4279.547	5878.881	8076.760	44
45	386.5056	525.8587	718.9048	986.6386	1358.230	1874.165	2590.565	3585.129	4965.274	6879.291	9531.577	45
46	418.4261	574.1860	791.7953	1096.169	1522.218	2118.806	2954.244	4123.898	5760.718	8049.770	11248.26	46
47	452.9002	626.8628	871.9749	1217.747	1705.884	2395.251	3368.838	4743.482	6683.433	9419.231	13273.95	47
48	490.1322	684.2804	960.1723	1352.700	1911.590	2707.633	3841.475	5456.005	7753.782	11021.50	15664.26	48
49	530.3427	746.8657	1057.190	1502.497	2141.981	3060.626	4380.282	6275.406	8995.387	12896.16	18484.83	49
50	573.7702	815.0836	1163.909	1668.771	2400.018	3459.507	4994.521	7217.716	10435.65	15089.50	21813.09	50

Table III
Future Value of Annuity of $1

n	19%	20%	21%	22%	23%	24%	25%	26%	28%	30%	32%	n
1	1.00000	1.00000	1.00000	1.00000	1.00000	1.00000	1.00000	1.00000	1.00000	1.00000	1.00000	1
2	2.19000	2.20000	2.21000	2.22000	2.23000	2.24000	2.25000	2.26000	2.28000	2.30000	2.32000	2
3	3.60610	3.64000	3.67410	3.70840	3.74290	3.77760	3.81250	3.84760	3.91840	3.99000	4.06240	3
4	5.29126	5.36800	5.44566	5.52425	5.60377	5.68422	5.76562	5.84798	6.01555	6.18700	6.36237	4
5	7.29660	7.44160	7.58925	7.73958	7.89263	8.04844	8.20703	8.36845	8.69991	9.04310	9.39833	5
6	9.68295	9.92992	10.18299	10.44229	10.70794	10.98006	11.25879	11.54425	12.13588	12.75603	13.40579	6
7	12.52271	12.91590	13.32142	13.73959	14.17077	14.61528	15.07349	15.54575	16.53393	17.58284	18.69564	7
8	15.90203	16.49908	17.11892	17.76231	18.43004	19.12294	19.84186	20.58765	22.16343	23.85769	25.67825	8
9	19.92341	20.79890	21.71389	22.67001	23.66895	24.71245	25.80232	26.94043	29.36919	32.01500	34.89529	9
10	24.70886	25.95868	27.27381	28.65742	30.11281	31.64344	33.25290	34.94495	38.59256	42.61950	47.06178	10
11	30.40355	32.15042	34.00131	35.96205	38.03876	40.23787	42.56613	45.03063	50.39847	56.40535	63.12155	11
12	37.18022	39.58050	42.14158	44.87370	47.78767	50.89495	54.20766	57.73860	65.51005	74.32695	84.32045	12
13	45.24446	48.49660	51.99132	55.74591	59.77883	64.10974	68.75958	73.75063	84.85286	97.62504	112.3030	13
14	54.84091	59.19592	63.90949	69.01001	74.52796	80.49608	86.94947	93.92580	109.6117	127.9126	149.2399	14
15	66.26068	72.03511	78.33049	85.19221	92.66940	100.8151	109.6868	119.3465	141.3029	167.2863	197.9967	15
16	79.85021	87.44213	95.77989	104.9345	114.9834	126.0108	138.1086	151.3766	181.8677	218.4722	262.3557	16
17	96.02175	105.9306	116.8937	129.0201	142.4295	157.2534	173.6357	191.7345	233.7907	285.0139	347.3095	17
18	115.2659	128.1167	142.4413	158.4045	176.1883	195.9942	218.0446	242.5855	300.2521	371.5180	459.4485	18
19	138.1664	154.7400	173.3540	194.2535	217.7116	244.0328	273.5558	306.6577	385.3227	483.9734	607.4721	19
20	165.4180	186.6880	210.7584	237.9893	268.7853	303.6006	342.9447	387.3887	494.2131	630.1655	802.8631	20
21	197.8474	225.0256	256.0176	291.3469	331.6059	377.4648	429.6809	489.1098	633.5927	820.2151	1060.779	21
22	236.4385	271.0307	310.7813	356.4432	408.8753	469.0563	538.1011	617.2783	811.9987	1067.280	1401.229	22
23	282.3618	326.2369	377.0454	435.8608	503.9166	582.6298	673.6264	778.7707	1040.358	1388.464	1850.622	23
24	337.0105	392.4842	457.2249	532.7501	620.8174	723.4610	843.0330	982.2511	1332.659	1806.003	2443.821	24
25	402.0425	471.9811	554.2422	650.9551	764.6055	898.0916	1054.791	1238.636	1706.803	2348.803	3226.844	25
26	479.4306	567.3773	671.6330	795.1653	941.4647	1114.634	1319.489	1561.682	2185.708	3054.444	4260.434	26
27	571.5224	681.8528	813.6759	971.1016	1159.002	1383.146	1650.361	1968.719	2798.706	3971.778	5624.772	27
28	681.1116	819.2233	985.5479	1185.744	1426.572	1716.101	2063.952	2481.586	3583.344	5164.311	7425.699	28
29	811.5228	984.0680	1193.513	1447.608	1755.683	2128.965	2580.939	3127.798	4587.680	6714.604	9802.923	29
30	966.7122	1181.882	1445.151	1767.081	2160.491	2640.916	3227.174	3942.026	5873.231	8729.985	12940.86	30
31	1151.387	1419.258	1749.632	2156.839	2658.404	3275.736	4034.968	4967.953	7518.735	11349.98	17082.93	31
32	1371.151	1704.109	2118.055	2632.344	3270.836	4062.913	5044.710	6260.620	9624.981	14755.98	22550.47	32
33	1632.670	2045.931	2563.847	3212.460	4024.129	5039.012	6306.887	7889.382	12320.98	19183.77	29767.62	33
34	1943.877	2456.118	3103.254	3920.201	4950.678	6249.375	7884.609	9941.621	15771.85	24939.90	39294.26	34
35	2314.214	2948.341	3755.938	4783.645	6090.334	7750.225	9856.761	12527.44	20188.97	32422.87	51869.43	35
36	2754.914	3539.009	4545.685	5837.047	7492.111	9611.279	12321.95	15785.58	25842.88	42150.73	68468.64	36
37	3279.348	4247.811	5501.279	7122.197	9216.297	11918.99	15403.44	19890.83	33079.88	54796.95	90379.61	37
38	3903.424	5098.374	6657.547	8690.080	11337.05	14780.54	19255.30	25063.44	42343.25	71237.03	119302.1	38
39	4646.075	6119.048	8056.632	10602.90	13945.57	18328.87	24070.12	31580.94	54200.36	92609.14	157479.8	39
40	5529.829	7343.858	9749.525	12936.54	17154.05	22728.80	30088.66	39792.98	69377.46	120392.9	207874.3	40
41	6581.496	8813.629	11797.93	15783.57	21100.48	28184.72	37611.82	50140.16	88804.15	156511.7	274395.0	41
42	7832.981	10577.36	14276.49	19256.96	25954.59	34950.05	47015.77	63177.60	113670.3	203466.3	362202.5	42
43	9322.247	12693.83	17275.55	23494.49	31925.14	43339.06	58770.72	79604.77	145499.0	264507.2	478108.2	43
44	11094.47	15233.59	20904.42	28664.28	39268.92	53741.43	73464.40	100303.0	186239.7	343860.3	631103.9	44
45	13203.42	18281.31	25295.35	34971.42	48301.77	66640.38	91831.50	126382.8	238387.8	447019.4	833058.1	45
46	15713.07	21938.57	30608.37	42666.13	59412.18	82635.07	114790.4	159243.3	305137.4	581126.2	1099637.7	46
47	18699.56	26327.29	37037.13	52053.68	73077.98	102468.5	143489.0	200647.6	390576.9	755465.1	1451522.8	47
48	22253.48	31593.74	44815.92	63506.49	89886.92	127061.9	179362.2	252817.0	499939.5	982105.6	1916011.1	48
49	26482.64	37913.49	54228.27	77478.92	110561.9	157557.8	224203.8	318550.4	639923.5	1276738.3	2529135.6	49
50	31515.34	45497.19	65617.20	94525.28	135992.2	195372.6	280255.7	401374.5	819103.1	1659760.7	3338460.0	50

Table IV
Present Value of Annuity of $1

n	8%	9%	10%	11%	12%	13%	14%	15%	16%	17%	18%	n
1	0.92593	0.91743	0.90909	0.90090	0.89286	0.88496	0.87719	0.86957	0.86207	0.85470	0.84746	1
2	1.78326	1.75911	1.73554	1.71252	1.69005	1.66810	1.64666	1.62571	1.60523	1.58521	1.56564	2
3	2.57710	2.53129	2.48685	2.44371	2.40183	2.36115	2.32163	2.28323	2.24589	2.20958	2.17427	3
4	3.31213	3.23972	3.16987	3.10245	3.03735	2.97447	2.91371	2.85498	2.79818	2.74324	2.69006	4
5	3.99271	3.88965	3.79079	3.69590	3.60478	3.51723	3.43308	3.35216	3.27429	3.19935	3.12717	5
6	4.62288	4.48592	4.35526	4.23054	4.11141	3.99755	3.88867	3.78448	3.68474	3.58918	3.49760	6
7	5.20637	5.03295	4.86842	4.71220	4.56376	4.42261	4.28830	4.16042	4.03857	3.92238	3.81153	7
8	5.74664	5.53482	5.33493	5.14612	4.96764	4.79877	4.63886	4.48732	4.34359	4.20716	4.07757	8
9	6.24689	5.99525	5.75902	5.53705	5.32825	5.13166	4.94637	4.77158	4.60654	4.45057	4.30302	9
10	6.71008	6.41766	6.14457	5.88923	5.65022	5.42624	5.21612	5.01877	4.83323	4.65860	4.49409	10
11	7.13896	6.80519	6.49506	6.20652	5.93770	5.68694	5.45273	5.23371	5.02864	4.83641	4.65601	11
12	7.53608	7.16073	6.81369	6.49236	6.19437	5.91765	5.66029	5.42062	5.19711	4.98839	4.79322	12
13	7.90378	7.48690	7.10336	6.74987	6.42355	6.12181	5.84236	5.58315	5.34233	5.11828	4.90951	13
14	8.24424	7.78615	7.36669	6.98187	6.62817	6.30249	6.00207	5.72448	5.46753	5.22930	5.00806	14
15	8.55948	8.06069	7.60608	7.19087	6.81086	6.46238	6.14217	5.84737	5.57546	5.32419	5.09158	15
16	8.85137	8.31256	7.82371	7.37916	6.97399	6.60388	6.26506	5.95423	5.66850	5.40529	5.16235	16
17	9.12164	8.54363	8.02155	7.54879	7.11963	6.72909	6.37286	6.04716	5.74870	5.47461	5.22233	17
18	9.37189	8.75563	8.20141	7.70162	7.24967	6.83991	6.46742	6.12797	5.81785	5.53385	5.27316	18
19	9.60360	8.95011	8.36492	7.83929	7.36578	6.93797	6.55037	6.19823	5.87746	5.58449	5.31624	19
20	9.81815	9.12855	8.51356	7.96333	7.46944	7.02475	6.62313	6.25933	5.92884	5.62777	5.35275	20
21	10.01680	9.29224	8.64869	8.07507	7.56200	7.10155	6.68696	6.31246	5.97314	5.66476	5.38368	21
22	10.20074	9.44243	8.77154	8.17574	7.64465	7.16951	6.74294	6.35866	6.01133	5.69637	5.40990	22
23	10.37106	9.58021	8.88322	8.26643	7.71843	7.22966	6.79206	6.39884	6.04425	5.72340	5.43212	23
24	10.52876	9.70661	8.98474	8.34814	7.78432	7.28288	6.83514	6.43377	6.07263	5.74649	5.45095	24
25	10.67478	9.82258	9.07704	8.42174	7.84314	7.32998	6.87293	6.46415	6.09709	5.76623	5.46691	25
26	10.80998	9.92897	9.16095	8.48806	7.89566	7.37167	6.90608	6.49056	6.11818	5.78311	5.48043	26
27	10.93516	10.02658	9.23722	8.54780	7.94255	7.40856	6.93515	6.51353	6.13636	5.79753	5.49189	27
28	11.05108	10.11613	9.30657	8.60162	7.98442	7.44120	6.96066	6.53351	6.15204	5.80985	5.50160	28
29	11.15841	10.19828	9.36961	8.65011	8.02181	7.47009	6.98304	6.55088	6.16555	5.82039	5.50983	29
30	11.25778	10.27365	9.42691	8.69379	8.05518	7.49565	7.00266	6.56598	6.17720	5.82939	5.51681	30
31	11.34980	10.34280	9.47901	8.73315	8.08499	7.51828	7.01988	6.57911	6.18724	5.83709	5.52272	31
32	11.43500	10.40624	9.52638	8.76860	8.11159	7.53830	7.03498	6.59053	6.19590	5.84366	5.52773	32
33	11.51389	10.46444	9.56943	8.80054	8.13535	7.55602	7.04823	6.60046	6.20336	5.84928	5.53197	33
34	11.58693	10.51784	9.60857	8.82932	8.15656	7.57170	7.05985	6.60910	6.20979	5.85409	5.53557	34
35	11.65457	10.56682	9.64416	8.85524	8.17550	7.58557	7.07005	6.61661	6.21534	5.85820	5.53862	35
36	11.71719	10.61176	9.67651	8.87859	8.19241	7.59785	7.07899	6.62314	6.22012	5.86171	5.54120	36
37	11.77518	10.65299	9.70592	8.89963	8.20751	7.60872	7.08683	6.62881	6.22424	5.86471	5.54339	37
38	11.82887	10.69082	9.73265	8.91859	8.22099	7.61833	7.09371	6.63375	6.22779	5.86727	5.54525	38
39	11.87858	10.72552	9.75696	8.93567	8.23303	7.62684	7.09975	6.63805	6.23086	5.86946	5.54682	39
40	11.92461	10.75736	9.77905	8.95105	8.24378	7.63438	7.10504	6.64178	6.23350	5.87133	5.54815	40
41	11.96723	10.78657	9.79914	8.96491	8.25337	7.64104	7.10969	6.64502	6.23577	5.87294	5.54928	41
42	12.00670	10.81337	9.81740	8.97740	8.26194	7.64694	7.11376	6.64785	6.23774	5.87430	5.55024	42
43	12.04324	10.83795	9.83400	8.98865	8.26959	7.65216	7.11733	6.65030	6.23943	5.87547	5.55105	43
44	12.07707	10.86051	9.84909	8.99878	8.27642	7.65678	7.12047	6.65244	6.24089	5.87647	5.55174	44
45	12.10840	10.88120	9.86281	9.00791	8.28252	7.66086	7.12322	6.65429	6.24214	5.87733	5.55232	45
46	12.13741	10.90018	9.87528	9.01614	8.28796	7.66448	7.12563	6.65591	6.24323	5.87806	5.55281	46
47	12.16427	10.91760	9.88662	9.02355	8.29282	7.66768	7.12774	6.65731	6.24416	5.87868	5.55323	47
48	12.18914	10.93358	9.89693	9.03022	8.29716	7.67052	7.12960	6.65853	6.24497	5.87922	5.55359	48
49	12.21216	10.94823	9.90630	9.03624	8.30104	7.67302	7.13123	6.65959	6.24566	5.87967	5.55389	49
50	12.23348	10.96168	9.91481	9.04165	8.30450	7.67524	7.13266	6.66051	6.24626	5.88006	5.55414	50

Table IV
Present Value of Annuity of $1

n	19%	20%	21%	22%	23%	24%	25%	26%	28%	30%	32%	n
1	0.84034	0.83333	0.82645	0.81967	0.81301	0.80645	0.80000	0.79365	0.78125	0.76923	0.75758	1
2	1.54650	1.52778	1.50946	1.49153	1.47399	1.45682	1.44000	1.42353	1.39160	1.36095	1.33150	2
3	2.13992	2.10648	2.07393	2.04224	2.01137	1.98130	1.95200	1.92344	1.86844	1.81611	1.76629	3
4	2.63859	2.58873	2.54044	2.49364	2.44827	2.40428	2.36160	2.32019	2.24097	2.16624	2.09567	4
5	3.05763	2.99061	2.92598	2.86364	2.80347	2.74538	2.68928	2.63507	2.53201	2.43557	2.34521	5
6	3.40978	3.32551	3.24462	3.16692	3.09225	3.02047	2.95142	2.88498	2.75938	2.64275	2.53425	6
7	3.70570	3.60459	3.50795	3.41551	3.32704	3.24232	3.16114	3.08331	2.93702	2.80211	2.67746	7
8	3.95437	3.83716	3.72558	3.61927	3.51792	3.42122	3.32891	3.24073	3.07579	2.92470	2.78595	8
9	4.16333	4.03097	3.90543	3.78628	3.67310	3.56550	3.46313	3.36566	3.18421	3.01900	2.86815	9
10	4.33893	4.19247	4.05408	3.92318	3.79927	3.68186	3.57050	3.46481	3.26892	3.09154	2.93041	10
11	4.48650	4.32706	4.17692	4.03540	3.90185	3.77569	3.65640	3.54350	3.33509	3.14734	2.97759	11
12	4.61050	4.43922	4.27845	4.12737	3.98524	3.85136	3.72512	3.60595	3.38679	3.19026	3.01332	12
13	4.71471	4.53268	4.36235	4.20277	4.05304	3.91239	3.78010	3.65552	3.42718	3.22328	3.04040	13
14	4.80228	4.61057	4.43170	4.26456	4.10816	3.96160	3.82408	3.69485	3.45873	3.24867	3.06091	14
15	4.87586	4.67547	4.48901	4.31522	4.15298	4.00129	3.85926	3.72607	3.48339	3.26821	3.07644	15
16	4.93770	4.72956	4.53637	4.35673	4.18941	4.03330	3.88741	3.75085	3.50265	3.28324	3.08822	16
17	4.98966	4.77463	4.57551	4.39077	4.21904	4.05911	3.90993	3.77052	3.51769	3.29480	3.09713	17
18	5.03333	4.81219	4.60786	4.41866	4.24312	4.07993	3.92794	3.78613	3.52945	3.30369	3.10389	18
19	5.07003	4.84350	4.63460	4.44152	4.26270	4.09672	3.94235	3.79851	3.53863	3.31053	3.10901	19
20	5.10086	4.86958	4.65669	4.46027	4.27862	4.11026	3.95388	3.80834	3.54580	3.31579	3.11288	20
21	5.12677	4.89132	4.67495	4.47563	4.29156	4.12117	3.96311	3.81615	3.55141	3.31984	3.11582	21
22	5.14855	4.90943	4.69004	4.48822	4.30208	4.12998	3.97049	3.82234	3.55579	3.32296	3.11805	22
23	5.16685	4.92453	4.70251	4.49854	4.31063	4.13708	3.97639	3.82725	3.55921	3.32535	3.11973	23
24	5.18223	4.93710	4.71282	4.50700	4.31759	4.14281	3.98111	3.83115	3.56188	3.32719	3.12101	24
25	5.19515	4.94759	4.72134	4.51393	4.32324	4.14742	3.98489	3.83425	3.56397	3.32861	3.12198	25
26	5.20601	4.95632	4.72838	4.51962	4.32784	4.15115	3.98791	3.83670	3.56560	3.32970	3.12271	26
27	5.21513	4.96360	4.73420	4.52428	4.33158	4.15415	3.99033	3.83865	3.56688	3.33054	3.12326	27
28	5.22280	4.96967	4.73901	4.52810	4.33462	4.15657	3.99226	3.84020	3.56787	3.33118	3.12369	28
29	5.22924	4.97472	4.74298	4.53123	4.33709	4.15853	3.99381	3.84143	3.56865	3.33168	3.12400	29
30	5.23466	4.97894	4.74627	4.53379	4.33909	4.16010	3.99505	3.84240	3.56926	3.33206	3.12425	30
31	5.23921	4.98245	4.74898	4.53590	4.34073	4.16137	3.99604	3.84318	3.56973	3.33235	3.12443	31
32	5.24303	4.98537	4.75122	4.53762	4.34205	4.16240	3.99683	3.84379	3.57010	3.33258	3.12457	32
33	5.24625	4.98781	4.75308	4.53903	4.34313	4.16322	3.99746	3.84428	3.57039	3.33275	3.12467	33
34	5.24895	4.98984	4.75461	4.54019	4.34401	4.16389	3.99797	3.84467	3.57062	3.33289	3.12475	34
35	5.25122	4.99154	4.75588	4.54114	4.34472	4.16443	3.99838	3.84497	3.57080	3.33299	3.12481	35
36	5.25312	4.99295	4.75692	4.54192	4.34530	4.16486	3.99870	3.84522	3.57094	3.33307	3.12486	36
37	5.25472	4.99412	4.75779	4.54256	4.34578	4.16521	3.99896	3.84541	3.57104	3.33313	3.12489	37
38	5.25607	4.99510	4.75850	4.54308	4.34616	4.16549	3.99917	3.84556	3.57113	3.33318	3.12492	38
39	5.25720	4.99592	4.75909	4.54351	4.34647	4.16572	3.99934	3.84569	3.57119	3.33321	3.12494	39
40	5.25815	4.99660	4.75958	4.54386	4.34672	4.16590	3.99947	3.84578	3.57124	3.33324	3.12495	40
41	5.25895	4.99717	4.75998	4.54415	4.34693	4.16605	3.99957	3.84586	3.57128	3.33326	3.12496	41
42	5.25962	4.99764	4.76032	4.54438	4.34710	4.16617	3.99966	3.84592	3.57132	3.33328	3.12497	42
43	5.26019	4.99803	4.76059	4.54458	4.34723	4.16627	3.99973	3.84597	3.57134	3.33329	3.12498	43
44	5.26066	4.99836	4.76082	4.54473	4.34734	4.16634	3.99978	3.84601	3.57136	3.33330	3.12498	44
45	5.26106	4.99863	4.76101	4.54486	4.34743	4.16641	3.99983	3.84604	3.57138	3.33331	3.12499	45
46	5.26140	4.99886	4.76116	4.54497	4.34751	4.16646	3.99986	3.84606	3.57139	3.33331	3.12499	46
47	5.26168	4.99905	4.76129	4.54506	4.34757	4.16650	3.99989	3.84608	3.57140	3.33332	3.12499	47
48	5.26191	4.99921	4.76140	4.54513	4.34762	4.16653	3.99991	3.84610	3.57140	3.33332	3.12499	48
49	5.26211	4.99934	4.76149	4.54519	4.34766	4.16656	3.99993	3.84611	3.57141	3.33332	3.12500	49
50	5.26228	4.99945	4.76156	4.54524	4.34769	4.16658	3.99994	3.84612	3.57141	3.33333	3.12500	50

Table V
Areas Under the Normal Curve

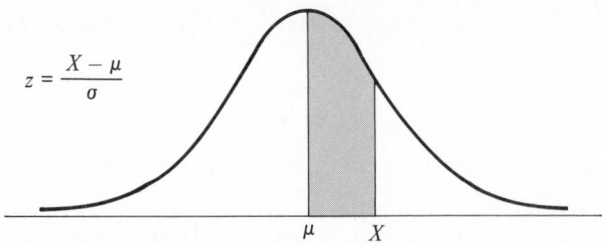

$$z = \frac{X - \mu}{\sigma}$$

z	.00	.01	.02	.03	.04	.05	.06	.07	.08	.09
.00	.00000	.00399	.00798	.01197	.01595	.01994	.02392	.02790	.03188	.03586
.10	.03983	.04379	.04776	.05172	.05567	.05962	.06356	.06749	.07142	.07534
.20	.07926	.08317	.08706	.09095	.09483	.09871	.10257	.10642	.11026	.11409
.30	.11791	.12172	.12551	.12930	.13307	.13683	.14058	.14431	.14803	.15173
.40	.15542	.15910	.16276	.16640	.17003	.17364	.17724	.18082	.18438	.18793
.50	.19146	.19497	.19847	.20194	.20540	.20884	.21226	.21566	.21904	.22240
.60	.22575	.22907	.23237	.23565	.23891	.24215	.24537	.24857	.25175	.25490
.70	.25803	.26115	.26424	.26730	.27035	.27337	.27637	.27935	.28230	.28523
.80	.28814	.29103	.29389	.29673	.29954	.30234	.30510	.30785	.31057	.31327
.90	.31594	.31859	.32121	.32381	.32639	.32894	.33147	.33397	.33645	.33891
1.00	.34134	.34375	.34613	.34849	.35083	.35314	.35543	.35769	.35993	.36214
1.10	.36433	.36650	.36864	.37076	.37285	.37493	.37697	.37900	.38100	.38297
1.20	.38493	.38686	.38877	.39065	.39251	.39435	.39616	.39796	.39973	.40147
1.30	.40320	.40490	.40658	.40824	.40988	.41149	.41308	.41465	.41620	.41773
1.40	.41924	.42073	.42219	.42364	.42506	.42647	.42785	.42922	.43056	.43189
1.50	.43319	.43448	.43574	.43699	.43822	.43943	.44062	.44179	.44295	.44408
1.60	.44520	.44630	.44738	.44845	.44950	.45053	.45154	.45254	.45352	.45448
1.70	.45543	.45637	.45728	.45818	.45907	.45994	.46079	.46164	.46246	.46327
1.80	.46407	.46485	.46562	.46637	.46711	.46784	.46856	.46926	.46994	.47062
1.90	.47128	.47193	.47257	.47320	.47381	.47441	.47500	.47558	.47615	.47670
2.00	.47725	.47778	.47831	.47882	.47932	.47982	.48030	.48077	.48124	.48169
2.10	.48213	.48257	.48300	.48341	.48382	.48422	.48461	.48500	.48537	.48574
2.20	.48610	.48645	.48679	.48713	.48745	.48777	.48809	.48840	.48870	.48899
2.30	.48928	.48956	.48983	.49010	.49036	.49061	.49086	.49111	.49134	.49158
2.40	.49180	.49202	.49224	.49245	.49266	.49286	.49305	.49324	.49343	.49361
2.50	.49379	.49396	.49413	.49430	.49446	.49461	.49477	.49491	.49506	.49520
2.60	.49534	.49547	.49560	.49573	.49585	.49598	.49609	.49621	.49632	.49643
2.70	.49653	.49664	.49674	.49683	.49693	.49702	.49711	.49720	.49728	.49736
2.80	.49744	.49752	.49760	.49767	.49774	.49781	.49788	.49795	.49801	.49807
2.90	.49813	.49819	.49825	.49831	.49836	.49841	.49846	.49851	.49856	.49860
3.00	.49865	.49869	.49874	.49878	.49882	.49886	.49889	.49893	.49896	.49900
3.10	.49903	.49906	.49910	.49913	.49916	.49918	.49921	.49924	.49926	.49929
3.20	.49931	.49934	.49936	.49938	.49940	.49942	.49944	.49946	.49948	.49950
3.30	.49952	.49953	.49955	.49957	.49958	.49960	.49961	.49962	.49964	.49965
3.40	.49966	.49968	.49969	.49970	.49971	.49972	.49973	.49974	.49975	.49976

Table VI
Table of Random Numbers

	1–6	7–12	13–18	19–24	25–30	31–36	37–42	43–45
1	72 74 52	98 14 60	80 18 28	14 39 12	03 19 20	73 79 24	94 36 56	28 73 00
2	46 75 44	80 81 02	49 44 11	56 07 71	93 09 97	23 11 36	07 34 24	41 56 33
3	70 63 10	66 89 99	03 81 38	82 69 21	98 61 75	31 77 18	57 91 28	33 84 79
4	72 43 78	62 94 00	13 39 86	85 90 48	58 87 86	21 67 67	56 34 35	53 89 94
5	08 28 63	97 31 43	01 26 27	55 40 15	69 20 19	34 40 09	72 78 53	95 04 84
6	43 28 75	98 11 96	24 90 32	85 34 06	92 34 67	17 40 76	68 56 90	23 05 21
7	16 29 11	41 51 00	50 61 18	30 29 03	38 28 76	94 31 67	68 34 93	67 70 58
8	67 12 67	54 76 91	58 49 56	19 52 83	06 35 23	77 87 76	72 38 54	57 98 04
9	50 72 29	93 66 07	30 67 30	96 23 71	67 22 82	23 64 86	89 13 42	35 48 66
10	51 69 88	41 34 56	60 56 78	14 74 14	99 66 59	14 79 31	45 59 24	27 86 62
11	28 30 28	23 52 89	86 83 60	03 45 03	42 10 67	87 26 99	03 44 41	37 05 71
12	10 75 80	57 12 05	55 55 28	28 90 42	57 21 41	81 31 56	24 18 80	14 26 78
13	92 45 09	64 81 18	92 58 26	42 38 43	93 21 43	62 90 43	39 40 45	70 28 96
14	93 30 37	04 83 25	93 08 10	66 45 56	09 31 80	19 97 83	53 43 25	44 58 00
15	83 16 68	19 59 91	62 46 50	79 85 21	17 85 20	87 52 97	14 10 73	57 36 52
16	88 34 85	93 12 59	49 26 44	76 30 96	39 70 47	62 11 15	35 35 07	36 18 48
17	54 33 51	76 52 48	18 65 14	61 86 53	44 51 71	86 92 09	13 57 80	85 05 66
18	16 26 56	80 52 21	98 07 13	07 50 76	34 17 56	16 99 17	12 87 10	61 95 43
19	08 22 14	10 81 85	44 43 49	68 73 63	79 17 88	55 32 31	34 84 72	82 40 71
20	43 26 21	33 38 60	54 97 39	75 87 56	60 59 41	17 40 76	68 56 90	23 05 21
21	16 92 07	38 74 46	87 78 35	96 49 86	41 88 32	94 31 67	68 34 93	67 70 58
22	75 37 44	38 93 60	13 55 18	71 31 55	52 56 15	77 87 76	72 38 54	57 98 04
23	89 15 30	41 81 34	63 35 62	26 76 73	53 52 84	48 66 60	79 40 43	07 71 77
24	09 67 10	04 14 75	66 42 49	48 37 91	06 35 98	29 55 13	44 96 29	38 28 27
25	70 31 80	76 93 17	42 86 19	71 77 06	62 04 08	69 56 11	04 46 75	66 56 55
26	27 25 34	21 69 61	52 78 15	72 97 72	83 48 52	12 67 43	88 17 40	10 56 51
27	39 58 46	35 82 83	33 66 15	85 96 52	49 80 40	77 22 76	01 87 99	99 35 91
28	64 22 03	61 41 09	12 17 15	79 72 31	15 72 05	43 74 74	67 21 35	11 12 26
29	06 14 07	62 22 52	86 87 11	84 61 62	53 79 56	22 98 21	75 94 90	69 00 65
30	84 91 06	46 81 80	34 86 75	91 24 82	50 47 57	51 70 21	52 71 47	21 58 71
31	53 44 58	83 09 16	25 27 20	02 17 61	96 50 16	18 51 33	50 95 62	70 84 64
32	14 38 29	28 65 03	89 91 37	89 44 83	93 00 32	44 67 76	52 71 92	51 58 80
33	12 11 59	93 45 15	22 68 17	77 88 01	47 99 26	54 71 70	87 04 83	83 28 81
34	57 11 18	82 71 46	51 54 16	17 27 41	41 54 45	83 67 99	47 71 43	69 89 67
35	89 95 74	44 72 43	81 57 46	99 03 76	59 73 18	43 18 30	48 73 48	03 83 27
36	71 37 38	55 24 48	22 04 20	24 47 42	21 55 94	48 96 24	48 46 63	29 88 10
37	55 21 51	51 69 78	38 82 10	03 67 61	37 00 61	79 29 76	41 56 98	48 84 98
38	45 11 59	05 58 91	99 50 70	45 80 59	42 74 23	23 88 82	85 04 22	58 49 57
39	93 72 34	38 08 74	88 83 58	71 78 04	18 16 93	90 24 83	61 52 95	86 28 99
40	62 28 90	08 87 98	52 39 47	43 97 83	56 77 65	39 70 27	35 59 72	22 37 86
41	91 47 87	96 82 82	80 19 47	83 71 96	60 59 41	98 29 02	65 82 60	62 86 74
42	94 10 02	00 32 63	71 96 58	79 47 01	73 74 11	39 74 15	67 23 74	70 55 38
43	56 47 41	52 95 53	81 11 28	90 81 47	49 29 86	36 81 87	00 91 71	81 69 48
44	41 26 17	32 46 73	07 79 24	35 59 97	62 33 68	61 85 62	20 22 95	83 00 93
45	19 89 51	24 85 43	11 36 15	18 53 32	95 16 40	14 06 69	97 61 15	34 76 85
46	89 23 60	87 38 01	97 18 84	44 36 11	96 37 20	13 03 37	62 50 06	97 26 05
47	62 21 30	79 75 97	30 50 32	08 85 71	72 52 44	48 66 91	41 37 02	44 22 10
48	18 17 58	40 03 40	88 83 28	43 92 84	47 90 87	21 81 56	11 29 31	31 35 74
49	55 73 85	28 03 11	13 39 27	25 80 04	31 45 87	65 91 49	98 32 61	98 14 70
50	68 21 91	45 71 11	20 29 22	57 73 72	63 71 96	39 89 92	42 71 35	32 15 69

Table VII
Conversion Factors for Average Cumulative Cost or Time

Units	80%	81%	82%	83%	84%	85%	86%	87%	88%	89%	90%	91%	92%	93%	94%	95%	Units
1	1.0000	1.0000	1.0000	1.0000	1.0000	1.0000	1.0000	1.0000	1.0000	1.0000	1.0000	1.0000	1.0000	1.0000	1.0000	1.0000	1
2	.8000	.8100	.8200	.8300	.8400	.8500	.8600	.8700	.8800	.8900	.9000	.9100	.9200	.9300	.9400	.9500	2
3	.7021	.7161	.7301	.7443	.7586	.7729	.7874	.8019	.8166	.8314	.8462	.8612	.8762	.8913	.9066	.9219	3
4	.6400	.6561	.6724	.6889	.7056	.7225	.7396	.7569	.7744	.7921	.8100	.8281	.8464	.8649	.8836	.9025	4
5	.5956	.6131	.6308	.6488	.6671	.6857	.7045	.7237	.7432	.7629	.7830	.8033	.8240	.8449	.8662	.8877	5
6	.5617	.5800	.5987	.6178	.6372	.6570	.6771	.6977	.7186	.7399	.7616	.7837	.8061	.8290	.8522	.8758	6
7	.5345	.5535	.5729	.5927	.6130	.6337	.6548	.6764	.6985	.7210	.7439	.7674	.7913	.8157	.8405	.8659	7
8	.5120	.5314	.5514	.5718	.5927	.6141	.6361	.6585	.6815	.7050	.7290	.7536	.7787	.8044	.8306	.8574	8
9	.4929	.5127	.5331	.5540	.5754	.5974	.6200	.6431	.6668	.6911	.7161	.7416	.7677	.7945	.8219	.8499	9
10	.4765	.4966	.5172	.5385	.5604	.5828	.6059	.6296	.6540	.6790	.7047	.7310	.7581	.7858	.8142	.8433	10
11	.4621	.4824	.5033	.5249	.5471	.5699	.5935	.6177	.6426	.6682	.6946	.7216	.7494	.7780	.8073	.8374	11
12	.4493	.4698	.4909	.5127	.5352	.5584	.5823	.6070	.6324	.6585	.6854	.7131	.7416	.7709	.8011	.8320	12
13	.4379	.4585	.4798	.5018	.5246	.5480	.5723	.5973	.6231	.6497	.6771	.7054	.7345	.7645	.7954	.8271	13
14	.4276	.4483	.4697	.4919	.5149	.5386	.5631	.5885	.6146	.6417	.6696	.6983	.7280	.7586	.7901	.8226	14
15	.4182	.4390	.4606	.4829	.5060	.5300	.5547	.5804	.6069	.6343	.6626	.6918	.7220	.7531	.7853	.8184	15
16	.4096	.4305	.4521	.4746	.4979	.5220	.5470	.5729	.5997	.6274	.6561	.6857	.7164	.7481	.7807	.8145	16
17	.4017	.4226	.4443	.4669	.4903	.5146	.5398	.5660	.5930	.6211	.6501	.6801	.7112	.7433	.7765	.8109	17
18	.3944	.4153	.4371	.4598	.4833	.5078	.5332	.5595	.5868	.6151	.6445	.6748	.7063	.7389	.7726	.8074	18
19	.3876	.4086	.4304	.4532	.4768	.5014	.5269	.5535	.5810	.6096	.6392	.6699	.7017	.7347	.7689	.8042	19
20	.3812	.4022	.4241	.4470	.4707	.4954	.5211	.5478	.5755	.6043	.6342	.6652	.6974	.7308	.7654	.8012	20
21	.3753	.3963	.4183	.4411	.4650	.4898	.5156	.5424	.5704	.5994	.6295	.6608	.6933	.7271	.7620	.7983	21
22	.3697	.3907	.4127	.4356	.4595	.4844	.5104	.5374	.5655	.5947	.6251	.6567	.6895	.7235	.7589	.7955	22
23	.3644	.3855	.4075	.4305	.4544	.4794	.5055	.5326	.5609	.5903	.6209	.6527	.6858	.7202	.7559	.7929	23
24	.3595	.3805	.4026	.4256	.4496	.4747	.5008	.5281	.5565	.5861	.6169	.6489	.6823	.7170	.7530	.7904	24
25	.3548	.3759	.3979	.4209	.4450	.4701	.4964	.5238	.5523	.5821	.6131	.6453	.6789	.7139	.7503	.7880	25
26	.3503	.3714	.3934	.4165	.4406	.4658	.4922	.5197	.5483	.5782	.6094	.6419	.6758	.7110	.7476	.7858	26
27	.3461	.3672	.3892	.4123	.4365	.4617	.4881	.5157	.5445	.5746	.6059	.6386	.6727	.7082	.7451	.7836	27
28	.3421	.3631	.3852	.4083	.4325	.4578	.4843	.5120	.5409	.5711	.6026	.6355	.6698	.7055	.7427	.7815	28
29	.3382	.3593	.3813	.4045	.4287	.4541	.4806	.5084	.5374	.5677	.5994	.6324	.6669	.7029	.7404	.7794	29
30	.3346	.3556	.3777	.4008	.4251	.4505	.4771	.5049	.5341	.5645	.5963	.6295	.6642	.7004	.7381	.7775	30
31	.3310	.3521	.3741	.3973	.4216	.4470	.4737	.5016	.5308	.5614	.5933	.6267	.6616	.6980	.7360	.7756	31
32	.3277	.3487	.3707	.3939	.4182	.4437	.4704	.4984	.5277	.5584	.5905	.6240	.6591	.6957	.7339	.7738	32
33	.3244	.3454	.3675	.3907	.4150	.4405	.4673	.4953	.5247	.5555	.5877	.6214	.6566	.6935	.7319	.7720	33
34	.3213	.3423	.3644	.3875	.4119	.4374	.4643	.4924	.5219	.5527	.5851	.6189	.6543	.6913	.7299	.7703	34
35	.3184	.3393	.3613	.3845	.4089	.4345	.4613	.4895	.5191	.5501	.5825	.6165	.6520	.6892	.7281	.7687	35
36	.3155	.3364	.3584	.3816	.4060	.4316	.4585	.4868	.5164	.5475	.5800	.6141	.6498	.6872	.7262	.7671	36
37	.3127	.3336	.3556	.3788	.4032	.4289	.4558	.4841	.5138	.5449	.5776	.6118	.6477	.6852	.7245	.7655	37
38	.3100	.3309	.3529	.3761	.4005	.4262	.4532	.4815	.5113	.5425	.5753	.6096	.6456	.6833	.7227	.7640	38
39	.3075	.3283	.3503	.3735	.3979	.4236	.4506	.4790	.5088	.5401	.5730	.6075	.6436	.6814	.7211	.7625	39
40	.3050	.3258	.3478	.3710	.3954	.4211	.4481	.4766	.5065	.5378	.5708	.6054	.6416	.6796	.7194	.7611	40
41	.3026	.3234	.3453	.3685	.3929	.4187	.4457	.4742	.5042	.5356	.5687	.6033	.6397	.6779	.7178	.7597	41
42	.3002	.3210	.3430	.3661	.3906	.4163	.4434	.4719	.5019	.5335	.5666	.6014	.6379	.6762	.7163	.7584	42
43	.2979	.3187	.3407	.3638	.3883	.4140	.4411	.4697	.4997	.5313	.5646	.5994	.6361	.6745	.7148	.7570	43
44	.2958	.3165	.3384	.3616	.3860	.4118	.4389	.4675	.4976	.5293	.5626	.5976	.6343	.6729	.7133	.7558	44
45	.2936	.3143	.3363	.3594	.3838	.4096	.4368	.4654	.4956	.5273	.5607	.5957	.6326	.6713	.7119	.7545	45
46	.2915	.3123	.3342	.3573	.3817	.4075	.4347	.4634	.4936	.5254	.5588	.5940	.6309	.6698	.7105	.7533	46
47	.2895	.3102	.3321	.3552	.3797	.4055	.4327	.4614	.4916	.5235	.5570	.5922	.6293	.6682	.7091	.7521	47
48	.2876	.3082	.3301	.3532	.3777	.4035	.4307	.4594	.4897	.5216	.5552	.5905	.6277	.6668	.7078	.7509	48
49	.2857	.3063	.3282	.3513	.3757	.4015	.4288	.4575	.4879	.5198	.5535	.5889	.6262	.6653	.7065	.7498	49
50	.2838	.3044	.3263	.3494	.3738	.3996	.4269	.4557	.4860	.5180	.5518	.5873	.6246	.6639	.7052	.7486	50

Table VIII
Conversion Factors for Average Incremental Cost or Time

Units	80%	81%	82%	83%	84%	85%	86%	87%	88%	89%	90%	91%	92%	93%	94%	95%	Units
1	1.0000	1.0000	1.0000	1.0000	1.0000	1.0000	1.0000	1.0000	1.0000	1.0000	1.0000	1.0000	1.0000	1.0000	1.0000	1.0000	1
2	.6000	.6200	.6400	.6600	.6800	.7000	.7200	.7400	.7600	.7800	.8000	.8200	.8400	.8600	.8800	.9000	2
3	.5063	.5282	.5504	.5729	.5957	.6187	.6421	.6658	.6898	.7141	.7386	.7635	.7886	.8140	.8398	.8658	3
4	.4537	.4762	.4992	.5227	.5467	.5713	.5963	.6218	.6478	.6743	.7014	.7289	.7570	.7856	.8146	.8442	4
5	.4182	.4409	.4643	.4884	.5130	.5384	.5643	.5910	.6183	.6463	.6749	.7043	.7343	.7650	.7965	.8286	5
6	.3919	.4148	.4383	.4626	.4877	.5135	.5402	.5675	.5957	.6247	.6546	.6852	.7167	.7491	.7822	.8163	6
7	.3713	.3941	.4178	.4422	.4676	.4937	.5208	.5488	.5776	.6074	.6381	.6698	.7025	.7361	.7707	.8063	7
8	.3546	.3773	.4009	.4255	.4509	.4774	.5047	.5331	.5626	.5930	.6244	.6569	.6904	.7251	.7609	.7978	8
9	.3405	.3632	.3869	.4114	.4370	.4636	.4913	.5199	.5497	.5805	.6126	.6457	.6801	.7156	.7524	.7904	9
10	.3286	.3512	.3746	.3993	.4249	.4516	.4794	.5084	.5385	.5698	.6023	.6361	.6710	.7073	.7449	.7839	10
11	.3181	.3405	.3641	.3886	.4144	.4411	.4691	.4983	.5286	.5603	.5932	.6274	.6630	.7000	.7384	.7782	11
12	.3090	.3313	.3547	.3793	.4049	.4319	.4599	.4892	.5199	.5518	.5850	.6197	.6558	.6933	.7323	.7729	12
13	.3007	.3230	.3464	.3708	.3966	.4234	.4517	.4811	.5119	.5441	.5777	.6127	.6493	.6873	.7269	.7681	13
14	.2934	.3155	.3388	.3633	.3889	.4159	.4441	.4738	.5047	.5370	.5709	.6063	.6432	.6818	.7220	.7638	14
15	.2867	.3087	.3319	.3563	.3820	.4090	.4373	.4669	.4980	.5307	.5648	.6005	.6377	.6767	.7173	.7598	15
16	.2806	.3026	.3256	.3500	.3756	.4026	.4309	.4608	.4920	.5248	.5591	.5950	.6327	.6719	.7131	.7560	16
17	.2750	.2968	.3199	.3442	.3698	.3968	.4252	.4550	.4864	.5192	.5538	.5900	.6279	.6676	.7091	.7525	17
18	.2699	.2916	.3145	.3388	.3644	.3913	.4197	.4496	.4811	.5142	.5488	.5853	.6235	.6635	.7054	.7493	18
19	.2650	.2867	.3096	.3337	.3593	.3862	.4147	.4446	.4762	.5093	.5443	.5808	.6193	.6597	.7019	.7462	19
20	.2607	.2821	.3049	.3290	.3545	.3815	.4100	.4400	.4715	.5049	.5399	.5767	.6154	.6560	.6986	.7432	20
21	.2564	.2779	.3006	.3247	.3501	.3771	.4055	.4356	.4673	.5007	.5358	.5729	.6117	.6525	.6955	.7406	21
22	.2526	.2738	.2965	.3205	.3460	.3729	.4013	.4314	.4632	.4966	.5319	.5691	.6082	.6494	.6926	.7379	22
23	.2488	.2701	.2927	.3167	.3420	.3689	.3974	.4275	.4593	.4929	.5283	.5656	.6049	.6462	.6897	.7354	23
24	.2455	.2666	.2890	.3129	.3383	.3652	.3937	.4238	.4556	.4893	.5248	.5622	.6017	.6434	.6871	.7331	24
25	.2421	.2632	.2857	.3095	.3348	.3616	.3901	.4202	.4521	.4858	.5215	.5591	.5988	.6405	.6845	.7309	25
26	.2390	.2600	.2823	.3061	.3314	.3583	.3867	.4169	.4489	.4826	.5183	.5561	.5958	.6378	.6821	.7286	26
27	.2361	.2570	.2793	.3030	.3282	.3550	.3835	.4137	.4456	.4795	.5153	.5531	.5931	.6353	.6797	.7266	27
28	.2334	.2542	.2764	.3000	.3252	.3520	.3804	.4106	.4426	.4765	.5124	.5504	.5905	.6328	.6775	.7246	28
29	.2306	.2514	.2735	.2971	.3223	.3490	.3775	.4076	.4397	.4737	.5097	.5477	.5879	.6305	.6754	.7227	29
30	.2281	.2487	.2708	.2944	.3195	.3462	.3746	.4049	.4369	.4709	.5069	.5451	.5855	.6282	.6732	.7209	30
31	.2256	.2463	.2683	.2918	.3168	.3435	.3719	.4021	.4343	.4683	.5044	.5426	.5832	.6259	.6713	.7190	31
32	.2234	.2438	.2658	.2892	.3143	.3410	.3694	.3996	.4316	.4658	.5020	.5409	.5809	.6239	.6693	.7174	32
33	.2210	.2416	.2634	.2869	.3118	.3384	.3668	.3970	.4292	.4633	.4995	.5380	.5787	.6219	.6675	.7157	33
34	.2190	.2393	.2612	.2844	.3094	.3361	.3644	.3947	.4268	.4610	.4973	.5358	.5766	.6198	.6657	.7141	34
35	.2169	.2372	.2589	.2823	.3072	.3337	.3621	.3923	.4245	.4587	.4950	.5336	.5746	.6180	.6639	.7125	35
36	.2149	.2351	.2569	.2801	.3049	.3315	.3599	.3900	.4222	.4565	.4929	.5316	.5726	.6161	.6622	.7111	36
37	.2129	.2332	.2548	.2780	.3028	.3294	.3576	.3879	.4201	.4543	.4909	.5296	.5707	.6144	.6606	.7096	37
38	.2112	.2312	.2528	.2760	.3008	.3272	.3556	.3858	.4180	.4523	.4888	.5276	.5689	.6126	.6590	.7081	38
39	.2093	.2295	.2510	.2741	.2988	.3253	.3536	.3838	.4160	.4503	.4868	.5257	.5670	.6109	.6574	.7068	39
40	.2077	.2276	.2491	.2721	.2969	.3233	.3516	.3818	.4140	.4484	.4850	.5239	.5653	.6092	.6560	.7054	40
41	.2059	.2259	.2473	.2704	.2950	.3214	.3496	.3798	.4121	.4465	.4831	.5221	.5636	.6077	.6545	.7042	41
42	.2044	.2242	.2457	.2685	.2932	.3196	.3479	.3781	.4103	.4447	.4814	.5204	.5620	.6062	.6530	.7029	42
43	.2028	.2227	.2439	.2669	.2915	.3178	.3460	.3762	.4084	.4428	.4795	.5187	.5603	.6046	.6517	.7016	43
44	.2012	.2210	.2423	.2652	.2897	.3161	.3443	.3744	.4067	.4412	.4780	.5171	.5588	.6031	.6503	.7004	44
45	.1999	.2195	.2408	.2636	.2881	.3144	.3426	.3728	.4051	.4395	.4762	.5155	.5572	.6017	.6490	.6993	45
46	.1984	.2181	.2392	.2620	.2865	.3128	.3409	.3711	.4033	.4378	.4747	.5139	.5558	.6004	.6477	.6981	46
47	.1970	.2166	.2378	.2605	.2849	.3112	.3393	.3694	.4017	.4363	.4730	.5124	.5543	.5989	.6465	.6969	47
48	.1956	.2152	.2363	.2590	.2834	.3096	.3378	.3679	.4002	.4346	.4716	.5109	.5529	.5976	.6452	.6959	48
49	.1944	.2139	.2349	.2576	.2820	.3081	.3362	.3664	.3987	.4332	.4701	.5095	.5515	.5964	.6441	.6948	49
50	.1931	.2125	.2335	.2561	.2805	.3067	.3347	.3649	.3971	.4317	.4686	.5080	.5502	.5950	.6428	.6938	50

Table IX
Conversion Factors for Total Cumulative Cost or Time

Units	80%	81%	82%	83%	84%	85%	86%	87%	88%	89%	90%	91%	92%	93%	94%	95%	Units
1	1.0000	1.0000	1.0000	1.0000	1.0000	1.0000	1.0000	1.0000	1.0000	1.0000	1.0000	1.0000	1.0000	1.0000	1.0000	1.0000	1
2	1.6000	1.6200	1.6400	1.6600	1.6800	1.7000	1.7200	1.7400	1.7600	1.7800	1.8000	1.8200	1.8400	1.8600	1.8800	1.9000	2
3	2.1063	2.1482	2.1904	2.2329	2.2757	2.3187	2.3621	2.4058	2.4498	2.4941	2.5386	2.5835	2.6286	2.6740	2.7198	2.7658	3
4	2.5600	2.6244	2.6896	2.7556	2.8224	2.8900	2.9584	3.0276	3.0976	3.1684	3.2400	3.3124	3.3856	3.4596	3.5344	3.6100	4
5	2.9782	3.0653	3.1539	3.2440	3.3354	3.4284	3.5227	3.6186	3.7159	3.8147	3.9149	4.0167	4.1199	4.2246	4.3309	4.4386	5
6	3.3701	3.4801	3.5922	3.7066	3.8231	3.9419	4.0629	4.1861	4.3116	4.4394	4.5695	4.7019	4.8366	4.9737	5.1131	5.2549	6
7	3.7414	3.8742	4.0100	4.1488	4.2907	4.4356	4.5837	4.7349	4.8892	5.0468	5.2076	5.3717	5.5391	5.7098	5.8838	6.0612	7
8	4.0960	4.2515	4.4109	4.5743	4.7416	4.9130	5.0884	5.2680	5.4518	5.6398	5.8320	6.0286	6.2295	6.4349	6.6447	6.8590	8
9	4.4365	4.6147	4.7978	4.9857	5.1786	5.3766	5.5797	5.7879	6.0015	6.2203	6.4446	6.6743	6.9096	7.1505	7.3971	7.6494	9
10	4.7651	4.9659	5.1724	5.3850	5.6035	5.8282	6.0591	6.2963	6.5400	6.7901	7.0469	7.3104	7.5806	7.8578	8.1420	8.4333	10
11	5.0832	5.3064	5.5365	5.7736	6.0179	6.2693	6.5282	6.7946	7.0686	7.3504	7.6401	7.9378	8.2436	8.5578	8.8804	9.2115	11
12	5.3922	5.6377	5.8912	6.1529	6.4228	6.7012	6.9881	7.2838	7.5885	7.9022	8.2251	8.5575	8.8994	9.2511	9.6127	9.9844	12
13	5.6929	5.9607	6.2376	6.5237	6.8194	7.1246	7.4398	7.7649	8.1004	8.4463	8.8028	9.1702	9.5487	9.9384	10.3396	10.7525	13
14	5.9863	6.2762	6.5764	6.8870	7.2083	7.5405	7.8839	8.2387	8.6051	8.9833	9.3737	9.7765	10.1919	10.6202	11.0616	11.5163	14
15	6.2730	6.5849	6.9083	7.2433	7.5903	7.9495	8.3212	8.7056	9.1031	9.5140	9.9385	10.3770	10.8296	11.2969	11.7789	12.2761	15
16	6.5536	6.8875	7.2339	7.5933	7.9659	8.3521	8.7521	9.1664	9.5951	10.0388	10.4976	10.9720	11.4623	11.9688	12.4920	13.0321	16
17	6.8286	7.1843	7.5538	7.9375	8.3357	8.7489	9.1773	9.6214	10.0815	10.5580	11.0514	11.5620	12.0902	12.6364	13.2011	13.7846	17
18	7.0985	7.4759	7.8683	8.2763	8.7001	9.1402	9.5970	10.0715	10.5626	11.0722	11.6002	12.1473	12.7137	13.2999	13.9065	14.5339	18
19	7.3635	7.7626	8.1779	8.6100	9.0594	9.5264	10.0117	10.5156	11.0388	11.5815	12.1445	12.7281	13.3330	13.9596	14.6084	15.2801	19
20	7.6242	8.0447	8.4828	8.9390	9.4139	9.9079	10.4217	10.9556	11.5103	12.0864	12.6844	13.3048	13.9484	14.6156	15.3070	16.0233	20
21	7.8806	8.3226	8.7834	9.2637	9.7640	10.2850	10.8272	11.3912	11.9776	12.5871	13.2202	13.8777	14.5601	15.2681	16.0025	16.7639	21
22	8.1332	8.5964	9.0799	9.5842	10.1100	10.6579	11.2285	11.8226	12.4408	13.0837	13.7521	14.4468	15.1683	15.9175	16.6951	17.5018	22
23	8.3820	8.8665	9.3726	9.9009	10.4520	11.0268	11.6259	12.2501	12.9001	13.5766	14.2804	15.0124	15.7732	16.5637	17.3848	18.2372	23
24	8.6275	9.1331	9.6616	10.2138	10.7903	11.3920	12.0196	12.6739	13.3557	14.0659	14.8052	15.5746	16.3749	17.2071	18.0719	18.9703	24
25	8.8696	9.3963	9.9473	10.5233	11.1251	11.7536	12.4097	13.0941	13.8078	14.5517	15.3267	16.1337	16.9737	17.8476	18.7564	19.7012	25
26	9.1086	9.6563	10.2296	10.8294	11.4565	12.1119	12.7964	13.5110	14.2567	15.0343	15.8450	16.6898	17.5695	18.4854	19.4385	20.4298	26
27	9.3447	9.9133	10.5089	11.1324	11.7847	12.4669	13.1799	13.9247	14.7023	15.5138	16.3603	17.2429	18.1626	19.1207	20.1182	21.1564	27
28	9.5781	10.1675	10.7853	11.4324	12.1099	12.8189	13.5603	14.3353	15.1449	15.9903	16.8727	17.7933	18.7531	19.7535	20.7957	21.8810	28
29	9.8087	10.4189	11.0588	11.7295	12.4322	13.1671	13.9378	14.7429	15.5846	16.4640	17.3824	18.3410	19.3410	20.3840	21.4711	22.6037	29
30	10.0368	10.6676	11.3296	12.0239	12.7517	13.5141	14.3124	15.1478	16.0215	16.9349	17.8893	18.8861	19.9265	21.0122	22.1443	23.3246	30
31	10.2624	10.9139	11.5979	12.3157	13.0685	13.8576	14.6843	15.5499	16.4558	17.4032	18.3937	19.4287	20.5097	21.6381	22.8156	24.0436	31
32	10.4858	11.1577	11.8637	12.6049	13.3828	14.1986	15.0537	15.9495	16.8874	17.8690	18.8957	19.9690	21.0906	22.2620	23.4849	24.7610	32
33	10.7068	11.3993	12.1271	12.8918	13.6946	14.5370	15.4205	16.3465	17.3166	18.3323	19.3952	20.5070	21.6693	22.8839	24.1524	25.4767	33
34	10.9258	11.6386	12.3883	13.1762	14.0040	14.8731	15.7849	16.7412	17.7434	18.7933	19.8925	21.0428	22.2459	23.5037	24.8181	26.1908	34
35	11.1427	11.8758	12.6472	13.4585	14.3112	15.2068	16.1470	17.1335	18.1679	19.2520	20.3875	21.5764	22.8205	24.1217	25.4820	26.9033	35
36	11.3576	12.1109	12.9041	13.7386	14.6161	15.5383	16.5069	17.5235	18.5901	19.7085	20.8804	22.1080	23.3931	24.7378	26.1442	27.6144	36
37	11.5705	12.3441	13.1589	14.0166	14.9189	15.8677	16.8645	17.9114	19.0102	20.1628	21.3713	22.6376	23.9638	25.3522	26.8048	28.3240	37
38	11.7817	12.5753	13.4117	14.2926	15.2197	16.1949	17.2201	18.2972	19.4282	20.6151	21.8601	23.1652	24.5327	25.9648	27.4638	29.0321	38
39	11.9910	12.8048	13.6627	14.5667	15.5185	16.5202	17.5737	18.6810	19.8442	21.0654	22.3469	23.6909	25.0997	26.5757	28.1212	29.7389	39
40	12.1987	13.0324	13.9118	14.8388	15.8154	16.8435	17.9253	19.0628	20.2582	21.5138	22.8319	24.2148	25.6650	27.1849	28.7772	30.4443	40
41	12.4046	13.2583	14.1591	15.1092	16.1104	17.1649	18.2749	19.4426	20.6703	21.9603	23.3150	24.7369	26.2286	27.7926	29.4317	31.1485	41
42	12.6090	13.4825	14.4048	15.3777	16.4036	17.4845	18.6228	19.8207	21.0806	22.4050	23.7964	25.2573	26.7906	28.3988	30.0847	31.8514	42
43	12.8118	13.7052	14.6487	15.6446	16.6951	17.8023	18.9688	20.1969	21.4890	22.8478	24.2759	25.7760	27.3509	29.0034	30.7364	32.5530	43
44	13.0130	13.9262	14.8910	15.9098	16.9848	18.1184	19.3131	20.5713	21.8957	23.2890	24.7539	26.2931	27.9097	29.6065	31.3867	33.2534	44
45	13.2129	14.1457	15.1318	16.1734	17.2729	18.4331	19.6557	20.9441	22.3008	23.7285	25.2301	26.8086	28.4669	30.2082	32.0357	33.9527	45
46	13.4113	14.3638	15.3710	16.4354	17.5594	18.7456	19.9966	21.3152	22.7041	24.1663	25.7048	27.3225	29.0227	30.8086	32.6834	34.6508	46
47	13.6083	14.5804	15.6088	16.6959	17.8443	19.0568	20.3359	21.6846	23.1058	24.6026	26.1778	27.8349	29.5770	31.4075	33.3299	35.3477	47
48	13.8039	14.7956	15.8451	16.9549	18.1277	19.3664	20.6737	22.0525	23.5060	25.0372	26.6494	28.3458	30.1299	32.0051	33.9751	36.0436	48
49	13.9983	15.0095	16.0800	17.2125	18.4097	19.6745	21.0099	22.4189	23.9047	25.4704	27.1195	28.8553	30.6814	32.6015	34.6192	36.7384	49
50	14.1914	15.2220	16.3135	17.4686	18.6902	19.9812	21.3446	22.7838	24.3018	25.9021	27.5881	29.3633	31.2316	33.1965	35.2620	37.4322	50

GLOSSARY

The number in parentheses after each term refers to the chapter in which the term is described.

abnormal spoiled unit cost *(6)* The manufacturing costs incurred in making products that are lost or spoiled in the production process.

absorption costing *(11)* A product costing method in which all costs of production, direct and indirect, fixed and variable, are included in the costs of products. Also called full costing.

accelerated cost recovery system (ACRS) *(16)* A system of asset depreciation required for tax reporting purposes for assets acquired after December 31, 1980.

accounting information *(1)* Financial information that is relevant, timely, and accurate.

accounting rate of return (ARR) *(15)* A method of capital expenditure investment analysis that uses accounting measures of income and investment as the basis for evaluating investment projects.

accuracy *(1)* A characteristic of accounting information referring to the correctness of accounting information, free from error.

activity costing *(2,10)* The process of determining costs for activities of a business other than manufacturing.

actual cost *(2,11)* The cost actually incurred in producing a product or providing a service. Also called historical cost.

actual cost transfer price *(12)* A price assigned to products or services transferred between segments of an organization. The price is based on the actual cost of making the product or providing the service.

actual hours *(9)* The number of direct labor hours actually worked during some reporting period. Usually reported in a labor summary report.

administrative expense budget *(7)* Estimated administrative expenses for a specified time period, such as a month or a year.

allocation *(2)* The process of assigning common costs to cost objectives in some systematic manner in accordance with the matching principle. *(17)* One of the three basic objectives of public finance, it deals with providing socially desirable goods and services in the right amount. (See also cost allocation.)

allocation base *(20)* An activity or service measure used for allocating costs to cost objectives.

alternative choice decision *(10)* A decision involving the choice between two or more decision alternatives or courses of action.

application base *(20)* A measure of some activity, such as direct labor hours, units of production, sales revenue, or machine hours, used to compute an overhead application rate.

assets employed *(12)* An asset base used to measure performance of a segment of an organization. The base includes all assets except those not employed in the normal course of business activities.

audit trail *(4)* The interrelated evidence consisting of accounting reports, ledger and journal entries, journal memoranda, and source documents used by accountants to trace transactions through the accounting system to their source.

average cost *(5)* An inventory valuation method used to assign production costs to units in a process costing system (also called **weights average inventory method**).

average cumulative cost *(25)* The average unit

919

cost of all units produced at some specific volume of production in a production environment in which a learning effect occurs.

average incremental cost *(25)* In a learning curve environment, the average unit cost of the incremental units that are produced.

average standard contribution margin *(22)* The average contribution margin provided by the expected product sales mix.

average standard cost of inputs *(22)* The average unit cost of production inputs at the standard mix of inputs.

bailout *(15)* A capital budgeting project evaluation method that measures how quickly the project's investment can be recovered from the combination of cash savings and the salvage value of the investment at any point in time.

basic standards *(8)* Long-term standards created for a period of 2 to 5 years or more. Used as a benchmark for long-term comparison.

benefit-cost analysis *(2,10)* The comparison of costs and benefits in evaluating alternative courses of action. *(17)* The formal project evaluation phase of budgeting using the federal government planning, programming, budgeting system (PPBS).

bill of materials *(8)* A list of materials and their quantities required for the production of a specific product.

break-even point *(3)* The activity level that yields zero profit. Revenue equals total costs.

budget *(7)* A comprehensive quantative plan for utilizing the resources of an entity for some specified period of time.

budget entity *(7)* Any accounting entity, such as a firm, division, department, or project, for which a budget is prepared.

budget performance report *(7,9)* An internal accounting report that shows the difference between actual results budgeted data.

budget review process *(7)* The process of evaluating budget proposals and arriving at the master budget.

budget variance *(6,9)* The difference between budgeted data and actual results.

budget variance report *(7,9)* An internal report that shows the difference between budget data and actual results.

budgeted activity level *(20)* The estimated amount of activity for the coming accounting period expressed in terms of the application base; for example, 10,000 direct labor hours. The budgeted activity level is estimated before the accounting period begins.

budgeted balance sheet *(7)* A balance sheet prepared for a future time period, usually as part of a financial budget.

budgeted hours *(9)* The number of direct labor hours budgeted before the accounting period begins. Usually used in creating the manufacturing overhead rate and in computing manufacturing overhead volume variances in a standard costing system.

budgeted income statement *(7)* Estimated revenues and expenses for an entity for some specified time period in the form of a pro forma income statement.

budgeted overhead cost *(7,20)* The estimated amount of overhead costs determined before the accounting period begins. Used in the computation of a predetermined overhead rate.

budgeted overhead rate *(4,7,20)* A rate for applying overhead to production during the accounting period; for example, $5 per machine hour. The rate is determined before the accounting period begins. Also called a predetermined overhead rate.

budgeted statement of changes in financial position *(7)* An estimated statement of changes in financial position for some specific future point in time, usually prepared as part of a master budget.

by-product *(21)* A product of relatively small economic value that results from the production of a main product or group of products; e.g., particle board made from sawdust in the production of lumber.

capacity costs *(2)* Cost required to provide and operate a production facility, sometimes called occupancy costs.

capacity variance *(9)* The amount of overhead variance that occurs because the actual level of activity is different from the budgeted level of activity.

capital budgeting *(15)* The systematic process of identifying and evaluating capital investment projects to arrive at a capital expenditure budget.

capital expenditure budget *(7)* The report identifying an organization's plans for investing in capital projects with lives typically exceeding 1 accounting year and representing relatively large expenditures.

capital rationing *(16)* The process of selecting the more desirable projects from a series of acceptable investments.

carrying costs *(13)* Costs such as inventory storage and handling costs that are essential in maintaining an inventory of goods ready for sale or for use in the production process.

cash budget *(7)* Estimated cash receipts and disbursements of an entity for some specified time period, starting with the expected beginning cash balance and ending with the expected ending cash balance.

central limit theorem *(23)* A statistical concept that describes the probability function of a large number of sample means obtained from a population.

Certificate in Management Accounting (CMA) *(1)* A certificate granted by the Institute of Management Accounting to candidates who have successfully completed a rigorous professional examination administered by the Institute and have met certain work experience requirements.

certified public accountant (CPA) *(1)* A professional accountant who has passed a professional examination, has obtained practical experience, has satisfied other requirements, and is certified to practice public accounting and to audit financial statements in his state of residence.

clearing account *(19)* An account used to accumulate costs until they can be distributed to various cost objectives or expense accounts. The Payroll account is an example. Also called a holding account.

cluster sample *(23)* A sample obtained by dividing the population to be sampled into clusters and using all elements of randomly selected clusters for performing statistical tests.

coefficient of correlation *(24)* A statistic known as r whose value ranges from -1 to $+1$ and that explains the strength of the relationship between two sets of data. If r has a value close to -1 or $+1$ it

represents a strong relationship; a value close to zero represents a weak relationship.

coefficient of determination *(24)* A statistic, known as r^2 that is obtained by squaring the coefficient of correlation. Its value ranges from zero to 1 and it measures the strength of the relationship between two sets of data, with the stronger relationship designated by values closer to 1 and the weaker relationship designated by values closer to zero.

coefficient of nondetermination *(24)* A statistic calculated as $1 - r^2$ where r^2 is the coefficient of determination. The coefficient of nondetermination explains random fluctuation in a set of data and fluctuations caused by variables other than the independent variable.

committed fixed costs *(3,7)* The fixed costs of providing production facilities and other relatively long-term commitments or resources. Fixed costs that cannot be easily or quickly eliminated.

common cost *(2)* A cost that is not identifiable with a single cost objective but instead is shared by, or common to, more than one cost objective; e.g., the salary of a production plant manager shared by all producing departments in the manufacturing plant.

complementary projects *(16)* Capital projects that complement one another, requiring the investment in one if the other is to be acquired.

constant percentage method *(21)* A method of allocating joint cost that results in each product in a joint product group providing the same percentage gross margin; also called the gross profit method.

constraint *(25)* An element in a linear programming problem that may limit some component of the solution to the problem. Constraints often define an upper or lower limit on some resource involved in the analysis.

contribution approach *(11)* A cost reporting approach that highlights cost behavior characteristics rather than functional cost characteristics. Variable costs are deducted from sales to determine the amount contributed toward covering fixed costs and providing profit.

contribution approach pricing *(14)* A form of cost-plus pricing using variable costs plus a percentage as the basis for setting the selling price of products or services.

contribution margin *(3,11)* The difference between the selling price and the variable cost of a product or service. Both the per-unit manufacturing and nonmanufacturing variable costs are deducted from the selling price to determine the contribution margin. In aggregate contribution margin is the difference between total sales and total variable costs.

contribution margin ratio *(3)* The contribution margin expressed as a percentage of sales or selling price.

contribution margin variance *(22)* A measure of the difference between the standard contribution margin and the actual contribution margin generated by a product for some time period.

contributory pension plan *(19)* A retirement plan to which employees contribute a portion of their salary or wage in addition to the contribution made by the employer.

control *(1,7)* The concept of monitoring activities and taking action to correct undesirable performance, often using budgets as a basis for measuring performance.

control *(7)* The process of monitoring activities and taking necessary actions to ensure that goals and objectives are achieved.

control account *(2)* An account whose balance the total of all balances in accounts of a related subsidiary ledger. Accounts receivable is the control account for the individual accounts of amounts owed by customers.

controllable cost *(2,3,12)* A cost over which a manager has direct control or significant influence.

controllable variance *(9)* The difference between actual manufacturing overhead and a flexible overhead budget based on actual output in the two-variance method of overhead variance analysis. Equal to the sum of the spending and efficiency variances in a three-way overhead variance analysis.

conversion cost *(2)* Direct labor cost and manufacturing overhead cost combined.

correlation analysis *(24)* See **regression-correlation analysis.**

cost *(2)* The amount of resource given up for some product or service.

cost accounted for *(5)* The section of a cost of production report that shows the disposition of

costs that occurred in the process center during the reporting period. Typically costs are transferred to the next process center or remain in the process center's ending work in process inventory.

cost accounting *(1)* The process of determining the cost of some product or activity.

cost accounting data base *(1)* The set of cost accounting data that comprises the cost data used for both internal and external accounting reports.

Cost Accounting Standards Board (CASB) *(1)* A five-member board created by Congress to establish cost accounting standards and procedures for accounting for the costs of goods and services provided under contracts negotiated with the federal government.

cost accounting system *(1)* The set of concepts and procedures that are used to accumulate the cost accounting data base.

cost after split-off *(21)* The joint-product production cost that occurs after the split-off point and therefore is identifiable with a specific product.

cost allocation *(2,4,20)* The process of assigning common costs to cost objectives in accordance with the matching concept.

cost analyzing *(1)* A basic activity in cost accounting dealing with the systematic evaluation of cost data to solve problems and to provide relevant information.

cost behavior *(2,3)* The way a cost changes with respect to changes in the level of activity. Usually classified as fixed, variable, semifixed, semivariable, or mixed.

cost-benefit analysis *(1,2,10)* The process of analyzing the benefits derived from some project or activity with the cost necessary to do it. To be acceptable the benefits must be greater than the costs.

cost of capital *(15)* The amount that an organization pays for the capital that it uses.

cost center *(12)* A responsibility center in which managers are held responsible for the costs under their control.

cost elements *(4)* The three basic components of product cost: direct materials, direct labor, and manufacturing overhead.

cost of estimation error *(16)* The cost that arises from incorrectly estimating the value of variables used in management decision making.

cost indifference point *(10)* The activity level at which the total costs of two alternatives are identical. At this level of activity managers are indifferent between the two alternatives in terms of cost.

cost of goods manufactured *(2)* The cost of the products transferred from work in process inventory to finished goods inventory during a period. Usually reported in a cost-of-goods-manufactured schedule showing beginning work in process, current-period production costs, and ending work in process.

cost of goods sold *(2)* An expense made up of the cost of products that have been sold and are no longer assets of the selling entity.

cost of goods sold budget *(7)* A budget showing the expected cost of goods sold for a future period.

cost measuring *(1)* A basic activity of cost accounting dealing with the determination of costs for some specific product or activity.

cost of one spoiled unit *(6)* The cost of producing one unit to the point in the production process where the spoilage is identified.

cost-plus pricing *(14)* A type of pricing model using costs plus an amount or percentage as the basis for determining the price.

cost of production report *(5)* A report used to summarize production costs in a process center of a process costing system.

cost recording *(1)* The process of recording cost data in the formal accounting records of an organization.

cost reporting *(1)* Communicating cost information in the form of internal and external reports.

costs to account for *(5)* The section of the cost of production report that reports the production costs incurred in the process center during the period.

cost-volume-profit (CVP) analysis *(3)* Analyses that deal with how costs and profits change in relation to changes in the volume of activity.

cost-volume-profit chart *(3)* A graphic presentation of cost-volume-profit relationships. Often called a CVP chart. Frequently useful for presenting complex cost relationships.

CVP diagram *(3)* A diagram of cost-volume-profit relationships, showing the break-even point and other aspects of CVP analysis. Also called a CVP chart.

currently attainable standards *(8)* Standards that describe desired levels of performance but that reflect the problems of the operating environment, such as machine breakdowns.

daily time ticket *(4, 19)* A document used by employees to record how they spent their workday. A source document used to identify labor cost with cost objectives.

data *(1)* The basic facts and figures that constitute a data base; the building blocks of an information system.

data base *(1)* The foundation of data supporting an information system or a portion of an information system; the data drawn on by users to meet information needs.

decentralization *(12)* The process of delegating decision authority to various levels in the organization.

decision model *(1)* A description of how a particular decision is made.

decision theory *(1)* The body of knowledge concerning the process of decision making.

defective units *(18)* Manufactured units that do not satisfy the company's standards of quality. Sometimes such units are scrapped and other times they are reworked.

delegation *(12)* The process of assigning decision authority and responsibility to managers of various segments of an organization.

demand *(14)* The total amount of product or service all purchasers are willing to buy at all possible prices.

demand curve *(14)* A graph of demand showing the amount buyers in aggregate are willing to buy at all possible prices.

demand elasticity *(14)* A measure of the way demand for goods or services changes with changing prices. If demand is elastic, a decrease in price results in higher revenue because demand increases more than enough to offset the lower price. The opposite is true of inelastic demand.

departmental job cost sheet *(4)* A job cost sheet that identifies manufacturing costs by department or production function as well as by cost elements.

departmental overhead rates *(20)* Manufacturing overhead rates created for individual departments or groups of departments rather than one overhead rate for an entire production plant. The purpose of departmental rates is to do a better job of matching overhead costs with the revenues generated by the sale of products.

dependent variable *(24)* The variable whose value is to be predicted by means of a linear regression line and that depends on the values of the independent variable.

differential cost *(10)* A cost that differs between decision alternatives.

direct allocation *(20)* A method of allocating service department overhead costs directly to producing departments without any allocation to other service departments.

direct costing *(11)* See **variable costing.**

direct labor *(2,4)* Labor that is directly identifiable with a specific product or activity.

direct labor budget *(7)* Estimated direct labor costs and quantities of an entity for some time period.

direct materials *(2,4)* Raw materials used in the production process that can be identified with specific products.

direct materials budget *(7)* A formal plan describing the use of direct materials for some specific time period. Part of the master budget.

discounted cash flows (DCF) *(15)* Capital budgeting and other types of analyses that rely on the time value of money. All cash flows are discounted at some interest rate to their present value.

discretionary fixed cost *(3,7)* Fixed costs that can be eliminated at managements' discretion in a relatively short period of time; e.g.; some administrative salaries, research and development, and new systems development.

dispersion *(23)* A measure of the amount by which data fluctuate about some measure of central tendency.

distribution *(17)* A basic objective of public finance concerned with who should receive the economic benefits of society and in what amount.

division contribution report *(11)* A contribution report identifying the amount of contribution margin provided by each division of a company.

division income statement *(12)* An income statement identifying net income by division.

dynamic budget *(9)* See **flexible budget.**

economic order quantity (EOQ) *(13)* The optimum order size that results in the lowest total inventory cost for some specific inventory item.

efficiency constant *(25)* A constant numeric value, expressed as a percentage, used to calculate the average incremental time or cost of the next doubling in production in a learning curve situation. Calculated as $2 \times$ Learning rate $- 1$.

efficiency variance *(9)* The difference in variable manufacturing overhead caused by using more or fewer hours than standard. Also used to describe labor variances caused by using more or fewer hours than standard.

elastic demand *(10,14)* Demand for goods and services that reacts to a price decrease by increasing more than enough to offset the revenue lost from lowering the price.

employee benefits *(19)* Compensation for employees other than salary and wages including paid vacations, holidays, insurance programs, education programs, and recreation programs.

ending inventory budget *(7)* The budgeted amounts of ending inventory for all inventory items.

engineering standards *(8)* Very tight standards assuming no production problems. Sometimes called ideal standards.

equivalent units *(5)* A measure of the amount of production in a process center. The amount of equivalent whole units that would have been produced if all efforts had been devoted to starting and completing units rather than completing units in beginning inventory and starting units in ending inventory.

estimated activity level *(4,20)* See **budgeted activity level.**

estimated overhead cost *(4,20)* See **budgeted overhead cost.**

estimated value at split-off method *(21)* A method of allocating joint costs based on the estimated market value of joint products at the point of split-off.

expected contribution margin *(22)* The contribution margin expected from sales based on the expected mix of product sales. The same as the weighted average contribution margin except the expected contribution margin is based on expected data rather than on historical data.

expected standard deviation *(23)* The standard deviation computed from expected data, measuring the amount of fluctuation around the expected value.

expected value *(23)* A mean computed from expected data whose probability of occurrence has been specified.

external reporting *(1)* See **financial accounting.**

factory burden *(2,4)* See **manufacturing overhead.**

factory overhead rate *(4,20)* See **manufacturing overhead rate.**

favorable variance *(8,9,22)* The amount by which standard costs exceed actual costs. Any variance in which actual cost is less than expected cost.

feasible solution space *(25)* In a linear programming problem, the area within which all possible solutions to a problem may lie.

Federal Trade Commission (FTC) An agency of the federal government primarily involved in ensuring the use of fair practices in business and trade activities. The Robinson-Patman Act and lines of business reporting are administered by the FTC.

FICA tax *(19)* Social security tax required to be withheld from employees with an equal amount matched and paid by employers.

financial accounting *(1)* Accounting for the financial affairs of entities for the purpose of reporting such affairs to those outside the entity. Also called external reporting.

Financial Accounting Standards Board (FASB) *(1)* An independent rule-making body charged with issuing financial accounting rules known as Standards.

financial budget *(7)* The set of budgets including capital expenditures budget, cash budget, budgeted balance sheet, and budgeted statement of changes in financial position.

finished goods *(2)* Products in a manufacturing firm that have been completed and are ready for sale.

first in, first out (FIFO) *(5,6)* The inventory valuation method that assumes that the inventory acquired earliest is the first to be used or sold. The method refers to the flow of costs rather than to the physical flow of goods.

fiscal policy *(17)* Pertains to the taxing and spending actions of government. One of the two instruments of economic stabilization policy.

fixed budget *(7,9)* A budget prepared for a single expected level of activity. Also called a static budget.

fixed cost *(2,3)* A cost that does not change with the level of activity. Described by the general formula Y = a.

fixed efficiency variance *(9)* The fixed portion of the manufacturing overhead variance that results from using more or fewer hours than standard to produce a product. Computed by multiplying the fixed part of the manufacturing overhead rate times the difference between standard and actual hours.

fixed overhead *(7,9)* The portion of manufacturing overhead that does not change with changing levels of activity.

flexible budget *(9)* A budget prepared for more than one level of activity, covering several levels within the relevant range of activity. Also called a dynamic budget.

fringe benefits *(19)* See **employee benefits.**

full costing *(11)* See **absorption costing.**

functional budget *(17)* See **line budget.**

funded pension plan *(19)* A retirement plan that includes an investment fund from whose income retirement benefits are paid.

FUTA tax *(19)* Unemployment tax required by the Federal Unemployment Tax Act, imposed on employers and payable to the federal and state governments.

gross margin method *(21)* See **equal percentage method.**

gross payroll *(19)* The total payroll expense for a period, computed as the wage rate multiplied by the time worked. The amount of pay from which employee withholdings are deducted to arrive at net pay.

gross profit allocation method *(21)* A method of assigning joint product costs to products so that each product contributes an equal percentage gross margin on sales.

gross profit method *(21)* See **equal percentage method.**

high-cost input *(22)* An input used in a multiple resource production process that costs more than the average standard cost of inputs.

high-low method *(3)* A method of estimating the fixed and variable cost components of a mixed cost. Based on the difference between the highest and lowest costs experienced in a specific time period and the difference in activity level.

high-profit product *(22)* A product that provides a profit or contribution margin that is higher than the average profit or contribution margin provided by all products.

holding account *(19)* An account in which costs are accumulated until they can be distributed to other accounts. An example is the payroll account whose balance is distributed to work in process, overhead, and expense accounts.

historical costs *(2)* Costs that have already occurred. Also called actual costs.

ideal standards *(8)* Very tight, hard-to-achieve standards assuming ideal production conditions.

incentive plans *(19)* An arrangement for rewarding employees who exceed specified performance, resulting in the payment of bonuses, extra pay, time off, or other benefits.

incremental budget *(17)* A budget that is prepared merely by changing or incrementing the last budget by a certain percentage or amount.

incremental cost *(10)* Costs that differ between decision alternatives.

independent variable *(24)* The variable whose value is used in linear regression analysis to predict the value of the dependent variable.

indirect costs *(2)* Costs that cannot be identified directly with a cost objective.

indirect labor *(2,4)* Manufacturing labor that cannot be identified directly with products.

indirect material *(2,4)* Material necessary for the production process, but not identifiable with specific product.

inelastic demand *(10,14)* Demand for products or services that reacts to price increases with a relatively small decrease in the quantity demanded. When demand is inelastic, a price increase will cause a decline in demand that is not sufficient to offset the additional revenue from the price increase.

inferior goods *(14)* Products whose demand is the inverse of normal products. Price increases cause an increase in demand, and price decreases cause a decrease in demand.

information *(1)* Data assembled in usable form. It should increase a person's knowledge or decrease the risk of making an incorrect decision.

information overload *(10)* A situation in which a manager receives more information than can be assimilated logically into a decision analysis.

internal rate of return (IRR) *(15)* The interest rate that discounts the cash inflows from a project to the present value, which is identical to the present value of the cash outflows of that project.

internal reporting *(1)* See **managerial accounting.**

Internal Revenue Service (IRS) *(1)* The tax-collecting agency of the U.S. government, responsible for enforcing federal tax laws. IRS regulations affect some accounting procedures.

inventoriable cost *(2)* Necessary cost of production that increases the value of a product and becomes part of the cost of the product.

inventory acquisition *(18)* All activities necessary to purchase and receive inventory and move it into the inventory storage area.

inventory control *(13)* The process of planning, monitoring and efficiently managing inventory.

inventory distribution *(18)* All activities associated with transferring raw materials into production.

inventory ledger card *(18)* An individual inventory account.

investment center *(12)* A form of responsibility center in which managers are held responsible for the return on assets invested in that segment of the organization.

investment tax credit *(16)* A feature of federal tax laws designed to stimulate capital investment by allowing a tax reduction equal to a percentage of the purchase price of qualified capital assets.

job order cost sheet *(4)* A document used to accumulate manufacturing cost data for a particular job in a job order costing system.

job cost sheet *(4)* A report used to summarize the production costs for a specific production job in a job order costing system.

job number *(4)* An identification number assigned to each job cost sheet. The number may be designed to allow accountants to analyze costs easily in a variety of ways.

job order costing *(4)* A cost accounting system used to accumulate costs for products produced in batches or intermittent production runs. Job order production is characterized by an identifiable starting and completion time for the batch of production. Production costs are summarized on a job cost sheet.

job time ticket *(4, 19)* A source document used to identify labor costs with cost objectives. Employees prepare this document for each job on which they work.

joint cost *(21)* Production costs associated with joint products before the split-off point and allocated to products by means such as the gross margin method or the physical units method.

joint cost allocation *(21)* The process of assigning joint costs to products in a systematic and logical manner that satisfies the matching principle.

joint product *(21)* A product that results from a production process in which two or more different products are manufactured.

joint production process *(21)* A production process that yields two or more different products.

judgmental sample *(23)* A sample selected from a population without the use of statistical methods but based instead on judgment. A judgmental sample may be biased rather than random and may be smaller or larger than necessary to satisfy specific confidence levels.

kinked demand curve *(14)* A demand curve occurring in oligopolistic markets in which the action of one supplier causes a kink or sharp break in the demand curve for products of other suppliers.

labor distribution report *(4, 19)* A report summarizing the use of labor for some time period, such as a week or month.

labor efficiency variance *(8, 22)* A variance caused by using more or fewer labor hours than standard.

labor mix variance *(22)* The amount of labor variance that results from changing the mix of labor inputs from the standard mix.

labor rate variance *(8, 22)* The amount of labor variance that results from paying labor more or less than the standard rate.

labor recapitulation report *(19)* A labor report that summarizies the cost and use of labor for some specific time period.

last in, first out (LIFO) *(15)* Inventory valuation method that assumes that the goods purchased most recently are the first ones sold. The method refers to the flow of inventory costs and not to the physical flow of the goods.

lead time *(13)* The time between placing and receiving an order.

lead time demand *(13)* The amount of inventory required during lead time.

learning curve *(25)* A graph or function that increases at a decreasing rate. It indicates the cost effect of labor becoming more efficient as new tasks and processes are learned.

learning curve cost *(3, 25)* A class of semivariable costs that increase at a decreasing rate, such as labor costs resulting during a period when a new task is being learned.

learning rate *(25)* The rate at which learning takes place, expressed as a percentage that determines the shape of the learning curve.

least-squares regression line *(24)* See **regression line.**

line of best fit *(24)* The straight line that minimizes the absolute distance between the line and the set of data points used in the analysis. Also called the least squares regression line.

line budget *(17)* A budget prepared along organizational or functional lines, such as marketing, administrative, and manufacturing.

line-program budget *(17)* A budget in a matrix form that combines line budgeting and program budgeting.

linear programming *(25)* A mathematical technique for optimizing production or other problems with linear constraints and a linear objective function. May be used for either maximization or minimization problems.

loss leader *(14)* A product priced very low, perhaps below cost, intended to attract customers to the business to buy products at normal price as well as the loss leader items.

lost unit cost *(6)* The cost of manufacturing units that are identified as spoiled or lost units.

low-cost input *(22)* In a multiple resource production process, an input that costs less than the average cost of all inputs at the standard mix.

low-profit item *(22)* A product whose profit or contribution margin is less than the average profit or contribution margin at the standard sales mix.

make-buy decision *(10)* A decision involving the choice between buying a product or service or producing it.

manageable costs *(3)* A cost over which managers have a significant amount of control.

management by objective *(8)* A management method whereby managers establish specific performance criteria and investigate situations only when actual performance varies significantly from the performance criteria. Also called management by exception.

managerial accounting *(1)* The accounting and reporting of information to managers within the organization. Also called internal reporting.

manufacturing contribution margin *(11)* The difference between sales and the variable manufacturing expenses.

manufacturing overhead *(2)* All necessary costs of manufacturing other than direct labor and direct materials. The indirect costs of manufacturing.

manufacturing overhead applied *(4,20)* The account used to accumulate the amount of overhead applied to production. The account normally has a credit balance. The term also refers to the amount of overhead charged to a particular cost objective.

manufacturing overhead budget *(7)* The estimated amount of manufacturing overhead costs for an entity for a specific time period. Estimated indirect manufacturing costs, both fixed and variable.

manufacturing overhead control *(4,20)* The account used to accumulate actual manfacturing overhead costs as they are incurred. The account normally has a debit balance.

manufacturing overhead rate *(4,20)* A predetermined rate used for applying manufacturing overhead costs to products, for example, $6 per direct labor hour.

manufacturing overhead variance analysis *(9)* The systematic process of analyzing the difference between actual manufacturing overhead and applied manufacturing overhead. The two-variance and three-variance methods are common ways of analyzing overhead variances.

margin of safety ratio *(3)* A measure of the relative amount that actual activity differs from break-even activity. The difference is expressed as a ratio of actual activity, with a range of possible values from $-(\infty)$ to $+1$. Values above zero indicate the firm is operating above the break-even point.

marginal cost *(14)* The amount of increase in total cost caused by a one-unit increase in output.

marginal revenue *(14)* The amount of increase in total revenue caused by a one-unit increase in sales.

market equilibrium *(14)* The intersection of the supply and demand curves; it occurs when the amount buyers are willing to buy at a particular price coincides with the amount sellers are willing to supply at that price.

market penetration *(14)* A strategy for introducing new products to the market by pricing them low enough to ensure widespread distribution and a significant market share.

market price *(12)* The price for some product or service determined by market mechanisms external to the business.

market price transfer price *(12)* A price, determined by the market place, that one segment of an organization charges another segment of the organization for some good or service.

marketing expense budget *(7)* Estimated marketing costs of an entity for a specific time period.

marketing variances *(22)* Variances from standard or budget for marketing activities.

master budget *(7)* The total budget package of an organization, including both the operating and financial budgets. Sometimes referred to as the profit plan.

matching principle *(2)* Accounting concept requiring the reporting of expenses in the same period in which the related revenues are earned. The expenses are said to be matched with the revenues to arrive at a proper measure of income.

material mix variance *(22)* The amount of material variance caused by using a different proportion of material inputs than the standard mix.

material price variance *(8,22)* A variance caused by paying more or less than the standard price for a raw material.

material quantity variance *(8,22)* A variance caused by using more or less material than the standard quantity.

material substitution variance *(8)* A material price variance caused by substituting one material in the production process for another material.

material use variance *(8)* See **material quantity variance.**

material yield variance *(22)* A material variance caused by using more or fewer total inputs than defined by standard quantities.

materials budget *(7)* Estimated materials costs and quantities for an entity for some specified period.

materials handling costs *(18)* The costs associated with acquiring and distributing materials.

materials requisition *(4,18)* A document sent to the inventory storeroom area to start raw materials into the production process.

materials requisition summary report *(18)* An internal report summarizing material requisitions for some specific period of time.

mean *(23)* A measure of central tendency calculated by adding all items in a set of data and dividing by the number of items.

measures of central tendency *(23)* Statistics that describe average characteristics of a set of data, such as the mean, the median, or the mode.

measures of dispersion *(23)* Statistics that describe how data fluctuate around some measure of central tendency.

median *(23)* A measure of central tendency calculated as the middle value of an ordered set of data.

mixed cost *(3)* A cost composed of both fixed and variable cost components. Described by the general equation $Y = a + bX$. Y is the total cost, a is the fixed component, and b is the variable cost per unit of activity.

mode *(23)* A measure of central tendency representing the value of a set of data that occurs most frequently.

modified cost *(12)* A form of transfer price based on cost and modified to reflect special conditions or management's attitudes.

modified cost transfer price *(12)* A price charged by one segment of an organization to another seg-

ment of the organization for some good or service. The transfer price is based on some cost such as actual product cost as a base and then modified by some amount or percentage to meet management objectives.

modified price transfer price *(12)* A transfer price based on market price and adjusted to reflect such factors as the absence of marketing costs in interdivisional sales.

monetary policy *(17)* Deals with the quantity of money and the cost of money in the economy. One of the two instruments of economic stabilization policy.

monopolistic competition *(14)* A market in which there are many suppliers of similar, but not identical, products.

monopoly *(14)* A market with only one supplier.

multiple-alternative choice decision *(10)* A decision involving more than two alternative courses of action.

multiple linear regression *(24)* A statistical technique using two or more independent variables to predict the value of one dependent variable.

multiyear costing *(17)* The process of identifying costs with a project for the life of the project rather than just the next budget year. An element of PPBS.

mutually exclusive projects *(16)* Capital investments that require the rejection of one project if another is selected, because both cannot be adopted. An example is the construction of an office building or a factory on a parcel of land that will accommodate only one of the structures.

negative correlation *(24)* The relationship described by the coefficient of correlation when increases in the values of the independent variable are accompanied by decreases in the values of the dependent variable.

negotiated transfer price *(12)* A form of transfer price in which the buying and selling parties negotiate the transfer price.

net assets *(12)* An asset base used in evaluating segments of an organization. It is gross assets less any contra asset accounts such as accumulated depreciation.

net pay *(19)* Gross pay less withholding items. The amount actually paid to employees.

net present value (NPV) *(15)* A capital budgeting analysis method that is used to discount all cash inflows and outflows from a project to their present value. The firm's cost of capital or target rate of return is used as the interest rate.

net realizable value *(21)* The market value of a product less all costs to complete, market, or distribute the product.

net realizable value at split-off point *(21)* A joint cost allocation process that allocates joint costs in proportion to the joint product's net realizable value at the point of split-off.

nonmanufacturing activities *(12)* All activities other than manufacturing, e.g., marketing, accounting, and administration.

normal capacity *(9,11,20)* The expected activity level for the accounting period assuming normal operating conditions. The activity level is expressed in units of output, direct labor hours, machine hours, or some other measure of activity.

normal curve *(23)* See **normal distribution.**

normal distribution *(23)* A symmetrical bell-shaped curve describing the normal probability distribution found in many types of statistical data.

normal lost units *(6)* Spoiled or lost units that occur in the normal production process and, therefore, are included as part of the normal cost of producing good units.

normal spoilage *(6)* See **normal lost units.**

normal spoiled unit cost *(6)* The cost associated with normal spoilage.

not-for-profit sector *(17)* The sector of the economy comprising governments, universities, charities, and other organizations that provide services to the public without attempting to generate a profit.

objective function *(25)* The function in a linear programming problem that is to be maximized or minimized.

occupancy costs *(2)* See **capacity costs.**

oligopoly *(14)* A market in which there are several large sellers that dominate the market and compete with one another.

operating budget *(7)* The set of budgets for the normal operations of a business, including all activities involved in generating operating income.

operational goals *(7)* Organization goals that are expressed in specific, measurable terms, such as a return of owners' equity greater than 10 percent, or a cost reduction of $40,000 per year.

opportunity cost *(10)* The benefit forgone by rejecting one alternative so that another can be accepted.

ordering costs *(13)* The total cost associated with ordering a particular inventory item, typically including the costs of obtaining current prices, securing order approval, preparing purchase documents, and receiving the order.

overapplied overhead *(4,20)* The amount by which applied overhead exceeds actual overhead.

overhead *(2,4,20)* See **manufacturing overhead.**

overhead application base *(20)* The activity measure that is used to apply manufacturing overhead to production.

overhead rate *(20)* A predetermined rate that is used to apply manufacturing overhead to products. The rate is composed of an amount and a base; for example, $6 per direct labor hour.

participative budgeting *(7)* The process of preparing the budget using input from managers who are held responsible for budget performance.

payback *(15)* A capital budgeting analysis method that is used to determine how long it will take to recover the initial investment of a proposed project.

payback reciprocal *(15)* A capital budgeting evaluation method used to estimate the internal rate of return. Payback reciprocal is computed by dividing the payback period into 1.

payroll taxes *(4,19)* Taxes on the wages of employees that must be paid by employers. Included are the employer's share of FICA taxes, federal and state unemployment taxes, and workmen's compensation taxes.

perfectly competitive market *(14)* A market in which there are many buyers and sellers, none of whom can affect the market price by their individual actions. The product or service sold in the market is homogeneous, resources can flow freely into and out of the market, and all market participants have perfect knowledge of prices and costs.

performance reporting *(7,8,9,11,12,22)* The comparison of actual results with the expected results embodied in the budget, often resulting in the reporting of variances.

period costs *(2)* The cost of goods and services that are recorded as expenses in the period in which they are consumed.

periodic inventory system *(2)* A method of accounting for inventories in which the inventory account is adjusted only at year-end after a physical count of the inventory. Inventory purchases are recorded in a purchases account and the cost of goods sold is determined at the end of the accounting period by summing beginning inventory and purchases and subtracting ending inventory.

perpetual inventory system *(2)* A method of accounting for inventories in which all inventory increases and decreases are recorded directly in the inventory account. Cost of goods sold is determined at the time of sale.

physical units allocation method *(21)* See **physical units method.**

physical units method *(21)* A method of joint cost allocation that assigns an equal amount of joint costs to each unit of joint product manufactured.

planning *(1,7)* The process of developing the set of budgets used in achieving organizational goals. A design or scheme for achieving specific goals or objectives.

planning, programming, budgeting system (PPBS) *(17)* A comprehensive review, evaluation, and preparation process first initiated in the federal government in 1965 and subsequently used in similar forms in various state and local governments.

population *(23)* Any set of data or events from which a sample is to be taken for statistical measurement. Also called a universe.

positive correlation *(23)* The relationship described by the coefficient of correlation when increases in the values of the independent variable are accompanied by increases in the values of the dependent variable.

predetermined overhead rate *(20)* See **budgeted overhead rate.**

present value (PV) *(15)* The current value of an amount to be received in the future.

price follower *(14)* A firm in an oligopolistic market that sets its prices by following the pricing pattern of a price leader in the market.

price indifference point *(10)* The activity level at which the new price produces a profit identical to the profit generated by the old price and activity level.

price leader *(14)* A firm in an oligopolistic market that sets its product prices. Other firms in the market follow the price leader.

price skimming *(14)* A marketing strategy for introducing a new product by setting an initially high price in order to benefit from buyers willing to pay the high price in order to acquire the product.

pricing *(14)* The process of assigning a selling price to products or services sold by the organization.

pricing decisions *(10,14)* The process of establishing prices for the products or services provided by the company.

prime cost *(2)* Direct materials cost and direct labor cost combined.

private sector *(17)* The sector of the economy consisting of privately owned organizations primarily engaged in providing services and selling products to earn profits.

probability *(23)* The chance that a given event will occur, expressed as a decimal ranging from 0 to 1, with 0 meaning that the event cannot occur and 1 indicating that it will occur with certainty.

probability distribution *(23)* A mathematical expression of the likelihood of events taking place, used in making statistical measurements and drawing inferences.

problem definition *(1)* The process of determining precisely what problem is being addressed.

process center *(5,6)* A separate identifiable production activity characterized by homogeneous output and by work that is identical for each unit.

process costing *(4,5)* A cost accounting system used to accumulate costs of products manufactured in continuous flow production processes. There is no identifiable starting and completion time for production activity, so production costs must be summarized periodically in cost of production reports.

product contribution report *(11)* A contribution report that identifies the amount of contribution margin provided by each product.

product cost *(2)* All costs, both direct and indirect, of producing a product in a manufacturing firm or the cost of acquiring a product in a merchandising business and making it ready for sale.

production department *(20)* A department that is directly involved in furthering the production of products by performing some production process, such as drilling, assembly, or finishing.

product group decision *(21)* A joint product production or sales decision that affects all products in the joint product group.

product profitability report *(12)* A report identifying profit by product.

production mix variance *(22)* A measure of the dollar amount of variance caused by changing from the standard mix of production inputs to some other mix.

production quantity budget *(7)* Estimated production quantities and costs for an entity for some specified period of time.

profit center *(12)* A form of responsibility center in which managers are held responsible for both expenses and revenues.

profit plan *(7)* A company's total budget used in achieving a desired profit goal. Sometimes the term refers only to the operating budget, and sometimes it is used synonymously with the term master budget.

profit-volume chart *(3)* A special form of cost-volume-profit chart that highlights the break-even point and profit. The horizontal center line of the chart is the zero profit line.

profitability index (PI) *(15)* The ratio of the present value of cash inflows to the present value of cash outflows. A capital budgeting evaluation method that adjusts for the dollar amount of projects.

program accounting *(17)* An accounting system with an ability to attach accounting data to specific programs to show the resources used or budgeted for each objective.

program budget *(17)* A budget prepared for programs or outputs of an organization.

prorated lost units cost *(6)* The increase in the cost of good units caused by normal spoilage or lost units.

prorated spoiled units cost *(6)* See **prorated lost units cost.**

public finance *(17)* The entire area of government economic activity including resource allocation, income distribution to people, and the financing function of government.

public sector *(17)* The portion of the not-for-profit sector consisting of publicly owned organizations and institutions, such as city governments, state universities, federal parks, and others whose purpose is to provide services to the public without earning a profit.

purchase order *(4, 18)* A business document prepared by the purchasing department to order some resource or service.

purchase price *(14)* The amount paid for some resource acquired by a firm.

purchase requisition *(4, 18)* A business document indicating that some item or service needs to be ordered.

purchasing agent *(18)* The individual who has responsibility for all purchasing activities.

quantity variance *(8)* See **material quantity variance.**

random sample *(23)* A sample taken from a population in such a way that every item in the population has an equal chance of being included in the sample.

range *(23)* The difference between the highest and lowest value in a set of data, indicating how much the data are dispersed.

raw materials *(2)* The basic materials used in production by a manufacturing firm. Most raw materials are direct materials, but some are indirect materials.

raw materials budget *(7)* See **materials budget.**

receiving report *(4, 18)* A business document indicating the receipt of some item or items and the amount received.

reciprocal allocation *(20)* A method of allocating service department costs to producing departments; requires the use of linear algebra.

regression analysis *(24)* See **regression-correlation analysis.**

regression-correlation analysis *(24)* The analysis of statistical data performed by calculating a regression line, the coefficient of correlation, and the coefficient of determination, and then interpreting the results of the calculations.

regression line *(24)* A straight line that best fits through a set of data by minimizing the absolute distances between the data points and the line. Also called the line of best fit and the least-squares regression line.

regression line equation *(24)* The equation that describes mathematically the intercept and slope of the regression line.

reinvestment rate *(15, 16)* The rate at which cash inflows from capital projects can be invested.

relevance *(1)* The characteristic of accounting information requiring that information meets the needs of users.

relevant cost *(10)* A cost useful in the decision-making process; it has two characteristics: it is an expected future cost and a differential cost.

relevant range assumption *(3,9)* The assumption that the identified behavior pattern of a cost may exist only for a certain range of activity. At an activity level above or below the relevant range the cost may have a different behavior pattern.

reorder point *(13)* The inventory level at which a new order is placed for some specific inventory item.

residual income *(12)* The difference between actual net income and a specified target net income.

responsibility accounting *(12)* The process of reporting on how well managers meet their responsibilities.

responsibility center *(12)* Clearly identified segment of an organization in which managers are held responsible for the performance in the organizational segment. Cost centers, profit centers, and investment centers are the three common forms of responsibility centers.

return on investment *(12)* A measure of the amount earned on an investment project.

returned materials report *(18)* An internal report that shows the cost and quantity of unused materials returned to inventory from production activities.

Robinson-Patman Act *(1)* A federal law that prohibits discriminatory pricing of products or services except in certain special situations.

safety stock *(13)* An additional amount of inventory in excess of lead-time demand intended to minimize or eliminate the possibility of a stockout.

sales budget *(7)* Estimate of sales volume of an entity for some specified period of time. Prepared first because most other budgets are derived, at least in part, from the sales budget.

sales mix variance *(22)* A measure of the profit consequences of selling products in different amounts from the standard sales mix.

sales quantity variance *(22)* A measure of the amount of variance in profits caused by selling more or less units than standard.

sales region contribution report *(11)* A report showing the amount of contribution margin provided by each sales region of a company.

sales value method *(21)* A method of joint cost allocation that assigns joint costs to products in proportion to the sales value of each joint product.

sample *(23)* A set of data collected from a population so that a set is representative of the population.

sample size *(23)* The number of items to be included in a statistical sample in order to achieve a desired statistical requirement, such as a 95 percent probability of making an estimate accurately.

scatter diagram *(3)* A chart or graph used to plot cost data that may provide managers with a visual representation of cost trends or patterns.

schedule of equivalent units *(5)* A portion of a cost of production report that shows the physical quantity of output for the process center for the reporting period, with partially completed units expressed as equivalent whole units.

scrap material *(18)* Salable material that results from the production process and is not suitable to be returned to inventory and reissued.

Securities and Exchange Commission (SEC) *(1)* A regulatory body of the United States government charged with overseeing the operation of stock markets and regulation of public corporations.

segment reports *(11,12)* Reports that identify costs, revenues, profits, contribution margin, or other variables for parts or segments of an organization.

selling expense budget *(7)* See **marketing expense budget.**

selling price *(14)* The amount charged by an organization for some product or resource that it sells to others.

semifixed cost *(3)* A cost that increases with activity in jumps or steps. It remains constant for a range of activity and then jumps to a higher amount. Also called a step function cost.

semivariable cost *(3)* A cost that increases continuously, but not proportionately, with activity. Learning curve costs increase at a decreasing rate. Other semivariable costs increase at an increasing rate.

sensitivity analysis *(16)* The process of determining how sensitive the output of a model is to changes in the inputs or changes in the model parameters.

service department *(20)* A department, such as maintenance or inventory storeroom, that facilitates or supports production activities, but is not directly involved in producing products.

shadow price *(25)* The marginal cost or benefit of one unit of resource defined by a constraint in a linear programming problem.

shortage costs *(13)* The cost of running out of an inventory item.

simple linear regression *(24)* Regression analysis involving one dependent variable and one independent variable.

simplex method *(25)* A mathematical method for systematically solving linear programming problems.

single-product decision *(21)* A joint product production or sales decision that affects only one of the joint products.

special order *(10,14)* An order that has characteristics different from regular orders. Typically, a one-time order that provides the opportunity to utilize unused capacity.

special order decisions *(10,14)* A decision about whether to accept or reject a special order.

spending variance *(9)* The difference between actual manufacturing overhead cost and a flexible budget based on actual inputs. One of the variances isolated by using the three-variance method.

split-off point *(21)* The point in the production process when a by-product separates from the main product or when joint products become identifiable as separate products.

spoiled unit cost *(6)* The cost of spoiled or lost units.

stabilization *(17)* An objective of public finance aimed at keeping the economy running smoothly with acceptable growth and few economic fluctuations. Fiscal and monetary policy are the two instruments of stabilization.

standard cost *(8)* A carefully predetermined cost. A measure of what a cost should be.

standard cost transfer price *(12)* A transfer price based on the standard cost of the good or service transferred between business segments.

standard deviation *(23)* A measure of dispersion describing the variation of data from their mean.

standard error of the estimate *(24)* A statistical measure of the amount of dispersion exhibited by a set of data about the regression line of the data.

standard error of the mean *(23)* A statistical measure of the dispersion among the means of several samples taken from the same population. Based on the central limit theorem, the standard error can be computed as σ/n where σ is the population standard deviation and n is the sample size.

standard hours *(9)* The number of hours that should have been worked given the standard number of hours per unit and the quantity of output manufactured during the period.

standard setting *(8)* The process of establishing standard costs.

standards committee *(8)* A group of people within an organization whose function is to establish standards and reevaluate them periodically.

static budget *(7,9)* See **fixed budget.**

statistic *(23)* Any item of information that describes some characteristic of a subject under investigation.

steady state *(25)* The point on a learning curve when no more learning takes place and each subsequent repetition of the learned task requires as much time or cost as the previous repetition.

step function cost *(3)* A cost that remains fixed for a given range of activity but makes incremental jumps as some activity level is reached, whereupon it again remains fixed for a new range of activity.

stockholders' equity *(12)* Capital stock plus retained earnings, used as a base in evaluating performance.

stockout *(13)* The zero inventory level for some specific inventory when there is demand for the item.

stockout costs *(13)* The cost associated with running out of inventory which includes lost sales, customer ill will, and production inefficiencies.

stores ledger card *(18)* See **inventory ledger card.**

stratified sample *(23)* A sample taken from a population divided into two or more sub-populations, or strata, with each subset sampled randomly. Stratified sampling often permits drawing inferences with smaller samples than is possible without stratification.

subsidiary ledger *(2,4)* The set of individual accounts whose balances are summarized in a control account in the general ledger, e.g., individual accounts receivable for each customer that sum to the balance in the control account for accounts receivable.

summary product cost report *(5)* A product cost report used in a process costing system that summarizes the manufacturing costs for all process centers used in the production of a particular product.

sunk cost *(10)* A cost that has already been incurred and cannot be changed and therefore is not relevant to the decision process.

supply *(14)* The total amount all suppliers are willing to sell at each possible selling price.

supply curve *(14)* A graphic presentation of the amount of goods in aggregate suppliers are willing to sell at each possible selling price.

systematic sample *(23)* A statistical sample taken by selecting every *n*th item from a population. Systematic sampling may yield a random sample with some population but it may also yield a biased sample under some circumstances.

target income *(3,10,12,14)* A desired level of income expressed as an amount or a percentage of investment or sales.

target profit pricing *(14)* The process of establishing prices based on desired profit levels.

target profit transfer price *(12)* A transfer price based on covering all costs and providing a desired level of income.

tax incentives *(16)* Features of the tax laws de-

signed to encourage or promote certain desirable activities such as saving or capital investment. The investment tax credit is an example.

theoretical standards *(8)* See **engineering standards.**

three-alternative decisions *(10)* A decision involving three alternative courses of action.

three-variance analysis *(9)* A method of overhead variance analysis that isolates three variances — spending, efficiency, and volume.

time assumption *(3)* The assumption that cost behavior patterns may change over time and an identified pattern may be valid only for a specific period of time.

time value of money *(15)* The notion that money in the present is worth more than money in the future, and the cost of waiting for future money requires payment in the form of interest.

timeliness *(1)* An information characteristic requiring that accounting information be very current.

total cost of spoiled units *(6)* The total costs associated with the production of units that are identified as spoiled or lost.

total cumulative cost *(25)* The total cost of manufacturing a particular number of units in a production environment with a learning curve effect.

total gross assets *(12)* An asset base comprised of total assets without deducting contra-asset accounts, used to measure business performance.

total incremental cost *(25)* The amount of incremental cost incurred in manufacturing a particular additional quantity of a product.

total net assets *(12)* Total assets less any contra asset accounts, such as accumulated depreciation.

total net assets employed *(12)* Total assets less contra asset accounts less any assets not currently employed in generating net income.

transfer price *(12)* The process of pricing the transfer of goods and services between segments of an organization.

trend *(24)* The tendency of some events or data to move in an upward or downward direction and to continue doing so for a time. The trend may be measured by regression or other methods and used to predict future values of the data.

two-alternative decisions *(10)* A decision that involves selecting one of two alternatives being evaluated.

two-variance method *(9)* A method of overhead variance analysis that isolates two variances — controllable and volume.

underapplied overhead *(4,20)* The amount by which actual overhead exceeds applied overhead.

unfavorable variance *(7,8,9,22)* The amount by which actual costs exceed budgeted costs or standard costs. Any variance in which actual cost is greater than standard cost.

unit cost *(2,3)* The cost of one unit of product. Typically an average unit cost of producing the product during some time period, such as a month.

units accounted for *(5)* The portion of a cost of production report that identifies the disposition of units in production in the process center during the period.

units of output method *(21)* See **physical units method.**

units of production method *(21)* See **physical units method.**

units to account for *(5)* The portion of a cost of production report that identifies the number of units that must be accounted for in the process center during the period.

universe *(23)* See **population.**

variable cost *(2,3)* A cost that increases proportionately with the level of activity. Described by the equation $Y = bX$ where Y is total cost and b is the variable cost per unit of activity.

variable costing *(11)* A product costing method that includes all variable costs of manufacturing in the cost of the product and excludes any fixed costs. Also called direct costing.

variable efficiency variance *(9)* The variable portion of the overhead variance that is caused by using more or less hours than standard to manufacture products.

variable overhead *(7,9)* The portion of manufacturing overhead costs that vary directly with the level of activity.

variance *(23)* A measure of dispersion describing the fluctuation of data about their mean. *(7,8,9)* Difference between expected and actual performance.

variance analysis *(8,9,22)* The systematic process of identifying, reporting, and explaining variances.

venture capital *(16)* Capital invested in high-risk ventures with potentially high returns.

vested benefits *(19)* Portion of a retirement plan which is designated as belonging to and must be paid to the employee even if he leaves employment prior to retirement.

volume variance *(9)* The amount of overhead variance caused by operating at an activity level different from budgeted. The difference between applied overhead and a budget based on actual output.

withholdings *(19)* Amounts deducted from gross payroll and paid to various recipients such as governments, unions, and insurance companies.

work in process *(2)* Inventory that is in the process of being manufactured. Partially completed inventory.

yield variance *(16)* The difference between the standard and actual output obtained from a given amount of inputs.

zero-base budgeting *(17)* A method of budget review and evaluation that requires all projects and programs, new and old, to justify all resources. Each project starts the budget evaluation process without a resource commitment even if it is an ongoing project.

KEY FIGURES

CHAPTER 4

Ex.	4-2	b. Applied overhead, $227,500; d. Actual MOH $6.25 per DLH
Ex.	4-3	Total unit cost, $23.90
Ex.	4-4	Total unit cost, $79.355
Ex.	4-5	b. $9,583.50
Ex.	4-6	a. Underapplied overhead, $3,200
Ex.	4-7	Total unit cost, $21.21
Ex.	4-8	d. WIP, $181.600; Finished goods, $71,800; CGS $502,600
Ex.	4-9	Total cost per unit, $170.19
Ex.	4-10	Applied overhead, $19,250
Ex.	4-12	a. $316,800; d. $360,000
P.	4-2	a. Underapplied, $170,000; c. Total applied overhead, $620,000
P.	4-3	a. $177; c. $173
P.	4-4	c. DLH overapplied, $24,000; MH underapplied, $13,500
P.	4-5	b. $9.51 per hr
P.	4-6	b. Cost per unit, $315; d. MOH per unit, $88
P.	4-7	c. Total for Job No. 457, $637.50
P.	4-8	a. Total unit cost, $4,060; b. Gross margin, 18.8%
P.	4-9	a. 3. Unit cost, $72,50
P.	4-10	c. Product price, $14.10
P.	4-11	d. Average unit cost, $35.70; f. Underapplied overhead, $9,000
P.	4-12	Total unit cost, $95; c. Ending WIP, $13,037
P.	4-14	a. Prime cost, $618,800; c. Average cost per unit, $846.61
Case	4-1	a. WIP Control, $12,740; e. Ending WIP, $17,590; h. Expected profit, $47,364
Case	4-2	Cost of typing one line: a. $.14; c. $.1275

CHAPTER 5

Ex.	5-1	Equivalent units of conversion, 3,900
Ex.	5-2	Total unit cost, $16.10
Ex.	5-3	Cost transferred out, $25,878
Ex.	5-4	Equivalent units of conversion, 7,600
Ex.	5-5	Total unit cost, $8.66
Ex.	5-6	Cost of ending inventory, $10,820
Ex.	5-7	Second process center equivalent units of conversion, 65,400
Ex.	5-8	Third process center equivalent units of conversion, 5,850
Ex.	5-9	Current period unit cost, $3.40
Ex.	5-10	Cost transferred out, 79,860
Ex.	5-11	Unit cost of beginning inventory, $3.00; Ending WIP, $3,530
Ex.	5-12	Cost of ending inventory, $8,500
Ex.	5-13	Cost of ending inventory, $56,680
Ex.	5-14	Distilling department: Unit cost, $25.00; Ending WIP, $4,750
Ex.	5-15	Ending WIP, $77,200
Ex.	5-16	Cost of ending work in process with FIFO, $79,030
P.	5-1	Cost of ending inventory, $16,500
P.	5-2	Current period unit cost, $7.35
P.	5-3	Cost transferred out, $77,200
P.	5-4	Average unit cost in the finishing department, $13.19
P.	5-5	Average unit cost, $7.70
P.	5-6	Cost transferred out of fabricating, $110,000; Assembly ending WIP, $29,925
P.	5-7	Cost of ending inventory, $34,100
P.	5-8	Cost transferred out of process center 3, $115,217
P.	5-9	Current period unit cost in process center 2, $7.20
P.	5-10	Cost of ending work in process in August, $18,333
P.	5-11	Average cost per equivalent unit: Grinding, $.90; Assembling, $2.40
P.	5-12	Current period unit cost in April, $28.20; May ending WIP, $88,540
Case	5-1	a. Cost transferred out of assembly in October, $121,200; d. Retail price, $39.45

CHAPTER 6

Ex.	6-1	Material equivalent units, 15,000
Ex.	6-2	Cost per unit, $219
Ex.	6-3	Cost transferred out, $45,000
Ex.	6-4	Item C, conversion equivalent units, 8,075
Ex.	6-5	Cost of ending work in process, $11,780
Ex.	6-6	Debit Cash, $8,400
Ex.	6-7	Debit Abnormal Spoilage Loss, $7,100
Ex.	6-9	a. Total cost of spoiled units, $25,650
Ex.	6-10	Cost per unit, $6.00
Ex.	6-11	Total spoiled unit cost, $4,500
Ex.	6-12	Prorated spoiled unit cost, $1.20
Ex.	6-13	Cost transferred out, $126,614
Ex.	6-14	Cost of ending work in process, $20,150
Ex.	6-15	f. Increase in unit cost, $.72
P.	6-1	Cost transferred out, $115,462
P.	6-2	Cost of ending work in process, $5,765
P.	6-3	d. Total cost of normal spoilage, $660
P.	6-4	Prorated spoiled unit cost, $1.10; Unit cost transferred out, $23.20
P.	6-5	Total spoiled unit cost, $12,250
P.	6-7	h. Cost transferred out, $65,450
P.	6-8	Unit cost of materials, $5.80

P.   6-9   Abnormal spoilage loss, $1,700
P.   6-10   a. Normal spoilage, loss at beginning, $47,400
P.   6-11   Cost transferred out of machining, $360,000
P.   6-12   b. Total cost per equivalent unit, $6.15 d. Average cost per unit, $6.40
Case   6-1   e. Total cost to account for, $684,800

CHAPTER 7

Ex.   7-1   Total year's sales, $1,586,760; Cash collection, 4th quarter, $470,440
Ex.   7-2   total year's sales, $66,150; Cash receipts, 4th quarter, $19,467
Ex.   7-3   Total purchases in units, 13,600
Ex.   7-4   Total manufacturing overhead, August, $52,625
Ex.   7-5   Total labor cost, $1,003,200
Ex.   7-6   Total cost of materials, $3,784,000
Ex.   7-7   Total labor cost, $412,800
Ex.   7-8   Total direct materials cost, $126,752
Ex.   7-9   Total direct labor cost, $67,104
Ex.   7-10   Total cost of purchases, $92,860
Ex.   7-11   a. Total overhead, $3,540
Ex.   7-12   Total cost of goods sold, $74,250
Ex.   7-13   Total selling expenses, $728,600
Ex.   7-14   Total April cash receipts, $388,800
Ex.   7-15   c. Total cash balance, $21,880
P.   7-1   Total requirements: Tubing 244,600 ft; Vinyl, 291,720 sq ft
P.   7-2   Total gross margin: Sales manager, $52,200; Production manager, $48,000
P.   7-3   b. Direct labor cost, $36,549; d. Selling price, $4.04 per unit
P.   7-4   Sept: a. materials required, $5,250; c. Cash collection, $9,720
P.   7-5   a. Net income, $30,359; c. Selling price must increase 2.7%
P.   7-6   b. Total direct labor cost, $990,000; d. Total MOH variance, $4,600 U
P.   7-7   1986 net income: $60 price, $130,000; $80 price, $128,000
P.   7-8   h. Cost of goods sold, $809,000; j. Net income, $21,000
P.   7-9   e. Direct labor budget, $882,000 f. Finished goods inventory, $1,984,000
P.   7-10   Ending cash balance, $101,000
P.   7-11   a. Net income, $15,590; b. Marginal income, $25,600; Room rate, $5.40
Case   7-1   a. Total sales, $295,000; f. MOH rate, $4.00 per DLH j. Net income, $26,173

CHAPTER 8

Ex.   8-1   Quantity variance, $150 F
Ex.   8-2   Rate variance, $930 U
Ex.   8-3   Price variance, $150 U
Ex.   8-5   Total labor variance, $5,000 U
Ex.   8-7   Quantity variance, $12.60 F
Ex.   8-8   Total price variance, $96 F
Ex.   8-9   Total rate variance, $33 F
Ex.   8-10   Total efficiency variance, $27 U
Ex.   8-11   Debit cost of goods sold, $154,500
Ex.   8-12   d. $370 F; f. $45,340
Ex.   8-13   a. $540 U; c. $315 U
P.   8-1   Material quantity variance: Wire, $360 U; Cores, $300 U
P.   8-2   Labor rate variance, $5.50 U; Material price variance, $6 U
P.   8-3   c. Net income, $360,000
P.   8-4   Price variances: Vinyl, $14 F; Paste, $3 U; Total rate variance, $6 U
P.   8-5   Greenway: Actual labor rate, $6.95; Actual spraying time, 801 hr; Material price variance, $460 F; Labor rate variance, $1,120.15 U
P.   8-6   Standard cost of coat, $270; Total material variance, $1 U; Rate variance, $49 U
P.   8-7   c. Credit cost of goods sold, $92
P.   8-8   b. Total price variance, $1,305 F; c. Total rate variance, $134 U e. Cost of PR17: $6.9625 / sq mi
P.   8-9   Debit cost of goods sold, $4,270 of quantity variance; $3,480 of rate variance
P.   8-10   b. Material price variance, $950 U; c. Total rate variance, $550 U
P.   8-11   a. Total equivalent units: Materials, 10,000; Labor, 10,300; b. Materials price variance, $11,000 U; Labor rate variance, $5,575 U; MOH variance, $6,180 U
Case   8-1   Boat windshield: Current cost of production, $400,000; Proposed by union, $418,600; Proposed automated, $375,000
Case   8-2   Net income: Current, $128,660; Steam, $440,580; Chemical, $378,084

CHAPTER 9

Ex.   9-1   Net income at $150,000 of sales, $8,500
Ex.   9-2   Total variance, $3,665 F
Ex.   9-4   Break-even sales, $180,000
Ex.   9-5   a. $8 per DLH; d. $126,000; e. $80,000
Ex.   9-6   Volume variance, $4,400 U

Ex.	9-7	Efficiency variance, 5,850 U
Ex.	9-8	b. $12.50
Ex.	9-11	Variable efficiency variance $2,000 F; Fixed efficiency variance, $1,200 F
Ex.	9-12	a. Variable MOH rate, $5.00 per DLH; b. Controllable variance, $650 U
P.	9-1	Net income at $100,000 of sales, $1,400
P.	9-2	b. MOH rate, $6.92 per DLH
P.	9-3	Volume variance, $1,600 F
P.	9-4	Efficiency variance, $6,400 U
P.	9-5	Total variance, $18,000 F
P.	9-6	a. $26,000 hr; d. $82,000
P.	9-7	Spending variance $9,400 F; Capacity variance $11,000 U
P.	9-9	b. 19,000 DLH; c. $95,000; e. 21,000 DLH
P.	9-10	a. 50,000 DLH; c. 46,000 DLH; d. $414,000; g. Spending variance, $8,000 F
P.	9-11	c. Total labor rate variance, $550 U; Controllable variance, $24 U

CHAPTER 10

Ex.	10-1	Cost indifference point, 140,000 tons
Ex.	10-2	Price indifference point, 45,000 hot dogs
Ex.	10-3	Cost of incorrect decision, $37,500
Ex.	10-4	Per-unit cost savings, $.15
Ex.	10-5	Per-unit profit form special order, $34.95
Ex.	10-6	Break-even point, conventional, 35,714 pounds
Ex.	10-7	Cost indifference point, 3,500 units
Ex.	10-8	Price indifference point, 120,000 units
Ex.	10-9	Increase in profit from purchase, $60,500
Ex.	10-10	First cost indifference point, 280,000 ft of coil
P.	10-1	Cost indifference point, 18,000 patrol hours
P.	10-2	d. Profit from order, $700
P.	10-3	c. Decrease in profit, $17,400
P.	10-4	Cost indifference point, 44,000 student requests
P.	10-5	Break-even, automated, 3,500 outboard motors
P.	10-6	b. Cost savings, $16,000
P.	10-7	b. Expected 1985 profit, $14,000
P.	10-8	Price indifference point, 16,667 units
P.	10-9	d. Cost of using the more costly system, $40,400
P.	10-10	Total cost to make, $178,800
P.	10-11	Average maximum amount per ton, $44
P.	10-12	Incremental cost using overtime, $124,750
Case 10-1		b. Price indifference point, 349,398 pages

CHAPTER 11

Ex.	11-1	Contribution for sporting goods, $.40 per sales dollar
Ex.	11-2	Divisional contribution, $5,500
Ex.	11-3	Eastern region contribution, $71,900
Ex.	11-4	Net income, $680,000
Ex.	11-5	Net income, $705,000
Ex.	11-6	Difference in net income, $21,000
Ex.	11-7	Net income, $103,000
Ex.	11-8	1985 cost of goods sold, $1,153,000
Ex.	11-9	Variable costing net income, $543,000
Ex.	11-10	Answer to number 3 is d
Ex.	11-11	Difference in net income, $20,000
P.	11-1	Contribution of the bumper division, $223,000
P.	11-2	Division contribution, $45,000
P.	11-3	Southern region contribution, $217,000
P.	11-4	Absorption costing net income, $195,000
P.	11-5	Division contribution, $26,500
P.	11-6	Absorption costing net income is lower by $20,000
P.	11-7	Absorption costing product cost, $21 per unit
P.	11-8	Absorption costing net income for year 3, $412,000
P.	11-9	1983 variable costing net income, $7,000
P.	11-10	Year 3 absorption costing net income, $219,000
P.	11-11	Variable costing net income, $79,500
P.	11-12	Cereals product contribution, $403,000
P.	11-13	Total labor hours required for production, 140,000
Case 11-1		1983 net income using variable costing, $207,300

CHAPTER 12

Ex.	12-1	Return on total gross assets, 10%
Ex.	12-2	Part b residual income, $80,000
Ex.	12-3	Net income for the year, $60,000
Ex.	12-4	Return on average owners' equity, 40%
Ex.	12-5	Return on net assets, 12.5%
Ex.	12-6	Gross assets, $625,000
Ex.	12-7	Total cost transfer price: Part c, $59.00
Ex.	12-8	Part b transfer price, $71.25
Ex.	12-9	Profit for the month of April, $765
P.	12-1	Residual income ranges, $24,000

P.   12-2   Total accumulated depreciation, $350,000

P.   12-3   ROI for Y using gross assets employed, 10.3%

P.   12-4   ROI Southern Division using gross assets, 3.5%

P.   12-5   Residual income for division A, $30,000

P.   12-7   ROI on the average owners' equity balance, 20.7

P.   12-9   Part g target profit transfer price, $58.98

P.   12-10 Target profit transfer price; Part e, $37.20 per tree

Case 12-1   Total charge to Students Services using core hours, $75,000

CHAPTER 13

Ex.   13-1   Number of orders per year, 5
Ex.   13-2   EOQ, $8,400 units
Ex.   13-3   Number of orders per year, 20
Ex.   13-4   Total cost of inventory, $22,768.57
Ex.   13-5   Reorder point, 2,600 units
Ex.   13-6   EOQ, $5,000
Ex.   13-7   Demand, 25,000 units
Ex.   13-8   30,000 unit EOQ, 5,657 units; Cost of estimation error, $8.83
Ex.   13-9   EOQ for 900 units, 73; Cost of error in demand estimate $29.29
Ex.   13-10 EOQ at 10%, 5,933 units; Cost of estimation error, $56.19
Ex.   13-11 EOQ at 18%, 82 units; Cost of incorrect carrying cost, $454.39
Ex.   13-12 EOQ at 12%, 129 units; Cost of estimation error, $693.02
Ex.   13-13 EOQ at $120 unit cost, 1,102; Cost of estimation error, $27.42
Ex.   13-14 EOQ at $120 units cost, 1,075 units; Cost of error, $57.38
Ex.   13-15 Expected stockout cost, $540; Safety stock, 15 units
Ex.   13-16 Expected stockout cost, $840; Safety stock, 70 units

P.   13-1   EOQ, 5,657 units; Reorder point, 650 units

P.   13-2   a. 1,309 units; c. 660 gal; e. $166.32

P.   13-3   a. 500 gal; d. $1,653.41

P.   13-4   a. 3,367 units; c. $18,300

P.   13-5   a. 100 units; Gross margin: b. $92,700; c. $91,700

P.   13-6   a. 200 cartons; c. 175 cartons; e. $1.143.33; g. $1,184

P.   13-7   a. 500 units; d. $5,400

P.   13-8   a. 600 units; c. $2,100; e. 463 units; f. $6,900

Case 13-1   Ordering cost, $20 per order; 1985 storage costs, $85,500

CHAPTER 14

Ex.   14-2   Market equilibrium, 50 million pounds at $10 per pound
Ex.   14-3   Market equilibrium, 45 million bu at $7.50 per bu; elasticity, 3.33
Ex.   14-4   b. Net income, 9,200
Ex.   14-5   a. Total revenue at 24 units, $2,040; b. Price, $85 per unit
Ex.   14-6   Large wok selling price, $8.28 per unit
Ex.   14-7   b. Full cost, $35 per hr
Ex.   14-8   Selling price, $38
Ex.   14-9   b. Loss on special order, $2,500
Ex.   14-10 Price: a. $304; c. $288
Ex.   14-11 a. $1.75 per lesson; b. 7 students
Ex.   14-12 a. Profit from special order, $6,000

P.   14-1   b. Net income, $1,016,000

P.   14-3   Market equilibrium, 67.11 kg at $12.57 per kg

P.   14-4   b. 4 units; c. Elasticity, 1.4 or 1.7 depending on approach used

P.   14-5   Exterior, $7.00 per gal; Undercoat, $6.09 per gal; Net income, $192,500

P.   14-6   Year 2 net income with $60 price, $140,000; $90 price, $150,000

P.   14-7   a. Annual cost, 9.9%; b. Income, 11.4%; Loan rate 14.25%

P.   14-8   a. $.99 per lb

P.   14-9   a. Regular, $22 per case; Heavy-duty, $30 per case; Total contribution margin, $840

P.   14-10 a. Contract price $804,000; b. WIP inventory, $137,100

Case 14-1   Standard material cost: Hygreen, $1.80; Banweed, $1.95; Setup cost: Hygreen $7.00; Banweed, $6.70; e. Total bid, $368.35; f. Total cost of contract, $8,159

CHAPTER 15

Ex.   15-1   IRR, 16%
Ex.   15-2   IRR, 15%
Ex.   15-3   IRR, 15.6%
Ex.   15-4   IRR, 22%
Ex.   15-5   NPV, −$1,661.50
Ex.   15-6   NPV, $466.40
Ex.   15-7   NPV, $911.50; IRR, 28%
Ex.   15-8   Payback: A, 4.2 years; B, 4.75 years
Ex.   15-10 Payback reciprocal: X, 22.7; Y, 20.4
Ex.   15-11 Cost of capital, 22%; Payback, 4.7 years
Ex.   15-12 Project life, 19 years; Cost of capital, 18%
Ex.   15-13 ARR: a. 17.4%; b. 22.2%

P.	22-3	Material mix variance, $187 F
P.	22-4	Labor yield variance, $9,375 F
P.	22-5	Total labor variance, $221 F
P.	22-6	Total material mix variance, $275.50 U
P.	22-7	Actual material cost, $.7859 per loaf
P.	22-8	Total variance, $3,140 U
P.	22-9	Sales mix variance, $272.33 F
P.	22-10	Material yield variance, $2,308.80 U
Case	22-1	Material quantity variance, $8,000 U

CHAPTER 23

Ex.	23-1	Mean, 47 hours; Median, 43
Ex.	23-2	Mean, 64.08 units; Standard deviation, 19.08
Ex.	23-3	Mean, $244; Standard deviation, 59.48
Ex.	23-4	a. 68.26%; b. 15.87% d. 13.59%
Ex.	23-5	Expected sales, $710
Ex.	23-6	Expected gain, $2,925,000
Ex.	23-7	Expected value, 154.50; Expected standard deviation, 17.53
P.	23-1	Line A: Mean 156; Standard deviation, 24.35
P.	23-2	Devil's Hole: a. $1,485 and $390.19; c. 32%
P.	23-3	Cost per day, $4
P.	23-4	True population mean, 716.05
P.	23-5	b. Error, ±36; c. 22
P.	23-6	a. 28.43%; d. 162
P.	23-7	c. $248,500
Case	23-1	a. Probable sales, year 3, $435,500

CHAPTER 24

Note: Your solutions may differ due to rounding of calculations.

Ex.	24-1	b. $407,650
Ex.	24-2	b. $1.29; a. $139.19
Ex.	24-3	b. −1.45; a. 16.11
Ex.	24-4	a. 27.66; Standard error, 6.06
Ex.	24-5	r^2, .63714
Ex.	24-6	a. Y = $197.47
Ex.	24-7	a. Y = $203.00; r^2, .998157
Ex.	24-8	Railroad paneling, $10,476.00
Ex.	24-9	a. 1. $14,000
P.	24-1	Y = $141.96 + $1.30X; Std. error, $20.98
P.	24-2	Std. error, $4.75; r^2, .23243; d. $11.81

P.	24-3	Y = $141.96 + $1.30 X; r^2, .96794
P.	24-4	b. $3,246.00; c. r^2 = .91336
P.	24-5	b. r^2, .883235; c. $631.67
P.	24-6	c. Direct cost, $2,613.42; Maintenance, $1,275
P.	24-7	c. 756,320 units, $90,632.00; d. $17,184.00
P.	24-8	c. 1,317 permits
P.	24-16	a. $150,000 decrease
Case	24-1	a. r^2 = .71320; b. Std. error, $1,754.97 c. $30,700.84 to $46,016.76

CHAPTER 25

Ex.	25-1	Price per unit, $47.03
Ex.	25-3	Incremental time, 102.2 hr
Ex.	25-4	b. $1,357,550
Ex.	25-5	b. Average cumulative time, 89.2 hr; 17th unit, 80.1 hr
Ex.	25-6	b. Total cumulative time, 409.6 hr
Ex.	25-7	Total cost, $1,741.20
Ex.	25-8	a. 84 percent; b. 62.73 hr per unit
Ex.	25-10	b. Optimal contribution margin, $270
Ex.	25-11	c. Forming, 28 hr; Assembly, 16 hr; d. Finishing, 1 hr
Ex.	25-12	Optimal contribution margin, $3,750
Ex.	25-13	b. Optimal contribution margin, $904; c. $14
P.	25-1	Average cumulative cost for all units, $10.76
P.	25-2	a. $3,368.90; b. $67.38; e. $61.30
P.	25-3	b. Total prime cost, $1,757,312; Selling price, $658.98
P.	25-4	a. Total time, 2,382.6 hr; c. 2.20 hr; d. 3,005.7 hr
P.	25-5	b. Total cumulative cost, $3,427.15; c. $38,701
P.	25-6	a. 1.7 hr; c. 3.21 hr; d. 2,109 hr
P.	25-8	Corner c, $284
P.	25-9	Optimal contribution margin, $12,000
P.	25-10	b. 150 alpha, 225 beta; c. 300 alpha, 100 beta
P.	25-11	a. 300 rolls commercial, 450 rolls residential
P.	25-12	a. 1. 5,000 bikes, no chairs, CM, $20,000; $20,000; a. 2. $1 per DLH
Case	25-1	Learning rate, 89 percent

INDEX

INDEX